ERISA

The Law and the Code

Annotated

Including Excerpts From the Public Health Service Act

2011 Edition

Related Titles from BNA Books

Employee Benefits Law
by ABA Section of Labor & Employment Law

ERISA Class Exemptions
by Donald J. Myers and Michael B. Richman

ERISA Fiduciary Law
Edited by Susan P. Serota and Frederick A. Brodie

ERISA Litigation
by Jayne E. Zanglein and Susan J. Stabile

ERISA Regulations
Edited by Eric H. Rubin, Michael G. Kushner, and
Sharon F. Fountain

Section 409A Handbook
by Regina Olshan and Erica F. Schohn

Reductions in Force in Employment Law
by Ethan Lipsig, Mary C. Dollarhide, and Brit K. Seifert

Uniformed Services Employment and Reemployment
Rights Act
Editors-in-Chief Gerorge R. Wood and Ossai Miazad

ERISA

The Law and the Code

Annotated

Including Excerpts From the Public Health Service Act

2011 Edition

Current Through October 14, 2011

Edited by

Sharon F. Fountain, Esq.

BNA Tax & Accounting
Arlington, VA

BNA Books, *A Division of BNA,* Arlington, VA

Published by BNA Books
1801 S. Bell Street, Arlington, VA 22202
bna.com/bnabooks

International Standard Serial Number: 1050-4230
ISBN: 978-1-57018-966-1
Library of Congress Catalog Number: 90-644912

Printed in the United States of America

Introduction

Development of the Law

The Employee Retirement Income Security Act (ERISA) (Pub. L. No. 93-406) was signed into law in 1974, following years of deliberation and intensive debate. ERISA and the related Internal Revenue Code (IRC) sections have been amended frequently since that time, as outlined below.

2011

Congress enacted several amendments to the Patient Protection and Affordable Care Act, 2010 (PPACA) (Pub. L. No. 111-148). For example, IRC §36B, which was added to the tax Code by PPACA, allows a refundable credit to help individuals and families pay for health insurance premiums. IRC §36B was amended by the Medicare and Medicaid Extenders Act of 2010 (Pub. L. No. 111-309), the Comprehensive 1099 Taxpayer Protection and Repayment of Exchange Subsidy Overpayments Act of 2011 (Pub. L. No. 112-9), and the Department of Defense and Full-Year Continuing Appropriations Act, 2011 (Pub. L. No. 112-10). In addition to amending IRC §36B, Pub. L. No. 112-10 repealed the provisions of PPACA that required employers to offer free choice vouchers to certain low-income employees to use to purchase health insurance through a state health care exchange.

In an effort to stimulate the economy by increasing the take-home pay of employees, Congress reduced payroll taxes. The Social Security payroll tax was 12.4% of taxable earnings, with 6.2% paid by the employer and 6.2% paid by the employee. The Tax Relief, Unemployment Insurance Reauthorization, and Job Creation Act of 2010 (Pub. L. No. 111-312) temporarily reduced the employee's share of the Social Security payroll tax to 4.2% for 2011.

2010

The Patient Protection and Affordable Care Act (PPACA) (Pub. L. No. 111-148), which was intended to increase the number of Americans with health insurance, changed many of the rules that govern the U.S. health care system. The law's reach extends to the states, employers, health care insurers, and most individual taxpayers.

PPACA made significant changes to the Public Health Service Act (PHSA) that added requirements for group health plans, including insured and self-insured plans, although some employer plans are grandfathered. All of the individual and group market reforms in part A of title XXVII of PHSA, as amended by PPACA, apply to group health plans and to health insurance issuers in the group market as if the provisions were included in ERISA and the tax Code. Because these provisions are included by reference in ERISA, participants have a private right of action to enforce them.

The law's effective dates are spread over several years. Some provisions are effective for plan years beginning after September 23, 2010 (for example, the ban on annual and lifetime limits). The individual mandate for coverage and the requirement that larger employers must provide coverage to their employees or pay a tax are effective in 2014. In 2018, the excise tax on high-cost employer coverage becomes effective. Delayed effective dates apply to collectively bargained plans.

PPACA was amended by the Health Care and Education Reconciliation Act of 2010 (Pub. L. No. 111-152) and by two other laws (Pub. L. No. 111-159 and Pub. L. No. 111-173).

Amendments were made to the funding provisions of ERISA and the tax Code by the Preservation of Access to Care for Medicare Beneficiaries and Pension Relief Act of 2010 (Pub. L. No. 111-192).

2009

In an effort to avoid a more serious recession, Congress passed the American Recovery and Reinvestment Act of 2009 (ARRA) (Pub. L. No. 111-5). In addition to provisions intended to stimulate the economy, Division B, Title VII of the Act amended the Emergency Economic Stabilization Act of 2008 by adding new standards for executive compensation and corporate governance that apply to entities that received taxpayer money under the Treasury Department's Troubled Asset Relief Program, such as restrictions on bonuses and golden parachute payments. ARRA also included a temporary subsidy for the cost of health care continuation coverage for eligible individuals and parity for transit benefits, in addition to other changes.

Two laws—the TAA Health Coverage Improvement Act of 2009 (Pub. L. No. 111-5), also part of ARRA, and the Children's Health Insurance Program Reauthorization Act of 2009 (Pub. L. No. 111-3)—amended ERISA §701.

The Worker, Retiree, and Employer Recovery Act of 2008 (Pub. L. No. 110-458) made extensive technical corrections to ERISA and the IRC related to changes made by the Pension Protection Act of 2006.

2008

Congress made changes to the rules governing taxation of executive compensation. The Emergency Economic Stabilization Act of 2008 (Pub. L. No. 110-343), which was intended to restore liquidity and stability to the U.S. financial system, added significant restrictions on the executive compensation that may be offered by the financial institutions participating in the "troubled assets" program created by the Act. The restrictions are designed to limit and discourage participating institutions from paying excessive compensation to senior executive officers. Also, the Act added IRC §457A, which applies principles similar to IRC §409A to nonqualified deferred compensation plans sponsored by certain foreign corporations and partnerships. IRC §457A applies the "substantial risk of forfeiture" standard to the taxation of nonqualified deferred compensation from those foreign entities and incorporates by reference many of the provisions of IRC §409A. In addition, the Act expands the mental health parity requirements for private insurance plans that offer mental health benefits and applies similar requirements to services for substance use disorders.

Other amending legislation includes the Genetic Information Nondiscrimination Act of 2008 (Pub. L. No. 110-233) (prohibits health insurers and employers from discriminating based on genetic information), the Heroes Earnings Assistance and Relief Tax Act of 2008 (Pub. L. No. 110-245) (includes tax breaks and penalty-free withdrawals from pension plans and IRAs for military personnel), and Michelle's Law (Pub. L. No. 110-381) (requires continued coverage of dependent students during a medically necessary leave of absence from school).

Other amendments were made by the Housing and Economic Recovery Act of 2008 (Pub. L. No. 110-289) and the Fostering Connections to Success and Increasing Adoptions Act of 2008 (Pub. L. No. 110-351).

2007

Congress modified some of the changes to the tax Code and ERISA that it made in the Pension Protection Act of 2006 (see "2006" below for discussion of the Pension Protection Act of 2006) in the U.S. Troop Readiness, Veterans' Care, Katrina Recovery, and Iraq Accountability Appropriations Act, 2007 (Pub. L. No. 110-28), title VI.

In Pub. L. No. 110-28, Congress made changes to the rules that apply when a multiemployer plan revokes its election to not be treated as a multiemployer plan or when a defined benefit plan transfers excess assets to a retiree medical account in order to fund retiree health benefits. Also, Congress extended the alternative deficit reduction contribution rules, which gave commercial passenger airlines, and catering services to commercial passenger airlines, the option of paying a reduced additional required contribution by amortizing unfunded plan liability over 17 plan years.

2006

Faced with terminations of large defined benefit pension plans, funding shortfalls in many other pension plans and some well-publicized corporate scandals that cost employees their retirement savings, Congress responded to these threats to the pension system by passing a comprehensive benefits law, the Pension Protection Act of 2006 (PPA) (Pub. L. No. 109-280). PPA replaced the prior funding rules for single-employer defined benefit plans in ERISA and the tax Code, effective after 2007, with new minimum required contribution rules, notice requirements, and restrictions that apply to "at-risk" plans, and made changes to the funding rules for multiemployer plans.

In addition, PPA made permanent pension and individual retirement account (IRA) provisions enacted in the Economic Growth and Tax Relief Reconciliation Act of 2001 (Pub. L. No. 107-16), which were set to expire after 2010.

While the primary emphasis of PPA was on defined benefit plan funding, PPA contained significant provisions related to defined contribution plans, the Pension Benefit Guaranty Corporation, fiduciaries, contributions, health benefits, distributions and rollovers, cash balance plans, IRAs, and other matters. Also, PPA permitted plans to continue to use corporate bond rates, rather than 30-year Treasury rates, for plan funding for the 2006 and 2007 plan years.

Two other laws enacted in 2006 changed some of the rules for IRAs. Beginning after December 31, 2009, the Tax Increase Prevention and Reconciliation Act of 2005 (Pub. L. No. 109-22), which was enacted May 17, 2006, eliminated the modified adjusted gross income limit on conversions of traditional IRAs to Roth IRAs and permits married taxpayers filing a separate return to convert amounts in a traditional IRA into a Roth IRA.

Congress addressed health savings accounts (HSAs) in the Tax Relief and Health Care Act of 2006 (Pub. L. No. 109-432). Taxpayers may transfer funds tax free from a flexible spending arrangement or health reimbursement arrangement to an HSA; deduct HSA contributions, subject to certain limitations; and make a one-time, tax-free distribution from an IRA to an HSA. Congress modified the rules that determine when an employer is subject to the excise tax for failing to make comparable HSA contributions for non-highly compensated employees.

Also enacted in 2006, the Heroes Earned Retirement Opportunities Act (Pub. L. No. 109-227) allows typically nontaxable combat pay to count as taxable income for purposes of calculating allowable IRA contributions under IRC §219.

2005

Much of the federal legislation concerning benefit plans focused on participants affected by Hurricanes Katrina, Rita, and Wilma. The Gulf Opportunity Zone Act of 2005 (GOZA) (Pub. L. No. 109-135) codified and expanded relief provided in an earlier act, the Katrina Emergency Tax Relief Act of 2005 (Pub. L. No. 109-73). GOZA includes an exception to the §72(t) early distribution tax for distributions related to the hurricanes, allows participants to recontribute certain distributions from retirement plans and eases the plan loan rules.

GOZA affects taxation of nonqualified deferred compensation under IRC §409A. GOZA provides that the additional tax and interest under IRC §409A is not treated as regular tax for alternative minimum tax purposes and that the funding rules in IRC §409A(b) relating to offshore trusts and financial triggers are effective January 1, 2005.

The Deficit Reduction Act of 2005 (Pub. L. No. 109-171) amended Title IV of ERISA, which deals with plan termination insurance. The Act increases the per participant premium that must be paid by single and multiemployer plans and adds a new premium charge for certain terminated single-employer plans and a special rule for plans terminated in bankruptcy reorganization.

2004

Marking a busy year for benefits legislation, three statutes were enacted. The American Jobs Creation Act of 2004 (AJCA) (Pub. L. No. 108-357), the Working Families Tax Relief Act of 2004 (Pub. L. No. 108-311), and the Pension

Funding Equity Act of 2004 (Pub. L. No. 108-218) made extensive changes to the law of employee benefits, particularly to executive compensation. AJCA added IRC §409A, which creates another layer of rules on top of the pre-existing law governing nonqualified deferred compensation plans. IRC §409A contains a structure of rules that restrict when a participant may make an initial deferral election or receive distributions; prohibit accelerated distributions; limit a participant's ability to make a "subsequent election" that would delay or change the form of a distribution; immediately tax "off-shore" rabbi trusts and plans that provide for funding or increased security due to a change in the employer's financial health; and impose new reporting and withholding requirements.

The Pension Funding Equity Act amended ERISA and the IRC to lower certain employer contributions to underfunded plans, generally for the 2004 and 2005 plan years, by permitting plans to use higher interest rate assumptions based on long-term corporate bonds. In addition, the Act provided airlines and steel manufacturers with relief for up to two plan years from contributions for underfunded plans and permitted certain multiemployer plan sponsors to defer a charge for net experience loss.

Other changes to the law of employee benefits included an exclusion from wages and employment taxes for certain executive compensation; an excise tax on stock-based compensation from certain expatriated corporations; and a modification of the retiree health care minimum cost requirement when employers transfer excess pension assets to pay group health plan-liabilities.

2003

The Medicare Prescription Drug, Improvement, and Modernization Act of 2003 (Pub. L. No. 108-173) created health savings accounts (HSAs) that provide tax-favored treatment for current medical expenses, as well as a tax-favored vehicle for saving for future medical expenses. HSAs are tax-exempt trusts or custodial accounts created exclusively to pay for the qualified medical expenses of the account holder and his or her family. HSAs are subject to rules similar to those applicable to individual retirement arrangements.

The Military Family Tax Relief Act of 2003 (Pub. L. No. 108-121) expanded the tax relief available to members of the armed services and their families under IRC §7508. The Act granted extensions of time to persons deployed outside the United States away from the individual's permanent duty station while participating in military "contingency operations," as designated by the Secretary of Defense. The Act extended the time period for actions such as making a tax-qualified contribution to an individual retirement account. The Act also provided that dependent care assistance benefits provided to a member of the uniformed services by reason of the member's status or service as a member of the uniformed services are excludible from gross income as a qualified military benefit.

2002

The Job Creation and Worker Assistance Act of 2002 (JCWAA) (Pub. L. No. 107-147) contained several changes that affected employee benefit plans, including temporary funding relief for defined benefit plans, an extension for medical savings accounts and corrections to the Economic Growth and Tax Relief Reconciliation Act of 2001 (EGTRRA) (Pub. L. No. 107-6).

The Sarbanes-Oxley Act of 2002 (Pub. L. No. 107-204) contained some key provisions related to employee benefit plans, including requiring plan administrators to provide participants with advance notice of any "blackout" periods during which participants may not self-direct the investments in their accounts within a defined contribution plan or receive plan loans or distributions. The Act also imposed new penalties for violations of ERISA's reporting and disclosure rules.

The Trade Act of 2002 (Pub. L. No. 107-210) expanded the benefits available to workers displaced by import competition or shifts of production to other countries. The Trade Act also provided a first-time benefit to certain workers who are receiving trade adjustment assistance, in the form of a tax credit for 65% of the premiums paid by these workers for certain types of medical coverage (including COBRA coverage) for themselves and their families. The Trade Act included additional help for eligible workers through grants to state programs that may be used to assist in obtaining medical coverage (including COBRA coverage). In addition, to give workers who did not elect COBRA another chance to make an election after becoming eligible for the new tax credit (or for state assistance in obtaining coverage), the Trade Act created a new, second COBRA election period for workers who are receiving trade adjustment assistance.

2001

The Economic Growth and Tax Relief Reconciliation Act of 2001 (EGTRRA) (Pub. L. No. 107-16) included much of the pension reform package that Congress had been working on for the previous several years.

Sunset Provision: To comply with the Congressional Budget Act of 1974, §901 of EGTRRA provided that all provisions of, and amendments made by, EGTRRA generally would not have applied for taxable, plan, or limitation years beginning after December 31, 2010, unless renewed by Congress. The Pension Protection Act of 2006 (Pub. L. No. 109-280), §811, repealed the EGTRRA sunset provision as it applied to pensions and individual retirement accounts. Subsequently, the Tax Relief, Unemployment Insurance Reauthorization, and Job Creation Act of 2010 (Pub. L. No. 111-312), §101(a), extended the EGTRRA sunset to December 31, 2012.

Public Law No. 107-22 renamed "education individual retirement accounts" as "Coverdell education savings accounts."

2000

The Consolidated Appropriations Act of 2001 (Pub. L. No. 106-554) included the Community Renewal Tax Relief Act of 2000, which made many technical corrections to the IRC in the areas of qualified plans and individual retirement accounts (IRAs). Specifically, the Community Renewal Tax Relief Act retroactively treated nontaxable salary reduction amounts used for qualified transportation fringe benefits as compensation for purposes of qualified retirement plans; permitted lump-sum distributions from a terminated 401(k) plan to include distributions from annuity contracts; and clarified that IRA contributions for a non-working (or lesser-earning) spouse cannot exceed the couple's combined earned income.

The Consolidated Appropriations Act also enacted the Medicare, Medicaid and SCHIP Benefits Improvement and Protection Act of 2000, which amended ERISA §4022A to increase by more than 100% the maximum Pension Benefit Guaranty Corporation guarantees for multiemployer pension plans that terminate without sufficient assets to pay benefits.

1999

The Tax Relief Extension Act of 1999 (Pub. L. No. 106-170) amended IRC §420(c)(3) to reflect minimum cost requirements for the transfer of excess pension assets to retiree health accounts and the calculation of minimum cost requirements. For qualified transfers occurring after December 17, 1999, the applicable employer cost is determined according to employer cost and not the benefits provided. The Act also made conforming amendments to ERISA and the IRC and extended certain expiring tax and employee benefits provisions.

1998

Four statutes were enacted that contained significant employee benefit provisions. The Transportation Equity Act for the 21st Century (Pub. L. No. 105-178) clarified that metro transit vouchers provided pursuant to a qualified transportation fringe benefit program could be provided on a salary-reduction basis. The Act also increased the monthly value of transit passes and parking that could be provided tax free by an employer to an employee.

The Child Support Performance and Incentive Act of 1998 (Pub. L. No. 105-200) required that all health care plans recognize a national medical support notice. The Act amended ERISA to provide that such notices are to be considered qualified medical child support orders with which plan administrators must comply.

The Internal Revenue Service Restructuring and Reform Act of 1998 (Pub. L. No. 105-206) made numerous technical changes in the areas of regular IRAs, Roth IRAs, and SIMPLE IRAs. The Act also made certain §401(k) plan distributions ineligible for rollover treatment.

Finally, the Tax and Trade Relief Extension Act of 1998 (Pub. L. No. 105-277) increased the deduction for health insurance for self-employed individuals and made certain technical changes to the rules of IRC §221 regarding the deductibility of interest on qualified educational loans. Part of that legislation, the Women's Health and Cancer Rights Act, added §713 to ERISA, granting certain rights under group health plans for reconstructive surgery following a mastectomy.

1997

The Taxpayer Relief Act of 1997 (Pub. L. No. 105-34) and the Balanced Budget Act of 1997 (Pub. L. No. 105-33) became law. The Taxpayer Relief Act, among other things, created the Roth IRA, from which distributions are nontaxable; allowed taxpayers to save for a child's higher education through Educational IRAs; and repealed the excise tax on excess retirement distributions and accumulations. The Balanced Budget Act introduced the Medicare+Choice MSA (later renamed the Medicare Advantage MSA). Other benefits legislation enacted in 1997 included Pub. L. No. 105-72, making certain amendments to ERISA §3(38)(B), and the SAVER Act (Pub. L. No. 105-92), requiring the Labor Department to host a national conference on retirement policy.

1996

The Small Business Job Protection Act of 1996 (SBJPA) (Pub. L. No. 104-188) created a new type of simplified employee retirement plan, known as the SIMPLE plan, for the employees of certain small employers. SIMPLE plans can be maintained in either IRA or §401(k) form. The SBJPA also enacted a wide variety of pension simplification measures.

The Health Insurance Portability and Accountability Act (HIPAA) (Pub. L. No. 104-191) authorized the establishment of MSAs as a means of allowing employees to save for medical expenses on a tax-favored basis. HIPAA also permitted certain long-term care insurance and services to be treated as provided under an accident or health plan for tax purposes. Finally, HIPAA added rules for the application and enforcement of certain group health plan portability, access, and renewability requirements.

The Departments of Veterans Affairs and Housing and Urban Development, and Independent Agencies Appropriations Act of 1997 (Pub. L. No. 104-204) added mental health parity provisions and provisions regarding the minimum hospital stay for newborns and mothers to the health care portability, access, and renewability requirements of the IRC and ERISA. Other minor changes in the employee benefits area were made by Pub. L. No. 104-193, the Personal Responsibility and Work Opportunity Reconciliation Act of 1996 (the welfare reform bill).

1995

The Self-Employed Health Insurance Act of 1995 (Pub. L. No. 104-7) made the deduction for the health insurance costs of self-employed individuals permanent and increased the allowable deduction. In addition, the State Taxation of

Pension Income Act of 1995 (Pub. L. No. 104-95) amended Title 4 of the *United States Code* to limit the ability of states to tax the retirement income of certain nonresidents.

1994

The Retirement Protection Act of 1994 (RPA) (Pub. L. No. 103-465) significantly tightened the funding rules for underfunded defined benefit pensions. The RPA also extended the sunset date through the year 2000 for IRC §420 (later extended through 2013 by Pub. L. No. 108-218), which allows the transfer of certain excess pension assets from defined benefit plans to individual medical accounts within such plans. In addition, the Pension Annuitants' Protection Act (Pub. L. No. 103-401) clarified that individuals and the Labor Department could bring suit for a failure to provide the annuitized benefits called for under ERISA to former participants and beneficiaries of terminated defined benefit plans. Also, the Social Security Administrative Reform Act of 1994 (Pub. L. No. 103-296) established the Social Security Administration as an independent federal agency and made appropriate conforming changes to the IRC.

1993

The Omnibus Budget Reconciliation Act of 1993 (OBRA '93) (Pub. L. No. 103-66) lowered the amount of compensation that could be taken into account in calculating benefit accruals or allocations under qualified plans. OBRA '93 extended retroactively the income tax exclusion for employer-provided educational assistance and the health insurance deduction for self-employed individuals. The law changed the fringe benefit treatment of moving expenses and required group health plans to honor child medical support orders.

1992

The Unemployment Compensation Amendments of 1992 (UCA) (Pub. L. No. 102-318) allowed any portion of most distributions from a qualified pension plan or annuity or a tax-sheltered annuity to be rolled over tax free into an IRA or another qualified plan or annuity. The law required qualified plans to permit participants to elect to have any distribution eligible for rollover treatment transferred directly to an eligible transferee plan designated by the participant.

The Comprehensive National Energy Policy Act of 1992 (Pub. L. No. 102-486) included a provision on the funding of health benefits for retired coal miners. The law required companies that were party to labor agreements with the United Mine Workers of America as far back as 1950 to cover retiree health costs. In addition, excess union pension funds and interest on monies in the abandoned mine land reclamation fund were required by the Act to be transferred to the union's health benefit fund. Also, the law allowed excess assets in qualified black lung benefit trusts to be used to pay accident and health premiums for retired miners. Another provision of the law expanded the exclusion from taxable income for employer-provided transit subsidies while limiting the exclusion for employer-provided parking.

1991

The Rural Telephone Cooperative Associations ERISA Amendments Act of 1991 (Pub. L. No. 102-89) removed from ERISA's definition of "multiple employer welfare arrangements" the welfare plans of rural telephone cooperative associations.

Emergency supplemental appropriations legislation (Pub. L. No. 102-229) created ERISA §4001(a)(14)(C). The provision was aimed specifically at preventing Carl Icahn, chairman and chief executive officer of Trans World Airlines Inc., from escaping responsibility for TWA's pension plan underfunding.

While the Federal Deposit Insurance Corporation Improvement Act of 1991 (Pub. L. No. 102-242) did not amend ERISA or its corresponding tax code sections, it did contain provisions affecting employee benefit plans. The Act allowed pass-through coverage by the Federal Deposit Insurance Corporation (FDIC) for benefit plan assets placed in well-capitalized financial institutions. However, pass-through coverage for bank investment contracts was eliminated. The Act also specified that the FDIC and other successors to failed financial institutions have the same obligation under ERISA §602 to offer COBRA continuation group health coverage to former employees as the failed institution would have had if not for its failure.

The Tax Extension Act of 1991 (Pub. L. No. 102-227) extended for six months certain expiring tax provisions, including the provisions covering employer-provided educational assistance, group legal services plans, and health insurance costs of self-employed individuals. However, the six months lapsed without the provisions being extended again or made permanent; the provisions expired at the end of June 1992. (The exclusion for educational assistance was extended several times, then made permanent and broadened to include graduate education in Pub. L. No. 107-16.)

1990

The Omnibus Budget Reconciliation Act of 1990 (OBRA '90) (Pub. L. No. 101-508) extended the sunset date for the IRC's tax breaks for tuition assistance and group legal service plans, increased the excise tax on reversions of excess assets to employers from plan terminations, raised plan termination insurance premiums, permitted the transfer of some excess assets to retiree health accounts, and made a number of technical changes. Also, Pub. L. No. 101-540 amended Title I of ERISA to expand the definition of "employer securities" to include interests in certain publicly traded partnerships.

1989

Public Law No. 101-140 increased the public debt limit and repealed IRC §89. The Omnibus Budget Reconciliation Act of 1989 (OBRA '89) (Pub. L. No. 101-239) modified COBRA health care continuation coverage rules and made numerous technical corrections to prior laws. The law also amended civil penalties for fiduciary violations and repealed or limited a number of provisions on employee stock ownership plans.

1988

The Technical and Miscellaneous Revenue Act of 1988 (TAMRA) (Pub. L. No. 100-647) included a number of provisions affecting employee benefits. TAMRA amended the tax sanctions for violation of the COBRA requirements; increased the excise tax on reversions of excess plan assets; made certain clarifying amendments to pension rules; and amended IRC §457 (relating to unfunded deferred compensation arrangements for employees of governmental units and tax-exempt organizations).

1987

The Omnibus Budget Reconciliation Act of 1987 (OBRA '87) (Pub. L. No. 100-203) tightened the funding requirements for defined benefit pension plans and increased the premium that single-employer defined benefit plans must pay to guarantee a certain level of benefits.

1986

The Consolidated Omnibus Budget Reconciliation Act of 1986 (COBRA) (Pub. L. No. 99-272) included provisions requiring the continuation of employer-sponsored group health insurance for certain individuals and their dependents. In addition, Title XI of the law amended the single-employer pension plan provisions of ERISA. Title XI is cited as the Single-Employer Pension Plan Amendments Act of 1986.

The Tax Reform Act of 1986 (Pub. L. No. 99-514) made extensive changes affecting employee pension and welfare benefit plans, including amendments to the rules on nondiscrimination, coverage, participation, Social Security integration, vesting, and distributions.

The Omnibus Budget Reconciliation Act of 1986 (OBRA '86) (Pub. L. No. 99-509) required continued benefit accruals or allocations for employees who continue to work beyond normal retirement age and stipulated that employers must offer health insurance coverage to retirees and dependents who otherwise would lose coverage because the employer filed for Chapter 11 bankruptcy.

1984

The Deficit Reduction Act (Pub. L. No. 98-369) added and amended tax code provisions in such areas as fringe benefits, cafeteria plans, and employee welfare plans. The Retirement Equity Act (REA) (Pub. L. No. 98-397) amended both tax code and ERISA provisions on vesting, participation, and joint and survivor annuities.

1982

A bill was introduced in the House to reduce the contribution and benefit limits for qualified corporate plans; modify the rules for integration with Social Security; tighten the rules for loans from plans to key employees; and limit the estate tax exclusion for retirement annuities paid to beneficiaries, among other changes. Those proposals were modified and rolled into a revenue raising package introduced in an attempt to reduce budget deficits. The revenue package became the Tax Equity and Fiscal Responsibility Act of 1982 (Pub. L. No. 97-248).

1981

A series of savings incentive bills was introduced in Congress. Proposals were made to raise the limits on deductible contributions to IRAs and Keogh plans; encourage the adoption of employee stock ownership plans; and change the tax treatment of stock options. The retirement plan proposals and other savings incentive provisions eventually were consolidated, and became part of the Economic Recovery Tax Act (Pub. L. No. 97-34).

1980

The first major changes in benefits law were enacted in the Multiemployer Pension Plan Amendments Act of 1980 (Pub. L. No. 96-364). Although ERISA itself remained virtually untouched for six years, a number of changes affecting pension and benefit plans were enacted through various tax laws that amended the qualified plan provisions of the IRC.

Organization of This Book

Part 1 contains the text of the Employee Retirement Income Security Act of 1974 (ERISA), as amended, including ERISA sections that parallel Internal Revenue Code sections. Following each ERISA section is a complete statutory history of the section, including provisions of amending statutes that relate to the section.

Part 2 contains pertinent sections of the Internal Revenue Code, as amended. A statutory history that tracks all amendments made since 2001 follows each Code section. The statutory history includes provisions of amending statutes that relate to the section.

Part 3 contains selected provisions of the Public Health Service Act, as amended by the Patient Protection and Affordable Care Act (PPACA) (enacted March 23, 2010) and other legislation. Following each PHSA section is a statutory history of the section, including provisions of amending statutes that relate to the section.

Part 4 contains selected provisions of the Public Health Service Act as they appeared prior to enactment of PPACA.

Part 5 is the health care provisions (Part Eight) of the report of the Joint Committee on Taxation entitled *General Explanation of Tax Legislation Enacted in the 111th Congress* (March 2011).

Part 6 contains an index to ERISA and the Code (Parts 1 and 2) and a separate index to the Public Health Service Act as amended by PPACA and other legislation (Part 3). The index to ERISA and the Code is cross-indexed to Treasury, Department of Labor, Pension Benefit Guaranty Corporation, and Department of Health and Human Services regulations printed in *ERISA Regulations*, 2012 Edition (BNA), edited by Eric H. Rubin, Esq., Sharon F. Fountain, Esq., and Michael G. Kushner, Esq. *ERISA Regulations* is published annually.

The text of ERISA and the Code is current through October 14, 2011. Small amounts of text of ERISA and the Code that were deleted by the changes made by recent legislation are set forth in ~~strikeout~~ mode. Text of ERISA or the Code that was added by recent legislation appears in *italics*. Editor's notes containing amendment, effective date, and other useful information are at the beginning of the section or subsection of ERISA, the Code, or PHSA to which they pertain.

Contents

Part 1—Text of ERISA

Part 2—IRC Excerpts

Part 3—PHSA Excerpts After PPACA

Part 4—PHSA Excerpts Prior to PPACA

Part 5—Reports

Part 6—Indexes

Section

29 U.S.C. ERISA

Title 29—Labor

Chapter 18—Employee Retirement Income Security Program

Title I—Protection of Employee Benefit Rights

Subtitle A—General Provisions

Subtitle B—Regulatory Provisions

Part 1—Reporting and Disclosure

Section

29 U.S.C. ERISA

Part 2—Participation and Vesting

Part 3—Funding

Section
29 U.S.C. ERISA

Part 4—Fiduciary Responsibility

Part 5—Administration and Enforcement

Section

29 U.S.C. ERISA

Section
29 U.S.C. ERISA

Title III—Jurisdiction, Administration, Enforcement; Joint Pension Task Force, etc.

Subtitle A—Jurisdiction, Administration, and Enforcement

Section
29 U.S.C. ERISA

Subtitle B—Coverage

Subtitle C—Terminations

Subtitle D—Liability

Section

29 U.S.C. ERISA

Subtitle E—Special Provisions for Multiemployer Plans

Part 1—Employer Withdrawals

Section
29 U.S.C. ERISA

Part 2—Merger or Transfer of Plan Assets or Liabilities

Part 3—Reorganization; Minimum Contribution Requirement for Multiemployer Plans

Part 4—Financial Assistance

IRC Section

26 U.S.C.

IRC Section
26 U.S.C.

IRC Section
26 U.S.C.

IRC Section
26 U.S.C.

Subpart B—Special Rules

Subpart C—Special Rules for Multiemployer Plans

Subpart D—Treatment of Welfare Benefit Funds

IRC Section
26 U.S.C.

IRC Section

26 U.S.C.

IRC Section
26 U.S.C.

IRC Section

26 U.S.C.

IRC Section
26 U.S.C.

Chapter 43—Qualified Pension, etc., Plans

Chapter 45—Provisions Relating to Expatriated Entities

IRC Section
26 U.S.C.

IRC Section
26 U.S.C.

IRC Section
26 U.S.C.

IRC Section

26 U.S.C.

IRC Section
26 U.S.C.

IRC Section
26 U.S.C.

Editor's Note: The following are selected provisions of the Public Health Service Act as amended by the Patient Protection and Affordable Care Act and other legislation. See Part 3 for the full text of these provisions.

Section

42 U.S.C.   PHSA

Title 42—Public Health and Welfare

Section

Section

Public Health Service Act, Selected Provisions
Prior to PPACA
Finding List

Editor's Note: The following are selected provisions of the Public Health Service Act as they appeared prior to enactment of the Patient Protection and Affordable Care Act. See Part 4 for the full text of these provisions.

Part 1

Text of ERISA

ERISA Finding List

Section

29 U.S.C. ERISA

Section

29 U.S.C. ERISA

Part 4—Fiduciary Responsibility

Part 5—Administration and Enforcement

Section

29 U.S.C. ERISA

Part 6—Continuation Coverage and Additional Standards
for Group Health Plans

Part 7—Group Health Plan Requirements

Subpart A—Requirements Relating to Portability,
Access, and Renewability

Section
29 U.S.C. ERISA

Title III—Jurisdiction, Administration, Enforcement; Joint Pension Task Force, etc.

Subtitle A—Jurisdiction, Administration, and Enforcement

Section

29 U.S.C. ERISA

Section
29 U.S.C. ERISA

Subtitle B—Coverage

Subtitle C—Terminations

Subtitle D—Liability

Section
29 U.S.C. ERISA

Editor's Note

This is the text of ERISA, as amended by various public laws, current through October 14, 2011.

Title II of ERISA contains amendments to the Internal Revenue Code, which are included in part 2 of this book. ERISA's other titles are reprinted here. Text within subsections of ERISA that was deleted by the changes made by recent legislation is set forth in ~~strikeout~~ mode. Certain sections or subsections of ERISA that were repealed or amended appear in full with an editor's note. Provisions that were added by recent legislation are in italics. Editor's notes appear at the beginning of the section or subsection of ERISA to which they pertain.

ERISA sections are followed by a complete statutory history of the section, including certain provisions of amending statutes that relate to the section.

ERISA is codified at Title 29 of the U.S. Code. For the U.S. Code section numbers and the table of contents, see ERISA Finding List above.

SEC. 1. SHORT TITLE AND TABLE OF CONTENTS.

This Act may be cited as the "Employee Retirement Income Security Act of 1974."

Title I—Protection of Employee Benefit Rights

Subtitle A—General Provisions

SEC. 2. CONGRESSIONAL FINDINGS AND DECLARATION OF POLICY.

(a) Benefit Plans as Affecting Interstate Commerce and the Federal Taxing Power.—The Congress finds that the growth in size, scope, and numbers of employee benefit plans in recent years has been rapid and substantial; that the operational scope and economic impact of such plans is increasingly interstate; that the continued well-being and security of millions of employees and their dependents are directly affected by these plans; that they are affected with a national public interest; that they have become an important factor affecting the stability of employment and the successful development of industrial relations; that they have become an important factor in commerce because of the interstate character of their activities, and of the activities of their participants, and the employers, employee organizations, and other entities by which they are established or maintained; that a large volume of the activities of such plans is carried on by means of the mails and instrumentalities of interstate commerce; that owing to the lack of employee information and adequate safeguards concerning their operation, it is desirable in the interests of employees and their beneficiaries, and to provide for the general welfare and the free flow of commerce, that disclosure be made and safeguards be provided with respect to the establishment, operation, and administration of such plans; that they substantially affect the revenues of the United States because they are afforded preferential Federal tax treatment; that despite the enormous growth in such plans many employees with long years of employment are losing anticipated retirement benefits owing to the lack of vesting provisions in such plans; that owing to the inadequacy of current minimum standards, the soundness and stability of plans with respect to adequate funds to pay promised benefits may be endangered; that owing to the termination of plans before requisite funds have been accumulated, employees and their beneficiaries have been deprived of anticipated benefits; and that it is therefore desirable in the interests of employees and their beneficiaries, for the protection of the revenue of the United States, and to provide for the free flow of commerce, that minimum standards be provided assuring the equitable character of such plans and their financial soundness.

(b) Protection of Interstate Commerce and Beneficiaries by Reporting Disclosure and Reporting, Setting Standards of Conduct, etc., for Fiduciaries.—It is hereby declared to be the policy of this chapter to protect interstate commerce and the interests of participants in employee benefit plans and their beneficiaries, by requiring the disclosure and reporting to participants and beneficiaries of financial and other information with respect thereto, by establishing standards of conduct, responsibility, and obligation for fiduciaries of employee benefit plans, and by providing for appropriate remedies, sanctions, and ready access to the Federal courts.

(c) Protection of Interstate Commerce, the Federal Taxing Power, and Beneficiaries by Vesting of Accrued Benefits, Setting Minimum Standards of Funding, Requiring Termination Insurance.—It is hereby further declared to be the policy of this chapter to protect interstate commerce, the Federal taxing power, and the interests of participants in private pension plans and their beneficiaries by improving the equitable character and the soundness of such plans by requiring them to vest the accrued benefits of employees with significant periods of service, to meet minimum standards of funding, and by requiring plan termination insurance.

29 USC SEC. 1001a. ADDITIONAL CONGRESSIONAL FINDINGS AND DECLARATION OF POLICY.

(a) Effects of multiemployer pension plans.—The Congress finds that—

(1) multiemployer pension plans have a substantial impact on interstate commerce and are affected with a national public interest;

(2) multiemployer pension plans have accounted for a substantial portion of the increase in private pension plan coverage over the past three decades;

(3) the continued well-being and security of millions of employees, retirees, and their dependents are directly affected by multiemployer pension plans; and

(4)(A) withdrawals of contributing employers from a multiemployer pension plan frequently result in substantially increased funding obligations for employers who continue to contribute to the plan, adversely affecting the plan, its participants and beneficiaries, and labor-management relations, and

(B) in a declining industry, the incidence of employer withdrawals is higher and the adverse effects described in subparagraph (A) are exacerbated.

(b) Modification of multiemployer plan termination insurance provisions and replacement of program.—The Congress further finds that—

(1) it is desirable to modify the current multiemployer plan termination insurance provisions in order to increase the likelihood of protecting plan participants against benefit losses; and

(2) it is desirable to replace the termination insurance program for multiemployer pension plans with an insolvency-based benefit protection program that will enhance the financial soundness of such plans, place primary emphasis on plan continuation, and contain program costs within reasonable limits.

(c) Policy.—It is hereby declared to be the policy of this Act—

(1) to foster and facilitate interstate commerce,

(2) to alleviate certain problems which tend to discourage the maintenance and growth of multiemployer pension plans,

(3) to provide reasonable protection for the interests of participants and beneficiaries of financially distressed multiemployer pension plans, and

(4) to provide a financially self-sufficient program for the guarantee of employee benefits under multiemployer plans.

Amendments to 29 USC §1001a
Multiemployer Pension Plan Amendments Act of 1980 (Pub. L. No. 96-364), as follows:
- 29 USC §1001a was added by Act §3. Eff. Sept. 26, 1980. *Note:* 29 USC §1001a was enacted as part of the Multiemployer Pension Plan Amendments Act of 1980, and not as part of the Employee Retirement Income Security Act of 1974.

---

29 USC SEC. 1001b. FINDINGS AND DECLARATION OF POLICY.

(a) Findings.—The Congress finds that—

(1) single-employer defined benefit pension plans have a substantial impact on interstate commerce and are affected with a national interest;

(2) the continued well-being and retirement income security of millions of workers, retirees, and their dependents are directly affected by such plans;

(3) the existence of a sound termination insurance system is fundamental to the retirement income security of participants and beneficiaries of such plans; and

(4) the current termination insurance system in some instances encourages employers to terminate pension plans, evade their obligations to pay benefits, and shift unfunded pension liabilities onto the termination insurance system and the other premium-payers.

(b) Additional findings.—The Congress further finds that modification of the current termination insurance system and an increase in the insurance premium for single-employer defined benefit pension plans—

(1) is desirable to increase the likelihood that full benefits will be paid to participants and beneficiaries of such plans;

(2) is desirable to provide for the transfer of liabilities to the termination insurance system only in cases of severe hardship;

(3) is necessary to maintain the premium costs of such system at a reasonable level; and

(4) is necessary to finance properly current funding deficiencies and future obligations of the single-employer pension plan termination insurance system.

(c) Declaration of policy.—It is hereby declared to be the policy of this title—

(1) to foster and facilitate interstate commerce;

(2) to encourage the maintenance and growth of single-employer defined benefit pension plans;

(3) to increase the likelihood that participants and beneficiaries under single-employer defined benefit pension plans will receive their full benefits;

(4) to provide for the transfer of unfunded pension liabilities onto the single-employer pension plan termination insurance system only in cases of severe hardship;

(5) to maintain the premium costs of such system at a reasonable level; and

(6) to assure the prudent financing of current funding deficiencies and future obligations of the single-employer pension plan termination insurance system by increasing termination insurance premiums.

Amendments to 29 USC §1001b
Single-Employer Pension Plan Amendments Act of 1986 (Pub. L. No. 99-272), as follows:
• 29 USC §1001b was added by Act §11002. Eff. Jan. 1, 1986, with some exceptions. *Note:* 29 USC §1001b was enacted as part of the Multiemployer Pension Plan Amendments Act of 1980, and not as part of the Employee Retirement Income Security Act of 1974.

SEC. 3. DEFINITIONS.

For purposes of this title:

(1) The terms "employee welfare benefit plan" and "welfare plan" mean any plan, fund, or program which was heretofore or is hereafter established or maintained by an employer or by an employee organization, or by both, to the extent that such plan, fund, or program was established or is maintained for the purpose of providing for its participants or their beneficiaries, through the purchase of insurance or otherwise, (A) medical, surgical, or hospital care or benefits, or benefits in the event of sickness, accident, disability, death or unemployment, or vacation benefits, apprenticeship or other training programs, or day care centers, scholarship funds, or prepaid legal services, or (B) any benefit described in section 302(c) of the Labor Management Relations Act, 1947 (other than pensions on retirement or death, and insurance to provide such pensions).

(2)(A) Except as provided in subparagraph (B), the terms "employee pension benefit plan" and "pension plan" mean any plan, fund, or program which was heretofore or is hereafter established or maintained by an employer or by an employee organization, or by both, to the extent that by its express terms or as a result of surrounding circumstances such plan, fund, or program—

(i) provides retirement income to employees, or

(ii) results in a deferral of income by employees for periods extending to the termination of covered employment or beyond, regardless of the method of calculating the contributions made to the plan, the method of calculating the benefits

under the plan or the method of distributing benefits from the plan.

A distribution from a plan, fund, or program shall not be treated as made in a form other than retirement income or as a distribution prior to termination of covered employment solely because such distribution is made to an employee who has attained age 62 and who is not separated from employment at the time of such distribution.

(B) The Secretary may by regulation prescribe rules consistent with the standards and purposes of this chapter providing one or more exempt categories under which—

(i) severance pay arrangements, and

(ii) supplemental retirement income payments, under which the pension benefits of retirees or their beneficiaries are supplemented to take into account some portion or all of the increases in the cost of living (as determined by the Secretary of Labor) since retirement, shall, for purposes of this title, be treated as welfare plans rather than pension plans. In the case of any arrangement or payment a principal effect of which is the evasion of the standards or purposes of this Act applicable to pension plans, such arrangement or payment shall be treated as a pension plan.

An applicable voluntary early retirement incentive plan (as defined in section 457(e)(11)(D)(ii) of the Internal Revenue Code of 1986) making payments or supplements described in section 457(e)(11)(D)(i) of such Code, and an applicable employment retention plan (as defined in section 457(f)(4)(C) of such Code) making payments of benefits described in section 457(f)(4)(A) of such Code, shall, for purposes of this title, be treated as a welfare plan (and not a pension plan) with respect to such payments and supplements.

(3) The term "employee benefit plan" or "plan" means an employee welfare benefit plan or an employee pension benefit plan or a plan which is both an employee welfare benefit plan and an employee pension benefit plan.

(4) The term "employee organization" means any labor union or any organization of any kind, or any agency or employee representation committee, association, group, or plan, in which employees participate and which exists for the purpose, in whole or in part, of dealing with employers concerning an employee benefit plan, or other matters incidental to employment relationships; or any employees' beneficiary association organized for the purpose in whole or in part, of establishing such a plan.

(5) The term "employer" means any person acting directly as an employer, or indirectly in the interest of an employer, in relation to an employee benefit plan; and includes a group or association of employers acting for an employer in such capacity.

(6) The term "employee" means any individual employed by an employer.

(7) The term "participant" means any employee or former employee of an employer, or any member or former member of an employee organization, who is or may become eligible to receive a benefit of any type from an employee benefit plan which covers employees of such employer or members of such organization, or whose beneficiaries may be eligible to receive any such benefit.

(8) The term "beneficiary" means a person designated by a participant, or by the terms of an employee benefit plan, who is or may become entitled to a benefit thereunder.

(9) The term "person" means an individual, partnership, joint venture, corporation, mutual company, joint-stock company, trust, estate, unincorporated organization, association, or employee organization.

(10) The term "State" includes any State of the United States, the District of Columbia, Puerto Rico, the Virgin Islands, American Samoa, Guam, Wake Island, and the Canal Zone. The term "United States" when used in the geographic sense means the States and the Outer Continental Shelf lands defined in the Outer Continental Shelf Lands Act (43 U.S.C. 1331-1343).

(11) The term "commerce" means trade, traffic, commerce, transportation, or communication between any State and any place outside thereof.

(12) The term "industry or activity affecting commerce" means any activity, business, or industry in commerce or in which a labor dispute would hinder or obstruct commerce or the free flow of commerce, and includes any activity or industry "affecting commerce" within the meaning of the Labor Management Relations Act, 1947, or the Railway Labor Act.

(13) The term "Secretary" means the Secretary of Labor.

(14) The term "party in interest" means, as to an employee benefit plan—

(A) any fiduciary (including, but not limited to, any administrator, officer, trustee, or custodian), counsel, or employee of such employee benefit plan;

(B) a person providing services to such plan;

(C) an employer any of whose employees are covered by such plan;

(D) an employee organization any of whose members are covered by such plan;

(E) an owner, direct or indirect, of 50 percent or more of—

(i) the combined voting power of all classes of stock entitled to vote or the total value of shares of all classes of stock of a corporation.[,]

(ii) the capital interest or the profits interest of a partnership, or

(iii) the beneficial interest of a trust or unincorporated enterprise, which is an employer or an employee organization described in subparagraph (C) or (D);

(F) a relative (as defined in paragraph (15)) of any individual described in subparagraph (A), (B), (C), or (E);

(G) a corporation, partnership, or trust or estate of which (or in which) 50 percent or more of—

(i) the combined voting power of all classes of stock entitled to vote or the total value of shares of all classes of stock of such corporation,

(ii) the capital interest or profits interest of such partnership, or

(iii) the beneficial interest of such trust or estate,

is owned directly or indirectly, or held by persons described in subparagraph (A), (B), (C), (D), or (E);

(H) an employee, officer, director (or an individual having powers or responsibilities similar to those of officers or directors), or a 10 percent or more shareholder directly or indirectly, of a person described in subparagraph (B), (C), (D), (E), or (G), or of the employee benefit plan; or

(I) a 10 percent or more (directly or indirectly in capital or profits) partner or joint venturer of a person described in subparagraph (B), (C), (D), (E), or (G).

The Secretary, after consultation and coordination with the Secretary of the Treasury, may by regulation prescribe a percentage lower than 50 percent for subparagraph (E) and (G) and lower than 10 percent for subparagraph (H) or (I). The Secretary may prescribe regulations for determining the ownership (direct or indirect) of profits and beneficial interests, and the manner in which indirect stockholdings are taken into account. Any person who is a party in interest with respect to a plan to which a trust described in section 501(c)(22) of title 26 is permitted to make payments under section 4223 shall be treated as a party in interest with respect to such trust.

(15) The term "relative" means a spouse, ancestor, lineal descendant, or spouse of a lineal descendant.

(16)(A) The term "administrator" means—

(i) the person specifically so designated by the terms of the instrument under which the plan is operated;

(ii) if an administrator is not so designated, the plan sponsor; or

(iii) in the case of a plan for which an administrator is not designated and a plan sponsor cannot be identified, such other person as the Secretary may by regulation prescribe.

(B) The term "plan sponsor" means—

(i) the employer in the case of an employee benefit plan established or maintained by a single employer,

(ii) the employee organization in the case of a plan established or maintained by an employee organization, or

(iii) in the case of a plan established or maintained by two or more employers or jointly by one or more employers and one or more employee organizations, the association, committee, joint board of trustees, or other similar group of representatives of the parties who establish or maintain the plan.

(17) The term "separate account" means an account established or maintained by an insurance company under which income, gains, and losses, whether or not realized, from assets allocated to such account, are, in accordance with the applicable contract, credited to or charged against such account without regard to other income, gains, or losses of the insurance company.

(18) The term "adequate consideration" when used in part 4 of subtitle B means (A) in the case of a security for which there is a generally recognized market, either (i) the price of the security prevailing on a national securities exchange which is registered under section 6 of the Securities Exchange Act of 1934, or (ii) if the security is not traded on such a national securities exchange, a price not less favorable to the plan than the offering price for the security as established by the current bid and asked prices quoted by persons independent of the issuer and of any party in interest; and (B) in the case of an asset other than a security for which there is a generally recognized market, the fair market value of the asset as determined in good faith by the trustee or named fiduciary pursuant to the terms of the plan and in accordance with regulations promulgated by the Secretary.

(19) The term "nonforfeitable" when used with respect to a pension benefit or right means a claim obtained by a participant or his beneficiary to that part of an immediate or deferred benefit under a pension plan which arises from the participant's service, which is unconditional, and which is legally enforceable against the plan. For purposes of this paragraph, a right to an accrued benefit derived from employer contributions shall not be treated as forfeitable merely because the plan contains a provision described in section 203(a)(3).

(20) The term "security" has the same meaning as such term has under section 2(1) of the Securities Act of 1933 (15 U.S.C. 77b(1)).

(21)(A) Except as otherwise provided in subparagraph (B), a person is a fiduciary with respect to a plan to the extent (i) he exercises any discretionary authority or discretionary control respecting management of such plan or exercises any authority or control respecting management or disposition of its assets, (ii) he renders investment advice for a fee or other compensation, direct or indirect, with respect to any moneys or other property of such plan, or has any authority or responsibility to do so, or (iii) he has any discretionary authority or discretionary responsibility in the administration of such plan. Such term includes any person designated under section 405(c)(1)(B).

(B) If any money or other property of an employee benefit plan is invested in securities issued by an investment company registered under the Investment Company Act of 1940, such investment shall not by itself cause such investment company or such investment company's investment adviser or principal underwriter to be deemed to be a fiduciary or a party in interest as those terms are defined in this title, except insofar as such investment company or its investment adviser or principal underwriter acts in connection with an employee benefit plan covering employees of the investment company, the investment adviser, or its principal underwriter. Nothing contained in this subparagraph shall limit the duties imposed on such investment company, investment adviser, or principal underwriter by any other law.

(22) The term "normal retirement benefit" means the greater of the early retirement benefit under the plan, or the benefit under the plan commencing at normal retirement age. The normal retirement benefit shall be determined without regard to—

(A) medical benefits, and

(B) disability benefits not in excess of the qualified disability benefit.

For purposes of this paragraph, a qualified disability benefit is a disability benefit provided by a plan which does not exceed the benefit which would be provided for the participant if he separated from the service at normal retirement age. For purposes of this paragraph, the early retirement benefit under a plan shall be determined without regard to any benefit under the plan which the Secretary of the Treasury finds to be a benefit described in section 204(b)(1)(G).

(23) The term "accrued benefit" means—

(A) in the case of a defined benefit plan, the individual's accrued benefit determined under the plan and, except as provided in section 204(c)(3), expressed in the form of an annual benefit commencing at normal retirement age, or

(B) in the case of a plan which is an individual account plan, the balance of the individual's account.

The accrued benefit of an employee shall not be less than the amount determined under section 204(c)(2)(B) with respect to the employee's accumulated contribution.

(24) The term "normal retirement age" means the earlier of—

(A) the time a plan participant attains normal retirement age under the plan, or

(B) the later of—

(i) the time a plan participant attains age 65, or

(ii) the 5th anniversary of the time a plan participant commenced participation in the plan.

(25) The term "vested liabilities" means the present value of the immediate or deferred benefits available at normal retirement age for participants and their beneficiaries which are nonforfeitable.

(26) The term "current value" means fair market value where available and otherwise the fair value as determined in good faith by a trustee or a named fiduciary (as defined in section 402(a)(2)) pursuant to the terms of the plan and in accordance with regulations of the Secretary, assuming an orderly liquidation at the time of such determination.

(27) The term "present value", with respect to a liability, means the value adjusted to reflect anticipated events. Such adjustments shall conform to such regulations as the Secretary of the Treasury may prescribe.

(28) The term "normal service cost" or "normal cost" means the annual cost of future pension benefits and administrative expenses assigned, under an actuarial cost method, to years subsequent to a particular valuation date of a pension plan. The Secretary of the Treasury may prescribe regulations to carry out this paragraph.

(29) The term "accrued liability" means the excess of the present value, as of a particular valuation date of a pension plan, of the projected future benefits cost and administrative expenses for all plan participants and beneficiaries over the present value of future contributions for the normal cost of all applicable plan participants and beneficiaries. The Secretary of the Treasury may prescribe regulations to carry out this paragraph.

(30) The term "unfunded accrued liability" means the excess of the accrued liability, under an actuarial cost method which so provides, over the present value of the assets of a pension plan. The Secretary of the Treasury may prescribe regulations to carry out this paragraph.

(31) The term "advance funding actuarial cost method" or "actuarial cost method" means a recognized actuarial technique utilized for establishing the amount and incidence of the annual actuarial cost of pension plan benefits and expenses. Acceptable actuarial cost methods shall include the accrued benefit cost method (unit credit method), the entry age normal cost method, the individual level premium cost method, the aggregate cost method, the attained age normal cost method, and the frozen initial liability cost method. The terminal funding cost method and the current funding (pay-as-you-go) cost method are not acceptable actuarial cost methods. The Secretary of the Treasury shall issue regulations to further define acceptable actuarial cost methods.

(32) The term "governmental plan" means a plan established or maintained for its employees by the Government of the United States, by the government of any State or political subdivision thereof, or by any agency or instrumentality of any of the foregoing. The term "governmental plan" also includes any plan to which the Railroad Retirement Act of 1935 or 1937 applies, and which is financed by contributions required under that Act and any plan of an international organization which is exempt from taxation under the provisions of the International Organizations Immunities Act (59 Stat. 669). The term "governmental plan" includes a plan which is established and maintained by an Indian tribal government (as defined in section 7701(a)(40)), a subdivision of an Indian tribal government (determined in accordance with section 7871(d)), or an agency or instrumentality of either, and all of the participants of which are employees of such entity substantially all of whose services as such an employee are in the performance of essential governmental functions but not in the performance of commercial activities (whether or not an essential government function)[.]

(33)(A) The term "church plan" means a plan established and maintained (to the extent required in clause (ii) of subparagraph (B)) for its employees (or their beneficiaries) by a church or by a convention or association of churches which is exempt from tax under section 501 of title 26.

(B) The term "church plan" does not include a plan—

(i) which is established and maintained primarily for the benefit of employees (or their beneficiaries) of such church or convention or association of churches who are employed in connection with one or more unrelated trades or businesses (within the meaning of section 513 of title 26), or

(ii) if less than substantially all of the individuals included in the plan are individuals described in subparagraph (A) or in clause (ii) of subparagraph (C) (or their beneficiaries).

(C) For purposes of this paragraph—

(i) A plan established and maintained for its employees (or their beneficiaries) by a church or by a convention or association of churches includes a plan maintained by an organization, whether a civil law corporation or otherwise, the principal purpose or function of which is the administration or funding of a plan or program for the provision of retirement benefits or welfare benefits, or both, for the employees of a church or a convention or association of churches, if such organization is controlled by or associated with a church or a convention or association of churches.

(ii) The term employee of a church or a convention or association of churches includes—

(I) a duly ordained, commissioned, or licensed minister of a church in the exercise of his ministry, regardless of the source of his compensation;

(II) an employee of an organization, whether a civil law corporation or otherwise, which is exempt from tax under section 501 of title 26 and which is controlled by or associated with a church or a convention or association of churches; and

(III) an individual described in clause (v).

(iii) A church or a convention or association of churches which is exempt from tax under section 501 of title 26 shall be deemed the employer of any individual included as an employee under clause (ii).

(iv) An organization, whether a civil law corporation or otherwise, is associated with a church or a convention or association of churches if it shares common religious bonds and convictions with that church or convention or association of churches.

(v) If an employee who is included in a church plan separates from the service of a church or a convention or association of churches or an organization, whether a civil law corporation or otherwise, which is exempt from tax under section 501 of title 26 and which is controlled by or associated with a church or a convention or association of churches, the church plan shall not fail to meet the requirements of this paragraph merely because the plan—

(I) retains the employee's accrued benefit or account for the payment of benefits to the employee or his beneficiaries pursuant to the terms of the plan; or

(II) receives contributions on the employee's behalf after the employee's separation from such service, but only for a period of 5 years after such separation, unless the employee is disabled (within the meaning of the disability provisions of the church plan or, if there are no such provisions in the church plan, within the meaning of section 72(m)(7) of title 26 at the time of such separation from service.

(D)(i) If a plan established and maintained for its employees (or their beneficiaries) by a church or by a convention or association of churches which is exempt from tax under section 501 of title 26 fails to meet one or more of the requirements of this paragraph and corrects its failure to meet such requirements within the correction period, the plan shall be deemed to meet the requirements of this paragraph for the year in which the correction was made and for all prior years.

(ii) If a correction is not made within the correction period, the plan shall be deemed not to meet the requirements of this paragraph beginning with the date on which the earliest failure to meet one or more of such requirements occurred.

(iii) For purposes of this subparagraph, the term "correction period" means—

(I) the period ending 270 days after the date of mailing by the Secretary of the Treasury of a notice of default with respect to the plan's failure to meet one or more of the requirements of this paragraph; or

(II) any period set by a court of competent jurisdiction after a final determination that the plan fails to meet such requirements, or, if the court does not specify such period, any reasonable period determined by the Secretary of the Treasury on the basis of all the facts and circumstances, but in any event not less than 270 days after the determination has become final; or

(III) any additional period which the Secretary of the Treasury determines is reasonable or necessary for the correction of the default, whichever has the latest ending date.

(34) The term "individual account plan" or "defined contribution plan" means a pension plan which provides for an individual account for each participant and for benefits based solely upon the amount contributed to the participant's account, and any income, expenses, gains, and losses, and any forfeitures of accounts of other participants which may be allocated to such participant's account.

(35) The term "defined benefit plan" means a pension plan other than an individual account plan; except that a pension plan which is not an individual account plan and which provides a benefit derived from employer contributions which is based partly on the balance of the separate account of a participant—

(A) for the purposes of section 202, shall be treated as an individual account plan, and

(B) for the purposes of paragraph (23) of this section and section 204, shall be treated as an individual account plan to the extent benefits are based upon the separate account of a participant and as a defined benefit plan with respect to the remaining portion of benefits under the plan.

(36) The term "excess benefit plan" means a plan maintained by an employer solely for the purpose of providing benefits for certain employees in excess of the limitations on contributions and benefits imposed by section 415 of title 26 on plans to which that section applies, without regard to whether the plan is funded. To the extent that a separable part of a plan (as determined by the Secretary of Labor) maintained

by an employer is maintained for such purpose, that part shall be treated as a separate plan which is an excess benefit plan.

(37)(A) The term "multiemployer plan" means a plan—

(i) to which more than one employer is required to contribute,

(ii) which is maintained pursuant to one or more collective bargaining agreements between one or more employee organizations and more than one employer, and

(iii) which satisfies such other requirements as the Secretary may prescribe by regulation.

(B) For purposes of this paragraph, all trades or businesses (whether or not incorporated) which are under common control within the meaning of section 4001(b)(1) are considered a single employer.

(C) Notwithstanding subparagraph (A), a plan is a multiemployer plan on and after its termination date if the plan was a multiemployer plan under this paragraph for the plan year preceding its termination date.

(D) For purposes of this title, notwithstanding the preceding provisions of this paragraph, for any plan year which began before the date of the enactment of the Multiemployer Pension Plan Amendments Act of 1980, the term "multiemployer plan" means a plan described in section 3(37) of this Act as in effect immediately before such date.

(E) Within one year after the date of the enactment of the Multiemployer Pension Plan Amendments Act of 1980 [enacted Sept. 26, 1980], a multiemployer plan may irrevocably elect, pursuant to procedures established by the corporation and subject to the provisions of sections 4403[4303](b) and (c), that the plan shall not be treated as a multiemployer plan for all purposes under this chapter or the Internal Revenue Code of 1954 if for each of the last 3 plan years ending prior to the effective date of the Multiemployer Pension Plan Amendments Act of 1980—

(i) the plan was not a multiemployer plan because the plan was not a plan described in section 3(37)(A)(iii) of this Act and section 414(f)(1)(C) of the Internal Revenue Code of 1954 (as such provisions were in effect on the day before the date of the enactment of the Multiemployer Pension Plan Amendments Act of 1980 [enacted Sept. 26, 1980]); and

(ii) the plan had been identified as a plan that was not a multiemployer plan in substantially all its filings with the corporation, the Secretary of Labor and the Secretary of the Treasury.

(F)(i) For purposes of this title a qualified football coaches plan—

(I) shall be treated as a multiemployer plan to the extent not inconsistent with the purposes of this subparagraph; and

(II) notwithstanding section 401(k)(4)(B) of the Internal Revenue Code of 1986 may include a qualified cash and deferred arrangement.

(ii) For purposes of this subparagraph, the term "qualified football coaches plan" means any defined contribution plan which is established and maintained by an organization—

(I) which is described in section 501(c) of such Code;

(II) the membership of which consists entirely of individuals who primarily coach football as full-time employees of 4-year colleges or universities described in section 170(b)(1)(A)(ii) of such Code; and

(III) which was in existence on September 18, 1986.

(G)(i) Within 1 year after the enactment of the Pension Protection Act of 2006—

(I) an election under subparagraph (E) may be revoked, pursuant to procedures prescribed by the Pension Benefit Guaranty Corporation, if, for each of the 3 plan years prior to the date of the enactment of that Act, the plan would have been a multiemployer plan but for the election under subparagraph (E), and

(II) a plan that meets the criteria in clauses (i) and (ii) of subparagraph (A) of this paragraph or that is described in clause (vi) may, pursuant to procedures prescribed by the Pension Benefit Guaranty Corporation, elect to be a multiemployer plan, if—

(aa) for each of the 3 plan years immediately preceding the first plan year for which the election under this paragraph is effective with respect to the plan, the plan has met those criteria or is so described,

(bb) substantially all of the plan's employer contributions for each of those plan years were made or required to be made by organizations that were exempt from tax under section 501 of the Internal Revenue Code of 1986, and

(cc) the plan was established prior to September 2, 1974.

(ii) An election under this subparagraph shall be effective for all purposes under this Act and under the Internal Revenue Code of 1986, starting with any plan year beginning on or after January 1, 1999, and ending before January 1, 2008, as designated by the plan in the election made under clause (i)(II).

(iii) Once made, an election under this subparagraph shall be irrevocable, except that a plan described in clause (i)(II) shall cease to be a multiemployer plan as of the plan year beginning immediately after the first plan year for which the majority of its employer contributions were made or required to be made by organizations that were not exempt from tax under section 501 of the Internal Revenue Code of 1986.

(iv) The fact that a plan makes an election under clause (i)(II) does not imply that the plan was not a multiemployer plan prior to the date of the election or would not be a multiemployer plan without regard to the election.

(v)(I) No later than 30 days before an election is made under this subparagraph, the plan administrator shall provide notice of the pending election to each plan participant and beneficiary, each labor organization representing such participants or beneficiaries, and each employer that has an obligation to contribute to the plan, describing the principal differences between the guarantee programs under title IV and the benefit restrictions under this title for single employer and multiemployer plans, along with such other information as the plan administrator chooses to include.

(II) Within 180 days after the date of enactment of the Pension Protection Act of 2006, the Secretary shall prescribe a model notice under this clause.

(III) A plan administrator's failure to provide the notice required under this subparagraph shall be treated for purposes of section 502(c)(2) as a failure or refusal by the plan administrator to file the annual report required to be filed with the Secretary under section 101(b)(1).

(vi) A plan is described in this clause if it is a plan sponsored by an organization which is described in section 501(c)(5) of the Internal Revenue Code of 1986 and exempt from tax under section 501(a) of such Code and which was established in Chicago, Illinois, on August 12, 1881.

(vii) For purposes of this Act and the Internal Revenue Code of 1986, a plan making an election under this subparagraph shall be treated as maintained pursuant to a collective bargaining agreement if a collective bargaining agreement, expressly or otherwise, provides for or permits employer contributions to the plan by one or more employers that are signatory to such agreement, or participation in the plan by one or more employees of an employer that is signatory to such agreement, regardless of whether the plan was created, established, or maintained for such employees by virtue of another document that is not a collective bargaining agreement.

(38) The term "investment manager" means any fiduciary (other than a trustee or named fiduciary, as defined in section 402(a)(2))—

(A) who has the power to manage, acquire, or dispose of any asset of a plan;

(B) who (i) is registered as an investment adviser under the Investment Advisers Act of 1940; (ii) is not registered as an investment adviser under such Act by reason of paragraph (1) of section 203(A)(a) of such Act, is registered as an investment adviser under the laws of the State (referred to in such paragraph (1)) in which it maintains its principal office and place of business, and, at the time the fiduciary last filed the registration form most recently filed by the fiduciary with such State in order to maintain the fiduciary's registration under the laws of such State, also filed a copy of such form with the Secretary; (iii) is a bank, as defined in that Act; or (iv) is an insurance company qualified to perform services described in subparagraph (A) under the laws of more than one State; and

(C) has acknowledged in writing that he is a fiduciary with respect to the plan.

(39) The terms "plan year" and "fiscal year of the plan" mean, with respect to a plan, the calendar, policy, or fiscal year on which the records of the plan are kept.

(40)(A) The term "multiple employer welfare arrangement" means an employee welfare benefit plan, or any other arrangement (other than an employee welfare benefit plan), which is established or maintained for the purpose of offering or providing any benefit described in paragraph (1) to the employees of two or more employers (including one or more self-employed individuals), or to their beneficiaries, except that such term does not include any such plan or other arrangement which is established or maintained—

(i) under or pursuant to one or more agreements which the Secretary finds to be collective bargaining agreements,

(ii) by a rural electric cooperative, or

(iii) by a rural telephone cooperative association.

(B) For purposes of this paragraph—

(i) two or more trades or businesses, whether or not incorporated, shall be deemed a single employer if such trades or businesses are within the same control group,

(ii) the term "control group" means a group of trades or businesses under common control,

(iii) the determination of whether a trade or business is under "common control" with another trade or business shall be determined under regulations of the Secretary applying principles similar to the principles applied in determining whether employees of two or more trades or businesses are treated as employed by a single employer under section 4001(b), except that, for purposes of this paragraph, common control shall not be based on an interest of less than 25 percent,

(iv) the term "rural electric cooperative" means—

(I) any organization which is exempt from tax under section 501(a) of title 26 and which is engaged primarily in providing electric service on a mutual or cooperative basis, and

(II) any organization described in paragraph (4) or (6) of section 501(c) of title 26 which is exempt from tax under section 501(a) of title 26 and at least 80 percent of the members of which are organizations described in subclause (I), and

(v) the term "rural telephone cooperative association" means an organization described in paragraph (4) or (6) of section 501(c) of title 26 which is exempt from tax under section 501(a) of title 26 and at least 80 percent of the members of which are organizations engaged primarily in providing telephone service to rural areas of the United States on a mutual, cooperative, or other basis.

(41) Single-Employer Plan.—The term "single-employer plan" means an employee benefit plan other than a multiemployer plan.

(41)[42] The term "single-employer plan" means a plan which is not a multiemployer plan.

(42)[43] the term "plan assets" means plan assets as defined by such regulations as the Secretary may prescribe, except that under such regulations the assets of any entity shall not be treated as plan assets if, immediately after the most recent acquisition of any equity interest in the entity, less than 25 percent of the total value of each class of equity interest in the entity is held by benefit plan investors. For purposes of determinations pursuant to this paragraph, the value of any equity interest held by a person (other than such a benefit plan investor) who has discretionary authority or control with respect to the assets of the entity or any person who provides investment advice for a fee (direct or indirect) with respect to such assets, or any affiliate of such a person, shall be disregarded for purposes of calculating the 25 percent threshold. An entity shall be considered to hold plan assets only to the extent of the percentage of the equity interest held by benefit plan investors. For purposes of this paragraph, the term "benefit plan investor" means an employee benefit plan subject to part 4, any plan to which section 4975 of the Internal Revenue Code of 1986 applies, and any entity whose underlying assets include plan assets by reason of a plan's investment in such entity.

Amendments to ERISA §3
Worker, Retiree, and Employer Recovery Act of 2008 (Pub. L. No. 110-458), as follows:

● ERISA §3(37)(G) was amended by Act §111(c) by striking "paragraph" in cls. (ii), (iii), and (v)(I) and inserting "subparagraph"; striking "subclause (i)(II)" in cl. (iii) and inserting "clause (i)(II)"; striking "subparagraph" in cl. (v)(II) and inserting "clause"; and by striking "section 101(b)(4)" in cl. (v)(III) and inserting "section 101(b)(1)". Eff. Aug 17, 2006, as if included in §1106 of Pub. L. No. 109-280.

Small Business and Work Opportunity Tax Act of 2007 (Pub. L. No. 110-28), as follows:

● ERISA §3(37)(G) was amended by Act §6611(a)(1) and (b)(1) in subsec. (G)(i)(II)(aa) by deleting "for each of the 3 plan years immediately before the date of the enactment of the Pension Protection Act of 2006," and adding "for each of the 3 plan years immediately preceding the first plan year for which the election under this paragraph is effective with respect to the plan,"; in subsec. (G)(ii) by deleting "starting with the first plan year ending after the date of the enactment of the Pension Protection Act of 2006.", and adding "starting with any plan year beginning on or after January 1, 1999, and ending before January 1, 2008, as designated by the plan in the election made under clause (i)(II)."; in subsec. (G)(vi), by deleting "is a plan—(I) that was established in Chicago, Illinois, on August 12, 1881; and (II) sponsored by an organization described in §501(c)(5) of the Internal Revenue Code of 1986 and exempt from tax under §501(a) of such Code."; and adding "if it is a plan sponsored by an organization which is described in §501(c)(5) of the Internal Revenue Code of 1986 and exempt from tax under §501(a) of such Code and which was established in Chicago, Illinois, on August 12, 1881"; and adding "(vii) For purposes of this Act and the Internal Revenue Code of 1986, a plan making an election under this subparagraph shall be treated as maintained pursuant to a collective bargaining agreement if a collective bargaining agreement, expressly or otherwise, provides for or permits employer contributions to the plan by one or more employers that are signatory to such agreement, or participation in the plan by one or more employees of an employer that is signatory to such agreement, regardless of whether the plan was created, established, or maintained for such employees by virtue of another document that is not a collective bargaining agreement." Eff. Aug. 17, 2006, as if included in Pub. L. No. 109-280.

Pension Protection Act of 2006 (Pub. L. No. 109-280), as follows:

● ERISA §3(2)(A) was amended by Act §905(a) by adding a new sentence at the end. Eff. for distributions in plan years beginning after Dec. 31, 2006.

● ERISA §3(2)(B) was amended by Act §1104(c) by adding a new sentence at the end. Eff. for plan years ending after Aug. 17, 2006.

● ERISA §3(32) was amended by Act §906(a)(2)(A) by adding a new sentence at the end. Eff. for plan years beginning on or after Aug. 17, 2006.

● ERISA §3(37)(G) was added by Act §1106(a). Eff. Aug. 17, 2006.

● ERISA §3(42) was added by Act §611(f). Eff. for transactions occuring after Aug. 17, 2006.

● **Other Provision.** Act §1104(d)(4) provides:

(4) Construction.—Nothing in the amendments made by this section shall alter or affect the construction of the Internal Revenue Code of 1986, the Employee Retirement Income Security Act of 1974, or the Age Discrimination in Employment Act of 1967 as applied to any plan, arrangement, or conduct to which such amendments do not apply.

ERISA Amendments of 1997 (Pub. L. No. 105-72), as follows:

● ERISA §3(38)(B) was amended by adding introductory provisions and cls. (i) and (ii); redesignating former cl. (ii) and (iii) as (iii) and (iv), respectively; and striking former introductory provisions and cl. (i), which read as follows: "who is (i) registered as an investment adviser under the Investment Advisers Act of 1940 or under the laws of any State;". Eff. July 8, 1997.

National Securities Markets Improvement Act of 1996 (Pub. L. No. 104-290), as follows:

● ERISA §3(38)(B) was amended by Act §308(b) by temporarily inserting "or under the laws of any State" after "1940" and before "; (ii) is a bank,". Eff. 270 days after Oct. 11, 1996, but ending two years after Oct. 11, 1996. Superseded by Pub. L. No. 105-72.

Rural Telephone Cooperative Associations ERISA Amendments Act of 1991 (Pub. L. No. 102-89), as follows:

● ERISA §3(40)(A)(iii) and (B)(v) was amended by Act §2 by adding cl. (iii) at the end of subparagraph (A), and cl. (v) at the end of subpara. (B). Eff. Aug. 14, 1991.

Omnibus Budget Reconciliation Act of 1990 (Pub. L. No. 101-508), as follows:

● ERISA §3(41) was added by Act §12002(b)(2)(C). Eff. Oct. 1, 1990.

Omnibus Budget Reconciliation Act of 1989 (Pub. L. No. 101-239), as follows:

● ERISA §3(14), 3(33), 3(36), 3(40)(B)(iv) were amended by Act §7891(a)(1) substituting "Internal Revenue Code of 1986" for "Internal Revenue Code of 1954", which for purposes of codification was translated as "title 26". Eff. as if included in Pub. L. No. 99-514.

● ERISA §3(23) was amended by Act §7881(m)(2)(D) by inserting at the end "The accrued benefit of an employee shall not be less than the amount determined under section 1054(c)(2)(B) of this title with respect to the employee's accumulated contribution." Eff. as if included in Pub. L. No. 100-203, see Act §7882.

● ERISA §3(24)(B) was amended by Act §7871(b)(2). Eff. as if included in Pub. L. No. 99-509. ERISA §3(24)(B) prior to amendment:

   (B) the latest of—
      (i) the time a plan participant attains age 65,
      (ii) in the case of a plan participant who commences participation in the plan within 5 years before attaining normal retirement age under the plan, the 5th anniversary of the time the plan participant commences participation in the plan, or
      (iii) in the case of a plan participant not described in clause (ii), the 10th anniversary of the time the plan participant commences participation in the plan.

● ERISA §3(33)(D)(iii) was amended by Act §7894(a)(1)(A) by substituting "Secretary of the Treasury" for "Secretary" in subcls. (I)–(III). Eff. as if included in Pub. L. No. 96-364, see Act §7894(a)(1)(B).

● ERISA §3(37)(B) was amended by Act §7893(a) by substituting "section 4001(b)(1)" for "section 4001(c)(1)". Eff. as if included in Pub. L. No. 99-272, title XI.

● ERISA §3(37)(F)(i)(II) was amended by Act §7894(a)(2)(A)(i) by substituting "the Internal Revenue Code of 1986" for "such Code", which for purposes of codification was translated as "title 26". Eff. as if included in Pub. L. No. 96-364, §407.

● ERISA §3(37)(F)(ii) was amended by Act §7894(a)(2)(A)(ii)–(iii) by inserting "of such Code" after "section 501(c)" in subcl. (I) and in subcl. (II) after "section 170 (b)(1)(A)(ii)". For purposes of codification, these amendments were translated as "of title 26". Eff. as if included in Pub. L. No. 100-202, §136.

● ERISA §3(39) was amended by Act §7894(a)(3) by substituting "mean, with respect to a plan, the calendar" for "mean with respect to a plan, calendar".

● ERISA §3(41) was added by Act §7894(a)(4). Eff. as if originally included in Pub. L. No. 93-406.

Omnibus Budget Reconciliation Act of 1987 (Pub. L. No. 100-202), as follows:

● ERISA §3(37)(F) was added by Act §136(a). Eff. for years beginning after Dec. 22, 1987.

Omnibus Budget Reconciliation Act of 1986 (Pub. L. No. 99-509), as follows:

● ERISA §3(24)(B) was amended by Act §9204. Eff. for plan years beginning on or after Jan. 1, 1988, for service performed on or after that date. ERISA §3(24)(B) prior to amendment:

   (B) the later of—
      (i) the time a plan participant attains age 65, or
      (ii) the 10th anniversary of the time a plan participant commenced participation in the plan.

Tax Reform Act of 1986 (Pub. L. No. 99-514), as follows:

● ERISA §3(37)(A) was amended by Act §1879, to read "means a plan" after repealing the amendment made by Pub. L. No. 99-272, which had substituted "means a pension plan" for "means a plan". Eff. Jan. 1, 1986.

Omnibus Budget Reconciliation Act of 1986 (Pub. L. No. 99-272), as follows:

● ERISA §3(37)(A) was amended by Act §11016 by substituting "means a pension plan" for "means a plan". Eff. Jan. 1, 1986, but repealed by Pub. L. No. 99-514.

Multiple Employer Welfare Arrangements Act of 1983 (Pub. L. No. 97-473), as follows:

● ERISA §3(40) was added by Act §302. Eff. Jan. 14, 1983.

Multiemployer Pension Plan Amendments Act of 1980 (Pub. L. No. 96-364), as follows:

● ERISA §3(2) amended by Act §409 by designating existing provisions as subpara. (A), inserting exception for subpara. (B), substituting "(i)" for "(A)" and "(ii)" for "(B)", and adding subpara. (B). Eff. Sept. 26, 1980.

● ERISA §3(14) was amended by Act §305 by inserting provisions respecting a trust described in IRC §501(c)(2). Eff. Sept. 26, 1980.

● ERISA §3(33) was amended by Act §407(a) by substituting provisions defining "church plan" as a plan established and maintained (to the extent required in cl. (ii) of subpara. (B)) for employees or beneficiaries by a church, etc., exempt from tax under section 501 of title 26, for provisions defining "church plan" as a plan established and maintained for employees by a church, etc., exempt from tax under section 501 of title 26, or a plan in existence on Jan. 1, 1974, established and maintained by a church, etc., for employees and employees of agencies of the church, etc. Eff. Jan. 1, 1974.

● ERISA §3(37) was amended by Act §302(a) by substantially revising definition of term "multiemployer plan" by, among other changes, restructuring subpara. (A), resulting in elimination of provisions covering amount of contributions and payment of benefits, and subpara. (B), resulting in elimination of provisions reworking amount of contributions for subsequent plan years, and adding subparas. (C)–(E). Eff. Sept. 26, 1980.

SEC. 4. COVERAGE.

(a) Except as provided in subsection (b) or (c) and in sections 201, 301, and 401, this title shall apply to any employee benefit plan if it is established or maintained—

(1) by any employer engaged in commerce or in any industry or activity affecting commerce; or

(2) by any employee organization or organizations representing employees engaged in commerce or in any industry or activity affecting commerce; or

(3) by both.

(b) The provisions of this title shall not apply to any employee benefit plan if—

(1) such plan is a governmental plan (as defined in section 3(32));

(2) such plan is a church plan (as defined in section 3(33)) with respect to which no election has been made under section 410(d) of title 26;

(3) such plan is maintained solely for the purpose of complying with applicable workmen's compensation laws or unemployment compensation or disability insurance laws;

(4) such plan is maintained outside of the United States primarily for the benefit of persons substantially all of whom are nonresident aliens; or

(5) such plan is an excess benefit plan (as defined in section 3(36)) and is unfunded.

The provisions of part 7 of subtitle B shall not apply to a health insurance issuer (as defined in section 733(b)(2)) solely by reason of health insurance coverage (as defined in section 733(b)(1)) provided by such issuer in connection with a group health plan (as defined in section 733(a)(1)) if the provisions of this title do not apply to such group health plan.

(c) If a pension plan allows an employee to elect to make voluntary employee contributions to accounts and annuities as provided in section 408(q) of the Internal Revenue Code of 1986, such accounts and annuities (and contributions thereto) shall not be treated as part of such plan (or as a separate pension plan) for purposes of any provision of this title other than section 403(c), 404, or 405 (relating to exclusive benefit, and fiduciary and co-fiduciary responsibilities) and part 5 (relating to administration and enforcement). Such provisions shall apply to such accounts and annuities in a manner similar to their application to a simplified employee pension under section 408(k) of the Internal Revenue Code of 1986.

Amendments to ERISA §4

Job Creation and Worker Assistance Act of 2002 (Pub. L. No. 107-147), as follows:
- ERISA §4(c) was amended by Act §411 by inserting "and part 5 of subtitle B of this subchapter (relating to administration and enforcement)" after "co-fiduciary responsibilities)" and "Such provisions shall apply to such accounts and annuities in a manner similar to their application to a simplified employee pension under section 408(k) of title 26." at end. Eff. for plan years after Dec. 31, 2002.

Economic Growth and Tax Relief Reconciliation Act of 2001 (Pub. L. No. 107-16), as follows:
- ERISA §4(a) was amended by Act §§602(b)(2) and 901 by temporarily inserting "or (c)" after "subsection (b)" in introductory provisions. Eff. between Jan. 1, 2003, and Dec. 31, 2010. See note below on sunset rule.
- ERISA §4(c) was amended by Act §§602(b)(2) and 901 by temporarily adding subsec. (c). Eff. between Jan. 1, 2003, and Dec. 31, 2010. See note below on sunset rule.
- **Sunset Rule.** To comply with the Congressional Budget Act of 1974, §901 of Pub. L. 107-16 provides that all provisions of, and amendments made by, the Act will not apply to taxable, plan, or limitation years beginning after December 31, 2010. *But see* Pension Protection Act of 2006 (Pub. L. No. 109-280), §811 (sunset rule of Pub. L. No. 107-16 does not apply to the provisions of, and the amendments made by, Pub. L. No. 107-16, §§601-666 (relating to modifications to pensions and retirement income arrangement provisions)).

Departments of Veterans Affairs and HUD and Independent Agencies Appropriations Act of 1997 (Pub. L. No. 104-204), as follows:
- ERISA §4(b) was amended by the Act in concluding provisions by making technical amendment to references in ERISA as originally passed which appear in text as references to ERISA §733. Eff. Jan. 1, 1998.

Health Insurance Portability and Accountability Act of 1996 (Pub. L. No. 104-191), as follows:
- ERISA §4(b) was amended by Act §101(d) by inserting at the end "The provisions of part 7 of subtitle B of this subchapter shall not apply to a health insurance issuer (as defined in §733(b)(2) of this title) solely by reason of health insurance coverage (as defined in §733(b)(1) of this title) provided by such issuer in connection with a group health plan (as defined in §733(a)(1) of this title) if the provisions of this subchapter do not apply to such group health plan." Eff. June 30. 1997.

Omnibus Budget Reconciliation Act of 1989 (Pub. L. No. 101-239), as follows:
- ERISA §4(b)(2) was amended by Act §7891(a)(1) by substituting "Internal Revenue Code of 1986" for "Internal Revenue Code of 1954", which for purposes of codification was translated as "title 26". Eff. as if included in Pub. L. No. 99-514.

Subtitle B—Regulatory Provisions

Part 1—Reporting and Disclosure

SEC. 101. DUTY OF DISCLOSURE AND REPORTING.

(a) Summary Plan Description and Information to be Furnished to Participants and Beneficiaries.—The administrator of each employee benefit plan shall cause to be furnished in accordance with section 104(b) to each participant covered under the plan and to each beneficiary who is receiving benefits under the plan—

(1) a summary plan description described in section 102(a)(1); and

(2) the information described in subsection (f) and sections 104(b)(3) and 105(a) and (c).

(b) Plan Description, Modifications and Changes, and Reports to be Filed With Secretary of Labor.—The administrator shall, in accordance with section 104(a), file with the Secretary—

(1) the annual report containing information required by section 103; and

(2) terminal and supplementary reports as required by subsection (c) of this section.

(c) Terminal and Supplementary Reports.—

(1) Each administrator of an employee pension benefit plan which is winding up its affairs (without regard to the number of participants remaining in the plan) shall, in accordance with regulations prescribed by the Secretary, file such terminal reports as the Secretary may consider necessary. A copy of such report shall also be filed with the Pension Benefit Guaranty Corporation.

(2) The Secretary may require terminal reports to be filed with regard to any employee welfare benefit plan which is winding up its affairs in accordance with regulations promulgated by the Secretary.

(3) The Secretary may require that a plan described in paragraph (1) or (2) file a supplementary or terminal report with the annual report in the year such plan is terminated and that a copy of such supplementary or terminal report in the case of a plan described in paragraph (1) be also filed with the Pension Benefit Guaranty Corporation.

(d) Notice of Failure to Meet Minimum Funding Standards.—

(1) In general.—If an employer maintaining a plan other than a multiemployer plan fails to make a required installment or other payment required to meet the minimum funding standard under section 302 to a plan before the 60th day following the due date for such installment or other payment, the employer shall notify each participant and beneficiary (including an alternate payee as defined in section 206(d)(3)(K)) of such plan of such failure. Such notice shall be made at such time and in such manner as the Secretary may prescribe.

(2) Subsection not to apply if waiver pending.—This subsection shall not apply to any failure if the employer has filed a waiver request under section 1083 of this title with respect to the plan year to which the required installment relates, except that if the waiver request is denied, notice under paragraph (1) shall be provided within 60 days after the date of such denial.

(3) Definitions.—For purposes of this subsection, the terms "required installment" and "due date" have the same meanings given such terms by section 303(j) of this title.

(e) Notice of Transfer of Excess Pension Assets to Health Benefits Accounts.—

(1) Notice to participants.—Not later than 60 days before the date of a qualified transfer by an employee pension benefit plan of excess pension assets to a health benefits account, the administrator of the plan shall notify (in such manner as the Secretary may prescribe) each participant and beneficiary under the plan of such transfer. Such notice shall include information with respect to the amount of excess pension assets, the portion to be transferred, the amount of health benefits liabilities expected to be provided with the assets transferred, and the amount of pension benefits of the participant which will be nonforfeitable immediately after the transfer.

(2) Notice to secretaries, administrator, and employee organizations.—

(A) In general.—Not later than 60 days before the date of any qualified transfer by an employee pension benefit plan of excess pension assets to a health benefits account, the employer maintaining the plan from which the transfer is made shall provide the Secretary, the Secretary of the Treasury, the administrator, and each employee organization representing participants in the plan a written notice of such transfer. A copy of such notice shall be available for inspection in the principal office of the administrator.

(B) Information relating to transfer.—Such notice shall identify the plan from which the transfer is made, the amount of the transfer, a detailed accounting of assets projected to be held by the plan immediately before and immediately after the transfer, and the current liabilities under the plan at the time of the transfer.

(C) Authority for additional reporting requirements.—The Secretary may prescribe such additional reporting requirements as may be necessary to carry out the purposes of this section.

(3) Definitions.—For purposes of paragraph (1), any term used in such paragraph which is also used in section 420 of the Internal Revenue Code of 1986 (as in effect on the date of the enactment of the Pension Protection Act of 2006) shall have the same meaning as when used in such section.

(f) Defined Benefit Plan Funding Notices.—

(1) In general.—The administrator of a defined benefit plan to which title IV applies shall for each plan year provide a plan funding notice to the Pension Benefit Guaranty Corporation, to each plan participant and beneficiary, to each labor organization representing such participants or beneficiaries, and, in the case of a multiemployer plan, to each employer that has an obligation to contribute to the plan.

(2) Information contained in notices.—

(A) Identifying information.—Each notice required under paragraph (1) shall contain identifying information, including the name of the plan, the address and phone number of the plan administrator and the plan's principal administrative officer, each plan sponsor's employer identification number, and the plan number of the plan.

(B) Specific information.—A plan funding notice under paragraph (1) shall include—

(i)(I) in the case of a single-employer plan, a statement as to whether the plan's funding target attainment percentage (as defined in section 303(d)(2)) for the plan year to which the notice relates, and for the 2 preceding plan years, is at least 100 percent (and, if not, the actual percentages), or

(II) in the case of a multiemployer plan, a statement as to whether the plan's funded percentage (as defined in section 305(i)) for the plan year to which the notice relates, and for the 2 preceding plan years, is at least 100 percent (and, if not, the actual percentages),

(ii)(I) in the case of a single-employer plan, a statement of—

(aa) the total assets (separately stating the prefunding balance and the funding standard carryover balance) and liabilities of the plan, determined in the same manner as under section 303, for the plan year to which the notice relates and for the 2 preceding plan years, as reported in the annual report for each such plan year, and

(bb) the value of the plan's assets and liabilities for the plan year to which the notice relates as of the last day of the plan year to which the notice relates determined using the asset valuation under subclause (II) of section 4006(a)(3)(E)(iii) and the interest rate under section 4006(a)(3)(E)(iv), and

(II) in the case of a multiemployer plan, a statement, for the plan year to which the notice relates and the preceding 2 plan years, of the value of the plan assets (determined both in the same manner as under section 304 and under the rules of subclause (I)(bb)) and the value of the plan liabilities (determined in the same manner as under section 304 except that the method specified in section 305(i)(8) shall be used),

(iii) a statement of the number of participants who are—

(I) retired or separated from service and are receiving benefits,

(II) retired or separated participants entitled to future benefits, and

(III) active participants under the plan,

(iv) a statement setting forth the funding policy of the plan and the asset allocation of investments under the plan (expressed as percentages of total assets) as of the end of the plan year to which the notice relates,

(v) in the case of a multiemployer plan, whether the plan was in critical or endangered status under section 305 for such plan year and, if so—

(I) a statement describing how a person may obtain a copy of the plan's funding improvement or rehabilitation plan, as appropriate, adopted under section 305 and the actuarial and financial data that demonstrate any action taken by the plan toward fiscal improvement, and

(II) a summary of any funding improvement plan, rehabilitation plan, or modification thereof adopted under section 305 during the plan year to which the notice relates,

(vi) in the case of any plan amendment, scheduled benefit increase or reduction, or other known event taking effect in the current plan year and having a material effect on plan liabilities or assets for the year (as defined in regulations by the Secretary), an explanation of the amendment, schedule increase or reduction, or event, and a projection to the end of such plan year of the effect of the amendment, scheduled increase or reduction, or event on plan liabilities,

(vii)(I) in the case of a single-employer plan, a summary of the rules governing termination of single-employer plans under subtitle C of title IV, or

(II) in the case of a multiemployer plan, a summary of the rules governing reorganization or insolvency, including the limitations on benefit payments,

(viii) a general description of the benefits under the plan which are eligible to be guaranteed by the Pension Benefit Guaranty Corporation, along with an explanation of the limitations on the guarantee and the circumstances under which such limitations apply,

(ix) a statement that a person may obtain a copy of the annual report of the plan filed under section 104(a) upon request, through the Internet website of the Department of Labor, or through an Intranet website maintained by the applicable plan sponsor (or plan administrator on behalf of the plan sponsor), and

(x) if applicable, a statement that each contributing sponsor, and each member of the contributing sponsor's controlled group, of the single-employer plan was required to provide the information under section 4010 for the plan year to which the notice relates.

(C) Other information.—Each notice under paragraph (1) shall include—

(i) in the case of a multiemployer plan, a statement that the plan administrator shall provide, upon written request, to any labor organization representing plan participants and beneficiaries and any employer that has an obligation to contribute to the plan, a copy of the annual report filed with the Secretary under section 104(a), and

(ii) any additional information which the plan administrator elects to include to the extent not inconsistent with regulations prescribed by the Secretary.

(3) Time for providing notice.—

(A) In general.—Any notice under paragraph (1) shall be provided not later than 120 days after the end of the plan year to which the notice relates.

(B) Exception for small plans.—In the case of a small plan (as such term is used under section 303(g)(2)(B)) any notice under paragraph (1) shall be provided upon filing of the annual report under section 104(a).

(4) Form and manner.—Any notice under paragraph (1)—

(A) shall be provided in a form and manner prescribed in regulations of the Secretary,

(B) shall be written in a manner so as to be understood by the average plan participant, and

(C) may be provided in written, electronic, or other appropriate form to the extent such form is reasonably accessible to persons to whom the notice is required to be provided.

Editor's Note

ERISA §101(g), below, as amended by Pub. L. No. 111-148, §6606, is effective March 23, 2010.

(g) Reporting by Certain Arrangements.—The Secretary shall, by regulation, require multiple employer welfare arrangements providing benefits consisting of medical care (within the meaning of section 733(a)(2)) which are not group health plans to register with the Secretary prior to operating in a State and may, by regulation, require such multiple employer welfare arrangements to report, not more frequently than annually, in such form and such manner as the Secretary may require for the purpose of determining the extent to which the requirements of part 7 are being carried out in connection with such benefits.

(h) Simple Retirement Accounts.—

(1) No employer reports.—Except as provided in this subsection, no report shall be required under this section by an employer maintaining a qualified salary reduction arrangement under section 408(p) of the Internal Revenue Code of 1986.

(2) Summary description.—The trustee of any simple retirement account established pursuant to a qualified salary reduction arrangement under section 408(p) of such Code shall provide to the employer maintaining the arrangement each year a description containing the following information:

(A) The name and address of the employer and the trustee.

(B) The requirements for eligibility for participation.

(C) The benefits provided with respect to the arrangement.

(D) The time and method of making elections with respect to the arrangement.

(E) The procedures for, and effects of, withdrawals (including rollovers) from the arrangement.

(3) Employee notification.—The employer shall notify each employee immediately before the period for which an election described in section 408(p)(5)(C) of such Code may be made of the employee's opportunity to make such election. Such notice shall include a copy of the description described in paragraph (2).

(i) Notice of Blackout Periods to Participant or Beneficiary Under Individual Account Plan.—

(1) Duties of plan administrator.—In advance of the commencement of any blackout period with respect to an individual account plan, the plan administrator shall notify the plan participants and beneficiaries who are affected by such action in accordance with this subsection.

(2) Notice requirements.—

(A) In general.—The notices described in paragraph (1) shall be written in a manner calculated to be understood by the average plan participant and shall include—

(i) the reasons for the blackout period,

(ii) an identification of the investments and other rights affected,

(iii) the expected beginning date and length of the blackout period,

(iv) in the case of investments affected, a statement that the participant or beneficiary should evaluate the appropriateness of their current investment decisions in light of their inability to direct or diversify assets credited to their accounts during the blackout period, and

(v) such other matters as the Secretary may require by regulation.

(B) Notice to participants and beneficiaries.—Except as otherwise provided in this subsection, notices described in paragraph (1) shall be furnished to all participants and beneficiaries under the plan to whom the blackout period applies at least 30 days in advance of the blackout period.

(C) Exception to 30-day notice requirement.—In any case in which—

(i) a deferral of the blackout period would violate the requirements of subparagraph (A) or (B) of section 404(a)(1), and a fiduciary of the plan reasonably so determines in writing, or

(ii) the inability to provide the 30-day advance notice is due to events that were unforeseeable or circumstances beyond the reasonable control of the plan administrator, and a fiduciary of the plan reasonably so determines in writing,

subparagraph (B) shall not apply, and the notice shall be furnished to all participants and beneficiaries under the plan to whom the blackout period applies as soon as reasonably possible under the circumstances unless such a notice in advance of the termination of the blackout period is impracticable.

(D) Written notice.—The notice required to be provided under this subsection shall be in writing, except that such notice may be in electronic or other form to the extent that such form is reasonably accessible to the recipient.

(E) Notice to issuers of employer securities subject to blackout period.—In the case of any blackout period in connection with an individual account plan, the plan administrator shall provide timely notice of such blackout period to the issuer of any employer securities subject to such blackout period.

(3) Exception for blackout periods with limited applicability.—In any case in which the blackout period applies only to 1 or more participants or beneficiaries in connection with a merger, acquisition, divestiture, or similar transaction involving the plan or plan sponsor and occurs solely in connection with becoming or ceasing to be a participant or beneficiary under the plan by reason of such merger, acquisition, divestiture, or transaction, the requirement of this subsection that the notice be provided to all participants and beneficiaries shall be treated as met if the notice required under paragraph (1) is provided to such participants or beneficiaries to whom the blackout period applies as soon as reasonably practicable.

(4) Changes in length of blackout period.—If, following the furnishing of the notice pursuant to this subsection, there is a change in the beginning date or length of the blackout period (specified in such notice pursuant to paragraph (2)(A)(iii)), the administrator shall provide affected participants and beneficiaries notice of the change as soon as reasonably practicable. In relation to the extended blackout period, such notice shall meet the requirements of paragraph (2)(D) and shall specify any material change in the matters referred to in clauses (i) through (v) of paragraph (2)(A).

(5) Regulatory exceptions.—The Secretary may provide by regulation for additional exceptions to the requirements of this subsection which the Secretary determines are in the interests of participants and beneficiaries.

(6) Guidance and model notices.—The Secretary shall issue guidance and model notices which meet the requirements of this subsection.

(7) Blackout period.—For purposes of this subsection—

(A) In general.—The term "blackout period" means, in connection with an individual account plan, any period for which any ability of participants or beneficiaries under the plan, which is otherwise available under the terms of such plan, to direct or diversify assets credited to their accounts, to obtain loans from the plan, or to obtain distributions from the plan is temporarily suspended, limited, or restricted, if such suspension, limitation, or restriction is for any period of more than 3 consecutive business days.

(B) Exclusions.—The term "blackout period" does not include a suspension, limitation, or restriction—

(i) which occurs by reason of the application of the securities laws (as defined in section 3(a)(47) of the Securities Exchange Act of 1934),

(ii) which is a change to the plan which provides for a regularly scheduled suspension, limitation, or restriction which is disclosed to participants or beneficiaries through any summary of

material modifications, any materials describing specific investment alternatives under the plan, or any changes thereto, or

(iii) which applies only to 1 or more individuals, each of whom is the participant, an alternate payee (as defined in section 206(d)(3)(K)), or any other beneficiary pursuant to a qualified domestic relations order (as defined in section 206(d)(3)(B)(i)).

(8) Individual account plan.—

(A) In general.—For purposes of this subsection, the term "individual account plan" shall have the meaning provided such term in section 3(34), except that such term shall not include a one-participant retirement plan.

(B) One-participant retirement plan.—For purposes of subparagraph (A), the term "one-participant retirement plan" means a retirement plan that on the first day of the plan year—

(i) covered only one individual (or the individual and the individual's spouse) and the individual (or the individual and the individual's spouse) owned 100 percent of the plan sponsor (whether or not incorporated), or

(ii) covered only one or more partners (or partners and their spouses) in the plan sponsor.

(j) Notice of Funding-Based Limitation on Certain Forms of Distribution.—The plan administrator of a single-employer plan shall provide a written notice to plan participants and beneficiaries within 30 days—

(1) after the plan has become subject to a restriction described in paragraph (1) or (3) of section 206(g),

(2) in the case of a plan to which section 206(g)(4) applies, after the valuation date for the plan year described in section 206(g)(4)(A) for which the plan's adjusted funding target attainment percentage for the plan year is less than 60 percent (or, if earlier, the date such percentage is deemed to be less than 60 percent under section 206(g)(7)), and

(3) at such other time as may be determined by the Secretary of the Treasury.

The notice required to be provided under this subsection shall be in writing, except that such notice may be in electronic or other form to the extent that such form is reasonably accessible to the recipient. The Secretary of the Treasury, in consultation with the Secretary, shall have the authority to prescribe rules applicable to the notices required under this subsection.

(k) Multiemployer Plan Information Made Available on Request.—

(1) In general.—Each administrator of a multiemployer plan shall, upon written request, furnish to any plan participant or beneficiary, employee representative, or any employer that has an obligation to contribute to the plan—

(A) a copy of any periodic actuarial report (including any sensitivity testing) received by the plan for any plan year which has been in the plan's possession for at least 30 days,

(B) a copy of any quarterly, semi-annual, or annual financial report prepared for the plan by any plan investment manager or advisor or other fiduciary which has been in the plan's possession for at least 30 days, and

(C) a copy of any application filed with the Secretary of the Treasury requesting an extension under section 304 of this Act or section 431(d) of the Internal Revenue Code of 1986 and the determination of such Secretary pursuant to such application.

(2) Compliance.—Information required to be provided under paragraph (1)—

(A) shall be provided to the requesting participant, beneficiary, or employer within 30 days after the request in a form and manner prescribed in regulations of the Secretary,

(B) may be provided in written, electronic, or other appropriate form to the extent such form is reasonably accessible to persons to whom the information is required to be provided, and

(C) shall not—

(i) include any individually identifiable information regarding any plan participant, beneficiary, employee, fiduciary, or contributing employer, or

(ii) reveal any proprietary information regarding the plan, any contributing employer, or entity providing services to the plan.

Subparagraph (C)(i) shall not apply to individually identifiable information with respect to any plan investment manager or adviser, or with respect to any other person (other than an employee of the plan) preparing a financial report required to be included under paragraph (1)(B).

(3) Limitations.—In no case shall a participant, beneficiary, or employer be entitled under this subsection to receive more than one copy of any report or application described in paragraph (1) during any one 12-month period. The administrator may make a reasonable charge to cover copying, mailing, and other costs of furnishing copies of information pursuant to paragraph (1). The Secretary may by regulations prescribe the maximum amount which will constitute a reasonable charge under the preceding sentence.

(*l*) Notice of Potential Withdrawal Liability.—

(1) In general.—The plan sponsor or administrator of a multiemployer plan shall, upon written request, furnish to any employer who has an obligation to contribute to the plan a notice of—

(A) the estimated amount which would be the amount of such employer's withdrawal liability under part 1 of subtitle E of title IV if such employer withdrew on the last day of the plan year preceding the date of the request, and

(B) an explanation of how such estimated liability amount was determined, including the actuarial assumptions and methods used to determine the value of the plan liabilities and assets, the data regarding employer contributions, unfunded vested benefits, annual changes in the plan's unfunded vested benefits, and the application of any relevant limitations on the estimated withdrawal liability.

For purposes of subparagraph (B), the term "employer contribution" means, in connection with a participant, a contribution made by an employer as an employer of such participant.

(2) Compliance.—Any notice required to be provided under paragraph (1)—

(A) shall be provided in a form and manner prescribed in regulations of the Secretary to the requesting employer within—

(i) 180 days after the request, or

(ii) subject to regulations of the Secretary, such longer time as may be necessary in the case of a plan that determines withdrawal liability based on any method described under paragraph (4) or (5) of section 4211(c); and

(B) may be provided in written, electronic, or other appropriate form to the extent such form is reasonably accessible to employers to whom the information is required to be provided.

(3) Limitations.—In no case shall an employer be entitled under this subsection to receive more than one notice described in paragraph (1) during any one 12-month period. The person required to provide such notice may make a reasonable charge to cover copying, mailing, and other costs of furnishing such notice pursuant to paragraph (1). The Secretary may by regulations prescribe the maximum amount which will constitute a reasonable charge under the preceding sentence.

(m) Notice of Right To Divest.—Not later than 30 days before the first date on which an applicable individual of an applicable individual account plan is eligible to exercise the right under section 204(j) to direct the proceeds from the divestment of employer securities with respect to any type of contribution, the administrator shall provide to such individual a notice—

(1) setting forth such right under such section, and

(2) describing the importance of diversifying the investment of retirement account assets.

The notice required by this subsection shall be written in a manner calculated to be understood by the average plan participant and may be delivered in written, electronic, or other appropriate form to the extent that such form is reasonably accessible to the recipient.

(n) Cross References.—For regulations relating to coordination of reports to the Secretaries of Labor and the Treasury, see section 3004.

Amendments to ERISA §101

Patient Protection and Affordable Care Act, 2010 (Pub. L. No. 111-148), as follows:

- ERISA §101(g) was amended by Act §6606 by striking "Secretary may" and inserting "Secretary shall" and inserting "to register with the Secretary prior to operating in a State and may, by regulation, require such multiple employer welfare arrangements" after "not group health plans". Eff. Mar. 23, 2010.

Worker, Retiree, and Employer Recovery Act of 2008 (Pub. L. No. 110-458), as follows:

- ERISA §101(f)(2)(B)(ii)(I)(aa) was amended by Act §105(a)(1) by striking "for which the latest annual report filed under section 104(a) was filed" and inserting "to which the notice relates". Eff. for plan years beginning after Dec. 31, 2007, as if included in §501 of Pub. L. No. 109-280.

- ERISA §101(f)(2)(B)(ii)(II) was amended by Act §105(a)(2) by striking subclause (II) and replacing it. Eff. for plan years beginning after Dec. 31, 2007, as if included in §501 of Pub. L. No. 109-280. ERISA §101(f)(2)(B)(ii)(II) prior to amendment:

    (II) in the case of a multiemployer plan, a statement of the value of the plan's assets and liabilities for the plan year to which the notice relates as the last day of such plan year and the preceding 2 plan years,

- ERISA §101(i)(8)(B) was amended by Act §105(g). Eff. as if included in §509 of Pub. L. No. 109-280. ERISA §101(i)(8)(B) prior to amendment:

    (B) One-participant retirement plan.—For purposes of subparagraph (A), the term "one-participant retirement plan" means a retirement plan that—

    (i) on the first day of the plan year—

    (I) covered only one individual (or the individual and the individual's spouse) and the individual (or the individual and the individual's spouse) owned 100 percent of the plan sponsor (whether or not incorporated), or

    (II) covered only one or more partners (or partners and their spouses) in the plan sponsor, and

    (ii) does not cover a business that leases employees.

- ERISA §101(j) was amended by Act §101(c)(1)(A) by striking "section 206(g)(4)(B)" and inserting "section 206(g)(4)(A)", and adding at the end the following: "The Secretary of the Treasury, in consultation with the Secretary, shall have the authority to prescribe rules applicable to the notices required under this subsection." Eff. for plan years beginning after Dec. 31, 2007, as if included in §103 of Pub. L. No. 109-280.

- ERISA §101(k)(2) was amended by Act §105(b)(1) by adding a flush sentence. Eff. for plan years beginning after Dec. 31, 2007, as if included in §502 of Pub. L. No. 109-280.

- Act §101(c)(3) amended Pub. L. No. 109-280, §§103(c)(2)(A)(ii) and 113(b)(2)(A)(ii) by striking "subsection" and inserting "section", and striking "subparagraph" and inserting "paragraph".

- Act §105(c)(2) amended Pub. L. No. 109-280, §503(e) by striking "section 101(f)" and inserting "section 104(d)".

Pension Protection Act of 2006 (Pub. L. No. 109-280), as follows:

- ERISA §101(a)(2) was amended by Act §503(c)(2) by adding "subsection (f) and" before "Secs. 104(b)(3) and 105(a) and (c)." Eff. for plan years beginning after Dec. 31, 2007.

- ERISA §101(d)(3) was amended by Act §107(a)(1) (redesignated as §108(a)(1) by Pub. L. No. 111-192, §202(a)) by substituting "§303(j)" for "§302(e)." Eff. generally for plan years beginning after 2007; delayed effective date for "eligible cooperative plans" until the earlier of the first plan year that the plan ceases to be an eligible cooperative plan, or Jan. 1, 2017.

- ERISA §101(e)(3) was amended by Act §107(a)(11) (redesignated as §108(a)(11) by Pub. L. No. 111-192, §202(a)) by substituting "Pension Protection Act of 2006" for "American Jobs Creation Act of 2004." Eff. generally for plan years beginning after 2007; delayed effective date for "eligible cooperative plans" until the earlier of the first plan year that the plan ceases to be an eligible cooperative plan, or Jan. 1, 2017.

- ERISA §101(f) was added by Act §501(a) by replacing ERISA §101(f), which was added by Pub. L. No. 108-218. Act §501(d) contained a transition rule that any requirement under ERISA §101(f) (as amended) to report the funding target attainment percentage or funded percentage of a plan with respect to any plan year beginning before Jan. 1, 2008, will be treated as met if the plan reports: (A) in the case of a plan year beginning in 2006, the funded current liability percentage (as defined in Act §302(d)(8)) of the plan for such plan year, and (B) in the case of a plan year beginning in 2007, the funding target attainment percentage or funded percentage as determined using such methods of estimation as the Secretary of the Treasury may provide. Eff. for plan years after Dec. 31, 2007. ERISA §101(f) prior to amendment (applicable to plan years beginning after Dec. 31, 2004, and until plan years beginning before Jan. 1, 2008):

    (f) Multiemployer Defined Benefit Plan Funding Notices.—

    (1) In general.—The administrator of a defined benefit plan which is a multiemployer plan shall for each plan year provide a plan funding notice to each plan participant and beneficiary, to each labor organization representing such participants or beneficiaries, to each employer that has an obligation to contribute under the plan, and to the Pension Benefit Guaranty Corporation.

    (2) Information contained in notices.—

    (A) Identifying information.—Each notice required under paragraph (1) shall contain identifying information, including the name of the plan, the address and phone number of the plan administrator and the plan's principal administrative officer, each plan sponsor's employer identification number, and the plan number of the plan.

    (B) Specific information.—A plan funding notice under paragraph (1) shall include—

    (i) a statement as to whether the plan's funded current liability percentage (as defined in section 302(d)(8)(B)) for the plan year to which the notice relates is at least 100 percent (and, if not, the actual percentage);

    (ii) a statement of the value of the plan's assets, the amount of benefit payments, and the ratio of the assets to the payments for the plan year to which the notice relates;

    (iii) a summary of the rules governing insolvent multiemployer plans, including the limitations on benefit payments and any potential benefit reductions and suspensions (and the potential effects of such limitations, reductions, and suspensions on the plan); and

    (iv) a general description of the benefits under the plan which are eligible to be guaranteed by the Pension Benefit Guaranty Corporation, along wth an explanation of the limitations on the guarantee and the circumstances under which such limitations apply.

    (C) Other information.—Each notice under paragraph (1) shall include any additional information which the plan administrator elects to include to the extent not inconsistent with regulations prescribed by the Secretary.

    (3) Time for providing notice.—

    Any notice under paragraph (1) shall be provided no later than two months after the deadline (including extensions) for filing the annual report for the plan year to which the notice relates.

    (4) Form and manner.—Any notice under paragraph (1)—

    (A) shall be provided in a form and manner prescribed in regulations of the Secretary,

    (B) shall be written in a manner so as to be understood by the average plan participant, and

    (C) may be provided in written, electronic, or other appropriate form to the extent such form is reasonably accessible to persons to whom the notice is required to be provided.

- ERISA §101(i)(8)(B) was amended by Act §509(a) by striking cls. (i)–(iv), redesignating cl. (v) as (ii), and inserting new cl. (i). Eff. Jan. 26, 2003, as if included in Pub. L. No. 107-204, §306. ERISA §101(i)(8)(B) prior to amendment:

   (B) One-participant retirement plan

   For purposes of subparagraph (A), the term 'one-participant retirement plan' means a retirement plan that—

   (i) on the first day of the plan year—

   (I) covered only the employer (and the employer's spouse) and the employer owned the entire business (whether or not incorporated), or

   (II) covered only one or more partners (and their spouses) in a business partnership (including partners in an S or C corporation (as defined in section 1361(a) of title 26)),

   (ii) meets the minimum coverage requirements of section 410(b) of title 26 (as in effect on July 30, 2002) without being combined with any other plan of the business that covers the employees of the business,

   (iii) does not provide benefits to anyone except the employer (and the employer's spouse) or the partners (and their spouses),

   (iv) does not cover a business that is a member of an affiliated service group, a controlled group of corporations, or a group of businesses under common control, and

   (v) does not cover a business that leases employees.

- ERISA §§101(j), (k), (*l*), (n) were amended by Act §§103(b)(1), 502(a)(1), 502(b)(1), and 507(a) by redesignating former (j) as (k), and adding new (j). Eff. for plan years beginning after Dec. 31, 2007, for §101(j)–(*l*); and for plan years beginning after Dec. 31, 2006, for §101(m)–(n). Act §103(c)(2) provides a delayed effective date for collective bargaining agreements for ERISA §101(j), and a delayed effective date for "eligible cooperative plans" until the earlier of the first plan year that the plan ceases to be an eligible cooperative plan, or Jan. 1, 2017.

- **Other Provision—Effective Date.** Act §103(c)(2) provides:

   (2) Collective bargaining exception.—In the case of a plan maintained pursuant to 1 or more collective bargaining agreements between employee representatives and 1 or more employers ratified before January 1, 2008, the amendments made by this section shall not apply to plan years beginning before the earlier of—

   (A) the later of—

   (i) the date on which the last collective bargaining agreement relating to the plan terminates (determined without regard to any extension thereof agreed to after the date of the enactment of this Act), or

   (ii) the first day of the first plan year to which the amendments made by this subsection would (but for this subparagraph) apply, or

   (B) January 1, 2010.

   For purposes of subparagraph (A)(i), any plan amendment made pursuant to a collective bargaining agreement relating to the plan which amends the plan solely to conform to any requirement added by this section shall not be treated as a termination of such collective bargaining agreement.

- **Other Provision—Effective Date.** Act §104 provides:

   SEC. 104. SPECIAL RULES FOR MULTIPLE EMPLOYER PLANS OF CERTAIN COOPERATIVES.

   (a) **General Rule.**—Except as provided in this section, if a plan in existence on July 26, 2005, was an eligible cooperative plan for its plan year which includes such date, the amendments made by this subtitle and subtitle B shall not apply to plan years beginning before the earlier of—

   (1) the first plan year for which the plan ceases to be an eligible cooperative plan, or

   (2) January 1, 2017.

   (b) **Interest Rate.**—In applying section 302(b)(5)(B) of the Employee Retirement Income Security Act of 1974 and section 412(b)(5)(B) of the Internal Revenue Code of 1986 (as in effect before the amendments made by this subtitle and subtitle B) to an eligible cooperative plan for plan years beginning after December 31, 2007, and before the first plan year to which such amendments apply, the third segment rate determined under

section 303(h)(2)(C)(iii) of such Act and section 430(h)(2)(C)(iii) of such Code (as added by such amendments) shall be used in lieu of the interest rate otherwise used.

(c) **Eligible Cooperative Plan Defined.**—For purposes of this section, a plan shall be treated as an eligible cooperative plan for a plan year if the plan is maintained by more than 1 employer and at least 85 percent of the employers are—

   (1) rural cooperatives (as defined in section 401(k)(7)(B) of such Code without regard to clause (iv) thereof), or

   (2) organizations which are—

   (A) cooperative organizations described in section 1381(a) of such Code which are more than 50-percent owned by agricultural producers or by cooperatives owned by agricultural producers, or

   (B) more than 50-percent owned, or controlled by, one or more cooperative organizations described in subparagraph (A).

A plan shall also be treated as an eligible cooperative plan for any plan year for which it is described in section 210(a) of the Employee Retirement Income Security Act of 1974 and is maintained by a rural telephone cooperative association described in section 3(40)(B)(v) of such Act.

- **Other Provision.** Act §503(e) provides:

   (e) Model Form.—Not later than 1 year after the date of the enactment of this Act, the Secretary of Labor shall publish a model form for providing the statements, schedules, and other material required to be provided under section 101(f) of the Employee Retirement Income Security Act of 1974, as amended by this section. The Secretary of Labor may promulgate any interim final rules as the Secretary determines appropriate to carry out the provisions of this subsection.

- **Other Provision.** See Note under "Preservation of Access to Case for Medicare Beneficiaries and Pension Relief Act of 2010" for Act §107. Prior Act §107 was redesignated as Act §108 by Pub. L. No. 111-192, §202(a).

American Jobs Creation Act of 2004 (Pub. L. No. 108-357), as follows:

- ERISA §101(e)(3) was amended by Act §709(a)(1) by substituting "October 22, 2004" for "April 10, 2004". Eff. Dec. 31, 2004.

Pension Funding Equity Act of 2004 (Pub. L. No. 108-218), as follows:

- ERISA §101(e)(3) was amended by Act §204(b)(1) by substituting "April 10, 2004" for "December 17, 1999". Eff. for plan years beginning after Dec. 31, 2004.

- ERISA §101(f) was amended by Act §103(a) by adding (f). Eff. for plan years beginning after Dec. 31, 2004, and before Jan. 1, 2008. ERISA §101(f) prior to amendment and replacement by Pub. L. No. 109-280:

   (f) **Multiemployer defined benefit plan funding notices.**—

   (1) In general.—The administrator of a defined benefit plan which is a multiemployer plan shall for each plan year provide a plan funding notice to each plan participant and beneficiary, to each labor organization representing such participants or beneficiaries, to each employer that has an obligation to contribute under the plan, and to the Pension Benefit Guaranty Corporation.

   (2) Information contained in notices

   (A) Identifying information.—Each notice required under paragraph (1) shall contain identifying information, including the name of the plan, the address and phone number of the plan administrator and the plan's principal administrative officer, each plan sponsor's employer identification number, and the plan number of the plan.

   (B) Specific information.—A plan funding notice under paragraph (1) shall include—

   (i) a statement as to whether the plan's funded current liability percentage (as defined in section 302(d)(8)(B) of this title) for the plan year to which the notice relates is at least 100 percent (and, if not, the actual percentage);

   (ii) a statement of the value of the plan's assets, the amount of benefit payments, and the ratio of the assets to the payments for the plan year to which the notice relates;

(iii) a summary of the rules governing insolvent multiemployer plans, including the limitations on benefit payments and any potential benefit reductions and suspensions (and the potential effects of such limitations, reductions, and suspensions on the plan); and
(iv) a general description of the benefits under the plan which are eligible to be guaranteed by the Pension Benefit Guaranty Corporation, along with an explanation of the limitations on the guarantee and the circumstances under which such limitations apply.
(C) Other information.—Each notice under paragraph (1) shall include any additional information which the plan administrator elects to include to the extent not inconsistent with regulations prescribed by the Secretary.
(3) Time for providing notice.—Any notice under paragraph (1) shall be provided no later than two months after the deadline (including extensions) for filing the annual report for the plan year to which the notice relates.
(4) Form and manner.—Any notice under paragraph (1)—
(A) shall be provided in a form and manner prescribed in regulations of the Secretary,
(B) shall be written in a manner so as to be understood by the average plan participant, and
(C) may be provided in written, electronic, or other appropriate form to the extent such form is reasonably accessible to persons to whom the notice is required to be provided.

Sarbanes-Oxley Act of 2002 (Pub. L. No. 107-204), as follows:
• ERISA §101(i) was added by Act §306 by adding subsec. (i) and redesignating subsec. (h) relating to cross reference as (j). Eff. 180 days after July 30, 2002.

Tax Relief Extension Act of 1999 (Pub. L. No. 106-170), as follows:
• ERISA §101(e)(3) was amended by Act §535(a) by substituting "December 17, 1999" for "January 1, 1995". Eff. for qualified transfers occurring after Dec. 17, 1999.

Child Support Performance and Incentive Act of 1998 (Pub. L. No. 105-200), as follows:
• ERISA §101(f) was amended by Act §401(h)(1)(B) by striking subsec. (f) relating to information necessary to comply with Medicare and Medicaid Coverage Data Bank requirements. Eff. Oct. 2, 1996, as if included in Pub. L. No. 104-226.

Taxpayer Relief Act of 1997 (Pub. L. No. 105-34), as follows:
• ERISA §101(b) was amended by Act §1503(a) by redesignating paras. (4) and (5) as (1) and (2), respectively, and striking former paras. (1)–(3). Eff. Aug. 5, 1997. ERISA §101(b)(1)–(3) prior to amendment:
(1) the summary plan description described in section 102(a)(1) of this title;
(2) a plan description containing the matter required in section 102(b) of this title;
(3) modifications and changes referred to in section 102(a)(2) of this title;.

Departments of Veterans Affairs and HUD and Independent Agencies Appropriations Act of 1997 (Pub. L. No. 104-204), as follows:
• ERISA §101(g) amended by Act §603(b) that making technical amendment to reference in original act which appears in text as reference to section 733 of this title. Eff. Jan. 1, 1998.

Health Insurance Portability and Accountability Act of 1996 (Pub. L. No. 104-191), as follows:
• ERISA §101(g) was redesignated by Act §101(e)(1)(B) as subsec. (h) and new (g) was added. Eff. June 30, 1997.

Small Business Job Protection Act of 1996 (Pub. L. No. 104-188), as follows:
• ERISA §101(g) was added by Act §1421(d)(1) by redesignating former subsec. (g), relating to cross references, as (h). Eff. Jan. 1, 1997.

Retirement Protection Act of 1994 (Pub. L. No. 103-465), as follows:
• ERISA §101(e)(3) was amended by Act §731(c) by substituting "1995" for "1991". Eff. Dec. 8, 1994.

Omnibus Budget Reconciliation Act of 1993 (Pub. L. No. 103-66), as follows:

• ERISA §101(f) was added and former (f) was redesignated as (g) by Act §4310(b). Eff. Aug. 10, 1993.

Omnibus Budget Reconciliation Act of 1990 (Pub. L. No. 101-508), as follows:
• ERISA §101(e) was added and former (e) was redesignated Act §12012(d)(1). Eff. Nov. 5, 1990.

Omnibus Budget Reconciliation Act of 1989 (Pub. L. No. 101-239), as follows:
• ERISA §101(a)(2) was amended by Act §7894(b)(2) by substituting "sections" for "section". Eff. as if included in Pub. L. No. 100-203.
• ERISA §101(d)(1) was amended by Act §7881(b)(5)(A) by substituting "an employer maintaining a plan" for "an employer of a plan". Eff. for plan years after 1987.

Agricultural Reconciliation Act of 1987 (Pub. L. 100-203), as follows:
• ERISA §101(d) was added and former (d) was redesignated as (e) by Act §304(d). Eff. for plan years after 1987.

SEC. 102. SUMMARY PLAN DESCRIPTION.

(a) A summary plan description of any employee benefit plan shall be furnished to participants and beneficiaries as provided in section 104(b). The summary plan description shall include the information described in subsection (b), shall be written in a manner calculated to be understood by the average plan participant, and shall be sufficiently accurate and comprehensive to reasonably apprise such participants and beneficiaries of their rights and obligations under the plan. A summary of any material modification in the terms of the plan and any change in the information required under subsection (b) shall be written in a manner calculated to be understood by the average plan participant and shall be furnished in accordance with section 104(b)(1).

(b) The summary plan description shall contain the following information: The name and type of administration of the plan; in the case of a group health plan (as defined in section 733(a)(1)), whether a health insurance issuer (as defined in section 733(b)(2)) is responsible for the financing or administration (including payment of claims) of the plan and (if so) the name and address of such issuer; the name and address of the person designated as agent for the service of legal process, if such person is not the administrator; the name and address of the administrator; names, titles and addresses of any trustee or trustees (if they are persons different from the administrator); a description of the relevant provisions of any applicable collective bargaining agreement; the plan's requirements respecting eligibility for participation and benefits; a description of the provisions providing for nonforfeitable pension benefits; circumstances which may result in disqualification, ineligibility, or denial or loss of benefits; the source of financing of the plan and the identity of any organization through which benefits are provided; the date of the end of the plan year and whether the records of the plan are kept on a calendar, policy, or fiscal year basis; the procedures to be followed in presenting claims for benefits under the plan including the office at the Department of Labor through which participants and beneficiaries may seek assistance or information regarding their rights under this Act and the Health Insurance Portability and Accountability Act of 1996 with respect to health benefits that are offered through a group health plan (as defined in section 733(a)(1)), the remedies available under the plan for the redress of claims which are denied in whole or in part (including procedures required under section 503 of this Act), and if the employer so elects for purposes of complying with §701(f)(3)(B)(i), the model notice applicable to the State in which the participants and beneficiaries reside.

Amendments to ERISA §102

Childen's Health Insurance Program Reauthorization Act of 2009 (Pub. L. No. 111-3), as follows:

● ERISA §102(b) was amended by Act §311(b)(1)(B)(i) by striking "and the remedies" and inserting ", the remedies". See Effective Date Note below.

● ERISA §102(b) was amended by Act §311(b)(1)(B)(ii) by inserting before the period ", and if the employer so elects for purposes of complying with section 701(f)(3)(B)(i), the model notice applicable to the State in which the participants and beneficiaries reside". See Effective Date Note below.

● **Effective Date Note.** Act §3 provides:

(a) **General Effective Date.**—Unless otherwise provided in this Act, subject to subsections (b) through (d), this Act (and the amendments made by this Act) shall take effect on April 1, 2009, and shall apply to child health assistance and medical assistance provided on or after that date.

(b) **Exception for State Legislation.**—In the case of a State plan under title XIX or State child health plan under XXI of the Social Security Act, which the Secretary of Health and Human Services determines requires State legislation in order for the respective plan to meet one or more additional requirements imposed by amendments made by this Act, the respective plan shall not be regarded as failing to comply with the requirements of such title solely on the basis of its failure to meet such an additional requirement before the first day of the first calendar quarter beginning after the close of the first regular session of the State legislature that begins after the date of enactment of this Act. For purposes of the previous sentence, in the case of a State that has a 2-year legislative session, each year of the session shall be considered to be a separate regular session of the State legislature.

(c) **Coordination of CHIP Funding for Fiscal Year 2009.**—Notwithstanding any other provision of law, insofar as funds have been appropriated under section 2104(a)(11), 2104(k), or 2104(l) of the Social Security Act, as amended by section 201 of Public Law 110-173, to provide allotments to States under CHIP for fiscal year 2009—

(1) any amounts that are so appropriated that are not so allotted and obligated before April 1, 2009 are rescinded; and

(2) any amount provided for CHIP allotments to a State under this Act (and the amendments made by this Act) for such fiscal year shall be reduced by the amount of such appropriations so allotted and obligated before such date.

(d) **Reliance on Law.**—With respect to amendments made by this Act (other than title VII) that become effective as of a date—

(1) such amendments are effective as of such date whether or not regulations implementing such amendments have been issued; and

(2) Federal financial participation for medical assistance or child health assistance furnished under title XIX or XXI, respectively, of the Social Security Act on or after such date

by a State in good faith reliance on such amendments before the date of promulgation of final regulations, if any, to carry out such amendments (or before the date of guidance, if any, regarding the implementation of such amendments) shall not be denied on the basis of the State's failure to comply with such regulations or guidance.

Taxpayer Relief Act of 1997 (Pub. L. No. 105-34), as follows:

● ERISA §102 was amended by Act §1503(b)(2)(B) by substituting "Summary plan description" for "Plan description and summary plan description" in section headline. Eff. Aug. 5, 1997.

● ERISA §102(a) was amended by Act §1503(b)(1) by striking "(1)" after subsec. designation and striking para. (2). Eff. Aug. 5, 1997. ERISA §102(a) prior to amendment:

(a) A plan description (containing the information required by subsection (b) of this section) of any employee benefit plan shall be prepared on forms prescribed by the Secretary, and shall be filed with the Secretary as required by section 104(a)(1) of this title. Any material modification in the terms of the plan and any change in the information described in subsection (b) of this section shall be filed in accordance with section 104(a)(1)(D) of this title.

● ERISA §102(b) was amended by Act §1503(b)(2)(A) by substituting "The summary plan description shall contain" for "The plan description and summary plan description shall contain". Eff. Aug. 5, 1997.

Departments of Veterans Affairs and HUD and Independent Agencies Appropriations Act of 1997 (Pub. L. No. 104-204), as follows:

● ERISA §102(b) was amended by Act §603(b) by making technical amendments to references which appeared in text as references to section 733. Eff. with respect to group health plans for plan years beginning on or after Jan. 1, 1998.

Health Insurance Portability and Accountability Act of 1996 (Pub. L. No. 104-191), as follows:

● ERISA §102(b) was amended by Act §101(c) by inserting "in the case of a group health plan (as defined in section 733(a)(1) of this title), whether a health insurance issuer (as defined in section 733(b)(2) of this title) is responsible for the financing or administration (including payment of claims) of the plan and (if so) the name and address of such issuer;" after "type of administration of the plan;" and "including the office at the Department of Labor through which participants and beneficiaries may seek assistance or information regarding their rights under this chapter and the Health Insurance Portability and Accountability Act of 1996 with respect to health benefits that are offered through a group health plan (as defined in section 733(a)(1) of this title)" after "presenting claims for benefits under the plan". Eff. with respect to group health plans for plan years beginning after June 30, 1997.

SEC. 103. ANNUAL REPORTS.

(a) Publication and Filing.—

(1)(A) An annual report shall be published with respect to every employee benefit plan to which this part applies. Such report shall be filed with the Secretary in accordance with section 104(a), and shall be made available and furnished to participants in accordance with section 104(b).

(B) The annual report shall include the information described in subsections (b) and (c) and where applicable subsections (d), (e), and (f) and shall also include—

(i) a financial statement and opinion, as required by paragraph (3) of this subsection, and

(ii) an actuarial statement and opinion, as required by paragraph (4) of this subsection.

(2) If some or all of the information necessary to enable the administrator to comply with the requirements of this title is maintained by—

(A) an insurance carrier or other organization which provides some or all of the benefits under the plan, or holds assets of the plan in a separate account,

(B) a bank or similar institution which holds some or all of the assets of the plan in a common or collective trust or a separate trust, or custodial account, or

(C) a plan sponsor as defined in section 3(16)(B),

such carrier, organization, bank, institution, or plan sponsor shall transmit and certify the accuracy of such information to the administrator within 120 days after the end of the plan year (or such other date as may be prescribed under regulations of the Secretary).

(3)(A) Except as provided in subparagraph (C), the administrator of an employee benefit plan shall engage, on behalf of all plan participants, an independent qualified public accountant, who shall conduct such an examination of any financial statements of the plan, and of other books and records of the plan, as the accountant may deem necessary to enable the accountant to form an opinion as to whether the financial statements and schedules required to be included in the annual report by subsection (b) of this section are presented fairly in conformity with generally accepted accounting principles applied on a basis consistent with that of the preceding year. Such examination shall be conducted in accordance with generally accepted auditing standards, and shall involve such tests of the books and records of the plan as are considered necessary by the independent qualified public accountant. The independent qualified public accountant shall also offer his opinion as to whether the separate schedules specified in subsection (b)(3) of this section and the summary material required under section 104(b)(3) present fairly and in all material respects the information contained therein when considered in conjunction with the financial statements taken as a whole. The opinion by the independent qualified public accountant shall be made a part of the annual report. In a case where a plan is not required to file an annual report, the requirements of this paragraph shall not apply. In a case where by reason of section 104(a)(2) a plan is required only to file a simplified annual report, the Secretary may waive the requirements of this paragraph.

(B) In offering his opinion under this section the accountant may rely on the correctness of any actuarial matter certified to by an enrolled actuary, if he so states his reliance.

(C) The opinion required by subparagraph (A) need not be expressed as to any statements required by subsection (b)(3)(G) prepared by a bank or similar institution or insurance carrier regulated and supervised and subject to periodic examination by a State or Federal agency if such statements are certified by the bank, similar institution, or insurance carrier as accurate and are made a part of the annual report.

(D) For purposes of this title, the term "qualified public accountant" means—

(i) a person who is a certified public accountant, certified by a regulatory authority of a State;

(ii) a person who is a licensed public accountant, licensed by a regulatory authority of a State; or

(iii) a person certified by the Secretary as a qualified public accountant in accordance with regulations published by him for a person who practices in States where there is no certification or licensing procedure for accountants.

(4)(A) The administrator of an employee pension benefit plan subject to the reporting requirement of subsection (d) of this section shall engage, on behalf of all plan participants, an enrolled actuary who shall be responsible for the preparation of the materials comprising the actuarial statement required under subsection (d) of this section. In a case where a plan is not required to file an annual report, the requirement of this paragraph shall not apply, and, in a case where by reason of section 104(a)(2), a plan is required only to file a simplified report, the Secretary may waive the requirement of this paragraph.

(B) The enrolled actuary shall utilize such assumptions and techniques as are necessary to enable him to form an opinion as to whether the contents of the matters reported under subsection (d) of this section—

(i) are in the aggregate reasonably related to the experience of the plan and to reasonable expectations; and

(ii) represent his best estimate of anticipated experience under the plan.

The opinion by the enrolled actuary shall be made with respect to, and shall be made a part of, each annual report.

(C) For purposes of this title, the term "enrolled actuary" means an actuary enrolled under subtitle C of title III of this Act.

(D) In making a certification under this section the enrolled actuary may rely on the correctness of any accounting matter under section 103(b) as to which any qualified public accountant has expressed an opinion, if he so states his reliance.

(b) Financial Statement.—An annual report under this section shall include a financial statement containing the following information:

(1) With respect to an employee welfare benefit plan: a statement of assets and liabilities; a statement of changes in fund balance; and a statement of changes in financial position. In the notes to financial statements, disclosures concerning the following items shall be considered by the accountant: a description of the plan including any significant changes in the plan made during the period and the impact of such changes on benefits; a description of material lease commitments, other commitments, and contingent liabilities; a description of agreements and transactions with persons known to be parties in interest; a general description of priorities upon termination of the plan; information concerning whether or not a tax ruling or determination letter has been obtained; and any other matters necessary to fully and fairly present the financial statements of the plan.

(2) With respect to an employee pension benefit plan: a statement of assets and liabilities, and a statement of changes in net assets available for plan benefits which shall include details of revenues and expenses and other changes aggregated by general source and application. In the notes to financial statements, disclosures concerning the following items shall be considered by the accountant: a description of the plan including any significant changes in the plan made during the period and the impact of such changes on benefits; the funding policy (including policy with respect to prior service cost), and any changes in such policies during the year; a description of any significant changes in plan benefits made during the period; a description of material lease commitments, other commitments, and contingent liabilities; a description of agreements and transactions with persons known to be parties in interest; a general description of priorities upon termination of the plan; information concerning whether or not a tax ruling or determination letter has been obtained; and any other matters necessary to fully and fairly present the financial statements of such pension plan.

(3) With respect to all employee benefit plans, the statement required under paragraph (1) or (2) shall have attached the following information in separate schedules:

(A) a statement of the assets and liabilities of the plan aggregated by categories and valued at their current value, and the same data displayed in comparative form for the end of the previous fiscal year of the plan;

(B) a statement of receipts and disbursements during the preceding twelve-month period aggregated by general sources and applications;

(C) a schedule of all assets held for investment purposes aggregated and identified by issuer, borrower, or lessor, or similar party to the transaction (including a notation as to whether such party is known to be a party in interest), maturity date, rate of interest, collateral, par or maturity value, cost, and current value;

(D) a schedule of each transaction involving a person known to be party in interest, the identity of such party in interest and his relationship or that of any other party in interest to the plan, a description of each asset to which the transaction relates; the purchase or selling price in case of a sale or purchase, the rental in case of a lease, or the interest rate and maturity date in case of a loan; expenses incurred in connection with the transaction; the cost of the asset, the current value of the asset, and the net gain (or loss) on each transaction;

(E) a schedule of all loans or fixed income obligations which were in default as of the close of the plan's fiscal year or were classified during the year as uncollectible and the following information with respect to each loan on such schedule (including a notation as to whether parties involved are known to be parties in interest): the original principal amount of the loan, the amount of principal and interest received during the reporting year, the unpaid balance, the identity and address of the obligor, a detailed description of the loan (including date of making and maturity, interest rate, the type and value of collateral, and other material terms), the amount of principal and interest overdue (if any) and an explanation thereof;

(F) a list of all leases which were in default or were classified during the year as uncollectible; and the following information with respect to each lease on such schedule (including a notation as to whether parties involved are known to be parties in interest): the type of property leased (and, in the case of fixed assets such as land, buildings, leasehold, and so forth, the location of the property), the identity of the lessor or lessee from or to whom the plan is leasing, the relationship of such lessors and lessees, if any, to the plan, the employer, employee organization, or any other party in interest, the terms of the lease regarding rent, taxes, insurance, repairs, expenses, and renewal options; the date the leased property was purchased and its cost, the date the property was leased and its approximate value at such date, the gross rental receipts during the reporting period, expenses paid for the leased property during the reporting period, the net receipts from the lease, the amounts in arrears, and a statement as to what steps have been taken to collect amounts due or otherwise remedy the default;

(G) if some or all of the assets of a plan or plans are held in a common or collective trust maintained by a bank or similar institution or in a separate account maintained by an insurance carrier or a separate trust maintained by a bank as trustee, the report shall include the most recent annual statement of assets and liabilities of such common or collective trust, and in the case of a separate account or a separate trust, such other information as is required by the administrator in order to comply with this subsection; and

(H) a schedule of each reportable transaction, the name of each party to the transaction (except that,

ERISA Sec. 103(b)(3)(H)

in the case of an acquisition or sale of a security on the market, the report need not identify the person from whom the security was acquired or to whom it was sold) and a description of each asset to which the transaction applies; the purchase or selling price in case of a sale or purchase, the rental in case of a lease, or the interest rate and maturity date in case of a loan; expenses incurred in connection with the transaction; the cost of the asset, the current value of the asset, and the net gain (or loss) on each transaction. For purposes of the preceding sentence, the term "reportable transaction" means a transaction to which the plan is a party if such transaction is—

(i) a transaction involving an amount in excess of 3 percent of the current value of the assets of the plan;

(ii) any transaction (other than a transaction respecting a security) which is part of a series of transactions with or in conjunction with a person in a plan year, if the aggregate amount of such transactions exceeds 3 percent of the current value of the assets of the plan;

(iii) a transaction which is part of a series of transactions respecting one or more securities of the same issuer, if the aggregate amount of such transactions in the plan year exceeds 3 percent of the current value of the assets of the plan; or

(iv) a transaction with or in conjunction with a person respecting a security, if any other transaction with or in conjunction with such person in the plan year respecting a security is required to be reported by reason of clause (i).

(4) The Secretary may, by regulation, relieve any plan from filing a copy of a statement of assets and liabilities (or other information) described in paragraph (3)(G) if such statement and other information is filed with the Secretary by the bank or insurance carrier which maintains the common or collective trust or separate account.

(c) **Information to Be Furnished by Administrator.**—The administrator shall furnish as a part of a report under this section the following information:

(1) The number of employees covered by the plan.

(2) The name and address of each fiduciary.

(3) Except in the case of a person whose compensation is minimal (determined under regulations of the Secretary) and who performs solely ministerial duties (determined under such regulations), the name of each person (including but not limited to, any consultant, broker, trustee, accountant, insurance carrier, actuary, administrator, investment manager, or custodian who rendered services to the plan or who had transactions with the plan) who received directly or indirectly compensation from the plan during the preceding year for services rendered to the plan or its participants, the amount of such compensation, the nature of his services to the plan or its participants, his relationship to the employer of the employees covered by the plan, or the employee organization, and any other office, position, or employment he holds with any party in interest.

(4) An explanation of the reason for any change in appointment of trustee, accountant, insurance carrier, enrolled actuary, administrator, investment manager, or custodian.

(5) Such financial and actuarial information including but not limited to the material described in subsections (b) and (d) of this section as the Secretary may find necessary or appropriate.

(d) **Actuarial Statement.**—With respect to an employee pension benefit plan (other than (A) a profit sharing, savings, or other plan, which is an individual account plan, (B) a plan described in section 301(b), or (C) a plan described both in section 4021(b) and in paragraph (1), (2), (3), (4), (5), (6), or (7) of section 301(a)) an annual report under this section for a plan year shall include a complete actuarial statement applicable to the plan year which shall include the following:

(1) The date of the plan year, and the date of the actuarial valuation applicable to the plan year for which the report is filed.

(2) The date and amount of the contribution (or contributions) received by the plan for the plan year for which the report is filed and contributions for prior plan years not previously reported.

(3) The following information applicable to the plan year for which the report is filed: the normal costs or target normal costs, the accrued liabilities or funding target, an identification of benefits not included in the calculation; a statement of the other facts and actuarial assumptions and methods used to determine costs, and a justification for any change in actuarial assumptions or cost methods; and the minimum contribution required under section 302.

(4) The number of participants and beneficiaries, both retired and nonretired, covered by the plan.

(5) The current value of the assets accumulated in the plan, and the present value of the assets of the plan used by the actuary in any computation of the amount of contributions to the plan required under section 302 and a statement explaining the basis of such valuation of present value of assets.

(6) Information required in regulations of the Pension Benefit Guaranty Corporation with respect to:

(A) the current value of the assets of the plan,

(B) the present value of all nonforfeitable benefits for participants and beneficiaries receiving payments under the plan,

(C) the present value of all nonforfeitable benefits for all other participants and beneficiaries,

(D) the present value of all accrued benefits which are not nonforfeitable (including a separate accounting of such benefits which are benefit commitments, as defined in section 4001(a)(16)), and

(E) the actuarial assumptions and techniques used in determining the values described in subparagraphs (A) through (D).

(7) A certification of the contribution necessary to reduce the minimum required contribution determined under section 303, or the accumulated funding deficiency determined under section 304 to zero.

(8) A statement by the enrolled actuary—

(A) that to the best of his knowledge the report is complete and accurate, and

(B) the applicable requirements of sections 303(h) and 304(c)(3) (relating to reasonable actuarial assumptions and methods) have been complied with.

(9) A copy of the opinion required by subsection (a)(4).

(10) A statement by the actuary which discloses—

(A) any event which the actuary has not taken into account, and

(B) any trend which, for purposes of the actuarial assumptions used, was not assumed to continue in the future,

but only if, to the best of the actuary's knowledge, such event or trend may require a material increase in plan costs or required contribution rates.

(11) If the current value of the assets of the plan is less than 70 percent of—

(A) in the case of a single-employer plan, the funding target (as defined in section 303(d)(1)) of the plan, or

(B) in the case of a multiemployer plan, the current liability (as defined in section 304(c)(6)(D)) under the plan,

the percentage which such value is of the amount described in subparagraph (A) or (B).

(12) A statement explaining the actuarial assumptions and methods used in projecting future retirements and forms of benefit distributions under the plan.

(13) Such other information regarding the plan as the Secretary may by regulation require.

(14) Such other information as may be necessary to fully and fairly disclose the actuarial position of the plan.

Such actuary shall make an actuarial valuation of the plan for every third plan year, unless he determines that a more frequent valuation is necessary to support his opinion under subsection (a)(4) of this section.

(e) Statement From Insurance Company, Insurance Service, or Other Similar Organizations Which Sell or Guarantee Plan Benefits.—If some or all of the benefits under the plan are purchased from and guaranteed by an insurance company, insurance service, or other similar organization, a report under this section shall include a statement from such insurance company, service, or other similar organization covering the plan year and enumerating—

(1) the premium rate or subscription charge and the total premium or subscription charges paid to each such carrier, insurance service, or other similar organization and the approximate number of persons covered by each class of such benefits; and

(2) the total amount of premiums received, the approximate number of persons covered by each class of benefits, and the total claims paid by such company, service, or other organization; dividends or retroactive rate adjustments, commissions, and administrative service or other fees or other specific acquisition costs paid by such company, service, or other organization; any amounts held to provide benefits after retirement; the remainder of such premiums; and the names and addresses of the brokers, agents, or other persons to whom commissions or fees were paid, the amount paid to each, and for what purpose. If any such company, service, or other organization does not maintain separate experience records covering the specific groups it serves, the report shall include in lieu of the information required by the foregoing provisions of this paragraph (A) a statement as to the basis of its premium rate or subscription charge, the total amount of premiums or subscription charges received from the plan, and a copy of the financial report of the company, service, or other organization and (B) if such company, service, or organization incurs specific costs in connection with the acquisition or retention of any particular plan or plans, a detailed statement of such costs.

(f) Additional Information With Respect to Defined Benefit Plans.—

(1) Liabilities under 2 or more plans.—

(A) In general.—In any case in which any liabilities to participants or their beneficiaries under a defined benefit plan as of the end of a plan year consist (in whole or in part) of liabilities to such participants and beneficiaries under 2 or more pension plans as of immediately before such plan year, an annual report under this section for such plan year shall include the funded percentage of each of such 2 or more pension plans as of the last day of such plan year and the funded percentage of the plan with respect to which the annual report is filed as of the last day of such plan year.

(B) Funded percentage.—For purposes of this paragraph, the term "funded percentage"—

(i) in the case of a single-employer plan, means the funding target attainment percentage, as defined in section 303(d)(2), and

ERISA Sec. 103(f)(1)(B)(i)

(ii) in the case of a multiemployer plan, has the meaning given such term in section 305(i)(2).

(2) Additional information for multiemployer plans.—With respect to any defined benefit plan which is a multiemployer plan, an annual report under this section for a plan year shall include, in addition to the information required under paragraph (1), the following, as of the end of the plan year to which the report relates:

(A) The number of employers obligated to contribute to the plan.

(B) A list of the employers that contributed more than 5 percent of the total contributions to the plan during such plan year.

(C) The number of participants under the plan on whose behalf no contributions were made by an employer as an employer of the participant for such plan year and for each of the 2 preceding plan years.

(D) The ratios of—

(i) the number of participants under the plan on whose behalf no employer had an obligation to make an employer contribution during the plan year, to

(ii) the number of participants under the plan on whose behalf no employer had an obligation to make an employer contribution during each of the 2 preceding plan years.

(E) Whether the plan received an amortization extension under section 304(d) of this Act or section 431(d) of the Internal Revenue Code of 1986 for such plan year and, if so, the amount of the difference between the minimum required contribution for the year and the minimum required contribution which would have been required without regard to the extension, and the period of such extension.

(F) Whether the plan used the shortfall funding method (as such term is used in section 305) for such plan year and, if so, the amount of the difference between the minimum required contribution for the year and the minimum required contribution which would have been required without regard to the use of such method, and the period of use of such method.

(G) Whether the plan was in critical or endangered status under section 305 for such plan year, and if so, a summary of any funding improvement or rehabilitation plan (or modification thereto) adopted during the plan year, and the funded percentage of the plan.

(H) The number of employers that withdrew from the plan during the preceding plan year and the aggregate amount of withdrawal liability assessed, or estimated to be assessed, against such withdrawn employers.

(I) In the case of a multiemployer plan that has merged with another plan or to which assets and liabilities have been transferred, the actuarial valuation of the assets and liabilities of each affected plan during the year preceding the effective date of the merger or transfer, based upon the most recent data available as of the day before the first day of the plan year, or other valuation method performed under standards and procedures as the Secretary may prescribe by regulation.

Amendments to ERISA §103

Worker, Retiree, and Employer Recovery Act of 2008 (Pub. L. No. 110-458), as follows:

● ERISA §103(d)(3) was amended by Act §101(d)(1)(A)(i) by striking "the normal costs, the accrued liabilities" and inserting "the normal costs or target normal costs, the accrued liabilities or funding target". Eff. for plan years beginning after 2007, as if included in §107 of Pub. L. No. 109-280.

● ERISA §103(d)(7) was amended by Act §101(d)(1)(A)(ii). Eff. for plan years beginning after 2007, as if included in §107 of Pub. L. No. 109-280. ERISA §103(d)(7) prior to amendment:

(7) A certification of the contribution necessary to reduce the accumulated funding deficiency to zero.

Pension Protection Act of 2006 (Pub. L. No. 109-280), as follows:

● ERISA §103(a)(1)(B) was amended by Act §503(a)(1) by substituting "subsections (d), (e), and (f)" for "subsections (d) and (e)". Eff. for plan years beginning after Dec. 31, 2007.

● ERISA §103(d)(8)(B) was amended by Act §107(a)(2) (redesignated as §108(a)(2) by Pub. L. No. 111-192, §202(a)) by substituting "the applicable requirements of §§303(h) and 304(c)(3)" for "the requirements of Sec. 302(c)(3)". Eff. for plan years beginning after 2007. There is a delayed effective date for "eligible cooperative plans" until the earlier of the first plan year that the plan ceases to be an eligible cooperative plan, or Jan. 1, 2017.

● ERISA §103(d)(11) was amended by Act §107(a)(3) (redesignated as §108(a)(3) by Pub. L. No. 111-192, §202(a)) by replacing former para. (11) with new para. (11). Eff. for plan years beginning after 2007. There is a delayed effective date for "eligible cooperative plans" until the earlier of the first plan year that the plan ceases to be an eligible cooperative plan, or Jan. 1, 2017. ERISA §103(d)(11) prior to amendment:

(11) If the current value of the assets of the plan is less than 70 percent of the current liability under the plan (within the meaning of Sec. 302(d)(7)), the percentage which such value is of such liability.

● ERISA §103(d)(12)–(14) were amended by Act §503(b) by redesignating (12)–(13) as (13)–(14), and adding a new para. (12). Eff. for plan years beginning after 2007.

● ERISA §103(f), added by Act §503(a)(1)(B). Eff. for plan years after 2007.

Omnibus Budget Reconciliation Act of 1989 (Pub. L. No. 101-239), as follows:

● ERISA §103(d)(11) was amended by Act §7881(j) by substituting "70 percent" for "60 percent" and "the percentage which such value is of such liability." for "such percentage". Eff. as if included in Pub. L. No. 100-203.

Omnibus Budget Reconciliation Act of 1987 (Pub. L. No. 100-203), as follows:

● ERISA §103(d)(11)–(13) were amended by Act §9342(a) by adding para. (11) and redesignating former paras. (11)–(12) as (12)–(13), respectively. Eff. Jan. 1, 1988.

Consolidated Omnibus Budget Reconciliation Act of 1986 (Pub. L. No. 99-272), as follows:

● ERISA §103(d)(6) was amended by Act §11016(b). Eff. Jan. 1, 1986. ERISA §103(d)(6) prior to amendment:

(6) The present value of all of the plan's liabilities for nonforfeitable pension benefits allocated by the termination priority categories as set forth in section 4044 of this title, and

the actuarial assumptions used in these computations. The Secretary shall establish regulations defining (for purposes of this section) "termination priority categories" and acceptable methods, including approximate methods, for allocating the plan's liabilities to such termination priority categories.

Multiemployer Pension Plan Amendments Act of 1980 (Pub. L. No. 96-364), as follows:

● ERISA §103(d)(10) was added and former paras. (10)–(11) were redesignated as (11)–(12), respectively, by Act §307. Eff. Sept. 26, 1980.

SEC. 104. FILING WITH SECRETARY AND FURNISHING INFORMATION TO PARTICIPANTS AND CERTAIN EMPLOYERS.

(a) Filing of Annual Report, With Secretary.—

(1) The administrator of any employee benefit plan subject to this part shall file with the Secretary the annual report for a plan year within 210 days after the close of such year (or within such time as may be required by regulations promulgated by the Secretary in order to reduce duplicative filing). The Secretary shall make copies of such annual reports available for inspection in the public document room of the Department of Labor.

(2)(A) With respect to annual reports required to be filed with the Secretary under this part, he may by regulation prescribe simplified annual reports for any pension plan which covers less than 100 participants.

(B) Nothing contained in this paragraph shall preclude the Secretary from requiring any information or data from any such plan to which this part applies where he finds such data or information is necessary to carry out the purposes of this title nor shall the Secretary be precluded from revoking provisions for simplified reports for any such plan if he finds it necessary to do so in order to carry out the objectives of this title.

(3) The Secretary may by regulation exempt any welfare benefit plan from all or part of the reporting and disclosure requirements of this title, or may provide for simplified reporting and disclosure if he finds that such requirements are inappropriate as applied to welfare benefit plans.

(4) The Secretary may reject any filing under this section—

(A) if he determines that such filing is incomplete for purposes of this part; or

(B) if he determines that there is any material qualification by an accountant or actuary contained in an opinion submitted pursuant to section 103(a)(3)(A) or section 103(a)(4)(B).

(5) If the Secretary rejects a filing of a report under paragraph (4) and if a revised filing satisfactory to the Secretary is not submitted within 45 days after

the Secretary makes his determination under paragraph (4) to reject the filing, and if the Secretary deems it in the best interest of the participants, he may take any one or more of the following actions—

(A) retain an independent qualified public accountant (as defined in section 103(a)(3)(D)) on behalf of the participants to perform an audit,

(B) retain an enrolled actuary (as defined in section 103(a)(4)(C) of this Act) on behalf of the plan participants, to prepare an actuarial statement,

(C) bring a civil action for such legal or equitable relief as may be appropriate to enforce the provisions of this part, or

(D) take any other action authorized by this title.

The administrator shall permit such accountant or actuary to inspect whatever books and records of the plan are necessary for such audit. The plan shall be liable to the Secretary for the expenses for such audit or report, and the Secretary may bring an action against the plan in any court of competent jurisdiction to recover such expenses.

(6) The administrator of any employee benefit plan subject to this part shall furnish to the Secretary, upon request, any documents relating to the employee benefit plan, including but not limited to, the latest summary plan description (including any summaries of plan changes not contained in the summary plan description), and the bargaining agreement, trust agreement, contract, or other instrument under which the plan is established or operated.

(b) Publication of Summary Plan Description and Annual Report to Participants and Beneficiaries of Plan.—Publication of the summary plan descriptions and annual reports shall be made to participants and beneficiaries of the particular plan as follows:

(1) The administrator shall furnish to each participant, and each beneficiary receiving benefits under the plan, a copy of the summary plan description, and all modifications and changes referred to in section 102(a)—

(A) within 90 days after he becomes a participant, or (in the case of a beneficiary) within 90 days after he first receives benefits, or

(B) if later, within 120 days after the plan becomes subject to this part.

The administrator shall furnish to each participant, and each beneficiary receiving benefits under the plan, every fifth year after the plan becomes subject to this part an updated summary plan description described in section 102(a) which integrates all plan amendments made within such five-year period, except that in a case where no amendments have been made to a plan during such five-year period this sentence shall not apply. Notwithstanding the foregoing, the administrator shall furnish to each participant, and to each beneficiary receiving benefits under the plan, the summary plan description described in section 102 every tenth year after the plan becomes subject to this part. If there is a modification or change described in section 102(a) (other than a material reduction in covered services or benefits provided in the case of a group health plan (as defined in section 733(a)(1))), a summary description of such modification or change shall be furnished not later than 210 days after the end of the plan year in which the change is adopted to each participant, and to each beneficiary who is receiving benefits under the plan. If there is a modification or change described in section 102(a) that is a material reduction in covered services or benefits provided under a group health plan (as defined in section 733(a)(1)), a summary description of such modification or change shall be furnished to participants and beneficiaries not later than 60 days after the date of the adoption of the modification or change. In the alternative, the plan sponsors may provide such description at regular intervals of not more than 90 days. The Secretary shall issue regulations within 180 days after August 21, 1996, [the date of enactment of the Health Insurance Portability and Accountability Act of 1996], providing alternative mechanisms to delivery by mail through which group health plans (as so defined) may notify participants and beneficiaries of material reductions in covered services or benefits.

(2) The administrator shall make copies of the latest updated summary plan description and the latest annual report and the bargaining agreement, trust agreement, contract, or other instruments under which the plan was established or is operated available for examination by any plan participant or beneficiary in the principal office of the administrator and in such other places as may be necessary to make available all pertinent information to all participants (including such places as the Secretary may prescribe by regulations).

(3) Within 210 days after the close of the fiscal year of the plan, the administrator (other than an administrator of a defined benefit plan to which the requirements of section 101(f) applies) shall furnish to each participant, and to each beneficiary receiving benefits under the plan, a copy of the statements and schedules, for such fiscal year, described in subparagraphs (A) and (B) of section 103(b)(3) and such other material (including the percentage determined under section 103(d)(11)) as is necessary to fairly summarize the latest annual report.

(4) The administrator shall, upon written request of any participant or beneficiary, furnish a copy of the latest updated summary, [so in original; comma probably should not appear] plan description, and the latest annual report, any terminal report, the bargaining agreement, trust agreement, contract, or other instruments under which the plan is established or operated. The administrator may make a reasonable

charge to cover the cost of furnishing such complete copies. The Secretary may by regulation prescribe the maximum amount which will constitute a reasonable charge under the preceding sentence.

(5) Identification and basic plan information and actuarial information included in the annual report for any plan year shall be filed with the Secretary in an electronic format which accommodates display on the Internet, in accordance with regulations which shall be prescribed by the Secretary. The Secretary shall provide for display of such information included in the annual report, within 90 days after the date of the filing of the annual report, on an Internet website maintained by the Secretary and other appropriate media. Such information shall also be displayed on any Intranet website maintained by the plan sponsor (or by the plan administrator on behalf of the plan sponsor) for the purpose of communicating with employees and not the public, in accordance with regulations which shall be prescribed by the Secretary.

(c) Statement of Rights.—The Secretary may by regulation require that the administrator of any employee benefit plan furnish to each participant and to each beneficiary receiving benefits under the plan a statement of the rights of participants and beneficiaries under this title.

(d) Furnishing Summary Plan Information to Employers and Employee Representatives of Multiemployer Plans.—

(1) In general.—With respect to a multiemployer plan subject to this section, within 30 days after the due date under subsection (a)(1) for the filing of the annual report for the fiscal year of the plan, the administrators shall furnish to each employee organization and to each employer with an obligation to contribute to the plan a report that contains—

(A) a description of the contribution schedules and benefit formulas under the plan, and any modification to such schedules and formulas, during such plan year;

(B) the number of employers obligated to contribute to the plan;

(C) a list of the employers that contributed more than 5 percent of the total contributions to the plan during such plan year;

(D) the number of participants under the plan on whose behalf no contributions were made by an employer as an employer of the participant for such plan year and for each of the 2 preceding plan years;

(E) whether the plan was in critical or endangered status under section 305 for such plan year and, if so, include—

(i) a list of the actions taken by the plan to improve its funding status; and

(ii) a statement describing how a person may obtain a copy of the plan's funding improvement or rehabilitation plan, as applicable, adopted under section 305 and the actuarial and financial data that demonstrate any action taken by the plan toward fiscal improvement;

(F) the number of employers that withdrew from the plan during the preceding plan year and the aggregate amount of withdrawal liability assessed, or estimated to be assessed, against such withdrawn employers, as reported on the annual report for the plan year to which the report under this subsection relates;

(G) in the case of a multiemployer plan that has merged with another plan or to which assets and liabilities have been transferred, the actuarial valuation of the assets and liabilities of each affected plan during the year preceding the effective date of the merger or transfer, based upon the most recent data available as of the day before the first day of the plan year, or other valuation method performed under standards and procedures as the Secretary may prescribe by regulation;

(H) a description as to whether the plan—

(i) sought or received an amortization extension under section 304(d) of this Act or section 431(d) of the Internal Revenue Code of 1986 for such plan year; or

(ii) used the shortfall funding method (as such term is used in section 305) for such plan year; and

(I) notification of the right under this section of the recipient to a copy of the annual report filed with the Secretary under subsection (a), summary plan description, summary of any material modification of the plan, upon written request, but that—

(i) in no case shall a recipient be entitled to receive more than one copy of any such document described during any one 12-month period; and

(ii) the administrator may make a reasonable charge to cover copying, mailing, and other costs of furnishing copies of information pursuant to this subparagraph.

(2) **Effect of subsection.**—Nothing in this subsection waives any other provision under this title requiring plan administrators to provide, upon request, information to employers that have an obligation to contribute under the plan.

(e) **Cross References.**—For regulations respecting coordination of reports to the Secretaries of Labor and the Treasury, see section 3004.

Amendments to ERISA §104

Worker, Retiree, and Employer Recovery Act of 2008 (Pub. L. No. 110-458), as follows:

● ERISA §104(b)(3) was amended by Act §105(c)(1)(A) by striking "section 103(f)" and inserting "section 101(f)", and striking "the administrators" and inserting "the administrator" [Ed. Note: second amendment could not be made]. Eff. for plan years

after 2007 as if included in amendments made by §503 of Pub. L. No. 109-280.

● ERISA §104(d)(1)(E)(ii) was amended by Act §105(c)(1)(B) by inserting "funding" after "plan's". Eff. for plan years after 2007 as if included in amendments made by §503 of Pub. L. No. 109-280.

Pension Protection Act of 2006 (Pub. L. No. 109-280), as follows:

● ERISA §104(b)(3) was amended by Act §503(c)(1) by adding "(other than an administrator of a defined benefit plan to which the requirements of section 103(f) applies)" after "the administrator". Eff. for plan years after 2007.

● ERISA §104(b)(5) was added by Act §504(a). Eff. for plan years after 2007.

● ERISA §104(d) was amended by Act §503(d)(2) by redesignating (d) as (e), and inserting new (d). Eff. for plan years after 2007. ERISA §104(d) prior to amendment:

> **(d) Cross References.**—For regulations respecting coordination of reports to the Secretary of Labor and the Treasury, see section 30004.

Taxpayer Relief Act of 1997 (Pub. L. No. 105-34), as follows:

● ERISA §104(a)(1) was amended by Act §1503(c)(1) by substituting provisions for former provisions requiring filing of annual report, plan description, summary plan description, as well as modifications and changes in plan descriptions. Eff. Aug. 5, 1997.

● ERISA §104(a)(6) was amended by Act §1503(c)(2)(A) by adding para. (6). Eff. Aug. 5, 1997.

● ERISA §104(b)(1) was amended by Act §1503(d)(1) by substituting "section 102(a) of this title" for "section 102(a)(1) of this title" wherever appearing. Eff. Aug. 5, 1997.

● ERISA §104(b)(2) was amended by Act ERISA §1503(d)(2) by substituting "the latest updated summary plan description and" for "the plan description and". Eff. Aug. 5, 1997.

● ERISA §104(b)(4) was amended by Act §1503(d)(3) by striking "plan description" before ", latest annual report". Eff. Aug. 5, 1997.

Departments of Veterans Affairs and HUD and Independent Agencies Appropriations Act of 1997 (Pub. L. No. 104-204), as follows:

● ERISA §104(b)(1) was amended by Act §603(b) by technical amendments to references in original act which appear in text as references to ERISA §733. Eff. with respect to group health plans for plan years beginning on or after Jan. 1, 1998.

Health Insurance Portability and Accountability Act of 1996 (Pub. L. No. 104-191), as follows:

● ERISA §104(b)(1) was amended by Act §101(c)(1), in the flush language, by substituting "102(a)(1) of this title (other than a material reduction in covered services or benefits provided in the case of a group health plan (as defined in §733(a)(1) of this title))," for "102(a)(1) of this title," and inserting at end "If there is a modification or change described in section 102(a)(1) of this title that is a material reduction in covered services or benefits provided under a group health plan (as defined in section 733(a)(1) of this title), a summary description of such modification or change shall be furnished to participants and beneficiaries not later than 60 days after the date of the adoption of the modification or change. In the alternative, the plan sponsors may provide such description at regular intervals of not more than 90 days. The Secretary shall issue regulations within 180 days after August 21, 1996, providing alternative mechanisms to delivery by mail through which group health plans (as so defined) may notify participants and beneficiaries of material reductions in covered services or benefits." Eff. for group health plans for plan years beginning after June 30, 1997.

Omnibus Budget Reconciliation Act of 1989 (Pub. L. No. 101-239), as follows:

● ERISA §104(a)(5)(B) was amended by Act §7894(b)(3) by substituting a comma for period at end. Eff. as if originally included in Pub. L. No. 93-406, see Act §7894(i).

● ERISA §104(b)(1) as amended by Act §7894(b)(4) by striking comma after "summary". Eff. as if originally included in Pub. L. No. 93-406, see Act §7894(i).

Omnibus Budget Reconciliation Act of 1987 (Pub. L. No. 100-203), as follows:

ERISA Sec. 104(e)

- ERISA §104(b)(3) was amended by Act §9342(a)(2) by inserting "(including the percentage determined under section 103(d)(11) of this title)" after "material". Eff. with respect to reports required to be filed after Dec. 31, 1987.

Consolidated Omnibus Budget Reconciliation Act of 1986 (Pub. L. No. 99-272), as follows:

- ERISA §104(a)(2)(A) was amended by Act §11016(b)(2) by striking provision permitting the Secretary to waive or modify the requirements of ERISA §103(d)(6) if he found that the interests of the plan participants were not harmed and the expense of compliance was not justified by the needs of the participants, PBGC, and the Department of Labor for some portion or all of the information otherwise required under ERISA §103(d)(6). Eff. effective Jan. 1, 1986.

SEC. 105. REPORTING OF PARTICIPANT'S BENEFIT RIGHTS.

(a) Requirements To Provide Pension Benefit Statements.—

(1) Requirements.—

(A) Individual account plan.—The administrator of an individual account plan (other than a one-participant retirement plan described in section 101(i)(8)(B)) shall furnish a pension benefit statement—

(i) at least once each calendar quarter to a participant or beneficiary who has the right to direct the investment of assets in his or her account under the plan,

(ii) at least once each calendar year to a participant or beneficiary who has his or her own account under the plan but does not have the right to direct the investment of assets in that account, and

(iii) upon written request to a plan beneficiary not described in clause (i) or (ii).

(B) Defined benefit plan.—The administrator of a defined benefit plan (other than a one-participant retirement plan described in section 101(i)(8)(B)) shall furnish a pension benefit statement—

(i) at least once every 3 years to each participant with a nonforfeitable accrued benefit and who is employed by the employer maintaining the plan at the time the statement is to be furnished, and

(ii) to a participant or beneficiary of the plan upon written request.

Information furnished under clause (i) to a participant may be based on reasonable estimates determined under regulations prescribed by the Secretary, in consultation with the Pension Benefit Guaranty Corporation.

(2) Statements.—

(A) In general.—A pension benefit statement under paragraph (1)—

(i) shall indicate, on the basis of the latest available information—

(I) the total benefits accrued, and

(II) the nonforfeitable pension benefits, if any, which have accrued, or the earliest date on which benefits will become nonforfeitable,

(ii) shall include an explanation of any permitted disparity under section 401(l) of the Internal Revenue Code of 1986 or any floor-offset arrangement that may be applied in determining any accrued benefits described in clause (i),

(iii) shall be written in a manner calculated to be understood by the average plan participant, and

(iv) may be delivered in written, electronic, or other appropriate form to the extent such form is reasonably accessible to the participant or beneficiary.

(B) Additional information.—In the case of an individual account plan, any pension benefit statement under clause (i) or (ii) of paragraph (1)(A) shall include—

(i) the value of each investment to which assets in the individual account have been allocated, determined as of the most recent valuation date under the plan, including the value of any assets held in the form of employer securities, without regard to whether such employer securities were contributed by the plan sponsor or acquired at the direction of the plan or of the participant or beneficiary, and

(ii) in the case of a pension benefit statement under paragraph (1)(A)(i)—

(I) an explanation of any limitations or restrictions on any right of the participant or beneficiary under the plan to direct an investment,

(II) an explanation, written in a manner calculated to be understood by the average plan participant, of the importance, for the long-term retirement security of participants and beneficiaries, of a well-balanced and diversified investment portfolio, including a statement of the risk that holding more than 20 percent of a portfolio in the security of one entity (such as employer securities) may not be adequately diversified, and

(III) a notice directing the participant or beneficiary to the Internet website of the Department of Labor for sources of information on individual investing and diversification.

(C) Alternative notice.—The requirements of subparagraph (A)(i)(II) are met if, at least annually and in accordance with requirements of the Secretary, the plan—

(i) updates the information described in such paragraph which is provided in the pension benefit statement, or

(ii) provides in a separate statement such information as is necessary to enable a participant or beneficiary to determine their nonforfeitable vested benefits.

(3) Defined benefit plans.—

(A) Alternative notice.—In the case of a defined benefit plan, the requirements of paragraph (1)(B)(i) shall be treated as met with respect to a participant if at least once each year the administrator provides to the participant notice of the availability of the pension benefit statement and the ways in which the participant may obtain such statement. Such notice may be delivered in written, electronic, or other appropriate form to the extent such form is reasonably accessible to the participant.

(B) Years in which no benefits accrue.—The Secretary may provide that years in which no employee or former employee benefits (within the meaning of section 410(b) of the Internal Revenue Code of 1986) under the plan need not be taken into account in determining the 3-year period under paragraph (1)(B)(i).

(b) Limitation on Number of Statements.—In no case shall a participant or beneficiary of a plan be entitled to more than 1 statement described in subparagraph (A)(iii) or (B)(ii) of subsection (a)(1), whichever is applicable, in any 12-month period.

(c) Individual Statement Furnished by Administrator to Participants Setting Forth Information in Administrator's Internal Revenue Registration Statement and Notification of Forfeitable Benefits.—Each administrator required to register under section 6057 of title 26 shall, before the expiration of the time prescribed for such registration, furnish to each participant described in subsection (a)(2)(C) of such section, an individual statement setting forth the information with respect to such participant required to be contained in the registration statement required by section 6057(a)(2) of title 26. Such statement shall also include a notice to the participant of any benefits which are forfeitable if the participant dies before a certain date.

(d) [Repealed.]

Amendments to ERISA §105
Pension Protection Act of 2006 (Pub. L. No. 109-280), as follows:
● ERISA §105(a) was amended by Act §508(a)(1). Eff. for plan years beginning after Dec. 31, 2006. ERISA §105(a) prior to amendment:
    (a) Statement furnished by administrator to participants and beneficiaries.—Each administrator of an employee pension benefit plan shall furnish to any plan participant or beneficiary who so requests in writing, a statement indicating, on the basis of the latest available information—
      (1) the total benefits accrued, and
      (2) the nonforfeitable pension benefits, if any, which have accrued, or the earliest date on which benefits will become nonforfeitable.
● ERISA §105(b) was amended by Act §508(a)(2)(B). Eff. generally for plan years beginning after Dec. 31, 2006. ERISA §105(b) prior to amendment:

(b) One-per-Year Limit on Reports.—In no case shall a participant or beneficiary be entitled under this section to receive more than one report described in subsection (a) during any one 12-month period.
● ERISA §105(d) was stricken by Act §508(a)(2)(A). Eff. for plan years beginning after Dec. 31, 2006. ERISA §105(d) prior to being stricken:
    (d) Plans to Which More than One Unaffiliated Employer Is Required to Contribute; Regulations.—Subsection (a) of this section shall apply to a plan to which more than one unaffiliated employer is required to contribute only to the extent provided in regulations prescribed by the Secretary in coordination with the Secretary of the Treasury.
Omnibus Budget Reconciliation Act of 1989 (Pub. L. No. 101-239), as follows:
● ERISA §105(b) was amended by Act §7894(b)(5) by substituting "12-month" for "12 month". Eff. as if originally included in Pub. L. No. 93-406.
● ERISA §105(c) was amended by Act §7891(a)(1) by substituting "Internal Revenue Code of 1986" for "Internal Revenue Code of 1954", which for purposes of codification was translated as "title 26". Eff. as if originally included in Pub. L. No. 99-514.
Retirement Equity Act of 1984 (Pub. L. No. 98-397), as follows:
● ERISA §105(c) was amended by Act §106 by inserting at the end "Such statement shall also include a notice to the participant of any benefits which are forfeitable if the participant dies before a certain date." Eff. for plan years beginning after Dec. 31, 1984.

SEC. 106. REPORTS MADE PUBLIC INFORMATION.

(a) Except as provided in subsection (b), the contents of the annual reports, statements, and other documents filed with the Secretary pursuant to this part shall be public information and the Secretary shall make any such information and data available for inspection in the public document room of the Department of Labor. The Secretary may use the information and data for statistical and research purposes, and compile and publish such studies, analyses, reports, and surveys based thereon as he may deem appropriate.

(b) Information described in sections 105(a) and 105(c) with respect to a participant may be disclosed only to the extent that information respecting that participant's benefits under title II of the Social Security Act may be disclosed under such Act.

Amendments to ERISA §106
Taxpayer Relief Act of 1997 (Pub. L. No. 105-34), as follows:
● ERISA §106(a) was amended by Act §1503(d)(4) by striking "descriptions," before "annual reports," . Eff. Aug. 5, 1997.
Omnibus Budget Reconciliation Act of 1989 (Pub. L. No. 101-239), as follows:
● ERISA §106(b) was amended by Act §7894(b)(6) by substituting "sections" for "section". Eff. as if included in Pub. L. No. 93-406.

SEC. 107. RETENTION OF RECORDS.

Every person subject to a requirement to file any report or to certify any information therefor under this title or who would be subject to such a requirement but for an exemption or simplified reporting requirement under section 104(a)(2) or (3) of this title shall maintain records on the matters of which disclosure is required which will provide in sufficient detail the necessary basic information and data from which the documents thus required may be verified, explained, or clarified, and checked for accuracy and completeness, and shall include vouchers, worksheets, receipts, and applicable resolutions, and shall keep such records available for examination for a period of not less than six years after the filing date of the documents based on the information which they contain, or six years after the date on which such documents would have been filed but for an exemption or simplified reporting requirement under section 104(a)(2) or (3).

Amendments to ERISA §107

Taxpayer Relief Act of 1997 (Pub. L. No. 105-34), as follows:
● ERISA §107 was amended by Act §1503(d)(5) by striking "description or" after "requirement to file any". Eff. Aug. 5, 1997.

SEC. 108. RELIANCE ON ADMINISTRATIVE INTERPRETATIONS.

In any criminal proceeding under section 501 based on any act or omission in alleged violation of this part or section 412, no person shall be subject to any liability or punishment for or on account of the failure of such person to (1) comply with this part or section 412, if he pleads and proves that the act or omission complained of was in good faith, in conformity with, and in reliance on any regulation or written ruling of the Secretary, or (2) publish and file any information required by any provision of this part if he pleads and proves that he published and filed such information in good faith, and in conformity with any regulation or written ruling of the Secretary issued under this part regarding the filing of such reports. Such a defense, if established, shall be a bar to the action or proceeding, notwithstanding that (A) after such act or omission, such interpretation or opinion is modified or rescinded or is determined by judicial authority to be invalid or of no legal effect, or (B) after publishing or filing the annual reports and other reports required by this title, such publication or filing is determined by judicial authority not to be in conformity with the requirements of this part.

Amendments to ERISA §108

Taxpayer Relief Act of 1997 (Pub. L. No. 105-34), as follows:
● ERISA §108(2)(B) was amended by Act §1503(d)(6) by substituting "annual reports" for "plan descriptions, annual reports,". Eff. Aug. 5, 1997.

Omnibus Budget Reconciliation Act of 1989 (Pub. L. No. 101-239), as follows:

● ERISA §108 was amended by Act §7894(b)(7) by substituting "act or omission" for "act of omission" before "complained of". Eff. as if originally included in Pub. L. No. 93-406.

SEC. 109. FORMS.

(a) Information Required on Forms.—Except as provided in subsection (b) of this section, the Secretary may require that any information required under this title to be submitted to him, including but not limited to the information required to be filed by the administrator pursuant to section 103(b)(3) and (c), must be submitted on such forms as he may prescribe.

(b) Information Not Required on Forms.—The financial statement and opinion required to be prepared by an independent qualified public accountant pursuant to section 103(a)(3)(A), the actuarial statement required to be prepared by an enrolled actuary pursuant to section 103(a)(4)(A) and the summary plan description required by section 102(a) shall not be required to be submitted on forms.

(c) Format and Content of Summary Plan Description, Annual Report, etc., Required to Be Furnished to Plan Participants and Beneficiaries.— The Secretary may prescribe the format and content of the summary plan description, the summary of the annual report described in section 104(b)(3) and any other report, statements or documents (other than the bargaining agreement, trust agreement, contract, or other instrument under which the plan is established or operated), which are required to be furnished or made available to plan participants and beneficiaries receiving benefits under the plan.

SEC. 110. ALTERNATIVE METHODS OF COMPLIANCE.

(a) The Secretary on his own motion or after having received the petition of an administrator may prescribe an alternative method for satisfying any requirement of this part with respect to any pension plan, or class of pension plans, subject to such requirement if he determines—

(1) that the use of such alternative method is consistent with the purposes of this title and that it provides adequate disclosure to the participants and beneficiaries in the plan, and adequate reporting to the Secretary,

(2) that the application of such requirement of this part would—

(A) increase the costs to the plan, or—

(B) impose unreasonable administrative burdens with respect to the operation of the plan, having regard to the particular characteristics of the plan or the type of plan involved; and

(3) that the application of this part would be adverse to the interests of plan participants in the aggregate.

(b) An alternative method may be prescribed under subsection (a) by regulation or otherwise. If an alternative method is prescribed other than by regulation, the Secretary shall provide notice and an opportunity for interested persons to present their views, and shall publish in the Federal Register the provisions of such alternative method.

SEC. 111. REPEAL AND EFFECTIVE DATE.

(a)(1) The Welfare and Pension Plans Disclosure Act is repealed except that such Act shall continue to apply to any conduct and events which occurred before the effective date of this part.

(2)(A) Section 664 of title 18, United States Code, is amended by striking out "any such plan subject to the provisions of the Welfare and Pension Plans Disclosure Act" and inserting in lieu thereof "any employee benefit plan subject to any provision of title I of the Employee Retirement Income Security Act of 1974".

(B)(i) Section 1027 of such title 18 is amended by striking out "Welfare and Pension Plans Disclosure Act" and inserting in lieu thereof "title I of the Employee Retirement Income Security Act of 1974", and by striking out "Act" each place it appears and inserting in lieu thereof "title".

(ii) The heading for such section is amended by striking out "WELFARE AND PENSION PLANS DISCLOSURE ACT" and inserting in lieu thereof "EMPLOYEE RETIREMENT INCOME SECURITY ACT OF 1974".

(iii) The table of sections of chapter 47 of such title 18 is amended by striking out "Welfare and Pension Plans Disclosure Act" in the item relating to section 1027 and inserting in lieu thereof "Employee Retirement Income Security Act of 1974".

(C) Section 1954 of such title 18 is amended by striking out "any plan subject to the provisions of the Welfare and Pension Plans Disclosure Act as amended" and inserting in lieu thereof "any employee welfare benefit plan or employee pension benefit plan, respectively, subject to any provision of title I of the Employee Retirement Income Security Act of 1974"; and by striking out "sections 3(3) and 5(b)(1) and (2) of the Welfare and Pension Plans Disclosure Act, as amended" and inserting in lieu thereof "sections 3(4) and (3)(16)[3(16)] of the Employee Retirement Income Security Act of 1974".

(D) Section 211 of the Labor-Management Reporting and Disclosure Act of 1959 (29 U.S.C. 441) is amended by striking out "Welfare and Pension Plans Disclosure Act" and inserting in lieu thereof "Employee Retirement Income Security Act of 1974".

(b)(1) Except as provided in paragraph (2), this part (including the amendments and repeals made by subsection (a)) shall take effect on January 1, 1975.

(2) In the case of a plan which has a plan year which begins before January 1, 1975, and ends after December 31, 1974, the Secretary may postpone by regulation the effective date of the repeal of any provision of the Welfare and Pension Plans Disclosure Act (and of any amendment made by subsection (a)(2)) and the effective date of any provision of this part, until the beginning of the first plan year of such plan which begins after January 1, 1975.

(c) The provisions of this title authorizing the Secretary to promulgate regulations shall take effect on the date of enactment of this Act.

(d) Subsections (b) and (c) shall not apply with respect to amendments made to this part in provisions enacted after the date of the enactment of this Act [enacted Sept. 2, 1974].

Amendment to ERISA §111

Omnibus Budget Reconciliation Act of 1989 (Pub. L. No. 101-239), as follows:

● ERISA §111(d) was added by Act §7894(h)(1). Eff. as if included in Pub. L. No. 93-406.

Part 2—Participation and Vesting

SEC. 201. COVERAGE.

This part shall apply to any employee benefit plan described in section 4(a) (and not exempted under section 4(b)) other than—

(1) an employee welfare benefit plan;

(2) a plan which is unfunded and is maintained by an employer primarily for the purpose of providing deferred compensation for a select group of management or highly compensated employees;

(3)(A) a plan established and maintained by a society, order, or association described in section 501(c)(8) or (9) of title 26 if no part of the contributions to or under such plan are made by employers of participants in such plan, or

(B) a trust described in section 501(c)(18) of title 26;

(4) a plan which is established and maintained by a labor organization described in section 501(c)(5) of title 26 and which does not at any time after the date of enactment of this Act provide for employer contributions;

(5) any agreement providing payments to a retired partner or a deceased partner's successor in interest, as described in section 736 of title 26;

(6) an individual retirement account or annuity described in section 408 of title 26 or a retirement bond described in section 409 of title 26 (as effective for obligations issued before January 1, 1984);

(7) an excess benefit plan; or

(8) any plan, fund or program under which an employer, all of whose stock is directly or indirectly owned by employees, former employees or their beneficiaries, proposes through an unfunded arrangement to compensate retired employees for benefits which were forfeited by such employees under a pension plan maintained by a former employer prior to the date such pension plan became subject to this Act.

Amendments to ERISA §201

Omnibus Budget Reconciliation Act of 1989 (Pub. L. No. 101-239), as follows:

• ERISA §201(3)(A), (4), (5) were amended by Act §7891(a)(1) by substituting "Internal Revenue Code of 1986" for "Internal Revenue Code of 1954", which for purposes of codification was translated as "title 26". Eff. as if included in Pub. L. No. 99-514.

• ERISA §201(6) was amended by Act §7891(a)(1) by substituting "§408 of the Internal Revenue Code of 1986" for "§408 of the Internal Revenue Code of 1954", which for purposes of codification was translated as "section 408 of title 26". Eff. as if included in Pub. L. No. 99-514.

Omnibus Budget Reconciliation Act of 1989 (Pub. L. No. 101-239), as follows:

• ERISA §201 was amended by Act §7894(c)(11)(A) by substituting "§409 of title 26 (as effective for obligations issued before Jan. 1, 1984)" for "§409 of title 26". Eff. as if included in Pub. L. No. 98-369.

• ERISA §201 was amended by Act §7894(c)(1)(A)(i) by striking "or" after semicolon at end. Eff. as if included in Pub. L. No. 96-364.

• ERISA §201(7) was amended by Act §7894(c)(1)(A)(ii) by substituting "plan; or" for "plan." Eff. as if included in Pub. L. No. 96-364.

• ERISA §201(8) was amended by Act §7894(c)(1)(A)(iii) by substituting "any plan" for "Any plan". Eff. as if included in Pub. L. No. 96-364.

Multiemployer Pension Plan Amendments Act of 1980 (Pub. L. No. 96-364), as follows:

• ERISA §201(8) was added by Act §411(a). Eff. Sept. 26, 1980.

SEC. 202. MINIMUM PARTICIPATION STANDARDS.

(a)(1)(A) No pension plan may require, as a condition of participation in the plan, that an employee complete a period of service with the employer or employers maintaining the plan extending beyond the later of the following dates—

(i) the date on which the employee attains the age of 21; or

(ii) the date on which he completes 1 year of service.

(B)(i) In the case of any plan which provides that after not more than 2 years of service each participant has a right to 100 percent of his accrued benefit under the plan which is nonforfeitable at the time such benefit accrues, clause (ii) of sub-

paragraph (A) shall be applied by substituting "2 years of service" for "1 year of service".

(ii) In the case of any plan maintained exclusively for employees of an educational organization (as defined in section 170(b)(1)(A)(ii) of title 26) by an employer which is exempt from tax under section 501(a) of title 26, which provides that each participant having at least 1 year of service has a right to 100 percent of his accrued benefit under the plan which is nonforfeitable at the time such benefit accrues, clause (i) of subparagraph (A) shall be applied by substituting "26" for "21". This clause shall not apply to any plan to which clause (i) applies.

(2) No pension plan may exclude from participation (on the basis of age) employees who have attained a specified age.

(3)(A) For purposes of this section, the term "year of service" means a 12-month period during which the employee has not less than 1,000 hours of service. For purposes of this paragraph, computation of any 12-month period shall be made with reference to the date on which the employee's employment commenced, except that, in accordance with regulations prescribed by the Secretary, such computation may be made by reference to the first day of a plan year in the case of an employee who does not complete 1,000 hours of service during the 12-month period beginning on the date his employment commenced.

(B) In the case of any seasonal industry where the customary period of employment is less than 1,000 hours during a calendar year, the term "year of service" shall be such period as may be determined under regulations prescribed by the Secretary.

(C) For purposes of this section, the term "hour of service" means a time of service determined under regulations prescribed by the Secretary.

(D) For purposes of this section, in the case of any maritime industry, 125 days of service shall be treated as 1,000 hours of service. The Secretary may prescribe regulations to carry out the purposes of this subparagraph.

(4) A plan shall be treated as not meeting the requirements of paragraph (1) unless it provides that any employee who has satisfied the minimum age and service requirements specified in such paragraph, and who is otherwise entitled to participate in the plan, commences participation in the plan no later than the earlier of—

(A) the first day of the first plan year beginning after the date on which such employee satisfied such requirements, or

(B) the date 6 months after the date on which he satisfied such requirements,

unless such employee was separated from the service before the date referred to in subparagraph (A) or (B), whichever is applicable.

(b)(1) Except as otherwise provided in paragraphs (2), (3), and (4), all years of service with the employer or employers maintaining the plan shall be taken into account in computing the period of service for purposes of subsection (a)(1).

(2) In the case of any employee who has any 1-year break in service (as defined in section 203(b)(3)(A)) under a plan to which the service requirements of clause (i) of subsection (a)(1)(B) apply, if such employee has not satisfied such requirements, service before such break shall not be required to be taken into account.

(3) In computing an employee's period of service for purposes of subsection (a)(1) in the case of any participant who has any 1-year break in service (as defined in section 203(b)(3)(A)), service before such break shall not be required to be taken into account under the plan until he has completed a year of service (as defined in subsection (a)(3)) after his return.

(4)(A) For purposes of paragraph (1), in the case of a nonvested participant, years of service with the employer or employers maintaining the plan before any period of consecutive 1-year breaks in service shall not be required to be taken into account in computing the period of service if the number of consecutive 1-year breaks in service within such period equals or exceeds the greater of—

   (i) 5, or

   (ii) the aggregate number of years of service before such period.

(B) If any years of service are not required to be taken into account by reason of a period of breaks in service to which subparagraph (A) applies, such years of service shall not be taken into account in applying subparagraph (A) to a subsequent period of breaks in service.

(C) For purposes of subparagraph (A), the term "nonvested participant" means a participant who does not have any nonforfeitable right under the plan to an accrued benefit derived from employer contributions.

(5)(A) In the case of each individual who is absent from work for any period—

   (i) by reason of the pregnancy of the individual,

   (ii) by reason of the birth of a child of the individual,

   (iii) by reason of the placement of a child with the individual in connection with the adoption of such child by such individual, or

   (iv) for purposes of caring for such child for a period beginning immediately following such birth or placement,

the plan shall treat as hours of service solely for purposes of determining under this subsection whether a 1-year break in service (as defined in section 203(b)(3)(A)) has occurred, the hours described in subparagraph (B).

(B) The hours described in this subparagraph are—

   (i) the hours of service which otherwise would normally have been credited to such individual but for such absence, or

   (ii) in any case in which the plan is unable to determine the hours described in clause (i), 8 hours of service per day of such absence,

except that the total number of hours treated as hours of service under this subparagraph by reason of any such pregnancy or placement shall not exceed 501 hours.

(C) The hours described in subparagraph (B) shall be treated as hours of service as provided in this paragraph—

   (i) only in the year in which the absence from work begins, if a participant would be prevented from incurring a 1-year break in service in such year solely because the period of absence is treated as hours of service as provided in subparagraph (A); or

   (ii) in any other case, in the immediately following year.

(D) For purposes of this paragraph, the term "year" means the period used in computations pursuant to section 202(a)(3)(A).

(E) A plan may provide that no credit will be given pursuant to this paragraph unless the individual furnishes to the plan administrator such timely information as the plan may reasonably require to establish—

   (i) that the absence from work is for reasons referred to in subparagraph (A), and

   (ii) the number of days for which there was such an absence.

Amendments to ERISA §202

Omnibus Budget Reconciliation Act of 1989 (Pub. L. No. 101-239), as follows:

● ERISA §202(a)(1)(B)(i) was amended by Act §7861(a)(2), which made technical corrections to directory language of Pub. L. No. 99-514. Eff. as if included in that act.

● ERISA §202(a)(1)(B)(ii) was amended by Act §7894(c)(2)(A) by substituting "educational organization" for "educational institution". Eff. as if included in Pub. L. No. 93-406.

● ERISA §202 was amended by Act §7891(a)(1) by substituting "Internal Revenue Code of 1986" for "Internal Revenue Code of 1954", which for purposes of codification was translated as "title 26". Eff. as if included in Pub. L. No. 99-514.

● ERISA §202(a)(2) was amended by Act §7892(a) by striking a comma after "specified age". Eff. as if included in Pub. L. No. 99-509.

● ERISA §202(b)(2) was amended by Act §7894(c)(2)(B) by substituting "a plan" for "the plan". Eff. as if included in Pub. L. No. 93-406.

Tax Reform Act of 1986 (Pub. L. No. 99-514), as follows:
- ERISA §202(a)(1)(B)(i) was amended by Act §7861(a)(2) by substituting "2 years of service" for "3 years of service" in two places. Eff. for plan years after 1988, with special rule for collectively bargained plans with agreements ratified before March 1, 1986, and inapplicable to employees who did not have one hour of service in any plan year to which the amendment applied.

Omnibus Budget Reconciliation Act of 1986 (Pub. L. No. 99-509), as follows:
- ERISA §202(a)(2) was amended by Act §9203(a)(1) by substituting a period for "unless—(A) the plan is a—(i) defined benefit plan, or (ii) target benefit plan (as defined under regulations prescribed by the Secretary of the Treasury), and (B) such employees begin employment with the employer after they have attained a specified age which is not more than 5 years before the normal retirement age under the plan." Eff. for plan years after Jan. 1, 1988.

Retirement Equity Act of 1984 (Pub. L. No. 98-397), as follows:
- ERISA §202(a)(1) was amended by Act §102(a) by substituting "21" for "25" in subpara. (A)(i) and " '26' for '21' " for " '30' for '25' " in subpara. (B)(ii). Eff. for plan years beginning after 1984.
- ERISA §202(b)(4) was amended by Act §102(d)(1). Eff. for plan years beginning after 1984. ERISA §202(b)(4) prior to amendment:

  (4) In the case of an employee who does not have any nonforfeitable right to an accrued benefit derived from employer contributions, years of service with the employer or employers maintaining the plan before a break in service shall not be required to be taken into account in computing the period of service for purposes of subsection (a)(1) of this section if the number of consecutive 1-year breaks in service equals or exceeds the aggregate number of such years of service before such break. Such aggregate number of years of service before such break shall be deemed not to include any years of service not required to be taken into account under this paragraph by reason of any prior break in service.

- ERISA §202(b)(5) was added by Act §102(e)(1). Eff. for plan years beginning after 1984.

SEC. 203. MINIMUM VESTING STANDARDS.

(a) Nonforfeitability Requirements.—Each pension plan shall provide that an employee's right to his normal retirement benefit is nonforfeitable upon the attainment of normal retirement age and in addition shall satisfy the requirements of paragraphs (1) and (2) of this subsection.

(1) A plan satisfies the requirements of this paragraph if an employee's rights in his accrued benefit derived from his own contributions are nonforfeitable.

(2)(A)(i) In the case of a defined benefit plan, a plan satisfies the requirements of this paragraph if it satisfies the requirements of clause (ii) or (iii).

(ii) A plan satisfies the requirements of this clause if an employee who has completed at least 5 years of service has a nonforfeitable right to 100 percent of the employee's accrued benefit derived from employer contributions.

(iii) A plan satisfies the requirements of this clause if an employee has a nonforfeitable right to

a percentage of the employee's accrued benefit derived from employer contributions determined under the following table:

Years of service	The nonforfeitable percentage is:
3	20
4	40
5	60
6	80
7 or more	100

(B)(i) In the case of an individual account plan, a plan satisfies the requirements of this paragraph if it satisfies the requirements of clause (ii) or (iii).

(ii) A plan satisfies the requirements of this clause if an employee who has completed at least 3 years of service has a nonforfeitable right to 100 percent of the employee's accrued benefit derived from employer contributions.

(iii) A plan satisfies the requirements of this clause if an employee has a nonforfeitable right to a percentage of the employee's accrued benefit derived from employer contributions determined under the following table:

Years of service	The nonforfeitable percentage is:
2	20
3	40
4	60
5	80
6 or more	100

(3)(A) A right to an accrued benefit derived from employer contributions shall not be treated as forfeitable solely because the plan provides that it is not payable if the participant dies (except in the case of a survivor annuity which is payable as provided in section 205).

(B) A right to an accrued benefit derived from employer contributions shall not be treated as forfeitable solely because the plan provides that the payment of benefits is suspended for such period as the employee is employed, subsequent to the commencement of payment of such benefits—

(i) in the case of a plan other than a multiemployer plan, by an employer who maintains the plan under which such benefits were being paid; and

(ii) in the case of a multiemployer plan, in the same industry, in the same trade or craft, and the same geographic area covered by the plan, as when such benefits commenced.

The Secretary shall prescribe such regulations as may be necessary to carry out the purposes of this subparagraph, including regulations with respect to the meaning of the term "employed".

(C) A right to an accrued benefit derived from employer contributions shall not be treated as forfeitable solely because plan amendments may be given retroactive application as provided in section 302(d)(2).

(D)(i) A right to an accrued benefit derived from employer contributions shall not be treated as forfeitable solely because the plan provides that, in the case of a participant who does not have a nonforfeitable right to at least 50 percent of his accrued benefit derived from employer contributions, such accrued benefit may be forfeited on account of the withdrawal by the participant of any amount attributable to the benefit derived from mandatory contributions (as defined in the last sentence of section 204(c)(2)(C)) made by such participant.

(ii) Clause (i) shall not apply to a plan unless the plan provides that any accrued benefit forfeited under a plan provision described in such clause shall be restored upon repayment by the participant of the full amount of the withdrawal described in such clause plus, in the case of a defined benefit plan, interest.

Such interest shall be computed on such amount at the rate determined for purposes of section 204(c)(2)(C) (if such subsection applies) on the date of such repayment (computed annually from the date of such withdrawal). The plan provision required under this clause may provide that such repayment must be made (I) in the case of a withdrawal on account of separation from service, before the earlier of 5 years after the first date on which the participant is subsequently re-employed by the employer, or the close of the first period of 5 consecutive 1-year breaks in service commencing after the withdrawal; or (II) in the case of any other withdrawal, 5 years after the date of the withdrawal.

(iii) In the case of accrued benefits derived from employer contributions which accrued before the date of the enactment of this Act, a right to such accrued benefit derived from employer contributions shall not be treated as forfeitable solely because the plan provides that an amount of such accrued benefit may be forfeited on account of the withdrawal by the participant of an amount attributable to the benefit derived from mandatory contributions, made by such participant before the date of the enactment of this Act if such amount forfeited is proportional to such amount withdrawn. This clause shall not apply to any plan to which any mandatory contribution is made after the date of the enactment of this Act. The Secretary of the Treasury shall prescribe such regulations as may be necessary to carry out the purposes of this clause.

(iv) For purposes of this subparagraph, in the case of any class-year plan, a withdrawal of employee contributions shall be treated as a withdrawal of such contributions on a plan-year-by-plan-year basis in succeeding order of time.

(v) Cross Reference.—For nonforfeitability where the employee has a nonforfeitable right to at least 50 percent of his accrued benefit, see section 206(c).

(E)(i) A right to an accrued benefit derived from employer contributions under a multiemployer plan shall not be treated as forfeitable solely because the plan provides that benefits accrued as a result of service with the participant's employer before the employer had an obligation to contribute under the plan may not be payable if the employer ceases contributions to the multiemployer plan.

(ii) A participant's right to an accrued benefit derived from employer contributions under a multiemployer plan shall not be treated as forfeitable solely because—

(I) the plan is amended to reduce benefits under section 4244A or 4281, or

(II) benefit payments under the plan may be suspended under section 4245 or 4281.

(F) A matching contribution (within the meaning of section 401(m) of the Internal Revenue Code of 1986) shall not be treated as forfeitable merely because such contribution is forfeitable if the contribution to which the matching contribution relates is treated as an excess contribution under section 401(k)(8)(B) of such Code, an excess deferral under section 402(g)(2)(A) of such Code, an erroneous automatic contribution under section 414(w) of such Code, or an excess aggregate contribution under section 401(m)(6)(B) of such Code.

(4) [Repealed.]

(b) Computation of Service.—

(1) In computing the period of service under the plan for purposes of determining the nonforfeitable percentage under subsection (a)(2), all of an employee's years of service with the employer or employers maintaining the plan shall be taken into account, except that the following may be disregarded:

(A) years of service before age 18,[;]

(B) years of service during a period for which the employee declined to contribute to a plan requiring employee contributions,[;]

(C) years of service with an employer during any period for which the employer did not maintain the plan or a predecessor plan, defined by the Secretary of the Treasury;

(D) service not required to be taken into account under paragraph (3);

ERISA Sec. 203(b)(1)(D)

(E) years of service before January 1, 1971, unless the employee has had at least 3 years of service after December 31, 1970;

(F) years of service before this part first applies to the plan if such service would have been disregarded under the rules of the plan with regard to breaks in service, as in effect on the applicable date; and

(G) in the case of a multiemployer plan, years of service—

(i) with an employer after—

(I) a complete withdrawal of such employer from the plan (within the meaning of section 4203), or

(II) to the extent permitted by regulations prescribed by the Secretary of the Treasury, a partial withdrawal described in section 4205(b)(2)(A)(i) in connection with the decertification of the collective bargaining representative; and

(ii) with any employer under the plan after the termination date of the plan under section 4048.

(2)(A) For purposes of this section, except as provided in subparagraph (C), the term "year of service" means a calendar year, plan year, or other 12-consecutive-month period designated by the plan (and not prohibited under regulations prescribed by the Secretary) during which the participant has completed 1,000 hours of service.

(B) For purposes of this section, the term "hour of service" has the meaning provided by section 202(a)(3)(C).

(C) In the case of any seasonal industry where the customary period of employment is less than 1,000 hours during a calendar year, the term "year of service" shall be such period as determined under regulations of the Secretary.

(D) For purposes of this section, in the case of any maritime industry, 125 days of service shall be treated as 1,000 hours of service. The Secretary may prescribe regulations to carry out the purposes of this subparagraph.

(3)(A) For purposes of this paragraph, the term "1-year break in service" means a calendar year, plan year, or other 12-consecutive-month period designated by the plan (and not prohibited under regulations prescribed by the Secretary) during which the participant has not completed more than 500 hours of service.

(B) For purposes of paragraph (1), in the case of any employee who has any 1-year break in service, years of service before such break shall not be required to be taken into account until he has completed a year of service after his return.

(C) For purposes of paragraph (1), in the case of any participant in an individual account plan or an insured defined benefit plan which satisfies the requirements of subsection 204(b)(1)(F) who has 5 consecutive 1-year breaks in service, years of service after such 5-year period shall not be required to be taken into account for purposes of determining the nonforfeitable percentage of his accrued benefit derived from employer contributions which accrued before such 5-year period.

(D)(i) For purposes of paragraph (1), in the case of a nonvested participant, years of service with the employer or employers maintaining the plan before any period of consecutive 1-year breaks in service shall not be required to be taken into account if the number of consecutive 1-year breaks in service within such period equals or exceeds the greater of—

(I) 5, or

(II) the aggregate number of years of service before such period.

(ii) If any years of service are not required to be taken into account by reason of a period of breaks in service to which clause (i) applies, such years of service shall not be taken into account in applying clause (i) to a subsequent period of breaks in service.

(iii) For purposes of clause (i), the term "nonvested participant" means a participant who does not have any nonforfeitable right under the plan to an accrued benefit derived from employer contributions.

(E)(i) In the case of each individual who is absent from work for any period—

(I) by reason of the pregnancy of the individual,

(II) by reason of the birth of a child of the individual,

(III) by reason of the placement of a child with the individual in connection with the adoption of such child by such individual, or

(IV) for purposes of caring for such child for a period beginning immediately following such birth or placement,

the plan shall treat as hours of service, solely for purposes of determining under this paragraph whether a 1-year break in service has occurred, the hours described in clause (ii).

(ii) The hours described in this clause are—

(I) the hours of service which otherwise would normally have been credited to such individual but for such absence, or

(II) in any case in which the plan is unable to determine the hours described in subclause (I), 8 hours of service per day of absence,

except that the total number of hours treated as hours of service under this clause by reason of such pregnancy or placement shall not exceed 501 hours.

(iii) The hours described in clause (ii) shall be treated as hours of service as provided in this subparagraph—

(I) only in the year in which the absence from work begins, if a participant would be prevented from incurring a 1-year break in service in such year solely because the period of absence is treated as hours of service as provided in clause (i); or

(II) in any other case, in the immediately following year.

(iv) For purposes of this subparagraph, the term "year" means the period used in computations pursuant to paragraph (2).

(v) A plan may provide that no credit will be given pursuant to this subparagraph unless the individual furnishes to the plan administrator such timely information as the plan may reasonably require to establish—

(I) that the absence from work is for reasons referred to in clause (i), and

(II) the number of days for which there was such an absence.

(4) Cross References.—

(A) For definitions of "accrued benefit" and "normal retirement age", see sections 3(23) and (24).

(B) For effect of certain cash out distributions, see section 204(d)(1).

(c) Plan Amendments Altering Vesting Schedule.—

(1)(A) A plan amendment changing any vesting schedule under the plan shall be treated as not satisfying the requirements of subsection (a)(2) if the nonforfeitable percentage of the accrued benefit derived from employer contributions (determined as of the later of the date such amendment is adopted, or the date such amendment becomes effective) of any employee who is a participant in the plan is less than such nonforfeitable percentage computed under the plan without regard to such amendment.

(B) A plan amendment changing any vesting schedule under the plan shall be treated as not satisfying the requirements of subsection (a)(2) unless each participant having not less than 3 years of service is permitted to elect, within a reasonable period after adoption of such amendment, to have his nonforfeitable percentage computed under the plan without regard to such amendment.

(2) Subsection (a) shall not apply to benefits which may not be provided for designated employees in the event of early termination of the plan under provisions of the plan adopted pursuant to regulations prescribed by the Secretary of the Treasury to preclude the discrimination prohibited by section 401(a)(4) of title 26.

(3)(A) The requirements of subsection (a)(2) shall be treated as satisfied in the case of a class-year plan if such plan provides that 100 percent of each employee's right to or derived from the contributions of the employer on the employee's behalf with respect to any plan year is nonforfeitable not later than when such participant was performing services for the employer as of the close of each of 5 plan years (whether or not consecutive) after the plan year for which the contributions were made.

(B) For purposes of subparagraph (A) if—(i) any contributions are made on behalf of a participant with respect to any plan year, and (ii) before such participant meets the requirements of subparagraph (A), such participant was not performing services for the employer as of the close of any 5 consecutive plan years after such plan year, then the plan may provide that the participant forfeits any right to or derived from the contributions made with respect to such plan year.

(C) For purposes of this part, the term "class year plan" means a profit-sharing, stock bonus, or money purchase plan which provides for the separate nonforfeitability of employees' rights to or derived from the contributions for each plan year.

(d) Nonforfeitable Benefits After Lesser Period and in Greater Amounts Than Required.—A pension plan may allow for nonforfeitable benefits after a lesser period and in greater amounts than are required by this part.

(e) Consent for Distribution; Present Value; Covered Distributions.—

(1) If the present value of any nonforfeitable benefit with respect to a participant in a plan exceeds $5,000, the plan shall provide that such benefit may not be immediately distributed without the consent of the participant.

(2) For purposes of paragraph (1), the present value shall be calculated in accordance with section 205(g)(3).

(3) This subsection shall not apply to any distribution of dividends to which section 404(k) of title 26 applies.

(4) A plan shall not fail to meet the requirements of this subsection if, under the terms of the plan, the present value of the nonforfeitable accrued benefit is determined without regard to that portion of such benefit which is attributable to rollover contributions (and earnings allocable thereto). For purposes of this subparagraph, the term "rollover contributions" means any rollover contribution under sections 402(c), 403(a)(4), 403(b)(8), 408(d)(3)(A)(ii), and 457(e)(16) of the Internal Revenue Code of 1986.

(f) Special Rules for Plans Computing Accrued Benefits by Reference to Hypothetical Account Balance or Equivalent Amounts.—

(1) In general.—An applicable defined benefit plan shall not be treated as failing to meet—

(A) subject to paragraph (2), the requirements of subsection (a)(2), or

(B) the requirements of section 204(c) or 205(g), or the requirements of subsection (e), with respect to accrued benefits derived from employer contributions.

(2) 3-year vesting.—In the case of an applicable defined benefit plan, such plan shall be treated as meeting the requirements of subsection (a)(2) only if an employee who has completed at least 3 years of service has a nonforfeitable right to 100 percent of the employee's accrued benefit derived from employer contributions.

(3) Applicable defined benefit plan and related rules.—

For purposes of this subsection—

(A) In general.—The term "applicable defined benefit plan" means a defined benefit plan under which the accrued benefit (or any portion thereof) is calculated as the balance of a hypothetical account maintained for the participant or as an accumulated percentage of the participant's final average compensation.

(B) Regulations to include similar plans.—The Secretary of the Treasury shall issue regulations which include in the definition of an applicable defined benefit plan any defined benefit plan (or any portion of such a plan) which has an effect similar to an applicable defined benefit plan.

Amendments to ERISA §203

Worker, Retiree, and Employer Recovery Act of 2008 (Pub. L. No. 110-458), as follows:

● ERISA §203(f)(1)(B) was amended by Act §107(a)(1). Eff. as if included in Title VII of Pub. L. No. 109-280. ERISA §203(f)(1)(B) prior to amendment:

(B) the requirements of section 204(c) or section 205(g) with respect to contributions other than employee contributions, solely because the present value of the accrued benefit (or any portion thereof) of any participant is, under the terms of the plan, equal to the amount expressed as the balance in the hypothetical account described in paragraph (3) or as an accumulated percentage of the participant's final average compensation.

Pension Protection Act of 2006 (Pub. L. No. 109-280), as follows

● ERISA §203(a)(2) was replaced by Act §904(b)(1). Eff. for plan years after Dec. 31, 2006, with a transition rule for collective bargaining agreements, see Act §904(c)(2). The amendment applies to an employee once that employee has one hour of service under the plan in any plan year to which the amendment applies. ERISA §203(a)(2) prior to amendment:

(2) Except as provided in paragraph (4), a plan satisfies the requirements of this paragraph if it satisfies the requirements of subparagraph (A) or (B).

(A) A plan satisfies the requirements of this subparagraph if an employee who has completed at least 5 years of service has a nonforfeitable right to 100 percent of the employee's accrued benefit derived from employer contributions.

(B) A plan satisfies the requirements of this subparagraph if an employee has a nonforfeitable right to a percentage of

the employee's accrued benefit derived from employer contributions determined under the following table:

Years of service	The nonforfeitable percentage is:
3	20
4	40
5	60
6	80
7 or more	100

● ERISA §203(a)(3)(C) was amended by Act §107(a)(4) (redesignated as §108(a)(4) by Pub. L. No. 111-192, §202(a)) by substituting "§302(d)(2)" for "§302(c)(8)". Eff. for plan years beginning after 2007. For "eligible cooperative plans," the effective date is the earlier of the date they cease to be eligible or Jan. 1, 2017.

● ERISA §203(a)(3)(F) was amended by Act §902(d)(2)(E) by adding "an erroneous automatic contribution under §414(w) of such Code," after "§402(g)(2)(A) of such Code". Eff. for plan years beginning after Dec. 31, 2007.

● ERISA §203(a)(4) was stricken by Act §904(b)(2). Eff. generally for plan years beginning after 2006, with a transition rule for collective bargaining agreements, see Act §904(c)(2). The amendment applies to an employee once that employee has one hour of service under the plan in any plan year to which the amendment applies. ERISA §203(a)(4) prior to amendment:

(4) In the case of matching contributions (as defined in section 401(m)(4)(A) of title 26), paragraph (2) shall be applied—

(A) by substituting "3 years" for "5 years" in subparagraph (A), and

(B) by substituting the following table for the table contained in subparagraph (B):

Years of service	The nonforfeitable percentage is:
2	20
3	40
4	60
5	80
6 or more	100

● ERISA §203(f) was added by Act §701(a)(2). Eff for distributions made after Aug. 17, 2006, with a transition rule for collective bargaining agreements, see Act §701(e).

● **Other Provision.** Act §701(d)–(e) provides:

(d) No Inference.—Nothing in the amendments made by this section shall be construed to create an inference with respect to—

(1) the treatment of applicable defined benefit plans or conversions to applicable defined benefit plans under §§204(b)(1)(H) of the Employee Retirement Income Security Act of 1974, 4(i)(1) of the Age Discrimination in Employment Act of 1967, and 411(b)(1)(H) of the Internal Revenue Code of 1986, as in effect before such amendments, or

(2) the determination of whether an applicable defined benefit plan fails to meet the requirements of §§203(a)(2), 204(c), or 204(g) of the Employee Retirement Income Security Act of 1974 or §§411(a)(2), 411(c), or 417(e) of such Code, as in effect before such amendments, solely because the present value of the accrued benefit (or any portion thereof) of any participant is, under the terms of the plan, equal to the amount expressed as the balance in a hypothetical account or as an accumulated percentage of the participant's final average compensation.

For purposes of this subsection, the term "applicable defined benefit plan" has the meaning given such term by §203(f)(3) of the Employee Retirement Income Security Act of 1974 and §411(a)(13)(C) of such Code, as in effect after such amendments.

(e) Effective Date.—

(1) General.—The amendments made by this section shall apply to periods beginning on or after June 29, 2005.

(2) Present Value of Accrued Benefit.—The amendments made by subsections (a)(2) and (b)(2) shall apply to distributions made after the date of the enactment of this Act.

(3) Vesting and Interest Credit Requirements.—In the case of a plan in existence on June 29, 2005, the requirements of clause (i) of §411(b)(5)(B) of the Internal Revenue Code of 1986, clause (i) of §204(b)(5)(B) of the Employee Retirement Income Security Act of 1974, and clause (i) of §4(i)(10)(B) of the Age Discrimination in Employment Act of 1967 (as added by this Act) and the requirements of §203(f)(2) of the Employee Retirement Income Security Act of 1974 and §411(a)(13)(B) of the Internal Revenue Code of 1986 (as so added) shall, for purposes of applying the amendments made by subsections (a) and (b), apply to years beginning after December 31, 2007, unless the plan sponsor elects the application of such requirements for any period after June 29, 2005, and before the first year beginning after December 31, 2007.

(4) Special Rule for Collectively Bargained Plans.—In the case of a plan maintained pursuant to 1 or more collective bargaining agreements between employee representatives and 1 or more employers ratified on or before the date of the enactment of this Act, the requirements described in paragraph (3) shall, for purposes of applying the amendments made by subsections (a) and (b), not apply to plan years beginning before—

(A) the earlier of—

(i) the date on which the last of such collective bargaining agreements terminates (determined without regard to any extension thereof on or after such date of enactment), or

(ii) January 1, 2008, or

(B) January 1, 2010.

(5) Conversions.—The requirements of clause (ii) of §411(b)(5)(B) of the Internal Revenue Code of 1986, clause (ii) of §204(b)(5)(B) of the Employee Retirement Income Security Act of 1974, and clause (ii) of §4(i)(10)(B) of the Age Discrimination in Employment Act of 1967 (as added by this Act), shall apply to plan amendments adopted after, and taking effect after, June 29, 2005, except that the plan sponsor may elect to have such amendments apply to plan amendments adopted before, and taking effect after, such date.

● **Other Provision.** Act §904(c) contains the following transition rule:

(4) Special Rule for Stock Ownership Plans.—Notwithstanding paragraph (1) or (2), in the case of an employee stock ownership plan (as defined in §4975(e)(7) of the Internal Revenue Code of 1986) which had outstanding on September 26, 2005, a loan incurred for the purpose of acquiring qualifying employer securities (as defined in §4075(e)(8) of such Code), the amendments made by this section shall not apply to any plan year beginning before the earlier of—

(A) the date on which the loan is fully repaid, or (B) the date on which the loan was, as of September 26, 2005, scheduled to be fully repaid.

Working Families Tax Relief Act of 2004 (Pub. L. No. 108-311), as follows:

● ERISA §203(a)(4)(B) was amended by Act §408(b)(8) by substituting "6 or more" for "6" in table. Eff. Oct. 4, 2004.

Economic Growth and Tax Relief Reconciliation Act of 2001 (Pub. L. No. 107-16), as follows:

● ERISA §203(a)(2) was amended by Act §§633(b)(1), 901 by temporarily substituting "Except as provided in paragraph (4), a plan" for "A plan" in introductory provisions. Eff. between Jan. 1, 2002, and Dec. 31, 2010. See note below on sunset rule.

● ERISA §203(a)(4) was amended by Act §§633(b)(2), 901 by temporarily adding para. (4). Eff. between Jan. 1, 2002, and Dec. 31, 2010. See note below on sunset rule.

● ERISA §203(e)(4) was amended by Act §§648(a)(2), 901 by temporarily adding para. (4). Eff. between Jan. 1, 2002, and Dec. 31, 2010. See note below on sunset rule.

● **Sunset Rule.** To comply with the Congressional Budget Act of 1974, §901 of Pub. L. No. 107-16 provides that all provisions of,

and amendments made by, the Act will not apply to taxable, plan, or limitation years beginning after December 31, 2010. *But see* Pension Protection Act of 2006 (Pub. L. No. 109-280), §811 (sunset rule of Pub. L. No. 107-16 does not apply to the provisions of, and the amendments made by, Pub. L. No. 107-16, §§601–666 (relating to modifications to pensions and retirement income arrangement provisions)).

Taxpayer Relief Act of 1997 (Pub. L. No. 105-34), as follows:

● ERISA §203(e)(1) was amended by Act §1071(b)(1) by substituting "$5,000" for "$3,500". Eff. Aug. 5, 2005.

Small Business Job Protection Act of 1996 (Pub. L. No. 104-188), as follows:

● ERISA §203(a)(2) was amended by Act §1442(b)(1) by substituting "subparagraph (A) or (B)" for "subparagraph (A), (B), or (C)" in introductory provisions. Eff. for plan years beginning on or after the earlier of (1) the later of (A) Jan. 1, 1997, or (B) the date on which the last of the collective bargaining agreements under which the plan is maintained ends, or (2) Jan. 1, 1999; amendment is inapplicable to individual who does not have more than one hour of service under the plan on or after the first day of the first plan year to which the amendment applies.

● ERISA §203(a)(2)(C) was amended by Act §1442(b)(2) by striking subpara. (C). Eff. for plan years beginning on or after the earlier of (1) the later of (A) Jan. 1, 1997, or (B) the date on which the last of the collective bargaining agreements under which the plan is maintained ends, or (2) Jan. 1, 1999; amendment is inapplicable to individual who does not have more than one hour of service under the plan on or after the first day of the first plan year to which the amendment applies. ERISA §203(a)(2)(C) prior to amendment:

(C) A plan satisfies the requirements of this subparagraph if—

(i) the plan is a multiemployer plan (within the meaning of §3(37)), and

(ii) under the plan—

(I) an employee who is covered pursuant to a collective bargaining agreement described in §3(37)(A)(ii) of this title and who has completed at least 10 years of service has a nonforfeitable right to 100 percent of the employee's accrued benefit derived from employer contributions, and

(II) the requirements of subparagraph (A) or (B) are met with respect to employees not described in subclause (I).

Retirement Protection Act of 1994 (Pub. L. No. 103-465), as follows:

● ERISA §203(e)(2) was amended by Act §767(c). Eff. for plan and limitation years after Dec. 31, 1994, although an employer may elect to treat such amendment as effective on or after Dec. 8, 1994. ERISA §203(e)(2) prior to amendment:

(2)

(A) For purposes of paragraph (1), the present value shall be calculated—

(i) by using an interest rate no greater than the applicable interest rate if the vested accrued benefit (using such rate) is not in excess of $25,000, and

(ii) by using an interest rate no greater than 120 percent of the applicable interest rate if the vested accrued benefit exceeds $25,000 (as determined under clause (i)).

In no event shall the present value determined under subclause (II) be less than $25,000.

(B) For purposes of subparagraph (A), the term "applicable interest rate" means the interest rate which would be used (as of the date of the distribution) by the Pension Benefit Guaranty Corporation for purposes of determining the present value of a lump sum distribution on plan termination.

Omnibus Budget Reconciliation Act of 1989 (Pub. L. No. 101-239), as follows:

● ERISA §203(a)(2) was amended by Act §7861(a)(1)(A) by substituting "satisfies the requirements" for "satisfies the following requirements" in introductory provisions. Eff. as if originally included in Pub. L. No. 99-514.

● ERISA §203(a)(2)(C)(ii)(I) was amended by Act §7861(a)(1)(B) by substituting "§3(37)(A)(ii) of this title" for "§414(f)(1)(B)". Eff. as if originally included in Pub. L. No. 99-514.

● ERISA §203(a)(3)(D)(v) was amended by Act §7894(c)(3) by substituting "nonforfeitability" for "nonforfeitably". Eff. as if originally in Pub. L. No. 93-406.

ERISA Sec. 203(f)(3)(B)

- ERISA §203(a)(3)(F) was added by Act §7861(a)(5)(B). Eff. as if included in Pub. L. No. 99-514.
- ERISA §203(b)(1)(A) was amended by Act §7861(a)(6)(B). Eff. as if included in Pub. L. No. 99-514. ERISA §203(b)(1)(A) prior to amendment:

    (A) years of service before age 18, except that in case of a plan which does not satisfy subparagraph (A) or (B) of subsection (a)(2) of this section, the plan may not disregard any such year of service during which the employee was a participant;.

- ERISA §203(c)(2) was amended by Act §7891(a)(1) by substituting "Internal Revenue Code of 1986" for "Internal Revenue Code of 1954", which for purposes of codification was translated as "title 26". Eff. as if included in Pub. L. No. 99-514.
- ERISA §203(e)(1) was amended by Act §7862(d)(10) by substituting "nonforfeitable benefit" for "vested accrued benefit", but could not be executed because the language "vested accrued benefit" did not appear after the amendment made by §7862(d)(5) (see note below). Eff. as if included in Pub. L. No. 99-514.
- ERISA §203(e)(1) was amended by Act §7862(d)(5). Eff. as if included in Pub. L. No. 99-514.
- ERISA §203(e)(1) prior to amendment:

    (1) If the present value of any vested accrued benefit exceeds $3,500, a pension plan shall provide that such benefit may not be immediately distributed without the consent of the participant.

- ERISA §203(e)(2) was amended by Act §7891(b)(1), (2) by realigning margins of subparas. (A) and (B) and striking subpara. (B) heading, "Applicable interest rate". Eff. as if included in Pub. L. No. 99-514.
- ERISA §203(e)(3) was amended by Act §7891(a)(1) by substituting "Internal Revenue Code of 1986" for "Internal Revenue Code of 1954", which for purposes of codification was translated as "title 26". Eff. as if included in Pub. L. No. 99-514.

Tax Reform Act of 1986 (Pub. L. No. 99-514), as follows:

- ERISA §203(a)(2) was amended by Act §1113(e)(1) by substituting provisions covering 5-year vesting, 3- to 7-year vesting, and multiemployer plans, for former provisions which covered 10-year vesting, 5- to 15-year vesting, and the "rule of 45" under which a plan satisfied the requirements of this paragraph if an employee who had completed at least 5 years of service and with respect to whom the sum of his age and years of service equaled or exceeded 45 had a right to a percentage of his accrued benefits derived from employer contributions. Eff. for plan years after 1988, with special rule for collective bargaining agreements.
- ERISA §203(a)(3)(D)(ii) was amended by Act §1898(a)(4)(B)(i) by inserting the last sentence and striking former last sentence which read as follows: "In the case of a defined contribution plan the plan provision required under this clause may provide that such repayment must be made before the participant has any 1-year break in service commencing after the withdrawal." Eff. as if included in Pub. L. No. 98-397.
- ERISA §203(c)(1)(B) was amended by Act §1113(e)(4)(A) by substituting "3 years" for "5 years". Eff. for plan years after 1988, with special rule for collective bargaining agreements.
- ERISA §203(c)(3) (which provided for class year vesting) was stricken by Act §1113(e)(2). Eff. for plan years after 1988, with special rule for collective bargaining agreements.
- ERISA §203(c)(3) was amended by Act §1898(a)(1)(B). Generally effective for plan years beginning after Oct. 22, 1986. ERISA §203(c)(3) prior to amendment:

    (3) The requirements of subsection (a)(2) of this section shall be deemed to be satisfied in the case of a class year plan if such plan provides that 100 percent of each employee's right to or derived from the contributions of the employer on his behalf with respect to any plan year are nonforfeitable not later than the end of the 5th year following the plan year for which such contributions were made. For purposes of this part, the term "class year plan" means a profit sharing, stock bonus, or money purchase plan which provides for the separate nonforfeitability of employees' rights to or derived from the contributions for each plan year.

- ERISA §203(e)(1) was amended by Act §1898(d)(1)(B), as amended by Pub. L. No. 101-239, §7862(d)(4). Eff. as if included in Pub. L. No. 98-397. ERISA §203(e)(1) prior to amendment:

    (1) If the present value of any accrued benefit exceeds $3,500, such benefit shall not be treated as nonforfeitable if the plan provides that the present value of such benefit could be immediately distributed without the consent of the participant.

- ERISA §203(e)(2) was amended by Act §1139(c)(1). Eff. for distributions in plan years beginning after Dec. 31, 1984, and before Jan. 1, 1987, if such distributions were made in accordance with the regulations issued under the Retirement Equity Act of 1984. ERISA §203(e)(2) prior to amendment:

    (2) For purposes of paragraph (1), the present value shall be calculated by using an interest rate not greater than the interest rate which would be used (as of the date of the distribution) by the Pension Benefit Guaranty Corporation for purposes of determining the present value of a lump sum distribution on plan termination.

- ERISA §203(x)(3) was added by Act §1898(d)(2)(B). Eff. as if included in Pub. L. No. 98-397.

Retirement Equity Act of 1984 (Pub. L. No. 98-397), as follows:

- ERISA §203(b)(1)(A) was amended by Act §102(b) by substituting "18" for "22". Eff. for plan years beginning after 1984.
- ERISA §203(b)(3)(C) was amended by Act §102(c) by substituting "5 consecutive 1-year breaks in service" for "any 1-year break in service" and substituting "such 5-year period" for "such break" in two places. Eff. for plan years beginning after 1984.
- ERISA §203(b)(3)(D) was amended by Act §102(d)(2). Eff. for plan years beginning after 1984. ERISA §203(b)(3)(D) prior to amendment:

    (D) For purposes of paragraph (1), in the case of a participant who, under the plan, does not have any nonforfeitable right to an accrued benefit derived from employer contributions, years of service before any 1-year break in service shall not be required to be taken into account if the number of consecutive 1-year breaks in service equals or exceeds the aggregate number of such years of service prior to such break. Such aggregate number of years of service before such break shall be deemed not to include any years of service not required to be taken into account under this subparagraph by reason of any prior break in service.

- ERISA §203(b)(3)(E) was added by Act §102(e)(2). Eff. for plan years beginning after 1984.
- ERISA §203(e) was added by Act §105(a). Eff. for plan years beginning after 1984.

Multiemployer Pension Plan Amendments Act of 1980 (Pub. L. No. 96-364), as follows:

- ERISA §203(a)(3)(E) was added by Act §303(1). Eff. Sept. 26, 1980.
- ERISA §203(b)(1)(G) was added by Act §303(2)–(4). Eff. Sept. 26, 1980.

SEC. 204. BENEFIT ACCRUAL REQUIREMENTS.

(a) Satisfaction of Requirements by Pension Plans.—Each pension plan shall satisfy the requirements of subsection (b)(3), and—

(1) in the case of a defined benefit plan, shall satisfy the requirements of subsection (b)(1); and

(2) in the case of a defined contribution plan, shall satisfy the requirements of subsection (b)(2).

(b) Enumeration of Plan requirements.—

(1)(A) A defined benefit plan satisfies the requirements of this paragraph if the accrued benefit to which each participant is entitled upon his separation from the service is not less than—

(i) 3 percent of the normal retirement benefit to which he would be entitled at the normal retirement age if he commenced participation at the earliest possible entry age under the plan and served continuously until the earlier of age 65 or the normal retirement age specified under the plan, multiplied by

(ii) the number of years (not in excess of 33⅓) of his participation in the plan.

In the case of a plan providing retirement benefits based on compensation during any period, the normal retirement benefit to which a participant would be entitled shall be determined as if he continued to earn annually the average rate of compensation which he earned during consecutive years of service, not in excess of 10, for which his compensation was the highest. For purposes of this subparagraph, social security benefits and all other relevant factors used to compute benefits shall be treated as remaining constant as of the current year for all years after current year.

(B) A defined benefit plan satisfies the requirements of this paragraph of a particular plan year if under the plan the accrued benefit payable at the normal retirement age is equal to the normal retirement benefit and the annual rate at which any individual who is or could be a participant can accrue the retirement benefits payable at normal retirement age under the plan for any later plan year is not more than 133⅓ percent of the annual rate at which he can accrue benefits for any plan year beginning on or after such particular plan year and before such later plan year. For purposes of this subparagraph—

(i) any amendment to the plan which is in effect for the current year shall be treated as in effect for all other plan years;

(ii) any change in an accrual rate which does not apply to any individual who is or could be a participant in the current year shall be disregarded;

(iii) the fact that benefits under the plan may be payable to certain employees before normal retirement age shall be disregarded; and

(iv) social security benefits and all other relevant factors used to compute benefits shall be treated as remaining constant as of the current year for all years after the current year.

(C) A defined benefit plan satisfies the requirements of this paragraph if the accrued benefit to which any participant is entitled upon his separation from the service is not less than a fraction of the annual benefit commencing at normal retirement age to which he would be entitled under the plan as in effect on the date of his separation if he continued to earn annually until normal retirement age the same rate of compensation upon which his normal retirement benefit would be computed under the plan, determined as if he had attained normal retirement age on the date any such determi-

nation is made (but taking into account no more than the 10 years of service immediately preceding his separation from service). Such fraction shall be a fraction, not exceeding 1, the numerator of which is the total number of his years of participation in the plan (as of the date of his separation from the service) and the denominator of which is the total number of years he would have participated in the plan if he separated from the service at the normal retirement age. For purposes of this subparagraph, social security benefits and all other relevant factors used to compute benefits shall be treated as remaining constant as of the current year for all years after such current year.

(D) Subparagraphs (A), (B), and (C) shall not apply with respect to years of participation before the first plan year to which this section applies but a defined benefit plan satisfies the requirements of this subparagraph with respect to such years of participation only if the accrued benefit of any participant with respect to such years of participation is not less than the greater of—

(i) his accrued benefit determined under the plan, as in effect from time to time prior to the date of the enactment of this Act, or

(ii) an accrued benefit which is not less than one-half of the accrued benefit to which such participant would have been entitled if subparagraph (A), (B), or (C) applied with respect to such years of participation.

(E) Notwithstanding subparagraphs (A), (B), and (C) of this paragraph, a plan shall not be treated as not satisfying the requirements of this paragraph solely because the accrual of benefits under the plan does not become effective until the employee has two continuous years of service. For purposes of this subparagraph, the term "year of service" has the meaning provided by section 202(a)(3)(A).

(F) Notwithstanding subparagraphs (A), (B), and (C), a defined benefit plan satisfies the requirements of this paragraph if such plan—

(i) is funded exclusively by the purchase of insurance contracts, and

(ii) satisfies the requirements of paragraphs (2) and (3) of section 301(b) (relating to certain insurance contract plans), but only if an employee's accrued benefit as of any applicable date is not less than the cash surrender value his insurance contracts would have on such applicable date if the requirements of paragraphs (4), (5), and (6) of section 301(b) were satisfied.

(G) Notwithstanding the preceding subparagraphs, a defined benefit plan shall be treated as not satisfying the requirements of this paragraph if the participant's accrued benefit is reduced on account of any increase in his age or service. The preceding sentence shall not apply to benefits under the plan commencing before benefits payable under title II of the Social Security Act which benefits under the plan—

(i) do not exceed social security benefits, and

(ii) terminate when such social security benefits commence.

(H)(i) Notwithstanding the preceding subparagraphs, a defined benefit plan shall be treated as not satisfying the requirements of this paragraph if, under the plan, an employee's benefit accrual is ceased, or the rate of an employee's benefit accrual is reduced, because of the attainment of any age.

(ii) A plan shall not be treated as failing to meet the requirements of this subparagraph solely because the plan imposes (without regard to age) a limitation on the amount of benefits that the plan provides or a limitation on the number of years of service or years of participation which are taken into account for purposes of determining benefit accrual under the plan.

(iii) In the case of any employee who, as of the end of any plan year under a defined benefit plan, has attained normal retirement age under such plan—

(I) if distribution of benefits under such plan with respect to such employee has commenced as of the end of such plan year, then any requirement of this subparagraph for continued accrual of benefits under such plan with respect to such employee during such plan year shall be treated as satisfied to the extent of the actuarial equivalent of in-service distribution of benefits, and

(II) if distribution of benefits under such plan with respect to such employee has not commenced as of the end of such year in accordance with section 206(a)(3), and the payment of benefits under such plan with respect to such employee is not suspended during such plan year pursuant to section 203(a)(3)(B), then any requirement of this subparagraph for continued accrual of benefits under such plan with respect to such employee during such plan year shall be treated as satisfied to the extent of any adjustment in the benefit payable under the plan during such plan year attributable to the delay in the distribution of benefits after the attainment of normal retirement age.

The preceding provisions of this clause shall apply in accordance with regulations of the Secretary of the Treasury. Such regulations may provide for the application of the preceding provisions of this clause, in the case of any such employee, with respect to any period of time within a plan year.

(iv) Clause (i) shall not apply with respect to any employee who is a highly compensated employee (within the meaning of section 414(q) of the Internal Revenue Code of 1986) to the extent provided in regulations prescribed by the Secretary of the Treasury for purposes of precluding discrimination in favor of highly compensated employees within the meaning of subchapter D of chapter 1 of the Internal Revenue Code of 1986.

(v) A plan shall not be treated as failing to meet the requirements of clause (i) solely because the subsidized portion of any early retirement benefit is disregarded in determining benefit accruals.

(vi) Any regulations prescribed by the Secretary of the Treasury pursuant to clause (v) of section 411(b)(1)(H) of the Internal Revenue Code of 1986 shall apply with respect to the requirements of this sub-paragraph in the same manner and to the same extent as such regulations apply with respect to the requirements of such section 411(b)(1)(H).

(2)(A) A defined contribution plan satisfies the requirements of this paragraph if, under the plan, allocations to the employee's account are not ceased, and the rate at which amounts are allocated to the employee's account is not reduced, because of the attainment of any age.

(B) A plan shall not be treated as failing to meet the requirements of subparagraph (A) solely because the subsidized portion of any early retirement benefit is disregarded in determining benefit accruals.

(C) Any regulations prescribed by the Secretary of the Treasury pursuant to subparagraphs (B) and (C) of section 411(b)(2) of the Internal Revenue Code of 1986 shall apply with respect to the requirements of this paragraph in the same manner and to the same extent as such regulations apply with respect to the requirements of such section 411(b)(2).

(3) A plan satisfies the requirements of this paragraph if—

(A) in the case of a defined benefit plan, the plan requires separate accounting for the portion of each employee's accrued benefit derived from any voluntaryemployee contributions permitted under the plan; and

(B) in the case of any plan which is not a defined benefit plan, the plan requires separate accounting for each employee's accrued benefit.

(4)(A) For purposes of determining an employee's accrued benefit, the term "year of participation" means a period of service (beginning at the earliest date on which the employee is a participant in the plan and which is included in a period of service required to be taken into account under section 202(b)) as determined without regard to section 202(b)(5) as determined under regulations prescribed by the Secretary which provide for the calculation of such period on any reasonable and consistent basis.

(B) For purposes of this paragraph, except as provided in subparagraph (C), in the case of any employee whose customary employment is less than full time, the calculation of such employee's service on any basis which provides less than a ratable portion of the accrued benefit to which he would be entitled under the plan if his customary employment were full time shall not be treated as made on a reasonable and consistent basis.

(C) For purposes of this paragraph, in the case of any employee whose service is less than 1,000 hours during any calendar year, plan year or other 12-consecutive-month period designated by the plan (and not prohibited under regulations prescribed by the Secretary) the calculation of his period of service shall not be treated as not made on a reasonable and consistent basis merely because such service is not taken into account.

(D) In the case of any seasonal industry where the customary period of employment is less than 1,000 hours during a calendar year, the term "year of participation" shall be such period as determined under regulations prescribed by the Secretary.

(E) For purposes of this subsection in the case of any maritime industry, 125 days of service shall be treated as a year of participation. The Secretary may prescribe regulations to carry out the purposes of this subparagraph.

(5) Special rules relating to age.—

(A) Comparison to similarly situated younger individual.—

(i) In general.—A plan shall not be treated as failing to meet the requirements of paragraph (1)(H)(i) if a participant's accrued benefit, as determined as of any date under the terms of the plan, would be equal to or greater than that of any similarly situated, younger individual who is or could be a participant.

(ii) Similarly situated.—For purposes of this subparagraph, a participant is similarly situated to any other individual if such participant is identical to such other individual in every respect (including period of service, compensation, position, date of hire, work history, and any other respect) except for age.

(iii) Disregard of subsidized early retirement benefits.—In determining the accrued benefit as of any date for purposes of this subparagraph, the subsidized portion of any early retirement benefit or retirement-type subsidy shall be disregarded.

(iv) Accrued benefit.—For purposes of this subparagraph, the accrued benefit may, under the terms of the plan, be expressed as an annuity payable at normal retirement age, the balance of a hypothetical account, or the current value of the accumulated percentage of the employee's final average compensation.

(B) Applicable defined benefit plans.—

(i) Interest credits.—

(I) In general.—An applicable defined benefit plan shall be treated as failing to meet the requirements of paragraph (1)(H) unless the terms of the plan provide that any interest credit (or an equivalent amount) for any plan year shall be at a rate which is not greater than a market rate of return. A plan shall not be treated as failing to meet the requirements of this subclause merely because the plan provides for a reasonable minimum guaranteed rate of return or for a rate of return that is equal to the greater of a fixed or variable rate of return.

(II) Preservation of capital.—An applicable defined benefit plan shall be treated as failing to meet the requirements of paragraph (1)(H) unless the plan provides that an interest credit (or equivalent amount) of less than zero shall in no event result in the account balance or similar amount being less than the aggregate amount of contributions credited to the account.

(III) Market rate of return.—The Secretary of the Treasury may provide by regulation for rules governing the calculation of a market rate of return for purposes of subclause (I) and for permissible methods of crediting interest to the account (including fixed or variable interest rates) resulting in effective rates of return meeting the requirements of subclause (I).

(ii) Special rule for plan conversions.—If, after June 29, 2005, an applicable plan amendment is adopted, the plan shall be treated as failing to meet the requirements of paragraph (1)(H) unless the requirements of clause (iii) are met with respect to each individual who was a participant in the plan immediately before the adoption of the amendment.

(iii) Rate of benefit accrual.—Subject to clause (iv), the requirements of this clause are met with respect to any participant if the accrued benefit of the participant under the terms of the plan as in effect after the amendment is not less than the sum of—

(I) the participant's accrued benefit for years of service before the effective date of the amendment, determined under the terms of the plan as in effect before the amendment, plus

(II) the participant's accrued benefit for years of service after the effective date of the amendment, determined under the terms of the plan as in effect after the amendment.

(iv) Special rules for early retirement subsidies.—For purposes of clause (iii)(I), the plan shall credit the accumulation account or similar amount with the amount of any early retirement benefit or retirement-type subsidy for the plan year in which the participant retires if, as of such time, the participant has met the age, years of service, and other requirements under the plan for entitlement to such benefit or subsidy.

(v) Applicable plan amendment.—For purposes of this subparagraph—

(I) In general.—The term "applicable plan amendment" means an amendment to a defined benefit plan which has the effect of converting the plan to an applicable defined benefit plan.

(II) Special rule for coordinated benefits.—If the benefits of 2 or more defined benefit plans established or maintained by an employer are coordinated in such a manner as to have the effect of the adoption of an amendment described in subclause (I), the sponsor of the defined benefit plan or plans providing for such coordination shall be treated as having adopted such a plan amendment as of the date such coordination begins.

(III) Multiple amendments.—The Secretary of the Treasury shall issue regulations to prevent the avoidance of the purposes of this subparagraph through the use of 2 or more plan amendments rather than a single amendment.

(IV) Applicable defined benefit plan.—For purposes of this subparagraph, the term "applicable defined benefit plan" has the meaning given such term by section 203(f)(3).

(vi) Termination requirements.—An applicable defined benefit plan shall not be treated as meeting the requirements of clause (i) unless the plan provides that, upon the termination of the plan—

(I) if the interest credit rate (or an equivalent amount) under the plan is a variable rate, the rate of interest used to determine accrued benefits under the plan shall be equal to the average of the rates of interest used under the plan during the 5-year period ending on the termination date, and

(II) the interest rate and mortality table used to determine the amount of any benefit under the plan payable in the form of an annuity payable at normal retirement age shall be the rate and table specified under the plan for such purpose as of the termination date, except that if such interest rate is a variable rate, the interest rate shall be determined under the rules of subclause (I).

(C) Certain offsets permitted.—A plan shall not be treated as failing to meet the requirements of paragraph (1)(H)(i) solely because the plan provides offsets against benefits under the plan to the extent such offsets are otherwise allowable in applying the requirements of section 401(a) of the Internal Revenue Code of 1986.

(D) Permitted disparities in plan contributions or benefits.—A plan shall not be treated as failing to meet the requirements of paragraph (1)(H) solely because the plan provides a disparity in contributions or benefits with respect to which the requirements of section 401(l) of the Internal Revenue Code of 1986 are met.

(E) Indexing permitted.—

(i) In general.—A plan shall not be treated as failing to meet the requirements of paragraph (1)(H) solely because the plan provides for indexing of accrued benefits under the plan.

(ii) Protection against loss.—Except in the case of any benefit provided in the form of a variable annuity, clause (i) shall not apply with respect to any indexing which results in an accrued benefit less than the accrued benefit determined without regard to such indexing.

(iii) Indexing.—For purposes of this subparagraph, the term "indexing" means, in connection with an accrued benefit, the periodic adjustment of the accrued benefit by means of the application of a recognized investment index or methodology.

(F) Early retirement benefit or retirement-type subsidy.—For purposes of this paragraph, the terms "early retirement benefit" and "retirement-type subsidy" have the meaning given such terms in subsection (g)(2)(A).

(G) Benefit accrued to date.—For purposes of this paragraph, any reference to the accrued benefit shall be a reference to such benefit accrued to date.

(c) Employees' Accrued Benefits Derived from Employer and Employee Contributions.—

(1) For purposes of this section and section 203 an employee's accrued benefit derived from employer contributions as of any applicable date is the excess (if any) of the accrued benefit for such employee as of such applicable date over the accrued benefit derived from contributions made by such employee as of such date.

(2)(A) In the case of a plan other than a defined benefit plan, the accrued benefit derived from contributions made by an employee as of any applicable date is—

(i) except as provided in clause (ii), the balance of the employee's separate account consisting only of his contributions and the income, expenses, gains, and losses attributable thereto, or

(ii) if a separate account is not maintained with respect to an employee's contributions under such a plan, the amount which bears the same ratio to his total accrued benefit as the total amount of the employee's contributions (less withdrawals) bears to the sum of such contributions and the contributions made on his behalf by the employer (less withdrawals).

(B) Defined benefit plans.—In the case of a defined benefit plan, the accrued benefit derived from contributions made by an employee as of any applicable date is the amount equal to the employee's accumulated contributions expressed as an annual benefit commencing at normal retirement age, using an interest rate which would be used under the plan under section 205(g)(3) (as of the determination date).

(C) For purposes of this subsection, the term "accumulated contributions" means the total of—

(i) all mandatory contributions made by the employee,

(ii) interest (if any) under the plan to the end of the last plan year to which section 203(a)(2) does not apply (by reason of the applicable effective date), and

(iii) interest on the sum of the amounts determined under clauses (i) and (ii) compounded annually—

(I) at the rate of 120 percent of the Federal mid-term rate (as in effect under section 1274 of the Internal Revenue Code of 1986 for the 1st month of a plan year for the period beginning with the 1st plan year to which subsection (a)(2) applies by reason of the applicable effective date) and ending with the date on which the determination is being made, and

(II) at the interest rate which would be used under the plan under section 205(g)(3) (as of the determination date) for the period beginning with the determination date and ending on the date on which the employee attains normal retirement age.

For purposes of this subparagraph, the term "mandatory contributions" means amounts contributed to the plan by the employee which are required as a condition of employment, as a condition of participation in such plan, or as a condition of obtaining benefits under the plan attributable to employer contributions.

(D) The Secretary of the Treasury is authorized to adjust by regulation the conversion factor described in subparagraph (B) from time to time as he may deem necessary. No such adjustment shall be effective for a plan year beginning before the expiration of 1 year after such adjustment is determined and published.

(3) For purposes of this section, in the case of any defined benefit plan, if an employee's accrued benefit is to be determined as an amount other than an annual benefit commencing at normal retirement age, or if the accrued benefit derived from contributions made by an employee is to be determined with respect to a benefit other than an annual benefit in the form of a single life annuity (without ancillary benefits) commencing at normal retirement age, the employee's accrued benefit, or the accrued benefits derived from contributions made by an employee, as the case may be, shall be the actuarial equivalent of such benefit or amount determined under paragraph (1) or (2).

(4) In the case of a defined benefit plan which permits voluntary employee contributions, the portion of an employee's accrued benefit derived from such contributions shall be treated as an accrued benefit derived from employee contributions under a plan other than a defined benefit plan.

(d) Employee Service Which May Be Disregarded in Determining Employees' Accrued Benefits Under Plan.—Notwithstanding section 203(b)(1), for purposes of determining the employee's accrued benefit under the plan, the plan may disregard service performed by the employee with respect to which he has received—

(1) a distribution of the present value of his entire nonforfeitable benefit if such distribution was in an amount (not more than the dollar amount under section 203(e)(1)) permitted under regulations prescribed by the Secretary of the Treasury, or

(2) a distribution of the present value of his nonforfeitable benefit attributable to such service which he elected to receive.

Paragraph (1) shall apply only if such distribution was made on termination of the employee's participation in the plan. Paragraph (2) shall apply only if such distribution was made on termination of the employee's participation in the plan or under such other circumstances as may be provided under regulations prescribed by the Secretary of the Treasury.

(e) Opportunity to Repay Full Amount of Distributions Which Have Been Reduced Through Disregarded Employee Service.—For purposes of determining the employee's accrued benefit, the plan shall not disregard service as provided in subsection (d) unless the plan provides an opportunity for the participant to repay the full amount of a distribution described in subsection (d) with, in the case of a defined benefit plan, interest at the rate determined for purposes of subsection (c)(2)(C) and provides that upon such repayment the employee's accrued benefit shall be recomputed by taking into account service so disregarded. This subsection shall apply only in the case of a participant who—

(1) received such a distribution in any plan year to which this section applies, which distribution was less than the present value of his accrued benefit,

(2) resumes employment covered under the plan, and

(3) repays the full amount of such distribution with, in the case of a defined benefit plan, interest at the rate determined for purposes of subsection (c)(2)(C).

The plan provision required under this subsection may provide that such repayment must be made (A) in the case of a withdrawal on account of separation from service, before the earlier of 5 years after the first date on which the participant is subsequently re-employed by the employer, or the close of the first period of 5 consecutive 1-year breaks in service commencing after the withdrawal; or (B) in the case of any other withdrawal, 5 years after the date of the withdrawal.

(f) Employer Treated as Maintaining a Plan.—For the purposes of this part, an employer shall be treated as maintaining a plan if any employee of such employer accrues benefits under such plan by reason of service with such employer.

(g) Decrease of Accrued Benefits Through Amendment of Plan.—

(1) The accrued benefit of a participant under a plan may not be decreased by an amendment of the plan, other than an amendment described in section 302(d)(2) or 4281.

(2) For purposes of paragraph (1), a plan amendment which has the effect of—

(A) eliminating or reducing an early retirement benefit or a retirement-type subsidy (as defined in regulations), or

(B) eliminating an optional form of benefit,

with respect to benefits attributable to service before the amendment shall be treated as reducing accrued benefits. In the case of a retirement-type subsidy, the preceding sentence shall apply only with respect to a participant who satisfies (either before or after the amendment) the preamendment conditions for the subsidy. The Secretary of the Treasury shall by regulations provide that this paragraph shall not apply to any plan amendment which reduces or eliminates benefits or subsidies which create significant burdens or complexities for the plan and plan participants, unless such amendment adversely affects the rights of any participant in a more than de minimis manner. The Secretary of the Treasury may by regulations provide that this subparagraph shall not apply to a plan amendment described in subparagraph (B) (other than a plan amendment having an effect described in subparagraph (A)).

(3) For purposes of this subsection, any—

(A) tax credit employee stock ownership plan (as defined in section 409(a) of title 26, or

(B) employee stock ownership plan (as defined in section 4975(e)(7) of title 26),

shall not be treated as failing to meet the requirements of this subsection merely because it modifies distribution options in a nondiscriminatory manner.

(4)(A) A defined contribution plan (in this subparagraph referred to as the "transferee plan") shall not be treated as failing to meet the requirements of this subsection merely because the transferee plan does not provide some or all of the forms of distribution previously available under another defined contribution plan (in this subparagraph referred to as the "transferor plan") to the extent that—

(i) the forms of distribution previously available under the transferor plan applied to the account of a participant or beneficiary under the transferor plan that was transferred from the transferor plan to the transferee plan pursuant to a direct transfer rather than pursuant to a distribution from the transferor plan;

(ii) the terms of both the transferor plan and the transferee plan authorize the transfer described in clause (i);

(iii) the transfer described in clause (i) was made pursuant to a voluntary election by the participant or beneficiary whose account was transferred to the transferee plan;

(iv) the election described in clause (iii) was made after the participant or beneficiary received a notice describing the consequences of making the election; and

(v) the transferee plan allows the participant or beneficiary described in clause (iii) to receive any distribution to which the participant or beneficiary is entitled under the transferee plan in the form of a single sum distribution.

(B) Subparagraph (A) shall apply to plan mergers and other transactions having the effect of a direct transfer, including consolidations of benefits attributable to different employers within a multiple employer plan.

(5) Except to the extent provided in regulations promulgated by the Secretary of the Treasury, a defined contribution plan shall not be treated as failing to meet the requirements of this subsection merely because of the elimination of a form of distribution previously available thereunder. This paragraph shall not apply to the elimination of a form of distribution with respect to any participant unless—

(A) a single sum payment is available to such participant at the same time or times as the form of distribution being eliminated; and

(B) such single sum payment is based on the same or greater portion of the participant's account as the form of distribution being eliminated.

(h) Notice of Significant Reduction in Benefit Accruals.—

(1) An applicable pension plan may not be amended so as to provide for a significant reduction in the rate of future benefit accrual unless the plan administrator provides the notice described in paragraph (2) to each applicable individual (and to each employee organization representing applicable individuals) and to each employer who has an obligation to contribute to the plan.

(2) The notice required by paragraph (1) shall be written in a manner calculated to be understood by the average plan participant and shall provide sufficient information (as determined in accordance with regulations prescribed by the Secretary of the Treasury) to allow applicable individuals to understand the effect of the plan amendment. The Secretary of the Treasury may provide a simplified form of notice for, or exempt from any notice requirement, a plan—

(A) which has fewer than 100 participants who have accrued a benefit under the plan, or

(B) which offers participants the option to choose between the new benefit formula and the old benefit formula.

(3) Except as provided in regulations prescribed by the Secretary of the Treasury, the notice required by paragraph (1) shall be provided within a reasonable time before the effective date of the plan amendment.

(4) Any notice under paragraph (1) may be provided to a person designated, in writing, by the person to which it would otherwise be provided.

(5) A plan shall not be treated as failing to meet the requirements of paragraph (1) merely because notice is provided before the adoption of the plan amendment if no material modification of the amendment occurs before the amendment is adopted.

(6)(A) In the case of any egregious failure to meet any requirement of this subsection with respect to any plan amendment, the provisions of the applicable pension plan shall be applied as if such plan amendment entitled all applicable individuals to the greater of—

(i) the benefits to which they would have been entitled without regard to such amendment, or

(ii) the benefits under the plan with regard to such amendment.

(B) For purposes of subparagraph (A), there is an egregious failure to meet the requirements of this subsection if such failure is within the control of the plan sponsor and is—

(i) an intentional failure (including any failure to promptly provide the required notice or information after the plan administrator discovers an unintentional failure to meet the requirements of this subsection),

(ii) a failure to provide most of the individuals with most of the information they are entitled to receive under this subsection, or

(iii) a failure which is determined to be egregious under regulations prescribed by the Secretary of the Treasury.

(7) The Secretary of the Treasury may by regulations allow any notice under this subsection to be provided by using new technologies.

(8) For purposes of this subsection—

(A) The term "applicable individual" means, with respect to any plan amendment—

(i) each participant in the plan; and

(ii) any beneficiary who is an alternate payee (within the meaning of section 206(d)(3)(K)) under an applicable qualified domestic relations order (within the meaning of section 206(d)(3)(B)(i)),

whose rate of future benefit accrual under the plan may reasonably be expected to be significantly reduced by such plan amendment.

(B) The term "applicable pension plan" means—

(i) any defined benefit plan; or

(ii) an individual account plan which is subject to the funding standards of section 412 of the Internal Revenue Code of 1986.

(9) For purposes of this subsection, a plan amendment which eliminates or reduces any early retirement benefit or retirement-type subsidy (within the meaning of subsection (g)(2)(A)) shall be treated as having the effect of reducing the rate of future benefit accrual.

(i) Prohibition on Benefit Increases Where Plan Sponsor Is in Bankruptcy.—

(1) In the case of a plan described in paragraph (3) which is maintained by an employer that is a debtor in a case under title 11, United States Code, or similar Federal or State law, no amendment of the plan which increases the liabilities of the plan by reason of—

(A) any increase in benefits,

(B) any change in the accrual of benefits, or

(C) any change in the rate at which benefits become nonforfeitable under the plan, with respect to employees of the debtor, shall be effective prior to the effective date of such employer's plan of reorganization.

(2) Paragraph (1) shall not apply to any plan amendment that—

(A) the Secretary of the Treasury determines to be reasonable and that provides for only de minimis increases in the liabilities of the plan with respect to employees of the debtor,

(B) only repeals an amendment described in section 302(d)(2),

(C) is required as a condition of qualification under part I of subchapter D of chapter 1 of the Internal Revenue Code of 1986, or

(D) was adopted prior to, or pursuant to a collective bargaining agreement entered into prior to, the date on which the employer became a debtor in a case under title 11, United States Code, or similar Federal or State law.

(3) This subsection shall apply only to plans (other than multiemployer plans) covered under section 4021 of this Act for which the funding target

attainment percentage (as defined in section 303(d)(2)) is less than 100 percent after taking into account the effect of the amendment.

(4) For purposes of this subsection, the term "employer" has the meaning set forth in section 302(b)(1), without regard to section 302(b)(2).

(j) Diversification Requirements for Certain Individual Account Plans.—

(1) In general.—An applicable individual account plan shall meet the diversification requirements of paragraphs (2), (3), and (4).

(2) Employee contributions and elective deferrals invested in employer securities.—In the case of the portion of an applicable individual's account attributable to employee contributions and elective deferrals which is invested in employer securities, a plan meets the requirements of this paragraph if the applicable individual may elect to direct the plan to divest any such securities and to reinvest an equivalent amount in other investment options meeting the requirements of paragraph (4).

(3) Employer contributions invested in employer securities.—In the case of the portion of the account attributable to employer contributions other than elective deferrals which is invested in employer securities, a plan meets the requirements of this paragraph if each applicable individual who—

(A) is a participant who has completed at least 3 years of service, or

(B) is a beneficiary of a participant described in subparagraph (A) or of a deceased participant,

may elect to direct the plan to divest any such securities and to reinvest an equivalent amount in other investment options meeting the requirements of paragraph (4).

(4) Investment options.—

(A) In general.—The requirements of this paragraph are met if the plan offers not less than 3 investment options, other than employer securities, to which an applicable individual may direct the proceeds from the divestment of employer securities pursuant to this subsection, each of which is diversified and has materially different risk and return characteristics.

(B) Treatment of certain restrictions and conditions.—

(i) Time for making investment choices.—A plan shall not be treated as failing to meet the requirements of this paragraph merely because the plan limits the time for divestment and reinvestment to periodic, reasonable opportunities occurring no less frequently than quarterly.

(ii) Certain restrictions and conditions not allowed.—Except as provided in regulations, a plan

shall not meet the requirements of this paragraph if the plan imposes restrictions or conditions with respect to the investment of employer securities which are not imposed on the investment of other assets of the plan.

This subparagraph shall not apply to any restrictions or conditions imposed by reason of the application of securities laws.

(5) Applicable individual account plan.—For purposes of this subsection—

(A) In general.—The term "applicable individual account plan" means any individual account plan (as defined in section 3(34)) which holds any publicly traded employer securities.

(B) Exception for certain ESOPs.—Such term does not include an employee stock ownership plan if—

(i) there are no contributions to such plan (or earnings thereunder) which are held within such plan and are subject to subsection (k) or (m) of section 401 of the Internal Revenue Code of 1986, and

(ii) such plan is a separate plan (for purposes of section 414(l) of such Code) with respect to any other defined benefit plan or individual account plan maintained by the same employer or employers.

(C) Exception for one participant plans.—Such term shall not include a one-participant retirement plan (as defined in section 101(i)(8)(B)).

(D) Certain plans treated as holding publicly traded employer securities.—

(i) In general.—Except as provided in regulations or in clause (ii), a plan holding employer securities which are not publicly traded employer securities shall be treated as holding publicly traded employer securities if any employer corporation, or any member of a controlled group of corporations which includes such employer corporation, has issued a class of stock which is a publicly traded employer security.

(ii) Exception for certain controlled groups with publicly traded securities.—Clause (i) shall not apply to a plan if—

(I) no employer corporation, or parent corporation of an employer corporation, has issued any publicly traded employer security, and

(II) no employer corporation, or parent corporation of an employer corporation, has issued any special class of stock which grants particular rights to, or bears particular risks for, the holder or issuer with respect to any corporation described in clause (i) which has issued any publicly traded employer security.

(iii) Definitions.—For purposes of this subparagraph, the term—

(I) "controlled group of corporations" has the meaning given such term by section 1563(a) of the Internal Revenue Code of 1986, except that "50 percent" shall be substituted for "80 percent" each place it appears,

(II) "employer corporation" means a corporation which is an employer maintaining the plan, and

(III) "parent corporation" has the meaning given such term by section 424(e) of such Code.

(6) Other definitions.—For purposes of this paragraph—

(A) Applicable individual.—The term "applicable individual" means—

(i) any participant in the plan, and

(ii) any beneficiary who has an account under the plan with respect to which the beneficiary is entitled to exercise the rights of a participant.

(B) Elective deferral.—The term "elective deferral" means an employer contribution described in section 402(g)(3)(A) of the Internal Revenue Code of 1986.

(C) Employer security.—The term "employer security" has the meaning given such term by section 407(d)(1).

(D) Employee stock ownership plan.—The term "employee stock ownership plan" has the meaning given such term by section 4975(e)(7) of such Code.

(E) Publicly traded employer securities.—The term "publicly traded employer securities" means employer securities which are readily tradable on an established securities market.

(F) Year of service.—The term "year of service" has the meaning given such term by section 203(b)(2).

(7) Transition rule for securities attributable to employer contributions.—

(A) Rules phased in over 3 years.—

(i) In general.—In the case of the portion of an account to which paragraph (3) applies and which consists of employer securities acquired in a plan year beginning before January 1, 2007, paragraph (3) shall only apply to the applicable percentage of such securities. This subparagraph shall be applied separately with respect to each class of securities.

(ii) Exception for certain participants aged 55 or over.—Clause (i) shall not apply to an applicable individual who is a participant who has attained age 55 and completed at least 3 years of service before the first plan year beginning after December 31, 2005.

(B) Applicable percentage.—For purposes of subparagraph (A), the applicable percentage shall be determined as follows:

Plan year to which paragraph (3) applies:	The applicable percentage is:
1st	33
2d	66
3d	100

(k) Cross Reference.—For special rules relating to plan provisions adopted to preclude discrimination, see section 203(c)(2).

Amendments to ERISA §204

Worker, Retiree, and Employer Recovery Act of 2008 (Pub. L. No. 110-458), as follows:

- ERISA §204(b)(5) was amended by Act §107(a)(2) by striking "clause" in subpara. (A)(iii) and inserting "subparagraph", and inserting "otherwise" before "allowable" in subpara. (C). Eff. for periods beginning on or after June 29, 2005, as if included in Title VII of Pub. L. No. 109-280.
- ERISA §204(b)(5)(B)(i)(II) was amended by Act §107(a)(3). Eff. for periods beginning on or after June 29, 2005, as if included in Title VII of Pub. L. No. 109-280. ERISA §204(b)(5)(B)(i)(II) prior to amendment:

  (II) Preservation of capital.—An interest credit (or an equivalent amount) of less than zero shall in no event result in the account balance or similar amount being less than the aggregate amount of contributions credited to the account.

Pension Protection Act of 2006 (Pub. L. No. 109-280), as follows:

- ERISA §204(b)(5) was added by Act §701(a)(1). Eff. generally after June 29, 2005, with a transition rule for collectively bargained plans.
- ERISA §204(g)(1) was amended by Act §107(a)(5) (redesignated as §108(a)(5) by Pub. L. No. 111-192, §202(a)) by substituting "§302(d)(2)" for "§302(c)(8)". Eff. for plan years beginning after 2007.
- ERISA §204(h)(1) was amended by Act §503(c)(1) by adding "and to each employer who has an obligation to contribute to the plan" at the end. Eff. for plan years beginning after Dec. 31, 2007.
- ERISA §204(i)(2)(B) was amended by Act §107(a)(6) (redesignated as §108(a)(6) by Pub. L. No. 111-192, §202(a)) by substituting "§302(d)(2)" for "§302(c)(8)". Eff. for plan years beginning after 2007.
- ERISA §204(i)(3) was amended by Act §107(a)(7) (redesignated as §108(a)(7) by Pub. L. No. 111-192, §202(a)) by substituting "funding target attainment percentage (as defined in §303(d)(2))" for "funded current liability percentage (within the meaning of §302(d)(8) of this Act)". Eff. for plan years beginning after 2007.
- ERISA §204(i)(4) was amended by Act §107(a)(8) (redesignated as §108(a)(8) by Pub. L. No. 111-192, §202(a)) by substituting "§302(b)(1), without regard to §302(b)(2)" for "§302(c)(11)(A), without regard to §302(c)(11)(B)". Eff. for plan years beginning after 2007.
- ERISA §204(j)–(k) was amended by Act §901(b)(1) by redesignating former (j) as (k), and inserting new (j). Eff. for plan years beginning after 2006.
- **Other Provision.** Act §402(g)(4) provides:

  (4) **Notice.**—In the case of a plan amendment adopted in order to comply with this section, any notice required under section 204(h) of such Act or section 4980F(e) of such Code shall be provided within 15 days of the effective date of such plan amendment. This subsection shall not apply to any plan unless such plan is maintained pursuant to one or more collective bargaining agreements between employee representatives and 1 or more employers.
- **Other Provision.** Additional effective date rules are in Act §701(e):

(e) Effective Date.—

(1) In general.—The amendments made by this section shall apply to periods beginning on or after June 29, 2005.

(2) Present value of accrued benefit.—The amendments made by subsections (a)(2) and (b)(2) shall apply to distributions made after the date of the enactment of this Act.

(3) Vesting and interest credit requirements.—In the case of a plan in existence on June 29, 2005, the requirements of clause (i) of section 411(b)(5)(B) of the Internal Revenue Code of 1986, clause (i) of section 204(b)(5)(B) of the Employee Retirement Income Security Act of 1974, and clause (i) of section 4(i)(10)(B) of the Age Discrimination in Employment Act of 1967 (as added by this Act) and the requirements of 203(f)(2) of the Employee Retirement Income Security Act of 1974 and section 411(a)(13)(B) of the Internal Revenue Code of 1986 (as so added) shall, for purposes of applying the amendments made by subsections (a) and (b), apply to years beginning after December 31, 2007, unless the plan sponsor elects the application of such requirements for any period after June 29, 2005, and before the first year beginning after December 31, 2007.

(4) Special rule for collectively bargained plans.—In the case of a plan maintained pursuant to 1 or more collective bargaining agreements between employee representatives and 1 or more employers ratified on or before the date of the enactment of this Act, the requirements described in paragraph (3) shall, for purposes of applying the amendments made by subsections (a) and (b), not apply to plan years beginning before—

(A) the earlier of—

(i) the date on which the last of such collective bargaining agreements terminates (determined without regard to any extension thereof on or after such date of enactment), or

(ii) January 1, 2008, or

(B) January 1, 2010.

(5) Conversions.—The requirements of clause (ii) of section 411(b)(5)(B) of the Internal Revenue Code of 1986, clause (ii) of section 204(b)(5)(B) of the Employee Retirement Income Security Act of 1974, and clause (ii) of section 4(i)(10)(B) of the Age Discrimination in Employment Act of 1967 (as added by this Act), shall apply to plan amendments adopted after, and taking effect after, June 29, 2005, except that the plan sponsor may elect to have such amendments apply to plan amendments adopted before, and taking effect after, such date.

Job Creation and Worker Assistance Act of 2002 (Pub. L. No. 107-147), as follows:

● ERISA §204(h)(9) was amended by Act §411(u)(2) by striking "significantly" before "reduces" and before "reducing". Eff. as if included in Pub. L. No. 107-16.

Economic Growth and Tax Relief Reconciliation Act of 2001 (Pub. L. No. 107-16), as follows:

● ERISA §204(g)(2) was amended by Act §§645(b)(2), 901 by temporarily inserting after second sentence "The Secretary of the Treasury shall by regulations provide that this paragraph shall not apply to any plan amendment which reduces or eliminates benefits or subsidies which create significant burdens or complexities for the plan and plan participants, unless such amendment adversely affects the rights of any participant in a more than de minimis manner." Eff. after June 1, 2001, and before Dec. 31, 2010. See note below on sunset rule.

● ERISA §204(g)(4), (5), were amended by Act §§645(a)(2), 901 by temporarily adding paras. (4) and (5). Eff. after Dec. 31, 2001, and before Dec. 31, 2010. See note below on sunset rule.

● ERISA §204(h) was amended by Act §§659(b), 901 by temporarily amending subsec. (h). Eff. after June 1, 2001, and before Dec. 31, 2010. See note below on sunset rule. ERISA §204(h) prior to amendment:

(h)

(1) A plan described in paragraph (2) may not be amended so as to provide for a significant reduction in the rate of future benefit accrual, unless, after adoption of the plan amendment and not less than 15 days before the effective date of the plan amendment, the plan administrator pro-

vides a written notice, setting forth the plan amendment and its effective date, to—

(A) each participant in the plan,

(B) each beneficiary who is an alternate payee (within the meaning of section 206(d)(3)(K) of this title) under an applicable qualified domestic relations order (within the meaning of section 206(d)(3)(B)(i) of this title), and

(C) each employee organization representing participants in the plan,

except that such notice shall instead be provided to a person designated, in writing, to receive such notice on behalf of any person referred to in subparagraph (A), (B), or (C).

(2) A plan is described in this paragraph if such plan is—

(A) a defined benefit plan, or

(B) an individual account plan which is subject to the funding standards of section 302 of this title.

● **Sunset Rule.** To comply with the Congressional Budget Act of 1974, §901 of Pub. L. No. 107-16 provides that all provisions of, and amendments made by, the Act will not apply to taxable, plan, or limitation years beginning after December 31, 2010. *But see* Pension Protection Act of 2006 (Pub. L. No. 109-280), §811 (sunset rule of Pub. L. No. 107-16 does not apply to the provisions of, and the amendments made by, Pub. L. No. 107-16, §§601–666 (relating to modifications to pensions and retirement income arrangement provisions)).

Taxpayer Relief Act of 1997 (Pub. L. No.105-34), as follows:

● ERISA §204(d)(1) amended by Act §1071(b) by substituting "the dollar limit under §206(e)(1)" for "$3,500". Eff. after Aug. 5, 1997.

Retirement Protection Act of 1994 (Pub. L. No. 103-465), as follows:

● ERISA §204(i), (j), were amended by Act §766(a) by adding subsec. (i) and redesignating former subsec. (i) as (j). Eff. for plan amendments adopted on or after Dec. 8, 1994.

Omnibus Budget Reconciliation Act of 1989 (Pub. L. No. 101-239), as follows:

● ERISA §204(b)(1)(A) was amended by Act §7894(c)(4) by substituting "subparagraph" for "suparagraph" in last sentence. Eff. as if included in Pub. L. No. 93-406.

● ERISA §204(b)(1)(E) was amended by Act §7894(c)(5) by substituting "term 'year of service' " for "term 'years of service' ". Eff. as if included in Pub. L. No. 93-406.

● ERISA §204(b)(2)(B) was amended by Act §7871(a)(1) by redesignating former subpara. (C) as (B) and striking former subpara. (B). Eff. as if included in Pub. L. No. 99-509. ERISA §204(b)(2)(B) prior to amendment:

(B) Subparagraph (A) shall not apply with respect to any employee who is a highly compensated employee (within the meaning of section 414(q) of title 26) to the extent provided in regulations prescribed by the Secretary of the Treasury for purposes of precluding discrimination in favor of highly compensated employees within the meaning of subchapter D of chapter 1 of title 26.

● ERISA §204(b)(2)(C) was amended by Act §7871(a) by substituting "subparagraphs (B) and (C)" for "subparagraphs (C) and (D)"; and redesignating former subpara. (D) as (C) and former subpara. (C) as (B). Eff. as if originally included in Pub. L. No. 99-509.

● ERISA §204(b)(2)(D) was amended by Act §7871(a)(1) by redesignating former subpara. (D) as (C). Eff. as if included in Pub. L. No. 99-509.

● ERISA §204(c)(2)(B) was amended by Act §7881(m)(2)(B) by inserting a heading and amending text generally. Eff. as if included in Pub. L. No. 100-203. ERISA §204(c)(2)(B) prior to amendment:

(B)

(i) In the case of a defined benefit plan providing an annual benefit in the form of a single life annuity (without ancillary benefits) commencing at normal retirement age, the accrued benefit derived from contributions made by an employee as of any applicable date is the annual benefit equal to the employee's accumulated contributions multiplied by the appropriate conversion factor.

(ii) For purposes of clause (i), the term "appropriate conversion factor" means the factor necessary to convert an amount equal to the accumulated contributions to a single life annuity (without ancillary benefits) commencing at normal retirement age and shall be 10 percent for a normal retirement age of 65 years. For other normal retirement ages the conversion factor shall be determined in accordance with regulations prescribed by the Secretary of the Treasury or his delegate.

- ERISA §204(c)(2)(C)(iii) was amended by Act §7881(m)(2)(A). Eff. as if included in Pub. L. No. 100-203. ERISA §204(c)(2)(C)(iii) prior to amendment:

    (iii) interest on the sum of the amounts determined under clauses (i) and (ii) compounded annually at the rate of 120 percent of the Federal mid-term rate (as in effect under section 1274 of title 26 for the 1st month of a plan year) from the beginning of the first plan year to which section 203(a)(2) of this title applies (by reason of the applicable effective date) to the date upon which the employee would attain normal retirement age.

- ERISA §204(c)(2)(E) was stricken by Act §7881(m)(2)(C). Eff. as if included in Pub. L. No. 100-203. ERISA §204(c)(2)(E) prior to amendment:

    (E) The accrued benefit derived from employee contributions shall not exceed the greater of—
    (i) the employee's accrued benefit under the plan, or
    (ii) the accrued benefit derived from employee contributions determined as though the amounts calculated under clauses (ii) and (iii) of subparagraph (C) were zero.

- ERISA §204(d) was amended by Act §7894(c)(6) by removing the indentation of the term "Paragraph" where first appearing in concluding provisions. Eff. as if included in Pub. L. No. 93-406.
- ERISA §204(g)(3)(A) was amended by Act §7891(a)(1) by substituting "Internal Revenue Code of 1986" for "Internal Revenue Code of 1954", which for purposes of codification was translated as "title 26". Eff. as if included in Pub. L. No. 99-514.
- ERISA §204(h) was amended by Act §7862(b)(1)(A) by making technical correction to directory language of Pub. L. No. 99-514, §1879(u)(1). Eff. as if included in Pub. L. No. 99-514.
- ERISA §204(h)(2) was amended by Act §7862(b)(2) to adjust the left-hand margin of introductory provisions to full measure. Eff. as if included in Pub. L. No. 99-514.

Omnibus Budget Reconciliation Act of 1987 (Pub. L. No. 100-203), as follows:

- ERISA §204(c)(2)(C)(iii) was amended by Act §9346(a)(1) by substituting "120 percent of the Federal mid-term rate (as in effect under §1274 of title 26 for the 1st month of a plan year)" for "5 percent per annum". Eff. for plan years after 1987.
- ERISA §204(c)(2)(D) was amended by Act §9346(a)(2) by striking ", clause (iii) of subparagraph (C), or both," before "from time to time" in first sentence and striking second sentence, which read: "The rate of interest shall bear the relationship to 5 percent which the Secretary of the Treasury determines to be comparable to the relationship which the long-term money rates and investment yields for the last period of 10 calendar years ending at least 12 months before the beginning of the plan year bear to the long-term money rates and investment yields for the 10-calendar year period 1964 through 1973." Eff. for plan years after 1987.

Omnibus Budget Reconciliation Act of 1986 (Pub. L. No. 99-509), as follows:

- ERISA §204(a) was amended by Act §9202(a)(1). Eff. after Jan. 1, 1988, for employees who have one hour of service in any plan year to which the amendment applies, and with a special rule for collectively bargained plans. ERISA §204(a) prior to amendment:

    (a) Each pension plan shall satisfy the requirements of subsection (b)(2) of this section, and in the case of a defined benefit plan shall also satisfy the requirements of subsection (b)(1) of this section.

- ERISA §204(b)(1)(H) was added by Act §9202(a)(2). Eff. after Jan. 1, 1988, for employees who have one hour of service in any plan year to which the amendment applies, and with a special rule for collectively bargained plans.
- ERISA §204(b)(2)–(4) were amended by Act §9202(a)(3) by adding para. (2) and redesignating former paras. (2) and (3) as (3) and (4), respectively. Eff. after Jan. 1, 1988, for employees

who have one hour of service in any plan year to which the amendment applies, and with a special rule for collectively bargained plans.

Tax Reform Act of 1986 (Pub. L. No. 99-514), as follows:

- ERISA §204(e) was amended by Act §1898(a)(4)(B)(ii) by inserting last sentence and striking former last sentence, which read: "In the case of a defined contribution plan, the plan provision required under this subsection may provide that such repayment must be made before the participant has 5 consecutive 1-year breaks in service commencing after such withdrawal." Eff. as if included in Pub. L. No. 98-397.
- ERISA §204(g)(1) was amended by Act §1898(f)(2) by inserting reference to §1441. Eff. as if included in Pub. L. No. 98-397.
- ERISA §204(g)(3) was added by Act §1898(f)(1)(B). Eff. as if included in Pub. L. No. 98-397.
- ERISA §204(h) was amended by Act §1879(u)(1) (and later amended by Pub. L. No. 101-239, §7862(b)(1)(A)), by designating existing provisions as para. (1); substituting "plan described in paragraph (2)" for "single-employer plan"; redesignating former paras. (1)–(3) as subparas. (A)–(C), respectively; substituting "subparagraph (A), (B), or (C)" for "paragraph (1), (2), or (3)" in concluding provisions; and adding para. (2). Eff. as if included in Pub. L. No. 99-272.
- ERISA §204(h) was added by Act §1113(e) and former subsec. (h) was redesignated as (i). Eff. for plan years beginning after 1988.
- ERISA §204(i) was amended by Act §1113(e)(4)(B) by striking reference to class year plans under ERISA §203(c)(3). Eff. for plan years beginning after 1988.

Consolidated Omnibus Budget Reconciliation Act of 1985 (Pub. L. No. 99-272), as follows:

- ERISA §204 was amended by Act §11006(a) by redesignating former subsec. (h) as (i). Eff. after 1985.

Retirement Equity Act of 1984 (Pub. L. No. 98-397), as follows:

- ERISA §204(b)(3)(A) was amended by Act §102 by inserting ", 102(b)(5) of this title" after "section 102(b) of this title". Eff. after 1984.
- ERISA §204(d)(1) was amended by Act §105(b) by substituting "$3,500" for "$1,750". Eff. after 1984.
- ERISA §204(e) was amended by Act §102(f) by substituting "5 consecutive 1-year breaks in service" for "any 1-year break in service". Eff. after 1984.
- ERISA §204(g) was amended by Act §301(a)(2) by designating existing provisions as para. (1) and adding para. (2). Eff. after 1984.

SEC. 205. REQUIREMENT OF JOINT AND SURVIVOR ANNUITY AND PRERETIREMENT SURVIVOR ANNUITY.

(a) Required Contents for Applicable Plans.— Each pension plan to which this section applies shall provide that—

(1) in the case of a vested participant who does not die before the annuity starting date, the accrued benefit payable to such participant shall be provided in the form of a qualified joint and survivor annuity, and

(2) in the case of a vested participant who dies before the annuity starting date and who has a surviving spouse, a qualified preretirement survivor annuity shall be provided to the surviving spouse of such participant.

(b) Applicable Plans.—

(1) This section shall apply to—

(A) any defined benefit plan,

ERISA Sec. 205(b)(1)(A)

(B) any individual account plan which is subject to the funding standards of section 302, and

(C) any participant under any other individual account plan unless—

(i) such plan provides that the participant's nonforfeitable accrued benefit (reduced by any security interest held by the plan by reason of a loan outstanding to such participant) is payable in full, on the death of the participant, to the participant's surviving spouse (or, if there is no surviving spouse or the surviving spouse consents in the manner required under subsection (c)(2), to a designated beneficiary),

(ii) such participant does not elect the payment of benefits in the form of a life annuity, and

(iii) with respect to such participant, such plan is not a direct or indirect transferee (in a transfer after December 31, 1984) of a plan which is described in subparagraph (A) or (B) or to which this clause applied with respect to the participant.

Clause (iii) of subparagraph (C) shall apply only with respect to the transferred assets (and income therefrom) if the plan separately accounts for such assets and any income therefrom.

(2)(A) In the case of—

(i) a tax credit employee stock ownership plan (as defined in section 409(a) of title 26, or

(ii) an employee stock ownership plan (as defined in section 4975(e)(7) of title 26), subsection (a) shall not apply to that portion of the employee's accrued benefit to which the requirements of section 409(h) of title 26 apply.

(B) Subparagraph (A) shall not apply with respect to any participant unless the requirements of clause [clauses] (i), (ii), and (iii) of paragraph (1)(C) are met with respect to such participant.

[3](4) This section shall not apply to a plan which the Secretary of the Treasury or his delegate has determined is a plan described in section 404(c) of the Internal Revenue Code of 1986 (or a continuation thereof) in which participation is substantially limited to individuals who, before January 1, 1976, ceased employment covered by the plan.

(4) A plan shall not be treated as failing to meet the requirements of paragraph (1)(C) or (2) merely because the plan provides that benefits will not be payable to the surviving spouse of the participant unless the participant and such spouse had been married throughout the 1-year period ending on the earlier of the participant's annuity starting date or the date of the participant's death.

(c) **Plans Meeting Requirements of Section.—**

(1) A plan meets the requirements of this section only if—

(A) under the plan, each participant—

(i) may elect at any time during the applicable election period to waive the qualified joint and survivor annuity form of benefit or the qualified preretirement survivor annuity form of benefit (or both),

(ii) if the participant elects a waiver under clause (i), may elect the qualified optional survivor annuity at any time during the applicable election period, and

(iii) may revoke any such election at any time during the applicable election period, and

(B) the plan meets the requirements of paragraphs (2), (3), and (4).

(2) Each plan shall provide that an election under paragraph (1)(A)(i) shall not take effect unless—

(A)(i) the spouse of the participant consents in writing to such election, (ii) such election designates a beneficiary (or a form of benefits) which may not be changed without spousal consent (or the consent of the spouse expressly permits designations by the participant without any requirement of further consent by the spouse), and (iii) the spouse's consent acknowledges the effect of such election and is witnessed by a plan representative or a notary public, or

(B) it is established to the satisfaction of a plan representative that the consent required under subparagraph (A) may not be obtained because there is no spouse, because the spouse cannot be located, or because of such other circumstances as the Secretary of the Treasury may by regulations prescribe.

Any consent by a spouse (or establishment that the consent of a spouse may not be obtained) under the preceding sentence shall be effective only with respect to such spouse.

(3)(A) Each plan shall provide to each participant, within a reasonable period of time before the annuity starting date (and consistent with such regulations as the Secretary of the Treasury may prescribe) a written explanation of—

(i) the terms and conditions of the qualified joint and survivor annuity and of the qualified optional survivor annuity,

(ii) the participant's right to make, and the effect of, an election under paragraph (1) to waive the joint and survivor annuity form of benefit,

(iii) the rights of the participant's spouse under paragraph (2), and

(iv) the right to make, and the effect of, a revocation of an election under paragraph (1).

(B)(i) Each plan shall provide to each participant, within the applicable period with respect to such participant (and consistent with such regulations as the Secretary may prescribe), a written explanation with respect to the qualified preretirement survivor annuity comparable to that required under subparagraph (A).

(ii) For purposes of clause (i), the term "applicable period" means, with respect to a participant, whichever of the following periods ends last:

(I) The period beginning with the first day of the plan year in which the participant attains age 32 and ending with the close of the plan year preceding the plan year in which the participant attains age 35.

(II) A reasonable period after the individual becomes a participant.

(III) A reasonable period ending after paragraph (5) ceases to apply to the participant.

(IV) A reasonable period ending after section 205 [this section] applies to the participant.

In the case of a participant who separates from service before attaining age 35, the applicable period shall be a reasonable period after separation

(4) Each plan shall provide that, if this section applies to a participant when part or all of the participant's accrued benefit is to be used as security for a loan, no portion of the participant's accrued benefit may be used as security for such loan unless—

(A) the spouse of the participant (if any) consents in writing to such use during the 90-day period ending on the date on which the loan is to be so secured, and

(B) requirements comparable to the requirements of paragraph (2) are met with respect to such consent.

(5)(A) The requirements of this subsection shall not apply with respect to the qualified joint and survivor annuity form of benefit or the qualified preretirement survivor annuity form of benefit, as the case may be, if such benefit may not be waived (or another beneficiary selected) and if the plan fully subsidizes the costs of such benefit.

(B) For purposes of subparagraph (A), a plan fully subsidizes the costs of a benefit if under the plan the failure to waive such benefit by a participant would not result in a decrease in any plan benefits with respect to such participant and would not result in increased contributions from such participant.

(6) If a plan fiduciary acts in accordance with part 4 of this subtitle in—

(A) relying on a consent or revocation referred to in paragraph (1)(A), or

(B) making a determination under paragraph (2),

then such consent, revocation, or determination shall be treated as valid for purposes of discharging the

plan from liability to the extent of payments made pursuant to such Act.

(7) For purposes of this subsection, the term "applicable election period" means—

(A) in the case of an election to waive the qualified joint survivor annuity form of benefit, the 180-day period ending on the annuity starting date, or

(B) in the case of an election to waive the qualified preretirement survivor annuity, the period which begins on the first day of the plan year in which the participant attains age 35 and ends on the date of the participant's death.

In the case of a participant who is separated from service, the applicable election period under subparagraph (B) with respect to benefits accrued before the date of such separation from service shall not begin later than such date.

(8) Notwithstanding any other provision of this subsection—

(A)(i) A plan may provide the written explanation described in paragraph (3)(A) after the annuity starting date. In any case to which this subparagraph applies, the applicable election period under paragraph (7) shall not end before the 30th day after the date on which such explanation is provided.

(ii) The Secretary of the Treasury may by regulations limit the application of clause (i), except that such regulations may not limit the period of time by which the annuity starting date precedes the provision of the written explanation other than by providing that the annuity starting date may not be earlier than termination of employment.

(B) A plan may permit a participant to elect (with any applicable spousal consent) to waive any requirement that the written explanation be provided at least 30 days before the annuity starting date (or to waive the 30-day requirement under sub-paragraph (A)) if the distribution commences more than 7 days after such explanation is provided.

(d)(1) "Qualified Joint and Survivor Annuity" Defined.—For purposes of this section, the term "qualified joint and survivor annuity" means an annuity—

(A) for the life of the participant with a survivor annuity for the life of the spouse which is not less than 50 percent of (and is not greater than 100 percent of) the amount of the annuity which is payable during the joint lives of the participant and the spouse, and

(B) which is the actuarial equivalent of a single annuity for the life of the participant.

Such term also includes any annuity in a form having the effect of an annuity described in the preceding sentence.

(2)(A) For purposes of this section, the term "qualified optional survivor annuity" means an annuity—

(i) for the life of the participant with a survivor annuity for the life of the spouse which is equal to the applicable percentage of the amount of the annuity which is payable during the joint lives of the participant and the spouse, and

(ii) which is the actuarial equivalent of a single annuity for the life of the participant.

Such term also includes any annuity in a form having the effect of an annuity described in the preceding sentence.

(B)(i) For purposes of subparagraph (A), if the survivor annuity percentage—

(I) is less than 75 percent, the applicable percentage is 75 percent, and

(II) is greater than or equal to 75 percent, the applicable percentage is 50 percent.

(ii) For purposes of clause (i), the term "survivor annuity percentage" means the percentage which the survivor annuity under the plan's qualified joint and survivor annuity bears to the annuity payable during the joint lives of the participant and the spouse.

(e) "Qualified Preretirement Survivor Annuity" Defined.—For purposes of this section—

(1) Except as provided in paragraph (2), the term "qualified preretirement survivor annuity" means a survivor annuity for the life of the surviving spouse of the participant if—

(A) the payments to the surviving spouse under such annuity are not less than the amounts which would be payable as a survivor annuity under the qualified joint and survivor annuity under the plan (or the actuarial equivalent thereof) if—

(i) in the case of a participant who dies after the date on which the participant attained the earliest retirement age, such participant had retired with an immediate qualified joint and survivor annuity on the day before the participant's date of death, or

(ii) in the case of a participant who dies on or before the date on which the participant would have attained the earliest retirement age, such participant had—

(I) separated from service on the date of death,

(II) survived to the earliest retirement age,

(III) retired with an immediate qualified joint and survivor annuity at the earliest retirement age, and

(IV) died on the day after the day on which such participant would have attained the earliest retirement age, and

(B) under the plan, the earliest period for which the surviving spouse may receive a payment under such annuity is not later than the month in which the participant would have attained the earliest retirement age under the plan.

In the case of an individual who separated from service before the date of such individual's death, subparagraph (A)(ii)(I) shall not apply.

(2) In the case of any individual account plan or participant described in subparagraph (B) or (C) of subsection (b)(1), the term "qualified preretirement survivor annuity" means an annuity for the life of the surviving spouse the actuarial equivalent of which is not less than 50 percent of the portion of the account balance of the participant (as of the date of death) to which the participant had a nonforfeitable right (within the meaning of section 203).

(3) For purposes of paragraphs (1) and (2), any security interest held by the plan by reason of a loan outstanding to the participant shall be taken into account in determining the amount of the qualified preretirement survivor annuity.

(f) Marriage Requirements for Plan.—

(1) Except as provided in paragraph (2), a plan may provide that a qualified joint and survivor annuity (or a qualified preretirement survivor annuity) will not be provided unless the participant and spouse had been married throughout the 1-year period ending on the earlier of—

(A) the participant's annuity starting date, or

(B) the date of the participant's death.

(2) For purposes of paragraph (1), if—

(A) a participant marries within 1 year before the annuity starting date, and

(B) the participant and the participant's spouse in such marriage have been married for at least a 1-year period ending on or before the date of the participant's death,

such participant and such spouse shall be treated as having been married throughout the 1-year period ending on the participant's annuity starting date.

(g) Distribution of Present Value of Annuity; Written Consent; Determination of Present Value.—

(1) A plan may provide that the present value of a qualified joint and survivor annuity or a qualified preretirement survivor annuity will be immediately distributed if such value does not exceed the amount that can be distributed without the participant's consent under section 203(e). No distribution may be made under the preceding sentence after the annuity starting date unless the participant and the spouse of the participant (or where the participant has died, the surviving spouse) consent in writing to such distribution.

(2) If—

(A) the present value of the qualified joint and survivor annuity or the qualified preretirement survivor annuity exceeds the amount that can be distributed without the participant's consent under section 203(e), and

(B) the participant and the spouse of the participant (or where the participant has died, the surviving spouse) consent in writing to the distribution, the plan may immediately distribute the present value of such annuity.

(3)(A) For purposes of paragraphs (1) and (2), the present value shall not be less than the present value calculated by using the applicable mortality table and the applicable interest rate.

(B) For purposes of subparagraph (A)—

(i) The term "applicable mortality table" means a mortality table, modified as appropriate by the Secretary of the Treasury, based on the mortality table specified for the plan year under subparagraph (A) of section 303(h)(3) (without regard to subparagraph (C) or (D) of such section).

(ii) The term "applicable interest rate" means the adjusted first, second, and third segment rates applied under rules similar to the rules of section 303(h)(2)(C) for the month before the date of the distribution or such other time as the Secretary of the Treasury may by regulations prescribe.

(iii) For purposes of clause (ii), the adjusted first, second, and third segment rates are the first, second, and third segment rates which would be determined under section 303(h)(2)(C) if—

(I) section 303(h)(2)(D) were applied by substituting the average yields for the month described in clause (ii) for the average yields for the 24-month period described in such section,

(II) section 303(h)(2)(G)(i)(II) were applied by substituting "section 205(g)(3)(A)(ii)(II)" for "section 302(b)(5)(B)(ii)(II)", and

(III) the applicable percentage under section 303(h)(2)(G) were determined in accordance with the following table:

In the case of plan years beginning in:	The applicable percentage is:
2008	20 percent
2009	40 percent
2010	60 percent
2011	80 percent

(h) Definitions.—For purposes of this section—

(1) the term "vested participant" means any participant who has a nonforfeitable right (within the meaning of section 3(19)) to any portion of such participant's accrued benefit.

(2)(A) The term "annuity starting date" means—

(i) the first day of the first period for which an amount is payable as an annuity, or

(ii) in the case of a benefit not payable in the form of an annuity, the first day on which all events have occurred which entitle the participant to such benefit.

(B) For purposes of subparagraph (A), the first day of the first period for which a benefit is to be received by reason of disability shall be treated as the annuity starting date only if such benefit is not an auxiliary benefit.

(3) The term "earliest retirement age" means the earliest date on which, under the plan, the participant could elect to receive retirement benefits.

(i) Increased Costs From Providing Annuity.—A plan may take into account in any equitable manner (as determined by the Secretary of the Treasury) any increased costs resulting from providing a qualified joint or survivor annuity or a qualified preretirement survivor annuity.

(j) Use of Participant's Accrued Benefit as Security for Loan as Not Preventing Distribution.—If the use of any participant's accrued benefit (or any portion thereof) as security for a loan meets the requirements of subsection (c)(4), nothing in this section shall prevent any distribution required by reason of a failure to comply with the terms of such loan.

(k) Spousal Consent.—No consent of a spouse shall be effective for purposes of subsection (g)(1) or (g)(2) (as the case may be) unless requirements comparable to the requirements for spousal consent to an election under subsection (c)(1)(A) are met.

(*l*) Regulations; Consultation of Secretary of the Treasury with Secretary of Labor.—In prescribing regulations under this section, the Secretary of the Treasury shall consult with the Secretary of Labor.

Amendments to ERISA §205

Worker, Retiree, and Employer Recovery Act of 2008 (Pub. L. No. 110-458), as follows:

● ERISA §205(g)(3)(B)(iii)(II) was amended by Act §103(b)(1) by striking "section 205(g)(3)(B)(iii)(II)" and inserting "section 205(g)(3)(A)(ii)(II)". Eff. for plan years beginning after Dec. 31, 2007, as if included in Pub. L. No. 109-280, §302.

Pension Protection Act of 2006 (Pub. L. No. 109-280), as follows:

● ERISA §205(c)(1)(A) was amended by Act §1004(b). Eff. generally for plan years beginning after 2007. ERISA §205(c)(1)(A) prior to amendment:

　(A) Under the plan, each participant—
　　(i) may elect at any time during the applicable election period to waive the qualified joint and survivor annuity form of benefit or the qualified preretirement survivor annuity form of benefit (or both), and
　　(ii) may revoke any such election at any time during the applicable election period, and.

● ERISA §205(c)(3(A)(i) was amended by Act §1004(b)(3) by adding "and of the qualified optional survivor annuity" after "annuity". Eff. generally for plan years after 2007, with a collective bargaining transition rule.

- ERISA §205(c)(7)(A) was amended by Act §1101(a)(2)(A) by substituting "180-day" for "90 day". Eff. for years after 2006.
- ERISA §205(d) was amended by Act §1004(b)(2) by inserting "1" after "(d)", and redesignating paras. (1) and (2) as subparas. (A) and (B), respectively. Eff. generally for plan years after 2007.
- ERISA §205(g)(3) was amended by Act §302(a). Eff. for plan years beginning after 2007. ERISA §205(g)(3) prior to amendment:

(3) Determination of present value.—

(A) In general.—(i) Present value.—Except as provided in subparagraph (B), for purposes of paragraphs (1) and (2), the present value shall not be less than the present value calculated by using the applicable mortality table and the applicable interest rate.

(ii) Definitions.—For purposes of clause (i)—

(I) Applicable mortality table.—The term "applicable mortality table" means the table prescribed by the Secretary of the Treasury. Such table shall be based on the prevailing commissioners' standard table (described in section 807(d)(5)(A) of title 26) used to determine reserves for group annuity contracts issued on the date as of which present value is being determined (without regard to any other subparagraph of section 807(d)(5) of such title).

(II) Applicable interest rate.—The term "applicable interest rate" means the annual rate of interest on 30-year Treasury securities for the month before the date of distribution or such other time as the Secretary of the Treasury may by regulations prescribe.

(B) Exception.—In the case of a distribution from a plan that was adopted and in effect prior to December 8, 1994, the present value of any distribution made before the earlier of—

(i) the later of when a plan amendment applying subparagraph (A) is adopted or made effective, or

(ii) the first day of the first plan year beginning after December 31, 1999, shall be calculated, for purposes of paragraphs (1) and (2), using the interest rate determined under the regulations of the Pension Benefit Guaranty Corporation for determining the present value of a lump sum distribution on plan termination that were in effect on September 1, 1993, and using the provisions of the plan as in effect on the day before December 8, 1994; but only if such provisions of the plan met the requirements of this paragraph as in effect on the day before December 8, 1994.

Job Creation and Worker Assistance Act of 2002 (Pub. L. No. 107-147), as follows:

- ERISA §205(g)(1) was amended by Act §411(r)(2)(A) by substituting "exceed the amount that can be distributed without the participant's consent under section 203(e) of this title" for "exceed the dollar limit under section 203(e)(1) of this title". Eff. as if included in Pub. L. No. 107-16.
- ERISA §205(g)(2)(A) was amended by Act §411(r)(2)(B) by substituting "exceeds the amount that can be distributed without the participant's consent under section 203(e) of this title" for "exceeds the dollar limit under section 203(e)(1) of this title". Eff. as if included in Pub. L. No. 107-16.

Taxpayer Relief Act of 1997 (Pub. L. No. 105-34), as follows:

- ERISA §205(c)(8)(A)(ii) was amended by Act §1601(d)(5) by substituting "Secretary of the Treasury" for "Secretary". Eff. for plan years beginning after Aug. 5, 1997.
- ERISA §205(g)(1), (2)(A) were amended by Act §1071(b)(2) by substituting "the dollar limit under section 203(e)(1) of this title" for "$3,500". Eff. for plan years beginning after Aug. 5, 1997.

Small Business Job Protection Act of 1996 (Pub. L. No. 104-88), as follows:

- ERISA §205(c)(8) was added by Act §1451(b). Eff. for plan years beginning after 1996.

Retirement Protection Act of 1994 (Pub. L. No. 103-465), as follows:

- ERISA §205(g)(3) was amended by Act §767. Eff. for plan and limitation years after 1994. ERISA §205(g)(3) prior to amendment:

(3)(A) For purposes of paragraphs (1) and (2), the present value shall be calculated—

(i) by using an interest rate no greater than the applicable interest rate if the vested accrued benefit (using such rate) is not in excess of $25,000, and

(ii) by using an interest rate no greater than 120 percent of the applicable interest rate if the vested accrued benefit exceeds $25,000 (as determined under clause (i)). In no event shall the present value determined under subclause (II) be less than $25,000.

(B) For purposes of subparagraph (A), the term "applicable interest rate" means the interest rate which would be used (as of the date of the distribution) by the Pension Benefit Guaranty Corporation for purposes of determining the present value of a lump sum distribution on plan termination.

Omnibus Budget Reconciliation Act of 1989 (Pub. L. No. 101-239), as follows:

- ERISA §205(b)(1)(C)(i) was amended by Act §7862(d)(7) by making a technical correction to directory language of Pub. L. No. 99-514, §1898(b)(7)(B). Eff. as if included in Pub. L. No. 99-514.
- ERISA §205(b)(2)(A)(i) was amended by Act §7891(a)(1) by substituting "Internal Revenue Code of 1986" for "Internal Revenue Code of 1954", which for purposes of codification was translated as "title 26". Eff. as if included in Pub. L. No. 99-514.
- ERISA §205(b)(3)–(4), were amended by Act §7862(d)(9) by amending directory language of Pub. L. No. 99-514, §1898(b)(14)(B); and redesignating para. (3), as added by Pub. L. No. 99-514, §1898(b)(14)(B), as para. (4). Eff. as if included in Pub. L. No. 99-514.
- ERISA §205 was amended by Act §§7861(d)(2), 7891(c), by realigning margins of para. (3), as added by Pub. L. No. 99-514, §1145(b), and redesignating para. (3) as (4). Eff. as if included in Pub. L. No. 99-514.
- ERISA §205(c)(3)(B)(ii) was amended by Act §7862(d)(1)(B) by inserting at the end "In the case of a participant who separates from service before attaining age 35, the applicable period shall be a reasonable period after separation." Eff. as if included in Pub. L. No. 99-514.
- ERISA §205(c)(3)(B)(ii)(IV) was amended by Act §7862(d)(6) by substituting "after this section" for "after section 401(a)(11) of this title". Eff. as if included in Pub. L. No. 99-514.
- ERISA §205(c)(3)(B)(ii)(V) was stricken by Act §7862(d)(1)(B). Eff. as if included in the Tax Reform Act of 1986 (Pub. L. No. 99-514). ERISA §205(c)(3)(B)(ii)(V) prior to amendment:

(V) A reasonable period after separation from service in case of a participant who separates before attaining age 35.

- ERISA §205(c)(6) was amended by Act §7894(c)(7)(A) by substituting "such Act" for "such act". Eff. as if included in Pub. L. No. 98-397.
- ERISA §205(e)(2) was amended by Act §7862(d)(8) by substituting "nonforfeitable right (within the meaning of §203 of this title)" for "nonforfeitable accrued benefit". Eff. as if included in Pub. L. No. 99-514.
- ERISA §205(g)(3)(A) was amended by Act §7891(b)(3) by realigning margins of subpara. (A). Eff. as if included in Pub. L. No. 99-514.
- ERISA §205(h)(1) was amended by Act §§7862(d)(3)(A), 7891(e)(1), by amending para. (1) identically, substituting "The term" for "the term" and "benefit." for "benefit,". Eff. as if included in Pub. L. No. 99-514.
- ERISA §205(h)(3) was amended by Act §§7862(d)(3)(B), 7891(e)(2), by amending para. (3) identically, substituting "The term" for "the term". Eff. as if included in Pub. L. No. 99-514.

Tax Reform Act of 1986 (Pub. L. No. 99-514), as follows:

- ERISA §205(a)(1) was amended by Act §1898(b)(3)(B) by substituting "who does not die before the annuity starting date" for "who retires under the plan". Eff. as if included in Pub. L. No. 98-397.
- ERISA §205(b)(1) was amended by Act §1898(b)(2)(B)(ii) by inserting at the end "Clause (iii) of subparagraph (C) shall apply only with respect to the transferred assets (and income therefrom) if the plan separately accounts for such assets and any income therefrom." Eff. as if included in Pub. L. No. 98-397.

- ERISA §205(b)(1)(C)(i) was amended by Act §1898(b)(13)(B) by substituting "(c)(2)" for "(c)(2)(A)". Act §1898(b)(7)(B) was later amended by Pub. L. No. 101-239, §7862(d)(7), which inserted "(reduced by any security interest held by the plan by reason of a loan outstanding to such participant)". Eff. as if included in Pub. L. No. 98-397.
- ERISA §205(b)(1)(C)(iii) was amended by Act §1898(b)(2)(B)(i) by substituting "a direct or indirect transferee (in a transfer after December 31, 1984)" for "a transferee". Eff. as if included in Pub. L. No. 98-397.
- ERISA §205(b)(3) was amended by Act §1898(b)(14)(B), as amended by Pub. L. No. 101-239 §7862(d)(9)(A), which added para. (3) relating to treatment of a plan as meeting requirements of para. (1)(C) or (2) of subsec. (b). Pub. L. No. 99-514, §1145(b), added para. (3) relating to applicability of this section to plans described in IRC §404(c). Eff. as if included in Pub. L. No. 98-397.
- ERISA §205(c)(1)(B) was added by Act §1898(b)(4)(B)(i) by substituting "paragraphs (2), (3), and (4)" for "paragraphs (2) and (3)". Eff. Aug. 18, 1985.
- ERISA §205(c)(2)(A) was amended by Act §1898(b)(6)(B). Eff. Oct. 22, 1986. ERISA §205(c)(2)(A) prior to amendment:
  (A) the spouse of the participant consents in writing to such election, and the spouse's consent acknowledges the effect of such election and is witnessed by a plan representative or a notary public, or".
- ERISA §205(c)(3)(B) was amended by Act §1898(b)(5)(B). Eff. as if included in Pub. L. No. 98-397. ERISA §205(c)(3)(B) prior to amendment:
  (B) Each plan shall provide to each participant, within the period beginning with the first day of the plan year in which the participant attains age 32 and ending with the close of the plan year preceding the plan year in which the participant attains age 35 (and consistent with such regulations as the Secretary of the Treasury may prescribe), a written explanation with respect to the qualified preretirement survivor annuity comparable to that required under subparagraph (A).
- ERISA §205(c)(4) was added by Act §1898(b)(4)(B)(ii) and former para. (4) was redesignated (5). Eff. Aug. 18, 1985.
- ERISA §205(c)(5) was added by Act §1898(b)(4)(B)(ii) and former paras. (4) and (5) were redesignated as paras. (5) and (6), respectively. Eff. Aug. 18, 1985.
- ERISA §205(c)(5)(A) was amended by Act §1898(b)(11)(B) by inserting "if such benefit may not be waived (or another beneficiary selected) and". Eff. as if included in Pub. L. No. 98-397.
- ERISA §205(c)(6)–(7) was added by Act §1898(b)(4)(B)(ii) and former paras. (5) and (6) were redesignated as (6) and (7), respectively. Eff. Aug. 18, 1985.
- ERISA §205(e)(1) was amended by Act §1898(b)(1)(B) by inserting at the end "In the case of an individual who separated from service before the date of such individual's death, subparagraph (A)(ii)(I) shall not apply." Eff. as if included in Pub. L. No. 98-397.
- ERISA §205(e)(2) was amended by Act §1898(b)(9)(B)(i) by substituting "the portion of the account balance of the participant (as of the date of death) to which the participant had a nonforfeitable accrued benefit" for "the account balance of the participant as of the date of death". Eff. as if included in Pub. L. No. 98-397.
- ERISA §205(e)(3) was added by Act §1898(b)(9)(B)(ii). Eff. as if included in Pub. L. No. 98-397.
- ERISA §205(g)(3) was amended by Act §1139(c)(2). Eff. for distributions in plan years beginning after 1984, although amendments do not apply after 1984 and before 1987, if the distributions were made pursuant to regulations under Pub. L. No. 98-3974. ERISA §205(g)(3) prior to amendment:
  (3) For purposes of paragraphs (1) and (2), the present value of a qualified joint and survivor annuity or a qualified preretirement survivor annuity shall be determined as of the date of the distribution and by using an interest rate not greater than the interest rate which would be used (as of the date of the distribution) by the Pension Benefit Guaranty Corporation for purposes of determining the present value of a lump sum distribution on plan termination.
- ERISA §205(h)(1) was amended by Act §1898(b)(8)(B) by substituting "such participant's accrued benefit" for "the accrued

benefit derived from employer contributions". Eff. Oct. 22, 1986.
- ERISA §205(h)(2) was amended by Act §1898(b)(12)(B). Eff. as if included in Pub. L. No. 98-397. ERISA §205(h)(2) prior to amendment:
  (2) the term "annuity starting date" means the first day of the first period for which an amount is received as an annuity (whether by reason of retirement or disability), and.
- ERISA §205(j) was redesignated as (k) and new (j) was inserted by Act §1898(b)(4)(B)(iii). Eff. Aug. 18, 1985.
- ERISA §205(k) was redesignated as (*l*) and new (k) was inserted by Act §1898(b)(10)(B). Eff. as if included in Pub. L. No. 98-397.

Retirement Equity Act of 1984 (Pub. L. No. 98-397), as follows:
- ERISA §205(a) was amended by Act §103(a) by substituting provisions relating to provisions to be included in applicable plans for former provisions relating to form of payment of annuity benefits. Eff. after 1984.
- ERISA §205(b) was amended by Act §103 by substituting provisions relating to applicable plans under this section for former provisions relating to plans providing for payment of benefits before normal retirement age. Eff. after 1984.
- ERISA §205(c) was amended by Act §103 by substituting provisions relating to conditions under which plans meet the requirements of this section for former provisions relating to election of qualified joint and survivor annuity form. Eff. after 1984.
- ERISA §205(d) was amended by Act §103 by substituting provisions defining "qualified joint and survivor annuity" for former provisions relating to the participant's spouse not being entitled to receive survivor annuity. Eff. after 1984.
- ERISA §205(e) was amended by Act §103 by substituting provisions defining "qualified preretirement survivor annuity" for former provisions relating to election to take annuity. Eff. after 1984.
- ERISA §205(f) was amended by Act §103 by substituting provisions to the effect that plans may provide that annuities will not be provided unless the participant and spouse had been married for a certain 1-year period, for former provisions relating to plan provisions which render election or revocation ineffective if participant dies within period of up to 2 years following the date of election or revocation. Eff. after 1984.
- ERISA §205(g) was amended by Act §103 by substituting provisions relating to plan provisions for immediate distribution of present value if such value does not exceed $3,500 and for written consent from the participant and spouse for former provisions setting forth definitions. Eff. after 1984.
- ERISA §205(h) was amended by Act §103 by substituting provisions setting forth definitions for former provisions relating to increased costs resulting from providing joint and survivor annuity benefits. Eff. after 1984.
- ERISA §205(i) was amended by Act §103 by substituting provisions relating to increased costs resulting from providing annuities under applicable plans for former provisions setting forth the effective date of this section.
- ERISA §205(j) was added by Act §103. Eff. after 1984.

SEC. 206. FORM AND PAYMENT OF BENEFITS.

(a) Commencement Date for Payment of Benefits.—Each pension plan shall provide that unless the participant otherwise elects, the payment of benefits under the plan to the participant shall begin not later than the 60th day after the latest of the close of the plan year in which—

(1) occurs the date on which the participant attains the earlier of age 65 or the normal retirement age specified under the plan,

(2) occurs the 10th anniversary of the year in which the participant commenced participation in the plan, or

(3) the participant terminates his service with the employer.

In the case of a plan which provides for the payment of an early retirement benefit, such plan shall provide that a participant who satisfied the service requirements for such early retirement benefit, but separated from the service (with any nonforfeitable right to an accrued benefit) before satisfying the age requirement for such early retirement benefit, is entitled upon satisfaction of such age requirement to receive a benefit not less than the benefit to which he would be entitled at the normal retirement age, actuarially reduced under regulations prescribed by the Secretary of the Treasury.

(b) Decrease in Plan Benefits by Reason of Increases in Benefit Levels Under Social Security Act or Railroad Retirement Act of 1937.—If—

(1) a participant or beneficiary is receiving benefits under a pension plan, or

(2) a participant is separated from the service and has nonforfeitable rights to benefits,

a plan may not decrease benefits of such a participant by reason of any increase in the benefit levels payable under title II of the Social Security Act or the Railroad Retirement Act of 1937, or any increase in the wage base under such title II, if such increase takes place after the date of the enactment of this Act or (if later) the earlier of the date of first entitlement of such benefits or the date of such separation.

(c) Forfeiture of Accrued Benefits Derived From Employer Contributions.—No pension plan may provide that any part of a participant's accrued benefit derived from employer contributions (whether or not otherwise nonforfeitable) is forfeitable solely because of withdrawal by such participant of any amount attributable to the benefit derived from contributions made by such participant. The preceding sentence shall not apply (1) to the accrued benefit of any participant unless, at the time of such withdrawal, such participant has a nonforfeitable right to at least 50 percent of such accrued benefit, or (2) to the extent that an accrued benefit is permitted to be forfeited in accordance with section 203(a)(3)(D)(iii).

(d) Assignment or Alienation of Plan Benefits.—

(1) Each pension plan shall provide that benefits provided under the plan may not be assigned or alienated.

(2) For the purposes of paragraph (1) of this subsection, there shall not be taken into account any voluntary and revocable assignment of not to exceed 10 percent of any benefit payment, or of any irrevocable assignment or alienation of benefits executed before the date of enactment of this Act. The preceding sentence shall not apply to any assignment or alienation made for the purposes of defraying plan administration costs. For purposes of this paragraph a loan made to a participant or beneficiary shall not be treated as anassignment or alienation if such loan is secured by the participant's accrued nonforfeitable benefit and is exempt from the tax imposed by section 4975 of title 26 (relating to tax on prohibited transactions) by reason of section 4975(d)(1) of title 26.

(3)(A) Paragraph (1) shall apply to the creation, assignment, or recognition of a right to any benefit payable with respect to a participant pursuant to a domestic relations order, except that paragraph (1) shall not apply if the order is determined to be a qualified domestic relations order. Each pension plan shall provide for the payment of benefits in accordance with the applicable requirements of any qualified domestic relations order.

(B) For purposes of this paragraph—

(i) the term "qualified domestic relations order" means a domestic relations order—

(I) which creates or recognizes the existence of an alternate payee's right to, or assigns to an alternate payee the right to, receive all or a portion of the benefits payable with respect to a participant under a plan, and

(II) with respect to which the requirements of subparagraphs (C) and (D) are met, and

(ii) the term "domestic relations order" means any judgment, decree, or order (including approval of a property settlement agreement) which—

(I) relates to the provision of child support, alimony payments, or marital property rights to a spouse, former spouse, child, or other dependent of a participant, and

(II) is made pursuant to a State domestic relations law (including a community property law).

(C) A domestic relations order meets the requirements of this subparagraph only if such order clearly specifies—

(i) the name and the last known mailing address (if any) of the participant and the name and mailing address of each alternate payee covered by the order,

(ii) the amount or percentage of the participant's benefits to be paid by the plan to each such alternate payee, or the manner in which such amount or percentage is to be determined,

(iii) the number of payments or period to which such order applies, and

(iv) each plan to which such order applies.

(D) A domestic relations order meets the requirements of this subparagraph only if such order—

(i) does not require a plan to provide any type or form of benefit, or any option, not otherwise provided under the plan,

(ii) does not require the plan to provide increased benefits (determined on the basis of actuarial value), and

(iii) does not require the payment of benefits to an alternate payee which are required to be paid to another alternate payee under another order previously determined to be a qualified domestic relations order.

(E)(i) A domestic relations order shall not be treated as failing to meet the requirements of clause (i) of subparagraph (D) solely because such order requires that payment of benefits be made to an alternate payee—

(I) in the case of any payment before a participant has separated from service, on or after the date on which the participant attains (or would have attained) the earliest retirement age,

(II) as if the participant had retired on the date on which such payment is to begin under such order (but taking into account only the present value of benefits actually accrued and not taking into account the present value of any employer subsidy for early retirement), and

(III) in any form in which such benefits may be paid under the plan to the participant (other than in the form of a joint and survivor annuity with respect to the alternate payee and his or her subsequent spouse).

For purposes of subclause (II), the interest rate assumption used in determining the present value shall be the interest rate specified in the plan or, if no rate is specified, 5 percent.

(ii) For purposes of this subparagraph, the term "earliest retirement age" means the earlier of—

(I) the date on which the participant is entitled to a distribution under the plan, or

(II) the later of the date the participant attains age 50 or the earliest date on which the participant could begin receiving under the plan if the participant separated from service.

(F) To the extent provided in any qualified domestic relations order—

(i) the former spouse of a participant shall be treated as a surviving spouse of such participant for purposes of section 205 (and any spouse of the participant shall not be treated as a spouse of the participant for such purposes), and

(ii) if married for at least 1 year, the surviving former spouse shall be treated as meeting the requirements of section 205(f).

(G)(i) In the case of any domestic relations order received by a plan—

(I) the plan administrator shall promptly notify the participant and each alternate payee of the receipt of such order and the plan's procedures for determining the qualified status of domestic relations orders, and

(II) within a reasonable period after receipt of such order, the plan administrator shall determine whether such order is a qualified domestic relations order and notify the participant and each alternate payee of such determination.

(ii) Each plan shall establish reasonable procedures to determine the qualified status of domestic relations orders and to administer distributions under such qualified orders. Such procedures—

(I) shall be in writing,

(II) shall provide for the notification of each person specified in a domestic relations order as entitled to payment of benefits under the plan (at the address included in the domestic relations order) of such procedures promptly upon receipt by the plan of the domestic relations order, and

(III) shall permit an alternate payee to designate a representative for receipt of copies of notices that are sent to the alternate payee with respect to a domestic relations order.

(H)(i) During any period in which the issue of whether a domestic relations order is a qualified domestic relations order is being determined (by the plan administrator, by a court of competent jurisdiction, or otherwise), the plan administrator shall separately account for the amounts (hereinafter in this subparagraph referred to as the "segregated amounts") which would have been payable to the alternate payee during such period if the order had been determined to be a qualified domestic relations order.

(ii) If within the 18-month period described in clause (v) the order (or modification thereof) is determined to be a qualified domestic relations order, the plan administrator shall pay the segregated amounts (including any interest thereon) to the person or persons entitled thereto.

(iii) If within the 18-month period described in clause (v)—

(I) it is determined that the order is not a qualified domestic relations order, or

(II) the issue as to whether such order is a qualified domestic relations order is not resolved,

then the plan administrator shall pay the segregated amounts (including any interest thereon) to the person or persons who would have been entitled to such amounts if there had been no order.

(iv) Any determination that an order is a qualified domestic relations order which is made after the close of the 18-month period described in clause (v) shall be applied prospectively only.

(v) For purposes of this subparagraph, the 18-month period described in this clause is the 18-

month period beginning with the date on which the first payment would be required to be made under the domestic relations order.

(I) If a plan fiduciary acts in accordance with part 4 of this subtitle in—

(i) treating a domestic relations order as being (or not being) a qualified domestic relations order, or

(ii) taking action under subparagraph (H),

then the plan's obligation to the participant and each alternate payee shall be discharged to the extent of any payment made pursuant to such Act.

(J) A person who is an alternate payee under a qualified domestic relations order shall be considered for purposes of any provision of this Act a beneficiary under the plan. Nothing in the preceding sentence shall permit a requirement under section 4001 of the payment of more than 1 premium with respect to a participant for any period.

(K) The term "alternate payee" means any spouse, former spouse, child, or other dependent of a participant who is recognized by a domestic relations order as having a right to receive all, or a portion of, the benefits payable under a plan with respect to such participant.

(L) This paragraph shall not apply to any plan to which paragraph (1) does not apply.

(M) Payment of benefits by a pension plan in accordance with the applicable requirements of a qualified domestic relations order shall not be treated as garnishment for purposes of section 303(a) of the Consumer Credit Protection Act.

(N) In prescribing regulations under this paragraph, the Secretary shall consult with the Secretary of the Treasury.

(4) Paragraph (1) shall not apply to any offset of a participant's benefits provided under an employee pension benefit plan against an amount that the participant is ordered or required to pay to the plan if—

(A) the order or requirement to pay arises—

(i) under a judgment of conviction for a crime involving such plan,

(ii) under a civil judgment (including a consent order or decree) entered by a court in an action brought in connection with a violation (or alleged violation) of part 4 of this subtitle, or

(iii) pursuant to a settlement agreement between the Secretary and the participant, or a settlement agreement between the Pension Benefit Guaranty Corporation and the participant, in connection with a violation (or alleged violation) of part 4 of this subtitle by a fiduciary or any other person,

(B) the judgment, order, decree, or settlement agreement expressly provides for the offset of all or part of the amount ordered or required to be paid to the plan against the participant's benefits provided under the plan, and

(C) in a case in which the survivor annuity requirements of section 205 apply with respect to distributions from the plan to the participant, if the participant has a spouse at the time at which the offset is to be made—

(i) either—

(I) such spouse has consented in writing to such offset and such consent is witnessed by a notary public or representative of the plan (or it is established to the satisfaction of a plan representative that such consent may not be obtained by reason of circumstances described in section 205(c)(2)(B)), or

(II) an election to waive the right of the spouse to a qualified joint and survivor annuity or a qualified preretirement survivor annuity is in effect in accordance with the requirements of section 205(c),

(ii) such spouse is ordered or required in such judgment, order, decree, or settlement to pay an amount to the plan in connection with a violation of part 4 of this subtitle, or

(iii) in such judgment, order, decree, or settlement, such spouse retains the right to receive the survivor annuity under a qualified joint and survivor annuity provided pursuant to section 205(a)(1) and under a qualified preretirement survivor annuity provided pursuant to section 205(a)(2), determined in accordance with paragraph (5).

A plan shall not be treated as failing to meet the requirements of section 205 solely by reason of an offset under this paragraph.

(5)(A) The survivor annuity described in paragraph (4)(C)(iii) shall be determined as if—

(i) the participant terminated employment on the date of the offset,

(ii) there was no offset,

(iii) the plan permitted commencement of benefits only on or after normal retirement age,

(iv) the plan provided only the minimum-required qualified joint and survivor annuity, and

(v) the amount of the qualified preretirement survivor annuity under the plan is equal to the amount of the survivor annuity payable under the minimum-required qualified joint and survivor annuity.

(B) For purposes of this paragraph, the term "minimum-required qualified joint and survivor annuity" means the qualified joint and survivor annuity which is theactuarial equivalent of the participant'saccrued benefit (within the meaning of section 3(23)) and under which the survivor annuity is 50 percent of the amount of the annuity which is payable during the joint lives of the participant and the spouse.

(e) Limitation on Distributions Other Than Life Annuities Paid by the Plan.—

(1) **In general.**—Notwithstanding any other provision of this part, the fiduciary of a pension plan that is subject to the additional funding requirements of section 303(j)(4) shall not permit a prohibited payment to be made from a plan during a period in which such plan has a liquidity shortfall (as defined in section 303(j)(4)(E)(i)).

(2) **Prohibited payment.**—For purposes of paragraph (1), the term "prohibited payment" means—

(A) any payment, in excess of the monthly amount paid under a single life annuity (plus any social security supplements described in the last sentence of section 204(b)(1)(G)), to a participant or beneficiary whose annuity starting date (as defined in section 205(h)(2)), that occurs during the period referred to in paragraph (1),

(B) any payment for the purchase of an irrevocable commitment from an insurer to pay benefits, and

(C) any other payment specified by the Secretary of the Treasury by regulations.

(3) **Period of shortfall.**—For purposes of this subsection, a plan has a liquidity shortfall during the period that there is an underpayment of an installment under section 303(j)(3) by reason of section 303(j)(4)(A).

(4) **Coordination with other provisions.**—Compliance with this subsection shall not constitute a violation of any other provision of this Act.

(f) Missing Participants in Terminated Plans.—In the case of a plan covered by section 4050, upon termination of the plan, benefits of missing participants shall be treated in accordance with section 4050.

(g) Funding-Based Limits on Benefits and Benefit Accruals Under Single-Employer Plans.—

(1) Funding-based limitation on shutdown benefits and other unpredictable contingent event benefits under single-employer plans.—

(A) In general.—If a participant of a defined benefit plan which is a single-employer plan is entitled to an unpredictable contingent event benefit payable with respect to any event occurring during any plan year, the plan shall provide that such benefit may not be provided if the adjusted funding target attainment percentage for such plan year—

(i) is less than 60 percent, or

(ii) would be less than 60 percent taking into account such occurrence.

(B) Exemption.—Subparagraph (A) shall cease to apply with respect to any plan year, effective as of the first day of the plan year, upon payment by the plan sponsor of a contribution (in addition to any minimum required contribution under section 303) equal to—

(i) in the case of subparagraph (A)(i), the amount of the increase in the funding target of the plan (under section 303) for the plan year attributable to the occurrence referred to in subparagraph (A), and

(ii) in the case of subparagraph (A)(ii), the amount sufficient to result in an adjusted funding target attainment percentage of 60 percent.

(C) Unpredictable contingent event benefit.—For purposes of this paragraph, the term "unpredictable contingent event benefit" means any benefit payable solely by reason of—

(i) a plant shutdown (or similar event, as determined by the Secretary of the Treasury), or

(ii) an event other than the attainment of any age, performance of any service, receipt or derivation of any compensation, or occurrence of death or disability.

(2) **Limitations on plan amendments increasing liability for benefits.—**

(A) In general.—No amendment to a defined benefit plan which is a single-employer plan which has the effect of increasing liabilities of the plan by reason of increases in benefits, establishment of new benefits, changing the rate of benefit accrual, or changing the rate at which benefits become nonforfeitable may take effect during any plan year if the adjusted funding target attainment percentage for such plan year is—

(i) less than 80 percent, or

(ii) would be less than 80 percent taking into account such amendment.

(B) Exemption.—Subparagraph (A) shall cease to apply with respect to any plan year, effective as of the first day of the plan year (or if later, the effective date of the amendment), upon payment by the plan sponsor of a contribution (in addition to any minimum required contribution under section 303) equal to—

(i) in the case of subparagraph (A)(i), the amount of the increase in the funding target of the plan (under section 303) for the plan year attributable to the amendment, and

(ii) in the case of subparagraph (A)(ii), the amount sufficient to result in an adjusted funding target attainment percentage of 80 percent.

(C) Exception for certain benefit increases.—Subparagraph (A) shall not apply to any amendment which provides for an increase in benefits under a formula which is not based on a participant's compensation, but only if the rate of such increase is not in excess of the contemporaneous rate of increase in average wages of participants covered by the amendment.

(3) Limitations on accelerated benefit distributions.—

(A) Funding percentage less than 60 percent.—A defined benefit plan which is a single-employer plan shall provide that, in any case in which the plan's adjusted funding target attainment percentage for a plan year is less than 60 percent, the plan may not pay any prohibited payment after the valuation date for the plan year.

(B) Bankruptcy.—A defined benefit plan which is a single-employer plan shall provide that, during any period in which the plan sponsor is a debtor in a case under title 11, United States Code, or similar Federal or State law, the plan may not pay any prohibited payment. The preceding sentence shall not apply on or after the date on which the enrolled actuary of the plan certifies that the adjusted funding target attainment percentage of such plan is not less than 100 percent.

(C) Limited payment if percentage at least 60 percent but less than 80 percent.—

(i) In general.—A defined benefit plan which is a single-employer plan shall provide that, in any case in which the plan's adjusted funding target attainment percentage for a plan year is 60 percent or greater but less than 80 percent, the plan may not pay any prohibited payment after the valuation date for the plan year to the extent the amount of the payment exceeds the lesser of—

(I) 50 percent of the amount of the payment which could be made without regard to this subsection, or

(II) the present value (determined under guidance prescribed by the Pension Benefit Guaranty Corporation, using the interest and mortality assumptions under section 205(g)) of the maximum guarantee with respect to the participant under section 4022.

(ii) One-time application.—

(I) In general.—The plan shall also provide that only 1 prohibited payment meeting the requirements of clause (i) may be made with respect to any participant during any period of consecutive plan years to which the limitations under either subparagraph (A) or (B) or this subparagraph applies.

(II) Treatment of beneficiaries.—For purposes of this clause, a participant and any beneficiary on his behalf (including an alternate payee, as defined in section 206(d)(3)(K)) shall be treated as 1 par-

ticipant. If the accrued benefit of a participant is allocated to such an alternate payee and 1 or more other persons, the amount under clause (i) shall be allocated among such persons in the same manner as the accrued benefit is allocated unless the qualified domestic relations order (as defined in section 206(d)(3)(B)(i)) provides otherwise.

(D) Exception.—This paragraph shall not apply to any plan for any plan year if the terms of such plan (as in effect for the period beginning on September 1, 2005, and ending with such plan year) provide for no benefit accruals with respect to any participant during such period.

(E) Prohibited payment.—For purpose of this paragraph, the term "prohibited payment" means—

(i) any payment, in excess of the monthly amount paid under a single life annuity (plus any social security supplements described in the last sentence of section 204(b)(1)(G)), to a participant or beneficiary whose annuity starting date (as defined in section 205(h)(2)) occurs during any period a limitation under subparagraph (A) or (B) is in effect,

(ii) any payment for the purchase of an irrevocable commitment from an insurer to pay benefits, and

(iii) any other payment specified by the Secretary of the Treasury by regulations.

Such term shall not include the payment of a benefit which under section 203(e) may be immediately distributed without the consent of the participant.

(4) Limitation on benefit accruals for plans with severe funding shortfalls.—

(A) In general.—A defined benefit plan which is a single-employer plan shall provide that, in any case in which the plan's adjusted funding target attainment percentage for a plan year is less than 60 percent, benefit accruals under the plan shall cease as of the valuation date for the plan year.

(B) Exemption.—Subparagraph (A) shall cease to apply with respect to any plan year, effective as of the first day of the plan year, upon payment by the plan sponsor of a contribution (in addition to any minimum required contribution under section 303) equal to the amount sufficient to result in an adjusted funding target attainment percentage of 60 percent.

(5) Rules relating to contributions required to avoid benefit limitations.—

(A) Security may be provided.—

(i) In general.—For purposes of this subsection, the adjusted funding target attainment percentage shall be determined by treating as an asset of the plan any security provided by a plan sponsor in a form meeting the requirements of clause (ii).

(ii) Form of security.—The security required under clause (i) shall consist of—

(I) a bond issued by a corporate surety company that is an acceptable surety for purposes of section 412 of this Act,

(II) cash, or United States obligations which mature in 3 years or less, held in escrow by a bank or similar financial institution, or

(III) such other form of security as is satisfactory to the Secretary of the Treasury and the parties involved.

(iii) Enforcement.—Any security provided under clause (i) may be perfected and enforced at any time after the earlier of—

(I) the date on which the plan terminates,

(II) if there is a failure to make a payment of the minimum required contribution for any plan year beginning after the security is provided, the due date for the payment under section 303(j), or

(III) if the adjusted funding target attainment percentage is less than 60 percent for a consecutive period of 7 years, the valuation date for the last year in the period.

(iv) Release of security.—The security shall be released (and any amounts thereunder shall be refunded together with any interest accrued thereon) at such time as the Secretary of the Treasury may prescribe in regulations, including regulations for partial releases of the security by reason of increases in the adjusted funding target attainment percentage.

(B) Prefunding balance or funding standard carryover balance may not be used.—No prefunding balance or funding standard carryover balance under section 303(f) may be used under paragraph (1), (2), or (4) to satisfy any payment an employer may make under any such paragraph to avoid or terminate the application of any limitation under such paragraph.

(C) Deemed reduction of funding balances.—

(i) In general.—Subject to clause (iii), in any case in which a benefit limitation under paragraph (1), (2), (3), or (4) would (but for this subparagraph and determined without regard to paragraph (1)(B), (2)(B), or (4)(B)) apply to such plan for the plan year, the plan sponsor of such plan shall be treated for purposes of this Act as having made an election under section 303(f) to reduce the prefunding balance or funding standard carryover balance by such amount as is necessary for such benefit limitation to not apply to the plan for such plan year.

(ii) Exception for insufficient funding balances.—Clause (i) shall not apply with respect to a benefit limitation for any plan year if the applica-

tion of clause (i) would not result in the benefit limitation not applying for such plan year.

(iii) Restrictions of certain rules to collectively bargained plans.—With respect to any benefit limitation under paragraph (1), (2), or (4), clause (i) shall only apply in the case of a plan maintained pursuant to 1 or more collective bargaining agreements between employee representatives and 1 or more employers.

(6) New plans.—Paragraphs (1), (2), and (4) shall not apply to a plan for the first 5 plan years of the plan. For purposes of this paragraph, the reference in this paragraph to a plan shall include a reference to any predecessor plan.

(7) Presumed underfunding for purposes of benefit limitations.—

(A) Presumption of continued underfunding.—In any case in which a benefit limitation under paragraph (1), (2), (3), or (4) has been applied to a plan with respect to the plan year preceding the current plan year, the adjusted funding target attainment percentage of the plan for the current plan year shall be presumed to be equal to the adjusted funding target attainment percentage of the plan for the preceding plan year until the enrolled actuary of the plan certifies the actual adjusted funding target attainment percentage of the plan for the current plan year.

(B) Presumption of underfunding after 10th month.—In any case in which no certification of the adjusted funding target attainment percentage for the current plan year is made with respect to the plan before the first day of the 10th month of such year, for purposes of paragraphs (1), (2), (3), and (4), such first day shall be deemed, for purposes of such paragraph, to be the valuation date of the plan for the current plan year and the plan's adjusted funding target attainment percentage shall be conclusively presumed to be less than 60 percent as of such first day.

(C) Presumption of underfunding after 4th month for nearly underfunded plans.—In any case in which—

(i) a benefit limitation under paragraph (1), (2), (3), or (4) did not apply to a plan with respect to the plan year preceding the current plan year, but the adjusted funding target attainment percentage of the plan for such preceding plan year was not more than 10 percentage points greater than the percentage which would have caused such paragraph to apply to the plan with respect to such preceding plan year, and

(ii) as of the first day of the 4th month of the current plan year, the enrolled actuary of the plan has not certified the actual adjusted funding target attainment percentage of the plan for the current plan year,

ERISA Sec. 206(g)(7)(C)(ii)

until the enrolled actuary so certifies, such first day shall be deemed, for purposes of such paragraph, to be the valuation date of the plan for the current plan year and the adjusted funding target attainment percentage of the plan as of such first day shall, for purposes of such paragraph, be presumed to be equal to 10 percentage points less than the adjusted funding target attainment percentage of the plan for such preceding plan year.

(8) Treatment of plan as of close of prohibited or cessation period.—For purposes of applying this part—

(A) Operation of plan after period.—Unless the plan provides otherwise, payments and accruals will resume effective as of the day following the close of the period for which any limitation of payment or accrual of benefits under paragraph (3) or (4) applies.

(B) Treatment of affected benefits.—Nothing in this paragraph shall be construed as affecting the plan's treatment of benefits which would have been paid or accrued but for this subsection.

(9) Terms relating to funding target attainment percentage.—For purposes of this subsection—

(A) In general.—The term "funding target attainment percentage" has the same meaning given such term by section 303(d)(2).

(B) Adjusted funding target attainment percentage.—The term "adjusted funding target attainment percentage" means the funding target attainment percentage which is determined under subparagraph (A) by increasing each of the amounts under subparagraphs (A) and (B) of section 303(d)(2) by the aggregate amount of purchases of annuities for employees other than highly compensated employees (as defined in section 414(q) of the Internal Revenue Code of 1986) which were made by the plan during the preceding 2 plan years.

(C) Application to plans which are fully funded without regard to reductions for funding balances.—

(i) In general.—In the case of a plan for any plan year, if the funding target attainment percentage is 100 percent or more (determined without regard to the reduction in the value of assets under section 303(f)(4)), the funding target attainment percentage for purposes of subparagraphs (A) and (B) shall be determined without regard to such reduction.

(ii) Transition rule.—Clause (i) shall be applied to plan years beginning after 2007 and before 2011 by substituting for "100 percent" the applicable percentage determined in accordance with the following table:

In the case of any applicable plan year beginning in—	The applicable percentage is—
2008	92
2009	94
2010	96

(iii) Limitation.—Clause (ii) shall not apply with respect to any plan year beginning after 2008 unless the funding target attainment percentage (determined without regard to the reduction in the value of assets under section 303(f)(4)) of the plan for each preceding plan year beginning after 2007 was not less than the applicable percentage with respect to such preceding plan year determined under clause (ii).

Editor's Note

ERISA §206(g)(9)(D), below, was added by Pub. L. No. 111-192, §203(a)(1), effective generally for plan years beginning on or after October 1, 2008, except that for plans for which the valuation date is not the first day of the plan year, the amendment is effective for plan years beginning after December 31, 2007. See amendment notes for details.

(D) Special rule for certain years.—Solely for purposes of any applicable provision—

(i) In general.—For plan years beginning on or after October 1, 2008, and before October 1, 2010, the adjusted funding target attainment percentage of a plan shall be the greater of—

(I) such percentage, as determined without regard to this subparagraph, or

(II) the adjusted funding target attainment percentage for such plan for the plan year beginning after October 1, 2007, and before October 1, 2008, as determined under rules prescribed by the Secretary of the Treasury.

(ii) Special rule.—In the case of a plan for which the valuation date is not the first day of the plan year—

(I) clause (i) shall apply to plan years beginning after December 31, 2007, and before January 1, 2010, and

(II) clause (i)(II) shall apply based on the last plan year beginning before November 1, 2007, as determined under rules prescribed by the Secretary of the Treasury.

(iii) Applicable provision.—For purposes of this subparagraph, the term "applicable provision" means—

(I) paragraph (3), but only for purposes of applying such paragraph to a payment which, as determined under rules prescribed by the Secretary of the Treasury, is a payment under a social security leveling option which accelerates payments under the plan before, and reduces payments after, a participant starts receiving social security benefits in order to provide substantially similar aggregate payments both before and after such benefits are received, and

(II) paragraph (4).

(10) Secretarial authority for plans with alternate valuation date.—In the case of a plan which has designated a valuation date other than the first day of the plan year, the Secretary of the Treasury may prescribe rules for the application of this subsection which are necessary to reflect the alternate valuation date.

(11) Special rule for 2008.—For purposes of this subsection, in the case of plan years beginning in 2008, the funding target attainment percentage for the preceding plan year may be determined using such methods of estimation as the Secretary of the Treasury may provide.

Amendments to ERISA §206

Preservation of Access to Care for Medicare Beneficiaries and Pension Relief Act of 2010 (Pub. L. No. 111-192), as follows:

- ERISA §206(g)(9)(D) was added by Act §203(a)(1). Eff. generally for plan years beg. on or after Oct. 1, 2008, except that for plans for which the valuation date is not the first day of the plan year, amendment is effective for plan years beg. after Dec. 31, 2007.
- **Other Provision.** Act §202(b) provides:
  (b) Interaction With WRERA Rule.—Section 203 of the Worker, Retiree, and Employer Recovery Act of 2008 shall apply to a plan for any plan year in lieu of the amendments made by this section applying to sections 206(g)(4) of the Employee Retirement Income Security Act of 1974 and 436(e) of the Internal Revenue Code of 1986 only to the extent that such section produces a higher adjusted funding target attainment percentage for such plan for such year.
- **Other Provision.** Act §202(a) renumbered Pub. L. No. 109-280, §107(a)(9), (10), as §108(a)(9), (10). See notes below to Pub. L. No. 109-280.

Worker, Retiree, and Employer Recovery Act of 2008 (Pub. L. No. 110-458), as follows:

- ERISA §206(g)(1)(B)(ii) was amended by Act §101(c)(1)(B) by striking "a funding" and inserting "an adjusted funding". Eff. for plan years beginning after 2007, as if included in Pub. L. No. 109-280, §103.
- ERISA §206(g)(1)(C) was amended by Act §101(c)(1)(C) by inserting "benefit" after "event" in the heading. Eff. for plan years beginning after 2007, as if included in Pub. L. No. 109-280, §103.
- ERISA §206(g)(3)(E) was amended by Act §101(c)(1)(D) by adding at the end: "Such term shall not include the payment of a benefit which under section 203(e) may be immediately distributed without the consent of the participant." Eff. for plan years beginning after 2007, as if included in Pub. L. No. 109-280, §103.
- ERISA §206(g)(5)(A)(iv) was amended by Act §101(c)(1)(E) by inserting "adjusted" before "funding". Eff. for plan years beginning after 2007, as if included in Pub. L. No. 109-280, §103.
- ERISA §206(g)(9)(C) was amended by Act §101(c)(1)(F) by striking "without regard to this subparagraph" and inserting

"without regard to the reduction in the value of assets under section 303(f)(4)" in cl. (iii); and inserting "beginning" before "after" each place it appears in cl. (iii). Eff. for plan years beginning after 2007, as if included in Pub. L. No. 109-280, §103.

- ERISA §206(g)(10) was redesignated by Act §101(c)(1)(G) as para. (11) and new para. (10) was added. Eff. for plan years beginning after 2007, as if included in Pub. L. No. 109-280, §103.
- Act §101(c)(3) amended Pub. L. No. 109-280, §§103(c)(2)(A)(ii) and 113(b)(2)(A)(ii) by striking "subsection" and inserting "section", and striking "subparagraph" and inserting "paragraph".
- **Other Provision.** Act §203 provides:

SEC. 203.—TEMPORARY MODIFICATION OF APPLICATION OF LIMITATION ON BENEFIT ACCRUALS.

In the case of the first plan year beginning during the period beginning on October 1, 2008, and ending on September 30, 2009, sections 206(g)(4)(A) of the Employee Retirement Income Security Act of 1974 (29 U.S.C. 1056(g)(4)(A)) and 436(e)(1) of the Internal Revenue Code of 1986 shall be applied by substituting the plan's adjusted funding target attainment percentage for the preceding plan year for such percentage for such plan year but only if the adjusted funding target attainment percentage for the preceding plan year is greater.

Pension Protection Act of 2006 (Pub. L. No. 109-280), as follows:

- ERISA §206(e)(1) was amended by Act §107(a)(9) (redesignated as §108(a)(9) by Pub. L. No. 111-192, §202(a)) by substituting "§303(j)(4)" for "§302(d)" and "§303(j)(4)(E)(i)" for "§302(e)(5)". Eff. for plan years beginning after 2007.
- ERISA §206(e)(3) was amended by Act §107(a)(10) (redesignated as §108(a)(10) by Pub. L. No. 111-192, §202(a)) by substituting "§303(j)(3) by reason of §303(j)(4)(A)" for "§302(e) by reason of paragraph (5)(A) thereof". Eff. for plan years beginning after 2007.
- ERISA §206(f) was amended by Act §410(b) by substituting "4050" for "title IV" and deleting "the plan shall provide that,". Eff. for distributions after final regulations implementing ERISA §§4050(c) and (d) are issued.
- ERISA §206(g) was added by Act §103(a). Eff. generally for plan years after 2007, although collective bargaining agreements have transition rules.
- **Other Provision—Effective Date.** Act §103(c)(2) provides:
  (2) Collective bargaining exception.—In the case of a plan maintained pursuant to 1 or more collective bargaining agreements between employee representatives and 1 or more employers ratified before January 1, 2008, the amendments made by this section shall not apply to plan years beginning before the earlier of—
    (A) the later of—
      (i) the date on which the last collective bargaining agreement relating to the plan terminates (determined without regard to any extension thereof agreed to after the date of the enactment of this Act), or
      (ii) the first day of the first plan year to which the amendments made by this subsection would (but for this subparagraph) apply, or
    (B) January 1, 2010.
  For purposes of subparagraph (A)(i), any plan amendment made pursuant to a collective bargaining agreement relating to the plan which amends the plan solely to conform to any requirement added by this section shall not be treated as a termination of such collective bargaining agreement.

Taxpayer Relief Act of 1997 (Pub. L. No. 105-34), as follows:

- ERISA §206(d)(4)–(5) were added by Act §1502(a). Eff. Aug. 5, 1997.

Retirement Protection Act of 1994 (Pub. L. No. 103-465), as follows:

- ERISA §206(e) was added by Act §761(a)(9)(B)(i). Eff. for plan years after 1994.
- ERISA §206(f) was added by Act §776(c)(2). Eff. for distributions in plan years beginning on or after Jan. 1, 1996.

ERISA Sec. 206(g)(11)

Omnibus Budget Reconciliation Act of 1989 (Pub. L. No. 101-239), as follows:
- ERISA §206(a)(1) was amended by Act §7894(c)(8) by inserting "occurs" before "the date". Eff. as if included in Pub. L. No. 93-406.
- ERISA §206(d)(2) was amended by Act §7891(a)(1) by substituting "Internal Revenue Code of 1986" for "Internal Revenue Code of 1954", which for purposes of codification was translated as "title 26". Eff. as if included in Pub. L. No. 99-514.
- ERISA §206(d)(3)(I) was amended by Act §7894(c)(9)(A) by substituting "such Act" for "such act". Eff. as if included in Pub. L. No. 103-465.

Tax Reform Act of 1986 (Pub. L. No. 99-514), as follows:
- ERISA §206(d)(3)(E)(i) was amended by Act §1898(c)(7)(B)(iii) by substituting "A" for "In the case of any payment before a participant has separated from service, a" in introductory provisions and inserting "in the case of any payment before a participant has separated from service," in subcl. (I). Eff. as if included in Pub. L. No. 103-465.
- ERISA §206(d)(3)(E)(ii) was amended by Act §1898(c)(7)(B)(iv). Eff. as if included in Pub. L. No. 103-465. ERISA §206(d)(3)(E)(ii) prior to amendment:
  (ii) For purposes of this subparagraph, the term "earliest retirement age" has the meaning given such term by section 1055(h)(3) of this section, except that in the case of any individual account plan, the earliest retirement age shall be the date which is 10 years before the normal retirement age.
- ERISA §206(d)(3)(F)(i) was amended by Act §1898(c)(6)(B) by inserting "(and any spouse of the participant shall not be treated as a spouse of the participant for such purposes)". Eff. as if included in Pub. L. No. 103-465.
- ERISA §206(d)(3)(F)(ii) was amended by Act §1898(c)(7)(B)(i) by inserting "surviving" before "former spouse". Eff. as if included in Pub. L. No. 103-465.
- ERISA §206(d)(3)(G)(i)(I) was amended by Act §1898(c)(7)(B)(ii) by substituting "each" for "any other". Eff. as if included in Pub. L. No. 103-465.
- ERISA §206(d)(3)(H)(i) was amended by Act §1898(c)(2)(B)(i) by substituting "shall separately account for the amounts (hereinafter in this subparagraph referred to as the 'segregated amounts')" for "shall segregate in a separate account in the plan or in an escrow account the amounts". Eff. as if included in Pub. L. No. 103-465.
- ERISA §206(d)(3)(H)(ii)–(iii) was amended by Act §1898(c)(2)(B)(ii)–(iii) by substituting "the 18-month period described in clause (v)" for "18 months" and "including any interest" for "plus any interest". Eff. as if included in Pub. L. No. 103-465.
- ERISA §206(d)(3)(H)(iv) was amended by Act §1898(c)(2)(B)(iv) by inserting "described in clause (v)". Eff. as if included in Pub. L. No. 103-465.
- ERISA §206(d)(3)(H)(v) was added by Act §1898(c)(2)(B)(v). Eff. as if included in Pub. L. No. 103-465.
- ERISA §206(d)(3)(L) was redesignated as (N) and new (L) was added by Act §1898(c)(4)(B). Eff. as if included in Pub. L. No. 103-465.
- ERISA §206(d)(3)(M) was added by Act §1898(c)(5). Eff. as if included in Pub. L. No. 103-465.

Retirement Equity Act of 1984 (Pub. L. No. 98-397), as follows:
- ERISA §206(d)(3) was added by Act §104(a). Eff. Jan. 1, 1985.

SEC. 207. TEMPORARY VARIANCES FROM CERTAIN VESTING REQUIREMENTS. [Repealed.]

In the case of any plan maintained on January 1, 1974, if not later than 2 years after September 2, 1974, the administrator petitions the Secretary, the Secretary may prescribe an alternate method which shall be treated as satisfying the requirements of section 203(a)(2) or 204(b)(1) (other than subparagraph (D) thereof) of this title or both for a period of not more than 4 years. The Secretary may prescribe such alternate method only when he finds that—

(1) the application of such requirements would increase the costs of the plan to such an extent that there would result a substantial risk to the voluntary continuation of the plan or a substantial curtailment of benefit levels or the levels of employees' compensation.

(2) the application of such requirements or discontinuance of the plan would be adverse to the interests of plan participants in the aggregate, and

(3) a waiver or extension of time granted under section 303 or 304 of this title would be inadequate.

In the case of any plan with respect to which an alternate method has been prescribed under the preceding provisions of this subsection for a period of not more than 4 years, if, not later than 1 year before the expiration of such period, the administrator petitions the Secretary for an extension of such alternate method, and the Secretary makes the findings required by the preceding sentence, such alternate method may be extended for not more than 3 years.

Amendments to ERISA §207 [Repealed.]
Pension Protection Act of 2006 (Pub. L. No. 109-280), as follows:
- ERISA §207 was repealed by Act §107(d) (redesignated as §108(d) by Pub. L. No. 111-192, §202(a)). Eff. for years after 2007.

SEC. 208. MERGERS AND CONSOLIDATIONS OF PLANS OR TRANSFERS OF PLAN ASSETS.

A pension plan may not merge or consolidate with, or transfer its assets or liabilities to, any other plan after the date of the enactment of this Act, unless each participant in the plan would (if the plan then terminated) receive a benefit immediately after the merger, consolidation, or transfer which is equal to or greater than the benefit he would have been entitled to receive immediately before the merger, consolidation, or transfer (if the plan had then terminated). The preceding sentence shall not apply to any transaction to the extent that participants either before or after the transaction are covered under a multiemployer plan to which title IV of this Act applies.

Amendments to ERISA §208
Multiemployer Pension Plan Amendments Act of 1980 (Pub. L. No. 96-364), as follows:
- ERISA §208 was amended by Act §402(b)(1) by substituting provisions respecting applicability of preceding sentence to transactions under a covered multiemployer plan to which subchapter III applies, for provisions relating to applicability of paragraph to a multiemployer plan only to extent determined by Corporation. Eff. Sept. 26, 1980.

SEC. 209. RECORDKEEPING AND REPORTING REQUIREMENTS.

(a)(1) Except as provided by paragraph (2) every employer shall, in accordance with such regulations as the Secretary may prescribe, maintain records with respect to each of his employees sufficient to determine the benefits due or which may become due to such employees. The plan administrator shall make a report, in such manner and at such time as may be provided in regulations prescribed by the Secretary, to each employee who is a participant under the plan and who—

(A) requests such report, in such manner and at such time as may be provided in such regulations,

(B) terminates his service with the employer, or

(C) has a 1-year break in service (as defined in section 203(b)(3)(A)).

The employer shall furnish to the plan administrator the information necessary for the administrator to make the reports required by the preceding sentence. Not more than one report shall be required under subparagraph (A) in any 12-month period. Not more than one report shall be required under subparagraph (C) with respect to consecutive 1-year breaks in service. The report required under this paragraph shall be in the same form, and contain the same information, as periodic benefit statements under section 105(a).

(2) If more than one employer adopts a plan, each such employer shall furnish to the plan administrator the information necessary for the administrator to maintain the records, and make the reports, required by paragraph (1). Such administrator shall maintain the records, and make the reports, required by paragraph (1).

(b) If any person who is required, under subsection (a), to furnish information or maintain records for any plan year fails to comply with such requirement, he shall pay to the Secretary a civil penalty of $10 for each employee with respect to whom such failure occurs, unless it is shown that such failure is due to reasonable cause.

Amendments to ERISA §209

Worker, Retiree, and Employer Recovery Act of 2008 (Pub. L. No. 110-458), as follows:

- ERISA §209(a)(1) was amended by Act §105(f)(1) by striking "regulations prescribed by the Secretary" and inserting "such regulations as the Secretary may prescribe", and by striking "The report required under this paragraph shall be sufficient to inform the employee of his accrued benefits under the plan and the percentage of such benefits which are nonforfeitable under the plan." and inserting "The report required under this paragraph shall be in the same form, and contain the same information, as periodic benefit statements under section 105(a)." Eff. for plan years beginning after Dec. 31, 2006, as if included in Pub. L. No. 109-280, §508.

- ERISA §209(a)(2) was amended by Act §105(f)(2). Eff. for plan years beginning after Dec. 31, 2006, as if included in Pub. L. No. 109-280, §508. ERISA §209(a)(2) prior to amendment:

  (2) If more than one employer adopts a plan, each such employer shall, in accordance with regulations prescribed by the Secretary, furnish to the plan administrator the information necessary for the administrator to maintain the records and make the reports required by paragraph (1). Such admin-

istrator shall maintain the records and, to the extent provided under regulations prescribed by the Secretary, make the reports, required by paragraph (1).

SEC. 210. MULTIPLE EMPLOYER PLANS AND OTHER SPECIAL RULES.

(a) **Plans Maintained by More Than One Employer.**—Notwithstanding any other provision of this part or part 3, the following provisions of this subsection shall apply to a plan maintained by more than one employer:

(1) Section 202 shall be applied as if all employees of each of the employers were employed by a single employer.

(2) Sections 203 and 204 shall be applied as if all such employers constituted a single employer, except that the application of any rules with respect to breaks in service shall be made under regulations prescribed by the Secretary.

(3) The minimum funding standard provided by section 302 shall be determined as if all participants in the plan were employed by a single employer.

(b) **Maintenance of Plan of Predecessor Employer.**—For purposes of this part and part 3—

(1) in any case in which the employer maintains a plan of a predecessor employer, service for such predecessor shall be treated as service for the employer, and

(2) in any case in which the employer maintains a plan which is not the plan maintained by a predecessor employer, service for such predecessor shall, to the extent provided in regulations prescribed by the Secretary of the Treasury, be treated as service for the employer.

(c) **Plan Maintained by Controlled Group of Corporations.**—For purposes of sections 202, 203, and 204, all employees of all corporations which are members of a controlled group of corporations (within the meaning of section 1563(a) of the Internal Revenue Code of 1986, determined without regard to section 1563(a)(4) and (e)(3)(C) of such Code) shall be treated as employed by a single employer. With respect to a plan adopted by more than one such corporation, the minimum funding standard of section 302 shall be determined as if all such employers were a single employer, and allocated to each employer in accordance with regulations prescribed by the Secretary of the Treasury.

(d) **Plan of Trades or Businesses Under Common Control.**—For purposes of sections 202, 203, and 204, under regulations prescribed by the Secretary of the Treasury, all employees of trades or businesses (whether or not incorporated) which are under common control shall be treated as employed by a single employer. The regulations prescribed under this sub-section shall be based on principles similar to the principles which apply in the case of subsection (c).

(e) Special Rules for Eligible Combined Defined Benefit Plans and Qualified Cash or Deferred Arrangements.—

(1) General rule.—Except as provided in this subsection, this Act shall be applied to any defined benefit plan or applicable individual account plan which are part of an eligible combined plan in the same manner as if each such plan were not a part of the eligible combined plan. In the case of a termination of the defined benefit plan and the applicable defined contribution plan forming part of an eligible combined plan, the plan administrator shall terminate each such plan separately.

(2) Eligible combined plan.—For purposes of this subsection—

(A) In general.—The term "eligible combined plan" means a plan—

(i) which is maintained by an employer which, at the time the plan is established, is a small employer,

(ii) which consists of a defined benefit plan and an applicable individual account plan each of which qualifies under section 401(a) of the Internal Revenue Code of 1986,

(iii) the assets of which are held in a single trust forming part of the plan and are clearly identified and allocated to the defined benefit plan and the applicable individual account plan to the extent necessary for the separate application of this Act under paragraph (1), and

(iv) with respect to which the benefit, contribution, vesting, and nondiscrimination requirements of subparagraphs (B), (C), (D), (E), and (F) are met.

For purposes of this subparagraph, the term "small employer" has the meaning given such term by section 4980D(d)(2) of the Internal Revenue Code of 1986, except that such section shall be applied by substituting "500" for "50" each place it appears.

(B) Benefit requirements.—

(i) In general.—The benefit requirements of this subparagraph are met with respect to the defined benefit plan forming part of the eligible combined plan if the accrued benefit of each participant derived from employer contributions, when expressed as an annual retirement benefit, is not less than the applicable percentage of the participant's final average pay. For purposes of this clause, final average pay shall be determined using the period of consecutive years (not exceeding 5) during which the participant had the greatest aggregate compensation from the employer.

(ii) Applicable percentage.—For purposes of clause (i), the applicable percentage is the lesser of—

(I) 1 percent multiplied by the number of years of service with the employer, or

(II) 20 percent.

(iii) Special rule for applicable defined benefit plans.—If the defined benefit plan under clause (i) is an applicable defined benefit plan as defined in section 203(f)(3)(B) which meets the interest credit requirements of section 204(b)(5)(B)(i), the plan shall be treated as meeting the requirements of clause (i) with respect to any plan year if each participant receives pay credit for the year which is not less than the percentage of compensation determined in accordance with the following table:

If the participant's age as of the beginning of the year is—	The applicable percentage is—
30 or less	2
Over 30 but less than 40	4
40 or over but less than 50	6
50 or over	8

(iv) Years of service.—For purposes of this subparagraph, years of service shall be determined under the rules of paragraphs (1), (2), and (3) of section 203(b), except that the plan may not disregard any year of service because of a participant making, or failing to make, any elective deferral with respect to the qualified cash or deferred arrangement to which subparagraph (C) applies.

(C) Contribution requirements.—

(i) In general.—The contribution requirements of this subparagraph with respect to any applicable individual account plan forming part of an eligible combined plan are met if—

(I) the qualified cash or deferred arrangement included in such plan constitutes an automatic contribution arrangement, and

(II) the employer is required to make matching contributions on behalf of each employee eligible to participate in the arrangement in an amount equal to 50 percent of the elective contributions of the employee to the extent such elective contributions do not exceed 4 percent of compensation.

Rules similar to the rules of clauses (ii) and (iii) of section 401(k)(12)(B) of the Internal Revenue Code of 1986 shall apply for purposes of this clause.

(ii) Nonelective contributions.—An applicable individual account plan shall not be treated as failing to meet the requirements of clause (i) because the employer makes nonelective contributions under the plan but such contributions shall not be taken into account in determining whether the requirements of clause (i)(II) are met.

(D) Vesting requirements.—The vesting requirements of this subparagraph are met if—

(i) in the case of a defined benefit plan forming part of an eligible combined plan an employee who has completed at least 3 years of service has a nonforfeitable right to 100 percent of the employee's accrued benefit under the plan derived from employer contributions, and

(ii) in the case of an applicable individual account plan forming part of eligible combined plan—

(I) an employee has a nonforfeitable right to any matching contribution made under the qualified cash or deferred arrangement included in such plan by an employer with respect to any elective contribution, including matching contributions in excess of the contributions required under subparagraph (C)(i)(II), and

(II) an employee who has completed at least 3 years of service has a nonforfeitable right to 100 percent of the employee's accrued benefit derived under the arrangement from nonelective contributions of the employer.

For purposes of this subparagraph, the rules of section 203 shall apply to the extent not inconsistent with this subparagraph.

(E) Uniform provision of contributions and benefits.—In the case of a defined benefit plan or applicable individual account plan forming part of an eligible combined plan, the requirements of this subparagraph are met if all contributions and benefits under each such plan, and all rights and features under each such plan, must be provided uniformly to all participants.

(F) Requirements must be met without taking into account social security and similar contributions and benefits or other plans.—

(i) In general.—The requirements of this subparagraph are met if the requirements of clauses (ii) and (iii) are met.

(ii) Social Security and similar contributions.—The requirements of this clause are met if—

(I) the requirements of subparagraphs (B) and (C) are met without regard to section 401(l) of the Internal Revenue Code of 1986, and

(II) the requirements of sections 401(a)(4) and 410(b) of the Internal Revenue Code of 1986 are met with respect to both the applicable defined contribution plan and defined benefit plan forming part of an eligible combined plan without regard to section 401(l) of the Internal Revenue Code of 1986.

(iii) Other plans and arrangements.—The requirements of this clause are met if the applicable defined contribution plan and defined benefit plan forming part of an eligible combined plan meet the requirements of sections 401(a)(4) and 410(b) of the Internal Revenue Code of 1986 without being combined with any other plan.

(3) Automatic contribution arrangement.— For purposes of this subsection—

(A) In general.—A qualified cash or deferred arrangement shall be treated as an automatic contribution arrangement if the arrangement—

(i) provides that each employee eligible to participate in the arrangement is treated as having elected to have the employer make elective contributions in an amount equal to 4 percent of the employee's compensation unless the employee specifically elects not to have such contributions made or to have such contributions made at a different rate, and

(ii) meets the notice requirements under subparagraph (B).

(B) Notice requirements.—

(i) In general.—The requirements of this subparagraph are met if the requirements of clauses (ii) and (iii) are met.

(ii) Reasonable period to make election.—The requirements of this clause are met if each employee to whom subparagraph (A)(i) applies—

(I) receives a notice explaining the employee's right under the arrangement to elect not to have elective contributions made on the employee's behalf or to have the contributions made at a different rate, and

(II) has a reasonable period of time after receipt of such notice and before the first elective contribution is made to make such election.

(iii) Annual notice of rights and obligations.— The requirements of this clause are met if each employee eligible to participate in the arrangement is, within a reasonable period before any year, given notice of the employee's rights and obligations under the arrangement.

The requirements of this subparagraph shall not be treated as met unless the requirements of clauses (i) and (ii) of section 401(k)(12)(D) of the Internal Revenue Code of 1986 are met with respect to the notices described in clauses (ii) and (iii) of this subparagraph.

(4) Coordination with other requirements.—

(A) Treatment of separate plans.—The except clause in section 3(35) shall not apply to an eligible combined plan.

(B) Reporting.—An eligible combined plan shall be treated as a single plan for purposes of section 103.

ERISA Sec. 210(e)(4)(B)

(5) Applicable individual account plan.—For purposes of this subsection—

(A) In general.—The term "applicable individual account plan" means an individual account plan which includes a qualified cash or deferred arrangement.

(B) Qualified cash or deferred arrangement.—The term "qualified cash or deferred arrangement" has the meaning given such term by section 401(k)(2) of the Internal Revenue Code of 1986.

(6) [Redesignated.]

Amendments to ERISA §210

Worker, Retiree, and Employer Recovery Act of 2008 (Pub. L. No. 110-458), as follows:

● ERISA §210(e)(1) was amended by Act §109(c)(2) by adding at the end: "In the case of a termination of the defined benefit plan and the applicable defined contribution plan forming part of an eligible combined plan, the plan administrator shall terminate each such plan separately." Eff. for plan years beginning after 2009, as if included in Pub. L. No. 109-280, §903.

● ERISA §210(e)(3) was stricken and paras. (4), (5), and (6) were redesignated as paras. (3), (4), and (5), respectively. Eff. for plan years beginning after 2009, as if included in Pub. L. No. 109-280, §903. ERISA §210(e)(3) prior to repeal:

    (3) Nondiscrimination requirements for qualified cash or deferred arrangement.—

      (A) In general.—A qualified cash or deferred arrangement which is included in an applicable individual account plan forming part of an eligible combined plan shall be treated as meeting the requirements of section 401(k)(3)(A)(ii) of the Internal Revenue Code of 1986 if the requirements of paragraph (2) are met with respect to such arrangement.

      (B) Matching contributions.—In applying section 401(m)(11) of such Code to any matching contribution with respect to a contribution to which paragraph (2)(C) applies, the contribution requirement of paragraph (2)(C) and the notice requirements of paragraph (5)(B) shall be substituted for the requirements otherwise applicable under clauses (i) and (ii) of section 401(m)(11)(A) of such Code.

Pension Protection Act of 2006 (Pub. L. No. 109-280), as follows:

● ERISA §210 (heading) was amended by Act §903(b)(2)(A) by adding "and other special rules". Eff. for plan years beginning after Dec. 31, 2009.

● ERISA §210(3) was added by Act §903(b)(1). Eff. for plan years beginning after Dec. 31, 2009.

Omnibus Budget Reconciliation Act of 1989 (Pub. L. No. 101-239), as follows:

● ERISA §210(c) was amended by Act §7894(c)(10) by substituting "and (e)(3)(C) of such Code" for "and (e)(3)(C) of such code", which for purposes of codification was translated as "and (e)(3)(C) of title 26". Eff. as if included in Pub. L. No. 93-406.

● ERISA §210 was amended by Act §7891(a)(1) by substituting "Internal Revenue Code of 1986" for "Internal Revenue Code of 1954", which for purposes of codification was translated as "title 26". Effective as if included in Pub. L. No. 99-514.

SEC. 211. EFFECTIVE DATES.

(a) Except as otherwise provided in this section, this part shall apply in the case of plan years beginning after the date of the enactment of this Act.

(b)(1) Except as otherwise provided in subsection (d), sections 205, 206(d), and 208 shall apply with respect to plan years beginning after December 31, 1975.

(2) Except as otherwise provided in subsections (c) and (d) in the case of a plan in existence on January 1, 1974, this part shall apply in the case of plan years beginning after December 31, 1975.

(c)(1) In the case of a plan maintained on January 1, 1974, pursuant to one or more agreements which the Secretary finds to be collective bargaining agreements between employee organizations and one or more employers, no plan shall be treated as not meeting the requirements of sections 204 and 205 solely by reason of a supplementary or special plan provision (within the meaning of paragraph (2)) for any plan year before the year which begins after the earlier of—

(A) the date on which the last of such agreements relating to the plan terminates (determined without regard to any extension thereof agreed to after the date of the enactment of this Act), or

(B) December 31, 1980.

For purposes of subparagraph (A) and section 307(c), any plan amendment made pursuant to a collective bargaining agreement relating to the plan which amends the plan solely to conform to any requirement contained in this Act or the Internal Revenue Code of 1954 shall not be treated as a termination of such collective bargaining agreement. This paragraph shall not apply unless the Secretary determines that the participation and vesting rules in effect on the date of enactment of this Act are not less favorable to participants, in the aggregate, than the rules provided under sections 202, 203, and 204.

(2) For purposes of paragraph (1), the term "supplementary or special plan provision" means any plan provision which—

(A) provides supplementary benefits, not in excess of one-third of the basic benefit, in the form of an annuity for the life of the participant, or

(B) provides that, under a contractual agreement based on medical evidence as to the effects of working in an adverse environment for an extended period of time, a participant having 25 years of service is to be treated as having 30 years of service.

(3) This subsection shall apply with respect to a plan if (and only if) the application of this subsection results in a later effective date for this part than the effective date required by subsection (b).

(d) If the administrator of a plan elects under section 1017(d) of this Act to make applicable to a plan year and to all subsequent plan years the provisions of title 26 relating to participation, vesting, funding, and form of benefit, this part shall apply to the first plan year to which such election applies and to all subsequent plan years.

(e)(1) No pension plan to which section 202 applies may make effective any plan amendment with respect to breaks in service (which amendment is made or becomes effective after January 1, 1974, and before the date on which section 202 first becomes effective with respect to such plan) which provides that any employee's participation in the plan would commence at any date later than the later of—

(A) the date on which his participation would commence under the break in service rules of section 202(b), or

(B) the date on which his participation would commence under the plan as in effect on January 1, 1974.

(2) No pension plan to which section 203 applies may make effective any plan amendment with respect to breaks in service (which amendment is made or becomes effective after January 1, 1974, and before the date on which section 203 first becomes effective with respect to such plan) if such amendment provides that the nonforfeitable benefit derived from employer contributions to which any employee would be entitled is less than the lesser of the nonforfeitable benefit derived from employer contributions to which he would be entitled under—

(A) the break in service rules of section 202(b)(3), or

(B) the plan as in effect on January 1, 1974.

Subparagraph (B) shall not apply if the break in service rules under the plan would have been in violation of any law or rule of law in effect on January 1, 1974.

(f) The preceding provisions of this section shall not apply with respect to amendments made to this part in provisions enacted after the date of enactment of this Act.

Amendments to ERISA §211

Omnibus Budget Reconciliation Act of 1989 (Pub. L. No. 101-239), as follows:
- ERISA §211(c)(1), (d), were amended by Act §7891(a)(1) by substituting "Internal Revenue Code of 1986" for "Internal Revenue Code of 1954". Eff. as if included in Pub. L. No. 99-514.
- ERISA §211(f) was added by Act §7894(h)(2). Eff. as if included in Pub. L. No. 93-406.

Consolidated Omnibus Budget Reconciliation Act of 1986 (Pub. L. No. 99-272), as follows:
- ERISA §211(c)(1) was amended by Act §11015 by making a technical amendment to the reference to §308(c) of this title to reflect the renumbering of the corresponding section of the original act. Eff. on or after April 7, 1986.

Part 3—Funding

SEC. 301. COVERAGE.

(a) Plans Excepted From Applicability of This Part.—This part shall apply to any employee pension benefit plan described in section 4(a), (and not exempted under section 4(b)), other than—

(1) an employee welfare benefit plan;

(2) an insurance contract plan described in subsection (b);

(3) a plan which is unfunded and is maintained by an employer primarily for the purpose of providing deferred compensation for a select group of management or highly compensated employees;

(4)(A) a plan which is established and maintained by a society, order, or association described in section 501(c)(8) or (9) of title 26, if no part of the contributions to or under such plan are made by employers of participants in such plan; or

(B) a trust described in section 501(c)(18) of title 26;

(5) a plan which has not at any time after the date of enactment of this Act provided for employer contributions;

(6) an agreement providing payments to a retired partner or deceased partner or a deceased partner's successor in interest as described in section 736 of title 26;

(7) an individual retirement account or annuity as described in section 408(a) of the Internal Revenue Code of 1954, or a retirement bond described in section 409 of the Internal Revenue Code of 1954 (as effective for obligations issued before January 1, 1984);

(8) an individual account plan (other than a money purchase plan) and a defined benefit plan to the extent it is treated as an individual account plan (other than a money purchase plan) under section 3(35)(B) of this title;

(9) an excess benefit plan; or

(10) any plan, fund or program under which an employer, all of whose stock is directly or indirectly owned by employees, former employees or their beneficiaries, proposes through an unfunded arrangement to compensate retired employees for benefits which were forfeited by such employees under a pension plan maintained by a former employer prior to the date such pension plan became subject to this Act.

(b) "Insurance Contract Plan" Defined.—For the purposes of paragraph (2) of subsection (a) a plan is an "insurance contract plan" if—

(1) the plan is funded exclusively by the purchase of individual insurance contracts,

(2) such contracts provide for level annual premium payments to be paid extending not later than the retirement age for each individual participating in the plan, and commencing with the date the individual became a participant in the plan (or, in the case of an increase in benefits, commencing at the time such increase becomes effective),

ERISA Sec. 301(b)(2)

(3) benefits provided by the plan are equal to the benefits provided under each contract at normal retirement age under the plan and are guaranteed by an insurance carrier (licensed under the laws of a State to do business with the plan) to the extent premiums have been paid,

(4) premiums payable for the plan year, and all prior plan years under such contracts have been paid before lapse or there is reinstatement of the policy,

(5) no rights under such contracts have been subject to a security interest at any time during the plan year, and

(6) no policy loans are outstanding at any time during the plan year.

A plan funded exclusively by the purchase of group insurance contracts which is determined under regulations prescribed by the Secretary of the Treasury to have the same characteristics as contracts described in the preceding sentence shall be treated as a plan described in this subsection.

(c) Applicability of This Part to Terminated Multiemployer Plans.—This part applies, with respect to a terminated multiemployer plan to which section 4021 applies, until the last day of the plan year in which the plan terminates, within the meaning of section 4041A(a)(2).

(d) [Repealed.]

Amendments to ERISA §301

Pension Protection Act of 2006 (Pub. L. No. 109-280), as follows:
- ERISA §301(d) was stricken by Act §201(c)(1). Eff. generally for plan years beginning after 2007. ERISA §301(d) prior to amendment:
   (d) Financial Assistance From Pension Benefit Guaranty Corporation.—Any amount of any financial assistance from the Pension Benefit Guaranty Corporation to any plan, and any repayment of such amount, shall be taken into account under this section in such manner as determined by the Secretary of the Treasury.
- **Other Provision.** Act §221(c)(1), provides:
   (c) Sunset.
   (1) In general.—Except as provided in this subsection, notwithstanding any other provision of this Act, the provisions of, and the amendments made by, sections 201(b), 202, and 212 shall not apply to plan years beginning after December 31, 2014.

Omnibus Budget Reconciliation Act of 1989 (Pub. L. No. 101-239), as follows:
- ERISA §301(a)(4)(A), (6) were amended by Act §7891(a)(1) by substituting "Internal Revenue Code of 1986" for "Internal Revenue Code of 1954", which for purposes of codification was translated as "title 26". Eff. as if included in Pub. L. No. 99-514.
- ERISA §301(a)(7) was amended by Act §7894(d)(4)(A) by substituting "§409 of title 26 (as effective for obligations issued before January 1, 1984)" for "§409 of title 26". Eff. as if included in Pub. L. No. 96-364.
- ERISA §301(a)(8) was amended by Act §7894(d)(1)(A)(i) by striking "or" after semicolon at end. Eff. as if included in Pub. L. No. 96-364.
- ERISA §301(a)(9) was amended by Act §7894(d)(1)(A)(ii) by substituting ";" for period at end. Eff. as if included in Pub. L. No. 96-364.

- ERISA §301(a)(10) was amended by Act §7894(d)(1)(A)(iii) by substituting "any" for "Any". Eff. as if included in Pub. L. No. 96-364.

Multiemployer Pension Plan Amendments Act of 1980 (Pub. L. No. 96-364), as follows:
- ERISA §301(a)(10) was added by Act §411(b). Eff. Sept. 26, 1980.
- ERISA §301(c), (d) were added by Act §304(a). Eff. Sept. 26, 1980.

> ### *Editor's Note*
>
> **Caution:** Pursuant to Pub. L. No. 109-280, §221(c), in general, the amendments to ERISA §302 made by Pub. L. No. 109-280, §202(d) and (e), will not apply to plan years beginning after December 31, 2014. See amendment notes for details.

SEC. 302. MINIMUM FUNDING STANDARDS.

(a) Requirement To Meet Minimum Funding Standard.—

(1) In general.—A plan to which this part applies shall satisfy the minimum funding standard applicable to the plan for any plan year.

(2) Minimum funding standard.—For purposes of paragraph (1), a plan shall be treated as satisfying the minimum funding standard for a plan year if—

(A) in the case of a defined benefit plan which is a single-employer plan, the employer makes contributions to or under the plan for the plan year which, in the aggregate, are not less than the minimum required contribution determined under section 303 for the plan for the plan year,

(B) in the case of a money purchase plan which is a single-employer plan, the employer makes contributions to or under the plan for the plan year which are required under the terms of the plan, and

(C) in the case of a multiemployer plan, the employers make contributions to or under the plan for any plan year which, in the aggregate, are sufficient to ensure that the plan does not have an accumulated funding deficiency under section 304 as of the end of the plan year.

(b) Liability for Contributions.—

(1) In general.—Except as provided in paragraph (2), the amount of any contribution required by this section (including any required installments under paragraphs (3) and (4) of section 303(j)) shall be paid by the employer responsible for making contributions to or under the plan.

(2) Joint and several liability where employer member of controlled group.—If the employer referred to in paragraph (1) is a member of a controlled group, each member of such group shall be jointly and severally liable for payment of such contributions.

(3) Multiemployer plans in critical status.— Paragraph (1) shall not apply in the case of a multiemployer plan for any plan year in which the plan is in critical status pursuant to section 305. This paragraph shall only apply if the plan sponsor adopts a rehabilitation plan in accordance with section 305(e) and complies with the terms of such rehabilitation plan (and any updates or modifications of the plan).

(c) Variance From Minimum Funding Standards.—

(1) Waiver in case of business hardship.—

(A) In general.—If—

(i) an employer is (or in the case of a multiemployer plan, 10 percent or more of the number of employers contributing to or under the plan are) unable to satisfy the minimum funding standard for a plan year without temporary substantial business hardship (substantial business hardship in the case of a multiemployer plan), and

(ii) application of the standard would be adverse to the interests of plan participants in the aggregate,

the Secretary of the Treasury may, subject to subparagraph (C), waive the requirements of subsection (a) for such year with respect to all or any portion of the minimum funding standard. The Secretary of the Treasury shall not waive the minimum funding standard with respect to a plan for more than 3 of any 15 (5 of any 15 in the case of a multiemployer plan) consecutive plan years.

(B) Effects of waiver.—If a waiver is granted under subparagraph (A) for any plan year—

(i) in the case of a single-employer plan, the minimum required contribution under section 303 for the plan year shall be reduced by the amount of the waived funding deficiency and such amount shall be amortized as required under section 303(e), and

(ii) in the case of a multiemployer plan, the funding standard account shall be credited under section 304(b)(3)(C) with the amount of the waived funding deficiency and such amount shall be amortized as required under section 304(b)(2)(C).

(C) Waiver of amortized portion not allowed.— The Secretary of the Treasury may not waive under subparagraph (A) any portion of the minimum funding standard under subsection (a) for a plan year which is attributable to any waived funding deficiency for any preceding plan year.

(2) Determination of business hardship.— For purposes of this subsection, the factors taken into account in determining temporary substantial business hardship (substantial business hardship in the case of a multiemployer plan) shall include (but shall not be limited to) whether or not—

(A) the employer is operating at an economic loss,

(B) there is substantial unemployment or underemployment in the trade or business and in the industry concerned,

(C) the sales and profits of the industry concerned are depressed or declining, and

(D) it is reasonable to expect that the plan will be continued only if the waiver is granted.

(3) Waived funding deficiency.— For purposes of this part, the term "waived funding deficiency" means the portion of the minimum funding standard under subsection (a) (determined without regard to the waiver) for a plan year waived by the Secretary of the Treasury and not satisfied by employer contributions.

(4) Security for waivers for single-employer plans, consultations.—

(A) Security may be required.—

(i) In general.—Except as provided in subparagraph (C), the Secretary of the Treasury may require an employer maintaining a defined benefit plan which is a single-employer plan (within the meaning of section 4001(a)(15)) to provide security to such plan as a condition for granting or modifying a waiver under paragraph (1).

(ii) Special rules.—Any security provided under clause (i) may be perfected and enforced only by the Pension Benefit Guaranty Corporation, or at the direction of the Corporation, by a contributing sponsor (within the meaning of section 4001(a)(13)), or a member of such sponsor's controlled group (within the meaning of section 4001(a)(14)).

(B) Consultation with the pension benefit guaranty corporation.—Except as provided in subparagraph (C), the Secretary of the Treasury shall, before granting or modifying a waiver under this subsection with respect to a plan described in subparagraph (A)(i)—

(i) provide the Pension Benefit Guaranty Corporation with—

(I) notice of the completed application for any waiver or modification, and

(II) an opportunity to comment on such application within 30 days after receipt of such notice, and

(ii) consider—

(I) any comments of the Corporation under clause (i)(II), and

(II) any views of any employee organization (within the meaning of section 3(4)) representing participants in the plan which are submitted in writing to the Secretary of the Treasury in connection with such application.

Information provided to the Corporation under this subparagraph shall be considered tax return information and subject to the safeguarding and reporting requirements of section 6103(p) of the Internal Revenue Code of 1986.

(C) Exception for certain waivers.—

(i) In general.—The preceding provisions of this paragraph shall not apply to any plan with respect to which the sum of—

(I) the aggregate unpaid minimum required contributions for the plan year and all preceding plan years, and

(II) the present value of all waiver amortization installments determined for the plan year and succeeding plan years under section 303(e)(2), is less than $1,000,000.

(ii) Treatment of waivers for which applications are pending.—The amount described in clause (i)(I) shall include any increase in such amount which would result if all applications for waivers of the minimum funding standard under this subsection which are pending with respect to such plan were denied.

(iii) Unpaid minimum required contribution.— For purposes of this subparagraph—

(I) In general.—The term "unpaid minimum required contribution" means, with respect to any plan year, any minimum required contribution under section 303 for the plan year which is not paid on or before the due date (as determined under section 303(j)(1)) for the plan year.

(II) Ordering rule.—For purposes of subclause (I), any payment to or under a plan for any plan year shall be allocated first to unpaid minimum required contributions for all preceding plan years on a first-in, first-out basis and then to the minimum required contribution under section 303 for the plan year.

(5) Special rules for single-employer plans.—

(A) Application must be submitted before date 2½ months after close of year.—In the case of a single-employer plan, no waiver may be granted under this subsection with respect to any plan for any plan year unless an application therefor is submitted to the Secretary of the Treasury not later than the 15th day of the 3rd month beginning after the close of such plan year.

(B) Special rule if employer is member of controlled group.—In the case of a single-employer plan, if an employer is a member of a controlled

group, the temporary substantial business hardship requirements of paragraph (1) shall be treated as met only if such requirements are met—

(i) with respect to such employer, and

(ii) with respect to the controlled group of which such employer is a member (determined by treating all members of such group as a single employer).

The Secretary of the Treasury may provide that an analysis of a trade or business or industry of a member need not be conducted if such Secretary determines such analysis is not necessary because the taking into account of such member would not significantly affect the determination under this paragraph.

(6) Advance notice.—

(A) In general.—The Secretary of the Treasury shall, before granting a waiver under this subsection, require each applicant to provide evidence satisfactory to such Secretary that the applicant has provided notice of the filing of the application for such waiver to each affected party (as defined in section 4001(a)(21)). Such notice shall include a description of the extent to which the plan is funded for benefits which are guaranteed under title IV and for benefit liabilities.

(B) Consideration of relevant information.—The Secretary of the Treasury shall consider any relevant information provided by a person to whom notice was given under subparagraph (A).

(7) Restriction on plan amendments.—

(A) In general.—No amendment of a plan which increases the liabilities of the plan by reason of any increase in benefits, any change in the accrual of benefits, or any change in the rate at which benefits become nonforfeitable under the plan shall be adopted if a waiver under this subsection or an extension of time under section 304(d) is in effect with respect to the plan, or if a plan amendment described in subsection (d)(2) which reduces the accrued benefit of any participant has been made at any time in the preceding 12 months (24 months in the case of a multiemployer plan). If a plan is amended in violation of the preceding sentence, any such waiver, or extension of time, shall not apply to any plan year ending on or after the date on which such amendment is adopted.

(B) Exception.—Subparagraph (A) shall not apply to any plan amendment which—

(i) the Secretary of the Treasury determines to be reasonable and which provides for only de minimis increases in the liabilities of the plan,

(ii) only repeals an amendment described in subsection (d)(2), or

(iii) is required as a condition of qualification under part I of subchapter D of chapter 1 of the Internal Revenue Code of 1986.

(8) Cross reference.—For corresponding duties of the Secretary of the Treasury with regard to implementation of the Internal Revenue Code of 1986, see section 412(c) of such Code.

(d) Miscellaneous Rules.—

(1) Change in method or year.—If the funding method or a plan year for a plan is changed, the change shall take effect only if approved by the Secretary of the Treasury.

(2) Certain retroactive plan amendments.—For purposes of this section, any amendment applying to a plan year which—

(A) is adopted after the close of such plan year but no later than 2½ months after the close of the plan year (or, in the case of a multiemployer plan, no later than 2 years after the close of such plan year),

(B) does not reduce the accrued benefit of any participant determined as of the beginning of the first plan year to which the amendment applies, and

(C) does not reduce the accrued benefit of any participant determined as of the time of adoption except to the extent required by the circumstances,

shall, at the election of the plan administrator, be deemed to have been made on the first day of such plan year. No amendment described in this paragraph which reduces the accrued benefits of any participant shall take effect unless the plan administrator files a notice with the Secretary of the Treasury notifying him of such amendment and such Secretary has approved such amendment, or within 90 days after the date on which such notice was filed, failed to disapprove such amendment. No amendment described in this subsection shall be approved by the Secretary of the Treasury unless such Secretary determines that such amendment is necessary because of a temporary substantial business hardship (as determined under subsection (c)(2)) or a substantial business hardship (as so determined) in the case of a multiemployer plan and that a waiver under subsection (c) (or, in the case of a multiemployer plan, any extension of the amortization period under section 304(d)) is unavailable or inadequate.

(3) Controlled group.—For purposes of this section, the term "controlled group" means any group treated as a single employer under subsection (b), (c), (m), or (o) of section 414 of the Internal Revenue Code of 1986.

Amendments to ERISA §302

Worker, Retiree, and Employer Recovery Act of 2008 (Pub. L. No. 110-458), as follows:

- ERISA §302(b)(3) was amended by Act §102(b)(1)(A) was amended by striking "the plan adopts" and inserting "the plan sponsor adopts". Eff. for plan years beginning after 2007, as if included in Pub. L. No. 109-280, §202.
- ERISA §302(c)(1)(A)(i) was amended by Act §101(a)(1)(A) by striking "the plan is" and inserting "the plan are". Eff. for plan

years beginning after 2007, as if included in Pub. L. No. 109-280, §101.

- ERISA §302(c)(7)(A) was amended by Act §101(a)(1)(B) by inserting "which reduces the accrued benefit of any participant" after "subsection (d)(2)". Eff. for plan years beginning after 2007, as if included in Pub. L. No. 109-280, §101.
- ERISA §302(d)(1) was amended by Act §101(a)(1)(C) by striking ", the valuation date,". Eff. for plan years beginning after 2007, as if included in Pub. L. No. 109-280, §101.

Pension Protection Act of 2006 (Pub. L. No. 109-280), as follows:

- ERISA §302 was added by Act §§101(b) and 202(d). Eff. for plan years beginning after 2007. Act §104 has a delayed effective date for "eligible cooperative plans" until the earlier of the plan year that such a plan is ineligible, or Jan. 1, 2017. Act §105 provides temporary relief for certain PBGC settlement plans. Act §106 contains rules applicable to certain government contractors. Act §115 provides modified transition rules to the pension funding requirements applicable to certain passenger bus companies. Act §§202(f)(3) and 206 provide special rules for certain multiemployer plans. Act §221(c) provides that changes made by Act §§201(b), 202, and 212 will not apply to plan years beginning after 2014.
- Prior ERISA §302 was repealed by Act §101(a). Eff. for plan years beginning after 2007. See below for text of repealed ERISA §302.
- ERISA §302(b)(3) was added by Act §202(d). Eff. generally for plan years beginning after 2007.
- **Other Provision.** Act §201(b), as amended by Pub. L. No. 110-458, §102(a) (see above), provides:
  (b) Shortfall Funding Method.—
    (1) In general.—A multiemployer plan meeting the criteria of paragraph (2) may adopt, use, or cease using, the shortfall funding method and such adoption, use, or cessation of use of such method, shall be deemed approved by the Secretary of the Treasury under section 302(d)(1) of the Employee Retirement Income Security Act of 1974 and section 412(d)(1) of the Internal Revenue Code of 1986.
    (2) Criteria.—A multiemployer pension plan meets the criteria of this clause if—
      (A) the plan has not adopted, or ceased using, the shortfall funding method during the 5-year period ending on the day before the date the plan is to use the method under paragraph (1); and
      (B) the plan is not operating under an amortization period extension under section 304(d) of such Act and did not operate under such an extension during such 5-year period.
    (3) Shortfall funding method defined.—For purposes of this subsection, the term "shortfall funding method" means the shortfall funding method described in Treasury Regulations section 1.412(c)(1)-2 (26 CFR §1.412(c)(1)-2).
    (4) Benefit restrictions to apply.—The benefit restrictions under section 302(c)(7) of such Act and section 412(c)(7) of such Code shall apply during any period a multiemployer plan is on the shortfall funding method pursuant to this subsection.
    (5) Use of shortfall method not to preclude other options.— Nothing in this subsection shall be construed to affect a multiemployer plan's ability to adopt the shortfall funding method with the Secretary's permission under otherwise applicable regulations or to affect a multiemployer plan's right to change funding methods, with or without the Secretary's consent, as provided in applicable rules and regulations.
- **Other Provision.** Act §202(f) provides:
  (f) Effective Dates.—
    (1) In general.—The amendments made by this section shall apply with respect to plan years beginning after 2007.
    (2) Special rule for certain notices.—In any case in which a plan's actuary certifies that it is reasonably expected that a multiemployer plan will be in critical status under section 305(b)(3) of the Employee Retirement Income Security Act of 1974, as added by this section, with respect to the first plan year beginning after 2007, the notice required under subparagraph (D) of such section may be provided at any time after the date of enactment, so long as it is provided on or before the last date for providing the notice under such subparagraph.

(3) Special rule for certain restored benefits.—In the case of a multiemployer plan—

(A) with respect to which benefits were reduced pursuant to a plan amendment adopted on or after January 1, 2002, and before June 30, 2005, and

(B) which, pursuant to the plan document, the trust agreement, or a formal written communication from the plan sponsor to participants provided before June 30, 2005, provided for the restoration of such benefits, the amendments made by this section shall not apply to such benefit restorations to the extent that any restriction on the providing or accrual of such benefits would otherwise apply by reason of such amendments.

• **Other Provision.** Act §221(c) provides:

(c) **Sunset.**

(1) In general.—Except as provided in this subsection, notwithstanding any other provision of this Act, the provisions of, and the amendments made by, sections 201(b), 202, and 212 shall not apply to plan years beginning after December 31, 2014.

(2) Funding Improvement and Rehabilitation Plans.—If a plan is operating under a funding improvement or rehabilitation plan under section 305 of such Act or 432 of such Code for its last years beginning before January 1, 2015, such plan shall continue to operate under such funding improvement or rehabilitation plan during any period after December 31, 2014, such funding improvement or rehabilitation plan is in effect and all provisions of such Act or Code relating to the operation of such funding improvement or rehabilitation plan shall continue in effect during such period.

SEC. 302. MINIMUM FUNDING STANDARDS. [Repealed.]

(a) **Avoidance of Accumulated Funding Deficiency.—**

(1) Every employee pension benefit plan subject to this part shall satisfy the minimum funding standard (or the alternative minimum funding standard under section 305) for any plan year to which this part applies. A plan to which this part applies shall have satisfied the minimum funding standard for such plan for a plan year if as of the end of such plan year the plan does not have an accumulated funding deficiency.

(2) For the purposes of this part, the term "accumulated funding deficiency" means for any plan the excess of the total charges to the funding standard account for all plan years (beginning with the first plan year to which this part applies) over the total credits to such account for such years or, if less, the excess of the total charges to the alternative minimum funding standard account for such plan years over the total credits to such account for such years.

(3) In any plan year in which a multiemployer plan is in reorganization, the accumulated funding deficiency of the plan shall be determined under section 4243.

(b) **Funding Standard Account.—**

(1) Each plan to which this part applies shall establish and maintain a funding standard account. Such account shall be credited and charged solely as provided in this section.

(2) For a plan year, the funding standard account shall be charged with the sum of—

(A) the normal cost of the plan for the plan year,

(B) the amounts necessary to amortize in equal annual installments (until fully amortized)—

(i) in the case of a plan in existence on January 1, 1974, the unfunded past service liability under the plan on the first day of the first plan year to which this part applies, over a period of 40 plan years,

(ii) in the case of a plan which comes into existence after January 1, 1974, the unfunded past service liability under the

plan on the first day of the first plan year to which this part applies, over a period of 30 plan years,

(iii) [Repealed] (iii) separately, with respect to each plan year, the net increase (if any) in unfunded past service liability under the plan arising from plan amendments adopted in such year, over a period of 30 plan years,

(iv) separately, with respect to each plan year, the net experience loss (if any) under the plan, over a period of 5 plan years (15 plan years in the case of a multiemployer plan), and

(v) separately, with respect to each plan year, the net loss (if any) resulting from changes in actuarial assumptions used under the plan, over a period of 10 plan years (30 plan years in the case of a multiemployer plan),

(C) the amount necessary to amortize each waived funding deficiency (within the meaning of section 303(c)) for each prior plan year in equal annual installments (until fully amortized) over a period of 5 plan years (15 plan years in the case of a multiemployer plan),

(D) the amount necessary to amortize in equal annual installments (until fully amortized) over a period of 5 plan years any amount credited to the funding standard account under paragraph (3)(D), and

(E) the amount necessary to amortize in equal annual installments (until fully amortized) over a period of 20 years the contributions which would be required to be made under the plan but for the provisions of subsection (c)(7)(A)(i)(I).

(3) For a plan year, the funding standard account shall be credited with the sum of—

(A) the amount considered contributed by the employer to or under the plan for the plan year,

(B) the amount necessary to amortize in equal annual installments (until fully amortized)—

(i) separately, with respect to each plan year, the net decrease (if any) in unfunded past service liability under the plan arising from plan amendments adopted in such year, over a period of 30 plan years,

(ii) separately, with respect to each plan year, the net experience gain (if any) under the plan, over a period of 5 plan years (15 plan years in the case of a multiemployer plan), and

(iii) separately, with respect to each plan year, the net gain (if any) resulting from changes in actuarial assumptions used under the plan, over a period of 10 plan years (30 plan years in the case of a multiemployer plan),

(C) the amount of the waived funding deficiency (within the meaning of section 303(c)) for the plan year, and

(D) in the case of a plan year for which the accumulated funding deficiency is determined under the funding standard account if such plan year follows a plan year for which such deficiency was determined under the alternative minimum funding standard, the excess (if any) of any debit balance in the funding standard account (determined without regard to this subparagraph) over any debit balance in the alternative minimum funding standard account.

(4) Under regulations prescribed by the Secretary of the Treasury, amounts required to be amortized under paragraph (2) or paragraph (3), as the case may be—

(A) may be combined into one amount under such paragraph to be amortized over a period determined on the basis of the remaining amortization period for all items entering into such combined amount, and

(B) may be offset against amounts required to be amortized under the other such paragraph, with the resulting amount to be amortized over a period determined on the basis of the remaining amortization periods for all items entering into whichever of the two amounts being offset is the greater.

(5) Interest.—

(A) In general.—The funding standard account (and items therein) shall be charged or credited (as determined under regulations prescribed by the Secretary of the Treasury) with interest at the appropriate rate consistent with the rate or rates of interest used under the plan to determine costs.

(B) Required change of interest rate.—For purposes of determining a plan's current liability and for purposes of determining a plan's required contribution under section 302(d) for any plan year—

(i) In general.—If any rate of interest used under the plan to determine cost is not within the permissible range, the plan shall establish a new rate of interest within the permissible range.

(ii) Permissible range.—For purposes of this subparagraph—

(I) In general.—Except as provided in subclause (II or III), the term "permissible range" means a rate of interest which is not more than 10 percent above, and not more than 10 percent below, the weighted average of the rates of interest on 30-year Treasury securities during the 4-year period ending on the last day before the beginning of the plan year.

(II) Special rule for years 2004, 2005, 2006, and 2007.—In the case of plan years beginning after December 31, 2003, and before January 1, 2008, the term "permissible range" means a rate of interest which is not above, and not more than 10 percent below, the weighted average of the rates of interest on amounts invested conservatively in long-term investment grade corporate bonds during the 4-year period ending on the last day before the beginning of the plan year. Such rates shall be determined by the Secretary of the Treasury on the basis of 2 or more indices that are selected periodically by the Secretary of the Treasury and that are in the top 3 quality levels available. The Secretary of the Treasury shall make the permissible range, and the indices and methodology used to determine the average rate, publicly available.

(III) Secretarial authority.—If the Secretary finds that the lowest rate of interest permissible under subclause (I) or (II) is unreasonably high, the Secretary may prescribe a lower rate of interest, except that such rate may not be less than 80 percent of the average rate determined under such subclause.

(iii) Assumptions.—Notwithstanding subsection (c)(3)(A)(i), the interest rate used under the plan shall be—

(I) determined without taking into account the experience of the plan and reasonable expectations, but

(II) consistent with the assumptions which reflect the purchase rates which would be used by insurance companies to satisfy the liabilities under the plan.

(6) In the case of a plan which, immediately before the date of the enactment of the Multiemployer Pension Plan Amendments Act of 1980, was a multiemployer plan (within the meaning of section 3(37) as in effect immediately before such date)—

(A) any amount described in paragraph (2)(B)(ii), (2)(B)(iii), or (3)(B)(i) of this subsection which arose in a plan year beginning before such date shall be amortized in equal annual installments (until fully amortized) over 40 plan years, beginning with the plan year in which the amount arose;

(B) any amount described in paragraph (2)(B)(iv) or (3)(B)(ii) of this subsection which arose in a plan year beginning before such date shall be amortized in equal annual installments (until fully amortized) over 20 plan years, beginning with the plan year in which the amount arose;

(C) any change in past service liability which arises during the period of 3 plan years beginning on or after such date, and results from a plan amendment adopted before such date, shall be amortized in equal annual installments (until fully amortized) over 40 plan years, beginning with the plan year in which the change arises; and

(D) any change in past service liability which arises during the period of 2 plan years beginning on or after such date, and results from the changing of a group of participants from one benefit level toanother benefit level under a schedule of plan benefits which—

(i) was adopted before such date, and

(ii) was effective for any plan participant before the beginning of the first plan year beginning on or after such date,

shall be amortized in equal annual installments (until fully amortized) over 40 plan years, beginning with the plan year in which the increase arises.

(7) For purposes of this part—

(A) Any amount received by a multiemployer plan in payment of all or part of an employer's withdrawal liability under part 1 of subtitle E of title IV shall be considered an amount contributed by the employer to or under the plan. The Secretary of the Treasury may prescribe by regulation additional charges and credits to a multiemployer plan's funding standard account to the extent necessary to prevent withdrawal liability payments from being unduly reflected as advance funding for plan liabilities.

(B) If a plan is not in reorganization in the plan year but was in reorganization in the immediately preceding plan year, any balance in the funding standard account at the close of such immediately preceding plan year—

(i) shall be eliminated by an offsetting credit or charge (as the case may be), but

(ii) shall be taken into account in subsequent plan years by being amortized in equal annual installments (until fully amortized) over 30 plan years.

The preceding sentence shall not apply to the extent of any accumulated funding deficiency under section 418B(a) of title 26 as of the end of the last plan year that the plan was in reorganization.

(C) Any amount paid by a plan during a plan year to the Pension Benefit Guaranty Corporation pursuant to section 4222 or to a fund exempt under section 501(c)(22) of title 26 pursuant to section 4223 shall reduce the amount of contributions considered received by the plan for the plan year.

(D) Any amount paid by an employer pending a final determination of the employer's withdrawal liability under part 1 of subtitle E of title IV and subsequently refunded to the employer by the plan shall be charged to the funding standard account in accordance with regulations prescribed by the Secretary.

(E) For purposes of the full funding limitation under subsection (c)(7), unless otherwise provided by the plan, the accrued liability under a multiemployer plan shall not include benefits which are not nonforfeitable under the plan after the termination of the plan (taking into consideration section 411(d)(3) of title 26).

(F) Election for deferral of charge for portion of net experience loss.—

(i) In general.—With respect to the net experience loss of an eligible multiemployer plan for the first plan year beginning after December 31, 2001, the plan sponsor may elect to defer up to 80 percent of the amount otherwise required to be charged under paragraph (2)(B)(iv) for any plan year beginning after June 30, 2003, and before July 1, 2005, to any plan year selected by the plan from either of the 2 immediately succeeding plan years;

(ii) Interest.—For the plan year to which a charge is deferred pursuant to an election under clause (i), the funding standard account shall be charged with interest on the deferred charge for the period of deferral at the rate determined under section 304(a) for multiemployer plans.

(iii) Restrictions on benefit increases.—No amendment which increases the liabilities of the plan by reason of any increase in benefits, any change in the accrual of benefits, or any change in the rate at which benefits become nonforfeitable under the plan shall be adopted during any period for which a charge is deferred pursuant to an election under clause (i), unless—

(I) the plan's enrolled actuary certifies (in such form and manner prescribed by the Secretary of the Treasury) that the amendment provides for an increase in annual contributions which will exceed the increase in annual charges to the funding standard account attributable to such amendment, or

(II) the amendment is required by a collective bargaining agreement which is in effect on the date of enactment of this subparagraph.

ERISA Sec. 302 [Repealed]

If a plan is amended during any such plan year in violation of the preceding sentence, any election under this paragraph shall not apply to any such plan year ending on or after the date on which such amendment is adopted.

(iv) Eligible multiemployer plan.—For purposes of this subparagraph, the term "eligible multiemployer plan" means a multiemployer plan—

(I) which had a net investment loss for the first plan year beginning after December 31, 2001, of at least 10 percent of the average fair market value of the plan assets during the plan year, and

(II) with respect to which the plan's enrolled actuary certifies (not taking into account the application of this subparagraph), on the basis of the actuarial assumptions used for the last plan year ending before the date of the enactment of this subparagraph, that the plan is projected to have an accumulated funding deficiency (within the meaning of subsection (a)(2)) for any plan year beginning after June 30, 2003, and before July 1, 2006.

For purposes of subclause (I), a plan's net investment loss shall be determined on the basis of the actual loss and not under any actuarial method used under subsection (c)(2).

(v) Exception to treatment of eligible multiemployer plan.— In no event shall a plan be treated as an eligible multiemployer plan under clause (iv) if—

(I) for any taxable year beginning during the 10-year period preceding the first plan year for which an election is made under clause (i), any employer required to contribute to the plan failed to timely pay any excise tax imposed under section 4971 of the Internal Revenue Code of 1986 with respect to the plan,

(II) for any plan year beginning after June 30, 1993, and before the first plan year for which an election is made under clause (i), the average contribution required to be made by all employers to the plan does not exceed 10 cents per hour or no employer is required to make contributions to the plan, or

(III) with respect to any of the plan years beginning after June 30, 1993, and before the first plan year for which an election is made under clause (i), a waiver was granted under section 303 of this Act or section 412(d) of the Internal Revenue Code of 1986 with respect to the plan or an extension of an amortization period was granted under section 304 of this Act or section 412(e) of such Code with respect to the plan.

(vi) Notice.—If a plan sponsor makes an election under this subparagraph or section 412(b)(7)(F) of the Internal Revenue Code of 1986 for any plan year, the plan administrator shall provide, within 30 days of filing the election for such year, written notice of the election to participants and beneficiaries, to each labor organization representing such participants or beneficiaries, to each employer that has an obligation to contribute under the plan, and to the Pension Benefit Guaranty Corporation. Such notice shall include with respect to any election the amount of any charge to be deferred and the period of the deferral. Such notice shall also include the maximum guaranteed monthly benefits which the Pension Benefit Guaranty Corporation would pay if the plan terminated while underfunded.

(vii) Election.—An election under this subparagraph shall be made at such time and in such manner as the Secretary of the Treasury may prescribe.

(c) Methods.—

(1) For purposes of this part, normal costs, accrued liability, past service liabilities, and experience gains and losses shall be determined under the funding method used to determine costs under the plan.

(2)(A) For purposes of this part, the value of the plan's assets shall be determined on the basis of any reasonable actuarial method of valuation which takes into account fair market value and which is permitted under regulations prescribed by the Secretary of the Treasury.

(B) For purposes of this part, the value of a bond or other evidence of indebtedness which is not in default as to principal or interest may, at the election of the plan administrator, be determined on an amortized basis running from initial cost at

purchase to par value at maturity or earliest call date. Any election under this subparagraph shall be made at such time and in such manner as the Secretary of the Treasury shall by regulations provide, shall apply to all such evidences of indebtedness, and may be revoked only with the consent of the Secretary of the Treasury. In the case of a plan other than a multiemployer plan, this subparagraph shall not apply, but the Secretary of the Treasury may by regulations provide that the value of any dedicated bond portfolio of such plan shall be determined by using the interest rate under subsection (b)(5).

(3) For purposes of this section, all costs, liabilities, rates of interest, and other factors under the plan shall be determined on the basis of actuarial assumptions and methods—

(A) in the case of—

(i) a plan other than a multiemployer plan, each of which is reasonable (taking into account the experience of the plan and reasonable expectations) or which, in the aggregate, result in a total contribution equivalent to that which would be determined if each such assumption and method were reasonable, or

(ii) a multiemployer plan, which, in the aggregate, are reasonable (taking into account the experiences of the plan and reasonable expectations), and

(B) which, in combination, offer the actuary's best estimate of anticipated experience under the plan.

(4) For purposes of this section, if—

(A) a change in benefits under the Social Security Act or in other retirement benefits created under Federal or State law, or

(B) a change in the definition of the term "wages" under section 3121 of title 26, or a change in the amount of such wages taken into account under regulations prescribed for purposes of section 401(a)(5) of title 26, results in an increase or decrease in accrued liability under a plan, such increase or decrease shall be treated as an experience loss or gain.

(5)(A) In general.—If the funding method for a plan is changed, the new funding method shall become the funding method used to determine costs and liabilities under the plan only if the change is approved by the Secretary of the Treasury. If the plan year for a plan is changed, the new plan year shall become the plan year for the plan only if the change is approved by the Secretary of the Treasury.

(B) Approval required for certain changes in assumptions by certain single-employer plans subject to additional funding requirement.—

(i) In general.—No actuarial assumption (other than the assumptions described in subsection (d)(7)(C)) used to determine the current liability for a plan to which this subparagraph applies may be changed without the approval of the Secretary of the Treasury.

(ii) Plans to which subparagraph applies.—This subparagraph shall apply to a plan only if—

(I) the plan is a defined benefit plan (other than a multiemployer plan) to which title IV applies;

(II) the aggregate unfunded vested benefits as of the close of the preceding plan year (as determined under section 4006(a)(3)(E)(iii)) of such plan and all other plans maintained by the contributing sponsors (as defined in section 4001(a)(13)) and members of such sponsors' controlled groups (as defined in section 4001(a)(14)) which arecovered by title IV (disregarding plans with no unfunded vested benefits) exceed $50,000,000; and

(III) the change in assumptions (determined after taking into account any changes in interest rate and mortality table) results in a decrease in the unfunded current liability of the plan for the current plan year that exceeds $50,000,000, or that exceeds $5,000,000 and that is 5 percent or more of the current liability of the plan before such change.

(6) If, as of the close of a plan year, a plan would (without regard to this paragraph) have an accumulated funding deficiency (determined without regard to the alternative minimum funding standard account permitted under section 305) in excess of the full funding limitation—

(A) the funding standard account shall be credited with the amount of such excess, and

(B) all amounts described in paragraphs (2), (B), (C), and (D) and (3)(B) of subsection (b) which are required to be amortized shall be considered fully amortized for purposes of such paragraphs.

(7) Full-funding limitation.—

(A) In general.—For purposes of paragraph (6), the term "full-funding limitation" means the excess (if any) of—

(i) the lesser of—

(I) in the case of plan years beginning before January 1, 2004, the applicable percentage of current liability (including the expected increase in current liability due to benefits accruing during the plan year), or

(II) the accrued liability (including normal cost) under the plan (determined under the entry age normal funding method if such accrued liability cannot be directly calculated under the funding method used for the plan), over

(ii) the lesser of—

(I) the fair market value of the plan's assets, or

(II) the value of such assets determined under paragraph (2).

(B) Current liability.—For purposes of subparagraph (D) and subclause (I) of subparagraph (A)(i), the term "current liability" has the meaning given such term by subsection (d)(7) (without regard to subparagraphs (C) and (D) thereof) and using the rate of interest used under subsection (b)(5)(B).

(C) Special rule for paragraph (6)(B).—For purposes of paragraph (6)(B), subparagraph (A)(i) shall be applied without regard to subclause (I) thereof.

(D) Regulatory authority.—The Secretary of the Treasury may by regulations provide—

(i) for adjustments to the percentage contained in subparagraph (A)(i) to take into account the respective ages or lengths of service of the participants, and

(ii) alternative methods based on factors other than current liability for the determination of the amount taken into account under subparagraph (A)(i).

(E) Minimum amount.—

(i) In general.—In no event shall the full-funding limitation determined under subparagraph (A) be less than the excess (if any) of—

(I) 90 percent of the current liability of the plan (including the expected increase in current liability due to benefits accruing during the plan year), over

(II) the value of the plan's assets determined under paragraph (2).

(ii) Current liability; assets.—For purposes of clause (i)—

(I) the term "current liability" has the meaning given such term by subsection (d)(7) (without regard to subparagraph (D) thereof), and

(II) assets shall not be reduced by any credit balance in the funding standard account.

(F) Applicable Percentage.—For purposes of subparagraph (A)(i)(I), the applicable percentage shall be determined in accordance with the following table:

In the case of any applicable plan year beginning in—	The applicable percentage is—
2002	165
2003	170

(8) For purposes of this part, any amendment applying to a plan year which—

(A) is adopted after the close of such plan year but no later than 2½ months after the close of the plan year (or, in the case of a

multiemployer plan, no later than 2 years after the close of such plan year),

(B) does not reduce the accrued benefit of any participant determined as of the beginning of the first plan year to which the amendment applies, and

(C) does not reduce the accrued benefit of any participant determined as of the time of adoption except to the extent required by the circumstances,

shall, at the election of the plan administrator, be deemed to have been made on the first day of such plan year. No amendment described in this paragraph which reduces the accrued benefits of any participant shall take effect unless the plan administrator files a notice with the Secretary notifying him of such amendment and the Secretary has approved such amendment or, within 90 days after the date on which such notice was filed, failed to disapprove such amendment. No amendment described in this subsection shall be approved by the Secretary unless he determines that such amendment is necessary because of a substantial business hardship (as determined under section 303(b)) and that waiver under section 303(a) is unavailable or inadequate.

(9)(A) For purposes of this part, a determination of experience gains and losses and a valuation of the plan's liability shall be made not less frequently than once every year, except that such determination shall be made more frequently to the extent required in particular cases under regulations prescribed by the Secretary of the Treasury.

(B)(i) Except as provided in clause (ii), the valuation referred to in subparagraph (A) shall be made as of a date within the plan year to which the valuation refers or within one month prior to the beginning of such year.

(ii) The valuation referred to in subparagraph (A) may be made as of a date within the plan year prior to the year to which the valuation refers if, as of such date, the value of the assets of the plan are not less than 100 percent of the plan's current liability (as defined in paragraph (7)(B)).

(iii) Information under clause (ii) shall, in accordance with regulations, be actuarially adjusted to reflect significant differences in participants.

(iv) Limitation.—A change in funding method to use a prior year valuation, as provided in clause (ii), may not be made unless as of the valuation date within the prior plan year, the value of the assets of the plan are not less than 125 percent of the plan's current liability (as defined in paragraph (7)(B)).

(10) For purposes of this section—

(A) In the case of a defined benefit plan other than a multiemployer plan, anycontributions for a plan year made by an employer during the period—

(i) beginning on the day after the last day of such plan year, and

(ii) ending on the date which is $8^{1}/^{2}$ months after the close of the plan year, shall be deemed to have been made on such last day.

(B) In the case of a plan not described in subparagraph (A), any contributions for a plan year made by an employer after the last day of such plan year, but not later than two and one-half months after such day, shall be deemed to have been made on such last day. For purposes of this subparagraph, such two and one-half month period may be extended for not more than six months under regulations prescribed by the Secretary of the Treasury.

(11) Liability for contributions.—

(A) In general.—Except as provided in subparagraph (B), the amount of any contribution required by this section and any required installments under subsection (e) shall be paid by the employer responsible for contributing to or under the plan the amount described in subsection (b)(3)(A).

(B) Joint and several liability where employer member of controlled group.—

(i) In general.—In the case of a plan other than a multiemployer plan, if the employer referred to in subparagraph (A) is a member of a controlled group, each member of such group shall

ERISA Sec. 302 [Repealed]

be jointly and severally liable for payment of such contribution or required installment.

(ii) Controlled group.—For purposes of clause (i), the term "controlled group" means any group treated as a single employer under subsection (b), (c), (m), or (o) of section 414 of the Internal Revenue Code of 1986.

(12) Anticipation of benefit increases effective in the future.—In determining projected benefits, the funding method of a collectively bargained plan described in section 413(a) of the Internal Revenue Code of 1986 (other than a multiemployer plan) shall anticipate benefit increases scheduled to take effect during the term of the collective bargaining agreement applicable to the plan.

(d) Additional Funding Requirements for Plans Which Are Not Multiemployer Plans.—

(1) In general.—In the case of a defined benefit plan (other than a multiemployer plan) to which this subsection applies under paragraph (9) for any plan year, the amount charged to the funding standard account for such plan year shall be increased by the sum of—

(A) the excess (if any) of—

(i) the deficit reduction contribution determined under paragraph (2) for such plan year, over

(ii) the sum of the charges for such plan year under subsection (b)(2), reduced by the sum of the credits for such plan year under subparagraph (B) of subsection (b)(3), plus

(B) the unpredictable contingent event amount (if any) for such plan year.

Such increase shall not exceed the amount which, after taking into account charges (other than the additional charge under this subsection) and credits under subsection (b), is necessary to increase the funded current liability percentage (taking into account the expected increase in current liability due to benefits accruing during the plan year) to 100 percent.

(2) Deficit reduction contribution.—For purposes of paragraph (1), the deficit reduction contribution determined under this paragraph for any plan year is the sum of—

(A) the unfunded old liability amount,

(B) the unfunded new liability amount,

(C) the expected increase in current liability due to benefits accruing during the plan year, and

(D) the aggregate of the unfunded mortality increase amounts.

(3) Unfunded old liability amount.—For purposes of this subsection—

(A) In general.—The unfunded old liability amount with respect to any plan for any plan year is the amount necessary to amortize the unfunded old liability under the plan in equal annual installments over a period of 18 plan years (beginning with the 1st plan year beginning after December 31, 1988).

(B) Unfunded old liability.—The term "unfunded old liability" means the unfunded current liability of the plan as of the beginning of the 1st plan year beginning after December 31, 1987 (determined without regard to any plan amendment increasing liabilities adopted after October 16, 1987).

(C) Special rules for benefit increases under existing collective bargaining agreements.—

(i) In general.—In the case of a plan maintained pursuant to 1 or more collective bargaining agreements between employee representatives and the employer ratified before October 29, 1987, the unfunded old liability amount with respect to such plan for any plan year shall be increased by the amount necessary to amortize the unfunded existing benefit increase liability in equal annual installments over a period of 18 plan years beginning with—

(I) the plan year in which the benefit increase with respect to such liability occurs, or

(II) if the taxpayer elects, the 1st plan year beginning after December 31, 1988.

(ii) Unfunded existing benefit increase liabilities.—For purposes of clause (i), the unfunded existing benefit increase liabil-

ity means, with respect to any benefit increase under the agreements described in clause (i) which takes effect during or after the 1st plan year beginning after December 31, 1987, the unfunded current liability determined—

(I) by taking into account only liabilities attributable to such benefit increase, and

(II) by reducing (but not below zero) the amount determined under paragraph (8)(A)(ii) by the current liability determined without regard to such benefit increase.

(iii) Extensions, modifications, etc. not taken into account.—For purposes of this subparagraph, any extension, amendment, or other modification of an agreement after October 28, 1987, shall not be taken into account.

(D) Special rule for required changes in actuarial assumptions.—

(i) In general.—The unfunded old liability amount with respect to any plan for any plan year shall be increased by the amount necessary to amortize the amount of additional unfunded old liability under the plan in equal annual installments over a period of 12 plan years (beginning with the first plan year beginning after December 31, 1994).

(ii) Additional unfunded old liability.—For purposes of clause (i), the term "additional unfunded old liability" means the amount (if any) by which—

(I) the current liability of the plan as of the beginning of the first plan year beginning after December 31, 1994, valued using the assumptions required by paragraph (7)(C) as in effect for plan years beginning after December 31, 1994, exceeds

(II) the current liability of the plan as of the beginning of such first plan year, valued using the same assumptions used under subclause (I) (other than the assumptions required by paragraph (7)(C)), using the prior interest rate, and using such mortality assumptions as were used to determine current liability for the first plan year beginning after December 31, 1992.

(iii) Prior interest rate.—For purposes of clause (ii), the term "prior interest rate" means the rate of interest that is the same percentage of the weighted average under subsection (b)(5)(B)(ii)(I) for the first plan year beginning after December 31, 1994, as the rate of interest used by the plan to determine current liability for the first plan year beginning after December 31, 1992, is of the weighted average under subsection (b)(5)(B)(ii)(I) for such first plan year beginning after December 31, 1992.

(E) Optional rule for additional unfunded old liability.—

(i) In general.—If an employer makes an election under clause (ii), the additional unfunded old liability for purposes of subparagraph (D) shall be the amount (if any) by which—

(I) the unfunded current liability of the plan as of the beginning of the first plan year beginning after December 31, 1994, valued using the assumptions required by paragraph (7)(C) as in effect for plan years beginning after December 31, 1994, exceeds—

(II) the unamortized portion of the unfunded old liability under the plan as of the beginning of the first plan year beginning after December 31, 1994.

(ii) Election.—

(I) An employer may irrevocably elect to apply the provisions of this subparagraph as of the beginning of the first plan year beginning after December 31, 1994.

(II) If an election is made under this clause, the increase under paragraph (1) for any plan year beginning after December 31, 1994, and before January 1, 2002, to which this subsection applies (without regard to this subclause) shall not be less than the increase that would be required under paragraph (1) if the provisions of this title as in effect for the last plan year beginning before January 1, 1995, had remained in effect.

(4) Unfunded new liability amount.—For purposes of this subsection—

(A) In general.—The unfunded new liability amount with respect to any plan for any plan year is the applicable percentage of the unfunded new liability.

(B) Unfunded new liability.—The term "unfunded new liability" means the unfunded current liability of the plan for the plan year determined without regard to—

(i) the unamortized portion of the unfunded old liability, the unamortized portion of the additional unfunded old liability, the unamortized portion of each unfunded mortality increase, and the unamortized portion of the unfunded existing benefit increase liability, and

(ii) the liability with respect to any unpredictable contingent event benefits (without regard to whether the event has occurred).

(C) Applicable percentage.—The term "applicable percentage" means, with respect to any plan year, 30 percent, reduced by the product of—

(i) .40 multiplied by

(ii) the number of percentage points (if any) by which the funded current liability percentage exceeds 60 percent.

(5) Unpredictable contingent event amount.—

(A) In general.—The unpredictable contingent event amount with respect to a plan for any plan year is an amount equal to the greatest of—

(i) the applicable percentage of the product of—

(I) 100 percent, reduced (but not below zero) by the funded current liability percentage for the plan year, multiplied by

(II) the amount of unpredictable contingent event benefits paid during the plan year, including (except as provided by the Secretary of the Treasury) any payment for the purchase of an annuity contract for a participant or beneficiary with respect to such benefits,

(ii) the amount which would be determined for the plan year if the unpredictable contingent event benefit liabilities were amortized in equal annual installments over 7 plan years (beginning with the plan year in which such event occurs), or

(iii) the additional amount that would be determined under paragraph (4)(A) if the unpredictable contingent event benefit liabilities were included in unfunded new liability notwithstanding paragraph (4)(B)(ii).

(B) Applicable percentage.—

In the case of plan years beginning in:	The applicable percentage is:
1989 and 1990	5
1991	10
1992	15
1993	20
1994	30
1995	40
1996	50
1997	60
1998	70
1999	80
2000	90
2001 and thereafter	100

(C) Paragraph not to apply to existing benefits.—This paragraph shall not apply to unpredictable contingent event benefits (and liabilities attributable thereto) for which the event occurred before the first plan year beginning after December 31, 1988.

(D) Special rule for first year of amortization.—Unless the employer elects otherwise, the amount determined under subparagraph (A) for the plan year in which the event occurs shall be equal to 150 percent of the amount determined under subparagraph (A)(i). The amount under subparagraph (A)(ii) for subsequent plan years in the amortization period shall be adjusted in the manner provided by the Secretary of the Treasury to reflect the application of this subparagraph.

(E) Limitation.—The present value of the amounts described in subparagraph (A) with respect to any one event shall not exceed the unpredictable contingent event benefit liabilities attributable to that event.

(6) Special rules for small plans.—

(A) Plans with 100 or fewer participants.—This subsection shall not apply to any plan for any plan year if on each day during the preceding plan year such plan had no more than 100 participants.

(B) Plans with more than 100 but not more than 150 participants.—In the case of a plan to which subparagraph (A) does not apply and which on each day during the preceding plan year had no more than 150 participants, the amount of the increase under paragraph (1) for such plan year shall be equal to the product of—

(i) such increase determined without regard to this subparagraph, multiplied by

(ii) 2 percent for the highest number of participants in excess of 100 on any such day.

(C) Aggregation of plans.—For purposes of this paragraph, all defined benefit plans maintained by the same employer (or any member of such employer's controlled group) shall be treated as 1 plan, but only employees of such employer or member shall be taken into account.

(7) Current liability.— For purposes of this subsection—

(A) In general.—The term "current liability" means all liabilities to participants and their beneficiaries under the plan.

(B) Treatment of unpredictable contingent event benefits.—

(i) In general.—For purposes of subparagraph (A), any unpredictable contingent event benefit shall not be taken into account until the event on which the benefit is contingent occurs.

(ii) Unpredictable contingent event benefit.—The term "unpredictable contingent event benefit" means any benefit contingent on an event other than—

(I) age, service, compensation, death, or disability, or

(II) an event which is reasonably and reliably predictable (as determined by the Secretary of the Treasury).

(C) Interest rate and mortality assumptions used.—Effective for plan years beginning after December 31, 1994—

(i) Interest rate.—

(I) In general.—The rate of interest used to determine current liability under this subsection shall be the rate of interest used under subsection (b)(5), except that the highest rate in the permissible range under subparagraph (B)(ii) thereof shall not exceed the specified percentage under subclause (II) of the weighted average referred to in such subparagraph.

(II) Specified percentage.—For purposes of subclause (I), the specified percentage shall be determined as follows:

In the case of plan years beginning in calendar year:	The specified percentage is:
1995	109
1996	108
1997	107
1998	106
1999 and thereafter	105

(III) Special rule for 2002 and 2003.—For a plan year beginning in 2002 or 2003, notwithstanding subclause (I), in the case that the rate of interest used under subsection (b)(5) exceeds the highest rate permitted under subclause (I), the rate of interest

ERISA Sec. 302 [Repealed]

used to determine current liability under this subsection may exceed the rate of interest otherwise permitted under subclause (I); except that such rate of interest shall not exceed 120 percent of the weighted average referred to in subsection (b)(5)(B)(ii).

(IV) Special rule for 2004, 2005, 2006, and 2007.—For plan years beginning in 2004, 2005, 2006, or 2007, notwithstanding subclause (I), the rate of interest used to determine current liability under this subsection shall be the rate of interest under subsection (b)(5).

(ii) Mortality tables.—

(I) Commissioners' standard table.—In the case of plan years beginning before the first plan year to which the first tables prescribed under subclause (II) apply, the mortality table used in determining current liability under this subsection shall be the table prescribed by the Secretary of the Treasury which is based on the prevailing commissioners' standard table (described in section 807(d)(5)(A) of the Internal Revenue Code of 1986) used to determine reserves for group annuity contracts issued on January 1, 1993.

(II) Secretarial authority.—The Secretary of the Treasury may by regulation prescribe for plan years beginning after December 31, 1999, mortality tables to be used in determining current liability under this subsection. Such tables shall be based upon the actual experience of pension plans and projected trends in such experience. In prescribing such tables, the Secretary of the Treasury shall take into account results of available independent studies of mortality of individuals covered by pension plans.

(III) Periodic review.—The Secretary of the Treasury shall periodically (at least every 5 years) review any tables in effect under this subsection and shall, to the extent the Secretary determines necessary, by regulation update the tables to reflect the actual experience of pension plans and projected trends in such experience.

(iii) Separate mortality tables for the disabled.—Notwithstanding clause (ii)—

(I) In general.—In the case of plan years beginning after December 31, 1995, the Secretary of the Treasury shall establish mortality tables which may be used (in lieu of the tables under clause (ii)) to determine current liability under this subsection for individuals who are entitled to benefits under the plan on account of disability. Such Secretary shall establish separate tables for individuals whose disabilities occur in plan years beginning before January 1, 1995, and for individuals whose disabilities occur in plan years beginning on or after such date.

(II) Special rule for disabilities occurring after 1994.—In the case of disabilities occurring in plan years beginning after December 31, 1994, the tables under subclause (I) shall apply only with respect to individuals described in such subclause who are disabled within the meaning of title II of the Social Security Act and the regulations thereunder.

(III) Plan years beginning in 1995.—In the case of any plan year beginning in 1995, a plan may use its own mortality assumptions for individuals who are entitled to benefits under the plan on account of disability.

(D) Certain service disregarded.—

(i) In general.—In the case of a participant to whom this subparagraph applies, only the applicable percentage of the years of service before such individual became a participant shall be taken into account in computing the current liability of the plan.

(ii) Applicable percentage.—For purposes of this subparagraph, the applicable percentage shall be determined as follows:

If the years of participation are:	The percentage is:
1	20
2	40
3	60

If the years of participation are:	The percentage is:
4	80
5 or more	100

(iii) Participants to whom subparagraph applies.—This subparagraph shall apply to any participant who, at the time of becoming a participant—

(I) has not accrued any other benefit under any defined benefit plan (whether or not terminated) maintained by the employer or a member of the same controlled group of which the employer is a member,

(II) who first becomes a participant under the plan in a plan year beginning after December 31, 1987, and

(III) has years of service greater than the minimum years of service necessary for eligibility to participate in the plan.

(iv) Election.—An employer may elect not to have this subparagraph apply. Such an election, once made, may be revoked only with the consent of the Secretary of the Treasury.

(8) Other definitions.—For purposes of this subsection—

(A) Unfunded current liability.—The term "unfunded current liability" means, with respect to any plan year, the excess (if any) of—

(i) the current liability under the plan, over

(ii) value of the plan's assets determined under subsection (c)(2).

(B) Funded current liability percentage.—The term "funded current liability percentage" means, with respect to any plan year, the percentage which—

(i) the amount determined under subparagraph (A)(ii), is of

(ii) the current liability under the plan.

(C) Controlled group.—The term "controlled group" means any group treated as a single employer under subsections (b), (c), (m), and (o) of section 414 of the Internal Revenue Code of 1986.

(D) Adjustments to prevent omissions and duplications.—The Secretary of the Treasury shall provide such adjustments in the unfunded old liability amount, the unfunded new liability amount, the unpredictable contingent event amount, the current payment amount, and any other charges or credits under this section as are necessary to avoid duplication or omission of any factors in the determination of such amounts, charges, or credits.

(E) Deduction for credit balances.—For purposes of this subsection, the amount determined under subparagraph (A)(ii) shall be reduced by any credit balance in the funding standard account. The Secretary of the Treasury may provide for such reduction for purposes of any other provision which references this subsection.

(9) Applicability of subsection.—

(A) In general.—Except as provided in paragraph (6)(A), this subsection shall apply to a plan for any plan year if its funded current liability percentage for such year is less than 90 percent.

(B) Exception for certain plans at least 80 percent funded.—Subparagraph (A) shall not apply to a plan for a plan year if—

(i) the funded current liability percentage for the plan year is at least 80 percent, and

(ii) such percentage for each of the 2 immediately preceding plan years (or each of the 2d and 3d immediately preceding plan years) is at least 90 percent.

(C) Funded current liability percentage.—For purposes of subparagraphs (A) and (B), the term "funded current liability percentage" has the meaning given such term by paragraph (8)(B), except that such percentage shall be determined for any plan year—

(i) without regard to paragraph (8)(E), and

(ii) by using the rate of interest which is the highest rate allowable for the plan year under paragraph (7)(C).

ERISA Sec. 302 [Repealed]

(D) Transition rules.—For purposes of this paragraph:

(i) Funded percentage for years before 1995.—The funded current liability percentage for any plan year beginning before January 1, 1995, shall be treated as not less than 90 percent only if for such plan year the plan met one of the following requirements (as in effect for such year):

(I) The full-funding limitation under subsection (c)(7) for the plan was zero.

(II) The plan had no additional funding requirement under this subsection (or would have had no such requirement if its funded current liability percentage had been determined under subparagraph (C)).

(III) The plan's additional funding requirement under this subsection did not exceed the lesser of 0.5 percent of current liability or $5,000,000.

(ii) Special rule for 1995 and 1996.—For purposes of determining whether subparagraph (B) applies to any plan year beginning in 1995 or 1996, a plan shall be treated as meeting the requirements of subparagraph (B)(ii) if the plan met the requirements of clause (i) of this subparagraph for any two of the plan years beginning in 1992, 1993, and 1994 (whether or not consecutive).

(10) Unfunded mortality increase amount.—

(A) In general.—The unfunded mortality increase amount with respect to each unfunded mortality increase is the amount necessary to amortize such increase in equal annual installments over a period of 10 plan years (beginning with the first plan year for which a plan uses any new mortality table issued under paragraph (7)(C)(ii)(II) or (III)).

(B) Unfunded mortality increase.—For purposes of subparagraph (A), the term "unfunded mortality increase" means an amount equal to the excess of—

(i) the current liability of the plan for the first plan year for which a plan uses any new mortality table issued under paragraph (7)(C)(ii)(II) or (III), over

(ii) the current liability of the plan for such plan year which would have been determined if the mortality table in effect for the preceding plan year had been used.

(11) Phase-in of increases in funding required by Retirement Protection Act of 1994.—

(A) In general.—For any applicable plan year, at the election of the employer, the increase under paragraph (1) shall not exceed the greater of—

(i) the increase that would be required under paragraph (1) if the provisions of this title as in effect for plan years beginning before January 1, 1995, had remained in effect, or

(ii) the amount which, after taking into account charges (other than the additional charge under this subsection) and credits under subsection (b), is necessary to increase the funded current liability percentage (taking into account the expectedincrease in current liability due to benefits accruing during the plan year) for the applicable plan year to a percentage equal to the sum of the initial funded current liability percentage of the plan plus the applicable number of percentage points for such applicable plan year.

(B) Applicable number of percentage points.—

(i) Initial funded current liability percentage of 75 percent or less.—Except as provided in clause (ii), for plans with an initial funded current liability percentage of 75 percent or less, the applicable number of percentage points for the applicable plan year is:

In the case of plan years beginning in—	The applicable-number of percentage points is—
1995	3
1996	6
1997	9
1998	12
1999	15
2000	19
2001	24

(ii) Other cases.—In the case of a plan to which this clause applies, the applicable number of percentage points for any such applicable plan year is the sum of—

(I) 2 percentage points;

(II) the applicable number of percentage points (if any) under this clause for the preceding applicable plan year;

(III) the product of .10 multiplied by the excess (if any) of (a) 85 percentage points over (b) the sum of the initial funded current liability percentage and the number determined under subclause (II);

(IV) for applicable plan years beginning in 2000, 1 percentage point; and

(V) for applicable plan years beginning in 2001, 2 percentage points.

(iii) Plans to which clause (ii) applies.—

(I) In general.—Clause (ii) shall apply to a plan for an applicable plan year if the initial funded current liability percentage of such plan is more than 75 percent.

(II) Plans initially under clause (i).—In the case of a plan which (but for this subclause) has an initial funded current liability percentage of 75 percent or less, clause (ii) (and not clause (i)) shall apply to such plan with respect to applicable plan years beginning after the first applicable plan year for which the sum of the initial funded current liability percentage and the applicable number of percentage points (determined under clause (i)) exceeds 75 percent. For purposes of applying clause (ii) to such a plan, the initial funded current liability percentage of such plan shall be treated as being the sum referred to in the preceding sentence.

(C) Definitions.—For purposes of this paragraph—

(i) The term "applicable plan year" means a plan year beginning after December 31, 1994, and before January 1, 2002.

(ii) The term "initial funded current liability percentage" means the funded current liability percentage as of the first day of the first plan year beginning after December 31, 1994.

(12) Election for certain plans.—

(A) In general.—In the case of a defined benefit plan established and maintained by an applicable employer, if this subsection did not apply to the plan for the plan year beginning in 2000 (determined without regard to paragraph (6)), then, at the election of the employer, the increased amount under paragraph (1) for any applicable plan year shall be the greater of—

(i) 20 percent of the increased amount under paragraph (1) determined without regard to this paragraph, or

(ii) the increased amount which would be determined under paragraph (1) if the deficit reduction contribution under paragraph (2) for the applicable plan year were determined without regard to subparagraphs (A), (B), and (D) of paragraph (2).

(B) Restrictions on benefit increases.—No amendment which increases the liabilities of the plan by reason of any increase in benefits, any change in the accrual of benefits, or any change in the rate at which benefits become nonforfeitable under the plan shall be adopted during any applicable plan year, unless—

(i) the plan's enrolled actuary certifies (in such form and manner prescribed by the Secretary of the Treasury) that the

ERISA Sec. 302 [Repealed]

amendment provides for an increase in annual contributions which will exceed the increase in annual charges to the funding standard account attributable to such amendment, or

(ii) the amendment is required by a collective bargaining agreement which is in effect on the date of enactment of this subparagraph.

If a plan is amended during any applicable plan year in violation of the preceding sentence, any election under this paragraph shall not apply to any applicable plan year ending on or after the date on which such amendment is adopted.

(C) Applicable employer.—For purposes of this paragraph, the term "applicable employer" means an employer which is—

(i) a commercial passenger airline,

(ii) primarily engaged in the production or manufacture of a steel mill product or the processing of iron ore pellets, or

(iii) an organization described in section 501(c)(5) of the Internal Revenue Code of 1986 and which established the plan to which this paragraph applies on June 30, 1955.

(D) Applicable plan year.—For purposes of this paragraph—

(i) In general.—The term "applicable plan year" means any plan year beginning after December 27, 2003, and before December 28, 2005, for which the employer elects the application of this paragraph.

(ii) Limitation on number of years which may be elected.— An election may not be made under this paragraph with respect to more than 2 plan years.

(E) Notice requirements for plans electing alternative deficit reduction contributions.—

(i) In general.—If an employer elects an alternative deficit reduction contribution under this paragraph and section 412(l)(12) of the Internal Revenue Code of 1986 for any year, the employer shall provide, within 30 days of filing the election for such year, written notice of the election to participants and beneficiaries and to the Pension Benefit Guaranty Corporation.

(ii) Notice to participants and beneficiaries.—The notice under clause (i) to participants and beneficiaries shall include with respect to any election—

(I) the due date of the alternative deficit reduction contribution and the amount by which such contribution was reduced from the amount which would have been owed if the election were not made, and

(II) a description of the benefits under the plan which are eligible to be guaranteed by the Pension Benefit GuarantyCorporation and an explanation of thelimitations on the guarantee and the circumstances under which such limitations apply, including the maximum guaranteed monthly benefits which the Pension Benefit Guaranty Corporation would pay if the plan terminated while underfunded.

(iii) Notice to PBGC.—The notice under clause (i) to the Pension Benefit Guaranty Corporation shall include—

(I) the information described in clause (ii)(I),

(II) the number of years it will take to restore the plan to full funding if the employer only makes the required contributions, and

(III) information as to how the amount by which the plan is underfunded compares with the capitalization of the employer making the election.

(F) Election.—An election under this paragraph shall be made at such time and in such manner as the Secretary of the Treasury may prescribe.

(e) Quarterly Contributions Required.—

(1) In general.—If a defined benefit plan (other than a multiemployer plan) which has a funded current liability percentage (as defined in subsection (d)(8)) for the preceding plan year of less than 100 percent fails to pay the full amount of a required installment for the plan year, then the rate of interest charged to the funding standard account under subsection (b)(5) with respect to the amount of the underpayment for the period of the underpayment shall be equal to the greater of—

(A) 175 percent of the Federal mid-term rate (as in effect under section 1274 of the Internal Revenue Code of 1986 for the 1st month of such plan year), or

(B) the rate of interest used under the plan in determining costs (including adjustments under subsection (b)(5)(B)).

(2) Amount of underpayment, period of underpayment.— For purposes of paragraph (1)—

(A) Amount.—The amount of the underpayment shall be the excess of—

(i) the required installment, over

(ii) the amount (if any) of the installment contributed to or under the plan on or before the due date for the installment.

(B) Period of underpayment.—The period for which any interest is charged under this subsection with respect to any portion of the underpayment shall run from the due date for the installment to the date on which such portion is contributed to or under the plan (determined without regard to subsection (c)(10)).

(C) Order of crediting contributions.—For purposes of subparagraph (A)(ii), contributions shall be credited against unpaid required installments in the order in which such installments are required to be paid.

(3) Number of required installments; due dates.—For purposes of this subsection—

(A) Payable in 4 installments.—There shall be 4 required installments for each plan year.

(B)Time for payment of installments.—

In the case of the following required installments:	The due date is:
1st	April 15
2nd	July 15
3rd	October 15
4th	January 15 of the following year.

(4) Amount of required installment.—For purposes of this subsection—

(A) In general.—The amount of any required installment shall be the applicable percentage of the required annual payment.

(B) Required annual payment.—For purposes of subparagraph (A), the term "required annual payment" means the lesser of—

(i) 90 percent of the amount required to be contributed to or under the plan by the employer for the plan year under section 412 of the Internal Revenue Code of 1986 (without regard to any waiver under subsection (d) thereof), or

(ii) 100 percent of the amount so required for the preceding plan year.

Clause (ii) shall not apply if the preceding plan year was not a year of 12 months.

(C) Applicable percentage.—For purposes of subparagraph (A), the applicable percentage shall be determined in accordance with the following table:

For plan years beginning in:	The applicable percentage is:
1989	6.25
1990	12.50
1991	18.75
1992 and thereafter	25.00

(D) Special rules for unpredictable contingent event benefits.— In the case of a plan to which subsection (d) applies for any calendar year and which has any unpredictable contingent event benefit liabilities—

(i) Liabilities not taken into account.—Such liabilities shall not be taken into account in computing the required annual payment under subparagraph (B).

(ii) Increase in installments.—Each required installment shall be increased by the greatest of—

(I) the unfunded percentage of the amount of benefits described in subsection (d)(5)(A)(i) paid during the 3-month period preceding the month in which the due date for such installment occurs,

(II) 25 percent of the amount determined under subsection (d)(5)(A)(ii) for the plan year, or

(III) 25 percent of the amount determined under subsection (d)(5)(A)(iii) for the plan year.

(iii) Unfunded percentage.—For purposes of clause (ii)(I), the term "unfunded percentage" means the percentage determined under subsection (d)(5)(A)(i)(I) for the plan year.

(iv) Limitation on increase.—In no event shall the increases under clause (ii) exceed the amount necessary to increase the funded current liability percentage (within the meaning of subsection (d)(8)(B)) for the plan year to 100 percent.

(5) Liquidity requirement.—

(A) In general.—A plan to which this paragraph applies shall be treated as failing to pay the full amount of any required installment to the extent that the value of the liquid assets paid in such installment is less than the liquidity shortfall (whether or not such liquidity shortfall exceeds the amount of such installment required to be paid but for this paragraph).

(B) Plans to which paragraph applies.—This paragraph shall apply to a defined benefit plan (other than a multiemployer plan or a plan described in subsection (d)(6)(A)) which—

(i) is required to pay installments under this subsection for a plan year, and

(ii) has a liquidity shortfall for any quarter during such plan year.

(C) Period of underpayment.—For purposes of paragraph (1), any portion of an installment that is treated as not paid under subparagraph (A) shall continue to be treated as unpaid until the close of the quarter in which the due date for such installment occurs.

(D) Limitation on increase.—If the amount of any required installment is increased by reason of subparagraph (A), in no event shall such increase exceed the amount which, when added to prior installments for the plan year, is necessary to increase the funded current liability percentage (taking into account the expected increase in current liability due to benefits accruing during the plan year) to 100 percent.

(E) Definitions.—For purposes of this paragraph—

(i) Liquidity shortfall.—The term "liquidity shortfall" means, with respect to any required installment, an amount equal to the excess (as of the last day of the quarter for which such installment is made) of the base amount with respect to such quarter over the value (as of such last day) of the plan's liquid assets.

(ii) Base amount.—

(I) In general.—The term "base amount" means, with respect to any quarter, an amount equal to 3 times the sum of the adjusted disbursements from the plan for the 12 months ending on the last day of such quarter.

(II) Special rule.—If the amount determined under subclause (I) exceeds an amount equal to 2 times the sum of the adjusted disbursements from the plan for the 36 months ending on the last day of the quarter and an enrolled actuary certifies to the satisfaction of the Secretary of the Treasury that such excess is the result of nonrecurring circumstances, the base amount with respect to such quarter shall be determined without regard to amounts related to those nonrecurring circumstances.

(iii) Disbursements from the plan.—The term "disbursements from the plan" means all disbursements from the trust, including purchases of annuities, payments of single sums and other benefits, and administrative expenses.

(iv) Adjusted disbursements.—The term "adjusted disbursements" means disbursements from the plan reduced by the product of—

(I) the plan's funded current liability percentage (as defined in subsection (d)(8)) for the plan year, and

(II) the sum of the purchases of annuities, payments of single sums, and such other disbursements as the Secretary of the Treasury shall provide in regulations.

(v) Liquid assets.—The term "liquid assets" means cash, marketable securities and such other assets as specified by the Secretary of the Treasury in regulations.

(vi) Quarter.—The term "quarter" means, with respect to any required installment, the 3-month period preceding the month in which the due date for such installment occurs.

(F) Regulations.—The Secretary of the Treasury may prescribe such regulations as are necessary to carry out this paragraph.

(6) Fiscal years and short years.—

(A) Fiscal years.—In applying this subsection to a plan year beginning on any date other than January 1, there shall be substituted for the months specified in this subsection, the months which correspond thereto.

(B) Short plan year.—This section shall be applied to plan years of less than 12 months in accordance with regulations prescribed by the Secretary of the Treasury.

(7) Special rule for 2002.—In any case in which the interest rate used to determine current liability is determined under subsection (d)(7)(C)(i)(III), for purposes of applying paragraphs (1) and (4)(B)(ii) for plan years beginning in 2002, the current liability for the preceding plan year shall be redetermined using 120 percent as the specified percentage determined under subsection (d)(7)(C)(i)(II).

(f) Imposition of Lien Where Failure to Make Required Contributions.—

(1) In general.—In the case of a plan covered under section 4021 of this Act, if—

(A) any person fails to make a required installment under subsection (e) or any other payment required under this section before the due date for such installment or other payment, and

(B) the unpaid balance of such installment or other payment (including interest), when added to the aggregate unpaid balance of all preceding such installments or other payments for which payment was not made before the due date (including interest), exceeds $1,000,000,

then there shall be a lien in favor of the plan in the amount determined under paragraph (3) upon all property and rights to property, whether real or personal, belonging to such person and any other person who is a member of the same controlled group of which such person is a member.

(2) Plans to which subsection applies.—This subsection shall apply to a defined benefit plan (other than a multiemployer plan) for any plan year for which the funded current liability percentage (within the meaning of subsection (d)(8)(B)) of such plan is less than 100 percent.

(3) Amount of lien.—For purposes of paragraph (1), the amount of the lien shall be equal to the aggregate unpaid balance of required installments and other payments required under this section (including interest)—

(A) for plan years beginning after 1987, and

(B) for which payment has not been made before the due date.

(4) Notice of failure; lien.—

(A) Notice of failure.—A person committing a failure described in paragraph (1) shall notify the Pension Benefit Guaranty Corporation of such failure within 10 days of the due date for the required installment or other payment.

(B) Period of lien.—The lien imposed by paragraph (1) shall arise on the due date for the required installment or other payment and shall continue until the last day of the first plan year in which the plan ceases to be described in paragraph

ERISA Sec. 302 [Repealed]

(1)(B). Such lien shall continue to run without regard to whether such plan continues to be described in paragraph (2) during the period referred to in the preceding sentence.

(C) Certain rules to apply.—Any amount with respect to which a lien is imposed under paragraph (1) shall be treated as taxes due and owing the United States and rules similar to the rules of subsections (c), (d), and (e) of section 4068 shall apply with respect to a lien imposed by subsection (a) and the amount with respect to such lien.

(5) Enforcement.—Any lien created under paragraph (1) may be perfected and enforced only by the Pension Benefit Guaranty Corporation, or at the direction of the Pension Benefit Guaranty Corporation, by the contributing sponsor (or any member of the controlled group of the contributing sponsor).

(6) Definitions.—For purposes of this subsection—

(A) Due date; required installment.—The terms "due date," and "required installment" have the meanings given such terms by subsection (e), except that in the case of a payment other than a required installment, the due date shall be the date such payment is required to be made under this section.

(B) Controlled group.—The term "controlled group" means any group treated as a single employer under sub-sections (b), (c), (m), and (o) of section 414 of the Internal Revenue Code of 1986.

(g) Qualified Transfers to Health Benefit Accounts.—For purposes of this section, in the case of a qualified transfer (as defined in section 420 of the Internal Revenue Code of 1986)—

(1) any assets transferred in a plan year on or before the valuation date for such year (and any income allocable thereto) shall, for purposes of subsection (c)(7), be treated as assets in the plan as of the valuation date for such year, and

(2) the plan shall be treated as having a net experience loss under subsection (b)(2)(B)(iv) in an amount equal to the amount of such transfer (reduced by any amounts transferred back to the plan under section 420(c)(1)(B) of such Code) and for which amortization charges begin for the first plan year after the plan year in which such transfer occurs, except that such subsection shall be applied to such amount by substituting "10 plan years" for "5 plan years".

(h) Cross Reference.—For alternative amortization method for certain multiemployer plans see section 1013(d) of this Act.

Amendments to ERISA §302 [Repealed.]

Preservation of Access to Care for Medicare Beneficiaries and Pension Relief Act of 2010 (Pub. L. No. 111-192), as follows:

• **Other Provision.** Act §202(a) provided (effective as if included in the Pension Protection Act (Pub. L. No. 109-280)):

(a) In General.—Title I of the Pension Protection Act of 2006 is amended by redesignating section 107 as section 108 and by inserting the following after section 106:

SEC. 107. APPLICATION OF EXTENDED AMORTIZATION PERIODS TO PLANS WITH DELAYED EFFECTIVE DATE.

(a) In General.—If the plan sponsor of a plan to which section 104, 105, or 106 of this Act applies elects to have this section apply for any eligible plan year (in this section referred to as an "election year"), section 302 of the Employee Retirement Income Security Act of 1974 and section 412 of the Internal Revenue Code of 1986 (as in effect before the amendments made by this subtitle and subtitle B) shall apply to such year in the manner described in subsection (b) or (c), whichever is specified in the election. All references in this section to "such Act" or "such Code" shall be to such Act or such Code as in effect before the amendments made by this subtitle and subtitle B.

(b) Application of 2 and 7 Rule.—In the case of an election year to which this subsection applies—

(1) 2-year lookback for determining deficit reduction contributions for certain plans.—For purposes of applying section 302(d)(9) of such Act and section 412(*l*)(9) of such Code, the funded current liability percentage (as defined in subparagraph (C) thereof) for such plan for such plan year shall be such funded current liability percentage of such plan for the second plan year preceding the first election year of such plan.

(2) Calculation of deficit reduction contribution.—For purposes of applying section 302(d) of such Act and section 412(*l*) of such Code to a plan to which such sections apply (after taking into account paragraph (1))—

(A) in the case of the increased unfunded new liability of the plan, the applicable percentage described in section 302(d)(4)(C) of such Act and section 412(*l*)(4)(C) of such Code shall be the third segment rate described in sections 104(b), 105(b), and 106(b) of this Act, and

(B) in the case of the excess of the unfunded new liability over the increased unfunded new liability, such applicable percentage shall be determined without regard to this section.

(c) Application of 15-year Amortization.—In the case of an election year to which this subsection applies, for purposes of applying section 302(d) of such Act and section 412(*l*) of such Code—

(1) in the case of the increased unfunded new liability of the plan, the applicable percentage described in section 302(d)(4)(C) of such Act and section 412(*l*)(4)(C) of such Code for any pre-effective date plan year beginning with or after the first election year shall be the ratio of—

(A) the annual installments payable in each year if the increased unfunded new liability for such plan year were amortized over 15 years, using an interest rate equal to the third segment rate described in sections 104(b), 105(b), and 106(b) of this Act, to

(B) the increased unfunded new liability for such plan year, and

(2) in the case of the excess of the unfunded new liability over the increased unfunded new liability, such applicable percentage shall be determined without regard to this section.

(d) Election.—

(1) In general.—The plan sponsor of a plan may elect to have this section apply to not more than 2 eligible plan years with respect to the plan, except that in the case of a plan to which section 106 of this Act applies, the plan sponsor may only elect to have this section apply to 1 eligible plan year.

(2) Amortization schedule.—Such election shall specify whether the rules under subsection (b) or (c) shall apply to an election year, except that if a plan sponsor elects to have this section apply to 2 eligible plan years, the plan sponsor must elect the same rule for both years.

(3) Other rules.—Such election shall be made at such time, and in such form and manner, as shall be prescribed by the Secretary of the Treasury, and may be revoked only with the consent of the Secretary of the Treasury.

(e) Definitions.—For purposes of this section—

(1) Eligible plan year.—For purposes of this subparagraph, the term "eligible plan year" means any plan year beginning in 2008, 2009, 2010, or 2011, except that a plan year beginning in 2008 shall only be treated as an eligible plan year if the due date for the payment of the minimum required contribution for such plan year occurs on or after the date of the enactment of this clause.

(2) Pre-effective date plan year.—The term "pre-effective date plan year" means, with respect to a plan, any plan year prior to the first year in which the amendments made by this subtitle and subtitle B apply to the plan.

(3) Increased unfunded new liability.—The term "increased unfunded new liability" means, with respect to a year, the excess (if any) of the unfunded new liability over the amount of unfunded new liability determined as if the value of the plan's assets determined under subsection 302(c)(2) of such Act and section 412(c)(2) of such Code equaled the product of the current liability of the plan for the year multiplied by the funded current liability percentage (as defined in section 302(d)(8)(B) of such Act and 412(*l*)(8)(B) of such Code) of the plan for the second plan year preceding the first election year of such plan.

(4) Other definitions.—The terms "unfunded new liability" and "current liability" shall have the meanings set forth in section 302(d) of such Act and section 412(*l*) of such Code.

Pension Protection Act of 2006 (Pub. L. No. 109-280), as follows:

● ERISA §302 was repealed by Act §101(a). Eff. for plan years beginning after 2007.

● ERISA §302(b)(5)(B)(ii)(II), was amended by Act §301(a)(1), which substituted "2005, 2006, and 2007" for "and 2005" in the heading, and "2008" for "2006" in the text, effective Aug. 17, 2006.

● ERISA §302(d)(7)(C)(i)(IV), was amended by Act §301(a)(2), which substituted "2005, 2006, and 2007" for "and 2005" in the heading and ", 2005, 2006, or 2007" for "and 2005" in the text, effective Aug. 17, 2006.

● **Other Provision—Effective Date.** Act §104 (as amended by Pub. L. No. 111-192, §202(b)) provides:

SEC. 104. SPECIAL RULES FOR MULTIPLE EMPLOYER PLANS OF CERTAIN COOPERATIVES.

    (a) General Rule.—Except as provided in this section, if a plan in existence on July 26, 2005, was an eligible cooperative plan or an eligible charity plan for its plan year which includes such date, the amendments made by this subtitle and subtitle B shall not apply to plan years beginning before the earlier of—

        (1) the first plan year for which the plan ceases to be an eligible cooperative plan or an eligible charity plan, or

        (2) January 1, 2017.

    (b) Interest Rate.—In applying section 302(b)(5)(B) of the Employee Retirement Income Security Act of 1974 and section 412(b)(5)(B) of the Internal Revenue Code of 1986 (as in effect before the amendments made by this subtitle and subtitle B) to an eligible cooperative plan or an eligible charity plan for plan years beginning after December 31, 2007, and before the first plan year to which such amendments apply, the third segment rate determined under section 303(h)(2)(C)(iii) of such Act and section 430(h)(2)(C)(iii) of such Code (as added by such amendments) shall be used in lieu of the interest rate otherwise used.

    (c) Eligible Cooperative Plan Defined.—For purposes of this section, a plan shall be treated as an eligible cooperative plan for a plan year if the plan is maintained by more than 1 employer and at least 85 percent of the employers are—

        (1) rural cooperatives (as defined in section 401(k)(7)(B) of such Code without regard to clause (iv) thereof), or

        (2) organizations which are—

            (A) cooperative organizations described in section 1381(a) of such Code which are more than 50-percent owned by agricultural producers or by cooperatives owned by agricultural producers, or

            (B) more than 50-percent owned, or controlled by, one or more cooperative organizations described in subparagraph (A).

A plan shall also be treated as an eligible cooperative plan for any plan year for which it is described in section 210(a) of the Employee Retirement Income Security Act of 1974 and is maintained by a rural telephone cooperative association described in section 3(40)(B)(v) of such Act.

    (d) Eligible Charity Plan Defined.—For purposes of this section, a plan shall be treated as an eligible charity plan for a plan year if the plan is maintained by more than one employer determined without regard to section 414(c) of the Internal Revenue Code) and 100 percent of the employers are described in section 501(c)(3) of such Code.

Note: Act §104, as amended by Pub. L. No. 111-192, §202(b), is effective according to Pub. L. No. 111-192, §202(c):

    (c) Effective Date.—

        (1) In general.—The amendment made by subsection (a) shall take effect as if included in the Pension Protection Act of 2006.

        (2) Eligible charity plan.—The amendments made by subsection (b) shall apply to plan years beginning after December 31, 2007, except that a plan sponsor may elect to apply such amendments to plan years beginning after December 31, 2008. Any such election shall be made at such time, and in such form and manner, as shall be prescribed by the Secretary of the Treasury, and may be revoked only with the consent of the Secretary of the Treasury.

Gulf Opportunity Zone Act of 2005 (Pub. L. No. 109-135), as follows:

● ERISA §302(e)(4)(B)(i) was amended by Act §412(x)(2) by substituting "subsection (d)" for "subsection (c)". Eff. Dec. 21, 2005.

Pension Funding Equity Act of 2004 (Pub. L. No. 108-218), as follows:

● ERISA §302(b)(5)(B)(ii)(I) was amended by Act §101(a)(1)(C) by inserting "or (III)" after "subclause (II)". Eff. for plan years after 2003.

● ERISA §302(b)(5)(B)(ii)(II) was redesignated as (III) and new subcl. (II) was added by Act §101(a)(1)(A). Eff. for plan years after 2003.

● ERISA §302(b)(5)(B)(ii)(III), as redesignated, was amended by Act §101(a)(1)(A), (B) by inserting "or (II)" after "subclause (I)" the first place appearing, and substituting "such subclause" for "subclause (I)" the second place appearing. Eff. for plan years after 2003.

● ERISA §302(b)(7)(F) was added by Act §104(a)(1). Eff. for plan years after 2003.

● ERISA §302(d)(7)(C)(i)(IV) was added by Act §101(a)(2). Eff. for plan years after 2003.

● ERISA §302(d)(12) was added by Act §102(a). Eff. for plan years after 2003.

● ERISA §302(e)(7) was amended by Act §101(a)(3) by amending the heading and text of para. (7). Prior to amendment, text consisted of subparas. (A) and (B) relating to special rules for 2002 and 2004, respectively. Eff. for plan years after 2003.

Job Creation and Worker Assistance Act of 2002 (Pub. L. No. 107-147), as follows:

● ERISA §302(c)(9)(B)(ii) was amended by Act §411(v)(2)(A) by substituting "100 percent" for "125 percent". Eff. after Dec. 31, 2001, and before Dec. 31, 2010.

● ERISA §302(c)(9)(B)(iv) was added by Act §411(v)(2)(B). Eff. after Dec. 31, 2001, and before Dec. 31, 2010.

● ERISA §302(d)(7)(C)(i)(III) was added by Act §405(b)(1). Eff. after Dec. 31, 2001, and before Dec. 31, 2010.

● ERISA §302(e)(7) was added by Act §405(b)(2). Eff. after Dec. 31, 2001, and before Dec. 31, 2010.

Economic Growth and Tax Relief Reconciliation Act of 2001 (Pub. L. No. 107-16), as follows:

● ERISA §302(c)(7)(A)(i)(I) was amended by Act §§651(b)(1), 901 by temporarily substituting "in the case of plan years beginning before January 1, 2004, the applicable percentage" for "the applicable percentage". Eff. after Dec. 31, 2001, and before Dec. 31, 2010. See note below on sunset rule.

● ERISA §302(c)(7)(F) was amended by Act §§651(b)(2), 901 by temporarily reenacting heading without change and amending text of subpara. (F) by substituting applicable percentages 165 and 170 in the case of any plan year beginning in calendar year 2002 and 2003, respectively, for applicable percentages 155, 160, 165, and 170 in the case of any plan year beginning in 1999 or 2000, 2001 or 2002, 2003 or 2004, and 2005 and succeeding years, respectively. Eff. after Dec. 31, 2001, and before Dec. 31, 2010. See note below on sunset rule.

● ERISA §302(c)(9) was amended by Act §§661(b), 901 by temporarily designating existing provisions as subpara. (A) and adding subpara. (B). Eff. after Dec. 31, 2001, and before Dec. 31, 2010. See note below on sunset rule.

● **Sunset Rule.** To comply with the Congressional Budget Act of 1974, §901 of Pub. L. No. 107-16 provides that all provisions of, and amendments made by, the Act will not apply to taxable, plan, or limitation years beginning after December 31, 2010. *But see* Pension Protection Act of 2006 (Pub. L. No. 109-280), §811 (sunset rule of Pub. L. No. 107-16 does not apply to the provisions of, and the amendments made by, Pub. L. No. 107-16, §§601-666 (relating to modifications to pensions and retirement income arrangement provisions)).

Taxpayer Relief Act of 1997 (Pub. L. No. 105-34), as follows:

● ERISA §302(b)(2)(E) was added by Act §1521(c)(2). Eff. for plan years after Dec. 31, 1998.

● ERISA §302(c)(7)(A)(i)(I) was amended by Act §1521(b)(A) by substituting "the applicable percentage" for "150 percent". Eff. for plan years after Dec. 31, 1998.

● ERISA §302(c)(7)(D) was amended by Act §1521(c)(3)(B) by inserting "and" at end of cl. (i), substituting a period for "and" at end of cl. (ii), and striking cl. (iii) which read: "the treatment under this section of contributions which would be required to be made under the plan but for the provisions of subparagraph (A)(i)(I)." Eff. for plan years after Dec. 31, 1998.

● ERISA §302(c)(7)(F) was added by Act §1521(b)(B). Eff. for plan years after Dec. 31, 1998.

● ERISA §302(e)(5)(E)(ii)(II) was amended by Act §1604(b)(2)(B) by substituting "subclause (I)" for "clause (i)". Eff. for plan years after Dec. 31, 1994.

Retirement Protection Act of 1994 (Pub. L. No. 103-465), as follows:

● ERISA §302(c)(5) was amended by Act §762(a) by designating existing provisions as subpara. (A), inserting heading, and adding subpara. (B). Eff. after 1994.

● ERISA §302(c)(7)(A)(i) was amended by Act §761(a)(10)(A) by inserting "(including the expected increase in current liability due to benefits accruing during the plan year)" after "current liability". Eff. after 1994.

● ERISA §302(c)(7)(B) was amended by Act §761(a)(10)(C) by amending heading and text of subpara. (B). Eff. after 1994. ERISA §302(c)(7)(B) prior to amendment:

> (B) For purposes of subparagraphs (A) and (D), the term "current liability" has the meaning given such term by subsection (d)(7) of this section (without regard to subparagraph (D) thereof).

● ERISA §302(c)(7)(E) was added by Act §761(a)(10)(B). Eff. after 1994.

● ERISA §302(c)(12) was added by Act §763(a). Eff. after 1994.

● ERISA §302(d)(1) was amended by Act §761(a)(1)(A), (2)(B) by substituting "to which this subsection applies under paragraph (9)" for "which has an unfunded current liability" in introductory provisions and substituting last sentence for one which read "Such increase shall not exceed the amount necessary to increase the funded current liability percentage to 100 percent." Eff. after 1994.

● ERISA §302(d)(1)(A)(ii) was amended by Act §761(a)(2)(A). Eff. after 1994. ERISA §302(d)(1)(A)(ii) prior to amendment:

> (ii) the sum of the charges for such plan year under subparagraphs (B) (other than clauses (iv) and (v) thereof), (C), and (D) of subsection (b)(2) of this section, reduced by the sum of the credits for such plan year under subparagraph (B)(i) of subsection (b)(3) of this section, plus.

● ERISA §302(d)(2)(C)–(D) were added by Act §761(a)(3), (7)(B)(i). Eff. after 1994.

● ERISA §302(d)(3)(D), (E) were added by Act §761(a)(4)(A). Eff. after 1994.

● ERISA §302(d)(4)(B)(i) was amended by Act §761(a)(4)(B), (7)(B)(iii) by inserting ", the additional unfunded old liability, the unamortized portion of each unfunded mortality increase," after "the unfunded old liability". Eff. after 1994.

● ERISA §302(d)(4)(C) was amended by Act §761(a)(5) by substituting ".40" for ".25" in cl. (i) and "60" for "35" in cl. (ii). Eff. after 1994.

● ERISA §302(d)(5)(A) was amended by Act §761(a)(6)(A)(i) by substituting "greatest of" for "greater of" in introductory provisions. Eff. after 1994.

● ERISA §302(d)(5)(A)(iii) was added by Act §761(a)(6)(A)(ii)–(iv). Eff. after 1994.

● ERISA §302(d)(5)(E) was added by Act §761(a)(6)(B). Eff. after 1994.

● ERISA §302(d)(7)(C) was amended by Act §761(a)(7)(A) by amending heading and text of subpara. (C). Eff. after 1994. ERISA §302(d)(7)(C) prior to amendment:

> (C) The rate of interest used to determine current liability shall be the rate of interest used under subsection (b)(5) of this section.

● ERISA §302(d)(9)–(11) were added by Act §761(a)(1)(B), (7)(B)(ii), (8). Eff. after 1994.

● ERISA §302(e)(1) was amended by Act §764(a), in introductory provisions, by inserting "which has a funded current liability percentage (as defined in subsection (d)(8) of this section) for the preceding plan year of less than 100 percent" before "fails to pay" and substituting "the plan year" for "any plan year". Eff. after 1994.

● ERISA §302(e)(4)(D)(ii) was amended by Act §761(a)(6)(C)(i) by substituting "greatest of" for "greater of" in introductory provisions. Eff. after 1994.

● ERISA §302(e)(4)(D)(ii)(III) was added by Act §761(a)(6)(C)(ii)–(iv). Eff. after 1994.

● ERISA §302(e)(5)–(6) were amended by Act §761(a)(9)(A) by redesignating former para. (5) as (6) and adding new para. (5). Eff. after 1994.

● ERISA §302(f)(1) was amended by Act §768(b)(1) by substituting "covered under section 4021 of this title" for "to which this section applies" in introductory provisions. Eff. after 1994.

● ERISA §302(f)(3) was amended by Act §768(b)(2) by amending heading and text of para. (3). Eff. after 1994. ERISA §302(f)(3) prior to amendment:

> (3) For purposes of paragraph (1), the amount of the lien shall be equal to the lesser of—
>
> (A) the amount by which the unpaid balances described in paragraph (1)(B)(including interest) exceed $1,000,000, or
>
> (B) the aggregate unpaid balance of required installments and other payments required under this section (including interest)—
>
> (i) for plan years beginning after 1987, and
>
> (ii) for which payment has not been made before the due date.

● ERISA §302(f)(4)(B) was amended by Act §768(b)(3) by striking "60th day following the" before "due date". Eff. after 1994.

Omnibus Budget Reconciliation Act of 1990 (Pub. L. No. 101-508), as follows:

● ERISA §302(g)–(h) were amended by Act §12012(c) by adding subsec. (g) and redesignating former subsec. (g) as (h). Eff. Nov. 5, 1990.

Omnibus Budget Reconciliation Act of 1989 (Pub. L. No. 101-239), as follows:

● ERISA §302(b)(3)(B)(iii) was amended by Act §7894(d)(2) by substituting a comma for period at end. Eff. as if included in Pub. L. No. 93-406.

● ERISA §302(b)(5) was amended by Act §7881(d)(2)(B) by striking introductory provision which read: "For purposes of determining a plan's current liability and for purposes of determining a plan's required contribution under section 412(l) of title 26 for any plan year—". Eff. as if included in Pub. L. No. 100-203.

● ERISA §302(b)(5)(B) was amended by Act §7881(d)(2)(A) by inserting introductory provision "For purposes of determining a plan's current liability and for purposes of determining a plan's required contribution under subsection (d) of this section for any plan year—". Eff. as if included in Pub. L. No. 100-203.

● ERISA §302(b)(5)(B)(ii)(I) was amended by Act §7881(d)(2)(C) by substituting "the weighted average of the rates" for "average rate". Eff. as if included in Pub. L. No. 100-203.

● ERISA §302(b)(5)(B)(iii) was amended by Act §7881(d)(1)(B) by striking "for purposes of this section and for purposes of determining current liability," before "the interest rate" in introductory provisions. Eff. as if included in Pub. L. No. 100-203.

● ERISA §302(b)(7)(B), (E) were amended by Act §7891(a)(1) by substituting "Internal Revenue Code of 1986" for "Internal Revenue Code of 1954", which for purposes of codification was translated as "title 26". Eff. as if originally included in Pub. L. No. 99-514.

● ERISA §302(c)(3) was amended by Act §7881(d)(4) by realigning margins. Eff. as if originally included in Pub. L. No. 100-203.

● ERISA §302(c)(4)(B) was amended by Act §7891(a)(1) by substituting "Internal Revenue Code of 1986" for "Internal Revenue Code of 1954", which for purposes of codification was translated as "title 26". Eff. as if originally included in Pub. L. No. 99-514.

● ERISA §302(c)(6) was amended by Act §7894(d)(5) by substituting "section 305 of this title" for "subsection (g) of this section". Eff. as if originally included in Pub. L. No. 93-406.

● ERISA §302(c)(7) was amended by Act §7892(b) by realigning margins. Eff. as if originally included in Pub. L. No. 100-203.

● ERISA §302(c)(9) was amended by Act §7881(a)(6)(B) by substituting "every year" for "every 3 years". Eff. as if originally included in Pub. L. No. 100-203.

● ERISA §302(c)(10)(A) was amended by Act §7881(b)(1)(B) by inserting "defined benefit" before "plan other". Eff. as if originally included in Pub. L. No. 100-203.

● ERISA §302(c)(10)(B) was amended by Act §7881(b)(2)(B) by substituting "plan not described in subparagraph (A)" for "multiemployer plan". Eff. as if originally included in Pub. L. No. 100-203.

- ERISA §302(d)(3)(C)(ii)(II) was amended by Act §7881(a)(1)(B) by inserting "(but not below zero)" after "reducing". Eff. as if originally included in Pub. L. No. 100-203.
- ERISA §302(d)(4)(B)(i), was amended by Act §7881(a)(2)(B) by inserting "and the unamortized portion of the unfunded existing benefit increase liability" after "liability". Eff. as if originally included in Pub. L. No. 100-203.
- ERISA §302(d)(5)(C) was amended by Act §7881(a)(3)(B) by substituting "the first plan year beginning after December 31, 1988" for "October 17, 1987". Eff. as if originally included in Pub. L. No. 100-203.
- ERISA §302(d)(7)(D)(iii)(III) was added by Act §7881(a)(4)(B)(i). Eff. as if originally included in Pub. L. No. 100-203.
- ERISA §302(d)(7)(D)(iv) was added by Act §7881(a)(4)(B)(ii). Eff. as if originally included in Pub. L. No. 100-203.
- ERISA §302(d)(8)(A)(ii) was amended by Act §7881(a)(5)(B)(i) by striking "reduced by any credit balance in the funding standard account" after "this section". Eff. as if originally included in Pub. L. No. 100-203.
- ERISA §302(d)(8)(E) was added by Act §7881(a)(5)(B)(ii). Eff. as if originally included in Pub. L. No. 100-203.
- ERISA §302(e)(1) was amended by Act §7881(b)(3)(B) by inserting "defined benefit" before "plan (other". Eff. as if originally included in Pub. L. No. 100-203.
- ERISA §302(e)(1)(B) was amended by Act §7881(b)(6)(B)(i). Eff. as if originally included in Pub. L. No. 100-203. ERISA §302(e)(1)(B) prior to amendment:

    (B) the rate under subsection (b)(5) of this section.
- ERISA §302(e)(4)(D) was amended by Act §7881(b)(4)(B). Eff. as if originally included in Pub. L. No. 100-203. ERISA §302(e)(4)(D) prior to amendment:

    (D) In the case of a plan with any unpredictable contingent event benefit liabilities—

    (i) such liabilities shall not be taken into account in computing the required annual payment under subparagraph (B), and

    (ii) each required installment shall be increased by the greater of—

    (I) the amount of benefits described in subsection (d)(5)(A)(i) of this section paid during the 3-month period preceding the month in which the due date for such installment occurs, or

    (II) 25 percent of the amount determined under subsection (d)(5)(A)(ii) of this section for the plan year.

Technical and Miscellaneous Revenue Act of 1988 (Pub. L. No. 100-647), as follows:

- ERISA §302(d)(3)(C) was amended by Act §2005(a)(2)(B) by substituting "October 29" for "October 17" in cl. (i) and "October 28" for "October 16" in cl. (iii). Eff. as if originally included in Pub. L. No. 100-203.
- ERISA §302(d)(3)(B) was to be amended by Act §2005(d)(2) by striking "October 17, 1987" in cl. (i) and inserting in lieu thereof "October 29, 1987", and by striking out "October 16, 1987" in cl. (iii) and inserting in lieu thereof "October 28, 1987", but the amendment could not be executed because the section did not contain cls. (i) and (iii). Eff. as if originally included in Pub. L. No. 100-203.

Omnibus Budget Reconciliation Act of 1987 (Pub. L. No. 100-203), as follows:

- ERISA §302(b)(2)(B)(iv), (C), (3)(B)(ii) were amended by Act §9307(a)(2)(A) by substituting "5 plan years (15 plan years in the case of a multiemployer plan)" for "15 plan years". Eff. after 1987.
- ERISA §302(b)(2)(B)(v), (3)(B)(iii) were amended by Act §9307(a)(2)(B) by substituting "10 plan years (30 plan years in the case of a multiemployer plan)" for "30 plan years". Eff. after 1987.
- ERISA §302(b)(5) was amended by Act §9307(e)(2). Eff. after 1987. ERISA §302(b)(5) prior to amendment:

    (5) The funding standard account (and items therein) shall be charged or credited (as determined under regulations prescribed by the Secretary of the Treasury) with interest at the

appropriate rate consistent with the rate or rates of interest used under the plan to determine costs.

- ERISA §302(c)(2)(B) was amended by Act §9303(d)(2) by inserting at end "In the case of a plan other than a multiemployer plan, this subparagraph shall not apply, but the Secretary of the Treasury may by regulations provide that the value of any dedicated bond portfolio of such plan shall be determined by using the interest rate under subsection (b)(5) of this section." Eff. after 1988.
- ERISA §302(c)(3) was amended by Act §9307(b)(2). Eff. after 1987. ERISA §302(c)(3) prior to amendment:

    (3) For purposes of this part, all costs, liabilities, rates of interest, and other factors under the plan shall be determined on the basis of actuarial assumptions and methods which, in the aggregate, are reasonable (taking into account the experience of the plan and reasonable expectations) and which, in combination, offer the actuary's best estimate of anticipated experience under the plan.
- ERISA §302(c)(7) was amended by Act §9301(b). Eff. after 1987. ERISA §302(c)(7) prior to amendment:

    (7) For purposes of paragraph (6), the term "full funding limitation" means the excess (if any) of—

    (A) the accrued liability (including normal cost) under the plan (determined under the entry age normal funding method if such accrued liability cannot be directly calculated under the funding method used for the plan), over

    (B) the lesser of the fair market value of the plan's assets or the value of such assets determined under paragraph (2).
- ERISA §302(c)(10) was amended by Act §9304(a)(2). Eff. after 1987. ERISA §302(c)(10) prior to amendment:

    (10) For purposes of this part, any contributions for a plan year made by an employer after the last day of such plan year, but not later than 2 months after such day, shall be deemed to have been made on such last day. For purposes of this paragraph, such 2 month period may be extended for not more than 6 months under regulations prescribed by the Secretary of the Treasury.
- ERISA §302(c)(11) was added by Act §9305(b)(2). Eff. after 1987.
- ERISA §302(d) was redesignated as subsec. (e) by Act §9303(b)(1). Eff. after 1988.
- ERISA §302(e) was redesignated as subsec. (f) and new subsec. (e) was added by Act §9304(b)(2). Eff. after 1987.
- ERISA §302(f) was redesignated as subsec. (g) and new subsec. (F) was added by Act §9304(e)(2). Eff. after 1987.

Multiemployer Pension Plan Amendments Act of 1980 (Pub. L. No. 96-364), as follows:

- ERISA §302(a)(3) was added by Act §304(b)(3). Eff. Sept. 26, 1980.
- ERISA §302(b)(2) was amended by Act §304(b)(1) by striking from para. (B)(ii) and (iii) "(40 plan years in the case of a multiemployer plan)" after "30 plan years"; and, from para. (B)(iv), "(20 plan years in the case of a multiemployer plan)" after "15 plan years". Eff. Sept. 26, 1980.
- ERISA §302(b)(3) was amended by Act §304(b)(1) by striking from para. (B)(i) "(40 plan years in the case of a multiemployer plan)" after "30 plan years"; and, from para. (B)(ii) "(20 plan years in the case of a multiemployer plan)" after "15 plan years". Eff. Sept. 26, 1980.
- ERISA §302(b)(6)–(7) were added by Act §304(b)(2). Eff. Sept. 26, 1980.

SEC. 303. MINIMUM FUNDING STANDARDS FOR SINGLE-EMPLOYER DEFINED BENEFIT PENSION PLANS.

(a) Minimum Required Contribution.—For purposes of this section and section 302(a)(2)(A), except as provided in subsection (f), the term "minimum required contribution" means, with respect to any plan year of a single-employer plan—

(1) in any case in which the value of plan assets of the plan (as reduced under subsection (f)(4)(B)) is less than the funding target of the plan for the plan year, the sum of—

(A) the target normal cost of the plan for the plan year,

(B) the shortfall amortization charge (if any) for the plan for the plan year determined under subsection (c), and

(C) the waiver amortization charge (if any) for the plan for the plan year as determined under subsection (e); or

(2) in any case in which the value of plan assets of the plan (as reduced under subsection (f)(4)(B)) equals or exceeds the funding target of the plan for the plan year, the target normal cost of the plan for the plan year reduced (but not below zero) by such excess.

(b) Target Normal Cost.—For purposes of this section:

(1) In general.—Except as provided in subsection (i)(2) with respect to plans in at-risk status, the term "target normal cost" means, for any plan year, the excess of—

(A) the sum of—

(i) the present value of all benefits which are expected to accrue or to be earned under the plan during the plan year, plus

(ii) the amount of plan-related expenses expected to be paid from plan assets during the plan year, over

(B) the amount of mandatory employee contributions expected to be made during the plan year.

(2) Special rule for increase in compensation.— For purposes of this subsection, if any benefit attributable to services performed in a preceding plan year is increased by reason of any increase in compensation during the current plan year, the increase in such benefit shall be treated as having accrued during the current plan year.

Editor's Note

ERISA §303(c)(1), below, was amended by Pub. L. No. 111-192, §201(a)(3)(A), effective for plan years beginning after December 31, 2007.

(c) Shortfall Amortization Charge.—

(1) In general.—For purposes of this section, the shortfall amortization charge for a plan for any plan year is the aggregate total (not less than zero) of any shortfall amortization base which has not been fully amortized under this subsection.

(2) Shortfall amortization installment.—For purposes of paragraph (1)—

(A) Determination.—The shortfall amortization installments are the amounts necessary to amortize the shortfall amortization base of the plan for any plan year in level annual installments over the 7-plan-year period beginning with such plan year.

(B) Shortfall installment.—The shortfall amortization installment for any plan year in the 7-plan-year period under subparagraph (A) with respect to any shortfall amortization base is the annual installment determined under subparagraph (A) for that year for that base.

(C) Segment rates.—In determining any shortfall amortization installment under this paragraph, the plan sponsor shall use the segment rates determined under subparagraph (C) of subsection (h)(2), applied under rules similar to the rules of subparagraph (B) of subsection (h)(2).

Editor's Note

ERISA §303(c)(2)(D), below, was added by Pub. L. No. 111-192, §201(a), effective for plan years beginning after December 31, 2007.

(D) Special election for eligible plan years.—

(i) In general.—If a plan sponsor elects to apply this subparagraph with respect to the shortfall amortization base of a plan for any eligible plan year (in this subparagraph and paragraph (7) referred to as an "election year"), then, notwithstanding subparagraphs (A) and (B)—

(I) the shortfall amortization installments with respect to such base shall be determined under clause (ii) or (iii), whichever is specified in the election, and

(II) the shortfall amortization installment for any plan year in the 9-plan-year period described in clause (ii) or the 15-plan-year period described in clause (iii), respectively, with respect to such shortfall amortization base is the annual installment determined under the applicable clause for that year for that base.

(ii) 2 plus 7 amortization schedule.—The shortfall amortization installments determined under this clause are—

(I) in the case of the first 2 plan years in the 9-plan-year period beginning with the election year, interest on the shortfall amortization base of the plan for the election year (determined using the effective interest rate for the plan for the election year), and

(II) in the case of the last 7 plan years in such 9-plan-year period, the amounts necessary to amortize the remaining balance of the shortfall amortization base of the plan for the election year in level annual installments over such last 7 plan years (using the segment rates under subparagraph (C) for the election year).

(iii) 15-year amortization.—The shortfall amortization installments determined under this subparagraph are the amounts necessary to amortize the shortfall amortization base of the plan for the election year in level annual installments over the 15-plan-year period beginning with the election year (using the segment rates under subparagraph (C) for the election year).

(iv) Election.—

(I) In general.—The plan sponsor of a plan may elect to have this subparagraph apply to not more than 2 eligible plan years with respect to the plan, except that in the case of a plan described in section 106 of the Pension Protection Act of 2006, the plan sponsor may only elect to have this subparagraph apply to a plan year beginning in 2011.

(II) Amortization schedule.—Such election shall specify whether the amortization schedule under clause (ii) or (iii) shall apply to an election year, except that if a plan sponsor elects to have this subparagraph apply to 2 eligible plan years, the plan sponsor must elect the same schedule for both years.

(III) Other rules.—Such election shall be made at such time, and in such form and manner, as shall be prescribed by the Secretary of the Treasury, and may be revoked only with the consent of the Secretary of the Treasury. The Secretary of the Treasury shall, before granting a revocation request, provide the Pension Benefit Guaranty Corporation an opportunity to comment on the conditions applicable to the treatment of any portion of the election year shortfall amortization base that remains unamortized as of the revocation date.

(v) Eligible plan year. —For purposes of this subparagraph, the term "eligible plan year" means any plan year beginning in 2008, 2009, 2010, or 2011, except that a plan year shall only be treated as an eligible plan year if the due date under subsection (j)(1) for the payment of the minimum required contribution for such plan year occurs on or after the date of the enactment of this subparagraph.

(vi) Reporting.—A plan sponsor of a plan who makes an election under clause (i) shall—

(I) give notice of the election to participants and beneficiaries of the plan, and

(II) inform the Pension Benefit Guaranty Corporation of such election in such form and manner as the Director of the Pension Benefit Guaranty Corporation may prescribe.

(vii) Increases in required installments in certain cases.—For increases in required contributions in cases of excess compensation or extraordinary dividends or stock redemptions, see paragraph (7).

(3) Shortfall amortization base.—For purposes of this section, the shortfall amortization base of a plan for a plan year is—

(A) the funding shortfall of such plan for such plan year, minus

(B) the present value (determined using the segment rates determined under subparagraph (C) of subsection (h)(2), applied under rules similar to the rules of subparagraph (B) of subsection (h)(2)) of the aggregate total of the shortfall amortization installments and waiver amortization installments which have been determined for such plan year and any succeeding plan year with respect to the shortfall amortization bases and waiver amortization bases of the plan for any plan year preceding such plan year.

(4) Funding shortfall.—For purposes of this section, the funding shortfall of a plan for any plan year is the excess (if any) of—

(A) the funding target of the plan for the plan year, over

(B) the value of plan assets of the plan (as reduced under subsection (f)(4)(B)) for the plan year which are held by the plan on the valuation date.

(5) Exemption from new shortfall amortization base.—

(A) In general.—In any case in which the value of plan assets of the plan (as reduced under subsection (f)(4)(A)) is equal to or greater than the funding target of the plan for the plan year, the shortfall amortization base of the plan for such plan year shall be zero.

(B) Transition rule.—

(i) In general.—Except as provided in clause (iii), in the case of plan years beginning after 2007 and before 2011, only the applicable percentage of the funding target shall be taken into account under paragraph (3)(A) in determining the funding shortfall for purposes of paragraph (3)(A) and subparagraph (A).

(ii) Applicable percentage.—For purposes of subparagraph (A), the applicable percentage shall be determined in accordance with the following table:

In the case of a plan year beginning in calendar year:	The applicable percentage is:
2008	92

In the case of a plan year beginning in calendar year:	The applicable percentage is:
2009	94
2010	96

(iii) Transition relief not available for new or deficit reduction plans.—Clause (i) shall not apply to a plan—

(I) which was not in effect for a plan year beginning in 2007, or

(II) which was in effect for a plan year beginning in 2007 and which was subject to section 302(d) (as in effect for plan years beginning in 2007) for such year, determined after the application of paragraphs (6) and (9) thereof.

(iv) **[Redesignated.]**

(6) Early deemed amortization upon attainment of funding target.—In any case in which the funding shortfall of a plan for a plan year is zero, for purposes of determining the shortfall amortization charge for such plan year and succeeding plan years, the shortfall amortization bases for all preceding plan years (and all shortfall amortization installments determined with respect to such bases) shall be reduced to zero.

> ***Editor's Note***
>
> ERISA §303(c)(7), below, was added by Pub. L. No. 111-192, §201(a)(2), effective for years beginning after December 31, 2007.

---

(7) Increases in alternate required installments in cases of excess compensation or extraordinary dividends or stock redemptions.—

(A) In general.—If there is an installment acceleration amount with respect to a plan for any plan year in the restriction period with respect to an election year under paragraph (2)(D), then the shortfall amortization installment otherwise determined and payable under such paragraph for such plan year shall, subject to the limitation under subparagraph (B), be increased by such amount.

(B) Total installments limited to shortfall base.— Subject to rules prescribed by the Secretary of the Treasury, if a shortfall amortization installment with respect to any shortfall amortization base for an election year is required to be increased for any plan year under subparagraph (A)—

(i) such increase shall not result in the amount of such installment exceeding the present value of such installment and all succeeding installments with respect to such base (determined without regard to such increase but after application of clause (ii)), and

(ii) subsequent shortfall amortization installments with respect to such base shall, in reverse order of the otherwise required installments, be reduced to the extent necessary to limit the present value of such subsequent shortfall amortization installments (after application of this paragraph) to the present value of the remaining unamortized shortfall amortization base.

(C) Installment acceleration amount.—For purposes of this paragraph—

(i) In general.—The term "installment acceleration amount" means, with respect to any plan year in a restriction period with respect to an election year, the sum of—

(I) the aggregate amount of excess employee compensation determined under subparagraph (D) with respect to all employees for the plan year plus

(II) the aggregate amount of extraordinary dividends and redemptions determined under subparagraph (E) for the plan year.

(ii) Annual limitation.—The installment acceleration amount for any plan year shall not exceed the excess (if any) of—

(I) the sum of the shortfall amortization installments for the plan year and all preceding plan years in the amortization period elected under paragraph (2)(D) with respect to the shortfall amortization base with respect to an election year, determined without regard to paragraph (2)(D) and this paragraph, over

(II) the sum of the shortfall amortization installments for such plan year and all such preceding plan years, determined after application of paragraph (2)(D) (and in the case of any preceding plan year, after application of this paragraph).

(iii) Carryover of excess installment acceleration amounts.—

(I) In general.—If the installment acceleration amount for any plan year (determined without regard to clause (ii)) exceeds the limitation under clause (ii), then, subject to subclause (II), such excess shall be treated as an installment acceleration amount with respect to the succeeding plan year.

(II) Cap to apply.—If any amount treated as an installment acceleration amount under subclause (I) or this subclause with respect [to] any succeeding plan year, when added to other installment acceleration amounts (determined without regard to clause (ii)) with respect to the plan year, exceeds the limitation under clause (ii), the portion of such amount representing such excess shall be treated as an installment acceleration amount with respect to the next succeeding plan year.

(III) Limitation on years to which amounts carried for.—No amount shall be carried under subclause (I) or (II) to a plan year which begins after the first plan year following the last plan year in the restriction period (or after the second plan year following such last plan year in the case of an election year with respect to which 15-year amortization was elected under paragraph (2)(D)).

(IV) Ordering rules.—For purposes of applying subclause (II), installment acceleration amounts for the plan year (determined without regard to any carryover under this clause) shall be applied first against the limitation under clause (ii) and then carryovers to such plan year shall be applied against such limitation on a first-in, first-out basis.

(D) Excess employee compensation.—For purposes of this paragraph—

(i) In general.—The term "excess employee compensation" means, with respect to any employee for any plan year, the excess (if any) of—

(I) the aggregate amount includible in income under chapter 1 of the Internal Revenue Code of 1986 for remuneration during the calendar year in which such plan year begins for services performed by the employee for the plan sponsor (whether or not performed during such calendar year), over

(II) $1,000,000.

(ii) Amounts set aside for nonqualified deferred compensation.—If during any calendar year assets are set aside or reserved (directly or indirectly) in a trust (or other arrangement as determined by the Secretary of the Treasury), or transferred to such a trust or other arrangement, by a plan sponsor for purposes of paying deferred compensation of an employee under a nonqualified deferred compensation plan (as defined in section 409A of such Code) of the plan sponsor, then, for purposes of clause (i), the amount of such assets shall be treated as remuneration of the employee includible in income for the calendar year unless such amount is otherwise includible in income for such year. An amount to which the preceding sentence applies shall not be taken into account under this paragraph for any subsequent calendar year.

(iii) Only remuneration for certain post-2009 services counted.—Remuneration shall be taken into account under clause (i) only to the extent attributable to services performed by the employee for the plan sponsor after February 28, 2010.

(iv) Exception for certain equity payments.—

(I) In general.—There shall not be taken into account under clause (i)(I) any amount includible in income with respect to the granting after February 28, 2010, of service recipient stock (within the meaning of section 409A of the Internal Revenue Code of 1986) that, upon such grant, is subject to a substantial risk of forfeiture (as defined under section 83(c)(1) of such Code) for at least 5 years from the date of such grant.

(II) Secretarial authority.—The Secretary of the Treasury may by regulation provide for the application of this clause in the case of a person other than a corporation.

(v) Other exceptions.—The following amounts includible in income shall not be taken into account under clause (i)(I):

(I) Commissions.—Any remuneration payable on a commission basis solely on account of income directly generated by the individual performance of the individual to whom such remuneration is payable.

(II) Certain payments under existing contracts.—Any remuneration consisting of nonqualified deferred compensation, restricted stock, stock options, or stock appreciation rights payable or granted under a written binding contract that was in effect on March 1, 2010, and which was not modified in any material respect before such remuneration is paid.

(vi) Self-employed individual treated as employee.—The term "employee" includes, with respect to a calendar year, a self-employed individual who is treated as an employee under section 401(c) of such Code for the taxable year ending during such calendar year, and the term "compensation" shall include earned income of such individual with respect to such self-employment.

(vii) Indexing of amount.—In the case of any calendar year beginning after 2010, the dollar amount under clause (i)(II) shall be increased by an amount equal to—

(I) such dollar amount, multiplied by

(II) the cost-of-living adjustment determined under section 1(f)(3) of such Code for the calendar year, determined by substituting "calendar year 2009" for "calendar year 1992" in subparagraph (B) thereof. If the amount of any increase under clause (i) is not a multiple of $1,000, such increase shall be rounded to the next lowest multiple of $1,000.

(E) Extraordinary dividends and redemptions.—

(i) In general.—The amount determined under this subparagraph for any plan year is the excess (if any) of the sum of the dividends declared during the plan year by the plan sponsor plus the aggregate amount paid for the redemption of stock of the plan sponsor redeemed during the plan year over the greater of—

(I) the adjusted net income (within the meaning of section 4043) of the plan sponsor for the preceding plan year, determined without regard to any

ERISA Sec. 303(c)(7)(E)(i)(I)

reduction by reason of interest, taxes, depreciation, or amortization, or

(II) in the case of a plan sponsor that determined and declared dividends in the same manner for at least 5 consecutive years immediately preceding such plan year, the aggregate amount of dividends determined and declared for such plan year using such manner.

(ii) Only certain post-2009 dividends and redemptions counted.—For purposes of clause (i), there shall only be taken into account dividends declared, and redemptions occurring, after February 28, 2010.

(iii) Exception for intra-group dividends.— Dividends paid by one member of a controlled group (as defined in section 302(d)(3)) to another member of such group shall not be taken into account under clause (i).

(iv) Exception for certain redemptions.—Redemptions that are made pursuant to a plan maintained with respect to employees, or that are made on account of the death, disability, or termination of employment of an employee or shareholder, shall not be taken into account under clause (i).

(v) Exception for certain preferred stock.—

(I) In general.—Dividends and redemptions with respect to applicable preferred stock shall not be taken into account under clause (i) to the extent that dividends accrue with respect to such stock at a specified rate in all events and without regard to the plan sponsor's income, and interest accrues on any unpaid dividends with respect to such stock.

(II) Applicable preferred stock.—For purposes of subclause (I), the term "applicable preferred stock" means preferred stock which was issued before March 1, 2010 (or which was issued after such date and is held by an employee benefit plan subject to the provisions of this title).

(F) Other definitions and rules.—For purposes of this paragraph—

(i) Plan sponsor.—The term "plan sponsor" includes any member of the plan sponsor's controlled group (as defined in section 302(d)(3)).

(ii) Restriction period.—The term "restriction period" means, with respect to any election year—

(I) except as provided in subclause (II), the 3-year period beginning with the election year (or, if later, the first plan year beginning after December 31, 2009), and

(II) if the plan sponsor elects 15-year amortization for the shortfall amortization base for the election year, the 5-year period beginning with the election year (or, if later, the first plan year beginning after December 31, 2009).

(iii) Elections for multiple plans.—If a plan sponsor makes elections under paragraph (2)(D)

with respect to 2 or more plans, the Secretary of the Treasury shall provide rules for the application of this paragraph to such plans, including rules for the ratable allocation of any installment acceleration amount among such plans on the basis of each plan's relative reduction in the plan's shortfall amortization installment for the first plan year in the amortization period described in subparagraph (A) (determined without regard to this paragraph).

(iv) Mergers and acquisitions.—The Secretary of the Treasury shall prescribe rules for the application of paragraph (2)(D) and this paragraph in any case where there is a merger or acquisition involving a plan sponsor making the election under paragraph (2)(D).

(d) Rules Relating to Funding Target.—For purposes of this section—

(1) Funding target.—Except as provided in subsection (i)(1) with respect to plans in at-risk status, the funding target of a plan for a plan year is the present value of all benefits accrued or earned under the plan as of the beginning of the plan year.

(2) Funding target attainment percentage.— The "funding target attainment percentage" of a plan for a plan year is the ratio (expressed as a percentage) which—

(A) the value of plan assets for the plan year (as reduced under subsection (f)(4)(B)), bears to

(B) the funding target of the plan for the plan year (determined without regard to subsection (i)(1)).

(e) Waiver Amortization Charge.—

(1) Determination of waiver amortization charge.—The waiver amortization charge (if any) for a plan for any plan year is the aggregate total of the waiver amortization installments for such plan year with respect to the waiver amortization bases for each of the 5 preceding plan years.

(2) Waiver amortization installment.—For purposes of paragraph (1)—

(A) Determination.—The waiver amortization installments are the amounts necessary to amortize the waiver amortization base of the plan for any plan year in level annual installments over a period of 5 plan years beginning with the succeeding plan year.

(B) Waiver installment.—The waiver amortization installment for any plan year in the 5-year period under subparagraph (A) with respect to any waiver amortization base is the annual installment determined under subparagraph (A) for that year for that base.

(3) Interest rate.—In determining any waiver amortization installment under this subsection, the plan sponsor shall use the segment rates determined under subparagraph (C) of subsection (h)(2), applied under rules similar to the rules of subparagraph (B) of subsection (h)(2).

(4) Waiver amortization base.—The waiver amortization base of a plan for a plan year is the amount of the waived funding deficiency (if any) for such plan year under section 302(c).

(5) Early deemed amortization upon attainment of funding target.—In any case in which the funding shortfall of a plan for a plan year is zero, for purposes of determining the waiver amortization charge for such plan year and succeeding plan years, the waiver amortization bases for all preceding plan years (and all waiver amortization installments determined with respect to such bases) shall be reduced to zero.

(f) Reduction of Minimum Required Contribution by Prefunding Balance and Funding Standard Carryover Balance.—

(1) Election to maintain balances.—

(A) Prefunding balance.—The plan sponsor of a single-employer plan may elect to maintain a prefunding balance.

(B) Funding standard carryover balance.—

(i) In general.—In the case of a single-employer plan described in clause (ii), the plan sponsor may elect to maintain a funding standard carryover balance, until such balance is reduced to zero.

(ii) Plans maintaining funding standard account in 2007.—A plan is described in this clause if the plan—

(I) was in effect for a plan year beginning in 2007, and

(II) had a positive balance in the funding standard account under section 302(b) as in effect for such plan year and determined as of the end of such plan year.

(2) Application of balances.—A prefunding balance and a funding standard carryover balance maintained pursuant to this paragraph—

(A) shall be available for crediting against the minimum required contribution, pursuant to an election under paragraph (3),

(B) shall be applied as a reduction in the amount treated as the value of plan assets for purposes of this section, to the extent provided in paragraph (4), and

(C) may be reduced at any time, pursuant to an election under paragraph (5).

(3) Election to apply balances against minimum required contribution.—

(A) In general.—Except as provided in subparagraphs (B) and (C), in the case of any plan year in which the plan sponsor elects to credit against the minimum required contribution for the current plan year all or a portion of the prefunding balance or the funding standard carryover balance for the current plan year (not in excess of such minimum required contribution), the minimum required contribution for the plan year shall be reduced as of the first day of the plan year by the amount so credited by the plan sponsor. For purposes of the preceding sentence, the minimum required contribution shall be determined after taking into account any waiver under section 302(c).

(B) Coordination with funding standard carryover balance.—To the extent that any plan has a funding standard carryover balance greater than zero, no amount of the prefunding balance of such plan may be credited under this paragraph in reducing the minimum required contribution.

(C) Limitation for underfunded plans.—The preceding provisions of this paragraph shall not apply for any plan year if the ratio (expressed as a percentage) which—

(i) the value of plan assets for the preceding plan year (as reduced under paragraph (4)(C)), bears to

(ii) the funding target of the plan for the preceding plan year (determined without regard to subsection (i)(1)),

is less than 80 percent. In the case of plan years beginning in 2008, the ratio under this subparagraph may be determined using such methods of estimation as the Secretary of the Treasury may prescribe.

Editor's Note

ERISA §303(f)(3)(D), below, was added by Pub. L. No. 111-192, §204(a), effective generally for plan years beginning after August 31, 2009, except that for plans for which the valuation date is not the first day of the plan year, the amendment is effective for plan years beginning after December 31, 2008.

(D) Special rule for certain years of plans maintained by charities.—

(i) In general.—For purposes of applying subparagraph (C) for plan years beginning after August 31, 2009, and before September 1, 2011, the ratio determined under such subparagraph for the preceding plan year shall be the greater of—

(I) such ratio, as determined without regard to this subparagraph, or

(II) the ratio for such plan for the plan year beginning after Aught 31, 2007, and before September 1, 2008, as determined under rules prescribed by the Secretary of the Treasury.

(ii) Special rule.—In the case of a plan for which the valuation date is not the first day of the plan year.—

(I) clause (i) shall apply to plan years beginning after December 31, 2008, and before January 1, 2011, and

(II) clause (i)(II) shall apply based on the last plan year beginning before September 1, 2007, as determined under rules prescribed by the Secretary of the Treasury.

(iii) Limitation to charities.—This subparagraph shall not apply to any plan unless such plan is maintained exclusively by one or more organizations described in section 501(c)(3) of the Internal Revenue Code of 1986.

(4) Effect of balances on amounts treated as value of plan assets.—In the case of any plan maintaining a prefunding balance or a funding standard carryover balance pursuant to this subsection, the amount treated as the value of plan assets shall be deemed to be such amount, reduced as provided in the following subparagraphs:

(A) Applicability of shortfall amortization base.—For purposes of subsection (c)(5), the value of plan assets is deemed to be such amount, reduced by the amount of the prefunding balance, but only if an election under paragraph 3 applying any portion of the prefunding balance in reducing the minimum required contribution is in effect for the plan year.

(B) Determination of excess assets, funding shortfall, and funding target attainment percentage.—

(i) In general.—For purposes of subsections (a), (c)(4)(B), and (d)(2)(A), the value of plan assets is deemed to be such amount, reduced by the amount of the prefunding balance and the funding standard carryover balance.

(ii) Special rule for certain binding agreements with pbgc.—For purposes of subsection (c)(4)(B), the value of plan assets shall not be deemed to be reduced for a plan year by the amount of the specified balance if, with respect to such balance, there is in effect for a plan year a binding written agreement with the Pension Benefit Guaranty Corporation which provides that such balance is not available to reduce the minimum required contribution for the plan year. For purposes of the preceding sentence, the term "specified balance" means the prefunding balance or the funding standard carryover balance, as the case may be.

(C) Availability of balances in plan year for crediting against minimum required contribution.—For purposes of paragraph (3)(C)(i) of this subsection, the value of plan assets is deemed to be such

amount, reduced by the amount of the prefunding balance.

(5) Election to reduce balance prior to determinations of value of plan assets and crediting against minimum required contribution.—

(A) In general.—The plan sponsor may elect to reduce by any amount the balance of the prefunding balance and the funding standard carryover balance for any plan year (but not below zero). Such reduction shall be effective prior to any determination of the value of plan assets for such plan year under this section and application of the balance in reducing the minimum required contribution for such plan for such plan year pursuant to an election under paragraph (2).

(B) Coordination between prefunding balance and funding standard carryover balance.—To the extent that any plan has a funding standard carryover balance greater than zero, no election may be made under subparagraph (A) with respect to the prefunding balance.

(6) Prefunding balance.—

(A) In general.—A prefunding balance maintained by a plan shall consist of a beginning balance of zero, increased and decreased to the extent provided in subparagraphs (B) and (C), and adjusted further as provided in paragraph (8).

(B) Increases.—

(i) In general.—As of the first day of each plan year beginning after 2008, the prefunding balance of a plan shall be increased by the amount elected by the plan sponsor for the plan year. Such amount shall not exceed the excess (if any) of—

(I) the aggregate total of employer contributions to the plan for the preceding plan year, over—

(II) the minimum required contribution for such preceding plan year.

(ii) Adjustments for interest.—Any excess contributions under clause (i) shall be properly adjusted for interest accruing for the periods between the first day of the current plan year and the dates on which the excess contributions were made, determined by using the effective interest rate for the preceding plan year and by treating contributions as being first used to satisfy the minimum required contribution.

(iii) Certain contributions necessary to avoid benefit limitations disregarded.—The excess described in clause (i) with respect to any preceding plan year shall be reduced (but not below zero) by the amount of contributions an employer would be required to make under paragraph (1), (2), or (4) of section 206(g) to avoid a benefit limitation which would otherwise be imposed under such paragraph for the preceding plan year. Any contribution which may be taken into account in satisfying the requirements of more than 1 of such paragraphs shall be taken into account only once for purposes of this clause.

(C) Decrease.—The prefunding balance of a plan shall be decreased (but not below zero) by—

(i) as of the first day of each plan year after 2008, the amount of such balance credited under paragraph (2) (if any) in reducing the minimum required contribution of the plan for the preceding plan year, and

(ii) as of the time specified in paragraph (5)(A), any reduction in such balance elected under paragraph (5).

(7) **Funding standard carryover balance.**—

(A) In general.—A funding standard carryover balance maintained by a plan shall consist of a beginning balance determined under subparagraph (B), decreased to the extent provided in subparagraph (C), and adjusted further as provided in paragraph (8).

(B) Beginning balance.—The beginning balance of the funding standard carryover balance shall be the positive balance described in paragraph (1)(B)(ii)(II).

(C) Decreases.—The funding standard carryover balance of a plan shall be decreased (but not below zero) by—

(i) as of the first day of each plan year after 2008, the amount of such balance credited under paragraph (2) (if any) in reducing the minimum required contribution of the plan for the preceding plan year, and

(ii) as of the time specified in paragraph (5)(A), any reduction in such balance elected under paragraph (5).

(8) **Adjustments for investment experience.**— In determining the prefunding balance or the funding standard carryover balance of a plan as of the first day of the plan year, the plan sponsor shall, in accordance with regulations prescribed by the Secretary of the Treasury, adjust such balance to reflect the rate of return on plan assets for the preceding plan year. Notwithstanding subsection (g)(3), such rate of return shall be determined on the basis of fair market value and shall properly take into account, in accordance with such regulations, all contributions, distributions, and other plan payments made during such period.

(9) **Elections.**—Elections under this subsection shall be made at such times, and in such form and manner, as shall be prescribed in regulations of the Secretary of the Treasury.

(g) **Valuation of Plan Assets and Liabilities.**—

(1) **Timing of determinations.**—Except as otherwise provided under this subsection, all determinations under this section for a plan year shall be made as of the valuation date of the plan for such plan year.

(2) **Valuation date.**—For purposes of this section—

(A) In general.—Except as provided in subparagraph (B), the valuation date of a plan for any plan year shall be the first day of the plan year.

(B) Exception for small plans.—If, on each day during the preceding plan year, a plan had 100 or fewer participants, the plan may designate any day during the plan year as its valuation date for such plan year and succeeding plan years. For purposes of this subparagraph, all defined benefit plans which are single-employer plans and are maintained by the same employer (or any member of such employer's controlled group) shall be treated as 1 plan, but only participants with respect to such employer or member shall be taken into account.

(C) Application of certain rules in determination of plan size.—For purposes of this paragraph—

(i) Plans not in existence in preceding year.— In the case of the first plan year of any plan, subparagraph (B) shall apply to such plan by taking into account the number of participants that the plan is reasonably expected to have on days during such first plan year.

(ii) Predecessors.—Any reference in subparagraph (B) to an employer shall include a reference to any predecessor of such employer.

(3) **Determination of value of plan assets.**—For purposes of this section—

(A) In general.—Except as provided in subparagraph (B), the value of plan assets shall be the fair market value of the assets.

(B) Averaging allowed.—A plan may determine the value of plan assets on the basis of the averaging of fair market values, but only if such method—

(i) is permitted under regulations prescribed by the Secretary of the Treasury,

(ii) does not provide for averaging of such values over more than the period beginning on the last day of the 25th month preceding the month in which the valuation date occurs and ending on the valuation date (or a similar period in the case of a valuation date which is not the 1st day of a month), and

(iii) does not result in a determination of the value of plan assets which, at any time, is lower than 90 percent or greater than 110 percent of the fair market value of such assets at such time.

Any such averaging shall be adjusted for contributions, distributions, and expected earnings (as determined by the plan's actuary on the basis of an assumed earnings rate specified by the actuary but not in excess of the third segment rate applicable under subsection (h)(2)(C)(iii)), as specified by the Secretary of the Treasury.

(4) Accounting for contribution receipts.—For purposes of determining the value of assets under paragraph (3)—

(A) Prior year contributions.—If—

(i) an employer makes any contribution to the plan after the valuation date for the plan year in which the contribution is made, and

(ii) the contribution is for a preceding plan year,

the contribution shall be taken into account as an asset of the plan as of the valuation date, except that in the case of any plan year beginning after 2008, only the present value (determined as of the valuation date) of such contribution may be taken into account. For purposes of the preceding sentence, present value shall be determined using the effective interest rate for the preceding plan year to which the contribution is properly allocable.

(B) Special rule for current year contributions made before valuation date.—If any contributions for any plan year are made to or under the plan during the plan year but before the valuation date for the plan year, the assets of the plan as of the valuation date shall not include—

(i) such contributions, and

(ii) interest on such contributions for the period between the date of the contributions and the valuation date, determined by using the effective interest rate for the plan year.

(h) Actuarial Assumptions and Methods.—

(1) In general.—Subject to this subsection, the determination of any present value or other computation under this section shall be made on the basis of actuarial assumptions and methods—

(A) each of which is reasonable (taking into account the experience of the plan and reasonable expectations), and

(B) which, in combination, offer the actuary's best estimate of anticipated experience under the plan.

(2) Interest rates.—

(A) Effective interest rate.—For purposes of this section, the term "effective interest rate" means, with respect to any plan for any plan year, the single rate of interest which, if used to determine the present value of the plan's accrued or earned benefits referred to in subsection (d)(1), would result in an amount equal to the funding target of the plan for such plan year.

(B) Interest rates for determining funding target.—For purposes of determining the funding tar-

get and normal cost of a plan for any plan year, the interest rate used in determining the present value of the benefits of the plan shall be—

(i) in the case of benefits reasonably determined to be payable during the 5-year period beginning on the first day of the plan year, the first segment rate with respect to the applicable month,

(ii) in the case of benefits reasonably determined to be payable during the 15-year period beginning at the end of the period described in clause (i), the second segment rate with respect to the applicable month, and

(iii) in the case of benefits reasonably determined to be payable after the period described in clause (ii), the third segment rate with respect to the applicable month.

(C) Segment rates.—For purposes of this paragraph—

(i) First segment rate.—The term "first segment rate" means, with respect to any month, the single rate of interest which shall be determined by the Secretary of the Treasury for such month on the basis of the corporate bond yield curve for such month, taking into account only that portion of such yield curve which is based on bonds maturing during the 5-year period commencing with such month.

(ii) Second segment rate.—The term "second segment rate" means, with respect to any month, the single rate of interest which shall be determined by the Secretary of the Treasury for such month on the basis of the corporate bond yield curve for such month, taking into account only that portion of such yield curve which is based on bonds maturing during the 15-year period beginning at the end of the period described in clause (i).

(iii) Third segment rate.—The term "third segment rate" means, with respect to any month, the single rate of interest which shall be determined by the Secretary of the Treasury for such month on the basis of the corporate bond yield curve for such month, taking into account only that portion of such yield curve which is based on bonds maturing during periods beginning after the period described in clause (ii).

(D) Corporate bond yield curve.—For purposes of this paragraph—

(i) In general.—The term "corporate bond yield curve" means, with respect to any month, a yield curve which is prescribed by the Secretary of the Treasury for such month and which reflects the average, for the 24-month period ending with the month preceding such month, of monthly yields on investment grade corporate bonds with varying maturities and that are in the top 3 quality levels available.

(ii) Election to use yield curve.—Solely for purposes of determining the minimum required contribution under this section, the plan sponsor may, in lieu of the segment rates determined under subparagraph (C), elect to use interest rates under the corporate bond yield curve. For purposes of the preceding sentence such curve shall be determined without regard to the 24-month averaging described in clause (i). Such election, once made, may be revoked only with the consent of the Secretary of the Treasury.

(E) Applicable month.—For purposes of this paragraph, the term "applicable month" means, with respect to any plan for any plan year, the month which includes the valuation date of such plan for such plan year or, at the election of the plan sponsor, any of the 4 months which precede such month. Any election made under this subparagraph shall apply to the plan year for which the election is made and all succeeding plan years, unless the election is revoked with the consent of the Secretary of the Treasury.

(F) Publication requirements.—The Secretary of the Treasury shall publish for each month the corporate bond yield curve (and the corporate bond yield curve reflecting the modification described in section 205(g)(3)(B)(iii)(I) for such month) and each of the rates determined under subparagraph (C) for such month. The Secretary of the Treasury shall also publish a description of the methodology used to determine such yield curve and such rates which is sufficiently detailed to enable plans to make reasonable projections regarding the yield curve and such rates for future months based on the plan's projection of future interest rates.

(G) Transition rule.—

(i) In general.—Notwithstanding the preceding provisions of this paragraph, for plan years beginning in 2008 or 2009, the first, second, or third segment rate for a plan with respect to any month shall be equal to the sum of—

(I) the product of such rate for such month determined without regard to this subparagraph, multiplied by the applicable percentage, and

(II) the product of the rate determined under the rules of section 302(b)(5)(B)(ii)(II) (as in effect for plan years beginning in 2007), multiplied by a percentage equal to 100 percent minus the applicable percentage.

(ii) Applicable percentage.—For purposes of clause (i), the applicable percentage is 33⅓-percent for plan years beginning in 2008 and 66⅔-percent for plan years beginning in 2009.

(iii) New plans ineligible.—Clause (i) shall not apply to any plan if the first plan year of the plan begins after December 31, 2007.

(iv) Election.—The plan sponsor may elect not to have this subparagraph apply. Such election, once made, may be revoked only with the consent of the Secretary of the Treasury.

(3) Mortality tables.—

(A) In general.—Except as provided in subparagraph (C) or (D), the Secretary of the Treasury shall by regulation prescribe mortality tables to be used in determining any present value or making any computation under this section. Such tables shall be based on the actual experience of pension plans and projected trends in such experience. In prescribing such tables, the Secretary of the Treasury shall take into account results of available independent studies of mortality of individuals covered by pension plans.

(B) Periodic revision.—The Secretary of the Treasury shall (at least every 10 years) make revisions in any table in effect under subparagraph (A) to reflect the actual experience of pension plans and projected trends in such experience.

(C) Substitute mortality table.—

(i) In general.—Upon request by the plan sponsor and approval by the Secretary of the Treasury, a mortality table which meets the requirements of clause (iii) shall be used in determining any present value or making any computation under this section during the period of consecutive plan years (not to exceed 10) specified in the request.

(ii) Early termination of period.—Notwithstanding clause (i), a mortality table described in clause (i) shall cease to be in effect as of the earliest of—

(I) the date on which there is a significant change in the participants in the plan by reason of a plan spinoff or merger or otherwise, or

(II) the date on which the plan actuary determines that such table does not meet the requirements of clause (iii).

(iii) Requirements.—A mortality table meets the requirements of this clause if—

(I) there is a sufficient number of plan participants, and the pension plans have been maintained for a sufficient period of time, to have credible information necessary for purposes of subclause (II), and

(II) such table reflects the actual experience of the pension plans maintained by the sponsor and projected trends in general mortality experience.

(iv) All plans in controlled group must use separate table.—Except as provided by the Secretary of the Treasury, a plan sponsor may not use a mortality table under this subparagraph for any plan maintained by the plan sponsor unless—

(I) a separate mortality table is established and used under this subparagraph for each other plan maintained by the plan sponsor and if the plan sponsor is a member of a controlled group, each member of the controlled group, and

(II) the requirements of clause (iii) are met separately with respect to the table so established for each such plan, determined by only taking into account the participants of such plan, the time such plan has been in existence, and the actual experience of such plan.

(v) Deadline for submission and disposition of application.—

(I) Submission.—The plan sponsor shall submit a mortality table to the Secretary of the Treasury for approval under this subparagraph at least 7 months before the 1st day of the period described in clause (i).

(II) Disposition.—Any mortality table submitted to the Secretary of the Treasury for approval under this subparagraph shall be treated as in effect as of the 1st day of the period described in clause (i) unless the Secretary of the Treasury, during the 180-day period beginning on the date of such submission, disapproves of such table and provides the reasons that such table fails to meet the requirements of clause (iii). The 180-day period shall be extended upon mutual agreement of the Secretary of the Treasury and the plan sponsor.

(D) Separate mortality tables for the disabled.—Notwithstanding subparagraph (A)—

(i) In general.—The Secretary of the Treasury shall establish mortality tables which may be used (in lieu of the tables under subparagraph (A)) under this subsection for individuals who are entitled to benefits under the plan on account of disability. The Secretary of the Treasury shall establish separate tables for individuals whose disabilities occur in plan years beginning before January 1, 1995, and for individuals whose disabilities occur in plan years beginning on or after such date.

(ii) Special rule for disabilities occurring after 1994.—In the case of disabilities occurring in plan years beginning after December 31, 1994, the tables under clause (i) shall apply only with respect to individuals described in such subclause who are disabled within the meaning of title II of the Social Security Act and the regulations thereunder.

(iii) Periodic revision.—The Secretary of the Treasury shall (at least every 10 years) make revisions in any table in effect under clause (i) to reflect the actual experience of pension plans and projected trends in such experience.

(4) Probability of benefit payments in the form of lump sums or other optional forms.—For purposes of determining any present value or making any computation under this section, there shall be taken into account—

(A) the probability that future benefit payments under the plan will be made in the form of optional forms of benefits provided under the plan (including lump sum distributions, determined on the basis of the plan's experience and other related assumptions), and

(B) any difference in the present value of such future benefit payments resulting from the use of actuarial assumptions, in determining benefit payments in any such optional form of benefits, which are different from those specified in this subsection.

(5) Approval of large changes in actuarial assumptions.—

(A) In general.—No actuarial assumption used to determine the funding target for a plan to which this paragraph applies may be changed without the approval of the Secretary of the Treasury.

(B) Plans to which paragraph applies.—This paragraph shall apply to a plan only if—

(i) the plan is a single-employer plan to which title IV applies,

(ii) the aggregate unfunded vested benefits as of the close of the preceding plan year (as determined under section 4006(a)(3)(E)(iii)) of such plan and all other plans maintained by the contributing sponsors (as defined in section 4001(a)(13)) and members of such sponsors' controlled groups (as defined in section 4001(a)(14)) which are covered by title IV (disregarding plans with no unfunded vested benefits) exceed $50,000,000, and

(iii) the change in assumptions (determined after taking into account any changes in interest rate and mortality table) results in a decrease in the funding shortfall of the plan for the current plan year that exceeds $50,000,000, or that exceeds $5,000,000 and that is 5 percent or more of the funding target of the plan before such change.

(i) Special Rules for At-Risk Plans.—

(1) Funding target for plans in at-risk status.—

(A) In general.—In the case of a plan which is in at-risk status for a plan year, the funding target of the plan for the plan year shall be equal to the sum of—

(i) the present value of all benefits accrued or earned under the plan as of the beginning of the plan year, as determined by using the additional actuarial assumptions described in subparagraph (B), and

(ii) in the case of a plan which also has been in at-risk status for at least 2 of the 4 preceding plan years, a loading factor determined under subparagraph (C).

(B) Additional actuarial assumptions.—The actuarial assumptions described in this subparagraph are as follows:

(i) All employees who are not otherwise assumed to retire as of the valuation date but who will be eligible to elect benefits during the plan year and the 10 succeeding plan years shall be assumed to retire at the earliest retirement date under the plan but not before the end of the plan year for which the at-risk funding target and at-risk target normal cost are being determined.

(ii) All employees shall be assumed to elect the retirement benefit available under the plan at the assumed retirement age (determined after application of clause (i)) which would result in the highest present value of benefits.

(C) Loading factor.—The loading factor applied with respect to a plan under this paragraph for any plan year is the sum of—

(i) $700, times the number of participants in the plan, plus

(ii) 4 percent of the funding target (determined without regard to this paragraph) of the plan for the plan year.

(2) Target normal cost of at-risk plans.—In the case of a plan which is in at-risk status for a plan year, the target normal cost of the plan for such plan year shall be equal to the sum of—

(A) the excess of—

(i) the sum of—

(I) the present value of all benefits which are expected to accrue or to be earned under the plan during the plan year, determined using the additional actuarial assumptions described in paragraph (1)(B), plus

(II) the amount of plan-related expenses expected to be paid from plan assets during the plan year, over

(ii) the amount of mandatory employee contributions expected to be made during the plan year, plus

(B) in the case of a plan which also has been in at-risk status for at least 2 of the 4 preceding plan years, a loading factor equal to 4 percent of the amount determined under subsection (b)(1)(A)(i) with respect to the plan for the plan year.

(3) Minimum amount.—In no event shall—

(A) the at-risk funding target be less than the funding target, as determined without regard to this subsection, or

(B) the at-risk target normal cost be less than the target normal cost, as determined without regard to this subsection.

(4) Determination of at-risk status.—For purposes of this subsection—

(A) In general.—A plan is in at-risk status for a plan year if—

(i) the funding target attainment percentage for the preceding plan year (determined under this section without regard to this subsection) is less than 80 percent, and

(ii) the funding target attainment percentage for the preceding plan year (determined under this section by using the additional actuarial assumptions described in paragraph (1)(B) in computing the funding target) is less than 70 percent.

(B) Transition rule.—In the case of plan years beginning in 2008, 2009, and 2010, subparagraph (A) shall be applied by substituting the following percentages for "80 percent":

(i) 65 percent in the case of 2008.

(ii) 70 percent in the case of 2009.

(iii) 75 percent in the case of 2010.

In the case of plan years beginning in 2008, the funding target attainment percentage for the preceding plan year under subparagraph (A)(ii) may be determined using such methods of estimation as the Secretary of the Treasury may provide.

(C) Special rule for employees offered early retirement in 2006.—

(i) In general.—For purposes of subparagraph (A)(ii), the additional actuarial assumptions described in paragraph (1)(B) shall not be taken into account with respect to any employee if—

(I) such employee is employed by a specified automobile manufacturer,

(II) such employee is offered a substantial amount of additional cash compensation, substantially enhanced retirement benefits under the plan, or materially reduced employment duties on the condition that by a specified date (not later than December 31, 2010) the employee retires (as defined under the terms of the plan),

(III) such offer is made during 2006 and pursuant to a bona fide retirement incentive program and requires, by the terms of the offer, that such offer can be accepted not later than a specified date (not later than December 31, 2006), and

(IV) such employee does not elect to accept such offer before the specified date on which the offer expires.

(ii) Specified automobile manufacturer.—For purposes of clause (i), the term "specified automobile manufacturer" means—

(I) any manufacturer of automobiles, and

(II) any manufacturer of automobile parts which supplies such parts directly to a manufacturer of automobiles and which, after a transaction or series of transactions ending in 1999, ceased to be a member of a controlled group which included such manufacturer of automobiles.

ERISA Sec. 303(i)(4)(C)(ii)(II)

(5) Transition between applicable funding targets and between applicable target normal costs.—

(A) In general.—In any case in which a plan which is in at-risk status for a plan year has been in such status for a consecutive period of fewer than 5 plan years, the applicable amount of the funding target and of the target normal cost shall be, in lieu of the amount determined without regard to this paragraph, the sum of—

(i) the amount determined under this section without regard to this subsection, plus

(ii) the transition percentage for such plan year of the excess of the amount determined under this subsection (without regard to this paragraph) over the amount determined under this section without regard to this subsection.

(B) Transition percentage.—For purposes of subparagraph (A), the transition percentage shall be determined in accordance with the following table:

If the consecutive number of years (including the plan year) the plan is in at-risk status is—	The transition percentage is—
1	20
2	40
3	60
4	80

(C) Years before effective date.—For purposes of this paragraph, plan years beginning before 2008 shall not be taken into account.

(6) Small plan exception.—If, on each day during the preceding plan year, a plan had 500 or fewer participants, the plan shall not be treated as in at-risk status for the plan year. For purposes of this paragraph, all defined benefit plans (other than multiemployer plans) maintained by the same employer (or any member of such employer's controlled group) shall be treated as 1 plan, but only participants with respect to such employer or member shall be taken into account and the rules of subsection (g)(2)(C) shall apply.

(j) Payment of Minimum Required Contributions.—

(1) In general.—For purposes of this section, the due date for any payment of any minimum required contribution for any plan year shall be 8½-months after the close of the plan year.

(2) Interest.—Any payment required under paragraph (1) for a plan year that is made on a date other than the valuation date for such plan year shall be adjusted for interest accruing for the period between the valuation date and the payment date, at the effective rate of interest for the plan for such plan year.

(3) Accelerated quarterly contribution schedule for underfunded plans.—

(A) Failure to timely make required installment.—In any case in which the plan has a funding shortfall for the preceding plan year, the employer maintaining the plan shall make the required installments under this paragraph and if the employer fails to pay the full amount of a required installment for the plan year, then the amount of interest charged under paragraph (2) on the underpayment for the period of underpayment shall be determined by using a rate of interest equal to the rate otherwise used under paragraph (2) plus 5 percentage points. In the case of plan years beginning in 2008, the funding shortfall for the preceding plan year may be determined using such methods of estimation as the Secretary of the Treasury may provide.

(B) Amount of underpayment, period of underpayment.—For purposes of subparagraph (A)—

(i) Amount.—The amount of the underpayment shall be the excess of—

(I) the required installment, over

(II) the amount (if any) of the installment contributed to or under the plan on or before the due date for the installment.

(ii) Period of underpayment.—The period for which any interest is charged under this paragraph with respect to any portion of the underpayment shall run from the due date for the installment to the date on which such portion is contributed to or under the plan.

(iii) Order of crediting contributions.—For purposes of clause (i)(II), contributions shall be credited against unpaid required installments in the order in which such installments are required to be paid.

(C) Number of required installments; due dates.—For purposes of this paragraph—

(i) Payable in 4 installments.—There shall be 4 required installments for each plan year.

(ii) Time for payment of installments.—The due dates for required installments are set forth in the following table:

In the case of the following required installment:	The due date is:
1st	April 15
2nd	July 15
3rd	October 15
4th	January 15 of the following year

(D) Amount of required installment.—For purposes of this paragraph—

(i) In general.—The amount of any required installment shall be 25 percent of the required annual payment.

(ii) Required annual payment.—For purposes of clause (i), the term "required annual payment" means the lesser of—

(I) 90 percent of the minimum required contribution (determined without regard to this subsection) to the plan for the plan year under this section, or

(II) 100 percent of the minimum required contribution (determined without regard to this subsection or to any waiver under section 302(c)) to the plan for the preceding plan year.

Subclause (II) shall not apply if the preceding plan year referred to in such clause was not a year of 12 months.

(E) Fiscal years, short years, and years with alternate valuation date.—

(i) Fiscal years.—In applying this paragraph to a plan year beginning on any date other than January 1, there shall be substituted for the months specified in this paragraph, the months which correspond thereto.

(ii) Short plan year.—This subparagraph shall be applied to plan years of less than 12 months in accordance with regulations prescribed by the Secretary of the Treasury.

(iii) Plan with alternate valuation date.—The Secretary of the Treasury shall prescribe regulations for the application of this paragraph in the case of a plan which has a valuation date other than the first day of the plan year.

Editor's Note

ERISA §303(j)(3)(F), below, was added by Pub. L. No. 111-192, §201(a)(3)(B), effective for plan years beginning after December 31, 2007.

(F) Quarterly contributions not to include certain increased contributions.—Subparagraph (D) shall be applied without regard to any increase under subsection (c)(7).

(4) Liquidity requirement in connection with quarterly contributions.—

(A) In general.—A plan to which this paragraph applies shall be treated as failing to pay the full amount of any required installment under paragraph (3) to the extent that the value of the liquid assets paid in such installment is less than the liquidity shortfall (whether or not such liquidity shortfall exceeds the amount of such installment required to be paid but for this paragraph).

(B) Plans to which paragraph applies.—This paragraph shall apply to a plan (other than a plan described in subsection (g)(2)(B)) which—

(i) is required to pay installments under paragraph (3) for a plan year, and

(ii) has a liquidity shortfall for any quarter during such plan year.

(C) Period of underpayment.—For purposes of paragraph (3)(A), any portion of an installment that is treated as not paid under subparagraph (A) shall continue to be treated as unpaid until the close of the quarter in which the due date for such installment occurs.

(D) Limitation on increase.—If the amount of any required installment is increased by reason of subparagraph (A), in no event shall such increase exceed the amount which, when added to prior installments for the plan year, is necessary to increase the funding target attainment percentage of the plan for the plan year (taking into account the expected increase in funding target due to benefits accruing or earned during the plan year) to 100 percent.

(E) Definitions.—For purposes of this paragraph—

(i) Liquidity shortfall.—The term "liquidity shortfall" means, with respect to any required installment, an amount equal to the excess (as of the last day of the quarter for which such installment is made) of—

(I) the base amount with respect to such quarter, over

(II) the value (as of such last day) of the plan's liquid assets.

(ii) Base amount.—

(I) In general.—The term "base amount" means, with respect to any quarter, an amount equal to 3 times the sum of the adjusted disbursements from the plan for the 12 months ending on the last day of such quarter.

(II) Special rule.—If the amount determined under subclause (I) exceeds an amount equal to 2 times the sum of the adjusted disbursements from the plan for the 36 months ending on the last day of the quarter and an enrolled actuary certifies to the satisfaction of the Secretary of the Treasury that such excess is the result of nonrecurring circumstances, the base amount with respect to such quarter shall be determined without regard to amounts related to those nonrecurring circumstances.

(iii) Disbursements from the plan.—The term "disbursements from the plan" means all disbursements from the trust, including purchases of annuities, payments of single sums and other benefits, and administrative expenses.

(iv) Adjusted disbursements.—The term "adjusted disbursements" means disbursements from the plan reduced by the product of—

(I) the plan's funding target attainment percentage for the plan year, and

(II) the sum of the purchases of annuities, payments of single sums, and such other disbursements as the Secretary of the Treasury shall provide in regulations.

(v) Liquid assets.—The term "liquid assets" means cash, marketable securities, and such other assets as specified by the Secretary of the Treasury in regulations.

(vi) Quarter.—The term "quarter" means, with respect to any required installment, the 3-month period preceding the month in which the due date for such installment occurs.

(F) Regulations.—The Secretary of the Treasury may prescribe such regulations as are necessary to carry out this paragraph.

(k) Imposition of Lien Where Failure to Make Required Contributions.—

(1) In general.—In the case of a plan to which this subsection applies (as provided under paragraph (2)), if—

(A) any person fails to make a contribution payment required by section 302 and this section before the due date for such payment, and

(B) the unpaid balance of such payment (including interest), when added to the aggregate unpaid balance of all preceding such payments for which payment was not made before the due date (including interest), exceeds $1,000,000, then there shall be a lien in favor of the plan in the amount determined under paragraph (3) upon all property and rights to property, whether real or personal, belonging to such person and any other person who is a member of the same controlled group of which such person is a member.

(2) Plans to which subsection applies.—This subsection shall apply to a single-employer plan covered under section 4021 for any plan year for which the funding target attainment percentage (as defined in subsection (d)(2)) of such plan is less than 100 percent.

(3) Amount of lien.—For purposes of paragraph (1), the amount of the lien shall be equal to the aggregate unpaid balance of contribution payments required under this section and section 302 for which payment has not been made before the due date.

(4) Notice of failure; lien.—

(A) Notice of failure.—A person committing a failure described in paragraph (1) shall notify the Pension Benefit Guaranty Corporation of such failure within 10 days of the due date for the required contribution payment.

(B) Period of lien.—The lien imposed by paragraph (1) shall arise on the due date for the required contribution payment and shall continue until the last day of the first plan year in which the plan ceases to be described in paragraph (1)(B). Such lien shall continue to run without regard to whether such plan continues to be described in paragraph (2) during the period referred to in the preceding sentence.

(C) Certain rules to apply.—Any amount with respect to which a lien is imposed under paragraph (1) shall be treated as taxes due and owing the United States and rules similar to the rules of subsections (c), (d), and (e) of section 4068 shall apply with respect to a lien imposed by subsection (a) and the amount with respect to such lien.

(5) Enforcement.—Any lien created under paragraph (1) may be perfected and enforced only by the Pension Benefit Guaranty Corporation, or at the direction of the Pension Benefit Guaranty Corporation, by the contributing sponsor (or any member of the controlled group of the contributing sponsor).

(6) Definitions.—For purposes of this subsection—

(A) Contribution payment.—The term "contribution payment" means, in connection with a plan, a contribution payment required to be made to the plan, including any required installment under paragraphs (3) and (4) of subsection (j).

(B) Due date; required installment.—The terms "due date" and "required installment" have the meanings given such terms by subsection (j).

(C) Controlled group.—The term "controlled group" means any group treated as a single employer under subsections (b), (c), (m), and (o) of section 414 of the Internal Revenue Code of 1986.

(*l*) Qualified Transfers to Health Benefit Accounts.—In the case of a qualified transfer (as defined in section 420 of the Internal Revenue Code of 1986), any assets so transferred shall not, for purposes of this section, be treated as assets in the plan.

Amendments to ERISA §303

Preservation of Access to Care for Medicare Beneficiaries and Pension Relief Act of 2010 (Pub. L. No. 111-192), as follows:

● ERISA §303(c)(1) was amended by Act §201(a)(3)(A) by striking "the shortfall amortization bases for such plan year and each of the 6 preceding plan years" and inserting "any shortfall amortization base which has not been fully amortized under this section". Eff. for plan years begining after Dec. 31, 2007.

● ERISA §303(c)(2)(D) was added by Act §201(a)(1). Eff. for plan years begining after Dec. 31, 2007.

● ERISA §303(c)(7) was added by Act §201(a)(1). Eff. for plan years begining after Dec. 31, 2007.

● ERISA §303(f)(3)(D) was added by Act §204(a). Eff. generally for plan years beginning after Aug. 31, 2009, except that for plans for which the valuation date is not the first day of the plan year, amendment is effective for plan years beginning after Dec. 31, 2008.

● ERISA §303(j)(3)(F) was added by Act §201(a)(3)(B). Eff. for plan years beginning after Dec. 31, 2007.

Worker, Retiree, and Employer Recovery Act of 2008 (Pub. L. No. 110-458), as follows:

● ERISA §303(b) was amended by Act §101(b)(1)(A). Eff. for plan years beginning after Dec. 31, 2008. ERISA §303(b) prior to amendment:

> **(b) Target Normal Cost.**—For purposes of this section, except as provided in subsection (i)(2) with respect to plans in at-risk status, the term "target normal cost" means, for any plan year, the present value of all benefits which are expected to accrue or to be earned under the plan during the plan year. For purposes of this subsection, if any benefit attributable to services performed in a preceding plan year is increased by reason of any increase in compensation during the current plan year, the increase in such benefit shall be treated as having accrued during the current plan year.

● ERISA §303(c)(5)(B)(i) was amended by Act §202(a)(2). Eff. for plan years beginning after 2007, as if included in Pub. L. No. 109-280, §102. ERISA §303(c)(5)(B)(i) prior to amendment:

> (i) In general.—Except as provided in clauses (iii) and (iv), in the case of plan years beginning after 2007 and before 2011, only the applicable percentage of the funding target shall be taken into account under paragraph (3)(A) in determining the funding shortfall for the plan year for purposes of subparagraph (A).

● ERISA §303(c)(5)(B)(iii) was amended by Act §101(b)(1)(B) by inserting "beginning" before "after 2008". [ERISA §303(c)(5)(B)(iii) was repealed by Act §202(a)(1), see below.]

● ERISA §303(c)(5)(B) was amended by Act §202(a)(1) by striking cl. (iii) and redesignating cl. (iv) and cl. (iii). Eff. for plan years beginning after 2007, as if included in Pub. L. No. 109-280, §102. ERISA §303(c)(5)(B)(iii), as amended by Act §(b)(1)(B), prior to repeal:

> (iii) Limitation.—Clause (i) shall not apply with respect to any plan year beginning after 2008 unless the shortfall amortization base for each of the preceding years beginning after 2007 was zero (determined after application of this subparagraph).

● ERISA §303(c)(5)(B)(iv)(II) was amended by Act §101(b)(1)(C) by inserting "for such year" after "beginning in 2007)". [Prior to redesignation by Act §202(a)(1), see above.]

● ERISA §303(f)(4)(A) was amended by Act §101(b)(1)(D) by striking "paragraph (2)" and inserting "paragraph (3)". Eff. for plan years beginning after 2007, as if included in Pub. L. No. 109-280, §102.

● ERISA §303(g)(3)(B) was amended by Act §121(a) by amending the last sentence. Eff. for plan years beginning after 2007, as if included in Pub. L. No. 109-280, §102. Last sentence prior to amendment:

> Any such averaging shall be adjusted for contributions and distributions (as provided by the Secretary of the Treasury).

● ERISA §303(h)(2)(F) was amended by Act §101(b)(1)(E) by striking "section 205(g)(3)(B)(iii)(I)) for such month" and inserting "section 205(g)(3)(B)(iii)(I) for such month)", and striking "subparagraph (B)" and inserting "subparagraph (C)". Eff. for plan years beginning after 2007, as if included in Pub. L. No. 109-280, §102.

● ERISA §303(i)(2)(A) was amended by Act §101(b)(1)(F)(i)(I). Eff. for plan years beginning after Dec. 31, 2008. ERISA §303(i)(2)(A) prior to amendment:

> (A) the present value of all benefits which are expected to accrue or be earned under the plan during the plan year, determined using the additional actuarial assumptions described in paragraph (1)(B), plus

● ERISA §303(i)(2)(B) was amended by Act §101(b)(1)(F)(i)(II) by striking "the target normal cost (determined without regard to this paragraph) of the plan for the plan year" and inserting "the amount determined under subsection (b)(1)(A)(i) with respect to the plan for the plan year". Eff. for plan years beginning after Dec. 31, 2008.

● ERISA §303(i)(4)(B) was amended by Act §101(b)(1)(F)(ii) by striking "subparagraph (A)(ii)" in the last sentence and inserting

"subparagraph (A)". Eff. for plan years beginning after 2007, as if included in Pub. L. No. 109-280, §102.

● ERISA §303(j)(3)(A) was amended by Act §101(b)(1)(G)(i) by adding at the end: "In the case of plan years beginning in 2008, the funding shortfall for the preceding plan year may be determined using such methods of estimation as the Secretary of the Treasury may provide." Eff. for plan years beginning after 2007, as if included in Pub. L. No. 109-280, §102.

● ERISA §303(j)(3)(E) was amended by Act §101(b)(1)(G)(iii) in the heading by striking "and short years" and inserting ", short years, and years with alternate valuation date". Eff. for plan years beginning after 2007, as if included in Pub. L. No. 109-280, §102.

● ERISA §303(j)(3)(E)(iii) was added by Act §101(b)(1)(G)(ii). Eff. for plan years beginning after 2007, as if included in Pub. L. No. 109-280, §102.

● ERISA §303(k)(6)(B) was amended by Act §101(b)(1)(H) by striking ", except" and all that follows and inserting a period. Eff. for plan years beginning after 2007, as if included in Pub. L. No. 109-280, §102.

● **Other Provision.** Act §101(b)(3)(B) provides:

> (B) ELECTION FOR EARLIER APPLICATION.—The amendments made by such paragraphs shall apply to a plan for the first plan year beginning after December 31, 2007, if the plan sponsor makes the election under this subparagraph. An election under this subparagraph shall be made at such time and in such manner as the Secretary of the Treasury or the Secretary's delegate may prescribe, and, once made, may be revoked only with the consent of the Secretary.

Pension Protection Act of 2006 (Pub. L. No. 109-280), as follows:

● ERISA §303 was added by Act §102(a). Eff. for plan years after 2007.

● Prior ERISA §303 was repealed by Act §101(a). Eff. for plan years beginning after 2007. See below for text of repealed ERISA §303.

SEC. 303. VARIANCE FROM MINIMUM FUNDING STANDARD. [Repealed.]

(a) Waiver of Requirements in Event of Business Hardship.— If an employer, or in the case of a multiemployer plan, 10 percent or more of the number of employers contributing to or under the plan are unable to satisfy the minimum funding standard for a plan year without temporary substantial business hardship (substantial business hardship in the case of a multiemployer plan) and if application of the standard would be adverse to the interests of plan participants in the aggregate, the Secretary of the Treasury may waive the requirements of section 302(a) for such year with respect to all or any portion of the minimum funding standard other than the portion thereof determined under section 302(b)(2)(C). The Secretary of the Treasury shall not waive the minimum funding standard with respect to a plan for more than 3 of any 15 (5 of any 15 in the case of a multiemployer plan) consecutive plan years. The interest rate used for purposes of computing the amortization charge described in subsection (b)(2)(C) for any plan year shall be—

(1) in the case of a plan other than a multiemployer plan, the greater of (A) 150 percent of the Federal mid-term rate (as in effect under section 1274 of the Internal Revenue Code of 1986 for the 1st month of such plan year), or (B) the rate of interest used under the plan in determining costs (including adjustments under section 302(b)(5)(B)), and

(2) in the case of a multiemployer plan, the rate determined under section 6621(b) of such Code.

(b) Matters Considered in Determining Business Hardship.— For purposes of this part, the factors taken into account in determining temporary substantial business hardship (substantial business hardship in the case of a multiemployer plan) shall include (but shall not be limited to) whether—

(1) the employer is operating at an economic loss,

(2) there is substantial unemployment or underemployment in the trade or business and in the industry concerned,

(3) the sales and profits of the industry concerned are depressed or declining, and

(4) it is reasonable to expect that the plan will be continued only if the waiver is granted.

(c) For purposes of this part, the term "waived funding deficiency" means the portion of the minimum funding standard (determined without regard to subsection (b)(3)(C) of section 302) for a plan year waived by the Secretary of the Treasury and not satisfied by employer contributions.

(d) Special Rules.—

(1) Application must be submitted before date 2 months after close of year.—In the case of a plan other than a multiemployer plan, no waiver may be granted under this section with respect to any plan for any plan year unless an application therefor is submitted to the Secretary of the Treasury not later than the 15th day of the 3rd month beginning after the close of such plan year.

(2) Special rule if employer is member of controlled group.—

(A) In general.—In the case of a plan other than a multiemployer plan, if an employer is a member of a controlled group, the temporary substantial business hardship requirements of subsection (a) shall be treated as met only if such requirements are met—

(i) with respect to such employer, and

(ii) with respect to the controlled group of which such employer is a member (determined by treating all members of such group as a single employer).

The Secretary of the Treasury may provide that an analysis of a trade or business or industry of a member need not be conducted if the Secretary of the Treasury determines such analysis is not necessary because the taking into account of such member would not significantly affect the determination under this subsection.

(B) Controlled group.—For purposes of subparagraph (A), the term "controlled group" means any group treated as a single employer under subsection (b), (c), (m), or (o) of section 414 of the Internal Revenue Code of 1986.

(e) Notice of Filing Application for Waiver.—

(1) The Secretary of the Treasury shall, before granting a waiver under this section, require each applicant to provide evidence satisfactory to such Secretary that the applicant has provided notice of the filing of the application for such waiver to each employee organization representing employees covered by the affected plan, and each affected party (as defined in section 4001(a)(21)) other than the Pension Benefit Guaranty Corporation. Such notice shall include a description of the extent to which the plan is funded for benefits which are guaranteed under title IV and for benefit liabilities.

(2) The Secretary of the Treasury shall consider any relevant information provided by a person to whom notice was given under paragraph (1).

(f) Cross Reference.—For corresponding duties of the Secretary of the Treasury with regard to implementation of the Internal Revenue Code of 1986, see section 412(d) of such Code.

Amendments to ERISA §303 [Repealed.]

Pension Protection Act of 2006 (Pub. L. No. 109-280), as follows:

● ERISA §303 was repealed bt Act §101(a). Eff. for plan years beg. after 2007.

Omnibus Budget Reconciliation Act of 1989 (Pub. L. No. 101-239), as follows:

● ERISA §303(a) was amended by Act §7881(b)(7) by redesignating paras. (A) and (B) as paras. (1) and (2), respectively; realign-

ing margins; redesignating cls. (i) and (ii) as subparas. (A) and (B), respectively, of para. (1); and making technical correction to reference to IRC §6621(b) in para. (2) resulting in no change in text. Eff. as if included in Pub. L. No. 100-203.

● ERISA §303(a)(1)(B) was amended by Act §7881(b)(6)(B)(ii) by inserting "(including adjustments under section 302(b)(5)(B) of this title)" after "costs". Eff. as if included in Pub. L. No. 100-203.

● ERISA §303(e)(1) was amended by Act §7881(c)(2) by substituting "for benefit liabilities" for "the benefit liabilities" in last sentence. Eff. as if included in Pub. L. No. 100-203.

● ERISA §303(f) was amended by Act §7891(a)(1) by substituting "Internal Revenue Code of 1986" for "Internal Revenue Code of 1954" and by Act §7881(b)(8) by transferring subsec. (f) to follow immediately after subsec. (e). Eff. as if included in Pub. L. No. 99-514.

Omnibus Budget Reconciliation Act of 1987 (Pub. L. No. 100-203), as follows:

● ERISA §303(a) was amended by Act §9306(a)(2)(B) by substituting "temporary substantial business hardship (substantial business hardship in the case of a multiemployer plan)" for "substantial business hardship"; by Act §9306(b)(2) by substituting "more than 3 of any 15 (5 of any 15 in the case of a multiemployer plan)" for "more than 5 of any 15"; by Act §9306(c)(2)(A) by substituting "The interest rate used for purposes of computing the amortization charge described in subsection (b)(2)(C) of this section for any plan year shall be—" and paras. (A) and (B) for "The interest rate used for purposes of computing the amortization charge described in section 302(b)(2)(C) of this title for a variance granted under this subsection shall be the rate determined under section 6621(b) of title 26." Eff. after 1987.

● ERISA §303(b) was amended by Act §9306(a)(2)(B) by substituting "temporary substantial business hardship (substantial business hardship in the case of a multiemployer plan)" for "substantial business hardship". Eff. after 1987.

● ERISA §303(d)(1) was amended by Act §9306(a)(2)(A) by adding new subsec. (d)(1) and redesignating former subsec. (d) as (f). Eff. after 1987.

● ERISA §303(d)(2) was added by Act §9306(a)(2)(C). Eff. after 1987.

● ERISA §303(e)(1) was amended by Act §9306(d)(2) by substituting "plan, and each affected party (as defined in section 4001(a)(21) of this title) other than the Pension Benefit Guaranty Corporation. Such notice shall include a description of the extent to which the plan is funded for benefits which are guaranteed under subchapter III of this chapter and the benefit liabilities." for "plan." Eff. after 1987.

● ERISA §303(f) was amended by Act §9306(a)(2)(A) by redesignating former subsec. (d) as (f). Eff. after 1987.

Consolidated Omnibus Budget Reconciliation Act of 1986 (Pub. L. No. 99-272), as follows:

● ERISA §303 was amended by Act §11015(b)(1)(A) by inserting the provision that the interest rate used for purposes of computing the amortization charge described in ERISA §302(b)(2)(C) for a variance granted under this subsection is the rate determined under IRC §6621(b).

● ERISA §303(e) was added by Act §11016(c)(2). Eff. Jan. 1, 1986.

Editor's Note

Caution: Pursuant to Pub. L. No. 109-280, §221(c), the provisions of Pub. L. No. 109-280, §201(b) (shortfall funding method), will not apply to plan years beginning after December 31, 2014. See amendment notes for details.

SEC. 304. MINIMUM FUNDING STANDARDS FOR MULTIEMPLOYER PLANS

(a) In General.—For purposes of section 302, the accumulated funding deficiency of a multiemployer plan for any plan year is—

(1) except as provided in paragraph (2), the amount, determined as of the end of the plan year, equal to the excess (if any) of the total charges to the funding standard account of the plan for all plan years (beginning with the first plan year for which this part applies to the plan) over the total credits to such account for such years, and

(2) if the multiemployer plan is in reorganization for any plan year, the accumulated funding deficiency of the plan determined under section 4243.

(b) Funding Standard Account.—

(1) Account required.—Each multiemployer plan to which this part applies shall establish and maintain a funding standard account. Such account shall be credited and charged solely as provided in this section.

(2) Charges to account.—For a plan year, the funding standard account shall be charged with the sum of—

(A) the normal cost of the plan for the plan year,

(B) the amounts necessary to amortize in equal annual installments (until fully amortized)—

(i) in the case of a plan which comes into existence on or after January 1, 2008, the unfunded past service liability under the plan on the first day of the first plan year to which this section applies, over a period of 15 plan years,

(ii) separately, with respect to each plan year, the net increase (if any) in unfunded past service liability under the plan arising from plan amendments adopted in such year, over a period of 15 plan years,

(iii) separately, with respect to each plan year, the net experience loss (if any) under the plan, over a period of 15 plan years, and

(iv) separately, with respect to each plan year, the net loss (if any) resulting from changes in actuarial assumptions used under the plan, over a period of 15 plan years,

(C) the amount necessary to amortize each waived funding deficiency (within the meaning of section 302(c)(3)) for each prior plan year in equal annual installments (until fully amortized) over a period of 15 plan years,

(D) the amount necessary to amortize in equal annual installments (until fully amortized) over a period of 5 plan years any amount credited to the funding standard account under section 302(b)(3)(D) (as in effect on the day before the date of the enactment of the Pension Protection Act of 2006), and

(E) the amount necessary to amortize in equal annual installments (until fully amortized) over a period of 20 years the contributions which would be required to be made under the plan but for the provisions of section 302(c)(7)(A)(i)(I) (as in effect on the day before the date of the enactment of the Pension Protection Act of 2006).

(3) Credits to account.—For a plan year, the funding standard account shall be credited with the sum of—

(A) the amount considered contributed by the employer to or under the plan for the plan year,

(B) the amount necessary to amortize in equal annual installments (until fully amortized)—

(i) separately, with respect to each plan year, the net decrease (if any) in unfunded past service liability under the plan arising from plan amendments adopted in such year, over a period of 15 plan years,

(ii) separately, with respect to each plan year, the net experience gain (if any) under the plan, over a period of 15 plan years, and

(iii) separately, with respect to each plan year, the net gain (if any) resulting from changes in actuarial assumptions used under the plan, over a period of 15 plan years,

(C) the amount of the waived funding deficiency (within the meaning of section 302(c)(3)) for the plan year, and

(D) in the case of a plan year for which the accumulated funding deficiency is determined under the funding standard account if such plan year follows a plan year for which such deficiency was determined under the alternative minimum funding standard under section 305 (as in effect on the day before the date of the enactment of the Pension Protection Act of 2006), the excess (if any) of any debit balance in the funding standard account (determined without regard to this subparagraph) over any debit balance in the alternative minimum funding standard account.

(4) Special rule for amounts first amortized in plan years before 2008.—In the case of any amount amortized under section 302(b) (as in effect on the day before the date of the enactment of the Pension Protection Act of 2006) over any period beginning with a plan year beginning before 2008, in lieu of the amortization described in paragraphs (2)(B) and (3)(B), such amount shall continue to be amortized under such section as so in effect.

(5) Combining and offsetting amounts to be amortized.—Under regulations prescribed by the Secretary of the Treasury, amounts required to be amortized under paragraph (2) or paragraph (3), as the case may be—

(A) may be combined into one amount under such paragraph to be amortized over a period determined on the basis of the remaining amortization period for all items entering into such combined amount, and

(B) may be offset against amounts required to be amortized under the other such paragraph, with the resulting amount to be amortized over a period determined on the basis of the remaining amortization periods for all items entering into whichever of the two amounts being offset is the greater.

(6) Interest.—The funding standard account (and items therein) shall be charged or credited (as determined under regulations prescribed by the Secretary of the Treasury) with interest at the appropriate rate consistent with the rate or rates of interest used under the plan to determine costs.

(7) Special rules relating to charges and credits to funding standard account.—For purposes of this part—

(A) Withdrawal liability.—Any amount received by a multiemployer plan in payment of all or part of an employer's withdrawal liability under part 1 of subtitle E of title IV shall be considered an amount contributed by the employer to or under the plan. The Secretary of the Treasury may prescribe by regulation additional charges and credits to a multiemployer plan's funding standard account to the extent necessary to prevent withdrawal liability payments from being unduly reflected as advance funding for plan liabilities.

(B) Adjustments when a multiemployer plan leaves reorganization.—If a multiemployer plan is not in reorganization in the plan year but was in reorganization in the immediately preceding plan year, any balance in the funding standard account at the close of such immediately preceding plan year—

(i) shall be eliminated by an offsetting credit or charge (as the case may be), but

(ii) shall be taken into account in subsequent plan years by being amortized in equal annual installments (until fully amortized) over 30 plan years.

The preceding sentence shall not apply to the extent of any accumulated funding deficiency under section 4243(a) as of the end of the last plan year that the plan was in reorganization.

(C) Plan payments to supplemental program or withdrawal liability payment fund.—Any amount paid by a plan during a plan year to the Pension Benefit Guaranty Corporation pursuant to section 4222 of this Act or to a fund exempt under section 501(c)(22) of the Internal Revenue Code of 1986 pursuant to section 4223 of this Act shall reduce the amount of contributions considered received by the plan for the plan year.

(D) Interim withdrawal liability payments.—Any amount paid by an employer pending a final determination of the employer's withdrawal liability under part 1 of subtitle E of title IV and subsequently refunded to the employer by the plan shall be charged to the funding standard account in accordance with regulations prescribed by the Secretary of the Treasury.

(E) Election for deferral of charge for portion of net experience loss.—If an election is in effect under section 302(b)(7)(F) (as in effect on the day before the date of the enactment of the Pension Protection Act of 2006) for any plan year, the funding standard account shall be charged in the plan year to which the portion of the net experience loss deferred by such election was deferred with the amount so deferred (and paragraph (2)(B)(iii) shall not apply to the amount so charged).

(F) Financial assistance.—Any amount of any financial assistance from the Pension Benefit Guaranty Corporation to any plan, and any repayment of such amount, shall be taken into account under this section and section 302 in such manner as is determined by the Secretary of the Treasury.

(G) Short-term benefits.—To the extent that any plan amendment increases the unfunded past service liability under the plan by reason of an increase in benefits which are not payable as a life annuity but are payable under the terms of the plan for a period that does not exceed 14 years from the effective date of the amendment, paragraph (2)(B)(ii) shall be applied separately with respect to such increase in unfunded past service liability by substituting the number of years of the period during which such benefits are payable for "15".

(8) Special relief rules.—Notwithstanding any other provision of this subsection—

(A) Amortization of net investment losses.—

(i) In general.—A multiemployer plan with respect to which the solvency test under subparagraph (C) is met may treat the portion of any experience loss or gain attributable to net investment losses incurred in either or both of the first two plan years ending after August 31, 2008, as an item separate from other experience losses, to be amortized in equal annual installments (until fully amortized) over the period —

(I) beginning with the plan year in which such portion is first recognized in the actuarial value of assets, and

(II) ending with the last plan year in the 30-plan year period beginning with the plan year in which such net investment loss was incurred.

(ii) Coordination with extensions.—If this subparagraph applies for any plan year—

(I) no extension of the amortization period under clause (i) shall be allowed under subsection (d), and

(II) if an extension was granted under subsection (d) for any plan year before the election to have this subparagraph apply to the plan year, such extension shall not result in such amortization period exceeding 30 years.

(iii) Net investment losses.—For purposes of this subparagraph—

(I) In general.—Net investment losses shall be determined in the manner prescribed by the Secretary of the Treasury on the basis of the difference between actual and expected returns (including any difference attributable to any criminally fraudulent investment arrangement).

(II) Criminally fraudulent investment arrangements.—The determination as to whether an arrangement is a criminally fraudulent investment arrangement shall be made under rules substantially similar to the rules prescribed by the Secretary of the Treasury for purposes of section 165 of the Internal Revenue Code of 1986.

(B) Expanded smoothing period.—

(i) In general.—A multiemployer plan with respect to which the solvency test under subparagraph (C) is met may change its asset valuation method in a manner which—

(I) spreads the difference between expected and actual returns for either or both of the first 2 plan years ending after August 31, 2008, over a period of not more than 10 years,

(II) provides that for either or both of the first 2 plan years beginning after August 31, 2008, the value of plan assets at any time shall not be less than 80 percent or greater than 130 percent of the fair market value of such assets at such time, or

(III) makes both changes described in subclauses (I) and (II) to such method.

(ii) Asset valuation methods.—If this subparagraph applies for any plan year—

(I) the Secretary of the Treasury shall not treat the asset valuation method of the plan as unreasonable solely because of the changes in such method described in clause (i), and

(II) such changes shall be deemed approved by such Secretary under section 302(d)(1) and section 412(d)(1) of such Code.

(iii) Amortization of reduction in unfunded accrued liability.—If this subparagraph and subparagraph (A) both apply for any plan year, the plan shall treat any reduction in unfunded accrued liability resulting from the application of this subparagraph as a separate experience amortization base, to be amortized in equal annual installments (until fully amortized) over a period of 30 plan years rather than the period such liability would otherwise be amortized over.

(C) Solvency test.—The solvency test under this paragraph is met only if the plan actuary certifies that the plan is projected to have sufficient assets to timely pay expected benefits and anticipated expenditures over the amortization period, taking into account the changes in the funding standard account under this paragraph.

(D) Restriction on benefit increases.—If subparagraph (A) or (B) apply to a multiemployer plan for any plan year, then, in addition to any other applicable restrictions on benefit increases, a plan amendment increasing benefits may not go into effect during either of the 2 plan years immediately following such plan year unless—

(i) the plan actuary certifies that—

(I) any such increase is paid for out of additional contributions not allocated to the plan immediately before the application of this paragraph to the plan, and

(II) the plan's funded percentage and projected credit balances for such 2 plan years are reasonably expected to be at least as high as such percentage and balances would have been if the benefit increase had not been adopted, or

(ii) the amendment is required as a condition of qualification under part I of subchapter D of chapter 1 of the Internal Revenue Code of 1986 or to comply with other applicable law.

(E) Reporting.—A plan sponsor of a plan to which this paragraph applies shall—

(i) give notice of such application to participants and beneficiaries of the plan, and

(ii) inform the Pension Benefit Guaranty Corporation of such application in such form and manner as the Director of the Pension Benefit Guaranty Corporation may prescribe.

(c) Additional Rules.—

(1) Determinations to be made under funding method.—For purposes of this part, normal costs, accrued liability, past service liabilities, and experience gains and losses shall be determined under the funding method used to determine costs under the plan.

(2) Valuation of assets.—

(A) In general.—For purposes of this part, the value of the plan's assets shall be determined on the basis of any reasonable actuarial method of valuation which takes into account fair market value and which is permitted under regulations prescribed by the Secretary of the Treasury.

(B) Election with respect to bonds.—The value of a bond or other evidence of indebtedness which is not in default as to principal or interest may, at the election of the plan administrator, be determined on an amortized basis running from initial cost at purchase to par value at maturity or earliest call date. Any election under this subparagraph shall be made at such time and in such manner as the Secretary of the Treasury shall by regulations provide, shall apply to all such evidences of indebtedness, and may be revoked only with the consent of such Secretary.

(3) Actuarial assumptions must be reasonable.—For purposes of this section, all costs, liabilities, rates of interest, and other factors under the plan shall be determined on the basis of actuarial assumptions and methods—

(A) each of which is reasonable (taking into account the experience of the plan and reasonable expectations), and

(B) which, in combination, offer the actuary's best estimate of anticipated experience under the plan.

(4) Treatment of certain changes as experience gain or loss.—For purposes of this section, if—

(A) a change in benefits under the Social Security Act or in other retirement benefits created under Federal or State law, or

(B) a change in the definition of the term "wages" under section 3121 of the Internal Revenue Code

of 1986, or a change in the amount of such wages taken into account under regulations prescribed for purposes of section 401(a)(5) of such Code,

results in an increase or decrease in accrued liability under a plan, such increase or decrease shall be treated as an experience loss or gain.

(5) Full funding.—If, as of the close of a plan year, a plan would (without regard to this paragraph) have an accumulated funding deficiency in excess of the full funding limitation—

(A) the funding standard account shall be credited with the amount of such excess, and

(B) all amounts described in subparagraphs (B), (C), and (D) of subsection (b)(2) and subparagraph (B) of subsection (b)(3) which are required to be amortized shall be considered fully amortized for purposes of such subparagraphs.

(6) Full-funding limitation.—

(A) In general.—For purposes of paragraph (5), the term "full-funding limitation" means the excess (if any) of—

(i) the accrued liability (including normal cost) under the plan (determined under the entry age normal funding method if such accrued liability cannot be directly calculated under the funding method used for the plan), over

(ii) the lesser of—

(I) the fair market value of the plan's assets, or

(II) the value of such assets determined under paragraph (2).

(B) Minimum amount.—

(i) In general.—In no event shall the full-funding limitation determined under subparagraph (A) be less than the excess (if any) of—

(I) 90 percent of the current liability of the plan (including the expected increase in current liability due to benefits accruing during the plan year), over

(II) the value of the plan's assets determined under paragraph (2).

(ii) Assets.—For purposes of clause (i), assets shall not be reduced by any credit balance in the funding standard account.

(C) Full funding limitation.—For purposes of this paragraph, unless otherwise provided by the plan, the accrued liabilityunder a multiemployer plan shall not include benefits which are not nonforfeitable under the plan after the termination of the plan (taking into consideration section 411(d)(3) of the Internal Revenue Code of 1986).

(D) Current liability.—For purposes of this paragraph—

(i) In general.—The term "current liability" means all liabilities to employees and their beneficiaries under the plan.

(ii) Treatment of unpredictable contingent event benefits.—For purposes of clause (i), any benefit contingent on an event other than—

(I) age, service, compensation, death, or disability, or

(II) an event which is reasonably and reliably predictable (as determined by the Secretary of the Treasury),

shall not be taken into account until the event on which the benefit is contingent occurs.

(iii) Interest rate used.—The rate of interest used to determine current liability under this paragraph shall be the rate of interest determined under subparagraph (E).

(iv) Mortality tables.—

(I) Commissioners' standard table.—In the case of plan years beginning before the first plan year to which the first tables prescribed under subclause (II) apply, the mortality table used in determining current liability under this paragraph shall be the table prescribed by the Secretary of the Treasury which is based on the prevailing commissioners'' standard table (described in section 807(d)(5)(A) of the Internal Revenue Code of 1986) used to determine reserves for group annuity contracts issued on January 1, 1993.

(II) Secretarial authority.—The Secretary of the Treasury may by regulation prescribe for plan years beginning after December 31, 1999, mortality tables to be used in determining current liability under this subsection. Such tables shall be based upon the actual experience of pension plans and projected trends in such experience. In prescribing such tables, such Secretary shall take into account results of available independent studies of mortality of individuals covered by pension plans.

(v) Separate mortality tables for the disabled.—Notwithstanding clause (iv)—

(I) In general.—The Secretary of the Treasury shall establish mortality tables which may be used (in lieu of the tables under clause (iv)) to determine current liability under this subsection for individuals who are entitled to benefits under the plan on account of disability. Such Secretary shall establish separate tables for individuals whose disabilities occur in plan years beginning before January 1, 1995, and for individuals whose disabilities occur in plan years beginning on or after such date.

(II) Special rule for disabilities occurring after 1994.—In the case of disabilities occurring in plan years beginning after December 31, 1994, the tables under subclause (I) shall apply only with respect to individuals described in such subclause who are disabled within the meaning of title II of the Social Security Act and the regulations thereunder.

(vi) Periodic review.—The Secretary of the Treasury shall periodically (at least every 5 years) review any tables in effect under this subparagraph and shall, to the extent such Secretary determines necessary, by regulation update the tables to reflect the actual experience of pension plans and projected trends in such experience.

(E) Required change of interest rate.—For purposes of determining a plan's current liability for purposes of this paragraph—

(i) In general.—If any rate of interest used under the plan under subsection (b)(6) to determine cost is not within the permissible range, the plan shall establish a new rate of interest within the permissible range.

(ii) Permissible range.—For purposes of this subparagraph—

(I) In general.—Except as provided in subclause (II), the term "permissible range" means a rate of interest which is not more than 5 percent above, and not more than 10 percent below, the weighted average of the rates of interest on 30-year Treasury securities during the 4-year period ending on the last day before the beginning of the plan year.

(II) Secretarial authority.—If the Secretary of the Treasury finds that the lowest rate of interest permissible under subclause (I) is unreasonably high, such Secretary may prescribe a lower rate of interest, except that such rate may not be less than 80 percent of the average rate determined under such subclause.

(iii) Assumptions.—Notwithstanding paragraph (3)(A), the interest rate used under the plan shall be—

(I) determined without taking into account the experience of the plan and reasonable expectations, but

(II) consistent with the assumptions which reflect the purchase rates which would be used by insurance companies to satisfy the liabilities under the plan.

(7) Annual valuation.—

(A) In general.—For purposes of this section, a determination of experience gains and losses and a valuation of the plan's liability shall be made not less frequently than once every year, except that such determination shall be made more frequently to the extent required in particular cases under regulations prescribed by the Secretary of the Treasury.

(B) Valuation date.—

(i) Current year.—Except as provided in clause (ii), the valuation referred to in subparagraph (A) shall be made as of a date within the plan year to which the valuation refers or within one month prior to the beginning of such year.

(ii) Use of prior year valuation.—The valuation referred to in subparagraph (A) may be made as of a date within the plan year prior to the year to which the valuation refers if, as of such date, the value of the assets of the plan are not less than 100 percent of the plan's current liability (as defined in paragraph (6)(D) without regard to clause (iv) thereof).

(iii) Adjustments.—Information under clause (ii) shall, in accordance with regulations, be actuarially adjusted to reflect significant differences in participants.

(iv) Limitation.—A change in funding method to use a prior year valuation, as provided in clause (ii), may not be made unless as of the valuation date within the prior plan year, the value of the assets of the plan are not less than 125 percent of the plan's current liability (as defined in paragraph (6)(D) without regard to clause (iv) thereof).

(8) Time when certain contributions deemed made.—For purposes of this section, any contributions for a plan year made by an employer after the last day of such plan year, but not later than two and one-half months after such day, shall be deemed to have been made on such last day. For purposes of this subparagraph, such two and one-half month period may be extended for not more than six months under regulations prescribed by the Secretary of the Treasury.

(d) Extension of Amortization Periods for Multiemployer Plans.—

(1) Automatic extension upon application by certain plans.—

(A) In general.—If the plan sponsor of a multiemployer plan—

(i) submits to the Secretary of the Treasury an application for an extension of the period of years required to amortize any unfunded liability described in any clause of subsection (b)(2)(B) or described in subsection (b)(4), and

(ii) includes with the application a certification by the plan's actuary described in subparagraph (B),

the Secretary of the Treasury shall extend the amortization period for the period of time (not in excess of 5 years) specified in the application. Such extension shall be in addition to any extension under paragraph (2).

(B) Criteria.—A certification with respect to a multiemployer plan is described in this subparagraph if the plan's actuary certifies that, based on reasonable assumptions—

(i) absent the extension under subparagraph (A), the plan would have an accumulated funding

deficiency in the current plan year or any of the 9 succeeding plan years,

(ii) the plan sponsor has adopted a plan to improve the plan's funding status,

(iii) the plan is projected to have sufficient assets to timely pay expected benefits and anticipated expenditures over the amortization period as extended, and

(iv) the notice required under paragraph (3)(A) has been provided.

(C) Termination.—The preceding provisions of this paragraph shall not apply with respect to any application submitted after December 31, 2014.

(2) Alternative extension.—

(A) In general.—If the plan sponsor of a multiemployer plan submits to the Secretary of the Treasury an application for an extension of the period of years required to amortize any unfunded liability described in any clause of subsection (b)(2)(B) or described in subsection (b)(4), the Secretary of the Treasury may extend the amortization period for a period of time (not in excess of 10 years reduced by the number of years of any extension under paragraph (1) with respect to such unfunded liability) if the Secretary of the Treasury makes the determination described in subparagraph (B). Such extension shall be in addition to any extension under paragraph (1).

(B) Determination.—The Secretary of the Treasury may grant an extension under subparagraph (A) if such Secretary determines that—

(i) such extension would carry out the purposes of this Act and would provide adequate protection for participants under the plan and their beneficiaries, and

(ii) the failure to permit such extension would—

(I) result in a substantial risk to the voluntary continuation of the plan, or a substantial curtailment of pension benefit levels or employee compensation, and

(II) be adverse to the interests of plan participants in the aggregate.

(C) Action by secretary of the treasury.—The Secretary of the Treasury shall act upon any application for an extension under this paragraph within 180 days of the submission of such application. If such Secretary rejects the application for an extension under this paragraph, such Secretary shall provide notice to the plan detailing the specific reasons for the rejection, including references to the criteria set forth above.

(3) Advance notice.—

(A) In general.—The Secretary of the Treasury shall, before granting an extension under this subsection, require each applicant to provide evidence satisfactory to such Secretary that the applicant has provided notice of the filing of the application for such extension to each affected party (as defined in section 4001(a)(21)) with respect to the affected plan. Such notice shall include a description of the extent to which the plan is funded for benefits which are guaranteed under title IV and for benefit liabilities.

(B) Consideration of relevant information.—The Secretary of the Treasury shall consider any relevant information provided by a person to whom notice was given under paragraph (1).

Amendments to ERISA §304

Preservation of Access to Care for Medicare Beneficiaries and Pension Relief Act of 2010 (Pub. L. No. 111-192), as follows:
- ERISA §304(b)(8) was added by Act §211(a)(1). See effective date below.
- Effective Date. Act §211(b) provides:
  (b) Effective Dates.—
  (1) In general.—The amendments made by this section shall take effect as of the first day of the first plan year ending after August 31, 2008, except that any election a plan makes pursuant to this section that affects the plan's funding standard account for the first plan year beginning after August 31, 2008, shall be disregarded for purposes of applying the provisions of section 305 of the Employee Retirement Income Security Act of 1974 and section 432 of the Internal Revenue Code of 1986 to such plan year.
  (2) Restrictions on benefit increases.—Notwithstanding paragraph (1), the restrictions on plan amendments increasing benefits in sections 304(b)(8)(D) of such Act and 431(b)(8)(D) of such Code, as added by this section, shall take effect on the date of enactment of this Act.

Pension Protection Act of 2006 (Pub. L. No. 109-280), as follows:
- ERISA §304 was added by Act §201(a). Eff. for plan years after 2007. For eligible cooperative plans, plan amendments are delayed until the earlier of when such a plan is no longer eligible or Jan. 1, 2017.
- ERISA §304, as in effect before 2007, was repealed by Act §101(a). Eff. for plan years after 2007. See below for text of repealed ERISA §304.
- Other Provision. Act §201(b) provides:
  (b) Shortfall Funding Method.—
  (1) In general.—A multiemployer plan meeting the criteria of paragraph (2) may adopt, use, or cease using, the shortfall funding method and such adoption, use, or cessation of use of such method, shall be deemed approved by the Secretary of the Treasury under section 302(d)(1) of the Employee Retirement Income Security Act of 1974 and section 412(d)(1) of the Internal Revenue Code of 1986.
  (2) Criteria.—A multiemployer pension plan meets the criteria of this clause if—
    (A) the plan has not used the shortfall funding method during the 5-year period ending on the day before the date the plan is to use the method under paragraph (1); and
    (B) the plan is not operating under an amortization period extension under section 304(d) of such Act and did not operate under such an extension during such 5-year period.
  (3) Shortfall funding method defined.—For purposes of this subsection, the term "shortfall funding method" means the shortfall funding method described in Treasury Regulations section 1.412(c)(1)-2 (26 CFR 1.412(c)(1)-2).
  (4) Benefit restrictions to apply.—The benefit restrictions under section 302(c)(7) of such Act and section 412(c)(7) of such Code shall apply during any period a multiemployer plan is on the shortfall funding method pursuant to this subsection.

(5) Use of shortfall method not to preclude other options.—Nothing in this subsection shall be construed to affect a multiemployer plan's ability to adopt the shortfall funding method with the Secretary's permission under otherwise applicable regulations or to affect a multiemployer plan's right to change funding methods, with or without the Secretary's consent, as provided in applicable rules and regulations.
- **Other Provision—Sunset.** Act §221(c), provides:
  (c) Sunset.—
  (1) In general.—Except as provided in this subsection, notwithstanding any other provision of this Act, the provisions of, and the amendments made by, sections 201(b), 202, and 212 shall not apply to plan years beginning after December 31, 2014.
  (2) Funding Improvement and Rehabilitation Plans.—If a plan is operating under a funding improvement or rehabilitation plan under section 305 of such Act or 432 of such Code for its last years beginning before January 1, 2015, such plan shall continue to operate under such funding improvement or rehabilitation plan during any period after December 31, 2014, such funding improvement or rehabilitation plan is in effect and all provisions of such Act or Code relating to the operation of such funding improvement or rehabilitation plan shall continue in effect during such period.

SEC. 304. EXTENSION OF AMORTIZATION PERIODS. [Repealed.]

(a) Determinations by Secretary in Granting Extension.—The period of years required to amortize any unfunded liability (described in any clause of subsection (b)(2)(B) of section 302) of any plan may be extended by the Secretary for a period of time (not in excess of 10 years) if he determines that such extension would carry out the purposes of this Act and would provide adequate protection for participants under the plan and their beneficiaries and if he determines that the failure to permit such extension would—

(1) result in—

(A) a substantial risk to the voluntary continuation of the plan, or

(B) a substantial curtailment of pension benefit levels or employee compensation, and

(2) be adverse to the interests of plan participants in the aggregate.

In the case of a plan other than a multiemployer plan, the interest rate applicable for any plan year under any arrangement entered into by the Secretary in connection with an extension granted under this subsection shall be the greater of (A) 150 percent of the Federal mid-term rate (as in effect under section 1274 of the Internal Revenue Code of 1986 for the 1st month of such plan year), or (B) the rate of interest used under the plan in determining costs. In the case of a multiemployer plan, such rate shall be the rate determined under section 6621(b) of such Code.

(b) Amendment of Plan.—

(1) No amendment of the plan which increases the liabilities of the plan by reason of any increase in benefits, any change in the accrual of benefits, or any change in the rate at which benefits become nonforfeitable under the plan shall be adopted if a waiver under section 303(a) or an extension of time under subsection (a) of this section is in effect with respect to the plan, or if a plan amendment described in section 302(c)(8) has been made at any time in the preceding 12 months (24 months in the case of a multiemployer plan). If a plan is amended in violation of the preceding sentence, any such waiver, or extension of time, shall not apply to any plan year ending on or after the date on which such amendment is adopted.

(2) Paragraph (1) shall not apply to any plan amendment which—

(A) the Secretary determines to be reasonable and which provides for only de minimis increases in the liabilities of the plan,

(B) only repeals an amendment described in section 302(c)(8), or

(C) is required as a condition of qualification under part I of subchapter D, of chapter 1, of title 26.

(c) Notice for Filing Application for Extension.—

(1) The Secretary of the Treasury shall, before granting an extension under this section, require each applicant to provide evidence satisfactory to such Secretary that the applicant has provided notice of the filing of the application for such extension to each employee organization representing employees covered by the affected plan.

(2) The Secretary of the Treasury shall consider any relevant information provided by a person to whom notice was given under paragraph (1).

Amendments to ERISA §304 [Repealed.]

Pension Protection Act of 2006 (Pub. L. No. 109-280), as follows:
- ERISA §304, as in effect before 2007, was repealed by Act §201(a). Eff. for plan years after 2007.

Omnibus Budget Reconciliation Act of 1989 (Pub. L. No. 101-239), as follows:
- ERISA §304(b)(2)(A) was amended by Act §7894(d)(3) by substituting a comma for period at end. Eff. as if originally included in Pub. L. No. 93-406.
- ERISA §304(b)(2)(C) was amended by Act §7891(a)(1) by substituting "Internal Revenue Code of 1986" for "Internal Revenue Code of 1954", which for purposes of codification was translated as "title 26". Eff. as if included in Pub. L. No. 99-514.

Omnibus Budget Reconciliation Act of 1987 (Pub. L. No. 100-203), as follows:
- ERISA §304(a) was amended by Act §9306(c)(2)(B) by amending the last sentence generally. Eff. for applications submitted after Dec. 17, 1987. Prior to amendment, the last sentence read as follows:
  The interest rate applicable under any arrangement entered into by the Secretary in connection with an extension granted under this subsection shall be the rate determined under section 6621(b) of title 26.

Consolidated Omnibus Budget Reconciliation Act of 1986 (Pub. L. No. 99-272), as follows:
- ERISA §304(a) was amended by Act §11015(b)(1)(B) by inserting a provision that the interest rate applicable under any arrangement entered into by the Secretary in connection with an extension granted under this subsection be the rate determined under IRC §6621(b). Eff. Jan. 1, 1986.
- ERISA §304(c) was amended by Act §11016(c)(3) by adding subsec. (c). Eff. Jan. 1, 1986.

> ### Editor's Note
>
> **Caution:** Pursuant to Pub. L. No. 109-280, §221(c), the amendments to ERISA §305 made by Pub. L. No. 109-280, §202(a) will not apply to plan years beginning after December 31, 2014. See amendment notes for details.

SEC. 305. ADDITIONAL FUNDING RULES FOR MULTIEMPLOYER PLANS IN ENDANGERED STATUS OR CRITICAL STATUS

(a) General Rule.—For purposes of this part, in the case of a multiemployer plan in effect on July 16, 2006—

(1) if the plan is in endangered status—

(A) the plan sponsor shall adopt and implement a funding improvement plan in accordance with the requirements of subsection (c), and

(B) the requirements of subsection (d) shall apply during the funding plan adoption period and the funding improvement period, and

(2) if the plan is in critical status—

(A) the plan sponsor shall adopt and implement a rehabilitation plan in accordance with the requirements of subsection (e), and

(B) the requirements of subsection (f) shall apply during the rehabilitation plan adoption period and the rehabilitation period.

(b) Determination of Endangered and Critical Status.—For purposes of this section—

(1) Endangered status.—A multiemployer plan is in endangered status for a plan year if, as determined by the plan actuary under paragraph (3), the plan is not in critical status for the plan year and, as of the beginning of the plan year, either—

(A) the plan's funded percentage for such plan year is less than 80 percent, or

(B) the plan has an accumulated funding deficiency for such plan year, or is projected to have such an accumulated funding deficiency for any of the 6 succeeding plan years, taking into account any extension of amortization periods under section 304(d).

For purposes of this section, a plan shall be treated as in seriously endangered status for a plan year if the plan is described in both subparagraphs (A) and (B).

(2) Critical status.—A multiemployer plan is in critical status for a plan year if, as determined by the plan actuary under paragraph (3), the plan is described in 1 or more of the following subparagraphs as of the beginning of the plan year:

(A) A plan is described in this subparagraph if—

(i) the funded percentage of the plan is less than 65 percent, and

(ii) the sum of—

(I) the fair market value of plan assets, plus

(II) the present value of the reasonably anticipated employer contributions for the current plan year and each of the 6 succeeding plan years, assuming that the terms of all collective bargaining agreements pursuant to which the plan is maintained for the current plan year continue in effect for succeeding plan years,

is less than the present value of all nonforfeitable benefits projected to be payable under the plan during the current plan year and each of the 6 succeeding plan years (plus administrative expenses for such plan years).

(B) A plan is described in this subparagraph if—

(i) the plan has an accumulated funding deficiency for the current plan year, not taking into account any extension of amortization periods under section 304(d), or

(ii) the plan is projected to have an accumulated funding deficiency for any of the 3 succeeding plan years (4 succeeding plan years if the funded percentage of the plan is 65 percent or less), not taking into account any extension of amortization periods under section 304(d).

(C) A plan is described in this subparagraph if—

(i)(I) the plan's normal cost for the current plan year, plus interest (determined at the rate used for determining costs under the plan) for the current plan year on the amount of unfunded benefit liabilities under the plan as of the last date of the preceding plan year, exceeds

(II) the present value of the reasonably anticipated employer and employee contributions for the current plan year,

(ii) the present value, as of the beginning of the current plan year, of nonforfeitable benefits of inactive participants is greater than the present value of nonforfeitable benefits of active participants, and

(iii) the plan has an accumulated funding deficiency for the current plan year, or is projected to have such a deficiency for any of the 4 succeeding plan years, not taking into account any extension of amortization periods under section 304(d).

(D) A plan is described in this subparagraph if the sum of—

(i) the fair market value of plan assets, plus

(ii) the present value of the reasonably anticipated employer contributions for the current plan year and each of the 4 succeeding plan years, assuming that the terms of all collective bargaining agreements pursuant to which the plan is maintained for the current plan year continue in effect for succeeding plan years,

is less than the present value of all benefits projected to be payable under the plan during the current plan year and each of the 4 succeeding plan years (plus administrative expenses for such plan years).

(3) Annual certification by plan actuary.—

(A) In general.—Not later than the 90th day of each plan year of a multiemployer plan, the plan actuary shall certify to the Secretary of the Treasury and to the plan sponsor—

(i) whether or not the plan is in endangered status for such plan year and whether or not the plan is or will be in critical status for such plan year, and

(ii) in the case of a plan which is in a funding improvement or rehabilitation period, whether or not the plan is making the scheduled progress in meeting the requirements of its funding improvement or rehabilitation plan.

(B) Actuarial projections of assets and liabilities.—

(i) In general.—In making the determinations and projections under this subsection, the plan actuary shall make projections required for the current and succeeding plan years of the current value of the assets of the plan and the present value of all liabilities to participants and beneficiaries under the plan for the current plan year as of the beginning of such year. The actuary's projections shall be based on reasonable actuarial estimates, assumptions, and methods that, except as provided in clause (iii), offer the actuary's best estimate of anticipated experience under the plan. The projected present value of liabilities as of the beginning of such year shall be determined based on the most recent of either—

(I) the actuarial statement required under section 103(d) with respect to the most recently filed annual report, or

(II) the actuarial valuation for the preceding plan year.

(ii) Determinations of future contributions.— Any actuarial projection of plan assets shall assume—

(I) reasonably anticipated employer contributions for the current and succeeding plan years, assuming that the terms of the one or more collective bargaining agreements pursuant to which the plan is maintained for the current plan year continue in effect for succeeding plan years, or

(II) that employer contributions for the most recent plan year will continue indefinitely, but only if the plan actuary determines there have been no significant demographic changes that would make such assumption unreasonable.

(iii) Projected industry activity.—Any projection of activity in the industry or industries covered by the plan, including future covered employment and contribution levels, shall be based on information provided by the plan sponsor, which shall act reasonably and in good faith.

(C) Penalty for failure to secure timely actuarial certification.—Any failure of the plan's actuary to certify the plan's status under this subsection by the date specified in subparagraph (A) shall be treated for purposes of section 502(c)(2) as a failure or refusal by the plan administrator to file the annual report required to be filed with the Secretary under section 101(b)(1).

ERISA Sec. 305(b)(3)(C)

(D) Notice.—

(i) In general.—In any case in which it is certified under subparagraph (A) that a multiemployer plan is or will be in endangered or critical status for a plan year, the plan sponsor shall, not later than 30 days after the date of the certification, provide notification of the endangered or critical status to the participants and beneficiaries, the bargaining parties, the Pension Benefit Guaranty Corporation, and the Secretary.

(ii) Plans in critical status.—If it is certified under subparagraph (A) that a multiemployer plan is or will be in critical status, the plan sponsor shall include in the notice under clause (i) an explanation of the possibility that—

(I) adjustable benefits (as defined in subsection (e)(8)) may be reduced, and

(II) such reductions may apply to participants and beneficiaries whose benefit commencement date is on or after the date such notice is provided for the first plan year in which the plan is in critical status.

(iii) Model notice.—The Secretary of the Treasury, in consultation with the Secretary, shall prescribe a model notice that a multiemployer plan may use to satisfy the requirements under clause (ii).

(c) Funding Improvement Plan Must Be Adopted for Multiemployer Plans in Endangered Status.—

(1) In general.—In any case in which a multiemployer plan is in endangered status for a plan year, the plan sponsor, in accordance with this subsection—

(A) shall adopt a funding improvement plan not later than 240 days following the required date for the actuarial certification of endangered status under subsection (b)(3)(A), and

(B) within 30 days after the adoption of the funding improvement plan—

(i) shall provide to the bargaining parties 1 or more schedules showing revised benefit structures, revised contribution structures, or both, which, if adopted, may reasonably be expected to enable the multiemployer plan to meet the applicable benchmarks in accordance with the funding improvement plan, including—

(I) one proposal for reductions in the amount of future benefit accruals necessary to achieve the applicable benchmarks, assuming no amendments increasing contributions under the plan (other than amendments increasing contributions necessary to achieve the applicable benchmarks after amendments have reduced future benefit accruals to the maximum extent permitted by law), and

(II) one proposal for increases in contributions under the plan necessary to achieve the applicable

benchmarks, assuming no amendments reducing future benefit accruals under the plan, and

(ii) may, if the plan sponsor deems appropriate, prepare and provide the bargaining parties with additional information relating to contribution rates or benefit reductions, alternative schedules, or other information relevant to achieving the applicable benchmarks in accordance with the funding improvement plan.

For purposes of this section, the term "applicable benchmarks" means the requirements applicable to the multiemployer plan under paragraph (3) (as modified by paragraph (5)).

(2) Exception for years after process begins.— Paragraph (1) shall not apply to a plan year if such year is in a funding plan adoption period or funding improvement period by reason of the plan being in endangered status for a preceding plan year. For purposes of this section, such preceding plan year shall be the initial determination year with respect to the funding improvement plan to which it relates.

(3) Funding improvement plan.—For purposes of this section—

(A) In general.—A funding improvement plan is a plan which consists of the actions, including options or a range of options to be proposed to the bargaining parties, formulated to provide, based on reasonably anticipated experience and reasonable actuarial assumptions, for the attainment by the plan during the funding improvement period of the following requirements:

(i) Increase in plan's funding percentage.—The plan's funded percentage as of the close of the funding improvement period equals or exceeds a percentage equal to the sum of—

(I) such percentage as of the beginning of such period, plus

(II) 33 percent of the difference between 100 percent and the percentage under subclause (I).

(ii) Avoidance of accumulated funding deficiencies.—No accumulated funding deficiency for any plan year during the funding improvement period (taking into account any extension of amortization periods under section 304(d)).

(B) Seriously endangered plans.—In the case of a plan in seriously endangered status, except as provided in paragraph (5), subparagraph (A)(i)(II) shall be applied by substituting "20 percent" for "33 percent".

(4) Funding improvement period.—For purposes of this section—

(A) In general.—The funding improvement period for any funding improvement plan adopted pursuant to this subsection is the 10-year period beginning on the first day of the first plan year of the multiemployer plan beginning after the earlier of—

(i) the second anniversary of the date of the adoption of the funding improvement plan, or

(ii) the expiration of the collective bargaining agreements in effect on the due date for the actuarial certification of endangered status for the initial determination year under subsection (b)(3)(A) and covering, as of such due date, at least 75 percent of the active participants in such multiemployer plan.

(B) Seriously endangered plans.—In the case of a plan in seriously endangered status, except as provided in paragraph (5), subparagraph (A) shall be applied by substituting "15-year period" for "10-year period".

(C) Coordination with changes in status.—

(i) Plans no longer in endangered status.—If the plan's actuary certifies under subsection (b)(3)(A) for a plan year in any funding plan adoption period or funding improvement period that the plan is no longer in endangered status and is not in critical status, the funding plan adoption period or funding improvement period, whichever is applicable, shall end as of the close of the preceding plan year.

(ii) Plans in critical status.—If the plan's actuary certifies under subsection (b)(3)(A) for a plan year in any funding plan adoption period or funding improvement period that the plan is in critical status, the funding plan adoption period or funding improvement period, whichever is applicable, shall end as of the close of the plan year preceding the first plan year in the rehabilitation period with respect to such status.

(D) Plans in endangered status at end of period.— If the plan's actuary certifies under subsection (b)(3)(A) for the first plan year following the close of the period described in subparagraph (A) that the plan is in endangered status, the provisions of this subsection and subsection (d) shall be applied as if such first plan year were an initial determination year, except that the plan may not be amended in a manner inconsistent with the funding improvement plan in effect for the preceding plan year until a new funding improvement plan is adopted.

(5) Special rules for seriously endangered plans more than 70 percent funded.—

(A) In general.—If the funded percentage of a plan in seriously endangered status was more than 70 percent as of the beginning of the initial determination year—

(i) paragraphs (3)(B) and (4)(B) shall apply only if the plan's actuary certifies, within 30 days after the certification under subsection (b)(3)(A) for the initial determination year, that, based on the

terms of the plan and the collective bargaining agreements in effect at the time of such certification, the plan is not projected to meet the requirements of paragraph (3)(A) (without regard to paragraphs (3)(B) and (4)(B)), and

(ii) if there is a certification under clause (i), the plan may, in formulating its funding improvement plan, only take into account the rules of paragraph (3)(B) and (4)(B) for plan years in the funding improvement period beginning on or before the date on which the last of the collective bargaining agreements described in paragraph (4)(A)(ii) expires.

(B) Special rule after expiration of agreements.— Notwithstanding subparagraph (A)(ii), if, for any plan year ending after the date described in subparagraph (A)(ii), the plan actuary certifies (at the time of the annual certification under subsection (b)(3)(A) for such plan year) that, based on the terms of the plan and collective bargaining agreements in effect at the time of that annual certification, the plan is not projected to be able to meet the requirements of paragraph (3)(A) (without regard to paragraphs (3)(B) and (4)(B)), paragraphs (3)(B) and (4)(B) shall continue to apply for such year.

(6) Updates to funding improvement plan and schedules.—

(A) Funding improvement plan.—The plan sponsor shall annually update the funding improvement plan and shall file the update with the plan's annual report under section 104.

(B) Schedules.—The plan sponsor shall annually update any schedule of contribution rates provided under this subsection to reflect the experience of the plan.

(C) Duration of schedule.—A schedule of contribution rates provided by the plan sponsor and relied upon by bargaining parties in negotiating a collective bargaining agreement shall remain in effect for the duration of that collective bargaining agreement.

(7) Imposition of default schedule where failure to adopt funding improvement plan.—

(A) In general.—If—

(i) a collective bargaining agreement providing for contributions under a multiemployer plan that was in effect at the time the plan entered endangered status expires, and

(ii) after receiving one or more schedules from the plan sponsor under paragraph (1)(B), the bargaining parties with respect to such agreement fail to adopt a contribution schedule with terms consistent with the funding improvement plan and a schedule from the plan sponsor,

the plan sponsor shall implement the schedule described in paragraph (1)(B)(i)(I) beginning on the date specified in subparagraph (B).

ERISA Sec. 305(c)(7)(A)(ii)

(B) Date of implementation.—The date specified in this subparagraph is the date which is 180 days after the date on which the collective bargaining agreement described in subparagraph (A) expires.

(C) Failure to make scheduled contributions.— Any failure to make a contribution under a schedule of contribution rates provided under this paragraph shall be treated as a delinquent contribution under section 515 and shall be enforceable as such.

(8) Funding plan adoption period.—For purposes of this section, the term "funding plan adoption period" means the period beginning on the date of the certification under subsection (b)(3)(A) for the initial determination year and ending on the day before the first day of the funding improvement period.

(d) Rules for Operation of Plan During Adoption and Improvement Periods.—

(1) Special rules for plan adoption period.— During the funding plan adoption period—

(A) the plan sponsor may not accept a collective bargaining agreement or participation agreement with respect to the multiemployer plan that provides for—

(i) a reduction in the level of contributions for any participants,

(ii) a suspension of contributions with respect to any period of service, or

(iii) any new direct or indirect exclusion of younger or newly hired employees from plan participation,

(B) no amendment of the plan which increases the liabilities of the plan by reason of any increase in benefits, any change in the accrual of benefits, or any change in the rate at which benefits become nonforfeitable under the plan may be adopted unless the amendment is required as a condition of qualification under part I of subchapter D of chapter 1 of the Internal Revenue Code of 1986 or to comply with other applicable law, and

(C) in the case of a plan in seriously endangered status, the plan sponsor shall take all reasonable actions which are consistent with the terms of the plan and applicable law and which are expected, based on reasonable assumptions, to achieve—

(i) an increase in the plan's funded percentage, and

(ii) postponement of an accumulated funding deficiency for at least 1 additional plan year.

Actions under subparagraph (C) include applications for extensions of amortization periods under section 304(d), use of the shortfall funding method in making funding standard account computations, amendments to the plan's benefit structure, reductions in future benefit accruals, and other reasonable actions consistent with the terms of the plan and applicable law.

(2) Compliance with funding improvement plan.—

(A) In general.—A plan may not be amended after the date of the adoption of a funding improvement plan so as to be inconsistent with the funding improvement plan.

(B) No reduction in contributions.—A plan sponsor may not during any funding improvement period accept a collective bargaining agreement or participation agreement with respect to the multiemployer plan that provides for—

(i) a reduction in the level of contributions for any participants,

(ii) a suspension of contributions with respect to any period of service, or

(iii) any new direct or indirect exclusion of younger or newly hired employees from plan participation.

(C) Special rules for benefit increases.—A plan may not be amended after the date of the adoption of a funding improvement plan so as to increase benefits, including future benefit accruals, unless the plan actuary certifies that the benefit increase is consistent with the funding improvement plan and is paid for out of contributions not required by the funding improvement plan to meet the applicable benchmark in accordance with the schedule contemplated in the funding improvement plan.

(e) Rehabilitation Plan Must Be Adopted for Multiemployer Plans in Critical Status.—

(1) In general.—In any case in which a multiemployer plan is in critical status for a plan year, the plan sponsor, in accordance with this subsection—

(A) shall adopt a rehabilitation plan not later than 240 days following the required date for the actuarial certification of critical status under subsection (b)(3)(A), and

(B) within 30 days after the adoption of the rehabilitation plan—

(i) shall provide to the bargaining parties 1 or more schedules showing revised benefit structures, revised contribution structures, or both, which, if adopted, may reasonably be expected to enable the multiemployer plan to emerge from critical status in accordance with the rehabilitation plan, and

(ii) may, if the plan sponsor deems appropriate, prepare and provide the bargaining parties with additional information relating to contribution rates or benefit reductions, alternative schedules, or other information relevant to emerging from critical status in accordance with the rehabilitation plan.

The schedule or schedules described in subparagraph (B)(i) shall reflect reductions in future benefit accruals and adjustable benefits, and increases in contributions, that the plan sponsor determines are reasonably necessary to emerge from critical status. One schedule shall be designated as the default schedule and such schedule shall assume that there are no increases in contributions under the plan other than the increases necessary to emerge from critical status after future benefit accruals and other benefits (other than benefits the reduction or elimination of which are not permitted under section 204(g)) have been reduced to the maximum extent permitted by law.

(2) Exception for years after process begins.— Paragraph (1) shall not apply to a plan year if such year is in a rehabilitation plan adoption period or rehabilitation period by reason of the plan being in critical status for a preceding plan year. For purposes of this section, such preceding plan year shall be the initial critical year with respect to the rehabilitation plan to which it relates.

(3) Rehabilitation plan.—For purposes of this section—

(A) In general.—A rehabilitation plan is a plan which consists of—

(i) actions, including options or a range of options to be proposed to the bargaining parties, formulated, based on reasonably anticipated experience and reasonable actuarial assumptions, to enable the plan to cease to be in critical status by the end of the rehabilitation period and may include reductions in plan expenditures (including plan mergers and consolidations), reductions in future benefit accruals or increases in contributions, if agreed to by the bargaining parties, or any combination of such actions, or

(ii) if the plan sponsor determines that, based on reasonable actuarial assumptions and upon exhaustion of all reasonable measures, the plan can not reasonably be expected to emerge from critical status by the end of the rehabilitation period, reasonable measures to emerge from critical status at a later time or to forestall possible insolvency (within the meaning of section 4245).

A rehabilitation plan must provide annual standards for meeting the requirements of such rehabilitation plan. Such plan shall also include the schedules required to be provided under paragraph (1)(B)(i) and if clause (ii) applies, shall set forth the alternatives considered, explain why the plan is not reasonably expected to emerge from critical status by the end of the rehabilitation period, and specify when, if ever, the plan is expected to emerge from critical status in accordance with the rehabilitation plan.

(B) Updates to rehabilitation plan and schedules.—

(i) Rehabilitation plan.—The plan sponsor shall annually update the rehabilitation plan and

shall file the update with the plan's annual report under section 104.

(ii) Schedules.—The plan sponsor shall annually update any schedule of contribution rates provided under this subsection to reflect the experience of the plan.

(iii) Duration of schedule.—A schedule of contribution rates provided by the plan sponsor and relied upon by bargaining parties in negotiating a collective bargaining agreement shall remain in effect for the duration of that collective bargaining agreement.

(C) Imposition of default schedule where failure to adopt rehabilitation plan.—

(i) In general.—If—

(I) a collective bargaining agreement providing for contributions under a multiemployer plan that was in effect at the time the plan entered critical status expires, and

(II) after receiving one or more schedules from the plan sponsor under paragraph (1)(B), the bargaining parties with respect to such agreement fail to adopt a contribution schedule with terms consistent with the rehabilitation plan and a schedule from the plan sponsor under paragraph (1)(B)(i),

the plan sponsor shall implement the default schedule described in the last sentence of paragraph (1) beginning on the date specified in clause (ii).

(ii) Date of implementation.—The date specified in this clause is the date which is 180 days after the date on which the collective bargaining agreement described in clause (i) expires.

(iii) Failure to make scheduled contributions.—Any failure to make a contribution under a schedule of contribution rates provided under this subsection shall be treated as a delinquent contribution under section 515 and shall be enforceable as such.

(4) Rehabilitation period.—For purposes of this section—

(A) In general.—The rehabilitation period for a plan in critical status is the 10-year period beginning on the first day of the first plan year of the multiemployer plan following the earlier of—

(i) the second anniversary of the date of the adoption of the rehabilitation plan, or

(ii) the expiration of the collective bargaining agreements in effect on the due date for the actuarial certification of critical status for the initial critical year under subsection (a)(1) and covering, as of such date at least 75 percent of the active participants in such multiemployer plan.

If a plan emerges from critical status as provided under subparagraph (B) before the end of such 10-

year period, the rehabilitation period shall end with the plan year preceding the plan year for which the determination under subparagraph (B) is made.

(B) Emergence.—A plan in critical status shall remain in such status until a plan year for which the plan actuary certifies, in accordance with subsection (b)(3)(A), that the plan is not projected to have an accumulated funding deficiency for the plan year or any of the 9 succeeding plan years, without regard to the use of the shortfall method but taking into account any extension of amortization periods under section 304(d).

(5) **Rehabilitation plan adoption period.**—For purposes of this section, the term "rehabilitation plan adoption period" means the period beginning on the date of the certification under subsection (b)(3)(A) for the initial critical year and ending on the day before the first day of the rehabilitation period.

(6) **Limitation on reduction in rates of future accruals.**—Any reduction in the rate of future accruals under the default schedule described in the last sentence of paragraph (1) shall not reduce the rate of future accruals below—

(A) a monthly benefit (payable as a single life annuity commencing at the participant's normal retirement age) equal to 1 percent of the contributions required to be made with respect to a participant, or the equivalent standard accrual rate for a participant or group of participants under the collective bargaining agreements in effect as of the first day of the initial critical year, or

(B) if lower, the accrual rate under the plan on such first day.

The equivalent standard accrual rate shall be determined by the plan sponsor based on the standard or average contribution base units which the plan sponsor determines to be representative for active participants and such other factors as the plan sponsor determines to be relevant. Nothing in this paragraph shall be construed as limiting the ability of the plan sponsor to prepare and provide the bargaining parties with alternative schedules to the default schedule that establish lower or higher accrual and contribution rates than the rates otherwise described in this paragraph.

(7) **Automatic employer surcharge.**—

(A) Imposition of surcharge.—Each employer otherwise obligated to make contributions for the initial critical year shall be obligated to pay to the plan for such year a surcharge equal to 5 percent of the contributions otherwise required under the applicable collective bargaining agreement (or other agreement pursuant to which the employer contributes). For each succeeding plan year in which the plan is in critical status for a consecutive period of years beginning with the initial critical year, the surcharge shall be 10 percent of the contributions otherwise so required.

(B) Enforcement of surcharge.—The surcharges under subparagraph (A) shall be due and payable on the same schedule as the contributions on which the surcharges are based. Any failure to make a surcharge payment shall be treated as a delinquent contribution under section 515 and shall be enforceable as such.

(C) Surcharge to terminate upon collective bargaining agreement renegotiation.—The surcharge under this paragraph shall cease to be effective with respect to employees covered by a collective bargaining agreement (or other agreement pursuant to which the employer contributes), beginning on the effective date of a collective bargaining agreement (or other such agreement) that includes terms consistent with a schedule presented by the plan sponsor under paragraph (1)(B)(i), as modified under subparagraph (B) of paragraph (3).

(D) Surcharge not to apply until employer receives notice.—The surcharge under this paragraph shall not apply to an employer until 30 days after the employer has been notified by the plan sponsor that the plan is in critical status and that the surcharge is in effect.

(E) Surcharge not to generate increased benefit accruals.—Notwithstanding any provision of a plan to the contrary, the amount of any surcharge under this paragraph shall not be the basis for any benefit accrual under the plan.

(8) **Benefit adjustments.**—

(A) Adjustable benefits.—

(i) In general.—Notwithstanding section 204(g), the plan sponsor shall, subject to the notice requirements in subparagraph (C), make any reductions to adjustable benefits which the plan sponsor deems appropriate, based upon the outcome of collective bargaining over the schedule or schedules provided under paragraph (1)(B)(i).

(ii) Exception for retirees.—Except in the case of adjustable benefits described in clause (iv)(III), the plan sponsor of a plan in critical status shall not reduce adjustable benefits of any participant or beneficiary whose benefit commencement date is before the date on which the plan provides notice to the participant or beneficiary under subsection (b)(3)(D) for the initial critical year.

(iii) Plan sponsor flexibility.—The plan sponsor shall include in the schedules provided to the bargaining parties an allowance for funding the benefits of participants with respect to whom contributions are not currently required to be made, and shall reduce their benefits to the extent permitted under this title and considered appropriate by the plan sponsor based on the plan's then current overall funding status.

(iv) Adjustable benefit defined.—For purposes of this paragraph, the term "adjustable benefit" means—

(I) benefits, rights, and features under the plan, including post-retirement death benefits, 60-month guarantees, disability benefits not yet in pay status, and similar benefits,

(II) any early retirement benefit or retirement-type subsidy (within the meaning of section 204(g)(2)(A)) and any benefit payment option (other than the qualified joint and survivor annuity), and

(III) benefit increases that would not be eligible for a guarantee under section 4022A on the first day of initial critical year because the increases were adopted (or, if later, took effect) less than 60 months before such first day.

(B) Normal retirement benefits protected.—Except as provided in subparagraph (A)(iv)(III), nothing in this paragraph shall be construed to permit a plan to reduce the level of a participant's accrued benefit payable at normal retirement age.

(C) Notice requirements.—

(i) In general.—No reduction may be made to adjustable benefits under subparagraph (A) unless notice of such reduction has been given at least 30 days before the general effective date of such reduction for all participants and beneficiaries to—

(I) plan participants and beneficiaries,

(II) each employer who has an obligation to contribute (within the meaning of section 4212(a)) under the plan, and

(III) each employee organization which, for purposes of collective bargaining, represents plan participants employed by such an employer.

(ii) Content of notice.—The notice under clause (i) shall contain—

(I) sufficient information to enable participants and beneficiaries to understand the effect of any reduction on their benefits, including an estimate (on an annual or monthly basis) of any affected adjustable benefit that a participant or beneficiary would otherwise have been eligible for as of the general effective date described in clause (i), and

(II) information as to the rights and remedies of plan participants and beneficiaries as well as how to contact the Department of Labor for further information and assistance where appropriate.

(iii) Form and manner.—Any notice under clause (i)—

(I) shall be provided in a form and manner prescribed in regulations of the Secretary of the Treasury, in consultation with the Secretary,

(II) shall be written in a manner so as to be understood by the average plan participant, and

(III) may be provided in written, electronic, or other appropriate form to the extent such form is reasonably accessible to persons to whom the notice is required to be provided.

The Secretary of the Treasury shall in the regulations prescribed under subclause (I) establish a model notice that a plan sponsor may use to meet the requirements of this subparagraph.

(9) Adjustments disregarded in withdrawal liability determination.—

(A) Benefit reductions.—Any benefit reductions under this subsection shall be disregarded in determining a plan's unfunded vested benefits for purposes of determining an employer's withdrawal liability under section 4201.

(B) Surcharges.—Any surcharges under paragraph (7) shall be disregarded in determining the allocation of unfunded vested benefits to an employer under section 4211, except for purposes of determining the unfunded vested benefits attributable to an employer under section 4211(c)(4) or a comparable method approved under section 4211(c)(5).

(C) Simplified calculations.—The Pension Benefit Guaranty Corporation shall prescribe simplified methods for the application of this paragraph in determining withdrawal liability.

(f) Rules for Operation of Plan During Adoption and Rehabilitation Period.—

(1) Compliance with rehabilitation plan.—

(A) In general.—A plan may not be amended after the date of the adoption of a rehabilitation plan under subsection (e) so as to be inconsistent with the rehabilitation plan.

(B) Special rules for benefit increases.—A plan may not be amended after the date of the adoption of a rehabilitation plan under subsection (e) so as to increase benefits, including future benefit accruals, unless the plan actuary certifies that such increase is paid for out of additional contributions not contemplated by the rehabilitation plan, and, after taking into account the benefit increase, the multiemployer plan still is reasonably expected to emerge from critical status by the end of the rehabilitation period on the schedule contemplated in the rehabilitation plan.

(2) Restriction on lump sums and similar benefits.—

(A) In general.—Effective on the date the notice of certification of the plan's critical status for the initial critical year under subsection (b)(3)(D) is sent, and notwithstanding section 204(g), the plan shall not pay—

(i) any payment, in excess of the monthly amount paid under a single life annuity (plus any social security supplements described in the last sentence of section 204(b)(1)(G)), to a participant or beneficiary whose annuity starting date (as defined in section 205(h)(2)) occurs after the date such notice is sent,

    (ii) any payment for the purchase of an irrevocable commitment from an insurer to pay benefits, and

    (iii) any other payment specified by the Secretary of the Treasury by regulations.

(B) Exception.—Subparagraph (A) shall not apply to a benefit which under section 203(e) may be immediately distributed without the consent of the participant or to any makeup payment in the case of a retroactive annuity starting date or any similar payment of benefits owed with respect to a prior period.

(3) Adjustments disregarded in withdrawal liability determination.—Any benefit reductions under this subsection shall be disregarded in determining a plan's unfunded vested benefits for purposes of determining an employer's withdrawal liability under section 4201.

(4) Special rules for plan adoption period.— During the rehabilitation plan adoption period—

(A) the plan sponsor may not accept a collective bargaining agreement or participation agreement with respect to the multiemployer plan that provides for—

    (i) a reduction in the level of contributions for any participants,

    (ii) a suspension of contributions with respect to any period of service, or

    (iii) any new direct or indirect exclusion of younger or newly hired employees from plan participation, and

(B) no amendment of the plan which increases the liabilities of the plan by reason of any increase in benefits, any change in the accrual of benefits, or any change in the rate at which benefits become nonforfeitable under the plan may be adopted unless the amendment is required as a condition of qualification under part I of subchapter D of chapter 1 of the Internal Revenue Code of 1986 or to comply with other applicable law.

(g) Expedited Resolution of Plan Sponsor Decisions.—If, within 60 days of the due date for adoption of a funding improvement plan under subsection (c) or a rehabilitation plan under subsection (e), the plan sponsor of a plan in endangered status or a plan in critical status has not agreed on a funding improvement plan or rehabilitation plan, then any member of the board or group that constitutes the plan sponsor may require that the plan sponsor enter into an expedited dispute resolution procedure for the development and adoption of a funding improvement plan or rehabilitation plan.

(h) Nonbargained Participation.—

(1) Both bargained and nonbargained employee-participants.—In the case of an employer that contributes to a multiemployer plan with respect to both employees who are covered by one or more collective bargaining agreements and employees who are not so covered, if the plan is in endangered status or in critical status, benefits of and contributions for the nonbargained employees, including surcharges on those contributions, shall be determined as if those nonbargained employees were covered under the first to expire of the employer's collective bargaining agreements in effect when the plan entered endangered or critical status.

(2) Nonbargained employees only.—In the case of an employer that contributes to a multiemployer plan only with respect to employees who are not covered by a collective bargaining agreement, this section shall be applied as if the employer were the bargaining party, and its participation agreement with the plan were a collective bargaining agreement with a term ending on the first day of the plan year beginning after the employer is provided the schedule or schedules described in subsections (c) and (e).

(i) Definitions; Actuarial Method.—For purposes of this section—

(1) Bargaining party.—The term "bargaining party" means—

    (A)(i) except as provided in clause (ii), an employer who has an obligation to contribute under the plan; or

    (ii) in the case of a plan described under section 404(c) of the Internal Revenue Code of 1986, or a continuation of such a plan, the association of employers that is the employer settlor of the plan; and

(B) an employee organization which, for purposes of collective bargaining, represents plan participants employed by an employer who has an obligation to contribute under the plan.

(2) Funded percentage.—The term "funded percentage" means the percentage equal to a fraction—

(A) the numerator of which is the value of the plan's assets, as determined under section 304(c)(2), and

(B) the denominator of which is the accrued liability of the plan, determined using actuarial assumptions described in section 304(c)(3).

(3) Accumulated funding deficiency.—The term "accumulated funding deficiency" has the meaning given such term in section 304(a).

(4) Active participant.—The term "active participant" means, in connection with a multiemployer plan, a participant who is in covered service under the plan.

(5) Inactive participant.—The term "inactive participant" means, in connection with a multiemployer plan, a participant, or the beneficiary or alternate payee of a participant, who—

(A) is not in covered service under the plan, and

(B) is in pay status under the plan or has a nonforfeitable right to benefits under the plan.

(6) Pay status.—A person is in pay status under a multiemployer plan if—

(A) at any time during the current plan year, such person is a participant or beneficiary under the plan and is paid an early, late, normal, or disability retirement benefit under the plan (or a death benefit under the plan related to a retirement benefit), or

(B) to the extent provided in regulations of the Secretary of the Treasury, such person is entitled to such a benefit under the plan.

(7) Obligation to contribute.—The term "obligation to contribute" has the meaning given such term under section 4212(a).

(8) Actuarial method.—Notwithstanding any other provision of this section, the actuary's determinations with respect to a plan's normal cost, actuarial accrued liability, and improvements in a plan's funded percentage under this section shall be based upon the unit credit funding method (whether or not that method is used for the plan's actuarial valuation).

(9) Plan sponsor.—In the case of a plan described under section 404(c) of the Internal Revenue Code of 1986, or a continuation of such a plan, the term "plan sponsor" means the bargaining parties described under paragraph (1).

(10) Benefit commencement date.—The term "benefit commencement date" means the annuity starting date (or in the case of a retroactive annuity starting date, the date on which benefit payments begin).

Amendments to ERISA §305

Worker, Retiree, and Employer Recovery Act of 2008 (Pub. L. No. 110-458), as follows:

- ERISA §305(b)(3)(C) was amended by Act §102(b)(1)(B) by striking "section 101(b)(4)" and inserting "section 101(b)(1)". Eff. for plan years beginning after 2007, as if included in Pub. L. No. 109-280, §202.
- ERISA §305(b)(3)(D)(iii) was amended by Act §102(b)(1)(C) by striking "The Secretary" and inserting "The Secretary of the Treasury, in consultation with the Secretary". Eff. for plan years beginning after 2007, as if included in Pub. L. No. 109-280, §202.
- ERISA §305(c)(7)(A)(ii) was amended by Act §102(b)(1)(D)(i) by striking "to agree on" and all that followed and inserting "to adopt a contribution schedule with terms consistent with the funding improvement plan and a schedule from the plan sponsor,". Eff. for plan years beginning after 2007, as if included in Pub. L. No. 109-280, §202. ERISA §305(c)(7)(A)(ii) prior to amendment:
   (ii) after receiving one or more schedules from the plan sponsor under paragraph (1)(B), the bargaining parties with respect to such agreement fail to agree on changes to contribution or benefit schedules necessary to meet the applicable benchmarks in accordance with the funding improvement plan,
- ERISA §305(c)(7)(B) was amended by Act §102(b)(1)(D)(ii). Eff. for plan years beginning after 2007, as if included in Pub. L. No. 109-280, §202. ERISA §305(c)(7)(B) prior to repeal:
   (B) Date of implementation.—The date specified in this subparagraph is the earlier of the date—
      (i) on which the Secretary certifies that the parties are at an impasse, or
      (ii) which is 180 days after the date on which the collective bargaining agreement described in subparagraph (A) expires.
- ERISA §305(c)(7)(C) was added by Act §102(b)(1)(D)(iii). Eff. for plan years beginning after 2007, as if included in Pub. L. No. 109-280, §202.
- ERISA §305(e)(3)(C)(i)(II) was amended by Act §102(b)(1)(E)(i)(I) by striking all that followed "to adopt a" and inserting "to adopt a contribution schedule with terms consistent with the rehabilitation plan and a schedule from the plan sponsor under paragraph (1)(B)(i),". Eff. for plan years beginning after 2007, as if included in Pub. L. No. 109-280, §202.
- ERISA §305(e)(3)(C)(ii) was amended by Act §102(b)(1)(E)(i)(II). Eff. for plan years beginning after 2007, as if included in Pub. L. No. 109-280, §202. ERISA §305(e)(3)(C)(ii) prior to amendment:
   (ii) Date of implementation.—The date specified in this clause is the earlier of the date—
      (I) on which the Secretary certifies that the parties are at an impasse, or
      (II) which is 180 days after the date on which the collective bargaining agreement described in clause (i) expires.
- ERISA §305(e)(3)(C)(iii) was added by Act §102(b)(1)(E)(i)(III). Eff. for plan years beginning after 2007, as if included in Pub. L. No. 109-280, §202.
- ERISA §305(e)(4)(A)(ii) was amended by Act §102(b)(1)(E)(ii)(I) by striking "the date of". Eff. for plan years beginning after 2007, as if included in Pub. L. No. 109-280, §202.
- ERISA §305(e)(4)(B) was amended by Act §102(b)(1)(E)(ii)(II) by striking "and taking" and inserting "but taking". Eff. for plan years beginning after 2007, as if included in Pub. L. No. 109-280, §202.
- ERISA §305(e)(6) was amended by Act §102(b)(1)(E)(iii) by striking "paragraph (1)(B)(i)" and inserting "the last sentence of paragraph (1)", and by striking "established" and inserting "establish". Eff. for plan years beginning after 2007, as if included in Pub. L. No. 109-280, §202.
- ERISA §305(e)(8)(C)(iii) was amended by Act §102(b)(1)(E)(iv) by striking "the Secretary" in cl. (I) and inserting "the Secretary of the Treasury, in consultation with the Secretary". Eff. for plan years beginning after 2007, as if included in Pub. L. No. 109-280, §202.
- ERISA §305(e)(9)(B) was amended by Act §102(b)(1)(E)(v) by striking "an employer's withdrawal liability" and inserting "the allocation of unfunded vested benefits to an employer". Eff. for plan years beginning after 2007, as if included in Pub. L. No. 109-280, §202.
- ERISA §305(f)(2)(A)(i) was amended by Act §102(b)(1)(F) by adding at the end: "to a participant or beneficiary whose annuity starting date (as defined in section 205(h)(2)) occurs after the date such notice is sent,". Eff. for plan years beginning after 2007, as if included in Pub. L. No. 109-280, §202.
- ERISA §305(g) was amended by Act §102(b)(1)(G) by inserting "under subsection (c)" after "funding improvement plan" the first place it appeared. Eff. for plan years beginning after 2007, as if included in Pub. L. No. 109-280, §202.

Pension Protection Act of 2006 (Pub. L. No. 109-280), as follows:

- ERISA §305 was added by Act §202(a). Eff. generally for plan years after 2007. For eligible cooperative plans, plan amendments are delayed until the earlier of when such a plan is no longer eligible or Jan. 1, 2017. Act §202(f) applied special rules for certain notices and restored benefits. If a multiemployer

ERISA Sec. 305(i)(10)

plan's actuary certifies that the plan is reasonably expected to be in critical status under ERISA §305(b)(3), as added by the Act, for the first plan year beginning after 2007, the notice requirement under subparagraph (D) may be provided at any time after the date of enactment, so long as it is provided on or before the last date for providing the notice under the subparagraph. For a multiemployer plan the benefits of which were reduced by a plan amendment adopted on or after Jan. 1, 2002, and before June 30, 2005, and which, pursuant to the plan document, the trust agreement, or a formal written communication from the plan sponsor to participants approved before June 30, 2005, providing for the restoration of such benefits, ERISA §305 shall not apply to such benefit restoration to the extent that any restriction on the provision or accrual of such benefits otherwise would apply by reason of such amendments. See below for repealed ERISA §305.

● **Other Provision—Sunset.** Act §221(c), provides:

   (c) Sunset.—

     (1) In general.—Except as provided in this subsection, notwithstanding any other provision of this Act, the provisions of, and the amendments made by, sections 201(b), 202, and 212 shall not apply to plan years beginning after December 31, 2014.

     (2) Funding Improvement and Rehabilitation Plans.—If a plan is operating under a funding improvement or rehabilitation plan under section 305 or such Act or 432 of such Code for its last year beginning before January 1, 2015, such plan shall continue to operate under such funding improvement or rehabilitation plan during any period after December 31, 2014, such funding improvement or rehabilitation plan is in effect and all provisions of such Act or Code relating to the operation of such funding improvement or rehabilitation plan shall continue in effect during such period.

SEC. 305. ALTERNATIVE MINIMUM FUNDING STANDARD. [Repealed.]

(a) Maintenance of Account.—A plan which uses a funding method that requires contributions in all years not less than those required under the entry age normal funding method may maintain an alternative minimum funding standard account for any plan year. Such account shall be credited and charged solely as provided in this section.

(b) Operation of Account.—For a plan year the alternative minimum funding standard accounts shall be—

   (1) charged with the sum of—

   (A) the lesser of normal cost under the funding method used under the plan or normal cost determined under the unit credit method,

   (B) the excess, if any, of the present value of accrued benefits under the plan over the fair market value of the assets, and

   (C) an amount equal to the excess, if any, of credits to the alternative minimum funding standard account for all prior plan years over charges to such account for all such years, and

   (2) credited with the amount considered contributed by the employer to or under the plan (within the meaning of section 302(c)(10)) for the plan year.

(c) Interest.—The alternative minimum funding standard account (and items therein) shall be charged or credited with interest in the manner provided under section 302(b)(5) with respect to the funding standard account.

Amendments to ERISA §305 [Repealed.]
Pension Protection Act of 2006 (Pub. L. No. 109-280), as follows:
● ERISA §305, as in effect before 2007, was repealed by Act §101(a). Eff. for plan years after 2007.

● ERISA §305 (new) was added. Eff. generally for plan years after 2007. See ERISA §305 in this chapter.

SEC. 306. SECURITY FOR WAIVERS OF MINIMUM FUNDING STANDARD AND EXTENSIONS OF AMORTIZATION PERIOD. [Repealed.]

(a) Security May Be Required.—

   (1) In general.—Except as provided in subsection (c), the Secretary of the Treasury may require an employer maintaining a defined benefit plan which is a single-employer plan (within the meaning of section 4001(a)(15)) to provide security to such plan as a condition for granting or modifying a waiver under section 303 or an extension under section 304.

   (2) Special rules.—Any security provided under paragraph (1) may be perfected and enforced only by the Pension Benefit Guaranty Corporation or, at the direction of the Corporation, by a contributing sponsor (within the meaning of section 4001(a)(13)) or a member of such sponsor's controlled group (within the meaning of section 4001(a)(14)).

(b) Consultation With the Pension Benefit Guaranty Corporation.—Except as provided in subsection (c), the Secretary of the Treasury shall, before granting or modifying a waiver under section 303 or an extension under section 304 with respect to a plan described in subsection (a)(1)—

   (1) provide the Pension Benefit Guaranty Corporation with—

   (A) notice of the completed application for any waiver, extension, or modification, and

   (B) an opportunity to comment on such application within 30 days after receipt of such notice, and

   (2) consider—

   (A) any comments of the Corporation under paragraph (1)(B), and

   (B) any views of any employee organization representing participants in the plan which are submitted to the Secretary of the Treasury in connection with such application.

Information provided to the Corporation under this subsection shall be considered tax return information and subject to the safeguarding and reporting requirements of section 6103(p) of the Internal Revenue Code of 1954.

(c) Exception for Certain Waivers and Extensions.—

   (1) In general.—The preceding provisions of this section shall not apply to any plan with respect to which the sum of—

   (A) the outstanding balance of the accumulated funding deficiencies (within the meaning of section 302(a)(2) of this Act and section 412(a) of the Internal Revenue Code of 1954) of the plan,

   (B) the outstanding balance of the amount of waived funding deficiencies of the plan waived under section 303 of this Act or section 412(d) of such Code, and

   (C) the outstanding balance of the amount of decreases in the minimum funding standard allowed under section 304 of this Act or section 412(e) of such Code is less than $1,000,000.

   (2) Accumulated funding deficiencies.—For purposes of paragraph (1)(A), accumulated funding deficiencies shall include any increase in such amount which would result if all applications for waivers of the minimum funding standard under section 303 of this Act or section 412(d) of the Internal Revenue Code of 1954 and for extensions of the amortization period under section 304 of this Act or section 412(e) of such Code which are pending with respect to such plan were denied.

Amendments to ERISA §306 [Repealed.]

Pension Protection Act of 2006 (Pub. L. No. 109-280), as follows:

● ERISA §306, as in effect before 2007, was repealed by Act §101(a). Eff. for plan years after 2007. For eligible cooperative plans, plan amendments are delayed until the earlier of when such a plan is no longer eligible, or Jan. 1, 2017.

Omnibus Budget Reconciliation Act of 1989 (Pub. L. No. 101-239), as follows:

● ERISA §306(b)–(c) were amended by Act §7891(f) by substituting "Internal Revenue Code of 1986" for "Internal Revenue Code of 1954", which for purposes of codification was translated as "title 26". Effective as if included in Pub. L. No. 99-514.

Omnibus Budget Reconciliation Act of 1987 (Pub. L. No. 100-203), as follows:

● ERISA §306(c)(1) was amended by Act §9306(e)(2) by substituting "$1,000,000" for "$2,000,000". Eff. for any application submitted after Dec. 17, 1987.

SEC. 307. SECURITY REQUIRED UPON ADOPTION OF PLAN AMENDMENT RESULTING IN SIGNIFICANT UNDERFUNDING. [Repealed.]

(a) In General.—If—

(1) a defined benefit plan (other than a multiemployer plan) to which the requirements of section 302 apply adopts an amendment an effect of which is to increase current liability under the plan for a plan year, and

(2) the funded current liability percentage of the plan for the plan year in which the amendment takes effect is less than 60 percent, including the amount of the unfunded current liability under the plan attributable to the plan amendment,

the contributing sponsor (or any member of the controlled group of the contributing sponsor) shall provide security to the plan.

(b) Form of Security.—The security required under subsection (a) shall consist of—

(1) a bond issued by a corporate surety company that is an acceptable surety for purposes of section 412,

(2) cash, or United States obligations which mature in 3 years or less, held in escrow by a bank or similar financial institution, or

(3) such other form of security as is satisfactory to the Secretary of the Treasury and the parties involved.

(c) Amount of Security.—The security shall be in an amount equal to the excess of—

(1) the lesser of—

(A) the amount of additional plan assets which would be necessary to increase the funded current liability percentage under the plan to 60 percent, including the amount of the unfunded current liability under the plan attributable to the plan amendment, or

(B) the amount of the increase in current liability under the plan attributable to the plan amendment and any other plan amendments adopted after December 22, 1987, and before such plan amendment, over

(2) $10,000,000.

(d) Release of Security.—The security shall be released (and any amounts thereunder shall be refunded together with any interest accrued thereon) at the end of the first plan year which ends after the provision of the security and for which the funded current liability percentage under the plan is not less than 60 percent. The Secretary of the Treasury may prescribe regulations for partial releases of the security by reason of increases in the funded current liability percentage.

(e) Notice.—A contributing sponsor which is required to provide security under subsection (a) shall notify the Pension Benefit Guaranty Corporation within 30 days after the amendment requiring such security takes effect. Such notice shall contain such information as the Corporation may require.

(f) Definitions.—For purposes of this section, the terms "current liability", "funded current liability percentage", and "unfunded current liability" shall have the meanings given such terms by section 302(d), except that in computing unfunded current liability there shall not be taken into account any unamortized portion of the unfunded old liability amount as of the close of the plan year.

Amendments to ERISA §307 [Repealed.]

Pension Protection Act of 2006 (Pub. L. No. 109-280), as follows:

● ERISA §307, as in effect before 2007, was repealed by Act §101(a). Eff. for plan years after 2007. For eligible cooperative plans, plan amendments are delayed until the earlier of when such a plan is no longer eligible, or Jan. 1, 2017.

Omnibus Budget Reconciliation Act of 1989 (Pub. L. No. 101-239), as follows:

● ERISA §307(a)(1) was amended by Act §7881(i)(4)(B) by inserting "to which the requirements of section 302 of this title apply" after "multiemployer plan)". Eff., except as otherwise provided, as if included in Pub. L. No. 100-203, see Act §7882.

● ERISA §307(c)(1)(B) was amended by Act §7881(i)(1)(B) by inserting "and any other plan amendments adopted after December 22, 1987, and before such plan amendment" without specifying where such language was to be inserted, and was executed by making the insertion after "to the plan amendment", as the probable intent of Congress. Eff., except as otherwise provided, as if included in Pub. L. No. 100-203, see Act §7882.

● ERISA §307(d) was amended by Act §7881(i)(2) by inserting "of the Treasury" after "Secretary". Eff., except as otherwise provided, as if included in Pub. L. No. 100-203, see Act §7882.

● ERISA §307(e)–(f) were amended by Act §7881(i)(3)(A) by redesignating former subsec. (e) as (f) and adding new (e). Eff., except as otherwise provided, as if included in Pub. L. No. 100-203, and applicable to plan amendments adopted after Dec. 22, 1987, except that, in the case of a plan maintained pursuant to one or more collective bargaining agreements between employee representatives and one or more employers ratified before Dec. 22, 1987, this section not applicable to plan amendments adopted pursuant to collective bargaining agreements ratified before Dec. 22, 1987.

SEC. 308. EFFECTIVE DATES. [Repealed.]

(a) Except as otherwise provided in this section, this part shall apply in the case of plan years beginning after the date of the enactment of this Act.

(b) Except as otherwise provided in subsections (c) and (d), in the case of a plan in existence on January 1, 1974, this part shall apply in the case of plan years beginning after December 31, 1975.

(c)(1) In the case of a plan maintained on January 1, 1974, pursuant to one or more agreements which the Secretary finds to be collective bargaining agreements between employee representatives and one or more employers, this part shall apply only with respect to plan years beginning after the earlier of the date specified in subparagraph (A) or (B) of section 211(c)(1).

(2) This subsection shall apply with respect to a plan if (and only if) the application of this subsection results in a later effective date for this part than the effective date required by subsection (b).

(d) In the case of a plan the administrator of which elects under section 1017(d) of this Act to have the provisions of title 26 relating to participation, vesting, funding, and form of benefit to apply to a plan year and to all subsequent plan years, this part shall apply to plan years beginning on the earlier of the first plan year to which such election applies or the first plan year determined under subsections (a), (b), and (c) of this section.

(e) In the case of a plan maintained by a labor organization which is exempt from tax under section 501(c)(5) of title 26 exclusively for the benefit of its employees and their beneficiaries, this part shall be applied by substituting for the term "December 31, 1975" in subsection (b), the earlier of—

(1) the date on which the second convention of such labor organization held after the date of the enactment of this Act ends, or

(2) December 31, 1980,

but in no event shall a date earlier than the later of December 31, 1975, or the date determined under subsection (c) be substituted.

(f) The preceding provisions of this section shall not apply with respect to amendments made to this part in provisions enacted after the date of the enactment of this Act.

Amendments to ERISA §308 [Repealed.]

Pension Protection Act of 2006 (Pub. L. No. 109-280), as follows:
● ERISA §308, as in effect before 2007, was repealed by Act §101(a). Eff. for plan years after 2007. **Caution:** For eligible cooperative plans, plan amendments are delayed until the earlier of when such a plan is no longer eligible, or Jan. 1, 2017.

Omnibus Budget Reconciliation Act of 1989 (Pub. L. No. 101-239), as follows:
● ERISA §308(f) was added by Act §7894(h)(3). Eff. as if originally included in Pub. L. No. 93-406.
● Renumbered. ERISA §308 was originally numbered as ERISA §306, then renumbered as §307 by Pub. L. No. 99-272, and then renumbered as §308 by Pub. L. No. 100-203.

Part 4—Fiduciary Responsibility

SEC. 401. COVERAGE.

(a) Scope of Coverage.—This part shall apply to any employee benefit plan described in section 4(a) (and not exempted under section 4(b)), other than—

(1) a plan which is unfunded and is maintained by an employer primarily for the purpose of providing deferred compensation for a select group of management or highly compensated employees; or

(2) any agreement described in section 736 of title 26, which provides payments to a retired partner or deceased partner or a deceased partner's successor in interest.

(b) Securities of Policies Deemed to Be Included in Plan Assets.—For purposes of this part:

(1) In the case of a plan which invests in any security issued by an investment company registered under the Investment Company Act of 1940, the assets of such plan shall be deemed to include such security but shall not, solely by reason of such investment, be deemed to include any assets of such investment company.

(2) In the case of a plan to which a guaranteed benefit policy is issued by an insurer, the assets of such plan shall be deemed to include such policy, but shall not, solely by reason of the issuance of such policy, be deemed to include any assets of such insurer. For purposes of this paragraph:

(A) The term "insurer" means an insurance company, insurance service, or insurance organization, qualified to do business in a State.

(B) The term "guaranteed benefit policy" means an insurance policy or contract to the extent that such policy or contract provides for benefits the amount of which is guaranteed by the insurer. Such term includes any surplus in a separate account, but excludes any other portion of a separate account.

(c) Clarification of Application of ERISA to Insurance Company General Accounts.

(1)(A) Not later than June 30, 1997, the Secretary shall issue proposed regulations to provide guidance for the purpose of determining, in cases where an insurer issues 1 or more policies to or for the benefit of an employee benefit plan (and such policies are supported by assets of such insurer's general account), which assets held by the insurer (other than plan assets held in its separate accounts) constitute assets of the plan for purposes of this part and section 4975 of the Internal Revenue Code of 1986 and to provide guidance with respect to the application of this title to the general account assets of insurers.

(B) The proposed regulations under subparagraph (A) shall be subject to public notice and comment until September 30, 1997.

(C) The Secretary shall issue final regulations providing the guidance described in subparagraph (A) not later than December 31, 1997.

(D) Such regulations shall only apply with respect to policies which are issued by an insurer on or before December 31, 1998, to or for the benefit of an employee benefit plan which is supported by assets of such insurer's general account. With respect to policies issued on or before December 31, 1998, such regulations shall take effect at the end of the 18-month period following the date on which such regulations become final.

(2) The Secretary shall ensure that the regulations issued under paragraph (1)—

(A) are administratively feasible, and

(B) protect the interests and rights of the plan and of its participants and beneficiaries (including meeting the requirements of paragraph (3)).

(3) The regulations prescribed by the Secretary pursuant to paragraph (1) shall require, in connection with any policy issued by an insurer to or for the benefit of an employee benefit plan to the extent that the policy is not a guaranteed benefit policy (as defined in subsection (b)(2)(B))—

(A) that a plan fiduciary totally independent of the insurer authorize the purchase of such policy (unless such purchase is a transaction exempt under section 408(b)(5)),

(B) that the insurer describe (in such form and manner as shall be prescribed in such regulations), in annual reports and in policies issued to the policyholder after the date on which such regulations are issued in final form pursuant to paragraph (1)(C)—

(i) a description of the method by which any income and expenses of the insurer's general account are allocated to the policy during the term of the policy and upon the termination of the policy, and

(ii) for each report, the actual return to the plan under the policy and such other financial information as the Secretary may deem appropriate for the period covered by each such annual report,

(C) that the insurer disclose to the plan fiduciary the extent to which alternative arrangements supported by assets of separate accounts of the insurer (which generally hold plan assets) are available, whether there is a right under the policy to transfer funds to a separate account and the terms governing any such right, and the extent to which support by assets of the insurer's general account and support by assets of separate accounts of the insurer might pose differing risks to the plan, and

(D) that the insurer manage those assets of the insurer which are assets of such insurer's general account (irrespective of whether any such assets are plan assets) with the care, skill, prudence, and diligence under the circumstances then prevailing that a prudent man acting in a like capacity and familiar with such matters would use in the conduct of an enterprise of a like character and with like aims, taking into account all obligations supported by such enterprise.

(4) Compliance by the insurer with all requirements of the regulations issued by the Secretary pursuant to paragraph (1) shall be deemed compliance by such insurer with sections 404, 406, and 407 with respect to those assets of the insurer's general account which support a policy described in paragraph (3).

(5)(A) Subject to subparagraph (B), any regulations issued under paragraph (1) shall not take effect before the date on which such regulations become final.

(B) No person shall be subject to liability under this part or section 4975 of the Internal Revenue Code of 1986 for conduct which occurred before the date which is 18 months following the date described in subparagraph (A) on the basis of a claim that the assets of an insurer (other than plan assets held in a separate account) constitute assets of the plan, except—

(i) as otherwise provided by the Secretary in regulations intended to prevent avoidance of the regulations issued under paragraph (1), or

(ii) as provided in an action brought by the Secretary pursuant to paragraph (2) or (5) of section 502(a) for a breach of fiduciary responsibilities which would also constitute a violation of Federal or State criminal law.

The Secretary shall bring a cause of action described in clause (ii) if a participant, beneficiary, or fiduciary demonstrates to the satisfaction of the Secretary that a breach described in clause (ii) has occurred.

(6) Nothing in this subsection shall preclude the application of any Federal criminal law.

(7) For purposes of this subsection, the term "policy" includes a contract.

Amendments to ERISA §401

Small Business Job Protection Act of 1996 (Pub. L. No. 104-188), as follows:

● ERISA §401(c) was added by Act §1460(a). Eff. Jan. 1, 1975, but not for civil actions commenced before Nov. 7, 1995. In addition, plan amendments were not required to be made before the first day of the plan year beginning on or after Jan. 1, 1998.

Omnibus Budget Reconciliation Act of 1989 (Pub. L. No. 101-239), as follows:

● ERISA §401(a)(2) was amended by Act §7891(a)(1) by substituting "Internal Revenue Code of 1986" for "Internal Revenue Code of 1954", which for purposes of codification was translated as "title 26". Eff. as if included in Pub. L. 99-514.

SEC. 402. ESTABLISHMENT OF PLAN.

(a) Named Fiduciaries.—

(1) Every employee benefit plan shall be established and maintained pursuant to a written instrument. Such instrument shall provide for one or more named fiduciaries who jointly or severally shall have authority to control and manage the operation and administration of the plan.

(2) For purposes of this title, the term "named fiduciary" means a fiduciary who is named in the plan instrument, or who, pursuant to a procedure specified in the plan, is identified as a fiduciary (A) by a person who is an employer or employee organization with respect to the plan or (B) by such an employer and such an employee organization acting jointly.

(b) Requisite Features of Plan.—Every employee benefit plan shall—

(1) provide a procedure for establishing and carrying out a funding policy and method consistent with the objectives of the plan and the requirements of this title,

(2) describe any procedure under the plan for the allocation of responsibilities for the operation and

administration of the plan (including any procedure described in section 405(c)(1)),

(3) provide a procedure for amending such plan, and for identifying the persons who have authority to amend the plan, and

(4) specify the basis on which payments are made to and from the plan.

(c) Optional Features of Plan.—Any employee benefit plan may provide—

(1) that any person or group of persons may serve in more than one fiduciary capacity with respect to the plan (including service both as trustee and administrator);

(2) that a named fiduciary, or a fiduciary designated by a named fiduciary pursuant to a plan procedure described in section 405(c)(1), may employ one or more persons to render advice with regard to any responsibility such fiduciary has under the plan; or

(3) that a person who is a named fiduciary with respect to control or management of the assets of the plan may appoint an investment manager or managers to manage (including the power to acquire and dispose of) any assets of a plan.

SEC. 403. ESTABLISHMENT OF TRUST.

(a) Benefit Plan Assets to Be Held in Trust; Authority of Trustees.—Except as provided in subsection (b), all assets of an employee benefit plan shall be held in trust by one or more trustees. Such trustee or trustees shall be either named in the trust instrument or in the plan instrument described in section 402(a) or appointed by a person who is a named fiduciary, and upon acceptance of being named or appointed, the trustee or trustees shall have exclusive authority and discretion to manage and control the assets of the plan, except to the extent that—

(1) the plan expressly provides that the trustee or trustees are subject to the direction of a named fiduciary who is not a trustee, in which case the trustees shall be subject to proper directions of such fiduciary which are made in accordance with the terms of the plan and which are not contrary to this Act, or

(2) authority to manage, acquire, or dispose of assets of the plan is delegated to one or more investment managers pursuant to section 402(c)(3).

(b) Exceptions.—The requirements of subsection (a) of this section shall not apply—

(1) to any assets of a plan which consist of insurance contracts or policies issued by an insurance company qualified to do business in a State;

(2) to any assets of such an insurance company or any assets of a plan which are held by such an insurance company;

(3) to a plan—

(A) some or all of the participants of which are employees described in section 401(c)(1) of the Internal Revenue Code of 1986; or

(B) which consists of one or more individual retirement accounts described in section 408 of the Internal Revenue Code of 1986,

to the extent that such plan's assets are held in one or more custodial accounts which qualify under section 401(f) or 408(h) of such Code, whichever is applicable.

(4) to a plan which the Secretary exempts from the requirement of subsection (a) and which is not subject to any of the following provisions of this Act;

(A) part 2 of this subtitle [ERISA §201 et seq.],

(B) part 3 of this subtitle [ERISA §301 et seq.], or

(C) title IV of this Act; or

(5) to a contract established and maintained under section 403(b) of title 26 to the extent that the assets of the contract are held in one or more custodial accounts pursuant to section 403(b)(7) of such Code.

(6) Any plan, fund or program under which an employer, all of whose stock is directly or indirectly owned by employees, former employees or their beneficiaries, proposes through an unfunded arrangement to compensate retired employees for benefits which were forfeited by such employees under a pension plan maintained by a former employer prior to the date such pension plan became subject to this Act.

(c) Assets of Plan Not to Inure to Benefit of Employer; Allowable Purposes of Holding Plan Assets.—

(1) Except as provided in paragraph (2), (3), or (4) or subsection (d), or under section 4042 and 4044 (relating to termination of insured plans), or under section 420 of the Internal Revenue Code of 1986 (as in effect on the date of enactment of the Pension Protection Act of 2006), the assets of a plan shall never inure to the benefit of any employer and shall be held for the exclusive purposes of providing benefits to participants in the plan and their beneficiaries and defraying reasonable expenses of administering the plan.

(2)(A) In the case of a contribution, or a payment of withdrawal liability under part 1 of subtitle E of title IV [ERISA §4201 et seq.]—

(i) if such contribution or payment is made by an employer to a plan (other than a multiemployer plan) by a mistake of fact, paragraph (1) shall not prohibit the return of such contribution to the employer within one year after the payment of the contribution, and

(ii) if such contribution or payment is made by an employer to a multiemployer plan by a mistake of fact or law (other than a mistake relating to whether the plan is described in section 401(a) of title 26 or the trust which is part of such plan is exempt from taxation under section 501(a) of title 26), paragraph (1) shall not prohibit the return of such contribution or payment to the employer within 6 months after the plan administrator determines that the contribution was made by such a mistake.

(B) If a contribution is conditioned on initial qualification of the plan under section 401 or 403(a) of the Internal Revenue Code of 1986, and if the plan receives an adverse determination with respect to its initial qualification, then paragraph (1) shall not prohibit the return of such contribution to the employer within one year after such determination, but only if the application for the determination is made by the time prescribed by law for filing the employer's return for the taxable year in which such plan was adopted, or such later date as the Secretary of the Treasury may prescribe.

(C) If a contribution is conditioned upon the deductibility of the contribution under section 404 of title 26, then, to the extent the deduction is disallowed, paragraph (1) shall not prohibit the return to the employer of such contribution (to the extent disallowed) within one year after the disallowance of the deduction.

(3) In the case of a withdrawal liability payment which has been determined to be an overpayment, paragraph (1) shall not prohibit the return of such payment to the employer within 6 months after the date of such determination.

(d) **Termination of Plan.—**

(1) Upon termination of a pension plan to which section 4021 does not apply at the time of termination and to which this part applies (other than a plan to which no employer contributions have been made) the assets of the plan shall be allocated in accordance with the provisions of section 4044 of this Act, except as otherwise provided in regulations of the Secretary.

(2) The assets of a welfare plan which terminates shall be distributed in accordance with the terms of the plan, except as otherwise provided in regulations of the Secretary.

Amendments to ERISA §403

Pension Protection Act of 2006 (Pub. L. No. 109-280), as follows:

- ERISA §403(c)(1) was amended by Act §107(a)(11) (redesignated as §108(a)(11) by Pub. L. No. 111-192, §202(a)) by substituting "Pension Protection Act of 2006" for "American Jobs Creation Act of 2004". Eff. for plan years beginning after 2007. "Eligible cooperative plans" have a delayed effective date until the earlier of the date the plans are no longer eligible, or Jan. 1, 2017.

American Jobs Creation Act of 2004 (Pub. L. No. 108-357), as follows:

- ERISA §403(c)(1) was amended by Act §709(a)(2) by substituting "October 22, 2004" for "April 10, 2004". Eff. Oct. 22, 2004.

Pension Funding Equity Act of 2004 (Pub. L. No. 108-218), as follows:

- ERISA §403(c)(1) was amended by Act §204(b)(2) by substituting "April 10, 2004" for "December 17, 1999". Eff. April 10, 2004.

Tax Relief Extension Act of 1999 (Pub. L. No. 106-170), as follows:

- ERISA §403(c)(1) was amended by Act §35(a)(2)(B) by substituting "December 17, 1999" for "January 1, 1995". Eff. Dec. 17, 1999.

Retirement Protection Act of 1994 (Pub. L. No. 103-465), as follows:

- ERISA §403(c)(1) was amended by Act §731(c)(4)(B) by substituting "1995" for "1991". Eff. Jan. 1, 1995.

Omnibus Budget Reconciliation Act of 1990 (Pub. L. No. 101-508), as follows:

- ERISA §403(c)(1) was amended by Act §12012(a) by inserting ", 420 of title 26 (as in effect on January 1, 1991)" after "insured plans". Eff. Nov. 5, 1990.

Omnibus Budget Reconciliation Act of 1989 (Pub. L. No. 101-239), as follows:

- ERISA §403(b)(3), (5), (c)(2)(A)(ii), (C) were amended by Act §7891(a)(1) by substituting "Internal Revenue Code of 1986" for "Internal Revenue Code of 1954", which for purposes of codification was translated as "title 26". Eff. as if included in Pub. L. No. 99-514.
- ERISA §403(b)(3) was amended by Act §7894(e)(3) by redesignating cls. (i)–(ii) as subparas. (A)–(B), respectively; and in redesignated subpara. (B), by striking "to the extent" and all that follows through "applicable" and by adding at the end, after and below redesignated subpara. (B) "to the extent that such plan's assets are held in one or more custodial accounts which qualify under section section 401(f) or 408(h) of such Code, whichever is applicable." Eff. as if originally included in Pub. L. No. 93-406.
- ERISA §403(c)(2)(A) was amended by Act §7894(e)(1)(A), in introductory provisions, by making technical amendment to reference to part 1 of subtitle E of subchapter III of this chapter to correct reference to corresponding part of original Act, requiring no change in text; and in cls. (i) and (ii), inserted "if such contribution or payment is" before "made by an employer". Eff. as if originally included in Pub. L. No. 96-364.
- ERISA §403(c)(3)–(4) were amended by Act §7881(k) by redesignating para. (4) as (3) and striking former para. (3). Eff. as if included in Pub. L. No. 100-203. ERISA §403(c)(3) prior to amendment:

  (3) In the case of a contribution which would otherwise be an excess contribution (as defined in section 4979(c) of title 26) paragraph (1) shall not prohibit a correcting distribution with respect to such contribution from the plan to the employer to the extent permitted in such section to avoid payment of an excise tax on excess contributions under such section.

Omnibus Budget Reconciliation Act of 1987 (Pub. L. No. 100-203), as follows:

- ERISA §403(c)(2)(B) was amended by Act §9343(c)(1). Eff. Dec. 22, 1987. ERISA §403(c)(2)(B) prior to amendment:

  (B) If a contribution is conditioned on qualification of the plan under section 401, 403(a), or 405(a) of title 26, and if the plan does not qualify, then paragraph (1) shall not prohibit the return of such contributions to the employer within one year after the date of denial of qualification of the plan.

- ERISA §403(c)(3) was amended by Act §9343(c)(2) by substituting "section 4979(c) of title 26" for "section 4972(b) of title 26". Eff. Dec. 22, 1987.

Multiemployer Pension Plan Amendments Act of 1980 (Pub. L. No. 96-364), as follows:

- ERISA §403(a)(1) was amended by Act §402(b)(2) by substituting "chapter" for "subchapter". Eff. Sept. 26, 1980.
- ERISA §403(b)(6) was added by Act §411(c). Eff. Sept. 26, 1980.
- ERISA §403(c)(1) was amended by Act §310(1) by inserting reference to para. (4). Eff. Sept. 26, 1980.

● ERISA §403(c)(2)(A) was amended by Act §410(a) by substituting provisions relating to contributions or payments of withdrawal liability under part 1 of subtitle E of subchapter III of this chapter made by an employer to a plan by a mistake of fact, and by an employer to a multiemployer plan by a mistake of fact or law, for provisions relating to contributions made by an employer by a mistake of fact. Eff. Jan. 1, 1975.

● ERISA §403(c)(4) was added by Act §310(2). Eff. Sept. 26, 1980.

SEC. 404. FIDUCIARY DUTIES.

(a) Prudent Man Standard of Care.—

(1) Subject to sections 403(c) and (d), 4042, and 4044, a fiduciary shall discharge his duties with respect to a plan solely in the interest of the participants and beneficiaries and—

(A) for the exclusive purpose of:

(i) providing benefits to participants and their beneficiaries; and

(ii) defraying reasonable expenses of administering the plan;

(B) with the care, skill, prudence, and diligence under the circumstances then prevailing that a prudent man acting in a like capacity and familiar with such matters would use in the conduct of an enterprise of a like character and with like aims;

(C) by diversifying the investments of the plan so as to minimize the risk of large losses, unless under the circumstances it is clearly prudent not to do so; and

(D) in accordance with the documents and instruments governing the plan insofar as such documents and instruments are consistent with the provisions of this title and title IV.

(2) In the case of an eligible individual account plan (as defined in section 407(d)(3)), the diversification requirement of paragraph (1)(C) and the prudence requirement (only to the extent that it requires diversification) of paragraph (1)(B) is not violated by acquisition or holding of qualifying employer real property or qualifying employer securities (as defined in section 407(d)(4) and (5)).

(b) Indicia of Ownership of Assets Outside Jurisdiction of District Courts.—Except as authorized by the Secretary by regulation, no fiduciary may maintain the indicia of ownership of any assets of a plan outside the jurisdiction of the district courts of the United States.

(c) Control of Assets by Participant or Beneficiary.—

(1)(A) In the case of a pension plan which provides for individual accounts and permits a participant or beneficiary to exercise control over assets in his account, if a participant or beneficiary exercises control over the assets in his account (as determined under regulations of the Secretary)—

(i) such participant or beneficiary shall not be deemed to be a fiduciary by reason of such exercise, and

(ii) no person who is otherwise a fiduciary shall be liable under this part for any loss, or by reason of any breach, which results from such participant's, or beneficiary's exercise of control, except that this clause shall not apply in connection with such participant or beneficiary for any blackout period during which the ability of such participant or beneficiary to direct the investment of the assets in his or her account is suspended by a plan sponsor or fiduciary.

(B) If a person referred to in subparagraph (A)(ii) meets the requirements of this title in connection with authorizing and implementing the blackout period, any person who is otherwise a fiduciary shall not be liable under this title for any loss occurring during such period.

(C) For purposes of this paragraph, the term "blackout period" has the meaning given such term by section 101(i)(7).

(2) In the case of a simple retirement account established pursuant to a qualified salary reduction arrangement under section 408(p) of the Internal Revenue Code of 1986, a participant or beneficiary shall, for purposes of paragraph (1), be treated as exercising control over the assets in the account upon the earliest of—

(A) an affirmative election among investment options with respect to the initial investment of any contribution,

(B) a rollover to any other simple retirement account or individual retirement plan, or

(C) one year after the simple retirement account is established.

No reports, other than those required under section 101(g), shall be required with respect to a simple retirement account established pursuant to such a qualified salary reduction arrangement.

(3) In the case of a pension plan which makes a transfer to an individual retirement account or annuity of a designated trustee or issuer under section 401(a)(31)(B) of the Internal Revenue Code of 1986, the participant or beneficiary shall, for purposes of paragraph (1), be treated as exercising control over the assets in the account or annuity upon—

(A) the earlier of—

(i) a rollover of all or a portion of the amount to another individual retirement account or annuity; or

(ii) one year after the transfer is made; or

(B) a transfer that is made in a manner consistent with guidance provided by the Secretary.

(4)(A) In any case in which a qualified change in investment options occurs in connection with an individual account plan, a participant or beneficiary shall not be treated for purposes of paragraph (1) as not exercising control over the assets in his account in connection with such change if the requirements of subparagraph (C) are met in connection with such change.

(B) For purposes of subparagraph (A), the term "qualified change in investment options" means, in connection with an individual account plan, a change in the investment options offered to the participant or beneficiary under the terms of the plan, under which—

(i) the account of the participant or beneficiary is reallocated among one or more remaining or new investment options which are offered in lieu of one or more investment options offered immediately prior to the effective date of the change, and

(ii) the stated characteristics of the remaining or new investment options provided under clause (i), including characteristics relating to risk and rate of return, are, as of immediately after the change, reasonably similar to those of the existing investment options as of immediately before the change.

(C) The requirements of this subparagraph are met in connection with a qualified change in investment options if—

(i) at least 30 days and no more than 60 days prior to the effective date of the change, the plan administrator furnishes written notice of the change to the participants and beneficiaries, including information comparing the existing and new investment options and an explanation that, in the absence of affirmative investment instructions from the participant or beneficiary to the contrary, the account of the participant or beneficiary will be invested in the manner described in subparagraph (B),

(ii) the participant or beneficiary has not provided to the plan administrator, in advance of the effective date of the change, affirmative investment instructions contrary to the change, and

(iii) the investments under the plan of the participant or beneficiary as in effect immediately prior to the effective date of the change were the product of the exercise by such participant or beneficiary of control over the assets of the account within the meaning of paragraph (1).

(5) Default investment arrangements.—

(A) In general.—For purposes of paragraph (1), a participant or beneficiary in an individual account plan meeting the notice requirements of subparagraph (B) shall be treated as exercising control over the assets in the account with respect to the amount of contributions and earnings which, in the absence of an investment election by the participant or beneficiary, are invested by the plan in accordance with regulations prescribed by the Secretary. The regulations under this subparagraph shall provide guidance on the appropriateness of designating default investments that include a mix of asset classes consistent with capital preservation or long-term capital appreciation, or a blend of both.

(B) Notice requirements.—

(i) In general.—The requirements of this subparagraph are met if each participant or beneficiary—

(I) receives, within a reasonable period of time before each plan year, a notice explaining the employee's right under the plan to designate how contributions and earnings will be invested and explaining how, in the absence of any investment election by the participant, such contributions and earnings will be invested, and

(II) has a reasonable period of time after receipt of such notice and before the beginning of the plan year to make such designation.

(ii) Form of notice.—The requirements of clauses (i) and (ii) of section 401(k)(12)(D) of the Internal Revenue Code of 1986 shall apply with respect to the notices described in this subparagraph.

(d)(1) If, in connection with the termination of a pension plan which is a single-employer plan, there is an election to establish or maintain a qualified replacement plan, or to increase benefits, as provided under section 4980(d) of the Internal Revenue Code of 1986, a fiduciary shall discharge the fiduciary's duties under this title and title IV in accordance with the following requirements:

(A) In the case of a fiduciary of the terminated plan, any requirement—

(i) under section 4980(d)(2)(B) of such Code with respect to the transfer of assets from the terminated plan to a qualified replacement plan, and

(ii) under section 4980(d)(2)(B)(ii) or 4980(d)(3) of such Code with respect to any increase in benefits under the terminated plan.

(B) In the case of a fiduciary of a qualified replacement plan, any requirement—

(i) under section 4980(d)(2)(A) of such Code with respect to participation in the qualified replacement plan of active participants in the terminated plan.

(ii) under section 4980(d)(2)(B) of such Code with respect to the receipt of assets from the terminated plan, and

ERISA Sec. 404(d)(1)(B)(ii)

(iii) under section 4980(d)(2)(C) of such Code with respect to the allocation of assets to participants of the qualified replacement plan.

(2) For purposes of this subsection—

(A) any term used in this subsection which is also then used in section 4980(d) of the Internal Revenue Code of 1986 shall have the same meaning as when used in such section, and

(B) any reference to this subsection in the Internal Revenue Code of 1986 should be a reference to such Code as in effect immediately after the enactment of the Omnibus Budget Reconciliation Act of 1990 [enacted Nov. 5, 1990].

Amendments to ERISA §404

Worker, Retiree, and Employer Recovery Act of 2008 (Pub. L. No. 110-458), as follows:

● ERISA §404(c)(5) was amended by Act §106(d) by striking "participant" each place it appeared and inserting "participant or beneficiary". Eff. for plan years beginning after Dec. 31, 2006, as if included in Pub. L. No. 109-280, §624.

Pension Protection Act of 2006 (Pub. L. No. 109-280), as follows:

● ERISA §404(c)(1) was amended by Act §621(a)(1) by redesignating (A) and (B) as cls. (i) and (ii), respectively; inserting "(A)" after para. (c)(1); adding to redesignated cl. (ii), before the period, "except that this clause shall not apply in connection with such participant or beneficiary for any blackout period during which the ability of such participant or beneficiary to direct the investment of the assets in his or her account is suspended by a plan sponsor or fiduciary"; and adding subparas. (B) and (C). Eff. for plan years beginning after 2007, with a transition rule for collective bargaining agreements.

● ERISA §404(c)(4) was added by Act §621(a)(2). Eff. for plan years beginning after 2007, with a transition rule for collective bargaining agreements.

● ERISA §404(c)(5) was added by Act §624(a). Eff. for plan years beginning after 2006.

Job Creation and Worker Assistance Act of 2002 (Pub. L. No. 107-147), as follows:

● ERISA §404(c)(3)(A) was amended by Act §411(t)(1) by striking "the earlier of" after "the earlier of" in introductory provisions. Eff. for taxable, plan, and limitation years between March 5, 2005, and Dec. 31, 2010.

● ERISA §404(c)(3)(B) was amended by Act §411(t)(2) by substituting "a transfer that" for "if the transfer". Eff. for taxable, plan, and limitation years between March 5, 2005, and Dec. 31, 2010.

Economic Growth and Tax Relief Reconciliation Act of 2001 (Pub. L. No. 107-16), as follows:

● ERISA §404(c)(3) was amended by Act §§657(c)(1), 901 by temporarily adding para. (3). Eff. for taxable, plan, and limitation years between March 5, 2005, and Dec. 31, 2010. See note below on sunset rule.

● **Sunset Rule.** To comply with the Congressional Budget Act of 1974, §901 of Pub. L. No. 107-16 provides that all provisions of, and amendments made by, the Act will not apply to taxable, plan, or limitation years beginning after December 31, 2010. *But see* Pension Protection Act of 2006 (Pub. L. No. 109-280), §811 (sunset rule of Pub. L. No. 107-16 does not apply to the provisions of, and the amendments made by, Pub. L. No. 107-16, §§601–666 (relating to modifications to pensions and retirement income arrangement provisions)).

Small Business Job Protection Act of 1996 (Pub. L. No. 104-188), as follows:

● ERISA §404(c) was amended by Act §1421(d)(2) by designating existing provisions as para. (1); redesignating former paras. (1) and (2) as subparas. (A) and (B), respectively; and adding para.

(2). Eff. for taxable years beginning after Dec. 31, 1996, see Act §1421(e).

Omnibus Budget Reconciliation Act of 1990 (Pub. L. No. 101-508), as follows:

● ERISA §404(a)(1)(D) was amended by Act §12002(b)(2)(A) by substituting "and subchapter III" for "or subchapter III". Eff. Nov. 5, 1990.

● ERISA §404(d) was added by Act §12002(b)(1). Eff. for reversions occurring after Sept. 30, 1990, but not applicable to any reversion after Sept. 30, 1990, if (1) in the case of plans subject to subchapter III of this chapter, notice of intent to terminate under such subchapter was provided to participants (or if no participants, to PBGC) before Oct. 1, 1990, (2) in the case of plans subject to subchapter I of this chapter (and not subchapter III), notice of intent to reduce future accruals under section 204(h) of this title was provided to participants in connection with termination before Oct. 1, 1990, (3) in the case of plans not subject to subchapter I or III of this chapter, a request for a determination letter with respect to termination was filed with Secretary of the Treasury or Secretary's delegate before Oct. 1, 1990, or (4) in the case of plans not subject to subchapter I or III of this chapter and having only one participant, a resolution terminating the plan was adopted by employer before Oct. 1, 1990.

Multiemployer Pension Plan Amendments Act of 1980 (Pub. L. No. 96-364), as follows;

● ERISA §404(a)(1)(D) was amended by Act §309 by inserting a reference to subchapter III of this chapter. Eff. Sept. 26, 1980.

SEC. 405. LIABILITY FOR BREACH BY CO-FIDUCIARY.

(a) Circumstances Giving to Liability.—In addition to any liability which he may have under any other provision of this part, a fiduciary with respect to a plan shall be liable for a breach of fiduciary responsibility of another fiduciary with respect to the same plan in the following circumstances:

(1) if he participates knowingly in, or knowingly undertakes to conceal, an act or omission of such other fiduciary, knowing such act or omission is a breach;

(2) if, by his failure to comply with section 404(a)(1) in the administration of his specific responsibilities which give rise to his status as a fiduciary, he has enabled such other fiduciary to commit a breach; or

(3) if he has knowledge of a breach by such other fiduciary, unless he makes reasonable efforts under the circumstances to remedy the breach.

(b) Assets Held by Two or More Trustees.—

(1) Except as otherwise provided in subsection (d) and in section 403(a)(1) and (2), if the assets of a plan are held by two or more trustees—

(A) each shall use reasonable care to prevent a co-trustee from committing a breach; and

(B) they shall jointly manage and control the assets of the plan, except that nothing in this subparagraph (B) shall preclude any agreement, authorized by the trust instrument, allocating specific responsibilities, obligations, or duties among trustees, in which event a trustee to whom certain responsibilities, obligations, or duties have not been allocated shall not be liable by reason of this subparagraph (B) either individually or as a trustee for any loss resulting to the plan arising from the acts or omissions on the part of another trustee to whom such responsibilities, obligations, or duties have been allocated.

(2) Nothing in this subsection shall limit any liability that a fiduciary may have under subsection (a) or any other provision of this part.

(3)(A) In the case of a plan the assets of which are held in more than one trust, a trustee shall not be liable under paragraph (1) except with respect to an act or omission of a trustee of a trust of which he is a trustee.

(B) No trustee shall be liable under this subsection for following instructions referred to in section 403(a)(1).

(c) Allocation of Fiduciary Responsibility; Designated Persons to Carry Out Fiduciary Responsibilities.—

(1) The instrument under which a plan is maintained may expressly provide for procedures (A) for allocating fiduciary responsibilities (other than trustee responsibilities) among named fiduciaries, and (B) for named fiduciaries to designate persons other than named fiduciaries to carry out fiduciary responsibilities (other than trustee responsibilities) under the plan.

(2) If a plan expressly provides for a procedure described in paragraph (1), and pursuant to such procedure any fiduciary responsibility of a named fiduciary is allocated to any person, or a person is designated to carry out any such responsibility, then such named fiduciary shall not be liable for an act or omission of such person in carrying out such responsibility except to the extent that—

(A) the named fiduciary violated section 404(a)(1)—

(i) with respect to such allocation or designation,

(ii) with respect to the establishment or implementation of the procedure under paragraph (1), or

(iii) in continuing the allocation or designation; or

(B) the named fiduciary would otherwise be liable in accordance with subsection (a).

(3) For purposes of this subsection, the term "trustee responsibility" means any responsibility provided in the plan's trust instrument (if any) to manage or control the assets of the plan, other than a power under the trust instrument of a named fiduciary to appoint an investment manager in accordance with section 402(c)(3).

(d) Investment Managers.—

(1) If an investment manager or managers have been appointed under section 402(c)(3), then, notwithstanding subsections (a)(2) and (3) and subsection (b), no trustee shall be liable for the acts or omissions of such investment manager or managers, or be under an obligation to invest or otherwise manage any asset of the plan which is subject to the management of such investment manager.

(2) Nothing in this subsection shall relieve any trustee of any liability under this part for any act of such trustee.

SEC. 406. PROHIBITED TRANSACTIONS.

(a) Transactions Between Plan and Party in Interest.—Except as provided in section 408:

(1) A fiduciary with respect to a plan shall not cause the plan to engage in a transaction, if he knows or should know that such transaction constitutes a direct or indirect—

(A) sale or exchange, or leasing, of any property between the plan and a party in interest;

(B) lending of money or other extension of credit between the plan and a party in interest;

(C) furnishing of goods, services, or facilities between the plan and a party in interest;

(D) transfer to, or use by or for the benefit of, a party in interest, of any assets of the plan; or

(E) acquisition, on behalf of the plan, of any employer security or employer real property in violation of section 407(a).

(2) No fiduciary who has authority or discretion to control or manage the assets of a plan shall permit the plan to hold any employer security or employer real property if he knows or should know that holding such security or real property violates section 407(a).

(b) Transactions Between Plan and Fiduciary.—A fiduciary with respect to a plan shall not—

(1) deal with the assets of the plan in his own interest or for his own account,

(2) in his individual or in any other capacity act in any transaction involving the plan on behalf of a party (or represent a party) whose interests are adverse to the interests of the plan or the interests of its participants or beneficiaries, or

(3) receive any consideration for his own personal account from any party dealing with such plan in connection with a transaction involving the assets of the plan.

(c) Transfer of Real or Personal Property to Plan by Party in Interest.—A transfer of real or personal property by a party in interest to a plan shall be treated as a sale or exchange if the property is subject to a mortgage or similar lien which the plan assumes or if it is subject to a mortgage or similar lien which a party-in-interest placed on the property within the 10-year period ending on the date of the transfer.

SEC. 407. LIMITATION WITH RESPECT TO ACQUISITION AND HOLDING OF EMPLOYER SECURITIES AND EMPLOYER REAL PROPERTY BY CERTAIN PLANS.

(a) **Percentage Limitation.**—Except as otherwise provided in this section and section 414:

(1) A plan may not acquire or hold—

(A) any employer security which is not a qualifying employer security, or

(B) any employer real property which is not qualifying employer real property.

(2) A plan may not acquire any qualifying employer security or qualifying employer real property, if immediately after such acquisition the aggregate fair market value of employer securities and employer real property held by the plan exceeds 10 percent of the fair market value of the assets of the plan.

(3)(A) After December 31, 1984, a plan may not hold any qualifying employer securities or qualifying employer real property (or both) to the extent that the aggregate fair market value of such securities and property determined on December 31, 1984, exceeds 10 percent of the greater of—

(i) the fair market value of the assets of the plan, determined on December 31, 1984, or

(ii) the fair market value of the assets of the plan determined on January 1, 1975.

(B) Subparagraph (A) of this paragraph shall not apply to any plan which on any date after December 31, 1974, and before January 1, 1985, did not hold employer securities or employer real property (or both) the aggregate fair market value of which determined on such date exceeded 10 percent of the greater of—

(i) the fair market value of the assets of the plan, determined on such date, or

(ii) the fair market value of the assets of the plan determined on January 1, 1975.

(4)(A) After December 31, 1979, a plan may not hold any employer securities or employer real property in excess of the amount specified in regulations under subparagraph (B). This subparagraph shall not apply to a plan after the earliest date after December 31, 1974, on which it complies with such regulations.

(B) Not later than December 31, 1976, the Secretary shall prescribe regulations which shall have the effect of requiring that a plan divest itself of 50 percent of the holdings of employer securities and employer real property which the plan would be required to divest before January 1, 1985, under paragraph (2) or subsection (c) (whichever is applicable).

(b) **Exception.—**

(1) Subsection (a) of this section shall not apply to any acquisition or holding of qualifying employer securities or qualifying employer real property by an eligible individual account plan.

(2)(A) If this paragraph applies to an eligible individual account plan, the portion of such plan which consists of applicable elective deferrals (and earnings allocable thereto) shall be treated as a separate plan—

(i) which is not an eligible individual account plan, and

(ii) to which the requirements of this section apply.

(B)(i) This paragraph shall apply to any eligible individual account plan if any portion of the plan's applicable elective deferrals (or earnings allocable thereto) are required to be invested in qualifying employer securities or qualifying employer real property or both—

(I) pursuant to the terms of the plan, or

(II) at the direction of a person other than the participant on whose behalf such elective deferrals are made to the plan (or a beneficiary).

(ii) This paragraph shall not apply to an individual account plan for a plan year if, on the last day of the preceding plan year, the fair market value of the assets of all individual account plans maintained by the employer equals not more than 10 percent of the fair market value of the assets of all pension plans (other than multiemployer plans) maintained by the employer.

(iii) This paragraph shall not apply to an individual account plan that is an employee stock ownership plan as defined in section 4975(e)(7) of the Internal Revenue Code of 1986.

(iv) This paragraph shall not apply to an individual account plan if, pursuant to the terms of the plan, the portion of any employee's applicable elective deferrals which is required to be invested in qualifying employer securities and qualifying employer real property for any year may not exceed 1 percent of the employee's compensation which is taken into account under the plan in determining the maximum amount of the employee's applicable elective deferrals for such year.

(C) For purposes of this paragraph, the term "applicable elective deferral" means any elective deferral (as defined in section 402(g)(3)(A) of the Internal Revenue Code of 1986) which is made pursuant to a qualified cash or deferred arrangement as defined in section 401(k) of the Internal Revenue Code of 1986.

(3) Cross References.—

(A) For exemption from diversification requirements for holding of qualifying employer securities and qualifying employer real property by eligible individual account plans, see section 404(a)(2).

(B) For exemption from prohibited transactions for certain acquisitions of qualifying employer securities and qualifying employer real property which are not in violation of the 10 percent limitation, see section 408(e).

(C) For transitional rules respecting securities or real property subject to binding contracts in effect on June 30, 1974, see section 414(c).

(D) For diversification requirements for qualifying employer securities held in certain individual account plans, see section 204(j).

(c) Election.—

(1) A plan which makes the election, under paragraph (3) shall be treated as satisfying the requirement of subsection (a)(3) if and only if employer securities held on any date after December 31, 1974 and before January 1, 1985 have a fair market value, determined as of December 31, 1974, not in excess of 10 percent of the lesser of—

(A) the fair market value of the assets of the plan determined on such date (disregarding any portion of the fair market value of employer securities which is attributable to appreciation of such securities after December 31, 1974) but not less than the fair market value of plan assets on January 1, 1975, or

(B) an amount equal to the sum of (i) the total amount of the contributions to the plan received after December 31, 1974, and prior to such date, plus (ii) the fair market value of the assets of the plan, determined on January 1, 1975.

(2) For purposes of this subsection, in the case of an employer security held by a plan after January 1, 1975, the ownership of which is derived from ownership of employer securities held by the plan on January 1, 1975, or from the exercise of rights derived from such ownership, the value of such security held after January 1, 1975, shall be based on the value as of January 1, 1975, of the security from which ownership was derived. The Secretary shall prescribe regulations to carry out this paragraph.

(3) An election under this paragraph may not be made after December 31, 1975. Such an election shall be made in accordance with regulations prescribed by the Secretary, and shall be irrevocable. A plan may make an election under this paragraph only if on January 1, 1975, the plan holds no employer real property. After such election and before January 1, 1985 the plan may not acquire any employer real property.

(d) Definitions.—For purposes of this section—

(1) The term "employer security" means a security issued by an employer of employees covered by the plan, or by an affiliate of such employer. A contract to which section 408(b)(5) applies shall not be treated as a security for purposes of this section.

(2) The term "employer real property" means real property (and related personal property) which is leased to an employer of employees covered by the plan, or to an affiliate of such employer. For purposes of determining the time at which a plan acquires employer real property for purposes of this section, such property shall be deemed to be acquired by the plan on the date on which the plan acquires the property or on the date on which the lease to the employer (or affiliate) is entered into, whichever is later.

(3)(A) The term "eligible individual account plan" means an individual account plan which is (i) a profit-sharing, stock bonus, thrift, or savings plan; (ii) an employee stock ownership plan; or (iii) a money purchase plan which was in existence on the date of enactment of this Act and which on such date invested primarily in qualifying employer securities. Such term excludes an individual retirement account or annuity described in section 408 of title 26.

(B) Notwithstanding subparagraph (A), a plan shall be treated as an eligible individual account plan with respect to the acquisition or holding of qualifying employer real property or qualifying employer securities only if such plan explicitly provides for acquisition and holding of qualifying employer securities or qualifying employer real property (as the case may be). In the case of a plan in existence on the date of enactment of this Act, this subparagraph shall not take effect until January 1, 1976.

(C) The term "eligible individual account plan" does not include any individual account plan the benefits of which are taken into account in determining the benefits payable to a participant under any defined benefit plan.

(4) The term "qualifying employer real property" means parcels of employer real property—

(A) if a substantial number of the parcels are dispersed geographically;

(B) if each parcel of real property and the improvements thereon are suitable (or adaptable without excessive cost) for more than one use;

(C) even if all of such real property is leased to one lessee (which may be an employer, or an affiliate of an employer); and

(D) if the acquisition and retention of such property comply with the provisions of this part (other than section 404(a)(1)(B) to the extent it requires diversification, and sections 404(a)(1)(C), 406, and subsection (a) of this section).

ERISA Sec. 407(d)(4)(D)

(5) The term "qualifying employer security" means an employer security which is—

(A) stock,

(B) a marketable obligation (as defined in subsection (e)), or

(C) an interest in a publicly traded partnership (as defined in section 7704(b) of the Internal Revenue Code of 1986), but only if such partnership is an existing partnership as defined in section 10211(c)(2)(A) of the Revenue Act of 1987 (Public Law 100-203).

After December 17, 1987, in the case of a plan other than an eligible individual account plan, an employer security described in subparagraph (A) or (C) shall be considered a qualifying employer security only if such employer security satisfies the requirements of subsection (f)(1).

(6) The term "employee stock ownership plan" means an individual account plan—

(A) which is a stock bonus plan which is qualified, or a stock bonus plan and money purchase plan both of which are qualified, under section 401 of title 26, and which is designed to invest primarily in qualifying employer securities, and

(B) which meets such other requirements as the Secretary of the Treasury may prescribe by regulation.

(7) A corporation is an affiliate of an employer if it is a member of any controlled group of corporations (as defined in section 1563(a) of title 26, except that "applicable percentage" shall be substituted for "80 percent" wherever the latter percentage appears in such section) of which the employer who maintains the plan is a member. For purposes of the preceding sentence, the term "applicable percentage" means 50 percent, or such lower percentage as the Secretary may prescribe by regulation. A person other than a corporation shall be treated as an affiliate of an employer to the extent provided in regulations of the Secretary. An employer which is a person other than a corporation shall be treated as affiliated with another person to the extent provided by regulations of the Secretary. Regulations under this paragraph shall be prescribed only after consultation and coordination with the Secretary of the Treasury.

(8) The Secretary may prescribe regulations specifying the extent to which conversions, splits, the exercise of rights, and similar transactions are not treated as acquisitions.

(9) For purposes of this section, an arrangement which consists of a defined benefit plan and an individual account plan shall be treated as 1 plan if the benefits of such individual account plan are taken into account in determining the benefits payable under such defined benefit plan.

(e) Marketable Obligations.—For purposes of subsection (d)(5), the term "marketable obligation" means a bond, debenture, note, or certificate, or other evidence of indebtedness (hereinafter in this subsection referred to as "obligation") if—

(1) such obligation is acquired—

(A) on the market, either (i) at the price of the obligation prevailing on a national securities exchange which is registered with the Securities and Exchange Commission, or (ii) if the obligation is not traded on such a national securities exchange, at a price not less favorable to the plan than the offering price for the obligation as established by current bid and asked prices quoted by persons independent of the issuer;

(B) from an underwriter, at a price (i) not in excess of the public offering price for the obligation as set forth in a prospectus or offering circular filed with the Securities and Exchange Commission, and (ii) at which a substantial portion of the same issue is acquired by persons independent of the issuer; or

(C) directly from the issuer, at a price not less favorable to the plan than the price paid currently for a substantial portion of the same issue by persons independent of the issuer;

(2) immediately following acquisition of such obligation—

(A) not more than 25 percent of the aggregate amount of obligations issued in such issue and outstanding at the time of acquisition is held by the plan, and

(B) at least 50 percent of the aggregate amount referred to in subparagraph (A) is held by persons independent of the issuer; and

(3) immediately following acquisition of the obligation, not more than 25 percent of the assets of the plan is invested in obligations of the employer or an affiliate of the employer.

(f) Maximum Percentage of Stock Held by Plan; Time of Holding or Acquisition; Necessity of Legal Binding Contract.—

(1) Stock satisfies the requirements of this paragraph if, immediately following the acquisition of such stock—

(A) no more than 25 percent of the aggregate amount of stock of the same class issued and outstanding at the time of acquisition is held by the plan, and

(B) at least 50 percent of the aggregate amount referred to in subparagraph (A) is held by persons independent of the issuer.

(2) Until January 1, 1993, a plan shall not be treated as violating subsection (a) solely by holding stock which fails to satisfy the requirements of paragraph (1) if such stock—

(A) has been so held since December 17, 1987, or

(B) was acquired after December 17, 1987, pursuant to a legally binding contract in effect on December 17, 1987, and has been so held at all times after the acquisition.

Amendments to ERISA §407

Pension Protection Act of 2006 (Pub. L. No. 109-280), as follows:
- ERISA §407(b)(3)(D) was added by Act §901(b)(2). Eff. for plan years beginning after 2006, with a transition rule for collectively bargained agreements and a special rule for employee stock ownership plans (ESOPs). The ESOP special rule in Act §901(c) provides that the amendments apply to plan years beginning after the earlier of Dec. 31, 2007, or the first date on which the fair market value of such securities exceeds the guaranteed minimum value. The special rule applies to employer securities that are attributable to employer contributions other than elective deferrals, and that, on Sept. 17, 2003, consist of preferred stock, and are within an ESOP, the terms of which provide that the value of the securities cannot be less than the guaranteed minimum value specified by the plan on such date.

Economic Growth and Tax Relief Extension Act of 2001 (Pub. L. No. 107-16), as follows:
- ERISA §407(b)(2)–(3) were amended by Act §655(a). Eff. as if included in Pub. L. No. 105-34.

Taxpayer Relief Act of 1997 (Pub. L. No. 105-34), as follows:
- ERISA §407(b)(2), (3) were amended by Act §1524(a) by adding new para. (2) and redesignating former para. (2) as (3). Eff. after 1998.

Pub. L. No. 101-540, as follows:
- ERISA §407(d)(5) was amended by Act §1. Eff. Jan. 1, 1987. ERISA §407(d)(5) prior to amendment:
  > (5) The term "qualifying employer security" means an employer security which is stock or a marketable obligation (as defined in subsection (e) of this section). After December 17, 1987, in the case of a plan other than an eligible individual account plan, stock shall be considered a qualifying employer security only if such stock satisfies the requirements of subsection (f)(1) of this section.

Omnibus Budget Reconciliation Act of 1989 (Pub. L. No. 101-239), as follows:
- ERISA §407(d)(3)(A), (6)(A), (7) were amended by Act §7891(a)(1) by substituting "Internal Revenue Code of 1986" for "Internal Revenue Code of 1954", which for purposes of codification was translated as "title 26". Eff. as if included in Pub. L. No. 99-514.
- ERISA §407(d)(3)(C) was amended by Act §7881(*l*)(1) by realigning the margin. Eff. as if included in Pub. L. No. 100-203.
- ERISA §407(d)(6)(A) was amended by Act §7894(e)(2) by substituting "money purchase plan" for "money purchase" and "employer securities" for "employee securities". Eff. as if originally included in Pub. L. No. 93-406.
- ERISA §407(d)(9) was amended by Act §7881(*l*)(2) by substituting "such individual account plan" for "such arrangement" and realigning the margin. Eff. as if originally included in Pub. L. No. 93-406.
- ERISA §407(f)(1) was amended by Act §7881(*l*)(3)(A), (4) by substituting "paragraph" for "subsection" and "if, immediately following the acquisition of such stock" for "if". Eff. as if included in Pub. L. No. 100-203.
- ERISA §407(f)(3) was amended by Act §7881(*l*)(3)(B) by striking para. (3). Eff. as if included in Pub. L. No. 100-203. ERISA §407(f)(3):
  > (3) After December 17, 1987, no plan may acquire stock which does not satisfy the requirements of paragraph (1) unless the acquisition is made pursuant to a legally binding contract in effect on such date.

Omnibus Budget Reconciliation Act of 1987 (Pub. L. No. 100-203), as follows:
- ERISA §407(d)(3)(C) was added by Act §9345(a)(1). Eff. after Dec. 17, 1987.
- ERISA §407(d)(5) was amended by Act §9345(b)(1) by inserting at end "After December 17, 1987, in the case of a plan other than an eligible individual account plan, stock shall be considered a qualifying employer security only if such stock satisfies the requirements of subsection (f)(1) of this section." Eff. after Dec. 17, 1987.
- ERISA §407(d)(9) was added by Act §9345(a)(2). Eff. after Dec. 17, 1987.
- ERISA §407(f) was added by Act §9345(b)(2). Eff. after Dec. 17, 1987.

SEC. 408. EXEMPTIONS FROM PROHIBITED TRANSACTIONS.

(a) Grant of Exemptions.—The Secretary shall establish an exemption procedure for purposes of this subsection. Pursuant to such procedure, he may grant a conditional or unconditional exemption of any fiduciary or transaction, or class of fiduciaries or transactions, from all or part of the restrictions imposed by sections 406 and 407(a). Action under this subsection may be taken only after consultation and coordination with the Secretary of the Treasury. An exemption granted under this section shall not relieve a fiduciary from any other applicable provision of this Act. The Secretary may not grant an exemption under this subsection unless he finds that such exemption is—

(1) administratively feasible,

(2) in the interests of the plan and of its participants and beneficiaries, and

(3) protective of the rights of participants and beneficiaries of such plan.

Before granting an exemption under this subsection from section 406(a) or 407(a), the Secretary shall publish notice in the Federal Register of the pendency of the exemption, shall require that adequate notice be given to interested persons, and shall afford interested persons opportunity to present views. The Secretary may not grant an exemption under this subsection from section 406(b) unless he affords an opportunity for a hearing and makes a determination on the record with respect to the findings required by paragraphs (1), (2), and (3) of this subsection.

(b) Enumeration of Transactions Exempted From Section 406 Prohibitions.—The prohibitions provided in section 406 shall not apply to any of the following transactions:

(1) Any loans made by the plan to parties in interest who are participants or beneficiaries of the plan if such loans (A) are available to all such participants and beneficiaries on a reasonably equivalent basis, (B) are not made available to highly compensated employees (within the meaning of section 414(q) of the Internal Revenue Code of 1986) in an amount greater than the amount made available to other employees, (C) are made in accordance with specific provisions regarding such loans set forth in the plan, (D) bear a reasonable rate of interest, and (E) are adequately secured. A loan made by a plan shall not

fail to meet the requirements of the preceding sentence by reason of a loan repayment suspension described under section 414(u)(4) of title 26.

(2) Contracting or making reasonable arrangements with a party in interest for office space, or legal, accounting, or other services necessary for the establishment or operation of the plan, if no more than reasonable compensation is paid therefor.

(3) A loan to an employee stock ownership plan (as defined in section 407(d)(6)), if—

(A) such loan is primarily for the benefit of participants and beneficiaries of the plan, and

(B) such loan is at an interest rate which is not in excess of a reasonable rate.

If the plan gives collateral to a party in interest for such loan, such collateral may consist only of qualifying employer securities (as defined in section 407(d)(5)).

(4) The investment of all or part of a plan's assets in deposits which bear a reasonable interest rate in a bank or similar financial institution supervised by the United States or a State, if such bank or other institution is a fiduciary of such plan and if—

(A) the plan covers only employees of such bank or other institution and employees of affiliates of such bank or other institution, or

(B) such investment is expressly authorized by a provision of the plan or by a fiduciary (other than such bank or institution or affiliate thereof) who is expressly empowered by the plan to so instruct the trustee with respect to such investment.

(5) Any contract for life insurance, health insurance, or annuities with one or more insurers which are qualified to do business in a State, if the plan pays no more than adequate consideration, and if each such insurer orinsurers is—

(A) the employer maintaining the plan, or

(B) a party in interest which is wholly owned (directly or indirectly) by the employer maintaining the plan, or by any person which is a party in interest with respect to the plan, but only if the total premiums and annuity considerations written by such insurers for life insurance, health insurance, or annuities for all plans (and their employers) with respect to which such insurers are parties in interest (not including premiums or annuity considerations written by the employer maintaining the plan) do not exceed 5 percent of the total premiums and annuity considerations written for all lines of insurance in that year by such insurers (not including premiums or annuity considerations written by the employer maintaining the plan).

(6) The providing of any ancillary service by a bank or similar financial institution supervised by the United States or a State, if such bank or other institution is a fiduciary of such plan, and if—

(A) such bank or similar financial institution has adopted adequate internal safeguards which assure that the providing of such ancillary service is consistent with sound banking and financial practice, as determined by Federal or State supervisory authority, and

(B) the extent to which such ancillary service is provided is subject to specific guidelines issued by such bank or similar financial institution (as determined by the Secretary after consultation with Federal and State supervisory authority), and adherence to such guidelines would reasonably preclude such bank or similar financial institution from providing such ancillary service (i) in an excessive or unreasonable manner, and (ii) in a manner that would be inconsistent with the best interests of participants and beneficiaries of employee benefit plans.

Such ancillary services shall not be provided at more than reasonable compensation.

(7) The exercise of a privilege to convert securities, to the extent provided in regulations of the Secretary, but only if the plan receives no less than adequate consideration pursuant to such conversion.

(8) Any transaction between a plan and (i) a common or collective trust fund or pooled investment fund maintained by a party in interest which is a bank or trust company supervised by a State or Federal agency or (ii) a pooled investment fund of an insurance company qualified to do business in a State, if—

(A) the transaction is a sale or purchase of an interest in the fund,

(B) the bank, trust company, or insurance company receives not more than reasonable compensation, and

(C) such transaction is expressly permitted by the instrument under which the plan is maintained, or by a fiduciary (other than the bank, trust company, or insurance company, or an affiliate thereof) who has authority to manage and control the assets of the plan.

(9) The making by a fiduciary of a distribution of the assets of the plan in accordance with the terms of the plan if such assets are distributed in the same manner as provided under section 4044 of this Act (relating to allocation of assets).

(10) Any transaction required or permitted under part 1 of subtitle E of title IV.

(11) A merger of multiemployer plans, or the transfer of assets or liabilities between multiemployer plans, determined by the Pension Benefit Guaranty Corporation to meet the requirements of section 4231.

(12) The sale by a plan to a party in interest on or after December 18, 1987, of any stock, if—

(A) the requirements of paragraphs (1) and (2) of subsection (e) are met with respect to such stock,

(B) on the later of the date on which the stock was acquired by the plan, or January 1, 1975, such stock constituted a qualifying employer security (as defined in section 407(d)(5) as then in effect), and

(C) such stock does not constitute a qualifying employer security (as defined in section 407(d)(5) as in effect at the time of the sale).

(13) Any transfer made before January 1, 2014, of excess pension assets from a defined benefit plan to a retiree health account in a qualified transfer permitted under section 420 of the Internal Revenue Code of 1986 (as in effect on the date of the enactment of the Pension Protection Act of 2006 [enacted Aug. 17, 2006]).

(14) Any transaction in connection with the provision of investment advice described in section 3(21)(A)(ii) to a participant or beneficiary of an individual account plan that permits such participant or beneficiary to direct the investment of assets in their individual account, if—

(A) the transaction is—

(i) the provision of the investment advice to the participant or beneficiary of the plan with respect to a security or other property available as an investment under the plan,

(ii) the acquisition, holding, or sale of a security or other property available as an investment under the plan pursuant to the investment advice, or

(iii) the direct or indirect receipt of fees or other compensation by the fiduciary adviser or an affiliate thereof (or any employee, agent, or registered representative of the fiduciary adviser or affiliate) in connection with the provision of the advice or in connection with an acquisition, holding, or sale of a security or other property available as an investment under the plan pursuant to the investment advice; and

(B) the requirements of subsection (g) are met.

(15)(A) Any transaction involving the purchase or sale of securities, or other property (as determined by the Secretary), between a plan and a party in interest (other than a fiduciary described in section 3(21)(A)) with respect to a plan if—

(i) the transaction involves a block trade,

(ii) at the time of the transaction, the interest of the plan (together with the interests of any other plans maintained by the same plan sponsor), does not exceed 10 percent of the aggregate size of the block trade,

(iii) the terms of the transaction, including the price, are at least as favorable to the plan as an arm's length transaction, and

(iv) the compensation associated with the purchase and sale is not greater than the compensation

associated with an arm's length transaction with an unrelated party.

(B) For purposes of this paragraph, the term "block trade" means any trade of at least 10,000 shares or with a market value of at least $200,000 which will be allocated across two or more unrelated client accounts of a fiduciary.

(16) Any transaction involving the purchase or sale of securities, or other property (as determined by the Secretary), between a plan and a party in interest if—

(A) the transaction is executed through an electronic communication network, alternative trading system, or similar execution system or trading venue subject to regulation and oversight by—

(i) the applicable Federal regulating entity, or

(ii) such foreign regulatory entity as the Secretary may determine by regulation,

(B) either—

(i) the transaction is effected pursuant to rules designed to match purchases and sales at the best price available through the execution system in accordance with applicable rules of the Securities and Exchange Commission or other relevant governmental authority, or

(ii) neither the execution system nor the parties to the transaction take into account the identity of the parties in the execution of trades,

(C) the price and compensation associated with the purchase and sale are not greater than the price and compensation associated with an arm's length transaction with an unrelated party,

(D) if the party in interest has an ownership interest in the system or venue described in subparagraph (A), the system or venue has been authorized by the plan sponsor or other independent fiduciary for transactions described in this paragraph, and

(E) not less than 30 days prior to the initial transaction described in this paragraph executed through any system or venue described in subparagraph (A), a plan fiduciary is provided written or electronic notice of the execution of such transaction through such system or venue.

(17)(A) Transactions described in subparagraphs (A), (B), and (D) of section 406(a)(1) between a plan and a person that is a party in interest other than a fiduciary (or an affiliate) who has or exercises any discretionary authority or control with respect to the investment of the plan assets involved in the transaction or renders investment advice (within the meaning of section 3(21)(A)(ii)) with respect to those assets, solely by reason of providing services to the plan or solely by reason of a relationship to such a service provider described in subparagraph (F), (G), (H), or (I) of section 3(14), or both, but only if in connection

ERISA Sec. 408(b)(17)(A)

with such transaction the plan receives no less, nor pays no more, than adequate consideration.

(B) For purposes of this paragraph, the term "adequate consideration" means—

(i) in the case of a security for which there is a generally recognized market—

(I) the price of the security prevailing on a national securities exchange which is registered under section 6 of the Securities Exchange Act of 1934, taking into account factors such as the size of the transaction and marketability of the security, or

(II) if the security is not traded on such a national securities exchange, a price not less favorable to the plan than the offering price for the security as established by the current bid and asked prices quoted by persons independent of the issuer and of the party in interest, taking into account factors such as the size of the transaction and marketability of the security, and

(ii) in the case of an asset other than a security for which there is a generally recognized market, the fair market value of the asset as determined in good faith by a fiduciary or fiduciaries in accordance with regulations prescribed by the Secretary.

(18) Foreign exchange transactions.—Any foreign exchange transactions, between a bank or broker-dealer (or any affiliate ofeither), and a plan (as defined in section 3(3)) with respect to which such bank orbroker-dealer (or affiliate) is a trustee, custodian, fiduciary, or other party in interest, if—

(A) the transaction is in connection with the purchase, holding, or sale of securities or other investment assets (other than a foreign exchange transaction unrelated to any other investment in securities or other investment assets),

(B) at the time the foreign exchange transaction is entered into, the terms of the transaction are not less favorable to the plan than the terms generally available in comparable arm's length foreign exchange transactions between unrelated parties, or the terms afforded by the bank or broker-dealer (or any affiliate of either) in comparable arm's-length foreign exchange transactions involving unrelated parties,

(C) the exchange rate used by such bank or broker-dealer (or affiliate) for a particular foreign exchange transaction does not deviate by more than 3 percent from the interbank bid and asked rates for transactions of comparable size and maturity at the time of the transaction as displayed on an independent service that reports rates of exchange in the foreign currency market for such currency, and

(D) the bank or broker-dealer (or any affiliate of either) does not have investment discretion, or provide investment advice, with respect to the transaction.

(19) Cross trading.—Any transaction described in sections 406(a)(1)(A) and 406(b)(2) involving the purchase and sale of a security between a plan and any other account managed by the same investment manager, if—

(A) the transaction is a purchase or sale, for no consideration other than cash payment against prompt delivery of a security for which market quotations are readily available,

(B) the transaction is effected at the independent current market price of the security (within the meaning of section 270.17a-7(b) of title 17, Code of Federal Regulations),

(C) no brokerage commission, fee (except for customary transfer fees, the fact of which is disclosed pursuant to subparagraph (D)), or other remuneration is paid in connection with the transaction,

(D) a fiduciary (other than the investment manager engaging in the cross-trades or any affiliate) for each plan participating in the transaction authorizes in advance of any cross-trades (in a document that is separate from any other written agreement of the parties) the investment manager to engage in cross trades at the investment manager's discretion, after such fiduciary has received disclosure regarding the conditions under which cross trades may take place (but only if such disclosure is separate from any other agreement or disclosure involving the asset management relationship), including the written policies and procedures of the investment manager described in subparagraph (H),

(E) each plan participating in the transaction has assets of at least $100,000,000, except that if the assets of a plan are invested in a master trust containing the assets of plans maintained by employers in the same controlled group (as defined in section 407(d)(7)), the master trust has assets of at least $100,000,000,

(F) the investment manager provides to the plan fiduciary who authorized cross trading under subparagraph (D) a quarterly report detailing all cross trades executed by the investment manager in which the plan participated during such quarter, including the following information, as applicable: (i) the identity of each security bought or sold; (ii) the number of shares or units traded; (iii) the parties involved in the cross-trade; and (iv) trade price and the method used to establish the trade price,

(G) the investment manager does not base its fee schedule on the plan's consent to cross trading, and no other service (other than the investment opportunities and cost savings available through a cross trade) is conditioned on the plan's consent to cross trading,

(H) the investment manager has adopted, and cross-trades are effected in accordance with, written cross-trading policies and procedures that are fair and equitable to all accounts participating in the cross-trading program, and that include a description of the manager's pricing policies and procedures, and the manager's policies and procedures for allocating cross trades in an objective manner among accounts participating in the cross-trading program, and

(I) the investment manager has designated an individual responsible for periodically reviewing such purchases and sales to ensure compliance with the written policies and procedures described in subparagraph (H), and following such review, the individual shall issue an annual written report no later than 90 days following the period to which it relates signed under penalty of perjury to the plan fiduciary who authorized cross trading under subparagraph (D) describing the steps performed during the course of the review, the level of compliance, and any specific instances of non-compliance.

The written report under subparagraph (I) shall also notify the plan fiduciary of the plan's right to terminate participation in the investment manager's cross-trading program at any time.

(20)(A) Except as provided in subparagraphs (B) and (C), a transaction described in section 406(a) in connection with the acquisition, holding, or disposition of any security or commodity, if the transaction is corrected before the end of the correction period.

(B) Subparagraph (A) does not apply to any transaction between a plan and a plan sponsor or its affiliates that involves the acquisition or sale of an employer security (as defined in section 407(d)(1)) or the acquisition, sale, or lease of employer real property (as defined in section 407(d)(2)).

(C) In the case of any fiduciary or other party in interest (or any other person knowingly participating in such transaction), subparagraph (A) does not apply to any transaction if, at the time the transaction occurs, such fiduciary or party in interest (or other person) knew (or reasonably should have known) that the transaction would (without regard to this paragraph) constitute a violation of section 406(a).

(D) For purposes of this paragraph, the term "correction period" means, in connection with a fiduciary or party in interest (or other person knowingly participating in the transaction), the 14-day period beginning on the date on which such fiduciary or party in interest (or other person) discovers, or reasonably should have discovered, that the transaction would (without regard to this paragraph) constitute a violation of section 406(a).

(E) For purposes of this paragraph—

(i) The term "security" has the meaning given such term by section 475(c)(2) of the Internal Revenue Code of 1986 (without regard to subparagraph (F)(iii) and the last sentence thereof).

(ii) The term "commodity" has the meaning given such term by section 475(e)(2) of such Code (without regard to subparagraph (D)(iii) thereof).

(iii) The term "correct" means, with respect to a transaction—

(I) to undo the transaction to the extent possible and in any case to make good to the plan or affected account any losses resulting from the transaction, and

(II) to restore to the plan or affected account any profits made through the use of assets of the plan.

(c) Fiduciary Benefits and Compensation Not Prohibited by Section 406.—Nothing in section 406 shall be construed to prohibit any fiduciary from—

(1) receiving any benefit to which he may be entitled as a participant or beneficiary in the plan, so long as the benefit is computed and paid on a basis which is consistent with the terms of the plan as applied to all other participants and beneficiaries;

(2) receiving any reasonable compensation for services rendered, or for the reimbursement of expenses properly and actually incurred, in the performance of his duties with the plan; except that no person so serving who already receives full-time pay from an employer or an association of employers, whose employees are participants in the plan, or from an employee organization whose members are participants in such plan shall receive compensation from such plan, except for reimbursement of expenses properly and actually incurred; or

(3) serving as a fiduciary in addition to being an officer, employee, agent, or other representative of a party in interest.

(d) Owner-Employees; Family Members; Shareholder Employees.—

(1) Section 407(b) and subsections (b), (c), and (e) of this section shall not apply to a transaction in which a plan directly or indirectly—

(A) lends any part of the corpus or income of the plan to,

(B) pays any compensation for personal services rendered to the plan to, or

(C) acquires for the plan any property from, or sells any property to,

any person who is with respect to the plan an owner-employee (as defined in section 401(c)(3) of the Internal Revenue Code of 1986), a member of the family (as defined in section 267(c)(4) of such Code) of any such owner-employee, or any corporation in which any such owner-employee owns, directly or indirectly, 50 percent or more of the total combined voting power of all classes of stock entitled to vote or 50 percent or more of the total value of shares of all classes of stock of the corporation.

(2)(A) For purposes of paragraph (1), the following shall be treated as owner-employees:

(i) A shareholder-employee.

(ii) A participant or beneficiary of an individual retirement plan (as defined in section 7701(a)(37) of the Internal Revenue Code of 1986).

(iii) An employer or association of employees which establishes such an individual retirement plan under section 408(c) of such Code.

(B) Paragraph (1)(C) shall not apply to a transaction which consists of a sale of employer securities to an employee stock ownership plan (as defined in section 407(d)(6) by a shareholder-employee, a member of the family (as defined in section 267(c)(4) of such Code) of any such owner-employee, or a corporation in which such a shareholder-employee owns stock representing a 50 percent or greater interest described in paragraph (1).

(C) For purposes of paragraph (1)(A), the term "owner-employee" shall only include a person described in clause (ii) or (iii) of subparagraph (A).

(3) For purposes of paragraph (2), the term "shareholder-employee" means an employee or officer of an S corporation (as defined in section 1361(a)(1) of such Code) who owns (or is considered as owning within the meaning of section 318(a)(1) of such Code) more than 5 percent of the outstanding stock of the corporation on any day during the taxable year of such corporation.

(e) Acquisition or Sale by Plan of Qualifying Employer Securities; Acquisition, Sale, or Lease by Plan of Qualifying Employer Real Property.—Sections 406 and 407 shall not apply to the acquisition or sale by a plan of qualifying employer securities (as defined in section 407(d)(5)) or acquisition, sale or lease by a plan of qualifying employer real property (as defined in section 407(d)(4))—

(1) if such acquisition, sale, or lease is for adequate consideration (or in the case of a marketable obligation, at a price not less favorable to the plan than the price determined under section 407(e)(1)),

(2) if no commission is charged with respect thereto, and

(3) if—

(A) the plan is an eligible individual account plan (as defined in section 407(d)(3)), or

(B) in the case of an acquisition or lease of qualifying employer real property by a plan which is not an eligible individual account plan, or of an acquisition of qualifying employer securities by such a plan, the lease or acquisition is not prohibited by section 407(a).

(f) Applicability of Statutory Prohibitions to Mergers or Transfers.—Section 406(b)(2) shall not apply to any merger or transfer described in subsection (b)(11).

(g) Provision of Investment Advice to Participant and Beneficiaries.—

(1) In general.—The prohibitions provided in section 406 shall not apply to transactions described in subsection (b)(14) if the investment advice provided by a fiduciary adviser is provided under an eligible investment advice arrangement.

(2) Eligible investment advice arrangement.—For purposes of this subsection, the term "eligible investment advice arrangement" means an arrangement—

(A) which either—

(i) provides that any fees (including any commission or other compensation) received by the fiduciary adviser for investment advice or with respect to the sale, holding, or acquisition of any security or other property for purposes of investment of plan assets do not vary depending on the basis of any investment option selected, or

(ii) uses a computer model under an investment advice program meeting the requirements of paragraph (3) in connection with the provision of investment advice by a fiduciary adviser to a participant or beneficiary, and

(B) with respect to which the requirements of paragraph (4), (5), (6), (7), (8), and (9) are met.

(3) Investment advice program using computer model.—

(A) In general.—An investment advice program meets the requirements of this paragraph if the requirements of subparagraphs (B), (C), and (D) are met.

(B) Computer model.—The requirements of this subparagraph are met if the investment advice provided under the investment advice program is provided pursuant to a computer model that—

(i) applies generally accepted investment theories that take into account the historic returns of different asset classes over defined periods of time,

(ii) utilizes relevant information about the participant, which may include age, life expectancy, retirement age, risk tolerance, other assets or sources of income, and preferences as to certain types of investments,

(iii) utilizes prescribed objective criteria to provide asset allocation portfolios comprised of investment options available under the plan,

(iv) operates in a manner that is not biased in favor of investments offered by the fiduciary adviser or a person with a material affiliation or contractual relationship with the fiduciary adviser, and

(v) takes into account all investment options under the plan in specifying how a participant's account balance should be invested and is not inappropriately weighted with respect to any investment option.

(C) Certification.—

(i) In general.—The requirements of this subparagraph are met with respect to any investment advice program if an eligible investment expert certifies, prior to the utilization of the computer model and in accordance with rules prescribed by the Secretary, that the computer model meets the requirements of subparagraph (B).

(ii) Renewal of certifications.—If, as determined under regulations prescribed by the Secretary, there are material modifications to a computer model, the requirements of this subparagraph are met only if a certification described in clause (i) is obtained with respect to the computer model as so modified.

(iii) Eligible investment expert.—The term "eligible investment expert" means any person—

(I) which meets such requirements as the Secretary may provide, and

(II) does not bear any material affiliation or contractual relationship with any investment adviser or a related person thereof (or any employee, agent, or registered representative of the investment adviser or related person).

(D) Exclusivity of recommendation.—The requirements of this subparagraph are met with respect to any investment advice program if—

(i) the only investment advice provided under the program is the advice generated by the computer model described in subparagraph (B), and

(ii) any transaction described in subsection (b)(14)(A)(ii) occurs solely at the direction of the participant or beneficiary.

Nothing in the preceding sentence shall preclude the participant or beneficiary from requesting investment advice other than that described in subparagraph (A), but only if such request has not been solicited by any person connected with carrying out the arrangement.

(4) Express authorization by separate fiduciary.—The requirements of this paragraph are met with respect to an arrangement if the arrangement is expressly authorized by a plan fiduciary other than the person offering the investment advice program, any person providing investment options under the plan, or any affiliate of either.

(5) Annual audit.—The requirements of this paragraph are met if an independent auditor, who has appropriate technical training or experience and proficiency and so represents in writing—

(A) conducts an annual audit of the arrangement for compliance with the requirements of this subsection, and

(B) following completion of the annual audit, issues a written report to the fiduciary who authorized use of the arrangement which presents its specific findings regarding compliance of the arrangement with the requirements of this subsection.

For purposes of this paragraph, an auditor is considered independent if it is not related to the person offering the arrangement to the plan and is not related to any person providing investment options under the plan.

(6) Disclosure.—The requirements of this paragraph are met if—

(A) the fiduciary adviser provides to a participant or a beneficiary before the initial provision of the investment advice with regard to any security or other property offered as an investment option, a written notification (which may consist of notification by means of electronic communication)—

(i) of the role of any party that has a material affiliation or contractual relationship with the fiduciary adviser in the development of the investment advice program and in the selection of investment options available under the plan,

(ii) of the past performance and historical rates of return of the investment options available under the plan,

(iii) of all fees or other compensation relating to the advice that the fiduciary adviser or any affiliate thereof is to receive (including compensation provided by any third party) in connection with the provision of the advice or in connection with the sale, acquisition, or holding of the security or other property,

(iv) of any material affiliation or contractual relationship of the fiduciary adviser or affiliates thereof in the security or other property,

(v) the manner, and under what circumstances, any participant or beneficiary information provided under the arrangement will be used or disclosed,

(vi) of the types of services provided by the fiduciary adviser in connection with the provision of investment advice by the fiduciary adviser,

(vii) that the adviser is acting as a fiduciary of the plan in connection with the provision of the advice, and

(viii) that a recipient of the advice may separately arrange for the provision of advice by another adviser, that could have no material affiliation with and receive no fees or other compensation in connection with the security or other property, and

(B) at all times during the provision of advisory services to the participant or beneficiary, the fiduciary adviser—

(i) maintains the information described in subparagraph (A) in accurate form and in the manner described in paragraph (8),

(ii) provides, without charge, accurate information to the recipient of the advice no less frequently than annually,

(iii) provides, without charge, accurate information to the recipient of the advice upon request of the recipient, and

(iv) provides, without charge, accurate information to the recipient of the advice concerning any material change to the information required to be provided to the recipient of the advice at a time reasonably contemporaneous to the change in information.

(7) Other conditions.—The requirements of this paragraph are met if—

(A) the fiduciary adviser provides appropriate disclosure, in connection with the sale, acquisition, or holding of the security or other property, in accordance with all applicable securities laws,

(B) the sale, acquisition, or holding occurs solely at the direction of the recipient of the advice,

(C) the compensation received by the fiduciary adviser and affiliates thereof in connection with the sale, acquisition, or holding of the security or other property is reasonable, and

(D) the terms of the sale, acquisition, or holding of the security or other property are at least as favorable to the plan as an arm's length transaction would be.

(8) Standards for presentation of information.—

(A) In general.—The requirements of this paragraph are met if the notification required to be provided to participants and beneficiaries under paragraph (6)(A) is written in a clear and conspicuous manner and in a manner calculated to be understood by the average plan participant and is sufficiently accurate and comprehensive to reasonably apprise such participants and beneficiaries of the information required to be provided in the notification.

(B) Model form for disclosure of fees and other compensation.—The Secretary shall issue a model form for the disclosure of fees and other compensation required in paragraph (6)(A)(iii) which meets the requirements of subparagraph (A).

(9) Maintenance for 6 years of evidence of compliance.—The requirements of this paragraph are met if a fiduciary adviser who has provided advice referred to in paragraph (1) maintains, for a period of not less than 6 years after the provision of the advice, any records necessary for determining whether the requirements of the preceding provisions of this subsection and of subsection (b)(14) have been met. A transaction prohibited under section 406 shall not be considered to have occurred solely because the records are lost or destroyed prior to the end of the 6-year period due to circumstances beyond the control of the fiduciary adviser.

(10) Exemption for plan sponsor and certain other fiduciaries.—

(A) In general.—Subject to subparagraph (B), a plan sponsor or other person who is a fiduciary (other than a fiduciary adviser) shall not be treated as failing to meet the requirements of this part solely by reason of the provision of investment advice referred to in section 3(21)(A)(ii) (or solely by reason of contracting for or otherwise arranging for the provision of the advice), if—

(i) the advice is provided by a fiduciary adviser pursuant to an eligible investment advice arrangement between the plan sponsor or other fiduciary and the fiduciary adviser for the provision by the fiduciary adviser of investment advice referred to in such section,

(ii) the terms of the eligible investment advice arrangement require compliance by the fiduciary adviser with the requirements of this subsection, and

(iii) the terms of the eligible investment advice arrangement include a written acknowledgment by the fiduciary adviser that the fiduciary adviser is a fiduciary of the plan with respect to the provision of the advice.

(B) Continued duty of prudent selection of adviser and periodic review.—Nothing in subparagraph (A) shall be construed to exempt a plan sponsor or other person who is a fiduciary from any requirement of this part for the prudent selection and periodic review of a fiduciary adviser with whom the plan sponsor or other person enters into an eligible investment advice arrangement for the provision of investment advice referred to in section 3(21)(A)(ii). The plan sponsor or other person who is a fiduciary has no duty under this part to monitor the specific investment advice given by the fiduciary adviser to any particular recipient of the advice.

(C) Availability of plan assets for payment for advice.—Nothing in this part shall be construed to preclude the use of plan assets to pay for reasonable expenses in providing investment advice referred to in section 3(21)(A)(ii).

(11) Definitions.—For purposes of this subsection and subsection (b)(14)—

(A) Fiduciary adviser.—The term "fiduciary adviser" means, with respect to a plan, a person who is a fiduciary of the plan by reason of the provision of investment advice referred to in section 3(21)(A)(ii) by the person to a participant or beneficiary of the plan and who is—

(i) registered as an investment adviser under the Investment Advisers Act of 1940 (15 U.S.C. 80b-1 et seq.) or under the laws of the State in which the fiduciary maintains its principal office and place of business,

(ii) a bank or similar financial institution referred to in subsection (b)(4) or a savings association (as defined in section 3(b)(1) of the Federal Deposit Insurance Act (12 U.S.C. 1813(b)(1)), but only if the advice is provided through a trust department of the bank or similar financial institution or savings association which is subject to periodic examination and review by Federal or State banking authorities,

(iii) an insurance company qualified to do business under the laws of a State,

(iv) a person registered as a broker or dealer under the Securities Exchange Act of 1934 (15 U.S.C. 78a et seq.),

(v) an affiliate of a person described in any of clauses (i) through (iv), or

(vi) an employee, agent, or registered representative of a person described in clauses (i) through (v) who satisfies the requirements of applicable insurance, banking, and securities laws relating to the provision of the advice.

For purposes of this part, a person who develops the computer model described in paragraph (3)(B) or markets the investment advice program or computer model shall be treated as a person who is a fiduciary of the plan by reason of the provision of investment advice referred to in section 3(21)(A)(ii) to a participant or beneficiary and shall be treated as a fiduciary adviser for purposes of this subsection and subsection (b)(14), except that the Secretary may prescribe rules under which only 1 fiduciary adviser may elect to be treated as a fiduciary with respect to the plan.

(B) Affiliate.—The term "affiliate" of another entity means an affiliated person of the entity (as defined in section 2(a)(3) of the Investment Company Act of 1940 (15 U.S.C. 80a-2(a)(3))).

(C) Registered representative.—The term "registered representative" of another entity means a person described in section 3(a)(18) of the Securities Exchange Act of 1934 (15 U.S.C. 78c(a)(18)) (substituting the entity for the broker or dealer referred to in such section) or a person described in section 202(a)(17) of the Investment Advisers Act

of 1940 (15 U.S.C. 80b-2(a)(17)) (substituting the entity for the investment adviser referred to in such section).

Amendments to ERISA §408

Worker, Retiree, and Employer Recovery Act of 2008 (Pub. L. No. 110-458), as follows:

- ERISA §408(g)(3)(D)(ii) was amended by Act §106(a)(1)(A) by striking "subsection (b)(14)(B)(ii)" and inserting "subsection (b)(14)(A)(ii)". Eff. for investment advice with respect to plan assets that is provided after Dec. 31, 2006, and rendered for a fee or other compensation, as if included in Pub. L. No. 109-280, §601.
- ERISA §408(g)(6)(A)(i) was amended by Act §106(a)(1)(B) by striking "financial adviser" and inserting "fiduciary adviser". Eff. for investment advice with respect to plan assets that is provided after Dec. 31, 2006, and rendered for a fee or other compensation, as if included in Pub. L. No. 109-280, §601.
- ERISA §408(g)(11)(A) was amended by Act §106(a)(1)(C) by striking "the participant" and inserting "a participant"; and striking "section 408(b)(4)" in cl. (ii) and inserting "subsection (b)(4)". Eff. for investment advice with respect to plan assets that is provided after Dec. 31, 2006, and rendered for a fee or other compensation, as if included in Pub. L. No. 109-280, §601.
- ERISA §408(b)(18)(C) was amended by Act §106(b)(1) by striking "or less". Eff. for transactions occurring after Aug. 17, 2006, as if included in Pub. L. No. 109-280, §611.

Pension Protection Act of 2006 (Pub. L. No. 109-280), as follows:

- ERISA §408(b)(13) was amended by Act §107(a)(11) (redesignated as §108(a)(11) by Pub. L. No. 111-192, §202(a)) by substituting "Pension Protection Act of 2006" for "American Jobs Creation Act of 2004". Eff. for plan years after 2007, with a delayed effective date for amendments for "eligible cooperative plans" until the earlier of the first plan year the plan ceases to be eligible, or Jan. 1, 2017.
- ERISA §408(b)(14) was added by Act §601(a)(1). Eff. for investment advice with respect to plan assets that is provided after Dec. 31, 2006, and rendered for a fee or other compensation.
- ERISA §408(b)(15) was added by Act §611(a)(1). Eff. for transactions occurring after Aug. 17, 2006.
- ERISA §408(b)(16) was added by Act §611(c)(1). Eff. for transactions occurring after Aug. 17, 2006.
- ERISA §408(b)(17) was added by Act §611(d)(1). Eff. for transactions occurring after Aug. 17, 2006.
- ERISA §408(b)(18) was added by Act §611(c)(1). Eff. for transactions occurring after Aug. 17, 2006.
- ERISA §408(b)(19) was added by Act §611(g)(1). Eff. for transactions occurring after Aug. 17, 2006.
- ERISA §408(b)(20) was added by Act §612(a). Eff. for a transaction that a fiduciary or disqualified person discovers or should have discovered after Aug. 17, 2006, constitutes a prohibited transaction.
- ERISA §408(g) was added by Act §601(a)(2). Eff. for investment advice with respect to plan assets that is provided after Dec. 31, 2006, and rendered for a fee or other compensation. See Act §601(c), in note above.
- **Other Provision.** Act §601 coordination provision:

  (c) Coordination With Existing Exemptions.—Any exemption under section 408(b) of ERISA and section 4975(d) of the Internal Revenue Code of 1986 provided by the amendments made by this section shall not in any manner alter existing individual or class exemptions, provided by statute or administrative action.

American Jobs Creation Act of 2004 (Pub. L. No. 108-357), as follows:

- ERISA §408(b)(13) was amended by Act §709(a)(3) by substituting "October 22, 2004" for "April 10, 2004". Eff. Oct. 22, 2004.

Pension Funding Equity Act of 2004 (Pub. L. No. 108-218), as follows:

- ERISA §408 was amended by Act 204(b)(3) by substituting "January 1, 2014" for "January 1, 2006" and "April 10, 2004" for "December 17, 1999". Eff. April 10, 2004.

Economic Growth and Tax Relief Reconciliation Act of 2001 (Pub. L. No. 107-16), as follows:

- ERISA §408(d)(2)(C) was amended by Act §§612(b), 901 by temporarily adding subpara. (C). Eff. after 2001, and until Dec. 31, 2010. See note below on sunset rule.
- **Sunset Rule.** To comply with the Congressional Budget Act of 1974, §901 of Pub. L. No. 107-16 provides that all provisions of, and amendments made by, the Act will not apply to taxable, plan, or limitation years beginning after December 31, 2010. *But see* Pension Protection Act of 2006 (Pub. L. No. 109-280), §811 (sunset rule of Pub. L. No. 107-16 does not apply to the provisions of, and the amendments made by, Pub. L. No. 107-16, §§601–666 (relating to modifications to pensions and retirement income arrangement provisions)).

Tax Relief Extension Act of 1999 (Pub. L. No. 106-170), as follows:

- ERISA 408(b)(13) was amended by Act §535(a)(2)(C) by substituting "made before January 1, 2006" for "in a taxable year beginning before January 1, 2001" and "December 17, 1999" for "January 1, 1995". Eff. Dec. 17, 1999.

Taxpayer Relief Act of 1997 (Pub. L. No. 105-34), as follows:

- ERISA §408(d) was amended by Act §1506(b)(2) by substituting existing provisions for provisions exempting transactions involving an owner-employee, a member of the family, or a corporation controlled by any such owner-employee through the ownership, directly or indirectly, of 50 percent or more of the total combined voting power of all classes of stock entitled to vote or 50 percent or more of the total value of shares of all classes of stock of the corporation. Eff. Aug. 5, 1997.

Small Business Job Protection Act of 1996 (Pub. L. No. 104-188), as follows:

- ERISA §408(b)(1) was amended by Act §1704(n)(2) by inserting at the end "A loan made by a plan shall not fail to meet the requirements of the preceding sentence by reason of a loan repayment suspension described under section 414(u)(4) of title 26." Eff. Aug. 20, 1996.

Retirement Protection Act of 1994 (Pub. L. No. 103-465), as follows:

- ERISA §408(b)(13) was amended by Act §731(c)(4)(C) by substituting "2001" for "1996" and "1995" for "1991". Eff. Dec. 8, 1994.

Omnibus Budget Reconciliation Act of 1990 (Pub. L. No. 101-508), as follows:

- ERISA §408(b)(13) was added by Act §12012(b). Eff. Nov. 5, 1990.

Omnibus Budget Reconciliation Act of 1989 (Pub. L. No. 101-239), as follows:

- ERISA §408(b)(12) was added by Act §7881(l)(5). Eff. as if included in Pub. L. No. 100-203.
- ERISA §408(d) was amended by Act §7891(a)(1), in last sentence, by substituting "section 401(c)(3) of the Internal Revenue Code of 1986" for "section 401(c)(3) of the Internal Revenue Code of 1954", which for purposes of codification was translated as "section 401(c)(3) of title 26"; by Act §7891(a)(2), in last sentence, by substituting "section 408 of the Internal Revenue Code of 1986" for "section 408 of the Internal Revenue Code of 1954" and "section 408(c) of the Internal Revenue Code of 1986" for "section 408(c) of such Code" which for purposes of codification were translated as "section 408 of title 26" and "section 408(c) of title 26", respectively; Act §7894(e)(4)(A), in last sentence, by substituting "individual retirement account or individual retirement annuity described in section 408 of title 26 or a retirement bond described in section 409 of title 26 (as effective for obligations issued before January 1, 1984)" for "individual retirement account, individual retirement annuity, or an individual retirement bond (as defined in section 408 or 409 of title 26)" and "section 408(c) of such Code" for "section 408(c) of such code", which for purposes of codification was translated as "section 408(c) of title 26". Eff. as if included in Pub. L. No. 99-514.

Tax Reform Act of 1986 (Pub. L. No. 99-514), as follows:

- ERISA §408(b)(1)(B) was amended by Act §1114(b)(15)(B) by substituting "highly compensated employees (within the meaning of section 414(q) of title 26)" for "highly compensated employees, officers, or shareholders". Eff. after Dec. 31, 1988.

- ERISA §408(d), was amended by Act §1898(i)(1) by striking "(a)," before "(b)," in introductory provisions. Eff. Oct. 22, 1986.

Subchapter S Revision Act of 1982 (Pub. L. No. 97-354), as follows:

- ERISA §408(d) was amended by Act §5(a)(43) by substituting "section 1379 of title 26 as in effect on the day before the date of the enactment of the Subchapter S Revision Act of 1982" for "section 1379 of title 26". Eff. Oct. 19, 1982.

Multiemployer Pension Plan Amendments Act of 1980 (Pub. L. No. 96-364), as follows:

- ERISA §408(b)(10)–(11) were added by Act §308(a). Eff. Sept. 26, 1980.

- ERISA §408(f) was added by Act §308(b). Eff. Sept. 26, 1980.

SEC. 409. LIABILITY FOR BREACH OF FIDUCIARY DUTY.

(a) Any person who is a fiduciary with respect to a plan who breaches any of the responsibilities, obligations, or duties imposed upon fiduciaries by this title shall be personally liable to make good to such plan any losses to the plan resulting from each such breach, and to restore to such plan any profits of such fiduciary which have been made through use of assets of the plan by the fiduciary, and shall be subject to such other equitable or remedial relief as the court may deem appropriate, including removal of such fiduciary. A fiduciary may also be removed for a violation of section 411 of this Act.

(b) No fiduciary shall be liable with respect to a breach of fiduciary duty under this title if such breach was committed before he became a fiduciary or after he ceased to be a fiduciary.

SEC. 410. EXCULPATORY PROVISIONS; INSURANCE.

(a) Except as provided in sections 405(b)(1) and 405(d), any provision in an agreement or instrument which purports to relieve a fiduciary from responsibility or liability for any responsibility, obligation, or duty under this part shall be void as against public policy.

(b) Nothing in this subpart [part] shall preclude—

(1) a plan from purchasing insurance for its fiduciaries or for itself to cover liability or losses occurring by reason of the act or omission of a fiduciary, if such insurance permits recourse by the insurer against the fiduciary in the case of a breach of a fiduciary obligation by such fiduciary;

(2) a fiduciary from purchasing insurance to cover liability under this part from and for his own account; or

(3) an employer or an employee organization from purchasing insurance to cover potential liability of one or more persons who serve in a fiduciary capacity with regard to an employee benefit plan.

SEC. 411. PERSONS PROHIBITED FROM HOLDING CERTAIN POSITIONS.

(a) Conviction or Imprisonment.—No person who has been convicted of, or has been imprisoned as a result of his conviction of, robbery, bribery, extortion, embezzlement, fraud, grand larceny, burglary, arson, a felony violation of Federal or State law involving substances defined in section 102(6) of the Comprehensive Drug Abuse Prevention and Control Act of 1970, murder, rape, kidnapping, perjury, assault with intent to kill, any crime described in section 9(a)(1) of the Investment Company Act of 1940 (15 U.S.C. 80a-9(a)(1)), a violation of any provision of this Act, a violation of section 302 of the Labor-Management Relations Act, 1947 (29 U.S.C. 186), a violation of chapter 63 of title 18, United States Code, a violation of section 874, 1027, 1503, 1505, 1506, 1510, 1951, or 1954 of title 18, United States Code, a violation of the Labor-Management Reporting and Disclosure Act of 1959 (29 U.S.C. 401), any felony involving abuse or misuse of such person's position or employment in a labor organization or employee benefit plan to seek or obtain an illegal gain at the expense of the members of the labor organization or the beneficiaries of the employee benefit plan, or conspiracy to commit any such crimes or attempt to commit any such crimes, or a crime in which any of the foregoing crimes is an element, shall serve or be permitted to serve—

(1) as an administrator, fiduciary, officer, trustee, custodian, counsel, agent, employee, or representative in any capacity of any employee benefit plan,

(2) as a consultant or adviser to an employee benefit plan, including but not limited to any entity whose activities are in whole or substantial part devoted to providing goods or services to any employee benefit plan, or

(3) in any capacity that involves decision making authority or custody or control of the moneys, funds, assets, or property of any employee benefit plan,

during or for the period of thirteen years after such conviction or after the end of such imprisonment, whichever is later, unless the sentencing court on the motion of the person convicted set a lesser period of at least three years after such conviction or after the end of such imprisonment, whichever is later, or unless prior to the end of such period, in the case of a person so convicted or imprisoned (A) his citizenship rights, having been revoked as a result of such conviction, have been fully restored, or (B) if the offense is a Federal offense, the sentencing judge or, if the offense is a State or local offense, the United States district court for the district in which the offense was

committed, pursuant to sentencing guidelines and policy statements under section 994(a) of title 28, United States Code, determines that such person's service in any capacity referred to in paragraphs (1) through (3) would not be contrary to the purposes of this title. Prior to making any such determination the court shall hold a hearing and shall give notice to [of] such proceeding by certified mail to the Secretary of Labor and to State, county, and Federal prosecuting officials in the jurisdiction or jurisdictions in which such person was convicted. The court's determination in any such proceeding shall be final. No person shall knowingly hire, retain, employ, or otherwise place any other person to serve in any capacity in violation of this subsection. Notwithstanding the preceding provisions of this subsection, no corporation or partnership will be precluded from acting as an administrator, fiduciary, officer, trustee, custodian, counsel, agent, or employee of any employee benefit plan or as a consultant to any employee benefit plan without a notice, hearing, and determination by such court that such service would be inconsistent with the intention of this section.

(b) Penalty.—Any person who intentionally violates this section shall be fined not more than $10,000 or imprisoned for not more than five years, or both.

(c) Definitions.—For the purpose of this section:

(1) A person shall be deemed to have been "convicted" and under the disability of "conviction" from the date of the judgment of the trial court, regardless of whether that judgment remains under appeal.

(2) The term "consultant" means any person who, for compensation, advises or represents an employee benefit plan or who provides other assistance to such plan, concerning the establishment or operation of such plan.

(3) A period of parole or supervised release shall not be considered as part of a period of imprisonment.

(d) Salary of Person Barred From Employee Benefit Plan Office During Appeal From Conviction.— Whenever any person—

(1) by operation of this section, has been barred from office or other position in an employee benefit plan as a result of a conviction, and

(2) has filed an appeal of that conviction,

any salary which would be otherwise due such person by virtue of such office or position, shall be placed in escrow by the individual or organization responsible for payment of such salary. Payment of such salary into escrow shall continue for the duration of the appeal or for the period of time during which such salary would be otherwise due, whichever is shorter.

Upon the final reversal of such person's conviction on appeal, the amounts in escrow shall be paid to such person. Upon the final sustaining of that person's conviction on appeal, the amounts in escrow shall be returned to the individual or organization responsible for payments of those amounts. Upon final reversal of such person's conviction, such person shall no longer be barred by this statute [section] from assuming any position from which such person was previously barred.

Amendments to ERISA §411

Sentencing Act of 1987 (Pub. L. No. 100-182), as follows:
- ERISA §411(a) was amended by Act §15(b), in concluding provisions, by substituting "if the offense is a Federal offense, the sentencing judge or, if the offense is a State or local offense, the United States district court for the district in which the offense was committed, pursuant to sentencing guidelines and policy statements under section 994(a) of title 28," for "the United States Parole Commission", "court shall" for "Commission shall"; "court's" for "Commission's", "such court" for "such Parole Commission"; and "a hearing" for "an administrative hearing". Eff. for offenses committed after Dec. 7, 1987.

Criminal Justice Act Revisions of 1984 (Pub. L. No. 98-473), as follows:
- ERISA §411(a) was amended by Act §229 by substituting "if the offense is a Federal offense, the sentencing judge or, if the offense is a State or local offense, on motion of the United States Department of Justice, the district court of the United States for the district in which the offense was committed, pursuant to sentencing guidelines and policy statements issued pursuant to section 994(a) of title 28," for "the Board of Parole of the United States Justice Department"; "court" and "court's" for "Board" and "Board's", respectively; and "a" for "an administrative". Except for the last substitution, amendments incapable of execution in view of the amendment by Act §802 (see notes below), which became effective prior to the effective date of the amendment by Act §229. Eff. Oct. 12, 1984.
- ERISA §411(a) was amended by Act §802(a), in amending provisions after "the Labor-Management Reporting and Disclosure Act of 1959 (29 U.S.C. 401)," generally, by inserting provisions relating to abuse or misuse of employment in a labor organization or employee benefit plan; in cl. (1), by substituting "employee, or representative in any capacity" for "or employee"; in cl. (2), by substituting "consultant or adviser to an" for "consultant to any"; by adding cl. (3); by substituting "the period of thirteen years" for "five years", "unless the sentencing court on the motion of the person convicted sets a lesser period of at least three years after such conviction or after the end of such imprisonment, whichever is later, or unless prior to the end of such period," for "unless prior to the end of such five-year period,"; in cl. (B), by substituting "the United States Parole Commission" for "the Board of Parole of the United States Department of Justice" and "paragraphs (1) through (3)" for "paragraph (1) or (2)"; and in provisions following cl. (B), by substituting "Commission" and "Commission's" for "Board" and "Board's", respectively; by inserting provision of notice to the Secretary of Labor; and by substituting "hire, retain, employ, or otherwise place any other person to serve in any capacity" for "permit any other person to serve in any capacity referred to in paragraph (1) or (2)" and "Parole Commission" for "Board of Parole". Eff. Oct. 12, 1984.
- ERISA §411(b) was amended by Act §802(b) by substituting "five years" for "one year". Eff. Oct. 12, 1984.
- ERISA §411(c)(1) was amended by Act §802(c) by substituting ", appeal" for "or the date of the final sustaining of such judgment on appeal, whichever is the later event". Eff. Oct. 12, 1984.
- ERISA §411(c)(3) was amended by Act §230 by inserting "or supervised release" after "parole". Eff. Nov. 1, 1987.
- ERISA §411(d) was added by Act §802(d). Eff. Oct. 12, 1984.

SEC. 412. BONDING.

(a) Requisite Bonding of Plan Officials.—Every fiduciary of an employee benefit plan and every person who handles funds or other property of such a plan (hereafter in this section referred to as "plan official") shall be bonded as provided in this section; except that—

(1) where such plan is one under which the only assets from which benefits are paid are the general assets of a union or of an employer, the administrator, officers, and employees of such plan shall be exempt from the bonding requirements of this section,

(2) no bond shall be required of any entity which is registered as a broker or a dealer under section 15(b) of the Securities Exchange Act of 1934 (15 U.S.C. 78o(b)) if the broker or dealer is subject to the fidelity bond requirements of a self-regulatory organization (within the meaning of section 3(a)(26) of such Act (15 U.S.C. 78c(a)(26)).

(3) no bond shall be required of a fiduciary (or of any director, officer, or employee of such fiduciary) if such fiduciary—

(A) is a corporation organized and doing business under the laws of the United States or of any State;

(B) is authorized under such laws to exercise trust powers or to conduct an insurance business;

(C) is subject to supervision or examination by Federal or State authority; and

(D) has at all times a combined capital and surplus in excess of such a minimum amount as may be established by regulations issued by the Secretary, which amount shall be at least $1,000,000. Paragraph (2) shall apply to a bank or other financial institution which is authorized to exercise trust powers and the deposits of which are not insured by the Federal Deposit Insurance Corporation, only if such bank or institution meets bonding or similar requirements under State law which the Secretary determines are at least equivalent to those imposed on banks by Federal law.

The amount of such bond shall be fixed at the beginning of each fiscal year of the plan. Such amount shall be not less than 10 per centum of the amount of funds handled. In no case shall such bond be less than $1,000 nor more than $500,000, except that the Secretary, after due notice and opportunity for hearing to all interested parties, and after consideration of the record, may prescribe an amount in excess of $500,000, subject to the 10 per centum limitation of the preceding sentence. For purposes of fixing the amount of such bond, the amount of funds handled shall be determined by the funds handled by the person, group, or class to be covered by such bond and by their predecessor or predecessors, if any, during the preceding reporting year, or if the plan has no preceding reporting year, the amount of funds to be handled during the current reporting year by such person, group, or class, estimated as provided in regulations of the Secretary. Such bond shall provide protection to the plan against loss by reason of acts of fraud or dishonesty on the part of the plan official, directly or through connivance with others. Any bond shall have as surety thereon a corporate surety company which is an acceptable surety on Federal bonds under authority granted by the Secretary of the Treasury pursuant to sections 6 through 13 of title 6, United States Code. Any bond shall be in a form or of a type approved by the Secretary, including individual bonds or schedule or blanket forms of bonds which cover a group or class.

In the case of a plan that holds employer securities (within the meaning of section 407(d)(1)), this subsection shall be applied by substituting "$1,000,000" for "$500,000" each place it appears.

(b) Unlawful Acts.—It shall be unlawful for any plan official to whom subsection (a) applies, to receive, handle, disburse, or otherwise exercise custody or control of any of the funds or other property of any employee benefit plan, without being bonded as required by subsection (a) and it shall be unlawful for any plan official of such plan, or any other person having authority to direct the performance of such functions, to permit such functions, or any of them, to be performed by any plan official, with respect to whom the requirements of subsection (a) have not been met.

(c) Conflict of Interest Prohibited in Procuring Bonds.—It shall be unlawful for any person to procure any bond required by subsection (a) from any surety or other company or through any agent or broker in whose business operations such plan or any party in interest in such plan has any control or significant financial interest, direct or indirect.

(d) Exclusiveness of Statutory Basis for Bonding Requirement for Persons Handling Funds or Other Property of Employee Benefit Plans.—Nothing in any other provision of law shall require any person, required to be bonded as provided in subsection (a) because he handles funds or other property of an employee benefit plan, to be bonded insofar as the handling by such person of the funds or other property of such plan is concerned.

(e) Regulations.—The Secretary shall prescribe such regulations as may be necessary to carry out the provisions of this section including exempting a plan from the requirements of this section where he finds that (1) other bonding arrangements or (2) the overall financial condition of the plan would be adequate to protect the interests of the beneficiaries and participants. When, in the opinion of the Secretary, the administrator of a plan offers adequate evidence of the financialresponsibility of the plan, or that other bonding arrangements would provide adequate protection of the beneficiaries and participants, he may exempt such plan from the requirements of this section.

SEC. 413. LIMITATION OF ACTIONS.

No action may be commenced under this title with respect to a fiduciary's breach of any responsibility, duty, or obligation under this part, or with respect to a violation of this part, after the earlier of—

(1) six years after (A) the date of the last action which constituted a part of the breach or violation, or (B) in the case of an omission, the latest date on which the fiduciary could have cured the breach or violation, or

(2) three years after the earliest date on which the plaintiff had actual knowledge of the breach or violation

except that in the case of fraud or concealment, such action may be commenced not later than six years after the date of discovery of such breach or violation.

SEC. 414. EFFECTIVE DATE.

(a) Except as provided in subsections (b), (c), and (d), this part shall take effect on January 1, 1975.

(b)(1) The provisions of this part authorizing the Secretary to promulgate regulations shall take effect on the date of enactment of this Act.

(2) Upon application of a plan, the Secretary may postpone until not later than January 1, 1976, the applicability of any provision of sections 402, 403 (other than 403(c)), 405 (other than 405(a) and (d)), and 410(a), as it applies to any plan in existence on the date of enactment of this Act if he determines such postponement is (A) necessary to amend the instrument establishing the plan under which the plan is maintained and (B) not adverse to the interest of participants and beneficiaries.

(3) This part shall take effect on the date of enactment of this Act with respect to a plan which terminates after June 30, 1974, and before January 1, 1975, and to which at the time of termination section 4021 applies.

(c) Sections 406 and 407(a) (relating to prohibited transactions) shall not apply—

(1) until June 30, 1984, to a loan of money or other extension of credit between a plan and a party in interest under a binding contract in effect on July 1, 1974 (or pursuant to renewals of such a contract), if such loan or other extension of credit remains at least as favorable to the plan as an arm's-length transaction with an unrelated party would be, and if the execution of the contract, the making of the loan, or the extension of credit was not, at the time of such execution, making, or extension, a prohibited transaction (within the meaning of section 503(b) of the Internal Revenue Code of 1954 or the corresponding provisions of prior law);

(2) until June 30, 1984, to a lease or joint use of property involving the plan and a party in interest pursuant to a binding contract in effect on July 1, 1974 (or pursuant to renewals of such a contract), if such lease or joint use remains at least as favorable to the plan as an arm's-length transaction with an unrelated party would be and if the execution of the contract was not, at the time of such execution, a prohibited transaction (within the meaning of section 503(b) of the Internal Revenue Code of 1986 or the corresponding provisions of prior law);

(3) until June 30, 1984, to the sale, exchange, or other disposition of property described in paragraph (2) between a plan and a party in interest if—

(A) in the case of a sale, exchange, or other disposition of the property by the plan to the party in interest, the plan receives an amount which is not less than the fair market value of the property at the time of such disposition; and

(B) in the case of the acquisition of the property by the plan, the plan pays an amount which is not in excess of the fair market value of the property at the time of such acquisition;

(4) until June 30, 1977, to the provision of services, to which paragraphs (1), (2), and (3) do not apply between a plan and a party in interest—

(A) under a binding contract in effect on July 1, 1974 (or pursuant to renewals of such contract), or

(B) if the party in interest ordinarily and customarily furnished such services on June 30, 1974, if

such provision of services remains at least as favorable to the plan as an arm's-length transaction with an unrelated party would be and if such provision of services was not, at the time of such provision, a prohibited transaction (within the meaning of section 503(b) of the Internal Revenue Code of 1954) or the corresponding provisions of prior law; or

(5) the sale, exchange, or other disposition of property which is owned by a plan on June 30, 1974, and all times thereafter, to a party in interest, if such plan is required to dispose of such property in order to comply with the provisions of section 407(a) (relating to the prohibition against holding excess employer securities and employer real property), and if the plan receives not less than adequate consideration.

(d) Any election, or failure to elect, by a disqualified person under section 2003(c)(1)(B) of this Act shall be treated for purposes of this part (but not for purposes of section 514) as an act or omission occurring before the effective date of this part.

(e) The preceding provisions of this section shall not apply with respect to amendments made to this part in provisions enacted after the date of the enactment of this Act.

Amendments to ERISA §414

Omnibus Budget Reconciliation Act of 1989 (Pub. L. No. 101-239), as follows:

- ERISA §414(c)(2) was amended by Act §7894(e)(6) by substituting "Internal Revenue Code of 1986" for "Internal Revenue Code of 1954", which for purposes of codification was translated as "title 26", and substituting "or the corresponding provisions of prior law)" for ") provisions of prior law". Eff. as if originally included in Pub. L. No. 93-406.
- ERISA §414(e) was added by Act §7894(h)(4). Eff. as if originally included in Pub. L. No. 93-406.

Part 5—Administration and Enforcement

Editor's Note

ERISA §501, below, as amended by Pub. L. No. 111-148, §6601, is effective March 23, 2010.

SEC. 501. CRIMINAL PENALTIES.

(a) Any person who willfully violates any provision of part 1 of this subtitle, or any regulation or order issued under any such provision, shall upon conviction be fined not more than $100,000 or imprisoned not more than 10 years, or both; except that in the case of such violation by a person not an individual, the fine imposed upon such person shall be a fine not exceeding $500,000.

(b) Any person that violates section 519 shall upon conviction be imprisoned not more than 10 years or fined under title 18, United States Code, or both.

Amendments to ERISA §501

Patient Protection and Affordable Care Act, 2010 (Pub. L. No. 111-148), as follows:
- ERISA §501 was amended by Act §6601(b) inserting "(a)" before "Any person"; and by adding at the end "(b) Any person that violates section 519 shall upon conviction be imprisoned not more than 10 years or fined under title 18, United States Code, or both.". Eff. Mar. 23, 2010.

Sarbanes-Oxley Act of 2002 (Pub. L. No. 107-204), as follows:
- ERISA §501 was amended by Act §904 by substituting "$100,000" for "$5,000", "10 years" for "one year", and "$500,000" for "$100,000". Eff. July 30, 2002.

> ### *Editor's Note*
>
> **Caution:** Pursuant to Pub. L. No. 109-280, §221(c), the amendments to ERISA §502 made by Pub. L. No. 109-280, §202(b) and (c) will not apply to plan years beginning after December 31, 2014. See amendment notes for details.

SEC. 502. CIVIL ENFORCEMENT.

(a) Persons Empowered to Bring Civil Action.—A civil action may be brought—

(1) by a participant or beneficiary—

(A) for the relief provided for in subsection (c) of this section, or

(B) to recover benefits due to him under the terms of his plan, to enforce his rights under the terms of the plan, or to clarify his rights to future benefits under the terms of the plan;

(2) by the Secretary, or by a participant, beneficiary or fiduciary for appropriate relief under section 409;

(3) by a participant, beneficiary, or fiduciary (A) to enjoin any act or practice which violates any provision of this title or the terms of the plan, or (B) to obtain other appropriate equitable relief (i) to redress such violations or (ii) to enforce any provisions of this title or the terms of the plan;

(4) by the Secretary, or by a participant, or beneficiary for appropriate relief in the case of a violation of 105(c);

(5) except as otherwise provided in subsection (b), by the Secretary (A) to enjoin any act or practice which violates any provision of this title, or (B) to obtain other appropriate equitable relief (i) to redress such violation or (ii) to enforce any provision of this title;

(6) by the Secretary to collect any civil penalty under paragraph (2), (4), (5), (6), (7), (8), or (9) of subsection (c) or under subsection (i) or (*l*);

(7) by a State to enforce compliance with a qualified medical child support order (as defined in section 609(a)(2)(A));

(8) by the Secretary, or by an employer or other person referred to in section 101(f)(1), (A) to enjoin any act or practice which violates subsection (f) of section 101, or (B) to obtain appropriate equitable relief (i) to redress such violation or (ii) to enforce such subsection;

(9) in the event that the purchase of an insurance contract or insurance annuity in connection with termination of an individual's status as a participant covered under a pension plan with respect to all or any portion of the participant's pension benefit under such plan constitutes a violation of part 4 of this title [subtitle] or the terms of the plan, by the Secretary, by any individual who was a participant or beneficiary at the time of the alleged violation, or by a fiduciary, to obtain appropriate relief, including the posting of security if necessary, to assure receipt by the participant or beneficiary of the amounts provided or to be provided by such insurance contract or annuity, plus reasonable prejudgment interest on such amounts; or

(10) in the case of a multiemployer plan that has been certified by the actuary to be in endangered or critical status under section 305, if the plan sponsor—

(A) has not adopted a funding improvement or rehabilitation plan under that section by the deadline established in such section, or

(B) fails to update or comply with the terms of the funding improvement or rehabilitation plan in accordance with the requirements of such section,

by an employer that has an obligation to contribute with respect to the multiemployer plan or an employee organization that represents active participants in the multiemployer plan, for an order compelling the plan sponsor to adopt a funding improvement or rehabilitation plan or to update or comply with the terms of the funding improvement or rehabilitation plan in accordance with the requirements of such section and the funding improvement or rehabilitation plan.

(b) Plans Qualified Under Internal Revenue Code; Maintenance of Actions Involving Delinquent Contributions.—

(1) In the case of a plan which is qualified under section 401(a), 403(a), or 405(a) of title 26 (or with respect to which an application to so qualify has been filed and has not been finally determined) the Secretary may exercise his authority under subsection (a)(5) with respect to a violation of, or the enforcement of, parts 2 and 3 of this subtitle (relating to participation, vesting, and funding) only if—

(A) requested by the Secretary of the Treasury, or

(B) one or more participants, beneficiaries, or fiduciaries, of such plan request in writing (in such manner as the Secretary shall prescribe by regulation) that he exercise such authority on their behalf. In the case of such a request under this paragraph he may exercise such authority only if he determines that such violation affects, or such enforcement is necessary to protect, claims of participants or beneficiaries to benefits under the plan.

(2) The Secretary shall not initiate an action to enforce section 515.

(3) Except as provided in subsections (c)(9) and (a)(6) (with respect to collecting civil penalties under subsection (c)(9)), the Secretary is not authorized to enforce under this part any requirement of part 7 against a health insurance issuer offering health insurance coverage in connection with a group health plan (as defined in section 733(a)(1)). Nothing in this paragraph shall affect the authority of the Secretary to issue regulations to carry out such part.

(c) Administrator's Refusal to Supply Requested Information; Penalty for Failure to Provide Annual Report in Complete Form.—

(1) Any administrator (A) who fails to meet the requirements of paragraph (1) or (4) of section 606, section 101(e)(1), section 101(f), or section 105(a) with respect to a participant or beneficiary, or (B) who fails or refuses to comply with a request for any information which such administrator is required by this title to furnish to a participant or beneficiary (unless such failure or refusal results from matters reasonably beyond the control of the administrator) by mailing the material requested to the last known address of the requesting participant or beneficiary within 30 days after such request may in the court's discretion be personally liable to such participant or beneficiary in the amount of up to $100 a day from the date of such failure or refusal, and the court may in its discretion order such other relief as it deems proper. For purposes of this paragraph, each violation described in subparagraph (A) with respect to any single participant, and each violation described in subparagraph (B) with respect to any single participant or beneficiary, shall be treated as a separate violation.

(2) The Secretary may assess a civil penalty against any plan administrator of up to $1,000 a day from the date of such plan administrator's failure or refusal to file the annual report required to be filed with the Secretary under section 101(b)(1). For purposes of this paragraph, an annual report that has been rejected under section 104(a)(4) for failure to provide material information shall not be treated as having been filed with the Secretary.

(3) Any employer maintaining a plan who fails to meet the notice requirement of section 101(d) with respect to any participant or beneficiary or who fails to meet the requirements of section 101(e)(2) with respect to any person or who fails to meet the requirements of section 302(d)(12)(E) with respect to any person may in the court's discretion be liable to such participant or beneficiary or to such person in the amount of up to $100 a day from the date of such failure, and the court may in its discretion order such other relief as it deems proper.

(4) The Secretary may assess a civil penalty of not more than $1,000 a day for each violation by any person of subsection (j), (k), or (*l*) of section 101 or section 514(e)(3).

(5) The Secretary may assess a civil penalty against any person of up to $1,000 a day from the date of the person's failure or refusal to file the information required to be filed by such person with the Secretary under regulations prescribed pursuant to section 101(g).

(6) If, within 30 days of a request by the Secretary to a plan administrator for documents under section 104(a)(6), the plan administrator fails to furnish the material requested to the Secretary, the Secretary may assess civil penalty against the plan administrator of up to $100 a day from the date of such failure (but in no event in excess of $1,000 per request). No penalty shall be imposed under this paragraph for any failure resulting from matters reasonably beyond the control of the plan administrator.

(7) The Secretary may assess a civil penalty against a plan administrator of up to $100 a day from the date of the plan administrator's failure or refusal to provide notice to participants and beneficiaries in accordance with subsection (i) or (m) of section 101. For purposes of this paragraph, each violation with respect to any single participant or beneficiary shall be treated as a separate violation.

(8) The Secretary may assess against any plan sponsor of a multiemployer plan a civil penalty of not more than $1,100 per day—

(A) for each violation by such sponsor of the requirement under section 305 to adopt by the deadline established in that section a funding improvement plan or rehabilitation plan with respect to a multiemployer plan which is in endangered or critical status, or

(B) in the case of a plan in endangered status which is not in seriously endangered status, for failure by the plan to meet the applicable benchmarks under section 305 by the end of the funding improvement period with respect to the plan.

(9)(A) The Secretary may assess a civil penalty against any employer of up to $100 a day from the date of the employer's failure to meet the notice requirement of section 701(f)(3)(B)(i)(I). For purposes of this subparagraph, each violation with respect to any single employee shall be treated as a separate violation.

(B) The Secretary may assess a civil penalty against any plan administrator of up to $100 a day from the date of the plan administrator's failure to timely provide to any State the information required to be disclosed under section 701(f)(3)(B)(ii). For purposes of this subparagraph, each violation with respect to any single participant or beneficiary shall be treated as a separate violation.

(10) Secretarial enforcement authority relating to use of genetic information.—

(A) General rule.—The Secretary may impose a penalty against any plan sponsor of a group health plan, or any health insurance issuer offering health insurance coverage in connection with the plan, for any failure by such sponsor or issuer to meet the requirements of subsection (a)(1)(F), (b)(3), (c), or (d) of section 702 or section 701 or 702(b)(1) with respect to genetic information, in connection with the plan.

(B) Amount.—

(i) In general.—The amount of the penalty imposed by subparagraph (A) shall be $100 for each day in the noncompliance period with respect to each participant or beneficiary to whom such failure relates.

(ii) Noncompliance period.—For purposes of this paragraph, the term "noncompliance period" means, with respect to any failure, the period—

(I) beginning on the date such failure first occurs; and

(II) ending on the date the failure is corrected.

(C) Minimum penalties where failure discovered.—Notwithstanding clauses (i) and (ii) of subparagraph (D):

(i) In general.—In the case of 1 or more failures with respect to a participant or beneficiary—

(I) which are not corrected before the date on which the plan receives a notice from the Secretary of such violation; and

(II) which occurred or continued during the period involved;

the amount of penalty imposed by subparagraph (A) by reason of such failures with respect to such participant or beneficiary shall be not less than $2,500.

(ii) Higher minimum penalty where violations are more than de minimis.—To the extent violations for which any person is liable under this paragraph for any year are more than de minimis, clause (i) shall be applied by substituting "$15,000" for "$2,500" with respect to such person.

(D) Limitations.—

(i) Penalty not to apply where failure not discovered exercising reasonable diligence.—No penalty shall be imposed by subparagraph (A) on any failure during any period for which it is established to the satisfaction of the Secretary that the person otherwise liable for such penalty did not know, and exercising reasonable diligence would not have known, that such failure existed.

(ii) Penalty not to apply to failures corrected within certain periods.—No penalty shall be imposed by subparagraph (A) on any failure if—

(I) such failure was due to reasonable cause and not to willful neglect; and

(II) such failure is corrected during the 30-day period beginning on the first date the person otherwise liable for such penalty knew, or exercising reasonable diligence would have known, that such failure existed.

(iii) Overall limitation for unintentional failures.—In the case of failures which are due to reasonable cause and not to willful neglect, the penalty imposed by subparagraph (A) for failures shall not exceed the amount equal to the lesser of—

(I) 10 percent of the aggregate amount paid or incurred by the plan sponsor (or predecessor plan sponsor) during the preceding taxable year for group health plans; or

(II) $500,000.

(E) Waiver by Secretary.—In the case of a failure which is due to reasonable cause and not to willful neglect, the Secretary may waive part or all of the penalty imposed by subparagraph (A) to the extent that the payment of such penalty would be excessive relative to the failure involved.

(F) Definitions.—Terms used in this paragraph which are defined in section 733 shall have the meanings provided such terms in such section.

(10)[(11)] The Secretary and the Secretary of Health and Human Services shall maintain such ongoing consultation as may be necessary and appropriate to coordinate enforcement under this subsection with enforcement under section 1144(c)(8) of the Social Security Act.

(d) Status of Employee Benefit Plan as Entity.—

(1) An employee benefit plan may sue or be sued under this title as an entity. Service of summons, subpoena, or other legal process of a court upon a trustee or an administrator of an employee benefit plan in his capacity as such shall constitute service upon the employee benefit plan. In a case where a plan has not designated in the summary plan description of the plan an individual as agent for the service of legal process, service upon the Secretary shall constitute such service. The Secretary, not later than 15 days after receipt of service under the preceding sentence, shall notify the administrator or any trustee of the plan of receipt of such service.

(2) Any money judgment under this title against an employee benefit plan shall be enforceable only against the plan as an entity and shall not be enforceable against any other person unless liability against such person is established in his individual capacity under this title.

(e) Jurisdiction.—

(1) Except for actions under subsection (a)(1)(B) of this section, the district courts of the United States shall have exclusive jurisdiction of civil actions under this title brought by the Secretary or by a participant, beneficiary, fiduciary, or any person referred to in section 101(f)(1). State courts of competent jurisdiction and district courts of the United States shall have concurrent jurisdiction of actions under paragraphs (1)(B) and (7) of subsection (a).

(2) Where an action under this title is brought in a district court of the United States, it may be brought in the district where the plan is administered, where the breach took place, or where a defendant resides or may be found, and process may be served in any other district where a defendant resides or may be found.

(f) Amount in Controversy; Citizenship of Parties.—The district courts of the United States shall have jurisdiction, without respect to the amount in controversy or the citizenship of the parties, to grant the relief provided for in subsection (a) of this section in any action.

(g) Attorney's Fees and Costs; Awards in Actions Involving Delinquent Contributions.—

(1) In any action under this title (other than an action described in paragraph (2)) by a participant, beneficiary, or fiduciary, the court in its discretion may allow a reasonable attorney's fee and costs of action to either party.

(2) In any action under this title by a fiduciary for or on behalf of a plan to enforce section 515 in which a judgment in favor of the plan is awarded, the court shall award the plan—

(A) the unpaid contributions,

(B) interest on the unpaid contributions,

(C) an amount equal to the greater of—

(i) interest on the unpaid contributions, or

(ii) liquidated damages provided for under the plan in an amount not in excess of 20 percent (or such higher percentage as may be permitted under Federal or State law) of the amount determined by the court under subparagraph (A),

(D) reasonable attorney's fees and costs of the action, to be paid by the defendant, and

(E) such other legal or equitable relief as the court deems appropriate.

For purposes of this paragraph, interest on unpaid contributions shall be determined by using the rate provided under the plan, or, if none, the rate prescribed under section 6621 of title 26.

(h) Service Upon Secretary of Labor and Secretary of the Treasury.—A copy of the complaint in any action under this title by a participant, beneficiary, or fiduciary (other than an action brought by one or more participants or beneficiaries under subsection (a)(1)(B) which is solely for the purpose of recovering benefits due such participants under the terms of the plan) shall be served upon the Secretary and the Secretary of the Treasury by certified mail. Either Secretary shall have the right in his discretion to intervene in any action, except that the Secretary of the Treasury may not intervene in any action under part 4 of this subtitle. If the Secretary brings an action under subsection (a) on behalf of a participant or beneficiary, he shall notify the Secretary of the Treasury.

(i) Administrative Assessment of Civil Penalty.—In the case of a transaction prohibited by section 406 by a party in interest with respect to a plan to which this part applies, the Secretary may assess a civil penalty against such party in interest. The amount of such penalty may not exceed 5 percent of the amount involved in each such transaction (as defined in section 4975(f)(4) of the Internal Revenue Code of 1986) for each year or part thereof during which the prohibited transaction continues, except that, if the transaction is not corrected (in such manner as the Secretary shall prescribe in regulations which shall be consistent with section 4975(f)(5) of such Code) within 90 days after notice from the Secretary (or such longer period as the Secretary may permit), such penalty may be in an amount not more than 100 percent of the amount involved. This subsection shall not apply to a transaction with respect to a plan described in section 4975(e)(1) of such Code.

(j) Direction and Control of Litigation by Attorney General.—In all civil actions under this title, attorneys appointed by the Secretary may represent the Secretary (except as provided in section 518(a) of title 28, United States Code), but all such litigation shall be subject to the direction and control of the Attorney General.

(k) Jurisdiction of Action Against Secretary of Labor.—Suits by an administrator, fiduciary, participant, or beneficiary of an employee benefit plan to review a final order of the Secretary, to restrain the Secretary from taking any action contrary to the provisions of this Act, or to compel him to take action required under this title, may be brought in the district court of the United States for the district where the plan has its principal office, or in the United States District Court for the District of Columbia.

(*l*) Civil Penalties on Violations by Fiduciaries.—

(1) In the case of—

(A) any breach of fiduciary responsibility under (or other violation of) part 4 by a fiduciary, or

(B) any knowing participation in such a breach or violation by any other person,

the Secretary shall assess a civil penalty against such fiduciary or other person in an amount equal to 20 percent of the applicable recovery amount.

(2) For purposes of paragraph (1), the term "applicable recovery amount" means any amount which is recovered from a fiduciary or other person with respect to a breach or violation described in paragraph (1)—

(A) pursuant to any settlement agreement with the Secretary, or

(B) ordered by a court to be paid by such fiduciary or other person to a plan or its participants and beneficiaries in a judicial proceeding instituted by the Secretary under subsection (a)(2) or (a)(5).

(3) The Secretary may, in the Secretary's sole discretion, waive or reduce the penalty under paragraph (1) if the Secretary determines in writing that—

(A) the fiduciary or other person acted reasonably and in good faith, or

(B) it is reasonable to expect that the fiduciary or other person will not be able to restore all losses to the plan (or to provide the relief ordered pursuant to subsection (a)(9)) without severe financial hardship unless such waiver or reduction is granted.

(4) The penalty imposed on a fiduciary or other person under this subsection with respect to any transaction shall be reduced by the amount of any penalty or tax imposed on such fiduciary or other person with respect to such transaction under subsection (i) of this section and section 4975 of the Internal Revenue Code of 1986.

(m) Penalty for Improper Distribution.—In the case of a distribution to a pension plan participant or beneficiary in violation of section 206(e) by a plan fiduciary, the Secretary shall assess a penalty against such fiduciary in an amount equal to the value of the distribution. Such penalty shall not exceed $10,000 for each such distribution.

Amendments to ERISA §502

Children's Health Insurance Program Reauthorization Act of 2009 (Pub. L. No. 111-3), as follows:

- ERISA §502(a)(6) was amended by Act §311(b)(1)(E)(i) by striking "or (8)" and inserting "(8), or (9)". See Effective Date Note, below.
- ERISA §502(c) was amended by Act §311(b)(1)(E)(ii) by redesignating para. (9) as para. (10)[(11)] and adding new para. (9). See Effective Date Note, below.
- **Effective Date Note.** Act §3 provides:

  SEC. 3. GENERAL EFFECTIVE DATE; EXCEPTION FOR STATE LEGISLATION; CONTINGENT EFFECTIVE DATE; RELIANCE ON LAW.

  (a) **General Effective Date.**—Unless otherwise provided in this Act, subject to subsections (b) through (d), this Act (and the amendments made by this Act) shall take effect on April 1, 2009, and shall apply to child health assistance and medical assistance provided on or after that date.

(b) **Exception for State Legislation.**—In the case of a State plan under title XIX or State child health plan under XXI of the Social Security Act, which the Secretary of Health and Human Services determines requires State legislation in order for the respective plan to meet one or more additional requirements imposed by amendments made by this Act, the respective plan shall not be regarded as failing to comply with the requirements of such title solely on the basis of its failure to meet such an additional requirement before the first day of the first calendar quarter beginning after the close of the first regular session of the State legislature that begins after the date of enactment of this Act. For purposes of the previous sentence, in the case of a State that has a 2-year legislative session, each year of the session shall be considered to be a separate regular session of the State legislature.

(c) **Coordination of CHIP Funding for Fiscal Year 2009.**— Notwithstanding any other provision of law, insofar as funds have been appropriated under section 2104(a)(11), 2104(k), or 2104(l) of the Social Security Act, as amended by section 201 of Public Law 110-173, to provide allotments to States under CHIP for fiscal year 2009—

(1) any amounts that are so appropriated that are not so allotted and obligated before April 1, 2009 are rescinded; and

(2) any amount provided for CHIP allotments to a State under this Act (and the amendments made by this Act) for such fiscal year shall be reduced by the amount of such appropriations so allotted and obligated before such date.

(d) **Reliance on Law.**—With respect to amendments made by this Act (other than title VII) that become effective as of a date—

(1) such amendments are effective as of such date whether or not regulations implementing such amendments have been issued; and

(2) Federal financial participation for medical assistance or child health assistance furnished under title XIX or XXI, respectively, of the Social Security Act on or after such date by a State in good faith reliance on such amendments before the date of promulgation of final regulations, if any, to carry out such amendments (or before the date of guidance, if any, regarding the implementation of such amendments) shall not be denied on the basis of the State's failure to comply with such regulations or guidance.

Worker, Retiree, and Employer Recovery Act of 2008 (Pub. L. No. 110-458), as follows:

- ERISA §502(c)(2) was amended by Act §102(b)(1)(H) by striking "101(b)(4)" and inserting "101(b)(1)". Eff. for plan years beginning after 2007, as if included in Pub. L. No. 109-280, §202.
- ERISA §502(c)(4) was amended by Act §101(c)(1)(H) by striking "by any person" and all that followed the period and inserting "by any person of subsection (j), (k), or (l) of section 101 or section 514(e)(3)". Eff. for plan years beginning after Dec. 31, 2007, as if included in Pub. L. No. 109-280, §103.
- ERISA §502(c)(8)(A) was amended by Act §102(b)(1)(I) by inserting "plan" after multiemployer. Eff. for plan years beginning after 2007, as if included in Pub. L. No. 109-280, §202.

Genetic Information Nondiscrimination Act of 2008 (Pub. L. No. 110-233), as follows:

- ERISA §502(a)(6) was amended by Act §101(e)(1) by striking "(7), or (8)" and inserting "(7), (8), or (9)". Eff. with respect to group health plans for plan years beginning after the date that is one year after the date of enactment (date of enactment: May 21, 2008), see Act §101(f)(2).
- ERISA §502(b)(3) was amended by Act §101(e)(2) by striking "The Secretary" and inserting "Except as provided in subsections (c)(9) and (a)(6) (with respect to collecting civil penalties under subsection (c)(9)), the Secretary". Eff. with respect to group health plans for plan years beginning after the date that is one year after the date of enactment (date of enactment: May 21, 2008), see Act §101(f)(2).
- ERISA §502(c)(9) was redesignated as para. (10) and new para. 9 was added by Act §101(e)(3). Eff. with respect to group health plans for plan years beginning after the date that is one year after the date of enactment (date of enactment: May 21, 2008), see Act §101(f)(2).
- **Other Provision.** Act §101(f)(1) provides:

(1) Regulations.—The Secretary of Labor shall issue final regulations not later than 12 months after the date of enactment [May 21, 2008] of this Act to carry out the amendments made by this section.

Pension Protection Act of 2006 (Pub. L. No. 109-280), as follows:

● ERISA §502(a)(6) was amended by Act §202(b)(1) by substituting "(6), (7), or (8)" for "(6) or (7)". Eff. for years plan years beginning after 2007, but not for plan years beginning after Dec. 31, 2014.

● ERISA §502(a)(8), (9), (10) were amended by Act §202(c) by deleting "or" at the end of (8) and substituting "j or" for the period at the end of (9) and adding (10). Eff. after 2007, and before 2015.

● ERISA §502(c)(1) was amended by Act §508(a)(2)(C) by substituting "§101(f), or §105(a)" for "or §101(f)". Eff. after 2007, and before 2015.

● ERISA §502(c)(4) was amended by Act §§103(b), 502(a)(2), 502(b)(2), and 902(f)(2), which replaced the existing para. (4). Eff. for plan years after 2007. ERISA §502(c)(4) prior to amendment:

(4) The Secretary may access a civil penalty of not more than $1,000 a day for each violation by any person of, §302(b)(7)(F)(vi), or §514(e)(3).

● ERISA §502(c)(7) was amended by Act §507(b) by substituting "subsection (i) or (m) of section 101" for "§101(i)". Eff. for plan years beginning after 2006. However, Act §507(d)(2) provided a transition rule that a notice under ERISA §101(m) that would otherwise be required to be provided before the 90th day after the date of enactment of the Act, would not have to be provided until the 90th day after the Act's enactment.

● ERISA §502(c)(8)–(9) were amended by Act §202(b) by redesignating former (8) as (9), and adding a new (8). Eff. for plan years after 2007, and before 2015.

● **Other Provision—Effective Date.** Act §103(c)(2) provides:

(2) Collective bargaining exception.—In the case of a plan maintained pursuant to 1 or more collective bargaining agreements between employee representatives and 1 or more employers ratified before January 1, 2008, the amendments made by this section shall not apply to plan years beginning before the earlier of—

(A) the later of—

(i) the date on which the last collective bargaining agreement relating to the plan terminates (determined without regard to any extension thereof agreed to after the date of the enactment of this Act), or

(ii) the first day of the first plan year to which the amendments made by this subsection would (but for this subparagraph) apply, or

(B) January 1, 2010.

For purposes of subparagraph (A)(i), any plan amendment made pursuant to a collective bargaining agreement relating to the plan which amends the plan solely to conform to any requirement added by this section shall not be treated as a termination of such collective bargaining agreement.

● **Other Provision.** Act §206 provided a special rule:

SEC. 206. SPECIAL RULE FOR CERTAIN BENEFITS FUNDED UNDER AN AGREEMENT APPROVED BY THE PENSION BENEFIT GUARANTY CORPORATION.
In the case of a multiemployer plan that is a party to an agreement that was approved by the Pension Benefit Guaranty Corporation prior to June 30, 2005, and that—

(1) increases benefits, and

(2) provides for special withdrawal liability rules under section 4203(f) of the Employee Retirement Income Security Act of 1974 (29 U.S.C. 1383), the amendments made by sections 201, 202, 211, and 212 of this Act shall not apply to the benefit increases under any plan amendment adopted prior to June 30, 2005, that are funded pursuant to such agreement if the plan is funded in compliance with such agreement (and any amendments thereto).

● **Other Provision.** Act §221(c)(1), provides:

(c) Sunset.

(1) In general.—Except as provided in this subsection, notwithstanding any other provision of this Act, the provisions of, and the amendments made by, sections 201(b),

202, and 212 shall not apply to plan years beginning after December 31, 2014.

Pension Funding Equity Act of 2004 (Pub. L. No. 108-218), as follows:

● ERISA §502(c)(1) was amended by Act §103(b) by substituting ", 101(e)(1) of this title, or section 101(f) of this title" for "or section 101(e)(1) of this title". Eff. after 2004.

● ERISA §502(c)(3) was amended by Act §102(d) by inserting "or who fails to meet the requirements of section 302(d)(12)(E) of this title with respect to any person" after "101(e)(2) of this title with respect to any person". Eff. after 2004.

● ERISA §502(c)(4) was amended by Act §104(a)(2). Eff. after 2004. ERISA §502(c)(4) prior to amendment:

(4) The Secretary may assess a civil penalty of not more than $1,000 for each violation by any person of section 101(f)(1) of this title.

Sarbanes-Oxley Act of 2002 (Pub. L. No. 107-204), as follows:

● ERISA §502(a)(6) was amended by Act §306(b)(3)(A) by substituting "(5), (6), or (7)" for "(5), or (6)". Eff. Jan. 30, 2003.

● ERISA §502(c)(7)–(8) were amended by Act §306(b)(3)(B), (C) by adding new para. (7) and redesignating former para. (7) as (8). Eff. Jan. 30, 2003.

Taxpayer Relief Act of 1997 (Pub. L. No. 105-34), as follows:

● ERISA §502(a)(6) was amended by Act §1503(d)(7) by substituting "(5), or (6)" for "or (5)". Eff. after 1997.

● ERISA §502(c)(6)–(7) were amended by Act §1503(c)(2)(B) by adding new para. (6) and redesignating former para. (6) as (7). Eff. after 1997.

Health Insurance Portability and Accountability Act of 1996 (Pub. L. No. 104-191), as follows:

● ERISA §502(a)(6) was amended by Act §101(e)(2)(A)(i) by substituting "under paragraph (2), (4), or (5) of subsection (c) of this section or under subsection (i) or (l) of this section" for "under subsection (c)(2) or (i) or (l) of this section". Eff. June 30, 1997.

● ERISA §502(b)(3) was added by Act §101(b). Eff. June 30, 1997.

● ERISA §502(c)(1) was amended by Act §101(e)(2)(B) by inserting at end "For purposes of this paragraph, each violation described in subparagraph (A) with respect to any single participant, and each violation described in subparagraph (B) with respect to any single participant or beneficiary, shall be treated as a separate violation." Eff. June 30, 1997.

● ERISA §502(c)(4)–(6) were amended by Act §101(e)(2)(A)(ii) by striking "For purposes of this paragraph, each violation described in subparagraph (A) with respect to any single participant, and each violation described in subparagraph (B) with respect to any single participant or beneficiary, shall be treated as a separate violation. The Secretary and" after "section 101(f)(1) of this title."; and redesignating "the Secretary of Health and Human Services shall maintain such ongoing consultation as may be necessary and appropriate to coordinate enforcement under this subsection with enforcement under section 1320b-14(c)(8) of title 42." as para. (6); inserting "The Secretary and" before "the Secretary of Health and Human Services"; and adding para. (5). Eff. June 30, 1997.

Departments of Veterans Affairs and HUD and Independent Agencies Appropriations Act of 1997 (Pub. L. No. 104-204), as follows:

● ERISA §502(b)(3) was amended by Act §603(b) by making a technical amendment to ERISA as amended by HIPAA to the reference to §733. Eff. Jan. 1, 1998.

Pension Annuitants Protection Act of 1994 (Pub. L. No. 103-401), as follows:

● ERISA §502(a)(9) was added by Act §2. Eff. for legal actions brought after May 31, 1993.

● ERISA §502(l)(3)(B) was amended by Act §3 by inserting "(or to provide the relief ordered pursuant to subsection (a)(9) of this section)" after "to restore all losses to the plan". Eff. for legal actions brought after May 31, 1993.

Retirement Protection Act of 1994 (Pub. L. No. 103-465), as follows:

● ERISA §502(m) was added by Act §761. Eff. after Dec. 31, 1994.

Omnibus Budget Reconciliation Act of 1993 (Pub. L. No. 103-66), as follows:

• ERISA §502(a)(7)–(8) were added by Act §4301(c)(1). Eff. Aug. 10, 1993.

• ERISA §502(c)(4) was added by Act §4301(c)(2). Eff. Aug. 10, 1993.

• §502(e)(1) was amended by Act §4301(c)(3) by substituting in first sentence "fiduciary, or any person referred to in section 101(f)(1) of this title" for "or fiduciary" and in second sentence "paragraphs (1)(B) and (7) of subsection (a)" for "subsection (a)(1)(B)". Eff. Aug. 10, 1993.

Omnibus Budget Reconciliation Act of 1990 (Pub. L. No. 101-508), as follows:

• ERISA §502(c)(1) was amended by Act §12012(d)(2)(A) by inserting "or section 101(e)(1) of this title" after "section 606 of this title". Eff. Nov. 5, 1990.

• ERISA §502(c)(3) was amended by Act §12012(d)(2)(B) by inserting "or who fails to meet the requirements of section 101(e)(2) of this title with respect to any person" after first reference to "beneficiary" and "or to such person" after second reference to "beneficiary". Eff. Nov. 5, 1990.

Omnibus Budget Reconciliation Act of 1989 (Pub. L. No. 101-239), as follows:

• ERISA §502(a)(6) was amended by Act §7881(j)(2) by substituting "subsection (c)(2) or (i)" for "subsection (i)"; and by Act §2101(b) by inserting "or (l)" after "subsection (i)". Eff. as if included in Pub. L. No. 100-203.

• ERISA §502(b)(1) was amended by Act §7894(f)(1) by substituting "respect" for "respct" before "to a violation" in introductory provisions; and by Act §7891(a)(1) by substituting "Internal Revenue Code of 1986" for "Internal Revenue Code of 1954", which for purposes of codification was translated as "title 26". Eff. as if included in Pub. L. No. 99-514.

• ERISA §502(c)(2) was amended by Act §7881(j)(3) by inserting "against any plan administrator" after "civil penalty" and substituted "such plan administrator's" for "a plan administrator's". Eff. as if included in Pub. L. No. 100-203.

• ERISA §502(c)(3) was amended by Act §7881(b)(5)(B) by adding para. (3). Eff. as if included in Pub. L. No. 100-203.

• ERISA §502(g)(2) was amended by Act §7891(a)(1) by substituting "Internal Revenue Code of 1986" for "Internal Revenue Code of 1954", which for purposes of codification was translated as "title 26". Eff. as if included in Pub. L. No. 99-514.

• ERISA §502(l) was added by Act §2101(a). Eff. Dec. 19, 1989.

Omnibus Budget Reconciliation Act of 1987 (Pub. L. No. 100-203), as follows:

• ERISA §502(c) was amended by Act §9342(c) by designated existing provision as para. (1), redesignating as cls. (A)–(B) former cls. (1)–(2), and adding para. (2). Eff. after Dec. 31, 1987.

• ERISA §502(i) was amended by Act §9344 by amended second sentence. Eff. after 1987. Prior to amendment, second sentence read:

> The amount of such penalty may not exceed 5 percent of the amount involved (as defined in section 4975(f)(4) of title 26); except that if the transaction is not corrected (in such manner as the Secretary shall prescribe by regulation, which regulations shall be consistent with section 4975(f)(5) of title 26) within 90 days after notice from the Secretary (or such longer period as the Secretary may permit), such penalty may be in an amount not more than 100 percent of the amount involved.

Consolidated Omnibus Budget Reconciliation Act of 1986 (Pub. L. No. 99-272), as follows:

• ERISA §502(c) was amended by Act §10002(b) by inserting "(1) who fails to meet the requirements of paragraph (1) or (4) of section 1166 of this title with respect to a participant or beneficiary, or (2)". Eff. July 1, 1986.

Multiemployer Pension Plan Amendments Act of 1980 (Pub. L. No. 96-364), as follows:

• ERISA §502(b) was amended by Act §306(b)(1) by redesignated existing provisions as para. (1)(A) and (B) and adding para. (2). Eff. Sept. 26, 1980.

• ERISA §502(g) was amended by Act §306(b)(2) by redesignated existing provisions as para. (1), inserting exception for actions under para. (2), and adding para. (2). Eff. Sept. 26, 1980.

SEC. 503. CLAIMS PROCEDURE.

In accordance with regulations of the Secretary, every employee benefit plan shall—

(1) provide adequate notice in writing to any participant or beneficiary whose claim for benefits under the plan has been denied, setting forth the specific reasons for such denial, written in a manner calculated to be understood by the participant, and

(2) afford a reasonable opportunity to any participant whose claim for benefits has been denied for a full and fair review by the appropriate named fiduciary of the decision denying the claim.

SEC. 504. INVESTIGATIVE AUTHORITY.

(a) Investigation and Submission of Reports, Books, etc.—The Secretary shall have the power, in order to determine whether any person has violated or is about to violate any provision of this title or any regulation or order thereunder—

(1) to make an investigation, and in connection therewith to require the submission of reports, books, and records, and the filing of data in support of any information required to be filed with the Secretary under this title, and

(2) to enter such places, inspect such books and records and question such persons as he may deem necessary to enable him to determine the facts relative to such investigation, if he has reasonable cause to believe there may exist a violation of this title or any rule or regulation issued thereunder or if the entry is pursuant to an agreement with the plan.

The Secretary may make available to any person actually affected by any matter which is the subject of an investigation under this section, and to any department or agency of the United States, information concerning any matter which may be the subject of such investigation; except that any information obtained by the Secretary pursuant to section 6103(g) of title 26 shall be made available only in accordance with regulations prescribed by the Secretary of the Treasury.

(b) Frequency of Submission of Books and Records.—The Secretary may not under the authority of this section require any plan to submit to the Secretary any books or records of the plan more than once in any 12 month period, unless the Secretary has reasonable cause to believe there may exist a violation of this title or any regulation or order thereunder.

(c) Other Provisions Applicable to Relating to Attendance of Witnesses and Production of Books,

Records, etc.—For the purposes of any investigation provided for in this title, the provisions of sections 9 and 10 (relating to the attendance of witnesses and the production of books, records, and documents) of the Federal Trade Commission Act (15 U.S.C. 49, 50) are hereby made applicable (without regard to any limitation in such sections respecting persons, partnerships, banks, or common carriers) to the jurisdiction, powers, and duties of the Secretary or any officers designated by him. To the extent he considers appropriate, the Secretary may delegate his investigative functions under this section with respect to insured banks acting as fiduciaries of employee benefit plans to the appropriate Federal banking agency (as defined in section 3(q) of the Federal Deposit Insurance Act (12 U.S.C. 1813(q)).

Editor's Note

ERISA §504(d) and (e), below, added by Pub. L. No. 111-148, §6607, are effective March 23, 2010.

(d) The Secretary may promulgate a regulation that provides an evidentiary privilege for, and provides for the confidentiality of communications between or among, any of the following entities or their agents, consultants, or employees:

(1) A State insurance department.

(2) A State attorney general.

(3) The National Association of Insurance Commissioners.

(4) The Department of Labor.

(5) The Department of the Treasury.

(6) The Department of Justice.

(7) The Department of Health and Human Services.

(8) Any other Federal or State authority that the Secretary determines is appropriate for the purposes of enforcing the provisions of this title.

(e) The privilege established under subsection (d) shall apply to communications related to any investigation, audit, examination, or inquiry conducted or coordinated by any of the agencies. A communication that is privileged under subsection (d) shall not waive any privilege otherwise available to the communicating agency or to any person who provided the information that is communicated.

Amendments to ERISA §504

Patient Protection and Affordable Care Act, 2010 (Pub. L. No. 111-148), as follows:

● ERISA §504(d) and (e) were added by Act §6607. Eff. Mar. 23, 2010.

Omnibus Budget Reconciliation Act of 1989 (Pub. L. No. 101-239), as follows:

● ERISA §504(a) was amended by Act §7891(a)(1) by substituting "Internal Revenue Code of 1986" for "Internal Revenue Code of 1954", which for purposes of codification was translated as "title 26". Eff. as if included in Pub. L. No. 99-514.

SEC. 505. REGULATIONS.

Subject to title III and section 109, the Secretary may prescribe such regulations as he finds necessary or appropriate to carry out the provisions of this title. Among other things, such regulations may define accounting, technical and trade terms used in such provisions; may prescribe forms; and may provide for the keeping of books and records, and for the inspection of such books and records (subject to section 504(a) and (b)).

SEC. 506. COORDINATION AND RESPONSIBILITY OF AGENCIES ENFORCING EMPLOYEE RETIREMENT INCOME SECURITY ACT AND RELATED FEDERAL LAWS.

(a) Coordination With Other Agencies and Departments.—In order to avoid unnecessary expense and duplication of functions among Government agencies, the Secretary may make such arrangements or agreements for cooperation or mutual assistance in the performance of his functions under this title and the functions of any such agency as he may find to be practicable and consistent with law. The Secretary may utilize, on a reimbursable or other basis, the facilities or services of any department, agency, or establishment of the United States or of any State or political subdivision of a State, including the services of any of its employees, with the lawful consent of such department, agency, or establishment; and each department, agency, or establishment of the United States is authorized and directed to cooperate with the Secretary and, to the extent permitted by law, to provide such information and facilities as he may request for his assistance in the performance of his functions under this title. The Attorney General or his representative shall receive from the Secretary for appropriate action such evidence developed in the performance of his functions under this title as may be found to warrant consideration for criminal prosecution under the provisions of this title or other Federal law.

(b) Responsibility for Detecting and Investigating Civil and Criminal Violations of Employee Retirement Income Security Act and Related Federal Laws.—The Secretary shall have the responsibility and authority to detect and investigate and refer, where appropriate, civil and criminal violations related to the provisions of this title and other related Federal laws, including the detection, investigation, and appropriate referrals of related violations of title 18 of the United States Code. Nothing in this subsection shall be construed to preclude other appropriate Federal agencies from detecting and investigating civil and criminal violations of this title and other related Federal laws.

(c) Coordination of Enforcement With States With Respect to Certain Arrangements.—A State may enter into an agreement with the Secretary for delegation to the State of some or all of the Secretary's authority under sections 502 and 504 to enforce the requirements under part 7 in connection with multiple employer welfare arrangements, providing medical care (within the meaning of section 733(a)(2)), which are not group health plans.

Amendments to ERISA §506

Departments of Veterans Affairs and HUD and Independent Agencies Appropriations Act of 1997 (Pub. L. No. 104-204), as follows:

● ERISA §506(c) was amended by Act §603(b)(3)(F) by making a technical amendment to reference in original Act which appears in text as reference to §733 of this title. Eff. with respect to group health plans for plan years beginning on or after Jan. 1, 1998.

Health Insurance Portability and Accountability Act of 1986 (Pub. L. No. 104-191), as follows:

● ERISA §506(c) was added by Act §101(e)(3). Eff. with respect to group health plans for plan years beginning after June 30, 1997.

Comprehensive Crime Control Act of 1984 (Pub. L. No. 98-473), as follows:

● ERISA §506(a) was amended by Act §805 by designating existing provisions as subsec. (a), adding subsec. (b), and amending section catchline. Eff. Oct. 12, 1984.

SEC. 507. ADMINISTRATION.

(a) Subchapter II of chapter 5, and chapter 7, of title 5, United States Code (relating to administrative procedure), shall be applicable to this title.

(b) [Omitted.]

(c) No employee of the Department of Labor or the Department of the Treasury shall administer or enforce this title or the Internal Revenue Code of 1986 with respect to any employee benefit plan under which he is a participant or beneficiary, any employee organization of which he is a member, or any employer organization in which he has an interest. This subsection does not apply to an employee benefit plan which covers only employees of the United States.

Amendments to ERISA §507

Omnibus Budget Reconciliation Act of 1989 (Pub. L. No. 101-239), as follows:

● ERISA §507(c) was amended by Act §7891(a) by substituting "Internal Revenue Code of 1986" for "Internal Revenue Code of 1954", which for codification purposes was translated as "title 26". Eff. as if included in Pub. L. No. 99-514.

SEC. 508. APPROPRIATIONS.

There are hereby authorized to be appropriated such sums as may be necessary to enable the Secretary to carry out his functions and duties under this Act.

SEC. 509. SEPARABILITY.

If any provision of this Act, or the application of such provision to any person or circumstances, shall be held invalid, the remainder of this Act, or the application of such provision to persons or circumstances other than those as to which it is held invalid, shall not be affected thereby.

SEC. 510. INTERFERENCE WITH PROTECTED RIGHTS.

It shall be unlawful for any person to discharge, fine, suspend, expel, discipline, or discriminate against a participant or beneficiary for exercising any right to which he is entitled under the provisions of an employee benefit plan, this title, section 3001, or the Welfare and Pension Plans Disclosure Act, or for the purpose of interfering with the attainment of any right to which such participant may become entitled under the plan, this title, or the Welfare and Pension Plans Disclosure Act. It shall be unlawful for any person to discharge, fine, suspend, expel, or discriminate against any person because he has given information or has testified or is about to testify in any inquiry or proceeding relating to this Act or the Welfare and Pension Plans Disclosure Act. In the case of a multiemployer plan, it shall be unlawful for the plan sponsor or any other person to discriminate against any contributing employer for exercising rights under this Act or for giving information or testifying in any inquiry or proceeding relating to this Act before Congress. The provisions of section 502 shall be applicable in the enforcement of this section.

Amendments to ERISA §510

Pension Protection Act of 2006 (Pub. L. No. 109-280), as follows:

● ERISA §510 was amended by Act §205 by inserting the sentence: "In the case of a multiemployer plan, it shall be unlawful for the plan sponsor or any other person to discriminate against any contributing employer for exercising rights under this Act or for giving information or testifying in any inquiry or proceeding relating to this Act before Congress." before "The provisions of §502 . . .". Eff. Aug. 17, 2006.

SEC. 511. COERCIVE INTERFERENCE.

It shall be unlawful for any person through the use of fraud, force, violence, or threat of the use of force or violence, to restrain, coerce, intimidate, or attempt to restrain, coerce, or intimidate any participant or beneficiary for the purpose of interfering with or preventing the exercise of any right to which he is or may become entitled under the plan, this title, section 3001, or the Welfare and Pension Plans Disclosure Act. Any person who willfully violates this section shall be fined $100,000 or imprisoned for not more than 10 years, or both.

Amendments to ERISA §511

Pension Protection Act of 2006 (Pub. L. No. 109-280), as follows:

• ERISA §511 was amended by Act §623(a) by substituting "$100,000" for "$10,000" and "10 years" for "one year". Eff. for violations occurring on and after Aug. 17, 2006.

SEC. 512. ADVISORY COUNCIL ON EMPLOYEE WELFARE AND PENSION BENEFIT PLANS.

(a) Establishment; Membership; Terms; Appointment and Reappointment; Vacancies; Quorum.—

(1) There is hereby established an Advisory Council on Employee Welfare and Pension Benefit Plans (hereinafter in this section referred to as the "Council") consisting offifteen members appointed by the Secretary. Not more than eight members of the Council shall be members of the same political party.

(2) Members shall be persons qualified to appraise the programs instituted under this Act.

(3) Of the members appointed, three shall be representatives of employee organizations (at least one of whom shall be representative of any organization members of which are participants in a multiemployer plan); three shall be representatives of employers (at least one of whom shall be representative of employers maintaining or contributing to multiemployer plans); three representatives shall be appointed from the general public, one of whom shall be a person representing those receiving benefits from a pension plan; and there shall be one representative each from the fields of insurance, corporate trust, actuarial counseling, investment counseling, investment management, and the accounting field.

(4) Members shall serve for terms of three years except that of those first appointed, five shall be appointed for terms of one year, five shall be appointed for terms of two years, and five shall be appointed for terms of three years. A member may be reappointed. A member appointed to fill a vacancy shall be appointed only for the remainder of such term. A majority of members shall constitute a quorum and action shall be taken only by a majority vote of those present and voting.

(b) Duties and Functions.—It shall be the duty of the Council to advise the Secretary with respect to the carrying out of his functions under this Act and to submit to the Secretary recommendations with respect thereto. The Council shall meet at least four times each year and at such other times as the Secretary requests. In his annual report submitted pursuant to section 513(b), the Secretary shall include each recommendation which he has received from the Council during the preceding calendar year.

(c) Executive Secretary; Secretarial and Clerical Services.—The Secretary shall furnish to the Council an executive secretary and such secretarial, clerical, and other services as are deemed necessary to conduct its business. The Secretary may call upon other agencies of the Government for statistical data, reports, and other information which will assist the Council in the performance of its duties.

(d) Compensation.—

(1) Members of the Council shall each be entitled to receive the daily equivalent of the annual rate of basic pay in effect for grade GS-18 of the General Schedule for each day (including travel time) during which they are engaged in the actual performance of duties vested in the Council.

(2) While away from their homes or regular places of business in the performance of services for Council, members of the Council shall be allowed travel expenses, including per diem in lieu of subsistence, in the same manner as persons employed intermittently in the Government service are allowed expenses under section 5703(b) of title 5 of the United States Code.

(e) Termination.—Section 14(a) of the Federal Advisory Committee Act (relating to termination) shall not apply to the Council.

SEC. 513. RESEARCH, STUDIES, AND REPORTS.

(a) Authorization to Undertake Research and Surveys.—

(1) The Secretary is authorized to undertake research and surveys and in connection therewith to collect, compile, analyze and publish data, information, and statistics relating to employee benefit plans, including retirement, deferred compensation, and welfare plans, and types of plans not subject to this Act.

(2) The Secretary is authorized and directed to undertake research studies relating to pension plans, including but not limited to (A) the effects of this title upon the provisions and costs of pension plans, (B) the role of private pensions in meeting the economic security needs of the Nation, and (C) the operation of private pension plans including types and levels of benefits, degree of reciprocity or portability, and financial and actuarial characteristics and practices, and methods of encouraging the growth of the private pension system.

(3) The Secretary may, as he deems appropriate or necessary, undertake other studies relating to employee benefit plans, the matters regulated by this title, and the enforcement procedures provided for under this title.

(4) The research, surveys, studies, and publications referred to in this subsection may be conducted directly, or indirectly through grant or contract arrangements.

(b) Submission of Annual Report to Congress; Contents.—The Secretary shall submit annually a report to the Congress covering his administration of this title for the preceding year, and including (1) an explanation of any variances or extensions granted under section 110, 207, 303, or 304 and the projected date for terminating the variance; (2) the status of cases in enforcement status; (3) recommendations received from the Advisory Council during the preceding year; and (4) such information, data, research findings, studies, and recommendations for further legislation in connection with the matters covered by this title as he may find advisable.

(c) Cooperation With Congress.—The Secretary is authorized and directed to cooperate with the Congress and its appropriate committees, subcommittees, and staff in supplying data and any other information, and personnel and services, required by the Congress in any study, examination, or report by the Congress relating to pension benefit plans established or maintained by States or their political subdivisions.

SEC. 514. OTHER LAWS.

(a) Supersedure; Effective Date.—Except as provided in subsection (b) of this section, the provisions of this title and title IV shall supersede any and all State laws insofar as they may now or hereafter relate to any employee benefit plan described in section 4(a) and not exempt under section 4(b). This section shall take effect on January 1, 1975.

(b) Construction and Application.—

(1) This section shall not apply with respect to any cause of action which arose, or any act or omission which occurred, before January 1, 1975.

(2)(A) Except as provided in subparagraph (B), nothing in this title shall be construed to exempt or relieve any person from any law of any State which regulates insurance, banking, or securities.

(B) Neither an employee benefit plan described in section 4(a), which is not exempt under section 4(b) (other than a plan established primarily for the purpose of providing death benefits), nor any trust established under such a plan, shall be deemed to be an insurance company or other insurer, bank, trust company, or investment company or to be engaged in the business of insurance or banking for purposes of any law of any State purporting to regulate insurance companies, insurance contracts, banks, trust companies, or investment companies.

(3) Nothing in this section shall be construed to prohibit use by the Secretary of services or facilities of a State agency as permitted under section 506 of this Act.

(4) Subsection (a) shall not apply to any generally applicable criminal law of a State.

(5)(A) Except as provided in subparagraph (B), subsection (a) shall not apply to the Hawaii Prepaid Health Care Act (Haw. Rev. Stat. sections 393-1 through 393-51).

(B) Nothing in subparagraph (A) shall be construed to exempt from subsection (a)—

(i) any State tax law relating to employee benefit plans, or

(ii) any amendment of the Hawaii Prepaid Health Care Act enacted after September 2, 1974, to the extent it provides for more than the effective administration of such Act as in effect on such date.

(C) Notwithstanding subparagraph (A), parts 1 and 4 of this subtitle, and the preceding sections of this part to the extent they govern matters which are governed by the provisions of such parts 1 and 4, shall supersede the Hawaii Prepaid Health Care Act (as in effect on or after the date of the enactment of this paragraph [enacted Jan. 14, 1983]), but the Secretary may enter into cooperative arrangements under this paragraph and section 506 with officials of the State of Hawaii to assist them in effectuating the policies of provisions of such Act which are superseded by such parts 1 and 4 and the preceding sections of this part.

(6)(A) Notwithstanding any other provision of this section—

(i) in the case of an employee welfare benefit plan which is a multiple employer welfare arrangement and is fully insured (or which is a multiple employer welfare arrangement subject to an exemption under subparagraph (B)), any law of any State which regulates insurance may apply to such arrangement to the extent that such law provides—

(I) standards, requiring the maintenance of specified levels of reserves and specified levels of contributions, which any such plan, or any trust established under such a plan, must meet in order to be considered under such law able to pay benefits in full when due, and

(II) provisions to enforce such standards, and

(ii) in the case of any other employee welfare benefit plan which is a multiple employer welfare arrangement, in addition to this title, any law of any State which regulates insurance may apply to the extent not inconsistent with the preceding sections of this title.

(B) The Secretary may, under regulations which may be prescribed by the Secretary, exempt from

ERISA Sec. 514(b)(6)(B)

subparagraph (A)(ii), individually or by class, multiple employer welfare arrangements which are not fully insured. Any such exemption may be granted with respect to any arrangement or class of arrangements only if such arrangement or each arrangement which is a member of such class meets the requirements of section 3(1) and section 4 necessary to be considered an employee welfare benefit plan to which this title applies.

(C) Nothing in subparagraph (A) shall affect the manner or extent to which the provisions of this title apply to an employee welfare benefit plan which is not a multiple employer welfare arrangement and which is a plan, fund, or program participating in, subscribing to, or otherwise using a multiple employer welfare arrangement to fund or administer benefits to such plan's participants and beneficiaries.

(D) For purposes of this paragraph, a multiple employer welfare arrangement shall be considered fully insured only if the terms of the arrangement provide for benefits the amount of all of which the Secretary determines are guaranteed under a contract, or policy of insurance, issued by an insurance company, insurance service, or insurance organization, qualified to conduct business in a State.

(7) Subsection (a) shall not apply to qualified domestic relations orders (within the meaning of section 206(d)(3)(B)(i)), qualified medical child support orders (within the meaning of section 609(a)(2)(A), and the provisions of law referred to in section 609(a)(2)(B)(ii) to the extent they apply to qualified medical child support orders.

(8) Subsection (a) of this section shall not be construed to preclude any State cause of action—

(A) with respect to which the State exercises its acquired rights under section 609(b)(3) with respect to a group health plan (as defined in section 607(1)), or

(B) for recoupment of payment with respect to items or services pursuant to a State plan for medical assistance approved under title XIX of the Social Security Act which would not have been payable if such acquired rights had been executed before payment with respect to such items or services by the group health plan.

(9) For additional provisions relating to group health plans, see section 731.

(c) **Definitions.**—For purposes of this section:

(1) The term "State law" includes all laws, decisions, rules, regulations, or other State action having the effect of law, of any State. A law of the United States applicable only to the District of Columbia shall be treated as a State law rather than a law of the United States.

(2) The term "State" includes a State, any political subdivisions thereof, or any agency or instrumentality of either, which purports to regulate, directly or indirectly, the terms and conditions of employee benefit plans covered by this title.

(d) **Alteration, Amendment, Modification, Invalidation, Impairment, or Supersedure of Any Law of the United States Prohibited.**—Nothing in this title shall be construed to alter, amend, modify, invalidate, impair, or supersede any law of the United States (except as provided in sections 111 and 507(b)) or any rule or regulation issued under any such law.

(e)(1) Notwithstanding any other provision of this section, this title shall supersede any law of a State which would directly or indirectly prohibit or restrict the inclusion in any plan of an automatic contribution arrangement. The Secretary may prescribe regulations which would establish minimum standards that such an arrangement would be required to satisfy in order for this subsection to apply in the case of such arrangement.

(2) For purposes of this subsection, the term "automatic contribution arrangement" means an arrangement—

(A) under which a participant may elect to have the plan sponsor make payments as contributions under the plan on behalf of the participant, or to the participant directly in cash,

(B) under which a participant is treated as having elected to have the plan sponsor make such contributions in an amount equal to a uniform percentage of compensation provided under the plan until the participant specifically elects not to have such contributions made (or specifically elects to have such contributions made at a different percentage), and

(C) under which such contributions are invested in accordance with regulations prescribed by the Secretary under section 404(c)(5).

(3)(A) The plan administrator of an automatic contribution arrangement shall, within a reasonable period before such plan year, provide to each participant to whom the arrangement applies for such plan year notice of the participant's rights and obligations under the arrangement which—

(i) is sufficiently accurate and comprehensive to apprise the participant of such rights and obligations, and

(ii) is written in a manner calculated to be understood by the average participant to whom the arrangement applies.

(B) A notice shall not be treated as meeting the requirements of subparagraph (A) with respect to a participant unless—

(i) the notice includes an explanation of the participant's right under the arrangement not to have elective contributions made on the participant's behalf (or to elect to have such contributions made at a different percentage),

(ii) the participant has a reasonable period of time, after receipt of the notice described in clause (i) and before the first elective contribution is made, to make such election, and

(iii) the notice explains how contributions made under the arrangement will be invested in the absence of any investment election by the participant.

Amendments to ERISA §514

Patient Protection and Affordable Care Act, 2010 (Pub. L. No. 111-148), as follows:
- **Other Provision.** Act §1560(b) provides:
  (b) Rule of Construction Regarding Hawaii's Prepaid Health Care Act—Nothing in this title (or an amendment made by this title) shall be construed to modify or limit the application of the exemption for Hawaii's Prepaid Health Care Act (Haw. Rev. Stat. 393-1 et seq.) as provided for under section 514(b)(5) of the Employee Retirement Income Security Act of 1974 (29 U.S.C. 1144(b)(5)).

Pension Protection Act of 2006 (Pub. L. No. 109-280), as follows:
- ERISA §514(e) was added by Act §902(f)(1). Eff. Aug. 17, 2006.

Child Support Performance and Incentive Act of 1998 (Pub. L. No. 105-200), as follows:
- ERISA §514(b)(7) was amended by Act §401(h)(2)(A)(ii) by substituting "they apply to" for "enforced by". Eff. as if included in Pub. L. No. 103-66.

Departments of Veterans Affairs and HUD and Independent Agencies Appropriations Act of 1997 (Pub. L. No. 104-204), as follows:
- ERISA §514(b)(9) was amended by Act §603(b)(3)(G) by making a technical amendment to a reference in original Act which appears in text as reference to section 731 of this title. Eff. Jan. 1, 1998.

Health Insurance Portability and Accountability Act of 1996 (Pub. L. No. 104-191), as follows:
- ERISA §514(b)(9) was added by Act §101(f)(1). Eff. June 30, 1997.

Omnibus Budget Reconciliation Act of 1993 (Pub. L. No. 103-66), as follows:
- ERISA §514(b)(7) was amended by Act §4301(c)(4)(A), as amended by Pub. L. No. 105-200, by inserting ", orders (within the meaning of §609(a)(2)(A) of this title, and the provisions of law referred to in §609(a)(2)(B)(ii) of this title to the extent enforced by qualified medical child support orders" before period at end. Eff. Aug. 10, 1993.
- ERISA §514(b)(8) was amended by Act §4301(c)(4)(B). Eff. Aug. 10, 1993. ERISA §514(b)(8) prior to amendment:
  (8) Subsection (a) of this section shall not apply to any State law mandating that an employee benefit plan not include any provision which has the effect of limiting or excluding coverage or payment for any health care for an individual who would otherwise be covered or entitled to benefits or services under the terms of the employee benefit plan, because that individual is provided, or is eligible for, benefits or services pursuant to a plan under title XIX of the Social Security Act, to the extent such law is necessary for the State to be eligible to receive reimbursement under title XIX of that Act.

Omnibus Budget Reconciliation Act of 1989 (Pub. L. No. 101-239), as follows:
- ERISA §514(b)(5)(C) was amended by Act §7894(f)(2)(A) by substituting "by such parts 1 and 4 and the preceding sections of this part" for "by such parts". Eff. as if included in Pub. L. No. 97-473.
- ERISA §514(b)(6)(B) was amended by Act §7894(f)(3)(A) by substituting "section 3(1)" for "section 3(l)". Eff. as if included in Pub. L. No. 97-473.

Consolidated Omnibus Budget Reconciliation Act of 1986 (Pub. L. No. 99-272), as follows:
- ERISA §514(b)(8) was added by Act §9503(d)(1). Eff. July 1, 1986.

Retirement Equity Act of 1984 (Pub. L. No. 98-397), as follows:
- ERISA §514(b)(7) was added by Act §104(b). Eff. Aug. 23, 1984.

Pub. L. No. 97-493, as follows:
- ERISA §514(b)(5) was added by Act §301(a). Eff. Jan. 14, 1983.
- ERISA §514(b)(6) was added by Act §302(b). Eff. Jan. 14, 1983.

SEC. 515. DELINQUENT CONTRIBUTIONS.

Every employer who is obligated to make contributions to a multiemployer plan under the terms of the plan or under the terms of a collectively bargained agreement shall, to the extent not inconsistent with law, make such contributions in accordance with the terms and conditions of such plan or such agreement.

SEC. 516. OUTREACH TO PROMOTE RETIREMENT INCOME SAVINGS.

(a) In General.—The Secretary shall maintain an ongoing program of outreach to the public designed to effectively promote retirement income savings by the public.

(b) Methods.—The Secretary shall carry out the requirements of subsection (a) by means which shall ensure effective communication to the public, including publication of public service announcements, public meetings, creation of educational materials, and establishment of a site on the Internet.

(c) Information to Be Made Available.—The information to be made available by the Secretary as part of the program of outreach required under subsection (a) shall include the following:

(1) a description of the vehicles currently available to individuals and employers for creating and maintaining retirement income savings, specifically including information explaining to employers, in simple terms, the characteristics and operation of the different retirement savings vehicles, including the steps to establish each such vehicle; and

(2) information regarding matters relevant to establishing retirement income savings, such as—

(A) the forms of retirement income savings;

(B) the concept of compound interest;

(C) the importance of commencing savings early in life;

(D) savings principles;

(E) the importance of prudence and diversification in investing;

(F) the importance of the timing of investments; and

ERISA Sec. 516(c)(2)(F)

(G) the impact on retirement savings of life's uncertainties, such as living beyond one's life expectancy.

(d) Establishment of Site on the Internet.—The Secretary shall establish a permanent site on the Internet concerning retirement income savings. The site shall contain at least the following information:

(1) a means for individuals to calculate their estimated retirement savings needs, based on their retirement income goal as a percentage of their preretirement income;

(2) a description in simple terms of the common types of retirement income savings arrangements available to both individuals and employers (specifically including small employers), including information on the amount of money that can be placed into a given vehicle, the tax treatment of the money, the amount of accumulation possible through different typical investment options and interest rate projections, and a directory of resources of more descriptive information;

(3) materials explaining to employers in simple terms, the characteristics and operation of the different retirement savings arrangements for their workers and what the basic legal requirements are under this Act and the Internal Revenue Code of 1986, including the steps to establish each such arrangement;

(4) copies of all educational materials developed by the Department of Labor, and by other Federal agencies in consultation with such Department, to promote retirement income savings by workers and employers; and

(5) links to other sites maintained on the Internet by governmental agencies and nonprofit organizations that provide additional detail on retirement income savings arrangements and related topics on savings or investing.

(e) Coordination.—The Secretary shall coordinate the outreach program under this section with similar efforts undertaken by other public and private entities.

SEC. 517. NATIONAL SUMMIT ON RETIREMENT SAVINGS.

(a) Authority to Call Summit.—Not later than July 15, 1998, the President shall convene a National Summit on Retirement Income Savings at the White House, to be co-hosted by the President and the Speaker and the Minority Leader of the House of Representatives and the Majority Leader and Minority Leader of the Senate. Such a National Summit shall be convened thereafter in 2001 and 2005 on or after September 1 of each year involved. Such a National Summit shall—

(1) advance the public's knowledge and understanding of retirement savings and its critical importance to the future well-being of American workers and their families;

(2) facilitate the development of a broad-based, public education program to encourage and enhance individual commitment to a personal retirement savings strategy;

(3) develop recommendations for additional research, reforms, and actions in the field of private pensions and individual retirement savings; and

(4) disseminate the report of, and information obtained by, the National Summit and exhibit materials and works of the National Summit.

(b) Planning and Direction.—The National Summit shall be planned and conducted under the direction of the Secretary, in consultation with, and with the assistance of, the heads of such other Federal departments and agencies as the President may designate. Such assistance may include the assignment of personnel. The Secretary shall, in planning and conducting the National Summit, consult with the congressional leaders specified in subsection (e)(2). The Secretary shall also, in carrying out the Secretary's duties under this subsection, consult and coordinate with at least one organization made up of private sector businesses and associations partnered with Government entities to promote long-term financial security in retirement through savings.

(c) Purpose of National Summit.—The purpose of the National Summit shall be—

(1) to increase the public awareness of the value of personal savings for retirement;

(2) to advance the public's knowledge and understanding of retirement savings and its critical importance to the future well-being of American workers and their families;

(3) to facilitate the development of a broad-based, public education program to encourage and enhance individual commitment to a personal retirement savings strategy;

(4) to identify the problems workers have in setting aside adequate savings for retirement;

(5) to identify the barriers which employers, especially small employers, face in assisting their workers in accumulating retirement savings;

(6) to examine the impact and effectiveness of individual employers to promote personal savings for retirement among their workers and to promote participation in company savings options;

(7) to examine the impact and effectiveness of government programs at the Federal, State, and local levels to educate the public about, and to encourage, retirement income savings;

(8) to develop such specific and comprehensive recommendations for the legislative and executive branches of the Government and for private sector action as may be appropriate for promoting private pensions and individual retirement savings; and

(9) to develop recommendations for the coordination of Federal, State, and local retirement income savings initiatives among the Federal, State, and local levels of government and for the coordination of such initiatives.

(d) Scope of National Summit.—The scope of the National Summit shall consist of issues relating to individual and employer-based retirement savings and shall not include issues relating to the old-age, survivors, and disability insurance program under title II of the Social Security Act.

(e) National Summit Participants.—

(1) In general.—To carry out the purposes of the National Summit, the National Summit shall bring together—

(A) professionals and other individuals working in the fields of employee benefits and retirement savings;

(B) Members of Congress and officials in the executive branch;

(C) representatives of State and local governments;

(D) representatives of private sector institutions, including individual employers, concerned about promoting the issue of retirement savings and facilitating savings among American workers; and

(E) representatives of the general public.

(2) Statutorily required participation.—The participants in the National Summit shall include the following individuals or theirdesignees:

(A) the Speaker and the Minority Leader of the House of Representatives;

(B) the Majority Leader and the Minority Leader of the Senate;

(C) the Chairman and ranking Member of the Committee on Education and the Workforce of the House of Representatives;

(D) the Chairman and ranking Member of the Committee on Labor and Human Resources of the Senate;

(E) the Chairman and ranking Member of the Special Committee on Aging of the Senate;

(F) the Chairman and ranking Member of the Subcommittees on Labor, Health and Human Services, and Education of the Senate and House of Representatives; and

(G) the parties referred to in subsection (b).

(3) Additional participants.—

(A) In general.—There shall be not more than 200 additional participants. Of such additional participants—

(i) one-half shall be appointed by the President, in consultation with the elected leaders of the President's party in Congress (either the Speaker of the House of Representatives or the Minority Leader of the House of Representatives, and either the Majority Leader or the Minority Leader of the Senate; and

(ii) one-half shall be appointed by the elected leaders of Congress of the party to which the President does not belong (one-half of that allotment to be appointed by either the Speaker of the House of Representatives or the Minority Leader of the House of Representatives, and one-half of that allotment to be appointed by either the Majority Leader or the Minority Leader of the Senate).

(B) Appointment requirements.—The additional participants described in subparagraph (A) shall be—

(i) appointed not later than January 31, 1998;

(ii) selected without regard to political affiliation or past partisan activity; and

(iii) representative of the diversity of thought in the fields of employee benefits and retirement income savings.

(4) Presiding officers.—The National Summit shall be presided over equally by representatives of the executive and legislative branches.

(f) National Summit Administration.—

(1) Administration.—In administering this section, the Secretary shall—

(A) request the cooperation and assistance of such other Federal departments and agencies and other parties referred to in subsection (b) as may be appropriate in the carrying out of this section;

(B) furnish all reasonable assistance to State agencies, area agencies, and other appropriate organizations to enable them to organize and conduct conferences in conjunction with the National Summit;

(C) make available for public comment a proposed agenda for the National Summit that reflects to the greatest extent possible the purposes for the National Summit set out in this section;

(D) prepare and make available background materials for the use of participants in the National Summit that the Secretary considers necessary; and

(E) appoint and fix the pay of such additional personnel as may be necessary to carry out the provisions of this section without regard to provisions of title 5, United States Code, governing appointments in the competitive service, and without regard to chapter 51 and subchapter III of chapter 53 of such title relating to classification and General Schedule pay rates.

(2) Duties.—The Secretary shall, in carrying out the responsibilities and functions of the Secretary under this section, and as part of the National Summit, ensure that—

(A) the National Summit shall be conducted in a manner that ensures broad participation of Federal, State, and local agencies and private organizations, professionals, and others involved in retirement income savings and provides a strong basis for assistance to be provided under paragraph (1)(B);

(B) the agenda prepared under paragraph (1)(C) for the National Summit is published in the Federal Register; and

(C) the personnel appointed under paragraph (1)(E) shall be fairly balanced in terms of points of views represented and shall be appointed without regard to political affiliation or previous partisan activities.

(3) Nonapplication of FACA.—The provisions of the Federal Advisory Committee Act (5 U.S.C. App.) shall not apply to the National Summit.

(g) Report.—The Secretary shall prepare a report describing the activities of the National Summit and shall submit the report to the President, the Speaker and Minority Leader of the House of Representatives, the Majority and Minority Leaders of the Senate, and the chief executive officers of the States not later than 90 days after the date on which the National Summit is adjourned.

(h) Definition.—For purposes of this section, the term "State" means a State, the District of Columbia, the Commonwealth of Puerto Rico, the Commonwealth of the Northern Mariana Islands, Guam, the Virgin Islands, American Samoa, and any other territory or possession of the United States.

(i) Authorization of Appropriations.—

(1) In general.—There is authorized to be appropriated for fiscal years beginning on or after October 1, 1997, such sums as are necessary to carry out this section.

(2) Authorization to accept private contributions.—In order to facilitate the National Summit as a public-private partnership, the Secretary may accept private contributions, in the form of money, supplies, or services, to defray the costs of the National Summit.

(j) Financial Obligation for Fiscal Year 1998.— The financial obligation for the Department of Labor for fiscal year 1998 shall not exceed the lesser of—

(1) one-half of the costs of the National Summit; or

(2) $250,000.

The private sector organization described in subsection (b) and contracted with by the Secretary shall be obligated for the balance of the cost of the National Summit.

(k) Contracts.—The Secretary may enter into contracts to carry out the Secretary's responsibilities under this section. The Secretary shall enter into a contract on a sole-source basis to ensure the timely completion of the National Summit in fiscal year 1998.

SEC. 518. AUTHORITY TO POSTPONE CERTAIN DEADLINES BY REASON OF PRESIDENTIALLY DECLARED DISASTER OR TERRORISTIC OR MILITARY ACTIONS.

In the case of a pension or other employee benefit plan, or any sponsor, administrator, participant, beneficiary, or other person with respect to such plan, affected by a Presidentially declared disaster (as defined in section 1033(h)(3) of the Internal Revenue Code of 1986) or a terroristic or military action (as defined in section 692(c)(2) of such Code), the Secretary may, notwithstanding any other provision of law, prescribe, by notice or otherwise, a period of up to 1 year which may be disregarded in determining the date by which any action is required or permitted to be completed under this Act. No plan shall be treated as failing to be operated in accordance with the terms of the plan solely as the result of disregarding any period by reason of the preceding sentence.

Editor's Note

ERISA §519, below, added by Pub. L. No. 111-148, §6601, is effective March 23, 2010.

SEC. 519. PROHIBITION ON FALSE STATEMENTS AND REPRESENTATIONS.

No person, in connection with a plan or other arrangement that is multiple employer welfare arrangement described in section 3(40), shall make a false statement or false representation of fact, knowing it to be false, in connection with the marketing or sale of such plan or arrangement, to any employee, any member of an employee organization, any beneficiary, any employer, any employee organization, the Secretary, or any State, or the representative or agent of any such person, State, or the Secretary, concerning—

(1) the financial condition or solvency of such plan or arrangement;

(2) the benefits provided by such plan or arrangement;

(3) the regulatory status of such plan or other arrangement under any Federal or State law governing collective bargaining, labor management relations, or intern union affairs; or

(4) the regulatory status of such plan or other arrangement regarding exemption from state regulatory authority under this Act.

This section shall not apply to any plan or arrangement that does not fall within the meaning of the term "multiple employer welfare arrangement" under section 3(40)(A).

Amendments to ERISA §519

Patient Protection and Affordable Care Act, 2010 (Pub. L. No. 111-148), as follows:

• ERISA §519 was added by Act §6601(a). Eff. Mar. 23, 2010.

> *Editor's Note*
>
> ERISA §520, below, added by Pub. L. No. 111-148, §6604(a), is effective March 23, 2010.

SEC. 520. APPLICABILITY OF STATE LAW TO COMBAT FRAUD AND ABUSE.

The Secretary may, for the purpose of identifying, preventing, or prosecuting fraud and abuse, adopt regulatory standards establishing, or issue an order relating to a specific person establishing, that a person engaged in the business of providing insurance through a multiple employer welfare arrangement described in section 3(40) is subject to the laws of the States in which such person operates which regulate insurance in such State, notwithstanding section 514(b)(6) of this Act or the Liability Risk Retention Act of 1986, and regardless of whether the law of the State is otherwise preempted under any of such provisions. This section shall not apply to any plan or arrangement that does not fall within the meaning of the term "multiple employer welfare arrangement" under section 3(40)(A).

Amendments to ERISA §520

Patient Protection and Affordable Care Act, 2010 (Pub. L. No. 111-148), as follows:

• ERISA §520 was added by Act §6604(a). Eff. Mar. 23, 2010.

> *Editor's Note*
>
> ERISA §521, below, added by Pub. L. No. 111-148, §6605(a), is effective March 23, 2010.

SEC. 521. ADMINISTRATIVE SUMMARY CEASE AND DESIST ORDERS AND SUMMARY SEIZURE ORDERS AGAINST MULTIPLE EMPLOYER WELFARE ARRANGEMENTS IN FINANCIALLY HAZARDOUS CONDITION.

(a) In General.—The Secretary may issue a cease and desist (ex parte) order under this title if it appears to the Secretary that the alleged conduct of a multiple employer welfare arrangement described in section 3(40), other than a plan or arrangement described in subsection (g), is fraudulent, or creates an immediate danger to the public safety or welfare, or is causing or can be reasonably expected to cause significant, imminent, and irreparable public injury.

(b) Hearing.—A person that is adversely affected by the issuance of a cease and desist order under subsection (a) may request a hearing by the Secretary regarding such order. The Secretary may require that a proceeding under this section, including all related information and evidence, be conducted in a confidential manner.

(c) Burden of Proof.—The burden of proof in any hearing conducted under subsection (b) shall be on the party requesting the hearing to show cause why the cease and desist order should be set aside.

(d) Determination.—Based upon the evidence presented at a hearing under subsection (b), the cease and desist order involved may be affirmed, modified, or set aside by the Secretary in whole or in part.

(e) Seizure.—The Secretary may issue a summary seizure order under this title if it appears that a multiple employer welfare arrangement is in a financially hazardous condition.

(f) Regulations.—The Secretary may promulgate such regulations or other guidance as may be necessary or appropriate to carry out this section.

(g) Exception.—This section shall not apply to any plan or arrangement that does not fall within the meaning of the term "multiple employer welfare arrangement" under section 3(40)(A).

Amendments to ERISA §521

Patient Protection and Affordable Care Act, 2010 (Pub. L. No. 111-148), as follows:

• ERISA §521 was added by Act §6605(a). Eff. Mar. 23, 2010.

Part 6—Continuation Coverage and Additional Standards for Group Health Plans

SEC. 601. PLANS MUST PROVIDE CONTINUATION COVERAGE TO CERTAIN INDIVIDUALS.

(a) In General.—The plan sponsor of each group health plan shall provide, in accordance with this part, that each qualified beneficiary who would lose coverage under the plan as a result of a qualifying event is entitled, under the plan, to elect, within the election period, continuation coverage under the plan.

(b) Exception for Certain Plans.—Subsection (a) shall not apply to any group health plan for any calendar year if all employers maintaining such plan normally employed fewer than 20 employees on a typical business day during the preceding calendar year.

Amendment to ERISA §601

Omnibus Budget Reconciliation Act of 1989 (Pub. L. No. 101-239), as follows:

● ERISA §601(b) was amended by Act §§7862(c)(1)(B), 7891(a)(1) by striking at the end: "Under regulations, rules similar to the rules of subsections (a) and (b) of section 52 of title 26 (relating to employers under common control) shall apply for purposes of this subsection." Eff. for years beginning after 1986. Also, Act §7891(a)(1) substituted "Internal Revenue Code of 1986" for "Internal Revenue Code of 1954", which for purposes of codification was translated as "title 26". Eff. as if included in Pub. L. No. 99-514.

SEC. 602. CONTINUATION COVERAGE.

For purposes of section 601, the term "continuation coverage" means coverage under the plan which meets the following requirements:

(1) Type of benefit coverage.—The coverage must consist of coverage which, as of the time the coverage is being provided, is identical to the coverage provided under the plan to similarly situated beneficiaries under the plan with respect to whom a qualifying event has not occurred. If coverage is modified under the plan for any group of similarly situated beneficiaries, such coverage shall also be modified in the same manner for all individuals who are qualified beneficiaries under the plan pursuant to this part in connection with such group.

(2) Period of coverage.—The coverage must extend for at least the period beginning on the date of the qualifying event and ending not earlier than the earliest of the following:

(A) Maximum required period.—

(i) General rule for terminations and reduced hours.—In the case of a qualifying event described in section 603(2), except as provided in clause (ii), the date which is 18 months after the date of the qualifying event.

(ii) Special rule for multiple qualifying events.—If a qualifying event (other than a qualifying event described in section 603(6)) occurs during the 18 months after the date of a qualifying event described in section 603(2), the date which is 36 months after the date of the qualifying event described in section 603(2).

(iii) Special rule for certain bankruptcy proceedings.—In the case of a qualifying event described in section 603(6) (relating to bankruptcy proceedings), the date of the death of the covered employee or qualified beneficiary (described in section 607(3)(C)(iii)), or in the case of the surviving spouse or dependent children of the covered employee, 36 months after the date of the death of the covered employee.

(iv) General rule for other qualifying events.— In the case of a qualifying event not described in section 603(2) or 603(6), the date which is 36 months after the date of the qualifying event.

Editor's Note

ERISA §602(2)(A)(v) and (vi), below, were amended by Pub. L. No. 111-344, §116(a), effective for periods of coverage which would (without regard to the amendments made by that section) end on or after December 31, 2010.

(v) Special rule for PBGC recipients.—In the case of a qualifying event described in section 603(2) with respect to a covered employee who (as of such qualifying event) has a nonforfeitable right to a benefit any portion of which is to be paid by the Pension Benefit Guaranty Corporation under title IV, notwithstanding clause (i) or (ii), the date of the death of the covered employee, or in the case of the surviving spouse or dependent children of the covered employee, 24 months after the date of the death of the covered employee. The preceding sentence shall not require any period of coverage to extend beyond December 31, 2010 *February 12, 2011*.

(vi) Special rule for TAA-eligible individuals.—In the case of a qualifying event described in section 603(2) with respect to a covered employee who is (as of the date that the period of coverage would, but for this clause or clause (vii), otherwise terminate under clause (i) or (ii)) a TAA-eligible individual (as defined in section 605(b)(4)(B)), the period of coverage shall not terminate by reason of clause (i) or (ii), as the case may be, before the later of the date specified in such clause or the date on which such individual ceases to be such a TAA-eligible individual. The preceding sentence shall not require any period of coverage to extend beyond December 31, 2010 *February 12, 2011*.

(vii) Medicare entitlement followed by qualifying event.—In the case of a qualifying event described in section 603(4) that occurs less than 18 months after the date the covered employee became entitled to benefits under title XVIII of the Social Security Act, the period of coverage for qualified beneficiaries other than covered employees shall not terminate under this subparagraph before the close of the 36-month period beginning on the date the covered employee became so entitled.

(viii) Special rule for disability.—In the case of a qualified beneficiary who is determined, under title II or XVI of the Social Security Act, to have been disabled at any time during the first 60 days of continuation coverage under this part, any reference in clause (i) or (ii) to 18 months is deemed a reference to 29 months (with respect to all qualified beneficiaries), but only if the qualified beneficiary has provided notice of such determination under section 606(3) before the end of such 18 months.

(B) End of plan.—The date on which the employer ceases to provide any group health plan to any employee.

(C) Failure to pay premium.—The date on which coverage ceases under the plan by reason of a failure to make timely payment of any premium required under the plan with respect to the qualified beneficiary. The payment of any premium (other than any payment referred to in the last sentence of paragraph (3)) shall be considered to be timely if made within 30 days after the date due or within such longer period as applies to or under the plan.

(D) Group health plan coverage or Medicare entitlement.—The date on which the qualified beneficiary first becomes, after the date of the election—

(i) covered under any other group health plan (as an employee or otherwise) which does not contain any exclusion, or limitation with respect to any preexisting condition of such beneficiary (other than such an exclusion or limitation which does not apply to (or is satisfied by) such beneficiary by reason of chapter 100 of the Internal Revenue Code of 1986, part 7 of this subtitle, or title XXVII of the Public Health Service Act), or

(ii) in the case of a qualified beneficiary other than a qualified beneficiary described in section 607(3)(C), entitled to benefits under title XVIII of the Social Security Act.

(E) Termination of extended coverage for disability.—In the case of a qualified beneficiary who is disabled at any time during the first 60 days of continuation coverage under this part, the month that begins more than 30 days after the date of the final determination under title II or XVI of the Social Security Act that the qualified beneficiary is no longer disabled.

(3) Premium requirements.—The plan may require payment of a premium for any period of continuation coverage, except that such premium—

(A) shall not exceed 102 percent of the applicable premium for such period, and

(B) may, at the election of the payor, be made in monthly installments.

In no event may the plan require the payment of any premium before the day which is 45 days after the day on which the qualified beneficiary made the initial election for continuation coverage. In the case of an individual described in the last sentence of paragraph (2)(A), any reference in subparagraph (A) of this paragraph to "102 percent" is deemed a reference to "150 percent" for any month after the 18th month of continuation coverage described in clause (i) or (ii) of paragraph (2)(A).

(4) No requirement of insurability.—The coverage may not be conditioned upon, or discriminate on the basis of lack of, evidence of insurability.

(5) Conversion option.—In the case of a qualified beneficiary whose period of continuation coverage expires under paragraph (2)(A), the plan must, during the 180-day period ending on such expiration date, provide to the qualified beneficiary the option of enrollment under a conversion health plan otherwise generally available under the plan.

Amendments to ERISA §602

Omnibus Trade Act of 2010 (Pub. L. No. 111-344), as follows:
- ERISA §602(2)(A)(v) was amended by Act §116(a)(1) by striking "December 31, 2010" and inserting "February 12, 2011". Eff. for periods of coverage which would (without regard to the amendments made by that section) end on or after Dec. 31, 2010.
- ERISA §602(2)(A)(vi) was amended by Act §116(a)(2) by striking "December 31, 2010" and inserting "February 12, 2011". Eff. for periods of coverage which would (without regard to the amendments made by that section) end on or after Dec. 31, 2010.

TAA Health Coverage Improvement Act of 2009 (Pub. L. No. 111-5), as follows:
- ERISA §602(2)(A)(v) was amended by Act §1899F(a)(1) by moving clause (v) to after clause (iv) and before flush left sentence beginning with "In the case of a qualified beneficiary". See Effective Date Note below.
- ERISA §602(2)(A) was amended by Act §1899F(a)(2) by striking "In the case of a qualified beneficiary" and inserting "(vi) Special rule for disability.—In the case of a qualified beneficiary". See Effective Date Note below.
- ERISA §602(2)(A) was amended by Act §1899F(a)(3) by redesignating clauses (v) and (vi), as amended, as clauses (vii) and (viii), respectively, and inserting new clauses (v) and (vi). See Effective Date Note below.
- **Effective Date Note.**—Amendments made by Act §1899F apply to periods of coverage which would (without regard to the amendments made by the section) end on or after the date of enactment of the Act (enacted: February 17, 2009). Act §1899F(d).

Health Insurance Portability and Accountability Act of 1996 (Pub. L. No. 104-191), as follows:
- ERISA §602(2)(A) was amended by Act §421(b)(1)(A), in closing provisions, by substituting "In the case of a qualified beneficiary" for "In the case of an individual" and "at any time during the first 60 days of continuation coverage under this part" for "at the time of a qualifying event described in section 603(2) of this title", striking "with respect to such event" after "(ii) to 18 months", and inserting "(with respect to all qualified beneficiaries)" after "29 months". Eff. Jan. 1, 1997, regardless of whether qualifying event occurred before, on, or after such date.
- ERISA §602(2)(D)(i) was amended by Act §421(b)(1)(B) by inserting "(other than such an exclusion or limitation which does not apply to (or is satisfied by) such beneficiary by reason of chapter 100 of title 26, part 7 of this subtitle, or title XXVII of the Public Health Service Act [42 U.S.C. 300gg et seq.])" before "or" at the end. Eff. Jan. 1, 1997, regardless of whether qualifying event occurred before, on, or after such date.
- ERISA §602(2)(E) was amended by Act §421(b)(1)(C) by substituting "at any time during the first 60 days of continuation

coverage under this part" for "at the time of a qualifying event described in section 603(2) of this title". Eff. Jan. 1, 1997, regardless of whether qualifying event occurred before, on, or after such date.

Small Business Job Protection Act of 1996 (Pub. L. No. 104-188), as follows:

- ERISA §602(2)(A)(v) was amended by Act §1704(g)(1)(B). Eff. for plan years after Dec. 31, 1989. ERISA §602(2)(A)(v) prior to amendment:

  (v) Qualifying event involving medicare entitlement.—In the case of an event described in section 603(4) of this title (without regard to whether such event is a qualifying event), the period of coverage for qualified beneficiaries other than the covered employee for such event or any subsequent qualifying event shall not terminate before the close of the 36-month period beginning on the date the covered employee becomes entitled to benefits under title XVIII of the Social Security Act.

Omnibus Budget Reconciliation Act of 1989 (Pub. L. No. 101-239), as follows:

- ERISA §602(2)(A) was amended by Act §6703(a)(1) by inserting after and below cl. (iv): "In the case of an individual who is determined, under title II or XVI of the Social Security Act, to have been disabled at the time of a qualifying event described in section 603(2) of this title, any reference in clause (i) or (ii) to 18 months with respect to such event is deemed a reference to 29 months, but only if the qualified beneficiary has provided notice of such determination under section 606(3) of this title before the end of such 18 months." Eff. for plan years beginning on or after Dec. 19, 1989.

- ERISA §602(2)(A)(iii) was amended by Act §7871(c) by substituting "described in section 603(6)" for "described in 603(6)". Eff. for plan years beginning on or after Dec. 19, 1989.

- ERISA §602(2)(A)(v) was amended by Act §7862(c)(5)(B), which directed the insertion of cl. (v) "at the end" of para. (2)(A), but was executed by inserting cl. (v) after cl. (iv), to reflect the probable intent of Congress. Eff. for plan years beginning on or after Dec. 19, 1989.

- ERISA §602(2)(D) was amended by Act §7862(c)(3)(B) by substituting "entitlement" for "eligibility" in heading and inserting "which does not contain any exclusion or limitation with respect to any preexisting condition of such beneficiary" after "or otherwise)" in cl. (i). Eff. for plan years beginning on or after Dec. 31, 1989.

- ERISA §602(2)(E) was added by Act §6703(a)(2). Eff. for plan years beginning on or after Dec. 19, 1989.

- ERISA §602(3) was amended by Act §7862(c)(4)(A) by substituting "In no event may the plan require the payment of any premium before the day which is 45 days after the day on which the qualified beneficiary made the initial election for continuation coverage." for last sentence of para. (3), but was executed by making the substitution for the following sentence: "If an election is made after the qualifying event, the plan shall permit payment for continuation coverage during the period preceding the election to be made within 45 days of the date of the election.", notwithstanding the sentence added at the end of para. (3) by Act §6703(b). Act §6703(b) inserted at the end "In the case of an individual described in the last sentence of paragraph (2)(A), any reference in subparagraph (A) of this paragraph to '102 percent' is deemed a reference to '150 percent' for any month after the 18th month of continuation coverage described in clause (i) or (ii) of paragraph (2)(A)." Eff. for plan years beginning on or after Dec. 31, 1989.

Tax Reform Act of 1986 (Pub. L. No. 99-514), as follows:

- ERISA §602(1) was amended by Act §1895(d)(1)(B) by inserting "If coverage is modified under the plan for any group of similarly situated beneficiaries, such coverage shall also be modified in the same manner for all individuals who are qualified beneficiaries under the plan pursuant to this part in connection with such group." Eff. July 1, 1986, as if included in Pub. L. No. 99-272.

- ERISA §602(2)(A) was amended by Act §1895(d)(2)(B). Eff. July 1, 1986, as if included in Pub. L. No. 99-272. ERISA §602(2)(A) prior to amendment:

  (A) Maximum period.—In the case of—

(i) a qualifying event described in section 603(2) of this title (relating to terminations and reduced hours), the date which is 18 months after the date of the qualifying event, and

(ii) any qualifying event not described in clause (i), the date which is 36 months after the date of the qualifying event.

- ERISA §602(2)(C) was amended by Act §1895(d)(3)(B) by inserting "The payment of any premium (other than any payment referred to in the last sentence of paragraph (3)) shall be considered to be timely if made within 30 days after the date due or within such longer period as applies to or under the plan." Eff. July 1, 1986, as if included in Pub. L. No. 99-272.

- ERISA §602(2)(D) was amended by Act §1895(d)(4)(B)(ii)–(iii) by substituting "Group health plan coverage or Medicare eligibility" for "Reemployment or Medicare eligibility" as heading and substituting "covered under any other group health plan (as an employee or otherwise)" for "a covered employee under any other group health plan" in cl. (i). Eff. July 1, 1986, as if included in Pub. L. No. 99-272.

- ERISA §602(2)(E) was stricken by Act §1895(d)(4)(B)(i). Eff. July 1, 1986, as if included in Pub. L. No. 99-272. ERISA §602(2)(E) prior to amendment:

  (E) In the case of an individual who is a qualified beneficiary by reason of being the spouse of a covered employee, the date on which the beneficiary remarries and becomes covered under a group health plan.

Omnibus Budget Reconciliation Act of 1986 (Pub. L. No. 99-509), as follows:

- ERISA §602(2)(A)(ii) was amended by Act §9501(b)(1)(B)(i) by inserting "(other than a qualifying event described in section 603(6) of this title)". Eff. July 1, 1986, as if included in Pub. L. No. 99-272.

- ERISA §602(2)(A)(iii) was added by Act §9501(b)(1)(B)(iv) and former cl. (iii) was redesignated as (iv). Eff. July 1, 1986, as if included in Pub. L. No. 99-272.

- ERISA §602(2)(A)(iv) was amended by Act §9501(b)(1)(B)(ii)–(iii) by redesignating former cl. (iii) as (iv) and inserting "or 603(6)". Eff. July 1, 1986, as if included in Pub. L. No. 99-272.

- ERISA §602(2)(D)(ii) was amended by Act §9501(b)(2)(B) by inserting "in the case of a qualified beneficiary other than a qualified beneficiary described in section 607(3)(C) of this title" before "entitled". Eff. July 1, 1986, as if included in Pub. L. No. 99-272.

SEC. 603. QUALIFYING EVENT.

For purposes of this part, the term "qualifying event" means, with respect to any covered employee, any of the following events which, but for the continuation coverage required under this part, would result in the loss of coverage of a qualified beneficiary:

(1) The death of the covered employee.

(2) The termination (other than by reason of such employee's gross misconduct), or reduction of hours, of the covered employee's employment.

(3) The divorce or legal separation of the covered employee from the employee's spouse.

(4) The covered employee becoming entitled to benefits under title XVIII of the Social Security Act.

(5) A dependent child ceasing to be a dependent child under the generally applicable requirements of the plan.

(6) A proceeding in a case under title 11, United States Code, commencing on or after July 1, 1986, with respect to the employer from whose employment the covered employee retired at any time.

In the case of an event described in paragraph (6), a loss of coverage includes a substantial elimination of coverage with respect to a qualified beneficiary described in section 607(3)(C) within one year before or after the date of commencement of the proceeding.

Amendments to ERISA §603

Omnibus Budget Reconciliation Act of 1986 (Pub. L. No. 99-509), as follows:

● ERISA §603 was added by Act §9501(a)(2) and the last sentence was amended. Eff. as if included in Pub. L. No. 99-272.

SEC. 604. APPLICABLE PREMIUM.

For purposes of this part—

(1) In general.—The term "applicable premium" means, with respect to any period of continuation coverage of qualified beneficiaries, the cost to the plan for such period of the coverage for similarly situated beneficiaries with respect to whom a qualifying event has not occurred (without regard to whether such cost is paid by the employer or employee).

(2) Special rule for self-insured plans.—To the extent that a plan is a self-insured plan—

(A) In general.—Except as provided in subparagraph (B), the applicable premium for any period of continuation coverage of qualified beneficiaries shall be equal to a reasonable estimate of the cost of providing coverage for such period for similarly situated beneficiaries which—

(i) is determined on an actuarial basis, and

(ii) takes into account such factors as the Secretary may prescribe in regulations.

(B) Determination on basis of past cost.—If an administrator elects to have this subparagraph apply, the applicable premium for any period of continuation coverage of qualified beneficiaries shall be equal to—

(i) the cost to the plan for similarly situated beneficiaries for the same period occurring during the preceding determination period under paragraph (3), adjusted by

(ii) the percentage increase or decrease in the implicit price deflator of the gross national product (calculated by the Department of Commerce and published in the Survey of Current Business) for the 12-month period ending on the last day of the sixth month of such preceding determination period.

(C) Subparagraph (B) not to apply where significant change.—An administrator may not elect to have subparagraph (B) apply in any case in which there is any significant difference, between the determination period and the preceding determination period, in coverage under, or in employees covered by, the plan. The determination under the preceding sentence for any determination period shall be made at the same time as the determination under paragraph (3).

(3) Determination period.—The determination of any applicable premium shall be made for a period of 12 months and shall be made before the beginning of such period.

SEC. 605. ELECTION.

(a) In General.—For purposes of this part—

(1) Election period.—The term "election period" means the period which—

(A) begins not later than the date on which coverage terminates under the plan by reason of a qualifying event,

(B) is of at least 60 days' duration, and

(C) ends not earlier than 60 days after the later of—

(i) the date described in subparagraph (A), or

(ii) in the case of any qualified beneficiary who receives notice under section 606(4), the date of such notice.

(2) Effect of election on other beneficiaries.—Except as otherwise specified in an election, any election of continuation coverage by a qualified beneficiary described in subparagraph (A)(i) or (B) of section 607(3) shall be deemed to include an election of continuation coverage on behalf of any other qualified beneficiary who would lose coverage under the plan by reason of the qualifying event. If there is a choice among types of coverage under the plan, each qualified beneficiary is entitled to make a separate selection among such types of coverage.

(b) Temporary Extension of COBRA Election Period for Certain Individuals.—

(1) In general.—In the case of a nonelecting TAA-eligible individual and notwithstanding subsection (a), such individual may elect continuation coverage under this part during the 60-day period that begins on the first day of the month in which the individual becomes a TAA-eligible individual, but only if such election is made not later than 6 months after the date of the TAA-related loss of coverage.

(2) Commencement of coverage; no reachback.—Any continuation coverage elected by a TAA-eligible individual under paragraph (1) shall commence at the beginning of the 60-day election period described in such paragraph and shall not include any period prior to such 60-day election period.

(3) Preexisting conditions.—With respect to an individual who elects continuation coverage pursuant to paragraph (1), the period—

(A) beginning on the date of the TAA-related loss of coverage, and

(B) ending on the first day of the 60-day election period described in paragraph (1),

shall be disregarded for purposes of determining the 63-day periods referred to in section 701(c)(2), section 2701(c)(2) of the Public Health Service Act, and section 9801(c)(2) of the Internal Revenue Code of 1986.

(4) Definitions.—For purposes of this subsection:

(A) Nonelecting TAA-eligible individual.—The term "nonelecting TAA-eligible individual" means a TAA eligible individual who—

(i) has a TAA-related loss of coverage; and

(ii) did not elect continuation coverage under this part during the TAA-related election period.

(B) TAA-eligible individual.—The term "TAA-eligible individual" means—

(i) an eligible TAA recipient (as defined in paragraph (2) of section 35(c) of the Internal Revenue Code of 1986), and

(ii) an eligible alternative TAA recipient (as defined in paragraph (3) of such section).

(C) TAA-related election period.—The term "TAA-related election period" means, with respect to a TAA-related loss of coverage, the 60-day election period under this part which is a direct consequence of such loss.

(D) TAA-related loss of coverage.—The term "TAA-related loss of coverage" means, with respect to an individual whose separation from employment gives rise to being an TAA-eligible individual, the loss of health benefits coverage associated with such separation.

Amendments to ERISA §605

Trade Act of 2002 (Pub. L. No. 107-210), as follows:
• ERISA §605 was amended by Act §203(e)(1) by designating existing provisions as subsec. (a), inserting heading, and adding subsec. (b). Eff. Nov. 6, 2002.

Tax Reform Act of 1986 (Pub. L. No. 99-514), as follows:
• ERISA §605(2) was amended by Act §1895(d)(5)(B) by inserting "of continuation coverage" after "any election" and inserting at the end "If there is a choice among types of coverage under the plan, each qualified beneficiary is entitled to make a separate selection among such types of coverage." Eff. as if included in Pub. L. No. 99-272.

SEC. 606. NOTICE REQUIREMENTS.

(a) In General.—In accordance with regulations prescribed by the Secretary—

(1) the group health plan shall provide, at the time of commencement of coverage under the plan, written notice to each covered employee and spouse of the employee (if any) of the rights provided under this subsection [part],

(2) the employer of an employee under a plan must notify the administrator of a qualifying event described in paragraph (1), (2), (4), or (6) of section 603 within 30 days (or, in the case of a group health plan which is a multiemployer plan, such longer period of time as may be provided in the terms of the plan) of the date of the qualifying event,

(3) each covered employee or qualified beneficiary is responsible for notifying the administrator of the occurrence of any qualifying event described in paragraph (3) or (5) of section 603 within 60 days after the date of the qualifying event and each qualified beneficiary who is determined, under title II or XVI of the Social Security Act, to have been disabled at any time during the first 60 days of continuation coverage under this part is responsible for notifying the plan administrator of such determination within 60 days after the date of the determination and for notifying the plan administrator within 30 days after the date of any final determination under such title or titles that the qualified beneficiary is no longer disabled, and

(4) the administrator shall notify—

(A) in the case of a qualifying event described in paragraph (1), (2), (4), or (6) of section 603, any qualified beneficiary with respect to such event, and

(B) in the case of a qualifying event described in paragraph (3) or (5) of section 603 where the covered employee notifies the administrator under paragraph (3), any qualified beneficiary with respect to such event,

of such beneficiary's rights under this subsection [part].

(b) Alternative Means of Compliance With Requirement for Notification of Multiemployer Plans by Employers.—The requirements of subsection (a)(2) shall be considered satisfied in the case of a multiemployer plan in connection with a qualifying event described in paragraph (2) of section 603 if the plan provides that the determination of the occurrence of such qualifying event will be made by the plan administrator.

(c) Rules Relating to Notification of Qualified Beneficiaries by Plan Administrator.—For purposes of subsection (a)(4), any notification shall be made within 14 days (or, in the case of a group health plan which is a multiemployer plan, such longer period of time as may be provided in the terms of the plan) of the date on which the administrator is notified under paragraph (2) or (3), whichever is applicable, and any such notification to an individual who is a qualified beneficiary as the spouse of the covered employee shall be treated as notification to all other qualified beneficiaries residing with such spouse at the time such notification is made.

Amendments to ERISA §606

Health Insurance Portability and Accountability Act of 1996 (Pub. L. No. 104-191), as follows:

- ERISA §606(a)(3) was amended by Act §421(b)(2) by substituting "at any time during the first 60 days of continuation coverage under this part" for "at the time of a qualifying event described in section 603(2) of this title". Eff. Jan. 1, 1997.

Omnibus Budget Reconciliation Act of 1989 (Pub. L. No. 101-239), as follows:

- ERISA §606 was amended by Act §7891(d)(1)(A)(ii) by designating first sentence as subsec. (a), adding subsec. (b), designating second sentence as subsec. (c), and substituting "For purposes of subsection (a)(4) of this section" for "For purposes of paragraph (4)". Eff. Jan. 1, 1990.
- ERISA §606 was amended by Act §7891(d)(1)(A)(i)(II) by inserting in last sentence "(or, in the case of a group health plan which is a multiemployer plan, such longer period of time as may be provided in the terms of the plan)" after "14 days". Eff. Jan. 1, 1990.
- ERISA §606 was amended by Act §7891(d)(1)(A)(i)(I) by inserting "(or, in the case of a group health plan which is a multiemployer plan, such longer period of time as may be provided in the terms of the plan)" after "30 days" in para. (2). Eff. Jan. 1, 1990.
- ERISA §606 was amended by Act §6703(c) by inserting "and each qualified beneficiary who is determined, under title II or XVI of the Social Security Act, to have been disabled at the time of a qualifying event described in section 603(2) of this title is responsible for notifying the plan administrator of such determination within 60 days after the date of the determination and for notifying the plan administrator within 30 days after the date of any final determination under such title or titles that the qualified beneficiary is no longer disabled" before comma in para. (3). Eff. Dec. 19, 1989.

Omnibus Budget Reconciliation Act of 1986 (Pub. L. No. 99-509), as follows:

- ERISA §606(2) was amended by Act §9501(d)(2) by substituting "(4), or (6)" for "or (4)". Eff. July 1, 1986, as if included in Pub. L. No. 99-272.
- ERISA §606(4)(A) was amended by Act §9501(d)(2) by substituting "(4), or (6)" for "or (4)". Eff. July 1, 1986, as if included in Pub. L. No. 99-272.

Tax Reform Act of 1986 (Pub. L. No. 99-514), as follows:

- ERISA §606(3) was amended by Act §1895(d)(6)(B) by inserting "within 60 days after the date of the qualifying event". Eff. Oct. 22, 1986.

SEC. 607. DEFINITIONS AND SPECIAL RULES.

For purposes of this part—

(1) Group health plan.—The term "group health plan" means an employee welfare benefit plan providing medical care (as defined in section 213(d) of title 26) to participants or beneficiaries directly or through insurance, reimbursement, or otherwise. Such term shall not include any plan substantially all of the coverage under which is for qualified long-term care services as defined in section 7702(B) of such Code.

(2) Covered employee.—The term "covered employee" means an individual who is (or was) provided coverage under a group health plan by virtue of the performance of services by the individual for one or more persons maintaining the plan (including as an employee defined in section 401(c)(1) of the Internal Revenue Code of 1986).

(3) Qualified beneficiary.—

(A) In general.—The term "qualified beneficiary" means, with respect to a covered employee under a group health plan, any other individual who, on the day before the qualifying event for that employee, is a beneficiary under the plan—

(i) as the spouse of the covered employee, or

(ii) as the dependent child of the employee.

Such term shall also include a child who is born to or placed for adoption with the covered employee during the period of continuation coverage under this part.

(B) Special rule for terminations and reduced employment.—In the case of a qualifying event described in section 603(2), the term "qualified beneficiary" includes the covered employee.

(C) Special rule for retirees and widows.—In the case of a qualifying event described in section 603(6), the term "qualified beneficiary" includes a covered employee who had retired on or before the date of substantial elimination of coverage and any other individual who, on the day before such qualifying event, is a beneficiary under the plan—

(i) as the spouse of the covered employee,

(ii) as the dependent child of the employee, or

(iii) as the surviving spouse of the covered employee.

(4) Employer.—Subsection (n) (relating to leased employees) and subsection (t) (relating to application of controlled group rules to certain employee benefits) of section 414 of the Internal Revenue Code of 1986 shall apply for purposes of this part in the same manner and to the same extent as such subsections apply for purposes of section 106 of such Code. Any regulations prescribed by the Secretary pursuant to the preceding sentence shall be consistent and coextensive with any regulations prescribed for similar purposes by the Secretary of the Treasury (or such Secretary's delegate) under such subsections.

(5) Optional extension of required period.—A group health plan shall not be treated as failing to meet the requirements of this part solely because the plan provides both—

(A) that the period of extended coverage referred to in section 602(2) commences with the date of the loss of coverage, and

(B) that the applicable notice period provided under section 606(a)(2) commences with the date of the loss of coverage.

Amendments to ERISA §607

Health Insurance Portability and Accountability Act of 1996 (Pub. L. No. 104-191), as follows:

● ERISA §607(1) was amended by Act §321(d)(2) by inserting at the end "Such term shall not include any plan substantially all of the coverage under which is for qualified long-term care services (as defined in §7702B(c) of title 26)." Eff. for contracts issued after Dec. 31, 1996.

● ERISA §607(3)(A) was amended by Act §421(b)(3) by inserting at the end "Such term shall also include a child who is born to or placed for adoption with the covered employee during the period of continuation coverage under this part." Eff. Jan. 1, 1997.

Omnibus Budget Reconciliation Act of 1989 (Pub. L. No. 101-239), as follows:

● ERISA §607 was amended by Act §7891(d)(2)(B)(i)(I) by inserting "and special rules" after "Definitions" in section catch-line. Eff. Jan. 1, 1990.

● ERISA §607(1) was amended by Act §7862(c)(6)(A), which repealed §3011(b)(6) of Pub. L. No. 100-647 (see note below). Eff. as if included in Pub. L. No. 100-647.

● ERISA §607(1) was amended by Act §7891(a)(1) by substituting "Internal Revenue Code of 1986" for "Internal Revenue Code of 1954", which for purposes of codification was translated as "title 26". Eff. as if included in Pub. L. No. 99-514.

● ERISA §607(2) was amended by Act §7862(c)(2)(A) by substituting "the performance of services by the individual for 1 or more persons maintaining the plan (including as an employee defined in §401(c)(1) of title 26)" for "the individual's employment or previous employment with an employer". Eff. as if included in Pub. L. No. 100-647.

● ERISA §607(5) was added by Act §7891(d)(2)(B)(i)(II). Eff. Jan. 1, 1990.

Technical and Miscellaneous Revenue Act of 1988 (Pub. L. No. 100-647), as follows:

● ERISA §607(1) was amended by Act §3011(b)(6) by substituting "section 162(i)(2) of title 26" for "section 162(i)(3) of title 26", but was repealed by §7862(c)(6)(A) of Pub. L. No. 101-239 (see note above). Eff. for taxable years after Dec. 31, 1988, but did not apply to any plan for any plan year to which IRC §162(k), did not apply by reason of §10001(e)(2) of Pub. L. No. 99-272.

Tax Reform Act of 1986 (Pub. L. No. 99-514), as follows:

● ERISA §607(1) was amended by Act §1895(d)(8). ERISA §607(1) prior to amendment:

The term "group health plan" means an employee welfare benefit plan that is a group health plan (within the meaning of §162(i)(3) of title 26).

Eff. as if included in Pub. L. No. 99-272.

● ERISA §607(4) was added by Act §1895(d)(9)(A). Eff. as if included in Pub. L. No. 99-272.

Omnibus Budget Reconciliation Act of 1986 (Pub. L. No. 99-509), as follows:

● ERISA §607(3)(C) was added by Act §9501(c)(2). Eff. as if included in Pub. L. No. 99-272.

SEC. 608. REGULATIONS.

The Secretary may prescribe regulations to carry out the provisions of this part.

SEC. 609. ADDITIONAL STANDARDS FOR GROUP HEALTH PLANS.

(a) Group Health Plan Coverage Pursuant to Medical Child Support Orders.—

(1) In general.—Each group health plan shall provide benefits in accordance with the applicable requirements of any qualified medical child support order. A qualified medical child support order with respect to any participant or beneficiary shall be deemed to apply to each group health plan which has received such order, from which the participant or beneficiary is eligible to received benefits, and with respect to which the requirements of paragraph (4) are met.

(2) Definitions.—For purposes of this subsection—

(A) Qualified medical child support order.—The term "qualified medical child support order" means a medical child support order—

(i) which creates or recognizes the existence of an alternate recipient's right to, or assigns to an alternate recipient the right to, receive benefits for which a participant or beneficiary is eligible under a group health plan, and

(ii) with respect to which the requirements of paragraphs (3) and (4) are met.

(B) Medical child support order.—The term "medical child support order" means any judgment, decree, or order (including approval of a settlement agreement) which—

(i) provides for child support with respect to a child of a participant under a group health plan or provides for health benefit coverage to such a child is made pursuant to a State domestic relations law (including a community property law), and relates to benefits under such plan, or

(ii) is made pursuant to a law relating to medical child support described in section 1908 of the Social Security Act (as added by section 13822 [13623(b)] of the Omnibus Budget Reconciliation Act of 1993) with respect to a group health plan,

if such judgment, decree, or order—

(I) is issued by a court of competent jurisdiction or

(II) is issued through an administrative process established under State law and has the force and effect of law under applicable State law. For purposes of this subparagraph, an administrative notice which is issued pursuant to an administrative process referred to in subclause (II) of the preceding sentence and which has the effect of an order described in clause (i) or (ii) of the preceding sentence shall be treated as such an order.

(C) Alternate recipient.—The term "alternate recipient" means any child of a participant who is recognized under a medical child support order as having a right to enrollment under a group health plan with respect to such participant.

(D) Child.—The term "child" includes any child adopted by, or placed for adoption with, a participant of a group health plan.

(3) Information to be included in qualified order.—A medical child support order meets the requirements of this paragraph only if such order clearly specifies—

(A) the name and the last known mailing address (if any) of the participant and the name and mailing address of each alternate recipient covered by the order, except that, to the extent provided in the order, the name and mailing address of an official of state or a political subdivision thereof may be substituted for the mailing address of any such alternate recipient.

(B) a reasonable description of the type of coverage to be provided by the plan to each such alternate recipient, or the manner in which such type of coverage is to be determined, and

(C) the period to which such order applies.

(4) Restriction on new types or forms of benefits.—A medical child support order meets the requirements of this paragraph only if such order does not require a plan to provide any type or form of benefit, or any option, not otherwise provided under the plan, except to the extent necessary to meet the requirements of a law relating to medical child support described in section 1908 of the Social Security Act (as added by section 13822 [13623(b)] of the Omnibus Budget Reconciliation Act of 1993).

(5) Procedural requirements.—

(A) Timely notifications and determinations.—In the case of any medical child support order received by a group health plan—

(i) the plan administrator shall promptly notify the participant and each alternate recipient of the receipt of such order and the plan's procedures for determining whether medical child support orders are qualified medical child support orders, and

(ii) within a reasonable period after receipt of such order, the plan administrator shall determine whether such order is a qualified medical child support order and notify the participant and each alternate recipient of such determination.

(B) Establishment of procedures for determining qualified status of orders.—Each group health plan shall establish reasonable procedures to determine whether medical child support orders are qualified medical child support orders and to administer the provision of benefits under such qualified orders. Such procedures—

(i) shall be in writing,

(ii) shall provide for the notification of each person specified in a medical child support order as eligible to receive benefits under the plan (at the address included in the medical child support order) of such procedures promptly upon receipt by the plan of the medical child support order, and

(iii) shall permit an alternate recipient to designate a representative for receipt of copies of notices that are sent to the alternate recipient with respect to a medical child support order.

(C) National medical support notice deemed to be a qualified medical child support order.—

(i) In general.—If the plan administrator of a group health plan which is maintained by the employer of a noncustodial parent of a child or to which such an employer contributes receives an appropriately completed National Medical Support Notice promulgated pursuant to section 401(b) of the Child Support Performance and Incentive Act of 1998 in the case of such child, and the Notice meets the requirements of paragraphs (3) and (4), the Notice shall be deemed to be a qualified medical child support order in the case of such child.

(ii) Enrollment of Child in Plan.—In any case in which an appropriately completed National Medical Support Notice is issued in the case of a child of a participant under a group health plan who is a noncustodial parent of the child, and the Notice is deemed under clause (i) to be a qualified medical child support order, the plan administrator, within 40 business days after the date of the Notice, shall—

(I) notify the State agency issuing the Notice with respect to such child whether coverage of the child is available under the terms of the plan and, if so, whether such child is covered under the plan and either the effective date of the coverage or, if necessary, any steps to be taken by the custodial parent (or by the official of a State or political subdivision thereof substituted for the name of such child pursuant to paragraph (3)(A)) to effectuate the coverage; and

(II) provide to the custodial parent (or such substituted official) a description of the coverage available and any forms or documents necessary to effectuate such coverage.

(iii) Rule of Construction.—Nothing in this subparagraph shall be construed as requiring a group health plan, upon receipt of a National Medical Support Notice, to provide benefits under the plan (or eligibility for such benefits) in addition to benefits (or eligibility for benefits) provided under the terms of the plan as of immediately before receipt of such Notice.

(6) Actions taken by fiduciaries.—If a plan fiduciary acts in accordance with part 4 of this subtitle in treating a medical child support order as being (or not being) a qualified medical child support order, then the plan's obligation to the participant and each alternate recipient shall be discharged to the extent of any payment made pursuant to such act of the fiduciary.

(7) Treatment of alternate recipients.—

(A) Treatment as beneficiary generally.—A person who is an alternate recipient under a qualified medical child support order shall be considered a beneficiary under the plan for purposes of any provision of this Act.

(B) Treatment as participant for purposes of reporting and disclosure requirements.—A person who is an alternate recipient under any medical child support order shall be considered a participant under the plan for purposes of the reporting and disclosure requirements of part 1.

(8) **Direct provision of benefits provided to alternate recipients.**—Any payment for benefits made by a group health plan pursuant to a medical child support order in reimbursement for expenses paid by an alternate recipient or an alternate recipient's custodial parent or legal guardian shall be made to the alternate recipient or the alternate recipient's custodial parent or legal guardian.

(9) **Payment to State official treated as satisfaction of plan's obligation to make payment to alternate recipient.**—Payment of benefits by a group health plan to an official of a State or political subdivision thereof whose names and addresses have been substituted for the address of an alternate recipient in a qualified medical child support order, pursuant to paragraph (3)(A), shall be treated, for purposes of this title, as payment of benefits to the alternate recipient.

(b) **Rights of States With Respect to Group Health Plans Where Participants or Beneficiaries Thereunder Are Eligible for Medicaid Benefits.**—

(1) **Compliance by plans with assignment of rights.**—A group health plan shall provide that payment for benefits with respect to a participant under the plan will be made in accordance with any assignment of rights made by or on behalf of such participant or a beneficiary of the participant as required by a State plan for medical assistance approved under title XIX of the Social Security Act pursuant to section 1912(a)(1)(A) of such Act (as in effect on the date of the enactment of the Omnibus Budget Reconciliation Act of 1993 [enacted Aug. 10, 1993]).

(2) **Enrollment and provision of benefits without regard to Medicaid eligibility.**—A group health plan shall provide that, in enrolling an individual as a participant or beneficiary or in determining or making any payments for benefits of an individual as a participant or beneficiary, the fact that the individual is eligible for or is provided medical assistance under a State plan for medical assistance approved under title XIX of the Social Security Act will not be taken into account.

(3) **Acquisition by States of rights of third parties.**—A group health plan shall provide that, to the extent that payment has been made under a State plan for medical assistance approved under title XIX of the Social Security Act in any case in which a group health plan has a legal liability to make payment for items or services constituting such assistance, payment for benefits under the plan will be made in accordance with any State law which provides that the State has acquired the rights with respect to a participant to such payment for such items or services.

(c) **Group Health Plan Coverage of Dependent Children in Cases of Adoption.**—

(1) **Coverage effective upon placement for adoption.**—In any case in which a group health plan provides coverage for dependent children of participants or beneficiaries, such plan shall provide benefits to dependent children placed with participants or beneficiaries for adoption under the same terms and conditions as apply in the case of dependent children who are natural children of participants or beneficiaries under the plan, irrespective of whether the adoption has become final.

(2) **Restrictions based on preexisting conditions at time of placement for adoption prohibited.**—A group health plan may not restrict coverage under the plan of any dependent child adopted by a participant or beneficiary, or placed with a participant or beneficiary for adoption, solely on the basis of a preexisting condition of such child at the time that such child would otherwise become eligible for coverage under the plan, if the adoption or placement for adoption occurs while the participant or beneficiary is eligible for coverage under the plan.

(3) **Definitions.**—For purposes of this subsection—

(A) Child.—The term "child" means, in connection with any adoption, or placement for adoption, of the child, an individual who has not attained age 18 as of the date of such adoption or placement for adoption.

(B) Placement for adoption.—The term "placement", or being "placed", for adoption, in connection with any placement for adoption of a child with any person, means the assumption and retention by such person of a legal obligation for total or partial support of such child in anticipation of adoption of such child. The child's placement with such person terminates upon the termination of such legal obligation.

(d) **Continued Coverage of Costs of a Pediatric Vaccine Under Group Health Plans.**—A group health plan may not reduce its coverage of the costs of pediatric vaccines (as defined under section 1928(h)(6) of the Social Security Act as amended by section 13830 [13631(b)] of the Omnibus Budget Reconciliation Act of 1993) below the coverage it provided as of May 1, 1993.

(e) **Regulations.**—Any regulations prescribed under this section shall be prescribed by the Secretary of Labor, in consultation with the Secretary of Health and Human Services.

Amendments to ERISA §609

Child Support Performance and Incentive Act of 1998 (Pub. L. No. 105-200), as follows:

- ERISA §609(a)(2)(B)(ii) was amended by Act §401(h)(2)(A)(iii) by substituting "is made pursuant to" for "enforces". Eff. as if included in Pub. L. No. 103-66.
- ERISA §609(a)(2)(D) was added by Act §401(h)(2)(B). Eff. as if included in Pub. L. No. 103-66.
- ERISA §609(a)(5)(C) was added by Act §401(d). Eff. as if included in Pub. L. No. 103-66.
- ERISA §609(a)(9) was amended by Act §401(h)(3)(A) by substituting "the address of an alternate recipient" for "the name and address of an alternate recipient". Eff. as if included in §5611(b) of Pub. L. No. 105-33.

Taxpayer Relief Act of 1997 (Pub. L. No. 105-33), as follows:

- ERISA §609(a)(1) was amended by Act §5613(b) by inserting at the end: "A qualified medical child support order with respect to any participant or beneficiary shall be deemed to apply to each group health plan which has received such order, from which the participant or beneficiary is eligible to receive benefits, and with respect to which the requirements of paragraph (4) are met." Eff. Aug. 5, 1997.
- ERISA §609(a)(2)(B) was amended by Act §5612(a) by inserting at the end of concluding provisions: "For purposes of this subparagraph, an administrative notice which is issued pursuant to an administrative process referred to in subclause (II) of the preceding sentence and which has the effect of an order described in clause (i) or (ii) of the preceding sentence shall be treated as such an order." Eff. as if included in Pub. L. No. 104-193.
- ERISA §609(a)(3)(A) was amended by Act §5611(a) by inserting at the end "except that, to the extent provided in the order, the name and mailing address of an official of a State or a political subdivision thereof may be substituted for the mailing address of any such alternate recipient," . Eff. Aug. 5, 1997.
- ERISA §609(a)(3)(B) was amended by Act §5613(a)(1)–(2) by striking "by the plan" after "to be provided" and inserting "and" at end. Eff. Aug. 5, 1997.
- ERISA §609(a)(3)(C) was amended by Act §5613(a)(3) by substituting a period for ", and" at end. Eff. Aug. 5, 1997.
- ERISA §609(a)(3)(D) was stricken by Act §5613(a)(4). Eff. Aug. 5, 1997. ERISA §609(a)(3)(D) prior to amendment:
  (D) each plan to which such order applies.
- ERISA §609(a)(9) was added by Act §5611(b). Eff. Aug. 5, 1997.

Personal Responsibility and Work Opportunity Reconciliation Act of 1996 (Pub. L. No. 104-193), as follows:

- ERISA §609(a)(2)(B) was amended by Act §381(a) by substituting "which—" for "issued by a court of competent jurisdiction which—" in introductory provisions, substituting a comma for a period at end of cl. (ii), and inserting concluding provisions after cl. (ii). Eff. Aug. 22, 1996, although amendments could be delayed until Jan. 1, 1997.

Part 7—Group Health Plan Requirements

Subpart A—Requirements Relating to Portability, Access, and Renewability

SEC. 701. INCREASED PORTABILITY THROUGH LIMITATION ON PREEXISTING CONDITION EXCLUSIONS.

(a) Limitation on Preexisting Condition Exclusion Period; Crediting for Periods of Previous Coverage.—Subject to subsection (d), a group health plan, and a health insurance issuer offering group health coverage, may, with respect to a participant or beneficiary, impose a preexisting condition exclusion only if—

(1) such exclusion relates to a condition (whether physical or mental), regardless of the cause of the condition, for which medical advice, diagnosis, care, or treatment was recommended or received within the 6-month period ending on the enrollment date;

(2) such exclusion extends for a period of not more than 12 months (or 18 months in the case of a late enrollee) after the enrollment date; and

(3) the period of any such preexisting condition exclusion is reduced by the length of the aggregate of the periods of creditable coverage (if any, as described in subsection (c)(1)) applicable to the participant or beneficiary as of the enrollment date.

(b) Definitions.—For purposes of this part—

(1) Preexisting condition exclusion.—

(A) In general.—The term "preexisting condition exclusion" means, with respect to coverage, a limitation or exclusion of benefits relating to a condition based on the fact that the condition was present before the date of enrollment for such coverage, whether or not any medical advice, diagnosis, care, or treatment was recommended or received before such date.

(B) Treatment of genetic information.—Genetic information shall not be treated as a condition described in subsection (a)(1) in the absence of a diagnosis of the condition related to such information.

(2) Enrollment date.—The term "enrollment date" means, with respect to an individual covered under a group health plan, or health insurance coverage, the date of enrollment of the individual in the plan or, if earlier, the first day of the waiting period for such enrollment.

(3) Late enrollee.—The term "late enrollee" means, with respect to coverage under a group health plan, a participant or beneficiary who enrolls under the plan other than during—

(A) the first period in which the individual is eligible to enroll under the plan, or

(B) a special enrollment period under subsection (f).

(4) Waiting period.—The term "waiting period" means, with respect to a group health plan and an individual who is a potential participant or beneficiary in the plan, the period that must pass with respect to the individual before the individual is eligible to be covered for benefits under the terms of the plan.

(c) Rules Relating to Crediting Previous Coverage.—

(1) Creditable coverage defined.—For purposes of this part, the term "creditable coverage" means, with respect to an individual, coverage of the individual under any of the following:

(A) A group health plan.

(B) Health insurance coverage.

(C) Part A or part B of title XVIII of the Social Security Act.

(D) Title XIX of the Social Security Act, other than coverage consisting solely of benefits under section 1928.

(E) Chapter 55 of title 10, United States Code.

(F) A medical care program of the Indian Health Service or of a tribal organization.

(G) A State health benefits risk pool.

(H) A health plan offered under chapter 89 of title 5, United States Code.

(I) A public health plan (as defined in regulations).

(J) A health benefit plan under section 5(e) of the Peace Corps Act (22 U.S.C. 2504(e)).

Such term does not include coverage consisting solely of coverage of excepted benefits (as defined in section 733(c)).

(2) Not counting periods before significant breaks in coverage.—

(A) In general.—A period of creditable coverage shall not be counted, with respect to enrollment of an individual under a group health plan, if, after such period and before the enrollment date, there was a 63-day period during all of which the individual was not covered under any creditable coverage.

(B) Waiting period not treated as a break in coverage.—For purposes of subparagraph (A) and subsection (d)(4), any period that an individual is in a waiting period for any coverage under a group health plan (or for group health insurance coverage) or is in an affiliation period (as defined in subsection (g)(2)) shall not be taken into account in determining the continuous period under subparagraph (A).

Editor's Note

ERISA §701(c)(2)(C), below, was amended by Pub. L. No. 111-344, §114(b), effective for plan years beginning after December 31, 2010.

(C) TAA-eligible individuals.—In the case of plan years beginning before ~~January 1, 2011~~ *February 13, 2011*—

(i) TAA pre-certification period rule.—In the case of a TAA-eligible individual, the period be-

ginning on the date the individual has a TAA-related loss of coverage and ending on the date that is 7 days after the date of the issuance by the Secretary (or by any person or entity designated by the Secretary) of a qualified health insurance costs credit eligibility certificate for such individual for purposes of section 7527 of the Internal Revenue Code of 1986 shall not be taken into account in determining the continuous period under subparagraph (A).

(ii) Definitions.—The terms "TAA-eligible individual" and "TAA-related loss of coverage" have the meanings given such terms in section 605(b)(4).

(3) Method of crediting coverage.—

(A) Standard method.—Except as otherwise provided under subparagraph (B), for purposes of applying subsection (a)(3), a group health plan, and a group health insurance issuer offering group health insurance coverage, shall count a period of creditable coverage without regard to the specific benefits coverage offered during the period.

(B) Election of alternative method.—A group health plan, or a health insurance issuer offering group health insurance coverage, may elect to apply subsection (a)(3) based on coverage of any benefits within each of several classes or categories of benefits specified in regulations rather than as provided under subparagraph (A). Such election shall be made on a uniform basis for all participants and beneficiaries. Under such election a group health plan or issuer shall count a period of creditable coverage with respect to any class or category of benefits if any level of benefits is covered within such class or category.

(C) Plan notice.—In the case of an election with respect to a group health plan under subparagraph (B) (whether or not health insurance coverage is provided in connection with such plan), the plan shall—

(i) prominently state in any disclosure statements concerning the plan, and state to each enrollee at the time of enrollment under the plan, that the plan has made such election, and

(ii) include in such statements a description of the effect of this election.

(4) Establishment of period.—Periods of creditable coverage with respect to an individual shall be established through presentation of certifications described in subsection (e) or in such other manner as may be specified in regulations.

(d) Exceptions.—

(1) Exclusion not applicable to certain newborns.—Subject to paragraph (4), a group health plan, and a health insurance issuer offering group health insurance coverage, may not impose any preexisting condition exclusion in the case of an individual who, as of the last day of the 30-day period beginning with the date of birth, is covered under creditable coverage.

(2) Exclusion not applicable to certain adopted children.—Subject to paragraph (4), a group health plan, and a health insurance issuer offering group health insurance coverage, may not impose any preexisting condition exclusion in the case of a child who is adopted or placed for adoption before attaining 18 years of age and who, as of the last day of the 30-day period beginning on the date of the adoption or placement for adoption, is covered under creditable coverage. The previous sentence shall not apply to coverage before the date of such adoption or placement for adoption.

(3) Exclusion not applicable to pregnancy.—A group health plan, and a health insurance issuer offering group health insurance coverage, may not impose any preexisting condition exclusion relating to pregnancy as a preexisting condition.

(4) Loss if break in coverage.—Paragraphs (1) and (2) shall no longer apply to an individual after the end of the first 63-day period during all of which the individual was not covered under any creditable coverage.

(e) Certifications and Disclosure of Coverage.—

(1) Requirement for certification of period of creditable coverage.—

(A) In general.—A group health plan, and a health insurance issuer offering group health insurance coverage, shall provide the certification described in subparagraph (B)—

(i) at the time an individual ceases to be covered under the plan or otherwise becomes covered under a COBRA continuation provision,

(ii) in the case of an individual becoming covered under such a provision, at the time the individual ceases to be covered under such provision, and

(iii) on the request on behalf of an individual made not later than 24 months after the date of cessation of the coverage described in clause (i) or (ii), whichever is later.

The certification under clause (i) may be provided, to the extent practicable, at a time consistent with notices required under any applicable COBRA continuation provision.

(B) Certification.—The certification described in this subparagraph is a written certification of—

(i) the period of creditable coverage of the individual under such plan and the coverage (if any) under such COBRA continuation provision, and

(ii) the waiting period (if any) (and affiliation period, if applicable) imposed with respect to the individual for any coverage under such plan.

(C) Issuer compliance.—To the extent that medical care under a group health plan consists of group health insurance coverage, the plan is deemed to have satisfied the certification requirement under this paragraph if the issuer provides for such certification in accordance with this paragraph.

(2) Disclosure of information on previous benefits.—In the case of an election described in subsection (c)(3)(B) by a group health plan or health insurance issuer, if the plan enrolls an individual for coverage under the plan and the individual provides a certification of coverage of the individual under paragraph (1)—

(A) upon request of such plan, the entity which issued the certification provided by the individual shall promptly disclose to such requesting plan information on coverage of classes and categories of health benefits available under such entity's plan, and

(B) such entity may charge the requesting plan or issuer for the reasonable cost of disclosing such information.

(3) Regulations.—The Secretary shall establish rules to prevent an entity's failure to provide information under paragraph (1) or (2) with respect to previous coverage of an individual from adversely affecting any subsequent coverage of the individual under another group health plan or health insurance coverage.

(f) Special Enrollment Periods.—

(1) Individuals losing other coverage.—A group health plan, and a health insurance issuer offering group health insurance coverage in connection with a group health plan, shall permit an employee who is eligible, but not enrolled, for coverage under the terms of the plan (or a dependent of such an employee if the dependent is eligible, but not enrolled, for coverage under such terms) to enroll for coverage under the terms of the plan if each of the following conditions is met:

(A) The employee or dependent was covered under a group health plan or had health insurance coverage at the time coverage was previously offered to the employee or dependent.

(B) The employee stated in writing at such time that coverage under a group health plan or health insurance coverage was the reason for declining enrollment, but only if the plan sponsor or issuer (if applicable) required such a statement at such time and provided the employee with notice of such requirement (and the consequences of such requirement) at such time.

(C) The employee's or dependent's coverage described in subparagraph (A)—

(i) was under a COBRA continuation provision and the coverage under such provision was exhausted; or

(ii) was not under such a provision and either the coverage was terminated as a result of loss of eligibility for the coverage (including as a result of legal separation, divorce, death, termination of employment, or reduction in the number of hours of employment) or employer contributions toward such coverage were terminated.

(D) Under the terms of the plan, the employee requests such enrollment not later than 30 days after the date of exhaustion of coverage described in subparagraph (C)(i) or termination of coverage or employer contribution described in subparagraph (C)(ii).

(2) For dependent beneficiaries.—

(A) In general.—If—

(i) a group health plan makes coverage available with respect to a dependent of an individual,

(ii) the individual is a participant under the plan (or has met any waiting period applicable to becoming a participant under the plan and is eligible to be enrolled under the plan but for a failure to enroll during a previous enrollment period), and

(iii) a person becomes such a dependent of the individual through marriage, birth, or adoption or placement for adoption,

the group health plan shall provide for a dependent special enrollment period described in subparagraph (B) during which the person (or, if not otherwise enrolled, the individual) may be enrolled under the plan as a dependent of the individual, and in the case of the birth or adoption of a child, the spouse of the individual may be enrolled as a dependent of the individual if such spouse is otherwise eligible forcoverage.

(B) Dependent special enrollment period.—A dependent special enrollment period under this subparagraph shall be a period of not less than 30 days and shall begin on the later of—

(i) the date dependent coverage is made available, or

(ii) the date of the marriage, birth, or adoption or placement for adoption (as the case may be) described in subparagraph (A)(iii).

(C) No waiting period.—If an individual seeks coverage of a dependent during the first 30 days of such a dependent special enrollment period, the coverage of the dependent shall become effective—

(i) in the case of marriage, not later than the first day of the first month beginning after the date the completed request for enrollment is received;

(ii) in the case of a dependent's birth, as of the date of such birth; or

(iii) in the case of a dependent's adoption or placement for adoption, the date of such adoption or placement for adoption.

Editor's Note

ERISA §701(f)(3), below, was added by Pub. L. No. 111-3, §311(b)(1)(A). The model notices in this subsection are effective as of February 4, 2010. See amendment notes for details.

(3) Special rules for application in case of Medicaid and CHIP.—

(A) In general.—A group health plan, and a health insurance issuer offering group health insurance coverage in connection with a group health plan, shall permit an employee who is eligible, but not enrolled, for coverage under the terms of the plan (or a dependent of such an employee if the dependent is eligible, but not enrolled, for coverage under such terms) to enroll for coverage under the terms of the plan if either of the following conditions is met:

(i) Termination of Medicaid or CHIP coverage.—The employee or dependent is covered under a Medicaid plan under title XIX of the Social Security Act or under a State child health plan under title XXI of such Act and coverage of the employee or dependent under such a plan is terminated as a result of loss of eligibility for such coverage and the employee requests coverage under the group health plan (or health insurance coverage) not later than 60 days after the date of termination of such coverage.

(ii) Eligibility for employment assistance under Medicaid or CHIP.—The employee or dependent becomes eligible for assistance, with respect to coverage under the group health plan or health insurance coverage, under such Medicaid plan or State child health plan (including under any waiver or demonstration project conducted under or in relation to such a plan), if the employee requests coverage under the group health plan or health insurance coverage not later than 60 days after the date the employee or dependent is determined to be eligible for such assistance.

(B) Coordination with Medicaid and CHIP.—

(i) Outreach to employees regarding availability of Medicaid and CHIP coverage.—

(I) In general.—Each employer that maintains a group health plan in a State that provides medical assistance under a State Medicaid plan under title XIX of the Social Security Act, or child health assistance under a State child health plan under title XXI of such Act, in the form of premium assistance for the purchase of coverage under a group health plan, shall provide to each employee a written notice informing the employee of potential opportunities then currently available in the State in which the employee resides for premium assistance under such plans for health coverage of the employee or the employee's dependents.

(II) Model notice.—Not later than 1 year after the date of enactment of the Children's Health Insurance Program Reauthorization Act of 2009 [enacted Feb. 4, 2009], the Secretary and the Secretary of Health and Human Services, in consultation with Directors of State Medicaid agencies under title XIX of the Social Security Act and Directors of State CHIP agencies under title XXI of such Act, shall jointly develop national and State-specific model notices for purposes of subparagraph (A). The Secretary shall provide employers with such model notices so as to enable employers to timely comply with the requirements of subparagraph (A). Such model notices shall include information regarding how an employee may contact the State in which the employee resides for additional information regarding potential opportunities for such premium assistance, including how to apply for such assistance.

(III) Option to provide concurrent with provision of plan materials to employee.—An employer may provide the model notice applicable to the State in which an employee resides concurrent with the furnishing of materials notifying the employee of health plan eligibility, concurrent with materials provided to the employee in connection with an open season or election process conducted under the plan, or concurrent with the furnishing of the summary plan description as provided in section 104(b).

(ii) Disclosure about group health plan benefits to states for Medicaid and CHIP eligible individuals.—In the case of a participant or beneficiary of a group health plan who is covered under a Medicaid plan of a State under title XIX of the Social Security Act or under a State child health plan under title XXI of such Act, the plan administrator of the group health plan shall disclose to the State, upon request, information about the benefits available under the group health plan in sufficient specificity, as determined under regulations of the Secretary of Health and Human Services in consultation with the Secretary that require use of the model coverage coordination disclosure form developed under section 311(b)(1)(C) of the Children's Health Insurance Program Reauthorization Act of 2009, so as to permit the State to make a determination (under paragraph (2)(B), (3), or (10) of section 2105(c) of the Social Security Act or otherwise) concerning the cost-effectiveness of the State providing medical or child health assistance through premium assistance for the purchase of coverage under such group health plan and in order for the State to provide supplemental benefits required under paragraph (10)(E) of such section or other authority.

(g) Use of Affiliation Period by HMOs as Alternative to Preexisting Condition Exclusion.—

(1) In general.—In the case of a group health plan that offers medical care through health insurance cov-

erage offered by a health maintenance organization, the plan may provide for an affiliation period with respect to coverage through the organization only if—

(A) no preexisting condition exclusion is imposed with respect to coverage through the organization,

(B) the period is applied uniformly without regard to any health status-related factors, and

(C) such period does not exceed 2 months (or 3 months in the case of a late enrollee).

(2) Affiliation period.—

(A) Defined.—For purposes of this section, the term "affiliation period" means a period which, under the terms of the health insurance coverage offered by the health maintenance organization, must expire before the health insurance coverage becomes effective. The organization is not required to provide health care services or benefits during such period and no premium shall be charged to the participant or beneficiary for any coverage during that period.

(B) Beginning.—Such period shall begin on the enrollment date.

(C) Runs concurrently with waiting periods.— Any such affiliation period shall run concurrently with any waiting period under the plan.

(3) Alternative Methods.—A health maintenance organization described in paragraph (1) may use alternative methods, from those described in such paragraph, to address adverse selection as approved by the State insurance commissioner or official or officials designated by the State to enforce the requirements of part A of title XXVII of the Public Health Service Act for the State involved with respect to such issuer.

Amendments to ERISA §701

Omnibus Trade Act of 2010 (Pub. L. No. 111-344), as follows:
● ERISA §701(c)(2)(C) was amended by Act §114(b) by striking "January 1, 2011" and inserting "February 13, 2011". Eff. for plan years begining after Dec. 31, 2010.

TAA Health Coverage Improvement Act of 2009 (Pub. L. No. 111-5), as follows:
● ERISA §701(c)(2)(C) was added by Act, Div. B, §1899D(b). Eff. for plan years beg. after date of enactment [enacted: Feb. 17, 2009].

Children's Health Insurance Program Reauthorization Act of 2009, Pub. L. No. 111-3, as follows:
● ERISA §701(f) was amended by Act §311(b)(1)(A) by adding para. (3). See Effective Date Note, below.
● **Effective Date Note:** Act §3 provides:
   SEC. 3. GENERAL EFFECTIVE DATE; EXCEPTION FOR STATE LEGISLATION; CONTINGENT EFFECTIVE DATE; RELIANCE ON LAW.
   (a) General Effective Date.—Unless otherwise provided in this Act, subject to subsections (b) through (d), this Act (and the amendments made by this Act) shall take effect on April 1, 2009, and shall apply to child health assistance and medical assistance provided on or after that date.
   (b) Exception for State Legislation.—In the case of a State plan under title XIX or State child health plan under XXI of

the Social Security Act, which the Secretary of Health and Human Services determines requires State legislation in order for the respective plan to meet one or more additional requirements imposed by amendments made by this Act, the respective plan shall not be regarded as failing to comply with the requirements of such title solely on the basis of its failure to meet such an additional requirement before the first day of the first calendar quarter beginning after the close of the first regular session of the State legislature that begins after the date of enactment of this Act. For purposes of the previous sentence, in the case of a State that has a 2-year legislative session, each year of the session shall be considered to be a separate regular session of the State legislature.

(c) Coordination of CHIP Funding for Fiscal Year 2009.— Notwithstanding any other provision of law, insofar as funds have been appropriated under section 2104(a)(11), 2104(k), or 2104(l) of the Social Security Act, as amended by section 201 of Public Law 110-173, to provide allotments to States under CHIP for fiscal year 2009—

(1) any amounts that are so appropriated that are not so allotted and obligated before April 1, 2009 are rescinded; and

(2) any amount provided for CHIP allotments to a State under this Act (and the amendments made by this Act) for such fiscal year shall be reduced by the amount of such appropriations so allotted and obligated before such date.

(d) Reliance on Law.—With respect to amendments made by this Act (other than title VII) that become effective as of a date—

(1) such amendments are effective as of such date whether or not regulations implementing such amendments have been issued; and

(2) Federal financial participation for medical assistance or child health assistance furnished under title XIX or XXI, respectively, of the Social Security Act on or after such date by a State in good faith reliance on such amendments before the date of promulgation of final regulations, if any, to carry out such amendments (or before the date of guidance, if any, regarding the implementation of such amendments) shall not be denied on the basis of the State's failure to comply with such regulations or guidance.

• **Other Provision.** Act §311(b)(1)(C) and (D) provide:

(C) Working group to develop model coverage coordination disclosure form.—

(i) Medicaid, CHIP, and employer-sponsored coverage coordination working group.—

(I) In general.—Not later than 60 days after the date of enactment of this Act, the Secretary of Health and Human Services and the Secretary of Labor shall jointly establish a Medicaid, CHIP, and Employer-Sponsored Coverage Coordination Working Group (in this subparagraph referred to as the "Working Group"). The purpose of the Working Group shall be to develop the model coverage coordination disclosure form described in subclause (II) and to identify the impediments to the effective coordination of coverage available to families that include employees of employers that maintain group health plans and members who are eligible for medical assistance under title XIX of the Social Security Act or child health assistance or other health benefits coverage under title XXI of such Act.

(II) Model coverage coordination disclosure form described.—The model form described in this subclause is a form for plan administrators of group health plans to complete for purposes of permitting a State to determine the availability and cost-effectiveness of the coverage available under such plans to employees who have family members who are eligible for premium assistance offered under a State plan under title XIX or XXI of such Act and to allow for coordination of coverage for enrollees of such plans. Such form shall provide the following information in addition to such other information as the Working Group determines appropriate:

(aa) A determination of whether the employee is eligible for coverage under the group health plan.

(bb) The name and contract information of the plan administrator of the group health plan.

(cc) The benefits offered under the plan.

(dd) The premiums and cost-sharing required under the plan.

(ee) Any other information relevant to coverage under the plan.

(ii) Membership.—The Working Group shall consist of not more than 30 members and shall be composed of representatives of—

(I) the Department of Labor;

(II) the Department of Health and Human Services;

(III) State directors of the Medicaid program under title XIX of the Social Security Act;

(IV) State directors of the State Children's Health Insurance Program under title XXI of the Social Security Act;

(V) employers, including owners of small businesses and their trade or industry representatives and certified human resource and payroll professionals;

(VI) plan administrators and plan sponsors of group health plans (as defined in section 607(1) of the Employee Retirement Income Security Act of 1974);

(VII) health insurance issuers; and

(VIII) children and other beneficiaries of medical assistance under title XIX of the Social Security Act or child health assistance or other health benefits coverage under title XXI of such Act.

(iii) Compensation.—The members of the Working Group shall serve without compensation.

(iv) Administrative support.—The Department of Health and Human Services and the Department of Labor shall jointly provide appropriate administrative support to the Working Group, including technical assistance. The Working Group may use the services and facilities of either such Department, with or without reimbursement, as jointly determined by such Departments.

(v) Report.—

(I) Report by working group to the secretaries.—Not later than 18 months after the date of the enactment of this Act, the Working Group shall submit to the Secretary of Labor and the Secretary of Health and Human Services the model form described in clause (i)(II) along with a report containing recommendations for appropriate measures to address the impediments to the effective coordination of coverage between group health plans and the State plans under titles XIX and XXI of the Social Security Act.

(II) Report by secretaries to the congress.—Not later than 2 months after receipt of the report pursuant to subclause (I), the Secretaries shall jointly submit a report to each House of the Congress regarding the recommendations contained in the report under such subclause.

(vi) Termination.—The Working Group shall terminate 30 days after the date of the issuance of its report under clause (v).

(D) Effective dates.—The Secretary of Labor and the Secretary of Health and Human Services shall develop the initial model notices under section 701(f)(3)(B)(i)(II) of the Employee Retirement Income Security Act of 1974, and the Secretary of Labor shall provide such notices to employers, not later than the date that is 1 year after the date of enactment of this Act, and each employer shall provide the initial annual notices to such employer's employees beginning with the first plan year that begins after the date on which such initial model notices are first issued. The model coverage coordination disclosure form developed under subparagraph (C) shall apply with respect to requests made by States beginning with the first plan year that begins after the date on which such model coverage coordination disclosure form is first issued.

Departments of Veterans Affairs and HUD and Independent Agencies Appropriations Act of 1997 (Pub. L. No. 104-204), as follows:

• ERISA §701(c)(1) was amended by Act §603(b)(3)(H) by making a technical amendment to reference in original act which appears in text as reference to §733 of this title. Eff. with respect to group health plans for plan years beginning on and after Jan. 1, 1998.

SEC. 702. PROHIBITING DISCRIMINATION AGAINST INDIVIDUAL PARTICIPANTS AND BENEFICIARIES BASED ON HEALTH STATUS.

(a) In Eligibility to Enroll.—

(1) In general.—Subject to paragraph (2), a group health plan, and a health insurance issuer offering group health insurance coverage in connection with a group health plan, may not establish rules for eligibility (including continued eligibility) of any individual to enroll under the terms of the plan based on any of the following health status-related factors in relation to the individual or a dependent of the individual:

(A) Health status.

(B) Medical condition (including both physical and mental illnesses).

(C) Claims experience.

(D) Receipt of health care.

(E) Medical history.

(F) Genetic information.

(G) Evidence of insurability (including conditions arising out of acts of domestic violence).

(H) Disability.

(2) No application to benefits or exclusions.— To the extent consistent with §9801, paragraph (1) shall not be construed—

(A) to require a group health plan, or a group health insurance coverage, to provide particular benefits other than those provided under the terms of such plan or coverage; or

(B) to prevent such a plan or coverage from establishing limitations or restrictions on the amount, level, extent, or nature of the benefits or coverage for similarly situated individuals enrolled in the plan or coverage.

(3) Construction.—For purposes of paragraph (1), rules for eligibility to enroll under a plan include rules defining any applicable waiting periods for such enrollment.

(b) In Premium Contributions.—

(1) In general.—A group health plan, and a health insurance issuer offering health insurance coverage in connection with a group health plan, may not require any individual (as a condition of enrollment or continued enrollment under the plan) to pay a premium or contribution which is greater than such premium or contribution for a similarly situated individual enrolled in the plan on the basis of any health status-related factor in relation to the individual or to an individual enrolled under the plan as a dependent of the individual.

(2) Construction.—Nothing in paragraph (1) shall be construed—

(A) to restrict the amount that an employer may be charged for coverage under a group health plan except as provided in paragraph (3); or

(B) to prevent a group health plan, and a health insurance issuer offering group health insurance coverage, from establishing premium discounts or rebates or modifying otherwise applicable copayments or deductibles in return for adherence to programs of health promotion and disease prevention.

(3) No group-based discrimination on basis of genetic information.—

(A) In general.—For purposes of this section, a group health plan, and a health insurance issuer offering group health insurance coverage in connection with a group health plan, may not adjust premium or contribution amounts for the group covered under such plan on the basis of genetic information.

(B) Rule of construction.—Nothing in subparagraph (A) or in paragraphs (1) and (2) of subsection (d) shall be construed to limit the ability of a health insurance issuer offering health insurance coverage in connection with a group health plan to increase the premium for an employer based on the manifestation of a disease or disorder of an individual who is enrolled in the plan. In such case, the manifestation of a disease or disorder in one individual cannot also be used as genetic information about other group members and to further increase the premium for the employer.

(c) Genetic Testing.—

(1) Limitation on requesting or requiring genetic testing.—A group health plan, and a health insurance issuer offering health insurance coverage in connection with a group health plan, shall not request or require an individual or a family member of such individual to undergo a genetic test.

(2) Rule of construction.—Paragraph (1) shall not be construed to limit the authority of a health care professional who is providing health care services to an individual to request that such individual undergo a genetic test.

(3) Rule of construction regarding payment.—

(A) In general.—Nothing in paragraph (1) shall be construed to preclude a group health plan, or a health insurance issuer offering health insurance coverage in connection with a group health plan, from obtaining and using the results of a genetic test in making a determination regarding payment (as such term is defined for the purposes of applying the regulations promulgated by the Secretary of Health and Human Services under part C of title XI of the Social Security Act and section 264 of the Health Insurance Portability and Accountability Act of 1996, as may be revised from time to time) consistent with subsection (a).

(B) Limitation.—For purposes of subparagraph (A), a group health plan, or a health insurance issuer offering health insurance coverage in connection with a group health plan, may request only the minimum amount of information necessary to accomplish the intended purpose.

(4) **Research exception.**—Notwithstanding paragraph (1), a group health plan, or a health insurance issuer offering health insurance coverage in connection with a group health plan, may request, but not require, that a participant or beneficiary undergo a genetic test if each of the following conditions is met:

(A) The request is made, in writing, pursuant to research that complies with part 46 of title 45, Code of Federal Regulations, or equivalent Federal regulations, and any applicable State or local law or regulations for the protection of human subjects in research.

(B) The plan or issuer clearly indicates to each participant or beneficiary, or in the case of a minor child, to the legal guardian of such beneficiary, to whom the request is made that—

(i) compliance with the request is voluntary; and

(ii) non-compliance will have no effect on enrollment status or premium or contribution amounts.

(C) No genetic information collected or acquired under this paragraph shall be used for underwriting purposes.

(D) The plan or issuer notifies the Secretary in writing that the plan or issuer is conducting activities pursuant to the exception provided for under this paragraph, including a description of the activities conducted.

(E) The plan or issuer complies with such other conditions as the Secretary may by regulation require for activities conducted under this paragraph.

(d) **Prohibition on Collection of Genetic Information.—**

(1) **In general.**—A group health plan, and a health insurance issuer offering health insurance coverage in connection with a group health plan, shall not request, require, or purchase genetic information for underwriting purposes (as defined in section 733).

(2) **Prohibition on collection of genetic information prior to enrollment.**—A group health plan, and a health insurance issuer offering health insurance coverage in connection with a group health plan, shall not request, require, or purchase genetic information with respect to any individual prior to such individual's enrollment under the plan or coverage in connection with such enrollment.

(3) **Incidental collection.**—If a group health plan, or a health insurance issuer offering health insurance coverage in connection with a group health plan, obtains genetic information incidental to the requesting, requiring, or purchasing of other information concerning any individual, such request, requirement, or purchase shall not be considered a violation of paragraph (2) if such request, requirement, or purchase is not in violation of paragraph (1).

(e) **Application to All Plans.**—The provisions of subsections (a)(1)(F), (b)(3), (c), and (d), and subsection (b)(1) and section 701 with respect to genetic information, shall apply to group health plans and health insurance issuers without regard to section 732(a).

(f) **Genetic Information of a Fetus or Embryo.—** Any reference in this part to genetic information concerning an individual or family member of an individual shall—

(1) with respect to such an individual or family member of an individual who is a pregnant woman, include genetic information of any fetus carried by such pregnant woman; and

(2) with respect to an individual or family member utilizing an assisted reproductive technology, include genetic information of any embryo legally held by the individual or family member.

Amendments to ERISA §702

Genetic Information Nondiscrimination Act of 2008 (Pub. L. No. 110-233), as follows:

● ERISA §702(b)(2)(A) was amended by Act §101(a)(1) by inserting before the semicolon "except as provided in paragraph (3)". Eff. with respect to group health plans for plan years beginning after the date that is one year after the date of enactment (date of enactment: May 21, 2008), see Act §101(f)(2).

● ERISA §702(b)(3) was added by Act §101(a)(2). Eff. with respect to group health plans for plan years beginning after the date that is one year after the date of enactment (date of enactment: May 21, 2008), see Act §101(f)(2).

● ERISA §702(c)–(e) were added by Act §101(b). Eff. with respect to group health plans for plan years beginning after the date that is one year after the date of enactment (date of enactment: May 21, 2008), see Act §101(f)(2).

● ERISA §702(f) was added by Act §101(c). Eff. with respect to group health plans for plan years beginning after the date that is one year after the date of enactment (date of enactment: May 21, 2008), see Act §101(f)(2).

● **Other Provision.** Act §101(f)(1) provides:

(1) Regulations.—The Secretary of Labor shall issue final regulations not later than 12 months after the date of enactment [May 21, 2008] of this Act to carry out the amendments made by this section.

SEC. 703. GUARANTEED RENEWABILITY IN MULTIEMPLOYER PLANS AND MULTIPLE EMPLOYER WELFARE ARRANGEMENTS.

A group health plan which is a multiemployer plan or which is a multiple employer welfare arrangement may not deny an employer whose employees are covered under such a plan continued access to the same or different coverage under the terms of such a plan, other than—

(1) for nonpayment of contributions;

(2) for fraud or other intentional misrepresentation of material fact by the employer;

(3) for noncompliance with material plan provisions;

(4) because the plan is ceasing to offer any coverage in a geographic area;

(5) in the case of a plan that offers benefits through a network plan, there is no longer any individual enrolled through the employer who lives, resides, or works in the service area of the network plan and the plan applies this paragraph uniformly without regard to the claims experience of employers or any health status-related factor in relation to such individuals or their dependents; and

(6) for failure to meet the terms of an applicable collective bargaining agreement, to renew a collective bargaining or other agreement requiring or authorizing contributions to the plan, or to employ employees covered by such an agreement.

Subpart B—Other Requirements

SEC. 711. STANDARDS RELATING TO BENEFITS FOR MOTHERS AND NEWBORNS.

(a) Requirements for Minimum Hospital Stay Following Birth.—

(1) In general.—A group health plan, and a health insurance issuer offering group health insurance coverage, may not—

(A) except as provided in paragraph (2)—

(i) restrict benefits for any hospital length of stay in connection with childbirth for the mother or newborn child, following a normal vaginal delivery, to less than 48 hours, or

(ii) restrict benefits for any hospital length of stay in connection with childbirth for the mother or newborn child, following a cesarean section, to less than 96 hours; or

(B) require that a provider obtain authorization from the plan or the issuer for prescribing any length of stay required under subparagraph (A) (without regard to paragraph (2)).

(2) Exception.—Paragraph (1)(A) shall not apply in connection with any group health plan or health insurance issuer in any case in which the decision to discharge the mother or her newborn child prior to the expiration of the minimum length of stay otherwise required under paragraph (1)(A) is made by an attending provider in consultation with the mother.

(b) Prohibitions.—A group health plan, and a health insurance issuer offering group health insurance coverage in connection with a group health plan, may not—

(1) deny to the mother or her newborn child eligibility, or continued eligibility, to enroll or to renew coverage under the terms of the plan, solely for the purpose of avoiding the requirements of this section;

(2) provide monetary payments or rebates to mothers to encourage such mothers to accept less than the minimum protections available under this section;

(3) penalize or otherwise reduce or limit the reimbursement of an attending provider because such provider provided care to an individual participant or beneficiary in accordance with this section;

(4) provide incentives (monetary or otherwise) to an attending provider to induce such provider to provide care to an individual participant or beneficiary in a manner inconsistent with this section; or

(5) subject to subsection (c)(3), restrict benefits for any portion of a period within a hospital length of stay required under subsection (a) in a manner which is less favorable than the benefits provided for any preceding portion of such stay.

(c) Rules of Construction.—

(1) Nothing in this section shall be construed to require a mother who is a participant or beneficiary—

(A) to give birth in a hospital; or

(B) to stay in the hospital for a fixed period of time following the birth of her child.

(2) This section shall not apply with respect to any group health plan, or any group health insurance coverage offered by a health insurance issuer, which does not provide benefits for hospital lengths of stay in connection with childbirth for a mother or her newborn child.

(3) Nothing in this section shall be construed as preventing a group health plan or issuer from imposing deductibles, coinsurance, or other cost-sharing in relation to benefits for hospital lengths of stay in connection with childbirth for a mother or newborn

child under the plan (or under health insurance coverage offered in connection with a group health plan), except that such coinsurance or other cost-sharing for any portion of a period within a hospital length of stay required under subsection (a) may not be greater than such coinsurance or cost-sharing for any preceding portion of such stay.

(d) Notice Under Group Health Plan.—The imposition of the requirements of this section shall be treated as a material modification in the terms of the plan described in section 102(a)(1), for purposes of assuring notice of such requirements under the plan; except that the summary description required to be provided under the last sentence of section 104(b)(1) with respect to such modification shall be provided by not later than 60 days after the first day of the first plan year in which such requirements apply.

(e) Level and Type of Reimbursements.—Nothing in this section shall be construed to prevent a group health plan or a health insurance issuer offering group health insurance coverage from negotiating the level and type of reimbursement with a provider for care provided in accordance with this section.

(f) Preemption; Exception for Health Insurance Coverage in Certain States.—

(1) In general.—The requirements of this section shall not apply with respect to health insurance coverage if there is a State law (as defined in section 731(d)(1)) for a State that regulates such coverage that is described in any of the following subparagraphs:

(A) Such State law requires such coverage to provide for at least a 48-hour hospital length of stay following a normal vaginal delivery and at least a 96-hour hospital length of stay following a cesarean section.

(B) Such State law requires such coverage to provide for maternity and pediatric care in accordance with guidelines established by the American College of Obstetricians and Gynecologists, the American Academy of Pediatrics, or other established professional medical associations.

(C) Such State law requires, in connection with such coverage for maternity care, that the hospital length of stay for such care is left to the decision of (or required to be made by) the attending provider in consultation with the mother.

(2) Construction.—Section 731(a)(1) shall not be construed as superseding a State law described in paragraph (1).

Amendments to ERISA §711
Departments of Veterans Affairs and HUD and Independent Agencies Appropriations Act of 1997 (Pub. L. No. 104-204), as follows:
● ERISA §711 was added by Act §603(a)(5). Eff. Jan. 1, 1998.

SEC. 712. PARITY IN MENTAL HEALTH AND SUBSTANCE USE DISORDER BENEFITS.

(a) In General.—

(1) Aggregate lifetime limits.—In the case of a group health plan (or health insurance coverage offered in connection with such a plan) that provides both medical and surgical benefits and mental health or substance use disorder benefits—

(A) No lifetime limit.—If the plan or coverage does not include an aggregate lifetime limit on substantially all medical and surgical benefits, the plan or coverage may not impose any aggregate lifetime limit on mental health or substance use disorder benefits.

(B) Lifetime limit.—If the plan or coverage includes an aggregate lifetime limit on substantially all medical and surgical benefits (in this paragraph referred to as the "applicable lifetime limit"), the plan or coverage shall either—

(i) apply the applicable lifetime limit both to the medical and surgical benefits to which it otherwise would apply and to mental health and substance abuse disorder benefits and not distinguish in the application of such limit between such medical and surgical benefits and mental health and substance use disorder benefits; or

(ii) not include any aggregate lifetime limit on mental health or substance use disorder benefits that is less than the applicable lifetime limit.

(C) Rule in case of different limits.—In the case of a plan or coverage that is not described in subparagraph (A) or (B) and that includes no or different aggregate lifetime limits on different categories of medical and surgical benefits, the Secretary shall establish rules under which subparagraph (B) is applied to such plan or coverage with respect to mental health and substance use disorder benefits by substituting for the applicable lifetime limit an average aggregate lifetime limit that is computed taking into account the weighted average of the aggregate lifetime limits applicable to such categories.

(2) Annual limits.—In the case of a group health plan (or health insurance coverage offered in connection with such a plan) that provides both medical and surgical benefits and mental health or substance use disorder benefits—

(A) No annual limit.—If the plan or coverage does not include an annual limit on substantially all medical and surgical benefits, the plan or coverage may not impose any annual limit on mental health or substance use disorder benefits.

(B) Annual limit.—If the plan or coverage includes an annual limit on substantially all medical and surgical benefits (in this paragraph referred to as the "applicable annual limit"), the plan or coverage shall either—

(i) apply the applicable annual limit both to medical and surgical benefits to which it otherwise would apply and to mental health and substance use disorder benefits and not distinguish in the application of such limit between such medical and surgical benefits and mental health and substance use disorder benefits; or

(ii) not include any annual limit on mental health or substance use disorder benefits that is less than the applicable annual limit.

(C) Rule in case of different limits.—In the case of a plan or coverage that is not described in subparagraph (A) or (B) and that includes no or different annual limits on different categories of medical and surgical benefits, the Secretary shall establish rules under which subparagraph (B) is applied to such plan or coverage with respect to mental health and substance use disorder benefits by substituting for the applicable annual limit an average annual limit that is computed taking into account the weighted average of the annual limits applicable to such categories.

(3) Financial requirements and treatment limitations.—

(A) In general.—In the case of a group health plan (or health insurance coverage offered in connection with such a plan) that provides both medical and surgical benefits and mental health or substance use disorder benefits, such plan or coverage shall ensure that—

(i) the financial requirements applicable to such mental health or substance use disorder benefits are no more restrictive than the predominant financial requirements applied to substantially all medical and surgical benefits covered by the plan (or coverage), and there are no separate cost sharing requirements that are applicable only with respect to mental health or substance use disorder benefits; and

(ii) the treatment limitations applicable to such mental health or substance use disorder benefits are no more restrictive than the predominant treatment limitations applied to substantially all medical and surgical benefits covered by the plan (or coverage) and there are no separate treatment limitations that are applicable only with respect to mental health or substance use disorder benefits.

(B) Definitions.—In this paragraph:

(i) Financial requirement.—The term "financial requirement" includes deductibles, copayments, coinsurance, and out-of-pocket expenses, but excludes an aggregate lifetime limit and an annual limit subject to paragraphs (1) and (2),

(ii) Predominant.—A financial requirement or treatment limit is considered to be predominant if it is the most common or frequent of such type of limit or requirement.

(iii) Treatment limitation.—The term "treatment limitation" includes limits on the frequency of treatment, number of visits, days of coverage, or other similar limits on the scope or duration of treatment.

(4) Availability of plan information.—The criteria for medical necessity determinations made under the plan with respect to mental health or substance use disorder benefits (or the health insurance coverage offered in connection with the plan with respect to such benefits) shall be made available by the plan administrator (or the health insurance issuer offering such coverage) in accordance with regulations to any current or potential participant, beneficiary, or contracting provider upon request. The reason for any denial under the plan (or coverage) of reimbursement or payment for services with respect to mental health or substance use disorder benefits in the case of any participant or beneficiary shall, on request or as otherwise required, be made available by the plan administrator (or the health insurance issuer offering such coverage) to the participant or beneficiary in accordance with regulations.

(5) Out-of-network providers.—In the case of a plan or coverage that provides both medical and surgical benefits and mental health or substance use disorder benefits, if the plan or coverage provides coverage for medical or surgical benefits provided by out-of-network providers, the plan or coverage shall provide coverage for mental health or substance use disorder benefits provided by out-of-network providers in a manner that is consistent with the requirements of this section.

(b) Construction.—Nothing in this section shall be construed—

(1) as requiring a group health plan (or health insurance coverage offered in connection with such a plan) to provide any mental health or substance use disorder benefits; or

(2) in the case of a group health plan (or health insurance coverage offered in connection with such a plan) that provides mental health or substance use disorder benefits, as affecting the terms and conditions of the plan or coverage relating to such benefits under the plan or coverage, except as provided in subsection (a).

(c) Exemptions.—

(1) Small employer exemption.—

(A) In general.—This section shall not apply to any group health plan (and group health insurance coverage offered in connection with a group health plan) for any plan year of a small employer.

(B) Small employer.—For purposes of subparagraph (A), the term "small employer" means, in connection with a group health plan with respect to a calendar year and a plan year, an employer who employed an average of at least 2 (or 1 in the case of an employer residing in a State that permits small groups to include a single individual) but not more than 50 employees on business days during the preceding calendar year.

(C) Application of certain rules in determination of employer size.—For purposes of this paragraph—

(i) Application of aggregation rule for employers.—Rules similar to the rules under subsections (b), (c), (m), and (o) of section 414 of the Internal Revenue Code of 1986 shall apply for purposes of treating persons as a single employer.

(ii) Employers not in existence in preceding year.—In the case of an employer which was not in existence throughout the preceding calendar year, the determination of whether such employer is a small employer shall be based on the average number of employees that it is reasonably expected such employer will employ on business days in the current calendar year.

(iii) Predecessors.—Any reference in this paragraph to an employer shall include a reference to any predecessor of such employer.

(2) Cost exemption.—

(A) In general.—With respect to a group health plan (or health insurance coverage offered in connection with such a plan), if the application of this section to such plan (or coverage) results in an increase for the plan year involved of the actual total costs of coverage with respect to medical and surgical benefits and mental health and substance use disorder benefits under the plan (as determined and certified under subparagraph (C)) by an amount that exceeds the applicable percentage described in subparagraph (B) of the actual total plan costs, the provisions of this section shall not apply to such plan (or coverage) during the following plan year, and such exemption shall apply to the plan (or coverage) for 1 plan year. An employer may elect to continue to apply mental health and substance use disorder parity pursuant to this section with respect to the group health plan (or coverage) involved regardless of any increase in total costs.

(B) Applicable percentage.—With respect to a plan (or coverage), the applicable percentage described in this subparagraph shall be—

(i) 2 percent in the case of the first plan year in which this section is applied; and

(ii) 1 percent in the case of each subsequent plan year.

(C) Determinations by actuaries.—Determinations as to increases in actual costs under a plan (or coverage) for purposes of this section shall be made and certified by a qualified and licensed actuary who is a member in good standing of the American Academy of Actuaries. All such determinations shall be in a written report prepared by the actuary. The report, and all underlying documentation relied upon by the actuary, shall be maintained by the group health plan or health insurance issuer for a period of 6 years following the notification made under subparagraph (E).

(D) 6-month determinations.—If a group health plan (or a health insurance issuer offering coverage in connection with a group health plan) seeks an exemption under this paragraph, determinations under subparagraph (A) shall be made after such plan (or coverage) has complied with this section for the first 6 months of the plan year involved.

(E) Notification.—

(i) In general.—A group health plan (or a health insurance issuer offering coverage in connection with a group health plan) that, based upon a certification described under subparagraph (C), qualifies for an exemption under this paragraph, and elects to implement the exemption, shall promptly notify the Secretary, the appropriate State agencies, and participants and beneficiaries in the plan of such election.

(ii) Requirement.—A notification to the Secretary under clause (i) shall include—

(I) a description of the number of covered lives under the plan (or coverage) involved at the time of the notification, and as applicable, at the time of any prior election of the cost exemption under this paragraph by such plan (or coverage);

(II) for both the plan year upon which a cost exemption is sought and the year prior, a description of the actual total costs of coverage with respect to medical and surgical benefits and mental health and substance use disorder benefits under the plan; and

(III) for both the plan year upon which a cost exemption is sought and the year prior, the actual total costs of coverage with respect to mental health and substance use disorder benefits under the plan.

(iii) Confidentiality.—A notification to the Secretary under clause (i) shall be confidential. The Secretary shall make available, upon request and on not more than an annual basis, an anonymous itemization of such notifications, that includes—

(I) a breakdown of States by the size and type of employers submitting such notification; and

(II) a summary of the data received under clause (ii).

(F) Audits by appropriate agencies.—To determine compliance with this paragraph, the Secretary may audit the books and records of a group health plan or health insurance issuer relating to an exemption, including any actuarial reports prepared pursuant to subparagraph (C), during the 6 year period following the notification of such exemption under subparagraph (E). A State agency receiving a notification under subparagraph (E) may also conduct such an audit with respect to an exemption covered by such notification.

(d) Separate Application to Each Option Offered.—In the case of a group health plan that offers a participant or beneficiary two or more benefit package options under the plan, the requirements of this section shall be applied separately with respect to each such option.

(e) Definitions.—For purposes of this section:

(1) Aggregate lifetime limit.—The term "aggregate lifetime limit" means, with respect to benefits under a group health plan or health insurance coverage, a dollar limitation on the total amount that may be paid with respect to such benefits under the plan or health insurance coverage with respect to an individual or other coverage unit.

(2) Annual limit.—The term "annual limit" means, with respect to benefits under a group health plan or health insurance coverage, a dollar limitation on the total amount of benefits that may be paid with respect to such benefits in a 12-month period under the plan or health insurance coverage with respect to an individual or other coverage unit.

(3) Medical or surgical benefits.—The term "medical or surgical benefits" means benefits with respect to medical or surgical services, as defined under the terms of the plan or coverage (as the case may be), but does not include mental health or substance use disorder benefits.

(4) Mental health benefits.—The term "mental health or substance use disorder benefits" means benefits with respect to services for mental health conditions, as defined under the terms of the plan and in accordance with applicable Federal and State law.

(5) Substance use disorder benefits.—The term "substance use disorder benefits" means benefits with respect to services for substance use disorders, as defined under the terms of the plan and in accordance with applicable Federal and State law.

(f) Secretary Report.—The Secretary shall, by January 1, 2012, and every two years thereafter, submit to the appropriate committees of Congress a report on compliance of group health plans (and health insurance coverage offered in connection with such plans) with the requirements of this section. Such report shall include the results of any surveys or audits on compliance of group health plans (and health insurance coverage offered in connection with such plans) with such requirements and an analysis of the reasons for any failures to comply.

(g) Notice and Assistance.—The Secretary, in cooperation with the Secretaries of Health and Human Services and Treasury, as appropriate, shall publish and widely disseminate guidance and information for group health plans, participants and beneficiaries, applicable State and local regulatory bodies, and the National Association of Insurance Commissioners concerning the requirements of this section and shall provide assistance concerning such requirements and the continued operation of applicable State law. Such guidance and information shall inform participants and beneficiaries of how they may obtain assistance under this section, including, where appropriate, assistance from State consumer and insurance agencies.

Amendments to ERISA §712

Emergency Economic Stabilization Act of 2008 (Pub. L. No. 110-343), as follows:

- ERISA §712, heading, was amended by Act, Div. C, §712(g)(1)(A). See effective date below. Heading prior to amendment:

    SEC. 712. PARITY IN THE APPLICATION OF CERTAIN LIMITS TO MENTAL HEALTH BENEFITS.

- ERISA §712(a)(3)(5) were added by Act, Div. C, §512(a)(1). See effective date below.

- ERISA §712(b)(2) was amended by Act, Div. C, §512(a)(2). See effective date below. ERISA §712(b)(2) prior to amendment:

    (2) in the case of a group health plan (or health insurance coverage offered in connection with such a plan) that provides mental health benefits, as affecting the terms and conditions (including cost sharing, limits on numbers of visits or days of coverage, and requirements relating to medical necessity) relating to the amount, duration, or scope of mental health benefits under the plan or coverage, except as specifically provided in subsection (a) (in regard to parity in the imposition of aggregate lifetime limits and annual limits for mental health benefits).

- ERISA §712(c)(1)(B) was amended by Act, Div. C, §512(a)(3)(A) by inserting "(or 1 in the case of an employer residing in a State that permits small groups to include a single individual)" after "at least 2" the first place it appeared; and by striking "and who employs at least 2 employees on the first day of the plan year". See effective date below.

- ERISA §712(c)(2) was amended by Act, Div. C, §512(a)(3)(B). See effective date below. ERISA §712(c)(2) prior to amendment:

    (2) Increased cost exemption.—This section shall not apply with respect to a group health plan (or health insurance coverage offered in connection with a group health plan) if the application of this section to such plan (or to such coverage) results in an increase in the cost under the plan (or for such coverage) of at least 1 percent.

- ERISA §712(e)(4) was amended, and (5) was added, by Act, Div. C, §512(a)(4). See effective date below. ERISA §712(e)(4) prior to amendment:

    (4) Mental health benefits.—The term "mental health benefits" means benefits with respect to mental health services, as defined under the terms of the plan or coverage (as the case may be), but does not include benefits with respect to treatment of substance abuse or chemical dependency.

- ERISA §712(f) was amended, and (g) was added, by Act, Div. C, §512(a)(5) and (6). See effective date below. ERISA §712(f) prior to amendment:

(f) Sunset.—This section shall not apply to benefits for services furnished—

(1) on or after January 1, 2008, and before the date for the enactment of the Heroes Earnings Assistance and Relief Tax Act of 2008, and (2) after December 31, 2008.

• ERISA §712(a)(1)(B)(i), (a)(1)(C), (a)(2)(B)(i) and (a)(2)(C) were amended by Act, Div. C, §512(a)(7) by striking "mental health benefits" and inserting "mental health and substance use disorder benefits" each place it appeared. See effective date below.

• ERISA §712 was amended by Act, Div. C, §512(a)(8) by striking "mental health benefits" and inserting "mental health or substance use disorder benefits" each place it appeared other than ERISA §712(a)(1)(B)(i), (a)(1)(C), (a)(2)(B)(i) and (a)(2)(C). See effective date below.

• **Other Provisions. Act,** Div. C, §512(d)(f):

(d) **Regulations.**—Not later than 1 year after the date of enactment of this Act, the Secretaries of Labor, Health and Human Services, and the Treasury shall issue regulations to carry out the amendments made by subsections (a), (b), and (c), respectively.

(e) **Effective Date.**—

(1) In General..—The amendments made by this section shall apply with respect to group health plans for plan years beginning after the date that is 1 year after the date of enactment of this Act, regardless of whether regulations have been issued to carry out such amendments by such effective date, except that the amendments made by subsections (a)(5), (b)(5), and (c)(5), relating to striking of certain sunset provisions, shall take effect on January 1, 2009.

(2) Special Rule for Collective Bargaining Agreements.—In the case of a group health plan maintained pursuant to one or more collective bargaining agreements between employee representatives and one or more employers ratified before the date of the enactment of this Act, the amendments made by this section shall not apply to plan years beginning before the later of—

(A) the date on which the last of the collective bargaining agreements relating to the plan terminates (determined without regard to any extension thereof agreed to after the date of the enactment of this Act), or

(B) January 1, 2009. For purposes of subparagraph (A), any plan amendment made pursuant to a collective bargaining agreement relating to the plan which amends the plan solely to conform to any requirement added by this section shall not be treated as a termination of such collective bargaining agreement.

(f) **Assuring Coordination.**—The Secretary of Health and Human Services, the Secretary of Labor, and the Secretary of the Treasury may ensure, through the execution or revision of an interagency memorandum of understanding among such Secretaries, that—

(1) regulations, rulings, and interpretations issued by such Secretaries relating to the same matter over which two or more such Secretaries have responsibility under this section (and the amendments made by this section) are administered so as to have the same effect at all times; and

(2) coordination of policies relating to enforcing the same requirements through such Secretaries in order to have a coordinated enforcement strategy that avoids duplication of enforcement efforts and assigns priorities in enforcement.

Heroes Earnings Assistance and Relief Tax Act of 2008 (Pub. L. No. 110-245), as follows:

• ERISA §712(f) was amended by Act §401(b). Enacted June 17, 2008, although amendment applies to services furnished "on or after January 1, 2008, and before the date of the enactment of the Heroes Earnings Assistance and Relief Tax Act of 2008, and (2) after December 31, 2008." ERISA §712(f) prior to amendment:

(f) **Sunset.** This section shall not apply to benefits for services furnished after December 31, 2007.

Tax Relief and Health Care Act of 2006 (Pub. L. No. 109-432), as follows:

• ERISA §712(f) was amended by Act §115(b) by extending the sunset to Dec. 31, 2007. Eff. Dec. 20, 2006.

Retirement Preservation Act of 2006 (Pub. L. No. 109-151), as follows:

• ERISA §712(f) was amended by Act §1(a) by substituting "December 31, 2006" for "December 31, 2005". Eff. Dec. 30, 2005.

Working Families Tax Relief Act of 2004 (Pub. L. No. 108-311), as follows:

• ERISA §712(f) was amended by Act §302(b) by substituting "after December 31, 2005" for "on or after December 31, 2004". Eff. Oct. 4, 2004.

Mental Health Parity Reauthorization Act of 2003 (Pub. L. No. 108-197), as follows:

• ERISA §712(f) was amended by Act §2(a) by substituting "December 31, 2004" for "December 31, 2003". Eff. Dec. 19, 2003.

Mental Health Parity Reauthorization Act of 2002 (Pub. L. No. 107-313), as follows:

• ERISA §712(f) was amended by Act §2(a) by substituting "December 31, 2003" for "December 31, 2002". Eff. Dec. 2, 2002.

Departments of Labor, Health and Human Services, and Education, and Related Agencies Appropriations Act of 2002 (Pub. L. No. 107-116), as follows:

• ERISA §712(f) was amended by Act §701(a) by substituting "December 31, 2002" for "September 30, 2001". Eff. Jan. 10, 2002.

Departments of Veterans Affairs and HUD and Independent Agencies Appropriations Act of 1997 (Pub. L. No. 104-204), as follows:

• ERISA §712(f) was added by Act §702(c). Eff. with respect to group health plans for plan years beginning on or after Jan. 1, 1998.

SEC. 713. REQUIRED COVERAGE FOR RECONSTRUCTIVE SURGERY FOLLOWING MASTECTOMIES.

(a) In General.—A group health plan, and a health insurance issuer providing health insurance coverage in connection with a group health plan, that provides medical and surgical benefits with respect to a mastectomy shall provide, in a case of a participant or beneficiary who is receiving benefits in connection with a mastectomy and who elects breast reconstruction in connection with such mastectomy, coverage for—

(1) all stages of reconstruction of the breast on which the mastectomy has been performed;

(2) surgery and reconstruction of the other breast to produce a symmetrical appearance; and

(3) prostheses and physical complications of mastectomy, including lymphedemas;

in a manner determined in consultation with the attending physician and the patient. Such coverage may be subject to annual deductibles and coinsurance provisions as may be deemed appropriate and as are consistent with those established for other benefits under the plan or coverage. Written notice of the availability of such coverage shall be delivered to the participant upon enrollment and annually thereafter.

(b) Notice.—A group health plan, and a health insurance issuer providing health insurance coverage in connection with a group health plan shall provide notice to each participant and beneficiary under such plan regarding the coverage required by this section in accordance with regulations promulgated by the Secretary. Such notice shall be in writing and prominently positioned in any literature or correspondence made available or distributed by the plan or issuer and shall be transmitted—

(1) in the next mailing made by the plan or issuer to the participant or beneficiary;

(2) as part of any yearly informational packet sent to the participant or beneficiary; or

(3) not later than January 1, 1999, whichever is earlier.

(c) Prohibitions.—A group health plan, and a health insurance issuer offering group health insurance coverage in connection with a group health plan, may not—

(1) deny to a patient eligibility, or continued eligibility, to enroll or to renew coverage under the terms of the plan, solely for the purpose of avoiding the requirements of this section; and

(2) penalize or otherwise reduce or limit the reimbursement of an attending provider, or provide incentives (monetary or otherwise) to an attending provider, to induce such provider to provide care to an individual participant or beneficiary in a manner inconsistent with this section.

(d) Rule of Construction.—Nothing in this section shall be construed to prevent a group health plan or a health insurance issuer offering group health insurance coverage from negotiating the level and type of reimbursement with a provider for care provided in accordance with this section.

(e) Preemption, Relation to State Laws.—

(1) In general.—Nothing in this section shall be construed to preempt any State law in effect on the date of enactment of this section with respect to health insurance coverage that requires coverage of at least the coverage of reconstructive breast surgery otherwise required under this section.

(2) ERISA.—Nothing in this section shall be construed to affect or modify the provisions of section 514 with respect to group health plans.

Amendments to ERISA §713

Tax and Trade Relief Extension Act of 1998 (Pub. L. No. 105-277), as follows:

• ERISA §713 was added by Act §902(a). Eff. for plan years beginning on or after Oct. 21, 1998, with a special rule for collective bargaining agreements, see Act §902(c)(2).

SEC. 714. COVERAGE OF DEPENDENT STUDENTS ON MEDICALLY NECESSARY LEAVE OF ABSENCE.

(a) Medically Necessary Leave of Absence.—In this section, the term "medically necessary leave of absence" means, with respect to a dependent child described in subsection (b)(2) in connection with a group health plan or health insurance coverage offered in connection with such plan, a leave of absence of such child from a postsecondary educational institution (including an institution of higher education as defined in section 102 of the Higher Education Act of 1965), or any other change in enrollment of such child at such an institution, that—

(1) commences while such child is suffering from a serious illness or injury;

(2) is medically necessary; and

(3) causes such child to lose student status for purposes of coverage under the terms of the plan or coverage.

(b) Requirement To Continue Coverage.—

(1) In general.—In the case of a dependent child described in paragraph (2), a group health plan, or a health insurance issuer that provides health insurance coverage in connection with a group health plan, shall not terminate coverage of such child under such plan or health insurance coverage due to a medically necessary leave of absence before the date that is the earlier of—

(A) the date that is 1 year after the first day of the medically necessary leave of absence; or

(B) the date on which such coverage would otherwise terminate under the terms of the plan or health insurance coverage.

(2) Dependent child described.—A dependent child described in this paragraph is, with respect to a group health plan or health insurance coverage offered in connection with the plan, a beneficiary under the plan who—

(A) is a dependent child, under the terms of the plan or coverage, of a participant or beneficiary under the plan or coverage; and

(B) was enrolled in the plan or coverage, on the basis of being a student at a postsecondary educational institution (as described in subsection (a)), immediately before the first day of the medically necessary leave of absence involved.

(3) Certification by physician.—Paragraph (1) shall apply to a group health plan or health insurance coverage offered by an issuer in connection with such plan only if the plan or issuer of the coverage has received written certification by a treating physician of the dependent child which states that the child is suffering from a serious illness or injury and that the leave of absence (or other change of enrollment) described in subsection (a) is medically necessary.

(c) Notice.—A group health plan, and a health insurance issuer providing health insurance coverage in connection with a group health plan, shall include, with any notice regarding a requirement for certification of student status for coverage under the plan or coverage, a description of the terms of this section for continued coverage during medically necessary leaves of absence. Such description shall be in language which is understandable to the typical plan participant.

(d) No Change in Benefits.—A dependent child whose benefits are continued under this section shall be entitled to the same benefits as if (during the medically necessary leave of absence) the child continued to be a covered student at the institution of higher education and was not on a medically necessary leave of absence.

(e) Continued Application in Case of Changed Coverage.—If—

(1) a dependent child of a participant or beneficiary is in a period of coverage under a group health plan or health insurance coverage offered in connection with such a plan, pursuant to a medically necessary leave of absence of the child described in subsection (b);

(2) the manner in which the participant or beneficiary is covered under the plan changes, whether through a change in health insurance coverage or health insurance issuer, a change between health insurance coverage and self-insured coverage, or otherwise; and

(3) the coverage as so changed continues to provide coverage of beneficiaries as dependent children,

this section shall apply to coverage of the child under the changed coverage for the remainder of the period of the medically necessary leave of absence of the dependent child under the plan in the same manner as it would have applied if the changed coverage had been the previous coverage.

Amendments to ERISA §714

Michelle's Law (Pub. L. No. 110-381), as follows:
- ERISA §714 was added by Act §2(a)(1). Eff. for plan years beginning on or after one year after date of enactment [enacted: Oct. 9, 2008] and to medically necessary leaves of absence beginning during such plan years.

> *Editor's Note*
>
> ERISA §715, below, added by Pub. L. No. 111-148, §1563(e) (as redesignated by Pub. L. No. 111-148, §10107(b)(1)), is effective March 23, 2010.

SEC. 715. ADDITIONAL MARKET REFORMS.

(a) General Rule.—Except as provided in subsection (b)—

(1) the provisions of part A of title XXVII of the Public Health Service Act (as amended by the Patient Protection and Affordable Care Act) shall apply to group health plans, and health insurance issuers providing health insurance coverage in connection with group health plans, as if included in this subpart; and

(2) to the extent that any provision of this part conflicts with a provision of such part A with respect to group health plans, or health insurance issuers providing health insurance coverage in connection with group health plans, the provisions of such part A shall apply.

(b) Exception.—Notwithstanding subsection (a), the provisions of sections 2716 and 2718 of title XXVII of the Public Health Service Act (as amended by the Patient Protection and Affordable Care Act) shall not apply with respect to self-insured group health plans, and the provisions of this part shall continue to apply to such plans as if such sections of the Public Health Service Act (as so amended) had not been enacted.

Amendments to ERISA §715

Patient Protection and Affordable Care Act, 2010 (Pub. L. No. 111-148), as follows:
- ERISA §715 was added by Act §1563(e) (as redesignated by Act §10107(b)(1)). Eff. Mar. 23, 2010.

Subpart C—General Provisions

SEC. 731. PREEMPTION; STATE FLEXIBILITY; CONSTRUCTION.

(a) Continued Applicability of State Law with Respect to Health Insurance Issuers.—

(1) In general.—Subject to paragraph (2) and except as provided in subsection (b), this part shall not be construed to supersede any provision of State law which establishes, implements, or continues in effect any standard or requirement solely relating to health insurance issuers in connection with group health insurance coverage except to the extent that such standard or requirement prevents the application of a requirement of this part.

(2) Continued preemption with respect to group health plans.—Nothing in this part shall be construed to affect or modify the provisions of section 514 with respect to group health plans.

(b) Special Rules in Case of Portability Requirements.—

(1) In general.—Subject to paragraph (2), the provisions of this part relating to health insurance coverage offered by a health insurance issuer supersede any provision of State law which establishes, implements, or continues in effect a standard or requirement applicable to imposition of a preexisting condition exclusion specifically governed by section 701 which differs from the standards or requirements specified in such section.

(2) Exceptions.—Only in relation to health insurance coverage offered by a health insurance issuer, the provisions of this part do not supersede any provision of State law to the extent that such provision—

(i) substitutes for the reference to "6-month period" in section 701(a)(1) a reference to any shorter period of time;

(ii) substitutes for the reference to "12 months" and "18 months" in section 701(a)(2) a reference to any shorter period of time;

(iii) substitutes for the references to "63 days" in sections 701(c)(2)(A) and (d)(4)(A) a reference to any greater number of days;

(iv) substitutes for the reference to "30-day period" in sections 701(b)(2) and (d)(1) a reference to any greater period;

(v) prohibits the imposition of any preexisting condition exclusion in cases not described in section 701(d) or expands the exceptions described in such section;

(vi) requires special enrollment periods in addition to those required under section 701(f); or

(vii) reduces the maximum period permitted in an affiliation period under section 701(g)(1)(B).

(c) Rules of Construction.—Except as provided in section 711, nothing in this part shall be construed as requiring a group health plan or health insurance coverage to provide specific benefits under the terms of such plan or coverage.

(d) Definitions.—For purposes of this section—

(1) State law.—The term "State law" includes all laws, decisions, rules, regulations, or other State action having the effect of law, of any State. A law of the United States applicable only to the District of Columbia shall be treated as a State law rather than a law of the United States.

(2) State.—The term "State" includes a State, the Northern Mariana Islands, any political subdivisions of a State or such Islands, or any agency or instrumentality of either.

Amendments to ERISA §731

Departments of Veterans Affairs and HUD and Independent Agencies Appropriations Act of 1997 (Pub. L. No. 104-204), as follows:
- ERISA §731 was renumbered by Act §603(a)(3) (originally numbered §704). Eff. Jan. 1, 1998.
- ERISA §731(c) was amended by Act §603(b)(1) by substituting "Except as provided in §711 of this title, nothing" for "Nothing". Eff. for group health plan years beginning on or after Jan. 1, 1998.

Health Insurance Portability and Accountability Act of 1996 (Pub. L. No. 104-191), as follows:

- ERISA §731 was added by Act §101(a), but originally numbered as §704. Eff. generally with respect to group health plans for plan years beginning after June 30, 1997, see Act §101(g).

SEC. 732. SPECIAL RULES RELATING TO GROUP HEALTH PLANS.

(a) General Exception for Certain Small Group Health Plans.—The requirements of this part (other than section 711) shall not apply to any group health plan (and group health insurance coverage offered in connection with a group health plan) for any plan year if, on the first day of such plan year, such plan has less than 2 participants who are current employees.

(b) Exception for Certain Benefits.—The requirements of this part shall not apply to any group health plan (and group health insurance coverage) in relation to its provision of excepted benefits described in section 733(c)(1).

(c) Exception for Certain Benefits if Certain Conditions Met.—

(1) Limited, excepted benefits.—The requirements of this part shall not apply to any group health plan (and group health insurance coverage offered in connection with a group health plan) in relation to its provision of excepted benefits described in section 733(c)(2) if the benefits—

(A) are provided under a separate policy, certificate, or contract of insurance; or

(B) are otherwise not an integral part of the plan.

(2) Noncoordinated, excepted benefits.—The requirements of this part shall not apply to any group health plan (and group health insurance coverage offered in connection with a group health plan) in relation to its provision of excepted benefits described in section 733(c)(3) if all of the following conditions are met:

(A) The benefits are provided under a separate policy, certificate, or contract of insurance.

(B) There is no coordination between the provision of such benefits and any exclusion of benefits under any group health plan maintained by the same plan sponsor.

(C) Such benefits are paid with respect to an event without regard to whether benefits are provided with respect to such an event under any group health plan maintained by the same plan sponsor.

(3) Supplemental excepted benefits.—The requirements of this part shall not apply to any group health plan (and group health insurance coverage) in relation to its provision of excepted benefits described in section 733(c)(4) if the benefits are provided under a separate policy, certificate, or contract of insurance.

(d) Treatment of Partnerships.—For purposes of this part—

(1) Treatment as a group health plan.—Any plan, fund, or program which would not be (but for this subsection) an employee welfare benefit plan and which is established or maintained by a partnership, to the extent that such plan, fund, or program provides medical care (including items and services paid for as medical care) to present or former partners in the partnership or to their dependents (as defined under the terms of the plan, fund, or program), directly or through insurance, reimbursement, or otherwise, shall be treated (subject to paragraph (2)) as an employee welfare benefit plan which is a group health plan.

(2) Employer.—In the case of a group health plan, the term "employer" also includes the partnership in relation to any partner.

(3) Participants of group health plans.—In the case of a group health plan, the term "participant" also includes—

(A) in connection with a group health plan maintained by a partnership, an individual who is a partner in relation to the partnership, or

(B) in connection with a group health plan maintained by a self-employed individual (under which one or more employees are participants), the self-employed individual, if such individual is, or may become, eligible to receive a benefit under the plan or such individual's beneficiaries may be eligible to receive any such benefit.

Amendments to ERISA §732

Departments of Veterans Affairs and HUD and Independent Agencies Appropriations Act of 1997 (Pub. L. No. 104-204), as follows:

● ERISA §732 was renumbered from §705 by Act §603(a)(3). Eff. with respect to group health plans for plan years beginning on and after Jan. 1, 1998.

● ERISA §732(a) was amended by Act §603(b)(2) by inserting "(other than section 1185 of this title)" after "part". Eff. Jan. 1, 1998.

● ERISA §732(b), (c)(1)–(3) were amended by Act §603(b)(3)(I)–(L) by making a technical amendment to references in original Act which appear in text as references to §733 of this title. Eff. for plan years beginning on or after Jan. 1, 1998.

Health Insurance Portability and Accountability Act of 1996 (Pub. L. No. 104-191), as follows:

● ERISA §732 was added by Act §101(a), but originally numbered as §705. Eff. with respect to group health plans for plan years beginning after June 30, 1997.

SEC. 733. DEFINITIONS.

(a) Group Health Plan.—For purposes of this part—

(1) In general.—The term "group health plan" means an employee welfare benefit plan to the extent that the plan provides medical care (as defined in paragraph (2) and including items and services paid for as medical care) to employees or their dependents (as defined under the terms of the plan) directly or through insurance, reimbursement, or otherwise.

(2) Medical care.—The term "medical care" means amounts paid for—

(A) the diagnosis, cure, mitigation, treatment, or prevention of disease, or amounts paid for the purpose of affecting any structure or function of the body,

(B) amounts paid for transportation primarily for and essential to medical care referred to in subparagraph (A), and

(C) amounts paid for insurance covering medical care referred to in subparagraphs (A) and (B).

(b) Definitions Relating to Health Insurance.—For purposes of this part—

(1) Health insurance coverage.—The term "health insurance coverage" means benefits consisting of medical care (provided directly, through insurance or reimbursement, or otherwise and including items and services paid for as medical care) under any hospital or medical service policy or certificate, hospital or medical service plan contract, or health maintenance organization contract offered by a health insurance issuer.

(2) Health insurance issuer.—The term "health insurance issuer" means an insurance company, insurance service, or insurance organization (including a health maintenance organization, as defined in paragraph (3)) which is licensed to engage in the business of insurance in a State and which is subject to State law which regulates insurance (within the meaning of section 514(b)(2)). Such term does not include a group health plan.

(3) Health maintenance organization.—The term "health maintenance organization" means—

(A) a Federally qualified health maintenance organization (as defined in section 1301(a) of the Public Health Service Act (42 U.S.C. 300e(a))),

(B) an organization recognized under State law as a health maintenance organization, or

(C) a similar organization regulated under State law for solvency in the same manner and to the same extent as such a health maintenance organization.

(4) Group health insurance coverage.—The term "group health insurance coverage" means, in connection with a group health plan, health insurance coverage offered in connection with such plan.

(c) Excepted Benefits.—For purposes of this part, the term "excepted benefits" means benefits under one or more (or any combination thereof) of the following:

(1) Benefits not subject to requirements.—

(A) Coverage only for accident, or disability income insurance, or any combination thereof.

(B) Coverage issued as a supplement to liability insurance.

(C) Liability insurance, including general liability insurance and automobile liability insurance.

(D) Workers' compensation or similar insurance.

(E) Automobile medical payment insurance.

(F) Credit-only insurance.

(G) Coverage for on-site medical clinics.

(H) Other similar insurance coverage, specified in regulations, under which benefits for medical care are secondary or incidental to other insurance benefits.

(2) Benefits not subject to requirements if offered separately.—

(A) Limited scope dental or vision benefits.

(B) Benefits for long-term care, nursing home care, home health care, community-based care, or any combination thereof.

(C) Such other similar, limited benefits as are specified in regulations.

(3) Benefits not subject to requirements if offered as independent, noncoordinated benefits.—

(A) Coverage only for a specified disease or illness.

(B) Hospital indemnity or other fixed indemnity insurance.

(4) Benefits not subject to requirements if offered as separate insurance policy.—Medicare supplemental health insurance (as defined under section 1882(g)(1) of the Social Security Act), coverage supplemental to the coverage provided under chapter 55 of title 10, United States Code, and similar supplemental coverage provided to coverage under a group health plan.

(d) Other Definitions.—For purposes of this part—

(1) COBRA continuation provision.—The term "COBRA continuation provision" means any of the following:

(A) Part 6 of this subtitle.

(B) Section 4980B, of the Internal Revenue Code of 1986, other than subsection (f)(1) of such section insofar as it relates to pediatric vaccines.

(C) Title XXII of the Public Health Service Act.

(2) Health status-related factor.—The term "health status-related factor" means any of the factors described in section 702(a)(1).

(3) Network plan.—The term "network plan" means health insurance coverage offered by a health insurance issuer under which the financing and delivery of medical care (including items and services paid for as medical care) are provided, in whole or in part, through a defined set of providers under contract with the issuer.

(4) Placed for adoption defined.—The term "placement", or being "placed", for adoption, has the meaning given such term in section 609(c)(3)(B).

(5) Family member.—The term "family member" means, with respect to an individual—

(A) a dependent (as such term is used for purposes of section 701(f)(2)) of such individual, and

(B) any other individual who is a first-degree, second-degree, third-degree, or fourth-degree relative of such individual or of an individual described in subparagraph (A).

(6) Genetic information.—

(A) In general.—The term "genetic information" means, with respect to any individual, information about—

(i) such individual's genetic tests,

(ii) the genetic tests of family members of such individual, and

(iii) the manifestation of a disease or disorder in family members of such individual.

(B) Inclusion of genetic services and participation in genetic research.—Such term includes, with respect to any individual, any request for, or receipt of, genetic services, or participation in clinical research which includes genetic services, by such individual or any family member of such individual.

(C) Exclusions.—The term "genetic information" shall not include information about the sex or age of any individual.

(7) Genetic test.—

(A) In general.—The term "genetic test" means an analysis of human DNA, RNA, chromosomes, proteins, or metabolites, that detects genotypes, mutations, or chromosomal changes.

(B) Exceptions.—The term "genetic test" does not mean—

(i) an analysis of proteins or metabolites that does not detect genotypes, mutations, or chromosomal changes; or

(ii) an analysis of proteins or metabolites that is directly related to a manifested disease, disorder, or pathological condition that could reasonably be detected by a health care professional with appropriate training and expertise in the field of medicine involved.

(8) Genetic services.—The term "genetic services" means—

(A) a genetic test;

ERISA Sec. 733(d)(8)(A)

(B) genetic counseling (including obtaining, interpreting, or assessing genetic information); or

(C) genetic education.

(9) Underwriting purposes.—The term "underwriting purposes" means, with respect to any group health plan, or health insurance coverage offered in connection with a group health plan—

(A) rules for, or determination of, eligibility (including enrollment and continued eligibility) for benefits under the plan or coverage;

(B) the computation of premium or contribution amounts under the plan or coverage;

(C) the application of any pre-existing condition exclusion under the plan or coverage; and

(D) other activities related to the creation, renewal, or replacement of a contract of health insurance or health benefits.

Amendments to ERISA §733

Genetic Information Nondiscrimination Act of 2008 (Pub. L. No. 110-233), as follows:

- ERISA §733(d)(5)–(9) were added by Act §101(d). Eff. with respect to group health plans for plan years beginning after the date that is one year after the date of enactment (date of enactment: May 21, 2008), see Act §101(f)(2).
- **Other Provision.** Act §101(f)(1) provides:

  (1) Regulations.—The Secretary of Labor shall issue final regulations not later than 12 months after the date of enactment [May 21, 2008] of this Act to carry out the amendments made by this section.

SEC. 734. REGULATIONS.

The Secretary, consistent with §104 of the Health Care Portability and Accountability Act of 1996, may promulgate such regulations as may be necessary or appropriate to carry out the provisions of this part. The Secretary may promulgate any interim final rules as the Secretary deems are appropriate to carry out this part.

Title II—Amendments to the Internal Revenue Code Relating to Retirement Plans

---

Editor's Note

Title II of ERISA amends the Internal Revenue Code. Code provisions relevant to pension and benefit plans appear in Part 2 of this volume. Title II of ERISA is not reprinted here.

Title III—Jurisdiction, Administration, Enforcement; Joint Pension Task Force, etc.

Subtitle A—Jurisdiction, Administration, and Enforcement

SEC. 3001. PROCEDURES IN CONNECTION WITH THE ISSUANCE OF CERTAIN DETERMINATION LETTERS BY THE SECRETARY OF THE TREASURY COVERING QUALIFICATIONS UNDER 26 USCS §§1 ET SEQ.

(a) Additional Material Required of Applicants.—Before issuing an advance determination of whether a pension, profit-sharing, or stock bonus plan, a trust which is a part of such a plan, or an annuity or bond purchase plan meets the requirements of part I of subchapter D of chapter 1 of title 26, the Secretary of the Treasury shall require the person applying for the determination to provide, in addition to any material and information necessary for such determination, such other material and information as may reasonably be made available at the time such application is made as the Secretary of Labor may require under title I of this Act for the administration of that title. The Secretary of the Treasury shall also require that the applicant provide evidence satisfactory to the Secretary that the applicant has notified each employee who qualifies as an interested party (within the meaning of regulations prescribed under section 7476(b)(1) of such Code (relating to declaratory judgments in connection with the qualification of certain retirement plans)) of the application for a determination.

(b) Opportunity to Comment on Application.—

(1) Whenever an application is made to the Secretary of the Treasury for a determination of whether a pension, profit-sharing, or stock bonus plan, a trust which is a part of such a plan, or an annuity or bond purchase plan meets the requirements of part I of subchapter D of chapter 1 of title 26, the Secretary shall upon request afford an opportunity to comment on the application at any time within 45 days after receipt thereof to—

(A) any employee or class of employee qualifying as an interested party within the meaning of the regulations referred to in subsection (a)[,]

(B) the Secretary of Labor, and

(C) the Pension Benefit Guaranty Corporation.

(2) The Secretary of Labor may not request an opportunity to comment upon such an application unless he has been requested in writing to do so by the Pension Benefit Guaranty Corporation or by the lesser of—

(A) 10 employees, or

(B) 10 percent of the employees

who qualify as interested parties within the meaning of the regulations referred to in subsection (a). Upon receiving such a request, the Secretary of Labor shall furnish a copy of the request to the Secretary of the Treasury within 5 days (excluding Saturdays, Sundays, and legal public holidays (as set forth in section 6103 of title 5, United States Code)).

(3) Upon receiving such a request from the Secretary of Labor, the Secretary of the Treasury shall furnish to the Secretary of Labor such information held by the Secretary of the Treasury relating to the application as the Secretary of Labor may request.

(4) The Secretary of Labor shall, within 30 days after receiving a request from the Pension Benefit Guaranty Corporation or from the necessary number of employees who qualify as interested parties, notify the Secretary of the Treasury, the Pension Benefit Guaranty Corporation, and such employees with respect to whether he is going to comment on the application to which the request relates and with respect to any matters raised in such request on which he is not going to comment. If the Secretary of Labor indicates in the notice required under the preceding sentence that he is not going to comment on all or part of the matters raised in such request, the Secretary of the Treasury shall afford the corporation, and such employees, an opportunity to comment on the application with respect to any matter on which the Secretary of Labor has declined to comment.

(c) Intervention by Pension Benefit Guaranty Corporation or Secretary of Labor Into Declaratory Judgment Action Under 26 USC Section 7476; Action by Corporation Authorized.—The Pension Benefit Guaranty Corporation and, upon petition of a group of employees referred to in subsection (b)(2), the Secretary of Labor, may intervene in any action brought for declaratory judgment under section 7476 of the Internal Revenue Code of 1954 in accordance with the provisions of such section. The Pension Benefit Guaranty Corporation is permitted to bring an action under such section 7476 under such rules as may be prescribed by the United States Tax Court.

(d) Notification and Information by Secretary of the Treasury to Secretary of Labor Upon Issuance by Secretary of the Treasury of a Determination Letter to Applicant.—If the Secretary of the Treasury determines that a plan or trust to which this section applies meets the applicable requirements of part I of subchapter D of chapter 1 of title 26 and issues a determination letter to the applicant, the Secretary shall notify the Secretary of Labor of his determination and furnish such information and material relating to the application and determination held by the Secretary of the Treasury as the Secretary of Labor may request for the proper administration of title I of this Act. The Secretary of Labor shall accept

the determination of the Secretary of the Treasury as prima facie evidence of initial compliance by the plan with the standards of parts 2, 3, and 4 of subtitle B of title I of this Act. The determination of the Secretary of the Treasury shall not be prima facie evidence on issues relating solely to part 4 of subtitle B of title I. If an application for such a determination is withdrawn, or if the Secretary of the Treasury issues a determination that the plan or trust does not meet the requirements of such part I, the Secretary shall notify the Secretary of Labor of the withdrawal or determination.

(e) Effective Date.—This section does not apply with respect to an application for any plan received by the Secretary of the Treasury before the date on which section 410 of title 26 applies to the plan, or on which such section will apply if the plan is determined by the Secretary to be a qualified plan.

Amendments to ERISA §3001

Omnibus Budget Reconciliation Act of 1989 (Pub. L. No. 101-239), as follows:

• ERISA §3001(a), (b)(1), (c)–(e) were amended by Act §7891(a)(1) by substituting "Internal Revenue Code of 1986" for "Internal Revenue Code of 1954", which for purposes of codification was translated as "title 26". Eff. as if included in Pub. L. No. 99-415.

Omnibus Budget Reconciliation Act of 1987 (Pub. L. No. 100-203), as follows:

• ERISA §3001(d) was amended by Act §9343(b) by inserting after second sentence: "The determination of the Secretary of the Treasury shall not be prima facie evidence on issues relating solely to part 4 of subtitle B of subchapter I of this chapter."

SEC. 3002. PROCEDURES WITH RESPECT TO CONTINUED COMPLIANCE WITH INTERNAL REVENUE REQUIREMENTS RELATING TO PARTICIPATION, VESTING, AND FUNDING STANDARDS.

(a) Notification by Secretary of the Treasury to Secretary of Labor of Issuance of a Preliminary Notice of Intent to Disqualify or of Commencement of Proceedings to Determine Satisfaction of Requirements.—In carrying out the provisions of part I of subchapter D of chapter 1 of title 26 with respect to whether a plan or a trust meets the requirements of section 410(a) or 411 of title 26 (relating to minimum participation standards and minimum vesting standards, respectively), the Secretary of the Treasury shall notify the Secretary of Labor when the Secretary of the Treasury issues a preliminary notice of intent to disqualify related to the plan or trust or, if earlier, at the time of commencing any proceeding to determine whether the plan or trust satisfies such requirements. Unless the Secretary of the Treasury finds that the collection of a tax imposed under title 26 is in jeopardy, the Secretary of the Treasury shall not issue a determination that the plan or trust does not satisfy the requirements of such section until the expiration of a period of 60 days after the date on which he notifies the Secretary of Labor of such review. The Secretary of the Treasury, in his discretion, may extend the 60-day period referred to in the preceding sentence if he determines that such an extension would enable the Secretary of Labor to obtain compliance with such requirements by the plan within the extension period. Except as otherwise provided in this Act, the Secretary of Labor shall not generally apply part 2 of title I of this Act to any plan or trust subject to sections 410(a) and 411 of title 26, but shall refer alleged general violations of the vesting or participation standards to the Secretary of the Treasury. (The preceding sentence shall not apply to matters relating to individuals benefits.)

(b) Notification to Secretary of Labor Before Secretary of the Treasury Sends Notice of Deficiency Under Code Section 4971; Waiver of Imposition of Tax; Requests for Investigation; Consultation.— Unless the Secretary of the Treasury finds that the collection of a tax is in jeopardy, in carrying out the provisions of section 4971 of title 26 (relating to taxes on the failure to meet minimum funding standards), the Secretary of the Treasury shall notify the Secretary of Labor before sending a notice of deficiency with respect to any tax imposed under that section on an employer, and, in accordance with the provisions of subsection (d) of that section, afford the Secretary of Labor anopportunity to comment on the imposition of the tax in the case. The Secretary of the Treasury may waive the imposition of the tax imposed under section 4971(b) of title 26 in appropriate cases. Upon receiving a written request from the Secretary of Labor or from the Pension Benefit Guaranty Corporation, the Secretary of the Treasury shall cause an investigation to be commenced expeditiously with respect to whether the tax imposed under section 4971 of title 26 should be applied with respect to any employer to which the request relates. The Secretary of the Treasury and the Secretary of Labor shall consult with each other from time to time with respect to the provisions of section 412 of title 26 (relating to minimum funding standards) and with respect to the funding standards applicable under title I of this Act in order to coordinate the rules applicable under such standards.

(c) Extended Application of Regulations Prescribed by Secretary of the Treasury Relating to Minimum Participation Standards, Minimum Vesting Standards, and Minimum Funding Standards.— Regulations prescribed by the Secretary of the Treasury under sections 410(a), 411, and 412 of title 26 (relating to minimum participation standards, minimum vesting standards, and minimum funding standards, respectively) shall also apply to the minimum participation, vesting, and funding standards set forth in parts 2 and 3 of subtitle B of title I of this Act. Except as otherwise expressly provided in this Act,

the Secretary of Labor shall not prescribe other regulations under such parts, or apply the regulations prescribed by the Secretary of the Treasury under sections 410(a), 411, 412 of title 26 and applicable to the minimum participation, vesting, and funding standards under such parts in a manner inconsistent with the way such regulations apply under sections 410(a), 411, and 412 of title 26.

(d) Opportunity Afforded Secretary of the Treasury to Intervene in Cases Involving Construction or Application of Minimum Standards; Review of Briefs Filed by Pension Benefit Guaranty Corporation or Secretary of Labor.— The Secretary of Labor and the Pension Benefit Guaranty Corporation, before filing briefs in any case involving the construction or application of minimum participation standards, minimum vesting standards, or minimum funding standards under title I of this Act, shall afford the Secretary of the Treasury a reasonable opportunity to review any such brief. The Secretary of the Treasury shall have the right to intervene in any such case.

(e) Consultative Requirements Respecting Promulgation of Proposed or Final Regulations.— The Secretary of the Treasury shall consult with the Pension Benefit Guaranty Corporation with respect to any proposed or final regulation authorized by subpart C of part I of subchapter D of chapter 1 of title 26, or by sections 4241 through 4245 of this Act, before publishing any such proposed or final regulation.

Amendments to ERISA §3002
Omnibus Budget Reconciliation Act of 1989 (Pub. L. No. 101-239), as follows:
● ERISA §3002(a)–(c) and (e) were amended by Act §7891(a)(1) by substituting "tax imposed under the Internal Revenue Code of 1986" for "tax imposed under the Internal Revenue Code of 1954" and "Internal Revenue Code of 1986" for "Internal Revenue Code of 1954", which for purposes of codification was translated as "title 26.". Eff., except as otherwise provided, as if included in Pub. L. No. 99-514, see Act §7891(f).

Multiemployer Pension Plan Amendments Act of 1980 (Pub. L. No. 96-364), as follows:
● ERISA §3002(e) was added by Act §402(b)(3). Eff. Sept. 26, 1980, except as specifically provided, see ERISA §4402(e).

Other Provision: The Pension Protection Act of 2006 (Pub. L. No. 109-280), §1101, provides:
  SEC. 1101. EMPLOYEE PLANS COMPLIANCE RESOLUTION SYSTEM.
    (a) In General.—The Secretary of the Treasury shall have full authority to establish and implement the Employee Plans Compliance Resolution System (or any successor program) and any other employee plans correction policies, including the authority to waive income, excise, or other taxes to ensure that any tax, penalty, or sanction is not excessive and bears a reasonable relationship to the nature, extent, and severity of the failure.
    (b) Improvements.—The Secretary of the Treasury shall continue to update and improve the Employee Plans Compliance Resolution System (or any successor program), giving special attention to—
      (1) increasing the awareness and knowledge of small employers concerning the availability and use of the program;
      (2) taking into account special concerns and circumstances that small employers face with respect to compliance and correction of compliance failures;

(3) extending the duration of the self-correction period under the Self-Correction Program for significant compliance failures;

(4) expanding the availability to correct insignificant compliance failures under the Self-Correction Program during audit; and

(5) assuring that any tax, penalty, or sanction that is imposed by reason of a compliance failure is not excessive and bears a reasonable relationship to the nature, extent, and severity of the failure.

SEC. 3003. PROCEDURES IN CONNECTION WITH PROHIBITED TRANSACTIONS.

(a) Notification to Secretary of Labor; Opportunity to Comment on Imposition of Tax Under Code Section 4975; Waiver; Requests for Investigations.—Unless the Secretary of the Treasury finds that the collection of a tax is in jeopardy, in carrying out the provisions of section 4975 of title 26 (relating to tax on prohibited transactions) the Secretary of the Treasury shall, in accordance with the provisions of subsection (h) of such section, notify the Secretary of Labor before sending a notice of deficiency with respect to the tax imposed by subsection (a) or (b) of such section, and, in accordance with the provisions of subsection (h) of such section, afford the Secretary an opportunity to comment on the imposition of the tax in any case. The Secretary of the Treasury shall have authority to waive the imposition of the tax imposed under section 4975(b) in appropriate cases. Upon receiving a written request from the Secretary of Labor or from the Pension Benefit Guaranty Corporation, the Secretary of the Treasury shall cause an investigation to be carried out with respect to whether the tax imposed by section 4975 of title 26 should be applied to any person referred to in the request.

(b) Consultation.—The Secretary of the Treasury and the Secretary of Labor shall consult with each other from time to time with respect to the provisions of section 4975 of title 26 (relating to tax on prohibited transactions) and with respect to the provisions of title I of this Act relating to prohibited transactions and exemptions therefrom in order to coordinate the rules applicable under such standards.

(c) Transmission of Information to Secretary of the Treasury.—Whenever the Secretary of Labor obtains information indicating that a party-in-interest or disqualified person is violating section 406 of this Act, he shall transmit such information to the Secretary of the Treasury.

Amendment to ERISA §3003

Omnibus Budget Reconciliation Act of 1989 (Pub. L. No. 101-239), as follows:

• ERISA §3003(a)–(b) were amended by Act §7891(a)(1) by substituting "Internal Revenue Code of 1986" for "Internal Revenue Code of 1954", which for purposes of codification was translated as "title 26". Eff., except as otherwise provided, as if included in Pub. L. No. 99-514, see Act §7891(f).

SEC. 3004. COORDINATION BETWEEN THE DEPARTMENT OF THE TREASURY AND THE DEPARTMENT OF LABOR.

(a) Whenever in this Act or in any provision of law amended by this Act the Secretary of the Treasury and the Secretary of Labor are required to carry out provisions relating to the same subject matter (as determined by them) they shall consult with each other and shall develop rules, regulations, practices, and forms which, to the extent appropriate for the efficient administration of such provisions, are designed to reduce duplication of effort, duplication of reporting, conflicting or overlapping requirements, and the burden of compliance with such provisions by plan administrators, employers, and participants and beneficiaries.

(b) In order to avoid unnecessary expense and duplication of functions among Government agencies, the Secretary of the Treasury and the Secretary of Labor may make such arrangements or agreements for cooperation or mutual assistance in the performance of their functions under this Act, and the functions of any such agency as they find to be practicable and consistent with law. The Secretary of the Treasury and the Secretary of Labor may utilize, on a reimbursable or other basis, the facilities or services, of any department, agency, or establishment of the United States or of any State or political subdivision of a State, including the services, of any of its employees, with the lawful consent of such department, agency, or establishment; and each department, agency, or establishment of the United States is authorized and directed to cooperate with the Secretary of the Treasury and the Secretary of Labor and, to the extent permitted by law, to provide such information and facilities as they may request for their assistance in the performance of their functions under this Act. The Attorney General or his representative shall receive from the Secretary of the Treasury and the Secretary of Labor for appropriate action such evidence developed in the performance of their functions under this Act as may be found to warrant consideration for criminal prosecution under the provisions of this title or other Federal law.

Subtitle B—Joint Pension, Profit-Sharing, and Employee Stock Ownership Plan Task Force; Studies

Part 1—Joint Pension, Profit-Sharing, and Employee Stock Ownership Plan Task Force

SEC. 3021. ESTABLISHMENT.

The staffs of the Committee on Ways and Means and the Committee on Education and Labor of the House of Representatives, the Joint Committee on Taxation, and the Committee on Finance and the Committee on Labor and Human Resources of the Senate shall carry out the duties assigned under this title to the Joint Pension, Profit-Sharing, and Employee Stock Ownership Plan Task Force. By agreement among the chairmen of such Committees, the Joint Pension, Profit-Sharing, and Employee Stock Ownership Plan Task Force shall be furnished with office space, clerical personnel, and such supplies and equipment as may be necessary for the Joint Pension, Profit-Sharing, and Employee Stock Ownership Plan Task Force to carry out its duties under this title.

Amendments to ERISA §3021

Tax Reform Act of 1976 (Pub. L. No. 94-455), as follows:
● ERISA §3021 was amended by Act §803(i)(2)(A)(iii) by substituting "Joint Pension, Profit-Sharing, and Employee Stock Ownership Plan Task Force" for "Joint Pension Task Force" wherever appearing. Eff. for taxable years beginning after 1974, see Act §803(j).

SEC. 3022. DUTIES.

(a) The Joint Pension, Profit-Sharing, and Employee Stock Ownership Plan Task Force shall, within 24 months after September 2, 1974, make a full study and review of—

(1) the effect of the requirements of section 411 of title 26 and of section 203 of this Act to determine the extent of discrimination, if any, among employees in various age groups resulting from the application of such requirements;

(2) means of providing for the portability of pension rights among different pension plans;

(3) the appropriate treatment under title IV of this Act (relating to termination insurance) of plans established and maintained by small employers;

(4) the broadening of stock ownership, particularly with regard to employee stock ownership plans (as defined in section 4975(e)(7) of the title 26 and section 407(d)(6) of the Act) and all other alternative methods for broadening stock ownership to the American labor force and others;

(5) the effects and desirability of the Federal preemption of State and local law with respect to matters relating to pension and similar plans; and

(6) such other matter as any of the committees referred to in section 3021 may refer to it.

(b) The Joint Pension, Profit-Sharing, and Employee Stock Ownership Plan Task Force shall report the results of its study and review to each of the committees referred to in section 3021.

Amendments to ERISA §3022

Omnibus Budget Reconciliation Act of 1989 (Pub. L. No. 101-239), as follows:
● ERISA §3022(a)(1), (4) were amended by Act §7891(a)(1) by substituting "Internal Revenue Code of 1986" for "Internal Revenue Code of 1954", which for purposes of codification was translated as "title 26". Eff. as if included in Pub. L. No. 99-514, see Act §7891(f).

Tax Reform Act of 1976 (Pub. L. No. 94-455), as follows:
● ERISA §3022(a) was amended by Act §803(i)(1), (2)(A)(iii) by substituting "Joint Pension, Profit-Sharing, and Employee Stock Ownership Plan Task Force" for "Joint Pension Task Force" in provision preceding para. (1), redesignating paras. (4) and (5) as (5) and (6), respectively, and adding para. (4). Eff. for taxable years beginning after 1974, see Act §803(j).
● ERISA §3022(b) was amended by Act §803(i)(2)(A)(iii) by substituting "Joint Pension, Profit-Sharing, and Employee Stock Ownership Plan Task Force" for "Joint Pension Task Force". Eff. for taxable years beginning after 1974, see Act §803(j).

Part 2—Other Studies

SEC. 3031. CONGRESSIONAL STUDY.

(a) The Committee on Education and Labor and the Committee on Ways and Means of the House of Representatives and the Committee on Finance and the Committee on Labor and Human Resources of the Senate shall study retirement plans established and maintained or financed (directly and indirectly) by the Government of the United States, by any State (including the District of Columbia) or political subdivision thereof, or by any agency or instrumentality of any of the foregoing. Such study shall include an analysis of—

(1) the adequacy of existing levels of participation, vesting, and financing arrangements,

(2) existing fiduciary standards, and

(3) the necessity for Federal legislation and standards with respect to such plans.

In determining whether any such plan is adequately financed, each committee shall consider the necessity for minimum funding standards, as well as the taxing power of the government maintaining the plan.

(b) Not later than December 31, 1976, the Committee on Education and Labor and the Committee on Ways and Means shall each submit to the House of

Representatives the results of the studies conducted under this section, together with such recommendations as they deem appropriate. The Committee on Finance and the Committee on Labor and Human Resources shall each submit to the Senate the results of the studies conducted under this section together with such recommendations as they deem appropriate not later than such date.

SEC. 3032. PROTECTION FOR EMPLOYEES UNDER FEDERAL PROCUREMENT, CONSTRUCTION, AND RESEARCH CONTRACTS AND GRANTS.

(a) **Study and Investigation by Secretary of Labor.**—The Secretary of Labor shall, during the 2-year period beginning on September 2, 1974, conduct a full and complete study and investigation of the steps necessary to be taken to insure that professional, scientific, and technical personnel and others working in associated occupations employed under Federal procurement, construction, or research contracts or grants will, to the extent feasible, be protected against forfeitures of pension or retirement rights or benefits, otherwise provided, as a consequence of job transfers or loss of employment resulting from terminations or modifications of Federal contracts, grants, or procurement policies. The Secretary of Labor shall report the results of his study and investigation to the Congress within 2 years after September 2, 1974. The Secretary of Labor is authorized, to the extent provided by law, to obtain the services of private research institutions and such other persons by contract or other arrangement as he determines necessary in carrying out the provisions of this section.

(b) **Consultation.**—In the course of conducting the study and investigation described in subsection (a) of this section, and in developing the regulations referred to in subsection (c) of this section, the Secretary of Labor shall consult—

(1) with appropriate professional societies, business organizations, and labor organizations, and

(2) with the heads of interested Federal departments and agencies.

(c) **Regulations.**—Within 1 year after the date on which he submits his report to the Congress under subsection (a) of this section, the Secretary of Labor shall, if he determines it to be feasible, develop regulations which will provide the protection of pension and retirement rights and benefits referred to in subsection (a) of this section.

(d) **Congressional Review of Regulations; Resolution of Disapproval.**—

(1) Any regulations developed pursuant to subsection (c) of this section shall take effect if, and only if—

(A) the Secretary of Labor, not later than the day which is 3 years after September 2, 1974, delivers a copy of such regulations to the House of Representatives and a copy to the Senate, and

(B) before the close of the 120-day period which begins on the day on which the copies of such regulations are delivered to the House of Representatives and to the Senate, neither the House of Representatives nor the Senate adopts, by an affirmative vote of a majority of those present and voting in that House, a resolution of disapproval.

(2) For purposes of this subsection, the term "resolution of disapproval" means only a resolution of either House of Congress, the matter after the resolving clause of which is as follows: "That the ____ does not favor the taking effect of the regulations transmitted to the Congress by the Secretary of Labor on ____ ", the first blank space therein being filled with the name of the resolving House and the second blank space therein being filled with the day and year.

(3) A resolution of disapproval in the House of Representatives shall be referred to the Committee on Education and Labor. A resolution of disapproval in the Senate shall be referred to the Committee on Labor and Human Resources.

(4) (A) If the committee to which a resolution of disapproval has been referred has not reported it at the end of 7 calendar days after its introduction, it is in order to move either to discharge the committee from further consideration of the resolution or to discharge the committee from further consideration of any other resolution of disapproval which has been referred to the committee.

(B) A motion to discharge may be made only by an individual favoring the resolution, is highly privileged (except that it may not be made after the committee has reported a resolution of disapproval), and debate thereon shall be limited to not more than 1 hour, to be divided equally between those favoring and those opposing the resolution. An amendment to the motion is not in order, and it is not in order to move to reconsider the vote by which the motion is agreed to or disagreed to.

(C) If the motion to discharge is agreed to or disagreed to, the motion may not be renewed, nor may another motion to discharge the committee be made with respect to any other resolution of disapproval.

(5)(A) When the committee has reported, or has been discharged from further consideration of, a resolution of disapproval, it is at any time thereafter in order (even though a previous motion to the same effect has been disagreed to) to move to proceed to the consideration of the resolution. The motion is highly privileged and is not debatable. An amendment to the motion is not in order, and it is not in order to move to reconsider the vote by which the motion is agreed to or disagreed to.

(B) Debate on the resolution of disapproval shall be limited to not more than 10 hours, which shall be divided equally between those favoring and those opposing the resolution. A motion further to limit debate is not debatable. An amendment to, or motion to recommit, the resolution is not in order, and it is not in order to move to reconsider the vote by which the resolution is agreed to or disagreed to.

(6)(A) Motions to postpone, made with respect to the discharge from committee or the consideration of a resolution of disapproval, and motions to proceed to the consideration of other business, shall be decided without debate.

(B) Appeals from the decisions of the Chair relating to the application of the rules of the House of Representatives or the Senate, as the case may be, to the procedure relating to any resolution of disapproval shall be decided without debate.

(7) Whenever the Secretary of Labor transmits copies of the regulations to the Congress, a copy of such regulations shall be delivered to each House of Congress on the same day and shall be delivered to the Clerk of the House of Representatives if the House is not in session and to the Secretary of the Senate if the Senate is not in session.

(8) The 120-day period referred to in paragraph (1) shall be computed by excluding—

(A) the days on which either House is not in session because of an adjournment of more than 3 days to a day certain or an adjournment of the Congress sine die, and

(B) any Saturday and Sunday, not excluded under subparagraph (A), when either House is not in session.

(9) This subsection is enacted by the Congress—

(A) as an exercise of the rulemaking power of the House of Representatives and the Senate, respectively, and as such they are deemed a part of the rules of each House, respectively, but applicable only with respect to the procedure to be followed in that House in the case of resolutions of disapproval described in paragraph (2); and they supersede other rules only to the extent that they are inconsistent therewith; and

(B) with full recognition of the constitutional right of either House to change the rules (so far as relating to the procedure of that House) at any time, in the same manner and to the same extent as in the case of any other rule of that House.

Subtitle C—Enrollment of Actuaries

SEC. 3041. JOINT BOARD FOR THE ENROLLMENT OF ACTUARIES.

The Secretary of Labor and the Secretary of the Treasury shall, not later than the last day of the first calendar month beginning after the date of the enactment of this Act, establish a Joint Board for the Enrollment of Actuaries (hereinafter in this part [subtitle] referred to as the "Joint Board").

SEC. 3042. ENROLLMENT BY BOARD; STANDARDS AND QUALIFICATIONS; SUSPENSION OR TERMINATION OF ENROLLMENT.

(a) The Joint Board shall, by regulations, establish reasonable standards and qualifications for persons performing actuarial services with respect to plans to which this Act applies and, upon application by any individual, shall enroll such individual if the Joint Board finds that such individual satisfies such standards and qualifications. With respect to individuals applying for enrollment before January 1, 1976, such standards and qualifications shall include a requirement for an appropriate period of responsible actuarial experience relating to pension plans. With respect to individuals applying for enrollment on or after January 1, 1976, such standards and qualifications shall include—

(1) education and training in actuarial mathematics and methodology, as evidenced by—

(A) a degree in actuarial mathematics or its equivalent from an accredited college or university,

(B) successful completion of an examination in actuarial mathematics and methodology to be given by the Joint Board, or

(C) successful completion of other actuarial examinations deemed adequate by the Joint Board, and

(2) an appropriate period of responsible actuarial experience.

Notwithstanding the preceding provisions of this subsection, the Joint Board may provide for the temporary enrollment for the period ending on January 1, 1976, of actuaries under such interim standards as it deems adequate.

(b) The Joint Board may, after notice and an opportunity for a hearing, suspend or terminate the enrollment of an individual under this section if the Joint Board finds that such individual—

(1) has failed to discharge his duties under this Act, or

(2) does not satisfy the requirements for enrollment as in effect at the time of his enrollment.

The Joint Board may also, after notice and opportunity for hearing, suspend or terminate the temporary enrollment of an individual who fails to discharge his duties under this Act or who does not satisfy the interim enrollment standards.

Title IV—Plan Termination Insurance

Subtitle A—Pension Benefit Guaranty Corporation

SEC. 4001. DEFINITIONS.

(a) For purposes of this title, the term—

(1) "administrator" means the person or persons described in paragraph (16) of section 3 of this Act;

(2) "substantial employer", for any plan year of a single-employer plan, means one or more persons—

(A) who are contributing sponsors of the plan in such plan year,

(B) who, at any time during such plan year, are members of the same controlled group, and

(C) whose required contributions to the plan for each plan year constituting one of—

(i) the two immediately preceding plan years, or

(ii) the first two of the three immediately preceding plan years,

total an amount greater than or equal to 10 percent of all contributions required to be paid to or under the plan for such plan year;

(3) "multiemployer plan" means a plan—

(A) to which more than one employer is required to contribute,

(B) which is maintained pursuant to one or more collective bargaining agreements between one or more employee organizations and more than one employer, and

(C) which satisfies such other requirements as the Secretary of Labor may prescribe by regulation,

except that, in applying this paragraph—

(i) a plan shall be considered a multiemployer plan on and after its termination date if the plan was a multiemployer plan under this paragraph for the plan year preceding such termination, and

(ii) for any plan year which began before the date of the enactment of the Multiemployer Pension Plan Amendments Act of 1980, the term "multiemployer plan" means a plan described in section 414(f) of title 26 as in effect immediately before such date;

(4) "corporation", except where the context clearly requires otherwise, means the Pension Benefit Guaranty Corporation established under section 4002;

(5) "fund" means the appropriate fund established under section 4005;

(6) "basic benefits" means benefits guaranteed under section 4022 (other than under section

4022(c)), or under section 4022A (other than under section 4022A(g));

(7) "non-basic benefits" means benefits guaranteed under section 4022(c) or 4022A(g);

(8) "nonforfeitable benefit" means, with respect to a plan, a benefit for which a participant has satisfied the conditions for entitlement under the plan or the requirements of this Act (other than submission of a formal application, retirement, completion of a required waiting period, or death in the case of a benefit which returns all or a portion of a participant's accumulated mandatory employee contributions upon the participant's death), whether or not the benefit may subsequently be reduced or suspended by a plan amendment, an occurrence of any condition, or operation of this Act or title 26;

(9) "reorganization index" means the amount determined under section 4241(b);

(10) "plan sponsor" means, with respect to a multiemployer plan—

(A) the plan's joint board of trustees, or

(B) if the plan has no joint board of trustees, the plan administrator;

(11) "contribution base unit" means a unit with respect to which an employer has an obligation to contribute under a multiemployer plan, as defined in regulations prescribed by the Secretary of the Treasury;

(12) "outstanding claim for withdrawal liability" means a plan's claim for the unpaid balance of the liability determined under part 1 of subtitle E for which demand has been made, valued in accordance with regulations prescribed by the corporation;

(13) "contributing sponsor", of a single-employer plan, means a person described in section 302(b)(1) of this Act (without regard to section 302(b)(2) of this Act) or section 412(b)(1) of the Internal Revenue Code of 1986 (without regard to section 412(b)(2) of such Code).[;]

(14) in the case of a single-employer plan—

(A) "controlled group" means, in connection with any person, a group consisting of such person and all other persons under common control with such person;

(B) the determination of whether two or more persons are under "common control" shall be made under regulations of the corporation which are consistent and coextensive with regulations prescribed by the Secretary of the Treasury under subsections (b) and (c) of section 414 of title 26; and

(C)(i) notwithstanding any other provision of this title, during any period in which an individual possesses, directly or indirectly, the power to direct

ERISA Sec. 4001(a)(14)(C)(i)

or cause the direction of the management and policies of an affected air carrier of which he is the accountable owner, whether through the ownership of voting securities, by contract, or otherwise, the affected air carrier shall be considered to be under common control not only with those persons described in subparagraph (B), but also with all related persons; and

(ii) for purposes of this subparagraph, the term—

(I) "affected air carrier" means an air carrier, as defined in section 101(3) of the Federal Aviation Act of 1958, that holds a certificate of public convenience and necessity under section 401 of such Act for route number 147, as of November 12, 1991;

(II) "related person" means any person which has under common control (as determined under subparagraph (B)) with an affected air carrier on October 10, 1991, or any successor to such related person;

(III) "accountable owner" means any individual who on October 10, 1991, owned directly or indirectly through the application of section 318 of the Internal Revenue Code of 1986 more than 50 percent of the total voting power of the stock of an affected air carrier;

(IV) "successor" means any person that acquires, directly or indirectly through the application of section 318 of the Internal Revenue Code of 1986, more than 50 percent of the total voting power of the stock of a related person, more than 50 percent of the total value of securities (as defined in section 3(20) of this Act) of the related person, more than 50 percent of the total value of the assets of the related person, or any person into which such related person shall be merged or consolidated; and

(V) "individual" means a living human being.

(15) "single-employer plan" means any defined benefit plan (as defined in section 3(35)) which is not a multiemployer plan;

(16) "benefit liabilities" means the benefits of employees and their beneficiaries under the plan (within the meaning of section 401(a)(2) of the Internal Revenue Code of 1986);

(17) "amount of unfunded guaranteed benefits", of a participant or beneficiary as of any date under a single-employer plan, means an amount equal to the excess of—

(A) the actuarial present value (determined as of such date on the basis of assumptions prescribed by the corporation for purposes of section 4044) of the benefits of the participant or beneficiary under the plan which are guaranteed under section 4022, over

(B) the current value (as of such date) of the assets of the plan which are required to be allocated to those benefits under section 4044;

(18) "amount of unfunded benefit liabilities" means, as of any date, the excess (if any) of—

(A) the value of the benefit liabilities under the plan (determined as of such date on the basis of assumptions prescribed by the corporation for purposes of section 4044), over

(B) the current value (as of such date) of the assets of the plan;

(19) "outstanding amount of benefit liabilities" means, with respect to any plan, the excess (if any) of—

(A) the value of the benefit liabilities under the plan (determined as of the termination date on the basis of assumptions prescribed by the corporation for purposes of section 4044), over

(B) the value of the benefit liabilities which would be so determined by only taking into account benefits which are guaranteed under section 4022 or to which assets of the plan are allocated under section 4044;

(20) "person" has the meaning set forth in section 3(9);

(21) "affected party" means, with respect to a plan—

(A) each participant in the plan,

(B) each beneficiary under the plan who is a beneficiary of a deceased participant or who is an alternate payee (within the meaning of section 206(d)(3)(K)) under an applicable qualified domestic relations order (within the meaning of section 206(d)(3)(B)(i)),

(C) each employee organization representing participants in the plan, and

(D) the corporation,

except that, in connection with any notice required to be provided to the affected party, if an affected party has designated, in writing, a person to receive such notice on behalf of the affected party, any reference to the affected party shall be construed to refer to such person.

(b)(1) An individual who owns the entire interest in an unincorporated trade or business is treated as his own employer, and a partnership is treated as the employer of each partner who is an employee within the meaning of section 401(c)(1) of title 26. For purposes of this title, under regulations prescribed by the corporation, all employees of trades or businesses (whether or not incorporated) which are under common control shall be treated as employed by a single employer and all such trades and businesses as a single employer. The regulations prescribed under the preceding sentence shall be consistent and coextensive with regulations prescribed for similar purposes by the Secretary of the Treasury under section 414(c) of title 26.

(2) For purposes of subtitle E—

(A) except as otherwise provided in subtitle E, contributions or other payments shall be considered made under a plan for a plan year if they are made within the period prescribed under section 412(c)(10) of title 26 (determined, in the case of a terminated plan, as if the plan had continued beyond the termination date), and

(B) the term "Secretary of the Treasury" means the Secretary of the Treasury or such Secretary's delegate.

Amendments to ERISA §4001

Pension Protection Act of 2006 (Pub. L. No. 109-280), as follows:

● ERISA §4001(a)(13) was amended by Act §107(b)(1) (redesignated as §108(b)(1) by Pub. L. No. 111-192, §202(a)). Eff. for plan years beginning after Dec. 31, 2007. *Note*: Act §104, provides a delayed effective date for amendments made by Act §§101–116, for "eligible cooperative plans" until the earlier of the first plan year that the plan ceases to be an eligible cooperative plan, or Jan. 1, 2017. ERISA §4001(a)(13) prior to amendment:

> (13) "contributing sponsor", of a single-employer plan, means a person described in §302(c)(11)(A) of this Act (without regard to §302(c)(11)(B) of this Act) or §412(c)(11)(A) of the Internal Revenue Code of 1986 (without regard to §412(c)(11)(B) of such Code).

Uruguay Round Agreements Act of 1994 (Pub. L. No. 103-465), as follows:

● ERISA §4001(a)(13) was amended by Act §761(a)(11) substituting "means a person described in section 1082(c)(11)(A) of this title (without regard to section 1082(c)(11)(B) of this title) or section 412(c)(11)(A) of title 26 (without regard to section 412(c)(11)(B) of such title)." for "means a person—(A) who is responsible, in connection with such plan, for meeting the funding requirements under section 1082 of this title or section 412 of title 26, or (B) who is a member of the controlled group of a person described in subparagraph (A), has been responsible for meeting such funding requirements, and has employed a significant number (as may be defined in regulations of the corporation) of participants under such plan while such person was so responsible;". Eff. Dec. 8, 1994.

Operation Desert Shield/Desert Storm Act (Pub. L. No. 102-229), as follows:

● ERISA§4001(a)(14)(A) was amended by Act §214 striking "and" at the end of subpara. (A), adding "and" at the end of subpara. (B) and adding subpara. (C).

Omnibus Budget Reconciliation Act of 1989 (Pub. L. No. 101-239), as follows:

● ERISA §4001(a)(8), (a)(13)(A), (a)(14)(B), (b)(1), and (b)(2) were amended by Act §7891(a)(1) to substitute "Internal Revenue Code of 1986" for "Internal Revenue Code of 1954", which for purposes of codification was translated as "title 26". Eff., except as otherwise provided, as if included in the provision of Pub. L. No. 99-514 to which it relates, see Act §7891(f).

Agricultural Reconciliation Act of 1987 (Pub. L. No. 100-203), as follows:

● ERISA §4001(a)(16) was amended by Act §9312(b)(4). Eff. with respect to (A) plan terminations under ERISA §4041(c) with respect to which notices of intent to terminate are provided under ERISA §4041(a)(2) after Dec. 17, 1987, and (B) plan terminations with respect to which proceedings are instituted by the PBGC under ERISA §4042 after Dec. 17, 1987. ERISA §4001(a)(16) prior to amendment:

> (16) "benefit commitments", to a participant or beneficiary as of any date under a single-employer plan, means all benefits provided by the plan with respect to the participant or beneficiary which—
> (A) are guaranteed under section 1322 of this title,
> (B) would be guaranteed under section 1322 of this title, but for the operation of subsection 1322(b) of this title, or
> (C) constitute—
> (i) early retirement supplements or subsidies, or
> (ii) plant closing benefits, irrespective of whether any such supplements, subsidies, or benefits are benefits guaranteed under section 1322 of this title, if the participant or beneficiary has satisfied, as of such date, all of the conditions required of him or her under the provisions of the plan to establish entitlement to the benefits, except for the submission of a formal application, retirement, completion of a required waiting period subsequent to application for benefits, or designation of a beneficiary;.

● ERISA §4001(a)(18) was amended by Act §9313(a)(2)(F). Eff. with respect to plan terminations under ERISA §4041 with respect to which notices of intent to terminate are provided under ERISA §4041(a)(2) after Dec. 17, 1987. ERISA §4001(a)(18) prior to amendment:

> (18) "amount of unfunded benefit commitments", of a participant or beneficiary as of any date under a single-employer plan, means an amount equal to the excess of—
> (A) the actuarial present value (determined as of such date on the basis of assumptions prescribed by the corporation for purposes of section 1344 of this title) of the benefit commitments to the participant or beneficiary under the plan, over
> (B) the current value (as of such date) of the assets of the plan which are required to be allocated to those benefit commitments under section 1344 of this title;.

● ERISA §4001(a)(19) was amended by Act §9312(b)(5). Eff. with respect to (A) plan terminations under ERISA §4041(c) with respect to which notices of intent to terminate are provided under ERISA §4041(a)(2) after Dec. 17, 1987, and (B) plan terminations with respect to which proceedings are instituted by the PBGC. ERISA §4001(a)(19) prior to amendment:

> (19) "outstanding amount of benefit commitments", of a participant or beneficiary under a terminated single-employer plan, means the excess of—
> (A) the actuarial present value (determined as of the termination date on the basis of assumptions prescribed by the corporation for purposes of section 1344 of this title) of the benefit commitments to such participant or beneficiary under the plan, over
> (B) the actuarial present value (determined as of such date on the basis of assumptions prescribed by the corporation for purposes of section 1344 of this title) of the benefits of such participant or beneficiary which are guaranteed under section 1322 of this title or to which assets of the plan are required to be allocated under section 1344 of this title;.

Consolidated Omnibus Budget Reconciliation Act of 1985 (Pub. L. No. 99-272), as follows:

● ERISA §4001(a)(2) was amended by Act §11004(a)(1). Eff. Jan. 1, 1986, with some exceptions, see Act §11019. ERISA §4001(a)(2) prior to amendment:

> (2) "substantial employer" means for any plan year an employer or beneficiary (treating employers who are members of the same affiliated group, within the meaning of section 1563(a) of the Internal Revenue Code of 1986, determined without regard to section 1563(a)(4) and (e)(3)(C) of such Code, as one employer) who has made contributions to or under a plan under which more than one employer (other than a multiemployer plan) makes contributions for each of—
> (A) the two immediately preceding plan years, or
> (B) the second and third preceding plan years, equaling or exceeding 10 percent of all employer contributions paid to or under the plan for each such year;.

● ERISA §4001(a)(11) was amended by Act §11004(a)(2) by striking out "and". Eff. Jan. 1, 1986, with some exceptions, see Act §11019.

• ERISA §4001(a)(12) was amended by Act §11004(a)(3) by striking out "corporation." and inserting "corporation;". Eff. in general as of Jan. 1, 1986, except with respect to terminations for which (1) notices of intent to terminate were filed with the PBGC under ERISA §4041 before such date, or (2) proceedings were commenced under ERISA §4042 before such date. Transition rules also apply.

• ERISA §4001(a)(12)–(21) were added by Act §11004(a)(4). Eff. in general as of Jan. 1, 1986, except for terminations for which (1) notices of intent to terminate were filed with the PBGC under ERISA §4041 before such date, or (2) proceedings were commenced under ERISA §4042 before such date. Transition rules also apply.

• ERISA §4001(b) was amended by Act §11004(b) by designating existing provisions as para. (1), adding para. (2), and striking amendments by Pub. L. No. 96-364, §402(a)(1)(F), which had been executed by designating existing provisions as para. (1) and adding paras. (2) through (4) as follows:

    (2) For purposes of this title, "single-employer plan means, except as otherwise specifically provided in this title, any plan which is not a multiemployer plan.

    (3) For purposes of this title, except as otherwise provided in this title, contributions or other payments shall be considered made under a plan for a plan year if they are made within the period prescribed under section 412(c)(10) of the Internal Revenue Code of 1986.

    (4) For purposes of subtitle E, "Secretary of the Treasury" means the Secretary of the Treasury or such Secretary's delegate.

See amendment note for the Multiemployer Pension Plan Amendments Act of 1980, below.

Multiemployer Pension Plan Amendments Act of 1980 (Pub. L. No. 96-364), as follows:

• ERISA §4001(a)(2) was amended by Act §402(a)(1)(A) by inserting "(other than a multiemployer plan)" after "more than one employer". Eff. Sept. 26, 1980, except as specifically provided, see ERISA §4402(e).

• ERISA §4001(a)(3) was amended by Act §402(a)(1)(B) by replacing subsec. (a)(3). Eff. Sept. 26, 1980, except as specifically provided, see ERISA §4402(e). ERISA §4001(a)(3) prior to amendment:

    (3) "multiemployer plan" means a multiemployer plan as defined in section 414(f) of the Internal Revenue Code of 1986 (as added by this Act but without regard to whether such section is in effect on the date of enactment of this Act;.

• ERISA §4001(a)(6) was replaced by Act §402(a)(1)(C). Eff. Sept. 26, 1980, except as specifically provided, see ERISA §4402(e). ERISA §4001(a)(6) prior to amendment:

    (6) "basic benefits" means benefits guaranteed under section 4022 other than under section 4022(c); and.

• ERISA §4001(a)(7) was amended by Act §402(a)(1)(D) by striking the period and inserting "or 4022A(g);". Eff. Sept. 26, 1980, except as specifically provided, see ERISA §4402(e).

• ERISA §4001(a)(8)–(12) were added by Act §402(a)(1)(E). Eff. Sept. 26, 1980, except as specifically provided, see ERISA §4402(e).

• ERISA §4001(c)[(b)] was amended by Act §402(a)(1)(F) by designating existing provisions as para. (1) and adding paras. (2) through (4), notwithstanding directory language that paras. (2) through (4) be added at end of subsec. (c)(1) as redesignated. Paras. (2) through (4) were struck by Pub. L. No. 99-272, §11004(b), see above.

SEC. 4002. PENSION BENEFIT GUARANTY CORPORATION.

(a) Establishment Within the Department of Labor.—There is established within the Department of Labor a body corporate to be known as the Pension Benefit Guaranty Corporation. In carrying out its functions under this title, the corporation shall be administered by a Director, who shall be appointed by the President, by and with the advice and consent of the Senate, and who shall act in accordance with the policies established by the board. The purposes of this title, which are to be carried out by the corporation, are—

    (1) to encourage the continuation and maintenance of voluntary private pension plans for the benefit of their participants,

    (2) to provide for the timely and uninterrupted payment of pension benefits to participants and beneficiaries under plans to which this title applies, and

    (3) to maintain premiums established by the corporation under section 4006 at the lowest level consistent with carrying out its obligations under this title.

(b) Powers of Corporation.—To carry out the purposes of this title, the corporation has the powers conferred on a nonprofit corporation under the District of Columbia Nonprofit Corporation Act and, in addition to any specific power granted to the corporation elsewhere in this title or under that Act, the corporation has the power—

    (1) to sue and be sued, complain and defend, in its corporate name and through its own counsel, in any court, State or Federal;

    (2) to adopt, alter, and use a corporate seal, which shall be judicially noticed;

    (3) to adopt, amend, and repeal, by the board of directors, bylaws, rules, and regulations relating to the conduct of its business and the exercise of all other rights and powers granted to it by this Act and such other bylaws, rules and regulations as may be necessary to carry out the purposes of this title;

    (4) to conduct its business (including the carrying on of operations and the maintenance of offices) and to exercise all other rights and powers granted to it by this Act in any State or other jurisdiction without regard to qualification, licensing, or other requirements imposed by law in such State or other jurisdiction;

    (5) to lease, purchase, accept gifts or donations of, or otherwise to acquire, to own, hold, improve, use, or otherwise deal in or with, and to sell, convey, mortgage, pledge, lease, exchange, or otherwise dispose of, any property, real, personal, or mixed, or any interest therein wherever situated;

    (6) to appoint and fix the compensation of such officers, attorneys, employees, and agents as may be required, to determine their qualifications, to define their duties, and, to the extent desired by the corporation, require bonds for them and fix the penalty thereof, and to appoint and fix the compensation of experts and consultants in accordance with the provisions of section 3109 of title 5, United States Code;

    (7) to utilize the personnel and facilities of any other agency or department of the United States Government, with or without reimbursement, with the consent of the head of such agency or department; and

(8) to enter into contracts, to execute instruments, to incur liabilities, and to do any and all other acts and things as may be necessary or incidental to the conduct of its business and the exercise of all other rights and powers granted to the corporation by this Act.

(c) [Omitted.]

(d) Board of Directors; Compensation; Reimbursement for Expenses.—The board of directors of the corporation consists of the Secretary of the Treasury, the Secretary of Labor, and the Secretary of Commerce. Members of the board shall serve without compensation, but shall be reimbursed for travel, subsistence, and other necessary expenses incurred in the performance of their duties as members of the board. The Secretary of Labor is the chairman of the board of directors.

(e) Meetings.—The board of directors shall meet at the call of its chairman, or as otherwise provided by the bylaws of the corporation.

(f) Adoption of Bylaws; Amendment; Alteration; Publication in the Federal Register.—As soon as practicable, but not later than 180 days after the date of enactment of this Act, the board of directors shall adopt initial bylaws and rules relating to the conduct of the business of the corporation. Thereafter, the board of directors may alter, supplement, or repeal any existing bylaw or rule, and may adopt additional bylaws and rules from time to time as may be necessary. The chairman of the board shall cause a copy of the bylaws of the corporation to be published in the Federal Register not less often than once each year.

(g) Exemption From Taxation.—

(1) The corporation, its property, its franchise, capital, reserves, surplus, and its income (including, but not limited to, any income of any fund established under section 4005), shall be exempt from all taxation now or hereafter imposed by the United States (other than taxes imposed under chapter 21 of title 26, relating to Federal Insurance Contributions Act and chapter 23 of title 26, relating to Federal Unemployment Tax Act) or by any State or local taxing authority, except that any real property and any tangible personal property (other than cash and securities) of the corporation shall be subject to State and local taxation to the same extent according to its value as other real and tangible personal property is taxed.

(2) The receipts and disbursements of the corporation in the discharge of its functions shall be included in the totals of the budget of the United States Government. The United States is not liable for any obligation or liability incurred by the corporation.

(3) [Omitted.]

(h) Advisory Committee to Corporation.—

(1) There is established an advisory committee to the corporation, for the purpose of advising the corporation as to its policies and procedures relating to (A) the appointment of trustees in termination proceedings, (B) investment of moneys, (C) whether plans being terminated should be liquidated immediately or continued in operation under a trustee, and (D) such other issues as the corporation may request from time to time. The advisory committee may also recommend persons for appointment as trustees in termination proceedings, make recommendations with respect to the investment of moneys in the funds, and advise the corporation as to whether a plan subject to being terminated should be liquidated immediately or continued in operation under a trustee.

(2) The advisory committee consists of seven members appointed, from among individuals recommended by the board of directors, by the President. Of the seven members, two shall represent the interests of employee organizations, two shall represent the interests of employers who maintain pension plans, and three shall represent the interests of the general public. The President shall designate one member as chairman at the time of the appointment of that member.

(3) Members shall serve for terms of 3 years each, except that, of the members first appointed, one of the members representing the interests of employee organizations, one of the members representing the interests of employers, and one of the members representing the interests of the general public shall be appointed for terms of 2 years each, one of the members representing the interests of the general public shall be appointed for a term of 1 year, and the other members shall be appointed to full 3-year terms. The advisory committee shall meet at least six times each year and at such other times as may be determined by the chairman or requested by any three members of the advisory committee.

(4) Members shall be chosen on the basis of their experience with employeeorganizations, with employers who maintain pension plans, with the administration of pension plans, or otherwise on account of outstanding demonstrated ability in related fields. Of the members serving on the advisory committee at any time, no more than four shall be affiliated with the same political party.

(5) An individual appointed to fill a vacancy occurring other than by the expiration of a term of office shall be appointed only for the unexpired term of the member he succeeds. Any vacancy occurring in the office of a member of the advisory committee shall be filled in the manner in which that office was originally filled.

(6) The advisory committee shall appoint and fix the compensation of such employees as it determines necessary to discharge its duties, including experts and consultants in accordance with the provisions of section 3109 of title 5, United States Code. The corporation shall furnish to the advisory committee such professional, secretarial, and other services as the committee may request.

(7) Members of the advisory committee shall, for each day (including travel time) during which they are attending meetings or conferences of the committee or otherwise engaged in the business of the committee, be compensated at a rate fixed by the corporation which is not in excess of the daily equivalent of the annual rate of basic pay in effect for grade GS-18 of the General Schedule, and while away from their homes or regular places of business they may be allowed travel expenses, including per diem in lieu of subsistence, as authorized by section 5703 of title 5, United States Code.

(8) The Federal Advisory Committee Act does not apply to the advisory committee established by this subsection.

(i) Special Rules Regarding Disasters, etc.—In the case of a pension or other employee benefit plan, or any sponsor, administrator, participant, beneficiary, or other person with respect to such plan, affected by a Presidentially declared disaster (as defined in section 1033(h)(3) of the Internal Revenue Code of 1986) or a terroristic or military action (as defined in section 692(c)(2) of such Code), the corporation may, notwithstanding any other provision of law, prescribe, by notice or otherwise, a period of up to 1 year which may be disregarded in determining the date by which any action is required or permitted to be completed under this Act. No plan shall be treated as failing to be operated in accordance with the terms of the plan solely as the result of disregarding any period by reason of the preceding sentence.

Amendments to ERISA §4002

Pension Protection Act of 2006 (Pub. L. No. 109-280), as follows:

● ERISA §4002(a) was amended by Act §411(a)(1) by striking the second sentence and adding a new second sentence. Eff. Aug. 17, 2006. Second sentence prior to amendment:

In carrying out its functions under this title, the corporation shall be administered by the chairman of the board of directors in accordance with policies established by the board.

● **Other Provision**. Act §411. Director of the Pension Benefit Guaranty Corporation.

(c) Jurisdiction of Nomination.—

(1) In general.—The Committee on Finance of the Senate and the Committee on Health, Education, Labor, and Pensions of the Senate shall have joint jurisdiction over the nomination of a person nominated by the President to fill the position of Director of the Pension Benefit Guaranty Corporation under section 4002 of the Employee Retirement Income Security Act of 1974 (29 U.S.C. 1302) (as amended by this Act), and if one committee votes to order reported such a nomination, the other shall report within 30 calendar days, or be automatically discharged.

(2) Rulemaking of the senate.—This subsection is enacted by Congress—

(A) as an exercise of rulemaking power of the Senate, and as such it is deemed a part of the rules of the Senate, but applicable only with respect to the procedure to be followed in the Senate in the case of a nomination described in

such sentence, and it supersedes other rules only to the extent that it is inconsistent with such rules; and

(B) with full recognition of the constitutional right of the Senate to change the rules (so far as relating to the procedure of the Senate) at any time, in the same manner and to the same extent as in the case of any other rule of the Senate.

(d) Transition.—The term of the individual serving as Executive Director of the Pension Benefit Guaranty Corporation on the date of enactment of this Act shall expire on such date of enactment. Such individual, or any other individual, may serve as interim Director of such Corporation until an individual is appointed as Director of such Corporation under section 4002 of the Employee Retirement Income Security Act of 1974 (29 U.S.C. 1302) (as amended by this Act).

Victims of Terrorism Tax Relief Act of 2001 (Pub. L. No. 107-134), as follows:

● ERISA §4002(i) was added by Act §112(c)(2). Eff. for disasters and terroristic or military actions occurring on or after Sept. 11, 2001, with respect to any action of the Secretary of the Treasury, the Secretary of Labor, or the PBGC occurring on or after Jan. 23, 2002.

Omnibus Budget Reconciliation Act of 1989 (Pub. L. No. 101-239), as follows:

● ERISA §4002(g)(1) was amended by Act §7891(a)(1) by substituting "Internal Revenue Code of 1986" for "Internal Revenue Code of 1954", which for purposes of codification was translated as "title 26". Eff. as if included in the provision of Pub. L. No. 99-514 to which it relates. See §7891(f) of Pub. L. No. 101-239.

Multiemployer Pension Plan Amendments Act of 1980 (Pub. L. No. 96-364), as follows:

● ERISA §4002(b)(3) was amended by Act §403(l) by inserting "and such bylaws, rules, and regulations as may be necessary to carry out the purposes of this title" after "Act". Eff. Sept. 26, 1980, as provided in ERISA §4402(e), except as specifically provided.

● ERISA §4002(g)(2) was amended by Act §406(a) by substituting subsec. [(f)](g)(2) for the following: "The receipts and disbursements of the corporation in the discharge of its functions shall not be included in the totals of the budget of the United States Government and shall be exempt from any general limitations imposed by statute on budget outlays of the United States. Except as explicitly provided in this title, the United States is not liable for any obligation or liability incurred by the corporation." Eff. for fiscal years beginning after Sept. 26, 1980, as provided in ERISA §4402(e), except as specifically provided.

Tax Reform Act of 1976 (Pub. L. No. 94-455), as follows:

● ERISA §4002(g)(1) was amended by Act §1510(b) by inserting "by the United States (other than taxes imposed under chapter 21 of the Internal Revenue Code of 1954, relating to Federal Insurance Contributions Act, and chapter 23 of such Code, relating to Federal Unemployment Tax Act) or" immediately after "imposed". Eff. Sept. 2, 1974.

SEC. 4003. OPERATION OF CORPORATION.

(a) Investigatory Authority; Audit of Statistically Significant Number of Terminating Plans.—The corporation may make such investigations as it deems necessary to enforce any provision of this title or any rule or regulation thereunder, and may require or permit any person to file with it a statement in writing, under oath or otherwise as the corporation shall determine, as to all the facts and circumstances concerning the matter to be investigated. The corporation shall annually audit a statistically significant number of plans terminating under section 4041(b) to determine whether participants and beneficiaries have received their benefit commitments and whether section 4050(a) has been satisfied. Each audit shall include a statistically significant number of participants and beneficiaries.

(b) Discovery Powers Vested in Board Members or Officers Designated by the Chairman.—For the purpose of any such investigation, or any other proceeding under this title, the Director, any member of the board of directors of the corporation, or any officer designated by the Director or chairman may administer oaths and affirmations, subpoena witnesses, compel their attendance, take evidence, and require the production of any books, papers, correspondence, memoranda, or other records which the corporation deems relevant or material to the inquiry.

(c) Contempt.—In case of contumacy by, or refusal to obey a subpoena issued to, any person, the corporation may invoke the aid of any court of the United States within the jurisdiction of which such investigation or proceeding is carried on, or where such person resides or carries on business, in requiring the attendance and testimony of witnesses and the production of books, papers, correspondence, memoranda, and other records. The court may issue an order requiring such person to appear before the corporation, or member or officer designated by the corporation, and to produce records or to give testimony related to the matter under investigation or in question. Any failure to obey such order of the court may be punished by the court as a contempt thereof. All process in any such case may be served in the judicial district in which such person is an inhabitant or may be found.

(d) Cooperation With Other Government Agencies.—In order to avoid unnecessary expense and duplication of functions among government agencies, the corporation may make such arrangements or agreements for cooperation or mutual assistance in the performance of its functions under this title as is practicable and consistent with law. The corporation may utilize the facilities or services any department, agency, or establishment of the United States or of any State or political subdivision of a State, including the services of any of its employees, with the lawful consent of such department, agency, or establishment. The head of each department, agency, or establishment of the United States shall cooperate with the corporation and, to the extent permitted by law, provide such information and facilities as it may request for its assistance in the performance of its functions under this title. The Attorney General or his representative shall receive from the corporation for appropriate action such evidence developed in the performance of its functions under this title as may be found to warrant consideration for criminal prosecution under the provisions of this or any other Federal law.

(e) Civil Actions by Corporation; Jurisdiction; Process; Expeditious Handling of Case; Costs; Limitations on Actions.—

(1) Civil actions may be brought by the corporation for appropriate relief, legal or equitable or both, to enforce (A) the provisions of this title, and (B) in the case of a plan which is covered under this title (other than a multiemployer plan) and for which the conditions for imposition of a lien described in section 303(k)(1)(A) and (B) of this Act or section 430(k)(1)(A) and (B) of the Internal Revenue Code of 1986 have been met, section 302 of this Act and section 412 of such Code.

(2) Except as otherwise provided in this title, where such an action is brought in a district court of the United States, it may be brought in the district where the plan is administered, where the violation took place, or where a defendant resides or may be found, and process may be served in any other district where a defendant resides or may be found.

(3) The district courts of the United States shall have jurisdiction of actions brought by the corporation under this title without regard to the amount in controversy in any such action.

(4) [Repealed.]

(5) In any action brought under this title, whether to collect premiums, penalties, and interest under section 4007 or for any other purpose, the court may award to the corporation all or a portion of the costs of litigation incurred by the corporation in connection with such action.

(6)(A) Except as provided in subparagraph (C), an action under this subsection may not be brought after the later of—

    (i) 6 years after the date on which the cause of action arose, or

    (ii) 3 years after the applicable date specified in subparagraph (B).

B(i) Except as provided in clause (ii), the applicable date specified in this subparagraph is the earliest date on which the corporation acquired or should have acquired actual knowledge of the existence of such cause of action.

    (ii) If the corporation brings the action as a trustee, the applicable date specified in this subparagraph is the date on which the corporation became a trustee with respect to the plan if such date is later than the date described in clause (i).

(C) In the case of fraud or concealment, the period described in subparagraph (A)(ii) shall be extended to 6 years after the applicable date specified in subparagraph (B).

(f) Civil Actions Against the Corporation; Appropriate Court; Award of Costs and Expenses; Limitation on Actions; Jurisdiction; Removal of Actions.—

(1) Except with respect to withdrawal liability disputes under part 1 of subtitle E, any person who is a fiduciary, employer, contributing sponsor, member of a contributing sponsor's controlled group, participant, or beneficiary, and is adversely affected by any action of the corporation with respect to a plan in which such person has an interest, or who is an employee organization representing such a participant or beneficiary so adversely affected for purposes of collective bargaining with respect to such plan, may bring an action against the corporation for appropriate equitable relief in the appropriate court.

(2) For purposes of this subsection, the term "appropriate court" means—

(A) the United States district court before which proceedings under section 4041 or 4042 are being conducted,

(B) if no such proceedings are being conducted, the United States district court for the judicial district in which the plan has its principal office, or

(C) the United States District Court for the District of Columbia.

(3) In any action brought under this subsection, the court may award all or a portion of the costs and expenses incurred in connection with such action to any party who prevails or substantially prevails in such action.

(4) This subsection shall be the exclusive means for bringing actions against the corporation under this title, including actions against the corporation in its capacity as a trustee under section 4042 or 4049.

(5)(A) Except as provided in subparagraph (C), an action under this subsection may not be brought after the later of—

(i) 6 years after the date on which the cause of action arose, or

(ii) 3 years after the applicable date specified in subparagraph (B).

(B)(i) Except as provided in clause (ii), the applicable date specified in this subparagraph is the earliest date on which the plaintiff acquired or should have acquired actual knowledge of the existence of such cause of action.

(ii) In the case of a plaintiff who is a fiduciary bringing the action in the exercise of fiduciary duties, the applicable date specified in this subparagraph is the date on which the plaintiff became a fiduciary with respect to the plan if such date is later than the date specified in clause (i).

(C) In the case of fraud or concealment, the period described in subparagraph (A)(ii) shall be extended to 6 years after the applicable date specified in subparagraph (B).

(6) The district courts of the United States have jurisdiction of actions brought under this subsection without regard to the amount in controversy.

(7) In any suit, action, or proceeding in which the corporation is a party, or intervenes under section 4301, in any State court, the corporation may, without bond or security, remove such suit, action, or proceeding from the State court to the United States district court for the district or division in which such suit, action, or proceeding is pending by following any procedure for removal now or hereafter in effect.

Amendments to ERISA §4003

Pension Protection Act of 2006 (Pub. L. No. 109-280), as follows:

• ERISA §4003(b) was amended by Act §411(a)(2)(A)–(B) by substituting "under this title, the Director, any member" for "under this title, any member" and "designated by the Director or chairman" for "designated by the chairman". Eff. Aug. 17, 2006.

• ERISA §4003(e)(1) was amended by Act §107(b)(2) (redesignated as §108(b)(2) by Pub. L. No. 111-192, §202(a)) by substituting "§303(k)(1)(A) and (B)" for "§302(f)(1)(A) and (B)" and "§430(k)(1)(A) and (B)" for "§412(n)(1)(A) and (B)". Eff. for plan years beginning after 2007. Act §104 provides a delayed effective date for amendments made by §§101–116 for "eligible cooperative plan" until the earlier of the first plan year that the plan ceases to be an eligible cooperative plan, or Jan. 1, 2017.

Uruguay Round Agreements Act of 1994 (Pub. L. No. 103-465), as follows:

• ERISA §4003(a) was amended by Act §776(b)(1) by inserting "and whether §1350(a) of this title has been satisfied" before period at end of second sentence. Eff. with respect to distributions that occur in plan years commencing on or after Jan. 1, 1996, see Act §776(e).

• ERISA §4003(e)(1) was amended by Act §773(a) by inserting "(A)" after "enforce" and substituting ", and" and cl. (B) for period at end. Eff. for installments and other payments required under ERISA §302 or IRC §412 that become due on or after the date of the enactment of this Act, Dec. 8, 1994, see Act §773(b).

Consolidated Omnibus Budget Reconciliation Act of 1985 (Pub. L. No. 99-272), as follows:

• ERISA §4003(a) was amended by Act §11016(c)(5) by inserting at the end the sentence: "The corporation shall annually audit a statistically significant number of plans terminating under §4041(b) to determine whether participants and beneficiaries have received their benefit commitments. Each audit shall include a statistically significant number of participants and beneficiaries." Eff. Jan. 1, 1986, with certain exceptions, see Act §11019 of Pub. L. 99-272.

• ERISA §4003(e)(6) was amended by Act §11014(b)(2) by adding para. (6). Eff. with respect to actions filed after the date of the enactment, Apr. 7, 1986, see Act §11014(b)(3).

• ERISA §4003(f) was amended by Act §11014(b)(1). Eff. with respect to actions filed after the date of the enactment, Apr. 7, 1986. ERISA §4003(f) prior to amendment:

(f) Except as provided in §1451(a)(2) of this title, any participant, beneficiary, plan administrator, or employee adversely affected by any action of the corporation, or by a receiver or trustee appointed by the corporation, with respect to a plan in which such participant, beneficiary, plan administrator or employer has an interest, may bring an action against the corporation, receiver, or trustee in the appropriate court. For purposes of this subsection the term "appropriate court" means the United States district court before which proceedings under §1341 or 1342 of this title are being conducted, or if no such proceedings are being conducted the United States district court for the district in which the plan has its principal office, or the United States district court for the District of Columbia. The district courts of the United States have jurisdiction of actions brought under this subsection without regard to the amount in controversy. In any suit, action, or proceeding in which the corporation is a party, or intervenes under §1451 of this title, in any State court, the corporation may, without bond or security, remove such suit, action, or proceeding from the State court to the United States District Court for the district or division embracing the place where the same is pending by following any procedure for removal now or hereafter in effect.

Trademark Clarification Act of 1984 (Pub. L. No. 98-620), as follows:
- ERISA §4003(e)(4) was repealed by Act §402(33). Amendment not applicable to cases pending on Nov. 8, 1984. See §403 of the Act for applicability.

Multiemployer Pension Plan Amendments Act of 1980 (Pub. L. No. 96-364), as follows:
- ERISA §4003(a) was amended by Act §402(a)(2)(A) by substituting "enforce" for "determine whether any person has violated or is about to violate". Eff. Sept. 26, 1980, except as specifically provided.
- ERISA §4003(e)(1) was amended by Act §402(a)(2)(B) by substituting "enforce" for "redress violations of". Eff. Sept. 26, 1980, except as specifically provided.
- ERISA §4003(f) was amended by Act §402(a)(2)(C) by inserting at the end: "In any suit, action, or proceeding in which the corporation is a party, or intervenes under section 4301, in any State court, the corporation may, without bond or security, remove such suit, action, or proceeding from the State court to the United States District Court for the district or division embracing the place where the same is pending by following any procedure for removal now or hereafter in effect." Eff. Sept. 26, 1980, except as specifically provided.
- ERISA §4003(f) was amended by Act §403(k) by substituting "Except as provided in §4301(a)(2), any" for "Any". Eff. Sept. 26, 1980, except as specifically provided.

SEC. 4004. [Repealed.]

Amendments to ERISA §4004 [Repealed.]

Consolidated Omnibus Budget Reconciliation Act of 1985 (Pub. L. No. 99-272), as follows:
- ERISA §4004 was repealed by Act §11016(c)(6). Eff. Jan. 1, 1986, with certain exceptions, see Act §11019. The section provided for a receiver to take control of a terminated plan and its assets.

SEC. 4005. PENSION BENEFIT GUARANTY FUNDS.

(a) Establishment of Four Revolving Funds on Books of Treasury of the United States.—There are established on the books of the Treasury of the United States four revolving funds to be used by the corporation in carrying out its duties under this title. One of the funds shall be used with respect to basic benefits guaranteed under section 4022, one of the funds shall be used with respect to basic benefits guaranteed under section 4022A, one of the funds shall be used with respect to nonbasic benefits guaranteed under section 4022 (if any), and the remaining fund shall be used with respect to nonbasic benefits guaranteed under section 4022A (if any), other than subsection (g)(2) thereof (if any). Whenever in this title reference is made to the term "fund" the reference shall be considered to refer to the appropriate fund established under this subsection.

(b) Credits to Funds; Availability of Funds; Investment of Moneys in Excess of Current Needs.—

(1) Each fund established under this section shall be credited with the appropriate portion of—

(A) funds borrowed under subsection (c),

(B) premiums, penalties, interest, and charges collected under this title,

(C) the value of the assets of a plan administered under section 4042 by a trustee to the extent that they exceed the liabilities of such plan,

(D) the amount of any employer liability payments collected under subtitle D, to the extent that such payments exceed liabilities of the plan (taking into account all other plan assets),

(E) earnings on investments of the fund or on assets credited to the fund under this subsection,

(F) attorney's fees awarded to the corporation, and

(G) receipts from any other operations under this title.

(2) Subject to the provisions of subsection (a), each fund shall be available—

(A) for making such payments as the corporation determines are necessary to pay benefits guaranteed under section 4022 or 4022A of this title or benefits payable under section 4050 of this title,

(B) to purchase assets from a plan being terminated by the corporation when the corporation determines such purchase will best protect the interests of the corporation, participants in the plan being terminated, and other insured plans,

(C) to repay to the Secretary of the Treasury such sums as may be borrowed (together with interest thereon) under subsection (c),

(D) to pay the operational and administrative expenses of the corporation, including reimbursement of the expenses incurred by the Department of the Treasury in maintaining the funds, and the Comptroller General in auditing the corporation, and

(E) to pay to participants and beneficiaries the estimated amount of benefits which are guaranteed by the corporation under this title and the estimated amount of other benefits to which plan assets are allocated under section 4044, under single-employer plans which are unable to pay benefits when due or which are abandoned.

(3) Whenever the corporation determines that the moneys of any fund are in excess of current needs, it may request the investment of such amounts as it determines advisable by the Secretary of the Treasury in obligations issued or guaranteed by the United States but, until all borrowings under subsection (c) have been repaid, the obligations in which such excess moneys are invested may not yield a rate of return in excess of the rate of interest payable on such borrowings.

(c) Authority to Issue Notes or Other Obligations; Purchase by Secretary of the Treasury as Public Debt Transaction.—The corporation is authorized to issue to the Secretary of the Treasury notes or other obligations in an aggregate amount of not to exceed $100,000,000, in such forms and denominations, bearing such maturities, and subject to such terms and conditions as may be prescribed by the Secretary of the Treasury. Such notes or other obligations shall bear interest at a rate determined by the Secretary of the Treasury, taking into consideration the current average market yield on outstanding marketable obligations of the United States of comparable maturities during the monthpreceding the issuance of such notes or other obligations of the corporation. The Secretary of the Treasury is authorized and directed to purchase any notes or other obligations issued by the corporation under this subsection, and for that purpose he is authorized to use as a public debt transaction the proceeds from the sale of any securities issued under the Second Liberty Bond Act, as amended, and the purposes for which securities may be issued under that Act, as amended, are extended to include any purchase of such notes and obligations. The Secretary of the Treasury may at any time sell any of the notes or other obligations acquired by him under this subsection. All redemptions, purchases, and sales by the Secretary of the Treasury of such notes or other obligations shall be treated as public debt transactions of the United States.

(d) Establishment of Fifth Fund; Purpose; Availability, etc.—

(1) A fifth fund shall be established for the reimbursement of uncollectible withdrawal liability under section 4222, and shall be credited with the appropriate—

(A) premiums, penalties, and interest charges collected under this title, and

(B) earnings on investments of the fund or on assets credited to the fund.

The fund shall be available to make payments pursuant to the supplemental program established under section 4222, including those expenses and other charges determined to be appropriate by the corporation.

(2) The corporation may invest amounts of the fund in such obligations as the corporation considers appropriate.

(e) Establishment of Sixth Fund; Purpose, Availability, etc.—

(1) A sixth fund shall be established for the supplemental benefit guarantee program provided under section 4022A(g)(2).

(2) Such fund shall be credited with the appropriate—

(A) premiums, penalties, and interest charges collected under section 4022A(g)(2), and

(B) earnings on investments of the fund or on assets credited to the fund.

The fund shall be available for makingpayments pursuant to the supplemental benefit guarantee program established under section 4022A(g)(2) including those expenses and other charges determined to be appropriate by the corporation.

(3) The corporation may invest amounts of the fund in such obligations as the corporation considers appropriate.

(f) Deposit of Premiums Into Separate Revolving Fund.—

(1) A seventh fund shall be established and credited with—

(A) premiums, penalties, and interest charges collected under section 4006(a)(3)(A)(i) (not described in subparagraph (B)) to the extent attributable to the amount of the premium in excess of $8.50,

(B) premiums, penalties, and interest charges collected under section 4006(a)(3)(E), and

(C) earnings on investments of the fund or on assets credited to the fund.

(2) Amounts in the fund shall be available for transfer to other funds established under this section with respect to a single-employer plan but shall not be available to pay—

(A) administrative costs of the corporation, or

(B) benefits under any plan which was terminated before October 1, 1988, unless no other amounts are available for such payment.

(3) The corporation may invest amounts of the fund in such obligations as the corporation considers appropriate.

(g) Other Use of Funds; Deposits of Repayments.—

(1) Amounts in any fund established under this section may be used only for the purposes for which such fund was established and may not be used to make loans to (or on behalf of) any other fund or to finance any other activity of the corporation.

(2) None of the funds borrowed under subsection (c) may be used to make loans to (or on behalf of) any fund other than a fund described in the second sentence of subsection (a).

(3) Any repayment to the corporation of any amount paid out of any fund in connection with a multiemployer plan shall be deposited in such fund.

(h) Voting by Corporation of Stock Paid as Liability.—Any stock in a person liable to the corporation under this title which is paid to the corporation by such person or a member of such person's controlled group in satisfaction of such person's liability under this title may be voted only by the custodial trustees or outside money managers of the corporation.

Amendments to ERISA §4005

Uruguay Round Agreements Act of 1994 (Pub. L. No. 103-465), as follows:

- ERISA §4005(b)(2)(A) was amended by Act §776(b)(2) by inserting "or benefits payable under §4050" after "§4022A". Eff. with respect to distributions that occur in plan years commencing after final regulations implementing these provisions are prescribed by PBGC, see Act §776(e).

Agricultural Reconciliation Act of 1987 (Pub. L. No. 100-203), as follows:

- ERISA §4005(f), (g) were amended by Act §9331(d) by adding new subsec. (f) and redesignating former subsec. (f) as subsec. (g) and former subsec. (g) as subsec. (h). Eff. for fiscal years beginning after Sept. 30, 1988, see Act §9331(f)(2).
- ERISA §4005(h) (as redesignated) was amended by Act §9312(c)(4) by striking "or fiduciaries with respect to trusts to which the requirements of §4049 apply". Eff. for plan terminations under ERISA §4041(c) for which notices of intent to terminate are provided under ERISA §4041(a)(2) after Dec. 17, 1987, and plan terminations for which proceedings are instituted by PBGC under ERISA §4042 after that date. See Act §9312(d)(1), as amended.

Consolidated Omnibus Budget Reconciliation Act of 1985 (Pub. L. No. 99-272), as follows:

- ERISA §4005(b)(1) was amended by Act §11016(a)(2) by striking "and" at the end of subpara. (E); adding new subpara. (F); and redesignating former subpara. (F) as subpara. (G). Eff. Jan. 1, 1986, except as specifically provided, see Act §11019.
- ERISA §4005(b)(2) was amended by Act §11016(a)(1) by striking "and" at the end of subpara. (C); striking the period at the end of subpara. (D); and inserting ", and"; and adding new subpara. (E). Eff. Jan. 1, 1986, except as specifically provided, see Act §11019.
- ERISA §4005(g) was added by Act §11016(c)(7). Eff. Jan. 1, 1986, except as specifically provided, see Act §11019.

Multiemployer Pension Plan Amendments Act of 1980 (Pub. L. No. 96-364), as follows:

- ERISA §4005(a) was amended by Act §403(a)(1) by substituting:
  "One of the funds shall be used with respect to basic benefits guaranteed under §4022, one of the funds shall be used with respect to basic benefits guaranteed under §4022A, one of the funds shall be used with respect to nonbasic benefits guaranteed under §4022 (if any), and the remaining fund shall be used with respect to nonbasic benefits guaranteed under §4022A (if any), other than subsection (g)(2) thereof (if any)." for "One of the funds shall be used in connection with benefits guaranteed under §§4022 and 4023 (but not non-basic benefits) with respect to plans other than multiemployer plans, one of the funds shall be used with respect to such benefits guaranteed under such sections (other than non-basic benefits) for multiemployer plans, one of the funds shall be used with respect to nonbasic benefits, if any are guaranteed by the corporation under §4022, for plans which are not multiemployer plans, and the remaining fund shall be used with respect to non-basic benefits, if any are guaranteed by the corporation under §4022, for multiemployer plans." Eff. Sept. 26, 1980, except as specifically provided.
- ERISA §4005(b)(2)(A) was amended by Act §403(a)(2) by inserting "or 4022A". Eff. Sept. 26, 1980, except as specifically provided.
- ERISA §4005(b)(2)(B) was stricken by Act §403(a)(3). Eff. Sept. 26, 1980, except as specifically provided. ERISA §4005(b)(2)(B) prior to being stricken:

(B) for making such payments as the corporation determines are necessary under §4023,

- ERISA §4005(b)(2) was amended by Act §403(a)(3) by redesignating subparas. (C), (D), and (E) as subparas. (B), (C), and (D), respectively. Eff. Sept. 26, 1980, except as specifically provided.
- ERISA §4005(b)(2) was amended by Act §403(a)(4) by adding subsecs. (d), (e), and (f). Eff. Sept. 26, 1980, except as specifically provided.

SEC. 4006. PREMIUM RATES.

(a) Schedule for Premium Rates and Bases for Application; Establishment, Coverage, etc.—

(1) The corporation shall prescribe such schedules of premium rates and bases for the application of those rates as may be necessary to provide sufficient revenue to the fund for the corporation to carry out its functions under this title. The premium rates charged by the corporation for any period shall be uniform for all plans, other than multiemployer plans, insured by the corporation with respect to basic benefits guaranteed by it under section 4022, and shall be uniform for all multiemployer plans with respect to basic benefits guaranteed by it under section 4022A.

(2) The corporation shall maintain separate schedules of premium rates, and bases for the application of those rates, for—

(A) basic benefits guaranteed by it under section 4022 for single-employer plans,

(B) basic benefits guaranteed by it under section 4022A for multiemployer plans,

(C) nonbasic benefits guaranteed by it under section 4022 for single-employer plans,

(D) nonbasic benefits guaranteed by it under section 4022A for multiemployer plans, and

(E) reimbursements of uncollectible withdrawal liability under section 4222.

The corporation may revise such schedules whenever it determines that revised schedules are necessary. Except as provided in section 4022A(f), in order to place a revised schedule described in subparagraph (A) or (B) in effect, the corporation shall proceed in accordance with subsection (b)(1), and such schedule shall apply only to plan years beginning more than 30 days after the date on which a joint resolution approving such revised schedule is enacted.

(3)(A) Except as provided in subparagraph (C), the annual premium rate payable to the corporation by all plans for basic benefits guaranteed under this title is—

(i) in the case of a single-employer plan, for plan years beginning after December 31, 2005, an amount equal to the sum of $30 plus the additional premium (if any) determined under subparagraph

ERISA Sec. 4006(a)(3)(A)(i)

(E) for each individual who is a participant in such plan during the plan year;

(ii) in the case of a multiemployer plan, for the plan year within which the date of enactment of the Multiemployer Pension Plan Amendments Act of 1980 [enacted Sept. 26, 1980] falls, an amount for each individual who is a participant in such plan for such plan year equal to the sum of—

(I) 50 cents, multiplied by a fraction the numerator of which is the number of months in such year ending on or before such date and the denominator of which is 12, and

(II) $1.00, multiplied by a fraction equal to 1 minus the fraction determined under clause (i),

(iii) in the case of a multiemployer plan for plan years after the date of enactment of the Multiemployer Pension Plan Amendments Act of 1980 [enacted Sept. 26, 1980] and before January 1, 2006, an amount equal to—

(I) $1.40 for each participant, for the first, second, third, and fourth plan years,

(II) $1.80 for each participant, for the fifth and sixth plan years,

(III) $2.20 for each participant, for the seventh and eighth plan years, and

(IV) $2.60 for each participant, for the ninth plan year, and for each succeeding plan year or

(iv) in the case of a multiemployer plan, for plan years beginning after December 31, 2005, $8.00 for each individual who is a participant in such plan during the applicable plan year.

(B) The corporation may prescribe by regulation the extent to which the rate described in subparagraph (A)(i) applies more than once for any plan year to an individual participating in more than one plan maintained by the same employer, and the corporation may prescribe regulations under which the rate described in clause (iii) or (iv) of subparagraph (A) will not apply to the same participant in any multiemployer plan more than once for any plan year.

(C)(i) If the sum of—

(I) the amounts in any fund for basic benefits guaranteed for multiemployer plans, and

(II) the value of any assets held by the corporation for payment of basic benefits guaranteed for multiemployer plans, is for any calendar year less than 2 times the amount of basic benefits guaranteed by the corporation under this title for multiemployer plans which were paid out of any such fund or assets during the preceding calendar year, the annual premium rates under subparagraph (A) shall be increased to the next highest premium level necessary to insure that such sum will be at

least 2 times greater than such amount during the following calendar year.

(ii) If the board of directors of the corporation determines that an increase in the premium rates under subparagraph (A) is necessary to provide assistance to plans which are receiving assistance under section 4261 and to plans the board finds are reasonably likely to require such assistance, the board may order such increase in the premium rates.

(iii) The maximum annual premium rate which may be established under this subparagraph is $2.60 for each participant.

(iv) The provisions of this subparagraph shall not apply if the annual premium rate is increased to a level in excess of $2.60 per participant under any other provisions of this title.

(D)(i) Not later than 120 days before the date on which an increase under subparagraph (C)(ii) is to become effective, the corporation shall publish in the Federal Register a notice of the determination described in subparagraph (C)(ii), the basis for the determination, the amount of the increase in the premium, and the anticipated increase in premium income that would result from the increase in the premium rate. The notice shall invite public comment, and shall provide for a public hearing if one is requested. Any such hearing shall be commenced not later than 60 days before the date on which the increase is to become effective.

(ii) The board of directors shall review the hearing record established under clause (i) and shall, not later than 30 days before the date on which the increase is to become effective, determine (after consideration of the comments received) whether the amount of the increase should be changed and shall publish its determination in the Federal Register.

(E)(i) Except as provided in subparagraph (H), the additional premium determined under this subparagraph with respect to any plan for any plan year shall be an amount equal to the amount determined under clause (ii) divided by the number of participants in such plan as of the close of the preceding plan year.

(ii) The amount determined under this clause for any plan year shall be an amount equal to $9.00 for each $1,000 (or fraction thereof) of unfunded vested benefits under the plan as of the close of the preceding plan year.

(iii) For purposes of clause (ii), the term "unfunded vested benefits" means, for a plan year, the excess (if any) of—

(I) the funding target of the plan as determined under section 303(d) for the plan year by only taking into account vested benefits and by using the interest rate described in clause (iv), over

(II) the fair market value of plan assets for the plan year which are held by the plan on the valuation date.

(iv) The interest rate used in valuing benefits for purposes of subclause (I) of clause (iii) shall be equal to the first, second, or third segment rate for the month preceding the month in which the plan year begins, which would be determined under section 303(h)(2)(C) if section 303(h)(2)(D) were applied by using the monthly yields for the month preceding the month in which the plan year begins on investment grade corporate bonds with varying maturities and in the top 3 quality levels rather than the average of such yields for a 24-month period.

(F) For each plan year beginning in a calendar year after 2006, there shall be substituted for the premium rate specified in clause (i) of subparagraph (A) an amount equal to the greater of—

(i) the product derived by multiplying the premium rate specified in clause (i) of subparagraph (A) by the ratio of—

(I) the national average wage index (as defined in section 209(k)(1) of the Social Security Act) for the first of the 2 calendar years preceding the calendar year in which such plan year begins, to

(II) the national average wage index (as so defined) for 2004; and

(ii) the premium rate in effect under clause (i) of subparagraph (A) for plan years beginning in the preceding calendar year.

If the amount determined under this subparagraph is not a multiple of $1, such product shall be rounded to the nearest multiple of $1.

(G) For each plan year beginning in a calendar year after 2006, there shall be substituted for the premium rate specified in clause (iv) of subparagraph (A) an amount equal to the greater of—

(i) the product derived by multiplying the premium rate specified in clause (iv) of subparagraph (A) by the ratio of—

(I) the national average wage index (as defined in section 209(k)(1) of the Social Security Act) for the first of the 2 calendar years preceding the calendar year in which such plan year begins, to

(II) the national average wage index (as so defined) for 2004; and

(ii) the premium rate in effect under clause (iv) of subparagraph (A) for plan years beginning in the preceding calendar year.

If the amount determined under this subparagraph is not a multiple of $1, such product shall be rounded to the nearest multiple of $1.

(H)(i) In the case of an employer who has 25 or fewer employees on the first day of the plan year, the additional premium determined under subparagraph (E) for each participant shall not exceed $5 multiplied by the number of participants in the plan as of the close of the preceding plan year.

(ii) For purposes of clause (i), whether an employer has 25 or fewer employees on the first day of the plan year is determined by taking into consideration all of the employees of all members of the contributing sponsor's controlled group. In the case of a plan maintained by two or more contributing sponsors, the employees of all contributing sponsors and their controlled groups shall be aggregated for purposes of determining whether the 25-or-fewer-employees limitation has been satisfied.

(4) The corporation may prescribe, subject to the enactment of a joint resolution in accordance with this section or section 4022A(f), alternative schedules of premium rates, and bases for the application of those rates, for basic benefits guaranteed by it under sections 4022 and 4022A based, in whole or in part, on the risks insured by the corporation in each plan.

(5)(A) In carrying out its authority under paragraph (1) to establish schedules of premium rates, and bases for the application of those rates, for nonbasic benefits guaranteed under sections 4022 and 4022A, the premium rates charged by the corporation for any period for nonbasic benefits guaranteed shall—

(i) be uniform by category of nonbasic benefits guaranteed,

(ii) be based on the risks insured in each category, and

(iii) reflect the experience of the corporation (including experience which may be reasonably anticipated) in guaranteeing such benefits.

(B) Notwithstanding subparagraph (A), premium rates charged to any multiemployer plan by the corporation for any period for supplemental guarantees under section 4022A(g)(2) may reflect any reasonable considerations which the corporation determines to be appropriate.

(6)(A) In carrying out its authority under paragraph (1) to establish premium rates and bases for basic benefits guaranteed under section 4022 with respect to single-employer plans, the corporation shall establish such rates and bases in coverage schedules in accordance with the provisions of this paragraph.

(B) The corporation may establish annual premiums for single-employer plans composed of the sum of—

(i) a charge based on a rate applicable to the excess, if any, of the present value of the basic benefits of the plan which are guaranteed over the value of the assets of the plan, not in excess of 0.1 percent, and

(ii) an additional charge based on a rate applicable to the present value of the basic benefits of the plan which are guaranteed.

The rate for the additional charge referred to in clause (ii) shall be set by the corporation for every year at a level which the corporation estimates will yield total revenue approximately equal to the total revenue to be derived by the corporation from the charges referred to in clause (i) of this subparagraph.

(C) The corporation may establish annual premiums for single-employer plans based on—

(i) the number of participants in a plan, but such premium rates shall not exceed the rates described in paragraph (3),

(ii) unfunded basic benefits guaranteed under this title, but such premium rates shall not exceed the limitations applicable to charges referred to in subparagraph (B)(i), or

(iii) total guaranteed basic benefits, but such premium rates shall not exceed the rates for additional charges referred to in subparagraph (B)(ii).

If the corporation uses two or more of the rate bases described in this subparagraph, the premium rates shall be designed to produce approximately equal amounts of aggregate premium revenue from each of the rate bases used.

(D) For purposes of this paragraph, the corporation shall by regulation define the terms "value of assets" and "present value of the benefits of the plan which are guaranteed" in a manner consistent with the purposes of this title and the provisions of this section.

(7) Premium Rate for Certain Terminated Single-Employer Plans.—

(A) In general.—If there is a termination of a single-employer plan under clause (ii) or (iii) of section 4041(c)(2)(B) or section 4042, there shall be payable to the corporation, with respect to each applicable 12-month period, a premium at a rate equal to $1,250 multiplied by the number of individuals who were participants in the plan immediately before the termination date. Such premium shall be in addition to any other premium under this section.

(B) Special rule for plans terminated in bankruptcy reorganization.—In the case of a single-employer plan terminated under section 4041(c)(2)(B)(ii) or under section 4042 during pendency of any bankruptcy reorganization proceeding under chapter 11 of title 11, United States Code, or under any similar law of a State or a political subdivision of a State (or a case described in section 4041(c)(2)(B)(i) filed by or against such person has been converted, as of such date, to such a case in which reorganization is sought), subparagraph (A) shall not apply to such plan until the date

of the discharge or dismissal of such person in such case.

(C) Applicable 12-month period.—For purposes of subparagraph (A)—

(i) In general.—The term "applicable 12-month period" means—

(I) the 12-month period beginning with the first month following the month in which the termination date occurs, and

(II) each of the first two 12-month periods immediately following the period described in subclause (I).

(ii) Plans terminated in bankruptcy reorganization.—In any case in which the requirements of subparagraph (B) are met in connection with the termination of the plan with respect to 1 or more persons described in such subparagraph, the 12-month period described in clause (i)(I) shall be the 12-month period beginning with the first month following the month which includes the earliest date as of which each such person is discharged or dismissed in the case described in such clause in connection with such person.

(D) Coordination with section 4007.—

(i) Notwithstanding section 4007—

(I) premiums under this paragraph shall be due within 30 days after the beginning of any applicable 12-month period, and

(II) the designated payor shall be the person who is the contributing sponsor as of immediately before the termination date.

(ii) The fifth sentence of section 4007(a) shall not apply in connection with premiums determined under this paragraph.

(E) **[Repealed.]**

(b) Revised Schedule; Congressional Procedures Applicable.—

(1) In order to place a revised schedule (other than a schedule described in subsection (a)(2)(C), (D), or (E) in effect, the corporation shall transmit the proposed schedule, its proposed effective date, and the reasons for its proposal to the Committee on Ways and Means and the Committee on Education and Labor of the House of Representatives and to the Committee on Finance and the Committee on Labor and Human Resources of the Senate.

(2) The succeeding paragraphs of this subsection are enacted by Congress as an exercise of the rule-making power of the Senate and the House of Representatives, respectively, and as such they shall be deemed a part of the rules of each House, respectively, but applicable only with respect to the procedure to be followed in that House in the case of resolutions described in paragraph (3). They shall supersede other rules only to the extent that they are inconsistent therewith. They are enacted with full recognition of the constitutional right of either House to change the rules (so far as relating to the procedure of that House) at any time, in the same manner and to the same extent as in the case of any rule of that House.

(3) For the purpose of the succeeding paragraphs of this subsection, "resolution" means only a joint resolution, the matter after the resolving clause of which is as follows: "The proposed revised schedule transmitted to Congress by the Pension Benefit Guaranty Corporation on is hereby approved.", the blank space therein being filled with the date on which the corporation's message proposing the rate was delivered.

(4) A resolution shall be referred to the Committee on Ways and Means and the Committee on Education and Labor of the House of Representatives and to the Committee on Finance and the Committee on Labor and Human Resources of the Senate.

(5) If a committee to which has been referred a resolution has not reported it before the expiration of 10 calendar days after its introduction, it shall then (but not before) be in order to move to discharge the committee from further consideration of that resolution, or to discharge the committee from further consideration of any other resolution with respect to the proposed adjustment which has been referred to the committee. The motion to discharge may be made only by a person favoring the resolution, shall be highly privileged (except that it may not be made after the committee has reported a resolution with respect to the same proposed rate), and debate thereon shall be limited to not more than 1 hour, to be divided equally between those favoring and those opposing the resolution. An amendment to the motion is not in order, and it is not in order to move to reconsider the vote by which the motion is agreed to or disagreed to. If the motion to discharge is agreed to or disagreed to, the motion may not be renewed, nor may another motion to discharge the committee be made with respect to any other resolution with respect to the same proposed rate.

(6) When a committee has reported, or has been discharged from further consideration of a resolution, it is at any time thereafter in order (even though a previous motion to the same effect has been disagreed to) to move to proceed to the consideration of the resolution. The motion is highly privileged and is not debatable. An amendment to the motion is not in order, and it is not in order to move to reconsider the vote by which the motion is agreed to or disagreed to. Debate on the resolution shall be limited to not more than 10 hours, which shall be divided equally between those favoring and those opposing the resolution. A motion further to limit debate is not debatable. An amendment to, or motion to recommit, the resolution is not in order, and it is not in order to move to

reconsider the vote by which the resolution is agreed to or disagreed to.

(7) Motions to postpone, made with respect to the discharge from committee, or the consideration of, a resolution and motions to proceed to the consideration of other business shall be decided without debate. Appeals from the decisions of the Chair relating to the application of the rules of the Senate or the House of Representatives, as the case may be, to the procedure relating to a resolution shall be decided without debate.

(c) **Rates for Plans for Basic Benefits.—**

(1) Except as provided in subsection (a)(3), and subject to paragraph (2), the rate for all plans for basic benefits guaranteed under this title with respect to plan years ending after September 2, 1974, is—

(A) in the case of a plan which was not a multiemployer plan in a plan year—

(i) with respect to each plan year beginning before January 1, 1978, an amount equal to $1 for each individual who was a participant in such plan during the plan year,

(ii) with respect to each plan year beginning after December 31, 1977, and before January 1, 1986, an amount equal to $2.60 for each individual who was a participant in such plan during the plan year,

(iii) with respect to each plan year beginning after December 31, 1985, and before January 1, 1988, an amount equal to $8.50 for each individual who was a participant in such plan during the plan year, and

(iv) with respect to each plan year beginning after December 31, 1987, and before January 1, 1991, an amount equal to $16 for each individual who was a participant in such plan during the plan year, and

(B) in the case of each plan which was a multiemployer plan in a plan year, an amount equal to 50 cents for each individual who was a participant in such plan during the plan year.

(2) The rate applicable under this subsection for the plan year preceding September 1, 1975, is the product of—

(A) the rate described in the preceding sentence; and

(B) a fraction—

(i) the numerator of which is the number of calendar months in the plan year which ends after September 2, 1974, and before the date on which the new plan year commences, and

(ii) the denominator of which is 12.

Amendments to ERISA §4006
Worker, Retiree, and Employer Recovery Act of 2008 (Pub. L. No. 110-458), as follows:

ERISA Sec. 4006(c)(2)(B)(ii)

- ERISA §4006(a)(3)(A)(i) was amended by Act §104(a) by striking "1990" and inserting "2005". Eff. as if included in Pub. L. No. 109-280, §401.

Pension Protection Act of 2006 (Pub. L. No. 109-280), as follows:

- ERISA §4006(a)(3)(E)(i) was amended by Act §405(a)(1) by substituting "Except as provided in subparagraph (H), the additional" for "The additional". Eff. for plan years beginning after Dec. 31, 2006.
- ERISA §4006(a)(3)(E)(iii)(V) was amended by Act §301(a)(3) by substituting "2008" for "2006". Eff. Aug. 17, 2006.
- ERISA §4006(a)(3)(E)(iii) and (iv) were amended by Act §401(a)(1). Eff. for plan years beginning after 2007. ERISA §4006(a)(3)(E)(iii) and (iv) prior to amendment:

    (iii) For purposes of clause (ii)—

    (I) Except as provided in subclause (II) or (III), the term "unfunded vested benefits" means the amount which would be the unfunded current liability (within the meaning of section 302(d)(8)(A) if only vested benefits were taken into account.

    (II) The interest rate used in valuing vested benefits for purposes of subclause (I) shall be equal to the applicable percentage of the annual yield on 30-year Treasury securities for the month preceding the month in which the plan year begins. For purposes of this subclause, the applicable percentage is 80 percent for plan years beginning before July 1, 1997, 85 percent for plan years beginning after June 30, 1997, and before the 1st plan year to which the first tables prescribed under section 302(d)(7)(C)(ii)(II) apply, and 100 percent for such 1st plan year and subsequent plan years.

    (III) In the case of any plan year for which the applicable percentage under subclause (II) is 100 percent, the value of the plan's assets used in determining unfunded current liability under subclause (I) shall be their fair market value.

    (IV) In the case of plan years beginning after December 31, 2001, and before January 1, 2004, subclause (II) shall be applied by substituting "100 percent" for "85 percent". Subclause (III) shall be applied for such years without regard to the preceding sentence. Any reference to this clause or this subparagraph by any other sections or subsections (other than sections 4005, 4010, 4011, and 4043) shall be treated as a reference to this clause or this subparagraph without regard to this subclause.

    (V) In the case of plan years beginning after December 31, 2003, and before January 1, 2006, the annual yield taken into account under subclause (II) shall be the annual rate of interest determined by the Secretary of the Treasury on amounts invested conservatively in long-term investment grade corporate bonds for the month preceding the month in which the plan year begins. For purposes of the preceding sentence, the Secretary of the Treasury shall determine such rate of interest on the basis of 2 or more indices that are selected periodically by the Secretary of the Treasury and that are in the top 3 quality levels available. The Secretary of the Treasury shall make the permissible range, and the indices and methodology used to determine the rate, publicly available.

    (IV) No premium shall be determined under this subparagraph for any plan year if, as of the close of the preceding plan year, contributions to the plan for the preceding plan year were not less than the full funding limitation for the preceding plan year under section 412(c)(7) of the Internal Revenue Code of 1986.

- ERISA §4006(a)(3)(H) was added by Act §405(a)(2). Eff. for plan years beginning after Dec. 31, 2006.
- ERISA §4006(a)(7)(C)(ii) was amended by Act §401(b)(2)(A) by substituting "subparagraph (B)" for "subparagraph (B)(i)(I)". Eff. for plan terminated after Dec. 31, 2005, as if included in the Deficit Reduction Act of 2005 (Pub. L. No. 109-171).
- ERISA §4006(a)(7)(E) was repealed by Act §401(b)(1). ERISA §4006(a)(7)(E) prior to repeal:

    (E) Termination. Subparagraph (A) shall not apply with respect to any plan terminated after Dec. 31, 2010.

- ERISA §4006(a)(7)(C)(ii) was amended by Act §401(b)(2)(A) by substituting "subparagraph (B)" for "subparagraph

(B)(i)(I)". Eff. for plan terminated after Dec. 31, 2005, as if included in the Deficit Reduction Act of 2005 (Pub. L. No. 109-171), except as provided in Pub. L. No. 109-171, §8101(d)(2)(B):

    (B) Special rule for plans terminated in bankruptcy.—The amendment made by subsection (b) shall not apply to a termination of a single-employer plan that is terminated during the pendency of any bankruptcy reorganization proceeding under chapter 11 of title 11, United States Code (or under any similar law of a State or political subdivision of a State), if the proceeding is pursuant to a bankruptcy filing occurring before October 18, 2005.

- **Other Provision.** Act §115(a)–(c):

SEC. 115. MODIFICATION OF TRANSITION RULE TO PENSION FUNDING REQUIREMENTS.

    (a) In General.—In the case of a plan that—

    (1) was not required to pay a variable rate premium for the plan year beginning in 1996,

    (2) has not, in any plan year beginning after 1995, merged with another plan (other than a plan sponsored by an employer that was in 1996 within the controlled group of the plan sponsor), and

    (3) is sponsored by a company that is engaged primarily in the interurban or interstate passenger bus service, the rules described in subsection (b) shall apply for any plan year beginning after December 31, 2007.

    (b) Modified Rules.—The rules described in this subsection are as follows:

    (1) For purposes of section 430(j)(3) of the Internal Revenue Code of 1986 and section 303(j)(3) of the Employee Retirement Income Security Act of 1974, the plan shall be treated as not having a funding shortfall for any plan year.

    (2) For purposes of—

    (A) determining unfunded vested benefits under section 4006(a)(3)(E)(iii) of such Act, and

    (B) determining any present value or making any computation under section 412 of such Code or section 302 of such Act, the mortality table shall be the mortality table used by the plan.

    (3) Section 430(c)(5)(B) of such Code and section 303(c)(5)(B) of such Act (relating to phase-in of funding target for exemption from new shortfall amortization base) shall each be applied by substituting "2012" for "2011" therein and by substituting for the table therein the following:

In the case of a plan year

beginning in calendar year	applicable percentage is:
2008	90 percent
2009	92 percent
2010	94 percent
2011	96 percent.

    (c) Definitions.—Any term used in this section which is also used in section 430 of such Code or section 303 of such Act shall have the meaning provided such term in such section. If the same term has a different meaning in such Code and such Act, such term shall, for purposes of this section, have the meaning provided by such Code when applied with respect to such Code and the meaning provided by such Act when applied with respect to such Act. * * *

- **Other Provision.** Act §402(g)(2)(B):

    (B) Termination premium.—In applying section 4006(a)(7)(A) of the Employee Retirement Income Security Act of 1974 to an eligible plan during any period in which an election under subsection (a)(1) is in effect—

    (i) "$2,500" shall be substituted for "$1,250" in such section if such plan terminates during the 5-year period beginning on the first day of the first applicable plan year with respect to such plan, and

    (ii) such section shall be applied without regard to subparagraph (B) of section 8101(d)(2) of the Deficit Reduction Act of 2005 (relating to special rule for plans terminated in bankruptcy).

The substitution described in clause (i) shall not apply with respect to any plan if the Secretary of Labor determines that such plan terminated as a result of extraordinary circumstances such as a terrorist attack or other similar event.

Deficit Reduction Act of 2005 (Pub. L. No. 109-171), as follows:

● ERISA §4006(a)(3)(A)(i) was amended by Act §8101(a)(1)(A) by substituting "$30" for "$19". Eff. for plan years beginning after Dec. 31, 2005, see Act §8101(d)(1).

● ERISA §4006(a)(3)(A)(iii) was amended by Act §8101(a)(2)(A)(i)(I) by adding "and before January 1, 2006," after "Act of 1980". Eff. for plan years beginning after Dec. 31, 2005, see Act §8101(d)(1).

● ERISA §4006(a)(3)(F) was added by Act §8101(a)(1)(B). Eff. for plan years beginning after Dec. 31, 2005, see Act §8101(d)(1).

● ERISA §4006(a)(3)(A) was amended by Act §8101(a)(2)(A)(i)(II) by substituting ", or" for the period at the end of cl. (iii) and adding cl. (iv). Eff. for plan years beginning after Dec. 31, 2005, see Act §8101(d)(1).

● ERISA §4006(a)(3)(G) was added by Act §8101(a)(2)(B). Eff. for plan years beginning after Dec. 31, 2005, see Act §8101(d)(1).

● ERISA §4006(a)(7) was added by Act §8101(b). Eff. for plans terminated after Dec. 31, 2005, except as provided by Act §8101(d)(2)(B):

(B) Special rule for plans terminated in bankruptcy.—The amendment made by subsection (b) shall not apply to a termination of a single-employer plan that is terminated during the pendency of any bankruptcy reorganization proceeding under chapter 11 of title 11, United States Code (or under any similar law of a State or political subdivision of a State), if the proceeding is pursuant to a bankruptcy filing occurring before October 18, 2005.

Working Families Tax Relief Act of 2004 (Pub. L. No. 108-311), as follows:

● ERISA §4006(a)(3)(E)(iii)(IV) was amended by Act §403(d)(1) by adding in last sentence "or this subparagraph" after "this clause" in two places. Eff. Mar. 9, 2002.

● ERISA §4006(a)(3)(E)(iii)(IV) was amended by Act §403(d)(2) by adding "(other than sections 4005, 4010, 4011, and 4043)" after "subsections". Eff. Mar. 9, 2002.

Pension Funding Equity Act of 2004 (Pub. L. No. 108-218), as follows:

● ERISA §4006(a)(3)(E)(iii)(V) was added by Act §101(a)(4). Eff. for plan years beginning after Dec. 31, 2003.

● **Other Provision.** Act §101(c) (as amended by Pub. L. No. 109-280, §301(c)):

(c) **Provisions relating to plan amendments.**

(1) In general. If this subsection applies to any plan or annuity contract amendment—

(A) such plan or contract shall be treated as being operated in accordance with the terms of the plan or contract during the period described in paragraph (2)(B)(i), and

(B) except as provided by the Secretary of the Treasury, such plan shall not fail to meet the requirements of section 411(b)(6) of the Internal Revenue Code of 1986 and section 204(g) of the Employee Retirement Income Security Act of 1974 by reason of such amendment.

(2)Amendments to which section applies.

(A) In general. This subsection shall apply to any amendment to any plan or annuity contract which is made—

(i) pursuant to any amendment made by this section, and

(ii) on or before the last day of the first plan year beginning on or after January 1, 2008.

(B) Conditions. This subsection shall not apply to any plan or annuity contract unless—

(i) during the period beginning on the date the amendment described in subparagraph (A)(i) takes effect and ending on the date described in subparagraph (A)(ii) (or, if earlier, the date the plan or contract amendment is adopted), the plan or contract is operated as if such plan or contract amendment were in effect; and

(ii) such plan or contract amendment applies retroactively for such period.

● **Other Provision.** Act §101(d)(2) and (3):

(2) Lookback rules.—For purposes of applying subsections (d)(9)(B)(ii) and (e)(1) of section 302 of the Employee Retirement Income Security Act of 1974 and subsections (l)(9)(B)(ii) and (m)(1) of section 412 of the Internal Revenue Code of 1986 to plan years beginning after December 31, 2003, the amendments made by this section may be applied as if such amendments had been in effect for all prior plan years. The Secretary of the Treasury may prescribe simplified assumptions which may be used in applying the amendments made by this section to such prior plan years.

(3) Transition rule for section 415 limitation.—In the case of any participant or beneficiary receiving a distribution after December 31, 2003 and before January 1, 2005, the amount payable under any form of benefit subject to section 417(e)(3) of the Internal Revenue Code of 1986 and subject to adjustment under section 415(b)(2)(B) of such Code shall not, solely by reason of the amendment made by subsection (b)(4), be less than the amount that would have been so payable had the amount payable been determined using the applicable interest rate in effect as of the last day of the last plan year beginning before January 1, 2004.

Job Creation and Worker Assistance Act of 2002 (Pub. L. No. 107-147), as follows:

● ERISA §4006(a)(3)(E)(iii) was amended by Act §405(c) by adding subcl. (IV). Effective Mar. 9, 2002.

Uruguay Round Agreements Act of 1994 (Pub. L. No. 103-465), as follows:

● ERISA §4006(a)(3)(E)(iii)(I) was amended by Act §774(b)(2)(A) by inserting "or (III)" after "subclause (II)". Eff. for plan years beginning after Dec. 8, 1994, see Act §774(b)(3).

● ERISA §4006(a)(3)(E)(iii)(II) was amended by Act §774(b)(1)(A) by substituting "the applicable percentage" for "80 percent" and inserting at the end "For purposes of this subclause, the applicable percentage is 80 percent for plan years beginning before July 1, 1997, 85 percent for plan years beginning after June 30, 1997, and before the 1st plan year to which the first tables prescribed under section 1082(d)(7)(C)(ii)(II) of this title apply, and 100 percent for such 1st plan year and subsequent plan years." Eff. for plan years beginning after Dec. 8, 1994, see Act §774(b)(3).

● ERISA §4006(a)(3)(E)(iii) was amended by Act §774(b)(2)(B) by adding subcl. (III). Eff. for plan years beginning after Dec. 8, 1994, see Act §774(b)(3).

● ERISA §4006(a)(3)(E) was amended by Act §774(a)(1) by repealing cl. (iv) and redesignating former cl. (v) as cl. (iv). Eff. for plan years beginning after Dec. 8, 1994, see Act §774(b)(3). ERISA §4006(a)(3)(E)(iv) prior to repeal:

(iv)

(I) Except as provided in this clause, the aggregate increase in the premium payable with respect to any participant by reason of this subparagraph shall not exceed $53.

(II) If an employer made contributions to a plan during 1 or more of the 5 plan years preceding the 1st plan year to which this subparagraph applies in an amount not less than the maximum amount allowable as a deduction with respect to such contributions under section 404 of title 26, the dollar amount in effect under subclause (I) for the 1st 5 plan years to which this subparagraph applies shall be reduced by $3 for each plan year for which such contributions were made in such amount.

Omnibus Budget Reconciliation Act of 1990 (Pub. L. No. 101-508), as follows:

● ERISA §4006(a)(3)(A)(i) was amended by Act §12021(a)(1) by substituting "for plan years beginning after December 31, 1990, an amount equal to the sum of $19" for "for plan years beginning after December 31, 1987, an amount equal to the sum of $16". Eff. for plan years beginning after Dec. 31, 1990, see Act §12021(c).

● ERISA §4006(a)(3)(E)(ii) was amended by Act §12021(b)(1) by substituting "$9.00" for "$6.00". Eff. for plan years beginning after Dec. 31, 1990, see Act §12021(c).

● ERISA §4006(a)(3)(E)(iv)(I) was amended by Act §12021(b)(2) by substituting "$53" for "$34". Eff. for plan years beginning after Dec. 31, 1990, see Act §12021(c).

● ERISA §4006(c)(1)(A)(iv) was added by Act §12021(a)(2). Eff. for plan years beginning after Dec. 31, 1990, see Act §12021(c).

Omnibus Budget Reconciliation Act of 1989 (Pub. L. No. 101-239), as follows:

- ERISA §4006(a)(3)(E) was amended by Act §7881(h)(1) by adding cl. (v). Eff., except as otherwise provided, as if included in the provision of Pub. L. No. 100-203, §§9302–9346, to which it relates.
- ERISA §4006(c)(1)(A)(iii) was amended by Act §7881(h)(2) by realigning the margin. Eff., except as otherwise provided, as if included in the provision of Pub. L. No. 100-203, §§9302–9346, to which it relates.

Omnibus Budget Reconciliation Act of 1987 (Pub. L. No. 100-203), as follows:

- ERISA §4006(a)(3)(A)(i) was amended by Act §9331(a) by substituting "for plan years beginning after December 31, 1987, an amount equal to the sum of $16 plus the additional premium (if any) determined under subparagraph (E)" for "for plan years beginning after December 31, 1985, an amount equal to $8.50". Eff. for plan years beginning after Dec. 31, 1987, see Act §9331(f)(1).
- ERISA §4006(a)(3)(E) was added by Act §9331(b). Eff. for plan years beginning after Dec. 31, 1987, see Act §9331(f)(1).
- ERISA §4006(c)(1)(A) was amended by Act §9331(e) by striking "and" at end of cl. (i), inserting "and before January 1, 1986," in cl. (i)[(ii)], and adding cl. (iii). Eff. for plan years beginning after Dec. 31, 1987, see Act §9331(f)(1).

Consolidated Omnibus Budget Reconciliation Act of 1985 (Pub. L. No. 99-272), as follows:

- ERISA §4006(a)(1) was amended by Act §11005(b)(1) by striking "In establishing annual premiums with respect to plans, other than multiemployer plans, paragraphs (5) and (6) of this subsection (as in effect before the enactment of the Multiemployer Pension Plan Amendments Act of 1980) shall continue to apply." Eff. Sept. 26, 1980, see Act §11005(d)(2).
- ERISA §4006(a)(2) was amended by Act §11005(c)(1) by substituting "a joint resolution approving such revised schedule is enacted" for "the Congress approves such revised schedule by a concurrent resolution". Eff. for plan years commencing after Dec. 31, 1985, see Act §11005(d)(1).
- ERISA §4006(a)(3)(A)(i) was amended by Act §11005(a)(1) by substituting "for plan years beginning after December 31, 1985, an amount equal to $8.50" for "for plan years beginning after December 31, 1977, an amount equal to $2.60". Eff. for plan years commencing after Dec. 31, 1985, see Act §11005(d)(1).
- ERISA §4006(a)(4) was amended by Act §11005(c)(2) by substituting "the enactment of a joint resolution" for "approval by the Congress". Eff. for plan years commencing after Dec. 31, 1985, see Act §11005(d)(1).
- ERISA §4006(a)(6) was added by Act §11005(b)(2). Eff. Sept. 26, 1980, see Act §11005(d)(2).
- ERISA §4006(b)(3) was amended by Act §11005(c)(3) by substituting "joint" for "concurrent" and "The" for "That the Congress favors the" and inserted "is hereby approved". Eff. for plan years commencing after Dec. 31, 1985, see Act §11005(d)(1).
- ERISA §4006(c)(1)(A) was amended by Act §11005(a)(2). Eff. for plan years commencing after Dec. 31, 1985, see Act §11005(d)(1). ERISA §4006(c)(1)(A) prior to amendment:

  (A) in the case of each plan which was not a multiemployer plan in a plan year, an amount equal to $1 for each individual who was a participant in such plan during the plan year, and.

Multiemployer Pension Plan Amendments Act of 1980 (Pub. L. No. 96-364), as follows:

- ERISA §4006(a) was amended by Act §105(a). Eff. Sept. 26, 1980. ERISA §4006(a) prior to amendment:

  (a)(1) The corporation shall prescribe such insurance premium rates and such coverage schedules for the application of those rates as may be necessary to provide sufficient revenue to the fund for the corporation to carry out its functions under this title. The premium rates charged by the corporation for any period shall be uniform for all plans, other than multiemployer plans insured by the corporation, with respect to basic benefits guaranteed by it under section 4022, and shall be uniform for all multiemployer plans with respect to basic benefits guaranteed by it under such section. The premium rates charged by the corporation for any period for non-basic benefits guaranteed by

it shall be uniform by category of non-basic benefit guaranteed, shall be based on the risk insured in each category, and shall reflect the experience of the corporation (including reasonably anticipated experience) in guaranteeing such benefits.

(2) The corporation shall maintain separate coverage schedules for—

(A) basic benefits guaranteed by it under section 4022 for—

   (i) plans which are multiemployer plans, and

   (ii) plans which are not multiemployer plans,

(B) employers insured under section 4023 against liability under subtitle D of this title, and

(C) non-basic benefits.

Except as provided in paragraph (3), the corporation may revise such schedules whenever it determines that revised rates are necessary, but a revised schedule described in subparagraph (A) shall apply only to plan years beginning more than 30 days after the date on which the Congress approves such revised schedule by a concurrent resolution.

(3) Except as provided in paragraph (4), the rate for all plans for benefits guaranteed under section 4022 (other than non-basic benefits) with respect to plan years ending no more than 35 months after the effective date of this title is—

(A) in the case of each plan which is not a multiemployer plan, an amount equal to one dollar for each individual who is a participant in such plan at any time during the plan year; and

(B) in the case of a multiemployer plan, an amount equal to fifty cents for each individual who is a participant in such plan at any time during such plan year.

The rate applicable under this paragraph to any plan the plan year of which does not begin on the date of enactment of this Act is a fraction of the rate described in the preceding sentence, the numerator of which is the number of months which end before the date on which the new plan year commences and the denominator of which is 12. The corporation is authorized to prescribe regulations under which the rate described in subparagraph (B) will not apply to the same participant in any multiemployer plan more than once for any plan year.

(4) Upon notification filed with the corporation not less than 60 days after the date on which the corporation publishes the rates applicable under paragraph (5), at the election of a plan the rate applicable to that plan with respect to the second full plan year to which this section applies beginning after the date of enactment of this Act shall be the greater of—

(A) an alternative rate determined under paragraph (5), or

(B) one-half of the rate applicable to the plan under paragraph (3).

In the case of a multiemployer plan, the rate prescribed by this paragraph (at the election of a plan) for the second full plan year is also the applicable rate for plan years succeeding the second full plan year and ending before the full plan year first commencing after December 31, 1977.

(5) In carrying out its authority under paragraph (1) to establish premium rates and bases for basic benefits guaranteed under section 4022 the corporation shall establish such rates and bases in coverage schedules for plan years beginning 24 months or more after the date of enactment of this Act in accordance with the provisions of this paragraph. The corporation shall publish the rate schedules first applicable under this paragraph in the Federal Register not later than 270 days after the date of enactment of this Act.

(A) The corporation may establish annual premiums composed of—

(i) a rate applicable to the excess, if any, of the present value of the basic benefits of the plan which are guaranteed over the value of the assets of the plan, not in excess of 0.1 percent for plans which are not multiemployer plans and not in excess of 0.025 percent for multiemployer plans, and

(ii) an additional charge based on the rate applicable to the present value of the basic benefits of the plan which are guaranteed, determined separately for multiemployer plans and for plans which are not multiemployer plans.

The rate for the additional charge referred to in clause (ii) shall be set by the corporation for every year at a level (determined separately for multiemployer plans and for plans which are not multiemployer plans) which the corporation estimates will yield total revenue approximately equal to the total revenue to be derived by the corporation from the premiums referred to in clause (i) of this subparagraph.

(B) The corporation may establish annual premiums based on—

(i) the number of participants in a plan, but such premium rates shall not exceed the rates described in paragraph (3),

(ii) unfunded basic benefits guaranteed under this title, but such premium rates shall not exceed the limitations applicable under subparagraph (A)(i), or

(iii) total guaranteed basic benefits, but such premium rates may not exceed the rates determined under subparagraph (A)(ii).

If the corporation uses 2 or more of the rate bases described in this subparagraph, the premium rates shall be designed to produce approximately equal amounts of aggregate premium revenue from each of the rate bases used.

(6) The corporation shall by regulation define the terms "value of the assets" and "present value of the benefits of the plan which are guaranteed" in a manner consistent with the purposes of this title and the provisions of this section.

- ERISA §4006(b)(1) was amended by Act §105(b) by substituting "(C), (D), or (E)" for "(B) or (C)", "revised schedule" for "revised coverage schedule", and "Human Resources" for "Public Welfare". Eff. Sept. 26, 1980.

- ERISA §4006(b)(3) was amended by Act §105 by substituting "revised schedule" for "revised coverage schedule". Eff. Sept. 26, 1980.

- ERISA §4006(b)(4) was amended by Act §105 by substituting "Human Resources" for "Public Welfare". Eff. Sept. 26, 1980.

- ERISA §4006(c) was added by Act §105(c). Eff. Sept. 26, 1980.

SEC. 4007. PAYMENT OF PREMIUMS.

(a) Premiums Payable When Due; Accrual; Waiver or Reduction.—The designated payor of each plan shall pay the premiums imposed by the corporation under this title with respect to that plan when they are due. Premiums under this title are payable at the time, and on an estimated, advance, or other basis, as determined by the corporation. Premiums imposed by this title on the date of enactment (applicable to that portion of any plan year during which such date occurs) are due within 30 days after such date. Premiums imposed by this title on the first plan year commencing after the date of enactment of this Act are due within 30 days after such plan year commences. Premiums shall continue to accrue until a plan's assets are distributed pursuant to a termination procedure, or until a trustee is appointed pursuant to section 4042, whichever is earlier. The corporation may waive or reduce premiums for a multiemployer plan for any plan year during which such plan receives financial assistance from the corporation under section 4261, except that any amount so waived or reduced shall be treated as financial assistance under such section.

(b)(1) Late Payment Charge; Waiver.—If any basic benefit premium is not paid when it is due the corporation is authorized to assess a late payment charge of not more than 100 percent of the premium payment which was not timely paid. The preceding sentence shall not apply to any payment of premium

made within 60 days after the date on which payment is due, if before such date, the designated payor obtains a waiver from the corporation based upon a showing of substantial hardship arising from the timely payment of the premium. The corporation is authorized to grant a waiver under this subsection upon application made by the designated payor, but the corporation may not grant a waiver if it appears that the plan administrator will be unable to pay the premium within 60 days after the date on which it is due. If any premium is not paid by the last date prescribed for a payment, interest on the amount of such premium at the rate imposed under section 6601(a) of title 26 (relating to interest on underpayment, nonpayment, or extensions of time for payment of tax) shall be paid for the period from such last date to the date paid.

(2) The corporation is authorized to pay, subject to regulations prescribed by the corporation, interest on the amount of any overpayment of premium refunded to a designated payor. Interest under this paragraph shall be calculated at the same rate and in the same manner as interest is calculated for underpayments under paragraph (1).

(c) Civil Action to Recover Premium Penalty and Interest.—If any designated payor fails to pay a premium when due, the corporation is authorized to bring a civil action in any district court of the United States within the jurisdiction of which the plan assets are located, the plan is administered, or in which a defendant resides or is found for the recovery of the amount of the premium penalty, and interest, and process may be served in any other district. The district courts of the United States shall have jurisdiction over actions brought under this subsection by the corporation without regard to the amount in controversy.

(d) Basic Benefits Guarantee Not Stopped by Designated Payor's Failure to Pay Premiums When Due.—The corporation shall not cease to guarantee basic benefits onaccount of the failure of a designated payor to pay any premium when due.

(e) Designated Payor.—

(1) For purposes of this section, the term "designated payor" means—

(A) the contributing sponsor or plan administrator in the case of a single-employer plan, and

(B) the plan administrator in the case of a multiemployer plan.

(2) If the contributing sponsor of any single-employer plan is a member of a controlled group, each member of such group shall be jointly and severally liable for any premiums required to be paid by such contributing sponsor. For purposes of the preceding sentence, the term "controlled group" means any group treated as a single employer under subsection (b), (c), (m), or (o) of section 414 of the Internal Revenue Code of 1986.

ERISA Sec. 4007(e)(2)

Amendments to ERISA §4007
Pension Protection Act of 2006 (Pub. L. No. 109-280), as follows:
● ERISA §4007(b) was amended by Act §406(a)(1) by striking "(b)" and inserting "(b)(1)" and adding para. (b)(2). Eff. for interest accruing for periods beginning not earlier than Aug. 17, 2006, see Act §406(b).
Omnibus Budget Reconciliation Act of 1989 (Pub. L. No. 101-239), as follows:
● ERISA §4007(b) was amended by Act §7891(a)(1) by substituting "Internal Revenue Code of 1986" for "Internal Revenue Code of 1954", which for purposes of codification was translated as "title 26". Eff., except as otherwise provided, as if included in the provision Pub. L. No. 99-514 to which such amendment relates, see Act §7891(f).
Omnibus Budget Reconciliation Act of 1987 (Pub. L. No. 100-203), as follows:
● ERISA §4007(a)–(d) were amended by Act §9331(c)(1) by substituting "designated payor" for "plan administrator" wherever appearing. Eff. for plan years beginning after Dec. 31, 1987, see Act §9331(f)(1).
● ERISA §4007(e) was added by Act §9331(c)(2). Eff. for plan years beginning after Dec. 31, 1987, see Act §9331(f)(1).
Multiemployer Pension Plan Amendments Act of 1980 (Pub. L. No. 96-364), as follows:
● ERISA §4007(a) was amended by Act §402(a)(3) by inserting at the end: "The corporation may waive or reduce premiums for a multiemployer plan for any plan year during which such plan receives financial assistance from the corporation under §4261, except that any amount so waived or reduced shall be treated as financial assistance under such section." Eff. Sept. 26, 1980.
● ERISA §4007(a) was amended by Act §403(b) by striking the second sentence: "Any employer obtaining contingent liability coverage under §4023 shall pay the premiums imposed by the corporation under that section when due." Eff. Sept. 26, 1980.

SEC. 4008. ANNUAL REPORT BY THE CORPORATION.

(a) As soon as practicable after the close of each fiscal year the corporation shall transmit to the President and the Congress a report relative to the conduct of its business under this title for that fiscal year. The report shall include financial statements setting forth the finances of the corporation at the end of such fiscal year and the result of its operations (including the source and application of its funds) for the fiscal year and shall include an actuarial evaluation of the expected operations and status of the funds established under section 4005 for the next five years (including a detailed statement of the actuarial assumptions and methods used in making such evaluation).

(b) The report under subsection (a) shall include.—

(1) a summary of the Pension Insurance Modeling System microsimulation model, including the specific simulation parameters, specific initial values, temporal parameters, and policy parameters used to calculate the financial statements for the corporation;

(2) a comparison of—

(A) the average return on investments earned with respect to assets invested by the corporation for the year to which the report relates; and

(B) an amount equal to 60 percent of the average return on investment for such year in the Standard & Poor's 500 Index, plus 40 percent of the average return on investment for such year in the Lehman Aggregate Bond Index (or in a similar fixed income index); and

(3) a statement regarding the deficit or surplus for such year that the corporation would have had if the corporation had earned the return described in paragraph (2)(B) with respect to assets invested by the corporation.

Amendments to ERISA §4008
Pension Protection Act of 2006 (Pub. L. No. 109-280), as follows:
● ERISA §4008 was amended by Act §412(1) by substituting "(a) As soon as practicable" for "As soon as practicable". Eff. Aug. 17, 2006.
● ERISA §4008(b) was added by Act §412(2). Eff. Aug. 17, 2006.

SEC. 4009. PORTABILITY ASSISTANCE.

The corporation shall provide advice and assistance to individuals with respect to evaluating the economic desirability of establishing individual retirement accounts or other forms of individual retirement savings for which a deduction is allowable under section 219 of the Internal Revenue Code of 1986 and with respect to evaluating the desirability, in particular cases, of transferring amounts representing an employee's interest in a qualified plan to such an account upon the employee's separation from service with an employer.

Amendments to ERISA §4009
Omnibus Budget Reconciliation Act of 1989 (Pub. L. No. 101-239), as follows:
● ERISA §4009 was amended by Act §3111(a) by substituting "Internal Revenue Code of 1986" for "Internal Revenue Code of 1954", which for purposes of codification was translated as "title 26". Eff., except as otherwise provided, as if included in the provision of Pub. L. No. 99-514 to which such amendment relates, see Act §7891(f).

SEC. 4010. AUTHORITY TO REQUIRE CERTAIN INFORMATION.

(a) Information Required.—Each person described in subsection (b) shall provide the corporation annually, on or before a date specified by the corporation in regulations, with—

(1) such records, documents, or other information that the corporation specifies in regulations as necessary to determine the liabilities and assets of plans covered by this title; and

(2) copies of such person's audited (or, if unavailable, unaudited) financial statements, and such other

financial information as the corporation may prescribe in regulations.

(b) Persons Required to Provide Information.— The persons covered by subsection (a) are each contributing sponser, and each member of a contributing sponsor's controlled group, of a single-employer plan covered by this title, if—

(1) the funding target attainment percentage (as defined in subsection (d)) at the end of the preceding plan year of a plan maintained by the contributing sponsor or any member of his controlled group is less than 80 percent;

(2) the conditions for imposition of a lien described in section 303(k)(1)(A) and (B) of this Act or section 430(k)(1)(A) and (B) of the Internal Revenue Code of 1986 have been met with respect to any plan maintained by the contributing sponsor or any member of its controlled group; or

(3) minimum funding waivers in excess of $1,000,000 have been granted with respect to any plan maintained by the contributing sponsor or any member of its controlled group, and any portion thereof is still outstanding.

(c) Information Exempt From Disclosure Requirements.—Any information or documentary material submitted to the corporation pursuant to this section shall be exempt from disclosure under section 552 of title 5, United States Code, and no such information or documentary material may be made public, except as may be relevant to any administrative or judicial action or proceeding. Nothing in this section is intended to prevent disclosure to either body of Congress or to any duly authorized committee or subcommittee of the Congress.

(d) Additional Information Required.—

(1) In general.—The information submitted to the corporation under subsection (a) shall include—

(A) the amount of benefit liabilities under the plan determined using the assumptions used by the corporation in determining liabilities;

(B) the funding target of the plan determined as if the plan has been in at-risk status for at least 5 plan years; and

(C) the funding target attainment percentage of the plan.

(2) Definitions.—For purposes of this subsection:

(A) Funding target.—The term "funding target" has the meaning provided under section 303(d)(1).

(B) Funding target attainment percentage.—The term "funding target attainment percentage" has the meaning provided under section 303(d)(2).

(C) At-risk status.—The term "at-risk status" has the meaning provided in section 303(i)(4).

(e) Notice to Congress.—The corporation shall, on an annual basis, submit to the Committee on Health, Education, Labor, and Pensions and the Committee on Finance of the Senate and the Committee on Education and the Workforce and the Committee on Ways and Means of the House of Representatives, a summary report in the aggregate of the information submitted to the corporation under this section.

Amendments to ERISA §4010

Worker, Retiree, and Employer Recovery Act of 2008 (Pub. L. No. 110-458), as follows:

● ERISA §4010(d)(2)(B) was amended by Act §105(d) by striking "section 302(d)(2)" and inserting "section 303(d)(2)". Eff. for years beginning after 2007, as if included in Pub. L. No. 109-280, §505.

Pension Protection Act of 2006 (Pub. L. No. 109-280), as follows:

● ERISA §4010(b)(1) was amended by Act §505(a). Eff. for plan years beginning after 2007, see Act §505(c). ERISA §4010(b)(1) prior to amendment:

(1) the aggregate unfunded vested benefits at the end of the preceding plan year (as determined under §4006(a)(3)(E)(iii) of plans maintained by the contributing sponsor and the members of its controlled group exceed $50,000,000 (disregarding plans with no unfunded vested benefits);.

● ERISA §4010(b)(2) was amended by Act §107(b)(3) (redesignated as §108(b)(3) by Pub. L. No. 111-192, §202(a)) by substituting "303(k)(1)(A) and (B)" for "302(f)(1)(A) and (B)" and substituting "430(k)(1)(A) and (B)" for "412(n)(1)(A) and (B)". Eff. for plan years beginning after 2007, see Act §107(e).

● ERISA §4010(d)–(e) were added by Act §505(a). Eff. for years beginning after 2007, see Act §505(c).

SEC. 4011. NOTICE TO PARTICIPANTS. [Repealed.]

(a) In General.—The plan administrator of a plan subject to the additional premium under section 4006(a)(3)(E) shall provide, in a form and manner and at such time as prescribed in regulations of the corporation, notice to plan participants and beneficiaries of the plan's funding status and the limits on the corporation's guaranty should the plan terminate while underfunded. Such notice shall be written in a manner so as to be understood by the average plan participant.

(b) Exception.—Subsection (a) shall not apply to any plan to which section 302(d) does not apply for the plan year by reason of paragraph (9) thereof.

Amendments to ERISA §4011 [Repealed.]

Pension Protection Act of 2006 (Pub. L. No. 109-280), as follows:

● ERISA §4011 was repealed by Act §501(b)(1). Eff. for plan years beginning after 2006, subject to a transition rule, see Act §501(d).

Subtitle B—Coverage

SEC. 4021. COVERAGE.

(a) Plans Covered.—Except as provided in subsection (b), this title applies to any plan (including a successor plan) which, for a plan year—

(1) is an employee pension benefit plan (as defined in paragraph (2) of section 3 of this Act) established or maintained—

(A) by an employer engaged in commerce or in any industry or activity affecting commerce, or

(B) by any employee organization, or organization representing employees, engaged in commerce or in any industry or activity affecting commerce, or

(C) by both,

which has, in practice, met the requirements of part I of subchapter D of chapter 1 of the Internal Revenue Code of 1986 (as in effect for the preceding 5 plan years of the plan) applicable to plans described in paragraph (2) for the preceding 5 plan years; or

(2) is, or has been determined by the Secretary of the Treasury to be, a plan described in section 401(a) of title 26, or which meets, or has been determined by the Secretary of the Treasury to meet, the requirements of section 404(a)(2) of title 26.

For purposes of this title, a successor plan is considered to be a continuation of a predecessor plan. For this purpose, unless otherwise specifically indicated in this title, a successor plan is a plan which covers a group of employees which includes substantially the same employees as a previously established plan, and provides substantially the same benefits as that plan provided.

(b) Plans Not Covered.—This section does not apply to any plan—

(1) which is an individual account plan, as defined in paragraph (34) of section 3 of this Act,

(2) established and maintained for its employees by the Government of the United States, by the government of any State or political subdivision thereof, or by any agency or instrumentality of any of the foregoing, or to which the Railroad Retirement Act of 1935 or 1937 applies and which is financed by contributions required under that Act or which is described in the last sentence of section 3(32)[,]

(3) which is a church plan as defined in section 414(e) of title 26, unless that plan has made an election under section 410(d) of title 26, and has notified the corporation in accordance with procedures prescribed by the corporation, that it wishes to have the provisions of this part apply to it,

(4)(A) established and maintained by a society, order, or association described in section 501(c)(8) or (9) of title 26, if no part of the contributions to or under the plan is made by employers of participants in the plan, or

(B) of which a trust described in section 501(c)(18) of such Code is a part;

(5) which has not at any time after the date of enactment of this Act provided for employer contributions;

(6) which is unfunded and which is maintained by an employer primarily for the purpose of providing deferred compensation for a select group of management or highly compensated employees;

(7) which is established and maintained outside of the United States primarily for the benefit of individuals substantially all of whom are nonresident aliens;

(8) which is maintained by an employer solely for the purpose of providing benefits for certain employees in excess of the limitations on contributions and benefits imposed by section 415 of title 26 on plans to which that section applies, without regard to whether the plan is funded, and, to the extent that a separable part of a plan (as determined by the corporation) maintained by an employer is maintained for such purpose, that part shall be treated for purposes of this title, as a separate plan which is an excess benefit plan;

(9) which is established and maintained exclusively for substantial owners;

(10) of an international organization which is exempt from taxation under the International Organizations Immunities Act;

(11) maintained solely for the purpose of complying with applicable workmen's compensation laws or unemployment compensation or disability insurance laws;

(12) which is a defined benefit plan, to the extent that it is treated as an individual account plan under paragraph (35)(B) of section 3 of this Act; or

(13) established and maintained by a professional service employer which does not at any time after the date of enactment of this Act have more than 25 active participants in the plan.

(14) [Deleted.]

(c) Definitions.—

(1) For purposes of subsection (b)(1), the term "individual account plan" does not include a plan under which a fixed benefit is promised if the employer or his representative participated in the determination of that benefit.

(2) For purposes of this paragraph and for purposes of subsection (b)(13)—

(A) the term "professional service employer" means any proprietorship, partnership, corporation, or other association or organization (i) owned or controlled by professional individuals or by executors or administrators of professional individuals, (ii) the principal business of which is the performance of professional services, and

(B) the term "professional individuals" includes but is not limited to, physicians, dentists, chiropractors, osteopaths, optometrists, other licensed practitioners of the healing arts, attorneys at law, public accountants, public engineers, architects, draftsmen, actuaries, psychologists, social or physical scientists, and performing artists.

(3) In the case of a plan established and maintained by more than one professional service employer, the plan shall not be treated as a plan described in subsection (b)(13) if, at any time after the date of enactment of this Act the plan has more than 25 active participants.

(d) For purposes of subsection (b)(9), the term "substantial owner" means an individual who, at any time during the 60-month period ending on the date the determination is being made—

(1) owns the entire interest in an unincorporated trade or business,

(2) in the case of a partnership, is a partner who owns, directly or indirectly, more than 10 percent of either the capital interest or the profits interest in such partnership, or

(3) in the case of a corporation, owns, directly or indirectly, more than 10 percent in value of either the voting stock of that corporation or all the stock of that corporation.

For purposes of paragraph (3), the constructive ownership rules of section 1563(e) of the Internal Revenue Code of 1986 (other than paragraph (3)(C) thereof) shall apply, including the application of such rules under section 414(c) of such Code.

Amendments to ERISA §4021

Worker, Retiree, and Employer Recovery Act of 2008 (Pub. L. No. 110-458), as follows:
● ERISA §4021(b) was amended by Act §109(d)(2) by inserting "or" at the end of para. (12); striking "; or" at end of para. (13) and inserting a period; and striking para. (14). Eff. as if included in Pub. L. No. 109-280, §906. ERISA §4021(b)(14) prior to repeal:

(14) established and maintained by an Indian tribal government (as defined in section 7701(a)(40) of the Internal Revenue Code of 1986), a subdivision of an Indian tribal government (determined in accordance with section 7871(d) of such Code), or an agency or instrumentality of either, and all of the participants of which are employees of such entity substantially all of whose services as such an employee are in the performance of essential governmental functions but not in the performance of commercial activities (whether or not an essential government function).

Pension Protection Act of 2006 (Pub. L. No. 109-280), as follows:
● ERISA §4021(b)(2) was amended by Act §906(a)(2)(B) by adding "or which is described in the last sentence of section 3(32)" to the last sentence. Eff. for any year beginning on or after Aug. 17, 2006, see Act §906(c).
● ERISA §4021(b)(9) was amended by Act §407(c)(1)(B) by striking "as defined in section 4022(b)(6)". Eff. Jan. 1, 2006, see Act §407(d).
● ERISA §4021(b)(12)–(14) was amended by Act §906(b)(2)(A)–(C) by striking "or" at the end of para. (12); substituting "plan; or" for "plan." in para. (13); and adding para. (14). Eff. for any year beginning on or after Aug. 17, 2006, see Act §906(c).
● ERISA §4021(d) was added by Act §407(c)(1)(B). Eff. Jan. 1, 2006, see Act §407(d).

Omnibus Budget Reconciliation Act of 1989 (Pub. L. No. 101-239), as follows:

● ERISA §4021(a) was amended by Act §7894(g)(3)(A) by substituting "this subchapter applies" for "this section applies" in introductory provisions. Eff., except as otherwise provided, as if included in the provision of Pub. L. No. 99-514 to which such amendment relates, see Act §7891(f).
● ERISA §4021(a)(1), (2), (b)(3), (b)(4)(A), (b)(8) were amended by Act §7891(a)(1) by substituting "Internal Revenue Code of 1986" for "Internal Revenue Code of 1954", which for purposes of codification was translated as "title 26". Eff., except as otherwise provided, as if included in the provision of Pub. L. No. 99-514 to which such amendment relates, see Act §7891(f).

Multiemployer Pension Plan Amendments Act of 1980 (Pub. L. No. 96-364), as follows:
● ERISA §4021(a) was amended by Act §402(a)(4) by inserting "unless otherwise specifically indicated in this subchapter," after "For this purpose,". Eff. Sept. 26, 1980.

SEC. 4022. SINGLE-EMPLOYER PLAN BENEFITS GUARANTEED.

(a) Nonforfeitable Benefits.—Subject to the limitations contained in subsection (b), the corporation shall guarantee in accordance with this section the payment of all nonforfeitable benefits (other than benefits becoming nonforfeitable solely on account of the termination of a plan) under a single-employer plan which terminates at a time when this title applies to it.

(b) Exceptions.—

(1) Except to the extent provided in paragraph (7)—

(A) no benefits provided by a plan which has been in effect for less than 60 months at the time the plan terminates shall be guaranteed under this section, and

(B) any increase in the amount of benefits under a plan resulting from a plan amendment which was made, or became effective, whichever is later, within 60 months before the date on which the plan terminates shall be disregarded.

(2) For purposes of this subsection, the time a successor plan (within the meaning of section 4021(a)) has been in effect includes the time a previously established plan (within the meaning of section 4021(a)) was in effect. For purposes of determining what benefits are guaranteed under this section in the case of a plan to which section 4021 does not apply on the day after the date of enactment of this Act, the 60-month period referred to in paragraph (1) shall be computed beginning on the first date on which such section does apply to the plan.

(3) The amount of monthly benefits described in subsection (a) provided by a plan, which are guaranteed under this section with respect to a participant, shall not have an actuarial value which exceeds the actuarial value of a monthly benefit in the form of a life annuity commencing at age 65 equal to the lesser of—

(A) his average monthly gross income from his employer during the 5 consecutive calendar year period (or, if less, during the number of calendar years in such period in which he actively participates in the plan) during which his gross income from that employer was greater than during any other such period with that employer determined by dividing $^1/^{12}$ of the sum of all such gross income by the number of such calendar years in which he had such gross income, or

(B) $750 multiplied by a fraction, the numerator of which is the contribution and benefit base (determined under section 230 of the Social Security Act) in effect at the time the plan terminates and the denominator of which is such contribution and benefit base in effect in calendar year 1974.

The provisions of this paragraph do not apply to nonbasic benefits. The maximum guaranteed monthly benefit shall not be reduced solely on account of the age of a participant in the case of a benefit payable by reason of disability that occurred on or before the termination date, if the participant demonstrates to the satisfaction of the corporation that the Social Security Administration has determined that the participant satisfies the definition of disability under title II or XVI of the Social Security Act, and the regulations thereunder. If a benefit payable by reason of disability is converted to an early or normal retirement benefit for reasons other than a change in the health of the participant, such early or normal retirement benefit shall be treated as a continuation of the benefit payable by reason of disability and this subparagraph shall continue to apply.

(4)(A) The actuarial value of a benefit, for purposes of this subsection, shall be determined in accordance with regulations prescribed by the corporation.

(B) For purposes of paragraph (3)—

(i) the term "gross income" means "earned income" within the meaning of section 911(b) of title 26 (determined without regard to any community property laws),

(ii) in the case of a participant in a plan under which contributions are made by more than one employer, amounts received as gross income from any employer under that plan shall be aggregated with amounts received from any other employer under that plan during the same period, and

(iii) any non-basic benefit shall be disregarded.

(5)(A) For purposes of this paragraph, the term "majority owner" means an individual who, at any time during the 60-month period ending on the date the determination is being made—

(i) owns the entire interest in an unincorporated trade or business,

(ii) in the case of a partnership, is a partner who owns, directly or indirectly, 50 percent or more of either the capital interest or the profits interest in such partnership, or

(iii) in the case of a corporation, owns, directly or indirectly, 50 percent or more in value of either the voting stock of that corporation or all the stock of that corporation.

For purposes of clause (iii), the constructive ownership rules of section 1563(e) of the Internal Revenue Code of 1986 (other than paragraph (3)(C) thereof) shall apply, including the application of such rules under section 414(c) of such Code.

(B) In the case of a participant who is a majority owner, the amount of benefits guaranteed under this section shall equal the product of—

(i) a fraction (not to exceed 1) the numerator of which is the number of years from the later of the effective date or the adoption date of the plan to the termination date, and the denominator of which is 10, and

(ii) the amount of benefits that would be guaranteed under this section if the participant were not a majority owner.

(6)(A) No benefits accrued under a plan after the date on which the Secretary of the Treasury issues notice that he has determined that any trust which is a part of a plan does not meet the requirements of section 401(a) of title 26, or that the plan does not meet the requirements of section 404(a)(2) of title 26, are guaranteed under this section unless such determination is erroneous. This subparagraph does not apply if the Secretary subsequently issues a notice that such trust meets the requirements of section 401(a) of title 26 or that the plan meets the requirements of section 404(a)(2) of title 26 and if the Secretary determines that the trust or plan has taken action necessary to meet such requirements during the period between the issuance of the notice referred to in the preceding sentence and the issuance of the notice referred to in this sentence.

(B) No benefits accrued under a plan after the date on which an amendment of the plan is adopted which causes the Secretary of the Treasury to determine that any trust under the plan has ceased to meet the requirements of section 401(a) of title 26 or that the plan has ceased to meet the requirements of section 404(a)(2) of title 26, are guaranteed under this section unless such determination is erroneous. This subparagraph shall not apply if the amendment is revoked as of the date it was first effective or amended to comply with such requirements.

(7) Benefits described in paragraph (1) are guaranteed only to the extent of the greater of—

(A) 20 percent of the amount which, but for the fact that the plan or amendment has not been in effect for 60 months or more, would be guaranteed under this section, or

(B) $20 per month,

multiplied by the number of years (but not more than 5) the plan or amendment, as the case may be, has been in effect. In determining how many years a plan or amendment has been in effect for purposes of this paragraph, the first 12 months beginning with the date on which the plan or amendment is made or first becomes effective (whichever is later) constitutes one year, and each consecutive period of 12 months thereafter constitutes an additional year. This paragraph does not apply to benefits payable under a plan unless the corporation finds substantial evidence that the plan was terminated for a reasonable business purpose and not for the purpose of obtaining the payment of benefits by the corporation under this title.

(8) If an unpredictable contingent event benefit (as defined in section 206(g)(1)) is payable by reason of the occurrence of any event, this section shall be applied as if a plan amendment had been adopted on the date such event occurred.

(c) Payment by Corporation to Participants and Beneficiaries of Recovery Percentage of Outstanding Amount of Benefit Liabilities.—

(1) In addition to benefits paid under the preceding provisions of this section with respect to a terminated plan, the corporation shall pay the portion of the amount determined under paragraph (2) which is allocated with respect to each participant under section 4044(a). Such payment shall be made to such participant or to such participant's beneficiaries (including alternate payees, within the meaning of section 206(d)(3)(K)).

(2) The amount determined under this paragraph is an amount equal to the product derived by multiplying—

(A) the outstanding amount of benefit liabilities under the plan (including interest calculated from the termination date), by

(B) the applicable recovery ratio.

(3)(A) In general.—Except as provided in subparagraph (C), the term "recovery ratio" means the ratio which—

(i) the sum of the values of all recoveries under section 4062, 4063, or 4064, determined by the corporation in connection with plan terminations described under subparagraph (B), bears to

(ii) the sum of all unfunded benefit liabilities under such plans as of the termination date in connection with any such prior termination.

(B) A plan termination described in this subparagraph is a termination with respect to which—

(i) the corporation has determined the value of recoveries under section 4062, 4063, or 4064 and

(ii) notices of intent to terminate were provided (or in the case of a termination by the corporation, a notice of determination under section 4042 was

issued) during the 5-Federal fiscal year period ending with the third fiscal year preceding the fiscal year in which occurs the date of the notice of intent to terminate (or the notice of determination under section 4042) with respect to the plan termination for which the recovery ratio is being determined.

(C) In the case of a terminated plan with respect to which the outstanding amount of benefit liabilities exceeds $20,000,000, for purposes of this section, the term "recovery ratio" means, with respect to the termination of such plan, the ratio of—

(i) the value of the recoveries of the corporation under section 4062, 4063, or 4064 in connection with such plan, to

(ii) the amount of unfunded benefit liabilities under such plan as of the termination date.

(4) Determinations under this subsection shall be made by the corporation. Such determinations shall be binding unless shown by clear and convincing evidence to be unreasonable.

(d) Authorization to Guarantee Other Classes of Benefits.—The corporation is authorized to guarantee the payment of such other classes of benefits and to establish the terms and conditions under which such other classes of benefits are guaranteed as it determines to be appropriate.

(e) Nonforfeitability of Preretirement Survivor Annuity.—For purposes of subsection (a), a qualified preretirement survivor annuity (as defined in section 205(e)(1)) with respect to a participant under a terminated single-employer plan shall not be treated as forfeitable solely because the participant has not died as of the termination date.

(f) Effective Date of Plan Amendments.—For purposes of this section, the effective date of a plan amendment described in section 204(i)(1) shall be the effective date of the plan of reorganization of the employer described in section 204(i)(1) or, if later, the effective date stated in such amendment.

(g) Bankruptcy Filing Substituted for Termination Date.—If a contributing sponsor of a plan has filed or has had filed against such person a petition seeking liquidation or reorganization in a case under title 11, United States Code, or under any similar Federal law or law of a State or political subdivision, and the case has not been dismissed as of the termination date of the plan, then this section shall be applied by treating the date such petition was filed as the termination date of the plan.

(h) Special Rule for Plans Electing Certain Funding Requirements.—If any plan makes an election under section 402(a)(1) of the Pension Protection Act of 2006 and is terminated effective before the end of the 10-year period beginning on the first day of the first applicable plan year—

(1) this section shall be applied—

(A) by treating the first day of the first applicable plan year as the termination date of the plan, and

(B) by determining the amount of guaranteed benefits on the basis of plan assets and liabilities as of such assumed termination date, and

(2) notwithstanding section 4044(a), plan assets shall first be allocated to pay the amount, if any, by which—

(A) the amount of guaranteed benefits under this section (determined without regard to paragraph (1) and on the basis of plan assets and liabilities as of the actual date of plan termination), exceeds

(B) the amount determined under paragraph (1).

Amendments to ERISA §4022

Pension Protection Act of 2006 (Pub. L. No. 109-280), as follows:
● ERISA §4022(b)(5) was amended by Act §407(a). Eff. for plan terminations under ERISA §4041(c) for which notices of intent to terminate are provided under ERISA §4041(a)(2) after Dec. 31, 2005, and under ERISA §4042 for which notices of determination are provided after such date, see Act §407(d). ERISA §4022(b)(5) prior to amendment:
(5)
(A) For purposes of this subchapter, the term "substantial owner" means an individual who—
(i) owns the entire interest in an unincorporated trade or business,
(ii) in the case of a partnership, is a partner who owns, directly or indirectly, more than 10 percent of either the capital interest or the profits interest in such partnership, or
(iii) in the case of a corporation, owns, directly or indirectly, more than 10 percent in value of either the voting stock of that corporation or all the stock of that corporation. For purposes of clause (iii) the constructive ownership rules of section 1563(e) of title 26 shall apply (determined without regard to section 1563(e)(3)(C)). For purposes of this subchapter an individual is also treated as a substantial owner with respect to a plan if, at any time within the 60 months preceding the date on which the determination is made, he was a substantial owner under the plan.
(B) In the case of a participant in a plan under which benefits have not been increased by reason of any plan amendments and who is covered by the plan as a substantial owner, the amount of benefits guaranteed under this section shall not exceed the product of—
(i) a fraction (not to exceed 1) the numerator of which is the number of years the substantial owner was an active participant in the plan, and the denominator of which is 30, and
(ii) the amount of the substantial owner's monthly benefits guaranteed under subsection (a) of this section (as limited under paragraph (3) of this subsection).
(C) In the case of a participant in a plan, other than a plan described in subparagraph (B), who is covered by the plan as a substantial owner, the amount of the benefit guaranteed under this section shall, under regulations prescribed by the corporation, treat each benefit increase attributable to a plan amendment as if it were provided under a new plan. The benefits guaranteed under this section with respect to all such amendments shall not exceed the amount which would be determined under subparagraph (B) if subparagraph (B) applied.
● ERISA §4022(b)(8) was added by Act §403(a). Eff. for benefits that become payable as a result of an event which occurs after July 26, 2005, see Act §403(b).
● ERISA §4022(c)(3)(A) was amended by Act §408(b)(1). Eff. for any termination for which notices of intent to terminate are

provided (or in the case of a termination by the PBGC, a notice of determination under ERISA §4042 is issued) on Sept. 16, 2006, or thereafter, see Act §408(c). ERISA §4022(c)(3)(A) prior to amendment:
(3)(A) Except as provided in subparagraph (C), for purposes of this subsection, the term "recovery ratio" means the average ratio, with respect to prior plan terminations described in subparagraph (B), of—
(i) the value of the recovery of the corporation under section 1362, 1363, or 1364 of this title in connection with such prior terminations, to
(ii) the amount of unfunded benefit liabilities under such plans as of the termination date in connection with such prior terminations.
● ERISA §4022(c)(3)(B)(ii) was amended by Act §408(a). Eff. for a termination for which notices of intent to terminate are provided (or in the case of a termination by the PBGC, a notice of determination under ERISA §4042 is issued) on or after 30 days after Aug. 17, 2006, see Act §408(c). ERISA §4022(c)(3)(B)(ii) prior to amendment:
(ii) notices of intent to terminate were provided after December 17, 1987, and during the 5-Federal fiscal year period ending with the fiscal year preceding the fiscal year in which occurs the date of the notice of intent to terminate with respect to the plan termination for which the recovery ratio is being determined.
● ERISA §4022(g) was added by Act §404(a). Eff. for proceedings initiated under title 11, United States Code, or under any similar federal law, or law of a state or political subdivision, on Sept. 16, 2006, or thereafter, see Act §404(c).
● ERISA §4022(h) was added by Act §402(g)(2)(A). Eff. for plan years ending after Aug. 17, 2006, see Act §402(j).

Uruguay Round Agreements Act (1994)(Pub. L. No. 103-465), as follows:
● ERISA §4022(b)(3) was amended by Act §777(a) by inserting two sentences at the end. Eff. for plan terminations under ERISA §4041(c) for which notices of intent to terminate are provided under ERISA §4041(a)(2), or under ERISA §4042 for proceedings instituted by the PBGC, on or after the date of enactment of the Act [Dec. 8, 1994], see Act §777(b).
● ERISA §4022(f) was added by Act §766(c). Eff. for plan amendments adopted on or after Dec. 8, 1994, see Act §766(d).

Omnibus Budget Reconciliation Act of 1989 (Pub. L. No. 101-239), as follows:
● ERISA §4022(a) was amended by Act §7894(g)(3)(B) by substituting "this subchapter" for "section 1321 of this title". Eff., except as otherwise provided, as if originally included in the provision of Pub. L. No. 93-406, to which it relates, see Act §7894(i).
● ERISA §4022(b)(2) was amended by Act §7894(g)(1) by substituting "60-month" for "60 month". Eff., except as otherwise provided, as if originally included in the provision of Pub. L. No. 93-406, to which it relates, see Act §7894(i).
● ERISA §4022(b)(4)(B)(i), (b)(5)(A), (b)(6) was amended by Act §7891(a)(1) by substituting "Internal Revenue Code of 1986" for "Internal Revenue Code of 1954", which for purposes of codification was translated as "title 26" thus requiring no change in text. Eff., except as otherwise provided, as if included in the provision of Pub. L. No. 99-514, to which it relates, see Act §7891(f).
● ERISA §4022(c)(1) was amended by Act §7881(f)(11) by substituting "under section 1344(a) of this title. Such payment shall be made to such participant" for "under section 1344(a) of this title, to such participant". Eff., except as otherwise provided, as if included in the provision of Pub. L. No. 100-203, §§9302–9346, to which it relates, see Act §7882.
● ERISA §4022 was amended by Act §7881(f)(4) by striking "(in the case of a deceased participant)" before "to such participant's beneficiaries". Eff., except as otherwise provided, as if included in the provision of Pub. L. No. 100-203, §§9302–9346, to which it relates, see Act §7882.
● ERISA §4022(c)(3)(B)(ii) was amended by Act §7881(f)(5) by inserting before period at end ", and during the 5-Federal fiscal year period ending with the fiscal year preceding the fiscal year in which occurs the date of the notice of intent to terminate with

respect to the plan termination for which the recovery ratio is being determined". Eff., except as otherwise provided, as if included in the provision of Pub. L. No. 100-203, §§9302–9346, to which it relates, see Act §7882.

Omnibus Budget Reconciliation Act of 1987 (Pub. L. No. 100-203), as follows:

● ERISA §4022(c)–(e) was amended by Act §9312(b)(3) by redesignating former subsecs. (c) and (d) as (d) and (e), respectively; and adding new subsec. (c). Eff. for plan terminations under ERISA §4041 to which notices of intent to terminate are provided under ERISA §1341(a)(2) after Dec. 17, 1987, and plan terminations with respect to which proceedings are instituted by the PBGC under ERISA §4042 after that date, see Act §9312(b)(3)(B) and (d)(1), as amended.

Consolidated Omnibus Budget Reconciliation Act of 1985 (Pub. L. No. 99-272), as follows:

● ERISA §4022(b)(7) was amended by Act §11016(c)(8), in provisions following subpara. (B) substituted "12 months beginning with" for "12 months following". Eff. Jan. 1, 1986, with certain exceptions, see Act §11019.

● ERISA §4022(d) was added by Act §11016(c)(9). Eff. Jan. 1, 1986, with certain exceptions, see Act §11019.

Multiemployer Pension Plan Amendments of 1980 (Pub. L. No. 96-364), as follows:

● ERISA §4022(a) was amended by Act §403(c)(2) by inserting ", in accordance with this section," after "guarantee" and "single-employer" before "plan which", and struck out "the terms of" after "under". Eff. Sept. 26, 1980.

● ERISA §4022(b)(1) was amended by Act §403(c)(3), (c)(4) by substituting "(7)" for "(8)", striking para. (5), and redesignating former paras. (6)–(8) as (5)–(7), respectively. Eff. Sept. 26, 1980. ERISA §4022(b)(5) prior to being stricken:

> **(5)** Notwithstanding paragraph (3), no person shall receive from the corporation for basic benefits with respect to a participant an amount, or amounts, with an actuarial value which exceeds a monthly benefit in the form of a life annuity commencing at age 65 equal to the amount determined under paragraph (3)(B) at the time of the last plan termination.

SEC. 4022A. MULTIEMPLOYER PLAN BENEFITS GUARANTEED.

(a) Benefits of Covered Plans.—The corporation shall guarantee, in accordance with this section, the payment of all nonforfeitable benefits (other than benefits becoming nonforfeitable solely on account of the termination of a plan) under a multiemployer plan—

(1) to which this title applies, and

(2) which is insolvent under section 4245(b) or 4281(d)(2).

(b) Benefits or Benefit Increases Not Eligible for Guarantee.—

(1)(A) For purposes of this section, a benefit or benefit increase which has been in effect under a plan for less than 60 months is not eligible for the corporation's guarantee. For purposes of this paragraph, any month of any plan year during which the plan was insolvent or terminated (within the meaning of section 4041A(a)(2)) shall not be taken into account.

(B) For purposes of this section, a benefit or benefit increase which has been in effect under a plan for less than 60 months before the first day of the plan year for which an amendment reducing the

benefit or the benefit increase is taken into account under section 4244A(a)(2) in determining the minimum contribution requirement for the plan year under section 4243(b) is not eligible for the corporation's guarantee.

(2) For purposes of this section—

(A) the date on which a benefit or a benefit increase under a plan is first in effect is the later of—

(i) the date on which the documents establishing or increasing the benefit were executed, or

(ii) the effective date of the benefit or benefit increase;

(B) the period of time for which a benefit or a benefit increase has been in effect under a successor plan includes the period of time for which the benefit or benefit increase was in effect under a previously established plan; and

(C) in the case of a plan to which section 4021 did not apply on September 3, 1974, the time periods referred to in this section are computed beginning on the date on which section 4021 first applies to the plan.

(c) Determinations Respecting Amount of Guarantee.—

(1) Except as provided in subsection (g), the monthly benefit of a participant or a beneficiary which is guaranteed under this section by the corporation with respect to a plan is the product of—

(A) 100 percent of the accrual rate up to $11, plus 75 percent of the lesser of—

(i) $33, or

(ii) the accrual rate, if any, in excess of $11, and

(B) the number of the participant's years of credited service.

(2) For purposes of this section, the accrual rate is—

(A) the monthly benefit of the participant or beneficiary which is described in subsection (a) and which is eligible for the corporation's guarantee under subsection (b), except that such benefit shall be—

(i) no greater than the monthly benefit which would be payable under the plan at normal retirement age in the form of a single life annuity, and

(ii) determined without regard to any reduction under section 411(a)(3)(E) of title 26; divided by

(B) the participant's years of credited service.

(3) For purposes of this subsection—

(A) a year of credited service is a year in which the participant completed—

(i) a full year of participation in the plan, or

(ii) any period of service before participation which is credited for purposes of benefit accrual as the equivalent of a full year of participation;

(B) any year for which the participant is credited for purposes of benefit accrual with a fraction of the equivalent of a full year of participation shall be counted as such a fraction of a year of credited service; and

(C) years of credited service shall be determined by including service which may otherwise be disregarded by the plan under section 411(a)(3)(E) of title 26.

(d) Amount of Guarantee of Reduced Benefit.—In the case of a benefit which has been reduced under section 411(a)(3)(E) of title 26, the corporation shall guarantee the lesser of—

(1) the reduced benefit, or

(2) the amount determined under subsection (c).

(e) Ineligibility of Benefits for Guarantee.—The corporation shall not guarantee benefits under a multiemployer plan which, under section 4022(b)(6), would not be guaranteed under a single-employer plan.

(f) Study, Report, etc., Respecting Premium Increase in Existing Basic-Benefit Guarantee Levels; Congressional Procedures Applicable for Revision of Schedules.—

(1) No later than 5 years after the date of the enactment of the Multiemployer Pension Plan Amendments Act of 1980, and at least every fifth year thereafter, the corporation shall—

(A) conduct a study to determine—

(i) the premiums needed to maintain the basic-benefit guarantee levels for multiemployer plans described in subsection (c), and

(ii) whether the basic-benefit guarantee levels for multiemployer plans may beincreased without increasing the basic-benefit premiums for multiemployer plans under this title; and

(B) report such determinations to the Committee on Ways and Means and the Committee on Education and Labor of the House of Representatives and to the Committee on Finance and the Committee on Labor and Human Resources of the Senate.

(2)(A) If the last report described in paragraph (1) indicates that a premium increase is necessary to support the existing basic-benefit guarantee levels for multiemployer plans, the corporation shall transmit to the Committee on Ways and Means and the Committee on Education and Labor of the House of Representatives and to the Committee on Finance and the Committee on Labor and Human Resources of the Senate by March 31 of any calendar year in which congressional action under this subsection is requested—

(i) a revised schedule of basic-benefit guarantees for multiemployer plans which would be necessary in the absence of an increase in premiums approved in accordance with section 4006(b),

(ii) a revised schedule of basic-benefit premiums for multiemployer plans which is necessary to support the existing basic-benefit guarantees for such plans, and

(iii) a revised schedule of basic-benefit guarantees for multiemployer plans for which the schedule of premiums necessary is higher than the existing premium schedule for such plans but lower than the revised schedule of premiums for such plans specified in clause (ii), together with such schedule of premiums.

(B) The revised schedule of increased premiums referred to in subparagraph (A)(ii) or (A)(iii) shall go into effect as approved by the enactment of a joint resolution.

(C) If an increase in premiums is not so enacted, the revised guarantee schedule described in subparagraph (A)(i) shall go into effect on the first day of the second calendar year following the year in which such revised guarantee schedule was submitted to the Congress.

(3)(A) If the last report described in paragraph (1) indicates that basic-benefitguarantees for multiemployer plans can be increased without increasing the basic-benefit premiums for multiemployer plans under this title, the corporation shall submit to the Committee on Ways and Means and the Committee on Education and Labor of the House of Representatives and to the Committee on Finance and the Committee on Labor and Human Resources of the Senate by March 31 of the calendar year in which congressional action under this paragraph is requested—

(i) a revised schedule of increases in the basic-benefit guarantees which can be supported by the existing schedule of basic-benefit premiums for multiemployer plans, and

(ii) a revised schedule of basic-benefit premiums sufficient to support the existing basic-benefit guarantees.

(B) The revised schedules referred to in subparagraph (A)(1) or subparagraph (A)(ii) shall go into effect as approved by the enactment of a joint resolution.

(4)(A) The succeeding subparagraphs of this paragraph are enacted by the Congress as an exercise of the rulemaking power of the Senate and the House of Representatives, respectively, and as such they shall be deemed a part of the rules of each House, respectively, but applicable only with respect to the procedure to be followed in that House in the case of joint resolutions (as defined in subparagraph (B)). Such subparagraphs shall supersede other rules only to the extent that they are inconsistent therewith. They are enacted with full recognition of theconstitutional right of either House to change the rules (so far as relating to the procedure of that House) at any time, in the same manner, and to the same extent as in the case of any rule of that House.

(B) For purposes of this subsection, "joint resolution" means only a joint resolution, the matter after the resolving clause of which is as follows: "The proposed schedule described in transmitted to the Congress by the Pension Benefit Guaranty Corporation on is hereby approved.", the first blank space therein being filled with "section 4022A(f)(2)(A)(ii) of the Employee Retirement Income Security Act of 1974", "section 4022A(f)(2)(A)(iii) of the Employee Retirement Income Security Act of 1974", "section 4022A(f)(3)(A)(i) of the Employee Retirement Income Security Act of 1974", or "section 4022A(f)(3)(A)(ii) of the Employee Retirement Income Security Act of 1974" (whichever is applicable), and the second blank space therein being filled with the date on which the corporation's message proposing the revision was submitted.

(C) The procedure for disposition of a joint resolution shall be the procedure described in section 4006(b)(4) through (7).

(g) Guarantee of Payment of Other Classes of Benefits and Establishment of Terms and Conditions of Guarantee; Promulgation of Regulations for Establishment of Supplemental Program to Guarantee Benefits Otherwise Ineligible; Status of Benefits; Applicability of Revised Schedule of Premiums.—

(1) The corporation may guarantee the payment of such other classes of benefits under multiemployer plans, and establish the terms and conditions under which those other classes of benefits are guaranteed, as it determines to be appropriate.

(2)(A) The corporation shall prescribe regulations to establish a supplemental program to guarantee benefits under multiemployer plans which would be guaranteed under this section but for the limitations in subsection (c). Such regulations shall be proposed by the corporation no later than the end of the 18th calendar month following the date of the enactment of the Multiemployer Pension Plan Amendments Act of 1980. The regulations shall make coverage under the supplemental program available no later than January 1, 1983. Any election to participate in the supplemental program shall be on a voluntary basis, and a plan electing such coverage shall continue to pay the premiums required under section 4006(a)(2)(B) to the revolving fund used pursuant to section 4005 in connection with benefits otherwise guaranteed under this section. Any such election shall be irrevocable, except to the extent otherwise provided by regulations prescribed by the corporation.

(B) The regulations prescribed under this paragraph shall provide—

(i) that a plan must elect coverage under the supplemental program within the time permitted by the regulations;

(ii) unless the corporation determines otherwise, that a plan may not elect supplemental coverage unless the value of the assets of the plan as of the end of the plan year preceding the plan year in which the election must be made is an amount equal to 15 times the total amount of the benefit payments made under the plan for that year; and

(iii) such other reasonable terms and conditions for supplemental coverage, including funding standards and any other reasonable limitations with respect to plans or benefits covered or to means of program financing, as the corporation determines are necessary and appropriate for a feasible supplemental program consistent with the purposes of this title.

(3) Any benefits guaranteed under this subsection shall be considered nonbasic benefits for purposes of this title.

(4)(A) No revised schedule of premiums under this subsection, after the initial schedule, shall go into effect unless—

(i) the revised schedule is submitted to the Congress, and

(ii) a joint resolution described in subparagraph (B) is not enacted before the close of the 60th legislative day after such schedule is submitted to the Congress.

(B) For purposes of subparagraph (A), a joint resolution described in this subparagraph is a joint resolution the matter after the resolving clause of which is as follows: "The revised premium schedule transmitted to the Congress by the Pension Benefit Guaranty Corporation under section 4022A(g)(4) of the Employee Retirement Income Security Act of 1974 on is hereby disapproved.", the blank space therein being filled with the date on which the revised schedule was submitted.

(C) For purposes of subparagraph (A), the term "legislative day" means any calendar day other than a day on which either House is not in session because of a sine die adjournment or an adjournment of more than 3 days to a day certain.

(D) The procedure for disposition of a joint resolution described in subparagraph (B) shall be the procedure described in paragraphs (4) through (7) of section 4006(b).

(5) Regulations prescribed by the corporation to carry out the provisions of this subsection, may, to the extent provided therein, supersede the requirements of sections 4245, 4261, and 4281, and the requirements of section 418E of title 26, but only with respect to benefits guaranteed under this subsection.

(h) Applicability to Nonforfeitable Benefits Accrued as of July 30, 1980; Manner and Extent of Guarantee.—

(1) Except as provided in paragraph (3), subsections (b) and (c) shall not apply with respect to the nonforfeitable benefits accrued as of July 29, 1980, with respect to a participant or beneficiary under a multiemployer plan (1) who is in pay status on July 29, 1980, or (2) who is within 36 months of the normal retirement age and has a nonforfeitable right to a pension as of that date.

(2) The benefits described in paragraph (1) shall be guaranteed by the corporation in the same manner and to the same extent as benefits are guaranteed by the corporation under section 4022 (without regard to this section).

(3) This subsection does not apply with respect to a plan for plan years following a plan year—

(A) in which the plan has terminated within the meaning of section 4041A(a)(2), or

(B) in which it is determined by the corporation that substantially all the employers have withdrawn from the plan pursuant to an agreement or arrangement to withdraw.

Amendments to ERISA §4022A

Pub. L. No. 106-554, as follows:
- ERISA §4022A(c)(1) was amended by Act §951(a)(1) by substituting "$11" for "$5" in two places. Eff. Dec. 21, 2000, provided that: "The amendments made by this section shall apply to any multiemployer plan that has not received financial assistance (within the meaning of §4261 of the Employee Retirement Income Security Act of 1974 within the 1-year period ending on the date of the enactment [Dec. 21, 2000]." Act §951(b).
- ERISA §4022A(c)(1)(A)(i) was amended by Act §951(a)(2) by substituting "$33" for "$15". Eff. Dec. 21, 2000, provided that: "The amendments made by this section shall apply to any multiemployer plan that has not received financial assistance (within the meaning of §4261 of the Employee Retirement Income Security Act of 1974 within the 1-year period ending on the date of the enactment [Dec. 21, 2000]." Act §951(b).
- ERISA §4022A(c)(2)–(6) were amended by Act §951(a)(3) by redesignating paras. (3) and (4) as (2) and (3), respectively, and striking former paras. (2), (5), and (6). Eff. Dec. 21, 2000, provided that: "The amendments made by this section shall apply to any multiemployer plan that has not received financial assistance (within the meaning of §4261 of the Employee Retirement Income Security Act of 1974 within the 1-year period ending on the date of the enactment [Dec. 21, 2000]." Act §951(b).

Omnibus Budget Reconciliation Act of 1989 (Pub. L. No. 101-239), as follows:
- ERISA §4022A(a)(1) was amended by Act §7894(g)(3)(C)(i) by substituting "this title" for "section 4021". Eff. as if originally included in §102 of Pub. L. No. 96-364 (enacted Sept. 26, 1980), see Act §7894(i).
- ERISA §4022A(c)(3)(A)(ii), (4)(C), (5)(A)(ii), (6), (d), (g)(5) were amended by Act §7891(a)(1) by substituting "Internal Revenue Code of 1986" for "Internal Revenue Code of 1954", which for purposes of codification was translated as "title 26".

Eff., except as otherwise provided, as if included in the provision of Pub. L. No. 99-514, to which such amendment relates, see Act §7891(f).
- ERISA §4022A(f)(2)(B) was amended by Act §7893(b) by substituting "the enactment" for "the the enactment". Eff. as if included in the provision of Pub. L. No. 99-272, title XI, to which such amendment relates, see Act §7893(h).

Consolidated Omnibus Budget Reconciliation Act of 1985 (Pub. L. No. 99-272), as follows:
- ERISA §4022A(f)(2)(B) was amended by Act §11005(c)(4) by substituting "the enactment of a joint resolution" for "Congress by concurrent resolution". Eff. for plan years commencing after Dec. 31, 1985.
- ERISA §4022(f)(2)(C) was amended by Act §11005(c)(5) by substituting "so enacted" for "approved". Eff. for plan years commencing after Dec. 31, 1985, see Act §11005(d)(1).
- ERISA §4022A(f)(3)(B) was amended by Act §11005(c)(6) by substituting "enactment of a joint resolution" for "Congress by concurrent resolution". Eff. for plan years commencing after Dec. 31, 1985, Act §11005(d)(1).
- ERISA §4022A(f)(4)(A) was amended by Act §11005(c)(7) by substituting "joint" for "concurrent". Eff. for plan years commencing after Dec. 31, 1985, Act §11005(d)(1).
- ERISA §4022A(f)(4)(B) was amended by Act §11005(c)(8) by substituting "joint" for "concurrent" in two places and "The" for "That the Congress favors the" and inserting "is hereby approved". Eff. for plan years commencing after Dec. 31, 1985, Act §11005(d)(1).
- ERISA §4022A(f)(4)(C) was amended by Act §11005(c)(9) by substituting "joint" for "concurrent". Eff. for plan years commencing after Dec. 31, 1985, Act §11005(d)(1).
- ERISA §4022A(g)(4)(A)(ii) was amended by Act §11005(c)(10) by substituting "joint" for "concurrent" and "enacted" for "adopted". Eff. for plan years commencing after Dec. 31, 1985, Act §11005(d)(1).
- ERISA §4022A(g)(4)(B) was amended by Act §11005(c)(11) by substituting "joint" for "concurrent" in two places and "The" for "That the Congress disapproves the" and inserted "is hereby disapproved". Eff. for plan years commencing after Dec. 31, 1985, Act §11005(d)(1).
- ERISA §4022A(g)(4)(D) was amended by Act §11005(c)(12) by substituting "joint" for "concurrent". Eff. for plan years commencing after Dec. 31, 1985, Act §11005(d)(1).

SEC. 4022B. AGGREGATE LIMIT ON BENEFITS GUARANTEED; CRITERIA APPLICABLE.

(a) Notwithstanding sections 4022 and 4022A, no person shall receive from the corporation pursuant to a guarantee by the corporation of basic benefits with respect to a participant under all multiemployer and single employer plans an amount, or amounts, with an actuarial value which exceeds the actuarial value of a monthly benefit in the form of a life annuity commencing at age 65 equal to the amount determined under section 4022(b)(3)(B) as of the date of the last plan termination.

(b) For purposes of this section—

(1) the receipt of benefits under a multiemployer plan receiving financial assistance from the corporation shall be considered the receipt of amounts from the corporation pursuant to a guarantee by the corporation of basic benefits except to the extent provided in regulations prescribed by the corporation, and

(2) the date on which a multiemployer plan, whether or not terminated, begins receiving financial assistance from the corporation shall be considered a date of plan termination.

SEC. 4023. PLAN FIDUCIARIES.

Notwithstanding any other provision of this Act, a fiduciary of a plan to which section 4021 applies is not in violation of the fiduciary's duties as a result of any act or of any withholding of action required by this title.

Subtitle C—Terminations

SEC. 4041. TERMINATION OF SINGLE-EMPLOYER PLANS.

(a) General Rules Governing Single-Employer Plan Terminations.—

(1) Exclusive means of plan termination.—Except in the case of a termination for which proceedings are otherwise instituted by the corporation as provided in section 4042, a single-employer plan may be terminated only in a standard termination under subsection (b) or a distress termination under subsection (c).

(2) 60-day notice of intent to terminate.—Not less than 60 days before the proposed termination date of a standard termination under subsection (b) or a distress termination under subsection (c), the plan administrator shall provide to each affected party (other than the corporation in the case of a standard termination) a written notice of intent to terminate stating that such termination is intended and the proposed termination date. The written notice shall include any related additional information required by regulations of the corporation.

(3) Adherence to collective bargaining agreements.—The corporation shall not proceed with a termination of a plan under this section if the termination would violate the terms and conditions of an existing collective bargaining agreement. Nothing in the preceding sentence shall be construed as limiting the authority of the corporation to institute proceedings to involuntarily terminate a plan under section 4042.

(b) Standard Termination of Single-Employer Plans.—

(1) General requirements.—A single employer plan may terminate under a standard termination only if—

(A) the plan administrator provides the 60-day advance notice of intent to terminate to affected parties required under subsection (a)(2),

(B) the requirements of subparagraphs (A) and (B) of paragraph (2) are met,

(C) the corporation does not issue a notice of noncompliance under subparagraph (C) of paragraph (2), and

(D) when the final distribution of assets occurs, the plan is sufficient for benefit liabilities (determined as of the termination date).

(2) Termination procedure.—

(A) Notice to the corporation.—As soon as practicable after the date on which the notice of intent to terminate is provided pursuant to subsection (a)(2), the plan administrator shall send a notice to the corporation setting forth—

(i) certification by an enrolled actuary—

(I) of the projected amount of the assets of the plan (as of the proposed date of final distribution of assets),

(II) of the actuarial present value (as of such date) of the benefit liabilities (determined as of the proposed termination date) under the plan, and

(III) that the plan is projected to be sufficient (as of such proposed date of final distribution) for such benefit liabilities,

(ii) such information as the corporation may prescribe in regulations as necessary to enable the corporation to make determinations under subparagraph (C), and

(iii) certification by the plan administrator that—

(I) the information on which the enrolled actuary based the certification under clause (i) is accurate and complete, and

(II) the information provided to the corporation under clause (ii) is accurate and complete.

Clause (i) and clause (iii)(I) shall not apply to a plan described in section 412(i) of the Internal Revenue Code of 1986.

(B) Notice to participants and beneficiaries of benefit commitments [liabilities].—No later than the date on which a notice is sent by the plan administrator under subparagraph (A), the plan administrator shall send a notice to each person who is a participant or beneficiary under the plan—

(i) specifying the amount of the benefit liabilities (if any) attributable to such person as of the proposed termination date, and the benefit form on the basis of which such amount is determined, and

(ii) including the following information used in determining such benefit liabilities:

(I) the length of service,

(II) the age of the participant or beneficiary,

(III) wages,

(IV) the assumptions, including the interest rate, and

(V) such other information as the corporation may require.

ERISA Sec. 4041(b)(2)(B)(ii)(V)

Such notice shall be written in such manner as is likely to be understood by the participant or beneficiary and as may be prescribed in regulations of the corporation.

(C) Notice from the corporation of noncompliance.—

(i) In general.—Within 60 days after receipt of the notice under subparagraph (A), the corporation shall issue a notice of noncompliance to the plan administrator if—

(I) it determines, based on the notice sent under paragraph (2)(A) of subsection (b), that there is reason to believe that the plan is not sufficient for benefit liabilities,

(II) it otherwise determines, on the basis of information provided by affected parties or otherwise obtained by the corporation, that there is reason to believe that the plan is not sufficient for benefit liabilities, or

(III) it determines that any other requirement of subparagraph (A) or (B) of this paragraph or of subsection (a)(2) has not been met, unless it further determines that the issuance of such notice would be inconsistent with the interests of participants and beneficiaries.

(ii) Extension.—The corporation and the plan administrator may agree to extend the 60-day period referred to in clause (i) by a written agreement signed by the corporation and the plan administrator before the expiration of the 60-day period. The 60-day period shall be extended as provided in the agreement and may be further extended by subsequent written agreements signed by the corporation and the plan administrator made before the expiration of a previously agreed upon extension of the 60-day period. Any extension may be made upon such terms and conditions (including the payment of benefits) as are agreed upon by the corporation and the plan administrator.

(D) Final distribution of assets in absence of notice of noncompliance.—The plan administrator shall commence the final distribution of assets pursuant to the standard termination of the plan as soon as practicable after the expiration of the 60-day (or extended) period referred to in subparagraph (C), but such final distributions may occur only if—

(i) the plan administrator has not received during such period a notice of noncompliance from the corporation under subparagraph (C), and

(ii) when such final distribution occurs, the plan is sufficient for benefit liabilities (determined as of the termination date).

(3) **Methods of final distribution of assets.—**

(A) In general.—In connection with any final distribution of assets pursuant to the standard termination of the plan under this subsection, the plan administrator shall distribute the assets in accordance with section 4044. In distributing such assets, the plan administrator shall—

(i) purchase irrevocable commitments from an insurer to provide all benefit liabilities under the plan, or

(ii) in accordance with the provisions of the plan and any applicable regulations, otherwise fully provide all benefit liabilities under the plan. A transfer of assets to the corporation in accordance with section 4050 on behalf of a missing participant shall satisfy this subparagraph with respect to such participant.

(B) Certification to the corporation of final distribution of assets.—Within 30 days after the final distribution of assets is completed pursuant to the standard termination of the plan under this subsection, the plan administrator shall send a notice to the corporation certifying that the assets of the plan have been distributed in accordance with the provisions of subparagraph (A) so as to pay all benefit liabilities under the plan[.]

(4) **Continuing authority.**—Nothing in this section shall be construed to preclude the continued exercise by the corporation, after the termination date of a plan terminated in a standard termination under this subsection, of its authority under section 4003 with respect to matters relating to the termination. A certification under paragraph (3)(B) shall not affect the corporation's obligations under section 4022.

(5) **Special rule for certain plans where cessation or change in membership of a controlled group.—**

(A) In general.—Except as provided in subparagraphs (B) and (D), if—

(i) there is transaction or series of transactions which result in a person ceasing to be a member of a controlled group, and

(ii) such person immediately before the transaction or series of transactions maintained a single-employer plan which is a defined benefit plan which is fully funded,

then the interest rate used in determining whether the plan is sufficient for benefit liabilities or to otherwise assess plan liabilities for purposes of this subsection or section 4042(a)(4) shall be not less than the interest rate used in determining whether the plan is fully funded.

(B) Limitations.—Subparagraph (A) shall not apply to any transaction or series of transactions unless—

(i) any employer maintaining the plan immediately before or after such transaction or series of transactions—

(I) has an outstanding senior unsecured debt instrument which is rated investment grade by each of the nationally recognized statistical rating organizations for corporate bonds that has issued a credit rating for such instrument, or

(II) if no such debt instrument of such employer has been rated by such an organization but 1 or more of such organizations has made an issuer credit rating for such employer, all such organizations which have so rated the employer have rated such employer investment grade, and

(ii) the employer maintaining the plan after the transaction or series of transactions employs at least 20 percent of the employees located in the United States who were employed by such employer immediately before the transaction or series of transactions.

(C) Fully funded.—For purposes of subparagraph (A), a plan shall be treated as fully funded with respect to any transaction or series of transactions if—

(i) in the case of a transaction or series of transactions which occur in a plan year beginning before January 1, 2008, the funded current liability percentage determined under section 302(d) for the plan year is at least 100 percent, and

(ii) in the case of a transaction or series of transactions which occur in a plan year beginning on or after such date, the funding target attainment percentage determined under section 303 is, as of the valuation date for such plan year, at least 100 percent.

(D) 2 year limitation.—Subparagraph (A) shall not apply to any transaction or series of transactions if the plan referred to in subparagraph (A)(ii) is terminated under section 4041(c) or 4042 after the close of the 2-year period beginning on the date on which the first such transaction occurs.

(c) Distress Termination of Single-Employer Plans.—

(1) In general.—A single-employer plan may terminate under a distress termination only if—

(A) the plan administrator provides the 60-day advance notice of intent to terminate to affected parties required under subsection (a)(2),

(B) the requirements of subparagraph (A) of paragraph (2) are met, and

(C) the corporation determines that the requirements of subparagraphs (B) and (D) of paragraph (2) are met.

(2) Termination requirements.—

(A) Information submitted to the corporation.— As soon as practicable after the date on which the notice of intent to terminate is provided pursuant to

subsection (a)(2), the plan administrator shall provide the corporation, in such form as may be prescribed by the corporation in regulations, the following information:

(i) such information as the corporation may prescribe by regulation as necessary to make determinations under subparagraph (B) and paragraph (3);

(ii) unless the corporation determines the information is not necessary for purposes of paragraph (3)(A) or section 4062, certification by an enrolled actuary of—

(I) the amount (as of the proposed termination date and, if applicable, the proposed distribution date) of the current value of the assets of the plan,

(II) the actuarial present value (as of such dates) of the benefit liabilities under the plan,

(III) whether the plan is sufficient for benefit liabilities as of such dates,

(IV) the actuarial present value (as of such dates) of benefits under the plan guaranteed under section 4022, and

(V) whether the plan is sufficient for guaranteed benefits as of such dates;

(iii) in any case in which the plan is not sufficient for benefit liabilities as of such date—

(I) the name and address of each participant and beneficiary under the plan as of such date, and

(II) such other information as shall be prescribed by the corporation by regulation as necessary to enable the corporation to be able to make payments to participants and beneficiaries as required under section 4022(c); and

(iv) certification by the plan administrator that—

(I) the information on which the enrolled actuary based the certifications under clause (ii) is accurate and complete, and

(II) the information provided to the corporation under clauses (i) and (iii) is accurate and complete.

Clause (ii) and clause (iv)(I) shall not apply to a plan described in section 412(i) of the Internal Revenue Code of 1986.

(B) Determination by the corporation of necessary distress criteria.—Upon receipt of the notice of intent to terminate required under subsection (a)(2) and the information required under subparagraph (A), the corporation shall determine whether the requirements of this subparagraph are met as provided in clause (i), (ii), or (iii). The requirements of this subparagraph are met if each person who is (as of the proposed termination date) a contributing sponsor of such plan or a member of such spon-

ERISA Sec. 4041(c)(2)(B)

sor's controlled group meets the requirements of any of the following clauses:

(i) Liquidation in bankruptcy or insolvency proceedings.—The requirements of this clause are met by a person if—

(I) such person has filed or has had filed against such person, as of the proposed termination date, a petition seeking liquidation in a case under title 11, United States Code, or under any similar Federal law or law of a State or political subdivision of a State (or a case described in clause (ii) filed by or against such person has been converted, as of such date, to a case in which liquidation is sought), and

(II) such case has not, as of the termination date, been dismissed.

(ii) Reorganization in bankruptcy or insolvency proceedings.—The requirements of this clause are met by a person if—

(I) such person has filed, or has had filed against such person, as of the proposed termination date, a petition seeking reorganization in a case under title 11, United States Code, or under any similar law of a State or political subdivision of a State (or a case described in clause (i) filed by or against such person has been converted, as of such date, to such a case in which reorganization is sought),

(II) such case has not, as of the proposed termination date, been dismissed,

(III) such person timely submits to the corporation any request for the approval of the bankruptcy court (or other appropriate court in a case under such similar law of a State or political subdivision) of the plan termination, and

(IV) the bankruptcy court (or such other appropriate court) determines that, unless the plan is terminated, such person will be unable to pay all its debts pursuant to a plan of reorganization and will be unable to continue in business outside the chapter 11 reorganization process and approves the termination.

(iii) Termination required to enable payment of debts while staying in business or to avoid unreasonably burdensome pension costs caused by declining workforce.—The requirements of this clause are met by a person if such person demonstrates to the satisfaction of the corporation that—

(I) unless a distress termination occurs, such person will be unable to pay such person's debts when due and will be unable to continue in business, or

(II) the costs of providing pension coverage have become unreasonably burdensome to such person, solely as a result of a decline of such person's workforce covered as participants under

all single-employer pension plans of which such person is a contributing sponsor.

(C) Notification of determinations by the corporation.—The corporation shall notify the plan administrator as soon as practicable of its determinations made pursuant to subparagraph (B).

(D) Disclosure of termination information.—

(i) In general.—A plan administrator that has filed a notice of intent to terminate under subsection (a)(2) shall provide to an affected party any information provided to the corporation under subparagraph (A) or the regulations under subsection (a)(2) not later than 15 days after—

(I) receipt of a request from the affected party for the information; or

(II) the provision of new information to the corporation relating to a previous request.

(ii) Confidentiality.—

(I) In general.—The plan administrator shall not provide information under clause (i) in a form that includes any information that may directly or indirectly be associated with, or otherwise identify, an individual participant or beneficiary.

(II) Limitation.—A court may limit disclosure under this subparagraph of confidential information described in section 552(b) of title 5, United States Code, to any authorized representative of the participants or beneficiaries that agrees to ensure the confidentiality of such information.

(iii) Form and manner of information; charges.—

(I) Form and manner.—The corporation may prescribe the form and manner of the provision of information under this subparagraph, which shall include delivery in written, electronic, or other appropriate form to the extent that such form is reasonably accessible to individuals to whom the information is required to be provided.

(II) Reasonable charges.—A plan administrator may charge a reasonable fee for any information provided under this subparagraph in other than electronic form.

(iv) Authorized representative.—For purposes of this subparagraph, the term "authorized representative" means any employee organization representing participants in the pension plan.

(3) Termination procedure.—

(A) Determinations by the corporation relating to plan sufficiency for guaranteed benefits and for benefit liabilities.—If the corporation determines that the requirements for a distress termination set forth in paragraphs (1) and (2) are met, the corporation shall—

(i) determine that the plan is sufficient for guaranteed benefits (as of the termination date) or that the corporation is unable to make such determination on the basis of information made available to the corporation,

(ii) determine that the plan is sufficient for benefit liabilities (as of the termination date) or that the corporation is unable to make such determination on the basis of information made available to the corporation, and

(iii) notify the plan administrator of the determinations made pursuant to this subparagraph as soon as practicable.

(B) Implementation of termination.—After the corporation notifies the plan administrator of its determinations under subparagraph (A), the termination of the plan shall be carried out as soon as practicable, as provided in clause (i), (ii), or (iii).

(i) Cases of sufficiency for benefit liabilities.— In any case in which the corporation determines that the plan is sufficient for benefit liabilities, the plan administrator shall proceed to distribute the plan's assets, and make certification to the corporation with respect to such distribution, in the manner described in subsection (b)(3), and shall take such other actions as may be appropriate to carry out the termination of the plan.

(ii) Cases of sufficiency for guaranteed benefits without a finding of sufficiency for benefit liabilities.—In any case in which the corporation determines that the plan is sufficient for guaranteed benefits, but further determines that it is unable to determine that the plan is sufficient for benefit liabilities on the basis of the information made available to it, the plan administrator shall proceed to distribute the plan's assets in the manner described in subsection (b)(3), make certification to the corporation that the distribution has occurred, and take such actions as may be appropriate to carry out the termination of the plan.

(iii) Cases without any finding of sufficiency.—In any case in which the corporation determines that it is unable to determine that the plan is sufficient for guaranteed benefits on the basis of the information made available to it, the corporation shall commence proceedings in accordance with section 4042.

(C) Finding after authorized commencement of termination that plan is unable to pay benefits.—

(i) Findings with respect to benefit liabilities which are not guaranteed benefits.—If, after the plan administrator has begun to terminate the plan as authorized under subparagraph (B)(i), the plan administrator finds that the plan is unable, or will be unable, to pay benefit liabilities which are not benefits guaranteed by the corporation under section 4022, the plan administrator shall notify the corporation of such finding as soon as practicable thereafter.

(ii) Finding with respect to guaranteed benefits.—If, after the plan administrator has begun to terminate the plan as authorized by subparagraph (B)(i) or (ii), the plan administrator finds that the plan is unable, or will be unable, to pay all benefits under the plan which are guaranteed by the corporation under section 4022, the plan administrator shall notify the corporation of such finding as soon as practicable thereafter. If the corporation concurs in the finding of the plan administrator (or the corporation itself makes such a finding), the corporation shall institute appropriate proceedings under section 4042.

(D) Administration of the plan during interim period.—

(i) In general.—The plan administrator shall—

(I) meet the requirements of clause (ii) for the period commencing on the date on which the plan administrator provides a notice of distress termination to the corporation under subsection (a)(2) and ending on the date on which the plan administrator receives notification from the corporation of its determinations under subparagraph (A), and

(II) meet the requirements of clause (ii) commencing on the date on which the plan administrator or the corporation makes a finding under subparagraph (C)(ii).

(ii) Requirements.—The requirements of this clause are met by the plan administrator if the plan administrator—

(I) refrains from distributing assets or taking any other actions to carry out the proposed termination under this subsection,

(II) pays benefits attributable to employer contributions, other than death benefits, only in the form of an annuity,

(III) does not use plan assets to purchase irrevocable commitments to provide benefits from an insurer, and

(IV) continues to pay all benefit liabilities under the plan, but, commencing on the proposed termination date, limits the payment of benefits under the plan to those benefits which are guaranteed by the corporation under section 4022 or to which assets are required to be allocated under section 4044.

In the event the plan administrator is later determined not to have met the requirements for distress termination, any benefits which are not paid solely by reason of compliance with subclause (IV) shall be due and payable immediately (together with interest, at a reasonable rate, in accordance with regulations of the corporation).

(d) Sufficiency.—For purposes of this section—

(1) Sufficiency for benefit liabilities.—A single employer plan is sufficient for benefit liabilities if there is no amount of unfunded benefit liabilities under the plan.

(2) Sufficiency for guaranteed benefits.—A single-employer plan is sufficient for guaranteed benefits if there is no amount of unfunded guaranteed benefits under the plan.

(e) Limitation on the Conversion of a Defined Benefit Plan to a Defined Contribution Plan.—The adoption of an amendment to a plan which causes the plan to become a plan described in section 4021(b)(1) constitutes a termination of the plan. Such an amendment may take effect only after the plan satisfies the requirements for standard termination under subsection (b) or distress termination under subsection (c).

Amendments to ERISA §4041

Worker, Retiree, and Employer Recovery Act of 2008 (Pub. L. No. 110-458), as follows:

- ERISA §4041(b)(5)(A) was amended by Act §104(d) by striking "subparagraph (B)" and inserting "subparagraphs (B) and (D)". Eff. as if included in Pub. L. No. 109-280, §409.
- ERISA §4041(c)(2)(D)(i) was amended by Act §105(e)(1) by striking "subsection (a)(2)" second place it appeared and inserting "subparagraph (A) or the regulations under subsection (a)(2)". Eff. as if included in Pub. L. No. 109-280, §506.

Pension Protection Act of 2006 (Pub. L. No. 109-280), as follows:

- ERISA §4041(b)(5) was added by Act §409(a). Eff. for any transaction or series of transactions occurring on and after Aug. 17, 2006, see Act §409(b).
- ERISA §4041(c)(1)(C) was amended by Act §506(a)(2) by substituting "subparagraphs (B) and (D)" for "subparagraph (B)". Eff. generally for any plan termination under title IV of ERISA for which the notice of intent to terminate (or in the case of a PBGC termination, a notice of determination under ERISA §4042) occurs after Aug. 17, 2006, see Act §506(c)(1).
- ERISA §4041(c)(2)(D) was added by Act §506(a)(1). Eff. generally for any plan termination under title IV of ERISA for which the notice of intent to terminate (or in the case of a PBGC termination, a notice of determination under ERISA §4042) occurs after Aug. 17, 2006, see Act §506(c)(1).
- **Transition Rule.** Act §506(c)(2):
  (2) Transition Rule. If notice under section 4041(c)(2)(D) or 4042(c)(3) of the Employee Retirement Income Security Act of 1974 (as added by this section) would otherwise be required to be provided before the 90th day after the date of the enactment of this Act, such notice shall not be required to be provided until such 90th day.

Uruguay Round Agreements Act (1994) (Pub. L. No. 103-465), as follows:

- ERISA §4041(b)(2)(C)(i) was amended by Act §778(a)(1)(A)–(B) by adding new subcl. (I); striking former subcl. (I); and striking the period at the end of subcl. (II) and inserting ", or". Eff. for any plan termination under ERISA §4041(b) for which the PBGC has not, as of Dec. 8, 1994, issued a notice of noncompliance that has become final or otherwise issued a final determination that the plan termination is nullified, see Act §778(a)(1). ERISA §4041(b)(2)(C)(i)(I) prior to amendment:
  (I) It has reason to believe that any requirement of subsection (a)(2) of this section or subparagraph (A) or (B) has not been met, or.
- ERISA §4041(b)(2)(C)(i)(III) was added by Act §778(a)(1)(B)–(C). Eff. for any plan termination under ERISA §4041(b) for which the PBGC has not, as of Dec. 8, 1994, issued a notice of noncompliance that has become final or otherwise issued a final determination that the plan termination is nullified, see Act §778(a)(1).
- ERISA §4041(b)(3)(A)(ii) was amended by Act §776(b)(3) by inserting at the end "A transfer of assets to the corporation in

accordance with §4050 on behalf of a missing participant shall satisfy this subparagraph with respect to such participant." Eff. with respect to distributions that occur in plan years commencing on or after July 1, 1996, see Act §776(e).

- ERISA §4041(c)(2)(B)(i)(I) was amended by Act §778(b)(1) by inserting "Federal law or" after "under any similar". Eff. as if included in Pub. L. No. 99-272, title XI.

Omnibus Budget Reconciliation Act of 1989 (Pub. L. No. 101-239), as follows:

- ERISA §4041(b)(3)(B) was amended by Act §7881(g)(4) by inserting a period at end. Eff., except as otherwise provided, as if included in the provision of Pub. L. No. 100-203, §§9302–9346, to which it relates, see Act §7882.
- ERISA §4041(c)(2)(A)(ii) was amended by Act §7881(g)(3), in introductory provisions, by inserting "unless the corporation determines the information is not necessary for purposes of paragraph (3)(A) or §4062," before "certification"; in subcl. (I), by inserting "and, if applicable, the proposed distribution date" after "termination date"; and in subcls. (II)–(V), by substituting "dates" for "date". Eff., except as otherwise provided, as if included in the provision of Pub. L. No. 100-203, §§9302–9346, to which it relates, see Act §7882.
- ERISA §4041(c)(2)(A)(iii)(II) was amended by Act §7881(f)(7)(A)–(B) by striking "(or its designee under §4049(b))" before "to be able" and substituting "§4022(c) of this title" for "§4049". Eff., except as otherwise provided, as if included in the provision of Pub. L. No. 100-203, §§9302–9346, to which it relates, see Act §7882.
- ERISA §4041(c)(2)(B) was amended by Act §7881(g)(2) by substituting "(as of the proposed termination date)" for "(as of the termination date)". Eff., except as otherwise provided, as if included in the provision of Pub. L. No. 100-203, §§9302–9346, to which it relates, see Act §7882.
- ERISA §4041(c)(3)(C)(i) was amended by Act §7881(f)(7)(C) by striking at end "If the corporation concurs in the finding of the plan administrator (or the corporation itself makes such a finding) the corporation shall take the actions set forth in subparagraph (B)(ii)(II) relating to the trust established for purposes of §4049." Eff., except as otherwise provided, as if included in the provision of Pub. L. No. 100-203, §§9302–9346, to which it relates, see Act §7882.
- ERISA §4041(c)(3)(D)(ii)(I) was amended by Act §7893(d)(2) by substituting "under this subsection" for "of this subsection". Eff. as if included in the provision of Pub. L. No. 99-272, title XI, to which such it relates, see Act §7893(h).
- ERISA §4041(d)(1) was amended by Act §7881(g)(1) by substituting "sufficient for benefit liabilities" for "sufficient for benefit commitments". Eff., except as otherwise provided, as if included in the provision of Pub. L. No. 100-203, §§9302–9346, to which it relates, see Act §7882.

Omnibus Budget Reconciliation Act of 1987 (Pub. L. No. 100-203), as follows:

- ERISA §4041(b)(1)(D) was amended by Act §9313(a)(1). Eff. for plan terminations under ERISA §4041 for which notices of intent to terminate are provided under ERISA §4041(a)(2) after Dec. 17, 1987, see Act §9313(c). ERISA §4041(b)(1)(D) prior to amendment:
  (D) when the final distribution of assets occurs, the plan is sufficient for benefit commitments (determined as of the termination date).
- ERISA §4041(b)(2)(A), (2)(C), (2)(D), and (3) were amended by Act §9313(a)(2)(A) by substituting "benefit liabilities" for "benefit commitments". Eff. for plan terminations under ERISA §4041 for which notices of intent to terminate are provided under ERISA §4041(a)(2) after Dec. 17, 1987, see Act §9313(c).
- ERISA §4041(b)(2)(A)(iii) was amended by Act §9314(a)(1)(A) by adding new cl. (iii) and a sentence to the end (flush), "Clause (i) and clause (iii)(I) shall not apply to a plan described in §412(i) of the Internal Revenue Code of 1986." Eff. Dec. 22, 1987. ERISA §4041(b)(2)(A)(iii) prior to amendment:
  (iii) certification by the plan administrator that the information on which the enrolled actuary based the certification under clause (i) and the information provided to the corporation under clause (ii) are accurate and complete.
- ERISA §4041(b)(2)(B) was amended by Act §9313(a)(2)(B) by substituting "the amount of the benefit liabilities (if any) attrib-

utable to such person" for "the amount of such person's benefit commitments (if any)" in cl. (i); and "such benefit liabilities" for "such benefit commitments" in cl. (ii). Eff. for plan terminations under ERISA §4041 for which notices of intent to terminate are provided under ERISA §4041(a)(2) after Dec. 17, 1987, see Act §9313(c).

• ERISA §4041(b)(3)(A)(i) was amended by Act §9313(a)(2)(C)(i) by striking cl. (i) and adding new cl. (i). Eff. for plan terminations under ERISA §4041 for which notices of intent to terminate are provided under ERISA §4041(a)(2) after Dec. 17, 1987, see Act §9313(c). ERISA §4041(b)(3)(A)(i) prior to amendment:

> (i) purchase irrevocable commitments from an insurer to provide the benefit liabilities under the plan and all other benefits (if any) under the plan to which assets are required to be allocated under section 1344 of this title, or.

• ERISA §4041(b)(3)(A)(ii) was amended by Act §9313(a)(2)(C)(i) by striking cl. (ii) and adding new cl. (ii). Eff. for plan terminations under ERISA §4041 for which notices of intent to terminate are provided under ERISA §4041(a)(2) after Dec. 17, 1987, see Act §9313(c). ERISA §4041(b)(3)(A)(ii) prior to amendment:

> (ii) in accordance with the provisions of the plan and any applicable regulations of the corporation, otherwise fully provide the benefit liabilities under the plan and all other benefits (if any) under the plan to which assets are required to be allocated under section 4044.

• ERISA §4041(b)(3)(B) was amended by Act §9313(a)(2)(C)(ii) by substituting "so as to pay all benefit liabilities under the plan" for "so as to pay the benefit liabilities under the plan and all other benefits under the plan to which assets are required to be allocated under §4044." Eff. for plan terminations under ERISA §4041 for which notices of intent to terminate are provided under ERISA §4041(a)(2) after Dec. 17, 1987, see Act §9313(c).

• ERISA §4041(c)(2)(A) was amended by Act §9314(a)(1)(B) by inserting at the end "Clause (ii) and clause (iv)(I) shall not apply to a plan described in §412(i) of title 26." Eff. Dec. 22, 1987.

• ERISA §4041(c)(2)(A)(ii) was amended by Act §9313(a)(2)(D) by substituting "benefit liabilities" for "benefit commitments" in subcls. (II) and (III). Eff. for plan terminations under ERISA §4041 for which notices of intent to terminate are provided under ERISA §4041(a)(2) after Dec. 17, 1987, see Act §9313(c).

• ERISA §4041(c)(2)(A)(iii) was amended by Act §9313(a)(2)(D) by substituting "benefit liabilities" for "benefit commitments" in introductory provision. Eff. for plan terminations under ERISA §4041 for which notices of intent to terminate are provided under ERISA §4041(a)(2) after Dec. 17, 1987, see Act §9313(c).

• ERISA §4041(c)(2)(A)(iv) was amended by Act §9314(a)(2)(A) by striking cl. (iv) and adding new cl. (iv). ERISA §4041(c)(2)(A)(iv) prior to amendment:

> (iv) certification by the plan administrator that the information on which the enrolled actuary based the certifications under clause (ii) and the information provided to the corporation under clauses (i) and (iii) are accurate and complete.

• ERISA §4041(c)(2)(B) was amended by Act §9313(b)(1)(A) by substituting "a member" for "a substantial member" in introductory provisions. Eff. for plan terminations under ERISA §4041 for which notices of intent to terminate are provided under ERISA §4041(a)(2) after Dec. 17, 1987, see Act §9313(c).

• ERISA §4041(c)(2)(B)(i)(I)—(II) were amended by Act §9313(b)(3), as amended by Pub. L. No. 101-239, §7881(g)(5), by substituting "proposed termination date" for "termination date". Eff. for plan terminations under ERISA §4041 for which notices of intent to terminate are provided under ERISA §4041(a)(2) after Dec. 17, 1987, see Act §9313(c).

• ERISA §4041(c)(2)(B)(i)(I) was amended by Act §9313(b)(4) by inserting "(or a case described in clause (ii) filed by or against such person has been converted, as of such date, to a case in which liquidation is sought)". Eff. for plan terminations under ERISA §4041 for which notices of intent to terminate are provided under ERISA §4041(a)(2) after Dec. 17, 1987, see Act §9313(c).

• ERISA §4041(c)(2)(B)(ii)(I) was amended by Act §9313(b)(3), as amended by Pub. L. 101-239, §7881(g)(5), by substituting

"proposed termination date" for "termination date". Eff. for plan terminations under ERISA §4041 for which notices of intent to terminate are provided under ERISA §4041(a)(2) after Dec. 17, 1987, see Act §9313(c).

• ERISA §4041(c)(2)(B)(ii)(II) was amended by Act §9313(b)(5)(A) by striking "and" at the end. Eff. for plan terminations under ERISA §4041 for which notices of intent to terminate are provided under ERISA §4041(a)(2) after Dec. 17, 1987, see Act §9313(c).

• ERISA §4041(c)(2)(B)(i)—(ii) were amended by Act §9313(b)(3) by substituting "proposed termination date" for "termination date". Eff. for plan terminations under ERISA §4041 for which notices of intent to terminate are provided under ERISA §4041(a)(2) after Dec. 17, 1987, see Act §9313(c).

• ERISA §4041(c)(2)(B)(ii)(III) was amended by Act §9313(b)(5)(C) by adding subcl. (III) and redesignating former subcl. (III) as (IV). Eff. for plan terminations under ERISA §4041 for which notices of intent to terminate are provided under ERISA §4041(a)(2) after Dec. 17, 1987, see Act §9313(c).

• ERISA §4041(c)(2)(B)(ii)(IV) was amended by Act §9313(b)(2), (5)(B), (D) by redesignating former subcl. (III) as (IV) and substituting "(or such other appropriate court) determines that, unless the plan is terminated, such person will be unable to pay all its debts pursuant to a plan of reorganization and will be unable to continue in business outside the chapter 11 reorganization process and approves the termination" for "(or other appropriate court in a case under such similar law of a State or political subdivision) approves the termination". Eff. for plan terminations under ERISA §4041 for which notices of intent to terminate are provided under ERISA §4041(a)(2) after Dec. 17, 1987, see Act §9313(c).

• ERISA §4041(c)(2)(C)—(D) were amended by Act §9313(b)(1)(B) by redesignating former subpara. (D) as (C) and striking out former subpara. (C). Eff. for plan terminations under ERISA §4041 for which notices of intent to terminate are provided under ERISA §4041(a)(2) after Dec. 17, 1987, see Act §9313(c). ERISA §4041(c)(2)(C) prior to amendment:

> (C) For purposes of subparagraph (B), the term "substantial member" of a controlled group means a person whose assets comprise 5 percent or more of the total assets of the controlled group as a whole.

• ERISA §4041(c)(3)(A) was amended by Act §9313(a)(2)(D) by substituting "benefit liabilities" for "benefit commitments" in heading and in cl. (ii). Eff. for plan terminations under ERISA §4041 for which notices of intent to terminate are provided under ERISA §4041(a)(2) after Dec. 17, 1987, see Act §9313(c).

• ERISA §4041(c)(3)(B)(i) was amended by Act §9313(a)(2)(D) by substituting in heading and text "benefit liabilities" for "benefit commitments". Eff. for plan terminations under ERISA §4041 for which notices of intent to terminate are provided under ERISA §4041(a)(2) after Dec. 17, 1987, see Act §9313(c).

• ERISA §4041(c)(3)(B)(ii) was amended by Act §9313(a)(2)(D) by substituting in heading and text "benefit liabilities" for "benefit commitments". Eff. for plan terminations under ERISA §4041 for which notices of intent to terminate are provided under ERISA §4041(a)(2) after Dec. 17, 1987, see Act §9313(c).

• ERISA §4041(c)(3)(B)(ii) was amended by Act §9312(c)(1) by striking former subcl. (II); striking "the plan, and" at the end of subcl. (I) and inserting "plan."; and by striking "available to it—" and all that follows through "the plan administrator" and inserting "available to it, the plan administrator". Eff. for plan terminations under ERISA §4041(c) for which notices of intent to terminate are provided under ERISA §4041(a)(2) after Dec. 17, 1987, and plan terminations the proceedings for which are instituted by the PBGC under ERISA §4042 after that date, see Act §9312(d)(1). ERISA §4041(c)(3)(B)(ii)(II) prior to being stricken:

> (II) the corporation shall establish a separate trust in connection with the plan for purposes of section 4049.

• ERISA §4041(c)(3)(B)(iii) was amended by Act §9312(c)(2) by striking former subcl. (II); by striking "§4042, and" at the end of subcl. (I) and inserting "§4042."; and by striking "available to it—" and all that follows through "the corporation" in subcl. (I) and inserting "available to it, the corporation". Eff. for plan terminations under ERISA §4041(c) for which notices of intent to terminate are provided under ERISA §4041(a)(2) after Dec.

ERISA Sec. 4041(e)

17, 1987, and plan terminations the proceedings for which are instituted by the PBGC under ERISA §4042 after that date, see Act §9312(d)(1). ERISA §4041(c)(3)(B)(iii)(II) prior to being stricken:

(II) the corporation shall establish a separate trust in connection with the plan for purposes of §4049 of this title unless the corporation determines that all benefit commitments under the plan are benefits guaranteed by the corporation under section 4022.

- ERISA §4041(c)(3)(C)(i) was amended by Act §9313(a)(2)(D) by substituting in heading and text "benefit liabilities" for "benefit commitments". Eff. for plan terminations under ERISA §4041 for which notices of intent to terminate are provided under ERISA §4041(a)(2) after Dec. 17, 1987, see Act §9313(c).

- ERISA §4041(c)(3)(D)(ii)(IV) was amended by Act §9313(a)(2)(D) by substituting "benefit liabilities" for "benefit commitments". Eff. for plan terminations under ERISA §4041 for which notices of intent to terminate are provided under ERISA §4041(a)(2) after Dec. 17, 1987, see Act §9313(c).

- ERISA §4041(d)(1) was amended by Act §9313(a)(2)(E) by substituting "no amount of unfunded benefit liabilities" for "no amount of unfunded benefit commitments", and in heading, "benefit liabilities" for "benefit commitments". Eff. for plan terminations under ERISA §4041 for which notices of intent to terminate are provided under ERISA §4041(a)(2) after Dec. 17, 1987, see Act §9313(c).

Consolidated Omnibus Budget Reconciliation Act of 1985 (Pub. L. No. 99-272), as follows:

- ERISA §4041(a)–(c) were stricken and replaced with new subsecs. (a)–(c) by Act §11007(a). Eff. Jan. 1, 1986, subject to exceptions and transition rules, see Act §11019 (see note below). ERISA §4041(a)–(c) prior to amendment:

(a) Before the effective date of the termination of a single-employer plan, the plan administrator shall file a notice with the corporation that the plan is to be terminated on a proposed date (which may not be earlier than 10 days after the filing of the notice), and for a period of 90 days after the proposed termination date the plan administrator shall pay no amount pursuant to the termination procedure of the plan unless, before the expiration of such period, he receives a notice of sufficiency under subsection (b). Upon receiving such a notice, the plan administrator may proceed with the termination of the plan in a manner consistent with this subtitle.

(b) If the corporation determines that, after application of section 4044, the assets held under the plan are sufficient to discharge when due all obligations of the plan with respect to basic benefits, it shall notify the plan administrator of such determination as soon as practicable.

(c) If, within such 90-day period, the corporation finds that it is unable to determine that, if the assets of the plan are allocated in accordance with the provisions of section 4044, the assets held under the plan are sufficient to discharge when due all obligations of the plan with respect to basic benefits, it shall notify the plan administrator within such 90-day period of that finding. When the corporation issues a notice under this subsection, it shall commence proceedings in accordance with the provisions of section 4042. Upon receiving a notice under this subsection, the plan administrator shall refrain from taking any action under the proposed termination.

- ERISA §4041(d) was amended by Act §11007(b). Eff. Jan. 1, 1986, subject to exceptions and transition rules, see Act §11019 (see note below). ERISA §4041(d) prior to amendment:

(d) The corporation and the plan administrator may agree to extend the 90-day period provided by this section by a written agreement signed by the corporation and the plan administrator before the expiration of the 90-day period, or the corporation may apply to an appropriate court (as defined in section 4042(g)) for an order extending the 90-day period provided by this section. The 90-day period shall be extended as provided in the agreement or in any court order obtained by the corporation. The 90-day period may be further extended by subsequent written agreements signed by the corporation and the plan administrator made before the expiration of a previously agreed upon extension of the 90-day period, or by subsequent order of the court. Any extension may be made upon such terms and conditions (including the payment of

benefits) as are agreed upon by the corporation and the plan administrator or as specified in the court order.

- ERISA §4041(e) was stricken by Act §11009(b) and former subsec. (f) was redesignated as subsec. (e). Eff. Jan. 1, 1986, subject to exceptions and transition rules, see Act §11019 (see note below). ERISA §4041(e) prior to amendment:

(e) If, after the plan administrator has begun to terminate the plan as authorized by this section, the corporation or the plan administrator finds that the plan is unable, or will be unable, to pay basic benefits when due, the plan administrator shall notify the corporation of such finding as soon as practicable thereafter. If the corporation makes such a finding or concurs with the finding of the plan administrator, it shall institute appropriate proceedings under section 4042. The plan administrator terminating a plan shall furnish such reports to the corporation as it may require for purposes of its duties under this section.

- ERISA §4041(e) (prior to redesignation, (f), see above) was amended by Act §11008(b). Eff. Jan. 1, 1986, subject to exceptions and transition rules, see Act §11019 (see note below). ERISA §4041(e) prior to this amendment:

(e) For purposes of subsection (a), a plan with respect to which basic benefits are guaranteed shall be treated as terminated upon the adoption of an amendment to such plan, if, after giving effect to such amendment, the plan is a plan described in section 4021(b)(1).

- **Effective Date Provision.** Act §11019 provides:

SEC. 11019. EFFECTIVE DATE OF TITLE; TEMPORARY PROCEDURES.

(a) **In General.**—Except as otherwise provided in this title, the amendments made by this title shall be effective as of January 1, 1986, except that such amendments shall not apply with respect to terminations for which—

(1) notices of intent to terminate were filed with the Pension Benefit Guaranty Corporation under §4041 of the Employee Retirement Income Security Act of 1974 before such date, or

(2) proceedings were commenced under §4042 of such Act before such date.

(b) **Transitional Rules.**—

(1) In general.—In the case of a single-employer plan termination for which a notice of intent to terminate was filed with the Pension Benefit Guaranty Corporation under §4041 of the Employee Retirement Income Security Act of 1974 (as in effect before the amendments made by this title) on or after January 1, 1986, but before the date of the enactment of this Act, the amendments made by this title shall apply with respect to such termination, as modified by paragraphs (2) and (3).

(2) Deemed compliance with notice requirements.—The requirements of subsections (a)(2), (b)(1)(A), and (c)(1)(A) of §4041 of the Employee Retirement Income Security Act of 1974 (as amended by this title) shall be considered to have been met with respect to a termination described in paragraph (1) if—

(A) the plan administrator provided notice to the participants in the plan regarding the termination in compliance with applicable regulations of the Pension Benefit Guaranty Corporation as in effect on the date of the notice, and

(B) the notice of intent to terminate provided to the Pension Benefit Guaranty Corporation in connection with the termination was filed with the Corporation not less than 10 days before the proposed date of termination specified in the notice.

For purposes of §4041 of such Act (as amended by this title), the proposed date of termination specified in the notice of intent to terminate referred to in subparagraph (B) shall be considered the proposed termination date.

(3) Special termination procedures.—

(A) In general.—This paragraph shall apply with respect to any termination described in paragraph (1) if, within 90 days after the date of enactment of this Act [Apr. 7, 1986], the plan administrator notifies the Corporation in writing—

(i) that the plan administrator wishes the termination to proceed as a standard termination under §4041(b) of the

Employee Retirement Income Security Act of 1974 (as amended by this title) in accordance with subparagraph (B),

(ii) that the plan administrator wishes the termination to proceed as a distress termination under §4041(c) of such Act (as amended by this title) in accordance with subparagraph (C), or

(iii) that the plan administrator wishes to stop the termination proceedings in accordance with subparagraph (D).

(B) Terminations proceeding as standard termination.—

(i) Terminations for which sufficiency notices have not been issued.—

(I) In general.—In the case of a plan termination described in paragraph (1) with respect to which the Corporation has been provided the notification described in subparagraph (A)(i) and with respect to which a notice of sufficiency has not been issued by the Corporation before the date of the enactment of this Act, if, during the 90-day period commencing on the date of the notice required in subclause (II), all benefit commitments under the plan have been satisfied, the termination shall be treated as a standard termination under §4041(b) of such Act (as amended by this title).

(II) Special notice regarding sufficiency for terminations for which notices of sufficiency have not been issued as of date of enactment.—In the case of a plan termination described in paragraph (1) with respect to which the Corporation has been provided the notification described in subparagraph (A)(i) and with respect to which a notice of sufficiency has not been issued by the Corporation before the date of the enactment of this Act, the Corporation shall make the determinations described in §4041(c)(3)(A)(i) and (ii) (as amended by this title) and notify the plan administrator of such determinations as provided in §4041(c)(3)(A)(iii) (as amended by this title).

(ii) Terminations for which notices of sufficiency have been issued.—In the case of a plan termination described in paragraph (1) with respect to which the Corporation has been provided the notification described in subparagraph (A)(i) and with respect to which a notice of sufficiency has been issued by the Corporation before the date of the enactment of this Act, clause (i)(I) shall apply, except that the 90-day period referred to in clause (i)(I) shall begin on the date of the enactment of this Act.

(C) Terminations proceeding as distress termination.—In the case of a plan termination described in paragraph (1) with respect to which the Corporation has been provided the notification described in subparagraph (A)(ii), if the requirements of §4041(c)(2)(B) of such Act (as amended by this title) are met, the termination shall be treated as a distress termination under §4041(c) of such Act (as amended by this title).

(D) Termination of proceedings by plan administrator.—

(i) In general.—Except as provided in clause (ii), in the case of a plan termination described in paragraph (1) with respect to which the Corporation has been provided the notification described in subparagraph (A)(iii), the termination shall not take effect.

(ii) Terminations with respect to which final distribution of assets has commenced.—Clause (i) shall not apply with respect to a termination with respect to which the final distribution of assets has commenced before the date of the enactment of this Act unless, within 90 days after the date of the enactment of this Act, the plan has been restored in accordance with procedures issued by the Corporation pursuant to subsection (c).

(E) Authority of corporation to extend 90-day periods to permit standard termination.—The Corporation may, on a case-by-case basis in accordance with subsection (c), provide for extensions of the applicable 90-day period referred to in clause (i) or (ii) of subparagraph (B) if it is demonstrated to the satisfaction of the Corporation that—

(i) the plan could not otherwise, pursuant to the preceding provisions of this paragraph, terminate in a termination treated as a standard termination under §4041(b) of

the Employee Retirement Income Security Act of 1974 (as amended by this title), and

(ii) the extension would result in a greater likelihood that benefit commitments under the plan would be paid in full, except that any such period may not be so extended beyond one year after the date of the enactment of this Act.

(c) Authority To Prescribe Temporary Procedures.—The Pension Benefit Guaranty Corporation may prescribe temporary procedures for purposes of carrying out the amendments made by this title during the 180-day period beginning on the date described in subsection (a).

Multiemployer Pension Plan Amendments Act of 1980 (Pub. L. No. 96-364), as follows:

● ERISA §4041(a) was amended by Act §403(d)(2) by inserting "single-employer" after "termination of a". Eff. Sept. 26, 1980, except as specifically provided, see ERISA §4402(e).

● ERISA §4041(g) was stricken by Act §403(d)(3). Eff. Sept. 26, 1980, except as specifically provided, see ERISA §4402(e).

SEC. 4041A. TERMINATION OF MULTIEMPLOYER PLANS.

(a) **Determination Factors.**—Termination of a multiemployer plan under this section occurs as a result of—

(1) the adoption after the date of enactment of the Multiemployer Pension Plan Amendments Act of 1980 [enacted Sept. 26, 1980] of a plan amendment which provides that participants will receive no credit for any purpose under the plan for service with any employer after the date specified by such amendment;

(2) the withdrawal of every employer from the plan, within the meaning of section 4203 or the cessation of the obligation of all employers to contribute under the plan; or

(3) the adoption of an amendment to the plan which causes the plan to become a plan described in section 4021(b)(1).

(b) **Date of Termination.—**

(1) The date on which a plan terminates under paragraph (1) or (3) of subsection (a) is the later of—

(A) the date on which the amendment is adopted, or

(B) the date on which the amendment takes effect.

(2) The date on which a plan terminates under paragraph (2) of subsection (a) is the earlier of—

(A) the date on which the last employer withdraws, or

(B) the first day of the first plan year for which no employer contributions were required under the plan.

(c) **Duties of Plan Sponsor of Amended Plans.—** Except as provided in subsection (f)(1), the plan sponsor of a plan which terminates under paragraph (2) of subsection (a) shall—

(1) limit the payment of benefits to benefits which are nonforfeitable under the plan as of the date of the termination, and

(2) pay benefits attributable to employer contributions, other than death benefits, only in the form of an annuity, unless the plan assets are distributed in full satisfaction of all nonforfeitable benefits under the plan.

(d) Duties of Plan Sponsor of Nonoperative Plan.—The plan sponsor of a plan which terminates under paragraph (2) of subsection (a) shall reduce benefits and suspend benefit payments in accordance with section 4281.

(e) Amount of Contribution of Employer Under Amended Plan for Each Plan Year Subsequent to Plan Termination Date.—In the case of a plan which terminates under paragraph (1) or (3) of subsection (a), the rate of an employer's contributions under the plan for each plan year beginning on or after the plan termination date shall equal or exceed the highest rate of employer contributions at which the employer had an obligation to contribute under the plan in the 5 preceding plan years ending on or before the plan termination date, unless the corporation approves a reduction in the rate based on a finding that the plan is or soon will be fully funded.

(f) Payment of Benefits; Reporting Requirements for Terminated Plans and Rules and Standards for Administration of Such Plans.—

(1) The plan sponsor of a terminated plan may authorize the payment other than in the form of an annuity of a participant's entire nonforfeitable benefit attributable to employer contributions, other than a death benefit, if the value of the entire nonforfeitable benefit does not exceed $1,750. The corporation may authorize the payment of benefits under the terms of a terminated plan other than nonforfeitable benefits, or the payment other than in the form of an annuity of benefits having a value greater than $1,750, if the corporation determines that such payment is not adverse to the interest of the plan's participants and beneficiaries generally and does not unreasonably increase the corporation's risk of loss with respect to the plan.

(2) The corporation may prescribe reporting requirements for terminated plans, and rules and standards for the administration of such plans, which the corporation considers appropriate to protect the interests of plan participants and beneficiaries or to prevent unreasonable loss to the corporation.

SEC. 4042. INSTITUTION OF TERMINATION PROCEEDINGS BY THE CORPORATION.

(a) Authority to Institute Proceedings to Terminate Plan.—The corporation may institute proceedings under this section to terminate a plan whenever it determines that—

(1) the plan has not met the minimum funding standard required under section 412 of title 26, or has

been notified by the Secretary of the Treasury that a notice of deficiency under section 6212 of title 26 has been mailed with respect to the tax imposed under section 4971(a) of title 26,

(2) the plan will be unable to pay benefits when due,

(3) the reportable event described in section 4043(c)(7) has occurred, or

(4) the possible long-run loss of the corporation with respect to the plan may reasonably be expected to increase unreasonably if the plan is not terminated.

The corporation shall as soon as practicable institute proceedings under this section to terminate a single-employer plan whenever the corporation determines that the plan does not have assets available to pay benefits which are currently due under the terms of the plan. The corporation may prescribe a simplified procedure to follow in terminating small plans as long as that procedure includes substantial safeguards for the rights of the participants and beneficiaries under the plans, and for the employers who maintain such plans (including the requirement for a court decree under subsection (c)). Notwithstanding any other provision of this title, the corporation is authorized to pool assets of terminated plans for purposes of administration, investment, payment of liabilities of all such terminated plans, and such other purposes as it determines to be appropriate in the administration of this title.

(b) Appointment of Trustee.—

(1) Whenever the corporation makes a determination under subsection (a) with respect to a plan or is required under subsection (a) to institute proceedings under this section, it may, upon notice to the plan, apply to the appropriate United States district court for the appointment of a trustee to administer the plan with respect to which the determination is made pending the issuance of a decree under subsection (c) ordering the termination of the plan. If within 3 business days after the filing of an application under this subsection, or such other period as the court may order, the administrator of the plan consents to the appointment of a trustee, or fails to show why a trustee should not be appointed, the court may grant the application and appoint a trustee to administer the plan in accordance with its terms until the corporation determines that the plan should be terminated or that termination is unnecessary. The corporation may request that it be appointed as trustee of a plan in any case.

(2) Notwithstanding any other provision of this title—

(A) upon the petition of a plan administrator or the corporation, the appropriate United States district court may appoint a trustee in accordance with the provisions of this section if the interests of the plan participants would be better served by the appointment of the trustee, and

(B) upon the petition of the corporation, the appropriate United States district court shall appoint a trustee proposed by the corporation for a multiemployer plan which is in reorganization or to which section 4041A(d) applies, unless such appointment would be adverse to the interests of the plan participants and beneficiaries in the aggregate.

(3) The corporation and plan administrator may agree to the appointment of a trustee without proceeding in accordance with the requirements of paragraphs (1) and (2).

(c) Adjudication That Plan Must Be Terminated.—

(1) If the corporation is required under subsection (a) of this section to commence proceedings under this section with respect to a plan or, after issuing a notice under this section to a plan administrator, has determined that the plan should be terminated, it may, upon notice to the plan administrator, apply to the appropriate United States district court for a decree adjudicating that the plan must be terminated in order to protect the interests of the participants or to avoid any unreasonable deterioration of the financial condition of the plan or any unreasonable increase in the liability of the fund. If the trustee appointed under subsection (b) disagrees with the determination of the corporation under the preceding sentence he may intervene in the proceeding relating to the application for the decree, or make application for such decree himself. Upon granting a decree for which the corporation or trustee has applied under this subsection the court shall authorize the trustee appointed under subsection (b) (or appoint a trustee if one has not been appointed under such subsection and authorize him) to terminate the plan in accordance with the provisions of this subtitle. If the corporation and the plan administrator agree that a plan should be terminated and agree to the appointment of a trustee without proceeding in accordance with the requirements of this subsection (other than this sentence) the trustee shall have the power described in subsection (d)(1) and, in addition to any other duties imposed on the trustee under law or by agreement between the corporation and the plan administrator, the trustee is subject to the duties described in subsection (d)(3). Whenever a trustee appointed under this title is operating a plan with discretion as to the date upon which final distribution of the assets is to be commenced, the trustee shall notify the corporation at least 10 days before the date on which he proposes to commence such distribution.

(2) In the case of a proceeding initiated under this section, the plan administrator shall provide the corporation, upon the request of the corporation, the information described in clauses (ii), (iii), and (iv) of section 4041(c)(2)(A).

(3) Disclosure of termination information.—

(A) In general.—

(i) Information from plan sponsor or administrator.—A plan sponsor or plan administrator of a single-employer plan that has received a notice from the corporation of a determination that the plan should be terminated under this section shall provide to an affected party any information provided to the corporation in connection with the plan termination.

(ii) Information from corporation.—The corporation shall provide a copy of the administrative record, including the trusteeship decision record of a termination of a plan described under clause (i).

(B) Timing of disclosure.—The plan sponsor, plan administrator, or the corporation, as applicable, shall provide the information described in subparagraph (A) not later than 15 days after—

(i) receipt of a request from an affected party for such information; or

(ii) in the case of information described under subparagraph (A)(i), the provision of any new information to the corporation relating to a previous request by an affected party.

(C) Confidentiality.—

(i) In general.—The plan administrator, the plan sponsor, or the corporation shall not provide information under subparagraph (A) in a form which includes any information that may directly or indirectly be associated with, or otherwise identify, an individual participant or beneficiary.

(ii) Limitation.—A court may limit disclosure under this paragraph of confidential information described in section 552(b) of title 5, United States Code, to authorized representatives (within the meaning of section 4041(c)(2)(D)(iv)) of the participants or beneficiaries that agree to ensure the confidentiality of such information.

(D) Form and manner of information; charges.—

(i) Form and manner.—The corporation may prescribe the form and manner of the provision of information under this paragraph, which shall include delivery in written, electronic, or other appropriate form to the extent that such form is reasonably accessible to individuals to whom the information is required to be provided.

(ii) Reasonable charges.—A plan sponsor may charge a reasonable fee for any information provided under this paragraph in other than electronic form.

(d) Powers of Trustee.—

(1)(A) A trustee appointed under subsection (b) shall have the power—

(i) to do any act authorized by the plan or this title to be done by the plan administrator or any trustee of the plan;

(ii) to require the transfer of all (or any part) of the assets and records of the plan to himself as trustee;

(iii) to invest any assets of the plan which he holds in accordance with the provisions of the plan, regulations of the corporation, and applicable rules of law;

(iv) to limit payment of benefits under the plan to basic benefits or to continue payment of some or all of the benefits which were being paid prior to his appointment;

(v) in the case of a multiemployer plan, to reduce benefits or suspend benefit payments under the plan, give appropriate notices, amend the plan, and perform other acts required or authorized by subtitle (E) to be performed by the plan sponsor or administrator;

(vi) to do such other acts as he deems necessary to continue operation of the plan without increasing the potential liability of the corporation, if such acts may be done under the provisions of the plan; and

(vii) to require the plan sponsor, the plan administrator, any contributing or withdrawn employer, and any employee organization representing plan participants to furnish any information with respect to the plan which the trustee may reasonably need in order to administer the plan.

If the court to which application is made under subsection (c) dismisses the application with prejudice, or if the corporation fails to apply for a decree under subsection (c) within 30 days after the date on which the trustee is appointed under subsection (b), the trustee shall transfer all assets and records of the plan held by him to the plan administrator within 3 business days after such dismissal or the expiration of such 30-day period, and shall not be liable to the plan or any other person for his acts as trustee except for willful misconduct, or for conduct in violation of the provisions of part 4 of subtitle B of title I of this Act (except as provided in subsection (d)(1)(A)(v)). The 30-day period referred to in this subparagraph may be extended as provided by agreement between the plan administrator and the corporation or by court order obtained by the corporation.

(B) If the court to which an application is made under subsection (c) issues the decree requested in such application, in addition to the powers described in subparagraph (A), the trustee shall have the power—

(i) to pay benefits under the plan in accordance with the requirements of this title;

(ii) to collect for the plan any amounts due the plan, including but not limited to the power to collect from the persons obligated to meet the requirements of section 302 or the terms of the plan;

(iii) to receive any payment made by the corporation to the plan under this title;

(iv) to commence, prosecute, or defend on behalf of the plan any suit or proceeding involving the plan;

(v) to issue, publish, or file such notices, statements, and reports as may be required by the corporation or any order of the court;

(vi) to liquidate the plan assets;

(vii) to recover payments under section 4045(a); and

(viii) to do such other acts as may be necessary to comply with this title or any order of the court and to protect the interests of plan participants and beneficiaries.

(2) As soon as practicable after his appointment, the trustee shall give notice to interested parties of the institution of proceedings under this title to determine whether the plan should be terminated or to terminate the plan, whichever is applicable. For purposes of this paragraph, the term "interested party" means—

(A) the plan administrator,

(B) each participant in the plan and each beneficiary of a deceased participant,

(C) each employer who may be subject to liability under section 4062, 4063, or 4064,

(D) each employer who is or may be liable to the plan under [section] part 1 of subtitle E,

(E) each employer who has an obligation to contribute, within the meaning of section 4212(a), under a multiemployer plan, and

(F) each employee organization which, for purposes of collective bargaining, represents plan participants employed by an employer described in subparagraph (C), (D), or (E).

(3) Except to the extent inconsistent with the provisions of this Act, or as may be otherwise ordered by the court, a trustee appointed under this section shall be subject to the same duties as those of a trustee under section 704 of title 11, United States Code, and shall be, with respect to the plan, a fiduciary within the meaning of paragraph (21) of section 3 of this Act and under section 4975(e) of title 26 (except to the extent that the provisions of this title are inconsistent with the requirements applicable under part 4 of subtitle B of title I of this Act and of such section 4975).

(e) Filing of Application Notwithstanding Pendency of Other Proceedings.—An application by the corporation under this section may be filed notwithstanding the pendency in the same or any other court of any bankruptcy, mortgage foreclosure, or equity receivership proceeding, or any proceeding to reorganize, conserve, or liquidate such plan or its property, or any proceeding to enforce a lien against property of the plan.

(f) Exclusive Jurisdiction; Stay of Other Proceedings.—Upon the filing of an application for the appointment of a trustee or the issuance of a decree under this section, the court to which an application is made shall have exclusive jurisdiction of the plan involved and its property wherever located with the powers, to the extent consistent with the purposes of this section, of a court of the United States having jurisdiction over cases under chapter 11 of title 11. Pending an adjudication under subsection (c) of this section such court shall stay, and upon appointment by it of a trustee, as provided in this section such court shall continue the stay of, any pending mortgage foreclosure, equity receivership, or other proceeding to reorganize, conserve, or liquidate the plan or its property and any other suit against any receiver, conservator, or trustee of the plan or its property. Pending such adjudication and upon the appointment by it of such trustee, the court may stay any proceeding to enforce a lien against property of the plan or any other suit against the plan.

(g) Venue.—An action under this subsection may be brought in the judicial district where the plan administrator resides or does business or where any asset of the plan is situated. A district court in which such action is brought may issue process with respect to such action in any other judicial district.

(h) Compensation of Trustee and Professional Service Personnel Appointed or Retained by Trustee.—

(1) The amount of compensation paid to each trustee appointed under the provisions of this title shall require the prior approval of the corporation, and, in the case of a trustee appointed by a court, the consent of that court.

(2) Trustees shall appoint, retain, and compensate accountants, actuaries, and other professional service personnel in accordance with regulations prescribed by the corporation.

Amendments to ERISA §4042

Worker, Retiree, and Employer Recovery Act of 2008 (Pub. L. No. 110-458), as follows:

- ERISA §4042(c)(3)(C)(i) was amended by Act §105(e)(2) by striking "and plan sponsor" and inserting ", the plan sponsor, or the corporation", and striking "subparagraph (A)(i)" and inserting "subparagraph (A)". Eff. as if included in Pub. L. No. 109-280, §506.

Pension Protection Act of 2006 (Pub. L. No. 109-280), as follows:

- ERISA §4042(c)(7) was amended by Act §407(c)(2) by substituting "section 4021(d)" for "section 4022(b)(6)". Eff. Jan. 1, 2006, see Act §407(d).
- ERISA §4042(c) was amended by Act §506(b)(1)(A) by substituting "(c)(1) If the" for "(c) If the". Eff. for any plan termination under ERISA title IV for which the notice of intent to terminate (or in the case of a termination by the PBGC, a notice of determination under ERISA §4042) occurs after Aug. 17, 2006, see Act §506(c)(1).
- ERISA §4042(c)(3) was redesignated as (c)(2) and new (c)(3) was added by Act §506(b)(1). Eff. for any plan termination under

ERISA title IV for which the notice of intent to terminate (or in the case of a termination by the PBGC, a notice of determination under ERISA §4042) occurs after Aug. 17, 2006, see Act §506(c)(1).

- **Transition Rule.** Act §506(c):
  (2) Transition rule—If notice under section 4041(c)(2)(D) or 4042(c)(3) of the Employee Retirement Income Security Act of 1974 (as added by this section) would otherwise be required to be provided before the 90th day after the date of the enactment of this Act, such notice shall not be required to be provided until such 90th day.

- **Temporary Relief.** Act §105.
  SEC. 105. TEMPORARY RELIEF FOR CERTAIN PBGC SETTLEMENT PLANS.
  (a) General Rule.—Except as provided in this section, if a plan in existence on July 26, 2005, was a PBGC settlement plan as of such date, the amendments made by this subtitle and subtitle B shall not apply to plan years beginning before January 1, 2014.
  (b) Interest Rate.—In applying §302(b)(5)(B) of the Employee Retirement Income Security Act of 1974 and §412(b)(5)(B) of the Internal Revenue Code of 1986 (as in effect before the amendments made by this subtitle and subtitle B), to a PBGC settlement plan for plan years beginning after December 31, 2007, and before January 1, 2014, the third segment rate determined under §303(h)(2)(C)(iii) of such Act and §430(h)(2)(C)(iii) of such Code (as added by such amendments) shall be used in lieu of the interest rate otherwise used.
  (c) PBGC Settlement Plan.—For purposes of this section, the term "PBGC settlement plan" means a defined benefit plan (other than a multiemployer plan) to which §302 of such Act and §412 of such Code apply and —
  (1) which was sponsored by an employer which was in bankruptcy, giving rise to a claim by the Pension Benefit Guaranty Corporation of not greater than $150,000,000, and the sponsorship of which was assumed by another employer that was not a member of the same controlled group as the bankrupt sponsor and the claim of the Pension Benefit Guaranty Corporation was settled or withdrawn in connection with the assumption of such sponsorship, or
  (2) which, by agreement with the Pension Benefit Guaranty Corporation, was spun off from a plan subsequently terminated by such Corporation under §4042 of the Employee Retirement Income Security Act of 1974.

Uruguay Round Agreements Act (1994)(Pub. L. No. 103-465), as follows:

- ERISA §4042(a)(3) was amended by Act §771(e)(2) by substituting "1343(c)(7)" for "1343(b)(7)". Eff. for events occurring 60 days or more after Dec. 8, 1994, see Act §771(f).

Omnibus Budget Reconciliation Act of 1989 (Pub. L. No. 101-239), as follows:

- ERISA §4042(a) was amended by Act §7893(e) by inserting a period after "terms of the plan" at the end of the second sentence. Eff. as if included in Pub. L. No. 99-272, title XI, to which it relates, see Act §7893(h).
- ERISA §4042(a)(1), (d)(3) were amended by Act §7891(a)(1) by substituting "Internal Revenue Code of 1986" for "Internal Revenue Code of 1954", which for purposes of codification was translated as "title 26". Eff., except as otherwise provided, as if included in the provision of Pub. L. No. 99-514, to which it relates, see Act §7891(f).

Omnibus Budget Reconciliation Act of 1987 (Pub. L. No. 100-203), as follows:

- ERISA §4042(a)(third sentence) was amended by Act §9314(b), as amended by Pub. L. No. 101-239, §7881(g)(7). Eff. Dec. 22, 1987. ERISA §4042(a) (third sentence) prior to amendment:
  The corporation is authorized to pool the assets of terminated plans for purposes of administration and such other purposes, ,not inconsistent with its duties to the plan participants and the employer maintaining the plan under this subchapter, as it determines to be required for the efficient administration of this subchapter.
- ERISA §4042(c)(3) was added by Act §9314(b). Eff. Dec. 22, 1987.

- ERISA §4042(i) was repealed by Act §9312(c)(3). Eff. for plan terminations under ERISA §4041 for which notices of intent to terminate are provided under ERISA §4041(a)(2) after Dec. 17, 1987, and plan terminations for which proceedings are instituted by the PBGC under this section after that date, see Act §9312(d)(1), as amended. ERISA §4042(i) prior to repeal:

  (i) In any case in which a plan is terminated under this section in a termination proceeding initiated by the corporation pursuant to subsection (a) of this section, the corporation shall establish a separate trust in connection with the plan for purposes of section 4049, unless the corporation determines that all benefit commitments under the plan are benefits guaranteed by the corporation under section 4022 or that there is no amount of unfunded benefit commitments under the plan.

Consolidated Omnibus Budget Reconciliation Act of 1985 (Pub. L. No. 99-272), as follows:

- ERISA §4042 (heading) was amended by Act §11010(c) by substituting "Institution of termination proceedings by the corporation" for "Termination by corporation". Eff., Jan. 1, 1986, except as otherwise provided, see Act §11019.
- ERISA §4042(a) was amended by Act §11010(a)(1)(B) to add a paragraph following para. (4). Eff. Jan. 1, 1986, except as otherwise provided, see Act §11019.
- ERISA §4042(a)(2) was amended by Act §11010(a)(1)(A) by substituting "will be" for "is". Eff. Jan. 1, 1986, except as otherwise provided, see Act §11019.
- ERISA §4042(b)(1) was amended by Act §11010(a)(2)(A) by inserting "or is required under subsection (a) of this section to institute proceedings under this section,". Eff. Jan. 1, 1986, except as otherwise provided, see Act §11019.
- ERISA §4042(c) was amended by Act §11010(a)(2)(B) by substituting "is required under subsection (a) of this section to commence proceedings under this section with respect to a plan or, after issuing a notice under this section to a plan administrator," for "has issued a notice under this section to a plan administrator and (whether or not a trustee has been appointed under subsection (b) of this section)". Eff. Jan. 1, 1986, except as otherwise provided, see Act §11019.
- ERISA §4042(d)(1)(B)(ii) was amended by Act §11016(c)(10) by inserting ", including but not limited to the power to collect from the persons obligated to meet the requirements of §302 or the terms of the plan". Eff. Jan. 1, 1986, except as otherwise provided, see Act §11019.
- ERISA §4042(d)(3) was amended by Act §11016(c)(11) by substituting "those of a trustee under section 704 of title 11" for "a trustee appointed under §75 of title 11". Eff. Jan. 1, 1986, except as otherwise provided, see Act §11019.
- ERISA §4042(i) was added by Act §11010(b). Eff. Jan. 1, 1986, except as otherwise provided, see Act §11019.

Multiemployer Pension Plan Amendments Act of 1980 (Pub. L. No. 96-364), as follows:

- ERISA §4042(a) was amended by Act §402(a)(6)(A) by substituting "terminated plans" for "such small plans". Eff. Sept. 26, 1980, except as specifically provided, see ERISA §4402(e).
- ERISA §4042(b) was amended by Act §402(a)(6)(B) by redesignating provision as para. (1) and adding paras. (2) and (3). Eff. Sept. 26, 1980, except as specifically provided, see ERISA §4402(e).
- ERISA §4042(c) was amended by Act §402(a)(6)(C), (D) substituting "unreasonable" for "further" wherever appearing, and "of the participants or" for "of the participants and". Eff. Sept. 26, 1980, except as specifically provided, see ERISA §4402(e).
- ERISA §4042(d)(1)(A) was amended by Act §402(a)(6)(E) by adding cls. (v) and (vii) and redesignating former cl. (v) as (vi). Eff. Sept. 26, 1980, except as specifically provided, see ERISA §4402(e).
- ERISA §4042(d)(1)–(2) were amended by Act §402(a)(6)(F), (G) in subparas. (1)(B)(i) and (B)(iv) by substituting in cl. (i) "requirements of this subchapter" for "allocation requirements of §4044" and in cl. (iv), deleting ", except to the extent that the corporation is an adverse party in a suit or proceeding" following "involving the plan"; in subpara. (2)(B), deleting "and" following "participant,"; in subpara. (2)(C) substituting a comma for the concluding period; and adding subparas. (2)(D)–(F). Eff. Sept. 26, 1980, except as specifically provided, see Act ERISA §4402(e).

- ERISA §4042(d)(2)(D)–(F) were added by Act §402(a)(6)(H)–(J).

Bankruptcy Reform Act of 1978 (Pub. L. No. 95-598), as follows:

- ERISA §4042(f) was amended by Act §321 by substituting "of a court of the United States having jurisdiction over cases under chapter 11 of title 11" for "of a court of bankruptcy and of a court in a proceeding under chapter X of the Bankruptcy Act" in first sentence and striking "bankruptcy," before "mortgage foreclosure" in second sentence. Eff. Oct. 1, 1979, see Act §402(a).

SEC. 4043. REPORTABLE EVENTS.

(a) Notification That Event Has Occurred.— Within 30 days after the plan administrator or the contributing sponsor knows or has reason to know that a reportable event described in subsection (c) has occurred, he shall notify the corporation that such event has occurred, unless a notice otherwise required under this subsection has already been provided with respect to such event. The corporation is authorized to waive the requirement of the preceding sentence with respect to any or all reportable events with respect to any plan, and to require the notification to be made by including the event in the annual report made by the plan.

(b) Notification That Event Is About to Occur.—

(1) The requirements of this subsection shall be applicable to a contributing sponsor if, as of the close of the preceding plan year—

(A) the aggregate unfunded vested benefits (as determined under section 4006(a)(3)(E)(iii)) of plans subject to this title which are maintained by such sponsor and members of such sponsor's controlled groups (disregarding plans with no unfunded vested benefits) exceed $50,000,000, and

(B) the funded vested benefit percentage for such plans is less than 90 percent.

For purposes of subparagraph (B), the funded vested benefit percentage means the percentage which the aggregate value of the assets of such plans bears to the aggregate vested benefits of such plans (determined in accordance with section 4006(a)(3)(E)(iii)).

(2) This subsection shall not apply to an event if the contributing sponsor, or the member of the contributing sponsor's controlled group to which the event relates, is—

(A) a person subject to the reporting requirements of section 13 or 15(d) of the Securities Exchange Act of 1934, or

(B) a subsidiary (as defined for purposes of such Act) of a person subject to such reporting requirements.

(3) No later than 30 days prior to the effective date of an event described in paragraph (9), (10), (11),

(12), or (13) of subsection (c), a contributing sponsor to which the requirements of this subsection apply shall notify the corporation that the event is about to occur.

(4) The corporation may waive the requirement of this subsection with respect to any or all reportable events with respect to any contributing sponsor.

(c) Enumeration of Reportable Events.—For purposes of this section a reportable event occurs—

(1) when the Secretary of the Treasury issues notice that a plan has ceased to be a plan described in section 4021(a)(2), or when the Secretary of Labor determines the plan is not in compliance with title I of this Act;

(2) when an amendment of the plan is adopted if, under the amendment, the benefit payable with respect to any participant may be decreased;

(3) when the number of active participants is less than 80 percent of the number of such participants at the beginning of the plan year, or is less than 75 percent of the number of such participants at the beginning of the previous plan year;

(4) when the Secretary of the Treasury determines that there has been a termination or partial termination of the plan within the meaning of section 411(d)(3) of title 26, but the occurrence of such a termination or partial termination does not, by itself, constitute or require a termination of a plan under this title;

(5) when the plan fails to meet the minimum funding standards under section 412 of such Code (without regard to whether the plan is a plan described in section 4021(a)(2) of this Act) or under section 302 of this Act;

(6) when the plan is unable to pay benefits thereunder when due;

(7) when there is a distribution under the plan to a participant who is a substantial owner as defined in section 4021(d) if—

(A) such distribution has a value of $10,000 or more;

(B) such distribution is not made by reason of the death of the participant; and

(C) immediately after the distribution, the plan has nonforfeitable benefits which are not funded;

(8) when a plan merges, consolidates, or transfers its assets under section 208 of this Act, or when an alternative method of compliance is prescribed by the Secretary of Labor under section 110 of this Act;

(9) when, as a result of an event, a person ceases to be a member of the controlled group;

(10) when a contributing sponsor or a member of a contributing sponsor's controlled group liquidates

in a case under title 11, United States Code, or under any similar Federal law or law of a State or political subdivision of a State;

(11) when a contributing sponsor or a member of a contributing sponsor's controlled group declares an extraordinary dividend (as defined in section 1059(c) of the Internal Revenue Code of 1986) or redeems, in any 12-month period, an aggregate of 10 percent or more of the total combined voting power of all classes of stock entitled to vote, or an aggregate of 10 percent or more of the total value of shares of all classes of stock, of a contributing sponsor and all members of its controlled group;

(12) when, in any 12-month period, an aggregate of 3 percent or more of the benefit liabilities of a plan covered by this title and maintained by a contributing sponsor or a member of its controlled group are transferred to a person that is not a member of the controlled group or to a plan or plans maintained by a person or persons that are not such a contributing sponsor or a member of its controlled group; or

(13) when any other event occurs that may be indicative of a need to terminate the plan and that is prescribed by the corporation in regulations.

For purposes of paragraph (7), all distributions to a participant within any 24-month period are treated as a single distribution.

(d) Notification to Corporation by Secretary of the Treasury.—The Secretary of the Treasury shall notify the corporation—

(1) whenever a reportable event described in paragraph (1), (4), or (5) of subsection (c) occurs, or

(2) whenever any other event occurs which the Secretary of the Treasury believes indicates that the plan may not be sound.

(e) Notification to Corporation by Secretary of Labor.—The Secretary of Labor shall notify the corporation—

(1) whenever a reportable event described in paragraph (1), (5), or (8) of subsection (c) occurs, or

(2) whenever any other event occurs which the Secretary of Labor believes indicates that the plan may not be sound.

(f) Disclosure Exemption.—Any information or documentary material submitted to the corporation pursuant to this section shall be exempt from disclosure under section 552 of title 5, United States Code, and no such information or documentary material may be made public, except as may be relevant to any administrative or judicial action or proceeding. Nothing in this section is intended to prevent disclosure to either body of Congress or to any duly authorized committee or subcommittee of the Congress.

Amendments to ERISA §4043
Pension Protection Act of 2006 (Pub. L. No. 109-280), as follows:

• ERISA §4043(c)(7) was amended by Act §407(c)(2) by substituting "section 4021(d)" for "section 4022(b)(6)". Eff. Jan. 1, 2006, see Act §407(d)(2).

Uruguay Round Agreements Act, 1994 (Pub. L. No. 103-465), as follows:

• ERISA §4043(a) was amended by Act §771(a), (e)(1), in first sentence, by inserting "or the contributing sponsor" after "administrator", substituting "subsection (c)" for "subsection (b)", and inserting before period at end ", unless a notice otherwise required under this subsection has already been provided with respect to such event", and striking the last sentence, which read: "Whenever an employer making contributions under a plan to which section 1321 of this title applies knows or has reason to know that a reportable event has occurred he shall notify the plan administrator immediately." Eff. for events occurring 60 days or more after Dec. 8, 1994, see Act §771(f).

• ERISA §4043 was amended by Act §771(b) by redesignating subsec. (b) as (c) and adding new subsec. (b). Eff. for events occurring 60 days or more after Dec. 8, 1994, see Act §771(f).

• ERISA §4043(c)(8)–(13) were amended by Act §771(c) by striking "or" at end of para. (8); adding paras. (9)–(13); and repealing former para. (9). Eff. for events occurring 60 days or more after Dec. 8, 1994, see Act §771(f). ERISA §4043(c)(9) prior to repeal:

(9) when any other event occurs which the corporation determines may be indicative of a need to terminate the plan.

• ERISA §4043(d), (e) were amended by Act §771(b), (e)(1) by redesignating subsecs. (c) and (d) as (d) and (e), respectively; and substituting "subsection (c)" for "subsection (b)" in para. (1) of each subsec. Eff. for events occurring 60 days or more after Dec. 8, 1994, see Act §771(f).

• ERISA §4043(f) was added by Act §771(d). Eff. for events occurring 60 days or more after Dec. 8, 1994, see Act §771(f).

Omnibus Budget Reconciliation Act of 1989 (Pub. L. No. 101-239), as follows:

• ERISA §4043(b)(4) was amended by Act §7891(a)(1) by substituting "Internal Revenue Code of 1986" for "Internal Revenue Code of 1954", which for purposes of codification was translated as "title 26". Eff., except as otherwise provided, as if included in the provision of Pub. L. No. 99-514, to which it relates, see Act §7891(f).

SEC. 4044. ALLOCATION OF ASSETS.

(a) Order of Priority of Participants and Beneficiaries.—In the case of the termination of a single-employer plan, the plan administrator shall allocate the assets of the plan (available to provide benefits) among the participants and beneficiaries of the plan in the following order:

(1) First, to that portion of each individual's accrued benefit which is derived from the participant's contributions to the plan which were not mandatory contributions.

(2) Second, to that portion of each individual's accrued benefit which is derived from the participant's mandatory contributions.

(3) Third, in the case of benefits payable as an annuity—

(A) in the case of the benefit of a participant or beneficiary which was in pay status as of the beginning of the 3-year period ending on the termination date of the plan, to each such benefit, based on the provisions of the plan (as in effect during the

5-year period ending on such date) under which such benefit would be the least,

(B) in the case of a participant's or beneficiary's benefit (other than a benefit described in subparagraph (A)) which would have been in pay status as of the beginning of such 3-year period if the participant had retired prior to the beginning of the 3-year period and if his benefits had commenced (in the normal form of annuity under the plan) as of the beginning of such period, to each such benefit based on the provisions of the plan (as in effect during the 5-year period ending on such date) under which such benefit would be the least.

For purposes of subparagraph (A), the lowest benefit in pay status during a 3-year period shall be considered the benefit in pay status for such period.

(4) Fourth—

(A) to all other benefits (if any) of individuals under the plan guaranteed under this title (determined without regard to section 4022B(a)), and

(B) to the additional benefits (if any) which would be determined under subparagraph (A) if section 4022(b)(5)(B) did not apply.

For purposes of this paragraph, section 4021 shall be applied without regard to subsection (c) thereof.

(5) Fifth, to all other nonforfeitable benefits under the plan.

(6) Sixth, to all other benefits under the plan.

(b) Adjustment of Allocations; Reallocations; Mandatory Contributions; Establishment of Subclasses and Categories.—For purposes of subsection (a)—

(1) The amount allocated under any paragraph of subsection (a) with respect to any benefit shall be properly adjusted for any allocation of assets with respect to that benefit under a prior paragraph of subsection (a).

(2) If the assets available for allocation under any paragraph of subsection (a) (other than paragraphs (4), (5), and (6)) are insufficient to satisfy in full the benefits of all individuals which are described in that paragraph, the assets shall be allocated pro rata among such individuals on the basis of the present value (as of the termination date) of their respective benefits described in that paragraph.

(3) If assets available for allocation under paragraph (4) of subsection (a) are insufficient to satisfy in full the benefits of all individuals who are described in that paragraph, the assets shall be allocated first to benefits described in subparagraph (A) of that paragraph. Any remaining assets shall then be allocated to benefits described in subparagraph (B) of that paragraph. If assets allocated to such subparagraph (B) are insufficient to satisfy in full the benefits described in that subparagraph, the assets shall be allocated pro

rata among individuals on the basis of the present value (as of the termination date) of their respective benefits described in that subparagraph.

(4) This paragraph applies if the assets available for allocation under paragraph (5) of subsection (a) are not sufficient to satisfy in full the benefits of individuals described in that paragraph.

(A) If this paragraph applies, except as provided in subparagraph (B), the assets shall be allocated to the benefits of individuals described in such paragraph (5) on the basis of the benefits of individuals which would have been described in such paragraph (5) under the plan as in effect at the beginning of the 5-year period ending on the date of plan termination.

(B) If the assets available for allocation under subparagraph (A) are sufficient to satisfy in full the benefits described in such subparagraph (without regard to this subparagraph), then for purposes of subparagraph (A), benefits of individuals described in such subparagraph shall be determined on the basis of the plan as amended by the most recent plan amendment effective during such 5-year period under which the assets available for allocation are sufficient to satisfy in full the benefits of individuals described in subparagraph (A) and any assets remaining to be allocated under such subparagraph shall be allocated under subparagraph (A) on the basis of the plan as amended by the next succeeding plan amendment effective during such period.

(5) If the Secretary of Treasury determines that the allocation made pursuant to this section (without regard to this paragraph) results in discrimination prohibited by section 401(a)(4) of title 26 then, if required to prevent the disqualification of the plan (or any trust under the plan) under section 401(a) or 403(a) of title 26, the assets allocated under subsection (a)(4)(B), (a)(5), and (a)(6) shall be reallocated to the extent necessary to avoid such discrimination.

(6) The term "mandatory contributions" means amounts contributed to the plan by a participant which are required as a condition of employment, as a condition of participation in such plan, or as a condition of obtaining benefits under the plan attributable to employer contributions. For this purpose, the total amount of mandatory contributions of a participant is the amount of such contributions reduced (but not below zero) by the sum of the amounts paid or distributed to him under the plan before its termination.

(7) A plan may establish subclasses and categories within the classes described in paragraphs (1) through (6) of subsection (a) in accordance with regulations prescribed by the corporation.

(c) Increase or Decrease in Value of Assets.—Any increase or decrease in the value of the assets of a single-employer plan occurring during the period beginning on the later of (1) the date a trustee is appointed under section 4042(b) or (2) the date on which the plan is terminated is to be allocated between the plan and the corporation in the manner determined by the court (in the case of a court-appointed trustee) or as agreed upon by the corporation and the plan administrator in any other case. Any increase or decrease in the value of the assets of a single-employer plan occurring after the date on which the plan is terminated shall be credited to, or suffered by, the corporation.

(d) Distribution of Residual Assets; Restrictions on Reversions Pursuant to Recently Amended Plans; Assets Attributable to Employee Contributions; Calculation of Remaining Assets.—

(1) Subject to paragraph (3), any residual assets of a single-employer plan may be distributed to the employer if—

(A) all liabilities of the plan to participants and their beneficiaries have been satisfied,

(B) the distribution does not contravene any provision of law, and

(C) the plan provides for such a distribution in these circumstances.

(2)(A) In determining the extent to which a plan provides for the distribution of plan assets to the employer for purposes of paragraph (1)(C), any such provision, and any amendment increasing the amount which may be distributed to the employer, shall not be treated as effective before the end of the fifth calendar year following the date of the adoption of such provision or amendment.

(B) A distribution to the employer from a plan shall not be treated as failing to satisfy the requirements of this paragraph if the plan has been in effect for fewer than 5 years and the plan has provided for such a distribution since the effective date of the plan.

(C) Except as otherwise provided in regulations of the Secretary of the Treasury, in any case in which a transaction described in section 208 occurs, subparagraph (A) shall continue to apply separately with respect to the amount of any assets transferred in such transaction.

(D) For purposes of this subsection, the term "employer" includes any member of the controlled group of which the employer is a member. For purposes of the preceding sentence, the term "controlled group" means any group treated as a single employer under subsection (b), (c), (m) or (o) of section 414 of the Internal Revenue Code of 1986.

(3)(A) Before any distribution from a plan pursuant to paragraph (1), if any assets of the plan attributable to employee contributions remain after satisfaction of all liabilities described in subsection (a),

ERISA Sec. 4044(d)(3)(A)

such remaining assets shall be equitably distributed to the participants who made such contributions or their beneficiaries (including alternate payees, within the meaning of section 206(d)(3)(K)).

(B) For purposes of subparagraph (A), the portion of the remaining assets which are attributable to employee contributions shall be an amount equal to the product derived by multiplying—

(i) the market value of the total remaining assets, by

(ii) a fraction—

(I) the numerator of which is the present value of all portions of the accrued benefits with respect to participants which are derived from participants' mandatory contributions (referred to in subsection (a)(2)), and

(II) the denominator of which is the present value of all benefits with respect to which assets are allocated under paragraphs (2) through (6) of subsection (a).

(C) For purposes of this paragraph, each person who is, as of the termination date—

(i) a participant under the plan, or

(ii) an individual who has received, during the 3-year period ending with the termination date, a distribution from the plan of such individual's entire nonforfeitable benefit in the form of a single sum distribution in accordance with section 203(e) or in the form of irrevocable commitments purchased by the plan from an insurer to provide such nonforfeitable benefit,

shall be treated as a participant with respect to the termination, if all or part of the nonforfeitable benefit with respect to such person is or was attributable to participants' mandatory contributions (referred to in subsection (a)(2)).

(4) Nothing in this subsection shall be construed to limit the requirements of section 4980(d) of the Internal Revenue Code of 1986 (as in effect immediately after the enactment of the Omnibus Budget Reconciliation Act of 1990) or §404(d) of this Act with respect to any distribution of residual assets of a single-employer plan to the employer.

(e) Bankruptcy Filing Substituted for Termination Date.—If a contributing sponsor of a plan has filed or has had filed against such person a petition seeking liquidation or reorganization in a case under title 11, United States Code, or under any similar Federal law or law of a State or political subdivision, and the case has not been dismissed as of the termination date of the plan, then subsection (a)(3) shall be applied by treating the date such petition was filed as the termination date of the plan.

(f) Valuation of Section 4062(c) Liability for Determining Amounts Payable by Corporation to Participants and Beneficiaries.—

(1) In general.—In the case of a terminated plan, the value of the recovery of liability under section 4062(c) allocable as a plan asset under this section for purposes of determining the amount of benefits payable by the corporation shall be determined by multiplying—

(A) the amount of liability under section 4062(c) as of the termination date of the plan, by

(B) the applicable section 4062(c) recovery ratio.

(2) Section 4062(c) recovery ratio.—For purposes of this subsection—

(A) In general.—Except as provided in subparagraph (C), the "term section 4062(c) recovery ratio" means the ratio which—

(i) the sum of the values of all recoveries under section 4062(c) determined by the corporation in connection with plan terminations described under subparagraph (B), bears to

(ii) the sum of all the amounts of liability under section 4062(c) with respect to such plans as of the termination date in connection with any such prior termination.

(B) Prior terminations.—A plan termination described in this subparagraph is a termination with respect to which—

(i) the value of recoveries under section 4062(c) have been determined by the corporation, and

(ii) notices of intent to terminate were provided (or in the case of a termination by the corporation, a notice of determination under section 4042 was issued) during the 5-Federal fiscal year period ending with the third fiscal year preceding the fiscal year in which occurs the date of the notice of intent to terminate (or the notice of determination under section 4042) with respect to the plan termination for which the recovery ratio is being determined.

(C) Exception.—In the case of a terminated plan with respect to which the outstanding amount of benefit liabilities exceeds $20,000,000, the term "section 4062(c) recovery ratio" means, with respect to the termination of such plan, the ratio of—

(i) the value of the recoveries on behalf of the plan under section 4062(c), to

(ii) the amount of the liability owed under section 4062(c) as of the date of plan termination to the trustee appointed under section 4042(b) or (c).

(3) Subsection not to apply.—This subsection shall not apply with respect to the determination of—

(A) whether the amount of outstanding benefit liabilities exceeds $20,000,000, or

(B) the amount of any liability under section 4062 to the corporation or the trustee appointed under section 4042(b) or (c).

(4) Determinations.—Determinations under this subsection shall be made by the corporation. Such determinations shall be binding unless shown by clear and convincing evidence to be unreasonable.

Amendments to ERISA §4044

Worker, Retiree, and Employer Recovery Act of 2008 (Pub. L. No. 110-458), as follows:

● ERISA §4044(e), as added by Pub. L. No. 109-280, §408(b)(2), was redesignated as para. (f) by Act §104(c). Eff. as if included in Pub. L. No. 109-280, §408.

Pension Protection Act of 2006 (Pub. L. No. 109-280), as follows:

● ERISA §4044(a)(4)(B) was amended by Act §407(b)(1) by substituting "§4022(b)(5)(B)" for "§4022(b)(5)". Eff. for plan terminations under ERISA §4041(c) for which notices of intent to terminate are provided under ERISA §4041(a)(2) after Dec. 31, 2005, and under ERISA §4042 for which notices of determination are provided after such date, see Act §407(d)(1).

● ERISA §4044(b)(2) was amended by Act §407(b)(2)(A) by substituting "(4), (5)," for "(5)". Eff. for plan terminations under ERISA §4041(c) for which notices of intent to terminate are provided under ERISA §4041(a)(2) after Dec. 31, 2005, and under ERISA §4042 for which notices of determination are provided after such date, see Act §407(d)(1).

● ERISA §4044(b) was amended by Act §407(b) by redesignating subparas. (3)–(6) as (4)–(7) and adding new subpara. (3). Eff. for plan terminations under ERISA §4041(c) for which notices of intent to terminate are provided under ERISA §4041(a)(2) after Dec. 31, 2005, and under ERISA §4042 for which notices of determination are provided after such date, see Act §407(d)(1).

● ERISA §4044(e)[f] was added by Act §404(b). Eff. for proceedings initiated under title 11, United States Code, or under any similar Federal law or law of a State or political subdivision, on or after Sept. 16, 2006, see Act §404(c).

Omnibus Budget Reconciliation Act of 1990 (Pub. L. No. 101-508), as follows:

● ERISA §4044(d)(4) was added by Act §12002(b)(2)(B). See effective date provision in note below.

● **Effective Date Provision.**

> **SEC. 12003. EFFECTIVE DATE.**
> **(a) In General.**—Except as provided in subsection (b), the amendments made by this subtitle shall apply to reversions occurring after September 30, 1990.
> **(b) Exception.**—The amendments made by this subtitle shall not apply to any reversion after September 30, 1990, if—
> (1) in the case of plans subject to title IV of the Employee Retirement Income Security Act of 1974, a notice of intent to terminate under such title was provided to participants (or if no participants, to the Pension Benefit Guaranty Corporation) before October 1, 1990,
> (2) in the case of plans subject to title I (and not to title IV) of such Act, a notice of intent to reduce future accruals under section 204(h) of such Act was provided to participants in connection with the termination before October 1, 1990,
> (3) in the case of plans not subject to title I or IV of such Act, a request for a determination letter with respect to the termination was filed with the Secretary of the Treasury or the Secretary's delegate before October 1, 1990, or
> (4) in the case of plans not subject to title I or IV of such Act and having only 1 participant, a resolution terminating the plan was adopted by the employer before October 1, 1990.

Omnibus Budget Reconciliation Act of 1989 (Pub. L. No. 101-239), as follows:

● ERISA §4044(a)(1) was amended by Act §7894(g)(2) by substituting "accrued" for "accured". Eff., except as otherwise provided, as if originally included in the provision of the Pub. L. No. 93-406, to which it relates, see Act §7894(i).

● ERISA §4044(b)(4) was amended by Act §7891(a)(1) by substituting "Internal Revenue Code of 1986" for "Internal Revenue Code of 1954", which for purposes of codification was translated as "title 26". Eff., except as otherwise provided, as if

included in the provision of Pub. L. No. 99-514, to which it relates, see Act §7891(f).

Omnibus Budget Reconciliation Act of 1987 (Pub. L. No. 11-203), as follows:

● ERISA §4044(b)(4) was amended by Act §9311(c) by striking reference to §405(a) of title 26. Eff., except as otherwise provided, for plan terminations under ERISA §4041 for which notices of intent to terminate are provided under ERISA §4041(a)(2) after Dec. 17, 1987, and plan terminations for which proceedings are instituted by the PBGC under ERISA §4042 after Dec. 17, 1987, see Act §9311(d).

● ERISA §4044(d)(1) was amended by Act §9311(b)(1) by substituting "Subject to paragraph (3), any" for "Any". Eff., except as otherwise provided, for plan terminations under ERISA §4041 for which notices of intent to terminate are provided under ERISA §4041(a)(2) after Dec. 17, 1987, and plan terminations for which proceedings are instituted by the PBGC under ERISA §4042 after Dec. 17, 1987, see Act §9311(d).

● ERISA §4044(d)(2) was redesignated as para. (3) and new para. (2) was added by Act §9311(a)(1)(A)–(B). Eff., except as otherwise provided, for plan terminations under ERISA §4041 for which notices of intent to terminate are provided under ERISA §4041(a)(2) after Dec. 17, 1987, and plan terminations for which proceedings are instituted by the PBGC under ERISA §4042 after Dec. 17, 1987.

● ERISA §4044(d)(3), as redesignated, was amended by Act §9311(b)(2), as amended by Pub. L. No. 101-239, §7881(e)(3). Eff., except as otherwise provided, for plan terminations under ERISA §4041 for which notices of intent to terminate are provided under ERISA §4041(a)(2) after Dec. 17, 1987, and plan terminations for which proceedings are instituted by the PBGC under ERISA §4042 after Dec. 17, 1987, see Act 9311(d). ERISA §4044(d)(3) prior to amendment:

> **(3)** Notwithstanding the provisions of paragraph (1), if any assets of the plan attributable to employee contributions, remain after all liabilities of the plan to participants and their beneficiaries have been satisfied, such assets shall be equitably distributed to the employees who made such contributions (or their beneficiaries) in accordance with their rate of contributions.

Consolidated Omnibus Budget Reconciliation Act of 1985 (Pub. L. No. 99-272), as follows:

● ERISA §4044(a) was amended by Act §11016(c)(12), in provision preceding para. (1) by striking "defined benefit" after "single-employer". Eff. Jan. 1, 1986, except as otherwise provided, see Act §11019.

● ERISA §4044(a)(4)(A) was amended by Act §11016(c)(13)(A) by substituting "section 1322b(a)" for "section 1322(b)(5)". Eff. Jan. 1, 1986, except as otherwise provided, see Act §11019.

● ERISA §4044(a)(4)(B) was amended by Act §11016(c)(13)(B) by substituting "section 1322(b)(5)" for "section 1322(b)(6)". Eff. Jan. 1, 1986, except as otherwise provided, see Act §11019.

Multiemployer Pension Plan Amendments Act of 1980 (Pub. L. No. 96-364), as follows:

● ERISA §4044(a) was amended by Act §402(a)(7)(A) by inserting "single-employer" before "defined benefit". Eff. Sept. 26, 1980, except as otherwise provided, see Act ERISA §4402(e).

● ERISA §4044(c) was amended by Act §402(a)(7)(B) by inserting "single-employer" before "plan occurring" wherever appearing. Eff. Sept. 26, 1980, except as otherwise provided, see Act ERISA §4402(e).

● ERISA §4044(d)(1) was amended by Act §402(a)(7)(C) by inserting "single-employer" after "assets of a". Eff. Sept. 26, 1980, except as otherwise provided, see Act ERISA §4402(e).

SEC. 4045. RECAPTURE OF PAYMENTS.

(a) Authorization to Recover Benefits.—Except as provided in subsection (c), the trustee is authorized to recover for the benefit of a plan from a participant the recoverable amount (as defined in subsection (b)) of all payments from the plan to him which commenced within the 3-year period immediately preceding the time the plan is terminated.

(b) Recoverable Amount.—For purposes of subsection (a) the recoverable amount is the excess of the amount determined under paragraph (1) over the amount determined under paragraph (2).

(1) The amount determined under this paragraph is the sum of the amount of the actual payments received by the participant within the 3-year period.

(2) The amount determined under this paragraph is the sum of—

(A) the sum of the amount such participant would have received during each consecutive 12-month period within the 3 years if the participant received the benefit in the form described in paragraph (3),

(B) the sum for each of the consecutive 12-month periods of the lesser of—

(i) the excess, if any, of $10,000 over the benefit in the form described in paragraph (3), or

(ii) the excess of the actual payment, if any, over the benefit in the form described in paragraph (3), and

(C) the present value at the time of termination of the participant's future benefits guaranteed under this title as if the benefits commenced in the form described in paragraph (3).

(3) The form of benefit for purposes of this subsection shall be the monthly benefit the participant would have received during the consecutive 12-month period, if he had elected at the time of the first payment made during the 3-year period, to receive his interest in the plan as a monthly benefit in the form of a life annuity commencing at the time of such first payment.

(c) Payments Made on or After Death or Disability of Participant; Waiver of Recovery in Case of Hardship.—

(1) In the event of a distribution described in section 4043(b)(7) the 3-year period referred to in subsection (b) shall not end sooner than the date on which the corporation is notified of the distribution.

(2) The trustee shall not recover any payment made from a plan after or on account of the death of a participant, or to a participant who is disabled (within the meaning of section 72(m)(7) of title 26).

(3) The corporation is authorized to waive, in whole or in part, the recovery of any amount which the trustee is authorized to recover for the benefit of a plan under this section in any case in which it determines that substantial economic hardship would result to the participant or his beneficiaries from whom such amount is recoverable.

Amendments to ERISA §4045
Omnibus Budget Reconciliation Act of 1989 (Pub. L. No. 101-239), as follows:

● ERISA §4045(c)(2) was amended by Act §11891(a)(1) by substituting "Internal Revenue Code of 1986" for "Internal Revenue Code of 1954", which for purposes of codification was translated as "title 26". Eff., except as otherwise provided, as if included in the provision of Pub. L. No. 99-514, to which it relates, see Act §7891(f).

SEC. 4046. REPORTS TO TRUSTEE.

The corporation and the plan administrator of any plan to be terminated under this subtitle shall furnish to the trustee such information as the corporation or the plan administrator has and, to the extent practicable, can obtain regarding—

(1) the amount of benefits payable with respect to each participant under a plan to be terminated,

(2) the amount of basic benefits guaranteed under section 4022 or 4022A which are payable with respect to each participant in the plan,

(3) the present value, as of the time of termination, of the aggregate amount of basic benefits payable under section 4022 or 4022A (determined without regard to section 4022B),

(4) the fair market value of the assets of the plan at the time of termination,

(5) the computations under section 4044, and all actuarial assumptions under which the items described in paragraphs (1) through (4) were computed, and

(6) any other information with respect to the plan the trustee may require in order to terminate the plan.

Amendments to ERISA §4046
Multiemployer Pension Plan Amendments Act of 1980 (Pub. L. No. 96-364), as follows:
● ERISA §4046(2) was amended by Act §403(e)(1) by inserting "basic" before "benefits" and "or 4022a" after "4022". Eff. Sept. 26, 1980, except as otherwise provided, see ERISA §4402(e).
● ERISA §4046(3) was amended by Act §403(e) inserting "basic" before "benefits" and "or 4022a" after "4022", and substituting "4022b" for "4022(b)(5)". Eff. Sept. 26, 1980, except as otherwise provided, see ERISA §4402(e).

SEC. 4047. RESTORATION OF PLANS.

Whenever the corporation determines that a plan which is to be terminated under section 4041 or 4042, or which is in the process of being terminated under section 4041 or 4042, should not be terminated under section 4041 or 4042 as a result of such circumstances as the corporation determines to be relevant, the corporation is authorized to cease any activities undertaken to terminate the plan, and to take whatever action is necessary and within its power to restore the plan to its status prior to the determination that the plan was to be terminated under section 4041 or 4042. In the case of a plan which has been terminated under section 4041 or 4042 the corporation is authorized in any such case in which the corporation determines such action to be appropriate and consistent with its duties under this title, to take such action as may be necessary to restore the plan to its pretermination status, including, but not limited to, the transfer to the employer or a plan administrator of control of part or all of the remaining assets and liabilities of the plan.

Amendments to ERISA §4047

Omnibus Budget Reconciliation Act of 1989 (Pub. L. No. 101-239), as follows:

● ERISA §4047 was amended by Act §7893(g)(1) by striking "under this subtitle" before "should not be terminated". Eff. as if included in the provision of Pub. L. No. 99-272, title XI, to which it relates, see Act §7893(h).

Consolidated Omnibus Budget Reconciliation Act of 1985 (Pub. L. No. 99-272), as follows:

● ERISA §4047 was amended by Act §11016(a)(3) by inserting "under §4041 or 4042 of this title" after "terminated" in four places and substituting "§4041 or 4042 of this title the corporation" for "§4042 the corporation". Eff. Jan. 1, 1986, except as otherwise provided, see Act §11019.

SEC. 4048. TERMINATION DATE.

(a) For purposes of this title the termination date of a single-employer plan is—

(1) in the case of a plan terminated in a standard termination in accordance with the provisions of section 4041(b), the termination date proposed in the notice provided under section 4041(a)(2),

(2) in the case of a plan terminated in a distress termination in accordance with the provisions of section 4041(c), the date established by the plan administrator and agreed to by the corporation,

(3) in the case of a plan terminated in accordance with the provisions of section 4042, the date established by the corporation and agreed to by the plan administrator, or

(4) in the case of a plan terminated under section 4041(c) or 4042 in any case in which no agreement is reached between the plan administrator and the corporation (or the trustee), the date established by the court.

(b) For purposes of this title, the date of termination of a multiemployer plan is—

(1) in the case of a plan terminated in accordance with the provisions of section 4041A, the date determined under subsection (b) of that section; or

(2) in the case of a plan terminated in accordance with the provisions of section 4042, the date agreed to between the plan administrator and the corporation

(or the trustee appointed under section 4042(b)(2), if any), or, if no agreement is reached, the date established by the court.

Amendments to ERISA §4048

Consolidated Omnibus Budget Reconciliation Act of 1985 (Pub. L. No. 99-272), as follows:

● ERISA §4048(a) was amended by Act §11016(a)(4) in provisions preceding para. (1) by substituting "termination date" for "date of termination"; redesignating former paras. (1)–(3) as (2)–(4), respectively; adding new para. (1); in para. (2), as redesignated, inserting "in a distress termination" after "terminated" and substituting "§4041(c)" for "§4041"; and in para. (4), as redesignated, substituting "under §4041(c) or 4042" for "in accordance with the provisions of either section". Eff. Jan. 1, 1986, except as otherwise provided, see Act §11019.

Multiemployer Pension Plan Amendments Act of 1980 (Pub. L. No. 96-364), as follows:

● ERISA §4048(a) was amended by Act §402(a)(8) by inserting "(a)" before "For", and inserting "single-employer plan". Eff. Sept. 26, 1980, except as otherwise provided, see ERISA §4402(e).

SEC. 4049. DISTRIBUTION TO PARTICIPANTS AND BENEFICIARIES OF LIABILITY PAYMENTS TO SECTION 4049 TRUST. [Repealed.]

(a) Trust requirements. The requirements of this section apply to a trust established by the corporation in connection with a terminated plan pursuant to section 4041(c)(3)(B)(ii) or (iii) or 4042(i). The trust shall be used exclusively for—

(1) receiving liability payments under section 4062(c) from the persons who were (as of the termination date) contributing sponsors of the terminated plan and members of their controlled groups,

(2) making distributions as provided in this section to the persons who were (as of the termination date) participants and beneficiaries under the terminated plan, and

(3) defraying the reasonable administrative expenses incurred in carrying out responsibilities under this section.

The trust shall be maintained for such period of time as is necessary to receive all liability payments required to be made to the trust under section 4062(c) with respect to the terminated plan and to make all distributions required to be made to participants and beneficiaries under this section with respect to the terminated plan. Reasonable administrative expenses incurred in carrying out the responsibilities under this section prior to the receipt of any liability payments under section 4062(c) shall be paid by the persons described in section 4062(a) in accordance with procedures which shall be prescribed by the corporation by regulation, and the amount of the liability determined under section 4062(c) shall be reduced by the amount of such expenses so paid.

(b) Designation of fiduciary by the corporation.

(1) Purposes for designation of fiduciary.

(A) Collection of liability. The corporation shall designate a fiduciary (within the meaning of section 3(21)) to serve as trustee of the trust for purposes of conducting negotiations and assessing and collecting liability pursuant to section 4062(c).

(B) Administration of trust.

(i) Corporation's functions. Except as provided in clause (ii), the corporation shall serve as trustee of the trust for purposes of administering the trust, including making distributions from the trust to participants and beneficiaries.

(ii) Designation of fiduciary if cost-effective. If the corporation determines that it would be cost-effective to do so, it may designate a fiduciary (within the meaning of section 3(21)), including the fiduciary designated under subparagraph (A), to perform the functions described in clause (i).

(2) Fiduciary requirements. A fiduciary designated under paragraph (1) shall be—

(A) independent of each contributing sponsor of the plan and the members of such sponsor's controlled group, and

(B) subject to the requirements of part 4 of subtitle B of title I (other than section 406(a)) as if such trust were a plan subject to such part.

(c) Distributions from trust.

(1) In general. Not later than 30 days after the end of each liability payment year (described in section 4062(e)(3)) with respect to a terminated single-employer plan, the corporation, or its designee under subsection (b), shall distribute from the trust maintained pursuant to subsection (a) to each person who was (as of the termination date) a participant or beneficiary under the plan—

(A) in any case not described in subparagraph (B), an amount equal to the outstanding amount of benefit commitments to such person under the plan (including interest calculated from the termination date), to the extent not previously paid under this paragraph, or

(B) in any case in which the balance in the trust at the end of such year which is in cash or may be prudently converted to cash (after taking into account liability payments received under subsection (a)(1) and administrative expenses paid under subsection (a)(3)) is less than the total of all amounts described in subparagraph (A) in connection with all persons who were (as of the termination date) participants and beneficiaries under the terminated plan, the product derived by multiplying—

(i) the amount described in subparagraph (A) in connection with each such person, by

(ii) a fraction—

(I) the numerator of which is such balance in the trust, and

(II) the denominator of which is equal to the total of all amounts described in subparagraph (A) in connection with all persons who were (as of the termination date) participants and beneficiaries under the terminated plan.

(2) Carry-over of minimal payment amounts. The corporation, or its designee under subsection (b), may withhold a payment to any person under this subsection in connection with any liability payment year (other than the last liability payment year with respect to which payments under paragraph (1) are payable) if such payment does not exceed $100. In any case in which such a payment is so withheld, the payment to such person in connection with the next following liability payment year shall be increased by the amount of such withheld payment.

(d) Regulations. The corporation may issue such regulations as it considers necessary to carry out the purposes of this section.

Amendments to ERISA §4049 [Repealed.]
Omnibus Budget Reconciliation Act of 1987 (Pub. L. No. 100-203), as follows:
• ERISA §4049 was repealed by Act §9312(a). Eff. for certain plan terminations occurring on or before Dec. 17, 1987, see Act §9312(d)(1).

SEC. 4050. MISSING PARTICIPANTS.

(a) General Rule.—

(1) Payment to the corporation.—A plan administrator satisfies section 4041(b)(3)(A) in the case of a missing participant only if the plan administrator—

(A) transfers the participant's designated benefit to the corporation or purchases an irrevocable commitment from an insurer in accordance with clause (i) of section 4041(b)(3)(A), and

(B) provides the corporation such information and certifications with respect to such designated benefits or irrevocable commitments as the corporation shall specify.

(2) Treatment of transferred assets.—A transfer to the corporation under this section shall be treated as a transfer of assets from a terminated plan to the corporation as trustee, and shall be held with assets of terminated plans for which the corporation is trustee under section 4042, subject to the rules set forth in that section.

(3) Payment by the corporation.—After a missing participant whose designated benefit was transferred to the corporation is located—

(A) in any case in which the plan could have distributed the benefit of the missing participant in a single sum without participant or spousal consent under section 205(g), the corporation shall pay the participant or beneficiary a single sum benefit equal to the designated benefit paid the corporation plus interest as specified by the corporation, and

(B) in any other case, the corporation shall pay a benefit based on the designated benefit and the assumptions prescribed by the corporation at the time that the corporation received the designated benefit.

The corporation shall make payments under subparagraph (B) available in the same forms and at the same times as a guaranteed benefit under section 4022 would be available to be paid, except that the corporation may make a benefit available in the form of a single sum if the plan provided a single sum benefit (other than a single sum described in subsection (b)(2)(A)).

(b) Definitions.—For purposes of this section—

(1) Missing participant.—The term "missing participant" means a participant or beneficiary under a terminating plan whom the plan administrator cannot locate after a diligent search.

(2) Designated benefit.—The term "designated benefit" means the single sum benefit the participant would receive—

(A) under the plan's assumptions, in the case of a distribution that can be made without participant or spousal consent under section 205(g);

(B) under the assumptions of the corporation in effect on the date that the designated benefit is transferred to the corporation, in the case of a plan that does not pay any single sums other than those described in subparagraph (A); or

(C) under the assumptions of the corporation or of the plan, whichever provides the higher single sum, in the case of a plan that pays a single sum other than those described in subparagraph (A).

(c) Multiemployer Plans.—The corporation shall prescribe rules similar to the rules in subsection (a) for multiemployer plans covered by this title that terminate under section 4041A.

(d) Plans Not Otherwise Subject to Title.—

(1) Transfer to corporation.—The plan administrator of a plan described in paragraph (4) may elect to transfer a missing participant's benefits to the corporation upon termination of the plan.

(2) Information to the corporation.—To the extent provided in regulations, the plan administrator of a plan described in paragraph (4) shall, upon termination of the plan, provide the corporation information with respect to benefits of a missing participant if the plan transfers such benefits—

(A) to the corporation, or

(B) to an entity other than the corporation or a plan described in paragraph (4)(B)(ii).

(3) Payment by the corporation.—If benefits of a missing participant were transferred to the corporation under paragraph (1), the corporation shall, upon location of the participant or beneficiary, pay to the participant or beneficiary the amount transferred (or the appropriate survivor benefit) either—

(A) in a single sum (plus interest), or

(B) in such other form as is specified in regulations of the corporation.

(4) Plans described.—A plan is described in this paragraph if—

(A) the plan is a pension plan (within the meaning of section 3(2))—

(i) to which the provisions of this section do not apply (without regard to this subsection),

(ii) which is not a plan described in paragraph (2), (3), (4), (6), (7), (8), (9), (10), or (11) of section 4021(b), and

(iii) which, was a plan described in section 401(a) of the Internal Revenue Code of 1986 which includes a trust exempt from tax under section 501(a) of such Code, and

(B) at the time the assets are to be distributed upon termination, the plan—

(i) has missing participants, and

(ii) has not provided for the transfer of assets to pay the benefits of all missing participants to another pension plan (within the meaning of section 3(2)).

(5) Certain provisions not to apply.—Subsections (a)(1) and (a)(3) shall not apply to a plan described in paragraph (4).

(e) Regulatory Authority.—The corporation shall prescribe such regulations as are necessary to carry out the purposes of this section, including rules relating to what will be considered a diligent search, the amount payable to the corporation, and the amount to be paid by the corporation.

Amendments to ERISA §4050

Worker, Retiree, and Employer Recovery Act of 2008 (Pub. L. No. 110-458), as follows:

- ERISA §4050(d)(4)(A) was amended by Act §104(e) by striking "and" at end of cl. (i); amending cl. (ii); and adding cl. (iii). Eff. as if included in Pub. L. No. 109-280, §410. ERISA §4050(d)(4)(A)(ii) prior to amendment:

    (ii) which is not a plan described in paragraphs (2) through (11) of section 4021(b), and

Pension Protection Act of 2006 (Pub. L. No. 109-280), as follows:

- ERISA §4050(c) was amended by Act §410(a) by redesignating subsec. (c) as subsec. (e) and adding new subsecs. (c) and (d). Eff. for distributions made before final regulations implementing ERISA §4050(c) and (d), as added by Act §410(a), respectively, are prescribed.

Subtitle D—Liability

SEC. 4061. AMOUNTS PAYABLE BY CORPORATION.

The corporation shall pay benefits under a single-employer plan terminated under this title subject to the limitations and requirements of subtitle B of this title. The corporation shall provide financial assistance to pay benefits under a multiemployer plan which is insolvent under section 4245 or 4281(d)(2)(A), subject to the limitations and requirements of subtitles B, C, and E of this title. Amounts guaranteed by the corporation under sections 4022 and 4022A shall be paid by the corporation only out of the appropriate fund. The corporation shall make payments under the supplemental program to reimburse multiemployer plans for uncollectible withdrawal liability only out of the fund established under section 4005(e).

Amendments to ERISA §4061

Multiemployer Pension Plan Amendments Act of 1980 (Pub. L. No. 96-364), as follows:

- ERISA §4061 was amended by Act §403(f). Eff. Sept. 26, 1980, except as otherwise provided, see ERISA §4402. ERISA §4061 prior to amendment:

    The corporation shall pay benefits under a plan terminated under this title subject to the limitations and requirements of subtitle B of this title. Amounts guaranteed by the corporation under section 4022 shall be paid by the corporation out of the appropriate fund.

SEC. 4062. LIABILITY FOR TERMINATION OF SINGLE-EMPLOYER PLANS UNDER A DISTRESS TERMINATION OR A TERMINATION BY CORPORATION.

(a) In General.—In any case in which a single-employer plan is terminated in a distress termination under section 4041(c) or a termination otherwise instituted by the corporation under section 4042, any person who is, on the termination date, a contributing sponsor of the plan or a member of such a contributing sponsor's controlled group shall incur liability under this section. The liability under this section of all such persons shall be joint and several. The liability under this section consists of—

(1) liability to the corporation, to the extent provided in subsection (b), and

(2) liability to the trustee appointed under subsection (b) or (c) of section 4042 to the extent provided in subsection (c).

(b) Liability to the Corporation.—

(1) Amount of liability.—

(A) In general.—Except as provided in subparagraph (B), the liability to the corporation of a person described in subsection (a) shall be the total amount of the unfunded benefit liabilities (as of the termination date) to all participants and beneficiaries under the plan, together with interest (at a reasonable rate) calculated from the termination date in accordance with regulations prescribed by the corporation.

(B) Special rule in case of subsequent insufficiency.—For purposes of subparagraph (A), in any case described in section 4041(c)(3)(C)(ii), actuarial present values shall be determined as of the date of the notice to the corporation (or the finding by the corporation) described in such section.

(2) Payment of liability.—

(A) In general.—Except as provided in subparagraph (B), the liability to the corporation under this subsection shall be due and payable to the corporation as of the termination date, in cash or securities acceptable to the corporation.

(B) Special rule.—Payment of so much of the liability under paragraph (1)(A) as exceeds 30 percent of the collective net worth of all persons described in subsection (a)(including interest) shall be made under commercially reasonable terms prescribed by the corporation. The parties involved shall make a reasonable effort to reach

agreement on such commercially reasonable terms. Any such terms prescribed by the corporation shall provide for deferral of 50 percent of any amount of liability otherwise payable for any year under this subparagraph if a person subject to such liability demonstrates to the satisfaction of the corporation that no person subject to such liability has any individual pre-tax profits for such person's fiscal year ending during such year.

(3) Alternative arrangements.—The corporation and any person liable under this section may agree to alternative arrangements for the satisfaction of liability to the corporation under this subsection.

(c) Liability to Section 4042 Trustee.—A person described in subsection (a) shall be subject to liability under this subsection to the trustee appointed under subsection (b) or (c) of section 4042. The liability of such person under this subsection shall consist of—

(1) the sum of the shortfall amortization charge (within the meaning of section 303(c)(1) of this Act and 430(d)(1) of the Internal Revenue Code of 1986) with respect to the plan (if any) for the plan year in which the termination date occurs, plus the aggregate total of shortfall amortization installments (if any) determined for succeeding plan years under section 303(c)(2) of this Act and section 430(d)(2) of such Code (which, for purposes of this subparagraph, shall include any increase in such sum which would result if all applications for waivers of the minimum funding standard under section 302(c) of this Act and section 412(c) of such Code which are pending with respect to such plan were denied and if no additional contributions (other than those already made by the termination date) were made for the plan year in which the termination date occurs or for any previous plan year), and

(2) the sum of the waiver amortization charge (within the meaning of section 303(e)(1) of this Act and 430(e)(1) of the Internal Revenue Code of 1986) with respect to the plan (if any) for the plan year in which the termination date occurs, plus the aggregate total of waiver amortization installments (if any) determined for succeeding plan years under section 303(e)(2) of this Act and section 430(e)(2) of such Code.

(d) Definitions.—

(1) Collective net worth of persons subject to liability.—

(A) In general.—The collective net worth of persons subject to liability in connection with a plan termination consists of the sum of the individual net worths of all persons who—

(i) have individual net worths which are greater than zero, and

(ii) are (as of the termination date) contributing sponsors of the terminated plan or members of their controlled groups.

(B) Determination of net worth.—For purposes of this paragraph, the net worth of a person is—

(i) determined on whatever basis best reflects, in the determination of the corporation, the current status of the person's operations and prospects at the time chosen for determining the net worth of the person, and

(ii) increased by the amount of any transfers of assets made by the person which are determined by the corporation to be improper under the circumstances, including any such transfers which would be inappropriate under title 11, United States Code, if the person were a debtor in a case under chapter 7 of such title.

(C) Timing of determination.—For purposes of this paragraph, determinations of net worth shall be made as of a day chosen by the corporation (during the 120-day period ending with the termination date) and shall be computed without regard to any liability under this section.

(2) **Pre-tax profits.**—The term "pre-tax profits" means—

(A) except as provided in subparagraph (B), for any fiscal year of any person, such person's consolidated net income (excluding any extraordinary charges to income and including any extraordinary credits to income) for such fiscal year, as shown on audited financial statements prepared in accordance with generally accepted accounting principles, or

(B) for any fiscal year of an organization described in section 501(c) of title 26, the excess of income over expenses (as such terms are defined for such organizations under generally accepted accounting principles),

before provision for or deduction of Federal or other income tax, any contribution to any single-employer plan of which such person is a contributing sponsor at any time during the period beginning on the termination date and ending with the end of such fiscal year, and any amounts required to be paid for such fiscal year under this section. The corporation may by regulation require such information to be filed on such forms as may be necessary to determine the existence and amount of such pre-tax profits.

(3) **[Repealed.]**

(e) **Treatment of Substantial Cessation of Operations.**—If an employer ceases operations at a facility in any location and, as a result of such cessation of operations, more than 20 percent of the total number of his employees who are participants under a plan established and maintained by him are separated from employment, the employer shall be treated with respect to that plan as if he were a substantial employer under a plan under which more than one employer makes contributions and the provisions of sections 4063, 4064, and 4065 shall apply.

Amendments to ERISA §4062

Pension Protection Act of 2006 (Pub. L. No. 109-280), as follows:

● ERISA §4062(c)(1)–(3) were deleted by Act §107(b)(4) (redesignated as §108(b)(4) by Pub. L. No. 111-192, §202(a)) and paras. (c)(1) and (2) were added. Eff. for plan years beginning after 2007, see Act §107(e). ERISA §4062(c)(1)–(3) prior to amendment:

(1) the outstanding balance of the accumulated funding deficiencies (within the meaning of section 302(a)(2) of this Act and section 412(a) of the Internal Revenue Code of 1986) of the plan (if any) (which, for purposes of this subparagraph, shall include the amount of any increase in such accumulated funding deficiencies of the plan which would result if all pending applications for waivers of the minimum funding standard under section 303 of this Act or section 412(d) of such Code and for extensions of the amortization period under section 304 of this Act with respect to such plan were denied and if no additional contributions (other than those already made by the termination date) were made for the plan year in which the termination date occurs or for any previous plan year),

(2) the outstanding balance of the amount of waived funding deficiencies of the plan waived before such date under section 303 of this Act or section 412(d) of such Code (if any), and

(3) the outstanding balance of the amount of decreases in the minimum funding standard allowed before such date under section 304 of this Act or section 412(e) of such Code (if any), together with interest (at a reasonable rate) calculated from the termination date in accordance with regulations prescribed by the corporation. The liability under this subsection shall be due and payable to such trustee as of the termination date, in cash or securities acceptable to such trustee.

Omnibus Budget Reconciliation Act of 1989 (Pub. L. No. 101-239), as follows:

● ERISA §4062(a) was amended by Act §7881(f)(2) by inserting "and" at end of para. (1); redesignating para. (3) as (2); substituting "subsection (c)" for "subsection (d)" in para. (2) as redesignated; and striking former para. (2). Eff., except as otherwise provided, as if included in the provision of Pub. L. No. 100-203 to which it relates, see Act §7882. ERISA §4062(a)(2) prior to amendment:

(2) liability to the trust established pursuant to section 4041(c)(3)(B)(ii) or (iii) or section 4042(i), to the extent provided in subsection (c) of this section, and

● ERISA §4062(b)(2)(B) was amended by Act §7881(f)(10)(A) by substituting "so much of the liability under paragraph (1)(A) as exceeds 30 percent of the collective net worth of all persons described in subsection (a) of this section (including interest)" for "the liability under paragraph (1)(A)(ii)". Eff., except as otherwise provided, as if included in the provision of Pub. L. No. 100-203 to which it relates, see Act §7882.

● ERISA §4062(c)(1), (d)(2)(B) were amended by Act §7891(a)(1) by substituting "Internal Revenue Code of 1986" for "Internal Revenue Code of 1954", which for purposes of codification was translated as "title 26". Eff., except as otherwise provided, as if included in the provision of Pub. L. No. 99-514, to which it relates, see Act §7891(f).

● Act §7881(f)(10)(B) amended Pub. L. 100-203, §9312(b)(2)(B)(ii). Eff., except as otherwise provided, as if included in the provision of Pub. L. No. 100-203 to which it relates, see Act §7882.

Omnibus Budget Reconciliation Act of 1987 (Pub. L. No. 100-203), as follows:

● ERISA §4062(b)(1)(A) was amended by Act §9312(b)(2)(A). Eff. for plan terminations under ERISA §4041 for which notices of intent to terminate are provided under ERISA §4041(a)(2) after Dec. 17, 1987, and plan terminations for which proceedings are instituted by the PBGC under ERISA §4042 after that date, see Act §9312(d)(1). ERISA §4062(b)(1)(A) prior to amendment:

(A) In General. Except as provided in subparagraph (B), the liability to the corporation of a person described in subsection (a) of this section shall consist of the sum of—

(i) the lesser of—
(I) the total amount of unfunded guaranteed benefits (as of the termination date) of all participants and beneficiaries under the plan, or
(II) 30 percent of the collective net worth of all persons described in subsection (a) of this section, and
(ii) the excess (if any) of—
(I) 75 percent of the amount described in clause (i)(I), over
(II) the amount described in clause (i)(II),
together with interest (at a reasonable rate) calculated from the termination date in accordance with regulations prescribed by the corporation.

- ERISA §4062 was amended by Act §9312(b)(1) by striking subsec. (c) and by redesignating former subsecs. (d), (e), and (f) as subsecs. (c), (d), and (e), respectively. Eff. for plan terminations under ERISA §4041 for which notices of intent to terminate are provided under ERISA §4041(a)(2) after Dec. 17, 1987, and plan terminations for which proceedings are instituted by the PBGC under ERISA §4042 after that date, see Act §9312(d)(1). ERISA §4062(c) prior to being stricken:

(c) Liability to section 4049 trust.
(1) Amount of liability.
(A) In general. In any case in which there is an outstanding amount of benefit commitments under section 4041(c) or 4042, a person described in subsection (a) shall be subject to liability under this subsection to the trust established under section 4041(c)(3)(B)(ii) or (iii) or section 4042(i) in connection with the terminated plan. Except as provided in subparagraph (B), the liability of such person under this subsection shall consist of the lesser of—
(i) 75 percent of the total outstanding amount of benefit commitments under the plan, or
(ii) 15 percent of the actuarial present value (determined as of the termination date on the basis of assumptions prescribed by the corporation for purposes of §4044) of all benefit commitments under the plan.
(B) Special rule in case of subsequent insufficiency. For purposes of subparagraph (A)—
(i) Plans insufficient for guaranteed benefits. In any case described in section 4041(c)(3)(C)(ii), actuarial present values shall be determined as of the date of the notice to the corporation (or the finding by the corporation) described in such section.
(ii) Plans sufficient for guaranteed benefits but insufficient for benefit entitlements. In any case described in section 4041(c)(3)(C)(i) but not described in section 4041(c)(3)(C)(ii), actuarial present values shall be determined as of the date on which the final distribution of assets is completed.
(2) Payment of liability.
(A) General rule. Except as otherwise provided in this paragraph, payment of a person's liability under this subsection shall be made for liability payment years under commercially reasonable terms prescribed by the fiduciary designated by the corporation pursuant to section 4049(b)(1)(A). Such fiduciary and the liable persons assessed liability under this subsection shall make a reasonable effort to reach agreement on such commercially reasonable terms.
(B) Special rule for plans with low amounts of liability. In any case in which the amount described in paragraph (1)(A) is less than $100,000, the requirements of subparagraph (A) may be satisfied by payment of such liability over 10 liability payment years in equal annual installments (with interest at the rate determined under section 6621(b) of the Internal Revenue Code of 1986. The corporation may, by regulation, increase the dollar amount referred to in this subparagraph as it determines appropriate, taking into account reasonable administrative costs of trusts established under section 4041(c)(3)(B)(ii) or (iii) or section 4042(i).
(C) Deferral of payments. The terms for payment provided for under subparagraph (A) or (B) shall also provide for deferral of 75 percent of any amount of liability otherwise payable for any liability payment year if a person subject to such liability demonstrates to the satisfaction of the corporation that no person subject to such liability has any individual pre-tax profits for such person's fiscal year ending during such year. The amount of liability so deferred is payable only after payment in full of any amount of liability under subsection (b) in connection with the termination of the same plan which has been deferred pursuant to terms provided for under subsection (b)(2)(B).

- ERISA §4062(d)(3) was stricken by Act §9312(b)(2)(B)(ii), as amended by Pub. L. No. 101-239, §7881(f)(10)(B). Eff. for plan terminations under ERISA §4041 for which notices of intent to terminate are provided under ERISA §4041(a)(2) after Dec. 17, 1987, and plan terminations for which proceedings are instituted by the PBGC under ERISA §4042 after that date, see §9312(d)(1) of Pub. L. No. 100-203, as amended. ERISA §4062(d)(3) prior to amendment:
(3) The liability payment years in connection with a terminated plan consist of the consecutive one-year periods following the last plan year preceding the termination date, excluding the first such year in any case in which the first such year ends less than 180 days after the termination date.

Consolidated Omnibus Budget Reconciliation Act of 1985 (Pub. L. No. 99-272), as follows:

- ERISA §4062(f), as redesignated, was amended by Act §11011(a)(2) by substituting "Liability for termination of single-employer plans under a distress termination or a termination by the corporation" for "Liability of employer". Eff. Jan. 1, 1986, except as otherwise provided, see Act §11019.
- ERISA §4062(a)–(d) were amended by Act §11011(a)(2). ERISA §4062(a)–(d) prior to amendment:
(a) This section applies to any employer who maintained a single-employer plan at the time it was terminated, but does not apply
(1) to an employer who maintained a plan with respect to which he paid the annual premium described in section 4006(a)(2)(B) for each of the 5 plan years immediately preceding the plan year during which the plan terminated unless the conditions imposed by the corporation on the payment of coverage under section 4023 do not permit such coverage to apply under the circumstances, or
(2) to the extent of any liability arising out of the insolvency of an insurance company with respect to an insurance contract.
(b) Any employer to which this section applies shall be liable to the corporation, in an amount equal to the lesser of —
(1) the excess of—
(A) the current value of the plan's benefits guaranteed under this title on the date of termination over
(B) the current value of the plan's assets allocable to such benefits on the date of termination, or
(2) 30 percent of the net worth of the employer determined as of a day, chosen by the corporation but not more than 120 days prior to the date of termination, computed without regard to any liability under this section.
(c) For purposes of subsection (b)(2) the net worth of an employer is —
(1) determined on whatever basis best reflects, in the determination of the corporation, the current status of the employer's operations and prospects at the time chosen for determining the net worth of the employer, and
(2) increased by the amount of any transfers of assets made by the employer determined by the corporation to be improper under the circumstances, including any such transfers which would be inappropriate under title 11 of the United States Code if the employer were a debtor in a case under chapter 7 of such title.
(d) For purposes of this section the following rules apply in the case of certain corporate reorganizations:
(1) If an employer ceases to exist by reason of a reorganization which involves a mere change in identity, form, or place of organization, however effected, a successor corporation resulting from such reorganization shall be treated as the employer to whom this section applies.
(2) If an employer ceases to exist by reason of a liquidation into a parent corporation, the parent corporation shall be treated as the employer to whom this section applies.
(3) If an employer ceases to exist by reason of a merger, consolidation, or division, the successor corporation or cor-

ERISA Sec. 4062(e)

porations shall be treated as the employer to whom this section applies.

- ERISA §4062(e) was amended by Act §11011(a) by adding subsec. (e) and redesignating former subsec. (e) as subsec. (f). Eff. Jan. 1, 1986, except as otherwise provided, see Act §11019.

Multiemployer Pension Plan Amendments Act of 1980 (Pub. L. No. 96-364), as follows:

- ERISA §4062(a) was amended by Act §403(g) by substituting "single-employer plan" for "plan (other than a multiemployer plan)". Eff. Sept. 26, 1980, except as otherwise provided, see ERISA §4402(e).

Pub. L. No. 95-598 (1978), as follows:

- ERISA §4062(c)(2) was amended by Act §321(b) by substituting "title 11" and "a debtor in a case under chapter 7 of such title" for "the Bankruptcy Act" and "the subject of a proceeding under that Act", respectively. Eff. Oct. 1, 1979, see Act §402(a).

SEC. 4063. LIABILITY OF SUBSTANTIAL EMPLOYER FOR WITHDRAWAL FROM SINGLE-EMPLOYER PLANS UNDER MULTIPLE CONTROLLED GROUPS.

(a) Single-employer Plans With Two or More Contributing Sponsors.—Except as provided in subsection (d), the plan administrator of a single-employer plan which has two or more contributing sponsors at least two of whom are not under common control—

(1) shall notify the corporation of the withdrawal during a plan year of a substantial employer for such plan year from the plan, within 60 days after such withdrawal, and

(2) request that the corporation determine the liability of all persons with respect to the withdrawal of the substantial employer.

The corporation shall, as soon as practicable thereafter, determine whether there is liability resulting from the withdrawal of the substantial employer and notify the liable persons of such liability.

(b) Computation of Liability.—Except as provided in subsection (c), any one or more contributing sponsors who withdraw, during a plan year for which they constitute a substantial employer, from a single-employer plan which has two or more contributing sponsors at least two of whom are not under common control, shall, upon notification of such contributing sponsors by the corporation as provided by subsection (a), be liable, together with the members of their controlled groups, to the corporation in accordance with the provisions of section 4062 and this section. The amount of liability shall be computed on the basis of an amount determined by the corporation to be the amount described in section 4062 for the entire plan, as if the plan had been terminated by the corporation on the date of the withdrawal referred to in subsection (a)(1), multiplied by a fraction—

(1) the numerator of which is the total amount required to be contributed to the plan by such contributing sponsors for the last 5 years ending prior to the withdrawal, and

(2) the denominator of which is the total amount required to be contributed to the plan by all contributing sponsors for such last 5 years.

In addition to and in lieu of the manner prescribed in the preceding sentence, the corporation may also determine such liability on any other equitable basis prescribed by the corporation in regulations. Any amountcollected by the corporation under this subsection shall be held in escrow subject to disposition in accordance with the provisions of paragraphs (2) and (3) of subsection (c).

(c) Bond in Lieu of Payment of Liability 5-year Termination Period.—

(1) In lieu of payment of a contributing sponsor's liability under this section, the contributing sponsor may be required to furnish a bond to the corporation in an amount not exceeding 150 percent of his liability to insure payment of his liability under this section. The bond shall have as surety thereon a corporate surety company which is an acceptable surety on Federal bonds under authority granted by the Secretary of the Treasury under sections 6 through 13 of title 6, United States Code. Any such bond shall be in a form or of a type approved by the Secretary including individual bonds or schedule or blanket forms of bonds which cover a group or class.

(2) If the plan is not terminated under section 4041(c) or 4042 within the 5-year period commencing on the day of withdrawal, the liability is abated and any payment held in escrow shall be refunded without interest (or the bond canceled) in accordance with bylaws or rules prescribed by the corporation.

(3) If the plan terminates under section 4041(c) or 4042 within the 5-year period commencing on the day of withdrawal, the corporation shall—

(A) demand payment or realize on the bond and hold such amount in escrow for the benefit of the plan;

(B) treat any escrowed payments under this section as if they were plan assets and apply them in a manner consistent with this subtitle; and

(C) refund any amount to the contributing sponsor which is not required to meet any obligation of the corporation with respect to the plan.

(d) Alternate Appropriate Procedure.—The provisions of this subsection apply in the case of a withdrawal described in subsection (a), and the provisions of subsections (b) and (c) shall not apply, if the corporation determines that the procedure provided for under this subsection is consistent with the purposes of this section and section 4064 and is more appropriate in the particular case. Upon a showing by the plan administrator of the plan that the withdrawal from the plan by one or more contributing sponsors has resulted, or will result, in a significant reduction in the amount of aggregate contributions to or under the plan, the corporation may—

(1) require the plan fund to be equitably allocated between those participants no longer working in covered service under the plan as a result of the withdrawal, and those participants who remain in covered service under the plan;

(2) treat that portion of the plan funds allocable under paragraph (1) to participants no longer in covered service as a plan termination under section 4042; and

(3) treat that portion of the plan fund allocable to participants remaining in covered service as a separate plan.

(e) Indemnity Agreement.—The corporation is authorized to waive the application of the provisions of subsections (b), (c), and (d) of this section whenever it determines that there is an indemnity agreement in effect among contributing sponsors under the plan which is adequate to satisfy the purposes of this section and of section 4064.

Amendments to ERISA §4063

Consolidated Omnibus Budget Reconciliation Act of 1985 (Pub. L. No. 99-272), as follows:

- ERISA §4063 (heading) was amended by Act §11016(a)(5)(A)(vi) by inserting "from single-employer plans under multiple controlled groups". Eff. Jan. 1, 1986, except as otherwise provided, see Act §11019.
- ERISA §4063(a) was amended by Act §11016(a)(5)(A)(i) by substituting, in introductory para., "single-employer plan which has two or more contributing sponsors at least two of whom are not under common control" for "plan under which more than one employer makes contributions (other than a multiemployer plan)"; in para. (1), substituting "withdrawal during a plan year of a substantial employer for such plan year" for "withdrawal of a substantial employer"; in para. (2), substituting "of all persons with respect to the withdrawal of the substantial employer" for "of such employer under this subtitle with respect to such withdrawal"; and, in concluding provision, substituting "whether there is liability resulting from the withdrawal of the substantial employer" for "whether such employer is liable for any amount under this subtitle with respect to the withdrawal" and "notify the liable persons" for "notify such employer". Eff. Jan. 1, 1986, except as otherwise provided, see Act §11019.
- ERISA §4063(b) was amended by Act §11016(a)(5)(A)(ii), in introductory para., by substituting "any one or more contributing sponsors who withdraw, during a plan year for which they constitute a substantial employer, from a single-employer plan which has two or more contributing sponsors at least two of whom are not under common control, shall, upon notification of such contributing sponsors by the corporation as provided by subsection (a) of this section, be liable, together with the members of their controlled groups," for "an employer who withdraws from a plan to which §4021 of this title applies, during a plan year for which he was a substantial employer, and who is notified by the corporation as provided by subsection (a) of this section, shall be liable", and "amount of liability" for "amount of such employer's liability", and "the withdrawal referred to in subsection (a)(1) of this section" for "the employer's withdrawal"; in para. (1), substituting "such contributing sponsors" for "such employer"; in para. (2), substituting "all contributing sponsors" for "all employers"; and, in concluding provision, substituting "such liability" for "the liability of each such employer". Eff. Jan. 1, 1986, except as otherwise provided, see Act §11019.
- ERISA §4063(c)(1) was amended by Act §11016(a)(5)(A)(iii)(I) by substituting "of a contributing sponsor's liability under this section, the contributing sponsor" for "of his liability under this

section the employer". Eff. Jan. 1, 1986, except as otherwise provided, see Act §11019.
- ERISA §4063(c)(2) was amended by Act §11016(a)(5)(A)(iii)(II) by inserting "under section 1341(c) or 1342 of this title", and substituting "liability is" for "liability of such employer is" and "(or the bond cancelled)" for "to the employer (or his bond cancelled)". Eff. Jan. 1, 1986, except as otherwise provided, see Act §11019.
- ERISA §4063(c)(3) was amended by Act §11016(a)(5)(A)(iii)(III), in introductory para., by inserting "under section 1341(c) or 1342 of this title" and, in subpara. (C), substituting "contributing sponsor" for "employer". Eff. Jan. 1, 1986, except as otherwise provided, see Act §11019.
- ERISA §4063(d) was amended by Act §11016(a)(5)(A)(iv), in introductory para., by substituting "of the plan that the withdrawal from the plan by one or more contributing sponsors" for "of a plan (other than a multiemployer plan) that the withdrawal from the plan by any employer or employers" and striking "by employers" after "contributions to or under the plan"; in para. (1), substituting "the withdrawal" for "their employer's withdrawal"; and in para. (2), substituting "plan terminated under §4042 of this title" for "termination". Eff. Jan. 1, 1986, with certain exceptions, see Act §11019.
- ERISA §4063(e) was amended by Act §11016(a)(5)(A)(v) by striking "to any employer or plan administrator" before "whenever it determines" and substituting "contributing sponsors" for "all other employers". Eff. Jan. 1, 1986, except as otherwise provided, see Act §11019.

Multiemployer Pension Plan Amendments Act of 1980 (Pub. L. No. 96-364), as follows:
- ERISA §4063(a) and (h) were amended by Act §403(h) by inserting "(other than a multiemployer plan)". Eff. Sept. 26, 1980, except as otherwise provided, see ERISA §4402(e).

SEC. 4064. LIABILITY ON TERMINATION OF SINGLE-EMPLOYER PLANS UNDER MULTIPLE CONTROLLED GROUPS.

(a) This section applies to all contributing sponsors of a single-employer plan which has two or more contributing sponsors at least two of whom are not under common control at the time such plan is terminated under section 4041(c) or 4042, or who, at any time within the 5 plan years preceding the date of termination, made contributions under the plan.

(b) The corporation shall determine the liability with respect to each contributing sponsor and each member of its controlled group in a manner consistent with section 4062, except that the amount of liability determined under section 4062(b)(1) with respect to the entire plan shall be allocated to each controlled group by multiplying such amount by a fraction—

(1) the numerator of which is the amount required to be contributed to the plan for the last 5 plan years ending prior to the termination date by persons in such controlled group as contributing sponsors, and

(2) the denominator of which is the total amount required to be contributed to the plan for such last 5 plan years by all persons as contributing sponsors,

and section 4068(a) shall be applied separately with respect to each controlled group. The corporation may also determine the liability of each such contributing sponsor and member of its controlled group on any other equitable basis prescribed by the corporation in regulations.

Amendments to ERISA §4064

Omnibus Budget Reconciliation Act of 1989 (Pub. L. No. 101-239), as follows:

● ERISA §4064(b) was amended by Act §7881(f)(3)(A) by substituting "§4068(a)" for "clauses (i)(II) and (ii) of §4062(b)(1)(A)". Eff., except as otherwise provided, as if included in the provision of Pub. L. 100-203, §§9302–9346, to which the amendment relates, see Act §7882.

Omnibus Budget Reconciliation Act of 1987 (Pub. L. No. 100-203), as follows:

● ERISA §4064(b) was amended by Act §9312(b)(2)(C)(i) by substituting material for the material preceding the sentence beginning "The corporation may also—". Eff. for plan terminations under ERISA §4041 for which notices of intent to terminate were provided under ERISA §4041(a)(2) after Dec. 17, 1987, and plan terminations for which proceedings are instituted by PBGC under ERISA §4042 after that date, see Act §9312(d)(1). Deleted material:

> The corporation shall determine the liability with respect to each contributing sponsor and each member of its controlled group in a manner consistent with section 4062, except that—
>> (1) the amount of the liability determined under section 4062(b)(1) of this title with respect to the entire plan—
>> (A) shall be determined without regard to clauses (i)(II) and (ii) of section 4062(b)(1)(A) of this title, and
>> (B) shall be allocated to each controlled group by multiplying such amount by a fraction—
>> (i) the numerator of which is the amount required to be contributed to the plan for the last 5 plan years ending prior to the termination date by persons in such controlled group as contributing sponsors, and
>> (ii) the denominator of which is the total amount required to be contributed to the plan for such last 5 plan years by all persons as contributing sponsors, and clauses (i)(II) and (ii) of section 4062(b)(1)(A) shall be applied separately with respect to each such controlled group, and
>> (2) the amount of the liability determined under section 4062(c)(1) of this title with respect to the entire plan shall be allocated to each controlled group by multiplying such amount by the fraction described in paragraph (1)(B) in connection with such controlled group.

Consolidated Omnibus Budget Reconciliation Act of 1985 (Pub. L. No. 99-272), as follows:

● ERISA §4064(a) was amended by Act §11016(a)(5)(B)(i)(I) by substituting "all contributing sponsors of a single-employer plan which has two or more contributing sponsors at least two of whom are not under common control" for "all employers who maintain a plan under which more than one employer makes contributions (other than a multiemployer plan)". Eff. Jan. 1, 1986, except as otherwise provided, see Act §11019.

● ERISA §4064(b) was amended by Act §11016(a)(5)(B)(i)(II) by inserting "under section 4041(c) or 4042" after "terminated". Eff. Jan. 1, 1986, except as otherwise provided, see Act §11019.

● ERISA §4064(b) was amended by Act §11016(a)(5)(B)(ii). Eff. Jan. 1, 1986, except as otherwise provided, see Act §11019. ERISA §4064(b) prior to amendment:

> (b) The corporation shall determine the liability of each such employer in a manner consistent with section 4062 except that the amount of the liability determined under section 4062(b)(1) with respect to the entire plan shall be allocated to each employer by multiplying such amounts by a fraction—
> (1) the numerator of which is the amount required to be contributed to the plan by each employer for the last 5 plan years ending prior to the termination, and
> (2) the denominator of which is the total amount required to be contributed to the plan by all such employers for such last 5 years, and the limitation described in section 4062(b)(2) shall be applied separately to each employer. The corporation may also determine the liability of each such employer on any

other equitable basis prescribed by the corporation in regulations.

Multiemployer Pension Plan Amendments Act of 1980 (Pub. L. No. 96-364), as follows:

● ERISA §4064(a) was amended by Act §403(i) by inserting "(other than a multiemployer plan)". Eff. Sept. 26, 1980, except as otherwise provided, see ERISA §4402(e).

SEC. 4065. ANNUAL REPORT OF PLAN ADMINISTRATOR.

For each plan year for which section 4021 applies to a plan, the plan administrator shall file with the corporation, on a form prescribed by the corporation, an annual report which identifies the plan and plan administrator and which includes—

(1) a copy of each notification required under section 4063 with respect to such year,

(2) a statement disclosing whether any reportable event (described in section 4043(b)) occurred during the plan year except to the extent the corporation waives such requirement, and

(3) in the case of a multiemployer plan, information with respect to such plan which the corporation determines is necessary for the enforcement of subtitle E and requires by regulation, which may include—

(A) a statement certified by the plan's enrolled actuary of—

(i) the value of all vested benefits under the plan as of the end of the plan year, and

(ii) the value of the plan's assets as of the end of the plan year;

(B) a statement certified by the plan sponsor of each claim for outstanding withdrawal liability (within the meaning of section 4001(a)(12)) and its value as of the end of that plan year and as of the end of the preceding plan year; and

(C) the number of employers having an obligation to contribute to the plan and the number of employers required to make withdrawal liability payments.

The report shall be filed within 6 months after the close of the plan year to which it relates. The corporation shall cooperate with the Secretary of the Treasury and the Secretary of Labor in an endeavor to coordinate the timing and content, and possibly obtain the combination, of reports under this section with reports required to be made by plan administrators to such Secretaries.

Amendments to ERISA §4065

Multiemployer Pension Plan Amendments Act of 1980 (Pub. L. No. 96-364), as follows:

● ERISA §4065 was amended by Act §106, in para. (1), by striking "and" following "year,"; in para. (2) by substituting "except to the extent the corporation waives such requirement, and" for the period at the end; and adding para. (3). Eff. Sept. 26, 1980, except as otherwise provided, see ERISA §4402(e).

SEC. 4066. ANNUAL NOTIFICATION TO SUBSTANTIAL EMPLOYERS.

The plan administrator of each single-employer plan which has at least two contributing sponsors at least two of whom are not under common control shall notify, within 6 months after the close of each plan year, any contributing sponsor of the plan who is described in section 4001(a)(2) that such contributing sponsor (along or together with members of such contributing sponsor's controlled group) constitutes a substantial employer for that year.

Amendments to ERISA §4066

Omnibus Budget Reconciliation Act of 1989 (Pub. L. No. 101-239), as follows:

● ERISA §4066 was amended by Act §7893(g)(2) by inserting "any" before "contributing sponsor" the first place it appears. Eff. as if included in the provision of Pub. L. No. 99-272, to which it relates, see Act §7893(h)

Consolidated Omnibus Budget Reconciliation Act of 1985 (Pub. L. No. 99-272), as follows:

● ERISA §4066 was amended by Act §11016(a)(5)(C) by substituting "each single-employer plan which has at least two contributing sponsors at least two of whom are not under common control" for "each plan under which contributions are made by more than one employer (other than a multiemployer plan)"; substituting "contributing sponsor of the plan" for "any employer making contributions under that plan"; and substituting "that such contributing sponsor (alone or together with members of such contributing sponsor's controlled group) constitutes a substantial employer" for "that he is a substantial employer". Eff. Jan. 1, 1986, except as otherwise provided, see Act §11019.

Multiemployer Pension Plan Amendments Act of 1980 (Pub. L. No. 96-354), as follows:

● ERISA §4066 was amended by Act §403(j) by inserting "(other than a multiemployer plan)". Eff. Sept. 26, 1980, except as otherwise provided, see ERISA §4402(e).

SEC. 4067. RECOVERY OF LIABILITY FOR PLAN TERMINATION.

The corporation is authorized to make arrangements with any contributing sponsors and members of their controlled groups who are or may become liable under section 4062, 4063, or 4064 for payment of their liability, including arrangements for deferred payment of amounts of liability to the corporation accruing as of the termination date on such terms and for such periods as the corporation deems equitable and appropriate.

Amendments to ERISA §4067

Omnibus Budget Reconciliation Act of 1987 (Pub. L. No. 100-203), as follows:

● ERISA §4067 was amended by Act §9313(b)(6) by striking "controlled groups who are" and inserting "controlled groups who are or may become". Eff. for plan terminations under ERISA §4041 for which notices of intent to terminate were provided under ERISA §4041(a)(2) after Dec. 17, 1987, see Act §9313(c).

Consolidated Omnibus Budget Reconciliation Act of 1985 (Pub. L. No. 99-272), as follows:

● ERISA §4066 was amended by Act §11016(a)(6)(A), in the heading, by striking "employer"; by substituting "contributing sponsors and members of their controlled groups" for "employer or employers"; and by inserting "of amounts of liability to the corporation accruing as of the termination date" after "deferred payment". Eff. Jan. 1, 1986, except as otherwise provided, see Act §11019.

SEC. 4068. LIEN FOR LIABILITY.

(a) Creation of Lien.—If any person liable to the corporation under section 4062, 4063, or 4064 neglects or refuses to pay, after demand, the amount of such liability (including interest), there shall be a lien in favor of the corporation in the amount of such liability (including interest) upon all property and rights to property, whether real or personal, belonging to such person, except that such lien may not be in an amount in excess of 30 percent of the collective net worth of all persons described in section 4062(a)[.]

(b) Term of Lien.—The lien imposed by subsection (a) arises on the date of termination of a plan, and continues until the liability imposed under sectuib 4062, 4063, or 4064 is satisfied or becomes unenforceable by reason of lapse of time.

(c) Priority.—

(1) Except as otherwise provided under this section, the priority of a lien imposed under subsection (a) shall be determined in the same manner as under section 6323 of title 26 (as in effect on the date of the enactment of the Single-Employer Pension Plan Amendments Act of 1986). Such section 6323 shall be applied for purposes of this section by disregarding subsection (g)(4) and by substituting—

(A) "lien imposed by section 4068 of the Employee Retirement Income Security Act of 1974" for "lien imposed by section 6321" each place it appears in subsections (a), (b), (c)(1), (c)(4)(B), (d), (e), and (h)(5);

(B) "the corporation" for "the Secretary" in subsections (a) and (b)(9)(C);

(C) "the payment of the amount on which the section 4068(a) lien is based" for "the collection of any tax under this title" in subsection (b)(3);

(D) "a person whose property is subject to the lien" for "the taxpayer" in subsections (b)(8), (c)(2)(A)(i) (the first place it appears), (c)(2)(A)(ii), (c)(2)(B), (c)(4)(B), and (c)(4)(C) (in the matter preceding clause (i));

(E) "such person" for "the taxpayer" in subsections (c)(2)(A)(i) (the second place it appears) and (c)(4)(C)(ii);

(F) "payment of the loan value of the amount on which the lien is based is made to the corporation" for "satisfaction of a levy pursuant to section 6332(b)" in subsection (b)(9)(C);

(G) "section 4068(a) lien" for "tax lien" each place it appears in subsections (c)(1), (c)(2)(A), (c)(2)(B), (c)(3)(B)(iii), (c)(4)(B), (d), and (h)(5); and

(H) "the date on which the lien is first filed" for the "date of the assessment of the tax" in subsection (g)(3)(A).

(2) In a case under title 11 of the United States Code or in insolvency proceedings, the lien imposed under subsection (a) shall be treated in the same manner as a tax due and owing to the United States for purposes of title 11 of section 3713 of title 31 of the United States Code.

(3) For purposes of applying section 6323(a) of title 26 to determine the priority between the lien imposed under subsection (a) and a Federal tax lien, each lien shall be treated as a judgment lien arising as of the time notice of such lien is filed.

(4) For purposes of this subsection, notice of the lien imposed by subsection (a) shall be filed in the same manner as under section 6323(f) and (g) of title 26.

(d) Civil Action; Limitation Period.—

(1) In any case where there has been a refusal or neglect to pay the liability imposed under section 4062, 4063, or 4064, the corporation may bring civil action in a district court of the United States to enforce the lien of the corporation under this section with respect to such liability or to subject any property, of whatever nature, of the liable person, or in which he has any right, title, or interest to the payment of such liability.

(2) The liability imposed by section 4062, 4063, or 4064 may be collected by a proceeding in court if the proceeding is commenced within 6 years after the date upon which the plan was terminated or prior to the expiration of any period for collection agreed upon in writing by the corporation and the liable person before the expiration of such 6-year period. The period of limitations provided under this paragraph shall be suspended for the period the assets of the liable person are in the control or custody of any court of the United States, or of any State, or of the District of Columbia, and for 6 months thereafter, and for any period during which the liable person is outside the United States if such period of absence is for a continuous period of at least 6 months.

(e) Release of Subordination.—If the corporation determines that release of the lien or subordination of the lien to any other creditor of the liable person would not adversely affect the collection of the liability imposed under section 4062, 4063, or 4064, or that the amount realizable by the corporation from the property to which the lien attaches will ultimately be increased by such release or subordination, and that the ultimate collection of the liability will be facilitated by such release or subordination, the corporation may issue a certificate of release or subordination of the lien with respect to such property, or any part thereof.

(f) Definitions.—For purposes of this section—

(1) The collective net worth of persons subject to liability in connection with a plan termination shall be determined as provided in section 4062(d)(1).

(2) The term "pre-tax profits" has the meaning provided in section 4062(d)(2).

Amendments to ERISA §4068

Omnibus Budget Reconciliation Act of 1989 (Pub. L. No. 101-239), as follows:

● ERISA §4068(a) was amended by Act §7881(f)(12) by striking "to the extent such amount does not exceed 30 percent of the collective net worth of all persons described in section 1362(a) of this title" after "the amount of such liability"; and substituting "in the amount of such liability (including interest) upon all property and rights to property, whether real or personal, belonging to such person, except that such lien may not be in an amount in excess of 30 percent of the collective net worth of all persons described in §4062(a)" for "to the extent such amount does not exceed 30 percent of the collective net worth of all persons described in §4062(a) upon all property and rights to property, whether real or personal, belonging to such person." Eff., except as otherwise provided, as if included in the provision of Pub. L. 100-203, §§9302–9346, to which it relates, see Act §7882.

● ERISA §4068(a) was amended by Act §7881(f)(3)(B) by striking "The preceding provisions of this subsection shall be applied in a manner consistent with the provisions of §4064(d) of this title relating to treatment of multiple controlled groups." Eff., except as otherwise provided, as if included in the provision of Pub. L. 100-203, §§9302–9346, to which it relates, see Act §7882.

● ERISA §4068(c) was amended by Act §7891(a)(1), in paras. (1), (3), and (4), by substituting "Internal Revenue Code of 1986" for "Internal Revenue Code of 1954", which for purposes of codification was translated as "title 26". Eff., except as otherwise provided, as if included in the provision of Pub. L. No. 99-514, to which it relates, see Act §7891(f).

● ERISA §4068(c)(2) was amended by Act §7894(g)(4)(A) by substituting "section 3713 of title 31" for "section 3466 of the Revised Statutes (31 U.S.C. 191)". Eff., except as otherwise provided, as if included in the provision of Pub. L. No. 93-406, to which it relates, see Act §7894(i).

● ERISA §4068(f) was added by Act §7881(f)(10)(C). Eff., except as otherwise provided, as if included in the provision of Pub. L. No. 100-203, §§9302–9346, to which it relates, see Act §7882.

Omnibus Budget Reconciliation Act of 1987 (Pub. L. No. 100-203), as follows:

● ERISA §4068(a) was amended by Act §9312(b)(2)(B)(i) by substituting "to the extent such amount does not exceed 30 percent of the collective net worth of all persons described in section 1362(a) of this title" for "to the extent of an amount equal to the unpaid amount described in §4062(b)(1)(A)(i)" in two places. Eff. for plan terminations under ERISA §4041 for which notices of intent to terminate are provided under ERISA §4041(a)(2) after Dec. 17, 1987, and plan terminations for which proceedings are instituted by the PBGC under ERISA §4042 after that date, see Act §9312(d)(1), as amended.

● ERISA §4068(a) was amended by Act §9312(b)(2)(C)(ii) by inserting at end "The preceding provisions of this subsection shall be applied in a manner consistent with the provisions of §4064(d) relating to treatment of multiple controlled groups."

Eff. for plan terminations under ERISA §4041 for which notices of intent to terminate are provided under ERISA §4041(a)(2) after Dec. 17, 1987, and plan terminations for which proceedings are instituted by the PBGC under ERISA §4042 after that date, see Act §9312(d)(1), as amended.

Consolidated Omnibus Budget Reconciliation Act of 1985 (Pub. L. No. 99-272), as follows:

• ERISA §4068 (heading) was amended by Act §11016(a)(6)(B)(i) by striking "of employer" after "liability". Eff. Jan. 1, 1986, except as otherwise provided, see Act §11019.

• ERISA §4068(a) was amended by Act §11016(a)(6)(B)(ii) by substituting "person" for "employer or employers" in the first place it appears; "neglects or refuses" for "neglect or refuse"; and "such person" for "such employer or employers"; and inserting "to the extent of an amount equal to the unpaid amount described in §4062(b)(1)(A)(i)" after "corporation" the second place it appears. Eff. Jan. 1, 1986, except as otherwise provided, see Act §11019.

• ERISA §4068(c)(1) was amended by Act §11016(a)(6)(B)(vi) by substituting new para. (1) for former para. (1). Eff. Jan. 1, 1986, except as otherwise provided, see Act §11019. ERISA §4068(c)(1) prior to amendment:

  (1) Except as otherwise provided under this section, the priority of the lien imposed under subsection (a) of this section shall be determined in the same manner as under section 6323 of title 26. Such section 6323 shall be applied by substituting "lien imposed by section 4068 of the Employee Retirement Income Security Act of 1974" for "lien imposed by section 6321"; "corporation" for "Secretary or his delegate"; "employer liability lien" for "tax lien"; "employer" for "taxpayer"; "lien arising under section 4068(a) of the Employee Retirement Income Security Act of 1974" for "assessment of the tax"; and "payment of the loan value is made to the corporation" for "satisfaction of a levy pursuant to section 6332(b)"; each place such terms appear.

• ERISA §4068(d)(1), (2) were amended by Act §11016(a)(6)(B)(iii), (iv) by substituting "liable person" for "employer" wherever appearing. Eff. Jan. 1, 1986, except as otherwise provided, see Act §11019.

• ERISA §4068(e) was amended by Act §11016(a)(6)(B)(v), (c)(14) by striking ", with the consent of the board of directors," after "corporation determines" and substituting "liable person" for "employer or employers". Eff. Jan. 1, 1986, except as otherwise provided, see Act §11019.

Pub. L. No. 95-598, as follows:

• ERISA §4068(c)(2) was amended by substituting "a case under title 11 or in" and "title 11" for "the case of bankruptcy or" and "the Bankruptcy Act". Eff. Oct. 1, 1979, see Act §402(a).

SEC. 4069. TREATMENT OF TRANSACTIONS TO EVADE LIABILITY; EFFECT OF CORPORATE REORGANIZATION.

(a) Treatment of Transactions to Evade Liability.—If a principal purpose of any person in entering into any transaction is to evade liability to which such person would be subject under this subtitle and the transaction becomes effective within five years before the termination date of the termination on which such liability would be based, then such person and the members of such person's controlled group (determined as of the termination date) shall be subject to liability under this subtitle in connection with such termination as if such person were a contributing sponsor of the terminated plan as of the termination date. This subsection shall not cause any person to be liable under this subtitle in connection with such plan

termination for any increases or improvements in the benefits provided under the plan which are adopted after the date on which the transaction referred to in the preceding sentence becomes effective.

(b) Effect of Corporate Reorganization.—For purposes of this subtitle, the following rules apply in the case of certain corporate reorganizations:

(1) Change of identity, form, etc.—If a person ceases to exist by reason of a reorganization which involves a mere change in identity, form, or place of organization, however effected, a successor corporation resulting from such reorganization shall be treated as the person to whom this subtitle applies.

(2) Liquidation into parent corporation.—If a person ceases to exist by reason of liquidation into a parent corporation, the parent corporation shall be treated as the person to whom this subtitle applies.

(3) Merger, consolidation, or division.—If a person ceases to exist by reason of a merger, consolidation, or division, the successor corporation or corporations shall be treated as the person to whom this subtitle applies.

SEC. 4070. ENFORCEMENT AUTHORITY RELATING TO TERMINATIONS OF SINGLE-EMPLOYER PLANS.

(a) In General.—Any person who is with respect to a single-employer plan a fiduciary, contributing sponsor, member of a contributing sponsor's controlled group, participant, or beneficiary, and is adversely affected by an act or practice of any party (other than the corporation) in violation of any provision of section 4041, 4042, 4062, 4063, 4064, or 4069, or who is an employee organization representing such a participant or beneficiary so adversely affected for purposes of collective bargaining with respect to such plan, may bring an action—

(1) to enjoin such act or practice, or

(2) to obtain other appropriate equitable relief (A) to redress such violation or (B) to enforce such provision.

(b) Status of Plan as Party to Action and With Respect to Legal Process.—A single-employer plan may be sued under this section as an entity. Service of summons, subpoena, or other legal process of a court upon a trustee or an administrator of a single-employer plan in such trustee's or administrator's capacity as such shall constitute service upon the plan. If a plan has not designated in the summary plan description of the plan an individual as agent for the service of legal process, service upon any contributing sponsor of the plan shall constitute such service. Any money judgment under this section against a single-employer plan shall be enforceable only against the plan as an entity and shall not be enforceable against any other person unless liability against such person is established in such person's individual capacity.

(c) Jurisdiction and Venue.—The district courts of the United States shall have exclusive jurisdiction of civil actions under this section. Such actions may be brought in the district where the plan is administered, where the violation took place, or where a defendant resides or may be found, and process may be served in any other district where a defendant resides or may be found. The district courts of the United States shall have jurisdiction, without regard to the amount in controversy or the citizenship of the parties, to grant the relief provided for in subsection (a) in any action.

(d) Right of Corporation to Intervene.—A copy of the complaint or notice of appeal in any action under this section shall be served upon the corporation by certified mail. The corporation shall have the right in its discretion to intervene in any action.

(e) Awards of Costs and Expenses.—

(1) **General rule.**—In any action brought under this section, the court in its discretion may award all or a portion of the costs and expenses incurred in connection with such action, including reasonable attorney's fees, to any party who prevails or substantially prevails in such action.

(2) **Exemption for plans.**—Notwithstanding the preceding provisions of this subsection, no plan shall be required in any action to pay any costs and expenses (including attorney's fees).

(f) Limitation on Actions.—

(1) **In general.**—Except as provided in paragraph (3), an action under this section may not be brought after the later of—

(A) 6 years after the date on which the cause of action arose, or

(B) 3 years after the applicable date specified in paragraph (2).

(2) **Applicable date.**—

(A) General rule.—Except as provided in subparagraph (B), the applicable date specified in this paragraph is the earliest date on which the plaintiff acquired or should have acquired actual knowledge of the existence of such cause of action.

(B) Special rule for plaintiffs who are fiduciaries.—In the case of a plaintiff who is a fiduciary bringing the action in the exercise of fiduciary duties, the applicable date specified in this paragraph is the date on which the plaintiff became a fiduciary with respect to the plan if such date is later than the date described in subparagraph (A).

(3) **Cases of fraud or concealment.**—In the case of fraud or concealment, the period described in paragraph (1)(B) shall be extended to 6 years after the applicable date specified in paragraph (2).

Amendments to ERISA §4070
Omnibus Budget Reconciliation Act of 1989 (Pub. L. No. 101-239), as follows:

• ERISA §4070(a) was amended by Act §7881(f)(8) by striking "1349," preceding "4062". Eff., except as otherwise provided, as if included in the provision of Pub. L. No. 100-203, §§9302–9346, to which it relates, see Act §7882.

SEC. 4071. PENALTY FOR FAILURE TO TIMELY PROVIDE REQUIRED INFORMATION.

The corporation may assess a penalty, payable to the corporation, against any person who fails to provide any notice or other material information required under this subtitle or subtitle A, B, or C, or section 303(k)(4) or any regulations prescribed under any such subtitle or such section, within the applicable time limit specified therein. Such penalty shall not exceed $1,000 for each day for which such failure continues.

Amendments to ERISA §4071
Pension Protection Act of 2006 (Pub. L. No. 109-280), as follows:
• ERISA §4071 was amended by Act §107(b)(5) (redesignated as §108(b)(5) by Pub. L. No. 111-192, §202(a)) by striking "302(f)(4)" and inserting "303(k)(4)".
Worker, Retiree, and Employer Recovery Act of 2008 (Pub. L. No. 110-458), as follows:
• ERISA §4071 was amended by Act §101(d)(1)(B) by striking "as section 303(k)(4) or 307(e)" and inserting "or section 303(k)(4)". Eff. for plan years beginning after 2007, as if included in Pub. L. No. 109-280, §107.
Omnibus Budget Reconciliation Act of 1989 (Pub. L. No. 101-239), as follows:
• ERISA §4071 was amended by Act §7881(i)(3)(B) by substituting ", subtitle A, B, or C of this subchapter, as §1082(f)(4) or 1085b(e) of this title" for "or subtitle A, B, or C" and inserting "or such section" after "such subtitle". Eff., except as otherwise provided, as if included in the provision of Pub. L. No. 100-203, §§9302–9346, to which it relates, see Act §7882.

Subtitle E—Special Provisions For Multiemployer Plans

Part 1—Employer Withdrawals

SEC. 4201. WITHDRAWAL LIABILITY ESTABLISHED; CRITERIA AND DEFINITIONS.

(a) If an employer withdraws from a multiemployer plan in a complete withdrawal or a partial withdrawal, then the employer is liable to the plan in the amount determined under this part to be the withdrawal liability.

(b) For purposes of subsection (a)—

(1) The withdrawal liability of an employer to a plan is the amount determined under section 4211 to be the allocable amount of unfunded vested benefits, adjusted—

(A) first, by any de minimis reduction applicable under section 4209,

(B) next, in the case of a partial withdrawal, in accordance with section 4206,

(C) then, to the extent necessary to reflect the limitation on annual payments under section 4219(c)(1)(B), and

(D) finally, in accordance with section 4225.

(2) The term "complete withdrawal" means a complete withdrawal described in §4203.

(3) The term "partial withdrawal" means a partial withdrawal described in section 4205.

SEC. 4202. DETERMINATION AND COLLECTION OF LIABILITY; NOTIFICATION OF EMPLOYER.

When an employer withdraws from a multiemployer plan, the plan sponsor, in accordance with this part, shall—

(1) determine the amount of the employer's withdrawal liability,

(2) notify the employer of the amount of the withdrawal liability, and

(3) collect the amount of the withdrawal liability from the employer.

SEC. 4203. COMPLETE WITHDRAWAL.

(a) **Determinative Factors.**—For purposes of this part, a complete withdrawal from a multiemployer plan occurs when an employer—

(1) permanently ceases to have an obligation to contribute under the plan, or

(2) permanently ceases all covered operations under the plan.

(b) **Building and Construction Industry.—**

(1) Notwithstanding subsection (a), in the case of an employer that has an obligation to contribute under a plan for work performed in the building and construction industry, a complete withdrawal occurs only as described in paragraph (2), if—

(A) substantially all the employees with respect to whom the employer has an obligation to contribute under the plan perform work in the building and construction industry, and

(B) the plan—

(i) primarily covers employees in the building and construction industry, or

(ii) is amended to provide that this subsection applies to employers described in this paragraph.

(2) A withdrawal occurs under this paragraph if—

(A) an employer ceases to have an obligation to contribute under the plan, and

(B) the employer—

(i) continues to perform work in the jurisdiction of the collective bargaining agreement of the type for which contributions were previously required, or

(ii) resumes such work within 5 years after the date on which the obligation to contribute under the plan ceases, and does not renew the obligation at the time of the resumption.

(3) In the case of a plan terminated by mass withdrawal (within the meaning of section 4041A(a)(2)), paragraph (2) shall be applied by substituting "3 years" for "5 years" in subparagraph (B)(ii).

(c) **Entertainment Industry.—**

(1) Notwithstanding subsection (a), in the case of an employer that has an obligation to contribute under a plan for work performed in the entertainment industry, primarily on a temporary or project-by-project basis, if the plan primarily covers employees in the entertainment industry, a complete withdrawal occurs only as described in subsection (b)(2) applied by substituting "plan" for "collective bargaining agreement" in subparagraph (B)(i) thereof.

(2) For purposes of this subsection, the term "entertainment industry" means—

(A) theater, motion picture (except to the extent provided in regulations prescribed by the corporation), radio, television, sound or visual recording, music, and dance, and

(B) such other entertainment activities as the corporation may determine to be appropriate.

(3) The corporation may by regulation exclude a group or class of employers described in the preceding sentence from the application of this subsection if the corporation determines that such exclusion is necessary—

(A) to protect the interest of the plan's participants and beneficiaries, or

(B) to prevent a significant risk of loss to the corporation with respect to the plan.

(4) A plan may be amended to provide that this subsection shall not apply to a group or class of employers under the plan.

(d) **Other Determinative Factors.—**

(1) Notwithstanding subsection (a), in the case of an employer who—

(A) has an obligation to contribute under a plan described in paragraph (2) primarily for work described in such paragraph, and

(B) does not continue to perform work within the jurisdiction of the plan,

a complete withdrawal occurs only as described in paragraph (3).

(2) A plan is described in this paragraph if substantially all of the contributions required under the plan are made by employers primarily engaged in the long and short haul trucking industry, the household goods moving industry, or the public warehousing industry.

(3) A withdrawal occurs under this paragraph if—

(A) an employer permanently ceases to have an obligation to contribute under the plan or permanently ceases all covered operations under the plan, and

(B) either—

(i) the corporation determines that the plan has suffered substantial damage to its contribution base as a result of such cessation, or

(ii) the employer fails to furnish a bond issued by a corporate surety company that is an acceptable surety for purposes of section 412, or an amount held in escrow by a bank or similar financial institution satisfactory to the plan, in an amount equal to 50 percent of the withdrawal liability of the employer.

(4) If, after an employer furnishes a bond or escrow to a plan under paragraph (3)(B)(ii), the corporation determines that the cessation of the employer's obligation to contribute under the plan (considered together with any cessations by other employers), or cessation of covered operations under the plan, has resulted in substantial damage to the contribution base of the plan, the employer shall be treated as having withdrawn from the plan on the date on which the obligation to contribute or covered operations ceased, and such bond or escrow shall be paid to the plan. The corporation shall not make a determination under this paragraph more than 60 months after the date on which such obligation to contribute or covered operations ceased.

(5) If the corporation determines that the employer has no further liability under the plan either—

(A) because it determines that the contribution base of the plan has not suffered substantial damage as a result of the cessation of the employer's obligation to contribute or cessation of covered operations (considered together with any cessation of contribution obligation, or of covered operations, with respect to other employers), or

(B) because it may not make a determination under paragraph (4) because of the last sentence thereof, then the bond shall be canceled or the escrow refunded.

(6) Nothing in this subsection shall be construed as a limitation on the amount of the withdrawal liability of any employer.

(e) Date of Complete Withdrawal.—For purposes of this part, the date of a complete withdrawal is the date of the cessation of the obligation to contribute or the cessation of covered operations.

(f) Special Liability Withdrawal Rules for Industries Other Than Construction and Entertainment Industries; Procedures Applicable to Amend Plans.—

(1) The corporation may prescribe regulations under which plans in industries other than the construction or entertainment industries may be amended to provide for special withdrawal liability rules similar to the rules described in subsections (b) and (c).

(2) Regulations under paragraph (1) shall permit use of special withdrawal liability rules—

(A) only in industries (or portions thereof) in which, as determined by the corporation, the characteristics that would make use of such rules appropriate are clearly shown, and

(B) only if the corporation determines, in each instance in which special withdrawal liability rules are permitted, that use of such rules will not pose a significant risk to the corporation under this title.

Amendments to ERISA §4203

Pension Protection Act of 2006 (Pub. L. No. 109-280), as follows:

● **Other Provision**. Act §206 provides:

> SEC. 206. SPECIAL RULE FOR CERTAIN BENEFITS FUNDED UNDER AN AGREEMENT APPROVED BY THE PENSION BENEFIT GUARANTY CORPORATION.
>
> In the case of a multiemployer plan that is a party to an agreement that was approved by the Pension Benefit Guaranty Corporation prior to June 30, 2005, and that—
>
> (1) increases benefits, and
>
> (2) provides for special withdrawal liability rules under §4203(f) of the Employee Retirement Income Security Act of 1974 (29 U.S.C. 1383),
>
> the amendments made by §§201, 202, 211, and 212 of this Act shall not apply to the benefit increases under any plan amendment adopted prior to June 30, 2005, that are funded pursuant to such agreement if the plan is funded in compliance with such agreement (and any amendments thereto).

SEC. 4204. SALE OF ASSETS.

(a) Complete or Partial Withdrawal Not Occurring as a Result of Sale and Subsequent Cessation of Covered Operations or Cessation of Obligation to Contribute to Covered Operations; Continuation of Liability of Seller.—

(1) A complete or partial withdrawal of an employer (hereinafter in this section referred to as the "seller") under this section does not occur solely because, as a result of a bona fide, arm's-length sale of assets to an unrelated party (hereinafter in this section referred to as the "purchaser"), the seller ceases covered operations or ceases to have an obligation to contribute for such operations, if—

(A) the purchaser has an obligation to contribute to the plan with respect to the operations for substantially the same number of contribution base units for which the seller had an obligation to contribute to the plan;

(B) the purchaser provides to the plan for a period of 5 plan years commencing with the first plan year beginning after the sale of assets, a bond issued by a corporate surety company that is an acceptable surety for purposes of section 412 of this Act, or an amount held in escrow by a bank or similar financial institution satisfactory to the plan, in an amount equal to the greater of—

(i) the average annual contribution required to be made by the seller with respect to the operations under the plan for the 3 plan years preceding the plan year in which the sale of the employer's assets occurs, or

(ii) the annual contribution that the seller was required to make with respect to the operations under the plan for the last plan year before the plan year in which the sale of the assets occurs,

which bond or escrow shall be paid to the plan if the purchaser withdraws from the plan, or fails to make a contribution to the plan when due, at any time during the first 5 plan years beginning after the sale; and

(C) the contract for sale provides that, if the purchaser withdraws in a complete withdrawal, or a partial withdrawal with respect to operations, during such first 5 plan years, the seller is secondarily liable for any withdrawal liability it would have had to the plan with respect to the operations (but for this section) if the liability of the purchaser with respect to the plan is not paid.

(2) If the purchaser—

(A) withdraws before the last day of the fifth plan year beginning after the sale, and

(B) fails to make any withdrawal liability payment when due,

then the seller shall pay to the plan an amount equal to the payment that would have been due from the seller but for this section.

(3)(A) If all, or substantially all, of the seller's assets are distributed, or if the seller is liquidated before the end of the 5 plan year period described in paragraph (1)(C), then the seller shall provide a bond or amount in escrow equal to the present value of the withdrawal liability the seller would have had but for this subsection.

(B) If only a portion of the seller's assets are distributed during such period, then a bond or escrow shall be required, in accordance with regulations prescribed by the corporation, in a manner consistent with subparagraph (A).

(4) The liability of the party furnishing a bond or escrow under this subsection shall be reduced, upon payment of the bond or escrow to the plan, by the amount thereof.

(b) Liability of Purchaser.—

(1) For the purposes of this part, the liability of the purchaser shall be determined as if the purchaser had been required to contribute to the plan in the year of the sale and the 4 plan years preceding the sale the amount the seller was required to contribute for such operations for such 5 plan years.

(2) If the plan is in reorganization in the plan year in which the sale of assets occurs, the purchaser shall furnish a bond or escrow in an amount equal to 200 percent of the amount described in subsection (a)(1)(B).

(c) Variances or Exemptions From Continuation of Liability of Seller; Procedures Applicable.—The corporation may by regulation vary the standards in subparagraphs (B) and (C) of subsection (a)(1) if the variance would more effectively or equitably carry out the purposes of this title. Before it promulgates such regulations, the corporation may grant individual or class variances or exemptions from the requirements of such subparagraphs if the particular case warrants it. Before granting such an individual or class variance or exemption, the corporation—

(1) shall publish notice in the Federal Register of the pendency of the variance or exemption,

(2) shall require that adequate notice be given to interested persons, and

(3) shall afford interested persons an opportunity to present their views.

(d) "Unrelated Party" Defined.—For purposes of this section, the term "unrelated party" means a purchaser or seller who does not bear a relationship to the seller or purchaser, as the case may be, that is described in section 267(b) of title 26, or that is described in regulations prescribed by the corporation applying principles similar to the principles of such section.

Amendments to ERISA §4204

Omnibus Budget Reconciliation Act of 1989 (Pub. L. No. 101-239), as follows:

• ERISA §4204(d) was amended by Act §7891(a)(1) by substituting "Internal Revenue Code of 1986" for "Internal Revenue Code of 1954", which for purposes of codification was translated as "title 26". Eff., except as otherwise provided, as if included in the provision of Pub. L. No. 100-203, §§9302–9346, to which it relates, see Act §7882.

SEC. 4205. PARTIAL WITHDRAWALS.

(a) Determinative Factors.—Except as otherwise provided in this section, there is a partial withdrawal by an employer from a plan on the last day of a plan year if for such plan year—

(1) there is a 70-percent contribution decline, or

(2) there is a partial cessation of the employer's contribution obligation.

(b) Criteria Applicable.—For purposes of subsection (a)—

(1)(A) There is a 70-percent contribution decline for any plan year if during each plan year in the 3-year testing period the employer's contribution base units do not exceed 30 percent of the employer's contribution base units for the high base year.

(B) For purposes of subparagraph (A)—

(i) The term "3-year testing period" means the period consisting of the plan year and the immediately preceding 2 plan years.

(ii) The number of contribution base units for the high base year is the average number of such units for the 2 plan years for which the employer's contribution base units were the highest within the 5 plan years immediately preceding the beginning of the 3-year testing period.

(2)(A) There is a partial cessation of the employer's contribution obligation for the plan year if, during such year—

(i) the employer permanently ceases to have an obligation to contribute under one or more but fewer than all collective bargaining agreements under which the employer has been obligated to contribute under the plan but continues to perform work in the jurisdiction of the collective bargaining agreement of the type for which contributions were previously required or transfers such work to another location or to an entity or entities owned or controlled by the employer, or

(ii) an employer permanently ceases to have an obligation to contribute under the plan with respect to work performed at one or more but fewer than all of its facilities, but continues to perform work at the facility of the type for which the obligation to contribute ceased.

(B) For purposes of subparagraph (A), a cessation of obligations under a collective bargaining agreement shall not be considered to have occurred solely because, with respect to the same plan, one agreement that requires contributions to the plan has been substituted for another agreement.

(c) Retail Food Industry.—

(1) In the case of a plan in which a majority of the covered employees are employed in the retail food industry, the plan may be amended to provide that this section shall be applied with respect to such plan—

(A) by substituting "35 percent" for "70 percent" in subsections (a) and (b), and

(B) by substituting "65 percent" for "30 percent" in subsection (b).

(2) Any amendment adopted under paragraph (1) shall provide rules for the equitable reduction of withdrawal liability in any case in which the number of the plan's contribution base units, in the 2 plan years following the plan year of withdrawal of the employer, is higher than such number immediately after the withdrawal.

(3) Section 4208 shall not apply to a plan which has been amended under paragraph (1).

(d) Continuation of Liability of Employer for Partial Withdrawal Under Amended Plan.—In the case of a plan described in section 404(c) of title 26, or a continuation thereof, the plan may be amended to provide rules setting forth other conditions consistent with the purposes of this Act under which an employer has liability for partial withdrawal.

Amendments to ERISA §4205

Pension Protection Act of 2006 (Pub. L. No. 109-280), as follows:

• ERISA §4205(b)(2)(A)(i) was amended by Act §204(b)(1) by adding "or to an entity or entities owned or controlled by the employer, or" after "to another location". Eff. for work transferred on or after Aug. 17, 2006, see Act §204(b)(2).

Omnibus Budget Reconciliation Act of 1989 (Pub. L. No. 101-239), as follows:

• ERISA §4205(d) was amended by Act §39 substituted "Internal Revenue Code of 1986" for "Internal Revenue Code of 1954", which for purposes of codification was translated as "title 26". Eff., except as otherwise provided, as if included in the provision of Pub. L. No. 100-203, §§9302–9346, to which it relates, see Act §7882.

Multiemployer Pension Plan Amendments Act of 1980 (Pub. L. No. 96-364), §108(c)(2)(A) through (e) contain special rules for the application of ERISA §4205:

(2)(A) For the purpose of applying section 4205 of the Employee Retirement Income Security Act of 1974 in the case of an employer described in subparagraph (B)—
(i) "more than 75 percent" shall be substituted for "70 percent" in subsections (a) and (b) of such section,
"25 percent or less" shall be substituted for "30 percent" in subsection (b) of such section, and
(iii) the number of contribution units for the high base year shall be the average annual number of such units for calendar years 1970 and 1971.
(B) An employer is described in this subparagraph if—
(i) the employer is engaged in the trade or business of shipping bulk cargoes in the Great Lakes Maritime Industry, and whose fleet consists of vessels the gross registered tonnage of which was at least 7,800, as stated in the American Bureau of Shipping Record, and
(ii) whose fleet during any 5 years from the period 1970 through and including 1979 has experienced a 33 percent or more increase in the contribution units as measured from the average annual contribution units for the calendar years 1970 and 1971.
(3)(A) For the purpose of determining the withdrawal liability of an employer under title IV of the Employee Retirement Income Security Act of 1974 from a plan that terminates while the plan is insolvent (within the meaning of section 4245 of such Act), the plan's unfunded vested benefits shall be reduced by an amount equal to the sum of all overburden credits that were applied in determining the plan's accumulated funding deficiency for all plan years preceding the first plan year in which the plan is insolvent, plus interest thereon.
(B) The provisions of subparagraph (A) apply only if—
(i) the plan would have been eligible for the overburden credit in the last plan year beginning before the date of the enact-

ment of this Act, if §4243 of the Employee Retirement Income Security Act of 1974 had been in effect for that plan year, and

(ii) the Pension Benefit Guaranty Corporation determines that the reduction of unfunded vested benefits under subparagraph (A) would not significantly increase the risk of loss to the corporation.

(4) In the case of an employer who withdrew before the date of enactment of this Act from a multiemployer plan covering employees in the seagoing industry (as determined by the corporation), sections 4201 through 4219 of the Employee Retirement Income Security Act of 1974, as added by this Act, are effective as of May 3, 1979. For the purpose of applying section 4217 for purposes of the preceding sentence, the date "May 2, 1979," shall be substituted for "April 28, 1980," and the date "May 3,1979" shall be substituted for "April 29, 1980". For purposes of this paragraph, terms which are used in title IV of the Employee Retirement Income Security Act of 1974, or in regulations prescribed under that title, and which are used in the preceding sentence have the same meaning as when used in that Act or those regulations. For purposes of this paragraph, the term "employer" includes only a substantial employer covering employees in the seagoing industry (as so determined) in connection with ports on the West Coast of the United States, but does not include an employer who withdrew from a plan because of a change in the collective bargaining representative.

(d) For purposes of section 4205 of the Employee Retirement Income Security Act of 1974—

(1) subsection (a)(l) of such section shall not apply to any plan year beginning before April 29,1982,

(2) subsection (a)(2) of such section shall not apply with respect to any cessation of contribution obligations occurring before April 29, 1980, and

(3) in applying subsection (b) of such section, the employer's contribution base units for any plan year ending before April 29, 1980, shall be deemed to be equal to the employer's contribution base units for the last plan year ending before such date.

(e)(l) In the case of a partial withdrawal under section 4205 of the Employee Retirement Income Security Act of 1974, an employer who—

(A) before December 13,1979, had publicly announced the total cessation of covered operations at a facility in a State (and such cessation occurred within 12 months after the announcement)

(B) had not been obligated to make contributions to the plan on behalf of the employees at such facility for more than 8 years before the discontinuance of contributions, and

(C) after the discontinuance of contributions does not within 1 year after the date of the partial withdrawal perform work in the same State of the type for which contributions were previously required, shall be liable under such section with respect to such partial withdrawal in an amount not greater than the amount determined under paragraph (2).

(2) The amount determined under this paragraph is the excess (if any) of—

(A) the present value (on the withdrawal date) of the benefits under the plan which—

(i) were vested on the withdrawal date (or, if earlier, at the time of separation from service with the employer at the facility),

(ii) were accrued by employees who on December 13, 1979 (or, if earlier, at the time of separation from service with the employer at the facility), were employed at the facility, and

(iii) are attributable to service with the withdrawing employer, over

(B)(i) the sum of—

(I) all employer contributions to the plan on behalf of employees at the facility before the withdrawal date,

(II) interest (to the withdrawal date) on amounts described in subclause (I), and

(III) $100,000, reduced by

(ii) the sum of—

(I) the benefits paid under the plan on or before the withdrawal date with respect to former employees who separated from employment at the facility, and

(II) interest (to the withdrawal date) on amounts described in subclause (I).

(3) For purposes of paragraph (2)—

(A) actuarial assumptions shall be those used in the last actuarial report completed before December 13,1979,

(B) the term "withdrawal date" means the date on which the employer ceased work at the facility of the type for which contributions were previously required, and

(C) the term "facility" means the facility referred to in paragraph (1).

Pub. L. No. 98-369, Div. A, §558(b)(2), amended Pub. L. No. 96-364, §108(d) (see note above) to provide:

For purposes of §4205 of the Employee Retirement Income Security Act of 1974—

(1) subsection (a)(1) of such section shall not apply to any plan year beginning before September 26, 1982,

(2) subsection (a)(2) of such section shall not apply with respect to any cessation of contribution obligations occurring before September 26, 1980, and

(3) in applying subsection (b) of such section, the employer's contribution base units for any plan year ending before September 26, 1980, shall be deemed to be equal to the employer's contribution base units for the last plan year ending before such date.

SEC. 4206. ADJUSTMENT FOR PARTIAL WITHDRAWAL; DETERMINATION OF AMOUNT; REDUCTION FOR PARTIAL WITHDRAWAL LIABILITY; PROCEDURES APPLICABLE.

(a) The amount of an employer's liability for a partial withdrawal, before the application of sections 4219(c)(1) and 4225, is equal to the product of—

(1) the amount determined under §4211, and adjusted under §4209 if appropriate, determined as if the employer had withdrawn from the plan in a complete withdrawal—

(A) on the date of the partial withdrawal, or

(B) in the case of a partial withdrawal described in section 4205(a)(1) (relating to 70-percent contribution decline), on the last day of the first plan year in the 3-year testing period,

multiplied by

(2) a fraction which is 1 minus a fraction—

(A) the numerator of which is the employer's contribution base units for the plan year following the plan year in which the partial withdrawal occurs, and

(B) the denominator of which is the average of the employer's contribution base units for—

(i) except as provided in clause (ii), the 5 plan years immediately preceding the plan year in which the partial withdrawal occurs, or

(ii) in the case of a partial withdrawal described in section 4205(a)(1) (relating to 70-percent contribution decline), the 5 plan years immediately preceding the beginning of the 3-year testing period.

(b)(1) In the case of an employer that has withdrawal liability for a partial withdrawal from a plan, any withdrawal liability of that employer for a partial or complete withdrawal from that plan in a subsequent plan year shall be reduced by the amount of any partial withdrawal liability (reduced by any abatement or reduction of such liability) of the employer with respect to the plan for a previous plan year.

(2) The corporation shall prescribe such regulations as may be necessary to provide for proper adjustments in the reduction provided by paragraph (1) for—

(A) changes in unfunded vested benefits arising after the close of the prior year for which partial withdrawal liability was determined,

(B) changes in contribution base units occurring after the close of the prior year for which partial withdrawal liability was determined, and

(C) any other factors for which it determines adjustment to be appropriate,

so that the liability for any complete or partial withdrawal in any subsequent year (after the application of the reduction) properly reflects the employer's share of liability with respect to the plan.

SEC. 4207. REDUCTION OR WAIVER OF COMPLETE WITHDRAWAL LIABILITY; PROCEDURES AND STANDARDS APPLICABLE.

(a) The corporation shall provide by regulation for the reduction or waiver of liability for a complete withdrawal in the event that an employer who was withdrawn from a plan subsequently resumes covered operations under the plan or renews an obligation to contribute under the plan, to the extent that the corporation determines that reduction or waiver of withdrawal liability is consistent with the purposes of this Act.

(b) The corporation shall prescribe by regulation a procedure and standards for the amendment of plans to provide alternative rules for the reduction or waiver of liability for a complete withdrawal in the event that an employer who has withdrawn from the plan subsequently resumes covered operations or renews an obligation to contribute under the plan. The rules may apply only to the extent that the rules are consistent with the purposes of this Act.

SEC. 4208. REDUCTION OF PARTIAL WITHDRAWAL LIABILITY.

(a) Obligation of Employer for Payments for Partial Withdrawal for Plan Years Beginning After the Second Consecutive Plan Year Following the Partial Withdrawal Year; Criteria Applicable; Furnishing of Bond in Lieu of Payment of Partial Withdrawal Liability.—

(1) If, for any 2 consecutive plan years following the plan year in which an employer has partially withdrawn from a plan under section 4205(a)(1) (referred to elsewhere in this section as the "partial withdrawal year"), the number of contribution base units with respect to which the employer has an obligation to contribute under the plan for each such year is not less than 90 percent of the total number of contribution base units with respect to which the employer had an obligation to contribute under the plan for the high base year (within the meaning of section 4205(b)(1)(B)(ii)), then the employer shall have no obligation to make payments with respect to such partial withdrawal (other than delinquent payments) for plan years beginning after the second consecutive plan year following the partial withdrawal year.

(2)(A) For any plan year for which the number of contribution base units with respect to which an employer who has partially withdrawn under section 4205(a)(1) has an obligation to contribute under the plan equals or exceeds the number of units for the highest year determined under paragraph (1) without regard to "90 percent of", the employer may furnish (in lieu of payment of the partial withdrawal liability determined under section 4206) a bond to plan in the amount determined by the plan sponsor (not exceeding 50 percent of the annual payment otherwise required).

(B) If the plan sponsor determines under paragraph (1) that the employer has no further liability to the plan for the partial withdrawal, then the bond shall be canceled.

(C) If the plan sponsor determines under paragraph (1) that the employer continues to have liability to the plan for the partial withdrawal, then—

(i) the bond shall be paid to the plan,

(ii) the employer shall immediately be liable for the outstanding amount of liability due with respect to the plan year for which the bond was posted, and

(iii) the employer shall continue to make the partial withdrawal liability payments as they are due.

(b) Obligation of Employer for Payments for Partial Withdrawal for Plan Years Beginning After the Second Consecutive Plan Year; Other Criteria Applicable.—If—

(1) for any 2 consecutive plan years following a partial withdrawal under section 4205(a)(1), the number of contribution base units with respect to which the employer has an obligation to contribute for each such year exceeds 30 percent of the total number of contribution base units with respect to which the employer has an obligation to contribute for the high base year (within the meaning of section 4205(b)(1)(B)(ii)), and

(2) the total number of contribution base units with respect to which all employersunder the plan have obligations to contribute in each of such 2 consecutive years is not less than 90 percent of the total number of contribution base units for which all employers had obligations to contribute in the partial withdrawal plan year;

then, the employer shall have no obligation to make payments with respect to such partial withdrawal (other than delinquent payments) for plan years beginning after the second such consecutive plan year.

(c) Pro Rata Reduction of Amount of Partial Withdrawal Liability Payment of Employer for Plan Year Following Partial Withdrawal Year.—In any case in which, in any plan year following a partial withdrawal under section 4205(a)(1), the number of contribution base units with respect to which the employer has an obligation to contribute for such year equals or exceeds 110 percent (or such other percentage as the plan may provide by amendment and which is not prohibited under regulations prescribed by the corporation) of the number of contribution base units with respect to which the employer has an obligation to contribute in the partial withdrawal year, then the amount of the employer's partial withdrawal liability payment for such year shall be reduced pro rata, in accordance with regulations prescribed by the corporation.

(d) Building and Construction Industry; Entertainment Industry.—

(1) An employer to whom section 4202(b) (relating to the building and construction industry) applies is liable for a partial withdrawal only if the employer's obligation to contribute under the plan is continued for no more than an insubstantial portion of its work in the craft and area jurisdiction of the collective bargaining agreement of the type for which contributions are required.

(2) An employer to whom section 4202(c) (relating to the entertainment industry) applies shall have no liability for a partial withdrawal except under the conditions and to the extent prescribed by the corporation by regulation.

(e) Reduction or Elimination of Partial Withdrawal Liability Under Any Conditions; Criteria; Procedures Applicable.—

(1) The corporation may prescribe regulations providing for the reduction or elimination of partial withdrawal liability under any conditions with respect to which the corporation determines that reduction or elimination of partial withdrawal liability is consistent with the purposes of this Act.

(2) Under such regulations, reduction of withdrawal liability shall be provided only with respect to subsequent changes in the employer's contributions for the same operations, or under the same collective bargaining agreement, that gave rise to the partial withdrawal, and changes in the employer's contribution base units with respect to other facilities or other

collective bargaining agreements shall not be taken into account.

(3) The corporation shall prescribe by regulation a procedure by which a plan may by amendment adopt rules for the reduction or elimination of partial withdrawal liability under any other conditions, subject to the approval of the corporation based on its determination that adoption of such rules by the plan is consistent with the purposes of this Act.

SEC. 4209. DE MINIMIS RULE.

(a) Reduction of Unfunded Vested Benefits Allocable to Employer Withdrawn From Plan.—Except in the case of a plan amended under subsection (b), the amount of the unfunded vested benefits allocable under section 4211 to an employer who withdraws from a plan shall be reduced by the smaller of—

(1) ¾ of 1 percent of the plan's unfunded vested obligations (determined as of the end of the plan year ending before the date of withdrawal), or

(2) $50,000,

reduced by the amount, if any, by which the unfunded vested benefits allowable to the employer, determined without regard to this subsection, exceeds $100,000.

(b) Amendment of Plan for Reduction of Amount of Unfunded Vested Benefits Allocable to Employer Withdrawn From Plan.—A plan may be amended to provide for the reduction of the amount determined under section 4211 by not more than the greater of—

(1) the amount determined under subsection (a), or

(2) the lesser of—

(A) the amount determined under subsection (a)(1), or

(B) $100,000,

reduced by the amount, if any, by which the amount determined under section 4211 for the employer, determined without regard to this subsection, exceeds $150,000.

(c) Nonapplicability.—This section does not apply—

(1) to an employer who withdraws in a plan year in which substantially all employers withdraw from the plan, or

(2) in any case in which substantially all employers withdraw from the plan during a period of one or more plan years pursuant to an agreement or arrangement to withdraw, to an employer who withdraws pursuant to such agreement or arrangement.

(d) Presumption of Employer Withdrawal From Plan Pursuant to Agreement or Arrangement Ap-

plicable in Action or Proceeding to Determine or Collect Withdrawal Liability.—In any action or proceeding to determine or collect withdrawal liability, if substantially all employers have withdrawn from a plan within a period of 3 plan years, an employer who has withdrawn from such plan during such period shall be presumed to have withdrawn from the plan pursuant to an agreement or arrangement, unless the employer proves otherwise by a preponderance of the evidence.

SEC. 4210. NONAPPLICABILITY OF WITHDRAWAL LIABILITY FOR CERTAIN TEMPORARY CONTRIBUTION OBLIGATION PERIODS; EXCEPTION.

(a) An employer who withdraws from a plan in complete or partial withdrawal is not liable to the plan if the employer—

(1) first had an obligation to contribute to the plan after the date of the enactment of the Multiemployer Pension Plan Amendments Act of 1980,

(2) had an obligation to contribute to the plan for no more than the lesser of—

(A) 6 consecutive plan years preceding the date on which the employer withdraws, or

(B) the number of years required for vesting under the plan,

(3) was required to make contributions to the plan for each such plan year in an amount equal to less than 2 percent of the sum of all employer contributions made to the plan for each such year, and

(4) has never avoided withdrawal liability because of the application of this section with respect to the plan.

(b) Subsection (a) shall apply to an employer with respect to a plan only if—

(1) the plan is amended to provide that subsection (a) applies;

(2) the plan provides, or is amended to provide, that the reduction under section 411(a)(3)(E) of title 26 applies with respect to the employees of the employer; and

(3) the ratio of the assets of the plan for the plan year preceding the first plan year for which the employer was required to contribute to the plan to the benefit payments made during that plan year was at least 8 to 1.

Amendments to ERISA §4210

Pension Protection Act of 2006 (Pub. L. No. 109-280), as follows:

● ERISA §4210(b)(1) was stricken and former (b)(2)–(4) were redesignated as (b)(1)–(3) by Act §204(c)(1)(A)–(B). Eff. for plan withdrawals occurring on or after Jan. 1, 2007, see Act §204(c)(3). ERISA §4210(b)(1) prior to being stricken:

(1) the plan is not a plan which primarily covers employees in the building and construction industry.

Omnibus Budget Reconciliation Act of 1989 (Pub. L. No. 101-239), as follows:

● ERISA §4210(b)(3) was amended by Act §7891(a)(1) by substituting "Internal Revenue Code of 1986" for "Internal Revenue Code of 1954", which for purposes of codification was translated as "title 26". Eff., except as otherwise provided, as if included in the provision of Pub. L. No. 100-203, §§9302–9346, to which it relates, see Act §7882.

SEC. 4211. METHODS FOR COMPUTING WITHDRAWAL LIABILITY.

(a) Determination of Amount of Unfunded Vested Benefits Allocable to Employer Withdrawn From Plan.—The amount of the unfunded vested benefits allocable to an employer that withdraws from a plan shall be determined in accordance with subsection (b), (c), or (d) of this section.

(b) Factors Determining Computation of Amount of Unfunded Vested BenefitsAllocable to Employer Withdrawn From Plan.—

(1) Except as provided in subsections (c) and (d), the amount of unfunded vested benefits allocable to an employer that withdraws is the sum of—

(A) the employer's proportional share of the unamortized amount of the change in the plan's unfunded vested benefits for plan years ending after September 25, 1980, as determined under paragraph (2),

(B) the employer's proportional share, if any, of the unamortized amount of the plan's unfunded vested benefits at the end of the plan year ending before September 26, 1980, as determined under paragraph (3); and

(C) the employer's proportional share of the unamortized amounts of the reallocated unfunded vested benefits (if any) as determined under paragraph (4).

If the sum of the amounts determined with respect to an employer under paragraphs (2), (3), and (4) is negative, the unfunded vested benefits allocable to the employer shall be zero.

(2)(A) An employer's proportional share of the unamortized amount of the change in the plan's unfunded vested benefits for plan years ending after September 25, 1980, is the sum of the employer's proportional shares of the unamortized amount of the change in unfunded vested benefits for each plan year in which the employer has an obligation to contribute under the plan ending—

(i) after such date, and

(ii) before the plan year in which the withdrawal of the employer occurs.

(B) The change in a plan's unfunded vested benefits for a plan year is the amount by which—

ERISA Sec. 4211(b)(2)(B)

(i) the unfunded vested benefits at the end of the plan year; exceeds

(ii) the sum of—

(I) the unamortized amount of the unfunded vested benefits for the last plan year ending before September 26, 1980, and

(II) the sum of the unamortized amounts of the change in unfunded vested benefits for each plan year ending after September 25, 1980, and preceding the plan year for which the change is determined.

(C) The unamortized amount of the change in a plan's unfunded vested benefits with respect to a plan year is the change in unfunded vested benefits for the plan year, reduced by 5 percent of such change for each succeeding plan year.

(D) The unamortized amount of the unfunded vested benefits for the last plan year ending before September 26, 1980, is the amount of the unfunded vested benefits as of the end of that plan year reduced by 5 percent of such amount for each succeeding plan year.

(E) An employer's proportional share of the unamortized amount of a change in unfunded vested benefits is the product of—

(i) the unamortized amount of such change (as of the end of the plan year preceding the plan year in which the employer withdraws); multiplied by

(ii) a fraction—

(I) the numerator of which is the sum of the contributions required to be made under the plan by the employer for the year in which such change arose and for the 4 preceding plan years, and

(II) the denominator of which is the sum for the plan year in which such change arose and the 4 preceding plan years of all contributions made by employers who had an obligation to contribute under the plan for the plan year in which such change arose reduced by the contributions made in such years by employers who had withdrawn from the plan in the year in which the change arose.

(3) An employer's proportional share of the unamortized amount of the plan's unfunded vested benefits for the last plan year ending before September 26, 1980, is the product of—

(A) such unamortized amount; multiplied by—

(B) a fraction—

(i) the numerator of which is the sum of all contributions required to be made by the employer under the plan for the most recent 5 plan years ending before September 26, 1980, and

(ii) the denominator of which is the sum of all contributions made for the most recent 5 plan years

ending before September 26, 1980, by all employers—

(I) who had an obligation to contribute under the plan for the first plan year ending on or after such date, and

(II) who had not withdrawn from the plan before such date.

(4)(A) An employer's proportional share of the unamortized amount of the reallocated unfunded vested benefits is the sum of the employer's proportional shares of the unamortized amount of the reallocated unfunded vested benefits for each plan year ending before the plan year in which the employer withdrew from the plan.

(B) Except as otherwise provided in regulations prescribed by the corporation, the reallocated unfunded vested benefits for a plan year is the sum of—

(i) any amount which the plan sponsor determines in that plan year to be uncollectible for reasons arising out of cases or proceedings under title 11, United States Code, or similar proceedings,

(ii) any amount which the plan sponsor determines in that plan year will not be assessed as a result of the operation of section 4209, section 4219(c)(1)(B), or section 4225 against an employer to whom a notice described in section 4219 has been sent, and

(iii) any amount which the plan sponsor determines to be uncollectible or unassessable in that plan year for other reasons under standards not inconsistent with regulations prescribed by the corporation.

(C) The unamortized amount of the reallocated unfunded vested benefits with respect to a plan year is the reallocated unfunded vested benefits for the plan year, reduced by 5 percent of such reallocated unfunded vested benefits for each succeeding plan year.

(D) An employer's proportional share of the unamortized amount of the reallocated unfunded vested benefits with respect to a plan year is the product of—

(i) the unamortized amount of the reallocated unfunded vested benefits (as of the end of the plan year preceding the plan year in which the employer withdraws); multiplied by

(ii) the fraction defined in paragraph (2)(E)(ii).

(c) Amendment of Multiemployer Plan for Determination Respecting Amount of Unfunded Vested Benefits Allocable to Employer Withdrawn From Plan; Factors Determining Computation of Amount.—

(1) A multiemployer plan, other than a plan which primarily covers employees in the building and con-

struction industry, may be amended to provide that the amount of unfunded vested benefits allocable to an employer that withdraws from the plan is an amount determined under paragraph (2), (3), (4), or (5) of this subsection, rather than under subsection (b) or (d). A plan prescribed in section 4203(b)(1)(B)(i) (relating to the building and construction industry) may be amended, to the extent provided in regulations prescribed by the corporation, to provide that the amount of the unfunded vested benefits allocable to an employer not described in section 4203(b)(1)(A) shall be determined in a manner different from that provided in subsection (b).

(2)(A) The amount of the unfunded vested benefits allocable to any employer under this paragraph is the sum of the amounts determined under subparagraphs (B) and (C).

(B) The amount determined under this subparagraph is the product of—

(i) the plan's unfunded vested benefits as of the end of the last plan year ending before September 26, 1980, reduced as if those obligations were being fully amortized in level annual installments over 15 years beginning with the first plan year ending on or after such date; multiplied by

(ii) a fraction—

(I) the numerator of which is the sum of all contributions required to be made by the employer under the plan for the last 5 plan years ending before September 26, 1980, and

(II) the denominator of which is the sum of all contributions made for the last 5 plan years ending before September 26, 1980, by all employers who had an obligation to contribute under the plan for the first plan year ending after September 25, 1980, and who had not withdrawn from the plan before such date.

(C) The amount determined under this subparagraph is the product of—

(i) an amount equal to—

(I) the plan's unfunded vested benefits as of the end of the plan year preceding the plan year in which the employer withdraws, less

(II) the sum of the value as of such date of all outstanding claims for withdrawal liability which can reasonably be expected to be collected, with respect to employers withdrawing before such plan year, and that portion of the amount determined under subparagraph (B)(i) which is allocable to employers who have an obligation to contribute under the plan in the plan year preceding the plan year in which the employer withdraws and who also had an obligation to contribute under the plan for the first plan year ending after September 25, 1980, multiplied by

(ii) a fraction—

(I) the numerator of which is the total amount required to be contributed under the plan by the employer for the last 5 plan years ending before the date on which the employer withdraws, and

(II) the denominator of which is the total amount contributed under the plan by all employers for the last 5 plan years ending before the date on which the employer withdraws, increased by the amount of any employer contributions owed with respect to earlier periods which were collected in those plan years, and decreased by any amount contributed by an employer who withdrew from the plan under this part during those plan years.

(D) The corporation may by regulation permit adjustments in any denominator under this section, consistent with the purposes of this title, where such adjustment would be appropriate to ease administrative burdens of plan sponsors in calculating such denominators.

(3) The amount of the unfunded vested benefits allocable to an employer under this paragraph is the product of—

(A) the plan's unfunded vested benefits as of the end of the plan year preceding the plan year in which the employer withdraws, less the value as of the end of such year of all outstanding claims for withdrawal liability which can reasonably be expected to be collected from employers withdrawing before such year; multiplied by

(B) a fraction—

(i) the numerator of which is the total amount required to be contributed by the employer under the plan for the last 5 plan years ending before the withdrawal, and

(ii) the denominator of which is the total amount contributed under the plan by all employers for the last 5 plan years ending before the withdrawal, increased by any employer contributions owed with respect to earlier periods which were collected in those plan years, and decreased by any amount contributed to the plan during those plan years by employers who withdrew from the plan under this section during those plan years.

(4)(A) The amount of the unfunded vested benefits allocable to an employer under this paragraph is equal to the sum of—

(i) the plan's unfunded vested benefits which are attributable to participants' service with the employer (determined as of the end of the plan year preceding the plan year in which the employer withdraws), and

(ii) the employer's proportional share of any unfunded vested benefits which are not attributable to service with the employer or other employers who are obligated to contribute under the plan in

ERISA Sec. 4211(c)(4)(A)(ii)

the plan year preceding the plan year in which the employer withdraws (determined as of the end of the plan year preceding the plan year in which the employer withdraws).

(B) The plan's unfunded vested benefits which are attributable to participants' service with the employer is the amount equal to the value of nonforfeitable benefits under the plan which are attributable to participants' service with such employer (determined under plan rules not inconsistent with regulations of the corporation) decreased by the share of plan assets determined under subparagraph (C) which is allocated to the employer as provided under subparagraph (D).

(C) The value of plan assets determined under this subparagraph is the value of plan assets allocated to nonforfeitable benefits which are attributable to service with the employers who have an obligation to contribute under the plan in the plan year preceding the plan year in which the employer withdraws, which is determined by multiplying—

(i) the value of the plan assets as of the end of the plan year preceding the plan year in which the employer withdraws, by

(ii) a fraction—

(I) the numerator of which is the value of nonforfeitable benefits which are attributable to service with such employers, and

(II) the denominator of which is the value of all nonforfeitable benefits under the plan

as of the end of the plan year.

(D) The share of plan assets, determined under subparagraph (C), which is allocated to the employer shall be determined in accordance with one of the following methods which shall be adopted by the plan by amendment:

(i) by multiplying the value of plan assets determined under subparagraph (C) by a fraction—

(I) the numerator of which is the value of the nonforfeitable benefits which are attributable to service with the employer, and

(II) the denominator of which is the value of the nonforfeitable benefits which are attributable to service with all employers who have an obligation to contribute under the plan in the plan year preceding the plan year in which the employer withdraws;

(ii) by multiplying the value of plan assets determined under subparagraph (C) by a fraction—

(I) the numerator of which is the sum of all contributions (accumulated with interest) which have been made to the plan by the employer for the plan year preceding the plan year in which the employer withdraws and all preceding plan years; and

(II) the denominator of which is the sum of all contributions (accumulated with interest) which have been made to the plan (for the plan year preceding the plan year in which the employer withdraws and all preceding plan years) by all employers who have an obligation to contribute to the plan for the plan year preceding the plan year in which the employer withdraws; or

(iii) by multiplying the value of plan assets under subparagraph (C) by a fraction—

(I) the numerator of which is the amount determined under clause (ii)(I) of this subparagraph, less the sum of benefit payments (accumulated with interest) made to participants (and their beneficiaries) for the plan years described in such clause (ii)(I) which are attributable to service with the employer; and

(II) the denominator of which is the amount determined under clause (ii)(II) of this subparagraph, reduced by the sum of benefit payments (accumulated with interest) made to participants (and their beneficiaries) for the plan years described in such clause (ii)(II) which are attributable to service with respect to the employers described in such clause (ii)(II).

(E) The amount of the plan's unfunded vested benefits for a plan year preceding the plan year in which an employer withdraws, which is not attributable to service with employers who have an obligation to contribute under the plan in the plan year preceding the plan year in which such employer withdraws, is equal to—

(i) an amount equal to—

(I) the value of all nonforfeitable benefits under the plan at the end of such plan year, reduced by

(II) the value of nonforfeitable benefits under the plan at the end of such plan year which are attributable to participants' service with employers who have an obligation to contribute under the plan for such plan year; reduced by

(ii) an amount equal to—

(I) the value of the plan assets as of the end of such plan year, reduced by

(II) the value of plan assets as of the end of such plan year as determined under subparagraph (C); reduced by

(iii) the value of all outstanding claims for withdrawal liability which can reasonably be expected to be collected with respect to employers withdrawing before the year preceding the plan year in which the employer withdraws.

(F) The employer's proportional share described in subparagraph (A)(ii) for a plan year is the amount determined under subparagraph (E) for the employer, but not in excess of an amount which bears the same ratio to the sum of the amounts determined under subparagraph (E) for all employers under the plan as the amount determined under subparagraph (C) for the employer bears to the sum of the amounts determined under subparagraph (C) for all employers under the plan.

(G) The corporation may prescribe by regulation other methods which a plan may adopt for allocating assets to determine the amount of the unfunded vested benefits attributable to service with the employer and to determine the employer's share of unfunded vested benefits not attributable to service with employers who have an obligation to contribute under the plan in the plan year in which the employer withdraws.

(5)(A) The corporation shall prescribe by regulation a procedure by which a plan may, by amendment, adopt any other alternative method for determining an employer's allocable share of unfunded vested benefits under this section, subject to the approval of the corporation based on its determination that adoption of the method by the plan would not significantly increase the risk of loss to plan participants and beneficiaries or to the corporation.

(B) The corporation may prescribe by regulation standard approaches for alternative methods, other than those set forth in the preceding paragraphs of this subsection, which a plan may adopt under subparagraph (A), for which the corporation may waive or modify the approval requirements of subparagraph (A). Any alternative method shall provide for the allocation of substantially all of a plan's unfunded vested benefits among employers who have an obligation to contribute under the plan.

(C) Unless the corporation by regulation provides otherwise, a plan may be amended to provide that a period of more than 5 but not more than 10 plan years may be used for determining the numerator and denominator of any fraction which is used under any method authorized under this section for determining an employer's allocable share of unfunded vested benefits under this section.

(D) The corporation may by regulation permit adjustments in any denominator under this section, consistent with the purposes of this title, where such adjustment would be appropriate to ease administrative burdens of plan sponsors in calculating such denominators.

(E) Fresh start option.—Notwithstanding paragraph (1), a plan may be amended to provide that the withdrawal liability method described in subsection (b) shall be applied by substituting the plan year which is specified in the amendment and for which the plan has no unfunded vested benefits for the plan year ending before September 26, 1980.

(d) Method of Calculating Allocable Share of Employer of Unfunded Vested Benefits Set Forth in Subsection (c)(3) of this Section; Applicability of Certain Statutory Provisions.—

(1) The method of calculating an employer's allocable share of unfunded vested benefits set forth in subsection (c)(3) shall be the method for calculating an employer's allocable share of unfunded vested benefits under a plan to which section 404(c) of title 26, or a continuation of such a plan, applies, unless the plan is amended to adopt another method authorized under subsection (b) or (c).

(2) Sections 4204, 4209, 4219(c)(1)(B), and 4225 shall not apply with respect to the withdrawal of an employer from a plan described in paragraph (1) unless the plan is amended to provide that any of such sections apply.

(e) Reduction of Liability of Withdrawn Employer in Case of Transfer of Liabilities to Another Plan Incident to Withdrawal or Partial Withdrawal of Employer.—In the case of a transfer of liabilities to another plan incident to an employer's withdrawal or partial withdrawal, the withdrawn employer's liability under this part shall be reduced in an amount equal to the value, as of the end of the last plan year ending on or before the date of the withdrawal, of the transferred unfunded vested benefits.

(f) Computations Applicable in Case of Withdrawal Following Merger of Multiemployer Plans.—In the case of a withdrawal following a merger of multiemployer plans, subsection (b), (c) or (d) shall be applied in accordance with regulations prescribed by the corporation; except that, if a withdrawal occurs in the first plan year beginning after a merger of multiemployer plans, the determination under this section shall be made as if each of the multiemployer plans had remained separate plans.

Amendments to ERISA §4211

Pension Protection Act of 2006 (Pub. L. No. 109-280), as follows:

● ERISA §4211(c)(5)(E) was added by Act §204(c)(2). Eff. for plan withdrawals occurring on or after Jan. 1, 2007, see Act §204(c)(3).

Omnibus Budget Reconciliation Act of 1989 (Pub. L. No. 101-239), as follows:

● ERISA §4211(d)(1) was amended by Act §7891(a)(1) by substituting "Internal Revenue Code of 1986" for "Internal Revenue Code of 1954", which for purposes of codification was translated as "title 26". Eff., except as otherwise provided, as if included in the provision of Pub. L. No. 100-203, §§9302–9346, to which it relates, see Act §7882.

Deficit Reduction Act of 1984 (Pub. L. No. 98-369), as follows:

● ERISA §4211(b)–(c) were amended by Act §558(b)(1)(A)–(B) by substituting "September 25, 1980" for "April 28, 1980" and "September 26, 1980" for "April 29, 1980" wherever appearing.

SEC. 4212. OBLIGATION TO CONTRIBUTE.

(a) "Obligation to Contribute" Defined.—For purposes of this part, the term "obligation to contribute" means an obligation to contribute arising—

(1) under one or more collective bargaining (or related) agreements, or

(2) as a result of a duty under applicable labor-management relations law, but

does not include an obligation to pay withdrawal liability under this section or to pay delinquent contributions.

(b) Payments of Withdrawal Liability Not Considered Contributions.—Payments of withdrawal liability under this part shall not be considered contributions for purposes of this part.

(c) Transactions to Evade or Avoid Liability.—If a principal purpose of any transaction is to evade or avoid liability under this part, this part shall be applied (and liability shall be determined and collected) without regard to such transaction.

SEC. 4213. ACTUARIAL ASSUMPTIONS.

(a) Use by Plan Actuary in Determining Unfunded Vested Benefits of a Plan for Computing Withdrawal Liability of Employer.—The corporation may prescribe by regulation actuarial assumptions which may be used by a plan actuary in determining the unfunded vested benefits of a plan for purposes of determining an employer's withdrawal liability under this part. Withdrawal liability under this part shall be determined by each plan on the basis of—

(1) actuarial assumptions and methods which, in the aggregate, are reasonable (taking into account the experience of the plan and reasonable expectations) and which, in combination, offer the actuary's best estimate of anticipated experience under the plan, or

(2) actuarial assumptions and methods set forth in the corporation's regulations for purposes of determining an employer's withdrawal liability.

(b) Factors Determinative of Unfunded Vested Benefits of Plan for Computing Withdrawal Liability of Employer.—In determining the unfunded vested benefits of a plan for purposes of determining an employer's withdrawal liability under this part, the plan actuary may—

(1) rely on the most recent complete actuarial valuation used for purposes of §412 of title 26 and

reasonable estimates for the interim years of the unfunded vested benefits, and

(2) in the absence of complete data, rely on the data available or on data secured by a sampling which can reasonably be expected to be representative of the status of the entire plan.

(c) Determination of Amount of Unfunded Vested Benefits.—For purposes of this part, the term "unfunded vested benefits" means with respect to a plan, an amount equal to—

(A) the value of nonforfeitable benefits under the plan, less

(B) the value of the assets of the plan.

SEC. 4214. APPLICATION OF PLAN AMENDMENTS; EXCEPTION.

(a) No plan rule or amendment adopted after January 31, 1981, under section 4209 or 4211(c) may be applied without the employer's consent with respect to liability for a withdrawal or partial withdrawal which occurred before the date on which the rule or amendment was adopted.

(b) All plan rules and amendments authorized under this part shall operate and be applied uniformly with respect to each employer, except that special provisions may be made to take into account the creditworthiness of an employer. The plan sponsor shall give notice to all employers who have an obligation to contribute under the plan and to all employee organizations representing employees covered under the plan of any plan rules or amendments adopted pursuant to this section.

SEC. 4215. PLAN NOTIFICATION TO CORPORATION OF POTENTIALLY SIGNIFICANT WITHDRAWALS.

The corporation may, by regulation, require the plan sponsor of a multiemployer plan to provide notice to the corporation when the withdrawal from the plan by any employer has resulted, or will result, in a significant reduction in the amount of aggregate contributions under the plan made by employers.

SEC. 4216. SPECIAL RULES FOR PLANS UNDER SECTION 404(c) OF TITLE 26.

(a) Amount of Withdrawal Liability; Determinative Factors.—In the case of a plan described in subsection (b)—

(1) if an employer withdraws prior to a termination described in section 4041A(a)(2), the amount of withdrawal liability to be paid in any year by such employer shall be an amount equal to the greater of—

(A) the amount determined under section 4219(c)(1)(C)(i), or

(B) the product of—

(i) the number of contribution base units for which the employer would have been required to make contributions for the prior plan year if the employer had not withdrawn, multiplied by

(ii) the contribution rate for the plan year which would be required to meet the amortization schedules contained in section 4243(d)(3)(B)(ii) (determined without regard to any limitation on such rate otherwise provided by this title)

except that an employer shall not be required to pay an amount in excess of the withdrawal liability computed with interest; and

(2) the withdrawal liability of an employer who withdraws after December 31, 1983, as a result of a termination described in section 4041A(a)(2) which is agreed to by the labor organization that appoints the employee representative on the joint board of trustees which sponsors the plan, shall be determined under subsection (c) if—

(A) as a result of prior employer withdrawals in any plan year commencing after January 1, 1980, the number of contribution base units is reduced to less than 67 percent of the average number of such units for the calendar years 1974 through 1979; and

(B) at least 50 percent of the withdrawal liability attributable to the first 33 percent decline described in subparagraph (A) has been determined by the plan sponsor to be uncollectible within the meaning of regulations of the corporation of general applicability; and

(C) the rate of employer contributions under the plan for each plan year following the first plan year beginning after the date of enactment of the Multiemployer Pension Plan Amendments Act of 1980 and preceding the termination date equals or exceeds the rate described in section 4243(d)(3).

(b) Covered Plans.—A plan is described in this subsection if—

(1) it is a plan described in section 404(c) of title 26 or a continuation thereof; and

(2) participation in the plan is substantially limited to individuals who retired prior to January 1, 1976.

(c) Amount of Liability of Employer; "A Year of Signatory Service" Defined.—

(1) The amount of an employer's liability under this paragraph is the product of—

(A) the amount of the employer's withdrawal liability determined without regard to this section, and

(B) the greater of 90 percent, or a fraction—

(i) the numerator of which is an amount equal to the portion of the plan's unfunded vested benefits that is attributable to plan participants who

have a total of 10 or more years of signatory service, and

(ii) the denominator of which is an amount equal to the total unfunded vested benefits of the plan.

(2) For purposes of paragraph (1), the term "a year of signatory service" means a year during any portion of which a participant was employed for an employer who was obligated to contribute in that year, or who was subsequently obligated to contribute.

Amendments to ERISA §4216

Omnibus Budget Reconciliation Act of 1989 (Pub. L. No. 101-239), as follows:

• ERISA §4216(b) was amended by Act §7891(a)(1) by substituting "Internal Revenue Code of 1986" for "Internal Revenue Code of 1954", which for purposes of codification was translated as "title 26". Eff., except as otherwise provided, as if included in the provision of Pub. L. No. 100-203, §§9302–9346, to which it relates, see Act §7882.

SEC. 4217. APPLICATION OF PART IN CASE OF CERTAIN PRE-1980 WITHDRAWALS; ADJUSTMENT OF COVERED PLAN.

(a) For the purpose of determining the amount of unfunded vested benefits allocable to an employer for a partial or complete withdrawal from a plan which occurs after September 25, 1980, and for the purpose of determining whether there has been a partial withdrawal after such date, the amount of contributions, and the number of contribution base units, of such employer properly allocable—

(1) to work performed under a collective bargaining agreement for which there was a permanent cessation of the obligation to contribute before September 26, 1980, or

(2) to work performed at a facility at which all covered operations permanently ceased before September 26, 1980, or for which there was a permanent cessation of the obligation to contribute before that date,

shall not be taken into account.

(b) A plan may, in a manner not inconsistent with regulations, which shall be prescribed by the corporation, adjust the amount of unfunded vested benefits allocable to other employers under a plan maintained by an employer described in subsection (a).

Amendments to ERISA §4217

Deficit Reduction Act of 1984 (Pub. L. No. 98-369), as follows:

• ERISA §4217(a) was amended by Act §558(b), in introductory matter, by substituting "September 25, 1980" for "April 28, 1980" and, in paras. (1)–(2), by substituting "September 26, 1980" for "April 29, 1980".

SEC. 4218. WITHDRAWAL NOT TO OCCUR MERELY BECAUSE OF CHANGE IN BUSINESS FORM OR SUSPENSION OF CONTRIBUTIONS DURING LABOR DISPUTE.

Notwithstanding any other provision of this part, an employer shall not be considered to have withdrawn from a plan solely because—

(1) an employer ceases to exist by reason of—

(A) a change in corporate structure described in section 4069(b), or

(B) a change to an unincorporated form of business enterprise,

if the change causes no interruption in employer contributions or obligations to contribute under the plan, or

(2) an employer suspends contributions under the plan during a labor dispute involving its employees.

For purposes of this part, a successor or parent corporation or other entity resulting from any such change shall be considered the original employer.

Amendments to ERISA §4218

Omnibus Budget Reconciliation Act of 1989 (Pub. L. No. 101-239), as follows:
• ERISA §4218(1)(A) was amended by Act §7893(f) by substituting "§4069(b)" for "§4062(d)". Pub. L. No. 99-514, §1879(u)(4) made an identical amendment. Eff. as if included in the provision of Pub. L. No. 99-272, title XI, to which it relates, see Act §7893(h).

SEC. 4219. NOTICE, COLLECTION, ETC., OF WITHDRAWAL LIABILITY.

(a) Furnishing of Information by Employer for Plan Sponsor.—An employer shall, within 30 days after a written request from the plan sponsor, furnish such information as the plan sponsor reasonably determines to be necessary to enable the plan sponsor to comply with the requirements of this part.

(b) Notification, Demand for Payment, and Review Upon Complete or Partial Withdrawal by Employer.—

(1) As soon as practicable after an employer's complete or partial withdrawal, the plan sponsor shall—

(A) notify the employer of—

(i) the amount of the liability, and

(ii) the schedule for liability payments, and

(B) demand payment in accordance with the schedule.

(2)(A) No later than 90 days after the employer receives the notice described in paragraph (1), the employer—

(i) may ask the plan sponsor to review any specific matter relating to the determination of the employer's liability and the schedule of payments,

(ii) may identify any inaccuracy in the determination of the amount of the unfunded vested benefits allocable to the employer, and

(iii) may furnish any additional relevant information to the plan sponsor.

(B) After a reasonable review of any matter raised, the plan sponsor shall notify the employer of—

(i) the plan sponsor's decision,

(ii) the basis for the decision, and

(iii) the reason for any change in the determination of the employer's liability or schedule of liability payments.

(c) Payment Requirements; Amounts, etc.—

(1)(A)(i) Except as provided in subparagraphs (B) and (D) of this paragraph and in paragraphs (4) and (5), an employer shall pay the amount determined under section 4211, adjusted if appropriate first under section 4209 and then under section 4206 over the period of years necessary to amortize the amount in level annual payments determined under subparagraph (C), calculated as if the first payment were made on the first day of the plan year following the plan year in which the withdrawal occurs and as if each subsequent payment were made on the first day of each subsequent plan year. Actual payment shall commence in accordance with paragraph (2).

(ii) The determination of the amortization period described in clause (i) shall be based on the assumptions used for the most recent actuarial valuation for the plan.

(B) In any case in which the amortization period described in subparagraph (A) exceeds 20 years, the employer's liability shall be limited to the first 20 annual payments determined under subparagraph (C).

(C)(i) Except as provided in subparagraph (E), the amount of each annual payment shall be the product of—

(I) the average annual number of contribution base units for the period of 3 consecutive plan years, during the period of 10 consecutive plan years ending before the plan year in which the withdrawal occurs, in which the number of contribution base units for which the employer had an obligation to contribute under the plan is the highest, and

(II) the highest contribution rate at which the employer had an obligation to contribute under the plan during the 10 plan years ending with the plan year in which the withdrawal occurs.

For purposes of the preceding sentence, a partial withdrawal described in section 4205(a)(1) shall be deemed to occur on the last day of the first year of the 3-year testing period described in section 4205(b)(1)(B)(i).

(ii)(I) A plan may be amended to provide that for any plan year ending before 1986 the amount of each annual payment shall be (in lieu of the amount determined under clause (i)) the average of the required employer contributions under the plan for the period of 3 consecutive plan years (during the period of 10 consecutive plan years ending with the plan year preceding the plan year in which the withdrawal occurs) for which such required contributions were the highest.

(II) Subparagraph (B) shall not apply to any plan year to which this clause applies.

(III) This clause shall not apply in the case of any withdrawal described in subparagraph (D).

(IV) If under a plan this clause applies to any plan year but does not apply to the next plan year, this clause shall not apply to any plan year after such next plan year.

(V) For purposes of this clause, the term "required contributions" means, for any period, the amounts which the employer was obligated to contribute for such period (not taking into account any delinquent contribution for any other period).

(iii) A plan may be amended to provide that for the first plan year ending on or after September 26, 1980, the number "5" shall be substituted for the number "10" each place it appears in clause (i) or clause (ii) (whichever is appropriate). If the plan is so amended, the number "5" shall be increased by one for each succeeding plan year until the number "10" is reached.

(D) In any case in which a multiemployer plan terminates by the withdrawal of every employer from the plan, or in which substantially all the employers withdraw from a plan pursuant to an agreement or arrangement to withdraw from the plan—

(i) the liability of each such employer who has withdrawn shall be determined (or redetermined) under this paragraph without regard to subparagraph (B), and

(ii) notwithstanding any other provision of this part, the total unfunded vested benefits of the plan

shall be fully allocated among all such employers in a manner not inconsistent with regulations which shall be prescribed by the corporation.

Withdrawal by an employer from a plan, during a period of 3 consecutive plan years within which substantially all the employers who have an obligation to contribute under the plan withdraw, shall be presumed to be a withdrawal pursuant to an agreement or arrangement, unless the employer proves otherwise by a preponderance of the evidence.

(E) In the case of a partial withdrawal described in section 4205(a), the amount of each annual payment shall be the product of—

(i) the amount determined under subparagraph (C) (determined without regard to this subparagraph), multiplied by

(ii) the fraction determined under section 4206(a)(2).

(2) Withdrawal liability shall be payable in accordance with the schedule set forth by the plan sponsor under subsection (b)(1) beginning no later than 60 days after the date of the demand notwithstanding any request for review or appeal of determinations of the amount of such liability or of the schedule.

(3) Each annual payment determined under paragraph (1)(C) shall be payable in 4 equal installments due quarterly, or at other intervals specified by plan rules. If a payment is not made when due, interest on the payment shall accrue from the due date until the date on which the payment is made.

(4) The employer shall be entitled to prepay the outstanding amount of the unpaid annual withdrawal liability payments determined under paragraph (1)(C), plus accrued interest, if any, in whole or in part, without penalty. If the prepayment is made pursuant to a withdrawal which is later determined to be part of a withdrawal described in paragraph (1)(D), the withdrawal liability of the employer shall not be limited to the amount of the prepayment.

(5) In the event of a default, a plan sponsor may require immediate payment of the outstanding amount of an employer's withdrawal liability, plus accrued interest on the total outstanding liability from the due date of the first payment which was not timely made. For purposes of this section, the term "default" means—

(A) the failure of an employer to make, when due, any payment under this section, if the failure is not cured within 60 days after the employer receives written notification from the plan sponsor of such failure, and

(B) any other event defined in rules adopted by the plan which indicates a substantial likelihood that an employer will be unable to pay its withdrawal liability.

(6) Except as provided in paragraph (1)(A)(ii), interest under this subsection shall be charged at rates

based on prevailing market rates for comparable obligations, in accordance with regulations prescribed by the corporation.

(7) A multiemployer plan may adopt rules for other terms and conditions for the satisfaction of an employer's withdrawal liability if such rules—

(A) are consistent with this Act, and

(B) are not inconsistent with regulations of the corporation.

(8) In the case of a terminated multiemployer plan, an employer's obligation to make payments under this section ceases at the end of the plan year in which the assets of the plan (exclusive of withdrawal liability claims) are sufficient to meet all obligations of the plan, as determined by the corporation.

(d) Applicability of Statutory Prohibitions.—The prohibitions provided in section 406(a) do not apply to any action required or permitted under this part.

Amendments to ERISA §4219

Deficit Reduction Act of 1984 (Pub. L. No. 98-369), as follows:
● ERISA §4219(c)(1)(C)(iii) was amended by Act §558(b)(1)(B) by substituting "September 26, 1980" for "April 29, 1980".

SEC. 4220. APPROVAL OF AMENDMENTS.

(a) Amendment of Covered Multiemployer Plan; Procedures Available.—Except as provided in subsection (b), if an amendment to a multiemployer plan authorized by any preceding section of this part is adopted more than 36 months after the effective date of this section, the amendment shall be effective only if the corporation approves the amendment, or, within 90 days after the corporation receives notice and a copy of the amendment from the plan sponsor, fails to disapprove the amendment.

(b) Amendment Respecting Methods for Computing Withdrawal Liability.—An amendment permitted by section 4211(c)(5) may be adopted only in accordance with that section.

(c) Criteria for Disapproval by Corporation.—The corporation shall disapprove an amendment referred to in subsection (a) or (b) only if the corporation determines that the amendment creates an unreasonable risk of loss to plan participants and beneficiaries or to the corporation.

SEC. 4221. RESOLUTION OF DISPUTES.

(a) Arbitration Proceedings; Matters Subject to Arbitration, Procedures Applicable, etc.—

(1) Any dispute between an employer and the plan sponsor of a multiemployer plan concerning a determination made under sections 4201 through 4219

shall be resolved through arbitration. Either party may initiate the arbitration proceeding within a 60-day period after the earlier of—

(A) the date of notification to the employer under section 4219(b)(2)(B), or

(B) 120 days after the date of the employer's request under section 4219(b)(2)(A).

The parties may jointly initiate arbitration within the 180-day period after the date of the plan sponsor's demand under section 4219(b)(1).

(2) An arbitration proceeding under this section shall be conducted in accordance with fair and equitable procedures to be promulgated by the corporation. The plan sponsor may purchase insurance to cover potential liability of the arbitrator. If the parties have not provided for the costs of the arbitration, including arbitrator's fees, by agreement, the arbitrator shall assess such fees. The arbitrator may also award reasonable attorney's fees.

(3)(A) For purposes of any proceeding under this section, any determination made by a plan sponsor under sections 4201 through 4219 and section 4225 is presumed correct unless the party contesting the determination shows by a preponderance of the evidence that the determination was unreasonable or clearly erroneous.

(B) In the case of the determination of a plan's unfunded vested benefits for a plan year, the determination is presumed correct unless a party contesting the determination shows by a preponderance of evidence that—

(i) the actuarial assumptions and methods used in the determination were, in the aggregate, unreasonable (taking into account the experience of the plan and reasonable expectations), or

(ii) the plan's actuary made a significant error in applying the actuarial assumptions or methods.

(b) Alternative Collection Proceedings; Civil Action Subsequent to Arbitration Award; Conduct of Arbitration Proceedings.—

(1) If no arbitration proceeding has been initiated pursuant to subsection (a), the amounts demanded by the plan sponsor under section 4219(b)(1) shall be due and owing on the schedule set forth by the plan sponsor. The plan sponsor may bring an action in a State or Federal court of competent jurisdiction for collection.

(2) Upon completion of the arbitration proceedings in favor of one of the parties, any party thereto may bring an action, no later than 30 days after the issuance of an arbitrator's award, in an appropriate United States district court in accordance with section 4301 to enforce, vacate, or modify the arbitrator's award.

(3) Any arbitration proceedings under this section shall, to the extent consistent with this title, be conducted in the same manner, subject to the same limitations, carried out with the same powers (including subpoena power), and enforced in United States courts as an arbitration proceeding carried out under title 9, United States Code.

(c) Presumption Respecting Finding of Fact by Arbitration.—In any proceeding under subsection (b), there shall be a presumption, rebuttable only by a clear preponderance of the evidence, that the findings of fact made by the arbitrator were correct.

(d) Payments by Employer Prior and Subsequent to Determination by Arbitrator; Adjustments; Failure of Employer to Make Payments.—Payments shall be made by an employer in accordance with the determinations made under this part until the arbitrator issues a final decision with respect to the determination submitted for arbitration, with any necessary adjustments in subsequent payments for overpayments or underpayments arising out of the decision of the arbitrator with respect to the determination. If the employer fails to make timely payment in accordance with such final decision, the employer shall be treated as being delinquent in the making of a contribution required under the plan (within the meaning of section 515).

(e) Procedures Applicable to Certain Disputes.—

(1) In general.—If—

(A) a plan sponsor of a plan determines that—

(i) a complete or partial withdrawal of an employer has occurred, or

(ii) an employer is liable for withdrawal liability payments with respect to the complete or partial withdrawal of an employer from the plan,

(B) such determination is based in whole or in part on a finding by the plan sponsor under §4212(c) that a principal purpose of a transaction that occurred before January 1, 1999, was to evade or avoid withdrawal liability under this subtitle, and

(C) such transaction occurred at least 5 years before the date of the complete or partial withdrawal, then the special rules under paragraph (2) shall be used in applying subsections (a) and (d) of this section and §4219(c) to the employer.

(2) Special rules.—

(A) Determination.—Notwithstanding subsection (a)(3)—

(i) a determination by the plan sponsor under paragraph (1)(B) shall not be presumed to be correct, and

(ii) the plan sponsor shall have the burden to establish, by a preponderance of the evidence, the elements of the claim under §4212(c) that a principal purpose of the transaction was to evade or avoid withdrawal liability under this subtitle.

Nothing in this subparagraph shall affect the burden of establishing any other element of a claim for withdrawal liability under this subtitle.

(B) Procedure.—Notwithstanding subsection (d) and §4219(c), if an employer contests the plan sponsor's determination under paragraph (1) through an arbitration proceeding pursuant to subsection (a), or through a claim brought in a court of competent jurisdiction, the employer shall not be obligated to make any withdrawal liability payments until a final decision in the arbitration proceeding, or in court, upholds the plan sponsor's determination.

(f) Procedures Applicable to Certain Disputes.—

(1) In general.—If—

(A) a plan sponsor of a plan determines that—

(i) a complete or partial withdrawal of an employer has occurred, or

(ii) an employer is liable for withdrawal liability payments with respect to such complete or partial withdrawal, and

(B) such determination is based in whole or in part on a finding by the plan sponsor under section 4212(c) that a principal purpose of any transaction which occurred after December 31, 1998, and at least 5 years (2 years in the case of a small employer) before the date of the complete or partial withdrawal was to evade or avoid withdrawal liability under this subtitle,

then the person against which the withdrawal liability is assessed based solely on the application of section 4212(c) may elect to use the special rule under paragraph (2) in applying subsection (d) of this section and section 4219(c) to such person.

(2) Special rule.—Notwithstanding subsection (d) and section 4219(c), if an electing person contests the plan sponsor's determination with respect to withdrawal liability payments under paragraph (1) through an arbitration proceeding pursuant to subsection (a), through an action brought in a court of competent jurisdiction for review of such an arbitration decision, or as otherwise permitted by law, the electing person shall not be obligated to make the withdrawal liability payments until a final decision in the arbitration proceeding, or in court, upholds the plan sponsor's determination, but only if the electing person—

(A) provides notice to the plan sponsor of its election to apply the special rule in this paragraph within 90 days after the plan sponsor notifies the electing person of its liability by reason of the application of section 4212(c); and

(B) if a final decision in the arbitration proceeding, or in court, of the withdrawal liability dispute has not been rendered within 12 months from the date of such notice, the electing person provides to the plan, effective as of the first day following the 12-month period, a bond issued by a corporate surety company that is an acceptable surety for purposes of section 412 of this Act, or an amount held in escrow by a bank or similar financial institution satisfactory to the plan, in an amount equal to the sum of the withdrawal liability payments that would otherwise be due under subsection (d) and section 4219(c) for the 12-month period beginning with the first anniversary of such notice. Such bond or escrow shall remain in effect until there is a final decision in the arbitration proceeding, or in court, of the withdrawal liability dispute, at which time such bond or escrow shall be paid to the plan if such final decision upholds the plan sponsor's determination.

(3) Definition of small employer.—For purposes of this subsection—

(A) In general.—The term "small employer" means any employer which, for the calendar year in which the transaction referred to in paragraph (1)(B) occurred and for each of the 3 preceding years, on average—

(i) employs not more than 500 employees, and

(ii) is required to make contributions to the plan for not more than 250 employees.

(B) Controlled group.—Any group treated as a single employer under subsection (b)(1) of section 4001, without regard to any transaction that was a basis for the plan's finding under section 4212, shall be treated as a single employer for purposes of this subparagraph.

(4) Additional security pending resolution of dispute.—If a withdrawal liability dispute to which this subsection applies is not concluded by 12 months after the electing person posts the bond or escrow described in paragraph (2), the electing person shall, at the start of each succeeding 12-month period, provide an additional bond or amount held in escrow equal to the sum of the withdrawal liability payments that would otherwise be payable to the plan during that period.

(5) The liability of the party furnishing a bond or escrow under this subsection shall be reduced, upon the payment of the bond or escrow to the plan, by the amount thereof.

(g) [Redesignated.]

Amendments to ERISA §4221
Worker, Retiree, and Employer Recovery Act of 2008 (Pub. L. No. 110-458), as follows:
- ERISA §4221(e) was repealed and subsecs. (f) and (g) were redesignated as subsecs. (e) and (f), respectively, by Act §105(b)(2). Eff. for plan years beginning after Dec. 31, 2007, as if included in Pub. L. No. 109-280, §502. ERISA §4221(e) prior to repeal:

(e) Furnishing of Information by Plan Sponsor to Employer Respecting Computation of Withdrawal Liability of Employer; Fees.—If any employer requests in writing that the plan sponsor make available to the employer general information necessary for the employer to compute its withdrawal liability with respect to the plan (other than information which is unique to that employer), the plan sponsor shall furnish the information to the employer without charge. If any employer requests in writing that the plan sponsor make an estimate of such employer's potential withdrawal liability with respect to the plan or to provide information unique to that employer, the plan sponsor may require the employer to pay the reasonable cost of making such estimate or providing such information.

Pension Protection Act of 2006 (Pub. L. No. 109-280), as follows:
- ERISA §4221(g) was added by Act §204(d)(1). Eff. for any person that receives a notification under ERISA §4219(b)(1) on or after Aug. 17, 2006, with respect to a transaction that occurred after Dec. 31, 1998, see Act §204(d)(2).

Pension Funding Equity Act of 2004 (Pub. L. No. 108-218), as follows:
- ERISA §4221(f) was added by Act §202(a). Eff. for any employer that receives a notification under ERISA §4219(b)(1) after Oct. 31, 2003, Act §202(b).

SEC. 4222. REIMBURSEMENTS FOR UNCOLLECTIBLE WITHDRAWAL LIABILITY.

(a) Required Supplemental Program to Reimburse for Payments Due From Employers Uncollectible as a Result of Employer Involvement in Bankruptcy Case or Proceedings; Program Participation, Premiums, etc.—By May 1, 1982, the corporation shall establish by regulation a supplemental program to reimburse multiemployer plans for withdrawal liability payments which are due from employers and which are determined to be uncollectible for reasons arising out of cases or proceedings involving the employers under title 11, United States Code, or similar cases or proceedings. Participation in the supplemental program shall be on a voluntary basis, and a plan which elects coverage under the program shall pay premiums to the corporation in accordance with a premium schedule which shall be prescribed from time to time by the corporation. The premium schedule shall contain such rates and bases for the application of such rates as the corporation considers to be appropriate.

(b) Discretionary Supplemental Program to Reimburse for Payments Due From Employers Uncollectible for Other Appropriate Reasons.—The corporation may provide under the program for reimbursement of amounts of withdrawal liability determined to be uncollectible for any other reasons the corporation considers appropriate.

(c) Payment of Cost of Program.—The cost of the program (including such administrative and legal costs as the corporation considers appropriate) may be paid only out of premiums collected under such program.

(d) Terms and Conditions, Limitations, etc., of Supplemental Program.—The supplemental program may be offered to eligible plans on such terms and conditions, and with such limitations with respect to the payment of reimbursements (including the exclusion of de minimis amounts of uncollectible employer liability, and the reduction or elimination of reimbursements which cannot be paid from collected premiums) and such restrictions on withdrawal from the program, as the corporation considers necessary and appropriate.

(e) Arrangements by Corporation with Private Insurers for Implementation of Program; Election of Coverage by Participating Plans With Private Insurers.—The corporation may enter into arrangements with private insurers to carry out in whole or in part the program authorized by this section and may require plans which elect coverage under the program to elect coverage by those private insurers.

SEC. 4223. WITHDRAWAL LIABILITY PAYMENT FUND.

(a) Establishment of or Participation in Fund by Plan Sponsors.—The plan sponsors of multiemployer plans may establish or participate in a withdrawal liability payment fund.

(b) Definitions.—For purposes of this section, the term "withdrawal liability payment fund", and the term "fund", mean a trust which—

(1) is established and maintained under section 501(c)(22) of title 26,

(2) maintains agreements which cover a substantial portion of the participants who are in multiemployer plans which (under the rules of the trust instrument) are eligible to participate in the fund,

(3) is funded by amounts paid by the plans which participate in the fund, and

(4) is administered by a Board of Trustees, and in the administration of the fund there is equal representation of—

(A) trustees representing employers who are obligated to contribute to the plans participating in the fund, and

(B) trustees representing employees who are participants in plans which participate in the fund.

(c) Payments to Plan; Amount; Criteria, etc.—

(1) If an employer withdraws from a plan which participates in a withdrawal liability payment fund, then, to the extent provided in the trust, the fund shall pay to that plan—

(A) the employer's unattributable liability,

(B) the employer's withdrawal liability payments which would have been due but for section 4208, 4209, 4219, or 4225,

(C) the employer's withdrawal liability payments to the extent they are uncollectible.

(2) The fund may provide for the payment of the employer's attributable liability if the fund—

(A) provides for the payment of both the attributable and the unattributable liability of the employer in a single payment, and

(B) is subrogated to all rights of the plan against the employer.

(3) For purposes of this section, the term—

(A) "attributable liability" means the excess, if any, determined under the provisions of a plan not inconsistent with regulations of the corporation, of—

(i) the value of vested benefits accrued as a result of service with the employer, over

(ii) the value of plan assets attributed to the employer, and

(B) "unattributable liability" means the excess of withdrawal liability over attributable liability.

Such terms may be further defined, and the manner in which they shall be applied may be prescribed, by the corporation by regulation.

(4)(A) The trust of a fund shall be maintained for the exclusive purpose of paying—

(i) any amount described in paragraph (1) and paragraph (2), and

(ii) reasonable and necessary administrative expenses in connection with the establishment and operation of the trust and the processing of claims against the fund.

(B) The amounts paid by a plan to a fund shall be deemed a reasonable expense of administering the plan under sections 403(c)(1) and 404(a)(1)(A)(ii), and the payments made by a fund to a participating plan shall be deemed services necessary for the operation of the plan within the meaning of section 408(b)(2) or within the meaning of section 4975(d)(2) of title 26.

(d) Application of Payments by Plan.—

(1) For purposes of this part—

(A) only amounts paid by the fund to a plan under subsection (c)(1)(A) shall be credited to withdrawal liability otherwise payable by the employer, unless the plan otherwise provides, and

(B) any amounts paid by the fund under subsection (c) to a plan shall be treated by the plan as a payment of withdrawal liability to such plan.

(2) For purposes of applying provisions relating to the funding standard accounts (and minimum contribution requirements), amounts paid from the plan to the fund shall be applied to reduce the amount treated as contributed to the plan.

(e) Subrogation of Fund to Rights of Plan.—The fund shall be subrogated to the rights of the plan against the employer that has withdrawn from the plan for amounts paid by a fund to a plan under—

(1) subsection (c)(1)(A), to the extent not credited under subsection (d)(1)(A), and

(2) subsection (c)(1)(C).

(f) Discharge of Rights of Fiduciary of Fund; Standards Applicable, etc.—Notwithstanding any other provision of this Act, a fiduciary of the fund shall discharge the fiduciary's duties with respect to the fund in accordance with the standards for fiduciaries prescribed by this Act (to the extent not inconsistent with the purposes of this section), and in accordance with the documents and instruments governing the fund insofar as such documents and instruments are consistent with the provisions of this Act (to the extent not inconsistent with the purposes of this section). The provisions of the preceding sentence shall supersede any and all State laws relating to fiduciaries insofar as they may now or hereafter relate to a fund to which this section applies.

(g) Prohibition on Payments From Fund to Plan Where Certain Labor Negotiations Involve Employer Withdrawn or Partially Withdrawn From Plan and Continuity of Labor Organization Representing Employees Continues.—No payments shall be made from a fund to a plan on the occasion of a withdrawal or partial withdrawal of an employer from such plan if the employees representing the withdrawn contribution base units continue, after such withdrawal, to be represented under section 9 of the National Labor Relations Act (or other applicable labor laws) in negotiations with such employer by the labor organization which represented such employees immediately preceding such withdrawal.

(h) Purchase of Insurance by Employer.—Nothing in this section shall be construed to prohibit the purchase of insurance by an employer from any other person, to limit the circumstances under which such insurance would be payable, or to limit in any way the terms and conditions of such insurance.

(i) Promulgation of Regulations for Establishment and Maintenance of Fund.—The corporation may provide by regulation rules not inconsistent with this section governing the establishment and maintenance of funds, but only to the extent necessary to carry out the purposes of this part (other than section 4222).

Amendments to ERISA §4223

Omnibus Budget Reconciliation Act of 1989 (Pub. L. No. 101-239), as follows:

• ERISA §4223(b)(1), (c)(4)(B) were amended by Act §7891(a)(1) by substituting "Internal Revenue Code of 1986" for "Internal Revenue Code of 1954", which for purposes of codification was translated as "title 26". Eff., except as otherwise provided, as if included in the provision of Pub. L. No. 99-514, to which it relates, see Act §7891(f).

SEC. 4224. ALTERNATIVE METHOD OF WITHDRAWAL LIABILITY PAYMENTS.

A multiemployer plan may adopt rules providing for other terms and conditions for the satisfaction of an employer's withdrawal liability if such rules are consistent with this Act and with such regulations as may be prescribed by the corporation.

SEC. 4225. LIMITATION ON WITHDRAWAL LIABILITY.

(a) Unfunded Vested Benefits Allocable to Employer in Bona Fide Sale of Assets of Employer in Arms-Length Transaction to Unrelated Party; Maximum Amount; Determinative Factors.—

(1) In the case of bona fide sale of all or substantially all of the employer's assets in an arm's-length transaction to an unrelated party (within the meaning of section 4204(d)), the unfunded vested benefits allocable to an employer (after the application of all sections of this part having a lower number designation than this section), other than an employer undergoing reorganization under title 11, United States Code, or similar provisions of State law, shall not exceed the greater of—

(A) a portion (determined under paragraph (2)) of the liquidation or dissolution value of the employer (determined after the sale or exchange of such assets), or

(B) in the case of a plan using the attributable method of allocating withdrawal liability, the unfunded vested benefits attributable to employees of the employer.

(2) For purposes of paragraph (1), the portion shall be determined in accordance with the following table:

If the liquidation or distribution value of the employer after the sale or exchange is—	The portion is—
Not more than $5,000,000	30 percent of the amount
More than $5,000,000, but not more than $10,000,000	$1,500,000, plus 35 percent of the amount in excess of $5,000,000
More than $10,000,000, but not more than $15,000,000	$3,250,000, plus 40 percent of the amount in excess of $10,000,000

If the liquidation or distribution value of the employer after the sale or exchange is—	The portion is—
More than $15,000,000, but not more than $17,500,000	$5,250,000, plus 45 percent of the amount in excess of $15,000,000
More than $17,500,000, but not more than $20,000,000	$6,375,000, plus 50 percent of the amount in excess of $17,500,000
More than $20,000,000, but not more than $22,500,000	$7,625,000, plus 60 percent of the amount in excess of $20,000,000
More than $22,500,000, but not more than $25,000,000	$9,125,000, plus 70 percent of the amount in excess of $22,500,000
More than $25,000,000	$10,875,000, plus 80 percent of the amount in excess of $25,000,000

(b) Unfunded Vested Benefits Allocable to Insolvent Employer Undergoing Liquidations or Dissolution; Maximum Amount; Determinative Factors.—In the case of an insolvent employer undergoing liquidation or dissolution, the unfunded vested benefits allocable to that employer shall not exceed an amount equal to the sum of—

(1) 50 percent of the unfunded vested benefits allocable to the employer (determined without regard to this section), and

(2) that portion of 50 percent of the unfunded vested benefits allocable to the employer (as determined under paragraph (1)) which does not exceed the liquidation or dissolution value of the employer determined—

(A) as of the commencement of liquidation or dissolution, and

(B) after reducing the liquidation or dissolution value of the employer by the amount determined under paragraph (1).

(c) Property Not Subject to Enforcement of Liability; Precondition.—To the extent that the withdrawal liability of an employer is attributable to his obligation to contribute to or under a plan as an individual (whether as a sole proprietor or as a member of a partnership), property which may be exempt from the estate under section 522 of title 11, United States Code, or under similar provisions of law, shall not be subject to enforcement of such liability.

(d) Insolvency of Employer; Liquidation or Dissolution Value of Employer.—For purposes of this section—

(1) an employer is insolvent if the liabilities of the employer, including withdrawal liability under the plan (determined without regard to subsection (b)),

exceed the assets of the employer (determined as of the commencement of the liquidation or dissolution), and

(2) the liquidation or dissolution value of the employer shall be determined without regard to such withdrawal liability.

(e) One or More Withdrawals of Employer Attributable to Same Sale, Liquidation, or Dissolution.—In the case of one or more withdrawals of an employer attributable to the same sale, liquidation, or dissolution, under regulations prescribed by the corporation—

(1) all such withdrawals shall be treated as a single withdrawal for the purpose of applying this section, and

(2) the withdrawal liability of the employer to each plan shall be an amount which bears the same ratio to the present value of the withdrawal liability payments to all plans (after the application of the preceding provisions of this section) as the withdrawal liability of the employer to such plan (determined without regard to this section) bears to the withdrawal liability of the employer to all such plans (determined without regard to this section).

Amendments to ERISA §4225

Pension Protection Act of 2006 (Pub. L. No. 109-280), as follows:

- ERISA §4225(a)(1)(B) was amended by Act §204(a)(2) by substituting "in the case of a plan using the attributable method of allocating withdrawal liability, the unfunded vested benefits attributable to employees of the employer." for "the unfunded vested benefits attributable to employees of the employer." Eff. for sales occurring on or after Jan. 1, 2007, see Act §204(a)(3).
- ERISA §4225(a)(2) was amended by Act §204(a)(1). Eff. for sales occurring on or after Jan. 1, 2007, see Act §204(a)(3). ERISA §4225(a)(2) prior to amendment:

  (2) For purposes of paragraph (1), the portion shall be determined in accordance with the following table:

If the liquidation or distribution value of the employer after the sale or exchange is—	The portion is—
Not more than 2,000,000	30 percent of the amount
More than $2,000,000, but not more than $4,000,000	$600,000, plus 35 percent of the amount in excess of $2,000,000
More than $4,000,000, but not more than $6,000,000	$1,300,000, plus 40 percent of the amount in excess of $4,000,000
More than $6,000,000, but not more than $7,000,000	$2,100,000, plus 45 percent of the amount in excess of $6,000,000
More than $7,000,000, but not more than $8,000,000	$2,550,000, plus 50 percent of the amount in excess of $7,000,000

ERISA Sec. 4225(e)(2)

If the liquidation or distribution value of the employer after the sale or exchange is—	The portion is—
More than $8,000,000, but not more than $9,000,000	$3,050,000, plus 60 percent of the amount in excess of $8,000,000
More than $9,000,000, but not more than $10,000,000	3,650,000, plus 70 percent of the amount in excess of $9,000,000
More than $10,000,000	$4,350,000, plus 80 percent of the amount in excess of $10,000,000

Part 2—Merger or Transfer of Plan Assets or Liabilities

SEC. 4231. MERGERS AND TRANSFERS BETWEEN MULTIEMPLOYER PLANS.

(a) Authority of Plan Sponsor.—Unless otherwise provided in regulations prescribed by the corporation, a plan sponsor may not cause a multiemployer plan to merge with one or more multiemployer plans, or engage in a transfer of assets and liabilities to or from another multiemployer plan, unless such merger or transfer satisfies the requirements of subsection (b).

(b) Criteria.—A merger or transfer satisfies the requirements of this section if—

(1) in accordance with regulations of the corporation, the plan sponsor of a multiemployer plan notifies the corporation of a merger with or transfer of plan assets or liabilities to another multiemployer plan at least 120 days before the effective date of the merger or transfer;

(2) no participant's or beneficiary's accrued benefit will be lower immediately after the effective date of the merger or transfer than the benefit immediately before that date;

(3) the benefits of participants and beneficiaries are not reasonably expected to be subject to suspension under section 4245; and

(4) an actuarial valuation of the assets and liabilities of each of the affected plans has been performed during the plan year preceding the effective date of the merger or transfer, based upon the most recent data available as of the day before the start of that plan year, or other valuation of such assets and liabilities performed under such standards and procedures as the corporation may prescribe by regulation.

(c) Actions Not Deemed Violations of Section 406(a) or (b)(2).—The merger of multiemployer plans or the transfer of assets or liabilities between multiemployer plans, shall be deemed not to consti-

tute a violation of the provisions of section 406(a) or section 406(b)(2) if the corporation determines that the merger or transfer otherwise satisfies the requirements of this section.

(d) Nature of Plan to Which Liabilities Are Transferred.—A plan to which liabilities are transferred under this section is a successor plan for purposes of section 4022A(b)(2)(B).

SEC. 4232. TRANSFERS BETWEEN A MULTIEMPLOYER PLAN AND A SINGLE-EMPLOYER PLAN.

(a) General Authority.—A transfer of assets or liabilities between, or a merger of, a multiemployer plan and a single-employer plan shall satisfy the requirements of this section.

(b) Accrued Benefit of Participant or Beneficiary Not Lower Immediately After Effective Date of Transfer or Merger.—No accrued benefit of a participant or beneficiary may be lower immediately after the effective date of a transfer or merger described in subsection (a) than the benefit immediately before that date.

(c) Liability of Multiemployer Plan to Corporation Where Single-Employer Plan Terminates Within 60 Months After Effective Date of Transfer; Amount of Liability; Exemption, etc.—

(1) Except as provided in paragraphs (2) and (3), a multiemployer plan which transfers liabilities to a single-employer plan shall be liable to the corporation if the single-employer plan terminates within 60 months after the effective date of the transfer. The amount of liability shall be the lesser of—

(A) the amount of the plan asset insufficiency of the terminated single-employer plan, less 30 percent of the net worth of the employer who maintained the single-employer plan, determined in accordance with section 4062 or 4064, or

(B) the value, on the effective date of the transfer, of the unfunded benefits transferred to the single-employer plan which are guaranteed under section 4022.

(2) A multiemployer plan shall be liable to the corporation as provided in paragraph (1) unless, within 180 days after the corporation receives an application (together with such information as the corporation may reasonably require for purposes of such application) from the multiemployer plan sponsor for a determination under this paragraph—

(A) the corporation determines that the interests of the plan participants and beneficiaries and of the corporation are adequately protected, or

(B) fails to make any determination regarding the adequacy with which such interests are protected with respect to such transfer of liabilities.

If, after the receipt of such application, the corporation requests from the plan sponsor additional information necessary for the determination, the running of the 180-day period shall be suspended from the date of such request until the receipt by the corporation of the additional information requested. The corporation may by regulation prescribe procedures and standards for the issuance of determinations under this paragraph. This paragraph shall not apply to any application submitted less than 180 days after the date of enactment of the Multiemployer Pension Plan Amendments Act of 1980.

(3) A multiemployer plan shall not be liable to the corporation as provided in paragraph (1) in the case of a transfer from the multiemployer plan to a single-employer plan of liabilities which accrued under a single-employer plan which merged with the multiemployer plan, if, the value of liabilities transferred to the single-employer plan does not exceed the value of the liabilities for benefits which accrued before the merger, and the value of the assets transferred to the single-employer plan is substantially equal to the value of the assets which would have been in the single-employer plan if the employer had maintained and funded it as a separate plan under which no benefits accrued after the date of the merger.

(4) The corporation may make equitable arrangements with multiemployer plans which are liable under this subsection forsatisfaction of their liability.

(d) Guarantee of Benefits Under Single-Employer Plan.—Benefits under a single-employer plan to which liabilities are transferred in accordance with this section are guaranteed under section 4022 to the extent provided in that section as of the effective date of the transfer and the plan is a successor plan.

(e) Transfer of Liabilities by Multiemployer Plan to Single-Employer Plan.—

(1) Except as provided in paragraph (2), a multiemployer plan may not transfer liabilities to a single-employer plan unless the plan sponsor of the plan to which the liabilities would be transferred agrees to the transfer.

(2) In the case of a transfer described in subsection (c)(3), paragraph (1) of this subsection is satisfied by the advance agreement to the transfer by the employer who will be obligated to contribute to the single-employer plan.

(f) Additional Requirements by Corporation for Protection of Interest of Plan Participants, Beneficiaries and Corporation; Approval by Corporation of Transfer of Assets or Liabilities to Single-Employer Plan From Plan in Reorganization; Covered Transfers in Connection With Termination.—

(1) The corporation may prescribe by regulation such additional requirements with respect to the transfer of assets or liabilities as may be necessary to protect the interests of plan participants and beneficiaries and the corporation.

(2) Except as otherwise determined by the corporation, a transfer of assets or liabilities to a single-employer plan from a plan in reorganization under section 4241 is not effective unless the corporation approves such transfer.

(3) No transfer to which this section applies, in connection with a termination described in section 4041A(a)(2) shall be effective unless the transfer meets such requirements as may be established by the corporation to prevent an increase in the risk of loss to thecorporation.

SEC. 4233. PARTITION.

(a) Authority of Corporation.—The corporation may order the partition of a multiemployer plan in accordance with this section.

(b) Authority of Plan Sponsor Upon Application to Corporation for Partition Order; Procedures Applicable to Corporation.—A plan sponsor may apply to the corporation for an order partitioning a plan. The corporation may not order the partition of a plan except upon notice to the plan sponsor and the participants and beneficiaries whose vested benefits will be affected by the partition of the plan, and upon finding that—

(1) a substantial reduction in the amount of aggregate contributions under the plan has resulted or will result from a case or proceeding under title 11, United States Code, with respect to an employer;

(2) the plan is likely to become insolvent;

(3) contributions will have to be increased significantly in reorganization to meet the minimum contribution requirement and prevent insolvency; and

(4) partition would significantly reduce the likelihood that the plan will become insolvent.

(c) Authority of Corporation Notwithstanding Pendency of Partition Proceeding.—The corporation may order the partition of a plan notwithstanding the pendency of a proceeding described in subsection (b)(1).

(d) Scope of Partition Order.—The corporation's partition order shall provide for a transfer of no more than the nonforfeitable benefits directly attributable to service with the employer referred to in subsection (b)(1) and an equitable share of assets.

(e) Nature of Plan Created by Partition.—The plan created by the partition is—

(1) a successor plan to which section 4022A applies, and

(2) a terminated multiemployer plan to which section 4041A(d) applies, with respect to which only the employer described in subsection (b)(1) has withdrawal liability, and to which section 4068 applies.

(f) Authority of Corporation to Obtain Decree Partitioning Plan and Appointing Trustee for Ter-

ERISA Sec. 4233(f)

minated Portion of Partitioned Plans.—The corporation may proceed under section 4042(c) through (h) for a decree partitioning a plan and appointing a trustee for the terminated portion of a partitioned plan. The court may order the partition of a plan upon making the findings described in subsection (b)(1) through (4), and subject to the conditions set forth in subsections (c) through (e).

SEC. 4234. ASSET TRANSFER RULES.

(a) Applicability and Scope.—A transfer of assets from a multiemployer plan to another plan shall comply with asset-transfer rules which shall be adopted by the multiemployer plan and which—

(1) do not unreasonably restrict the transfer of plan assets in connection with the transfer of plan liabilities, and

(2) operate and are applied uniformly with respect to each proposed transfer, except that the rules may provide for reasonable variations taking into account the potential financial impact of a proposed transfer on the multiemployer plan.

Plan rules authorizing asset transfers consistent with the requirements of section 4232(c)(3) shall be considered to satisfy the requirements of this subsection.

(b) Exemption of De Minimis Transfers.—The corporation shall prescribe regulations which exempt de minimis transfers of assets from the requirements of this part.

(c) Written Reciprocity Agreements.—This part shall not apply to transfers of assets pursuant to written reciprocity agreements, except to the extent provided in regulations prescribed by the corporation.

SEC. 4235. TRANSFERS PURSUANT TO CHANGE IN BARGAINING REPRESENTATIVE.

(a) Authority to Transfer From Old Plan to New Plan Pursuant to Employee Participation in Another Multiemployer Plan After Certified Change of Representative.—In any case in which an employer has completely or partially withdrawn from a multiemployer plan (hereafter in this section referred to as the "old plan") as a result of a certified change of collective bargaining representative occurring after September 25, 1980, if participants of the old plan who are employed by the employer will, as a result of that change, participate in another multiemployer plan (hereafter in this section referred to as the "new plan"), the old plan shall transfer assets and liabilities to the new plan in accordance with this section.

(b) Notification by Employer of Plan Sponsor of Old Plan; Notification by Plan Sponsor of Old Plan of Employer and Plan Sponsor of New Plan; Appeal by Plan to Prevent Transfer; Further Proceedings.—

(1) The employer shall notify the plan sponsor of the old plan of a change in multiemployer plan par-

ticipation described in subsection (a) no later than 30 days after the employer determines that the change will occur.

(2) The plan sponsor of the old plan shall—

(A) notify the employer of—

(i) the amount of the employer's withdrawal liability determined under part 1 with respect to the withdrawal,

(ii) the old plan's intent to transfer to the new plan the nonforfeitable benefits of the employees who are no longer working in covered service under the old plan as a result of the change of bargaining representative, and

(iii) the amount of assets and liabilities which are to be transferred to the new plan, and

(B) notify the plan sponsor of the new plan of the benefits, assets, and liabilities which will be transferred to the new plan.

(3) Within 60 days after receipt of the notice described in paragraph (2)(B), the new plan may file an appeal with the corporation to prevent the transfer. The transfer shall not be made if the corporation determines that the new plan would suffer substantial financial harm as a result of the transfer. Upon notification described in paragraph (2), if—

(A) the employer fails to object to the transfer within 60 days after receipt of the notice described in paragraph (2)(A), or

(B) the new plan either—

(i) fails to file such an appeal, or

(ii) the corporation, pursuant to such an appeal, fails to find that the new plan would suffer substantial financial harm as a result of the transfer described in the notice under paragraph (2)(B) within 180 days after the date on which the appeal is filed,

then the plan sponsor of the old plan shall transfer the appropriate amount of assets and liabilities to the new plan.

(c) Reduction of Amount of Withdrawal Liability of Employer Upon Transfer of Appropriate Amount of Assets and Liabilities by Plan Sponsor of Old Plan to New Plan.—If the plan sponsor of the old plan transfers the appropriate amount of assets and liabilities under this section to the new plan, then the amount of the employer's withdrawal liability (as determined under section 4201(b) without regard to such transfer and this section) with respect to the old plan shall be reduced by the amount by which—

(1) the value of the unfunded vested benefits allocable to the employer which were transferred by the plan sponsor of the old plan to the new plan, exceeds

(2) the value of the assets transferred.

(d) Escrow Payments by Employer Upon Complete or Partial Withdrawal and Prior to Trans-

fer.—In any case in which there is a complete or partial withdrawal described in subsection (a), if—

(1) the new plan files an appeal with the corporation under subsection (b)(3), and

(2) the employer is required by section 4219 to begin making payments of withdrawal liability before the earlier of—

(A) the date on which the corporation finds that the new plan would not suffer substantial financial harm as a result of the transfer, or

(B) the last day of the 180-day period beginning on the date on which the new plan files its appeal,

then the employer shall make such payments into an escrow held by a bank or similar financial institution satisfactory to the old plan. If the transfer is made, the amounts paid into the escrow shall be returned to the employer. If the transfer is not made, the amounts paid into the escrow shall be paid to the old plan and credited against the employer's withdrawal liability.

(e) Prohibition on Transfer of Assets to New Plan by Plan Sponsor of Old Plan; Exemptions.—

(1) Notwithstanding subsection (b), the plan sponsor shall not transfer any assets to the new plan if—

(A) the old plan is in reorganization (within the meaning of section 4241(a)), or

(B) the transfer of assets would cause the old plan to go into reorganization (within the meaning of section 4241(a)).

(2) In any case in which a transfer of assets from the old plan to the new plan is prohibited by paragraph (1), the plan sponsor of the old plan shall transfer—

(A) all nonforfeitable benefits described in subsection (b)(2), if the value of such benefits does not exceed the withdrawal liability of the employer with respect to such withdrawal, or

(B) such nonforfeitable benefits having a value equal to the withdrawal liability of the employer, if the value of such benefits exceeds the withdrawal liability of the employer.

(f) Agreement Between Plan Sponsors of Old Plan and New Plan to Transfer in Compliance With Other Statutory Provisions; Reduction of Withdrawal Liability of Employer From Old Plan; Amount of Withdrawal Liability of Employer to New Plan.—

(1) Notwithstanding subsections (b) and (e), the plan sponsors of the old plan and the new plan may agree to a transfer of assets and liabilities that complies with sections 4231 and 4234, rather than this section, except that the employer's liability with respect to the withdrawal from the old plan shall be reduced under subsection (c) as if assets and liabilities had been transferred in accordance with this section.

(2) If the employer withdraws from the new plan within 240 months after the effective date of a transfer of assets and liabilities described in this section, the amount of the employer's withdrawal liability to the new plan shall be the greater of—

(A) the employer's withdrawal liability determined under part 1 with respect to the new plan, or

(B) the amount by which the employer's withdrawal liability to the old plan was reduced under subsection (c), reduced by 5 percent for each 12-month period following the effective date of the transfer and ending before the date of the withdrawal from the new plan.

(g) Definitions.—For purposes of this section—

(1) "appropriate amount of assets" means the amount by which the value of the nonforfeitable benefits to be transferred exceeds the amount of the employer's withdrawal liability to the old plan (determined under part 1 without regard to section 4211(e)), and

(2) "certified change of collective bargaining representative" means a change of collective bargaining representative certified under the Labor-Management Relations Act, 1947, or the Railway Labor Act.

Amendments to ERISA §4235

Deficit Reduction Act of 1984 (Pub. L. No. 98-369), as follows:
● ERISA §4235(a) was amended by Act §558(b)(1)(A) by substituting "September 25, 1980" for "April 28, 1980".

Part 3—Reorganization; Minimum Contribution Requirement for Multiemployer Plans

SEC. 4241. REORGANIZATION STATUS.

(a) Reorganization Index of Plan for Plan Year Greater Than Zero.—A multiemployer plan is in reorganization for a plan year if the plan's reorganization index for that year is greater than zero.

(b) Determination of Reorganization Index of Plan Year; Applicable Factors, Definitions, etc.—

(1) A plan's reorganization index for any plan year is the excess of—

(A) the vested benefits charge for such year, over

(B) the net charge to the funding standard account for such year.

(2) For purposes of this part, the net charge to the funding standard account for any plan year is the excess (if any) of—

(A) the charges to the funding standard account for such year under section 412(b)(2) of title 26, over

(B) the credits to the funding standard account under Section 412(b)(3)(B) of title 26.

(3) For purposes of this part, the vested benefits charge for any plan year is the amount which would be necessary to amortize the plan's unfunded vested benefits as of the end of the base plan year in equal annual installments—

(A) over 10 years, to the extent such benefits are attributable to persons in pay status, and

(B) over 25 years, to the extent such benefits are attributable to other participants.

(4)(A) The vested benefits charge for a plan year shall be based on an actuarial valuation of the plan as of the end of the base plan year, adjusted to reflect—

(i) any—

(I) decrease of 5 percent or more in the value of plan assets, or increase of 5 percent or more in the number of persons in pay status, during the period beginning on the first day of the plan year following the base plan year and ending on the adjustment date, or

(II) at the election of the plan sponsor, actuarial valuation of the plan as of the adjustment date or any later date not later than the last day of the plan year for which the determination is being made,

(ii) any change in benefits under the plan which is not otherwise taken into account under this subparagraph and which is pursuant to any amendment—

(I) adopted before the end of the plan year for which the determination is being made, and

(II) effective after the end of the base plan year and on or before the end of the plan year referred to in subclause (I), and

(iii) any other event (including an event described in subparagraph (B)(i)(I)) which, as determined in accordance with regulations prescribed by the Secretary, would substantially increase the plan's vested benefit charge.

(B)(i) In determining the vested benefits charge for a plan year following a plan year in which the plan was not in reorganization, any change in benefits which—

(I) results from the changing of a group of participants from one benefit level to another benefit level under a schedule of plan benefits as a result of changes in a collective bargaining agreement, or

(II) results from any other change in a collective bargaining agreement,

shall not be taken into account except to the extent provided in regulations prescribed by the Secretary of the Treasury.

(ii) Except as otherwise determined by the Secretary of the Treasury, in determining the vested benefits charge for any plan year following any plan year in which the plan was in reorganization, any change in benefits—

(I) described in clause (i)(I), or

(II) described in clause (i)(II) as determined under regulations prescribed by the Secretary of the Treasury,

shall, for purposes of subparagraph (A)(ii), be treated as a change in benefits pursuant to an amendment to a plan.

(5)(A) For purposes of this part, the base plan year for any plan year is—

(i) if there is a relevant collective bargaining agreement, the last plan year ending at least 6 months before the relevant effective date, or

(ii) if there is no relevant collective bargaining agreement, the last plan year ending at least 12 months before the beginning of the plan year.

(B) For purposes of this part, a relevant collective bargaining agreement is a collective bargaining agreement—

(i) which is in effect for at least 6 months during the plan year, and

(ii) which has not been in effect for more than 36 months as of the end of the plan year.

(C) For purposes of this part, the relevant effective date is the earliest of the effective dates for the relevant collective bargaining agreements.

(D) For purposes of this part, the adjustment date is the date which is—

(i) 90 days before the relevant effective date, or

(ii) if there is no relevant effective date, 90 days before the beginning of the plan year.

(6) For purposes of this part, the term "person in pay status" means—

(A) a participant or beneficiary on the last day of the base plan year who, at any time during such year, was paid an early, late, normal, or disability retirement benefit (or a death benefit related to a retirement benefit), and

(B) to the extent provided in regulations prescribed by the Secretary of the Treasury, any other person who is entitled to such a benefit under the plan.

(7) For purposes of paragraph (3)—

(A) in determining the plan's unfunded vested benefits, plan assets shall first be allocated to the vested benefits attributable to persons in pay status, and

(B) the vested benefits charge shall be determined without regard to reductions in accrued benefits under section 4244A which are first effective in the plan year.

(8) For purposes of this part, any outstanding claim for withdrawal liability shall not be considered a plan asset, except as otherwise provided in regulations prescribed by the Secretary of the Treasury.

(9) For purposes of this part, the term "unfunded vested benefits" means with respect to a plan, an amount (determined in accordance with regulations prescribed by the Secretary of the Treasury) equal to—

(A) the value of nonforfeitable benefits under the plan, less

(B) the value of assets of the plan.

(c) Payment of Benefits to Participants.—Except as provided in regulations prescribed by the corporation, while a plan is in reorganization a benefit with respect to a participant (other than a death benefit) which is attributable to employer contributions and which has a value of more than $1,750 may not be paid in a form other than an annuity which (by itself or in combination with social security, railroad retirement, or workers' compensation benefits) provides substantially level payments over the life of the participant.

(d) Terminated Multiemployer Plans.—Any multiemployer plan which terminates under section 4041A(a)(2) shall not be considered in reorganization after the last day of the plan year in which the plan is treated as having terminated.

Amendments to ERISA §4241
Omnibus Budget Reconciliation Act of 1989 (Pub. L. No. 101-239), as follows:

• ERISA §4241(b)(2)(A) was amended by Act §7891(a)(1) by substituting "Internal Revenue Code of 1986" for "Internal Revenue Code of 1954", which for purposes of codification was translated as "title 26". Eff., except as otherwise provided, as if included in the provision of Pub. L. No. 99-514, to which it relates, see Act §7891(f).

SEC. 4242. NOTICE OF REORGANIZATION AND FUNDING REQUIREMENTS.

(a)(1) If—

(A) a multiemployer plan is in reorganization for a plan year, and

(B) section 4243 would require an increase in contributions for such plan year, the plan sponsor shall notify the persons described in paragraph (2) that the plan is in reorganization and that, if contributions to the plan are not increased, accrued benefits under the plan may be reduced or an excise tax may be imposed (or both such reduction and imposition may occur).

(2) The persons described in this paragraph are—

(A) each employer who has an obligation to contribute under the plan (within the meaning of section 4201(h)(5)), and

(B) each employee organization which, for purposes of collective bargaining, represents plan participants employed by such an employer.

(3) The determination under paragraph (1)(B) shall be made without regard to the overburden credit provided by section 4244.

(b) The corporation may prescribe additional or alternative requirements for assuring, in the case of a plan with respect to which notice is required by subsection (a)(1), that the persons described in subsection (a)(2)—

(1) receive appropriate notice that the plan is in reorganization,

(2) are adequately informed of the implications of reorganization status, and

(3) have reasonable access to information relevant to the plan's reorganization status.

SEC. 4243. MINIMUM CONTRIBUTION REQUIREMENT.

(a) Maintenance of Funding Standard Account; Amount of Accumulated Funding Deficiency.—

(1) For any plan year for which a plan is in reorganization—

(A) the plan shall continue to maintain its funding standard account while it is in reorganization, and

(B) the plan's accumulated funding deficiency under section 304(a) for such plan year shall be equal to the excess (if any) of—

(i) the sum of the minimum contribution requirement for such plan year (taking into account any overburden credit under section 4244(a)) plus the plan's accumulated funding deficiency for the preceding plan year (determined under this section if the plan was in reorganization during such year or under §304(a) if the plan was not in reorganization), over

(ii) amounts considered contributed by employers to or under the plan for the plan year (increased by any amount waived under subsection (f) for the plan year).

(2) For purposes of paragraph (1), withdrawal liability payments (whether or not received) which are due with respect to withdrawals before the end of the base plan year shall be considered amounts contributed by the employer to or under the plan if, as of the adjustment date, it was reasonable for the plan sponsor to anticipate that such payments would be made during the plan year.

(b) Determination of Amount; Applicable Factors.—

(1) Except as otherwise provided in this section, for purposes of this part the minimum contribution requirement for a plan year in which a plan is in reorganization is an amount equal to the excess of—

(A) the sum of—

(i) the plan's vested benefits charge for the plan year, and

(ii) the increase in normal cost for the plan year determined under the entry age normal funding method which is attributable to plan amendments adopted while the plan was in reorganization, over

(B) the amount of the overburden credit (if any) determined under section 4244 for the plan year.

(2) If the plan's current contribution base for the plan year is less than the plan's valuation contribution base for the plan year, the minimum contribution requirement for such plan year shall be equal to the product of the amount determined under paragraph (1) (after any adjustment required by this part other than this paragraph) and a fraction—

(A) the numerator of which is the plan's current contribution base for the plan year, and

(B) the denominator of which is the plan's valuation contribution base for the plan year.

(3)(A) If the vested benefits charge for a plan year of a plan in reorganization is less than the plan's cash-flow amount for the plan year, the plan's minimum contribution requirement for the plan year is the amount determined under paragraph (1) (determined before the application of paragraph (2)) after substituting the term "cash-flow amount" for the term "vested benefits charge" in paragraph (1)(A).

(B) For purposes of subparagraph (A), a plan's cash-flow amount for a plan year is an amount equal to—

(i) the amount of the benefits payable under the plan for the base plan year, plus the amount of the plan's administrative expenses for the base plan year, reduced by

(ii) the value of the available plan assets for the base plan year determined under regulations prescribed by the Secretary of the Treasury,

adjusted in a manner consistent with section 4241(b)(4).

(c) Current Contributions Base; Valuation Contribution Base.—

(1) For purposes of this part, a plan's current contribution base for a plan year is the number of contribution base units with respect to which contributions are required to be made under the plan for that plan year, determined in accordance with regulations prescribed by the Secretary of the Treasury.

(2)(A) Except as provided in subparagraph (B), for purposes of this part a plan's valuation contribu-

tion base is the number of contribution base units for which contributions were received for the base plan year—

(i) adjusted to reflect declines in the contribution base which have occurred (or could reasonably be anticipated) as of the adjustment date for the plan year referred to in paragraph (1),

(ii) adjusted upward (in accordance with regulations prescribed by the Secretary of the Treasury) for any contribution base reduction in the base plan year caused by a strike or lockout or by unusual events, such as fire, earthquake, or severe weather conditions, and

(iii) adjusted (in accordance with regulations prescribed by the Secretary of the Treasury) for reductions in the contribution base resulting from transfers of liabilities.

(B) For any plan year—

(i) in which the plan is insolvent (within the meaning of section 4245(b)(1), and

(ii) beginning with the first plan year beginning after the expiration of all relevant collective bargaining agreements which were in effect in the plan year in which the plan became insolvent,

the plan's valuation contribution base is the greater of the number of contribution base units for which contributions were received for the first or second plan year preceding the first plan year in which the plan is insolvent, adjusted as provided in clause (ii) or (iii) of subparagraph (A).

(d) Maximum Amount; Amount of Funding Standard Requirement; Applicability to Plan Amendments Increasing Benefits.—

(1) Under regulations prescribed by the Secretary of the Treasury, the minimum contribution requirement applicable to any plan for any plan year which is determined under subsection (b) (without regard to subsection (b)(2)) shall not exceed an amount which is equal to the sum of—

(A) the greater of—

(i) the funding standard requirement for such plan year, or

(ii) 107 percent of—

(I) if the plan was not in reorganization in the preceding plan year, the funding standard requirement for such preceding plan year, or

(II) if the plan was in reorganization in the preceding plan year, the sum of the amount determined under this subparagraph for the preceding plan year and the amount (if any) determined under subparagraph (B) for the preceding plan year, plus

(B) if for the plan year a change in benefits is first required to be considered in computing the charges under section 412(b)(2)(A) or (B) of title 26, the sum of—

(i) the increase in normal cost for a plan year determined under the entry age normal funding method due to increases in benefits described in section 4241(b)(4)(A)(ii) (determined without regard to section 4241(b)(4)(B)(i)), and

(ii) the amount necessary to amortize in equal annual installments the increase in the value of vested benefits under the plan due to increases in benefits described in clause (i) over—

(I) 10 years, to the extent such increase in value is attributable to persons in pay status, or

(II) 25 years, to the extent such increase in value is attributable to other participants.

(2) For purposes of paragraph (1), the funding standard requirement for any plan year is an amount equal to the net charge to the funding standard account for such plan year (as defined in section 4241(b)(2)).

(3)(A) In the case of a plan described in section 4216(b), if a plan amendment which increases benefits is adopted after January 1, 1980—

(i) paragraph (1) shall apply only if the plan is a plan described in subparagraph (B), and

(ii) the amount under paragraph (1) shall be determined without regard to paragraph (1)(B).

(B) A plan is described in this subparagraph if—

(i) the rate of employer contributions under the plan for the first plan year beginning on or after the date on which an amendment increasing benefits is adopted, multiplied by the valuation contribution base for that plan year, equals or exceeds the sum of—

(I) the amount that would be necessary to amortize fully, in equal annual installments, by July 1, 1986, the unfunded vested benefits attributable to plan provisions in effect on July 1, 1977 (determined as of the last day of the base plan year); and

(II) the amount that would be necessary to amortize fully, in equal annual installments, over the period described in subparagraph (C), beginning with the first day of the first plan year beginning on or after the date on which the amendment is adopted, the unfunded vested benefits (determined as of the last day of the base plan year) attributable to each plan amendment after July 1, 1977; and

(ii) the rate of employer contributions for each subsequent plan year is not less than the lesser of—

(I) the rate which when multiplied by the valuation contribution base for that subsequent plan year produces the annual amount that would be necessary to complete the amortization schedule described in clause (i), or

(II) the rate for the plan year immediately preceding such subsequent plan year, plus 5 percent of such rate.

(C) The period determined under this subparagraph is the lesser of—

(i) 12 years, or

(ii) a period equal in length to the average of the remaining expected lives of all persons receiving benefits under the plan.

(4) Paragraph (1) shall not apply with respect to a plan, other than a plan described in paragraph (3), for the period of consecutive plan years in each of which the plan is in reorganization, beginning with a plan year in which occurs the earlier of the date of the adoption or the effective date of any amendment of the plan which increases benefits with respect to service performed before the plan year in which the adoption of the amendment occurred.

(e) **Adjustment of Vested Benefits Charge.**—In determining the minimum contribution requirement with respect to a plan for a plan year under subsection (b), the vested benefits charge may be adjusted to reflect a plan amendment reducing benefits under section 412(c)(8) of title 26.

(f) **Waiver of Accumulated Funding Deficiency.**—

(1) The Secretary of the Treasury may waive any accumulated funding deficiency under this section in accordance with the provisions of section 302(c).

(2) Any waiver under paragraph (1) shall not be treated as a waived funding deficiency (within the meaning of section 302(c)(3)).

(g) **Statutory Methods Applicable for Determinations.**—For purposes of making any determination under this part, the requirements of section 304(c)(3) shall apply.

Amendments to ERISA §4243

Pension Protection Act of 2006 (Pub. L. No. 109-280), as follows:

● ERISA §4243(a)(1)(B) was amended by Act §107(b)(6) (redesignated as §108(b)(6) by Pub. L. No. 111-192, §202(a)) by substituting "§304(a)" for "§302(a)". Eff. for plan years beginning after 2007, see Act §107(e).

● ERISA §4243(f)(1) was amended by Act §107(b)(7) (redesignated as §108(b)(7) by Pub. L. No. 111-192, §202(a)) by substituting "§302(c)" for "§303(a)". Eff. for plan years beginning after 2007, see Act §107(e).

● ERISA §4243(f)(2) was amended by Act §107(b)(8) (redesignated as §108(b)(8) by Pub. L. No. 111-192, §202(a)) by substituting "§302(c)(3)" for "§303(c)". Eff. for plan years beginning after 2007, see Act §107(e).

● ERISA §4243(g) was amended by Act §107(b)(9) (redesignated as §108(b)(9) by Pub. L. No. 111-192, §202(a)) by substituting "304(c)(3)" for "§302(c)(3)". Eff. for plan years beginning after 2007, see Act §107(e).

● **Other Provision—Effective Date.** Act §104 provides a delayed effective date for amendments made by Act §§101–116 for "eligible cooperative plans" until the earlier of the first plan year that the plan ceases to be an eligible cooperative plan, or Jan. 1, 2017.

Omnibus Budget Reconciliation Act of 1989 (Pub. L. No. 101-239), as follows:

● ERISA §4243(d)(1)(B), (e) were amended by Act §7891(a)(1) by substituting "Internal Revenue Code of 1986" for "Internal Revenue Code of 1954", which for purposes of codification was translated as "title 26". Eff., except as otherwise provided, as if included in the provision of Pub. L. No. 99-514, to which it relates, see Act §7891(f).

SEC. 4244. OVERBURDEN CREDIT AGAINST MINIMUM CONTRIBUTION REQUIREMENT.

(a) Applicability of Overburden Credit to Determinations.—For purposes of determining the minimum contribution requirement under section 4243 (before the application of section 4243(b)(2) or (d)) the plan sponsor of a plan which is overburdened for the plan year shall apply an overburden credit against the plan's minimum contribution requirement for the plan year (determined without regard to section 4243(b)(2) or (d) and without regard to this section).

(b) Determination of Overburden Status of Plan.—A plan is overburdened for a plan year if—

(1) the average number of pay status participants under the plan in the base plan year exceeds the average of the number of active participants in the base plan year and the 2 plan years preceding the base plan year, and

(2) the rate of employer contributions under the plan equals or exceeds the greater of—

(A) such rate for the preceding plan year, or

(B) such rate for the plan year preceding the first year in which the plan is in reorganization.

(c) Amount of Overburden Credit.—The amount of the overburden credit for a plan year is the product of—

(1) one-half of the average guaranteed benefit paid for the base plan year, and

(2) the overburden factor for the plan year.

The amount of the overburden credit for a plan year shall not exceed the amount of the minimum contribution requirement for such year (determined without regard to this section).

(d) Amount of Overburden Factor.—For purposes of this section, the overburden factor of a plan for the plan year is an amount equal to—

(1) the average number of pay status participants for the base plan year, reduced by

(2) the average of the number of active participants for the base plan year and for each of the 2 plan years preceding the base plan year.

(e) Definitions; Determinative Factors.—For purposes of this section—

(1) The term "pay status participant" means, with respect to a plan, a participant receiving retirement benefits under the plan.

(2) The number of active participants for a plan year shall be the sum of—

(A) the number of active employees who are participants in the plan and on whose behalf contributions are required to be made during the plan year;

(B) the number of active employees who are not participants in the plan but who are in an employment unit covered by a collective bargaining agreement which requires the employees' employer to contribute to the plan, unless service in such employment unit was never covered under the plan or a predecessor thereof, and

(C) the total number of active employees attributed to employers who made payments to the plan for the plan year of withdrawal liability pursuant to part 1, determined by dividing—

(i) the total amount of such payments, by

(ii) the amount equal to the total contributions received by the plan during the plan year divided by the average number of active employees who were participants in the plan during the plan year.

The Secretary of the Treasury shall by regulation provide alternative methods of determining active participants where (by reason of irregular employment, contributions on a unit basis, or otherwise) this paragraph does not yield a representative basis for determining the credit.

(3) The term "average number" means, with respect to pay status participants for a plan year, a number equal to one-half the sum of—

(A) the number with respect to the plan as of the beginning of the plan year, and

(B) the number with respect to the plan as of the end of the plan year.

(4) The average guaranteed benefit paid is 12 times the average monthly pension payment guaranteed under section 4022A(c)(1) determined under the provisions of the plan in effect at the beginning of the first plan year in which the plan is in reorganization and without regard to section 4022A(c)(2).

(5) The first year in which the plan is in reorganization is the first of a period of 1 or more consecutive plan years in which the plan has been in reorganization not taking into account any plan years the plan was in reorganization prior to any period of 3 or more consecutive plan years in which the plan was not in reorganization.

(f) Eligibility of Plan for Overburden Credit for Plan Year.—

(1) Notwithstanding any other provision of this section, a plan is not eligible for an overburden credit for a plan year if the Secretary of the Treasury finds that the plan's current contribution base for the plan year was reduced, without a corresponding reduction in the plan's unfunded vested benefits attributable to pay status participants, as a result of a change in an agreement providing for employer contributions under the plan.

(2) For purposes of paragraph (1), a complete or partial withdrawal of an employer (within the meaning of part 1) does not impair a plan's eligibility for an overburden credit, unless the Secretary of the Treasury finds that a contribution base reduction described in paragraph (1) resulted from a transfer of liabilities to another plan in connection with the withdrawal.

(g) Overburden Credit Where Two or More Multiemployer Plans Merge.—Notwithstanding any other provision of this section, if 2 or more multiemployer plans merge, the amount of the overburden credit which may be applied under this section with respect to the plan resulting from the merger for any of the 3 plan years ending after the effective date of the merger shall not exceed the sum of the used overburden credit for each of the merging plans for its last plan year ending before the effective date of the merger. For purposes of the preceding sentence, the used overburden credit is that portion of the credit which does not exceed the excess of the minimum contribution requirement (determined without regard to any overburden requirement under this section) over the employer contributions required under the plan.

SEC. 4244A. ADJUSTMENTS IN ACCRUED BENEFITS.

(a) Amendment of Multiemployer Plan in Reorganization to Reduce or Eliminate Accrued Benefits Attributable to Employer Contributions Ineligible for Guarantee of Corporation; Adjustment of Vested Benefits Charge to Reflect Plan Amendment.—

(1) Notwithstanding sections 203 and 204, a multiemployer plan in reorganization may be amended in accordance with this section, to reduce or eliminate accrued benefits attributable to employer contributions which, under section 4022A(b), are not eligible for the corporation's guarantee. The preceding sentence shall only apply to accrued benefits under plan amendments (or plans) adopted after March 26, 1980, or under collective bargaining agreements entered into after March 26, 1980.

(2) In determining the minimum contribution requirement with respect to a plan for a plan year under section 4243(b), the vested benefits charge may be adjusted to reflect a plan amendment reducing benefits under this section or section 412(c)(8) of title 26, but only if the amendment is adopted and effective no later than 2½ months after the end of the plan year, or within such extended period as the Secretary of the

Treasury may prescribe by regulation under section 412(c)(10) of title 26.

(b) Reduction of Accrued Benefits; Notice by Plan Sponsor to Plan Participants and Beneficiaries.—

(1) Accrued benefits may not be reduced under this section unless—

(A) notice has been given, at least 6 months before the first day of the plan year in which the amendment reducing benefits is adopted, to—

(i) plan participants and beneficiaries,

(ii) each employer who has an obligation to contribute (within the meaning of section 4212(a)) under the plan, and

(iii) each employee organization which, for purposes of collective bargaining, represents plan participants employed by such an employer,

that the plan is in reorganization and that, if contributions under the plan are not increased, accrued benefits under the plan will be reduced or an excise tax will be imposed on employers;

(B) in accordance with regulations prescribed by the Secretary of the Treasury—

(i) any category of accrued benefits is not reduced with respect to inactive participants to a greater extent proportionally than such category of accrued benefits is reduced with respect to active participants,

(ii) benefits attributable to employer contributions other than accrued benefits and the rate of future benefit accruals are reduced at least to an extent equal to the reduction in accrued benefits of inactive participants, and

(iii) in any case in which the accrued benefit of a participant or beneficiary is reduced by changing the benefit form or the requirements which the participant or beneficiary must satisfy to be entitled to the benefit, such reduction is not applicable to—

(I) any participant or beneficiary in pay status on the effective date of the amendment, or the beneficiary of such a participant, or

(II) any participant who has attained normal retirement age, or who is within 5 years of attaining normal retirement age, on the effective date of the amendment, or the beneficiary of any such participant; and

(C) the rate of employer contributions for the plan year in which the amendment becomes effective and for all succeeding plan years in which the plan is in reorganization equals or exceeds the greater of—

(i) the rate of employer contributions, calculated without regard to the amendment, for the plan year in which the amendment becomes effective, or

(ii) the rate of employer contributions for the plan year preceding the plan year in which the amendment becomes effective.

(2) The plan sponsors shall include in any notice required to be sent to plan participants and beneficiaries under paragraph (1) information as to the rights and remedies of plan participants and beneficiaries as well as how to contact the Department of Labor for further information and assistance where appropriate.

(c) Recoupment by Plan of Excess Benefit Payment.—A plan may not recoup a benefit payment which is in excess of the amount payable under the plan because of an amendment retroactively reducing accrued benefits under this section.

(d) Amendment of Plan to Increase or Restore Accrued Benefits Previously Reduced or Rate of Future Benefit Accruals; Conditions, Applicable Factors, etc.—

(1)(A) A plan which has been amended to reduce accrued benefits under this section may be amended to increase or restore accrued benefits, or the rate of future benefit accruals, only if the plan is amended to restore levels of previously reduced accrued benefits of inactive participants and of participants who are within 5 years of attaining normal retirement age to at least the same extent as any such increase in accrued benefits or in the rate of future benefit accruals.

(B) For purposes of this subsection, in the case of a plan which has been amended under this section to reduce accrued benefits—

(i) an increase in a benefit, or in the rate of future benefit accruals, shall be considered a benefit increase to the extent that the benefit, or the accrual rate, is thereby increased above the highest benefit level, or accrual rate, which was in effect under the terms of the plan before the effective date of the amendment reducing accrued benefits, and

(ii) an increase in a benefit, or in the rate of future benefit accruals, shall be considered a benefit restoration to the extent that the benefit, or the accrual rate, is not thereby increased above the highest benefit level, or accrual rate, which was in effect under the terms of the plan immediately before the effective date of the amendment reducing accrued benefits.

(2) If a plan is amended to partially restore previously reduced accrued benefit levels, or the rate of future benefit accruals, the benefits of inactive participants shall be restored in at least the same proportions as other accrued benefits which are restored.

(3) No benefit increase under a plan may take effect in a plan year in which an amendment reducing accrued benefits under the plan, in accordance with this section, is adopted or first becomes effective.

(4) A plan is not required to make retroactive benefit payments with respect to that portion of an accrued benefit which was reduced and subsequently restored under this section.

(e) "Inactive Participant" Defined.—For purposes of this section, "inactive participant" means a person not in covered service under the plan who is in pay status under the plan or who has a nonforfeitable benefit under the plan.

(f) Promulgation of Rules; Contents, etc.—The Secretary of the Treasury may prescribe rules under which, notwithstanding any other provision of this section, accrued benefit reductions or benefit increases for different participant groups may be varied equitably to reflect variations in contribution rates and other relevant factors reflecting differences in negotiated levels of financial support for plan benefit obligations.

Amendments to ERISA §4244A

Omnibus Budget Reconciliation Act of 1989 (Pub. L. No. 101-239), as follows:

• ERISA §4243(a)(2) was amended by Act §7891(a)(1) by substituting "Internal Revenue Code of 1986" for "Internal Revenue Code of 1954", which for purposes of codification was translated as "title 26". Eff., except as otherwise provided, as if included in the provision of Pub. L. No. 99-514, to which it relates, see Act §7891(f).

SEC. 4245. INSOLVENT PLANS.

(a) Suspension of Payments of Benefits; Conditions, Amount, etc.—Notwithstanding sections 203 and 204, in any case in which benefit payments under an insolvent multiemployer plan exceed the resource benefit level, any such payments of benefits which are not basic benefits shall be suspended, in accordance with this section, to the extent necessary to reduce the sum of such payments and the payments of such basic benefits to the greater of the resource benefit level or the level of basic benefits, unless an alternative procedure is prescribed by the corporation under section 4022A(g)(5).

(b) Determination of Insolvency Status for Plan Year; Definitions.—For purposes of this section, for a plan year—

(1) a multiemployer plan is insolvent if the plan's available resources are not sufficient to pay benefits under the plan when due for the plan year, or if the plan is determined to be insolvent under subsection (d);

(2) "resource benefit level" means the level of monthly benefits determined under subsections (c)(1) and (3) and (d)(3) to be the highest level which can be paid out of the plan's available resources;

(3) "available resources" means the plan's cash, marketable assets, contributions, withdrawal liability

payments, and earnings, less reasonable administrative expenses and amounts owed for such plan year to the corporation under section 4261(b)(2); and

(4) "insolvency year" means a plan year in which a plan is insolvent.

(c) Determination by Plan Sponsor in Reorganization of Resource Benefit Level of Plan for Each Insolvency Year; Uniform Application of Suspension of Benefits; Adjustments of Benefit Payments.—

(1) The plan sponsor of a plan in reorganization shall determine in writing the plan's resource benefit level for each insolvency year, based on the plan sponsor's reasonable projection of the plan's available resources and the benefits payable under the plan.

(2) The suspension of benefit payments under this section shall, in accordance with regulations prescribed by the Secretary of the Treasury, apply in substantially uniform proportions to the benefits of all persons in pay status (within the meaning of section 4241(b)(6)) under the plan, except that the Secretary of the Treasury may prescribe rules under which benefit suspensions for different participant groups may be varied equitably to reflect variations in contribution rates and other relevant factors including differences in negotiated levels of financial support for plan benefit obligations.

(3) Notwithstanding paragraph (2), if a plan sponsor determines in writing a resource benefit level for a plan year which is below the level of basic benefits, the payment of all benefits other than basic benefits must be suspended for that plan year.

(4)(A) If, by the end of an insolvency year, the plan sponsor determines in writing that the plan's available resources in that insolvency year could have supported benefit payments above the resource benefit level for that insolvency year, the plan sponsor shall distribute the excess resources to the participants and beneficiaries who received benefit payments from the plan in that insolvency year, in accordance with regulations prescribed by the Secretary of the Treasury.

(B) For purposes of this paragraph, the term "excess resources" means available resources above the amount necessary to support the resource benefit level, but no greater than the amount necessary to pay benefits for the plan year at the benefit levels under the plan.

(5) If, by the end of an insolvency year, any benefit has not been paid at the resource benefit level, amounts up to the resource benefit level which were unpaid shall be distributed to the participants and beneficiaries, in accordance with regulations prescribed by the Secretary of the Treasury, to the extent possible taking into account the plan's total available resources in that insolvency year.

(6) Except as provided in paragraph (4) or (5), a plan is not required to make retroactive benefit payments with respect to that portion of a benefit which was suspended under this section.

(d) Applicability and Determinations Respecting Plan Assets; Time for Determinations of Resource Benefit Level and Levels of Basic Benefits.—

(1) As of the end of the first plan year in which a plan is in reorganization, and at least every 3 plan years thereafter (unless the plan is no longer in reorganization), the plan sponsor shall compare the value of plan assets (determined in accordance with section 4243(b)(3)(B)(ii)) for that plan year with the total amount of benefit payments made under the plan for that plan year. Unless the plan sponsor determines that the value of plan assets exceeds 3 times the total amount of benefit payments, the plan sponsor shall determine whether the plan will be insolvent in any of the next 5 plan years. If the plan sponsor makes such a determination that the plan will be insolvent in any of the next 5 plan years, the plan sponsor shall make the comparison under this paragraph at least annually until the plan sponsor makes a determination that the plan will not be insolvent in any of the next 5 plan years.

(2) If, at any time, the plan sponsor of a plan in reorganization reasonably determines, taking into account the plan's recent and anticipated financial experience, that the plan's available resources are not sufficient to pay benefits under the plan when due for the next plan year, the plan sponsor shall make such determination available to interested parties.

(3) The plan sponsor of a plan in reorganization shall determine in writing for each insolvency year the resource benefit level and the level of basic benefits no later than 3 months before the insolvency year.

(e) Notice, etc., Requirements of Plan Sponsor in Reorganization Regarding Insolvency and Resource Benefit Levels.—

(1) If the plan sponsor of a plan in reorganization determines under subsection (d)(1) or (2) that the plan may become insolvent (within the meaning of subsection (b)(1)), the plan sponsor shall—

(A) notify the Secretary of the Treasury, the corporation, the parties described in section 4242(a)(2), and the plan participants and beneficiaries of that determination, and

(B) inform the parties described in section 4242(a)(2) and the plan participants and beneficiaries that if insolvency occurs certain benefit payments will be suspended, but that basic benefits will continue to be paid.

(2) No later than 2 months before the first day of each insolvency year, the plan sponsor of a plan in reorganization shall notify the Secretary of the Trea-

ERISA Sec. 4245(e)(2)

sury, the corporation, and the parties described in paragraph (1)(B) of the resource benefit level determined in writing for that insolvency year.

(3) In any case in which the plan sponsor anticipates that the resource benefit level for an insolvency year may not exceed the level of basic benefits, the plan sponsor shall notify the corporation.

(4) Notice required by this subsection shall be given in accordance with regulations prescribed by the corporation, except that notice to the Secretary of the Treasury shall be given in accordance with regulations prescribed by the Secretary of the Treasury.

(5) The corporation may prescribe a time other than the time prescribed by this section for the making of a determination or the filing of a notice under this section.

(f) Financial Assistance from Corporation; Conditions and Criteria Applicable.—

(1) If the plan sponsor of an insolvent plan, for which the resource benefit level is above the level of basic benefits, anticipates that, for any month in an insolvency year, the plan will not have funds sufficient to pay basic benefits, the plan sponsor may apply for financial assistance from the corporation under section 4261.

(2) A plan sponsor who has determined a resource benefit level for an insolvency year which is below the level of basic benefits shall apply for financial assistance from the corporation under section 4261.

Amendments to ERISA §4245

Pension Protection Act of 2006 (Pub. L. No. 109-280), as follows:

• ERISA §4245(d)(1) was amended by Act §203(a)(1) by substituting "5 plan years" for "3 plan years"; and by Act §203(a)(2) by inserting at the end the sentence: "If the plan sponsor makes such a determination that the plan will be insolvent in any of the next 5 plan years, the plan sponsor shall make the comparison under this paragraph at least annually until the plan sponsor makes a determination that the plan will not be insolvent in any of the next 5 plan years." Eff. for determinations made in plan years beginning after 2007, see Act §203(b).

Multiemployer Pension Plan Amendments Act of 1980 (Pub. L. No. 96-364), §108(c)(3), provides:

• Act §108(c)(3) provides:

(3)

(A) For the purpose of determining the withdrawal liability of an employer under title IV of the Employee Retirement Income Security Act of 1974 from a plan that terminates while the plan is insolvent (within the meaning of §4245 of such Act), the plan's unfunded vested benefits shall be reduced by an amount equal to the sum of all overburden credits that were applied in determining the plan's accumulated funding deficiency for all plan years preceding the first plan year in which the plan is insolvent, plus interest thereon.

(B) The provisions of subparagraph (A) apply only if—

(i) the plan would have been eligible for the overburden credit in the last plan year beginning before the date of the enactment of this Act [date of enactment: Sept. 26, 1980], if §4243 of the Employee Retirement Income Security Act of 1974 had been in effect for that plan year, and

(ii) the Pension Benefit Guaranty Corporation determines that the reduction of unfunded vested benefits under subparagraph

(A) would not significantly increase the risk of loss to the corporation.

Part 4—Financial Assistance

SEC. 4261. ASSISTANCE BY CORPORATION.

(a) Authority; Procedure Applicable; Amount.— If, upon receipt of an application for financial assistance under section 4245(f) or section 4281(d), the corporation verifies that the plan is or will be insolvent and unable to pay basic benefits when due, the corporation shall provide the plan financial assistance in an amount sufficient to enable the plan to pay basic benefits under the plan.

(b) Conditions; Repayment Terms.—

(1) Financial assistance shall be provided under such conditions as the corporation determines are equitable and are appropriate to prevent unreasonable loss to the corporation with respect to the plan.

(2) A plan which has received financial assistance shall repay the amount of such assistance to the corporation on reasonable terms consistent with regulations prescribed by the corporation.

(c) Assistance Pending Final Determination of Application.—Pending determination of the amount described in subsection (a), the corporation may provide financial assistance in such amounts as it considers appropriate in order to avoid undue hardship to plan participants and beneficiaries.

Part 5—Benefits After Termination

SEC. 4281. BENEFITS UNDER CERTAIN TERMINATED PLANS.

(a) Amendment of Plan by Plan Sponsor to Reduce Benefits, and Suspension of Benefit Payments.—Notwithstanding sections 203 and 204, the plan sponsor of a terminated multiemployer plan to which section 4041A(d) applies shall amend the plan to reduce benefits, and shall suspend benefit payments, as required by this section.

(b) Determinations Respecting Value of Nonforfeitable Benefits Under Terminated Plan and Value of Assets of Plan.—

(1) The value of nonforfeitable benefits under a terminated plan referred to in subsection (a), and the value of the plan's assets, shall be determined in writing, in accordance with regulations prescribed by the corporation, as of the end of the plan year during which section 4041A(d) becomes applicable to the plan, and each plan year thereafter.

(2) For purposes of this section, plan assets include outstanding claims for withdrawal liability (within the meaning of section 4001(a)(12)).

(c) Amendment of Plan by Plan Sponsor to Reduce Benefits for Conservation of Assets; Factors Applicable.—

(1) If, according to the determination made under subsection (b), the value of nonforfeitable benefits exceeds the value of the plan's assets, the plan sponsor shall amend the plan to reduce benefits under the plan to the extent necessary to ensure that the plan's assets are sufficient, as determined and certified in accordance with regulations prescribed by the corporation, to discharge when due all of the plan's obligations with respect to nonforfeitable benefits.

(2) Any plan amendment required by this subsection shall, in accordance with regulations prescribed by the Secretary of the Treasury—

(A) reduce benefits only to the extent necessary to comply with paragraph (1);

(B) reduce accrued benefits only to theextent that those benefits are not eligible for the corporation's guarantee under section 4022A(b);

(C) comply with the rules for and limitations on benefit reductions under a plan in reorganization, as prescribed in section 4244A, except to the extent that the corporation prescribes other rules and limitations in regulations under this section; and

(D) take effect no later than 6 months after the end of the plan year for which it is determined that the value of nonforfeitable benefits exceeds the value of the plan's assets.

(d) Suspension of Benefit Payments; Determinative Factors; Powers and Duties of Plan Sponsor; Retroactive Benefit Payments.—

(1) In any case in which benefit payments under a plan which is insolvent under paragraph (2)(A) exceed the resource benefit level, any such payments which are not basic benefits shall be suspended, in accordance with this subsection, to the extent necessary to reduce the sum of such payments and such basic benefits to the greater of the resource benefit level or the level of basic benefits, unless an alternative procedure is prescribed by the corporation in connection with a supplemental guarantee program established under section 4022A(g)(2).

(2) For the purposes of this subsection, for a plan year—

(A) a plan is insolvent if—

(i) the plan has been amended to reduce benefits to the extent permitted by subsection (c), and

(ii) the plan's available resources are not sufficient to pay benefits under the plan when due for the plan year; and

(B) "resource benefit level" and "available resources" have the meanings set forth in paragraphs (2) and (3), respectively, of section 4245(b).

(3) The plan sponsor of a plan which is insolvent (within the meaning of paragraph (2)(A)) shall have the powers and duties of the plan sponsor of a plan in reorganization which is insolvent (within the meaning of section 4245(b)(1)), except that regulations governing the plan sponsor's exercise of those powers and duties under this section shall beprescribed by the corporation, and the corporation shall prescribe by regulation notice requirements which assure that plan participants and beneficiaries receive adequate notice of benefit suspensions.

(4) A plan is not required to make retroactive benefit payments with respect to that portion of a benefit which was suspended under this subsection, except that the provisions of section 4245(c)(4) and (5) shall apply in the case of plans which are insolvent under paragraph (2)(A), in connection with the plan year during which such section 4041A(d) first became applicable to the plan and every year thereafter, in the same manner and to the same extent as such provisions apply to insolvent plans in reorganization under section 4245, in connection with insolvency years under such section 4245.

Part 6—Enforcement

SEC. 4301. CIVIL ACTIONS.

(a) Persons Entitled to Maintain Actions.—

(1) A plan fiduciary, employer, plan participant, or beneficiary, who is adversely affected by the act or omission of any party under this subtitle with respect to a multiemployer plan, or an employee organization which represents such a plan participant or beneficiary for purposes of collective bargaining, may bring an action for appropriate legal or equitable relief, or both.

(2) Notwithstanding paragraph (1), this section does not authorize an action against the Secretary of the Treasury, the Secretary of Labor, or the corporation.

(b) Failure of Employer to Make Withdrawal Liability Payment Within Prescribed Time.—In any action under this section to compel an employer to pay withdrawal liability, any failure of the employer to make any withdrawal liability payment within the time prescribed shall be treated in the same manner as a delinquent contribution (within the meaning of section 515).

(c) Jurisdiction of Federal and State Courts.— The district courts of the United States shall have exclusive jurisdiction of an action under this section without regard to the amount in controversy, except that State courts of competent jurisdiction shall have concurrent jurisdiction over an action brought by a plan fiduciary to collect withdrawal liability.

(d) Venue and Service of Process.—An action under this section may be brought in the district where the plan is administered or where a defendant resides or does business, and process may be served in any district where a defendant resides, does business, or may be found.

(e) Costs and Expenses.—In any action under this section, the court may award all or a portion of the costs and expenses incurred in connection with such action, including reasonable attorney's fees, to the prevailing party.

(f) Time Limitations.—An action under this section may not be brought after the later of—

(1) 6 years after the date on which the cause of action arose, or

(2) 3 years after the earliest date on which the plaintiff acquired or should have acquired actual knowledge of the existence of such cause of action; except that in the case of fraud or concealment, such action may be brought not later than 6 years after the date of discovery of the existence of such cause of action.

(g) Service of Complaint on Corporation; Intervention by Corporation.—A copy of the complaint in any action under this section or section 4221 shall be served upon the corporation by certified mail. The corporation may intervene in any such action.

SEC. 4302. PENALTY FOR FAILURE TO PROVIDE NOTICE.

Any person who fails, without reasonable cause, to provide a notice required under this subtitle or any implementing regulations shall be liable to the corporation in an amount up to $100 for each day for which such failure continues. The corporation may bring a civil action against any such person in the United States District Court for the District of Columbia or in any district court of the United States within the jurisdiction of which the plan assets are located, the plan is administered, or a defendant resides or does business, and process may be served in any district where a defendant resides, does business, or may be found.

SEC. 4303. ELECTION OF PLAN STATUS.

(a) Authority, Time, and Criteria.—Within one year after the date of the enactment of the Multiemployer Pension Plan Amendments Act of 1980, a multiemployer plan may irrevocably elect, pursuant to procedures established by the corporation, that the plan shall not be treated as a multiemployer plan for any purpose under this Act or title 26 if for each of the last 3 plan years ending prior to the effective date of the Multiemployer Pension Plan Amendments Act of 1980—

(1) the plan was not a multiemployer plan because the plan was not a plan described in section 3(37)(A)(iii) of this Act and section 414(f)(1)(C) of title 26 (as such provisions were in effect on the day

before the date of the enactment of the Multiemployer Pension Plan Amendments Act of 1980); and

(2) the plan had been identified as a plan that was not a multiemployer plan in substantially all its filings with the corporation, the Secretary of Labor and the Secretary of the Treasury.

(b) Requirements.—An election described in subsection (a) shall be effective only if—

(1) the plan is amended to provide that it shall not be treated as a multiemployer plan for all purposes under this Act and title 26, and

(2) written notice of the amendment is provided to the corporation within 60 days after the amendment is adopted.

(c) Effective Date.—An election described in subsection (a) shall be treated as being effective as of the date of the enactment of the Multiemployer Pension Plan Amendments Act of 1980.

Subtitle F—Transition Rules and Effective Dates

SEC. 4402. EFFECTIVE DATE; SPECIAL RULES.

(a) The provisions of this title take effect on September 2, 1974.

(b) Notwithstanding the provisions of subsection (a), the corporation shall pay benefits guaranteed under this title with respect to any plan—

(1) which is not a multiemployer plan,

(2) which terminates after June 30, 1974, and before the date of enactment of this Act,

(3) to which section 4021 would apply if that section were effective beginning on July 1, 1974, and

(4) with respect to which a notice is filed with the Secretary of Labor and received by him not later than 10 days after the date of enactment of this Act, except that, for reasonable cause shown, such notice may be filed with the Secretary of Labor and received by him not later than October 31, 1974, stating that the plan is a plan described in paragraphs (1), (2), and (3).

The corporation shall not pay benefits guaranteed under this title with respect to a plan described in the preceding sentence unless the corporation finds substantial evidence that the plan was terminated for a reasonable business purpose and not for the purpose of obtaining the payment of benefits by the corporation under this title or for the purpose of avoiding the liability which might be imposed under subtitle D if the plan terminated on or after September 2, 1974. The provisions of subtitle D do not apply in the case of such plan which terminates before September 2, 1974. For purposes of determining whether a plan is a plan described in paragraph (2), the provisions of section 4048 shall not apply, but the corporation shall make the determination on the basis of the date on which benefits ceased to accrue or on any other reasonable basis consistent with the purposes of this subsection.

(c)(1) Except as provided in paragraphs (2), (3), and (4), the corporation shall not pay benefits guaranteed under this title with respect to a multiemployer plan which terminates before August 1, 1980. Whenever the corporation exercises the authority granted under paragraph (2) or (3), the corporation shall notify the Committee on Education and Labor and the Committee on Ways and Means of the House of Representatives, and the Committee on Labor and Human Resources and the Committee on Finance of the Senate.

(2) The corporation may, in its discretion, pay benefits guaranteed under this title with respect to a multiemployer plan which terminates after the date of enactment of this Act and before August 1, 1980, if—

(A) the plan was maintained during the 60 months immediately preceding the date on which the plan terminates, and

(B) the corporation determines that the payment by the corporation of benefits guaranteed under this title with respect to that plan will not jeopardize the payments the corporation anticipates it may be required to make in connection with benefits guaranteed under this title with respect to multiemployer plans which terminate after July 31, 1980.

(3) Notwithstanding any provision of section 4021 or 4022 which would prevent such payments, the corporation, in carrying out its authority under paragraph (2), may pay benefits guaranteed under this title with respect to a multiemployer plan described in paragraph (2) in any case in which those benefits would otherwise not be payable if—

(A) the plan has been in effect for at least 5 years,

(B) the plan has been in substantial compliance with the funding requirements for a qualified plan with respect to the employees and former employees in those employment units on the basis of which the participating employers have contributed to the plan for the preceding 5 years, and

(C) the participating employers and employee organization or organizations had no reasonable recourse other than termination.

(4) If the corporation determines, under paragraph (2) or (3), that it will pay benefits guaranteed under this title with respect to a multiemployer plan which terminates before August 1, 1980, the corporation—

(A) may establish requirements for the continuation of payments which commenced before January 2, 1974, with respect to retired participants under the plan,

(B) may not, notwithstanding any other provision of this title, make payments with respect to any participant under such a plan who, on January 1, 1974, was receiving payment of retirement benefits, in excess of the amounts and rates payable with respect to such participant on that date,

(C) may not make any payments with respect to benefits guaranteed under this title in connection with such a plan which are derived, directly or indirectly, from amounts borrowed under section 4005(c), and

(D) shall review from time to time payments made under the authority granted to it by paragraphs (2) and (3), and reduce or terminate such payments to the extent necessary to avoid jeopardizing the ability of the corporation to make payments of benefits guaranteed under this title in connection with multiemployer plans which terminate after July 31, 1980, without increasing premium rates for such plans.

(d) Notwithstanding any other provision of this title, guaranteed benefits payable by the corporation pursuant to its discretionary authority under this section shall continue to be paid at the level guaranteed under section 4022, without regard to any limitation on payment under subparagraph (C) or (D) of subsection (c)(4).

(e)(1) Except as provided in paragraphs (2), (3), and (4), the amendments to this Act made by the Multiemployer Pension Plan Amendments Act of 1980 shall take effect on the date of the enactment of that Act.

(2)(A) Except as provided in this paragraph, part 1 of subtitle E, relating to withdrawal liability, takes effect on September 26, 1980.

(B) For purposes of determining withdrawal liability under part 1 of subtitle E, an employer who has withdrawn from a plan shall be considered to have withdrawn from a multiemployer plan if, at the time of the withdrawal, the plan was a multiemployer plan as defined in section 4001(a)(3) as in effect at the time of the withdrawal.

(3) Sections 4241 through 4245, relating to multiemployer plan reorganization, shall take effect, with respect to each plan, on the first day of the first plan year beginning on or after the earlier of—

(A) the date on which the last collective bargaining agreement providing for employer contributions under the plan, which was in effect on the date of the enactment of the Multiemployer Pension Plan Amendments Act of 1980, expires, without regard to extensions agreed to on or after the date of the enactment of that Act, or

(B) 3 years after the date of the enactment of the Multiemployer Pension Plan Amendments Act of 1980.

(4) Section 4235 shall take effect on September 26, 1980.

(f)(1) In the event that before the date of enactment of the Multiemployer Pension Plan Amendments Act of 1980, the corporation has determined that—

(A) an employer has withdrawn from a multiemployer plan under section 4063, and

(B) the employer is liable to the corporation under such section, the corporation shall retain the amount of liability paid to it or furnished in the form of a bond and shall pay such liability to the plan in the event the plan terminates in accordance with section 4041A(a)(2) before the earlier of September 26, 1985, or the day after the 5-year period commencing on the date of such withdrawal.

(2) In any case in which the plan is not so terminated within the period described in paragraph (1), the liability of the employer is abated and any payment held in escrow shall be refunded without interest to the employer or the employer's bond shall be canceled.

(g)(1) In any case in which an employer or employers withdrew from a multiemployer plan before the effective date of part 1 of subtitle E, the corporation may—

(A) apply section 4063(d), as in effect before the amendments made by the Multiemployer Pension Plan Amendments Act of 1980, to such plan,

(B) assess liability against the withdrawn employer with respect to the resulting terminated plan,

(C) guarantee benefits under the terminated plan under section 4022, as in effect before such amendments, and

(D) if necessary, enforce such action through suit brought under section 4003.

(2) The corporation shall use the revolving fund used by the corporation with respect to basic benefits guaranteed under section 4022A in guaranteeing benefits under a terminated plan described in this subsection.

(h)(1) In the case of an employer who entered into a collective bargaining agreement—

(A) which was effective on January 12, 1979, and which remained in effect through May 15, 1982, and

(B) under which contributions to a multiemployer plan were to cease on January 12, 1982, any withdrawal liability incurred by the employer pursuant to part 1 of subtitle E as a result of the complete or partial withdrawal of the employer from the multiemployer plan before January 16, 1982, shall be void.

(2) In any case in which—

(A) an employer engaged in the grocery wholesaling business—

(i) had ceased all covered operations under a multiemployer plan before June 30, 1981, and had relocated its operations to a new facility in another State, and

(ii) had notified a local union representative on May 14, 1980, that the employer had tentatively decided to discontinue operations and relocate to a new facility in another State, and

(B) all State and local approvals with respect to construction of and commencement of operations at the new facility had been obtained, a contract for construction had been entered into, and construction of the new facility had begun before September 26, 1980, any withdrawal liability incurred by the employer pursuant to part 1 of subtitle E as a result of the complete or partial withdrawal of the employer from the multiemployer plan before June 30, 1981, shall be void.

(i) The preceding provisions of this section shall not apply with respect to amendments made to this title in provisions enacted after October 22, 1986.

Amendments to ERISA §4402

Omnibus Budget Reconciliation Act of 1989 (Pub. L. No. 101-239), as follows:
- ERISA §4402(h)(1)(B) was amended by Act §7862(a) by substituting "before January 16, 1982" for "before January 12, 1982" in concluding provisions. Eff. as if included in the provision of Pub. L. No. 99-514 to which it relates, see Act §7863.
- ERISA §4402(i) was added by Act §7894(h)(5)(A). Act §7894(h)(5)(B) provided that: "The amendment made by subparagraph (A) [amending this section] shall take effect as if originally included in the Reform Act [Pub. L. No. 99-514]." Eff. as if originally included in the provision of Pub. L. No. 93-406 to which such amendment relates, see Act §7894(i).

Tax Reform Act of 1986 (Pub. L. No. 99-514), as follows:
- ERISA §4402(h) was added by Act §1852(i). Eff., except as otherwise provided, as if included in the provisions of Pub. L. No. 98-369, Division A, to which it relates, see Act §1881.

Deficit Reduction Act of 1984 (Pub. L. No. 98-369), as follows:
- ERISA §4402(e)(2)(A), (4) were amended by Act §558(b)(1)(B) by substituting "September 26, 1980" for "April 29, 1980".
- ERISA §4402(f)(1) was amended by Act §558(b)(1)(C) by substituting "September 26, 1985" for "April 29, 1985".

Multiemployer Pension Plan Amendments Act of 1980 (Pub. L. No. 96-364), as follows:
- ERISA §4082 was redesignated as ERISA §4402 by Act §108(a). Eff. Sept. 26, 1980, except as otherwise provided, see ERISA §4402(e).
- ERISA §4402(d) was replaced by new subsec. (d) by Act §108(b). Eff. Sept. 26, 1980, except as otherwise provided, see ERISA §4402(e).
- ERISA §4402(e) was replaced by new subsec. (e) by Act §108(c)(1). Eff. Sept. 26, 1980, except as otherwise provided, see ERISA §4402(e).
- ERISA §4402(f), (g) were added by Act §108(c)(1). Eff. Sept. 26, 1980, except as otherwise provided, see ERISA §4402(e).

Pub. L. No. 96-293, as follows:
- ERISA §4082(c)(1), (2), (4) were amended by Act §1(1) by substituting "August 1, 1980" for "July 1, 1980". Eff. June 28, 1980.
- ERISA §4082(c)(2)(B), (4)(D) were amended by Act §1(2) by substituting "July 31, 1980" for "June 30, 1980". Eff. June 28, 1980.

Pub. L. 96-239, as follows:
- ERISA §4082(c)(1), (2), (4) were amended by Act §1(1) by substituting "July 1, 1980" for "May 1, 1980". Eff. April 30, 1980.
- ERISA §4082(c)(2)(B), (4)(D) were amended by Act §1(2) by substituting "June 30, 1980" or "April 30, 1980". Eff. April 30, 1980.

Pub. L. No. 96-24, as follows:
- ERISA §4082(c)(1), (2), (4) were amended by Act §1(1) by substituting "May 1, 1980" for "July 1, 1979". Eff. June 19, 1979.
- ERISA §4082(c)(2)(B), (4)(D) were amended by Act §2(1) by substituting "April 30, 1980" for "June 30, 1979". Eff. June 19, 1979.

Pub. L. No. 95-214, as follows:
- ERISA §4082(c)(1) was amended by Act §1(a)(1) by substituting "July 1, 1979" for "January 1, 1978". Eff. June 19, 1979.
- ERISA §4082(c)(2) (former) was amended by Act §1(a)(2) by substituting "July 1, 1979" for "January 1, 1978" in provisions preceding subpara. (A). Eff. June 19, 1979.

- ERISA §4082(c)(2)(B) was amended by Act §1(a)(3) by substituting "June 30, 1979" for "December 31, 1977". Eff. June 19, 1979.
- ERISA §4082(c)(4) was amended by Act §1(a)(4) by substituting "July 1, 1979" for "January 1, 1978" in provisions preceding subpara. (A). Eff. June 19, 1979.
- ERISA §4082(c)(4)(D) was amended by Act §1(a)(5) by substituting "June 30, 1979" for "December 31, 1977". Eff. June 19, 1979.
- ERISA §4082(d), (e) was added by Act §1(b). Eff. June 19, 1979.

Part 2

IRC Excerpts

IRC Finding List

IRC Section
26 U.S.C.

IRC Section
26 U.S.C.

IRC Section
26 U.S.C.

Subpart B—Special Rules

Subpart C—Special Rules for Multiemployer Plans

Subpart D—Treatment of Welfare Benefit Funds

IRC Section

26 U.S.C.

IRC Section
26 U.S.C.

IRC Section
26 U.S.C.

IRC Section
26 U.S.C.

IRC Section
26 U.S.C.

IRC Section
26 U.S.C.

IRC Section

26 U.S.C.

IRC Section
26 U.S.C.

IRC Section
26 U.S.C.

IRC Section
26 U.S.C.

IRC Section
26 U.S.C.

Editor's Note

Part 2 contains excerpts from the Internal Revenue Code (IRC), as amended by various public laws, current through October 14, 2011. Text within subsections of the IRC that was deleted by recent legislation is set forth in ~~strikeout~~ mode. Certain sections of the IRC that were repealed appear in full with an editor's note. Provisions that were added by recent legislation are in *italics*. Editor's notes appear at the beginning of the section or subsection of the IRC to which they pertain.

Following the IRC sections are amendment notes for amendments made in 2001 or later.

These provisions of the IRC are codified in Title 26 of the *U.S. Code*. For a complete list of IRC provisions excerpted here, see the IRC Finding List on the previous pages.

Subtitle A—Income Taxes

Chapter 1—Normal Taxes and Surtaxes
* * *

Subchapter A—Determination of Tax Liability
* * *

Part IV—Credits Against Tax

Subpart A—Nonrefundable Personal Credits

SEC. 25B. ELECTIVE DEFERRALS AND IRA CONTRIBUTIONS BY CERTAIN INDIVIDUALS

(a) **Allowance of Credit**.—In the case of an eligible individual, there shall be allowed as a credit against the tax imposed by this subtitle for the taxable year an amount equal to the applicable percentage of so much of the qualified retirement savings contributions of the eligible individual for the taxable year as do not exceed $2,000.

(b) **Applicable Percentage**.—For purposes of this section—

(1) **Joint returns**.—In the case of a joint return, the applicable percentage is—

(A) if the adjusted gross income of the taxpayer is not over $30,000, 50 percent,

(B) if the adjusted gross income of the taxpayer is over $30,000 but not over $32,500, 20 percent,

(C) if the adjusted gross income of the taxpayer is over $32,500 but not over $50,000, 10 percent, and

(D) if the adjusted gross income of the taxpayer is over $50,000, zero percent.

(2) **Other returns**.—In the case of—

(A) a head of household, the applicable percentage shall be determined under paragraph (1) except that such paragraph shall be applied by substituting for each dollar amount therein (as adjusted under paragraph (3)) a dollar amount equal to 75 percent of such dollar amount, and

(B) any taxpayer not described in paragraph (1) or subparagraph (A), the applicable percentage shall be determined under paragraph (1) except that such paragraph shall be applied by substituting for each dollar amount therein (as adjusted under paragraph (3)) a dollar amount equal to 50 percent of such dollar amount.

(3) **Inflation adjustment**.—In the case of any taxable year beginning in a calendar year after 2006, each of the dollar amount[s] in paragraph (1) shall be increased by an amount equal to—

(A) such dollar amount, multiplied by

(B) the cost-of-living adjustment determined under section 1(f)(3) for the calendar year in which the taxable year begins, determined by substituting "calendar year 2005" for "calendar year 1992" in subparagraph (B) thereof.

Any increase determined under the preceding sentence shall be rounded to the nearest multiple of $500.

(c) **Eligible Individual**.—For purposes of this section—

(1) **In general**.—The term "eligible individual" means any individual if such individual has attained the age of 18 as of the close of the taxable year.

(2) **Dependents and full-time students not eligible**.—The term "eligible individual" shall not include—

(A) any individual with respect to whom a deduction under section 151 is allowed to another taxpayer for a taxable year beginning in the calendar year in which such individual's taxable year begins, and

(B) any individual who is a student (as defined in section 152(f)(2)).

(d) **Qualified Retirement Savings Contributions**.—For purposes of this section—

(1) **In general**.—The term "qualified retirement savings contributions" means, with respect to any taxable year, the sum of—

(A) the amount of the qualified retirement contributions (as defined in section 219(e)) made by the eligible individual,

(B) the amount of—

(i) any elective deferrals (as defined in section 402(g)(3)) of such individual, and

(ii) any elective deferral of compensation by such individual under an eligible deferred compensation plan (as defined in section 457(b)) of an eligible employer described in section 457(e)(1)(A), and

(C) the amount of voluntary employee contributions by such individual to any qualified retirement plan (as defined in section 4974(c)).

(2) Reduction for certain distributions.—

(A) In general.—The qualified retirement savings contributions determined under paragraph (1) shall be reduced (but not below zero) by the aggregate distributions received by the individual during the testing period from any entity of a type to which contributions under paragraph (1) may be made. The preceding sentence shall not apply to the portion of any distribution which is not includible in gross income by reason of a trustee-to-trustee transfer or a rollover distribution.

(B) Testing period.—For purposes of subparagraph (A), the testing period, with respect to a taxable year, is the period which includes—

(i) such taxable year,

(ii) the 2 preceding taxable years, and

(iii) the period after such taxable year and before the due date (including extensions) for filing the return of tax for such taxable year.

(C) Excepted distributions.—There shall not be taken into account under subparagraph (A)—

(i) any distribution referred to in section 72(p), 401(k)(8), 401(m)(6), 402(g)(2), 404(k), or 408(d)(4), and

(ii) any distribution to which section 408A(d)(3) applies.

(d) Treatment of distributions received by spouse of individual.—For purposes of determining distributions received by an individual under subparagraph (A) for any taxable year, any distribution received by the spouse of such individual shall be treated as received by such individual if such individual and spouse file a joint return for such taxable year and for the taxable year during which the spouse receives the distribution.

(e) Adjusted Gross Income.—For purposes of this section, adjusted gross income shall be determined without regard to sections 911, 931, and 933.

(f) Investment in the Contract.—Notwithstanding any other provision of law, a qualified retirement savings contribution shall not fail to be included in determining the investment in the contract for purposes of section 72 by reason of the credit under this section.

Editor's Note

Caution: IRC §25B(g), as follows, was amended by Pub. L. No. 109-135 and sunsets effective for taxable, plan, or limitation years beginning after December 31, 2012. See Pub. L. No. 109-135, §402(i)(3)(H), in the amendment notes, below.

(g) Limitation Based on Amount of Tax.—In the case of a taxable year to which section 26(a)(2) does not apply, the credit allowed under subsection (a) for the taxable year shall not exceed the excess of—

(1) the sum of the regular tax liability (as defined in section 26(b)) plus the tax imposed by section 55, over

---

Editor's Note

Caution: IRC §25B(g)(2), as follows, prior to amendment by Pub. L. No. 111-312, applies to tax years beginning on or before December 31, 2011. For sunset provision, see the amendment notes to this section for Pub. L. No. 111-148, as follows.

---

(2) the sum of the credits allowable under this subpart (other than this section and sections 25A(i), 25D, 30, 30B, and 30D) and section 27 for the taxable year.

Editor's Note

Caution: IRC §25B(g)(2), as follows, as amended by Pub. L. No. 111-312, applies to tax years beginning after December 31, 2011. For sunset provision, see the amendment notes to this section for Pub. L. No. 111-148, as amended by Pub. L. No. 111-312.

---

(2) the sum of the credits allowable under this subpart (other than this section and sections 23, 25A(i), 25D, 30, 30B, and 30D) and section 27 for the taxable year.

(h) [Repealed.]

Recent Amendments to IRC §25B

Tax Relief, Unemployment Insurance Reauthorization, and Job Creation Act of 2010 (Pub. L. No. 111-312), as follows:

● IRC §25B(g)(2) was amended by Act §101(b)(1) to read as such provision would read if the Patient Protection and Affordable Care Act (Pub. L. No. 111-148), §10909 had not been enacted. Eff. for tax years beginning after Dec. 31, 2011. See note below on sunset provision.

Patient Protection and Affordable Care Act, 2010 (Pub. L. No. 111-148), as follows:
● IRC §25B(g)(2) was amended by Act §10909(b)(2)(D) by striking "23,". Eff. for taxable years beginning after Dec. 31, 2009.
● **Sunset Provision.** Act §10909(c), as amended by Pub. L. No. 111-312, §101(b)(1), provides:
    (c) Sunset Provision. Each provision of law amended by this section is amended to read as such provision would read if this section had never been enacted. The amendments made by the preceding sentence shall apply to taxable years beginning after December 31, 2011.

American Recovery and Reinvestment Tax Act of 2009 (Pub. L. No. 111-5), as follows:
● IRC §25B(g)(2) was amended by Act, Div. B, §1004(b)(4) by inserting "25A(i)," after "23,". Eff. for tax years beginning after Dec. 31, 2008.
● IRC §25B(g)(2) was amended by Act, Div. B, §1142(b)(1)(C) by inserting "30," after "25D,". Eff. for vehicles acquired after date of enactment [enacted: Feb. 17, 2009]. For a transition rule, see Act, Div. B, §1142(d).
● IRC §25B(g)(2) was amended by Act, Div. B, §1144(b)(1)(C) by inserting "30B," after "30,". Eff. for tax years beginning after Dec. 31, 2008.

Energy Improvement and Extension Act of 2008 (Pub. L. No. 110-343), as follows:
● IRC §25B(g)(2) was amended by Act, Div. B, §106(e)(2)(C), by striking "section 23" and inserting "sections 23 and 25D". Eff. for tax years beginning after Dec. 31, 2007.
● IRC §25B(g)(2), as amended by Act, Div. B, §106(e)(2)(C), was amended by Act, Div. B, §205(d)(1)(C), by striking "and 25D" and inserting ", 25D, and 30D". Eff. for tax years beginning after Dec. 31, 2008.

Pension Protection Act of 2006 (Pub. L. No. 109-280), as follows:
● IRC §25B(b) was amended by Act §833(a). Eff. tax years beginning after 2006. IRC §25B(b) prior to amendment:
    (b) Applicable percentage.—For purposes of this section, the applicable percentage is the percentage determined in accordance with the following table: [*Ed. Note:* see table on the next page.]
● IRC §25B was amended by Act §812 by striking subsec. (h). Eff. Aug. 17, 2006. IRC §25B prior to being stricken:
    (h) Termination.—This section shall not apply to taxable years beginning after December 31, 2006.
● **Other Provision.** Act §811 provides:
    SEC. 811. PENSIONS AND INDIVIDUAL RETIRE-MENT ARRANGEMENT PROVISIONS OF ECO-NOMIC GROWTH AND TAX RELIEF RECONCILIA-TION ACT OF 2001 MADE PERMANENT.
    Title IX of the Economic Growth and Tax Relief Reconciliation Act of 2001 shall not apply to the provisions of, and amendments made by, subtitles A through F of title VI [§§601–666] of such Act (relating to pension and individual retirement arrangement provisions).

Gulf Opportunity Zone Act of 2005 (Pub. L. No. 109-135), as follows:
● IRC §25B(g) was amended by Act §402(i)(3)(D) by substituting "In the case of a taxable year to which section 26(a)(2) does not apply, the credit" for "The credit" in the matter preceding para. (1). Eff. tax years beginning after Dec. 31, 2005.
● **Sunset Provision.** Act §402(i)(3)(H) provides:
    (H) Application of EGTRRA Sunset.—The amendments made by this paragraph (and each part thereof) shall be subject to title IX of the Economic Growth and Tax Relief Reconciliation Act of 2001 in the same manner as the provisions of such Act to which such amendment (or part thereof) relates.
    [*Ed. Note:* see note below for sunset rule on Pub. L. No. 107-16, §901, as amended by Pub. L. No. 111-312, §101(a)(1), and Pub. L. No. 109-280, §811.]

Working Families Tax Relief Act of 2004 (Pub. L. No. 108-311), as follows:
● IRC §25B(c)(2)(B) was amended by Act §207(4) by substituting "152(f)(2)" for "151(c)(4)". Eff. for tax years beginning after Dec. 31, 2004.

Job Creation and Worker Assistance Act of 2002 (Pub. L. No. 107-147), as follows:
● IRC §25B(d)(2)(A) was amended by Act §411(m). Eff. for tax years beginning after Dec. 31, 2001, as if included in the provision of Pub. L. No. 107-16 to which it relates. IRC §25B(d)(2)(A) prior to amendment:
    (A) In general.—The qualified retirement savings contributions determined under paragraph (1) shall be reduced (but not below zero) by the sum of—
    (i) any distribution from a qualified retirement plan (as defined in §4974(c)), or from an eligible deferred compensation plan (as defined in §457(b)), received by the individual during the testing period which is includible in gross income, and
    (ii) any distribution from a Roth IRA or a Roth account received by the individual during the testing period which is not a qualified rollover contribution (as defined in §408A(e)) to a Roth IRA or a rollover under §402(c)(8)(B) to a Roth account.
● IRC §25B(g)–(h) were amended by Act §417(1) by redesignating subsec. (g) (relating to termination) as subsec. (h). Eff. Mar. 9, 2002.

● **Applicability Rule.** Act §601(b)(2) provides that amendments made by §§201(b), 202(f) and 618(b) of Pub. L. No. 107-16 shall not apply to taxable years beginning during 2002 and 2003.

Economic Growth and Tax Relief Reconciliation Act of 2001 (Pub. L. No. 107-16), as follows:
● IRC §25B was amended by Act §618(b)(1) by adding new subsec. (g). Eff. for tax years beginning after Dec. 31, 2001.
● **Sunset Provision.** Act §901, as amended by Pub. L. No. 111-312, §101(a)(1), provides the sunset rule below. But see Pub. L. No. 109-280, §811, and Pub. L. No. 111-148, §10909(c), as amended by Pub. L. No. 111-312, §101(b)(1).

    SEC. 901. SUNSET OF PROVISIONS OF ACT.

    (a) **In general.** All provisions of, and amendments made by, this Act shall not apply—

    (1) to taxable, plan, or limitation years beginning after December 31, 2012, or

    (2) in the case of title V, to estates of decedents dying, gifts made, or generation skipping transfers, after December 31, 2012.

    (b) **Application of certain laws.**—The Internal Revenue Code of 1986 and the Employee Retirement Income Security Act of 1974 shall be applied and administered to years, estates, gifts, and transfers described in subsection (a) as if the provisions and amendments described in subsection (a) had never been enacted.

IRC Sec. 25B(h)

Former Sec. 25B(b)

Adjusted Gross Income

Joint return		Head of a household		All other cases		Applicable percentage
Over	Not over	Over	Not over	Over	Not over	
	$30,000		$22,500		$15,000	50
30,000	32,500	22,500	24,375	15,000	16,250	20
32,500	50,000	24,375	37,500	16,250	25,000	10
50,000		37,500		25,000		0

SEC. 26. LIMITATION BASED ON TAX LIABILITY; DEFINITION OF TAX LIABILITY.

(a) Limitation Based on Amount of Tax.—

> ***Editor's Note***
>
> **Caution:** IRC §26(a)(1), as follows, prior to amendment by Pub. L. No. 111-312, applies to tax years beginning on or before December 31, 2011. For sunset provision, see the amendment notes to this section for Pub. L. No. 111-148, as amended by Pub. L. No. 111-312.

(1) In general.—*The aggregate amount of credits allowed by this subpart (other than sections 24, 25A(i), 25B, 25D, 30, 30B, and 30D) for the taxable year shall not exceed the excess (if any) of—*

(A) the taxpayer's regular tax liability for the taxable year, over

(B) the tentative minimum tax for the taxable year (determined without regard to the alternative minimum tax foreign tax credit).

For purposes of subparagraph (B), the taxpayer's tentative minimum tax for any taxable year beginning during 1999 shall be treated as being zero.

> ***Editor's Note***
>
> **Caution:** IRC §26(a)(1), as follows, as amended by Pub. L. No. 111-312, applies to tax years beginning after December 31, 2011. For sunset provision, see the amendment notes to this section for Pub. L. No. 111-148, as amended by Pub. L. No. 111-312.

(1) In general.—*The aggregate amount of credits allowed by this subpart (other than sections 23, 24, 25A(i), 25B, 25D, 30, 30B, and 30D) for the taxable year shall not exceed the excess (if any) of—*

(A) the taxpayer's regular tax liability for the taxable year, over

(B) the tentative minimum tax for the taxable year (determined without regard to the alternative minimum tax foreign tax credit).

For purposes of subparagraph (B), the taxpayer's tentative minimum tax for any taxable year beginning during 1999 shall be treated as being zero.

(2) Special rule for taxable years 2000 through 2011.—For purposes of any taxable year beginning during 2000, 2001, 2002, 2003, 2004, 2005, 2006, 2007, 2008, 2009, 2010, or 2011, the aggregate amount of credits allowed by this subpart for the taxable year shall not exceed the sum of—

(A) The taxpayer's regular tax liability for the taxable year reduced by the foreign tax credit allowable under section 27(a), and

(B) The tax imposed by section 55(a) for the taxable year.

(b) Regular Tax Liability. For purposes of this part—

(1) In general. The term "regular tax liability" means the tax imposed by this chapter for the taxable year.

(2) Exception for certain taxes. For purposes of paragraph (1), any tax imposed by any of the following provisions shall not be treated as tax imposed by this chapter:

* * *

(C) subsection (m)(5)(B), (q), (t), or (v) of section 72 (relating to additional taxes on certain distributions),

* * *

(E) section 530(d)(4) (relating to additional tax on certain distributions from Coverdell education savings accounts),

* * *

(Q) section 220(f)(4) (relating to additional tax on Archer MSA distributions not used for qualified medical expenses),

* * *

(S) sections 106(e)(3)(A)(ii), 223(b)(8)(B)(i)(II), and 408(d)(9)(D)(i)(II) (relating to certain failures to maintain high deductible health plan coverage),

* * *

(U) section 223(f)(4) (relating to additional tax on health savings account distributions not used for qualified medical expenses), and

(V) subsections (a)(1)(B)(i) and (b)(4)(A) of section 409A (relating to interest and additional tax with respect to certain deferred compensation).

* * *

(X) section 457A(c)(1)(B) (relating to determinability of amounts of compensation).

(c) Tentative Minimum Tax. For purposes of this part, the term "tentative minimum tax" means the amount determined under section 55(b)(1).

Recent Amendments to IRC §26

Tax Relief, Unemployment Insurance Reauthorization, and Job Creation Act of 2010 (Pub. L. No. 111-312), as follows:

- IRC §26(a)(1) was amended by Act §101(b)(1) to read as such provision would read if the Patient Protection and Affordable Care Act (Pub. L. No. 111-148), §10909, had not been enacted. Eff. for tax years beginning after Dec. 31, 2011. See note below on sunset provision.
- IRC §26(a)(2) was amended by striking "or 2009" and inserting "2009, 2010, or 2011", and by striking "2009" in the heading and inserting "2011". Eff. for taxable years beginning after Dec. 31, 2009.
- **Sunset Provision.** Act §101 provides:
  SEC. 101. TEMPORARY EXTENSION OF 2001 TAX RELIEF.
  (a) Temporary Extension.—
  (b)(1) In general.—Section 901 of the Economic Growth and Tax Relief Reconciliation Act of 2001 [Pub. L. No. 107-16] is amended by striking "December 31, 2010" both places it appears and inserting "December 31, 2012".
  (2) Effective date.—The amendment made by this subsection shall take effect as if included in the enactment of the Economic Growth and Tax Relief Reconciliation Act of 2001.
  (c) Separate Sunset for Expansion of Adoption Benefits Under the Patient Protection and Affordable Care Act [Pub. L. No. 111-148]—
  (1) In general.—Subsection (c) of section 10909 of the Patient Protection and Affordable Care Act is amended to read as follows:
  "(c) Sunset Provision.—Each provision of law amended by this section is amended to read as such provision would read if this section had never been enacted. The amendments made by the preceding sentence shall apply to taxable years beginning after December 31, 2011."
  (2) Conforming amendment.—Subsection (d) of section 10909 of such Act is amended by striking "The amendments" and inserting "Except as provided in subsection (c), the amendments".

Patient Protection and Affordable Care Act, 2010 (Pub. L. No. 111-148), as follows:

- IRC §26(a)(1) was amended by Act §10909(b)(2)(E) by striking "23,". Eff. for taxable years beginning after Dec. 31, 2009.
- **Sunset Provision.** Act §10909(c), as amended by Pub. L. No. 111-312, §101(b)(1), provides:
  (c) Sunset Provision. Each provision of law amended by this section is amended to read as such provision would read if this section had never been enacted. The amendments made by the preceding sentence shall apply to taxable years beginning after December 31, 2011.

American Recovery and Reinvestment Act of 2009 (Pub. L. No. 111-5), as follows:

- IRC §26(a)(1) was amended by Act, Div. B, §1004(b)(3) by inserting "25A(i)," after "24,". Eff. for tax years beginning after Dec. 31, 2008.
- IRC §26(a)(1) was amended by Act, Div. B, §1142(b)(1)(D) by inserting "30," after "25D,". Eff. for vehicles acquired after Feb. 17, 2009.
- IRC §26(a)(1), as amended by the Act, was amended by Act, Div. B, §1144(b)(1)(D) by inserting "30B," after "30,". Eff. for tax years beginning after Dec. 31, 2008.
- IRC §26(a)(2) was amended by Act, Div. B, §1011(a) by substituting "2008, or 2009" for "or 2008" and by substituting "2009" for "2008" in the heading. Eff. for tax years beginning after Dec. 31, 2008.

Energy Improvement and Extension Act of 2008 (Pub. L. No. 110-343), as follows:

- IRC §26(a)(1) was amended by Act, Div. B, §106(e)(2)(D) by striking "and 25B" and inserting "25B, and 25D". Eff. for tax years beginning after Dec. 31 2007.
- IRC §26(a)(1), as amended by the Act, was amended by Act, Div. B, §205(d)(1)(D), by striking "and 25D" and inserting "25D, and 30D". Eff. for tax years beginning after Dec. 31, 2008.

Tax Extenders and Alternative Minimum Tax Relief Act of 2008 (Pub. L. No. 110-343), as follows:

- IRC §26(a)(2) was amended by Act, Div. C, §101(a)(1)–(2) by striking "or 2007" and inserting "2007, or 2008", and by striking "2007" in the heading and inserting "2008". Eff. for tax years beginning after Dec. 31, 2007.
- IRC §26(b)(2), as amended by Pub. L. No. 110-289, was amended by Act, Div. C, §801(b) by striking "and" at the end of subpara. (V), striking the period at the end of subpara. (W) and inserting ", and", and adding new subpara. (X). Eff. generally for amounts deferred which are attributable to services performed after Dec. 31, 2008. See Act §801(d)(2) for a special rule.

Housing Assistance Tax Act of 2008 (Pub. L. No. 110-289), as follows:

- IRC §26(b)(2) was amended by Act §3011(b)(1) by striking "and" at the end of subpara. (U), striking the period and inserting ", and" at the end of subpara. (V) and inserting new subpara. (W). Eff. for residences purchased on or after Apr. 9, 2008, in tax years ending on or after such date.

Tax Technical Corrections Act of 2007 (Pub. L. No. 110-172), as follows:

- IRC §26(b)(2)(S)–(T) were amended by Act §11(a)(3) by redesignating subparas. (S) and (T) as subparas. (U) and (V), respectively, and by adding new subparas. (S) and (T). Eff. Dec. 29, 2007.

Tax Increase Prevention Act of 2007 (Pub. L. No. 110-166), as follows:

- IRC §26(a)(2) was amended by Act §3(a) in the heading by substituting "2007" for "2006" in the heading. Eff. for tax years beginning after Dec. 31, 2006.
- IRC §26(a)(2) was amended by Act §3(a) by substituting "2006, or 2007" for "or 2006". Eff. for tax years beginning after Dec. 31, 2006.

Tax Increase Prevention and Reconciliation Act of 2005 (Pub. L. No. 109-222), as follows:

- IRC §26(a)(2) was amended by Act §302(a)(1) by substituting "2006" for "2005" in the heading. Eff. for tax years beginning after Dec. 31, 2005.
- IRC §26(a)(2) was amended by Act §302(a)(2) by substituting "2005, or 2006" for "or 2005". Eff. for tax years beginning after Dec. 31, 2005.

Gulf Opportunity Zone Act of 2005 (Pub. L. No. 109-135), as follows:

- IRC §26(b)(2)(E) was amended by Act §412(c) by substituting "§530(d)(4)" for "§530(d)(3)". Eff. Dec. 21, 2005.
- IRC §26(b)(2) was amended by Act §403(hh) by striking the comma at the end of subpara. (R), by substituting ", and" for the period at the end of subpara. (S), and by adding subpara. (T). Eff. generally for amounts deferred after Dec. 31, 2004, as if included in the provision of Pub. L. No. 108-357 to which it relates.

Working Families Tax Relief Act of 2004 (Pub. L. No. 108-311), as follows:

- IRC §26(a)(2) was amended by Act §312(a)(1)–(2) by substituting "Rule for taxable years 2000 through 2005.—" for "Rule for 2000, 2001, 2002, and 2003.—" in the heading, and by substituting "2003, 2004, or 2005" for "or 2003". Eff. for tax years beginning after Dec. 31, 2003.
- IRC §26(b)(2) was amended by Act §408(a)(5)(A) by substituting "Medicare Advantage MSA" for "Medicare+Choice MSA". Eff. Oct. 4, 2004.
- IRC §26(b)(2)(Q)–(S) were amended by Act §401(a)(1) by striking "and" at the end of subpara. (Q), by substituting ", and" for the period at the end of subpara. (R), and adding new subpara. (S). Eff. for tax years beginning after Dec. 31, 2003, as if included in Pub. L. No. 108-173, §1201.
- **Applicability Rule.** Act §312(b)(2) provides that amendments made by §§201(b), 202(f) and 618(b) of Pub. L. No. 107-16 shall not apply to tax years beginning during 2004 or 2005.

Job Creation and Worker Assistance Act of 2002 (Pub. L. No. 107-147), as follows:

- IRC §26(a)(2) was amended by Act §601(a) by substituting "Rule for 2000, 2001, 2002, and 2003. —" for "Rule for 2000 and 2001. —" and by substituting "during 2000, 2001, 2002, or 2003," for "during 2000 or 2001,". Eff. for tax years beginning after Dec. 31, 2001.
- IRC §26(b)(2) was amended by Act §415(a) by striking "and" at the end of subpara. (P), substituting ", and" for the period at the end of subpara. (Q), and adding subpara. (R). Eff. for tax years beginning after Dec. 31, 1998, as if included in Pub. L. No. 105-33, §4006.
- **Applicability Rule.** Act §601(b)(2) provides that amendments made by Pub. L. No. 107-16, §§201(b), 202(f), and 618(b) shall not apply to tax years beginning during 2002 and 2003.

Pub. L. No. 107-22, as follows:

- IRC §26(b)(2)(E) was amended by Act §1(b)(2)(A) by substituting "Coverdell education savings" for "education individual retirement". Eff. Jul. 26, 2001.

Economic Growth and Tax Relief Reconciliation Act of 2001 (Pub. L. No. 107-16), as follows:

- IRC §26(a)(1) was amended by Act §201(b)(2)(D) by inserting "(other than §24)" after "this subpart". Eff. for tax years beginning after Dec. 31, 2001. [*Ed. Note: But see* "Applicability Rule" notes above regarding Pub. L. No. 107-147, §601(b)(2), and Pub. L. No. 108-311, §312(b)(2).]
- IRC §26(a)(1) was amended by Act §202(f)(2)(C) by substituting "§§23 and 24" for "§24". Eff. for tax years beginning after Dec. 31, 2001. [*Ed. Note: But see* "Applicability Rule" notes above regarding Pub. L. No. 107-147, §601(b)(2), and Pub. L. No. 108-311, §312(b)(2).]
- IRC §26(a)(1), as amended by Act §§201(b)(2)(D) and 202(f)(2)(C), was amended by Act §618(b)(2)(C) by substituting ", 24, and 25B" for "and 24". [*Ed. Note: But see* "Applicability Rule" notes above regarding Pub. L. No. 107-147, §601(b)(2), and Pub. L. No. 108-311, §312(b)(2).]
- **Sunset Provision.** Act §901, as amended by Pub. L. No. 111-312, §101(a)(1), provides the sunset rule below. But see Pub. L. No. 109-280, §811, and Pub. L. No. 111-148, §10909(c), as amended by Pub. L. No. 111-312, §101(b)(1).

> **SEC. 901. SUNSET OF PROVISIONS OF ACT.**
>
> (a) **In general.** All provisions of, and amendments made by, this Act shall not apply—
>
> (1) to taxable, plan, or limitation years beginning after December 31, 2012, or
>
> (2) in the case of title V, to estates of decedents dying, gifts made, or generation skipping transfers, after December 31, 2012.
>
> (b) **Application of certain laws.**—The Internal Revenue Code of 1986 and the Employee Retirement Income Security Act of 1974 shall be applied and administered to years, estates, gifts, and transfers described in subsection (a) as if the provisions and amendments described in subsection (a) had never been enacted.

* * *

Subpart C—Refundable Credits

* * *

SEC. 35. HEALTH INSURANCE COSTS OF ELIGIBLE INDIVIDUALS.

Editor's Note

IRC §35(a)(1), as follows, was amended by Pub. L. No. 111-344, effective for coverage months beginning after December 31, 2010.

(a) **In General.**—In the case of an individual, there shall be allowed as a credit against the tax imposed by subtitle A an amount equal to 65 percent (80 percent in the case of eligible coverage months beginning before ~~January 1, 2011~~ *February 13, 2011*) of the amount paid by the taxpayer for coverage of the taxpayer and qualifying family members under qualified health insurance for eligible coverage months beginning in the taxable year.

(b) Eligible Coverage Month.—For purposes of this section—

(1) In general.—The term "eligible coverage month" means any month if—

(A) as of the first day of such month, the taxpayer—

(i) is an eligible individual,

(ii) is covered by qualified health insurance, the premium for which is paid by the taxpayer,

(iii) does not have other specified coverage, and

(iv) is not imprisoned under Federal, State, or local authority, and

(B) such month begins more than 90 days after the date of the enactment of the Trade Act of 2002.

(2) Joint returns.—In the case of a joint return, the requirements of paragraph (1)(A) shall be treated as met with respect to any month if at least 1 spouse satisfies such requirements.

(c) Eligible Individual.—For purposes of this section—

(1) In general.—The term "eligible individual" means—

(A) an eligible TAA recipient,

(B) an eligible alternative TAA recipient, and

(C) an eligible PBGC pension recipient.

(2) Eligible TAA recipient.—

(A) In general.—Except as provided in subparagraph (B), the term "eligible TAA recipient" means, with respect to any month, any individual who is receiving for any day of such month a trade readjustment allowance under chapter 2 of title II of the Trade Act of 1974 or who would be eligible to receive such allowance if section 231 of such Act were applied without regard to subsection (a)(3)(B) of such section. An individual shall continue to be treated as an eligible TAA recipient during the first month that such individual would otherwise cease to be an eligible TAA recipient by reason of the preceding sentence.

Editor's Note

IRC §35(c)(2)(B), as follows, was amended by Pub. L. No. 111-344, applicable to coverage months beginning after December 31, 2010.

(B) Special rule.—In the case of any eligible coverage month beginning after the date of the enactment of this paragraph and before ~~January 1, 2011~~ *February 13, 2011*, the term "eligible TAA recipient" means, with respect to any month, any individual who—

(i) is receiving for any day of such month a trade readjustment allowance under chapter 2 of title II of the Trade Act of 1974,

(ii) would be eligible to receive such allowance except that such individual is in a break in training provided under a training program approved under section 236 of such Act that exceeds the period specified in section 233(e) of such Act, but is within the period for receiving such allowances provided under section 233(a) of such Act, or

(iii) is receiving unemployment compensation (as defined in section 85(b)) for any day of such month and who would be eligible to receive such allowance for such month if section 231 of such Act were applied without regard to subsections (a)(3)(B) and (a)(5) thereof.

An individual shall continue to be treated as an eligible TAA recipient during the first month that such individual would otherwise cease to be an eligible TAA recipient by reason of the preceding sentence.

(3) Eligible alternative TAA recipient.—The term "eligible alternative TAA recipient" means, with respect to any month, any individual who—

(A) is a worker described in section 246(a)(3)(B) of the Trade Act of 1974 who is participating in the program established under section 246(a)(1) of such Act, and

(B) is receiving a benefit for such month under section 246(a)(2) of such Act.

An individual shall continue to be treated as an eligible alternative TAA recipient during the first month that such individual would otherwise cease to be an eligible alternative TAA recipient by reason of the preceding sentence.

(4) Eligible PBGC pension recipient.—The term "eligible PBGC pension recipient" means, with respect to any month, any individual who—

(A) has attained age 55 as of the first day of such month, and

(B) is receiving a benefit for such month any portion of which is paid by the Pension Benefit Guaranty Corporation under title IV of the Employee Retirement Income Security Act of 1974.

IRC Sec. 35(c)(4)(B)

(d) Qualifying Family Member.—For purposes of this section—

(1) In general.—The term "qualifying family member" means—

(A) the taxpayer's spouse, and

(B) any dependent of the taxpayer with respect to whom the taxpayer is entitled to a deduction under section 151(c).

Such term does not include any individual who has other specified coverage.

(2) Special dependency test in case of divorced parents, etc.—If section 152(e) applies to any child with respect to any calendar year, in the case of any taxable year beginning in such calendar year, such child shall be treated as described in paragraph (1)(B) with respect to the custodial parent (as defined in section 152(e)(4)(A)) and not with respect to the non-custodial parent.

(e) Qualified Health Insurance.—For purposes of this section—

(1) In general.—The term "qualified health insurance" means any of the following:

(A) Coverage under a COBRA continuation provision (as defined in section 9832(d)(1)).

(B) State-based continuation coverage provided by the State under a State law that requires such coverage.

(C) Coverage offered through a qualified State high risk pool (as defined in section 2744(c)(2) of the Public Health Service Act).

(D) Coverage under a health insurance program offered for State employees.

(E) Coverage under a State-based health insurance program that is comparable to the health insurance program offered for State employees.

(F) Coverage through an arrangement entered into by a State and—

(i) a group health plan (including such a plan which is a multiemployer plan as defined in section 3(37) of the Employee Retirement Income Security Act of 1974),

(ii) an issuer of health insurance coverage,

(iii) an administrator, or

(iv) an employer.

(G) Coverage offered through a State arrangement with a private sector health care coverage purchasing pool.

(H) Coverage under a State-operated health plan that does not receive any Federal financial participation.

(I) Coverage under a group health plan that is available through the employment of the eligible individual's spouse.

(J) In the case of any eligible individual and such individual's qualifying family members, coverage under individual health insurance if the eligible individual was covered under individual health insurance during the entire 30-day period that ends on the date that such individual became separated from the employment which qualified such individual for—

(i) in the case of an eligible TAA recipient, the allowance described in subsection (c)(2),

(ii) in the case of an eligible alternative TAA recipient, the benefit described in subsection (c)(3)(B), or

(iii) in the case of any eligible PBGC pension recipient, the benefit described in subsection (c)(4)(B).

For purposes of this subparagraph, the term "individual health insurance" means any insurance which constitutes medical care offered to individuals other than in connection with a group health plan and does not include Federal- or State-based health insurance coverage.

Editor's Note

IRC §35(e)(1)(K), as follows, was amended by Pub. L. No. 111-344, effective for coverage months beginning after December 31, 2010.

(K) In the case of eligible coverage months beginning before ~~January 1, 2011~~ *February 13, 2012,* coverage under an employee benefit plan funded by a voluntary employees' beneficiary association (as defined in section 501(c)(9)) established pursuant to an order of a bankruptcy court, or by agreement with an authorized representative, as provided in section 1114 of title 11, United States Code.

(2) Requirements for State-based coverage.—

(A) In general.—The term "qualified health insurance" does not include any coverage described in subparagraphs (B) through (H) of paragraph (1) unless the State involved has elected to have such coverage treated as qualified health insurance under this section and such coverage meets the following requirements:

(i) Guaranteed issue.—Each qualifying individual is guaranteed enrollment if the individual pays the premium for enrollment or provides a qualified health insurance costs credit eligibility certificate described in section 7527 and pays the remainder of such premium.

(ii) No imposition of preexisting condition exclusion.—No pre-existing condition limitations are imposed with respect to any qualifying individual.

(iii) Nondiscriminatory premium.—The total premium (as determined without regard to any subsidies) with respect to a qualifying individual may not be greater than the total premium (as so determined) for a similarly situated individual who is not a qualifying individual.

(iv) Same benefits.—Benefits under the coverage are the same as (or substantially similar to) the benefits provided to similarly situated individuals who are not qualifying individuals.

(B) Qualifying individual.—For purposes of this paragraph, the term "qualifying individual" means—

(i) an eligible individual for whom, as of the date on which the individual seeks to enroll in the coverage described in subparagraphs (B) through (H) of paragraph (1), the aggregate of the periods of creditable coverage (as defined in section 9801(c)) is 3 months or longer and who, with respect to any month, meets the requirements of clauses (iii) and (iv) of subsection (b)(1)(A); and

(ii) the qualifying family members of such eligible individual.

(3) Exception.—The term "qualified health insurance" shall not include—

(A) a flexible spending or similar arrangement, and

(B) any insurance if substantially all of its coverage is of excepted benefits described in section 9832(c).

(f) Other Specified Coverage.—For purposes of this section, an individual has other specified coverage for any month if, as of the first day of such month—

(1) Subsidized coverage.—

(A) In general.—Such individual is covered under any insurance which constitutes medical care (except insurance substantially all of the coverage of which is of excepted benefits described in section 9832(c)) under any health plan maintained by any employer (or former employer) of the taxpayer or the taxpayer's spouse and at least 50 percent of the cost of such coverage (determined under section 4980B) is paid or incurred by the employer.

(B) Eligible alternative TAA recipients.—In the case of an eligible alternative TAA recipient, such individual is either—

(i) eligible for coverage under any qualified health insurance (other than insurance described in subparagraph (A), (B), or (F) of subsection (e)(1)) under which at least 50 percent of the cost of coverage (determined under section 4980B(f)(4)) is paid or incurred by an employer (or former employer) of the taxpayer or the taxpayer's spouse, or

(ii) covered under any such qualified health insurance under which any portion of the cost of coverage (as so determined) is paid or incurred by an employer (or former employer) of the taxpayer or the taxpayer's spouse.

(C) Treatment of cafeteria plans.—For purposes of subparagraphs (A) and (B), the cost of coverage shall be treated as paid or incurred by an employer to the extent the coverage is in lieu of a right to receive cash or other qualified benefits under a cafeteria plan (as defined in section 125(d)).

(2) Coverage under Medicare, Medicaid, or SCHIP.—Such individual—

(A) is entitled to benefits under part A of title XVIII of the Social Security Act or is enrolled under part B of such title, or

(B) is enrolled in the program under title XIX or XXI of such Act (other than under section 1928 of such Act).

(3) Certain other coverage.—Such individual—

(A) is enrolled in a health benefits plan under chapter 89 of title 5, United States Code, or

(B) is entitled to receive benefits under chapter 55 of title 10, United States Code.

(g) Special Rules.—

(1) Coordination with advance payments of credit.—With respect to any taxable year, the amount which would (but for this subsection) be allowed as a credit to the taxpayer under subsection (a) shall be reduced (but not below zero) by the aggregate amount paid on behalf of such taxpayer under section 7527 for months beginning in such taxable year.

(2) Coordination with other deductions.—Amounts taken into account under subsection (a) shall not be taken into account in determining any deduction allowed under section 162(l) or 213.

(3) Medical and Health Savings Accounts.—Amounts distributed from an Archer MSA (as defined in section 220(d)) or from a health savings account (as defined in section 223(d)) shall not be taken into account under subsection (a).

(4) Denial of credit to dependents.—No credit shall be allowed under this section to any individual with respect to whom a deduction under section 151 is allowable to another taxpayer for a taxable year beginning in the calendar year in which such individual's taxable year begins.

(5) Both spouses eligible individuals.—The spouse of the taxpayer shall not be treated as a qualifying family member for purposes of subsection (a), if—

(A) the taxpayer is married at the close of the taxable year,

(B) the taxpayer and the taxpayer's spouse are both eligible individuals during the taxable year, and

IRC Sec. 35(g)(5)(B)

(C) the taxpayer files a separate return for the taxable year.

(6) Marital status; certain married individuals living apart.—Rules similar to the rules of paragraphs (3) and (4) of section 21(e) shall apply for purposes of this section.

(7) Insurance which covers other individuals.—For purposes of this section, rules similar to the rules of section 213(d)(6) shall apply with respect to any contract for qualified health insurance under which amounts are payable for coverage of an individual other than the taxpayer and qualifying family members.

(8) Treatment of payments.—For purposes of this section—

(A) Payments by Secretary.—Payments made by the Secretary on behalf of any individual under section 7527 (relating to advance payment of credit for health insurance costs of eligible individuals) shall be treated as having been made by the taxpayer on the first day of the month for which such payment was made.

(B) Payments by taxpayer.—Payments made by the taxpayer for eligible coverage months shall be treated as having been made by the taxpayer on the first day of the month for which such payment was made.

Editor's Note

IRC §35(g)(9), below, as amended by Pub. L. No. 111-144, is effective for tax years ending after February 17, 2009.

---

(9) COBRA premium assistance.— In the case of an assistance eligible individual who receives premium reduction for COBRA continuation coverage under section 3001(a) of title III of division B of the American Recovery and Reinvestment Act of 2009 for any month during the taxable year, such individual shall not be treated as an eligible individual, a certified individual, or a qualifying family member for purposes of this section or section 7527 with respect to such month.

Editor's Note

IRC §35(g)(10) (as added by Pub. L. No. 111-5), below, was amended by Pub. L. No. 111-344, effective for months beginning after December 31, 2010.

---

(10) Continued qualification of family members after certain events.—In the case of eligible coverage months beginning before *February 13, 2011*—

(A) Medicare eligibility.—In the case of any month which would be an eligible coverage month with respect to an eligible individual but for subsection (f)(2)(A), such month shall be treated as an eligible coverage month with respect to such eligible individual solely for purposes of determining the amount of the credit under this section with respect to any qualifying family members of such individual (and any advance payment of such credit under section 7527). This subparagraph shall only apply with respect to the first 24 months after such eligible individual is first entitled to the benefits described in subsection (f)(2)(A).

(B) Divorce.—In the case of the finalization of a divorce between an eligible individual and such individual's spouse, such spouse shall be treated as an eligible individual for purposes of this section and section 7527 for a period of 24 months beginning with the date of such finalization, except that the only qualifying family members who may be taken into account with respect to such spouse are those individuals who were qualifying family members immediately before such finalization.

(C) Death.—In the case of the death of an eligible individual—

(i) any spouse of such individual (determined at the time of such death) shall be treated as an eligible individual for purposes of this section and section 7527 for a period of 24 months beginning with the date of such death, except that the only qualifying family members who may be taken into account with respect to such spouse are those individuals who were qualifying family members immediately before such death, and

(ii) any individual who was a qualifying family member of the decedent immediately before such death (or, in the case of an individual to whom paragraph (4) applies, the taxpayer to whom the deduction under section 151 is allowable) shall be treated as an eligible individual for purposes of this section and section 7527 for a period of 24 months beginning with the date of such death, except that in determining the amount of such credit only such qualifying family member may be taken into account.

(10)[(11)] Regulations.—The Secretary may prescribe such regulations and other guidance as may be necessary or appropriate to carry out this section, section 6050T, and section 7527.

Recent Amendments to IRC §35

Omnibus Trade Act of 2010 (Pub. L. No. 111-344), as follows:
- IRC §35(a) was amended by Act §111(a) by striking "January 1, 2011" and inserting "February 13, 2011". Eff. for coverage months beginning after Dec. 31, 2010.
- IRC §35(c)(2)(B) was amended by Act §113(a) by striking "January 1, 2011" and inserting "February 13, 2011". Eff. for coverage months beginning after Dec. 31, 2010.

• IRC §35(e)(1)(K) was amended by Act §117(a) by striking "January 1, 2011" and inserting "February 13, 2012". Eff. for coverage months beginning after Dec. 31, 2010.

• IRC §35(g)(10) (as added by Pub. L. No. 111-5) was amended by Act §115(a) by striking "January 1, 2011" and inserting "February 13, 2011". Eff. for months beginning after Dec. 31, 2010.

Temporary Extension Act of 2010 (Pub. L. No. 111-144), as follows:

• IRC §35(g)(9) was amended by Act §3(b)(5)(A) by substituting "section 3001(a) of title III of division B of the American Recovery and Reinvestment Act of 2009" for "section 3002(a) of the Health Insurance Assistance for the Unemployed Act of 2009". Eff. as if included in the provisions of Pub. L. No. 111-5, Div. B, §3001, to which it relates [effective for taxable years ending after date of enactment of Pub. L. No. 111-5 (date of enactment: Feb. 17, 2009)].

TAA Health Coverage Improvement Act of 2009 (Pub. L. No. 111-5), as follows:

• IRC §35(a) was amended by Act, Div. B, §1899A(a)(1) by inserting "(80 percent in the case of eligible coverage months beginning before January 1, 2011)" after "65 percent". Eff. for coverage months beginning on or after the first day of the first month beginning 60 days after date of enactment [enacted: Feb. 17, 2009].

• IRC §35(c)(2) was amended by Act, Div. B, §1899C. Eff. for coverage months beginning after date of enactment [enacted: Feb. 17, 2009]. IRC §35(c)(2) prior to amendment:

  (2) Eligible TAA recipient.—The term "eligible TAA recipient" means, with respect to any month, any individual who is receiving for any day of such month a trade readjustment allowance under chapter 2 of title II of the Trade Act of 1974 or who would be eligible to receive such allowance if section 231 of such Act were applied without regard to subsection (a)(3)(B) of such section. An individual shall continue to be treated as an eligible TAA recipient during the first month that such individual would otherwise cease to be an eligible TAA recipient by reason of the preceding sentence.

• IRC §35(e)(1)(K) was added by Act, Div. B, §1899G(a). Eff. for coverage months beginning after date of enactment [enacted: Feb. 17, 2009].

• IRC §35(g)(9)–(10) were amended by Act, Div. B, §1899E(a) by redesignating para. (9) as para. (10) and by adding a new para. (9). Eff. for months beginning after Dec. 31, 2009.

• IRC §35(g)(9)–(10) were amended by Act, Div. B, §3001(a)(14)(A) by redesignating para. (9) as para. (10)[11] and by adding a new para. (9). Eff. for taxable years ending after date of enactment [enacted: Feb. 17, 2009].

Tax Technical Corrections Act of 2007 (Pub. L. No. 110-172), as follows:

• IRC §35(d)(2) was amended by Act §11(a)(5) by striking "paragraph (2) or (4) of" before "section 152(e)" and by substituting "(as defined in section 152(e)(4)(A))" for "(within the meaning of section 152(e)(1))". Eff. date of enactment [enacted: Dec. 29, 2007].

Working Families Tax Relief Act of 2004 (Pub. L. No. 108-311), as follows:

• IRC §35(g)(3) was amended by Act §401(a)(2). IRC §35(g)(3) prior to amendment:

  (3) MSA distributions.—Amounts distributed from an Archer MSA (as defined in section 220(d)) shall not be taken into account under subsection (a). Eff. as if included in Pub. L. No. 108-173, §1201 [eff. tax years beginning after Dec. 31, 2003].

* * *

Editor's Note

Caution: IRC §36B, below, added by Pub. L. No. 111-148, §1401, and amended by Pub. L. No. 111-148 and Pub. L. No. 111-152, is effective for taxable years ending after December 31, 2013.

SEC. 36B. REFUNDABLE CREDIT FOR COVERAGE UNDER A QUALIFIED HEALTH PLAN.

(a) **In General.**—In the case of an applicable taxpayer, there shall be allowed as a credit against the tax imposed by this subtitle for any taxable year an amount equal to the premium assistance credit amount of the taxpayer for the taxable year.

(b) **Premium Assistance Credit Amount.**—For purposes of this section—

(1) **In general.**—The term "premium assistance credit amount" means, with respect to any taxable year, the sum of the premium assistance amounts determined under paragraph (2) with respect to all coverage months of the taxpayer occurring during the taxable year.

(2) **Premium assistance amount.**—The premium assistance amount determined under this subsection with respect to any coverage month is the amount equal to the lesser of—

(A) the monthly premiums for such month for 1 or more qualified health plans offered in the individual market within a State which cover the taxpayer, the taxpayer's spouse, or any dependent (as defined in section 152) of the taxpayer and which were enrolled in through an Exchange established by the State under 1311 of the Patient Protection and Affordable Care Act, or

(B) the excess (if any) of—

(i) the adjusted monthly premium for such month for the applicable second lowest cost silver plan with respect to the taxpayer, over

(ii) an amount equal to 1/12 of the product of the applicable percentage and the taxpayer's household income for the taxable year.

(3) **Other terms and rules relating to premium assistance amounts.**—For purposes of paragraph (2)—

(A) Applicable percentage.—

(i) In general.—Except as provided in clause (ii), the applicable percentage for any taxable year shall be the percentage such that the applicable percentage for any taxpayer whose household income is within an income tier specified in the following table shall increase, on a sliding scale in a linear manner, from the initial premium percent-

IRC Sec. 36B(b)(3)(A)(i)

age to the final premium percentage specified in   such table for such income tier:

In the case of household income (expressed as a percent of poverty line) within the following income tier:	The initial premium percentage is—	The final premium percentage is—
Up to 133%	2.0%	2.0%
133% up to 150%	3.0%	4.0%
150% up to 200%	4.0%	6.3%
200% up to 250%	6.3%	8.05%
250% up to 300%	8.05%	9.5%
300% up to 400%	9.5%	9.5%

(ii) Indexing.—

(I) In general.—Subject to subclause (II), in the case of taxable years beginning in any calendar year after 2014, the initial and final applicable percentages under clause (i) (as in effect for the preceding calendar year after application of this clause) shall be adjusted to reflect the excess of the rate of premium growth for the preceding calendar year over the rate of income growth for the preceding calendar year.

(II) Additional adjustment.—Except as provided in subclause (III), in the case of any calendar year after 2018, the percentages described in subclause (I) shall, in addition to the adjustment under subclause (I), be adjusted to reflect the excess (if any) of the rate of premium growth estimated under subclause (I) for the preceding calendar year over the rate of growth in the consumer price index for the preceding calendar year.

(III) Failsafe.—Subclause (II) shall apply for any calendar year only if the aggregate amount of premium tax credits under this section and cost-sharing reductions under section 1402 of the Patient Protection and Affordable Care Act for the preceding calendar year exceeds an amount equal to 0.504 percent of the gross domestic product for the preceding calendar year.

(B) Applicable second lowest cost silver plan.— The applicable second lowest cost silver plan with respect to any applicable taxpayer is the second lowest cost silver plan of the individual market in the rating area in which the taxpayer resides which—

(i) is offered through the same Exchange through which the qualified health plans taken into account under paragraph (2)(A) were offered, and

(ii) provides—

(I) self-only coverage in the case of an applicable taxpayer—

(aa) whose tax for the taxable year is determined under section 1(c) (relating to unmarried individuals other than surviving spouses and heads of households) and who is not allowed a deduction under section 151 for the taxable year with respect to a dependent, or

(bb) who is not described in item (aa) but who purchases only self-only coverage, and

(II) family coverage in the case of any other applicable taxpayer.

If a taxpayer files a joint return and no credit is allowed under this section with respect to 1 of the spouses by reason of subsection (e), the taxpayer shall be treated as described in clause (ii)(I) unless a deduction is allowed under section 151 for the taxable year with respect to a dependent other than either spouse and subsection (e) does not apply to the dependent.

(C) Adjusted monthly premium.—The adjusted monthly premium for an applicable second lowest cost silver plan is the monthly premium which would have been charged (for the rating area with respect to which the premiums under paragraph (2)(A) were determined) for the plan if each individual covered under a qualified health plan taken into account under paragraph (2)(A) were covered by such silver plan and the premium was adjusted only for the age of each such individual in the manner allowed under section 2701 of the Public Health Service Act. In the case of a State participating in the wellness discount demonstration project under section 2705(d) of the Public Health Service Act, the adjusted monthly premium shall be determined without regard to any premium discount or rebate under such project.

(D) Additional benefits.—If—

(i) a qualified health plan under section 1302(b)(5) of the Patient Protection and Affordable

Care Act offers benefits in addition to the essential health benefits required to be provided by the plan, or

(ii) a State requires a qualified health plan under section 1311(d)(3)(B) of such Act to cover benefits in addition to the essential health benefits required to be provided by the plan,

the portion of the premium for the plan properly allocable (under rules prescribed by the Secretary of Health and Human Services) to such additional benefits shall not be taken into account in determining either the monthly premium or the adjusted monthly premium under paragraph (2).

(E) Special rule for pediatric dental coverage.— For purposes of determining the amount of any monthly premium, if an individual enrolls in both a qualified health plan and a plan described in section 1311(d)(2)(B)(ii)(I) of the Patient Protection and Affordable Care Act for any plan year, the portion of the premium for the plan described in such section that (under regulations prescribed by the Secretary) is properly allocable to pediatric dental benefits which are included in the essential health benefits required to be provided by a qualified health plan under section 1302(b)(1)(J) of such Act shall be treated as a premium payable for a qualified health plan.

(c) Definition and Rules Relating to Applicable Taxpayers, Coverage Months, and Qualified Health Plan.—For purposes of this section—

(1) Applicable taxpayer.

(A) In general.—The term "applicable taxpayer" means, with respect to any taxable year, a taxpayer whose household income for the taxable year equals or exceeds 100 percent but does not exceed 400 percent of an amount equal to the poverty line for a family of the size involved.

(B) Special rule for certain individuals lawfully present in the united states.—If—

(i) a taxpayer has a household income which is not greater than 100 percent of an amount equal to the poverty line for a family of the size involved, and

(ii) the taxpayer is an alien lawfully present in the United States, but is not eligible for the medicaid program under title XIX of the Social Security Act by reason of such alien status,

the taxpayer shall, for purposes of the credit under this section, be treated as an applicable taxpayer with a household income which is equal to 100 percent of the poverty line for a family of the size involved.

(C) Married couples must file joint return.—If the taxpayer is married (within the meaning of section 7703) at the close of the taxable year, the taxpayer

shall be treated as an applicable taxpayer only if the taxpayer and the taxpayer's spouse file a joint return for the taxable year.

(D) Denial of credit to dependents.—No credit shall be allowed under this section to any individual with respect to whom a deduction under section 151 is allowable to another taxpayer for a taxable year beginning in the calendar year in which such individual's taxable year begins.

(2) Coverage month.—For purposes of this subsection—

(A) In general.—The term "coverage month" means, with respect to an applicable taxpayer, any month if—

(i) as of the first day of such month the taxpayer, the taxpayer's spouse, or any dependent of the taxpayer is covered by a qualified health plan described in subsection (b)(2)(A) that was enrolled in through an Exchange established by the State under section 1311 of the Patient Protection and Affordable Care Act, and

(ii) the premium for coverage under such plan for such month is paid by the taxpayer (or through advance payment of the credit under subsection (a) under section 1412 of the Patient Protection and Affordable Care Act).

(B) Exception for minimum essential coverage.—

(i) In general.—The term "coverage month" shall not include any month with respect to an individual if for such month the individual is eligible for minimum essential coverage other than eligibility for coverage described in section 5000A(f)(1)(C) (relating to coverage in the individual market).

(ii) Minimum essential coverage.—The term "minimum essential coverage" has the meaning given such term by section 5000A(f).

(C) Special rule for employer-sponsored minimum essential coverage.—For purposes of subparagraph (B)—

(i) Coverage must be affordable.—Except as provided in clause (iii), an employee shall not be treated as eligible for minimum essential coverage if such coverage—

(I) consists of an eligible employer-sponsored plan (as defined in section 5000A(f)(2)), and

(II) the employee's required contribution (within the meaning of section 5000A(e)(1)(B)) with respect to the plan exceeds 9.5 percent of the applicable taxpayer's household income.

This clause shall also apply to an individual who is eligible to enroll in the plan by reason of a relationship the individual bears to the employee.

(ii) Coverage must provide minimum value.— Except as provided in clause (iii), an employee

IRC Sec. 36B(c)(2)(C)(ii)

shall not be treated as eligible for minimum essential coverage if such coverage consists of an eligible employer-sponsored plan (as defined in section 5000A(f)(2)) and the plan's share of the total allowed costs of benefits provided under the plan is less than 60 percent of such costs.

(iii) Employee or family must not be covered under employer plan.—Clauses (i) and (ii) shall not apply if the employee (or any individual described in the last sentence of clause (i)) is covered under the eligible employer-sponsored plan or the grandfathered health plan.

(iv) Indexing.—In the case of plan years beginning in any calendar year after 2014, the Secretary shall adjust the 9.5 percent under clause (i)(II) in the same manner as the percentages are adjusted under subsection (b)(3)(A)(ii).

> ### Editor's Note
>
> IRC §36B(c)(2)(D) was added by Pub. L. No. 111-148 and stricken by Pub. L. No. 112-10, applicable to tax years beginning after December 31, 2013.

(D) [Stricken.]

(3) Definitions and other rules.—

(A) Qualified health plan.—The term "qualified health plan" has the meaning given such term by section 1301(a) of the Patient Protection and Affordable Care Act, except that such term shall not include a qualified health plan which is a catastrophic plan described in section 1302(e) of such Act.

(B) Grandfathered health plan.—The term "grandfathered health plan" has the meaning given such term by section 1251 of the Patient Protection and Affordable Care Act.

(d) Terms Relating to Income and Families.—For purposes of this section—

(1) Family size.—The family size involved with respect to any taxpayer shall be equal to the number of individuals for whom the taxpayer is allowed a deduction under section 151 (relating to allowance of deduction for personal exemptions) for the taxable year.

(2) Household income.—

(A) Household income.—The term "household income" means, with respect to any taxpayer, an amount equal to the sum of—

(i) the modified adjusted gross income of the taxpayer, plus

(ii) the aggregate modified adjusted gross incomes of all other individuals who—

(I) were taken into account in determining the taxpayer's family size under paragraph (1), and

(II) were required to file a return of tax imposed by section 1 for the taxable year.

(B) Modified adjusted gross income.—The term "modified adjusted gross income" means adjusted gross income increased by—

(i) any amount excluded from gross income under section 911, and

(ii) any amount of interest received or accrued by the taxpayer during the taxable year which is exempt from tax.

(3) Poverty level.—

(A) In general.—The term "poverty line" has the meaning given that term in section 2110(c)(5) of the Social Security Act (42 U.S.C. 1397jj(c)(5)).

(B) Poverty line used.—In the case of any qualified health plan offered through an Exchange for coverage during a taxable year beginning in a calendar year, the poverty line used shall be the most recently published poverty line as of the 1st day of the regular enrollment period for coverage during such calendar year.

(e) Rules for Individuals Not Lawfully Present.—

(1) In general.—If 1 or more individuals for whom a taxpayer is allowed a deduction under section 151 (relating to allowance of deduction for personal exemptions) for the taxable year (including the taxpayer or his spouse) are individuals who are not lawfully present—

(A) the aggregate amount of premiums otherwise taken into account under clauses (i) and (ii) of subsection (b)(2)(A) shall be reduced by the portion (if any) of such premiums which is attributable to such individuals, and

(B) for purposes of applying this section, the determination as to what percentage a taxpayer's household income bears to the poverty level for a family of the size involved shall be made under one of the following methods:

(i) A method under which—

(I) the taxpayer's family size is determined by not taking such individuals into account, and

(II) the taxpayer's household income is equal to the product of the taxpayer's household income (determined without regard to this subsection) and a fraction—

(aa) the numerator of which is the poverty line for the taxpayer's family size determined after application of subclause (I), and

(bb) the denominator of which is the poverty line for the taxpayer's family size determined without regard to subclause (I).

(ii) A comparable method reaching the same result as the method under clause (i).

(2) Lawfully present.—For purposes of this section, an individual shall be treated as lawfully present only if the individual is, and is reasonably expected to be for the entire period of enrollment for which the credit under this section is being claimed, a citizen or national of the United States or an alien lawfully present in the United States.

(3) Secretarial authority.—The Secretary of Health and Human Services, in consultation with the Secretary, shall prescribe rules setting forth the methods by which calculations of family size and household income are made for purposes of this subsection. Such rules shall be designed to ensure that the least burden is placed on individuals enrolling in qualified health plans through an Exchange and taxpayers eligible for the credit allowable under this section.

(f) Reconciliation of Credit and Advance Credit.—

(1) In general.—The amount of the credit allowed under this section for any taxable year shall be reduced (but not below zero) by the amount of any advance payment of such credit under section 1412 of the Patient Protection and Affordable Care Act.

(2) Excess advance payments.—

(A) In general.—If the advance payments to a taxpayer under section 1412 of the Patient Protection and Affordable Care Act for a taxable year exceed the credit allowed by this section (determined without regard to paragraph (1)), the tax imposed by this chapter for the taxable year shall be increased by the amount of such excess.

Editor's Note

Caution: IRC §36B(f)(2)(B)(i), below, as amended by Pub. L. No. 112-9, applies to tax years ending after December 31, 2013.

(B) Limitation on increase.—

(i) *In general.—In the case of a taxpayer whose household income is less than 400 percent of the poverty line for the size of the family involved for the taxable year, the amount of the increase under subparagraph (A) shall in no event exceed the applicable dollar amount determined in accordance with the following table (one-half of such amount in the case of a taxpayer whose tax is determined under section 1(c) for the taxable year):*

If the household income (expressed as a percent of poverty line) is:	*The applicable dollar amount is:*
Less than 200%	*$ 600*
At least 200% but less than 300%	*$1,500*
At least 300% but less than 400%	*$2,500.*

Editor's Note

Caution: IRC §36B(f)(2)(B)(ii), below, as amended by Pub. L. No. 111-309, applies to taxable years beginning after December 31, 2013.

(ii) Indexing of amount.—In the case of any calendar year beginning after 2014, each of the dollar amounts *in the table contained* under clause (i) shall be increased by an amount equal to—

(I) such dollar amount, multiplied by

(II) the cost-of-living adjustment determined under section 1(f)(3) for the calendar year, determined by substituting "calendar year 2013" for "calendar year 1992" in subparagraph (B) thereof.

If the amount of any increase under clause (i) is not a multiple of $50, such increase shall be rounded to the next lowest multiple of $50.

(3) Information requirement.—Each Exchange (or any person carrying out 1 or more responsibilities of an Exchange under section 1311(f)(3) or 1321(c) of the Patient Protection and Affordable Care Act) shall provide the following information to the Secretary and to the taxpayer with respect to any health plan provided through the Exchange:

(A) The level of coverage described in section 1302(d) of the Patient Protection and Affordable Care Act and the period such coverage was in effect.

(B) The total premium for the coverage without regard to the credit under this section or cost-sharing reductions under section 1402 of such Act.

(C) The aggregate amount of any advance payment of such credit or reductions under section 1412 of such Act.

(D) The name, address, and TIN of the primary insured and the name and TIN of each other individual obtaining coverage under the policy.

IRC Sec. 36B(f)(3)(D)

(E) Any information provided to the Exchange, including any change of circumstances, necessary to determine eligibility for, and the amount of, such credit.

(F) Information necessary to determine whether a taxpayer has received excess advance payments.

(g) Regulations.—The Secretary shall prescribe such regulations as may be necessary to carry out the provisions of this section, including regulations which provide for—

(1) the coordination of the credit allowed under this section with the program for advance payment of the credit under section 1412 of the Patient Protection and Affordable Care Act, and

(2) the application of subsection (f) where the filing status of the taxpayer for a taxable year is different from such status used for determining the advance payment of the credit.

Amendments to IRC §36B

Department of Defense and Full-Year Continuing Appropriations Act, 2011 (Pub. L. No. 112-10), as follows:

● IRC §36B(c)(2) was amended by Act §1858(b)(1) by striking subpara. (D). Eff. as if included in the provision of, and the amendments made by, Pub. L. No. 111-148 to which it relates [Ed. Note: effective for tax years beginning after Dec. 31, 2013]. IRC §36B(c)(2) prior to being stricken:

(D) Exception for individual receiving free choice vouchers.—The term "coverage month" shall not include any month in which such individual has a free choice voucher provided under section 10108 of the Patient Protection and Affordable Care Act.

Comprehensive 1099 Taxpayer Protection and Repayment of Exchange Subsidy Overpayments Act of 2011 (Pub. L. No. 112-9), as follows:

● IRC §36B(f)(2)(B)(i) was amended by Act §4(a). Eff. for tax years ending after Dec. 31, 2013. IRC §36B(f)(2)(B)(i) prior to amendment:

(i) In general.—In the case of a taxpayer whose household income is less than 500 percent of the poverty line for the size of the family involved for the taxable year, the amount of the increase under subparagraph (A) shall in no event exceed the applicable dollar amount determined in accordance with the following table (one-half of such amount in the case of a taxpayer whose tax is determined under section 1(c) for the taxable year):

If the household income (expressed as a percentage of poverty line) is:	The applicable dollar amount is:
Less than 200%	$ 600
At least 200% but less than 250%	$1,000
At least 250% but less than 300%	$1,500
At least 300% but less than 350%	$2,000
At least 350% but less than 400%	$2,500
At least 400% but less than 450%	$3,000
At least 450% but less than 500%	$3,500

Medicare and Medicaid Extenders Act of 2010 (Pub. L. No. 111-309), as follows:

● IRC §36B(f)(2)(B) was amended by Act §208(a) as precedes clause (ii). Eff. for tax years beginning after Dec. 31, 2013.

● IRC §36B(f)(2)(B)(ii) was amended by Act §208(b) by inserting "in the table contained" after "each of the dollar amounts". Eff. for tax years beginning after Dec. 31, 2013.

Health Care and Education Reconciliation Act of 2010 (Pub. L. No. 111-152), as follows:

● IRC §36B(b)(3)(A) was amended in cl. (i) by Act §1001(a)(1)(A) by substituting "for any taxable year shall be the percentage such that the applicable percentage for any taxpayer whose household income is within an income tier specified in the following table shall increase, on a sliding scale in a linear manner, from the initial premium percentage to the final premium percentage specified in such table for such income tier:

"In the case of household income (expressed as a percent of poverty line) within the following income tier:	The initial premium percentage is—	The final premium percentage is—
Up to 133%	2.0%	2.0%
133% up to 150%	3.0%	4.0%
150% up to 200%	4.0%	6.3%
200% up to 250%	6.3%	8.05%
250% up to 300%	8.05%	9.5%
300% up to 400%	9.5%	9.5%"

for "with respect to any taxpayer for any taxable year is equal to 2.8 percent, increased by the number of percentage points (not greater than 7) which bears the same ratio to 7 percentage points as—(I) the taxpayer's household income for the taxable year in excess of 100 percent of the poverty line for a family of the size involved, bears to (II) an amount equal to 200 percent of the poverty line for a family of the size involved".

Eff. on date of enactment of this Act [enacted: Mar. 30, 2010].

- IRC §36B(b)(3)(A) was amended by §1001(a)(1)(B) by striking clauses (ii) and (iii) and by adding clause (ii). Eff. on date of enactment of this Act [enacted: Mar. 30, 2010]. IRC §36B(b)(3)(A)(ii) and (iii) prior to amendment:

   (ii) Special rule for taxpayers under 133 percent of poverty line.—If a taxpayer's household income for the taxable year equals or exceeds 100 percent, but not more than 133 percent, of the poverty line for a family of the size involved, the taxpayer's applicable percentage shall be 2 percent.

   (iii) Indexing.—In the case of taxable years beginning in any calendar year after 2014, the Secretary shall adjust the initial and final applicable percentages under clause (i), and the 2 percent under clause (ii), for the calendar year to reflect the excess of the rate of premium growth between the preceding calendar year and 2013 over the rate of income growth for such period.

- IRC §36B(c)(2)(C)(i)(II) was amended by Act §1001(a)(2)(A) by substituting "9.5 percent" for "9.8 percent". Eff. on date of enactment of this Act [enacted: Mar. 30, 2010].
- IRC §36B(c)(2)(C)(iv) was amended by Act §1001(a)(2)(A), amended clause (iv) by substituting "9.8 percent" for "9.5 percent". Eff. on date of enactment of this Act [enacted: Mar. 30, 2010].
- IRC §36B(c)(2)(C)(iv) was amended by Act §1001(a)(2)(B) by substituting "(b)(3)(A)(ii)" for "(b)(3)(A)(iii)". Eff. on date of enactment of this Act [enacted: Mar. 30, 2010].
- IRC §36B(d)(2)(A)(i)–(ii) were amended by Act §1004(a)(1)(A) by substituting "modified adjusted gross" for "modified gross" each place it appeared. Eff. on date of enactment of this Act [enacted: Mar. 30, 2010].
- IRC §36B(d)(2)(B) was amended by Act §1004(a)(2)(A). Eff. on date of enactment of this Act [enacted: Mar. 30, 2010]. IRC §36B(d)(2)(B) prior to amendment:

   (B) Modified Gross Income.—The term "modified gross income" means gross income—
   (i) decreased by the amount of any deduction allowable under paragraph (1), (3), (4), or (10) of section 62(a),
   (ii) increased by the amount of interest received or accrued during the taxable year which is exempt from tax imposed by this chapter, and
   (iii) determined without regard to sections 911, 931, and 933.

- IRC §36B(f)(3) was added by Act §1004(c). Eff. on date of enactment of this Act [enacted: Mar. 30, 2010].

Patient Protection and Affordable Care Act, 2010 (Pub. L. No. 111-148), as follows:
- IRC §36B was added by Act §1401(a). Eff. for taxable years ending after Dec. 31, 2013.
- IRC §36B(b)(3)(A)(ii) was amended by Act §10105(a) striking "is in excess of" and inserting "equals or exceeds". Eff. for taxable years ending after Dec. 31, 2013.
- IRC §36B(c)(1)(A) was amended by Act §10105(b) by inserting "equals or" before "exceeds". Eff. for taxable years ending after Dec. 31, 2013.
- IRC §36B(c)(2)(C)(iv) was amended by Act §10105(c) by striking "subsection (b)(3)(A)(ii)" and inserting "subsection (b)(3)(A)(iii)". Eff. for taxable years ending after Dec. 31, 2013.
- IRC §36B(c)(2)(D) was added by Act §10108(h)(1). Eff. for taxable years ending after Dec. 31, 2013.

---

* * *

Subpart D—Business Related Credits

SEC. 45E. SMALL EMPLOYER PENSION PLAN STARTUP COSTS.

(a) General Rule.—For purposes of section 38, in the case of an eligible employer, the small employer pension plan startup cost credit determined under this section for any taxable year is an amount equal to 50 percent of the qualified startup costs paid or incurred by the taxpayer during the taxable year.

(b) Dollar Limitation. The amount of the credit determined under this section for any taxable year shall not exceed—

   (1) $500 for the first credit year and each of the 2 taxable years immediately following the first credit year, and

   (2) zero for any other taxable year.

(c) Eligible Employer. For purposes of this section—

   (1) In general. The term "eligible employer" has the meaning given such term by section 408(p)(2)(C)(i).

   (2) Requirement for new qualified employer plans. Such term shall not include an employer if, during the 3-taxable year period immediately preceding the 1st taxable year for which the credit under this section is otherwise allowable for a qualified employer plan of the employer, the employer or any member of any controlled group including the employer (or any predecessor of either) established or maintained a qualified employer plan with respect to which contributions were made, or benefits were accrued, for substantially the same employees as are in the qualified employer plan.

(d) Other Definitions. For purposes of this section—

   (1) Qualified startup costs.

   (A) In general. The term "qualified startup costs" means any ordinary and necessary expenses of an eligible employer which are paid or incurred in connection with—

      (i) the establishment or administration of an eligible employer plan, or

      (ii) the retirement-related education of employees with respect to such plan.

   (B) Plan must have at least 1 participant. Such term shall not include any expense in connection with a plan that does not have at least 1 employee eligible to participate who is not a highly compensated employee.

   (2) Eligible employer plan. The term "eligible employer plan" means a qualified employer plan within the meaning of section 4972(d).

   (3) First credit year. The term "first credit year" means—

   (A) the taxable year which includes the date that the eligible employer plan to which such costs relate becomes effective, or

   (B) at the election of the eligible employer, the taxable year preceding the taxable year referred to in subparagraph (A).

(e) Special Rules. For purposes of this section—

(1) Aggregation rules. All persons treated as a single employer under subsection (a) or (b) of section 52, or subsection (m) or (o) of section 414, shall be treated as one person. All eligible employer plans shall be treated as 1 eligible employer plan.

(2) Disallowance of deduction. No deduction shall be allowed for that portion of the qualified start-up costs paid or incurred for the taxable year which is equal to the credit determined under subsection (a).

(3) Election not to claim credit. This section shall not apply to a taxpayer for any taxable year if such taxpayer elects to have this section not apply for such taxable year.

Amendments to §45E

Pension Protection Act (Pub. L. No. 109-280) as follows:

• **Sunset Provision.** Act §811, provides:

> **SEC. 811. PENSIONS AND INDIVIDUAL RETIRE-MENT ARRANGEMENT PROVISIONS OF ECO-NOMIC GROWTH AND TAX RELIEF RECONCILIA-TION ACT OF 2001 MADE PERMANENT.**
>
> Title IX of the Economic Growth and Tax Relief Reconciliation Act of 2001 [Pub. L. No. 107-16] shall not apply to the provisions of, and amendments made by, subtitles A through F [§§601–666] of title VI of such Act (relating to pension and individual retirement arrangement provisions).

Job Creation and Worker Assistance Act of 2002 (Pub. L. No. 107-147), as follows:

• IRC §45E(e)(1) was amended by Act §411(n)(1) by substituting "(m)" for "(n)". Eff. as if included in the provision of Pub. L. No. 107-16 to which it relates [§619; eff. for costs paid or incurred in tax years beginning after Dec. 31, 2001, for qualified employer plans first effective after such date].

Economic Growth and Tax Relief Reconciliation Act of 2001 (Pub. L. No. 107-16), as follows:

• IRC §45E was added by Act §619(a). Eff. for costs paid or incurred in tax years beginning after Dec. 31, 2001, for qualified employer plans first effective after such date. [*Ed. Note:* Pub. L. No. 107-147, §411(n)(2), amended Pub. L. No. 107-16, §619(d), by substituting "first effective" for "established".]

• **Sunset Provision.** Act §901, as amended by Pub. L. No. 111-312, §101(a)(1), provides the sunset rule below. But see Pub. L. No. 109-280, §811, and Pub. L. No. 111-148, §10909(c), as amended by Pub. L. No. 111-312, §101(b)(1).

> **SEC. 901. SUNSET OF PROVISIONS OF ACT.**
>
> **(a) In general.** All provisions of, and amendments made by, this Act shall not apply—
>
> **(1)** to taxable, plan, or limitation years beginning after December 31, 2012, or
>
> **(2)** in the case of title V, to estates of decedents dying, gifts made, or generation skipping transfers, after December 31, 2012.
>
> **(b) Application of certain laws.**—The Internal Revenue Code of 1986 and the Employee Retirement Income Security Act of 1974 shall be applied and administered to years, estates, gifts, and transfers described in subsection (a) as if the provisions and amendments described in subsection (a) had never been enacted.

---

* * *

> ***Editor's Note***
>
> IRC §45R, as follows, was added and amended by Pub. L. No. 111-148, effective for amounts paid or incurred in taxable years beginning after December 31, 2009.

SEC. 45R. EMPLOYEE HEALTH INSURANCE EXPENSES OF SMALL EMPLOYERS.

(a) General Rule.—For purposes of section 38, in the case of an eligible small employer, the small employer health insurance credit determined under this section for any taxable year in the credit period is the amount determined under subsection (b).

(b) Health Insurance Credit Amount.—Subject to subsection (c), the amount determined under this subsection with respect to any eligible small employer is equal to 50 percent (35 percent in the case of a tax-exempt eligible small employer) of the lesser of—

(1) the aggregate amount of nonelective contributions the employer made on behalf of its employees during the taxable year under the arrangement described in subsection (d)(4) for premiums for qualified health plans offered by the employer to its employees through an Exchange, or

(2) the aggregate amount of nonelective contributions which the employer would have made during the taxable year under the arrangement if each employee taken into account under paragraph (1) had enrolled in a qualified health plan which had a premium equal to the average premium (as determined by the Secretary of Health and Human Services) for the small group market in the rating area in which the employee enrolls for coverage.

(c) Phaseout of Credit Amount Based on Number of Employees and Average Wages.—The amount of the credit determined under subsection (b) without regard to this subsection shall be reduced (but not below zero) by the sum of the following amounts:

(1) Such amount multiplied by a fraction the numerator of which is the total number of full-time equivalent employees of the employer in excess of 10 and the denominator of which is 15.

(2) Such amount multiplied by a fraction the numerator of which is the average annual wages of the employer in excess of the dollar amount in effect under subsection (d)(3)(B) and the denominator of which is such dollar amount.

(d) Eligible Small Employer.—For purposes of this section—

(1) In general.—The term "eligible small employer" means, with respect to any taxable year, an employer—

(A) which has no more than 25 full-time equivalent employees for the taxable year,

(B) the average annual wages of which do not exceed an amount equal to twice the dollar amount in effect under paragraph (3)(B) for the taxable year, and

(C) which has in effect an arrangement described in paragraph (4).

(2) Full-time equivalent employees.—

(A) In general.—The term "full-time equivalent employees" means a number of employees equal to the number determined by dividing—

(i) the total number of hours of service for which wages were paid by the employer to employees during the taxable year, by

(ii) 2,080.

Such number shall be rounded to the next lowest whole number if not otherwise a whole number.

(B) Excess hours not counted.—If an employee works in excess of 2,080 hours of service during any taxable year, such excess shall not be taken into account under subparagraph (A).

(C) Hours of service.—The Secretary, in consultation with the Secretary of Labor, shall prescribe such regulations, rules, and guidance as may be necessary to determine the hours of service of an employee, including rules for the application of this paragraph to employees who are not compensated on an hourly basis.

(3) Average annual wages.—

(A) In general.—The average annual wages of an eligible small employer for any taxable year is the amount determined by dividing—

(i) the aggregate amount of wages which were paid by the employer to employees during the taxable year, by

(ii) the number of full-time equivalent employees of the employee determined under paragraph (2) for the taxable year.

Such amount shall be rounded to the next lowest multiple of $1,000 if not otherwise such a multiple.

(B) Dollar amount.—For purposes of paragraph (1)(B) and subsection (c)(2)—

(i) 2010, 2011, 2012, and 2013—The dollar amount in effect under this paragraph for taxable years beginning in 2010, 2011, 2012, or 2013 is $25,000.

(ii) Subsequent Years.—In the case of a taxable year beginning in a calendar year after 2013, the dollar amount in effect under this paragraph shall be equal to $25,000, multiplied by the cost-of-living adjustment under section 1(f)(3) for the calendar year, determined by substituting "calendar year 2012" for "calendar year 1992" in subparagraph (B) thereof.

(4) Contribution arrangement.—An arrangement is described in this paragraph if it requires an eligible small employer to make a nonelective contribution on behalf of each employee who enrolls in a qualified health plan offered to employees by the employer through an exchange in an amount equal to a uniform percentage (not less than 50 percent) of the premium cost of the qualified health plan.

(5) Seasonal worker hours and wages not counted.—For purposes of this subsection—

(A) In general.—The number of hours of service worked by, and wages paid to, a seasonal worker of an employer shall not be taken into account in determining the full-time equivalent employees and average annual wages of the employer unless the worker works for the employer on more than 120 days during the taxable year.

(B) Definition of seasonal workers.—The term "seasonal worker" means a worker who performs labor or services on a seasonal basis as defined by the Secretary of Labor, including workers covered by section 500.20(s)(1) of title 29, Code of Federal Regulations and retail workers employed exclusively during holiday seasons.

(e) Other Rules and Definitions.—For purposes of this section—

(1) Employee.—

(A) Certain employees excluded.—The term "employee" shall not include—

(i) an employee within the meaning of section 401(c)(1),

(ii) any 2-percent shareholder (as defined in section 1372(b)) of an eligible small business which is an S corporation,

(iii) any 5-percent owner (as defined in section 416(i)(1)(B)(i)) of an eligible small business, or

(iv) any individual who bears any of the relationships described in subparagraphs (A) through (G) of section 152(d)(2) to, or is a dependent described in section 152(d)(2)(H) of, an individual described in clause (i), (ii), or (iii).

(B) Leased employees.—The term "employee" shall include a leased employee within the meaning of section 414(n).

(2) Credit period.—The term "credit period" means, with respect to any eligible small employer, the 2-consecutive-taxable year period beginning with the 1st taxable year in which the employer (or any predecessor) offers 1 or more qualified health plans to its employees through an Exchange.

(3) Nonelective contribution.—The term "nonelective contribution" means an employer contribution other than an employer contribution pursuant to a salary reduction arrangement.

IRC Sec. 45R(e)(3)

(4) Wages.—The term "wages" has the meaning given such term by section 3121(a) (determined without regard to any dollar limitation contained in such section).

(5) Aggregation and other rules made applicable.—

(A) Aggregation rules.—All employers treated as a single employer under subsection (b), (c), (m), or (o) of section 414 shall be treated as a single employer for purposes of this section.

(B) Other rules.—Rules similar to the rules of subsections (c), (d), and (e) of section 52 shall apply.

(f) Credit Made Available to Tax-Exempt Eligible Small Employers.—

(1) In general.—In the case of a tax-exempt eligible small employer, there shall be treated as a credit allowable under subpart C (and not allowable under this subpart) the lesser of—

(A) the amount of the credit determined under this section with respect to such employer, or

(B) the amount of the payroll taxes of the employer during the calendar year in which the taxable year begins.

(2) Tax-exempt eligible small employer.—For purposes of this section, the term "tax-exempt eligible small employer" means an eligible small employer which is any organization described in section 501(c) which is exempt from taxation under section 501(a).

(3) Payroll taxes.—For purposes of this subsection—

(A) In general.—The term "payroll taxes" means—

(i) amounts required to be withheld from the employees of the tax-exempt eligible small employer under section 3401(a),

(ii) amounts required to be withheld from such employees under section 3101(b), and

(iii) amounts of the taxes imposed on the tax-exempt eligible small employer under section 3111(b).

(B) Special rule.—A rule similar to the rule of section 24(d)(2)(C) shall apply for purposes of subparagraph (A).

(g) Application of Section for Calendar Years 2010, 2011, 2012, and 2013.—In the case of any taxable year beginning in 2010, 2011, 2012, or 2013, the following modifications to this section shall apply in determining the amount of the credit under subsection (a):

(1) No credit period required.—The credit shall be determined without regard to whether the taxable

year is in a credit period and for purposes of applying this section to taxable years beginning after 2013, no credit period shall be treated as beginning with a taxable year beginning before 2014.

(2) Amount of credit.—The amount of the credit determined under subsection (b) shall be determined—

(A) by substituting "35 percent (25 percent in the case of a tax-exempt eligible small employer)" for "50 percent (35 percent in the case of a tax-exempt eligible small employer)",

(B) by reference to an eligible small employer's nonelective contributions for premiums paid for health insurance coverage (within the meaning of section 9832(b)(1)) of an employee, and

(C) by substituting for the average premium determined under subsection (b)(2) the amount the Secretary of Health and Human Services determines is the average premium for the small group market in the State in which the employer is offering health insurance coverage (or for such area within the State as is specified by the Secretary).

(3) Contribution arrangement.—An arrangement shall not fail to meet the requirements of subsection (d)(4) solely because it provides for the offering of insurance outside of an Exchange.

(h) Insurance Definitions.—Any term used in this section which is also used in the Public Health Service Act or subtitle A of title I of the Patient Protection and Affordable Care Act shall have the meaning given such term by such Act or subtitle.

(i) Regulations.—The Secretary shall prescribe such regulations as may be necessary to carry out the provisions of this section, including regulations to prevent the avoidance of the 2-year limit on the credit period through the use of successor entities and the avoidance of the limitations under subsection (c) through the use of multiple entities.

Amendments to IRC §45R

Patient Protection and Affordable Care Act, 2010 (Pub. L. No. 111-148), as follows:
- IRC §45R was added by Act §1421(a). Eff. for amounts paid or incurred in tax years beginning after Dec. 31, 2009, Act §1421(f), as amended by Act §10105(e)(4).
- IRC §45R(d)(3)(B) was amended by Act §10105(e)(1). Eff. for amounts paid or incurred in tax years beginning after Dec. 31, 2009, Act §1421(f), as amended by Act §10105(e)(4). IRC §45R(d)(3)(B) prior to amendment:
  (B) Dollar Amount.—For purposes of paragraph (1)(B)—
  (i) 2011, 2012, AND 2013—The dollar amount in effect under this paragraph for taxable years beginning in 2011, 2012, or 2013 is $20,000.
  (ii) Subsequent Years.—In the case of a taxable year beginning in a calendar year after 2013, the dollar amount in effect under this paragraph shall be equal to $20,000, multiplied by the cost-of-living adjustment determined under section 1(f)(3) for the calendar year, determined by substituting "calendar year 2012" for "calendar year 1992" in subparagraph (B) thereof.

• IRC §45R(g) was amended by Act §10105(e)(2) by striking "2011" both places it appeared and inserting "2010, 2011". Eff. for amounts paid or incurred in tax years beginning after Dec. 31, 2009, Act §1421(f), as amended by Act §10105(e)(4).

* * *

Subchapter B—Computation of Taxable Income

Part I—Definition of Gross Income, Adjusted Gross Income, Taxable Income, etc.

SEC. 61. GROSS INCOME DEFINED.

(a) **General Definition**.—Except as otherwise provided in this subtitle, gross income means all income from whatever source derived, including (but not limited to) the following items:

(1) Compensation for services, including fees, commissions, fringe benefits, and similar items;

(2) Gross income derived from business;

(3) Gains derived from dealings in property;

(4) Interest;

(5) Rents;

(6) Royalties;

(7) Dividends;

(8) Alimony and separate maintenance payments;

(9) Annuities;

(10) Income from life insurance and endowment contracts;

(11) Pensions;

(12) Income from discharge of indebtedness;

(13) Distributive share of partnership gross income;

(14) Income in respect of a decedent; and

(15) Income from an interest in an estate or trust.

(b) **Cross References**.—For items specifically included in gross income, see part II (section 71 and following). For items specifically excluded from gross income, see part III (section 101 and following).

SEC. 62. ADJUSTED GROSS INCOME DEFINED.

(a) **General Rule**.—For purposes of this subtitle, the term "adjusted gross income" means, in the case of an individual, gross income minus the following deductions:

(1) **Trade and business deductions**.—The deductions allowed by this chapter (other than by part VII of this subchapter) which are attributable to a trade or business carried on by the taxpayer, if such trade or business does not consist of the performance of services by the taxpayer as an employee.

(2) **Certain trade and business deductions of employees.—**

(A) Reimbursed expenses of employees.—The deductions allowed by part VI (section 161 and following) which consist of expenses paid or incurred by the taxpayer, in connection with the performance by him of services as an employee, under a reimbursement or other expense allowance arrangement with his employer. The fact that the reimbursement may be provided by a third party shall not be determinative of whether or not the preceding sentence applies.

(B) Certain expenses of performing artists.—The deductions allowed by section 162 which consist of expenses paid or incurred by a qualified performing artist in connection with the performances by him of services in the performing arts as an employee.

(C) Certain expenses of officials.—The deductions allowed by section 162 which consist of expenses paid or incurred with respect to services performed by an official as an employee of a State or a political subdivision thereof in a position compensated in whole or in part on a fee basis.

Editor's Note

IRC §62(a)(2)(D), as follows, was amended by Pub. L. No. 111-312, effective for tax years beginning after December 31, 2009.

(D) Certain expenses of elementary and secondary school teachers.—In the case of taxable years beginning during 2002, 2003, 2004, 2005, 2006, 2007, 2008, ~~or 2009~~ *2009, 2010, or 2011*, the deductions allowed by section 162 which consist of expenses, not in excess of $250, paid or incurred by an eligible educator in connection with books, supplies (other than nonathletic supplies for courses of instruction in health or physical education), computer equipment (including related software and services) and other equipment, and supplementary materials used by the eligible educator in the classroom.

(E) Certain expenses of members of reserve components of the Armed Forces of the United States.—The deductions allowed by section 162 which consist of expenses, determined at a rate not in excess of the rates for travel expenses (including per diem in lieu of subsistence) authorized for employees of agencies under subchapter I of chapter 57 of title 5, United States Code, paid or incurred by the taxpayer in connection with the performance of services by such taxpayer as a member of a reserve component of the Armed Forces of the United States for any period during which such individual is more than 100 miles away from home in connection with such services.

(3) Losses from sale or exchange of property.— The deductions allowed by part VI (section 161 and following) as losses from the sale or exchange of property.

(4) Deductions attributable to rents and royalties.—The deductions allowed by part VI (section 161 and following), by section 212 (relating to expenses for production of income), and by section 611 (relating to depletion) which are attributable to property held for the production of rents or royalties.

(5) Certain deductions of life tenants and income beneficiaries of property.—In the case of a life tenant of property, or an income beneficiary of property held in trust, or an heir, legatee, or devisee of an estate, the deduction for depreciation allowed by section 167 and the deduction allowed by section 611.

(6) Pension, profit-sharing and annuity plans of self-employed individuals.—In the case of an individual who is an employee within the meaning of section 401(c)(1), the deduction allowed by section 404.

(7) Retirement savings.—The deduction allowed by section 219 (relating to deduction for certain retirement savings).

(8) [Repealed.]

(9) Penalties forfeited because of premature withdrawal of funds from time savings accounts or deposits.—The deductions allowed by section 165 for losses incurred in any transaction entered into for profit, though not connected with a trade or business, to the extent that such losses include amounts forfeited to a bank, mutual savings bank, savings and loan association, building and loan association, cooperative bank or homestead association as a penalty for premature withdrawal of funds from a time savings account, certificate of deposit, or similar class of deposit.

(10) Alimony.—The deduction allowed by section 215.

(11) Reforestation expenses.—The deduction allowed by section 194.

(12) Certain required repayments of supplemental unemployment compensation benefits.— The deduction allowed by section 165 for the repayment to a trust described in paragraph (9) or (17) of section 501(c) of supplemental unemployment compensation benefits received from such trust if such repayment is required because of the receipt of trade readjustment allowances under section 231 or 232 of the Trade Act of 1974 (19 U.S.C. 2291 and 2292).

(13) Jury duty pay remitted to employer.—Any deduction allowable under this chapter by reason of an individual remitting any portion of any jury pay to such individual's employer in exchange for payment by the employer of compensation for the period such individual was performing jury duty. For purposes of the preceding sentence, the term "jury pay" means any payment received by the individual for the discharge of jury duty.

(14) Deduction for clean-fuel vehicles and certain refueling property.—The deduction allowed by section 179A.

(15) Moving expenses.—The deduction allowed by section 217.

(16) Archer MSAs.—The deduction allowed by section 220.

(17) Interest on education loans.—The deduction allowed by section 221.

Editor's Note

Caution: IRC §62(a)(18), as follows, was added by Pub. L. No. 107-16. For sunset provision, see the amendment notes to this section on Pub. L. No. 107-16.

---

(18) Higher education expenses.—The deduction allowed by section 222.

(19) Health Savings Accounts.—The deduction allowed by section 223.

(20) Costs involving discrimination suits, etc.— Any deduction allowable under this chapter for attorney fees and court costs paid by, or on behalf of, the taxpayer in connection with any action involving a claim of unlawful discrimination (as defined in subsection (e)) or a claim of a violation of subchapter III of chapter 37 of title 31, United States Code or a claim made under section 1862(b)(3)(A) of the Social Security Act (42 U.S.C. 1395y(b)(3)(A)). The preceding sentence shall not apply to any deduction in excess of the amount includible in the taxpayer's gross income for the taxable year on account of a judgment or settlement (whether by suit or agreement and whether as lump sum or periodic payments) resulting from such claim.

* * *

Nothing in this section shall permit the same item to be deducted more than once.

(b) Qualified Performing Artist.—

(1) In general.—For purposes of subsection (a)(2)(B), the term "qualified performing artist" means, with respect to any taxable year, any individual if—

(A) such individual performed services in the performing arts as an employee during the taxable year for at least 2 employers,

(B) the aggregate amount allowable as a deduction under section 162 in connection with the performance of such services exceeds 10 percent of such individual's gross income attributable to the performance of such services, and

(C) the adjusted gross income of such individual for the taxable year (determined without regard to subsection (a)(2)(B)) does not exceed $16,000.

(2) Nominal employer not taken into account.—An individual shall not be treated as performing services in the performing arts as an employee for any employer during any taxable year unless the amount received by such individual from such employer for the performance of such services during the taxable year equals or exceeds $200.

(3) Special rules for married couples.—

(A) In general.—Except in the case of a husband and wife who lived apart at all times during the taxable year, if the taxpayer is married at the close of the taxable year, subsection (a)(2)(B) shall apply only if the taxpayer and his spouse file a joint return for the taxable year.

(B) Application of paragraph (1).—In the case of a joint return—

(i) paragraph (1) (other than subparagraph (C) thereof) shall be applied separately with respect to each spouse, but

(ii) paragraph (1)(C) shall be applied with respect to their combined adjusted gross income.

(C) Determination of marital status.—For purposes of this subsection, marital status shall be determined under section 7703(a).

(D) Joint return.—For purposes of this subsection, the term "joint return" means the joint return of a husband and wife made under section 6013.

(c) Certain Arrangements Not Treated as Reimbursement Arrangements.—For purposes of subsection (a)(2)(A), an arrangement shall in no event be treated as a reimbursement or other expense allowance arrangement if—

(1) such arrangement does not require the employee to substantiate the expenses covered by the arrangement to the person providing the reimbursement, or

(2) such arrangement provides the employee the right to retain any amount in excess of the substantiated expenses covered under the arrangement.

The substantiation requirements of the preceding sentence shall not apply to any expense to the extent that substantiation is not required under section 274(d) for such expense by reason of the regulations prescribed under the 2nd sentence thereof.

(d) Definition; Special Rules.—

(1) Eligible educator.—

(A) In general.—For purposes of subsection (a)(2)(D), the term "eligible educator" means, with respect to any taxable year, an individual who is a kindergarten through grade 12 teacher, instructor, counselor, principal, or aide in a school for at least 900 hours during a school year.

(B) School.—The term "school" means any school which provides elementary education or secondary education (kindergarten through grade 12), as determined under State law.

(2) Coordination with exclusions.—A deduction shall be allowed under subsection (a)(2)(D) for expenses only to the extent the amount of such expenses exceeds the amount excludable under section 135, 529(c)(1), or 530(d)(2) for the taxable year.

(e) Unlawful Discrimination Defined.—For purposes of subsection (a)(20), the term "unlawful discrimination" means an act that is unlawful under any of the following:

(1) Section 302 of the Civil Rights Act of 1991 (2 U.S.C. 1202).

(2) Section 201, 202, 203, 204, 205, 206, or 207 of the Congressional Accountability Act of 1995 (2 U.S.C. 1311, 1312, 1313, 1314, 1315, 1316, or 1317).

(3) The National Labor Relations Act (29 U.S.C. 151 et seq.).

(4) The Fair Labor Standards Act of 1938 (29 U.S.C. 201 et seq.).

(5) Section 4 or 15 of the Age Discrimination in Employment Act of 1967 (29 U.S.C. 623 or 633a).

(6) Section 501 or 504 of the Rehabilitation Act of 1973 (29 U.S.C. 791 or 794).

(7) Section 510 of the Employee Retirement Income Security Act of 1974 (29 U.S.C. 1140).

(8) Title IX of the Education Amendments of 1972 (20 U.S.C. 1681 et seq.).

(9) The Employee Polygraph Protection Act of 1988 (29 U.S.C. 2001 et seq.).

(19) The Worker Adjustment and Retraining Notification Act (29 U.S.C. 2102 et seq.).

(11) Section 105 of the Family and Medical Leave Act of 1993 (29 U.S.C. 2615).

(12) Chapter 43 of title 38, United States Code (relating to employment and reemployment rights of members of the uniformed services).

(13) Section 1977, 1979, or 1980 of the Revised Statutes (42 U.S.C. 1981, 1983, or 1985).

(14) Section 703, 704, or 717 of the Civil Rights Act of 1964 (42 U.S.C. 2000e-2, 2000e-3, or 2000e-16).

(15) Section 804, 805, 806, 808, or 818 of the Fair Housing Act (42 U.S.C. 3604, 3605, 3606, 3608, or 3617).

IRC Sec. 62(e)(15)

(16) Section 102, 202, 302, or 503 of the Americans with Disabilities Act of 1990 (42 U.S.C. 12112, 12132, 12182, or 12203).

(17) Any provision of Federal law (popularly known as whistleblower protection provisions) prohibiting the discharge of an employee, the discrimination against an employee, or any other form of retaliation or reprisal against an employee for asserting rights or taking other actions permitted under Federal law.

(18) Any provision of Federal, State, or local law, or common law claims permitted under Federal, State, or local law—

    (i) providing for the enforcement of civil rights, or

    (ii) regulating any aspect of the employment relationship, including claims for wages, compensation, or benefits, or prohibiting the discharge of an employee, the discrimination against an employee, or any other form of retaliation or reprisal against an employee for asserting rights or taking other actions permitted by law.

Recent Amendments to IRC §62 (As Excerpted)

Tax Relief, Unemployment Insurance Reauthorization, and Job Creation Act of 2010 (Pub. L. No. 111-312), as follows:

- IRC §62(a)(2)(D) was amended by Act §721(a) by striking "or 2009" and inserting "2009, 2010, or 2011". Eff. for tax years beginning after Dec. 31, 2009.
- **Sunset Provision of Economic Growth and Tax Relief Reconciliation Act of 2001.** Act §101(a) provides:

  (a) Temporary Extension.—

  (1) In general.—Section 901 of the Economic Growth and Tax Relief Reconciliation Act of 2001 is amended by striking "December 31, 2010" both places it appears and inserting "December 31, 2012".

  (2) Effective date.—The amendment made by this subsection shall take effect as if included in the enactment of the Economic Growth and Tax Relief Reconciliation Act of 2001.

Emergency Economic Stabilization Act of 2008 (Pub. L. No. 110-343), as follows:

- IRC §62(a)(2)(D) was amended by Act, Div. C, §203(a), by striking "or 2007" and inserting "2007, 2008, or 2009". Eff. for tax years beginning after Dec. 31, 2007.

Tax Relief and Health Care Act of 2006 (Pub. L. No. 109-432), as follows:

- IRC §62(a)(2)(D) was amended by Act, Div. A, §108(a), by substituting "2005, 2006, or 2007" for "or 2005". Eff. for tax years beginning after Dec. 31, 2005.
- IRC §61(a) was amended by Act, Div. A, §406(a)(3) by adding new para. (21). Eff. for information provided on or after Dec. 20, 2006.

Gulf Opportunity Zone Act of 2005 (Pub. L. No. 109-135), as follows:

- IRC §61(a)(19)–(20) was amended by Act §412(q)(1) by redesignating para. (19) (relating to costs involving discrimination suits), as added by Pub. L. No. 108-357, §703, as para. (20). Eff. Dec. 21, 2005.
- IRC §61(e) was amended by Act §412(q)(2) by substituting "subsection (a)(20)" for "subsection (a)(19)". Eff. Dec. 21, 2005.

American Jobs Creation Act of 2004 (Pub. L. No. 108-357), as follows:

- IRC §61(a) was amended by Act §703(a) by adding new para. (19)[20]. Eff. for fees and costs paid after Oct. 22, 2004, with respect to any judgment or settlement occurring after such date.

- IRC §62 was amended by Act §703(b) by adding new subsec. (e) at the end. Eff. for fees and costs paid after Oct. 22, 2004, with respect to any judgment or settlement occurring after such date.

Working Families Tax Relief Act of 2004 (Pub. L. No. 108-311), as follows:

- IRC §62(a)(2)(D) was amended by Act §307(a) by substituting ", 2003, 2004, or 2005" for "or 2003". Eff. for expenses paid or incurred in tax years beginning after Dec. 31, 2003.

Medicare Prescription Drug, Improvement, and Modernization Act of 2003 (Pub. L. No. 108-173), as follows:

- IRC §62(a) was amended by Act §1201(b) by adding new para. (19). Eff. for tax years beginning after Dec. 31, 2003.

Military Family Tax Relief Act of 2003 (Pub. L. No. 108-121), as follows:

- IRC §62(a)(2) was amended by Act §109(b) by adding new subpara. (E). Eff. for amounts paid or incurred in tax years beginning after Dec. 31, 2002.

Job Creation and Worker Assistance Act of 2002 (Pub. L. No. 107-147), as follows:

- IRC §62(a)(2) was amended by Act §406(a) by adding new subpara. (D). Eff. for tax years beginning after Dec. 31, 2001.
- IRC §62 was amended by Act §406(b) by adding new subsec. (d). Eff. for tax years beginning after Dec. 31, 2001.

Economic Growth and Tax Relief Reconciliation Act of 2001 (Pub. L. No. 107-16), as follows:

- IRC §62(a) was amended by Act §431(b) by adding new para. (18). Eff. for payments made in tax years beginning after Dec. 31, 2001.
- **Sunset Provision.** Act §901, as amended by Pub. L. No. 111-312, §101(a)(1), provides the sunset rule below. But see Pub. L. No. 109-280, §811, and Pub. L. No. 111-148, §10909(c), as amended by Pub. L. No. 111-312, §101(b)(1).

  SEC. 901. SUNSET OF PROVISIONS OF ACT.

  (a) In general. All provisions of, and amendments made by, this Act shall not apply—

  (1) to taxable, plan, or limitation years beginning after December 31, 2012, or

  (2) in the case of title V, to estates of decedents dying, gifts made, or generation skipping transfers, after December 31, 2012.

  (b) Application of certain laws.—The Internal Revenue Code of 1986 and the Employee Retirement Income Security Act of 1974 shall be applied and administered to years, estates, gifts, and transfers described in subsection (a) as if the provisions and amendments described in subsection (a) had never been enacted.

Part II—Items Specifically Included in Gross Income

* * *

SEC. 72. ANNUITIES; CERTAIN PROCEEDS OF ENDOWMENT AND LIFE INSURANCE CONTRACTS.

Editor's Note

IRC §72(a), below, was amended by Pub. L. No. 111-240, effective for amounts received in tax years beginning after December 31, 2010.

(a) General Rules for Annuities.—

    (1) Income inclusion.—Except as otherwise provided in this chapter, gross income includes any amount received as an annuity (whether for a period certain or during one or more lives) under an annuity, endowment, or life insurance contract.

(2) Partial annuitization.—If any amount is received as an annuity for a period of 10 years or more or during one or more lives under any portion of an annuity, endowment, or life insurance contract—

(A) such portion shall be treated as a separate contract for purposes of this section,

(B) for purposes of applying subsections (b), (c), and (e), the investment in the contract shall be allocated pro rata between each portion of the contract from which amounts are received as an annuity and the portion of the contract from which amounts are not received as an annuity, and

(C) a separate annuity starting date under subsection (c)(4) shall be determined with respect to each portion of the contract from which amounts are received as an annuity.

(b) Exclusion Ratio.—

(1) In general.—Gross income does not include that part of any amount received as an annuity under an annuity, endowment, or life insurance contract which bears the same ratio to such amount as the investment in the contract (as of the annuity starting date) bears to the expected return under the contract (as of such date).

(2) Exclusion limited to investment.—The portion of any amount received as an annuity which is excluded from gross income under paragraph (1) shall not exceed the unrecovered investment in the contract immediately before the receipt of such amount.

(3) Deduction where annuity payments cease before entire investment recovered.—

(A) In general.—If—

(i) after the annuity starting date, payments as an annuity under the contract cease by reason of the death of an annuitant, and

(ii) as of the date of such cessation, there is unrecovered investment in the contract,

the amount of such unrecovered investment (in excess of any amount specified in subsection (e)(5) which was not included in gross income) shall be allowed as a deduction to the annuitant for his last taxable year.

(B) Payments to other persons.—In the case of any contract which provides for payments meeting the requirements of subparagraphs (B) and (C) of subsection (c)(2), the deduction under subparagraph (A) shall be allowed to the person entitled to such payments for the taxable year in which such payments are received.

(C) Net operating loss deductions provided.—For purposes of section 172, a deduction allowed under this paragraph shall be treated as if it were attributable to a trade or business of the taxpayer.

(4) Unrecovered investment.—For purposes of this subsection, the unrecovered investment in the contract as of any date is—

(A) the investment in the contract (determined without regard to subsection (c)(2)) as of the annuity starting date, reduced by

(B) the aggregate amount received under the contract on or after such annuity starting date and before the date as of which the determination is being made, to the extent such amount was excludable from gross income under this subtitle.

(c) Definitions.—

(1) Investment in the contract.—For purposes of subsection (b), the investment in the contract as of the annuity starting date is—

(A) (A) the aggregate amount of premiums or other consideration paid for the contract, minus

(B) the aggregate amount received under the contract before such date, to the extent that such amount was excludable from gross income under this subtitle or prior income tax laws.

(2) Adjustment in investment where there is refund feature.—If—

(A) the expected return under the contract depends in whole or in part on the life expectancy of one or more individuals;

(B) the contract provides for payments to be made to a beneficiary (or to the estate of an annuitant) on or after the death of the annuitant or annuitants; and

(C) such payments are in the nature of a refund of the consideration paid,

then the value (computed without discount for interest) of such payments on the annuity starting date shall be subtracted from the amount determined under paragraph (1). Such value shall be computed in accordance with actuarial tables prescribed by the Secretary. For purposes of this paragraph and of subsection (e)(2)(A), the term "refund of the consideration paid" includes amounts payable after the death of an annuitant by reason of a provision in the contract for a life annuity with minimum period of payments certain, but (if part of the consideration was contributed by an employer) does not include that part of any payment to a beneficiary (or to the estate of the annuitant) which is not attributable to the consideration paid by the employee for the contract as determined under paragraph (1)(A).

(3) Expected return.—For purposes of subsection (b), the expected return under the contract shall be determined as follows:

(A) Life expectancy.—If the expected return under the contract, for the period on and after the annuity starting date, depends in whole or in part on the life expectancy of one or more individuals, the expected return shall be computed with reference to actuarial tables prescribed by the Secretary.

(B) Installment payments.—If subparagraph (A) does not apply, the expected return is the aggregate

IRC Sec. 72(c)(3)(B)

of the amounts receivable under the contract as an annuity.

(4) Annuity starting date.—For purposes of this section, the annuity starting date in the case of any contract is the first day of the first period for which an amount is received as an annuity under the contract; except that if such date was before January 1, 1954, then the annuity starting date is January 1, 1954.

(d) Special Rules for Qualified Employer Retirement Plans.—

(1) Simplified method of taxing annuity payments.—

(A) In general.—In the case of any amount received as an annuity under a qualified employer retirement plan—

(i) subsection (b) shall not apply, and

(ii) the investment in the contract shall be recovered as provided in this paragraph.

(B) Method of recovering investment in contract.—

(i) In general.—Gross income shall not include so much of any monthly annuity payment under a qualified employer retirement plan as does not exceed the amount obtained by dividing—

(I) the investment in the contract (as of the annuity starting date), by

(II) the number of anticipated payments determined under the table contained in clause (iii) (or, in the case of a contract to which subsection (c)(3)(B) applies, the number of monthly annuity payments under such contract).

(ii) Certain rules made applicable.—Rules similar to the rules of paragraphs (2) and (3) of subsection (b) shall apply for purposes of this paragraph.

(iii) Number of anticipated payments.—If the annuity is payable over the life of a single individual, the number of anticipated payments shall be determined as follows:

If the age of the annuitant on the annuity starting date is:	The number of anticipated payments is:
Not more than 55	360
More than 55 but not more than 60	310
More than 60 but not more than 65	260
More than 65 but not more than 70	210
More than 70	160

(iv) Number of anticipated payments where more than one life.—If the annuity is payable over

the lives of more than 1 individual, the number of anticipated payments shall be determined as follows:

If the combined ages of the annuitants are:	The number is:
Not more than 110	410
More than 110 but not more than 120	360
More than 120 but not more than 130	310
More than 130 but not more than 140	260
More than 140	210

(C) Adjustment for refund feature not applicable.—For purposes of this paragraph, investment in the contract shall be determined under subsection (c)(1) without regard to subsection (c)(2).

(D) Special rule where lump sum paid in connection with commencement of annuity payments.—If, in connection with the commencement of annuity payments under any qualified employer retirement plan, the taxpayer receives a lump sum payment—

(i) such payment shall be taxable under subsection (e) as if received before the annuity starting date, and

(ii) the investment in the contract for purposes of this paragraph shall be determined as if such payment had been so received.

(E) Exception.—This paragraph shall not apply in any case where the primary annuitant has attained age 75 on the annuity starting date unless there are fewer than 5 years of guaranteed payments under the annuity.

(F) Adjustment where annuity payments not on monthly basis.—In any case where the annuity payments are not made on a monthly basis, appropriate adjustments in the application of this paragraph shall be made to take into account the period on the basis of which such payments are made.

(G) Qualified employer retirement plan.—For purposes of this paragraph, the term "qualified employer retirement plan" means any plan or contract described in paragraph (1), (2), or (3) of section 4974(c).

(2) Treatment of employee contributions under defined contribution plans.—For purposes of this section, employee contributions (and any income allocable thereto) under a defined contribution plan may be treated as a separate contract.

(e) Amounts Not Received as Annuities.—

(1) Application of subsection.—

(A) In general.—This subsection shall apply to any amount which—

(i) is received under an annuity, endowment, or life insurance contract, and

(ii) is not received as an annuity, if no provision of this subtitle (other than this subsection) applies with respect to such amount.

(B) Dividends.—For purposes of this section, any amount received which is in the nature of a dividend or similar distribution shall be treated as an amount not received as an annuity.

(2) General rule.—Any amount to which this subsection applies—

(A) if received on or after the annuity starting date, shall be included in gross income, or

(B) if received before the annuity starting date—

(i) shall be included in gross income to the extent allocable to income on the contract, and

(ii) shall not be included in gross income to the extent allocable to the investment in the contract.

(3) Allocation of amounts to income and investment.—For purposes of paragraph (2)(B)—

(A) Allocation to income.—Any amount to which this subsection applies shall be treated as allocable to income on the contract to the extent that such amount does not exceed the excess (if any) of—

(i) the cash value of the contract (determined without regard to any surrender charge) immediately before the amount is received, over

(ii) the investment in the contract at such time.

(B) Allocation to investment.—Any amount to which this subsection applies shall be treated as allocable to investment in the contract to the extent that such amount is not allocated to income under subparagraph (A).

(4) Special rules for application of paragraph (2)(B).—For purposes of paragraph (2)(B)—

(A) Loans treated as distributions.—If, during any taxable year, an individual—

(i) receives (directly or indirectly) any amount as a loan under any contract to which this subsection applies, or

(ii) assigns or pledges (or agrees to assign or pledge) any portion of the value of any such contract,

such amount or portion shall be treated as received under the contract as an amount not received as an annuity. The preceding sentence shall not apply for purposes of determining investment in the contract, except that the investment in the contract shall be increased by any amount included in gross income by reason of the amount treated as received under the preceding sentence.

(B) Treatment of policyholder dividends.—Any amount described in paragraph (1)(B) shall not be included in gross income under paragraph (2)(B)(i) to the extent such amount is retained by the insurer as a premium or other consideration paid for the contract.

(C) Treatment of transfers without adequate consideration.—

(i) In general.—If an individual who holds an annuity contract transfers it without full and adequate consideration, such individual shall be treated as receiving an amount equal to the excess of—

(I) the cash surrender value of such contract at the time of transfer, over

(II) the investment in such contract at such time,

under the contract as an amount not received as an annuity.

(ii) Exception for certain transfers between spouses or former spouses.—Clause (i) shall not apply to any transfer to which section 1041(a) (relating to transfers of property between spouses or incident to divorce) applies.

(iii) Adjustment to investment in contract of transferee.—If under clause (i) an amount is included in the gross income of the transferor of an annuity contract, the investment in the contract of the transferee in such contract shall be increased by the amount so included.

(5) Retention of existing rules in certain cases.—

(A) In general.—In any case to which this paragraph applies—

(i) paragraphs (2)(B) and (4)(A) shall not apply, and

(ii) if paragraph (2)(A) does not apply,

the amount shall be included in gross income, but only to the extent it exceeds the investment in the contract.

(B) Existing contracts.—This paragraph shall apply to contracts entered into before August 14, 1982. Any amount allocable to investment in the contract after August 13, 1982, shall be treated as from a contract entered into after such date.

(C) Certain life insurance and endowment contracts.—Except as provided in paragraph (10) and except to the extent prescribed by the Secretary by regulations, this paragraph shall apply to any amount not received as an annuity which is received under a life insurance or endowment contract.

(D) Contracts under qualified plans.—Except as provided in paragraph (8), this paragraph shall apply to any amount received—

IRC Sec. 72(e)(5)(D)

(i) from a trust described in section 401(a) which is exempt from tax under section 501(a),

(ii) from a contract—

(I) purchased by a trust described in clause (i),

(II) purchased as part of a plan described in section 403(a),

(III) described in section 403(b), or

(IV) provided for employees of a life insurance company under a plan described in section 818(a)(3), or

(iii) from an individual retirement account or an individual retirement annuity.

Any dividend described in section 404(k) which is received by a participant or beneficiary shall, for purposes of this subparagraph, be treated as paid under a separate contract to which clause (ii)(I) applies.

(E) Full refunds, surrenders, redemptions, and maturities.—This paragraph shall apply to—

(i) any amount received, whether in a single sum or otherwise, under a contract in full discharge of the obligation under the contract which is in the nature of a refund of the consideration paid for the contract, and

(ii) any amount received under a contract on its complete surrender, redemption, or maturity.

In the case of any amount to which the preceding sentence applies, the rule of paragraph (2)(A) shall not apply.

(6) **Investment in the contract**.—For purposes of this subsection, the investment in the contract as of any date is—

(A) the aggregate amount of premiums or other consideration paid for the contract before such date, minus

(B) the aggregate amount received under the contract before such date, to the extent that such amount was excludable from gross income under this subtitle or prior income tax laws.

(7) **[Repealed.]**

(8) **Extension of paragraph (2)(B) to qualified plans.—**

(A) In general.—Notwithstanding any other provision of this subsection, in the case of any amount received before the annuity starting date from a trust or contract described in paragraph (5)(D), paragraph (2)(B) shall apply to such amounts.

(B) Allocation of amount received.—For purposes of paragraph (2)(B), the amount allocated to the investment in the contract shall be the portion of the amount described in subparagraph (A) which bears the same ratio to such amount as the investment in the contract bears to the account balance. The determination under the preceding sentence shall be made as of the time of the distribution or at such other time as the Secretary may prescribe.

(C) Treatment of forfeitable rights.—If an employee does not have a nonforfeitable right to any amount under any trust or contract to which subparagraph (A) applies, such amount shall not be treated as part of the account balance.

(D) Investment in the contract before 1987.—In the case of a plan which on May 5, 1986, permitted withdrawal of any employee contributions before separation from service, subparagraph (A) shall apply only to the extent that amounts received before the annuity starting date (when increased by amounts previously received under the contract after December 31, 1986) exceed the investment in the contract as of December 31, 1986.

(9) **Extension of paragraph (2)(B) to qualified tuition programs and educational individual retirement accounts**.—Notwithstanding any other provision of this subsection, paragraph (2)(B) shall apply to amounts received under a qualified tuition program (as defined in section 529(b)) or under a Coverdell education savings account (as defined in section 530(b)). The rule of paragraph (8)(B) shall apply for purposes of this paragraph.

(10) **Treatment of modified endowment contracts.—**

(A) In general.—Notwithstanding paragraph (5)(C), in the case of any modified endowment contract (as defined in section 7702A)—

(i) paragraphs (2)(B) and (4)(A) shall apply, and

(ii) in applying paragraph (4)(A), "any person" shall be substituted for "an individual".

(B) Treatment of certain burial contracts.—Notwithstanding subparagraph (A), paragraph (4)(A) shall not apply to any assignment (or pledge) of a modified endowment contract if such assignment (or pledge) is solely to cover the payment of expenses referred to in section 7702(e)(2)(C)(iii) and if the maximum death benefit under such contract does not exceed $25,000.

(11) **Special rules for certain combination contracts providing long-term care insurance**.—Notwithstanding paragraphs (2), (5)(C), and (10), in the case of any charge against the cash value of an annuity contract or the cash surrender value of a life insurance contract made as payment for coverage under a qualified long-term care insurance contract which is part of or a rider on such annuity or life insurance contract—

(A) the investment in the contract shall be reduced (but not below zero) by such charge, and

(B) such charge shall not be includible in gross income.

(12) Anti-abuse rules.—

(A) In general.—For purposes of determining the amount includible in gross income under this subsection—

(i) all modified endowment contracts issued by the same company to the same policyholder during any calendar year shall be treated as 1 modified endowment contract, and

(ii) all annuity contracts issued by the same company to the same policyholder during any calendar year shall be treated as 1 annuity contract.

The preceding sentence shall not apply to any contract described in paragraph (5)(D).

(B) Regulatory authority.—The Secretary may by regulations prescribe such additional rules as may be necessary or appropriate to prevent avoidance of the purposes of this subsection through serial purchases of contracts or otherwise.

(f) Special Rules for Computing Employees' Contributions.—In computing, for purposes of subsection (c)(1)(A), the aggregate amount of premiums or other consideration paid for the contract, and for purposes of subsection (e)(6), the aggregate premiums or other consideration paid, amounts contributed by the employer shall be included, but only to the extent that—

(1) such amounts were includible in the gross income of the employee under this subtitle or prior income tax laws; or

(2) if such amounts had been paid directly to the employee at the time they were contributed, they would not have been includible in the gross income of the employee under the law applicable at the time of such contribution.

Paragraph (2) shall apply to amounts which were contributed by the employer after December 31, 1962, and which would not have been includible in the gross income of the employee by reason of the application of section 911 if such amounts had been paid directly to the employee at the time of contribution. The preceding sentence shall not apply to amounts which were contributed by the employer, as determined under regulations prescribed by the Secretary, to provide pension or annuity credits, to the extent such credits are attributable to services performed before January 1, 1963, and are provided pursuant to pension or annuity plan provisions in existence on March 12, 1962, and on that date applicable to such services, or to the extent such credits are attributable to services performed as a foreign missionary (within the meaning of section 403(b)(2)(D)(iii), as in effect before the enactment of the Economic Growth and Tax Relief Reconciliation Act of 2001).

(g) Rules for Transferee Where Transfer Was for Value.—Where any contract (or any interest therein) is transferred (by assignment or otherwise) for a valuable consideration, to the extent that the contract (or interest therein) does not, in the hands of the transferee, have a basis which is determined by reference to the basis in the hands of the transferor, then—

(1) for purposes of this section, only the actual value of such consideration, plus the amount of the premiums and other consideration paid by the transferee after the transfer, shall be taken into account in computing the aggregate amount of the premiums or other consideration paid for the contract;

(2) for purposes of subsection (c)(1)(B), there shall be taken into account only the aggregate amount received under the contract by the transferee before the annuity starting date, to the extent that such amount was excludable from gross income under this subtitle or prior income tax laws; and

(3) the annuity starting date is January 1, 1954, or the first day of the first period for which the transferee received an amount under the contract as an annuity, whichever is the later.

For purposes of this subsection, the term "transferee" includes a beneficiary of, or the estate of, the transferee.

(h) Option to Receive Annuity in Lieu of Lump Sum.—If—

(1) a contract provides for payment of a lump sum in full discharge of an obligation under the contract, subject to an option to receive an annuity in lieu of such lump sum;

(2) the option is exercised within 60 days after the day on which such lump sum first became payable; and

(3) part or all of such lump sum would (but for this subsection) be includible in gross income by reason of subsection (e)(1),

then, for purposes of this subtitle, no part of such lump sum shall be considered as includible in gross income at the time such lump sum first became payable.

(i) [Repealed.]

(j) Interest.—Notwithstanding any other provision of this section, if any amount is held under an agreement to pay interest thereon, the interest payments shall be included in gross income.

(k) [Repealed.]

(*l*) Face-Amount Certificates.—For purposes of this section, the term "endowment contract" includes a face-amount certificate, as defined in section 2(a)(15) of the Investment Company Act of 1940 (15 U.S.C., section 80a-2), issued after December 31, 1954.

IRC Sec. 72(l)

(m) Special Rules Applicable to Employee Annuities and Distributions Under Employee Plans.—

(1) [Repealed.]

(2) Computation of consideration paid by the employee.—In computing—

(A) the aggregate amount of premiums or other consideration paid for the contract for purposes of subsection (c)(1)(A) (relating to the investment in the contract), and

(B) the aggregate premiums or other consideration paid for purposes of subsection (e)(6) (relating to certain amounts not received as an annuity),

any amount allowed as a deduction with respect to the contract under section 404 which was paid while the employee was an employee within the meaning of section 401(c)(1) shall be treated as consideration contributed by the employer, and there shall not be taken into account any portion of the premiums or other consideration for the contract paid while the employee was an owner-employee which is properly allocable (as determined under regulations prescribed by the Secretary) to the cost of life, accident, health, or other insurance.

(3) Life insurance contracts.—

(A) This paragraph shall apply to any life insurance contract—

(i) purchased as a part of a plan described in section 403(a), or

(ii) purchased by a trust described in section 401(a) which is exempt from tax under section 501(a) if the proceeds of such contract are payable directly or indirectly to a participant in such trust or to a beneficiary of such participant.

(B) Any contribution to a plan described in subparagraph (A)(i) or a trust described in subparagraph (A)(ii) which is allowed as a deduction under section 404, and any income of a trust described in subparagraph (A)(ii), which is determined in accordance with regulations prescribed by the Secretary to have been applied to purchase the life insurance protection under a contract described in subparagraph (A), is includible in the gross income of the participant for the taxable year when so applied.

(C) In the case of the death of an individual insured under a contract described in subparagraph (A), an amount equal to the cash surrender value of the contract immediately before the death of the insured shall be treated as a payment under such plan or a distribution by such trust, and the excess of the amount payable by reason of the death of the insured over such cash surrender value shall not be includible in gross income under this section and shall be treated as provided in section 101.

(4) [Repealed.]

(5) Penalties applicable to certain amounts received by 5-percent owners.—

(A) This paragraph applies to amounts which are received from a qualified trust described in section 401(a) or under a plan described in section 403(a) at any time by an individual who is, or has been, a 5-percent owner, or by a successor of such an individual, but only to the extent such amounts are determined, under regulations prescribed by the Secretary, to exceed thebenefits provided for such individual under the plan formula.

(B) If a person receives an amount to which this paragraph applies, his tax under this chapter for the taxable year in which such amount is received shall be increased by an amount equal to 10 percent of the portion of the amount so received which is includible in his gross income for such taxable year.

(C) For purposes of this paragraph, the term "5-percent owner" means any individual who, at any time during the 5 plan years preceding the plan year ending in the taxable year in which the amount is received, is a 5-percent owner (as defined in section 416(i)(1)(B)).

(6) Owner-employee defined.—For purposes of this subsection, the term "owner-employee" has the meaning assigned to it by section 401(c)(3) and includes an individual for whose benefit an individual retirement account or annuity described in section 408(a) or (b) is maintained. For purposes of the preceding sentence, the term "owner-employee" shall include an employee within the meaning of section 401(c)(1).

(7) Meaning of disabled.—For purposes of this section, an individual shall be considered to be disabled if he is unable to engage in any substantial gainful activity by reason of any medically determinable physical or mental impairment which can be expected to result in death or to be of long continued and indefinite duration. An individual shall not be considered to be disabled unless he furnishes proof of the existence thereof in such form and manner as the Secretary may require.

(8) [Repealed.]

(9) [Repealed.]

(10) Determination of investment in the contract in the case of qualified domestic relations orders.—Under regulations prescribed by the Secretary, in the case of a distribution or payment made to an alternate payee who is the spouse or former spouse of the participant pursuant to a qualified domestic relations order (as defined in section 414(p)), the investment in the contract as of the date prescribed in such regulations shall be allocated on a pro rata basis between the present value of such distribution or payment and the present value of all other benefits payable with respect to the participant to which such order relates.

IRC Sec. 72(m)

(n) Annuities Under Retired Serviceman's Family Protection Plan or Survivor Benefit Plan.—Subsection (b) shall not apply in the case of amounts received after December 31, 1965, as an annuity under chapter 73 of title 10 of the United States Code, but all such amounts shall be excluded from gross income until there has been so excluded (under section 122(b)(1) or this section, including amounts excluded before January 1, 1966) an amount equal to the consideration for the contract (as defined by section 122(b)(2)), plus any amount treated pursuant to section 101(b)(2)(D) (as in effect on the day before the date of the enactment of the Small Business Job Protection Act of 1996) as additional consideration paid by the employee. Thereafter all amounts so received shall be included in gross income.

(o) Special Rules for Distributions From Qualified Plans to Which Employee Made Deductible Contributions.—

(1) Treatment of contributions.—For purposes of this section and sections 402 and 403, notwithstanding section 414(h), any deductible employee contribution made to a qualified employer plan or government plan shall be treated as an amount contributed by the employer which is not includible in the gross income of the employee.

(2) [Repealed.]

(3) Amounts constructively received.—

(A) In general.—For purposes of this subsection, rules similar to the rules provided by subsection (p) (other than the exception contained in paragraph (2) thereof) shall apply.

(B) Purchase of life insurance.—To the extent any amount of accumulated deductible employee contributions of an employee are applied to the purchase of life insurance contracts, such amount shall be treated as distributed to the employee in the year so applied.

(4) Special rule for treatment of rollover amounts.—For purposes of sections 402(c), 403(a)(4), 403(b)(8), 408(d)(3), and 457(e)(16), the Secretary shall prescribe regulations providing for such allocations of amounts attributable to accumulated deductible employee contributions, and for such other rules, as may be necessary to ensure that such accumulated deductible employee contributions do not become eligible for additional tax benefits (or freed from limitations) through the use of rollovers.

(5) Definitions and special rules.—For purposes of this subsection—

(A) Deductible employee contributions.—The term "deductible employee contributions" means any qualified voluntary employee contribution (as defined in section 219(e)(2)) made after December 31, 1981, in a taxable year beginning after such date and made for a taxable year beginning before January 1, 1987, and allowable as a deduction under section 219(a) for such taxable year.

(B) Accumulated deductible employee contributions.—The term "accumulated deductible employee contributions" means the deductible employee contributions—

(i) increased by the amount of income and gain allocable to such contributions, and

(ii) reduced by the sum of the amount of loss and expense allocable to such contributions and the amounts distributed with respect to the employee which are attributable to such contributions (or income or gain allocable to such contributions).

(C) Qualified employer plan.—The term "qualified employer plan" has the meaning given to such term by subsection (p)(3)(A)(i).

(D) Government plan.—The term "government plan" has the meaning given such term by subsection (p)(3)(B).

(6) Ordering rules.—Unless the plan specifies otherwise, any distribution from such plan shall not be treated as being made from the accumulated deductible employee contributions until all other amounts to the credit of the employee have been distributed.

(p) Loans Treated as Distributions.—For purposes of this section—

(1) Treatment as distributions.—

(A) Loans.—If during any taxable year a participant or beneficiary receives (directly or indirectly) any amount as a loan from a qualified employer plan, such amount shall be treated as having been received by such individual as a distribution under such plan.

(B) Assignments or pledges.—If during any taxable year a participant or beneficiary assigns (or agrees to assign) or pledges (or agrees to pledge) any portion of his interest in a qualified employer plan, such portion shall be treated as having been received by such individual as a loan from such plan.

(2) Exception for certain loans.—

(A) General rule.—Paragraph (1) shall not apply to any loan to the extent that such loan (when added to the outstanding balance of all other loans from such plan whether made on, before, or after August 13, 1982), does not exceed the lesser of—

(i) $50,000, reduced by the excess (if any) of—

(I) the highest outstanding balance of loans from the plan during the 1-year period ending on the day before the date on which such loan was made, over

(II) the outstanding balance of loans from the plan on the date on which such loan was made, or

IRC Sec. 72(p)(2)(A)(i)(II)

(ii) the greater of (I) one-half of the present value of the nonforfeitable accrued benefit of the employee under the plan, or (II) $10,000.

For purposes of clause (ii), the present value of the nonforfeitable accrued benefit shall be determined without regard to any accumulated deductible employee contributions (as defined in subsection (o)(5)(B)).

(B) Requirement that loan be repayable within 5 years.—

(i) In general.—Subparagraph (A) shall not apply to any loan unless such loan, by its terms, is required to be repaid within 5 years.

(ii) Exception for home loans.—Clause (i) shall not apply to any loan used to acquire any dwelling unit which within a reasonable time is to be used (determined at the time the loan is made) as the principal residence of the participant.

(C) Requirement of level amortization.—Except as provided in regulations, this paragraph shall not apply to any loan unless substantially level amortization of such loan (with payments not less frequently than quarterly) is required over the term of the loan.

(D) Related employers and related plans.—For purposes of this paragraph—

(i) the rules of subsections (b), (c), and (m) of section 414 shall apply, and

(ii) all plans of an employer (determined after the application of such subsections) shall be treated as 1 plan.

(3) Denial of interest deductions in certain cases.—

(A) In general.—No deduction otherwise allowable under this chapter shall be allowed under this chapter for any interest paid or accrued on any loan to which paragraph (1) does not apply by reason of paragraph (2) during the period described in subparagraph (B).

(B) Period to which subparagraph (A) applies.—For purposes of subparagraph (A), the period described in this subparagraph is the period—

(i) on or after the 1st day on which the individual to whom the loan is made is a key employee (as defined in section 416(i)), or

(ii) such loan is secured by amounts attributable to elective deferrals described in subparagraph (A) or (C) of section 402(g)(3).

(4) Qualified employer plan, etc.—For purposes of this subsection—

(A) Qualified employer plan.—

(i) In general.—The term "qualified employer plan" means—

(I) a plan described in section 401(a) which includes a trust exempt from tax under section 501(a),

(II) an annuity plan described in section 403(a), and

(III) a plan under which amounts are contributed by an individual's employer for an annuity contract described in section 403(b).

(ii) Special rule.—The term "qualified employer plan" shall include any plan which was (or was determined to be) a qualified employer plan or a government plan.

(B) Government plan.—The term "government plan" means any plan, whether or not qualified, established and maintained for its employees by the United States, by a State or political subdivision thereof, or by an agency or instrumentality of any of the foregoing.

(5) Special rules for loans, etc., from certain contracts.—For purposes of this subsection, any amount received as a loan under a contract purchased under a qualified employer plan (and any assignment or pledge with respect to such a contract) shall be treated as a loan under such employer plan.

(q) 10-percent Penalty for Premature Distribution From Annuity Contracts.—

(1) Imposition of penalty.—If any taxpayer receives any amount under an annuity contract, the taxpayer's tax under this chapter for the taxable year in which such amount is received shall be increased by an amount equal to 10 percent of the portion of such amount which is includible in gross income.

(2) Subsection not to apply to certain distributions.—Paragraph (1) shall not apply to any distribution—

(A) made on or after the date on which the taxpayer attains age 59½,

(B) commencing on or after the death of the holder (or, where the holder is not an individual, the death of the primary annuitant (as defined in subsection (s)(6)(B)),

(C) attributable to the taxpayer's becoming disabled within the meaning of subsection (m)(7),

(D) which is a part of a series of substantially equal periodic payments (not less frequently than annually) made for the life (or life expectancy) of the taxpayer or the joint lives (or joint life expectancies) of such taxpayer and his designated beneficiary,

(E) from a plan, contract, account, trust, or annuity described in subsection (e)(5)(D),

(F) allocable to investment in the contract before August 14, 1982,

(G) under a qualified funding asset (within the meaning of section 130(d), but without regard to whether there is a qualified assignment),

(H) to which subsection (t) applies (without regard to paragraph (2) thereof),

(I) under an immediate annuity contract (within the meaning of section 72(u)(4)), or

(J) which is purchased by an employer upon the termination of a plan described in section 401(a) or 403(a) and which is held by the employer until such time as the employee separates from service.

(3) Change in substantially equal payments.—If—

(A) paragraph (1) does not apply to a distribution by reason of paragraph (2)(D), and

(B) the series of payments under such paragraph are subsequently modified (other than by reason of death or disability)—

(i) before the close of the 5-year period beginning on the date of the first payment and after the taxpayer attains age 59½, or

(ii) before the taxpayer attains age 59½,

the taxpayer's tax for the 1st taxable year in which such modification occurs shall be increased by an amount, determined under regulations, equal to the tax which (but for paragraph (2)(D)) would have been imposed, plus interest for the deferral period (within the meaning of subsection (t)(4)(B)).

(r) Certain Railroad Retirement Benefits Treated as Received Under Employer Plans.—

(1) In general.—Notwithstanding any other provision of law, any benefit provided under the Railroad Retirement Act of 1974 (other than a tier 1 railroad retirement benefit) shall be treated for purposes of this title as a benefit provided under an employer plan which meets the requirements of section 401(a).

(2) Tier 2 taxes treated as contributions.—

(A) In general.—For purposes of paragraph (1)—

(i) the tier 2 portion of the tax imposed by section 3201 (relating to tax on employees) shall be treated as an employee contribution,

(ii) the tier 2 portion of the tax imposed by section 3211 (relating to tax on employee representatives) shall be treated as an employee contribution, and

(iii) the tier 2 portion of the tax imposed by section 3221 (relating to tax on employers) shall be treated as an employer contribution.

(B) Tier 2 portion.—For purposes of subparagraph (A)—

(i) After 1984.—With respect to compensation paid after 1984, the tier 2 portion shall be the taxes imposed by sections 3201(b), 3211(b), and 3221(b).

(ii) After September 30, 1981, and before 1985—With respect to compensation paid before 1985 for services rendered after September 30, 1981, the tier 2 portion shall be—

(I) so much of the tax imposed by section 3201 as is determined at the 2 percent rate, and

(II) so much of the taxes imposed by sections 3211 and 3221 as is determined at the 11.75 percent rate.

With respect to compensation paid for services rendered after December 31, 1983 and before 1985, subclause (I) shall be applied by substituting "2.75 percent" for "2 percent", and subclause (II) shall be applied by substituting "12.75 percent" for "11.75 percent".

(iii) Before October 1, 1981.—With respect to compensation paid for services rendered during any period before October 1, 1981, the tier 2 portion shall be the excess (if any) of—

(I) the tax imposed for such period by section 3201, 3211, or 3221, as the case may be (other than any tax imposed with respect to man-hours), over

(II) the tax which would have been imposed by such section for such period had the rates of the comparable taxes imposed by chapter 21 for such period applied under such section.

(C) Contributions not allocable to supplemental annuity or windfall benefits.—For purposes of paragraph (1), no amount treated as an employee contribution under this paragraph shall be allocated to—

(i) any supplemental annuity paid under section 2(b) of the Railroad Retirement Act of 1974, or

(ii) any benefit paid under section 3(h), 4(e), or 4(h) of such Act.

(3) Tier 1 railroad retirement benefit.—For purposes of paragraph (1), the term "tier 1 railroad retirement benefit" has the meaning given such term by section 86(d)(4).

(s) Required Distributions Where Holder Dies Before Entire Interest Is Distributed.—

(1) In general.—A contract shall not be treated as an annuity contract for purposes of this title unless it provides that—

(A) if any holder of such contract dies on or after the annuity starting date and before the entire interest in such contract has been distributed, the remaining portion of such interest will be distributed at least as rapidly as under the method of distributions being used as of the date of his death, and

(B) if any holder of such contract dies before the annuity starting date, the entire interest in such contract will be distributed within 5 years after the death of such holder.

(2) Exception for certain amounts payable over life of beneficiary.—If—

IRC Sec. 72(s)(2)

(A) any portion of the holder's interest is payable to (or for the benefit of) a designated beneficiary,

(B) such portion will be distributed (in accordance with regulations) over the life of such designated beneficiary (or over a period not extending beyond the life expectancy of such beneficiary), and

(C) such distributions begin not later than 1 year after the date of the holder's death or such later date as the Secretary may by regulations prescribe,

then for purposes of paragraph (1), the portion referred to in subparagraph (A) shall be treated as distributed on the day on which such distributions begin.

(3) Special rule where surviving spouse beneficiary.—If the designated beneficiary referred to in paragraph (2)(A) is the surviving spouse of the holder of the contract, paragraphs (1) and (2) shall be applied by treating such spouse as the holder of such contract.

(4) Designated beneficiary.—For purposes of this subsection, the term "designated beneficiary" means any individual designated a beneficiary by the holder of the contract.

(5) Exception for certain annuity contracts.— This subsection shall not apply to any annuity contract—

(A) which is provided—

(i) under a plan described in section 401(a) which includes a trust exempt from tax under section 501, or

(ii) under a plan described in section 403(a),

(B) which is described in section 403(b),

(C) which is an individual retirement annuity or provided under an individual retirement account or annuity, or

(D) which is a qualified funding asset (as defined in section 130(d), but without regard to whether there is a qualified assignment).

(6) Special rule where holder is corporation or other non-individual.—

(A) In general.—For purposes of this subsection, if the holder of the contract is not an individual, the primary annuitant shall be treated as the holder of the contract.

(B) Primary annuitant.—For purposes of subparagraph (A), the term "primary annuitant" means the individual, the events in the life of whom are of primary importance in affecting the timing or amount of the payout under the contract.

(7) Treatment of changes in primary annuitant where holder of contract is not an individual.—For purposes of this subsection, in the case of a holder of an annuity contract which is not an individual, if there is a change in a primary annuitant (as defined in paragraph (6)(B)), such change shall be treated as the death of the holder.

(t) 10-Percent Additional Tax on Early Distributions From Qualified Retirement Plans.—

(1) Imposition of additional tax.—If any taxpayer receives any amount from a qualified retirement plan (as defined in section 4974(c)), the taxpayer's tax under this chapter for the taxable year in which such amount is received shall be increased by an amount equal to 10 percent of the portion of such amount which is includible in gross income.

(2) Subsection not to apply to certain distributions.—Except as provided in paragraphs (3) and (4), paragraph (1) shall not apply to any of the following distributions:

(A) In general.—Distributions which are—

(i) made on or after the date on which the employee attains age 59½,

(ii) made to a designated beneficiary (or to the estate of the employee) on or after the death of the employee,

(iii) attributable to the employee's being disabled within the meaning of subsection (m)(7),

(iv) part of a series of substantially equal periodic payments (not less frequently than annually) made for the life (or life expectancy) of the employee or the joint lives (or joint life expectancies) of such employee and his designated beneficiary,

(v) made to an employee after separation from service after attainment of age 55,

(vi) dividends paid with respect to stock of a corporation which are described in section 404(k) or,

(vii) made on account of a levy under section 6331 on the qualified retirement plan.

(B) Medical expenses.—Distributions made to the employee (other than distributions described in subparagraph (A), (C), or (D)) to the extent such distributions do not exceed the amount allowable as a deduction under section 213 to the employee for amounts paid during the taxable year for medical care (determined without regard to whether the employee itemizes deductions for such taxable year).

(C) Payments to alternate payees pursuant to qualified domestic relations orders.—Any distribution to an alternate payee pursuant to a qualified domestic relations order (within the meaning of section 414(p)(1)).

(D) Distributions to unemployed individuals for health insurance premiums—

(i) In general.—Distributions from an individual retirement plan to an individual after separation from employment—

(I) if such individual has received unemployment compensation for 12 consecutive weeks under any Federal or State unemployment compensation law by reason of such separation,

(II) if such distributions are made during any taxable year during which such unemployment compensation is paid or the succeeding taxable year, and

(III) to the extent such distributions do not exceed the amount paid during the taxable year for insurance described in section 213(d)(1)(D) with respect to the individual and the individual's spouse and dependents (as defined in section 152, determined without regard to subsections (b)(1), (b)(2), and (d)(1)(B) thereof).

(ii) Distributions after reemployment.—Clause (i) shall not apply to any distribution made after the individual has been employed for at least 60 days after the separation from employment to which clause (i) applies.

(iii) Self-employed individuals.—To the extent provided in regulations, a self-employed individual shall be treated as meeting the requirements of clause (i)(I) if, under Federal or State law, the individual would have received unemployment compensation but for the fact the individual was self-employed.

(E) Distributions from individual retirement plans for higher education expenses.—Distributions to an individual from an individual retirement plan to the extent such distributions do not exceed the qualified higher education expenses (as defined in paragraph (7)) of the taxpayer for the taxable year. Distributions shall not be taken into account under the preceding sentence if such distributions are described in subparagraph (A), (C), or (D) or to the extent paragraph (1) does not apply to such distributions by reason of subparagraph (B).

(F) Distributions from certain plans for first home purchases.—Distributions to an individual from an individual retirement plan which are qualified first-time homebuyer distributions (as defined in paragraph (8)). Distributions shall not be taken into account under the preceding sentence if such distributions are described in subparagraph (A), (C), (D), or (E) or to the extent paragraph (1) does not apply to such distributions by reason of subparagraph (B).

(G) Distributions from retirement plans to individuals called to active duty.—

(i) In general.—Any qualified reservist distribution.

(ii) Amount distributed may be repaid.—Any individual who receives a qualified reservist distribution may, at any time during the 2-year period beginning on the day after the end of the active duty period, make one or more contributions to an individual retirement plan of such individual in an aggregate amount not to exceed the amount of such distribution. The dollar limitations otherwise applicable to contributions to individual retirement plans shall not apply to any contribution made pursuant to the preceding sentence. No deduction shall be allowed for any contribution pursuant to this clause.

(iii) Qualified reservist distribution.—For purposes of this subparagraph, the term "qualified reservist distribution" means any distribution to an individual if—

(I) such distribution is from an individual retirement plan, or from amounts attributable to employer contributions made pursuant to elective deferrals described in subparagraph (A) or (C) of section 402(g)(3) or section 501(c)(18)(D)(iii),

(II) such individual was (by reason of being a member of a reserve component (as defined in section 101 of title 37, United States Code)) ordered or called to active duty for a period in excess of 179 days or for an indefinite period, and

(III) such distribution is made during the period beginning on the date of such order or call and ending at the close of the active duty period.

(iv) Application of subparagraph.—This subparagraph applies to individuals ordered or called to active duty after September 11, 2001. In no event shall the 2-year period referred to in clause (ii) end on or before the date which is 2 years after the date of the enactment of this subparagraph.

(3) Limitations.—

(A) Certain exceptions not to apply to individual retirement plans.—Subparagraphs (A)(v) and (C) of paragraph (2) shall not apply to distributions from an individual retirement plan.

(B) Periodic payments under qualified plans must begin after separation.—Paragraph (2)(A)(iv) shall not apply to any amount paid from a trust described in section 401(a) which is exempt from tax under section 501(a) or from a contract described in section 72(e)(5)(D)(ii) unless the series of payments begins after the employee separates from service.

(4) Change in substantially equal payments.—

(A) In general.—If—

(i) paragraph (1) does not apply to a distribution by reason of paragraph (2)(A)(iv), and

(ii) the series of payments under such paragraph are subsequently modified (other than by reason of death or disability)—

(I) before the close of the 5-year period beginning with the date of the first payment and after the employee attains age 59½, or

(II) before the employee attains age 59½,

IRC Sec. 72(t)(4)(A)(ii)(II)

the taxpayer's tax for the 1st taxable year in which such modification occurs shall be increased by an amount, determined under regulations, equal to the tax which (but for paragraph (2)(A)(iv)) would have been imposed, plus interest for the deferral period.

(B) Deferral period.—For purposes of this paragraph, the term "deferral period" means the period beginning with the taxable year in which (without regard to paragraph (2)(A)(iv)) the distribution would have been includible in gross income and ending with the taxable year in which the modification described in subparagraph (A) occurs.

(5) **Employee.**—For purposes of this subsection, the term "employee" includes any participant, and in the case of an individual retirement plan, the individual for whose benefit such plan was established.

(6) **Special rules for simple retirement accounts.**—In the case of any amount received from a simple retirement account (within the meaning of section 408 (p)) during the 2-year period beginning on the date such individual first participated in any qualified salary reduction arrangement maintained by the individual's employer under section 408(p)(2), paragraph (1) shall be applied by substituting "25 percent" for "10 percent".

(7) **Qualified higher education expenses.**—For purposes of paragraph (2)(E)—

(A) In general.—The term "qualified higher education expenses" means qualified higher education expenses (as defined in section 529(e)(3)) for education furnished to—

(i) the taxpayer,

(ii) the taxpayer's spouse, or

(iii) any child (as defined in section 152(f)(1) or grandchild of the taxpayer or the taxpayer's spouse, at an eligible educational institution (as defined in section 529(e)(5)).

(B) Coordination with other benefits.—The amount of qualified higher education expenses for any taxable year shall be reduced as provided in section 25A(g)(2).

(8) **Qualified first-time homebuyer distributions.**—For purposes of paragraph (2)(F)—

(A) In general.—The term "qualified first-time homebuyer distribution" means any payment or distribution received by an individual to the extent such payment or distribution is used by the individual before the close of the 120th day after the day on which such payment or distribution is received to pay qualified acquisition costs with respect to a principal residence of a first-time homebuyer who is such individual, the spouse of such individual, or any child, grandchild, or ancestor of such individual or the individual's spouse.

(B) Lifetime dollar limitation.—The aggregate amount of payments or distributions received by an individual which may be treated as qualified first-time homebuyer distributions for any taxable year shall not exceed the excess (if any) of—

(i) $10,000, over

(ii) the aggregate amounts treated as qualified first-time homebuyer distributions with respect to such individual for all prior taxable years.

(C) Qualified acquisition costs.—For purposes of this paragraph, the term "qualified acquisition costs" means the costs of acquiring, constructing, or reconstructing a residence. Such term includes any usual or reasonable settlement, financing, or other closing costs.

(D) First-time homebuyer; other definitions.—For purposes of this paragraph—

(i) First-time homebuyer.—The term "first-time homebuyer" means any individual if—

(I) such individual (and if married, such individual's spouse) had no present ownership interest in a principal residence during the 2-year period ending on the date of acquisition of the principal residence to which this paragraph applies, and

(II) subsection (h) or (k) of section 1034 (as in effect on the day before the date of the enactment of this paragraph) did not suspend the running of any period of time specified in section 1034 (as so in effect) with respect to such individual on the day before the date the distribution is applied pursuant to subparagraph (A).

(ii) Principal Residence.—The term "principal residence" has the same meaning as when used in section 121.

(iii) Date of acquisition.—The term "date of acquisition" means the date—

(I) on which a binding contract to acquire the principal residence to which subparagraph (A) applies is entered into, or

(II) on which construction or reconstruction of such a principal residence is commenced.

(E) Special rule where delay in acquisition.—If any distribution from any individual retirement plan fails to meet the requirements of subparagraph (A) solely by reason of a delay or cancellation of the purchase or construction of the residence, the amount of the distribution may be contributed to an individual retirement plan as provided in section 408(d)(3)(A)(i) (determined by substituting "120th day" for "60th day" in such section), except that—

(i) section 408(d)(3)(B) shall not be applied to such contribution, and

(ii) such amount shall not be taken into account in determining whether section 408(d)(3)(B) applies to any other amount.

(9) Special rule for rollovers to section 457 plans. For purposes of this subsection, a distribution from an eligible deferred compensation plan (as defined in section 457(b)) of an eligible employer described in section 457(e)(1)(A) shall be treated as a distribution from a qualified retirement plan described in section 4974(c)(1) to the extent that such distribution is attributable to an amount transferred to an eligible deferred compensation plan from a qualified retirement plan (as defined in section 4974(c)).

(10) Distributions to qualified public safety employees in governmental plans.—

(A) In general.—In the case of a distribution to a qualified public safety employee from a governmental plan (within the meaning of section 414(d)) which is a defined benefit plan, paragraph (2)(A)(v) shall be applied by substituting "age 50" for "age 55".

(B) Qualified public safety employee.—For purposes of this paragraph, the term "qualified public safety employee" means any employee of a State or political subdivision of a State who provides police protection, firefighting services, or emergency medical services for any area within the jurisdiction of such State or political subdivision.

(u) Treatment of Annuity Contracts Not Held by Natural Persons.—

(1) In general.—If any annuity contract is held by a person who is not a natural person—

(A) such contract shall not be treated as an annuity contract for purposes of this subtitle (other than subchapter L), and

(B) the income on the contract for any taxable year of the policyholder shall be treated as ordinary income received or accrued by the owner during such taxable year.

For purposes of this paragraph, holding by a trust or other entity as an agent for a natural person shall not be taken into account.

(2) Income on the contract.—

(A) In general.—For purposes of paragraph (1), the term "income on the contract" means, with respect to any taxable year of the policyholder, the excess of—

(i) the sum of the net surrender value of the contract as of the close of the taxable year plus all distributions under the contract received during the taxable year or any prior taxable year, reduced by

(ii) the sum of the amount of net premiums under the contract for the taxable year and prior taxable years and amounts includible in gross income for prior taxable years with respect to such contract under this subsection.

Where necessary to prevent the avoidance of this subsection, the Secretary may substitute "fair mar-

ket value of the contract" for "net surrender value of the contract" each place it appears in the preceding sentence.

(B) Net premiums.—For purposes of this paragraph, the term "net premiums" means the amount of premiums paid under the contract reduced by any policyholder dividends.

(3) Exceptions.—This subsection shall not apply to any annuity contract which—

(A) is acquired by the estate of a decedent by reason of the death of the decedent,

(B) is held under a plan described in section 401(a) or 403(a), under a program described in section 403(b), or under an individual retirement plan,

(C) is a qualified funding asset (as defined in section 130(d), but without regard to whether there is a qualified assignment),

(D) is purchased by an employer upon the termination of a plan described in section 401(a) or 403(a) and is held by the employer until all amounts under such contract are distributed to the employee for whom such contract was purchased or the employee's beneficiary, or

(E) is an immediate annuity.

(4) Immediate annuity.—For purposes of this subsection, the term "immediate annuity" means an annuity—

(A) which is purchased with a single premium or annuity consideration,

(B) the annuity starting date (as defined in subsection (c)(4)) of which commences no later than 1 year from the date of the purchase of the annuity, and

(C) which provides for a series of substantially equal periodic payments (to be made not less frequently than annually) during the annuity period.

(v) 10-Percent Additional Tax for Taxable Distributions From Modified Endowment Contracts.—

(1) Imposition of additional tax.—If any taxpayer receives any amount under a modified endowment contract (as defined in section 7702A), the taxpayer's tax under this chapter for the taxable year in which such amount is received shall be increased by an amount equal to 10 percent of the portion of such amount which is includible in gross income.

(2) Subsection not to apply to certain distributions.—Paragraph (1) shall not apply to any distribution—

(A) made on or after the date on which the taxpayer attains age 59½,

(B) which is attributable to the taxpayer's becoming disabled (within the meaning of subsection (m)(7)), or

(C) which is part of a series of substantially equal periodic payments (not less frequently than annually) made for the life (or life expectancy) of the taxpayer or the joint lives (or joint life expectancies) of such taxpayer and his beneficiary.

(w) Application of Basis Rules to Nonresident Aliens.—

(1) In general.—Notwithstanding any other provision of this section, for purposes of determining the portion of any distribution which is includible in gross income of a distributee who is a citizen or resident of the United States, the investment in the contract shall not include any applicable nontaxable contributions or applicable nontaxable earnings.

(2) Applicable nontaxable contribution.—For purposes of this subsection, the term "applicable nontaxable contribution" means any employer or employee contribution—

(A) which was made with respect to compensation—

(i) for labor or personal services performed by an employee who, at the time the labor or services were performed, was a nonresident alien for purposes of the laws of the United States in effect at such time, and

(ii) which is treated as from sources without the United States, and

(B) which was not subject to income tax (and would have been subject to income tax if paid as cash compensation when the services were rendered) under the laws of the United States or any foreign country.

(3) Applicable nontaxable earnings.—For purposes of this subsection, the term "applicable nontaxable earnings" means earnings—

(A) which are paid or accrued with respect to any employer or employee contribution which was made with respect to compensation for labor or personal services performed by an employee,

(B) with respect to which the employee was at the time the earnings were paid or accrued a nonresident alien for purposes of the laws of the United States, and

(C) which were not subject to income tax under the laws of the United States or any foreign country.

(4) Regulations.—The Secretary shall prescribe such regulations as may be necessary to carry out the provisions of this subsection, including regulations treating contributions and earnings as not subject to tax under the laws of any foreign country where appropriate to carry out the purposes of this subsection.

(x) Cross Reference.—For limitation on adjustments to basis of annuity contracts sold, see section 1021.

Recent Amendments to IRC §72

Tax Relief, Unemployment Insurance Reauthorization, and Job Creation Act of 2010 (Pub. L. No. 111-312), as follows:
- Sunset Provision to Economic Growth and Tax Relief Reconciliation Act of 2001 (Pub. L. No. 107-16). Act §101(a) provides:
  (a) Temporary Extension.—
  (1) In general.—Section 901 of the Economic Growth and Tax Relief Reconciliation Act of 2001 is amended by striking "December 31, 2010" both places it appears and inserting "December 31, 2012".
  (2) Effective date.—The amendment made by this subsection shall take effect as if included in the enactment of the Economic Growth and Tax Relief Reconciliation Act of 2001.

Small Business Jobs Act of 2010 (Pub. L. No. 111-240), as follows:
- IRC §72(a) was amended by Act §2113(a). Eff. for taxable years beginning after Dec. 31, 2010. IRC §72(a) prior to amendment:
  (a) General Rule for Annuities.—Except as otherwise provided in this chapter, gross income includes any amount received as an annuity (whether for a period certain or during one or more lives) under an annuity, endowment, or life insurance contract.

Worker, Retiree, and Employer Recovery Act of 2008 (Pub. L. No. 110-458), as follows:
- IRC §72(t)(2)(G)(iv) was amended by Act §108(e) [relating to Pub. L. No. 109-280, §827], prior to amendment by Pub. L. No. 110-245, by inserting "on or" before "before". Eff. as if included in Pub. L. No. 109-280, §827 [eff. for distributions after Sept. 11, 2001].

Heroes Earnings Assistance and Relief Tax Act of 2008 (Pub. L. No. 110-245), as follows:
- IRC §72(t)(2)(G)(iv) was amended by Act §107(a) by striking ", and before December 31, 2007". Eff. for individuals ordered or called to duty on or after Dec. 31, 2007.

Pension Protection Act of 2006 (Pub. L. No. 109-280), as follows:
- IRC §72(e) was amended by Act §844(a) by redesignating para. (11) as para. (12) and adding new para. (11). Eff. for contracts issued after Dec. 31, 1996, but only with respect to tax years beginning after Dec. 31, 2009.
- IRC §72(t)(2) was amended by Act §827(a) by adding new subpara. (G). Eff. for distributions after Sept. 11, 2001. See Act §827(c)(2) for waiver provisions.
- IRC §72(t) was amended by Act §828(a) by adding new para. (10). Eff. for distributions after Aug. 17, 2006.
- Sunset Provision. Act §811, provides:
  SEC. 811. PENSIONS AND INDIVIDUAL RETIREMENT ARRANGEMENT PROVISIONS OF ECONOMIC GROWTH AND TAX RELIEF RECONCILIATION ACT OF 2001 MADE PERMANENT.
  Title IX of the Economic Growth and Tax Relief Reconciliation Act of 2001 [Pub. L. No. 107-16] shall not apply to the provisions of, and amendments made by, subtitles A through F [§§601–666] of title VI of such Act (relating to pension and individual retirement arrangement provisions).

American Jobs Creation Act of 2004 (Pub. L. No. 108-357), as follows:
- IRC §72(w) was amended by Act §906(a) by redesignating subsec. (w) as subsec. (x) and adding new subsec. (w). Eff. for distributions on or after Oct. 22, 2004.

Working Families Tax Relief Act of 2004 (Pub. L. No. 108-311), as follows:
- IRC §72(f) was amended by Act §408(a)(4) by substituting "Economic Growth and Tax Relief Reconciliation Act of 2001)" for "Economic Growth and Tax Relief Reconciliation Act of 2001". Eff. Oct. 4, 2004.
- IRC §72(t)(2)(D)(i)(III) was amended by Act §207(6) by inserting ", determined without regard to subsections (b)(1), (b)(2), and (d)(1)(B) thereof" after "section 152". Eff. for tax years beginning after Dec. 31, 2004.
- IRC §72(t)(7)(A)(iii) was amended by Act §207(7) by substituting "152(f)(1)" for "151(c)(3)". Eff. tax years beginning after Dec. 31, 2004.

Railroad Retirement and Survivors' Improvement Act of 2001 (Pub. L. No. 107-90), as follows:

● IRC §72(r)(2)(B)(i) was amended by Act §204(e)(2) by substituting "3211(b)" for "3211(a)(2)". Eff. calendar years beginning after Dec. 31, 2001.

Pub. L. No. 107-22, as follows:

● IRC §72(e)(9) was amended by Act §1(b)(1)(A) by substituting "a Coverdell education savings" for "an education individual retirement". Eff. Jul. 26, 2001.

● IRC §72(e)(9) was amended by Act §1(b)(3)(A) in the heading by substituting "Coverdell education savings" for "education individual retirement". Eff. Jul. 26, 2001.

Economic Growth and Tax Relief Reconciliation Act of 2001 (Pub. L. No. 107-16), as follows:

● IRC §72(e)(9) was amended by Act §402(a)(4)(A) by substituting "qualified tuition" for "qualified State tuition" each place it appeared. Eff. tax years beginning after Dec. 31, 2001.

● IRC §72(e)(9) was amended by Act §402(a)(4)(B) in the heading by substituting "qualified tuition" for "qualified State tuition". Eff. tax years beginning after Dec. 31, 2001.

● IRC §72(f) was amended by Act §632(a)(3)(A) by substituting "§403(b)(2)(D)(iii), as in effect before the enactment of the Economic Growth and Tax Relief Reconciliation Act of 2001)" for "§403(b)(2)(D)(iii))". Eff. years beginning after Dec. 31, 2001.

● IRC §72(o)(4) was amended by Act §641(e)(1) by substituting "403(b)(8), 408(d)(3), and 457(e)(16)" for "and 408(d)(3)". Eff. generally for distributions after Dec. 31, 2001. See Act §641(f)(3) for a special rule.

● IRC §72(t) was amended by Act §641(a)(2)(C) by adding new para. (9). Eff. generally for distributions after Dec. 31, 2001. See Act §641(f)(3) for a special rule.

● **Sunset Provision.** Act §901, as amended by Pub. L. No. 111-312, §101(a)(1), provides the sunset rule below. But see Pub. L. No. 109-280, §811, and Pub. L. No. 111-148, §10909(c), as amended by Pub. L. No. 111-312, §101(b)(1).

> **SEC. 901. SUNSET OF PROVISIONS OF ACT.**
>
> **(a) In general.** All provisions of, and amendments made by, this Act shall not apply—
>
> **(1)** to taxable, plan, or limitation years beginning after December 31, 2012, or
>
> **(2)** in the case of title V, to estates of decedents dying, gifts made, or generation skipping transfers, after December 31, 2012.
>
> **(b) Application of certain laws.**—The Internal Revenue Code of 1986 and the Employee Retirement Income Security Act of 1974 shall be applied and administered to years, estates, gifts, and transfers described in subsection (a) as if the provisions and amendments described in subsection (a) had never been enacted.

* * *

SEC. 79. GROUP-TERM LIFE INSURANCE PURCHASED FOR EMPLOYEES.

(a) General Rule.—There shall be included in the gross income of an employee for the taxable year an amount equal to the cost of group-term life insurance on his life provided for part or all of such year under a policy (or policies) carried directly or indirectly by his employer (or employers); but only to the extent that such cost exceeds the sum of—

(1) the cost of $50,000 of such insurance, and

(4) the amount (if any) paid by the employee toward the purchase of such insurance.

(b) Exceptions.—Subsection (a) shall not apply to—

(1) the cost of group-term life insurance on the life of an individual which is provided under a policy carried directly or indirectly by an employer after such individual has terminated his employment with such employer and is disabled (within the meaning of section 72(m)(7)),

(2) the cost of any portion of the group-term life insurance on the life of an employee provided during part or all of the taxable year of the employee under which—

(A) the employer is directly or indirectly the beneficiary, or

(B) a person described in section 170(c) is the sole beneficiary,

for the entire period during such taxable year for which the employee receives such insurance, and

(3) the cost of any group-term life insurance which is provided under a contract to which section 72(m)(3) applies.

(c) Determination of Cost of Insurance.—For purposes of this section and section 6052, the cost of group-term insurance on the life of an employee provided during any period shall be determined on the basis of uniform premiums (computed on the basis of 5-year age brackets) prescribed by regulations by the Secretary.

(d) Nondiscrimination Requirements.—

(1) In general.—In the case of a discriminatory group-term life insurance plan—

(A) subsection (a)(1) shall not apply with respect to any key employee, and

(B) the cost of group term life insurance on the life of any key employee shall be the greater of—

(i) such cost determined without regard to subsection (c), or

(ii) such cost determined with regard to subsection (c).

(2) Discriminatory group-term life insurance plan.—For purposes of this subsection, the term "discriminatory group-term life insurance plan" means any plan of an employer for providing group-term life insurance unless—

(A) the plan does not discriminate in favor of key employees as to eligibility to participate, and

(B) the type and amount of benefits available under the plan do not discriminate in favor of participants who are key employees.

(3) Nondiscriminatory eligibility classification.—

(A) In general.—A plan does not meet requirements of subparagraph (A) of paragraph (2) unless—

(i) such plan benefits 70 percent or more of all employees of the employer,

(ii) at least 85 percent of all employees who are participants under the plan are not key employees,

(iii) such plan benefits such employees as qualify under a classification set up by the employer and found by the Secretary not to be discriminatory in favor of key employees, or

(iv) in the case of a plan which is part of a cafeteria plan, the requirements of section 125 are met.

(B) Exclusion of certain employees.—For purposes of subparagraph (A), there may be excluded from consideration—

(i) employees who have not completed 3 years of service;

(ii) part-time or seasonal employees;

(iii) employees not included in the plan who are included in a unit of employees covered by an agreement between employee representatives and one or more employers which the Secretary finds to be a collective bargaining agreement, if the benefits provided under the plan were the subject of good faith bargaining between such employee representatives and such employer or employers; and

(iv) employees who are nonresident aliens and who receive no earned income (within the meaning of section 911(d)(2)) from the employer which constitutes income from sources within the United States (within the meaning of section 861(a)(3)).

(4) Nondiscriminatory benefits.—A plan does not meet the requirements of paragraph (2)(B) unless all benefits available to participants who are key employees are available to all other participants.

(5) Special rule.—A plan shall not fail to meet the requirements of paragraph (2)(B) merely because the amount of life insurance on behalf of the employees under the plan bears a uniform relationship to the total compensation or basic or regular rate of compensation of such employees.

(6) Key employee defined.—For purposes of this subsection, the term "key employee" has the meaning given to such term by paragraph (1) of section 416(i). Such term also includes any former employee if such employee when he retired or separated from service was a key employee.

(7) Exemption for church plans.—

(A) In general.—This subsection shall not apply to a church plan maintained for church employees.

(B) Definitions.—For purposes of subparagraph (A), the terms "church plan" and "church employee" have the meaning given such terms by paragraphs (1) and (3)(B) of section 414(e), respectively, except that—

(i) section 414(e) shall be applied by substituting "section 501(c)(3)" for "section 501" each place it appears, and

(ii) the term "church employee" shall not include an employee of—

(I) an organization described in section 170(b)(1)(A)(ii) above the secondary school level (other than a school for religious training),

(II) an organization described in section 170(b)(1)(A)(iii), and

(III) an organization described in section 501(c)(3), the basis of the exemption for which is substantially similar to the basis for exemption of an organization described in subclause (II).

(8) Treatment of former employees.—To the extent provided in regulations, this subsection shall be applied separately with respect to former employees.

(e) Employee Includes Former Employee.—For purposes of this section, the term "employee" includes a former employee.

* * *

SEC. 83. PROPERTY TRANSFERRED IN CONNECTION WITH PERFORMANCE OF SERVICES.

(a) General Rule.—If, in connection with the performance of services, property is transferred to any person other than the person for whom such services are performed, the excess of—

(1) the fair market value of such property (determined without regard to any restriction other than a restriction which by its terms will never lapse) at the first time the rights of the person having the beneficial interest in such property are transferable or are not subject to a substantial risk of forfeiture, whichever occurs earlier, over

(2) the amount (if any) paid for such property,

shall be included in the gross income of the person who performed such services in the first taxable year in which the rights of the person having the beneficial interest in such property are transferable or are not subject to a substantial risk of forfeiture, whichever is applicable. The preceding sentence shall not apply if such person sells or otherwise disposes of such property in an arm's length transaction before his rights in such property become transferable or not subject to a substantial risk of forfeiture.

(b) Election to Include in Gross Income in Year of Transfer.—

(1) In general.—Any person who performs services in connection with which property is transferred to any person may elect to include in his gross income for the taxable year in which such property is transferred, the excess of—

(A) the fair market value of such property at the time of transfer (determined without regard to any restriction other than a restriction which by its terms will never lapse), over

(B) the amount (if any) paid for such property.

If such election is made, subsection (a) shall not apply with respect to the transfer of such property, and if such property is subsequently forfeited, no deduction shall be allowed in respect of such forfeiture.

(2) Election.—An election under paragraph (1) with respect to any transfer of property shall be made in such manner as the Secretary prescribes and shall be made not later than 30 days after the date of suchtransfer. Such election may not be revoked except with the consent of the Secretary.

(c) Special Rules.—For purposes of this section—

(1) Substantial risk of forfeiture.—The rights of a person in property are subject to a substantial risk of forfeiture if such person's rights to full enjoyment of such property are conditioned upon the future performance of substantial services by any individual.

(2) Transferability of property.—The rights of a person in property are transferable only if the rights in such property of any transferee are not subject to a substantial risk of forfeiture.

(3) Sales which may give rise to suit under section 16(b) of the Securities Exchange Act of 1934.—So long as the sale of property at a profit could subject a person to suit under section 16(b) of the Securities Exchange Act of 1934, such person's rights in such property are—

(A) subject to a substantial risk of forfeiture, and

(B) not transferable.

(4) For purposes of determining an individual's basis in property transferred in connection with the performances of services, rules similar to the rules of section 72(w) shall apply.

(d) Certain Restrictions Which Will Never Lapse.—

(1) Valuation.—In the case of property subject to a restriction which by its terms will never lapse, and which allows the transferee to sell such property only at a price determined under a formula, the price so determined shall be deemed to be the fair market value of the property unless established to the contrary by the Secretary, and the burden of proof shall be on the Secretary with respect to such value.

(2) Cancellation.—If, in the case of property subject to a restriction which by its terms will never lapse, the restriction is canceled, then, unless the taxpayer establishes—

(A) that such cancellation was not compensatory, and

(B) that the person, if any, who would be allowed a deduction if the cancellation were treated as compensatory, will treat the transaction as not compensatory, as evidenced in such manner as the Secretary shall prescribe by regulations,

the excess of the fair market value of the property (computed without regard to the restrictions) at the time of cancellation over the sum of—

(C) the fair market value of such property (computed by taking the restriction into account) immediately before the cancellation, and

(D) the amount, if any, paid for the cancellation,

shall be treated as compensation for the taxable year in which such cancellation occurs.

(e) Applicability of Section.—This section shall not apply to—

(1) a transaction to which section 421 applies,

(2) a transfer to or from a trust described in section 401(a) or a transfer under an annuity plan which meets the requirements of section 404(a)(2),

(3) the transfer of an option without a readily ascertainable fair market value,

(4) the transfer of property pursuant to the exercise of an option with a readily ascertainable fair market value at the date of grant, or

(5) group-term life insurance to which section 79 applies.

(f) Holding Period.—In determining the period for which the taxpayer has held property to which subsection (a) applies, there shall be included only the period beginning at the first time his rights in such property are transferable or are not subject to a substantial risk of forfeiture, whichever occurs earlier.

(g) Certain Exchanges.—If property to which subsection (a) applies is exchanged for property subject to restrictions and conditions substantially similar to those to which the property given in such exchange was subject, and if section 354, 355, 356, or 1036 (or so much of section 1031 as relates to section 1036) applied to such exchange, or if such exchange was pursuant to the exercise of a conversion privilege—

(1) such exchange shall be disregarded for purposes of subsection (a), and

(2) the property received shall be treated as property to which subsection (a) applies.

(h) Deduction by Employer.—In the case of a transfer of property to which this section applies or a cancellation of a restriction described in subsection (d), there shall be allowed as a deduction under section 162, to the person for whom were performed the services in connection with which such property was transferred, an amount equal to the amount included under subsection (a), (b), or (d)(2) in the gross income of the person who performed such services. Such deduction shall be allowed for the taxable year of such person in which or with which ends the taxable year in which such amount is included in the gross income of the person who performed such services.

(i) [Repealed.]

IRC Sec. 83(i)

Recent Amendments to IRC §83

American Jobs Creation Act of 2004 (Pub. L. No. 108-357), as follows:

• IRC §83(c) was amended by Act §906(b) by adding new para. (4). Eff. for distributions on or after Oct. 22, 2004.

* * *

SEC. 86. SOCIAL SECURITY AND TIER 1 RAILROAD RETIREMENT BENEFITS.

(a) In General.—

(1) In general.—Except as provided in paragraph (2), gross income for the taxable year of any taxpayer described in subsection (b) (notwithstanding section 207 of the Social Security Act) includes social security benefits in an amount equal to the lesser of—

(A) one-half of the social security benefits received during the taxable year, or

(b) one-half of the excess described in subsection (b)(1).

(2) Additional amount.—In the case of a taxpayer with respect to whom the amount determined under subsection (b)(1)(A) exceeds the adjusted base amount, the amount included in gross income under this section shall be equal to the lesser of—

(A) the sum of—

(i) 85 percent of such excess, plus

(ii) the lesser of the amount determined under paragraph (1) or an amount equal to one-half of the difference between the adjusted base amount and the base amount of the taxpayer, or

(B) 85 percent of the social security benefits received during the taxable year.

(b) Taxpayers to Whom Subsection (a) Applies.—

(1) In general.—A taxpayer is described in this subsection if—

(A) the sum of—

(i) the modified adjusted gross income of the taxpayer for the taxable year, plus

(ii) one-half of the social security benefits received during the taxable year, exceeds

(b) the base amount.

(2) Modified adjusted gross income.—For purposes of this subsection, the term "modified adjusted gross income" means adjusted gross income—

Editor's Note

Caution: IRC §86(b)(2)(A), as follows, was amended by Pub. L. No. 107-16. For sunset provision, see the amendment notes to this section for Pub. L. No. 107-16.

(A) determined without regard to this section and sections 135, 137, 199, 221, 222, 911, 931, and 933, and

(B) increased by the amount of interest received or accrued by the taxpayer during the taxable year which is exempt from tax.

(c) Base Amount and Adjusted Base Amount.—For purposes of this section—

(1) Base amount.—The term "base amount" means—

(A) except as otherwise provided in this paragraph, $25,000,

(B) $32,000 in the case of a joint return, and

(C) zero in the case of a taxpayer who—

(i) is married as of the close of the taxable year (within the meaning of section 7703) but does not file a joint return for such year, and

(ii) does not live apart from his spouse at all times during the taxable year.

(2) Adjusted base amount.—The term "adjusted base amount" means—

(A) except as otherwise provided in this paragraph, $34,000,

(B) $44,000 in the case of a joint return, and

(C) zero in the case of a taxpayer described in paragraph (1)(C).

(d) Social Security Benefit.—

(1) In general.—For purposes of this section, the term "social security benefit" means any amount received by the taxpayer by reason of entitlement to—

(A) a monthly benefit under title II of the Social Security Act, or

(B) a tier 1 railroad retirement benefit.

(2) Adjustment for repayments during year.—

(A) In general.—For purposes of this section, the amount of social security benefits received during any taxable year shall be reduced by any repayment made by the taxpayer during the taxable year of a social security benefit previously received by the taxpayer (whether or not such benefit was received during the taxable year).

(B) Denial of deduction.—If (but for this subparagraph) any portion of the repayments referred to in subparagraph (A) would have been allowable as a deduction for the taxable year under section 165, such portion shall be allowable as a deduction only to the extent it exceeds the social security benefits received by the taxpayer during the taxable year (and not repaid during such taxable year).

(3) Workmen's compensation benefits substituted for social security benefits.—For purposes of this section, if, by reason of section 224 of the Social Security Act (or by reason of section 3(a)(1) of the Railroad Retirement Act of 1974), any social security benefit is reduced by reason of the receipt of a benefit under a workmen's compensation act, the term "social security benefit" includes that portion of such benefit received under the workmen's compensation act which equals such reduction.

(4) Tier 1 railroad retirement benefit.—For purposes of paragraph (1), the term "tier 1 railroad retirement benefit" means—

(A) the amount of the annuity under the Railroad Retirement Act of 1974 equal to the amount of the benefit to which the taxpayer would have been entitled under the Social Security Act if all of the service after December 31, 1936, of the employee (on whose employment record the annuity is being paid) had been included in the term "employment" as defined in the Social Security Act, and

(B) a monthly annuity amount under section 3(f)(3) of the Railroad Retirement Act of 1974.

(5) Effect of early delivery of benefit checks.—For purposes of subsection (a), in any case where section 708 of the Social Security Act causes social security benefit checks to be delivered before the end of the calendar month for which they are issued, the benefits involved shall be deemed to have been received in the succeeding calendar month.

(e) Limitation on Amount Included Where Taxpayer Receives Lump-Sum Payment.—

(1) Limitation.—If—

(A) any portion of a lump-sum payment of social security benefits received during the taxable year is attributable to prior taxable years, and

(B) the taxpayer makes an election under this subsection for the taxable year,

then the amount included in gross income under this section for the taxable year by reason of the receipt of such portion shall not exceed the sum of the increases in gross income under this chapter for prior taxable years which would result solely from taking into account such portion in the taxable years to which it is attributable.

(2) Special rules.—

(A) Year to which benefit attributable.—For purposes of this subsection, a social security benefit is attributable to a taxable year if the generally applicable payment date for such benefit occurred during such taxable year.

(B) Election.—An election under this subsection shall be made at such time and in such manner as the Secretary shall by regulations prescribe. Such election, once made, may be revoked only with the consent of the Secretary.

(f) Treatment as Pension or Annuity for Certain Purposes.—For purposes of—

(1) section 22(c)(3)(A) (relating to reduction for amounts received as pension or annuity),

(2) section 32(c)(2) (defining earned income),

(3) section 219(f)(1) (defining compensation), and

(4) section 911(b)(1) (defining foreign earned income), any social security benefit shall be treated as an amount received as a pension or annuity.

Recent Amendments to IRC §86

American Jobs Creation Act of 2004 (Pub. L. No. 108-357), as follows:
● IRC §86(b)(2)(A) was amended by Act §102(d)(1) by inserting "199," before "221". Eff. tax years beginning after Dec. 31, 2004.

Economic Growth and Tax Relief Reconciliation Act of 2001 (Pub. L. No. 107-16), as follows:
● IRC §86(b)(2) was amended by Act §431(c)(1) by inserting "222," after "221,". Eff. for payments made in tax years beginning after Dec. 31, 2001.
● Sunset Provision. Act §901, as amended by Pub. L. No. 111-312, §101(a)(1), provides the sunset rule below. But see Pub. L. No. 109-280, §811, and Pub. L. No. 111-148, §10909(c), as amended by Pub. L. No. 111-312, §101(b)(1).
   SEC. 901. SUNSET OF PROVISIONS OF ACT.
   (a) In general. All provisions of, and amendments made by, this Act shall not apply—
   (1) to taxable, plan, or limitation years beginning after December 31, 2012, or
   (2) in the case of title V, to estates of decedents dying, gifts made, or generation skipping transfers, after December 31, 2012.
   (b) Application of certain laws.—The Internal Revenue Code of 1986 and the Employee Retirement Income Security Act of 1974 shall be applied and administered to years, estates, gifts, and transfers described in subsection (a) as if the provisions and amendments described in subsection (a) had never been enacted.

---

* * *

Part III—Items Specifically Excluded From Gross Income

SEC. 101. CERTAIN DEATH BENEFITS.

(a) Proceeds of Life Insurance Contracts Payable by Reason of Death.—

(1) General rule.—Except as otherwise provided in paragraph (2), subsection (d), subsection (f), and subsection (j), gross income does not include amounts received (whether in a single sum or otherwise) under a life insurance contract, if such amounts are paid by reason of the death of the insured.

(2) Transfer for valuable consideration.—In the case of a transfer for a valuable consideration, by assignment or otherwise, of a life insurance contract or any interest therein, the amount excluded from gross income by paragraph (1) shall not exceed an amount equal to the sum of the actual value of such consideration and the premiums and other amounts subsequently paid by the transferee. The preceding sentence shall not apply in the case of such a transfer—

(A) if such contract or interest therein has a basis for determining gain or loss in the hands of a transferee determined in whole or in part by reference to such basis of such contract or interest therein in the hands of the transferor, or

(B) if such transfer is to the insured, to a partner of the insured, to a partnership in which the insured is a partner, or to a corporation in which the insured is a shareholder or officer.

The term "other amounts" in the first sentence of this paragraph includes interest paid or accrued by the transferee on indebtedness with respect to such contract or any interest therein if such interest paid or accrued is not allowable as a deduction by reason of section 264(a)(4).

(b) [Repealed.]

(c) Interest.—If any amount excluded from gross income by subsection (a) is held under an agreement to pay interest thereon, the interest payments shall be included in gross income.

(d) Payment of Life Insurance Proceeds at a Date Later Than Death.—

(1) General rule.—The amounts held by an insurer with respect to any beneficiary shall be prorated (in accordance with such regulations as may be prescribed by the Secretary) over the period or periods with respect to which such payments are to be made. There shall be excluded from the gross income of such beneficiary in the taxable year received any amount determined by such proration. Gross income includes, to the extent not excluded by the preceding sentence, amounts received under agreements to which this subsection applies.

(2) Amount held by an insurer.—An amount held by an insurer with respect to any beneficiary shall mean an amount to which subsection (a) applies which is—

(A) held by any insurer under an agreement provided for in the life insurance contract, whether as an option or otherwise, to pay such amount on a date or dates later than the death of the insured, and

(B) equal to the value of such agreement to such beneficiary

(i) as of the date of death of the insured (as if any option exercised under the life insurance contract were exercised at such time), and

(ii) as discounted on the basis of the interest rate used by the insurer in calculating payments

under the agreement and mortality tables prescribed by the Secretary.

(3) Application of subsection.—This subsection shall not apply to any amount to which subsection (c) is applicable.

(e) [Repealed.]

(f) Proceeds of Flexible Premium Contracts Issued Before January 1, 1985 Payable by Reason of Death.—

(1) In general.—Any amount paid by reason of the death of the insured under a flexible premium life insurance contract issued before January 1, 1985 shall be excluded from gross income only if—

(A) under such contract—

(i) the sum of the premiums paid under such contract does not at any time exceed the guideline premium limitation as of such time, and

(ii) any amount payable by reason of the death of the insured (determined without regard to any qualified additional benefit) is not at any time less than the applicable percentage of the cash value of such contract at such time, or

(B) by the terms of such contract, the cash value of such contract may not at any time exceed the net single premium with respect to the amount payable by reason of the death of the insured (determined without regard to any qualified additional benefit) at such time.

(2) Guideline premium limitation.—For purposes of this subsection—

(A) Guideline premium limitation.—The term "guideline premium limitation" means, as of any date, the greater of—

(i) the guideline single premium, or

(ii) the sum of the guideline level premiums to such date.

(B) Guideline single premium.—The term "guideline single premium" means the premium at issue with respect to future benefits under the contract (without regard to any qualified additional benefit), and with respect to any charges for qualified additional benefits, at the time of a determination under subparagraph (A) or (E) and which is based on—

(i) the mortality and other charges guaranteed under the contract, and

(ii) interest at the greater of an annual effective rate of 6 percent or the minimum rate or rates guaranteed upon issue of the contract.

(C) Guideline level premium.—The term "guideline level premium" means the level annual amount, payable over the longest period permitted under the contract (but ending not less than 20 years from date of issue or not later than age 95, if earlier), computed on the same basis as the guideline single premium, except that subparagraph (B)(ii) shall be applied by substituting "4 percent" for "6 percent".

(D) Computational rules.—In computing the guideline single premium or guideline level premium under subparagraph (B) or (C)—

(i) the excess of the amount payable by reason of the death of the insured (determined without regard to any qualified additional benefit) over the cash value of the contract shall be deemed to be not greater than such excess at the time the contract was issued,

(ii) the maturity date shall be the latest maturity date permitted under the contract, but not less than 20 years after the date of issue or (if earlier) age 95, and

(iii) the amount of any endowment benefit (or sum of endowment benefits) shall be deemed not to exceed the least amount payable by reason of the death of the insured (determined without regard to any qualified additional benefit) at any time under the contract.

(E) Adjustments.—The guideline single premium and guideline level premium shall be adjusted in the event of a change in the future benefits or any qualified additional benefit under the contract which was not reflected in any guideline single premiums or guideline level premium previously determined.

(3) Other definitions and special rules.—For purposes of this subsection—

(A) Flexible premium life insurance contract.— The terms "flexible premium life insurance contract" and "contract" mean a life insurance contract (including any qualified additional benefits) which provides for the payment of one or more premiums which are not fixed by the insurer as to both timing and amount. Such terms do not include that portion of any contract which is treated under State law as providing any annuity benefits other than as a settlement option.

(B) Premiums paid.—The term "premiums paid" means the premiums paid under the contract less any amounts (other than amounts includible in gross income) to which section 72(e) applies. If, in order to comply with the requirements of paragraph (1)(A), any portion of any premium paid during any contract year is returned by the insurance company (with interest) within 60 days after the end of a contract year—

(i) the amount so returned (excluding interest) shall be deemed to reduce the sum of the premiums paid under the contract during such year, and

(ii) notwithstanding the provisions of section 72(e), the amount of any interest so returned shall be includible in the gross income of the recipient.

(C) Applicable percentage.—The term "applicable percentage" means—

(i) 140 percent in the case of an insured with an attained age at the beginning of the contract year of 40 or less, and

(ii) in the case of an insured with an attained age of more than 40 as of the beginning of the contract year, 140 percent reduced (but not below 105 percent) by one percent for each year in excess of 40.

(D) Cash value.—The cash value of any contract shall be determined without regard to any deduction for any surrender charge or policy loan.

(E) Qualified additional benefits.—The term "qualified additional benefits" means any—

(i) guaranteed insurability,

(ii) accidental death benefit,

(iii) family term coverage, or

(iv) waiver of premium.

(F) Premium payments not disqualifying contract.—The payment of a premium which would result in the sum of the premiums paid exceeding the guideline premium limitation shall be disregarded for purposes of paragraph (1)(A)(i) if the amount of such premium does not exceed the amount necessary to prevent the termination of the contract without cash value on or before the end of the contract year.

(G) Net single premium.—In computing the net single premium under paragraph (1)(B)—

(i) the mortality basis shall be that guaranteed under the contract (determined by reference to the most recent mortality table allowed under all State laws on the date of issuance),

(ii) interest shall be based on the greater of—

(I) an annual effective rate of 4 percent (3 percent for contracts issued before July 1, 1983), or

(II) the minimum rate or rates guaranteed upon issue of the contract, and

(iii) the computational rules of paragraph (2)(D) shall apply, except that the maturity date referred to in clause (ii) thereof shall not be earlier than age 95.

(H) Correction of errors.—If the taxpayer establishes to the satisfaction of the Secretary that—

(i) the requirements described in paragraph (1) for any contract year was not satisfied due to reasonable error, and

(ii) reasonable steps are being taken to remedy the error,

the Secretary may waive the failure to satisfy such requirements.

IRC Sec. 101(f)(3)(H)(ii)

(I) Regulations.—The Secretary shall prescribe such regulations as may be necessary or appropriate to carry out the purposes of this subsection.

(g) Treatment of Certain Accelerated Death Benefits.—

(1) In general.—For purposes of this section, the following amounts shall be treated as an amount paid by reason of the death of an insured:

(A) Any amount received under a life insurance contract on the life of an insured who is a terminally ill individual.

(B) Any amount received under a life insurance contract on the life of an insured who is a chronically ill individual.

(2) Treatment of viatical settlements.—

(A) In general.—If any portion of the death benefit under a life insurance contract on the life of an insured described in paragraph (1) is sold or assigned to a viatical settlement provider, the amount paid for the sale or assignment of such portion shall be treated as an amount paid under the life insurance contract by reason of the death of such insured.

(B) Viatical settlement provider.—

(i) In general.—The term "viatical settlement provider" means any person regularly engaged in the trade or business of purchasing, or taking assignments of, life insurance contracts on the lives of insured described in paragraph (1) if—

(I) such person is licensed for such purposes (with respect to insureds described in the same subparagraph of paragraph (1) as the insured) in the State in which the insured resides, or

(II) in the case of an insured who resides in a State not requiring the licensing of such persons for such purposes with respect to such insured, such person meets the requirements of clause (ii) or (iii), whichever applies to such insured.

(ii) Terminally ill insureds.—A person meets the requirements of this clause with respect to an insured who is a terminally ill individual if such person—

(I) meets the requirements of sections 8 and 9 of the Viatical Settlements Model Act of the National Association of Insurance Commissioners, and

(II) meets the requirements of the Model Regulations of the National Association of Insurance Commissioners (relating to standards for evaluation of reasonable payments) in determining amounts paid by such person in connection with such purchases or assignments.

(iii) Chronically ill insureds.—A person meets the requirements of this clause with respect to an insured who is a chronically ill individual if such person—

(I) meets requirements similar to the requirements referred to in clause (ii)(I), and

(II) meets the standards (if any) of the National Association of Insurance Commissioners for evaluating the reasonableness of amounts paid by such person in connection with such purchases or assignments with respect to chronically ill individuals.

(3) Special rules for chronically ill insureds.—In the case of an insured who is a chronically ill individual—

(A) In general.—Paragraphs (1) and (2) shall not apply to any payment received for any period unless—

(i) such payment is for costs incurred by the payee (not compensated for by insurance or otherwise) for qualified long-term care services provided for the insured for such period, and

(ii) the terms of the contract giving rise to such payment satisfy—

(I) the requirements of section 7702B(b)(1)(B), and

(II) the requirements (if any) applicable under subparagraph (B).

For purposes of the preceding sentence, the rule of section 7702B(b)(2)(B) shall apply.

(B) Other requirements.—The requirements applicable under this subparagraph are—

(i) those requirements of section 7702B(g) and section 4980C which the Secretary specifies as applying to such a purchase, assignment, or other arrangement,

(ii) standards adopted by the National Association of Insurance Commissioners which specifically apply to chronically ill individuals (and, if such standards are adopted, the analogous requirements specified under clause (i) shall cease to apply), and

(iii) standards adopted by the State in which the policyholder resides (and if such standards are adopted, the analogous requirements specified under clause (i) and (subject to section 4980C(f)) standards under clause (ii), shall cease to apply).

(C) Per diem payments.—A payment shall not fail to be described in subparagraph (A) by reason of being made on a per diem or other periodic basis without regard to the expenses incurred during the period to which the payment relates.

(D) Limitation on exclusion for periodic payments.—For limitation on amount of periodic payments which are treated as described in paragraph (1), see section 7702B(d).

(4) Definitions.—For purposes of this subsection—

(A) Terminally ill individual.—The term "terminally ill individual" means an individual who has been certified by a physician as having an illness or physical condition which can reasonably be expected to result in death in 24 months or less after the date of the certification.

(B) Chronically ill individual.—The term "chronically ill individual" has the meaning given such term by section 7702B(c)(2); except that such term shall not include a terminally ill individual.

(C) Qualified long-term care services.—The term "qualified long-term care services" has the meaning given such term by section 7702B(c).

(D) Physician.—The term "physician" has the meaning given to such term by section 1861(r)(1) of the Social Security Act (42 U.S.C. 1395x(r)(1)).

(5) Exception for business-related policies.—This subsection shall not apply in the case of any amount paid to any taxpayer other than the insured if such taxpayer has an insurable interest with respect to the life of the insured by reason of the insured being a director, officer, or employee of the taxpayer or by reason of the insured being financially interested in any trade or business carried on by the taxpayer.

(h) Survivor Benefits for Public Safety Officers Killed in the Line of Duty.—

(1) In general.—Gross income shall not include any amount paid as a survivor annuity on account of the death of a public safety officer (as such term is defined in section 1204 of the Omnibus Crime Control and Safe Streets Act of 1968) killed in the line of duty—

(A) if such annuity is provided, under a governmental plan which meets the requirements of section 401(a), to the spouse (or a former spouse) of the public safety officer or to a child of such officer; and

(B) to the extent such annuity is attributable to such officer's service as a public safety officer.

(2) Exceptions.—Paragraph (1) shall not apply with respect to the death of any public safety officer if, as determined in accordance with the provisions of the Omnibus Crime Control and Safe Streets Acts of 1968—

(A) the death was caused by the intentional misconduct of the officer or by such officer's intention to bring about such officer's death;

(B) the officer was voluntarily intoxicated (as defined in section 1204 of such Act) at the time of death;

(C) the officer was performing such officer's duties in a grossly negligent manner at the time of death; or

(D) the payment is to an individual whose actions were a substantial contributing factor to the death of the officer.

(i) Certain Employee Death Benefits Payable by Reason of Death of Certain Terrorist Victims or Astronauts.—

(1) In general.—Gross income does not include amounts (whether in a single sum or otherwise) paid by an employer by reason of the death of an employee who is a specified terrorist victim (as defined in section 692(d)(4)).

(2) Limitation.—

(A) In general.—Subject to such rules as the Secretary may prescribe, paragraph (1) shall not apply to amounts which would have been payable after death if the individual had died other than as a specified terrorist victim (as so defined).

(B) Exception.—Subparagraph (A) shall not apply to incidental death benefits paid from a plan described in section 401(a) and exempt from tax under section 501(a).

(3) Treatment of self-employed individuals.—For purposes of paragraph (1), the term "employee" includes a self-employed individual (as defined in section 401(c)(1)).

(4) Relief with respect to astronauts.—The provisions of this subsection shall apply to any astronaut whose death occurs in the line of duty.

(j) Treatment of Certain Employer-Owned Life Insurance Contracts.—

(1) General rule.—In the case of an employer-owned life insurance contract, the amount excluded from gross income of an applicable policyholder by reason of paragraph (1) of subsection (a) shall not exceed an amount equal to the sum of the premiums and other amounts paid by the policyholder for the contract.

(2) Exceptions.—In the case of an employer-owned life insurance contract with respect to which the notice and consent requirements of paragraph (4) are met, paragraph (1) shall not apply to any of the following:

(A) Exceptions based on insured's status.—Any amount received by reason of the death of an insured who, with respect to an applicable policyholder—

(i) was an employee at any time during the 12-month period before the insured's death, or

(ii) is, at the time the contract is issued—

(I) a director,

(II) a highly compensated employee within the meaning of section 414(q) (without regard to paragraph (1)(B)(ii) thereof), or

IRC Sec. 101(j)(2)(A)(ii)(II)

(III) a highly compensated individual within the meaning of section 105(h)(5), except that "35 percent" shall be substituted for "25 percent" in subparagraph (C) thereof.

(B) Exception for amounts paid to insured's heirs.—Any amount received by reason of the death of an insured to the extent—

(i) the amount is paid to a member of the family (within the meaning of section 267(c)(4)) of the insured, any individual who is the designated beneficiary of the insured under the contract (other than the applicable policyholder), a trust established for the benefit of any such member of the family or designated beneficiary, or the estate of the insured, or

(ii) the amount is used to purchase an equity (or capital or profits) interest in the applicable policyholder from any person described in clause (i).

(3) Employer-owned life insurance contract.—

(A) In general.—For purposes of this subsection, the term "employer-owned life insurance contract" means a life insurance contract which—

(i) is owned by a person engaged in a trade or business and under which such person (or a related person described in subparagraph (B)(ii)) is directly or indirectly a beneficiary under the contract, and

(ii) covers the life of an insured who is an employee with respect to the trade or business of the applicable policyholder on the date the contract is issued.

For purposes of the preceding sentence, if coverage for each insured under a master contract is treated as a separate contract for purposes of sections 817(h), 7702, and 7702A, coverage for each such insured shall be treated as a separate contract.

(B) Applicable policyholder.—For purposes of this subsection—

(i) In general.—The term "applicable policyholder" means, with respect to any employer-owned life insurance contract, the person described in subparagraph (A)(i) which owns the contract.

(ii) Related persons.—The term "applicable policyholder" includes any person which—

(I) bears a relationship to the person described in clause (i) which is specified in section 267(b) or 707(b)(1), or

(II) is engaged in trades or businesses with such person which are under common control (within the meaning of subsection (a) or (b) of section 52).

(4) Notice and consent requirements.—The notice and consent requirements of this paragraph are met if, before the issuance of the contract, the employee—

(A) is notified in writing that the applicable policyholder intends to insure the employee's life and the maximum face amount for which the employee could be insured at the time the contract was issued,

(B) provides written consent to being insured under the contract and that such coverage may continue after the insured terminates employment, and

(C) is informed in writing that an applicable policyholder will be a beneficiary of any proceeds payable upon the death of the employee.

(5) Definitions.—For purposes of this subsection—

(A) Employee.—The term "employee" includes an officer, director, and highly compensated employee (within the meaning of section 414(q)).

(B) Insured.—The term "insured" means, with respect to an employer-owned life insurance contract, an individual covered by the contract who is a United States citizen or resident. In the case of a contract covering the joint lives of 2 individuals, references to an insured include both of the individuals.

Recent Amendments to IRC §101

Pension Protection Act of 2006 (Pub. L. No. 109-280), as follows:
- IRC §101(a)(1) was amended by Act §863(c)(1) by substituting "subsection (f), and subsection (j)" for "and subsection (f)". Eff. for life insurance contracts issued after Aug. 17, 2006, except for a contract issued after such date pursuant to an exchange described in IRC §1035 for a contract issued on or prior to that date. For purposes of the preceding sentence, any material increase in the death benefit or other material change shall cause the contract to be treated as a new contract except that, in the case of a master contract (within the meaning of IRC §264(f)(4)(E)), the addition of covered lives shall be treated as a new contract only with respect to such additional covered lives.
- IRC §101 was amended by Act §863(a) by adding new subsec. (j). Eff. for life insurance contracts issued after Aug. 17, 2006, except for a contract issued after such date pursuant to an exchange described in IRC §1035 for a contract issued on or prior to that date. For purposes of the preceding sentence, any material increase in the death benefit or other material change shall cause the contract to be treated as a new contract except that, in the case of a master contract (within the meaning of IRC §264(f)(4)(E)), the addition of covered lives shall be treated as a new contract only with respect to such additional covered lives.

Military Family Tax Relief Act of 2003 (Pub. L. No. 108-121), as follows:
- IRC §101(i) was amended by Act §110(b)(1) by adding new para. (4). Eff. for amounts paid after Dec. 31, 2002, with respect to deaths occurring after such date.
- IRC §101(i) was amended by Act §110(b)(2) inserting in the heading "Or Astronauts" after "Victims". Eff. for amounts paid after Dec. 31, 2002, with respect to deaths occurring after such date.

Victims of Terrorism Tax Relief Act of 2001 (Pub. L. No. 107-134), as follows:
- IRC §101 was amended by Act §102(a) by adding new subsec. (i). Eff. for tax years ending before, on, or after Sept. 11, 2001.

See Act §102(b)(2) for waiver provision.

---

* * *

SEC. 104. COMPENSATION FOR INJURIES OR SICKNESS.

(a) In General.—Except in the case of amounts attributable to (and not in excess of) deductions allowed under section 213 (relating to medical, etc., expenses) for any prior taxable year, gross income does not include—

(1) amounts received under workmen's compensation acts as compensation for personal injuries or sickness;

(2) the amount of any damages (other than punitive damages) received (whether by suit or agreement and whether as lump sums or as periodic payments) on account of personal physical injuries or physical sickness;

(3) amounts received through accident or health insurance (or through an arrangement having the effect of accident or health insurance) for personal injuries or sickness (other than amounts received by an employee, to the extent such amounts (A) are attributable to contributions by the employer which were not includible in the gross income of the employee, or (B) are paid by the employer);

(4) amounts received as a pension, annuity, or similar allowance for personal injuries or sickness resulting from active service in the armed forces of any country or in the Coast and Geodetic Survey or the Public Health Service, or as a disability annuity payable under the provisions of section 808 of the Foreign Service Act of 1980; and

(5) amounts received by an individual as disability income attributable to injuries incurred as a direct result of a terroristic or military action (as defined in section 692(c)(2)).

For purposes of paragraph (3), in the case of an individual who is, or has been, an employee within the meaning of section 401(c)(1) (relating to self-employed individuals), contributions made on behalf of such individual while he was such an employee to a trust described in section 401(a) which is exempt from tax under section 501(a), or under a plan described in section 403(a), shall, to the extent allowed as deductions under section 404, be treated as contributions by the employer which were not includible in the gross income of the employee. For purposes of paragraph (2), emotional distress shall not be treated as a physical injury or physical sickness. The preceding sentence shall not apply to an amount of damages not in excess of the amount paid for medical care (described in subparagraph (A) or (B) of section 213(d)(1)) attributable to emotional distress.

(b) Termination of Application of Subsection (a)(4) in Certain Cases.—

(1) In general.—Subsection (a)(4) shall not apply in the case of any individual who is not described in paragraph (2).

(2) Individuals to whom subsection (a)(4) continues to apply.—An individual is described in this paragraph if—

(A) on or before September 24, 1975, he was entitled to receive any amount described in subsection (a)(4),

(B) on September 24, 1975, he was a member of any organization (or reserve component thereof) referred to in subsection (a)(4) or under a binding written commitment to become such a member,

(C) he receives an amount described in subsection (a)(4) by reason of a combat-related injury, or

(D) on application therefor, he would be entitled to receive disability compensation from the Veterans' Administration.

(3) Special rules for combat-related injuries.—For purposes of this subsection, the term "combat-related injury" means personal injury or sickness—

(A) which is incurred—

(i) as a direct result of armed conflict,

(ii) while engaged in extra hazardous service, or

(iii) under conditions simulating war; or

(B) which is caused by an instrumentality of war.

In the case of an individual who is not described in subparagraph (A) or (B) of paragraph (2), except as provided in paragraph (4), the only amounts taken into account under subsection (a)(4) shall be the amounts which he receives by reason of a combat-related injury.

(4) Amount excluded to be not less than veterans' disability compensation.—In the case of any individual described in paragraph (2), the amounts excludable under subsection (a)(4) for any period with respect to any individual shall not be less than the maximum amount which such individual, on application therefor, would be entitled to receive as disability compensation from the Veterans' Administration.

(c) Application of Prior Law in Certain Cases.—The phrase "(other than punitive damages)" shall not apply to punitive damages awarded in a civil action—

(1) which is a wrongful death action, and

(2) with respect to which applicable State law (as in effect on September 13, 1995 and without regard to any modification after such date) provides, or has been construed to provide by a court of competent jurisdiction pursuant to a decision issued on or before September 13, 1995, that only punitive damages may be awarded in such an action.

IRC Sec. 104(c)(2)

This subsection shall cease to apply to any civil action filed on or after the first date on which the applicable State law ceases to provide (or is no longer construed to provide) the treatment described in paragraph (2).

(d) Cross References.—

(1) For exclusion from employee's gross income of employer contributions to accident and health plans, see section 106.

(2) For exclusion of part of disability retirement pay from the application of subsection (a)(4) of this section, see section 1403 of title 10, United States Code (relating to career compensation laws).

Recent Amendments to IRC §104

Victims of Terrorism Tax Relief Act of 2001 (Pub. L. No. 107-134), as follows:

- IRC §104(a)(5) was amended by Act §113(a) by substituting "a terroristic or military action (as defined in §692(c)(2))" for "a violent attack which the Secretary of State determines to be a terrorist attack and which occurred while such individual was an employee of the United States engaged in the performance of his official duties outside the United States." Eff. tax years ending on or after Sept. 11, 2001.

SEC. 105. AMOUNTS RECEIVED UNDER ACCIDENT AND HEALTH PLANS.

(a) Amounts Attributable to Employer Contributions.—Except as otherwise provided in this section, amounts received by an employee through accident or health insurance for personal injuries or sickness shall be included in gross income to the extent such amounts (1) are attributable to contributions by the employer which were not includible in the gross income of the employee, or (2) are paid by the employer.

> ### Editor's Note
>
> IRC §105(b), below, as amended by Pub. L. No. 111-148, §1004(d)(1), is effective March 30, 2010.

(b) Amounts Expended for Medical Care.—Except in the case of amounts attributable to (and not in excess of) deductions allowed under section 213 (relating to medical, etc., expenses) for any prior taxable year, gross income does not include amounts referred to in subsection (a) if such amounts are paid, directly or indirectly, to the taxpayer to reimburse the taxpayer for expenses incurred by him for the medical care (as defined in section 213(d)) of the taxpayer, his spouse, his dependents (as defined in section 152, determined without regard to subsections (b)(1), (b)(2), and (d)(1)(B) thereof), and any child (as defined in section 152(f)(1)) of the taxpayer who as of the end of the taxable year has not attained age 27. Any child to whom section 152(e) applies shall be treated as a dependent of both parents for purposes of this subsection.

(c) Payments Unrelated to Absence From Work.—Gross income does not include amounts referred to in subsection (a) to the extent such amounts—

(1) constitute payment for the permanent loss or use of a member or function of the body, or the permanent disfigurement, of the taxpayer, his spouse, or a dependent (as defined in section 152, determined without regard to subsections (b)(1), (b)(2), and (d)(1)(B) thereof), and

(2) are computed with reference to the nature of the injury without regard to the period the employee is absent from work.

(d) [Repealed.]

(e) Accident and Health Plans.—For purposes of this section and section 104—

(1) amounts received under an accident or health plan for employees, and

(2) amounts received from a sickness and disability fund for employees maintained under the law of a State, or the District of Columbia,

shall be treated as amounts received through accident or health insurance.

(f) Rules for Application of Section 213.—For purposes of section 213(a) (relating to medical, dental, etc., expenses) amounts excluded from gross income under subsection (c) or (d) shall not be considered as compensation (by insurance or otherwise) for expenses paid for medical care.

(g) Self-Employed Individual Not Considered an Employee.—For purposes of this section, the term "employee" does not include an individual who is an employee within the meaning of section 401(c)(1) (relating to self-employed individuals).

(h) Amount Paid to Highly Compensated Individuals Under a Discriminatory Self-Insured Medical Expense Reimbursement Plan.—

(1) In general.—In the case of amounts paid to a highly compensated individual under a self-insured medical reimbursement plan which does not satisfy the requirements of paragraph (2) for a plan year, subsection (b) shall not apply to such amounts to the extent they constitute an excess reimbursement of such highly compensated individual.

(2) Prohibition of discrimination.—A self-insured medical reimbursement plan satisfies the requirements of this paragraph only if—

(A) the plan does not discriminate in favor of highly compensated individuals as to eligibility to participate; and

(B) the benefits provided under the plan do not discriminate in favor of participants who are highly compensated individuals.

(3) Nondiscriminatory eligibility classification.—

(A) In general.—A self-insured medical reimbursement plan does not satisfy the requirements of subparagraph (A) of paragraph (2) unless such plan benefits—

(i) 70 percent or more of all employees, or 80 percent or more of all the employees who are eligible to benefit under the plan if 70 percent or more of all employees are eligible to benefit under the plan; or

(ii) such employees as qualify under a classification set up by the employer and found by the Secretary not to be discriminatory in favor of highly compensated individuals.

(B) Exclusion of certain employees.—For purposes of subparagraph (A), there may be excluded from consideration—

(i) employees who have not completed 3 years of service;

(ii) employees who have not attained age 25;

(iii) part-time or seasonal employees;

(iv) employees not included in the plan who are included in a unit of employees covered by an agreement between employee representatives and one or more employers which the Secretary finds to be a collective bargaining agreement, if accident and health benefits were the subject of good faith bargaining between such employee representatives and such employer or employers; and

(v) employees who are nonresident aliens and who receive no earned income (within the meaning of section 911(d)(2)) from the employer which constitutes income from sources within the United States (within the meaning of section 861(a)(3)).

(4) Nondiscriminatory benefits.—A self-insured medical reimbursement plan does not meet the requirements of subparagraph (B) of paragraph (2) unless all benefits provided for participants who are highly compensated individuals are provided for all other participants.

(5) Highly compensated individual defined.—For purposes of this subsection, the term "highly compensated individual" means an individual who is—

(A) one of the 5 highest paid officers,

(B) a shareholder who owns (with the application of section 318) more than 10 percent in value of the stock of the employer, or

(C) among the highest paid 25 percent of all employees (other than employees described in paragraph (3)(B) who are not participants).

(6) Self-insured medical reimbursement plan.—The term "self-insured medical reimburse-

ment plan" means a plan of an employer to reimburse employees for expenses referred to in subsection (b) for which reimbursement is not provided under a policy of accident or health insurance.

(7) Excess reimbursement of highly compensated individual.—For purposes of this section, the excess reimbursement of a highly compensated individual which is attributable to a self-insured medical reimbursement plan is—

(A) in the case of a benefit available to highly compensated individuals but not to all other participants (or which otherwise fails to satisfy the requirements of paragraph (2)(B)), the amount reimbursed under the plan to the employee with respect to such benefit, and

(B) in the case of benefits (other than benefits described in subparagraph (A)) paid to a highly compensated individual by a plan which fails to satisfy the requirements of paragraph (2), the total amount reimbursed to the highly compensated individual for the plan year, multiplied by fraction—

(i) the numerator of which is the total amount reimbursed to all participants who are highly compensated individuals under the plan for the plan year, and

(ii) the denominator of which is the total amount reimbursed to all employees under the plan for such plan year.

In determining the fraction under subparagraph (B), there shall not be taken into account any reimbursement which is attributable to a benefit described in subparagraph (A).

(8) Certain controlled groups, etc.—All employees who are treated as employed by a single employer under subsection (b), (c), or (m) of section 414 shall be treated as employed by a single employer for purposes of this section.

(9) Regulation.—The Secretary shall prescribe such regulations as may be necessary to carry out the provisions of this section.

(10) Time of inclusion.—Any amount paid for a plan year that is included in income by reason of this subsection shall be treated as received or accrued in the taxable year of the participant in which the plan year ends.

(i) Sick Pay Under Railroad Unemployment Insurance Act.—Notwithstanding any other provision of law, gross income includes benefits paid under section 2(a) of the Railroad Unemployment Insurance Act for days of sickness; except to the extent such sickness (as determined in accordance with standards prescribed by the Railroad Retirement Board) is the result of on-the-job injury.

(j) Special Rule for Certain Governmental Plans.—

(1) In general.—For purposes of subsection (b), amounts paid (directly or indirectly) to the taxpayer from an accident or health plan described in paragraph (2) shall not fail to be excluded from gross income solely because such plan, on or before January 1, 2008, provides for reimbursements of health care expenses of a deceased plan participant's beneficiary.

(2) Plan described.—An accident or health plan is described in this paragraph if such plan is funded by a medical trust that is established in connection with a public retirement system and that—

(A) has been authorized by a State legislature, or

(B) has received a favorable ruling from the Internal Revenue Service that the trust's income is not includible in gross income under section 115.

Recent Amendments to IRC §105

Health Care and Education Reconciliation Act of 2010 (Pub. L. No. 111-152), as follows:

● IRC §105(b) was amended by Act §1004(d)(1) by substituting in the first sentence "his dependents" for "and his dependents" and by inserting ", and any child (as defined in section 152(f)(1)) of the taxpayer who as of the end of the taxable year has not attained age 27". Eff. on date of the enactment of this Act [enacted: Mar. 30, 2010].

Worker, Retiree, and Employer Recovery Act of 2008 (Pub. L. No. 110-458), as follows:

● IRC §105(j) was added by Act §124(a). Eff. for payments before, on, or after the date of enactment [enacted: Dec. 23, 2008].

Working Families Tax Relief Act of 2004 (Pub. L. No. 108-311), as follows:

● IRC §105(b), (c)(1) were amended by Act §207(9) by inserting ", determined without regard to subsections (b)(1), (b)(2), and (d)(1)(B) thereof" after "§152". Eff. for tax years beginning after Dec. 31, 2004.

SEC. 106. CONTRIBUTIONS BY EMPLOYER TO ACCIDENT AND HEALTH PLANS.

(a) General Rule.—Except as otherwise provided in this section, gross income of an employee does not include employer-provided coverage under an accident or health plan.

(b) Contributions to Archer MSAs—

(1) In general.—In the case of an employee who is an eligible individual, amounts contributed by such employee's employer to any Archer MSA of such employee shall be treated as employer-provided coverage for medical expenses under an accident or health plan to the extent such amounts do not exceed the limitation under section 220(b)(1) (determined without regard to this subsection) which is applicable to such employee for such taxable year.

(2) No constructive receipt.—No amount shall be included in the gross income of any employee solely because the employee may choose between the contributions referred to in paragraph (1) and em-

ployer contributions to another health plan of the employer.

(3) Special rule for deduction of employer contributions.—Any employer contribution to an Archer MSA, if otherwise allowable as a deduction under this chapter, shall be allowed only for the taxable year in which paid.

(4) Employer MSA contributions required to be shown on return.—Every individual required to file a return under section 6012 for the taxable year shall include on such return the aggregate amount contributed by employers to the Archer MSAs of such individual or such individual's spouse for such taxable year.

(5) MSA contributions not part of COBRA coverage.—Paragraph (1) shall not apply for purposes of section 4980B.

(6) Definitions.—For purposes of this subsection, the terms "eligible individual" and "Archer MSA" have the respective meanings given to such terms by section 220.

(7) Cross reference.—For penalty on failure by employer to make comparable contributions to the Archer MSAs of comparable employees, see section 4980E.

(c) Inclusion of Long-term Care Benefits Provided Through Flexible Spending Arrangements.—

(1) In general.—Effective on and after January 1, 1997, gross income of an employee shall include employer-provided coverage for qualified long-term care services (as defined in section 7702B(c)) to the extent that such coverage is provided through a flexible spending or similar arrangement.

(2) Flexible spending arrangement.—For purposes of this subsection, a flexible spending arrangement is a benefit program which provides employees with coverage under which—

(A) specified incurred expenses may be reimbursed (subject to reimbursement maximums and other reasonable conditions), and

(B) the maximum amount of reimbursement which is reasonably available to a participant for such coverage is less than 500 percent of the value of such coverage.

In the case of an insured plan, the maximum amount reasonably available shall be determined on the basis of the underlying coverage.

(d) Contributions to Health Savings Account.—

(1) In general.—In the case of an employee who is an eligible individual (as defined in section 223(c)(1)), amounts contributed by such employee's employer to any health savings account (as defined in section 223(d)) of such employee shall be treated as employer-provided coverage for medical expenses under an accident or health plan to the extent such amounts do not exceed the limitation under section 223(b) (determined without regard to this subsection) which is applicable to such employee for such taxable year.

(2) Special rules.—Rules similar to the rules of paragraphs (2), (3), (4), and (5) of subsection (b) shall apply for purposes of this subsection.

(3) Cross reference.—For penalty on failure by employer to make comparable contributions to the health savings accounts of comparable employees, see section 4980G.

(e) FSA and HRA Terminations to Fund HSAs.—

(1) In general.—A plan shall not fail to be treated as a health flexible spending arrangement or health reimbursement arrangement under this section or section 105 merely because such plan provides for a qualified HSA distribution.

(2) Qualified HSA distribution.—The term "qualified HSA distribution" means a distribution from a health flexible spending arrangement or health reimbursement arrangement to the extent that such distribution—

(A) does not exceed the lesser of the balance in such arrangement on September 21, 2006, or as of the date of such distribution, and

(B) is contributed by the employer directly to the health savings account of the employee before January 1, 2012.

Such term shall not include more than 1 distribution with respect to any arrangement.

(3) Additional tax for failure to maintain high deductible health plan coverage.—

(A) In general.—If, at any time during the testing period, the employee is not an eligible individual, then the amount of the qualified HSA distribution—

(i) shall be includible in the gross income of the employee for the taxable year in which occurs the first month in the testing period for which such employee is not an eligible individual, and

(ii) the tax imposed by this chapter for such taxable year on the employee shall be increased by 10 percent of the amount which is so includible.

(B) Exception for disability or death.—Clauses (i) and (ii) of subparagraph (A) shall not apply if the employee ceases to be an eligible individual by reason of the death of the employee or the employee becoming disabled (within the meaning of section 72(m)(7)).

(4) Definitions and special rules.—For purposes of this subsection—

(A) Testing period.—The term "testing period" means the period beginning with the month in which the qualified HSA distribution is contributed to the health savings account and ending on the last day of the 12th month following such month.

(B) Eligible individual.—The term "eligible individual" has the meaning given such term by section 223(c)(1).

(C) Treatment as rollover contribution.—A qualified HSA distribution shall be treated as a rollover contribution described in section 223(f)(5).

(5) Tax treatment relating to distributions.—For purposes of this title—

(A) In general.—A qualified HSA distribution shall be treated as a payment described in subsection (d).

(B) Comparability excise tax.—

(i) In general.—Except as provided in clause (ii), section 4980G shall not apply to qualified HSA distributions.

(ii) Failure to offer to all employees.—In the case of a qualified HSA distribution to any employee, the failure to offer such distribution to any eligible individual covered under a high deductible health plan of the employer shall (notwithstanding section 4980G(d)) be treated for purposes of section 4980G as a failure to meet the requirements of section 4980G(b).

Editor's Note

IRC §106(f), as follows, was added by Pub. L. No. 111-148, §9003, effective for expenses incurred with respect to taxable years beginning after December 31, 2010.

(f) Reimbursements for Medicine Restricted to Prescribed Drugs and Insulin.—For purposes of this section and section 105, reimbursement for expenses incurred for a medicine or a drug shall be treated as a reimbursement for medical expenses only if such medicine or drug is a prescribed drug (determined without regard to whether such drug is available without a prescription) or is insulin.

Recent Amendments to IRC §106

Patient Protection and Affordable Care Act, 2010 (Pub. L. No. 111-148), as follows:

● IRC §106(f) was added by Act §9003(c). Eff. for expenses incurred with respect to taxable years beginning after Dec. 31, 2010.

Tax Relief and Health Care Act of 2006 (Pub. L. No. 109-432), as follows:

● IRC §106 was amended by Act, Div. A, §302(a), by adding new subsec. (e). Eff. for distributions on or after Dec. 20, 2006.

Medicare Prescription Drug, Improvement, and Modernization Act of 2003 (Pub. L. No. 108-173), as follows:

• IRC §106 was amended by Act §1201(d)(1) by adding new subsec. (d). Eff. tax years beginning after Dec. 31, 2003.

* * *

SEC. 117. QUALIFIED SCHOLARSHIPS.

(a) General Rule.—Gross income does not include any amount received as a qualified scholarship by an individual who is a candidate for a degree at an educational organization described in section 170(b)(1)(A)(ii).

(b) Qualified Scholarship.—For purposes of this section—

(1) In general.—The term "qualified scholarship" means any amount received by an individual as a scholarship or fellowship grant to the extent the individual establishes that, in accordance with the conditions of the grant, such amount was used for qualified tuition and related expenses.

(2) Qualified tuition and related expenses.—For purposes of paragraph (1), the term "qualified tuition and related expenses" means—

(A) tuition and fees required for the enrollment or attendance of a student at an educational organization described in section 170(b)(1)(A)(ii), and

(B) fees, books, supplies, and equipment required for courses of instruction at such an educational organization.

Editor's Note

Caution: IRC §117(c), as follows, was amended by Pub. L. No. 107-16. For sunset provision, see the amendment notes to this section for Pub. L. No. 107-16.

(c) Limitation.—

(1) In general.—Except as provided in paragraph (2), subsections (a) and (d) shall not apply to that portion of any amount received which represents payment for teaching, research, or other services by the student required as a condition for receiving the qualified scholarship or qualified tuition reduction.

(2) Exceptions.—Paragraph (1) shall not apply to any amount received by an individual under—

(A) the National Health Service Corps Scholarship Program under section 338A(g)(1)(A) of the Public Health Service Act, or

(B) the Armed Forces Health Professions Scholarship and Financial Assistance Program under subchapter I of chapter 105 of title 10, United States Code.

(d) Qualified Tuition Reduction.—

(1) In general.—Gross income shall not include any qualified tuition reduction.

(2) Qualified tuition reduction.—For purposes of this subsection, the term "qualified tuition reduction" means the amount of any reduction in tuition provided to an employee of an organization described in section 170(b)(1)(A)(ii) for the education (below the graduate level) at such organization (or another organization described in section 170(b)(1)(A)(ii)) of—

(A) such employee, or

(B) any person treated as an employee (or whose use is treated as an employee use) under the rules of section 132(h).

(3) Reduction must not discriminate in favor of highly compensated, etc.—Paragraph (1) shall apply with respect to any qualified tuition reduction provided with respect to any highly compensated employee only if such reduction is available on substantially the same terms to each member of a group of employees which is defined under a reasonable classification set up by the employer which does not discriminate in favor of highly compensated employees (within the meaning of section 414(q)). For purposes of this paragraph, the term "highly compensated employee" has the meaning given such term by section 414(q).

(5)[(4)] Special rules for teaching and research assistants.—In the case of the education of an individual who is a graduate student at an educational organization described in section 170(b)(1)(A)(ii) and who is engaged in teaching or research activities for such organization, paragraph (2) shall be applied as if it did not contain the phrase "(below the graduate level)".

Recent Amendments to IRC §117

Economic Growth and Tax Relief Reconciliation Act of 2001 (Pub. L. No. 107-16), as follows:
• IRC §117(c) was amended by Act §413(a). Eff. for amounts received in tax years beginning after Dec. 31, 2001. IRC §117(c) prior to amendment:
   (c) Limitation.—Subsections (a) and (d) shall not apply to that portion of any amount received which represents payment for teaching, research, or other services by the student required as a condition for receiving the qualified scholarship or qualified tuition reduction.
• **Sunset Provision.** Act §901, as amended by Pub. L. No. 111-312, §101(a)(1), provides the sunset rule below. But see Pub. L. No. 109-280, §811, and Pub. L. No. 111-148, §10909(c), as amended by Pub. L. No. 111-312, §101(b)(1).
   SEC. 901. SUNSET OF PROVISIONS OF ACT.
   (a) In general. All provisions of, and amendments made by, this Act shall not apply—
   (1) to taxable, plan, or limitation years beginning after December 31, 2012, or
   (2) in the case of title V, to estates of decedents dying, gifts made, or generation skipping transfers, after December 31, 2012.
   (b) Application of certain laws.—The Internal Revenue Code of 1986 and the Employee Retirement Income Security Act of 1974 shall be applied and administered to years, estates, gifts, and transfers described in subsection (a) as if the provisions and amendments described in subsection (a) had

never been enacted.

* * *

SEC. 119. MEALS OR LODGING FURNISHED FOR THE CONVENIENCE OF THE EMPLOYER.

(a) Meals and Lodging Furnished to Employee, His Spouse, and His Dependents Pursuant to Employment.—There shall be excluded from gross income of an employee the value of any meals or lodging furnished to him, his spouse, or any of his dependents by or on behalf of his employer for the convenience of the employer, but only if—

(1) in the case of meals, the meals are furnished on the business premises of the employer, or

(2) in the case of lodging, the employee is required to accept such lodging on the business premises of his employer as a condition of his employment.

(b) Special Rules.—For purposes of subsection (a)—

(1) Provisions of employment contract or State statute not to be determinative.—In determining whether meals or lodging are furnished for the convenience of the employer, the provisions of an employment contract or of a State statute fixing terms of employment shall not be determinative of whether the meals or lodging are intended as compensation.

(2) Certain factors not taken into account with respect to meals.—In determining whether meals are furnished for the convenience of the employer, the fact that a charge is made for such meals, and the fact that the employee may accept or decline such meals, shall not be taken into account.

(3) Certain fixed charges for meals.—

(A) In general.—If—

(i) an employee is required to pay on a periodic basis a fixed charge for his meals, and

(ii) such meals are furnished by the employer for the convenience of the employer,

there shall be excluded from the employee's gross income an amount equal to such fixed charge.

(B) Application of subparagraph (A).—Subparagraph (A) shall apply—

(i) whether the employee pays the fixed charge out of his stated compensation or out of his own funds, and

(ii) only if the employee is required to make the payment whether he accepts or declines the meals.

(4) Meals furnished to employees on business premises where meals of most employees are otherwise excludable.—All meals furnished on the business premises of an employer to such employer's employees shall be treated as furnished for the convenience of the employer if, without regard to this paragraph, more than half of the employees to whom such meals are furnished on such premises are furnished such meals for the convenience of the employer.

(c) Employees Living in Certain Camps.—

(1) In general.—In the case of an individual who is furnished lodging in a camp located in a foreign country by or on behalf of his employer, such camp shall be considered to be part of the business premises of the employer.

(2) Camp.—For purposes of this section, a camp constitutes lodging which is—

(A) provided by or on behalf of the employer for the convenience of the employer because the place at which such individual renders services is in a remote area where satisfactory housing is not available on the open market,

(B) located, as near as practicable, in the vicinity of the place at which such individual renders services, and

(C) furnished in a common area (or enclave) which is not available to the public and which normally accommodates 10 or more employees.

(d) Lodging Furnished by Certain Educational Institutions to Employees.—

(1) In general.—In the case of an employee of an educational institution, gross income shall not include the value of qualified campus lodging furnished to such employee during the taxable year.

(2) Exception in cases of inadequate rent.— Paragraph (1) shall not apply to the extent of the excess of—

(A) the lesser of—

(i) 5 percent of the appraised value of the qualified campus lodging, or

(ii) the average of the rentals paid by individuals (other than employees or students of the educational institution) during such calendar year for lodging provided by the educational institution which is comparable to the qualified campus lodging provided to the employee, over

(B) the rent paid by the employee for the qualified campus lodging during such calendar year.

The appraised value under subparagraph (A)(i) shall be determined as of the close of the calendar year in which the taxable year begins, or, in the case of a rental period not greater than 1 year, at any time during the calendar year in which such period begins.

(3) Qualified campus lodging.—For purposes of this subsection, the term "qualified campus lodging" means lodging to which subsection (a) does not apply and which is—

(A) located on, or in the proximity of, a campus of the educational institution, and

(B) furnished to the employee, his spouse, and any of his dependents by or on behalf of such institution for use as a residence.

(4) Educational institution, etc.—For purposes of this subsection—

(A) In general.—The term "educational institution" means—

(i) an institution described in section 170(b)(1)(A)(ii) (or an entity organized under State law and composed of public institutions so described), or

(ii) an academic health center.

(B) Academic health center.—For purposes of subparagraph (A), the term "academic health center" means and entity—

(i) which is described in section 170(b)(1)(A)(iii),

(ii) which receives (during the calendar year in which the taxable year of the taxpayer begins) payments under subsection (d)(5)(B) or (h) of section 1886 of the Social Security Act (relating to graduate medical education), and

(iii) which has as one of its principal purposes or functions the providing and teaching of basic and clinical medical science and research with the entity's own faculty.

SEC. 120. AMOUNTS RECEIVED UNDER QUALIFIED GROUP LEGAL SERVICES PLANS.

(a) Exclusion by Employee for Contributions and Legal Services Provided by Employer.—Gross income of an employee, his spouse, or his dependents, does not include—

(1) amounts contributed by an employer on behalf of an employee, his spouse, or his dependent under a qualified group legal services plan (as defined in subsection (b)); or

(2) the value of legal service provided, or amounts paid for legal services, under a qualified group legal services plan (as defined in subsection (b)) to, or with respect to, an employee, his spouse, or his dependents.

No exclusion shall be allowed under this section with respect to an individual for any taxable year to the extent that the value of insurance (whether through an insurer or self-insurance) against legal costs incurred by the individual (or his spouse or dependents) provided under a qualified group legal services plan exceeds $70.

(b) Qualified Group Legal Services Plan.—For purposes of this section, a qualified group legal services plan is a separate written plan of an employer for the exclusive benefit of his employees or their spouses or dependents to provide such employees, spouse, or dependents with specified benefits consisting of personal legal services through prepayment of, or provision in advance for, legal fees in whole or in part by the employer, if the plan meets the requirements of subsection (c).

(c) Requirements.—

(1) Discrimination.—The contributions or benefits provided under the plan shall not discriminate in favor of employees who are highly compensated employees (within the meaning of section 414(q)).

(2) Eligibility.—The plan shall benefit employees who qualify under a classification set up by the employer and found by the Secretary not to be discriminatory in favor of employees who are described in paragraph (1). For purposes of this paragraph, there shall be excluded from consideration employees not included in the plan who are included in a unit of employees covered by an agreement which the Secretary of Labor finds to be a collective bargaining agreement between employee representatives and one or more employers, if there is evidence that group legal services plan benefits were the subject of good faith bargaining between such employee representatives and such employer or employers.

(3) Contribution limitation.—Not more than 25 percent of the amounts contributed under the plan during the year may be provided for the class of individuals who are shareholders or owners (or their spouses or dependents), each of whom (on any day of the year) owns more than 5 percent of the stock or of the capital or profits interest in the employer.

(4) Notification.—The plan shall give notice to the Secretary, in such manner as the Secretary may by regulations prescribe, that it is applying for recognition of the status of a qualified group legal services plan.

(5) Contributions.—Amounts contributed under the plan shall be paid only (A) to insurance companies, or to organizations or persons that provide personal legal services, or indemnification against the cost of personal legal services, in exchange for a prepayment or a payment of a premium, (B) to organizations or trusts described in section 501(c)(20), (C) to organizations described in section 501(c) which are permitted by that section to receive payments from an employer for support of one or more qualified group legal services plan or plans, except that such organizations shall pay or credit the contribution to an organization or trust described in section 501(c)(20), (D) as prepayments to providers of legal services under the plan, or (E) a combination of the above.

(d) Other Definitions and Special Rules.—For purposes of this section—

(1) Employee.—The term "employee" includes, for any year, an individual who is an employee within the meaning of section 401(c)(1) (relating to self-employed individuals).

(2) Employer.—An individual who owns the entire interest in an unincorporated trade or business shall be treated as his own employer. A partnership shall be treated as the employer of each partner who is an employee within the meaning of paragraph (1).

(3) Allocations.—Allocations of amounts contributed under the plan shall be made in accordance with regulations prescribed by the Secretary and shall take into account the expected relative utilization of benefits to be provided from such contributions or plan assets and the manner in which any premium or other charge was developed.

(4) Dependent.—The term "dependent" has the meaning given to it by section 152 (determined without regard to subsections (b)(1), (b)(2), and (d)(1)(B) thereof).

(5) Exclusive benefit.—In the case of a plan to which contributions are made by more than one employer, in determining whether the plan is for the exclusive benefit of an employer's employees or their spouses or dependents, the employees of any employer who maintains the plan shall be considered to be the employees of each employer who maintains the plan.

(6) Attribution rules.—For purposes of this section—

(A) ownership of stock in a corporation shall be determined in accordance with the rules and provided under subsections (d) and (e) of section 1563 (without regard to section 1563(e)(3)(C)), and

(B) the interest of an employee in a trade or business which is not incorporated shall be determined in accordance with regulations prescribed by the Secretary, which shall be based on principles similar to the principles which apply in the case of subparagraph (A).

(7) Time of notice to secretary.—A plan shall not be a qualified group legal services plan for any period prior to the time notification was provided to the Secretary in accordance with subsection (c)(4), if such notice is given after the time prescribed by the Secretary by regulations for giving such notice.

(e) Termination.—This section and section 501(c)(20) shall not apply to taxable years beginning after June 30, 1992.

(f) Cross Reference.—For reporting and record-keeping requirements, see section 6039D.

Recent Amendments to IRC §120

Working Families Tax Relief Act of 2004 (Pub. L. No. 108-311), as follows:

● IRC §120(d)(4) was amended by Act §207(10) by inserting "(determined without regard to subsections (b)(1), (b)(2), and (d)(1)(B) thereof)" after "§152". Eff. for tax years beginning after Dec. 31, 2004.

---

* * *

SEC. 122. CERTAIN REDUCED UNIFORMED SERVICES RETIREMENT PAY.

(a) General Rule.—In the case of a member or former member of the uniformed services of the United States, gross income does not include the amount of any reduction in his retired or retainer pay pursuant to the provisions of chapter 73 of title 10, United States Code.

(b) Special Rule.—

(1) Amount excluded from gross income.—In the case of any individual referred to in subsection (a), all amounts received after December 31, 1965, as retired or retainer pay shall be excluded from gross income until there has been so excluded an amount equal to the consideration for the contract. The preceding sentence shall apply only to the extent that the amounts received would, but for such sentence, be includible in gross income.

(2) Consideration for the contract.—For purposes of paragraph (1) and section 72(n), the term "consideration for the contract" means, in respect of any individual, the sum of—

(A) the total amount of the reductions before January 1, 1966, in his retired or retainer pay by reason of an election under chapter 73 of title 10 of the United States Code, and

(B) any amounts deposited at any time by him pursuant to section 1438 or 1452(d) of such title 10.

* * *

SEC. 125. CAFETERIA PLANS.

(a) In General.—Except as provided in subsection (b), no amount shall be included in the gross income of a participant in a cafeteria plan solely because, under the plan, the participant may choose among the benefits of the plan.

(b) Exception for Highly Compensated Participants and Key Employees.—

(1) Highly compensated participants.—In the case of a highly compensated participant, subsection (a) shall not apply to any benefit attributable to a plan year for which the plan discriminates in favor of—

(A) highly compensated individuals as to eligibility to participate, or

(B) highly compensated participants as to contributions and benefits.

IRC Sec. 125(b)(1)(B)

(2) Key employees.—In the case of a key employee (within the meaning of section 416(i)(1)), subsection (a) shall not apply to any benefit attributable to a plan [year] for which the statutory nontaxable benefits provided to key employees exceed 25 percent of the aggregate of such benefits provided for all employees under the plan. For purposes of the preceding sentence, statutory nontaxable benefits shall be determined without regard to the second sentence of subsection (f).

(3) Year of inclusion.—For purposes of determining the taxable year of inclusion, any benefit described in paragraph (1) or (2) shall be treated as received or accrued in the taxable year of the participant or key employee in which the plan year ends.

(c) Discrimination as to Benefits or Contributions.—For purposes of subparagraph (B) of subsection (b)(1), a cafeteria plan does not discriminate where qualified benefits and total benefits (or employer contributions allocable to statutory nontaxable benefits and employer contributions for total benefits) do not discriminate in favor of highly compensated participants.

(d) Cafeteria Plan Defined.—For purposes of this section.—

(1) In general.—The term "cafeteria plan" means a written plan under which—

(A) all participants are employees, and

(B) the participants may choose among 2 or more benefits consisting of cash and qualified benefits.

(2) Deferred compensation plans excluded.—

(A) In general.—The term "cafeteria plan" does not include any plan which provides for deferred compensation.

(B) Exception for cash and deferred arrangements.—Subparagraph (A) shall not apply to a profit-sharing or stock bonus plan or rural cooperative plan (within the meaning of section 401(k)(7)) which includes a qualified cash or deferred arrangement (as defined in section 401(k)(2)) to the extent of amounts which a covered employee may elect to have the employer pay as contributions to a trust under such plan on behalf of the employee.

(C) Exception for certain plans maintained by educational institutions.—Subparagraph (A) shall not apply to a plan maintained by an educational organization described in section 170(b)(1)(A)(ii) to the extent of amounts which a covered employee may elect to have the employer pay as contributions for post-retirement group life insurance if—

(i) all contributions for such insurance must be made before retirement, and

(ii) such life insurance does not have a cash surrender value at any time.

For purposes of section 79, any life insurance described in the preceding sentence shall be treated as group-term life insurance.

(D) Exception for Health Savings Accounts.—Subparagraph (A) shall not apply to a plan to the extent of amounts which a covered employee may elect to have the employer pay as contributions to a health savings account established on behalf of the employee.

(e) Highly Compensated Participant and Individual Defined.—For purposes of this section—

(1) Highly compensated participant.—The term "highly compensated participant" means a participant who is—

(A) an officer,

(B) a shareholder owning more than 5 percent of the voting power or value of all classes of stock of the employer,

(C) highly compensated, or

(D) a spouse or dependent (within the meaning of section 152, determined without regard to subsections (b)(1), (b)(2), and (d)(1)(B) thereof) of an individual described in subparagraph (A), (B), or (C).

(2) Highly compensated individual.—The term "highly compensated individual" means an individual who is described in subparagraph (A), (B), (C), or (D) of paragraph (1).

Editor's Note

Caution: IRC §125(f), as follows, before amendment by Pub. L. No. 111-148, is effective for taxable years beginning on or before December 31, 2013.

(f) Qualified Benefits Defined.—For purposes of this section, the term "qualified benefit" means any benefit which, with the application of subsection (a), is not includible in the gross income of the employee by reason of an express provision of this chapter (other than section 106(b), 117, 127, or 132). Such term includes any group term life insurance which is includible in gross income only because it exceeds the dollar limitation of section 79 and such term includes any other benefit permitted under regulations. Such term shall not include any product which is advertised, marketed, or offered as long-term care insurance.

Editor's Note

Caution: IRC §125(f), below, as amended by Pub. L. No. 111-148, §1515(a)–(b), is effective for taxable years beginning after December 31, 2013.

(f) Qualified Benefits Defined.—For purposes of this section—

(1) In general.—The term "qualified benefit" means any benefit which, with the application of subsection (a), is not includible in the gross income of the employee by reason of an express provision of this chapter (other than section 106(b), 117, 127, or 132). Such term includes any group term life insurance which is includible in gross income only because it exceeds the dollar limitation of section 79 and such term includes any other benefit permitted under regulations.

(2) Long-term care insurance not qualified.—The term "qualified benefit" shall not include any product which is advertised, marketed, or offered as long-term care insurance.

(3) Certain exchange-participating qualified health plans not qualified.—

(A) In general.—The term "qualified benefit" shall not include any qualified health plan (as defined in section 1301(a) of the Patient Protection and Affordable Care Act) offered through an Exchange established under section 1311 of such Act.

(B) Exception for exchange-eligible employers.—Subparagraph (A) shall not apply with respect to any employee if such employee's employer is a qualified employer (as defined in section 1312(f)(2) of the Patient Protection and Affordable Care Act) offering the employee the opportunity to enroll through such an Exchange in a qualified health plan in a group market.

(g) Special Rules.—

(1) Collectively bargained plan not considered discriminatory.—For purposes of this section, a plan shall not be treated as discriminatory if the plan is maintained under an agreement which the Secretary finds to be a collective bargaining agreement between employee representatives and one or more employers.

(2) Health benefits.—For purposes of subparagraph (B) of subsection (b)(1), a cafeteria plan which provides health benefits shall not be treated as discriminatory if—

(A) contributions under the plan on behalf of each participant include an amount which—

(i) equals 100 percent of the cost of the health benefit coverage under the plan of the majority of the highly compensated participants similarly situated, or

(ii) equals or exceeds 75 percent of the cost of the health benefit coverage of the participant (similarly situated) having the highest cost health benefit coverage under the plan, and

(B) contributions or benefits under the plan in excess of those described in subparagraph (A) bear a uniform relationship to compensation.

(3) Certain participation eligibility rules not treated as discriminatory.—For purposes of subparagraph (A) of subsection (b)(1), a classification shall not be treated as discriminatory if the plan—

(A) benefits a group of employees described in section 410(b)(2)(A)(i), and

(B) meets the requirements of clauses (i) and (ii):

(i) No employee is required to complete more than 3 years of employment with the employer or employers maintaining the plan as a condition of participation in the plan, and the employment requirement for each employee is the same.

(ii) Any employee who has satisfied the employment requirement of clause (i) and who is otherwise entitled to participate in the plan commences participation no later than the first day of the first plan year beginning after the date the employment requirement was satisfied unless the employee was separated from service before the first day of that plan year.

(4) Certain controlled groups, etc.—All employees who are treated as employed by a single employer under subsection (b), (c), or (m) of section 414 shall be treated as employed by a single employer for purposes of this section.

(h) Special Rule for Unused Benefits in Health Flexible Spending Arrangements of Individuals Called to Active Duty.—

(1) In general.—For purposes of this title, a plan or other arrangement shall not fail to be treated as a cafeteria plan or health flexible spending arrangement merely because such arrangement provides for qualified reservist distributions.

(2) Qualified reservist distribution.—For purposes of this subsection, the term "qualified reservist distribution" means, [sic] any distribution to an individual of all or a portion of the balance in the employee's account under such arrangement if—

(A) such individual was (by reason of being a member of a reserve component (as defined in section 101 of title 37, United States Code)) ordered or called to active duty for a period in excess of 179 days or for an indefinite period, and

(B) such distribution is made during the period beginning on the date of such order or call and ending on the last date that reimbursements could otherwise be made under such arrangement for the plan year which includes the date of such order or call.

IRC Sec. 125(h)(2)(B)

(i) Cross Reference.—For reporting and recordkeeping requirements, see section 6039D.

(i) Limitation on Health Flexible Spending Arrangements.—

(1) In general.—For purposes of this section, if a benefit is provided under a cafeteria plan through employer contributions to a health flexible spending arrangement, such benefit shall not be treated as a qualified benefit unless the cafeteria plan provides that an employee may not elect for any taxable year to have salary reduction contributions in excess of $2,500 made to such arrangement.

(2) Adjustment for inflation.—In the case of any taxable year beginning after December 31, 2013, the dollar amount in paragraph (1) shall be increased by an amount equal to—

(A) such amount, multiplied by

(B) the cost-of-living adjustment determined under section 1(f)(3) for the calendar year in which such taxable year begins by substituting "calendar year 2012" for "calendar year 1992" in subparagraph (B) thereof.

If any increase determined under this paragraph is not a multiple of $50, such increase shall be rounded to the next lowest multiple of $50.

(j) Regulations.—The Secretary shall prescribe such regulations as may be necessary to carry out the provisions of this section.

(j) Simple Cafeteria Plans for Small Businesses.—

(1) In general.—An eligible employer maintaining a simple cafeteria plan with respect to which the requirements of this subsection are met for any year shall be treated as meeting any applicable nondiscrimination requirement during such year.

(2) Simple cafeteria plan.—For purposes of this subsection, the term "simple cafeteria plan" means a cafeteria plan—

(A) which is established and maintained by an eligible employer, and

(B) with respect to which the contribution requirements of paragraph (3), and the eligibility and participation requirements of paragraph (4), are met.

(3) Contribution requirements.—

(A) In general.—The requirements of this paragraph are met if, under the plan the employer is required, without regard to whether a qualified employee makes any salary reduction contribution, to make a contribution to provide qualified benefits under the plan on behalf of each qualified employee in an amount equal to—

(i) a uniform percentage (not less than 2 percent) of the employee's compensation for the plan year, or

(ii) an amount which is not less than the lesser of—

(I) 6 percent of the employee's compensation for the plan year, or

(II) twice the amount of the salary reduction contributions of each qualified employee.

(B) Matching contributions on behalf of highly compensated and key employees.—The requirements of subparagraph (A)(ii) shall not be treated as met if, under the plan, the rate of contributions with respect to any salary reduction contribution of a highly compensated or key employee at any rate of contribution is greater than that with respect to an employee who is not a highly compensated or key employee.

(C) Additional contributions.—Subject to subparagraph (B), nothing in this paragraph shall be treated as prohibiting an employer from making contributions to provide qualified benefits under the plan in addition to contributions required under subparagraph (A).

(D) Definitions.—For purposes of this paragraph—

(i) Salary reduction contribution.—The term "salary reduction contribution" means, with respect to a cafeteria plan, any amount which is contributed to the plan at the election of the employee and which is not includible in gross income by reason of this section.

(ii) Qualified employee.—The term "qualified employee" means, with respect to a cafeteria plan, any employee who is not a highly compensated or key employee and who is eligible to participate in the plan.

(iii) Highly compensated employee.—The term "highly compensated employee" has the meaning given such term by section 414(q).

(iv) Key employee.—The term "key employee" has the meaning given such term by section 416(i).

(4) Minimum eligibility and participation requirements.—

(A) In general.—The requirements of this paragraph shall be treated as met with respect to any year if, under the plan—

(i) all employees who had at least 1,000 hours of service for the preceding plan year are eligible to participate, and

(ii) each employee eligible to participate in the plan may, subject to terms and conditions applicable to all participants, elect any benefit available under the plan.

(B) Certain employees may be excluded.—For purposes of subparagraph (A)(i), an employer may elect to exclude under the plan employees—

(i) who have not attained the age of 21 before the close of a plan year,

(ii) who have less than 1 year of service with the employer as of any day during the plan year,

(iii) who are covered under an agreement which the Secretary of Labor finds to be a collective bargaining agreement if there is evidence that the benefits covered under the cafeteria plan were the subject of good faith bargaining between employee representatives and the employer, or

(iv) who are described in section 410(b)(3)(C) (relating to nonresident aliens working outside the United States).

A plan may provide a shorter period of service or younger age for purposes of clause (i) or (ii).

(5) Eligible employer.—For purposes of this subsection—

(A) In general.—The term "eligible employer" means, with respect to any year, any employer if such employer employed an average of 100 or fewer employees on business days during either of the 2 preceding years. For purposes of this subparagraph, a year may only be taken into account if the employer was in existence throughout the year.

(B) Employers not in existence during preceding year.—If an employer was not in existence throughout the preceding year, the determination under subparagraph (A) shall be based on the average number of employees that it is reasonably expected such employer will employ on business days in the current year.

(C) Growing employers retain treatment as small employer.—

(i) In general.—If—

(I) an employer was an eligible employer for any year (a "qualified year"), and

(II) such employer establishes a simple cafeteria plan for its employees for such year,

then, notwithstanding the fact the employer fails to meet the requirements of subparagraph (A) for any subsequent year, such employer shall be treated as an eligible employer for such subsequent year with respect to employees (whether or not employees during a qualified year) of any trade or business which was covered by the plan during any qualified year.

(ii) Exception.—This subparagraph shall cease to apply if the employer employs an average of 200 or more employees on business days during any year preceding any such subsequent year.

(D) Special rules.—

(i) Predecessors.—Any reference in this paragraph to an employer shall include a reference to any predecessor of such employer.

(ii) Aggregation rules.—All persons treated as a single employer under subsection (a) or (b) of section 52, or subsection (n) or (o) of section 414, shall be treated as one person.

(6) Applicable nondiscrimination requirement.—For purposes of this subsection, the term "applicable nondiscrimination requirement" means any requirement under subsection (b) of this section, section 79(d), section 105(h), or paragraph (2), (3), (4), or (8) of section 129(d).

(7) Compensation.—The term "compensation" has the meaning given such term by section 414(s).

IRC Sec. 125(j)(7)

(k) Cross Reference.—For reporting and record-keeping requirements, see section 6039D.

(*l*) Regulations.—The Secretary shall prescribe such regulations as may be necessary to carry out the provisions of this section.

Recent Amendments to IRC §125

Health Care and Education Reconciliation Act of 2010 (Pub. L. No. 111-152), as follows:
- IRC §125(i)(2), as added by Pub. L. No. 111-148, §9005, was amended by Act §1403(b)(1) by substituting "December 31, 2013" for "December 31, 2011". Eff. on date of enactment of this Act [enacted: Mar. 30, 2010].
- IRC §125(i)(2)(B), as added by Pub. L. No. 111-148, §9005, was amended by Act §1403(b)(2) by substituting "2012" for "2010". Eff. on date of enactment of this Act [enacted: Mar. 30, 2010].

Patient Protection and Affordable Care Act, 2010 (Pub. L. No. 111-148), as follows:
- IRC §125(f) was amended by Act §1515(a) and (b) by striking "For purposes of this section, the term" and inserting "For purposes of this section—(1) In General— The term"; by striking "Such term shall not include"; inserting "(2) Long-Term Care Insurance Not Qualified—The term 'qualified benefit' shall not include"; and adding (f)(3). Eff. for taxable years beginning after Dec. 31, 2013.
- IRC §125 was amended by Act §9005(a) by redesignating subsections (i) and (j) as subsections (j) and (k), respectively, and inserting new (i). Eff. for taxable years beginning after Dec. 31, 2010.
- IRC §125(i), as added by Act §9005(a), was amended by Act §10902(a). Eff. for taxable years beginning after Dec. 31, 2010. IRC §125(i) prior to amendment:
  (i) Limitation on Health Flexible Spending Arrangements.—For purposes of this section, if a benefit is provided under a cafeteria plan through employer contributions to a health flexible spending arrangement, such benefit shall not be treated as a qualified benefit unless the cafeteria plan provides that an employee may not elect for any taxable year to have salary reduction contributions in excess of $2,500 made to such arrangement.
- IRC §125 was amended by Act §9022(a) by redesignating subsecs. (j) and (k), as redesignated, as subsecs. (k) and (*l*), respec-

tively, and by inserting new subsec. (j). Eff. for taxable years beginning after Dec. 31, 2010.

Heroes Earnings Assistance and Relief Tax Act of 2008 (Pub. L. No. 110-245), as follows:
- IRC §125(h) was added and former (h) and (i) were redesignated as (i) and (j), respectively, by Act §114(a). Eff. for distributions made after enactment date, June 17, 2008, see Act §114(b).

Tax Technical Corrections Act of 2007 (Pub. L. No. 110-172), as follows:
- IRC §125(b)(2) was amended by Act §11(a)(12) by substituting "second sentence" for "last sentence". Eff. Dec. 29, 2007.

Working Families Tax Relief Act of 2004 (Pub. L. No. 108-311), as follows:
- IRC §125(e)(1)(D) was amended by Act §207(11) by inserting ", determined without regard to subsections (b)(1), (b)(2), and (d)(1)(B) thereof" after "§152". Eff. tax years beginning after Dec. 31, 2004.

Medicare Prescription Drug, Improvement, and Modernization Act of 2003 (Pub. L. No. 108-173), as follows:
- IRC §125(d)(2) was amended by Act §1201(i) by adding subpar. (D). Eff. tax years beginning after Dec. 31, 2003.

---

* * *

SEC. 127. EDUCATIONAL ASSISTANCE PROGRAMS.

(a) Exclusion From Gross Income.—

(1) In general.—Gross income of an employee does not include amounts paid or expenses incurred by the employer for educational assistance to the employee if the assistance is furnished pursuant to a program which is described in subsection (b).

(2) $5,250 maximum exclusion.—If, but for this paragraph, this section would exclude from gross income more than $5,250 of educational assistance furnished to an individual during a calendar year, this section shall apply only to the first $5,250 of such assistance so furnished.

(b) Educational Assistance Program.—

(1) In general.—For purposes of this section, an educational assistance program is a separate written plan of an employer for the exclusive benefit of his employees to provide such employees with educational assistance. The program must meet the requirements of paragraphs (2) through (6) of this subsection.

(2) Eligibility.—The program shall benefit employees who qualify under a classification set up by the employer and found by the Secretary not to be discriminatory in favor of employees who are highly compensated employees (within the meaning of section 414(q)) or their dependents. For purposes of this paragraph, there shall be excluded from consideration employees not included in the program who are included in a unit of employees covered by an agreement which the Secretary of Labor finds to be a collective bargaining agreement between employee representatives and one or more employers, if there is evidence that educational assistance benefits were the subject of good faith bargaining between such employee representatives and such employer or employers.

(3) Principal shareholders or owners.—Not more than 5 percent of the amounts paid or incurred by the employer for educational assistance during the year may be provided for the class of individuals who are shareholders or owners (or their spouses or dependents), each of whom (on any day of the year) owns more than 5 percent of the stock or of the capital or profits interest in the employer.

(4) Other benefits as an alternative.—A program must not provide eligible employees with a choice between educational assistance and other remuneration includible in gross income. For purposes of this section, the business practices of the employer (as well as the written program) will be taken into account.

(5) No funding required.—A program referred to in paragraph (1) is not required to be funded.

(6) Notification of employees.—Reasonable notification of the availability and terms of the program must be provided to eligible employees.

(c) Definitions; Special Rules.—For purposes of this section—

Editor's Note

Caution: IRC §127(c)(1), as follows, was amended by Pub. L. No. 107-16, §411(b). For sunset provision, see the amendment notes to this section on Pub. L. No. 107-16.

---

(1) Educational assistance.—The term "educational assistance" means—

(A) the payment, by an employer, of expenses incurred by or on behalf of an employee for education of the employee (including, but not limited to, tuition, fees, and similar payments, books, supplies, and equipment), and

(B) the provision, by an employer, of courses of instruction for such employee (including books, supplies, and equipment),

but does not include payment for, or the provision of, tools or supplies which may be retained by the employee after completion of a course of instruction, or meals, lodging, or transportation. The term "educational assistance" also does not include any payment for, or the provisions of any benefits with respect to any course or other education involving sports, games, or hobbies.

(2) Employee.—The term "employee" includes, for any year, an individual who is an employee within the meaning of section 401(c)(1) (relating to self-employed individuals).

(3) Employer.—An individual who owns the entire interest in an unincorporated trade or business shall be treated as his own employer. A partnership shall be treated as the employer of each partner who is an employee within the meaning of paragraph (2).

(4) Attribution rules.—

(A) Ownership of stock.—Ownership of stock in a corporation shall be determined in accordance with the rules provided under subsections (d) and (e) of section 1563 (without regard to section 1563(e)(3)(C)).

(B) Interest in unincorporated trade or business.— The interest of an employee in a trade or business which is not incorporated shall be determined in accordance with regulations prescribed by the Secretary, which shall be based on principles similar to principles which apply in the case of subparagraph (A).

(5) Certain tests not applicable.—An educational assistance program shall not be held or considered to fail to meet any requirements of subsection (b) merely because—

(A) of utilization rates for the different types of educational assistance made available under the program; or

(B) successful completion, or attaining a particular course grade, is required for or considered in determining reimbursement under the program.

(6) Relationship to current law.—This section shall not be construed to affect the deduction or inclusion in income of amounts (not within the exclusion under this section) which are paid or incurred, or received as reimbursement, for educational expenses under section 117, 162, or 212.

(7) Disallowance of excluded amounts as credit or deduction.—No deduction or credit shall be allowed to the employee under any other section of this chapter for any amount excluded from income by reason of this section.

Editor's Note

Caution: IRC §127(d) was stricken and IRC §127(e) was redesignated as IRC §127(d) by Pub. L. No. 107-16, §411(a). For sunset provision, see the amendment notes to this section on Pub. L. No. 107-16.

(d) Cross Reference.—For reporting and record-keeping requirements, see section 6039D.

Recent Amendments to IRC §127

Economic Growth and Tax Relief Reconciliation Act of 2001 (Pub. L. No. 107-16), as follows:

• IRC §127(c)(1), last sentence, was amended by Act §411(b) by striking ", and such term also does not include any payment for, or the provision of any benefits with respect to, any graduate level course of a kind normally taken by an individual pursuing a program leading to a law, business, medical, or other advanced academic or professional degree" at the end. Eff. with respect to expenses relating to courses beginning after Dec. 31, 2001.

- IRC §127(d) was stricken by Act §411(a). Eff. with respect to expenses relating to courses beginning after Dec. 31, 2001. IRC §127(d) prior to being stricken:
  (d) Termination.—This section shall not apply to expenses paid with respect to courses beginning after December 31, 2001.
- IRC §127(e) was redesignated as subsec. (d) by Act §411(a). Eff. with respect to expenses relating to courses beginning after Dec. 31, 2001.
- **Sunset Provision.** Act §901, as amended by Pub. L. No. 111-312, §101(a)(1), provides the sunset rule below. But see Pub. L. No. 109-280, §811, and Pub. L. No. 111-148, §10909(c), as amended by Pub. L. No. 111-312, §101(b)(1).

    SEC. 901. SUNSET OF PROVISIONS OF ACT.

    (a) In general. All provisions of, and amendments made by, this Act shall not apply—

    (1) to taxable, plan, or limitation years beginning after December 31, 2012, or

    (2) in the case of title V, to estates of decedents dying, gifts made, or generation skipping transfers, after December 31, 2012.

    (b) Application of certain laws.—The Internal Revenue Code of 1986 and the Employee Retirement Income Security Act of 1974 shall be applied and administered to years, estates, gifts, and transfers described in subsection (a) as if the provisions and amendments described in subsection (a) had never been enacted.

SEC. 129. DEPENDENT CARE ASSISTANCE PROGRAMS.

(a) Exclusion.—

(1) In general.—Gross income of an employee does not include amounts paid or incurred by the employer for dependent care assistance provided to such employee if the assistance is furnished pursuant to a program which is described in subsection (d).

(2) Limitation of exclusion.—

(A) In general.—The amount which may be excluded under paragraph (1) for dependent care assistance with respect to dependent care services provided during a taxable year shall not exceed $5,000 ($2,500 in the case of a separate return by a married individual).

(B) Year of inclusion.—The amount of any excess under subparagraph (A) shall be included in gross income in the taxable year in which the dependent care services were provided (even if payment of dependent care assistance for such services occurs in a subsequent taxable year).

(C) Marital status.—For purposes of this paragraph, marital status shall be determined under the rules of paragraphs (3) and (4) of section 21(e).

(b) Earned Income Limitation.—

(1) In general.—The amount excluded from the income of an employee under subsection (a) for any taxable year shall not exceed—

(A) in the case of an employee who is not married at the close of such taxable year, the earned income of such employee for such taxable year, or

(B) in the case of an employee who is married at the close of such taxable year, the lesser of—

(i) the earned income of such employee for such taxable year, or

(ii) the earned income of the spouse of such employee for such taxable year.

(2) Special rule for certain spouses.—For purposes of paragraph (1), the provisions of section 21(d)(2) shall apply in determining the earned income of a spouse who is a student or incapable of caring for himself.

(c) Payments to Related Individuals.—No amount paid or incurred during the taxable year of an employee by an employer in providing dependent care assistance to such employee shall be excluded under subsection (a) if such amount was paid or incurred to an individual—

(1) with respect to whom, for such taxable year, a deduction is allowable under section 151(c) (relating to personal exemptions for dependents) to such employee or the spouse of such employee, or

(2) who is a child of such employee (within the meaning of section 152(f)(1)) under the age of 19 at the close of such taxable year.

(d) Dependent Care Assistance Program.—

(1) In general.—For purposes of this section a dependent care assistance program is a separate written plan of an employer for the exclusive benefit of his employees to provide such employees with dependent care assistance which meets the requirements of paragraphs (2) through (8) of this subsection. If any plan would qualify as a dependent care assistance program but for a failure to meet the requirements of this subsection, then, notwithstanding such failure, such plan shall be treated as a dependent care assistance program in the case of employees who are not highly compensated employees.

(2) Discrimination.—The contributions or benefits provided under the plan shall not discriminate in favor of employees who are highly compensated employees (within the meaning of section 414(q)) or their dependents.

(3) Eligibility.—The program shall benefit employees who qualify under a classification system set up by the employer and found by the Secretary not to be discriminatory in favor of employees described in paragraph (2), or their dependents.

(4) Principal shareholders or owners.—Not more than 25 percent of the amounts paid or incurred by the employer for dependent care assistance during the year may be provided for the class of individuals who are shareholders or owners (or their spouses or dependents), each of whom (on any day of the year) owns more than 5 percent of the stock or of the capital or profits interest in the employer.

(5) No funding required.—A program referred to in paragraph (1) is not required to be funded.

(6) Notification of eligible employees.—Reasonable notification of the availability and terms of the program shall be provided to eligible employees.

(7) Statement of expenses.—The plan shall furnish to an employee, on or before January 31, a written statement showing the amounts paid or expenses incurred by the employer in providing dependent care assistance to such employee during the previous calendar year.

(8) Benefits.—

(A) In general.—A plan meets the requirements of this paragraph if the average benefits provided to employees who are not highly compensated employees under all plans of the employer is at least 55 percent of the average benefits provided to highly compensated employees under all plans of the employer.

(B) Salary reduction agreements.—For purposes of subparagraph (A), in the case of any benefits provided through a salary reduction agreement, a plan may disregard any employees whose compensation is less than $25,000. For purposes of this subparagraph, the term "compensation" has the meaning given such term by section 414(q)(4), except that, under rules prescribed by the Secretary, an employer may elect to determine compensation on any other basis which does not discriminate in favor of highly compensated employees.

(9) Excluded employees.—For purposes of paragraphs (3) and (8), there shall be excluded from consideration—

(A) subject to rules similar to the rules of section 410(b)(4), employees who have not attained the age of 21 and completed 1 year of service (as defined in section 410(a)(3)), and

(B) employees not included in a dependent care assistance program who are included in a unit of employees covered by an agreement which the Secretary finds to be a collective bargaining agreement between employee representatives and 1 or more employers, if there is evidence that dependent care benefits were the subject of good faith bargaining between such employee representatives and such employer or employers.

(e) Definitions and Special Rules.—For purposes of this section—

(1) Dependent care assistance.—The term "dependent care assistance" means the payment of, or provision of, those services which if paid for by the employee would be considered employment-related expenses under section 21(b)(2) (relating to expenses for household and dependent care services necessary for gainful employment).

(2) Earned income.—The term "earned income" shall have the meaning given such term in section 32(c)(2), but such term shall not include any amounts paid or incurred by an employer for dependent care assistance to an employee.

(3) Employee.—The term "employee" includes, for any year, an individual who is an employee within the meaning of section 401(c)(1) (relating to self-employed individuals).

(4) Employer.—An individual who owns the entire interest in an unincorporated trade or business shall be treated as his own employer. A partnership shall be treated as the employer of each partner who is an employee within the meaning of paragraph (3).

(5) Attribution rules.—

(A) Ownership of stock.—Ownership of stock in a corporation shall be determined in accordance with the rules provided under subsections (d) and (e) of section 1563 (without regard to section 1563(e)(3)(C)).

(B) Interest in unincorporated trade or business.—The interest of an employee in a trade or business which is not incorporated shall be determined in accordance with regulations prescribed by the Secretary, which shall be based on principles similar to the principles which apply in the case of subparagraph (A).

(6) Utilization test not applicable.—A dependent care assistance program shall not be held or considered to fail to meet any requirements of subsection (d) (other than paragraphs (4) and (8) thereof) merely because of utilization rates for the different types of assistance made available under the program.

(7) Disallowance of excluded amounts as credit or deduction.—No deduction or credit shall be allowed to the employee under any other section of this chapter for any amount excluded from the gross income of the employee by reason of this section.

(8) Treatment of onsite facilities.—In the case of an onsite facility maintained by an employer, except to the extent provided in regulations, the amount of dependent care assistance provided to an employee excluded with respect to any dependent shall be based on—

(A) utilization of the facility by a dependent of the employee, and

(B) the value of the services provided with respect to such dependent.

(9) Identifying information required with respect to service provider.—No amount paid or incurred by an employer for dependent care assistance provided to an employee shall be excluded from the gross income of such employee unless—

(A) the name, address, and taxpayer identification number of the person performing the services are included on the return to which the exclusion relates, or

IRC Sec. 129(e)(9)(A)

(B) if such person is an organization described in section 501(c)(3) and exempt from tax under section 501(a), the name and address of such person are included on the return to which the exclusion relates.

In the case of a failure to provide the information required under the preceding sentence, the preceding sentence shall not apply if it is shown that the taxpayer exercised due diligence in attempting to provide the information so required.

Recent Amendments to IRC §129

Working Families Tax Relief Act of 2004 (Pub. L. No. 108-311), as follows:
• IRC §129(c)(2) was amended by Act §207(12) by substituting "152(f)(1)" for "151(c)(3)". Eff. for tax years beginning after Dec. 31, 2004.

---

* * *

SEC. 132. CERTAIN FRINGE BENEFITS.

(a) Exclusion From Gross Income.—Gross income shall not include any fringe benefit which qualifies as a—

(1) no-additional-cost service,

(2) qualified employee discount,

(3) working condition fringe,

(4) de minimis fringe,

(5) qualified transportation fringe,

(6) qualified moving expense reimbursement,

(7) qualified retirement planning services, or

(8) qualified military base realignment and closure fringe.

(b) No-Additional-Cost Service Defined.—For purposes of this section, the term "no-additional-cost service" means any service provided by an employer to an employee for use by such employee if—

(1) such service is offered for sale to customers in the ordinary course of the line of business by the employer in which the employee is performing services, and

(2) the employer incurs no substantial additional cost (including forgone revenue) in providing such service to the employee (determined without regard to any amount paid by the employee for such service).

(c) Qualified Employee Discount Defined.—For purposes of this section—

(1) Qualified employee discount.—The term "qualified employee discount" means any employee discount with respect to qualified property or services to the extent such discount does not exceed—

(A) in the case of property, the gross profit percentage of the price at which the property is being offered by the employer to customers, or

(B) in the case of services, 20 percent of the price at which the services are being offered by the employer to customers.

(2) Gross profit percentage.—

(A) In general.—The term "gross profit percentage" means the percent which—

(i) the excess of the aggregate sales price of property sold by the employer to customers over the aggregate cost of such property to the employer, is of—

(ii) the aggregate sale price of such property.

(B) Determination of gross profit percentage.— Gross profit percentage shall be determined on the basis of—

(i) all property offered to customers in the ordinary course of the line of business of the employer in which the employee is performing services (or a reasonable classification of property selected by the employer), and

(ii) the employer's experience during a representative period.

(3) Employee discount defined.—The term "employee discount" means the amount by which—

(A) the price at which the property or services are provided by the employer to an employee for use by such employee, is less than

(B) the price at which such property or services are being offered by the employer to customers.

(4) Qualified property or services.—The term "qualified property or services" means any property (other than real property and other than personal property of a kind held for investment) or services which are offered for sale to customers in the ordinary course of the line of business of the employer in which the employee is performing services.

(d) Working Condition Fringe Defined.—For purposes of this section, the term "working condition fringe" means any property or services provided to an employee of the employer to the extent that, if the employee paid for such property or services, such payment would be allowable as a deduction under section 162 or 167.

(e) De Minimis Fringe Defined.—For purposes of this section—

(1) In general.—The term "de minimis fringe" means any property or service the value of which is (after taking into account the frequency with which similar fringes are provided by the employer to the employer's employees) so small as to make accounting for it unreasonable or administratively impracticable.

(2) Treatment of certain eating facilities.—The operation by an employer of any eating facility for employees shall be treated as a de minimis fringe if—

(A) such facility is located on or near the business premises of the employer, and

(B) revenue derived from such facility normally equals or exceeds the direct operating costs of such facility.

The preceding sentence shall apply with respect to any highly compensated employee only if access to the facility is available on substantially the same terms to each member of a group of employees which is defined under a reasonable classification set up by the employer which does not discriminate in favor of highly compensated employees. For purposes of subparagraph (B), an employee entitled under section 119 to exclude the value of a meal provided at such facility shall be treated as having paid an amount for such meal equal to the direct operating costs of the facility attributable to such meal.

(f) Qualified Transportation Fringe.—

(1) In general.—For purposes of this section, the term "qualified transportation fringe" means any of the following provided by an employer to an employee:

(A) Transportation in a commuter highway vehicle if such transportation is in connection with travel between the employee's residence and place of employment.

(B) Any transit pass.

(C) Qualified parking.

(D) Any qualified bicycle commuting reimbursement.

Editor's Note

IRC §132(f)(2), below, was amended by Pub. L. No. 111-312, effective for months after December 31, 2010.

---

(2) Limitation on exclusion.—The amount of the fringe benefits which are provided by an employer to any employee and which may be excluded from gross income under subsection (a)(5) shall not exceed—

(A) $100 per month in the case of the aggregate of the benefits described in subparagraphs (A) and (B) of paragraph (1),

(B) $175 per month in the case of qualified parking, and

(C) the applicable annual limitation in the case of any qualified bicycle commuting reimbursement.

In the case of any month beginning on or after the date of the enactment of this sentence and before ~~January 1, 2011~~ *January 1, 2012*, subparagraph (A) shall be applied as if the dollar amount therein were the same as the dollar amount in effect for such month under subparagraph (B).

(3) Cash reimbursements.—For purposes of this subsection, the term "qualified transportation fringe" includes a cash reimbursement by an employer to an employee for a benefit described in paragraph (1). The preceding sentence shall apply to a cash reimbursement for any transit pass only if a voucher or similar item which may be exchanged only for a transit pass is not readily available for direct distribution by the employer to the employee.

(4) No constructive receipt.—No amount shall be included in the gross income of an employee solely because the employee may choose between any qualified transportation fringe (other than a qualified bicycle commuting reimbursement) and compensation which would otherwise be includible in gross income of such employee.

(5) Definitions.—For purposes of this subsection—

(A) Transit pass.—The term "transit pass" means any pass, token, farecard, voucher, or similar item entitling a person to transportation (or transportation at a reduced price) if such transportation is—

(i) on mass transit facilities (whether or not publicly owned), or

(ii) provided by any person in the business of transporting persons for compensation or hire if such transportation is provided in a vehicle meeting the requirements of subparagraph (B)(i).

(B) Commuter highway vehicle.—The term "commuter highway vehicle" means any highway vehicle—

(i) the seating capacity of which is at least 6 adults (not including the driver), and

(ii) at least 80 percent of the mileage use of which can reasonably be expected to be—

(I) for purposes of transporting employees in connection with travel between their residences and their place of employment, and

(II) on trips during which the number of employees transported for such purposes is at least ½ of the adult seating capacity of such vehicle (not including the driver).

(C) Qualified parking.—The term "qualified parking" means parking provided to an employee on or near the business premises of the employer or on or near a location from which the employee commutes to work by transportation described in subparagraph (A), in a commuter highway vehicle, or by carpool. Such term shall not include any parking on or near property used by the employee for residential purposes.

(D) Transportation provided by employer.— Transportation referred to in paragraph (1)(A) shall be considered to be provided by an employer if such transportation is furnished in a commuter highway vehicle operated by or for the employer.

IRC Sec. 132(f)(5)(D)

(E) Employee.—For purposes of this subsection, the term "employee" does not include an individual who is an employee within the meaning of section 401(c)(1).

(F) Definitions related to bicycle commuting reimbursement.—

(i) Qualified bicycle commuting reimbursement.—The term "qualified bicycle commuting reimbursement" means, with respect to any calendar year, any employer reimbursement during the 15-month period beginning with the first day of such calendar year for reasonable expenses incurred by the employee during such calendar year for the purchase of a bicycle and bicycle improvements, repair, and storage, if such bicycle is regularly used for travel between the employee's residence and place of employment.

(ii) Applicable annual limitation.—The term "applicable annual limitation" means, with respect to any employee for any calendar year, the product of $20 multiplied by the number of qualified bicycle commuting months during such year.

(iii) Qualified bicycle commuting month.—The term "qualified bicycle commuting month" means, with respect to any employee, any month during which such employee—

(I) regularly uses the bicycle for a substantial portion of the travel between the employee's residence and place of employment, and

(II) does not receive any benefit described in subparagraph (A), (B), or (C) of paragraph (1).

(6) Inflation adjustment.—

(A) In general.—In the case of any taxable year beginning in a calendar year after 1999, the dollar amounts contained in subparagraphs (A) and (B) of paragraph (2) shall be increased by an amount equal to—

(i) such dollar amount, multiplied by

(ii) the cost-of-living adjustment determined under section 1(f)(3) for the calendar year in which the taxable year begins, by substituting "calendar year 1998" for "calendar year 1992".

In the case of any taxable year beginning in a calendar year after 2002, clause (ii) shall be applied by substituting "calendar year 2001" for "calendar year 1998" for purposes of adjusting the dollar amount contained in paragraph (2)(A).

(B) Rounding.—If any increase determined under subparagraph (A) is not a multiple of $5, such increase shall be rounded to the next lowest multiple of $5.

(7) Coordination with other provisions.—For purposes of this section, the terms "working condition fringe" and "de minimis fringe" shall not include any qualified transportation fringe (determined without regard to paragraph (2)).

(g) Qualified Moving Expense Reimbursement.—For purposes of this section, the term "qualified moving expense reimbursement" means any amount received (directly or indirectly) by an individual from an employer as a payment for (or a reimbursement of) expenses which would be deductible as moving expenses under section 217 if directly paid or incurred by the individual. Such term shall not include any payment for (or reimbursement of) an expense actually deducted by the individual in a prior taxable year.

(h) Certain Individuals Treated as Employees for Purposes of Subsections (a)(1) and (2).—For purposes of paragraphs (1) and (2) of subsection (a)—

(1) Retired and disabled employees and surviving spouse of employee treated as employee.—With respect to a line of business of an employer, the term "employee" includes—

(A) any individual who was formerly employed by such employer in such line of business and who separated from service with such employer in such line of business by reason of retirement or disability, and

(B) any widow or widower of any individual who died while employed by such employer in such line of business or while an employee within the meaning of subparagraph (A).

(2) Spouse and dependent children.—

(A) In general.—Any use by the spouse or a dependent child of the employee shall be treated as use by the employee.

(B) Dependent child.—For purposes of subparagraph (A), the term "dependent child" means any child (as defined in section 152(f)(1)) of the employee—

(i) who is a dependent of the employee, or

(ii) both of whose parents are deceased and who has not attained age 25.

For purposes of the preceding sentence, any child to whom section 152(e) applies shall be treated as the dependent of both parents.

(3) Special rule for parents in the case of air transportation.—Any use of air transportation by a parent of an employee (determined without regard to paragraph (1)(B)) shall be treated as use by the employee.

(i) Reciprocal Agreements.—For purposes of paragraph (1) of subsection (a), any service provided by an employer to an employee of another employer shall be treated as provided by the employer of such employee if—

(1) such service is provided pursuant to a written agreement between such employers, and

(2) neither of such employers incurs any substantial additional costs (including foregone revenue) in providing such service or pursuant to such agreement.

(j) Special Rules.—

(1) Exclusions under subsection (a)(1) and (2) apply to highly compensated employees only if no discrimination.—Paragraphs (1) and (2) of subsection (a) shall apply with respect to any fringe benefit described therein provided with respect to any highly compensated employee only if such fringe benefit is available on substantially the same terms to each member of a group of employees which is defined under a reasonable classification set up by the employer which does not discriminate in favor of highly compensated employees.

(2) Special rule for leased sections of department stores.—

(A) In general.—For purposes of paragraph (2) of subsection (a), in the case of a leased section of a department store—

(i) such section shall be treated as part of the line of business of the person operating the department store, and

(ii) employees in the leased section shall be treated as employees of the person operating the department store.

(B) Leased section of department store.—For purposes of subparagraph (A), a leased section of a department store is any part of the department store where over-the-counter sales of property are made under a lease or similar arrangement where it appears to the general public that individuals making such sales are employed by the person operating the department store.

(3) Auto salesmen.—

(A) In general.—For purposes of subsection (a)(3), qualified automobile demonstration use shall be treated as a working condition fringe.

(B) Qualified automobile demonstration use.— For purposes of subparagraph (A), the term "qualified demonstration use" means any use of an automobile by a full-time automobile salesman in the sales area in which the automobile dealer's sales office is located if—

(i) such use is provided primarily to facilitate the salesman's performance of services for the employer, and

(ii) there are substantial restrictions on the personal use of such automobile by such salesman.

(4) On-premises gyms and other athletic facilities.—

(A) In general.—Gross income shall not include the value of any on-premises athletic facility provided by an employer to his employees.

(B) On-premises athletic facility.—For purposes of this paragraph, the term "on-premises athletic facility" means any gym or other athletic facility—

(i) which is located on the premises of the employer,

(ii) which is operated by the employer, and

(iii) substantially all the use of which is by employees of the employer, their spouses, and their dependent children (within the meaning of subsection (h)).

(5) Special rule for affiliates of airlines.—

(A) In general.—If—

(i) a qualified affiliate is a member of an affiliated group another member of which operates an airline, and

(ii) employees of the qualified affiliate who are directly engaged in providing airline-related services are entitled to no-additional-cost service with respect to air transportation provided by such other member,

then for purposes of applying paragraph (1) of subsection (a) to such no-additional-cost service provided to such employees, such qualified affiliate shall be treated as engaged in the same line of business as such other member.

(B) Qualified affiliate.—For purposes of this paragraph, the term "qualified affiliate" means any corporation which is predominantly engaged in airline-related services.

(C) Airline-related services.—For purposes of this paragraph, the term "airline-related services" means any of the following services provided in connection with air transportation:

(i) Catering.

(ii) Baggage handling.

(iii) Ticketing and reservations.

(iv) Flight planning and weather analysis.

(v) Restaurants and gift shops located at an airport.

(vi) Such other similar services provided to the airline as the Secretary may prescribe.

(D) Affiliated group.—For purposes of this section, the term "affiliated group" has the meaning given such term by section 1504(a).

(6) Highly compensated employee.—For purposes of this section, the term "highly compensated employee" has the meaning given such term by section 414(q).

(7) Air cargo.—For purposes of subsection (b), the transportation of cargo by air and the transportation of passengers by air shall be treated as the same service.

IRC Sec. 132(j)(7)

(8) Application of section to otherwise taxable educational or training benefits.—Amounts paid or expenses incurred by the employer for education or training provided to the employee which are not excludable from gross income under section 127 shall be excluded from gross income under this section if (and only if) such amounts or expenses are a working condition fringe.

(k) Customers Not to Include Employees.—For purposes of this section (other than subsection (c)(2)), the term "customers" shall only include customers who are not employees.

(l) Section Not to Apply to Fringe Benefits Expressly for Elsewhere.—This section (other than subsections (e) and (g)) shall not apply to any fringe benefits of a type the tax treatment of which is provided for in any other section of this chapter.

(m) Qualified Retirement Planning Services.—

(1) In general.—For purposes of this section, the term "qualified retirement planning services" means any retirement planning advice or information provided to an employee and his spouse by an employer maintaining a qualified employer plan.

(2) Nondiscrimination rule.—Subsection (a)(7) shall apply in the case of highly compensated employees only if such services are available on substantially the same terms to each member of the group of employees normally provided education and information regarding the employer's qualified employer plan.

(3) Qualified employer plan.—For purposes of this subsection, the term "qualified employer plan" means a plan, contract, pension, or account described in section 219(g)(5).

(n) Qualified Military Base Realignment and Closure Fringe.—For purposes of this section—

(1) In general.—The term "qualified military base realignment and closure fringe" means 1 or more payments under the authority of section 1013 of the Demonstration Cities and Metropolitan Development Act of 1966 (42 U.S.C. 3374) (as in effect on the date of the enactment of this subsection) to offset the adverse effects on housing values as a result of a military base realignment or closure.

(2) Limitation.—With respect to any property, such term shall not include any payment referred to in paragraph (1) to the extent that the sum of all of such payments related to such property exceeds the maximum amount described in clause (1) of subsection (c) of such section (as in effect on such date).

(o) Regulations.—The Secretary shall prescribe such regulations as may be necessary or appropriate to carry out the purposes of this section.

Recent Amendments to IRC §132

Tax Relief, Unemployment Insurance Reauthorization, and Job Creation Act of 2010 (Pub. L. No. 111-312), as follows:

- IRC §132(f)(2) was amended by Act §727(a) by striking "January 1, 2011" and inserting "January 1, 2012". Eff. for months after Dec. 31, 2010.

American Recovery and Reinvestment Act of 2009 (Pub. L. No. 111-5), as follows:

- IRC §132(f)(2) was amended by Act, Div. B, §1151(a), by adding the flush sentence at the end. Eff. for months beginning on or after date of enactment [enacted: Feb. 17, 2009].

Energy Improvement and Extension Act of 2008 (Pub. L. No. 110-343), as follows:

- IRC §132(f)(1)(D) was added by Act, Div. B, §211(a). Eff. for tax years beginning after Dec. 31, 2008.
- IRC §132(f)(2) was amended by Act, Div. B, §211(b), by striking "and" at the end of subpara. (A), by striking the period at the end of subpara. (B) and inserting ", and", and adding at the end new para. (C). Eff. for tax years beginning after Dec. 31, 2008.
- IRC §132(f)(4) was amended by Act, Div. B, §211(d), by inserting "(other than a qualified bicycle commuting reimbursement)" after "qualified transportation fringe". Eff. for tax years beginning after Dec. 31, 2008.
- IRC §132(f)(5)(F) was added by Act, Div. B, §211(c). Eff. for tax years beginning after Dec. 31, 2008.

Pension Protection Act of 2006 (Pub. L. No. 109-280), as follows:

- **Sunset Provision.** Act §811, provides:
  > SEC. 811. PENSIONS AND INDIVIDUAL RETIRE-MENT ARRANGEMENT PROVISIONS OF ECONOMIC GROWTH AND TAX RELIEF RECONCILIATION ACT OF 2001 MADE PERMANENT.
  > Title IX of the Economic Growth and Tax Relief Reconciliation Act of 2001 [Pub. L. No. 107-16] shall not apply to the provisions of, and amendments made by, subtitles A through F [§§601–666] of title VI of such Act (relating to pension and individual retirement arrangement provisions).

Working Families Tax Relief Act of 2004 (Pub. L. No. 108-311), as follows:

- IRC §132(h)(2)(B) was amended by Act §207(13) by substituting "152(f)(1)" for "151(c)(3)". Eff. tax years beginning after Dec. 31, 2004.

Military Family Tax Relief Act of 2003 (Pub. L. No. 108-121), as follows:

- IRC §132(a) was amended by Act §103(a) by striking "or" at the end of para. (6); amending para. (7) by substituting ", or" for the period at the end; and adding new para. (8). Eff. for payments made after Nov. 11, 2003.
- IRC §132 was amended by Act §103(b) by redesignating subsec. (n) as (o) and adding a new subsec. (n). Eff. for payments made after Nov. 11, 2003.

Economic Growth and Tax Relief Reconciliation Act of 2001 (Pub. L. No. 107-16), as follows:

- IRC §132(a) was amended by Act §665(a) by striking "or" at the end of para. (5); amending para. (6) by substituting ", or" for the period at the end; and adding new para. (7). Eff. for years beginning after Dec. 31, 2001.
- IRC §132 was amended by Act §665(b) by redesignating subsec. (m) as (n) and adding a new subsec. (m). Eff. for years beginning after Dec. 31, 2001.
- **Sunset Provision.** Act §901, as amended by Pub. L. No. 111-312, §101(a)(1), provides the sunset rule below. But see Pub. L. No. 109-280, §811, and Pub. L. No. 111-148, §10909(c), as amended by Pub. L. No. 111-312, §101(b)(1).
  > SEC. 901. SUNSET OF PROVISIONS OF ACT.
  > (a) In general. All provisions of, and amendments made by, this Act shall not apply—
  > (1) to taxable, plan, or limitation years beginning after December 31, 2012, or
  > (2) in the case of title V, to estates of decedents dying, gifts made, or generation skipping transfers, after December 31, 2012.
  > (b) Application of certain laws.—The Internal Revenue Code of 1986 and the Employee Retirement Income Security Act of 1974 shall be applied and administered to years, estates, gifts, and transfers described in subsection (a) as if the provisions and amendments described in subsection (a) had

never been enacted.

* * *

SEC. 134. CERTAIN MILITARY BENEFITS.

(a) General rule. Gross income shall not include any qualified military benefit.

(b) Qualified Military Benefit. For purposes of this section—

(1) In general. The term "qualified military benefit" means any allowance or in-kind benefit (other than personal use of a vehicle) which—

(A) is received by any member or former member of the uniformed services of the United States or any dependent of such member by reason of such member's status or service as a member of such uniformed services, and

(B) was excludable from gross income on September 9, 1986, under any provision of law, regulation, or administrative practice which was in effect on such date (other than a provision of this title).

(2) No other benefit to be excludable except as provided by this title. Notwithstanding any other provision of law, no benefit shall be treated as a qualified military benefit unless such benefit—

(A) is a benefit described in paragraph (1), or

(B) is excludable from gross income under this title without regard to any provision of law which is not contained in this title and which is not contained in a revenue Act.

(3) Limitations on modifications.

(A) In general. Except as provided in subparagraphs (B) and (C) and paragraphs (4) and (5), no modification or adjustment of any qualified military benefit after September 9, 1986, shall be taken into account.

(B) Exception for certain adjustments to cash benefits. Subparagraph (A) shall not apply to any adjustment to any qualified military benefit payable in cash which—

(i) is pursuant to a provision of law or regulation (as in effect on September 9, 1986), and

(ii) is determined by reference to any fluctuation in cost, price, currency, or other similar index.

(C) Exception for death gratuity adjustments made by law. Subparagraph (A) shall not apply to any adjustment to the amount of death gratuity payable under chapter 75 of title 10, United States Code, which is pursuant to a provision of law enacted after September 9, 1986.

(4) Clarification of certain benefits. For purposes of paragraph (1), such term includes any dependent care assistance program (as in effect on the date of the enactment of this paragraph) for any individual described in paragraph (1)(A).

(5) Travel benefits under operation hero miles. The term "qualified military benefit" includes a travel benefit provided under section 2613 of title 10, United States Code (as in effect on the date of the enactment of this paragraph).

(6) Certain State payments. The term "qualified military benefit" includes any bonus payment by a State or political subdivision thereof to any member or former member of the uniformed services of the United States or any dependent of such member only by reason of such member's service in an combat zone (as defined in section 112(c)(2), determined without regard to the parenthetical).

Recent Amendments to §134

Heroes Earnings Assistance and Relief Tax Act of 2008 (Pub. L. No. 110-245), as follows:
- IRC §134(b)(6) was added by Act §112(a). Eff. for payments made before, on, or after the date of enactment [June 17, 2008], see Act §112(b).

Ronald W. Reagan National Defense Authorization Act for Fiscal Year 2005 (Pub. L. No. 108-375), as follows:
- IRC §134(b)(3)(A) was amended by Act §585(b)(2)(A) by substituting "paragraphs (4) and (5)" for "paragraph (4)". Eff. for travel benefits provided after Oct. 28, 2004.
- IRC §134(b)(5) was added by Act §585(b)(1). Eff. for travel benefits provided after Oct. 28, 2004.

Military Family Tax Relief Act of 2003 (Pub. L. No. 108-121), as follows:
- IRC §134(b)(3)(A) was amended by Act §102(b)(2) by substituting "subparagraphs (B) and (C)" for "subparagraph (B)". Eff. for deaths after Sept. 11, 2001.
- IRC §134(b)(3)(A) was amended by Act §106(b)(1) by inserting "and paragraph (4)" after "subparagraphs (B) and (C)". Eff. for taxable years beginning after Dec. 31, 2002.
- IRC §134(b)(3)(C) was added by Act §102(b)(1). Eff. for deaths after Sept. 11, 2001.
- IRC §134(b)(4) was added by Act §106(a). Eff. for taxable years beginning after Dec. 31, 2002.
- **Other Provision.** Act §106(d) provides:
  (d) No Inference.—No inference may be drawn from the amendments made by this section with respect to the tax treatment of any amounts under the program described in section 134(b)(4) of the Internal Revenue Code of 1986 (as added by this section) for any taxable year beginning before January 1, 2003.

SEC. 135. INCOME FROM UNITED STATES SAVINGS BONDS USED TO PAY HIGHER EDUCATION TUITION AND FEES.

(a) General Rule.—In the case of an individual who pays qualified higher education expenses during the taxable year, no amount shall be includible in gross income by reason of the redemption during such year of any qualified United States savings bond.

(b) Limitations.—

(1) Limitation where redemption proceeds exceed higher education expenses.—

(A) In general. If—

(i) the aggregate proceeds of qualified United States savings bonds redeemed by the taxpayer during the taxable year exceed

(ii) the qualified higher education expenses paid by the taxpayer during such taxable year,

the amount excludable from gross income under subsection (a) shall not exceed the applicable fraction of the amount excludable from gross income under subsection (a) without regard to this subsection.

(B) Applicable fraction.—For purposes of subparagraph (A), the term "applicable fraction" means the fraction the numerator of which is the amount described in subparagraph (A)(ii) and the denominator of which is the amount described in subparagraph (A)(i).

(2) Limitation based on modified adjusted gross income.—

(A) In general.—If the modified adjusted gross income of the taxpayer for the taxable year exceeds $40,000 ($60,000 in the case of a joint return), the amount which would (but for this paragraph) be excludable from gross income under subsection (a) shall be reduced (but not below zero) by the amount which bears the same ratio to the amount which would be so excludable as such excess bears to $15,000 ($30,000 in the case of a joint return).

(B) Inflation adjustment.—In the case of any taxable year beginning in a calendar year after 1990, the $40,000 and $60,000 amounts contained in subparagraph (A) shall be increased by an amount equal to—

(i) such dollar amount, multiplied by

(ii) the cost-of-living adjustment under section 1(f)(3) for the calendar year in which the taxable year begins, determined by substituting "calendar year 1989" for "calendar year 1992" in subparagraph (B) thereof.

(C) Rounding.—If any amount as adjusted under subparagraph (B) is not a multiple of $50, such amount shall be rounded to the nearest multiple of $50 (or if such amount is a multiple of $25, such amount shall be rounded to the next highest multiple of $50).

(c) Definitions.—For purposes of this section—

(1) Qualified United States savings bond.—The term "qualified United States savings bond" means any United States savings bond issued—

(A) after December 31, 1989,

(B) to an individual who has attained age 24 before the date of issuance, and

(C) at discount under section 3105 of title 31, United States Code.

(2) Qualified higher education expenses.—

(A) In general.—The term "qualified higher education expenses" means tuition and fees required for the enrollment or attendance of—

(i) the taxpayer,

(ii) the taxpayer's spouse, or

(iii) any dependent of the taxpayer with respect to whom the taxpayer is allowed a deduction under section 151,

at an eligible educational institution.

(B) Exception for education involving sports, etc.—Such term shall not include expenses with respect to any course or other education involving sports, games, or hobbies other than as part of a degree program.

(C) Contributions to qualified tuition program and Coverdell education savings accounts.—Such term shall include any contribution to a qualified tuition program (as defined in section 529) on behalf of a designated beneficiary (as defined in such section), or to a Coverdell education savings account (as defined in section 530) on behalf of an account beneficiary, who is an individual described in subparagraph (A); but there shall be no increase in the investment in the contract for purposes of applying section 72 by reason of any portion of such contribution which is not includible in gross income by reason of this subparagraph.

(3) Eligible educational institution.—The term "eligible educational institution" has the meaning given such term by section 529(e)(5).

(4) Modified adjusted gross income.—The term "modified adjusted gross income" means the adjusted gross income of the taxpayer for the taxable year determined—

Editor's Note

Caution: IRC §135(c)(4)(A), as follows, was amended by Pub. L. No. 107-16, §431(c)(1). For sunset provision, see the amendment notes to this section on Pub. L. No. 107-16.

(A) without regard to this section and sections 137, 199, 221, 222, 911, 931, and 933, and

(B) after the application of sections 86, 469, and 219.

(d) Special Rules.—

(1) Adjustment for certain scholarships and veterans benefits.—The amount of qualified higher education expenses otherwise taken into account under subsection (a) with respect to the education of an individual shall be reduced (before the application of subsection (b)) by the sum of the amounts received with respect to such individual for the taxable year as—

(A) a qualified scholarship which under section 117 is not includable in gross income,

(B) an educational assistance allowance under chapter 30, 31, 32, 34, or 35 of title 38, United States Code,

(C) a payment (other than a gift, bequest, devise, or inheritance within the meaning of section 102(a)) for educational expenses, or attributable to attendance at an eligible educational institution, which is exempt from income taxation by any law of the United States, or

(D) a payment, waiver, or reimbursement of qualified higher education expenses under a qualified tuition program (within the meaning of section 529(b)).

(2) Coordination with other higher education benefits.—The amount of the qualified higher education expenses otherwise taken into account under subsection (a) with respect to the education of an individual shall be reduced (before the application of subsection (b)) by—

Editor's Note

Caution: IRC §135(d)(2)(A), as follows, was amended by Pub. L. No. 107-16, §401(g)(2)(B). For sunset provision, see the amendment notes to this section on Pub. L. No. 107-16.

(A) the amount of such expenses which are taken into account in determining the credit allowed to the taxpayer or any other person under section 25A with respect to such expenses, and

(B) the amount of such expenses which are taken into account in determining the exclusion under sections 529(c)(3)(B) and 530(d)(2).

(3) No exclusion for married individuals filing separate returns.—If the taxpayer is a married individual (within the meaning of section 7703), this section shall apply only if the taxpayer and his spouse file a joint return for the taxable year.

(4) Regulations.—The Secretary may prescribe such regulations as may be necessary or appropriate to carry out this section, including regulations requiring record keeping and information reporting.

Recent Amendments to IRC §135

Pension Protection Act of 2006 (Pub. L. No. 109-280), as follows:
- **Other Provision.** Act §1304(a) provides:

(a) Permanent Extension of Modifications.—Section 901 of the Economic Growth and Tax Relief Reconciliation Act of 2001 [Pub. L. No. 107-16] (relating to sunset provisions) shall not apply to section 402 of such Act (relating to modifications to qualified tuition programs).

American Jobs Creation Act of 2004 (Pub. L. No. 108-357), as follows:
- IRC §135(c)(4)(A) was amended by Act §102(d)(1) by inserting "199," before "221". Eff. tax years beginning after Dec. 31, 2004.

Pub. L. No. 107-22, as follows:
- IRC §135(c)(2)(C) was amended by Act §1(b)(1)(B) by replacing "an education individual retirement" with "a Coverdell education savings". Effective Jul. 26, 2001.
- IRC §135(c)(2)(C) was amended by Act §1(b)(3)(B) by replacing in the heading "education individual retirement" with "Coverdell education savings". Effective Jul. 26, 2001.

Economic Growth and Tax Relief Reconciliation Act of 2001 (Pub. L. No. 107-16), as follows:
- IRC §135(c)(2)(C) was amended by Act §402(c)(4)(A) by replacing "qualified State tuition" with "qualified tuition". Eff. tax years beginning after Dec. 31, 2001.
- IRC §135(c)(2)(C) was amended by Act §402(a)(4)(B) by replacing "qualified State tuition" with "qualified tuition". Eff. tax years beginning after Dec. 31, 2001.
- IRC §135(c)(4)(A) was amended by Act §431(c)(1) by inserting "222," after "221,". Eff. for payments made in tax years beginning after Dec. 31, 2001.
- IRC §135(d)(2)(A) amended by Act §401(g)(2)(B) by replacing "allowable" with "allowed". Eff. tax years beginning after Dec. 31, 2001.
- IRC §135(d)(2)(B) amended by Act §402(b)(2)(A) by replacing "the exclusion under §530(d)(2)" with "the exclusions under §§529(c)(3)(B) and 530(d)(2)". Eff. tax years beginning after Dec. 31, 2001.
- IRC §135(d)(1)(D) amended by Act §402(a)(4)(A) by replacing "qualified State tuition" with "qualified tuition". Eff. tax years beginning after Dec. 31, 2001.
- **Sunset Provision.** Act §901, as amended by Pub. L. No. 111-312, §101(a)(1), provides the sunset rule below. But see Pub. L. No. 109-280, §811, and Pub. L. No. 111-148, §10909(c), as amended by Pub. L. No. 111-312, §101(b)(1).

    SEC. 901. SUNSET OF PROVISIONS OF ACT.

    (a) In general. All provisions of, and amendments made by, this Act shall not apply—

    (1) to taxable, plan, or limitation years beginning after December 31, 2012, or

    (2) in the case of title V, to estates of decedents dying, gifts made, or generation skipping transfers, after December 31, 2012.

    (b) Application of certain laws.—The Internal Revenue Code of 1986 and the Employee Retirement Income Security Act of 1974 shall be applied and administered to years, estates, gifts, and transfers described in subsection (a) as if the provisions and amendments described in subsection (a) had never been enacted.

---

* * *

SEC. 137. ADOPTION ASSISTANCE PROGRAMS.

Editor's Note

Caution: IRC §137(a), as follows, was amended by Pub. L. No. 107-16, §202(a)(2). For sunset provision, see the amendment notes to this section on Pub. L. No. 107-16.

(a) Exclusion.—

(1) In general.—Gross income of an employee does not include amounts paid or expenses incurred by the employer for qualified adoption expenses in connection with the adoption of a child by an employee if such amounts are furnished pursuant to an adoption assistance program.

> *Editor's Note*
>
> **Caution:** IRC §137(a)(2), as follows, as amended by Pub. L. No. 107-16, Pub. L. No. 107-147, and Pub. L. No. 111-148, but prior to amendment by Pub. L. No. 111-312, applies to tax years beginning on or before December 31, 2011. For sunset provisions, see the amendment notes to this section on Pub. L. No. 107-16 and Pub. L. No. 111-312.

(2) $13,170 exclusion for adoption of child with special needs regardless of expenses.—In the case of an adoption of a child with special needs which becomes final during a taxable year, the qualified adoption expenses with respect to such adoption for such year shall be increased by an amount equal to the excess (if any) of $13,170 over the actual aggregate qualified adoption expenses with respect to such adoption during such taxable year and all prior taxable years.

> *Editor's Note*
>
> **Caution:** IRC §137(a)(2), as follows, amended by Pub. L. No. 111-312, applies to tax years beginning after December 31, 2011. For sunset provisions, see the amendment notes to this section on Pub. L. No. 107-16 and Pub. L. No. 111-148.

(2) $10,000 exclusion for adoption of child with special needs regardless of expenses.—In the case of an adoption of a child with special needs which becomes final during a taxable year, the qualified adoption expenses with respect to such adoption for such year shall be increased by an amount equal to the excess (if any) of $10,000 over the actual aggregate qualified adoption expenses with respect to such adoption during such taxable year and all prior taxable years.

(b) Limitations.—

> *Editor's Note*
>
> **Caution:** IRC §137(b)(1), as follows, was amended by Pub. L. No. 107-16, Pub. L. No. 107-47, and Pub. L. No. 111-148, but prior to amendment by Pub. L. No. 111-312, applies to tax years beginning on or before December 31, 2011. For sunset provision, see the amendment notes on Pub. L. No. 107-16 and Pub. L. No. 111-148.

(1) Dollar limitation.—The aggregate of the amounts paid or expenses incurred which may be taken into account under subsection (a) for all taxable years with respect to the adoption of a child by the taxpayer shall not exceed $13,170.

> *Editor's Note*
>
> **Caution:** IRC §137(b)(1), as follows, as amended by Pub. L. No. 111-312, applies to tax years beginning after December 31, 2011. For sunset provisions, see the amendment notes to this section on Pub. L. No. 107-16 and Pub. L. No. 111-148.

(1) Dollar limitation.—The aggregate of the amounts paid or expenses incurred which may be taken into account under subsection (a) for all taxable years with respect to the adoption of a child by the taxpayer shall not exceed $10,000.

(2) Income limitation.—The amount excludable from gross income under subsection (a) for any taxable year shall be reduced (but not below zero) by an amount which bears the same ratio to the amount so excludable (determined without regard to this paragraph but with regard to paragraph (1)) as—

> *Editor's Note*
>
> **Caution:** IRC §137(b)(2)(A), as follows, was amended by Pub. L. No. 107-16. For sunset provision, see the amendment notes to this section on Pub. L. No. 107-16.

(A) the amount (if any) by which the taxpayer's adjusted gross income exceeds $150,000, bears to

(B) $40,000.

(3) Determination of adjusted gross income.— For purposes of paragraph (2), adjusted gross income shall be determined—

(A) without regard to this section and sections 199, 221, 222, 911, 931, and 933, and

(B) after the application of sections 86, 135, 219, and 469.

(c) Adoption Assistance Program.—For purposes of this section, an adoption assistance program is a separate written plan of an employer for the exclusive benefit of such employer's employees—

(1) under which the employer provides such employees with adoption assistance, and

(2) which meets requirements similar to the requirements of paragraphs (2), (3), (5), and (6) of section 127(b).

An adoption reimbursement program operated under section 1052 of title 10, United States Code (relating to armed forces) or section 514 of title 14, United States Code (relating to members of the Coast Guard) shall be treated as an adoption assistance program for purposes of this section.

(d) Qualified Adoption Expenses.—For purposes of this section, the term "qualified adoption expenses" has the meaning given such term by section 36C(d) (determined without regard to reimbursements under this section).

(d) Qualified Adoption Expenses.—For purposes of this section, the term "qualified adoption expenses" has the meaning given such term by section 23(d) (determined without regard to reimbursements under this section).

(e) Certain Rules to Apply.—Rules similar to the rules of subsections (e), (f), and (g) of section 36C shall apply for purposes of this section.

(e) Certain Rules to Apply.—Rules similar to the rules of subsections (e), (f), and (g) of section 23 shall apply for purposes of this section.

(f) Adjustments for Inflation.—

(1) Dollar limitations.—In the case of a taxable year beginning after December 31, 2010, each of the dollar amounts in subsections (a)(2) and (b)(1) shall be increased by an amount equal to—

(A) such dollar amount, multiplied by

(B) the cost-of-living adjustment determined under section 1(f)(3) for the calendar year in which the taxable year begins, determined by substituting "calendar year 2009" for "calendar year 1992" in subparagraph (B) thereof.

If any amount as increased under the preceding sentence is not a multiple of $10, such amount shall be rounded to the nearest multiple of $10.

(2) Income limitation.—In the case of a taxable year beginning after December 31, 2002, the dollar amount in subsection (b)(2)(A) shall be increased by an amount equal to—

(A) such dollar amount, multiplied by

IRC Sec. 137(f)(2)(A)

(B) the cost-of-living adjustment determined under section 1(f)(3) for the calendar year in which the taxable year begins, determined by substituting "calendar year 2001" for "calendar year 1992" in subparagraph thereof.

If any amount as increased under the preceding sentence is not a multiple of $10, such amount shall be rounded to the nearest multiple of $10.

Editor's Note

Caution: IRC §137(f), as follows, as amended by Pub. L. No. 111-148 and Pub. L. No. 111-312, applies to tax years beginning after December 31, 2011. For sunset provision, see amendment notes to this section on Pub. L. No. 111-148.

(f) Adjustments for Inflation.—*In the case of a taxable year beginning after December 31, 2002, each of the dollar amounts in subsection (a)(2) and paragraphs (1) and (2)(A) of subsection (b) shall be increased by an amount equal to*—

(1) such dollar amount, multiplied by

(2) the cost-of-living adjustment determined under section 1(f)(3) for the calendar year in which the taxable year begins, determined by substituting "calendar year 2001" for "calendar year 1992" in subparagraph (B) thereof.

If any amount as increased under the preceding sentence is not a multiple of $10, such amount shall be rounded to the nearest multiple of $10.

Recent Amendments of IRC §137

Tax Relief, Unemployment Insurance Reauthorization, and Job Creation Act of 2010 (Pub. L. No. 111-312), as follows:
• IRC §137(a)(2), (b)(1), (d), (e), and (f) were amended to read as each provision would read if the Patient Protection and Affordable Care Act (Pub. L. No. 111-148), §10909, had never been enacted. Eff. for tax years beginning after Dec. 31, 2011.
• **Sunset Provision for Patient Protection and Affordable Care Act, 2010 (Pub. L. No. 111-148).** Act §101(b) provides:
(b) Separate Sunset for Expansion of Adoption Benefits Under the Patient Protection and Affordable Care Act.—
(1) In general.—Subsection (c) of section 10909 of the Patient Protection and Affordable Care Act is amended to read as follows:
  "(c) Sunset Provision.—Each provision of law amended by this section is amended to read as such provision would read if this section had never been enacted. The amendments made by the preceding sentence shall apply to taxable years beginning after December 31, 2011."
(2) Conforming amendment.—Subsection (d) of section 10909 of such Act is amended by striking "The amendments" and inserting "Except as provided in subsection (c), the amendments".

Patient Protection and Affordable Care Act, 2010 (Pub. L. No. 111-148), as follows:
• IRC §137(a)(2) and (b)(1) were amended by Act §10909(a)(2)(A)–(B) by striking "$10,000" wherever it appeared and inserting "$13,170". Eff. for taxable years beginning after Dec. 31, 2009.

• IRC §137(d) was amended by striking "section 23(d)" and inserting "section 36C(d)". Eff. for taxable years beginning after Dec. 31, 2009.
• IRC §137(e) was amended by Act §1090(b)(2)(J)(ii) by striking "section 23" and inserting "section 36C". Eff. for taxable years beginning after Dec. 31, 2009.
• IRC §137(f) was amended by Act §10909(a)(2)(C). Eff. for taxable years beginning after Dec. 31, 2009. IRC §137(f) prior to amendment:
  (f) Coordination With Limitation on Number of Taxpayers Having Archer MSAs.—Subsection (i) of section 220 shall not apply to an individual with respect to a Medicare Advantage MSA, and Medicare Advantage MSAs shall not be taken into account in determining whether the numerical limitations under section 220(j) are exceeded.
• **Sunset Provision.** Act §10909(c), as amended by Pub. L. No. 111-312, §101(b)(1), provides:
  (c) Sunset Provision. Each provision of law amended by this section is amended to read as such provision would read if this section had never been enacted. The amendments made by the preceding sentence shall apply to taxable years beginning after December 31, 2011.

American Jobs Creation Act of 2004 (Pub. L. No. 108-357), as follows:
• IRC §137(b)(3)(A) was amended by Act §102(d)(1) by inserting "199," before "221". Eff. tax years beginning after Dec. 31, 2004.

Job Creation and Worker Assistance Act of 2002 (Pub. L. No. 107-147), as follows
• IRC §137(a) was amended by Act §411(c)(2)(B), as amended by Pub. L. No. 108-311, §403(e). Eff. tax years beginning after Dec. 31, 2002. IRC §137(a) prior to amendment:
  (a) In general.—Gross income of an employee does not include amounts paid or expenses incurred by the employer for adoption expenses in connection with the adoption of a child by an employee if such amounts are furnished pursuant to an adoption assistance program. The amount of the exclusion shall be—
  (1) in the case of an adoption of a child other than a child with special needs, the amount of the qualified adoption expense paid or incurred by the taxpayer, and
  (2) in the case of an adoption of a child with special needs, $10,000.
• IRC §137(b)(1) was amended by Act §411(c)(2)(B) by replacing "subsection (a)(1)" with "subsection (a)". Eff. tax years beginning after Dec. 31, 2001.
• IRC §137(f) was amended by Act §418(a)(2) by adding the flush sentence at the end. Eff. tax years beginning after Dec. 31, 2001, as if included in the provision of Pub. L. No. 107-16 to which it relates.

Economic Growth and Tax Relief Reconciliation Act of 2001 (Pub. L. No. 107-16), as follows
• IRC §137(a) was amended by Act §202(a)(2). Eff. tax years beginning after Dec. 31, 2002. IRC §137(a) prior to amendment:
  (a) In general.—Gross income of an employee does not include amounts paid or expenses incurred by the employer for qualified adoption expenses in connection with the adoption of a child by an employee is such amounts are furnished pursuant to an adoption assistance program.
• IRC §137(b)(1) was amended by Act §202(b)(1)(B)(i)–(iii) by replacing "$5,000" with "$10,000", by striking "($6,000, in the case of a child with special needs)" before the period, and by striking "subsection (a)" and inserting "subsection (a)(1)". Eff. tax years beginning after Dec. 31, 2001.
• IRC §137(b)(2)(A) was amended by Act §202(b)(2)(B) by replacing "$75,000" with "$150,000". Eff. tax years beginning after Dec. 31, 2001.
• IRC §137(b)(3) was amended by Act §431(c)(1) by inserting "222," after "221,". Eff. for payments made in tax years beginning after Dec. 31, 2001.
• IRC §137(f) was stricken by Act §202(d)(2). Eff. tax years beginning after Dec. 31, 2001. IRC §137(f) prior to being stricken:
  (f) Termination.—This section shall not apply to amounts paid or expenses incurred after December 31, 2001.

- IRC §137 was amended by Act §202(d) by adding new subsec. (f). Eff. tax years beginning after Dec. 31, 2001.
- **Sunset Provision.** Act §901, as amended by Pub. L. No. 111-312, §101(a)(1), provides the sunset rule below. But see Pub. L. No. 109-280, §811, and Pub. L. No. 111-148, §10909(c), as amended by Pub. L. No. 111-312, §101(b)(1).

> **SEC. 901. SUNSET OF PROVISIONS OF ACT.**
> **(a) In general.** All provisions of, and amendments made by, this Act shall not apply—
> **(1)** to taxable, plan, or limitation years beginning after December 31, 2012, or
> **(2)** in the case of title V, to estates of decedents dying, gifts made, or generation skipping transfers, after December 31, 2012.
> **(b) Application of certain laws.**—The Internal Revenue Code of 1986 and the Employee Retirement Income Security Act of 1974 shall be applied and administered to years, estates, gifts, and transfers described in subsection (a) as if the provisions and amendments described in subsection (a) had never been enacted.

SEC. 138. MEDICARE ADVANTAGE MSA.

(a) Exclusion.—Gross income shall not include any payment to the Medicare Advantage MSA of an individual by the Secretary of Health and Human Services under part C of title XVIII of the Social Security Act.

(b) Medicare Advantage MSA—For purposes of this section, the term "Medicare Advantage MSA" means an Archer MSA (as defined in section 220(d))—

(1) which is designated as a Medicare Advantage MSA,

(2) with respect to which no contribution may be made other than—

(A) a contribution made by the Secretary of Health and Human Services pursuant to part C of title XVIII of the Social Security Act, or

(B) a trustee-to-trustee transfer described in subsection (c)(4),

(3) the governing instrument of which provides that trustee-to-trustee transfers described in subsection (c)(4) may be made to and from such account, and

(4) which is established in connection with an MSA plan described in section 1859(b)(3) of the Social Security Act.

(c) Special Rules for Distributions.—

(1) Distributions for qualified medical expenses.—In applying section 220 to a Medicare Advantage MSA—

(A) qualified medical expenses shall not include amounts paid for medical care for any individual other than the account holder, and

(B) section 220(d)(2)(C) shall not apply.

(2) Penalty for distributions from Medicare Advantage MSA not used for qualified medical expenses if minimum balance not maintained.—

(A) In general.—The tax imposed by this chapter for any taxable year in which there is a payment or distribution from a Medicare Advantage MSA which is not used exclusively to pay the qualified medical expenses of the account holder shall be increased by 50 percent of the excess (if any) of—

(i) the amount of such payment or distribution, over

(ii) the excess (if any) of—

(I) the fair market value of the assets in such MSA as of the close of the calendar year preceding the calendar year in which the taxable year begins, over

(II) an amount equal to 60 percent of the deductible under the Medicare Advantage MSA plan covering the account holder as of January 1 of the calendar year in which the taxable year begins.

Section 220(f)(4) shall not apply to any payment or distribution from a Medicare Advantage MSA.

(B) Exceptions.—Subparagraph (A) shall not apply if the payment or distribution is made on or after the date the account holder—

(i) becomes disabled within the meaning of section 72(m)(7), or

(ii) dies.

(C) Special Rules.—For purposes of subparagraph (A)—

(i) all Medicare Advantage MSAs of the account holder shall be treated as 1 account,

(ii) all payments and distributions not used exclusively to pay the qualified medical expenses of the account holder during any taxable year shall be treated as 1 distribution, and

(iii) any distribution of property shall be taken into account at its fair market value on the date of the distribution.

(3) Withdrawal of erroneous contributions.—Section 220(f)(2) and paragraph (2) of this subsection shall not apply to any payment or distribution from a Medicare Advantage MSA to the Secretary of Health and Human Services of an erroneous contribution to such MSA and of the net income attributable to such contribution.

(4) Trustee-to-trustee transfers.—Section 220(f)(2) and paragraph (2) of this subsection shall not apply to any trustee-to-trustee transfer from a Medicare Advantage MSA of an account holder to another Medicare Advantage MSA of such account holder.

(d) Special Rules for Treatment of Account After Death of Account Holder.—In applying section 220(f)(8)(A) to an account which was a Medicare Advantage MSA of a decedent, the rules of section

220(f) shall apply in lieu of the rules of subsection (c) of this section with respect to the spouse as the account holder of such Medicare Advantage MSA.

(e) Reports.—In the case of a Medicare Advantage MSA, the report under section 220(h)—

(1) shall include the fair market value of the assets in such Medicare Advantage MSA as of the close of each calendar year, and

(2) shall be furnished to the account holder—

(A) not later than January 31 of the calendar year following the calendar year to which such reports relate, and

(B) in such manner as the Secretary prescribes in such regulations.

(f) Coordination With Limitation on Number of Taxpayers Having Archer MSAs.—Subsection (i) of section 220 shall not apply to an individual with respect to a Medicare Advantage MSA, and Medicare Advantage MSAs shall not be taken into account in determining whether the numerical limitations under section 220(j) are exceeded.

Recent Amendments to IRC §138

Working Families Tax Relief Act of 2004 (Pub. L. No. 108-311), as follows:
• IRC §138 was amended by Act §408(a)(5)(A) by substituting "Medicare Advantage MSA" for "Medicare+Choice MSA" each place it appeared in the text. Eff. Oct. 4, 2004.
• IRC §138 was amended by Act §408(a)(5)(B) by substituting "Medicare Advantage MSA" for "Medicare+Choice MSA" in the heading. Eff. Oct. 4, 2004.
• IRC §138(b) was amended by Act §408(a)(5)(C) by substituting "Medicare Advantage MSA" for "Medicare+Choice MSA" in the heading. Eff. Oct. 4, 2004.
• IRC §138(c)(2) was amended by Act §408(a)(5)(D) by substituting "Medicare Advantage MSA" for "Medicare+Choice MSA" in the heading. Eff. Oct. 4, 2004.
• IRC §138(c)(2)(C)(i) was amended by Act §408(a)(5)(E) by substituting "Medicare Advantage MSAs" for "Medicare+Choice MSAs". Eff. Oct. 4, 2004.
• IRC §138(f) was amended by Act §408(a)(5)(F) by substituting "Medicare Advantage MSAs" for "Medicare+Choice MSA's". Eff. Oct. 4, 2004.

* * *

SEC. 139B. BENEFITS PROVIDED TO VOLUNTEER FIREFIGHTERS AND EMERGENCY MEDICAL RESPONDERS.

(a) In General.—In the case of any member of a qualified volunteer emergency response organization, gross income shall not include—

(1) any qualified State and local tax benefit, and

(2) any qualified payment.

(b) Denial of Double Benefits.—In the case of any member of a qualified volunteer emergency response organization—

(1) the deduction under 164 shall be determined with regard to any qualified State and local tax benefit, and

(2) expenses paid or incurred by the taxpayer in connection with the performance of services as such a member shall be taken into account under section 170 only to the extent such expenses exceed the amount of any qualified payment excluded from gross income under subsection (a).

(c) Definitions.—For purposes of this section—

(1) Qualified state and local tax benefit.—The term "qualified state and local tax benefit" means any reduction or rebate of a tax described in paragraph (1), (2), or (3) of section 164(a) provided by a State or political division thereof on account of services performed as a member of a qualified volunteer emergency response organization.

(2) Qualified payment.—

(A) In general.—The term "qualified payment" means any payment (whether reimbursement or otherwise) provided by a State or political division thereof on account of the performance of services as a member of a qualified volunteer emergency response organization.

(B) Applicable dollar limitation.—The amount determined under subparagraph (A) for any taxable year shall not exceed $30 multiplied by the number of months during such year that the taxpayer performs such services.

(3) Qualified volunteer emergency response organization.—The term "qualified volunteer emergency response organization" means any volunteer organization—

(A) which is organized and operated to provide firefighting or emergency medical services for persons in the State or political subdivision, as the case may be, and

(B) which is required (by written agreement) by the State or political subdivision to furnish firefighting or emergency medical services in such State or political subdivision.

(d) Termination.—This section shall not apply with respect to taxable years beginning after December 31, 2010.

Recent Amendments to IRC §139B

Mortgage Forgiveness Debt Relief Act of 2007 (Pub. L. No. 110-142), as follows:

• IRC §139B was added by Act §5. Eff. for taxable years beginning after Dec. 31, 2007, see Act §5(c).

Editor's Note

IRC §139C, below, as amended by Pub. L. No. 111-144, §3, is effective February 17, 2009.

SEC. 139C. COBRA PREMIUM ASSISTANCE.

In the case of an assistance eligible individual (as defined in section 3001 of title III of division B of the American Recovery and Reinvestment Act of 2009), gross income does not include any premium reduction provided under subsection (a) of such section.

Amendments to IRC §139C

Temporary Extension Act of 2010 (Pub. L. No. 111-144), as follows:
• IRC §139C was amended by Act §3(b)(5)(B) by striking "section 3002 of the Health Insurance Assistance for the Unemployed Act of 2009" and inserting "section 3001 of title III of division B of the American Recovery and Reinvestment Act of 2009". Eff. as if included in the provisions of §3001 of Pub. L. No. 111-5, Div. B, to which it relates [eff. for taxable years ending after the date of the enactment of this Pub. L. No. 111-5 (enacted: Feb. 17, 2009)].

American Recovery and Reinvestment Tax Act of 2009 (Pub. L. No. 111-5), as follows:
• IRC §139C was added by Act Div. B, §3001(a)(15)(A). Eff. for tax years ending after Feb. 17, 2009.

Editor's Note

IRC §139D, below, was added by Pub. L. No. 111-148, §9021, effective for benefits and coverage provided after the date of the enactment (enacted: March 23, 2010).

SEC. 139D. INDIAN HEALTH CARE BENEFITS.

(a) General Rule.—Except as otherwise provided in this section, gross income does not include the value of any qualified Indian health care benefit.

(b) Qualified Indian Health Care Benefit.—For purposes of this section, the term "qualified Indian health care benefit" means—

(1) any health service or benefit provided or purchased, directly or indirectly, by the Indian Health Service through a grant to or a contract or compact with an Indian tribe or tribal organization, or through a third-party program funded by the Indian Health Service,

(2) medical care provided or purchased by, or amounts to reimburse for such medical care provided by, an Indian tribe or tribal organization for, or to, a member of an Indian tribe, including a spouse or dependent of such a member,

(3) coverage under accident or health insurance (or an arrangement having the effect of accident or health insurance), or an accident or health plan, provided by an Indian tribe or tribal organization for medical care to a member of an Indian tribe, include a spouse or dependent of such a member, and

(4) any other medical care provided by an Indian tribe or tribal organization that supplements, replaces, or substitutes for a program or service relating to medical care provided by the Federal government to Indian tribes or members of such a tribe.

(c) Definitions.—For purposes of this section—

(1) **Indian tribe.**—The term "Indian tribe" has the meaning given such term by section 45A(c)(6).

(2) **Tribal organization.**—The term "tribal organization" has the meaning given such term by section 4(l) of the Indian Self-Determination and Education Assistance Act.

(3) **Medical care.**—The term "medical care" has the same meaning as when used in section 213.

(4) **Accident or health insurance; accident or health plans.**—The terms "accident or health insurance" and "accident or health plan" have the same meaning as when used in section 105.

(5) **Dependent.**—The term "dependent" has the meaning given such term by section 152, determined without regard to subsections (b)(1), (b)(2), and (d)(1)(B) thereof.

(d) Denial of Double Benefit.—Subsection (a) shall not apply to the amount of any qualified Indian health care benefit which is not includible in gross income of the beneficiary of such benefit under any other provision of this chapter, or to the amount of any such benefit for which a deduction is allowed to such beneficiary under any other provision of this chapter.

Amendments to IRC §139D

Patient Protection and Affordable Care Act, 2010 (Pub. L. No. 111-148), as follows:

• IRC §139D was added by Act §9021(a). Eff. Mar. 23, 2010.

• **Other Provision.** Act §9021(d) provides:

(d) No Inference.—Nothing in the amendments made by this section shall be construed to create an inference with respect to the exclusion from gross income of—

(1) benefits provided by an Indian tribe or tribal organization that are not within the scope of this section, and

IRC Sec. 139D(d)

(2) benefits provided prior to the date of the enactment of this Act.

Editor's Note

IRC §139D[E], below, added by Pub. L. No. 111-148, §10108, to be effective for vouchers provided after December 31, 2013, was repealed by Pub. L. No. 112-10.

SEC. 139D[E]. FREE CHOICE VOUCHERS. [Repealed.]

Gross income shall not include the amount of any free choice voucher provided by an employer under section 10108 of the Patient Protection and Affordable Care Act to the extent that the amount of such voucher does not exceed the amount paid for a qualified health plan (as defined in section 1301 of such Act) by the taxpayer.

Amendments to IRC §139D[E] [Repealed.]

Department of Defense and Full-Year Continuing Appropriations Act, 2011 (Pub. L. No. 112-10), as follows:
• IRC §139D[E] was repealed by Act §1858(b)(2)(A). Eff. as if included in the provisions of, and the amendments made by, the Patient Protection and Affordable Care Act [Pub. L. No. 111-148] to which they relate.
Patient Protection and Affordable Care Act, 2010 (Pub. L. No. 111-148), as follows:
• IRC §139D was added by Act §10108(f)(1). Eff. for vouchers provided after Dec. 31, 2013. Note: This section most likely was intended to be IRC §139E.

---

* * *

Part V—Deductions for Personal Exemptions
* * *

SEC. 152. DEPENDENT DEFINED.

(a) In General.—For purposes of this subtitle, the term "dependent" means—

(1) a qualifying child, or

(2) a qualifying relative.

(b) Exceptions.—For purposes of this section—

(1) Dependents ineligible.—If an individual is a dependent of a taxpayer for any taxable year of such taxpayer beginning in a calendar year, such individual shall be treated as having no dependents for any taxable year of such individual beginning in such calendar year.

(2) Married dependents.—An individual shall not be treated as a dependent of a taxpayer under subsection (a) if such individual has made a joint return with the individual's spouse under section 6013

for the taxable year beginning in the calendar year in which the taxable year of the taxpayer begins.

(3) Citizens or nationals of other countries.—

(A) In general.—The term "dependent" does not include an individual who is not a citizen or national of the United States unless such individual is a resident of the United States or a country contiguous to the United States.

(B) Exception for adopted child.—Subparagraph (A) shall not exclude any child of a taxpayer (within the meaning of subsection (f)(1)(B)) from the definition of "dependent" if—

(i) for the taxable year of the taxpayer, the child has the same principal place of abode as the taxpayer and is a member of the taxpayer's household, and

(ii) the taxpayer is a citizen or national of the United States.

(c) Qualifying Child.—For purposes of this section—

(1) In general.—The term "qualifying child" means, with respect to any taxpayer for any taxable year, an individual—

(A) who bears a relationship to the taxpayer described in paragraph (2),

(B) who has the same principal place of abode as the taxpayer for more than one-half of such taxable year,

(C) who meets the age requirements of paragraph (3),

(D) who has not provided over one-half of such individual's own support for the calendar year in which the taxable year of the taxpayer begins, and

(E) who has not filed a joint return (other than only for a claim of refund) with the individual's spouse under section 6013 for the taxable year beginning in the calendar year in which the taxable year of the taxpayer begins.

(2) Relationship.—For purposes of paragraph (1)(A), an individual bears a relationship to the taxpayer described in this paragraph if such individual is—

(A) a child of the taxpayer or a descendant of such a child, or

(B) a brother, sister, stepbrother, or stepsister of the taxpayer or a descendant of any such relative.

(3) Age requirements.—

(A) In general.—For purposes of paragraph (1)(C), an individual meets the requirements of this paragraph if such individual is younger than the taxpayer claiming such individual as a qualifying child and—

(i) has not attained the age of 19 as of the close of the calendar year in which the taxable year of the taxpayer begins, or

(ii) is a student who has not attained the age of 24 as of the close of such calendar year.

(B) Special rule for disabled.—In the case of an individual who is permanently and totally disabled (as defined in section 22(e)(3)) at any time during such calendar year, the requirements of subparagraph (A) shall be treated as met with respect to such individual.

(4) In general.— Special rule relating to 2 or more who can claim the same qualifying child.—

(A) Except as provided in subparagraphs (B) and (C), if (but for this paragraph) an individual may be claimed as a qualifying child by 2 or more taxpayers for a taxable year beginning in the same calendar year, such individual shall be treated as the qualifying child of the taxpayer who is—

(i) a parent of the individual, or

(ii) if clause (i) does not apply, the taxpayer with the highest adjusted gross income for such taxable year.

(B) More than 1 parent claiming qualifying child.—If the parents claiming any qualifying child do not file a joint return together, such child shall be treated as the qualifying child of—

(i) the parent with whom the child resided for the longest period of time during the taxable year, or

(ii) if the child resides with both parents for the same amount of time during such taxable year, the parent with the highest adjusted gross income.

(C) No parent claiming qualifying child.—If the parents of an individual may claim such individual as a qualifying child but no parent so claims the individual, such individual may be claimed as the qualifying child of another taxpayer but only if the adjusted gross income of such taxpayer is higher than the highest adjusted gross income of any parent of the individual.

(d) Qualifying Relative.—For purposes of this section—

(1) In general.—The term "qualifying relative" means, with respect to any taxpayer for any taxable year, an individual—

(A) who bears a relationship to the taxpayer described in paragraph (2),

(B) whose gross income for the calendar year in which such taxable year begins is less than the exemption amount (as defined in section 151(d)),

(C) with respect to whom the taxpayer provides over one-half of the individual's support for the

calendar year in which such taxable year begins, and

(D) who is not a qualifying child of such taxpayer or of any other taxpayer for any taxable year beginning in the calendar year in which such taxable year begins.

(2) Relationship.—For purposes of paragraph (1)(A), an individual bears a relationship to the taxpayer described in this paragraph if the individual is any of the following with respect to the taxpayer:

(A) A child or a descendant of a child.

(B) A brother, sister, stepbrother, or stepsister.

(C) The father or mother, or an ancestor of either.

(D) A stepfather or stepmother.

(E) A son or daughter of a brother or sister of the taxpayer.

(F) A brother or sister of the father or mother of the taxpayer.

(G) A son-in-law, daughter-in-law, father-in-law, mother-in-law, brother-in-law, or sister-in-law.

(H) An individual (other than an individual who at any time during the taxable year was the spouse, determined without regard to section 7703, of the taxpayer) who, for the taxable year of the taxpayer, has the same principal place of abode as the taxpayer and is a member of the taxpayer's household.

(3) Special rule relating to multiple support agreements.—For purposes of paragraph (1)(C), over one-half of the support of an individual for a calendar year shall be treated as received from the taxpayer if—

(A) no one person contributed over one-half of such support,

(B) over one-half of such support was received from 2 or more persons each of whom, but for the fact that any such person alone did not contribute over one-half of such support, would have been entitled to claim such individual as a dependent for a taxable year beginning in such calendar year,

(C) the taxpayer contributed over 10 percent of such support, and

(D) each person described in subparagraph (B) (other than the taxpayer) who contributed over 10 percent of such support files a written declaration (in such manner and form as the Secretary may by regulations prescribe) that such person will not claim such individual as a dependent for any taxable year beginning in such calendar year.

(4) Special rule relating to income of handicapped dependents.—

(A) In general.—For purposes of paragraph (1)(B), the gross income of an individual who is permanently and totally disabled (as defined in section 22(e)(3)) at any time during the taxable year shall not include income attributable to services performed by the individual at a sheltered workshop if—

(i) the availability of medical care at such workshop is the principal reason for the individual's presence there, and

(ii) the income arises solely from activities at such workshop which are incident to such medical care.

(B) Sheltered workshop defined.—For purposes of subparagraph (A), the term "sheltered workshop" means a school—

(i) which provides special instruction or training designed to alleviate the disability of the individual, and

(ii) which is operated by an organization described in section 501(c)(3) and exempt from tax under section 501(a), or by a State, a possession of the United States, any political subdivision of any of the foregoing, the United States, or the District of Columbia.

(5) Special rules for support.—For purposes of this subsection—

(A) payments to a spouse which are includible in the gross income of such spouse under section 71 or 682 shall not be treated as a payment by the payor spouse for the support of any dependent, and

(B) in the case of the remarriage of a parent, support of a child received from the parent's spouse shall be treated as received from the parent.

(e) Special Rule for Divorced Parents, Etc.—

(1) In general.—Notwithstanding subsection (c)(1)(B), (c)(4), or (d)(1)(C), if—

(A) a child receives over one-half of the child's support during the calendar year from the child's parents—

(i) who are divorced or legally separated under a decree of divorce or separate maintenance,

(ii) who are separated under a written separation agreement, or

(iii) who live apart at all times during the last 6 months of the calendar year, and—

(B) such child is in the custody of 1 or both of the child's parents for more than one-half of the calendar year, such child shall be treated as being the qualifying child or qualifying relative of the noncustodial parent for a calendar year if the requirements described in paragraph (2) or (3) are met.

(2) Exception where custodial parent releases claim to exemption for the year.—For purposes of paragraph (1), the requirements described in this

paragraph are met with respect to any calendar year if—

(A) the custodial parent signs a written declaration (in such manner and form as the Secretary may by regulations prescribe) that such custodial parent will not claim such child as a dependent for any taxable year beginning in such calendar year, and

(B) the noncustodial parent attaches such written declaration to the noncustodial parent's return for the taxable year beginning during such calendar year.

(3) Exception for certain pre-1985 instruments.—

(A) In general.—For purposes of paragraph (1), the requirements described in this paragraph are met with respect to any calendar year if—

(i) a qualified pre-1985 instrument between the parents applicable to the taxable year beginning in such calendar year provides that the noncustodial parent shall be entitled to any deduction allowable under section 151 for such child, and

(ii) the noncustodial parent provides at least $600 for the support of such child during such calendar year.

For purposes of this subparagraph, amounts expended for the support of a child or children shall be treated as received from the noncustodial parent to the extent that such parent provided amounts for such support.

(B) Qualified pre-1985 instrument.—For purposes of this paragraph, the term "qualified pre-1985 instrument" means any decree of divorce or separate maintenance or written agreement—

(i) which is executed before January 1, 1985,

(ii) which on such date contains the provision described in subparagraph (A)(i), and

(iii) which is not modified on or after such date in a modification which expressly provides that this paragraph shall not apply to such decree or agreement.

(4) Custodial parent and noncustodial parent.—For purposes of this subsection—

(A) Custodial parent.—The term "custodial parent" means the parent having custody for the greater portion of the calendar year.

(B) Noncustodial parent.—The term "noncustodial parent" means the parent who is not the custodial parent.

(5) Exception for multiple-support agreement.—This subsection shall not apply in any case where over one-half of the support of the child is treated as having been received from a taxpayer under the provision of subsection (d)(3).

(6) Special rule for support received from new spouse of parent.—For purposes of this subsection, in the case of the remarriage of a parent, support of a child received from the parent's spouse shall be treated as received from the parent.

(f) Other Definitions and Rules.—For purposes of this section—

(1) Child defined.—

(A) In general.—The term "child" means an individual who is—

(i) a son, daughter, stepson, or stepdaughter of the taxpayer, or

(ii) an eligible foster child of the taxpayer.

(B) Adopted child.—In determining whether any of the relationships specified in subparagraph (A)(i) or paragraph (4) exists, a legally adopted individual of the taxpayer, or an individual who is lawfully placed with the taxpayer for legal adoption by the taxpayer, shall be treated as a child of such individual by blood.

(C) Eligible foster child.—For purposes of subparagraph (A)(ii), the term "eligible foster child" means an individual who is placed with the taxpayer by an authorized placement agency or by judgment, decree, or other order of any court of competent jurisdiction.

(2) Student defined.—The term "student" means an individual who during each of 5 calendar months during the calendar year in which the taxable year of the taxpayer begins—

(A) is a full-time student at an educational organization described in section 170(b)(1)(A)(ii), or

(B) is pursuing a full-time course of institutional on-farm training under the supervision of an accredited agent of aneducational organization described in section 170(b)(1)(A)(ii) or of a State or political subdivision of a State.

(3) Determination of household status.—An individual shall not be treated as a member of the taxpayer's household if at any time during the taxable year of the taxpayer the relationship between such individual and the taxpayer is in violation of local law.

(4) Brother and sister.—The terms "brother" and "sister" include a brother or sister by the half blood.

(5) Special support test in case of students.—For purposes of subsections (c)(1)(D) and (d)(1)(C), in the case of an individual who is—

(A) a child of the taxpayer, and

(B) a student,

amounts received as scholarships for study at an educational organization described in section 170(b)(1)(A)(ii) shall not be taken into account.

(6) Treatment of missing children.—

(A) In general.—Solely for the purposes referred to in subparagraph (B), a child of the taxpayer—

(i) who is presumed by law enforcement authorities to have been kidnapped by someone who is not a member of the family of such child or the taxpayer, and

(ii) who had, for the taxable year in which the kidnapping occurred, the same principal place of abode as the taxpayer for more than one-half of the portion of such year before the date of the kidnapping,

shall be treated as meeting the requirement of subsection (c)(1)(B) with respect to a taxpayer for all taxable years ending during the period that the child is kidnapped.

(B) Purposes.—Subparagraph (A) shall apply solely for purposes of determining—

(i) the deduction under section 151(c),

(ii) the credit under section 24 (relating to child tax credit),

(iii) whether an individual is a surviving spouse or a head of a household (as such terms are defined in section 2), and

(iv) the earned income credit under section 32.

(C) Comparable treatment of certain qualifying relatives.—For purposes of this section, a child of the taxpayer—

(i) who is presumed by law enforcement authorities to have been kidnapped by someone who is not a member of the family of such child or the taxpayer, and

(ii) who was (without regard to this paragraph) a qualifying relative of the taxpayer for the portion of the taxable year before the date of the kidnapping,

shall be treated as a qualifying relative of the taxpayer for all taxable years ending during the period that the child is kidnapped.

(D) Termination of treatment.—Subparagraphs (A) and (C) shall cease to apply as of the first taxable year of the taxpayer beginning after the calendar year in which there is a determination that the child is dead (or, if earlier, in which the child would have attained age 18).

(7) Cross references.—For provision treating child as dependent of both parents for purposes of certain provisions, see sections 105(b), 132(h)(2)(B), and 213(d)(5).

Recent Amendments to IRC §152

Fostering Connections to Success and Increasing Adoptions Act of 2008 (Pub. L. No. 110-351), as follows:

IRC Sec. 152(f)(7)

- IRC §152(c)(1)(C)–(E) was amended by Act §501(b) by striking "and" at the end of subpara. (C), by substituting ", and" for the period at the end of subpara. (D), and by adding subpara. (E). Eff. for tax years beginning after Dec. 31, 2008.
- IRC §152(c)(3)(A) was amended by Act §501(a) by inserting "is younger than the taxpayer claiming such individual as a qualifying child and" after "such individual". Eff. for tax years beginning after Dec. 31, 2008.
- IRC §152(c)(4) was amended by Act §501(c)(2)(B)(ii) in the heading by substituting "who can caim the same" for "claiming". Eff. for tax years beginning after Dec. 31, 2008.
- IRC §152(c)(4)(A) was amended by Act §501(c)(2)(B)(i) by substituting "Except as provided in subparagraphs (B) and (C), if (but for this paragraph) an individual may be claimed as a qualifying child by 2 or more taxpayers" for "Except as provided in subparagraph (B), if (but for this paragraph) an individual may be and is claimed as a qualifying child by 2 or more taxpayers". Eff. for tax years beginning after Dec. 31, 2008.
- IRC §152(c)(4)(C) was added by Act §501(c)(2)(A). Eff. for tax years beginning after Dec. 31, 2008.

Gulf Opportunity Zone Act of 2005 (Pub. L. No. 109-135), as follows:

- IRC §152(e) was amended by Act §404(a). Eff. tax years beginning after Dec. 31, 2004, as if included in the provision of Pub. L. No. 108-311 to which it relates. IRC §152(e) prior to amendment [*Ed. Note:* the version below never took effect]:

 (e) Special Rule for Divorced Parents.—

 (1) In General.—Notwithstanding subsection (c)(1)(B), (c)(4), or (d)(1)(C), if—

 (A) a child receives over one-half of the child's support during the calendar year from the child's parents—

 (i) who are divorced or legally separated under a decree of divorce or separate maintenance,

 (ii) who are separated under a written separation agreement, or

 (iii) who live apart at all times during the last 6 months of the calendar year, and

 (B) such child is in the custody of 1 or both of the child's parents for more than one-half of the calendar year, such child shall be treated as being the qualifying child or qualifying relative of the noncustodial parent for a calendar year if the requirements described in paragraph (2) are met.

 (2) Requirements.—For purposes of paragraph (1), the requirements described in this paragraph are met if—

 (A) a decree of divorce or separate maintenance or written separation agreement between the parents applicable to the taxable year beginning in such calendar year provides that—

 (i) the noncustodial parent shall be entitled to any deduction allowable under section 151 for such child, or

 (ii) the custodial parent will sign a written declaration (in such manner and form as the Secretary may prescribe) that such parent will not claim such child as a dependent for such taxable year, or

 (B) in the case of such an agreement executed before January 1, 1985, the noncustodial parent provides at least $600 for the support of such child during such calendar year.

 For purposes of subparagraph (B), amounts expended for the support of a child or children shall be treated as received from the noncustodial parent to the extent that such parent provided amounts for such support.

 (3) Custodial parent and noncustodial parent.—For purposes of this subsection—

 (A) Custodial parent.—The term "custodial parent" means the parent with whom a child shared the same principal place of abode for the greater portion of the calendar year.

 (B) Noncustodial parent.—The term "noncustodial parent" means the parent who is not the custodial parent.

 (4) Exception for multiple-support agreements.—This subsection shall not apply in any case where over one-half of the support of the child is treated as having been received from a taxpayer under the provision of subsection (d)(3).

Working Families Tax Relief Act of 2004 (Pub. L. No. 108-311), as follows:

- IRC §152 was amended by Act §201. Eff. for tax years beginning after Dec. 31, 2004. IRC §152 prior to amendment:

SEC. 152. DEPENDENT DEFINED.

(a) General definition.—For purposes of this subtitle, the term "dependent" means any of the following individuals over half of whose support, for the calendar year in which the taxable year of the taxpayer begins, was received from the taxpayer (or is treated under subsection (c) or (e) as received from the taxpayer):

(1) A son or daughter of the taxpayer, or a descendant of either,

(2) A stepson or stepdaughter of the taxpayer,

(3) A brother, sister, stepbrother, or stepsister of the taxpayer,

(4) The father or mother of the taxpayer, or an ancestor of either,

(5) A stepfather or stepmother of the taxpayer,

(6) A son or daughter of a brother or sister of the taxpayer,

(7) A brother or sister of the father or mother of the taxpayer,

(8) A son-in-law, daughter-in-law, father-in-law, mother-in-law, brother-in-law, or sister-in-law of the taxpayer, or

(9) An individual (other than an individual who at any time during the taxable year was the spouse, determined without regard to §7703, of the taxpayer) who, for the taxable year of the taxpayer, has as his principal place of abode the home of the taxpayer and is a member of the taxpayer's household.

(b) Rules relating to general definition.—For purposes of this section—

(1) The terms "brother" and "sister" include a brother or sister by the halfblood.

(2) In determining whether any of the relationships specified in subsection (a) or paragraph (1) of this subsection exists, a legally adopted child of an individual (and a child who is a member of an individual's household, if placed with such individual by an authorized placement agency for legal adoption by such individual), or a foster child of an individual (if such child satisfies the requirements of subsection (a)(9) with respect to such individual), shall be treated as a child of such individual by blood.

(3) The term "dependent" does not include any individual who is not a citizen or national of the United States unless such individual is a resident of the United States or of a country contiguous to the United States. The preceding sentence shall not exclude from the definition of "dependent" any child of the taxpayer legally adopted by him, if, for the taxable year of the taxpayer, the child has as his principal place of abode the home of the taxpayer and is a member of the taxpayer's household, and if the taxpayer is a citizen or national of the United States.

(4) A payment to a wife which is includible in the gross income of the wife under §71 or 682 shall not be treated as a payment by her husband for the support of any dependent.

(5) An individual is not a member of the taxpayer's household if at any time during the taxable year of the taxpayer the relationship between such individual and the taxpayer is in violation of local law.

(c) Multiple support agreements.—For purposes of subsection (a), over half of the support of an individual for a calendar year shall be treated as received from the taxpayer if—

(1) no one person contributed over half of such support;

(2) over half of such support was received from persons each of whom, but for the fact that he did not contribute over half of such support, would have been entitled to claim such individual as a dependent for a taxable year beginning in such calendar year;

(3) the taxpayer contributed over 10 percent of such support; and

(4) each person described in paragraph (2) (other than the taxpayer) who contributed over 10 percent of such support files a written declaration (in such manner and form as the Secretary may by regulations prescribe) that he will not claim such individual as a dependent for any taxable year beginning in such calendar year.

(d) Special support test in case of students.—For purposes of subsection (a), in the case of any individual who is—

(1) a son, stepson, daughter, or stepdaughter of the taxpayer (within the meaning of this section), and

(2) a student (within the meaning of §151(c)(4)), amounts received as scholarships for study at an educational organiza-

tion described in §170(b)(1)(A)(ii) shall not be taken into account in determining whether such individual received more than half of his support from the taxpayer.

(e) Support test in case of child of divorced parents, etc.—

(1) Custodial parent gets exemption.—

Except as otherwise provided in this subsection, if—

(A) a child (as defined in §151(c)(3)) receives over half of his support during the calendar year from his parents—

(i) who are divorced or legally separated under a decree of divorce or separate maintenance,

(ii) who are separated under a written separation agreement, or

(iii) who live apart at all times during the last 6 months of the calendar year, and

(B) such child is in the custody of one or both of his parents for more than one-half of the calendar year, such child shall be treated, for purposes of subsection (a), as receiving over half of his support during the calendar year from the parent having custody for a greater portion of the calendar year (hereinafter in this subsection referred to as the "custodial parent").

(2) Exception where custodial parent releases claim to exemption for the year.—A child of parents described in paragraph (1) shall be treated as having received over half of his support during a calendar year from the noncustodial parent if—

(A) the custodial parent signs a written declaration (in such manner and form as the Secretary may by regulations prescribe) that such custodial parent will not claim such child as a dependent for any taxable year beginning in such calendar year, and

(B) the noncustodial parent attaches such written declaration to the noncustodial parent's return for the taxable year beginning during such calendar year.

For purposes of this subsection, the term "noncustodial parent" means the parent who is not the custodial parent.

(3) Exception for multiple-support agreement.—This subsection shall not apply in any case where over half of the support of the child is treated as having been received from a taxpayer under the provisions of subsection (c).

(4) Exception for certain pre-1985 instruments.—

(A) In general.—A child of parents described in paragraph (1) shall be treated as having received over half his support during a calendar year from the noncustodial parent if—

(i) a qualified pre-1985 instrument between the parents applicable to the taxable year beginning in such calendar year provides that the noncustodial parent shall be entitled to any deduction allowable under section 151 for such child, and

(ii) the noncustodial parent provides at least $600 for the support of such child during such calendar year.

For purposes of this subparagraph, amounts expended for the support of a child or children shall be treated as received from the noncustodial parent to the extent that such parent provided amounts for such support.

(B) Qualified pre-1985 instrument.—For purposes of this paragraph, the term "qualified pre-1985 instrument" means any decree of divorce or separate maintenance or written agreement—

(i) which is executed before January 1, 1985,

(ii) which on such date contains the provision described in subparagraph (A)(i), and

(iii) which is not modified on or after such date in a modification which expressly provides that this paragraph shall not apply to such decree or agreement.

(5) Special rule for support received from new spouse of parent.—For purposes of this subsection, in the case of the remarriage of a parent, support of a child received from the parent's spouse shall be treated as received from the parent.

(6) Cross reference.—For provision treating child as dependent of both parents for purposes of medical expense deduction, see §213(d)(5).

* * *

Part VI—Itemized Deductions for Individuals and Corporations

* * *

SEC. 162. TRADE OR BUSINESS EXPENSES.

Editor's Note

The last sentence of IRC §162(a), below, was added by Pub. L. No. 111-148, §10108, to be effective for vouchers provided after December 31, 2013, and was stricken by Pub. L. No. 112-10.

(a) In General.—There shall be allowed as a deduction all the ordinary and necessary expenses paid or incurred during the taxable year in carrying on any trade or business, including—

(1) a reasonable allowance for salaries or other compensation for personal services actually rendered;

(2) traveling expenses (including amounts expended for meals and lodging other than amounts which are lavish or extravagant under the circumstances) while away from home in the pursuit of a trade or business; and

(3) rentals or other payments required to be made as a condition to the continued use or possession, for purposes of the trade or business, of property to which the taxpayer has not taken or is not taking title or in which he has no equity.

For purposes of the preceding sentence, the place of residence of a Member of Congress (including any Delegate and Resident Commissioner) within the State, congressional district, or possession which he represents in Congress shall be considered his home, but amounts expended by such Members within each taxable year for living expenses shall not be deductible for income tax purposes in excess of $3,000. For purposes of paragraph (2), the taxpayer shall not be treated as being temporarily away from home during any period of employment if such period exceeds 1 year. The preceding sentence shall not apply to any Federal employee during any period for which such employee is certified by the Attorney General (or the designee thereof) as traveling on behalf of the United States in temporary duty status to investigate or prosecute, or provide support services for the investigation or prosecution of, a Federal crime. ~~For purposes of paragraph (1), the amount of a free choice voucher provided under section 10108 of the Patient Protection and Affordable Care Act shall be treated as an amount for compensation for personal services actually rendered.~~

* * *

(h) State Legislators' Travel Expenses Away From Home.—

(1) In general.—For purposes of subsection (a), in the case of any individual who is a State legislator at any time during the taxable year and who makes an election under this subsection for the taxable year—

(A) the place of residence of such individual within the legislative district which he represented shall be considered his home,

(B) he shall be deemed to have expended for living expenses (in connection with his trade or business as a legislator) an amount equal to the sum of the amounts determined by multiplying each legislative day of such individual during the taxable year by the greater of—

(i) the amount generally allowable with respect to such day to employees of the State of which he is a legislator for per diem while away from home, to the extent such amount does not exceed 110 percent of the amount described in clause (ii) with respect to such day, or

(ii) the amount generally allowable with respect to such day to employees of the executive branch of the Federal Government for per diem while away from home but serving in the United States, and

(C) he shall be deemed to be away from home in the pursuit of a trade or business on each legislative day.

(2) Legislative days.—For purposes of paragraph (1), a legislative day during any taxable year for any individual shall be any day during such year on which—

(A) the legislature was in session (including any day in which the legislature was not in session for a period of 4 consecutive days or less), or

(B) the legislature was not in session but the physical presence of the individual was formally recorded at a meeting of a committee of such legislature.

(3) Election.—An election under this subsection for any taxable year shall be made at such time and in such manner as the Secretary shall by regulations prescribe.

(4) Section not to apply to legislators who reside near capitol.—For taxable years beginning after December 31, 1980, this subsection shall not apply to any legislator whose place of residence within the legislative district which he represents is 50 or fewer miles from the capitol building of the State.

(i) [Repealed.]

* * *

(*l*) Special Rules for Health Insurance Costs of Self-Employed Individuals.—

Editor's Note

IRC §162(*l*)(1), below, as amended by Pub. L. No. 111-152, §1004, is effective on the date of enactment of the Act (enacted: March 30, 2010).

---

(1) Allowance of deduction.—

In the case of a taxpayer who is an employee within the meaning of section 401(c)(1), there shall be allowed as a deduction under this section an amount equal to the amount paid during the taxable year for insurance which constitutes medical care for—

(A) the taxpayer,

(B) the taxpayer's spouse,

(C) the taxpayer's dependents, and

(D) any child (as defined in section 152(f)(1)) of the taxpayer who as of the end of the taxable year has not attained age 27.

(2) Limitations.—

(A) Dollar amount.—No deduction shall be allowed under paragraph (1) to the extent that the amount of such deduction exceeds the taxpayer's earned income (within the meaning of section 401(c) derived by the taxpayer from the trade or business with respect to which the plan providing the medical care coverage is established).

Editor's Note

IRC §162(l)(2)(B), below, as amended by Pub. L. No. 111-152, §1004, is effective on the date of enactment of the Act (enacted: March 30, 2010).

(B) Other coverage.—Paragraph (1) shall not apply to any taxpayer for any calendar month for which the taxpayer is eligible to participate in any subsidized health plan maintained by any employer of the taxpayer or of the spouse of, or any dependent, or individual described in subparagraph (D) of paragraph (1) with respect to, the taxpayer. The preceding sentence shall be applied separately with respect to—

(i) plans which include coverage for qualified long-term care services (as defined in section 7702B(c)) or are qualified long-term care insurance contracts (as defined in section 7702B(b)), and

(ii) plans which do not include such coverage and are not such contracts.

(C) Long-term care premiums.—In the case of a qualified long-term care insurance contract (as defined in section 7702B(b)), only eligible long-term care premiums (as defined in section 213(d)(10)) shall be taken into account under paragraph (1).

(3) Coordination with medical deduction.— Any amount paid by a taxpayer for insurance to which paragraph (1) applies shall not be taken into account in computing the amount allowable to the taxpayer as a deduction under section 213(a).

Editor's Note

IRC §162(*l*)(4), below, was amended by Pub. L. No. 111-240, applicable to taxable years beginning after December 31, 2009.

---

(4) Deduction not allowed for self-employment tax purposes.—The deduction allowable by reason of this subsection shall not be taken into account in determining an individual's net earnings from self-employment (within the meaning of section 1402(a)) for purposes of chapter 2 *for taxable years beginning before January 1, 2010, or after December 31, 2010.*

(5) Treatment of certain S corporation shareholders.—This subsection shall apply in the case of any individual treated as a partner under section 1372(a), except that—

(A) for purposes of this subsection, such individual's wages (as defined in section 3121) from the S corporation shall be treated as such individual's earned income (within the meaning of section 401(c)(1)), and

(B) there shall be such adjustments in the application of this subsection as the Secretary may by regulations prescribe.

(m) Certain Excessive Employee Remuneration.—

(1) In general.—In the case of any publicly held corporation, no deduction shall be allowed under this chapter for applicable employee remuneration with respect to any covered employee to the extent that the amount of such remuneration for the taxable year with respect to such employee exceeds $1,000,000.

(2) Publicly held corporation.—For purposes of this subsection, the term "publicly held corporation" means any corporation issuing any class of common equity securities required to be registered under section 12 of the Securities Exchange Act of 1934.

(3) Covered employee.—For purposes of this subsection, the term "covered employee" means any employee of the taxpayer if—

(A) as of the close of the taxable year, such employee is the chief executive officer of the taxpayer or is an individual acting in such a capacity, or

(B) the total compensation of such employee for the taxable year is required to be reported to shareholders under the Securities Exchange Act of 1934 by reason of such employee being among the 4 highest compensated officers for the taxable year (other than the chief executive officer).

(4) Applicable employee remuneration.—For purposes of this subsection—

(A) In general.—Except as otherwise provided in this paragraph, the term "applicable employee remuneration" means, with respect to any covered employee for any taxable year, the aggregate amount allowable as a deduction under this chapter for such taxable year (determined without regard to this subsection) for remuneration for services performed by such employee (whether or not during the taxable year).

(B) Exception for remuneration payable on commission basis.—The term "applicable employee remuneration" shall not include any remuneration payable on a commission basis solely on account of income generated directly by the individual performance of the individual to whom such remuneration is payable.

(C) Other performance-based compensation.— The term "applicable employee remuneration" shall not include any remuneration payable solely on account of the attainment of one or more performance goals, but only if—

(i) the performance goals are determined by a compensation committee of the board of directors of the taxpayer which is comprised solely of 2 or more outside directors,

(ii) the material terms under which the remuneration is to be paid, including the performance goals, are disclosed to shareholders and approved by a majority of the vote in a separate shareholder vote before the payment of such remuneration, and

(iii) before any payment of such remuneration, the compensation committee referred to in clause (i) certifies that the performance goals and any other material terms were in fact satisfied.

(D) Exception for existing binding contracts.— The term "applicable employee remuneration" shall not include any remuneration payable under a written binding contract which was in effect on February 17, 1993, and which was not modified thereafter in any material respect before such remuneration is paid.

(E) Remuneration.—For purposes of this paragraph, the term "remuneration" includes any remuneration (including benefits) in any medium other than cash, but shall not include—

(i) any payment referred to in so much of section 3121(a)(5) as precedes subparagraph (E) thereof, and

(ii) any benefit provided to or on behalf of an employee if at the time such benefit is provided it

IRC Sec. 162(m)(4)(E)(ii)

is reasonable to believe that the employee will be able to exclude such benefit from gross income under this chapter.

For purposes of clause (i), section 3121(a)(5) shall be applied without regard to section 3121(v)(1).

(F) Coordination with disallowed golden parachute payments.—The dollar limitation contained in paragraph (1) shall be reduced (but not below zero) by the amount (if any) which would have been included in the applicable employee remuneration of the covered employee for the taxable year but for being disallowed under section 280G.

(G) Coordination with excise tax on specified stock compensation.—The dollar limitation contained in paragraph (1) with respect to any covered employee shall be reduced (but not below zero) by the amount of any payment (with respect to such employee) of the tax imposed by section 4985 directly or indirectly by the expatriated corporation (as defined in such section) or by any member of the expanded affiliated group (as defined in such section) which includes such corporation.

(5) Special rule for application to employers participating in the troubled assets relief program.—

(A) In general.—In the case of an applicable employer, no deduction shall be allowed under this chapter—

(i) in the case of executive remuneration for any applicable taxable year which is attributable to services performed by a covered executive during such applicable taxable year, to the extent that the amount of such remuneration exceeds $500,000, or

(ii) in the case of deferred deduction executive remuneration for any taxable year for services performed during any applicable taxable year by a covered executive, to the extent that the amount of such remuneration exceeds $500,000 reduced (but not below zero) by the sum of—

(I) the executive remuneration for such applicable taxable year, plus

(II) the portion of the deferred deduction executive remuneration for such services which was taken into account under this clause in a preceding taxable year.

(B) Applicable employer.—For purposes of this paragraph—

(i) In general.—Except as provided in clause (ii), the term "applicable employer" means any employer from whom 1 or more troubled assets are acquired under a program established by the Secretary under section 101(a) of the Emergency Economic Stabilization Act of 2008 if the aggregate amount of the assets so acquired for all taxable years exceeds $300,000,000.

(ii) Disregard of certain assets sold through direct purchase.—If the only sales of troubled assets by an employer under the program described in clause (i) are through 1 or more direct purchases (within the meaning of section 113(c) of the Emergency Economic Stabilization Act of 2008), such assets shall not be taken into account under clause (i) in determining whether the employer is an applicable employer for purposes of this paragraph.

(iii) Aggregation rules.—Two or more persons who are treated as a single employer under subsection (b) or (c) of section 414 shall be treated as a single employer, except that in applying section 1563(a) for purposes of either such subsection, paragraphs (2) and (3) thereof shall be disregarded.

(C) Applicable taxable year.—For purposes of this paragraph, the term "applicable taxable year" means, with respect to any employer—

(i) the first taxable year of the employer—

(I) which includes any portion of the period during which the authorities under section 101(a) of the Emergency Economic Stabilization Act of 2008 are in effect (determined under section 120 thereof), and

(II) in which the aggregate amount of troubled assets acquired from the employer during the taxable year pursuant to such authorities (other than assets to which subparagraph (B)(ii) applies), when added to the aggregate amount so acquired for all preceding taxable years, exceeds $300,000,000, and

(ii) any subsequent taxable year which includes any portion of such period.

(D) Covered executive.—For purposes of this paragraph—

(i) In general.—The term "covered executive" means, with respect to any applicable taxable year, any employee—

(I) who, at any time during the portion of the taxable year during which the authorities under section 101(a) of the Emergency Economic Stabilization Act of 2008 are in effect (determined under section 120 thereof), is the chief executive officer of the applicable employer or the chief financial officer of the applicable employer, or an individual acting in either such capacity, or

(II) who is described in clause (ii).

(ii) Highest compensated employees.—An employee is described in this clause if the employee is 1 of the 3 highest compensated officers of the applicable employer for the taxable year (other than an individual described in clause (i)(I)), determined—

(I) on the basis of the shareholder disclosure rules for compensation under the Securities Exchange Act of 1934 (without regard to whether those rules apply to the employer), and

(II) by only taking into account employees employed during the portion of the taxable year described in clause (i)(I).

(iii) Employee remains covered executive.—If an employee is a covered executive with respect to an applicable employer for any applicable taxable year, such employee shall be treated as a covered executive with respect to such employer for all subsequent applicable taxable years and for all subsequent taxable years in which deferred deduction executive remuneration with respect to services performed in all such applicable taxable years would (but for this paragraph) be deductible.

(E) Executive remuneration.—For purposes of this paragraph, the term "executive remuneration" means the applicable employee remuneration of the covered executive, as determined under paragraph (4) without regard to subparagraphs (B), (C), and (D) thereof. Such term shall not include any deferred deduction executive remuneration with respect to services performed in a prior applicable taxable year.

(F) Deferred deduction executive remuneration.—For purposes of this paragraph, the term "deferred deduction executive remuneration" means remuneration which would be executive remuneration for services performed in an applicable taxable year but for the fact that the deduction under this chapter (determined without regard to this paragraph) for such remuneration is allowable in a subsequent taxable year.

(G) Coordination.—Rules similar to the rules of subparagraphs (F) and (G) of paragraph (4) shall apply for purposes of this paragraph.

(H) Regulatory authority.—The Secretary may prescribe such guidance, rules, or regulations as are necessary to carry out the purposes of this paragraph and the Emergency Economic Stabilization Act of 2008, including the extent to which this paragraph applies in the case of any acquisition, merger, or reorganization of an applicable employer.

Editor's Note

IRC §162(m)(6), below, added by Pub. L. No. 111-148, §9014, is effective for taxable years beginning after December 31, 2009, with respect to services performed after such date.

---

(6) Special rule for application to certain health insurance providers.—

(A) In general.—No deduction shall be allowed under this chapter—

(i) in the case of applicable individual remuneration which is for any disqualified taxable year beginning after December 31, 2012, and which is attributable to services performed by an applicable individual during such taxable year, to the extent that the amount of such remuneration exceeds $500,000, or

(ii) in the case of deferred deduction remuneration for any taxable year beginning after December 31, 2012, which is attributable to services performed by an applicable individual during any disqualified taxable year beginning after December 31, 2009, to the extent that the amount of such remuneration exceeds $500,000 reduced (but not below zero) by the sum of—

(I) the applicable individual remuneration for such disqualified taxable year, plus

(II) the portion of the deferred deduction remuneration for such services which was taken into account under this clause in a preceding taxable year (or which would have been taken into account under this clause in a preceding taxable year if this clause were applied by substituting "December 31, 2009" for "December 31, 2012" in the matter preceding subclause (I)).

(B) Disqualified taxable year.—For purposes of this paragraph, the term "disqualified taxable year" means, with respect to any employer, any taxable year for which such employer is a covered health insurance provider.

(C) Covered health insurance provider.—For purposes of this paragraph—

(i) In general.—The term "covered health insurance provider" means—

(I) with respect to taxable years beginning after December 31, 2009, and before January 1, 2013, any employer which is a health insurance issuer (as defined in section 9832(b)(2)) and which receives premiums from providing health insurance coverage (as defined in section 9832(b)(1)), and

(II) with respect to taxable years beginning after December 31, 2012, any employer which is a health insurance issuer (as defined in section 9832(b)(2)) and with respect to which not less than 25 percent of the gross premiums received from providing health insurance coverage (as defined in section 9832(b)(1)) is from minimum essential coverage (as defined in section 5000A(f)).

(ii) Aggregation rules.—Two or more persons who are treated as a single employer under subsection (b), (c), (m), or (o) of section 414 shall be treated as a single employer, except that in applying section 1563(a) for purposes of any such subsection, paragraphs (2) and (3) thereof shall be disregarded.

(D) Applicable individual remuneration.—For purposes of this paragraph, the term "applicable individual remuneration" means, with respect to any applicable individual for any disqualified taxable year, the aggregate amount allowable as a deduction under this chapter for such taxable year (determined without regard to this subsection) for remuneration (as defined in paragraph (4) without regard to subparagraphs (B), (C), and (D) thereof) for services performed by such individual (whether or not during the taxable year). Such term shall not include any deferred deduction remuneration with respect to services performed during the disqualified taxable year.

(E) Deferred deduction remuneration.—For purposes of this paragraph, the term "deferred deduction remuneration" means remuneration which would be applicable individual remuneration for services performed in a disqualified taxable year but for the fact that the deduction under this chapter (determined without regard to this paragraph) for such remuneration is allowable in a subsequent taxable year.

(F) Applicable individual.—For purposes of this paragraph, the term "applicable individual" means, with respect to any covered health insurance provider for any disqualified taxable year, any individual—

(i) who is an officer, director, or employee in such taxable year, or

(ii) who provides services for or on behalf of such covered health insurance provider during such taxable year.

(G) Coordination.—Rules similar to the rules of subparagraphs (F) and (G) of paragraph (4) shall apply for purposes of this paragraph.

(H) Regulatory authority.—The Secretary may prescribe such guidance, rules, or regulations as are necessary to carry out the purposes of this paragraph.

Editor's Note

Caution: IRC §162(n), as follows, applied to services provided after February 2, 1993, and on or before December 31, 1995. IRC §162(n) was added by Pub. L. No. 103-66, §13442(a), and extended by Pub. L. No. 104-7, §5.

(n) Special Rule for Certain Group Health Plans.—

(1) In general.—No deduction shall be allowed under this chapter to an employer for any amount paid or incurred in connection with a group health plan if the plan does not reimburse for inpatient hospital care services provided in the State of New York—

(A) except as provided in subparagraphs (B) and (C), at the same rate as licensed commercial insur-

ers are required to reimburse hospitals for such services when such reimbursement is not through such a plan,

(B) in the case of any reimbursement through a health maintenance organization, at the same rate as health maintenance organizations are required to reimburse hospitals for such services for individuals not covered by such a plan (determined without regard to any government-supported individuals exempt from such rate), or

(C) in the case of any reimbursement through any corporation organized under Article 43 of the New York State Insurance Law, at the same rate as any such corporation is required to reimburse hospitals for such services for individuals not covered by such a plan.

(2) State law exception.—Paragraph (1) shall not apply to any group health plan which is not required under the laws of the State of New York (determined without regard to this subsection or other provisions of Federal law) to reimburse at the rates provided in paragraph (1).

(3) Group health plan.—For purposes of this subsection, the term "group health plan" means a plan of, or contributed to by, an employer or employee organization (including a self-insured plan) to provide health care (directly or otherwise) to any employee, any former employee, the employer, or any other individual associated or formerly associated with the employer in a business relationship, or any member of their family.

* * *

(p) Treatment of Expenses of Members of Reserve Component of Armed Forces of the United States.—For purposes of subsection (a)(2), in the case of an individual who performs services as a member of a reserve component of the Armed Forces of the United States at any time during the taxable year, such individual shall be deemed to be away from home in the pursuit of a trade or business for any period during which such individual is away from home in connection with such service.

Recent Amendments to IRC §162 (As Excerpted)

Small Business Jobs Act of 2010 (Pub. L. No. 111-240), as follows:
- IRC §162(*l*)(4) was amended by Act §2042(a) by inserting "for taxable years beginning before January 1, 2010, or after December 31, 2010" before the period. Eff. for taxable years beginning after Dec. 31, 2009.

Health Care and Education Reconciliation Act of 2010 (Pub. L. No. 111-152), as follows:
- IRC §162(*l*)(1) was amended by Act §1004(d)(2). Eff. on date of enactment of this Act [enacted: Mar. 30, 2010]. IRC §162(*l*)(1) prior to amendment:
    (1) Allowance of deduction.—
    (A) In general.—In the case of an individual who is an employee within the meaning of section 401(c)(1), there shall be allowed as a deduction under this section an amount equal

to the applicable percentage of the amount paid during the taxable year for insurance which constitutes medical care for the taxpayer, his spouse, and dependents.

(B) Applicable percentage.—For purposes of subparagraph (A), the applicable percentage shall be determined under the following table:

For taxable years beginning in calendar year—	The applicable percentage is—
1999 through 2001	60
2002	70
2003 and thereafter	100

• IRC §162(*l*)(2)(B) was amended by Act §1004(d)(3) by inserting ", or any dependent, or individual described in subparagraph (D) of paragraph (1) with respect to," after "spouse of". Eff. on date of enactment of this Act [enacted: Mar. 30, 2010].

Patient Protection and Affordable Care Act, 2010 (Pub. L. No. 111-148), as follows:
• IRC §162(a) was amended by Act §10108(g)(1) to add a new sentence at the end. Eff. for vouchers provided after Dec. 31, 2013.
• IRC §162(m)(6) was added by Act §9014(a). Eff. for taxable years beginning after Dec. 31, 2009, with respect to services performed after such date.

Emergency Economic Stabilization Act of 2008 (Pub. L. No. 110-343), as follows:
• IRC §162(m)(5) was added by Act, Div. A, §302(a). Eff. for tax years ending on or after date of enactment [enacted: Oct. 3, 2008].
• **Other Provision.** Act, Div. A, §111, as amended by Pub. L. No. 111-5, Div. B, §7001.
  SEC. 111. EXECUTIVE COMPENSATION AND COR-PORATE GOVERNANCE.
  (a) Definitions.—For purposes of this section, the following definitions shall apply:
  (1) Senior executive officer.—The term "senior executive Officer" means an individual who is 1 of the top 5 most highly paid executives of a public company, whose compensation is required to be disclosed pursuant to the Securities Exchange Act of 1934, and any regulations issued thereunder, and non-public company counterparts.
  (2) Golden parachute payment.—The term "golden parachute payment" means any payment to a senior executive officer for departure from a company for any reason, except for payments for services performed or benefits accrued.
  (3) TARP recipient.—The term "TARP recipient" means any entity that has received or will receive financial assistance under the financial assistance provided under the TARP.
  (4) Commission.—The term "Commission" means the Securities and Exchange Commission.
  (5) Period in which obligation is outstanding; rule of construction.—For purposes of this section, the period in which any obligation arising from financial assistance provided under the TARP remains outstanding does not include any period during which the Federal Government only holds warrants to purchase common stock of the TARP recipient.
  (b) Executive Compensation and Corporate Governance.—
  (1) Establishment of standards.—During the period in which any obligation arising from financial assistance provided under the TARP remains outstanding, each TARP recipient shall be subject to—
  (A) the standards established by the Secretary under this section; and
  (B) the provisions of section 162(m)(5) of the Internal Revenue Code of 1986, as applicable.
  (2) Standards required.—The Secretary shall require each TARP recipient to meet appropriate standards for executive compensation and corporate governance.
  (3) Specific requirements.—The standards established under paragraph (2) shall include the following:
  (A) Limits on compensation that exclude incentives for senior executive officers of the TARP recipient to take unnecessary

and excessive risks that threaten the value of such recipient during the period in which any obligation arising from financial assistance provided under the TARP remains outstanding.
(B) A provision for the recovery by such TARP recipient of any bonus, retention award, or incentive compensation paid to a senior executive officer and any of the next 20 most highly-compensated employees of the TARP recipient based on statements of earnings, revenues, gains, or other criteria that are later found to be materially inaccurate.
(C) A prohibition on such TARP recipient making any golden parachute payment to a senior executive officer or any of the next 5 most highly-compensated employees of the TARP recipient during the period in which any obligation arising from financial assistance provided under the TARP remains outstanding.
(D)(i) A prohibition on such TARP recipient paying or accruing any bonus, retention award, or incentive compensation during the period in which any obligation arising from financial assistance provided under the TARP remains outstanding, except that any prohibition developed under this paragraph shall not apply to the payment of long-term restricted stock by such TARP recipient, provided that such long-term restricted stock—
(I) does not fully vest during the period in which any obligation arising from financial assistance provided to that TARP recipient remains outstanding;
(II) has a value in an amount that is not greater than of the total amount of annual compensation of the employee receiving the stock; and
(III) is subject to such other terms and conditions as the Secretary may determine is in the public interest.
(ii) The prohibition required under clause (i) shall apply as follows:
(I) For any financial institution that received financial assistance provided under the TARP equal to less than $25,000,000, the prohibition shall apply only to the most highly compensated employee of the financial institution.
(II) For any financial institution that received financial assistance provided under the TARP equal to at least $25,000,000, but less than $250,000,000, the prohibition shall apply to at least the 5 most highly-compensated employees of the financial institution, or such higher number as the Secretary may determine is in the public interest with respect to any TARP recipient.
(III) For any financial institution that received financial assistance provided under the TARP equal to at least $250,000,000, but less than $500,000,000, the prohibition shall apply to the senior executive officers and at least the 10 next most highly-compensated employees, or such higher number as the Secretary may determine is in the public interest with respect to any TARP recipient.
(IV) For any financial institution that received financial assistance provided under the TARP equal to $500,000,000 or more, the prohibition shall apply to the senior executive officers and at least the 20 next most highly-compensated employees, or such higher number as the Secretary may determine is in the public interest with respect to any TARP recipient.
(iii) The prohibition required under clause (i) shall not be construed to prohibit any bonus payment required to be paid pursuant to a written employment contract executed on or

IRC Sec. 162(p)

before February 11, 2009, as such valid employment contracts are determined by the Secretary or the designee of the Secretary.

(E) A prohibition on any compensation plan that would encourage manipulation of the reported earnings of such TARP recipient to enhance the compensation of any of its employees.

(F) A requirement for the establishment of a Board Compensation Committee that meets the requirements of subsection (c).

(4) Certification of compliance.—The chief executive officer and chief financial officer (or the equivalents thereof) of each TARP recipient shall provide a written certification of compliance by the TARP recipient with the requirements of this section—

(A) in the case of a TARP recipient, the securities of which are publicly traded, to the Securities and Exchange Commission, together with annual filings required under the securities laws; and

(B) in the case of a TARP recipient that is not a publicly traded company, to the Secretary.

(c) **Board Compensation Committee.**—

(1) Establishment of board required.—Each TARP recipient shall establish a Board Compensation Committee, comprised entirely of independent directors, for the purpose of reviewing employee compensation plans.

(2) Meetings.—The Board Compensation Committee of each TARP recipient shall meet at least semiannually to discuss and evaluate employee compensation plans in light of an assessment of any risk posed to the TARP recipient from such plans.

(3) Compliance by non-SEC registrants.—In the case of any TARP recipient, the common or preferred stock of which is not registered pursuant to the Securities Exchange Act of 1934, and that has received $25,000,000 or less of TARP assistance, the duties of the Board Compensation Committee under this subsection shall be carried out by the board of directors of such TARP recipient.

(d) **Limitation on Luxury Expenditures.**—The board of directors of any TARP recipient shall have in place a company-wide policy regarding excessive or luxury expenditures, as identified by the Secretary, which may include excessive expenditures on—

(1) entertainment or events;

(2) office and facility renovations;

(3) aviation or other transportation services; or

(4) other activities or events that are not reasonable expenditures for staff development, reasonable performance incentives, or other similar measures conducted in the normal course of the business operations of the TARP recipient.

(e) **Shareholder Approval of Executive Compensation.**—

(1) Annual shareholder approval of executive compensation.—Any proxy or consent or authorization for an annual or other meeting of the shareholders of any TARP recipient during the period in which any obligation arising from financial assistance provided under the TARP remains outstanding shall permit a separate shareholder vote to approve the compensation of executives, as disclosed pursuant to the compensation disclosure rules of the Commission (which disclosure shall include the compensation discussion and analysis, the compensation tables, and any related material).

(2) Nonbinding vote.—A shareholder vote described in paragraph (1) shall not be binding on the board of directors of a TARP recipient, and may not be construed as overruling a decision by such board, nor to create or imply any additional fiduciary duty by such board, nor shall such vote be construed to restrict or limit the ability of shareholders to make proposals for inclusion in proxy materials related to executive compensation.

(3) Deadline for rulemaking.—Not later than 1 year after the date of enactment of the American Recovery and Reinvestment Act of 2009, the Commission shall issue any final rules and regulations required by this subsection.

(f) **Review of Prior Payments to Executives.**—

(1) In general.—The Secretary shall review bonuses, retention awards, and other compensation paid to the senior ex-

ecutive officers and the next 20 most highly-compensated employees of each entity receiving TARP assistance before the date of enactment of the American Recovery and Reinvestment Act of 2009, to determine whether any such payments were inconsistent with the purposes of this section or the TARP or were otherwise contrary to the public interest.

(2) Negotiations for reimbursement.—If the Secretary makes a determination described in paragraph (1), the Secretary shall seek to negotiate with the TARP recipient and the subject employee for appropriate reimbursements to the Federal Government with respect to compensation or bonuses.

(g) **No Impediment to Withdrawal by TARP Recipients.**—Subject to consultation with the appropriate Federal banking agency (as that term is defined in section 3 of the Federal Deposit Insurance Act), if any, the Secretary shall permit a TARP recipient to repay any assistance previously provided under the TARP to such financial institution, without regard to whether the financial institution has replaced such funds from any other source or to any waiting period, and when such assistance is repaid, the Secretary shall liquidate warrants associated with such assistance at the current market price.

(h) **Regulations.**—The Secretary shall promulgate regulations to implement this section.

American Jobs Creation Act of 2004 (Pub. L. No. 108-357), as follows:

● IRC §162(m)(4) was amended by Act §802(b)(2) by adding new subpara. (G) at the end. Eff. Mar. 4, 2003, except that periods before such date shall not be taken into account in applying the periods in IRC §4985(a) and (e)(1), as added by Act §802(a).

● IRC §162(o) was amended by Act §318(b) by striking "Reimbursed" in the heading. Eff. tax years beginning after Dec. 31, 2003.

● IRC §162(o) was amended by Act §318(a) by redesignating para. (2) as para. (3) and adding new para. (2). Eff. tax years beginning after Dec. 31, 2003.

Military Family Tax Relief Act of 2003 (Pub. L. No. 108-121), as follows:

● IRC §162 was amended by Act §109(a) by redesignating subsec. (p) as subsec. (q) and adding new subsec. (p). Eff. for amounts paid or incurred in tax years beginning after Dec. 31, 2002.

———

* * *

SEC. 194A. CONTRIBUTIONS TO EMPLOYER LIABILITY TRUSTS.

(a) **Allowance of Deduction**.—There shall be allowed as a deduction for the taxable year an amount equal to the amount—

(1) which is contributed by an employer to a trust described in section 501(c)(22) (relating to withdrawal liability payment fund) which meets the requirements of section 4223(h) of the Employee Retirement Income Security Act of 1974, and

(2) which is properly allocable to such taxable year.

(b) **Allocation to Taxable Year**.—In the case of a contribution described in subsection (a) which relates to any specified period of time which includes more than one taxable year, the amount properly allocable to any taxable year in such period shall be determined by prorating such amounts to such taxable years under regulations prescribed by the Secretary.

(c) **Disallowance of Deduction**.—No deduction shall be allowed under subsection (a) with respect to any contribution described in subsection (a) which does not relate to any specified period of time.

* * *

Part VII—Additional Itemized Deductions for Individuals

* * *

SEC. 213. MEDICAL, DENTAL, ETC., EXPENSES.

Editor's Note

Caution: IRC §213(a), as follows, is effective for taxable years beginning on or before December 31, 2012.

(a) Allowance of Deduction.—There shall be allowed as a deduction the expenses paid during the taxable year, not compensated for by insurance or otherwise, for medical care of the taxpayer, his spouse, or a dependent (as defined in section 152, determined without regard to subsections (b)(1), (b)(2), and (d)(1)(B) thereof), to the extent that such expenses exceed 10 percent of adjusted gross income.

Editor's Note

Caution: IRC §213(a), below, as amended by Pub. L. No. 111-148, §9013, is effective for taxable years beginning after December 31, 2012.

(a) Allowance of Deduction.—There shall be allowed as a deduction the expenses paid during the taxable year, not compensated for by insurance or otherwise, for medical care of the taxpayer, his spouse, or a dependent (as defined in section 152, determined without regard to subsections (b)(1), (b)(2), and (d)(1)(B) thereof), to the extent that such expenses exceed 10 percent of adjusted gross income.

(b) Limitation With Respect to Medicine and Drugs.—An amount paid during the taxable year for medicine or a drug shall be taken into account under subsection (a) only if such medicine or drug is a prescribed drug or is insulin.

(c) Special Rule for Decedents.—

(1) Treatment of expenses paid after death.—For purposes of subsection (a), expenses for the medical care of the taxpayer which are paid out of his estate during the 1-year period beginning with the day after the date of his death shall be treated as paid by the taxpayer at the time incurred.

(2) Limitation.—Paragraph (1) shall not apply if the amount paid is allowable under section 2053 as a deduction in computing the taxable estate of the decedent, but this paragraph shall not apply if (within the time and in the manner and form prescribed by the Secretary) there is filed—

(A) a statement that such amount has not been allowed as a deduction under section 2053, and

(B) a waiver of the right to have such amount allowed at any time as a deduction under section 2053.

(d) Definitions.—For purposes of this section—

(1) The term "medical care" means amounts paid—

(A) for the diagnosis, cure, mitigation, treatment, or prevention of disease, or for the purpose of affecting any structure or function of the body,

(B) for transportation primarily for and essential to medical care referred to in subparagraph (A),

(C) for qualified long-term care services (as defined in section 7702B(c)), or

(D) for insurance (including amounts paid as premiums under part B of title XVIII of the Social Security Act, relating to supplementary medical insurance for the aged) covering medical care referred to in subparagraphs (A) and (B) or for any qualified long-term care insurance contract (as defined in section 7702B(b)).

In the case of a qualified long-term care insurance contract (as defined in section 7702B(b)), only eligible long-term care premiums (as defined in paragraph (10)) shall be taken into account under subparagraph (D).

(2) Amounts paid for certain lodging away from home treated as paid for medical care.—Amounts paid for lodging (not lavish or extravagant under the circumstances) while away from home primarily for and essential to medical care referred to in paragraph (1)(A) shall be treated as amounts paid for medical care if—

(A) the medical care referred to in paragraph (1)(A) is provided by a physician in a licensed hospital (or in a medical care facility which is related to, or the equivalent of, a licensed hospital), and

(B) there is no significant element of personal pleasure, recreation, or vacation in the travel away from home. The amount taken into account under the preceding sentence shall not exceed $50 for each night for each individual.

(3) Prescribed drug.—The term "prescribed drug" means a drug or biological which requires a prescription of a physician for its use by an individual.

(4) Physician.—The term "physician" has the meaning given to such term by section 1861(r) of the Social Security Act (42 U.S.C. 1395x(r)).

(5) Special rule in the case of child of divorced parents, etc.—Any child to whom section 152(e) applies shall be treated as a dependent of both parents for purposes of this section.

IRC Sec. 213(d)(5)

(6) In the case of an insurance contract under which amounts are payable for other than medical care referred to in subparagraphs (A), (B), and (C) of paragraph (1)—

(A) no amount shall be treated as paid for insurance to which paragraph (1)(D) applies unless the charge for such insurance is either separately stated in the contract, or furnished to the policyholder by the insurance company in a separate statement,

(B) the amount taken into account as the amount paid for such insurance shall not exceed such charge, and

(C) no amount shall be treated as paid for such insurance if the amount specified in the contract (or furnished to the policyholder by the insurance company in a separate statement) as the charge for such insurance is unreasonably large in relation to the total charges under the contract.

(7) Subject to the limitations of paragraph (6), premiums paid during the taxable year by a taxpayer before he attains the age of 65 for insurance covering medical care (within the meaning of subparagraphs (A), (B), and (C) of paragraph (1)) for the taxpayer, his spouse, or a dependent after the taxpayer attains the age of 65 shall be treated as expenses paid during the taxable year for insurance which constitutes medical care if premiums for such insurance are payable (on a level payment basis) under the contract for a period of 10 years or more or until the year in which the taxpayer attains the age of 65 (but in no case for a period of less than 5 years).

(8) The determination of whether an individual is married at any time during the taxable year shall be made in accordance with the provisions of section 6013(d) (relating to determination of status as husband and wife).

(9) Cosmetic surgery.—

(A) In general.—The term "medical care" does not include cosmetic surgery or other similar procedures, unless the surgery or procedure is necessary to ameliorate a deformity arising from, or directly related to, a congenital abnormality, a personal injury resulting from an accident or trauma, or disfiguring disease.

(B) Cosmetic surgery defined.—For purposes of this paragraph, the term "cosmetic surgery" means any procedure which is directed at improving the patient's appearance and does not meaningfully promote the proper function of the body or prevent or treat illness or disease.

(10) Eligible long-term care premiums.—

(A) In general.—For purposes of this section, the term "eligible long-term care premiums" means the amount paid during a taxable year for any qualified long-term care insurance contract (as de-

fined in section 7702B(b)) covering an individual, to the extent such amount does not exceed the limitation determined under the following table:

In the case of an individual with an attained age before the close of the taxable year of:	The limitation is:
40 or less	$ 200
More than 40 but not more than 50	$ 375
More than 50 but not more than 60	$ 750
More than 60 but not more than 70.	$2,000
More than 70	$2,500

(B) Indexing.—

(i) In general.—In the case of any taxable year beginning in a calendar year after 1997, each dollar amount contained in subparagraph (A) shall be increased by the medical care cost adjustment of such amount for such calendar year. If any increase determined under the preceding sentence is not a multiple of $10, such increase shall be rounded to the nearest multiple of $10.

(ii) Medical care cost adjustment.—For purposes of clause (i), the medical care cost adjustment for any calendar year is the percentage (if any) by which—

(I) the medical care component of the Consumer Price Index (as defined in section 1(f)(5)) for August of the preceding calendar year, exceeds

(II) such component for August of 1996. The Secretary shall, in consultation with the Secretary of Health and Human Services, prescribe an adjustment which the Secretary determines is more appropriate for purposes of this paragraph than the adjustment described in the preceding sentence, and the adjustment so prescribed shall apply in lieu of the adjustment described in the preceding sentence.

(11) Certain payments to relatives treated as not paid for medical care.—An amount paid for a qualified long-term care service (as defined in section 7702B(c)) provided to an individual shall be treated as not paid for medical care if such service is provided—

(A) by the spouse of the individual or by a relative (directly or through a partnership, corporation, or other entity) unless the service is provided by a licensed professional with respect to such service, or

(B) by a corporation or partnership which is related (within the meaning of section 267(b) or 707(b)) to the individual.

IRC Sec. 213(d)(6)

For purposes of this paragraph, the term "relative" means an individual bearing a relationship to the individual which is described in any of subparagraphs (A) through (G) of section 152(d)(2). This paragraph shall not apply for purposes of section 105(b) with respect to reimbursements through insurance.

(e) Exclusion of Amounts Allowed for Care of Certain Dependents.—Any expense allowed as a credit under section 21 shall not be treated as an expense paid for medical care.

Editor's Note

Caution: IRC §213(f), below, as added by Pub. L. No. 111-148, §9013, is effective for taxable years beginning after December 31, 2012.

(f) Special Rule for 2013, 2014, 2015, and 2016.— In the case of any taxable year beginning after December 31, 2012, and ending before January 1, 2017, subsection (a) shall be applied with respect to a taxpayer by substituting "7.5 percent" for "10 percent" if such taxpayer or such taxpayer's spouse has attained age 65 before the close of such taxable year.

(g) [Repealed.]

Recent Amendments to IRC §213

Patient Protection and Affordable Care Act, 2010 (Pub. L. No. 111-148), as follows:

- IRC §213(a) was amended by Act §9013(a) by substituting "10 percent" for "7.5 percent". Eff. for taxable years beginning after Dec. 31, 2012.
- IRC §213(f) was added by Act §9013(b). Eff. for taxable years beginning after Dec. 31, 2012.

Working Families Tax Relief Act of 2004 (Pub. L. No. 108-311), as follows:

- IRC §213(a) was amended by Act §207(17) by inserting ", determined without regard to subsections (b)(1), (b)(2), and (d)(1)(B) thereof" after "§152". Eff. tax years beginning after Dec. 31, 2004.
- IRC §213(d)(11) was amended by Act §207(18) by substituting "subparagraphs (A) through (G) of §152(d)(2)" for "paragraphs (1) through (8) of §152(a)". Eff. tax years beginning after Dec. 31, 2004.

---

* * *

SEC. 219. RETIREMENT SAVINGS.

(a) Allowance of Deduction.—In the case of an individual, there shall be allowed as a deduction an amount equal to the qualified retirement contributions of the individual for the taxable year.

(b) Maximum Amount of Deduction.—

(1) In general.—The amount allowable as a deduction under subsection (a) to any individual for any taxable year shall not exceed the lesser of—

(A) the deductible amount, or

(B) an amount equal to the compensation includible in the individual's gross income for such taxable year.

(2) Special rule for employer contributions under simplified employee pensions.—This section shall not apply with respect to an employer contribution to a simplified employee pension.

(3) Plans under section 501(c)(18).—Notwithstanding paragraph (1), the amount allowable as a deduction under subsection (a) with respect to any contributions on behalf of an employee to a plan described in section 501(c)(18) shall not exceed the lesser of—

(A) $7,000, or

(B) an amount equal to 25 percent of the compensation (as defined in section 415(c)(3)) includible in the individual's gross income for such taxable year.

(4) Special rule for simple retirement accounts.—This section shall not apply with respect to any amount contributed to a simple retirement account established under section 408(p).

(5) Deductible amount.—For purposes of paragraph (1)(A)—

(A) In general.—The deductible amount shall be determined in accordance with the following table:

For taxable years beginning in:	The deductible amount is:
2002 through 2004	$3,000
2005 through 2007	$4,000
2008 and thereafter	$5,000

(B) Catch-up contributions for individuals 50 or older.—

(i) In general.—In the case of an individual who has attained the age of 50 before the close of the taxable year, the deductible amount for such taxable year shall be increased by the applicable amount.

(ii) Applicable amount.—For purposes of clause (i), the applicable amount shall be the amount determined in accordance with the following table:

For taxable years beginning in:	The applicable amount is:
2002 through 2005	$ 500
2006 and thereafter	$1,000

(C) Catchup contributions for certain individuals.—

(i) In general.—In the case of an applicable individual who elects to make a qualified retirement contribution in addition to the deductible amount determined under subparagraph (A)—

IRC Sec. 219(b)(5)(C)(i)

(I) the deductible amount for any taxable year shall be increased by an amount equal to 3 times the applicable amount determined under subparagraph (B) for such taxable year, and

(II) subparagraph (B) shall not apply.

(ii) Applicable individual.—For purposes of this subparagraph, the term "applicable individual" means, with respect to any taxable year, any individual who was a qualified participant in a qualified cash or deferred arrangement (as defined in section 401(k)) of an employer described in clause (iii) under which the employer matched at least 50 percent of the employee's contributions to such arrangement with stock of such employer.

(iii) Employer described.—An employer is described in this clause if, in any taxable year preceding the taxable year described in clause (ii)—

(I) such employer (or any controlling corporation of such employer) was a debtor in a case under title 11 of the United States Code, or similar Federal or State law, and

(II) such employer (or any other person) was subject to an indictment or conviction resulting from business transactions related to such case.

(iv) Qualified participant.—For purposes of clause (ii), the term "qualified participant" means any applicable individual who was a participant in the cash or deferred arrangement described in such clause on the date that is 6 months before the filing of the case described in clause (iii).

(v) Termination.—This subparagraph shall not apply to taxable years beginning after December 31, 2009.

(D) Cost-of-living adjustment.—

(i) In general.—In the case of any taxable year beginning in a calendar year after 2008, the $5,000 amount under subparagraph (A) shall be increased by an amount equal to—

(I) such dollar amount, multiplied by

(II) the cost-of-living adjustment determined under section 1(f)(3) for the calendar year in which the taxable year begins, determined by substituting "calendar year 2007" for "calendar year 1992" in subparagraph (B) thereof.

(ii) Rounding rules.—If any amount after adjustment under clause (i) is not a multiple of $500, such amount shall be rounded to the next lower multiple of $500.

(c) Special Rules for Certain Married Individuals.—

(1) In general.—In the case of an individual to whom this paragraph applies for the taxable year, the limitation of paragraph (1) of subsection (b) shall be equal to the lesser of—

(A) the dollar amount in effect under subsection (b)(1)(A) for the taxable year, or

(B) the sum of—

(i) the compensation includible in such individual's gross income for the taxable year, plus

(ii) the compensation includible in the gross income of such individual's spouse for the taxable year reduced by—

(I) the amount allowed as a deduction under subsection (a) to such spouse for such taxable year,

(II) the amount of any designated nondeductible contribution (as defined in section 408(o)) on behalf of such spouse for such taxable year, and

(III) the amount of any contribution on behalf of such spouse to a Roth IRA under section 408A for such taxable year.

(2) Individuals to whom paragraph (1) applies.—Paragraph (1) shall apply to any individual if—

(A) such individual files a joint return for the taxable year, and

(B) the amount of compensation (if any) includible in such individual's gross income for the taxable year is less than the compensation includible in the gross income of such individual's spouse for the taxable year.

(d) Other Limitations and Restrictions.—

(1) Beneficiary must be under age 70½.—No deduction shall be allowed under this section with respect to any qualified retirement contribution for the benefit of an individual if such individual has attained age 70½ before the close of such individual's taxable year for which the contribution was made.

(2) Recontributed amounts.—No deduction shall be allowed under this section with respect to a rollover contribution described in section 402(c), 403(a)(4), 403(b)(8), 408(d)(3), or 457(e)(16).

(3) Amounts contributed under endowment contract.—In the case of an endowment contract described in section 408(b), no deduction shall be allowed under this section for that portion of the amounts paid under the contract for the taxable year which is properly allocable, under regulations prescribed by the Secretary, to the cost of life insurance.

(4) Denial of deduction for amount contributed to inherited annuities or accounts.—No deduction shall be allowed under this section with respect to any amount paid to an inherited individual retirement account or individual retirement annuity (within the meaning of section 408(d)(3)(C)(ii)).

(e) Qualified Retirement Contribution.—For purposes of this section, the term "qualified retirement contribution" means—

(1) any amount paid in cash for the taxable year by or on behalf of an individual to an individual retirement plan for such individual's benefit, and

(2) any amount contributed on behalf of any individual to a plan described in section 501(c)(18).

(f) Other Definitions and Special Rules.—

(1) Compensation.—For purposes of this section, the term "compensation" includes earned income (as defined in section 401(c)(2)). The term "compensation" does not include any amount received as a pension or annuity and does not include any amount received as deferred compensation. The term "compensation" shall include any amount includible in the individual's gross income under section 71 with respect to a divorce or separation instrument described in subparagraph (A) of section 71(b)(2). For purposes of this paragraph, section 401(c)(2) shall be applied as if the term trade or business for purposes of section 1402 included service described in subsection (c)(6). The term compensation includes any differential wage payment (as defined in section 3401(h)(2)).

(2) Married individuals.—The maximum deduction under subsection (b) shall be computed separately for each individual, and this section shall be applied without regard to any community property laws.

(3) Time when contributions deemed made.— For purposes of this section, a taxpayer shall be deemed to have made a contribution to an individual retirement plan on the last day of the preceding taxable year if the contribution is made on account of such taxable year and is made not later than the time prescribed by law for filing the return for such taxable year (not including extensions thereof).

(4) Reports.—The Secretary shall prescribe regulations which prescribe the time and the manner in which reports to the Secretary and plan participants shall be made by the plan administrator of a qualified employer or government plan receiving qualified voluntary employee contributions.

(5) Employer payments.—For purposes of this title, any amount paid by an employer to an individual retirement plan shall be treated as payment of compensation to the employee (other than a self-employed individual who is an employee within the meaning of section 401(c)(1)) includible in his gross income in the taxable year for which the amount was contributed, whether or not a deduction for such payment is allowable under this section to the employee.

(6) Excess contributions treated as contribution made during subsequent year for which there is an unused limitation.—

(A) In general.—If for the taxable year the maximum amount allowable as a deduction under this section for contributions to an individual retirement plan exceeds the amount contributed, then

the taxpayer shall be treated as having made an additional contribution for the taxable year in an amount equal to the lesser of—

(i) the amount of such excess, or

(ii) the amount of the excess contributions for such taxable year (determined under section 4973(b)(2) without regard to subparagraph (C) thereof).

(B) Amount contributed.—For purposes of this paragraph, the amount contributed—

(i) shall be determined without regard to this paragraph, and

(ii) shall not include any rollover contribution.

(C) Special rule where excess deduction was allowed for closed year.—Proper reduction shall be made in the amount allowable as a deduction by reason of this paragraph for any amount allowed as a deduction under this section for a prior taxable year for which the period for assessing deficiency has expired if the amount so allowed exceeds the amount which should have been allowed for such prior taxable year.

(7) Special Rule for Compensation Earned by Members of the Armed Forces for Service in a Combat Zone.—For purposed of subsections (b)(1)(B) and (c), the amount of compensation includible in an individual's gross income shall be determined without regard to section 112.

(8) Election not to deduct contributions.—For election not to deduct contributions to individual retirement plans, see section 408(o)(2)(B)(ii).

(g) Limitation on Deduction for Active Participants in Certain Pension Plans.—

(1) In general.—If (for any part of any plan year ending with or within a taxable year) an individual or the individual's spouse is an active participant, each of the dollar limitations contained in subsections (b)(1)(A) and (c)(1)(A) for such taxable year shall be reduced (but not below zero) by the amount determined under paragraph (2).

(2) Amount of reduction.—

(A) In general.—The amount determined under this paragraph with respect to any dollar limitation shall be the amount which bears the same ratio to such limitation as—

(i) the excess of—

(I) the taxpayer's adjusted gross income for such taxable year, over

(II) the applicable dollar amount, bears to

(ii) $10,000 ($20,000 in the case of a joint return for a taxable year beginning after December 31, 2006).

(B) No reduction below $200 until complete phase-out.—No dollar limitation shall be reduced

IRC Sec. 219(g)(2)(B)

below $200 under paragraph (1) unless (without regard to this subparagraph) such limitation is reduced to zero.

(C) Rounding.—Any amount determined under this paragraph which is not a multiple of $10 shall be rounded to the next lowest $10.

(3) Adjusted gross income; applicable dollar amount.—For purposes of this subsection—

(A) Adjusted gross income.—Adjusted gross income of any taxpayer shall be determined—

(i) after application of sections 86 and 469, and

Editor's Note

Caution: IRC §219(g)(3)(A)(ii), as follows, was amended by Pub. L. No. 107-16, §431(c)(1). For sunset provision, see the amendment notes to this section on Pub. L. No. 107-16.

(ii) without regard to sections 135, 137, 199, 221, 222, and 911 or the deduction allowable under this section.

(B) Applicable dollar amount—The term "applicable dollar amount" means the following:

(i) In the case of a taxpayer filing a joint return:

For taxable years beginning in:	The applicable dollar amount is:
1998	$50,000
1999	$51,000
2000	$52,000
2001	$53,000
2002	$54,000
2003	$60,000
2004	$65,000
2005	$70,000
2006	$75,000
2007 and thereafter	$80,000

(ii) In the case of any other taxpayer (other than a married individual filing a separate return):

For taxable years beginning in:	The applicable dollar amount is:
1998	$30,000
1999	$31,000
2000	$32,000
2001	$33,000
2002	$34,000
2003	$40,000
2004	$45,000
2005	$50,000

(iii) In the case of a married individual filing a separate return, zero.

(4) Special rule for married individuals filing separately and living apart.—A husband and wife who—

(A) file separate returns for any taxable year, and

(B) live apart at all times during such taxable year,

shall not be treated as married individuals for purposes of this subsection.

(5) Active participant.—For purposes of this subsection, the term "active participant" means, with respect to any plan year, an individual—

(A) who is an active participant in—

(i) a plan described in section 401(a) which includes a trust exempt from tax under section 501(a),

(ii) an annuity plan described in section 403(a),

(iii) a plan established for its employees by the United States, by a State or political subdivision thereof, or by an agency or instrumentality of any of the foregoing,

(iv) an annuity contract described in section 403(b),

(v) a simplified employee pension (within the meaning of section 408(k)),

(vi) any simple retirement account (within the meaning of section 408(p)), or

(B) who makes deductible contributions to a trust described in section 501(c)(18).

The determination of whether an individual is an active participant shall be made without regard to whether or not such individual's rights under a plan, trust, or contract are nonforfeitable. An eligible deferred compensation plan (within the meaning of section 457(b)) shall not be treated as a plan described in subparagraph (A)(iii).

(6) Certain individuals not treated as active participants.—For purposes of this subsection, any individual described in any of the following subparagraphs shall not be treated as an active participant for any taxable year solely because of any participation so described:

(A) Members of reserve components.—Participation in a plan described in subparagraph (A)(iii) of paragraph (5) by reason of service as a member of a reserve component of the Armed Forces (as defined in section 10101 of title 10), unless such individual has served in excess of 90 days on active duty (other than active duty for training) during the year.

(B) Volunteer firefighters.—A volunteer firefighter—

(i) who is a participant in a plan described in subparagraph (A)(iii) of paragraph (5) based on his activity as a volunteer firefighter, and

(ii) whose accrued benefit as of the beginning of the taxable year is not more than an annual benefit of $1,800 (when expressed as a single life annuity commencing at age 65).

(7) Special rule for spouses who are not active participants.—If this subsection applies to an individual for any taxable year solely because their spouse is an active participant, then, in applying this subsection to the individual (but not their spouse)—

(A) the applicable dollar amount under paragraph (3)(B)(i) shall be $150,000; and

(B) the amount applicable under paragraph (2)(A)(ii) shall be $10,000.

(8) Inflation adjustment.—In the case of any taxable year beginning in a calendar year after 2006, the dollar amount in the last row of the table contained in paragraph (3)(B)(i), the dollar amount in the last row of the table contained in paragraph (3)(B)(ii), and the dollar amount contained in paragraph (7)(A), shall each be increased by an amount equal to—

(A) such dollar amount, multiplied by

(B) the cost-of-living adjustment determined under section 1(f)(3) for the calendar year in which the taxable year begins, determined by substituting "calendar year 2005" for "calendar year 1992" in subparagraph (B) thereof.

Any increase determined under the preceding sentence shall be rounded to the nearest multiple of $1,000.

(h) Cross Reference.—For failure to provide required reports, see section 6652(g).

Recent Amendments to IRC §219

Heroes Earnings Assistance and Relief Tax Act of 2008 (Pub. L. No. 110-245), as follows:

● IRC §219(f)(1) was amended by Act §105(b)(2) by adding the following sentence at the end: "The term compensation includes any differential wage payment (as defined in section 3401(h)(2))." Eff. for years beginning after Dec. 31, 2008, see Act §105(b)(3).

Pension Protection Act of 2006 (Pub. L. No. 109-280), as follows:

● IRC §219(b)(5) was amended by Act §831(a) by redesignating subpara. (C) as subpara. (D) and by inserting a new subpara. (C). Eff. tax years beginning after Dec. 31, 2006.

● IRC §219(g) was amended by Act §833(b) by adding new para. (8). Eff. tax years beginning after 2006.

● **Sunset Provision.** Act §811, provides:

   SEC. 811. PENSIONS AND INDIVIDUAL RETIRE-MENT ARRANGEMENT PROVISIONS OF ECO-

NOMIC GROWTH AND TAX RELIEF RECONCILIA-TION ACT OF 2001 MADE PERMANENT.

Title IX of the Economic Growth and Tax Relief Reconciliation Act of 2001 [Pub. L. No. 107-16] shall not apply to the provisions of, and amendments made by, subtitles A through F [§§601–666] of title VI of such Act (relating to pension and individual retirement arrangement provisions).

Heroes Earned Retirement Opportunities Act (Pub. L. No. 109-227), as follows:

● IRC §219(f) was amended by Act §2(a) by redesignating para. (7) as para. (8) and by inserting new para. (7). Eff. tax years beginning after Dec. 31, 2003. See Act §2(c) for special rule.

American Jobs Creation Act of 2004 (Pub. L. No. 108-357), as follows:

● IRC §219(g)(3)(A)(ii) was amended by Act §102(d)(1) by inserting "199," before "221". Eff. for tax years beginning after Dec. 31, 2004.

Economic Growth and Tax Relief Reconciliation Act of 2001 (Pub. L. No. 107-16), as follows:

● IRC §219(b)(1)(A) was amended by Act §601(a)(1) by replacing "$2,000" with "the deductible amount". Eff. for tax years beginning after Dec. 31, 2001.

● IRC §219(b) was amended by Act §601(a)(2) by adding new para. (5). Eff. tax years beginning after Dec. 31, 2001.

● IRC §219(d)(2) was amended by Act §641(e)(2) by replacing "or 408(d)(3)" with "408(d)(3), or 457(e)(16)". Eff. generally for distributions after Dec. 31, 2001. See Act §641(f)(3) for special rule.

● IRC §219(g)(3) was amended by Act §431(c)(1) by inserting "222," after "221,". Eff. for payments made in tax years beginning after Dec. 31, 2001.

● **Sunset Provision.** Act §901, as amended by Pub. L. No. 111-312, §101(a)(1), provides the sunset rule below. But see Pub. L. No. 109-280, §811, §111-148, §10909(c), as amended by Pub. L. No. 111-312, §101(b)(1).

   SEC. 901. SUNSET OF PROVISIONS OF ACT.

   (a) In general. All provisions of, and amendments made by, this Act shall not apply—

   (1) to taxable, plan, or limitation years beginning after December 31, 2012, or

   (2) in the case of title V, to estates of decedents dying, gifts made, or generation skipping transfers, after December 31, 2012.

   (b) Application of certain laws.—The Internal Revenue Code of 1986 and the Employee Retirement Income Security Act of 1974 shall be applied and administered to years, estates, gifts, and transfers described in subsection (a) as if the provisions and amendments described in subsection (a) had never been enacted.

SEC. 220. ARCHER MSAs.

(a) Deduction Allowed.—In the case of an individual who is an eligible individual for any month during the taxable year, there shall be allowed as a deduction for the taxable year an amount equal to the aggregate amount paid in cash during such taxable year by such individual to an Archer MSA of such individual.

(b) Limitations.—

(1) In general.—The amount allowable as a deduction under subsection (a) to an individual for the taxable year shall not exceed the sum of the monthly limitations for months during such taxable year that the individual is an eligible individual.

(2) Monthly limitation.—The monthly limitation for any month is the amount equal to $1/12$ of—

(A) in the case of an individual who has self-only coverage under the high deductible health plan as of the first day of such month, 65 percent of the annual deductible under such coverage, and

(B) in the case of an individual who has family coverage under the high deductible health plan as of the first day of such month, 75 percent of the annual deductible under such coverage.

(3) Special rule for married individuals.—In the case of individuals who are married to each other, if either spouse has family coverage—

(A) both spouses shall be treated as having only such family coverage (and if such spouses each have family coverage under different plans, as having the family coverage with the lowest annual deductible), and

(B) the limitation under paragraph (1) (after the application of subparagraph (A) of this paragraph) shall be divided equally between them unless they agree on a different division.

(4) Deduction not to exceed compensation.—

(A) Employees.—The deduction allowed under subsection (a) for contributions as an eligible individual described in subclause (I) of subsection (c)(1)(A)(iii) shall not exceed such individual's wages, salaries, tips, and other employee compensation which are attributable to such individual's employment by the employer referred to in such subclause.

(B) Self-employed individuals.—The deduction allowed under subsection (a) for contributions as an eligible individual described in subclause (II) of subsection (c)(1)(A)(iii) shall not exceed such individual's earned income (as defined in section 401(c)(1)) derived by the taxpayer from the trade or business with respect to which the high deductible health plan is established.

(C) Community property laws not to apply.—The limitations under this paragraph shall be determined without regard to community property laws.

(5) Coordination with exclusion for employer contributions.—No deduction shall be allowed under this section for any amount paid for any taxable year to an Archer MSA of an individual if—

(A) any amount is contributed to any Archer MSA of such individual for such year which is excludable from gross income under section 106(b), or

(B) if such individual's spouse is covered under the high deductible health plan covering such individual, any amount is contributed for such year to any Archer MSA of such spouse which is so excludable.

(6) Denial of deduction to dependents.—No deduction shall be allowed under this section to any individual with respect to whom a deduction under section 151 is allowable to another taxpayer for a taxable year beginning in the calendar year in which such individual's taxable year begins.

(7) Medicare eligible individuals.—The limitation under this subsection for any month with respect to an individual shall be zero for the first month such individual is entitled to benefits under title XVIII of the Social Security Act and for each month thereafter.

(c) Definitions.—For purposes of this section—

(1) Eligible individual.—

(A) In general.—The term "eligible individual" means, with respect to any month, any individual if—

(i) such individual is covered under a high deductible health plan as of the 1st day of such month,

(ii) such individual is not, while covered under a high deductible health plan, covered under any health plan—

(I) which is not a high deductible health plan, and

(II) which provides coverage for any benefit which is covered under the high deductible health plan, and

(iii) (I) the high deductible health plan covering such individual is established and maintained by the employer of such individual or of the spouse of such individual and such employer is a small employer, or

(II) such individual is an employee (within the meaning of section 401(c)(1)) or the spouse of such an employee and the high deductible health plan covering such individual is not established or maintained by any employer of such individual or spouse.

(B) Certain coverage disregarded.—Subparagraph (A)(ii) shall be applied without regard to—

(i) coverage for any benefit provided by permitted insurance, and

(ii) coverage (whether through insurance or otherwise) for accidents, disability, dental care, vision care, or long-term care.

(C) Continued eligibility of employee and spouse establishing Archer MSAs.—If, while an employer is a small employer—

(i) any amount is contributed to an Archer MSA of an individual who is an employee of such employer or the spouse of such an employee, and

(ii) such amount is excludable from gross income under section 106(b) or allowable as a deduction under this section, such individual shall not cease to meet the requirement of subparagraph (A)(iii)(I) by reason of such employer ceasing to be a small employer so long as such employee continues to be an employee of such employer.

(D) Limitations on eligibility.—For limitations on number of taxpayers who are eligible to have Archer MSAs, see subsection (i).

IRC Sec. 220(b)(2)(A)

(2) High deductible health plan.—

(A) In general.—The term "high deductible health plan" means a health plan—

(i) in the case of self-only coverage, which has an annual deductible which is not less than $1,500 and not more than $2,250,

(ii) in the case of family coverage, which has an annual deductible which is not less than $3,000 and not more than $4,500, and

(iii) the annual out-of-pocket expenses required to be paid under the plan (other than for premiums) for covered benefits does not exceed—

(I) $3,000 for self-only coverage, and

(II) $5,500 for family coverage.

(B) Special rules.—

(i) Exclusion of certain plans.—Such term does not include a health plan if substantially all of its coverage is coverage described in paragraph (1)(B).

(ii) Safe harbor for absence of preventive care deductible.—A plan shall not fail to be treated as a high deductible health plan by reason of failing to have a deductible for preventive care if the absence of a deductible for such care is required by State law.

(3) Permitted insurance.—The term "permitted insurance" means—

(A) insurance if substantially all of the coverage provided under such insurance relates to—

(i) liabilities incurred under workers' compensation laws,

(ii) tort liabilities,

(iii) liabilities relating to ownership or use of property, or

(iv) such other similar liabilities as the Secretary may specify by regulations,

(B) insurance for a specified disease or illness, and

(C) insurance paying a fixed amount per day (or other period) of hospitalization.

(4) Small employer.—

(A) In general.—The term "small employer" means, with respect to any calendar year, any employer if such employer employed an average of 50 or fewer employees on business days during either of the 2 preceding calendar years. For purposes of the preceding sentence, a preceding calendar year may be taken into account only if the employer was in existence throughout such year.

(B) Employers not in existence in preceding year.—In the case of an employer which was not in existence throughout the 1st preceding calendar year, the determination under subparagraph (A) shall be based on the average number of employees that it is reasonably expected such employer will employ on business days in the current calendar year.

(C) Certain growing employers retain treatment as small employer.—The term "small employer" includes, with respect to any calendar year, any employer if—

(i) such employer met the requirement of subparagraph (A) (determined without regard to subparagraph (B)) for any preceding calendar year after 1996,

(ii) any amount was contributed to the Archer MSA of any employee of such employer with respect to coverage of such employee under a high deductible health plan of such employer during such preceding calendar year and such amount was excludable from gross income under section 106(b) or allowable as a deduction under this section, and

(iii) such employer employed an average of 200 or fewer employees on business days during each preceding calendar year after 1996.

(D) Special rules.—

(i) Controlled groups.—For purposes of this paragraph, all persons treated as a single employer under subsection (b), (c), (m), or (o) of section 414 shall be treated as 1 employer.

(ii) Predecessors.—Any reference in this paragraph to an employer shall include a reference to any predecessor of such employer.

(5) Family coverage.—The term "family coverage" means any coverage other than self-only coverage.

(d) Archer MSA.—For purposes of this section—

(1) Archer MSA.—The term "Archer MSA" means a trust created or organized in the United States as a medical savings account exclusively for the purpose of paying the qualified medical expenses of the account holder, but only if the written governing instrument creating the trust meets the following requirements:

(A) Except in the case of a rollover contribution described in subsection (f)(5), no contribution will be accepted—

(i) unless it is in cash, or

(ii) to the extent such contribution, when added to previous contributions to the trust for the calendar year, exceeds 75 percent of the highest annual limit deductible permitted under subsection (c)(2)(A)(ii) for such calendar year.

(B) The trustee is a bank (as defined in section 408(n)), an insurance company (as defined in sec-

IRC Sec. 220(d)(1)(B)

tion 816), or another person who demonstrates to the satisfaction of the Secretary that the manner in which such person will administer the trust will be consistent with the requirements of this section.

(C) No part of the trust assets will be invested in life insurance contracts.

(D) The assets of the trust will not be commingled with other property except in a common trust fund or common investment fund.

(E) The interest of an individual in the balance in his account is nonforfeitable.

(2) Qualified medical expenses.—

Editor's Note

The last sentence of IRC §220(d)(2)(A), below, as added by Pub. L. No. 111-148, §9003, is effective for amounts paid with respect to taxable years beginning after December 31, 2010.

(A) In general.—The term "qualified medical expenses" means, with respect to an account holder, amounts paid by such holder for medical care (as defined in section 213(d)) for such individual, the spouse of such individual, and any dependent (as defined in section 152, determined without regard to subsections (b)(1), (b)(2), and (d)(1)(B) thereof) of such individual, but only to the extent such amounts are not compensated for by insurance or otherwise. Such term shall include an amount paid for medicine or a drug only if such medicine or drug is a prescribed drug (determined without regard to whether such drug is available without a prescription) or is insulin.

(B) Health insurance may not be purchased from account.—

(i) In general.—Subparagraph (A) shall not apply to any payment for insurance.

(ii) Exceptions.—Clause (i) shall not apply to any expense for coverage under—

(I) a health plan during any period of continuation coverage required under any Federal law,

(II) a qualified long-term care insurance contract (as defined in section 7702B(b)), or

(III) a health plan during a period in which the individual is receiving unemployment compensation under any Federal or State law.

(C) Medical expenses of individuals who are not eligible individuals.—Subparagraph (A) shall apply to an amount paid by an account holder for medical care of an individual who is not described in clauses (i) and (ii) of subsection (c)(1)(A) for the month in which the expense for such care is incurred only if no amount is contributed (other than

a rollover contribution) to any Archer MSA of such account holder for the taxable year which includes such month. This subparagraph shall not apply to any expense for coverage described in subclause (I) or (III) of subparagraph (B)(ii).

(3) Account holder.—The term "account holder" means the individual on whose behalf the Archer MSA was established.

(4) Certain rules to apply.—Rules similar to the following rules shall apply for purposes of this section:

(A) Section 219(d)(2) (relating to no deduction for rollovers).

(B) Section 219(f)(3) (relating to time when contributions deemed made).

(C) Except as provided in section 106(b), section 219(f)(5) (relating to employer payments).

(D) Section 408(g) (relating to community property laws).

(E) Section 408(h) (relating to custodial accounts).

(e) Tax Treatment of Accounts.—

(1) In general.—An Archer MSA is exempt from taxation under this subtitle unless such account has ceased to be an Archer MSA. Notwithstanding the preceding sentence, any such account is subject to the taxes imposed by section 511 (relating to imposition of tax on unrelated business income of charitable, etc. organizations).

(2) Account terminations.—Rules similar to the rules of paragraphs (2) and (4) of section 408(e) shall apply to Archer MSAs, and any amount treated as distributed under such rules shall be treated as not used to pay qualified medical expenses.

(f) Tax Treatment of Distributions.—

(1) Amounts used for qualified medical expenses.—Any amount paid or distributed out of an Archer MSA which is used exclusively to pay qualified medical expenses of any account holder shall not be includible in gross income.

(2) Inclusion of amounts not used for qualified medical expenses.—Any amount paid or distributed out of an Archer MSA which is not used exclusively to pay the qualified medical expenses of the account holder shall be included in the gross income of such holder.

(3) Excess contributions returned before due date of return.—

(A) In general.—If any excess contribution is contributed for a taxable year to any Archer MSA of an individual, paragraph (2) shall not apply to distributions from the Archer MSAs of such individual (to the extent such distributions do not exceed the aggregate excess contributions to all such accounts of such individual for such year) if—

(i) such distribution is received by the individual on or before the last day prescribed by law (including extensions of time) for filing such individual's return for such taxable year, and

(ii) such distribution is accompanied by the amount of net income attributable to such excess contribution.

Any net income described in clause (ii) shall be included in the gross income of the individual for the taxable year in which it is received.

(B) Excess contribution.—For purposes of subparagraph (A), the term "excess contribution" means any contribution (other than a rollover contribution) which is neither excludable from gross income under section 106(b) nor deductible under this section.

(4) Additional tax on distributions not used for qualified medical expenses.—

Editor's Note

IRC §220(f)(4)(A), below, is effective for distributions made on or before December 31, 2010.

(A) In general.—The tax imposed by this chapter on the account holder for any taxable year in which there is a payment or distribution from an Archer MSA of such holder which is includible in gross income under paragraph (2) shall be increased by 15 percent of the amount which is so includible.

Editor's Note

IRC §220(f)(4)(A), below, as amended by Pub. L. No. 111-148, §9004, is effective for distributions made after December 31, 2010.

(A) In general.—The tax imposed by this chapter on the account holder for any taxable year in which there is a payment or distribution from an Archer MSA of such holder which is includible in gross income under paragraph (2) shall be increased by 20 percent of the amount which is so includible.

(B) Exception for disability or death.—Subparagraph (A) shall not apply if the payment or distribution is made after the account holder becomes disabled within the meaning of section 72(m)(7) or dies.

(C) Exception for distributions after Medicare eligibility.—Subparagraph (A) shall not apply to any

payment or distribution after the date on which the account holder attains the age specified in section 1811 of the Social Security Act.

(5) Rollover contribution.—An amount is described in this paragraph as a rollover contribution if it meets the requirements of subparagraphs (A) and (B).

(A) In general.—Paragraph (2) shall not apply to any amount paid or distributed from an Archer MSA to the account holder to the extent the amount received is paid into an Archer MSA or a health savings account (as defined in section 223(d)) for the benefit of such holder not later than the 60th day after the day on which the holder receives the payment or distribution.

(B) Limitation.—This paragraph shall not apply to any amount described in subparagraph (A) received by an individual from an Archer MSA if, at any time during the 1-year period ending on the day of such receipt, such individual received any other amount described in subparagraph (A) from an Archer MSA which was not includible in the individual's gross income because of the application of this paragraph.

(6) Coordination with medical expense deduction.—For purposes of determining the amount of the deduction under section 213, any payment or distribution out of an Archer MSA for qualified medical expenses shall not be treated as an expense paid for medical care.

(7) Transfer of account incident to divorce.— The transfer of an individual's interest in an Archer MSA to an individual's spouse or former spouse under a divorce or separation instrument described in subparagraph (A) of section 71(b)(2) shall not be considered a taxable transfer made by such individual notwithstanding any other provision of this subtitle, and such interest shall, after such transfer, be treated as an Archer MSA with respect to which such spouse is the account holder.

(8) Treatment after death of account holder.—

(A) Treatment if designated beneficiary is spouse.—If the account holder's surviving spouse acquires such holder's interest in an Archer MSA by reason of being the designated beneficiary of such account at the death of the account holder, such Archer MSA shall be treated as if the spouse were the account holder.

(B) Other cases.—

(i) In general.—If, by reason of the death of the account holder, any person acquires the account holder's interest in an Archer MSA in a case to which subparagraph (A) does not apply—

(I) such account shall cease to be an Archer MSA as of the date of death, and

(II) an amount equal to the fair market value of the assets in such account on such date shall be includible if such person is not the estate of such holder, in such person's gross income for the taxable year which includes such date, or if such person is the estate of such holder, in such holder's gross income for the last taxable year of such holder.

(ii) Special rules.—

(I) Reduction of inclusion for pre-death expenses.—The amount includible in gross income under clause (i) by any person (other than the estate) shall be reduced by the amount of qualified medical expenses which were incurred by the decedent before the date of the decedent's death and paid by such person within 1 year after such date.

(II) Deduction for estate taxes.—An appropriate deduction shall be allowed under section 691(c) to any person (other than the decedent or the decedent's spouse) with respect to amounts included in gross income under clause (i) by such person.

(g) Cost-of-Living Adjustment.—In the case of any taxable year beginning in a calendar year after 1998, each dollar amount in subsection (c)(2) shall be increased by an amount equal to—

(1) such dollar amount, multiplied by

(2) the cost-of-living adjustment determined under section 1(f)(3) for the calendar year in which such taxable year begins by substituting "calendar year 1997" for "calendar year 1992" in subparagraph (B) thereof.

If any increase under the preceding sentence is not a multiple of $50, such increase shall be rounded to the nearest multiple of $50.

(h) Reports.—The Secretary may require the trustee of an Archer MSA to make such reports regarding such account to the Secretary and to the account holder with respect to contributions, distributions, and such other matters as the Secretary determines appropriate. The reports required by this subsection shall be filed at such time and in such manner and furnished to such individuals at such time and in such manner as may be required by the Secretary.

(i) Limitation on Number of Taxpayers Having Archer MSAs.—

(1) In general.—Except as provided in paragraph (5), no individual shall be treated as an eligible individual for any taxable year beginning after the cut-off year unless—

(A) such individual was an active MSA participant for any taxable year ending on or before the close of the cut-off year, or

(B) such individual first became an active MSA participant for a taxable year ending after the cut-off year by reason of coverage under a high deductible health plan of an MSA-participating employer.

(2) Cut-off year.—For purposes of paragraph (1), the term "cut-off year" means the earlier of—

(A) calendar year 2007, or

(B) the first calendar year before 2007 for which the Secretary determines under subsection (j) that the numerical limitation for such year has been exceeded.

(3) Active MSA participant.—For purposes of this subsection—

(A) In general.—The term "active MSA participant" means, with respect to any taxable year, any individual who is the account holder of any Archer MSA into which any contribution was made which was excludable from gross income under section 106(b), or allowable as a deduction under this section, for such taxable year.

(B) Special rule for cut-off years before 2007.—In the case of a cut-off year before 2007—

(i) an individual shall not be treated as an eligible individual for any month of such year or an active MSA participant under paragraph (1)(A) unless such individual is, on or before the cut-off date, covered under a high deductible health plan, and

(ii) an employer shall not be treated as an MSA-participating employer unless the employer, on or before the cut-off date, offered coverage under a high deductible health plan to any employee.

(C) Cut-off date.—For purposes of subparagraph (B)—

(i) In general.—Except as otherwise provided in this subparagraph, the cut-off date is October 1 of the cut-off year.

(ii) Employees with enrollment periods after October 1.—In the case of an individual described in subclause (I) of subsection (c)(1)(A)(iii), if the regularly scheduled enrollment period for health plans of the individual's employer occurs during the last 3 months of the cut-off year, the cut-off date is December 31 of the cut-off year.

(iii) Self-employed individuals.—In the case of an individual described in subclause (II) of subsection (c)(1)(A)(iii), the cut-off date is November 1 of the cut-off year.

(iv) Special rules for 1997.—If 1997 is a cut-off year by reason of subsection (j)(1)(A)—

(I) each of the cut-off dates under clauses (i) and (iii) shall be 1 month earlier than the date determined without regard to this clause, and

(II) clause (ii) shall be applied by substituting "4 months" for "3 months".

(4) MSA-participating employer.—For purposes of this subsection, the term "MSA-participating employer" means any small employer if—

IRC Sec. 220(f)(8)(B)(i)(II)

(A) such employer made any contribution to the Archer MSA of any employee during the cut-off year or any preceding calendar year which was excludable from gross income under section 106(b), or

(B) at least 20 percent of the employees of such employer who are eligible individuals for any month of the cut-off year by reason of coverage under a high deductible health plan of such employer each made a contribution of at least $100 to theirArcher MSAs for any taxable year ending with or within the cut-off year which was allowable as a deduction under this section.

(5) Additional eligibility after cut-off year.—If the Secretary determines under subsection (j)(2)(A) that the numerical limit for the calendar year following a cut-off year described in paragraph (2)(B) has not been exceeded—

(A) this subsection shall not apply to any otherwise eligible individual who is covered under a high deductible health plan during the first 6 months of the second calendar year following the cut-off year (and such individual shall be treated as an active MSA participant for purposes of this subsection if a contribution is made to any Archer MSA with respect to such coverage), and

(B) any employer who offers coverage under a high deductible health plan to any employee during such 6-month period shall be treated as an MSA-participating employer for purposes of this subsection if the requirements of paragraph (4) are met with respect to such coverage.

For purposes of this paragraph, subsection (j)(2)(A) shall be applied for 1998 by substituting "750,000" for "600,000".

(j) Determination of Whether Numerical Limits Are Exceeded.—

(1) Determination of whether limit exceeded for 1997.—The numerical limitation for 1997 is exceeded if, based on the reports required under paragraph (4), the number of Archer MSAs established as of—

(A) April 30, 1997, exceeds 375,000, or

(B) June 30, 1997, exceeds 525,000.

(2) Determination of whether limit exceeded for 1998, 1999, 2001, 2002, 2004, 2005, or 2006.—

(A) In general.—The numerical limitation for 1998, 1999, 2001, 2002, 2004, 2005, or 2006 is exceeded if the sum of—

(i) the number of MSA returns filed on or before April 15 of such calendar year for taxable years ending with or within the preceding calendar year, plus

(ii) the Secretary's estimate (determined on the basis of the returns described in clause (i)) of the

number of MSA returns for such taxable years which will be filed after such date,

exceeds 750,000 (600,000 in the case of 1998). For purposes of the preceding sentence, the term "MSA return" means any return on which any exclusion is claimed under section 106(b) or any deduction is claimed under this section.

(B) Alternative computation of limitation.—The numerical limitation for 1998, 1999, 2001, 2002, 2004, 2005, or 2006 is also exceeded if the sum of—

(i) 90 percent of the sum determined under subparagraph (A) for such calendar year, plus

(ii) the product of 2.5 and the number of Archer MSAs established during the portion of such year preceding July 1 (based on the reports required under paragraph (4)) for taxable years beginning in such year, exceeds 750,000.

(C) No limitation for 2000 or 2003.—The numerical limitation shall not apply for 2000 or 2003.

(3) Previously uninsured individuals not included in determination.—

(A) In general.—The determination of whether any calendar year is a cut-off year shall be made by not counting the Archer MSA of any previously uninsured individual.

(B) Previously uninsured individual.—For purposes of this subsection, the term "previously uninsured individual" means, with respect to any Archer MSA, any individual who had no health plan coverage (other than coverage referred to in subsection (c)(1)(B)) at any time during the 6-month period before the date such individual's coverage under the high deductible health plan commences.

(4) Reporting by MSA trustees.—

(A) In general.—Not later than August 1 of 1997, 1998, 1999, 2001, 2002, 2004, 2005, and 2006, each person who is the trustee of an Archer MSA established before July 1 of such calendar year shall make a report to the Secretary (in such form and manner as the Secretary shall specify) which specifies—

(i) the number of Archer MSAs established before such July 1 (for taxable years beginning in such calendar year) of which such person is the trustee,

(ii) the name and TIN of the account holder of each such account, and

(iii) the number of such accounts which are accounts of previously uninsured individuals.

(B) Additional report for 1997.—Not later than June 1, 1997, each person who is the trustee of an Archer MSA established before May 1, 1997, shall

IRC Sec. 220(j)(4)(B)

make an additional report described in subparagraph (A) but only with respect to accounts established before May 1, 1997.

(C) Penalty for failure to file report.—The penalty provided in section 6693(a) shall apply to any report required by this paragraph, except that—

(i) such section shall be applied by substituting "$25" for "$50", and

(ii) the maximum penalty imposed on any trustee shall not exceed $5,000.

(D) Aggregation of accounts.—To the extent practical, in determining the number of Archer MSAs on the basis of the reports under this paragraph, all Archer MSAs of an individual shall be treated as one account and all accounts of individuals who are married to each other shall be treated as one account.

(5) Date of making determinations.—Any determination under this subsection that a calendar year is a cut-off year shall be made by the Secretary and shall be published not later than October 1 of such year.

Recent Amendments to IRC §220

Patient Protection and Affordable Care Act, 2010 (Pub. L. No. 111-148), as follows:

- IRC §220(d)(2)(A) was amended by Act, §9003(b) by adding to the end: "Such term shall include an amount paid for medicine or a drug only if such medicine or drug is a prescribed drug (determined without regard to whether such drug is available without a prescription) or is insulin." Eff. for amounts paid with respect to taxable years beginning after Dec. 31, 2010.
- IRC §220(f)(4)(A) was amended by Act, §9004(b) by substituting "20 percent" for "15 percent". Eff. for distributions made after Dec. 31, 2010.

Tax Relief and Health Care Act of 2006 (Pub. L. No. 109-432), as follows:

- IRC §220(i)(2) and (3)(B) were amended by Act, Division A, §117(a) by substituting "2007" for "2005" each place it appeared in the text and heading. Eff. Dec. 20, 2006.
- IRC §220(j)(2) was amended by Act, Division A, §117(b)(1) by substituting "2004, 2005, or 2006" for "or 2004" each place it appeared in the text and heading. Eff. Dec. 20, 2006.
- IRC §220(j)(4)(A) was amended by Act, Division A, §117(b)(2) by substituting "2004, 2005, and 2006" for "and 2004". Eff. Dec. 20, 2006.
- **Other Provision.** Act §117 contains the following filing deadlines:
    (c) **Time for Filing Reports, etc.—**
    (1) The report required by section 220(j)(4) of the Internal Revenue Code of 1986 to be made on August 1, 2005, or August 1, 2006, as the case may be, shall be treated as timely if made before the close of the 90-day period beginning on the date of the enactment of this Act [*Ed. Note:* December 20, 2006].
    (2) The determination and publication required by section 220(j)(5) of such Code with respect to calendar year 2005 or calendar year 2006, as the case may be, shall be treated as timely if made before the close of the 120-day period beginning on the date of the enactment of this Act. [*Ed. Note:* Dec. 20, 2006] If the determination under the preceding sentence is that 2005 or 2006 is a cut-off year under section 220(i) of such Code, the cut-off date under such section 220(i) shall be the last day of such 120-day period.

Working Families Tax Relief Act of 2004 (Pub. L. No. 108-311), as follows:

- IRC §220(d)(2)(A) was amended by Act §207(19) by inserting ", determined without regard to subsections (b)(1), (b)(2), and (d)(1)(B) thereof" after "§152". Eff. tax years beginning after Dec. 31, 2004.
- IRC §220(i)(2) and (i)(3)(B) were amended by Act §322(a) by substituting "2005" for "2003" each place it appeared in the text and headings. Eff. Jan. 1, 2004.
- IRC §220(j)(2) was amended by Act §322(b)(1) by substituting "2002, or 2004" for "or 2002" each place it appeared in the text and headings. Eff. Jan. 1, 2004.
- IRC §220(j)(2)(C) was amended by Act §322(b)(3). Eff. Jan. 1, 2004. IRC §220(j)(2)(C) prior to amendment:
    (C) No limitation for 2000.—The numerical limitation shall not apply for 2000.
- IRC §220(j)(4)(A) was amended by Act §322(b)(2) by substituting "2002, and 2004" for "and 2002". Eff. Jan. 1, 2004. See Act §322(d) for a special rule.

Medicare Prescription Drug, Improvement, and Modernization Act of 2003 (Pub. L. No. 108-173), as follows:

- IRC §220(f)(5)(A) was amended by Act §1201(c) by inserting "or a health savings account (as defined in §223(d))" after "paid into an Archer MSA". Eff. for tax years beginning after Dec. 31, 2003.

Job Creation and Worker Assistance Act of 2002 (Pub. L. No. 147), as follows:

- IRC §220(i)(2) and (3)(B) were amended by Act §612(a) by substituting "2003" for "2002" each place it appeared. Eff. Jan. 1, 2002.
- IRC §220(j)(2) was amended by Act §612(b)(1) by substituting "1998, 1999, 2001, or 2002" for "1998, 1999, or 2001" each place it appeared. Eff. Jan. 1, 2002.
- IRC §220(j)(4)(A) was amended by Act §612(b)(2) by substituting "2001, and 2002" for "and 2001". Eff. Jan. 1, 2002.

SEC. 221. INTEREST ON EDUCATION LOANS.

(a) Allowance of Deduction.—In the case of an individual, there shall be allowed as a deduction for the taxable year an amount equal to the interest paid by the taxpayer during the taxable year on any qualified education loan.

(b) Maximum Deduction.—

(1) In general.—Except as provided in paragraph (2), the deduction allowed by subsection (a) for the taxable year shall not exceed the amount determined in accordance with the following table:

In the case of taxable years beginning in:	The dollar amount is:
1998	$1,000
1999	$1,500
2000	$2,000
2001	$2,500

(2) Limitation based on modified adjusted gross income.—

(A) In general.—The amount which would (but for this paragraph) be allowable as a deduction under this section shall be reduced (but not below zero) by the amount determined under subparagraph (B).

(B) Amount of reduction.—The amount determined under this subparagraph is the amount which bears the same ratio to the amount which would be so taken into account as—

(i) the excess of—

(I) the taxpayer's modified adjusted gross income for such taxable year, over

(II) $50,000 ($100,000 in the case of a joint return), bears to

(ii) $15,000 ($30,000 in the case of a joint return).

(C) Modified adjusted gross income.—The term "modified adjusted gross income" means adjusted gross income determined—

(i) without regard to this section and sections 199, 222, 911, 931, and 933, and

(ii) after application of sections 86, 135, 137, 219, and 469.

(c) Dependents Not Eligible for Deduction.—No deduction shall be allowed by this section to an individual for the taxable year if a deduction under section 151 with respect to such individual is allowed to another taxpayer for the taxable year beginning in the calendar year in which such individual's taxable year begins.

(d) Definitions.—For purposes of this section—

(1) Qualified education loan.—The term "qualified education loan" means any indebtedness incurred to pay qualified higher education expenses—

(A) which are incurred by the taxpayer solely on behalf of the taxpayer, the taxpayer's spouse, or any dependent of the taxpayer as of the time the indebtedness was incurred,

(B) which are paid or incurred within a reasonable period of time before or after the indebtedness is incurred, and

(C) which are attributable to education furnished during a period during which the recipient was an eligible student.

Such term includes indebtedness used to refinance indebtedness which qualifies as a qualified education loan. The term "qualified education loan" shall not include any indebtedness owed to a person who is related (within the meaning of section 267(b) or 707(b)(1)) to the taxpayer or to any person by reason of a loan under any qualified employer plan (as defined in section 72(p)(4)) or under any contract referred to in section 72(p)(5).

(2) Qualified higher education expenses.—The term "qualified higher education expenses" means the cost of attendance (as defined in section 472 of the Higher Education Act of 1965, 20 U.S.C. 1087ll, as in effect on the day before the date of the enactment of the Taxpayer Relief Act of 1997) at an eligible educational institution, reduced by the sum of—

(A) the amount excluded from gross income under section 127, 135, 529, or 530 by reason of such expenses, and

(B) the amount of any scholarship, allowance, or payment described in section 25A(g)(2).

For purposes of the preceding sentence, the term "eligible educational institution" has the same meaning given such term by section 25A(f)(2), except that such term shall also include an institution conducting an internship or residency program leading to a degree or certificate awarded by an institution of higher education, a hospital, or a health care facility which offers postgraduate training.

(3) Eligible student.—The term "eligible student" has the meaning given such term by section 25A(b)(3).

(4) Dependent.—The term "dependent" has the meaning given such term by section 152 (determined without regard to subsections (b)(1), (b)(2), and (d)(1)(B) thereof).

IRC Sec. 221(d)(4)

Editor's Note

Caution: Former IRC §221(f) was redesignated as IRC §221(e), as follows, by Pub. L. No. 107-16, §412(a)(1). For sunset provision, see the amendment notes to this section on Pub. L. No. 107-16.

(e) Special Rules.—

(1) Denial of double benefit.—No deduction shall be allowed under this section for any amount for which a deduction is allowable under any other provision of this chapter.

(2) Married couples must file joint return.—If the taxpayer is married at the close of the taxable year, the deduction shall be allowed under subsection (a) only if the taxpayer and the taxpayer's spouse file a joint return for the taxable year.

(3) Marital status.—Marital status shall be determined in accordance with section 7703.

Editor's Note

Caution: Former IRC §221(g) was redesignated as IRC §221(f) by Pub. L. No. 107-16, §412(a)(1), and IRC §221(f)(1) was amended by Pub. L. No. 107-16, §412(b)(2). For sunset provision, see the amendment notes to this section on Pub. L. No. 107-16.

(f) Inflation Adjustments.—

Editor's Note

Caution: IRC §221(f)(1), as follows, was amended by Pub. L. No. 107-16. For sunset provision, see amendment notes to this section on Pub. L. No. 107-16.

---

(1) In general.—In the case of a taxable year beginning after 2002, the $50,000 and $100,000 amounts in subsection (b)(2) shall each be increased by an amount equal to—

(A) such dollar amount, multiplied by

(B) the cost-of-living adjustment determined under section 1(f)(3) for the calendar year in which the taxable year begins, determined by substituting "calendar year 2001" for "calendar year 1992" in subparagraph (B) thereof.

(2) Rounding.—If any amount as adjusted under paragraph (1) is not a multiple of $5,000, such amount shall be rounded to the next lowest multiple of $5,000.

Recent Amendments to §221

Pension Protection Act of 2006 (Pub. L. No. 109-280), as follows:
• **Other Provision.** Act §1304(a) provides:
(a) **Permanent Extension of Modifications.**—Section 901 of the Economic Growth and Tax Relief Reconciliation Act of 2001 [Pub. L. No. 107-16] (relating to sunset provisions) shall not apply to section 402 of such Act (relating to modifications to qualified tuition programs).

Gulf Opportunity Zone Act of 2005 (Pub. L. No. 109-135), as follows:
• IRC §221(d)(2) was amended by Act §412(t) by replacing "this Act" with "the Taxpayer Relief Act of 1997". Eff. Dec. 21, 2005.

American Jobs Creation Act of 2004 (Pub. L. No. 108-357), as follows:
• IRC §221(b)(2)(C)(i) was amended by Act §102(d)(2) by inserting "199," before "222". Eff. tax years beginning after Dec. 31, 2004.

Working Families Tax Relief Act of 2004 (Pub. L. No. 108-311), as follows:
• IRC §221(d)(4) was amended by Act §207(20), by inserting "(determined without regard to subsections (b)(1), (b)(2), and (d)(1)(B) thereof)" after "§152". Eff. tax years beginning after Dec. 31, 2004.

Economic Growth and Tax Relief Reconciliation Act of 2001 (Pub. L. No. 107-16), as follows:
• IRC §221(b)(2)(B) was amended by Act §412(b)(1) by replacing cls. (i)–(ii) with new cls. (i)–(ii). Eff. tax years ending after Dec. 31, 2001. IRC §221(b)(2)(B)(i)–(ii) prior to amendment:
(i) the excess of—
(I) the taxpayer's modified adjusted gross income for such taxable year, over
(II) $40,000 ($60,000 in the case of a joint return), bears to
(ii) $15,000.
• IRC §221(b)(2)(C) was amended by Act §431(c)(2) by inserting "222," before "911". Eff. for payments made in tax years beginning after Dec. 31, 2001.
• IRC §221(e)(2)(A) by Act §402(b)(2)(B) by inserting "529," after "135,". Eff. tax years beginning after Dec. 31, 2001.
• IRC §221, as amended by Act §402(b)(2)(B), was amended by Act §412(a)(1) by striking subsec. (d) and redesignating subsecs. (e), (f), and (g) as subsecs. (d), (e), and (f), respectively. Eff. with respect to any loan interest paid after Dec. 31, 2001, in tax years ending after such date. IRC §221(d) prior to being stricken:
(d) **Limit on period deduction allowed.**—A deduction shall be allowed under this section only with respect to interest paid on any qualified education loan during the first 60 months (whether or not consecutive) in which interest payments are required. For purposes of this paragraph, any loan and all refinancings of such loan shall be treated as 1 loan. Such 60 months shall be determined in the manner prescribed by the Secretary in the case of multiple loans which are refinanced by, or serviced as, a single loan and in the case of loans incurred before the date of the enactment of this section.
• IRC §221(f)(1), as amended, was amended by Act §412(b)(2) by substituting "$50,000 and $100,000 amounts", for "$40,000 and $60,000 amounts". Eff. for tax years ending after Dec. 31, 2001.
• **Sunset Provision.** Act §901, as amended by Pub. L. No. 111-312, §101(a)(1), provides the sunset rule below. But see Pub. L. No. 109-280, §811, and Pub. L. No. 111-148, §10909(c), as amended by Pub. L. No. 111-312, §101(b)(1).
SEC. 901. SUNSET OF PROVISIONS OF ACT.
(a) **In general.** All provisions of, and amendments made by, this Act shall not apply—
(1) to taxable, plan, or limitation years beginning after December 31, 2012, or
(2) in the case of title V, to estates of decedents dying, gifts made, or generation skipping transfers, after December 31, 2012.
(b) **Application of certain laws.**—The Internal Revenue Code of 1986 and the Employee Retirement Income Security

---

Act of 1974 shall be applied and administered to years, estates, gifts, and transfers described in subsection (a) as if the provisions and amendments described in subsection (a) had never been enacted.

Editor's Note

Caution: IRC §222, as follows, was added by Pub. L. No. 107-16. For sunset provision, see the amendment notes to this section for Pub. L. No. 107-16.

SEC. 222. QUALIFIED TUITION AND RELATED EXPENSES.

(a) Allowance of Deduction.—In the case of an individual, there shall be allowed as a deduction an amount equal to the qualified tuition and related expenses paid by the taxpayer during the taxable year.

(b) Dollar Limitations.—

(1) In general.—The amount allowed as a deduction under subsection (a) with respect to the taxpayer for any taxable year shall not exceed the applicable dollar limit.

(2) Applicable dollar limit.—

(A) 2002 and 2003.—In the case of a taxable year beginning in 2002 or 2003, the applicable dollar limit shall be equal to—

(i) in the case of a taxpayer whose adjusted gross income for the taxable year does not exceed $65,000 ($130,000 in the case of a joint return), $3,000, and—

(ii) in the case of any other taxpayer, zero.

(B) After 2003.—In the case of any taxable year beginning after 2003, the applicable dollar amount shall be equal to—

(i) in the case of a taxpayer whose adjusted gross income for the taxable year does not exceed $65,000 ($130,000 in the case of a joint return), $4,000,

(ii) in the case of a taxpayer not described in clause (i) whose adjusted gross income for the taxable year does not exceed $80,000 ($160,000 in the case of a joint return), $2,000, and

(iii) in the case of any other taxpayer, zero.

(C) Adjusted gross income.—For purposes of this paragraph, adjusted gross income shall be determined—

(i) without regard to this section and sections 199, 911, 931, and 933, and

(ii) after application of sections 86, 135, 137, 219, 221, and 469.

(c) No Double Benefit.—

(1) In general.—No deduction shall be allowed under subsection (a) for any expense for which a deduction is allowed to the taxpayer under any other provision of this chapter.

(2) Coordination with other education incentives.—

(A) Denial of deduction if credit elected.—No deduction shall be allowed under subsection (a) for a taxable year with respect to the qualified tuition and related expenses with respect to an individual if the taxpayer or any other person elects to have section 25A apply with respect to such individual for such year.

(B) Coordination with exclusions.—The total amount of qualified tuition and related expenses shall be reduced by the amount of such expenses taken into account in determining any amount excluded under section 135, 529(c)(1), or 530(d)(2). For purposes of the preceding sentence, the amount taken into account in determining the amount excluded under section 529(c)(1) shall not include that portion of the distribution which represents a return of any contributions to the plan.

(3) Dependents.—No deduction shall be allowed under subsection (a) to any individual with respect to whom a deduction under section 151 is allowable to another taxpayer for a taxable year beginning in the calendar year in which such individual's taxable year begins.

(d) Definitions and Special Rules.—For purposes of this section—

(1) Qualified tuition and related expenses.—The term "qualified tuition and related expenses" has the meaning given such term by section 25A(f). Such expenses shall be reduced in the same manner as under section 25A(g)(2).

(2) Identification requirement.—No deduction shall be allowed under subsection (a) to a taxpayer with respect to the qualified tuition and related expenses of an individual unless the taxpayer includes the name and taxpayer identification number of the individual on the return of tax for the taxable year.

(3) Limitation on taxable year of deduction.—

(A) In general.—A deduction shall be allowed under subsection (a) for qualified tuition and related expenses for any taxable year only to the extent such expenses are in connection with enrollment at an institution of higher education during the taxable year.

(B) Certain prepayments allowed.—Subparagraph (A) shall not apply to qualified tuition and related expenses paid during a taxable year if such expenses are in connection with an academic term beginning during such taxable year or during the first 3 months of the next taxable year.

(4) No deduction for married individuals filing separate returns.—If the taxpayer is a married individual (within the meaning of section 7703), this section shall apply only if the taxpayer and the taxpayer's spouse file a joint return for the taxable year.

(5) Nonresident aliens.—If the taxpayer is a nonresident alien individual for any portion of the taxable year, this section shall apply only if such individual is treated as a resident alien of the United States for purposes of this chapter by reason of an election under subsection (g) or (h) of section 6013.

(6) Regulations.—The Secretary may prescribe such regulations as may be necessary or appropriate to carry out this section, including regulations requiring recordkeeping and information reporting.

Editor's Note

IRC §222(e), below, was amended by Pub. L. No. 111-312, applicable to taxable years beginning after December 31, 2009.

(e) Termination.—This section shall not apply to taxable years beginning after ~~December 31, 2009~~ *December 31, 2011.*

Recent Amendments to IRC §222

Tax Relief, Unemployment Insurance Reauthorization, and Job Creation Act of 2010 (Pub. L. No. 111-312), as follows:
- IRC §222(e) was amended by Act §724(a) by striking "December 31, 2009" and inserting "December 31, 2011". Eff. for taxable years beginning after Dec. 31, 2009.

Emergency Economic Stabilization Act of 2008 (Pub. L. No. 110-343), as follows:
- IRC §222(e) was amended by Act, Div. C, §202(a), by striking "December 31, 2007" and inserting "December 31, 2009". Eff. for tax years beginning after Dec. 31, 2007.

Tax Relief and Health Care Act of 2006 (Pub. L. No. 109-432), as follows:
- IRC §222(b)(2)(B) was amended by Act, Div. A, §101(b)(1)–(2) by replacing "a taxable year beginning in 2004 or 2005" with "any taxable year beginning after 2003", and replacing "2004 and 2005" in the heading with "after 2003". Eff. tax years beginning after Dec. 31, 2005.
- IRC §222(e) was amended by Act, Division A, §101(a) by replacing "2005" with "2007". Eff. tax years beginning after Dec. 31, 2005.

American Jobs Creation Act of 2004 (Pub. L. No. 108-357), as follows:
- IRC §222(b)(2)(C)(i) was amended by Act §102(d)(3) by inserting "199," before "911". Eff. tax years beginning after Dec. 31, 2004.

Economic Growth and Tax Relief Reconciliation Act of 2001 (Pub. L. No. 107-16), as follows:
- Amended part VII of subchapter B of chapter 1 by redesignating IRC §222 as IRC §223 and inserting new IRC §222. Eff. for payments made in tax years beginning after Dec. 31, 2001.
- **Sunset Provision.** Act §901, as amended by Pub. L. No. 111-312, §101(a)(1), provides the sunset rule below. But see Pub. L. No. 109-280, §811, and Pub. L. No. 111-148, §10909(c), as amended by Pub. L. No. 111-312, §101(b)(1).
  SEC. 901. SUNSET OF PROVISIONS OF ACT.
  (a) In general. All provisions of, and amendments made by, this Act shall not apply—
  (1) to taxable, plan, or limitation years beginning after December 31, 2012, or

(2) in the case of title V, to estates of decedents dying, gifts made, or generation skipping transfers, after December 31, 2012.
(b) Application of certain laws.—The Internal Revenue Code of 1986 and the Employee Retirement Income Security Act of 1974 shall be applied and administered to years, estates, gifts, and transfers described in subsection (a) as if the provisions and amendments described in subsection (a) had never been enacted.

SEC. 223. HEALTH SAVINGS ACCOUNTS.

(a) Deduction Allowed.—In the case of an individual who is an eligible individual for any month during the taxable year, there shall be allowed as a deduction for the taxable year an amount equal to the aggregate amount paid in cash during such taxable year by or on behalf of such individual to a health savings account of such individual.

(b) Limitations.—

(1) In general.—The amount allowable as a deduction under subsection (a) to an individual for the taxable year shall not exceed the sum of the monthly limitations for months during such taxable year that the individual is an eligible individual.

(2) Monthly limitation.—The monthly limitation for any month is $1/12$ of—

(A) in the case of an eligible individual who has self-only coverage under a high deductible health plan as of the first day of such month, $2,250.

(B) in the case of an eligible individual who has family coverage under a high deductible health plan as of the first day of such month, $4,500.

(3) Additional contributions for individuals 55 or older.

(A) In general.—In the case of an individual who has attained age 55 before the close of the taxable year, the applicable limitation under subparagraphs (A) and (B) of paragraph (2) shall be increased by the additional contribution amount.

(B) Additional contribution amount.—For purposes of this section, the additional contribution amount is the amount determined in accordance with the following table:

For taxable years beginning in:	The additional contribution amount is:
2004	$500
2005	$600
2006	$700
2007	$800
2008	$900
2009 and thereafter	$1,000.

(4) Coordination with other contributions.—The limitation which would (but for this paragraph) apply under this subsection to an individual for any taxable year shall be reduced (but not below zero) by the sum of—

(A) the aggregate amount paid for such taxable year to Archer MSAs of such individual,

(B) the aggregate amount contributed to health savings accounts of such individual which is excludable from the taxpayer's gross income for such taxable year under section 106(d) (and such amount shall not be allowed as a deduction under subsection (a)). Subparagraph (A) shall not apply with respect to any individual to whom paragraph (5) applies, and

(C) the aggregate amount contributed to health savings accounts of such individual for such taxable year under section 408(d)(9) (and such amount shall not be allowed as a deduction under subsection (a)).

(5) Special rule for married individuals.—In the case of individuals who are married to each other, if either spouse has family coverage—

(A) both spouses shall be treated as having only such family coverage (and if such spouses each have family coverage under different plans, as having the family coverage with the lowest annual deductible), and

(B) the limitation under paragraph (1) (after the application of subparagraph (A) and without regard to any additional contribution amount under paragraph (3))—

(i) shall be reduced by the aggregate amount paid to Archer MSAs of such spouses for the taxable year, and

(ii) after such reduction, shall be divided equally between them unless they agree on a different division.

(6) Denial of deduction to dependents.—No deduction shall be allowed under this section to any individual with respect to whom a deduction under section 151 is allowable to another taxpayer for a taxable year beginning in the calendar year in which such individual's taxable year begins.

(7) Medicare eligible individuals.—The limitation under this subsection for any month with respect to an individual shall be zero for the first month such individual is entitled to benefits under title XVIII of the Social Security Act and for each month thereafter.

(8) Increase in limit for individuals becoming eligible individuals after the beginning of the year.—

(A) In general—For purposes of computing the limitation under paragraph (1) for any taxable year, an individual who is an eligible individual during the last month of such taxable year shall be treated—

(i) as having been an eligible individual during each of the months in such taxable year, and

(ii) as having been enrolled, during each of the months such individual is treated as an eligible individual solely by reason of clause (i), in the same high deductible health plan in which the individual was enrolled for the last month of such taxable year.

(B) Failure to maintain high deductible health plan coverage.—

(i) In general.—If, at any time during the testing period, the individual is not an eligible individual, then—

(I) gross income of the individual for the taxable year in which occurs the first month in the testing period for which such individual is not an eligible individual is increased by the aggregate amount of all contributions to the health savings account of the individual which could not have been made but for subparagraph (A), and

(II) the tax imposed by this chapter for any taxable year on the individual shall be increased by 10 percent of the amount of such increase.

(ii) Exception for disability or death.—Subclauses (I) and (II) of clause (i) shall not apply if the individual ceased to be an eligible individual by reason of the death of the individual or the individual becoming disabled (within the meaning of section 72(m)(7)).

(iii) Testing period.—The term "testing period" means the period beginning with the last month of the taxable year referred to in subparagraph (A) and ending on the last day of the 12th month following such month.

(c) Definitions and Special Rules.—For purposes of this section—

(1) Eligible individual.

(A) In general.—The term "eligible individual" means, with respect to any month, any individual if—

(i) such individual is covered under a high deductible health plan as of the 1st day of such month, and

(ii) such individual is not, while covered under a high deductible health plan, covered under any health plan—

(I) which is not a high deductible health plan, and

(II) which provides coverage for any benefit which is covered under the high deductible health plan.

(B) Certain coverage disregarded.—Subparagraph (A)(ii) shall be applied without regard to—

IRC Sec. 223(c)(1)(B)

(i) coverage for any benefit provided by permitted insurance,

(ii) coverage (whether through insurance or otherwise) for accidents, disability, dental care, vision care, or long-term care, and

(iii) for taxable years beginning after December 31, 2006, coverage under a health flexible spending arrangement during any period immediately following the end of a plan year of such arrangement during which unused benefits or contributions remaining at the end of such plan year may be paid or reimbursed to plan participants for qualified benefit expenses incurred during such period if—

(I) the balance in such arrangement at the end of such plan year is zero, or

(II) the individual is making a qualified HSA distribution (as defined in section 106(e)) in an amount equal to the remaining balance in such arrangement as of the end of such plan year, in accordance with rules prescribed by the Secretary.

(2) High deductible health plan.—

(A) In general.—The term "high deductible health plan" means a health plan—

(i) which has an annual deductible which is not less than—

(I) $1,000 for self-only coverage, and

(II) twice the dollar amount in subclause (I) for family coverage, and

(ii) the sum of the annual deductible and the other annual out-of-pocket expenses required to be paid under the plan (other than for premiums) for covered benefits does not exceed—

(I) $5,000 for self-only coverage, and

(II) twice the dollar amount in subclause (I) for family coverage.

(B) Exclusion of certain plans.—Such term does not include a health plan if substantially all of its coverage is coverage described in paragraph (1)(B).

(C) Safe harbor for absence of preventive care deductible.—A plan shall not fail to be treated as a high deductible health plan by reason of failing to have a deductible for preventive care (within the meaning of section 1871 of the Social Security Act, except as otherwise provided by the Secretary).

(D) Special rules for network plans.—In the case of a plan using a network of providers—

(i) Annual out-of-pocket limitation.—Such plan shall not fail to be treated as a high deductible health plan by reason of having an out-of-pocket limitation for services provided outside of such network which exceeds the applicable limitation under subparagraph (A)(ii).

(ii) Annual deductible.—Such plan's annual deductible for services provided outside of such network shall not be taken into account for purposes of subsection (b)(2).

(3) Permitted insurance.—The term "permitted insurance" means—

(A) insurance if substantially all of the coverage provided under such insurance relates to—

(i) liabilities incurred under workers' compensation laws,

(ii) tort liabilities,

(iii) liabilities relating to ownership or use of property, or

(iv) such other similar liabilities as the Secretary may specify by regulations,

(B) insurance for a specified disease or illness, and

(C) insurance paying a fixed amount per day (or other period) of hospitalization.

(4) Family coverage.—The term "family coverage" means any coverage other than self-only coverage.

(5) Archer MSA.—The term "Archer MSA" has the meaning given such term in section 220(d).

(d) Health Savings Account.—For purposes of this section—

(1) In general.—The term "health savings account" means a trust created or organized in the United States as a health savings account exclusively for the purpose of paying the qualified medical expenses of the account beneficiary, but only if the written governing instrument creating the trust meets the following requirements:

(A) Except in the case of a rollover contribution described in subsection (f)(5) or section 220(f)(5), no contribution will be accepted—

(i) unless it is in cash, or

(ii) to the extent such contribution, when added to previous contributions to the trust for the calendar year, exceeds the sum of—

(I) the dollar amount in effect under subsection (b)(2)(B), and

(II) the dollar amount in effect under subsection (b)(3)(B).

(B) The trustee is a bank (as defined in section 408(n)), an insurance company (as defined in section 816), or another person who demonstrates to the satisfaction of the Secretary that the manner in which such person will administer the trust will be consistent with the requirements of this section.

(C) No part of the trust assets will be invested in life insurance contracts.

(D) The assets of the trust will not be commingled with other property except in a common trust fund or common investment fund.

(E) The interest of an individual in the balance in his account is nonforfeitable.

(2) Qualified medical expenses.—

Editor's Note

The last sentence of IRC §223(d)(2)(A), below, added by Pub. L. No. 111-148, §9004(a), is effective for amounts paid with respect to taxable years beginning after December 31, 2010.

(A) In general.—The term "qualified medical expenses" means, with respect to an account beneficiary, amounts paid by such beneficiary for medical care (as defined in section 213(d) for such individual, the spouse of such individual, and any dependent (as defined in section 152, determined without regard to subsections (b)(1), (b)(2), and (d)(1)(B) thereof) of such individual, but only to the extent such amounts are not compensated for by insurance or otherwise. Such term shall include an amount paid for medicine or a drug only if such medicine or drug is a prescribed drug (determined without regard to whether such drug is available without a prescription) or is insulin.

(B) Health insurance may not be purchased from account.—Subparagraph (A) shall not apply to any payment for insurance.

(C) Exceptions.—Subparagraph (B) shall not apply to any expense for coverage under—

(i) a health plan during any period of continuation coverage required under any Federal law,

(ii) a qualified long-term care insurance contract (as defined in section 7702B(b)),

(iii) a health plan during a period in which the individual is receiving unemployment compensation under any Federal or State law, or

(iv) in the case of an account beneficiary who has attained the age specified in section 1811 of the Social Security Act, any health insurance other than a medicare supplemental policy (as defined in section 1882 of the Social Security Act).

(3) Account beneficiary.—The term "account beneficiary" means the individual on whose behalf the health savings account was established.

(4) Certain rules to apply.—Rules similar to the following rules shall apply for purposes of this section:

(A) Section 219(d)(2) (relating to no deduction for rollovers).

(B) Section 219(f)(3) (relating to time when contributions deemed made).

(C) Except as provided in section 106(d), section 219(f)(5) (relating to employer payments).

(D) Section 408(g) (relating to community property laws).

(E) Section 408(h) (relating to custodial accounts).

(e) Tax Treatment of Accounts.—

(1) In general.—A health savings account is exempt from taxation under this subtitle unless such account has ceased to be a health savings account. Notwithstanding the preceding sentence, any such account is subject to the taxes imposed by section 511 (relating to imposition of tax on unrelated business income of charitable, etc. organizations).

(2) Account terminations.—Rules similar to the rules of paragraphs (2) and (4) of section 408(e) shall apply to health savings accounts, and any amount treated as distributed under such rules shall be treated as not used to pay qualified medical expenses.

(f) Tax Treatment of Distributions.—

(1) Amounts used for qualified medical expenses.—Any amount paid or distributed out of a health savings account which is used exclusively to pay qualified medical expenses of any account beneficiary shall not be includible in gross income.

(2) Inclusion of amounts not used for qualified medical expenses.—Any amount paid or distributed out of a health savings account which is not used exclusively to pay the qualified medical expenses of the account beneficiary shall be included in the gross income of such beneficiary.

(3) Excess contributions returned before due date of return.—

(A) In general.—If any excess contribution is contributed for a taxable year to any health savings account of an individual, paragraph (2) shall not apply to distributions from the health savings accounts of such individual (to the extent such distributions do not exceed the aggregate excess contributions to all such accounts of such individual for such year) if—

(i) such distribution is received by the individual on or before the last day prescribed by law (including extensions of time) for filing such individual's return for such taxable year, and

(ii) such distribution is accompanied by the amount of net income attributable to such excess contribution.

Any net income described in clause (ii) shall be included in the gross income of the individual for the taxable year in which it is received.

(B) Excess contribution.—For purposes of subparagraph (A), the term "excess contribution"

IRC Sec. 223(f)(3)(B)

means any contribution (other than a rollover contribution described in paragraph (5) or section 220(f)(5)) which is neither excludable from gross income under section 106(d) nor deductible under this section.

(4) Additional tax on distributions not used for qualified medical expenses.—

> *Editor's Note*
>
> IRC §223(f)(4)(A), below, is effective for distributions made on or before December 31, 2010.

(A) In general.—The tax imposed by this chapter on the account beneficiary for any taxable year in which there is a payment or distribution from a health savings account of such beneficiary which is includible in gross income under paragraph (2) shall be increased by 10 percent of the amount which is so includible.

> *Editor's Note*
>
> IRC §223(f)(4)(A), below, as amended by Pub. L. No. 111-148, §9004, is effective for distributions made after December 31, 2010.

(A) In general.—The tax imposed by this chapter on the account beneficiary for any taxable year in which there is a payment or distribution from a health savings account of such beneficiary which is includible in gross income under paragraph (2) shall be increased by 20 percent of the amount which is so includible.

(B) Exception for disability or death.—Subparagraph (A) shall not apply if the payment or distribution is made after the account beneficiary becomes disabled within the meaning of section 72(m)(7) or dies.

(C) Exception for distributions after Medicare eligibility.—Subparagraph (A) shall not apply to any payment or distribution after the date on which the account beneficiary attains the age specified in section 1811 of the Social Security Act.

(5) Rollover contribution.—An amount is described in this paragraph as a rollover contribution if it meets the requirements of subparagraphs (A) and (B).

(A) In general.—Paragraph (2) shall not apply to any amount paid or distributed from a health savings account to the account beneficiary to the extent the amount received is paid into a health savings account for the benefit of such beneficiary not later than the 60th day after the day on which the beneficiary receives the payment or distribution.

(B) Limitation.—This paragraph shall not apply to any amount described in subparagraph (A) received by an individual from a health savings account if, at any time during the 1-year period ending on the day of such receipt, such individual received any other amount described in subparagraph (A) from a health savings account which was not includible in the individual's gross income because of the application of this paragraph.

(6) Coordination with medical expense deduction.—For purposes of determining the amount of the deduction under section 213, any payment or distribution out of a health savings account for qualified medical expenses shall not be treated as an expense paid for medical care.

(7) Transfer of account incident to divorce.—The transfer of an individual's interest in a health savings account to an individual's spouse or former spouse under a divorce or separation instrument described in subparagraph (A) of section 71(b)(2) shall not be considered a taxable transfer made by such individual notwithstanding any other provision of this subtitle, and such interest shall, after such transfer, be treated as a health savings account with respect to which such spouse is the account beneficiary.

(8) Treatment after death of account beneficiary.—

(A) Treatment if designated beneficiary is spouse.—If the account beneficiary's surviving spouse acquires such beneficiary's interest in a health savings account by reason of being the designated beneficiary of such account at the death of the account beneficiary, such health savings account shall be treated as if the spouse were the account beneficiary.

(B) Other cases.—

(i) In general.—If, by reason of the death of the account beneficiary, any person acquires the account beneficiary's interest in a health savings account in a case to which subparagraph (A) does not apply—

(I) such account shall cease to be a health savings account as of the date of death, and

(II) an amount equal to the fair market value of the assets in such account on such date shall be includible if such person is not the estate of such beneficiary, in such person's gross income for the taxable year which includes such date, or if such person is the estate of such beneficiary, in such beneficiary's gross income for the last taxable year of such beneficiary.

(ii) Special rules.—

(I) Reduction of inclusion for predeath expenses.—The amount includible in gross income under clause (i) by any person (other than the estate) shall be reduced by the amount of qualified medical expenses which were incurred by the decedent before the date of the decedent's death and paid by such person within 1 year after such date.

(II) Deduction for estate taxes.—An appropriate deduction shall be allowed under section 691(c) to any person (other than the decedent or the decedent's spouse) with respect to amounts included in gross income under clause (i) by such person.

(g) Cost-of-Living Adjustment.—

(1) In general.—Each dollar amount in subsections (b)(2) and (c)(2)(A) shall be increased by an amount equal to—

(A) such dollar amount, multiplied by

(B) the cost-of-living adjustment determined under section 1(f)(3) for the calendar year in which such taxable year begins determined by substituting for "calendar year 1992" in subparagraph (B) thereof—

(i) except as provided in clause (ii), "calendar year 1997", and

(ii) in the case of each dollar amount in subsection (c)(2)(A), "calendar year 2003".

In the case of adjustments made for any taxable year beginning after 2007, section 1(f)(4) shall be applied for purposes of this paragraph by substituting "March 31" for "August 31", and the Secretary shall publish the adjusted amounts under subsections (b)(2) and (c)(2)(A) for taxable years beginning in any calendar year no later than June 1 of the preceding calendar year.

(2) Rounding.—If any increase under paragraph (1) is not a multiple of $50, such increase shall be rounded to the nearest multiple of $50.

(h) Reports.—The Secretary may require—

(1) the trustee of a health savings account to make such reports regarding such account to the Secretary and to the account beneficiary with respect to contributions, distributions, the return of excess contributions, and such other matters as the Secretary determines appropriate, and

(2) any person who provides an individual with a high deductible health plan to make such reports to the Secretary and to the account beneficiary with respect to such plan as the Secretary determines appropriate.

The reports required by this subsection shall be filed at such time and in such manner and furnished to such individuals at such time and in such manner as may be required by the Secretary.

Recent Amendments to IRC §223

Patient Protection and Affordable Care Act, 2010 (Pub. L. No. 111-148), as follows:

• IRC §223(d)(2)(A) was amended by Act §9003(a) by adding at the end: "Such term shall include an amount paid for medicine or a drug only if such medicine or drug is a prescribed drug (determined without regard to whether such drug is available without a prescription) or is insulin." Eff. for amounts paid with respect to taxable years beginning after Dec. 31, 2010.
• IRC §223(f)(4)(A) was amended by Act §9004(a) substituting "20 percent" for "10 percent". Eff. for distributions made after Dec. 31, 2010.

Tax Relief and Health Care Act of 2006 (Pub. L. No. 109-432), as follows:
• IRC §223(b)(2)(A) was amended by Act, Division A, §303(a)(1) by substituting "$2,250." for "the lesser of —" and all that followed. Eff. tax years beginning after Dec. 31, 2006. IRC §223(b)(2)(A) prior to amendment:
    (A) in the case of an eligible individual who has self-only coverage under a high deductible health plan as of the first day of such month, the lesser of—
    (i) the annual deductible under such coverage, or
    (ii) $2,250, or
• IRC §223(b)(2)(B) was amended by Act, Division A, §303(a)(2) by substituting "$4,500." for "the lesser of —" and all that followed. Eff. tax years beginning after Dec. 31, 2006. IRC §223(b)(2)(B) prior to amendment:
    (B) in the case of an eligible individual who has family coverage under a high deductible health plan as of the first day of such month, the lesser of—
    (i) the annual deductible under such coverage, or
    (ii) $4,500.
• IRC §223(b)(4) was amended by Act, Division A, §307(b) by striking "and" at the end of subpara. (A); by substituting ", and" for the period at the end of subpara. (B); and by adding new subpara. (C). Eff. tax years beginning after Dec. 31, 2006.
• IRC §223(b) was amended by Act, Division A, §305(a) by adding new para. (8). Eff. tax years beginning after Dec. 31, 2006.
• IRC §223(c)(1)(B) was amended by Act, Division A, §302(b) by striking "and" at the end of cl. (i); by substituting ", and" for the period at the end of cl. (ii); and by adding new cl. (iii). Eff. Dec. 20, 2006.
• IRC §223(d)(1)(A)(ii)(I) was amended by Act, Division A, §303(b) by substituting "subsection (b)(2)(B)" for "subsection (b)(2)(B)(ii)". Eff. tax years beginning after Dec. 31, 2006.
• IRC §223(g)(1) was amended by Act, Division A, §304 by adding the flush sentence at the end. Eff. Dec. 20, 2006.

Gulf Opportunity Zone Act of 2005 (Pub. L. No. 109-135), as follows:
• IRC §223(d)(2)(A) was amended by Act §404(c) by inserting ", determined without regard to subsection (b)(1), (b)(2), and (d)(1)(B) thereof" after "§152". Eff. tax years beginning after Dec. 31, 2004, as if included in the provision of Pub. L. No. 108-311 to which it relates.

---

* * *

Part IX—Items Not Deductible
* * *

SEC. 264. CERTAIN AMOUNTS PAID IN CONNECTION WITH INSURANCE CONTRACTS.

(a) General Rule.—No deduction shall be allowed for—

(1) Premiums on any life insurance policy, or endowment or annuity contract, if the taxpayer is directly or indirectly a beneficiary under the policy or contract.

(2) Any amount paid or accrued on indebtedness incurred or continued to purchase or carry a single premium life insurance, endowment, or annuity contract.

(3) Except as provided in subsection (d), any amount paid or accrued on indebtedness incurred or continued to purchase or carry a life insurance, endowment, or annuity contract (other than a single premium contract or a contract treated as a single premium contract) pursuant to a plan of purchase which contemplates the systematic direct or indirect borrowing of part or all of the increases in the cash value of such contract (either from the insurer or otherwise).

(4) Except as provided in subsection (e), any interest paid or accrued on any indebtedness with respect to 1 or more life insurance policies owned by the taxpayer covering the life of any individual, or any endowment or annuity contracts owned by the taxpayer covering any individual. Paragraph (2) shall apply in respect of annuity contracts only as to contracts purchased after March 1, 1954. Paragraph (3) shall apply only in respect of contracts purchased after August 6, 1963. Paragraph (4) shall apply with respect to contracts purchased after June 20, 1986.

(b) Exceptions to Subsection (a)(1).—Subsection (a)(1) shall not apply to—

(1) any annuity contract described in section 72(s)(5), and

(2) any annuity contract to which section 72(u) applies.

(c) Contracts Treated as Single Premium Contracts.—For purposes of subsection (a)(2), a contract shall be treated as a single premium contract—

(1) if substantially all the premiums on the contract are paid within a period of 4 years from the date on which the contract is purchased, or

(2) if an amount is deposited after March 1, 1954, with the insurer for payment of a substantial number of future premiums on the contract.

(d) Exceptions.—Subsection (a)(3) shall not apply to any amount paid or accrued by a person during a taxable year on indebtedness incurred or continued as part of a plan referred to in subsection (a)(3)—

(1) if no part of 4 of the annual premiums due during the 7-year period (beginning with the date the first premium on the contract to which such plan relates was paid) is paid under such plan by means of indebtedness,

(2) if the total of the amounts paid or accrued by such person during such taxable year for which (without regard to this paragraph) no deduction would be allowable by reason of subsection (a)(3) does not exceed $100.

(3) if such amount was paid or accrued on indebtedness incurred because of an unforeseen substantial loss of income or unforeseen substantial increase in his financial obligations, or

(4) if such indebtedness was incurred in connection with his trade or business. For purposes of applying paragraph (1), if there is a substantial increase in the premiums on a contract, a new 7-year period described in such paragraph with respect to such contract shall commence on the date of first such increased premium is paid.

(e) Special Rules for Application of Subsection (a)(4).—

(1) Exception for key persons.—Subsection (a)(4) shall not apply to any interest paid or accrued on any indebtedness with respect to policies or contracts covering an individual who is a key person to the extent that the aggregate amount of such indebtedness with respect to policies and contracts covering such individual does not exceed $50,000.

(2) Interest rate cap on key persons and pre-1986 contracts.—

(A) In general.—No deduction shall be allowed by reason of paragraph (1) or the last sentence of subsection (a) with respect to interest paid or accrued for any month beginning after December 31, 1995, to the extent the amount of such interest exceeds the amount which would have been determined if the applicable rate of interest were used for such month.

(B) Applicable rate of interest.—For purposes of subparagraph (A)—

(i) In general.—The applicable rate of interest for any month is the rate of interest described as Moody's Corporate Bond Yield Average-Monthly Average Corporates as published by Moody's Investors Service, Inc., or any successor thereto, for such month.

(ii) Pre-1986 contracts.—In the case of indebtedness on a contract purchased on or before June 20, 1986—

(I) which is a contract providing a fixed rate of interest, the applicable rate of interest for any month shall be the Moody's rate described in clause (i) for the month in which the contract was purchased, or

(II) which is a contract providing a variable rate of interest, the applicable rate of interest for any month in an applicable period shall be such Moody's rate for the third month preceding the first month in such period.

For purposes of subclause (II), the term "applicable period" means the 12-month period beginning on the date the policy is issued (and each successive 12-month period thereafter) unless the taxpayer elects a number of months (not greater than 12) other than the 12-month period to be its applicable period. Such an election shall be made not later than the 90th day after the date of the enactment of this sentence and, if made, shall apply to the taxpayer's first taxable year ending on or after October 13, 1995, and all subsequent taxable years unless revoked with the consent of the Secretary.

(3) Key person.—For purposes of paragraph (1), the term "key person" means an officer or 20-percent owner, except that the number of individuals who may be treated as key persons with respect to any taxpayer shall not exceed the greater of—

(A) 5 individuals, or

(B) the lesser of 5 percent of the total officers and employees of the taxpayer or 20 individuals.

(4) 20-percent owner.—For purposes of this subsection, the term "20-percent owner" means—

(A) if the taxpayer is a corporation, any person who owns directly 20 percent or more of the outstanding stock of the corporation or stock possessing 20 percent or more of the total combined voting power of all stock of the corporation, or

(B) if the taxpayer is not a corporation, any person who owns 20 percent or more of the capital or profits interest in the taxpayer.

(5) Aggregation rules.—

(A) In general.—For purposes of paragraph (4)(A) and applying the $50,000 limitation in paragraph (1)—

(i) all members of a controlled group shall be treated as 1 taxpayer, and

(ii) such limitation shall be allocated among the members of such group in such manner as the Secretary may prescribe.

(B) Controlled group.—For purposes of this paragraph, all persons treated as a single employer under subsection (a) or (b) of section 52 or subsection (m) or (o) of section 414 shall be treated as members of a controlled group.

(f) Pro Rata Allocation of Interest Expense to Policy Cash Values.—

(1) In general.—No deduction shall be allowed for that portion of the taxpayer's interest expense which is allocable to unborrowed policy cash values.

(2) Allocation.—For purposes of paragraph (1), the portion of the taxpayer's interest expense which is allocable to unborrowed policy cash values is an amount which bears the same ratio to such interest expense as—

(A) the taxpayer's average unborrowed policy cash values of life insurance policies, and annuity and endowment contracts, issued after June 8, 1997, bears to

(B) the sum of—

(i) in the case of assets of the taxpayer which are life insurance policies or annuity or endow-

ment contracts, the average unborrowed policy cash values of such policies and contracts, and

(ii) in the case of assets of the taxpayer not described in clause (i), the average adjusted bases (within the meaning of section 1016) of such assets.

(3) Unborrowed policy cash value.—For purposes of this subsection, the term "unborrowed policy cash value" means, with respect to any life insurance policy or annuity or endowment contract, the excess of—

(A) the cash surrender value of such policy or contract determined without regard to any surrender charge, over

(B) the amount of any loan with respect to such policy or contract.

If the amount described in subparagraph (A) with respect to any policy or contract does not reasonably approximate its actual value, the amount taken into account under subparagraph (A) shall be the greater of the amount of the insurance company liability or the insurance company reserve with respect to such policy or contract (as determined for purposes of the annual statement approved by the National Association of Insurance Commissioners) or shall be such other amount as is determined by the Secretary.

(4) Exception for certain policies and contracts.—

(A) Policies and contracts covering 20-percent owners, officers, directors, and employees.—Paragraph (1) shall not apply to any policy or contract owned by an entity engaged in a trade or business if such policy or contract covers only 1 individual and if such individual is (at the time first covered by the policy or contract)—

(i) a 20-percent owner of such entity, or

(ii) an individual (not described in clause (i)) who is an officer, director, or employee of such trade or business.

A policy or contract covering a 20-percent owner of such entity shall not be treated as failing to meet the requirements of the preceding sentence by reason of covering the joint lives of such owner and such owner's spouse.

(B) Contracts subject to current income inclusion.—Paragraph (1) shall not apply to any annuity contract to which section 72(u) applies.

(C) Coordination with paragraph (2).—Any policy or contract to which paragraph (1) does not apply by reason of this paragraph shall not be taken into account under paragraph (2).

(D) 20-percent owner.—For purposes of subparagraph (A), the term "20-percent owner" has the meaning given such term by subsection (e)(4).

IRC Sec. 264(f)(4)(D)

(E) Master Contracts.—If coverage for each insured under a master contract is treated as a separate contract for purposes of sections 817(h), 7702, and 7702A, coverage for each such insured shall be treated as a separate contract for purposes of subparagraph (A). For purposes of the preceding sentence, the term "master contract" shall not include any group life insurance contract (as defined in section 848(e)(2)).

(5) Exception for policies and contracts held by natural persons; treatment of partnerships and S corporations.—

(A) Policies and contracts held by natural persons.—

(i) In general.—This subsection shall not apply to any policy or contract held by a natural person.

(ii) Exception where business is beneficiary.— If a trade or business is directly or indirectly the beneficiary under any policy or contract, such policy or contract shall be treated as held by such trade or business and not by a natural person.

(iii) Special rules.—

(I) Certain trades or businesses not taken into account.—Clause (ii) shall not apply to any trade or business carried on as a sole proprietorship and to any trade or business performing services as an employee.

(II) Limitation on unborrowed cash value.— The amount of the unborrowed cash value of any policy or contract which is taken into account by reason of clause (ii) shall not exceed the benefit to which the trade or business is directly or indirectly entitled under the policy or contract.

(iv) Reporting.—The Secretary shall require such reporting from policyholders and issuers as is necessary to carry out clause (ii).

(B) Treatment of partnerships and S corporations.—In the case of a partnership or S corporation, this subsection shall be applied at the partnership and corporate levels.

(6) Special rules.—

(A) Coordination with subsection (a) and section 265.—If interest on any indebtedness is disallowed under subsection (a) or section 265—

(i) such disallowed interest shall not be taken into account for purposes of applying this subsection, and

(ii) the amount otherwise taken into account under paragraph (2)(B) shall be reduced (but not below zero) by the amount of such indebtedness.

(B) Coordination with section 263A.—This subsection shall be applied before the application of section 263A (relating to capitalization of certain expenses where taxpayer produces property).

(7) Interest expense.—The term "interest expense" means the aggregate amount allowable to the taxpayer as a deduction for interest (within the meaning of section 265(b)(4)) for the taxable year (determined without regard to this subsection, section 265(b), and section 291).

(8) Aggregation rules.—

(A) In general.—All members of a controlled group (within the meaning of subsection (e)(5)(B)) shall be treated as 1 taxpayer for purposes of this subsection.

(B) Treatment of insurance companies.—This subsection shall not apply to an insurance company subject to tax under subchapter L, and subparagraph (A) shall be applied without regard to any member of an affiliated group which is an insurance company.

* * *

SEC. 274. DISALLOWANCE OF CERTAIN ENTERTAINMENT, ETC., EXPENSES.

(a) Entertainment, Amusement, Recreation.—

(1) In general.—No deduction otherwise allowable under this chapter shall be allowed for any item—

(A) Activity.—With respect to an activity which is of a type generally considered to constitute entertainment, amusement, or recreation, unless the taxpayer establishes that the item was directly related to, or, in the case of an item directly preceding or following a substantial and bona fide business discussion (including business meetings at a convention or otherwise), that such item was associated with, the active conduct of the taxpayer's trade or business, or

(B) Facility.—With respect to a facility used in connection with an activity referred to in subparagraph (A).

In the case of an item described in subparagraph (A), the deduction shall in no event exceed the portion of such item which meets the requirements of subparagraph (A).

(2) Special rules.—For purposes of applying paragraph (1)—

(A) Dues or fees to any social, athletic, or sporting club or organization shall be treated as items with respect to facilities.

(B) An activity described in section 212 shall be treated as a trade or business.

(C) In the case of a club, paragraph (1)(B) shall apply unless the taxpayer establishes that the facility was used primarily for the furtherance of the taxpayer's trade or business and that the item was directly related to the active conduct of such trade or business.

(3) Denial of deduction for club dues.—Notwithstanding the preceding provisions of this subsection, no deduction shall be allowed under this chapter for amounts paid or incurred for membership in any club organized for business, pleasure, recreation, or other social purpose.

(b) Gifts.—

(1) Limitation.—No deduction shall be allowed under section 162 or section 212 for any expense for gifts made directly or indirectly to any individual to the extent that such expense, when added to prior expenses of the taxpayer for gifts made to such individual during the same taxable year, exceeds $25. For purposes of this section, the term "gift" means any item excludable from gross income of the recipient under section 102 which is not excludable from his gross income under any other provision of this chapter, but such term does not include—

(A) an item having a cost to the taxpayer not in excess of $4.00 on which the name of the taxpayer is clearly and permanently imprinted and which is one of a number of identical items distributed generally by the taxpayer, or

(B) a sign, display rack, or other promotional material to be used on the business premises of the recipient.

(2) Special rules.—

(A) In the case of a gift by a partnership, the limitation contained in paragraph (1) shall apply to the partnership as well as to each member thereof.

(B) For purposes of paragraph (1), a husband and wife shall be treated as one taxpayer.

(c) Certain Foreign Travel.—

(1) In general.—In the case of any individual who travels outside the United States away from home in pursuit of a trade or business or in pursuit of an activity described in section 212, no deduction shall be allowed under section 162, or section 212 for that portion of the expenses of such travel otherwise allowable under such section which, under regulations prescribed by the Secretary, is not allocable to such trade or business or to such activity.

(2) Exception.—Paragraph (1) shall not apply to the expenses of any travel outside the United States away from home if—

(A) such travel does not exceed one week, or

(B) the portion of the time of travel outside the United States away from home which is not attributable to the pursuit of the taxpayer's trade or business or an activity described in section 212 is less than 25 percent of the total time on such travel.

(3) Domestic travel excluded.—For purposes of this subsection, travel outside the United States does not include any travel from one point in the United States to another point in the United States.

(d) Substantiation Required.—No deduction or credit shall be allowed—

(1) under section 162 or 212 for any traveling expense (including meals and lodging while away from home),

(2) for any item with respect to an activity which is of a type generally considered to constitute entertainment, amusement, or recreation, or with respect to a facility used in connection with such an activity,

(3) for any expense for gifts, or

(4) with respect to any listed property (as defined in section 280F(d)(4)),

unless the taxpayer substantiates by adequate records or by sufficient evidence corroborating the taxpayer's own statement (A) the amount of such expense or other item, (B) the time and place of the travel, entertainment, amusement, recreation, or use of the facility or property, or the date and description of the gift, (C) the business purpose of the expense or other item, and (D) the business relationship to the taxpayer of persons entertained, using the facility or property, or receiving the gift. The Secretary may by regulations provide that some or all of the requirements of the preceding sentence shall not apply in the case of an expense which does not exceed an amount prescribed pursuant to such regulations. This subsection shall not apply to any qualified nonpersonal use vehicle (as defined in subsection (i)).

(e) Specific Exceptions to Application of Subsection (a).—Subsection (a) shall not apply to—

(1) Food and beverages for employees.—Expenses for food and beverages (and facilities used in connection therewith) furnished on the business premises of the taxpayer primarily for his employees.

(2) Expenses treated as compensation.—

(A) In general.—Except as provided in subparagraph (B), expenses for goods, services, and facilities, to the extent that the expenses are treated by the taxpayer, with respect to the recipient of the entertainment, amusement, or recreation, as compensation to an employee on the taxpayer's return of tax under this chapter and as wages to such employee for purposes of chapter 24 (relating to withholding of income tax at source on wages).

(B) Specified individuals.—

(i) In general.—In the case of a recipient who is a specified individual, subparagraph (A) and paragraph (9) shall each be applied by substituting "to the extent that the expenses do not exceed the amount of the expenses which" for "to the extent that the expenses".

(ii) Specified individual.—For purposes of clause (i), the term "specified individual" means any individual who—

(I) is subject to the requirements of section 16(a) of the Securities Exchange Act of 1934 with

IRC Sec. 274(e)(2)(B)(ii)(I)

respect to the taxpayer or a related party to the taxpayer, or

(II) would be subject to such requirements if the taxpayer (or such related party) were an issuer of equity securities referred to in such section.

For purposes of this clause, a person is a related party with respect to another person if such person bears a relationship to such other person described in section 267(b) or 707(b).

(3) Reimbursed expenses.—Expenses paid or incurred by the taxpayer, in connection with the performance by him of services for another person (whether or not such other person is his employer), under a reimbursement or other expense allowance arrangement with such other person, but this paragraph shall apply—

(A) where the services are performed for an employer, only if the employer has not treated such expenses in the manner provided in paragraph (2), or

(B) where the services are performed for a person other than an employer, only if the taxpayer accounts (to the extent provided by subsection (d)) to such person.

(4) Recreational, etc., expenses for employees.—Expenses for recreational, social, or similar activities (including facilities therefor) primarily for the benefit of employees (other than employees who are highly compensated employees (within the meaning of section 414(q))). For purposes of this paragraph, an individual owning less than a 10-percent interest in the taxpayer's trade or business shall not be considered a shareholder or other owner, and for such purposes an individual shall be treated as owning any interest owned by a member of his family (within the meaning of section 267(c)(4)). This paragraph shall not apply for purposes of subsection (a)(3).

(5) Employees, stockholder, etc., business meetings.—Expenses incurred by a taxpayer which are directly related to business meetings of his employees, stockholders, agents, or directors.

(6) Meetings of business leagues, etc.—Expenses directly related and necessary to attendance at a business meeting or convention of any organization described in section 501(c)(6) (relating to business leagues, chambers of commerce, real estate boards, and boards of trade) and exempt from taxation under section 501(a).

(7) Items available to public.—Expenses for goods, services, and facilities made available by the taxpayer to the general public.

(8) Entertainment sold to customers.—Expenses for goods or services (including the use of facilities) which are sold by the taxpayer in a bona fide transaction for an adequate and full consideration in money or money's worth.

(9) Expenses includible in income of persons who are not employees.—Expenses paid or incurred by the taxpayer for goods, services, and facilities to the extent that the expenses are includible in the gross income of a recipient of the entertainment, amusement, or recreation who is not an employee of the taxpayer as compensation for services rendered or as a prize or award under section 74. The preceding sentence shall not apply to any amount paid or incurred by the taxpayer if such amount is required to be included (or would be so required except that the amount is less than $600) in any information return filed by such taxpayer under part III of subchapter A of chapter 61 and is not so included.

For purposes of this subsection, any item referred to in subsection (a) be treated as an expense.

(f) Interest, Taxes, Casualty Losses, etc.—This section shall not apply to any deduction allowable to the taxpayer without regard to its connection with his trade or business (or with his income-producing activity). In the case of a taxpayer which is not an individual, the preceding sentence shall be applied as if it were an individual.

(g) Treatment of Entertainment, etc., Type Facility.—For purposes of this chapter, if deductions are under subsection (a) with respect to any portion of a facility, such portion shall be treated as an asset which is used for personal, living, and family purposes (and not as an asset used in the trade or business).

(h) Attendance at Conventions, etc.—

(1) In general.—In the case of any individual who attends a convention, seminar, or similar meeting which is held outside the North American area, no deduction shall be allowed under section 162 for expenses allocable to such meeting unless the taxpayer establishes that the meeting is directly related to the active conduct of his trade or business and that, after taking into account in the manner provided by regulations prescribed by the Secretary—

(A) the purpose of such meeting and the activities taking place at such meeting,

(B) the purposes and activities of the sponsoring organizations or groups,

(C) the residences of the active members of the sponsoring organization and the places at which other meetings of the sponsoring organization or groups have been held or will be held, and

(D) such other relevant factors as the taxpayer may present,

it is as reasonable for the meeting to be held outside the North American area as within the North American area.

(2) Conventions on cruise ships.—In the case of any individual who attends a convention, seminar, or other meeting which is held on any cruise ship, no deduction shall be allowed under section 162 for expenses allocable to such meeting, unless the taxpayer meets the requirements of paragraph (5) and establishes that the meeting is directly related to the active conduct of his trade or business and that—

(A) the cruise ship is a vessel registered in the United States; and

(B) all ports of call of such cruise ship are located in the United States or in possessions of the United States.

With respect to cruises beginning in any calendar year, not more than $2,000 of the expenses attributable to an individual attending one or more meetings may be taken into account under section 162 by reason of the preceding sentence.

(3) Definitions.—For purposes of this subsection—

(A) North American area.—The term "North American area" means the United States, its possessions, and the Trust Territory of the Pacific Islands, and Canada and Mexico.

(B) Cruise ship.—The term "cruise ship" means any vessel sailing within or without the territorial waters of the United States.

(4) Subsection to apply to employer as well as to traveler.—

(A) Except as provided in subparagraph (B), this subsection shall apply to deductions otherwise allowable under section 162 to any person, whether or not such person is the individual attending the convention, seminar, or similar meeting.

(B) This subsection shall not deny a deduction to any person other than the individual attending the convention, seminar, or similar meeting with respect to any amount paid by such person to or on behalf of such individual if includible in the gross income of such individual. The preceding sentence shall not apply if the amount is required to be included in any information return filed by such person under part III of subchapter A of chapter 61 and is not so included.

(5) Reporting requirements.—No deduction shall be allowed under section 162 for expenses allocable to attendance at a convention, seminar, or similar meeting on any cruise ship unless the taxpayer claiming the deduction attaches to the return of tax on which the deduction is claimed—

(A) a written statement signed by the individual attending the meeting which includes—

(i) information with respect to the total days of the trip, excluding the days of transportation to and from the cruise ship port, and the number of hours of each day of the trip which such individual devoted to scheduled business activities,

(ii) a program of the scheduled business activities of the meeting, and

(iii) such other information as may be required in regulations prescribed by the Secretary; and

(B) a written statement signed by an officer of the organization or group sponsoring the meeting which includes—

(i) a schedule of the business activities of each day of the meeting,

(ii) the number of hours which the individual attending the meeting attended such scheduled business activities, and

(iii) such other information as may be required in regulations prescribed by the Secretary.

(6) Treatment of conventions in certain Caribbean countries.—

(A) In general.—For purposes of this subsection, the term "North American area" includes, with respect to any convention, seminar, or similar meeting, any beneficiary country if (as of the time such meeting begins)—

(i) there is in effect a bilateral or multilateral agreement described in subparagraph (C) between such country and the United States providing for the exchange of information between the United States and such country, and

(ii) there is not in effect a finding by the Secretary that the tax laws of such country discriminate against conventions held in the United States.

(B) Beneficiary country.—For purposes of this paragraph, the term "beneficiary country" has the meaning given to such term by section 212(a)(1)(A) of the Caribbean Basin Economic Recovery Act; except that such term shall include Bermuda.

(C) Authority to conclude exchange of information agreements.—

(i) In general.—The Secretary is authorized to negotiate and conclude an agreement for the exchange of information with any beneficiary country. Except as provided in clause (ii), an exchange of information agreement shall provide for the exchange of such information (not limited to information concerning nationals or residents of the United States or the beneficiary country) as may be necessary or appropriate to carry out and enforce the tax laws of the United States and the beneficiary country (whether criminal or civil proceedings), including information which may otherwise be subject to nondisclosure provisions of the local law of the beneficiary country such as provisions respecting bank secrecy and bearer shares. The exchange of information agreement shall be terminable by either country on reasonable notice and shall provide that information received by either country will be disclosed only to persons or authorities (including courts and administrative bod-

IRC Sec. 274(h)(6)(C)(i)

ies) involved in the administration or oversight of, or in the determination of appeals in respect of, taxes of the United States or the beneficiary country and will be used by such persons or authorities only for such purposes.

(ii) Nondisclosure of qualified confidential information sought for civil tax purposes.—An exchange of information agreement need not provide for the exchange of qualified confidential information which is sought only for civil tax purposes if—

(I) the Secretary of the Treasury, after making all reasonable efforts to negotiate an agreement which includes the exchange of such information, determines that such an agreement cannot be negotiated but that the agreement which was negotiated will significantly assist in the administration and enforcement of the tax laws of the United States, and

(II) the President determines that the agreement as negotiated is in the national security interest of the United States.

(iii) Qualified confidential information defined.—For purposes of this subparagraph, the term "qualified confidential information" means information which is subject to the nondisclosure provisions of any local law of the beneficiary country regarding bank secrecy or ownership of bearer shares.

(iv) Civil tax purposes.—For purposes of this subparagraph, the determination of whether information is sought only for civil tax purposes shall be made by the requesting party.

(D) Coordination with other provisions.—Any exchange of information agreement negotiated under subparagraph (C) shall be treated as an income tax convention for purposes of section 6103(k)(4). The Secretary may exercise his authority under subchapter A of chapter 78 to carry out any obligation of the United States under an agreement referred to in subparagraph (C).

(E) Determinations published in the Federal Register.—The following shall be published in the Federal Register—

(i) any determination by the President under subparagraph (C)(ii) (including the reasons for such determination),

(ii) any determination by the Secretary under subparagraph (C)(ii) (including the reasons for such determination), and

(iii) any finding by the Secretary under subparagraph (A)(ii) (and any termination thereof).

(7) Seminars, etc. for section 212 purposes.— No deduction shall be allowed under section 212 for expenses allocable to a convention, seminar, or similar meeting.

(i) Qualified Nonpersonal Use Vehicle.—For purposes of subsection (d), the term "qualified nonpersonal use vehicle" means any vehicle which, by reason of its nature, is not likely to be used more than a de minimis amount for personal purposes.

(j) Employee Achievement Awards.—

(1) General rule.—No deduction shall be allowed under section 162 or section 212 for the cost of an employee achievement award except to the extent that such cost does not exceed the deduction limitations of paragraph (2).

(2) Deduction limitations.—The deduction for the cost of an employee achievement award made by an employer to an employee—

(A) which is not a qualified plan award, when added to the cost to the employer for all other employee achievement awards made to such employee during the taxable year which are not qualified plan awards, shall not exceed $400, and

(B) which is a qualified plan award, when added to the cost to the employer for all other employee achievement awards made to such employee during the taxable year (including employee achievement awards which are not qualified plan awards), shall not exceed $1,600.

(3) Definitions.—For purposes of this subsection—

(A) Employee achievement award. The term "employee achievement award" means an item of tangible personal property which is—

(i) transferred by an employer to an employee for length of service achievement or safety achievement,

(ii) awarded as part of a meaningful presentation, and

(iii) awarded under conditions and circumstances that do not create a significant likelihood of the payment of disguised compensation.

(B) Qualified plan award.—

(i) In general.—The term "qualified plan award" means an employee achievement award awarded as part of an established written plan or program of the taxpayer which does not discriminate in favor of highly compensated employees (within the meaning of section 414(q)) as to eligibility or benefits.

(ii) Limitation.—An employee achievement award shall not be treated as a qualified plan award for any taxable year if the average cost of all employee achievement awards which are provided by the employer during the year, and which would be qualified plan awards but for this subparagraph, exceeds $400. For purposes of the preceding sentence, average cost shall be determined by including the entire cost of qualified plan awards, without taking into account employee achievement awards of nominal value.

(4) Special rules.—For purposes of this subsection—

(A) Partnerships.—In the case of an employee achievement award made by a partnership, the deduction limitations contained in paragraph (2) shall apply to the partnership as well as to each member thereof.

(B) Length of service awards.—An item shall not be treated as having been provided for length of service achievement if the item is received during the recipient's 1st 5 years of employment or if the recipient received a length of service achievement award (other than an award excludable under section 132(e)(1)) during that year or any of the prior 4 years.

(C) Safety achievement awards.—An item provided by an employer to an employee shall not be treated as having been provided for safety achievement if—

(i) during the taxable year, employee achievement awards (other than awards excludable under section 132(e)(1)) for safety achievement have previously been awarded by the employer to more than 10 percent of the employees of the employer (excluding employees described in clause (ii)), or

(ii) such item is awarded to a manager, administrator, clerical employee, or other professional employee.

(k) Business Meals.—

(1) In general.—No deduction shall be allowed under this chapter for the expense of any food or beverages unless—

(A) such expense is not lavish or extravagant under the circumstances, and

(B) the taxpayer (or an employee of the taxpayer) is present at the furnishing of such food or beverages.

(2) Exceptions.—Paragraph (1) shall not apply to—

(A) any expense described in paragraph (2), (3), (4), (7), (8), or (9) of subsection (e), and

(B) any other expense to the extent provided in regulations.

(*l*) Additional Limitations on Entertainment Tickets.—

(1) Entertainment tickets.—

(A) In general.—In determining the amount allowable as a deduction under this chapter for any ticket for any activity or facility described in subsection (d)(2), the amount taken into account shall not exceed the face value of such ticket.

(B) Exception for certain charitable sports events.—Subparagraph (A) shall not apply to any ticket for any sports event—

(i) which is organized for the primary purpose of benefiting an organization which is described in section 501(c)(3) and exempt from tax under section 501(a),

(ii) all of the net proceeds of which are contributed to such organization, and

(iii) which utilizes volunteers for substantially all of the work performed in carrying out such event.

(2) Skyboxes, etc.—In the case of a skybox or other private luxury box leased for more than 1 event, the amount allowable as a deduction under this chapter with respect to such events shall not exceed the sum of the face value of non-luxury seat tickets for the seats in such box covered by the lease. For purposes of the preceding sentence, or more related leases shall be treated as 1 lease.

(m) Additional Limitations on Travel Expenses.—

(1) Luxury water transportation.—

(A) In general.—No deduction shall be allowed under this chapter for expenses incurred for transportation by water to the extent such expenses exceed twice the aggregate per diem amounts for days of such transportation. For purposes of the preceding sentence, the term "per diem amounts" means the highest amount generally allowable with respect to a day to employees of the executive branch of the Federal Government for per diem while away from home but serving in the United States.

(B) Exceptions.—Subparagraph (A) shall not apply to—

(i) any expense allocable to a convention, seminar, or other meeting which is held on any cruise ship, and

(ii) any expense described in paragraph (2), (3), (4), (7), (8), or (9) of subsection (e).

(2) Travel as form of education.—No deduction shall be allowed under this chapter for expenses for travel as a form of education.

(3) Travel expenses of spouse, dependent, or others.—No deduction shall be allowed under this chapter (other than section 217) for travel expenses paid or incurred with respect to a spouse, dependent, or other individual accompanying the taxpayer (or an officer or employee of the taxpayer) on business travel, unless—

(A) the spouse, dependent, or other individual is an employee of the taxpayer,

(B) the travel of the spouse, dependent, or other individual is for a bona fide business purpose, and

(C) such expenses would otherwise be deductible by the spouse, dependent, or other individual.

(n) Only 50 Percent of Meal and Entertainment Expenses Allowed as Deduction.—

(1) In general.—The amount allowable as a deduction under this chapter for—

(A) any expense for food or beverages, and

(B) any item with respect to an activity which is of a type generally considered to constitute entertainment, amusement, or recreation, or with respect to a facility used in connection with such activity, shall not exceed 50 percent 5 of the amount of such expense or item which would (but for this paragraph) be allowable as a deduction under this chapter.

(2) Exceptions.—Paragraph (1) shall not apply to any expense if—

(A) such expense is described in paragraph (2), (3), (4), (7), (8), or (9) of subsection (e),

(B) in the case of an expense for food or beverages, such expense is excludable from the gross income of the recipient under section 132 by reason of subsection (e) thereof (relating to de minimis fringes),

(C) such expense is covered by a package involving a ticket described in subsection (l)(1)(B),

(D) in the case of an employer who pays or reimburses moving expenses of an employee, such expenses are includible in the income of the employee under section 82, or

(E) such expense is for food or beverages—

(i) required by any Federal law to be provided to crew members of a commercial vessel,

(ii) provided to crew members of a commercial vessel—

(I) which is operating on the Great Lakes, the Saint Lawrence Seaway, or any inland waterway of the United States, and

(II) which is of a kind which would be required by Federal law to provide food and beverages to crew members if it were operated at sea,

(iii) provided on an oil or gas platform or drilling rig if the platform or rig is located offshore, or

(iv) provided on an oil or gas platform or drilling rig, or at a support camp which is in proximity and integral to such platform or rig, if the platform or rig is located in the United States north of 54 degrees north latitude.

Clauses (i) and (ii) of subparagraph (E) shall not apply to vessels primarily engaged in providing luxury water transportation (determined under the principles of subsection (m)). In the case of the em-

ployee, the exception of subparagraph (A) shall not apply to expenses described in subparagraph (D).

(3) Special rule for individuals subject to federal hours of service.—

(A) In general.—In the case of any expenses for food or beverages consumed while away from home (within the meaning of section 162(a)(2)) by an individual during, or incident to, the period of duty subject to the hours of service limitations of the Department of Transportation, paragraph (1) shall be applied by substituting "the applicable percentage" for "50 percent".

(B) Applicable percentage.—For purposes of this paragraph, the term "applicable percentage" means the percentage determined under the following table:

For taxable years beginning in calendar year—	The applicable percentage is—
1998 or 1999	55
2000 or 2001	60
2002 or 2003	65
2004 or 2005	70
2006 or 2007	75
2008 or thereafter	80

(o) Regulatory Authority.—The Secretary shall prescribe such regulations as he may deem necessary to carry out the purposes of this section, including regulations prescribing whether subsection (a) or subsection (b) applies in cases where both such subsections would otherwise apply.

Recent Amendments to IRC §274

Gulf Opportunity Zone Act of 2005 (Pub. L. No. 109-135), as follows:

• IRC §274(e)(2)(B)(ii)(I) was amended by Act §403(mm)(1) by inserting "or a related party to the taxpayer" after "the taxpayer". Eff. for expenses incurred after Oct. 22, 2004, as if included in the provision of Pub. L. No. 108-357 to which it relates.

• IRC §274(e)(2)(B)(ii)(II) was amended by Act §403(mm)(2) by inserting "(or such related party)" after "the taxpayer". Eff. for expenses incurred after Oct. 22, 2004, as if included in the provision of Pub. L. No. 108-357 to which it relates.

• IRC §274(e)(2)(B)(ii) was amended by Act §403(mm)(3) by adding the flush sentence at the end. Eff. for expenses incurred after Oct. 22, 2004, as if included in the provision of Pub. L. No. 108-357 to which it relates.

American Jobs Creation Act of 2004 (Pub. L. No. 108-357), as follows:

• IRC §274(e)(2) was amended by Act §907(a). Eff. for expenses incurred after Oct. 22, 2004. IRC §274(e)(2) prior to amendment:

(2) Expenses treated as compensation.—Expenses for goods, services, and facilities, to the extent that the expenses are treated by the taxpayer, with respect to the recipient of the entertainment, amusement, or recreation, as compensation to an employee on the taxpayer's return of tax under this chapter and as wages to such employee for purposes of chapter 24

(relating to withholding of income tax at source on wages).

* * *

SEC. 280G. GOLDEN PARACHUTE PAYMENTS.

(a) General Rule.—No deduction shall be allowed under this chapter for any excess parachute payment.

(b) Excess Parachute Payment.—For purposes of this section—

(1) In general.—The term "excess parachute payment" means an amount equal to the excess of any parachute payment over the portion of the base amount allocated to such payment.

(2) Parachute payment defined.—

(A) In general.—The term "parachute payment" means any payment in the nature of compensation to (or for the benefit of) a disqualified individual if—

(i) such payment is contingent on a change—

(I) in the ownership or effective control of the corporation, or

(II) in the ownership of a substantial portion of the assets of the corporation, and

(ii) the aggregate present value of the payments in the nature of compensation to (or for the benefit of) such individual which are contingent on such change equals or exceeds an amount equal to 3 times the base amount.

For purposes of clause (ii), payments not treated as parachute payments under paragraph (4)(A), (5), or (6) shall not be taken into account.

(B) Agreements.—The term "parachute payment" shall also include any payment in the nature of compensation to (or for the benefit of) a disqualified individual if such payment is made pursuant to an agreement which violates any generally enforced securities laws or regulations. In any proceeding involving the issue of whether any payment made to a disqualified individual is a parachute payment on account of a violation of any generally enforced securities laws or regulations, the burden of proof with respect to establishing the occurrence of a violation of such a law or regulation shall be upon the Secretary.

(C) Treatment of certain agreements entered into within 1 year before change of ownership.—For purposes of subparagraph (A)(i), any payment pursuant to—

(i) an agreement entered into within 1 year before the change described in subparagraph (A)(i), or

(ii) an amendment made within such 1-year period of a previous agreement,

shall be presumed to be contingent on such change unless the contrary is established by clear and convincing evidence.

(3) Base amount.—

(A) In general.—The term "base amount" means the individual's annualized includible compensation for the base period.

(B) Allocation.—The portion of the base amount allocated to any parachute payment shall be an amount which bears the same ratio to the base amount as—

(i) the present value of such payment, bears to

(ii) the aggregate present value of all such payments.

(4) Treatment of amounts which taxpayer establishes as reasonable compensation.—In the case of any payment described in paragraph (2)(A)—

(A) the amount treated as a parachute payment shall not include the portion of such payment which the taxpayer establishes by clear and convincing evidence is reasonable compensation for personal services to be rendered on or after the date of the change described in paragraph (2)(A)(i), and

(B) the amount treated as an excess parachute payment shall be reduced by the portion of such payment which the taxpayer establishes by clear and convincing evidence is reasonable compensation for personal services actually rendered before the date of the change described in paragraph (2)(A)(i).

For purposes of subparagraph (B), reasonable compensation for services actually rendered before the date of the change described in paragraph (2)(A)(i) shall be first offset against the base amount.

(5) Exemption for small business corporations, etc.—

(A) In general.—Notwithstanding paragraph (2), the term "parachute payment" does not include—

(i) any payment to a disqualified individual with respect to a corporation which (immediately before the change described in paragraph (2)(A)(i)) was a small business corporation (as defined in section 1361(b) but without regard to paragraph (1)(C) thereof), and

(ii) any payment to a disqualified individual with respect to a corporation (other than a corporation described in clause (i)) if—

(I) immediately before the change described in paragraph (2)(A)(i), no stock in such corporation was readily tradable on an established securities market or otherwise, and

(II) the shareholder approval requirements of subparagraph (B) are met with respect to such payment.

IRC Sec. 280G(b)(5)(A)(ii)(II)

The Secretary may, by regulations, prescribe that the requirements of subclause (I) of clause (ii) are not met where a substantial portion of the assets of any entity consists (directly or indirectly) of stock in such corporation and interests in such other entity are readily tradable on an established securities market, or otherwise. Stock described in section 1504(a)(4) shall not be taken into account under clause (ii)(I) if the payment does not adversely affect the shareholder's redemption and liquidation rights.

(B) Shareholder approval requirements.—The shareholder approval requirements of this subparagraph are met with respect to any payment if—

(i) such payment was approved by a vote of the persons who owned, immediately before the change described in paragraph (2)(A)(i), more than 75 percent of the voting power of all outstanding stock of the corporation, and

(ii) there was adequate disclosure to shareholders of all material facts concerning all payments which (but for this paragraph) would be parachute payments with respect to a disqualified individual.

The regulations prescribed under subsection (a) shall include regulations providing for the application of this subparagraph in the case of shareholders which are not individuals (including the treatment of nonvoting interests in an entity which is a shareholder) and where an entity holds a de minimis amount of stock in the corporation.

(6) Exemption for payments under qualified plans.—Notwithstanding paragraph (2), the term "parachute payment" shall not include any payment to or from—

(A) a plan described in section 401(a) which includes a trust exempt from tax under section 501(a),

(B) an annuity plan described in section 403(a),

(C) a simplified employee pension (as defined in section 408(k)), or

(D) a simple retirement account described in section 408(p).

(c) Disqualified Individuals.—For purposes of this section, the term "disqualified individual" means any individual who is—

(1) an employee, independent contractor, or other person specified in regulations by the Secretary who performs personal services for any corporation, and

(2) is an officer, shareholder, or highly-compensated individual.

For purposes of this section, a personal service corporation (or similar entity) shall be treated as an individual. For purposes of paragraph (2), the term "highly-compensated individual" only includes an individual who is (or would be if the individual were

an employee) a member of the group consisting of the highest paid 1 percent of the employees of the corporation or, if less, the highest paid 250 employees of the corporation.

(d) Other Definitions and Special Rules.—For purposes of this section—

(1) Annualized includible compensation for base period.—The term "annualized includible compensation for the base period" means the average annual compensation which—

(A) was payable by the corporation with respect to which the change in ownership or control described in paragraph (2)(A) of subsection (b) occurs, and

(B) was includible in the gross income of the disqualified individual for taxable years in the base period.

(2) Base period.—The term "base period" means the period consisting of the most recent 5 taxable years ending before the date on which the change in ownership or control described in paragraph (2)(A) of subsection (b) occurs (or such portion of such period during which the disqualified individual performed personal services for the corporation).

(3) Property transfers.—Any transfer of property—

(A) shall be treated as a payment, and

(B) shall be taken into account as its fair market value.

(4) Present value.—Present value shall be determined by using a discount rate equal to 120 percent of the applicable Federal rate (determined under section 1274(d)), compounded semiannually.

(5) Treatment of affiliated groups.—Except as otherwise provided in regulations, all members of the same affiliated group (as defined in section 1504, determined without regard to section 1504(b)) shall be treated as 1 corporation for purposes of this section. Any person who is an officer of any member of such group shall be treated as an officer of such 1 corporation.

(e) Special Rule For Application To Employers Participating in the Troubled Assets Relief Program.—

(1) In general.—In the case of the severance from employment of a covered executive of an applicable employer during the period during which the authorities under section 101(a) of the Emergency Economic Stabilization Act of 2008 are in effect (determined under section 120 of such Act), this section shall be applied to payments to such executive with the following modifications:

(A) Any reference to a disqualified individual (other than in subsection (c)) shall be treated as a reference to a covered executive.

(B) Any reference to a change described in subsection (b)(2)(A)(i) shall be treated as a reference to an applicable severance from employment of a covered executive, and any reference to a payment contingent on such a change shall be treated as a reference to any payment made during an applicable taxable year of the employer on account of such applicable severance from employment.

(C) Any reference to a corporation shall be treated as a reference to an applicable employer.

(D) The provisions of subsections (b)(2)(C), (b)(4), (b)(5), and (d)(5) shall not apply.

(2) Definitions and special rules.—For purposes of this subsection:

(A) Definitions.—Any term used in this subsection which is also used in section 162(m)(5) shall have the meaning given such term by such section.

(B) Applicable severance from employment.— The term "applicable severance from employment" means any severance from employment of a covered executive—

(i) by reason of an involuntary termination of the executive by the employer, or

(ii) in connection with any bankruptcy, liquidation, or receivership of the employer.

(C) Coordination and other rules.—

(i) In General.—If a payment which is treated as a parachute payment by reason of this subsection is also a parachute payment determined without regard to this subsection, this subsection shall not apply to such payment.

(ii) Regulatory authority.—The Secretary may prescribe such guidance, rules, or regulations as are necessary—

(I) to carry out the purposes of this subsection and the Emergency Economic Stabilization Act of 2008, including the extent to which this subsection applies in the case of any acquisition, merger, or reorganization of an applicable employer,

(II) to apply this section and section 4999 in cases where one or more payments with respect to any individual are treated as parachute payments by reason of this subsection, and other payments with respect to such individual are treated as parachute payments under this section without regard to this subsection, and

(III) to prevent the avoidance of the application of this section through the mischaracterization of a severance from employment as other than an applicable severance from employment.

(f) Regulations.—The Secretary shall prescribe such regulations as may be necessary or appropriate to carry out the purposes of this section (including regulations for the application of this section in the case of

related corporations and in the case of personal service corporations).

Recent Amendments to IRC §280G

Emergency Economic Stabilization Act of 2008 (Pub. L. No. 110-343), as follows:

● IRC §280G(e) was redesignated as subsec. (f), and new subsec. (e) was added. Eff. for payments with respect to severances occurring during the period during which the authorities under Act, Div. A, §101(a) are in effect (determined under Act, Div. A, §120) (see below for text).

● **Other Provision.** Act, Div. A, §101 provides:

SEC. 101. PURCHASES OF TROUBLED ASSETS.

(a) Offices; Authority.—

(1) Authority.—The Secretary is authorized to establish the Troubled Asset Relief Program (or "TARP") to purchase, and to make and fund commitments to purchase, troubled assets from any financial institution, on such terms and conditions as are determined by the Secretary, and in accordance with this Act and the policies and procedures developed and published by the Secretary.

(2) Commencement of program.—Establishment of the policies and procedures and other similar administrative requirements imposed on the Secretary by this Act are not intended to delay the commencement of the TARP.

(3) Establishment of treasury office.—

(A) In general.—The Secretary shall implement any program under paragraph (1) through an Office of Financial Stability, established for such purpose within the Office of Domestic Finance of the Department of the Treasury, which office shall be headed by an Assistant Secretary of the Treasury, appointed by the President, by and with the advice and consent of the Senate, except that an interim Assistant Secretary may be appointed by the Secretary.

(B) Clerical amendments.—

(i) Title 5.—Section 5315 of title 5, United States Code, is amended in the item relating to Assistant Secretaries of the Treasury, by striking "(9)" and inserting "(10)".

(ii) Title 31.—Section 301(e) of title 31, United States Code, is amended by striking "9" and inserting "10".

(b) Consultation.—In exercising the authority under this section, the Secretary shall consult with the Board, the Corporation, the Comptroller of the Currency, the Director of the Office of Thrift Supervision, the Chairman of the National Credit Union Administration Board, and the Secretary of Housing and Urban Development.

(c) Necessary Actions.—The Secretary is authorized to take such actions as the Secretary deems necessary to carry out the authorities in this Act, including, without limitation, the following:

(1) The Secretary shall have direct hiring authority with respect to the appointment of employees to administer this Act.

(2) Entering into contracts, including contracts for services authorized by section 3109 of title 5, United States Code.

(3) Designating financial institutions as financial agents of the Federal Government, and such institutions shall perform all such reasonable duties related to this Act as financial agents of the Federal Government as may be required.

(4) In order to provide the Secretary with the flexibility to manage troubled assets in a manner designed to minimize cost to the taxpayers, establishing vehicles that are authorized, subject to supervision by the Secretary, to purchase, hold, and sell troubled assets and issue obligations.

(5) Issuing such regulations and other guidance as may be necessary or appropriate to define terms or carry out the authorities or purposes of this Act.

(d) Program Guidelines.—Before the earlier of the end of the 2-business-day period beginning on the date of the first purchase of troubled assets pursuant to the authority under this section or the end of the 45-day period beginning on the date of enactment of this Act, the Secretary shall publish program guidelines, including the following:

(1) Mechanisms for purchasing troubled assets.

IRC Sec. 280G(f)

(2) Methods for pricing and valuing troubled assets.

(3) Procedures for selecting asset managers.

(4) Criteria for identifying troubled assets for purchase.

(e) Preventing Unjust Enrichment.—In making purchases under the authority of this Act, the Secretary shall take such steps as may be necessary to prevent unjust enrichment of financial institutions participating in a program established under this section, including by preventing the sale of a troubled asset to the Secretary at a higher price than what the seller paid to purchase the asset. This subsection does not apply to troubled assets acquired in a merger or acquisition, or a purchase of assets from a financial institution in conservatorship or receivership, or that has initiated bankruptcy proceedings under title 11, United States Code.

• **Other Provision.** Act, Div. A, §120 provides:

SEC. 120. TERMINATION OF AUTHORITY.

(a) Termination.—The authorities provided under sections 101(a), excluding section 101(a)(3), and 102 shall terminate on December 31, 2009.

(b) Extension Upon Certification.—The Secretary, upon submission of a written certification to Congress, may extend the authority provided under this Act to expire not later than 2 years from the date of enactment of this Act. Such certification shall include a justification of why the extension is necessary to assist American families and stabilize financial markets, as well as the expected cost to the taxpayers for such an extension.

* * *

Subchapter C—Corporate Distributions and Adjustments
* * *

Subpart C—Definitions: Constructive Ownership of Stock

SEC. 318. CONSTRUCTIVE OWNERSHIP OF STOCK.

(a) General rule. For purposes of those provisions of this subchapter to which the rules contained in this section are expressly made applicable—

(1) Members of family.

(A) In general. An individual shall be considered as owning the stock owned, directly or indirectly, by or for—

(i) his spouse (other than a spouse who is legally separated from the individual under a decree of divorce or separate maintenance), and

(ii) his children, grandchildren, and parents.

(B) Effect of adoption. For purposes of subparagraph (A)(ii), a legally adopted child of an individual shall be treated as a child of such individual by blood.

(2) Attribution from partnerships, estates, trusts, and corporations.

(A) From partnerships and estates. Stock owned, directly or indirectly, by or for a partnership or estate shall be considered as owned proportionately by its partners or beneficiaries.

(B) From trusts.

(i) Stock owned, directly or indirectly, by or for a trust (other than an employees' trust described in section 401(a) which is exempt from tax under section 501(a) shall be considered as owned by its beneficiaries in proportion to the actuarial interest of such beneficiaries in such trust.

(ii) Stock owned, directly or indirectly, by or for any portion of a trust of which a person is considered the owner under subpart E of part I of subchapter J (relating to grantors and others treated as substantial owners) shall be considered as owned by such person.

(C) From corporations. If 50 percent or more in value of the stock in a corporation is owned, directly or indirectly, by or for any person, such person shall be considered as owning the stock owned, directly or indirectly, by or for such corporation, in that proportion which the value of the stock which such person so owns bears to the value of all the stock in such corporation.

(3) Attribution to partnerships, estates, trusts, and corporations.

(A) To partnerships and estates. Stock owned, directly or indirectly, by or for a partner or a beneficiary of an estate shall be considered as owned by the partnership or estate.

(B) To trusts.

(i) Stock owned directly or indirectly, by or for a beneficiary of a trust (other than an employees' trust described in section 401(a) which is exempt from tax under section 501(a) shall be considered as owned by the trust, unless such beneficiary's interest in the trust is a remote contingent interest. For purposes of this clause, a contingent interest of a beneficiary in a trust shall be considered remote if, under the maximum exercise of discretion by the trustee in favor of such beneficiary, the value of such interest, computed actuarially, is 5 percent or less of the value of the trust property.

(ii) Stock owned, directly or indirectly, by or for a person who is considered the owner of any portion of a trust under subpart E of part I of subchapter J (relating to grantors and others treated as substantial owners) shall be considered as owned by the trust.

(C) To corporations. If 50 percent or more in value of the stock in a corporation is owned, directly or indirectly, by or for any person, such corporation shall be considered as owning the stock owned, directly or indirectly, by or for such person.

(4) Options. If any person has an option to acquire stock, such stock shall be considered as owned by such person. For purposes of this paragraph, an option to acquire such an option, and each one of a series of such options, shall be considered as an option to acquire such stock.

(5) Operating rules.

(A) In general. Except as provided in subparagraphs (B) and (C), stock constructively owned by a person by reason of the application of paragraph (1), (2), (3), or (4), shall, for purposes of applying paragraphs (1), (2), (3), and (4), be considered as actually owned by such person.

(B) Members of family. Stock constructively owned by an individual by reason of the application of paragraph (1) shall not be considered as owned by him for purposes of again applying paragraph (1) in order to make another the constructive owner of such stock.

(C) Partnerships, estates, trusts, and corporations. Stock constructively owned by a partnership, estate, trust, or corporation by reason of the application of paragraph (3) shall not be considered as owned by it for purposes of applying paragraph (2) in order to make another the constructive owner of such stock.

(D) Option rule in lieu of family rule. For purposes of this paragraph, if stock may be considered as owned by an individual under paragraph (1) or (4), it shall be considered as owned by him under paragraph (4).

(E) S Corporation treated as partnership. For purposes of this subsection—

    (i) an S corporation shall be treated as a partnership, and

    (ii) any shareholder of the S corporation shall be treated as a partner of such partnership.

The preceding sentence shall not apply for purposes of determining whether stock in the S corporation is constructively owned by any person.

(b) Cross references. For provisions to which the rules contained in subsection (a) apply, see—

    (1) section 302 (relating to redemption of stock);

    (2) section 304 (relating to redemption by related corporations);

    (3) section 306(b)(1)(A) (relating to disposition of section 306 stock);

    (4) section 338(h)(3) (defining purchase);

    (5) section 382(*l*)(3) (relating to special limitations on net operating loss carryovers);

    (6) section 856(d) (relating to definition of rents from real property in the case of real estate investment trusts);

    (7) section 958(b) (relating to constructive ownership rules with respect to controlled foreign corporations); and

    (8) section 6038(d)(2) (relating to information with respect to certain foreign corporations).

Recent Amendments to §318

Gulf Opportunity Zone Act of 2005 (Pub. L. No. 109-135), as follows:

● IRC §318(b)(8) was amended by Act §412(u) by substituting "section 6038(d)(2)" for "section 6038(e)(2)". Eff. Dec. 21, 2005.

---

* * *

Subchapter D—Deferred Compensation, Etc.

Part I—Pension, Profit-Sharing, Stock Bonus Plans, etc.

Subpart A—General Rule

SEC. 401. QUALIFIED PENSION, PROFIT-SHARING, AND STOCK BONUS PLANS.

(a) Requirements for Qualification.—A trust created or organized in the United States and forming part of a stock bonus, pension, or profit-sharing plan of an employer for the exclusive benefit of his employees or their beneficiaries shall constitute a qualified trust under this section—

    (1) if contributions are made to the trust by such employer, or employees, or both, or by another employer who is entitled to deduct his contributions under section 404(a)(3)(B) (relating to deduction for contributions to profit-sharing and stock bonus plans), or by a charitable remainder trust pursuant to a qualified gratuitous transfer (as defined in section 664(g)(1)) for the purpose of distributing to such employees or their beneficiaries the corpus and income of the fund accumulated by the trust in accordance with such plan;

    (2) if under the trust instrument it is impossible, at any time prior to the satisfaction of all liabilities with respect to employees and their beneficiaries under the trust, for any part of the corpus or income to be (within the taxable year or thereafter) used for, or diverted to, purposes other than for the exclusive benefit of his employees or their beneficiaries but this paragraph shall not be construed, in the case of a multiemployer plan, to prohibit the return of a contribution within 6 months after the plan administrator determines that the contribution was made by a mistake of fact or law (other than a mistake relating to whether the plan is described in section 401(a) or the trust which is part of such plan is exempt from taxation under section 501(a), or the return of any withdrawal liability payment determined to be an overpayment within 6 months of such determination);

    (3) if the plan of which such trust is a part satisfies the requirements of section 410 (relating to minimum participation standards); and

IRC Sec. 401(a)(3)

(4) if the contributions or benefits provided under the plan do not discriminate in favor of highly compensated employees (within the meaning of section 414(q)). For purposes of this paragraph, there shall be excluded from consideration employees described in section 410(b)(3)(A) and (C).

(5) Special rules relating to nondiscrimination requirements.—

(A) Salaried or clerical employees.—A classification shall not be considered discriminatory within the meaning of paragraph (4) or section 410(b)(2)(A)(i) merely because it is limited to salaried or clerical employees.

(B) Contributions and benefits may bear uniform relationship to compensation.—A plan shall not be considered discriminatory within the meaning of paragraph (4) merely because the contributions or benefits of, or on behalf of, the employees under the plan bear a uniform relationship to the compensation (within the meaning of section 414(s)) of such employees.

(C) Certain disparity permitted.—A plan shall not be considered discriminatory within the meaning of paragraph (4) merely because the contributions or benefits of, or on behalf of, the employees under the plan favor highly compensated employees (as defined in section 414(q)) in the manner permitted under subsection (*l*).

(D) Integrated defined benefit plan.—

(i) In general.—A defined benefit plan shall not be considered discriminatory within the meaning of paragraph (4) merely because the plan provides that the employer-derived accrued retirement benefit for any participant under the plan may not exceed the excess (if any) of—

(I) the participant's final pay with the employer, over

(II) the employer-derived retirement benefit created under Federal law attributable to service by the participant with the employer.

For purposes of this clause, the employer-derived retirement benefit created under Federal law shall be treated as accruing ratably over 35 years.

(ii) Final pay.—For purposes of this subparagraph, the participant's final pay is the compensation (as defined in section 414(q)(4)) paid to the participant by the employer for any year—

(I) which ends during the 5-year period ending with the year in which the participant separated from service for the employer, and

(II) for which the participant's total compensation from the employer was highest.

(E) 2 or more plans treated as single plan.—For purposes of determining whether 2 or more plans

of an employer satisfy the requirements of paragraph (4) when considered as a single plan—

(i) Contributions.—If the amount of contributions on behalf of the employees allowed as a deduction under section 404 for the taxable year with respect to such plans, taken together, bears a uniform relationship to the compensation (within the meaning of section 414(s)) of such employees, the plans shall not be considered discriminatory merely because the rights of employees to, or derived from, the employer contributions under the separate plans do not become nonforfeitable at the same rate.

(ii) Benefits.—If the employees' rights to benefits under the separate plans do not become nonforfeitable at the same rate, but the levels of benefits provided by the separate plans satisfy the requirements of regulations prescribed by the Secretary to take account of the differences in such rates, the plans shall not be considered discriminatory merely because of the difference in such rates.

(F) Social Security Retirement Age.—For purposes of testing for discrimination under paragraph (4)—

(i) the social security retirement age (as defined in section 415(b)(8)) shall be treated as a uniform retirement age, and

(ii) subsidized early retirement benefits and joint and survivor annuities shall not be treated as being unavailable to employees on the same terms merely because such benefits or annuities are based in whole or in part on an employee's social security retirement age (as so defined).

(G) Governmental plans.—Paragraphs (3) and (4) shall not apply to a governmental plan (within the meaning of section 414(d)).

(6) A plan shall be considered as meeting the requirements of paragraph (3) during the whole of any taxable year of the plan if on one day in each quarter it satisfied such requirements.

(7) A trust shall not constitute a qualified trust under this section unless the plan of which such trust is a part satisfies the requirements of section 411 (relating to minimum vesting standards).

(8) A trust forming part of a defined benefit plan shall not constitute a qualified trust under this section unless the plan provides that forfeitures must not be applied to increase the benefits any employee would otherwise receive under the plan.

(9) Required distributions.—

(A) In general.—A trust shall not constitute a qualified trust under this subsection unless the plan provides that the entire interest of each employee—

(i) will be distributed to such employee not later than the required beginning date, or

(ii) will be distributed, beginning not later than the required beginning date, in accordance with regulations, over the life of such employee or over the lives of such employee and designated beneficiary (or over a period not extending beyond the life expectancy of such employee or the life expectancy of such employee and a designated beneficiary).

(B) Required distribution where employee dies before entire interest is distributed.—

(i) Where distributions have begun under subparagraph (A)(ii).—A trust shall not constitute a qualified trust under this section unless the plan provides that if—

(I) the distribution of the employee's interest has begun in accordance with subparagraph (A)(ii), and

(II) the employee dies before his entire interest has been distributed to him,

the remaining portion of such interest will be distributed at least as rapidly as under the method of distribution being used under subparagraph (A)(ii) as of the date of his death.

(ii) 5-year rule for other cases.—A trust shall not constitute a qualified trust under this section unless the plan provides that, if an employee dies before the distribution of the employee's interest has begun in accordance with subparagraph (A)(ii), the entire interest of the employee will be distributed within 5 years after the death of such employee.

(iii) Exception to the 5-year rule for certain amounts payable over life of beneficiary.—If—

(I) any portion of the employee's interest is payable to (or for the benefit of) a designated beneficiary,

(II) such portion will be distributed (in accordance with regulations) over the life of such designated beneficiary (or over a period not extending beyond the life expectancy of such beneficiary), and

(III) such distributions begin not later than 1 year after the date of the employee's death or such later date as the Secretary may by regulations prescribe,

for purposes of clause (ii), the portion referred to in subclause (I) shall be treated as distributed on the date on which such distribution began.

(iv) Special rules for surviving spouse of employee.—If the designated beneficiary referred to in clause (iii)(I) is the surviving spouse of the employee—

(I) the date on which the distributions are required to begin under clause (iii)(III) shall not be

earlier than the date on which the employee would have attained age 70½, and

(II) if the surviving spouse dies before the distributions to such spouse begin, this subparagraph shall be applied as if the surviving spouse were the employee.

(C) Required beginning date.—For purposes of this paragraph—

(i) In general.—The term "required beginning date" means April 1 of the calendar year following the later of—

(I) the calendar year in which the employee attains age 70½, or

(II) the calendar year in which the employee retires.

(ii) Exception.—Subclause (II) of clause (i) shall not apply—

(I) except as provided in section 409(d), in the case of an employee who is a 5-percent owner (as defined in section 416) with respect to the plan year ending in the calendar year in which the employee attains age 70½, or

(II) for purposes of section 408(a)(6) or (b)(3).

(iii) Actuarial Adjustment.—In the case of an employee to whom clause (i)(II) applies who retires in a calendar year after the calendar year in which the employee attains age 70½, the employee's accrued benefit shall be actuarially increased to take into account the period after age 70½ in which the employee was not receiving any benefits under the plan.

(iv) Exception for governmental and church plans.—Clauses (ii) and (iii) shall not apply in the case of a governmental plan or church plan. For purposes of this clause, the term "church plan" means a plan maintained by a church for church employees, and the term "church" means any church (as defined in section 3121(w)(3)(A)) or qualified church-controlled organization (as defined in section 3121(w)(3)(B)).

(D) Life expectancy.—For purposes of this paragraph, the life expectancy of an employee and the employee's spouse (other than in the case of a life annuity) may be redetermined but not more frequently than annually.

(E) Designated beneficiary.—For purposes of this paragraph, the term "designated beneficiary" means any individual designated as a beneficiary by the employee.

(F) Treatment of payments to children.—Under regulations prescribed by the Secretary, for purposes of this paragraph, any amount paid to a child shall be treated as if it had been paid to the surviving spouse if such amount will become payable to the surviving spouse upon such child reaching majority (or other designated event permitted under regulations.)

(G) Treatment of incidental death benefit distributions.—For purposes of this title, any distribution required under the incidental death benefit requirements of this subsection shall be treated as a distribution required under this paragraph.

(H) Temporary waiver of minimum required distribution.—

(i) In general.—The requirements of this paragraph shall not apply for calendar year 2009 to—

(I) a defined contribution plan which is described in this subsection or in section 403(a) or 403(b),

(II) a defined contribution plan which is an eligible deferred compensation plan described in section 457(b) but only if such plan is maintained by an employer described in section 457(e)(1)(A), or

(III) an individual retirement plan.

(ii) Special rules regarding waiver period.—For purposes of this paragraph—

(I) the required beginning date with respect to any individual shall be determined without regard to this subparagraph for purposes of applying this paragraph for calendar years after 2009, and

(II) if clause (ii) of subparagraph (B) applies, the 5-year period described in such clause shall be determined without regard to calendar year 2009.

(10) Other requirements.—

(A) Plans benefiting owner-employees.—In the case of any plan which provides contributions or benefits for employees some or all of whom are owner-employees (as defined in subsection (c)(3)), a trust forming part of such plan shall constitute a qualified trust under this section only if the requirements of subsection (d) are also met.

(B) Top-heavy plans.—

(i) In general.—In the case of any top-heavy plan, a trust forming part of such plan shall constitute a qualified trust under this section only if the requirements of section 416 are met.

(ii) Plans which may become top-heavy.—Except to the extent provided in regulations, a trust forming part of a plan (whether or not a top-heavy plan) shall constitute a qualified trust under this section only if such plan contains provisions—

(I) which will take effect if such plan becomes a top-heavy plan, and

(II) which meet the requirements of section 416.

(iii) Exemption for governmental plans.—This subparagraph shall not apply to any governmental plan.

(11) Requirement of joint and survivor annuity and preretirement survivor annuity.—

(A) In general.—In the case of any plan to which this paragraph applies, except as provided in section 417, a trust forming part of such plan shall not constitute a qualified trust under this section unless—

(i) In general.—In the case of a vested participant who does not die before the annuity starting date, the accrued benefit payable to such participant is provided in the form of a qualified joint and survivor annuity, and

(ii) in the case of a vested participant who dies before the annuity starting date and who has a surviving spouse, a qualified preretirement survivor annuity is provided to the surviving spouse of such participant.

(B) Plans to which this paragraph applies.—This paragraph shall apply to—

(i) any defined benefit plan,

(ii) any defined contribution plan which is subject to the funding standards of section 412, and

(iii) any participant under any other defined contribution plan unless—

(I) such plan provides that the participant's nonforfeitable accrued benefit (reduced by any security interest held by the plan by reason of a loan outstanding to such participant) is payable in full, on the death of the participant, to the participant's surviving spouse (or, if there is no surviving spouse or the surviving spouse consents in the manner required under section 417(a)(2), to a designated beneficiary),

(II) such participant does not elect a payment of benefits in the form of a life annuity, and

(III) with respect to such participant, such plan is not a direct or indirect transferee (in a transfer after December 31, 1984) of a plan which is described in clause (i) or (ii) or to which this clause applied with respect to the participant.

Clause (iii)(III) shall apply only with respect to the transferred assets (and income therefrom) if the plan separately accounts for such assets and any income therefrom.

(C) Exception for certain ESOP benefits.—

(i) In general.—In the case of—

(I) a tax credit employee stock ownership plan (as defined in section 409(a)), or

(II) an employee stock ownership plan (as defined in section 4975(e)(7)),

subparagraph (A) shall not apply to that portion of the employee's accrued benefit to which the requirements of section 409(h) apply.

(ii) Nonforfeitable benefit must be paid in full, etc.—In the case of any participant, clause (i) shall apply only if the requirements of subclauses (I), (II), and (III) of subparagraph (B)(iii) are met with respect to such participant.

(D) Special rule where participant and spouse married less than 1 year.—A plan shall not be treated as failing to meet the requirements of subparagraphs (B)(iii) or (C) merely because the plan provides that benefits will not be payable to the surviving spouse of the participant unless the participant and such spouse had been married throughout the 1-year period ending on the earlier of the participant's annuity starting date or the date of the participant's death.

(E) Exception for plans described in section 404(c).—This paragraph shall not apply to a plan which the Secretary has determined is a plan described in section 404(c) (or a continuation thereof) in which participation is substantially limited to individuals who, before January 1, 1976, ceased employment covered by the plan.

(F) Cross reference.—For—

(i) provisions under which participants may elect to waive the requirements of this paragraph, and

(ii) other definitions and special rules for purposes of this paragraph, see section 417.

(12) A trust shall not constitute a qualified trust under this section unless the plan of which such trust is a part provides that in the case of any merger or consolidation with, or transfer of assets or liabilities to, any other plan after September 2, 1974, each participant in the plan would (if the plan then terminated) receive a benefit immediately after the merger, consolidation, or transfer which is equal to or greater than the benefit he would have been entitled to receive immediately before the merger, consolidation, or transfer (if the plan had then terminated). The preceding sentence does not apply to any multiemployer plan with respect to any transaction to the extent that participants either before or after the transaction are covered under a multiemployer plan to which title IV of the Employee Retirement Income Security Act of 1974 applies.

(13) Assignment and alienation.—

(A) In general.—A trust shall not constitute a qualified trust under this section unless the plan of which such trust is a part provides that benefits provided under the plan may not be assigned or alienated. For purposes of the preceding sentence, there shall not be taken into account any voluntary and revocable assignment of not to exceed 10 percent of any benefit payment made by any participant who is receiving benefits under the plan unless the assignment or alienation is made for purposes of defraying plan administration costs.

For purposes of this paragraph a loan made to a participant or beneficiary shall not be treated as an assignment or alienation if such loan is secured by the participant's accrued nonforfeitable benefit and is exempt from the tax imposed by section 4975 (relating to tax on prohibited transactions) by reason of section 4975(d)(1). This paragraph shall take effect on January 1, 1976, and shall not apply to assignments which were irrevocable on September 2, 1974.

(B) Special rules for domestic relations orders.—Subparagraph (A) shall apply to the creation, assignment, or recognition of a right to any benefit payable with respect to a participant pursuant to a domestic relations order, except that subparagraph (A) shall not apply if the order is determined to be a qualified domestic relations order.

(C) Special rule for certain judgments and settlements.—Subparagraph (A) shall not apply to any offset of a participant's benefits provided under a plan against an amount that the participant is ordered or required to pay to the plan if—

(i) the order or requirement to pay arises—

(I) under a judgment of conviction for a crime involving such plan,

(II) under a civil judgment (including a consent order or decree) entered by a court in an action brought in connection with a violation (or alleged violation) of part 4 of subtitle B of title I of the Employee Retirement Income Security Act of 1974, or

(III) pursuant to a settlement agreement between the Secretary of Labor and the participant, or a settlement agreement between the Pension Benefit Guaranty Corporation and the participant, in connection with a violation (or alleged violation) of part 4 of such subtitle by a fiduciary or any other person,

(ii) the judgment, order, decree, or settlement agreement expressly provides for the offset of all or part of the amount ordered or required to be paid to the plan against the participant's benefits provided under the plan, and

(iii) in a case in which the survivor annuity requirements of section 401(a)(11) apply with respect to distributions from the plan to the participant, if the participant has a spouse at the time at which the offset is to be made—

(I) either such spouse has consented in writing to such offset and such consent is witnessed by a notary public or representative of the plan (or it is established to the satisfaction of a plan representative that such consent may not be obtained by reason of circumstances described in section 417(a)(2)(B)), or an election to waive the right of the spouse to either a qualified joint and survivor annuity or a qualified preretirement survivor annuity is in effect in accordance with the requirements of section 417(a),

(II) such spouse is ordered or required in such judgment, order, decree, or settlement to pay an amount to the plan in connection with a violation of part 4 of such subtitle, or

(III) in such judgment, order, decree, or settlement, such spouse retains the right to receive the survivor annuity under a qualified joint and survivor annuity provided pursuant to section 401(a)(11)(A)(i) and under a qualified preretirement survivor annuity provided pursuant to section 401(a)(11)(A)(ii), determined in accordance with subparagraph (D). A plan shall not be treated as failing to meet the requirements of this subsection, subsection (k), section 403(b), or section 409(d) solely by reason of an offset described in this subparagraph.

(D) Survivor annuity.—

(i) In general.—The survivor annuity described in subparagraph (C)(iii)(III) shall be determined as if—

(I) the participant terminated employment on the date of the offset,

(II) there was no offset,

(III) the plan permitted commencement of benefits only on or after normal retirement age,

(IV) the plan provided only the minimum-required qualified joint and survivor annuity, and

(V) the amount of the qualified preretirement survivor annuity under the plan is equal to the amount of the survivor annuity payable under the minimum-required qualified joint and survivor annuity.

(ii) Definition.—For purposes of this subparagraph, the term "minimum-required qualified joint and survivor annuity" means the qualified joint and survivor annuity which is the actuarial equivalent of the participant's accrued benefit (within the meaning of section 411(a)(7)) and under which the survivor annuity is 50 percent of the amount of the annuity which is payable during the joint lives of the participant and the spouse.

(14) A trust shall not constitute a qualified trust under this section unless the plan of which such trust is a part provides that, unless the participant otherwise elects, the payment of benefits under the plan to the participant will begin not later than the 60th day after the latest of the close of the plan year in which—

(A) the date on which the participant attains the earlier of age 65 or the normal retirement age specified under the plan,

(B) occurs the 10th anniversary of the year in which the participant commenced participation in the plan, or

(C) the participant terminates his service with the employer.

In the case of a plan which provides for the payment of an early retirement benefit, a trust forming a part of such plan shall not constitute a qualified trust under this section unless a participant who satisfied the service requirements for such early retirement benefit, but separated from the service (with any nonforfeitable right to an accrued benefit) before satisfying the age requirement for such early retirement benefit, is entitled upon satisfaction of such age requirement to receive a benefit not less than the benefit to which he would be entitled at the normal retirement age, actuarially reduced under regulations prescribed by the Secretary.

(15) A trust shall not constitute a qualified trust under this section unless under the plan of which such trust is a part—

(A) in the case of a participant or beneficiary who is receiving benefits under such plan, or

(B) in the case of a participant who is separated from the service and who has nonforfeitable rights to benefits,

such benefits are not decreased by reason of any increase in the benefit levels payable under title II of the Social Security Act or any increase in the wage base under such title II, if such increase takes place after September 2, 1974, or (if later) the earlier of the date of first receipt of such benefits or the date of such separation, as the case may be.

(16) A trust shall not constitute a qualified trust under this section if the plan of which such trust is a part provides for benefits or contributions which exceed the limitations of section 415.

(17) Compensation limit.—

(A) In general.—A trust shall not constitute a qualified trust under this section unless, under the plan of which the trust is a part, the annual compensation of each employee taken into account under the plan for any year does not exceed $200,000.

(B) Cost-of-living adjustment.—The Secretary shall adjust annually the $200,000 amount in subparagraph (A) for increases in the cost-of-living at the same time and in the same manner as adjustments under section 415(d); except that the base period shall be the calendar quarter beginning July 1, 2001, and any increase which is not a multiple of $5,000 shall be rounded to the next lowest multiple of $5,000.

(18) [Repealed.]

(19) A trust shall not constitute a qualified trust under this section if under the plan of which such trust is a part any part of a participant's accrued benefit derived from employer contributions (whether or not

otherwise nonforfeitable), is forfeitable solely because of withdrawal by such participant of any amount attributable to the benefit derived from contributions made by such participant. The preceding sentence shall not apply to the accrued benefit of any participant unless, at the time of such withdrawal, such participant has a nonforfeitable right to at least 50 percent of such accrued benefit (as determined under section 411). The first sentence of this paragraph shall not apply to the extent that an accrued benefit is permitted to be forfeited in accordance with section 411(a)(3)(D)(iii) (relating to proportional forfeitures of benefits accrued before September 2, 1974, in the event of withdrawal of certain mandatory contributions).

(20) A trust forming part of a pension plan shall not be treated as failing to constitute a qualified trust under this section merely because the pension plan of which such trust is a part makes 1 or more distributions within 1 taxable year to a distributee on account of a termination of the plan of which the trust is a part, or in the case of a profit-sharing or stock bonus plan, a complete discontinuance of contributions under such plan. This paragraph shall not apply to a defined benefit plan unless the employer maintaining such plan files a notice with the Pension Benefit Guaranty Corporation (at the time and in the manner prescribed by the Pension Benefit Guaranty Corporation) notifying the Corporation of such payment or distribution and the Corporation has approved such payment or distribution or, within 90 days after the date on which such notice was filed, has failed to disapprove such payment or distribution. For purposes of this paragraph, rules similar to the rules of section 402(a)(6)(B) (as in effect before its repeal by section 521 of the Unemployment Compensation Amendments of 1992) shall apply.

(21) **[Repealed.]**

(22) If a defined contribution plan (other than a profit sharing plan)—

(A) is established by an employer whose stock is not readily tradable on an established market, and

(B) after acquiring securities of the employer, more than 10 percent of the total assets of the plan are securities of the employer,

any trust forming part of such plan shall not constitute a qualified trust under this section unless the plan meets the requirements of subsection (e) of section 409. The requirements of subsection (e) of section 409 shall not apply to any employees of an employer who are participants in any defined contribution plan established and maintained by such employer if the stock of such employer is not readily tradable on an established market and the trade or business of such employer consists of publishing on a regular basis a newspaper for general circulation. For purposes of the preceding sentence, subsections (b), (c), (m), and (o) of section 414 shall not apply except for determining

whether stock of the employer is not readily tradable on an established market.

(23) A stock bonus plan shall not be treated as meeting the requirements of this section unless such plan meets the requirements of subsections (h) and (o) of section 409, except that in applying section 409(h) for purposes of this paragraph, the term "employer securities" shall include any securities of the employer held by the plan.

(24) Any group trust which otherwise meets the requirements of this section shall not be treated as not meeting such requirements on account of the participation or inclusion in such trust of the moneys of any plan or governmental unit described in section 818(a)(6).

(25) Requirement that actuarial assumptions be specified.—A defined benefit plan shall not be treated as providing definitely determinable benefits unless, whenever the amount of any benefit is to be determined on the basis of actuarial assumptions, such assumptions are specified in the plan in a way which precludes employer discretion.

(26) Additional participation requirements.—

(A) In general.—In the case of a trust which is part of a defined benefit plan, such trust shall not constitute a qualified trust under this subsection unless on each day of the plan year such trust benefits at least the lesser of—

(i) 50 employees of the employer, or

(ii) the greater of—

(I) 40 percent of all employees of the employer, or

(II) 2 employees (or if there is only 1 employee, such employee).

(B) Treatment of excludable employees.—

(i) In general.—A plan may exclude from consideration under this paragraph employees described in paragraphs (3) and (4)(A) of section 410(b).

(ii) Separate application for certain excludable employees.—If employees described in section 410(b)(4)(B) are covered under a plan which meets the requirements of subparagraph (A) separately with respect to such employees, such employees may be excluded from consideration in determining whether any plan of the employer meets such requirements if—

(I) the benefits for such employees are provided under the same plan as benefits for other employees,

(II) the benefits provided to such employees are not greater than comparable benefits provided to other employees under the plan, and

(III) no highly compensated employee (within the meaning of section 414(q)) is included in the group of such employees for more than 1 year.

IRC Sec. 401(a)(26)(B)(ii)(III)

(C) Special rule for collective bargaining units.— Except to the extent provided in regulations, a plan covering only employees described in section 410(b)(3)(A) may exclude from consideration any employees who are not included in the unit or units in which the covered employees are included.

(D) Paragraph not to apply to multiemployer plans.—Except to the extent provided in regulations, this paragraph shall not apply to employees in a multiemployer plan (within the meaning of section 414(f)) who are covered by collective bargaining agreements.

(E) Special rule for certain dispositions for acquisitions.—Rules similar to the rules of section 410(b)(6)(C) shall apply for purposes of this paragraph.

(F) Separate lines of business.—At the election of the employer and with the consent of the Secretary, this paragraph may be applied separately with respect to each separate line of business of the employer. For purposes of this paragraph, the term "separate line of business" has the meaning given such term by section 414(r) (without regard to paragraph 2(A) or (7) thereof).

(G) Exception for governmental plans.—This paragraph shall not apply to a governmental plan (within the meaning of section 414(d)).

(H) Regulations.—The Secretary may by regulation provide that any separate benefit structure, any separate trust, or any other separate arrangement is to be treated as a separate plan for purposes of applying this paragraph.

(27) Determinations as to profit-sharing plans.—

(A) Contributions need not be based on profits.— The determination of whether the plan under which any contributions are made is a profit-sharing plan shall be made without regard to current or accumulated profits of the employer and without regard to whether the employer is a tax-exempt organization.

(B) Plan must designate type.—In the case of a plan which is intended to be a money purchase pension plan or a profit-sharing plan, a trust forming part of such plan shall not constitute a qualified trust under this subsection unless the plan designates such intent at such time and in such manner as the Secretary may prescribe.

(28) Additional requirements relating to employee stock ownership plans.—

(A) In general.—In the case of a trust which is part of an employee stock ownership plan (within the meaning of section 4975(e)(7)) or a plan which meets the requirements of section 409(a), such trust shall not constitute a qualified trust under this section unless such plan meets the requirements of subparagraphs (B) and (C).

(B) Diversification of investments.—

(i) In general.—A plan meets the requirements of this subparagraph if each qualified participant in the plan may elect within 90 days after the close of each plan year in the qualified election period to direct the plan as to the investment of at least 25 percent of the participant's account in the plan (to the extent such portion exceeds the amount to which a prior election under this subparagraph applies). In the case of the election year in which the participant can make his last election, the preceding sentence shall be applied by substituting "50 percent" for "25 percent".

(ii) Method of meeting requirements.—A plan shall be treated as meeting the requirements of clause (i) if—

(I) the portion of the participant's account covered by the election under clause (i) is distributed within 90 days after the period during which the election may be made, or

(II) the plan offers at least 3 investment options (not inconsistent with regulations prescribed by the Secretary) to each participant making an election under clause (i) and within 90 days after the period during which the election may be made, the plan invests the portion of the participant's account covered by the election in accordance with such election.

(iii) Qualified participant.—For purposes of this subparagraph, the term "qualified participant" means any employee who has completed at least 10 years of participation under the plan and has attained age 55.

(iv) Qualified election period.—For purposes of this subparagraph, the term "qualified election period" means the 6-plan-year period beginning with the later of—

(I) the 1st plan year in which the individual first became a qualified participant, or

(II) the 1st plan year beginning after December 31, 1986.

For purposes of the preceding sentence, an employer may elect to treat an individual first becoming a qualified participant in the 1st plan year beginning in 1987 as having become a participant in the 1st plan year beginning in 1988.

(v) Exception.—This subparagraph shall not apply to an applicable defined contribution plan (as defined in paragraph (35)(E)).

(C) Use of independent appraiser.—A plan meets the requirements of this subparagraph if all valuations of employer securities which are not readily tradable on an established securities market with respect to activities carried on by the plan are by an independent appraiser. For purposes of the preceding sentence, the term "independent appraiser" means any appraiser meeting requirements similar to the requirements of the regulations prescribed under section 170(a)(1).

(29) Benefit limitations.—In the case of a defined benefit plan (other than a multiemployer plan) to which the requirements of section 412 apply, the trust of which the plan is a part shall not constitute a qualified trust under this subsection unless the plan meets the requirements of section 436.

(30) Limitations on elective deferrals.—In the case of a trust which is part of a plan under which elective deferrals (within the meaning of section 402(g)(3)) may be made with respect to any individual during a calendar year, such trust shall not constitute a qualified trust under this subsection unless the plan provides that the amount of such deferrals under such plan and all other plans, contracts, or arrangements of an employer maintaining such plan may not exceed the amount of the limitation in effect under section 402(g)(1)(A) for taxable years beginning in such calendar year.

(31) Direct transfer of eligible rollover distributions.—

(A) In general.—A trust shall not constitute a qualified trust under this section unless the plan of which such trust is a part provides that if the distributee of any eligible rollover distribution—

(i) elects to have such distribution paid directly to an eligible retirement plan, and

(ii) specifies the eligible retirement plan to which such distribution is to be paid (in such form and at such time as the plan administrator may prescribe), such distribution shall be made in the form of a direct trustee-to-trustee transfer to the eligible retirement plan so specified.

(B) Certain mandatory distributions.—

(i) In general.—In case of a trust which is part of an eligible plan, such trust shall not constitute a qualified trust under this section unless the plan of which such trust is a part provides that if—

(I) a distribution described in clause (ii) in excess of $1,000 is made, and

(II) the distributee does not make an election under subparagraph (A) and does not elect to receive the distribution directly,

the plan administrator shall make such transfer to an individual retirement plan of a designated trustee or issuer and shall notify the distributee in writing (either separately or as part of the notice under section 402(f)) that the distribution may be transferred to another individual retirement plan.

(ii) Eligible plan.—For purposes of clause (i) the term "eligible plan" means a plan which provides that any nonforfeitable accrued benefit for

which the present value (as determined under section 411(a)(11) does not exceed $5,000 shall be immediately distributed to the participant.

(C) Limitation.—Subparagraphs (A) and (B) shall apply only to the extent that the eligible rollover distribution would be includible in gross income if not transferred as provided in subparagraph (A) (determined without regard to sections 402(c), 403(a)(4), 403(b)(8), and 457(e)(16)). The preceding sentence shall not apply to such distribution if the plan to which such distribution is transferred—

(i) is a qualified trust which is part of a plan which is a defined contribution plan and agrees to separately account for amounts so transferred, including separately accounting for the portion of such distribution which is includible in gross income and the portion of such distribution which is not so includible, or

(ii) is an eligible retirement plan described in clause (i) or (ii) of section 402(c)(8)(B).

(D) Eligible rollover distribution.—For purposes of this paragraph, the term "eligible rollover distribution" has the meaning given such term by section 402(f)(2)(A).

(E) Eligible retirement plan.—For purposes of this paragraph, the term "eligible retirement plan" has the meaning given such term by section 402(c)(8)(B), except that a qualified trust shall be considered an eligible retirement plan only if it is a defined contribution plan, the terms of which permit the acceptance of rollover distributions.

(32) Treatment of failure to make certain payments if plan has liquidity shortfall.—

(A) In general.—A trust forming part of a pension plan to which section 430(j)(4) applies shall not be treated as failing to constitute a qualified trust under this section merely because such plan ceases to make any payment described in subparagraph (B) during any period that such plan has a liquidity shortfall (as defined in section 430(j)(4)).

(B) Payments described.—A payment is described in this subparagraph if such payment is—

(i) any payment, in excess of the monthly amount paid under a single life annuity (plus any social security supplements described in the last sentence of section 411(a)(9)), to a participant or beneficiary whose annuity starting date (as defined in section 417(f)(2)) occurs during the period referred to in subparagraph (A),

(ii) any payment for the purchase of an irrevocable commitment from an insurer to pay benefits, and

(iii) any other payment specified by the Secretary by regulations.

(C) Period of shortfall.—For purposes of this paragraph, a plan has a liquidity shortfall during

IRC Sec. 401(a)(32)(C)

the period that there is an underpayment of an installment under section 430(j)(3) by reason of section 430(j)(4)(A) thereof.

(33) Prohibition on benefit increases while sponsor is in bankruptcy.—

(A) In general.—A trust which is part of a plan to which this paragraph applies shall not constitute a qualified trust under this section if an amendment to such plan is adopted while the employer is a debtor in a case under title 11, United States Code, or similar Federal or State law, if such amendment increases liabilities of the plan by reason of—

(i) any increase in benefits,

(ii) any change in the accrual of benefits, or

(iii) any change in the rate at which benefits become nonforfeitable under the plan, with respect to employees of the debtor, and such amendment is effective prior to the effective date of such employer's plan of reorganization.

(B) Exceptions.—This paragraph shall not apply to any plan amendment if—

(i) the plan, were such amendment to take effect, would have a funding target attainment percentage (as defined in section 430(d)(2)) of 100 percent or more,

(ii) the Secretary determines that such amendment is reasonable and provides for only de minimis increases in the liabilities of the plan with respect to employees of the debtor,

(iii) such amendment only repeals an amendment described in section 412(d)(2), or

(iv) such amendment is required as a condition of qualification under this part.

(C) Plans to which this paragraph applies.—This paragraph shall apply only to plans (other than multiemployer plans) covered under section 4021 of the Employee Retirement Income Security Act of 1974.

(D) Employer.—For purposes of this paragraph, the term "employer" means the employer referred to in section 412(b)(1), without regard to section 412(b)(2).

(34) Benefits of missing participants on plan termination.—In the case of a plan covered by title IV of the Employee Retirement Income Security Act of 1974, a trust forming part of such plan shall not be treated as failing to constitute a qualified trust under this section merely because the pension plan of which such trust is a part, upon its termination, transfers benefits of missing participants to the Pension Benefit Guaranty Corporation in accordance with section 4050 of such Act.

(35) Diversification requirements for certain defined contribution plans.—

(A) In general.—A trust which is part of an applicable defined contribution plan shall not be treated as a qualified trust unless the plan meets the diversification requirements of subparagraphs (B), (C), and (D).

(B) Employee contributions and elective deferrals invested in employer securities.—In the case of the portion of an applicable individual's account attributable to employee contributions and elective deferrals which is invested in employer securities, a plan meets the requirements of this subparagraph if the applicable individual may elect to direct the plan to divest any such securities and to reinvest an equivalent amount in other investment options meeting the requirements of subparagraph (D).

(C) Employer contributions invested in employer securities.—In the case of the portion of the account attributable to employer contributions other than elective deferrals which is invested in employer securities, a plan meets the requirements of this subparagraph if each applicable individual who—

(i) is a participant who has completed at least 3 years of service, or

(ii) is a beneficiary of a participant described in clause (i) or of a deceased participant, may elect to direct the plan to divest any such securities and to reinvest an equivalent amount in other investment options meeting the requirements of subparagraph (D).

(D) Investment options.—

(i) In general.—The requirements of this subparagraph are met if the plan offers not less than 3 investment options, other than employer securities, to which an applicable individual may direct the proceeds from the divestment of employer securities pursuant to this paragraph, each of which is diversified and has materially different risk and return characteristics.

(ii) Treatment of certain restrictions and conditions.—

(I) Time for making investment choices.—A plan shall not be treated as failing to meet the requirements of this subparagraph merely because the plan limits the time for divestment and reinvestment to periodic, reasonable opportunities occurring no less frequently than quarterly.

(II) Certain restrictions and conditions not allowed.—Except as provided in regulations, a plan shall not meet the requirements of this subparagraph if the plan imposes restrictions or conditions with respect to the investment of employer securities which are not imposed on the investment of other assets of the plan. This subclause shall not apply to any restrictions or conditions imposed by reason of the application of securities laws.

(E) Applicable defined contribution plan.—For purposes of this paragraph—

(i) In general.—The term "applicable defined contribution plan" means any defined contribution plan which holds any publicly traded employer securities.

(ii) Exception for certain ESOPs.—Such term does not include an employee stock ownership plan if—

(I) there are no contributions to such plan (or earnings thereunder) which are held within such plan and are subject to subsection (k) or (m), and

(II) such plan is a separate plan for purposes of section 414(*l*) with respect to any other defined benefit plan or defined contribution plan maintained by the same employer or employers.

(iii) Exception for one participant plans.—Such term does not include a one-participant retirement plan.

(iv) One-participant retirement plan.—For purposes of clause (iii), the term "one-participant retirement plan" means a retirement plan that on the first day of the plan year—

(I) covered only one individual (or the individual and the individual's spouse) and the individual (or the individual and the individual's spouse) owned 100 percent of the plan sponsor (whether or not incorporated), or

(II) covered only one or more partners (or partners and their spouses) in the plan sponsor.

(F) Certain plans treated as holding publicly traded employer securities.—

(i) In general.—Except as provided in regulations or in clause (ii), a plan holding employer securities which are not publicly traded employer securities shall be treated as holding publicly traded employer securities if any employer corporation, or any member of a controlled group of corporations which includes such employer corporation, has issued a class of stock which is a publicly traded employer security.

(ii) Exception for certain controlled groups with publicly traded securities.—Clause (i) shall not apply to a plan if—

(I) no employer corporation, or parent corporation of an employer corporation, has issued any publicly traded employer security, and

(II) no employer corporation, or parent corporation of an employer corporation, has issued any special class of stock which grants particular rights to, or bears particular risks for, the holder or issuer with respect to any corporation described in clause (i) which has issued any publicly traded employer security.

(iii) Definitions.—For purposes of this subparagraph, the term—

(I) "controlled group of corporations" has the meaning given such term by section 1563(a), except that "50 percent" shall be substituted for "80 percent" each place it appears,

(II) "employer corporation" means a corporation which is an employer maintaining the plan, and

(III) "parent corporation" has the meaning given such term by section 424(e).

(G) Other definitions.—For purposes of this paragraph—

(i) Applicable individual.—The term "applicable individual" means—

(I) any participant in the plan, and

(II) any beneficiary who has an account under the plan with respect to which the beneficiary is entitled to exercise the rights of a participant.

(ii) Elective deferral.—The term "elective deferral" means an employer contribution described in section 402(g)(3)(A).

(iii) Employer security.—The term "employer security" has the meaning given such term by section 407(d)(1) of the Employee Retirement Income Security Act of 1974.

(iv) Employee stock ownership plan.—The term "employee stock ownership plan" has the meaning given such term by section 4975(e)(7).

(v) Publicly traded employer securities.—The term "publicly traded employer securities" means employer securities which are readily tradable on an established securities market.

(vi) Year of service.—The term "year of service" has the meaning given such term by section 411(a)(5).

(H) Transition rule for securities attributable to employer contributions.—

(i) Rules phased in over 3 years.—

(I) In general.—In the case of the portion of an account to which subparagraph (C) applies and which consists of employer securities acquired in a plan year beginning before January 1, 2007, subparagraph (C) shall only apply to the applicable percentage of such securities. This subparagraph shall be applied separately with respect to each class of securities.

(II) Exception for certain participants aged 55 or over.—Subclause (I) shall not apply to an applicable individual who is a participant who has attained age 55 and completed at least 3 years of service before the first plan year beginning after December 31, 2005.

IRC Sec. 401(a)(35)(H)(i)(II)

(ii) Applicable percentage.—For purposes of clause (i), the applicable percentage shall be determined as follows:

Plan year to which subparagraph (C) applies:	The applicable percentage is:
1st	33
2d	66
3d and following	100

(36) Distributions during working retirement.—A trust forming part of a pension plan shall not be treated as failing to constitute a qualified trust under this section solely because the plan provides that a distribution may be made from such trust to an employee who has attained age 62 and who is not separated from employment at the time of such distribution.

(37) Death benefits under USERRA-qualified active military service.—A trust shall not constitute a qualified trust unless the plan provides that, in the case of a participant who dies while performing qualified military service (as defined in section 414(u)), the survivors of the participant are entitled to any additional benefits (other than benefit accruals relating to the period of qualified military service) provided under the plan had the participant resumed and then terminated employment on account of death.

Paragraphs (11), (12), (13), (14), (15), (19), and (20) shall only apply in the case of a plan to which section 411 (relating to minimum vesting standards) applies without regard to subsection (e)(2) of such section.

(b) Certain Retroactive Changes in Plan.—A stock bonus, pension, profit-sharing, or annuity plan shall be considered as satisfying the requirements of subsection (a) for the period beginning with the date on which it was put into effect, or for the period beginning with the earlier of the date on which there was adopted or put into effect any amendment which caused the plan to fail to satisfy such requirements, and ending with the time prescribed by law for filing the return of the employer for his taxable year in which such plan or amendment was adopted (including extensions thereof) or such later time as the Secretary may designate, if all provisions of the plan which are necessary to satisfy such requirements are in effect by the end of such period and have been made effective for all purposes for the whole of such period.

(c) Definitions and Rules Relating to Self-Employed Individuals and Owner-Employees.—For purposes of this section—

(1) Self-employed individual treated as employee.—

(A) In general.—The term "employee" includes, for any taxable year, an individual who is a self-employed individual for such taxable year.

(B) Self-employed individual.—The term "self-employed individual" means, with respect to any taxable year, an individual who has earned income (as defined in paragraph (2)) for such taxable year. To the extent provided in regulations prescribed by the Secretary, such term also includes, for any taxable year—

(i) an individual who would be a self-employed individual within the meaning of the preceding sentence but for the fact that the trade or business carried on by such individual did not have net profits for the taxable year, and

(ii) an individual who has been a self-employed individual within the meaning of the preceding sentence for any prior taxable year.

(2) Earned income.—

(A) In general.—The term "earned income" means the net earnings from self-employment (as defined in section 1402(a)), but such net earnings shall be determined—

(i) only with respect to a trade or business in which personal services of the taxpayer are a material income-producing factor,

(ii) without regard to paragraphs (4) and (5) of section 1402(c),

(iii) in the case of any individual who is treated as an employee under sections 3121(d)(3)(A), (C), or (D), without regard to paragraph (2) of section 1402(c),

(iv) without regard to items which are not included in gross income for purposes of this chapter, and the deductions properly allocable to or chargeable against such items,

(v) with regard to the deductions allowed by section 404 to the taxpayer, and

(vi) with regard to the deduction allowed to the taxpayer by section 164(f).

For purposes of this subparagraph, section 1402, as in effect for a taxable year ending on December 31, 1962, shall be treated as having been in effect for all taxable years ending before such date. For purposes of this part only (other than sections 419 and 419A), this subparagraph shall be applied as if the term "trade or business" for purposes of section 1402 included service described in section 1402(c)(6).

(B) [Repealed.]

(C) Income from disposition of certain property.—For purposes of this section, the term "earned income" includes gains (other than any gain which is treated under any provision of this chapter as gain from the sale or exchange of a capital asset) and net earnings derived from the sale or other disposition of, the transfer of any interest in, or the licensing of the use of property (other than good will) by an individual whose personal efforts created such property.

(3) Owner-employee.—The term "owner-employee" means an employee who—

(A) owns the entire interest in an unincorporated trade or business, or

(B) in the case of a partnership, is a partner who owns more than 10 percent of either the capital interest or the profits interest in such partnership.

To the extent provided in regulations prescribed by the Secretary, such term also means an individual who has been an owner-employee within the meaning of the preceding sentence.

(4) Employer.—An individual who owns the entire interest in an unincorporated trade or business shall be treated as his own employer. A partnership shall be treated as the employer of each partner who is an employee within the meaning of paragraph (1).

(5) Contributions on behalf of owner-employees.—The term "contribution on behalf of an owner-employee" includes, except as the context otherwise requires, a contribution under a plan—

(A) by the employer for an owner-employee, and

(B) by an owner-employee as an employee.

(6) Special rule for certain fishermen.—For purposes of this subsection, the term "self-employed individual" includes an individual described in section 3121(b)(20) (related to certain fishermen).

(d) Contribution Limit on Owner-Employees.—A trust forming part of a pension or profit-sharing plan which provides contributions or benefits for employees some or all of whom are owner-employees shall constitute a qualified trust under this section only if, in addition to meeting the requirements of subsection (a), the plan provides that contributions on behalf of any owner-employee may be made only with respect to the earned income of such owner-employee which is derived from the trade or business with respect to which such plan is established.

(e) [Repealed.]

(f) Certain Custodial Accounts and Contracts.— For purposes of this title, a custodial account, an annuity contract, or a contract (other than a life, health or accident, property, casualty, or liability insurance contract) issued by an insurance company qualified to do business in a State shall be treated as a qualified trust under this section if—

(1) the custodial account or contract would, except for the fact that it is not a trust, constitute a qualified trust under this section, and

(2) in the case of a custodial account the assets thereof are held by a bank (as defined in section 408(n)) or another person who demonstrates, to the satisfaction of the Secretary, that the manner in which

he will hold the assets will be consistent with the requirements of this section.

For purposes of this title, in the case of a custodial account or contract treated as a qualified trust under this section by reason of this subsection, the person holding the assets of such account or holding such contract shall be treated as the trustee thereof.

(g) Annuity Defined.—For purposes of this section and sections 402, 403, and 404, the term "annuity" includes a face-amount certificate, as defined in section 2(a)(15) of the Investment Company Act of 1940 (15 U.S.C., section 80a-2); but does not include any contract or certificate issued after December 31, 1962, which is transferable, if any person other than the trustee of a trust described in section 401(a) which is exempt from tax under section 501(a) is the owner of such contract or certificate.

Editor's Note

IRC §401(h), below, as amended by Pub. L. No. 111-152, §1004, is effective on the date of enactment of the Act (enacted: March 30, 2010).

(h) Medical, etc., Benefits for Retired Employees and Their Spouses and Dependents.—Under regulations prescribed by the Secretary, and subject to the provisions of section 420, a pension or annuity plan may provide for the payment of benefits for sickness, accident hospitalization, and medical expenses of retired employees, their spouses and their dependents, but only if—

(1) such benefits are subordinate to the retirement benefits provided by the plan,

(2) a separate account is established and maintained for such benefit,

(3) the employer's contributions to such separate account are reasonable and ascertainable,

(4) it is impossible, at any time prior to the satisfaction of all liabilities under the plan to provide such benefits, for any part of the corpus or income of such separate account to be (within the taxable year or thereafter) used for, or diverted to, any purposes other than the providing of such benefits,

(5) not withstanding the provisions of subsection (a)(2), upon the satisfaction of all liabilities under the plan to provide such benefits, any amount remaining in such separate account must, under the terms of the plan, be returned to the employer, and

(6) in the case of an employee who is a key employee, a separate account is established and maintained for such benefits payable to such employee (and his spouse and dependents) and such benefits (to the extent attributable to plan years beginning after

March 31, 1984, for which the employee is a key employee) are only payable to such employee (and his spouse and dependents) from such separate account.

For purposes of paragraph (6), the term "key employee" means any employee, who at any time during the plan year or any preceding plan year during which contributions were made on behalf of such employee, is or was a key employee as defined in section 416(i). In no event shall the requirements of paragraph (1) be treated as met if the aggregate actual contributions for medical benefits, when added to actual contributions for life insurance protection under the plan, exceed 25 percent of the total actual contributions to the plan (other than contributions to fund past service credits) after the date on which the account is established. For purposes of this subsection, the term "dependent" shall include any individual who is a child (as defined in section 152(f)(1)) of a retired employee who as of the end of the calendar year has not attained age 27.

(i) Certain Union-Negotiated Pension Plans.—In the case of a trust forming part of a pension plan which has been determined by the Secretary to constitute a qualified trust under subsection (a) and to be exempt from taxation under section 501(a) for a period beginning after contributions were first made to or for such trust, if it is shown to the satisfaction of the Secretary that—

(1) such trust was created pursuant to a collective bargaining agreement between employee representatives and one or more employers,

(2) any disbursements of contributions, made to or for such trust before the time as of which the Secretary determined that the trust constituted a qualified trust, substantially complied with the terms of the trust, and the plan of which the trust is a part, as subsequently qualified, and

(3) before the time as of which the Secretary determined that the trust constitutes a qualified trust, the contributions to or for such trust were not used in a manner which would jeopardize the interests of its beneficiaries,

then such trust shall be considered as having constituted a qualified trust under subsection (a) and as having been exempt from taxation under section 501(a) for the period beginning on the date on which contributions were first made to or for such trust and ending on the date such trust first constituted (without regard to this subsection) a qualified trust under subsection (a).

(j) [Repealed.]

(k) Cash or Deferred Arrangements.—

(1) General rule.—A profit-sharing or stock bonus plan, a pre-ERISA money purchase plan, or a rural cooperative plan shall not be considered as not satisfying the requirements of subsection (a) merely because the plan includes a qualified cash or deferred arrangement.

(2) Qualified cash or deferred arrangement.—A qualified cash or deferred arrangement is any arrangement which is part of a profit-sharing or stock bonus plan, a pre-ERISA money purchase plan, or a rural cooperative plan which meets the requirements of subsection (a)—

(A) under which a covered employee may elect to have the employer make payments as contributions to a trust under the plan on behalf of the employee, or to the employee directly in cash;

(B) under which amounts held by the trust which are attributable to employer contributions made pursuant to the employee's election—

(i) may not be distributable to participants or other beneficiaries earlier than—

(I) severance from employment, death, or disability,

(II) an event described in paragraph (10),

(III) in the case of a profit-sharing or stock bonus plan, the attainment of age 59½,

(IV) in the case of contributions to a profit-sharing or stock bonus plan to which section 402(e)(3) applies, upon hardship of the employee, or

(V) in the case of a qualified reservist distribution (as defined in section 72(t)(2)(G)(iii)), the date on which a period referred to in subclause (III) of such section begins, and

(ii) will not be distributable merely by reason of the completion of a stated period of participation or the lapse of a fixed number of years;

(C) which provides that an employee's right to his accrued benefit derived from employer contributions made to the trust pursuant to his election is nonforfeitable, and

(D) which does not require, as a condition of participation in the arrangement, that an employee complete a period of service with the employer (or employers) maintaining the plan extending beyond the period permitted under section 410(a)(1) (determined without regard to subparagraph (B)(i) thereof).

(3) Application of participation and discrimination standards.—

(A) A cash or deferred arrangement shall not be treated as a qualified cash or deferred arrangement unless—

(i) those employees eligible to benefit under the arrangement satisfy the provisions of section 410(b)(1), and

(ii) the actual deferral percentage for eligible highly compensated employees (as defined in paragraph (5)) for the plan year bears a relationship to the actual deferral percentage for all other eligible employees for the preceding plan year which meets either of the following tests:

(I) The actual deferral percentage for the group of eligible highly compensated employees is not more than the actual deferral percentage of all other eligible employees multiplied by 1.25.

(II) The excess of the actual deferral percentage for the group of eligible highly compensated employees over that of all other eligible employees is not more than 2 percentage points, and the actual deferral percentage for the group of eligible highly compensated employees is not more than the actual deferral percentage of all other eligible employees multiplied by 2.

If 2 or more plans which include cash or deferred arrangements are considered as 1 plan for purposes of section 401(a)(4) or 410(b), the cash or deferred arrangements included in such plans shall be treated as 1 arrangement for purposes of this subparagraph.

If any highly compensated employee is a participant under 2 or more cash or deferred arrangements of the employer, for purposes of determining the deferral percentage with respect to such employee, all such cash or deferred arrangements shall be treated as 1 cash or deferred arrangement. An arrangement may apply clause (ii) by using the plan year rather than the preceding plan year if the employer so elects, except that if such an election is made, it may not be changed except as provided by the Secretary.

(B) For purposes of subparagraph (A), the actual deferral percentage for a specified group of employees for a plan year shall be the average of the ratios (calculated separately for each employee in such group) of—

(i) the amount of employer contributions actually paid over to the trust on behalf of each such employee for such plan year to

(ii) the employee's compensation for such plan year.

(C) A cash or deferred arrangement shall be treated as meeting the requirements of subsection (a)(4) with respect to contributions if the requirements of subparagraph (A)(ii) are met.

(D) For purposes of subparagraph (B), the employer contributions on behalf of any employee—

(i) shall include any employer contributions made pursuant to the employee's election under paragraph (2), and

(ii) under such rules as the Secretary may prescribe, may, at the election of the employer, include—

(I) matching contributions (as defined in 401(m)(4)(A)) which meet the requirements of paragraph (2)(B) and (C), and

(II) qualified nonelective contributions (within the meaning of section 401(m)(4)(C)).

(E) For purposes of this paragraph, in the case of the first plan year of any plan (other than a successor plan), the amount taken into account as the actual deferral percentage of nonhighly compensated employees for the preceding plan year shall be—

(i) 3 percent, or

(ii) if the employer makes an election under this subclause, the actual deferral percentage of nonhighly compensated employees determined for such first plan year.

(F) Special rule for early participation.—If an employer elects to apply section 410(b)(4)(B) in determining whether a cash or deferred arrangement meets the requirements of subparagraph (A)(i), the employer may, in determining whether the arrangement meets the requirements of subparagraph (A)(ii), exclude from consideration all eligible employees (other than highly compensated employees) who have not met the minimum age and service requirements of section 410(a)(1)(A).

(G) Governmental plan. A governmental plan (within the meaning of section 414(d)) shall be treated as meeting the requirements of this paragraph.

(4) Other requirements.—

(A) Benefits (other than matching contributions) must not be contingent on election to defer.—A cash or deferred arrangement of any employer shall not be treated as a qualified cash or deferred arrangement if any other benefit is conditioned (directly or indirectly) on the employee electing to have the employer make or not make contributions under the arrangement in lieu of receiving cash. The preceding sentence shall not apply to any matching contribution (as defined in section 401(m)) made by reason of such an election.

(B) Eligibility of state and local governments and tax-exempt organizations.—

(i) Tax-exempts eligible.—Except as provided in clause (ii), any organization exempt from tax under this subtitle may include a qualified cash or deferred arrangement as part of a plan maintained by it.

(ii) Governments ineligible.—A cash or deferred arrangement shall not be treated as a qualified cash or deferred arrangement if it is part of a plan maintained by a State or local government or political subdivision thereof, or any agency or instrumentality thereof. This clause shall not apply to a rural cooperative plan or to a plan of an employer described in clause (iii).

(iii) Treatment of Indian tribal governments.— An employer which is an Indian tribal government (as defined in section 7701(a)(40)), a subdivision of an Indian tribal government (determined in accordance with section 7871(d)), an agency or instrumentality of an Indian tribal government or subdivision thereof, or a corporation chartered under Federal, State, or tribal law which is owned in whole or in part by any of the foregoing may include a qualified cash or deferred arrangement as part of a plan maintained by the employer.

(C) Coordination with other plans.—Except as provided in section 401(m), any employer contribution made pursuant to an employee's election under a qualified cash or deferred arrangement shall not be taken into account for purposes of determining whether any other plan meets the requirements of section 401(a) or 410(b). This subparagraph shall not apply for purposes of determining whether a plan meets the average benefit requirement of section 410(b)(2)(A)(ii).

(5) Highly compensated employee.—For purposes of this subsection, the term "highly compensated employee" has the meaning given such term by section 414(q).

(6) Pre-ERISA money purchase plan.—For purposes of this subsection, the term "pre-ERISA money purchase plan" means a pension plan—

(A) which is a defined contribution plan (as defined in section 414(i)),

(B) which was in existence on June 27, 1974, and which, on such date, included a salary reduction arrangement, and

(C) under which neither the employee contributions nor the employer contributions may exceed the levels provided for by the contribution formula in effect under the plan on such date.

(7) Rural cooperative plan.—For purposes of this subsection—

(A) In general.—The term "rural cooperative plan" means any pension plan—

(i) which is a defined contribution plan (as defined in section 414(i)), and

(ii) which is established and maintained by a rural cooperative.

(B) Rural cooperative defined.—For purposes of subparagraph (A), the term "rural cooperative" means—

(i) any organization which—

(I) is engaged primarily in providing electric service on a mutual or cooperative basis, or

(II) is engaged primarily in providing electric service to the public in its area of service and which is exempt from tax under this subtitle or which is a State or local government (or an agency or instrumentality thereof), other than a municipality (or an agency or instrumentality thereof),

(ii) any organization described in paragraph (4) or (6) of section 501(c) and at least 80 percent of the members of which are organizations described in clause (i),

(iii) a cooperative telephone company described in section 501(c)(12),

(iv) any organization which—

(I) is a mutual irrigation or ditch company described in section 501(c)(12) (without regard to the 85 percent requirement thereof), or

(II) is a district organized under the laws of a State as a municipal corporation for the purpose of irrigation, water conservation, or drainage, and

(v) an organization which is a national association of organizations described in clause (i), (ii), (iii), or (iv).

(C) Special rule for certain distributions.—A rural cooperative plan which includes a qualified cash or deferred arrangement shall not be treated as violating the requirements of section 401(a) or of paragraph (2) merely by reason of a hardship distribution or a distribution to a participant after attainment of age 59½. For purposes of this section, the term "hardship distribution" means a distribution described in paragraph (2)(B)(i)(IV) (without regard to the limitation of its application to profit-sharing or stock bonus plans).

(8) Arrangement not disqualified if excess contributions distributed.—

(A) In general.—A cash or deferred arrangement shall not be treated as failing to meet the requirements of clause (ii) of paragraph (3)(A) for any plan year if, before the close of the following plan year—

(i) the amount of the excess contributions for such plan year (and any income allocable to such contributions through the end of such year) is distributed, or

(ii) to the extent provided in regulations, the employee elects to treat the amount of the excess contributions as an amount distributed to the employee and then contributed by the employee to the plan.

Any distribution of excess contributions (and income) may be made without regard to any other provision of law.

(B) Excess contributions.—For purposes of subparagraph (A), the term "excess contributions" means, with respect to any plan year, the excess of—

(i) the aggregate amount of employer contributions actually paid over to the trust on behalf of highly compensated employees for such plan year, over

(ii) the maximum amount of such contributions permitted under the limitations of clause (ii) of paragraph (3)(A) (determined by reducing contributions made on behalf of highly compensated employees in order of the actual deferral percentages beginning with the highest of such percentages).

(C) Method of distributing excess contributions.—Any distribution of the excess contributions for any plan year shall be made to highly compensated employees on the basis of the amount of contributions by, or on behalf of, each such employee.

(D) Additional tax under section 72(t) not to apply.—No tax shall be imposed under section 72(t) on any amount required to be distributed under this paragraph.

(E) Treatment of matching contributions forfeited by reason of excess deferral or contribution or a permissible withdrawal.—For purposes of paragraph (2)(C), a matching contribution (within the meaning of subsection (m)) shall not be treated as forfeitable merely because such contribution is forfeitable if the contribution to which the matching contribution relates is treated as an excess contribution under subparagraph (B), an excess deferral under section 402(g)(2)(A), a permissible withdrawal under section 414(w), or an excess aggregate contribution under section 401(m)(6)(B).

(F) Cross reference.—For excise tax on certain excess contributions, see section 4979.

(9) Compensation.—For purposes of this subsection, the term "compensation" has the meaning given such term by section 414(s).

(10) Distributions upon termination of plan.—

(A) In general.—An event described in this subparagraph is the termination of the plan without establishment or maintenance of another defined contribution plan (other than an employee stock ownership plan as defined in section 4975(e)(7)).

(B) Distributions must be lump sum distributions.

(i) In general.—A termination shall not be treated as described in subparagraph (A) with respect to any employee unless the employee receives a lump sum distribution by reason of the termination.

(ii) Lump sum distribution.—For purposes of this subparagraph, the term "lump sum distribution" has the meaning given such term by section 402(e)(4)(D) (without regard to subclauses (I), (II), (III), and (IV) of clause (i) thereof). Such term includes a distribution of an annuity contract from—

(I) a trust which forms a part of a plan described in section 401(a) and which is exempt from tax under section 501(a), or

(II) an annuity plan described in section 403(a).

(C) [Repealed.]

(11) Adoption of simple plan to meet nondiscrimination tests.—

(A) In general.—A cash or deferred arrangement maintained by an eligible employer shall be treated as meeting the requirements of paragraph (3)(A)(ii) if such arrangement meets—

(i) the contribution requirements of subparagraph (B),

(ii) the exclusive plan requirements of subparagraph (C), and

(iii) the vesting requirements of section 408(p)(3).

(B) Contribution requirements.—

(i) In general.—The requirements of this subparagraph are met if, under the arrangement—

(I) an employee may elect to have the employer make elective contributions for the year on behalf of the employee to a trust under the plan in an amount which is expressed as a percentage of compensation of the employee but which in no event exceeds the amount in effect under section 408(p)(2)(A)(ii).

(II) the employer is required to make a matching contribution to the trust for the year in an amount equal to so much of the amount the employee elects under subclause (I) as does not exceed 3 percent of compensation for the year, and

(III) no other contributions may be made other than contributions described in subclause (I) or (II).

(ii) Employer may elect 2-percent nonelective contribution.—An employer shall be treated as meeting the requirements of clause (i)(II) for any year if, in lieu of the contributions described in such clause, the employer elects (pursuant to the terms of the arrangement) to make nonelective contributions of 2 percent of compensation for each employee who is eligible to participate in the arrangement and who has at least $5,000 of compensation from the employer for the year. If an employer makes an election under this subparagraph for any year, the employer shall notify employees of such election within a reasonable period of time before the 60th day before the beginning of such year.

(iii) Administrative requirements.—

(I) In general.—Rules similar to the rules of subparagraphs (B) and (C) of section 408(p)(5) shall apply for purposes of this subparagraph.

(II) Notice of election period.—The requirements of this subparagraph shall not be treated as met with respect to any year unless the employer notifies each employee eligible to participate, within a reasonable period of time before the 60th day before the beginning of such year (and, for the first year the employee is so eligible, the 60th day before the first day such employee is so eligible), of the rules similar to the rules of section 408(p)(5)(C) which apply by reason of subclause (I).

(C) Exclusive plan requirement.—The requirements of this subparagraph are met for any year to which this paragraph applies if no contributions were made, or benefits were accrued, for services during such year under any qualified plan of the employer on behalf of any employee eligible to participate in the cash or deferred arrangement, other than contributions described in subparagraph (B).

(D) Definitions and special rule.—

(i) Definitions.—For purposes of this paragraph, any term used in this paragraph which is also used in section 408(p) shall have the meaning given such term by such section.

(ii) Coordination with top-heavy rules.—A plan meeting the requirements of this paragraph for any year shall not be treated as a top-heavy plan under section 416 for such year if such plan allows only contributions required under this paragraph.

(E) [Repealed.]

(12) Alternative methods of meeting nondiscrimination requirements.—

(A) In general.—A cash or deferred arrangement shall be treated as meeting the requirements of paragraph (3)(A)(ii) if such arrangement—

(i) meets the contribution requirements of subparagraph (B) or (C), and

(ii) meets the notice requirements of subparagraph (D).

(B) Matching contributions.—

(i) In general.—The requirements of this subparagraph are met if, under the arrangement, the employer makes matching contributions on behalf of each employee who is not a highly compensated employee in an amount equal to—

(I) 100 percent of the elective contributions of the employee to the extent such elective contributions do not exceed 3 percent of the employee's compensation, and

(II) 50 percent of the elective contributions of the employee to the extent that such elective contributions exceed 3 percent but do not exceed 5 percent of the employee's compensation.

(ii) Rate for highly compensated employees.—The requirements of this subparagraph are not met

if, under the arrangement, the rate of matching contribution with respect to any elective contribution of a highly compensated employee at any rate of elective contribution is greater than that with respect to an employee who is not a highly compensated employee.

(iii) Alternative plan designs.—If the rate of any matching contribution with respect to any rate of elective contribution is not equal to the percentage required under clause (i), an arrangement shall not be treated as failing to meet the requirements of clause (i) if—

(I) the rate of an employer's matching contribution does not increase as an employee's rate of elective contributions increase, and

(II) the aggregate amount of matching contributions at such rate of elective contribution is at least equal to the aggregate amount of matching contributions which would be made if matching contributions were made on the basis of the percentages described in clause (i).

(C) Nonelective contributions.—The requirements of this subparagraph are met if, under the arrangement, the employer is required, without regard to whether the employee makes an elective contribution or employee contribution, to make a contribution to a defined contribution plan on behalf of each employee who is not a highly compensated employee and who is eligible to participate in the arrangement in an amount equal to at least 3 percent of the employee's compensation.

(D) Notice requirement.—An arrangement meets the requirements of this paragraph if, under the arrangement, each employee eligible to participate is, within a reasonable period before any year, given written notice of the employee's rights and obligations under the arrangement which—

(i) is sufficiently accurate and comprehensive to appraise the employee of such rights and obligations, and

(ii) is written in a manner calculated to be understood by the average employee eligible to participate.

(E) Other requirements.—

(i) Withdrawal and vesting restrictions.—An arrangement shall not be treated as meeting the requirements of subparagraph (B) or (C) of this paragraph unless the requirements of subparagraphs (B) and (C) of paragraph (2) are met with respect to all employer contributions (including matching contributions) taken into account in determining whether the requirements of subparagraphs (B) and (C) of this paragraph are met.

(ii) Social Security and similar contributions not taken into account.—An arrangement shall not be treated as meeting the requirements of subparagraph (B) or (C) unless such requirements are met without regard to subsection (*l*), and, for purposes of subsection (*l*), employer contributions under subparagraph (B) or (C) shall not be taken into account.

(F) Other plans.—An arrangement shall be treated as meeting the requirements under subparagraph (A)(i) if any other plan maintained by the employer meets such requirements with respect to employees eligible under the arrangement.

(13) Alternative method for automatic contribution arrangements to meet nondiscrimination requirements.—

(A) In general.—A qualified automatic contribution arrangement shall be treated as meeting the requirements of paragraph (3)(A)(ii).

(B) Qualified automatic contribution arrangement.—For purposes of this paragraph, the term "qualified automatic contribution arrangement" means any cash or deferred arrangement which meets the requirements of subparagraphs (C) through (E).

(C) Automatic deferral.—

(i) In general.—The requirements of this subparagraph are met if, under the arrangement, each employee eligible to participate in the arrangement is treated as having elected to have the employer make elective contributions in an amount equal to a qualified percentage of compensation.

(ii) Election out.—The election treated as having been made under clause (i) shall cease to apply with respect to any employee if such employee makes an affirmative election—

(I) to not have such contributions made, or

(II) to make elective contributions at a level specified in such affirmative election.

(iii) Qualified percentage.—For purposes of this subparagraph, the term "qualified percentage" means, with respect to any employee, any percentage determined under the arrangement if such percentage is applied uniformly, does not exceed 10 percent, and is at least—

(I) 3 percent during the period ending on the last day of the first plan year which begins after the date on which the first elective contribution described in clause (i) is made with respect to such employee,

(II) 4 percent during the first plan year following the plan year described in subclause (I),

(III) 5 percent during the second plan year following the plan year described in subclause (I), and

(IV) 6 percent during any subsequent plan year.

(iv) Automatic deferral for current employees not required.—Clause (i) may be applied without taking into account any employee who—

(I) was eligible to participate in the arrangement (or a predecessor arrangement) immediately before the date on which such arrangement becomes a qualified automatic contribution arrangement (determined after application of this clause), and

(II) had an election in effect on such date either to participate in the arrangement or to not participate in the arrangement.

(D) Matching or nonelective contributions.—

(i) In general.—The requirements of this subparagraph are met if, under the arrangement, the employer—

(I) makes matching contributions on behalf of each employee who is not a highly compensated employee in an amount equal to the sum of 100 percent of the elective contributions of the employee to the extent that such contributions do not exceed 1 percent of compensation plus 50 percent of so much of such contributions as exceed 1 percent but do not exceed 6 percent of compensation, or

(II) is required, without regard to whether the employee makes an elective contribution or employee contribution, to make a contribution to a defined contribution plan on behalf of each employee who is not a highly compensated employee and who is eligible to participate in the arrangement in an amount equal to at least 3 percent of the employee's compensation.

(ii) Application of rules for matching contributions.—The rules of clauses (ii) and (iii) of paragraph (12)(B) shall apply for purposes of clause (i)(I).

(iii) Withdrawal and vesting restrictions.—An arrangement shall not be treated as meeting the requirements of clause (i) unless, with respect to employer contributions (including matching contributions) taken into account in determining whether the requirements of clause (i) are met—

(I) any employee who has completed at least 2 years of service (within the meaning of section 411(a)) has a nonforfeitable right to 100 percent of the employee's accrued benefit derived from such employer contributions, and

(II) the requirements of subparagraph (B) of paragraph (2) are met with respect to all such employer contributions.

(iv) Application of certain other rules.—The rules of subparagraphs (E)(ii) and (F) of paragraph (12) shall apply for purposes of subclauses (I) and (II) of clause (i).

(E) Notice requirements.—

(i) In general.—The requirements of this subparagraph are met if, within a reasonable period before each plan year, each employee eligible to participate in the arrangement for such year receives written notice of the employee's rights and obligations under the arrangement which—

(I) is sufficiently accurate and comprehensive to apprise the employee of such rights and obligations, and

(II) is written in a manner calculated to be understood by the average employee to whom the arrangement applies.

(ii) Timing and content requirements.—A notice shall not be treated as meeting the requirements of clause (i) with respect to an employee unless—

(I) the notice explains the employee's right under the arrangement to elect not to have elective contributions made on the employee's behalf (or to elect to have such contributions made at a different percentage),

(II) in the case of an arrangement under which the employee may elect among 2 or more investment options, the notice explains how contributions made under the arrangement will be invested in the absence of any investment election by the employee, and

(III) the employee has a reasonable period of time after receipt of the notice described in subclauses (I) and (II) and before the first elective contribution is made to make either such election.

(l) **Permitted Disparity in Plan Contributions or Benefits.**—

(1) In general.—The requirements of this subsection are met with respect to a plan if—

(A) in the case of a defined contribution plan, the requirements of paragraph (2) are met, and

(B) in the case of a defined benefit plan, the requirements of paragraph (3) are met.

(2) Defined contribution plan.—

(A) In general.—A defined contribution plan meets the requirements of this paragraph if the excess contribution percentage does not exceed the base contribution percentage by more than the lesser of—

(i) the base contribution percentage, or

(ii) the greater of—

(I) 5.7 percentage points, or

(II) the percentage equal to the portion of the rate of tax under section 3111(a) (in effect as of the beginning of the year) which is attributable to old-age insurance.

(B) Contribution percentages.—For purposes of this paragraph—

(i) Excess contribution percentage.—The term "excess contribution percentage" means the percentage of compensation which is contributed by the employer under the plan with respect to that portion of each participant's compensation in excess of the integration level.

(ii) Base contribution percentage.—The term "base contribution percentage" means the percentage of compensation contributed by the employer under the plan with respect to that portion of each participant's compensation not in excess of the integration level.

(3) Defined benefit plan.—A defined benefit plan meets the requirements of this paragraph if—

(A) Excess plans.—

(i) In general.—In the case of a plan other than an offset plan—

(I) the excess benefit percentage does not exceed the base benefit percentage by more than the maximum excess allowance,

(II) any optional form of benefit, preretirement benefit, actuarial factor, or other benefit or feature provided with respect to compensation in excess of the integration level is provided with respect to compensation not in excess of such level, and

(III) benefits are based on average annual compensation.

(ii) Benefit percentages.—For purposes of this subparagraph, the excess and base benefit percentages shall be computed in the same manner as the excess and base contribution percentages under paragraph (2)(B), except that such determination shall be made on the basis of benefits attributable to employer contributions rather than contributions.

(B) Offset plans.—In the case of an offset plan, the plan provides that—

(i) a participant's accrued benefit attributable to employer contributions (within the meaning of section 411(c)(1)) may not be reduced (by reason of the offset) by more than the maximum offset allowance, and

(ii) benefits are based on average annual compensation.

(4) Definitions relating to paragraph (3).—For purposes of paragraph (3)—

(A) Maximum excess allowance.—The maximum excess allowance is equal to—

(i) in the case of benefits attributable to any year of service with the employer taken into account under the plan, ¾ of a percentage point, and

(ii) in the case of total benefits, ¾ of a percentage point, multiplied by the participant's years of service (not in excess of 35) with the employer taken into account under the plan.

In no event shall the maximum excess allowance exceed the base benefit percentage.

(B) Maximum offset allowance.—The maximum offset allowance is equal to—

(i) in the case of benefits attributable to any year of service with the employer taken into account under the plan, ¾ percent of the participant's final average compensation, and

(ii) in the case of total benefits, ¾ percent of the participant's final average compensation, multiplied by the participant's years of service (not in excess of 35) with the employer taken into account under the plan.

In no event shall the maximum offset allowance exceed 50 percent of the benefit which would have accrued without regard to the offset reduction.

(C) Reductions.—

(i) In general.—The Secretary shall prescribe regulations requiring the reduction of the ¾ percentage factor under subparagraph (A) or (B)—

(I) in the case of a plan other than an offset plan which has an integration level in excess of covered compensation, or

(II) with respect to any participant in an offset plan who has final average compensation in excess of covered compensation.

(ii) Basis of reductions.—Any reductions under clause (i) shall be based on the percentages of compensation replaced by the employer-derived portions of primary insurance amounts under the Social Security Act for participants with compensation in excess of covered compensation.

(D) Offset plan.—The term "offset plan" means any plan with respect to which the benefit attributable to employer contributions for each participant is reduced by an amount specified in the plan.

(5) Other definitions and special rules.—For purposes of this subsection—

(A) Integration level.—

(i) In general.—The term "integration level" means the amount of compensation specified under the plan (by dollar amount or formula) at or below which the rate at which contributions or benefits are provided (expressed as a percentage) is less than such rate above such amount.

(ii) Limitation.—The integration level for any year may not exceed the contribution and benefit base in effect under section 230 of the Social Security Act for such year.

(iii) Level to apply to all participants.—A plan's integration level shall apply with respect to all participants in the plan.

(iv) Multiple integration levels.—Under rules prescribed by the Secretary, a defined benefit plan may specify multiple integration levels.

(B) Compensation.—The term "compensation" has the meaning given such term by section 414(s).

(C) Average annual compensation.—The term "average annual compensation" means the participant's highest average annual compensation for—

(i) any period of at least 3 consecutive years, or

(ii) if shorter, the participant's full period of service.

(D) Final average compensation.—

(i) In general.—The term "final average compensation" means the participant's average annual compensation for—

(I) the 3-consecutive year period ending with the current year, or

(II) if shorter, the participant's full period of service.

(ii) Limitation.—A participant's final average compensation shall be determined by not taking into account in any year compensation in excess of the contribution and benefit base in effect under section 230 of the Social Security Act for such year.

(E) Covered compensation.—

(i) In general.—The term "covered compensation" means, with respect to an employee, the average of the contribution and benefit bases in effect under section 230 of the Social Security Act for each year in the 35-year period ending with the year in which the employee attains the social security retirement age.

(ii) Computation for any year.—For purposes of clause (i), the determination for any year preceding the year in which the employee attains the social security retirement age shall be made by assuming that there is no increase in the bases described in clause (i) after the determination year and before the employee attains the social security retirement age.

(iii) Social Security retirement age.—For purposes of this subparagraph, the term "social security retirement age" has the meaning given such term by section 415(b)(8).

(F) Regulations.—The Secretary shall prescribe such regulations as are necessary or appropriate to carry out the purposes of this subsection, including—

(i) in the case of a defined benefit plan which provides for unreduced benefits commencing before the social security retirement age (as defined in section 415(b)(8)), rules providing for the reduction of the maximum excess allowance and the maximum offset allowance, and

(ii) in the case of an employee covered by 2 or more plans of the employer which fail to meet the requirements of subsection (a)(4) (without regard to this subsection), rules preventing the multiple use of the disparity permitted under this subsection with respect to any employee.

For purposes of clause (i), unreduced benefits shall not include benefits for disability (within the meaning of section 223(d) of the Social Security Act).

(6) Special rule for plan maintained by railroads.—In determining whether a plan which includes employees of a railroad employer who are entitled to benefits under the Railroad Retirement Act of 1974 meets the requirements of this subsection, rules similar to the rules set forth in this subsection shall apply. Such rules shall take into account the employer-derived portion of the employees' tier 2 railroad retirement benefits and any supplemental annuity under the Railroad Retirement Act of 1974.

(m) Nondiscrimination Test for Matching Contributions and Employee Contributions.—

(1) In general.—A defined contribution plan shall be treated as meeting the requirements of subsection (a)(4) with respect to the amount of any matching contribution or employee contribution for any plan year only if the contribution percentage requirement of paragraph (2) of this subsection is met for such plan year.

(2) Requirements.—

(A) Contribution percentage requirement.—A plan meets the contribution percentage requirement of this paragraph for any plan year only if the contribution percentage for eligible highly compensated employees for such plan year does not exceed the greater of—

(i) 125 percent of such percentage for all other eligible employees for the preceding plan year, or

(ii) the lesser of 200 percent of such percentage for all other eligible employees, or such percentage for all other eligible employees for the preceding plan year plus 2 percentage points.

This subparagraph may be applied by using the plan year rather than the preceding plan year if the employer so elects, except that if such an election is made, it may not be changed except as provided by the Secretary.

(B) Multiple plans treated as a single plan.—If two or more plans of an employer to which matching contributions, employee contributions, or elective deferrals are made are treated as one plan for purposes of section 410(b), such plans shall be treated as one plan for purposes of this subsection. If a highly compensated employee participates in two or more plans of an employer to which contributions to which this subsection applies are made, all such contributions shall be aggregated for purposes of this subsection.

(3) Contribution percentage.—For purposes of paragraph (2), the contribution percentage for a specified group of employees for a plan year shall be the average of the ratios (calculated separately for each employee in such group) of—

(A) the sum of the matching contributions and employee contributions paid under the plan on behalf of each such employee for such plan year, to—

(B) the employee's compensation (within the meaning of section 414(s)) for such plan year.

Under regulations, an employer may elect to take into account (in computing the contribution percentage) elective deferrals and qualified nonelective contributions under the plan or any other plan of the employer. If matching contributions are taken into account for purposes of subsection (k)(3)(A)(ii) for any plan year, such contributions shall not be taken into account under subparagraph (A) for such year. Rules similar to the rules of subsection (k)(3)(E) shall apply for purposes of this subsection.

(4) Definitions.—For purposes of this subsection—

(A) Matching contribution.—The term "matching contribution" means—

(i) any employer contribution made to a defined contribution plan on behalf of an employee on account of an employee contribution made by such employee, and

(ii) any employer contribution made to a defined contribution plan on behalf of an employee on account of an employee's elective deferral.

(B) Elective deferral.—The term "elective deferral" means any employer contribution described in section 402(g)(3).

(C) Qualified nonelective contributions.—The term "qualified nonelective contribution" means any employer contribution (other than a matching contribution) with respect to which—

(i) the employee may not elect to have the contribution paid to the employee in cash instead of being contributed to the plan, and

(ii) the requirements of subparagraphs (B) and (C) of subsection (k)(2) are met.

(5) Employees taken into consideration.—

(A) In general.—Any employee who is eligible to make an employee contribution (or, if the employer takes elective contributions into account, elective contributions) or to receive a matching contribution under the plan being tested under

IRC Sec. 401(l)(5)(F)(i)

paragraph (1) shall be considered an eligible employee for purposes of this subsection.

(B) Certain nonparticipant.—If an employee contribution is required as a condition of participation in the plan, any employee who would be a participant in the plan if such employee made such a contribution shall be treated as an eligible employee on behalf of whom no employer contributions are made.

(C) Special rule for early participation.—If an employer elects to apply section 10(b)(4)(B) in determining whether a plan meets the requirements of section 410(b), the employer may, in determining whether the plan meets the requirements of paragraph (2), exclude from consideration all eligible employees (other than highly compensated employees) who have not met the minimum age and service requirements of section 410(a)(1)(A).

(6) Plan not disqualified if excess aggregate contributions distributed before end of following plan year.—

(A) In general.—A plan shall not be treated as failing to meet the requirements of paragraph (1) for any plan year if, before the close of the following plan year, the amount of the excess aggregate contributions for such plan year (and any income allocable to such contributions through the end of such year) is distributed (or, if forfeitable, is forfeited). Such contributions (and such income) may be distributed without regard to any other provision of law.

(B) Excess aggregate contributions.—For purposes of subparagraph (A), the term "excess aggregate contributions" means, with respect to any plan year, the excess of—

(i) the aggregate amount of the matching contributions and employee contributions (and any qualified nonelective contribution or elective contribution taken into account in computing the contribution percentage) actually made on behalf of highly compensated employees for such plan year, over

(ii) the maximum amount of such contributions permitted under the limitations of paragraph (2)(A) (determined by reducing contributions made on behalf of highly compensated employees in order of their contribution percentages beginning with the highest of such percentages).

(C) Method of distributing excess aggregate contributions.—Any distribution of the excess aggregate contributions for any plan year shall be made to highly compensated employees on the basis of the amount of contributions on behalf of, or by, each such employee. Forfeitures of excess aggregate contributions may not be allocated to participants whose contributions are reduced under this paragraph.

(D) Coordination with subsection (k) and 402(g).—The determination of the amount of excess aggregate contributions with respect to a plan shall be made after—

(i) first determining the excess deferrals (within the meaning of section 402(g)), and

(ii) then determining the excess contributions under subsection (k).

(7) Treatment of distributions.—

(A) Additional tax of section 72(t) not applicable.—No tax shall be imposed under section 72(t) on any amount required to be distributed under paragraph (6).

(B) Exclusion of employee contributions.—Any distribution attributable to employee contributions shall not be included in gross income except to the extent attributable to income on such contributions.

(8) Highly compensated employee.—For purposes of this subsection, the term "highly compensated employee" has the meaning given to such term by section 414(q).

(9) Regulations.—The Secretary shall prescribe such regulations as may be necessary to carry out the purposes of this subsection and subsection (k) including regulations permitting appropriate aggregation of plans and contributions.

(10) Alternative method of satisfying tests.—A defined contribution plan shall be treated as meeting the requirements of paragraph (2) with respect to matching contributions if the plan—

(A) meets the requirements of subparagraph (B) of subsection (k)(11),

(B) meets the exclusive plan requirements of subsection (k)(11)(C), and

(C) meets the vesting requirements of section 408(p)(3).

(11) Additional alternative method of satisfying tests.—

(A) In general.—A defined contribution plan shall be treated as meeting the requirements of paragraph (2) with respect to matching contributions if the plan—

(i) meets the contribution requirements of subparagraph (B) or (C) of subsection (k)(12),

(ii) meets the notice requirements of subsection (k)(12)(D), and

(iii) meets the requirements of subparagraph (B).

(B) Limitation on matching contributions.—The requirements of this subparagraph are met if—

(i) matching contributions on behalf of any employee may not be made with respect to an em-

IRC Sec. 401(m)(11)(B)(i)

ployee's contributions or elective deferrals in excess of 6 percent of the employee's compensation,

(ii) the rate of an employer's matching contribution does not increase as the rate of an employee's contributions or elective deferrals increase, and

(iii) the matching contribution with respect to any highly compensated employee at any rate of an employee contribution or rate of elective deferral is not greater than that with respect to an employee who is not a highly compensated employee.

(12) Alternative method for automatic contribution arrangements.—A defined contribution plan shall be treated as meeting the requirements of paragraph (2) with respect to matching contributions if the plan—

(A) is a qualified automatic contribution arrangement (as defined in subsection (k)(13)), and

(B) meets the requirements of paragraph (11)(B).

(13) Cross reference.—For excise tax on certain excess contributions, see section 4979.

(n) Coordination With Qualified Domestic Relations Orders.—The Secretary shall prescribe such rules or regulations as may be necessary to coordinate the requirements of subsection (a)(13)(B) and section 414(p) (and the regulations issued by the Secretary of Labor thereunder) with the other provisions of this chapter.

(o) Cross Reference.—For exemption from tax of a trust qualified under this section, see section 501(a).

Recent Amendments to IRC §401

Health Care and Education Reconciliation Act of 2010 (Pub. L. No. 111-148), as follows:
- IRC §401(h) was amended by Act §1004(d)(5) to add the sentence at the end. Eff. on date of enactment of the Act [enacted: Mar. 30, 2010].

Worker, Retiree, and Employer Recovery Act of 2008 (Pub. L. No. 110-458), as follows:
- IRC §401(a)(9)(H) was added by Act §201(a). Eff. for calendar years beginning after Dec. 31, 2008.
- IRC §401(a)(29) was amended by Act §101(d)(2)(A) by striking "on plans in at-risk status" in the heading. Eff. as if included in Pub. L. No. 109-280, §114 [eff. for plan years beginning after 2007].
- IRC §401(a)(32)(C) was amended by Act §101(d)(2)(B)(i) by striking "section 430(j)" and inserting "section 430(j)(4)(A)", and by Act §101(d)(2)(B)(ii) by striking "paragraph (5)(A)" and inserting "section 430(j)(4)(A)". Eff. as if included in Pub. L. No. 109-280, §114 [eff. for plan years beginning after 2007].
- IRC §401(a)(33)(B)(iii) was amended by Act §101(d)(2)(C)(i) by striking "section 412(c)(2)" and inserting "section 412(d)(2)". Eff. as if included in Pub. L. No. 109-280, §114 [eff. for plan years beginning after 2007].
- IRC §401(a)(33)(D) was amended by Act §101(d)(2)(C)(ii) by striking "section 412(b)(2) (without regard to subparagraph (B) thereof)" and inserting "section 412(b)(1), without regard to section 412(b)(2)". Eff. as if included in Pub. L. No. 109-280, §114 [eff. for plan years beginning after 2007].
- IRC §401(a)(35)(E)(iv) was amended by Act §109(a). Eff. as if included in Pub. L. No. 109-280, §901 [eff. for plan years

beginning after 2006]. IRC §401(a)(35)(E)(iv) prior to amendment:

(iv) One-participant retirement plan. For purposes of clause (iii) , the term "one-participant retirement plan" means a retirement plan that—
(I) on the first day of the plan year covered only one individual (or the individual and the individual's spouse) and the individual owned 100 percent of the plan sponsor (whether or not incorporated), or covered only one or more partners (or partners and their spouses) in the plan sponsor,
(II) meets the minimum coverage requirements of section 410(b) without being combined with any other plan of the business that covers the employees of the business,
(III) does not provide benefits to anyone except the individual (and the individual's spouse) or the partners (and their spouses),
(IV) does not cover a business that is a member of an affiliated service group, a controlled group of corporations, or a group of businesses under common control, and
(V) does not cover a business that uses the services of leased employees (within the meaning of section 414(n)).
For purposes of this clause, the term "partner" includes a 2-percent shareholder (as defined in section 1372(b)) of an S corporation.
- IRC §401(k)(8)(E) was amended by Act §109(b)(2)(A) by striking "an erroneous automatic contribution" and inserting "a permissible withdrawal", and by striking "erroneous automatic contribution" in the heading and inserting "a permissible withdrawal". Eff. as if included in Pub. L. No. 109-280, §902 [eff. for plan years beginning after 2007].
- IRC §401(k)(13)(D)(i)(I) was amended by Act §109(b)(1) by striking "such compensation as exceeds 1 percent but does not" and inserting "such contributions as exceed 1 percent but do not". Eff. as if included in Pub. L. 109-280, §902 [eff. for plan years beginning after 2007].
- **Other Provision—Effective Date.** Act §101(d)(3) provides:
(3) Amendment to 2006 Act—Section 114 of the 2006 Act is amended by adding at the end the following new subsection:
(g) Effective Dates—
(1) In General.—The amendments made by this section shall apply to plan years beginning after 2007.
(2) Excise Tax.—The amendments made by subsection (e) shall apply to taxable years beginning after 2007, but only with respect to plan years described in paragraph (1) which end with or within any such taxable year.
- **Other Provision.** Act §201(c)(2) provides:
(2) Provisions relating to plan or contract amendments.—
(A) In general.—If this paragraph applies to any pension plan or contract amendment, such pension plan or contract shall not fail to be treated as being operated in accordance with the terms of the plan during the period described in subparagraph (B)(ii) solely because the plan operates in accordance with this section.
(B) Amendments to which paragraph applies.—
(i) In general.—This paragraph shall apply to any amendment to any pension plan or annuity contract which—
(I) is made pursuant to the amendments made by this section, and
(II) is made on or before the last day of the first plan year beginning on or after January 1, 2011. In the case of a governmental plan, subclause (II) shall be applied by substituting "2012" for "2011".
(ii) Conditions.—This paragraph shall not apply to any amendment unless during the period beginning on the effective date of the amendment and ending on December 31, 2009, the plan or contract is operated as if such plan or contract amendment were in effect.

Heroes Earnings Assistance and Relief Tax Act of 2008 (Pub. L. No. 110-245), as follows:
- IRC §401(a)(37) was added by Act §104(a). Eff., in general, with respect to deaths and disabilities occurring on or after Jan. 1, 2007, see Act §104(d)(1).
- **Other Provision.** Act §104(d)(2) provides:
(2) Provisions relating to plan amendments.—
(A) In general.—If this subparagraph applies to any plan or contract amendment, such plan or contract shall be treated as

being operated in accordance with the terms of the plan during the period described in subparagraph (B)(iii).

(B) Amendments to which subparagraph (A) applies.—

(i) In general.—Subparagraph (A) shall apply to any amendment to any plan or annuity contract which is made—

(I) pursuant to the amendments made by subsection (a) or pursuant to any regulation issued by the Secretary of the Treasury under subsection (a), and

(II) on or before the last day of the first plan year beginning on or after January 1, 2010.

In the case of a governmental plan (as defined in section 414(d) of the Internal Revenue Code of 1986), this clause shall be applied by substituting "2012" for "2010" in subclause (II).

(ii) Conditions.—This paragraph shall not apply to any amendment unless—

(I) the plan or contract is operated as if such plan or contract amendment were in effect for the period described in clause (iii), and

(II) such plan or contract amendment applies retroactively for such period.

(iii) Period described.—The period described in this clause is the period—

(I) beginning on the effective date specified by the plan, and

(II) ending on the date described in clause (i)(II) (or, if earlier, the date the plan or contract amendment is adopted).

Pension Protection Act of 2006 (Pub. L. No. 109-280), as follows:

- IRC §401(a)(5)(G) was amended by Act §861(a)(1) by substituting "§414(d))" for "§414(d)) maintained by a State or local government or political subdivision thereof (or agency or instrumentality thereof)" and by striking "State and Local" in the heading. Eff. for any year beginning after Aug. 17, 2006.

- IRC §401(a)(26)(G) was amended by Act §861(a)(1) by substituting "§414(d))" for "§414(d)) maintained by a State or local government or political subdivision thereof (or agency or instrumentality thereof)" and by substituting "Exception for" for "Exception for State and Local" in the heading. Eff. for any year beginning after Aug. 17, 2006.

- IRC §401(a)(28)(B) was amended by Act §901(a)(2)(A) by adding new cl. (v). Eff. generally for plan years beginning after Dec. 31, 2006. See Act §901(c) for a special rule.

- IRC §401(a)(29) was amended by Act §114(a)(1). Eff. Aug. 17, 2006 [for plan years beginning after 2007, effective date as amended by Pub. L. No. 110-458, §101(d)(3)]. IRC §401(a)(29) prior to amendment:

(29) Security required upon adoption of plan amendment resulting in significant underfunding.—

(A) In general.—If—

(i) a defined benefit plan (other than a multiemployer plan) to which the requirements of §412 apply adopts an amendment an effect of which is to increase current liability under the plan for a plan year, and

(ii) the funded current liability percentage of the plan for the plan year in which the amendment takes effect is less than 60 percent, including the amount of the unfunded current liability under the plan attributable to the plan amendment, the trust of which such plan is a part shall not constitute a qualified trust under this subsection unless such amendment does not take effect until the contributing sponsor (or any member of the controlled group of the contributing sponsor) provides security to the plan.

(B) Form of security.—The security required under subparagraph (A) shall consist of—

(i) a bond issued by a corporate surety company that is an acceptable surety for purposes of §412 of the Employee Retirement Income Security Act of 1974,

(ii) cash, or United States obligations which mature in 3 years or less, held in escrow by a bank or similar financial institution, or

(iii) such other form of security as is satisfactory to the Secretary and the parties involved.

(C) Amount of security.—The security shall be in an amount equal to the excess of—

(i) the lesser of—

(I) the amount of additional plan assets which would be necessary to increase the funded current liability percentage

under the plan to 60 percent, including the amount of the unfunded current liability under the plan attributable to the plan amendment, or

(II) the amount of the increase in current liability under the plan attributable to the plan amendment and any other plan amendments adopted after December 22, 1987, and before such plan amendment, over

(ii) $10,000,000.

(D) Release of security.—The security shall be released (and any amounts thereunder shall be refunded together with any interest accrued thereon) at the end of the first plan year which ends after the provision of the security and for which the funded current liability percentage under the plan is not less than 60 percent. The Secretary may prescribe regulations for partial releases of the security by reason of increases in the funded current liability percentage.

(E) Definitions.—For purposes of this paragraph, the terms "current liability", "funded current liability percentage", and "unfunded current liability" shall have the meanings given such terms by §412(l), except that in computing unfunded current liability there shall not be taken into account any unamortized portion of the unfunded old liability amount as of the close of the plan year.

- IRC §401(a)(32)(A) was amended by Act §114(a)(2)(A) by substituting "§430(j)(4)" for "412(m)(5)" each place it appeared. Eff. Aug. 17, 2006 [for plan years beginning after 2007, effective date as amended by Pub. L. No. 110-458, §101(d)(3)].

- IRC §401(a)(32)(C) was amended by Act §114(a)(2)(B) by substituting "§430(j)" for "§412(m)". Eff. Aug. 17, 2006 [for plan years beginning after 2007, effective date as amended by Pub. L. No. 110-458, §101(d)(3)].

- IRC §401(a)(33)(B)(i) was amended by Act §114(a)(3)(A) by substituting "funding target attainment percentage (as defined in §430(d)(2))" for "funded current liability percentage (within the meaning of §412(l)(8))". Eff. Aug. 17, 2006 [for plan years beginning after 2007, effective date as amended by Pub. L. No. 110-458, §101(d)(3)].

- IRC §401(a)(33)(B)(iii) was amended by Act §114(a)(3)(B) by substituting "§412(c)(2)" for "§412(c)(8)". Eff. Aug. 17, 2006 [for plan years beginning after 2007, effective date as amended by Pub. L. No. 110-458, §101(d)(3)].

- IRC §401(a)(33)(D) was amended by Act §114(a)(3)(C) by substituting "§412(b)(2) (without regard to subparagraph (B) thereof)" for "§412(c)(11) (without regard to subparagraph (B) thereof)". Eff. Aug. 17, 2006 [for plan years beginning after 2007, effective date as amended by Pub. L. No. 110-458, §101(d)(3)].

- IRC §401(a)(35) was amended by Act §901(a)(1) by adding new para. (35). Eff. generally for plan years beginning after Dec. 31, 2006, with a special rule for collectively bargained plans. See Act §901(c) for a special rule.

- IRC §401(a)(36) was amended by Act §905(b) by adding new para. (36). Eff. for distributions in plan years beginning after Dec. 31, 2006.

- IRC §401(k)(2)(B)(i) was amended by Act §827(b)(1) by striking "or" at the end of subcl. (III), by substituting "or" for "and" at the end of subcl. (IV), and by adding subcl. (V). Eff. for distributions after Sept. 11, 2001. See Act §827(c)(2) for waiver rule.

- IRC §401(k)(3)(G) was amended by Act §861(b)(3) by inserting "Governmental Plan.—" after "(G)". Eff. for any year beginning after Aug. 17, 2006.

- IRC §401(k)(3)(G) was amended by Act §861(a)(2) by striking "maintained by a State or local government or political subdivision thereof (or agency or instrumentality thereof)". Eff. for any year beginning after Aug. 17, 2006.

- IRC §401(k)(8)(A)(i) was amended by Act §902(e)(3)(B) by adding "through the end of such year" after "such contributions". Eff. for plan years beginning after Dec. 31, 2007.

- IRC §401(k)(8)(E) was amended by Act §902(d)(2)(C)–(D) by inserting "or erroneous automatic contribution" before the period in the heading, and by inserting "an erroneous automatic contribution under §414(w)," after "402(g)(2)(A),". Eff. for plan years beginning after Dec. 31, 2007.

- IRC §401(k) was amended by Act §902(a) by adding para. (13). Eff. for plan years beginning after Dec. 31, 2007.

IRC Sec. 401(o)

• IRC §401(m)(6)(A) was amended by Act §902(e)(3)(B)(ii) by adding "through the end of such year" after "to such contributions". Eff. for plan years beginning after Dec. 31, 2007.

• IRC §401(m) was amended by Act §902(b) by redesignating para. (12) as para. (13) and by adding a new para. (12). Effective for plan years beginning after Dec. 31, 2007.

• **Sunset Provision.** Act §811, provides:

SEC. 811. PENSIONS AND INDIVIDUAL RETIREMENT ARRANGEMENT PROVISIONS OF ECONOMIC GROWTH AND TAX RELIEF RECONCILIATION ACT OF 2001 MADE PERMANENT.

Title IX of the Economic Growth and Tax Relief Reconciliation Act of 2001 [Pub. L. No. 107-16] shall not apply to the provisions of, and amendments made by, subtitles A through F [§§601–666] of title VI of such Act (relating to pension and individual retirement arrangement provisions).

• **Other Provision—Effective Dates.** Act §901 provides:

(c) **Effective Dates.—**

(1) In General.—Except as provided in paragraphs (2) and (3), the amendments made by this section shall apply to plan years beginning after December 31, 2006.

(2) Special rule for collectively bargained agreements—In the case of a plan maintained pursuant to 1 or more collective bargaining agreements between employee representatives and 1 or more employers ratified on or before the date of the enactment of this Act, paragraph (1) shall be applied to benefits pursuant to, and individuals covered by, any such agreement by substituting for "December 31, 2006" the earlier of—

(A) the later of—

(i) December 31, 2007, or

(ii) the date on which the last of such collective bargaining agreements terminates (determined without regard to any extension thereof after such date of enactment), or

(B) December 31, 2008.

(3) Special rule for certain employer securities held in an ESOP—

(A) In general—In the case of employer securities to which this paragraph applies, the amendments made by this section shall apply to plan years beginning after the earlier of—

(i) December 31, 2007, or

(ii) the first date on which the fair market value of such securities exceeds the guaranteed minimum value described in subparagraph (B)(ii).

(B) Applicable securities—This paragraph shall apply to employer securities which are attributable to employer contributions other than elective deferrals, and which, on September 17, 2003—

(i) consist of preferred stock, and

(ii) are within an employee stock ownership plan (as defined in section 4975(e)(7) of the Internal Revenue Code of 1986), the terms of which provide that the value of the securities cannot be less than the guaranteed minimum value specified by the plan on such date.

(C) Coordination with transition rule—In applying section 401(a)(35)(H) of the Internal Revenue Code of 1986 and section 204(j)(7) of the Employee Retirement Income Security Act of 1974 (as added by this section) to employer securities to which this paragraph applies, the applicable percentage shall be determined without regard to this paragraph.

Working Families Tax Relief Act of 2004 (Pub. L. No. 108-311), as follows:

• IRC §401(a)(26)(C)–(I) was amended by Act §407(b) by striking subpara. (C) and redesignating subpara. (D) through (I) as subpara. (C) through (H), respectively. Eff. years beginning after Dec. 31, 1996, as if included in the provision of Pub. L. No. 104-188 to which it relates. IRC §401(a)(26)(C) prior to being stricken:

(C) Eligibility to participate.—In the case of contributions under §401(k) or 401(m), employees who are eligible to contribute (or may elect to have contributions made on their behalf) shall be treated as benefiting under the plan.

Job Creation and Worker Assistance Act of 2002 (Pub. L. No. 107-147), as follows:

• IRC §401(a)(30) was amended by Act §411(o)(2) by substituting "402(g)(1)(A)" for "402(g)(1)". Eff. for contributions in tax

years beginning after Dec. 31, 2001, as if included in the provision of Pub. L. No. 107-16 to which it relates.

• IRC §401(a)(31)(C)(i) was amended by Act §411(q)(1) by inserting "is a qualified trust which is part of a plan which is a defined contribution plan and" before "agrees". Eff. for distributions made after Dec. 31, 2001, as if included in the provision of Pub. L. No. 107-16 to which it relates.

Economic Growth and Tax Relief Reconciliation Act of 2001 (Pub. L. No. 107-16), as follows:

• IRC §401(a)(17) was amended by Act §611(c)(1) by substituting "$200,000" for "$150,000" each place it appeared. Eff. for years beginning after Dec. 31, 2001. See Act §611(i)(3) for a special rule.

• IRC §401(a)(17)(B) was amended by Act §611(c)(2) by substituting "July 1, 2001" for "October 1, 1993" and by substituting "$5,000" for "$10,000" each place it appeared. Eff. for years beginning after Dec. 31, 2001. See Act §611(i)(3) for a special rule.

• IRC §401(a)(31) was amended by Act §657(a)(2)(A) by substituting "Direct" for "Optional direct" in the heading of para. (31). Eff. for distributions made after final regulations are prescribed to implement Act §657(c)(2)(A).

• IRC §401(a)(31)(B) was amended by Act §641(e)(3) by substituting ", 403(a)(4), 403(b)(8), and 457(e)(16)" for "and 403(a)(4)". Eff. generally for distributions after Dec. 31, 2001. See Act §641(f)(3) for special rule.

• IRC §401(a)(31)(B) was amended by Act §643(b) by adding the sentence at the end. Eff. for distributions after Dec. 31, 2001.

• IRC §401(a)(31) was amended by Act §657(a)(1) by redesignating subparas. (B)–(D) as subparas. (C)–(E), respectively, and adding new subpara. (B). Eff. for distributions made after final regulations are prescribed to implement Act §657(c)(2)(A).

• IRC §401(a)(31)(C) was amended by Act §657(a)(2)(B), as redesignated by Act §657(a)(1), by substituting "Subparagraphs (A) and (B)" for "Subparagraph (A)". Eff. for distributions made after final regulations are prescribed to implement Act §657(c)(2)(A).

• IRC §401(c)(2)(A) was amended by Act §611(g)(1) by adding the sentence at the end. Eff. for years beginning after Dec. 31, 2001. See Act §611(i)(3) for special rule.

• IRC §401(k)(2)(B)(i)(I) was amended by Act §646(a)(1)(A) by substituting "severance from employment" for "separation from service". Eff. for distributions after Dec. 31, 2001.

• IRC §401(k)(10) was amended by Act §646(a)(1)(C)(iii) by striking "or disposition of assets or subsidiary" from the heading. Eff. for distributions after Dec. 31, 2001.

• IRC §401(k)(10)(A) was amended by Act §646(a)(1)(B). Eff. for distributions after Dec. 31, 2001. IRC §401(k)(10)(A) prior to amendment:

(A) In general.—The following events are described in this paragraph:

(i) Termination.—The termination of the plan without establishment or maintenance of another defined contribution plan (other than an employee stock ownership plan as defined in section 4975(e)(7)).

(ii) Disposition of assets.—The disposition by a corporation of substantially all of the assets (within the meaning of section 409(d)(2)) used by such corporation in a trade or business of such corporation, but only with respect to an employee who continues employment with the corporation acquiring such assets.

(iii) Disposition of subsidiary.—The disposition by a corporation of such corporation's interest in a subsidiary (within the meaning of section 409(d)(3)), but only with respect to an employee who continues employment with such subsidiary.

• IRC §401(k)(10)(B)(i) was amended by Act §646(a)(1)(C)(i) by substituting "A termination" for "An event" and substituting "the termination" for "the event". Eff. for distributions after Dec. 31, 2001.

• IRC §401(k)(10)(C) was amended by Act §646(a)(1)(C)(ii) by striking subpara. (C). Eff. for distributions after Dec. 31, 2001. IRC §401(k)(10)(C) prior to being stricken:

(C) Transferor corporation must maintain plan.—An event shall not be treated as described in clause (ii) or (iii) of subparagraph (A) unless the transferor corporation continues to maintain the plan after the disposition.

IRC Sec. 401(o)

- IRC §401(k)(11)(B)(i)(I) was amended by Act §611(f)(3)(A) by substituting "the amount in effect under §408(p)(2)(A)(ii)" for "$6,000". Eff. for years beginning after Dec. 31, 2001. See Act §611(i)(3) for special rule.
- IRC §401(k)(11)(E) was amended by Act §611(f)(3)(B) by striking subpara. (E). Eff. years beginning after Dec. 31, 2001. IRC §401(k)(11)(E) prior to amendment:
  (E) Cost-of-living adjustment—The Secretary shall adjust the $6,000 amount under subparagraph (B)(i)(I) at the same time and in the same manner as under section 408(p)(2)(E).
- IRC §401(m)(9) was amended by Act §666(a). Eff. years beginning after Dec. 31, 2001. IRC §401(m)(9) prior to amendment:
  (9) Regulations.—The Secretary shall prescribe such regulations as may be necessary to carry out the purposes of this subsection and subsection (k) including—
  (A) such regulations as may be necessary to prevent the multiple use of the alternative limitation with respect to any highly compensated employee, and
  (B) regulations permitting appropriate aggregation of plans and contributions.
  For purposes of the preceding sentence, the term "alternative limitation" means the limitation of section 401(k)(3)(A)(ii)(II) and the limitation of paragraph (2)(A)(ii) of this subsection.
- **Sunset Provision.** Act §901, as amended by Pub. L. No. 111-312, §101(a)(1), provides the sunset rule below. But see Pub. L. No. 109-280, §811, and Pub. L. No. 111-148, §10909(c), as amended by Pub. L. No. 111-312, §101(b)(1).
  SEC. 901. SUNSET OF PROVISIONS OF ACT.
  (a) In general. All provisions of, and amendments made by, this Act shall not apply—
  (1) to taxable, plan, or limitation years beginning after December 31, 2012, or
  (2) in the case of title V, to estates of decedents dying, gifts made, or generation skipping transfers, after December 31, 2012.
  (b) Application of certain laws.—The Internal Revenue Code of 1986 and the Employee Retirement Income Security Act of 1974 shall be applied and administered to years, estates, gifts, and transfers described in subsection (a) as if the provisions and amendments described in subsection (a) had never been enacted.

SEC. 402. TAXABILITY OF BENEFICIARY OF EMPLOYEES' TRUST.

(a) Taxability of Beneficiary of Exempt Trust.— Except as otherwise provided in this section, any amount actually distributed to any distributee by any employees' trust described in section 401(a) which is exempt from tax under section 501(a) shall be taxable to the distributee, in the taxable year of the distributee in which distributed, under section 72 (relating to annuities).

(b) Taxability of Beneficiary of Nonexempt Trust.—

(1) Contributions.—Contributions to an employees' trust made by an employer during a taxable year of the employer which ends with or within a taxable year of the trust for which the trust is not exempt from tax under section 501(a) shall be included in the gross income of the employee in accordance with section 83 (relating to property transferred in connection with performance of services), except that the value of the employee's interest in the trust shall be substituted for the fair market value of the property for purposes of applying such section.

(2) Distributions.—The amount actually distributed or made available to any distributee by any trust described in paragraph (1) shall be taxable to the distributee, in the taxable year in which so distributed or made available, under section 72 (relating to annuities), except that distributions of income of such trust before the annuity starting date (as defined in section 72(c)(4)) shall be included in the gross income of the employee without regard to section 72(e)(5) (relating to amounts not received as annuities).

(3) Grantor trusts.—A beneficiary of any trust described in paragraph (1) shall not be considered the owner of any portion of such trust under subpart E of part I of subchapter J (relating to grantors and others treated as substantial owners).

(4) Failure to meet requirements of section 410(b).—

(A) Highly compensated employees.—If 1 of the reasons a trust is not exempt from tax under section 501(a) is the failure of the plan of which it is a part to meet the requirements of section 401(a)(26) or 410(b), then a highly compensated employee shall, in lieu of the amount determined under paragraph (1) or (2) include in gross income for the taxable year with or within which the taxable year of the trust ends an amount equal to the vested accrued benefit of such employee (other than the employee's investment in the contract) as of the close of such taxable year of the trust.

(B) Failure to meet coverage tests.—If a trust is not exempt from tax under section 501(a) for any taxable year solely because such trust is part of a plan which fails to meet the requirements of section 401(a)(26) or 410(b), paragraphs (1) and (2) shall not apply by reason of such failure to any employee who was not a highly compensated employee during—

(i) such taxable year, or

(ii) any preceding period for which service was creditable to such employee under the plan.

(C) Highly compensated employee.—For purposes of this paragraph, the term "highly compensated employee" has the meaning given such term by section 414(q).

(c) Rules Applicable to Rollovers from Exempt Trusts.—

(1) Exclusion from income.—If—

(A) any portion of the balance to the credit of an employee in a qualified trust is paid to the employee in an eligible rollover distribution,

(B) the distributee transfers any portion of the property received in such distribution to an eligible retirement plan, and

(C) in the case of a distribution of property other than money, the amount so transferred consists of the property distributed,

then such distribution (to the extent so transferred) shall not be includible in gross income for the taxable year in which paid.

(2) Maximum amount which may be rolled over.—In the case of any eligible rollover distribution, the maximum amount transferred to which paragraph (1) applies shall not exceed the portion of such distribution which is includible in gross income (determined without regard to paragraph (1)). The preceding sentence shall not apply to such distribution to the extent—

(A) such portion is transferred in a direct trustee-to-trustee transfer to a qualified trust or to an annuity contract described in section 403(b) and such trust or contract provides for separate accounting for amounts so transferred (and earnings thereon), including separately accounting for the portion of such distribution which is includible in gross income and the portion of such distribution which is not so includible, or

(B) such portion is transferred to an eligible retirement plan described in clause (i) or (ii) of paragraph (8)(B).

In the case of a transfer described in subparagraph (A) or (B), the amount transferred shall be treated as consisting first of the portion of such distribution that is includible in gross income (determined without regard to paragraph (1)).

(3) Transfer must be made within 60 days of receipt.—

(A) In general.—Except as provided in subparagraph (B), paragraph (1) shall not apply to any transfer of a distribution made after the 60th day following the day on which the distributee received the property distributed.

(B) Hardship exception.—The Secretary may waive the 60-day requirement under subparagraph (A) where the failure to waive such requirement would be against equity or good conscience, including casualty, disaster, or other events beyond the reasonable control of the individual subject to such requirement.

(4) Eligible rollover distribution.—For purposes of this subsection, the term "eligible rollover distribution" means any distribution to an employee of all or any portion of the balance to the credit of the employee in a qualified trust; except that such term shall not include—

(A) any distribution which is one of a series of substantially equal periodic payments (not less frequently than annually) made—

(i) for the life (or life expectancy) of the employee or the joint lives (or joint life expectancies) of the employee and the employee's designated beneficiary, or

(ii) for a specified period of 10 years or more,

(B) any distribution to the extent such distribution is required under section 401(a)(9), and

(C) any distribution which is made upon hardship of the employee.

If all or any portion of a distribution during 2009 is treated as an eligible rollover distribution but would not be so treated if the minimum distribution requirements under section 401(a)(9) had applied during 2009, such distribution shall not be treated as an eligible rollover distribution for purposes of section 401(a)(31) or 3405(c) or subsection (f) of this section.

(5) Transfer treated as rollover contribution under section 408.—For purposes of this title, a transfer to an eligible retirement plan described in clause (i) or (ii) of paragraph (8)(B) resulting in any portion of a distribution being excluded from gross income under paragraph (1) shall be treated as a rollover contribution described in section 408(d)(3).

(6) Sales of distributed property.—For purposes of this subsection—

(A) Transfer of proceeds from sale of distributed property treated as transfer of distributed property.—The transfer of an amount equal to any portion of the proceeds from the sale of property received in the distribution shall be treated as the transfer of property received in the distribution.

(B) Proceeds attributable to increase in value.—The excess of fair market value of property on sale over its fair market value on distribution shall be treated as property received in the distribution.

(C) Designation where amount of distribution exceeds rollover contribution.—In any case where part or all of the distribution consists of property other than money—

(i) the portion of the money or other property which is to be treated as attributable to amounts not included in gross income, and

(ii) the portion of the money or other property which is to be treated as included in the rollover contribution,

shall be determined on a ratable basis unless the taxpayer designates otherwise. Any designation under this subparagraph for a taxable year shall be made not later than the time prescribed by law for filing the return for such taxable year (including extensions thereof). Any such designation, once made, shall be irrevocable.

(D) Nonrecognition of gain or loss.—No gain or loss shall be recognized on any sale described in subparagraph (A) to the extent that an amount equal to the proceeds is transferred pursuant to paragraph (1).

(7) Special rule for frozen deposits.—

(A) In general.—The 60-day period described in paragraph (3) shall not—

(i) include any period during which the amount transferred to the employee is a frozen deposit, or

(ii) end earlier than 10 days after such amount ceases to be a frozen deposit.

(B) Frozen deposits.—For purposes of this subparagraph, the term "frozen deposit" means any deposit which may not be withdrawn because of—

(i) the bankruptcy or insolvency of any financial institution, or

(ii) any requirement imposed by the State in which such institution is located by reason of the bankruptcy or insolvency (or threat thereof) of 1 or more financial institutions in such State.

A deposit shall not be treated as a frozen deposit unless on at least 1 day during the 60-day period described in paragraph (3) (without regard to this paragraph) such deposit is described in the preceding sentence.

(8) Definitions.—For purposes of this subsection—

(A) Qualified trust.—The term "qualified trust" means an employees' trust described in section 401(a) which is exempt from tax under section 501(a).

(B) Eligible retirement plan.—The term "eligible retirement plan" means—

(i) an individual retirement account described in section 408(a),

(ii) an individual retirement annuity described in section 408(b) (other than an endowment contract),

(iii) a qualified trust,

(iv) an annuity plan described in section 403(a),

(v) an eligible deferred compensation plan described in section 457(b) which is maintained by an eligible employer described in section 457(e)(1)(A), and

(vi) an annuity contract described in section 403(b).

If any portion of an eligible rollover distribution is attributable to payments or distributions from a designated Roth account (as defined in section 402A), an eligible retirement plan with respect to such portion shall include only another designated Roth account and a Roth IRA.

(9) Rollover where spouse receives distribution after death of employee.—If any distribution attributable to an employee is paid to the spouse of the employee after the employee's death, the preceding provisions of this subsection shall apply to such distribution in the same manner as if the spouse were the employee.

(10) Separate accounting.—Unless a plan described in clause (v) of paragraph (8)(B) agrees to separately account for amounts rolled into such plan from eligible retirement plans not described in such clause, the plan described in such clause may not accept transfers or rollovers from such retirement plans.

(11) Distributions to inherited individual retirement plan of nonspouse beneficiary.—

(A) In general.—If, with respect to any portion of a distribution from an eligible retirement plan described in paragraph (8)(B)(iii) of a deceased employee, a direct trustee-to-trustee transfer is made to an individual retirement plan described in clause (i) or (ii) of paragraph (8)(B) established for the purposes of receiving the distribution on behalf of an individual who is a designated beneficiary (as defined by section 401(a)(9)(E)) of the employee and who is not the surviving spouse of the employee—

(i) the transfer shall be treated as an eligible rollover distribution,

(ii) the individual retirement plan shall be treated as an inherited individual retirement account or individual retirement annuity (within the meaning of section 408(d)(3)(C)) for purposes of this title, and

(iii) section 401(a)(9)(B) (other than clause (iv) thereof) shall apply to such plan.

(B) Certain trusts treated as beneficiaries.—For purposes of this paragraph, to the extent provided in rules prescribed by the Secretary, a trust maintained for the benefit of one or more designated beneficiaries shall be treated in the same manner as a designated beneficiary.

(d) Taxability of Beneficiary of Certain Foreign Situs Trusts.—For purposes of subsections (a), (b), and (c), a stock bonus, pension, or profit-sharing trust which would qualify for exemption from tax under section 501(a) except for the fact that it is a trust created or organized outside the United States shall be treated as if it were a trust exempt from tax under section 501(a).

(e) Other Rules Applicable to Exempt Trusts.—

(1) Alternate payees.—

(A) Alternate payee treated as distributee.—For purposes of subsection (a) and section 72, an alternate payee who is the spouse or former spouse of the participant shall be treated as the distributee of any distribution or payment made to the alternate payee under a qualified domestic relations order (as defined in section 414(p)).

(B) Rollovers.—If any amount is paid or distributed to an alternate payee who is the spouse or former spouse of the participant by reason of any qualified domestic relations order (within the meaning of section 414(p)), subsection (c) shall

IRC Sec. 402(e)(1)(B)

apply to such distribution in the same manner as if such alternate payee were the employee.

(2) Distributions by United States to nonresident aliens.—The amount includible under subsection (a) in the gross income of a nonresident alien with respect to a distribution made by the United States in respect of services performed by an employee of the United States shall not exceed an amount which bears the same ratio to the amount includible in gross income without regard to this paragraph as—

(A) the aggregate basic pay paid by the United States to such employee for such services, reduced by the amount of such basic pay which was not includible in gross income by reason of being from sources without the United States, bears to

(B) the aggregate basic pay paid by the United States to such employee for such services.

In the case of distributions under the civil service retirement laws, the term "basic pay" shall have the meaning provided in section 8331(3) of title 5, United States Code.

(3) Cash or deferred arrangements.—For purposes of this title, contributions made by an employer on behalf of an employee to a trust which is a part of a qualified cash or deferred arrangement (as defined in section 401(k)(2)) or which is part of a salary reduction agreement under section 403(b) shall not be treated as distributed or made available to the employee nor as contributions made to the trust by the employee merely because the arrangement includes provisions under which the employee has an election whether the contribution will be made to the trust or received by the employee in cash.

(4) Net unrealized appreciation.—

(A) Amounts attributable to employee contributions.—For purposes of subsection (a) and section 72, in the case of a distribution other than a lump sum distribution, the amount actually distributed to any distributee from a trust described in subsection (a) shall not include any net unrealized appreciation in securities of the employer corporation attributable to amounts contributed by the employee (other than deductible employee contributions within the meaning of section 72(o)(5)). This subparagraph shall not apply to a distribution to which subsection (c) applies.

(B) Amounts attributable to employer contributions.—For purposes of subsection (a) and section 72, in the case of any lump sum distribution which includes securities of the employer corporation, there shall be excluded from gross income the net unrealized appreciation attributable to that part of the distribution which consists of securities of the employer corporation. In accordance with rules prescribed by the Secretary, a taxpayer may elect, on the return of tax on which a lump sum distribu-

tion is required to be included, not to have this subparagraph apply to such distribution.

(C) Determination of amounts and adjustments.—For purposes of subparagraphs (A) and (B), net unrealized appreciation and the resulting adjustments to basis shall be determined in accordance with regulations prescribed by the Secretary.

(D) Lump-sum distribution.—For purposes of this paragraph—

(i) In general.—The term "lump sum distribution" means the distribution or payment within one taxable year of the recipient of the balance to the credit of an employee which becomes payable to the recipient—

(I) on account of the employee's death,

(II) after the employee attains age 59½,

(III) on account of the employee's separation from service, or

(IV) after the employee has become disabled (within the meaning of section 72(m)(7)),

from a trust which forms a part of a plan described in section 401(a) and which is exempt from tax under section 501 or from a plan described in section 403(a). Subclause (III) of this clause shall be applied only with respect to an individual who is an employee without regard to section 401(c)(1), and subclause (IV) shall be applied only with respect to an employee within the meaning of section 401(c)(1). For purposes of this clause, a distribution to two or more trusts shall be treated as a distribution to one recipient. For purposes of this paragraph, the balance to the credit of the employee does not include the accumulated deductible employee contributions under the plan (within the meaning of section 72(o)(5)).

(ii) Aggregation of certain trusts and plans.—For purposes of determining the balance to the credit of an employee under clause (i)—

(I) all trusts which are part of a plan shall be treated as a single trust, all pension plans maintained by the employer shall be treated as a single plan, all profit-sharing plans maintained by the employer shall be treated as a single plan, and all stock bonus plans maintained by the employer shall be treated as a single plan, and

(II) trusts which are not qualified trusts under section 401(a) and annuity contracts which do not satisfy the requirements of section 404(a)(2) shall not be taken into account.

(iii) Community property laws.—The provisions of this paragraph shall be applied without regard to community property laws.

(iv) Amounts subject to penalty.—This paragraph shall not apply to amounts described in subparagraph (A) of section 72(m)(5) to the extent that section 72(m)(5) applies to such amounts.

IRC Sec. 402(e)(1)(B)

(v) Balance to credit of employee not to include amounts payable under qualified domestic relations order.—For purposes of this paragraph, the balance to the credit of an employee shall not include any amount payable to an alternate payee under a qualified domestic relations order (within the meaning of section 414(p)).

(vi) Transfers to cost-of-living arrangement not treated as distribution.—For purposes of this paragraph, the balance to the credit of an employee under a defined contribution plan shall not include any amount transferred from such defined contribution plan to a qualified cost-of-living arrangement (within the meaning of section 415(k)(2)) under a defined benefit plan.

(vii) Lump-sum distributions of alternate payees.—If any distribution or payment of the balance to the credit of an employee would be treated as a lump-sum distribution, then, for purposes of this paragraph, the payment under a qualified domestic relations order (within the meaning of section 414(p)) of the balance to the credit of an alternate payee who is the spouse or former spouse of the employee shall be treated as a lump-sum distribution. For purposes of this clause, the balance to the credit of the alternate payee shall not include any amount payable to the employee.

(E) Definitions relating to securities.—For purposes of this paragraph—

(i) Securities.—The term "securities" means only shares of stock and bonds or debentures issued by a corporation with interest coupons or in registered form.

(ii) Securities of the employer.—The term "securities of the employer corporation" includes securities of a parent or subsidiary corporation (as defined in subsections (e) and (f) of section 424) of the employer corporation.

(5) [Repealed.]

(6) Direct trustee-to-trustee transfers.—Any amount transferred in a direct trustee-to-trustee transfer in accordance with section 401(a)(31) shall not be includible in gross income for the taxable year of such transfer.

(f) Written Explanation to Recipients of Distributions Eligible for Rollover Treatment.—

(1) In general.—The plan administrator of any plan shall, within a reasonable period of time before making an eligible rollover distribution provide a written explanation to the recipient—

(A) of the provisions under which the recipient may have the distribution directly transferred to an eligible retirement plan, and that the automatic distribution by direct transfer applies to certain distributions in accordance with section 401(a)(31)(B),

(B) of the provision which requires the withholding of tax on the distribution if it is not directly transferred to an eligible retirement plan,

(C) of the provisions under which the distribution will not be subject to tax if transferred to an eligible retirement plan within 60 days after the date on which the recipient received the distribution,

(D) if applicable, of the provisions of subsections (d) and (e) of this section, and

(E) of the provisions under which distributions from the eligible retirement plan receiving the distribution may be subject to restrictions and tax consequences which are different from those applicable to distributions from the plan making such distribution.

(2) Definitions.—For purposes of this subsection—

(A) Eligible rollover distribution.—The term "eligible rollover distribution" has the same meaning as when used in subsection (c) of this section, paragraph (4) of section 403(a), subparagraph (A) of section 403(b)(8), or subparagraph (A) of section 457(e)(16). Such term shall include any distribution to a designated beneficiary which would be treated as an eligible rollover distribution by reason of subsection (c)(11), or section 403(a)(4)(B), 403(b)(8)(B), or 457(e)(16)(B), if the requirements of subsection (c)(11) were satisfied.

(B) Eligible retirement plan.—The term "eligible retirement plan" has the meaning given such term by subsection (c)(8)(B).

(g) Limitation on Exclusion for Elective Deferrals.—

(1) In general.—

(A) Limitation.—Notwithstanding subsections (e)(3) and (h)(1)(B), the elective deferrals of any individual for any taxable year shall be included in such individual's gross income to the extent the amount of such deferrals for the taxable year exceeds the applicable dollar amount. The preceding sentence shall not apply to the portion of such excess as does not exceed the designated Roth contributions of the individual for the taxable year.

(B) Applicable dollar amount.—For purposes of subparagraph (A), the applicable dollar amount shall be the amount determined in accordance with the following table:

For taxable years beginning in calendar year	The applicable dollar amount
2002	$11,000
2003	$12,000

IRC Sec. 402(g)(1)(B)

2004	$13,000
2005	$14,000
2006 or thereafter	$15,000

(C) Catch-up contributions.—In addition to subparagraph (A), in the case of an eligible participant (as defined in section 414(v)), gross income shall not include elective deferrals in excess of the applicable dollar amount under subparagraph (B) to the extent that the amount of such elective deferrals does not exceed the applicable dollar amount under section 414(v)(2)(B)(i) for the taxable year (without regard to the treatment of the elective deferrals by an applicable employer plan under section 414(v)).

(2) Distribution of excess deferrals.—

(A) In general.—If any amount (hereinafter in this paragraph referred to as "excess deferrals") is included in the gross income of an individual under paragraph (1) (or would be included but for the last sentence thereof) for any taxable year—

(i) not later than the 1st March 1 following the close of the taxable year, the individual may allocate the amount of such excess deferrals among the plans under which the deferrals were made and may notify each such plan of the portion allocated to it, and

(ii) not later than the 1st April 15 following the close of the taxable year, each such plan may distribute to the individual the amount allocated to it under clause (i) (and any income allocable to such amount through the end of such taxable year).

The distribution described in clause (ii) may be made notwithstanding any other provision of law.

(B) Treatment of distribution under section 401(k).—Except to the extent provided under rules prescribed by the Secretary, notwithstanding the distribution of any portion of an excess deferral from a plan under subparagraph (A)(ii), such portion shall, for purposes of applying section 401(k)(3)(A)(ii), be treated as an employer contribution.

(C) Taxation of distribution.—In the case of a distribution to which subparagraph (A) applies—

(i) except as provided in clause (ii), such distribution shall not be included in gross income, and

(ii) any income on the excess deferral shall, for purposes of this chapter, be treated as earned and received in the taxable year in which such income is distributed.

No tax shall be imposed under section 72(t) on any distribution described in the preceding sentence.

(D) Partial distributions.—If a plan distributes only a portion of any excess deferral and income

allocable thereto, such portion shall be treated as having been distributed ratably from the excess deferral and the income.

(3) Elective deferrals.—For purposes of this subsection, the term "elective deferrals" means, with respect to any taxable year, the sum of—

(A) any employer contribution under a qualified cash or deferred arrangement (as defined in section 401(k)) to the extent not includible in gross income for the taxable year under subsection (e)(3) (determined without regard to this subsection),

(B) any employer contribution to the extent not includible in gross income for the taxable year under subsection (h)(1)(B) (determined without regard to this subsection),

(C) any employer contribution to purchase an annuity contract under section 403(b) under a salary reduction agreement (within the meaning of section 3121(a)(5)(D)), and

(D) any elective employer contribution under section 408(p)(2)(A)(i).

An employer contribution shall not be treated as an elective deferral described in subparagraph (C) if under the salary reduction agreement such contribution is made pursuant to a one-time irrevocable election made by the employee at the time of initial eligibility to participate in the agreement or is made pursuant to a similar arrangement involving a one-time irrevocable election specified in regulations.

(4) Cost-of-living adjustment.—In the case of taxable years beginning after December 31, 2006, the Secretary shall adjust the $15,000 amount under paragraph (1)(B) at the same time and in the same manner as under section 415(d), except that the base period shall be the calendar quarter beginning July 1, 2005, and any increase under this paragraph which is not a multiple of $500 shall be rounded to the next lowest multiple of $500.

(5) Disregard of community property laws.—This subsection shall be applied without regard to community property laws.

(6) Coordination with section 72.—For purposes of applying section 72, any amount includible in gross income for any taxable year under this subsection but which is not distributed from the plan during such taxable year shall not be treated as investment in the contract.

(7) Special rule for certain organizations.—

(A) In general.—In the case of a qualified employee of a qualified organization, with respect to employer contributions described in paragraph (3)(C) made by such organization, the limitation of paragraph (1) for any taxable year shall be increased by whichever of the following is the least:

(i) $3,000,

IRC Sec. 402(g)(1)(B)

(ii) $15,000 reduced by the sum of—

(I) the amounts not included in gross income for prior taxable years by reason of this paragraph, plus

(II) the aggregate amount of designated Roth contributions (as defined in section 402A(c)) permitted for prior taxable years by reason of this paragraph, or

(iii) the excess of $5,000 multiplied by the number of years of service of the employee with the qualified organization over the employer contributions described in paragraph (3) made by the organization on behalf of such employee for prior taxable years (determined in the manner prescribed by the Secretary).

(B) Qualified organization.—For purposes of this paragraph, the term "qualified organization" means any educational organization, hospital, home health service agency, health and welfare service agency, church, or convention or association of churches. Such term includes any organization described in section 414(e)(3)(B)(ii). Terms used in this subparagraph shall have the same meaning as when used in section 415(c)(4) (as in effect before the enactment of the Economic Growth and Tax Relief Reconciliation Act of 2001).

(C) Qualified employee.—For purposes of this paragraph, the term "qualified employee" means any employee who has completed 15 years of service with the qualified organization.

(D) Years of service.—For purposes of this paragraph, the term "years of service" has the meaning given such term by section 403(b).

(8) Matching contributions on behalf of self-employed individuals not treated as elective employer contributions.—Except as provided in section 401(k)(3)(D)(ii), any matching contribution described in section 401(m)(4)(A) which is made on behalf of a self-employed individual (as defined in section 401(c)) shall not be treated as an elective employer contribution under a qualified cash or deferred arrangement (as defined in section 401(k)) for purposes of this title.

(h) Special Rules for Simplified Employee Pensions.—For purposes of this chapter—

(1) In general.—Except as provided in paragraph (2), contributions made by an employer on behalf of an employee to an individual retirement plan pursuant to a simplified employee pension (as defined in section 408(k))—

(A) shall not be treated as distributed or made available to the employee or as contributions made by the employee, and

(B) if such contributions are made pursuant to an arrangement under section 408(k)(6) under which

an employee may elect to have the employer make contributions to the simplified employee pension on behalf of the employee, shall not be treated as distributed or made available or as contributions made by the employee merely because the simplified employee pension includes provisions for such election.

(2) Limitations on employer contributions.—Contributions made by an employer to a simplified employee pension with respect to an employee for any year shall be treated as distributed or made available to such employee and as contributions made by the employee to the extent such contributions exceed the lesser of—

(A) 25 percent of the compensation (within the meaning of section 414(s)) from such employer includible in the employee's gross income for the year (determined without regard to the employer contributions to the simplified employee pension), or

(B) the limitation in effect under section 415(c)(1)(A), reduced in the case of any highly compensated employee (within the meaning of section 414(q)) by the amount taken into account with respect to such employee under section 408(k)(3)(D).

(3) Distributions.—Any amount paid or distributed out of an individual retirement plan pursuant to a simplified employee pension shall be included in gross income by the payee or distributee, as the case may be, in accordance with the provisions of section 408(d).

(i) Treatment of Self-Employed Individuals.—For purposes of this section, except as otherwise provided in subparagraph (A) of subsection (d)(4), the term "employee" includes a self-employed individual (as defined in section 401(c)(1)(B)) and the employer of such individual shall be the person treated as his employer under section 401(c)(4).

(j) Effect of Disposition of Stock by Plan on Net Unrealized Appreciation.—

(1) In general.—For purposes of subsection (e)(4), in the case of any transaction to which this subsection applies, the determination of net unrealized appreciation shall be made without regard to such transaction.

(2) Transaction to which subsection applies.— This subsection shall apply to any transaction in which—

(A) the plan trustee exchanges the plan's securities of the employer corporation for other such securities, or

(B) the plan trustee disposes of securities of the employer corporation and uses the proceeds of such disposition to acquire securities of the employer corporation within 90 days (or such longer

IRC Sec. 402(j)(2)(B)

period as the Secretary may prescribe), except that this subparagraph shall not apply to any employee with respect to whom a distribution of money was made during the period after such disposition and before such acquisition.

(k) Treatment of Simple Retirement Accounts.— Rules similar to the rules of paragraphs (1) and (3) of subsection (h) shall apply to contributions and distributions with respect to a simple retirement account under section 408(p).

(l) Distributions From Governmental Plans for Health and Long-Term Care Insurance.—

(1) In general.—In the case of an employee who is an eligible retired public safety officer who makes the election described in paragraph (6) with respect to any taxable year of such employee, gross income of such employee for such taxable year does not include any distribution from an eligible retirement plan maintained by the employer described in paragraph (4)(B) to the extent that the aggregate amount of such distributions does not exceed the amount paid by such employee for qualified health insurance premiums for such taxable year.

(2) Limitation.—The amount which may be excluded from gross income for the taxable year by reason of paragraph (1) shall not exceed $3,000.

(3) Distributions must otherwise be includible.—

(A) In general.—An amount shall be treated as a distribution for purposes of paragraph (1) only to the extent that such amount would be includible in gross income without regard to paragraph (1).

(B) Application of section 72.—Notwithstanding section 72, in determining the extent to which an amount is treated as a distribution for purposes of subparagraph (A), the aggregate amounts distributed from an eligible retirement plan in a taxable year (up to the amount excluded under paragraph (1)) shall be treated as includible in gross income (without regard to subparagraph (A)) to the extent that such amount does not exceed the aggregate amount which would have been so includible if all amounts to the credit of the eligible public safety officer in all eligible retirement plans maintained by the employer described in paragraph (4)(B) were distributed during such taxable year and all such plans were treated as 1 contract for purposes of determining under section 72 the aggregate amount which would have been so includible. Proper adjustments shall be made in applying section 72 to other distributions in such taxable year and subsequent taxable years.

(4) Definitions.—For purposes of this subsection—

(A) Eligible retirement plan.—For purposes of paragraph (1), the term "eligible retirement plan"

means a governmental plan (within the meaning of section 414(d)) which is described in clause (iii), (iv), (v), or (vi) of subsection (c)(8)(B).

(B) Eligible retired public safety officer.—The term "eligible retired public safety officer" means an individual who, by reason of disability or attainment of normal retirement age, is separated from service as a public safety officer with the employer who maintains the eligible retirement plan from which distributions subject to paragraph (1) are made.

(C) Public safety officer.—The term "public safety officer" shall have the same meaning given such term by section 1204(9)(A) of the Omnibus Crime Control and Safe Streets Act of 1968 (42 U.S.C. 3796b(9)(A)).

(D) Qualified health insurance premiums.—The term "qualified health insurance premiums" means premiums for coverage for the eligible retired public safety officer, his spouse, and dependents (as defined in section 152), by an accident or health plan or qualified long-term care insurance contract (as defined in section 7702B(b)).

(5) Special rules.—For purposes of this subsection—

(A) Direct payment to insurer required.—Paragraph (1) shall only apply to a distribution if payment of the premiums is made directly to the provider of the accident or health plan or qualified long-term care insurance contract by deduction from a distribution from the eligible retirement plan.

(B) Related plans treated as 1.—All eligible retirement plans of an employer shall be treated as a single plan.

(6) Election described.—

(A) In general.—For purposes of paragraph (1), an election is described in this paragraph if the election is made by an employee after separation from service with respect to amounts not distributed from an eligible retirement plan to have amounts from such plan distributed in order to pay for qualified health insurance premiums.

(B) Special rule.—A plan shall not be treated as violating the requirements of section 401, or as engaging in a prohibited transaction for purposes of section 503(b), merely because it provides for an election with respect to amounts that are otherwise distributable under the plan or merely because of a distribution made pursuant to an election described in subparagraph (A).

(7) Coordination with medical expense deduction.—The amounts excluded from gross income under paragraph (1) shall not be taken into account under section 213.

(8) Coordination with deduction for health insurance costs of self-employed individuals.—The amounts excluded from gross income under paragraph (1) shall not be taken into account under section 162(*l*).

Recent Amendments to IRC §402

Worker, Retiree, and Employer Recovery Act of 2008 (Pub. L. No. 110-458), as follows:
- IRC §402(c)(4) was amended by Act §201(b) by inserting a flush sentence. Eff. for calendar years beginning after Dec. 31, 2008. See Act §201(c)(2), below, for special effective date provision.
- IRC §402(c)(11) was amended by Act §108(f)(1) by inserting "described in paragraph (8)(B)(iii)" after "eligible retirement plan" in subpara. (A), and by striking "trust" before "designated beneficiary" in subpara. (B). Eff. as if included in Pub. L. No. 109-280, §829, [eff. for distributions after Dec. 31, 2006].
- IRC §402(c)(11)(A)(i) was amended by Act §108(f)(2)(B) by striking "for purposes of this subsection". Eff. with respect to plan years beginning after Dec. 31, 2009.
- IRC §402(f)(2)(A) was amended by Act §108(f)(2)(A) by adding a new sentence at the end. Eff. with respect to plan years beginning after Dec. 31, 2009.
- IRC §402(g)(2)(A)(ii) was amended by Act §109(b)(3) by inserting "through the end of such taxable year" after "such amount". Eff. as if included in Pub. L. No. 109-280, §902 [eff. for plan years beginning after Dec. 31, 2007].
- IRC §402(*l*)(1) was amended by Act §108(j)(1) by inserting "maintained by the employer described in paragraph (4)(B)" after "an eligible retirement plan", and by striking "of the employee, his spouse, or dependents (as defined in section 152)". Eff. as if included in Pub. L. No. 109-280, §845 [eff. for distributions in tax years beginning after Dec. 31, 2006].
- IRC §402(*l*)(3)(B) was amended by Act §108(j)(2) by striking "all amounts distributed from all eligible retirement plans were treated as 1 contract for purposes of determining the inclusion of such distribution under section 72" and inserting "all amounts to the credit of the eligible public safety officer in all eligible retirement plans maintained by the employer described in paragraph (4)(B) were distributed during such taxable year and all such plans were treated as 1 contract for purposes of determining under section 72 the aggregate amount which would have been so includible". Eff. as if included in Pub. L. No. 109-280, §845 [eff. for distributions in tax years beginning after Dec. 31, 2006].
- IRC §402(*l*)(4)(D) was amended by Act §108(j)(1)(B) by inserting "as defined in section 152" after "dependents", and striking "health insurance plan" and inserting "health plan". Eff. as if included in Pub. L. No. 109-280, §845 [eff. for distributions in tax years beginning after Dec. 31, 2006].
- IRC §402(*l*)(5)(A) was amended by Act §108(j)(1)(C) by striking "health insurance plan" and inserting "health plan". Eff. as if included in Pub. L. No. 109-280, §845 [eff. for distributions in tax years beginning after Dec. 31, 2006].
- **Other Provision—**Effective Date. Act §201(c)(2) provides:
  (2) Provisions relating to plan or contract amendments.—
  (A) In general.—If this paragraph applies to any pension plan or contract amendment, such pension plan or contract shall not fail to be treated as being operated in accordance with the terms of the plan during the period described in subparagraph (B)(ii) solely because the plan operates in accordance with this section.
  (B) Amendments to which paragraph applies.—
  (i) In general.—This paragraph shall apply to any amendment to any pension plan or annuity contract which—
  (I) is made pursuant to the amendments made by this section, and
  (II) is made on or before the last day of the first plan year beginning on or after January 1, 2011. In the case of a governmental plan, subclause (II) shall be applied by substituting "2012" for "2011".
  (ii) Conditions.—This paragraph shall not apply to any amendment unless during the period beginning on the effective date of the amendment and ending on December 31, 2009, the plan or contract is operated as if such plan or contract amendment were in effect.

Tax Technical Corrections Act of 2007 (Pub. L. No. 110-172), as follows:
- IRC §402(g)(7)(A)(ii)(II) was amended by substituting "permitted for prior taxable years by reason of this paragraph" for "for prior taxable years". Eff. as if included in Pub. L. No. 107-16, §617 [eff. for tax years beginning after Dec. 31, 2005].

Pension Protection Act of 2006 (Pub. L. No. 109-280), as follows:
- IRC §402(c)(2)(A) was amended by Act §822(a)(1)–(2), by replacing "which is part of a plan which is a defined contribution plan and which agrees to separately account" with "or to an annuity contract described in §403(b) and such trust or contract provides for separate accounting"; and by inserting "(and earnings thereon)" after "so transferred". Eff. tax years beginning after Dec. 31, 2006.
- IRC §402(c) was amended by Act §829(a)(1) by adding new para. (11). Eff. for distributions after Dec. 31, 2006.
- IRC §402 was amended by Act §845(a) by adding new subsec. (l). Eff. for distributions in tax years beginning after Dec. 31, 2006.
- **Sunset Provision.** Act §811, provides:
  SEC. 811. PENSIONS AND INDIVIDUAL RETIREMENT ARRANGEMENT PROVISIONS OF ECONOMIC GROWTH AND TAX RELIEF RECONCILIATION ACT OF 2001 MADE PERMANENT.
  Title IX of the Economic Growth and Tax Relief Reconciliation Act of 2001 [Pub. L. No. 107-16] shall not apply to the provisions of, and amendments made by, subtitles A through F [§§601–666] of title VI of such Act (relating to pension and individual retirement arrangement provisions).

Gulf Opportunity Zone Act of 2005 (Pub. L. No. 109-135), as follows:
- IRC §402(g)(1)(A) was amended by Act §407(a)(2) by inserting "to" after "shall not apply". Eff. for tax years beginning after Dec. 31, 2005, as if included in the provision of Pub. L. No. 107-16 to which it relates.
- IRC §402(g)(7)(A)(ii) was amended by Act §407(a)(1). Eff. for tax years beginning after Dec. 31, 2005, as if included in the provision of Pub. L. No. 107-16 to which it relates. IRC §402(g)(7)(A)(ii) prior to amendment:
  (ii) $15,000 reduced by amounts not included in gross income for prior taxable years by reason of this paragraph, or.

Job Creation and Worker Assistance Act of 2002 (Pub. L. No. 107-147), as follows:
- IRC §402(c)(2) was amended by Act §411(q)(2) by adding a sentence at the end. Eff. for distributions made after Dec. 31, 2001, as if included in the provision of Pub. L. No. 107-16 to which it relates.
- IRC §402(g)(1) was amended by Act §411(o)(1) by adding new subpara. (C). Eff. for contributions in tax years beginning after Dec. 31, 2001, as if included in the provision of Pub. L. No. 107-16 to which it relates.
- IRC §402(g)(7)(B) was amended by Act §411(p)(6) by replacing "2001." with "2001)." Eff. for years beginning after Dec. 31, 2001, as if included in the provision of Pub. L. No. 107-16 to which it relates.
- IRC §402(h)(2)(A) was amended by Act §411(l)(3) by replacing "15 percent" with "25 percent". Eff. for years beginning after Dec. 31, 2001, as if included in the provision of Pub. L. No. 107-16 to which it relates.

Economic Growth and Tax Relief Reconciliation Act of 2001 (Pub. L. No. 107-16), as follows:
- IRC §402(c)(2) was amended by Act §643(a) by adding a sentence at the end containing subparas. (A) and (B). Eff. for distributions after Dec. 31, 2001.
- IRC §402(c)(3) was amended by Act §644(a). Eff. for distributions after Dec. 31, 2001. IRC §402(c)(3) prior to amendment:
  (d) Transfer must be made within 60 days of receipt.— Paragraph (1) shall not apply to any transfer of a distribution made after the 60th day following the day on which the distribute received the property distributed.
- IRC §402(c)(4)(C) was amended by Act §636(b)(1). Eff. for distributions made after Dec. 31, 2001. IRC §402(c)(4)(C) prior to amendment:
  (C) any hardship distributions described in section 401(k)(2)(B)(i)(IV).

IRC Sec. 402(l)(8)

- IRC §402(c)(8)(B) was amended by Act §617(c) by adding a sentence at the end. Eff. for tax years beginning after Dec. 31, 2005.
- IRC §402(c)(8)(B) was amended by Act §641(a)(2)(A) by striking "and" at the end of cl. (iii) and inserting cl. (v). Eff. generally for distributions after Dec. 31, 2001. See Act §641(f)(3) for a special rule.
- IRC §402(c)(8)(B), as amended by Act 641(a), was amended by Act §641(b)(2) by striking "and" at the end of cl. (iv), replacing the period at the end of cl. (v) with ", and", and adding new cl. (vi). Eff. generally for distributions after Dec. 31, 2001. See Act §641(f)(3) for a special rule.
- IRC §402(c)(9) was amended by striking "; except that" and all that follows to the period at the end. Eff. generally for distributions after Dec. 31, 2001. See Act §641(f)(3) for special rule. IRC §402(c)(9) prior to amendment:

   (9) Rollover where spouse receives distributions after death of employee.—If any distribution attributable to an employee is paid to the spouse of the employee after the employee's death, the preceding provisions of this subsection shall apply to such distribution in the same manner as if the spouse were the employee; except that a trust or plan described in clause (iii) or (iv) of paragraph (8)(B) shall not be treated as an eligible retirement plan with respect to such distribution.

- IRC §402(c) was amended by Act §641(a)(2)(B) by adding new para. (10). Eff. generally for distributions after Dec. 31, 2001. See Act §641(f)(3) for special rule.
- IRC §402(f)(1) was amended by Act §641(c) by striking "and" at the end of subpara. (C) and the period at the end of subpara. (D), inserting ", and", and by adding (E). Eff. generally for distributions after Dec. 31, 2001. See Act §641(f)(3) for special rule.
- IRC §402(f)(1) was amended by Act §641(e)(5) by striking "from an eligible retirement plan" after "rollover distribution". Eff. generally for distributions after Dec. 31, 2001. See Act §641(f)(3) for special rule.
- IRC §402(f)(1)(A) was amended by Act §657(b) by inserting "and that the automatic distribution by direct transfer applies to certain distributions in accordance with §401(a)(31)(B)" before the comma at the end. Eff. for distributions made after final regulations are prescribed implementing Act §657(c)(2)(A).
- IRC §402(f)(1)(A) and (B) was amended by Act §641(e)(6) by replacing "another eligible retirement plan" with "an eligible retirement plan". Eff. generally for distributions after Dec. 31, 2001. See Act §641(f)(3) for special rule.
- IRC §402(f)(2)(A) was amended by Act §641(e)(4) by replacing "or paragraph (4) of §403(a)" with ", paragraph (4) of §403(a), subparagraph (A) of §403(b)(8), or subparagraph (A) of §457(e)(16)". Eff. generally for distributions after Dec. 31, 2001. See Act §641(f)(3) for special rule.
- IRC §402(g)(1) was amended by Act §611(d)(1). Eff. for years beginning after Dec. 31, 2001. See Act §611(i)(3) for a special rule. IRC §402(g)(1) prior to amendment:

   (1) In general.—Notwithstanding subsections (e)(3) and (H)(1)(B), the elective deferrals of any individual for any taxable year shall be included in such individual's gross income to the extend the amount of such deferrals for the taxable year exceeds $7,000.

- IRC §402(g)(1)(A), as added by Act §611(d)(1), was amended by Act §617(b)(1)–(2) by adding a sentence at the end, and inserting "(or would be included but for the last sentence thereof)" after "paragraph (1)" in para. (2)(A). Eff. for tax years beginning after Dec. 31, 2005.
- IRC §402(g)(5) was amended by Act §611(d)(2). Eff. for years beginning after Dec. 31, 2001. See Act §611(i)(3) for a special rule. IRC §402(g)(5) prior to amendment:

   (5) Cost-of-living adjustment.—The Secretary shall adjust the $7,000 amount under paragraph (1) at the same time and in the same manner as under section 415(d); except that any increase under this paragraph which is not a multiple of $500 shall be rounded to the next lowest multiple of $500.

- IRC §402(g), as amended by Act §611(d)(1)–(2), was amended by Act §611(d)(3)(A) by striking para. (4) and redesignating paras. (5), (6), (7), (8) and (9) as paras. (4), (5), (6), (7) and (8), respectively. Eff. for years beginning after Dec. 31, 2001. See Act §611(i)(3) for a special rule. Prior to being stricken:

   (4) Increase in limit for amounts contributed under section 403(b) contracts.—The limitation under paragraph (1) shall be increased (but not to an amount in excess of $9,500) by the amount of any employer contributions for the taxable year described in paragraph (3)(C).

- IRC §402(g)(7)(B), as redesignated by Act §611(c)(3), was amended by Act §632(a)(3)(G) by inserting "(as in effect before the enactment of the Economic Growth and Tax Relief Reconciliation Act of 2001[)]" before the period at the end. Eff. for years beginning after Dec. 31, 2001.
- **Sunset Provision.** Act §901, as amended by Pub. L. No. 111-312, §101(a)(1), provides the sunset rule below. But see Pub. L. No. 109-280, §811, and Pub. L. No. 111-148, §10909(c), as amended by Pub. L. No. 111-312, §101(b)(1).

   SEC. 901. SUNSET OF PROVISIONS OF ACT.

   (a) In general. All provisions of, and amendments made by, this Act shall not apply—

   (1) to taxable, plan, or limitation years beginning after December 31, 2012, or

   (2) in the case of title V, to estates of decedents dying, gifts made, or generation skipping transfers, after December 31, 2012.

   (b) Application of certain laws.—The Internal Revenue Code of 1986 and the Employee Retirement Income Security Act of 1974 shall be applied and administered to years, estates, gifts, and transfers described in subsection (a) as if the provisions and amendments described in subsection (a) had never been enacted.

SEC. 402A. OPTIONAL TREATMENT OF ELECTIVE DEFERRALS AS ROTH CONTRIBUTIONS.

(a) General Rule.—If an applicable retirement plan includes a qualified Roth contribution program—

(1) any designated Roth contribution made by an employee pursuant to the program shall be treated as an elective deferral for purposes of this chapter, except that such contribution shall not be excludable from gross income, and

(2) such plan (and any arrangement which is part of such plan) shall not be treated as failing to meet any requirement of this chapter solely by reason of including such program.

(b) Qualified Roth Contribution Program.—For purposes of this section—

(1) In general.—The term "qualified Roth contribution program" means a program under which an employee may elect to make designated Roth contributions in lieu of all or a portion of elective deferrals the employee is otherwise eligible to make under the applicable retirement plan.

(2) Separate accounting required.—A program shall not be treated as a qualified Roth contribution program unless the applicable retirement plan—

(A) establishes separate accounts ("designated Roth accounts") for the designated Roth contributions of each employee and any earnings properly allocable to the contributions, and

(B) maintains separate recordkeeping with respect to each account.

(c) Definitions and Rules Relating to Designated Roth Contributions.—For purposes of this section—

(1) Designated Roth contribution.—The term "designated Roth contribution" means any elective deferral which—

(A) is excludable from gross income of an employee without regard to this section, and

(B) the employee designates (at such time and in such manner as the Secretary may prescribe) as not being so excludable.

(2) Designation limits.—The amount of elective deferrals which an employee may designate under paragraph (1) shall not exceed the excess (if any) of—

(A) the maximum amount of elective deferrals excludable from gross income of the employee for the taxable year (without regard to this section), over

(B) the aggregate amount of elective deferrals of the employee for the taxable year which the employee does not designate under paragraph (1).

(3) Rollover contributions.—

(A) In general.—A rollover contribution of any payment or distribution from a designated Roth account which is otherwise allowable under this chapter may be made only if the contribution is to—

(i) another designated Roth account of the individual from whose account the payment or distribution was made, or

(ii) a Roth IRA of such individual.

(B) Coordination with limit.—Any rollover contribution to a designated Roth account under subparagraph (A) shall not be taken into account for purposes of paragraph (1).

Editor's Note

IRC §402A(c)(4) was added by Pub. L. No. 111-240, applicable to distributions after the date of enactment (September 27, 2010).

---

(4) Taxable rollovers to designated Roth accounts.—

(A) In general.—Notwithstanding sections 402(c), 403(b)(8), and 457(e)(16), in the case of any distribution to which this paragraph applies—

(i) there shall be included in gross income any amount which would be includible were it not part of a qualified rollover contribution,

(ii) section 72(t) shall not apply, and

(iii) unless the taxpayer elects not to have this clause apply, any amount required to be included in gross income for any taxable year beginning in 2010 by reason of this paragraph shall be so in-

cluded ratably over the 2-taxable-year period beginning with the first taxable year beginning in 2011.

Any election under clause (iii) for any distributions during a taxable year may not be changed after the due date for such taxable year.

(B) Distributions to which paragraph applies.—In the case of an applicable retirement plan which includes a qualified Roth contribution program, this paragraph shall apply to a distribution from such plan other than from a designated Roth account which is contributed in a qualified rollover contribution (within the meaning of section 408A(e)) to the designated Roth account maintained under such plan for the benefit of the individual to whom the distribution is made.

(C) Coordination with limit.—Any distribution to which this paragraph applies shall not be taken into account for purposes of paragraph (1).

(D) Other rules.—The rules of subparagraphs (D), (E), and (F) of section 408A(d)(3) (as in effect for taxable years beginning after 2009) shall apply for purposes of this paragraph.

(d) Distribution Rules.—For purposes of this title—

(1) Exclusion.—Any qualified distribution from a designated Roth account shall not be includible in gross income.

(2) Qualified distribution.—For purposes of this subsection—

(A) In general.—The term "qualified distribution" has the meaning given such term by section 408A(d)(2)(A) (without regard to clause (iv) thereof).

(B) Distributions within nonexclusion period.—A payment or distribution from a designated Roth account shall not be treated as a qualified distribution if such payment or distribution is made within the 5-taxable-year period beginning with the earlier of—

(i) the first taxable year for which the individual made a designated Roth contribution to any designated Roth account established for such individual under the same applicable retirement plan, or

(ii) if a rollover contribution was made to such designated Roth account from a designated Roth account previously established for such individual under another applicable retirement plan, the first taxable year for which the individual made a designated Roth contribution to such previously established account.

(C) Distributions of excess deferrals and contributions and earnings thereon.—The term "qualified distribution" shall not include any distribution of any excess deferral under section 402(g)(2) or any excess contribution under section 401(k)(8), and any income on the excess deferral or contribution.

(3) Treatment of distributions of certain excess deferrals.—Notwithstanding section 72, if any excess deferral under section 402(g)(2) attributable to a designated Roth contribution is not distributed on or before the 1st April 15 following the close of the taxable year in which such excess deferral is made, the amount of such excess deferral shall—

(A) not be treated as investment in the contract, and

(B) be included in gross income for the taxable year in which such excess is distributed.

(4) Aggregation rules.—Section 72 shall be applied separately with respect to distributions and payments from a designated Roth account and other distributions and payments from the plan.

Editor's Note

IRC §402A(e), below, was amended by Pub. L. No. 111-240, applicable to taxable years beginning after December 31, 2010.

(e) Other Definitions.—For purposes of this section—

(1) Applicable retirement plan.—The term "applicable retirement plan" means—

(A) an employees' trust described in section 401(a) which is exempt from tax under section 501(a), and

(B) a plan under which amounts are contributed by an individual's employer for an annuity contract described in section 403(b), *and*

(C) an eligible deferred compensation plan (as defined in section 457(b)) of an eligible employer described in section 457(e)(l)(A).

(2) Elective deferral.—The term "elective deferral" means—

(A) any elective deferral described in subparagraph (A) or (C) of section 402(g)(3), and

(B) any elective deferral of compensation by an individual under an eligible deferred compensation plan (as defined in section 457(b)) of an eligible employer described in section 457(e)(l)(A).

Recent Amendments to IRC §402A

Small Business Jobs Act of 2010 (Pub. L. No. 111-240), as follows:
- IRC §402A(c)(4) was added by Act §2112(a). Eff. for distributions after date of enactment [enacted: Sept. 27, 2010].
- IRC §402A(e)(1) was amended by Act §2111(a) by striking "and" at the end of subpara. (A), by striking the period at the end

of subpara. (B) and inserting ", and", and by adding (C) at the end. Eff. for taxable years beginning after Dec. 31, 2010.
- IRC §402A(e)(2) was amended by Act §2112(b). Eff. for taxable years beginning after Dec. 31, 2010. IRC §402A(e)(2) prior to amendment:
  (2) Elective deferral.—The term "elective deferral" means any elective deferral described in subparagraph (A) or (C) of section 402(g)(3).

Pension Protection Act of 2006 (Pub. L. No. 109-280), as follows:
- **Sunset Provision**. Act §811, provides:
  SEC. 811. PENSIONS AND INDIVIDUAL RETIREMENT ARRANGEMENT PROVISIONS OF ECONOMIC GROWTH AND TAX RELIEF RECONCILIATION ACT OF 2001 MADE PERMANENT.
  Title IX of the Economic Growth and Tax Relief Reconciliation Act of 2001 [Pub. L. No. 107-16] shall not apply to the provisions of, and amendments made by, subtitles A through F [§§601–666] of title VI of such Act (relating to pension and individual retirement arrangement provisions).

Economic Growth and Tax Relief Reconciliation Act of 2001 (Pub. L. No. 107-16), as follows:
- IRC §402A was added by Act §617(a). Eff. for tax years beginning after Dec. 31, 2005.
- **Sunset Provision**. Act §901, as amended by Pub. L. No. 111-312, §101(a)(1), provides the sunset rule below. But see Pub. L. No. 109-280, §811, and Pub. L. No. 111-148, §10909(c), as amended by Pub. L. No. 111-312, §101(b)(1).
  SEC. 901. SUNSET OF PROVISIONS OF ACT.
  (a) **In general.** All provisions of, and amendments made by, this Act shall not apply—
  (1) to taxable, plan, or limitation years beginning after December 31, 2012, or
  (2) in the case of title V, to estates of decedents dying, gifts made, or generation skipping transfers, after December 31, 2012.
  (b) **Application of certain laws.**—The Internal Revenue Code of 1986 and the Employee Retirement Income Security Act of 1974 shall be applied and administered to years, estates, gifts, and transfers described in subsection (a) as if the provisions and amendments described in subsection (a) had never been enacted.

SEC. 403. TAXATION OF EMPLOYEE ANNUITIES.

(a) Taxability of Beneficiary Under a Qualified Annuity Plan.—

(1) Distributee taxable under section 72.—If an annuity contract is purchased by an employer for an employee under a plan which meets the requirements of section 404(a)(2) (whether or not the employer deducts the amounts paid for the contract under such section), the amount actually distributed to any distributee under the contract shall be taxable to the distributee (in the year in which so distributed) under section 72 (relating to annuities).

(2) Special rule for health and long-term care insurance.—To the extent provided in section 402(l), paragraph (1) shall not apply to the amount distributed under the contract which is otherwise includible in gross income under this subsection.

(3) Self-employed individuals.—For purposes of this subsection, the term "employee" includes an individual who is an employee within the meaning of section 401(c)(1), and the employer of such individual is the person treated as his employer under section 401(c)(4).

(4) Rollover amounts.—

(A) General rule.—If—

(i) any portion of the balance to the credit of an employee in an employee annuity described in paragraph (1) is paid to him in an eligible rollover distribution (within the meaning of section 402(c)(4)),

(ii) the employee transfers any portion of the property he receives in such distribution to an eligible retirement plan, and

(iii) in the case of a distribution of property other than money, the amount so transferred consists of the property distributed,

then such distribution (to the extent so transferred) shall not be includible in gross income for the taxable year in which paid.

(B) Certain rules made applicable.—The rules of paragraphs (2) through (7) and (11) and (9) of section 402(c) and section 402(f) shall apply for purposes of Subparagraph (A).

(5) Direct trustee-to-trustee transfer.—Any amount transferred in a direct trustee-to-trustee transfer in accordance with section 401(a)(31) shall not be includible in gross income for the taxable year of such transfer.

(b) Taxability of Beneficiary Under Annuity Purchased by Section 501(c)(3) Organization or Public School.—

(1) General rule.—If—

(A) an annuity contract is purchased—

(i) for an employee by an employer described in section 501(c)(3) which is exempt from tax under section 501(a),

(ii) for an employee (other than an employee described in clause (i)), who performs services for an educational organization described in section 170(b)(1)(A)(ii), by an employer which is a State, a political subdivision of a State, or an agency or instrumentality of any one or more of the foregoing, or

(iii) for the minister described in section 414(e)(5)(A) by the minister or by an employer.

(B) such annuity contract is not subject to subsection (a),

(C) the employee's rights under the contract are nonforfeitable, except for failure to pay future premiums,

(D) except in the case of a contract purchased by a church, such contract is purchased under a plan which meets the nondiscrimination requirements of (paragraph 12), and

(E) in the case of a contract purchased under a salary reduction agreement, the contract meets the requirements of section 401(a)(30),

then contributions and other additions by such employer for such annuity contract shall be excluded from the gross income of the employee for the taxable year to the extent that the aggregate of such contributions and additions (when expressed as an annual addition (within the meaning of section 415(c)(2))) does not exceed the applicable limit under section 415. The amount actually distributed to any distributee under such contract shall be taxable to the distributee (in the year in which so distributed) under section 72 (relating to annuities). For purposes of applying the rules of this subsection to contributions and other additions by an employer for a taxable year, amounts transferred to a contract described in this paragraph by reason of a rollover contribution described in paragraph (8) of this subsection or section 408(d)(3)(A)(ii) shall not be considered contributed by such employer.

(2) Special rule for health and long-term care insurance.—To the extent provided in section 402(l), paragraph (1) shall not apply to the amount distributed under the contract which is otherwise includible in gross income under this subsection.

(3) Includable compensation.—For purposes of this subsection, the term "includable compensation" means, in the case of any employee, the amount of compensation which is received from the employer described in paragraph (1)(A), and which is includable in gross income (computed without regard to section 911) for the most recent period (ending not later than the close of the taxable year) which under paragraph (4) may be counted as one year of service, and which precedes the taxable year by no more than five years. Such term does not include any amount contributed by the employer for any annuity contract to which this subsection applies. Such term includes—

(A) any elective deferral (as defined in section 402(g)(3)), and

(B) any amount which is contributed or deferred by the employer at the election of the employee and which is not includible in the gross income of the employee by reason of section 125, 132(f)(4), or 457.

(4) Years of service.—In determining the number of years of service for purposes of this subsection, there shall be included—

(A) one year for each full year during which the individual was a full-time employee of the organization purchasing the annuity for him, and

(B) a fraction of a year (determined in accordance with regulations prescribed by the Secretary) for each full year during which such individual was a part-time employee of such organization and for each part of a year during which such individual was a full-time or part-time employee of such organization.

IRC Sec. 403(b)(4)(B)

In no case shall the number of years of service be less than one.

(5) Application to more than one annuity contract.—If for any taxable year of the employee this subsection applies to 2 or more annuity contracts purchased by the employer, such contracts shall be treated as one contract.

(6) [Repealed.]

(7) Custodial accounts for regulated investment company stock.—

(A) Amounts paid treated as contributions.—For purposes of this title, amounts paid by an employer described in paragraph (1)(A) to a custodial account which satisfies the requirements of section 401(f)(2) shall be treated as amounts contributed by him for an annuity contract for his employee if—

(i) the amounts are to be invested in regulated investment company stock to be held in that custodial account, and

(ii) under the custodial account no such amounts may be paid or made available to any distributee (unless such amount is a distribution to which section 72(t)(2)(G) applies) before the employee dies, attains age 59½, has a severance from employment, becomes disabled (within the meaning of section 72(m)(7)), or in the case of contributions made pursuant to a salary reduction agreement (within the meaning of section 3121(a)(5)(D)), encounters financial hardship.

(B) Account treated as plan.—For purposes of this title, a custodial account which satisfies the requirements of section 401(f)(2) shall be treated as an organization described in section 401(a) solely for purposes of subchapter F and subtitle F with respect to amounts received by it (and income from investment thereof).

(C) Regulated investment company.—For purposes of this paragraph, the term "regulated investment company" means a domestic corporation which is a regulated investment company within the meaning of section 851(a).

(8) Rollover amounts.—

(A) General rule.—If—

(i) any portion of the balance to the credit of an employee in an annuity contract described in paragraph (1) is paid to him in an eligible rollover distribution (within the meaning of section 402(c)(4)),

(ii) the employee transfers any portion of the property he receives in such distribution to an eligible retirement plan described in section 402(c)(8)(B), and

(iii) in the case of a distribution of property other than money, the property so transferred con-

sists of the property distributed, then such distribution (to the extent so transferred) shall not be includible in gross income for the taxable year in which paid.

(B) Certain rules made applicable.—The rules of paragraphs (2) through (7), (9), and (11) of section 402(c) and section 402(f) shall apply for purposes of subparagraph (A), except that section 402(f) shall be applied to the payor in lieu of the plan administrator.

(9) Retirement income accounts provided by churches, etc.—

(A) Amounts paid treated as contributions.—For purposes of this title—

(i) a retirement income account shall be treated as an annuity contract described in this subsection, and

(ii) amounts paid by an employer described in paragraph (1)(A) to a retirement income account shall be treated as amounts contributed by the employer for an annuity contract for the employee on whose behalf such account is maintained.

(B) Retirement income account.—For purposes of this paragraph, the term "retirement income account" means a defined contribution program established or maintained by a church, or a convention or association of churches, including an organization described in section 414(e)(3)(A), to provide benefits under section 403(b) for an employee described in paragraph (1) or his beneficiaries.

(10) Distribution requirements.—Under regulations prescribed by the Secretary, this subsection shall not apply to any annuity contract (or to any custodial account described in paragraph (7) or retirement income account described in paragraph (9)) unless requirements similar to the requirements of sections 401(a)(9) and 401(a)(31) are met (and requirements similar to the incidental death benefit requirements of section 401(a) are met) with respect to such annuity contract (or custodial account or retirement income account). Any amount transferred in a direct trustee-to-trustee transfer in accordance with section 401(a)(31) shall not be includible in gross income for the taxable year of the transfer.

(11) Requirement that distributions not begin before age 59½, severance fromemployment, death, or disability.—This subsection shall not apply to any annuity contract unless under such contract distributions attributable to contributions made pursuant to a salary reduction agreement (within the meaning of section 402(g)(3)(C)) may be paid only—

(A) when the employee attains age 59½, has a severance from employment, dies, or becomes disabled (within the meaning of section 72(m)(7)),

(B) in the case of hardship, or

(C) for distributions to which section 72(t)(2)(G) applies.

Such contract may not provide for the distribution of any income attributable to such contributions in the case of hardship.

(12) Nondiscrimination requirements.—

(A) In general.—For purposes of paragraph (1)(D), a plan meets the nondiscrimination requirements of this paragraph if—

(i) with respect to contributions not made pursuant to a salary reduction agreement, such plan meets the requirements of paragraphs (4), (5), (17), and (26) of section 401(a), section 401(m), and section 410(b) in the same manner as if such plan were described in section 401(a), and

(ii) all employees of the organization may elect to have the employer make contributions of more than $200 pursuant to a salary reduction agreement if any employee of the organization may elect to have the organization make contributions for such contracts pursuant to such agreement.

For purposes of clause (i), a contribution shall be treated as not made pursuant to a salary reduction agreement if under the agreement it is made pursuant to a 1-time irrevocable election made by the employee at the time of initial eligibility to participate in the agreement or is made pursuant to a similar arrangement involving a one-time irrevocable election specified in regulations. For purposes of clause (ii), there may be excluded any employee who is a participant in an eligible deferred compensation plan (within the meaning of section 457) or a qualified cash or deferred arrangement of the organization or another annuity contract described in this subsection. Any nonresident alien described in section 410(b)(3)(C) may also be excluded. Subject to the conditions applicable under section 410(b)(4), there may be excluded for purposes of this subparagraph employees who are students performing services described in section 3121(b)(10) and employees who normally work less than 20 hours per week.

(B) Church.—For purposes of paragraph (1)(D), the term "church" has the meaning given to such term by section 3121(w)(3)(A). Such term shall include any qualified church-controlled organization (as defined in section 3121(w)(3)(B)).

(C) State and local governmental plans.—For purposes of paragraph (1)(D), the requirements of subparagraph (A)(i) (other than those relating to section 401(a)(17)) shall not apply to a governmental plan (within the meaning of section 414(d)) maintained by a State or local government or political subdivision thereof (or agency or instrumentality thereof).

(13) Trustee-to-trustee transfers to purchase permissive service credit.—No amount shall be in-

cludible in gross income by reason of a direct trustee-to-trustee transfer to a defined benefit governmental plan (as defined in section 414(d)) if such transfer is—

(A) for the purchase of permissive service credit (as defined in section 415(n)(3)(A)) under such plan, or

(B) a repayment to which section 415 does not apply by reason of subsection (k)(3) thereof.

(14) Death benefits under USERRA-qualified active military service.—This subsection shall not apply to an annuity contract unless such contract meets the requirements of section 401(a)(37).

(c) Taxability of Beneficiary Under NonQualified Annuities or Under Annuities Purchased by Exempt Organizations.—Premiums paid by an employer for an annuity contract which is not subject to subsection (a) shall be included in the gross income of the employee in accordance with section 83 (relating to property transferred in connection with performance of services), except that the value of such contract shall be substituted for the fair market value of the property for purposes of applying such section. The preceding sentence shall not apply to that portion of the premiums paid which is excluded from gross income under subsection (b). In the case of any portion of any contract which is attributable to premiums to which this subsection applies, the amount actually paid or made available under such contract to any beneficiary which is attributable to such premiums shall be taxable to the beneficiary (in the year in which so paid or made available) under section 72 (relating to annuities).

Recent Amendments to IRC §403

Heroes Earnings Assistance and Relief Tax Act of 2008 (Pub. L. No. 110-245), as follows:

- IRC §403(b)(14) was added by Act §104(c)(2). Eff., in general, with respect to deaths and disabilities occurring on or after Jan. 1, 2007, see Act §104(d)(1).
- **Other Provision.** Act §104(d)(2) provides:
  (2) Provisions relating to plan amendments.—
  (A) In general.—If this subparagraph applies to any plan or contract amendment, such plan or contract shall be treated as being operated in accordance with the terms of the plan during the period described in subparagraph (B)(iii).
  (B) Amendments to which subparagraph (A) applies.—
  (i) In general.—Subparagraph (A) shall apply to any amendment to any plan or annuity contract which is made—
  (I) pursuant to the amendments made by subsection (a) or pursuant to any regulation issued by the Secretary of the Treasury under subsection (a), and
  (II) on or before the last day of the first plan year beginning on or after January 1, 2010.
  In the case of a governmental plan (as defined in section 414(d) of the Internal Revenue Code of 1986), this clause shall be applied by substituting "2012" for "2010" in subclause (II).
  (ii) Conditions.—This paragraph shall not apply to any amendment unless—
  (I) the plan or contract is operated as if such plan or contract amendment were in effect for the period described in clause (iii), and

(II) such plan or contract amendment applies retroactively for such period.

(iii) Period described.—The period described in this clause is the period—

(I) beginning on the effective date specified by the plan, and

(II) ending on the date described in clause (i)(II) (or, if earlier, the date the plan or contract amendment is adopted).

Pension Protection Act of 2006 (Pub. L. No. 109-280), as follows:

• IRC §403(a)(2) was amended by Act §845(b)(1) by adding new para. (2). Eff. for distributions in tax years beginning after Dec. 31, 2006.

• IRC §403(a)(4)(B) was amended by Act §829(a)(2) by inserting "and (11)" after "(7)". Eff. for distributions after Dec. 31, 2006.

• IRC §403(b)(7)(A)(ii) was amended by Act §827(b)(2) by inserting "(unless such amount is a distribution to which §72(t)(2)(G) applies)" after "distributee". Eff. for distributions after Sept. 11, 2001. See Act §827(c)(2) for waiver limits.

• IRC §403(b)(11) was amended by Act §827(b)(3) by striking "or" at the end of subpara. (A), striking the period at the end of subpara. (B) and adding new subpara. (C). Eff. for distributions after Sept. 11, 2001. See Act §827(c)(2) for waiver limits.

• IRC §403(b)(8)(B) was amended by Act §829(a)(3) by replacing "and (9)" with ", (9), and (11)". Eff. for distributions after Dec. 31, 2006.

• IRC §403(b) was amended by Act §845(b)(2) by inserting new para. (2). Eff. for distributions in tax years beginning after Dec. 31, 2006.

• **Sunset Provision.** Act §811, provides:

SEC. 811. PENSIONS AND INDIVIDUAL RETIRE-MENT ARRANGEMENT PROVISIONS OF ECO-NOMIC GROWTH AND TAX RELIEF RECONCILIA-TION ACT OF 2001 MADE PERMANENT.

Title IX of the Economic Growth and Tax Relief Reconciliation Act of 2001 [Pub. L. No. 107-16] shall not apply to the provisions of, and amendments made by, subtitles A through F [§§601–666] of title VI of such Act (relating to pension and individual retirement arrangement provisions).

Gulf Opportunity Zone Act of 2005 (Pub. L. No. 109-135), as follows:

• IRC §403(b)(9)(B) was amended by Act §412(w) by inserting "or" before "a convention". Eff. Dec. 21, 2005.

Working Families Tax Relief Act of 2004 (Pub. L. No. 108-311), as follows:

• IRC §403(a)(4)(B) was amended by Act §404(e). Eff. for distributions after Dec. 31, 2001, as if included in the provision of Pub. L. No. 107-16 to which it relates. IRC §403(a)(4)(B) prior to amendment:

(B) Certain rules made applicable.—Rules similar to the rules of paragraphs (2) through (7) of section 402(c) shall apply for purposes of subparagraph (A).

• IRC §403(b)(7)(A)(ii) was amended by Act §408(a)(11) by replacing "§3121(a)(1)(D)" with "§3121(a)(5)(D)". Eff. Oct. 4, 2004.

Job Creation and Worker Assistance Act of 2002 (Pub. L. No. 107-147), as follows:

• IRC §403(b)(1) was amended by Act §411(p)(1) by striking in the matter following (E) "then amounts contributed" and all that followed and inserting text. Eff. generally for years beginning after Dec. 31, 2001, as if included in the provision of Pub. L. No. 107-16 to which it relates. Matter that followed IRC §403(b)(1)(E) prior to amendment:

then amounts contributed by such employer for such annuity contract on or after such rights become nonforfeitable shall be excluded from the gross income of the employee for the taxable year to the extent that the aggregate of such amounts does not exceed the applicable limit under section 415. The amount actually distributed to any distributee under such contract shall be taxable to the distributee (in the year in which so distributed) under section 72 (relating to annuities). For purposes of applying the rules of this subsection to amounts contributed by an employer for a taxable year, amounts transferred to a contract described in this paragraph by reason of a rollover contribution described in this paragraph (8) of this subsection or section 408(d)(3)(A)(ii) shall not be considered contributed by such employer.

• IRC §403(b)(3) was amended by Act §411(p)(3)(A)–(B) by inserting ", and which precedes the taxable year by no more than five years" before the period at the end of the first sentence, and by striking "or any amount received by a former employee after the fifth taxable year following the taxable year in which such employee was terminated" in the second sentence after "this subsection applies". Eff. for years beginning after Dec. 31, 2001, as if included in the provision of Pub. L. No. 107-16 to which it relates.

• IRC §403(b)(6) was stricken by Act §411(p)(2). Eff. generally for years beginning after Dec. 31, 2001, as if included in the provision of Pub. L. No. 107-16 to which it relates. IRC §403(b)(6) prior to amendment:

(6) Forfeitable rights which become nonforfeitable.—For purposes of this subsection and section 72(f) (relating to special rules for computing employees' contributions to annuity contracts), if rights of the employee under an annuity contract described in subparagraphs (A) and (B) of paragraph (1) change from forfeitable to nonforfeitable rights, then the amount (determined without regard to this subsection) includible in gross income by reason of such change shall be treated as an amount contributed by the employer for such annuity contract as of the time such rights become nonforfeitable.

Economic Growth and Tax Relief Reconciliation Act of 2001 (Pub. L. No. 109-280), as follows:

• IRC §403(b) was amended by Act §632(a)(2)(A)–(C) by replacing "the exclusion allowance for such taxable year" in para. (1) with "the applicable limit under §415", by striking para. (2), and inserting "or any amount received by a former employee after the fifth taxable year following the taxable year in which such employee was terminated" before the period at the end of the second sentence of para. (3). Eff. for years beginning after Dec. 31, 2001. IRC §403(b) prior to being stricken:

(2) Exclusion allowance.—

(A) In general.—For purposes of this subsection, the exclusion allowance for any employee for the taxable year is an amount equal to the excess, if any, of—

(i) the amount determined by multiplying 20 percent of his includible compensation by the number of years of service, over

(ii) the aggregate of the amount contributed by the employer for annuity contracts and excludable from the gross income of the employee for any prior taxable year.

(B) Election to have allowance determined under section 415 rules.—In the case of an employee who makes an election under section 415(c)(4)(D) to have the provisions of section 415(c)(4)(C) (relating to special rule for section 403(b) contracts purchased by educational institutions, hospitals, home health service agencies, and certain churches, etc.) apply, the exclusion allowance for any such employee for the taxable year is the amount which could be contributed (under section 415 without regard to section 415(c)(8)[7]) by his employer under a plan described in section 403(a) if the annuity contract for the benefit of such employee were treated as a defined contribution plan maintained by the employer.

(C) Number of years of service for duly ordained, commissioned, or licensed ministers or lay employees.—For purposes of this subsection and section 415(c)(4)(A)—

(i) all years of service by—

(I) a duly ordained, commissioned, or licensed minister of a church, or

(II) a lay person, as an employee of a church (or convention or association of churches) or such organization described in section 414(e)(3)(B)(ii), shall be considered as years of service for 1 employer, and

(ii) all amounts contributed for annuity contracts by each such church (or convention or association of churches) or such organization during such years for such minister or lay person shall be considered to have been contributed by 1 employer. For purposes of the preceding sentence, the terms "church" and "convention or association of churches" have the same meaning as when used in section 414(e).

(D) Alternative exclusion allowance.—

(i) In general.—In the case of any individual described in subparagraph (C), the amount determined under subparagraph (A) shall not be less than the lesser of—

IRC Sec. 403(c)

(I) $3,000, or

(II) the includible compensation of such individual.

(ii) Subparagraph not to apply to individuals with adjusted gross income over $17,000.—This subparagraph shall not apply with respect to any individual whose adjusted gross income for such taxable year (determined separately and without regard to any community property laws) exceeds $17,000.

(iii) Special rule for foreign missionaries.—In the case of an individual described in subparagraph (C)(i) performing services outside the United States, there shall be included as includible compensation for any year under clause (i)(II) any amount contributed during such year by a church (or convention or association of churches) for an annuity contract with respect to such individual.

- IRC §403(b)(1) was amended by Act §642(b)(1) by replacing "§408(d)(3)(A)(iii)" with "§408(d)(3)(A)(ii)". Eff. for distributions after Dec. 31, 2001. See Act §642(c)(2) for a special rule.
- IRC §403(b)(7)(A)(ii) was amended by Act §646(a)(2)(A) by replacing "separates from service" with "has a severance from employment". Eff. for distributions after Dec. 31, 2001.
- IRC §403(b)(8)(A)(ii) was amended by Act §641(b)(1) by replacing "such distribution" and all that follows with "such distribution to an eligible retirement plan described in §402(c)(8)(B), and". Eff. generally for distributions after Dec. 31, 2001. See Act §641(f)(3) for special rule. IRC §403(b)(8)(A)(ii) prior to amendment:

    (ii) the employee transfers any portion of the property he receives in such distribution to an individual retirement plan or to an annuity contract described in paragraph (1), and.

- IRC §403(b)(8)(B) was amended by Act §641(e)(7). Eff. generally for distributions after Dec. 31, 2001. See Act §641(f)(3) for a special rule. IRC §403(b)(8)(B) prior to amendment:

    (B) Certain rules made applicable.—Rules similar to the rules of paragraphs (2) through (7) of section 402(c) (including paragraph (4)(C) thereof) shall apply for purposes of subparagraph (A).

- IRC §403(b)(11)(A) was amended by Act §646(a)(2)(A) by replacing "separates from service" with "has a severance from employment", and, in the heading, replacing "separation from service" with "severance from employment". Eff. for distributions after Dec. 31, 2001.
- IRC §403(b) was amended by Act §647(a) by adding new para. (13). Eff. for trustee-to-trustee transfers after Dec. 31, 2001.
- **Sunset Provision.** Act §901, as amended by Pub. L. No. 111-312, §101(a)(1), provides the sunset rule below. But see Pub. L. No. 109-280, §811, and Pub. L. No. 111-148, §10909(c), as amended by Pub. L. No. 111-312, §101(b)(1).

    SEC. 901. SUNSET OF PROVISIONS OF ACT.

    (a) In general. All provisions of, and amendments made by, this Act shall not apply—

    (1) to taxable, plan, or limitation years beginning after December 31, 2012, or

    (2) in the case of title V, to estates of decedents dying, gifts made, or generation skipping transfers, after December 31, 2012.

    (b) Application of certain laws.—The Internal Revenue Code of 1986 and the Employee Retirement Income Security Act of 1974 shall be applied and administered to years, estates, gifts, and transfers described in subsection (a) as if the provisions and amendments described in subsection (a) had never been enacted.

SEC. 404. DEDUCTION FOR CONTRIBUTIONS OF AN EMPLOYER TO AN EMPLOYEES' TRUST OR ANNUITY PLAN AND COMPENSATION UNDER A DEFERRED-PAYMENT PLAN.

(a) General Rule.—If contributions are paid by an employer to or under a stock bonus, pension, profit-sharing, or annuity plan, or if compensation is paid or accrued on account of any employee under a plan deferring the receipt of such compensation, such contributions or compensation shall not be deductible under this chapter; but, if they would otherwise be deductible, they shall be deductible under this section, subject, however, to the following limitations as to the amounts deductible in any year:

(1) Pension trusts.—

(A) In general.—In the taxable year when paid, if the contributions are paid into a pension trust (other than a trust to which paragraph (3) applies), and if such taxable year ends within or with a taxable year of the trust for which the trust is exempt under section 501(a), in the case of a defined benefit plan other than a multiemployer plan, in an amount determined under subsection (o), and in the case of any other plan in an amount determined as follows:

(i) the amount necessary to satisfy the minimum funding standard provided by section 412(a) for plan years ending within or with such taxable year (or for any prior plan year), if such amount is greater than the amount determined under clause (ii) or (iii) (whichever is applicable with respect to the plan),

(ii) the amount necessary to provide with respect to all of the employees under the trust remaining unfunded cost of their past and current service credits distributed as a level amount, or a level percentage of compensation, over the remaining future service of each such employee, as determined under regulations prescribed by the Secretary, but if such remaining unfunded cost with respect to any 3 individuals is more than 50 percent of such remaining unfunded cost, the amount of such unfunded cost attributable to such individuals shall be distributed over a period of at least 5 taxable years,

(iii) an amount equal to the normal cost of the plan, as determined under regulations prescribed by the Secretary, plus, if past service or other supplementary pension or annuity credits are provided by the plan, an amount necessary to amortize the unfunded costs attributable to such credits in equal annual payments (until fully amortized) over 10 years, as determined under regulations prescribed by the Secretary.

In determining the amount deductible in such year under the foregoing limitations the funding method and the actuarial assumptions used shall be those used for such year under section 431, and the maximum amount deductible for such year shall be an amount equal to the full funding limitation for such year determined under section 431.

(B) Special rule in case of certain amendments.—In the case of a multiemployer plan which the Secretary of Labor finds to be collectively bargained which makes an election under this subparagraph (in such manner and at such time as may be provided under the regulations prescribed by the Secretary), if the full funding limitation determined under section 431(c)(6) for such year is zero, if as a result of any plan amendment applying to such plan year, the amount determined under section 431(c)(6)(A)(ii) exceeds the amount determined under section 431(c)(6)(A)(i), and if the funding method and the actuarial assumptions used are those used for such year under section 431, the maximum amount deductible in such year under the limitations of this paragraph shall be an amount equal to the lesser of—

(i) the full funding limitation for such year determined by applying section 431(c)(6) but increasing the amount referred to in subparagraph (A) thereof by the decrease in the present value of all unamortized liabilities resulting from such amendment, or

(ii) the normal cost under the plan reduced by the amount necessary to amortize in equal annual installments over 10 years (until fully amortized) the decrease described in clause (i).

In the case of any election under this subparagraph, the amount deductible under the limitations of this paragraph with respect to any of the plan years following the plan year for which such election was made shall be determined as provided under such regulations as may be prescribed by the Secretary to carry out the purposes of this subparagraph.

(C) Certain collectively bargained plans.—In the case of a plan which the Secretary of Labor finds to be collectively bargained, established or maintained by an employer doing business in not less than 40 States and engaged in the trade or business of furnishing or selling services described in section 168(i)(10)(C), with respect to which the rates have been established or approved by a State or political subdivision thereof, by any agency or instrumentality of the United States, or by a public service or public utility commission or other similar body of any State or political subdivision thereof, and in the case of any employer which is a member of a controlled group with such employer, subparagraph (B) shall be applied by substituting for the words "plan amendment" the words "plan amendment or increase in benefits payable under title II of the Social Security Act". For purposes of this subparagraph, the term "controlled group" has the meaning provided by section 1563(a), determined without regard to section 1563(a)(4) and (e)(3)(C).

(D) Amount determined on basis of unfunded current liability.—In the case of a defined benefit plan which is a multiemployer plan, except as provided in regulations, the maximum amount deductible under the limitations of this paragraph shall not be less than the excess (if any) of—

(i) 140 percent of the current liability of the plan determined under section 431(c)(6)(D), over

(ii) the value of the plan's assets determined under section 431(c)(2).

(E) Carryover.—Any amount paid in a taxable year in excess of the amount deductible in such year under the foregoing limitations shall be deductible in the succeeding taxable years in order of time to the extent of the difference between the amount paid and deductible in each such succeeding year and the maximum amount deductible for such year under the foregoing limitations.

(2) Employees' annuities.—In the taxable year when paid, in an amount determined in accordance with paragraph (1), if the contributions are paid toward the purchase of retirement annuities, or retirement annuities and medical benefits as described in section 401(h), and such purchase is a part of a plan which meets the requirements of section 401(a)(3), (4), (5), (6), (7), (8), (9), (11), (12), (13), (14), (15), (16), (17), (19), (20), (22), (26), (27), (31), and (37) and, if applicable, the requirements of section 401(a)(10) and of section 401(d), and if refunds of premiums, if any, are applied within the current taxable year or next succeeding taxable year towards the purchase of such retirement annuities, or such retirement annuities and medical benefits.

(3) Stock bonus and profit-sharing trusts.—

(A) Limits on deductible contributions.—

(i) In general.—In the taxable year when paid, if the contributions are paid into a stock bonus or profit-sharing trust, and if such taxable year ends within or with a taxable year of the trust with respect to which the trust is exempt under section 501(a), in an amount not in excess of the greater of—

(I) 25 percent of the compensation otherwise paid or accrued during the taxable year to the beneficiaries under the stock bonus or profit-sharing plan, or

(II) the amount such employer is required to contribute to such trust under section 401(k)(11) for such year.

(ii) Carryover of excess contributions.—Any amount paid into the trust in any taxable year in excess of the limitation of clause (i) (or the corresponding provision of prior law) shall be deductible in the succeeding taxable years in order of time, but the amount so deductible under this clause in any 1 such succeeding taxable year together with the amount allowable under clause (i) shall not exceed the amount described in subclause (I) or (II) of clause (i), whichever is greater, with respect to such taxable year.

(iii) Certain retirement plans excluded.—For purposes of this subparagraph, the term "stock bonus or profit-sharing trust" shall not include any trust designed to provide benefits upon retirement and covering a period of years, if under the plan the amounts to be contributed by the employer can be determined actuarially as provided in paragraph (1).

(iv) 2 or more trusts treated as 1 trust.—If the contributions are made to 2 or more stock bonus or profit-sharing trusts, such trusts shall be considered a single trust for purposes of applying the limitations in this subparagraph.

(v) Defined contribution plans subject to the funding standards.—Except as provided by the Secretary, a defined contribution plan which is subject to the funding standards of section 412 shall be treated in the same manner as a stock bonus or profit-sharing plan for purposes of this subparagraph.

(B) Profit-sharing plan of affiliated group.—In the case of a profit-sharing plan, or a stock bonus plan in which contributions are determined with reference to profits, of a group of corporations which is an affiliated group within the meaning of section 1504, if any member of such affiliated group is prevented from making a contribution which it would otherwise have made under the plan, by reason of having no current or accumulated earnings or profits or because such earnings or profits are less than the contributions which it would otherwise have made, then so much of the contribution which such member was so prevented from making may be made, for the benefit of the employees of such member, by the other members of the group, to the extent of current or accumulated earnings or profits, except that such contribution by each such other member shall be limited, where the group does not file a consolidated return, to that proportion of its total current and accumulated earnings or profits remaining after adjustment for its contribution deductible without regard to this subparagraph which the total prevented contribution bears to the total current and accumulated earnings or profits of all the members of the group remaining after adjustment for all contributions deductible without regard to this subparagraph. Contributions made under the preceding sentence shall be deductible under subparagraph (A) of this paragraph by the employer making such contribution, and, for the purpose of determining amounts which may be carried forward and deducted under the second sentence of subparagraph (A) of this paragraph in succeeding taxable years, shall be deemed to have been made by the employer on behalf of whose employees such contributions were made.

(4) Trusts created or organized outside the United States.—If a stock bonus, pension, or profit-sharing trust would qualify for exemption under section 501(a) except for the fact that it is a trust created or organized outside the United States, contributions to such a trust by an employer which is a resident, or corporation, or other entity of the United States, shall be deductible under the preceding paragraphs.

(5) Other plans.—If the plan is not one included in paragraph (1), (2), or (3), in the taxable year in which an amount attributable to the contribution is includible in the gross income of employees participating in the plan, but, in the case of a plan in which more than one employee participates only if separate accounts are maintained for each employee. For purposes of this section, any vacation pay which is treated as deferred compensation shall be deductible for the taxable year of the employer in which paid to the employee.

(6) Time when contributions deemed made.—For purposes of paragraphs (1), (2), and (3), a taxpayer shall be deemed to have made a payment on the last day of the preceding taxable year if the payment is on account of such taxable year and is made not later than the time prescribed by law for filing the return for such taxable year (including extensions thereof).

(7) Limitation on deductions where combination of defined contribution plan and defined benefit plan.—

(A) In general.—If amounts are deductible under the foregoing paragraphs of this subsection (other than paragraph (5)) in connection with 1 or more defined contribution plans and 1 or more defined benefit plans or in connection with trusts or plans described in 2 or more of such paragraphs, the total amount deductible in a taxable year under such plans shall not exceed the greater of—

(i) 25 percent of the compensation otherwise paid or accrued during the taxable year to the beneficiaries under such plans, or

(ii) the amount of contributions made to or under the defined benefit plans to the extent such contributions do not exceed the amount of employer contributions necessary to satisfy the minimum funding standard provided by section 412 with respect to any such defined benefit plans for the plan year which ends with or within such taxable year (or for any prior plan year).

A defined contribution plan which is a pension plan shall not be treated as failing to provide definitely determinable benefits merely by limiting employer contributions to amounts deductible under this section. In the case of a defined benefit plan which is a single employer plan, the amount necessary to satisfy the minimum funding standard provided by section 412 shall not be less than the excess (if any) of the plan's funding target (as defined in section 430(d)(1)) over the value of the plan's assets (as determined under section 430(g)(3)).

(B) Carryover of contributions in excess of the deductible limit.—Any amount paid under the plans in any taxable year in excess of the limitation of subparagraph (A) shall be deductible in the succeeding taxable years in order of time, but the amount so deductible under this subparagraph in any 1 such succeeding taxable year together with the amount allowable under subparagraph (A) shall not exceed 25 percent of the compensation otherwise paid or accrued during such taxable year to the beneficiaries under the plans.

(C) Paragraph not to apply in certain cases.—

(i) Beneficiary test.—This paragraph shall not have the effect of reducing the amount otherwise deductible under paragraphs (1), (2), and (3), if no employee is a beneficiary under more than 1 trust or under a trust and an annuity plan.

(ii) Elective deferrals.—If, in connection with 1 or more defined contribution plans and 1 or more defined benefit plans, no amounts (other than elective deferrals (as defined in section 402(g)(3))) are contributed to any of the defined contribution plans for the taxable year, then subparagraph (A) shall not apply with respect to any of such defined contribution plans and defined benefit plans.

(iii) Limitation.—In the case of employer contributions to 1 or more defined contribution plans—

(I) if such contributions do not exceed 6 percent of the compensation otherwise paid or accrued during the taxable year to the beneficiaries under such plans, this paragraph shall not apply to such contributions or to employer contributions to the defined benefit plans to which this paragraph would otherwise apply by reason of contributions to the defined contribution plans, and

(II) if such contributions exceed 6 percent of such compensation, this paragraph shall be applied by only taking into account such contributions to the extent of such excess.

For purpose of this clause, amounts carried over from preceding taxable years under subparagraph (B) shall be treated as employer contributions to 1 or more defined contributions plans to the extent attributable to employer contributions to such plans in such preceding taxable years.

(iv) Guaranteed plans.—In applying this paragraph, any single-employer plan covered under section 4021 of the Employee Retirement Income Security Act of 1974 shall not be taken into account.

(v) Multiemployer plans.—In applying this paragraph, any multiemployer plan shall not be taken into account.

(D) Insurance contract plans.—For purposes of this paragraph, a plan described in section 412(e)(3) shall be treated as a defined benefit plan.

(8) Self-employed individuals.—In the case of a plan included in paragraph (1), (2), or (3) which provides contributions or benefits for employees some or all of whom are employees within the meaning of section 401(c)(1), for purposes of this section—

(A) the term "employee" includes an individual who is an employee within the meaning of section 401(c)(1), and the employer of such individual is the person treated as his employer under section 401(c)(4);

(B) the term "earned income" has the meaning assigned to it by section 401(c)(2);

(C) the contributions to such plan on behalf of an individual who is an employee within the meaning of section 401(c)(1) shall be considered to satisfy the conditions of section 162 or 212 to the extent that such contributions do not exceed the earned income of such individual (determined without regard to the deductions allowed by this section) derived from the trade or business with respect to which such plan is established, and to the extent that such contributions are not allocable (determined in accordance with regulations prescribed by the Secretary) to the purchase of life, accident, health or other insurance; and

(D) any reference to compensation shall, in the case of an individual who is an employee within the meaning of section 401(c)(1), be considered to be a reference to the earned income of such individual derived from the trade or business with respect to which the plan is established.

(9) Certain contributions to employee stock ownership plans.—

(A) Principal payments.—Notwithstanding the provisions of paragraphs (3) and (7), if contributions are paid into a trust which forms a part of an employee stock ownership plan (as described in section 4957(e)(7)), and such contributions are, on or before the time prescribed in paragraph (6), applied by the plan to the repayment of the principal of a loan incurred for the purpose of acquiring qualifying employer securities (as described in section 4975(e)(8)), such contributions shall be deductible under this paragraph for the taxable year determined under paragraph (6). The amount deductible under this paragraph shall not, however, exceed 25 percent of the compensation otherwise paid or accrued during the taxable year to the employees under such employee stock ownership plan. Any amount paid into such trust in any taxable year in excess of the amount deductible under this paragraph shall be deductible in the succeeding taxable years in order of time to the extent of the difference between the amount paid and deductible in each such succeeding year and the maximum amount deductible for such year under the preceding sentence.

(B) Interest payment.—Notwithstanding the provisions of paragraphs (3) and (7), if contributions are made to an employee stock ownership plan (described in subparagraph (A)) and such contributions are applied by the plan to the repayment of interest on a loan incurred for the purpose of acquiring qualifying employer securities (as described in subparagraph (A)), such contributions shall be deductible for the taxable year with respect to which such contributions are made as determined under paragraph (6).

(C) S corporations.—This paragraph shall not apply to an S corporation.

(D) Qualified Gratuitous Transfers.—A qualified gratuitous transfer (as defined in section 664(g)(1)) shall have no effect on the amount or amounts otherwise deductible under paragraph (3) or (7) or under this paragraph.

(10) Contributions by certain ministers to retirement income accounts.—In the case of contributions made by a minister described in section 414(e)(5) to a retirement income account described in section 403(b)(9) and not by a person other than such minister, such contributions—

(A) shall be treated as made to a trust which is exempt from tax under section 501(a) and which is part of a plan which is described in section 401(a), and

(B) shall be deductible under this subsection to the extent such contributions do not exceed the limit on elective deferrals under section 402(g) or the limit on annual additions under section 415.

For purposes of this paragraph, all plans in which the minister is a participant shall be treated as one plan.

(11) Determinations relating to deferred compensation.—For purposes of determining under this section—

(A) whether compensation of an employee is deferred compensation; and

(B) when deferred compensation is paid,

no amount shall be treated as received by the employee, or paid, until it is actually received by the employee.

(12) Definition of compensation.—For purposes of paragraphs (3), (7), (8), and (9) and subsection (h)(1)(C), the term "compensation" shall include amounts treated as "participant's compensation" under subparagraph (C) or (D) of section 415(c)(3).

(b) Method of Contributions, etc., Having the Effect of a Plan; Certain Deferred Benefits.—

(1) Methods of contributions, etc., having the effect of a plan.—If—

(A) there is no plan, but

(B) there is a method or arrangement of employer contributions or compensation which has the effect

of a stock bonus, pension, profit-sharing, or annuity plan, or other plan deferring the receipt of compensation (including a plan described in paragraph (2)),

subsection (a) shall apply as if there were such a plan.

(2) Plans providing certain deferred benefits.—

(A) In general.—For purposes of this section, any plan providing for deferred benefits (other than compensation) for employees, their spouses, or their dependents shall be treated as a plan deferring the receipt of compensation. In the case of such a plan, for purposes of this section, the determination of when an amount is includible in gross income shall be made without regard to any provisions of this chapter excluding such benefits from gross income.

(B) Exception.—Subparagraph (A) shall not apply to any benefit provided through a welfare benefit fund (as defined in section 419(e)).

(c) Certain Negotiated Plans.—If contributions are paid by an employer—

(1) under a plan under which such contributions are held in trust for the purpose of paying (either from principal or income or both) for the benefit of employees and their families and dependents at least medical or hospital care, or pensions on retirement or death of employees; and

(2) such plan was established prior to January 1, 1954, as a result of an agreement between employee representatives and the Government of the United States during a period of Government operation, under seizure powers, of a major part of the productive facilities of the industry in which such employer is engaged,

such contributions shall not be deductible under this section nor be made nondeductible by this section, but the deductibility thereof shall be governed solely by section 162 (relating to trade or business expenses). For purposes of this chapter and subtitle B, in the case of any individual who before July 1, 1974, was a participant in a plan described in the preceding sentence—

(A) such individual, if he is or was an employee within the meaning of section 401(c)(1), shall be treated (with respect to service covered by the plan) as being an employee other than an employee within the meaning of section 401(c)(1) and as being an employee of a participating employer under the plan,

(B) earnings derived from service covered by the plan shall be treated as not being earned income within the meaning of section 401(c)(2), and

(C) such individual shall be treated as an employee of a participating employer under the plan with respect to service before July 1, 1975, covered by the plan.

IRC Sec. 404(c)(2)(C)

Section 277 (relating to deductions incurred by certain membership organizations in transactions with members) does not apply to any trust described in this subsection. The first and third sentences of this subsection shall have no application with respect to amounts contributed to a trust on or after any date on which such trust is qualified for exemption from tax under section 501(a).

(d) Deductibility of Payments of Deferred Compensation, etc., to Independent Contractors.—If a plan would be described in so much of subsection (a) as precedes paragraph (1) thereof (as modified by subsection (b)) but for the fact that there is no employer-employee relationship, the contributions or compensation—

(1) shall not be deductible by the payor thereof under this chapter, but

(2) shall (if they would be deductible under this chapter but for paragraph (1)) be deductible under this subsection for the taxable year in which an amount attributable to the contribution or compensation is includible in the gross income of the persons participating in the plan.

(e) Contributions Allocable to Life Insurance Protection for Self-Employed Individuals.—In the case of a self-employed individual described in section 401(c)(1), contributions which are allocable (determined under regulations prescribed by the Secretary) to the purchase of life, accident, health, or other insurance shall not be taken into account under paragraph (1), (2), or (3) of subsection (a).

(f) [Repealed.]

(g) Certain Employer Liability Payments Considered as Contributions.—

(1) **In general.**—For purposes of this section, any amount paid by an employer under section 4041(b), 4062, 4063, or 4064, or part 1 of subtitle E of title IV of the Employee Retirement Income Security Act of 1974 shall be treated as a contribution to which this section applies by such employer to or under a stock bonus, pension, profit-sharing, or annuity plan.

(2) **Controlled group deductions.**—In the case of a payment described in paragraph (1) made by an entity which is liable because it is a member of a commonly controlled group of corporations, trades, or businesses, within the meaning of subsection (b) or (c) of section 414, the fact that the entity did not directly employ participants of the plan with respect to which the liability payment was made shall not affect the deductibility of a payment which otherwise satisfies the conditions of section 162 (relating to trade or business expenses) or section 212 (relating to expenses for the production of income).

(3) **Timing of deduction of contributions.**—

(A) In general.—Except as otherwise provided in this paragraph, any payment described in para-

graph (1) shall (subject to the last sentence of subsection (a)(1)(A)) be deductible under this section when paid.

(B) Contributions under standard terminations.— Subparagraph (A) shall not apply (and subsection (a)(1)(A) shall apply) to any payments described in paragraph (1) which are paid to terminate a plan under section 4041(b) of the Employee Retirement Income Security Act of 1974 to the extent such payments result in the assets of the plan being in excess of the total amount of benefits under such plan which are guaranteed by the Pension Benefit Guaranty Corporation under section 4022 of such Act.

(C) Contributions to certain trusts.—Subparagraph (A) shall not apply to any payment described in paragraph (1) which is made under section 4062(c) of such Act and such payment shall be deductible at such time as may be prescribed in regulations which are based on principles similar to the principles of subsection (a)(1)(A).

(4) **References to Employee Retirement Income Security Act of 1974.**—For purposes of this section, any reference to a section of the Employee Retirement Income Security Act of 1974 shall be treated as a reference to such section as in effect on the date of the enactment of the Retirement Protection Act of 1994.

(h) Special Rules for Simplified Employee Pensions.—

(1) **In general.**—Employee contributions to a simplified employee pension shall be treated as if they are made to a plan subject to the requirements of this section. Employer contributions to a simplified employee pension are subject to the following limitations:

(A) Contributions made for a year are deductible—

(i) in the case of a simplified employee pension maintained on a calendar year basis, for the taxable year with or within which the calendar year ends, or

(ii) in the case of a simplified employee pension which is maintained on the basis of the taxable year of the employer, for such taxable year.

(B) Contributions shall be treated for purposes of this subsection as if they were made for a taxable year if such contributions are made on account of such taxable year and are made not later than the time prescribed by law for filing the return for such taxable year (including extensions thereof).

(C) The amount deductible in a taxable year for a simplified employee pension shall not exceed 25 percent of the compensation paid to the employees during the calendar year ending with or within the taxable year (or during the taxable year in the case

IRC Sec. 404(c)(2)(C)

of a taxable year described in subparagraph (A)(ii)). The excess of the amount contributed over the amount deductible for a taxable year shall be deductible in the succeeding taxable years in order of time, subject to the 25 percent limit of the preceding sentence.

(2) Effect on certain trusts.—For any taxable year for which the employer has a deduction under paragraph (1), the otherwise applicable limitations in subsection (a)(3)(A) shall be reduced by the amount of the allowable deductions under paragraph (1) with respect to participants in the trust subject to subsection (a)(3)(A).

(3) Coordination with subsection (a)(7).—For purposes of subsection (a)(7), a simplified employee pension shall be treated as if it were a separate stock bonus or profit-sharing trust.

(i) [Repealed.]

(j) Special Rules Relating to Application With Section 415.—

(1) No deduction in excess of section 415 limitation.—In computing the amount of any deduction allowable under paragraph (1), (2), (3), (4), (7), or (9) of subsection (a) for any year—

(A) in the case of a defined benefit plan, there shall not be taken into account any benefits for any year in excess of any limitation on such benefits under section 415 for such year, or

(B) in the case of a defined contribution plan, the amount of any contributions otherwise taken into account shall be reduced by any annual additions in excess of the limitation under section 415 for such year.

(2) No advance funding of cost-of-living adjustments.—For purposes of clause (i), (ii) or (iii) of subsection (a)(1)(A), and in computing the full funding limitation, there shall not be taken into account any adjustments under section 415(d)(1) for any year before the year for which such adjustment first takes effect.

(k) Deduction for Dividends Paid on Certain Employer Securities.—

(1) General rule.—In the case of a C corporation, there shall be allowed as a deduction for a taxable year the amount of any applicable dividend paid in cash by such corporation with respect to applicable employer securities. Such deduction shall be in addition to the deductions allowed under subsection (a).

(2) Applicable dividend.—For purposes of this subsection—

(A) In general.—The term "applicable dividend" means any dividend which, in accordance with plan provisions—

(i) is paid in cash to the participants in the plan or their beneficiaries,

(ii) is paid to the plan and is distributed in cash to participants in the plan or their beneficiaries not later that 90 days after the close of the plan year in which paid,

(iii) is, at the election of such participants or their beneficiaries—

(I) payable as provided in clause (i) or (ii), or

(II) paid to the plan and reinvested in qualifying employer securities, or

(iv) is used to make payments on a loan described in subsection (a)(9) the proceeds of which were used to acquire the employer securities (whether or not allocated to participants) with respect to which the dividend is paid.

(B) Limitation on certain dividends.—A dividend described in subparagraph (A)(iv) which is paid with respect to any employer security which is allocated to a participant shall not be treated as an applicable dividend unless the plan provides that employer securities with a fair market value of not less than the amount of such dividend are allocated to such participant for the year which (but for subparagraph (A)) such dividend would have been allocated to such participant.

(3) Applicable employer securities.—For purposes of this subsection, the term "applicable employer securities" means, with respect to any dividend, employer securities which are held on the record date for such dividend by an employee stock ownership plan which is maintained by—

(A) the corporation paying such dividend, or

(B) any other corporation which is a member of a controlled group of corporations (within the meaning of section 409(l)(4)) which includes such corporation.

(4) Time for deduction.—

(A) In general.—The deduction under paragraph (1) shall be allowable in the taxable year of the corporation to which the dividend is paid or distributed to a participant or his beneficiary.

(B) Reinvestment dividends.—For purposes of subparagraph (A), an applicable dividend reinvested pursuant to clause (iii)(II) of paragraph (2)(A) shall be treated as paid in the taxable year of the corporation in which such dividend is reinvested in qualifying employer securities or in which the election under clause (iii) of paragraph (2)(A) is made, whichever is later.

(C) Repayment of loans.—In the case of an applicable dividend described in clause (iv) of paragraph (2)(A), the deduction under paragraph (1) shall be allowable in the taxable year of the corporation in which such dividend is used to repay the loan described in such clause.

(5) Other rules.—For purposes of this subsection—

(A) Disallowance of deduction.—The Secretary may disallow the deduction under paragraph (1) for any dividend if the Secretary determines that such dividend constitutes, in substance, an avoidance or evasion of taxation.

(B) Plan qualification.—A plan shall not be treated as violating the requirements of section 401, 409, or 4975(e)(7), or as engaging in a prohibited transaction for purposes of section 4975(d)(3), merely by reason of any payment or distribution described in paragraph (2)(A).

(6) Definitions.—For purposes of this subsection—

(A) Employer securities.—The term "employer securities" has the meaning given such term by section 409(l).

(B) Employee stock ownership plan.—The term "employee stock ownership plan" has the meaning given such term by section 4975(e)(7). Such term includes a tax credit employee stock ownership plan (as defined in section 409).

(7) Full vesting.—In accordance with section 411, an applicable dividend described in clause (iii)(II) of paragraph (2)(A) shall be subject to the requirements of section 411(a)(1).

(l) Limitation on Amount of Annual Compensation Taken Into Account.—For purposes of applying the limitations of this section, the amount of annual compensation of each employee taken into account under the plan for any year shall not exceed $200,000. The Secretary shall adjust the $200,000 amount at the same time, and by the same amount, as any adjustment under section 401(a)(17)(B). For purposes of clause (i), (ii), or (iii) of subsection (a)(1)(A), and in computing the full funding limitation, any adjustment under the preceding sentence shall not be taken into account for any year before the year for which such adjustment first takes effect.

(m) Special Rules for Simple Retirement Accounts.—

(1) In general.—Employer contributions to a simple retirement account shall be treated as if they are made to a plan subject to the requirements of this section.

(2) Timing.—

(A) Deduction.—Contributions described in paragraph (1) shall be deductible in the taxable year of the employer with or within which the calendar year for which the contributions were made ends.

(B) Contributions after end of year.—For purposes of this subsection, contributions shall be treated as made for a taxable year if they are made on account of the taxable year and are made not later than the time prescribed by law for filing the return for the taxable year (including extensions thereof).

(n) Elective Deferrals Not Taken Into Account for Purposes of Deduction Limits.—Elective deferrals (as defined in section 402(g)(3)) shall not be subject to any limitation contained in paragraph (3), (7), or (9) of subsection (a) or paragraph (1)(C) of subsection (h) and such elective deferrals shall not be taken into account in applying any such limitation to any other contributions.

(o) Deduction Limit for Single-Employer Plans.—For purposes of subsection (a)(1)(A)—

(1) In general.—In the case of a defined benefit plan to which subsection (a)(1)(A) applies (other than a multiemployer plan), the amount determined under this subsection for any taxable year shall be equal to the greater of—

(A) the sum of the amounts determined under paragraph (2) with respect to each plan year ending with or within the taxable year, or

(B) the sum of the minimum required contributions under section 430 for such plan years.

(2) Determination of amount.—

(A) In general.—The amount determined under this paragraph for any plan year shall be equal to the excess (if any) of—

(i) the sum of—

(I) the funding target for the plan year,

(II) the target normal cost for the plan year, and

(III) the cushion amount for the plan year, over

(ii) the value (determined under section 430(g)(3)) of the assets of the plan which are held by the plan as of the valuation date for the plan year.

(B) Special rule for certain employers.—If section 430(i) does not apply to a plan for a plan year, the amount determined under subparagraph (A)(i) for the plan year shall in no event be less than the sum of—

(i) the funding target for the plan year (determined as if section 430(i) applied to the plan), plus

(ii) the target normal cost for the plan year (as so determined).

(3) Cushion amount.—For purposes of paragraph (2)(A)(i)(III)—

(A) In general.—The cushion amount for any plan year is the sum of—

(i) 50 percent of the funding target for the plan year, and

(ii) the amount by which the funding target for the plan year would increase if the plan were to take into account—

(I) increases in compensation which are expected to occur in succeeding plan years, or

IRC Sec. 404(k)(5)(A)

(II) if the plan does not base benefits for service to date on compensation, increases in benefits which are expected to occur in succeeding plan years (determined on the basis of the average annual increase in benefits over the 6 immediately preceding plan years).

(B) Limitations.—

(i) In general.—In making the computation under subparagraph (A)(ii), the plan's actuary shall assume that the limitations under subsection (l) and section 415(b) shall apply.

(ii) Expected increases.—In the case of a plan year during which a plan is covered under section 4021 of the Employee Retirement Income Security Act of 1974, the plan's actuary may, notwithstanding subsection (l), take into account increases in the limitations which are expected to occur in succeeding plan years.

(4) Special rules for plans with 100 or fewer participants.—

(A) In general.—For purposes of determining the amount under paragraph (3) for any plan year, in the case of a plan which has 100 or fewer participants for the plan year, the liability of the plan attributable to benefit increases for highly compensated employees (as defined in section 414(q)) resulting from a plan amendment which is made or becomes effective, whichever is later, within the last 2 years shall not be taken into account in determining the target liability.

(B) Rule for determining number of participants.—For purposes of determining the number of plan participants, all defined benefit plans maintained by the same employer (or any member of such employer's controlled group (within the meaning of section 412(d)(3))) shall be treated as one plan, but only participants of such member or employer shall be taken into account.

(5) Special rule for terminating plans.—In the case of a plan which, subject to section 4041 of the Employee Retirement Income Security Act of 1974, terminates during the plan year, the amount determined under paragraph (2) shall in no event be less than the amount required to make the plan sufficient for benefit liabilities (within the meaning of section 4041(d) of such Act).

(6) Actuarial assumptions.—Any computation under this subsection for any plan year shall use the same actuarial assumptions which are used for the plan year under section 430.

(7) Definitions.—Any term used in this subsection which is also used in section 430 shall have the same meaning given such term by section 430.

Recent Amendments to IRC §404

Worker, Retiree, and Employer Recovery Act of 2008 (Pub. L. No. 110-458), as follows:

- IRC §404(a)(1)(D)(i) was amended by Act §108(b) by striking "431(c)(6)(C)" and inserting "431(c)(6)(D)". Eff. as if included in Pub. L. No. 109-280, §801 [eff. for years beginning after Dec. 31, 2007].
- IRC §404(a)(7)(A) was amended by Act §108(a)(2) by striking the next to last sentence, and striking "the plan's funding shortfall determined under section 430" in the last sentence and inserting "the excess (if any) of the plan's funding target (as defined in section 430(d)(1)) over the value of the plan's assets (as determined under section 430(g)(3))". Eff. as if included in Pub. L. No. 109-280, §801 [eff. for years beginning after Dec. 31, 2007]. Next to last sentence prior to amendment:

    For purposes of clause (ii), if paragraph (1)(D) applies to a defined benefit plan for any plan year, the amount necessary to satisfy the minimum funding standard provided by section 412 with respect to such plan for such plan year shall not be less than the unfunded current liability of such plan under section 412(l).

- IRC §404(a)(7)(C)(iii) was amended by Act §108(c). Eff. as if included in Pub. L. No. 109-280, §801 [eff. for years beginning after Dec. 31, 2007]. IRC §404(a)(7)(C)(iii) prior to amendment:

    (iii) Limitation.—In the case of employer contributions to 1 or more defined contribution plans, this paragraph shall only apply to the extent that such contributions exceed 6 percent of the compensation otherwise paid or accrued during the taxable year to the beneficiaries under such plans. For purposes of this clause, amounts carried over from preceding taxable years under subparagraph (B) shall be treated as employer contributions to 1 or more defined contributions to the extent attributable to employer contributions to such plans in such preceding taxable years.

- IRC §404(o)(2)(A)(ii) was amended by Act §108(a)(1)(A) by striking "430(g)(2)" and inserting "430(g)(3)". Eff. as if included in Pub. L. No. 109-280, §801 [eff. for years beginning after Dec. 31, 2007].
- IRC §404(o)(4)(B) was amended by Act §108(a)(1)(B) by striking "412(f)(4)" and inserting "412(d)(3)". Eff. as if included in Pub. L. No. 109-280, §801 [eff. for years beginning after Dec. 31, 2007].

Heroes Earnings Assistance and Relief Tax Act of 2008 (Pub. L. No. 110-245), as follows:

- IRC §404(a)(2) was amended by Act §104(c)(1) by striking "and (31)" and inserting "(31), and (37)". Eff., in general, with respect to deaths and disabilities occurring on or after Jan. 1, 2007, see Act §104(d)(1).
- **Other Provision.** Act §104(d)(2) provides:

    (2) Provisions relating to plan amendments.—

    (A) In general.—If this subparagraph applies to any plan or contract amendment, such plan or contract shall be treated as being operated in accordance with the terms of the plan during the period described in subparagraph (B)(iii).

    (B) Amendments to which subparagraph (A) applies.—

    (i) In general.—Subparagraph (A) shall apply to any amendment to any plan or annuity contract which is made—

    (I) pursuant to the amendments made by subsection (a) or pursuant to any regulation issued by the Secretary of the Treasury under subsection (a), and

    (II) on or before the last day of the first plan year beginning on or after January 1, 2010.

    In the case of a governmental plan (as defined in section 414(d) of the Internal Revenue Code of 1986), this clause shall be applied by substituting "2012" for "2010" in subclause (II).

    (ii) Conditions.—This paragraph shall not apply to any amendment unless—

    (I) the plan or contract is operated as if such plan or contract amendment were in effect for the period described in clause (iii), and

    (II) such plan or contract amendment applies retroactively for such period.

    (iii) Period described.—The period described in this clause is the period—

    (I) beginning on the effective date specified by the plan, and

    (II) ending on the date described in clause (i)(II) (or, if earlier, the date the plan or contract amendment is adopted).

Pension Protection Act of 2006 (Pub. L. No. 109-280), as follows:

IRC Sec. 404(o)(7)

- IRC §404(a)(1)(A) was amended by Act §801(a)(1) by inserting "in the case of a defined benefit plan other than a multiemployer plan, in an amount determined under subsection (o), and in the case of any other plan" after "§501(a),". Eff. for years beginning after Dec. 31, 2007.

- IRC §404(a)(1)(A) was amended by Act §801(c)(1) by replacing "§412" each place it appeared with "§431". Eff. for years beginning after Dec. 31, 2007.

- IRC §404(a)(1)(B) was amended by Act §801(c)(2)(A)–(E) by replacing "In the case of a plan" with "In the case of a multiemployer plan", by replacing "§412(c)(7)" each place it appeared with "§431(c)(6)", by replacing "§412(c)(7)(B)" with "§431(c)(6)(A)(ii)", by replacing "412(c)(7)(A)" with "§431(c)(6)(A)(i)", and by replacing "§412" with "§431". Eff. years beginning after Dec. 31, 2007.

- IRC §404(a)(7)(C) was amended by Act §801(b) by adding new cl. (iv). Eff. years beginning after Dec. 31, 2007.

- IRC §404(a)(7) was amended by Act §801(c)(3)(A)–(B) by adding a new sentence at the end of subpara. (A), by striking subpara. (D), and by inserting new subpara. (D). Eff. years beginning after Dec. 31, 2007. IRC §404(a)(7)(D) prior to amendment:

  > (D) section 412(i) plans.—For purposes of this paragraph, any plan described in section 412(i) shall be treated as a defined benefit plan.

- IRC §404(a)(1)(D)(i) was amended by Act §801(d)(1) by replacing "§412(*l*)" with "§412(*l*)(8)(A), except that §412(*l*)(8)(A) shall be applied for purposes of this clause by substituting '150 percent (140 percent in the case of a multiemployer plan) of current liability' for 'the current liability' in clause (i)". Eff. years beginning after Dec. 31, 2005.

- IRC §404(a)(1) was amended by Act §801(d)(2) by striking subpara. (F). Eff. years beginning after Dec. 31, 2005. IRC §404(a)(1)(F) prior to being stricken:

  > (F) Election to disregard modified interest rate.—An employer may elect to disregard subsections (b)(5)(B)(ii)(II) and (*l*)(7)(C)(i)(IV) of section 412 solely for purposes of determining the interest rate used in calculating the maximum amount of the deduction allowable under this paragraph.

- IRC §404(a)(1)(D), as amended by Act §801(d)(1), was amended by Act §802(a). Eff. years beginning after Dec. 31, 2005. IRC §404(a)(1)(D) prior to amendment:

  > (D) Special rule in case of certain plans.—
  > (i) In General.—In the case of any defined benefit plan, except as provided in regulations, the maximum amount deductible under the limitations of this paragraph shall not be less than the unfunded current liability determined under section 412(*l*)(8)(A), except that section 412(*l*)(8)(A) shall be applied for purposes of this clause by substituting "150 percent (140 percent in the case of a multiemployer plan) of current liability" for the "current liability" in clause (i).
  > (ii) Plans with 100 or less participants.—For purposes of this subparagraph, in the case of a plan which has 100 or less participants for the plan year, unfunded current liability shall not include the liability attributable to benefit increases for highly compensated employees (as defined in section 414(q)) resulting from a plan amendment which is made or becomes effective, whichever is later, within the last 2 years.
  > (iii) Rule for determining number of participants.—For purposes of determining the number of plan participants, all defined benefit plans maintained by the same employer (or any member of such employer's controlled group (within the meaning of section 412(*l*)(8)(C)) shall be treated as one plan, but only employees of such member or employer shall be taken into account.
  > (iv) Special rule for terminating plans.—In the case of a plan which, subject to section 4041 of the Employee Retirement Income Security Act of 1974, terminates during the plan year, clause (i) shall be applied by substituting for unfunded current liability the amount required to make the plan sufficient for benefit liabilities (within the meaning of section 4041(d) of such Act).

- IRC §404(a)(7)(C) was amended by Act §803(a) by adding after cl. (ii) new cl. (iii). Eff. for contributions for tax years beginning after Dec. 31, 2005.

- IRC §404(a)(7)(C), as amended by the Act §803(a), was amended by Act §803(b) by adding new cl. (v). Eff. for contributions for tax years beginning after Dec. 31, 2005.

- IRC §404 was amended by Act §801(a)(2) by inserting new subsec. (o). Eff. years beginning after Dec. 31, 2007.

- **Sunset Provision.** Act §811, provides:

  > **SEC. 811. PENSIONS AND INDIVIDUAL RETIREMENT ARRANGEMENT PROVISIONS OF ECONOMIC GROWTH AND TAX RELIEF RECONCILIATION ACT OF 2001 MADE PERMANENT.**
  > Title IX of the Economic Growth and Tax Relief Reconciliation Act of 2001 [Pub. L. No. 107-16] shall not apply to the provisions of, and amendments made by, subtitles A through F [§§601–666] of title VI of such Act (relating to pension and individual retirement arrangement provisions).

Pension Funding Equity Act of 2004 (Pub. L. No. 108-218), as follows:

- IRC §404(a)(1) was amended by Act §101(b)(5) by adding new subpara. (F). Eff. plan years beginning after Dec. 31, 2003.

Job Creation and Worker Assistance Act of 2002 (Pub. L. No. 107-147), as follows:

- IRC §404(a)(12) was amended by Act §411(*l*)(1) by replacing "(9)," with "(9) and subsection (h)(1)(C),". Eff. years beginning after Dec. 31, 2001, as if included in the provision of Pub. L. No.107-16 to which it relates.

- IRC §404(a)(7)(C) was amended by Act §411(l)(4). Eff. for years beginning after Dec. 31, 2001, as if included in the provision of Pub. L. No. 107-16 to which it relates. IRC §404(a)(7)(C) prior to amendment:

  > (C) Paragraph not to apply in certain cases.—This paragraph shall not have the effect of reducing the amount otherwise deductible under paragraphs (1), (2), and (3), if no employee is a beneficiary under more than 1 trust or under a trust and an annuity plan.

- IRC §404(a)(1)(D)(iv) was amended by Act §411(s) by replacing "Plans maintained by professional service employers" with "Special rule for terminating plans". Eff. plan years beginning after Dec. 31, 2001, as if included in the provision of Pub. L. No. 107-16 to which it relates.

- IRC §404(k) was amended by Act §411(w)(1)(A)–(D) by striking "during the taxable year" before "with respect to" in para. (1), by striking "(A)(iii)", by inserting "(A)(iv)" in para. (2)(B), by replacing "(iii)" with "(iv)" in para. (4)(B), by redesignating subpara. (B) of para. (4) as subpara. (C) of para. (4), and by inserting new subpara. (B) after subpara. (A). Eff. tax years beginning after Dec. 31, 2001, as if included in the provision of Pub. L. No. 107-16 to which it relates.

- IRC §404(k) was amended by Act §411(w)(2) by adding a new para. (7). Eff. tax years beginning after Dec. 31, 2001, as if included in the provision of Pub. L. No. 107-16 to which it relates

- IRC §404(n) was amended by Act §411(*l*)(2) by substituting "subsection (a) or paragraph (1)(C) of subsection (h)" for "subsection (a)". Eff. for years beginning after Dec. 31, 2001, as if included in the provision of Pub. L. No. 107-16 to which it relates.

Economic Growth and Tax Relief Reconciliation Act of 2001 (Pub. L. No. 107-16), as follows:

- IRC §404(a)(1)(A) was amended by Act §616(a)(2)(B)(i) by inserting "(other than a trust to which paragraph (3) applies)" after "pension trust". Eff. for years beginning after Dec. 31, 2001.

- IRC §404(a)(3)(A)(i)(I) was amended by Act §616(a)(1)(A) by replacing "15 percent" with "25 percent". Eff. years beginning after Dec. 31, 2001.

- IRC §404(a)(3)(A)(v) was amended by Act §616(a)(2)(A). Eff. for years beginning after Dec. 31, 2001. IRC §404(a)(3)(A)(v) prior to amendment:

  > (v) Pre-87 limitation carryforwards.—
  > (I) In general.—The limitation of clause (i) for any taxable year shall be increased by the unused pre-87 limitation carryforwards (but not to an amount in excess of 25 percent of the compensation described in clause (i)).
  > (II) Unused pre-87 limitation carryforwards.—For purposes of subclause (I), the term "unused pre-87 limitation carryforwards" means the amount by which the limitation of the first sentence of this subparagraph (as in effect on the day before the date of the enactment of the Tax Reform Act of 1986) for any taxable year beginning before January 1, 1987, exceeded

the amount paid to the trust for such taxable year (to the extent such excess was not taken into account in prior taxable years).

- IRC §404(a)(1)(A) was amended by Act §616(a)(2)(B)(i) by inserting "(other than a trust to which paragraph (3) applies)" after "pension trust". Effective for years beginning after Dec. 31, 2001.
- IRC §404(a) was amended by Act §616(b)(1) by adding new para. (12). Eff. years beginning after Dec. 31, 2001.
- IRC §404(a)(3)(B) was amended by Act §616(b)(2)(A) by striking the last sentence. Eff. years beginning after Dec. 31, 2001. IRC §404(a)(3)(B), last sentence, prior to being stricken:

  The term "compensation otherwise paid or accrued during the taxable year to all employees" shall include any amount with respect to which an election under section 415(c)(3)(C) is in effect, but only to the extent that any contribution with respect to such amount is nonforfeitable.

- IRC §404(a)(10)(B) was amended by Act §632(a)(3)(B) by striking ", the exclusion allowance under §403(b)(2)," after "§402(g),". Eff. years beginning after Dec. 31, 2001.
- IRC §404(a)(1)(D) was amended by Act §652(a). Eff. for plan years beginning after Dec. 31, 2001. IRC §404(a)(1)(D) prior to amendment:

  (D) Special rule in case of certain plans.—In the case of any defined benefit plan (other than a multiemployer plan) which has more than 100 participants for the plan year, except as provided in regulations, the maximum amount deductible under the limitations of this paragraph shall not be less than the unfunded current liability determined under section 412(*l*). For purposes of determining whether a plan has more than 100 participants, all defined benefit plans maintained by the same employer (or any member of such employer's controlled group (within the meaning of section 412(*l*)(8)(C)) shall be treated as 1 plan, but only employees of such member or employer shall be taken into account.

- IRC §404(h)(1)(C) was amended by Act §616(a)(1)(B) by replacing "15 percent", each place it appeared, with "25 percent". Eff. years beginning after Dec. 31, 2001.
- IRC §404(h)(2) was amended by Act §616(a)(2)(B)(ii) by replacing "stock bonus or profit-sharing trust" with "trust subject to subsection (a)(3)(A)". Eff. years beginning after Dec. 31, 2001.
- IRC §404(h)(2) was amended in the heading by Act §616(a)(2)(B)(iii) by replacing "Stock bonus and profit-sharing trust" with "Certain trusts". Eff. years beginning after Dec. 31, 2001.
- IRC §404(k)(2)(A) was amended by Act §662(a) by striking "or" at the end of cl. (ii), by redesignating cl. (iii) as cl. (iv), and by inserting after cl. (ii) new cl. (iii). Eff. tax years beginning after Dec. 31, 2001.
- IRC §404(k)(5)(A) was amended by Act §662(b) by inserting "avoidance or" before "evasion". Eff. tax years beginning after Dec. 31, 2001.
- IRC §404(l) was amended by Act §611(c)(1) by substituting "$200,000" for "$150,000" each place it appeared. Eff. years beginning after Dec. 31, 2001. See Act §611(i)(3) for a special rule.
- IRC §404 was amended by Act §614(a) by adding new subsec. (n). Eff. years beginning after Dec. 31, 2001.
- **Sunset Provision.** Act §901, as amended by Pub. L. No. 111-312, §101(a)(1), provides the sunset rule below. But see Pub. L. No. 109-280, §811, and Pub. L. No. 111-148, §10909(c), as amended by Pub. L. No. 111-312, §101(b)(1).

  SEC. 901. SUNSET OF PROVISIONS OF ACT.

  (a) In general. All provisions of, and amendments made by, this Act shall not apply—

  (1) to taxable, plan, or limitation years beginning after December 31, 2012, or

  (2) in the case of title V, to estates of decedents dying, gifts made, or generation skipping transfers, after December 31, 2012.

  (b) Application of certain laws.—The Internal Revenue Code of 1986 and the Employee Retirement Income Security Act of 1974 shall be applied and administered to years, estates, gifts, and transfers described in subsection (a) as if the

provisions and amendments described in subsection (a) had never been enacted.

SEC. 404A. DEDUCTION FOR CERTAIN FOREIGN DEFERRED COMPENSATION PLANS.

(a) General Rule.—Amounts paid or accrued by an employer under a qualified foreign plan—

(1) shall not be allowable as a deduction under this chapter, but

(2) if they would otherwise be deductible, shall be allowed as a deduction under this section for the taxable year for which such amounts are properly taken into account under this section.

(b) Rules for Qualified Funded Plans.—For purposes of this section—

(1) In general.—Except as otherwise provided in this section, in the case of a qualified funded plan contributions are properly taken into account for the taxable year in which paid.

(2) Payment after close of taxable year.—For purposes of paragraph (1), a payment made after the close of a taxable year shall be treated as made on the last day of such year if the payment is made—

(A) on account of such year, and

(B) not later than the time prescribed by law for filing the return for such year (including extensions thereof).

(3) Limitations.—In the case of a qualified funded plan, the amount allowable as a deduction for the taxable year shall be subject to—

(A) in the case of—

(i) a plan under which the benefits are fixed or determinable, limitations similar to those contained in clauses (ii) and (iii) of subparagraph (A) of section 404(a)(1) (determined without regard to the last sentence of such subparagraph (A)), or

(ii) any other plan, limitations similar to the limitations contained in paragraph (3) of section 404(a), and

(B) limitations similar to those contained in paragraph (7) of section 404(a).

(4) Carryover.—If—

(A) the aggregate of the contributions paid during the taxable year reduced by any contributions not allowable as a deduction under paragraphs (1) and (2) of subsection (g), exceeds

(B) the amount allowable as a deduction under subsection (a) (determined without regard to subsection (d)),

such excess shall be treated as an amount paid in the succeeding taxable year.

IRC Sec. 404A(b)(4)(B)

(5) Amounts must be paid to qualified trust, etc.—In the case of a qualified funded plan, a contribution shall be taken into account only if it is paid—

(A) to a trust (or the equivalent of a trust) which meets the requirements of section 401(a)(2),

(B) for a retirement annuity, or

(C) to a participant or beneficiary.

(c) Rules Relating to Qualified Reserve Plans.—For purposes of this section—

(1) In general.—In the case of a qualified reserve plan, the amount properly taken into account for the taxable year is the reasonable addition for such year to a reserve for the taxpayer's liability under the plan. Unless otherwise required or permitted in regulations prescribed by the Secretary, the reserve for the taxpayer's liability shall be determined under the unit credit method modified to reflect the requirements of paragraphs (3) and (4). All benefits paid under the plan shall be charged to the reserve.

(2) Income item.—In the case of a plan which is or has been a qualified reserve plan, an amount equal to that portion of any decrease for the taxable year in the reserve which is not attributable to the payment of benefits shall be included in gross income.

(3) Rights must be nonforfeitable, etc.—In the case of a qualified reserve plan, an item shall be taken into account for a taxable year only if—

(A) there is no substantial risk that the rights of the employee will be forfeited, and

(B) such item meets such additional requirements as the Secretary may by regulations prescribe as necessary or appropriate to ensure that the liability will be satisfied.

(4) Spreading of certain increases and decreases in reserves.—There shall be amortized over a 10-year period any increase or decrease to the reserve on account of—

(A) the adoption of the plan or a plan amendment,

(B) experience gains and losses, and

(C) any change in actuarial assumptions,

(D) changes in the interest rate under subsection (g)(3)(B), and

(E) such other factors as may be prescribed by regulations.

(d) Amounts Taken Into Account Must Be Consistent With Amounts Allowed Under Foreign Law.—

(1) General rule.—In the case of any plan, the amount allowed as a deduction under subsection (a) for any taxable year shall equal—

(A) the lesser of—

(i) the cumulative United States amount, or

(ii) the cumulative foreign amount, reduced by

(B) the aggregate amount determined under this section for all prior taxable years.

(2) Cumulative amounts defined.—For purposes of paragraph (1)—

(A) Cumulative United States amount.—The term "cumulative United States amount" means the aggregate amount determined with respect to the plan under this section for the taxable year and for all prior taxable years to which this section applies. Such determination shall be made for each taxable year without regard to the application of paragraph (1).

(B) Cumulative foreign amount.—The term "cumulative foreign amount" means the aggregate amount allowed as a deduction under the appropriate foreign tax laws for the taxable year and all prior taxable years to which this section applies.

(3) Effect on earnings and profits, etc.—In determining the earnings and profits and accumulated profits of any foreign corporation with respect to a qualified foreign plan, except as provided in regulations, the amount determined under paragraph (1) with respect to any plan for any taxable year shall in no event exceed the amount allowed as a deduction under the appropriate foreign tax laws for such taxable year.

(e) Qualified Foreign Plan.—For purposes of this section, the term "qualified foreign plan" means any written plan of an employer for deferring the receipt of compensation but only if—

(1) such plan is for the exclusive benefit of the employer's employees or their beneficiaries,

(2) 90 percent or more of the amounts taken into account for the taxable year under the plan are attributable to services—

(A) performed by nonresident aliens, and

(B) the compensation for which is not subject to tax under this chapter, and

(3) the employer elects (at such time and in such manner as the Secretary shall by regulations prescribe) to have this section apply to such plan.

(f) Funded and Reserve Plans.—For purposes of this section—

(1) Qualified funded plan.—The term "qualified funded plan" means a qualified foreign plan which is not a qualified reserve plan.

(2) Qualified reserve plan.—The term "qualified reserve plan" means a qualified foreign plan with respect to which an election made by the taxpayer is in effect for the taxable year. An election under the preceding sentence shall be made in such manner and form as the Secretary may by regulations prescribe and, once made, may be revoked only with the consent of the Secretary.

(g) Other Special Rules.—

(1) No deduction for certain amounts.—Except as provided in section 404(a)(5), no deduction shall be allowed under this section for any item to the extent such item is attributable to services—

(A) performed by a citizen or resident of the United States who is a highly compensated employee (within the meaning of section 414(q)), or

(B) performed in the United States the compensation for which is subject to tax under this chapter.

(2) Taxpayer must furnish information.—

(A) In general.—No deduction shall be allowed under this section with respect to any plan for any taxable year unless the taxpayer furnishes to the Secretary with respect to such plan (at such time as the Secretary may by regulations prescribe)—

(i) a statement from the foreign tax authorities specifying the amount of the deduction allowed in computing taxable income under foreign law for such year with respect to such plan,

(ii) if the return under foreign tax law shows the deduction for plan contributions or reserves as a separate, identifiable item, a copy of the foreign tax return for the taxable year, or

(iii) such other statement, return, or other evidence as the Secretary prescribes by regulation as being sufficient to establish the amount of the deduction under foreign law.

(B) Redetermination where foreign tax deduction is adjusted.—If the deduction under foreign tax law is adjusted, the taxpayers shall notify the Secretary of such adjustment on or before the date prescribed by regulations, and the Secretary shall redetermine the amount of the tax year or years affected. In any case described in the preceding sentence, rules similar to the rules of subsection (c) of section 905 shall apply.

(3) Actuarial assumptions must be reasonable; full funding.—

(A) In general.—Except as provided in subparagraph (B), principles similar to those set forth in paragraphs (3) and (6) of section 431(c) shall apply for purposes of this section.

(B) Interest rate for reserve plan.—

(i) In general.—In the case of a qualified reserve plan, in lieu of taking rates of interest into account under subparagraph (A), the rate of interest for the plan shall be the rate selected by the taxpayer which is within the permissible range.

(ii) Rate remains in effect so long as it falls within permissible range.—Any rate selected by the taxpayer for the plan under this subparagraph shall remain in effect for such plan until the first taxable year for which such rate is no longer within the permissible range. At such time, the taxpayer shall select a new rate of interest which is within the permissible range applicable at such time.

(iii) Permissible range.—For purposes of this subparagraph, the term "permissible range" means a rate of interest which is not more than 20 percent above, and not more than 20 percent below, the average rate of interest for long-term corporate bonds in the appropriate country for the 15-year period ending on the last day before the beginning of the taxable year.

(4) Accounting method.—Any change in the method (but not the actuarial assumptions) used to determine the amount allowed as a deduction under subsection (a) shall be treated as a change in accounting method under section 446(e).

(5) Section 481 applies to election.—For purposes of section 481, any election under this section shall be treated as a change in the taxpayer's method of accounting. In applying section 481 with respect to any such election, the period for taking into account any increase or decrease in accumulated profits, earnings and profits or taxable income resulting from the application of section 481(a)(2) shall be the year for which the election is made and the fourteen succeeding years.

(h) Regulations.—The Secretary shall prescribe such regulations as may be necessary to carry out the purposes of this section (including regulations providing for the coordination of the provisions of this section with section 404 in the case of a plan which has been subject to both of such sections).

Recent Amendments to IRC §404A

Pension Protection Act of 2006 (Pub. L. No. 109-280), as follows:
● IRC §404A(g)(3)(A) was amended by Act §801(c)(4) by substituting "paragraphs (3) and (6) of §431(c)" for "paragraphs (3) and (7) of §412(c)". Eff. years beginning after Dec. 31, 2007.

SEC. 405. QUALIFIED BOND PURCHASE PLANS. [REPEALED.]

SEC. 406. EMPLOYEES OF FOREIGN AFFILIATES COVERED BY SECTION 3121(*l*) AGREEMENTS.

(a) Treatment as Employees of American Employer.—For purposes of applying this part with respect to a pension, profit-sharing, or stock bonus plan described in section 401(a) or an annuity plan described in section 403(a) of an American employer (as defined in section 3121(h)), an individual who is a citizen or resident of the United States and who is an employee of a foreign affiliate (as defined in section 3121(*l*)(8)[(6)]) of such American employer shall be treated as an employee of such an American employer, if—

(1) such American employer has entered into an agreement under section 3121(*l*) which applies to the foreign affiliate of which such individual is an employee;

(2) the plan of such American employer expressly provides for contributions or benefits for individuals who are citizens or residents of the United States and who are employees of its foreign affiliates to which an agreement entered into by such American employer under section 3121(*l*) applies; and

(3) contributions under a funded plan of deferred compensation (whether or not a plan described in section 401(a) or 403(a)) are not provided by any other person with respect to the remuneration paid to such individual by the foreign affiliate.

(b) Special Rules for Application of Section 401(a).—

(1) Nondiscrimination requirements.—For purposes of applying section 401(a)(4) and section 410(b) with respect to an individual who is treated as an employee of an American employer under subsection (a)—

(A) if such individual is a highly compensated employee (within the meaning of section 414(q)), he shall be treated as having such capacity with respect to such American employer; and

(B) the determination of whether such individual is a highly compensated employee (as so defined) shall be made by treating such individual's total compensation (determined with the application of paragraph (2) of this subsection) as compensation paid by such American employer and by determining such individual's status with regard to such American employer.

(2) Determination of compensation.—For purposes of applying paragraph (5) of section 401(a) with respect to an individual who is treated as an employee of an American employer under subsection (a)—

(A) the total compensation of such individual shall be the remuneration paid to such individual by the foreign affiliate which would constitute his total compensation if his services had been performed for such American employer, and the basic or regular rate of compensation of such individual shall be determined under regulations prescribed by the Secretary; and

(B) such individual shall be treated as having paid the amount paid by such American employer which is equivalent to the tax imposed by section 3101.

(c) [Repealed.]

(d) Deductibility of Contributions.—For purposes of applying section 404 with respect to contributions made to or under a pension, profit-sharing, stock bonus, or annuity plan by an American employer, or by another taxpayer which is entitled to deduct its contributions under section 404(a)(3)(B), on behalf of an individual who is treated as an employee of such American employer under subsection (a)—

(1) except as provided in paragraph (2), no deduction shall be allowed to such American employer or to any other taxpayer which is entitled to deduct its contributions under such sections,

(2) there shall be allowed as a deduction to the foreign affiliate of which such individual is an employee an amount equal to the amount which (but for paragraph (1)) would be deductible under section 404 by the American employer if he were an employee of the American employer, and

(3) any reference to compensation shall be considered to be a reference to the total compensation of such individual (determined with the application of subsection (b)(2)).

Any amount deductible by a foreign affiliate under this subsection shall be deductible for its taxable year with or within which the taxable year of such American employer ends.

(e) Treatment as Employee Under Related Provisions.—An individual who is treated as an employee of an American employer under subsection (a) shall also be treated as an employee of such American employer, with respect to the plan described in subsection (a)(2), for purposes of applying the following provisions of this title:

(1) Section 72(f) (relating to special rules for computing employees' contributions).

(2) Section 2039 (relating to annuities).

SEC. 407. CERTAIN EMPLOYEES OF DOMESTIC SUBSIDIARIES ENGAGED IN BUSINESS OUTSIDE THE UNITED STATES.

(a) Treatment as Employees of Domestic Parent Corporation.—

(1) In general.—For purpose of applying this part with respect to a pension, profit-sharing, or stock bonus plan described in section 401(a) or an annuity plan described in section 403(a) of a domestic parent corporation, an individual who is a citizen or resident of the United States and who is an employee of a domestic subsidiary (within the meaning of paragraph (2)) of such domestic parent corporation shall be treated as an employee of such domestic parent corporation, if—

(A) the plan of such domestic parent corporation expressly provides for contributions or benefits for individuals who are citizens or residents of the United States and who are employees of its domestic subsidiaries; and

(B) contributions under a funded plan of deferred compensation (whether or not a plan described in section 401(a) or 403(a)) are not provided by any other person with respect to the remuneration paid to such individual by the domestic subsidiary.

(2) Definitions.—For purposes of this section—

(A) Domestic subsidiary.—A corporation shall be treated as a domestic subsidiary for any taxable year only if—

(i) such corporation is a domestic corporation 80 percent or more of the outstanding voting stock of which is owned by another domestic corporation;

(ii) 95 percent or more of its gross income for the three-year period immediately preceding the close of its taxable year which ends on or before the close of the taxable year of such other domestic corporation (or for such part of such period during which the corporation was in existence) was derived from sources without the United States; and

(iii) 90 percent or more of its gross income for such period (or such part) was derived from the active conduct of a trade or business.

If for the period (or part thereof) referred to in clauses (ii) and (iii) such corporation has no gross income, the provisions of clauses (ii) and (iii) shall be treated as satisfied if it is reasonable to anticipate that, with respect to the first taxable year thereafter for which such corporation has gross income, the provisions of such clauses will be satisfied.

(B) Domestic parent corporation.—The domestic parent corporation of any domestic subsidiary is the domestic corporation which owns 80 percent or more of the outstanding voting stock of such domestic subsidiary.

(b) Special Rules for Application of section 401(a).—

(1) Nondiscrimination requirements.—For purposes of applying section 401(a)(4) and section 410(b) with respect to an individual who is treated as an employee of a domestic parent corporation under subsection (a)—

(A) if such individual is a highly compensated employee (within the meaning of section 414(q)), he shall be treated as having such capacity with respect to such domestic parent corporation; and

(B) the determination of whether such individual is a highly compensated employee (as so defined) shall be made by treating such individual's total compensation (determined with the application of paragraph (2) of this subsection) as compensation paid by such domestic parent corporation and by determining such individual's status with regard to such domestic parent corporation.

(2) Determination of compensation.—For purposes of applying paragraph (5) of section 401(a) with respect to an individual who is treated as an employee of a domestic parent corporation under subsection (a), the total compensation of such individual shall be the remuneration paid to such individual by the domestic subsidiary which would constitute his total compensation if his services had been performed for such domestic parent corporation, and the basic or regular rate of compensation of such individual shall be determined under regulations prescribed by the Secretary.

(c) [Repealed.]

(d) Deductibility of Contributions.—For purposes of applying section 404 with respect to contributions made to or under a pension, profit-sharing, stock bonus, or annuity plan by a domestic parent corporation, or by another corporation which is entitled to deduct its contributions under section 404(a)(3)(B), on behalf of an individual who is treated as an employee of such domestic corporation under subsection (a)—

(1) except as provided in paragraph (2), no deduction shall be allowed to such domestic parent corporation or to any other corporation which is entitled to deduct its contributions under such sections,

(2) there shall be allowed as a deduction to the domestic subsidiary of which such individual is an employee an amount equal to the amount which (but for paragraph (1)) would be deductible under section 404 by the domestic parent corporation if he were an employee of the domestic parent corporation, and

(3) any reference to compensation shall be considered to be a reference to the total compensation of such individual (determined with the application of subsection (b)(2)).

Any amount deductible by a domestic subsidiary under this subsection shall be deductible for its taxable year with or within which the taxable year of such domestic parent corporation ends.

(e) Treatment as Employee Under Related Provisions.—An individual who is treated as an employee of a domestic parent corporation under subsection (a) shall also be treated as an employee of such domestic parent corporation, with respect to the plan described in subsection (a)(1)(A), for purposes of applying the following provisions of this title:

(1) Section 72(f) (relating to special rules for computing employees' contributions).

(2) Section 2039 (relating to annuities).

SEC. 408. INDIVIDUAL RETIREMENT ACCOUNTS.

(a) Individual Retirement Account.—For purposes of this section, the term "individual retirement account" means a trust created or organized in the United States for the exclusive benefit of an individual or his beneficiaries, but only if the written governing instrument creating the trust meets the following requirements:

IRC Sec. 408(a)

(1) Except in the case of a rollover contribution described in subsection (d)(3), in section 402(c), 403(a)(4), 403(b)(8), or 457(e)(16), no contribution will be accepted unless it is in cash, and contributions will not be accepted for the taxable year on behalf of any individual in excess of the amount in effect for such taxable year under section 219(b)(1)(A).

(2) The trustee is a bank (as defined in subsection (n)) or such other person who demonstrates to the satisfaction of the Secretary that the manner in which such other person will administer the trust will be consistent with the requirements of this section.

(3) No part of the trust funds will be invested in life insurance contracts.

(4) The interest of an individual in the balance in his account is nonforfeitable.

(5) The assets of the trust will not be commingled with other property except in a common trust fund or common investment fund.

(6) Under regulations prescribed by the Secretary, rules similar to the rules of section 401(a)(9) and the incidental death benefit requirements of section 401(a) shall apply to the distribution of the entire interest of an individual for whose benefit the trust is maintained.

(b) Individual Retirement Annuity.—For purposes of this section, the term "individual retirement annuity" means an annuity contract, or an endowment contract (as determined under regulations prescribed by the Secretary), issued by an insurance company which meets the following requirements:

(1) The contract is not transferable by the owner.

(2) Under the contract—

(A) the premiums are not fixed,

(B) the annual premium on behalf of any individual will not exceed the dollar amount in effect under section 219(b)(1)(A), and

(C) any refund of premiums will be applied before the close of the calendar year following the year of the refund toward the payment of future premiums or the purchase of additional benefits.

(3) Under regulations prescribed by the Secretary, rules similar to the rules of section 401(a)(9) and the incidental death benefit requirements of section 401(a) shall apply to the distribution of the entire interest of the owner.

(4) The entire interest of the owner is nonforfeitable.

Such term does not include such an annuity contract for any taxable year of the owner in which it is disqualified on the application of subsection (e) or for any subsequent taxable year. For purposes of this subsection, no contract shall be treated as an endowment contract if it matures later than the taxable year

in which the individual in whose name such contract is purchased attains age 70½; if it is not for the exclusive benefit of the individual in whose name it is purchased or his beneficiaries; or if the aggregate annual premiums under all such contracts purchased in the name of such individual for any taxable year exceed the dollar amount in effect under section 219(b)(1)(A).

(c) Accounts Established by Employers and Certain Associations of Employees.—A trust created or organized in the United States by an employer for the exclusive benefit of his employees or their beneficiaries, or by an association of employees (which may include employees within the meaning of section 401(c)(1)) for the exclusive benefit of its members or their beneficiaries, shall be treated as an individual retirement account (described in subsection (a)), but only if the written governing instrument creating the trust meets the following requirements:

(1) The trust satisfies the requirements of paragraphs (1) through (6) of subsection (a).

(2) There is a separate accounting for the interest of each employee or member (or spouse of an employee or member).

The assets of the trust may be held in a common fund for the account of all individuals who have an interest in the trust.

(d) Tax Treatment of Distributions.—

(1) In general.—Except as otherwise provided in this subsection, any amount paid or distributed out of an individual retirement plan shall be included in gross income by the payee or distributee, as the case may be, in the manner provided under section 72.

(2) Special rules for applying section 72.—For purposes of applying section 72 to any amount described in paragraph (1)—

(A) all individual retirement plans shall be treated as 1 contract,

(B) all distributions during any taxable year shall be treated as 1 distribution, and

(C) the value of the contract, income on the contract, and investment in the contract shall be computed as of the close of the calendar year in which the taxable year begins.

For purposes of subparagraph (C), the value of the contract shall be increased by the amount of any distributions during the calendar year.

(3) Rollover contribution.—An amount is described in this paragraph as a rollover contribution if it meets the requirements of subparagraphs (A) and (B).

(A) In general.—Paragraph (1) does not apply to any amount paid or distributed out of an individual retirement account or individual retirement annuity to the individual for whose benefit the account or annuity is maintained if—

(i) the entire amount received (including money and any other property) is paid into an individual retirement account or individual retirement annuity (other than an endowment contract) for the benefit of such individual not later than the 60th day after the day on which he receives the payment or distribution; or

(ii) the entire amount received (including money and any other property) is paid into an eligible retirement plan for the benefit of such individual not later than the 60th day after the date on which the payment or distribution is received, except that the maximum amount which may be paid into such plan may not exceed the portion of the amount received which is includible in gross income (determined without regard to this paragraph).

For purposes of clause (ii), the term "eligible retirement plan" means an eligible retirement plan described in clause (iii), (iv), (v) or (vi) of section 402(c)(8)(B).

(B) Limitation.—This paragraph does not apply to any amount described in subparagraph (A)(i) received by an individual from an individual retirement account or individual retirement annuity if at any time during the 1-year period ending on the day of such receipt such individual received any other amount described in that subparagraph from an individual retirement account or an individual retirement annuity which was not includible in his gross income because of the application of this paragraph.

(C) Denial of rollover treatment for inherited accounts, etc.—

(i) In general.—In the case of an inherited individual retirement account or individual retirement annuity—

(I) this paragraph shall not apply to any amount received by an individual from such an account or annuity (and no amount transferred from such account or annuity to another individual retirement account or annuity shall be excluded from gross income by reason of such transfer), and

(II) such inherited account or annuity shall not be treated as an individual retirement account or annuity for purposes of determining whether any other amount is a rollover contribution.

(ii) Inherited individual retirement account or annuity.—An individual retirement account or individual retirement annuity shall be treated as inherited if—

(I) the individual for whose benefit the account or annuity is maintained acquired such account by reason of the death of another individual, and

(II) such individual was not the surviving spouse of such other individual.

(D) Partial rollovers permitted.—

(i) In general.—If any amount paid or distributed out of an individual retirement account or individual retirement annuity would meet the requirements of subparagraph (A) but for the fact that the entire amount was not paid into an eligible plan as required by clause (i) or (ii) of subparagraph (A), such amount shall be treated as meeting the requirements of subparagraph (A) to the extent it is paid into an eligible plan referred to in such clause not later than the 60th day referred to in such clause.

(ii) Eligible plan.—For purposes of clause (i), the term "eligible plan" means any account, annuity, contract, or plan referred to in subparagraph (A).

(E) Denial of rollover treatment for required distributions.—This paragraph shall not apply to any amount to the extent such amount is required to be distributed under subsection (a)(6) or (b)(3).

(F) Frozen deposits.—For purposes of this paragraph, rules similar to the rules of section 402(c)(7) (relating to frozen deposits) shall apply.

(G) Simple retirement accounts.—In the case of any payment or distribution out of a simple retirement account (as defined in subsection (p)) to which section 72(t)(6) applies, this paragraph shall not apply unless such payment or distribution is paid into another simple retirement account.

(H) Application of section 72.—

(i) In general.—If—

(I) a distribution is made from an individual retirement plan, and

(II) a rollover contribution is made to an eligible retirement plan described in section 402(c)(8)(B)(iii), (iv), (v), or (vi) with respect to all or part of such distribution, then, notwithstanding paragraph (2), the rules of clause (ii) shall apply for purposes of applying section 72.

(ii) Applicable rules.—In the case of a distribution described in clause (i)—

(I) Section 72 shall be applied separately to such distribution,

(II) notwithstanding the pro rata allocation of income on, and investment in, the contract to distributions under section 72, the portion of such distribution rolled over to an eligible retirement plan described in clause (i) shall be treated as from income on the contract (to the extent of the aggregate income on the contract from all individual retirement plans of the distributee), and

(III) appropriate adjustments shall be made in applying section 72 to other distributions in such taxable year and subsequent taxable years.

IRC Sec. 408(d)(3)(H)(ii)(III)

(I) Waiver of 60-day requirement.—The Secretary may waive the 60-day requirement under subparagraphs (A) and (D) where the failure to waive such requirement would be against equity or good conscience, including casualty, disaster, or other events beyond the reasonable control of the individual subject to such requirement.

(4) Contributions returned before due date of return.—Paragraph (1) does not apply to the distribution of any contribution paid during a taxable year to an individual retirement account or for an individual retirement annuity if—

(A) such distribution is received on or before the day prescribed by law (including extensions of time) for filing such individual's return for such taxable year,

(B) no deduction is allowed under section 219 with respect to such contribution, and

(C) such distribution is accompanied by the amount of net income attributable to such contribution.

In the case of such a distribution, for purposes of section 61, any net income described in subparagraph (C) shall be deemed to have been earned and receivable in the taxable year in which such contribution is made.

(5) Distributions of excess contributions after due date for taxable year and certain excess rollover contributions.—

(A) In general.—In the case of any individual, if the aggregate contributions (other than rollover contributions) paid for any taxable year to an individual retirement account or for an individual retirement annuity do not exceed the dollar amount in effect under section 219(b)(1)(A), paragraph (1) shall not apply to the distribution of any such contribution to the extent that such contribution exceeds the amount allowable as a deduction under section 219 for the taxable year for which the contribution was paid—

(i) if such distribution is received after the date described in paragraph (4),

(ii) but only to the extent that no deduction has been allowed under section 219 with respect to such excess contribution.

If employer contributions on behalf of the individual are paid for the taxable year to a simplified employee pension, the dollar limitation of the preceding sentence shall be increased by the lesser of the amount of such contributions or the dollar limitation in effect under section 415(c)(1)(A) for such taxable year.

(B) Excess rollover contributions attributable to erroneous information.—If—

(i) the taxpayer reasonably relies on information supplied pursuant to subtitle F for determining the amount of a rollover contribution, but

(ii) the information was erroneous,

subparagraph (A) shall be applied by increasing the dollar limit set forth therein by that portion of the excess contribution which was attributable to such information.

For purposes of this paragraph, the amount allowable as a deduction under section 219 shall be computed without regard to section 219(g).

(6) Transfer of account incident to divorce.—The transfer of an individual's interest in an individual retirement account or an individual retirement annuity to his spouse or former spouse under a divorce or separation instrument described in subparagraph (A) of section 71(b)(2) is not to be considered a taxable transfer made by such individual notwithstanding any other provision of this subtitle, and such interest at the time of the transfer is to be treated as an individual retirement account of such spouse, and not of such individual. Thereafter such account or annuity for purposes of this subtitle is to be treated as maintained for the benefit of such spouse.

(7) Special rules for simplified employee pensions or simple retirement accounts.—

(A) Transfer or rollover of contributions prohibited until deferral test met.—Notwithstanding any other provision of this subsection or section 72(t), paragraph (1) and section 72(t)(1) shall apply to the transfer or distribution from a simplified employee pension of any contribution under a salary reduction arrangement described in subsection (k)(6) (or any income allocable thereto) before a determination as to whether the requirements of subsection (k)(6)(A)(iii) are met with respect to such contribution.

(B) Certain exclusions treated as deductions.—For purposes of paragraphs (4) and (5) and section 4973, any amount excludable or excluded from gross income under section 402(h) or 402(k) shall be treated as an amount allowable or allowed as a deduction under section 219.

(8) Distributions for charitable purposes.—

(A) In general.—So much of the aggregate amount of qualified charitable distributions with respect to a taxpayer made during any taxable year which does not exceed $100,000 shall not be includible in gross income of such taxpayer for such taxable year.

(B) Qualified charitable distribution.—For purposes of this paragraph, the term "qualified charitable distribution" means any distribution from an individual retirement plan (other than a plan described in subsection (k) or (p))—

(i) which is made directly by the trustee to an organization described in section 170(b)(1)(A) (other than any organization described in section 509(a)(3) or any fund or account described in section 4966(d)(2)), and

(ii) which is made on or after the date that the individual for whose benefit the plan is maintained has attained age 70½.

A distribution shall be treated as a qualified charitable distribution only to the extent that the distribution would be includible in gross income without regard to subparagraph (A).

(C) Contributions must be otherwise deductible.—For purposes of this paragraph, a distribution to an organization described in subparagraph (B)(i) shall be treated as a qualified charitable distribution only if a deduction for the entire distribution would be allowable under section 170 (determined without regard to subsection (b) thereof and this paragraph).

(D) Application of section 72.—Notwithstanding section 72, in determining the extent to which a distribution is a qualified charitable distribution, the entire amount of the distribution shall be treated as includible in gross income without regard to subparagraph (A) to the extent that such amount does not exceed the aggregate amount which would have been so includible if all amounts in all individual retirement plans of the individual were distributed during such taxable year and all such plans were treated as 1 contract for purposes of determining under section 72 the aggregate amount which would have been so includible. Proper adjustments shall be made in applying section 72 to other distributions in such taxable year and subsequent taxable years.

(E) Denial of deduction.—Qualified charitable distributions which are not includible in gross income pursuant to subparagraph (A) shall not be taken into account in determining the deduction under section 170.

Editor's Note

IRC §408(d)(8)(F), below, was amended by Pub. L. No. 111-312, generally applicable to distributions made in taxable years beginning after December 31, 2009. See the amendments notes to this section for Pub. L. No. 111-312, for a special effective date provision.

(F) Termination.—This paragraph shall not apply to distributions made in taxable years beginning after ~~December 31, 2009~~ *December 31, 2011.*

(9) Distribution for health savings account funding.—

(A) In general.—In the case of an individual who is an eligible individual (as defined in section 223(c)) and who elects the application of this paragraph for a taxable year, gross income of the individual for the taxable year does not include a qualified HSA funding distribution to the extent such distribution is otherwise includible in gross income.

(B) Qualified HSA funding distribution.—For purposes of this paragraph, the term "qualified HSA funding distribution" means a distribution from an individual retirement plan (other than a plan described in subsection (k) or (p)) of the employee to the extent that such distribution is contributed to the health savings account of the individual in a direct trustee-to-trustee transfer.

(C) Limitations.—

(i) Maximum dollar limitation.—The amount excluded from gross income by subparagraph (A) shall not exceed the excess of—

(I) the annual limitation under section 223(b) computed on the basis of the type of coverage under the high deductible health plan covering the individual at the time of the qualified HSA funding distribution, over

(II) in the case of a distribution described in clause (ii)(II), the amount of the earlier qualified HSA funding distribution.

(ii) One-time transfer.—

(I) In general.—Except as provided in subclause (II), an individual may make an election under subparagraph (A) only for one qualified HSA funding distribution during the lifetime of the individual. Such an election, once made, shall be irrevocable.

(II) Conversion from self-only to family coverage.—If a qualified HSA funding distribution is made during a month in a taxable year during which an individual has self-only coverage under a high deductible health plan as of the first day of the month, the individual may elect to make an additional qualified HSA funding distribution during a subsequent month in such taxable year during which the individual has family coverage under a high deductible health plan as of the first day of the subsequent month.

(D) Failure to maintain high deductible health plan coverage.—

(i) In general.—If, at any time during the testing period, the individual is not an eligible individual, then the aggregate amount of all contributions to the health savings account of the individual made under subparagraph (A)—

(I) shall be includible in the gross income of the individual for the taxable year in which occurs the first month in the testing period for which such individual is not an eligible individual, and

(II) the tax imposed by this chapter for any taxable year on the individual shall be increased by 10 percent of the amount which is so includible.

(ii) Exception for disability or death.—Subclauses (I) and (II) of clause (i) shall not apply if the individual ceased to be an eligible individual by reason of the death of the individual or the individual becoming disabled (within the meaning of section 72(m)(7)).

(iii) Testing period.—The term "testing period" means the period beginning with the month in which the qualified HSA funding distribution is contributed to a health savings account and ending on the last day of the 12th month following such month.

(E) Application of section 72.—Notwithstanding section 72, in determining the extent to which an amount is treated as otherwise includible in gross income for purposes of subparagraph (A), the aggregate amount distributed from an individual retirement plan shall be treated as includible in gross income to the extent that such amount does not exceed the aggregate amount which would have been so includible if all amounts from all individual retirement plans were distributed. Proper adjustments shall be made in applying section 72 to other distributions in such taxable year and subsequent taxable years.

(e) Tax Treatment of Accounts and Annuities.—

(1) Exemption from tax.—Any individual retirement account is exempt from taxation under this subtitle unless such account has ceased to be an individual retirement account by reason of paragraph (2) or (3). Notwithstanding the preceding sentence, any such account is subject to the taxes imposed by section 511 (relating to imposition of tax on unrelated business income of charitable, etc. organizations).

(2) Loss of exemption of account where employee engages in prohibited transaction.—

(A) In general.—If, during any taxable year of the individual for whose benefit any individual retirement account is established, that individual or his beneficiary engages in any transaction prohibited by section 4975 with respect to such account, such account ceases to be an individual retirement account as of the first day of such taxable year. For purposes of this paragraph—

(i) the individual for whose benefit any account was established is treated as the creator of such account, and

(ii) the separate account for any individual within an individual retirement account maintained by an employer or association of employees is treated as a separate individual retirement account.

(B) Account treated as distributing all its assets.—In any case in which any account ceases to be an individual retirement account by reason of subparagraph (A) as of the first day of any taxable

year, paragraph (1) of subsection (d) applies as if there were a distribution on such first day in an amount equal to the fair market value (on such first day) of all assets in the account (on such first day).

(3) Effect of borrowing on annuity contract.—If during any taxable year the owner of an individual retirement annuity borrows any money under or by use of such contract, the contract ceases to be an individual retirement annuity as of the first day of such taxable year. Such owner shall include in gross income for such year an amount equal to the fair market value of such contract as of such first day.

(4) Effect of pledging account as security.—If, during any taxable year of the individual for whose benefit an individual retirement account is established, that individual uses the account or any portion thereof as security for a loan, the portion so used is treated as distributed to that individual.

(5) Purchase of endowment contract by individual retirement account.—If the assets of an individual retirement account or any part of such assets are used to purchase an endowment contract for the benefit of the individual for whose benefit the account is established—

(A) to the extent that the amount of the assets involved in the purchase are not attributable to the purchase of life insurance, the purchase is treated as a rollover contribution described in subsection (d)(3), and

(B) to the extent that the amount of the assets involved in the purchase are attributable to the purchase of life, health, accident, or other insurance, such amounts are treated as distributed to that individual (but the provisions of subsection (f) do not apply).

(6) Commingling individual retirement account amounts in certain common trust funds and common investment funds.—Any common trust fund or common investment fund of individual retirement account assets which is exempt from taxation under this subtitle does not cease to be exempt on account of the participation or inclusion of assets of a trust exempt from taxation under section 501(a) which is described in section 401(a).

(f) [Repealed.]

(g) Community Property Laws.—This section shall be applied without regard to any community property laws.

(h) Custodial Accounts.—For purposes of this section, a custodial account shall be treated as a trust if the assets of such account are held by a bank (as defined in subsection (n)) or another person who demonstrates, to the satisfaction of the Secretary, that the manner in which he will administer the account will be consistent with the requirements of this section, and if the custodial account would, except for the fact that it is not a trust, constitute an individual retirement account described in subsection (a). For purposes of this title, in the case of a custodial account treated as a trust by reason of the preceding sentence, the custodian of such account shall be treated as the trustee thereof.

(i) Reports.—The trustee of an individual retirement account and the issuer of an endowment contract described in subsection (b) or an individual retirement annuity shall make such reports regarding such account, contract, or annuity to the Secretary and to the individual for whom the account, contract, or annuity is, or is to be, maintained with respect to the contributions (and the years to which they relate), distributions, aggregating $10 or more in any calendar year and such other matters as the Secretary may require. The reports required by this subsection—

(1) shall be filed at such time and in such manner as the Secretary prescribes, and

(2) shall be furnished to individuals—

(A) not later than January 31 of the calendar year following the calendar year to which such reports relate, and

(B) in such manner as the Secretary prescribes.

In the case of a simple retirement account under subsection (p), only one report under this subsection shall be required to be submitted each calendar year to the Secretary (at the time provided under paragraph (2)) but, in addition to the report under this subsection, there shall be furnished, within 30 days after each calendar year, to the individual on whose behalf the account is maintained a statement with respect to the account balance as of the close of, and the account activity during, such calendar year.

(j) Increase in Maximum Limitations for Simplified Employee Pensions.—In the case of any simplified employee pension, subsections (a)(1) and (b)(2) of this section shall be applied by increasing the amounts contained therein by the amount of the limitation in effect under section 415(c)(1)(A).

(k) Simplified Employee Pension Defined.—

(1) In general.—For purposes of this title, the term "simplified employee pension" means an individual retirement account or individual retirement annuity—

(A) with respect to which the requirements of paragraphs (2), (3), (4), and (5) of this subsection are met, and

(B) if such account or annuity is part of a top-heavy plan (as defined in section 416), with respect to which the requirements of section 416(c)(2) are met.

(2) Participation requirements.—This paragraph is satisfied with respect to a simplified employee pension for a year only if for such year the employer contributes to the simplified employee pension of each employee who—

(A) has attained age 21,

(B) has performed service for the employer during at least 3 of the immediately preceding 5 years, and

(C) received at least $450 in compensation (within the meaning of section 414(q)(4)) from the employer for the year.

For purposes of this paragraph, there shall be excluded from consideration employees described in subparagraph (A) or (C) of section 410(b)(3). For purposes of any arrangement described in subsection (k)(6), any employee who is eligible to have employer contributions made on the employee's behalf under such arrangement shall be treated as if such a contribution was made.

(3) Contributions may not discriminate in favor of the highly compensated, etc.—

(A) In general.—The requirements of this paragraph are met with respect to a simplified employee pension for a year if for such year the contributions made by the employer to simplified employee pensions for his employees do not discriminate in favor of any highly compensated employee (within the meaning of section 414(q)).

(B) Special rules.—For purposes of subparagraph (A), there shall be excluded from consideration employees described in subparagraph (A) or (C) of section 410(b)(3).

(C) Contributions must bear uniform relationship to compensation.—For purposes of subparagraph (A) and except as provided in subparagraph (D), employer contributions to simplified employee pensions (other than contributions under an arrangement described in paragraph (6)) shall be considered discriminatory unless contributions thereto bear a uniform relationship to the compensation (not in excess of the first $200,000) of each employee maintaining a simplified employee pension.

(D) Permitted disparity.—For purposes of subparagraph (C), the rules of section 401(*l*)(2) shall apply to contributions to simplified employee pensions (other than contributions under an arrangement described in paragraph (6)).

(4) Withdrawals must be permitted.—A simplified employee pension meets the requirements of this paragraph only if—

(A) employer contributions thereto are not conditioned on the retention in such pension of any portion of the amount contributed, and

(B) there is no prohibition imposed by the employer on withdrawals from the simplified employee pension.

(5) Contributions must be made under written allocation formula.—The requirements of this paragraph are met with respect to a simplified employee pension only if employer contributions to such pension are determined under a definite written allocation formula which specifies—

(A) the requirements which an employee must satisfy to share in an allocation, and

(B) the manner in which the amount allocated is computed.

(6) Employee may elect salary reduction arrangement.—

(A) Arrangements which qualify.—

(i) In general.—A simplified employee pension shall not fail to meet the requirements of this subsection for a year merely because, under the terms of the pension, an employee may elect to have the employer make payments—

(I) as elective employer contributions to the simplified employee pension on behalf of the employee, or

(II) to the employee directly in cash.

(ii) 50 percent of eligible employees must elect.—Clause (i) shall not apply to a simplified employee pension unless an election described in clause (i)(I) is made or is in effect with respect to not less than 50 percent of the employees of the employer eligible to participate.

(iii) Requirements relating to deferral percentage.—Clause (i) shall not apply to a simplified employee pension for any year unless the deferral percentage for such year of each highly compensated employee eligible to participate is not more than the product of—

(I) the average of the deferral percentages for such year of all employees (other than highly compensated employees) eligible to participate, multiplied by

(II) 1.25.

(iv) Limitations on elective deferrals.—Clause (i) shall not apply to a simplified employee pension unless the requirements of section 401(a)(30) are met.

(B) Exception where more than 25 employees.—This paragraph shall not apply with respect to any year in the case of a simplified employee pension maintained by an employer with more than 25 employees who were eligible to participate (or would have been required to be eligible to participate if a pension was maintained) at any time during the preceding year.

(C) Distributions of excess contributions.—

(i) In general.—Rules similar to the rules of section 401(k)(8) shall apply to any excess contribution under this paragraph. Any excess contribu-

tion under a simplified employee pension shall be treated as an excess contribution for purposes of section 4979.

(ii) Excess contribution.—For purposes of clause (i), the term "excess contribution" means, with respect to a highly compensated employee, the excess of elective employer contributions under this paragraph over the maximum amount of such contributions allowable under subparagraph (A)(iii).

(D) Deferral percentage.—For purposes of this paragraph, the deferral percentage for an employee for a year shall be the ratio of—

(i) the amount of elective employer contributions actually paid over to the simplified employee pension on behalf of the employee for the year, to

(ii) the employee's compensation (not in excess of the first $200,000) for the year.

(E) Exception for state and local and tax-exempt pensions.—This paragraph shall not apply to a simplified employee pension maintained by—

(i) a State or local government or political subdivision thereof, or any agency or instrumentality thereof, or

(ii) an organization exempt from tax under this title.

(F) Exception where pension does not meet requirements necessary to insure distribution of excess contributions.—This paragraph shall not apply with respect to any year for which the simplified employee pension does not meet such requirements as the Secretary may prescribe as are necessary to insure that excess contributions are distributed in accordance with subparagraph (C), including—

(i) reporting requirements, and

(ii) requirements which, notwithstanding paragraph (4), provide that contributions (and any income allocable thereto) may not be withdrawn from a simplified employee pension until a determination has been made that the requirements of subparagraph (A)(iii) have been met with respect to such contributions.

(G) Highly compensated employee.—For purposes of this paragraph, the term "highly compensated employee" has the meaning given such term by section 414(q).

(H) Termination.—This paragraph shall not apply to years beginning after December 31, 1996. The preceding sentence shall not apply to a simplified employee pension of an employer if the terms of simplified employee pensions of such employer, as in effect on December 31, 1996, provide that an employee may make the election described in subparagraph (A).

(7) Definitions.—For purposes of this subsection and subsection (*l*)—

(A) Employee, employer, or owner-employee.—The terms "employee", "employer", and "owner-employee" shall have the respective meanings given such terms by section 401(c).

(B) Compensation.—Except as provided in paragraph (2)(C), the term "compensation" has the meaning given such term by section 414(s).

(C) Year.—The term "year" means—

(i) the calendar year, or

(ii) if the employer elects, subject to such terms and conditions as the Secretary may prescribe, to maintain the simplified employee pension on the basis of the employer's taxable year.

(8) Cost-of-living adjustment.—The Secretary shall adjust the $450 amount in paragraph (2)(C) at the same time and in the same manner as under section 415(d) and shall adjust the $200,000 amount in paragraphs (3)(C) and (6)(D)(ii) at the same time, and by the same amount, as any adjustment under section 401(a)(17)(B); except that any increase in the $450 amount which is not a multiple of $50 shall be rounded to the next lowest multiple of $50.

(9) Cross reference.—For excise tax on certain excess contributions, see section 4979.

(*l*) Simplified Employer Reports.—

(1) In general. An employer who makes a contribution on behalf of an employee to a simplified employee pension shall provide such simplified reports with respect to such contributions as the Secretary may require by regulations. The reports required by this subsection shall be filed at such time and in such manner, and information with respect to such contributions shall be furnished to the employee at such time and in such manner, as may be required by regulations.

(2) Simple retirement accounts.—

(A) No employer reports.—Except as provided in this paragraph, no report shall be required under this section by an employer maintaining a qualified salary reduction arrangement under subsection (p).

(B) Summary description.—The trustee of any simple retirement account established pursuant to a qualified salary reduction arrangement under subsection (p) and the issuer of an annuity established under such an arrangement shall provide to the employer maintaining the arrangement, each year a description containing the following information:

(i) The name and address of the employer and the trustee or issuer.

(ii) The requirements for eligibility for participation.

(iii) The benefits provided with respect to the arrangement.

(iv) The time and method of making elections with respect to the arrangement.

(v) The procedures for, and effects of, withdrawals (including rollovers) from the arrangement.

(C) Employee notification.—The employer shall notify each employee immediately before the period for which an election described in subsection (p)(5)(C) may be made of the employee's opportunity to make such election. Such notice shall include a copy of the description described in subparagraph (B).

(m) Investment in Collectibles Treated as Distributions.—

(1) In general.—The acquisition by an individual retirement account or by an individually-directed account under a plan described in section 401(a) of any collectible shall be treated (for purposes of this section and section 402) as a distribution from such account in an amount equal to the cost to such account of such collectible.

(2) Collectible defined.—For purposes of this subsection, the term "collectible" means—

(A) any work of art,

(B) any rug or antique,

(C) any metal or gem,

(D) any stamp or coin,

(E) any alcoholic beverage, or

(F) any other tangible personal property specified by the Secretary for purposes of this subsection.

(3) Exception for certain coins and bullion.—For purposes of this subsection, the term "collectible" shall not include—

(A) any coin which is—

(i) a gold coin described in paragraph (7), (8), (9), or (10) of section 5112(a) of title 31, United States Code,

(ii) a silver coin described in section 5112(e) of title 31, United States Code,

(iii) a platinum coin described in section 5112(k) of title 31, United States Code, or

(iv) a coin issued under the laws of any State, or

(B) any gold, silver, platinum, or palladium bullion of a fineness equal to or exceeding the minimum fineness that a contract market (as described in section 7 of the Commodity Exchange Act, 7 U.S.C. 7) requires for metals which may be delivered in satisfaction of a regulated futures contract,

IRC Sec. 408(m)(3)(B)

if such bullion is in the physical possession of a trustee described under subsection (a) of this section.

(n) Bank.—For purposes of subsection (a)(2), the term "bank" means—

(1) any bank (as defined in section 581),

(2) an insured credit union (within the meaning of paragraph (6) or (7) of section 101 of the Federal Credit Union Act), and

(3) a corporation which, under the laws of the State of its incorporation, is subject to supervision and examination by the Commissioner of Banking or other officer of such State in charge of the administration of the banking laws of such State.

(o) Definitions and Rules Relating to Nondeductible Contributions to Individual Retirement Plans.—

(1) In general.—Subject to the provisions of this subsection, designated nondeductible contributions may be made on behalf of an individual to an individual retirement plan.

(2) Limits on amounts which may be contributed.—

(A) In general.—The amount of the designated nondeductible contributions made on behalf of any individual for any taxable year shall not exceed the nondeductible limit for such taxable year.

(B) Nondeductible limit.—For purposes of this paragraph—

(i) In general.—The term "non-deductible limit" means the excess of—

(I) the amount allowable as a deduction under section 219 (determined without regard to section 219(g)), over

(II) the amount allowable as a deduction under section 219 (determined with regard to section 219(g)).

(ii) Taxpayer may elect to treat deductible contributions as nondeductible.—If a taxpayer elects not to deduct an amount which (without regard to this clause) is allowable as a deduction under section 219 for any taxable year, the nondeductible limit for such taxable year shall be increased by such amount.

(C) Designated nondeductible contributions.—

(i) In general.—For purposes of this paragraph, the term "designated nondeductible contribution" means any contribution to an individual retirement plan for the taxable year which is designated (in such manner as the Secretary may prescribe) as a contribution for which a deduction is not allowable under section 219.

(ii) Designation.—Any designation under clause (i) shall be made on the return of tax imposed by chapter 1 for the taxable year.

(3) Time when contributions made.—In determining for which taxable year a designated nondeductible contribution is made, the rule of section 219(f)(3) shall apply.

(4) Individual required to report amount of designated nondeductible contributions.—

(A) In general.—Any individual who—

(i) makes a designated nondeductible contribution to any individual retirement plan for any taxable year, or

(ii) receives any amount from any individual retirement plan for any taxable year,

shall include on his return of the tax imposed by chapter 1 for such taxable year and any succeeding taxable year (or on such other form as the Secretary may prescribe for any such taxable year) information described in subparagraph (B).

(B) Information required to be supplied.—The following information is described in this subparagraph:

(i) The amount of designated nondeductible contributions for the taxable year.

(ii) The amount of distributions from individual retirement plans for the taxable year.

(iii) The excess (if any) of—

(I) the aggregate amount of designated nondeductible contributions for all preceding taxable years, over

(II) the aggregate amount of distributions from individual retirement plans which was excludable from gross income for such taxable years.

(iv) The aggregate balance of all individual retirement plans of the individual as of the close of the calendar year in which the taxable year begins.

(v) Such other information as the Secretary may prescribe.

(C) Penalty for reporting contributions not made.—For penalty where individual reports designated nondeductible contributions not made, see section 6693(b).

(p) Simple Retirement Accounts.—

(1) In general.—For purposes of this title, the term "simple retirement account" means an individual retirement plan (as defined in section 7701(a)(37))—

(A) with respect to which the requirements of paragraphs (3), (4), and (5) are met; and

(B) with respect to which the only contributions allowed are contributions under a qualified salary reduction arrangement.

(2) Qualified salary reduction arrangement.—

(A) In general.—For purposes of this subsection, the term "qualified salary reduction arrangement" means a written arrangement of an eligible employer under which—

(i) an employee eligible to participate in the arrangement may elect to have the employer make payments—

(I) as elective employer contributions to a simple retirement account on behalf of the employee, or

(II) to the employee directly in cash,

(ii) the amount which an employee may elect under clause (i) for any year is required to be expressed as a percentage of compensation and may not exceed a total of the applicable dollar amount for any year,

(iii) the employer is required to make a matching contribution to the simple retirement account for any year in an amount equal to so much of the amount the employee elects under clause (i)(I) as does not exceed the applicable percentage of compensation for the year, and

(iv) no contributions may be made other than contributions described in clause (i) or (iii).

(B) Employer may elect 2-percent nonelective contribution.—

(i) In general.—An employer shall be treated as meeting the requirements of subparagraph (A)(iii) for any year if, in lieu of the contributions described in such clause, the employer elects to make nonelective contributions of 2 percent of compensation for each employee who is eligible to participate in the arrangement and who has at least $5,000 of compensation from the employer for the year. If an employer makes an election under this subparagraph for any year, the employer shall notify employees of such election within a reasonable period of time before the 60-day period for such year under paragraph (5)(C).

(ii) Compensation limitation.—The compensation taken into account under clause (i) for any year shall not exceed the limitation in effect for such year under section 401(a)(17).

(C) Definitions.—For purposes of this subsection—

(i) Eligible employer.—

(I) In general.—The term "eligible employer" means, with respect to any year, an employer which had no more than 100 employees who received at least $5,000 of compensation from the employer for the preceding year.

(II) 2-year grace period.—An eligible employer who establishes and maintains a plan under this subsection for 1 or more years and who fails to be an eligible employer for any subsequent year shall be treated as an eligible employer for the 2 years following the last year the employer was an eligible employer. If such failure is due to any acquisition, disposition, or similar transaction involving an eligible employer, the preceding sentence shall not apply.

(ii) Applicable percentage.—

(I) In general.—The term "applicable percentage" means 3 percent.

(II) Election of lower percentage.—An employer may elect to apply a lower percentage (not less than 1 percent) for any year for all employees eligible to participate in the plan for such year if the employer notifies the employees of such lower percentage within a reasonable period of time before the 60-day election period for such year under paragraph (5)(C). An employer may not elect a lower percentage under this subclause for any year if that election would result in the applicable percentage being lower than 3 percent in more than 2 of the years in the 5-year period ending with such year.

(III) Special rule for years arrangement not in effect.—If any year in the 5-year period described in subclause (II) is a year prior to the first year for which any qualified salary reduction arrangement is in effect with respect to the employer (or any predecessor), the employer shall be treated as if the level of the employer matching contribution was at 3 percent of compensation for such prior year.

(D) Arrangement may be only plan of employer.—

(i) In general.—An arrangement shall not be treated as a qualified salary reduction arrangement for any year if the employer (or any predecessor employer) maintained a qualified plan with respect to which contributions were made, or benefits were accrued, for service in any year in the period beginning with the year such arrangement became effective and ending with the year for which the determination is being made. If only individuals other than employees described in subparagraph (A) of section 410(b)(3) are eligible to participate in such arrangement, then the preceding sentence shall be applied without regard to any qualified plan in which only employees so described are eligible to participate.

(ii) Qualified plan.—For purposes of this subparagraph, the term "qualified plan" means a plan, contract, pension, or trust described in subparagraph (A) or (B) of section 219(g)(5).

(iii) [Repealed.]

(E) Applicable dollar amount; cost-of-living adjustment.—

(i) In general.—For purposes of subparagraph (A)(ii), the applicable dollar amount shall be the amount determined in accordance with the following table:

For taxable years beginning in calendar year:	The applicable dollar amount:
2002	$ 7,000
2003	$ 8,000
2004	$ 9,000
2005 or thereafter	$10,000

(ii) Cost-of-living adjustment.—In the case of a year beginning after December 31, 2005, the Secretary shall adjust the $10,000 amount under clause (i) at the same time and in the same manner as under section 415(d), except that the base period taken into account shall be the calendar quarter beginning July 1, 2004, and any increase under this subparagraph which is not a multiple of $500 shall be rounded to the next lower multiple of $500.

(3) **Vesting requirements.**—The requirements of this paragraph are met with respect to a simple retirement account if the employee's rights to any contribution to the simple retirement account are nonforfeitable. For purposes of this paragraph, rules similar to the rules of subsection (k)(4) shall apply.

(4) **Participation requirements.**—

(A) In general.—The requirements of this paragraph are met with respect to any simple retirement account for a year only if, under the qualified salary reduction arrangement, all employees of the employer who—

(i) received at least $5,000 in compensation from the employer during any 2 preceding years, and

(ii) are reasonably expected to receive at least $5,000 in compensation during the year, are eligible to make the election under paragraph (2)(A)(i) or receive the nonelective contribution described in paragraph (2)(B).

(B) Excludable employees.—An employer may elect to exclude from the requirement under subparagraph (A) employees described in section 410(b)(3).

(5) **Administrative requirements.**—The requirements of this paragraph are met with respect to any simple retirement account if, under the qualified salary reduction arrangement—

(A) an employer must—

(i) make the elective employer contributions under paragraph (2)(A)(i) not later than the close of the 30-day period following the last day of the month with respect to which the contributions are to be made, and

(ii) make the matching contributions under paragraph (2)(A)(iii) or the nonelective contributions under paragraph (2)(B) not later than the date described in section 404(m)(2)(B),

(B) an employee may elect to terminate participation in such arrangement at any time during the year, except that if an employee so terminates, the arrangement may provide that the employee may not elect to resume participation until the beginning of the next year, and

(C) each employee eligible to participate may elect, during the 60-day period before the beginning of any year (and the 60-day period before the first day such employee is eligible to participate), to participate in the arrangement, or to modify the amounts subject to such arrangement, for such year.

(6) **Definitions.**—For purposes of this subsection—

(A) Compensation.—

(i) In general.—The term "compensation" means amounts described in paragraphs (3) and (8) of section 6051(a). For purposes of the preceding sentence, amounts described in section 6051(a)(3) shall be determined without regard to section 3401(a)(3).

(ii) Self-employed.—In the case of an employee described in subparagraph (B), the term "compensation" means net earnings from self-employment determined under section 1402(a) without regard to any contribution under this subsection. The preceding sentence shall be applied as if the term "trade or business" for purposes of section 1402 included service described in section 1402(c)(6).

(B) Employee.—The term "employee" includes an employee as defined in section 401(c)(1).

(C) Year.—The term "year" means the calendar year.

(7) **Use of designated financial institution.**—A plan shall not be treated as failing to satisfy the requirements of this subsection or any other provision of this title merely because the employer makes all contributions to the individual retirement accounts or annuities of a designated trustee or issuer. The preceding sentence shall not apply unless each plan participant is notified in writing (either separately or as part of the notice under subsection (*l*)(2)(C)) that the participant's balance may be transferred without cost or penalty to another individual account or annuity in accordance with subsection (d)(3)(G).

(8) **Coordination with maximum limitation under subsection (a)**—In the case of any simple retirement account, subsections (a)(1) and (b)(2) shall be applied by substituting "the sum of the dollar amount in effect under paragraph (2)(A)(ii) of this subsection

and the employer contribution required under subparagraph (A)(iii) or (B)(i) of paragraph (2)" for "the dollar amount in effect under section 219(b)(1)(A)."

(9) Matching contributions on behalf of self-employed individuals not treated as elective employer contributions.—Any matching contribution described in paragraph (2)(A)(iii) which is made on behalf of a self-employed individual (as defined in section 401(c)) shall not be treated as an elective employer contribution to a simple retirement account for purposes of this title.

(10) Special rules for acquisitions, dispositions, and similar transactions.—

(A) In general.—An employer which fails to meet any applicable requirement by reason of an acquisition, disposition, or similar transaction shall not be treated as failing to meet such requirement during the transition period if—

(i) the employer satisfies requirements similar to the requirements of section 410(b)(6)(C)(i)(II); and

(ii) the qualified salary reduction arrangement maintained by the employer would satisfy the requirements of this subsection after the transaction if the employer which maintained the arrangement before the transaction had remained a separate employer.

(B) Applicable Requirement.—For purposes of this paragraph, the term "applicable requirement" means—

(i) the requirement under paragraph (2)(A)(i) that an employer be an eligible employer;

(ii) the requirement under paragraph (2)(D) that an arrangement be the only plan of an employer; and

(iii) the participation requirements under paragraph (4).

(C) Transition Period.—For purposes of this paragraph, the term "transition period" means the period beginning on the date of any transaction described in subparagraph (A) and ending on the last day of the second calendar year following the calendar year in which such transaction occurs.

(q) Deemed IRAs under Qualified Employer Plans.—

(1) General rule.—If—

(A) a qualified employer plan elects to allow employees to make voluntary employee contributions to a separate account or annuity established under the plan, and

(B) under the terms of the qualified employer plan, such account or annuity meets the applicable requirements of this section or section 408A for an individual retirement account or annuity,

then such account or annuity shall be treated for purposes of this title in the same manner as an individual retirement plan and not as a qualified employer plan (and contributions to such account or annuity as contributions to an individual retirement plan and not to the qualified employer plan). For purposes of subparagraph (B), the requirements of subsection (a)(5) shall not apply.

(2) Special rules for qualified employer plans.—For purposes of this title, a qualified employer plan shall not fail to meet any requirement of this title solely by reason of establishing and maintaining a program described in paragraph (1).

(3) Definitions.—For purposes of this subsection–

(A) Qualified employer plan.—The term "qualified employer plan" has the meaning given such term by section 72(p)(4)(A)(i); except that such term shall also include an eligible deferred compensation plan (as defined in section 457(b)) of an eligible employer described in section 457(e)(1)(A).

(B) Voluntary employee contribution.—The term "voluntary employee contribution" means any contribution (other than a mandatory contribution within the meaning of section 411(c)(2)(C))—

(i) which is made by an individual as an employee under a qualified employer plan which allows employees to elect to make contributions described in paragraph (1), and

(ii) with respect to which the individual has designated the contribution as a contribution to which this subsection applies.

(r) Cross References.—

(1) For tax on excess contributions in individual retirement accounts or annuities, see section 4973.

(2) For tax on certain accumulations in individual retirement accounts or annuities, see section 4974.

Recent Amendments to IRC §408

Tax Relief, Unemployment Insurance Reauthorization, and Job Creation Act of 2010 (Pub. L. No. 111-312), as follows:

• IRC §408(d)(8)(F) was amended by Act §725(a) by striking "December 31, 2009" and inserting "December 31, 2011". See effective date below.

• **Effective Date.** Act §725(b) provides:

  (b) Effective Date; Special Rule.—

  (1) Effective date.—The amendment made by this section shall apply to distributions made in taxable years beginning after December 31, 2009.

  (2) Special rule.—For purposes of subsections (a)(6), (b)(3), and (d)(8) of section 408 of the Internal Revenue Code of 1986, at the election of the taxpayer (at such time and in such manner as prescribed by the Secretary of the Treasury) any qualified charitable distribution made after December 31, 2010, and before February 1, 2011, shall be deemed to have been made on December 31, 2010.

Tax Extenders and Alternative Minimum Tax Relief Act of 2008 (Pub. L. No. 110-343), as follows:

IRC Sec. 408(r)(2)

- IRC §408(d)(8)(F) was amended by Act, Div. C, §205(a), by striking "December 31, 2007" and inserting "December 31, 2009". Eff. for distributions made in tax years beginning after Dec. 31, 2007.

Tax Technical Corrections Act of 2007 (Pub. L. No. 110-172), as follows:

- IRC §408(d)(8)(D) was amended by Act §3(a) by substituting "all amounts in all individual retirement plans of the individual were distributed during such taxable year and all such plans were treated as 1 contract for purposes of determining under section 72 the aggregate amount which would have been so includible" for "all amounts distributed from all individual retirement plans were treated as 1 contract under paragraph (2)(A) for purposes of determining the inclusion of such distribution under section 72". Eff. as if included in Pub. L. No. 109-280, §1201 [eff. for distributions made in tax years beginning after Dec. 31, 2005].

Tax Relief and Health Care Act of 2006 (Pub. L. No. 109-432), as follows:

- IRC §408(d) was amended by Act §307(a) by adding new para. (9). Eff. tax years beginning after Dec. 31, 2006.

Pension Protection Act of 2006 (Pub. L. No. 109-280), as follows:

- IRC §408(d) was amended by Act §1201(a) by adding new para. (8). Eff. for distributions made in tax years beginning after Dec. 31, 2005.

- **Sunset Provision.** Act §811, provides:

  SEC. 811. PENSIONS AND INDIVIDUAL RETIRE-MENT ARRANGEMENT PROVISIONS OF ECO-NOMIC GROWTH AND TAX RELIEF RECONCILIA-TION ACT OF 2001 MADE PERMANENT.

  Title IX of the Economic Growth and Tax Relief Reconciliation Act of 2001 [Pub. L. No. 107-16] shall not apply to the provisions of, and amendments made by, subtitles A through F [§§601–666] of title VI of such Act (relating to pension and individual retirement arrangement provisions).

Working Families Tax Relief Act of 2004 (Pub. L. No. 108-311), as follows:

- IRC §408(a)(1) was amended by Act §408(a)(12) by substituting "457(e)(16)," for "457(e)(16)". Eff. Oct. 4, 2004.
- IRC §408(n)(2) was amended by Act §408(a)(13) by substituting "paragraph (6) or (7) of §101" for "§101(6)". Eff. Oct. 4, 2004.
- IRC §408(p)(6)(A)(i) was amended by Act §404(d) by adding a new sentence at the end. Eff. tax years beginning after Dec. 31, 2001, as if included in the provision of Pub. L. No. 107-16 to which it relates.

Job Creation and Worker Assistance Act of 2002 (Pub. L. No. 107-147), as follows:

- IRC §408(k)(2)(C) was amended by Act §411(j)(1)(A) by substituting "$450" for "$300" each place it appeared. Eff. years beginning after Dec. 31, 2001, as if included in the provision of Pub. L. No. 107-16 to which it relates.
- IRC §408(k)(8) was amended by Act §411(j)(1)(B) by substituting "$450" for "$300". Eff. years beginning after Dec. 31, 2001, as if included in the provision of Pub. L. No. 107-16 to which it relates.
- IRC §408(q)(3)(A) was amended by Act §411(i)(1). Eff. plan years beginning after Dec. 31, 2002, as if included in the provision of Pub. L. No. 107-16 to which it relates. IRC §408(q)(3)(A) prior to amendment:

  (A) Qualified employer plan.—The term "qualified employer plan" has the meaning given such term by section 72(p)(4); except such term shall not include a government plan which is not a qualified plan unless the plan is an eligible deferred compensation plan (as defined in section 457(b)).

Economic Growth and Tax Relief Reconciliation Act of 2001 (Pub. L. No. 107-16), as follows:

- IRC §408(a)(1) was amended by Act §601(b)(1) by substituting "on behalf of any individual in excess of the amount in effect for such taxable year under §219(b)(1)(A)" for "in excess of $2,000 on behalf of any individual". Eff. tax years beginning after Dec. 31, 2001.
- IRC §408(a)(1) was amended by Act §641(e)(8) by substituting "403(b)(8), or 457(e)(16)" for "or 403(b)(8),". Eff. generally for distributions after Dec. 31, 2001. See Act §641(f)(3) for a special rule.

- IRC §408(b) was amended by Act §601(b)(3) by substituting "the dollar amount in effect under §219(b)(1)(A)" for "$2,000" in the matter following para. (4). Eff. tax years beginning after Dec. 31, 2001.
- IRC §408(b)(2)(B) was amended by Act §601(b)(2) by substituting "the dollar amount in effect under §219(b)(1)(A)" for "$2,000". Eff. tax years beginning after Dec. 31, 2001.
- IRC §408(d)(3)(A) was amended by Act §642(a) by adding "or" at the end of cl. (i), by striking cls. (ii) and (iii), and by adding new cl. (ii) and a flush sentence. Eff. for distributions after Dec. 31, 2001. See Act §642(c)(2) for a special rule. IRC §408(d)(3)(A)(ii)–(iii) prior to being stricken:

  (ii) no amount in the account and no part of the value of the annuity is attributable to any source other than a rollover contribution (as defined in section 402) from an employee's trust described in section 401(a) which is exempt from tax under section 501(a) or from an annuity plan described in section 403(a) (and any earnings on such contribution), and the entire amount received (including property and other money) is paid (for the benefit of such individual) into another such trust or annuity plan not later than the 60th day on which the individual receives the payment or the distribution; or

  (iii)(I) the entire amount received (including money and other property) represents the entire interest in the account or the entire value of the annuity,

  (II) no amount in the account and no part of the value of the annuity is attributable to any source other than a rollover contribution from an annuity contract described in section 403(b) and any earnings on such rollover, and

  (III) the entire amount thereof is paid into another annuity contract described in section 403(b) (for the benefit of such individual) not later than the 60th day after he receives the payment or distribution.

- IRC §408(d)(3)(D)(i) was amended by Act §642(b)(2) by substituting "(i) or (ii)" for "(i), (ii), or (iii)". Eff. for distributions after Dec. 31, 2001. See Act §642(c)(2) for a special rule.
- IRC §408(d)(3)(G) was amended by Act §642(b)(3). Eff. for distributions after Dec. 31, 2001. See Act §642(c)(2) for a special rule. IRC §408(d)(3)(G) prior to amendment:

  (G) Simple retirement accounts.—This paragraph shall not apply to any amount paid or distributed out of a simple retirement account (as defined in subsection (p)) unless—
  (i) it is paid into another simple retirement account, or
  (ii) in the case of any payment or distribution to which section 72(t)(6) does not apply, it is paid into an individual retirement plan.

- IRC §408(d)(3) was amended by Act §643(c) by adding new subpara. (H). Eff. for distributions after Dec. 31, 2001.
- IRC §408(d)(3), as amended by the Act §643(c), was amended by Act §644(b) by adding new subpara. (I). Eff. for distributions after Dec. 31, 2001.
- IRC §408(j) was amended by Act §601(b)(4) by striking "$2,000" after "by the increasing the". Eff. for tax years beginning after Dec. 31, 2001.
- IRC §408(k) was amended by Act §611(c)(1) by substituting "$200,000" for "$150,000" each place it appeared. Eff. years beginning after Dec. 31, 2001. See Act §611(i)(3) for a special rule.
- IRC §408(p)(8) was amended by Act §601(b)(5) by substituting "the dollar amount in effect under §219(b)(1)(A)" for "$2,000". Eff. tax years beginning after Dec. 31, 2001.
- IRC §408(p)(2)(A)(ii) was amended by Act §611(f)(1) by substituting "the applicable dollar amount" for "$6,000". Eff. years beginning after Dec. 31, 2001. See Act §611(i)(3) for a special rule.
- IRC §408(p)(2)(E) was amended by Act §611(f)(2). Eff. years beginning after Dec. 31, 2001. See Act §611(i)(3) for a special rule. IRC §408(p)(2)(E) prior to amendment:

  (E) Cost-of-living adjustment.—The Secretary shall adjust the $6,000 amount in subparagraph (A)(II) at the same time and in the same manner as under section 415(d), except that the base period taken into account shall be the calendar quarter ending September 30, 1996, and any increase under this subparagraph which is not a multiple of $500 shall be rounded to the next lower multiple of $500.

- IRC §408(p)(6)(A)(ii) was amended by Act §611(g)(2) by adding a new sentence at the end. Eff. years beginning after Dec. 31, 2001. See Act §611(i)(3) for a special rule.

IRC Sec. 408(r)(2)

- IRC §408 was amended by Act §602(a) by redesignating subsec. (q) as subsec. (r) and by adding new subsec. (q). Eff. plan years beginning after Dec. 31, 2002.
- **Sunset Provision.** Act §901, as amended by Pub. L. No. 111-312, §101(a)(1), provides the sunset rule below. But see Pub. L. No. 109-280, §811, and Pub. L. No. 111-148, §10909(c), as amended by Pub. L. No. 111-312, §101(b)(1).

> **SEC. 901. SUNSET OF PROVISIONS OF ACT.**
> **(a) In general.** All provisions of, and amendments made by, this Act shall not apply—
> **(1)** to taxable, plan, or limitation years beginning after December 31, 2012, or
> **(2)** in the case of title V, to estates of decedents dying, gifts made, or generation skipping transfers, after December 31, 2012.
> **(b) Application of certain laws.**—The Internal Revenue Code of 1986 and the Employee Retirement Income Security Act of 1974 shall be applied and administered to years, estates, gifts, and transfers described in subsection (a) as if the provisions and amendments described in subsection (a) had never been enacted.

SEC. 408A. ROTH IRAs.

(a) General Rule.—Except as provided in this section, a Roth IRA shall be treated for purposes of this title in the same manner as an individual retirement plan.

(b) Roth IRA.—For purposes of this title, the term "Roth IRA" means an individual retirement plan (as defined in section 7701(a)(37)) which is designated (in such manner as the Secretary may prescribe) at the time of establishment of the plan as a Roth IRA. Such designation shall be made in such manner as the Secretary may prescribe.

(c) Treatment of Contributions.—

(1) No deduction allowed.—No deduction shall be allowed under section 219 for a contribution to a Roth IRA.

(2) Contribution limit.—The aggregate amount of contributions for any taxable year to all Roth IRAs maintained for the benefit of an individual shall not exceed the excess (if any) of—

(A) the maximum amount allowable as a deduction under section 219 with respect to such individual for such taxable year (computed without regard to subsection (d)(1) or (g) of such section), over

(B) the aggregate amount of contributions for such taxable year to all other individual retirement plans (other than Roth IRAs) maintained for the benefit of the individual.

(3) Limits based on modified adjusted gross income.—

(A) Dollar limit.—The amount determined under paragraph (2) for any taxable year shall not exceed an amount equal to the amount determined under paragraph (2)(A) for such taxable year, reduced (but not below zero) by the amount which bears the same ratio to such amount as—

(i) the excess of—

(I) the taxpayer's adjusted gross income for such taxable year, over

(II) the applicable dollar amount, bears to

(ii) $15,000 ($10,000 in the case of a joint return or a married individual filing a separate return).

The rules of subparagraphs (B) and (C) of section 219(g)(2) shall apply to any reduction under this subparagraph.

(B) Definitions.—For purposes of this paragraph—

(i) adjusted gross income shall be determined in the same manner as under section 219(g)(3), except that any amount included in gross income under subsection (d)(3) shall not be taken into account, and

(ii) the applicable dollar amount is—

(I) in the case of a taxpayer filing a joint return, $150,000,

(II) in the case of any other taxpayer (other than a married individual filing a separate return), $95,000, and

(III) in the case of a married individual filing a separate return, zero.

(C) Marital status.—Section 219(g)(4) shall apply for purposes of this paragraph.

(D) Inflation Adjustment.—In the case of any taxable year beginning in a calendar year after 2006, the dollar amounts in subclauses (I) and (II) of subparagraph (B)(ii) shall each be increased by an amount equal to—

(i) such dollar amount, multiplied by

(ii) the cost-of-living adjustment determined under section 1(f)(3) for the calendar year in which the taxable year begins, determined by substituting "calendar year 2005" for "calendar year 1992" in subparagraph (B) thereof.

Any increase determined under the preceding sentence shall be rounded to the nearest multiple of $1,000.

(4) Contributions permitted after age 70½— Contributions to a Roth IRA may be made even after the individual for whom the account is maintained has attained age 70½.

(5) Mandatory distribution rules not to apply before death.—Notwithstanding subsections (a)(6) and (b)(3) of section 408 (relating to required distributions), the following provisions shall not apply to any Roth IRA:

(A) Section 401(a)(9)(A).

(B) The incidental death benefit requirements of section 401(a).

(6) Rollover contributions.—

(A) In general.—No rollover contribution may be made to a Roth IRA unless it is a qualified rollover contribution.

(B) Coordination with limit.—A qualified rollover contribution shall not be taken into account for purposes of paragraph (2).

(7) Time when contributions made.—For purposes of this section, the rule of section 219(f)(3) shall apply.

(d) Distribution Rules.—For purposes of this title—

(1) Exclusion.—Any qualified distribution from a Roth IRA shall not be includible in gross income.

(2) Qualified distribution.—For purposes of this subsection—

(A) In general.—The term "qualified distribution" means any payment or distribution—

(i) made on or after the date on which the individual attains age 59½,

(ii) made to a beneficiary (or to the estate of the individual) on or after the death of the individual,

(iii) attributable to the individual's being disabled (within the meaning of section 72(m)(7)), or

(iv) which is a qualified special purpose distribution.

(B) Distributions within nonexclusion period.—A payment or distribution from a Roth IRA shall not be treated as a qualified distribution under subparagraph (A) if such payment or distribution is made within the 5-taxable year period beginning with the 1st taxable year for which the individual made a contribution to a Roth IRA (or such individual's spouse made a contribution to a Roth IRA) established for such individual.

(C) Distributions of excess contributions and earnings.—The term "qualified distribution" shall not include any distribution of any contribution described in section 408(d)(4) and any net income allocable to the contribution.

(3) Rollovers from an eligible retirement plan other than a Roth IRA.—

(A) In general.—Notwithstanding sections 402(c), 403(b)(8), 408(d)(3), and 457(e)(16), in the case of any distribution to which this paragraph applies—

(i) there shall be included in gross income any amount which would be includible were it not part of a qualified rollover contribution,

(ii) section 72(t) shall not apply, and

(iii) unless the taxpayer elects not to have this clause apply, any amount required to be included

in gross income for any taxable year beginning in 2010 by reason of this paragraph shall be so included ratably over the 2-taxable-year period beginning with the first taxable year beginning in 2011.

Any election under clause (iii) for any distributions during a taxable year may not be changed after the due date for such taxable year.

(B) Distributions to which paragraph applies.—This paragraph shall apply to a distribution from an eligible retirement plan (as defined by section 402(c)(8)(B)) maintained for the benefit of an individual which is contributed to a Roth IRA maintained for the benefit of such individual in a qualified rollover contribution. This paragraph shall not apply to a distribution which is a qualified rollover contribution from a Roth IRA or qualified rollover contribution from a designated Roth account which is a rollover contribution described in section 402A(c)(3)(A).

(C) Conversions.—The conversion of an individual retirement plan (other than a Roth IRA) to a Roth IRA shall be treated for purposes of this paragraph as a distribution to which this paragraph applies.

(D) Additional reporting requirements.—Trustees of Roth IRAs, trustees of individual retirement plans, persons subject to section 6047(d)(1), or all of the foregoing persons, whichever is appropriate, shall include such additional information in reports required under section 408(i) or 6047 as the Secretary may require to ensure that amounts required to be included in gross income under subparagraph (A) are so included.

(E) Special rules for contributions to which 2-year averaging applies.—In the case of a qualified rollover contribution to a Roth IRA of a distribution to which subparagraph (A)(iii) applied, the following rules shall apply:

(i) Acceleration of inclusion.—

(I) In general.—The amount otherwise required to be included in gross income for any taxable year beginning in 2010 or the first taxable year in the 2-year period under subparagraph (A)(iii) shall be increased by the aggregate distributions from Roth IRAs for such taxable year which are allocable under paragraph (4) to the portion of such qualified rollover contribution required to be included in gross income under subparagraph (A)(i).

(II) Limitation of aggregate amount included.—The amount required to be included in gross income for any taxable year under subparagraph (A)(iii) shall not exceed the aggregate amount required to be included in gross income under subparagraph (A)(iii) for all taxable years in the 2-year period (without regard to subclause (I)) reduced by amounts included for all preceding taxable years.

(ii) Death of distributee.—

(I) In general.—If the individual required to include amounts in gross income under such subparagraph dies before all of such amounts are included, all remaining amounts shall be included in gross income for the taxable year which includes the date of death.

(II) Special rule for surviving spouse.—If the spouse of the individual described in subclause (I) acquires the individual's entire interest in any Roth IRA to which such qualified rollover contribution is properly allocable, the spouse may elect to treat the remaining amounts described in subclause (I) as includible in the spouse's gross income in the taxable years of the spouse ending with or within the taxable years of such individual in which such amounts would otherwise have been includible. Any such election may not be made or changed after the due date for the spouse's taxable year which includes the date of death.

(F) Special rule for applying section 72.—

(i) In general.—If—

(I) any portion of a distribution from a Roth IRA is properly allocable to a qualified rollover contribution described in this paragraph, and

(II) such distribution is made within the 5-taxable year period beginning with the taxable year in which such contribution was made,

then section 72(t) shall be applied as if such portion were includible in gross income.

(ii) Limitation.—Clause (i) shall apply only to the extent of the amount of the qualified rollover contribution includible in gross income under subparagraph (A)(i).

(4) Aggregation and ordering rules.—

(A) Aggregation rules.—Section 408(d)(2) shall be applied separately with respect to Roth IRAs and other individual retirement plans.

(B) Reordering rules.—For purposes of applying this section and section 72 to any distribution from a Roth IRA, such distribution shall be treated as made—

(i) from contributions to the extent that the amount of such distribution, when added to all previous distributions from the Roth IRA, does not exceed the aggregate contributions to the Roth IRA, and

(ii) from such contributions in the following order:

(I) Contributions other than qualified rollover contributions to which paragraph (3) applies.

(II) Qualified rollover contributions to which paragraph (3) applies on a first-in, first-out basis.

Any distribution allocated to a qualified rollover contribution under clause (ii)(II) shall be allocated first to the portion of such contribution required to be included in gross income.

(5) Qualified special purpose distribution.— For purposes of this section, the term "qualified special purpose distribution" means any distribution to which subparagraph (F) of section 72(t)(2) applies.

(6) Taxpayer may make adjustments before due date.—

(A) In general.—Except as provided by the Secretary, if, on or before the due date for any taxable year, a taxpayer transfers in a trustee-to-trustee transfer any contribution to an individual retirement plan made during such taxable year from such plan to any other individual retirement plan, then, for purposes of this chapter, such contribution shall be treated as having been made to the transferee plan (and not the transferor plan).

(B) Special rules.—

(i) Transfer of earnings.—Subparagraph (A) shall not apply to the transfer of any contribution unless such transfer is accompanied by any net income allocable to such contribution.

(ii) No deduction.—Subparagraph (A) shall apply to the transfer of any contribution only to the extent no deduction was allowed with respect to the contribution to the transferor plan.

(7) Due date.—For purposes of this subsection, the due date for any taxable year is the date prescribed by law (including extensions of time) for filing the taxpayer's return for such taxable year.

(e) Qualified Rollover Contribution.—For purposes of this section—

(1) In general.—The term "qualified rollover Contribution" means a rollover contribution—

(A) to a Roth IRA from another such account,

(B) from an eligible retirement plan, but only if—

(i) in the case of an individual retirement plan, such rollover contribution meets the requirements of section 408(d)(3), and

(ii) in the case of any eligible retirement plan (as defined in section 402(c)(8)(B) other than clauses (i) and (ii) thereof), such rollover contribution meets the requirements of section 402(c), 403(b)(8), or 457(e)(16), as applicable.

For purposes of section 408(d)(3)(B), there shall be disregarded any qualified rollover contribution from an individual retirement plan (other than a Roth IRA) to a Roth IRA.

(2) Military death gratuity.—

(A) In general.—The term "qualified rollover Contribution" includes a contribution to a Roth IRA maintained for the benefit of an individual made before the end of the 1-year period beginning on the date on which such individual receives an amount under section 1477 of title 10, United States Code, or section 1967 of title 38 of such Code, with respect to a person, to the extent that such contribution does not exceed—

(i) the sum of the amounts received during such period by such individual under such sections with respect to such person, reduced by

(ii) the amounts so received which were contributed to a Coverdell education savings account under section 530(d)(9).

(B) Annual limit on number of rollovers not to apply.—Section 408(d)(3)(B) shall not apply with respect to amounts treated as a rollover by the subparagraph (A).

(C) Application of section 72.—For purposes of applying section 72 in the case of a distribution which is not a qualified distribution, the amount treated as a rollover by reason of subparagraph (A) shall be treated as investment in the contract.

(f) Individual Retirement Plan.—For purposes of this section—

(1) a simplified employee pension or a simple retirement account may not be designated as a Roth IRA, and

(2) contributions to any such pension or account shall not be taken into account for purposes of subsection (c)(2)(B).

Recent Amendments to IRC §408A

Worker, Retiree, and Employer Recovery Act of 2008 (Pub. L. No. 110-458), as follows:

- IRC §408A(c)(3)(B) was amended by Act §108(d)(1) by striking "an" before "eligible", striking "other than a Roth IRA", and adding a flush sentence . Eff. as if included in Pub. L. No. 109-280, §824 [eff. for distributions after Dec. 31, 2007].
- IRC §408A(c)(3)(C) was amended by Act §108(h)(1) by redesignating subpara. (C), as added by Pub. L. No. 109-280, §833(c), as subpara. (E). Eff. as if included in in Pub. L. No. 109-280, §833 [eff. for tax years beginning after 2006].
- IRC §408A(c)(3)(E) was redesignated by Act §108(h)(2) as subpara. (D), and amended by substituting "subparagraph (B)(ii)" for "subparagraph (C)(ii)". Eff. for tax years beginning after Dec. 31, 2009.
- IRC §408A(d)(3)(B) (as in effect after amendment by Pub. L. No. 109-280, §824(b)(2)(B)) was amended by Act §108(d)(2) by striking "(other than a Roth IRA)" and by adding a new sentence at the end. Eff. as if included in Pub. L. No. 109-280, §824 [eff. for distributions after Dec. 31, 2007].
- Other Provision. Act §125 provides:
  SEC. 125. ROLLOVER OF AMOUNTS RECEIVED IN AIRLINE CARRIER BANKRUPTCY TO ROTH IRAS.
  (a) General Rule—If a qualified airline employee receives any airline payment amount and transfers any portion of such amount to a Roth IRA within 180 days of receipt of such amount (or, if later, within 180 days of the date of the enactment of this Act), then such amount (to the extent so trans-

ferred) shall be treated as a qualified rollover contribution described in section 408A(e) of the Internal Revenue Code of 1986, and the limitations described in section 408A(c)(3) of such Code shall not apply to any such transfer.

(b) Definitions and Special Rules.—For purposes of this section—

(1) Airline payment amount.—

(A) In general.—The term "airline payment amount" means any payment of any money or other property which is payable by a commercial passenger airline carrier to a qualified airline employee—

(i) under the approval of an order of a Federal bankruptcy court in a case filed after September 11, 2001, and before January 1, 2007, and

(ii) in respect of the qualified airline employee's interest in a bankruptcy claim against the carrier, any note of the carrier (or amount paid in lieu of a note being issued), or any other fixed obligation of the carrier to pay a lump sum amount.

The amount of such payment shall be determined without regard to any requirement to deduct and withhold tax from such payment under sections 3102(a) and 3402(a).

(B) Exception.—An airline payment amount shall not include any amount payable on the basis of the carrier's future earnings or profits.

(2) Qualified airline employee.—The term "qualified airline employee" means an employee or former employee of a commercial passenger airline carrier who was a participant in a defined benefit plan maintained by the carrier which—

(A) is a plan described in section 401(a) of the Internal Revenue Code of 1986 which includes a trust exempt from tax under section 501(a) of such Code, and

(B) was terminated or became subject to the restrictions contained in paragraphs (2) and (3) of section 402(b) of the Pension Protection Act of 2006.

(3) Reporting requirements.—If a commercial passenger airline carrier pays 1 or more airline payment amounts, the carrier shall, within 90 days of such payment (or, if later, within 90 days of the date of the enactment of this Act), report—

(A) to the Secretary of the Treasury, the names of the qualified airline employees to whom such amounts were paid, and

(B) to the Secretary and to such employees, the years and the amounts of the payments.

Such reports shall be in such form, and contain such additional information, as the Secretary may prescribe.

(c) Effective Date.—This section shall apply to transfers made after the date of the enactment of this Act with respect to airline payment amounts paid before, on, or after such date.

Heroes Earnings Assistance and Relief Tax Act of 2008 (Pub. L. No. 110-245), as follows:

- IRC §408A(e), as in effect after amendment by Pub. L. No. 109-280, §824(a), was amended by Act §109(b). Eff. generally with respect to deaths from injuries occurring on or after June 17, 2008. For special applicability date, see below. IRC §408A(e) prior to amendment:
  (e) Qualified Rollover Contribution—For purposes of this section, the term "qualified rollover contribution" means a rollover contribution—
  (1) to a Roth IRA from another such account,
  (2) from an eligible retirement plan, but only if—
  (A) in the case of an individual retirement plan, such rollover contribution meets the requirements of section 408(d)(3), and
  (B) in the case of any eligible retirement plan (as defined in section 402(c)(8)(B) other than clauses (i) and (ii) thereof), such rollover contribution meets the requirements of section 402(c), 403(b)(8), or 457(e)(16), as applicable.
  For purposes of section 408(d)(3)(B), there shall be disregarded any qualified rollover contribution from an individual retirement plan (other than a Roth IRA) to a Roth IRA.
- IRC §408A(e), before amendment by Pub. L. No. 109-280, §824(a), was amended by Act §109(a). Eff. generally with respect to deaths from injuries occurring on or after June 17, 2008. For a special applicability rule, see below. IRC §408A(e) prior to amendment:
  (e) Qualified Rollover Contribution.—For purposes of this section, the term "qualified rollover contribution" means a

rollover contribution to a Roth IRA from another such account, or from an individual retirement plan, but only if such rollover contribution meets the requirements of section 408(d)(3). Such term includes a rollover contribution described in section 402A(c)(3)(A). For purposes of section 408(d)(3)(B), there shall be disregarded any qualified rollover contribution from an individual retirement plan (other than a Roth IRA) to a Roth IRA.

- **Other provision.** Act §109(d)(2)–(3) provide:

    (2) Application of amendments to deaths from injuries occurring on or after October 7, 2001, and before enactment.—The amendments made by this section shall apply to any contribution made pursuant to section 408A(e)(2) or 530(d)(5) of the Internal Revenue Code of 1986, as amended by this Act, with respect to amounts received under section 1477 of title 10, United States Code, or under section 1967 of title 38 of such Code, for deaths from injuries occurring on or after October 7, 2001, and before the date of the enactment of this Act if such contribution is made not later than 1 year after the date of the enactment of this Act.

    (3) Pension Protection Act changes.—Section 408A(e)(1) of the Internal Revenue Code of 1986 (as in effect after the amendments made by subsection (b)) shall apply to taxable years beginning after December 31, 2007.

Pension Protection Act of 2006 (Pub. L. No. 109-280), as follows:

- IRC §408A(c)(3)(B) (as in effect prior to Pub. L. No. 109-222) was amended by Act §824(b)(1)(A) by substituting "an eligible retirement plan (as defined by §402(c)(8)(B))" for "individual retirement plan". Eff. for distributions after Dec. 31, 2007.

- IRC §408A(c)(3)(B) (as in effect prior to Pub. L. No. 109-222) was amended by Act §824(b)(1)(B) by substituting in the heading "Eligible retirement plan" for "IRA" in the first place it appeared. Eff. for distributions after Dec. 31, 2007.

- IRC §408A(c)(3) was amended by Act §833(c) by adding new subpara. (C)[(D)] at the end. Eff. for tax years beginning after 2006.

- IRC §408A(d)(3) was amended by Act §824(b)(2)(A)–(E) by replacing "§408(d)(3)" in subpara. (A) with "§§402(c), 403(b)(8), 408(d)(3), and 457(e)(16)", by replacing in subpara. (B) "individual retirement plan" with "eligible retirement plan (as defined by §402(c)(8)(B))", by inserting "or 6047" after "408(i)" in subpara. (D), by replacing in subpara. (D) "or both" with "persons subject to §6047(d)(1), or all of the foregoing persons", and by replacing "IRA" the first place it appeared in the heading with "Eligible retirement plan". Eff. for distributions after Dec. 31, 2007.

- IRC §408A(e) was amended by Act §824(a). Eff. for distributions after Dec. 31, 2007. IRC §408A(e) prior to amendment:

    (e) Qualified rollover contribution.—For purposes of this section, the term "qualified rollover contribution" means a rollover contribution to a Roth IRA from another such account, or from an individual retirement plan, but only if such rollover contribution meets the requirements of section 408(d)(3). Such term includes a rollover contribution described in section 402A(c)(3)(A). For purposes of section 408(d)(3)(B), there shall be disregarded any qualified rollover contribution from an individual retirement plan (other than a Roth IRA) to a Roth IRA.

- **Sunset Provision.** Act §811, provides:

    SEC. 811. PENSIONS AND INDIVIDUAL RETIREMENT ARRANGEMENT PROVISIONS OF ECONOMIC GROWTH AND TAX RELIEF RECONCILIATION ACT OF 2001 MADE PERMANENT.
    Title IX of the Economic Growth and Tax Relief Reconciliation Act of 2001 [Pub. L. No. 107-16] shall not apply to the provisions of, and amendments made by, subtitles A through F [§§601–666] of title VI of such Act (relating to pension and individual retirement arrangement provisions).

Tax Increase Prevention and Reconciliation Act of 2005 (Pub. L. No. 109-222), as follows:

- IRC §408A(c)(3) was amended by Act §512(a)(1) by striking subpara. (B) and redesignating subparas. (C) and (D) as subparas. (B) and (C). Eff. tax years beginning after Dec. 31, 2009. IRC §408A(c)(3)(B) prior to being stricken:

    (B) Rollover from eligible retirement plan.—A taxpayer shall not be allowed to make a qualified rollover contribution to a Roth IRA from an an [sic] eligible retirement plan (as defined by section 402(c)(8)(B) other than a Roth IRA during any taxable year if, for the taxable year of the distribution to which such contribution relates—

        (i) the taxpayer's adjusted gross income exceeds $100,000, or

        (ii) the taxpayer is a married individual filing a separate return.

- IRC §408A(c)(3)(B)(i), as redesignated Act §512(a)(1), was amended by Act §512(a)(2) by substituting "except that any amount included in gross income under subsection (d)(3) shall not be taken into account, and" for "except that—" and all that follows. Eff. tax years beginning after Dec. 31, 2009. IRC §408A(c)(3)(B)(i) prior to being stricken:

        (i) adjusted gross income shall be determined in the same manner as under section 219(g)(3), except that—

        (I) any amount included in gross income under subsection (d)(3) shall not be taken into account; and

        (II) any amount included in gross income by reason of a required distribution under a provision described in paragraph (5) shall not be taken into account for purposes of subparagraph (B)(i), and

- IRC §408A(d)(3)(A)(iii) was amended by Act §512(b)(1). Eff. tax years beginning after Dec. 31, 2009. IRC §408A(d)(3)(A)(iii) prior to amendment:

        (iii) unless the taxpayer elects not to have this clause apply for any taxable year, any amount required to be included in gross income for such taxable year by reason of this paragraph for any distribution before January 1, 1999, shall be so included ratably over the 4-taxable year period beginning with such taxable year.

- IRC §408A(d)(3)(E)(i) was amended by Act §512(b)(2)(A). Eff. tax years beginning after Dec. 31, 2009. IRC §408A(d)(3)(E)(i) prior to amendment:

        (i) Acceleration of inclusion.—

        (I) In general.—The amount required to be included in gross income for each of the first 3 taxable years in the 4-year period under subparagraph (A)(iii) shall be increased by the aggregate distribution from Roth IRAs for such taxable year which are allocable under paragraph (4) to the portion of such qualified rollover contribution required to be included in gross income under subparagraph (A)(i).

        (II) Limitation on aggregate amount included.—The amount required to be included in gross income for any taxable year under subparagraph (A)(iii) shall not exceed the aggregate amount required to be included in gross income under subparagraph (A)(iii) for all taxable years in the 4-year period (without regard to subclause (I)) reduced by amounts included for all preceding taxable years.

- IRC §408A(d)(3)(E) was amended by Act §512(b)(2)(B) by striking in the heading "4-year" and inserting "2-year". Eff. tax years beginning after Dec. 31, 2009.

Economic Growth and Tax Relief Reconciliation Act of 2001 (Pub. L. No. 107-16), as follows:

- IRC §408A(e) was amended by Act §617(e)(1) by adding a new sentence after the first sentence. Eff. tax years beginning after Dec. 31, 2005.

- **Sunset Provision.** Act §901, as amended by Pub. L. No. 111-312, §101(a)(1), provides the sunset rule below. But see Pub. L. No. 109-280, §811, and Pub. L. No. 111-148, §10909(c), as amended by Pub. L. No. 111-312, §101(b)(1).

    SEC. 901. SUNSET OF PROVISIONS OF ACT.

    (a) In general. All provisions of, and amendments made by, this Act shall not apply—

    (1) to taxable, plan, or limitation years beginning after December 31, 2012, or

    (2) in the case of title V, to estates of decedents dying, gifts made, or generation skipping transfers, after December 31, 2012.

    (b) Application of certain laws.—The Internal Revenue Code of 1986 and the Employee Retirement Income Security Act of 1974 shall be applied and administered to years, estates, gifts, and transfers described in subsection (a) as if the provisions and amendments described in subsection (a) had never been enacted.

SEC. 409. QUALIFICATIONS FOR TAX CREDIT EMPLOYEE STOCK OWNERSHIP PLANS.

(a) Tax Credit Employee Stock Ownership Plan Defined.—Except as otherwise provided in this title, for purposes of this title, the term "tax credit employee stock ownership plan" means a defined contribution plan which—

(1) meets the requirements of section 401(a),

(2) is designed to invest primarily in employer securities, and

(3) meets the requirements of subsections (b), (c), (d), (e), (f), (g), (h), and (o) of this section.

(b) Required Allocation of Employer Securities.—

(1) In general.—A plan meets the requirements of this subsection if—

(A) the plan provides for the allocation for the plan year of all employer securities transferred to it or purchased by it (because of the requirements of section 41(c)(1)(B)) to the accounts of all participants who are entitled to share in such allocation, and

(B) for the plan year the allocation to each participant so entitled is an amount which bears substantially the same proportion to the amount of all such securities allocated to all such participants in the plan for that year as the amount of compensation paid to such participant during that year bears to the compensation paid to all such participants during that year.

(2) Compensation in excess of $100,000 disregarded.—For purposes of paragraph (1), compensation of any participant in excess of the first $100,000 per year shall be disregarded.

(3) Determination of compensation.—For purposes of this subsection, the amount of compensation paid to a participant for any period is the amount of such participant's compensation (within the meaning of section 415(c)(3)) for such period.

(4) Suspension of allocation in certain cases.—Notwithstanding paragraph (1), the allocation to the account of any participant which is attributable to the basic employee plan credit or the credit allowed under section 41 (relating to the employee stock ownership credit) may be extended over whatever period may be necessary to comply with the requirements of section 415.

(c) Participants Must Have Nonforfeitable Rights.—A plan meets the requirements of this subsection only if it provides that each participant has a nonforfeitable right to any employer security allocated to his account.

(d) Employer Securities Must Stay in the Plan.—A plan meets the requirements of this subsection only if it provides that no employer security allocated to a participant's account under subsection (b) (or allocated to a participant's account in connection with matched employer and employee contributions) may be distributed from that account before the end of the 84th month beginning after the month in which the security is allocated to the account. To the extent provided in the plan, the preceding sentence shall not apply in the case of—

(1) death, disability, separation from service, or termination of the plan;

(2) a transfer of a participant to the employment of an acquiring employer from the employment of the selling corporation in the case of a sale to the acquiring corporation of substantially all of the assets used by the selling corporation in a trade or business conducted by the selling corporation, or

(3) with respect to the stock of a selling corporation, a disposition of such selling corporation's interest in a subsidiary when the participant continues employment with such subsidiary.

This subsection shall not apply to any distribution required under section 401(a)(9) or to any distribution or reinvestment required under section 401(a)(28).

(e) Voting Rights.—

(1) In general.—A plan meets the requirements of this subsection if it meets the requirements of paragraph (2) or (3), whichever is applicable.

(2) Requirements where employer has a registration-type class of securities.—If the employer has a registration-type class of securities, the plan meets the requirements of this paragraph only if each participant or beneficiary in the plan is entitled to direct the plan as to the manner in which securities of the employer which are entitled to vote and are allocated to the account of such participant or beneficiary are to be voted.

(3) Requirement for other employers.—If the employer does not have a registration-type class of securities, the plan meets the requirements of this paragraph only if each participant or beneficiary in the plan is entitled to direct the plan as to the manner in which voting rights under securities of the employer which are allocated to the account of such participant or beneficiary are to be exercised with respect to any corporate matter which involves the voting of such shares with respect to the approval or disapproval of any corporate merger or consolidation, recapitalization, reclassification, liquidation, dissolution, sale of substantially all assets of a trade or business, or such similar transaction as the Secretary may prescribe in regulations.

(4) Registration-type class of securities defined.—For purposes of this subsection, the term "registration-type class of securities" means—

(A) a class of securities required to be registered under section 12 of the Securities Exchange Act of 1934, and

(B) a class of securities which would be required to be so registered except for the exemption from registration provided in subsection (g)(2)(H) of such section 12.

(5) 1 vote per participant.—A plan meets the requirements of paragraph (3) with respect to an issue if—

(A) the plan permits each participant 1 vote with respect to such issue, and

(B) the trustee votes the shares held by the plan in the proportion determined after application of subparagraph (A).

(f) Plan Must Be Established Before Employer's Due Date.—

(1) In general.—A plan meets the requirements of this subsection only if it is established on or before the due date (including any extension of such date) for the filing of the employer's tax return for the first taxable year of the employer for which an employee plan credit is claimed by the employer with respect to the plan.

(2) Special rule for first year.—A plan which otherwise meets the requirements of this section shall not be considered to have failed to meet the requirements of section 401(a) merely because it was not established by the close of the first taxable year of the employer for which an employee plan credit is claimed by the employer with respect to the plan.

(g) Transferred Amounts Must Stay in Plan Even Though Investment Credit Is Redetermined or Recaptured.—A plan meets the requirement of this subsection only if it provides that amounts which are transferred to the plan (because of the requirements of section 48(n)(1) or 41(c)(1)(B)) shall remain in the plan (and, if allocated under the plan, shall remain so allocated) even though part or all of the employee plan credit or the credit allowed under section 41 (relating to employee stock ownership credit) is recaptured or redetermined. For purposes of the preceding sentence, the references to section 48(n)(1) and the employee plan credit shall refer to such section and credit as in effect before the enactment of the Tax Reform Act of 1984.

(h) Right to Demand Employer Securities; Put Option.—

(1) In general.—A plan meets the requirements of this subsection if a participant who is entitled to a distribution from the plan—

(A) has a right to demand that his benefits be distributed in the form of employer securities, and

(B) if the employer securities are not readily tradable on an established market, has a right to require

that the employer repurchase employer securities under a fair valuation formula.

(2) Plan may distribute cash in certain cases.—

(A) In general.—A plan which otherwise meets the requirements of this subsection or of section 4975(e)(7) shall not be considered to have failed to meet the requirements of section 401(a) merely because under the plan the benefits may be distributed in cash or in the form of employer securities.

(B) Exception for certain plans restricted from distributing securities.—

(i) In general.—A plan to which this subparagraph applies shall not be treated as failing to meet the requirements of this subsection or section 401(a) merely because it does not permit a participant to exercise the right described in paragraph (1)(A) if such plan provides that the participant entitled to a distribution has a right to receive the distribution in cash, except that such plan may distribute employer securities subject to a requirement that such securities may be resold to the employer under terms which meet the requirements of paragraph (1)(B).

(ii) Applicable plans.—This subparagraph shall apply to a plan which otherwise meets the requirements of this subsection or section 4975(e)(7) and which is established and maintained by—

(I) an employer whose charter or bylaws restrict the ownership of substantially all outstanding employer securities to employees or to a trust described in section 401(a), or

(II) an S corporation.

(3) Special rule for banks.—In the case of a plan established and maintained by a bank (as defined in section 581) which is prohibited by law from redeeming or purchasing its own securities, the requirements of paragraph (1)(B) shall not apply if the plan provides that participants entitled to a distribution from the plan shall have a right to receive a distribution in cash.

(4) Put option period.—An employer shall be deemed to satisfy the requirements of paragraph (1)(B) if it provides a put option for a period of at least 60 days following the date of distribution of stock of the employer and, if the put option is not exercised within such 60-day period, for an additional period of at least 60 days in the following plan year (as provided in regulations promulgated by the Secretary).

(5) Payment requirement for total distribution.—If an employer is required to repurchase employer securities which are distributed to the employee as part of a total distribution, the requirements of paragraph (1)(B) shall be treated as met if—

(A) the amount to be paid for the employer securities is paid in substantially equal periodic payments (not less frequently than annually) over a period beginning not later than 30 days after the exercise of the put option described in paragraph (4) and not exceeding 5 years, and

(B) there is adequate security provided and reasonable interest paid on the unpaid amounts referred to in subparagraph (A).

For purposes of this paragraph, the term "total distribution" means the distribution within 1 taxable year to the recipient of the balance to the credit of the recipient's account.

(6) Payment requirement for installment distributions.—If an employer is required to repurchase employer securities as part of an installment distribution, the requirements of paragraph (1)(B) shall be treated as met if the amount to be paid for the employer securities is paid not later than 30 days after the exercise of the put option described in paragraph (4).

(7) Exception where employee elected diversification.—Paragraph (1)(A) shall not apply with respect to the portion of the participant's account which the employee elected to have reinvested under section 401(a)(28)(B) or subparagraph (B) or (C) of section 401(a)(35).

(i) Reimbursement for Expenses of Establishing and Administering Plan.—A plan which otherwise meets the requirements of this section shall not be treated as failing to meet such requirements merely because it provides that—

(1) Expenses of establishing plan.—As reimbursement for the expenses of establishing the plan, the employer may withhold from amounts due the plan for the taxable year for which the plan is established (or the plan may pay) so much of the amounts paid or incurred in connection with the establishment of the plan as does not exceed the sum of—

(A) 10 percent of the first $100,000 which the employer is required to transfer to the plan for that taxable year under section 41(c)(1)(B), and

(B) 5 percent of any amount so required to be transferred in excess of the first $100,000; and

(2) Administrative expenses.—As reimbursement for the expenses of administering the plan, the employer may withhold from amounts due the plan (or the plan may pay) so much of the amounts paid or incurred during the taxable year as expenses of administering the plan as does not exceed the lesser of—

(A) the sum of—

(i) 10 percent of the first $100,000 of the dividends paid to the plan with respect to stock of the employer during the plan year ending with or within the employer's taxable year, and

(ii) 5 percent of the amount of such dividends in excess of $100,000, or

(B) $100,000.

(j) Conditional Contributions to the Plan.—A plan which otherwise meets the requirements of this section shall not be treated as failing to satisfy such requirements (or as failing to satisfy the requirements of section 401(a) of this title or of section 403(c)(1) of the Employee Retirement Income Security Act of 1974) merely because of the return of a contribution (or a provision permitting such a return) if—

(1) the contribution to the plan is conditioned on a determination by the Secretary that such plan meets the requirements of this section,

(2) the application for a determination described in paragraph (1) is filed with the Secretary not later than 90 days after the date on which an employee plan credit is claimed, and

(3) the contribution is returned within 1 year after the date on which the Secretary issues notice to the employer that such plan does not satisfy the requirements of this section.

(k) Requirements Relating to Certain Withdrawals.—Notwithstanding any other law or rule of law—

(1) the withdrawal from a plan which otherwise meets with requirements of this section by the employer of an amount contributed for purposes of the matching employee plan credit shall not be considered to make the benefits forfeitable, and

(2) the plan shall not, by reason of such withdrawal, fail to be for the exclusive benefit of participants or their beneficiaries, if the withdrawn amounts were not matched by employee contributions or were in excess of the limitations of section 415. Any withdrawal described in the preceding sentence shall not be considered to violate the provisions of section 403(c)(1) of the Employee Retirement Income Security Act of 1974. For purposes of this subsection, the reference to the matching employee plan credit shall refer to such credit as in effect before the enactment of the Tax Reform Act of 1984.

(l) Employer Securities Defined.—For purposes of this section—

(1) In general.—The term "employer securities" means common stock issued by the employer (or by a corporation which is a member of the same controlled group) which is readily tradable on an established securities market.

(2) Special rule where there is no readily tradable common stock.—If there is no common stock which meets the requirements of paragraph (1), the term "employer securities" means common stock issued by the employer (or by a corporation which is a member of the same controlled group) having a combination of voting power and dividend rights equal to or in excess of—

(A) that class of common stock of the employer (or of any other such corporation) having the greatest voting power, and

(B) that class of common stock of the employer (or of any other such corporation) having the greatest dividend rights.

(3) Preferred stock may be issued in certain cases.—Noncallable preferred stock shall be treated as employer securities if such stock is convertible at any time into stock which meets the requirements of paragraph (1) or (2) (whichever is applicable) and if such conversion is at a conversion price which (as of the date of the acquisition by the tax credit employee stock ownership plan) is reasonable. For purposes of the preceding sentence, under regulations prescribed by the Secretary, preferred stock shall be treated as noncallable if after the call there will be a reasonable opportunity for a conversion which meets the requirements of the preceding sentence.

(4) Application to controlled group of corporations.—

(A) In general.—For purposes of this subsection, the term "controlled group of corporations" has the meaning given to such term by section 1563(a) (determined without regard to subsections (a)(4) and (e)(3)(C) of section 1563).

(B) Where common parent owns at least 50 percent of first tier subsidiary.—For purposes of subparagraph (A), if the common parent owns directly stock possessing at least 50 percent of the voting power of all classes of stock and at least 50 percent of each class of nonvoting stock in a first tier subsidiary, such subsidiary (and all other corporations below it in the chain which would meet the 80 percent test of section 1563(a) if the first tier subsidiary were the common parent) shall be treated as includible corporations.

(C) Where common parent owns 100 percent of first tier subsidiary.—For purposes of subparagraph (A), if the common parent owns directly stock possessing all of the voting power of all classes of stock and all of the nonvoting stock, in a first tier subsidiary, and if the first tier subsidiary owns directly stock possessing at least 50 percent of the voting power of all classes of stock, and at least 50 percent of each class of nonvoting stock, in a second tier subsidiary of the common parent, such second tier subsidiary (and all other corporations below it in the chain which would meet the 80 percent test of section 1563(a) if the second tier subsidiary were the common parent) shall be treated as includible corporations.

(5) Nonvoting common stock may be acquired in certain cases.—Nonvoting common stock of an employer described in the second sentence of section 401(a)(22) shall be treated as employer securities if an employer has a class of nonvoting common stock outstanding and the specific shares that the plan acquires have been issued and outstanding for at least 24 months.

(m) Nonrecognition of Gain or Loss on Contribution of Employer Securities to Tax Credit Employee Stock Ownership Plan.—No gain or loss shall be recognized to the taxpayer with respect to the transfer of employer securities to a tax credit employee stock ownership plan maintained by the taxpayer to the extent that such transfer is required under section 41(c)(1)(B), or subparagraph (A) or (B) of section 48(n)(1).

(n) Securities Received in Certain Transactions.—

(1) In general.—A plan to which section 1042 applies and an eligible worker-owned cooperative (within the meaning of section 1042(c)) shall provide that no portion of the assets of the plan or cooperative attributable to (or allocable in lieu of) employer securities acquired by the plan or cooperative in a sale to which section 1042 applies may accrue (or be allocated directly or indirectly under any plan of the employer meeting the requirements of section 401(a))—

(A) during the nonallocation period, for the benefit of—

(i) any taxpayer who makes an election under section 1042(a) with respect to employer securities,

(ii) any individual who is related to the taxpayer (within the meaning of section 267(b)), or

(B) for the benefit of any other person who owns (after application of section 318(a)) more than 25 percent of—

(i) any class of outstanding stock of the corporation which issued such employer securities or of any corporation which is a member of the same controlled group of corporations (within the meaning of subsection (*l*)(4)) as such corporation, or

(ii) the total value of any class of outstanding stock of any such corporation.

For purposes of subparagraph (B), section 318(a) shall be applied without regard to the employee trust exception in paragraph (2)(B)(i).

(2) Failure to meet requirements.—If a plan fails to meet the requirements of paragraph (1)—

(A) the plan shall be treated as having distributed to the person described in paragraph (1) the amount allocated to the account of such person in violation of paragraph (1) at the time of such allocation,

(B) the provisions of section 4979A shall apply, and

(C) the statutory period for the assessment of any tax imposed by section 4979A shall not expire before the date which is 3 years from the later of—

(i) the 1st allocation of employer securities in connection with a sale to the plan to which section 1042 applies, or

(ii) the date on which the Secretary is notified of such failure.

IRC Sec. 409(n)(2)(C)(ii)

(3) Definitions and special rules.—For purposes of this subsection—

(A) Lineal descendants.—Paragraph (1)(A)(ii) shall not apply to any individual if—

(i) such individual is a lineal descendant of the taxpayer, and

(ii) the aggregate amount allocated to the benefit of all such lineal descendants during the nonallocation period does not exceed more than 5 percent of the employer securities (or amounts allocated in lieu thereof) held by the plan which are attributable to a sale to the plan by any person related to such descendants (within the meaning of section 267(c)(4)) in a transaction to which section 1042 applied.

(B) 25-percent shareholders.—A person shall be treated as failing to meet the stock ownership limitation under paragraph (1)(B) if such person fails such limitation—

(i) at any time during the 1-year period ending on the date of sale of qualified securities to the plan or cooperative, or

(ii) on the date as of which qualified securities are allocated to participants in the plan or cooperative.

(C) Nonallocation period.—The term "nonallocation period" means the period beginning on the date of the sale of the qualified securities and ending on the later of—

(i) the date which is 10 years after the date of sale, or

(ii) the date of the plan allocation attributable to the final payment of acquisition indebtedness incurred in connection with such sale.

(o) Distribution and Payment Requirements.—A plan meets the requirements of this subsection if—

(1) Distribution requirement.—

(A) In general.—The plan provides that, if the participant and, if applicable pursuant to sections 401(a)(11) and 417, with the consent of the participant's spouse elects, the distribution of the participant's account balance in the plan will commence not later than 1 year after the close of the plan year—

(i) in which the participant separates from service by reason of the attainment of normal retirement age under the plan, disability, or death, or

(ii) which is the 5th plan year following the plan year in which the participant otherwise separates from service, except that this clause shall not apply if the participant is reemployed by the employer before distribution is required to begin under this clause.

(B) Exception for certain financed securities.—For purposes of this subsection, the account bal-

ance of a participant shall not include any employer securities acquired with the proceeds of the loan described in section 404(a)(9) until the close of the plan year in which such loan is repaid in full.

(C) Limited distribution period.—The plan provides that, unless the participant elects otherwise, the distribution of the participant's account balance will be in substantially equal periodic payments (not less frequently than annually) over a period not longer than the greater of—

(i) 5 years, or

(ii) in the case of a participant with an account balance in excess of $800,000, 5 years plus 1 additional year (but not more than 5 additional years) for each $160,000 or fraction thereof by which such balance exceeds $800,000.

(2) Cost-of-living adjustment.—The Secretary shall adjust the dollar amounts under paragraph (1)(C) at the same time and in the same manner as under section 415(d).

(p) Prohibited Allocation of Securities in an S Corporation.—

(1) In general.—An employee stock ownership plan holding employer securities consisting of stock in an S corporation shall provide that no portion of the assets of the plan attributable to (or allocable in lieu of) such employer securities may, during a nonallocation year, accrue (or be allocated directly or indirectly under any plan of the employer meeting the requirements of section 401(a)) for the benefit of any disqualified person.

(2) Failure to meet requirements.—

(A) In general.—If a plan fails to meet the requirements of paragraph (1), the plan shall be treated as having distributed to any disqualified person the amount allocated to the account of such person in violation of paragraph (1) at the time of such allocation.

(B) Cross reference.—For excise tax relating to violations of paragraph (1) and ownership of synthetic equity, see section 4979A.

(3) Nonallocation year.—For purposes of this subsection—

(A) In general.—The term "nonallocation year" means any plan year of an employee stock ownership plan if, at any time during such plan year—

(i) such plan holds employer securities consisting of stock in an S corporation, and

(ii) disqualified persons own at least 50 percent of the number of shares of stock in the S corporation.

(B) Attribution rules.—For purposes of subparagraph (A)—

(i) In general.—The rules of section 318(a) shall apply for purposes of determining ownership, except that—

(I) in applying paragraph (1) thereof, the members of an individual's family shall include members of the family described in paragraph (4)(D), and

(II) paragraph (4) thereof shall not apply.

(ii) Deemed-owned shares.—Notwithstanding the employee trust exception in section 318(a)(2)(B)(i), an individual shall be treated as owning deemed-owned shares of the individual.

Solely for purposes of applying paragraph (5), this subparagraph shall be applied after the attribution rules of paragraph (5) have been applied.

(4) Disqualified person.—For purposes of this subsection—

(A) In general.—The term "disqualified person" means any person if—

(i) the aggregate number of deemed-owned shares of such person and the members of such person's family is at least 20 percent of the number of deemed-owned shares of stock in the S corporation, or

(ii) in the case of a person not described in clause (i), the number of deemed-owned shares of such person is at least 10 percent of the number of deemed-owned shares of stock in such corporation.

(B) Treatment of family members.—In the case of a disqualified person described in subparagraph (A)(i), any member of such person's family with deemed-owned shares shall be treated as a disqualified person if not otherwise treated as a disqualified person under subparagraph (A).

(C) Deemed-owned shares.—

(i) In general.—The term "deemed-owned shares" means, with respect to any person—

(I) the stock in the S corporation constituting employer securities of an employee stock ownership plan which is allocated to such person under the plan, and

(II) such person's share of the stock in such corporation which is held by such plan but which is not allocated under the plan to participants.

(ii) Person's share of unallocated stock.—For purposes of clause (i)(II), a person's share of unallocated S corporation stock held by such plan is the amount of the unallocated stock which would be allocated to such person if the unallocated stock were allocated to all participants in the same proportions as the most recent stock allocation under the plan.

(D) Member of family.—For purposes of this paragraph, the term "member of the family" means, with respect to any individual—

(i) the spouse of the individual,

(ii) an ancestor or lineal descendant of the individual or the individual's spouse,

(iii) a brother or sister of the individual or the individual's spouse and any lineal descendant of the brother or sister, and

(iv) the spouse of any individual described in clause (ii) or (iii).

A spouse of an individual who is legally separated from such individual under a decree of divorce or separate maintenance shall not be treated as such individual's spouse for purposes of this subparagraph.

(5) Treatment of synthetic equity.—For purposes of paragraphs (3) and (4), in the case of a person who owns synthetic equity in the S corporation, except to the extent provided in regulations, the shares of stock in such corporation on which such synthetic equity is based shall be treated as outstanding stock in such corporation and deemed-owned shares of such person if such treatment of synthetic equity of 1 or more such persons results in—

(A) the treatment of any person as a disqualified person, or

(B) the treatment of any year as a nonallocation year.

For purposes of this paragraph, synthetic equity shall be treated as owned by a person in the same manner as stock is treated as owned by a person under the rules of paragraphs (2) and (3) of section 318(a). If, without regard to this paragraph, a person is treated as a disqualified person or a year is treated as a nonallocation year, this paragraph shall not be construed to result in the person or year not being so treated.

(6) Definitions.—For purposes of this subsection—

(A) Employee stock ownership plan.—The term "employee stock ownership plan" has the meaning given such term by section 4975(e)(7).

(B) Employer securities.—The term "employer security" has the meaning given such term by section 409(*l*).

(C) Synthetic equity.—The term "synthetic equity" means any stock option, warrant, restricted stock, deferred issuance stock right, or similar interest or right that gives the holder the right to acquire or receive stock of the S corporation in the future. Except to the extent provided in regulations, synthetic equity also includes a stock appreciation right, phantom stock unit, or similar right to a future cash payment based on the value of such stock or appreciation in such value.

(7) Regulations and guidance.—

(A) In general.—The Secretary shall prescribe such regulations as may be necessary to carry out the purposes of this subsection.

IRC Sec. 409(p)(7)(A)

(B) Avoidance evasion.—The Secretary may, by regulation or other guidance of general applicability, provide that a nonallocation year occurs in any case in which the principal purpose of the ownership structure of an S corporation constitutes an avoidance or evasion of this subsection.

(q) Cross References.—

(1) For requirements of allowance of employee plan credit, see section 48(n).

(2) For assessable penalties for failure to meet requirements of this section, or for failure to make contributions required with respect to the allowance of an employee plan credit or employee stock ownership credit, see section 6699.

(3) For requirements for allowance of an employee stock ownership credit, see section 41.

Recent Amendments to IRC §409

Pension Protection Act of 2006 (Pub. L. No. 109-280), as follows:

• IRC §409(h)(7) was amended by Act §901(a)(2)(B) by inserting "or subparagraph (B) or (C) of §401(a)(35)" before the period at the end. Eff. generally for plan years beginning after Dec. 31, 2006. See Act §901(c) for special effective date rule.

• **Sunset Provision.** Act §811, provides:

SEC. 811. PENSIONS AND INDIVIDUAL RETIREMENT ARRANGEMENT PROVISIONS OF ECONOMIC GROWTH AND TAX RELIEF RECONCILIATION ACT OF 2001 MADE PERMANENT.

Title IX of the Economic Growth and Tax Relief Reconciliation Act of 2001 [Pub. L. No. 107-16] shall not apply to the provisions of, and amendments made by, subtitles A through F [§§601–666] of title VI of such Act (relating to pension and individual retirement arrangement provisions).

Job Creation and Worker Assistance Act of 2002 (Pub. L. No. 107-147), as follows:

• IRC §409(o)(1)(C)(ii) was amended by Act §411(j)(2)(A)–(B) by replacing "$500,000", each place it appeared, with "$800,000", and by replacing "$100,000" with "$160,000". Eff. generally for years beginning after Dec. 31, 2001, as if included in the provision of Pub. L. No. 107-16 to which it relates.

Economic Growth Tax Relief Reconciliation Act of 2001 (Pub. L. No. 107-16), as follows:

• IRC §409 was amended by Act §656(a) by redesignating subsec. (p) as subsec. (q) and inserting after subsec. (o) new subsec. (p). Eff. generally for plan years beginning after Dec. 31, 2004. See Act §656(d)(2) for a special effective date rule.

• **Sunset Provision.** Act §901, as amended by Pub. L. No. 111-312, §101(a)(1), provides the sunset rule below. But see Pub. L. No. 109-280, §811, and Pub. L. No. 111-148, §10909(c), as amended by Pub. L. No. 111-312, §101(b)(1).

SEC. 901. SUNSET OF PROVISIONS OF ACT.

(a) **In general.** All provisions of, and amendments made by, this Act shall not apply—

(1) to taxable, plan, or limitation years beginning after December 31, 2012, or

(2) in the case of title V, to estates of decedents dying, gifts made, or generation skipping transfers, after December 31, 2012.

(b) **Application of certain laws.**—The Internal Revenue Code of 1986 and the Employee Retirement Income Security Act of 1974 shall be applied and administered to years, estates, gifts, and transfers described in subsection (a) as if the provisions and amendments described in subsection (a) had never been enacted.

SEC. 409A. INCLUSION IN GROSS INCOME OF DEFERRED COMPENSATION UNDER NONQUALIFIED DEFERRED COMPENSATION PLANS.

(a) Rules Relating to Constructive Receipt.—

(1) Plan failures.—

(A) Gross income inclusion.—

(i) In general.—If at any time during a taxable year a nonqualified deferred compensation plan—

(I) fails to meet the requirements of paragraphs (2), (3), and (4), or

(II) is not operated in accordance with such requirements,

all compensation deferred under the plan for the taxable year and all preceding taxable years shall be includible in gross income for the taxable year to the extent not subject to a substantial risk of forfeiture and not previously included in gross income.

(ii) Application only to affected participants.—Clause (i) shall only apply with respect to all compensation deferred under the plan for participants with respect to whom the failure relates.

(B) Interest and additional tax payable with respect to previously deferred compensation.—

(i) In general.—If compensation is required to be included in gross income under subparagraph (A) for a taxable year, the tax imposed by this chapter for the taxable year shall be increased by the sum of—

(I) the amount of interest determined under clause (ii), and

(II) an amount equal to 20 percent of the compensation which is required to be included in gross income.

(ii) Interest.—For purposes of clause (i), the interest determined under this clause for any taxable year is the amount of interest at the underpayment rate plus 1 percentage point on the underpayments that would have occurred had the deferred compensation been includible in gross income for the taxable year in which first deferred or, if later, the first taxable year in which such deferred compensation is not subject to a substantial risk of forfeiture.

(2) Distributions.—

(A) In general.—The requirements of this paragraph are met if the plan provides that compensation deferred under the plan may not be distributed earlier than—

(i) separation from service as determined by the Secretary (except as provided in subparagraph (B)(i)),

(ii) the date the participant becomes disabled (within the meaning of subparagraph (C)),

(iii) death,

(iv) a specified time (or pursuant to a fixed schedule) specified under the plan at the date of the deferral of such compensation,

(v) to the extent provided by the Secretary, a change in the ownership or effective control of the corporation, or in the ownership of a substantial portion of the assets of the corporation, or

(vi) the occurrence of an unforeseeable emergency.

(B) Special rules.—

(i) Specified employees.—In the case of any specified employee, the requirement of subparagraph (A)(i) is met only if distributions may not be made before the date which is 6 months after the date of separation from service (or, if earlier, the date of death of the employee). For purposes of the preceding sentence, a specified employee is a key employee (as defined in section 416(i) without regard to paragraph (5) thereof) of a corporation any stock in which is publicly traded on an established securities market or otherwise.

(ii) Unforeseeable emergency.—For purposes of subparagraph (A)(vi)—

(I) In general.—The term "unforeseeable emergency" means a severe financial hardship to the participant resulting from an illness or accident of the participant, the participant's spouse, or a dependent (as defined in section 152(a)) of the participant, loss of the participant's property due to casualty, or other similar extraordinary and unforeseeable circumstances arising as a result of events beyond the control of the participant.

(II) Limitation on distributions.—The requirement of subparagraph (A)(vi) is met only if, as determined under regulations of the Secretary, the amounts distributed with respect to an emergency do not exceed the amounts necessary to satisfy such emergency plus amounts necessary to pay taxes reasonably anticipated as a result of the distribution, after taking into account the extent to which such hardship is or may be relieved through reimbursement or compensation by insurance or otherwise or by liquidation of the participant's assets (to the extent the liquidation of such assets would not itself cause severe financial hardship).

(C) Disabled.—For purposes of subparagraph (A)(ii), a participant shall be considered disabled if the participant—

(i) is unable to engage in any substantial gainful activity by reason of any medically determinable physical or mental impairment which can be expected to result in death or can be expected to

last for a continuous period of not less than 12 months, or

(ii) is, by reason of any medically determinable physical or mental impairment which can be expected to result in death or can be expected to last for a continuous period of not less than 12 months, receiving income replacement benefits for a period of not less than 3 months under an accident and health plan covering employees of the participant's employer.

(3) Acceleration of benefits.—The requirements of this paragraph are met if the plan does not permit the acceleration of the time or schedule of any payment under the plan, except as provided in regulations by the Secretary.

(4) Elections.—

(A) In general.—The requirements of this paragraph are met if the requirements of subparagraphs (B) and (C) are met.

(B) Initial deferral decision.—

(i) In general.—The requirements of this subparagraph are met if the plan provides that compensation for services performed during a taxable year may be deferred at the participant's election only if the election to defer such compensation is made not later than the close of the preceding taxable year or at such other time as provided in regulations.

(ii) First year of eligibility.—In the case of the first year in which a participant becomes eligible to participate in the plan, such election may be made with respect to services to be performed subsequent to the election within 30 days after the date the participant becomes eligible to participate in such plan.

(iii) Performance-based compensation.—In the case of any performance-based compensation based on services performed over a period of at least 12 months, such election may be made no later than 6 months before the end of the period.

(C) Changes in time and form of distribution.— The requirements of this subparagraph are met if, in the case of a plan which permits under a subsequent election a delay in a payment or a change in the form of payment—

(i) the plan requires that such election may not take effect until at least 12 months after the date on which the election is made,

(ii) in the case of an election related to a payment not described in clause (ii), (iii), or (vi) of paragraph (2)(A), the plan requires that the payment with respect to which such election is made be deferred for a period of not less than 5 years from the date such payment would otherwise have been made, and

IRC Sec. 409A(a)(4)(C)(ii)

(iii) the plan requires that any election related to a payment described in paragraph (2)(A)(iv) may not be made less than 12 months prior to the date of the first scheduled payment under such paragraph.

(b) Rules Relating to Funding.—

(1) Offshore property in a trust.—In the case of assets set aside (directly or indirectly) in a trust (or other arrangement determined by the Secretary) for purposes of paying deferred compensation under a nonqualified deferred compensation plan, for purposes of section 83 such assets shall be treated as property transferred in connection with the performance of services whether or not such assets are available to satisfy claims of general creditors—

(A) at the time set aside if such assets (or such trust or other arrangement) are located outside of the United States, or

(B) at the time transferred if such assets (or such trust or other arrangement) are subsequently transferred outside of the United States.

This paragraph shall not apply to assets located in a foreign jurisdiction if substantially all of the services to which the nonqualified deferred compensation relates are performed in such jurisdiction.

(2) Employer's financial health.—In the case of compensation deferred under a nonqualified deferred compensation plan, there is a transfer of property within the meaning of section 83 with respect to such compensation as of the earlier of—

(A) the date on which the plan first provides that assets will become restricted to the provision of benefits under the plan in connection with a change in the employer's financial health, or

(B) the date on which assets are so restricted, whether or not such assets are available to satisfy claims of general creditors.

(3) Treatment of employer's defined benefit plan during restricted period.—

(A) In general.—If—

(i) during any restricted period with respect to a single-employer defined benefit plan, assets are set aside or reserved (directly or indirectly) in a trust (or other arrangement as determined by the Secretary) or transferred to such a trust or other arrangement for purposes of paying deferred compensation of an applicable covered employee under a nonqualified deferred compensation plan of the plan sponsor or member of a controlled group which includes the plan sponsor, or

(ii) a nonqualified deferred compensation plan of the plan sponsor or member of a controlled group which includes the plan sponsor provides that assets will become restricted to the provision of benefits under the plan to an applicable covered employee in connection with such restricted period (or other similar financial measure determined by the Secretary) with respect to the defined benefit plan, or assets are so restricted,

such assets shall, for purposes of section 83, be treated as property transferred in connection with the performance of services whether or not such assets are available to satisfy claims of general creditors. Clause (i) shall not apply with respect to any assets which are so set aside before the restricted period with respect to the defined benefit plan.

(B) Restricted period.—For purposes of this section, the term "restricted period" means, with respect to any plan described in subparagraph (A)—

(i) any period during which the plan is in at-risk status (as defined in section 430(i));

(ii) any period the plan sponsor is a debtor in a case under title 11, United States Code, or similar Federal or State law, and

(iii) the 12-month period beginning on the date which is 6 months before the termination date of the plan if, as of the termination date, the plan is not sufficient for benefit liabilities (within the meaning of section 4041 of the Employee Retirement Income Security Act of 1974).

(C) Special rule for payment of taxes on deferred compensation included in income.—If an employer provides directly or indirectly for the payment of any Federal, State, or local income taxes with respect to any compensation required to be included in gross income by reason of this paragraph—

(i) interest shall be imposed under subsection (a)(1)(B)(i)(I) on the amount of such payment in the same manner as if such payment was part of the deferred compensation to which it relates,

(ii) such payment shall be taken into account in determining the amount of the additional tax under subsection (a)(1)(B)(i)(II) in the same manner as if such payment was part of the deferred compensation to which it relates, and

(iii) no deduction shall be allowed under this title with respect to such payment.

(D) Other definitions.—For purposes of this section—

(i) Applicable covered employee.—The term "applicable covered employee" means any—

(I) covered employee of a plan sponsor,

(II) covered employee of a member of a controlled group which includes the plan sponsor, and

(III) former employee who was a covered employee at the time of termination of employment with the plan sponsor or a member of a controlled group which includes the plan sponsor.

(ii) Covered employee.—The term "covered employee" means an individual described in section 162(m)(3) or an individual subject to the requirements of section 16(a) of the Securities Exchange Act of 1934.

(4) Income inclusion for offshore trusts and employer's financial health.—For each taxable year that assets treated as transferred under this subsection remain set aside in a trust or other arrangement subject to paragraph (1), (2), or (3), any increase in value in, or earnings with respect to, such assets shall be treated as an additional transfer of property under this subsection (to the extent not previously included in income).

(5) Interest on tax liability payable with respect to transferred property.—

(A) In general.—If amounts are required to be included in gross income by reason of paragraph (1), (2), or (3) for a taxable year, the tax imposed by this chapter for such taxable year shall be increased by the sum of—

(i) the amount of interest determined under subparagraph (B), and

(ii) an amount equal to 20 percent of the amounts required to be included in gross income.

(B) Interest.—For purposes of subparagraph (A), the interest determined under this subparagraph for any taxable year is the amount of interest at the underpayment rate plus 1 percentage point on the underpayments that would have occurred had the amounts so required to be included in gross income by paragraph (1), (2), or (3) been includible in gross income for the taxable year in which first deferred or, if later, the first taxable year in which such amounts are not subject to a substantial risk of forfeiture.

(c) No Inference on Earlier Income Inclusion or Requirement of Later Inclusion.—Nothing in this section shall be construed to prevent the inclusion of amounts in gross income under any other provision of this chapter or any other rule of law earlier than the time provided in this section. Any amount included in gross income under this section shall not be required to be included in gross income under any other provision of this chapter or any other rule of law later than the time provided in this section.

(d) Other Definitions and Special Rules.—For purposes of this section—

(1) Nonqualified deferred compensation plan.—The term "nonqualified deferred compensation plan" means any plan that provides for the deferral of compensation, other than—

(A) a qualified employer plan, and

(B) any bona fide vacation leave, sick leave, compensatory time, disability pay, or death benefit plan.

(2) Qualified employer plan.—The term "qualified employer plan" means—

(A) any plan, contract, pension, account, or trust described in subparagraph (A) or (B) of section 219(g)(5) (without regard to subparagraph (A)(iii)),

(B) any eligible deferred compensation plan (within the meaning of section 457(b)), and

(C) any plan described in section 415(m).

(3) Plan includes arrangements, etc.—The term "plan" includes any agreement or arrangement, including an agreement or arrangement that includes one person.

(4) Substantial risk of forfeiture.—The rights of a person to compensation are subject to a substantial risk of forfeiture if such person's rights to such compensation are conditioned upon the future performance of substantial services by any individual.

(5) Treatment of earnings.—References to deferred compensation shall be treated as including references to income (whether actual or notional) attributable to such compensation or such income.

(6) Aggregation rules.—Except as provided by the Secretary, rules similar to the rules of subsections (b) and (c) of section 414 shall apply.

(e) Regulations.—The Secretary shall prescribe such regulations as may be necessary or appropriate to carry out the purposes of this section, including regulations—

(1) providing for the determination of amounts of deferral in the case of a nonqualified deferred compensation plan which is a defined benefit plan,

(2) relating to changes in the ownership and control of a corporation or assets of a corporation for purposes of subsection (a)(2)(A)(v),

(3) exempting arrangements from the application of subsection (b) if such arrangements will not result in an improper deferral of United States tax and will not result in assets being effectively beyond the reach of creditors,

(4) defining financial health for purposes of subsection (b)(2), and

(5) disregarding a substantial risk of forfeiture in cases where necessary to carry out the purposes of this section.

Amendments to IRC §409A

Worker, Retiree, and Employer Recovery Act of 2008 (Pub. L. No. 110-458), as follows:

● IRC §409A(b)(3)(A)(ii) was amended by Act §101(e) by inserting "to an applicable covered employee" after "under the plan". Eff. as if included in Pub. L. No. 109-280, §116 [eff. for transfers or other reservations of assets after Aug. 17, 2006].

Pension Protection Act of 2006 (Pub. L. No. 109-280), as follows:

• IRC §409A(b) was amended by Act §116(a) by redesignating paras. (3) and (4) as paras. (4) and (5), and inserting after para. (2) new para. (3). Eff. for transfers or other reservation of assets after Aug. 17, 2006.
• IRC §409A(b)(4)–(5), as redesignated by Act §116(a), were amended by Act §116(b) by replacing "paragraph (1) or (2)", each place it appeared, with "paragraph (1), (2), or (3)". Eff. for transfers or other reservation of assets after Aug. 17, 2006.

Gulf Opportunity Zone Act of 2005 (Pub. L. No. 109-135), as follows:
• IRC §409A(a)(4)(C)(ii) was amended by Act §403(hh)(2) by striking "first" before "payment with respect to which". Eff. generally for amounts deferred after Dec. 31, 2004, as if included in the provision of Pub. L. No. 108-357 to which it relates.

American Jobs Creation Act of 2004 (Pub. L. No. 108-357), as follows:
• IRC §409A was added by Act §885(a). Eff. generally for amounts deferred after Dec. 31, 2004. See Act §§885(d)(2)–(3), 885(e) and 885(f).

Subpart B—Special Rules

SEC. 410. MINIMUM PARTICIPATION STANDARDS.

(a) Participation.—

(1) Minimum age and service conditions.—

(A) General rule.—A trust shall not constitute a qualified trust under section 401(a) if the plan of which it is a part requires, as a condition of participation in the plan, that an employee complete a period of service with employer or employers maintaining the plan extending beyond the later of the following dates—

(i) the date on which the employee attains the age of 21; or

(ii) the date on which he completes 1 year of service.

(B) Special rules for certain plans.—

(i) In the case of any plan which provides that after not more than 2 years of service each participant has a right to 100 percent of his accrued benefit under the plan which is nonforfeitable (within the meaning of section 411) at the time such benefit accrues, clause (ii) of subparagraph (A) shall be applied by substituting "2 years of service" for "1 year of service".

(ii) In the case of any plan maintained exclusively for employees of an educational institution (as defined in section 170(b)(1)(A)(ii)) by an employer which is exempt from tax under section 501(a) which provides that each participant having at least 1 year of service has a right to 100 percent of his accrued benefit under the plan which is nonforfeitable (within the meaning of section 411) at the time such benefit accrues, clause (i) of subparagraph (A) shall be applied by substituting "26" for "21". This clause shall not apply to any plan to which clause (i) applies.

(2) Maximum age conditions.—A trust shall not constitute a qualified trust under section 401(a) if the

plan of which it is a part excludes from participation (on the basis of age) employees who have attained a specified age.

(3) Definition of year of service.—

(A) General rule.—For purposes of this subsection, the term "year of service" means a 12-month period during which the employee has not less than 1,000 hours of service. For purposes of this paragraph, computation of any 12-month period shall be made with reference to the date on which the employee's employment commenced, except that, under regulations prescribed by the Secretary of Labor, such computation may be made by reference to the first day of a plan year in the case of an employee who does not complete 1,000 hours of service during the 12-month period beginning on the date his employment commenced.

(B) Seasonal industries.—In the case of any seasonal industry where the customary period of employment is less than 1,000 hours during a calendar year, the term "year of service" shall be such period as may be determined under regulations prescribed by the Secretary of Labor.

(C) Hours of service.—For purposes of this subsection the term "hours of service" means a time of service determined under regulations prescribed by the Secretary of Labor.

(D) Maritime industries.—For purposes of this subsection, in the case of any maritime industry, 125 days of service shall be treated as 1,000 hours of service. The Secretary of Labor may prescribe regulations to carry out this subparagraph.

(4) Time of participation.—A plan shall be treated as not meeting the requirements of paragraph (1) unless it provides that any employee who has satisfied the minimum age and service requirements specified in such paragraph, and who is otherwise entitled to participate in the plan, commences participation in the plan no later than the earlier of—

(A) the first day of the first plan year beginning after the date on which such employee satisfied such requirements, or

(B) the date 6 months after the date on which he satisfied such requirements,

unless such employee was separated from the service before the date referred to in subparagraph (A) or (B), whichever is applicable.

(5) Breaks in service.—

(A) General rule.—Except as otherwise provided in subparagraphs (B), (C), and (D), all years of service with the employer or employers maintaining the plan shall be taken into account in computing the period of service for purposes of paragraph (1).

(B) Employees under 2-year 100 percent vesting.—In the case of any employee who has any

1-year break in service (as defined in section 411(a)(6)(A)) under a plan to which the service requirements of clause (i) of paragraph (1)(B) apply, if such employee has not satisfied such requirements, service before such break shall not be required to be taken into account.

(C) 1-year break in service.—In computing an employee's period of service for purposes of paragraph (1) in the case of any participant who has any 1-year break in service (as defined in section 411(a)(6)(A)), service before such break shall not be required to be taken into account under the plan until he has completed a year of service (as defined in paragraph (3)) after his return.

(D) Nonvested participants.—

(i) In general.—For purposes of paragraph (1), in the case of a nonvested participant, years of service with the employer or employers maintaining the plan before any period of consecutive 1-year breaks in service shall not be required to be taken into account in computing the period of service if the number of consecutive 1-year breaks in service within such period equals or exceeds the greater of—

(I) 5, or

(II) the aggregate number of years of service before such period.

(ii) Years of service not taken into account.—If any years of service are not required to be taken into account by reason of a period of breaks in service to which clause (i) applies, such years of service shall not be taken into account in applying clause (i) to a subsequent period of breaks in service.

(iii) Nonvested participant defined.—For purposes of clause (i), the term "nonvested participant" means a participant who does not have any nonforfeitable right under the plan to an accrued benefit derived from employer contributions.

(E) Special rule for maternity or paternity absences.—

(i) General rule.—In the case of each individual who is absent from work for any period—

(I) by reason of the pregnancy of the individual,

(II) by reason of the birth of a child of the individual,

(III) by reason of the placement of a child with the individual in connection with the adoption of such child by such individual, or

(IV) for purposes of caring for such child for a period beginning immediately following such birth or placement,

the plan shall treat as hours of service, solely for purposes of determining under this paragraph whether a 1-year break in service (as defined in section 411(a)(6)(A)) has occurred, the hours described in clause (ii).

(ii) Hours treated as hours of service.—The hours described in this clause are—

(I) the hours of service which otherwise would normally have been credited to such individual but for such absence, or

(II) in any case in which the plan is unable to determine the hours described in subclause (I), 8 hours of service per day of such absence,

except that the total number of hours treated as hours of service under this clause by reason of any such pregnancy or placement shall not exceed 501 hours.

(iii) Year to which hours are credited.—The hours described in clause (ii) shall be treated as hours of service as provided in this subparagraph—

(I) only in the year in which the absence from work begins, if a participant would be prevented from incurring a 1-year break in service in such year solely because the period of absence is treated as hours of service as provided in clause (i), or

(II) in any other case, in the immediately following year.

(iv) Year defined.—For purposes of this subparagraph, the term "year" means the period used in computations pursuant to paragraph (3).

(v) Information required to be filed.—A plan shall not fail to satisfy the requirements of this subparagraph solely because it provides that no credit will be given pursuant to this subparagraph unless the individual furnishes to the plan administrator such timely information as the plan may reasonably require to establish—

(I) that the absence from work is for reasons referred to in clause (i), and

(II) the number of days for which there was such an absence.

(b) Minimum Coverage Requirements.—

(1) In general.—A trust shall not constitute a qualified trust under section 401(a) unless such trust is designated by the employer as part of a plan which meets 1 of the following requirements:

(A) The plan benefits at least 70 percent of employees who are not highly compensated employees.

(B) The plan benefits—

(i) a percentage of employees who are not highly compensated employees which is at least 70 percent of

(ii) the percentage of highly compensated employees benefiting under the plan.

IRC Sec. 410(b)(1)(B)(ii)

(C) The plan meets the requirements of paragraph (2).

(2) Average benefit percentage test.—

(A) In general.—A plan shall be treated as meeting the requirements of this paragraph if—

(i) the plan benefits such employees as qualify under a classification set up by the employer and found by the Secretary not to be discriminatory in favor of highly compensated employees, and

(ii) the average benefit percentage for employees who are not highly compensated employees is at least 70 percent of the average benefit percentage for highly compensated employees.

(B) Average benefit percentage.—For purposes of this paragraph, the term "average benefit percentage" means, with respect to any group, the average of the benefit percentages calculated separately with respect to each employee in such group (whether or not a participant in any plan).

(C) Benefit percentage.—For purposes of this paragraph—

(i) In general.—The term "benefit percentage" means the employer-provided contribution or benefit of an employee under all qualified plans maintained by the employer, expressed as a percentage of such employee's compensation (within the meaning of section 414(s)).

(ii) Period for computing percentage.—At the election of an employer, the benefit percentage for any plan year shall be computed on the basis of contributions or benefits for—

(I) such plan year, or

(II) any consecutive plan year period (not greater than 3 years) which ends with such plan year and which is specified in such election.

An election under this clause, once made, may be revoked or modified only with the consent of the Secretary.

(D) Employees taken into account.—For purposes of determining who is an employee for purposes of determining the average benefit percentage under subparagraph (B)—

(i) except as provided in clause (ii), paragraph (4)(A) shall not apply, or

(ii) if the employer elects, paragraph (4)(A) shall be applied by using the lowest age and service requirements of all qualified plans maintained by the employer.

(E) Qualified plan.—For purposes of this paragraph, the term "qualified plan" means any plan which (without regard to this subsection) meets the requirements of section 401(a).

(3) Exclusion of certain employees.—For purposes of this subsection, there shall be excluded from consideration—

(A) employees who are included in a unit of employees covered by an agreement which the Secretary of Labor finds to be a collective bargaining agreement between employee representatives and one or more employers, if there is evidence that retirement benefits were the subject of good faith bargaining between such employee representatives and such employer or employers,

(B) in the case of a trust established or maintained pursuant to an agreement which the Secretary of Labor finds to be a collective bargaining agreement between air pilots represented in accordance with title II of the Railway Labor Act and one or more employers, all employees not covered by such agreement, and

(C) employees who are nonresident aliens and who receive no earned income (within the meaning of section 911(d)(2)) from the employer which constitutes income from sources within the United States (within the meaning of section 861(a)(3)).

Subparagraph (A) shall not apply with respect to coverage of employees under a plan pursuant to an agreement under such subparagraph. For purposes of subparagraph (B), management pilots who are not represented in accordance with title II of the Railway Labor Act shall be treated as covered by a collective bargaining agreement described in such subparagraph if the management pilots manage the flight operations of air pilots who are so represented and the management pilots are, pursuant to the terms of the agreement, included in the group of employees benefitting under the trust described in such subparagraph. Subparagraph (B) shall not apply in the case of a plan which provides contributions or benefits for employees whose principal duties are not customarily performed aboard an aircraft in flight (other than management pilots described in the preceding sentence).

(4) Exclusion of employees not meeting age and service requirements.—

(A) In general.—If a plan—

(i) prescribes minimum age and service requirements as a condition of participation, and

(ii) excludes all employees not meeting such requirements from participation,

then such employees shall be excluded from consideration for purposes of this subsection.

(B) Requirements may be met separately with respect to excluded group.—If employees not meeting the minimum age or service requirements of subsection (a)(1) (without regard to subparagraph (B) thereof) are covered under a plan of the employer which meets the requirements of paragraph (1) separately with respect to such employees, such employees may be excluded from consideration in determining whether any plan of the employer meets the requirements of paragraph (1).

(C) Requirements not treated as being met before entry date.—An employee shall not be treated as meeting the age and service requirements described in this paragraph until the first date on which, under the plan, any employee with the same age and service would be eligible to commence participation in the plan.

(5) Line of business exception.—

(A) In general.—If, under section 414(r), an employer is treated as operating separate lines of business for a year, the employer may apply the requirements of this subsection for such year separately with respect to employees in each separate line of business.

(B) Plan must be nondiscriminatory.—Subparagraph (A) shall not apply with respect to any plan maintained by an employer unless such plan benefits such employees as qualify under a classification set up by the employer and found by the Secretary not to be discriminatory in favor of highly compensated employees.

(6) Definitions and special rules.—For purposes of this subsection—

(A) Highly compensated employee.—The term "highly compensated employee" has the meaning given such term by section 414(q).

(B) Aggregation rules.—An employer may elect to designate—

(i) 2 or more trusts,

(ii) 1 or more trusts and 1 or more annuity plans, or

(iii) 2 or more annuity plans,

as part of 1 plan intended to qualify under section 401(a) to determine whether the requirements of this subsection are met with respect to such trusts or annuity plans. If an employer elects to treat any trusts or annuity plans as 1 plan under this subparagraph, such trusts or annuity plans shall be treated as 1 plan for purposes of section 401(a)(4).

(C) Special rules for certain dispositions or acquisitions.—

(i) In general.—If a person becomes, or ceases to be, a member of a group described in subsection (b), (c), (m), or (o) of section 414, then the requirements of this subsection shall be treated as having been met during the transition period with respect to any plan covering employees of such person or any other member of such group if—

(I) such requirements were met immediately before each such change, and

(II) the coverage under such plan is not significantly changed during the transition period (other than by reason of the change in members of a group) or such plan meets such other requirements as the Secretary may prescribe by regulation.

(ii) Transition period.—For purposes of clause (i), the term "transition period" means the period—

(I) beginning on the date of the change in members of a group, and

(II) ending on the last day of the 1st plan year beginning after the date of such change.

(D) Special rule for certain employee stock ownership plans.—A trust which is part of a tax credit employee stock ownership plan which is the only plan of an employer intended to qualify under section 401(a) shall not be treated as not a qualified trust under section 401(a) solely because it fails to meet the requirements of this subsection if—

(i) such plan benefits 50 percent or more of all the employees who are eligible under a nondiscriminatory classification under the plan, and

(ii) the sum of the amounts allocated to each participant's account for the year does not exceed 2 percent of the compensation of that participant for the year.

(E) Eligibility to contribute.—In the case of contributions which are subject to section 401(k) or 401(m), employees who are eligible to contribute (or elect to have contributions made on their behalf) shall be treated as benefiting under the plan (other than for purposes of paragraph (2)(A)(ii)).

(F) Employers with only highly compensated employees.—A plan maintained by an employer which has no employees other than highly compensated employees for any year shall be treated as meeting the requirements of this subsection for such year.

(G) Regulations.—The Secretary shall prescribe such regulations as may be necessary or appropriate to carry out the purposes of this subsection.

(c) Application of Participation Standards to Certain Plans.—

(1) The provisions of this section (other than paragraph (2) of this subsection) shall not apply to—

(A) a governmental plan (within the meaning of section 414(d)),

(B) a church plan (within the meaning of section 414(e)) with respect to which the election provided by subsection (d) of this section has not been made,

(C) a plan which has not at any time after September 2, 1974, provided for employer contributions, and

(D) a plan established and maintained by a society, order, or association described in section 501(c)(8) or (9) if no part of the contributions to or under such plan are made by employers of participants in such plan.

IRC Sec. 410(c)(1)(D)

(2) A plan described in paragraph (1) shall be treated as meeting the requirements of this section for purposes of section 401(a), except that in the case of a plan described in subparagraph (B), (C), or (D) of paragraph (1), this paragraph shall apply only if such plan meets the requirements of section 401(a)(3) (as in effect on September 1, 1974).

(d) Election by Church to Have Participation, Vesting, Funding, etc., Provisions Apply.—

(1) In general.—If the church or convention or association of churches which maintains any church plan makes an election under this subsection (in such form and manner as the Secretary may by regulations prescribe), then the provisions of this title relating to participation, vesting, funding, etc. (as in effect from time to time) shall apply to such church plan as if such provisions did not contain an exclusion for church plans.

(2) Election irrevocable.—An election under this subsection with respect to any church plan shall be binding with respect to such plan, and, once made, shall be irrevocable.

Recent Amendments to IRC §410

Pension Protection Act of 2006 (Pub. L. No. 109-280), as follows:
- IRC §410(b)(3) was amended by Act §402(h)(1) by replacing the last sentence with two new sentences. Eff. years beginning before, on or after Aug. 17, 2006. IRC §410(b)(3), last sentence, prior to being stricken:
  Subparagraph (B) shall not apply in the case of a plan which provides contributions or benefits for employees whose principal duties are not customarily performed aboard aircraft in flight.

SEC. 411. MINIMUM VESTING STANDARDS.

(a) General Rule.—A trust shall not constitute a qualified trust under section 401(a) unless the plan of which such trust is a part provides that an employee's right to his normal retirement benefit is nonforfeitable upon the attainment of normal retirement age (as defined in paragraph (8)) and in addition satisfies the requirements of paragraphs (1), (2), and (11) of this subsection and the requirements of subsection (b)(3), and also satisfied, in the case of a defined benefit plan, the requirements of subsection (b)(1) and, in the case of a defined contribution plan, the requirements of subsection (b)(2).

(1) Employee contributions.—A plan satisfies the requirements of this paragraph if an employee's rights in his accrued benefit derived from his own contributions are nonforfeitable.

(2) Employer contributions.—

(A) Defined benefit plans.—

(i) In general.—In the case of a defined benefit plan, a plan satisfies the requirements of this para-graph if it satisfies the requirements of clause (ii) or (iii).

(ii) 5-year vesting.—A plan satisfies the requirements of this clause if an employee who has completed at least 5 years of service has a nonforfeitable right to 100 percent of the employee's accrued benefit derived from employer contributions.

(iii) 3 to 7 year vesting.—A plan satisfies the requirements of this clause if an employee has a nonforfeitable right to a percentage of the employee's accrued benefit derived from employer contributions determined under the following table:

Years of service:	The nonforfeitable percentage is
3	20
4	40
5	60
6	80
7 or more	100

(B) Defined contribution plans.—

(i) In general.—In the case of a defined contribution plan, a plan satisfies the requirements of this paragraph if it satisfies the requirements of clause (ii) or (iii).

(ii) 3-year vesting.—A plan satisfies the requirements of this clause if an employee who has completed at least 3 years of service has a nonforfeitable right to 100 percent of the employee's accrued benefit derived from employer contributions.

(iii) 2 to 6 year vesting.—A plan satisfies the requirements of this clause if an employee has a nonforfeitable right to a percentage of the employee's accrued benefit derived from employer contributions determined under the following table:

Years of service:	The nonforfeitable percentage is:
2	20
3	40
4	60
5	80
6 or more	100

(3) Certain permitted forfeitures, suspensions, etc.—For purposes of this subsection—

(A) Forfeiture on account of death.—A right to an accrued benefit derived from employer contributions shall not be treated as forfeitable solely because the plan provides that it is not payable if the participant dies (except in the case of a survivor annuity which is payable as provided in section 401(a)(11)).

(B) Suspension of benefits from reemployment of retiree.—A right to an accrued benefit derived from employer contributions shall not be treated as forfeitable solely because the plan provides that the payment of benefits is suspended for such period as the employee is employed, subsequent to the commencement of payment of such benefits—

(i) in the case of a plan other than a multiemployer plan, by the employer who maintains the plan under which such benefits were being paid; and

(ii) in the case of a multiemployer plan, in the same industry, the same trade or craft, and the same geographic area covered by the plan as when such benefits commenced.

The Secretary of Labor shall prescribe such regulations as may be necessary to carry out the purposes of this subparagraph, including regulations with respect to the meaning of the term "employed".

(C) Effect of retroactive plan amendments.—A right to an accrued benefit derived from employer contributions shall not be treated as forfeitable solely because plan amendments may be given retroactive application as provided in section 412(d)(2).

(D) Withdrawal of mandatory contribution.—

(i) A right to an accrued benefit derived from employer contributions shall not be treated as forfeitable solely because the plan provides that, in the case of a participant who does not have a nonforfeitable right to at least 50 percent of his accrued benefit derived from employer contributions, such accrued benefit may be forfeited on account of the withdrawal by the participant of any amount attributable to the benefit derived from mandatory contributions (as defined in subsection (c)(2)(C)) made by such participant.

(ii) Clause (i) shall not apply to a plan unless the plan provides that any accrued benefit forfeited under a plan provision described in such clause shall be restored upon repayment by the participant of the full amount of the withdrawal described in such clause plus, in the case of a defined benefit plan, interest. Such interest shall be computed on such amount at the rate determined for purposes of subsection (c)(2)(C) on the date of such repayment (computed annually from the date of such withdrawal). The plan provision required under this clause may provide that such repayment must be made (I) in the case of a withdrawal on account of separation from service, before the earlier of 5 years after the first date on which the participant is subsequently re-employed by the employer, or the close of the first period of 5 consecutive 1-year breaks in service commencing after the withdrawal; or (II) in the case of any other withdrawal, 5 years after the date of the withdrawal.

(iii) In the case of accrued benefits derived from employer contributions which accrued before September 2, 1974, a right to such accrued benefit derived from employer contributions shall not be treated as forfeitable solely because the plan provides that an amount of such accrued benefit may be forfeited on account of the withdrawal by the participant of an amount attributable to the benefit derived from mandatory contributions (as defined in subsection (c)(2)(C)) made by such participant before September 2, 1974, if such amount forfeited is proportional to such amount withdrawn. This clause shall not apply to any plan to which any mandatory contribution is made after September 2, 1974. The Secretary shall prescribe such regulations as may be necessary to carry out the purposes of this clause.

(iv) For purposes of this subparagraph, in the case of any class-year plan, a withdrawal of employee contributions shall be treated as a withdrawal of such contributions on a plan year by plan year basis in succeeding order of time.

(v) For nonforfeitability where the employee has a nonforfeitable right to at least 50 percent of his accrued benefit, see section 401(a)(19).

(E) Cessation of contributions under a multiemployer plan.—A right to an accrued benefit derived from employer contributions under a multiemployer plan shall not be treated as forfeitable solely because the plan provides that benefits accrued as a result of service with the participant's employer before the employer had an obligation to contribute under the plan may not be payable if the employer ceases contributions to the multiemployer plan.

(F) Reduction and suspension of benefits by a multiemployer plan.—A participant's right to an accrued benefit derived from employer contributions under a multiemployer plan shall not be treated as forfeitable solely because—

(i) the plan is amended to reduce benefits under section 418D or under section 4281 of the Employee Retirement Income Security Act of 1974, or

(ii) benefit payments under the plan may be suspended under section 418E or under section 4281 of the Employee Retirement Income Security Act of 1974.

(G) Treatment of matching contributions forfeited by reason of excess deferral or contribution or permissible withdrawal.—A matching contribution (within the meaning of section 401(m)) shall not be treated as forfeitable merely because such contribution is forfeitable if the contribution to which the matching contribution relates is treated as an excess contribution under section 401(k)(8)(B), an excess deferral under section 402(g)(2)(A), a permissible withdrawal under sec-

IRC Sec. 411(a)(3)(G)

tion 414(w), or an excess aggregate contribution under section 401(m)(6)(B).

(4) Service included in determination of nonforfeitable percentage.—In computing the period of service under the plan for purposes of determining the nonforfeitable percentage under paragraph (2), all of an employee's years of service with the employer or employers maintaining the plan shall be taken into account, except that the following may be disregarded:

(A) years of service before age 18;

(B) years of service during a period for which the employee declined to contribute to a plan requiring employee contributions;

(C) years of service with an employer during any period for which the employer did not maintain the plan or a predecessor plan (as defined under regulations prescribed by the Secretary);

(D) service not required to be taken into account under paragraph (6);

(E) years of service before January 1, 1971, unless the employee has had at least 3 years of service after December 3, 1970;

(F) years of service before the first plan year to which this section applies, if such service would have been disregarded under the rules of the plan with regard to breaks in service as in effect on the applicable date; and

(G) in the case of a multiemployer plan, years of service—

(i) with an employer after—

(I) a complete withdrawal of that employer from the plan (within the meaning of section 4203 of the Employee Retirement Income Security Act of 1974), or

(II) to the extent permitted in regulations prescribed by the Secretary, a partial withdrawal described in section 4205(b)(2)(A)(i) of such Act in conjunction with the decertification of the collective bargaining representative, and

(ii) with any employer under the plan after the termination date of the plan under section 4048 of such Act.

(5) Year of service.—

(A) General rule.—For purposes of this subsection, except as provided in subparagraph (C), the term "year of service" means a calendar year, plan year, or other 12-consecutive month period designated by the plan (and not prohibited under regulations prescribed by the Secretary of Labor) during which the participant has completed 1,000 hours of service.

(B) Hours of service.—For purposes of this subsection, the term "hour of service" has the meaning provided by section 410(a)(3)(C).

(C) Seasonal industries.—In the case of any seasonal industry where the customary period of employment is less than 1,000 hours during a calendar year, the term "year of service" shall be such period as may be determined under regulations prescribed by the Secretary of Labor.

(D) Maritime industries.—For purposes of this subsection, in the case of any maritime industry, 125 days of service shall be treated as 1,000 hours of service. The Secretary of Labor may prescribe regulations to carry out the purposes of this subparagraph.

(6) Breaks in service.—

(A) Definition of 1-year break in service.—For purposes of this paragraph, the term "1-year break in service" means a calendar year, plan year, or other 12-consecutive month period designated by the plan (and not prohibited under regulations prescribed by the Secretary of Labor) during which the participant has not completed more than 500 hours of service.

(B) 1 year of service after 1-year break in service.—For purposes of paragraph (4), in the case of any employee who has any 1-year break in service, years of service before such break shall not be required to be taken into account until he has completed a year of service after his return.

(C) 5 consecutive 1-year breaks in service under defined contribution plan.—For purposes of paragraph (4), in the case of any participant in a defined contribution plan, or an insured defined benefit plan which satisfies the requirements of subsection (b)(1)(F), who has 5 consecutive 1-year breaks in service, years of service after such 5-year period shall not be required to be taken into account for purposes of determining the nonforfeitable percentage of his accrued benefit derived from employer contributions which accrued before such 5-year period.

(D) Nonvested participants.—

(i) In general.—For purposes of paragraph (4), in the case of a nonvested participant, years of service with the employer or employers maintaining the plan before any period of consecutive 1-year breaks in service shall not be required to be taken into account if the number of consecutive 1-year breaks in service within such period equals or exceeds the greater of—

(I) 5, or

(II) the aggregate number of years of service before such period.

(ii) Years of service not taken into account.—If any years of service are not taken into account by reason of a period of breaks in service to which clause (i) applies, such years of service shall not be taken into account in applying clause (i) to a subsequent period of breaks in service.

(iii) Nonvested participant defined.—For purposes of clause (i), the term "nonvested participant" means a participant who does not have any nonforfeitable right under the plan to an accrued benefit derived from employer contributions.

(E) Special rule for maternity or paternity absences.—

(i) General rule.—In the case of each individual who is absent from work for any period—

(I) by reason of the pregnancy of the individual,

(II) by reason of the birth of a child of the individual,

(III) by reason of the placement of a child with the individual in connection with the adoption of such child by such individual, or

(IV) for purposes of caring for such child for a period beginning immediately following such birth or placement,

the plan shall treat as hours of service, solely for purposes of determining under this paragraph whether a 1-year break in service has occurred, the hours described in clause (ii),

(ii) Hours treated as hours of service.—The hours described in this clause are—

(I) the hours of service which otherwise would normally have been credited to such individual but for such absence, or

(II) in any case in which the plan is unable to determine the hours described in subclause (I), 8 hours of service per day of absence,

except that the total number of hours treated as hours of service under this clause by reason of any such pregnancy or placement shall not exceed 501 hours.

(iii) Year to which hours are credited.—The hours described in clause (ii) shall be treated as hours of service as provided in this subparagraph—

(I) only in the year in which the absence from work begins, if a participant would be prevented from incurring a 1-year break in service in such year solely because the period of absence is treated as hours of service as provided in clause (i); or

(II) in any other case, in the immediately following year.

(iv) Year defined.—For purposes of this subparagraph, the term "year" means the period used in computations pursuant to paragraph (5).

(v) Information required to be filed.—A plan shall not fail to satisfy the requirements of this subparagraph solely because it provides that no credit will be given pursuant to this subparagraph unless the individual furnishes the plan administrator such timely information as the plan may reasonably require to establish—

(I) that the absence from work is for reasons referred to in clause (i), and

(II) the number of days for which there was an absence.

(7) Accrued benefit.—

(A) In general.—For purposes of this section, the term "accrued benefit" means—

(i) in the case of a defined benefit plan, the employee's accrued benefit determined under the plan and, except as provided in subsection (c)(3), expressed in the form of an annual benefit commencing at normal retirement age, or

(ii) in the case of a plan which is not a defined benefit plan, the balance of the employee's account.

(B) Effect of certain distributions.—Notwithstanding paragraph (4), for purposes of determining the employee's accrued benefit under the plan, the plan may disregard service performed by the employee with respect to which he has received—

(i) a distribution of the present value of his entire nonforfeitable benefit if such distribution was in an amount (not more than the dollar limit under section 411(a)(11)(A)) permitted under regulations prescribed by the Secretary, or

(ii) a distribution of the present value of his nonforfeitable benefit attributable to such service which he elected to receive.

Clause (i) of this subparagraph shall apply only if such distribution was made on termination of the employee's participation in the plan. Clause (ii) of this subparagraph shall apply only if such distribution was made on termination of the employee's participation in the plan or under such other circumstances as may be provided under regulations prescribed by the Secretary.

(C) Repayment of subparagraph (B) distributions.—For purposes of determining the employee's accrued benefit under a plan, the plan may not disregard service as provided in subparagraph (B) unless the plan provides an opportunity for the participant to repay the full amount of the distribution described in such subparagraph (B) with, in the case of a defined benefit plan, interest at the rate determined for purposes of subsection (c)(2)(C) and provides that upon such repayment the employee's accrued benefit shall be recomputed by taking into account service so disregarded. This subparagraph shall apply only in the case of a participant who—

(i) received such a distribution in any plan year to which this section applies, which distribution was less than the present value of his accrued benefit,

IRC Sec. 411(a)(7)(C)(i)

(ii) resumes employment covered under the plan, and

(iii) repays the full amount of such distribution with, in the case of a defined benefit plan, interest at the rate determined for purposes of subsection (c)(2)(C).

The plan provision required under this subparagraph may provide that such repayment must be made (I) in the case of a withdrawal on account of separation from service, before the earlier of 5 years after the first date on which the participant is subsequently re-employed by the employer, or the close of the first period of 5 consecutive 1-year breaks in service commencing after the withdrawal; or (II) in the case of any other withdrawal, 5 years after the date of the withdrawal.

(D) Accrued benefit attributable to employee contributions.—The accrued benefit of an employee shall not be less than the amount determined under subsection (c)(2)(B) with respect to the employee's accumulated contributions.

(8) **Normal retirement age**.—For purposes of this section, the term "normal retirement age" means the earlier of—

(A) the time a plan participant attains normal retirement age under the plan, or

(B) the later of—

(i) the time a plan participant attains age 65, or

(ii) the 5th anniversary of the time a plan participant commenced participation in the plan.

(9) **Normal retirement benefit**.—For purposes of this section, the term "normal retirement benefit" means the greater of the early retirement benefit under the plan, or the benefit under the plan commencing at normal retirement age. The normal retirement benefit shall be determined without regard to—

(A) medical benefits, and

(B) disability benefits not in excess of the qualified disability benefit.

For purposes of this paragraph, a qualified disability benefit is a disability benefit provided by a plan which does not exceed the benefit which would be provided for the participant if he separated from the service at normal retirement age. For purposes of this paragraph, the early retirement benefit under a plan shall be determined without regard to any benefits commencing before benefits payable under title II of the Social Security Act become payable which—

(i) do not exceed such social security benefits, and

(ii) terminate when such social security benefits commence.

(10) **Changes in vesting schedule**.—

(A) General rule.—A plan amendment changing any vesting schedule under the plan shall be treated as not satisfying the requirements of paragraph (2) if the nonforfeitable percentage of the accrued benefit derived from employer contributions (determined as of the later of the date such amendment is adopted, or the date such amendment becomes effective) of any employee who is a participant in the plan is less than such nonforfeitable percentage computed under the plan without regard to such amendment.

(B) Election of former schedule.—A plan amendment changing any vesting schedule under the plan shall be treated as not satisfying the requirements of paragraph (2) unless each participant having not less than 3 years of service is permitted to elect, within a reasonable period after the adoption of such amendment, to have his nonforfeitable percentage computed under the plan without regard to such amendment.

(11) **Restrictions on certain mandatory distributions.**—

(A) In general.—If the present value of any nonforfeitable accrued benefit exceeds $5,000, a plan meets the requirements of this paragraph only if such plan provides that such benefit may not be immediately distributed without the consent of the participant.

(B) Determination of present value.—For purposes of subparagraph (A), the present value shall be calculated in accordance with section 417(e)(3).

(C) Dividend distributions of ESOPs arrangement.—This paragraph shall not apply to any distribution of dividends to which section 404(k) applies.

(D) Special rule for rollover contributions.—A plan shall not fail to meet the requirements of this paragraph if, under the terms of the plan, the present value of the nonforfeitable accrued benefit is determined without regard to that portion of such benefit which is attributable to rollover contributions (and earnings allocable thereto). For purposes of this subparagraph, the term "rollover contributions" means any rollover contribution under sections 402(c), 403(a)(4), 403(b)(8), 408(d)(3)(A)(ii), and 457(e)(16).

(12) **[Stricken].**

(13) **Special rules for plans computing accrued benefits by reference to hypothetical account balance or equivalent amounts.**—

(A) In general.—An applicable defined benefit plan shall not be treated as failing to meet—

(i) subject to subparagraph (B), the requirements of subsection (a)(2), or

(ii) the requirements of subsection (a)(11) or (c), or the requirements of section 417(e), with respect to accrued benefits derived from employer contributions,

solely because the present value of the accrued benefit (or any portion thereof) of any participant is, under the terms of the plan, equal to the amount expressed as the balance in the hypothetical account described in subparagraph (C) or as an accumulated percentage of the participant's final average compensation.

(B) 3-year vesting.—In the case of an applicable defined benefit plan, such plan shall be treated as meeting the requirements of subsection (a)(2) only if an employee who has completed at least 3 years of service has a nonforfeitable right to 100 percent of the employee's accrued benefit derived from employer contributions.

(C) Applicable defined benefit plan and related rules.—For purposes of this subsection—

(i) In general.—The term "applicable defined benefit plan" means a defined benefit plan under which the accrued benefit (or any portion thereof) is calculated as the balance of a hypothetical account maintained for the participant or as an accumulated percentage of the participant's final average compensation.

(ii) Regulations to include similar plans.—The Secretary shall issue regulations which include in the definition of an applicable defined benefit plan any defined benefit plan (or any portion of such a plan) which has an effect similar to an applicable defined benefit plan.

(b) **Accrued Benefit Requirements.**—

(1) **Defined benefit plans.**—

(A) 3-percent method.—A defined benefit plan satisfies the requirements of this paragraph if the accrued benefit to which each participant is entitled upon his separation from the service is not less than—

(i) 3 percent of the normal retirement benefit to which he would be entitled if he commenced participation at the earliest possible entry age under the plan and served continuously until the earlier of age 65 or the normal retirement age specified under the plan, multiplied by

(ii) the number of years (not in excess of 33⅓) of his participation in the plan.

In the case of a plan providing retirement benefits based on compensation during any period, the normal retirement benefit to which a participant would be entitled shall be determined as if he continued to earn annually the average rate of compensation which he earned during consecutive years of service, not in excess of 10, for which his compensation was the highest. For purposes of this subparagraph, social security benefits and all other relevant factors used to compute benefits shall be treated as remaining con-

stant as of the current year for all years after such current year.

(B) 133⅓ percent rule.—A defined benefit plan satisfies the requirements of this paragraph for a particular plan year if under the plan the accrued benefit payable at the normal retirement age is equal to the normal retirement benefit and the annual rate at which any individual who is or could be a participant can accrue the retirement benefits payable at normal retirement age under the plan for any later plan year is not more than 133⅓ percent of the annual rate at which he can accrue benefits for any plan year beginning on or after such particular plan year and before such later plan year. For purposes of this subparagraph—

(i) any amendment to the plan which is in effect for the current year shall be treated as in effect for all other plan years;

(ii) any change in an accrual rate which does not apply to any individual who is or could be a participant in the current year shall be disregarded;

(iii) the fact that benefits under the plan may be payable to certain employees before normal retirement age shall be disregarded; and

(iv) social security benefits and all other relevant factors used to compute benefits shall be treated as remaining constant as of the current year for all years after the current year.

(C) Fractional rule.—A defined benefit plan satisfies the requirements of this paragraph if the accrued benefit to which any participant is entitled upon his separation from the service is not less than a fraction of the annual benefit commencing at normal retirement age to which he would be entitled under the plan as in effect on the date of his separation if he continued to earn annually until normal retirement age the same rate of compensation upon which his normal retirement benefit would be computed under the plan, determined as if he had attained normal retirement age on the date on which any such determination is made (but taking into account no more than the 10 years of service immediately preceding his separation from service). Such fraction shall be a fraction, not exceeding 1, the numerator of which is the total number of his years of participation in the plan (as of the date of his separation from the service) and the denominator of which is the total number of years he would have participated in the plan if he separated from the service at the normal retirement age. For purposes of this subparagraph, social security benefits and all other relevant factors used to compute benefits shall be treated as remaining constant as of the current year for all years after such current year.

(D) Accrual for service before effective date.—Subparagraphs (A), (B), and (C) shall not apply

IRC Sec. 411(b)(1)(D)

with respect to years of participation before the first plan year to which this section applies, but a defined benefit plan satisfies the requirements of this subparagraph with respect to such years of participation only if the accrued benefit of any participant with respect to such years of participation is not less than the greater of—

(i) his accrued benefit determined under the plan, as in effect from time to time prior to September 2, 1974, or

(ii) an accrued benefit which is not less than one-half of the accrued benefit to which such participant would have been entitled if subparagraph (A), (B), or (C) applied with respect to such years of participation.

(E) First two years of service.—Notwithstanding subparagraphs (A), (B), and (C) of this paragraph, a plan shall not be treated as not satisfying the requirements of this paragraph solely because the accrual of benefits under the plan does not become effective until the employee has two continuous years of service. For purposes of this subparagraph, the term "years of service" has the meaning provided by section 410(a)(3)(A).

(F) Certain insured defined benefit plans.—Notwithstanding subparagraphs (A), (B), and (C), a defined benefit plan satisfies the requirements of this paragraph if such plan—

(i) is funded exclusively by the purchase of insurance contracts, and

(ii) satisfies the requirements of subparagraphs (B) and (C) of section 412(e)(3) (relating to certain insurance contract plans),

but only if an employee's accrued benefit as of any applicable date is not less than the cash surrender value his insurance contracts would have on such applicable date if the requirements of subparagraphs (D), (E), and (F) of section 412(e)(3) were satisfied.

(G) Accrued benefit may not decrease on account of increasing age or service.—Notwithstanding the preceding subparagraphs, a defined benefit plan shall be treated as not satisfying the requirements of this paragraph if the participant's accrued benefit is reduced on account of any increase in his age or service. The preceding sentence shall not apply to benefits under the plan commencing before entitlement to benefits payable under title II of the Social Security Act which benefits under the plan—

(i) do not exceed such social security benefits, and

(ii) terminate when such social security benefits commence.

(H) Continued accrual beyond normal retirement age.—

(i) In general.—Notwithstanding the preceding subparagraphs, a defined benefit plan shall be treated as not satisfying the requirements of this paragraph if, under the plan, an employee's benefit accrual is ceased, or the rate of an employee's benefit accrual is reduced, because of the attainment of any age.

(ii) Certain limitations permitted.—A plan shall not be treated as failing to meet the requirements of this subparagraph solely because the plan imposes (without regard to age) a limitation on the amount of benefits that the plan provides or a limitation on the number of years of service or years of participation which are taken into account for purposes of determining benefit accrual under the plan.

(iii) Adjustments under plan for delayed retirement taken into account.—In the case of any employee who, as of the end of any plan year under a defined benefit plan, has attained normal retirement age under such plan—

(I) if distribution of benefits under such plan with respect to such employee has commenced as of the end of such plan year, then any requirement of this subparagraph for continued accrual of benefits under such plan with respect to such employee during such plan year shall be treated as satisfied to the extent of the actuarial equivalent of in-service distribution of benefits, and

(II) if distribution of benefits under such plan with respect to such employee has not commenced as of the end of such year in accordance with section 401(a)(14)(C), and the payment of benefits under such plan with respect to such employee is not suspended during such plan year pursuant to subsection (a)(3)(B), then any requirement of this subparagraph for continued accrual of benefits under such plan with respect to such employee during such plan year shall be treated as satisfied to the extent of any adjustment in the benefit payable under the plan during such plan year attributable to the delay in the distribution of benefits after the attainment of normal retirement age.

The preceding provisions of this clause shall apply in accordance with regulations of the Secretary. Such regulations may provide for the application of the preceding provisions of this clause, in the case of any such employee, with respect to any period of time within a plan year.

(iv) Disregard of subsidized portion of early retirement benefit.—A plan shall not be treated as failing to meet the requirements of clause (i) solely because the subsidized portion of any early retirement benefit is disregarded in determining benefit accruals.

(v) Coordination with other requirements.— The Secretary shall provide by regulation for the coordination of the requirements of this subparagraph with the requirements of subsection (a), sections 404, 410, and 415, and the provisions of this subchapter precluding discrimination in favor of highly compensated employees.

(2) Defined contribution plans.—

(A) In general.—A defined contribution plan satisfies the requirements of this paragraph if, under the plan, allocations to the employee's account are not ceased, and the rate at which amounts are allocated to the employee's account is not reduced, because of the attainment of any age.

(B) Application to target benefit plans.—The Secretary shall provide by regulation for the application of the requirements of this paragraph to target benefit plans.

(C) Coordination with other requirements.—The Secretary may provide by regulation for the coordination of the requirements of this paragraph with the requirements of subsection (a), sections 404, 410, and 415, and the provisions of this subchapter precluding discrimination in favor of highly compensated employees.

(3) Separate accounting required in certain cases.—A plan satisfies the requirements of this paragraph if—

(A) in the case of a defined benefit plan, the plan requires separate accounting for the portion of each employee's accrued benefit derived from any voluntary employee contributions permitted under the plan; and

(B) in the case of any plan which is not a defined benefit plan, the plan requires separate accounting for each employee's accrued benefit.

(4) Year of participation.—

(A) Definition.—For purposes of determining an employee's accrued benefit, the term "year of participation" means a period of service (beginning at the earliest date on which the employee is a participant in the plan and which is included in a period of service required to be taken into account under section 410(a)(5) determined without regard to section 410(a)(5)(E)) as determined under regulations prescribed by the Secretary of Labor which provide for the calculation of such period on any reasonable and consistent basis.

(B) Less than full time service.—For purposes of this paragraph, except as provided in subparagraph (C), in the case of any employee whose customary employment is less than full time, the calculation of such employee's service on any basis which provides less than a ratable portion of the accrued benefit to which he would be entitled under the plan if his customary employment were full time shall not be treated as made on a reasonable and consistent basis.

(C) Less than 1,000 hours of service during year.—For purposes of this paragraph, in the case of any employee whose service is less than 1,000 hours during any calendar year, plan year or other 12-consecutive month period designated by the plan (and not prohibited under regulations prescribed by the Secretary of Labor) the calculation of his period of service shall not be treated as not made on a reasonable and consistent basis solely because such service is not taken into account.

(D) Seasonal industries.—In the case of any seasonal industry where the customary period of employment is less than 1,000 hours during a calendar year, the term "year of participation" shall be such period as determined under regulations prescribed by the Secretary of Labor.

(E) Maritime industries.—For purposes of this subsection, in the case of any maritime industry, 125 days of service shall be treated as a year of participation. The Secretary of Labor may prescribe regulations to carry out the purposes of this subparagraph.

(5) Special rules relating to age.—

(A) Comparison to similarly situated younger individual.—

(i) In general.—A plan shall not be treated as failing to meet the requirements of paragraph (1)(H)(i) if a participant's accrued benefit, as determined as of any date under the terms of the plan, would be equal to or greater than that of any similarly situated, younger individual who is or could be a participant.

(ii) Similarly situated.—For purposes of this subparagraph, a participant is similarly situated to any other individual if such participant is identical to such other individual in every respect (including period of service, compensation, position, date of hire, work history, and any other respect) except for age.

(iii) Disregard of subsidized early retirement benefits.—In determining the accrued benefit as of any date for purposes of this subparagraph, the subsidized portion of any early retirement benefit or retirement-type subsidy shall be disregarded.

(iv) Accrued benefit.—For purposes of this subparagraph, the accrued benefit may, under the terms of the plan, be expressed as an annuity payable at normal retirement age, the balance of a hypothetical account, or the current value of the accumulated percentage of the employee's final average compensation.

(B) Applicable defined benefit plans.—

(i) Interest credits.—

(I) In general.—An applicable defined benefit plan shall be treated as failing to meet the requirements of paragraph (1)(H) unless the terms of the plan provide that any interest credit (or an equivalent amount) for any plan year shall be at a rate which is not greater than a market rate of return. A plan shall not be treated as failing to meet the requirements of this subclause merely because the plan provides for a reasonable minimum guaranteed rate of return or for a rate of return that is equal to the greater of a fixed or variable rate of return.

(II) Preservation of capital.—An applicable defined benefit plan shall be treated as failing to meet the requirements of paragraph (1)(H) unless the plan provides that an interest credit (or equivalent amount) of less than zero shall in no event result in the account balance or similar amount being less than the aggregate amount of contributions credited to the account.

(III) Market rate of return.—The Secretary may provide by regulation for rules governing the calculation of a market rate of return for purposes of subclause (I) and for permissible methods of crediting interest to the account (including fixed or variable interest rates) resulting in effective rates of return meeting the requirements of subclause (I).

(ii) Special rule for plan conversions.—If, after June 29, 2005, an applicable plan amendment is adopted, the plan shall be treated as failing to meet the requirements of paragraph (1)(H) unless the requirements of clause (iii) are met with respect to each individual who was a participant in the plan immediately before the adoption of the amendment.

(iii) Rate of benefit accrual.—Subject to clause (iv), the requirements of this clause are met with respect to any participant if the accrued benefit of the participant under the terms of the plan as in effect after the amendment is not less than the sum of—

(I) the participant's accrued benefit for years of service before the effective date of the amendment, determined under the terms of the plan as in effect before the amendment, plus

(II) the participant's accrued benefit for years of service after the effective date of the amendment, determined under the terms of the plan as in effect after the amendment.

(iv) Special rules for early retirement subsidies.—For purposes of clause (iii)(I), the plan shall credit the accumulation account or similar amount with the amount of any early retirement benefit or retirement-type subsidy for the plan year in which the participant retires if, as of such time, the participant has met the age, years of service, and other requirements under the plan for entitlement to such benefit or subsidy.

(v) Applicable plan amendment.—For purposes of this subparagraph—

(I) In general.—The term "applicable plan amendment" means an amendment to a defined benefit plan which has the effect of converting the plan to an applicable defined benefit plan.

(II) Special rule for coordinated benefits.—If the benefits of 2 or more defined benefit plans established or maintained by an employer are coordinated in such a manner as to have the effect of the adoption of an amendment described in subclause (I), the sponsor of the defined benefit plan or plans providing for such coordination shall be treated as having adopted such a plan amendment as of the date such coordination begins.

(III) Multiple amendments.—The Secretary shall issue regulations to prevent the avoidance of the purposes of this subparagraph through the use of 2 or more plan amendments rather than a single amendment.

(IV) Applicable defined benefit plan.—For purposes of this subparagraph, the term "applicable defined benefit plan" has the meaning given such term by section 411(a)(13).

(vi) Termination requirements.—An applicable defined benefit plan shall not be treated as meeting the requirements of clause (i) unless the plan provides that, upon the termination of the plan—

(I) if the interest credit rate (or an equivalent amount) under the plan is a variable rate, the rate of interest used to determine accrued benefits under the plan shall be equal to the average of the rates of interest used under the plan during the 5-year period ending on the termination date, and

(II) the interest rate and mortality table used to determine the amount of any benefit under the plan payable in the form of an annuity payable at normal retirement age shall be the rate and table specified under the plan for such purpose as of the termination date, except that if such interest rate is a variable rate, the interest rate shall be determined under the rules of subclause (I).

(C) Certain offsets permitted.—A plan shall not be treated as failing to meet the requirements of paragraph (1)(H)(i) solely because the plan provides offsets against benefits under the plan to the extent such offsets are otherwise allowable in applying the requirements of section 401(a).

(D) Permitted disparities in plan contributions or benefits.—A plan shall not be treated as failing to meet the requirements of paragraph (1)(H) solely because the plan provides a disparity in contributions or benefits with respect to which the requirements of section 401(l) are met.

(E) Indexing permitted.—

(i) In general.—A plan shall not be treated as failing to meet the requirements of paragraph

(1)(H) solely because the plan provides for indexing of accrued benefits under the plan.

(ii) Protection against loss.—Except in the case of any benefit provided in the form of a variable annuity, clause (i) shall not apply with respect to any indexing which results in an accrued benefit less than the accrued benefit determined without regard to such indexing.

(iii) Indexing.—For purposes of this subparagraph, the term "indexing" means, in connection with an accrued benefit, the periodic adjustment of the accrued benefit by means of the application of a recognized investment index or methodology.

(F) Early retirement benefit or retirement-type subsidy.—For purposes of this paragraph, the terms "early retirement benefit" and "retirement-type subsidy" have the meaning given such terms in subsection (d)(6)(B)(i).

(G) Benefit accrued to date.—For purposes of this paragraph, any reference to the accrued benefit shall be a reference to such benefit accrued to date.

(c) Allocation of Accrued Benefits Between Employer and Employee Contributions.—

(1) Accrued benefit derived from employer contributions.—For purposes of this section, an employee's accrued benefit derived from employer contributions as of any applicable date is the excess, if any, of the accrued benefit for such employee as of such applicable date over the accrued benefit derived from contributions made by such employee as of such date.

(2) Accrued benefit derived from employee contributions.—

(A) Plans other than defined benefit plans.—In the case of a plan other than a defined benefit plan, the accrued benefit derived from contributions made by an employee as of any applicable date is—

(i) except as provided in clause (ii), the balance of the employee's separate account consisting only of his contributions and the income, expenses, gains, and losses attributable thereto, or

(ii) if a separate account is not maintained with respect to an employee's contributions under such a plan, the amount which bears the same ratio to his total accrued benefit as the total amount of the employee's contributions (less withdrawals) bears to the sum of such contributions and the contributions made on his behalf by the employer (less withdrawals).

(B) Defined benefit plans.—In the case of a defined benefit plan, the accrued benefit derived from contributions made by an employee as of any applicable date is the amount equal to the employee's accumulated contributions expressed as an annual benefit commencing at normal retirement age, us-ing an interest rate which would be used under the plan under section 417(e)(3) (as of the determination date).

(C) Definition of accumulated contributions.—For purposes of this subsection, the term "accumulated contributions" means the total of—

(i) all mandatory contributions made by the employee,

(ii) interest (if any) under the plan to the end of the last plan year to which subsection (a)(2) does not apply (by reason of the applicable effective date), and

(iii) interest on the sum of the amounts determined under clauses (i) and (ii) compounded annually—

(I) at the rate of 120 percent of the Federal mid-term rate (as in effect under section 1274 for the 1st month of a plan year) for the period beginning with the 1st plan year to which subsection (a)(2) applies (by reason of the applicable effective date) and ending with the date on which the determination is being made, and

(II) at the interest rate which would be used under the plan under section 417(e)(3) (as of the determination date) for the period beginning with the determination date and ending on the date on which the employee attains normal retirement age. For purposes of this subparagraph, the term "mandatory contributions" means amounts contributed to the plan by the employee which are required as a condition of employment, as a condition of participation in such plan, or as a condition of obtaining benefits under the plan attributable to employer contributions.

(D) Adjustments.—The Secretary is authorized to adjust by regulation the conversion factor described in subparagraph (B) from time to time as he may deem necessary. No such adjustment shall be effective for a plan year beginning before the expiration of 1 year after such adjustment is determined and published.

(E) [Repealed.]

(3) Actuarial adjustment.—For purposes of this section, in the case of any defined benefit plan, if an employee's accrued benefit is to be determined as an amount other than an annual benefit commencing at normal retirement age, or if the accrued benefit derived from contributions made by an employee is to be determined with respect to a benefit other than an annual benefit in the form of a single life annuity (without ancillary benefits) commencing at normal retirement age, the employee's accrued benefit, or the accrued benefits derived from contributions made by an employee, as the case may be, shall be the actuarial equivalent of such benefit or amount determined under paragraph (1) or (2).

IRC Sec. 411(c)(3)

(d) Special Rules.—

(1) Coordination with section 401(a)(4).—A plan which satisfies the requirements of this section shall be treated as satisfying any vesting requirements resulting from the application of section 401(a)(4) unless—

(A) there has been a pattern of abuse under the plan (such as dismissal of employees before their accrued benefits become nonforfeitable) tending to discriminate in favor of employees who are highly compensated employees (within the meaning of section 414(q)), or

(B) there have been, or there is reason to believe there will be, an accrual of benefits or forfeitures tending to discriminate in favor of employees who are highly compensated employees (within the meaning of section 414(q)).

(2) Prohibited discrimination.—Subsection (a) shall not apply to benefits which may not be provided for designated employees in the event of early termination of the plan under provisions of the plan adopted pursuant to regulations prescribed by the Secretary to preclude the discrimination prohibited by section 401(a)(4).

(3) Termination or partial termination; discontinuance of contributions.—Notwithstanding the provisions of subsection (a), a trust shall not constitute a qualified trust under section 401(a) unless the plan of which such trust is a part provides that—

(A) upon its termination or partial termination, or

(B) in the case of a plan to which section 412 does not apply, upon complete discontinuance of contributions under the plan,

the rights of all affected employees to benefits accrued to the date of such termination, partial termination, or discontinuance, to the extent funded as of such date, or the amounts credited to the employees' accounts, are nonforfeitable. This paragraph shall not apply to benefits or contributions which, under provisions of the plan adopted pursuant to regulations prescribed by the Secretary to preclude the discrimination prohibited by section 401(a)(4), may not be used for designated employees in the event of early termination of the plan. For purposes of this paragraph, in the case of the complete discontinuance of contributions under a profit-sharing or stock bonus plan, such plan shall be treated as having terminated on the day on which the plan administrator notifies the Secretary (in accordance with regulations) of the discontinuance.

(4) [Repealed.]

(5) Treatment of voluntary employee contributions.—In the case of a defined benefit plan which permits voluntary employee contributions, the portion of an employee's accrued benefit derived from such contributions shall be treated as an accrued benefit derived from employee contributions under a plan other than a defined benefit plan.

(6) Accrued benefit not to be decreased by amendment.—

(A) In general.—A plan shall be treated as not satisfying the requirements of this section if the accrued benefit of a participant is decreased by an amendment of the plan, other than an amendment described in section 412(d)(2), or section 4281 of the Employee Retirement Income Security Act of 1974.

(B) Treatment of certain plan amendments.—For purposes of subparagraph (A), a plan amendment which has the effect of—

(i) eliminating or reducing an early retirement benefit or a retirement-type subsidy (as defined in regulations), or

(ii) eliminating an optional form of benefit,

with respect to benefits attributable to service before the amendment shall be treated as reducing accrued benefits. In the case of a retirement-type subsidy, the preceding sentence shall apply only with respect to a participant who satisfies (either before or after the amendment) the preamendment conditions for the subsidy. The Secretary shall by regulations provide that this subparagraph shall not apply to any plan amendment which reduces or eliminates benefits or subsidies which create significant burdens or complexities for the plan and plan participants, unless such amendment adversely affects the rights of any participant in a more than de minimis manner. The Secretary may by regulations provide that this subparagraph shall not apply to a plan amendment described in clause (ii) (other than a plan amendment having an effect described in clause (i)).

(C) Special rule for ESOPs.—For purposes of this paragraph, any—

(i) tax credit employee stock ownership plan (as defined in section 409(a)), or

(ii) employee stock ownership plan (as defined in section 4975(e)(7)),

shall not be treated as failing to meet the requirements of this paragraph merely because it modifies distribution options in a nondiscriminatory manner.

(D) Plan transfers.—

(i) In general.—A defined contribution plan (in this subparagraph referred to as the "transferee plan") shall not be treated as failing to meet the requirements of this subsection merely because the transferee plan does not provide some or all of the forms of distribution previously available under another defined contribution plan (in this subparagraph referred to as the "transferor plan") to the extent that—

(I) the forms of distribution previously available under the transferor plan applied to the account of a participant or beneficiary under the transferor plan that was transferred from the transferor plan to the transferee plan pursuant to a direct transfer rather than pursuant to a distribution from the transferor plan,

(II) the terms of both the transferor plan and the transferee plan authorize the transfer described in subclause (I),

(III) the transfer described in subclause (I) was made pursuant to a voluntary election by the participant or beneficiary whose account was transferred to the transferee plan,

(IV) the election described in subclause (III) was made after the participant or beneficiary received a notice describing the consequences of making the election, and

(V) the transferee plan allows the participant or beneficiary described in subclause (III) to receive any distribution to which the participant or beneficiary is entitled under the transferee plan in the form of a single sum distribution.

(ii) Special rule for mergers, etc.—Clause (i) shall apply to plan mergers and other transactions having the effect of a direct transfer, including consolidations of benefits attributable to different employers within a multiple employer plan.

(E) Elimination of form of distribution.—Except to the extent provided in regulations, a defined contribution plan shall not be treated as failing to meet the requirements of this section merely because of the elimination of a form of distribution previously available thereunder. This subparagraph shall not apply to the elimination of a form of distribution with respect to any participant unless—

(i) a single sum payment is available to such participant at the same time or times as the form of distribution being eliminated, and

(ii) such single sum payment is based on the same or greater portion of the participant's account as the form of distribution being eliminated.

(e) Application of Vesting Standards to Certain Plans.—

(1) The provisions of this section (other than paragraph (2)) shall not apply to—

(A) a governmental plan (within the meaning of section 414(d)),

(B) a church plan (within the meaning of section 414(e)) with respect to which the election provided by section 410(d) has not been made,

(C) a plan which has not, at any time after September 2, 1974, provided for employer contributions, and

(D) a plan established and maintained by a society, order, or association described in section 501(c)(8) or (9), if no part of the contributions to or under such plan are made by employers of participants in such plan.

(2) A plan described in paragraph (1) shall be treated as meeting the requirements of this section, for purposes of section 401(a), if such plan meets the vesting requirements resulting from the application of section 401(a)(4) and 401(a)(7) as in effect on September 1, 1974.

Recent Amendments to IRC §411

Worker, Retiree, and Employer Recovery Act of 2008 (Pub. L. No. 110-458), as follows:

● IRC §411(a)(3)(C) was amended by Act §101(d)(2)(D)(i) by substituting "section 412(d)(2)" for "section 412(c)(2)". Eff. as if included in Pub. L. No. 109-280, §114 [eff. for plan years beginning after 2007].

● IRC §411(a)(3)(G) was amended by Act §109(b)(2) by substituting "permissible withdrawal" for "erroneous automatic contribution" in the heading and by substituting "a permissible withdrawal" for "an erroneous automatic contribution". Eff. as if included in Pub. L. No. 109-280, §902 [eff. for plan years beginning after Dec. 31, 2007].

● IRC §411(a)(13)(A) was amended by Act §107(b)(2)(C) in the text following clause (ii) by substituting "subparagraph (C)" for "paragraph (3)". Eff. as if included in Pub. L. No. 109-280, §701 [eff. generally for distributions made after Aug. 17, 2006].

● IRC §411(a)(13)(A)(i) was amended by Act §107(b)(2)(A) by substituting "subparagraph (B)" for "paragraph (2)". Eff. as if included in Pub. L. No. 109-280, §701 [eff. generally for distributions made after Aug. 17, 2006].

● IRC §411(a)(13)(A)(ii) was amended by Act §107(b)(2)(B). Eff. as if included in Pub. L. No. 109-280, §701 [eff. generally for distributions made after Aug. 17, 2006]. IRC §411(a)(13)(A)(ii) prior to amendment:

(ii) the requirements of subsection (c) or section 417(e) with respect to contributions other than employee contributions,

● IRC §411(b)(5)(A)(iii) was amended by Act §107(b)(1)(A) by substituting "subparagraph" for "clause". Eff. as if included in Pub. L. No. 109-280, §701 [eff. generally for periods beginning on or after June 29, 2005].

● IRC §411(b)(5)(B)(i)(II) was amended by Act §107(b)(3). Eff. as if included in Pub. L. No. 109-280, §701 [eff. generally for periods beginning on or after June 29, 2005]. IRC §411(b)(5)(B)(i)(II) prior to amendment:

(II) Preservation of capital.—An interest credit (or an equivalent amount) of less than zero shall in no event result in the account balance or similar amount being less than the aggregate amount of contributions credited to the account.

● IRC §411(b)(5)(C) was amended by Act §107(b)(1)(B) by inserting "otherwise" before "allowable". Eff. as if included in Pub. L. No. 109-280, §701 [eff. generally for periods beginning on or after June 29, 2005].

● IRC §411(d)(6)(A) was amended by Act §101(d)(2)(D)(ii) by substituting "section 412(d)(2)" for "section 412(e)(2)". Eff. as if included in Pub. L. No. 109-280, §114 [eff. for plan years beginning after 2007].

Pension Protection Act of 2006 (Pub. L. No. 109-280), as follows:

● IRC §411(a)(2) was amended by Act §904(a)(1). Eff. generally for contributions for plan years beginning after Dec. 31, 2006. See Act §904(c) for special rules. IRC §411(a)(2) prior to amendment:

(2) Employer contributions.—Except as provided in paragraph (12), a plan satisfies the requirements of this paragraph if it satisfies the requirements of subparagraph (A) or (B).

(A) 5-year vesting.—A plan satisfies the requirements of this subparagraph if an employee who has completed at least 5 years of service has a nonforfeitable right to 100 percent of the employee's accrued benefit derived from employer contributions.

IRC Sec. 411(e)(2)

(B) 3 to 7 year vesting.—A plan satisfies the requirements of this subparagraph if an employee has a nonforfeitable right to a percentage of the employee's accrued benefit derived from employer contributions determined under the following table:

Years of service:	The nonforfeitable percentage is—
2	20
3	40
4	60
5	80
6 or more	100

- IRC §411(a)(3)(C) was amended by Act §114(b)(1) by replacing "§412(c)(8)" with "§412(c)(2)[412(d)(2)]". Eff. Aug. 17, 2006 [for plan years beginning after 2007, eff. date as amended by Pub. L. No. 110-458, §101(d)(3)].
- IRC §411(a)(3)(G) was amended by Act §902(d)(2)(A) by inserting "an erroneous automatic contribution under §414(w)," after "402(g)(2)(A),". Eff. plan years beginning after Dec. 31, 2007.
- IRC §411(a)(3)(G) was amended, in the heading, by Act §902(d)(2)(B) by inserting "or erroneous automatic contribution" before the period. Eff. plan years beginning after Dec. 31, 2007.
- IRC §411(a) was amended by Act §904(a)(2) by striking para. (12). Eff. generally for contributions for plan years beginning after Dec. 31, 2006. See Act §904(c) for special rules. IRC §411(a)(12) prior to being stricken:
  (12) Faster vesting for matching contributions.—In the case of matching contributions (as defined in section 401(m)(4)(A)), paragraph (2) shall be applied—
  (A) by substituting "3 years" for "5 years" in subparagraph (A), and
  (B) by substituting the following table for the table contained in subparagraph (B):

Years of service:	The nonforfeitable percentage is—
2	20
3	40
4	60
5	80
6 or more	100

- IRC §411(a) was amended by Act §701(b)(2) by adding new para. (13). Eff. generally for distributions made after Aug. 17, 2006. See Act §701(d) and (e)(3)-(5) for special rules.
- IRC §411(b)(1)(F) was amended by Act §114(b)(2) by striking "paragraphs (2) and (3) of section 412(i)" and inserting "subparagraphs (B) and (C) of section 412(e)(3)" in cl. (ii), and striking "paragraphs (4), (5), and (6) of section 412(i)" and inserting "subparagraphs (D), (E), and (F) of section 412(e)(3)". Eff. for plan years beginning after 2007 [eff. date as amended by Pub. L. No. 110-458, §101(d)(3)].
- IRC §411(b) was amended by Act §701(b)(1) by adding new para. (5). Eff. generally for periods beginning on or after June 29, 2005. See Act §701(d) and (e)(3)-(5) for special rules.
- IRC §411(d)(6)(A) was amended by Act §114(b)(3) by striking "section 412(c)(8)" and inserting "section 412(e)(2)". Eff. for plan years beginning after 2007 [eff. date as amended by Pub. L. No. 110-458, §101(d)(3)].
- **Sunset Provision.** Act §811, provides:
  SEC. 811. PENSIONS AND INDIVIDUAL RETIREMENT ARRANGEMENT PROVISIONS OF ECONOMIC GROWTH AND TAX RELIEF RECONCILIATION ACT OF 2001 MADE PERMANENT.
  Title IX of the Economic Growth and Tax Relief Reconciliation Act of 2001 [Pub. L. No. 107-16] shall not apply to the

provisions of, and amendments made by, subtitles A through F [§§601–666] of title VI of such Act (relating to pension and individual retirement arrangement provisions).

Working Families Tax Relief Act of 2004 (Pub. L. No. 108-311), as follows:

- IRC §411(a)(12)(B) was amended by Act §408(a)(14) by striking the last line of the table and adding a new line. Eff. Oct. 4, 2004. IRC §411(a)(12)(B) table, last line, prior to being stricken:

6	100

- IRC §411(b)(1)(F) was amended by Act §114(b)(2)(A)–(B) by replacing "paragraphs (2) and (3) of §412(i)" in cl. (ii) with "subparagraphs (B) and (C) of §412(e)(3)", and by replacing "paragraphs (4), (5), and (6) of §412(i)" with "subparagraphs (D), (E), and (F) of §412(e)(3)". Effective Aug. 17, 2006.
- IRC §411(d)(6)(A) was amended by Act §114(b)(3) by replacing "§412(c)(8)" with "§412(e)(2)[412(d)(2)]". Eff. Aug. 17, 2006.
- **Other Provision—** Effective Date. Act §101(c), as amended by Pub. L. No. 110-458, §103(a) and Pub. L. No. 109-280, §301(c), provides:
  (c) Provisions relating to plan amendments.—
  (1) In general.—If this subsection applies to any plan or annuity contract amendment—
  (A) such plan or contract shall be treated as being operated in accordance with the terms of the plan or contract during the period described in paragraph (2)(B)(i), and
  (B) except as provided by the Secretary of the Treasury, such plan shall not fail to meet the requirements of section 411(d)(6) of the Internal Revenue Code of 1986 and section 204(g) of the Employee Retirement Income Security Act of 1974 by reason of such amendment.
  (2) Amendments to which section applies.—
  (A) In general.—This subsection shall apply to any amendment to any plan or annuity contract which is made—
  (i) pursuant to any amendment made by this section, and
  (ii) on or before the last day of the first plan year beginning on or after January 1, 2009.
  (B) Conditions.—This subsection shall not apply to any plan or annuity contract amendment unless—
  (i) during the period beginning on the date the amendment described in subparagraph (A)(i) takes effect and ending on the date described in subparagraph (A)(ii) (or, if earlier, the date the plan or contract amendment is adopted), the plan or contract is operated as if such plan or contract amendment were in effect; and
  (ii) such plan or contract amendment applies retroactively for such period.

Economic Growth and Tax Relief Reconciliation Act of 2001 (Pub. L. No. 107-16), as follows:

- IRC §411(a) was amended by Act §633(a)(1)–(2) by replacing "A plan" in para. (2) with "Except as provided in paragraph (12), a plan", and by adding new para. (12). Eff. generally for contributions for plan years beginning after Dec. 31, 2001. [*Ed. Note*: see Act §633(c)(2)–(3) for special rules.]
- IRC §411(a)(11) was amended by Act §648(a)(1) by adding new subpara. (D). Eff. for distributions after Dec. 31, 2001.
- IRC §411(d)(6) was amended by Act §645(a)(1) by adding new subparas. (D) and (E). Eff. for years beginning after Dec. 31, 2001.
- IRC §411(d)(6)(B) was amended by Act §645(b)(1) by inserting a new sentence after the second sentence. Eff. June 7, 2001.
- **Sunset Provision.** Act §901, as amended by Pub. L. No. 111-312, §101(a)(1), provides the sunset rule below. But see Pub. L. No. 109-280, §811, and Pub. L. No. 111-148, §10909(c), as amended by Pub. L. No. 111-312, §101(b)(1).
  SEC. 901. SUNSET OF PROVISIONS OF ACT.
  (a) In general. All provisions of, and amendments made by, this Act shall not apply—
  (1) to taxable, plan, or limitation years beginning after December 31, 2012, or
  (2) in the case of title V, to estates of decedents dying, gifts made, or generation skipping transfers, after December 31, 2012.
  (b) Application of certain laws.—The Internal Revenue Code of 1986 and the Employee Retirement Income Security

Act of 1974 shall be applied and administered to years, estates, gifts, and transfers described in subsection (a) as if the provisions and amendments described in subsection (a) had never been enacted.

SEC. 412. MINIMUM FUNDING STANDARDS.

(a) Requirement to Meet Minimum Funding Standard.—

(1) In general.—A plan to which this section applies shall satisfy the minimum funding standard applicable to the plan for any plan year.

(2) Minimum funding standard.—For purposes of paragraph (1), a plan shall be treated as satisfying the minimum funding standard for a plan year if—

(A) in the case of a defined benefit plan which is not a multiemployer plan, the employer makes contributions to or under the plan for the plan year which, in the aggregate, are not less than the minimum required contribution determined under section 430 for the plan for the plan year,

(B) in the case of a money purchase plan which is not a multiemployer plan, the employer makes contributions to or under the plan for the plan year which are required under the terms of the plan, and

(C) in the case of a multiemployer plan, the employers make contributions to or under the plan for any plan year which, in the aggregate, are sufficient to ensure that the plan does not have an accumulated funding deficiency under section 431 as of the end of the plan year.

(b) Liability for Contributions.—

(1) In general.—Except as provided in paragraph (2), the amount of any contribution required by this section (including any required installments under paragraphs (3) and (4) of section 430(j)) shall be paid by the employer responsible for making contributions to or under the plan.

(2) Joint and several liability where employer member of controlled group.—If the employer referred to in paragraph (1) is a member of a controlled group, each member of such group shall be jointly and severally liable for payment of such contributions.

Editor's Note

Caution: IRC §412(b)(3), as follows, was added by Pub. L. No. 109-280, §212(c), generally applicable to plan years beginning after 2007. For the sunset provision of Pub. L. No. 109-280, §221(c), see the amendment notes to Pub. L. No. 109-280 for this section.

---

(3) Multiemployer plans in critical status.—Paragraph (1) shall not apply in the case of a mul-

tiemployer plan for any plan year in which the plan is in critical status pursuant to section 432. This paragraph shall only apply if the plan sponsor adopts a rehabilitation plan in accordance with section 432(e) and complies with such rehabilitation plan (and any modifications of the plan).

(c) Variance From Minimum Funding Standards.—

(1) Waiver in case of business hardship.—

(A) In general.—If—

(i) an employer is (or in the case of a multiemployer plan, 10 percent or more of the number of employers contributing to or under the plan are) unable to satisfy the minimum funding standard for a plan year without temporary substantial business hardship (substantial business hardship in the case of a multiemployer plan), and

(ii) application of the standard would be adverse to the interests of plan participants in the aggregate,

the Secretary may, subject to subparagraph (C), waive the requirements of subsection (a) for such year with respect to all or any portion of the minimum funding standard. The Secretary shall not waive the minimum funding standard with respect to a plan for more than 3 of any 15 (5 of any 15 in the case of a multiemployer plan) consecutive plan years.

(B) Effects of waiver.—If a waiver is granted under subparagraph (A) for any plan year—

(i) in the case of a defined benefit plan which is not a multiemployer plan, the minimum required contribution under section 430 for the plan year shall be reduced by the amount of the waived funding deficiency and such amount shall be amortized as required under section 430(e), and

(ii) in the case of a multiemployer plan, the funding standard account shall be credited under section 431(b)(3)(C) with the amount of the waived funding deficiency and such amount shall be amortized as required under section 431(b)(2)(C).

(C) Waiver of amortized portion not allowed.—The Secretary may not waive under subparagraph (A) any portion of the minimum funding standard under subsection (a) for a plan year which is attributable to any waived funding deficiency for any preceding plan year.

(2) Determination of business hardship.—For purposes of this subsection, the factors taken into account in determining temporary substantial business hardship (substantial business hardship in the case of a multiemployer plan) shall include (but shall not be limited to) whether or not—

(A) the employer is operating at an economic loss,

(B) there is substantial unemployment or underemployment in the trade or business and in the industry concerned,

IRC Sec. 412(c)(2)(B)

(C) the sales and profits of the industry concerned are depressed or declining, and

(D) it is reasonable to expect that the plan will be continued only if the waiver is granted.

(3) Waived funding deficiency.—For purposes of this section and part III of this subchapter, the term "waived funding deficiency" means the portion of the minimum funding standard under subsection (a) (determined without regard to the waiver) for a plan year waived by the Secretary and not satisfied by employer contributions.

(4) Security for waivers for single-employer plans, consultations.—

(A) Security may be required.—

(i) In general.—Except as provided in subparagraph (C), the Secretary may require an employer maintaining a defined benefit plan which is a single-employer plan (within the meaning of section 4001(a)(15) of the Employee Retirement Income Security Act of 1974) to provide security to such plan as a condition for granting or modifying a waiver under paragraph (1).

(ii) Special rules.—Any security provided under clause (i) may be perfected and enforced only by the Pension Benefit Guaranty Corporation, or at the direction of the Corporation, by a contributing sponsor (within the meaning of section 4001(a)(13) of the Employee Retirement Income Security Act of 1974), or a member of such sponsor's controlled group (within the meaning of section 4001(a)(14) of such Act).

(B) Consultation with the Pension Benefit Guaranty Corporation.—Except as provided in subparagraph (C), the Secretary shall, before granting or modifying a waiver under this subsection with respect to a plan described in subparagraph (A)(i)—

(i) provide the Pension Benefit Guaranty Corporation with—

(I) notice of the completed application for any waiver or modification, and

(II) an opportunity to comment on such application within 30 days after receipt of such notice, and

(ii) consider—

(I) any comments of the Corporation under clause (i)(II), and

(II) any views of any employee organization (within the meaning of section 3(4) of the Employee Retirement Income Security Act of 1974) representing participants in the plan which are submitted in writing to the Secretary in connection with suchapplication.

Information provided to the Corporation under this subparagraph shall be considered tax return informa-

tion and subject to the safeguarding and reporting requirements of section 6103(p).

(C) Exception for certain waivers.—

(i) In general.—The preceding provisions of this paragraph shall not apply to any plan with respect to which the sum of—

(I) the aggregate unpaid minimum required contributions (within the meaning of section 4971(c)(4)) for the plan year and all preceding plan years, and

(II) the present value of all waiver amortization installments determined for the plan year and succeeding plan years under section 430(e)(2), is less than $1,000,000.

(ii) Treatment of waivers for which applications are pending.—The amount described in clause (i)(I) shall include any increase in such amount which would result if all applications for waivers of the minimum funding standard under this subsection which are pending with respect to such plan were denied.

(5) Special rules for single-employer plans.—

(A) Application must be submitted before date 2½ months after close of year.—In the case of a defined benefit plan which is not a multiemployer plan, no waiver may be granted under this subsection with respect to any plan for any plan year unless an application therefor is submitted to the Secretary not later than the 15th day of the 3rd month beginning after the close of such plan year.

(B) Special rule if employer is member of controlled group.—In the case of a defined benefit plan which is not a multiemployer plan, if an employer is a member of a controlled group, the temporary substantial business hardship requirements of paragraph (1) shall be treated as met only if such requirements are met—

(i) with respect to such employer, and

(ii) with respect to the controlled group of which such employer is a member (determined by treating all members of such group as a single employer).

The Secretary may provide that an analysis of a trade or business or industry of a member need not be conducted if the Secretary determines such analysis is not necessary because the taking into account of such member would not significantly affect the determination under this paragraph.

(6) Advance notice.—

(A) In general.—The Secretary shall, before granting a waiver under this subsection, require each applicant to provide evidence satisfactory to the Secretary that the applicant has provided notice of the filing of the application for such waiver to each affected party (as defined in section 4001(a)(21) of the Employee Retirement Income Security Act of 1974). Such notice shall include a description of the extent to which the plan is funded for benefits which are guaranteed under title IV of the Employee Retirement Income Security Act of 1974 and for benefit liabilities.

(B) Consideration of relevant information.—The Secretary shall consider any relevant information provided by a person to whom notice was given under subparagraph (A).

(7) Restriction on plan amendments.—

(A) In general.—No amendment of a plan which increases the liabilities of the plan by reason of any increase in benefits, any change in the accrual of benefits, or any change in the rate at which benefits become nonforfeitable under the plan shall be adopted if a waiver under this subsection or an extension of time under section 431(d) is in effect with respect to the plan, or if a plan amendment described in subsection (d)(2) which reduces the accrued benefit of any participant has been made at any time in the preceding 12 months (24 months in the case of a multiemployer plan). If a plan is amended in violation of the preceding sentence, any such waiver, or extension of time, shall not apply to any plan year ending on or after the date on which such amendment is adopted.

(B) Exception.—Subparagraph (A) shall not apply to any plan amendment which—

(i) the Secretary determines to be reasonable and which provides for only de minimis increases in the liabilities of the plan,

(ii) only repeals an amendment described in subsection (d)(2), or

(iii) is required as a condition of qualification under part I of subchapter D, of chapter 1.

(d) Miscellaneous Rules.—

(1) Change in method or year.—If the funding method, or a plan year for a plan is changed, the change shall take effect only if approved by the Secretary.

(2) Certain retroactive plan amendments.—For purposes of this section, any amendment applying to a plan year which—

(A) is adopted after the close of such plan year but no later than 2½ months after the close of the plan year (or, in the case of a multiemployer plan, no later than 2 years after the close of such plan year),

(B) does not reduce the accrued benefit of any participant determined as of the beginning of the first plan year to which the amendment applies, and

(C) does not reduce the accrued benefit of any participant determined as of the time of adoption except to the extent required by the circumstances,

shall, at the election of the plan administrator, be deemed to have been made on the first day of such plan year. No amendment described in this paragraph which reduces the accrued benefits of any participant shall take effect unless the plan administrator files a notice with the Secretary notifying him of such amendment and the Secretary has approved such amendment, or within 90 days after the date on which such notice was filed, failed to disapprove such amendment. No amendment described in this subsection shall be approved by the Secretary unless the Secretary determines that such amendment is necessary because of a temporary substantial business hardship (as determined under subsection (c)(2)) or a substantial business hardship (as so determined) in the case of a multiemployer plan and that a waiver under subsection (c) (or, in the case of a multiemployer plan, any extension of the amortization period under section 431(d)) is unavailable or inadequate.

(3) Controlled group.—For purposes of this section, the term "controlled group" means any group treated as a single employer under subsection (b), (c), (m), or (o) of section 414.

(e) Plans to Which Section Applies.—

(1) In general.—Except as provided in paragraphs (2) and (4), this section applies to a plan if, for any plan year beginning on or after the effective date of this section for such plan under the Employee Retirement Income Security Act of 1974—

(A) such plan included a trust which qualified (or was determined by the Secretary to have qualified) under section 401(a), or

(B) such plan satisfied (or was determined by the Secretary to have satisfied) the requirements of section 403(a).

(2) Exceptions.—This section shall not apply to—

(A) any profit-sharing or stock bonus plan,

(B) any insurance contract plan described in paragraph (3),

(C) any governmental plan (within the meaning of section 414(d)),

(D) any church plan (within the meaning of section 414(e)) with respect to which the election provided by section 410(d) has not been made,

(E) any plan which has not, at any time after September 2, 1974, provided for employer contributions, or

(F) any plan established and maintained by a society, order, or association described in section 501(c)(8) or (9), if no part of the contributions to or under such plan are made by employers of participants in such plan.

No plan described in subparagraph (C), (D), or (F) shall be treated as a qualified plan for purposes of

IRC Sec. 412(e)(2)

section 401(a) unless such plan meets the requirements of section 401(a)(7) as in effect on September 1, 1974.

(3) Certain insurance contract plans.—A plan is described in this paragraph if—

(A) the plan is funded exclusively by the purchase of individual insurance contracts,

(B) such contracts provide for level annual premium payments to be paid extending not later than the retirement age for each individual participating in the plan, and commencing with the date the individual became a participant in the plan (or, in the case of an increase in benefits, commencing at the time such increase becomes effective),

(C) benefits provided by the plan are equal to the benefits provided under each contract at normal retirement age under the plan and are guaranteed by an insurance carrier (licensed under the laws of a State to do business with the plan) to the extent premiums have been paid,

(D) premiums payable for the plan year, and all prior plan years, under such contracts have been paid before lapse or there is reinstatement of the policy,

(E) no rights under such contracts have been subject to a security interest at any time during the plan year, and

(F) no policy loans are outstanding at any time during the plan year.

A plan funded exclusively by the purchase of group insurance contracts which is determined under regulations prescribed by the Secretary to have the same characteristics as contracts described in the preceding sentence shall be treated as a plan described in this paragraph.

(4) Certain terminated multiemployer plans.— This section applies with respect to a terminated multiemployer plan to which section 4021 of the Employee Retirement Income Security Act of 1974 applies until the last day of the plan year in which the plan terminates (within the meaning of section 4041A(a)(2) of such Act).

Recent Amendments to IRC §412

Worker, Retiree, and Employer Recovery Act of 2008 (Pub. L. No. 110-458), as follows:
- IRC §412(b)(3) was amended by Act §102(b)(2)(H) by substituting "plan sponsor adopts" for "plan adopts". Eff. as if included in Pub. L. 109-280, §112 [eff. generally for plan years beginning after 2007].
- IRC §412(c)(1)(A)(i) was amended by Act §101(a)(2)(A) by substituting "the plan are" for "the plan is". Eff. as if included in Pub. L. No. 109-280, §111 [eff. for plan years beginning after 2007].
- IRC §412(c)(7)(A) was amended by Act §101(a)(2)(B) by inserting "which reduces the accrued benefit of any participant" after "subsection (d)(2)". Eff. as if included in Pub. L. No. 109-280, §111 [eff. for plan years beginning after 2007].

- IRC §412(d)(1) was amended by Act §101(a)(2)(C) by striking "; the valuation date,". Eff. as if included in Pub. L. No. 109-280, §111 [eff. for plan years beginning after 2007].

Pension Protection Act of 2006 (Pub. L. No. 109-280), as follows:
- IRC §412 was amended by Act §111(a). Eff. plan years beginning after Dec. 31, 2007. For IRC §412 prior to amendment, see below in this chapter.
- IRC §412(b) was amended by Act §212(c) by adding new para. (3) at the end. Eff. generally with respect to plan years beginning after 2007. See Act §212(e)(2)–(3) for special rules.
- **Applicability Rule.** Act §206 provides:

    SEC. 206. SPECIAL RULE FOR CERTAIN BENEFITS FUNDED UNDER AN AGREEMENT APPROVED BY THE PENSION BENEFIT GUARANTY CORPORATION.

    In the case of a multiemployer plan that is a party to an agreement that was approved by the Pension Benefit Guaranty Corporation prior to June 30, 2005, and that—

    (1) increases benefits, and

    (2) provides for special withdrawal liability rules under section 4203(f) of the Employee Retirement Income Security Act of 1974 (29 U.S.C. 1383), the amendments made by sections 201, 202, 211, and 212 of this Act shall not apply to the benefit increases under any plan amendment adopted prior to June 30, 2005, that are funded pursuant to such agreement if the plan is funded in compliance with such agreement (and any amendments thereto).

- **Sunset Provision.** Act §221(c) provides:

    (C) Sunset.—

    (1) In general.—Except as provided in this subsection, notwithstanding any other provision of this Act, the provisions of, and the amendments made by, sections 201(b), 202, and 212 shall not apply to plan years beginning after December 31, 2014.

    (2) Funding improvement and rehabilitation plans.—If a plan is operating under a funding improvement or rehabilitation plan under section 305 of such Act or 432 or such Code for its last year beginning before January 1, 2015, such plan shall continue to operate under such funding improvement or rehabilitation plan during any period after December 31, 2014, such funding improvement or rehabilitation plan is in effect and all provisions of such Act or Code relating to the operation of such funding improvement or rehabilitation plan shall continue in effect during such period.

- **Sunset Provision.** Act §811, provides:

    SEC. 811. PENSIONS AND INDIVIDUAL RETIREMENT ARRANGEMENT PROVISIONS OF ECONOMIC GROWTH AND TAX RELIEF RECONCILIATION ACT OF 2001 MADE PERMANENT.

    Title IX of the Economic Growth and Tax Relief Reconciliation Act of 2001 [Pub. L. No. 107-16] shall not apply to the provisions of, and amendments made by, subtitles A through F [§§601–666] of title VI of such Act (relating to pension and individual retirement arrangement provisions).

SEC. 412. MINIMUM FUNDING STANDARDS. [Repealed.]

(a) General Rule.—Except as provided in subsection (h), this section applies to a plan if, for any plan year beginning on or after the effective date of this section for such plan—

(1) such plan included a trust which qualified (or was determined by the Secretary to have qualified) under section 401(a), or

(2) such plan satisfied (or was determined by the Secretary to have satisfied) the requirements of section 403(a).

A plan to which this section applies shall have satisfied the minimum funding standard for such plan for a plan year if as of the end of such plan year, the plan does not have an accumulated funding deficiency. For purposes of this section and section 4971, the term "accumulated funding deficiency" means for any plan the excess of the total charges to the funding standard account for all plan years (beginning with the first plan year to which this section applies) over the total credits to such account for such years or, if less, the excess of the total charges to the alternative minimum funding standard account for such plan years over the total credits to such account for such years. In any plan year in which a multiemployer plan is in reorganization, the accumulated funding deficiency of the plan shall be determined under section 418B.

(b) Funding Standard Account.—

(1) Account required.—Each plan to which this section applies shall establish and maintain a funding standard account. Such account shall be credited and charged solely as provided in this section.

(2) Charges to account.—For a plan year, the funding standard account shall be charged with the sum of—

(A) the normal cost of the plan for the plan year.

(B) the amounts necessary to amortize in equal annual installments (until fully amortized)—

(i) in the case of a plan in existence on January 1, 1974, the unfunded past service liability under the plan on the first day of the first plan year to which this section applies, over a period of 40 plan years,

(ii) in the case of a plan which comes into existence after January 1, 1974, the unfunded past service liability under the plan on the first day of the first plan year to which this section applies, over a period of 30 plan years,

(iii) separately, with respect to each plan year, the net increase (if any) in unfunded past service liability under the plan arising from plan amendments adopted in such year, over a period of 30 plan years,

(iv) separately, with respect to each plan year, the net experience loss (if any) under the plan, over a period of 5 plan years (15 plan years in the case of a multiemployer plan), and

(v) separately, with respect to each plan year, the net loss (if any) resulting from changes in actuarial assumptions used under the plan, over a period of 10 plan years (30 plan years in the case of a multiemployer plan),

(C) the amount necessary to amortize each waived funding deficiency (within the meaning of subsection (d)(3)) for each prior plan year in equal annual installments (until fully amortized) over a period of 5 plan years (15 plan years in the case of a multiemployer plan),

(D) the amount necessary to amortize in equal annual installments (until fully amortized) over a period of 5 plan years any amount credited to the funding standard account under paragraph (3)(D), and

(E) the amount necessary to amortize in equal annual installments (until fully amortized) over a period of 20 years the contributions which would be required to be made under the plan but for the provisions of subsection (c)(7)(A)(i)(I).

For additional requirements in the case of plans other than multiemployer plans, see subsection (l).

(3) Credits to account.—For a plan year, the funding standard account shall be credited with the sum of—

(A) the amount considered contributed by the employer to or under the plan for the plan year,

(B) the amount necessary to amortize in equal annual installments (until fully amortized)—

(i) separately, with respect to each plan year, the net decrease (if any) in unfunded past service liability under the plan arising from plan amendments adopted in such year, over a period of 30 plan years,

(ii) separately, with respect to each plan year, the net experience gain (if any) under the plan, over a period of 5 plan years (15 plan years in the case of a multiemployer plan), and

(iii) separately, with respect to each plan year, the net gain (if any) resulting from changes in actuarial assumptions used under the plan, over a period of 10 plan years (30 plan years in the case of a multiemployer plan),

(C) the amount of the waived funding deficiency (within the meaning of subsection (d)(3)) for the plan year, and

(D) in the case of a plan year for which the accumulated funding deficiency is determined under the funding standard account if such plan year follows a plan year for which such deficiency was determined under the alternative minimum funding standard, the excess (if any) of any debit balance in the funding standard account (determined without regard to this subparagraph) over any debit balance in the alternative minimum funding standard account.

(4) Combining and offsetting amounts to be amortized.— Under regulations prescribed by the Secretary, amounts required to be amortized under paragraph (2) or paragraph (3), as the case may be—

(A) may be combined into one amount under such paragraph to be amortized over a period determined on the basis of the remaining amortization period for all items entering into such combined amount, and

(B) may be offset against amounts required to be amortized under the other such paragraph, with the resulting amount to be amortized over a period determined on the basis of the remaining amortization periods for all items entering into whichever of the two amounts being offset is the greater.

(5) Interest.—

(A) In general.—The funding standard account (and items therein) shall be charged or credited (as determined under regulations prescribed by the Secretary) with interest at the appropriate rate consistent with the rate or rates of interest used under the plan to determine costs.

(B) Required change of interest rate.—For purposes of determining a plan's current liability and for purposes of determining a plan's required contribution under section 412(l) for any plan year—

(i) In general.—If any rate of interest used under the plan to determine cost is not within the permissible range, the plan shall establish a new rate of interest within the permissible range.

(ii) Permissible range.—For purposes of this subparagraph—

(I) In general.—Except as provided in subclause (II) or (III), the term "permissible range" means a rate of interest which is not more than 10 percent above, and not more than 10 percent below, the weighted average of the rates of interest on 30-year Treasury securities during the 4-year period ending on the last day before the beginning of the plan year.

(II) Special rule for years 2004, 2005, 2006, and 2007.—In the case of plan years beginning after December 31, 2003, and before January 1, 2008, the term "permissible range" means a rate of interest which is not above, and not more than 10 percent below, the weighted average of the rates of interest on amounts invested conservatively in long-term investment grade corporate bonds during the 4-year period ending on the last day before the beginning of the plan year. Such rates shall be determined by the Secretary on the basis of 2 or more indices that are selected periodically by the Secretary and that are in the top 3 quality levels available. The Secretary shall make the permissible range, and the indices and methodology used to determine the average rate, publicly available.

(III) Secretarial authority.—If the Secretary finds that the lowest rate of interest permissible under subclause (I) or (II) is unreasonably high, the Secretary may prescribe a lower rate of interest, except that such rate may not be less than 80 percent of the average rate determined under such subclause.

(iii) Assumptions.—Notwithstanding subsection (c)(3)(A)(i), the interest rate used under the plan shall be—

IRC Sec. 412 [Repealed]

(I) determined without taking into account the experience of the plan and reasonable expectations, but

(II) consistent with the assumptions which reflect the purchase rates which would be used by insurance companies to satisfy the liabilities under the plan.

(6) Certain amortization charges and credits.—In the case of a plan which, immediately before the date of the enactment of the Multiemployer Pension Plan Amendments Act of 1980, was a multiemployer plan (within the meaning of section 414(f) as in effect immediately before such date)—

(A) any amount described in paragraph (2)(B)(ii), (2)(B)(iii), or (3)(B)(i) of this subsection which arose in a plan year beginning before such date shall be amortized in equal annual installments (until fully amortized) over 40 plan years, beginning with the plan year in which the amount arose;

(B) any amount described in paragraph (2)(B)(iv) or (3)(B)(ii) of this subsection which arose in a plan year beginning before such date shall be amortized in equal annual installments (until fully amortized) over 20 plan years, beginning with the plan year in which the amount arose;

(C) any change in past service liability which arises during the period of 3 plan years beginning on or after such date, and results from a plan amendment adopted before such date, shall be amortized in equal annual installments (until fully amortized) over 40 plan years, beginning with the plan year in which the change arises; and

(D) any change in past service liability which arises during the period of 2 plan years beginning on or after such date, and results from the changing of a group of participants from one benefit level to another benefit level under a schedule of plan benefits which—

(i) was adopted before such date, and

(ii) was effective for any plan participant before the beginning of the first plan year beginning on or after such date,

shall be amortized in equal annual installments (until fully amortized) over 40 plan years, beginning with the plan year in which the change arises.

(7) Special rules for multiemployer plans.—For purposes of this section—

(A) Withdrawal liability.—Any amount received by a multiemployer plan in payment of all or part of an employer's withdrawal liability under part 1 of subtitle E of title IV of the Employee Retirement Income Security Act of 1974 shall be considered an amount contributed by the employer to or under the plan. The Secretary may prescribe by regulation additional charges and credits to a multiemployer plan's funding standard account to the extent necessary to prevent withdrawal liability payments from being unduly reflected as advance funding for plan liabilities.

(B) Adjustments when a multiemployer plan leaves reorganization.—If a multiemployer plan is not in reorganization in the plan year but was in reorganization in the immediately preceding plan year, any balance in the funding standard account at the close of such immediately preceding plan year—

(i) shall be eliminated by an offsetting credit or charge (as the case may be), but

(ii) shall be taken into account in subsequent plan years by being amortized in equal annual installments (until fully amortized) over 30 plan years.

The preceding sentence shall not apply to the extent of any accumulated funding deficiency under section 418B(a) as of the end of the last plan year that the plan was in reorganization.

(C) Plan payments to supplemental program or withdrawal liability payment fund.—Any amount paid by a plan during a plan year to the Pension Benefit Guaranty Corporation pursuant to section 4222 of such Act or to a fund exempt under section

501(c)(22) pursuant to section 4223 of such Act shall reduce the amount of contributions considered received by the plan for the plan year.

(D) Interim withdrawal liability payments.—Any amount paid by an employer pending a final determination of the employer's withdrawal liability under part 1 of subtitle E of title IV of such Act and subsequently refunded to the employer by the plan shall be charged to the funding standard account in accordance with regulations prescribed by the Secretary.

(E) For purposes of the full funding limitation under subsection (c)(7), unless otherwise provided by the plan, the accrued liability under a multiemployer plan shall not include benefits which are not nonforfeitable under the plan after the termination of the plan (taking into consideration section 411(d)(3)).

(F) Election for deferral of charge for portion of net experience loss.—

(i) In general.—With respect to the net experience loss of an eligible multiemployer plan for the first plan year beginning after December 31, 2001, the plan sponsor may elect to defer up to 80 percent of the amount otherwise required to be charged under paragraph (2)(B)(iv) for any plan year beginning after June 30, 2003, and before July 1, 2005, to any plan year selected by the plan from either of the 2 immediately succeeding plan years.

(ii) Interest.—For the plan year to which a charge is deferred pursuant to an election under clause (i), the funding standard account shall be charged with interest on the deferred charge for the period of deferral at the rate determined under subsection (d) for multiemployer plans.

(iii) Restrictions on benefit increases.—No amendment which increases the liabilities of the plan by reason of any increase in benefits, any change in the accrual of benefits, or any change in the rate at which benefits become nonforfeitable under the plan shall be adopted during any period for which a charge is deferred pursuant to an election under clause (i), unless—

(I) the plan's enrolled actuary certifies (in such form and manner prescribed by the Secretary) that the amendment provides for an increase in annual contributions which will exceed the increase in annual charges to the funding standard account attributable to such amendment, or

(II) the amendment is required by a collective bargaining agreement which is in effect on the date of enactment of this subparagraph.

If a plan is amended during any such plan year in violation of the preceding sentence, any election under this paragraph shall not apply to any such plan year ending on or after the date on which such amendment is adopted.

(iv) Eligible multiemployer plan.—For purposes of this subparagraph, the term "eligible multiemployer plan" means a multiemployer plan—

(I) which had a net investment loss for the first plan year beginning after December 31, 2001, of at least 10 percent of the average fair market value of the plan assets during the plan year, and

(II) with respect to which the plan's enrolled actuary certifies (not taking into account the application of this subparagraph), on the basis of the actuarial assumptions used for the last plan year ending before the date of the enactment of this subparagraph, that the plan is projected to have an accumulated funding deficiency (within the meaning of subsection (a)) for any plan year beginning after June 30, 2003, and before July 1, 2006.

For purposes of subclause (I), a plan's net investment loss shall be determined on the basis of the actual loss and not under any actuarial method under subsection (c)(2).

(v) Exception to treatment of eligible multiemployer plan.— In no event shall a plan be treated as an eligible multiemployer plan under clause (iv) if—

IRC Sec. 412 [Repealed]

(I) for any taxable year beginning during the 10-year period preceding the first plan year for which an election is made under clause (i), any employer required to contribute to the plan failed to timely pay any excise tax imposed under section 4971 with respect to the plan,

(II) for any plan year beginning after June 30, 1993, and before the first plan year for which an election is made under clause (i), the average contribution required to be made by all employers to the plan does not exceed 10 cents per hour or no employer is required to make contributions to the plan, or

(III) with respect to any of the plan years beginning after June 30, 1993, and before the first plan year for which an election is made under clause (i), a waiver was granted under section 412(d) or section 303 of the Employee Retirement Income Security Act of 1974 with respect to the plan or an extension of an amortization period was granted under subsection (e) or section 304 of such Act with respect to the plan.

(vi) Election.—An election under this subparagraph shall be made at such time and in such manner as the Secretary may prescribe.

(c) Special Rules.—

(1) Determinations to be made under funding method.—For purposes of this section, normal costs, accrued liability, past service liabilities, and experience gains and losses shall be determined under the funding method used to determine costs under the plan.

(2) Valuation of assets.—

(A) In general.—For purposes of this section, the value of the plan's assets shall be determined on the basis of any reasonable actuarial method of valuation which takes into account fair market value and which is permitted under regulations prescribed by the Secretary.

(B) Election with respect to bonds.—The value of a bond or other evidence of indebtedness which is not in default as to principal or interest may, at the election of the plan administrator, be determined on an amortized basis running from initial cost at purchase to par value at maturity or earliest call date. Any election under this subparagraph shall be made at such time and in such manner as the Secretary shall by regulations provide, shall apply to all such evidences of indebtedness, and may be revoked only with the consent of the Secretary. In the case of a plan other than a multiemployer plan, this subparagraph shall not apply, but the Secretary may by regulations provide that the value of any dedicated bond portfolio of such plan shall be determined by using the interest rate under subsection (b)(5).

(3) Actuarial assumptions must be reasonable.— For purposes of this section, all costs, liabilities, rates of interest, and other factors under the plan shall be determined on the basis of actuarial assumptions and methods—

(A) in the case of—

(i) a plan other than a multiemployer plan, each of which is reasonable (taking into account the experience of the plan and reasonable expectations) or which, in the aggregate, result in a total contribution equivalent to that which would be determined if each such assumption and method were reasonable, or

(ii) a multiemployer plan, which, in the aggregate, are reasonable (taking into account the experiences of the plan and reasonable expectations), and

(B) which, in combination, offer the actuary's best estimate of anticipated experience under the plan.

(4) Treatment of certain changes as experience gain or loss.—For purposes of this section, if—

(A) a change in benefits under the Social Security Act or in other retirement benefits created under Federal or State law, or

(B) a change in the definition of the term "wages" under section 3121, or a change in the amount of such wages taken into account under regulations prescribed for purposes of section

401(a)(5), results in an increase or decrease in accrued liability under a plan, such increase or decrease shall be treated as an experience loss or gain.

(5) Change in funding method or in plan year requires approval.—

(A) In general.—If the funding method for a plan is changed, the new funding method shall become the funding method used to determine costs and liabilities under the plan only if the change is approved by the Secretary. If the plan year for a plan is changed, the new plan year shall become the plan year for the plan only if the change is approved by the Secretary.

(B) Approval required for certain changes in assumptions by certain single-employer plans subject to additional funding requirement.—

(i) In general.—No actuarial assumption (other than the assumptions described in subsection (*l*)(7)(C)) used to determine the current liability for a plan to which this subparagraph applies may be changed without the approval of the Secretary.

(ii) Plans to which subparagraph applies.—This subparagraph shall apply to a plan only if—

(I) the plan is a defined benefit plan (other than a multiemployer plan) to which title IV of the Employee Retirement Income Security Act of 1974 applies;

(II) the aggregate unfunded vested benefits as of the close of the preceding plan year (as determined under section 4006(a)(3) (E)(iii) of the Employee Retirement Income Security Act of 1974) of such plan and all other plans maintained by the contributing sponsors (as defined in section 4001(a)(13) of such Act) and members of such sponsors' controlled groups (as defined in section 4001(a)(14) of such Act) which are covered by title IV of such Act (disregarding plans with no unfunded vested benefits) exceed $50,000,000; and

(III) the change in assumptions (determined after taking into account any changes in interest rate and mortality table) results in a decrease in the unfunded current liability of the plan for the current plan year that exceeds $50,000,000, or that exceeds $5,000,000 and that is 5 percent or more of the current liability of the plan before such change.

(6) Full funding.—If, as of the close of a plan year, a plan would (without regard to this paragraph) have an accumulated funding deficiency (determined without regard to the alternative minimum funding standard account permitted under subsection (g)) in excess of the full funding limitation—

(A) the funding standard account shall be credited with the amount of such excess, and

(B) all amounts described in paragraphs (2)(B), (C), and (D) and (3)(B) of subsection (b) which are required to be amortized shall be considered fully amortized for purposes of such paragraphs.

(7) Full-funding limitation.—

(A) In general.—For purposes of paragraph (6), the term "full-funding limitation" means the excess (if any) of—

(i) the lesser of—

(I) in the case of plan years beginning before January 1, 2004, the applicable percentage of current liability (including the expected increase in current liability due to benefits accruing during the plan year), or

(II) the accrued liability (including normal cost) under the plan (determined under the entry age normal funding method if such accrued liability cannot be directly calculated under the funding method used for the plan), over

(ii) the lesser of—

(I) the fair market value of the plan's assets, or

(II) the value of such assets determined under paragraph (2).

(B) Current liability.—For purposes of subparagraph (D) and subclause (I) of subparagraph (A)(i), the term "current liability"

IRC Sec. 412 [Repealed]

has the meaning given such term by subsection (*l*)(7) (without regard to subparagraphs (C) and (D) thereof) and using the rate of interest used under subsection (b)(5)(B).

(C) Special rule for paragraph (6)(B).—For purposes of paragraph (6)(B), subparagraph (A)(i) shall be applied without regard to subclause (I) thereof.

(D) Regulatory authority.—The Secretary may by regulations provide—

(i) for adjustments to the percentage contained in subparagraph (A)(i) to take into account the respective ages or lengths of service of the participants, and

(ii) alternative methods based on factors other than current liability for the determination of the amount taken into account under subparagraph (A)(i).

(E) Minimum amount.—

(i) In general.—In no event shall the full-funding limitation determined under subparagraph (A) be less than the excess (if any) of—

(I) 90 percent of the current liability of the plan (including the expected increase in current liability due to benefits accruing during the plan year), over

(II) the value of the plan's assets determined under paragraph (2).

(ii) Current liability; assets.—For purposes of clause (i)

(I) the term "current liability" has the meaning given such term by subsection (*l*)(7) (without regard to subparagraph (D) thereof), and

(II) assets shall not be reduced by any credit balance in the funding standard account.

(F) Applicable percentage.—For purposes of subparagraph (A)(i)(I), the applicable percentage shall be determined in accordance with the following table:

In the case of any plan year beginning in—	The applicable percentage is:
2002	160
2003	170

(8) **Certain retroactive plan amendments.**—For purposes of this section, any amendment applying to a plan year which—

(A) is adopted after the close of such plan year but no later than 2 and one-half months after the close of the plan year (or, in the case of a multiemployer plan, no later than 2 years after the close of such plan year),

(B) does not reduce the accrued benefit of any participant determined as of the beginning of the first plan year to which the amendment applies, and

(C) does not reduce the accrued benefit of any participant determined as of the time of adoption except to the extent required by the circumstances,

shall, at the election of the plan administrator, be deemed to have been made on the first day of such plan year. No amendment described in this paragraph which reduces the accrued benefits of any participant shall take effect unless the plan administrator files a notice with the Secretary of Labor notifying him of such amendment and the Secretary of Labor has approved such amendment, or within 90 days after the date on which such notice was filed, failed to disapprove such amendment. No amendment described in this subsection shall be approved by the Secretary of Labor unless he determines that such amendment is necessary because of a substantial business hardship (as determined under subsection (d)(2)) and that a waiver under subsection (d)(1) is unavailable or inadequate.

(9) **Annual valuation.**—

(A) In general.—For purposes of this section, a determination of experience gains and losses and a valuation of the plan's liability shall be made not less frequently than once every year, except that such determination shall be made more frequently to the extent required in particular cases under regulations prescribed by the Secretary.

(B) Valuation date.—

(i) Current year.—Except as provided in clause (ii), the valuation referred to in subparagraph (A) shall be made as of a date within the plan year to which the valuation refers or within one month prior to the beginning of such year.

(ii) Use of prior year valuation.—The valuation referred to in subparagraph (A) may be made as of a date within the plan year prior to the year to which the valuation refers if, as of such date, the value of the assets of the plan are not less than 100 percent of the plan's current liability (as defined in paragraph (7)(B)).

(iii) Adjustments.—Information under clause (ii) shall, in accordance with regulations, be actuarially adjusted to reflect significant differences in participants.

(iv) Limitation.—A change in funding method to use a prior year valuation, as provided in clause (ii), may not be made unless as of the valuation date within the prior plan year, the value of the assets of the plan are not less than 125 percent of the plan's current liability (as defined in paragraph (7)(B)).

(10) **Time when certain contributions deemed made.**—For purposes of this section—

(A) Defined benefit plans other than multiemployer plans.—In the case of a defined benefit plan other than a multiemployer plan, any contributions for a plan year made by an employer during the period—

(i) beginning on the day after the last day of such plan year, and

(ii) ending on the day which is 8½ months after the close of the plan year,

shall be deemed to have been made on such last day.

(B) Other plans.—In the case of a plan not described in subparagraph (A), any contributions for a plan year made by an employer after the last day of such plan year, but not later than two and one-half months after such day, shall be deemed to have been made on such last day. For purposes of this subparagraph, such two and one-half month period may be extended for not more than six months under regulations prescribed by the Secretary.

(11) **Liability for contributions.**—

(A) In general.—Except as provided in subparagraph (B), the amount of any contribution required by this section and any required installments under subsection (m) shall be paid by the employer responsible for contributing to or under the plan the amount described in subsection (b)(3)(A).

(B) Joint and several liability where employer member of controlled group.—

(i) In general.—In the case of a plan other than a multiemployer plan, if the employer referred to in subparagraph (A) is a member of a controlled group, each member of such group shall be jointly and severally liable for payment of such contribution or required installment.

(ii) Controlled group.—For purposes of clause (i), the term "controlled group" means any group treated as a single employer under subsection (b), (c), (m), or (o) of section 414.

(12) **Anticipation of benefit increases effective in the future.**—In determining projected benefits, the funding method of a collectively bargained plan described in section 413(a) (other than a multiemployer plan) shall anticipate benefit increases scheduled to take effect during the term of the collective bargaining agreement applicable to the plan.

IRC Sec. 412 [Repealed]

(d) Variance From Minimum Funding Standard.—

(1) Waiver in case of business hardship.—If an employer, or in the case of a multiemployer plan, 10 percent or more of the number of employers contributing to or under the plan, are unable to satisfy the minimum funding standard for a plan year without temporary substantial business hardship (substantial business hardship in the case of a multiemployer plan) and if application of the standard would be adverse to the interests of plan participants in the aggregate, the Secretary may waive the requirements of subsection (a) for such year with respect to all or any portion of the minimum funding standard other than the portion thereof determined under subsection (b)(2)(C). The Secretary shall not waive the minimum funding standards with respect to a plan for more than 3 of any 15 (5 of any 15 in the case of a multiemployer plan) consecutive plan years. The interest rate used for purposes of computing the amortization charge described in subsection (b)(2)(C) for any plan year shall be—

(A) in the case of a plan other than a multiemployer plan, the greater of (i) 150 percent of the Federal mid-term rate (as in effect under section 1274 for the 1st month of such plan year), or (ii) the rate of interest used under the plan in determining costs (including adjustments under subsection (b)(5)(B)), and

(B) in the case of a multiemployer plan, the rate determined under section 6621(b).

(2) Determination of business hardship.—For purposes of this section, the factors taken into account in determining temporary substantial business hardship (substantial business hardship in the case of a multiemployer plan) shall include (but shall not be limited to) whether or not—

(A) the employer is operating at an economic loss,

(B) there is substantial unemployment or underemployment in the trade or business and in the industry concerned,

(C) the sales and profits of the industry concerned are depressed or declining, and

(D) it is reasonable to expect that the plan will be continued only if the waiver is granted.

(3) Waived funding deficiency.— For purposes of this section, the term "waived funding deficiency" means the portion of the minimum funding standard (determined without regard to subsection (b)(3)(C)) for a plan year waived by the Secretary and not satisfied by employer contributions.

(4) Application must be submitted before date 2 1/2 months after close of year.—In the case of a plan other than a multiemployer plan, no waiver may be granted under this subsection with respect to any plan for any plan year unless an application therefor is submitted to the Secretary not later than the 15th day of the 3rd month beginning after the close of such plan year.

(5) Special rule if employer is member of controlled group.—

(A) In general.—In the case of a plan other than a multiemployer plan, if an employer is a member of a controlled group, the temporary substantial business hardship requirements of paragraph (1) shall be treated as met only if such requirements are met—

(i) with respect to such employer, and

(ii) with respect to the controlled group of which such employer is a member (determined by treating all members of such group as a single employer).

The Secretary may provide that an analysis of a trade or business or industry of a member need not be conducted if the Secretary determines such analysis is not necessary because the taking into account of such member would not significantly affect the determination under this subsection.

(B) Controlled group.—For purposes of subparagraph (A), the term "controlled group" means any group treated as a single employer under subsection (b), (c), (m), or (o) of sectio 414.

(e) Extension of Amortization Periods.—The period of years required to amortize any unfunded liability (described in any clause of subsection (b)(2)(B)) of any plan may be extended by the Secretary of Labor for a period of time (not in excess of 10 years) if he determines that such extension would carry out the purposes of the Employee Retirement Income Security Act of 1974 and would provide adequate protection for participants under the plan and their beneficiaries and if he determines that the failure to permit such extension would—

(1) result in—

(A) a substantial risk to the voluntary continuation of the plan, or

(B) a substantial curtailment of pension benefit levels or employee compensation, and

(2) be adverse to the interests of plan participants in the aggregate.

In the case of a plan other than a multiemployer plan, the interest rate applicable for any plan year under any arrangement entered into by the Secretary in connection with an extension granted under this subsection shall be the greater of (A) 150 percent of the Federal mid-term rate (as in effect under section 1274 for the 1st month of such plan year), or (B) the rate of interest used under the plan in determining costs. In the case of a multiemployer plan, such rate shall be the rate determined under section 6621(b).

(f) Requirements Relating to Waivers and Extensions.—

(1) Benefits may not be increased during waiver or extension period.—No amendment of the plan which increases the liabilities of the plan by reason of any increase in benefits, any change in the accrual of benefits, or any change in the rate at which benefits become nonforfeitable under the plan shall be adopted if a waiver under subsection (d)(1) or an extension of time under subsection (e) is in effect with respect to the plan, or if a plan amendment described in subsection (c)(8) has been made at any time in the preceding 12 months (24 months for multiemployer plans). If a plan is amended in violation of the preceding sentence, any such waiver or extension of time shall not apply to any plan year ending on or after the date on which such amendment is adopted.

(2) Exception.—Paragraph (1) shall not apply to any plan amendment which—

(A) the Secretary of Labor determines to be reasonable and which provides for only de minimis increases in the liabilities of the plan,

(B) only repeals an amendment described in subsection (c)(8), or

(C) is required as a condition of qualification under this part.

(3) Security for waivers and extensions; consultations.—

(A) Security may be required.—

(i) In general.—Except as provided in subparagraph (C), the Secretary may require an employer maintaining a defined benefit plan which is a single-employer plan (within the meaning of section 4001(a)(15) of the Employee Retirement Income Security Act of 1974) to provide security to such plan as a condition for granting or modifying a waiver under subsection (d) or an extension under subsection (e).

(ii) Special rules.—Any security provided under clause (i) may be perfected and enforced only by the Pension Benefit Guaranty Corporation, or at the direction of the Corporation, by a contributing sponsor (within the meaning of section 4001(a)(13) of such Act), or a member of such sponsor's controlled group (within the meaning of section 4001(a)(14) of such Act).

(B) Consultation with the Pension Benefit Guaranty Corporation.—Except as provided in subparagraph (C), the Secretary shall, before granting or modifying a waiver under subsection (d) or an extension under subsection (e) with respect to a plan described in subparagraph (A)(i)—

(i) provide the Pension Benefit Guaranty Corporation with—

(I) notice of the completed application for any waiver, extension, or modification, and

IRC Sec. 412 [Repealed]

(II) an opportunity to comment on such application within 30 days after receipt of such notice, and

(ii) consider—

(I) any comments of the Corporation under clause (i)(II), and

(II) any views of any employee organization (within the meaning of section 3(4) of the Employee Retirement Income Security Act of 1974) representing participants in the plan which are submitted in writing to the Secretary in connection with such application.

Information provided to the corporation under this subparagraph shall be considered tax return information and subject to the safeguarding and reporting requirements of section 6103(p).

(C) Exceptions for certain waivers and extensions.—

(i) In general. The preceding provisions of this paragraph shall not apply to any plan with respect to which the sum of—

(I) the outstanding balance of the accumulated funding deficiencies (within the meaning of subsection (a) and section 302(a) of such Act) of the plan,

(II) the outstanding balance of the amount of the waived funding deficiencies of the plan waived under subsection (d) or section 303 of such Act, and

(III) the outstanding balance of the amount of decreases in the minimum funding standard allowed under subsection (e) or section 304 of such Act, is less than $1,000,000.

(ii) Accumulated funding deficiencies.—For purposes of clause (i)(I), accumulated funding deficiencies shall include any increase in such amount which would result if all applications for waivers of the minimum funding standard under subsection (d) or section 303 of such Act and for extensions of the amortization period under subsection (e) or section 304 of such Act which are pending with respect to such plan were denied.

(4) Additional requirements.—

(A) Advance notice.—The Secretary shall, before granting a waiver under subsection (d) or an extension under subsection (e), require each applicant to provide evidence satisfactory to the Secretary that the applicant has provided notice of the filing of the application for such waiver or extension to each employee organization representing employees covered by the affected plan, and each participant, beneficiary, and alternate payee (within the meaning of section 414(p)(8)). Such notice shall include a description of the extent to which the plan is funded for benefits which are guaranteed under title IV of such Act and for benefit liabilities.

(B) Consideration of relevant information.—The Secretary shall consider any relevant information provided by a person to whom notice was given under subparagraph (A).

(g) Alternative Minimum Funding Standard.—

(1) In general.—A plan which uses a funding method that requires contributions in all years not less than those required under the entry age normal funding method may maintain an alternative minimum funding standard account for any plan year. Such account shall be credited and charged solely as provided in this subsection.

(2) Charges and credits to account.—For a plan year the alternative minimum funding standard account shall be—

(A) charged with the sum of—

(i) the lesser of normal cost under the funding method used under the plan or normal cost determined under the unit credit method,

(ii) the excess, if any, of the present value of accrued benefits under the plan over the fair market value of the assets, and

(iii) an amount equal to the excess (if any) of credits to the alternative minimum standard account for all prior plan years over charges to such account for all such years, and

(B) credited with the amount considered contributed by the employer to or under the plan for the plan year.

(3) Special rules.—The alternative minimum funding standard account (and items therein) shall be charged or credited with interest in the manner provided under subsection (b)(5) with respect to the funding standard account.

(h) Exceptions.—This section shall not apply to—

(1) any profit-sharing or stock bonus plan,

(2) any insurance contract plan described in subsection (i),

(3) any governmental plan (within the meaning of section 414(d)),

(4) any church plan (within the meaning of section 414(e)) with respect to which the election provided by section 410(d) has not been made,

(5) any plan which has not, at any time after September 2, 1974, provided for employer contributions, or

(6) any plan established and maintained by a society, order, or association described in section 501(c)(8) or (9), if no part of the contributions to or under such plan are made by employers of participants in such plan.

No plan described in paragraph (3), (4), or (6) shall be treated as a qualified plan for purposes of section 401(a) unless such plan meets the requirements of section 401(a)(7) as in effect on September 1, 1974.

(i) Certain Insurance Contract Plans.—A plan is described in this subsection if—

(1) the plan is funded exclusively by the purchase of individual insurance contracts,

(2) such contracts provided for level annual premium payments to be paid extending not later than the retirement age for each individual participating in the plan, and commencing with the date the individual became a participant in the plan (or, in the case of an increase in benefits, commencing at the time such increase becomes effective),

(3) benefits provided by the plan are equal to the benefits provided under each contract at normal retirement age under the plan and are guaranteed by an insurance carrier (licensed under the laws of a State to do business with the plan) to the extent premiums have been paid,

(4) premiums payable for the plan year, and all prior plan years, under such contracts have been paid before lapse or there is reinstatement of the policy,

(5) no rights under such contracts have been subject to a security interest at any time during the plan year, and

(6) no policy loans are outstanding at any time during the plan year.

A plan funded exclusively by the purchase of group insurance contracts which is determined under regulations prescribed by the Secretary to have the same characteristics as contracts described in the preceding sentence shall be treated as a plan described in this subsection.

(j) Certain Terminated Multiemployer Plans.—This section applies with respect to a terminated multiemployer plan to which section 4021 of the Employee Retirement Income Security Act of 1974 applies, until the last day of the plan year in which the plan terminates, within the meaning of section 4041A(a)(2) of that Act.

(k) Financial Assistance.—Any amount of any financial assistance from the Pension Benefit Guaranty Corporation to any plan, and any repayment of such amount, shall be taken into account under this section in such manner as determined by the Secretary.

(l) Additional Funding Requirements for Plans Which Are Not Multiemployer Plans.—

(1) In general.—In the case of a defined benefit plan (other than a multiemployer plan) to which this subsection applies under paragraph (9) for any plan year, the amount charged to the funding standard account for such plan year shall be increased by the sum of—

(A) the excess (if any) of—

(i) the deficit reduction contribution determined under paragraph (2) for such plan year, over

(ii) the sum of the charges for such plan year under subsection (b)(2), reduced by the sum of the credits for such plan year under subparagraph (B) of subsection (b)(3), plus

(B) the unpredictable contingent event amount (if any) for such plan year.

Such increase shall not exceed the amount which, after taking into account charges (other than the additional charge under this subsection) and credits under subsection (b), is necessary to increase the funded current liability percentage (taking into account the expected increase in current liability due to benefits accruing during the plan year) to 100 percent.

(2) Deficit reduction contribution.—For purposes of paragraph (1), the deficit reduction contribution determined under this paragraph for any plan year is the sum of—

(A) the unfunded old liability amount,

(B) the unfunded new liability amount.

(C) the expected increase in current liability due to benefits accruing during the plan year, and

(D) the aggregate of the unfunded mortality increase amounts.

(3) Unfunded old liability amount.—For purposes of this subsection—

(A) In general.—The unfunded old liability amount with respect to any plan for any plan year is the amount necessary to amortize the unfunded old liability under the plan in equal annual installments over a period of 18 plan years (beginning with the 1st plan year beginning after December 31, 1988).

(B) Unfunded old liability.—The term "unfunded old liability" means the unfunded current liability of the plan as of the beginning of the 1st plan year beginning after December 31, 1987 (determined without regard to any plan amendment increasing liabilities adopted after October 16, 1987).

(C) Special rules for benefit increases under existing collective bargaining agreements.—

(i) In general.—In the case of a plan maintained pursuant to 1 or more collective bargaining agreements between employee representatives and the employer ratified before October 29, 1987, the unfunded old liability amount with respect to such plan for any plan year shall be increased by the amount necessary to amortize the unfunded existing benefit increase liability in equal annual installments over a period of 18 plan years beginning with—

(I) the plan year in which the benefit increase with respect to such liability occurs, or

(II) if the taxpayer elects, the 1st plan year beginning after December 31, 1988.

(ii) Unfunded existing benefit increase liabilities.—For purposes of clause (i), the unfunded existing benefit increase liability means, with respect to any benefit increase under the agreements described in clause (i) which takes effect during or after the 1st plan year beginning after December 31, 1987, the unfunded current liability determined—

(I) by taking into account only liabilities attributable to such benefit increase, and

(II) by reducing (but not below zero) the amount determined under paragraph (8)(A)(ii) by the current liability determined without regard to such benefit increase.

(iii) Extensions, modifications, etc. not taken into account.—For purposes of this subparagraph, any extension, amendment, or other modification of an agreement after October 28, 1987, shall not be taken into account.

(D) Special rule for required changes in actuarial assumptions.—

(i) In general.—The unfunded old liability amount with respect to any plan for any plan year shall be increased by the amount necessary to amortize the amount of additional unfunded old liability under the plan in equal annual installments over a period of 12 plan years (beginning with the first plan year beginning after December 31, 1994).

(ii) Additional unfunded old liability.—For purposes of clause (i), the term "additional unfunded old liability" means the amount (if any) by which—

(I) the current liability of the plan as of the beginning of the first plan year beginning after December 31, 1994, valued using the assumptions required by paragraph (7)(C) as in effect for plan years beginning after December 31, 1994, exceeds

(II) the current liability of the plan as of the beginning of such first plan year, valued using the same assumptions used under subclause (I) (other than the assumptions required by paragraph (7)(C)), using the prior interest rate, and using such mortality assumptions as were used to determine current liability for the first plan year beginning after December 31, 1992.

(iii) Prior interest rate.—For purposes of clause (ii), the term "prior interest rate" means the rate of interest that is the same percentage of the weighted average under subsection (b)(5)(B)(ii)(I) for the first plan year beginning after December 31, 1994, as the rate of interest used by the plan to determine current liability for the first plan year beginning after December 31, 1992, is of the weighted average under subsection (b)(5)(B)(ii)(I) for such first plan year beginning after December 31, 1992.

(E) Optional rule for additional unfunded old liability.—

(i) In general.—If an employer makes an election under clause (ii), the additional unfunded old liability for purposes of subparagraph (D) shall be the amount (if any) by which—

(I) the unfunded current liability of the plan as of the beginning of the first plan year beginning after December 31, 1994, valued using the assumptions required by paragraph (7)(C) as in effect for plan years beginning after December 31, 1994, exceeds

(II) the unamortized portion of the unfunded old liability under the plan as of the beginning of the first plan year beginning after December 31, 1994.

(ii) Election.—

(I) An employer may irrevocably elect to apply the provisions of this subparagraph as of the beginning of the first plan year beginning after December 31, 1994.

(II) If an election is made under this clause, the increase under paragraph (1) for any plan year beginning after December 31, 1994, and before January 1, 2002, to which this subsection applies (without regard to this subclause) shall not be less than the increase that would be required under paragraph (1) if the provisions of this title as in effect for the last plan year beginning before January 1, 1995, had remained in effect.

(4) Unfunded new liability amount.—For purposes of this subsection—

(A) In general.—The unfunded new liability amount with respect to any plan for any plan year is the applicable percentage of the unfunded new liability.

(B) Unfunded new liability.—The term "unfunded new liability" means the unfunded current liability of the plan for the plan year determined without regard to—

(i) the unamortized portion of the unfunded old liability, the unamortized portion of the additional unfunded old liability, the

IRC Sec. 412 [Repealed]

unamortized portion of each unfunded mortality increase, and the unamortized portion of the unfunded existing benefit increase liability, and

(ii) the liability with respect to any unpredictable contingent event benefits (without regard to whether the event has occurred).

(C) Applicable percentage.—The term "applicable percentage" means, with respect to any plan year, 30 percent, reduced by the product of—

(i) .40 multiplied by

(ii) the number of percentage points (if any) by which the funded current liability percentage exceeds 60 percent.

(5) Unpredictable contingent event amount.—

(A) In general.—The unpredictable contingent event amount with respect to a plan for any plan year is an amount equal to the greatest of—

(i) the applicable percentage of the product of—

(I) 100 percent, reduced (but not below zero) by the funded current liability percentage for the plan year, multiplied by

(II) the amount of unpredictable contingent event benefits paid during the plan year, including (except as provided by the Secretary) any payment for the purchase of an annuity contract for a participant or beneficiary with respect to such benefits,

(ii) the amount which would be determined for the plan year if the unpredictable contingent event benefit liabilities were amortized in equal annual installments over 7 plan years (beginning with the plan year in which such event occurs), or

(iii) the additional amount that would be determined under paragraph (4)(A) if the unpredictable contingent event benefit liabilities were included in unfunded new liability notwithstanding paragraph (4)(B)(ii).

(B) Applicable percentage.—

In the case of plan years beginning in:	The applicable percentage is:
1989 and 1990	5
1991	10
1992	15
1993	20
1994	30
1995	40
1996	50
1997	60
1998	70
1999	80
2000	90
2001 and thereafter	100

(C) Paragraph not to apply to existing benefits.—This paragraph shall not apply to unpredictable contingent event benefits (and liabilities attributable thereto) for which the event occurred before the first plan year beginning after December 31, 1988.

(D) Special rule for first year of amortization.—Unless the employer elects otherwise, the amount determined under subparagraph (A) for the plan year in which the event occurs shall be equal to 150 percent of the amount determined under subparagraph (A)(i). The amount under subparagraph (A)(ii) for subsequent plan years in the amortization period shall be ad-

justed in the manner provided by the Secretary to reflect the application of this subparagraph.

(E) Limitation.—The present value of the amounts described in subparagraph (A) with respect to any one event shall not exceed the unpredictable contingent event benefit liabilities attributable to that event.

(6) Special rules for small plans.—

(A) Plans with 100 or fewer participants.—This subsection shall not apply to any plan for any plan year if on each day during the preceding plan year such plan had no more than 100 participants.

(B) Plans with more than 100 but not more than 150 participants.—In the case of a plan to which subparagraph (A) does not apply and which on each day during the preceding plan year had no more than 150 participants, the amount of the increase under paragraph (1) for such plan year shall be equal to the product of—

(i) such increase determined without regard to this subparagraph, multiplied by

(ii) 2 percent for the highest number of participants in excess of 100 on any such day.

(C) Aggregation of plans.—For purposes of this paragraph, all defined benefit plans maintained by the same employer (or any member of such employer's controlled group) shall be treated as 1 plan, but only employees of such employer or member shall be taken into account.

(7) Current liability.—For purposes of this subsection—

(A) In general.—The term "current liability" means all liabilities to employees and their beneficiaries under the plan.

(B) Treatment of unpredictable contingent event benefits.—

(i) In general.—For purposes of subparagraph (A), any unpredictable contingent event benefit shall not be taken into account until the event on which the benefit is contingent occurs.

(ii) Unpredictable contingent event benefit.—The term "unpredictable contingent event benefit" means any benefit contingent on an event other than—

(I) age, service, compensation, death, or disability, or

(II) an event which is reasonably and reliably predictable (as determined by the Secretary).

(C) Interest rate and mortality assumptions used.—Effective for plan years beginning after December 31, 1994—

(i) Interest rate.—

(I) In general.—The rate of interest used to determine current liability under this subsection shall be the rate of interest used under subsection (b)(5), except that the highest rate in the permissible range under subparagraph (B)(ii) thereof shall not exceed the specified percentage under subclause (II) of the weighted average referred to in such subparagraph.

(II) Specified percentage.—For purposes of subclause (I), the specified percentage shall be determined as follows:

In the case of plan years beginning in:	The applicable percentage is:
1995	109
1996	108
1997	107
1998	106
1999 and thereafter	105

(III) Special rule for 2002 and 2003.—For a plan year beginning in 2002 or 2003, notwithstanding subclause (I), in the case that the rate of interest used under subsection (b)(5) exceeds the highest rate permitted under subclause (I), the rate of interest used to determine current liability under this subsection may exceed the rate of interest otherwise permitted under subclause (I); except that such rate of interest shall not exceed 120 percent of the weighted average referred to in subsection (b)(5)(B)(ii).

(IV) Special rule for 2004, 2005, 2006, or 2007—For plan years beginning in 2004, 2005, 2006, or 2007 notwithstanding subclause (I), the rate of interest used to determine current liability under this subsection shall be the rate of interest under subsection (b)(5).

(ii) Mortality tables.—

(I) Commissioner's standard table.—In the case of plan years beginning before the first plan year to which the first tables prescribed under subclause (II) apply, the mortality table used in determining current liability under this subsection shall be the table prescribed by the Secretary which is based on the prevailing commissioners' standard table (described in section 807(d)(5)(A)) used to determine reserves for group annuity contracts issued on January 1, 1993.

(II) Secretarial authority.—The Secretary may by regulation prescribe for plan years beginning after December 31, 1999, mortality tables to be used in determining current liability under this subsection. Such tables shall be based upon the actual experience of pension plans and projected trends in such experience. In prescribing such tables, the Secretary shall take into account results of available independent studies of mortality of individuals covered by pension plans.

(III) Periodic review.—The Secretary shall periodically (at least every 5 years) review any tables in effect under this subsection and shall, to the extent the Secretary determines necessary, by regulation update the tables to reflect the actual experience of pension plans and projected trends in such experience.

(iii) Separate mortality tables for the disabled.—Notwithstanding clause (ii)—

(I) In general.—In the case of plan years beginning after December 31, 1995, the Secretary shall establish separate mortality tables which may be used (in lieu of the tables under clause (ii)) to determine current liability under this subsection for individuals who are entitled to benefits under the plan on account of disability. The Secretary shall establish separate tables for individuals whose disabilities occur in plan years beginning before January 1, 1995, and for individuals whose disabilities occur in plan years beginning on or after such date.

(II) Special rule for disabilities occurring after 1994.—In the case of disabilities occurring in plan years beginning after December 31, 1994, the tables under subclause (I) shall apply only with respect to individuals described in such subclause who are disabled within the meaning of title II of the Social Security Act and the regulations thereunder.

(III) Plan years beginning in 1995.—In the case of any plan year beginning in 1995, a plan may use its own mortality assumptions for individuals who are entitled to benefits under the plan on account of disability.

(D) Certain service disregarded.—

(i) In general.—In the case of a participant to whom this subparagraph applies, only the applicable percentage of the years of service before such individual became a participant shall be taken into account in computing the current liability of the plan.

(ii) Applicable percentage.—For purposes of this subparagraph, the applicable percentage shall be determined as follows:

In the case of plan years beginning in:	The applicable percentage is:
1	20
2	40
3	60
4	80
5 or more	100

(iii) Participants to whom subparagraph applies.—This subparagraph shall apply to any participant who, at the time of becoming a participant—

(I) has not accrued any other benefit under any defined benefit plan (whether or not terminated) maintained by the employer or a member of the same controlled group of which the employer is a member,

(II) who first becomes a participant under the plan in a plan year beginning after December 31, 1987, and

(III) has years of service greater than the minimum years of service necessary for eligibility to participate in the plan.

(iv) Election.—An employer may elect not to have this subparagraph apply. Such an election, once made, may be revoked only with the consent of the Secretary.

(8) Other definitions.—For purposes of this subsection—

(A) Unfunded current liability.—The term "unfunded current liability" means, with respect to any plan year, the excess (if any) of—

(i) the current liability under the plan, over

(ii) value of the plan's assets determined under subsection (c)(2).

(B) Funded current liability percentage.—The term "funded current liability percentage" means, with respect to any plan year, the percentage which—

(i) the amount determined under subparagraph (A)(ii), is of

(ii) the current liability under the plan.

(C) Controlled group.—The term "controlled group" means any group treated as a single employer under subsection (b), (c), (m), and (o) of section 414.

(D) Adjustments to prevent omissions and duplications.—The Secretary shall provide such adjustments in the unfunded old liability amount, the unfunded new liability amount, the unpredictable contingent event amount, the current payment amount, and any other charges or credits under this section as are necessary to avoid duplication or omission of any factors in the determination of such amounts, charges, or credits.

(E) Deduction for credit balances.—For purposes of this subsection, the amount determined under subparagraph (A)(ii) shall be reduced by any credit balance in the funding standard account. The Secretary may provide for such reduction for purposes of any other provision which references this subsection.

(9) Applicability of subsection.—

(A) In general.—Except as provided in paragraph (6)(A), this subsection shall apply to a plan for any plan year if its funded current liability percentage for such year is less than 90 percent.

(B) Exception for certain plans at least 80 percent funded.—Subparagraph (A) shall not apply to a plan for a plan year if—

(i) the funded current liability percentage for the plan year is at least 80 percent, and

(ii) such percentage for each of the 2 immediately preceding plan years (or each of the 2d and 3d immediately preceding plan years) is at least 90 percent.

(C) Funded current liability percentage.—For purposes of subparagraphs (A) and (B), the term "funded current liability percentage" has the meaning given such term by paragraph (8)(B),

IRC Sec. 412 [Repealed]

except that such percentage shall be determined for any plan year—

(i) without regard to paragraph (8)(E), and

(ii) by using the rate of interest which is the highest rate allowable for the plan year under paragraph (7)(C).

(D) Transition rules.—For purposes of this paragraph:

(i) Funded percentage for years before 1995.—The funded current liability percentage for any plan year beginning before January 1, 1995, shall be treated as not less than 90 percent only if for such plan year the plan met one of the following requirements (as in effect for such year):

(I) The full-funding limitation under subsection (c)(7) for the plan was zero.

(II) The plan had no additional funding requirement under this subsection (or would have had no such requirement if its funded current liability percentage had been determined under subparagraph (C)).

(III) The plan's additional funding requirement under this subsection did not exceed the lesser of 0.5 percent of current liability or $5,000,000.

(ii) Special rule for 1995 and 1996.—For purposes of determining whether subparagraph (B) applies to any plan year beginning in 1995 or 1996, a plan shall be treated as meeting the requirements of subparagraph (B)(ii) if the plan met the requirements of clause (i) of this subparagraph for any two of the plan years beginning in 1992, 1993, and 1994 (whether or not consecutive).

(10) Unfunded mortality increase amount.—

(A) In general.—The unfunded mortality increase amount with respect to each unfunded mortality increase is the amount necessary to amortize such increase in equal annual installments over a period of 10 plan years (beginning with the first plan year for which a plan uses any new mortality table issued under paragraph (7)(C)(ii)(II) or (III)).

(B) Unfunded mortality increase.—For purposes of subparagraph (A), the term "unfunded mortality increase" means an amount equal to the excess of—

(i) the current liability of the plan for the first plan year for which a plan uses any new mortality table issued under paragraph (7)(C)(ii)(II) or (III), over

(ii) the current liability of the plan for such plan year which would have been determined if the mortality table in effect for the preceding plan year had been used.

(11) Phase-in of increases in funding required by Retirement Protection Act of 1994.—

(A) In general.—For any applicable plan year, at the election of the employer, the increase under paragraph (1) shall not exceed the greater of—

(i) the increase that would be required under paragraph (1) if the provisions of this title as in effect for plan years beginning before January 1, 1995, had remained in effect, or

(ii) the amount which, after taking into account charges (other than the additional charge under this subsection) and credits under subsection (b), is necessary to increase the funded current liability percentage (taking into account the expected increase in current liability due to benefits accruing during the plan year) for the applicable plan year to a percentage equal to the sum of the initial funded current liability percentage of the plan plus the applicable number of percentage points for such applicable plan year.

(B) Applicable number of percentage points.—

(i) Initial funded current liability percentage of 75 percent or less.—Except as provided in clause (ii), for plans with an initial funded current liability percentage of 75 percent or less, the applicable number of percentage points for the applicable plan year is:

In the case of applicable plan years beginning in:	The applicable number of percentage is:
1995	3
1996	6
1997	9
1998	12
1999	15
2000	19
2001	24

(ii) Other cases.—In the case of a plan to which this clause applies, the applicable number of percentage points for any such applicable plan year is the sum of—

(I) 2 percentage points;

(II) the applicable number of percentage points (if any) under this clause for the preceding applicable plan year;

(III) the product of .10 multiplied by the excess (if any) of (a) 85 percentage points over (b) the sum of the initial funded current liability percentage and the number determined under subclause (II);

(IV) for applicable plan years beginning in 2000, 1 percentage point; and

(V) for applicable plan years beginning in 2001, 2 percentage points.

(iii) Plans to which clause (ii) applies.—

(I) In general.—Clause (ii) shall apply to a plan for an applicable plan year if the initial funded current liability percentage of such plan is more than 75 percent.

(II) Plans initially under clause (i).—In the case of a plan which (but for this subclause) has an initial funded current liability percentage of 75 percent or less, clause (ii) (and not clause (i)) shall apply to such plan with respect to applicable plan years beginning after the first applicable plan year for which the sum of the initial funded current liability percentage and the applicable number of percentage points (determined under clause (i)) exceeds 75 percent. For purposes of applying clause (ii) to such a plan, the initial funded current liability percentage of such plan shall be treated as being the sum referred to in the preceding sentence.

(C) Definitions.—For purposes of this paragraph:

(i) The term "applicable plan year" means a plan year beginning after December 31, 1994, and before January 1, 2002.

(ii) The term "initial funded current liability percentage" means the funded current liability percentage as of the first day of the first plan year beginning after December 31, 1994.

(12) Election for certain plans.—

(A) In general.—In the case of a defined benefit plan established and maintained by an applicable employer, if this subsection did not apply to the plan for the plan year beginning in 2000 (determined without regard to paragraph (6)), then, at the election of the employer, the increased amount under paragraph (1) for any applicable plan year shall be the greater of—

(i) 20 percent of the increased amount under paragraph (1) determined without regard to this paragraph, or

(ii) the increased amount which would be determined under paragraph (1) if the deficit reduction contribution under paragraph (2) for the applicable plan year were determined without regard to subparagraphs (A), (B), and (D) of paragraph (2).

(B) Restrictions on benefit increases.—No amendment which increases the liabilities of the plan by reason of any increase in benefits, any change in the accrual of benefits, or any change in the rate at which benefits become nonforfeitable under the plan shall be adopted during any applicable plan year, unless—

(i) the plan's enrolled actuary certifies (in such form and manner prescribed by the Secretary) that the amendment provides for an increase in annual contributions which will exceed the increase in annual charges to the funding standard account attributable to such amendment, or

(ii) the amendment is required by a collective bargaining agreement which is in effect on the date of enactment of this subparagraph.

If a plan is amended during any applicable plan year in violation of the preceding sentence, any election under this paragraph shall not apply to any applicable plan year ending on or after the date on which such amendment is adopted.

(C) Applicable employer.—For purposes of this paragraph, the term "applicable employer" means an employer which is—

(i) a commercial passenger airline,

(ii) primarily engaged in the production or manufacture of a steel mill product or the processing of iron ore pellets, or

(iii) an organization described in section 501(c)(5) and which established the plan to which this paragraph applies on June 30, 1955.

(D) Applicable plan year.—For purposes of this paragraph—

(i) In general.—The term "applicable plan year" means any plan year beginning after December 27, 2003, and beforeDecember 28, 2005, for which the employer elects the application of this paragraph.

(ii) Limitation on number of years which may be elected.— An election may not be made under this paragraph with respect to more than 2 plan years.

(E) Election.—An election under this paragraph shall be made at such time and in such manner as the Secretary may prescribe.

(m) Quarterly Contributions Required.—

(1) In general.—If a defined benefit plan (other than a multiemployer plan) which has a funded current liability percentage (as defined in subsection (l)(8)) for the preceding plan year of less than 100 percent fails to pay the full amount of a required installment for the plan year, then the rate of interest charged to the funding standard account under subsection (b)(5) with respect to the amount of the underpayment for the period of the underpayment shall be equal to the greater of—

(A) 175 percent of the Federal mid-term rate (as in effect under section 1274 for the 1st month of such plan year), or

(B) the rate of interest used under the plan in determining costs (including adjustments under subsection (b)(5)(B)).

(2) Amount of underpayment, period of underpayment.— For purposes of paragraph (1)—

(A) Amount.—The amount of the underpayment shall be the excess of—

(i) the required installment, over

(ii) the amount (if any) of the installment contributed to or under the plan on or before the due date for the installment.

(B) Period of underpayment.—The period for which interest is charged under this subsection with regard to any portion of the underpayment shall run from the due date for the installment to the date on which such portion is contributed to or under the plan (determined without regard to subsection (c)(10)).

(C) Order of crediting contributions.—For purposes of subparagraph (A)(ii), contributions shall be credited against unpaid required installments in the order in which such installments are required to be paid.

(3) Number of required installments; due dates.—For purposes of this subsection—

(A) Payable in 4 installments.—There shall be 4 required installments for each plan year.

(B) Time for payment of installments.—

In the case of the following required installments:	The due date is:
1st	April 15
2nd	July 15
3rd	October 15
4th	January 15 of the following year

(4) Amount of required installment.—For purposes of this subsection—

(A) In general.—The amount of any required installment shall be the applicable percentage of the required annual payment.

(B) Required annual payment.—For purposes of subparagraph (A), the term "required annual payment" means the lesser of—

(i) 90 percent of the amount required to be contributed to or under the plan by the employer for the plan year under section 412 (without regard to any waiver under subsection (d) thereof), or

(ii) 100 percent of the amount so required for the preceding plan year.

Clause (ii) shall not apply if the preceding plan year was not a year of 12 months.

(C) Applicable percentage.—For purposes of subparagraph (A), the applicable percentage shall be determined in accordance with the following table:

For plan years beginning in:	The applicable percentage is:
1989	6.25
1990	12.50
1991	18.75
1992 and thereafter	25.00

(D) Special rules for unpredictable contingent event benefits.— In the case of a plan to which subsection (l) applies for any calendar year and which has any unpredictable contingent event benefit liabilities—

(i) Liabilities not taken into account.—Such liabilities shall not be taken into account in computing the required annual payment under subparagraph (B).

(ii) Increase in installments.—Each required installment shall be increased by the greatest of—

(I) the unfunded percentage of the amount of benefits described in subsection (l)(5)(A)(i) paid during the 3-month period preceding the month in which the due date for such installment occurs,

(II) 25 percent of the amount determined under subsection (l)(5)(A)(ii) for the plan year, or

(III) 25 percent of the amount determined under subsection (l)(5)(A)(iii) for the plan year.

IRC Sec. 412 [Repealed]

(iii) Unfunded percentage.—For purposes of clause (ii)(I), the term "unfunded percentage" means the percentage determined under subsection (*l*)(5)(A)(i)(I) for the plan year.

(iv) Limitation on increase.—In no event shall the increases under clause (ii) exceed the amount necessary to increase the funded current liability percentage (within the meaning of subsection (*l*)(8)(B)) for the plan year to 100 percent.

(5) Liquidity requirement.—

(A) In general.—A plan to which this paragraph applies shall be treated as failing to pay the full amount of any required installment to the extent that the value of the liquid assets paid in such installment is less than the liquidity shortfall (whether or not such liquidity shortfall exceeds the amount of such installment required to be paid but for this paragraph).

(B) Plans to which paragraph applies.—This paragraph shall apply to a defined benefit plan (other than a multiemployer plan or a plan described in subsection (*l*)(6)(A)) which—

(i) is required to pay installments under this subsection for a plan year, and

(ii) has a liquidity shortfall for any quarter during such plan year.

(C) Period of underpayment.—For purposes of paragraph (1), any portion of an installment that is treated as not paid under subparagraph (A) shall continue to be treated as unpaid until the close of the quarter in which the due date for such installment occurs.

(D) Limitation on increase.—If the amount of any required installment is increased by reason of subparagraph (A), in no event shall such increase exceed the amount which, when added to prior installments for the plan year, is necessary to increase the funded current liability percentage (taking into account the expected increase in current liability due to benefits accruing during the plan year) to 100 percent.

(E) Definitions.—For purposes of this paragraph:

(i) Liquidity shortfall.—The term "liquidity shortfall" means, with respect to any required installment, an amount equal to the excess (as of the last day of the quarter for which such installment is made) of the base amount with respect to such quarter over the value (as of such last day) of the plan's liquid assets.

(ii) Base amount.—

(I) In general.—The term "base amount" means, with respect to any quarter, an amount equal to 3 times the sum of the adjusted disbursements from the plan for the 12 months ending on the last day of such quarter.

(II) Special rule.—If the amount determined under subclause (I) exceeds an amount equal to 2 times the sum of the adjusted disbursements from the plan for the 36 months ending on the last day of the quarter and an enrolled actuary certifies to the satisfaction of the Secretary that such excess is the result of nonrecurring circumstances, the base amount with respect to such quarter shall be determined without regard to amounts related to those nonrecurring circumstances.

(iii) Disbursements from the plan.—The term "disbursements from the plan" means all disbursements from the trust, including purchases of annuities, payments of single sums and other benefits, and administrative expenses.

(iv) Adjusted disbursements.—The term "adjusted disbursements" means disbursements from the plan reduced by the product of—

(I) the plan's funded current liability percentage (as defined in subsection (*l*)(8)) for the plan year, and

(II) the sum of the purchases of annuities, payments of single sums, and such other disbursements as the Secretary shall provide in regulations.

(v) Liquid assets.—The term "liquid assets" means cash, marketable securities and such other assets as specified by the Secretary in regulations.

(vi) Quarter.—The term "quarter" means, with respect to any required installment, the 3-month period preceding the month in which the due date for such installment occurs.

(F) Regulations.—The Secretary may prescribe such regulations as are necessary to carry out this paragraph.

(6) Fiscal years and short years.—

(A) Fiscal years.—In applying this subsection to a plan year beginning on any date other than January 1, there shall be substituted for the months specified in this subsection, the months which correspond thereto.

(B) Short plan year.—This subsection shall be applied to plan years of less than 12 months in accordance with regulations prescribed by the Secretary.

(7) Special rule for 2002.—In any case in which the interest rate used to determine current liability is determined under subsection (*l*)(7)(C)(i)(III), for purposes of applying paragraphs (1) and (4)(B)(ii) for plan years beginning in 2002, the current liability for the preceding plan year shall be redetermined using 120 percent as the specified percentage determined under subsection (*l*)(7)(C)(i)(II).

(n) Imposition of Lien Where Failure To Make Required Contributions.—

(1) In general.—In the case of a plan to which this section applies, if—

(A) any person fails to make a required installment under subsection (m) or any other payment required under this section before the due date for such installment or other payment, and

(B) the unpaid balance of such installment or other payment (including interest), when added to the aggregate unpaid balance of all preceding such installments or other payments for which payment was not made before the due date (including interest), exceeds $1,000,000,

then there shall be a lien in favor of the plan in the amount determined under paragraph (3) upon all property and rights to property, whether real or personal, belonging to such person and any other person who is a member of the same controlled group of which such person is a member.

(2) Plans to which subsection applies.—This subsection shall apply to a defined benefit plan (other than a multiemployer plan) for any plan year for which the funded current liability percentage (within the meaning of subsection (*l*)(8)(B)) of such plan is less than 100 percent. This subsection shall not apply to any plan to which section 4021 of the Employee Retirement Income Security Act of 1974 does not apply (as such section is in effect on the date of the enactment of the Retirement Protection Act of 1994).

(3) Amount of lien.—For purposes of paragraph (1), the amount of the lien shall be equal to the aggregate unpaid balance of required installments and other payments required under this section (including interest)—

(A) for plan years beginning after 1987, and

(B) for which payment has not been made before the due date.

(4) Notice of failure; lien.—

(A) Notice of failure.—A person committing a failure described in paragraph (1) shall notify the Pension Benefit Guaranty Corporation of such failure within 10 days of the due date for the required installment or other payment.

(B) Period of lien.—The lien imposed by paragraph (1) shall arise on the due date for the required installment or other payment and shall continue until the last day of the first plan year in which the plan ceases to be described in paragraph (1)(B). Such lien shall continue to run without regard to whether such plan continues to be described in paragraph (2) during the period referred to in the preceding sentence.

(C) Certain rules to apply.—Any amount with respect to which a lien is imposed under paragraph (1) shall be treated as taxes due and owing the United States and rules similar to the rules of subsections (c), (d), and (e) of section 4068 of the Employee Retirement Income Security Act of 1974 shall apply with respect to a lien imposed by subsection (a) and the amount with respect to such lien.

(5) Enforcement.—Any lien created under paragraph (1) may be perfected and enforced only by the Pension Benefit Guaranty Corporation, or at the direction of the Pension Benefit Guaranty Corporation, by the contributing sponsor (or any member of the controlled group of the contributing sponsor).

(6) Definitions.—For purposes of this subsection—

(A) Due date; required installment.—The terms "due date" and "required installment" have the meanings given such terms by subsection (m), except that in the case of a payment other than a required installment, the due date shall be the date such payment is required to be made under this section.

(B) Controlled group.—The term "controlled group" means any group treated as a single employer under subsections (b), (c), (m), and (o) of section 414.

Recent Amendments to IRC §412 [Repealed.]

Preservation of Access to Care for Medicare Beneficiaries and Pension Relief Act of 2010 (Pub. L. No. 111-192), as follows:
- **Other Provision; Amendment to the Pension Protection Act of 2006 (Pub. L. No. 109-280).** Act §202(a) provides, effective as if included in Pub. L. No. 109-280:
  (a) In General.—Title I of the Pension Protection Act of 2006 is amended by redesignating section 107 as section 108 and by inserting the following after section 106:
  SEC. 107. APPLICATION OF EXTENDED AMORTIZATION PERIODS TO PLANS WITH DELAYED EFFECTIVE DATE.
  (a) In General.—If the plan sponsor of a plan to which section 104, 105, or 106 of this Act applies elects to have this section apply for any eligible plan year (in this section referred to as an "election year"), section 302 of the Employee Retirement Income Security Act of 1974 and section 412 of the Internal Revenue Code of 1986 (as in effect before the amendments made by this subtitle and subtitle B) shall apply to such year in the manner described in subsection (b) or (c), whichever is specified in the election. All references in this section to "such Act" or "such Code" shall be to such Act or such Code as in effect before the amendments made by this subtitle and subtitle B.
  (b) Application of 2 and 7 Rule.—In the case of an election year to which this subsection applies—
  (1) 2-year lookback for determining deficit reduction contributions for certain plans.—For purposes of applying section 302(d)(9) of such Act and section 412(*l*)(9) of such Code, the funded current liability percentage (as defined in subparagraph (C) thereof) for such plan for such plan year shall be such funded current liability percentage of such plan for the second plan year preceding the first election year of such plan.
  (2) Calculation of deficit reduction contribution.—For purposes of applying section 302(d) of such Act and section 412(*l*) of such Code to a plan to which such sections apply (after taking into account paragraph (1))—
  (A) in the case of the increased unfunded new liability of the plan, the applicable percentage described in section 302(d)(4)(C) of such Act and section 412(*l*)(4)(C) of such Code shall be the third segment rate described in sections 104(b), 105(b), and 106(b) of this Act, and
  (B) in the case of the excess of the unfunded new liability over the increased unfunded new liability, such applicable percentage shall be determined without regard to this section.
  (c) Application of 15-year Amortization.—In the case of an election year to which this subsection applies, for purposes of applying section 302(d) of such Act and section 412(*l*) of such Code—
  (1) in the case of the increased unfunded new liability of the plan, the applicable percentage described in section

302(d)(4)(C) of such Act and section 412(*l*)(4)(C) of such Code for any pre-effective date plan year beginning with or after the first election year shall be the ratio of—
(A) the annual installments payable in each year if the increased unfunded new liability for such plan year were amortized over 15 years, using an interest rate equal to the third segment rate described in sections 104(b), 105(b), and 106(b) of this Act, to
(B) the increased unfunded new liability for such plan year, and
(2) in the case of the excess of the unfunded new liability over the increased unfunded new liability, such applicable percentage shall be determined without regard to this section.
(d) Election.—
(1) In general.—The plan sponsor of a plan may elect to have this section apply to not more than 2 eligible plan years with respect to the plan, except that in the case of a plan to which section 106 of this Act applies, the plan sponsor may only elect to have this section apply to 1 eligible plan year.
(2) Amortization schedule.—Such election shall specify whether the rules under subsection (b) or (c) shall apply to an election year, except that if a plan sponsor elects to have this section apply to 2 eligible plan years, the plan sponsor must elect the same rule for both years.
(3) Other rules.—Such election shall be made at such time, and in such form and manner, as shall be prescribed by the Secretary of the Treasury, and may be revoked only with the consent of the Secretary of the Treasury.
(e) Definitions.—For purposes of this section—
(1) Eligible plan year.—For purposes of this subparagraph, the term "eligible plan year" means any plan year beginning in 2008, 2009, 2010, or 2011, except that a plan year beginning in 2008 shall only be treated as an eligible plan year if the due date for the payment of the minimum required contribution for such plan year occurs on or after the date of the enactment of this clause.
(2) Pre-effective date plan year.—The term "pre-effective date plan year" means, with respect to a plan, any plan year prior to the first year in which the amendments made by this subtitle and subtitle B apply to the plan.
(3) Increased unfunded new liability.—The term "increased unfunded new liability" means, with respect to a year, the excess (if any) of the unfunded new liability over the amount of unfunded new liability determined as if the value of the plan's assets determined under subsection 302(c)(2) of such Act and section 412(c)(2) of such Code equaled the product of the current liability of the plan for the year multiplied by the funded current liability percentage (as defined in section 302(d)(8)(B) of such Act and 412(*l*)(8)(B) of such Code) of the plan for the second plan year preceding the first election year of such plan.
(4) Other definitions.—The terms "unfunded new liability" and "current liability" shall have the meanings set forth in section 302(d) of such Act and section 412(*l*) of such Code.

Pension Protection Act of 2006 (Pub. L. No. 109-280), as follows:
- IRC §412(b)(5)(B)(ii)(II) was amended by Act §301(b)(1)(A)–(B) by replacing "2006" with "2008", and, in the heading, by replacing "and 2005" with ", 2005, 2006, and 2007". Eff. Aug. 17, 2006.
- IRC §412(*l*)(7)(C)(i)(IV) was amended by Act §301(b)(2)(A)–(B) by replacing "or 2005" with ", 2005, 2006, or 2007" and, in the heading, by replacing "and 2005" with ", 2005, 2006, and 2007". Eff. Aug. 17, 2006.
- **Sunset Provision.** Act §811, provides:
  SEC. 811. PENSIONS AND INDIVIDUAL RETIREMENT ARRANGEMENT PROVISIONS OF ECONOMIC GROWTH AND TAX RELIEF RECONCILIATION ACT OF 2001 MADE PERMANENT.
  Title IX of the Economic Growth and Tax Relief Reconciliation Act of 2001 [Pub. L. No. 107-16] shall not apply to the provisions of, and amendments made by, subtitles A through F [§§601–666] of title VI of such Act (relating to pension and individual retirement arrangement provisions).

Gulf Opportunity Zone Act of 2005 (Pub. L. No. 109-135), as follows:

• IRC §412(m)(4)(B)(i) was amended by Act §412(x)(1) by replacing "subsection (c)" with "subsection (d)". Eff. Dec. 21, 2005.

Pension Funding Equity Act of 2004 (Pub. L. No. 108-218), as follows:

• IRC §412(b)(5)(B)(ii) was amended by Act §101(b)(1)(A) by redesignating subcl. (II) as subcl. (III), and by inserting after subcl. (I) new subcl. (II). Eff. plan years beginning after Dec. 31, 2003.

• IRC §412(b)(5)(B)(ii)(III), as redesignated by Act §101(b)(1)(A), was amended by Act §101(b)(1)(B)(i)–(ii) by inserting "or (II)" after "subclause (I)" the first place it appeared, and by striking "subclause (I)" the second place it appeared, and by inserting "such subclause". Eff. plan years beginning after Dec. 31, 2003.

• IRC §412(b)(5)(B)(ii)(I) was amended by Act §101(b)(1)(C) by inserting "or (III)" after "subclause (II)". Eff. plan years beginning after Dec. 31, 2003.

• IRC §412(b)(7) was amended by Act §104(b) by adding new subpara. (F). Eff. Apr. 10, 2004.

• IRC §412(*l*)(7)(c)(i) was amended by Act §101(b)(2) by adding new subcl. (IV). Eff. generally for plan years beginning after Dec. 31, 2003. [*Ed. Note:* see Act §101(c)(1)–(2) and (d)(2) for special rules.]

• IRC §412(*l*) was amended by Act §102(b) by adding new para. (12). Eff. Apr. 10, 2004.

• IRC §412(m)(7) was amended by Act §101(b)(3). Eff. generally for plan years beginning after Dec. 21, 2003. See Act §101(d)(2) for a special rule. IRC §412(m)(7) prior to amendment:

(7) Special rules for 2002 and 2004.—In any case in which the interest rate used to determine current liability is determined under subsection (i)(7)(C)(i)(III)—

(A) —For purposes of applying paragraphs (1) and (4)(B)(ii) for plan years beginning in 2002, the current liability for the preceding plan year shall be redetermined using 120 percent as the specified percentage determined under subsection (*l*)(7)(C)(i)(II).

(B) 2004.—For purposes of applying paragraphs (1) and (4)(B)(ii) for plan years beginning in 2004, the current liability for the preceding plan year shall be redetermined using 105 percent as the specified percentage determined under subsection (*l*)(7)(C)(i)(II).

Jobs Creation and Worker Assistance Act of 2002 (Pub. L. No. 107-147), as follows:

• IRC §412(c)(9)(B) was amended by Act §411(v)(1)(A)–(B) by replacing "125 percent" with "100 percent" in cl. (ii), and adding new cl. (iv). Eff. plan years beginning after Dec. 31, 2001, as if included in the provision of Pub. L. No. 107-16 to which it relates.

• IRC §412(*l*)(7)(C)(i) was amended by Act §405(a)(1) by adding new subcl. (III). Eff. Mar. 9, 2002.

• IRC §412(m) was amended by Act §405(a)(2) by adding new para. (7). Eff. Mar. 9, 2002.

Economic Growth and Tax Relief Reconciliation Act of 2001 (Pub. L. No. 107-16), as follows:

• IRC §412(c)(7)(A)(i)(1) was amended by Act §651(a)(1) by replacing "the applicable percentage" with "in the case of plan years beginning before January 1, 2004, the applicable percentage". Eff. plan years beginning after Dec. 31, 2001, as if included in the provision of Pub. L. No. 107-16 to which it relates.

• IRC §412(c)(7)(F) was amended by Act §651(a)(2). Eff. plan years beginning after Dec. 31, 2001, as if included in the provision of Pub. L. No. 107-16 to which it relates. IRC §412(c)(7)(F) prior to amendment:

(F) Applicable percentage.—For purposes of subparagraph (A)(i)(I), the applicable percentage shall be determined in accordance with the following table:

In the case of any plan year beginning in—	The applicable percentage is—
1999 or 2000	155
2001 or 2002	160
2003 or 2004	165
2005 and succeeding years	170

• IRC §412(c)(9) was amended by Act §661(a). Eff. plan years beginning after Dec. 31, 2001. IRC §412(c)(9) prior to amendment:

(9) Annual valuation.—For purposes of this section a determination of experience gains and losses and a valuation of the plan's liability shall be made not less frequently than once every year, except that such determination shall be made more frequently to the extent required in particular cases under regulations prescribed by the Secretary.

• **Sunset Provision.** Act §901, as amended by Pub. L. No. 111-312, §101(a)(1), provides the sunset rule below. But see Pub. L. No. 109-280, §811, and Pub. L. No. 111-148, §10909(c), as amended by Pub. L. No. 111-312, §101(b)(1).

SEC. 901. SUNSET OF PROVISIONS OF ACT.

(a) In general. All provisions of, and amendments made by, this Act shall not apply—

(1) to taxable, plan, or limitation years beginning after December 31, 2012, or

(2) in the case of title V, to estates of decedents dying, gifts made, or generation skipping transfers, after December 31, 2012.

(b) Application of certain laws.—The Internal Revenue Code of 1986 and the Employee Retirement Income Security Act of 1974 shall be applied and administered to years, estates, gifts, and transfers described in subsection (a) as if the provisions and amendments described in subsection (a) had never been enacted.

SEC. 413. COLLECTIVELY BARGAINED PLANS, ETC.

(a) Application of Subsection (b).—Subsection (b) applies to—

(1) a plan maintained pursuant to an agreement which the Secretary of Labor finds to be a collective-bargaining agreement between employee representatives and one or more employers, and

(2) each trust which is a part of such plan.

(b) General Rule.—If this subsection applies to a plan, notwithstanding any other provision of this title—

(1) Participation.—Section 410 shall be applied as if all employees of each of the employers who are parties to the collective-bargaining agreement and who are subject to the same benefit computation formula under the plan were employed by a single employer.

(2) Discrimination, etc.—Sections 401(a)(4) and 411(d)(3) shall be applied as if all participants who are subject to the same benefit computation formula and who are employed by employers who are parties to the collective-bargaining agreement were employed by a single employer.

(3) Exclusive benefit.—For purposes of section 401(a), in determining whether the plan of an employer is for the exclusive benefit of his employees and their beneficiaries, all plan participants shall be considered to be his employees.

(4) Vesting.—Section 411 (other than subsection (d)(3)) shall be applied as if all employers who have been parties to the collective-bargaining agreement constituted a single employer, except that the application of any rules with respect to breaks in service shall be made under regulations prescribed by the Secretary of Labor.

(5) Funding.—The minimum funding standard provided by section 412 shall be determined as if all participants in the plan were employed by a single employer.

(6) Liability for funding tax.—For a plan year the liability under section 4971 of each employer who is a party to the collective-bargaining agreement shall be determined in a reasonable manner not inconsistent with regulations prescribed by the Secretary—

(A) first on the basis of their respective delinquencies in meeting required employer contributions under the plan, and

(B) then on the basis of their respective liabilities for contributions under the plan.

For purposes of this subsection and the last sentence of section 4971(a), an employer's withdrawal liability under part 1 of subtitle E of title IV of the Employee Retirement Income Security Act of 1974 shall not be treated as a liability for contributions under the plan.

(7) Deduction limitations.—Each applicable limitation provided by section 404(a) shall be determined as if all participants in the plan were employed by a single employer. The amounts contributed to or under the plan by each employer who is a party to the agreement, for the portion of his taxable year which is included within such a plan year, shall be considered not to exceed such a limitation if the anticipated employer contributions for such plan year (determined in a manner consistent with the manner in which actual employer contributions for such plan year are determined) do not exceed such limitation. If such anticipated contributions exceed such a limitation, the portion of each such employer's contributions which is not deductible under section 404 shall be determined in accordance with regulations prescribed by the Secretary.

(8) Employees of labor unions.—For purposes of this subsection, employees of employee representatives shall be treated as employees of an employer described in subsection (a)(1) if such representatives meet the requirements of sections 401(a)(4) and 410 with respect to such employees.

(9) Plans covering a professional employee.—Notwithstanding subsection (a), in the case of a plan (and trust forming part thereof) which covers any professional employee, paragraph (1) shall be applied by substituting "section 410(a)" for "section 410", and paragraph (2) shall not apply.

(c) Plans Maintained by More Than One Employer.—In the case of a plan maintained by more than one employer—

(1) Participation.—Section 410(a) shall be applied as if all employees of each of the employers who maintain the plan were employed by a single employer.

(2) Exclusive benefit.—For purposes of section 401(a), in determining whether the plan of an employer is for the exclusive benefit of his employees and their beneficiaries all plan participants shall be considered to be his employees.

(3) Vesting.—Section 411 shall be applied as if all employers who maintain the plan constituted a single employer, except that the application of any rules with respect to breaks in service shall be made under regulations prescribed by the Secretary of Labor.

(4) Funding.—

(A) In general.—In the case of a plan established after December 31, 1988, each employer shall be treated as maintaining a separate plan for purposes of section 412 unless such plan uses a method for determining required contributions which provides that any employer contributes not less than the amount which would be required if such employer maintained a separate plan.

(B) Other plans.—In the case of a plan not described in subparagraph (A), the requirements of section 412 shall be determined as if all participants in the plan were employed by a single employer unless the plan administrator elects not later than the close of the first plan year of the plan beginning after the date of enactment of the Technical and Miscellaneous Revenue Act of 1988 to have the provisions of subparagraph (A) apply. An election under the preceding sentence shall take effect for the plan year in which made and, once made, may be revoked only with the consent of the Secretary.

(5) Liability for funding tax.—For a plan year the liability under section 4971 of each employer who maintains the plan shall be determined in a reasonable manner not inconsistent with regulations prescribed by the Secretary—

(A) first on the basis of their respective delinquencies in meeting required employer contributions under the plan, and

(B) then on the basis of their respective liabilities for contributions under the plan.

(6) Deduction limitations.—

(A) In general.—In the case of a plan established after December 31, 1988, each applicable limitation provided by section 404(a) shall be determined as if each employer were maintaining a separate plan.

(B) Other plans.—

(i) In general.—In the case of a plan not described in subparagraph (A), each applicable limi-

IRC Sec. 413(c)(6)(B)(i)

tation provided by section 404(a) shall be determined as if all participants in the plan were employed by a single employer, except that if an election is made under paragraph (4)(B), subparagraph (A) shall apply to such plan.

(ii) Special rule.—If this subparagraph applies, the amounts contributed to or under the plan by each employer who maintains the plan (for the portion of the taxable year included within a plan year) shall be considered not to exceed any such limitation if the anticipated employer contributions for such plan year (determined in a reasonable manner not inconsistent with regulations prescribed by the Secretary) do not exceed such limitation. If such anticipated contributions exceed such a limitation, the portion of each such employer's contributions which is not deductible under §404 shall be determined in accordance with regulations prescribed by the Secretary.

(7) Allocations.—

(A) In general.—Except as provided in subparagraph (B), allocations of amounts under paragraphs (4), (5), and (6) among the employers maintaining the plan shall not be inconsistent with regulations prescribed for this purpose by the Secretary.

(B) Assets and liabilities of plan.—For purposes of applying paragraphs (4)(A) and (6)(A), the assets and liabilities of each plan shall be treated as the assets and liabilities which would be allocated to a plan maintained by the employer if the employer withdrew from the multiple employer plan.

SEC. 414. DEFINITIONS AND SPECIAL RULES.

(a) Service for Predecessor Employer.—For purposes of this part—

(1) in any case in which the employer maintains a plan of a predecessor employer, service for such predecessor shall be treated as service for the employer, and

(2) in any case in which the employer maintains a plan which is not the plan maintained by a predecessor employer, service for such predecessor shall, to the extent provided in regulations prescribed by the Secretary, be treated as service for the employer.

(b) Employees of Controlled Group of Corporations.—For purposes of sections 401, 408(k), 408(p), 410, 411, 415, and 416, all employees of all corporations which are members of a controlled group of corporations (within the meaning of section 1563(a), determined without regard to section 1563(a)(4) and (e)(3)(C)) shall be treated as employed by a single employer. With respect to a plan adopted by more than one such corporation, the applicable limitations provided by section 404(a) shall be determined as if all such employers were a single employer, and allo-

cated to each employer in accordance with regulations prescribed by the Secretary.

(c) Employees of Partnerships, Proprietorships, etc., Which Are Under Common Control.—For purposes of sections 401, 408(k), 408(p), 410, 411, 415, and 416, under regulations prescribed by the Secretary, all employees of trades or businesses (whether or not incorporated) which are under common control shall be treated as employed by a single employer. The regulations prescribed under this subsection shall be based on principles similar to the principles which apply in the case of subsection (b).

(d) Governmental Plan.—For purposes of this part, the term "governmental plan" means a plan established and maintained for its employees by the Government of the United States, by the government of any State or political subdivision thereof, or by any agency or instrumentality of any of the foregoing. The term "governmental plan" also includes any plan to which the Railroad Retirement Act of 1935 or 1937 applies and which is financed by contributions required under that Act and any plan of an international organization which is exempt from taxation by reason of the International Organizations Immunities Act (59 Stat. 669).

The term "governmental plan" includes a plan which is established and maintained by an Indian tribal government (as defined in section 7701(a)(40)), a subdivision of an Indian tribal government (determined in accordance with section 7871(d)), or an agency or instrumentality of either, and all of the participants of which are employees of such entity substantially all of whose services as such an employee are in the performance of essential governmental functions but not in the performance of commercial activities (whether or not an essential government function).

(e) Church Plan.—

(1) In general.—For purposes of this part, the term "church plan" means a plan established and maintained (to the extent required in paragraph (2)(B)) for its employees (or their beneficiaries) by a church or by a convention or association of churches which is exempt from tax under section 501.

(2) Certain plans excluded.—The term "church plan" does not include a plan—

(A) which is established and maintained primarily for the benefit of employees (or their beneficiaries) of such church or convention or association of churches who are employed in connection with one or more unrelated trades or businesses (within the meaning of section 513); or

(B) if less than substantially all of the individuals included in the plan are individuals described in paragraph (1) or (3)(B) (or their beneficiaries).

(3) Definitions and other provisions.—For purposes of this subsection—

(A) Treatment as church plan.—A plan established and maintained for its employees (or their beneficiaries) by a church or by a convention or association of churches includes a plan maintained by an organization, whether a civil law corporation or otherwise, the principal purpose or function of which is the administration or funding of a plan or program for the provision of retirement benefits or welfare benefits, or both, for the employees of a church or a convention or association of churches, if such organization is controlled by or associated with a church or a convention or association of churches.

(B) Employee defined.—The term employee of a church or a convention or association of churches shall include—

(i) a duly ordained, commissioned, or licensed minister of a church in the exercise of his ministry, regardless of the source of his compensation;

(ii) an employee of an organization, whether a civil law corporation or otherwise, which is exempt from tax under section 501 and which is controlled by or associated with a church or a convention or association of churches; and

(iii) an individual described in subparagraph (E).

(C) Church treated as employer.—A church or a convention or association of churches which is exempt from tax under section 501 shall be deemed the employer of any individual included as an employee under subparagraph (B).

(D) Association with church.—An organization, whether a civil law corporation or otherwise, is associated with a church or a convention or association of churches if it shares common religious bonds and convictions with that church or convention or association of churches.

(E) Special rule in case of separation from plan.— If an employee who is included in a church plan separates from the service of a church or a convention or association of churches or an organization described in clause (ii) of paragraph (3)(B), the church plan shall not fail to meet the requirements of this subsection merely because the plan—

(i) retains the employee's accrued benefit or account for the payment of benefits to the employee or his beneficiaries pursuant to the terms of the plan; or

(ii) receives contributions on the employee's behalf after the employee's separation from such service, but only for a period of 5 years after such separation, unless the employee is disabled (within the meaning of the disability provisions of the church plan or, if there are no such provisions in the church plan, within the meaning of section 72(m)(7)) at the time of such separation from service.

(4) Correction of failure to meet church plan requirements.—

(A) In general.—If a plan established and maintained for its employees (or their beneficiaries) by a church or by a convention or association of churches which is exempt from tax under section 501 fails to meet one or more of the requirements of this subsection and corrects its failure to meet such requirements within the correction period, the plan shall be deemed to meet the requirements of this subsection for the year in which the correction was made and for all prior years.

(B) Failure to correct.—If a correction is not made within the correction period, the plan shall be deemed not to meet the requirements of this subsection beginning with the date on which the earliest failure to meet one or more of such requirements occurred.

(C) Correction period defined.—The term "correction period" means—

(i) the period ending 270 days after the date of mailing by the Secretary of a notice of default with respect to the plan's failure to meet one or more of the requirements of this subsection;

(ii) any period set by a court of competent jurisdiction after a final determination that the plan fails to meet such requirements, or, if the court does not specify such period, any reasonable period determined by the Secretary on the basis of all the facts and circumstances, but in any event not less than 270 days after the determination has become final; or

(iii) any additional period which the Secretary determines is reasonable or necessary for the correction of the default,

whichever has the latest ending date.

(5) Special rules for chaplains and self-employed ministers.—

(A) Certain ministers may participate.—For purposes of this part—

(i) In general.—A duly ordained, commissioned, or licensed minister of a church is described in paragraph (3)(B) if, in connection with the exercise of their ministry, the minister—

(I) is a self-employed individual (within the meaning of section 401(c)(1)(B), or

(II) is employed by an organization other than an organization which is described in section 501(c)(3) and with respect to which the minister shares common religious bonds.

(ii) Treatment as employer and employee.— For purposes of sections 403(b)(1)(A) and 404(a)(10), a minister described in clause (i)(I) shall be treated as employed by the minister's own employer which is an organization described in section 501(c)(3) and exempt from tax under section 501(a).

(B) Special rules for applying section 403(b) to self-employed ministers.—In the case of a minister described in subparagraph (A)(i)(I)—

(i) the minister's includible compensation under section 403(b)(3) shall be determined by reference to the minister's earned income (within the meaning of section 401(c)(2)) from such ministry rather than the amount of compensation which is received from an employer, and

(ii) the years (and portions of years) in which such minister was a self-employed individual (within the meaning of section 401(c)(1)(B)) with respect to such ministry shall be included for purposes of section 403(b)(4).

(C) Effect on non-denominational plans.—If a duly ordained, commissioned, or licensed minister of a church in the exercise of his or her ministry participates in a church plan (within the meaning of this section) and in the exercise of such ministry is employed by an employer not otherwise participating in such church plan, then such employer may exclude such minister from being treated as an employee of such employer for purposes of applying sections 401(a)(3), 401(a)(4), and 401(a)(5), as in effect on September 1, 1974, and sections 401(a)(4), 401(a)(5), 401(a)(26), 401(k)(3), 401(m), 403(b)(1)(D) (including section 403(b)(12)), and 410 to any stock bonus, pension, profit-sharing, or annuity plan (including an annuity described in section 403(b) or a retirement income account described in section 403(b)(9)). The Secretary shall prescribe such regulations as may be necessary or appropriate to carry out the purpose of, and prevent the abuse of, this subparagraph.

(D) Compensation taken into account only once.—If any compensation is taken into account in determining the amount of any contributions made to, or benefits to be provided under, any church plan, such compensation shall not also be taken into account in determining the amount of any contributions made to, or benefits to be provided under, any other stock bonus, pension, profit-sharing, or annuity plan which is not a church plan.

(E) Exclusion.—In the case of a contribution to a church plan made on behalf of a minister described in subparagraph (A)(i)(II), such contribution shall not be included in the gross income of the minister to the extent that such contribution would not be so included if the minister was an employee of a church.

(f) Multiemployer Plan.—

(1) Definition.—For purposes of this part, the term "multiemployer plan" means a plan—

(A) to which more than one employer is required to contribute,

(B) which is maintained pursuant to one or more collective bargaining agreements between one or more employee organizations and more than one employer, and

(C) which satisfies such other requirements as the Secretary of Labor may prescribe by regulation.

(2) Cases of common control.—For purposes of this subsection, all trades or businesses (whether or not incorporated) which are under common control within the meaning of subsection (c) are considered a single employer.

(3) Continuation of status after termination.—Notwithstanding paragraph (1), a plan is a multiemployer plan on and after its termination date under title IV of the Employee Retirement Income Security Act of 1974 if the plan was a multiemployer plan under this subsection for the plan year preceding its termination date.

(4) Transitional rule.—For any plan year which began before the date of the enactment of the Multiemployer Pension Plan Amendments Act of 1980, the term "multiemployer plan" means a plan described in this subsection as in effect immediately before that date.

(5) Special election.—Within one year after the date of the enactment of the Multiemployer Pension Plan Amendments Act of 1980, a multiemployer plan may irrevocably elect, pursuant to procedures established by the Pension Benefit Guaranty Corporation and subject to the provisions of section 4403(b) and (c) of the Employee Retirement Income Security Act of 1974, that the plan shall not be treated as a multiemployer plan for any purpose under such Act or this title, if for each of the last 3 plan years ending prior to the effective date of the Multiemployer Pension Plan Amendments Act of 1980—

(A) the plan was not a multiemployer plan because the plan was not a plan described in section 3(37)(A)(iii) of the Employee Retirement Income Security Act of 1974 and section 414(f)(1)(C) (as such provisions were in effect on the day before the date of the enactment of the Multiemployer Pension Plan Amendments Act of 1980); and

(B) the plan had been identified as a plan that was not a multiemployer plan in substantially all its filings with the Pension Benefit Guaranty Corporation, the Secretary of Labor and the Secretary.

(6) Election with regard to multiemployer status.—

(A) Within 1 year after the enactment of the Pension Protection Act of 2006—

(i) An election under paragraph (5) may be revoked, pursuant to procedures prescribed by the

Pension Benefit Guaranty Corporation, if, for each of the 3 plan years prior to the date of the enactment of that Act, the plan would have been a multiemployer plan but for the election under paragraph (5), and

(ii) a plan that meets the criteria in subparagraph (A) and (B) of paragraph (1) of this subsection or that is described in subparagraph (E) may, pursuant to procedures prescribed by the Pension Benefit Guaranty Corporation, elect to be a multiemployer plan, if—

(I) for each of the 3 plan years immediately preceding the first plan year for which the election under this paragraph is effective with respect to the plan, the plan has met those criteria or is so described,

(II) substantially all of the plan's employer contributions for each of those plan years were made or required to be made by organizations that were exempt from tax under section 501, and

(III) the plan was established prior to September 2, 1974.

(B) An election under this paragraph shall be effective for all purposes under this Act and under the Employee Retirement Income Security Act of 1974, starting with any plan year beginning on or after January 1, 1999, and ending before January 1, 2008, as designated by the plan in the election made under subparagraph (A)(ii).

(C) Once made, an election under this paragraph shall be irrevocable, except that a plan described in subparagraph (A)(ii) shall cease to be a multiemployer plan as of the plan year beginning immediately after the first plan year for which the majority of its employer contributions were made or required to be made by organizations that were not exempt from tax under section 501.

(D) The fact that a plan makes an election under subparagraph (A)(ii) does not imply that the plan was not a multiemployer plan prior to the date of the election or would not be a multiemployer plan without regard to the election.

(E) A plan is described in this subparagraph if it is a plan sponsored by an organization which is described in section 501(c)(5) and exempt from tax under section 501(a) and which was established in Chicago, Illinois, on August 12, 1881.

(F) Maintenance under collective bargaining agreement.—For purposes of this title and the Employee Retirement Income Security Act of 1974, a plan making an election under this paragraph shall be treated as maintained pursuant to a collective bargaining agreement if a collective bargaining agreement, expressly or otherwise, provides for or permits employer contributions to the plan by one or more employers that are signatory to such agreement, or participation in the plan by one or more employees of an employer that is signatory to such agreement, regardless of whether the plan was created, established, or maintained for such employees by virtue of another document that is not a collective bargaining agreement.

(g) Plan Administrator.—For purposes of this part, the term "plan administrator" means—

(1) the person specifically so designated by the terms of the instrument under which the plan is operated;

(2) in the absence of a designation referred to in paragraph (1)—

(A) in the case of a plan maintained by a single employer, such employer,

(B) in the case of a plan maintained by two or more employers or jointly by one or more employers and one or more employee organizations, the association, committee, joint board of trustees, or other similar group of representatives of the parties who maintained the plan, or

(C) in any case to which subparagraph (A) or (B) does not apply, such other person as the Secretary may by regulation, prescribe.

(h) Tax Treatment of Certain Contributions.—

(1) In general.—Effective with respect to taxable years beginning after December 31, 1973, for purposes of this title, any amount contributed—

(A) to an employees' trust described in section 401(a), or

(B) under a plan described in section 403(a),

shall not be treated as having been made by the employer if it is designated as an employee contribution.

(2) Designation by units of government.—For purposes of paragraph (1), in the case of any plan established by the government of any State or political subdivision thereof, or by any agency or instrumentality of any of the foregoing, or a governmental plan described in the last sentence of section 414(d) (relating to plans of Indian tribal governments), where the contributions of employing units are designated as employee contributions but where any employing unit picks up the contributions, the contributions so picked up shall be treated as employer contributions.

(i) Defined Contribution Plan.—For purposes of this part, the term "defined contribution plan" means a plan which provides for an individual account for each participant and for benefits based solely on the amount contributed to the participant's account, and any income, expenses, gains and losses, and any forfeitures of accounts of other participants which may be allocated to such participant's account.

IRC Sec. 414(i)

(j) Defined Benefit Plan.—For purposes of this part, the term "defined benefit plan" means any plan which is not a defined contribution plan.

(k) Certain Plans.—A defined benefit plan which provides a benefit derived from employer contributions which is based partly on the balance of the separate account of a participant shall—

(1) for purposes of section 410 (relating to minimum participation standards), be treated as a defined contribution plan,

(2) for purposes of sections 72(d) (relating to treatment of employee contributions as separate contract), 411(a)(7)(A) (relating to minimum vesting standards) 415 (relating to limitations on benefits and contributions under qualified plans), and 401(m) (relating to nondiscrimination tests for matching requirements and employee contributions), be treated as consisting of a defined contribution plan to the extent benefits are based on the separate account of a participant and as a defined benefit plan with respect to the remaining portion of benefits under the plan, and

(3) for purposes of section 4975 (relating to tax on prohibited transactions), be treated as a defined benefit plan.

(l) Merger and Consolidations of Plans or Transfers of Plan Assets.—

(1) In general.—A trust which forms a part of a plan shall not constitute a qualified trust under section 401 and a plan shall be treated as not described in section 403(a) unless in the case of any merger or consolidation of the plan with, or in the case of any transfer of assets or liabilities of such plan to, any other trust plan after September 2, 1974, each participant in the plan would (if the plan then terminated) receive a benefit immediately after the merger, consolidation, or transfer which is equal to or greater than the benefit he would have been entitled to receive immediately before the merger, consolidation, or transfer (if the plan had then terminated). The preceding sentence does not apply to any multiemployer plan with respect to any transaction to the extent that participants either before or after the transaction are covered under a multiemployer plan to which title IV of the Employee Retirement Income Security Act of 1974 applies.

(2) Allocation of assets in plan spin-offs, etc.—

(A) In general.—In the case of a plan spin-off of a defined benefit plan, a trust which forms part of—

(i) the original plan, or

(ii) any plan spun off from such plan, shall not constitute a qualified trust under this section unless the applicable percentage of excess assets are allocated to each of such plans.

(B) Applicable percentage.—For purposes of subparagraph (A), the term "applicable percentage"

means, with respect to each of the plans described in clauses (i) and (ii) of subparagraph (A), the percentage determined by dividing—

(i) the excess (if any) of—

(I) the sum of the funding target and target normal cost determined under section 430, over

(II) the amount of the assets required to be allocated to the plan after the spin-off (without regard to this paragraph), by—

(ii) the sum of the excess amounts determined separately under clause (i) for all such plans.

(C) Excess assets.—For purposes of subparagraph (A), the term "excess assets" means an amount equal to the excess (if any) of—

(i) the fair market value of the assets of the original plan immediately before the spin-off, over

(ii) the amount of assets required to be allocated after the spin-off to all plans (determined without regard to this paragraph).

(D) Certain spun-off plans not taken into account.—

(i) In general.—A plan involved in a spin-off which is described in clause (ii), (iii), or (iv) shall not be taken into account for purposes of this paragraph, except that the amount determined under subparagraph (C)(ii) shall be increased by the amount of assets allocated to such plan.

(ii) Plans transferred out of controlled groups.—A plan is described in this clause if, after such spin-off, such plan is maintained by an employer who is not a member of the same controlled group as the employer maintaining the original plan.

(iii) Plans transferred out of multiple employer plans.—A plan as described in this clause if, after the spin-off, any employer maintaining such plan (and any member of the same controlled group as such employer) does not maintain any other plan remaining after the spin-off which is also maintained by another employer (or member of the same controlled group as such other employer) which maintained the plan in existence before the spin-off.

(iv) Terminated plans.—A plan is described in this clause if, pursuant to the transaction involving the spin-off, the plan is terminated.

(v) Controlled group.—For purposes of this subparagraph, the term "controlled group" means any group treated as a single employer under subsection (b), (c), (m), or (o).

(E) Paragraph not to apply to multiemployer plans.—This paragraph does not apply to any multiemployer plan with respect to any spin-off to the extent that participants either before or after the spin-off are covered under a multiemployer plan to which title IV of the Employee Retirement Income Security Act of 1974 applies.

(F) Application to similar transaction.—Except as provided by the Secretary, rules similar to the rules of this paragraph shall apply to transactions similar to spin-offs.

(G) Special rules for bridge banks.—For purposes of this paragraph, in the case of a bridge depository institution established under section 11(i) of the Federal Deposit Insurance Act (12 U.S.C. 1821(i))—

(i) such bank shall be treated as a member of any controlled group which includes any insured bank (as defined in section 3(h) of such Act (12 U.S.C. 1813(h)))—

(I) which maintains a defined benefit plan,

(II) which is closed by the appropriate bank regulatory authorities, and

(III) any asset and liabilities of which are received by the bridge depository institution, and

(ii) the requirements of this paragraph shall not be treated as met with respect to such plan unless during the 180-day period beginning on the date such insured bank is closed—

(I) the bridge depository institution has the right to require the plan to transfer (subject to the provisions of this paragraph) not more than 50 percent of the excess assets (as defined in subparagraph (C)) to a defined benefit plan maintained by the bridge depository institution with respect to participants or former participants (including retirees and beneficiaries) in the original plan employed by the bridge depository institution or formerly employed by the closed bank, and

(II) no other merger, spin-off, termination, or similar transaction involving the portion of the excess assets described in subclause (I) may occur without the prior written consent of the bridge depository institution.

(m) Employees of an Affiliated Service Group.—

(1) In general.—For purposes of the employee benefit requirements listed in paragraph (4), except to the extent otherwise provided in regulations, all employees of the members of an affiliated service group shall be treated as employed by a single employer.

(2) Affiliated service group.—For purposes of this subsection, the term "affiliated service group" means a group consisting of a service organization (hereinafter in this paragraph referred to as the "first organization") and one or more of the following:

(A) any service organization which—

(i) is a shareholder or partner in the first organization, and

(ii) regularly performs services for the first organization or is regularly associated with the first organization in performing services for third persons, and

(B) any other organization if—

(i) a significant portion of the business of such organization is the performance of services (for the first organization, for organizations described in subparagraph (A), or for both) of a type historically performed in such service field by employees, and

(ii) 10 percent or more of the interests in such organization is held by persons who are highly compensated employees (within the meaning of section 414(q)) of the first organization or an organization described in subparagraph (A).

(3) Service organizations.—For purposes of this subsection, the term "service organization" means an organization the principal business of which is the performance of services.

(4) Employee benefit requirements.—For purposes of this subsection, the employee benefit requirements listed in this paragraph are—

(A) paragraphs (3), (4), (7), (16), (17), and (26) of section 401(a), and

(B) sections 408(k), 408(p), 410, 411, 415, and 416.

(5) Certain organizations performing management functions.—For purposes of this subsection, the term "affiliated service group" also includes a group consisting of—

(A) an organization the principal business of which is performing, on a regular and continuing basis, management functions for 1 organization (or for 1 organization and other organizations related to such 1 organization), and

(B) the organization (and related organizations) for which such functions are so performed by the organization described in subparagraph (A).

For purposes of this paragraph, the term "related organizations" has the same meaning as the term "related persons" when used in section 144(a)(3).

(6) Other definitions.—For purposes of this subsection—

(A) Organization defined.—The term "organization" means a corporation, partnership, or other organization.

(B) Ownership.—In determining ownership, the principles of section 318(a) shall apply.

(7) [Repealed.]

(n) Employee Leasing.—

(1) In general.—For purposes of the requirements listed in paragraph (3), with respect to any person (hereinafter in this subsection referred to as the "recipient") for whom a leased employee performs services—

(A) the leased employee shall be treated as an employee of the recipient, but

(B) contributions or benefits provided by the leasing organization which are attributable to services performed for the recipient shall be treated as provided by the recipient.

(2) Leased employee.—For purposes of paragraph (1), the term "leased employee" means any person who is not an employee of the recipient and who provides services to the recipient if—

(A) such services are provided pursuant to an agreement between the recipient and any other person (in this subsection referred to as the "leasing organization"),

(B) such person has performed such services for the recipient (or for the recipient and related persons) on a substantially full-time basis for a period of at least 1 year, and

(C) such services are performed under primary direction or control by the recipient.

(3) Requirements.—For purposes of this subsection, the requirements listed in this paragraph are—

(A) paragraphs (3), (4), (7), (16), (17), and (26) of section 401(a),

(B) sections 408(k), 410, 411, 415, and 416, and

(C) sections 79, 106, 117(d), 120, 125, 127, 129, 132, 137, 274(j), 505, and 4980B.

(4) Time when first considered as employee.—

(A) In general.—In the case of any leased employee, paragraph (1) shall apply only for purposes of determining whether the requirements listed in paragraph (3) are met for periods after the close of the period referred to in paragraph (2)(B).

(B) Years of service.—In the case of a person who is an employee of the recipient (whether by reason of this subsection or otherwise), for purposes of the requirements listed in paragraph (3), years of service for the recipient shall be determined by taking into account any period for which such employee would have been a leased employee but for the requirements of paragraph (2)(B).

(5) Safe harbor.—

(A) In general.—In the case of requirements described in subparagraphs (A) and (B) of paragraph (3), this subsection shall not apply to any leased employee with respect to services performed for a recipient if—

(i) such employee is covered by a plan which is maintained by the leasing organization and meets the requirements of subparagraph (B), and

(ii) leased employees (determined without regard to this paragraph) do not constitute more than 20 percent of the recipient's nonhighly compensated work force.

(B) Plan requirements.—A plan meets the requirements of this subparagraph if—

(i) such plan is a money purchase pension plan with a nonintegrated employer contribution rate for each participant of at least 10 percent of compensation,

(ii) such plan provides for full and immediate vesting, and

(iii) each employee of the leasing organization (other than employees who perform substantially all of their services for the leasing organization) immediately participates in such plan.

Clause (iii) shall not apply to any individual whose compensation from the leasing organization in each plan year during the 4-year period ending with the plan year is less than $1,000.

(C) Definitions.—For purposes of this paragraph—

(i) Highly compensated employee.—The term "highly compensated employee" has the meaning given such term by section 414(q).

(ii) Nonhighly compensated work force.—The term "nonhighly compensated work force" means the aggregate number of individuals (other than highly compensated employees)—

(I) who are employees of the recipient (without regard to this subsection) and have performed services for the recipient (or for the recipient and related persons) on a substantially full-time basis for a period of at least 1 year, or

(II) who are leased employees with respect to the recipient (determined without regard to this paragraph).

(iii) Compensation.—The term "compensation" has the same meaning as when used in section 415; except that such term shall include—

(I) any employer contribution under a qualified cash or deferred arrangement to the extent not included in gross income under section 402(e)(3) or 402(h)(1)(B),

(II) any amount which the employee would have received in cash but for an election under a cafeteria plan (within the meaning of section 125), and

(III) any amount contributed to an annuity contract described in section 403(b) pursuant to a salary reduction agreement (within the meaning of section 3121(a)(5)(D)).

(6) Other rules.—For purposes of this subsection—

(A) Related persons.—The term "related persons" has the same meaning as when used in section 144(a)(3).

(B) Employees of entities under common control.—The rules of subsections (b), (c), (m), and (o) shall apply.

(o) Regulations.—The Secretary shall prescribe regulations (which may provide rules in addition to the rules contained in subsections (m) and (n)) as may be necessary to prevent the avoidance of any employee benefit requirement listed in subsection (m)(4) or (n)(3) or any requirement under section 457 through the use of—

(1) separate organizations,

(2) employee leasing, or

(3) other arrangements.

The regulations prescribed under subsection (n) shall include provisions to minimize the recordkeeping requirements of subsection (n) in the case of an employer which has no top-heavy plans (within the meaning of section 416(g)) and which uses the services of persons (other than employees) for an insignificant percentage of the employer's total workload.

(p) Qualified Domestic Relations Order Defined.—For purposes of this subsection and section 401(a)(13)—

(1) In general.—

(A) Qualified domestic relations order.—The term "qualified domestic relations order" means a domestic relations order—

(i) which creates or recognizes the existence of an alternate payee's right to, or assigns to an alternate payee the right to, receive all or a portion of the benefits payable with respect to a participant under a plan, and

(ii) with respect to which the requirements of paragraphs (2) and (3) are met.

(B) Domestic relations order.—The term "domestic relations order" means any judgment, decree, or order (including approval of a property settlement agreement) which—

(i) relates to the provision of child support, alimony payments, or marital property rights to a spouse, former spouse, child, or other dependent of a participant, and

(ii) is made pursuant to a State domestic relations law (including a community property law).

(2) Order must clearly specify certain facts.—A domestic relations order meets the requirements of this paragraph only if such order clearly specifies—

(A) the name and last known mailing address (if any) of the participant and the name and mailing address of each alternate payee covered by the order,

(B) the amount or percentage of the participant's benefits to be paid by the plan to each such alternate payee, or the manner in which such amount or percentage is to be determined,

(C) the number of payments or period to which such order applies, and

(D) each plan to which such order applies.

(3) Order may not alter amount, form, etc., of benefits.—A domestic relations order meets the requirements of this paragraph only if such order—

(A) does not require a plan to provide any type or form of benefit, or any option, not otherwise provided under the plan,

(B) does not require the plan to provide increased benefits (determined on the basis of actuarial value), and

(C) does not require the payment of benefits to an alternate payee which are required to be paid to another alternate payee under another order previously determined to be a qualified domestic relations order.

(4) Exception for certain payments made after earliest retirement age.—

(A) In general.—A domestic relations order shall not be treated as failing to meet the requirements of subparagraph (A) of paragraph (3) solely because such order requires that payment of benefits be made to an alternate payee—

(i) in the case of any payment before a participant has separated from service, on or after the date on which the participant attains (or would have attained) the earliest retirement age,

(ii) as if the participant had retired on the date on which such payment is to begin under such order (but taking into account only the present value of the benefits actually accrued and not taking into account the present value of any employer subsidy for early retirement), and

(iii) in any form in which such benefits may be paid under the plan to the participant (other than in the form of a joint and survivor annuity with respect to the alternate payee and his or her subsequent spouse).

For purposes of clause (ii), the interest rate assumption used in determining the present value shall be the interest rate specified in the plan or, if no rate is specified, 5 percent.

(B) Earliest retirement age.—For purposes of this paragraph, the term "earliest retirement age" means the earlier of—

(i) the date on which the participant is entitled to a distribution under the plan, or

IRC Sec. 414(p)(4)(B)(i)

(ii) the later of—

(I) the date the participant attains age 50, or

(II) the earliest date on which the participant could begin receiving benefits under the plan if the participant separated from service.

(5) Treatment of former spouse as surviving spouse for purposes of determining survivor benefits.—To the extent provided in any qualified domestic relations order—

(A) the former spouse of a participant shall be treated as a surviving spouse of such participant for purposes of sections 401(a)(11) and 417 (and any spouse of the participant shall not be treated as a spouse of the participant for such purposes), and

(B) if married for at least 1 year, the surviving former spouse shall be treated as meeting the requirements of section 417(d).

(6) Plan procedures with respect to orders.—

(A) Notice and determination by administrator.— In the case of any domestic relations order received by a plan—

(i) the plan administrator shall promptly notify the participant and each alternate payee of the receipt of such order and the plan's procedures for determining the qualified status of domestic relations orders, and

(ii) within a reasonable period after receipt of such order, the plan administrator shall determine whether such order is a qualified domestic relations order and notify the participant of such determination.

(B) Plan to establish reasonable procedures.— Each plan shall establish reasonable procedures to determine the qualified status of domestic relations orders and to administer distributions under such qualified orders.

(7) Procedures for period during which determination is being made.—

(A) In general.—During any period in which the issue of whether a domestic relations order is a qualified domestic relations order is being determined (by the plan administrator, by a court of competent jurisdiction, or otherwise), the plan administrator shall separately account for the amounts (hereinafter in this paragraph referred to as the "segregated amounts") which would have been payable to the alternate payee during such period if the order had been determined to be a qualified domestic relations order.

(B) Payment to alternate payee if order determined to be qualified domestic relations order.—If within the 18-month period described in subparagraph (E) the order (or modification thereof) is determined to be a qualified domestic relations

order, the plan administrator shall pay the segregated amounts (including any interest thereon) to the person or persons entitled thereto.

(C) Payment to plan participant in certain cases.— If within the 18-month period described in subparagraph (E)—

(i) it is determined that the order is not a qualified domestic relations order, or

(ii) the issue as to whether such order is a qualified domestic relations order is not resolved,

then the plan administrator shall pay the segregated amounts (including any interest thereon) to the person or persons who would have been entitled to such amounts if there had been no order.

(D) Subsequent determination or order to be applied prospectively only.—Any determination that an order is a qualified domestic relations order which is made after the close of the 18-month period described in subparagraph (E) shall be applied prospectively only.

(E) Determination of 18-month period.—For purposes of this paragraph, the 18-month period described in this subparagraph is the 18-month period beginning with the date on which the first payment would be required to be made under the domestic relations order.

(8) Alternate payee defined.—The term "alternate payee" means any spouse, former spouse, child, or other dependent of a participant who is recognized by a domestic relations order as having a right to receive all, or a portion of, the benefits payable under a plan with respect to such participant.

(9) Subsection not to apply to plans to which section 401(a)(13) does not apply.—This subsection shall not apply to any plan to which section 401(a)(13) does not apply. For purposes of this title, except as provided in regulations, any distribution from an annuity contract under section 403(b) pursuant to a qualified domestic relations order shall be treated in the same manner as a distribution from a plan to which section 401(a)(13) applies.

(10) Waiver of certain distribution requirements.—With respect to the requirements of subsections (a) and (k) of section 401, section 403(b), section 409(d), and section 457(d), a plan shall not be treated as failing to meet such requirements solely by reason of payments to an alternative payee pursuant to a qualified domestic relations order.

(11) Application of rules to certain other plans.—For purposes of this title, a distribution or payment from a governmental plan (as defined in subsection (d)) or a church plan (as described in subsection (e)) or an eligible deferred compensation plan (within the meaning of section 457(b)) shall be treated as made pursuant to a qualified domestic relations order if it is made pursuant to a domestic relations order which meets the requirement of clause (i) of paragraph (1)(A).

(12) Tax treatment of payments from a section 457 plan.—If a distribution or payment from an eligible deferred compensation plan described in section 457(b) is made pursuant to a qualified domestic relations order, rules similar to the rules of section 402(e)(1)(A) shall apply to such distribution or payment.

(13) Consultation with the Secretary.—In prescribing regulations under this subsection and section 401(a)(13), the Secretary of Labor shall consult with the Secretary.

(q) Highly Compensated Employee.—

(1) In general.—The term "highly compensated employee" means any employee who—

(A) was a 5-percent owner at any time during the year or the preceding year, or

(B) for the preceding year—

(i) had compensation from the employer in excess of $80,000, and

(ii) if the employer elects the application of this clause for such preceding year, was in the top-paid group of employees for such preceding year.

The Secretary shall adjust the $80,000 amount under subparagraph (B) at the same time and in the same manner as under section 415(d), except that the base period shall be the calendar quarter ending September 30, 1996.

(2) 5-percent owner.—An employee shall be treated as a 5-percent owner for any year if at any time during such year such employee was a 5-percent owner (as defined in section 416(i)(1)) of the employer.

(3) Top-paid group.—An employee is in the top-paid group of employees for any year if such employee is in the group consisting of the top 20 percent of the employees when ranked on the basis of compensation paid during such year.

(4) Compensation.—For purposes of this subsection, the term "compensation" has the meaning given such term by section 415(c)(3).

(5) Excluded employees.—For purposes of subsection (r) and for purposes of determining the number of employees in the top-paid group, the following employees shall be excluded—

(A) employees who have not completed 6 months of service,

(B) employees who normally work less than 17½ hours per week,

(C) employees who normally work during not more than 6 months during any year,

(D) employees who have not attained age 21, and

(E) except to the extent provided in regulations, employees who are included in a unit of employees covered by an agreement which the Secretary of Labor finds to be a collective bargaining agreement between employee representatives and the employer.

Except as provided by the Secretary, the employer may elect to apply subparagraph (A), (B), (C), or (D) by substituting a shorter period of service, smaller number of hours or months, or lower age for the period of service, number of hours or months, or age (as the case may be) than that specified in such subparagraph.

(6) Former employees.—A former employee shall be treated as a highly compensated employee if—

(A) such employee was a highly compensated employee when such employee separated from service, or

(B) such employee was a highly compensated employee at any time after attaining age 55.

(7) Coordination with other provisions.—Subsections (b), (c), (m), (n), and (o) shall be applied before the application of this subsection.

(8) Special rule for nonresident aliens.—For purposes of this subsection and subsection (r), employees who are nonresident aliens and who receive no earned income (within the meaning of section 911(d)(2)) from the employer which constitutes income from sources within the United States (within the meaning of section 861(a)(3)) shall not be treated as employees.

(9) Certain employees not considered highly compensated and excluded employees under pre-ERISA rules for church plans.—In the case of a church plan (as defined in subsection (e)), no employee shall be considered an officer, a person whose principal duties consist of supervising the work of other employees, or a highly compensated employee for any year unless such employee is a highly compensated employee under paragraph (1) for such year.

(r) Special Rules for Separate Line of Business.—

(1) In general.—For purposes of sections 129(d)(8) and 410(b), an employer shall be treated as operating separate lines of business during any year if the employer for bona fide business reasons operates separate lines of business.

(2) Line of business must have 50 employees, etc.—A line of business shall not be treated as separate under paragraph (1) unless—

(A) such line of business has at least 50 employees who are not excluded under subsection (q)(5),

(B) the employer notifies the Secretary that such line of business is being treated as separate for purposes of paragraph (1), and

ERISA: The Law and the Code, 2011 Edition

(C) such line of business meets guidelines prescribed by the Secretary or the employer receives a determination from the Secretary that such line of business may be treated as separate for purposes of paragraph (1).

(3) Safe harbor rule.—

(A) In general.—The requirements of subparagraph (C) of paragraph (2) shall not apply to any line of business if the highly compensated employee percentage with respect to such line of business is—

(i) not less than one-half, and

(ii) not more than twice,

the percentage which highly compensated employees are of all employees of the employer. An employer shall be treated as meeting the requirements of clause (i) if at least 10 percent of all highly compensated employees of the employer perform services solely for such line of business.

(B) Determination may be based on preceding year.—The requirements of subparagraph (A) shall be treated as met with respect to any line of business if such requirements were met with respect to such line of business for the preceding year and if—

(i) no more than a de minimis number of employees were shifted to or from the line of business after the close of the preceding year, or

(ii) the employees shifted to or from the line of business after the close of the preceding year contained a substantially proportional number of highly compensated employees.

(4) Highly compensated employee percentage defined.—For purposes of this subsection, the term "highly compensated employee percentage" means the percentage which highly compensated employees performing services for the line of business are of all employees performing services for the line of business.

(5) Allocation of benefits to line of business.—For purposes of this subsection, benefits which are attributable to services provided to a line of business shall be treated as provided by such line of business.

(6) Headquarters personnel, etc.—The Secretary shall prescribe rules providing for—

(A) the allocation of headquarters personnel among the lines of business of the employer, and

(B) the treatment of other employees providing services for more than 1 line of business of the employer or not in lines of business meeting the requirements of paragraph (2).

(7) Separate operating units.—For purposes of this subsection, the term "separate line of business" includes an operating unit in a separate geographic area separately operated for a bona fide business reason.

(8) Affiliated service groups.—This subsection shall not apply in the case of any affiliated service group (within the meaning of section 414(m)).

(s) Compensation.—For purposes of any applicable provision—

(1) In general.—Except as provided in this subsection, the term "compensation" has the meaning given such term by section 415(c)(3).

(2) Employer may elect not to treat certain deferrals as compensation.—An employer may elect not to include as compensation any amount which is contributed by the employer pursuant to a salary reduction agreement and which is not includible in the gross income of an employee under section 125, 132(f)(4), 402(e)(3), 402(h), or 403(b).

(3) Alternative determination of compensation.—The Secretary shall by regulation provide for alternative methods of determining compensation which may be used by an employer, except that such regulations shall provide that an employer may not use an alternative method if the use of such method discriminates in favor of highly compensated employees (within the meaning of subsection (q)).

(4) Applicable provision.—For purposes of this subsection, the term "applicable provision" means any provision which specifically refers to this subsection.

(t) Application of Controlled Group Rules to Certain Employee Benefits.—

(1) In general.—All employees who are treated as employed by a single employer under subsection (b), (c), or (m) shall be treated as employed by a single employer for purposes of an applicable section. The provisions of subsection (o) shall apply with respect to the requirements of an applicable section.

(2) Applicable section.—For purposes of this subsection, the term "applicable section" means section 79, 106, 117(d), 120, 125, 127, 129, 132, 137, 274(j), 505, or 4980B.

(u) Special Rules Relating to Veterans' Reemployment Rights Under USERRA and to Differential Wage Payments to Members on Active Duty.—

(1) Treatment of certain contributions made pursuant to veterans' reemployment rights.—If any contribution is made by an employer or an employee under an individual account plan with respect to an employee, or by an employee to a defined benefit plan that provides for employee contributions, and such contribution is required by reason of such employee's rights under chapter 43 of title 38, United States Code, resulting from qualified military service, then—

(A) such contribution shall not be subject to any otherwise applicable limitation contained in sec-

IRC Sec. 414(r)(2)(C)

tion 402(g), 402(h), 403(b), 404(a), 404(h), 408, 415, or 457, and shall not be taken into account in applying such limitations to other contributions or benefits under such plan or any other plan, with respect to the year in which the contribution is made,

(B) such contribution shall be subject to the limitations referred to in subparagraph (A) with respect to the year to which the contribution relates (in accordance with rules prescribed by the Secretary), and

(C) such plan shall not be treated as failing to meet the requirements of section 401(a)(4), 401(a)(26), 401(k)(3), 401(k)(11), 401(k)(12), 401(m), 403(b)(12), 408(k)(3), 408 (k)(6), 408(p), 410(b), or 416 by reason of the making of (or the right to make) such contribution.

For purposes of the preceding sentence, any elective deferral or employee contribution made under paragraph (2) shall be treated as required by reason of the employee's rights under such chapter 43.

(2) Reemployment rights under USERRA with respect to elective deferrals.—

(A) In general.—For purposes of this subchapter and section 457, if an employee is entitled to the benefits of chapter 43 of title 38, United States Code, with respect to any plan which provides for elective deferrals, the employer sponsoring the plan shall be treated as meeting the requirements of such chapter 43 with respect to such elective deferrals only if such employer—

(i) permits such employee to make additional elective deferrals under such plan (in the amount determined under subparagraph (B) or such lesser amount as is elected by the employee) during the period which begins on the date of the reemployment of such employee with such employer and has the same length as the lesser of—

(I) the product of 3 and the period of qualified military service which resulted in such rights, and

(II) 5 years, and

(ii) makes a matching contribution with respect to any additional elective deferral made pursuant to clause (i) which would have been required had such deferral actually been made during the period of such qualified military service.

(B) Amount of make up required.—The amount determined under this subparagraph with respect to any plan is the maximum amount of the elective deferrals that the individual would have been permitted to make under the plan in accordance with the limitations referred to in paragraph (1)(A) during the period of qualified military service if the individual had continued to be employed by the employer during such period and received compensation as determined under paragraph (7).

Proper adjustment shall be made to the amount determined under the preceding sentence for any elective deferrals actually made during the period of such qualified military service.

(C) Elective deferral.—For purposes of this paragraph, the term "elective deferral" has the meaning given such term by section 402(g)(3); except that such term shall include any deferral of compensation under an eligible deferred compensation plan (as defined in section 457(b)).

(D) After-tax employee contributions.—References in subparagraphs (A) and (B) to elective deferrals shall be treated as including references to employee contributions.

(3) Certain retroactive adjustments not required.—For purposes of this subchapter and subchapter E, no provision of chapter 43 of title 38, United States Code, shall be construed as requiring—

(A) any crediting of earnings to an employee with respect to any contribution before such contribution is actually made, or

(B) any allocation of any forfeiture with respect to the period of qualified military service.

(4) Loan repayment suspensions permitted.—If any plan suspends the obligation to repay any loan made to an employee from such plan for any part of any period during which such employee is performing service in the uniformed services (as defined in chapter 43 of title 38, United States Code), whether or not qualified military service, such suspension shall not be taken into account for purposes of section 72(p), 401(a), or 4975(d)(1).

(5) Qualified military service.—or purposes of this subsection, the term "qualified military service" means any service in the uniformed services (as defined in chapter 43 of title 38, United States Code) by any individual if such individual is entitled to reemployment rights under such chapter withrespect to such service.

(6) Individual account plan.—For purposes of this subsection, the term "individual account plan" means any defined contribution plan (including any tax-sheltered annuity plan under section 403(b), any simplified employee pension under section 408(k), any qualified salary reduction arrangement under section 408(p), and any eligible deferred compensation plan (as defined in section 457(b)).

(7) Compensation.—For purposes of sections 403(b)(3), 415(c)(3), and 457(e)(5), an employee who is in qualified military service shall be treated as receiving compensation from the employer during such period of qualified military service equal to—

(A) the compensation the employee would have received during such period if the employee were not in qualified military service, determined based on the rate of pay the employee would have received from the employer but for absence during the period of qualified military service, or

(B) if the compensation the employee would have received during such period was not reasonably certain, the employee's average compensation from the employer during the 12-month period immediately preceding the qualified military service (or, if shorter, the period of employment immediately preceding the qualified military service).

(8) USERRA requirements for qualified retirement plans.—For purposes of this subchapter and section 457, an employer sponsoring a retirement plan shall be treated as meeting the requirements of chapter 43 of title 38, United States Code, only if each of the following requirements is met:

(A) An individual reemployed under such chapter is treated with respect to such plan as not having incurred a break in service with the employer maintaining the plan by reason of such individual's period of qualified military service.

(B) Each period of qualified military service served by an individual is, upon reemployment under such chapter, deemed with respect to such plan to constitute service with the employer maintaining the plan for the purpose of determining the nonforfeitability of the individual's accrued benefits under such plan and for the purpose of determining the accrual of benefits under such plan.

(C) An individual reemployed under such chapter is entitled to accrued benefits that are contingent on the making of, or derived from, employee contributions or elective deferrals only to the extent the individual makes payment to the plan with respect to such contributions or deferrals. No such payment may exceed the amount the individual would have been permitted or required to contribute had the individual remained continuously employed by the employer throughout the period of qualified military service. Any payment to such plan shall be made during the period beginning with the date of reemployment and whose duration is 3 times the period of the qualified military service (but not greater than 5 years).

(9) Treatment in the case of death or disability resulting from active military service.—

(A) In general.—For benefit accrual purposes, an employer sponsoring a retirement plan may treat an individual who dies or becomes disabled (as defined under the terms of the plan) while performing qualified military service with respect to the employer maintaining the plan as if the individual has resumed employment in accordance with the individual's reemployment rights under chapter 43 of title 38, United States Code, on the day preceding death or disability (as the case may be) and terminated employment on the actual date of death or disability. In the case of any such treatment, and

subject to subparagraphs (B) and (C), any full or partial compliance by such plan with respect to the benefit accrual requirements of paragraph (8) with respect to such individual shall be treated for purposes of paragraph (1) as if such compliance were required under such chapter 43.

(B) Nondiscrimination requirement.—Subparagraph (A) shall apply only if all individuals performing qualified military service with respect to the employer maintaining the plan (as determined under subsections (b), (c), (m), and (o)) who die or became disabled as a result of performing qualified military service prior to reemployment by the employer are credited with service and benefits on reasonably equivalent terms.

(C) Determination of benefits.—The amount of employee contributions and the amount of elective deferrals of an individual treated as reemployed under subparagraph (A) for purposes of applying paragraph (8)(C) shall be determined on the basis of the individual's average actual employee contributions or elective deferrals for the lesser of—

(i) the 12-month period of service with the employer immediately prior to qualified military service, or

(ii) if service with the employer is less than such 12-month period, the actual length of continuous service with the employer.

(10) Plans not subject to title 38.—This subsection shall not apply to any retirement plan to which chapter 43 of title 38, United States Code, does not apply.

(11) References.—For purposes of this section, any reference to chapter 43 of title 38, United States Code, shall be treated as a reference to such chapter as in effect on December 12, 1994 (without regard to any subsequent amendment).

(12) Treatment of differential wage payments.—

(A) In general.—Except as provided in this paragraph, for purposes of applying this title to a retirement plan to which this subsection applies—

(i) an individual receiving a differential wage payment shall be treated as an employee of the employer making the payment,

(ii) the differential wage payment shall be treated as compensation, and

(iii) the plan shall not be treated as failing to meet the requirements of any provision described in paragraph (1)(C) by reason of any contribution or benefit which is based on the differential wage payment.

(B) Special rule for distributions.—

(i) In general.—Notwithstanding subparagraph (A)(i), for purposes of section 401(k)(2)(B)(i)(I),

403(b)(7)(A)(ii), 403(b)(11)(A), or 457(d)(1)(A)(ii), an individual shall be treated as having been severed from employment during any period the individual is performing service in the uniformed services described in section 3401(h)(2)(A).

(ii) Limitation.—If an individual elects to receive a distribution by reason of clause (i), the plan shall provide that the individual may not make an elective deferral or employee contribution during the 6-month period beginning on the date of the distribution.

(C) Nondiscrimination requirement.—Subparagraph (A)(iii) shall apply only if all employees of an employer (as determined under subsections (b), (c), (m), and (o)) performing service in the uniformed services described in section 3401(h)(2)(A) are entitled to receive differential wage payments on reasonably equivalent terms and, if eligible to participate in a retirement plan maintained by the employer, to make contributions based on the payments on reasonably equivalent terms. For purposes of applying this subparagraph, the provisions of paragraphs (3), (4), and (5) of section 410(b) shall apply.

(D) Differential wage payment.—For purposes of this paragraph, the term "differential wage payment" has the meaning given such term by section 3401(h)(2).

(v) Catch-Up Contributions for Individuals Age 50 or Over.—

(1) In general.—An applicable employer plan shall not be treated as failing to meet any requirement of this title solely because the plan permits an eligible participant to make additional elective deferrals in any plan year.

(2) Limitation on amount of additional deferrals.—

(A) In general.—A plan shall not permit additional elective deferrals under paragraph (1) for any year in an amount greater than the lesser of—

(i) the applicable dollar amount, or

(ii) the excess (if any) of—

(I) the participant's compensation (as defined in section 415(c)(3)) for the year, over

(II) any other elective deferrals of the participant for such year which are made without regard to this subsection.

(B) Applicable dollar amount.—For purposes of this paragraph—

(i) In the case of an applicable employer plan other than a plan described in section 401(k)(11) or 408(p), the applicable dollar amount shall be determined in accordance with the following table:

For taxable years beginning in:	The applicable dollar amount is:
2002	$1,000
2003	$2,000
2004	$3,000
2005	$4,000
2006 and thereafter	$5,000

(ii) In the case of an applicable employer plan described in section 401(k)(11) or 408(p), the applicable dollar amount shall be determined in accordance with the following table:

For taxable years beginning in:	The applicable dollar amount is:
2002	$500
2003	$1,000
2004	$1,500
2005	$2,000
2006 and thereafter	$2,500

(C) Cost-of-living adjustment.—In the case of a year beginning after December 31, 2006, the Secretary shall adjust annually the $5,000 amount in subparagraph (B)(i) and the $2,500 amount in subparagraph (B)(ii) for increases in the cost-of-living at the same time and in the same manner as adjustments under section 415(d); except that the base period taken into account shall be the calendar quarter beginning July 1, 2005, and any increase under this subparagraph which is not a multiple of $500 shall be rounded to the next lower multiple of $500.

(D) Aggregation of plans.—For purposes of this paragraph, plans described in clauses (i), (ii), and (iv) of paragraph (6)(A) that are maintained by the same employer (as determined under subsection (b), (c), (m) or (o)) shall be treated as a single plan, and plans described in clause (iii) of paragraph (6)(A) that maintained by the same employer shall be treated as a single plan.

(3) Treatment of contributions.—In the case of any contribution to a plan under paragraph (1)—

(A) such contribution shall not, with respect to the year in which the contribution is made—

(i) be subject to any otherwise applicable limitation contained in sections 401(a)(30), 402(h), 403(b), 408, 415(c), and 457 (b)(2)(determined without regard to section 457 (b)(3)), or

(ii) be taken into account in applying such limitations to other contributions or benefits under such plan or any other such plan, and

(B) except as provided in paragraph (4), such plan shall not be treated as failing to meet the require-

IRC Sec. 414(v)(3)(B)

ments of section 401(a)(4), 401(k)(3), 401(k)(11), 403(b)(12), 408(k), 410(b), or 416 by reason of the making of (or the right to make) such contribution.

(4) Application of nondiscrimination rules.—

(A) In general.—An applicable employer plan shall be treated as failing to meet the nondiscrimination requirements under section 401(a)(4) with respect to benefits, rights, and features unless the plan allows all eligible participants to make the same election with respect to the additional elective deferrals under this subsection.

(B) Aggregation.—For purposes of subparagraph (A), all plans maintained by employers who are treated as a single employer under subsection (b), (c), (m), or (o) of section 414 shall be treated as 1 plan except that a plan described in clause (i) of section 410(b)(6)(C) shall not be treated as a plan of the employer until the expiration of the transition period with respect to such plan (as determined under clause (ii) of such section).

(5) Eligible participant.—For purposes of this subsection, the term "eligible participant" means, a participant in a plan—

(A) who would attain age 50 by the end of the taxable year, and

(B) with respect to whom no other elective deferrals may (without regard to this subsection) be made to the plan for the plan (or other applicable) year by reason of the application of any limitation or other restriction described in paragraph (3) or comparable limitation or restriction contained in the terms of the plan.

(6) Other definitions and rules.—For purposes of this subsection—

(A) Applicable employer plan.—The term "applicable employer plan" means

(i) an employees' trust described in section 401(a) which is exempt from tax under section 501(a),

(ii) a plan under which amounts are contributed by an individual's employer for an annuity contract described in section 403(b),

(iii) an eligible deferred compensation plan under section 457 of an eligible employer described in section 457(e)(1)(A), and

(iv) an arrangement meeting the requirements of section 408 (k) or (p).

(B) Elective deferral.—The term "elective deferral" has the meaning given such term by subsection (u)(2)(C).

(C) Exception for section 457 plans.—This subsection shall not apply to a participant for any year for which a higher limitation applies to the participant under section 457(b)(3).

(w) Special Rules for Certain Withdrawals From Eligible Automatic Contribution Arrangements.—

(1) In general.—If an eligible automatic contribution arrangement allows an employee to elect to make permissible withdrawals—

(A) the amount of any such withdrawal shall be includible in the gross income of the employee for the taxable year of the employee in which the distribution is made,

(B) no tax shall be imposed under section 72(t) with respect to the distribution, and

(C) the arrangement shall not be treated as violating any restriction on distributions under this title solely by reason of allowing the withdrawal.

In the case of any distribution to an employee by reason of an election under this paragraph, employer matching contributions shall be forfeited or subject to such other treatment as the Secretary may prescribe.

(2) Permissible withdrawal.—For purposes of this subsection—

(A) In general.—The term "permissible withdrawal" means any withdrawal from an eligible automatic contribution arrangement meeting the requirements of this paragraph which—

(i) is made pursuant to an election by an employee, and

(ii) consists of elective contributions described in paragraph (3)(B) (and earnings attributable thereto).

(B) Time for making election.—Subparagraph (A) shall not apply to an election by an employee unless the election is made no later than the date which is 90 days after the date of the first elective contribution with respect to the employee under the arrangement.

(C) Amount of distribution.—Subparagraph (A) shall not apply to any election by an employee unless the amount of any distribution by reason of the election is equal to the amount of elective contributions made with respect to the first payroll period to which the eligible automatic contribution arrangement applies to the employee and any succeeding payroll period beginning before the effective date of the election (and earnings attributable thereto).

(3) Eligible automatic contribution arrangement.—For purposes of this subsection, the term "eligible automatic contribution arrangement" means an arrangement under an applicable employer plan—

(A) under which a participant may elect to have the employer make payments as contributions under the plan on behalf of the participant, or to the participant directly in cash,

(B) under which the participant is treated as having elected to have the employer make such con-

IRC Sec. 414(v)(3)(B)

tributions in an amount equal to a uniform percentage of compensation provided under the plan until the participant specifically elects not to have such contributions made (or specifically elects to have such contributions made at a different percentage), and

(C) which meets the requirements of paragraph (4).

(4) Notice requirements.—

(A) In general.—The administrator of a plan containing an arrangement described in paragraph (3) shall, within a reasonable period before each plan year, give to each employee to whom an arrangement described in paragraph (3) applies for such plan year notice of the employee's rights and obligations under the arrangement which—

(i) is sufficiently accurate and comprehensive to apprise the employee of such rights and obligations, and

(ii) is written in a manner calculated to be understood by the average employee to whom the arrangement applies.

(B) Time and form of notice.—A notice shall not be treated as meeting the requirements of subparagraph (A) with respect to an employee unless—

(i) the notice includes an explanation of the employee's right under the arrangement to elect not to have elective contributions made on the employee's behalf (or to elect to have such contributions made at a different percentage),

(ii) the employee has a reasonable period of time after receipt of the notice described in clause (i) and before the first elective contribution is made to make such election, and

(iii) the notice explains how contributions made under the arrangement will be invested in the absence of any investment election by the employee.

(5) Applicable employer plan.—For purposes of this subsection, the term "applicable employer plan" means—

(A) an employees' trust described in section 401(a) which is exempt from tax under section 501(a),

(B) a plan under which amounts are contributed by an individual's employer for an annuity contract described in section 403(b),

(C) an eligible deferred compensation plan described in section 457(b) which is maintained by an eligible employer described in section 457(e)(1)(A),

(D) a simplified employee pension the terms of which provide for a salary reduction arrangement described in section 408(k)(6), and

(E) a simple retirement account (as defined in section 408(p)).

(6) Special rule.—A withdrawal described in paragraph (1) (subject to the limitation of paragraph (2)(C)) shall not be taken into account for purposes of section 401(k)(3) or for purposes of applying the limitation under section 402(g)(1).

(x) Special Rules for Eligible Combined Defined Benefit Plans and Qualified Cash or Deferred Arrangements.—

(1) General rule.—Except as provided in this subsection, the requirements of this title shall be applied to any defined benefit plan or applicable defined contribution plan which are part of an eligible combined plan in the same manner as if each such plan were not a part of the eligible combined plan. In the case of a termination of the defined benefit plan and the applicable defined contribution plan forming part of an eligible combined plan, the plan administrator shall terminate each such plan separately.

(2) Eligible combined plan.—For purposes of this subsection—

(A) In general.—The term "eligible combined plan" means a plan—

(i) which is maintained by an employer which, at the time the plan is established, is a small employer,

(ii) which consists of a defined benefit plan and an applicable defined contribution plan,

(iii) the assets of which are held in a single trust forming part of the plan and are clearly identified and allocated to the defined benefit plan and the applicable defined contribution plan to the extent necessary for the separate application of this title under paragraph (1), and

(iv) with respect to which the benefit, contribution, vesting, and nondiscrimination requirements of subparagraphs (B), (C), (D), (E), and (F) are met.

For purposes of this subparagraph, the term "small employer" has the meaning given such term by section 4980D(d)(2), except that such section shall be applied by substituting "500" for "50" each place it appears.

(B) Benefit requirements.—

(i) In general.—The benefit requirements of this subparagraph are met with respect to the defined benefit plan forming part of the eligible combined plan if the accrued benefit of each participant derived from employer contributions, when expressed as an annual retirement benefit, is not less than the applicable percentage of the participant's final average pay. For purposes of this clause, final average pay shall be determined using the period of consecutive years (not exceeding 5) during

IRC Sec. 414(x)(2)(B)(i)

which the participant had the greatest aggregate compensation from the employer.

(ii) Applicable percentage.—For purposes of clause (i), the applicable percentage is the lesser of—

(I) 1 percent multiplied by the number of years of service with the employer, or

(II) 20 percent.

(iii) Special rule for applicable defined benefit plans.—If the defined benefit plan under clause (i) is an applicable defined benefit plan as defined in section 411(a)(13)(B) which meets the interest credit requirements of section 411(b)(5)(B)(i), the plan shall be treated as meeting the requirements of clause (i) with respect to any plan year if each participant receives a pay credit for the year which is not less than the percentage of compensation determined in accordance with the following table:

If the participant's age as of the beginning of the year is —	The percentage is—
30 or less	2
Over 30 but less than 40	4
40 or over but less than 50	6
50 or over	8

(iv) Years of service.—For purposes of this subparagraph, years of service shall be determined under the rules of paragraphs (4), (5), and (6) of section 411(a), except that the plan may not disregard any year of service because of a participant making, or failing to make, any elective deferral with respect to the qualified cash or deferred arrangement to which subparagraph (C) applies.

(C) Contribution requirements.—

(i) In general.—The contribution requirements of this subparagraph with respect to any applicable defined contribution plan forming part of an eligible combined plan are met if—

(I) the qualified cash or deferred arrangement included in such plan constitutes an automatic contribution arrangement, and

(II) the employer is required to make matching contributions on behalf of each employee eligible to participate in the arrangement in an amount equal to 50 percent of the elective contributions of the employee to the extent such elective contributions do not exceed 4 percent of compensation.

Rules similar to the rules of clauses (ii) and (iii) of section 401(k)(12)(B) shall apply for purposes of this clause.

(ii) Nonelective contributions.—An applicable defined contribution plan shall not be treated as failing to meet the requirements of clause (i) be-

cause the employer makes nonelective contributions under the plan but such contributions shall not be taken into account in determining whether the requirements of clause (i)(II) are met.

(D) Vesting requirements.—The vesting requirements of this subparagraph are met if—

(i) in the case of a defined benefit plan forming part of an eligible combined plan an employee who has completed at least 3 years of service has a nonforfeitable right to 100 percent of the employee's accrued benefit under the plan derived from employer contributions, and

(ii) in the case of an applicable defined contribution plan forming part of eligible combined plan—

(I) an employee has a nonforfeitable right to any matching contribution made under the qualified cash or deferred arrangement included in such plan by an employer with respect to any elective contribution, including matching contributions in excess of the contributions required under subparagraph (C)(i)(II), and

(II) an employee who has completed at least 3 years of service has a nonforfeitable right to 100 percent of the employee's accrued benefit derived under the arrangement from nonelective contributions of the employer.

For purposes of this subparagraph, the rules of section 411 shall apply to the extent not inconsistent with this subparagraph.

(E) Uniform provision of contributions and benefits.—In the case of a defined benefit plan or applicable defined contribution plan forming part of an eligible combined plan, the requirements of this subparagraph are met if all contributions and benefits under each such plan, and all rights and features under each such plan, must be provided uniformly to all participants.

(F) Requirements must be met without taking into account social security and similar contributions and benefits or other plans.—

(i) In general.—The requirements of this subparagraph are met if the requirements of clauses (ii) and (iii) are met.

(ii) Social Security and similar contributions.—The requirements of this clause are met if—

(I) the requirements of subparagraphs (B) and (C) are met without regard to section 401(l), and

(II) the requirements of sections 401(a)(4) and 410(b) are met with respect to both the applicable defined contribution plan and defined benefit plan forming part of an eligible combined plan without regard to section 401(l).

(iii) Other plans and arrangements.—The requirements of this clause are met if the applicable defined contribution plan and defined benefit plan forming part of an eligible combined plan meet the requirements of sections 401(a)(4) and 410(b) without being combined with any other plan.

(3) Nondiscrimination requirements for qualified cash or deferred arrangement.—

(A) In general.—A qualified cash or deferred arrangement which is included in an applicable defined contribution plan forming part of an eligible combined plan shall be treated as meeting the requirements of section 401(k)(3)(A)(ii) if the requirements of paragraph (2)(C) are met with respect to such arrangement.

(B) Matching contributions.—In applying section 401(m)(11) to any matching contribution with respect to a contribution to which paragraph (2)(C) applies, the contribution requirement of paragraph (2)(C) and the notice requirements of paragraph (5)(B) shall be substituted for the requirements otherwise applicable under clauses (i) and (ii) of section 401(m)(11)(A).

(4) Satisfaction of top-heavy rules.—A defined benefit plan and applicable defined contribution plan forming part of an eligible combined plan for any plan year shall be treated as meeting the requirements of section 416 for the plan year.

(5) Automatic contribution arrangement.—For purposes of this subsection—

(A) In general.—A qualified cash or deferred arrangement shall be treated as an automatic contribution arrangement if the arrangement—

(i) provides that each employee eligible to participate in the arrangement is treated as having elected to have the employer make elective contributions in an amount equal to 4 percent of the employee's compensation unless the employee specifically elects not to have such contributions made or to have such contributions made at a different rate, and

(ii) meets the notice requirements under subparagraph (B).

(B) Notice requirements.—

(i) In general.—The requirements of this subparagraph are met if the requirements of clauses (ii) and (iii) are met.

(ii) Reasonable period to make election.—The requirements of this clause are met if each employee to whom subparagraph (A)(i) applies—

(I) receives a notice explaining the employee's right under the arrangement to elect not to have elective contributions made on the employee's behalf or to have the contributions made at a different rate, and

(II) has a reasonable period of time after receipt of such notice and before the first elective contribution is made to make such election.

(iii) Annual notice of rights and obligations.— The requirements of this clause are met if each employee eligible to participate in the arrangement is, within a reasonable period before any year, given notice of the employee's rights and obligations under the arrangement.

The requirements of clauses (i) and (ii) of section 401(k)(12)(D) shall be met with respect to the notices described in clauses (ii) and (iii) of this subparagraph.

(6) Coordination with other requirements.—

(A) Treatment of separate plans.—Section 414(k) shall not apply to an eligible combined plan.

(B) Reporting.—An eligible combined plan shall be treated as a single plan for purposes of sections 6058 and 6059.

(7) Applicable defined contribution plan.—For purposes of this subsection—

(A) In general.—The term "applicable defined contribution plan" means a defined contribution plan which includes a qualified cash or deferred arrangement.

(B) Qualified cash or deferred arrangement.—The term "qualified cash or deferred arrangement" has the meaning given such term by section 401(k)(2).

Recent Amendments to IRC §414

Worker, Retiree, and Employer Recovery Act of 2008 (Pub. L. No. 110-458), as follows:
- IRC §414(*l*)(2)(B)(i)(I) was amended by Act §101(d)(2)(E). Eff. as if included in Pub. L. No. 109-280, §114 [eff. for plan years beginning after 2007]. IRC §414(*l*)(2)(B)(i)(I) prior to amendment:

  (I) the amount determined under section 431(c)(6)(A)(i) in the case of a multiemployer plan (and the sum of the funding shortfall and target normal cost determined under section 430 in the case of any other plan), over
- IRC §414(w)(3)(B)–(D) was amended by Act §109(b)(4) by inserting "and" after the comma at the end of subpara. (B), striking subpara. (C), and redesignating subpara. (D) as (C). Eff. as if included in Pub. L. No. 109-280, §902 [eff. for plan years beginning after Dec. 31, 2007]. IRC §414(w)(3)(C) prior to amendment:

  (C) under which, in the absence of an investment election by the participant, contributions described in subparagraph (B) are invested in accordance with regulations prescribed by the Secretary of Labor under section 404(c)(5) of the Employee Retirement Income Security Act of 1974, and
- IRC §414(w)(5)(B)–(E) was amended by Act §109(b)(5) by striking "and" at the end of subpara. (B), substituting a comma for the period at the end of subpara. (C), and adding subpara. (D) and (E). Eff. as if included in Pub. L. No. 109-280, §902 [eff. for plan years beginning after Dec. 31, 2007].
- IRC §414(w)(6) was amended by Act §109(b)(6) by inserting "or for purposes of applying the limitation under section 402(g)(1)" before the period at the end. Eff. as if included in Pub. L. No. 109-280, §902 [eff. for plan years beginning after Dec. 31, 2007].
- IRC §414(x)(1) was amended by Act §109(c)(1) by adding the sentence at the end. Eff. as if included in Pub. L. No. 109-280, §903 [eff. for plan years beginning after Dec. 31, 2009].

Federal Housing Finance Regulatory Reform Act of 2008 (Pub. L. No. 110-289), as follows:
- IRC §414(*l*)(2)(G) was amended by Act Div. A, Title VI, §1604(b)(4) by striking "bridge bank" and inserting "bridge

IRC Sec. 414(x)(7)(B)

depository institution". This change was made everywhere "bridge bank" appeared, as the probable intent of Congress. Enacted July 30, 2008.

Heroes Earnings Assistance and Relief Tax Act of 2008 (Pub. L. No. 110-245), as follows:

- IRC §414(u) (heading) was amended by Act §105(b)(1)(B) by adding "and to Differential Wage Payments to Members on Active Duty" after "USERRA". Eff. for years beginning after 2008, see Act §105(b)(3).
- IRC §414(u)(9) was added by Act §104(b). Eff. with respect to deaths and disabilities occurring on or after Jan. 1, 2007, see Act §104(d)(1).
- IRC §414(u)(9) and (10) (former) were redesignated as (10) and (11), respectively. Eff. with respect to deaths and disabilities occurring on or after Jan. 1, 2007, see Act §104(d)(1).
- IRC §414(u)(12) was added by Act §105(b)(1). Eff. for years beginning after 2008, see Act §105(b)(3).
- **Other Provision.** Act §104(d)(2) provides:

    (2) Provisions relating to plan amendments.—
    (A) In general.—If this subparagraph applies to any plan or contract amendment, such plan or contract shall be treated as being operated in accordance with the terms of the plan during the period described in subparagraph (B)(iii).
    (B) Amendments to which subparagraph (A) applies.—
    (i) In general.—Subparagraph (A) shall apply to any amendment to any plan or annuity contract which is made—
    (I) pursuant to the amendments made by subsection (a) or pursuant to any regulation issued by the Secretary of the Treasury under subsection (a), and
    (II) on or before the last day of the first plan year beginning on or after January 1, 2010.
    In the case of a governmental plan (as defined in section 414(d) of the Internal Revenue Code of 1986), this clause shall be applied by substituting "2012" for "2010" in subclause (II).
    (ii) Conditions.—This paragraph shall not apply to any amendment unless—
    (I) the plan or contract is operated as if such plan or contract amendment were in effect for the period described in clause (iii), and
    (II) such plan or contract amendment applies retroactively for such period.
    (iii) Period described.—The period described in this clause is the period—
    (I) beginning on the effective date specified by the plan, and
    (II) ending on the date described in clause (i)(II) (or, if earlier, the date the plan or contract amendment is adopted).

- **Other Provision.** Act §105(c) provides:
    (c) Provisions Relating to Plan Amendments.—
    (1) In general.—If this subsection applies to any plan or annuity contract amendment, such plan or contract shall be treated as being operated in accordance with the terms of the plan or contract during the period described in paragraph (2)(B)(i).
    (2) Amendments to which section applies.—
    (A) In general.—This subsection shall apply to any amendment to any plan or annuity contract which is made—
    (i) pursuant to any amendment made by subsection (b)(1), and
    (ii) on or before the last day of the first plan year beginning on or after January 1, 2010.
    In the case of a governmental plan (as defined in section 414(d) of the Internal Revenue Code of 1986), this subparagraph shall be applied by substituting "2012" for "2010" in clause (ii).
    (B) Conditions.—This subsection shall not apply to any plan or annuity contract amendment unless—
    (i) during the period beginning on the date the amendment described in subparagraph (A)(i) takes effect and ending on the date described in subparagraph (A)(ii) (or, if earlier, the date the plan or contract amendment is adopted), the plan or contract is operated as if such plan or contract amendment were in effect, and
    (ii) such plan or contract amendment applies retroactively for such period.

U.S. Troop Readiness, Veterans' Care, Katrina Recovery, and Iraq Accountability Appropriations Act, 2007 (Pub. L. No. 110-28), as follows:

- IRC §414(f)(6)(A)(ii)(I), as amended by Pub. L. No. 109-280, §1106(b), was amended by Act §6611(a)(2)(A) by substituting "for each of the 3 plan years immediately preceding the first plan year for which the election under this paragraph is effective with respect to the plan," for "for each of the 3 plan years immediately before the date of enactment of the Pension Protection Act of 2006,". Eff. Aug. 17, 2006, as if included in §1106 of Pub. L. No. 109-280.
- IRC §414(f)(6)(B), as amended by Pub. L. No. 109-280, §1106(b), was amended by Act §6611(a)(2)(B) by substituting "starting with any plan year beginning on or after January 1, 1999, and ending before January 1, 2008, as designated by the plan in the election made under subparagraph (A)(ii)" for "starting with the first plan year ending after the date of the enactment of the Pension Protection Act of 2006". Eff. Aug. 17, 2006, as if included in §1106 of Pub. L. No. 109-280.
- IRC §414(f)(6)(E), as amended by Pub. L. No. 109-280, §1106(b), was amended by Act §6611(b)(2) by substituting "if it is a plan sponsored by an organization which is described in §501(c)(5) and exempt from tax under §501(a) and which was established in Chicago, Illinois, on August 12, 1881." for "if it is a plan—(i) that was established in Chicago, Illinois, on August 12, 1881; and (ii) sponsored by an organization described in §501(c)(5) and exempt from tax under §501(a)." Effective Aug. 17, 2006, as if included in §1106 of Pub. L. No. 109-280.
- IRC §414(f)(6)(F) was amended by Act §6611(a)(2)(C) by adding new subpara. (F). Eff. Aug. 17, 2006, as if included in §1106 of Pub. L. No. 109-280.

Pension Protection Act of 2006 (Pub. L. No. 109-280), as follows:

- IRC §414(d) was amended by Act §906(a)(1) by adding the new sentence at the end. Eff. for any year beginning on or after Aug. 17, 2006.
- IRC §414(f) was amended by Act §1106(b) by adding para. (6). Eff. Aug. 17, 2006.
- IRC §414(h)(2) was amended by Act §906(b)(1)(C) by inserting "or a governmental plan described in the last sentence of §414(d) (relating to plans of Indian tribal governments)," after "foregoing,". Eff. for any year beginning on or after Aug. 17, 2006.
- IRC §414(*l*)(2)(B)(i)(I) was amended by Act §114(c). Eff. Aug. 17, 2006 [for plan years beginning after 2007, eff. date as amended by Pub. L. No. 110-458, §101(d)(3)]. IRC §414(*l*)(2)(B)(i)(I) prior to amendment:
    (I) the amount determined under section 412(c)(7)(A)(i) with respect to the plan, over.
- IRC 414 was amended by Act §902(d)(1) by adding new subsec. (w). Eff. plan years beginning after Dec. 31, 2007.
- IRC 414 was amended by Act §903(a) by adding new subsec. (x). Eff. plan years beginning after Dec. 31, 2009.
- **Other Provision.** Act §865 provides:
    SEC. 865. GRANDFATHER RULE FOR CHURCH PLANS WHICH SELF-ANNUITIZE.
    (a) In General.—In the case of any plan year ending after the date of the enactment of this Act [August 17, 2006], annuity payments provided with respect to any account maintained for a participant or beneficiary under a qualified church plan shall not fail to satisfy the requirements of section 401(a)(9) of the Internal Revenue Code of 1986 merely because the payments are not made under an annuity contract purchased from an insurance company if such payments would not fail such requirements if provided with respect to a retirement income account described in section 403(b)(9) of such Code.
    (b) Qualified Church Plan.—For purposes of this section, the term "qualified church plan" means any money purchase pension plan described in section 401(a) of such Code which—
    (1) is a church plan (as defined in section 414(e) of such Code) with respect to which the election provided by section 410(d) of such Code has not been made, and
    (2) was in existence on April 17, 2002.

- **Sunset Provision.** Act §811, provides:
    SEC. 811. PENSIONS AND INDIVIDUAL RETIREMENT ARRANGEMENT PROVISIONS OF ECONOMIC GROWTH AND TAX RELIEF RECONCILIATION ACT OF 2001 MADE PERMANENT.

IRC Sec. 414(x)(7)(B)

Title IX of the Economic Growth and Tax Relief Reconciliation Act of 2001 [Pub. L. No. 107-16] shall not apply to the provisions of, and amendments made by, subtitles A through F [§§601–666] of title VI of such Act (relating to pension and individual retirement arrangement provisions).

Working Families Tax Relief Act of 2004 (Pub. L. No. 108-311), as follows:

• IRC §414(q)(7) was amended by Act §408(a)(15) by substituting "subsection" for "section". Eff. Oct. 4, 2004.

Job Creation and Worker Assistance Act of 2002 (Pub. L. No. 107-147), as follows:

• IRC §414(v)(2) was amended by Act §411(o)(3) by adding new subpara. (D). Eff. tax years beginning after Dec. 31, 2001, as if included in the provision of Pub. L. No. 107-16 to which it relates.

• IRC §414(v)(3)(A)(i) was amended by Act §411(o)(4) by substituting "§401(a)(30), 402(h), 403(b), 408, 415(c), and 457(b)(2) (determined without regard to §457(b)(3))" for "§402(g), 402(h), 403(b), 404(h), 408(k), 408(p), 415, or 457". Eff. tax years beginning after Dec. 31, 2001, as if included in the provision of Pub. L. No. 107-16 to which it relates.

• IRC §414(v)(3)(B) was amended by Act §411(o)(5) by substituting "§401(a)(4), 401(k)(3), 401(k)(11), 403(b)(12), 408(k), 410(b), or 416" for "§401(a)(4), 401(a)(26), 401(k)(3), 401(k)(11), 401(k)(12), 403(b)(12), 408(k), 408(p), 408B, 410(b), or 416". Eff. tax years beginning after Dec. 31, 2001, as if included in the provision of Pub. L. No. 107-16 to which it relates.

• IRC §414(v)(4)(B) was amended by Act §411(o)(6) by inserting before the period at the end ", except that a plan described in clause (i) of §410(b)(6)(C) shall not be treated as a plan of the employer until the expiration of the transition period with respect to such plan (as determined under clause (ii) of such section)". Eff. tax years beginning after Dec. 31, 2001, as if included in the provision of Pub. L. No. 107-16 to which it relates.

• IRC §414(v)(5) was amended by Act §411(o)(7)(A) by striking ", with respect to any plan year," after "means," in the matter preceding subpara. (A). Eff. tax years beginning after Dec. 31, 2001, as if included in the provision of Pub. L. No. 107-16 to which it relates.

• IRC §414(v)(5)(A) was amended by Act §411(o)(7)(B). Eff. tax years beginning after Dec. 31, 2001, as if included in the provision of Pub. L. No. 107-16 to which it relates. IRC §414(v)(5)(A) prior to amendment:

   (A) who has attained the age of 50 before the close of the plan year, and.

• IRC §414(v)(5)(B) was amended by Act §411(o)(7)(C) by substituting "plan (or other applicable) year" for "plan year". Eff. tax years beginning after Dec. 31, 2001, as if included in the provision of Pub. L. No. 107-16 to which it relates.

• IRC §414(v)(6)(C) was amended by Act §411(o)(8). Eff. tax years beginning after Dec. 31, 2001, as if included in the provision of Pub. L. No. 107-16 to which it relates. IRC §414(v)(6)(C) prior to amendment:

   (C) Exception for section 457 plans.—This subsection shall not apply to an applicable employer plan described in subparagraph (A)(iii) for any year to which section 457(b)(3) applies.

Economic Growth and Tax Relief Reconciliation Act of 2001 (Pub. L. No. 107-16), as follows:

• IRC §414(p)(10) was amended by Act §635(b) by substituting "§409(d), and §457(d)" for "and §409(d)". Eff. for transfers, distributions, and payments made after Dec. 31, 2001.

• IRC §414(p) was amended by Act §635(a) by substituting "certain other plans" for "governmental and church plans" in the heading, and by inserting "or an eligible deferred compensation plan (within the meaning of §457(b))" after "subsection (e))". Eff. for transfers, distributions, and payments made after Dec. 31, 2001.

• IRC §414 was amended by Act §635(c) by redesignating para. (12) as para. (13), and by adding new para. (12). Eff. for transfers, distributions, and payments made after Dec. 31, 2001.

• IRC §414 was amended by Act §631(a) by adding new subsec. (v) at the end. Eff. for contributions in tax years beginning after Dec. 31, 2001.

• **Sunset Provision.** Act §901, as amended by Pub. L. No. 111-312, §101(a)(1), provides the sunset rule below. But see Pub. L. No. 109-280, §811, and Pub. L. No. 111-148, §10909(c), as amended by Pub. L. No. 111-312, §101(b)(1).

   SEC. 901. SUNSET OF PROVISIONS OF ACT.

   (a) In general. All provisions of, and amendments made by, this Act shall not apply—

   (1) to taxable, plan, or limitation years beginning after December 31, 2012, or

   (2) in the case of title V, to estates of decedents dying, gifts made, or generation skipping transfers, after December 31, 2012.

   (b) Application of certain laws.—The Internal Revenue Code of 1986 and the Employee Retirement Income Security Act of 1974 shall be applied and administered to years, estates, gifts, and transfers described in subsection (a) as if the provisions and amendments described in subsection (a) had never been enacted.

SEC. 415. LIMITATIONS ON BENEFITS AND CONTRIBUTIONS UNDER QUALIFIED PLANS.

(a) General Rule.—

(1) Trusts.—A trust which is a part of a pension, profit-sharing, or stock bonus plan shall not constitute a qualified trust under section 401(a) if—

(A) in the case of a defined benefit plan, the plan provides for the payment of benefits with respect to a participant which exceeds the limitation of subsection (b), or

(B) in the case of a defined contribution plan, contributions and other additions under the plan with respect to any participant for any taxable year exceeds the limitation of subsection (c).

(C) [Repealed.]

(2) Section applies to certain annuities and accounts.—In the case of—

(A) an employee annuity plan described in section 403(a), or

(B) an annuity contract described in section 403(b), or

(C) a simplified employee pension described in section 408(k),

such a contract, plan, or pension shall not be considered to be described in section 403(a), 403(b), or 408(k), as the case may be, unless it satisfies the requirements of subparagraph (A) or subparagraph (B) of paragraph (1), whichever is appropriate, and has not been disqualified under subsection (g). In the case of an annuity contract described in section 403(b), the preceding sentence shall apply only to the portion of the annuity contract which exceeds the limitation of subsection (b) or the limitation of subsection (c), whichever is appropriate.

(b) Limitation for Defined Benefit Plans.—

(1) In general.—Benefits with respect to a participant exceed the limitation of this subsection if, when expressed as an annual benefit (within the meaning of paragraph (2)), such annual benefit is greater than the lesser of—

(A) 160,000, or

(B) 100 percent of the participant's average compensation for his high 3 years.

(2) Annual benefit.—

(A) In general.—For purposes of paragraph (1), the term "annual benefit" means a benefit payable annually in the form of a straight life annuity (with no ancillary benefits) under a plan to which employees do not contribute and under which no rollover contributions (as defined in sections 402(c), 403(a)(4), 403(b)(8), 408(d)(3), and 457(e)(16)) are made.

(B) Adjustment for certain other forms of benefit.—If the benefit under the plan is payable in any form other than the form described in subparagraph (A), or if the employees contribute to the plan or make rollover contributions (as defined in sections 402(c), 403(a)(4), 403(b)(8), 408(d)(3), and 457(e)(16)), the determinations as to whether the limitation described in paragraph (1) has been satisfied shall be made, in accordance with regulations prescribed by the Secretary, by adjusting such benefit so that it is equivalent to the benefit described in subparagraph (A). For purposes of this subparagraph, any ancillary benefit which is not directly related to retirement income benefits shall not be taken into account; and that portion of any joint and survivor annuity which constitutes a qualified joint and survivor annuity (as defined in section 417) shall not be taken into account.

(C) Adjustment to $160,000 limit where benefit begins before age 62—If the retirement income benefit under the plan begins before age 62, the determination as to whether the $160,000 limitation set forth in paragraph (1)(A) has been satisfied shall be made, in accordance with regulations prescribed by the Secretary, by reducing the limitation of paragraph (1)(A) so that such limitation (as so reduced) equals an annual benefit (beginning when such retirement income benefit begins) which is equivalent to a $160,000 annual benefit beginning at age 62.

(D) Adjustment to $160,000 limit where benefit begins after age 65.—If the retirement income benefit under the plan begins after age 65, the determination as to whether the $160,000 limitation set forth in paragraph (1)(A) has been satisfied shall be made, in accordance with regulations prescribed by the Secretary, by increasing the limitation of paragraph (1)(A) so that such limitation (as so increased) equals an annual benefit (beginning when such retirement income benefit begins) which is equivalent to a $160,000 annual benefit beginning at age 65.

(E) Limitation on certain assumptions.—

(i) For purposes of adjusting any limitation under subparagraph (C) and except as provided in clause (ii), for purposes of adjusting any benefit under subparagraph (B), the interest rate assumption shall not be less than the greater of 5 percent or the rate specified in the plan.

(ii) For purposes of adjusting any benefit under subparagraph (B) for any form of benefit subject to section 417(e)(3), the interest rate assumption shall not be less than the greatest of—

(I) 5.5 percent,

(II) the rate that provides a benefit of not more than 105 percent of the benefit that would be provided if the applicable interest rate (as defined in section 417(e)(3)) were the interest rate assumption, or

(III) the rate specified under the plan.

(iii) For purposes of adjusting any limitation under subparagraph (D), the interest rate assumption shall not be greater than the lesser of 5 percent or the rate specified in the plan.

(iv) For purposes of this subsection, no adjustments under subsection (d)(1) shall be taken into account before the year for which such adjustment first takes effect.

(v) For purposes of adjusting any benefit or limitation under subparagraph (B), (C), or (D), the mortality table used shall be the applicable mortality table (within the meaning of section 417(e)(3)(B)).

(vi) In the case of a plan maintained by an eligible employer (as defined in section 408(p)(2)(C)(i)), clause (ii) shall be applied without regard to subclause (II) thereof.

(F) [Repealed.]

(G) Special limitation for qualified police or firefighters.—In the case of a qualified participant, subparagraph (C) of this paragraph shall not apply.

(H) Qualified participant defined.—For purposes of subparagraph (G), the term "qualified participant" means a participant—

(i) in a defined benefit plan which is maintained by a State, Indian tribal government (as defined in section 7701(a)(40)), or any political subdivision thereof,

(ii) with respect to whom the period of service taken into account in determining the amount of the benefit under such defined benefit plan includes at least 15 years of service of the participant—

(I) as a full-time employee of any police department or fire department which is organized and operated by the State, Indian tribal government (as so defined), or any political subdivision maintaining such defined benefit plan to provide police protection, fire fighting services, or emergency medical services for any area within the jurisdiction of such State, Indian tribal government (as so defined), or any political subdivision, or

(II) as a member of the Armed Forces of the United States.

(I) Exemption for survivor and disability benefits provided under governmental plans.—Subparagraph (C) of this paragraph and paragraph (5) shall not apply to—

(i) income received from a governmental plan (as defined in section 414(d)) as a pension, annuity, or similar allowance as the result of the recipient becoming disabled by reason of personal injuries or sickness, or

(ii) amounts received from a governmental plan by the beneficiaries, survivors, or the estate of an employee as the result of the death of the employee.

(3) Average compensation for high 3 years.— For purposes of paragraph (1), a participant's high 3 years shall be the period of consecutive calendar years (not more than 3) during which the participant had the greatest aggregate compensation from the employer. In the case of an employee within the meaning of section 401(c)(1), the preceding sentence shall be applied by substituting for "compensation from the employer" the following "the participant's earned income (within the meaning of section 401(c)(2) but determined without regard to any exclusion under section 911)".

(4) Total annual benefit not in excess of $10,000.—Notwithstanding the preceding provisions of this subsection, the benefits payable with respect to a participant under any defined benefit plan shall be deemed not to exceed the limitation of this subsection if—

(A) the retirement benefits payable with respect to such participant under such plan and under all other defined benefit plans of the employer do not exceed $10,000 for the plan year, or for any prior plan year, and

(B) the employer has not at any time maintained a defined contribution plan in which the participant participated.

(5) Reduction for participation or service of less than 10 years.—

(A) Dollar limitation.—In the case of an employee who has less than 10 years of participation in a defined benefit plan, the limitation referred to in paragraph (1)(A) shall be the limitation determined under such paragraph (without regard to this paragraph) multiplied by a fraction—

(i) the numerator of which is the number of years (or part thereof) of participation in the defined benefit plan of the employer, and

(ii) the denominator of which is 10.

(B) Compensation and benefits limitations.—The provisions of subparagraph (A) shall apply to the limitation under paragraphs (1)(B) and (4), except that such subparagraph shall be applied with respect to years of service with an employer rather than years of participation in a plan.

(C) Limitation on reduction.—In no event shall subparagraph (A) or (B) reduce the limitations referred to in paragraphs (1) and (4) to an amount less than $\frac{1}{10}$ of such limitation (determined without regard to this paragraph).

(D) Application to changes in benefit structure.— To the extent provided in regulations, subparagraph (A) shall be applied separately with respect to each change in the benefit structure of a plan.

(6) Computation of benefits and contributions.—The computation of—

(A) benefits under a defined contribution plan, for purposes of section 401(a)(4),

(B) contributions made on behalf of a participant in a defined benefit plan, for purposes of section 401(a)(4), and

(C) contributions and benefits provided for a participant in a plan described in section 414(k), for purposes of this section

shall not be made on a basis inconsistent with regulations prescribed by the Secretary.

(7) Benefits under certain collectively bargained plans.—For a year, the limitation referred to in paragraph (1)(B) shall not apply to benefits with respect to a participant under a defined benefit plan (other than a multiemployer plan)—

(A) which is maintained for such year pursuant to a collective bargaining agreement between employee representatives and one or more employers,

(B) which, at all times during such year, has at least 100 participants,

(C) under which benefits are determined solely by reference to length of service, the particular years during which service was rendered, age at retirement, and date of retirement,

(D) which provide that an employee who has at least 4 years of service has a nonforfeitable right to 100 percent of his accrued benefit derived from employer contributions, and

(E) which requires, as a condition of participation in the plan, that an employee complete a period of not more than 60 consecutive days of service with the employer or employers maintaining the plan.

This paragraph shall not apply to a participant whose compensation for any 3 years during the 10-year period immediately preceding the year in which he

IRC Sec. 415(b)(7)(E)

separates from service exceeded the average compensation for such 3 years of all participants in such plan. This paragraph shall not apply to a participant for any period for which he is a participant under another plan to which this section applies which is maintained by an employer maintaining this plan. For any year for which the paragraph applies to benefits with respect to a participant, paragraph (1)(A) and subsection (d)(1)(A) shall be applied with respect to such participant by substituting one-half the amount otherwise applicable for such year under paragraph (1)(A) for "$160,000".

(8) Social Security retirement age defined.— For purposes of this subsection, the term "social security retirement age" means the age used as the retirement age under section 216(*l*)(2) of the Social Security Act, except that such section shall be applied—

(A) without regard to the age increase factor, and

(B) as if the early retirement age under section 216(*l*)(2) of such Act were 62.

(9) Special rule for commercial airline pilots.—

(A) In general.—Except as provided in subparagraph (B), in the case of any participant who is a commercial airline pilot, if, as of the time of the participant's retirement, regulations prescribed by the Federal Aviation Administration require an individual to separate from service as a commercial airline pilot after attaining any age occurring on or after age 60 and before age 62, paragraph (2)(C) shall be applied by substituting such age for age 62.

(B) Individuals who separate from service before age 60.—If a participant described in subparagraph (A) separates from service before age 60, the rules of paragraph (2)(C) shall apply.

(10) Special rule for State, Indian tribal, and local government plans.—

(A) Limitation to equal accrued benefit.—In the case of a plan maintained for its employees by any State or political subdivision thereof, or by any agency or instrumentality of the foregoing, or a governmental plan described in the last sentence of section 414(d) (relating to plans of Indian tribal governments), the limitation with respect to a qualified participant under this subsection shall not be less than the accrued benefit of the participant under the plan (determined without regard to any amendment of the plan made after October 14, 1987).

(B) Qualified participant.—For purposes of this paragraph, the term "qualified participant" means a participant who first became a participant in the plan maintained by the employer before January 1, 1990.

(C) Election.—

(i) In general.—This paragraph shall not apply to any plan unless each employer maintaining the plan elects before the close of the 1st plan year beginning after December 31, 1989, to have this subsection (other than paragraph (2)(G)) [applied].

(ii) Revocation of election.—An election under clause (i) may be revoked not later than the last day of the third plan year beginning after the date of the enactment of this clause. The revocation shall apply to all plan years to which the election applied and to all subsequent plan years. Any amount paid by a plan in a taxable year ending after the revocation shall be includible in income in such taxable year under the rules of this chapter in effect for such taxable year, except that, for purposes of applying the limitations imposed by this section, any portion of such amount which is attributable to any taxable year during which the election was in effect shall be treated as received in such taxable year.

(11) Special limitation rule for governmental and multiemployer plans.—In the case of a governmental plan (as defined in section 414(d)) or a multiemployer plan (as defined in section 414(f)), subparagraph (B) of paragraph (1) shall not apply. Subparagraph (B) of paragraph (1) shall not apply to a plan maintained by an organization described in section 3121(w)(3)(A) except with respect to highly compensated benefits. For purposes of this paragraph, the term "highly compensated benefits" means any benefits accrued for an employee in any year on or after the first year in which such employee is a highly compensated employee (as defined in section 414(q)) of the organization described in section 3121(w)(3)(A). For purposes of applying paragraph (1)(B) to highly compensated benefits, all benefits of the employee otherwise taken into account (without regard to this paragraph) shall be taken into account.

(c) Limitation for Defined Contribution Plans.—

(1) In general.—Contributions and other additions with respect to a participant exceed the limitation of this subsection if, when expressed as an annual addition (within the meaning of paragraph (2)) to the participant's account, such annual addition is greater than the lesser of—

(A) $40,000, or,

(B) 100 percent of the participant's compensation.

(2) Annual addition.—For purposes of paragraph (1), the term "annual addition" means the sum for any year of—

(A) employer contributions,

(B) the employee contributions, and

(C) forfeitures.

For the purposes of this paragraph, employee contributions under subparagraph (B) are determined without regard to any rollover contributions (as defined in sections 402(c), 403(a)(4), 403(b)(8), 408(d)(3), and 457(e)(16)) without regard to employee contributions to a simplified employee pension which are excludable from gross income under section 408(k)(6). Subparagraph (B) of paragraph (1) shall not apply to any contribution for medical benefits (within the meaning of section 419A(f)(2)) after separation from service which is treated as an annual addition.

(3) Participant's compensation.—For purposes of paragraph (1)—

(A) In general.—The term "participant's compensation" means the compensation of the participant from the employer for the year.

(B) Special rule for self-employed individuals.—In the case of an employee within the meaning of section 401(c)(1), subparagraph (A) shall be applied by substituting "the participant's earned income (within the meaning of section 401(c)(2) but determined without regard to any exclusion under section 911)" for "compensation of the participant from the employer".

(C) Special rules for permanent and total disability.—In the case of a participant in any defined contribution plan—

(i) who is permanently and totally disabled (as defined in section 22(e)(3)).

(ii) who is not a highly compensated employee (within the meaning of section 414(q)), and

(iii) with respect to whom the employer elects, at such time and in such manner as the Secretary may prescribe, to have this subparagraph apply,

the term "participant's compensation" means the compensation the participant would have received for the year if the participant was paid at the rate of compensation paid immediately before becoming permanently and totally disabled. This subparagraph shall apply only if contributions made with respect to amounts treated as compensation under this subparagraph are nonforfeitable when made. If a defined contribution plan provides for the continuation of contributions on behalf of all participants described in clause (i) for a fixed or determinable period, this subparagraph shall be applied without regard to clauses (ii) and (iii).

(D) Certain deferrals included.—The term "participant's compensation" shall include—

(i) any elective deferral (as defined in section 402(g)(3)), and

(ii) any amount which is contributed or deferred by the employer at the election of the employee and which is not includible in the gross income of the employee by reason of section 125, 132(f)(4), or 457.

(E) Annuity contracts.—In the case of an annuity contract described in section 403(b), the term "participant's compensation" means the participant's includible compensation determined under section 403(b)(3).

(4) [Repealed.]

(5) [Repealed.]

(6) Special rule for employee stock ownership plans.—If no more than one-third of the employer contributions to an employee stock ownership plan (as described in section 4975(e)(7)) for a year which are deductible under paragraph (9) of section 404(a) are allocated to highly compensated employees (within the meaning of section 414(q)), the limitations imposed by this section shall not apply to—

(A) forfeitures of employer securities (within the meaning of section 409) under such an employee stock ownership plan if such securities were acquired with the proceeds of a loan (as described in section 404(a)(9)(A)), or

(B) employer contributions to such an employee stock ownership plan which are deductible under section 404(a)(9)(B) and charged against the participant's account.

The amount of any qualified gratuitous transfer (as defined in section 664(g)(1)) allocated to a participant for any limitation year shall not exceed the limitations imposed by this section, but such amount shall not be taken into account in determining whether any other amount exceeds the limitations imposed by this section.

(7) Special rules relating to church plans.—

(A) Alternative contribution limitation.—

(i) In general.—Notwithstanding any other provision of this subsection, at the election of a participant who is an employee of a church or a convention orassociation of churches, including an organization described in section 414(e)(3)(B)(ii), contributions and other additions for an annuity contract or retirement income account described in section 403(b) with respect to such participant, when expressed as an annual addition to such participant's account, shall be treated as not exceeding the limitation of paragraph (1) if such annual addition is not in excess of $10,000.

(ii) $40,000 aggregate limitation.—The total amount of additions with respect to any participant which may be taken into account for purposes of this subparagraph for all years may not exceed $40,000.

(B) Number of years of service for duly ordained, commissioned, or licensed ministers or lay employees.—For purposes of this paragraph—

(i) all years of service by—

(I) a duly ordained, commissioned, or licensed minister of a church, or

IRC Sec. 415(c)(7)(B)(i)(I)

(II) a lay person,

as an employee of a church, a convention or association of churches, including an organization described in section 414(e)(3)(B)(ii), shall be considered as years of service for 1 employer, and

(ii) all amounts contributed for annuity contracts by each such church (or convention or association of churches) or such organization during such years for such minister or lay person shall be considered to have been contributed by 1 employer.

(C) Foreign missionaries—In the case of any individual described in subparagraph (B) performing services outside the United States, contributions and other additions for an annuity contract or retirement income account described in section 403(b) with respect to such employee, when expressed as an annual addition to such employee's account, shall not be treated as exceeding the limitation of paragraph (1) if such annual addition is not in excess of $3,000. This subparagraph shall not apply with respect to any taxable year to any individual whose adjusted gross income for such taxable year (determined separately and without regard to community property laws) exceeds $17,000.

(D) Annual addition.—For purposes of this paragraph, the term "annual addition" has the meaning given such term by paragraph (2).

(E) Church, convention or association of churches.—For purposes of this paragraph, the terms "church" and "convention or association of churches" have the same meaning as when used in section 414(e).

(d) Cost-of-Living Adjustments.

(1) **In general**.—The Secretary shall adjust annually—

(A) the $160,000 amount in subsection (b)(1)(A),

(B) in the case of a participant who separated from service, the amount taken into account under subsection (b)(1)(B), and

(C) the $40,000 amount in subsection (c)(1)(A),

for increases in the cost-of-living in accordance with regulations prescribed by the Secretary.

(2) **Method**.—The regulations prescribed under paragraph (1) shall provide for—

(A) an adjustment with respect to any calendar year based on the increase in the applicable index for the calendar quarter ending September 30 of the preceding calendar year over such index for the base period, and

(B) adjustment procedures which are similar to the procedures used to adjust benefit amounts under section 215(i)(2)(A) of the Social Security Act.

(3) **Base period**.—For purposes of paragraph (2)—

(A) $160,000 amount.—The base period taken into account for purposes of paragraph (1)(A) is the calendar quarter beginning July 1, 2001.

(B) Separations after December 31, 1994.—The base period taken into account for purposes of paragraph (1)(B) with respect to individuals separating from service with the employer after December 31, 1994, is the calendar quarter beginning July 1 of the calendar year preceding the calendar year in which such separation occurs.

(C) Separations before January 1, 1995.—The base period taken into account for purposes of paragraph (1)(B) with respect to individuals separating from service with the employer before January 1, 1995, is the calendar quarter beginning October 1 of the calendar year preceding the calendar year in which such separation occurs.

(D) $40,000 amount.—The base period taken into account for purposes of paragraph (1)(C) is the calendar quarter beginning July 1, 2001.

(4) Rounding.—

(A) $160,000 amount.—Any increase under subparagraph (A) of paragraph (1) which is not a multiple of $5,000 shall be rounded to the next lowest multiple of $5,000. This subparagraph shall also apply for purposes of any provision of this title that provides for adjustments in accordance with the method contained in this subsection, except to the extent provided in such provision.

(B) $40,000 amount.—Any increase under subparagraph (C) of paragraph (1) which is not a multiple of $1,000 shall be rounded to the next lowest multiple of $1,000.

(e) [Repealed.]

(f) Combining of Plans.—

(1) **In general**.—For purposes of applying the limitations of subsections (b) and (c)—

(A) all defined benefit plans (whether or not terminated) of an employer are to be treated as one defined benefit plan, and

(B) all defined contribution plans (whether or not terminated) of an employer are to be treated as one defined contribution plan.

(2) **Exception for multiemployer plans**.—Notwithstanding paragraph (1) and subsection (g), a multiemployer plan (as defined in section 414(f)) shall not be combined or aggregated—

(A) with any other plan which is not a multiemployer plan for purposes of applying subsection (b)(1)(B) to such other plan, or

(B) with any other multiemployer plan for purposes of applying the limitations established in this section.

(g) Aggregation of Plans.—Except as provided in subsection (f)(3), the Secretary, in applying the provisions of this section to benefits or contributions under more than one plan maintained by the same employer, and to any trust, contracts, accounts, or bonds referred to in subsection (a)(2), with respect to which the participant has the control required under section 414(b) or (c), as modified by subsection (h), shall, under regulations prescribed by the Secretary, disqualify one or more trusts, plans, contracts, accounts, or bonds, or any combination thereof until such benefits or contributions do not exceed the limitations contained in this section. In addition to taking into account such other factors as may be necessary to carry out the purposes of subsection (f), the regulations prescribed under this paragraph shall provide that no plan which has been terminated shall be disqualified until all other trusts, plans, contracts, accounts, or bonds have been disqualified.

(h) 50 Percent Control.—For purposes of applying subsections (b) and (c) of section 414 to this section, the phrase "more than 50 percent" shall be substituted for the phrase "at least 80 percent" each place it appears in section 1563(a)(1).

(i) Records Not Available for Past Periods.— Where for the period before January 1, 1976, or (if later) the first day of the first plan year of the plan, the records necessary for the application of this section are not available, the Secretary may by regulations prescribe alternative methods for determining the amounts to be taken into account for such period.

(j) Regulations; Definition of Year.—The Secretary shall prescribe such regulations as may be necessary to carry out the purposes of this section, including, but not limited to, regulations defining the term "year" for purposes of any provision of this section.

(k) Special Rules.—

(1) Defined benefit plan and defined contribution plan.—For purposes of this title, the term "defined contribution plan" or "defined benefit plan" means a defined contribution plan (within the meaning of section 414(i)) or a defined benefit plan (within the meaning of section 414(j)), whichever applies, which is—

(A) a plan described in section 401(a) which includes a trust which is exempt from tax under section 501(a),

(B) an annuity plan described in section 403(a),

(C) an annuity contract described in section 403(b) or

(D) a simplified employee pension.

(2) Contributions to provide cost-of-living protection under defined benefit plans.—

(A) In general.—In the case of a defined benefit plan which maintains a qualified cost-of-living arrangement—

(i) any contribution made directly by an employee under such an arrangement shall not be treated as an annual addition for purposes of subsection (c), and

(ii) any benefit under such arrangement which is allocable to an employer contribution which was transferred from a defined contribution plan and to which the requirements of subsection (c) were applied shall, for purposes of subsection (b), be treated as a benefit derived from an employee contribution (and subsection (c) shall not again apply to such contribution by reason of such transfer).

(B) Qualified cost-of-living arrangement defined.—For purposes of this paragraph, the term "qualified cost-of-living arrangement" means an arrangement under a defined benefit plan which—

(i) provides a cost-of-living adjustment to a benefit provided under such plan or a separate plan subject to the requirements of section 412, and

(ii) meets the requirements of subparagraphs (C), (D), (E), and (F) and such other requirements as the Secretary may prescribe.

(C) Determination of amount of benefit.—An arrangement meets the requirement of this subparagraph only if the cost-of-living adjustment of participants is based—

(i) on increases in the cost-of-living after the annuity starting date, and

(ii) on average cost-of-living increases determined by reference to 1 or more indexes prescribed by the Secretary, except that the arrangement may provide that the increase for any year will not be less than 3 percent of the retirement benefit (determined without regard to such increase).

(D) Arrangement elective; time for election.—An arrangement meets the requirements of this subparagraph only if it is elective, it is available under the same terms to all participants, and it provides that such election may at least be made in the year in which the participant—

(i) attains the earliest retirement age under the defined benefit plan (determined without regard to any requirement of separation from service), or

(ii) separates from service.

(E) Nondiscrimination requirements.—An arrangement shall not meet the requirements of this subparagraph if the Secretary finds that a pattern of discrimination exists with respect to participation.

(F) Special rules for key employees.—

(i) In general.—An arrangement shall not meet the requirements of this paragraph if any key employee is eligible to participate.

(ii) Key employee.—For purposes of this subparagraph, the term "key employee" has the meaning given such term by section 416(i)(1), except that in the case of a plan other than a top-heavy plan (within the meaning of section 416(g)), such term shall not include an individual who is a key employee solely by reason of section 416(i)(1)(A)(i).

(3) Repayments of cashouts under governmental plans.—In the case of any repayment of contributions (including interest thereon) to the governmental plan with respect to an amount previously refunded upon a forfeiture of service credit under the plan or under another governmental plan maintained by a State or local government employer within the same State, any such repayment shall not be taken into account for purposes of this section.

(4) Special rules for sections 403(b) and 408.—For purposes of this section, any annuity contract described in section 403(b) for the benefit of a participant shall be treated as a defined contribution plan maintained by each employer with respect to which the participant has the control required under subsection (b) or (c) of section 414 (as modified by subsection (h)). For purposes of this section, any contribution by an employer to a simplified employee pension plan for an individual for a taxable year shall be treated as an employer contribution to a defined contribution plan for such individual for such year.

(l) **Treatment of Certain Medical Benefits.**—

(1) In general.—For purposes of this section, contributions allocated to any individual medical benefit account which is part of a pension or annuity plan shall be treated as an annual addition to a defined contribution plan for purposes of subsection (c). Subparagraph (B) of subsection (c)(1) shall not apply to any amount treated as an annual addition under the preceding sentence.

(2) Individual medical benefit account.—For purposes of paragraph (1), the term "individual medical account" means any separate account—

(A) which is established for a participant under a pension or annuity plan, and

(B) from which benefits described in section 401(h) are payable solely to such participant, his spouse, or his dependents.

(m) Treatment of Qualified Governmental Excess Benefit Arrangements.—

(1) Governmental plan not affected.—In determining whether a governmental plan (as defined in section 414(d)) meets the requirements of this section, benefits provided under a qualified governmental excess benefit arrangement shall not be taken into account. Income accruing to a governmental plan (or to a trust that is maintained solely for the purpose of providing benefits under a qualified governmental excess benefit arrangement) in respect of a qualified governmental excess benefit arrangement shall constitute income derived from the exercise of an essential governmental function upon which such governmental plan (or trust) shall be exempt from tax under section 115.

(2) Taxation of participant.—For purposes of this chapter—

(A) the taxable year or years for which amounts in respect of a qualified governmental excess benefit arrangement are includible in gross income by a participant, and

(B) the treatment of such amounts when so includible by the participant, shall be determined as if such qualified governmental excess benefit arrangement were treated as a plan for the deferral of compensation which is maintained by a corporation not exempt from tax under this chapter and which does not meet the requirements for qualification under section 401.

(3) Qualified governmental excess benefit arrangement.—For purposes of this subsection, the term "qualified governmental excess benefit arrangement" means a portion of a governmental plan if—

(A) such portion is maintained solely for the purpose of providing to participants in the plan that part of the participant's annual benefit otherwise payable under the terms of the plan that exceeds the limitations on benefits imposed by this section,

(B) under such portion no election is provided at any time to the participant (directly or indirectly) to defer compensation, and

(C) benefits described in subparagraph (A) are not paid from a trust forming a part of such governmental plan unless such trust is maintained solely for the purpose of providing such benefits.

(n) Special Rules Relating to Purchase of Permissive Service Credit.—

(1) In general.—If a participant makes 1 or more contributions to a defined benefit governmental plan (within the meaning of section 414(d)) to purchase permissive service credit under such plan, then the requirements of this section shall be treated as met only if—

(A) the requirements of subsection (b) are met, determined by treating the accrued benefit derived from all such contributions as an annual benefit for purposes of subsection (b), or

(B) the requirements of subsection (c) are met, determined by treating all such contributions as annual additions for purposes of subsection (c).

(2) Application of limit.—For purposes of—

(A) applying paragraph (1)(A), the plan shall not fail to meet the reduced limit under subsection (b)(2)(C) solely by reason of this subsection, and

(B) applying paragraph (1)(B), the plan shall not fail to meet the percentage limitation under subsection (c)(1)(B) solely by reason of this subsection.

(3) Permissive service credit.—For purposes of this subsection—

(A) In general.—The term "permissive service credit" means service credit—

(i) recognized by the governmental plan for purposes of calculating a participant's benefit under the plan,

(ii) which such participant has not received under such governmental plan, and

(iii) which such participant may receive only by making a voluntary additional contribution, in an amount determined under such governmental plan, which does not exceed the amount necessary to fund the benefit attributable to such service credit.

Such term may include service credit for periods for which there is no performance of service, and, notwithstanding clause (ii), may include service credited in order to provide an increased benefit for service credit which a participant is receiving under the plan.

(B) Limitation on nonqualified service credit.—A plan shall fail to meet the requirements of this section if—

(i) more than 5 years of nonqualified service credit are taken into account for purposes of this subsection, or

(ii) any nonqualified service credit is taken into account under this subsection before the employee has at least 5 years of participation under the plan.

(C) Nonqualified service credit.—For purposes of subparagraph (B), the term "nonqualified service credit" means permissive service credit other than that allowed with respect to—

(i) service (including parental, medical, sabbatical, and similar leave) as an employee of the Government of the United States, any State or political subdivision thereof, or any agency or instrumentality of any of the foregoing (other than military service or service for credit which was obtained as a result of a repayment described in subsection (k)(3)),

(ii) service (including parental, medical, sabbatical, and similar leave) as an employee (other than as an employee described in clause (i)) of an educational organization described in section 170(b)(1)(A)(ii) which is a public, private, or sectarian school which provides elementary or secondary education (through grade 12), or a comparable level of education, as determined under the applicable law of the jurisdiction in which the service was performed,

(iii) service as an employee of an association of employees who are described in clause (i), or

(iv) military service (other than qualified military service under section 414(u)) recognized by such governmental plan. In the case of service described in clause (i), (ii), or (iii), such service will be nonqualified service if recognition of such service would cause a participant to receive a retirement benefit for the same service under more than one plan.

(D) Special rules for trustee-to-trustee transfers.—In the case of a trustee-to-trustee transfer to which section 403(b)(13)(A) or 457(e)(17)(A) applies (without regard to whether the transfer is made between plans maintained by the same employer)—

(i) the limitations of subparagraph (B) shall not apply in determining whether the transfer is for the purchase of permissive service credit, and

(ii) the distribution rules applicable under this title to the defined benefit governmental plan to which any amounts are so transferred shall apply to such amounts and any benefits attributable to such amounts.

Recent Amendments to §415

Worker, Retiree, and Employer Recovery Act of 2008 (Pub. L. No. 110-458), as follows:

- IRC §415(b)(2)(E)(v) was amended by Act §103(b)(2)(B)(i). Eff. generally for years beginning after Dec. 31, 2008. **[Note exception:** Pub. L. No. 110-458, §103(b)(2)(B)(ii)(II) provides that "A plan sponsor may elect to have the amendment made by clause [103(b)(2)(B)](i) apply to any year beginning after December 31, 2007, and before January 1, 2009, or to any portion of any such year."] IRC §415(b)(2)(E)(v) prior to amendment:

    (v) purposes of adjusting any benefit or limitation under subparagraph (B), (C), or (D), the mortality table used shall be the table prescribed by the Secretary. Such table shall be based on the prevailing commissioners' standard table (described in section 807(d)(5)(A)) used to determine reserves for group annuity contracts issued on the date the adjustment is being made (without regard to any other subparagraph of section 807(d)(5)).

- IRC §415(b)(2)(E)(vi) was added by Act §122(a). Eff. for years beginning after Dec. 31, 2008.
- IRC §415(f) was amended by Act §108(g) by striking para. (2) and redesignating para. (3) as para. (2). Eff. as if included in Pub. L. No. 109-280, §832 [eff. for years beginning after Dec. 31, 2005]. IRC §415(f)(2) prior to being stricken:

    (2) Annual compensation taken into account for defined benefit plans.—If the employer has more than one defined benefit plan—

    (A) subsection (b)(1)(B) shall be applied separately with respect to each such plan, but

    (B) in applying subsection (b)(1)(B) to the aggregate of such defined benefit plans for purposes of this subsection, the high 3 years of compensation taken into account shall be the period of consecutive calendar years (not more than 3) during which the individual had the greatest aggregate compensation from the employer.

Pension Protection Act 2006 (Pub. L. No. 109-280), as follows:

- IRC §415(b)(2)(E)(ii) was amended by Act §303(a). Eff. for distributions made in years beginning after Dec. 31, 2005. IRC §415(b)(2)(E)(ii) prior to amendment:

    (ii) For purposes of adjusting any benefit under subparagraph (B) for any form of benefit subject to section 417(e)(3), the applicable interest rate (as defined in section 417(e)(3)) shall be substituted for "5 percent" in clause (i), except that in the case of plan years beginning in 2004 or 2005, "5.5 percent" shall be substituted for "5 percent" in clause (i).

• IRC §415(b)(2)(H)(i) was amended by Act §906(b)(1)(A)(i) by substituting "State, Indian tribal government (as defined in §7701(a)(40)), or any political subdivision" for "State or political subdivision". Eff. for any year beginning on or after Aug. 17, 2006.

• IRC §415(b)(2)(H)(ii)(I) was amended by Act §906(b)(1)(A)(ii) by substituting "State, Indian tribal government (as so defined), or any political subdivision" for "State or political subdivision" each place it appeared. Eff. for any year beginning on or after Aug. 17, 2006.

• IRC §415(b)(3) was amended by Act §832(a) by striking "both was an active participant in the plan and" after "during which the participant". Eff. for years beginning after Dec. 31, 2005.

• IRC §415(b)[(10)] was amended by Act §906(b)(1)(B)(ii) by substituting in the heading "special rule for State, Indian tribal, and" for "Special rule for State and". [*Ed. Note*: Act §906(b)(1)(B)(ii) instructed the amendment to be made to IRC §415(b)(1).] Eff. any year beginning on or after Aug. 17, 2006.

• IRC §415(b)(10)(A) was amended by Act §906(b)(1)(B)(i) by inserting "or a governmental plan described in the last sentence of §414(d) (relating to plans of Indian tribal governments)," after "foregoing,". Eff. any year beginning on or after Aug. 17, 2006.

• IRC §415(b)(11) was amended by Act §867(a) by adding three sentences to the end. Eff. years beginning after Dec. 31, 2006.

• IRC §415(n)(1) was amended by Act §821(a)(1) by substituting "a participant" for "an employee". Eff. for permissive service credit contributions made in years beginning after Dec. 31, 1997, as if included in the amendments made by Pub. L. No. 105-34, §1526.

• IRC §415(n)(3)(A) was amended by Act §821(a)(2) by adding a new flush sentence at the end. Eff. for permissive service credit contributions made in years beginning after Dec. 31, 1997, as if included in the amendments made by Pub. L. No. 105-34, §1526.

• IRC §415(n)(3)(B) was amended by Act §821(c)(1) by striking "permissive service credit attributable to nonqualified service" each place it appeared in subpara. (B) and inserting "nonqualified service credit". Eff. for permissive service credit contributions made in years beginning after Dec. 31, 1997, as if included in the amendments made by Pub. L. No. 105-34, §1526.

• IRC §415(n)(3)(C) was amended by Act §821(c)(2) by substituting "(C) Nonqualified service credit.—For purposes of subparagraph (B), the term 'nonqualified service credit' means permissive service credit other than that allowed with respect to—" for "(C) Nonqualified service.—For purposes of subparagraph (B), the term 'nonqualified service' means service for which permissive service credit is allowed other than—". Eff. for permissive service credit contributions made in years beginning after Dec. 31, 1997, as if included in the amendments made by Pub. L. No. 105-34, §1526.

• IRC §415(n)(3)(C)(ii) was amended by Act §821(c)(3) by substituting "elementary or secondary education (through grade 12), or a comparable level of education, as determined under the applicable law of the jurisdiction in which the service was performed" for "elementary or secondary education (through grade 12), as determined under State law". Eff. for permissive service credit contributions made in years beginning after Dec. 31, 1997, as if included in the amendments made by Pub. L. No. 105-34, §1526.

• IRC §415(n)(3) was amended by Act §821(b) by adding new subpara. (D). Eff. for trustee-to-trustee transfers after Dec. 31, 2001, as if included in the amendments made by Pub. L. No. 107-16, §647.

• **Sunset Provision.** Act §811, provides:

> **SEC. 811. PENSIONS AND INDIVIDUAL RETIREMENT ARRANGEMENT PROVISIONS OF ECONOMIC GROWTH AND TAX RELIEF RECONCILIATION ACT OF 2001 MADE PERMANENT.**
>
> Title IX of the Economic Growth and Tax Relief Reconciliation Act of 2001 [Pub. L. No. 107-16] shall not apply to the provisions of, and amendments made by, subtitles A through F [§§601–666] of title VI of such Act (relating to pension and individual retirement arrangement provisions).

Gulf Opportunity Zone Act of 2005 (Pub. L. No. 109-135), as follows:

• IRC §415(c)(7)(C) was amended by Act §407(b) by replacing "the greater of "$3,000" and all that follows with "$3,000. This subparagraph shall not apply with respect to any taxable year to any individual whose adjusted gross income for such taxable year (determined separately and without regard to community property laws) exceeds $17,000.". Eff. tax years beginning after Dec. 31, 2001, as if included in the provision of Pub. L. No. 107-16 to which it relates. IRC §415(c)(7)(C) prior to amendment:

> (C) Foreign missionaries.—In the case of any individual described in subparagraph (B) performing services outside the United States, contributions and other additions for an annuity contract or retirement income account described in section 403(b) with respect to such employee, when expressed as an annual addition to such employee's account, shall not be treated as exceeding the limitation of paragraph (1) if such annual addition is not in excess of the greater of $3,000 or the employee's includible compensation determined under section 403(b)(3).

• IRC §415(*l*)(1) was amended by Act §412(y) by substituting "individual medical benefit account" for "individual medical account". Eff. Dec. 21, 2005.

• IRC §415(n)(3)(C) was amended by Act §412(z) in the material following cl. (iv) by substituting "clause" for "clauses". Effective Dec. 21, 2005.

Working Families Tax Relief Act of 2004 (Pub. L. No. 108-311), as follows:

• IRC §415(c)(7)(C) was amended by Act §408(a)(17) by substituting "subparagraph (B)" for "subparagraph (D)". Eff. Oct. 4, 2004.

• IRC §415(d)(4)(A) was amended by Act §404(b)(2) by adding the new sentence at the end. Eff. years beginning after Dec. 31, 2001, as if included in the provision of Pub. L. No. 107-16 to which it relates.

Pension Funding Equity Act of 2004 (Pub. L. No. 108-218), as follows:

• IRC §415(b)(2)(E)(ii) was amended by Act §101(b)(4) by adding ", except that in the case of plan years beginning in 2004 or 2005, '5.5 percent' shall be substituted for '5 percent' in clause (i)" before the period at the end. Eff. generally for plan years beginning after Dec. 31, 2003. [*Ed. Note:* see Act §101(d)(3) for a special rule.]

Job Creation and Worker Assistance Act of 2002 (Pub. L. No. 107-147), as follows:

• IRC §415(c)(7) was amended by Act §411(p)(4). Eff. years beginning after Dec. 31, 2001, as if included in the provision of Pub. L. No. 107-16 to which it relates. IRC §415(c)(7) prior to amendment:

> (7) Certain contributions by church plans not treated as exceeding limit.—
>
> (A) In general.—Notwithstanding any other provision of this subsection, at the election of a participant who is an employee of a church or a convention or association of churches, including an organization described in section 414(e)(3)(B)(ii), contributions and other additions for an annuity contract or retirement income account described in section 403(b) with respect to such participant, when expressed as an annual addition to such participant's account, shall be treated as not exceeding the limitation of paragraph (1) if such annual addition is not in excess of $10,000.
>
> (B) $40,000 Aggregate limitation.—The total amount of additions with respect to any participant which may be taken into account for purposes of this subparagraph for all years may not exceed $40,000.
>
> (C) Annual addition.—For purposes of this paragraph, the term 'annual addition' has the meaning given such term by paragraph (2).

Economic Growth and Tax Relief Reconciliation Act of 2001 (Pub. L. No. 107-16), as follows:

• IRC §415(a)(2) was amended by Act §632(a)(3)(C) by striking ", whichever is appropriate, and the amount of the contribution for such portion shall reduce the exclusion allowance as provided in §403(b)(2)" at the end. Eff. years beginning after Dec. 31, 2001.

• IRC §415(b)(1)(A) was amended by Act §611(a)(1)(A) by substituting "$160,000" for "$90,000". Eff. years ending after Dec. 31, 2001. [*Ed. Note:* see Act §611(I)(3) for a special rule.]

- IRC §415(b)(2)(A) was amended by Act §641(e)(9) by substituting "403(b)(8), 408(d)(3), and 457(e)(16)" for "and 408(d)(3)". Eff. generally for distributions after Dec. 31, 2001. [*Ed. Note:* see Act §641(f)(3) for a special rule.]
- IRC §415(b)(2)(B) was amended by Act §641(e)(9) by substituting "403(b)(8), 408(d)(3), and 457(e)(16)" for "and 408(d)(3)". Eff. generally for distributions after Dec. 31, 2001. [*Ed. Note:* see Act §641(f)(3) for a special rule.]
- IRC §415(b)(2)(C) was amended by Act §611(a)(1)(B) by substituting "$160,000" for "$90,000" in the heading and the text. Eff. years ending after Dec. 31, 2001. [*Ed. Note:* see Act §611(i)(3) for a special rule.]
- IRC §415(b)(2)(C) was amended by Act §611(a)(2) by substituting "age 62" for "the social security retirement age" each place it appeared in the heading and text, and by striking the second sentence. Eff. years ending after Dec. 31, 2001. [*Ed. Note:* see Act §611(i)(3) for a special rule.] IRC §415(b)(2)(C), second sentence, prior to being stricken:

    The reduction under this subparagraph shall be made in such manner as the Secretary may prescribe which is consistent with the reduction for old-age insurance benefits commencing before the social security retirement age under the Social Security Act.

- IRC §415(b)(2)(D) was amended by Act §611(a)(1)(B) by substituting "$160,000" for "$90,000" in the heading and the text. Eff. years ending after Dec. 31, 2001. [*Ed. Note:* see Act §611(i)(3) for a special rule.]
- IRC §415(b)(2)(D) was amended by Act §611(a)(3) by substituting "age 65" for "the social security retirement age" each place it appeared in the heading and text. Eff. years ending after Dec. 31, 2001. [*Ed. Note:* see Act §611(i)(3) for a special rule.]
- IRC §415(b)(2)(F) was amended by Act §611(a)(5)(A). Eff. years ending after Dec. 31, 2001. IRC §415(b)(2)(F) prior to being stricken:

    (F) Plans maintained by governments and tax exempt organizations.—In the case of a governmental plan (within the meaning of section 414(d)), a plan maintained by an organization (other than a governmental unit) exempt from tax under this subtitle, or a qualified merchant marine plan—
    (i) subparagraph (C) shall be applied—
    (I) by substituting "age 62" for "social security retirement age" each place it appears, and
    (II) as if the last sentence thereof read as follows: "The reduction under the subparagraph shall not reduce the limitation of paragraph (1)(A) below (i) $75,000 if the benefit begins at or after age 55, or (ii) if the benefit begins before age 55, the equivalent of the $75,000 limitation for age 55.", and
    (ii) subparagraph (D) shall be applied by substituting "age 65" for "social security retirement age" each place it appears. For purposes of this subparagraph, the term "qualified merchant marine plan" means a plan in existence on January 1, 1986, the participants in which are merchant marine officers holding licenses issued by the Secretary of Transportation under title 46, United States Code.

- IRC §415(b)(7) was amended by Act §611(a)(1)(C) by substituting "one-half the amount otherwise applicable for such year under paragraph (1)(A) for '$160,000' " for "the greater of $68,212 or one-half the amount otherwise applicable for such year under paragraph (1)(A) for '$90,000' ". Eff. years ending after Dec. 31, 2001. [*Ed. Note:* see Act §611(i)(3) for a special rule.]
- IRC §415(b)(7) was amended by Act §654(a)(2) by inserting "(other than a multiemployer plan)" after "defined benefit plan". Eff. years beginning after Dec. 31, 2001.
- IRC §415(b)(9) was amended by Act §611(a)(5)(B). Eff. years ending after Dec. 31, 2001. [*Ed. Note:* see Act §611(i)(3) for a special rule.] IRC §415(b)(9) prior to amendment:

    (9) Special Rule for Commercial Airline Pilots.—
    (A) In general.—Except as provided in subparagraph (B), in the case of any participant who is a commercial airline pilot—
    (i) the rule of paragraph (2)(F)(i)(II) shall apply, and
    (ii) if, as of the time of the participant's retirement, regulations prescribed by the Federal Aviation Administration require an individual to separate from service as a commercial airline pilot after attaining any age occurring on or after age 60 and before the social security retirement age, paragraph

    (2)(C) (after application of clause (i)) shall be applied by substituting such age for the social security retirement age.
    (B) Individuals who separate from service before age 60.—If a participant described in subparagraph (A) separates from service before age 60, the rules of paragraph (2)(F) shall apply.

- IRC §415(b)(10)(C)(i) was amended by Act §611(a)(5)(C) by striking "applied without regard to paragraph (2)(F)" after "(other than paragraph (2)(G))". Eff. years ending after Dec. 31, 2001. [*Ed. Note:* see Act §611(i)(3) for a special rule.]
- IRC §415(b)(11) was amended by Act §654(a)(1). Eff. years beginning after Dec. 31, 2001. IRC §415(b)(11) prior to amendment:

    (11) Joint Special limitation rule for governmental plans.—In the case of a governmental plan (as defined in section 414(d)), subparagraph (B) of paragraph (1) shall not apply.

- IRC §415(c)(1)(A) was amended by Act §611(b)(1) by substituting "$40,000" for "$30,000". Eff. years beginning after Dec. 31, 2001. [*Ed. Note:* see Act §611(i)(3) for a special rule.]
- IRC §415(c)(1)(B) was amended by Act §632(a)(1) by substituting "100 percent" for "25 percent". Eff. years beginning after Dec. 31, 2001.
- IRC §415(c)(2) was amended by Act §641(e)(10) by substituting "408(d)(3), and 457(e)(16)" for "and 408(d)(3)". Eff. generally for distributions after Dec. 31, 2001. [*Ed. Note:* see Act §641(f)(3) for a special rule.]
- IRC §415(c)(3) was amended by Act §632(a)(3)(D) by adding new subpara. (E). Eff. years beginning after Dec. 31, 2001.
- IRC §415(c) was amended by Act §632(a)(3)(E) by striking para. (4). Eff. years beginning after Dec. 31, 2001. IRC §415(c)(4) prior to being stricken:

    (4) Special election for section 403(b) contracts purchased by educational organizations, hospitals, home health service agencies, and certain churches, etc.—
    (A) In the case of amounts contributed for an annuity contract described in section 403(b) for the year in which occurs a participant's separation from the service with an educational organization, a hospital, a home health service agency, a health and welfare service agency, or a church, convention or association of churches, or an organization described in section 414(e)(3)(B)(ii), at the election of the participant there is substituted for the amount specified in paragraph (1)(B) the amount of the exclusion allowance which would be determined under section 403(b)(2) (without regard to this section) for the participant's taxable year in which such separation occurs if the participant's years of service were computed only by taking into account his service for the employer (as determined for purposes of section 403(b)(2)) during the period of years (not exceeding ten) ending on the date of such separation.
    (B) In the case of amounts contributed for an annuity contract described in section 403(b) for any year in the case of a participant who is an employee of an educational organization, a hospital, a home health service agency, a health and welfare service agency, or a church, convention or association of churches, or an organization described in section 414(e)(3)(B)(ii), at the election of the participant there is substituted for the amount specified in paragraph (1)(B) the least of—
    (i) 25 percent of the participant's includible compensation (as defined in section 403(b)(3)) plus $4,000,
    (ii) the amount of the exclusion allowance determined for the year under section 403(b)(2), or
    (iii) $15,000.
    (C) In the case of amounts contributed for an annuity contract described in section 403(b) for any year for a participant who is an employee of an educational organization, a hospital, a home health service agency, a health and welfare service agency, or a church, convention or association of churches, or an organization described in section 414(e)(3)(B)(ii), at the election of the participant the provisions of section 403(b)(2)(A) shall not apply.
    (D)(i) The provisions of this paragraph apply only if the participant elects its application at the time and in the manner provided under regulations prescribed by the Secretary. Not more than one election may be made under subparagraph (A)

IRC Sec. 415(n)(3)(D)(ii)

by any participant. A participant who elects to have the provisions of subparagraph (A), (B), or (C) of this paragraph apply to him may not elect to have any other subparagraph of this paragraph apply to him. Any election made under this paragraph is irrevocable.

(ii) For purposes of this paragraph the term "educational organization" means an educational organization described in section 170(b)(1)(A)(ii).

(iii) For purposes of this paragraph the term "home health service agency" means an organization described in subsection 501(c)(3) which is exempt from tax under section 501(a) and which has been determined by the Secretary of Health, Education, and Welfare to be a home health agency (as defined in section 1861(o) of the Social Security Act).

(iv) For purposes of this paragraph, the terms "church" and "convention or association of churches" have the same meaning as when used in section 414(e).

• IRC §415(c) was amended by Act §632(a)(3)(F) by amending para. (7). Eff. years beginning after Dec. 31, 2001. IRC §415(c) prior to amendment:

(7) Certain contributions by church plans not treated as exceeding limits.—

(A) Alternative exclusion allowance.—Any contribution or addition with respect to any participant, when expressed as an annual addition, which is allocable to the application of section 403(b)(2)(D) to such participant for such year, shall be treated as not exceeding the limitations of paragraph (1).

(B) Contributions not in excess of $40,000 ($10,000 per year).—

(i) In general.—Notwithstanding any other provision of this subsection, at the election of a participant who is an employee of a church, a convention or association of churches, including an organization described in section 414(e)(3)(B)(ii), contributions and other additions for an annuity contract or retirement income account described in section 403(b) with respect to such participant, when expressed as an annual addition to such participant's account, shall be treated as not exceeding the limitation of paragraph (1) if such annual addition is not in excess of $10,000.

(ii) $40,000 aggregate limitation.—The total amount of additions with respect to any participant which may be taken into account for purposes of this subparagraph for all years may not exceed $40,000.

(iii) No election if paragraph (4)(A) election made.—No election may be made under this subparagraph for any year if an election is made under paragraph (4)(A) for such year.

(C) Annual addition.—For purposes of this paragraph, the term "annual addition" has the meaning given such term by paragraph (2).

• IRC §415(d)(1)(A) was amended by Act §611(a)(4)(A) by substituting "$160,000" for "$90,000". Eff. years ending after Dec. 31, 2001.

• IRC §415(d)(1)(C) was amended by Act §611(b)(2)(A) by substituting "$40,000" for "$30,000". Eff. years beginning after Dec. 31, 2001. [Ed. Note: see Act §611(i)(3) for a special rule.]

• IRC §415(d)(3)(A) was amended by Act §611(a)(4)(B) by substituting "$160,000" for "$90,000" in the heading, and by substituting "July 1, 2001" for "October 1, 1986" in the text. Eff. years ending after Dec. 31, 2001.

• IRC §415(d)(3)(D) was amended by Act §611(b)(2)(B) by substituting "$40,000" for "$30,000" in the heading, by and substituting "July 1, 2001" for "October 1, 1993" in the text. Eff. years beginning after Dec. 31, 2001. [Ed. Note: see Act §611(i)(3) for a special rule.]

• IRC §415(d)(4) was amended by Act §611(h). Eff. years beginning after Dec. 31, 2001. See Act §611(i)(3) for a special rule. IRC §415(d)(4) prior to amendment:

(4) Rounding.—Any increase under subparagraph (A) or (C) of paragraph (1) which is not a multiple of $5,000 shall be rounded to the next lowest multiple of $5,000.

• IRC §415(f)(3) was amended by Act §654(b)(1) by adding para. (3). Eff. years beginning after Dec. 31, 2001.

• IRC §415(g) was amended by Act §654(b)(2) by substituting "Except as provided in subsection (f)(3), the Secretary" for "The Secretary". Eff. years beginning after Dec. 31, 2001.

• IRC §415(k)(4) was amended by Act §632(b)(1) by adding para. (4). Eff. generally for limitation years beginning after Dec. 31, 1999. [Ed. Note: see Act §632(b)(2)–(3) for special rules.]

• **Sunset Provision.** Act §901, as amended by Pub. L. No. 111-312, §101(a)(1), provides the sunset rule below. But see Pub. L. No. 109-280, §811, and Pub. L. No. 111-148, §10909(c), as amended by Pub. L. No. 111-312, §101(b)(1).

SEC. 901. SUNSET OF PROVISIONS OF ACT.

(a) In general. All provisions of, and amendments made by, this Act shall not apply—

(1) to taxable, plan, or limitation years beginning after December 31, 2012, or

(2) in the case of title V, to estates of decedents dying, gifts made, or generation skipping transfers, after December 31, 2012.

(b) Application of certain laws.—The Internal Revenue Code of 1986 and the Employee Retirement Income Security Act of 1974 shall be applied and administered to years, estates, gifts, and transfers described in subsection (a) as if the provisions and amendments described in subsection (a) had never been enacted.

SEC. 416. SPECIAL RULES FOR TOP-HEAVY PLANS.

(a) General Rule.—A trust shall not constitute a qualified trust under section 401(a) for any plan year if the plan of which it is a part is a top-heavy plan for such plan year unless such plan meets—

(1) the vesting requirements of subsection (b), and

(2) the minimum benefit requirements of subsection (c).

(b) Vesting Requirements.—

(1) **In general.**—A plan satisfies the requirements of this subsection if it satisfies the requirements of either of the following subparagraphs:

(A) 3-year vesting.—A plan satisfies the requirements of this subparagraph if an employee who has completed at least 3 years of service with the employer or employers maintaining the plan has a nonforfeitable right to 100 percent of his accrued benefit derived from employer contributions.

(B) 6-year graded vesting.—A plan satisfies the requirements of this subparagraph if an employee has a nonforfeitable right to a percentage of his accrued benefit derived from employer contributions determined under the following table:

Years of service:	The nonforfeitable percentage is:
2	20
3	40
4	60
5	80
6 or more	100

(2) **Certain rules made applicable.**—Except to the extent inconsistent with the provisions of this subsection, the rules of section 411 shall apply for purposes of this subsection.

(c) Plan Must Provide Minimum Benefits.—

(1) **Defined benefit plans.**—

(A) In general.—A defined benefit plan meets the requirements of this subsection if the accrued benefit derived from employer contributions of each participant who is a non-key employee, when expressed as an annual retirement benefit, is not less than the applicable percentage of the participant's average compensation for years in the testing period.

(B) Applicable percentage.—For purposes of subparagraph (A), the term "applicable percentage" means the lesser of—

(i) 2 percent multiplied by the number of years of service with the employer, or

(ii) 20 percent.

(C) Years of service.—For purposes of this paragraph—

(i) In general.—Except as provided in clause (ii) or (iii), years of service shall be determined under the rules of paragraphs (4), (5), and (6) of section 411(a).

(ii) Exception for years during which plan was not top-heavy.—A year of service with the employer shall not be taken into account under this paragraph if—

(I) the plan was not a top-heavy plan for any plan year ending during such year of service, or

(II) such year of service was completed in a plan year beginning before January 1, 1984.

(iii) Exception for plan under which no key employee (or former key employee) benefits for plan year.—For purposes of determining an employee's years of service with the employer, any service with the employer shall be disregarded to the extent that such service occurs during a plan year when the plan benefits (within the meaning of section 410(b)) no key employee or former key employee.

(D) Average compensation for high 5 years.—For purposes of this paragraph—

(i) In general.—A participant's testing period shall be the period of consecutive years (not exceeding 5) during which the participant had the greatest aggregate compensation from the employer.

(ii) Year must be included in year of service.—The years taken into account under clause (i) shall be properly adjusted for years not included in a year of service.

(iii) Certain years not taken into account.—Except to the extent provided in the plan, a year shall not be taken into account under clause (i) if—

(I) such year ends in a plan year beginning before January 1, 1984, or

(II) such year begins after the close of the last year in which the plan was a top-heavy plan.

(E) Annual retirement benefit.—For purposes of this paragraph, the term "annual retirement benefit" means a benefit payable annually in the form of a single life annuity (with no ancillary benefits) beginning at the normal retirement age under the plan.

(2) Defined contribution plans.—

(A) In general.—A defined contribution plan meets the requirements of the subsection if the employer contribution for the year for each participant who is a non-key employee is not less than 3 percent of such participant's compensation (within the meaning of section 415). Employer matching contributions (as defined in section 401(m)(4)(A)) shall be taken into account for purposes of this subparagraph (and any reduction under this sentence shall not be taken into account in determining whether section 401(k)(4)(A) applies).

(B) Special rule where maximum contribution less than 3 percent.—

(i) In general.—The percentage referred to in subparagraph (A) for any year shall not exceed the percentage at which contributions are made (or required to be made) under the plan for the year for the key employee for whom such percentage is the highest for the year.

(ii) Treatment of aggregation groups.—

(I) For purposes of this subparagraph, all defined contribution plans required to be included in an aggregation group under subsection (g)(2)(A)(i) shall be treated as one plan.

(II) This subparagraph shall not apply to any plan required to be included in an aggregation group if such plan enables a defined benefit plan required to be included in such group to meet the requirements of section 401(a)(4) or 410.

(d) [Repealed.]

(e) Plan Must Meet Requirements Without Taking Into Account Social Security and Similar Contributions and Benefits.—A top-heavy plan shall not be treated as meeting the requirement of subsection (b) or (c) unless such plan meets such requirement without taking into account contributions or benefits under chapter 2 (relating to tax on self-employment income), chapter 21 (relating to Federal Insurance Contributions Act), title II of the Social Security Act, or any other Federal or State law.

(f) Coordination Where Employer Has 2 or More Plans.—The Secretary shall prescribe such regulations as may be necessary or appropriate to carry out the purposes of this section where the employer has 2 or more plans including (but not limited to) regulations to prevent inappropriate omissions or required duplication of minimum benefits or contributions.

(g) Top-Heavy Plan Defined.—For purposes of this section—

IRC Sec. 416(g)

(1) In general.—

(A) Plans not required to be aggregated.—Except as provided in subparagraphs (B), the term "top-heavy plan" means, with respect to any plan year—

(i) any defined benefit plan if, as of the determination date, the present value of the cumulative accrued benefits under the plan for key employees exceeds 60 percent of the present value of the cumulative accrued benefits under the plan for all employees, and

(ii) any defined contribution plan if, as of the determination date, the aggregate of the accounts of key employees under the plan exceeds 60 percent of the aggregate of the accounts of all employees under such plan.

(B) Aggregated plans.—Each plan of an employer required to be included in an aggregation group shall be treated as a top-heavy plan if such group is a top-heavy group.

(2) Aggregation.—For purposes of this subsection—

(A) Aggregation group.—

(i) Required aggregation.—The term "aggregation group" means—

(I) each plan of the employer in which a key employee is a participant, and

(II) each other plan of the employer which enables any plan described in subclause (I) to meet the requirements of section 401(a)(4) or 410.

(ii) Permissive aggregation.—The employer may treat any plan not required to be included in an aggregation group under clause (i) as being part of such group if such group would continue to meet the requirements of sections 401(a)(4) and 410 with such plan being taken into account.

(B) Top-heavy group.—The term "top-heavy group" means any aggregation group if—

(i) the sum (as of the determination date) of—

(I) the present value of the cumulative accrued benefits for key employees under all defined benefit plans included in such group, and

(II) the aggregate of the accounts of key employees under all defined contribution plans included in such group,

(ii) exceeds 60 percent of a similar sum determined for all employees.

(3) Distributions during last year before determination date taken into account.—

(A) In general.—For purposes of determining—

(i) the present value of the cumulative accrued benefit for any employee, or

(ii) the amount of the account of any employee,

such present value or amount shall be increased by the aggregate distributions made with respect to such employee under the plan during the 1-year period ending on the determination date. The preceding sentence shall also apply to distributions under a terminated plan which if it had not been terminated would have been required to be included in an aggregation group.

(B) 5-year period in case of in-service distribution.—In the case of any distribution made for a reason other than severance from employment, death, or disability, subparagraph (A) shall be applied by substituting "5-year period" for "1-year period".

(4) Other special rules.—For purposes of this subsection—

(A) Rollover contributions to plan not taken into account.—Except to the extent provided in regulations, any rollover contribution (or similar transfer) initiated by the employee and made after December 31, 1983, to a plan shall not be taken into account with respect to the transferee plan for purposes of determining whether such plan is a top-heavy plan (or whether any aggregation group which includes such plan is a top-heavy group).

(B) Benefits not taken into account if employee ceases to be key employee.—If any individual is a non-key employee with respect to any plan for any plan year, but such individual was a key employee with respect to such plan for any prior plan year, any accrued benefit for such employee (and the account of such employee) shall not be taken into account.

(C) Determination date.—The term "determination date" means, with respect to any plan year—

(i) the last day of the preceding plan year, or

(ii) in the case of the first plan year of any plan, the last day of such plan year.

(D) Years.—To the extent provided in regulations, this section shall be applied on the basis of any year specified in such regulations in lieu of plan years.

(E) Benefits not taken into account if employee not employed for last year before determination date.—If any individual has not performed services for the employer maintaining the plan at any time during the 1-year period ending on the determination date, any accrued benefit for such individual (and account of such individual) shall not be taken into account.

(F) Accrued benefits treated as accruing ratably.— The accrued benefit of any employee (other than a key employee) shall be determined—

(i) under the method which is used for accrual purposes for all plans of the employer, or

(ii) if there is no method described in clause (i), as if such benefit accrued not more rapidly than the slowest accrual rate permitted under section 411(b)(1)(C).

(G) Simple retirement accounts.—The term "top-heavy plan" shall not include a simple retirement account under section 408(p).

(H) Cash or deferred arrangements using alternative methods of meeting nondiscrimination requirements.—The term "top-heavy plan" shall not include a plan which consists solely of—

(i) a cash or deferred arrangement which meets the requirements of section 401(k)(12) or 401(k)(13), and

(ii) matching contributions with respect to which the requirements of section 401(m)(11) or 401(m)(12) are met.

If, but for this subparagraph, a plan would be treated as a top-heavy plan because it is a member of an aggregation group which is a top-heavy group, contributions under the plan may be taken into account in determining whether any other plan meets the requirements of subsection (c)(2).

(h) [Repealed.]

(i) Definitions.—For purposes of this section—

(1) Key employee.—

(A) In general.—The term "key employee" means an employee who, at any time during the plan year is—

(i) an officer of the employer having an annual compensation greater than $130,000,

(ii) a 5-percent owner of the employer, or

(iii) a 1-percent owner of the employer having an annual compensation from the employer of more than $150,000.

For purposes of clause (i), no more than 50 employees (or, if lesser, the greater of 3 or 10 percent of the employees) shall be treated as officers. In the case of plan years beginning after December 31, 2002, the $130,000 amount in clause (i) shall be adjusted at the same time and in the same manner as under section 415(d), except that the base period shall be the calendar quarter beginning July 1, 2001, and any increase under this sentence which is not a multiple of $5,000 shall be rounded to the next lower multiple of $5,000. Such term shall not include any officer or employee of an entity referred to in section 414(d) (relating to governmental plans). For purposes of determining the number of officers taken into account under clause (i), employees described in section 414(q)(5) shall be excluded.

(B) Percentage owners.—

(i) 5-percent owner.—For purposes of this paragraph, the term "5-percent owner" means—

(I) if the employer is a corporation, any person who owns (or is considered as owning within the meaning of section 318) more than 5 percent of the outstanding stock of the corporation or stock possessing more than 5 percent of the total combined voting power of all stock of the corporation, or

(II) if the employer is not a corporation, any person who owns more than 5 percent of the capital or profits interest in the employer.

(ii) 1-percent owner.—For purposes of this paragraph, the term "1-percent owner" means any person who would be described in clause (i) if "1 percent" were substituted for "5 percent" each place it appears in clause (i).

(iii) Constructive ownership rules.—For purposes of this subparagraph—

(I) subparagraph (C) of section 318(a)(2) shall be applied by substituting "5 percent for "50 percent" and

(II) in the case of any employer which is not a corporation, ownership in such employer shall be determined in accordance with regulations prescribed by the Secretary which shall be based on principles similar to the principles of section 318 (as modified by subclause (I)).

(C) Aggregation rules do not apply for purposes of determining ownership in the employer.—The rules of subsections (b), (c), and (m) of section 414 shall not apply for purposes of determining ownership in the employer.

(D) Compensation.—For purposes of this paragraph, the term "compensation" has the meaning given such term by section 414(q)(4).

(2) Non-key employee.—The term "non-key employee" means any employee who is not a key employee.

(3) Self-employed individuals.—In the case of a self-employed individual described in section 401(c)(1)—

(A) such individual shall be treated as an employee, and

(B) such individual's earned income (within the meaning of section 401(c)(2)) shall be treated as compensation.

(4) Treatment of employees covered by collective bargaining agreements.—The requirements of subsections (b), (c), and (d) shall not apply with respect to any employee included in a unit of employees covered by an agreement which the Secretary of Labor finds to be a collective bargaining agreement between employee representatives and 1 or more employers if there is evidence that retirement benefits were the subject of good faith bargaining between such employee representatives and such employer or employers.

IRC Sec. 416(i)(4)

(5) Treatment of beneficiaries.—The terms "employee" and "key employee" include their beneficiaries.

(6) Treatment of simplified employee pensions.—

(A) Treatment as defined contribution plans.—A simplified employee pension shall be treated as a defined contribution plan.

(B) Election to have determinations based on employer contributions.—In the case of a simplified employee pension, at the election of the employer, paragraphs (1)(A)(ii) and (2)(B) of subsection (g) shall be applied by taking into account aggregate employer contributions in lieu of the aggregate of the accounts of employees.

Recent Amendments to IRC §416

Pension Protection Act of 2006 (Pub. L. No. 109-280), as follows:

• IRC §416(g)(4)(H)(i) was amended by Act §902(c)(1) by inserting "or 401(k)(13)" after "§401(k)(12)". Eff. plan years beginning after Dec. 31, 2007.
• IRC §416(g)(4)(H)(ii) was amended by Act §902(c)(2) by inserting "or 401(m)(12)" after "§401(m)(11)". Eff. plan years beginning after Dec. 31, 2007.
• Sunset Provision. Act §811, provides:
   SEC. 811. PENSIONS AND INDIVIDUAL RETIRE-MENT ARRANGEMENT PROVISIONS OF ECO-NOMIC GROWTH AND TAX RELIEF RECONCILIA-TION ACT OF 2001 MADE PERMANENT.
   Title IX of the Economic Growth and Tax Relief Reconciliation Act of 2001 [Pub. L. No. 107-16] shall not apply to the provisions of, and amendments made by, subtitles A through F [§§601–666] of title VI of such Act (relating to pension and individual retirement arrangement provisions).

Working Families Tax Relief Act of 2004 (Pub. L. No. 108-311), as follows:

• IRC §416(i)(1)(A) was amended by Act §408(a)(16) by substituting "In the case of plan years" for "in the case of plan years" in the matter following cl. (iii). Eff. Oct. 4, 2004.

Job Creation and Worker Assistance Act of 2002 (Pub. L. No. 107-147), as follows:

• IRC §416(c)(1)(C)(iii) was amended by Act §411(k)(1) by substituting in the heading "Exception for plan under which no key employee (or former key employee) benefits for plan year" for "Exception for frozen plan". Eff. years beginning after Dec. 31, 2001, as if included in the provision of Pub. L. No. 107-16 to which it relates.
• IRC §416(g)(3)(B) was amended by Act §411(k)(2) by substituting "severance from employment" for "separation from service". Eff. years beginning after Dec. 31, 2001, as if included in the provision of Pub. L. No. 107-16 to which it relates.

Economic Growth and Tax Relief Reconciliation Act of 2001 (Pub. L. No. 107-16), as follows:

• IRC §416(c)(1)(C)(i) was amended by Act §613(e) by substituting "clause (ii) or (iii)" for "clause (ii)". Eff. years beginning after Dec. 31, 2001.
• IRC §416(c)(1)(C) was amended by Act §613(e) by adding new cl. (iii). Eff. years beginning after Dec. 31, 2001.
• IRC §416(c)(2)(A) was amended by Act §613(b) by adding the sentence at the end. Eff. years beginning after Dec. 31, 2001.
• IRC §416(g)(3) was amended by Act §613(c)(1). Eff. years beginning after Dec. 31, 2001. IRC §416(g)(3) prior to amendment:
   (3) Distributions during last 5 years taken into account.—For purposes of determining—
   (A) the present value of the cumulative accrued benefit for any employee, or

(B) the amount of the account of any employee, such present value or amount shall be increased by the aggregate distributions made with respect to such employee under the plan during the 5-year period ending on the determination date. The preceding sentence shall also apply to distributions under a terminated plan which if it had not been terminated would have been required to be included in an aggregation group.

• IRC §416(g)(4)(E) was amended by Act §613(c)(2)(A) by substituting in the heading "last year before determination date" for "last 5 years", and by substituting in the text "1-year period" for "5-year period". Eff. years beginning after Dec. 31, 2001.
• IRC §416(g)(4) was amended by Act §613(d) by adding subpara. (H). Eff. years beginning after Dec. 31, 2001.
• IRC §416(i)(1)(A) was amended by Act §613(a)(1)(A) by striking "or any of the 4 preceding plan years" in the matter preceding cl. (i). Eff. years beginning after Dec. 31, 2001.
• IRC §416(i)(1)(A) was amended by Act §613(a)(1)(D) by striking the second sentence in the matter following clause (iii), as redesignated by Act §613(a)(1)(C), and by inserting a new sentence. Eff. years beginning after Dec. 31, 2001.
• IRC §416(i)(1)(A)(i) was amended by Act §613(a)(1)(B). Eff. years beginning after Dec. 31, 2001. IRC §416(i)(1)(A)(i) prior to amendment:
   (i) an officer of the employer having an annual compensation greater than 50 percent of the amount in effect under section 415(b)(1)(A) for any such plan year,.
• IRC §416(i)(1)(A)(ii)–(iv) was amended by Act §613(a)(1)(C) by striking cl. (ii), and by redesignating cls. (iii)–(iv) as cls. (ii)–(iii), respectively. Eff. years beginning after Dec. 31, 2001. IRC §416(i)(1)(A)(ii) prior to being stricken:
   (ii) 1 of the 10 employees having annual compensation from the employer of more than the limitation in effect under section 415(c)(1)(A) and owning (or considered as owning within the meaning of section 318) the largest interests in the employer,.
• IRC §416(i)(1)(B)(iii) was amended by Act §613(a)(2) by striking "and subparagraph (A)(ii)". Eff. years beginning after Dec. 31, 2001.
• Sunset Provision. Act §901, as amended by Pub. L. No. 111-312, §101(a)(1), provides the sunset rule below. But see Pub. L. No. 109-280, §811, and Pub. L. No. 111-148, §10909(c), as amended by Pub. L. No. 111-312, §101(b)(1).
   SEC. 901. SUNSET OF PROVISIONS OF ACT.
   (a) In general. All provisions of, and amendments made by, this Act shall not apply—
   (1) to taxable, plan, or limitation years beginning after December 31, 2012, or
   (2) in the case of title V, to estates of decedents dying, gifts made, or generation skipping transfers, after December 31, 2012.
   (b) Application of certain laws.—The Internal Revenue Code of 1986 and the Employee Retirement Income Security Act of 1974 shall be applied and administered to years, estates, gifts, and transfers described in subsection (a) as if the provisions and amendments described in subsection (a) had never been enacted.

SEC. 417. DEFINITIONS AND SPECIAL RULES FOR PURPOSES OF MINIMUM SURVIVOR ANNUITY REQUIREMENTS.

(a) Election to Waive Qualified Joint and Survivor Annuity or Qualified Preretirement Annuity.—

(1) In general.—A plan meets the requirements of section 401(a)(11) only if—

(A) under the plan, each participant—

(i) may elect at any time during the applicable election period to waive the qualified joint and survivor annuity form of benefit or the qualified preretirement survivor annuity form of benefit (or both),

(ii) if the participant elects a waiver under clause (i), may elect the qualified optional survivor annuity at any time during the applicable election period, and

(iii) may revoke any such election at any time during the applicable election period, and

(B) the plan meets the requirements of paragraphs (2), (3), and (4) of this subsection.

(2) Spouse must consent to election.—Each plan shall provide that an election under paragraph (1)(A)(i) shall not take effect unless—

(A)(i) the spouse of the participant consents in writing to such election,

(ii) such election designates a beneficiary (or a form of benefits) which may not be changed without spousal consent (or the consent of the spouse expressly permits designations by the participant without any requirement of further consent by the spouse), and

(iii) the spouse's consent acknowledges the effect of such election and is witnessed by a plan representative or a notary public, or

(B) it is established to the satisfaction of a plan representative that the consent required under subparagraph (A) may not be obtained because there is no spouse, because the spouse cannot be located, or because of such other circumstances as the Secretary may by regulations prescribe.

Any consent by a spouse (or establishment that the consent of a spouse may not be obtained) under the preceding sentence shall be effective only with respect to such spouse.

(3) Plan to provide written explanations.—

(A) Explanation of joint and survivor annuity.—Each plan shall provide to each participant, within a reasonable period of time before the annuity starting date (and consistent with such regulations as the Secretary may prescribe), a written explanation of—

(i) the terms and conditions of the qualified joint and survivor annuity and of the qualified optional survivor annuity,

(ii) the participant's right to make, and the effect of, an election under paragraph (1) to waive the joint and survivor annuity form of benefit,

(iii) the rights of the participant's spouse under paragraph (2), and

(iv) the right to make, and the effect of, a revocation of an election under paragraph (1).

(B) Explanation of qualified preretirement survivor annuity.—

(i) In general.—Each plan shall provide to each participant, within the applicable period with respect to such participant (and consistent with such regulations as the Secretary may prescribe), a written explanation with respect to the qualified preretirement survivor annuity comparable to that required under subparagraph (A).

(ii) Applicable period.—For purposes of clause (i), the term "applicable period" means, with respect to a participant, whichever of the following periods ends last:

(I) The period beginning with the first day of the plan year in which the participant attains age 32 and ending with the close of the plan year preceding the plan year in which the participant attains age 35.

(II) A reasonable period after the individual becomes a participant.

(III) A reasonable period ending after paragraph (5) ceases to apply to the participant.

(IV) A reasonable period ending after section 401(a)(11) applies to the participant.

In the case of a participant who separates from service before attaining age 35, the applicable period shall be a reasonable period after separation.

(4) Requirement of spousal consent for using plan assets as security for loans.—Each plan shall provide that, if section 401(a)(11) applies to a participant when part or all of the participant's accrued benefit is to be used as security for a loan, no portion of the participant's accrued benefit may be used as security for such loan unless—

(A) the spouse of the participant (if any) consents in writing to such use during the 90-day period ending on the date on which the loan is to be so secured, and

(B) requirements comparable to the requirements of paragraph (2) are met with respect to such consent.

(5) Special rule where plan fully subsidizes costs.—

(A) In general.—The requirements of this subsection shall not apply with respect to the qualified joint and survivor annuity form of benefit or the qualified preretirement survivor annuity form of benefit, as the case may be, if such benefit may not be waived (or another beneficiary selected) and if the plan fully subsidizes the costs of such benefit.

(B) Definition.—For purposes of subparagraph (A), a plan fully subsidizes the costs of a benefit if under the plan the failure to waive such benefit by a participant would not result in a decrease in any plan benefits with respect to such participant and would not result in increased contributions from such participant.

IRC Sec. 417(a)(5)(B)

(6) Applicable election period.—For purposes of this subsection, the term "applicable election period" means—

(A) in the case of an election to waive the qualified joint and survivor annuity form of benefit, the 180-day period ending on the annuity starting date, or

(B) in the case of an election to waive the qualified preretirement survivor annuity, the period which begins on the first day of the plan year in which the participant attains age 35 and ends on the date of the participant's death.

In the case of a participant who is separated from service, the applicable election period under subparagraph (B) with respect to benefits accrued before the date of such separation from service shall not begin later than such date.

(7) Special rules relating to time for written explanation.—Notwithstanding any other provision of this subsection—

(A) Explanation may be provided after annuity starting date.—

(i) In general.—A plan may provide the written explanation described in paragraph (3)(A) after the annuity starting date. In any case to which this subparagraph applies, the applicable election period under paragraph (6) shall not end before the 30th day after the date on which such explanation is provided.

(ii) Regulatory authority.—The Secretary may by regulations limit the application of clause (i), except that such regulations may not limit the period of time by which the annuity starting date precedes the provision of the written explanation other than by providing that the annuity starting date may not be earlier than termination of employment.

(B) Waiver of 30-day period.—A plan may permit a participant to elect (with any applicable spousal consent) to waive any requirement that the written explanation be provided at least 30 days before the annuity starting date (or to waive the 30-day requirement under subparagraph (A)) if the distribution commences more than 7 days after such explanation is provided.

(b) Definition of Qualified Joint and Survivor Annuity.—For purposes of this section and section 401(a)(11), the term "qualified joint and survivor annuity" means an annuity—

(1) for the life of the participant with a survivor annuity for the life of the spouse which is not less than 50 percent of (and is not greater than 100 percent of) the amount of the annuity which is payable during the joint lives of the participant and the spouse, and

(2) which is the actuarial equivalent of a single annuity for the life of the participant.

Such term also includes any annuity in a form having the effect of an annuity described in the preceding sentence.

(c) Definition of Qualified Preretirement Survivor Annuity.—For purposes of this section and section 401(a)(11)—

(1) In general.—Except as provided in paragraph (2), the term "qualified preretirement survivor annuity" means a survivor annuity for the life of the surviving spouse of the participant if—

(A) the payments to the surviving spouse under such an annuity are not less than the amount which would be payable as a survivor annuity under the qualified joint and survivor annuity under the plan (or the actuarial equivalent thereof)—

(i) in the case of a participant who dies after the date on which the participant attained the earliest retirement age, such participant had retired with an immediate qualified joint and survivor annuity on the day before the participant's date of death, or

(ii) in the case of a participant who dies on or before the date on which the participant would have attained the earliest retirement age, such participant had—

(I) separated from service on the date of death,

(II) survived to the earliest retirement age,

(III) retired with an immediate qualified joint and survivor annuity at the earliest retirement age, and

(IV) died on the day after the day on which such participant would have attained the earliest retirement age, and

(B) under the plan, the earliest period for which the surviving spouse may receive a payment under such annuity is not later than the month in which the participant would have attained the earliest retirement age under the plan.

In the case of an individual who separated from service before the date of such individual's death, subparagraph (A)(ii)(I) shall not apply.

(2) Special rule for defined contribution plans.—In the case of any defined contribution plan or participant described in clause (ii) or (iii) of section 401(a)(11)(B), the term "qualified preretirement survivor annuity" means an annuity for the life of the surviving spouse the actuarial equivalent of which is not less than 50 percent of the portion of the account balance of the participant (as of the date of death) to which the participant had a nonforfeitable right (within the meaning of section 411(a)).

(3) Security interests taken into account.—For purposes of paragraphs (1) and (2), any security interest held by the plan by reason of a loan outstanding to the participant shall be taken into account in determining the amount of the qualified preretirement survivor annuity.

(d) Survivor Annuities Need Not Be Provided if Participant and Spouse Married Less Than 1 Year.—

(1) In general.—Except as provided in paragraph (2), a plan shall not be treated as failing to meet the requirements of section 401(a)(11) merely because the plan provides that a qualified joint and survivor annuity (or a qualified preretirement survivor annuity) will not be provided unless the participant and spouse had been married throughout the 1-year period ending on the earlier of—

(A) the participant's annuity starting date, or

(B) the date of the participant's death.

(2) Treatment of certain marriages within 1 year of annuity starting date for purposes of qualified joint and survivor annuities.—For purposes of paragraph (1), if—

(A) a participant marries within 1 year before the annuity starting date, and

(B) the participant and the participant's spouse in such marriage have been married for at least a 1-year period ending on or before the date of the participant's death,

such participant and such spouse shall be treated as having been married throughout the 1-year period ending on the participant's annuity starting date.

(e) Restrictions on Cash-Outs.—

(1) Plan may require distribution if present value not in excess of dollar limit.—A plan may provide that the present value of a qualified joint and survivor annuity or a qualified preretirement survivor annuity will be immediately distributed if such value does not exceed the amount that can be distributed without the participant's consent under section 411(a)(11). No distribution may be made under the preceding sentence after the annuity starting date unless the participant and the spouse of the participant (or where the participant has died, the surviving spouse) consents in writing to such distribution.

(2) Plan may distribute benefit in excess of dollar limit only with consent.—If—

(A) the present value of the qualified joint and survivor annuity or the qualified preretirement survivor annuity exceeds the amount that can be distributed without the participant's consent under section 411(a)(11), and

(B) the participant and the spouse of the participant (or where the participant has died, the surviving spouse) consent in writing to the distribution,

the plan may immediately distribute the present value of such annuity.

(3) Determination of present value.—

(A) In general.—For purposes of paragraphs (1) and (2), the present value shall not be less than the present value calculated by using the applicable mortality table and the applicable interest rate.

(B) Applicable mortality table.—For purposes of subparagraph (A), the term "applicable mortality table" means a mortality table, modified as appropriate by the Secretary, based on the mortality table specified for the plan year under subparagraph (A) of section 430(h)(3) (without regard to subparagraph (C) or (D) of such section).

(C) Applicable interest rate.—For purposes of subparagraph (A), the term "applicable interest rate" means the adjusted first, second, and third segment rates applied under rules similar to the rules of section 430(h)(2)(C) for the month before the date of the distribution or such other time as the Secretary may by regulations prescribe.

(D) Applicable segment rates.—For purposes of subparagraph (C), the adjusted first, second, and third segment rates are the first, second, and third segment rates which would be determined under section 430(h)(2)(C) if—

(i) section 430(h)(2)(D) were applied by substituting the average yields for the month described in subparagraph (C) for the average yields for the 24-month period described in such section,

(ii) section 430(h)(2)(G)(i)(II) were applied by substituting "section 417(e)(3)(A)(ii)(II)" for "section 412(b)(5)(B)(ii)(II)", and

(iii) the applicable percentage under section 430(h)(2)(G) were determined in accordance with the following table:

In the case of plan years beginning in:	The applicable percentage is:
2008	20 percent
2009	40 percent
2010	60 percent
2011	80 percent

(f) Other Definitions and Special Rules.—For purposes of this section and section 401(a)(11)—

(1) Vested participant.—The term "vested participant" means any participant who has a nonforfeitable right (within the meaning of section 411(a)) to any portion of such participant's accrued benefit.

(2) Annuity starting date.—

(A) In general.—The term "annuity starting date" means—

(i) the first day of the first period for which an amount is payable as an annuity, or

(ii) in the case of a benefit not payable in the form of an annuity, the first day on which all events have occurred which entitle the participant to such benefit.

(B) **Special rule for disability benefits.**—For purposes of subparagraph (A), the first day of the first period for which a benefit is to be received by reason of disability shall be treated as the annuity starting date only if such benefit is not an auxiliary benefit.

(3) **Earliest retirement age.**—The term "earliest retirement age" means the earliest date on which, under the plan, the participant could elect to receive retirement benefits.

(4) **Plan may take into account increased costs.**—A plan may take into account in any equitable manner (as determined by the Secretary) any increased costs resulting from providing a qualified joint or survivor annuity or a qualified preretirement survivor annuity.

(5) **Distributions by reason of security interests.**—If the use of any participant's accrued benefit (or any portion thereof) as security for a loan meets the requirements of subsection (a)(4), nothing in this section or section 411(a)(11) shall prevent any distribution required by reason of a failure to comply with the terms of such loan.

(6) **Requirements for certain spousal consents.**—No consent of a spouse shall be effective for purposes of subsection (e)(1) or (e)(2) (as the case may be) unless requirements comparable to the requirements for spousal consent to an election under subsection (a)(1)(A) are met.

(7) **Consultation with the Secretary of Labor.**—In prescribing regulations under this section and section 401(a)(11), the Secretary shall consult with the Secretary of Labor.

(g) **Definition of Qualified Optional Survivor Annuity.**—

(1) **In general.**—For purposes of this section, the term "qualified optional survivor annuity" means an annuity—

(A) for the life of the participant with a survivor annuity for the life of the spouse which is equal to the applicable percentage of the amount of the annuity which is payable during the joint lives of the participant and the spouse, and

(B) which is the actuarial equivalent of a single annuity for the life of the participant.

Such term also includes any annuity in a form having the effect of an annuity described in the preceding sentence.

(2) **Applicable percentage.**—

(A) **In general.**—For purposes of paragraph (1), if the survivor annuity percentage—

(i) is less than 75 percent, the applicable percentage is 75 percent, and

(ii) is greater than or equal to 75 percent, the applicable percentage is 50 percent.

(B) **Survivor annuity percentage.**—For purposes of subparagraph (A), the term "survivor annuity percentage" means the percentage which the survivor annuity under the plan's qualified joint and survivor annuity bears to the annuity payable during the joint lives of the participant and the spouse.

Recent Amendments to IRC §417

Worker, Retiree, and Employer Recovery Act of 2008 (Pub. L. No. 110-458), as follows:

● IRC §417(e)(3)(D)(i) was amended by Act §103(b)(2)(A) by striking "clause (ii)" and substituting "subparagraph (C)". Eff. as if included in Pub. L. No. 109-280, §301 [eff. with respect to plan years beginning after Dec. 31, 2007].

Pension Protection Act of 2006 (Pub. L. No. 109-280), as follows:

● IRC §417(a)(1)(A) was amended by Act §1004(a)(1) by substituting a comma at the end for ", and" in cl. (i), redesignating cl. (ii) as cl. (iii), and by adding new cl. (ii). Eff. generally for plan years beginning after Dec. 31, 2007. [*Ed. Note*: see Act §1004(c)(2) for a special rule.]

● IRC §417(a)(3)(A)(i) was amended by Act §1004(a)(3) by inserting "and of the qualified optional survivor annuity" after "annuity". Eff. generally for plan years beginning after Dec. 31, 2007.

[*Ed. Note*: see Act §1004(c)(2) for a special rule.]

● IRC §417(a)(6)(A) was amended by Act §1102(a)(1)(A) by substituting "180-day" for "90-day". Eff. years beginning after Dec. 31, 2006.

● IRC §417(e)(3) was amended by Act §302(b). Eff. with respect to plan years beginning after Dec. 31, 2007. IRC §417(e)(3) prior to amendment:

(3) Determination of present value.—

(A) In general.—

(i) Present value.—Except as provided in subparagraph (B), for purposes of paragraphs (1) and (2), the present value shall not be less than the present value calculated by using the applicable mortality table and the applicable interest rate.

(ii) Definitions.—For purposes of clause (i)—

(I) Applicable mortality table.—The term "applicable mortality table" means the table prescribed by the Secretary. Such table shall be based on the prevailing commissioners' standard table (described in section 807(d)(5)(A)) used to determine reserves for group annuity contracts issued on the date as of which present value is being determined (without regard to any other subparagraph of section 807(d)(5)).

(II) Applicable interest rate.—The term "applicable interest rate" means the annual rate of interest on 30-year Treasury securities for the month before the date of distribution or such other time as the Secretary may by regulations prescribe.

(B) Exception.—In the case of a distribution from a plan that was adopted and in effect before the date of the enactment of the Retirement Protection Act of 1994, the present value of any distribution made before the earlier of—

(i) the later of the date a plan amendment applying subparagraph (A) is adopted or made effective, or

(ii) the first day of the first plan year beginning after December 31, 1999, shall be calculated, for purposes of paragraphs (1) and (2), using the interest rate determined under the regulations of the Pension Benefit Guaranty Corporation for determining the present value of a lump sum distribution on plan termination that were in effect on September 1, 1993, and using the provisions of the plan as in effect on the day before such date of enactment; but only if such provisions of the plan met the requirements of section 417(e)(3) as in effect on the day before such date of enactment.

● IRC §417 was amended by Act §1004(a)(2) by adding new subsec. (g) at the end. Eff. generally for plan years beginning after Dec. 31, 2007. [*Ed. Note*: see Act §1004(c)(2) for a special rule.]

• **Sunset Provision.** Act §811, provides:

SEC. 811. PENSIONS AND INDIVIDUAL RETIRE-MENT ARRANGEMENT PROVISIONS OF ECO-NOMIC GROWTH AND TAX RELIEF RECONCILIA-TION ACT OF 2001 MADE PERMANENT.

Title IX of the Economic Growth and Tax Relief Reconciliation Act of 2001 [Pub. L. No. 107-16] shall not apply to the provisions of, and amendments made by, subtitles A through F [§§601–666] of title VI of such Act (relating to pension and individual retirement arrangement provisions).

Job Creation and Worker Assistance Act of 2002 (Pub. L. No. 107-147), as follows:

• IRC §417(e)(1) was amended by Act §411(r)(1)(A) by substituting "exceed the amount that can be distributed without the participant's consent under §411(a)(11)" for "exceed the dollar limit under §411(a)(11)(A)". Eff. for distributions after Dec. 31, 2001, as if included in the provision of Pub. L. No. 107-16 to which it relates.

• IRC §417(e)(2)(A) was amended by Act §411(r)(1)(B) by substituting "exceeds the amount that can be distributed without the participant's consent under §411(a)(11)" for "exceeds the dollar limit under §411(a)(11)(A)". Eff. for distributions after Dec. 31, 2001, as if included in the provision of Pub. L. No. 107-16 to which it relates.

Economic Growth and Tax Relief Reconciliation Act of 2001 (Pub. L. No. 107-16), as follows:

• **Sunset Provision.** Act §901, as amended by Pub. L. No. 111-312, §101(a)(1), provides the sunset rule below. But see Pub. L. No. 109-280, §811, and Pub. L. No. 111-148, §10909(c), as amended by Pub. L. No. 111-312, §101(b)(1).

SEC. 901. SUNSET OF PROVISIONS OF ACT.

(a) In general. All provisions of, and amendments made by, this Act shall not apply—

(1) to taxable, plan, or limitation years beginning after December 31, 2012, or

(2) in the case of title V, to estates of decedents dying, gifts made, or generation skipping transfers, after December 31, 2012.

(b) Application of certain laws.—The Internal Revenue Code of 1986 and the Employee Retirement Income Security Act of 1974 shall be applied and administered to years, estates, gifts, and transfers described in subsection (a) as if the provisions and amendments described in subsection (a) had never been enacted.

Subpart C—Special Rules for Multiemployer Plans

SEC. 418. REORGANIZATION STATUS.

(a) General Rule.—A multiemployer plan is in reorganization for a plan year if the plan's reorganization index for that year is greater than zero.

(b) Reorganization Index.—For purposes of this subpart—

(1) In general.—A plan's reorganization index for any plan year is the excess of—

(A) the vested benefits charge for such year, over

(B) the net charge to the funding standard account for such year.

(2) Net charge to funding standard account.— The net charge to the funding standard account for any plan year is the excess (if any) of—

(A) the charges to the funding standard account for such year under section 412(b)(2), over

(B) the credits to the funding standard account under section 412(b)(3)(B).

(3) Vested benefits charge.—The vested benefits charge for any plan year is the amount which would be necessary to amortize the plan's unfunded vested benefits as of the end of the base plan year in equal annual installments—

(A) over 10 years, to the extent such benefits are attributable to persons in pay status, and

(B) over 25 years, to the extent such benefits are attributable to other participants.

(4) Determination of vested benefits charge.—

(A) In general.—The vested benefits charge for a plan year shall be based on an actuarial valuation of the plan as of the end of the base plan year, adjusted to reflect—

(i) any—

(I) decrease of 5 percent or more in the value of plan assets, or increase of 5 percent or more in the number of persons in pay status, during the period beginning on the first day of the plan year following the base plan year and ending on the adjustment date, or

(II) at the election of the plan sponsor, actuarial valuation of the plan as of the adjustment date or any later date not later than the last day of the plan year for which the determination is being made,

(ii) any change in benefits under the plan which is not otherwise taken into account under this subparagraph and which is pursuant to any amendment—

(I) adopted before the end of the plan year for which the determination is being made, and

(II) effective after the end of the base plan year and on or before the end of the plan year referred to in subclause (I), and

(iii) any other event (including an event described in subparagraph (B)(i)(I)) which, as determined in accordance with regulations prescribed by the Secretary, would substantially increase the plan's vested benefit charge.

(B) Certain changes in benefit levels.—

(i) In general.—In determining the vested benefits charge for a plan year following a plan year in which the plan was not in reorganization, any change in benefits which—

(I) results from the changing of a group of participants from one benefit level to another benefit level under a schedule of plan benefits as a result of changes in a collective bargaining agreement, or

(II) results from any change in a collective bargaining agreement, shall not be taken into account

IRC Sec. 418(b)(4)(B)(i)(II)

except to the extent provided in regulations prescribed by the Secretary.

(ii) Plan in reorganization.—Except as otherwise determined by the Secretary, in determining the vested benefits charge for any plan year following any plan year in which the plan was in reorganization, any change in benefits—

(I) described in clause (i)(I), or

(II) described in clause (i)(II) as determined under regulations prescribed by the Secretary, shall, for purposes of subparagraph (A)(ii), be treated as a change in benefits pursuant to an amendment to a plan.

(5) Base plan year.—

(A) In general.—The base plan year for any plan year is—

(i) if there is a relevant collective bargaining agreement, the last plan year ending at least 6 months before the relevant effective date, or

(ii) if there is no relevant collective bargaining agreement, the last plan year ending at least 12 months before the beginning of the plan year.

(B) Relevant collective bargaining agreement.—A relevant collective bargaining agreement is a collective bargaining agreement—

(i) which is in effect for at least 6 months during the plan year, and

(ii) which has not been in effect for more than 36 months as of the end of the plan year.

(C) Relevant effective date.—The relevant effective date is the earliest of the effective dates for the relevant collective bargaining agreements.

(D) Adjustment date.—The adjustment date is the date which is—

(i) 90 days before the relevant effective date, or

(ii) if there is no relevant effective date, 90 days before the beginning of the plan year.

(6) Person in pay status.—The term "person in pay status" means—

(A) a participant or beneficiary on the last day of the base plan year who, at any time during such year, was paid an early, late, normal, or disability retirement benefit (or a death benefit related to a retirement benefit), and

(B) to the extent provided in regulations prescribed by the Secretary, any other person who is entitled to such a benefit under the plan.

(7) Other definitions and special rules.—

(A) Unfunded vested benefits.—The term "unfunded vested benefits" means, in connection with a plan, an amount (determined in accordance with regulations prescribed by the Secretary) equal to—

(i) the value of vested benefits under the plan, less

(ii) the value of the assets of the plan.

(B) Vested benefits.—The term "vested benefits" means any nonforfeitable benefit (within the meaning of section 4001(a)(8) of the Employee Retirement Income Security Act of 1974).

(C) Allocation of assets.—In determining the plan's unfunded vested benefits, plan assets shall first be allocated to the vested benefits attributable to persons in pay status.

(D) Treatment of certain benefit reductions.—The vested benefits charge shall be determined without regard to reductions in accrued benefits under section 418D which are first effective in the plan year.

(E) Withdrawal liability.—For purposes of this part, any outstanding claim for withdrawal liability shall not be considered a plan asset, except as otherwise provided in regulations prescribed by the Secretary.

(c) Prohibition of Nonannuity Payments.—Except as provided in regulations prescribed by the Pension Benefit Guaranty Corporation, while a plan is in reorganization a benefit with respect to a participant (other than a death benefit) which is attributable to employer contributions and which has a value of more than $1,750 may not be paid in a form other than an annuity which (by itself or in combination with social security, railroad retirement, or workers' compensation benefits) provides substantially level payments over the life of the participant.

(d) Terminated Plans.—Any multiemployer plan which terminates under section 4041A(a)(2) of the Employee Retirement Income Security Act of 1974 shall not be considered in reorganization after the last day of the plan year in which the plan is treated as having terminated.

SEC. 418A. NOTICE OF REORGANIZATION AND FUNDING REQUIREMENTS.

(a) Notice Requirement.—

(1) In general.—If—

(A) a multiemployer plan is in reorganization for a plan year, and

(B) section 418B would require an increase in contributions for such plan year, the plan sponsor shall notify the persons described in paragraph (2) that the plan is in reorganization and that, if contributions to the plan are not increased, accrued benefits under the plan may be reduced or an excise tax may be imposed (or both such reduction and imposition may occur).

(2) Persons to whom notice is to be given.—The persons described in this paragraph are—

(A) each employer who has an obligation to contribute under the plan (within the meaning of section 4212(a) of the Employee Retirement Income Security Act of 1974), and

(B) each employee organization which, for purposes of collective bargaining, represents plan participants employed by such an employer.

(3) Overburden credit not taken into account.—The determination under paragraph (1)(B) shall be made without regard to the overburden credit provided by section 418C.

(b) Additional Requirements.—The Pension Benefit Guaranty Corporation may prescribe additional or alternative requirements for assuring, in the case of a plan with respect to which notice is required by subsection (a)(1), that the persons described in subsection (a)(2)—

(1) receive appropriate notice that the plan is in reorganization,

(2) are adequately informed of the implications of reorganization status, and

(3) have reasonable access to information relevant to the plan's reorganization status.

SEC. 418B. MINIMUM CONTRIBUTION REQUIREMENT.

(a) Accumulated Funding Deficiency in Reorganization.—

(1) In general.—For any plan year in which a multiemployer plan is in reorganization—

(A) the plan shall continue to maintain its funding standard account, and

(B) the plan's accumulated funding deficiency under section 412(a) for such plan year shall be equal to the excess (if any) of—

(i) the sum of the minimum contribution requirement for such plan year (taking into account any overburden credit under section 418C(a)) plus the plan's accumulated funding deficiency for the preceding plan year (determined under this section if the plan was in reorganization during such plan year or under section 412(a) if the plan was not in reorganization), over

(ii) amounts considered contributed by employers to or under the plan for the plan year (increased by any amount waived under subsection (f) for the plan year).

(2) Treatment of withdrawal liability payments.—For purposes of paragraph (1), withdrawal liability payments (whether or not received) which are due with respect to withdrawals before the end of the base plan year shall be considered amounts contributed by the employer to or under the plan if, as of the adjustment date, it was reasonable for the plan

sponsor to anticipate that such payments would be made during the plan year.

(b) Minimum Contribution Requirement.—

(1) In general.—Except as otherwise provided in this section for purposes of this subpart the minimum contribution requirement for a plan year in which a plan is in reorganization is an amount equal to the excess of—

(A) the sum of—

(i) the plan's vested benefits charge for the plan year; and

(ii) the increase in normal cost for the plan year determined under the entry age normal funding method which is attributable to plan amendments adopted while the plan was in reorganization, over

(B) the amount of the overburden credit (if any) determined under section 418C for the plan year.

(2) Adjustment for reductions in contribution base units.—If the plan's current contribution base for the plan year is less than the plan's valuation contribution base for the plan year, the minimum contribution requirement for such plan year shall be equal to the product of the amount determined under paragraph (1) (after any adjustment required by this subpart other than this paragraph) multiplied by a fraction—

(A) the numerator of which is the plan's current contribution base for the plan year, and

(B) the denominator of which is the plan's valuation contribution base for the plan year.

(3) Special rule where cash-flow amount exceeds vested benefits charge.—

(A) In general.—If the vested benefits charge for a plan year of a plan in reorganization is less than the plan's cash-flow amount for the plan year, the plan's minimum contribution requirement for the plan year is the amount determined under paragraph (1) (determined before the application of paragraph (2)) after substituting the term "cash-flow amount" for the term "vested benefits charge" in paragraph (1)(A).

(B) Cash-flow amount.—For purposes of subparagraph (A), a plan's cash-flow amount for a plan year is an amount equal to—

(i) the amount of the benefits payable under the plan for the base plan year, plus the amount of the plan's administrative expenses for the base plan year, reduced by

(ii) the value of the available plan assets for the base plan year determined under regulations prescribed by the Secretary, adjusted in a manner consistent with section 418(b)(4).

(c) Current Contribution Base; Valuation Contribution Base.—

IRC Sec. 418B(c)

(1) Current contribution base.—For purposes of this subpart, a plan's current contribution base for a plan year is the number of contribution base units with respect to which contributions are required to be made under the plan for that plan year determined in accordance with regulations prescribed by the Secretary.

(2) Valuation contribution base.—

(A) In general.—Except as provided in subparagraph (B), for purposes of this subpart a plan's valuation contribution base is the number of contribution base units for which contributions were received for the base plan year—

(i) adjusted to reflect declines in the contribution base which have occurred (or could reasonably be anticipated) as of the adjustment date for the plan year referred to in paragraph (1),

(ii) adjusted upward (in accordance with regulations prescribed by the Secretary) for any contribution base reduction in the base plan year caused by a strike or lockout or by unusual events, such as fire, earthquake, or severe weather conditions, and

(iii) adjusted (in accordance with regulations prescribed by the Secretary) for reductions in the contribution base resulting from transfers of liabilities.

(B) Insolvent plans.—For any plan year—

(i) in which the plan is insolvent (within the meaning of section 418E(b)(1)), and

(ii) beginning with the first plan year beginning after the expiration of all relevant collective bargaining agreements which were in effect in the plan year in which the plan became insolvent,

the plan's valuation contribution base is the greater of the number of contribution base units for which contributions were received for the first or second plan year preceding the first plan year in which the plan is insolvent, adjusted as provided in clause (ii) or (iii) of subparagraph (A).

(3) Contribution base unit.—For purposes of this subpart, the term "contribution base unit" means a unit with respect to which an employer has an obligation to contribute under a multiemployer plan (as defined in regulations prescribed by the Secretary).

(d) Limitation on Required Increases in Rate of Employer Contributions.—

(1) In general.—Under regulations prescribed by the Secretary, the minimum contribution requirement applicable to any plan for any plan year which is determined under subsection (b) (without regard to subsection (b)(2)) shall not exceed an amount which is equal to the sum of—

(A) the greater of—

(i) the funding standard requirement for such plan year, or

(ii) 107 percent of—

(I) if the plan was not in reorganization in the preceding plan year, the funding standard requirement for such preceding plan year, or

(II) if the plan was in reorganization in the preceding plan year, the sum of the amount determined under this subparagraph for the preceding plan year and the amount (if any) determined under subparagraph (B) for the preceding plan year, plus

(B) if for the plan year a change in benefits is first required to be considered in computing the charges under section 412(b)(2)(A) or (B), the sum of—

(i) the increase in normal cost for a plan year determined under the entry age normal funding method due to increases in benefits described in section 418(b)(4)(A)(ii) (determined without regard to section 418(b)(4)(B)(ii)), and

(ii) the amount necessary to amortize in equal annual installments the increase in the value of vested benefits under the plan due to increases in benefits described in clause (i) over—

(I) 10 years, to the extent such increase in value is attributable to persons in pay status, or

(II) 25 years, to the extent such increase in value is attributable to other participants.

(2) Funding standard requirement.—For purposes of paragraph (1), the funding standard requirement for any plan year is an amount equal to the net charge to the funding standard account for such plan year (as defined in section 418(b)(2)).

(3) Special rule for certain plans.—

(A) In general.—In the case of a plan described in section 4216(b) of the Employee Retirement Income Security Act of 1974, if a plan amendment which increases benefits is adopted after January 1, 1980—

(i) paragraph (1) shall apply only if the plan is a plan described in subparagraph (B), and

(ii) the amount under paragraph (1) shall be determined without regard to subparagraph (1)(B).

(B) Eligible plans.—A plan is described in this subparagraph if—

(i) the rate of employer contributions under the plan for the first plan year beginning on or after the date on which an amendment increasing benefits is adopted, multiplied by the valuation contribution base for that plan year, equals or exceeds the sum of—

(I) the amount that would be necessary to amortize fully, in equal annual installments, by July 1,

1986, the unfunded vested benefits attributable to plan provisions in effect on July 1, 1977 (determined as of the last day of the base plan year); and

(II) the amount that would be necessary to amortize fully, in equal annual installments, over the period described in subparagraph (C), beginning with the first day of the first plan year beginning on or after the date on which the amendment is adopted, the unfunded vested benefits (determined as of the last day of the base plan year) attributable to each plan amendment after July 1, 1977; and

(ii) the rate of employer contributions for each subsequent plan year is not less than the lesser of—

(I) the rate which when multiplied by the valuation contribution base for that subsequent plan year produces the annual amount that would be necessary to complete the amortization schedule described in clause (i), or

(II) the rate for the plan year immediately preceding such subsequent plan year, plus 5 percent of such rate.

(C) Period.—The period determined under this subparagraph is the lesser of—

(i) 12 years, or

(ii) a period equal in length to the average of the remaining expected lives of all persons receiving benefits under the plan.

(4) Exception in case of certain benefit increases.—Paragraph (1) shall not apply with respect to a plan, other than a plan described in paragraph (3), for the period of consecutive plan years in each of which the plan is in reorganization, beginning with a plan year in which occurs the earlier of the date of the adoption or the effective date of any amendment of the plan which increases benefits with respect to service performed before the plan year in which the adoption of the amendment occurred.

(e) Certain Retroactive Plan Amendments.—In determining the minimum contribution requirement with respect to a plan for a plan year under subsection (b), the vested benefits charge may be adjusted to reflect a plan amendment reducing benefits under section 412(c)(8).

(f) Waiver of Accumulated Funding Deficiency.—

(1) In general.—The Secretary may waive any accumulated funding deficiency under this section in accordance with the provisions of section 412(d)(1).

(2) Treatment of waiver.—Any waiver under paragraph (1) shall not be treated as a waived funding deficiency (within the meaning of section 412(d)(3)).

(g) Actuarial Assumptions Must Be Reasonable.—For purposes of making any determination under this subpart, the requirements of section 412(c)(3) shall apply.

SEC. 418C. OVERBURDEN CREDIT AGAINST MINIMUM CONTRIBUTION REQUIREMENT.

(a) General Rule.—For purposes of determining the contribution under section 418B (before the application of section 418B(b)(2) or (d)), the plan sponsor of a plan which is overburdened for the plan year shall apply an overburden credit against the plan's minimum contribution requirement for the plan year (determined without regard to section 418B(b)(2) or (d) and without regard to this section).

(b) Definition of Overburdened Plan.—A plan is overburdened for a plan year if—

(1) the average number of pay status participants under the plan in the base plan year exceeds the average of the number of active participants in the base plan year and the 2 plan years preceding the base plan year, and

(2) the rate of employer contributions under the plan equals or exceeds the greater of—

(A) such rate for the preceding plan year, or

(B) such rate for the plan year preceding the first year in which the plan is in reorganization.

(c) Amount of Overburden Credit.—The amount of the overburden credit for a plan year is the product of—

(1) one-half of the average guaranteed benefit paid for the base plan year, and

(2) the overburden factor for the plan year.

The amount of the overburden credit for a plan year shall not exceed the amount of the minimum contribution requirement for such year (determined without regard to this section).

(d) Overburden Factor.—For purposes of this section, the overburden factor of a plan for the plan year is an amount equal to—

(1) the average number of pay status participants for the base plan year, reduced by

(2) the average of the number of active participants for the base plan year and for each of the 2 plan years preceding the base plan year.

(e) Definitions.—For purposes of this section—

(1) Pay status participant.—The term "pay status participant" means, with respect to a plan, a participant receiving retirement benefits under the plan.

(2) Number of active participants.—The number of active participants for a plan year shall be the sum of—

(A) the number of active employees who are participants in the plan and on whose behalf contributions are required to be made during the plan year;

(B) the number of active employees who are not participants in the plan but who are in an employment unit covered by a collective bargaining agreement which requires the employees' employer to contribute to the plan unless service in such employment unit was never covered under the plan or a predecessor thereof, and

(C) the total number of active employees attributed to employers who made payments to the plan for the plan year of withdrawal liability pursuant to part 1 of subtitle E of title IV of the Employee Retirement Income Security Act of 1974, determined by dividing—

(i) the total amount of such payments, by

(ii) the amount equal to the total contributions received by the plan during the plan year divided by the average number of active employees who were participants in the plan during the plan year.

The Secretary shall by regulations provide alternative methods of determining active participants where (by reason of irregular employment, contributions on a unit basis, or otherwise) this paragraph does not yield a representative basis for determining the credit.

(3) **Average number.**—The term "average number" means, with respect to pay status participants for a plan year, a number equal to one-half the sum of—

(A) the number with respect to the plan as of the beginning of the plan year, and

(B) the number with respect to the plan as of the end of the plan year.

(4) **Average guaranteed benefit.**—The average guaranteed benefit paid is 12 times the average monthly pension payment guaranteed under section 4022A(c)(1) of the Employee Retirement Income Security Act of 1974 determined under the provisions of the plan in effect at the beginning of the first plan year in which the plan is in reorganization and without regard to section 4022A(c)(2).

(5) **First year in reorganization.**—The first year in which the plan is in reorganization is the first of a period of 1 or more consecutive plan years in which the plan has been in reorganization not taking into account any plan years the plan was in reorganization prior to any period of 3 or more consecutive plan years in which the plan was not in reorganization.

(f) No Overburden Credit in Case of Certain Reductions in Contributions.—

(1) **In general.**—Notwithstanding any other provision of this section, a plan is not eligible for an overburden credit for a plan year if the Secretary finds that the plan's current contribution base for any plan year was reduced, without a corresponding reduction in the plan's unfunded vested benefits attributable to pay status participants, as a result of a change in an agreement providing for employer contributions under the plan.

(2) **Treatment of certain withdrawals.**—For purposes of paragraph (1), a complete or partial withdrawal of an employer (within the meaning of part 1 of subtitle E of title IV of the Employee Retirement Income Security Act of 1974) does not impair a plan's eligibility for an overburden credit, unless the Secretary finds that a contribution base reduction described in paragraph (1) resulted from a transfer of liabilities to another plan in connection with the withdrawal.

(g) Mergers.—Notwithstanding any other provision of this section, if 2 or more multiemployer plans merge, the amount of the overburden credit which may be applied under this section with respect to the plan resulting from the merger for any of the 3 plan years ending after the effective date of the merger shall not exceed the sum of the used overburden credit for each of the merging plans for its last plan year ending before the effective date of the merger. For purposes of the preceding sentence, the used overburden credit is that portion of the credit which does not exceed the excess of the minimum contribution requirement determined without regard to any overburden credit under this section over the employer contributions required under the plan.

SEC. 418D. ADJUSTMENTS IN ACCRUED BENEFITS.

(a) Adjustments in Accrued Benefits.—

(1) **In general.**—Notwithstanding section 411, a multiemployer plan in reorganization may be amended, in accordance with this section, to reduce or eliminate accrued benefits attributable to employer contributions which, under section 4022A(b) of the Employee Retirement Income Security Act of 1974, are not eligible for the Pension Benefit Guaranty Corporation's guarantee. The preceding sentence shall only apply to accrued benefits under plan amendments (or plans) adopted after March 26, 1980, or under collective bargaining agreements entered into after March 26, 1980.

(2) **Adjustment of vested benefits charge.**—In determining the minimum contribution requirement with respect to a plan for a plan year under section 418B(b), the vested benefits charge may be adjusted to reflect a plan amendment reducing benefits under this section or section 412(c)(8), but only if the amendment is adopted and effective no later than 2½ months after the end of the plan year, or within such extended period as the Secretary may prescribe by regulations under section 412(c)(10).

(b) Limitation on Reduction.—

(1) **In general.**—Accrued benefits may not be reduced under this section unless—

(A) notice has been given, at least 6 months before the first day of the plan year in which the amendment reducing benefits is adopted, to—

(i) plan participants and beneficiaries.

(ii) each employer who has an obligation to contribute (within the meaning of section 4212(a) of the Employee Retirement Income Security Act of 1974) under the plan, and

(iii) each employee organization which, for purposes of collective bargaining, represents plan participants employed by such an employer, that the plan is in reorganization and that, if contributions under the plan are not increased, accrued benefits under the plan will be reduced or an excise tax will be imposed on employers;

(B) in accordance with regulations prescribed by the Secretary—

(i) any category of accrued benefits is not reduced with respect to inactive participants to a greater extent proportionally that such category of accrued benefits is reduced with respect to active participants,

(ii) benefits attributable to employer contributions other than accrued benefits and the rate of future benefit accruals are reduced at least to an extent equal to the reduction in accrued benefits of inactive participants, and

(iii) in any case in which the accrued benefit of a participant or beneficiary is reduced by changing the benefit form or the requirements which the participant or beneficiary must satisfy to be entitled to the benefit, such reduction is not applicable to—

(I) any participant or beneficiary in pay status on the effective date of the amendment, or the beneficiary of such a participant, or

(II) any participant who has attained normal retirement age, or who is within 5 years of attaining normal retirement age, on the effective date of the amendment, or the beneficiary of any such participant; and

(C) the rate of employer contributions for the plan year in which the amendment becomes effective and for all succeeding plan years in which the plan is in reorganization equals or exceeds the greater of—

(i) the rate of employer contributions, calculated without regard to the amendment, for the plan year in which the amendment becomes effective, or

(ii) the rate of employer contributions for the plan year preceding the plan year in which the amendment becomes effective.

(2) Information required to be included in notice.—The plan sponsors shall include in any notice required to be sent to plan participants and beneficiaries under paragraph (1) information as to the rights and remedies of plan participants and beneficiaries as well as how to contact the Department of Labor for further information and assistance where appropriate.

(c) No Recoupment.—A plan may not recoup a benefit payment which is in excess of the amount payable under the plan because of an amendment retroactively reducing accrued benefits under this section.

(d) Benefit Increases Under Multiemployer Plan in Reorganization.—

(1) Restoration of previously reduced benefits.—

(A) In general.—A plan which has been amended to reduce accrued benefits under this section may be amended to increase or restore accrued benefits, or the rate of future benefit accruals, only if the plan is amended to restore levels of previously reduced accrued benefits of inactive participants and of participants who are within 5 years of attaining normal retirement age to at least the same extent as any such increase in accrued benefits or in the rate of future benefit accruals.

(B) Benefit increases and benefit restorations.— For purposes of this subsection, in the case of a plan which has been amended under this section to reduce accrued benefits—

(i) an increase in a benefit, or in the rate of future benefit accruals, shall be considered a benefit increase to the extent that the benefit, or the accrual rate, is thereby increased above the highest benefit level, or accrual rate, which was in effect under the terms of the plan before the effective date of the amendment reducing accrued benefits, and

(ii) an increase in a benefit, or in the rate of future benefit accruals, shall be considered a benefit restoration to the extent that the benefit, or the accrual rate, is not thereby increased above the highest benefit level, or accrual rate, which was in effect under the terms of the plan immediately before the effective date of the amendment reducing accrued benefits.

(2) Uniformity in benefit restoration.—If a plan is amended to partially restore previously reduced accrued benefit levels, or the rate of future benefit accruals, the benefits of inactive participants shall be restored in at least the same proportions as other accrued benefits which are restored.

(3) No benefit increases in year of benefit reduction.—No benefit increase under a plan may take effect in a plan year in which an amendment reducing accrued benefits under the plan, in accordance with this section, is adopted or first becomes effective.

(4) Retroactive payments.—A plan is not required to make retroactive benefit payments with respect to that portion of an accrued benefit which was reduced and subsequently restored under this section.

IRC Sec. 418D(d)(4)

(e) **Inactive Participant.**—For purposes of this section, the term "inactive participant" means a person not in covered service under the plan who is in pay status under the plan or who has a nonforfeitable benefit under the plan.

(f) **Regulations.**—The Secretary may prescribe rules under which, notwithstanding any other provision of this section, accrued benefit reductions or benefit increases for different participant groups may be varied equitably to reflect variations in contribution rates and other relevant factors reflecting differences in negotiated levels of financial support for plan benefit obligations.

SEC. 418E. INSOLVENT PLANS.

(a) **Suspension of Certain Benefit Payments.**—Notwithstanding section 411, in any case in which benefit payments under an insolvent multiemployer plan exceed the resource benefit level, any such payments of benefits which are not basic benefits shall be suspended, in accordance with this section, to the extent necessary to reduce the sum of such payments and the payments of such basic benefits to the greater of the resource benefit level or the level of basic benefits, unless an alternative procedure is prescribed by the Pension Benefit Guaranty Corporation under section 4022A(g)(5) of the Employee Retirement Income Security Act of 1974.

(b) **Definitions.**—For purposes of this section, for a plan year—

(1) **Insolvency.**—A multiemployer plan is insolvent if the plan's available resources are not sufficient to pay benefits under the plan when due for the plan year, or if the plan is determined to be insolvent under subsection (d).

(2) **Resource benefit level.**—The term "resource benefit level" means the level of monthly benefits determined under subsections (c)(1) and (3) and (d)(3) to be the highest level which can be paid out of the plan's available resources.

(3) **Available resources.**—The term "available resources" means the plan's cash, marketable assets, contributions, withdrawal liability payments, and earnings, less reasonable administrative expenses and amounts owed for such plan year to the Pension Benefit Guaranty Corporation under section 4261(b)(2) of the Employee Retirement Income Security Act of 1974.

(4) **Insolvency year.**—The term "insolvency year" means a plan year in which a plan is insolvent.

(c) **Benefit Payments Under Insolvent Plans.**—

(1) **Determination of resource benefit level.**—The plan sponsor of a plan in reorganization shall determine in writing the plan's resource benefit level for each insolvency year, based on the plan sponsor's reasonable projection of the plan's available resources and the benefits payable under the plan.

(2) **Uniformity of the benefit suspension.**—The suspension of benefit payments under this section shall, in accordance with regulations prescribed by the Secretary, apply in substantially uniform proportions to the benefits of all persons in pay status (within the meaning of section 418(b)(6)) under the plan, except that the Secretary may prescribe rules under which benefit suspensions for different participant groups may be varied equitably to reflect variations in contribution rates and other relevant factors including differences in negotiated levels of financial support for plan benefit obligations.

(3) **Resource benefit level below level of basic benefits.**—Notwithstanding paragraph (2), if a plan sponsor determines in writing a resource benefit level for a plan year which is below the level of basic benefits, the payment of all benefits other than basic benefits shall be suspended for that plan year.

(4) **Excess resources.**—

(A) **In general.**—If, by the end of an insolvency year, the plan sponsor determines in writing that the plan's available resources in that insolvency year could have supported benefit payments above the resource benefit level for that insolvency year, the plan sponsor shall distribute the excess resources to the participants and beneficiaries who received benefit payments from the plan in that insolvency year, in accordance with regulations prescribed by the Secretary.

(B) **Excess resources.**—For purposes of this paragraph, the term "excess resources" means available resources above the amount necessary to support the resource benefit level, but no greater than the amount necessary to pay benefits for the plan year at the benefit levels under the plan.

(5) **Unpaid benefits.**—If, by the end of an insolvency year, any benefit has not been paid at the resource benefit level, amounts up to the resource benefit level which were unpaid shall be distributed to the participants and beneficiaries, in accordance with regulations prescribed by the Secretary, to the extent possible taking into account the plan's total available resources in that insolvency year.

(6) **Retroactive payments.**—Except as provided in paragraph (4) or (5), a plan is not required to make retroactive benefit payments with respect to that portion of a benefit which was suspended under this section.

(d) **Plan Sponsor Determination.**—

(1) **Triennial test.**—As of the end of the first plan year in which a plan is in reorganization, and at least every 3 plan years thereafter (unless the plan is no longer in reorganization), the plan sponsor shall compare the value of plan assets (determined in accordance with section 418B(b)(3)(B)(ii)) for that plan year with the total amount of benefit payments made under the plan for that plan year. Unless the plan

sponsor determines that the value of plan assets exceeds 3 times the total amount of benefit payments, the plan sponsor shall determine whether the plan will be insolvent in any of the next 5 plan years. If the plan sponsor makes such a determination that the plan will be insolvent in any of the next 5 plan years, the plan sponsor shall make the comparison under this paragraph at least annually until the plan sponsor makes a determination that the plan will not be insolvent in any of the next 5 plan years.

(2) Determination of insolvency.—If, at any time, the plan sponsor of a plan in reorganization reasonably determines, taking into account the plan's recent and anticipated financial experience, that the plan's available resources are not sufficient to pay benefits under the plan when due for the next plan year, the plan sponsor shall make such determination available to interested parties.

(3) Determination of resource benefit level.— The plan sponsor of a plan in reorganization shall determine in writing for each insolvency year the resource benefit level and the level of basic benefits no later than 3 months before the insolvency year.

(e) Notice Requirements.—

(1) Impending insolvency.—If the plan sponsor of a plan in reorganization determines under subsection (d)(1) or (2) that the plan may become insolvent (within the meaning of subsection (b)(1)), the plan sponsor shall—

(A) notify the Secretary, the Pension Benefit Guaranty Corporation, the parties described in section 418A(a)(2), and the plan participants and beneficiaries of that determination, and

(B) inform the parties described in section 418A(a)(2) and the plan participants and beneficiaries that if insolvency occurs certain benefit payments will be suspended, but that basic benefits will continue to be paid.

(2) Resource benefit level.—No later than 2 months before the first day of each insolvency year, the plan sponsor of a plan in reorganization shall notify the Secretary, the Pension Benefit Guaranty Corporation, the parties described in section 418A(a)(2), and the plan participants and beneficiaries of the resource benefit level determined in writing for that insolvency year.

(3) Potential need for financial assistance.—In any case in which the plan sponsor anticipates that the resource benefit level for an insolvency year may not exceed the level of basic benefits, the plan sponsor shall notify the Pension Benefit Guaranty Corporation.

(4) Regulations.—Notice required by this subsection shall be given in accordance with regulations prescribed by the Pension Benefit Guaranty Corporation, except that notice to the Secretary shall be given

in accordance with regulations prescribed by the Secretary.

(5) Corporation may prescribe time.—The Pension Benefit Guaranty Corporation may prescribe a time other than the time prescribed by this section for the making of a determination or the filing of a notice under this section.

(f) Financial Assistance.—

(1) Permissive application.—If the plan sponsor of an insolvent plan for which the resource benefit level is above the level of basic benefits anticipates that, for any month in an insolvency year, the plan will not have funds sufficient to pay basic benefits, the plan sponsor may apply for financial assistance from the Pension Benefit Guaranty Corporation under section 4261 of the Employee Retirement Income Security Act of 1974.

(2) Mandatory application.—A plan sponsor who has determined a resource benefit level for an insolvency year which is below the level of basic benefits shall apply for financial assistance from the Pension Benefit Guaranty Corporation under section 4261 of the Employee Retirement Income Security Act of 1974.

(g) Financial Assistance.—Any amount of any financial assistance from the Pension Benefit Guaranty Corporation to any plan, and any repayment of such amount, shall be taken into account under this subpart in such manner as determined by the Secretary.

Recent Amendments to IRC §418E

Pension Protection Act of 2006 (Pub. L. No. 109-280), as follows:
- IRC §418E(d)(1) was amended by Act §213(a) by substituting "5 plan years" for "3 plan years" the second place it appeared, and by adding the new sentence at the end. Eff. with respect to the determinations made in plan years beginning after 2007.

---

* * *

Subpart D—Treatment of Welfare Benefit Funds

SEC. 419. TREATMENT OF FUNDED WELFARE BENEFIT PLANS.

(a) General Rule.—Contributions paid or accrued by an employer to a welfare benefit fund—

(1) shall not be deductible under this chapter, but,

(2) if they would otherwise be deductible, shall (subject to the limitation of subsection (b)) be deductible under this section for the taxable year in which paid.

(b) Limitation.—The amount of the deduction allowable under subsection (a)(2) for any taxable year shall not exceed the welfare benefit fund's qualified cost for the taxable year.

(c) Qualified Cost.—For purposes of this section—

(1) In general.—Except as otherwise provided in this subsection, the term "qualified cost" means, with respect to any taxable year, the sum of—

(A) the qualified direct cost for such taxable year, and

(B) subject to the limitation of section 419A(b), any addition to a qualified asset account for the taxable year.

(2) Reduction for fund's after-tax income.—In the case of any welfare benefit fund, the qualified cost for any taxable year shall be reduced by such fund's after-tax income for such taxable year.

(3) Qualified direct cost.—

(A) In general.—The term "qualified direct cost" means, with respect to any taxable year, the aggregate amount (including administrative expenses) which would have been allowable as a deduction to the employer with respect to the benefits provided during the taxable year, if—

(i) such benefits were provided directly by the employer, and

(ii) the employer used the cash receipts and disbursements method of accounting.

(B) Time when benefits provided.—For purposes of subparagraph (A), a benefit shall be treated as provided when such benefit would be includible in the gross income of the employee if provided directly by the employer (or would be so includible but for any provision of this chapter excluding such benefit from gross income).

(C) 60-month amortization of child care facilities.—

(i) In general.—In determining qualified direct costs with respect to any child care facility for purposes of subparagraph (A), in lieu or depreciation the adjusted basis of such facility shall be allowable as a deduction ratably over a period of 60 months beginning with the month in which the facility is placed in service.

(ii) Child care facility.—The term "child care facility" means any tangible property which qualifies under regulations prescribed by the Secretary as a child care center primarily for children of employees of the employer; except that such term shall not include any property—

(I) not of a character subject to depreciation; or

(II) located outside the United States.

(4) After-tax income.—

(A) In general.—The term "after-tax income" means, with respect to any taxable year, the gross income of the welfare benefit fund reduced by the sum of—

(i) the deductions allowed by this chapter which are directly connected with the production of such gross income, and

(ii) the tax imposed by this chapter on the fund for the taxable year.

(B) Treatment of certain amounts.—In determining the gross income of any welfare benefit fund—

(i) contributions and other amounts received from employees shall be taken into account, but

(ii) contributions from the employer shall not be taken into account.

(5) Item only taken into account once.—No item may be taken into account more than once in determining the qualified cost of any welfare benefit fund.

(d) Carryover of Excess Contributions.—If—

(1) the amount of the contributions paid (or deemed paid under this subsection) by the employer during any taxable year to a welfare benefit fund exceeds

(2) the limitation of subsection (b),

such excess shall be treated as an amount paid by the employer to such fund during the succeeding year.

(e) Welfare Benefit Fund.—For purposes of this section—

(1) In general.—The term "welfare benefit fund" means any fund—

(A) which is part of a plan of an employer, and

(B) through which the employer provides welfare benefits to employees or their beneficiaries.

(2) Welfare benefit.—The term "welfare benefit" means any benefit other than a benefit with respect to which—

(A) section 83(h) applies,

(B) section 404 applies (determined without regard to section 404(b)(2)), or

(C) section 404A applies.

(3) Fund.—The term "fund" means—

(A) any organization described in paragraph (7), (9), (17), or (20) of section 501(c),

(B) any trust, corporation, or other organization not exempt from the tax imposed by this chapter, and

(C) to the extent provided in regulations, any account held for an employer by any person.

(4) Treatment of amounts held pursuant to certain insurance contracts.—

(A) In   general.—Notwithstanding   paragraph (3)(C), the term "fund" shall not include amounts held by an insurance company pursuant to an insurance contract if—

(i) such contract is a life insurance contract described in section 264(a)(1), or

(ii) such contract is a qualified nonguaranteed contract.

(B) Qualified nonguaranteed contract.—

(i) In general.—For purposes of this paragraph, the term "qualified nonguaranteed contract" means any insurance contract (including a reasonable premium stabilization reserve held thereunder) if—

(I) there is no guarantee of a renewal of such contract, and

(II) other than insurance protection, the only payments to which the employer or employees are entitled are experience rated refunds or policy dividends which are not guaranteed and which are determined by factors other than the amount of welfare benefits paid to (or on behalf of) the employees of the employer or their beneficiaries.

(ii) Limitation.—In the case of any qualified nonguaranteed contracts, subparagraph (A) shall not apply unless the amount of any experience rated refund or policy dividend payable to an employer with respect to a policy year is treated by the employer as received or accrued in the taxable year in which the policy year ends.

(f) Method of Contributions, etc., Having the Effect of a Plan.—If—

(1) there is no plan, but

(2) there is a method or arrangement of employer contributions or benefits which has the effect of a plan,

this section shall apply as if there were a plan.

(g) Extension to Plans for Independent Contractors.—If any fund would be a welfare benefit fund (as modified by subsection (f)) but for the fact that there is no employer-employee relationship—

(1) this section shall apply as if there were such a relationship, and

(2) any reference in this section to the employer shall be treated as a reference to the person for whom services are provided, and any reference in this section to an employee shall be treated as a reference to the person providing the services.

SEC. 419A. QUALIFIED ASSET ACCOUNT; LIMITATION ON ADDITIONS TO ACCOUNT.

(a) General Rule.—For purposes of this subpart and section 512, the term "qualified asset account" means any account consisting of assets set aside to provide for the payment of—

(1) disability benefits,

(2) medical benefits,

(3) SUB or severance pay benefits, or

(4) life insurance benefits.

(b) Limitation on Additions to Account.—No addition to any qualified asset account may be taken into account under section 419(c)(1)(B) to the extent such addition results in the amount in such account exceeding the account limit.

(c) Account Limit.—For purposes of this section—

(1) In general.—Except as otherwise provided in this subsection, the account limit for any qualified asset account for any taxable year is the amount reasonably and actuarially necessary to fund—

(A) claims incurred but unpaid (as of the close of such taxable year) for benefits referred to in subsection (a), and

(B) administrative costs with respect to such claims.

(2) Additional reserve for post-retirement medical and life insurance benefits.—The account limit for any taxable year may include a reserve funded over the working lives of the covered employees and actuarially determined on a level basis (using assumptions that are reasonable in the aggregate) as necessary for—

(A) post-retirement medical benefits to be provided to covered employees (determined on the basis of current medical costs), or

(B) post-retirement life insurance benefits to be provided to covered employees.

(3) Amount taken into account for SUB or severance pay benefits.—

(A) In general.—The account limit for any taxable year with respect to SUB or severance pay benefits is 75 percent of the average annual qualified direct costs for SUB or severance pay benefits for any 2 of the immediately preceding 7 taxable years (as selected by the fund).

(B) Special rule for certain new plans.—In the case of any new plan for which SUB or severance pay benefits are not available to any key employee, the Secretary shall, by regulations, provide for an interim amount to be taken into account under paragraph (1).

(4) Limitation on amounts to be taken into account.—

(A) Disability benefits.—For purposes of paragraph (1), disability benefits payable to any individual shall not be taken into account to the extent such benefits are payable at an annual rate in excess of the lower of—

(i) 75 percent of such individual's average compensation for his high 3 years (within the meaning of section 415(b)(3)), or

IRC Sec. 419A(c)(4)(A)(i)

(ii) the limitation in effect under section 415(b)(1)(A).

(B) Limitation on SUB or severance pay benefits.—For purposes of paragraph (3), any SUB or severance pay benefit payable to any individual shall not be taken into account to the extent such benefit is payable at an annual rate in excess of 150 percent of the limitation in effect under section 415(c)(1)(A).

(5) Special limitation where no actuarial certification.—

(A) In general.—Unless there is an actuarial certification of the account limit determined under this subsection for any taxable year, the account limit for such taxable year shall not exceed the sum of the safe harbor limits for such taxable year.

(B) Safe harbor limits.—

(i) Short-term disability benefits.—In the case of short-term disability benefits, the safe harbor limit for any taxable year is 17.5 percent of the qualified direct costs (other than insurance premiums) for the immediately preceding taxable year with respect to such benefits.

(ii) Medical benefits.—In the case of medical benefits, the safe harbor limit for any taxable year is 35 percent of the qualified direct costs (other than insurance premiums) for the immediately preceding taxable year with respect to medical benefits.

(iii) SUB or severance pay benefits.—In the case of SUB or severance pay benefits, the safe harbor limit for any taxable year is the amount determined under paragraph (3).

(iv) Long-term disability or life insurance benefits.—In the case of any long-term disability benefit or life insurance benefit, the safe harbor limit for any taxable year shall be the amount prescribed by regulations.

(6) Additional reserve for medical benefits of bona fide association plans.—

(A) In general.—An applicable account limit for any taxable year may include a reserve in an amount not to exceed 35 percent of the sum of—

(i) the qualified direct costs, and

(ii) the change in claims incurred but unpaid, for such taxable year with respect to medical benefits (other than post-retirement medical benefits).

(B) Applicable account limit.—For purposes of this subsection, the term "applicable account limit" means an account limit for a qualified asset account with respect to medical benefits provided through a plan maintained by a bona fide association (as defined in section 2791(d)(3) of the Public Health Service Act (42 U.S.C. 300gg-91(d)(3)).

(d) Requirement of Separate Accounts for Post-Retirement Medical or Life Insurance Benefits Provided to Key Employees.—

(1) In general.—In the case of any employee who is a key employee—

(A) a separate account shall be established for any medical benefits or life insurance benefits provided with respect to such employee after retirement, and

(B) medical benefits and life insurance benefits provided with respect to such employee after retirement may only be paid from such separate account.

The requirements of this paragraph shall apply to the first taxable year for which a reserve is taken into account under subsection (c)(2) and to all subsequent taxable years.

(2) Coordination with section 415.—For purposes of section 415, any amount attributable to medical benefits allocated to an account established under paragraph (1) shall be treated as an annual addition to a defined contribution plan for purposes of section 415(c). Subparagraph (B) of section 415(c)(1) shall not apply to any amount treated as an annual addition under the preceding sentence.

(3) Key employee.—For purposes of this section, the term "key employee" means any employee who, at any time during the plan year or any preceding plan year, is or was a key employee as defined in section 416(i).

(e) Special Limitations on Reserves for Medical Benefits or Life Insurance Benefits Provided to Retired Employees.—

(1) Reserve must be nondiscriminatory.—No reserve may be taken into account under subsection (c)(2) for post-retirement medical benefits or life insurance benefits to be provided to covered employees unless the plan meets the requirements of section 505(b) with respect to such benefits (whether or not such requirements apply to such plan). The preceding sentence shall not apply to any plan maintained pursuant to an agreement between employee representatives and 1 or more employers if the Secretary finds that such agreement is a collective bargaining agreement and that post-retirement medical benefits or life insurance benefits were the subject of good faith bargaining between such employee representatives and such employer or employers.

(2) Limitation on amount of life insurance benefits.—Life insurance benefits shall not be taken into account under subsection (c)(2) to the extent the aggregate amount of such benefits to be provided with respect to the employee exceeds $50,000.

(f) Definitions and Other Special Rules.—For purposes of this section—

(1) SUB or severance pay benefit.—The term "SUB or severance pay benefit" means—

(A) any supplemental unemployment compensation benefit (as defined in section 501(c)(17)(D)), and

(B) any severance pay benefit.

(2) Medical benefit.—The term "medical benefit" means a benefit which consists of the providing (directly or through insurance) of medical care (as defined in section 213(d)).

(3) Life insurance benefit.—The term "life insurance benefit" includes any other death benefit.

(4) Valuation.—For purposes of this section, the amount of the qualified asset account shall be the value of the assets in such account (as determined under regulations).

(5) Special rule for collective bargained and employee pay-all plans.—No account limits shall apply in the case of any qualified asset account under a separate welfare benefit fund—

(A) under a collective bargaining agreement, or

(B) an employee pay-all plan under section 501(c)(9) if—

(i) such plan has at least 50 employees (determined without regard to subsection (h)(1)), and

(ii) no employee is entitled to a refund with respect to amounts in the fund, other than a refund based on the experience of the entire fund.

(6) Exception for 10-or-more employer plans.—

(A) In general.—This subpart shall not apply in the case of any welfare benefit fund which is part of a 10 or more employer plan. The preceding sentence shall not apply to any plan which maintains experience-rating arrangements with respect to individual employers.

(B) 10 or more employer plan.—For purposes of subparagraph (A), the term "10 or more employer plan" means a plan—

(i) to which more than 1 employer contributes, and

(ii) to which no employer normally contributes more than 10 percent of the total contributions contributed under the plan by all employers.

(7) Adjustments for existing excess reserves.

(A) Increase in account limit.—The account limit for any of the first 4 taxable years to which this section applies shall be increased by the applicable percentage of any existing excess reserves.

(B) Applicable percentage.—For purposes of subparagraph (A)—

In the case of—	The applicable percentage is—
The first taxable year to which this section applies,	80
The second taxable year to which this section applies,	60
The third taxable year to which this section applies,	40
The fourth taxable year to which this section applies,	20

(C) Existing excess reserve.—For purposes of computing the increase under subparagraph (A) for any taxable year, the term "existing excess reserve" means the excess (if any) of—

(i) the amount of assets set aside at the close of the first taxable year ending after July 18, 1984, for purposes described in subsection (a), over

(ii) the account limit determined under this section (without regard to this paragraph) for the taxable year for which such increase is being computed.

(D) Funds to which paragraph applies.—This paragraph shall apply only to a welfare benefit fund which, as of July 18, 1984, had assets set aside for purposes described in subsection (a).

(g) Employer Taxed on Income of Welfare Benefit Fund in Certain Cases.—

(1) In general. In the case of any welfare benefit fund which is not an organization described in paragraph (7), (9), (17), or (20) of section 501(c), the employer shall include in gross income for any taxable year an amount equal to such fund's deemed unrelated income for the fund's taxable year ending within the employer's taxable year.

(2) Deemed unrelated income.—For purposes of paragraph (1), the deemed unrelated income of any welfare benefit fund shall be the amount which would have been itsunrelated business taxable income under section 512(a)(3) if such fund were an organization described in paragraph (7), (9), (17), or (20) of section 501(c).

(3) Coordination with section 419.—If any amount is included in the gross income of an employer for any taxable year under paragraph (1) with respect to any welfare benefit fund—

(A) the amount of the tax imposed by this chapter which is attributable to the amount so included shall be treated as a contribution paid to such welfare benefit fund on the last day of such taxable year, and

(B) the tax so attributable shall be treated as imposed on the fund for purposes of section 419(c)(4)(A).

(h) Aggregation Rules.—For purposes of this subpart—

IRC Sec. 419A(h)

(1) Aggregation of funds.—

(A) Mandatory aggregation.—For purposes of subsections (c)(4), (d)(2), and (e)(2), all welfare benefit funds of an employer shall be treated as 1 fund.

(B) Permissive aggregation for purposes not specified in subparagraph (A).—For purposes of this section (other than the provisions specified in subparagraph (A)), at the election of the employer, 2 or more welfare benefit funds of such employer may (to the extent not inconsistent with the purposes of this subpart and section 512) be treated as 1 fund.

(2) Treatment of related employers.—Rules similar to the rules of subsections (b), (c), (m), and (n) of section 414 shall apply.

(i) Regulations.—The Secretary shall prescribe such regulations as may be appropriate to carry out the purposes of this subpart. Such regulations may provide that the plan administrator of any welfare benefit fund which is part of a plan to which more than 1 employer contributes shall submit such information to the employers contributing to the fund as may be necessary to enable the employers to comply with the provisions of this section.

Recent Amendments to IRC §419A

Pension Protection Act of 2006 (Pub. L. No. 109-280), as follows:
● IRC §419A(c) was amended by Act §843(a) by adding new para. (6). Eff. tax years beginning after Dec. 31, 2006.

Subpart E—Treatment of Transfers to Retiree Health Accounts

SEC. 420. TRANSFERS OF EXCESS PENSION ASSETS TO RETIREE HEALTH ACCOUNTS.

(a) General Rule.—If there is a qualified transfer of any excess pension assets of a defined benefit plan to a health benefits account which is part of such plan—

(1) a trust which is part of such plan shall not be treated as failing to meet the requirements of subsection (a) or (h) of section 401 solely by reason of such transfer (or any other action authorized under this section),

(2) no amount shall be includible in the gross income of the employer maintaining the plan solely by reason of such transfer,

(3) such transfer shall not be treated—

(A) as an employer reversion for purposes of section 4980, or

(B) as a prohibited transaction for purposes of section 4975, and

(4) the limitations of subsection (d) shall apply to such employer.

(b) Qualified Transfer.—For purposes of this section—

(1) In general.—The term "qualified transfer" means a transfer—

(A) of excess pension assets of a defined benefit plan to a health benefits account which is part of such plan in a taxable year beginning after December 31, 1990,

(B) which does not contravene any other provision of law, and

(C) with respect to which the following requirements are met in connection with the plan—

(i) the requirements of subsection (c)(1),

(ii) the vesting requirements of subsection (c)(2), and

(iii) the minimum cost requirements of subsection (c)(3).

(2) Only 1 transfer per year.—

(A) In general.—No more than 1 transfer with respect to any plan during a taxable year may be treated as a qualified transfer for purposes of this section.

(B) Exception.—A transfer described in paragraph (4) shall not be taken into account for purposes of subparagraph (A).

(3) Limitation on amount transferred.—The amount of excess pension assets which may be transferred in a qualified transfer shall not exceed the amount which is reasonably estimated to be the amount the employer maintaining the plan will pay (whether directly or through reimbursement) out of such account during the taxable year of the transfer for qualified current retiree health liabilities.

(4) Special rule for 1990.—

(A) In general.—Subject to the provisions of subsection (c), a transfer shall be treated as a qualified transfer if such transfer—

(i) is made after the close of the taxable year preceding the employer's first taxable year beginning after December 31, 1990, and before the earlier of—

(I) the due date (including extensions) for the filing of the return of tax for such preceding taxable year, or

(II) the date such return is filed, and

(ii) does not exceed the expenditures of the employer for qualified current retiree health liabilities for such preceding taxable year.

(B) Deduction reduced.—The amount of the deductions otherwise allowable under this chapter to an employer for the taxable year preceding the employer's first taxable year beginning after December 31, 1990, shall be reduced by the amount of any qualified transfer to which this paragraph applies.

(C) Coordination with reduction rule.—Subsection (e)(1)(B) shall not apply to a transfer described in subparagraph (A).

(5) Expiration.—No transfer in any taxable year beginning after December 31, 2013, shall be treated as a qualified transfer.

(c) Requirements of Plans Transferring Assets.—

(1) Use of transferred assets.—

(A) In general.—Any assets transferred to a health benefits account in a qualified transfer (and any income allocable thereto) shall be used only to pay qualified current retiree health liabilities (other than liabilities of key employees not taken into account under subsection (e)(1)(D)) for the taxable year of the transfer (whether directly or through reimbursement). In the case of a qualified future transfer or collectively bargained transfer to which subsection (f) applies, any assets so transferred may also be used to pay liabilities described in subsection (f)(2)(C).

(B) Amounts not used to pay for health benefits.—

(i) In general.—Any assets transferred to a health benefits account in a qualified transfer (and any income allocable thereto) which are not used as provided in subparagraph (A) shall be transferred out of the account to the transferor plan.

(ii) Tax treatment of amounts.—Any amount transferred out of an account under clause (i)—

(I) shall not be includible in the gross income of the employer for such taxable year, but

(II) shall be treated as an employer reversion for purposes of section 4980 (without regard to subsection (d) thereof).

(C) Ordering rule.—For purposes of this section, any amount paid out of a health benefits account shall be treated as paid first out of the assets and income described in subparagraph (A).

(2) Requirements relating to pension benefits accruing before transfer.—

(A) In general.—The requirements of this paragraph are met if the plan provides that the accrued pension benefits of any participant or beneficiary under the plan become nonforfeitable in the same manner which would be required if the plan had terminated immediately before the qualified transfer (or in the case of a participant who separated during the 1-year period ending on the date of the transfer, immediately before such separation).

(B) Special rule for 1990.—In the case of a qualified transfer described in subsection (b)(4), the requirements of this paragraph are met with respect to any participant who separated from service during the taxable year to which such transfer relates by recomputing such participant's benefits as if subparagraph (A) had applied immediately before such separation.

(3) Minimum cost requirements.—

(A) In general.—The requirements of this paragraph are met if each group health plan or arrangement under which applicable health benefits are provided provides that the applicable employer cost for each taxable year during the cost maintenance period shall not be less than the higher of the applicable employer costs for each of the 2 taxable years immediately preceding the taxable year of the qualified transfer or, in the case of a transfer which involves a plan maintained by an employer described in subsection (f)(2)(E)(i)(III), if the plan meets the requirements of subsection (f)(2)(D)(i)(II).

(B) Applicable employer cost.—For purposes of this paragraph, the term "applicable cost" means, with respect to any taxable year, the amount determined by dividing—

(i) the qualified current retiree health liabilities of the employer for such taxable year determined—

(I) without regard to any reduction under subsection (e)(1)(B), and

(II) in the case of a taxable year in which there was no qualified transfer, in the same manner as if there had been such a transfer at the end of the taxable year, by

(ii) the number of individuals to whom coverage for applicable health benefits was provided during such taxable year.

(C) Election to compute cost separately.—An employer may elect to have this paragraph applied separately with respect to individuals eligible for benefits under title XVIII of the Social Security Act at any time during the taxable year and with respect to individuals not so eligible.

(D) Cost maintenance period.—For purposes of this paragraph, the term "cost maintenance period" means the period of 5 taxable years beginning with the taxable year in which the qualified transfer occurs. If a taxable year is in two or more overlapping cost maintenance periods, this paragraph shall be applied by taking into account the highest applicable employer cost required to be provided under subparagraph (A) for such taxable year.

(E) Regulations.—

(i) In general.—The Secretary shall prescribe such regulations as may be necessary to prevent an employer who significantly reduces retiree health coverage during the cost maintenance period from being treated as satisfying the minimum cost requirement of this subsection.

(ii) Insignificant cost reductions permitted.—

(I) In general.—An eligible employer shall not be treated as failing to meet the requirements of this paragraph for any taxable year if, in lieu of any reduction of retiree health coverage permitted under the regulations prescribed under clause (i), the employer reduces applicable employer cost by an amount not in excess of the reduction in costs which would have occurred if the employer had made the maximum permissible reduction in retiree health coverage under such regulations. In applying such regulations to any subsequent taxable year, any reduction in applicable employer cost under this clause shall be treated as if it were an equivalent reduction in retiree health coverage.

(II) Eligible employer.—For purposes of subclause (I), an employer shall be treated as an eligible employer for any taxable year if, for the preceding taxable year, the qualified current retiree health liabilities of the employer were at least 5 percent of the gross receipts of the employer. For purposes of this subclause, the rules of paragraphs (2), (3)(B), and (3)(C) of section 448(c) shall apply in determining the amount of an employer's gross receipts.

(d) Limitations on Employer.—For purposes of this title—

(1) Deduction limitations.—No deduction shall be allowed—

(A) for the transfer of any amount to a health benefits account in a qualified transfer (or any retransfer to the plan under subsection (c)(1)(B)),

(B) for qualified current retiree health liabilities paid out of the assets (and income) described in subsection (c)(1), or

(C) for any amounts to which subparagraph (B) does not apply and which are paid for qualified current retiree health liabilities for the taxable year to the extent such amounts are not greater than the excess (if any) of—

(i) the amount determined under subparagraph (A) (and income allocable thereto), over

(ii) the amount determined under subparagraph (B).

(2) No contributions allowed.—An employer may not contribute after December 31, 1990, any amount to a health benefits account or welfare benefit fund (as defined in section 419(e)(1)) with respect to qualified current retiree health liabilities for which transferred assets are required to be used under subsection (c)(1).

(e) Definition and Special Rules.—For purposes of this section—

(1) Qualified current retiree health liabilities.—For purposes of this section—

(A) In general.—The term "qualified current retiree health liabilities" means, with respect to any taxable year, the aggregate amounts (including administrative expenses) which would have been allowable as a deduction to the employer for such taxable year with respect to applicable health benefits provided during such taxable year if—

(i) such benefits were provided directly by the employer, and

(ii) the employer used the cash receipts and disbursements method of accounting.

For purposes of the preceding sentence, the rule of section 419(c)(3)(B) shall apply.

(B) Reductions for amounts previously set aside.—The amount determined under subparagraph (A) shall be reduced by the amount which bears the same ratio to such amount as—

(i) the value (as of the close of the plan year preceding the year of the qualified transfer) of the assets in all health benefits accounts or welfare benefit funds (as defined in section 419(e)(1)) set aside to pay for the qualified current retiree health liability, bears to

(ii) the present value of the qualified current retiree health liabilities for all plan years (determined without regard to this subparagraph).

(C) Applicable health benefits.—The term "applicable health benefits" means health benefits or coverage which are provided to—

(i) retired employees who, immediately before the qualified transfer, are entitled to receive such benefits upon retirement and who are entitled to pension benefits under the plan, and

(ii) their spouses and dependents.

(D) Key employees excluded.—If an employee is a key employee (within the meaning of section 416(i)(1)) with respect to any plan year ending in a taxable year, such employee shall not be taken into account in computing qualified current retiree health liabilities for such taxable year or in calculating applicable employer cost under subsection (c)(3)(B).

(2) Excess pension assets.—The term "excess pension assets" means the excess (if any) of—

(A) the lesser of—

(i) the fair market value of the plan's assets (reduced by the prefunding balance and funding standard carryover balance determined under section 430(f)), or

(ii) the value of plan assets as determined under section 430(g)(3) after reduction under section 430(f), over

(B) 125 percent of the sum of the funding target and the target normal cost determined under section 430 for such plan year.

(3) Health benefits account.—The term "health benefits account" means an account established and maintained under section 401(h).

(4) Coordination with section 430.—In the case of a qualified transfer, any assets so transferred shall not, for purposes of this section and section 430, be treated as assets in the plan.

(5) Application to multiemployer plans.—In the case of a multiemployer plan, this section shall be applied to any such plan—

(A) by treating any reference in this section to an employer as a reference to all employers maintaining the plan (or, if appropriate, the plan sponsor), and

(B) in accordance with such modifications of this section (and the provisions of this title relating to this section) as the Secretary determines appropriate to reflect the fact the plan is not maintained by a single employer.

(f) Qualified Transfers To Cover Future Retiree Health Costs and Collectively Bargained Retiree Health Benefits.—

(1) In general.—An employer maintaining a defined benefit plan (other than a multiemployer plan) may, in lieu of a qualified transfer, elect for any taxable year to have the plan make—

(A) a qualified future transfer, or

(B) a collectively bargained transfer.

Except as provided in this subsection, a qualified future transfer and a collectively bargained transfer shall be treated for purposes of this title and the Employee Retirement Income Security Act of 1974 as if it were a qualified transfer.

(2) Qualified future and collectively bargained transfers.—For purposes of this subsection—

(A) In general.—The terms "qualified future transfer" and "collectively bargained transfer" mean a transfer which meets all of the requirements for a qualified transfer, except that—

(i) the determination of excess pension assets shall be made under subparagraph (B),

(ii) the limitation on the amount transferred shall be determined under subparagraph (C),

(iii) the minimum cost requirements of subsection (c)(3) shall be modified as provided under subparagraph (D), and

(iv) in the case of a collectively bargained transfer, the requirements of subparagraph (E) shall be met with respect to the transfer.

(B) Excess pension assets.—

(i) In general.—In determining excess pension assets for purposes of this subsection, subsection (e)(2) shall be applied by substituting "120 percent" for "125 percent".

(ii) Requirement to maintain funded status.—If, as of any valuation date of any plan year in the transfer period, the amount determined under subsection (e)(2)(B) (after application of clause (i)) exceeds the amount determined under subsection (e)(2)(A), either—

(I) the employer maintaining the plan shall make contributions to the plan in an amount not less than the amount required to reduce such excess to zero as of such date, or

(II) there is transferred from the health benefits account to the plan an amount not less than the amount required to reduce such excess to zero as of such date.

(C) Limitation on amount transferred.—Notwithstanding subsection (b)(3), the amount of the excess pension assets which may be transferred—

(i) in the case of a qualified future transfer shall be equal to the sum of—

(I) if the transfer period includes the taxable year of the transfer, the amount determined under subsection (b)(3) for such taxable year, plus

(II) in the case of all other taxable years in the transfer period, the sum of the qualified current retiree health liabilities which the plan reasonably estimates, in accordance with guidance issued by the Secretary, will be incurred for each of such years, and

(ii) in the case of a collectively bargained transfer, shall not exceed the amount which is reasonably estimated, in accordance with the provisions of the collective bargaining agreement and generally accepted accounting principles, to be the amount the employer maintaining the plan will pay (whether directly or through reimbursement) out of such account during the collectively bargained cost maintenance period for collectively bargained retiree health liabilities.

(D) Minimum cost requirements.—

(i) In general.—The requirements of subsection (c)(3) shall be treated as met if—

(I) in the case of a qualified future transfer, each group health plan or arrangement under which applicable health benefits are provided provides applicable health benefits during the period beginning with the first year of the transfer period and ending with the last day of the 4th year following the transfer period such that the annual average amount of the applicable employer cost during such period is not less than the applicable employer cost determined under subsection (c)(3)(A) with respect to the transfer, and

(II) in the case of a collectively bargained transfer, each collectively bargained group health plan under which collectively bargained health benefits are provided provides that the collectively bargained employer cost for each taxable year during the collectively bargained cost maintenance period shall not be less than the amount specified by the collective bargaining agreement.

(ii) Election to maintain benefits for future transfers.—An employer may elect, in lieu of the requirements of clause (i)(I), to meet the requirements of subsection (c)(3) by meeting the requirements of such subsection (as in effect before the amendments made by section 535 of the Tax Relief Extension Act of 1999) for each of the years described in the period under clause (i)(I).

(iii) Collectively bargained employer cost.— For purposes of this subparagraph, the term "collectively bargained employer cost" means the average cost per covered individual of providing collectively bargained retiree health benefits as determined in accordance with the applicable collective bargaining agreement. Such agreement may provide for an appropriate reduction in the collectively bargained employer cost to take into account any portion of the collectively bargained retiree health benefits that is provided or financed by a government program or other source.

(E) Special rules for collectively bargained transfers.—

(i) In general.—A collectively bargained transfer shall only include a transfer which—

(I) is made in accordance with a collective bargaining agreement,

(II) before the transfer, the employer designates, in a written notice delivered to each employee organization that is a party to the collective bargaining agreement, as a collectively bargained transfer in accordance with this section, and

(III) involves a plan maintained by an employer which, in its taxable year ending in 2005, provided health benefits or coverage to retirees and their spouses and dependents under all of the benefit plans maintained by the employer, but only if the aggregate cost (including administrative expenses) of such benefits or coverage which would have been allowable as a deduction to the employer (if such benefits or coverage had been provided directly by the employer and the employer used the cash receipts and disbursements method of accounting) is at least 5 percent of the gross receipts of the employer (determined in accordance with the last sentence of subsection (c)(3)(E)(ii)(II)) for such taxable year, or a plan maintained by a successor to such employer.

(ii) Use of assets.—Any assets transferred to a health benefits account in a collectively bargained transfer (and any income allocable thereto) shall be used only to pay collectively bargained retiree health liabilities (other than liabilities of key employees not taken into account under paragraph (6)(B)(iii)) for the taxable year of the transfer or for any subsequent taxable year during the collectively bargained cost maintenance period (whether directly or through reimbursement).

(3) Coordination with other transfers.—In applying subsection (b)(3) to any subsequent transfer during a taxable year in a transfer period or collectively bargained cost maintenance period, qualified current retiree health liabilities shall be reduced by any such liabilities taken into account with respect to the qualified future transfer or collectively bargained transfer to which such period relates.

(4) Special deduction rules for collectively bargained transfers.—In the case of a collectively bargained transfer—

(A) the limitation under subsection (d)(1)(C) shall not apply, and

(B) notwithstanding subsection (d)(2), an employer may contribute an amount to a health benefits account or welfare benefit fund (as defined in section 419(e)(1)) with respect to collectively bargained retiree health liabilities for which transferred assets are required to be used under subsection (c)(1)(B), and the deductibility of any such contribution shall be governed by the limits applicable to the deductibility of contributions to a welfare benefit fund under a collective bargaining agreement (as determined under section 419A(f)(5)(A)) without regard to whether such contributions are made to a health benefits account or welfare benefit fund and without regard to the provisions of section 404 or the other provisions of this section.

The Secretary shall provide rules to ensure that the application of this paragraph does not result in a deduction being allowed more than once for the same contribution or for 2 or more contributions or expenditures relating to the same collectively bargained retiree health liabilities.

(5) Transfer period.—For purposes of this subsection, the term "transfer period" means, with respect to any transfer, a period of consecutive taxable years (not less than 2) specified in the election under paragraph (1) which begins and ends during the 10-taxable-year period beginning with the taxable year of the transfer.

(6) Terms relating to collectively bargained transfers.—For purposes of this subsection—

(A) Collectively bargained cost maintenance period.—The term "collectively bargained cost maintenance period" means, with respect to each covered retiree and his covered spouse and dependents, the shorter of—

(i) the remaining lifetime of such covered retiree and his covered spouse and dependents, or

(ii) the period of coverage provided by the collectively bargained health plan (determined as of the date of the collectively bargained transfer) with respect to such covered retiree and his covered spouse and dependents.

(B) Collectively bargained retiree health liabilities.—

(i) In general.—The term "collectively bargained retiree health liabilities" means the present value, as of the beginning of a taxable year and determined in accordance with the applicable collective bargaining agreement, of all collectively bargained health benefits (including administrative expenses) for such taxable year and all subsequent taxable years during the collectively bargained cost maintenance period.

(ii) Reduction for amounts previously set aside.—The amount determined under clause (i) shall be reduced by the value (as of the close of the plan year preceding the year of the collectively bargained transfer) of the assets in all health benefits accounts or welfare benefit funds (as defined in section 419(e)(1)) set aside to pay for the collectively bargained retiree health liabilities.

(iii) Key employees excluded.—If an employee is a key employee (within the meaning of section 416(I)(1)) with respect to any plan year ending in a taxable year, such employee shall not be taken into account in computing collectively bargained retiree health liabilities for such taxable year or in calculating collectively bargained employer cost under subsection (c)(3)(C).

(C) Collectively bargained health benefits.—The term "collectively bargained health benefits" means health benefits or coverage which are provided to—

(i) retired employees who, immediately before the collectively bargained transfer, are entitled to receive such benefits upon retirement and who are entitled to pension benefits under the plan, and their spouses and dependents, and

(ii) if specified by the provisions of the collective bargaining agreement governing the collectively bargained transfer, active employees who, following their retirement, are entitled to receive such benefits and who are entitled to pension benefits under the plan, and their spouses and dependents.

(D) Collectively bargained health plan.—The term "collectively bargained health plan" means a group health plan or arrangement for retired employees and their spouses and dependents that is maintained pursuant to 1 or more collective bargaining agreements.

Recent Amendments to IRC §420

Worker, Retiree, and Employer Recovery Act of 2008 (Pub. L. No. 110-458), as follows:

- IRC §420(c)(1)(A) was amended by Act §108(i)(1) by adding the sentence at the end. Eff. as if included in Pub. L. No. 109-280, §841 [eff. for transfers after Aug. 17, 2006].
- IRC §420(f)(2)(D)(i)(I) was amended by Act §108(i)(2) by striking "such" before "the applicable". Eff. as if included in Pub. L. No. 109-280, §841 [eff. for transfers after Aug. 17, 2006].

U.S. Troop Readiness, Veterans' Care, Katrina Recovery, and Iraq Accountability Appropriations Act, 2007 (Pub. L. No. 110-28), as follows:

- IRC §420(c)(3)(A) was amended by Act §6613(a) by substituting "transfer or, in the case of a transfer which involves a plan maintained by an employer described in subsection (f)(2)(E)(i)(III), if the plan meets the requirements of subsection (f)(2)(D)(i)(II)" for "transfer.". Eff. for transfers after May 25, 2007.
- IRC §420(e)(2)(B) was amended by Act §6612(b) by substituting "funding target" for "funding shortfall". Eff. Aug. 17, 2006, as if included in provision of Pub. L. No. 109-280 to which it relates.
- IRC §420(f)(2)(E)(i)(III) was amended by Act §6612(a) by substituting "subsection (c)(3)(E)(ii)(II)" for "subsection (c)(2)(E)(ii)(II)". Eff. for transfers after Aug. 17, 2006, as if included in the provision of Pub. L. No. 109-280 to which it relates.

Pension Protection Act of 2006 (Pub. L. No. 109-280), as follows:

- IRC §420(a) was amended by Act §842(a)(1) by striking "(other than a multiemployer plan)" after "defined benefit plan". Eff. for transfers made in tax years beginning after Dec. 31, 2006.
- IRC §420(e)(2) was amended by Act §114(d)(1). Eff. Aug. 17, 2006 [for plan years beginning after 2007, eff. date as amended by Pub. L. No. 110-458, §101(d)(3)]. IRC §420(e)(2) prior to amendment:
  (2) Excess pension assets.—The term "excess pension assets" means the excess (if any) of—
  (A) the amount determined under section 412(c)(7)(A)(ii), over
  (B) the greater of—
  (i) the amount determined under section 412(c)(7)(A)(i), or
  (ii) 125 percent of current liability (as defined in section 412(c)(7)(B)).
  The determination under this paragraph shall be made as of the most recent valuation date of the plan preceding the qualified transfer.
- IRC §420(e)(4) was amended by Act §114(d)(2). Eff. Aug. 17, 2006 [for plan years beginning after 2007, eff. date as amended by Pub. L. No. 110-458, §101(d)(3)]. IRC §420(e)(4) prior to amendment:
  (4) Coordination with section 412.—In the case of a qualified transfer to a health benefits account—
  (A) any assets transferred in a plan year on or before the valuation date for such year (and any income allocable thereto) shall, for purposes of section 412, be treated as assets in the plan as of the valuation date for such year, and
  (B) the plan shall be treated as having a net experience loss under section 412(b)(2)(B)(iv) in an amount equal to the amount of such transfer (reduced by any amounts transferred back to the pension plan under subsection (c)(1)(B)) and for which amortization charges begin for the first plan year after the plan year in which such transfer occurs, except that such section shall be applied to such amount by substituting "10 plan years" for "5 plan years".
- IRC §420(e) was amended by Act §842(a)(2) by adding para. (5). Eff. for transfers made in tax years beginning after Dec. 31, 2006.
- IRC §420 was amended by Act §841(a) by adding new subsec. (f). Eff. for transfers after Aug. 17, 2006.

IRC Sec. 420(f)(6)(D)

American Jobs Creation Act of 2004 (Pub. L. No. 108-357), as follows:

- IRC §420(c)(3)(E) was amended by Act §709(b) by substituting "(i) In general.—The Secretary" for "The Secretary", and by adding new cl. (ii). Eff. tax years ending after Oct. 22, 2004.

Pension Funding Equity Act of 2004 (Pub. L. No. 108-218), as follows:

- IRC §420(b)(5) was amended by Act §204(a) by substituting "December 31, 2013" for "December 31, 2005". Eff. Apr. 10, 2004.

Part II—Certain Stock Options

SEC. 421. GENERAL RULES.

(a) **Effect of Qualifying Transfer.**—If a share of stock is transferred to an individual in a transfer in respect of which the requirements of section 422(a) or 423(a) are met—

(1) no income shall result at the time of the transfer of such share to the individual upon his exercise of the option with respect to such share;

(2) no deduction under section 162 (relating to trade or business expenses) shall be allowable at any time to the employer corporation, a parent or subsidiary corporation of such corporation, or a corporation issuing or assuming a stock option in a transaction to which section 424(a) applies, with respect to the share so transferred; and

(3) no amount other than the price paid under the option shall be considered as received by any of such corporations for the share so transferred.

(b) **Effect of Disqualifying Disposition.**—If the transfer of a share of stock to an individual pursuant to his exercise of an option would otherwise meet the requirements of section 422(a) or 423(a) except that there is a failure to meet any of the holding period requirements of section 422(a)(1) or 423(a)(1), then any increase in the income of such individual or deduction from the income of his employer corporation for the taxable year in which such exercise occurred attributable to such disposition, shall be treated as an increase in income or a deduction from income in the taxable year of such individual or of such employer corporation in which such disposition occurred. No amount shall be required to be deducted and withheld under chapter 24 with respect to any increase in income attributable to a disposition described in the preceding sentence.

(c) **Exercise by Estate.**—

(1) **In general.**—If an option to which this part applies is exercised after the death of the employee by the estate of the decedent, or by a person who acquired the right to exercise such option by bequest or inheritance or by reason of the death of the decedent, the provisions of subsection (a) shall apply to the same extent as if the option had been exercised by the decedent, except that—

(A) the holding period and employment requirements of section 422(a) and 423(a) shall not apply, and

(B) any transfer by the estate of stock acquired shall be considered a disposition of such stock for purposes of section 423(c).

(2) **Deduction for estate tax.**—If an amount is required to be included under section 423(c) in gross income of the estate of the deceased employee or of a person described in paragraph (1), there shall be allowed to the estate or such person a deduction with respect to the estate tax attributable to the inclusion in the taxable estate of the deceased employee of the net value for estate tax purposes of the option. For this purpose, the deduction shall be determined under section 691(c) as if the option acquired from the deceased employee were an item of gross income in respect of the decedent under section 691 and as if the amount includible in gross income under section 423(c) were an amount included in gross income under section 691 in respect of such item of gross income.

(3) **Basis of shares acquired.**—In the case of a share of stock acquired by the exercise of an option to which paragraph (1) applies—

(A) the basis of such share shall include so much of the basis of the option as is attributable to such share; except that the basis of such share shall be reduced by the excess (if any) of (i) the amount which would have been includible in gross income under section 423(c) if the employee had exercised the option on the date of his death and had held the share acquired pursuant to such exercise at the time of his death, over (ii) the amount which is includible in gross income under such section; and

(B) the last sentence of section 423(c) shall apply only to the extent that the amount includible in gross income under such section exceeds so much of the basis of the option as is attributable to such share.

(d) **Certain Sales to Comply With Conflict-of-Interest Requirements.**—If—

(1) a share of stock is transferred to an eligible person (as defined in section 1043(b)(1)) pursuant to such person's exercise of an option to which this part applies, and

(2) such share is disposed of by such person pursuant to a certificate of divestiture (as defined in section 1043(b)(2)), such disposition shall be treated as meeting the requirements of section 422(a)(1) or 423(a)(1), whichever is applicable.

Recent Amendments to IRC §421

American Jobs Creation Act of 2004 (Pub. L. No. 108-357), as follows:

- IRC §421(b) was amended by Act §251(b) by adding a new sentence at the end. Eff. for stock acquired pursuant to options exercised after Oct. 22, 2004.

• IRC §421 was amended by Act §905(a) by adding para. (d). Eff. for sales after Oct. 22, 2004.

SEC. 422. INCENTIVE STOCK OPTIONS.

(a) In General.—Section 421(a) shall apply with respect to the transfer of a share of stock to an individual pursuant to his exercise of an incentive stock option if—

(1) no disposition of such share is made by him within 2 years from the date of the granting of the option nor within 1 year after the transfer of such share to him, and

(2) at all times during the period beginning on the date of the granting of the option and ending on the day 3 months before the date of such exercise, such individual was an employee of either the corporation granting such option, a parent or subsidiary corporation of such corporation, or a corporation or a parent or subsidiary corporation of such corporation issuing or assuming a stock option in a transaction to which section 424(a) applies.

(b) Incentive Stock Option.—For purposes of this part, the term "incentive stock option" means an option granted to an individual for any reason connected with his employment by a corporation, if granted by the employer corporation or its parent or subsidiary corporation, to purchase stock of any of such corporations, but only if—

(1) the option is granted pursuant to a plan which includes the aggregate number of shares which may be issued under options and the employees (or class of employees) eligible to receive options, and which is approved by the stockholders of the granting corporation within 12 months before or after the date such plan is adopted;

(2) such option is granted within 10 years from the date such plan is adopted, or the date such plan is approved by the stockholders, whichever is earlier;

(3) such option by its terms is not exercisable after the expiration of 10 years from the date such option is granted;

(4) the option price is not less than the fair market value of the stock at the time such option is granted;

(5) such option by its terms is not transferable by such individual otherwise than by will or the laws of descent and distribution, and is exercisable, during his lifetime, only by him; and

(6) such individual, at the time the option is granted, does not own stock possessing more than 10 percent of the total combined voting power of all classes of stock of the employer corporation or of its parent or subsidiary corporation.

Such term shall not include any option if (as of the time the option is granted) the terms of such option provide that it will not be treated as an incentive stock option.

(c) Special Rules.—

(1) Good faith efforts to value of stock.—If a share of stock is transferred pursuant to the exercise by an individual of an option which would fail to qualify as an incentive stock option under subsection (b) because there was a failure in an attempt, made in good faith, to meet the requirement of subsection (b)(4), the requirement of subsection (b)(4) shall be considered to have been met. To the extent provided in regulations by the Secretary, a similar rule shall apply for purposes of subsection (d).

(2) Certain disqualifying dispositions where amount realized is less than value at exercise.—If—

(A) an individual who has acquired a share of stock by the exercise of an incentive stock option makes a disposition of such share within either of the periods described in subsection (a)(1), and

(B) such disposition is a sale or exchange with respect to which a loss (if sustained) would be recognized to such individual,

then the amount which is includible in the gross income of such individual, and the amount which is deductible from the income of his employer corporation, as compensation attributable to the exercise of such option shall not exceed the excess (if any) of the amount realized on such sale or exchange over the adjusted basis of such share.

(3) Certain transfers by insolvent individuals.—If an insolvent individual holds a share of stock acquired pursuant to his exercise of an incentive stock option, and if such share is transferred to a trustee, receiver, or other similar fiduciary in any proceeding under title 11 or any other similar insolvency proceeding, neither such transfer, nor any other transfer of such share for the benefit of his creditors in such proceeding, shall constitute a disposition of such share for purposes of subsection (a)(1).

(4) Permissible provisions.—An option which meets the requirements of subsection (b) shall be treated as an incentive stock option even if—

(A) the employee may pay for the stock with stock of the corporation granting the option,

(B) the employee has a right to receive property at the time of exercise of the option, or

(C) the option is subject to any condition not inconsistent with the provisions of this subsection (b).

Subparagraph (B) shall apply to a transfer of property (other than cash) only if section 83 applies to the property so transferred.

(5) 10-percent shareholder rule.—Subsection (b)(6) shall not apply if at the time such option is granted the option price is at least 110 percent of the fair market value of the stock subject to the option and such option by its terms is not exercisable after the expiration of 5 years from the date such option is granted.

(6) Special rule when disabled.—For purposes of subsection (a)(2), in the case of an employee who is disabled (within the meaning of section 22(e)(3)), the 3-month period of subsection (a)(2) shall be 1 year.

(7) Fair market value.—For purposes of this section, the fair market value of stock shall be determined without regard to any restriction other than a restriction which, by its terms, will never lapse.

(d) $100,000 Per Year Limitation.—

(1) In general.—To the extent that the aggregate fair market value of stock with respect to which incentive stock options (determined without regard to this subsection) are exercisable for the 1st time by any individual during any calendar year (under all plans of the individual's employer corporation and its parent and subsidiary corporations) exceeds $100,000, such options shall be treated as options which are not incentive stock options.

(2) Ordering rule.—Paragraph (1) shall be applied by taking options into account in the order in which they were granted.

(3) Determination of fair market value.—For purposes of paragraph (1), the fair market value of any stock shall be determined as of the time the option with respect to such stock is granted.

SEC. 423. EMPLOYEE STOCK PURCHASE PLANS.

(a) General Rule.—Section 421(a) shall apply with respect to the transfer of a share of stock to an individual pursuant to his exercise of an option granted after December 31, 1963, under an employee stock purchase plan (as defined in subsection (b)) if—

(1) no disposition of such share is made by him within 2 years after the date of the granting of the option nor within 1 year after the transfer of such share to him; and

(2) at all times during the period beginning with the date of the granting of the option and ending on the day 3 months before the date of such exercise, he is an employee of the corporation granting such option, a parent or subsidiary corporation of such corporation, or a corporation or a parent or subsidiary corporation of such corporation issuing or assuming a stock option in a transaction to which section 424(a) applies.

(b) Employee Stock Purchase Plan.—For purposes of this part, the term "employee stock purchase plan" means a plan which meets the following requirements:

(1) the plan provides that options are to be granted only to employees of the employer corporation or of its parent or subsidiary corporation to purchase stock in any such corporation;

(2) such plan is approved by the stockholders of the granting corporation within 12 months before or after the date such plan is adopted;

(3) under the terms of the plan, no employee can be granted an option if such employee, immediately after the option is granted, owns stock possessing 5 percent or more of the total combined voting power or value of all classes of stock of the employer corporation or of its parent or subsidiary corporation. For purposes of this paragraph, the rules of section 424(d) shall apply in determining the stock ownership of an individual, and stock which the employee may purchase under outstanding options shall be treated as stock owned by the employee;

(4) under the terms of the plan, options are to be granted to all employees of any corporation whose employees are granted any of such options by reason of their employment by such corporation, except that there may be excluded—

(A) employees who have been employed less than 2 years,

(B) employees whose customary employment is 20 hours or less per week,

(C) employees whose customary employment is for not more than 5 months in any calendar year, and

(D) highly compensated employees (within the meaning of section 414(q));

(5) under the terms of the plan, all employees granted such options shall have the same rights and privileges, except that the amount of stock which may be purchased by any employee under such option may bear a uniform relationship to the total compensation, or the basic or regular rate of compensation, of employees, and the plan may provide that no employee may purchase more than a maximum amount of stock fixed under the plan;

(6) under the terms of the plan, the option price is not less than the lesser of—

(A) an amount equal to 85 percent of the fair market value of the stock at the time such option is granted, or

(B) an amount which under the terms of the option may not be less than 85 percent of the fair market value of the stock at the time such option is exercised;

(7) under the terms of the plan, such option cannot be exercised after the expiration of—

(A) 5 years from the date such option is granted, if, under the terms of such plan, the option price is to be not less than 85 percent of the fair market value of such stock at the time of the exercise of the option, or

(B) 27 months from the date such option is granted, if the option price is not determinable in the manner described in subparagraph (A);

(8) under the terms of the plan, no employee may be granted an option which permits his rights to purchase stock under all such plans of his employer corporation and its parent and subsidiary corporations to accrue at a rate which exceeds $25,000 of fair market value of such stock (determined at the time such option is granted) for each calendar year in which such option is outstanding at any time. For purposes of this paragraph—

(A) the right to purchase stock under an option accrues when the option (or any portion thereof) first becomes exercisable during the calendar year;

(B) the right to purchase stock under an option accrues at the rate provided in the option, but in no case may such rate exceed $25,000 of fair market value of such stock (determined at the time such option is granted) for any one calendar year; and

(C) a right to purchase stock which has accrued under one option granted pursuant to the plan may not be carried over to any other option; and

(9) under the terms of the plan, such option is not transferable by such individual otherwise than by will or the laws of descent and distribution, and is exercisable, during his lifetime, only by him.

For purposes of paragraphs (3) to (9), inclusive, where additional terms are contained in an offering made under a plan, such additional terms shall, with respect to options exercised under such offering, be treated as a part of the terms of such plan.

(c) Special Rule Where Option Price Is Between 85 Percent and 100 Percent of Value of Stock.—If the option price of a share of stock acquired by an individual pursuant to a transfer to which subsection (a) applies was less than 100 percent of the fair market value of such share at the time such option was granted, then, in the event of any disposition of such share by him which meets the holding period requirements of subsection (a), or in the event of his death (whenever occurring) while owning such share, there shall be included as compensation (and not as gain upon the sale or exchange of a capital asset) in his gross income, for the taxable year in which falls the date of such disposition or for the taxable year closing with his death, whichever applies, an amount equal to the lesser of—

(1) the excess of the fair market value of the share at the time of such disposition or death over the amount paid for the share under the option, or

(2) the excess of the fair market value of the share at the time the option was granted over the option price.

If the option price is not fixed or determinable at the time the option is granted, then for purposes of this subsection, the option price shall be determined as if the option were exercised at such time. In the case of the disposition of such share by the individual, the basis of the share in his hands at the time of such disposition shall be increased by an amount equal to the amount so includible in his gross income. No amount shall be required to be deducted and withheld under chapter 24 with respect to any amount treated as compensation under this subsection.

Recent Amendments to IRC §423

American Jobs Creation Act of 2004 (Pub. L. No. 108-357), as follows:

● IRC §423(c) was amended by Act §251(c) by adding a new sentence at the end. Eff. for stock acquired pursuant to options exercised after Oct. 22, 2004.

SEC. 424. DEFINITIONS AND SPECIAL RULES.

(a) Corporate Reorganizations, Liquidations, etc.—For purposes of this part, the term "issuing or assuming a stock option in a transaction to which section 424 applies" means a substitution of a new option for the old option, or an assumption of the old option, by an employer corporation, or a parent or subsidiary of such corporation, by reason of a corporate merger, consolidation, acquisition of property or stock, separation, reorganization, or liquidation, if—

(1) the excess of the aggregate fair market value of the shares subject to the option immediately after the substitution or assumption over the aggregate option price of such shares is not more than the excess of the aggregate fair market value of all shares subject to the option immediately before such substitution or assumption over the aggregate option price of such shares, and

(2) the new option or the assumption of the old option does not give the employee additional benefits which he did not have under the old option.

For purposes of this subsection, the parent-subsidiary relationship shall be determined at the time of any such transaction under this subsection.

(b) Acquisition of New Stock.—For purposes of this part, if stock is received by an individual in a distribution to which section 305, 354, 355, 356, or 1036 (or so much of section 1031 as relates to section 1036) applies, and such distribution was made with respect to stock transferred to him upon his exercise of the option, such stock shall be considered as having been transferred to him on his exercise of such option. A similar rule shall be applied in the case of a series of such distributions.

(c) Disposition.—

(1) In general.—Except as provided in paragraphs (2), (3), and (4), for purposes of this part, the term "disposition" includes a sale, exchange, gift, or a transfer of legal title, but does not include—

IRC Sec. 424(c)(1)

(A) a transfer from a decedent to an estate or a transfer by bequest or inheritance;

(B) an exchange to which section 354, 355, 356, or 1036 (or so much of section 1031 as relates to section 1036) applies; or

(C) a mere pledge or hypothecation.

(2) **Joint tenancy.**—The acquisition of a share of stock in the name of the employee and another jointly with the right of survivorship or a subsequent transfer of a share of stock into such joint ownership shall not be deemed a disposition, but a termination of such joint tenancy (except to the extent such employee acquires ownership of such stock) shall be treated as a disposition by him occurring at the time such joint tenancy is terminated.

(3) **Special rule where incentive stock is acquired through use of other statutory option stock.**—

(A) Nonrecognition sections not to apply.—If—

(i) there is a transfer of statutory option stock in connection with the exercise of any incentive stock option, and

(ii) the applicable holding period requirements (under section 422(a)(1) or 423(a)(1)) are not met before such transfer, then no section referred to in subparagraph (B) of paragraph (1) shall apply to such transfer.

(B) Statutory option stock.—For purpose of subparagraph (A), the term "statutory option stock" means any stock acquired through the exercise of an incentive stock option or an option granted under an employee stock purchase plan.

(4) **Transfers between spouses or incident to divorce.**—In the case of any transfer described in subsection (a) of section 1041—

(A) such transfer shall not be treated as a disposition for purposes of this part, and

(B) the same tax treatment under this part with respect to the transferred property shall apply to the transferee as would have applied to the transferor.

(d) **Attribution of Stock Ownership.**—For purposes of this part, in applying the percentage limitations of sections 422(b)(6) and 423(b)(3)—

(1) the individual with respect to whom such limitation is being determined shall be considered as owning the stock owned, directly or indirectly, by or for his brothers and sisters (whether by the whole or half blood), spouse, ancestors, and lineal descendants, and

(2) stock owned, directly or indirectly, by or for a corporation, partnership, estate, or trust, shall be considered as being owned proportionately by or for its shareholders, partners, or beneficiaries.

(e) **Parent Corporation.**—For purposes of this part, the term "parent corporation" means any corporation (other than the employer corporation) in an unbroken chain of corporations ending with the employer corporation if, at the time of the granting of the option, each of the corporations other than the employer corporation owns stock possessing 50 percent or more of the total combined voting power of all classes of stock in one of the other corporations in such chain.

(f) **Subsidiary Corporation.**—For purposes of this part, the term "subsidiary corporation" means any corporation (other than the employer corporation) in an unbroken chain of corporations beginning with the employer corporation if, at the time of the granting of the option, each of the corporations other than the last corporation in the unbroken chain owns stock possessing 50 percent or more of the total combined voting power of all classes of stock in one of the other corporations in such chain.

(g) **Special Rule for Applying Subsections (e) and (f).**—In applying subsections (e) and (f) for purposes of section 422(a)(2) and 423(a)(2), there shall be substituted for the term "employer corporation" wherever it appears in subsections (e) and (f) the term "grantor corporation", or the term "corporation issuing or assuming a stock option in a transaction to which section 424(a) applies", as the case may be.

(h) **Modification, Extension, or Renewal of Option.**—

(1) **In general.**—For purposes of this part, if the terms of any option to purchase stock are modified, extended, or renewed, such modification, extension, or renewal shall be considered as the granting of a new option.

(2) **Special rule for section 423 options.**—In the case of the transfer of stock pursuant to the exercise of an option to which section 423 applies and which has been so modified, extended, or renewed, the fair market value of such stock at the time of the granting of the option shall be considered as whichever of the following is the highest—

(A) the fair market value of such stock on the date of the original granting of the option,

(B) the fair market value of such stock on the date of the making of such modification, extension, or renewal, or

(C) the fair market value of such stock at the time of the making of any intervening modification, extension, or renewal.

(3) **Definition of modification.**—The term "modification" means any change in the terms of the option which gives the employee additional benefits under the option, but such term shall not include a change in the terms of the option—

(A) attributable to the issuance or assumption of an option under subsection (a);

(B) to permit the option to qualify under section 423(b)(9); or

(C) in the case of an option not immediately exercisable in full, to accelerate the time at which the option may be exercised.

(i) Stockholder Approval.—For purposes of this part, if the grant of an option is subject to approval by stockholders, the date of grant of the option shall be determined as if the option had not been subject to such approval.

(j) Cross References.—For provisions requiring the reporting of certain acts with respect to a qualified stock option, an incentive stock option, options granted under employer stock purchase plans, or a restricted stock option, see section 6039.

Part III—Rules Relating to Minimum Funding Standards and Benefit Limitations

Subpart A—Minimum Funding Standards for Pension Plans

SEC. 430. MINIMUM FUNDING STANDARDS FOR SINGLE-EMPLOYER DEFINED BENEFIT PENSION PLANS.

(a) Minimum Required Contribution.—For purposes of this section and section 412(a)(2)(A), except as provided in subsection (f), the term "minimum required contribution" means, with respect to any plan year of a defined benefit plan which is not a multiemployer plan—

(1) in any case in which the value of plan assets of the plan (as reduced under subsection (f)(4)(B)) is less than the funding target of the plan for the plan year, the sum of—

(A) the target normal cost of the plan for the plan year,

(B) the shortfall amortization charge (if any) for the plan for the plan year determined under subsection (c), and

(C) the waiver amortization charge (if any) for the plan for the plan year as determined under subsection (e);

(2) in any case in which the value of plan assets of the plan (as reduced under subsection (f)(4)(B)) equals or exceeds the funding target of the plan for the plan year, the target normal cost of the plan for the plan year reduced (but not below zero) by such excess.

(b) Target Normal Cost.—For purposes of this section:

(1) In general.—Except as provided in subsection (i)(2) with respect to plans in at-risk status, the term "target normal cost" means, for any plan year, the excess of—

(A) the sum of—

(i) the present value of all benefits which are expected to accrue or to be earned under the plan during the plan year, plus

(ii) the amount of plan-related expenses expected to be paid from plan assets during the plan year, over

(B) the amount of mandatory employee contributions expected to be made during the plan year.

(2) Special rule for increase in compensation.—For purposes of this subsection, if any benefit attributable to services performed in a preceding plan year is increased by reason of any increase in compensation during the current plan year, the increase in such benefit shall be treated as having accrued during the current plan year.

(c) Shortfall Amortization Charge.—

(1) In general.—For purposes of this section, the shortfall amortization charge for a plan for any plan year is the aggregate total (not less than zero) of the shortfall amortization installments for such plan year with respect to any shortfall amortization base which has not been fully amortized under this subsection.

(2) Shortfall amortization installment.—For purposes of paragraph (1)—

(A) Determination.—The shortfall amortization installments are the amounts necessary to amortize the shortfall amortization base of the plan for any plan year in level annual installments over the 7-plan-year period beginning with such plan year.

(B) Shortfall installment.—The shortfall amortization installment for any plan year in the 7-plan-year period under subparagraph (A) with respect to any shortfall amortization base is the annual installment determined under subparagraph (A) for that year for that base.

(C) Segment rates.—In determining any shortfall amortization installment under this paragraph, the plan sponsor shall use the segment rates determined under subparagraph (C) of subsection (h)(2), applied under rules similar to the rules of subparagraph (B) of subsection (h)(2).

(D) Special election for eligible plan years.—

(i) In general.—If a plan sponsor elects to apply this subparagraph with respect to the shortfall amortization base of a plan for any eligible plan year (in this subparagraph and paragraph (7) referred to as an "election year"), then, notwithstanding subparagraphs (A) and (B)—

(I) the shortfall amortization installments with respect to such base shall be determined under clause (ii) or (iii), whichever is specified in the election, and

(II) the shortfall amortization installment for any plan year in the 9-plan-year period described

IRC Sec. 430(c)(2)(D)(i)(II)

in clause (ii) or the 15-plan-year period described in clause (iii), respectively, with respect to such shortfall amortization base is the annual installment determined under the applicable clause for that year for that base.

(ii) 2 plus 7 amortization schedule.—The shortfall amortization installments determined under this clause are—

(I) in the case of the first 2 plan years in the 9-plan-year period beginning with the election year, interest on the shortfall amortization base of the plan for the election year (determined using the effective interest rate for the plan for the election year), and

(II) in the case of the last 7 plan years in such 9-plan-year period, the amounts necessary to amortize the remaining balance of the shortfall amortization base of the plan for the election year in level annual installments over such last 7 plan years (using the segment rates under subparagraph (C) for the election year).

(iii) 15-year amortization.—The shortfall amortization installments determined under this subparagraph are the amounts necessary to amortize the shortfall amortization base of the plan for the election year in level annual installments over the 15-plan-year period beginning with the election year (using the segment rates under subparagraph (C) for the election year).

(iv) Election.—

(I) In general.—The plan sponsor of a plan may elect to have this subparagraph apply to not more than 2 eligible plan years with respect to the plan, except that in the case of a plan described in section 106 of the Pension Protection Act of 2006, the plan sponsor may only elect to have this subparagraph apply to a plan year beginning in 2011.

(II) Amortization schedule.—Such election shall specify whether the amortization schedule under clause (ii) or (iii) shall apply to an election year, except that if a plan sponsor elects to have this subparagraph apply to 2 eligible plan years, the plan sponsor must elect the same schedule for both years.

(III) Other rules.—Such election shall be made at such time, and in such form and manner, as shall be prescribed by the Secretary, and may be revoked only with the consent of the Secretary. The Secretary shall, before granting a revocation request, provide the Pension Benefit Guaranty Corporation an opportunity to comment on the conditions applicable to the treatment of any portion of the election year shortfall amortization base that remains unamortized as of the revocation date.

(v) Eligible plan year.—For purposes of this subparagraph, the term "eligible plan year" means any plan year beginning in 2008, 2009, 2010, or 2011, except that a plan year shall only be treated as an eligible plan year if the due date under subsection (j)(1) for the payment of the minimum required contribution for such plan year occurs on or after the date of the enactment of this subparagraph.

(vi) Reporting.—A plan sponsor of a plan who makes an election under clause (i) shall—

(I) give notice of the election to participants and beneficiaries of the plan, and

(II) inform the Pension Benefit Guaranty Corporation of such election in such form and manner as the Director of the Pension Benefit Guaranty Corporation may prescribe.

(vii) Increases in required installments in certain cases.—For increases in required contributions in cases of excess compensation or extraordinary dividends or stock redemptions, see paragraph (7).

(3) Shortfall amortization base.—For purposes of this section, the shortfall amortization base of a plan for a plan year is—

(A) the funding shortfall of such plan for such plan year, minus

(B) the present value (determined using the segment rates determined under subparagraph (C) of subsection (h)(2), applied under rules similar to the rules of subparagraph (B) of subsection (h)(2)) of the aggregate total of the shortfall amortization installments and waiver amortization installments which have been determined for such plan year and any succeeding plan year with respect to the shortfall amortization bases and waiver amortization bases of the plan for any plan year preceding such plan year.

(4) Funding shortfall.—For purposes of this section, the funding shortfall of a plan for any plan year is the excess (if any) of—

(A) the funding target of the plan for the plan year, over

(B) the value of plan assets of the plan (as reduced under subsection (f)(4)(B)) for the plan year which are held by the plan on the valuation date.

(5) Exemption from new shortfall amortization base.—

(A) In general.—In any case in which the value of plan assets of the plan (as reduced under subsection (f)(4)(A)) is equal to or greater than the funding target of the plan for the plan year, the shortfall amortization base of the plan for such plan year shall be zero.

(B) Transition rule.—

(i) In general.—Except as provided in clause (iii), in the case of plan years beginning after 2007 and before 2011, only the applicable percentage of the funding target shall be taken into account under paragraph (3)(A) in determining the funding shortfall for purposes of paragraph (3)(A) and subparagraph (A).

(ii) Applicable percentage.—For purposes of subparagraph (A), the applicable percentage shall be determined in accordance with the following table:

In the case of a plan year beginning in calendar year:	The applicable percentage is:
2008	92
2009	94
2010	96

(iii) Transition relief not available for new or deficit reduction plans.—Clause (i) shall not apply to a plan—

(I) which was not in effect for a plan year beginning in 2007, or

(II) which was in effect for a plan year beginning in 2007 and which was subject to section 412(l) (as in effect for plan years beginning in 2007) for such year, determined after the application of paragraphs (6) and (9) thereof.

(6) Early deemed amortization upon attainment of funding target.—In any case in which the funding shortfall of a plan for a plan year is zero, for purposes of determining the shortfall amortization charge for such plan year and succeeding plan years, the shortfall amortization bases for all preceding plan years (and all shortfall amortization installments determined with respect to such bases) shall be reduced to zero.

(7) Increases in alternate required installments in cases of excess compensation or extraordinary dividends or stock redemptions.—

(A) In general.—If there is an installment acceleration amount with respect to a plan for any plan year in the restriction period with respect to an election year under paragraph (2)(D), then the shortfall amortization installment otherwise determined and payable under such paragraph for such plan year shall, subject to the limitation under subparagraph (B), be increased by such amount.

(B) Total installments limited to shortfall base.— Subject to rules prescribed by the Secretary, if a shortfall amortization installment with respect to any shortfall amortization base for an election year is required to be increased for any plan year under subparagraph (A)—

(i) such increase shall not result in the amount of such installment exceeding the present value of such installment and all succeeding installments

with respect to such base (determined without regard to such increase but after application of clause (ii)), and

(ii) subsequent shortfall amortization installments with respect to such base shall, in reverse order of the otherwise required installments, be reduced to the extent necessary to limit the present value of such subsequent shortfall amortization installments (after application of this paragraph) to the present value of the remaining unamortized shortfall amortization base.

(C) Installment acceleration amount.—For purposes of this paragraph—

(i) In general.—The term "installment acceleration amount" means, with respect to any plan year in a restriction period with respect to an election year, the sum of—

(I) the aggregate amount of excess employee compensation determined under subparagraph (D) with respect to all employees for the plan year, plus

(II) the aggregate amount of extraordinary dividends and redemptions determined under subparagraph (E) for the plan year.

(ii) Annual limitation.—The installment acceleration amount for any plan year shall not exceed the excess (if any) of—

(I) the sum of the shortfall amortization installments for the plan year and all preceding plan years in the amortization period elected under paragraph (2)(D) with respect to the shortfall amortization base with respect to an election year, determined without regard to paragraph (2)(D) and this paragraph, over

(II) the sum of the shortfall amortization installments for such plan year and all such preceding plan years, determined after application of paragraph (2)(D) (and in the case of any preceding plan year, after application of this paragraph).

(iii) Carryover of excess installment acceleration amounts.—

(I) In general.—If the installment acceleration amount for any plan year (determined without regard to clause (ii)) exceeds the limitation under clause (ii), then, subject to subclause (II), such excess shall be treated as an installment acceleration amount with respect to the succeeding plan year.

(II) Cap to apply.—If any amount treated as an installment acceleration amount under subclause (I) or this subclause with respect any succeeding plan year, when added to other installment acceleration amounts (determined without regard to clause (ii)) with respect to the plan year, exceeds the limitation under clause (ii), the portion of such amount representing such excess shall be treated as

IRC Sec. 430(c)(7)(C)(iii)(II)

an installment acceleration amount with respect to the next succeeding plan year.

(III) Limitation on years to which amounts carried for.—No amount shall be carried under subclause (I) or (II) to a plan year which begins after the first plan year following the last plan year in the restriction period (or after the second plan year following such last plan year in the case of an election year with respect to which 15-year amortization was elected under paragraph (2)(D)).

(IV) Ordering rules.—For purposes of applying subclause (II), installment acceleration amounts for the plan year (determined without regard to any carryover under this clause) shall be applied first against the limitation under clause (ii) and then carryovers to such plan year shall be applied against such limitation on a first-in, first-out basis.

(D) Excess employee compensation.—For purposes of this paragraph—

(i) In general.—The term "excess employee compensation" means, with respect to any employee for any plan year, the excess (if any) of—

(I) the aggregate amount includible in income under this chapter for remuneration during the calendar year in which such plan year begins for services performed by the employee for the plan sponsor (whether or not performed during such calendar year), over

(II) $1,000,000.

(ii) Amounts set aside for nonqualified deferred compensation.—If during any calendar year assets are set aside or reserved (directly or indirectly) in a trust (or other arrangement as determined by the Secretary), or transferred to such a trust or other arrangement, by a plan sponsor for purposes of paying deferred compensation of an employee under a nonqualified deferred compensation plan (as defined in section 409A) of the plan sponsor, then, for purposes of clause (i), the amount of such assets shall be treated as remuneration of the employee includible in income for the calendar year unless such amount is otherwise includible in income for such year. An amount to which the preceding sentence applies shall not be taken into account under this paragraph for any subsequent calendar year.

(iii) Only remuneration for certain post-2009 services counted.—Remuneration shall be taken into account under clause (i) only to the extent attributable to services performed by the employee for the plan sponsor after February 28, 2010.

(iv) Exception for certain equity payments.—

(I) In general.—There shall not be taken into account under clause (i)(I) any amount includible in income with respect to the granting after February 28, 2010, of service recipient stock (within the meaning of section 409A) that, upon such grant, is subject to a substantial risk of forfeiture (as defined under section 83(c)(1)) for at least 5 years from the date of such grant.

(II) Secretarial authority.—The Secretary may by regulation provide for the application of this clause in the case of a person other than a corporation.

(v) Other exceptions.—The following amounts includible in income shall not be taken into account under clause (i)(I):

(I) Commissions.—Any remuneration payable on a commission basis solely on account of income directly generated by the individual performance of the individual to whom such remuneration is payable.

(II) Certain payments under existing contracts.—Any remuneration consisting of nonqualified deferred compensation, restricted stock, stock options, or stock appreciation rights payable or granted under a written binding contract that was in effect on March 1, 2010, and which was not modified in any material respect before such remuneration is paid.

(vi) Self-employed individual treated as employee.—The term "employee" includes, with respect to a calendar year, a self-employed individual who is treated as an employee under section 401(c) for the taxable year ending during such calendar year, and the term "compensation" shall include earned income of such individual with respect to such self-employment.

(vii) Indexing of amount.—In the case of any calendar year beginning after 2010, the dollar amount under clause (i)(II) shall be increased by an amount equal to—

(I) such dollar amount, multiplied by

(II) the cost-of-living adjustment determined under section 1(f)(3) for the calendar year, determined by substituting "calendar year 2009" for "calendar year 1992" in subparagraph (B) thereof.

If the amount of any increase under clause (i) is not a multiple of $1,000, such increase shall be rounded to the next lowest multiple of $1,000.

(E) Extraordinary dividends and redemptions.—

(i) In general.—The amount determined under this subparagraph for any plan year is the excess (if any) of the sum of the dividends declared during the plan year by the plan sponsor plus the aggregate amount paid for the redemption of stock of the plan sponsor redeemed during the plan year over the greater of—

(I) the adjusted net income (within the meaning of section 4043 of the Employee Retirement Income Security Act of 1974) of the plan sponsor for the preceding plan year, determined without regard to any reduction by reason of interest, taxes, depreciation, or amortization, or

(II) in the case of a plan sponsor that determined and declared dividends in the same manner for at least 5 consecutive years immediately preceding such plan year, the aggregate amount of dividends determined and declared for such plan year using such manner.

(ii) Only certain post-2009 dividends and redemptions counted.—For purposes of clause (i), there shall only be taken into account dividends declared, and redemptions occurring, after February 28, 2010.

(iii) Exception for intra-group dividends.— Dividends paid by one member of a controlled group (as defined in section 412(d)(3)) to another member of such group shall not be taken into account under clause (i).

(iv) Exception for certain redemptions.—Redemptions that are made pursuant to a plan maintained with respect to employees, or that are made on account of the death, disability, or termination of employment of an employee or shareholder, shall not be taken into account under clause (i).

(v) Exception for certain preferred stock.—

(I) In general.—Dividends and redemptions with respect to applicable preferred stock shall not be taken into account under clause (i) to the extent that dividends accrue with respect to such stock at a specified rate in all events and without regard to the plan sponsor's income, and interest accrues on any unpaid dividends with respect to such stock.

(II) Applicable preferred stock.—For purposes of subclause (I), the term "applicable preferred stock" means preferred stock which was issued before March 1, 2010 (or which was issued after such date and is held by an employee benefit plan subject to the provisions of title I of Employee Retirement Income Security Act of 1974).

(F) Other definitions and rules.—For purposes of this paragraph—

(i) Plan sponsor.—The term "plan sponsor" includes any member of the plan sponsor's controlled group (as defined in section 412(d)(3)).

(ii) Restriction period.—The term "restriction period" means, with respect to any election year—

(I) except as provided in subclause (II), the 3-year period beginning with the election year (or, if later, the first plan year beginning after December 31, 2009), and

(II) if the plan sponsor elects 15-year amortization for the shortfall amortization base for the election year, the 5-year period beginning with the

election year (or, if later, the first plan year beginning after December 31, 2009).

(iii) Elections for multiple plans.—If a plan sponsor makes elections under paragraph (2)(D) with respect to 2 or more plans, the Secretary shall provide rules for the application of this paragraph to such plans, including rules for the ratable allocation of any installment acceleration amount among such plans on the basis of each plan's relative reduction in the plan's shortfall amortization installment for the first plan year in the amortization period described in subparagraph (A) (determined without regard to this paragraph).

(iv) Mergers and acquisitions.—The Secretary shall prescribe rules for the application of paragraph (2)(D) and this paragraph in any case where there is a merger or acquisition involving a plan sponsor making the election under paragraph (2)(D).

(d) Rules Relating to Funding Target.—For purposes of this section—

(1) Funding target.—Except as provided in subsection (i)(1) with respect to plans in at-risk status, the funding target of a plan for a plan year is the present value of all benefits accrued or earned under the plan as of the beginning of the plan year.

(2) Funding target attainment percentage.— The "funding target attainment percentage" of a plan for a plan year is the ratio (expressed as a percentage) which—

(A) the value of plan assets for the plan year (as reduced under subsection (f)(4)(B)), bears to

(B) the funding target of the plan for the plan year (determined without regard to subsection (i)(1)).

(e) Waiver Amortization Charge.—

(1) Determination of waiver amortization charge.—The waiver amortization charge (if any) for a plan for any plan year is the aggregate total of the waiver amortization installments for such plan year with respect to the waiver amortization bases for each of the 5 preceding plan years.

(2) Waiver amortization installment.—For purposes of paragraph (1)—

(A) Determination.—The waiver amortization installments are the amounts necessary to amortize the waiver amortization base of the plan for any plan year in level annual installments over a period of 5 plan years beginning with the succeeding plan year.

(B) Waiver installment.—The waiver amortization installment for any plan year in the 5-year period under subparagraph (A) with respect to any waiver amortization base is the annual installment determined under subparagraph (A) for that year for that base.

IRC Sec. 430(e)(2)(B)

(3) Interest rate.—In determining any waiver amortization installment under this subsection, the plan sponsor shall use the segment rates determined under subparagraph (C) of subsection (h)(2), applied under rules similar to the rules of subparagraph (B) of subsection (h)(2).

(4) Waiver amortization base.—The waiver amortization base of a plan for a plan year is the amount of the waived funding deficiency (if any) for such plan year under section 412(c).

(5) Early deemed amortization upon attainment of funding target.—In any case in which the funding shortfall of a plan for a plan year is zero, for purposes of determining the waiver amortization charge for such plan year and succeeding plan years, the waiver amortization bases for all preceding plan years (and all waiver amortization installments determined with respect to such bases) shall be reduced to zero.

(f) Reduction of Minimum Required Contribution by Prefunding Balance and Funding Standard Carryover Balance.—

(1) Election to maintain balances.—

(A) Prefunding balance.—The plan sponsor of a defined benefit plan which is not a multiemployer plan may elect to maintain a prefunding balance.

(B) Funding standard carryover balance.—

(i) In general.—In the case of a defined benefit plan (other than a multiemployer plan) described in clause (ii), the plan sponsor may elect to maintain a funding standard carryover balance, until such balance is reduced to zero.

(ii) Plans maintaining funding standard account in 2007.—A plan is described in this clause if the plan—

(I) was in effect for a plan year beginning in 2007, and

(II) had a positive balance in the funding standard account under section 412(b) as in effect for such plan year and determined as of the end of such plan year.

(2) Application of balances.—A prefunding balance and a funding standard carryover balance maintained pursuant to this paragraph—

(A) shall be available for crediting against the minimum required contribution, pursuant to an election under paragraph (3),

(B) shall be applied as a reduction in the amount treated as the value of plan assets for purposes of this section, to the extent provided in paragraph (4), and

(C) may be reduced at any time, pursuant to an election under paragraph (5).

(3) Election to apply balances against minimum required contribution.—

(A) In general.—Except as provided in subparagraphs (B) and (C), in the case of any plan year in which the plan sponsor elects to credit against the minimum required contribution for the current plan year all or a portion of the prefunding balance or the funding standard carryover balance for the current plan year (not in excess of such minimum required contribution), the minimum required contribution for the plan year shall be reduced as of the first day of the plan year by the amount so credited by the plan sponsor. For purposes of the preceding sentence, the minimum required contribution shall be determined after taking into account any waiver under section 412(c).

(B) Coordination with funding standard carryover balance.—To the extent that any plan has a funding standard carryover balance greater than zero, no amount of the prefunding balance of such plan may be credited under this paragraph in reducing the minimum required contribution.

(C) Limitation for underfunded plans.—The preceding provisions of this paragraph shall not apply for any plan year if the ratio (expressed as a percentage) which—

(i) the value of plan assets for the preceding plan year (as reduced under paragraph (4)(C)), bears to

(ii) the funding target of the plan for the preceding plan year (determined without regard to subsection (i)(1)), is less than 80 percent. In the case of plan years beginning in 2008, the ratio under this subparagraph may be determined using such methods of estimation as the Secretary may prescribe.

(D) Special rule for certain years of plans maintained by charities.—

(i) In general.—For purposes of applying subparagraph (C) for plan years beginning after August 31, 2009, and before September 1, 2011, the ratio determined under such subparagraph for the preceding plan year of a plan shall be the greater of—

(I) such ratio, as determined without regard to this subsection, or

(II) the ratio for such plan for the plan year beginning after August 31, 2007 and before September 1, 2008, as determined under rules prescribed by the Secretary.

(ii) Special rule.—In the case of a plan for which the valuation date is not the first day of the plan year—

(I) clause (i) shall apply to plan years beginning after December 31, 2007, and before January 1, 2010, and

(II) clause (i)(II) shall apply based on the last plan year beginning before September 1, 2007, as determined under rules prescribed by the Secretary.

(iii) Limitation to charities.—This subparagraph shall not apply to any plan unless such plan is maintained exclusively by one or more organizations described in section 501(c)(3).

(4) Effect of balances on amounts treated as value of plan assets.—In the case of any plan maintaining a prefunding balance or a funding standard carryover balance pursuant to this subsection, the amount treated as the value of plan assets shall be deemed to be such amount, reduced as provided in the following subparagraphs:

(A) Applicability of shortfall amortization base.—For purposes of subsection (c)(5), the value of plan assets is deemed to be such amount, reduced by the amount of the prefunding balance, but only if an election under paragraph (3) applying any portion of the prefunding balance in reducing the minimum required contribution is in effect for the plan year.

(B) Determination of excess assets, funding shortfall, and funding target attainment percentage.—

(i) In general.—For purposes of subsections (a), (c)(4)(B), and (d)(2)(A), the value of plan assets is deemed to be such amount, reduced by the amount of the prefunding balance and the funding standard carryover balance.

(ii) Special rule for certain binding agreements with PBGC.—For purposes of subsection (c)(4)(B), the value of plan assets shall not be deemed to be reduced for a plan year by the amount of the specified balance if, with respect to such balance, there is in effect for a plan year a binding written agreement with the Pension Benefit Guaranty Corporation which provides that such balance is not available to reduce the minimum required contribution for the plan year. For purposes of the preceding sentence, the term "specified balance" means the prefunding balance or the funding standard carryover balance, as the case may be.

(C) Availability of balances in plan year for crediting against minimum required contribution.— For purposes of paragraph (3)(C)(i) of this subsection, the value of plan assets is deemed to be such amount, reduced by the amount of the prefunding balance.

(5) Election to reduce balance prior to determinations of value of plan assets and crediting against minimum required contribution.—

(A) In general.—The plan sponsor may elect to reduce by any amount the balance of the prefunding balance and the funding standard carryover balance for any plan year (but not below zero). Such reduction shall be effective prior to any determination of the value of plan assets for such plan year under this section and application of the balance in reducing the minimum required contribution for such plan for such plan year pursuant to an election under paragraph (2).

(B) Coordination between prefunding balance and funding standard carryover balance.—To the extent that any plan has a funding standard carryover balance greater than zero, no election may be made under subparagraph (A) with respect to the prefunding balance.

(6) Prefunding balance.—

(A) In general.—A prefunding balance maintained by a plan shall consist of a beginning balance of zero, increased and decreased to the extent provided in subparagraphs (B) and (C), and adjusted further as provided in paragraph (8).

(B) Increases.—

(i) In general.—As of the first day of each plan year beginning after 2008, the prefunding balance of a plan shall be increased by the amount elected by the plan sponsor for the plan year. Such amount shall not exceed the excess (if any) of—

(I) the aggregate total of employer contributions to the plan for the preceding plan year, over—

(II) the minimum required contribution for such preceding plan year.

(ii) Adjustments for interest.—Any excess contributions under clause (i) shall be properly adjusted for interest accruing for the periods between the first day of the current plan year and the dates on which the excess contributions were made, determined by using the effective interest rate for the preceding plan year and by treating contributions as being first used to satisfy the minimum required contribution.

(iii) Certain contributions necessary to avoid benefit limitations disregarded.—The excess described in clause (i) with respect to any preceding plan year shall be reduced (but not below zero) by the amount of contributions an employer would be required to make under subsection (b), (c), or (e) of section 436 to avoid a benefit limitation which would otherwise be imposed under such paragraph for the preceding plan year. Any contribution which may be taken into account in satisfying the requirements of more than 1 of such paragraphs shall be taken into account only once for purposes of this clause.

(C) Decreases.—The prefunding balance of a plan shall be decreased (but not below zero) by—

(i) as of the first day of each plan year after 2008, the amount of such balance credited under paragraph (2) (if any) in reducing the minimum required contribution of the plan for the preceding plan year, and

(ii) as of the time specified in paragraph (5)(A), any reduction in such balance elected under paragraph (5).

(7) Funding standard carryover balance.—

(A) In general.—A funding standard carryover balance maintained by a plan shall consist of a beginning balance determined under subparagraph (B), decreased to the extent provided in subparagraph (C), and adjusted further as provided in paragraph (8).

(B) Beginning balance.—The beginning balance of the funding standard carryover balance shall be the positive balance described in paragraph (1)(B)(ii)(II).

(C) Decreases.—The funding standard carryover balance of a plan shall be decreased (but not below zero) by—

(i) as of the first day of each plan year after 2008, the amount of such balance credited under paragraph (2) (if any) in reducing the minimum required contribution of the plan for the preceding plan year, and

(ii) as of the time specified in paragraph (5)(A), any reduction in such balance elected under paragraph (5).

(8) Adjustments for investment experience.— In determining the prefunding balance or the funding standard carryover balance of a plan as of the first day of the plan year, the plan sponsor shall, in accordance with regulations prescribed by the Secretary, adjust such balance to reflect the rate of return on plan assets for the preceding plan year. Notwithstanding subsection (g)(3), such rate of return shall be determined on the basis of fair market value and shall properly take into account, in accordance with such regulations, all contributions, distributions, and other plan payments made during such period.

(9) Elections.—Elections under this subsection shall be made at such times, and in such form and manner, as shall be prescribed in regulations of the Secretary.

(g) Valuation of Plan Assets and Liabilities.—

(1) Timing of determinations.—Except as otherwise provided under this subsection, all determinations under this section for a plan year shall be made as of the valuation date of the plan for such plan year.

(2) Valuation date.—For purposes of this section—

(A) In general.—Except as provided in subparagraph (B), the valuation date of a plan for any plan year shall be the first day of the plan year.

(B) Exception for small plans.—If, on each day during the preceding plan year, a plan had 100 or fewer participants, the plan may designate any day during the plan year as its valuation date for such plan year and succeeding plan years. For purposes of this subparagraph, all defined benefit plans (other than multiemployer plans) maintained by the same employer (or any member of such employer's controlled group) shall be treated as 1 plan, but only participants with respect to such employer or member shall be taken into account.

(C) Application of certain rules in determination of plan size.—For purposes of this paragraph—

(i) Plans not in existence in preceding year.— In the case of the first plan year of any plan, subparagraph (B) shall apply to such plan by taking into account the number of participants that the plan is reasonably expected to have on days during such first plan year.

(ii) Predecessors.—Any reference in subparagraph (B) to an employer shall include a reference to any predecessor of such employer.

(3) Determination of value of plan assets.—For purposes of this section—

(A) In general.—Except as provided in subparagraph (B), the value of plan assets shall be the fair market value of the assets.

(B) Averaging allowed.—A plan may determine the value of plan assets on the basis of the averaging of fair market values, but only if such method—

(i) is permitted under regulations prescribed by the Secretary,

(ii) does not provide for averaging of such values over more than the period beginning on the last day of the 25th month preceding the month in which the valuation date occurs and ending on the valuation date (or a similar period in the case of a valuation date which is not the 1st day of a month), and

(iii) does not result in a determination of the value of plan assets which, at any time, is lower than 90 percent or greater than 110 percent of the fair market value of such assets at such time.

Any such averaging shall be adjusted for contributions, distributions, and expected earnings (as determined by the plan's actuary on the basis of an assumed earnings rate specified by the actuary but not in excess of the third segment rate applicable under subsection (h)(2)(C)(iii)), as specified by the Secretary.

(4) Accounting for contribution receipts.—For purposes of determining the value of assets under paragraph (3)—

(A) Prior year contributions.—If—

(i) an employer makes any contribution to the plan after the valuation date for the plan year in which the contribution is made, and

(ii) the contribution is for a preceding plan year,

the contribution shall be taken into account as an asset of the plan as of the valuation date, except that in the case of any plan year beginning after 2008, only the present value (determined as of the valuation date) of such contribution may be taken into account. For purposes of the preceding sentence, present value shall be determined using the effective interest rate for the preceding plan year to which the contribution is properly allocable.

(B) Special rule for current year contributions made before valuation date.—If any contributions for any plan year are made to or under the plan during the plan year but before the valuation date for the plan year, the assets of the plan as of the valuation date shall not include—

(i) such contributions, and

(ii) interest on such contributions for the period between the date of the contributions and the valuation date, determined by using the effective interest rate for the plan year.

(h) Actuarial Assumptions and Methods.—

(1) In general.—Subject to this subsection, the determination of any present value or other computation under this section shall be made on the basis of actuarial assumptions and methods—

(A) each of which is reasonable (taking into account the experience of the plan and reasonable expectations), and

(B) which, in combination, offer the actuary's best estimate of anticipated experience under the plan.

(2) Interest rates.—

(A) Effective interest rate.—For purposes of this section, the term "effective interest rate" means, with respect to any plan for any plan year, the single rate of interest which, if used to determine the present value of the plan's accrued or earned benefits referred to in subsection (d)(1), would result in an amount equal to the funding target of the plan for such plan year.

(B) Interest rates for determining funding target.—For purposes of determining the funding target and target normal cost of a plan for any plan year, the interest rate used in determining the present value of the benefits of the plan shall be—

(i) in the case of benefits reasonably determined to be payable during the 5-year period beginning on the first day of the plan year, the first segment rate with respect to the applicable month,

(ii) in the case of benefits reasonably determined to be payable during the 15-year period beginning at the end of the period described in clause (i), the second segment rate with respect to the applicable month, and

(iii) in the case of benefits reasonably determined to be payable after the period described in clause (ii), the third segment rate with respect to the applicable month.

(C) Segment rates.—For purposes of this paragraph—

(i) First segment rate.—The term "first segment rate" means, with respect to any month, the single rate of interest which shall be determined by the Secretary for such month on the basis of the corporate bond yield curve for such month, taking into account only that portion of such yield curve which is based on bonds maturing during the 5-year period commencing with such month.

(ii) Second segment rate.—The term "second segment rate" means, with respect to any month, the single rate of interest which shall be determined by the Secretary for such month on the basis of the corporate bond yield curve for such month, taking into account only that portion of such yield curve which is based on bonds maturing during the 15-year period beginning at the end of the period described in clause (i).

(iii) Third segment rate.—The term "third segment rate" means, with respect to any month, the single rate of interest which shall be determined by the Secretary for such month on the basis of the corporate bond yield curve for such month, taking into account only that portion of such yield curve which is based on bonds maturing during periods beginning after the period described in clause (ii).

(D) Corporate bond yield curve.—For purposes of this paragraph—

(i) In general.—The term "corporate bond yield curve" means, with respect to any month, a yield curve which is prescribed by the Secretary for such month and which reflects the average, for the 24-month period ending with the month preceding such month, of monthly yields on investment grade corporate bonds with varying maturities and that are in the top 3 quality levels available.

(ii) Election to use yield curve.—Solely for purposes of determining the minimum required contribution under this section, the plan sponsor may, in lieu of the segment rates determined under subparagraph (C), elect to use interest rates under the corporate bond yield curve. For purposes of the preceding sentence such curve shall be determined without regard to the 24-month averaging described in clause (i). Such election, once made, may be revoked only with the consent of the Secretary.

(E) Applicable month.—For purposes of this paragraph, the term "applicable month" means, with respect to any plan for any plan year, the month which includes the valuation date of such

IRC Sec. 430(h)(2)(E)

plan for such plan year or, at the election of the plan sponsor, any of the 4 months which precede such month. Any election made under this subparagraph shall apply to the plan year for which the election is made and all succeeding plan years, unless the election is revoked with the consent of the Secretary.

(F) Publication requirements.—The Secretary shall publish for each month the corporate bond yield curve (and the corporate bond yield curve reflecting the modification described in section 417(e)(3)(D)(i) for such month) and each of the rates determined under subparagraph (C) for such month. The Secretary shall also publish a description of the methodology used to determine such yield curve and such rates which is sufficiently detailed to enable plans to make reasonable projections regarding the yield curve and such rates for future months based on the plan's projection of future interest rates.

(G) Transition rule.—

(i) In general.—Notwithstanding the preceding provisions of this paragraph, for plan years beginning in 2008 or 2009, the first, second, or third segment rate for a plan with respect to any month shall be equal to the sum of—

(I) the product of such rate for such month determined without regard to this subparagraph, multiplied by the applicable percentage, and

(II) the product of the rate determined under the rules of section 412(b)(5)(B)(ii)(II) (as in effect for plan years beginning in 2007), multiplied by a percentage equal to 100 percent minus the applicable percentage.

(ii) Applicable percentage.—For purposes of clause (i), the applicable percentage is 33⅓ percent for plan years beginning in 2008 and 66⅔ percent for plan years beginning in 2009.

(iii) New plans ineligible.—Clause (i) shall not apply to any plan if the first plan year of the plan begins after December 31, 2007.

(iv) Election.—The plan sponsor may elect not to have this subparagraph apply. Such election, once made, may be revoked only with the consent of the Secretary.

(3) **Mortality tables.**—

(A) In general.—Except as provided in subparagraph (C) or (D), the Secretary shall by regulation prescribe mortality tables to be used in determining any present value or making any computation under this section. Such tables shall be based on the actual experience of pension plans and projected trends in such experience. In prescribing such tables, the Secretary shall take into account results of available independent studies of mortality of individuals covered by pension plans.

(B) Periodic revision.—The Secretary shall (at least every 10 years) make revisions in any table in effect under subparagraph (A) to reflect the actual experience of pension plans and projected trends in such experience.

(C) Substitute mortality table.—

(i) In general.—Upon request by the plan sponsor and approval by the Secretary, a mortality table which meets the requirements of clause (iii) shall be used in determining any present value or making any computation under this section during the period of consecutive plan years (not to exceed 10) specified in the request.

(ii) Early termination of period.—Notwithstanding clause (i), a mortality table described in clause (i) shall cease to be in effect as of the earliest of—

(I) the date on which there is a significant change in the participants in the plan by reason of a plan spinoff or merger or otherwise, or

(II) the date on which the plan actuary determines that such table does not meet the requirements of clause (iii).

(iii) Requirements.—A mortality table meets the requirements of this clause if—

(I) there is a sufficient number of plan participants, and the pension plans have been maintained for a sufficient period of time, to have credible information necessary for purposes of subclause (II), and

(II) such table reflects the actual experience of the pension plans maintained by the sponsor and projected trends in general mortality experience.

(iv) All plans in controlled group must use separate table.—Except as provided by the Secretary, a plan sponsor may not use a mortality table under this subparagraph for any plan maintained by the plan sponsor unless—

(I) a separate mortality table is established and used under this subparagraph for each other plan maintained by the plan sponsor and if the plan sponsor is a member of a controlled group, each member of the controlled group, and

(II) the requirements of clause (iii) are met separately with respect to the table so established for each such plan, determined by only taking into account the participants of such plan, the time such plan has been in existence, and the actual experience of such plan.

(v) Deadline for submission and disposition of application.—

(I) Submission.—The plan sponsor shall submit a mortality table to the Secretary for approval under this subparagraph at least 7 months before the 1st day of the period described in clause (i).

IRC Sec. 430(h)(2)(E)

(II) Disposition.—Any mortality table submitted to the Secretary for approval under this subparagraph shall be treated as in effect as of the 1st day of the period described in clause (i) unless the Secretary, during the 180-day period beginning on the date of such submission, disapproves of such table and provides the reasons that such table fails to meet the requirements of clause (iii). The 180-day period shall be extended upon mutual agreement of the Secretary and the plan sponsor.

(D) Separate mortality tables for the disabled.—Notwithstanding subparagraph (A)—

(i) In general.—The Secretary shall establish mortality tables which may be used (in lieu of the tables under subparagraph (A)) under this subsection for individuals who are entitled to benefits under the plan on account of disability. The Secretary shall establish separate tables for individuals whose disabilities occur in plan years beginning before January 1, 1995, and for individuals whose disabilities occur in plan years beginning on or after such date.

(ii) Special rule for disabilities occurring after 1994.—In the case of disabilities occurring in plan years beginning after December 31, 1994, the tables under clause (i) shall apply only with respect to individuals described in such subclause who are disabled within the meaning of title II of the Social Security Act and the regulations thereunder.

(iii) Periodic revision.—The Secretary shall (at least every 10 years) make revisions in any table in effect under clause (i) to reflect the actual experience of pension plans and projected trends in such experience.

(4) Probability of benefit payments in the form of lump sums or other optional forms.—For purposes of determining any present value or making any computation under this section, there shall be taken into account—

(A) the probability that future benefit payments under the plan will be made in the form of optional forms of benefits provided under the plan (including lump sum distributions, determined on the basis of the plan's experience and other related assumptions), and

(B) any difference in the present value of such future benefit payments resulting from the use of actuarial assumptions, in determining benefit payments in any such optional form of benefits, which are different from those specified in this subsection.

(5) Approval of large changes in actuarial assumptions.—

(A) In general.—No actuarial assumption used to determine the funding target for a plan to which this paragraph applies may be changed without the approval of the Secretary.

(B) Plans to which paragraph applies.—This paragraph shall apply to a plan only if—

(i) the plan is a defined benefit plan (other than a multiemployer plan) to which title IV of the Employee Retirement Income Security Act of 1974 applies,

(ii) the aggregate unfunded vested benefits as of the close of the preceding plan year (as determined under section 4006(a)(3)(E)(iii) of the Employee Retirement Income Security Act of 1974) of such plan and all other plans maintained by the contributing sponsors (as defined in section 4001(a)(13) of such Act) and members of such sponsors' controlled groups (as defined in section 4001(a)(14) of such Act) which are covered by title IV (disregarding plans with nonfunded vested benefits) exceed $50,000,000, and

(iii) the change in assumptions (determined after taking into account any changes in interest rate and mortality table) results in a decrease in the funding shortfall of the plan for the current plan year that exceeds $50,000,000, or that exceeds $5,000,000 and that is 5 percent or more of the funding target of the plan before such change.

(i) Special Rules for At-Risk Plans.—

(1) Funding target for plans in at-risk status.—

(A) In general.—In the case of a plan which is in at-risk status for a plan year, the funding target of the plan for the plan year shall be equal to the sum of—

(i) the present value of all benefits accrued or earned under the plan as of the beginning of the plan year, as determined by using the additional actuarial assumptions described in subparagraph (B), and

(ii) in the case of a plan which also has been in at-risk status for at least 2 of the 4 preceding plan years, a loading factor determined under subparagraph (C).

(B) Additional actuarial assumptions.—The actuarial assumptions described in this subparagraph are as follows:

(i) All employees who are not otherwise assumed to retire as of the valuation date but who will be eligible to elect benefits during the plan year and the 10 succeeding plan years shall be assumed to retire at the earliest retirement date under the plan but not before the end of the plan year for which the at-risk funding target and at-risk target normal cost are being determined.

(ii) All employees shall be assumed to elect the retirement benefit available under the plan at the assumed retirement age (determined after application of clause (i)) which would result in the highest present value of benefits.

IRC Sec. 430(i)(1)(B)(ii)

(C) Loading factor.—The loading factor applied with respect to a plan under this paragraph for any plan year is the sum of—

(i) $700, times the number of participants in the plan, plus

(ii) 4 percent of the funding target (determined without regard to this paragraph) of the plan for the plan year.

(2) Target normal cost of at-risk plans.—In the case of a plan which is in at-risk status for a plan year, the target normal cost of the plan for such plan year shall be equal to the sum of—

(A) the excess of—

(i) the sum of—

(I) the present value of all benefits which are expected to accrue or to be earned under the plan during the plan year, determined using the additional actuarial assumptions described in paragraph (1)(B), plus

(II) the amount of plan-related expenses expected to be paid from plan assets during the plan year, over

(ii) the amount of mandatory employee contributions expected to be made during the plan year, plus

(B) in the case of a plan which also has been in at-risk status for at least 2 of the 4 preceding plan years, a loading factor equal to 4 percent of the amount determined under subsection (b)(1)(A)(i) with respect to the plan for the plan year.

(3) Minimum amount.—In no event shall—

(A) the at-risk funding target be less than the funding target, as determined without regard to this subsection, or

(B) the at-risk target normal cost be less than the target normal cost, as determined without regard to this subsection.

(4) Determination of at-risk status.—For purposes of this subsection—

(A) In general.—A plan is in at-risk status for a plan year if—

(i) the funding target attainment percentage for the preceding plan year (determined under this section without regard to this subsection) is less than 80 percent, and

(ii) the funding target attainment percentage for the preceding plan year (determined under this section by using the additional actuarial assumptions described in paragraph (1)(B) in computing the funding target) is less than 70 percent.

(B) Transition rule.—In the case of plan year beginning in 2008, 2009, and 2010, subparagraph

(A)(i) shall be applied by substituting the following percentages for "80 percent":

(i) 65 percent in the case of 2008.

(ii) 70 percent in the case of 2009.

(iii) 75 percent in the case of 2010.

In the case of plan years beginning in 2008, the funding target attainment percentage for the preceding plan year under subparagraph (A) may be determined using such methods of estimation as the Secretary may provide.

(C) Special rule for employees offered early retirement in 2006.—

(i) In general.—For purposes of subparagraph (A)(ii), the additional actuarial assumptions described in paragraph (1)(B) shall not be taken into account with respect to any employee if—

(I) such employee is employed by a specified automobile manufacturer,

(II) such employee is offered a substantial amount of additional cash compensation, substantially enhanced retirement benefits under the plan, or materially reduced employment duties on the condition that by a specified date (not later than December 31, 2010) the employee retires (as defined under the terms of the plan),

(III) such offer is made during 2006 and pursuant to a bona fide retirement incentive program and requires, by the terms of the offer, that such offer can be accepted not later than a specified date (not later than December 31, 2006), and

(IV) such employee does not elect to accept such offer before the specified date on which the offer expires.

(ii) Specified automobile manufacturer.—For purposes of clause (i), the term "specified automobile manufacturer" means—

(I) any manufacturer of automobiles, and

(II) any manufacturer of automobile parts which supplies such parts directly to a manufacturer of automobiles and which, after a transaction or series of transactions ending in 1999 ceased to be a member of a controlled group which included such manufacturer of automobiles.

(5) Transition between applicable funding targets and between applicable target normal costs.—

(A) In general.—In any case in which a plan which is in at-risk status for a plan year has been in such status for a consecutive period of fewer than 5 plan years, the applicable amount of the funding target and of the target normal cost shall be, in lieu of the amount determined without regard to this paragraph, the sum of—

(i) the amount determined under this section without regard to this subsection, plus

IRC Sec. 430(i)(1)(C)

(ii) the transition percentage for such plan year of the excess of the amount determined under this subsection (without regard to this paragraph) over the amount determined under this section without regard to this subsection.

(B) Transition percentage.—For purposes of subparagraph (A), the transition percentage shall be determined in accordance with the following table:

If the consecutive number of years (including the plan year) the plan is in at-risk status is —	The transition percentage is—
1	20
2	40
3	60
4	80

(C) Years before effective date.—For purposes of this paragraph, plan years beginning before 2008 shall not be taken into account.

(6) **Small plan exception.**—If, on each day during the preceding plan year, a plan had 500 or fewer participants, the plan shall not be treated as in at-risk status for the plan year. For purposes of this paragraph, all defined benefit plans (other than multiemployer plans) maintained by the same employer (or any member of such employer's controlled group) shall be treated as 1 plan, but only participants with respect to such employer or member shall be taken into account and the rules of subsection (g)(2)(C) shall apply.

(j) **Payment of Minimum Required Contributions.**—

(1) **In general.**—For purposes of this section, the due date for any payment of any minimum required contribution for any plan year shall be 8½ months after the close of the plan year.

(2) **Interest.**—Any payment required under paragraph (1) for a plan year that is made on a date other than the valuation date for such plan year shall be adjusted for interest accruing for the period between the valuation date and the payment date, at the effective rate of interest for the plan for such plan year.

(3) **Accelerated quarterly contribution schedule for underfunded plans.**—

(A) Failure to timely make required installment.—In any case in which the plan has a funding shortfall for the preceding plan year, the employer maintaining the plan shall make the required installments under this paragraph and if the employer fails to pay the full amount of a required installment for the plan year, then the amount of interest charged under paragraph (2) on the underpayment for the period of underpayment shall be

determined by using a rate of interest equal to the rate otherwise used under paragraph (2) plus 5 percentage points. In the case of plan years beginning in 2008, the funding shortfall for the preceding plan year may be determined using such methods of estimation as the Secretary may provide.

(B) Amount of underpayment, period of underpayment.—For purposes of subparagraph (A)—

(i) Amount.—The amount of the underpayment shall be the excess of—

(I) the required installment, over

(II) the amount (if any) of the installment contributed to or under the plan on or before the due date for the installment.

(ii) Period of underpayment.—The period for which any interest is charged under this paragraph with respect to any portion of the underpayment shall run from the due date for the installment to the date on which such portion is contributed to or under the plan.

(iii) Order of crediting contributions.—For purposes of clause (i)(II), contributions shall be credited against unpaid required installments in the order in which such installments are required to be paid.

(C) Number of required installments; due dates.—For purposes of this paragraph—

(i) Payable in 4 installments.—There shall be 4 required installments for each plan year.

(ii) Time for payment of installments.—The due dates for required installments are set forth in the following table:

In the case of the following required installment:	The due date is:
1st	April 15
2nd	July 15
3rd	October 15
4th	January 15 of the following year

(D) Amount of required installment.—For purposes of this paragraph—

(i) In general.—The amount of any required installment shall be 25 percent of the required annual payment.

(ii) Required annual payment.—For purposes of clause (i), the term "required annual payment" means the lesser of—

(I) 90 percent of the minimum required contribution (determined without regard to this subsection) to the plan for the plan year under this section, or

IRC Sec. 430(j)(3)(D)(ii)(I)

(II) 100 percent of the minimum required contribution (determined without regard to this subsection or to any waiver under section 412(c)) to the plan for the preceding plan year.

Subclause (II) shall not apply if the preceding plan year referred to in such clause was not a year of 12 months.

(E) Fiscal years, short years, and years with alternate valuation date.—

(i) Fiscal years.—In applying this paragraph to a plan year beginning on any date other than January 1, there shall be substituted for the months specified in this paragraph, the months which correspond thereto.

(ii) Short plan year.—This subparagraph shall be applied to plan years of less than 12 months in accordance with regulations prescribed by the Secretary.

(iii) Plan with alternate valuation date.—The Secretary shall prescribe regulations for the application of this paragraph in the case of a plan which has a valuation date other than the first day of the plan year.

(F) Quarterly contributions not to include certain increased contributions.—Subparagraph (D) shall be applied without regard to any increase under subsection (c)(7).

(4) Liquidity requirement in connection with quarterly contributions.—

(A) In general.—A plan to which this paragraph applies shall be treated as failing to pay the full amount of any required installment under paragraph (3) to the extent that the value of the liquid assets paid in such installment is less than the liquidity shortfall (whether or not such liquidity shortfall exceeds the amount of such installment required to be paid but for this paragraph).

(B) Plans to which paragraph applies.—This paragraph shall apply to a plan (other than a plan described in subsection (g)(2)(B)) which—

(i) is required to pay installments under paragraph (3) for a plan year, and

(ii) has a liquidity shortfall for any quarter during such plan year.

(C) Period of underpayment.—For purposes of paragraph (3)(A), any portion of an installment that is treated as not paid under subparagraph (A) shall continue to be treated as unpaid until the close of the quarter in which the due date for such installment occurs.

(D) Limitation on increase.—If the amount of any required installment is increased by reason of subparagraph (A), in no event shall such increase exceed the amount which, when added to prior

installments for the plan year, is necessary to increase the funding target attainment percentage of the plan for the plan year (taking into account the expected increase in funding target due to benefits accruing or earned during the plan year) to 100 percent.

(E) Definitions.—For purposes of this paragraph—

(i) Liquidity shortfall.—The term "liquidity shortfall" means, with respect to any required installment, an amount equal to the excess (as of the last day of the quarter for which such installment is made) of—

(I) the base amount with respect to such quarter, over

(II) the value (as of such last day) of the plan's liquid assets.

(ii) Base amount.—

(I) In general.—The term "base amount" means, with respect to any quarter, an amount equal to 3 times the sum of the adjusted disbursements from the plan for the 12 months ending on the last day of such quarter.

(II) Special rule.—If the amount determined under subclause (I) exceeds an amount equal to 2 times the sum of the adjusted disbursements from the plan for the 36 months ending on the last day of the quarter and an enrolled actuary certifies to the satisfaction of the Secretary that such excess is the result of nonrecurring circumstances, the base amount with respect to such quarter shall be determined without regard to amounts related to those nonrecurring circumstances.

(iii) Disbursements from the plan.—The term "disbursements from the plan" means all disbursements from the trust, including purchases of annuities, payments of single sums and other benefits, and administrative expenses.

(iv) Adjusted disbursements.—The term "adjusted disbursements" means disbursements from the plan reduced by the product of—

(I) the plan's funding target attainment percentage for the plan year, and

(II) the sum of the purchases of annuities, payments of single sums, and such other disbursements as the Secretary shall provide in regulations.

(v) Liquid assets.—The term "liquid assets" means cash, marketable securities, and such other assets as specified by the Secretary in regulations.

(vi) Quarter.—The term "quarter" means, with respect to any required installment, the 3-month period preceding the month in which the due date for such installment occurs.

(F) Regulations.—The Secretary may prescribe such regulations as are necessary to carry out this paragraph.

(k) Imposition of Lien Where Failure to Make Required Contributions.—

(1) In general.—In the case of a plan to which this subsection applies (as provided under paragraph (2)), if—

(A) any person fails to make a contribution payment required by section 412 and this section before the due date for such payment, and

(B) the unpaid balance of such payment (including interest), when added to the aggregate unpaid balance of all preceding such payments for which payment was not made before the due date (including interest), exceeds $1,000,000,

then there shall be a lien in favor of the plan in the amount determined under paragraph (3) upon all property and rights to property, whether real or personal, belonging to such person and any other person who is a member of the same controlled group of which such person is a member.

(2) Plans to which subsection applies.—This subsection shall apply to a defined benefit plan (other than a multiemployer plan) covered under section 4021 of the Employee Retirement Income Security Act of 1974 for any plan year for which the funding target attainment percentage (as defined in subsection (d)(2)) of such plan is less than 100 percent.

(3) Amount of lien.—For purposes of paragraph (1), the amount of the lien shall be equal to the aggregate unpaid balance of contribution payments required under this section and section 412 for which payment has not been made before the due date.

(4) Notice of failure; lien.—

(A) Notice of failure.—A person committing a failure described in paragraph (1) shall notify the Pension Benefit Guaranty Corporation of such failure within 10 days of the due date for the required contribution payment.

(B) Period of lien.—The lien imposed by paragraph (1) shall arise on the due date for the required contribution payment and shall continue until the last day of the first plan year in which the plan ceases to be described in paragraph (1)(B). Such lien shall continue to run without regard to whether such plan continues to be described in paragraph (2) during the period referred to in the preceding sentence.

(C) Certain rules to apply.—Any amount with respect to which a lien is imposed under paragraph (1) shall be treated as taxes due and owing the United States and rules similar to the rules of subsections (c), (d), and (e) of section 4068 of the Employee Retirement Income Security Act of 1974 shall apply with respect to a lien imposed by subsection (a) and the amount with respect to such lien.

(5) Enforcement.—Any lien created under paragraph (1) may be perfected and enforced only by the Pension Benefit Guaranty Corporation, or at the direction of the Pension Benefit Guaranty Corporation, by the contributing sponsor (or any member of the controlled group of the contributing sponsor).

(6) Definitions.—For purposes of this subsection—

(A) Contribution payment.—The term "contribution payment" means, in connection with a plan, a contribution payment required to be made to the plan, including any required installment under paragraphs (3) and (4) of subsection (j).

(B) Due date; required installment.—The terms "due date" and "required installment" have the meanings given such terms by subsection (j).

(C) Controlled group.—The term "controlled group" means any group treated as a single employer under subsections (b), (c), (m), and (o) of section 414.

(*l*) Qualified Transfers to Health Benefit Accounts.—In the case of a qualified transfer (as defined in section 420), any assets so transferred shall not, for purposes of this section, be treated as assets in the plan.

Recent Amendments to IRC §430

Preservation of Access to Care for Medicare Beneficiaries and Pension Relief Act of 2010 (Pub. L. No. 111-192), as follows:

- IRC §430(c)(2)(D) was added by Act §201(b)(1). Eff. for plan years beginning after Dec. 31, 2007.
- IRC §430(c)(7) was added by Act §201(b)(2). Eff. for plan years beginning after Dec. 31, 2007.
- IRC §430(c)(1) was amended by Act §201(b)(3)(A) by striking "the shortfall amortization bases for such plan year and each of the 6 preceding plan years" and inserting "any shortfall amortization base which has not been fully amortized under this subsection". Eff. for plan years beginning after Dec. 31, 2007.
- IRC §430(f)(3)(D) was added by Act §204(b). Eff. generally for plan years beginning after Aug. 31, 2009; but eff. for plan years beginning after Dec. 31, 2008, for plans with a valuation date not the first day of the plan year.
- IRC §430(j)(3)(F) was added by Act §201(b)(3)(B). Eff. for plan years beginning after Dec. 31, 2007.

Worker, Retiree, and Employer Recovery Act of 2008 (Pub. L. No. 110-458), as follows:

- IRC §430(b) was amended by Act §101(b)(2)(A). Eff. generally for plan years beginning after Dec. 31, 2008. See Act §101(b)(3)(B), below, for special provision. IRC §430(b) prior to amendment:

    (b) Target Normal Cost.—For purposes of this section, except as provided in subsection (i)(2) with respect to plans in at-risk status, the term "target normal cost" means, for any plan year, the present value of all benefits which are expected to accrue or to be earned under the plan during the plan year. For purposes of this subsection, if any benefit attributable to services performed in a preceding plan year is increased by reason of any increase in compensation during the current plan year, the increase in such benefit shall be treated as having accrued during the current plan year.

- IRC §430(c)(5)(B)(i) was amended by Act §202(b)(2). Eff. as if included in Pub. L. No. 109-280, §112 [eff. with respect to plan years beginning after Dec. 31, 2007]. IRC §430(c)(5)(B)(i) prior to amendment:

    (i) In General.—Except as provided in clauses (iii) and (iv), in the case of plan years beginning after 2007 and before 2011,

IRC Sec. 430(*l*)

only the applicable percentage of the funding target shall be taken into account under paragraph (3)(A) in determining the funding shortfall for the plan year for purposes of subparagraph (A).

- IRC §430(c)(5)(B)(iii) was amended by Act §101(b)(2)(B) by inserting "beginning" before "after 2008". Eff. as if included in Pub. L. No. 109-280, §112 [eff. with respect to plan years beginning after Dec. 31, 2007].

- IRC §430(c)(5)(B)(iii) was stricken by Act §202(b)(1) and cl. (iv) was redesignated as cl. (iii). Eff. as if included in Pub. L. No. 109-280, §112 [eff. with respect to plan years beginning after Dec. 31, 2007]. IRC §430(c)(5)(B)(iii) prior to repeal:

  (iii) Limitation.—Clause (i) shall not apply with respect to any plan year beginning after 2008 unless the shortfall amortization base for each of the preceding years beginning after 2007 was zero (determined after application of this subparagraph).

- IRC §430(c)(5)(B)(iv)(II) was amended by Act §101(b)(2)(C) by inserting "for such year" after "beginning in 2007)". Eff. as if included in Pub. L. No. 109-280, §112 [eff. with respect to plan years beginning after Dec. 31, 2007].

- IRC §430(f)(3)(A) was amended by Act §101(b)(2)(D)(i)–(v) by striking "as of the first day of the plan year" the second place it appeared in the first sentence of para. (3)(A); by substituting "paragraph (3)" for "paragraph (2)" in para. (4)(A); substituting "subsection (b), (c), or (e) of section 436" for "paragraph (1), (2), or (4) of section 206(g)" in para. (6)(B)(iii); striking "the sum of" in para. (f)(6)(C); and striking "of the Treasury" in para. (8). Eff. as if included in Pub. L. No. 109-280, §112 [eff. with respect to plan years beginning after Dec. 31, 2007].

- IRC §430(g)(3)(B) was amended by Act §121(b) by amending the last sentence. Eff. as if included in Pub. L. No. 109-280, §112 [eff. with respect to plan years beginning after Dec. 31, 2007]. IRC §430(g)(3)(B), last sentence, prior to amendment:

  Any such averaging shall be adjusted for contributions and distributions (as provided by the Secretary).

- IRC §430(h)(2)(B) was amended by Act §101(b)(2)(E)(i)–(ii) by inserting "and target normal cost" after "funding target" and by substituting "benefits" for "liabilities". Eff. as if included in Pub. L. No. 109-280, §112 [eff. with respect to plan years beginning after Dec. 31, 2007].

- IRC §430(h)(2)(F) was amended by Act §101(b)(2)(E)(iii)–(iv) by substituting "section 417(e)(3)(D)(i) for such month)" for "section 417(e)(3)(D)(i)) for such month", and by substituting "subparagraph (C)" for "subparagraph (B)". Eff. as if included in Pub. L. No. 109-280, §112 [eff. with respect to plan years beginning after Dec. 31, 2007].

- IRC §430(i)(2)(A) was amended by Act §101(b)(2)(F)(i)(I). Eff. for plan years beginning after Dec. 31, 2008. See Act §101(b)(3)(B), below, for special provision. IRC §430(i)(2)(A) prior to amendment:

  (A) the present value of all benefits which are expected to accrue or be earned under the plan during the plan year, determined using the additional actuarial assumptions described in paragraph (1)(B), plus

- IRC §430(i)(2)(B) was amended by Act §101(b)(2)(F)(i)(II) by substituting "the amount determined under subsection (b)(1)(A)(i) with respect to the plan for the plan year" for "the target normal cost (determined without regard to this paragraph) of the plan for the plan year". Eff. generally for plan years beginning after Dec. 31, 2008. See Act §101(b)(3)(B), below, for special provision.

- IRC §430(i)(4)(B) was amended by Act §101(b)(2)(F)(ii) by substituting "subparagraph (A)" for "subparagraph (A)(ii)" in the last sentence. Eff. as if included in Pub. L. No. 109-280, §112 [eff. with respect to plan years beginning after Dec. 31, 2007]. See Act §101(b)(3)(B), below, for special provision.

- IRC §430(j)(3)(A) was amended by Act §101(b)(2)(G)(i) by adding the sentence at the end. Eff. as if included in Pub. L. No. 109-280, §112 [eff. with respect to plan years beginning after Dec. 31, 2007].

- IRC §430(j)(3)(D)(ii)(II) was amended by Act §101(b)(2)(G)(ii) by substituting "section 412(c)" for "section 302(c)". Eff. as if included in Pub. L. No. 109-280, §112 [eff. with respect to plan years beginning after Dec. 31, 2007].

- IRC §430(j)(3)(E) was amended by Act §101(b)(2)(G)(iv) by substituting ", Short Years, And Years With Alternate Valuation

Date" for "And Short Years" in the heading. Eff. as if included in Pub. L. No. 109-280, §112 [eff. with respect to plan years beginning after Dec. 31, 2007].

- IRC §430(j)(3)(E)(iii) was added by Act §101(b)(2)(G)(iii). Eff. as if included in Pub. L. No. 109-280, §112 [eff. with respect to plan years beginning after Dec. 31, 2007].

- IRC §430(k)(1) was amended by Act §101(b)(2)(H)(i) by inserting "(as provided under paragraph (2))" after "applies". Eff. as if included in Pub. L. No. 109-280, §112 [eff. with respect to plan years beginning after Dec. 31, 2007].

- IRC §430(k)(6)(B) was amended by Act §101(b)(2)(H)(ii) by substituting a period for ", except that in the case of a payment other than a required installment, the due date shall be the date such payment is required to be made under section 430". Eff. as if included in Pub. L. No. 109-280, §112 [eff. with respect to plan years beginning after Dec. 31, 2007].

- **Other Provision.** Act §101(b)(3)(B) provides:

  (B) Election for earlier application.—The amendments made by such paragraphs shall apply to a plan for the first plan year beginning after December 31, 2007, if the plan sponsor makes the election under this subparagraph. An election under this subparagraph shall be made at such time and in such manner as the Secretary of the Treasury or the Secretary's delegate may prescribe, and, once made, may be revoked only with the consent of the Secretary.

Pension Protection Act of 2006 (Pub. L. No. 109-280), as follows:

- IRC §430 was added by Act §112(a). Eff. plan years beginning after Dec. 31, 2007. [*Ed. Note*: see Act §§105 through 106 for special rules. For Act §104, see notes to ERISA §303.]

- [*Ed. Note*: see Act §115(a)–(c) for transition rule applicable to funding requirements.]

- **Multiple Employer Plans.** For Act §104, **Special Rules for Multiple Employer Plans of Certain Cooperatives**, as amended by Pub. L. No. 111-192, §202(b), see amendment notes to ERISA §303.

SEC. 431. MINIMUM FUNDING STANDARDS FOR MULTIEMPLOYER PLANS.

(a) In General.—For purposes of section 412, the accumulated funding deficiency of a multiemployer plan for any plan year is—

(1) except as provided in paragraph (2), the amount, determined as of the end of the plan year, equal to the excess (if any) of the total charges to the funding standard account of the plan for all plan years (beginning with the first plan year for which this part applies to the plan) over the total credits to such account for such years, and

(2) if the multiemployer plan is in reorganization for any plan year, the accumulated funding deficiency of the plan determined under section 4243 of the Employee Retirement Income Security Act of 1974.

(b) Funding Standard Account.—

(1) **Account required.**—Each multiemployer plan to which this part applies shall establish and maintain a funding standard account. Such account shall be credited and charged solely as provided in this section.

(2) **Charges to account.**—For a plan year, the funding standard account shall be charged with the sum of—

(A) the normal cost of the plan for the plan year,

(B) the amounts necessary to amortize in equal annual installments (until fully amortized)—

(i) in the case of a plan which comes into existence on or after January 1, 2008, the unfunded past service liability under the plan on the first day of the first plan year to which this section applies, over a period of 15 plan years,

(ii) separately, with respect to each plan year, the net increase (if any) in unfunded past service liability under the plan arising from plan amendments adopted in such year, over a period of 15 plan years,

(iii) separately, with respect to each plan year, the net experience loss (if any) under the plan, over a period of 15 plan years, and

(iv) separately, with respect to each plan year, the net loss (if any) resulting from changes in actuarial assumptions used under the plan, over a period of 15 plan years,

(C) the amount necessary to amortize each waived funding deficiency (within the meaning of section 412(c)(3)) for each prior plan year in equal annual installments (until fully amortized) over a period of 15 plan years,

(D) the amount necessary to amortize in equal annual installments (until fully amortized) over a period of 5 plan years any amount credited to the funding standard account under section 412(b)(3)(D) (as in effect on the day before the date of the enactment of the Pension Protection Act of 2006), and

(E) the amount necessary to amortize in equal annual installments (until fully amortized) over a period of 20 years the contributions which would be required to be made under the plan but for the provisions of section 412(c)(7)(A)(i)(I) (as in effect on the day before the date of the enactment of the Pension Protection Act of 2006).

(3) **Credits to account**.—For a plan year, the funding standard account shall be credited with the sum of—

(A) the amount considered contributed by the employer to or under the plan for the plan year,

(B) the amount necessary to amortize in equal annual installments (until fully amortized)—

(i) separately, with respect to each plan year, the net decrease (if any) in unfunded past service liability under the plan arising from plan amendments adopted in such year, over a period of 15 plan years,

(ii) separately, with respect to each plan year, the net experience gain (if any) under the plan, over a period of 15 plan years, and

(iii) separately, with respect to each plan year, the net gain (if any) resulting from changes in

actuarial assumptions used under the plan, over a period of 15 plan years,

(C) the amount of the waived funding deficiency (within the meaning of section 412(c)(3)) for the plan year, and

(D) in the case of a plan year for which the accumulated funding deficiency is determined under the funding standard account if such plan year follows a plan year for which such deficiency was determined under the alternative minimum funding standard under section 412(g) (as in effect on the day before the date of the enactment of the Pension Protection Act of 2006), the excess (if any) of any debit balance in the funding standard account (determined without regard to this subparagraph) over any debit balance in the alternative minimum funding standard account.

(4) **Special rule for amounts first amortized in plan years before 2008**.—In the case of any amount amortized under section 412(b) (as in effect on the day before the date of the enactment of the Pension Protection Act of 2006) over any period beginning with a plan year beginning before 2008 in lieu of the amortization described in paragraphs (2)(B) and (3)(B), such amount shall continue to be amortized under such section as so in effect.

(5) **Combining and offsetting amounts to be amortized**.—Under regulations prescribed by the Secretary, amounts required to be amortized under paragraph (2) or paragraph (3), as the case may be—

(A) may be combined into one amount under such paragraph to be amortized over a period determined on the basis of the remaining amortization period for all items entering into such combined amount, and

(B) may be offset against amounts required to be amortized under the other such paragraph, with the resulting amount to be amortized over a period determined on the basis of the remaining amortization periods for all items entering into whichever of the two amounts being offset is the greater.

(6) **Interest**.—The funding standard account (and items therein) shall be charged or credited (as determined under regulations prescribed by the Secretary of the Treasury) with interest at the appropriate rate consistent with the rate or rates of interest used under the plan to determine costs.

(7) **Special rules relating to charges and credits to funding standard account**.—For purposes of this part—

(A) Withdrawal liability.—Any amount received by a multiemployer plan in payment of all or part of an employer's withdrawal liability under part 1 of subtitle E of title IV of the Employee Retirement Income Security Act of 1974 shall be considered an amount contributed by the employer to or under

IRC Sec. 431(b)(7)(A)

the plan. The Secretary may prescribe by regulation additional charges and credits to a multiemployer plan's funding standard account to the extent necessary to prevent withdrawal liability payments from being unduly reflected as advance funding for plan liabilities.

(B) Adjustments when a multiemployer plan leaves reorganization.—If a multiemployer plan is not in reorganization in the plan year but was in reorganization in the immediately preceding plan year, any balance in the funding standard account at the close of such immediately preceding plan year—

(i) shall be eliminated by an offsetting credit or charge (as the case may be), but

(ii) shall be taken into account in subsequent plan years by being amortized in equal annual installments (until fully amortized) over 30 plan years.

The preceding sentence shall not apply to the extent of any accumulated funding deficiency under section 4243(a) of such Act as of the end of the last plan year that the plan was in reorganization.

(C) Plan payments to supplemental program or withdrawal liability payment fund.—Any amount paid by a plan during a plan year to the Pension Benefit Guaranty Corporation pursuant to section 4222 of such Act or to a fund exempt under section 501(c)(22) pursuant to section 4223 of such Act shall reduce the amount of contributions considered received by the plan for the plan year.

(D) Interim withdrawal liability payments.—Any amount paid by an employer pending a final determination of the employer's withdrawal liability under part 1 of subtitle E of title IV of such Act and subsequently refunded to the employer by the plan shall be charged to the funding standard account in accordance with regulations prescribed by the Secretary.

(E) Election for deferral of charge for portion of net experience loss.—If an election is in effect under section 412(b)(7)(F) (as in effect on the day before the date of the enactment of the Pension Protection Act of 2006) for any plan year, the funding standard account shall be charged in the plan year to which the portion of the net experience loss deferred by such election was deferred with the amount so deferred (and paragraph (2)(B)(iii) shall not apply to the amount so charged).

(F) Financial assistance.—Any amount of any financial assistance from the Pension Benefit Guaranty Corporation to any plan, and any repayment of such amount, shall be taken into account under this section and section 412 in such manner as is determined by the Secretary.

(G) Short-term benefits.—To the extent that any plan amendment increases the unfunded past ser-

vice liability under the plan by reason of an increase in benefits which are not payable as a life annuity but are payable under the terms of the plan for a period that does not exceed 14 years from the effective date of the amendment, paragraph (2)(B)(ii) shall be applied separately with respect to such increase in unfunded past service liability by substituting the number of years of the period during which such benefits are payable for "15".

(8) Special relief rules.—Notwithstanding any other provision of this subsection—

(A) Amortization of net investment losses.—

(i) In general.—A multiemployer plan with respect to which the solvency test under subparagraph (C) is met may treat the portion of any experience loss or gain attributable to net investment losses incurred in either or both of the first two plan years ending after August 31, 2008, as an item separate from other experience losses, to be amortized in equal annual installments (until fully amortized) over the period—

(I) beginning with the plan year in which such portion is first recognized in the actuarial value of assets, and

(II) ending with the last plan year in the 30-plan year period beginning with the plan year in which such net investment loss was incurred.

(ii) Coordination with extensions.—If this subparagraph applies for any plan year—

(I) no extension of the amortization period under clause (i) shall be allowed under subsection (d), and

(II) if an extension was granted under subsection (d) for any plan year before the election to have this subparagraph apply to the plan year, such extension shall not result in such amortization period exceeding 30 years.

(iii) Net investment losses.—For purposes of this subparagraph—

(I) In general.—Net investment losses shall be determined in the manner prescribed by the Secretary on the basis of the difference betweenactual and expected returns (including any difference attributable to any criminally fraudulent investment arrangement).

(II) Criminally fraudulent investment arrangements.—The determination as to whether an arrangement is a criminally fraudulent investment arrangement shall be made under rules substantially similar to the rules prescribed by the Secretary for purposes of section 165.

(B) Expanded smoothing period.—

(i) In general.—A multiemployer plan with respect to which the solvency test under subparagraph (C) is met may change its asset valuation method in a manner which—

(I) spreads the difference between expected and actual returns for either or both of the first 2 plan years ending after August 31, 2008, over a period of not more than 10 years,

(II) provides that for either or both of the first 2 plan years beginning after August 31, 2008, the value of plan assets at any time shall not be less than 80 percent or greater than 130 percent of the fair market value of such assets at such time, or

(III) makes both changes described in subclauses (I) and (II) to such method.

(ii) Asset valuation methods.—If this subparagraph applies for any plan year—

(I) the Secretary shall not treat the asset valuation method of the plan as unreasonable solely because of the changes in such method described in clause (i), and

(II) such changes shall be deemed approved by the Secretary under section 302(d)(1) of the Employee Retirement Income Security Act of 1974 and section 412(d)(1).

(iii) Amortization of reduction in unfunded accrued liability.—If this subparagraph and subparagraph (A) both apply for any plan year, the plan shall treat any reduction in unfunded accrued liability resulting from the application of this subparagraph as a separate experience amortization base, to be amortized in equal annual installments (until fully amortized) over a period of 30 plan years rather than the period such liability would otherwise be amortized over.

(C) Solvency test.—The solvency test under this paragraph is met only if the plan actuary certifies that the plan is projected to have sufficient assets to timely pay expected benefits and anticipated expenditures over the amortization period, taking into account the changes in the funding standard account under this paragraph.

(D) Restriction on benefit increases.—If subparagraph (A) or (B) apply to a multiemployer plan for any plan year, then, in addition to any other applicable restrictions on benefit increases, a plan amendment increasing benefits may not go into effect during either of the 2 plan years immediately following such plan year unless—

(i) the plan actuary certifies that—

(I) any such increase is paid for out of additional contributions not allocated to the plan immediately before the application of this paragraph to the plan, and

(II) the plan's funded percentage and projected credit balances for such 2 plan years are reasonably expected to be at least as high as such per-

centage and balances would have been if the benefit increase had not been adopted, or

(ii) the amendment is required as a condition of qualification under part I of subchapter D or to comply with other applicable law.

(E) Reporting.—A plan sponsor of a plan to which this paragraph applies shall—

(i) give notice of such application to participants and beneficiaries of the plan, and

(ii) inform the Pension Benefit Guaranty Corporation of such application in such form and manner as the Director of the Pension Benefit Guaranty Corporation may prescribe.

(c) Additional Rules.—

(1) Determinations to be made under funding method.—For purposes of this part, normal costs, accrued liability, past service liabilities, and experience gains and losses shall be determined under the funding method used to determine costs under the plan.

(2) Valuation of assets.—

(A) In general.—For purposes of this part, the value of the plan's assets shall be determined on the basis of any reasonable actuarial method of valuation which takes into account fair market value and which is permitted under regulations prescribed by the Secretary.

(B) Election with respect to bonds.—The value of a bond or other evidence of indebtedness which is not in default as to principal or interest may, at the election of the plan administrator, be determined on an amortized basis running from initial cost at purchase to par value at maturity or earliest call date. Any election under this subparagraph shall be made at such time and in such manner as the Secretary shall by regulations provide, shall apply to all such evidences of indebtedness, and may be revoked only with the consent of the Secretary.

(3) Actuarial assumptions must be reasonable.—For purposes of this section, all costs, liabilities, rates of interest, and other factors under the plan shall be determined on the basis of actuarial assumptions and methods—

(A) each of which is reasonable (taking into account the experience of the plan and reasonable expectations), and

(B) which, in combination, offer the actuary's best estimate of anticipated experience under the plan.

(4) Treatment of certain changes as experience gain or loss.—For purposes of this section, if—

(A) a change in benefits under the Social Security Act or in other retirement benefits created under Federal or State law, or

(B) a change in the definition of the term "wages" under section 3121, or a change in the amount of

IRC Sec. 431(c)(4)(B)

such wages taken into account under regulations prescribed for purposes of section 401(a)(5),

results in an increase or decrease in accrued liability under a plan, such increase or decrease shall be treated as an experience loss or gain.

(5) Full funding.—If, as of the close of a plan year, a plan would (without regard to this paragraph) have an accumulated funding deficiency in excess of the full funding limitation—

(A) the funding standard account shall be credited with the amount of such excess, and

(B) all amounts described in subparagraphs (B), (C), and (D) of subsection (b)(2) and subparagraph (B) of subsection (b)(3) which are required to be amortized shall be considered fully amortized for purposes of such subparagraphs.

(6) Full-funding limitation.—

(A) In general.—For purposes of paragraph (5), the term "full-funding limitation" means the excess (if any) of—

(i) the accrued liability (including normal cost) under the plan (determined under the entry age normal funding method if such accrued liability cannot be directly calculated under the funding method used for the plan), over

(ii) the lesser of—

(I) the fair market value of the plan's assets, or

(II) the value of such assets determined under paragraph (2).

(B) Minimum amount.—

(i) In general.—In no event shall the full-funding limitation determined under subparagraph (A) be less than the excess (if any) of—

(I) 90 percent of the current liability of the plan (including the expected increase in current liability due to benefits accruing during the plan year), over

(II) the value of the plan's assets determined under paragraph (2).

(ii) Assets.—For purposes of clause (i), assets shall not be reduced by any credit balance in the funding standard account.

(C) Full funding limitation.—For purposes of this paragraph, unless otherwise provided by the plan, the accrued liability under a multiemployer plan shall not include benefits which are not nonforfeitable under the plan after the termination of the plan (taking into consideration section 411(d)(3)).

(D) Current liability.—For purposes of this paragraph—

(i) In general.—The term "current liability" means all liabilities to employees and their beneficiaries under the plan.

(ii) Treatment of unpredictable contingent event benefits.—For purposes of clause (i), any benefit contingent on an event other than—

(I) age, service, compensation, death, or disability, or

(II) an event which is reasonably and reliably predictable (as determined by the Secretary),

shall not be taken into account until the event on which the benefit is contingent occurs.

(iii) Interest rate used.—The rate of interest used to determine current liability under this paragraph shall be the rate of interest determined under subparagraph (E).

(iv) Mortality tables.—

(I) Commissioners' standard table.—In the case of plan years beginning before the first plan year to which the first tables prescribed under subclause (II) apply, the mortality table used in determining current liability under this paragraph shall be the table prescribed by the Secretary which is based on the prevailing commissioners' standard table (described in section 807(d)(5)(A)) used to determine reserves for group annuity contracts issued on January 1, 1993.

(II) Secretarial authority.—The Secretary may by regulation prescribe for plan years beginning after December 31, 1999, mortality tables to be used in determining current liability under this subsection. Such tables shall be based upon the actual experience of pension plans and projected trends in such experience. In prescribing such tables, the Secretary shall take into account results of available independent studies of mortality of individuals covered by pension plans.

(v) Separate mortality tables for the disabled.—Notwithstanding clause (iv)—

(I) In general.—The Secretary shall establish mortality tables which may be used (in lieu of the tables under clause (iv)) to determine current liability under this subsection for individuals who are entitled to benefits under the plan on account of disability. The Secretary shall establish separate tables for individuals whose disabilities occur in plan years beginning before January 1, 1995, and for individuals whose disabilities occur in plan years beginning on or after such date.

(II) Special rule for disabilities occurring after 1994.—In the case of disabilities occurring in plan years beginning after December 31, 1994, the tables under subclause (I) shall apply only with respect to individuals described in such subclause who are disabled within the meaning of title II of the Social Security Act and the regulations thereunder.

(vi) Periodic review.—The Secretary shall periodically (at least every 5 years) review any tables in effect under this subparagraph and shall, to the extent such Secretary determines necessary, by regulation update the tables to reflect the actual experience of pension plans and projected trends in such experience.

(E) Required change of interest rate.—For purposes of determining a plan's current liability for purposes of this paragraph—

(i) In general.—If any rate of interest used under the plan under subsection (b)(6) to determine cost is not within the permissible range, the plan shall establish a new rate of interest within the permissible range.

(ii) Permissible range.—For purposes of this subparagraph—

(I) In general.—Except as provided in subclause (II), the term "permissible range" means a rate of interest which is not more than 5 percent above, and not more than 10 percent below, the weighted average of the rates of interest on 30-year Treasury securities during the 4-year period ending on the last day before the beginning of the plan year.

(II) Secretarial authority.—If the Secretary finds that the lowest rate of interest permissible under subclause (I) is unreasonably high, the Secretary may prescribe a lower rate of interest, except that such rate may not be less than 80 percent of the average rate determined under such subclause.

(iii) Assumptions.—Notwithstanding paragraph (3)(A), the interest rate used under the plan shall be—

(I) determined without taking into account the experience of the plan and reasonable expectations, but

(II) consistent with the assumptions which reflect the purchase rates which would be used by insurance companies to satisfy the liabilities under the plan.

(7) Annual valuation.—

(A) In general.—For purposes of this section, a determination of experience gains and losses and a valuation of the plan's liability shall be made not less frequently than once every year, except that such determination shall be made more frequently to the extent required in particular cases under regulations prescribed by the Secretary.

(B) Valuation date.—

(i) Current year.—Except as provided in clause (ii), the valuation referred to in subparagraph (A) shall be made as of a date within the plan year to which the valuation refers or within one month prior to the beginning of such year.

(ii) Use of prior year valuation.—The valuation referred to in subparagraph (A) may be made as of a date within the plan year prior to the year to which the valuation refers if, as of such date, the value of the assets of the plan are not less than 100 percent of the plan's current liability (as defined in paragraph (6)(D) without regard to clause (iv) thereof).

(iii) Adjustments.—Information under clause (ii) shall, in accordance with regulations, be actuarially adjusted to reflect significant differences in participants.

(iv) Limitation.—A change in funding method to use a prior year valuation, as provided in clause (ii), may not be made unless as of the valuation date within the prior plan year, the value of the assets of the plan are not less than 125 percent of the plan's current liability (as defined in paragraph (6)(D) without regard to clause (iv) thereof).

(8) Time when certain contributions deemed made.—For purposes of this section, any contributions for a plan year made by an employer after the last day of such plan year, but not later than two and one-half months after such day, shall be deemed to have been made on such last day. For purposes of this subparagraph, such two and one-half month period may be extended for not more than six months under regulations prescribed by the Secretary.

(d) Extension of Amortization Periods for Multiemployer Plans.—

(1) Automatic extension upon application by certain plans.—

(A) In general.—If the plan sponsor of a multiemployer plan—

(i) submits to the Secretary an application for an extension of the period of years required to amortize any unfunded liability described in any clause of subsection (b)(2)(B) or described in subsection (b)(4), and

(ii) includes with the application a certification by the plan's actuary described in subparagraph (B),

the Secretary shall extend the amortization period for the period of time (not in excess of 5 years) specified in the application. Such extension shall be in addition to any extension under paragraph (2).

(B) Criteria.—A certification with respect to a multiemployer plan is described in this subparagraph if the plan's actuary certifies that, based on reasonable assumptions—

(i) absent the extension under subparagraph (A), the plan would have an accumulated funding deficiency in the current plan year or any of the 9 succeeding plan years,

(ii) the plan sponsor has adopted a plan to improve the plan's funding status,

(iii) the plan is projected to have sufficient assets to timely pay expected benefits and anticipated

IRC Sec. 431(d)(1)(B)(iii)

expenditures over the amortization period as extended, and

(iv) the notice required under paragraph (3)(A) has been provided.

(C) Termination.—The preceding provisions of this paragraph shall not apply with respect to any application submitted after December 31, 2014.

(2) Alternative extension.—

(A) In general.—If the plan sponsor of a multiemployer plan submits to the Secretary an application for an extension of the period of years required to amortize any unfunded liability described in any clause of subsection (b)(2)(B) or described in subsection (b)(4), the Secretary may extend the amortization period for a period of time (not in excess of 10 years reduced by the number of years of any extension under paragraph (1) with respect to such unfunded liability) if the Secretary makes the determination described in subparagraph (B). Such extension shall be in addition to any extension under paragraph (1).

(B) Determination.—The Secretary may grant an extension under subparagraph (A) if the Secretary determines that—

(i) such extension would carry out the purposes of this Act and would provide adequate protection for participants under the plan and their beneficiaries, and

(ii) the failure to permit such extension would—

(I) result in a substantial risk to the voluntary continuation of the plan, or a substantial curtailment of pension benefit levels or employee compensation, and

(II) be adverse to the interests of plan participants in the aggregate.

(C) Action by Secretary.—The Secretary shall act upon any application for an extension under this paragraph within 180 days of the submission of such application. If the Secretary rejects the application for an extension under this paragraph, the Secretary shall provide notice to the plan detailing the specific reasons for the rejection, including references to the criteria set forth above.

(3) Advance notice.—

(A) In general.—The Secretary shall, before granting an extension under this subsection, require each applicant to provide evidence satisfactory to such Secretary that the applicant has provided notice of the filing of the application for such extension to each affected party (as defined in section 4001(a)(21) of the Employee Retirement Income Security Act of 1974) with respect to the affected plan. Such notice shall include a description of the extent to which the plan is funded for

benefits which are guaranteed under title IV of such Act and for benefit liabilities.

(B) Consideration of relevant information.—The Secretary shall consider any relevant information provided by a person to whom notice was given under paragraph (1).

Recent Amendments to IRC §431

Preservation of Access to Care for Medicare Beneficiaries and Pension Relief Act of 2010 (Pub. L. No. 111-192), as follows:
- IRC §431(b)(8) was added by Act §211(a)(2). Eff. generally on the first day of the first plan year ending after Aug. 31, 2008, except any election under this section that affects the plan's funding standard account for the first plan year beginning after Aug. 31, 2008, is disregarded for purposes of ERISA §305 and IRC §432 for such plan year. Restrictions on plan amendments increasing benefits in ERISA §304(b)(8)(D) and IRC §431(b)(8)(D) take effect on the date of enactment [date of enactment: June 25, 2010]. See Act §211(b).

Pension Protection Act of 2006 (Pub. L. No. 109-280), as follows:
- IRC §431 was added by Act §211(a). Eff. generally for plan years beginning after 2007. [*Ed. Note:* for transition relief for certain benefits funded under an agreement approved by the PBGC, see Act §206.]
- **Other Provision.** Act §211(b)(2) provides:
  (2) Special rule for certain amortization extensions.—If the Secretary of the Treasury grants an extension under section 304 of the Employee Retirement Income Security Act of 1974 and section 412(e) of the Internal Revenue Code of 1986 with respect to any application filed with the Secretary of the Treasury on or before June 30, 2005, the extension (and any modification thereof) shall be applied and administered under the rules of such sections as in effect before the enactment of this Act, including the use of the rate of interest determined under section 6621(b) of such Code.

> ### Editor's Note
>
> **Caution:** IRC §432, as follows, was added by the Pension Protection Act of 2006 (PPA) (Pub. L. No. 109-280), §212(a), generally applicable to plan years beginning after 2007. For sunset provision, see the amendment notes below.

SEC. 432. ADDITIONAL FUNDING RULES FOR MULTIEMPLOYER PLANS IN ENDANGERED STATUS OR CRITICAL STATUS.

(a) General Rule.—For purposes of this part, in the case of a multiemployer plan in effect on July 16, 2006—

(1) if the plan is in endangered status—

(A) the plan sponsor shall adopt and implement a funding improvement plan in accordance with the requirements of subsection (c), and

(B) the requirements of subsection (d) shall apply during the funding plan adoption period and the funding improvement period, and

(2) if the plan is in critical status—

(A) the plan sponsor shall adopt and implement a rehabilitation plan in accordance with the requirements of subsection (e), and

(B) the requirements of subsection (f) shall apply during the rehabilitation plan adoption period and the rehabilitation period.

(b) Determination of Endangered and Critical Status.—For purposes of this section—

(1) Endangered status.—A multiemployer plan is in endangered status for a plan year if, as determined by the plan actuary under paragraph (3), the plan is not in critical status for the plan year and, as of the beginning of the plan year, either—

(A) the plan's funded percentage for such plan year is less than 80 percent, or

(B) the plan has an accumulated funding deficiency for such plan year, or is projected to have such an accumulated funding deficiency for any of the 6 succeeding plan years, taking into account any extension of amortization periods under section 431(d).

For purposes of this section, a plan shall be treated as in seriously endangered status for a plan year if the plan is described in both subparagraphs (A) and (B).

(2) Critical status.—A multiemployer plan is in critical status for a plan year if, as determined by the plan actuary under paragraph (3), the plan is described in 1 or more of the following subparagraphs as of the beginning of the plan year:

(A) A plan is described in this subparagraph if—

(i) the funded percentage of the plan is less than 65 percent, and

(ii) the sum of—

(I) the fair market value of plan assets, plus

(II) the present value of the reasonably anticipated employer contributions for the current plan year and each of the 6 succeeding plan years, assuming that the terms of all collective bargaining agreements pursuant to which the plan is maintained for the current plan year continue in effect for succeeding plan years, is less than the present value of all nonforfeitable benefits projected to be payable under the plan during the current plan year and each of the 6 succeeding plan years (plus administrative expenses for such plan years).

(B) A plan is described in this subparagraph if—

(i) the plan has an accumulated funding deficiency for the current plan year, not taking into account any extension of amortization periods under section 431(d), or

(ii) the plan is projected to have an accumulated funding deficiency for any of the 3 succeeding plan years (4 succeeding plan years if the funded percentage of the plan is 65 percent or less), not taking into account any extension of amortization periods under section 431(d).

(C) A plan is described in this subparagraph if—

(i)

(I) the plan's normal cost for the current plan year, plus interest (determined at the rate used for determining costs under the plan) for the current plan year on the amount of unfunded benefit liabilities under the plan as of the last date of the preceding plan year, exceeds

(II) the present value of the reasonably anticipated employer and employee contributions for the current plan year,

(ii) the present value, as of the beginning of the current plan year, of nonforfeitable benefits of inactive participants is greater than the present value of nonforfeitable benefits of active participants, and

(iii) the plan has an accumulated funding deficiency for the current plan year, or is projected to have such a deficiency for any of the 4 succeeding plan years, not taking into account any extension of amortization periods under section 431(d).

(D) A plan is described in this subparagraph if the sum of—

(i) the fair market value of plan assets, plus

(ii) the present value of the reasonably anticipated employer contributions for the current plan year and each of the 4 succeeding plan years, assuming that the terms of all collective bargaining agreements pursuant to which the plan is maintained for the current plan year continue in effect for succeeding plan years,

is less than the present value of all benefits projected to be payable under the plan during the current plan year and each of the 4 succeeding plan years (plus administrative expenses for such plan years).

(3) Annual certification by plan actuary.—

(A) In general.—Not later than the 90th day of each plan year of a multiemployer plan, the plan actuary shall certify to the Secretary and to the plan sponsor—

(i) whether or not the plan is in endangered status for such plan year and whether or not the plan is or will be in critical status for such plan year, and

(ii) in the case of a plan which is in a funding improvement or rehabilitation period, whether or not the plan is making the scheduled progress in meeting the requirements of its funding improvement or rehabilitation plan.

(B) Actuarial projections of assets and liabilities.—

IRC Sec. 432(b)(3)(B)

(i) In general.—In making the determinations and projections under this subsection, the plan actuary shall make projections required for the current and succeeding plan years of the current value of the assets of the plan and the present value of all liabilities to participants and beneficiaries under the plan for the current plan year as of the beginning of such year. The actuary's projections shall be based on reasonable actuarial estimates, assumptions, and methods that, except as provided in clause (iii), offer the actuary's best estimate of anticipated experience under the plan. The projected present value of liabilities as of the beginning of such year shall be determined based on the most recent of either—

(I) the actuarial statement required under section 103(d) of the Employee Retirement Income Security Act of 1974 with respect to the most recently filed annual report, or

(II) the actuarial valuation for the preceding plan year.

(ii) Determinations of future contributions.—Any actuarial projection of plan assets shall assume—

(I) reasonably anticipated employer contributions for the current and succeeding plan years, assuming that the terms of the one or more collective bargaining agreements pursuant to which the plan is maintained for the current plan year continue in effect for succeeding plan years, or

(II) that employer contributions for the most recent plan year will continue indefinitely, but only if the plan actuary determines there have been no significant demographic changes that would make such assumption unreasonable.

(iii) Projected industry activity.—Any projection of activity in the industry or industries covered by the plan, including future covered employment and contribution levels, shall be based on information provided by the plan sponsor, which shall act reasonably and in good faith.

(C) Penalty for failure to secure timely actuarial certification.—Any failure of the plan's actuary to certify the plan's status under this subsection by the date specified in subparagraph (A) shall be treated for purposes of section 502(c)(2) of the Employee Retirement Income Security Act of 1974 as a failure or refusal by the plan administrator to file the annual report required to be filed with the Secretary under section 101(b)(1) of such Act.

(D) Notice.—

(i) In general.—In any case in which it is certified under subparagraph (A) that a multiemployer plan is or will be in endangered or critical status for a plan year, the plan sponsor shall, not later than 30 days after the date of the certification, provide

notification of the endangered or critical status to the participants and beneficiaries, the bargaining parties, the Pension Benefit Guaranty Corporation, and the Secretary of Labor.

(ii) Plans in critical status.—If it is certified under subparagraph (A) that a multiemployer plan is or will be in critical status, the plan sponsor shall include in the notice under clause (i) an explanation of the possibility that—

(I) adjustable benefits (as defined in subsection (e)(8)) may be reduced, and

(II) such reductions may apply to participants and beneficiaries whose benefit commencement date is on or after the date such notice is provided for the first plan year in which the plan is in critical status.

(iii) Model notice.—The Secretary, in consultation with the Secretary of Labor shall prescribe a model notice that a multiemployer plan may use to satisfy the requirements under clause (ii).

(c) Funding Improvement Plan Must Be Adopted for Multiemployer Plans in Endangered Status.—

(1) In general.—In any case in which a multiemployer plan is in endangered status for a plan year, the plan sponsor, in accordance with this subsection—

(A) shall adopt a funding improvement plan not later than 240 days following the required date for the actuarial certification of endangered status under subsection (b)(3)(A), and

(B) within 30 days after the adoption of the funding improvement plan—

(i) shall provide to the bargaining parties 1 or more schedules showing revised benefit structures, revised contribution structures, or both, which, if adopted, may reasonably be expected to enable the multiemployer plan to meet the applicable benchmarks in accordance with the funding improvement plan, including—

(I) one proposal for reductions in the amount of future benefit accruals necessary to achieve the applicable benchmarks, assuming no amendments increasing contributions under the plan (other than amendments increasing contributions necessary to achieve the applicable benchmarks after amendments have reduced future benefit accruals to the maximum extent permitted by law), and

(II) one proposal for increases in contributions under the plan necessary to achieve the applicable benchmarks, assuming no amendments reducing future benefit accruals under the plan, and

(ii) may, if the plan sponsor deems appropriate, prepare and provide the bargaining parties with additional information relating to contribution rates or benefit reductions, alternative schedules, or other information relevant to achieving the applicable benchmarks in accordance with the funding improvement plan.

For purposes of this section, the term "applicable benchmarks" means the requirements applicable to the multiemployer plan under paragraph (3) (as modified by paragraph (5)).

(2) Exception for years after process begins.—Paragraph (1) shall not apply to a plan year if such year is in a funding plan adoption period or funding improvement period by reason of the plan being in endangered status for a preceding plan year. For purposes of this section, such preceding plan year shall be the initial determination year with respect to the funding improvement plan to which it relates.

(3) Funding improvement plan.—For purposes of this section—

(A) In general.—A funding improvement plan is a plan which consists of the actions, including options or a range of options to be proposed to the bargaining parties, formulated to provide, based on reasonably anticipated experience and reasonable actuarial assumptions, for the attainment by the plan during the funding improvement period of the following requirements:

(i) Increase in plan's funding percentage.—The plan's funded percentage as of the close of the funding improvement period equals or exceeds a percentage equal to the sum of—

(I) such percentage as of the beginning of such period, plus

(II) 33 percent of the difference between 100 percent and the percentage under subclause (I).

(ii) Avoidance of accumulated funding deficiencies.—No accumulated funding deficiency for any plan year during the funding improvement period (taking into account any extension of amortization periods under section 431(d)).

(B) Seriously endangered plans.—In the case of a plan in seriously endangered status, except as provided in paragraph (5), subparagraph (A)(i)(II) shall be applied by substituting "20 percent" for "33 percent".

(4) Funding improvement period.—For purposes of this section—

(A) In general.—The funding improvement period for any funding improvement plan adopted pursuant to this subsection is the 10-year period beginning on the first day of the first plan year of the multiemployer plan beginning after the earlier of—

(i) the second anniversary of the date of the adoption of the funding improvement plan, or

(ii) the expiration of the collective bargaining agreements in effect on the due date for the actu-

arial certification of endangered status for the initial determination year under subsection (b)(3)(A) and covering, as of such due date, at least 75 percent of the active participants in such multiemployer plan.

(B) Seriously endangered plans.—In the case of a plan in seriously endangered status, except as provided in paragraph (5), subparagraph (A) shall be applied by substituting "15-year period" for "10-year period".

(C) Coordination with changes in status.—

(i) Plans no longer in endangered status.—If the plan's actuary certifies under subsection (b)(3)(A) for a plan year in any funding plan adoption period or funding improvement period that the plan is no longer in endangered status and is not in critical status, the funding plan adoption period or funding improvement period, whichever is applicable, shall end as of the close of the preceding plan year.

(ii) Plans in critical status.—If the plan's actuary certifies under subsection (b)(3)(A) for a plan year in any funding plan adoption period or funding improvement period that the plan is in critical status, the funding plan adoption period or funding improvement period, whichever is applicable, shall end as of the close of the plan year preceding the first plan year in the rehabilitation period with respect to such status.

(D) Plans in endangered status at end of period.—If the plan's actuary certifies under subsection (b)(3)(A) for the first plan year following the close of the period described in subparagraph (A) that the plan is in endangered status, the provisions of this subsection and subsection (d) shall be applied as if such first plan year were an initial determination year, except that the plan may not be amended in a manner inconsistent with the funding improvement plan in effect for the preceding plan year until a new funding improvement plan is adopted.

(5) Special rules for seriously endangered plans more than 70 percent funded.—

(A) In general.—If the funded percentage of a plan in seriously endangered status was more than 70 percent as of the beginning of the initial determination year—

(i) paragraphs (3)(B) and (4)(B) shall apply only if the plan's actuary certifies, within 30 days after the certification under subsection (b)(3)(A) for the initial determination year, that, based on the terms of the plan and the collective bargaining agreements in effect at the time of such certification, the plan is not projected to meet the requirements of paragraph (3)(A) (without regard to paragraphs (3)(B) and (4)(B)), and

(ii) if there is a certification under clause (i), the plan may, in formulating its funding improvement

IRC Sec. 432(c)(5)(A)(ii)

plan, only take into account the rules of paragraph (3)(B) and (4)(B) for plan years in the funding improvement period beginning on or before the date on which the last of the collective bargaining agreements described in paragraph (4)(A)(ii) expires.

(B) Special rule after expiration of agreements.—Notwithstanding subparagraph (A)(ii), if, for any plan year ending after the date described in subparagraph (A)(ii), the plan actuary certifies (at the time of the annual certification under subsection (b)(3)(A) for such plan year) that, based on the terms of the plan and collective bargaining agreements in effect at the time of that annual certification, the plan is not projected to be able to meet the requirements of paragraph (3)(A) (without regard to paragraphs (3)(B) and (4)(B)), paragraphs (3)(B) and (4)(B) shall continue to apply for such year.

(6) Updates to funding improvement plans and schedules.—

(A) Funding improvement plan.—The plan sponsor shall annually update the funding improvement plan and shall file the update with the plan's annual report under section 104 of the Employee Retirement Income Security Act of 1974.

(B) Schedules.—The plan sponsor shall annually update any schedule of contribution rates provided under this subsection to reflect the experience of the plan.

(C) Duration of schedule.—A schedule of contribution rates provided by the plan sponsor and relied upon by bargaining parties in negotiating a collective bargaining agreement shall remain in effect for the duration of that collective bargaining agreement.

(7) Imposition of default schedule where failure to adopt funding improvement plan.—

(A) In general.—If—

(i) a collective bargaining agreement providing for contributions under a multiemployer plan that was in effect at the time the plan entered endangered status expires, and

(ii) after receiving one or more schedules from the plan sponsor under paragraph (1)(B), the bargaining parties with respect to such agreement fail to adopt a contribution schedule with terms consistent with the funding improvement plan and a schedule from the plan sponsor,

the plan sponsor shall implement the schedule described in paragraph (1)(B)(i)(I) beginning on the date specified in subparagraph (B).

(B) Date of implementation.—The date specified in this subparagraph is the date which is 180 days after the date on which the collective bargaining agreement described in subparagraph (A) expires.

(8) Funding plan adoption period.—For purposes of this section, the term "funding plan adoption period" means the period beginning on the date of the certification under subsection (b)(3)(A) for the initial determination year and ending on the day before the first day of the funding improvement period.

(d) Rules for Operation of Plan During Adoption and Improvement Periods.—

(1) Special rules for plan adoption period.— During the funding plan adoption period—

(A) the plan sponsor may not accept a collective bargaining agreement or participation agreement with respect to the multiemployer plan that provides for—

(i) a reduction in the level of contributions for any participants,

(ii) a suspension of contributions with respect to any period of service, or

(iii) any new direct or indirect exclusion of younger or newly hired employees from plan participation,

(B) no amendment of the plan which increases the liabilities of the plan by reason of any increase in benefits, any change in the accrual of benefits, or any change in the rate at which benefits become nonforfeitable under the plan may be adopted unless the amendment is required as a condition of qualification under part I of subchapter D of chapter 1 or to comply with other applicable law, and

(C) in the case of a plan in seriously endangered status, the plan sponsor shall take all reasonable actions which are consistent with the terms of the plan and applicable law and which are expected, based on reasonable assumptions, to achieve—

(i) an increase in the plan's funded percentage, and

(ii) postponement of an accumulated funding deficiency for at least 1 additional plan year.

Actions under subparagraph (C) include applications for extensions of amortization periods under section 431(d), use of the shortfall funding method in making funding standard account computations, amendments to the plan's benefit structure, reductions in future benefit accruals, and other reasonable actions consistent with the terms of the plan and applicable law.

(2) Compliance with funding improvement plan.—

(A) In general.—A plan may not be amended after the date of the adoption of a funding improvement plan so as to be inconsistent with the funding improvement plan.

(B) No reduction in contributions.—A plan sponsor may not during any funding improvement period accept a collective bargaining agreement or participation agreement with respect to the multiemployer plan that provides for—

(i) a reduction in the level of contributions for any participants,

(ii) a suspension of contributions with respect to any period of service, or

(iii) any new direct or indirect exclusion of younger or newly hired employees from plan participation.

(C) Special rules for benefit increases.—A plan may not be amended after the date of the adoption of a funding improvement plan so as to increase benefits, including future benefit accruals, unless the plan actuary certifies that the benefit increase is consistent with the funding improvement plan and is paid for out of contributions not required by the funding improvement plan to meet the applicable benchmark in accordance with the schedule contemplated in the funding improvement plan.

(e) Rehabilitation Plan Must Be Adopted for Multiemployer Plans in Critical Status.—

(1) In general.—In any case in which a multiemployer plan is in critical status for a plan year, the plan sponsor, in accordance with this subsection—

(A) shall adopt a rehabilitation plan not later than 240 days following the required date for the actuarial certification of critical status under subsection (b)(3)(A), and

(B) within 30 days after the adoption of the rehabilitation plan—

(i) shall provide to the bargaining parties 1 or more schedules showing revised benefit structures, revised contribution structures, or both, which, if adopted, may reasonably be expected to enable the multiemployer plan to emerge from critical status in accordance with the rehabilitation plan, and

(ii) may, if the plan sponsor deems appropriate, prepare and provide the bargaining parties with additional information relating to contribution rates or benefit reductions, alternative schedules, or other information relevant to emerging from critical status in accordance with the rehabilitation plan.

The schedule or schedules described in subparagraph (B)(i) shall reflect reductions in future benefit accruals and adjustable benefits, and increases in contributions, that the plan sponsor determines are reasonably necessary to emerge from critical status. One schedule shall be designated as the default schedule and such schedule shall assume that there are no increases in contributions under the plan other than the increases necessary to emerge from critical status after future benefit accruals and other benefits (other than benefits the reduction or elimination of which are not permitted under section 411(d)(6)) have been reduced to the maximum extent permitted by law.

(2) Exception for years after process begins.—Paragraph (1) shall not apply to a plan year if such year is in a rehabilitation plan adoption period or rehabilitation period by reason of the plan being in critical status for a preceding plan year. For purposes of this section, such preceding plan year shall be the initial critical year with respect to the rehabilitation plan to which it relates.

(3) Rehabilitation plan.—For purposes of this section—

(A) In general.—A rehabilitation plan is a plan which consists of—

(i) actions, including options or a range of options to be proposed to the bargaining parties, formulated, based on reasonably anticipated experience and reasonable actuarial assumptions, to enable the plan to cease to be in critical status by the end of the rehabilitation period and may include reductions in plan expenditures (including plan mergers and consolidations), reductions in future benefit accruals or increases in contributions, if agreed to by the bargaining parties, or any combination of such actions, or

(ii) if the plan sponsor determines that, based on reasonable actuarial assumptions and upon exhaustion of all reasonable measures, the plan can not reasonably be expected to emerge from critical status by the end of the rehabilitation period, reasonable measures to emerge from critical status at a later time or to forestall possible insolvency (within the meaning of section 4245 of the Employee Retirement Income Security Act of 1974).

A rehabilitation plan must provide annual standards for meeting the requirements of such rehabilitation plan. Such plan shall also include the schedules required to be provided under paragraph (1)(B)(i) and if clause (ii) applies, shall set forth the alternatives considered, explain why the plan is not reasonably expected to emerge from critical status by the end of the rehabilitation period, and specify when, if ever, the plan is expected to emerge from critical status in accordance with the rehabilitation plan.

(B) Updates to rehabilitation plan and schedules.—

(i) Rehabilitation plan.—The plan sponsor shall annually update the rehabilitation plan and shall file the update with the plan's annual report under section 104 of the Employee Retirement Income Security Act of 1974.

(ii) Schedules.—The plan sponsor shall annually update any schedule of contribution rates provided under this subsection to reflect the experience of the plan.

(iii) Duration of schedule.—A schedule of contribution rates provided by the plan sponsor and relied upon by bargaining parties in negotiating a

IRC Sec. 432(e)(3)(B)(iii)

collective bargaining agreement shall remain in effect for the duration of that collective bargaining agreement.

(C) Imposition of default schedule where failure to adopt rehabilitation plan.—

(i) In general.—If—

(I) a collective bargaining agreement providing for contributions under a multiemployer plan that was in effect at the time the plan entered critical status expires, and

(II) after receiving one or more schedules from the plan sponsor under paragraph (1)(B), the bargaining parties with respect to such agreement fail to adopt a to adopt a [sic] contribution schedule with terms consistent with the rehabilitation plan and a schedule from the plan sponsor under paragraph (1)(B)(i),

the plan sponsor shall implement the default schedule described in the last sentence of paragraph (1) beginning on the date specified in clause (ii).

(ii) Date of implementation.—The date specified in this clause is the date which is 180 days after the date on which the collective bargaining agreement described in clause (i) expires.

(4) **Rehabilitation period**.—For purposes of this section—

(A) In general.—The rehabilitation period for a plan in critical status is the 10-year period beginning on the first day of the first plan year of the multiemployer plan following the earlier of—

(i) the second anniversary of the date of the adoption of the rehabilitation plan, or

(ii) the expiration of the collective bargaining agreements in effect on the due date for the actuarial certification of critical status for the initial critical year under subsection (a)(1) and covering, as of such date at least 75 percent of the active participants in such multiemployer plan.

If a plan emerges from critical status as provided under subparagraph (B) before the end of such 10-year period, the rehabilitation period shall end with the plan year preceding the plan year for which the determination under subparagraph (B) is made.

(B) Emergence.—A plan in critical status shall remain in such status until a plan year for which the plan actuary certifies, in accordance with subsection (b)(3)(A), that the plan is not projected to have an accumulated funding deficiency for the plan year or any of the 9 succeeding plan years, without regard to the use of the shortfall method but taking into account any extension of amortization periods under section 431(d).

(5) **Rehabilitation plan adoption period**.—For purposes of this section, the term "rehabilitation plan adoption period" means the period beginning on the date of the certification under subsection (b)(3)(A) for the initial critical year and ending on the day before the first day of the rehabilitation period.

(6) **Limitation on reduction in rates of future accruals**.—Any reduction in the rate of future accruals under the default schedule described in the last sentence of paragraph (1) shall not reduce the rate of future accruals below—

(A) a monthly benefit (payable as a single life annuity commencing at the participant's normal retirement age) equal to 1 percent of the contributions required to be made with respect to a participant, or the equivalent standard accrual rate for a participant or group of participants under the collective bargaining agreements in effect as of the first day of the initial critical year, or

(B) if lower, the accrual rate under the plan on such first day.

The equivalent standard accrual rate shall be determined by the plan sponsor based on the standard or average contribution base units which the plan sponsor determines to be representative for active participants and such other factors as the plan sponsor determines to be relevant. Nothing in this paragraph shall be construed as limiting the ability of the plan sponsor to prepare and provide the bargaining parties with alternative schedules to the default schedule that establish lower or higher accrual and contribution rates than the rates otherwise described in this paragraph.

(7) **Automatic employer surcharge**.—

(A) Imposition of surcharge.—Each employer otherwise obligated to make a contribution for the initial critical year shall be obligated to pay to the plan for such year a surcharge equal to 5 percent of the contribution otherwise required under the applicable collective bargaining agreement (or other agreement pursuant to which the employer contributes). For each succeeding plan year in which the plan is in critical status for a consecutive period of years beginning with the initial critical year, the surcharge shall be 10 percent of the contribution otherwise so required.

(B) Enforcement of surcharge.—The surcharges under subparagraph (A) shall be due and payable on the same schedule as the contributions on which the surcharges are based. Any failure to make a surcharge payment shall be treated as a delinquent contribution under section 515 of the Employee Retirement Income Security Act of 1974 and shall be enforceable as such.

(C) Surcharge to terminate upon collective bargaining agreement renegotiation.—The surcharge under this paragraph shall cease to be effective with respect to employees covered by a collective bargaining agreement (or other agreement pursuant to which the employer contributes), beginning on the effective date of a collective bargaining agreement (or other such agreement) that includes terms consistent with a schedule presented by the plan sponsor under paragraph (1)(B)(i), as modified under subparagraph (B) of paragraph (3).

(D) Surcharge not to apply until employer receives notice.—The surcharge under this paragraph shall not apply to an employer until 30 days after the employer has been notified by the plan sponsor that the plan is in critical status and that the surcharge is in effect.

(E) Surcharge not to generate increased benefit accruals.—Notwithstanding any provision of a plan to the contrary, the amount of any surcharge under this paragraph shall not be the basis for any benefit accrual under the plan.

(8) Benefit adjustments.—

(A) Adjustable benefits.—

(i) In general.—Notwithstanding section 411(d)(6), the plan sponsor shall, subject to the notice requirement under subparagraph (C), make any reductions to adjustable benefits which the plan sponsor deems appropriate, based upon the outcome of collective bargaining over the schedule or schedules provided under paragraph (1)(B)(i).

(ii) Exception for retirees.—Except in the case of adjustable benefits described in clause (iv)(III), the plan sponsor of a plan in critical status shall not reduce adjustable benefits of any participant or beneficiary whose benefit commencement date is before the date on which the plan provides notice to the participant or beneficiary under subsection (b)(3)(D) for the initial critical year.

(iii) Plan sponsor flexibility.—The plan sponsor shall include in the schedules provided to the bargaining parties an allowance for funding the benefits of participants with respect to whom contributions are not currently required to be made, and shall reduce their benefits to the extent permitted under this title and considered appropriate by the plan sponsor based on the plan's then current overall funding status.

(iv) Adjustable benefit defined.—For purposes of this paragraph, the term "adjustable benefit" means—

(I) benefits, rights, and features under the plan, including post-retirement death benefits, 60-month guarantees, disability benefits not yet in pay status, and similar benefits,

(II) any early retirement benefit or retirement-type subsidy (within the meaning of section 411(d)(6)(B)(i)) and any benefit payment option (other than the qualified joint and survivor annuity), and

(III) benefit increases that would not be eligible for a guarantee under section 4022A of the Em-

ployee Retirement Income Security Act of 1974 on the first day of initial critical year because the increases were adopted (or, if later, took effect) less than 60 months before such first day.

(B) Normal retirement benefits protected.—Except as provided in subparagraph (A)(iv)(III), nothing in this paragraph shall be construed to permit a plan to reduce the level of a participant's accrued benefit payable at normal retirement age.

(C) Notice requirements.—

(i) In general.—No reduction may be made to adjustable benefits under subparagraph (A) unless notice of such reduction has been given at least 30 days before the general effective date of such reduction for all participants and beneficiaries to—

(I) plan participants and beneficiaries,

(II) each employer who has an obligation to contribute (within the meaning of section 4212(a) of the Employee Retirement Income Security Act of 1974) under the plan, and

(III) each employee organization which, for purposes of collective bargaining, represents plan participants employed by such an employer.

(ii) Content of notice.—The notice under clause (i) shall contain—

(I) sufficient information to enable participants and beneficiaries to understand the effect of any reduction on their benefits, including an estimate (on an annual or monthly basis) of any affected adjustable benefit that a participant or beneficiary would otherwise have been eligible for as of the general effective date described in clause (i), and

(II) information as to the rights and remedies of plan participants and beneficiaries as well as how to contact the Department of Labor for further information and assistance where appropriate.

(iii) Form and manner.—Any notice under clause (i)—

(I) shall be provided in a form and manner prescribed in regulations of the Secretary, in consultation with the Secretary of Labor,

(II) shall be written in a manner so as to be understood by the average plan participant, and

(III) may be provided in written, electronic, or other appropriate form to the extent such form is reasonably accessible to persons to whom the notice is required to be provided.

the [sic] Secretary shall in the regulations prescribed under subclause (I) establish a model notice that a plan sponsor may use to meet the requirements of this subparagraph.

(9) Adjustments disregarded in withdrawal liability determination.—

IRC Sec. 432(e)(9)

(A) Benefit reductions.—Any benefit reductions under this subsection shall be disregarded in determining a plan's unfunded vested benefits for purposes of determining an employer's withdrawal liability under section 4201 of the Employee Retirement Income Security Act of 1974.

(B) Surcharges.—Any surcharges under paragraph (7) shall be disregarded in determining the allocation of unfunded vested benefits to an employer under section 4211 of such Act, except for purposes of determining the unfunded vested benefits attributable to an employer under section 4211(c)(4) of such Act or a comparable method approved under section 4211(c)(5) of such Act.

(C) Simplified calculations.—The Pension Benefit Guaranty Corporation shall prescribe simplified methods for the application of this paragraph in determiningwithdrawal liability.

(f) Rules for Operation of Plan During Adoption and Rehabilitation Period.—

(1) Compliance with rehabilitation plan.—

(A) In general.—A plan may not be amended after the date of the adoption of a rehabilitation plan under subsection (e) so as to be inconsistent with the rehabilitation plan.

(B) Special rules for benefit increases.—A plan may not be amended after the date of the adoption of a rehabilitation plan under subsection (e) so as to increase benefits, including future benefit accruals, unless the plan actuary certifies that such increase is paid for out of additional contributions not contemplated by the rehabilitation plan, and, after taking into account the benefit increase, the multiemployer plan still is reasonably expected to emerge from critical status by the end of the rehabilitation period on the schedule contemplated in the rehabilitation plan.

(2) Restriction on lump sums and similar benefits.—

(A) In general.—Effective on the date the notice of certification of the plan's critical status for the initial critical year under subsection (b)(3)(D) is sent, and notwithstanding section 411(d)(6), the plan shall not pay—

(i) any payment, in excess of the monthly amount paid under a single life annuity (plus any social security supplements described in the last sentence of section 411(a)(9)) to a participant or beneficiary whose annuity starting date (as defined in section 417(f)(2)) occurs after the date such notice is sent,

(ii) any payment for the purchase of an irrevocable commitment from an insurer to pay benefits, and

(iii) any other payment specified by the Secretary by regulations.

(B) Exception.—Subparagraph (A) shall not apply to a benefit which under section 411(a)(11) may be immediately distributed without the consent of the participant or to any makeup payment in the case of a retroactive annuity starting date or any similar payment of benefits owed with respect to a prior period.

(3) Adjustments disregarded in withdrawal liability determination.—Any benefit reductions under this subsection shall be disregarded in determining a plan's unfunded vested benefits for purposes of determining an employer's withdrawal liability under section 4201 of the Employee Retirement Income Security Act of 1974.

(4) Special rules for plan adoption period.—During the rehabilitation plan adoption period—

(A) the plan sponsor may not accept a collective bargaining agreement or participation agreement with respect to the multiemployer plan that provides for—

(i) a reduction in the level of contributions for any participants,

(ii) a suspension of contributions with respect to any period of service, or

(iii) any new direct or indirect exclusion of younger or newly hired employees from plan participation, and

(B) no amendment of the plan which increases the liabilities of the plan by reason of any increase in benefits, any change in the accrual of benefits, or any change in the rate at which benefits become nonforfeitable under the plan may be adopted unless the amendment is required as a condition of qualification under part I of subchapter D of chapter 1 or to comply with other applicable law.

(g) Expedited Resolution of Plan Sponsor Decisions.—If, within 60 days of the due date for adoption of a funding improvement plan under subsection (c) or a rehabilitation plan under subsection (e), the plan sponsor of a plan in endangered status or a plan in critical status has not agreed on a funding improvement plan or rehabilitation plan, then any member of the board or group that constitutes the plan sponsor may require that the plan sponsor enter into an expedited dispute resolution procedure for the development and adoption of a funding improvement plan or rehabilitation plan.

(h) Nonbargained Participation.—

(1) Both bargained and nonbargained employee-participants.—In the case of an employer that contributes to a multiemployer plan with respect to both employees who are covered by one or more collective bargaining agreements and employees who are not so covered, if the plan is in endangered status or in critical status, benefits of and contributions for the nonbargained employees, including surcharges on those contributions, shall be determined as if those nonbargained employees were covered under the first to expire of the employer's collective bargaining agreements in effect when the plan entered endangered or critical status.

(2) Nonbargained employees only.—In the case of an employer that contributes to a multiemployer plan only with respect to employees who are not covered by a collective bargaining agreement, this section shall be applied as if the employer were the bargaining party, and its participation agreement with the plan were a collective bargaining agreement with a term ending on the first day of the plan year beginning after the employer is provided the schedule or schedules described in subsections (c) and (e).

(i) Definitions; Actuarial Method.—For purposes of this section—

(1) Bargaining party.—The term "bargaining party" means—

(A) (i) except as provided in clause (ii), an employer who has an obligation to contribute under the plan; or

(ii) in the case of a plan described under section 404(c), or a continuation of such a plan, the association of employers that is the employer settlor of the plan; and

(B) an employee organization which, for purposes of collective bargaining, represents plan participants employed by an employer who has an obligation to contribute under the plan.

(2) Funded percentage.—The term "funded percentage" means the percentage equal to a fraction—

(A) the numerator of which is the value of the plan's assets, as determined under section 431(c)(2), and

(B) the denominator of which is the accrued liability of the plan, determined using actuarial assumptions described in section 431(c)(3).

(3) Accumulated funding deficiency.—The term "accumulated funding deficiency" has the meaning given such term in section 431(a).

(4) Active participant.—The term "active participant" means, in connection with a multiemployer plan, a participant who is in covered service under the plan.

(5) Inactive participant.—The term "inactive participant" means, in connection with a multiemployer plan, a participant, or the beneficiary or alternate payee of a participant, who—

(A) is not in covered service under the plan, and

(B) is in pay status under the plan or has a nonforfeitable right to benefits under the plan.

(6) Pay status.—A person is in pay status under a multiemployer plan if—

(A) at any time during the current plan year, such person is a participant or beneficiary under the plan and is paid an early, late, normal, or disability retirement benefit under the plan (or a death benefit under the plan related to a retirement benefit), or

(B) to the extent provided in regulations of the Secretary, such person is entitled to such a benefit under the plan.

(7) Obligation to contribute.—The term "obligation to contribute" has the meaning given such term under section 4212(a) of the Employee Retirement Income Security Act of 1974.

(8) Actuarial method.—Notwithstanding any other provision of this section, the actuary's determinations with respect to a plan's normal cost, actuarial accrued liability, and improvements in a plan's funded percentage under this section shall be based upon the unit credit funding method (whether or not that method is used for the plan's actuarial valuation).

(9) Plan sponsor. —For purposes of this section, section 431, and section 4971(g):

(A) In general.—The term "plan sponsor" means, with respect to any multiemployer plan, the association, committee, joint board of trustees, or other similar group of representatives of the parties who establish or maintain the plan.

(B) Special rule for section 404(c) plans.—In the case of a plan described in section 404(c) (or a continuation of such plan), such term means the bargaining parties described in paragraph (1).

(10) Benefit commencement date.—The term "benefit commencement date" means the annuity starting date (or in the case of a retroactive annuity starting date, the date on which benefit payments begin).

Recent Amendments to IRC §432

Worker, Retiree, and Employer Recovery Act of 2008 (Pub. L. No. 110-458), as follows:
- IRC §432(b)(3)(C) was amended by Act §102(b)(2)(A) by substituting "section 101(b)(1)" for "section 101(b)(4)". Eff. as if included in Pub. L. No. 109-280, §212 [eff. generally for plan years beginning after 2007].
- IRC §432(b)(3)(D)(iii) was amended by Act §102(b)(2)(B) by substituting "The Secretary, in consultation with the Secretary of Labor" for "The Secretary of Labor". Eff. as if included in Pub. L. No. 109-280, §212 [eff. generally for plan years beginning after 2007].
- IRC §432(c)(3)(A)(ii) was amended by Act §102(b)(2)(C)(i) by substituting "section 431(d)" for "section 304(d)". Eff. as if included in Pub. L. No. 109-280, §212 [eff. generally for plan years beginning after 2007].
- IRC §432(c)(7) was amended by Act §102(b)(2)(C)(ii)(I)–(II) by substituting "to adopt a contribution schedule with terms consistent with the funding improvement plan and a schedule from the plan sponsor," for "to agree on changes to contribution or benefit schedules necessary to meet the applicable benchmarks in accordance with the funding improvement plan," in para. (7)(A); and amending para. (7)(B). Eff. as if included in Pub. L. No. 109-280, §212 [eff. generally for plan years beginning after 2007]. IRC §432(c)(7)(B) prior to amendment:

(B) Date of implementation.—The date specified in this sub-paragraph is the earlier of the date—

(i) on which the Secretary of Labor certifies that the parties are at an impasse, or

(ii) which is 180 days after the date on which the collective bargaining agreement described in subparagraph (A) expires.

• IRC §432(e)(3)(C)(i)(II) was amended by Act §102(b)(2)(D)(i)(I) by substituting "to adopt a contribution schedule with terms consistent with the rehabilitation plan and a schedule from the plan sponsor under paragraph (1)(B)(i)," for "to adopt a contribution or benefit schedules with terms consistent with the rehabilitation plan and the schedule from the plan sponsor under paragraph (1)(B)(i)". Eff. as if included in Pub. L. No. 109-280, §212 [eff. generally for plan years beginning after 2007].

• IRC §432(e)(3)(C)(ii) was amended by Act §102(b)(2)(D)(i)(II). Eff. as if included in Pub. L. No. 109-280, §212 [eff. generally for plan years beginning after 2007]. IRC §432(e)(3)(C)(ii) prior to amendment:

(ii) Date of implementation.—The date specified in this clause is the earlier of the date—

(I) on which the Secretary of Labor certifies that the parties are at an impasse, or

(II) which is 180 days after the date on which the collective bargaining agreement described in clause (i) expires.

• IRC §432(e)(4)(A)(ii) was amended by Act §102(b)(2)(D)(ii)(I) by striking "the date of". Eff. as if included in Pub. L. No. 109-280, §212 [eff. generally for plan years beginning after 2007].

• IRC §432(e)(4)(B) was amended by Act §102(b)(2)(D)(ii)(II) by substituting "but taking" for "and taking". Eff. as if included in Pub. L. No. 109-280, §212 [eff. generally for plan years beginning after 2007].

• IRC §432(e)(6) was amended by Act §102(b)(2)(D)(iii) by substituting "the last sentence of paragraph (1)" for "paragraph (1)(B)(i)" and by substituting "establish" for "established" in §432(e)(6)(B). Eff. as if included in Pub. L. No. 109-280, §212 [eff. generally for plan years beginning after 2007].

• IRC §432(e)(8)(A)(i) was amended by Act §102(b)(2)(D)(iv)(I) by substituting "section 411(d)(6)" for "section 204(g)". Eff. as if included in Pub. L. No. 109-280, §212 [eff. generally for plan years beginning after 2007].

• IRC §432(e)(8)(C)(i)(II) was amended by Act §102(b)(2)(D)(iv)(II) by inserting "of the Employee Retirement Income Security Act of 1974" after "4212(a)". Eff. as if included in Pub. L. No. 109-280, §212 [eff. generally for plan years beginning after 2007].

• IRC §432(e)(8)(C)(iii)(I) was amended by Act §102(b)(2)(D)(iv)(III) by substituting "the Secretary, in consultation with the Secretary of Labor" for "the Secretary of Labor". Eff. as if included in Pub. L. No. 109-280, §212 [eff. generally for plan years beginning after 2007].

• IRC §432(e)(8)(C)(iii) was amended by Act §102(b)(2)(D)(iv)(IV) by substituting "the Secretary" for "the Secretary of Labor" in the last sentence. Eff. as if included in Pub. L. No. 109-280, §212 [eff. generally for plan years beginning after 2007].

• IRC §432(e)(9)(B) was amended by Act §102(b)(2)(D)(v) by substituting "the allocation of unfunded vested benefits to an employer" for "an employer's withdrawal liability". Eff. as if included in Pub. L. No. 109-280, §212 [eff. generally for plan years beginning after 2007].

• IRC §432(f)(2)(A)(i) was amended by Act §102(b)(2)(E) by substituting "section 411(a)(9)" for "section 411(b)(1)(A)" and by inserting "to a participant or beneficiary whose annuity starting date (as defined in section 417(f)(2)) occurs after the date such notice is sent". Eff. as if included in Pub. L. No. 109-280, §212 [eff. generally for plan years beginning after 2007].

• IRC §432(g) was amended by Act §102(b)(2)(F) inserting "under subsection (c)" after "funding improvement plan" the first place it appears. Eff. as if included in Pub. L. No. 109-280, §212 [eff. generally for plan years beginning after 2007].

• IRC §432(i)(3) was amended by Act §102(b)(2)(G)(i) by substituting "section 431(a)" for "section 412(a)". Eff. as if included in Pub. L. No. 109-280, §212 [eff. generally for plan years beginning after 2007].

• IRC §432(i)(9) was amended by Act §102(b)(2)(G)(ii). Eff. as if included in Pub. L. No. 109-280, §212 [eff. generally for plan years beginning after 2007]. IRC §432(i)(9) prior to amendment:

(9) Plan Sponsor.— In the case of a plan described under section 404(c), or a continuation of such a plan, the term "plan sponsor" means the bargaining parties described under paragraph (1).

• **Other Provision.** Act §204 provides:

SEC. 204. TEMPORARY DELAY OF DESIGNATION OF MULTIEMPLOYER PLANS AS IN ENDANGERED OR CRITICAL STATUS.

(a) In General.—Notwithstanding the actuarial certification under section 305(b)(3) of the Employee Retirement Income Security Act of 1974 and section 432(b)(3) of the Internal Revenue Code of 1986, if a plan sponsor of a multiemployer plan elects the application of this section, then, for purposes of section 305 of such Act and section 432 of such Code—

(1) the status of the plan for its first plan year beginning during the period beginning on October 1, 2008, and ending on September 30, 2009, shall be the same as the status of such plan under such sections for the plan year preceding such plan year, and

(2) in the case of a plan which was in endangered or critical status for the preceding plan year described in paragraph (1), the plan shall not be required to update its plan or schedules under section 305(c)(6) of such Act and section 432(c)(6) of such Code, or section 305(e)(3)(B) of such Act and section 432(e)(3)(B) of such Code, whichever is applicable, until the plan year following the first plan year described in paragraph (1).

If section 305 of the Employee Retirement Income Security Act of 1974 and section 432 of the Internal Revenue Code of 1986 did not apply to the preceding plan year described in paragraph (1), the plan actuary shall make a certification of the status of the plan under section 305(b)(3) of such Act and section 432(b)(3) of such Code for the preceding plan year in the same manner as if such sections had applied to such preceding plan year.

(b) Exception for Plans Becoming Critical During Election.—If—

(1) an election was made under subsection (a) with respect to a multiemployer plan, and

(2) such plan has, without regard to such election, been certified by the plan actuary under section 305(b)(3) of such Act and section 432(b)(3) of such Code to be in critical status for the first plan year described in subsection (a)(1),

then such plan shall be treated as a plan in critical status for such plan year for purposes of applying section 4971(g)(1)(A) of such Code, section 302(b)(3) of such Act (without regard to the second sentence thereof), and section 412(b)(3) of such Code (without regard to the second sentence thereof).

(c) Election and Notice.—

(1) Election.—An election under subsection (a) shall—

(A) be made at such time and in such manner as the Secretary of the Treasury or the Secretary's delegate may prescribe and, once made, may be revoked only with the consent of the Secretary, and

(B) if the election is made—

(i) before the date the annual certification is submitted to the Secretary or the Secretary's delegate under section 305(b)(3) of such Act and section 432(b)(3) of such Code, be included with such annual certification, and

(ii) after such date, be submitted to the Secretary or the Secretary's delegate not later than 30 days after the date of the election.

(2) Notice to participants.—

(A) In general.—Notwithstanding section 305(b)(3)(D) of such Act and section 431(b)(3)(D) of such Code, if the plan is neither in endangered nor critical status by reason of an election made under subsection (a)—

(i) the plan sponsor of a multiemployer plan shall not be required to provide notice under such sections, and

(ii) the plan sponsor shall provide to the participants and beneficiaries, the bargaining parties, the Pension Benefit Guaranty Corporation, and the Secretary of Labor a notice of the election and such other information as the Secretary of the

Treasury (in consultation with the Secretary of Labor) may require—

(I) if the election is made before the date the annual certification is submitted to the Secretary or the Secretary's delegate under section 305(b)(3) of such Act and section 432(b)(3) of such Code, not later than 30 days after the date of the certification, and

(II) if the election is made after such date, not later than 30 days after the date of the election.

(B) Notice of endangered status.—Notwithstanding section 305(b)(3)(D) of such Act and section 431(b)(3)(D) of such Code, if the plan is certified to be in critical status for any plan year but is in endangered status by reason of an election made under subsection (a), the notice provided under such sections shall be the notice which would have been provided if the plan had been certified to be in endangered status.

Pension Protection Act of 2006 (Pub. L. No. 109-280), as follows:

- IRC §432 was added by Act §212(a). Eff. generally for plan years beginning after 2007. For special rules, see Act §212(e)(2)–(3). For transition relief for certain benefits funded under an agreement approved by the PBGC, see Act §206.

- **Sunset Rule.** [*Ed. Note*: The provisions of and amendments made by Act §§201(b), 202, and 212 do not apply to plan years beginning after Dec. 31, 2014, except that if a plan is operating under a funding improvement or rehabilitation plan under Act §305 or IRC §432 for its last year beginning before Jan. 1, 2015, the plan will continue to operate under such funding improvement or rehabilitation plan during any period after Dec. 31, 2014, that such funding improvement or rehabilitation plan is in effect and all provisions of such Act or Code relating to the operation of the funding improvement or rehabilitation plan will continue in effect during such period. See Act §221(c), below.]

- **Other Provision.** Act §206, provides:

    SEC. 206. SPECIAL RULE FOR CERTAIN BENEFITS FUNDED UNDER AN AGREEMENT APPROVED BY THE PENSION BENEFIT GUARANTY CORPORATION.

    In the case of a multiemployer plan that is a party to an agreement that was approved by the Pension Benefit Guaranty Corporation prior to June 30, 2005, and that—

    (1) increases benefits, and

    (2) provides for special withdrawal liability rules under section 4203(f) of the Employee Retirement Income Security Act of 1974 (29 U.S.C. 1383),

    the amendments made by sections 201, 202, 211, and 212 of this Act shall not apply to the benefit increases under any plan amendment adopted prior to June 30, 2005, that are funded pursuant to such agreement if the plan is funded in compliance with such agreement (and any amendments thereto).

- **Other Provision.** Act §212(e)(2)–(3), as amended by Pub. L. No. 110-458, §102(b)(3)(C), provides:

    (2) Special rule for certain notices.—In any case in which a plan's actuary certifies that it is reasonably expected that a multiemployer plan will be in critical status under section 432(b)(3) of the Internal Revenue Code of 1986, as added by this section, with respect to the first plan year beginning after 2007, the notice required under subparagraph (D) of such section may be provided at any time after the date of enactment, so long as it is provided on or before the last date for providing the notice under such subparagraph.

    (3) Special rule for certain restored benefits.—In the case of a multiemployer plan—

    (A) with respect to which benefits were reduced pursuant to a plan amendment adopted on or after January 1, 2002, and before June 30, 2005, and

    (B) which, pursuant to the plan document, the trust agreement, or a formal written communication from the plan sponsor to participants provided before June 30, 2005, provided for the restoration of such benefits, the amendments made by this section shall not apply to such benefit restorations to the extent that any restriction on the providing or accrual of such benefits would otherwise apply by reason of such amendments.

- **Sunset Provision.** Act §221(c) provides:

(c) Sunset—

(1) In general.—Except as provided in this subsection, notwithstanding any other provision of this Act, the provisions of, and the amendments made by, sections 201(b), 202, and 212 shall not apply to plan years beginning after December 31, 2014.

(2) Funding improvement and rehabilitation plans.—If a plan is operating under a funding improvement or rehabilitation plan under section 305 of such Act or 432 of such Code for its last year beginning before January 1, 2015, such plan shall continue to operate under such funding improvement or rehabilitation plan during any period after December 31, 2014, such funding improvement or rehabilitation plan is in effect and all provisions of such Act or Code relating to the operation of such funding improvement or rehabilitation plan shall continue in effect during such period.

Subpart B—Benefit Limitations Under Single-Employer Plans

SEC. 436. FUNDING-BASED LIMITS ON BENEFITS AND BENEFIT ACCRUALS UNDER SINGLE-EMPLOYER PLANS.

(a) General Rule.—For purposes of section 401(a)(29), a defined benefit plan which is a single-employer plan shall be treated as meeting the requirements of this section if the plan meets the requirements of subsections (b), (c), (d), and (e).

(b) Funding-Based Limitation on Shutdown Benefits and Other Unpredictable Contingent Event Benefits Under Single-Employer Plans.—

(1) In general.—If a participant of a defined benefit plan which is a single-employer plan is entitled to an unpredictable contingent event benefit payable with respect to any event occurring during any plan year, the plan shall provide that such benefit may not be provided if the adjusted funding target attainment percentage for such plan year—

(A) is less than 60 percent, or

(B) would be less than 60 percent taking into account such occurrence.

(2) Exemption.—Paragraph (1) shall cease to apply with respect to any plan year, effective as of the first day of the plan year, upon payment by the plan sponsor of a contribution (in addition to any minimum required contribution under section 430) equal to—

(A) in the case of paragraph (1)(A), the amount of the increase in the funding target of the plan (under section 430) for the plan year attributable to the occurrence referred to in paragraph (1), and

(B) in the case of paragraph (1)(B), the amount sufficient to result in an adjusted funding target attainment percentage of 60 percent.

(3) Unpredictable contingent benefit.—For purposes of this subsection, the term "unpredictable contingent event benefit" means any benefit payable solely by reason of—

(A) a plant shutdown (or similar event, as determined by the Secretary), or

IRC Sec. 436(b)(3)(A)

(B) an event other than the attainment of any age, performance of any service, receipt or derivation of any compensation, or occurrence of death or disability.

(c) Limitations on Plan Amendments Increasing Liability for Benefits.—

(1) In general.—No amendment to a defined benefit plan which is a single-employer plan which has the effect of increasing liabilities of the plan by reason of increases in benefits, establishment of new benefits, changing the rate of benefit accrual, or changing the rate at which benefits become nonforfeitable may take effect during any plan year if the adjusted funding target attainment percentage for such plan year is—

(A) less than 80 percent, or

(B) would be less than 80 percent taking into account such amendment.

(2) Exemption.—Paragraph (1) shall cease to apply with respect to any plan year, effective as of the first day of the plan year (or if later, the effective date of the amendment), upon payment by the plan sponsor of a contribution (in addition to any minimum required contribution under section 430) equal to—

(A) in the case of paragraph (1)(A), the amount of the increase in the funding target of the plan (under section 430) for the plan year attributable to the amendment, and

(B) in the case of paragraph (1)(B), the amount sufficient to result in an adjusted funding target attainment percentage of 80 percent.

(3) Exception for certain benefit increases.—Paragraph (1) shall not apply to any amendment which provides for an increase in benefits under a formula which is not based on a participant's compensation, but only if the rate of such increase is not in excess of the contemporaneous rate of increase in average wages of participants covered by the amendment.

(d) Limitations on Accelerated Benefit Distributions.—

(1) Funding percentage less than 60 percent.—A defined benefit plan which is a single-employer plan shall provide that, in any case in which the plan's adjusted funding target attainment percentage for a plan year is less than 60 percent, the plan may not pay any prohibited payment after the valuation date for the plan year.

(2) Bankruptcy.—A defined benefit plan which is a single-employer plan shall provide that, during any period in which the plan sponsor is a debtor in a case under title 11, United States Code, or similar Federal or State law, the plan may not pay any prohibited payment. The preceding sentence shall not apply on or after the date on which the enrolled actuary of the

plan certifies that the adjusted funding target attainment percentage of such plan is not less than 100 percent.

(3) Limited payment if percentage at least 60 percent but less than 80 percent.—

(A) In general.—A defined benefit plan which is a single-employer plan shall provide that, in any case in which the plan's adjusted funding target attainment percentage for a plan year is 60 percent or greater but less than 80 percent, the plan may not pay any prohibited payment after the valuation date for the plan year to the extent the amount of the payment exceeds the lesser of—

(i) 50 percent of the amount of the payment which could be made without regard to this section, or

(ii) the present value (determined under guidance prescribed by the Pension Benefit Guaranty Corporation, using the interest and mortality assumptions under section 417(e)) of the maximum guarantee with respect to the participant under section 4022 of the Employee Retirement Income Security Act of 1974.

(B) One-time application.—

(i) In general.—The plan shall also provide that only 1 prohibited payment meeting the requirements of subparagraph (A) may be made with respect to any participant during any period of consecutive plan years to which the limitations under either paragraph (1) or (2) or this paragraph applies.

(ii) Treatment of beneficiaries.—For purposes of this subparagraph, a participant and any beneficiary on his behalf (including an alternate payee, as defined in section 414(p)(8)) shall be treated as 1 participant. If the accrued benefit of a participant is allocated to such an alternate payee and 1 or more other persons, the amount under subparagraph (A) shall be allocated among such persons in the same manner as the accrued benefit is allocated unless the qualified domestic relations order (as defined in section 414(p)(1)(A)) provides otherwise.

(4) Exception.—This subsection shall not apply to any plan for any plan year if the terms of such plan (as in effect for the period beginning on September 1, 2005, and ending with such plan year) provide for no benefit accruals with respect to any participant during such period.

(5) Prohibited payment.—For purpose of this subsection, the term "prohibited payment" means—

(A) any payment, in excess of the monthly amount paid under a single life annuity (plus any social security supplements described in the last sentence of section 411(a)(9)), to a participant or beneficiary whose annuity starting date (as defined in section 417(f)(2)) occurs during any period a limitation under paragraph (1) or (2) is in effect,

(B) any payment for the purchase of an irrevocable commitment from an insurer to pay benefits, and

(C) any other payment specified by the Secretary by regulations.

Such term shall not include the payment of a benefit which under section 411(a)(11) may be immediately distributed without the consent of the participant.

(e) Limitation on Benefit Accruals for Plans With Severe Funding Shortfalls.—

(1) In general.—A defined benefit plan which is a single-employer plan shall provide that, in any case in which the plan's adjusted funding target attainment percentage for a plan year is less than 60 percent, benefit accruals under the plan shall cease as of the valuation date for the plan year.

(2) Exemption.—Paragraph (1) shall cease to apply with respect to any plan year, effective as of the first day of the plan year, upon payment by the plan sponsor of a contribution (in addition to any minimum required contribution under section 430) equal to the amount sufficient to result in an adjusted funding target attainment percentage of 60 percent.

(f) Rules Relating to Contributions Required to Avoid Benefit Limitations.—

(1) Security may be provided.—

(A) In general.—For purposes of this section, the adjusted funding target attainment percentage shall be determined by treating as an asset of the plan any security provided by a plan sponsor in a form meeting the requirements of subparagraph (B).

(B) Form of security.—The security required under subparagraph (A) shall consist of—

(i) a bond issued by a corporate surety company that is an acceptable surety for purposes of section 412 of the Employee Retirement Income Security Act of 1974,

(ii) cash, or United States obligations which mature in 3 years or less, held in escrow by a bank or similar financial institution, or

(iii) such other form of security as is satisfactory to the Secretary and the parties involved.

(C) Enforcement.—Any security provided under subparagraph (A) may be perfected and enforced at any time after the earlier of—

(i) the date on which the plan terminates,

(ii) if there is a failure to make a payment of the minimum required contribution for any plan year beginning after the security is provided, the due date for the payment under section 430(j), or

(iii) if the adjusted funding target attainment percentage is less than 60 percent for a consecutive period of 7 years, the valuation date for the last year in the period.

(D) Release of security.—The security shall be released (and any amounts thereunder shall be refunded together with any interest accrued thereon) at such time as the Secretary may prescribe in regulations, including regulations for partial releases of the security by reason of increases in the adjusted funding target attainment percentage.

(2) Prefunding balance or funding standard carryover balance may not be used.—No prefunding balance or funding standard carryover balance under section 430(f) may be used under subsection (b), (c), or (e) to satisfy any payment an employer may make under any such subsection to avoid or terminate the application of any limitation under such subsection.

(3) Deemed reduction of funding balances.—

(A) In general.—Subject to subparagraph (C), in any case in which a benefit limitation under subsection (b), (c), (d), or (e) would (but for this subparagraph and determined without regard to subsection (b)(2), (c)(2), or (e)(2)) apply to such plan for the plan year, the plan sponsor of such plan shall be treated for purposes of this title as having made an election under section 430(f) to reduce the prefunding balance or funding standard carryover balance by such amount as is necessary for such benefit limitation to not apply to the plan for such plan year.

(B) Exception for insufficient funding balances.—Subparagraph (A) shall not apply with respect to a benefit limitation for any plan year if the application of subparagraph (A) would not result in the benefit limitation not applying for such plan year.

(C) Restrictions of certain rules to collectively bargained plans.—With respect to any benefit limitation under subsection (b), (c), or (e), subparagraph (A) shall only apply in the case of a plan maintained pursuant to 1 or more collective bargaining agreements between employee representatives and 1 or more employers.

(g) New Plans.—Subsections (b), (c), and (e) shall not apply to a plan for the first 5 plan years of the plan. For purposes of this subsection, the reference in this subsection to a plan shall include a reference to any predecessor plan.

(h) Presumed Underfunding for Purposes of Benefit Limitations.—

(1) Presumption of continued underfunding.—In any case in which a benefit limitation under subsection (b), (c), (d), or (e) has been applied to a plan with respect to the plan year preceding the current plan year, the adjusted funding target attainment percentage of the plan for the current plan year shall be presumed to be equal to the adjusted funding target attainment percentage of the plan for the preceding plan year until the enrolled actuary of the plan certifies the actual adjusted funding target attainment percentage of the plan for the current plan year.

IRC Sec. 436(h)(1)

(2) Presumption of underfunding after 10th month.—In any case in which no certification of the adjusted funding target attainment percentage for the current plan year is made with respect to the plan before the first day of the 10th month of such year, for purposes of subsections (b), (c), (d), and (e), such first day shall be deemed, for purposes of such subsection, to be the valuation date of the plan for the current plan year and the plan's adjusted funding target attainment percentage shall be conclusively presumed to be less than 60 percent as of such first day.

(3) Presumption of underfunding after 4th month for nearly underfunded plans.—In any case in which—

(A) a benefit limitation under subsection (b), (c), (d), or (e) did not apply to a plan with respect to the plan year preceding the current plan year, but the adjusted funding target attainment percentage of the plan for such preceding plan year was not more than 10 percentage points greater than the percentage which would have caused such subsection to apply to the plan with respect to such preceding plan year, and

(B) as of the first day of the 4th month of the current plan year, the enrolled actuary of the plan has not certified the actual adjusted funding target attainment percentage of the plan for the current plan year,

until the enrolled actuary so certifies, such first day shall be deemed, for purposes of such subsection, to be the valuation date of the plan for the current plan year and the adjusted funding target attainment percentage of the plan as of such first day shall, for purposes of such subsection, be presumed to be equal to 10 percentage points less than the adjusted funding target attainment percentage of the plan for such preceding plan year.

(i) Treatment of Plan as of Close of Prohibited or Cessation Period.—For purposes of applying this title—

(1) Operation of plan after period.—Unless the plan provides otherwise, payments and accruals will resume effective as of the day following the close of the period for which any limitation of payment or accrual of benefits under subsection (d) or (e) applies.

(2) Treatment of affected benefits.—Nothing in this subsection shall be construed as affecting the plan's treatment of benefits which would have been paid or accrued but for this section.

(j) Terms Relating to Funding Target Attainment Percentage.—For purposes of this section—

(1) In general.—The term "funding target attainment percentage" has the same meaning given such term by section 430(d)(2).

(2) Adjusted funding target attainment percentage.—The term "adjusted funding target attain-

ment percentage" means the funding target attainment percentage which is determined under paragraph (1) by increasing each of the amounts under subparagraphs (A) and (B) of section 430(d)(2) by the aggregate amount of purchases of annuities for employees other than highly compensated employees (as defined in section 414(q)) which were made by the plan during the preceding 2 plan years.

(3) Application to plans which are fully funded without regard to reductions for funding balances.—

(A) In general.—In the case of a plan for any plan year, if the funding target attainment percentage is 100 percent or more (determined without regard to the reduction in the value of assets under section 430(f)(4)), the funding target attainment percentage for purposes of paragraphs (1) and (2) shall be determined without regard to such reduction.

(B) Transition rule.—Subparagraph (A) shall be applied to plan years beginning after 2007 and before 2011 by substituting for "100 percent" the applicable percentage determined in accordance with the following table:

In the case of a plan year beginning in calendar year:	The applicable percentage is:
2008	92
2009	94
2010	96

(C) Limitation.—Subparagraph (B) shall not apply with respect to any plan year beginning after 2008 unless the funding target attainment percentage (determined without regard to the reduction in the value of assets under section 430(f)(4)) of the plan for each preceding plan year beginning after 2007 was not less than the applicable percentage with respect to such preceding plan year determined under subparagraph (B).

(3)[4] Special rule for certain years.—Solely for purposes of any applicable provision—

(A) In general.—For plan years beginning on or after October 1, 2008, and before October 1, 2010, the adjusted funding target attainment percentage of a plan shall be the greater of—

(i) such percentage, as determined without regard to this paragraph, or

(ii) the adjusted funding target attainment percentage for such plan for the plan year beginning after October 1, 2007, and before October 1, 2008, as determined under rules prescribed by the Secretary.

(B) Special rule.—In the case of a plan for which the valuation date is not the first day of the plan year—

(i) subparagraph (A) shall apply to plan years beginning after December 31, 2007, and before January 1, 2010, and

(ii) subparagraph (A)(ii) shall apply based on the last plan year beginning before November 1, 2007, as determined under rules prescribed by the Secretary.

(C) Applicable provision.—For purposes of this paragraph, the term "applicable Provision" means—

(i) subsection (d), but only for purposes of applying such paragraph to a payment which, as determined under rules prescribed by the Secretary, is a payment under a social security leveling option which accelerates payments under the plan before, and reduces payments after, a participant starts receiving social security benefits in order to provide substantially similar aggregate payments both before and after such benefits are received, and

(ii) subsection (e).

(k) Secretarial Authority for Plans with Alternate Valuation Date.—In the case of a plan which has designated a valuation date other than the first day of the plan year, the Secretary may prescribe rules for the application of this section which are necessary to reflect the alternate valuation date.

(*l*) Single-Employer Plan.—For purposes of this section, the term "single-employer plan" means a plan which is not a multiemployer plan.

(m) Special Rule for 2008.—For purposes of this section, in the case of plan years beginning in 2008, the funding target attainment percentage for the preceding plan year may be determined using such methods of estimation as the Secretary may provide.

Recent Amendments to IRC §436

Preservation of Access to Care for Medicare Beneficiaries and Pension Relief Act of 2010 (Pub. L. No. 111-192), as follows:

- IRC §436(j)(3)[4] was added by Act §203(a)(2). Eff. generally for plan years beginning on or after Oct. 1, 2008; eff. for plan years beginning after Dec. 31, 2007 for plans for which the valuation date is not the first day of the plan year. See Act §203(c).
- **Other Provision**. Act §203(b) provides:
  (b) Interaction With WRERA Rule.—Section 203 of the Worker, Retiree, and Employer Recovery Act of 2008 shall apply to a plan for any plan year in lieu of the amendments made by this section applying to sections 206(g)(4) of the Employee Retirement Income Security Act of 1974 and 436(e) of the Internal Revenue Code of 1986 only to the extent that such section produces a higher adjusted funding target attainment percentage for such plan for such year.

Worker, Retiree, and Employer Recovery Act of 2008 (Pub. L. No. 110-458), as follows:

- IRC §436(b)(2) was amended by Act §101(c)(2)(A)(i)–(ii) by substituting "section 430" for "section 303" in the matter preceding subpara. (A); and by substituting "an adjusted funding" for "a funding" in subpara. (2)(B). Eff. as if included in Pub. L. No. 109-280, §113 [eff. generally for plan years beginning after Dec. 31, 2007.

- IRC §436(b)(3) was amended by Act §101(c)(2)(B)(i)–(ii) by inserting "benefit" after "event"; and by substituting "an event" for "any event" in subpara. (3)(B). Eff. as if included in Pub. L. No. 109-280, §113 [eff. generally for plan years beginning after Dec. 31, 2007].

- IRC §436(d)(5) was amended by Act §101(c)(2)(C) by adding the flush sentence at the end. Eff. as if included in Pub. L. No. 109-280, §113 [eff. generally for plan years beginning after Dec. 31, 2007].

- IRC §436(f)(1)(D) was amended by Act §101(c)(2)(D)(i) by inserting "adjusted" before "funding". Eff. as if included in Pub. L. No. 109-280, §113 [eff. generally for plan years beginning after Dec. 31, 2007].

- IRC §436(f)(2) was amended by Act §101(c)(2)(D)(ii) by substituting "prefunding balance or funding standard carryover balance under section 430(f)" for "prefunding balance under section 430(f) or funding standard carryover balance". Eff. as if included in Pub. L. No. 109-280, §113 [eff. generally for plan years beginning after Dec. 31, 2007].

- IRC §436(j)(3)(A) was amended by Act §101(c)(2)(E)(i) by striking "without regard to this paragraph and", by substituting "section 430(f)(4)" for "section 430(f)(4)(A)", and by substituting "paragraphs (1) and (2)" for "paragraph (1)". Eff. as if included in Pub. L. No. 109-280, §113 [eff. generally for plan years beginning after Dec. 31, 2007].

- IRC §436(j)(3)(C) was amended by Act §101(c)(2)(E)(ii) by substituting "without regard to the reduction in the value of assets under section 430(f)(4)" for "without regard to this paragraph" and by inserting "beginning" before "after" each place it appears. Eff. as if included in Pub. L. No. 109-280, §113 [eff. generally for plan years beginning after Dec. 31, 2007].

- IRC §436(k) was redesignated, and new subsecs. (k) and (*l*) were added, by Act §101(c)(2)(F). Eff. as if included in Pub. L. No. 109-280, §113 [eff. generally for plan years beginning after Dec. 31, 2007].

Pension Protection Act of 2006 (Pub. L. No. 109-280), as follows:

- IRC §436 was added by Act §113(a)(1)(B). Eff. generally for plan years beginning after Dec. 31, 2007. [*Ed. Note*: For a transition rule for collectively bargained agreements, see Act §113(b)(2). For special rules for certain plans, see Act §§104 through 106.]

- **Other Provision—Effective Date.** Act §113(b)(2), as amended by Pub. L. No. 110-458, §101(c)(3), provides:
  (2) COLLECTIVE BARGAINING EXCEPTION—In the case of a plan maintained pursuant to 1 or more collective bargaining agreements between employee representatives and 1 or more employers ratified before January 1, 2008, the amendments made by this section shall not apply to plan years beginning before the earlier of—
  (A) the later of—
  (i) the date on which the last collective bargaining agreement relating to the plan terminates (determined without regard to any extension thereof agreed to after the date of the enactment of this Act), or
  (ii) the first day of the first plan year to which the amendments made by this section would (but for this paragraph) apply, or
  (B) January 1, 2010.
  For purposes of subparagraph (A)(i), any plan amendment made pursuant to a collective bargaining agreement relating to the plan which amends the plan solely to conform to any requirement added by this section shall not be treated as a termination of such collective bargaining agreement.

---

* * *

Subchapter E—Accounting Periods and Methods of Accounting
* * *

Part II—Methods of Accounting
* * *

Subpart B—Taxable Year for Which Items of Gross Income Included

* * *

SEC. 457. DEFERRED COMPENSATION PLANS OF STATE AND LOCAL GOVERNMENTS AND TAX-EXEMPT ORGANIZATIONS.

(a) Year of Inclusion in Gross Income.—

(1) In general.—Any amount of compensation deferred under an eligible deferred compensation plan, and any income attributable to the amounts so deferred, shall be includible in gross income only for the taxable year in which such compensation or other income—

(A) is paid to the participant or other beneficiary, in the case of a plan of an eligible employer described in subsection (e)(1)(A), and

(B) is paid or otherwise made available to the participant or other beneficiary, in the case of a plan of an eligible employer described in subsection (e)(1)(B).

(2) Special rule for rollover amounts.—To the extent provided in section 72(t)(9), section 72(t) shall apply to any amount includible in gross income under this subsection.

(3) Special rule for health and long-term care insurance.—In the case of a plan of an eligible employer described in subsection (e)(1)(A), to the extent provided in section 402(l), paragraph (1) shall not apply to amounts otherwise includible in gross income under this subsection.

(b) Eligible Deferred Compensation Plan Defined.—For purposes of this section, the term "eligible deferred compensation plan" means a plan established and maintained by an eligible employer—

(1) in which only individuals who perform service for the employer may be participants,

(2) which provides that (except as provided in paragraph (3)) the maximum amount which may be deferred under the plan for the taxable year (other than rollover amounts) shall not exceed the lesser of—

(A) the applicable dollar amount, or

(B) 100 percent of the participant's includible compensation,

(3) which may provide that, for 1 or more of the participant's last 3 taxable years ending before he attains normal retirement age under the plan, the ceiling set forth in paragraph (2) shall be the lesser of—

(A) twice the dollar amount in effect under subsection (b)(2)(A), or

(B) the sum of—

(i) the plan ceiling established for purposes of paragraph (2) for the taxable year (determined without regard to this paragraph), plus

(ii) so much of the plan ceiling established for purposes of paragraph (2) for taxable years before the taxable year as has not previously been used under paragraph (2) or this paragraph,

(4) which provides that compensation will be deferred for any calendar month only if an agreement providing for such deferral has been entered into before the beginning of such month,

(5) which meets the distribution requirements of subsection (d), and

(6) except as provided in subsection (g) which provides that—

(A) all amounts of compensation deferred under the plan,

(B) all property and rights purchased with such amounts, and

(C) all income attributable to such amounts, property, or rights,

shall remain (until made available to the participant or other beneficiary) solely the property and rights of the employer (without being restricted to the provision of benefits under the plan), subject only to the claims of the employer's general creditors.

A plan which is established and maintained by an employer which is described in subsection (e)(1)(A) and which is administered in a manner which is inconsistent with the requirements of any of the preceding paragraphs shall be treated as not meeting the requirements of such paragraph as of the 1st plan year beginning more than 180 days after the date of notification by the Secretary of the inconsistency unless the employer corrects the inconsistency before the 1st day of such plan year.

(c) Limitation.—The maximum amount of the compensation of any one individual which may be deferred under subsection (a) during any taxable year shall not exceed the amount in effect under subsection (b)(2)(A) (as modified by any adjustment provided under subsection (b)(3)).

(d) Distribution Requirements.—

(1) In general.—For purposes of subsection (b)(5), a plan meets the distribution requirements of this subsection if—

(A) under the plan amounts will not be made available to participants or beneficiaries earlier than—

(i) the calendar year in which the participant attains age 70½,

(ii) when the participant has a severance from employment with the employer, or

(iii) when the participant is faced with an unforeseeable emergency (determined in the manner prescribed by the Secretary in regulations),

(B) the plan meets the minimum distribution requirements of paragraph (2), and

(C) in the case of a plan maintained by an employer described in subsection (e)(1)(A), the plan meets requirements similar to the requirements of section 401(a)(31).

Any amount transferred in a direct trustee-to-trustee transfer in accordance with section 401(a)(31) shall not be includible in gross income for the taxable year of transfer.

(2) Minimum distribution requirements.—A plan meets the minimum distribution requirements of this paragraph if such plan meets the requirements of section 401(a)(9).

(3) Special rule for government plan.—An eligible deferred compensation plan of an employer described in subsection (e)(1)(A) shall not be treated as failing to meet the requirements of this subsection solely by reason of making a distribution described in subsection (e)(9)(A).

(e) Other Definitions and Special Rules.—For purposes of this section—

(1) Eligible employer.—The term "eligible employer" means—

(A) a State, political subdivision of a State, and any agency or instrumentality of a State or political subdivision of a State, and

(B) any other organization (other than a governmental unit) exempt from tax under this subtitle.

(2) Performance of service.—The performance of service includes performance of service as an independent contractor and the person (or governmental unit) for whom such services are performed shall be treated as the employer.

(3) Participant.—The term "participant" means an individual who is eligible to defer compensation under the plan.

(4) Beneficiary.—The term "beneficiary" means a beneficiary of the participant, his estate, or any other person whose interest in the plan is derived from the participant.

(5) Includible compensation.—The term "includible compensation" has the meaning given to the term "participant's compensation" by section 415(c)(3).

(6) Compensation taken into account at present value.—Compensation shall be taken into account at its present value.

(7) Community property laws.—The amount of includible compensation shall be determined without regard to any community property laws.

(8) Income attributable.—Gains from the disposition of property shall be treated as income attributable to such property.

(9) Benefits of tax exempt organization plans not treated as made available by reason of certain elections, etc.—In the case of an eligible deferred compensation plan of an employer described in subsection (e)(1)(B)—

(A) Total amount payable is dollar limit or less.—The total amount payable to a participant under the plan shall not be treated as made available merely because the participant may elect to receive such amount (or the plan may distribute such amount without the participant's consent) if—

(i) the portion of such amount which is not attributable to rollover contributions (as defined in section 411(a)(11)(D)) does not exceed the dollar limit under section 411(a)(11)(A), and

(ii) such amount may be distributed only if—

(I) no amount has been deferred under the plan with respect to such participant during the 2-year period ending on the date of the distribution, and

(II) there has been no prior distribution under the plan to such participant to which this subparagraph applied.

A plan shall not be treated as failing to meet the distribution requirements of subsection (d) by reason of a distribution to which this subparagraph applies.

(B) Election to defer commencement of distributions.—The total amount payable to a participant under the plan shall not be treated as made available merely because the participant may elect to defer commencement of distributions under the plan if—

(i) such election is made after amounts may be available under the plan in accordance with subsection (d)(1)(A) and before commencement of such distributions, and

(ii) the participant may make only 1 such election.

(10) Transfers between plans.—A participant shall not be required to include in gross income any portion of the entire amount payable to such participant solely by reason of the transfer of such portion from 1 eligible deferred compensation plan to another eligible deferred compensation plan.

(11) Certain plans excluded.—

(A) In general.—The following plans shall be treated as not providing for the deferral of compensation:

(i) Any bona fide vacation leave, sick leave, compensatory time, severance pay, disability pay, or death benefit plan.

(ii) Any plan paying solely length of service awards to bona fide volunteers (or their beneficiaries) on account of qualified services performed by such volunteers.

IRC Sec. 457(e)(11)(A)(ii)

(B) Special rules applicable to length of service award plans.—

(i) Bona fide volunteer.—An individual shall be treated as a bona fide volunteer for purposes of subparagraph (A)(ii) if the only compensation received by such individual for performing qualified services is in the form of—

(I) reimbursement for (or a reasonable allowance for) reasonable expenses incurred in the performance of such services, or

(II) reasonable benefits (including length of service awards), and nominal fees for such services, customarily paid by eligible employers in connection with the performance of such services by volunteers.

(ii) Limitation on accruals.—A plan shall not be treated as described in subparagraph (A)(ii) if the aggregate amount of length of service awards accruing with respect to any year of service for any bona fide volunteer exceeds $3,000.

(C) Qualified services.—For purposes of this paragraph, the term "qualified services" means fire fighting and prevention services, emergency medical services, and ambulance services.

(D) Certain voluntary early retirement incentive plans.—

(i) In general.—If an applicable voluntary early retirement incentive plan—

(I) makes payments or supplements as an early retirement benefit, a retirement-type subsidy, or a benefit described in the last sentence of section 411(a)(9), and

(II) such payments or supplements are made in coordination with a defined benefit plan which is described in section 401(a) and includes a trust exempt from tax under section 501(a) and which is maintained by an eligible employer described in paragraph (1)(A) or by an education association described in clause (ii)(II),

such applicable plan shall be treated for purposes of subparagraph (A)(i) as a bona fide severance pay plan with respect to such payments or supplements to the extent such payments or supplements could otherwise have been provided under such defined benefit plan (determined as if section 411 applied to such defined benefit plan).

(ii) Applicable voluntary early retirement incentive plan.—For purposes of this subparagraph, the term "applicable voluntary early retirement incentive plan" means a voluntary early retirement incentive plan maintained by—

(I) a local educational agency (as defined in section 9101 of the Elementary and Secondary Education Act of 1965 (20 U.S.C. 7801)), or

(II) an education association which principally represents employees of 1 or more agencies de-

scribed in subclause (I) and which is described in section 501(c)(5) or (6) and exempt from tax under section 501(a).

(12) Exception for nonelective deferred compensation of nonemployees.—

(A) In general.—This section shall not apply to nonelective deferred compensation attributable to services not performed as an employee.

(B) Nonelective deferred compensation.—For purposes of subparagraph (A), deferred compensation shall be treated as nonelective only if all individuals (other than those who have not satisfied any applicable initial service requirement) with the same relationship to the payor are covered under the same plan with no individual variations or options under the plan.

(13) Special rule for churches.—The term "eligible employer" shall not include a church (as defined in section 3121(w)(3)(A)) or qualified church-controlled organization (as defined in section 3121(w)(3)(B)).

(14) Treatment of qualified governmental excess benefit arrangements.—Subsections (b)(2) and (c)(1) shall not apply to any qualified governmental excess benefit arrangement (as defined in section 415(m)(3)), and benefits provided under such an arrangement shall not be taken into account in determining whether any other plan is an eligible deferred compensation plan.

(15) Applicable dollar amount.—

(A) In general.—The applicable dollar amount shall be the amount determined in accordance with the following table:

For taxable years beginning in calendar year:	The applicable dollar amount:
2002	$11,000
2003	$12,000
2004	$13,000
2005	$14,000
2006 or thereafter	$15,000

(B) Cost-of-living adjustments.—In the case of taxable years beginning after December 31, 2006, the Secretary shall adjust the $15,000 amount under subparagraph (A) at the same time and in the same manner as under section 415(d), except that the base period shall be the calendar quarter beginning July 1, 2005, and any increase under this paragraph which is not a multiple of $500 shall be rounded to the next lowest multiple of $500.

(16) Rollover amounts.—

(A) General rule.—In the case of an eligible deferred compensation plan established and maintained by an employer described in subsection (e)(1)(A), if—

(i) any portion of the balance to the credit of an employee in such plan is paid to such employee in an eligible rollover distribution (within the meaning of section 402(c)(4)).

(ii) the employee transfers any portion of the property such employee receives in such distribution to an eligible retirement plan described in section 402(c)(8)(B), and

(iii) in the case of a distribution of property other than money, the amount so transferred consists of the property distributed,

then such distribution (to the extent so transferred) shall not be includible in gross income for the taxable year in which paid.

(B) Certain rules made applicable.—The rules of paragraphs (2) through (7), (9), and (11) of section 402(c) and section 402(f) shall apply for purposes of subparagraph (A).

(C) Reporting.—Rollovers under this paragraph shall be reported to the Secretary in the same manner as rollovers from qualified retirement plans (as defined in section 4974(c)).

(17) Trustee-to-trustee transfers to purchase permissive service credit.—No amount shall be includible in gross income by reason of a direct trustee-to-trustee transfer to a defined benefit governmental plan (as defined in section 414(d)) if such transfer is—

(A) for the purchase of permissive service credit (as defined in section 415(n)(3)(A)) under such plan, or

(B) a repayment to which section 415 does not apply by reason of subsection (k)(3) thereof.

(18) Coordination with catch-up contributions for individuals age 50 or older.—In the case of an individual who is an eligible participant (as defined by section 414(v)) and who is a participant in an eligible deferred compensation plan of an employer described in paragraph (1)(A), subsections (b)(3) and (c) shall be applied by substituting for the amount otherwise determined under the applicable subsection the greater of—

(A) the sum of—

(i) the plan ceiling established for purposes of subsection (b)(2) (without regard to subsection (b)(3)), plus

(ii) the applicable dollar amount for the taxable year determined under section 414(v)(2)(B)(i), or

(B) the amount determined under the applicable subsection (without regard to this paragraph).

(f) Tax Treatment of Participants Where Plan or Arrangement of Employer Is Not Eligible.—

(1) In general.—In the case of a plan of an eligible employer providing for a deferral of compensation, if such plan is not an eligible deferred compensation plan, then—

(A) the compensation shall be included in the gross income of the participant or beneficiary for the 1st taxable year in which there is no substantial risk of forfeiture of the rights to such compensation, and

(B) the tax treatment of any amount made available under the plan to a participant or beneficiary shall be determined under section 72 (relating to annuities, etc.).

(2) Exceptions.—Paragraph (1) shall not apply to—

(A) a plan described in section 401(a) which includes a trust exempt from tax under section 501(a),

(B) an annuity plan or contract described in section 403,

(C) that portion of any plan which consists of a transfer of property described in section 83,

(D) that portion of any plan which consists of a trust to which section 402(b) applies,

(E) a qualified government excess benefit arrangement described in section 415(m), and

(F) that portion of any applicable employment retention plan described in paragraph (4) with respect to any participant.

(3) Definitions.—For purposes of this subsection—

(A) Plan includes arrangements, etc.—The term "plan" includes any agreement or arrangement.

(B) Substantial risk of forfeiture.—The rights of a person to compensation are subject to a substantial risk of forfeiture if such person's rights to such compensation are conditioned upon the future performance of substantial services by any individual.

(4) Employment retention plans.—For purposes of paragraph (2)(F)—

(A) In general.—The portion of an applicable employment retention plan described in this paragraph with respect to any participant is that portion of the plan which provides benefits payable to the participant not in excess of twice the applicable dollar limit determined under subsection (e)(15).

(B) Other rules.—

(i) Limitation.—Paragraph (2)(F) shall only apply to the portion of the plan described in subparagraph (A) for years preceding the year in which such portion is paid or otherwise made available to the participant.

(ii) Treatment.—A plan shall not be treated for purposes of this title as providing for the deferral of compensation for any year with respect to the portion of the plan described in subparagraph (A).

(C) Applicable employment retention plan.—The term "applicable employment retention plan" means an employment retention plan maintained by—

(i) a local educational agency (as defined in section 9101 of the Elementary and Secondary Education Act of 1965 (20 U.S.C. 7801), or

(ii) an education association which principally represents employees of 1 or more agencies described in clause (i) and which is described in section 501(c)(5) or (6) and exempt from taxation under section 501(a).

(D) Employment retention plan.—The term "employment retention plan" means a plan to pay, upon termination of employment, compensation to an employee of a local educational agency or education association described in subparagraph (C) for purposes of—

(i) retaining the services of the employee, or

(ii) rewarding such employee for the employee's service with 1 or more such agencies or associations.

(g) Governmental Plans Must Maintain Set-Asides for Exclusive Benefit of Participants.—

(1) In general.—A plan maintained by an eligible employer described in subsection (e)(1)(A) shall not be treated as an eligible deferred compensation plan unless all assets and income of the plan described in subsection (b)(6) are held in trust for the exclusive benefit of participants and their beneficiaries.

(2) Taxability of trusts and participants.—For purposes of this title—

(A) a trust described in paragraph (1) shall be treated as an organization exempt from taxation under section 501(a), and

(B) notwithstanding any other provision of this title, amounts in the trust shall be includible in the gross income of participants and beneficiaries only to the extent, and at the time, provided in this section.

(3) Custodial accounts and contracts.—For purposes of this subsection, custodial accounts and contracts described in section 401(f) shall be treated as trusts under rules similar to the rules under section 401(f).

(4) Death benefits under USERRA-qualified active military service.—A plan described in paragraph (1) shall not be treated as an eligible deferred compensation plan unless such plan meets the requirements of section 401(a)(37).

Recent Amendments to IRC §457

Heroes Earnings Assistance and Relief Tax Act of 2008 (Pub. L. No. 110-245), as follows:

● IRC §457(g)(4) was added by Act §104(c)(3). Eff. for deaths and disabilities occurring on or after Jan. 1, 2007, see Act §104(d)(1).
● **Other Provision.** Act §104(d)(2) provides:
  (2) Provisions relating to plan amendments.—
  (A) In general.—If this subparagraph applies to any plan or contract amendment, such plan or contract shall be treated as being operated in accordance with the terms of the plan during the period described in subparagraph (B)(iii).
  (B) Amendments to which subparagraph (A) applies.—
  (i) In general.—Subparagraph (A) shall apply to any amendment to any plan or annuity contract which is made—
  (I) pursuant to the amendments made by subsection (a) or pursuant to any regulation issued by the Secretary of the Treasury under subsection (a), and
  (II) on or before the last day of the first plan year beginning on or after January 1, 2010.
  In the case of a governmental plan (as defined in section 414(d) of the Internal Revenue Code of 1986), this clause shall be applied by substituting "2012" for "2010" in subclause (II).
  (ii) Conditions.—This paragraph shall not apply to any amendment unless—
  (I) the plan or contract is operated as if such plan or contract amendment were in effect for the period described in clause (iii), and
  (II) such plan or contract amendment applies retroactively for such period.
  (iii) Period described.—The period described in this clause is the period—
  (I) beginning on the effective date specified by the plan, and
  (II) ending on the date described in clause (i)(II) (or, if earlier, the date the plan or contract amendment is adopted).

Pension Protection Act of 2006 (Pub. L. No. 109-280), as follows:
● IRC §457(a) was amended by Act §845(b)(3) by adding new para. (3). Eff. for distributions in tax years beginning after December 31, 2006.
● IRC §457(e)(11) was amended by Act §1104(a)(1) by adding new subpara. (D). Eff. generally for tax years ending after Aug. 17, 2006. [Ed. Note: see Act §1104(d)(4) for a special rule.]
● IRC §457(e)(16)(B) was amended by Act §829(a)(4) by replacing "and (9)" with ", (9), and (11)". Eff. for distributions after Dec. 31, 2006.
● IRC §457(f)(2) was amended by Act §1104(b)(1) by striking "and" at the end of subpara. (D), by replacing the period at the end of subpara. (E) with ", and", and by adding new subpara. (F). Eff. tax years ending after Aug. 17, 2006. [Ed. Note: for a special rule, see Act §1104(d)(4).]
● IRC §457(f)(4) was amended by Act §1104(b)(2) by adding new para. (4). Eff. tax years ending after Aug. 17, 2006. [Ed. Note: for a special rule, see Act §1104(d)(4).]
● **Sunset Provision.** Act §811, provides;
  SEC. 811. PENSIONS AND INDIVIDUAL RETIREMENT ARRANGEMENT PROVISIONS OF ECONOMIC GROWTH AND TAX RELIEF RECONCILIATION ACT OF 2001 MADE PERMANENT.
  Title IX of the Economic Growth and Tax Relief Reconciliation Act of 2001 [Pub. L. No. 107-16] shall not apply to the provisions of, and amendments made by, subtitles A through F [§§601–666] of title VI of such Act (relating to pension and individual retirement arrangement provisions).

Job Creation and Worker Assistance Act of 2002 (Pub. L. No. 107-147), as follows:
● IRC §457(e)(5) was amended by Act §411(p)(5). Eff. years beginning after Dec. 31, 2001, as if included in the provision of Pub. L. No.107-16 to which it relates. IRC §457(e)(5) prior to amendment:
  (5) Includible compensation.—The term "includible compensation" means compensation for service performed for the employer which (taking into account the provisions of this section and other provisions of this chapter) is currently includible in gross income.
● IRC §457(e) was amended by Act §411(o)(9) by adding new para. (e). Eff. for contributions in tax years beginning after Dec. 31, 2001, as if included in the provision of Pub. L. No.107-16 to which it relates.

IRC Sec. 457(f)(4)(B)(ii)

Economic Growth and Tax Relief Reconciliation Act of 2001 (Pub. L. No. 107-16), as follows:

- IRC §457(a) was amended by Act §649(b)(1). Eff. for distributions after Dec. 31, 2001. IRC §457(a) prior to amendment:

  (a) Year of inclusion in gross income.—In the case of a participant in an eligible deferred compensation plan, any amount of compensation deferred under the plan, and any income attributable to the amounts so deferred, shall be includible in gross income only for the taxable year in which such compensation or other income is paid or otherwise made available to the participant or other beneficiary.

- IRC §457(b)(2) was amended by Act §641(a)(1)(B) by inserting "(other than rollover amounts)" after "taxable year". Eff. generally for distributions after Dec. 31, 2001. [*Ed. Note*: see Act §641(f)(3) for a special rule.]

- IRC §457(b)(2)(A) was amended by Act §611(e)(1)(A) by replacing "$7,500" with "the applicable dollar amount". Eff. years beginning after Dec. 31, 2001. [*Ed. Note*: see Act §611(i)(3) for a special rule.]

- IRC §457(b)(2)(B) was amended by Act §632(c)(1) by replacing "33⅓ percent" with "100 percent". Eff. years beginning after Dec. 31, 2001.

- IRC §457(b)(3)(A) was amended by Act §611(e)(1)(B) by replacing "$15,000" with "twice the dollar amount in effect under subsection (b)(2)(A)". Eff. years beginning after Dec. 31, 2001. [*Ed. Note*: see Act §611(i)(3) for a special rule.]

- IRC §457(c)(1) was amended by Act §611(e)(1)(A) by replacing "$7,500" with "the applicable dollar amount". Eff. years beginning after Dec. 31, 2001. [*Ed. Note*: see Act §611(i)(3) for a special rule.]

- IRC §457(c)(2) was amended by Act §611(d)(3)(B) by replacing "402(g)(8)(A)(iii)" with "402(g)(7)(A)(iii)". Eff. years beginning after Dec. 31, 2001. [*Ed. Note*: see Act §611(i)(3) for a special rule.]

- IRC §457(c), as amended by Act §611, was amended by Act §615(a). Eff. years beginning after Dec. 31, 2001. IRC §457(c) prior to amendment:

  (c) Individuals Who Are Participants in More Than 1 Plan.—

  (1) In general.—The maximum amount of the compensation of any one individual which may be deferred under subsection (a) during any taxable year shall not exceed the applicable dollar amount (as modified by any adjustment provided under subsection (b)(3)).

  (2) Coordination with certain other deferrals.—In applying paragraph (1) of this subsection—

  (A) any amount excluded from gross income under section 403(b) for the taxable year, and

  (B) any amount—

  (i) excluded from gross income under section 402(e)(3) or section 402(h)(1)(B) or (k) for the taxable year, or

  (ii) with respect to which a deduction is allowable by reason of a contribution to an organization described in section 501(c)(18) for the taxable year,

  shall be treated as an amount deferred under subsection (a). In applying section 402(g)(7)(A)(iii) or 403(b)(2)(A)(ii), an amount deferred under subsection (a) for any year of service shall be taken into account as if described in section 402(g)(3)(C) or 403(b)(2)(A)(ii), respectively. Subparagraph (B) shall not apply in the case of a participant in a rural cooperative plan (as defined in section 401(k)(7)).

- IRC §457(d)(1) was amended by Act §641(a)(1)(C) by striking "and" at the end of subpara. (A), by striking the period at the end of subpara. (B), by inserting ", and", and by adding new subpara. (C) and a new flush sentence. Eff. generally for distributions after Dec. 31, 2001. [*Ed. Note*: see Act §641(f)(3) for a special rule.]

- IRC §457(d)(1)(A)(ii) was amended by Act §646(a)(3) by replacing "is separated from service" with "has a severance from employment". Eff. for distributions after Dec. 31, 2001.

- IRC §457(d)(2) was amended by Act §649(a). Eff. for distributions after Dec. 31, 2001. IRC §457(d)(2) prior to amendment:

  (2) Minimum distribution requirements.—A plan meets the minimum distribution requirements of this paragraph if such plan meets the requirements of subparagraphs (A), (B), and (C):

(A) Application of section 401(a)(9).—A plan meets the requirements of this subparagraph if the plan meets the requirements of section 401(a)(9).

(B) Additional distribution requirements.—A plan meets the requirements of this subparagraph if—

(i) in the case of a distribution beginning before the death of the participant, such distribution will be made in a form under which—

(I) the amounts payable with respect to the participant will be paid at times specified by the Secretary which are not later than the time determined under section 401(a)(9)(G) (relating to incidental death benefits), and

(II) any amount not distributed to the participant during his life will be distributed after the death of the participant at least as rapidly as under the method of distributions being used under subclause (I) as of the date of his death, or

(ii) in the case of a distribution which does not begin before the death of the participant, the entire amount payable with respect to the participant will be paid during a period not to exceed 15 years (or the life expectancy of the surviving spouse if such spouse is the beneficiary).

(C) Nonincreasing benefits.—A plan meets the requirements of this subparagraph if any distribution payable over a period of more than 1 year can only be made in substantially nonincreasing amounts (paid not less frequently than annually).

- IRC §457(d) was amended by Act §649(b)(2)(B) by adding new para. (3). Eff. for distributions after Dec. 31, 2001.

- IRC §457(e)(9) was amended by Act §649(b)(2)(A) by amending the matter that preceded subpara. (A). Eff. for distributions after Dec. 31, 2001. IRC §457(e)(9) prior to amendment:

  (9) Benefits not treated as made available by reason of certain elections, etc.—

- IRC §457(e)(9)(A)(i) was amended by Act §648(b) by replacing "such amount" with "the portion of such amount which is not attributable to rollover contributions (as defined in §411(a)(11)(D))". Eff. for distributions after Dec. 31, 2001.

- IRC §457(e)(15) was amended by Act §611(e)(2). Eff. for years beginning after Dec. 31, 2001. See Act §611(i)(3) for a special rule. IRC §457(e)(15) prior to amendment:

  (15) Cost-of-living adjustment of maximum deferral amount.—The Secretary shall adjust the $7,500 amount specified in subsections (b)(2) and (c)(1) at the same time and in the same manner as under section 415(d), except that the base period shall be the calendar quarter ending September 30, 1994, and any increase under this paragraph which is not a multiple of $500 shall be rounded to the next lowest multiple of $500.

- IRC §457(e) was amended by Act §641(a)(1)(A) by adding new para. (16). Eff. generally for distributions after Dec. 31, 2001. [*Ed. Note*: see Act §641(f)(3) for a special rule.]

- IRC §457(e)(17) was amended by Act §647(b) by adding new para. (17). Eff. for trustee-to-trustee transfers after Dec. 31, 2001.

- **Sunset Provision.** Act §901, as amended by Pub. L. No. 111-312, §101(a)(1), provides the sunset rule below. But see Pub. L. No. 109-280, §811, and Pub. L. No. 111-148, §10909(c), as amended by Pub. L. No. 111-312, §101(b)(1).

  SEC. 901. SUNSET OF PROVISIONS OF ACT.

  (a) In general. All provisions of, and amendments made by, this Act shall not apply—

  (1) to taxable, plan, or limitation years beginning after December 31, 2012, or

  (2) in the case of title V, to estates of decedents dying, gifts made, or generation skipping transfers, after December 31, 2012.

  (b) Application of certain laws.—The Internal Revenue Code of 1986 and the Employee Retirement Income Security Act of 1974 shall be applied and administered to years, estates, gifts, and transfers described in subsection (a) as if the provisions and amendments described in subsection (a) had never been enacted.

SEC. 457A. NONQUALIFIED DEFERRED COMPENSATION FROM CERTAIN TAX INDIFFERENT PARTIES.

(a) In General.—Any compensation which is deferred under a nonqualified deferred compensation plan of a nonqualified entity shall be includible in gross income when there is no substantial risk of forfeiture of the rights to such compensation.

(b) Nonqualified Entity.—For purposes of this section, the term "nonqualified entity" means—

(1) any foreign corporation unless substantially all of its income is—

(A) effectively connected with the conduct of a trade or business in the United States, or

(B) subject to a comprehensive foreign income tax, and

(2) any partnership unless substantially all of its income is allocated to persons other than—

(A) foreign persons with respect to whom such income is not subject to a comprehensive foreign income tax, and

(B) organizations which are exempt from tax under this title.

(c) Determinability of Amounts of Compensation.—

(1) In general.—If the amount of any compensation is not determinable at the time that such compensation is otherwise includible in gross income under subsection (a)—

(A) such amount shall be so includible in gross income then determinable, and

(B) the tax imposed under this chapter for the taxable year in which such compensation is includible in gross income shall be increased by the sum of—

(i) the amount of interest determined under paragraph (2), and

(ii) an amount equal to 20 percent of the amount of such compensation.

(2) Interest.—For purposes of paragraph (1)(B)(i), the interest determined under this paragraph for any taxable year is the amount of interest at the underpayment rate under section 6621 plus 1 percentage point on the underpayments that would have occurred had the deferred compensation been includible in gross income for the taxable year in which first deferred or, if later, the first taxable year in which such deferred compensation is not subject to a substantial risk of forfeiture.

(d) Other Definitions and Special Rules.—For purposes of this section—

(1) Substantial risk of forfeiture.—

(A) In general.—The rights of a person to compensation shall be treated as subject to a substantial risk of forfeiture only if such person's rights to such compensation are conditioned upon the future performance of substantial services by any individual.

(B) Exception for compensation based on gain recognized on an investment asset.—

(i) In general.—To the extent provided in regulations prescribed by the Secretary, if compensation is determined solely by reference to the amount of gain recognized on the disposition of an investment asset, such compensation shall be treated as subject to a substantial risk of forfeiture until the date of such disposition.

(ii) Investment asset.—For purposes of clause (i), the term "investment asset" means any single asset (other than an investment fund or similar entity)—

(I) acquired directly by an investment fund or similar entity,

(II) with respect to which such entity does not (nor does any person related to such entity) participate in the active management of such asset (or if such asset is an interest in an entity, in the active management of the activities of such entity), and

(III) substantially all of any gain on the disposition of which (other than such deferred compensation) is allocated to investors in such entity.

(iii) Coordination with special rule.—Paragraph (3)(B) shall not apply to any compensation to which clause (i) applies.

(2) Comprehensive foreign income tax.—The term "comprehensive foreign income tax" means, with respect to any foreign person, the income tax of a foreign country if—

(A) such person is eligible for the benefits of a comprehensive income tax treaty between such foreign country and the United States, or

(B) such person demonstrates to the satisfaction of the Secretary that such foreign country has a comprehensive income tax.

(3) Nonqualified deferred compensation plan.—

(A) In general.—The term "nonqualified deferred compensation plan" has the meaning given such term under section 409A(d), except that such term shall include any plan that provides a right to compensation based on the appreciation in value of a specified number of equity units of the service recipient.

(B) Exception.—Compensation shall not be treated as deferred for purposes of this section if the service provider receives payment of such compensation not later than 12 months after the end of the taxable year of the service recipient during which the right to the payment of such compensation is no longer subject to a substantial risk of forfeiture.

(4) Exception for certain compensation with respect to effectively connected income.—In the case a foreign corporation with income which is taxable under section 882, this section shall not apply to compensation which, had such compensation had been paid in cash on the date that such compensation ceased to be subject to a substantial risk of forfeiture, would have been deductible by such foreign corporation against such income.

(5) Application of rules.—Rules similar to the rules of paragraphs (5) and (6) of section 409A(d) shall apply.

(e) Regulations.—The Secretary shall prescribe such regulations as may be necessary or appropriate to carry out the purposes of this section, including regulations disregarding a substantial risk of forfeiture in cases where necessary to carry out the purposes of this section.

Recent Amendments to IRC §457A

Tax Extenders and Alternative Minimum Tax Relief Act of 2008 (Pub. L. No. 110-343), as follows:

● IRC §457A was added by Act, Div. C, §801(a). Eff. generally for amounts deferred that are attributable to services performed after Dec. 31, 2008. See below for special effective date rule.

● **Special Effective Date Rule.** Act, Div. C, §801(d) provides:

(2) APPLICATION TO EXISTING DEFERRALS.—In the case of any amount deferred to which the amendments made by this section do not apply solely by reason of the fact that the amount is attributable to services performed before January 1, 2009, to the extent such amount is not includible in gross income in a taxable year beginning before 2018, such amounts shall be includible in gross income in the later of—

(A) the last taxable year beginning before 2018, or

(B) the taxable year in which there is no substantial risk of forfeiture of the rights to such compensation (determined in the same manner as determined for purposes of section 457A of the Internal Revenue Code of 1986, as added by this section).

(3) ACCELERATED PAYMENTS.—No later than 120 days after the date of the enactment of this Act, the Secretary shall issue guidance providing a limited period of time during which a nonqualified deferred compensation arrangement attributable to services performed on or before December 31, 2008, may, without violating the requirements of section 409A(a) of the Internal Revenue Code of 1986, be amended to conform the date of distribution to the date the amounts are required to be included in income.

(4) CERTAIN BACK-TO-BACK ARRANGEMENTS.—If the taxpayer is also a service recipient and maintains one or more nonqualified deferred compensation arrangements for its service providers under which any amount is attributable to services performed on or before December 31, 2008, the guidance issued under paragraph (4) shall permit such arrangements to be amended to conform the dates of distribution under such arrangement to the date amounts are required to be included in the income of such taxpayer under this subsection.

(5) ACCELERATED PAYMENT NOT TREATED AS MATERIAL MODIFICATION.—Any amendment to a nonqualified deferred compensation arrangement made pursuant to paragraph (4) or (5) shall not be treated as a material modification of the arrangement for purposes of section 409A of the Internal Revenue Code of 1986.

---

* * *

Subchapter F—Exempt Organizations

Part I—General Rule

SEC. 501. EXEMPTION FROM TAX ON CORPORATIONS, CERTAIN TRUSTS, ETC.

(a) Exemption From Taxation.—An organization described in subsection (c) or (d) or section 401(a) shall be exempt from taxation under this subtitle unless such exemption is denied under section 502 or 503.

(b) Tax on Unrelated Business Income and Certain Other Activities.—An organization exempt from taxation under subsection (a) shall be subject to tax to the extent provided in parts II, III, and VI of this subchapter, but (notwithstanding parts II, III, and VI of this subchapter) shall be considered an organization exempt from income taxes for the purpose of any law which refers to organizations exempt from income taxes.

(c) List of Exempt Organizations.—The following organizations are referred to in subsection (a):

(1) Any corporation organized under Act of Congress which is an instrumentality of the United States but only if such corporation—

(A) is exempt from Federal income taxes—

(i) under such Act as amended and supplemented before July 18, 1984, or

(ii) under this title without regard to any provision of law which is not contained in this title and which is not contained in a revenue Act, or

(B) is described in subsection (l).

(2) Corporations organized for the exclusive purpose of holding title to property, collecting income therefrom, and turning over the entire amount thereof, less expenses, to an organization which itself is exempt under this section. Rules similar to the rules of subparagraph (G) of paragraph (25) shall apply for purposes of this paragraph.

(3) Corporations, and any community chest, fund, or foundation, organized and operated exclusively for religious, charitable, scientific, testing for public safety, literary, or educational purposes, or to foster national or international amateur sports competition (but only if no part of its activities involve the provision of athletic facilities or equipment), or for the prevention of cruelty to children or animals, no part of the net earnings of which inures to the benefit of any private shareholder or individual, no substantial part of the activities of which is carrying on propaganda, or otherwise attempting to influence legislation (except as otherwise provided in subsection (h)), and which does not participate in, or intervene in (including the publishing or distributing of statements), any political campaign on behalf of (or in opposition to) any candidate for public office.

IRC Sec. 501(c)(3)

(4)(A) Civic leagues or organizations not organized for profit but operated exclusively for the promotion of social welfare, or local associations of employees, the membership of which is limited to the employees of a designated person or persons in a particular municipality, and the net earnings of which are devoted exclusively to charitable, educational, or recreational purposes.

(B) Subparagraph (A) shall not apply to an entity unless no part of the net earnings of such entity inures to the benefit of any private shareholder or individual.

(5) Labor, agricultural, or horticultural organizations.

(6) Business leagues, chambers of commerce, real-estate boards, boards of trade, or professional football leagues (whether or not administering a pension fund for football players) not organized for profit and no part of the net earnings of which inures to the benefit of any private shareholder or individual.

(7) Clubs organized for pleasure, recreation, and other nonprofitable purposes, substantially all of the activities of which are for such purposes and no part of the net earnings of which inures to the benefit of any private shareholder.

(8) Fraternal beneficiary societies, orders, or associations—

(A) operating under the lodge system or for the exclusive benefit of the members of a fraternity itself operating under the lodge system, and

(B) providing for the payment of life, sick, accident, or other benefits to the members of such society, order, or association or their dependents.

Editor's Note

IRC §501(c)(9), below, as amended by Pub. L. No. 111-152, §1004, is effective on the date of enactment of the Act (enacted: March 30, 2010).

---

(9) Voluntary employees' beneficiary associations providing for the payment of life, sick, accident, or other benefits to the members of such association or their dependents or designated beneficiaries, if no part of the net earnings of such association inures (other than through such payments) to the benefit of any private shareholder or individual. For purposes of providing for the payment of sick and accident benefits to members of such an association and their dependents, the term "dependent" shall include any individual who is a child (as defined in section 152(f)(1)) of a member who as of the end of calendar year has not attained age 27.

(10) Domestic fraternal societies, orders, or associations, operating under the lodge system—

(A) the net earnings of which are devoted exclusively to religious, charitable, scientific, literary, educational, and fraternal purposes, and

(B) which do not provide for the payment of life, sick, accident, or other benefits.

(11) Teachers' retirement fund associations of a purely local character, if—

(A) no part of their net earnings inures (other than through payment of retirement benefits) to the benefit of any private shareholder or individual, and

(B) the income consists solely of amounts received from public taxation, amounts received from assessments on the teaching salaries of members, and income in respect of investments.

(12)(A) Benevolent life insurance associations of a purely local character, mutual ditch or irrigation companies, mutual or cooperative telephone companies, or like organizations; but only if 85 percent or more of the income consists of amounts collected from members for the sole purpose of meeting losses and expenses.

(B) In the case of a mutual or cooperative telephone company, subparagraph (A) shall be applied without taking into account any income received or accrued—

(i) from a nonmember telephone company for the performance of communication services which involve members of the mutual or cooperative telephone company,

(ii) from qualified pole rentals,

(iii) from the sale of display listings in a directory furnished to the members of the mutual or cooperative telephone company, or

(iv) from the prepayment of a loan under section 306A, 306B, or 311 of the Rural Electrification Act of 1936 (as in effect on January 1, 1987).

(C) In the case of a mutual or cooperative electric company, subparagraph (A) shall be applied without taking into account any income received or accrued—

(i) from qualified pole rentals, or

(ii) from any provision or sale of electric energy transmission services or ancillary services if such services are provided on a nondiscriminatory open access basis under an open access transmission tariff approved or accepted by FERC or under an independent transmission provider agreement approved or accepted by FERC (other than income received or accrued directly or indirectly from a member),

(iii) from the provision or sale of electric energy distribution services or ancillary services if such services are provided on a nondiscriminatory open access basis to distribute electric energy not owned by the mutual or electric cooperative company—

(I) to end-users who are served by distribution facilities not owned by such company or any of its members (other than income received or accrued directly or indirectly from a member), or

(II) generated by a generation facility not owned or leased by such company or any of its members and which is directly connected to distribution facilities owned by such company or any of its members (other than income received or accrued directly or indirectly from a member),

(iv) from any nuclear decommissioning transaction, or

(v) from any asset exchange or conversion transaction.

(D) For purposes of this paragraph, the term "qualified pole rental" means any rental of a pole (or other structure used to support wires) if such pole (or other structure)—

(i) is used by the telephone or electric company to support one or more wires which are used by such company in providing telephone or electric services to its members, and

(ii) is used pursuant to the rental to support one or more wires (in addition to the wires described in clause (i)) for use in connection with the transmission by wire of electricity or of telephone or other communications.

For purposes of the preceding sentence, the term "rental" includes any sale of the right to use the pole (or other structure).

(E) For purposes of subparagraph (C)(ii), the term "FERC" means the Federal Energy Regulatory Commission and references to such term shall be treated as including the Public Utility Commission of Texas with respect to any ERCOT utility (as defined in section 212(k)(2)(B) of the Federal Power Act (16 U.S.C. 824k(k)(2)(B))).

(F) For purposes of subparagraph (C)(iv), the term "nuclear decommissioning transaction" means—

(i) any transfer into a trust, fund, or instrument established to pay any nuclear decommissioning costs if the transfer is in connection with the transfer of the mutual or cooperative electric company's interest in a nuclear power plant or nuclear power plant unit,

(ii) any distribution from any trust, fund, or instrument established to pay any nuclear decommissioning costs, or

(iii) any earnings from any trust, fund, or instrument established to pay any nuclear decommissioning costs.

(G) For purposes of subparagraph (C)(v), the term "asset exchange or conversion transaction" means

any voluntary exchange or involuntary conversion of any property related to generating, transmitting, distributing, or selling electric energy by a mutual or cooperative electric company, the gain from which qualifies for deferred recognition under section 1031 or 1033, but only if the replacement property acquired by such company pursuant to such section constitutes property which is used, or to be used, for—

(i) generating, transmitting, distributing, or selling electric energy, or

(ii) producing, transmitting, distributing, or selling natural as.

(H)(i) In the case of a mutual or cooperative electric company described in this paragraph or an organization described in section 1381(a)(2)(C), income received or accrued from a load loss transaction shall be treated as an amount collected from members for the sole purpose of meeting losses and expenses.

(ii) For purposes of clause (i), the term "load loss transaction" means any wholesale or retail sale of electric energy (other than to members) to the extent that the aggregate sales during the recovery period do not exceed the load loss mitigation sales limit for such period.

(iii) For purposes of clause (ii), the load loss mitigation sales limit for the recovery period is the sum of the annual load losses for each year of such period.

(iv) For purposes of clause (iii), a mutual or cooperative electric company's annual load loss for each year of the recovery period is the amount (if any) by which—

(I) the megawatt hours of electric energy sold during such year to members of such electric company are less than

(II) the megawatt hours of electric energy sold during the base year to such members.

(v) For purposes of clause (iv)(II), the term "base year" means—

(I) the calendar year preceding the start-up year, or

(II) at the election of the mutual or cooperative electric company, the second or third calendar years preceding the start-up year.

(vi) For purposes of this subparagraph, the recovery period is the 7-year period beginning with the start-up year.

(vii) For purposes of this subparagraph, the start-up year is the first year that the mutual or cooperative electric company offers nondiscriminatory open access or the calendar year which includes the date of the enactment of this subparagraph, if later, at the election of such company.

(viii) A company shall not fail to be treated as a mutual or cooperative electric company for purposes of this paragraph or as a corporation operating on a cooperative basis for purposes of section 1381(a)(2)(C) by reason of the treatment under clause (i).

(ix) For purposes of subparagraph (A), in the case of a mutual or cooperative electric company, income received, or accrued, indirectly from a member shall be treated as an amount collected from members for the sole purpose of meeting losses and expenses.

(13) Cemetery companies owned and operated exclusively for the benefit of their members or which are not operated for profit; and any corporation chartered solely for the purpose of the disposal of bodies by burial or cremation which is not permitted by its charter to engage in any business not necessarily incident to that purpose and no part of the net earnings of which inures to the benefit of any private shareholder or individual.

(14)(A) Credit unions without capital stock organized and operated for mutual purposes and without profit.

(B) Corporations or associations without capital stock organized before September 1, 1957, and operated for mutual purposes and without profit for the purpose of providing reserve funds for, and insurance of shares or deposits in—

(i) domestic building and loan associations,

(ii) cooperative banks without capital stock organized and operated for mutual purposes and without profit,

(iii) mutual savings banks not having capital stock represented by shares, or

(iv) mutual savings banks described in section 591(b)

(C) Corporations or associations organized before September 1, 1957, and operated for mutual purposes and without profit for the purpose of providing reserve funds for associations or banks described in clause (i), (ii), or (iii) of subparagraph (B); but only if 85 percent or more of the income is attributable to providing such reserve funds and to investments. This subparagraph shall not apply to any corporation or association entitled to exemption under subparagraph (B).

(15)(A) Insurance companies (as defined in section 816(a)) other than life (including interinsurers and reciprocal underwriters) if—

(i)(I) the gross receipts for the taxable year do not exceed $600,000, and

(II) more than 50 percent of such gross receipts consist of premiums, or

(ii) in the case of a mutual insurance company—

(I) the gross receipts of which for the taxable year do not exceed $150,000, and

(II) more than 35 percent of such gross receipts consist of premiums.

Clause (ii) shall not apply to a company if any employee of the company, or a member of the employee's family (as defined in section 2032A(e)(2)), is an employee of another company exempt from taxation by reason of this paragraph (or would be so exempt but for this sentence).

(B) For purposes of subparagraph (A), in determining whether any company or association is described in subparagraph (A), such company or association shall be treated as receiving during the taxable year amounts described in subparagraph (A) which are received during such year by all other companies or associations which are members of the same controlled group as the insurance company or association for which the determination is being made.

(C) For purposes of subparagraph (B), the term "controlled group" has the meaning given such term by section 831(b)(2)(B)(ii), except that in applying section 831(b)(2)(B)(ii) for purposes of this subparagraph, subparagraphs (B) and (C) of section 1563(b)(2) shall be disregarded.

(16) Corporations organized by an association subject to part IV of this subchapter or members thereof, for the purpose of financing the ordinary crop operations of such members or other producers, and operated in conjunction with such association. Exemption shall not be denied any such corporation because it has capital stock, if the dividend rate of such stock is fixed at not to exceed the legal rate of interest in the State of incorporation or 8 percent per annum, whichever is greater, on the value of the consideration for which the stock was issued, and if substantially all such stock (other than nonvoting preferred stock, the owners of which are not entitled or permitted to participate, directly or indirectly, in the profits of the corporation, on dissolution or otherwise, beyond the fixed dividends) is owned by such association, or members thereof; nor shall exemption be denied any such corporation because there is accumulated and maintained by it a reserve required by State law or a reasonable reserve for any necessary purpose.

(17)(A) A trust or trusts forming part of a plan providing for the payment of supplemental unemployment compensation benefits, if—

(i) under the plan, it is impossible, at any time prior to the satisfaction of all liabilities with respect to employees under the plan, for any part of the corpus or income to be (within the taxable year or thereafter) used for, or diverted to, any purpose other than the providing of supplemental unemployment compensation benefits,

(ii) such benefits are payable to employees under a classification which is set forth in the plan and which is found by the Secretary not to be discriminatory in favor of employees who are highly compensated employees (within the meaning of section 414(q)), and

(iii) such benefits do not discriminate in favor of employees who are highly compensated employees (within the meaning of section 414(q)). A plan shall not be considered discriminatory within the meaning of this clause merely because the benefits received under the plan bear a uniform relationship to the total compensation, or the basic or regular rate of compensation, of the employees covered by the plan.

(B) In determining whether a plan meets the requirements of subparagraph (A), any benefits provided under any other plan shall not be taken into consideration, except that a plan shall not be considered discriminatory—

(i) merely because the benefits under the plan which are first determined in a nondiscriminatory manner within the meaning of subparagraph (A) are then reduced by any sick, accident, or unemployment compensation benefits received under State or Federal law (or reduced by a portion of such benefits if determined in a nondiscriminatory manner), or

(ii) merely because the plan provides only for employees who are not eligible to receive sick, accident, or unemployment compensation benefits under State or Federal law the same benefits (or a portion of such benefits if determined in a nondiscriminatory manner) which such employees would receive under such laws if such employees were eligible for such benefits, or

(iii) merely because the plan provides only for employees who are not eligible under another plan (which meets the requirements of subparagraph (A)) of supplemental unemployment compensation benefits provided wholly by the employer the same benefits (or a portion of such benefits if determined in a nondiscriminatory manner) which such employees would receive under such other plan if such employees were eligible under such other plan, but only if the employees eligible under both plans would make a classification which would be nondiscriminatory within the meaning of subparagraph (A).

(C) A plan shall be considered to meet the requirements of subparagraph (A) during the whole of any year of the plan if on one day in each quarter it satisfies such requirements.

(D) The term "supplemental unemployment compensation benefits" means only—

(i) benefits which are paid to an employee because of his involuntary separation from the employment of the employer (whether or not such separation is temporary) resulting directly from a reduction in force, the discontinuance of a plant or operation, or other similar conditions, and

(ii) sick and accident benefits subordinate to the benefits described in clause (i).

(E) Exemption shall not be denied under subsection (a) to any organization entitled to such exemption as an association described in paragraph (9) of this subsection merely because such organization provides for the payment of supplemental unemployment benefits (as defined in subparagraph (D)(i)).

(18) A trust or trusts created before June 25, 1959, forming part of a plan providing for the payment of benefits under a pension plan funded only by contributions of employees, if—

(A) under the plan, it is impossible, at any time prior to the satisfaction of all liabilities with respect to employees under the plan, for any part of the corpus or income to be (within the taxable year or thereafter) used for, or diverted to, any purpose other than the providing of benefits under the plan,

(B) such benefits are payable to employees under a classification which is set forth in the plan and which is found by the Secretary not to be discriminatory in favor of employees who are highly compensated employees (within the meaning of section 414(q)),

(C) such benefits do not discriminate in favor of employees who are highly compensated employees (within the meaning of section 414(q)). A plan shall not be considered discriminatory within the meaning of this subparagraph merely because the benefits received under the plan bear a uniform relationship to the total compensation, or the basic or regular rate of compensation, of the employees covered by the plan, and

(D) in the case of a plan under which an employee may designate certain contributions as deductible—

(i) such contributions do not exceed the amount with respect to which a deduction is allowable under section 219(b)(3).

(ii) requirements similar to the requirements of section 401(k)(3)(A)(ii) are met with respect to such elective contributions,

(iii) such contributions are treated as elective deferrals for purposes of section 402(g) and

(iv) the requirements of section 401(a)(30) are met.

For purposes of subparagraph (D)(ii), rules similar to the rules of section 401(k)(8) shall apply. For purposes of section 4979, any excess contribution under clause (ii) shall be treated as an excess contribution under a cash or deferred arrangement.

IRC Sec. 501(c)(18)(D)(iv)

(19) A post or organization of past or present members of the Armed Forces of the United States, or an auxiliary unit or society of, or a trust or foundation for, any such post or organization—

(A) organized in the United States or any of its possessions,

(B) at least 75 percent of the members of which are past or present members of the Armed Forces of the United States and substantially all of the other members of which are individuals who are cadets or are spouses, widows, widowers, ancestors, or lineal descendants of past or present members of the Armed Forces of the United States or of cadets, and

(C) no part of the net earnings of which inures to the benefit of any private shareholder or individual.

(20) An organization or trust created or organized in the United States, the exclusive function of which is to form part of a qualified group legal services plan or plans, within the meaning of section 120. An organization or trust which receives contributions because of section 120(c)(5)(C) shall not be prevented from qualifying as an organization described in this paragraph merely because it provides legal services or indemnification against the cost of legal services unassociated with a qualified group legal services plan.

(21)(A) A trust or trusts established in writing, created or organized in the United States, and contributed to by any person (except an insurance company) if—

(i) the purpose of such trust or trusts is exclusively—

(I) to satisfy, in whole or in part, the liability of such person for, or with respect to, claims for compensation for disability or death due to pneumoconiosis under Black Lung Acts,

(II) to pay premiums for insurance exclusively covering such liability,

(III) to pay administrative and other incidental expenses of such trust in connection with the operation of the trust and the processing of claims against such person under Black Lung Acts, and

(IV) to pay accident or health benefits for retired miners and their spouses and dependents (including administrative and other incidental expenses of such trust in connection therewith) or premiums for insurance exclusively covering such benefits; and

(ii) no part of the assets of the trust may be used for, or diverted to, any purpose other than—

(I) the purposes described in clause (i),

(II) investment (but only to the extent that the trustee determines that a portion of the assets is not currently needed for the purposes described in clause (i)) in qualified investments, or

(III) payment into the Black Lung Disability Trust Fund established under section 9501, or into the general fund of the United States Treasury (other than in satisfaction of any tax or other civil or criminal liability of the person who established or contributed to the trust).

(B) No deduction shall be allowed under this chapter for any payment described in subparagraph (A)(i)(IV) from such trust.

(C) Payments described in subparagraph (A)(i)(IV) may be made from such trust during a taxable year only to the extent that the aggregate amount of such payments during such taxable year does not exceed the excess (if any), as of the close of the preceding taxable year, of—

(i) the fair market value of the assets of the trust, over

(ii) 110 percent of the present value of the liability described in subparagraph (A)(i)(I) of such person.

The determinations under the preceding sentence shall be made by an independent actuary using actuarial methods and assumptions (not inconsistent with the regulations prescribed under section 192(c)(1)(A)) each of which is reasonable and which are reasonable in the aggregate.

(D) For purposes of this paragraph:

(i) The term "Black Lung Acts" means part C of title IV of the Federal Mine Safety and Health Act of 1977, and any State law providing compensation for disability or death due to that pneumoconiosis.

(ii) The term "qualified investments" means—

(I) public debt securities of the United States,

(II) obligations of a State or local government which are not in default as to principal or interest, and

(III) time or demand deposits in a bank (as defined in section 581) or an insured credit union (within the meaning of section 101(7) of the Federal Credit Union Act, 12 U.S.C. 1752(7)) located in the United States.

(iii) The term "miner" has the same meaning as such term has when used in section 402(d) of the Black Lung Benefits Act (30 U.S.C. 902(d)).

(iv) The term "incidental expenses" includes legal, accounting, actuarial, and trustee expenses.

(22) A trust created or organized in the United States and established in writing by the plan sponsors of multiemployer plans if—

(A) the purpose of such trust is exclusively—

(i) to pay any amount described in section 4223(c) or (h) of the Employee Retirement Income Security Act of 1974, and

(ii) to pay reasonable and necessary administrative expenses in connection with the establishment and operation of the trust and the processing of claims against the trust,

(B) no part of the assets of the trust may be used for, or diverted to, any purpose other than—

(i) the purposes described in subparagraph (A), or

(ii) the investment in securities, obligations, or time or demand deposits described in clause (ii) of paragraph (21)(D),

(C) such trust meets the requirements of paragraphs (2), (3), and (4) of section 4223(b), 4223(h), or, if applicable, section 4223(c) of the Employee Retirement Income Security Act of 1974, and

(D) the trust instrument provides that, on dissolution of the trust, assets of the trust may not be paid other than to plans which have participated in the plan or, in the case of a trust established under section 4223(h) of such Act, to plans with respect to which employers have participated in the fund.

(23) Any association organized before 1880 more than 75 percent of the members of which are present or past members of the Armed Forces and a principal purpose of which is to provide insurance and other benefits to veterans or their dependents.

(24) A trust described in section 4049 of the Employee Retirement Income Security Act of 1974 (as in effect on the date of the enactment of the Single-Employer Pension Plan Amendments Act of 1986).

(25)(A) Any corporation or trust which—

(i) has no more than 35 shareholders or beneficiaries,

(ii) has only 1 class of stock or beneficial interest, and

(iii) is organized for the exclusive purposes of—

(I) acquiring real property and holding title to, and collecting income from, such property, and

(II) remitting the entire amount of income from such property (less expenses) to 1 or more organizations described in subparagraph (C) which are shareholders of such corporation or beneficiaries of such trust.

For purposes of clause (iii), the term "real property" shall not include any interest as a tenant in common (or similar interest) and shall not include any indirect interest.

(B) A corporation or trust shall be described in subparagraph (A) without regard to whether the corporation or trust is organized by 1 or more organizations described in subparagraph (C).

(C) An organization is described in this subparagraph if such organization is—

(i) a qualified pension, profit sharing, or stock bonus plan that meets the requirements of section 401(a),

(ii) a governmental plan (within the meaning of section 414(d)),

(iii) the United States, any State or political subdivision thereof, or any agency or instrumentality of any of the foregoing, or

(iv) any organization described in paragraph (3).

(D) A corporation or trust shall in no event be treated as described in subparagraph (A) unless such corporation or trust permits its shareholders or beneficiaries—

(i) to dismiss the corporation's or trust's investment adviser, following reasonable notice, upon a vote of the shareholders or beneficiaries holding a majority of interest in the corporation or trust, and

(ii) to terminate their interest in the corporation or trust by either, or both, of the following alternatives, as determined by the corporation or trust:

(I) by selling or exchanging their stock in the corporation or interest in the trust (subject to any Federal or State securities law) to any organization described in subparagraph (C) so long as the sale or exchange does not increase the number of shareholders or beneficiaries in such corporation or trust above 35, or

(II) by having their stock or interest redeemed by the corporation or trust after the shareholder or beneficiary has provided 90 days notice to such corporation or trust.

(E)(i) For purposes of this title—

(I) a corporation which is a qualified subsidiary shall not be treated as a separate corporation, and

(II) all assets, liabilities, and items of income, deduction, and credit of a qualified subsidiary shall be treated as assets, liabilities, and such items (as the case may be) of the corporation or trust described in subparagraph (A).

(ii) For purposes of this subparagraph, the term "qualified subsidiary" means any corporation if, at all times during the period such corporation was in existence, 100 percent of the stock of such corporation is held by the corporation or trust described in subparagraph (A).

(iii) For purposes of this subtitle, if any corporation which was a qualified subsidiary ceases to meet the requirements of clause (ii), such corporation shall be treated as a new corporation acquiring all of its assets (and assuming all of its liabilities) immediately before such cessation from the corporation or trust described in subparagraph (A) in exchange for its stock.

(F) For purposes of subparagraph (A), the term "real property" includes any personal property which is leased under, or in connection with, a lease of real property, but only if the rent attributable to such personal property (determined under the rules of section 856(d)(1)) for the taxable year does not exceed 15 percent of the total rent for the taxable year attributable to both the real and personal property leased under, or in connection with, such lease.

(G)(i) An organization shall not be treated as failing to be described in this paragraph merely by reason of the receipt of any otherwise disqualifying income which is incidentally derived from the holding of real property.

(ii) Clause (i) shall not apply if the amount of gross income described in such clause exceeds 10 percent of the organization's gross income for the taxable year unless the organization establishes to the satisfaction of the Secretary that the receipt of gross income described in clause (i) in excess of such limitation was inadvertent and reasonable steps are being taken to correct the circumstances giving rise to such income.

(26) Any membership organization if—

(A) such organization is established by a State exclusively to provide coverage for medical care (as defined in section 213(d)) on a not-for-profit basis to individuals described in subparagraph (B) through—

(i) insurance issued by the organization, or

(ii) a health maintenance organization under an arrangement with the organization,

(B) the only individuals receiving such coverage through the organization are individuals—

(i) who are residents of such State, and

(ii) who, by reason of the existence or history of a medical condition—

(I) are unable to acquire medical care coverage for such condition through insurance or from a health maintenance organization, or

(II) are able to acquire such coverage only at a rate which is substantially in excess of the rate for such coverage through the membership organization,

(C) the composition of the membership in such organization is specified by such State, and

(D) no part of the net earnings of the organization inures to the benefit of any private shareholder or individual.

A spouse and any qualifying child (as defined in section 24(c)) of an individual described in subparagraph (B) (without regard to this sentence) shall be treated as described in subparagraph (B).

(27)(A) Any membership organization if—

(i) such organization is established before June 1, 1996, by a State exclusively to reimburse its members for losses arising under workmen's compensation acts,

501(c)(27)(A)(ii) such State requires that the membership of such organization consist of—

(I) all persons who issue insurance covering workmen's compensation losses in such State, and

(II) all persons and governmental entities who self-insure against such losses, and

(iii) such organization operates as a non-profit organization by—

(I) returning surplus income to its members or workmen's compensation policyholders on a periodic basis, and

(II) reducing initial premiums in anticipation of investment income.

(B) Any organization (including a mutual insurance company) if—

(i) such organization is created by State law and is organized and operated under State law exclusively to—

(I) provide workmen's compensation insurance which is required by State law or with respect to which State law provides significant disincentives if such insurance is not purchased by an employer, and

(II) provide related coverage which is incidental to workmen's compensation insurance,

(ii) such organization must provide workmen's compensation insurance to any employer in the State (for employees in the State or temporarily assigned out-of-State) which seeks such insurance and meets other reasonable requirements relating thereto,

(iii)(I) the State makes a financial commitment with respect to such organization either by extending the full faith and credit of the State to the initial debt of such organization or by providing the initial operating capital of such organization, and

(II) in the case of periods after the date of enactment of this subparagraph, the assets of such organization revert to the State upon dissolution or State law does not permit the dissolution of such organization, and

(iv) the majority of the board of directors or oversight body of such organization are appointed by the chief executive officer or other executive branch official of the State, by the State legislature, or by both.

(28) The National Railroad Retirement Trust established under section 15(j) of the Railroad Retirement Act of 1974.

(29) Co-Op Health Insurance Issuers.—

(A) In General.—A qualified nonprofit health insurance issuer (within the meaning of section 1322 of the Patient Protection and Affordable Care Act) which has received a loan or grant under the CO-OP program under such section, but only with respect to periods for which the issuer is in compliance with the requirements of such section and any agreement with respect to the loan or grant.

(B) Conditions For Exemption.—Subparagraph (A) shall apply to an organization only if—

(i) the organization has given notice to the Secretary, in such manner as the Secretary may by regulations prescribe, that it is applying for recognition of its status under this paragraph,

(ii) except as provided in section 1322(c)(4) of the Patient Protection and Affordable Care Act, no part of the net earnings of which inures to the benefit of any private shareholder or individual,

(iii) no substantial part of the activities of which is carrying on propaganda, or otherwise attempting, to influence legislation, and

(iv) the organization does not participate in, or intervene in (including the publishing or distributing of statements), any political campaign on behalf of (or in opposition to) any candidate for public office.

* * *

Recent Amendments to IRC §501 (As Excerpted)

Health Care and Education Reconciliation Act of 2010 (Pub. L. No. 111-152), as follows:

● IRC §501(c)(9) was amended by Act §1004(d)(4) by adding the sentence at the end. Eff. on date of enactment [enacted: Mar. 30, 2010].

Pension Protection Act of 2006 (Pub. L. No. 109-280), as follows:

● IRC §501(c)(21)(C) was amended by Act §862(a) by amending the matter that precedes the last sentence. Eff. tax years beginning after Dec. 31, 2006. IRC §501(c)(21)(C), matter preceding last sentence, prior to amendment:

(C) Payments described in subparagraph (A)(i)(IV) may be made from such trust during a taxable year only to the extent that the aggregate amount of such payments during such taxable year does not exceed the lesser of—
(i) the excess (if any) (as of the close of the preceding taxable year) of—
(I) the fair market value of the assets of the trust, over
(II) 110 percent of the present value of the liability described in subparagraph (A)(i)(I) of such person, or
(ii) the excess (if any) of—
(I) the sum of a similar excess determined as of the close of the last taxable year ending before the date of the enactment of this subparagraph plus earnings thereon as of the close of the taxable year preceding the taxable year involved, over

(II) the aggregate payments described in subparagraph (A)(i)(IV) made from the trust during all taxable years beginning after the date of the enactment of this subparagraph.

● **Sunset Provision.** Act §811, provides:

SEC. 811. PENSIONS AND INDIVIDUAL RETIREMENT ARRANGEMENT PROVISIONS OF ECONOMIC GROWTH AND TAX RELIEF RECONCILIATION ACT OF 2001 MADE PERMANENT.

Title IX of the Economic Growth and Tax Relief Reconciliation Act of 2001 [Pub. L. No. 107-16] shall not apply to the provisions of, and amendments made by, subtitles A through F [§§601–666] of title VI of such Act (relating to pension and individual retirement arrangement provisions).

Economic Growth and Tax Relief Reconciliation Act of 2001 (Pub. L. No. 107-16), as follows:

● IRC §501(c)(18)(D)(iii) was amended by Act §611(d)(3)(C) by striking "(other than paragraph (4) thereof)" after "§402(g)". Eff. years beginning after Dec. 31, 2001. [*Ed. Note*: see Act §611(i)(3) for a special rule.]

● **Sunset Provision.** Act §901, as amended by Pub. L. No. 111-312, §101(a)(1), provides the sunset rule below. But see Pub. L. No. 109-280, §811, and Pub. L. No. 111-148, §10909(c), as amended by Pub. L. No. 111-312, §101(b)(1).

SEC. 901. SUNSET OF PROVISIONS OF ACT.

(a) In general. All provisions of, and amendments made by, this Act shall not apply—
(1) to taxable, plan, or limitation years beginning after December 31, 2012, or
(2) in the case of title V, to estates of decedents dying, gifts made, or generation skipping transfers, after December 31, 2012.

(b) Application of certain laws.—The Internal Revenue Code of 1986 and the Employee Retirement Income Security Act of 1974 shall be applied and administered to years, estates, gifts, and transfers described in subsection (a) as if the provisions and amendments described in subsection (a) had never been enacted.

---

* * *

SEC. 505. ADDITIONAL REQUIREMENTS FOR ORGANIZATIONS DESCRIBED IN PARAGRAPH (9), (17), OR (20) OF SECTION 501(c).

(a) Certain Requirements Must Be Met in the Case of Organizations Described in Paragraph (9) or (20) of Section 501(c).—

(1) Voluntary employees' beneficiary associations, etc.—An organization described in paragraph (9) or (20) of subsection (c) of section 501 which is part of a plan shall not be exempt from tax under section 501(a) unless such plan meets the requirements of subsection (b) of this section.

(2) Exception for collective bargaining agreements.—Paragraph (1) shall not apply to any organization which is part of a plan maintained pursuant to an agreement between employee representatives and 1 or more employers if the Secretary finds that such agreement is a collective bargaining agreement and that such plan was the subject of good faith bargaining between such employee representatives and such employer or employers.

(b) Nondiscrimination Requirements.—

(1) In general.—Except as otherwise provided in this subsection, a plan meets the requirements of this subsection only if—

(A) each class of benefits under the plan is provided under a classification of employees which is set forth in the plan and which is found by the Secretary not to be discriminatory in favor of employees who are highly compensated individuals, and

(B) in the case of each class of benefits, such benefits do not discriminate in favor of employees who are highly compensated individuals.

A life insurance, disability, severance pay, or supplemental unemployment compensation benefit shall not be considered to fail to meet the requirements of subparagraph (B) merely because the benefits available bear a uniform relationship to the total compensation, or the basic or regular rate of compensation, of employees covered by the plan.

(2) Exclusion of certain employees.—For purposes of paragraph (1), there may be excluded from consideration—

(A) employees who have not completed 3 years of service,

(B) employees who have not attained age 21,

(C) seasonal employees or less than half-time employees,

(D) employees not included in the plan who are included in a unit of employees covered by an agreement between employee representatives and 1 or more employers which the Secretary finds to be a collective bargaining agreement if the class of benefits involved was the subject of good faith bargaining between such employee representatives and such employer or employers, and

(E) employees who are nonresident aliens and who receive no earned income (within the meaning of section 911(d)(2)) from the employer which constitutes income from sources within the United States (within the meaning of section 861(a)(3)).

(3) Application of subsection where other nondiscrimination rules provided.—In the case of any benefit for which a provision of this chapter other than this subsection provides nondiscrimination rules, paragraph (1) shall not apply but the requirements of this subsection shall be met only if the nondiscrimination rules so provided are satisfied with respect to such benefit.

(4) Aggregation rules.—At the election of the employer, 2 or more plans of such employer may be treated as 1 plan for purposes of this subsection.

(5) Highly compensated individual.—For purposes of this subsection, the determination as to whether an individual is a highly compensated individual shall be made under rules similar to the rules for determining whether an individual is a highly compensated employee (within the meaning of section 414(q)).

(6) Compensation.—For purposes of this subsection, the term "compensation" has the meaning given such term by section 414(s).

(7) Compensation limit.—A plan shall not be treated as meeting the requirements of this subsection unless under the plan the annual compensation of each employee taken into account for any year does not exceed $200,000. The Secretary shall adjust the $200,000 amount at the same time, and by the same amount, as any adjustment under section 401(a)(17)(B). This paragraph shall not apply in determining whether the requirements of section 79(d) are met.

(c) Requirement That Organization Notify Secretary That It Is Applying for Tax-Exempt Status.—

(1) In general.—An organization shall not be treated as an organization described in paragraph (9), (17), or (20) of section 501(c)—

(A) unless it has given notice to the Secretary, in such manner as the Secretary may by regulation prescribe, that it is applying for recognition of such status, or

(B) for any period before the giving of such notice, if such notice is given after the time prescribed by the Secretary by regulations for giving notice under this subsection.

(2) Special rule for existing organizations.—In the case of any organization in existence on July 18, 1984, the time for giving notice under paragraph (1) shall not expire before the date 1 year after such date of the enactment.

Recent Amendments to IRC §505

Pension Protection Act of 2006 (Pub. L. No. 109-280), as follows:

● **Sunset Provision.** Act §811, provides:
    SEC. 811. PENSIONS AND INDIVIDUAL RETIREMENT ARRANGEMENT PROVISIONS OF ECONOMIC GROWTH AND TAX RELIEF RECONCILIATION ACT OF 2001 MADE PERMANENT.
    Title IX of the Economic Growth and Tax Relief Reconciliation Act of 2001 [Pub. L. No. 107-16] shall not apply to the provisions of, and amendments made by, subtitles A through F [§§601–666] of title VI of such Act (relating to pension and individual retirement arrangement provisions).

Economic Growth and Tax Relief Reconciliation Act of 2001 (Pub. L. No. 107-16), as follows:

● IRC §505(b)(7) was amended by Act §611(c)(1) by replacing "$150,000" each place it appeared with "$200,000". Eff. years beginning after Dec. 31, 2001. [*Ed. Note*: see Act §611(i)(3) for a special rule.]

● **Sunset Provision.** Act §901, as amended by Pub. L. No. 111-312, §101(a)(1), provides the sunset rule below. But see Pub. L. No. 109-280, §811, and Pub. L. No. 111-148, §10909(c), as amended by Pub. L. No. 111-312, §101(b)(1).
    SEC. 901. SUNSET OF PROVISIONS OF ACT.
    (a) In general. All provisions of, and amendments made by, this Act shall not apply—
    (1) to taxable, plan, or limitation years beginning after December 31, 2012, or
    (2) in the case of title V, to estates of decedents dying, gifts made, or generation skipping transfers, after December 31, 2012.

(b) Application of certain laws.—The Internal Revenue Code of 1986 and the Employee Retirement Income Security Act of 1974 shall be applied and administered to years, estates, gifts, and transfers described in subsection (a) as if the provisions and amendments described in subsection (a) had never been enacted.

* * *

Part III—Taxation of Business Income of Certain Exempt Organizations

SEC. 511. IMPOSITION OF TAX ON UNRELATED BUSINESS INCOME OF CHARITABLE, ETC., ORGANIZATIONS.

(a) Charitable, etc., Organizations Taxable at Corporation Rates.—

(1) Imposition of tax. There is hereby imposed for each taxable year on the unrelated business taxable income (as defined in section 512) of every organization described in paragraph (2) a tax computed as provided in section 11. In making such computation for purposes of this section, the term "taxable income" as used in section 11 shall be read as "unrelated business taxable income".

(2) Organizations subject to tax.

(A) Organizations described in sections 401(a) and 501(c).—The tax imposed by paragraph (1) shall apply in the case of any organization (other than a trust described in subsection (b) or an organization described in section 501(c)(1)) which is exempt, except as provided in this part or part II (relating to private foundations), from taxation under this subtitle by reason of section 501(a).

(B) State colleges and universities.—The tax imposed by paragraph (1) shall apply in the case of any college or university which is an agency or instrumentality of any government or any political subdivision thereof, or which is owned or operated by a government or any political subdivision thereof, or by any agency or instrumentality of one or more governments or political subdivisions. Such tax shall also apply in the case of any corporation wholly owned by one or more such colleges or universities.

(b) Tax on Charitable, etc., Trusts.—

(1) Imposition of tax.—There is hereby imposed for each taxable year on the unrelated business taxable income of every trust described in paragraph (2) a tax computed as provided in section 1(e). In making such computation for purposes of this section, the term "taxable income" as used in section 1 shall be read as "unrelated business taxable income" as defined in section 512.

(2) Charitable, etc., trusts subject to tax.—The tax imposed by paragraph (1) shall apply in the case of any trust which is exempt, except as provided in this part or part II (relating to private foundations),

from taxation under this subtitle by reason of section 501(a) and which, if it were not for such exemption, would be subject to subchapter J (section 641 and following, relating to estates, trusts, beneficiaries, and decedents).

(c) Special Rule for section 501(c)(2) Corporations.—If a corporation described in section 501(c)(2)—

(1) pays any amount of its net income for a taxable year to an organization exempt from taxation under section 501(a) (or which would pay such an amount but for the fact that the expenses of collecting its income exceed its income), and

(2) such corporation and such organization file a consolidated return for the taxable year, such corporation shall be treated, for purposes of the tax imposed by subsection (a), as being organized and operated for the same purposes as such organization, in addition to the purposes described in section 501(c)(2).

SEC. 512. UNRELATED BUSINESS TAXABLE INCOME.

(a) Definition.—For purposes of this title—

(1) General rule.—Except as otherwise provided in this subsection, the term "unrelated business taxable income" means the gross income derived by any organization from any unrelated trade or business (as defined in section 513) regularly carried on by it, less the deductions allowed by this chapter which are directly connected with the carrying on of such trade or business, both computed with the modifications provided in subsection (b).

(2) Special rule for foreign organizations.—In the case of an organization described in section 511 which is a foreign organization, the unrelated business taxable income shall be—

(A) its unrelated business taxable income which is derived from sources within the United States and which is not effectively connected with the conduct of a trade or business within the United States, plus

(B) its unrelated business taxable income which is effectively connected with the conduct of a trade or business within the United States.

(3) Special rules applicable to organizations described in paragraph (7), (9), (17), or (20) of section 501(c).—

(A) General rule.—In the case of an organization described in paragraph (7), (9), (17), or (20) of section 501(c), the term "unrelated business taxable income" means the gross income (excluding any exempt function income), less the deductions allowed by this chapter which are directly connected with the production of the gross income (excluding exempt function income), both computed with the modifications provided in paragraphs (6), (10), (11), and (12) of subsection (b). For purposes of the preceding sentence, the deductions provided by sections 243, 244, and 245 (relating to dividends received by corporations) shall be treated as not directly connected with the production of gross income.

(B) Exempt function income.—For purposes of subparagraph (A), the term "exempt function income" means the gross income from dues, fees, charges, or similar amounts paid by members of the organization as consideration for providing such members or their dependents or guests goods, facilities, or services in furtherance of the purposes constituting the basis for the exemption of the organization to which such income is paid. Such term also means all income (other than an amount equal to the gross income derived from any unrelated trade or business regularly carried on by such organization computed as if the organization were subject to paragraph (1)), which is set aside—

(i) for a purpose specified in section 170(c)(4), or

(ii) in the case of an organization described in paragraph (9), (17), or (20) of section 501(c), to provide for the payment of life, sick, accident, or other benefits, including reasonable costs of administration directly connected with a purpose described in clause (i) or (ii). If during the taxable year, an amount which is attributable to income so set aside is used for a purpose other than that described in clause (i) or (ii), such amount shall be included, under subparagraph (A), in unrelated business taxable income for the taxable year.

(C) Applicability to certain corporations described in section 501(c)(2).—In the case of a corporation described in section 501(c)(2), the income of which is payable to an organization described in paragraph (7), (9), (17), or (20) of section 501(c), subparagraph (A) shall apply as if such corporation were the organization to which the income is payable. For purposes of the preceding sentence, such corporation shall be treated as having exempt function income for a taxable year only if it files a consolidated return with such organization for such year.

(D) Nonrecognition of gain.—If property used directly in the performance of the exempt function of an organization described in paragraph (7), (9), (17), or (20) of section 501(c) is sold by such organization, and within a period beginning 1 year before the date of such sale, and ending 3 years after such date, other property is purchased and used by such organization directly in the performance of its exempt function, gain (if any) from such sale shall be recognized only to the extent that such organization's sales price of the old property exceeds the organization's cost of purchasing the other property. For purposes of this subparagraph,

the destruction in whole or in part, theft, seizure, requisition, or condemnation of property, shall be treated as the sale of such property, and rules similar to the rules provided by subsections (b), (c), (e), and (j) of section 1034 (as in effect on the day before the date of the enactment of the Taxpayer Relief Act of 1997) shall apply.

(E) Limitation on amount of set aside in the case of organizations described in paragraph (9), (17), or (20) of section 501(c).—

(i) In general.—In the case of any organization described in paragraph (9), (17), or (20) of section 501(c), a set-aside for any purpose specified in clause (ii) of subparagraph (B) may be taken into account under subparagraph (B) only to the extent that such set-aside does not result in an amount of assets set aside for such purpose in excess of the account limit determined under section 419A (without regard to subsection (f)(6) thereof) for the taxable year (not taking into account any reserve described in section 419A(c)(2)(A) for post-retirement medical benefits).

(ii) Treatment of existing reserves for post-retirement medical or life insurance benefits.—

(I) Clause (i) shall not apply to any income attributable to an existing reserve for post-retirement medical or life insurance benefits.

(II) For purposes of subclause (I), the term "reserve for post-retirement medical or life insurance benefits" means the greater of the amount of assets set aside for purposes of post-retirement medical or life insurance benefits to be provided to covered employees as of the close of the last plan year ending before the date of the enactment of the Tax Reform Act of 1984 or on July 18, 1984.

(III) All payments during plan years ending on or after the date of the enactment of the Tax Reform Act of 1984 of post-retirement medical benefits or life insurance benefits shall be charged against the reserve referred to in subclause (II). Except to the extent provided in regulations prescribed by the Secretary, all plans of an employer shall be treated as 1 plan for purposes of the preceding sentence.

(iii) Treatment of tax exempt organizations.— This subparagraph shall not apply to any organization if substantially all of the contributions to such organization are made by employers who were exempt from tax under this chapter throughout the 5-taxable year period ending with the taxable year in which the contributions are made.

(4) Special rule applicable to organizations described in section 501(c)(19).—In the case of an organization described in section 501(c)(19), the term "unrelated business taxable income" does not include any amount attributable to payments for life, sick, accident, or health insurance with respect to members of such organizations or their dependents which is set aside for the purpose of providing for the payment of insurance benefits or for a purpose specified in section 170(c)(4). If an amount set aside under the preceding sentence is used during the taxable year for a purpose other than a purpose described in the preceding sentence, such amount shall be included, under paragraph (1), in unrelated business taxable income for the taxable year.

(5) Definition of payments with respect to securities loans.—

(A) The term "payments with respect to securities loans" includes all amounts received in respect of a security (as defined in section 1236(c)) transferred by the owner to another person in a transaction to which section 1058 applies (whether or not title to the security remains in the name of the lender) including—

(i) amounts in respect of dividends, interest, or other distributions,

(ii) fees computed by reference to the period beginning with the transfer of securities by the owner and ending with the transfer of identical securities back to the transferor by the transferee and the fair market value of the security during such period,

(iii) income from collateral security for such loan, and

(iv) income from the investment of collateral security.

(B) Subparagraph (A) shall apply only with respect to securities transferred pursuant to an agreement between the transferor and the transferee which provides for—

(i) reasonable procedures to implement the obligation of the transferee to furnish to the transferor, for each business day during such period, collateral with a fair market value not less than the fair market value of the security at the close of business on the preceding business day,

(ii) termination of the loan by the transferor upon notice of not more than 5 business days, and

(iii) return to the transferor of securities identical to the transferred securities upon termination of the loan.

(b) Modifications.—The modifications referred to in subsection (a) are the following:

(1) There shall be excluded all dividends, interest, payments with respect to securities loans (as defined in subsection (a)(5)), amounts received or accrued as consideration for entering into agreements to make loans, and annuities, and all deductions directly connected with such income.

(2) There shall be excluded all royalties (including overriding royalties) whether measured by production or by gross or taxable income from the property, and all deductions directly connected with such income.

(3) In the case of rents—

(A) Except as provided in subparagraph (B), there shall be excluded—

(i) all rents from real property (including property described in section 1245(a)(3)(C)), and

(ii) all rents from personal property (including for purposes of this paragraph as personal property any property described in section 1245(a)(3)(B)) leased with such real property, if the rents attributable to such personal property are an incidental amount of the total rents received or accrued under the lease, determined at the time the personal property is placed in service.

(B) Subparagraph (A) shall not apply—

(i) if more than 50 percent of the total rent received or accrued under the lease is attributable to personal property described in subparagraph (A)(ii), or

(ii) if the determination of the amount of such rent depends in whole or in part on the income or profits derived by any person from the property leased (other than an amount based on a fixed percentage or percentages of receipts or sales).

(C) There shall be excluded all deductions directly connected with rents excluded under subparagraph (A).

(4) Notwithstanding paragraph (1), (2), (3), or (5), in the case of debt-financed property (as defined in section 514) there shall be included, as an item of gross income derived from an unrelated trade or business, the amount ascertained under section 514(a)(1), and there shall be allowed, as a deduction, the amount ascertained under section 514(a)(2).

(5) There shall be excluded all gains or losses from the sale, exchange, or other disposition of property other than—

(A) stock in trade or other property of a kind which would properly be includible in inventory if on hand at the close of the taxable year, or

(B) property held primarily for sale to customers in the ordinary course of the trade or business.

There shall also be excluded all gains or losses recognized, in connection with the organization's investment activities, from the lapse or termination of options to buy or sell securities (as defined in section 1236(c)) or real property and all gains or losses from the forfeiture of good-faith deposits (that are consistent with established business practice) for the purchase, sale, or lease of real property in connection with the organization's investment activities. This paragraph shall not apply with respect to the cutting of timber which is considered, on the application of section 631, as a sale or exchange of such timber.

(6) The net operating loss deduction provided in section 172 shall be allowed, except that—

(A) the net operating loss for any taxable year, the amount of the net operating loss carryback or carryover to any taxable year, and the net operating loss deduction for any taxable year shall be determined under section 172 without taking into account any amount of income or deduction which is excluded under this part in computing the unrelated business taxable income; and

(B) the terms "preceding taxable year" and "preceding taxable years" as used in section 172 shall not include any taxable year for which the organization was not subject to the provisions of this part.

(7) There shall be excluded all income derived from research for (A) the United States, or any of its agencies or instrumentalities, or (B) any State or political subdivision thereof; and there shall be excluded all deductions directly connected with such income.

(8) In the case of a college, university, or hospital, there shall be excluded all income derived from research performed for any person, and all deductions directly connected with such income.

(9) In the case of an organization operated primarily for purposes of carrying on fundamental research the results of which are freely available to the general public, there shall be excluded all income derived from research performed for any person, and all deductions directly connected with such income.

(10) In the case of any organization described in section 511(a), the deduction allowed by section 170 (relating to charitable etc. contributions and gifts) shall be allowed (whether or not directly connected with the carrying on of the trade or business), but shall not exceed 10 percent of the unrelated business taxable income computed without the benefit of this paragraph.

(11) In the case of any trust described in section 511(b), the deduction allowed by section 170 (relating to charitable etc. contributions and gifts) shall be allowed (whether or not directly connected with the carrying on of the trade or business), and for such purpose a distribution made by the trust to a beneficiary described in section 170 shall be considered as a gift or contribution. The deduction allowed by this paragraph shall be allowed with the limitations prescribed in section 170(b)(1)(A) and (B) determined with reference to the unrelated business taxable income computed without the benefit of this paragraph (in lieu of with reference to adjusted gross income).

(12) Except for purposes of computing the net operating loss under section 172 and paragraph (6), there shall be allowed a specific deduction of $1,000. In the case of a diocese, province of a religious order, or a convention or association of churches, there shall also be allowed, with respect to each parish, individual church, district, or other local unit, a specific deduction equal to the lower of—

(A) $1,000, or

(B) the gross income derived from any unrelated trade or business regularly carried on by such local unit.

(13) Special rules for certain amounts received from controlled entities.—

(A) In general.—If an organization (in this paragraph referred to as the "controlling organization") receives or accrues (directly or indirectly) a specified payment from another entity which it controls (in this paragraph referred to as the "controlled entity"), notwithstanding paragraphs (1), (2), and (3), the controlling organization shall include such payment as an item of gross income derived from an unrelated trade or business to the extent such payment reduces the net unrelated income of the controlled entity (or increases any net unrelated loss of the controlled entity). There shall be allowed all deductions of the controlling organization directly connected with amounts treated as derived from an unrelated trade or business under the preceding sentence.

(B) Net unrelated income or loss.—For purposes of this paragraph—

(i) Net unrelated income.—The term "net unrelated income" means—

(I) in the case of a controlled entity which is not exempt from tax under section 501(a), the portion of such entity's taxable income which would be unrelated business taxable income if such entity were exempt from tax under section 501(a) and had the same exempt purposes as the controlling organization, or

(II) in the case of a controlled entity which is exempt from tax under section 501(a), the amount of the unrelated business taxable income of the controlled entity.

(ii) Net unrelated loss.—The term "net unrelated loss" means the net operating loss adjusted under rules similar to the rules of clause (i).

(C) Specified payment.—For purposes of this paragraph, the term "specified payment" means any interest, annuity, royalty, or rent.

(D) Definition of control.—For purposes of this paragraph—

(i) Control.—The term "control" means—

(I) in the case of a corporation, ownership (by vote or value) of more than 50 percent of the stock in such corporation,

(II) in the case of a partnership, ownership of more than 50 percent of the profits interests or capital interests in such partnership, or

(III) in any other case, ownership of more than 50 percent of the beneficial interests in the entity.

IRC Sec. 512(b)(6)

(ii) Constructive ownership.—Section 318 (relating to constructive ownership of stock) shall apply for purposes of determining ownership of stock in a corporation. Similar principles shall apply for purposes of determining ownership of interests in any other entity.

(E) Paragraph to apply only to certain excess payments.—

(i) In general.—Subparagraph (A) shall apply only to the portion of a qualifying specified payment received or accrued by the controlling organization that exceeds the amount which would have been paid or accrued if such payment met the requirements prescribed under section 482.

(ii) Addition to tax for valuation misstatements.—The tax imposed by this chapter on the controlling organization shall be increased by an amount equal to 20 percent of the larger of—

(I) such excess determined without regard to any amendment or supplement to a return of tax, or

(II) such excess determined with regard to all such amendments and supplements.

(iii) Qualifying specified payment.—The term "qualifying specified payment" means a specified payment which is made pursuant to—

(I) a binding written contract in effect on the date of the enactment of this subparagraph, or

(II) a contract which is a renewal, under substantially similar terms, of a contract described in subclause (I).

> ### *Editor's Note*
>
> IRC §512(b)(13)(E)(iv), below, was amended by Pub. L. No. 111-312, applicable to payments received or accrued after December 31, 2009.

(iv) Termination.—This subparagraph shall not apply to payments received or accrued after ~~December 31, 2009~~ *December 31, 2011.*

(F) Related persons.—The Secretary shall prescribe such rules as may be necessary or appropriate to prevent avoidance of the purposes of this paragraph through the use of related persons.

(14) [Repealed.]

(15) Except as provided in paragraph (4), in the case of a trade or business—

(A) which consists of providing services under license issued by a Federal regulatory agency,

(B) which is carried on by a religious order or by an educational organization described in section 170(b)(1)(A)(ii) maintained by such religious order, and which was so carried on before May 27, 1959, and

(C) less than 10 percent of the net income of which for each taxable year is used for activities which are not related to the purpose constituting the basis for the religious order's exemption,

there shall be excluded all gross income derived from such trade or business and all deductions directly connected with the carrying on of such trade or business, so long as it is established to the satisfaction of the Secretary that the rates or other charges for such services are competitive with rates or other charges charged for similar services by persons not exempt from taxation.

(16) (A) Notwithstanding paragraph (5)(B), there shall be excluded all gains or losses from the sale, exchange, or other disposition of any real property described in subparagraph (B) if—

(i) such property was acquired by the organization from—

(I) a financial institution described in section 581 or 591(a) which is in conservatorship or receivership, or

(II) the conservator or receiver of such an institution (or any government agency or corporation succeeding to the rights or interests of the conservator or receiver),

(ii) such property is designated by the organization within the 9-month period beginning on the date of its acquisition as property held for sale, except that not more than one-half (by value determined as of such date) of property acquired in a single transaction may be so designated,

(iii) such sale, exchange, or disposition occurs before the later of—

(I) the date which is 30 months after the date of the acquisition of such property, or

(II) the date specified by the Secretary in order to assure an orderly disposition of property held by persons described in subparagraph (A), and

(iv) while such property was held by the organization, the aggregate expenditures on improvements and development activities included in the basis of the property are (or were) not in excess of 20 percent of the net selling price of such property.

(B) Property is described in this subparagraph if it is real property which—

(i) was held by the financial institution at the time it entered into conservatorship or receivership, or

(ii) was foreclosure property (as defined in section 514(c)(9)(H)(v)) which secured indebtedness held by the financial institution at such time.

For purposes of this subparagraph, real property includes an interest in a mortgage.

(17) Treatment of certain amounts derived from foreign corporations.—

(A) In general.—Notwithstanding paragraph (1), any amount included in gross income under section 951(a)(1)(A) shall be included as an item of gross income derived from an unrelated trade or business to the extent the amount so included is attributable to insurance income (as defined in section 953) which, if derived directly by the organization, would be treated as gross income from an unrelated trade or business. There shall be allowed all deductions directly connected with amounts included in gross income under the preceding sentence.

(B) Exception.—

(i) In general.—Subparagraph (A) shall not apply to income attributable to a policy of insurance or reinsurance with respect to which the person (directly or indirectly) insured is—

(I) such organization,

(II) an affiliate of such organization which is exempt from tax under section 501(a), or

(III) a director or officer of, or an individual who (directly or indirectly) performs services for, such organization or affiliate but only if the insurance covers primarily risks associated with the performance of services in connection with such organization or affiliate.

(ii) Affiliate.—For purposes of this subparagraph—

(I) In general.—The determination as to whether an entity is an affiliate of an organization shall be made under rules similar to the rules of section 168(h)(4)(B).

(II) Special rule.—Two or more organizations (and any affiliates of such organizations) shall be treated as affiliates if such organizations are colleges or universities described in section 170(b)(1)(A)(ii) or organizations described in section 170(b)(1)(A)(iii) and participate in an insurance arrangement that provides for any profits from such arrangement to be returned to the policyholders in their capacity as such.

(C) Regulations.—The Secretary shall prescribe such regulations as may be necessary or appropriate to carry out the purposes of this paragraph, including regulations for the application of this paragraph in the case of income paid through 1 or more entities or between 2 or more chains of entities.

* * *

(c) Special Rules for Partnerships.—

(1) In general.—If a trade or business regularly carried on by a partnership of which an organization is a member is an unrelated trade or business with respect to such organization, such organization in computing its unrelated business taxable income shall, subject to the exceptions, additions, and limitations contained in subsection (b), include its share (whether or not distributed) of the gross income of the partnership from such unrelated trade or business and its share of the partnership deductions directly connected with such gross income.

(2) Special rule where partnership year is different from organization's year.—If the taxable year of the organization is different from that of the partnership, the amounts to be included or deducted in computing the unrelated business taxable income under paragraph (1) shall be based upon the income and deductions of the partnership for any taxable year of the partnership ending within or with the taxable year of the organization.

(d) Treatment of Dues of Agricultural or Horticultural Organizations.—

(1) In general.—If—

(A) an agricultural or horticultural organization described in section 501(c)(5) requires annual dues to be paid in order to be a member of such organization, and

(B) the amount of such required annual dues does not exceed $100,

in no event shall any portion of such dues be treated as derived by such organization from an unrelated trade or business by reason of any benefits or privileges to which members of such organization are entitled.

(2) Indexation of $100 amount.—In the case of any taxable year beginning in a calendar year after 1995, the $100 amount in paragraph (1) shall be increased by an amount equal to—

(A) $100, multiplied by

(B) the cost-of-living adjustment determined under section 1(f)(3) for the calendar year in which the taxable year begins, by substituting "calendar year 1994" for "calendar year 1992" in subparagraph (B) thereof.

(3) Dues.—For purposes of this subsection, the term "dues" means any payment (whether or not designated as dues) which is required to be made in order to be recognized by the organization as a member of the organization.

(e) Special Rules Applicable to S Corporations.—

(1) In general.—If an organization described in section 1361(c)(2)(A)(vi) or section 1361(c)(6) holds stock in an S corporation—

(A) such interest shall be treated as an interest in an unrelated trade or business; and

(B) notwithstanding any other provision of this part—

(i) all items of income, loss, or deduction taken into account under section 1366(a), and

(ii) any gain or loss on the disposition of the stock in the S corporation

shall be taken into account in computing the unrelated business taxable income of such organization.

(2) Basis reduction.—Except as provided in regulations, for purposes of paragraph (1), the basis of any stock acquired by purchase (as defined in section 1361(e)(1)(C)) shall be reduced by the amount of any dividends received by the organization with respect to the stock.

(3) Exception for ESOPs.—This subsection shall not apply to employer securities (within the meaning of section 409(*l*)) held by an employee stock ownership plan described in section 4975(e)(7).

Recent Amendments to IRC §512 (as Excerpted)

Tax Relief, Unemployment Insurance Reauthorization, and Job Creation Act of 2010 (Pub. L. No. 111-312), as follows:
● IRC §512(b)(13)(E)(iv) was amended by Act §747(a) by striking "December 31, 2009" and inserting "December 31, 2011". Eff. for payments received or accrued after Dec. 31, 2009.

Tax Extenders and Alternative Minimum Tax Relief Act of 2008 (Pub. L. No. 110-343), as follows:
● IRC §512(b)(13)(E)(iv) was amended by Act, Div. C, §306(a) by striking "December 31, 2007" and inserting "December 31, 2009". Eff. for payments received or accrued after Dec. 31, 2007.

Pension Protection Act of 2006 (Pub. L. No. 109-290), as follows:
● IRC §512(b)(13) was amended by Act §1205(a) by redesignating subpara. (E) as subpara. (F), and by inserting new subpara. (E). Eff. for payments received or accrued after Dec. 31, 2005.

Gulf Opportunity Zone Act of 2005 (Pub. L. No. 109-135), as follows:
● IRC §512(b)(1) was amended by Act §412(dd) by replacing "§512(a)(5)" with "subsection (a)(5)". Eff. Dec. 21, 2005.
● IRC §512(b) was amended by Act §412(ee)(1)(A)–(B) by redesignating para. (18) as para. (19). Eff. Dec. 21, 2005.

American Job Creation Act of 2004 (Pub. L. No. 108-357), as follows:
● IRC §512(b) was amended by Act §319(c) by adding new para. (18). Eff. tax years beginning after Oct. 22, 2004.
● IRC §512(b) was amended by Act §702(a) by adding new para. (18)[(19)]. Eff. for any gain or loss on the sale, exchange, or other disposition of any property acquired by the taxpayer after Dec. 31, 2004. [*Ed. Note*: see Act §702(c) for a special rule.]
● IRC §512(e)(1) was amended by Act §233(d) by inserting "1361(c)(2)(A)(vi) or" before "1361(c)(6)". Eff. Oct. 22, 2004.

SEC. 513. UNRELATED TRADE OR BUSINESS.

(a) General Rule.—The term "unrelated trade or business" means, in the case of any organization subject to the tax imposed by section 511, any trade or business the conduct of which is not substantially related (aside from the need of such organization for income or funds or the use it makes of the profits derived) to the exercise or performance by such organization of its charitable, educational, or other purpose or function constituting the basis for its exemption under section 501 (or, in the case of an organization described in section 511(a)(2)(B), to the exercise or performance of any purpose or function described in section 501(c)(3)), except that such term does not include any trade or business—

(1) in which substantially all the work in carrying on such trade or business is performed for the organization without compensation; or

(2) which is carried on, in the case of an organization described in section 501(c)(3) or in the case of a college or university described in section 511(a)(2)(B), by the organization primarily for the convenience of its members, students, patients, officers, or employees, or, in the case of a local association of employees described in section 501(c)(4) organized before May 27, 1969, which is the selling by the organization of items of work-related clothes and equipment and items normally sold through vending machines, through food dispensing facilities, or by snack bars, for the convenience of its members at their usual places of employment; or

(3) which is the selling of merchandise, substantially all of which has been received by the organization as gifts or contributions.

(b) Special Rule for Trusts.—The term "unrelated trade or business" means, in the case of—

(1) a trust computing its unrelated business taxable income under section 512 for purposes of section 681; or

(2) a trust described in section 401(a), or section 501(c)(17), which is exempt from tax under section 501(a); any trade or business regularly carried on by such trust or by a partnership of which it is a member.

(c) Advertising, etc., Activities.—For purposes of this section, the term "trade or business" includes any activity which is carried on for the production of income from the sale of goods or the performance of services. For purposes of the preceding sentence, an activity does not lose identity as a trade or business merely because it is carried on within a larger aggregate of similar activities or within a larger complex of other endeavors which may, or may not, be related to the exempt purposes of the organization. Where an activity carried on for profit constitutes an unrelated trade or business, no part of such trade or business shall be excluded from such classification merely because it does not result in profit.

(d) Certain Activities of Trade Shows, State Fairs, etc.—

(1) General rule.—The term "unrelated trade or business" does not include qualified public entertainment activities of an organization described in paragraph (2)(C), or qualified convention and trade show activities of an organization described in paragraph (3)(C).

(2) Qualified public entertainment activities.—For purposes of this subsection—

(A) Public entertainment activity.—The term "public entertainment activity" means any enter-

IRC Sec. 513(d)(2)(A)

tainment or recreational activity of a kind traditionally conducted at fairs or expositions promoting agricultural and educational purposes, including, but not limited to, any activity one of the purposes of which is to attract the public to fairs or expositions or to promote the breeding of animals or the development of products or equipment.

(B) Qualified public entertainment activity.—The term "qualified public entertainment activity" means a public entertainment activity which is conducted by a qualifying organization described in subparagraph (C) in—

(i) conjunction with an international, national, State, regional, or local fair or exposition,

(ii) accordance with the provisions of State law which permit the activity to be operated or conducted solely by such an organization, or by an agency, instrumentality, or political subdivision of such State, or

(iii) accordance with the provisions of State law which permit such an organization to be granted a license to conduct not more than 20 days of such activity on payment to the State of a lower percentage of the revenue from such licensed activity than the State requires from organizations not described in section 501(c)(3), (4), or (5).

(C) Qualifying organization.—For purposes of this paragraph, the term "qualifying organization" means an organization which is described in section 501(c)(3), (4), or (5) which regularly conducts, as one of its substantial exempt purposes, an agricultural and educational fair or exposition.

(3) Qualified convention and trade show activities.—

(A) Convention and trade show activities.—The term "convention and trade show activity" means any activity of a kind traditionally conducted at conventions, annual meetings, or trade shows, including, but not limited to, any activity one of the purposes of which is to attract persons in an industry generally (without regard to membership in the sponsoring organization) as well as members of the public to the show for the purpose of displaying industry products or to stimulate interest in, and demand for, industry products or services, or to educate persons engaged in the industry in the development of new products and services or new rules and regulations affecting the industry.

(B) Qualified convention and trade show activity.—The term "qualified convention and trade show activity" means a convention and trade show activity carried out by a qualifying organization described in subparagraph (C) in conjunction with an international, national, State, regional, or local convention, annual meeting, or show conducted by an organization described in subparagraph (C) if

one of the purposes of such organization in sponsoring the activity is the promotion and stimulation of interest in, and demand for, the products and services of that industry in general or to educate persons in attendance regarding new developments or products and services related to the exempt activities of the organization, and the show is designed to achieve such purpose through the character of the exhibits and the extent of the industry products displayed.

(C) Qualifying organization.—For purposes of this paragraph, the term "qualifying organization" means an organization described in section 501(c)(3), (4), (5), or (6) which regularly conducts as one of its substantial exempt purposes a show which stimulates interest in, and demand for, the products of a particular industry or segment of such industry or which educates persons in attendance regarding new developments or products and services related to the exempt activities of the organization.

(4) Such activities not to affect exempt status.— An organization described in section 501(c)(3), (4), or (5) shall not be considered as not entitled to the exemption allowed under section 501(a) solely because of qualified public entertainment activities conducted by it.

(e) Certain Hospital Services.—In the case of a hospital described in section 170(b)(1)(A)(iii), the term "unrelated trade or business" does not include the furnishing of one or more of the services described in section 501(e)(1)(A) to one or more hospitals described in section 170(b)(1)(A)(iii) if—

(1) such services are furnished solely to such hospitals which have facilities to serve not more than 100 inpatients;

(2) such services, if performed on its own behalf by the recipient hospital, would constitute activities in exercising or performing the purpose or function constituting the basis for its exemption; and

(3) such services are provided at a fee or cost which does not exceed the actual cost of providing such services, such cost including straight line depreciation and a reasonable amount for return on capital goods used to provide such services.

(f) Certain Bingo Games.—

(1) In general.—The term "unrelated trade or business" does not include any trade or business which consists of conducting bingo games.

(2) Bingo game defined.—For purposes of paragraph (1), the term "bingo game" means any game of bingo—

(A) of a type in which usually—

(i) the wagers are placed,

(ii) the winners are determined, and

(iii) the distribution of prizes or other property is made, in the presence of all persons placing wagers in such game,

(B) the conducting of which is not an activity ordinarily carried out on a commercial basis, and

(C) the conducting of which does not violate any State or local law.

(g) Certain Pole Rentals.—In the case of a mutual or cooperative telephone or electric company, the term "unrelated trade or business" does not include engaging in qualified pole rentals (as defined in section 501(c)(12)(D)).

(h) Certain Distributions of Low Cost Articles Without Obligation to Purchase and Exchanges and Rentals of Member Lists.—

(1) In general.—In the case of an organization which is described in section 501 and contributions to which are deductible under paragraph (2) or (3) of section 170(c), the term "unrelated trade or business" does not include—

(A) activities relating to the distribution of low cost articles if the distribution of such articles is incidental to the solicitation of charitable contributions, or

(B) any trade or business which consists of—

(i) exchanging with another such organization names and addresses of donors to (or members of) such organization, or

(ii) renting such names and addresses to another such organization.

(2) Low cost article defined.—For purposes of this subsection—

(A) In general.—The term "low cost article" means any article which has a cost not in excess of $5 to the organization which distributes such item (or on whose behalf such item is distributed).

(B) Aggregation rule.—If more than 1 item is distributed by or on behalf of an organization to a single distributee in any calendar year, the aggregate of the items so distributed in such calendar year to such distributee shall be treated as 1 article for purposes of subparagraph (A).

(C) Indexation of $5 amount.—In the case of any taxable year beginning in a calendar year after 1987, the $5 amount in subparagraph (A) shall be increased by an amount equal to—

(i) $5, multiplied by

(ii) the cost-of-living adjustment determined under section 1(f)(3) for the calendar year in which the taxable year begins by substituting "calendar year 1987" for "calendar year 1992" in subparagraph (B) thereof.

(3) Distribution which is incidental to the solicitation of charitable contributions described.—For purposes of this subsection, any distribution of low cost articles by an organization shall be treated as a distribution incidental to the solicitation of charitable contributions only if—

(A) such distribution is not made at the request of the distributee,

(B) such distribution is made without the express consent of the distributee, and

(C) the articles so distributed are accompanied by—

(i) a request for a charitable contribution (as defined in section 170(c)) by the distributee to such organization, and

(ii) a statement that the distributee may retain the low cost article regardless of whether such distributee makes a charitable contribution to such organization.

(i) Treatment of Certain Sponsorship Payments.—

(1) In general.—The term "unrelated trade or business" does not include the activity of soliciting and receiving qualified sponsorship payments.

(2) Qualified sponsorship payments.—For purposes of this subsection—

(A) In general.—The term "qualified sponsorship payment" means any payment made by any person engaged in a trade or business with respect to which there is no arrangement or expectation that such person will receive any substantial return benefit other than the use or acknowledgment of the name or logo (or product lines) of such person's trade or business in connection with the activities of the organization that receives such payment. Such a use or acknowledgment does not include advertising such person's products or services (including messages containing qualitative or comparative language, price information, or other indications of savings or value, an endorsement, or an inducement to purchase, sell, or use such products or services).

(B) Limitations.—

(i) Contingent payments.—The term "qualified sponsorship payment" does not include any payment if the amount of such payment is contingent upon the level of attendance at one or more events, broadcast ratings, or other factors indicating the degree of public exposure to one or more events.

(ii) Safe harbor does not apply to periodicals and qualified convention and trade show activities.—The term "qualified sponsorship payment" does not include—

(I) any payment which entitles the payor to the use or acknowledgment of the name or logo (or product lines) of the payor's trade or business in

IRC Sec. 513(i)(2)(B)(ii)(I)

regularly scheduled and printed material published by or on behalf of the payee organization that is not related to and primarily distributed in connection with a specific event conducted by the payee organization, or

(II) any payment made in connection with any qualified convention or trade show activity (as defined in subsection (d)(3)(B)).

(3) Allocation of portions of single payment.— For purposes of this subsection, to the extent that a portion of a payment would (if made as a separate payment) be a qualified sponsorship payment, such portion of such payment and the other portion of such payment shall be treated as separate payments.

(j) Debt Management Plan Services.—The term "unrelated trade or business" includes the provision of debt management plan services (as defined in section 501(q)(4)(B)) by any organization other than an organization which meets the requirements of section 501(q).

Recent Amendments to IRC §513

Pension Protection Act of 2006 (Pub. L. No. 109-290), as follows:
• IRC §513 was amended by Act §1220(b) by adding new subsec. (j). Eff. generally for tax years beginning after Aug. 17, 2006. [*Ed. Note:* see Act §1220(c)(2) for a transition rule.]

SEC. 514. UNRELATED DEBT-FINANCED INCOME.

(a) Unrelated Debt-Financed Income and Deductions.—In computing under section 512 the unrelated business taxable income for any taxable year—

(1) Percentage of income taken into account.— There shall be included with respect to each debt-financed property as an item of gross income derived from an unrelated trade or business an amount which is the same percentage (but not in excess of 100 percent) of the total gross income derived during the taxable year from or on account of such property as (A) the average acquisition indebtedness (as defined in subsection (c)(7)) for the taxable year with respect to the property is of (B) the average amount (determined under regulations prescribed by the Secretary) of the adjusted basis of such property during the period it is held by the organization during such taxable year.

(2) Percentage of deductions taken into account.—There shall be allowed as a deduction with respect to each debt-financed property an amount determined by applying (except as provided in the last sentence of this paragraph) the percentage derived under paragraph (1) to the sum determined under paragraph (3). The percentage derived under this paragraph shall not be applied with respect to the deduction of any capital loss resulting from the car-

ryback or carryover of net capital losses under section 1212.

(3) Deductions allowable.—The sum referred to in paragraph (2) is the sum of the deductions under this chapter which are directly connected with the debt-financed property or the income therefrom, except that if the debt-financed property is of a character which is subject to the allowance for depreciation provided in section 167, the allowance shall be computed only by use of the straight-line method.

(b) Definition of Debt-Financed Property.—

(1) In general.—For purposes of this section, the term "debt-financed property" means any property which is held to produce income and with respect to which there is an acquisition indebtedness (as defined in subsection (c)) at any time during the taxable year (or, if the property was disposed of during the taxable year, with respect to which there was an acquisition indebtedness at any time during the 12-month period ending with the date of such disposition), except that such term does not include—

(A) (i) any property substantially all the use of which is substantially related (aside from the need of the organization for income or funds) to the exercise or performance by such organization of its charitable, educational, or other purpose or function constituting the basis for its exemption under section 501 (or, in the case of an organization described in section 511(a)(2)(B), to the exercise or performance of any purpose or function designated in section 501(c)(3)), or

(ii) any property to which clause (i) does not apply, to the extent that its use is so substantially related;

(B) except in the case of income excluded under section 512(b)(5), any property to the extent that the income from such property is taken into account in computing the gross income of any unrelated trade or business;

(C) any property to the extent that the income from such property is excluded by reason of the provisions of paragraph (7), (8), or (9) of section 512(b) in computing the gross income of any unrelated trade or business;

(D) any property to the extent that it is used in any trade or business described in paragraph (1), (2), or (3) of section 513(a); or

(E) any property the gain or loss from the sale, exchange, or other disposition of which would be excluded by reason of the provisions of section 512(b)(19) in computing the gross income of any unrelated trade or business.

For purposes of subparagraph (A), substantially all the use of a property shall be considered to be substantially related to the exercise or performance by an organization of its charitable, educational, or other purpose or function constituting the basis for its exemption under section 501 if such property is real property subject to a lease to a medical clinic entered into primarily for purposes which are substantially related (aside from the need of such organization for income or funds or the use it makes of the rents derived) to the exercise or performance by such organization of its charitable, educational, or other purpose or function constituting the basis for its exemption under section 501.

(2) Special rule for related uses.—For purposes of applying paragraphs (1)(A), (C), and (D), the use of any property by an exempt organization which is related to an organization shall be treated as use by such organization.

(3) Special rules when land is acquired for exempt use within 10 years.—

(A) Neighborhood land.—If an organization acquires real property for the principal purpose of using the land (commencing within 10 years of the time of acquisition) in the manner described in paragraph (1)(A) and at the time of acquisition the property is in the neighborhood of other property owned by the organization which is used in such manner, the real property acquired for such future use shall not be treated as debt-financed property so long as the organization does not abandon its intent to so use the land within the 10-year period. The preceding sentence shall not apply for any period after the expiration of the 10-year period, and shall apply after the first 5 years of the 10-year period only if the organization establishes to the satisfaction of the Secretary that it is reasonably certain that the land will be used in the described manner before the expiration of the 10-year period.

(B) Other cases.—If the first sentence of subparagraph (A) is inapplicable only because—

(i) the acquired land is not in the neighborhood referred to in subparagraph (A), or

(ii) the organization (for the period after the first 5 years of the 10-year period) is unable to establish to the satisfaction of the Secretary that it is reasonably certain that the land will be used in the manner described in paragraph (1)(A) before the expiration of the 10-year period, but the land is converted to such use by the organization within the 10-year period, the real property (subject to the provisions of subparagraph (D)) shall not be treated as debt-financed property for any period before such conversion. For purposes of this subparagraph, land shall not be treated as used in the manner described in paragraph (1)(A) by reason of the use made of any structure which was on the land when acquired by the organization.

(C) Limitations.—Subparagraphs (A) and (B)—

(i) shall apply with respect to any structure on the land when acquired by the organization, or to the land occupied by the structure, only if (and so long as) the intended future use of the land in the manner described in paragraph (1)(A) requires that the structure be demolished or removed in order to use the land in such manner;

(ii) shall not apply to structures erected on the land after the acquisition of the land; and

(iii) shall not apply to property subject to a lease which is a business lease (as defined in this section immediately before the enactment of the Tax Reform Act of 1976).

(D) Refund of taxes when subparagraph (B) applies.—If an organization for any taxable year has not used land in the manner to satisfy the actual use condition of subparagraph (B) before the time prescribed by law (including extensions thereof) for filing the return for such taxable year, the tax for such year shall be computed without regard to the application of subparagraph (B), but if and when such use condition is satisfied, the provisions of subparagraph (B) shall then be applied to such taxable year. If the actual use condition of subparagraph (B) is satisfied for any taxable year after such time for filing the return, and if credit or refund of any overpayment for the taxable year resulting from the satisfaction of such use condition is prevented at the close of the taxable year in which the use condition is satisfied, by the operation of any law or rule of law (other than chapter 74, relating to closing agreements and compromises), credit or refund of such overpayment may nevertheless be allowed or made if claim therefor is filed before the expiration of 1 year after the close of the taxable year in which the use condition is satisfied.

(E) Special rule for churches.—In applying this paragraph to a church or convention or association of churches, in lieu of the 10-year period referred to in subparagraphs (A) and (B) a 15-year period shall be applied, and subparagraphs (A) and (B)(ii) shall apply whether or not the acquired land meets the neighborhood test.

(c) Acquisition Indebtedness.—

(1) General rule. For purposes of this section, the term "acquisition indebtedness" means, with respect to any debt-financed property, the unpaid amount of—

(A) the indebtedness incurred by the organization in acquiring or improving such property;

(B) the indebtedness incurred before the acquisition or improvement of such property if such indebtedness would not have been incurred but for such acquisition or improvement; and

(C) the indebtedness incurred after the acquisition or improvement of such property if such indebtedness would not have been incurred but for such

IRC Sec. 514(c)(1)(C)

acquisition or improvement and the incurrence of such indebtedness was reasonably foreseeable at the time of such acquisition or improvement.

(2) Property acquired subject to mortgage, etc.—For purposes of this subsection—

(A) General rule.—Where property (no matter how acquired) is acquired subject to a mortgage or other similar lien, the amount of the indebtedness secured by such mortgage or lien shall be considered as an indebtedness of the organization incurred in acquiring such property even though the organization did not assume or agree to pay such indebtedness.

(B) Exceptions.—Where property subject to a mortgage is acquired by an organization by bequest or devise, the indebtedness secured by the mortgage shall not be treated as acquisition indebtedness during a period of 10 years following the date of the acquisition. If an organization acquires property by gift subject to a mortgage which was placed on the property more than 5 years before the gift, which property was held by the donor more than 5 years before the gift, the indebtedness secured by such mortgage shall not be treated as acquisition indebtedness during a period of 10 years following the date of such gift. This subparagraph shall not apply if the organization, in order to acquire the equity in the property by bequest, devise, or gift, assumes and agrees to pay the indebtedness secured by the mortgage, or if the organization makes any payment for the equity in the property owned by the decedent or the donor.

(C) Liens for taxes or assessments.—Where State law provides that—

(i) a lien for taxes, or

(ii) a lien for assessments, made by a State or a political subdivision thereof attaches to property prior to the time when such taxes or assessments become due and payable, then such lien shall be treated as similar to a mortgage (within the meaning of subparagraph (A)) but only after such taxes or assessments become due and payable and the organization has had an opportunity to pay such taxes or assessments in accordance with State law.

(3) Extension of obligations.—For purposes of this section, an extension, renewal, or refinancing of an obligation evidencing a pre-existing indebtedness shall not be treated as the creation of a new indebtedness.

(4) Indebtedness incurred in performing exempt purpose.—For purposes of this section, the term "acquisition indebtedness" does not include indebtedness the incurrence of which is inherent in the performance or exercise of the purpose or function constituting the basis of the organization's exemption, such as the indebtedness incurred by a credit union described in section 501(c)(14) in accepting deposits from its members.

(5) Annuities.—For purposes of this section, the term "acquisition indebtedness" does not include an obligation to pay an annuity which—

(A) is the sole consideration (other than a mortgage to which paragraph (2)(B) applies) issued in exchange for property if, at the time of the exchange, the value of the annuity is less than 90 percent of the value of the property received in the exchange,

(B) is payable over the life of one individual in being at the time the annuity is issued, or over the lives of two individuals in being at such time, and

(C) is payable under a contract which—

(i) does not guarantee a minimum amount of payments or specify a maximum amount of payments, and

(ii) does not provide for any adjustment of the amount of the annuity payments by reference to the income received from the transferred property or any other property.

(6) Certain Federal financing.—

(A) In general.—For purposes of this section, the term "acquisition indebtedness" does not include—

(i) an obligation, to the extent that it is insured by the Federal Housing Administration, to finance the purchase, rehabilitation, or construction of housing for low and moderate income persons, or

(ii) indebtedness incurred by a small business investment company licensed after the date of the enactment of the American Jobs Creation Act of 2004 under the Small Business Investment Act of 1958 if such indebtedness is evidenced by a debenture—

(I) issued by such company under section 303(a) of such Act, and

(II) held or guaranteed by the Small Business Administration.

(B) Limitation.—Subparagraph (A)(ii) shall not apply with respect to any small business investment company during any period that—

(i) any organization which is exempt from tax under this title (other than a governmental unit) owns more than 25 percent of the capital or profits interest in such company, or

(ii) organizations which are exempt from tax under this title (including governmental units other than any agency or instrumentality of the United States) own, in the aggregate, 50 percent or more of the capital or profits interest in such company.

(7) Average acquisition indebtedness.—For purposes of this section, the term "average acquisition indebtedness" for any taxable year with respect to a debt-financed property means the average amount, determined under regulations prescribed by the Secretary of the acquisition indebtedness during the period the property is held by the organization during the taxable year, except that for the purpose of computing the percentage of any gain or loss to be taken into account on a sale or other disposition of debt-financed property, such term means the highest amount of the acquisition indebtedness with respect to such property during the 12-month period ending with the date of the sale or other disposition.

(8) Securities subject to loans.—For purposes of this section—

(A) payments with respect to securities loans (as defined in section 512(a)(5)) shall be deemed to be derived from the securities loaned and not from collateral security or the investment of collateral security from such loans,

(B) any deductions which are directly connected with collateral security for such loan, or with the investment of collateral security, shall be deemed to be deductions which are directly connected with the securities loaned, and

(C) an obligation to return collateral security shall not be treated as acquisition indebtedness (as defined in paragraph (1)).

(9) Real property acquired by a qualified organization.—

(A) In general.—Except as provided in subparagraph (B), the term "acquisition indebtedness" does not, for purposes of this section, include indebtedness incurred by a qualified organization in acquiring or improving any real property. For purposes of this paragraph, an interest in a mortgage shall in no event be treated as real property.

(B) Exceptions.—The provisions of subparagraph (A) shall not apply in any case in which—

(i) the price for the acquisition or improvement is not a fixed amount determined as of the date of the acquisition or the completion of the improvement;

(ii) the amount of any indebtedness or any other amount payable with respect to such indebtedness, or the time for making any payment of any such amount, is dependent, in whole or in part, upon any revenue, income, or profits derived from such real property;

(iii) the real property is at any time after the acquisition leased by the qualified organization to the person selling such property to such organization or to any person who bears a relationship described in section 267(b) or 707(b) to such person;

(iv) the real property is acquired by a qualified trust from, or is at any time after the acquisition leased by such trust to, any person who—

(I) bears a relationship which is described in subparagraph (C), (E), or (G) of section 4975(e)(2) to any plan with respect to which such trust was formed, or

(II) bears a relationship which is described in subparagraph (F) or (H) of section 4975(e)(2) to any person described in subclause (I);

(v) any person described in clause (iii) or (iv) provides the qualified organization with financing in connection with the acquisition or improvement; or

(vi) the real property is held by a partnership unless the partnership meets the requirements of clauses (i) through (v) and unless—

(I) all of the partners of the partnership are qualified organizations,

(II) each allocation to a partner of the partnership which is a qualified organization is a qualified allocation (within the meaning of section 168(h)(6)), or

(III) such partnership meets the requirements of subparagraph (E).

For purposes of subclause (I) of clause (vi), an organization shall not be treated as a qualified organization if any income of such organization is unrelated business taxable income.

(C) Qualified organization.—For purposes of this paragraph, the term "qualified organization" means—

(i) an organization described in section 170(b)(1)(A)(ii) and its affiliated support organizations described in section 509(a)(3);

(ii) any trust which constitutes a qualified trust under section 401;

(iii) an organization described in section 501(c)(25); or

(iv) a retirement income account described in section 403(b)(9).

(D) Other pass-thru entities; tiered entities.—Rules similar to the rules of subparagraph (B)(vi) shall also apply in the case of any pass-thru entity other than a partnership and in the case of tiered partnerships and other entities.

(E) Certain allocations permitted.—

(i) In general.—A partnership meets the requirements of this subparagraph if—

(I) the allocation of items to any partner which is a qualified organization cannot result in such partner having a share of the overall partnership income for any taxable year greater than such partner's share of the overall partnership loss for the taxable year for which such partner's loss share will be the smallest, and

IRC Sec. 514(c)(9)(E)(i)(I)

(II) each allocation with respect to the partnership has substantial economic effect within the meaning of section 704(b)(2).

For purposes of this clause, items allocated under section 704(c) shall not be taken into account.

(ii) Special rules.—

(I) Chargebacks.—Except as provided in regulations, a partnership may without violating the requirements of this subparagraph provide for chargebacks with respect to disproportionate losses previously allocated to qualified organizations and disproportionate income previously allocated to other partners. Any chargeback referred to in the preceding sentence shall not be at a ratio in excess of the ratio under which the loss or income (as the case may be) was allocated.

(II) Preferred rates of return, etc.—To the extent provided in regulations, a partnership may without violating the requirements of this subparagraph provide for reasonable preferred returns or reasonable guaranteed payments.

(iii) Regulations.—The Secretary shall prescribe such regulations as may be necessary to carry out the purposes of this subparagraph, including regulations which may provide for exclusion or segregation of items.

(F) Special rules for organizations described in section 501(c)(25).—

(i) In general.—In computing under section 512 the unrelated business taxable income of a disqualified holder of an interest in an organization described in section 501(c)(25), there shall be taken into account—

(I) as gross income derived from an unrelated trade or business, such holder's pro rata share of the items of income described in clause (ii)(I) of such organization, and

(II) as deductions allowable in computing unrelated business taxable income, such holder's pro rata share of the items of deduction described in clause (ii)(II) of such organization.

Such amounts shall be taken into account for the taxable year of the holder in which (or with which) the taxable year of such organization ends.

(ii) Description of amounts.—For purposes of clause (i)—

(I) gross income is described in this clause to the extent such income would (but for this paragraph) be treated under subsection (a) as derived from an unrelated trade or business, and

(II) any deduction is described in this clause to the extent it would (but for this paragraph) be allowable under subsection (a)(2) in computing unrelated business taxable income.

(iii) Disqualified holder.—For purposes of this subparagraph, the term "disqualified holder" means any shareholder (or beneficiary) which is not described in clause (i) or (ii) of subparagraph (C).

(G) Special rules for purposes of the exceptions.—Except as otherwise provided by regulations—

(i) Small leases disregarded.—For purposes of clauses (iii) and (iv) of subparagraph (B), a lease to a person described in such clause (iii) or (iv) shall be disregarded if no more than 25 percent of the leasable floor space in a building (or complex of buildings) is covered by the lease and if the lease is on commercially reasonable terms.

(ii) Commercially reasonable financing.—Clause (v) of subparagraph (B) shall not apply if the financing is on commercially reasonable terms.

(H) Qualifying sales by financial institutions.—

(i) In general.—In the case of a qualifying sale by a financial institution, except as provided in regulations, clauses (i) and (ii) of subparagraph (B) shall not apply with respect to financing provided by such institution for such sale.

(ii) Qualifying sale.—For purposes of this clause, there is a qualifying sale by a financial institution if—

(I) a qualified organization acquires property described in clause (iii) from a financial institution and any gain recognized by the financial institution with respect to the property is ordinary income,

(II) the stated principal amount of the financing provided by the financial institution does not exceed the amount of the outstanding indebtedness (including accrued but unpaid interest) of the financial institution with respect to the property described in clause (iii) immediately before the acquisition referred to in clause (iii) or (v), whichever is applicable, and

(III) the present value (determined as of the time of the sale and by using the applicable Federal rate determined under section 1274(d)) of the maximum amount payable pursuant to the financing that is determined by reference to the revenue, income, or profits derived from the property cannot exceed 30 percent of the total purchase price of the property (including the contingent payments).

(iii) Property to which subparagraph applies.—Property is described in this clause if such property is foreclosure property, or is real property which—

(I) was acquired by the qualified organization from a financial institution which is in conservatorship or receivership, or from the conservator or receiver of such an institution, and

(II) was held by the financial institution at the time it entered into conservatorship or receivership.

(iv) Financial institution.—For purposes of this subparagraph, the term "financial institution" means—

(I) any financial institution described in section 581 or 591(a),

(II) any other corporation which is a direct or indirect subsidiary of an institution referred to in subclause (I) but only if, by virtue of being affiliated with such institution, such other corporation is subject to supervision and examination by a Federal or State agency which regulates institutions referred to in subclause (I), and

(III) any person acting as a conservator or receiver of an entity referred to in subclause (I) or (II) (or any government agency or corporation succeeding to the rights or interest of such person).

(v) Foreclosure property.—For purposes of this subparagraph, the term "foreclosure property" means any real property acquired by the financial institution as the result of having bid on such property at foreclosure, or by operation of an agreement or process of law, after there was a default (or a default was imminent) on indebtedness which such property secured.

(d) Basis of Debt-Financed Property Acquired in Corporate Liquidation.—For purposes of this subtitle, if the property was acquired in a complete or partial liquidation of a corporation in exchange for its stock, the basis of the property shall be the same as it would be in the hands of the transferor corporation, increased by the amount of gain recognized to the transferor corporation upon such distribution and by the amount of any gain to the organization which was included, on account of such distribution, in unrelated business taxable income under subsection (a).

(e) Allocation Rules.—Where debt-financed property is held for purposes described in subsection (b)(1)(A), (B), (C), or (D) as well as for other purposes, proper allocation shall be made with respect to basis, indebtedness, and income and deductions. The allocations required by this section shall be made in accordance with regulations prescribed by the Secretary to the extent proper to carry out the purposes of this section.

(f) Personal Property Leased With Real Property.—For purposes of this section, the term "real property" includes personal property of the lessor leased by it to a lessee of its real estate if the lease of such personal property is made under, or in connection with, the lease of such real estate.

(g) Regulations.—The Secretary shall prescribe such regulations as may be necessary or appropriate to carry out the purposes of this section, including regulations to prevent the circumvention of any provision of this section through the use of segregated asset accounts.

Recent Amendments to IRC §514

Pension Protection Act of 2006 (Pub. L. No. 109-290), as follows:
● IRC §514(c)(9)(C) was amended by Act §866(a) by striking "or" after cl. (ii), by replacing the period at the end of cl. (iii) with "; or", and by inserting new cl. (iv). Eff. for tax years beginning on or after Aug. 17, 2006.

Gulf Opportunity Zone Act of 2005 (Pub. L. No. 109-135), as follows:
● IRC §514(b)(1)(E) was amended by Act §412(ee)(2) by replacing "§512(b)(18)" with "§512(b)(19)". Eff. Dec. 21, 2005.

American Job Creation Act of 2004 (Pub. L. No. 108-357), as follows:
● IRC §514(b)(1) was amended by Act §702(b) by striking "or" at the end of subpara. (C), by replacing the period at the end of subpara. (D) with "; or", and by inserting new subpara. (E). Eff. for any gain or loss on the sale, exchange, or other disposition of any property acquired by the taxpayer after Dec. 31, 2004. [*Ed. Note:* see Act §702(c) for a special rule.]
● IRC §514(c)(6) was amended by Act §247(a). Eff. for indebtedness incurred after Oct. 22, 2004, by a small business investment company licensed after Oct. 22, 2004. IRC §514(c)(6) prior to amendment:

(6) Certain Federal financing.—For purposes of this section, the term "acquisition indebtedness" does not include an obligation, to the extent that it is insured by the Federal Housing Administration, to finance the purchase, rehabilitation, or construction of housing for low and moderate income persons.

---

* * *

Part VIII—Higher Education Savings Entities

SEC. 529. QUALIFIED TUITION PROGRAMS.

(a) General Rule.—A qualified tuition program shall be exempt from taxation under this subtitle. Notwithstanding the preceding sentence, such program shall be subject to the taxes imposed by section 511 (relating to imposition of tax on unrelated business income of charitable organizations).

(b) Qualified Tuition Program.—For purposes of this section—

(1) In general.—The term "qualified tuition program" means a program established and maintained by a State or agency or instrumentality thereof or by 1 or more eligible educational institutions—

(A) under which a person—

(i) may purchase tuition credits or certificates on behalf of a designated beneficiary which entitle the beneficiary to the waiver or payment of qualified higher education expenses of the beneficiary, or

(ii) in the case of a program established and maintained by a State or agency or instrumentality thereof, may make contributions to an account which is established for the purpose of meeting the qualified higher education expenses of the designated beneficiary of the account, and

(B) which meets the other requirements of this subsection.

Except to the extent provided in regulations, a program established and maintained by 1 or more eligible educational institutions shall not be treated as a qualified tuition program unless such program provides that amounts are held in a qualified trust and such program has received a ruling or determination that such program meets the applicable requirements for a qualified tuition program. For purposes of the preceding sentence, the term "qualified trust" means a trust which is created or organized in the United States for the exclusive benefit of designated beneficiaries and with respect to which the requirements of paragraphs (2) and (5) of section 408(a) are met.

(2) Cash contributions.—A program shall not be treated as a qualified tuition program unless it provides that purchases or contributions may only be made in cash.

(3) Separate accounting.—A program shall not be treated as a qualified tuition program unless it provides separate accounting for each designated beneficiary.

(4) No investment direction.—A program shall not be treated as a qualified tuition program unless it provides that any contributor to, or designated beneficiary under, such program may not directly or indirectly direct the investment of any contributions to the program (or any earnings thereon).

(5) No pledging of interest as security.—A program shall not be treated as a qualified tuition program if it allows any interest in the program or any portion thereof to be used as security for a loan.

(6) Prohibition on excess contribu-tions.—A program shall not be treated as a qualified tuition program unless it provides adequate safeguards to prevent contributions on behalf of a designated beneficiary in excess of those necessary to provide for the qualified higher education expenses of the beneficiary.

(c) Tax Treatment of Designated Beneficiaries and Contributors.—

(1) In general.—Except as otherwise provided in this subsection, no amount shall be includible in gross income of—

(A) a designated beneficiary under a qualified tuition program, or

(B) a contributor to such program on behalf of a designated beneficiary,

with respect to any distribution or earnings under such program.

(2) Gift tax treatment of contributions.—For purposes of chapters 12 and 13—

(A) In general.—Any contribution to a qualified tuition program on behalf of any designated beneficiary—

(i) shall be treated as a completed gift to such beneficiary which is not a future interest in property, and

(ii) shall not be treated as a qualified transfer under section 2503(e).

(B) Treatment of excess contributions.—If the aggregate amount of contributions described in subparagraph (A) during the calendar year by a donor exceeds the limitation for such year under section 2503(b), such aggregate amount shall, at the election of the donor, be taken into account for purposes of such section ratably over the 5-year period beginning with such calendar year.

(3) Distributions.—

(A) In general.—Any distribution under a qualified tuition program shall beincludible in the gross income of the distributee in the manner as provided under section 72 to the extent not excluded from gross income under any other provision of this chapter.

(B) Distributions for qualified higher education expenses.—For purposes of this paragraph—

(i) In-kind distributions.—No amount shall be includible in gross income under subparagraph (A) by reason of a distribution which consists of providing a benefit to the distributee which, if paid for by the distributee, would constitute payment of a qualified higher education expense.

(ii) Cash distributions.—In the case of distributions not described in clause (i), if—

(I) such distributions do not exceed the qualified higher education expenses (reduced by expenses described in clause (i)), no amount shall be includible in gross income, and

(II) in any other case, the amount otherwise includible in gross income shall be reduced by an amount which bears the same ratio to such amount as such expenses bear to such distributions.

(iii) Exception for institutional programs.—In the case of any taxable year beginning before January 1, 2004, clauses (i) and (ii) shall not apply with respect to any distribution during such taxable year under a qualified tuition program established and maintained by 1 or more eligible educational institutions.

(iv) Treatment as distributions.—Any benefit furnished to a designated beneficiary under a qualified tuition program shall be treated as a distribution to the beneficiary for purposes of this paragraph.

(v) Coordination with Hope and Lifetime Learning Credits.—The total amount of qualified higher education expenses with respect to an individual for the taxable year shall be reduced—

(I) as provided in section 25A(g)(2), and

(II) by the amount of such expenses which were taken into account in determining the credit allowed to the taxpayer or any other person under section 25A.

(vi) Coordination with Coverdell educational savings accounts.—If, with respect to an individual for any taxable year—

(I) the aggregate distributions to which clauses (i) and (ii) and section 530(d)(2)(A) apply, exceed

(II) the total amount of qualified higher education expenses otherwise taken into account under clauses (i) and (ii) (after the application of clause (v)) for such year,

the taxpayer shall allocate such expenses among such distributions for purposes of determining the amount of the exclusion under clauses (i) and (ii) and section 530(d)(2)(A).

(C) Change in beneficiaries or programs.—

(i) Rollovers.—Subparagraph (A) shall not apply to that portion of any distribution which, within 60 days of such distribution, is transferred—

(I) to another qualified tuition program for the benefit of the designated beneficiary, or

(II) to the credit of another designated beneficiary under a qualified tuition program who is a member of the family of the designated beneficiary with respect to which the distribution was made.

(ii) Change in designated beneficiaries.—Any change in the designated beneficiary of an interest in a qualified tuition program shall not be treated as a distribution for purposes of subparagraph (A) if the new beneficiary is a member of the family of the old beneficiary.

(iii) Limitation on certain rollovers.—Clause (i)(I) shall not apply to any transfer if such transfer occurs within 12 months from the date of a previous transfer to any qualified tuition program for the benefit of the designated beneficiary.

(D) Operating rules.—For purposes of applying section 72—

(i) to the extent provided by the Secretary, all qualified tuition programs of which an individual is a designated beneficiary shall be treated as one program,

(ii) except to the extent provided by the Secretary, all distributions during a taxable year shall be treated as one distribution, and

(iii) except to the extent provided by the Secretary, the value of the contract, income on the contract, and investment in the contract shall be computed as of the close of the calendar year in which the taxable year begins.

(4) Estate tax treatment.—

(A) In general.—No amount shall be includible in the gross estate of any individual for purposes of chapter 11 by reason of an interest in a qualified tuition program.

(B) Amounts includible in estate of designated beneficiary in certain cases.—Subparagraph (A) shall not apply to amounts distributed on account of the death of a beneficiary.

(C) Amounts includible in estate of donor making excess contributions.—In the case of a donor who makes the election described in paragraph (2)(B) and who dies before the close of the 5-year period referred to in such paragraph, notwithstanding subparagraph (A), the gross estate of the donor shall include the portion of such contributions properly allocable to periods after the date of death of the donor.

(5) Other gift tax rules.—For purposes of chapters 12 and 13—

(A) Treatment of distributions.—Except as provided in subparagraph (B), in no event shall a distribution from a qualified tuition program be treated as a taxable gift.

(B) Treatment of designation of new beneficiary.—The taxes imposed by chapters 12 and 13 shall apply to a transfer by reason of a change in the designated beneficiary under the program (or a rollover to the account of a new beneficiary) unless the new beneficiary is—

(i) assigned to the same generation as (or a higher generation than) the old beneficiary (determined in accordance with section 2651), and

(ii) a member of the family of the old beneficiary.

(6) Additional tax.—The tax imposed by section 530(d)(4) shall apply to any payment or distribution from a qualified tuition program in the same manner as such tax applied to a payment or distribution from a Coverdell education savings account. This paragraph shall not apply to any payment or distribution in any taxable year beginning before January 1, 2004, which is includible in gross income but used for qualified higher education expenses of the designated beneficiary.

(d) Reports.—Each officer or employee having control of the qualified tuition program or their designee shall make such reports regarding such program to the Secretary and to designated beneficiaries with respect to contributions, distributions, and such other matters as the Secretary may require. The reports required by this subsection shall be filed at such time and in such manner and furnished to such individuals at such time and in such manner as may be required by the Secretary.

(e) Other Definitions and Special Rules.—For purposes of this section—

(1) Designated beneficiary.—The term "designated beneficiary" means—

(A) the individual designated at the commencement of participation in the qualified tuition program as the beneficiary of amounts paid (or to be paid) to the program,

(B) in the case of a change in beneficiaries described in subsection (c)(3)(C), the individual who is the new beneficiary, and

(C) in the case of an interest in a qualified tuition program purchased by a State or local government (or agency or instrumentality thereof) or an organization described in section 501(c)(3) and exempt from taxation under section 501(a) as part of a scholarship program operated by such government or organization, the individual receiving such interest as a scholarship.

(2) Member of family.—The term "member of the family" means, with respect to any designated beneficiary—

(A) the spouse of such beneficiary;

(B) an individual who bears a relationship to such beneficiary which is described in subparagraphs (A) through (G) of section 152(d)(2);

(C) the spouse of any individual described in subparagraph (B); and

(D) any first cousin of such beneficiary.

(3) Qualified higher education expenses.—

(A) In general.—The term "qualified higher education expenses" means—

(i) tuition, fees, books, supplies, and equipment required for the enrollment or attendance of a designated beneficiary at an eligible educational institution;

(ii) expenses for special needs services in the case of a special needs beneficiary which are incurred in connection with such enrollment or attendance

(iii) expenses paid or incurred in 2009 or 2010 for the purchase of any computer technology or equipment (as defined in section 170(e)(6)(F)(i)) or Internet access and related services, if such technology, equipment, or services are to be used by the beneficiary and the beneficiary's family during any of the years the beneficiary is enrolled at an eligible educational institution.

Clause (iii) shall not include expenses for computer software designed for sports, games, or hobbies unless the software is predominantly educational in nature.

(B) Room and board included for students who are at least half-time.—

(i) In general.—In the case of an individual who is an eligible student (as defined in section 25A(b)(3)) for any academic period, such term shall also include reasonable costs for such period (as determined under the qualified tuition program) incurred by the designated beneficiary for room and board while attending such institution. For purposes of subsection (b)(6), a designated beneficiary shall be treated as meeting the requirements of this clause.

(ii) Limitation.—The amount treated as qualified higher education expenses by reason of clause (i) shall not exceed—

(I) the allowance (applicable to the student) for room and board included in the cost of attendance (as defined in section 472 of the Higher Education Act of 1965 (20 U.S.C. 1087*ll*), as in effect on the date of the enactment of the Economic Growth and Tax Relief Reconciliation Act of 2001) as determined by the eligible educational institution for such period, or

(II) if greater, the actual invoice amount the student residing in housing owned or operated by the eligible educational institution is charged by such institution for room and board costs for such period.

(4) Application of Section 514. An interest in a qualified tuition program shall not be treated as debt for purposes of section 514.

(5) Eligible educational institution.—The term "eligible educational institution" means an institution—

(A) which is described in section 481 of the Higher Education Act of 1965 (20 U.S.C. 1088), as in effect on the date of the enactment of this paragraph, and

(B) which is eligible to participate in a program under title IV of such Act.

(f) Regulations.—Notwithstanding any other provision of this section, the Secretary shall prescribe such regulations as may be necessary or appropriate to carry out the purposes of this section and to prevent abuse of such purposes, including regulations under chapters 11, 12, and 13 of this title.

Recent Amendments to IRC §529

American Recovery and Reinvestment Act of 2009 (Pub. L. No. 111-5), as follows:

● IRC §529(e)(3)(A)(i)–(iii) were amended by Act, Div. B, §1005(a) by striking "and" at the end of clause (i), striking the period at the end of clause (ii), and adding clause (iii) and the flush material at the end. Eff. for expenses paid or incurred after Dec. 31, 2008.

Pension Protection Act of 2006 (Pub. L. No. 109-280), as follows:

● IRC §529 was amended by Act §1304(b) by adding new subsec. (f). Eff. Aug. 17, 2006.

● **Other Provision.** Act §1304(a) provides:

    (a) Permanent Extension of Modifications.—Section 901 of the Economic Growth and Tax Relief Reconciliation Act of

2001 [Pub. L. No. 107-16] (relating to sunset provisions) shall not apply to section 402 of such Act (relating to modifications to qualified tuition programs).

Gulf Opportunity Zone Act of 2005 (Pub. L. No. 109-135), as follows:
• IRC §529(c)(6) was amended by Act §412(ee)(3) by replacing "education individual retirement account" with "Coverdell education savings account". Eff. Dec. 21, 2005.

Working Families Tax Relief Act of 2004 (Pub. L. No.108-311), as follows:
• IRC §529(c)(5)(B) was amended by Act §406(a). Eff. for transfers made after Oct. 5, 1997, as if included in the provision of Pub. L. No. 105-34 to which it relates. IRC §529(c)(5)(B) prior to amendment:
   (B) Treatment of designation of new beneficiary.—The taxes imposed by chapters 12 and 13 shall apply to a transfer by reason of a change in the designated beneficiary under the program (or a rollover to the account of a new beneficiary) only if the new beneficiary is a generation below the generation of the old beneficiary (determined in accordance with section 2651).
• IRC §529(e)(2)(B) was amended by Act §207(21) by replacing "paragraphs (1) through (8) of §152(a)" with "subparagraphs (A) through (G) of §152(d)(2)". Eff. tax years beginning after Dec. 31, 2004.

Job Creation and Worker Assistance Act of 2002 (Pub. L. No. 107-147), as follows:
• IRC §529(e)(3)(B)(i) was amended by Act §417(11) by replacing "subsection (b)(7)" with "subsection (b)(6)". Eff. Mar. 9, 2002.

Pub. L. No. 107-22, as follows:
• IRC §529(c)(3)(B)(vi) was amended by Act §1(b)(3)(C) in the heading by replacing "Education individual" with "Coverdell Education Savings". Eff. Jul. 26, 2001.

Economic Growth and Tax Relief Reconciliation Act of 2001 (Pub. L. No. 107-16), as follows:
• IRC §529 was amended by Act §402(a)(4)(D) in the heading by striking "STATE" following "QUALIFIED". Eff. tax years beginning after Dec. 31, 2001.
• IRC §529 was amended by Act §402(a)(4)(A) by replacing "qualified State tuition" each place it appeared with "qualified tuition". Eff. tax years beginning after Dec. 31, 2001.
• IRC §529(b) heading was amended by Act §402(a)(4)(C) by replacing "qualified state tuition" with "qualified tuition". Eff. tax years beginning after Dec. 31, 2001.
• IRC §529(b)(1) was amended by Act §402(a)(1) by inserting "or by 1 or more eligible educational institutions" after "maintained by a State or agency or instrumentality thereof" in the matter preceding subpara. (A), and by adding a new flush sentence at the end. Eff. tax years beginning after Dec. 31, 2001.
• IRC §529(b)(1)(A)(ii) was amended by Act §402(a)(2) by inserting "in the case of a program established and maintained by a State or agency or instrumentality thereof," before "may make". Eff. tax years beginning after Dec. 31, 2001.
• IRC §529 was amended by Act §402(a)(3)(A) by striking para. (3) and redesignating paras. (4) through (7) as paras. (3) through (6), respectively. Eff. tax years beginning after Dec. 31, 2001. IRC §529(b)(3) prior to being stricken:
   (3) Refunds.—A program shall not be treated as a qualified State tuition program unless it imposes a more than de minimis penalty on any refund of earnings from the account which are not—
   (A) used for qualified higher education expenses of the designated beneficiary,
   (B) made on account of the death or disability of the designated beneficiary, or
   (C) made on account of a scholarship (or allowance or payment described in section 135(d)(1)(B) or (C)) received by the designated beneficiary to the extent the amount of the refund does not exceed the amount of the scholarship, allowance, or payment.
• IRC §529(c)(3)(B) was amended by Act §402(b)(1). Eff. tax years beginning after Dec. 31, 2001. IRC §529(c)(3)(B) prior to amendment:
   (B) In-kind distributions.—Any benefit furnished to a designated beneficiary under a qualified tuition program shall be treated as a distribution to the beneficiary.

• IRC §529(c)(3)(C) was amended by Act §402(c)(3) by inserting in the heading "or programs" after "beneficiaries". Eff. tax years beginning after Dec. 31, 2001.
• IRC §529(c)(3)(C)(i) was amended by Act §402(c)(1) by replacing "transferred to the credit" with "transferred-(I) to another qualified tuition program for the benefit of the designated beneficiary, or (II) to the credit". Eff. tax years beginning after Dec. 31, 2001.
• IRC §529(c)(3)(C) was amended by Act §402(c)(2) by adding new cl. (iii). Eff. tax years beginning after Dec. 31, 2001.
• IRC §529(c)(3)(D)(ii) was amended by Act §402(g)(1) by inserting "except to the extent provided by the Secretary," before "all distributions". Eff. tax years beginning after Dec. 31, 2001.
• IRC §529(c)(3)(D)(iii) was amended by Act §402(g)(2) by inserting "except to the extent provided by the Secretary," before "the value". Eff. tax years beginning after Dec. 31, 2001.
• IRC §529(c) was amended by Act §402(a)(3)(B) by adding new para. (6). Eff. tax years beginning after Dec. 31, 2001.
• IRC §529(e)(2) was amended by Act §402(d) by striking "and" at the end of subpara. (B), by replacing the period at the end of subpara. (C) with "; and", and by adding new subpara. (D). Eff. tax years beginning after Dec. 31, 2001.
• IRC §529(e)(3)(A) was amended by Act §402(f). Eff. tax years beginning after Dec. 31, 2001. IRC §529(e)(3)(A) prior to amendment:
   (A) In general.—The term "qualified higher education expenses" means tuition, fees, books, supplies, and equipment required for the enrollment or attendance of a designated beneficiary at an eligible educational institution.
• IRC §529(e)(3)(B)(ii) was amended by Act §402(e). Eff. tax years beginning after Dec. 31, 2001. IRC §529(e)(3)(B)(ii) prior to amendment:
   (ii) Limitation.—The amount treated as qualified higher education expenses by reason of the preceding sentence shall not exceed the minimum amount (applicable to the student) included for room and board for such period in the cost of attendance (as defined in section 472 of the Higher Education Act of 1965, 20 U.S.C. 1087*ll*, as in effect on the date of the enactment of this paragraph) for the eligible educational institution for such period.
• Sunset Provision. Act §901, as amended by Pub. L. No. 111-312, §101(a)(1), provides the sunset rule below. But see Pub. L. No. 109-280, §811, and Pub. L. No. 111-148, §10909(c), as amended by Pub. L. No. 111-312, §101(b)(1).
   SEC. 901. SUNSET OF PROVISIONS OF ACT.
   (a) In general. All provisions of, and amendments made by, this Act shall not apply—
   (1) to taxable, plan, or limitation years beginning after December 31, 2012, or
   (2) in the case of title V, to estates of decedents dying, gifts made, or generation skipping transfers, after December 31, 2012.
   (b) Application of certain laws.—The Internal Revenue Code of 1986 and the Employee Retirement Income Security Act of 1974 shall be applied and administered to years, estates, gifts, and transfers described in subsection (a) as if the provisions and amendments described in subsection (a) had never been enacted.

SEC. 530. COVERDELL EDUCATION SAVINGS ACCOUNTS.

(a) General Rule.—A Coverdell education savings account shall be exempt from taxation under this subtitle. Notwithstanding the preceding sentence, the Coverdell education savings account shall be subject to the taxes imposed by section 511 (relating to imposition of tax on unrelated business income of charitable organizations).

(b) Definitions and Special Rules.—For purposes of this section—

(1) Coverdell education savings account.—The term "Coverdell education savings account" means a trust created or organized in the United States exclusively for the purpose of paying the qualified higher education expenses of an individual who is the designated beneficiary of the trust (and designated as a Coverdell education savings account at the time created or organized), but only if the written governing instrument creating the trust meets the following requirements:

(A) No contribution will be accepted—

(i) unless it is in cash,

(ii) after the date on which such beneficiary attains age 18, or

(iii) except in the case of rollover contributions, if such contribution would result in aggregate contributions for the taxable year exceeding $2,000.

(B) The trustee is a bank (as defined in section 408(n)) or another person who demonstrates to the satisfaction of the Secretary that the manner in which that person will administer the trust will be consistent with the requirements of this section or who has so demonstrated with respect to any individual retirement plan.

(C) No part of the trust assets will be invested in life insurance contracts.

(D) The assets of the trust shall not be commingled with other property except in a common trust fund or common investment fund.

(E) Except as provided in subsection (d)(7), any balance to the credit of the designated beneficiary on the date on which the beneficiary attains age 30 shall be distributed within 30 days after such date to the beneficiary or, if the beneficiary dies before attaining age 30, shall be distributed within 30 days after the date of death of such beneficiary.

The age limitations in subparagraphs (A)(ii) and (E), and paragraphs (5) and (6) of subsection (d), shall not apply to any designated beneficiary with special needs (as determined under regulations prescribed by the Secretary).

(2) Qualified education expenses.—

(A) In general.—The term "qualified education expenses" means—

(i) qualified higher education expenses (as defined in section 529(e)(3)), and

(ii) qualified elementary and secondary education expenses (as defined in paragraph (3)).

(B) Qualified tuition programs.—Such term shall include any contribution to a qualified tuition program (as defined in section 529(b)) on behalf of the designated beneficiary (as defined in section 529(e)(1)); but there shall be no increase in the investment in the contract for purposes of applying section 72 by reason of any portion of such contribution which is not includible in gross income by reason of subsection (d)(2).

(3) Qualified elementary and secondary education expenses.—

(A) In general.—The term "qualified elementary and secondary education expenses" means–

(i) expenses for tuition, fees, academic tutoring, special needs services in the case of a special needs beneficiary, books, supplies, and other equipment which are incurred in connection with the enrollment or attendance of the designated beneficiary of the trust as an elementary or secondary school student at a public, private, or religious school,

(ii) expenses for room and board, uniforms, transportation, and supplementary items and services (including extended day programs) which are required or provided by a public, private, or religious school in connection with such enrollment or attendance, and

(iii) expenses for the purchase of any computer technology or equipment (as defined in section 170(e)(6)(F)(i)) or Internet access and related services, if such technology, equipment, or services are to be used by the beneficiary and the beneficiary's family during any of the years the beneficiary is in school.

Clause (iii) shall not include expenses for computer software designed for sports, games, or hobbies unless the software is predominately educational in nature.

(B) School.—The term "school" means any school which provides elementary education or secondary education (kindergarten through grade 12), as determined under State law.

(4) Time when contributions deemed made.—An individual shall be deemed to have made a contribution to a Coverdell education savings account on the last day of the preceding taxable year if the contribution is made on account of such taxable year and is made not later than the time prescribed by law for filing the return for such taxable year (not including extensions thereof).

(c) Reduction in Permitted Contributions Based on Adjusted Gross Income.—

Editor's Note

Caution: IRC §530(c)(1), as follows, was amended by Pub. L. No. 107-16, §401(b)(1)–(2) and (e). For sunset provision, see the amendment notes to this section for Pub. L. No. 107-16.

---

(1) In general.—In the case of a contributor who is an individual, the maximum amount the contributor could otherwise make to an account under this section shall be reduced by an amount which bears the same ratio to such maximum amount as—

(A) the excess of—

(i) the contributor's modified adjusted gross income for such taxable year, over

(ii) $95,000 ($190,000 in the case of a joint return), bears to

(B) $15,000 ($30,000 in the case of a joint return).

(2) Modified adjusted gross income.—For purposes of paragraph (1), the term "modified adjusted gross income" means the adjusted gross income of the taxpayer for the taxable year increased by any amount excluded from gross income under section 911, 931, or 933.

(d) Tax Treatment of Distributions.—

(1) In general.—Any distribution shall be includible in the gross income of the distributee in the manner as provided in section 72.

Editor's Note

Caution: IRC §530(d)(2), as follows, was amended by Pub. L. No. 107-16, §401(c)(3)(A)–(B) and (g)(1), and by Pub. L. No. 108-311, §404(a), effective as if included in Pub. L. No. 107-16. For sunset provision, see the amendment notes to this section for Pub. L. No. 107-16.

---

(2) Distributions for qualified education expenses.—

(A) In general.—No amount shall be includible under paragraph (1) if the qualified education ex-

penses of the designated beneficiary during the taxable year are not less than the aggregate distributions during the taxable year.

(B) Distributions in excess of expenses.—If such aggregate distributions exceed such expenses during the taxable year, the amount includible in gross income under paragraph (1) shall be equal to the amount which bears the same ratio to the amount which would be includible in gross income under paragraph (1) (without regard to this subparagraph) as the qualified higher education expenses bear to such aggregate distributions.

(C) Coordination with Hope and Lifetime Learning credits and qualified tuition programs.—For purposes of subparagraph (A)—

(i) Credit coordination.—The total amount of qualified education expenses with respect to an individual for the taxable year shall be reduced—

(I) as provided in section 25A(g)(2), and

(II) by the amount of such expenses which were taken into account in determining the credit allowed to the taxpayer or any other person under section 25A.

(ii) Coordination with qualified tuition programs.—If, with respect to an individual for any taxable year.—

(I) the aggregate distributions during such year to which subparagraph (A) and section 529(c)(3)(B) apply, exceed

(II) the total amount of qualified education expenses (after the application of clause (i)) for such year,

the taxpayer shall allocate such expenses among such distributions for purposes of determining the amount of the exclusion under subparagraph (A) and section 529(c)(3)(B).

(D) Disallowance of excluded amounts as deduction, credit, or exclusion.—No deduction, credit, or exclusion shall be allowed to the taxpayer under any other section of this chapter for any qualified education expenses to the extent taken into account in determining the amount of the exclusion under this paragraph.

(3) Special rules for applying estate and gift taxes with respect to account.—Rules similar to the rules of paragraphs (2), (4), and (5) of section 529(c) shall apply for purposes of this section.

(4) Additional tax for distributions not used for educational expenses.—

(A) In general.—The tax imposed by this chapter for any taxable year on any taxpayer who receives a payment or distribution from a Coverdell education savings account which is includible in gross income shall be increased by 10 percent of the amount which is so includible.

IRC Sec. 530(d)(4)(A)

(B) Exceptions.—Subparagraph (A) shall not apply if the payment or distribution is—

(i) made to a beneficiary (or to the estate of the designated beneficiary) on or after the death of the designated beneficiary,

(ii) attributable to the designated beneficiary's being disabled (within the meaning of section 72(m)(7)),

(iii) made on account of a scholarship, allowance, or payment described in section 25A(g)(2) received by the designated beneficiary to the extent the amount of the payment or distribution does not exceed the amount of the scholarship, allowance, or payment,

(iv) made on account of the attendance of the designated beneficiary at the United States Military Academy, the United States Naval Academy, the United States Air Force Academy, the United States Coast Guard Academy, or the United States Merchant Marine Academy, to the extent that the amount of the payment or distribution does not exceed the costs of advanced education (as defined by section 2005(e)(3) of title 10, United States Code, as in effect on the date of the enactment of this section) attributable to such attendance, or

---

Editor's Note

Caution: Former IRC §530(d)(4)(B)(iv) was redesignated as IRC §530(d)(4)(B)(v) by Pub. L. No. 108-121, §107(a), and amended by Pub. L. No. 107-147, §411(f), effective as if included in Pub. L. No. 107-16. For sunset provision, see the amendment notes to this section for Pub. L. No. 107-16.

(v) an amount which is includible in gross income solely by application of paragraph (2)(C)(i)(II) for the taxable year.

Editor's Note

Caution: IRC §530(d)(4)(C) was amended by Pub. L. No. 107-16, §401(f)(2). For sunset provision, see the amendment notes to this section for Pub. L. No. 107-16.

(C) Contributions returned before certain date.—Subparagraph (A) shall not apply to the distribution of any contribution made during a taxable year on behalf of the designated beneficiary if—

(i) such distribution is made before the first day of the sixth month of the taxable year following the taxable year, and

(ii) such distribution is accompanied by the amount of net income attributable to such excess contribution.

Any net income described in clause (ii) shall be included in gross income for the taxable year in which such excess contribution was made.

(5) **Rollover contributions**.—Paragraph (1) shall not apply to any amount paid or distributed from a Coverdell education savings account to the extent that the amount received is paid, not later than the 60th day after the date of such payment or distribution, into another Coverdell education savings account for the benefit of the same beneficiary or a member of the family (within the meaning of section 529(e)(2)) of such beneficiary who has not attained age 30 as of such date. The preceding sentence shall not apply to any payment or distribution if it applied to any prior payment or distribution during the 12-month period ending on the date of the payment or distribution.

(6) **Change in beneficiary**.—Any change in the beneficiary of a Coverdell education savings account shall not be treated as a distribution for purposes of paragraph (1) if the new beneficiary is a member of the family (as so defined) of the old beneficiary and has not attained age 30 as of the date of such change.

(7) **Special rules for death and divorce**.—Rules similar to the rules of paragraphs (7) and (8) of section 220(f) shall apply. In applying the preceding sentence, members of the family (as so defined) of the designated beneficiary shall be treated in the same manner as the spouse under such paragraph (8).

(8) **Deemed distribution on required distribution date**.—In any case in which a distribution is required under subsection (b)(1)(E), any balance to the credit of a designated beneficiary as of the close of the 30-day period referred to in such subsection for making such distribution shall be deemed distributed at the close of such period.

(9) **Military death gratuity**.—

(A) In general.—For purposes of this section, the term "rollover contribution" includes a contribution to a Coverdell education savings account made before the end of the 1-year period beginning on the date on which the contributor receives an amount under section 1477 of title 10, United States Code, or section 1967 of title 38 of such Code, with respect to a person, to the extent that such contribution does not exceed—

(i) the sum of the amounts received during such period by such contributor under such sections with respect to such person, reduced by

(ii) the amounts so received which were contributed to a Roth IRA under section 408A(e)(2) or to another Coverdell education savings account.

(B) Annual limit on number of rollovers not to apply.—The last sentence of paragraph (5) shall not apply with respect to amounts treated as a rollover by the subparagraph (A).

(C) Application of section 72.—For purposes of applying section 72 in the case of a distribution which is includible in gross income under paragraph (1), the amount treated as a rollover by reason of subparagraph (A) shall be treated as investment in the contract.

(e) Tax Treatment of Accounts.—Rules similar to the rules of paragraphs (2) and (4) of section 408(e) shall apply to any Coverdell education savings account.

(f) Community Property Laws.—This section shall be applied without regard to any community property laws.

(g) Custodial Accounts.—For purposes of this section, a custodial account shall be treated as a trust if the assets of such account are held by a bank (as defined in section 408(n)) or another person who demonstrates, to the satisfaction of the Secretary, that the manner in which he will administer the account will be consistent with the requirements of this section, and if the custodial account would, except for the fact that it is not a trust, constitute an account described in subsection (b)(1). For purposes of this title, in the case of a custodial account treated as a trust by reason of the preceding sentence, the custodian of such account shall be treated as the trustee thereof.

(h) Reports.—The trustee of a Coverdell education savings account shall make such reports regarding such account to the Secretary and to the beneficiary of the account with respect to contributions, distributions, and such other matters as the Secretary may require. The reports required by this subsection shall be filed at such time and in such manner and furnished to such individuals at such time and in such manner as may be required.

Recent Amendments to IRC §530

Heroes Earnings Assistance and Relief Tax Act of 2008 (Pub. L. No. 110-245), as follows:
- IRC §530(d)(9) was added by Act §109(c). Eff. in general for deaths from injuries occurring on or after date of enactment [enacted: June 17, 2008].
- **Other Provision.** Act §109(d)(2) provides:
  (2) Application of amendments to deaths from injuries occurring on or after October 7, 2001, and before enactment.—
  The amendments made by this section shall apply to any contribution made pursuant to section 408A(e)(2) or 530(d)(5) of the Internal Revenue Code of 1986, as amended by this Act, with respect to amounts received under section 1477 of title 10, United States Code, or under section 1967 of title 38 of such Code, for deaths from injuries occurring on or after October 7, 2001, and before the date of the enactment of this Act if such contribution is made not later than 1 year after the date of the enactment of this Act.

Pension Protection Act of 2006 (Pub. L. No. 109-280), as follows:
- **Other Provision.** Act §1304(a) provides:
  (a) Permanent Extension of Modifications.—Section 901 of the Economic Growth and Tax Relief Reconciliation Act of 2001 [Pub. L. No. 107-16] (relating to sunset provisions) shall not apply to section 402 of such Act (relating to modifications to qualified tuition programs).

Gulf Opportunity Zone Act of 2005 (Pub. L. No. 109-135), as follows:

- IRC §530(b)(2)(A)(ii) was amended by Act §412(ff)(2) by replacing "paragraph (4)" with "paragraph (3)". Eff. Dec. 21, 2005.
- IRC §530(b) was amended by Act §412(ff)(1) by striking para. (3) and redesignating paras. (4) and (5) as paras. (3) and (4), respectively. Eff. Dec. 21, 2005. IRC §530(b)(3) prior to being stricken:
  (3) Eligible educational institution.—The term "eligible educational institution" has the meaning given such term by section 529(f)(5).

Working Families Tax Relief Act of 2004 (Pub. L. No. 108-311), as follows:
- IRC §530(d)(2)(C)(i) was amended by Act §404(a) by striking "higher" after "qualified". Eff. tax years beginning after Dec. 31, 2001, as if included in the provision of Pub. L. No. 107-16 to which it relates.
- IRC §530(d)(4)(B)(iii) was amended by Act §406(b) by replacing "account holder" with "designated beneficiary". Eff. tax years beginning after Dec. 31, 1997, as if included in the provision of Pub. L. No. 105-34 to which it relates.

Military Family Tax Relief Act of 2003 (Pub. L. No. 108-121), as follows:
- IRC §530(d)(4)(B) was amended by Act §107(a) by striking "or" at the end of cl. (iii), by redesignating cl. (iv) as cl. (v), and by inserting new clause (iv). Eff. tax years beginning after Dec. 31, 2002.

Job Creation and Worker Assistance Act of 2002 (Pub. L. No. 107-147), as follows:
- IRC §530(d)(4)(B)(v), as redesignated by Pub. L. No. 108-121, §107(a), was amended by Act §411(f) by replacing "because the taxpayer elected under paragraph (2)(C) to waive the application of paragraph (2)" with "by application of paragraph (2)(C)(i)(II)". Eff. tax years beginning after Dec. 31, 2001, as if included in the provision of Pub. L. No. 107-16 to which it relates.

Pub. L. No. 107-22, as follows:
- IRC §530 was amended by Act §1(a)(5) in the heading. Eff. July 26, 2001. IRC §530 heading prior to amendment:
  SEC. 530. EDUCATION INDIVIDUAL RETIREMENT ACCOUNTS.
- IRC §530 was amended by Act §1(a)(1) by replacing "an education individual retirement account" each place it appeared with "a Coverdell education savings account". Eff. July 26, 2001.
- IRC §530(a) was amended by Act §1(a)(2) by replacing "An education individual retirement account" with "A Coverdell education savings account", and by replacing "the education individual retirement account" with "the Coverdell education savings account". Eff. July 26, 2001.
- IRC §530(b)(1) was amended by Act §1(a)(3) by replacing "education individual retirement account" with "Coverdell education savings account", and by replacing "Education individual retirement account" with "Coverdell education savings account" in the heading. Eff. July 26, 2001.
- IRC §530(d)(5) was amended by Act §1(a)(4) by replacing "education individual retirement account" with "Coverdell education savings account". Eff. July 26, 2001.
- IRC §530(e) was amended by Act §1(a)(4) by substituting "Coverdell education savings account" for "education individual retirement account". Eff. July 26, 2001.

Economic Growth and Tax Relief Reconciliation Act of 2001 (Pub. L. No. 107-16), as follows:
- IRC §530(b)(1) was amended by Act §401(c)(3)(A) by striking "higher" after "qualified". Eff. tax years beginning after Dec. 31, 2001.
- IRC §530(b)(1) was amended by Act §401(d) by adding a new flush sentence at the end. Eff. tax years beginning after Dec. 31, 2001.
- IRC §530(b)(1)(A)(iii) was amended by Act §401(a)(1) by replacing "$500" with "$2,000". Eff. tax years beginning after Dec. 31, 2001.
- IRC §530(b)(2) was amended by Act §401(c)(1). Eff. tax years beginning after Dec. 31, 2001. IRC §530(b)(2) prior to amendment:
  (2) Qualified higher education expenses.—
  (A) In general.—The term "qualified higher education expenses" has the meaning given such term by section 529(e)(3), reduced as provided in section 25A(g)(2).

IRC Sec. 530(h)

(B) Qualified state tuition programs.—Such term shall include amounts paid or incurred to purchase tuition credits or certificates, or to make contributions to an account, under a qualified State tuition program (as defined in section 529(b)) for the benefit of the beneficiary of the account.

- IRC §530(b)(2)(B) was amended by Act §402(a)(4)(C) by striking "Qualified state tuition" and inserting "Qualified tuition" in the heading. Eff. tax years beginning after Dec. 31, 2001.
- IRC §530(b)(2)(B) was amended by Act §402(a)(4)(A) by striking "qualified State tuition" and inserting "qualified tuition". Eff. tax years beginning after Dec. 31, 2001.
- IRC §530(b) was amended by Act §401(c)(2) by adding new para. (4). Eff. tax years beginning after Dec. 31, 2001.
- IRC §530(b) was amended by Act §401(f)(1) by adding new para. (5). Eff. tax years beginning after Dec. 31, 2001.
- IRC §530(c)(1) was amended by Act §401(e) by substituting "In the case of a contributor who is an individual, the maximum amount the contributor" for "The maximum amount which a contributor". Eff. taxable years beginning after Dec. 31, 2001.
- IRC §530(c)(1)(A)(ii) was amended by Act §401(b)(1) by replacing "$150,000" with "$190,000". Eff. tax years beginning after Dec. 31, 2001.
- IRC §530(c)(1)(B) was amended by Act §401(b)(2) by replacing "$10,000" with "$30,000". Eff. tax years beginning after Dec. 31, 2001.
- IRC §530(d)(2) was amended by Act §401(c)(3)(B) by striking "higher" in the heading and text each place it appeared. Eff. tax years beginning after Dec. 31, 2001.
- IRC §530(d)(2)(C) was amended by Act §401(g)(1). Eff. tax years beginning after Dec. 31, 2001. IRC §530(d)(2)(C) prior to amendment:
  (C) Election to waive exclusion.—A taxpayer may elect to waive the application of this paragraph for any taxable year.
- IRC §530(d)(2)(D) was amended by Act §401(g)(2)(C) by replacing "or credit" with ", credit, or exclusion", and by replacing "credit or deduction" in the heading with "deduction, credit, or exclusion". Eff. tax years beginning after Dec. 31, 2001.
- IRC §530(d)(4)(C) heading was amended by Act §401(f)(2)(B) by replacing "due date of return" with "certain date". Eff. tax years beginning after Dec. 31, 2001.
- IRC §530(d)(4)(C)(i) was amended by Act §401(f)(2)(A). Eff. tax years beginning after Dec. 31, 2001. IRC §530(d)(4)(C)(i) prior to amendment:
  (i) such distribution is made on or before the day prescribed by law (including extensions of time) for filing the beneficiary's return of tax for the taxable year or, if the beneficiary is not required to file such a return, the 15th day of the 4th month of the taxable year following the taxable year, and.
- **Sunset Provision.** Act §901, as amended by Pub. L. No. 111-312, §101(a)(1), provides the sunset rule below. But see Pub. L. No. 109-280, §811, and Pub. L. No. 111-148, §10909(c), as amended by Pub. L. No. 111-312, §101(b)(1).
  SEC. 901. SUNSET OF PROVISIONS OF ACT.
  (a) In general. All provisions of, and amendments made by, this Act shall not apply—
  (1) to taxable, plan, or limitation years beginning after December 31, 2012, or
  (2) in the case of title V, to estates of decedents dying, gifts made, or generation skipping transfers, after December 31, 2012.
  (b) Application of certain laws.—The Internal Revenue Code of 1986 and the Employee Retirement Income Security Act of 1974 shall be applied and administered to years, estates, gifts, and transfers described in subsection (a) as if the provisions and amendments described in subsection (a) had never been enacted.

* * *

Subchapter N—Tax Based on Income From Sources Within or Without the United States
* * *

Part II—Nonresident Aliens and Foreign Corporations

Subpart A—Nonresident Alien Individuals
* * *

SEC. 871. TAX ON NONRESIDENT ALIEN INDIVIDUALS.

(a) Income Not Connected With United States Business.—30 percent tax.

(1) Income other than capital gains.—Except as provided in subsection (h), there is hereby imposed for each taxable year a tax of 30 percent of the amount received from sources within the United States by a nonresident alien individual as—

(A) interest (other than original issue discount as defined in section 1273), dividends, rents, salaries, wages, premiums, annuities, compensations, remunerations, emoluments, and other fixed or determinable annual or periodical gains, profits, and income,

(B) gains described in section 631(b) or (c), and gains on transfers described in section 1235 made on or before October 4, 1966,

(C) in the case of—

(i) a sale or exchange of an original issue discount obligation, the amount of the original issue discount accruing while such obligation was held by the nonresident alien individual (to the extent such discount was not theretofore taken into account under clause (ii)), and

(ii) a payment on an original issue discount obligation, an amount equal to the original issue discount accruing while such obligation was held by the nonresident alien individual (except that such original issue discount shall be taken into account under this clause only to the extent such discount was not theretofore taken into account under this clause and only to the extent that the tax thereon does not exceed the payment less the tax imposed by subparagraph (A) thereon), and

(D) gains from the sale or exchange after October 4, 1966, of patents, copyrights, secret processes and formulas, good will, trademarks, trade brands, franchises, and other like property, or of any interest in any such property, to the extent such gains are from payments which are contingent on the productivity, use, or disposition of the property or interest sold or exchanged,

but only to the extent the amount so received is not effectively connected with the conduct of a trade or business within the United States.

(2) Capital gains of aliens present in the United States 183 days or more.—In the case of a nonresident alien individual present in the United States for a period or periods aggregating 183 days or more during the taxable year, there is hereby imposed for such year a tax of 30 percent of the amount by which his gains, derived from sources within the United States, from the sale or exchange at any time during such year of capital assets exceed his losses, allocable to sources within the United States, from the sale or exchange at any time during such year of capital assets. For purposes of this paragraph, gains and losses shall be taken into account only if, and to the extent that, they would be recognized and taken into account if such gains and losses were effectively connected with the conduct of a trade or business within the United States, except that such gains and losses shall be determined without regard to section 1202 and such losses shall be determined without the benefits of the capital loss carryover provided in section 1212. Any gain or loss which is taken into account in determining the tax under paragraph (1) or subsection (b) shall not be taken into account in determining the tax under this paragraph. For purposes of the 183-day requirement of this paragraph, a nonresident alien individual not engaged in trade or business within the United States who has not established a taxable year for any prior period shall be treated as having a taxable year which is the calendar year.

(3) Taxation of social security benefits.—For purposes of this section and section 1441—

(A) 85 percent of any social security benefit (as defined in section 86(d)) shall be included in gross income (notwithstanding section 207 of the Social Security Act), and

(B) section 86 shall not apply.

For treatment of certain citizens of possessions of the United States, see section 932(c).

* * *

(f) Certain Annuities Received Under Qualified Plans.—

(1) In general.—For purposes of this section, gross income does not include any amount received as an annuity under a qualified annuity plan described in section 403(a)(1), or from a qualified trust described in section 401(a) which is exempt from tax under section 501(a), if—

(A) all of the personal services by reason of which the annuity is payable were either—

(i) personal services performed outside the United States by an individual who, at the time of performance of such personal services, was a nonresident alien, or

(ii) personal services described in section 864(b)(1) performed within the United States by such individual, and

(B) at the time the first amount is paid as an annuity under the annuity plan or by the trust, 90 percent or more of the employees for whom con-

tributions or benefits are provided under such annuity plan, or under the plan or plans of which the trust is a part, are citizens or residents of the United States.

(2) Exclusion.—Income received during the taxable year which would be excluded from gross income under this subsection but for the requirement of paragraph (1)(B) shall not be included in gross income if—

(A) the recipient's country of residence grants a substantially equivalent exclusion to residents and citizens of the United States; or

(B) the recipient's country of residence is a beneficiary developing country under title V of the Trade Act of 1974 (19 U.S.C. 2461 et seq.).

* * *

Recent Amendments to IRC §871 (as Excerpted)

Community Renewal Tax Relief Act of 2000 (Pub. L. No. 106-554), as follows:
- IRC §871(f)(2)(B) was amended by Act §319(11) by substituting "(19 U.S.C." for "19 U.S.C". Eff. Dec. 21, 2000.

IRS Restructuring and Reform Act of 1998 (Pub. L. No. 105-206), as follows:
- IRC §871(f)(2)(B) was amended by Act §6023(1) by substituting "19 U.S.C. 2461 et seq.)" for "(19 U.S.C. 2462)". Eff. Jul. 22, 1998.

Small Business Job Protection Act of 1996 (Pub. L. No. 104-188), as follows:
- IRC §871(f)(2)(B) was amended by Act §1954(b)(1) by substituting "under title V" for "within the meaning of section 502". Eff. Aug. 20, 1996.

Uruguay Round Agreements Act (Pub. L. No. 103-465), as follows:
- IRC §871(a)(3)(A) was amended by Act §733 by striking "one-half" and inserting "85 percent". Eff. for benefits paid after Dec. 31, 1994, in taxable years ending after such date.

Omnibus Budget Reconciliation Act of 1993 (Pub. L. No. 103-66), as follows:
- IRC §871(a)(2) was amended by Act §13113(d)(5) in the second sentence by inserting "such gains and losses shall be determined without regard to section 1202 and" after "except that". Eff. for stock issued after Aug. 10, 1993.

Unemployment Compensation Amendments of 1992 (Pub. L. No. 102-318), as follows:
- IRC §871(a)(1)(B) was amended by Act §521(b)(28) by striking "402(a)(2), 403(a)(2), or". Eff. for distributions after Dec. 31, 1992.

---

* * *

SEC. 877A. TAX RESPONSIBILITIES OF EXPATRIATION.

(a) General Rules.—For purposes of this subtitle—

(1) Mark to market.—All property of a covered expatriate shall be treated as sold on the day before the expatriation date for its fair market value.

(2) Recognition of gain or loss.—In the case of any sale under paragraph (1)—

(A) notwithstanding any other provision of this title, any gain arising from such sale shall be taken into account for the taxable year of the sale, and

IRC Sec. 877A(a)(2)(A)

(B) any loss arising from such sale shall be taken into account for the taxable year of the sale to the extent otherwise provided by this title, except that section 1091 shall not apply to any such loss.

Proper adjustment shall be made in the amount of any gain or loss subsequently realized for gain or loss taken into account under the preceding sentence, determined without regard to paragraph (3).

(3) Exclusion for certain gain.—

(A) In general.—The amount which would (but for this paragraph) be includible in the gross income of any individual by reason of paragraph (1) shall be reduced (but not below zero) by $600,000.

(B) Adjustment for inflation.—

(i) In general.—In the case of any taxable year beginning in a calendar year after 2008, the dollar amount in subparagraph (A) shall be increased by an amount equal to—

(I) such dollar amount, multiplied by

(II) the cost-of-living adjustment determined under section 1(f)(3) for the calendar year in which the taxable year begins, by substituting "calendar year 2007" for "calendar year 1992" in subparagraph (B) thereof.

(ii) Rounding.—If any amount as adjusted under clause (i) is not a multiple of $1,000, such amount shall be rounded to the nearest multiple of $1,000.

(b) Election To Defer Tax.—

(1) In general.—If the taxpayer elects the application of this subsection with respect to any property treated as sold by reason of subsection (a), the time for payment of the additional tax attributable to such property shall be extended until the due date of the return for the taxable year in which such property is disposed of (or, in the case of property disposed of in a transaction in which gain is not recognized in whole or in part, until such other date as the Secretary may prescribe).

(2) Determination of tax with respect to property.—For purposes of paragraph (1), the additional tax attributable to any property is an amount which bears the same ratio to the additional tax imposed by this chapter for the taxable year solely by reason of subsection (a) as the gain taken into account under subsection (a) with respect to such property bears to the total gain taken into account under subsection (a) with respect to all property to which subsection (a) applies.

(3) Termination of extension.—The due date for payment of tax may not be extended under this subsection later than the due date for the return of tax imposed by this chapter for the taxable year which includes the date of death of the expatriate (or, if earlier, the time that the security provided with re-

spect to the property fails to meet the requirements of paragraph (4), unless the taxpayer corrects such failure within the time specified by the Secretary).

(4) Security.—

(A) In general.—No election may be made under paragraph (1) with respect to any property unless adequate security is provided with respect to such property.

(B) Adequate security.—For purposes of subparagraph (A), security with respect to any property shall be treated as adequate security if—

(i) it is a bond which is furnished to, and accepted by, the Secretary, which is conditioned on the payment of tax (and interest thereon), and which meets the requirements of section 6325, or

(ii) it is another form of security for such payment (including letters of credit) that meets such requirements as the Secretary may prescribe.

(5) Waiver of certain rights.—No election may be made under paragraph (1) unless the taxpayer makes an irrevocable waiver of any right under any treaty of the United States which would preclude assessment or collection of any tax imposed by reason of this section.

(6) Elections.—An election under paragraph (1) shall only apply to property described in the election and, once made, is irrevocable.

(7) Interest.—For purposes of section 6601, the last date for the payment of tax shall be determined without regard to the election under this subsection.

(c) Exception for Certain Property.—Subsection (a) shall not apply—

(1) any deferred compensation item (as defined in subsection (d)(4)),

(2) any specified tax deferred account (as defined in subsection (e)(2)), and

(3) any interest in a nongrantor trust (as defined in subsection (f)(3)).

(d) Treatment   of   Deferred   Compensation Items.—

(1) Withholding on eligible deferred compensation items.—

(A) In general.—In the case of any eligible deferred compensation item, the payor shall deduct and withhold from any taxable payment to a covered expatriate with respect to such item a tax equal to 30 percent thereof.

(B) Taxable payment.—For purposes of subparagraph (A), the term "taxable payment" means with respect to a covered expatriate any payment to the extent it would be includible in the gross income of the covered expatriate if such expatriate continued to be subject to tax as a citizen or resident of the

United States. A deferred compensation item shall be taken into account as a payment under the preceding sentence when such item would be so includible.

(2) Other deferred compensation items.—In the case of any deferred compensation item which is not an eligible deferred compensation item—

(A)(i) with respect to any deferred compensation item to which clause (ii) does not apply, an amount equal to the present value of the covered expatriate's accrued benefit shall be treated as having been received by such individual on the day before the expatriation date as a distribution under the plan, and

(ii) with respect to any deferred compensation item referred to in paragraph (4)(D), the rights of the covered expatriate to such item shall be treated as becoming transferable and not subject to a substantial risk of forfeiture on the day before the expatriation date,

(B) no early distribution tax shall apply by reason of such treatment, and

(C) appropriate adjustments shall be made to subsequent distributions from the plan to reflect such treatment.

(3) Eligible deferred compensation items.—For purposes of this subsection, the term "eligible deferred compensation item" means any deferred compensation item with respect to which—

(A) the payor of such item is—

(i) a United States person, or

(ii) a person who is not a United States person but who elects to be treated as a United States person for purposes of paragraph (1) and meets such requirements as the Secretary may provide to ensure that the payor will meet the requirements of paragraph (1), and

(B) the covered expatriate—

(i) notifies the payor of his status as a covered expatriate, and

(ii) makes an irrevocable waiver of any right to claim any reduction under any treaty with the United States in withholding on such item.

(4) Deferred compensation item.—For purposes of this subsection, the term "deferred compensation item" means—

(A) any interest in a plan or arrangement described in section 219(g)(5),

(B) any interest in a foreign pension plan or similar retirement arrangement or program,

(C) any item of deferred compensation, and

(D) any property, or right to property, which the individual is entitled to receive in connection with

the performance of services to the extent not previously taken into account under section 83 or in accordance with section 83.

(5) Exception.—Paragraphs (1) and (2) shall not apply to any deferred compensation item to the extent attributable to services performed outside the United States while the covered expatriate was not a citizen or resident of the United States.

(6) Special rules.—

(A) Application of withholding rules.—Rules similar to the rules of subchapter B of chapter 3 shall apply for purposes of this subsection.

(B) Application of tax.—Any item subject to the withholding tax imposed under paragraph (1) shall be subject to tax under section 871.

(C) Coordination with other withholding requirements.—Any item subject to withholding under paragraph (1) shall not be subject to withholding under section 1441 or chapter 24.

(e) Treatment of Specified Tax Deferred Accounts.—

(1) Account treated as distributed.—In the case of any interest in a specified tax deferred account held by a covered expatriate on the day before the expatriation date—

(A) the covered expatriate shall be treated as receiving a distribution of his entire interest in such account on the day before the expatriation date,

(B) no early distribution tax shall apply by reason of such treatment, and

(C) appropriate adjustments shall be made to subsequent distributions from the account to reflect such treatment.

(2) Specified tax deferred account.—For purposes of paragraph (1), the term "specified tax deferred account" means an individual retirement plan (as defined in section 7701(a)(37)) other than any arrangement described in subsection (k) or (p) of section 408, a qualified tuition program (as defined in section 529), a Coverdell education savings account (as defined in section 530), a health savings account (as defined in section 223), and an Archer MSA (as defined in section 220).

(f) Special Rules for Nongrantor Trusts.—

(1) In general.—In the case of a distribution (directly or indirectly) of any property from a nongrantor trust to a covered expatriate—

(A) the trustee shall deduct and withhold from such distribution an amount equal to 30 percent of the taxable portion of the distribution, and

(B) if the fair market value of such property exceeds its adjusted basis in the hands of the trust, gain shall be recognized to the trust as if such

IRC Sec. 877A(f)(1)(B)

property were sold to the expatriate at its fair market value.

(2) Taxable portion.—For purposes of this subsection, the term "taxable portion" means, with respect to any distribution, that portion of the distribution which would be includible in the gross income of the covered expatriate if such expatriate continued to be subject to tax as a citizen or resident of the United States.

(3) Nongrantor trust.—For purposes of this subsection, the term "nongrantor trust" means the portion of any trust that the individual is not considered the owner of under subpart E of part I of subchapter J. The determination under the preceding sentence shall be made immediately before the expatriation date.

(4) Special rules relating to withholding.—For purposes of this subsection—

(A) rules similar to the rules of subsection (d)(6) shall apply, and

(B) the covered expatriate shall be treated as having waived any right to claim any reduction under any treaty with the United States in withholding on any distribution to which paragraph (1)(A) applies unless the covered expatriate agrees to such other treatment as the Secretary determines appropriate.

(5) Application.—This subsection shall apply to a nongrantor trust only if the covered expatriate was a beneficiary of the trust on the day before the expatriation date.

(g) Definitions and Special Rules Relating to Expatriation.—For purposes of this section—

(1) Covered expatriate.—

(A) In general.—The term "covered expatriate" means an expatriate who meets the requirements of subparagraph (A), (B), or (C) of section 877(a)(2).

(B) Exceptions.—An individual shall not be treated as meeting the requirements of subparagraph (A) or (B) of section 877(a)(2) if—

(i) the individual—

(I) became at birth a citizen of the United States and a citizen of another country and, as of the expatriation date, continues to be a citizen of, and is taxed as a resident of, such other country, and

(II) has been a resident of the United States (as defined in section 7701(b)(1)(A)(ii)) for not more than 10 taxable years during the 15-taxable year period ending with the taxable year during which the expatriation date occurs, or

(ii) (I) the individual's relinquishment of United States citizenship occurs before such individual attains age 18, and

(II) the individual has been a resident of the United States (as so defined) for not more than 10 taxable years before the date of relinquishment.

(C) Covered expatriates also subject to tax as citizens or residents.—In the case of any covered expatriate who is subject to tax as a citizen or resident of the United States for any period beginning after the expatriation date, such individual shall not be treated as a covered expatriate during such period for purposes of subsections (d)(1) and (f) and section 2801.

(2) Expatriate.—The term "expatriate" means—

(A) any United States citizen who relinquishes his citizenship, and

(B) any long-term resident of the United States who ceases to be a lawful permanent resident of the United States (within the meaning of section 7701(b)(6)).

(3) Expatriation date.—The term "expatriation date" means—

(A) the date an individual relinquishes United States citizenship, or

(B) in the case of a long-term resident of the United States, the date on which the individual ceases to be a lawful permanent resident of the United States (within the meaning of section 7701(b)(6)).

(4) Relinquishment of citizenship.—A citizen shall be treated as relinquishing his United States citizenship on the earliest of—

(A) the date the individual renounces his United States nationality before a diplomatic or consular officer of the United States pursuant to paragraph (5) of section 349(a) of the Immigration and Nationality Act (8 U.S.C. 1481(a)(5)),

(B) the date the individual furnishes to the United States Department of State a signed statement of voluntary relinquishment of United States nationality confirming the performance of an act of expatriation specified in paragraph (1), (2), (3), or (4) of section 349(a) of the Immigration and Nationality Act (8 U.S.C. 1481(a)(1)-(4)),

(C) the date the United States Department of State issues to the individual a certificate of loss of nationality, or

(D) the date a court of the United States cancels a naturalized citizen's certificate of naturalization.

Subparagraph (A) or (B) shall not apply to any individual unless the renunciation or voluntary relinquishment is subsequently approved by the issuance to the individual of a certificate of loss of nationality by the United States Department of State.

(5) Long-term resident.—The term "long-term resident" has the meaning given to such term by section 877(e)(2).

(6) Early distribution tax.—The term "early distribution tax" means any increase in tax imposed under section 72(t), 220(e)(4), 223(f)(4), 409A(a)(1)(B), 529(c)(6), or 530(d)(4).

(h) Other Rules.—

(1) Termination of deferrals, etc.—In the case of any covered expatriate, notwithstanding any other provision of this title—

(A) any time period for acquiring property which would result in the reduction in the amount of gain recognized with respect to property disposed of by the taxpayer shall terminate on the day before the expatriation date, and

(B) any extension of time for payment of tax shall cease to apply on the day before the expatriation date and the unpaid portion of such tax shall be due and payable at the time and in the manner prescribed by the Secretary.

(2) Step-up in basis.—Solely for purposes of determining any tax imposed by reason of subsection (a), property which was held by an individual on the date the individual first became a resident of the United States (within the meaning of section 7701(b)) shall be treated as having a basis on such date of not less than the fair market value of such property on such date.

The preceding sentence shall not apply if the individual elects not to have such sentence apply. Such an election, once made, shall be irrevocable.

(3) Coordination with section 684.—If the expatriation of any individual would result in the recognition of gain under section 684, this section shall be applied after the application of section 684.

(i) Regulations.—The Secretary shall prescribe such regulations as may be necessary or appropriate to carry out the purposes of this section.

Amendments to IRC §877A

Heroes Earnings Assistance and Relief Tax Act of 2008 (Pub. L. No. 110-245), as follows:
- IRC §877A was added by Act §301(a). Eff. for individuals whose expatriation date (as so defined) is on or after the date of enactment [enacted: June 17, 2008], see Act §301(g)(1).

---

* * *

Subchapter O—Gain or Loss on Disposition of Property
* * *

Part III—Common Nontaxable Exchanges
* * *

SEC. 1035. CERTAIN EXCHANGES OF INSURANCE POLICIES.

(a) General Rules.—No gain or loss shall be recognized on the exchange of—

(1) a contract of life insurance for another contract of life insurance or for an endowment or annuity contract or for a qualified long-term care insurance contract; or

(2) a contract of endowment insurance (A) for another contract of endowment insurance which provides for regular payments beginning at a date not later than the date payments would have begun under the contract exchanged, or (B) for an annuity contract, or (C) for a qualified long-term care insurance contract;

(3) an annuity contract for an annuity contract or for a qualified long-term care insurance contract; or

(4) a qualified long-term care insurance contract for a qualified long-term care insurance contract.

(b) Definitions. For the purpose of this section—

(1) Endowment contract. A contract of endowment insurance is a contract with an insurance company which depends in part on the life expectancy of the insured, but which may be payable in full in a single payment during his life.

(2) Annuity contract.—An annuity contract is a contract to which paragraph (1) applies but which may be payable during the life of the annuitant only in installments. For purposes of the preceding sentence, a contract shall not fail to be treated as an annuity contract solely because a qualified long-term care insurance contract is a part of or a rider on such contract.

(3) Life insurance contract.—A contract of life insurance is a contract to which paragraph (1) applies but which is not ordinarily payable in full during the life of the insured. For purposes of the preceding sentence, a contract shall not fail to be treated as a life insurance contract solely because a qualified long-term care insurance contract is a part of or a rider on such contract.

(c) Exchanges Involving Foreign Persons. To the extent provided in regulations, subsection (a) shall not apply to any exchange having the effect of transferring property to any person other than a United States person.

(d) Cross References.

(1) For rules relating to recognition of gain or loss where an exchange is not solely in kind, see subsections (b) and (c) of section 1031.

(2) For rules relating to the basis of property acquired in an exchange described in subsection (a), see subsection (d) of section 1031.

Recent Amendments to §1035

Pension Protection Act of 2006 (Pub. L. No. 109-280), as follows:
- IRC §1035(a)(1) was amended by Act §844(b)(3)(A) by inserting "or for a qualified long-term care insurance contract" before the semicolon at the end. Eff. for exchanges after Dec. 31, 2009.

IRC Sec. 1035(d)(2)

- IRC §1035(a)(2) was amended by Act §844(b)(3)(B) by inserting ", or (C) for a qualified long-term care insurance contract" before the semicolon at the end. Eff. for exchanges after Dec. 31, 2009.
- IRC §1035(a)(3) was amended by Act §844(b)(3)(C) by inserting "or for a qualified long-term care insurance contract" before the period at the end. Eff. for exchanges after Dec. 31, 2009.
- IRC §1035(a)(2)–(4) were amended by Act §844(b)(4) by striking "or" at the end of para. (2), by substituting "; or" for the period at the end of para. (3), and by adding para. (4). Eff. for exchanges after Dec. 31, 2009.
- IRC §1035(b)(2) was amended by Act §844(b)(1) by adding the sentence at the end. Eff. for exchanges after Dec. 31, 2009.
- IRC §1035(b)(3) was amended by Act §844(b)(2) by adding the sentence at the end. Eff. for exchanges after Dec. 31, 2009.

* * *

SEC. 1042. SALES OF STOCK TO EMPLOYEE STOCK OWNERSHIP PLANS OR CERTAIN COOPERATIVES.

(a) Nonrecognition of Gain.—If—

(1) the taxpayer or executor elects in such form as the Secretary may prescribe the application of this section with respect to any sale of qualified securities,

(2) the taxpayer purchases qualified replacement property within the replacement period, and

(3) the requirements of subsection (b) are met with respect to such sale,

then the gain (if any) on such sale which would be recognized as long-term capital gain shall be recognized only to the extent that the amount realized on such sale exceeds the cost to the taxpayer of such qualified replacement property.

(b) Requirements to Qualify for Nonrecognition.—A sale of qualified securities meets the requirements of this subsection if—

(1) Sale to employee organizations.—The qualified securities are sold to—

(A) an employee stock ownership plan (as defined in section 4975(e)(7)), or

(B) an eligible worker-owned cooperative.

(2) Plan must hold 30 percent of stock after sale.—The plan or cooperative referred to in paragraph (1) owns (after application of section 318(a)(4)), immediately after the sale, at least 30 percent of—

(A) each class of outstanding stock of the corporation (other than stock described in section 1504(a)(4)) which issued the qualified securities, or

(B) the total value of all outstanding stock of the corporation (other than stock described in section 1504(a)(4)).

(3) Written statement required.—

(A) In general.—The taxpayer files with the Secretary the written statement described in subparagraph (B).

(B) Statement.—A statement is described in this subparagraph if it is a verified written statement of—

(i) the employer whose employees are covered by the plan described in paragraph (1), or

(ii) any authorized officer of the cooperative described in paragraph (1),

consenting to the application of sections 4978 and 4979A with respect to such employer or cooperative.

(4) 3-year holding period.—The taxpayer's holding period with respect to the qualified securities is at least 3 years (determined as of the time of the sale).

(c) Definitions; Special Rules.—For purposes of this section—

(1) Qualified securities.—The term "qualified securities" means employer securities (as defined in section 409(l)) which—

(A) are issued by a domestic C Corporation that has no stock outstanding that are readily tradable on an established securities market, and

(B) were not received by the taxpayer in—

(i) a distribution from a plan described in section 401(a), or

(ii) a transfer pursuant to an option or other right to acquire stock to which section 83, 422, or 423 applied (or to which section 422 or 424 (as in effect on the day before the date of the enactment of the Revenue Reconciliation Act of 1990)) applied.

(2) Eligible worker-owned cooperative.—The term "eligible worker-owned cooperative" means any organization—

(A) to which part I of subchapter T applies,

(B) a majority of the membership of which is comprised of employees of such organization,

(C) a majority of the voting stock of which is owned by members,

(D) a majority of the board of directors of which is elected by the members on the basis of 1 person 1 vote, and

(E) a majority of the allocated earnings and losses of which are allocated to members on the basis of—

(i) patronage,

(ii) capital contributions, or

(iii) some combination of clauses (i) and (ii).

(3) Replacement period.—The term "replacement period" means the period which begins 3 months before the date on which the sale of qualified

securities occurs and which ends 12 months after the date of such sale.

(4) Qualified replacement property.—

(A) In general.—The term "qualified replacement property" means any security issued by a domestic operating corporation which—

(i) did not, for the taxable year preceding the taxable year in which such security was purchased, have passive investment income (as defined in section 1362(d)(3)(C)) in excess of 25 percent of the gross receipts of such corporation for such preceding taxable year, and

(ii) is not the corporation which issued the qualified securities which such security is replacing or a member of the same controlled group of corporations (within the meaning of section 1563(a)(1)) as such corporation.

For purposes of clause (i), income which is described in section 954(c)(3) (as in effect immediately before the Tax Reform Act of 1986) shall not be treated as passive investment income.

(B) Operating corporation.—For purposes of this paragraph—

(i) In general.—The term "operating corporation" means a corporation more than 50 percent of the assets of which were, at the time the security was purchased or before the close of the replacement period, used in the active conduct of the trade or business.

(ii) Financial institutions and insurance companies.—The term "operating corporation" shall include—

(I) any financial institution described in section 581, and

(II) an insurance company subject to tax under subchapter L.

(C) Controlling and controlled corporations treated as 1 corporation.—

(i) In general.—For purposes of applying this paragraph, if—

(I) the corporation issuing the security owns stock representing control of 1 or more other corporations,

(II) 1 or more other corporations own stock representing control of the corporation issuing the security, or

(III) both,

then all such corporations shall be treated as 1 corporation.

(ii) Control.—For purposes of clause (i), the term "control" has the meaning given such term by section 304(c). In determining control, there

shall be disregarded any qualified replacement property of the taxpayer with respect to the section 1042 sale being tested.

(D) Security defined.—For purposes of this paragraph the term "security" has the meaning given such term by section 165(g)(2), except that such term shall not include any security issued by a government or political subdivision thereof.

(5) Securities sold by underwriter.—No sale of securities by an underwriter to an employee stock ownership plan or eligible worker-owned cooperative in the ordinary course of his trade or business as an underwriter, whether or not guaranteed, shall be treated as a sale for purposes of subsection (a).

(6) Time for filing election.—An election under subsection (a) shall be filed not later than the last day prescribed by law (including extensions thereof) for filing the return of tax imposed by this chapter for the taxable year in which the sale occurs.

(7) Section not to apply to gain of C corporation.—Subsection (a) shall not apply to any gain on the sale of any qualified securities which is includible in the gross income of any C corporation.

(d) Basis of Qualified Replacement Property.— The basis of the taxpayer in qualified replacement property purchased by the taxpayer during the replacement period shall be reduced by the amount of gain not recognized by reason of such purchase and the application of subsection (a). If more than one item of qualified replacement property is purchased, the basis of each of such items shall be reduced by an amount determined by multiplying the total gain not recognized by reason of such purchase and the application of subsection (a) by a fraction—

(1) the numerator of which is the cost of such item of property, and

(2) the denominator of which is the total cost of all such items of property.

Any reduction in basis under this subsection shall not be taken into account for purposes of section 1278(a)(2)(A)(ii) (relating to definition of market discount).

(e) Recapture of Gain on Disposition of Qualified Replacement Property.—

(1) In general.—If a taxpayer disposes of any qualified replacement property, then, notwithstanding any other provision of this title, gain (if any) shall be recognized to the extent of the gain which was not recognized under subsection (a) by reason of the acquisition by such taxpayer of such qualified replacement property.

(2) Special rule for corporations controlled by the taxpayer.—If—

(A) a corporation issuing qualified replacement property disposes of a substantial portion of its assets other than in the ordinary course of its trade or business, and

(B) any taxpayer owning stock representing control (within the meaning of section 304(c)) of such corporation at the time of such disposition holds any qualified replacement property of such corporation at such time,

then the taxpayer shall be treated as having disposed of such qualified replacement property at such time.

(3) Recapture not to apply in certain cases.—Paragraph (1) shall not apply to any transfer of qualified replacement property—

(A) in any reorganization (within the meaning of section 368) unless the person making the election under subsection (a)(1) owns stock representing control in the acquiring or acquired corporation and such property is substituted basis property in the hands of the transferee,

(B) by reason of the death of the person making such election,

(C) by gift, or

(D) in any transaction to which section 1042(a) applies.

(f) Statute of Limitations.—If any gain is realized by the taxpayer on the sale or exchange of any qualified securities and there is in effect an election under subsection (a) with respect to such gain, then—

(1) the statutory period for the assessment of any deficiency with respect to such gain shall not expire before the expiration of 3 years from the date the Secretary is notified by the taxpayer (in such manner as the Secretary may by regulations prescribe) of—

(A) the taxpayer's cost of purchasing qualified replacement property which the taxpayer claims results in nonrecognition of any part of such gain,

(B) the taxpayer's intention not to purchase qualified replacement property within the replacement period, or

(C) a failure to make such purchase within the replacement period, and

(2) such deficiency may be assessed before the expiration of such 3-year period notwithstanding the provisions of any other law or rule of law which would otherwise prevent such assessment.

* * *

Subchapter S—Tax Treatment of S Corporations and Their Shareholders
* * *

Part III—Special Rules
* * *

SEC. 1372. PARTNERSHIP RULES TO APPLY FOR FRINGE BENEFIT PURPOSES.

(a) General Rule.—For purposes of applying the provisions of this subtitle which relate to employee fringe benefits—

(1) the S corporation shall be treated as a partnership, and

(2) any 2-percent shareholder of the S corporation shall be treated as a partner of such partnership.

(b) 2-Percent Shareholder Defined.—For purposes of this section, the term "2-percent shareholder" means any person who owns (or is considered as owning within the meaning of section 318) on any day during the taxable year of the S corporation more than 2 percent of the outstanding stock of such corporation or stock possessing more than 2 percent of the total combined voting power of all stock of such corporation.

* * *

Subchapter Y—Short-Term Regional Benefits
* * *

Part II—Tax Benefits for GO Zones

SEC. 1400M. DEFINITIONS.

For purposes of this part—

(1) Gulf Opportunity Zone.—The terms "Gulf Opportunity Zone" and "GO Zone" mean that portion of the Hurricane Katrina disaster area determined by the President to warrant individual or individual and public assistance from the Federal Government under the Robert T. Stafford Disaster Relief and Emergency Assistance Act by reason of Hurricane Katrina.

(2) Hurricane Katrina disaster area.—The term "Hurricane Katrina disaster area" means an area with respect to which a major disaster has been declared by the President before September 14, 2005, under section 401 of such Act by reason of Hurricane Katrina.

(3) Rita GO Zone.—The term "Rita GO Zone" means that portion of the Hurricane Rita disaster area determined by the President to warrant individual or individual and public assistance from the Federal Government under such Act by reason of Hurricane Rita.

(4) Hurricane Rita disaster area.—The term "Hurricane Rita disaster area" means an area with respect to which a major disaster has been declared by the President before October 6, 2005, under section 401 of such Act by reason of Hurricane Rita.

(5) Wilma GO Zone.—The term "Wilma GO Zone" means that portion of the Hurricane Wilma disaster area determined by the President to warrant individual or individual and public assistance from the Federal Government under such Act by reason of Hurricane Wilma.

(6) Hurricane Wilma disaster area.—The term "Hurricane Wilma disaster area" means an area with respect to which a major disaster has been declared by the President before November 14, 2005, under section 401 of such Act by reason of Hurricane Wilma.

Amendments to IRC §1400M

Gulf Opportunity Zone Act of 2005 (Pub. L. No. 109-135), as follows:
• IRC §1400M was added by Act §101(a). Eff. tax years ending on or after Aug. 28, 2005.

---

* * *

SEC. 1400Q. SPECIAL RULES FOR USE OF RETIREMENT FUNDS.

(a) Tax-Favored Withdrawals From Retirement Plans.—

(1) In general.—Section 72(t) shall not apply to any qualified hurricane distribution.

(2) Aggregate dollar limitation.—

(A) In general.—For purposes of this subsection, the aggregate amount of distributions received by an individual which may be treated as qualified hurricane distributions for any taxable year shall not exceed the excess (if any) of—

(i) $100,000, over

(ii) the aggregate amounts treated as qualified hurricane distributions received by such individual for all prior taxable years.

(B) Treatment of plan distributions.—If a distribution to an individual would (without regard to subparagraph (A)) be a qualified hurricane distribution, a plan shall not be treated as violating any requirement of this title merely because the plan treats such distribution as a qualified hurricane distribution, unless the aggregate amount of such distributions from all plans maintained by the employer (and any member of any controlled group which includes the employer) to such individual exceeds $100,000.

(C) Controlled group.—For purposes of subparagraph (B), the term "controlled group" means any group treated as a single employer under subsection (b), (c), (m), or (o) of section 414.

(3) Amount distributed may be repaid.—

(A) In general.—Any individual who receives a qualified hurricane distribution may, at any time during the 3-year period beginning on the day after the date on which such distribution was received, make one or more contributions in an aggregate amount not to exceed the amount of such distribution to an eligible retirement plan of which such individual is a beneficiary and to which a rollover contribution of such distribution could be made under section 402(c), 403(a)(4), 403(b)(8), 408(d)(3), or 457(e)(16), as the case may be.

(B) Treatment of repayments of distributions from eligible retirement plans other than IRAs.—For purposes of this title, if a contribution is made pursuant to subparagraph (A) with respect to a qualified hurricane distribution from an eligible retirement plan other than an individual retirement plan, then the taxpayer shall, to the extent of the amount of the contribution, be treated as having received the qualified hurricane distribution in an eligible rollover distribution (as defined in section 402(c)(4)) and as having transferred the amount to the eligible retirement plan in a direct trustee to trustee transfer within 60 days of the distribution.

(C) Treatment of repayments for distributions from IRAs.—For purposes of this title, if a contribution is made pursuant to subparagraph (A) with respect to a qualified hurricane distribution from an individual retirement plan (as defined by section 7701(a)(37)), then, to the extent of the amount of the contribution, the qualified hurricane distribution shall be treated as a distribution described in section 408(d)(3) and as having been transferred to the eligible retirement plan in a direct trustee to trustee transfer within 60 days of the distribution.

(4) Definitions.—For purposes of this subsection—

(A) Qualified hurricane distribution.—Except as provided in paragraph (2), the term "qualified hurricane distribution" means—

(i) any distribution from an eligible retirement plan made on or after August 25, 2005, and before January 1, 2007, to an individual whose principal place of abode on August 28, 2005, is located in the Hurricane Katrina disaster area and who has sustained an economic loss by reason of Hurricane Katrina,

(ii) any distribution (which is not described in clause (i)) from an eligible retirement plan made on or after September 23, 2005, and before January 1, 2007, to an individual whose principal place of abode on September 23, 2005, is located in the Hurricane Rita disaster area and who has sustained an economic loss by reason of Hurricane Rita, and

(iii) any distribution (which is not described in clause (i) or (ii)) from an eligible retirement plan made on or after October 23, 2005, and before January 1, 2007, to an individual whose principal place of abode on October 23, 2005, is located in

IRC Sec. 1400Q(a)(4)(A)(iii)

the Hurricane Wilma disaster area and who has sustained an economic loss by reason of Hurricane Wilma.

(B) Eligible retirement plan.—The term "eligible retirement plan" shall have the meaning given such term by section 402(c)(8)(B).

(5) Income inclusion spread over 3-year period.—

(A) In general.—In the case of any qualified hurricane distribution, unless the taxpayer elects not to have this paragraph apply for any taxable year, any amount required to be included in gross income for such taxable year shall be so included ratably over the 3- taxable year period beginning with such taxable year.

(B) Special rule.—For purposes of subparagraph (A), rules similar to the rules of subparagraph (E) of section 408A(d)(3) shall apply.

(6) Special rules.—

(A) Exemption of distributions from trustee to trustee transfer and withholding rules.—For purposes of sections 401(a)(31), 402(f), and 3405, qualified hurricane distributions shall not be treated as eligible rollover distributions.

(B) Qualified hurricane distributions treated as meeting plan distribution requirements.—For purposes this title, a qualified hurricane distribution shall be treated as meeting the requirements of sections 401(k)(2)(B)(i), 403(b)(7)(A)(ii), 403(b)(11), and 457(d)(1)(A).

(b) Recontributions of Withdrawals for Home Purchases.—

(1) Recontributions.—

(A) In general.—Any individual who received a qualified distribution may, during the applicable period, make one or more contributions in an aggregate amount not to exceed the amount of such qualified distribution to an eligible retirement plan (as defined in section 402(c)(8)(B)) of which such individual is a beneficiary and to which a rollover contribution of such distribution could be made under section 402(c), 403(a)(4), 403(b)(8), or 408(d)(3), as the case may be.

(B) Treatment of repayments.—Rules similar to the rules of subparagraphs (B) and (C) of subsection (a)(3) shall apply for purposes of this subsection.

(2) Qualified distribution.—For purposes of this subsection—

(A) In general.—The term "qualified distribution" means any qualified Katrina distribution, any qualified Rita distribution, and any qualified Wilma distribution.

(B) Qualified Katrina distribution.—The term "qualified Katrina distribution" means any distribution—

(i) described in section 401(k)(2)(B)(i)(IV), 403(b)(7)(A)(ii) (but only to the extent such distribution relates to financial hardship), 403(b)(11)(B), or 72(t)(2)(F),

(ii) received after February 28, 2005, and before August 29, 2005, and

(iii) which was to be used to purchase or construct a principal residence in the Hurricane Katrina disaster area, but which was not so purchased or constructed on account of Hurricane Katrina.

(C) Qualified Rita distribution.—The term "qualified Rita distribution" means any distribution (other than a qualified Katrina distribution)—

(i) described in section 401(k)(2)(B)(i)(IV), 403(b)(7)(A)(ii) (but only to the extent such distribution relates to financial hardship), 403(b)(11)(B), or 72(t)(2)(F),

(ii) received after February 28, 2005, and before September 24, 2005, and

(iii) which was to be used to purchase or construct a principal residence in the Hurricane Rita disaster area, but which was not so purchased or constructed on account of Hurricane Rita.

(D) Qualified Wilma distribution.—The term "qualified Wilma distribution" means any distribution (other than a qualified Katrina distribution or a qualified Rita distribution)—

(i) described in section 401(k)(2)(B)(i)(IV), 403(b)(7)(A)(ii) (but only to the extent such distribution relates to financial hardship), 403(b)(11)(B), or 72(t)(2)(F),

(ii) received after February 28, 2005, and before October 24, 2005, and

(iii) which was to be used to purchase or construct a principal residence in the Hurricane Wilma disaster area, but which was not so purchased or constructed on account of Hurricane Wilma.

(3) Applicable period.—For purposes of this subsection, the term "applicable period" means—

(A) with respect to any qualified Katrina distribution, the period beginning on August 25, 2005, and ending on February 28, 2006,

(B) with respect to any qualified Rita distribution, the period beginning on September 23, 2005, and ending on February 28, 2006, and

(C) with respect to any qualified Wilma distribution, the period beginning on October 23, 2005, and ending on February 28, 2006.

(c) Loans From Qualified Plans.—

(1) Increase in limit on loans not treated as distributions.—In the case of any loan from a qualified employer plan (as defined under section 72(p)(4)) to a qualified individual made during the applicable period—

(A) clause (i) of section 72(p)(2)(A) shall be applied by substituting "$100,000" for "$50,000", and

(B) clause (ii) of such section shall be applied by substituting "the present value of the nonforfeitable accrued benefit of the employee under the plan" for "one-half of the present value of the nonforfeitable accrued benefit of the employee under the plan".

(2) Delay of repayment.—In the case of a qualified individual with an outstanding loan on or after the qualified beginning date from a qualified employer plan (as defined in section 72(p)(4))—

(A) if the due date pursuant to subparagraph (B) or (C) of section 72(p)(2) for any repayment with respect to such loan occurs during the period beginning on the qualified beginning date and ending on December 31, 2006, such due date shall be delayed for 1 year,

(B) any subsequent repayments with respect to any such loan shall be appropriately adjusted to reflect the delay in the due date under paragraph (1) and any interest accruing during such delay, and

(C) in determining the 5-year period and the term of a loan under subparagraph (B) or (C) of section 72(p)(2), the period described in subparagraph (A) shall be disregarded.

(3) Qualified individual.—For purposes of this subsection—

(A) In general.—The term "qualified individual" means any qualified Hurricane Katrina individual, any qualified Hurricane Rita individual, and any qualified Hurricane Wilma individual.

(B) Qualified Hurricane Katrina individual.—The term "qualified Hurricane Katrina individual" means an individual whose principal place of abode on August 28, 2005, is located in the Hurricane Katrina disaster area and who has sustained an economic loss by reason of Hurricane Katrina.

(C) Qualified Hurricane Rita individual.—The term "qualified Hurricane Rita individual" means an individual (other than a qualified Hurricane Katrina individual) whose principal place of abode on September 23, 2005, is located in the Hurricane Rita disaster area and who has sustained an economic loss by reason of Hurricane Rita.

(D) Qualified Hurricane Wilma individual.—The term "qualified Hurricane Wilma individual" means an individual (other than a qualified Hurricane Katrina individual or a qualified Hurricane Rita individual) whose principal place of abode on October 23, 2005, is located in the Hurricane Wilma disaster area and who has sustained an economic loss by reason of Hurricane Wilma.

(4) Applicable period; qualified beginning date.—For purposes of this subsection—

(A) Hurricane Katrina.—In the case of any qualified Hurricane Katrina individual—

(i) the applicable period is the period beginning on September 24, 2005, and ending on December 31, 2006, and

(ii) the qualified beginning date is August 25, 2005.

(B) Hurricane Rita.—In the case of any qualified Hurricane Rita individual—

(i) the applicable period is the period beginning on the date of the enactment of this subsection and ending on December 31, 2006, and

(ii) the qualified beginning date is September 23, 2005.

(C) Hurricane Wilma.—In the case of any qualified Hurricane Wilma individual—

(i) the applicable period is the period beginning on the date of the enactment of this subparagraph and ending on December 31, 2006, and

(ii) the qualified beginning date is October 23, 2005.

(d) Provisions Relating to Plan Amendments.—

(1) In general.—If this subsection applies to any amendment to any plan or annuity contract, such plan or contract shall be treated as being operated in accordance with the terms of the plan during the period described in paragraph (2)(B)(i).

(2) Amendments to which subsectionapplies.—

(A) In general.—This subsection shall apply to any amendment to any plan or annuity contract which is made—

(i) pursuant to any provision of this section, or pursuant to any regulation issued by the Secretary or the Secretary of Labor under any provision of this section, and

(ii) on or before the last day of the first plan year beginning on or after January 1, 2007, or such later date as the Secretary may prescribe.

In the case of a governmental plan (as defined in section 414(d)), clause (ii) shall be applied by substituting the date which is 2 years after the date otherwise applied under clause (ii).

(B) Conditions.—This subsection shall not apply to any amendment unless—

(i) during the period—

(I) beginning on the date that this section or the regulation described in subparagraph (A)(i) takes effect (or in the case of a plan or contract amendment not required by this section or such regulation, the effective date specified by the plan), and

(II) ending on the date described in subparagraph (A)(ii) (or, if earlier, the date the plan or

IRC Sec. 1400Q(d)(2)(B)(i)(II)

contract amendment is adopted), the plan or contract is operated as if such plan or contract amendment were in effect; and

(ii) such plan or contract amendment applies retroactively for such period.

Amendments to IRC §1400Q

Heartland Disaster Tax Relief Act of 2008 (Pub. L. No. 110-343), as follows:
- For a special rule, see Act, Div. C, §702.

Heartland, Habitat, Harvest, and Horticulture Act of 2008 (Pub. L. No. 110-246), as follows:
- For a special rule, see Act §15345.

Gulf Opportunity Zone Act of 2005 (Pub. L. No. 109-135), as follows:
- IRC §1400Q was added by Act §201(a). Eff. Dec. 21, 2005.

---

* * *

SEC. 1400S. ADDITIONAL TAX RELIEF PROVISIONS

* * *

(c) Required Exercise of Authority Under Section 7508A.—In the case of any taxpayer determined by the Secretary to be affected by the Presidentially declared disaster relating to Hurricane Katrina, Hurricane Rita, or Hurricane Wilma, any relief provided by the Secretary under section 7508A shall be for a period ending not earlier than February 28, 2006.

* * *

Amendments to IRC §1400S (as Excerpted)

Gulf Opportunity Zone Act of 2005 (Pub. L. No. 109-135), as follows:
- IRC §1400S was added by Act §201(a). Eff. Dec. 21, 2005.

---

* * *

Chapter 6—Consolidated Returns
* * *

Subchapter B—Related Rules
* * *

Part II—Certain Controlled Corporations
* * *

SEC. 1563. DEFINITIONS AND SPECIAL RULES.

(a) Controlled Group of Corporations.—For purposes of this part, the term "controlled group of corporations" means any group of—

(1) Parent-subsidiary controlled group.—One or more chains of corporations connected through stock ownership with a common parent corporation if—

(A) stock possessing at least 80 percent of the total combined voting power of all classes of stock entitled to vote or at least 80 percent of the total value of shares of all classes of stock of each of the corporations, except the common parent corporation, is owned (within the meaning of subsection (d)(1)) by one or more of the other corporations; and

(B) the common parent corporation owns (within the meaning of subsection (d)(1)) stock possessing at least 80 percent of the total combined voting power of all classes of stock entitled to vote or at least 80 percent of the total value of shares of all classes of stock of at least one of the other corporations, excluding, in computing such voting power or value, stock owned directly by such other corporations.

(2) Brother-sister controlled group.—Two or more corporations if 5 or fewer persons who are individuals, estates, or trusts own (within the meaning of subsection (d)(2)) stock possessing more than 50 percent of the total combined voting power of all classes of stock entitled to vote or more than 50 percent of the total value of shares of all classes of stock of each corporation, taking into account the stock ownership of each such person only to the extent such stock ownership is identical with respect to each such corporation.

(3) Combined group.—Three or more corporations each of which is a member of a group of corporations described in paragraph (1) or (2), and one of which—

(A) is a common parent corporation included in a group of corporations described in paragraph (1), and also

(B) is included in a group of corporations described in paragraph (2).

(4) Certain insurance companies.—Two or more insurance companies subject to taxation under section 801 which are members of a controlled group of corporations described in paragraph (1), (2), or (3). Such insurance companies shall be treated as a controlled group of corporations separate from any other corporations which are members of the controlled group of corporations described in paragraph (1), (2), or (3).

(b) Component Member.—

(1) General rule.—For purposes of this part, a corporation is a component member of a controlled group of corporations on a December 31 of any taxable year (and with respect to the taxable year which includes such December 31) if such corporation—

(A) is a member of such controlled group of corporations on the December 31 included in such year and is not treated as an excluded member under paragraph (2), or

(B) is not a member of such controlled group of corporations on the December 31 included in such year but is treated as an additional member under paragraph (3).

(2) Excluded members.—A corporation which is a member of a controlled group of corporations on December 31 of any taxable year shall be treated as an excluded member of such group for the taxable year including such December 31 if such corporation—

(A) is a member of such group for less than one-half the number of days in such taxable year which precede such December 31,

(B) is exempt from taxation under section 501(a) (except a corporation which is subject to tax on its unrelated business taxable income under section 511) for such taxable year,

(C) is a foreign corporation subject to tax under section 881 for such taxable year,

(D) is an insurance company subject to taxation under section 801 (other than an insurance company which is a member of a controlled group described in subsection (a)(4)), or

(E) is a franchised corporation, as defined in subsection (f)(4).

(3) Additional members.—A corporation which—

(A) was a member of a controlled group of corporations at any time during a calendar year,

(B) is not a member of such group on December 31 of such calendar year, and

(C) is not described, with respect to such group, in subparagraph (B), (C), (D), or (E) of paragraph (2),

shall be treated as an additional member of such group on December 31 for its taxable year including such December 31 if it was a member of such group for one-half (or more) of the number of days in such taxable year which precede such December 31.

(4) Overlapping groups.—If a corporation is a component member of more than one controlled group of corporations with respect to any taxable year, such corporation shall be treated as a component member of only one controlled group. The determination as to the group of which such corporation is a component member shall be made under regulations prescribed by the Secretary which are consistent with the purposes of this part.

(c) Certain Stock Excluded.—

(1) General rule.—For purposes of this part, the term "stock" does not include—

(A) nonvoting stock which is limited and preferred as to dividends,

(B) treasury stock, and

(C) stock which is treated as "excluded stock" under paragraph (2).

(2) Stock treated as "excluded stock."—

(A) Parent-subsidiary controlled group.—For purposes of subsection (a)(1), if a corporation (referred to in this paragraph as "parent corporation") owns (within the meaning of subsections (d)(1) and (e)(4)), 50 percent or more of the total combined voting power of all classes of stock entitled to vote or 50 percent or more of the total value of shares of all classes of stock in another corporation (referred to in this paragraph as "subsidiary corporation"), the following stock of the subsidiary corporation shall be treated as excluded stock—

(i) stock in the subsidiary corporation held by a trust which is part of a plan of deferred compensation for the benefit of the employees of the parent corporation or the subsidiary corporation,

(ii) stock in the subsidiary corporation owned by an individual (within the meaning of subsection (d)(2)) who is a principal stockholder or officer of the parent corporation. For purposes of this clause, the term "principal stockholder" of a corporation means an individual who owns (within the meaning of subsection (d)(2)) 5 percent or more of the total combined voting power of all classes of stock entitled to vote or 5 percent or more of the total value of shares of all classes of stock in such corporation,

(iii) stock in the subsidiary corporation owned (within the meaning of subsection (d)(2)) by an employee of the subsidiary corporation if such stock is subject to conditions which run in favor of such parent (or subsidiary) corporation and which substantially restrict or limit the employee's right (or if the employee constructively owns such stock, the direct owner's right) to dispose of such stock, or

(iv) stock in the subsidiary corporation owned (within the meaning of subsection (d)(2)) by an organization (other than the parent corporation) to which section 501 (relating to certain educational and charitable organizations which are exempt from tax) applies and which is controlled directly or indirectly by the parent corporation or subsidiary corporation, by an individual, estate, or trust that is a principal stockholder (within the meaning of clause (ii)) of the parent corporation, or by an officer of the parent corporation, or by any combination thereof.

(B) Brother-sister controlled group.—For purposes of subsection (a)(2), if 5 or fewer persons who are individuals, estates, or trusts (referred to in this subparagraph as "common owners") own (within the meaning of subsection (d)(2)), 50 percent or more of the total combined voting power of all classes of stock entitled to vote or 50 percent or more of the total value of shares of all classes of stock in a corporation, the following stock of such corporation shall be treated as excluded stock—

IRC Sec. 1563(c)(2)(B)

(i) stock in such corporation held by an employees' trust described in section 401(a) which is exempt from tax under section 501(a), if such trust is for the benefit of the employees of such corporation,

(ii) stock in such corporation owned (within the meaning of subsection (d)(2)) by an employee of the corporation if such stock is subject to conditions which run in favor of any of such common owners (or such corporation) and which substantially restrict or limit the employee's right (or if the employee constructively owns such stock, the direct owner's right) to dispose of such stock. If a condition which limits or restricts the employee's right (or the direct owner's right) to dispose of such stock also applies to the stock held by any of the common owners pursuant to a bona fide reciprocal stock purchase arrangement, such condition shall not be treated as one which restricts or limits the employee's right to dispose of such stock, or

(iii) stock in such corporation owned (within the meaning of subsection (d)(2)) by an organization to which section 501 (relating to certain educational and charitable organizations which are exempt from tax) applies and which is controlled directly or indirectly by such corporation, by an individual, estate, or trust that is a principal stockholder (within the meaning of subparagraph (A)(ii)) of such corporation, by an officer of such corporation, or by any combination thereof.

(d) Rules for Determining Stock Ownership.—

(1) Parent-subsidiary controlled group.—For purposes of determining whether a corporation is a member of a parent-subsidiary controlled group of corporations (within the meaning of subsection (a)(1)), stock owned by a corporation means—

(A) stock owned directly by such corporation, and

(B) stock owned with the application of paragraphs (1), (2), and (3) of subsection (e).

(2) Brother-sister controlled group.—For purposes of determining whether a corporation is a member of a brother-sister controlled group of corporations (within the meaning of subsection (a)(2)), stock owned by a person who is an individual, estate, or trust means—

(A) stock owned directly by such person, and

(B) stock owned with the application of subsection (e).

(e) Constructive Ownership.—

(1) Options.—If any person has an option to acquire stock, such stock shall be considered as owned by such person. For purposes of this paragraph, an option to acquire such an option, and each one of a series of such options, shall be considered as an option to acquire such stock.

(2) Attribution from partnerships.—Stock owned, directly or indirectly, by or for a partnership shall be considered as owned by any partner having an interest of 5 percent or more in either the capital or profits of the partnership in proportion to his interest in capital or profits, whichever such proportion is the greater.

(3) Attribution from estates or trusts.—

(A) Stock owned, directly or indirectly, by or for an estate or trust shall be considered as owned by any beneficiary who has an actuarial interest of 5 percent or more in such stock, to the extent of such actuarial interest. For purposes of this subparagraph, the actuarial interest of each beneficiary shall be determined by assuming the maximum exercise of discretion by the fiduciary in favor of such beneficiary and the maximum use of such stock to satisfy his rights as a beneficiary.

(B) Stock owned, directly or indirectly, by or for any portion of a trust of which a person is considered the owner under subpart E of part I of subchapter J (relating to grantors and others treated as substantial owners) shall be considered as owned by such person.

(C) This paragraph shall not apply to stock owned by any employees' trust described in section 401(a) which is exempt from tax under section 501(a).

(4) Attribution from corporations.—Stock owned, directly or indirectly, by or for a corporation shall be considered as owned by any person who owns (within the meaning of subsection (d)) 5 percent or more in value of its stock in that proportion which the value of the stock which such person so owns bears to the value of all the stock in such corporation.

(5) Spouse.—An individual shall be considered as owning stock in a corporation owned, directly or indirectly, by or for his spouse (other than a spouse who is legally separated from the individual under a decree of divorce whether interlocutory or final, or a decree of separate maintenance), except in the case of a corporation with respect to which each of the following conditions is satisfied for its taxable year—

(A) The individual does not, at any time during such taxable year, own directly any stock in such corporation;

(B) The individual is not a director or employee and does not participate in the management of such corporation at any time during such taxable year;

(C) Not more than 50 percent of such corporation's gross income for such taxable year was derived from royalties, rents, dividends, interest, and annuities; and

(D) Such stock in such corporation is not, at any time during such taxable year, subject to conditions which substantially restrict or limit the spouse's right to dispose of such stock and which run in favor of the individual or his children who have not attained the age of 21 years.

(6) Children, grandchildren, parents, and grandparents.—

(A) Minor children.—An individual shall be considered as owning stock owned, directly or indirectly, by or for his children who have not attained the age of 21 years, and, if the individual has not attained the age of 21 years, the stock owned, directly or indirectly, by or for his parents.

(B) Adult children and grandchildren.—An individual who owns (within the meaning of subsection (d)(2), but without regard to this subparagraph) more than 50 percent of the total combined voting power of all classes of stock entitled to vote or more than 50 percent of the total value of shares of all classes of stock in a corporation shall be considered as owning the stock in such corporation owned, directly or indirectly, by or for his parents, grandparents, grandchildren, and children who have attained the age of 21 years.

(C) Adopted child.—For purposes of this section, a legally adopted child of an individual shall be treated as a child of such individual by blood.

(f) Other Definitions and Rules.—

(1) Employee defined.—For purposes of this section the term "employee" has the same meaning such term is given by paragraphs (1) and (2) of section 3121(d).

(2) Operating rules.—

(A) In general.—Except as provided in subparagraph (B), stock constructively owned by a person by reason of the application of paragraph (1), (2), (3), (4), (5), or (6) of subsection (e) shall, for purposes of applying such paragraphs, be treated as actually owned by such person.

(B) Members of family.—Stock constructively owned by an individual by reason of the application of paragraph (5) or (6) of subsection (e) shall not be treated as owned by him for purposes of again applying such paragraphs in order to make another the constructive owner of such stock.

(3) Special rules.—For purposes of this section—

(A) If stock may be considered as owned by a person under subsection (e)(1) and under any other paragraph of subsection (e), it shall be considered as owned by him under subsection (e)(1).

(B) If stock is owned (within the meaning of subsection (d)) by two or more persons, such stock shall be considered as owned by the person whose ownership of such stock results in the corporation being a component member of a controlled group. If by reason of the preceding sentence, a corporation would (but for this sentence) become a component member of two controlled groups, it shall be treated as a component member of one controlled group. The determination as to the group of which such corporation is a component member shall be made under regulations prescribed by the Secretary which are consistent with the purposes of this part.

(C) If stock is owned by a person within the meaning of subsection (d) and such ownership results in the corporation being a component member of a controlled group, such stock shall not be treated as excluded stock under subsection (c)(2), if by reason of treating such stock as excluded stock the result is that such corporation is not a component member of a controlled group of corporations.

(4) Franchised corporation.—If—

(A) a parent corporation (as defined in subsection (c)(2)(A)), or a common owner (as defined in subsection (c)(2)(B)), of a corporation which is a member of a controlled group of corporations is under a duty (arising out of a written agreement) to sell stock of such corporation (referred to in this paragraph as "franchised corporation") which is franchised to sell the products of another member, or the common owner, of such controlled group;

(B) such stock is to be sold to an employee (or employees) of such franchised corporation pursuant to a bona fide plan designated to eliminate the stock ownership of the parent corporation or of the common owner in the franchised corporation;

(C) such plan—

(i) provides a reasonable selling price for such stock, and

(ii) requires that a portion of the employee's share of the profits of such corporation (whether received as compensation or as a dividend) be applied to the purchase of such stock (or the purchase of notes, bonds, debentures, or other similar evidence of indebtedness of such franchised corporation held by such parent corporation or common owner);

(D) such employee (or employees) owns directly more than 20 percent of the total value of shares of all classes of stock in such franchised corporation;

(E) more than 50 percent of the inventory of such franchised corporation is acquired from members of the controlled group, the common owner, or both; and

(F) all of the conditions contained in subparagraphs (A), (B), (C), (D), and (E) have been met for one-half (or more) of the number of days preceding the December 31 included within the taxable year (or if the taxable year does not include December 31, the last day of such year) of the franchised corporation,

then such franchised corporation shall be treated as an excluded member of such group, under subsection (b)(2), for such taxable year.

IRC Sec. 1563(f)(4)(F)

(5) Brother-sister controlled group definition for provisions other than this part.—

(A) In general.—Except as specifically provided in an applicable provision, subsection (a)(2) shall be applied to an applicable provision as if it read as follows:

"(2) Brother-sister controlled group.—Two or more corporations if 5 or fewer persons who are individuals, estates, or trusts own (within the meaning of subsection (d)(2)) stock possessing—

(A) at least 80 percent of the total combined voting power of all classes of stock entitled to vote, or at least 80 percent of the total value of shares of all classes of stock, of each corporation, and

(B) more than 50 percent of the total combined voting power of all classes of stock entitled to vote or more than 50 percent of the total value of shares of all classes of stock of each corporation, taking into account the stock ownership of each such person only to the extent such stock ownership is identical with respect to each such corporation."

(B) Applicable provision.—For purposes of this paragraph, an applicable provision is any provision of law (other than this part) which incorporates the definition of controlled group of corporations under subsection (a).

Recent Amendments to IRC §1563

American Jobs Creation Act of 2004 (Pub. L. No. 108-357), as follows:

• IRC §1563(a)(2) was amended by Act §900(a) by replacing "possessing—" and all that follows through "(B)" with "possessing". Eff. tax years beginning after Oct. 22, 2004. IRC §1563(a)(2) prior to amendment:

(2) Brother-sister controlled group.—Two or more corporations if 5 or fewer persons who are individuals, estates, or trusts own (within the meaning of subsection (d)(2)) stock possessing—

(A) at least 80 percent of the total combined voting power of all classes of stock entitled to vote or at least 80 percent of the total value of shares of all classes of the stock of each corporation,

(B) more than 50 percent of the total combined voting power of all classes of stock entitled to vote or more than 50 percent of the total value of shares of all classes of stock of each corporation, taking into account the stock ownership of each such person only to the extent such stock ownership is identical with respect to each such corporation.

• IRC §1563(f) was amended by Act §900(b) by adding new para. (5). Eff. tax years beginning after Oct. 22, 2004.

---

* * *

Subtitle B—Estate and Gift Taxes

Chapter 11—Estate Tax

Subchapter A—Estates of Citizens or Residents

* * *

Part III—Gross Estate

* * *

SEC. 2039. ANNUITIES.

(a) In General.—The gross estate shall include the value of an annuity or other payment receivable by any beneficiary by reason of surviving the decedent under any form of contract or agreement entered into after March 3, 1931 (other than as insurance under policies on the life of the decedent), if, under such contract or agreement, an annuity or other payment was payable to the decedent, or the decedent possessed the right to receive such annuity or payment, either alone or in conjunction with another for his life or for any period not ascertainable without reference to his death or for any period which does not in fact end before his death.

(b) Amount Includible.—Subsection (a) shall apply to only such part of the value of the annuity or other payment receivable under such contract or agreement as is proportionate to that part of the purchase price therefor contributed by the decedent. For purposes of this section, any contribution by the decedent's employer or former employer to the purchase price of such contract or agreement (whether or not to an employee's trust or fund forming part of a pension, annuity, retirement, bonus or profit-sharing plan) shall be considered to be contributed by the decedent if made by reason of his employment.

* * *

Subtitle C—Employment Taxes

Chapter 21—Federal Insurance Contributions Act

* * *

Subchapter C—General Provisions

SEC. 3121. DEFINITIONS.

(a) Wages.—For purposes of this chapter, the term "wages" means all remuneration for employment, including the cash value of all remuneration (including benefits) paid in any medium other than cash; except that such term shall not include—

(1) in the case of the taxes imposed by sections 3101(a) and 3111(a), that part of the remuneration which, after remuneration (other than remuneration referred to in the succeeding paragraphs of this subsection) equal to the contribution and benefit base (as determined under section 230 of the Social Security Act) with respect to employment has been paid to an individual by an employer during a calendar year with respect to which such contribution and benefit base is effective, is paid to such individual by such employer during such calendar year. If an employer (hereinafter referred to as successor employer) during any calendar year acquires substantially all the property used in

the trade or business of another employer (hereinafter referred to as a predecessor), or used in a separate unit of a trade or business of a predecessor, and immediately after the acquisition employs in his trade or business an individual who immediately prior to the acquisition was employed in a trade or business of such predecessor, then, for the purpose of determining whether the successor employer has paid remuneration (other than remuneration referred to in the succeeding paragraphs of this subsection) with respect to employment equal to the Contribution and benefit base (as determined under section 230 of the Social Security Act) to such individual during such calendar year, any remuneration (other than remuneration referred to in the succeeding paragraphs of this subsection) with respect to employment paid (or considered under this paragraph as having been paid) to such individual by such predecessor during such calendar year and prior to such acquisition shall be considered as having been paid by such successor employer;

(2) the amount of any payment (including any amount paid by an employer for insurance or annuities, or into a fund, to provide for any such payment) made to, or on behalf of, an employee or any of his dependents under a plan or system established by an employer which makes provision for his employees generally (or for his employees generally and their dependents) or for a class or classes of his employees (or for a class or classes of his employees and their dependents), on account of—

(A) sickness or accident disability (but, in the case of payments made to an employee or any of his dependents, this subparagraph shall exclude from the term "wages" only payments which are received under a workmen's compensation law), or

(B) medical or hospitalization expenses in connections with sickness or accident disability, or

(C) death, except that this paragraph does not apply to a payment for group-term life insurance to the extent that such payment is includible in the gross income of the employee;

(3) [Repealed.]

(4) any payment on account of sickness or accident disability, or medical or hospitalization expenses in connection with sickness or accident disability, made by an employer to, or on behalf of, an employee after the expiration of 6 calendar months following the last calendar month in which the employee worked for such employer;

(5) any payment made to, or on behalf of, an employee or his beneficiary—

(A) from or to a trust described in section 401(a) which is exempt from tax under section 501(a) at the time of such payment unless such payment is made to an employee of the trust as remuneration for services rendered as such employee and not as a beneficiary of the trust,

(B) under or to an annuity plan which, at the time of such payment, is a plan described in section 403(a),

(C) under a simplified employee pension plan (as defined in section 408(k)(1)), other than any contributions described in section 408(k)(6),

(D) under or to an annuity contract described in section 403(b), other than a payment for the purchase of such contract which is made by reason of a salary reduction agreement (whether evidenced by a written instrument or otherwise),

(E) under or to an exempt governmental deferred compensation plan (as defined in subsection (v)(3)),

(F) to supplement pension benefits under a plan or trust described in any of the foregoing provisions of this paragraph to take into account some portion or all of the increase in the cost of living (as determined by the Secretary of Labor) since retirement but only if such supplemental payments are under a plan which is treated as a welfare plan under section 3(2)(B)(ii) of the Employee Retirement Income Security Act of 1974,

(G) under a cafeteria plan (within the meaning of section 125) if such payment would not be treated as wages without regard to such plan and it is reasonable to believe that (if section 125 applied for purposes of this section) section 125 would not treat any wages as constructively received,

(H) under an arrangement to which section 408(p) applies, other than any elective contributions under paragraph (2)(A)(i) thereof,

(I) under a plan described in section 457(e)(11)(A)(ii) and maintained by an eligible employer (as defined in section 457(e)(1));

(6) the payment by an employer (without deduction from the remuneration of the employee)—

(A) of the tax imposed upon an employee under section 3101, or

(B) of any payment required from an employee under a State unemployment compensation law,

with respect to remuneration paid to an employee for domestic service in a private home of the employer or for agricultural labor;

(7)(A) remuneration paid in any medium other than cash to an employee for service not in the course of the employer's trade or business or for domestic service in a private home of the employer;

(B) cash remuneration paid by an employer in any calendar year to an employee for domestic service in a private home of the employer (including domestic service on a farm operated for profit), if the cash remuneration paid in such year by the employer to the employee for such service is less than

IRC Sec. 3121(a)(7)(B)

the applicable dollar threshold (as defined in subsection (x)) for such year;

(C) cash remuneration paid by an employer in any calendar year to an employee for service not in the course of the employer's trade or business, if the cash remuneration paid in such year by the employer to the employee for such service is less than $100. As used in this subparagraph, the term "service not in the course of the employer's trade or business" does not include domestic service in a private home of the employer and does not include service described in subsection (g)(5);

(8)(A) remuneration paid in any medium other than cash for agricultural labor;

(B) cash remuneration paid by an employer in any calendar year to an employee for agricultural labor unless—

(i) the cash remuneration paid in such year by the employer to the employee for such labor is $150 or more, or

(ii) the employer's expenditures for agricultural labor in such year equal or exceed $2,500,

except that clause (ii) shall not apply in determining whether remuneration paid to an employee constitutes "wages" under this section if such employee (I) is employed as a hand harvest laborer and is paid on a piece rate basis in an operation which has been, and is customarily and generally recognized as having been, paid on a piece rate basis in the region of employment, (II) commutes daily from his permanent residence to the farm on which he is so employed, and (III) has been employed in agriculture less than 13 weeks during the preceding calendar year;

(9) [Repealed.]

(10) remuneration paid by an employer in any calendar year to an employee for service described in subsection (d)(3)(C) (relating to home workers), if the cash remuneration paid in such year by the employer to the employee for such service is less than $100;

(11) remuneration paid to or on behalf of an employee if (and to the extent that) at the time of the payment of such remuneration it is reasonable to believe that a corresponding deduction is allowable under section 217 (determined without regard to section 274(n));

(12) (A) tips paid in any medium other than cash;

(B) cash tips received by an employee in any calendar month in the course of his employment by an employer unless the amount of such cash tips is $20 or more;

(13) any payment or series of payments by an employer to an employee or any of his dependents which is paid—

(A) upon or after the termination of an employee's employment relationship because of (i) death, or (ii) retirement for disability, and

(B) under a plan established by the employer which makes provision for his employees generally or a class or classes of his employees (or for such employees or class or classes of employees and their dependents),

other than such payment or series of payments which would have been paid if the employee's employment relationship had not been so terminated;

(14) any payment made by an employer to a survivor or the estate of a former employee after the calendar year in which such employee died;

(15) any payment made by an employer to an employee, if at the time such payment is made such employee is entitled to disability insurance benefits under section 223(a) of the Social Security Act and such entitlement commenced prior to the calendar year in which such payment is made, and if such employee did not perform any services for such employer during the period for which such payment is made;

(16) remuneration is paid by an organization exempt from income tax under section 501(a) (other than an organization described in section 401(a)) or under section 521 in any calendar year to an employee for service rendered in the employ of such organization, if the remuneration paid in such year by the organization to the employee for such service is less than $100;

(17) any contribution, payment, or service provided by an employer which may be excluded from the gross income of an employee, his spouse, or his dependents, under the provisions of section 120 (relating to amounts received under qualified group legal services plans);

(18) any payment made, or benefit furnished, to or for the benefit of an employee if at the time of such payment or such furnishing it is reasonable to believe that the employee will be able to exclude such payment or benefit from income under section 127, 129, 134(b)(4), or 134(b)(5);

(19) the value of any meals or lodging furnished by or on behalf of the employer if at the time of such furnishing it is reasonable to believe that the employee will be able to exclude such items from income under section 119;

(20) any benefit provided to or on behalf of an employee if at the time such benefit is provided it is reasonable to believe that the employee will be able to exclude such benefit from income under section 74(c), 108(f)(4), 117, or 132;

(21) in the case of a member of an Indian tribe, any remuneration on which no tax is imposed by this chapter by reason of section 7873 (relating to income derived by Indians from exercise of fishing rights);

(22) remuneration on account of—

(A) a transfer of a share of stock to any individual pursuant to an exercise of an incentive stock option (as defined in section 422(b)) or under an employee stock purchase plan (as defined in section 423(b)), or (B) any disposition by the individual of such stock; or

(23) any benefit or payment which is excludable from the gross income of the employee under section 139B(b).

Nothing in the regulations prescribed for purposes of chapter 24 (relating to income tax withholding) which provides an exclusion from "wages" as used in such chapter shall be construed to require a similar exclusion from "wages" in the regulations prescribed for purposes of this chapter.

Except as otherwise provided in regulations prescribed by the Secretary, any third party which makes a payment included in wages solely by reason of the parenthetical matter contained in subparagraph (A) of paragraph (2) shall be treated for purposes of this chapter and chapter 22 as the employer with respect to such wages.

* * *

(v) Treatment of Certain Deferred Compensation and Salary Reduction Arrangements.—

(1) Certain employer contributions treated as wages.—Nothing in any paragraph of subsection (a) (other than paragraph (1)) shall exclude from the term "wages"—

(A) any employer contribution under a qualified cash or deferred arrangement (as defined in section 401(k)) to the extent not included in gross income by reason of section 402(e)(3) or consisting of designated Roth contributions (as defined in section 402A(c)), or

(B) any amount treated as an employer contribution under section 414(h)(2) where the pickup referred to in such section is pursuant to a salary reduction agreement (whether evidenced by a written instrument or otherwise).

(2) Treatment of certain nonqualified deferred compensation plans.—

(A) In general.—Any amount deferred under a nonqualified deferred compensation plan shall be taken into account for purposes of this chapter as of the later of—

(i) when services are performed, or

(ii) when there is no substantial risk of forfeiture of the rights to such amount.

The preceding sentence shall not apply to any excess parachute payment (as defined in section 280G(b)) or to any specified stock compensation (as defined in section 4985) on which tax is imposed by section 4985.

(B) Taxed only once.—Any amount taken into account as wages by reason of subparagraph (A)

(and the income attributable thereto) shall not thereafter be treated as wages for purposes of this chapter.

(C) Nonqualified deferred compensation plan.— For purposes of this paragraph, the term "nonqualified deferred compensation plan" means any plan or other arrangement for deferral of compensation other than a plan described in subsection (a)(5).

(3) Exempt governmental deferred compensation plan.—For purposes of subsection (a)(5), the term "exempt governmental deferred compensation plan" means any plan providing for deferral of compensation established and maintained for its employees by the United States, by a State or political subdivision thereof, or by an agency or instrumentality of any of the foregoing. Such term shall not include—

(A) any plan to which section 83, 402(b), 403(c), 457(a), or 457(f)(1) applies,

(B) any annuity contract described in section 403(b), and

(C) the Thrift Savings Fund (within the meaning of subchapter III of chapter 84 of title 5, United States Code).

* * *

(x) Applicable Dollar Threshold.—For purposes of subsection (a)(7)(B), the term "applicable dollar threshold" means $1,000. In the case of calendar years after 1995, the Commissioner of Social Security shall adjust such $1,000 amount at the same time and in the same manner as under section 215(a)(1)(B)(ii) of the Social Security Act with respect to the amounts referred to in section 215(a)(1)(B)(i) of such Act, except that, for purposes of this paragraph, 1993 shall be substituted for the calendar year referred to in section 215(a)(1)(B)(ii)(II) of such Act. If any amount as adjusted under the preceding sentence is not a multiple of $100, such amount shall be rounded to the next lowest multiple of $100.

* * *

(z) Treatment of Certain Foreign Persons as American Employers.—

(1) In general.—If any employee of a foreign person is performing services in connection with a contract between the United States Government (or any instrumentality thereof) and any member of any domestically controlled group of entities which includes such foreign person, such foreign person shall be treated for purposes of this chapter as an American employer with respect to such services performed by such employee.

(2) Domestically controlled group of entities.— For purposes of this subsection—

(A) In general.—The term "domestically controlled group of entities" means a controlled group of entities the common parent of which is a domestic corporation.

(B) Controlled group of entities.—The term "controlled group of entities" means a controlled group of corporations as defined in section 1563(a)(1), except that—

(i) "more than 50 percent" shall be substituted for "at least 80 percent" each place it appears therein, and

(ii) the determination shall be made without regard to subsections (a)(4) and (b)(2) of section 1563.

A partnership or any other entity (other than a corporation) shall be treated as a member of a controlled group of entities if such entity is controlled (within the meaning of section 954(d)(3)) by members of such group (including any entity treated as a member of such group by reason of this sentence).

(3) **Liability of common parent.**—In the case of a foreign person who is a member of any domestically controlled group of entities, the common parent of such group shall be jointly and severally liable for any tax under this chapter for which such foreign person is liable by reason of this subsection, and for any penalty imposed on such person by this title with respect to any failure to pay such tax or to file any return or statement with respect to such tax or wages subject to such tax. No deduction shall be allowed under this title for any liability imposed by the preceding sentence.

(4) **Provisions preventing double taxation.**—

(A) Agreements.—Paragraph (1) shall not apply to any services which are covered by an agreement under subsection (l).

(B) Equivalent foreign taxation.—Paragraph (1) shall not apply to any services if the employer establishes to the satisfaction of the Secretary that the remuneration paid by such employer for such services is subject to a tax imposed by a foreign country which is substantially equivalent to the taxes imposed by this chapter.

(5) **Cross reference.**—For relief from taxes in cases covered by certain international agreements, see sections 3101(c) and 3111(c).

Recent Amendments to IRC §3121 (as Excerpted)

Heroes Earnings Assistance and Relief Tax Act of 2008 (Pub. L. No. 110-245), as follows:
- IRC §3121(a)(21)–(22) were amended, and (23) was added, by Act §115(a)(1). Eff. as if included in Pub. L. No. 110-142, §5 [effective for taxable years beginning after Dec. 31, 2007], see Act §115(d).
- IRC §3121(z) was added by Act §302(a). Eff. for services performed in calendar months beginning more than 30 days after date of enactment [enacted: June 17, 2008], see Act §302(c).

Tax Technical Corrections Act of 2007 (Pub. L. No. 110-172), as follows:
- IRC §3121(v)(1)(A) was amended by Act §8(a)(2) by inserting "or consisting of designated Roth contributions (as defined in section 402A(c))" before the comma at the end. Eff. as if included in Pub. L. No. 106-17, §617.

Ronald W. Reagan National Defense Authorization Act for Fiscal Year 2005 (Pub. L. No. 108-375), as follows:
- IRC §3121(a)(18) was amended by Act §585(b)(2)(B) by replacing "or 134(b)(4)" with "134(b)(4), or 134(b)(5)". Eff. for travel benefits provided after Oct. 28, 2004.

American Jobs Creation Act of 2004 (Pub. L. No. 108-357), as follows:
- IRC §3121(a) was amended by Act §251(a)(1)(A) by striking "or" at the end of para. (20), by replacing the period at the end of para. (21) with "; or", and by inserting new para. (22). Eff. for stock acquired pursuant to options exercised after Oct. 22, 2004.
- IRC §3121(a)(20) was amended by Act §320(b)(1) by adding "108(f)(4)," after "74(c),". Eff. for amounts received by an individual in tax years beginning after Dec. 31, 2003.
- IRC §3121(v)(2)(A) was amended by Act §802(c)(1) by inserting before the period in the last sentence "or to any specified stock compensation (as defined in §4985) on which tax is imposed by §4985." Eff. generally Mar. 4, 2003, except that periods before Mar. 4, 2003, are not taken into account in applying IRC §4985(a) and (e)(A). See Act §802(d).

Social Security Protection Act of 2004 (Pub. L. No. 108-203), as follows:
- IRC §3121(a)(7)(B) was amended by Act §423(a) by replacing "described in subsection (g)(5)" with "on a farm operated for profit". Eff. Mar. 2, 2004.

Military Family Tax Relief Act of 2003 (Pub. L. No. 108-121), as follows:
- IRC §3121(a)(18) was amended by Act §106(b)(2) by replacing "or 129" with ", 129, or 134(b)(4)." Eff. tax years beginning after Dec. 31, 2002. See Act §106(d).

---

* * *

Chapter 24—Collection of Income Tax at Source on Wages

Subchapter A—Withholding from Wages

SEC. 3401. DEFINITIONS.

(a) **Wages.**—For purposes of this chapter, the term "wages" means all remuneration (other than fees paid to a public official) for services performed by an employee for his employer, including the cash value of all remuneration (including benefits) paid in any medium other than cash; except that such term shall not include remuneration paid—

(1) for active service performed in a month for which such employee is entitled to the benefits of section 112 (relating to certain combat zone compensation of members of the Armed Forces of the United States) to the extent remuneration for such service is excludable from gross income under such section; or

(2) for agricultural labor (as defined in section 3121(g)) unless the remuneration paid for such labor is wages (as defined in section 3121(a)); or

(3) for domestic service in a private home, local college club, or local chapter of a college fraternity or sorority; or

(4) for service not in the course of the employer's trade or business performed in any calendar quarter

by an employee, unless the cash remuneration paid for such service is $50 or more and such service is performed by an individual who is regularly employed by such employer to perform such service. For purposes of this paragraph, an individual shall be deemed to be regularly employed by an employer during a calendar quarter only if—

(A) on each of some 24 days during such quarter such individual performs for such employer for some portion of the day service not in the course of the employer's trade or business; or

(B) such individual was regularly employed (as determined under subparagraph (A)) by such employer in the performance of such service during the preceding calendar quarter; or

(5) for services by a citizen or resident of the United States for a foreign government or an international organization; or

(6) for such services, performed by a nonresident alien individual, as may be designated by regulations prescribed by the Secretary; or

(7) **[Repealed.]**

(8) (A) for services for an employer (other than the United States or any agency thereof)—

(i) performed by a citizen of the United States if, at the time of the payment of such remuneration, it is reasonable to believe that such remuneration will be excluded from gross income under section 911; or

(ii) performed in a foreign country or in a possession of the United States by such a citizen if, at the time of the payment of such remuneration, the employer is required by the law of any foreign country or possession of the United States to withhold income tax upon such remuneration; or

(B) for services for an employer (other than the United States or any agency thereof) performed by a citizen of the United States within a possession of the United States (other than Puerto Rico), if it is reasonable to believe that at least 80 percent of the remuneration to be paid to the employee by such employer during the calendar year will be for such services; or

(C) for services for an employer (other than the United States or any agency thereof) performed by a citizen of the United States within Puerto Rico, if it is reasonable to believe that during the entire calendar year the employee will be a bona fide resident of Puerto Rico; or

(D) for services for the United States (or any agency thereof) performed by a citizen of the United States within a possession of the United States to the extent the United States (or such agency) withholds taxes on such remuneration pursuant to an agreement with such possession; or

(9) for services performed by a duly ordained, commissioned, or licensed minister of a church in the exercise of his ministry or by a member of a religious order in the exercise of duties required by such order; or

(10) (A) for services performed by an individual under the age of 18 in the delivery or distribution of newspapers or shopping news, not including delivery or distribution to any point for subsequent delivery or distribution; or

(B) for services performed by an individual in, and at the time of, the sale of newspapers or magazines to ultimate consumers, under an arrangement under which the newspapers or magazines are to be sold by him at a fixed price, his compensation being based on the retention of the excess of such price over the amount at which the newspapers or magazines are charged to him, whether or not he is guaranteed a minimum amount of compensation for such services, or is entitled to be credited with the unsold newspapers or magazines turned back; or

(11) for services not in the course of the employer's trade or business, to the extent paid in any medium other than cash; or

(12) to, or on behalf of, an employee or his beneficiary—

(A) from or to a trust described in section 401(a) which is exempt from tax under section 501(a) at the time of such payment unless such payment is made to an employee of the trust as remuneration for services rendered as such employee and not as a beneficiary of the trust; or

(B) under or to an annuity plan which, at the time of such payment, is a plan described in section 403(a); or

(C) for a payment described in section 402(h)(1) and (2) if, at the time of such payment, it is reasonable to believe that the employee will be entitled to an exclusion under such section for payment; or

(D) under an arrangement to which section 408(p) applies, or

(E) under or to an eligible deferred compensation plan which, at the time of such payment, is a plan described in section 457(b) which is maintained by an eligible employer described in section 457(e)(1)(A), or

(13) pursuant to any provision of law other than section 5(c) or 6(1) of the Peace Corps Act, for service performed as a volunteer or volunteer leader within the meaning of such Act; or

(14) in the form of group-term life insurance on the life of an employee; or

(15) to or on behalf of an employee if (and to the extent that) at the time of the payment of such remu-

IRC Sec. 3401(a)(15)

2-414 ERISA: The Law and the Code, 2011 Edition

neration it is reasonable to believe that a corresponding deduction is allowable under section 217 (determined without regard to section 274(n)); or

(16) (A) as tips in any medium other than cash;

(B) as cash tips to an employee in any calendar month in the course of his employment by an employer unless the amount of such cash tips is $20 or more;

(17) for service described in section 3121(b)(20);

(18) for any payment made, or benefit furnished, to or for the benefit of an employee if at the time of such payment or such furnishing it is reasonable to believe that the employee will be able to exclude such payment or benefit from income under section 127, 129, 134(b)(4), or 134(b)(5);

(19) for any benefit provided to or on behalf of an employee if at the time such benefit is provided it is reasonable to believe that the employee will be able to exclude such benefit from income under section 74(c), 108(f)(4), 117, or 132;

(20) for any medical care reimbursement made to or for the benefit of an employee under a self-insured medical reimbursement plan (within the meaning of section 105(h)(6));

(21) for any payment made to or for the benefit of an employee if at the time of such payment it is reasonable to believe that the employee will be able to exclude such payment from income under section 106(b);

(22) any payment made to or for the benefit of an employee if at the time of such payment it is reasonable to believe that the employee will be able to exclude such payment from income under secton 106(d); or

(23) for any benefit or payment which is excludable from the gross income of the employee under section 139B(b).

The term "wages" includes any amount includible in gross income of an employee under section 409A and payment of such amount shall be treated as having been made in the taxable year in which the amount is so includible.

(b) Payroll Period.—For purposes of this chapter, the term "payroll period" means a period for which a payment of wages is ordinarily made to the employee by his employer, and the term "miscellaneous payroll period" means a payroll period other than a daily, weekly, biweekly, semimonthly, monthly, quarterly, semiannual or annual payroll period.

(c) Employee.—For purposes of this chapter, the term "employee" includes an officer, employee, or elected official of the United States, a State, or any political subdivision thereof, or the District of Columbia, or any agency or instrumentality of any one or more of the foregoing. The term "employee" also includes an officer of a corporation.

(d) Employer.—For purposes of this chapter, the term "employer" means the person for whom an individual performs or performed any service, of whatever nature, as the employee of such person, except that—

(1) if the person for whom the individual performs or performed the services does not have control of the payment of the wages for such services, the term "employer" (except for purposes of subsection (a)) means the person having control of the payment of such wages, and

(2) in the case of a person paying wages on behalf of a nonresident alien individual, foreign partnership, or foreign corporation, not engaged in trade or business within the United States, the term "employer" (except for purposes of subsection (a)) means such person.

(e) Number of Withholding Exemptions Claimed.—For purposes of this chapter, the term "number of withholding exemptions claimed" means the number of withholding exemptions claimed in a withholding exemption certificate in effect under section 3402(f), or in effect under the corresponding section of prior law, except that if no such certificate is in effect, the number of withholding exemptions claimed shall be considered to be zero.

(f) Tips.—For purposes of subsection (a), the term "wages" includes tips received by an employee in the course of his employment. Such wages shall be deemed to be paid at the time a written statement including such tips is furnished to the employer pursuant to section 6053(a) or (if no statement including such tips is so furnished) at the time received.

(g) Crew Leader Rules to Apply.—Rules similar to the rules of section 3121(o) shall apply for purposes of this chapter.

(h) Differential Wage Payments to Active Duty Members of the Uninformed Services.—

(1) In general.—For purposes of subsection (a), any differential wage payment shall be treated as a payment of wages by the employer to the employee.

(2) Differential wage payment.—For purposes of paragraph (1), the term "differential wage payment" means any payment which—

(A) is made by an employer to an individual with respect to any period during which the individual is performing service in the uniformed services (as defined in chapter 43 of title 38, United States Code) while on active duty for a period of more than 30 days, and

(B) represents all or a portion of the wages the individual would have received from the employer if the individual were performing service for the employer.

Recent Amendments to IRC §3401

Heroes Earnings Assistance and Relief Tax Act of 2008 (Pub. L. No. 110-245), as follows:

- IRC §3401(a)(23) was added by Act §115(c). Eff. as if included in Pub. L. No. 110-142, §5 [effective for taxable years beginning after Dec. 31, 2007], see Act §115(d).
- IRC §3401(h) was added by Act §105(a)(1). Eff. for remuneration paid after Dec. 31, 2008, see Act §105(a)(2).

Pension Protection Act of 2006 (Pub. L. No. 109-280), as follows:

- **Sunset Provision.** Act §811, provides:

   SEC. 811. PENSIONS AND INDIVIDUAL RETIREMENT ARRANGEMENT PROVISIONS OF ECONOMIC GROWTH AND TAX RELIEF RECONCILIATION ACT OF 2001 MADE PERMANENT.

   Title IX of the Economic Growth and Tax Relief Reconciliation Act of 2001 [Pub. L. No. 107-16] shall not apply to the provisions of, and amendments made by, subtitles A through F [§§601–666] of title VI of such Act (relating to pension and individual retirement arrangement provisions).

Gulf Opportunity Zone Act of 2005 (Pub. L. No. 109-135), as follows:

- IRC §3401(h) was redesignated as subsec. (g) by Act §412(tt). Eff. Dec. 21, 2005.

Ronald W. Reagan National Defense Authorization Act for Fiscal Year 2005 (Pub. L. No. 108-375), as follows:

- IRC §3401(a)(18) was amended by Act §585(b)(2)(B) by replacing "or 134(b)(4)" with "134(b)(4), or 134(b)(5)." Eff. for travel benefits provided after Oct. 28, 2004.

American Jobs Creation Act of 2004 (Pub. L. No. 108-357), as follows:

- IRC §3401(a) was amended by Act §885(b)(2) by adding at the end new flush sentence. Eff. generally for amounts deferred after Dec. 31, 2004. [*Ed. Note*: see Act §§885(d)(2) and (3) and (f).]
- IRC §3401(a)(19) was amended by Act §320(b)(4) by adding "108(f)(4)," after "74(c),". Eff. for amounts received by an individual in tax years beginning after Dec. 31, 2003.

Medicare Prescription Drug, Improvement, and Modernization Act of 2003 (Pub. L. No. 108-173), as follows:

- IRC §3401(a) was amended by Act §1201(d)(2)(C) by striking "or" at the end of para. (20), by replacing the period at the end of para. (21) with "; or", and by inserting new para. (22). Eff. tax years beginning after Dec. 31, 2003.

Military Family Tax Relief Act of 2003 (Pub. L. No. 108-121), as follows:

- IRC §3401(a)(18) was amended by Act §106(b)(4) by replacing "or 129" with ", 129, or 134(b)(4)". Eff. tax years beginning after Dec. 31, 2002. See Act §106(d).

Economic Growth and Tax Relief Reconciliation Act of 2001 (Pub. L. No. 107-16), as follows:

- IRC §3401(a)(12)(E) was added by Act §641(a)(1)(D)(i). Eff. generally for distributions after Dec. 31, 2001. [*Ed. Note*: see Act §641(f)(3).]
- **Sunset Provision.** Act §901, as amended by Pub. L. No. 111-312, §101(a)(1), provides the sunset rule below. But see Pub. L. No. 109-280, §811, and Pub. L. No. 111-148, §10909(c), as amended by Pub. L. No. 111-312, §101(b)(1).

   SEC. 901. SUNSET OF PROVISIONS OF ACT.

   (a) In general. All provisions of, and amendments made by, this Act shall not apply—

   (1) to taxable, plan, or limitation years beginning after December 31, 2012, or

   (2) in the case of title V, to estates of decedents dying, gifts made, or generation skipping transfers, after December 31, 2012.

   (b) Application of certain laws.—The Internal Revenue Code of 1986 and the Employee Retirement Income Security Act of 1974 shall be applied and administered to years, estates, gifts, and transfers described in subsection (a) as if the provisions and amendments described in subsection (a) had never been enacted.

* * *

SEC. 3405. SPECIAL RULES FOR PENSIONS, ANNUITIES, AND CERTAIN OTHER DEFERRED INCOME.

(a) Periodic Payments.—

(1) Withholding as if payment were wages.— The payor of any periodic payment (as defined in subsection (e)(2)) shall withhold from such payment the amount which would be required to be withheld from such payment if such payment were a payment of wages by an employer to an employee for the appropriate payroll period.

(2) Election of no withholding.—An individual may elect to have paragraph (1) not apply with respect to periodic payments made to such individual. Such an election shall remain in effect until revoked by such individual.

(3) When election takes effect.—Any election under this subsection (and any revocation of such an election) shall take effect as provided by subsection (f)(3) of section 3402 for withholding exemption certificates.

(4) Amount withheld where no withholding exemption certificate in effect.—In the case of any payment with respect to which a withholding exemption certificate is not in effect, the amount withheld under paragraph (1) shall be determined by treating the payee as a married individual claiming 3 withholding exemptions.

(b) Nonperiodic Distribution.—

(1) Withholding.—The payor of any nonperiodic distribution (as defined in subsection (e)(3)) shall withhold from such distribution an amount equal to 10 percent of such distribution.

(2) Election of no withholding.—

(A) In general.—An individual may elect not to have paragraph (1) apply with respect to any nonperiodic distribution.

(B) Scope of election.—An election under subparagraph (A)—

   (i) except as provided in clause (ii), shall be on a distribution-by-distribution basis, or

   (ii) to the extent provided in regulations, may apply to subsequent nonperiodic distributions made by the payor to the payee under the same arrangement.

(c) Eligible Rollover Distributions.—

(1) In general.—In the case of any designated distribution which is an eligible rollover distribution—

(A) subsections (a) and (b) shall not apply, and

(B) the payor of such distribution shall withhold from such distribution an amount equal to 20 percent of such distribution.

(2) Exception.—Paragraph (1)(B) shall not apply to any distribution if the distributee elects under section 401(a)(31)(A) to have such distribution paid directly to an eligible retirement plan.

(3) Eligible rollover distribution.—For purposes of this subsection, the term "eligible rollover distribution" has the meaning given such term by section 402(f)(2)(A).

(d) Liability for Withholding.—

(1) In general.—Except as provided in paragraph (2), the payor of a designated distribution (as defined in subsection (e)(1)) shall withhold, and be liable for, payment of the tax required to be withheld under this section.

(2) Plan administrator liable in certain cases.—

(A) In general.—In the case of any plan to which this paragraph applies, paragraph (1) shall not apply and the plan administrator shall withhold, and be liable for, payment of the tax unless the plan administrator—

(i) directs the payor to withhold such tax, and

(ii) provides the payor with such information as the Secretary may require by regulations.

(B) Plans to which paragraph applies.—This paragraph applies to any plan described in, or which at any time has been determined to be described in—

(i) section 401(a),

(ii) section 403(a),

(iii) section 301(d) of the Tax Reduction Act of 1975, or

(iv) section 457(b) and which is maintained by an eligible employer described in section 457(e)(1)(A).

(e) Definitions and Special Rules.—For purposes of this section—

(1) Designated distribution.—

(A) In general.—Except as provided in subparagraph (B), the term "designated distribution" means any distribution or payment from or under—

(i) an employer deferred compensation plan,

(ii) an individual retirement plan (as defined in section 7701(a)(37)), or

(iii) a commercial annuity.

(B) Exceptions.—The term "designated distribution" shall not include—

(i) any amount which is wages without regard to this section,

(ii) the portion of a distribution or payment which it is reasonable to believe is not includible in gross income,

(iii) any amount which is subject to withholding under subchapter A of chapter 3 (relating to withholding of tax on nonresident aliens and for-

eign corporations) by the person paying such amount or which would be so subject but for a tax treaty, or

(iv) any distribution described in section 404(k)(2).

For purposes of clause (ii), any distribution or payment from or under an individual retirement plan (other than a Roth IRA) shall be treated as includible in gross income.

(2) Periodic payment.—The term "periodic payment" means a designated distribution which is an annuity or similar periodic payment.

(3) Nonperiodic distribution.—The term "nonperiodic distribution" means any designated distribution which is not a periodic payment.

(4) [Repealed.]

(5) Employer deferred compensation plan.—The term "employer deferred compensation plan" means any pension, annuity, profit-sharing, or stock bonus plan or other plan deferring the receipt of compensation.

(6) Commercial annuity.—The term "commercial annuity" means an annuity, endowment, or life insurance contract issued by an insurance company licensed to do business under the laws of any State.

(7) Plan administrator.—The term "plan administrator" has the meaning given such term by section 414(g).

(8) Maximum amount withheld.—The maximum amount to be withheld under this section on any designated distribution shall not exceed the sum of the amount of money and the fair market value of other property (other than securities of the employer corporation) received in the distribution. No amount shall be required to be withheld under this section in the case of any designated distribution which consists only of securities of the employer corporation and cash (not in excess of $200) in lieu of fractional shares. For purposes of this paragraph, the term "securities of the employer corporation" has the meaning given such term by section 402(e)(4)(E).

(9) Separate arrangements to be treated separately.—If the payor has more than 1 arrangement under which designated distributions may be made to any individual, each such arrangement shall be treated separately.

(10) Time and manner of election.—

(A) In general.—Any election and any revocation under this section shall be made at such time and in such manner as the Secretary shall prescribe.

(B) Payor required to notify payee of rights to elect.—

(i) Periodic payments.—The payor of any periodic payment—

(I) shall transmit to the payee notice of the right to make an election under subsection (a) not earlier than 6 months before the first of such payments and not later than when making the first of such payments,

(II) if such a notice is not transmitted under subclause (I) when making such first payment, shall transmit such a notice when making such first payment, and

(III) shall transmit to payees, not less frequently than once each calendar year, notice of their rights to make elections under subsection (a) and to revoke such elections.

(ii) Nonperiodic distributions.—The payor of any nonperiodic distribution shall transmit to the payee notice of the right to make any election provided in subsection (b) at the time of the distribution (or at such earlier time as may be provided in regulations).

(iii) Notice.—Any notice transmitted pursuant to this subparagraph shall be in such form and contain such information as the Secretary shall prescribe.

(11) Withholding includes deduction.—The terms "withholding", "withhold", and "withheld" include "deducting", "deduct", and "deducted".

(12) Failure to provide correct TIN.—If—

(A) a payee fails to furnish his TIN to the payor in the manner required by the Secretary, or

(B) the Secretary notifies the payor before any payment or distribution that the TIN furnished by the payee is incorrect,

no election under section (a)(2) or (b)(2) shall be treated as in effect and subsection (a)(4) shall not apply to such payee.

(13) Election may not be made with respect to certain payments outside of the United States or its possessions.—

(A) In general.—Except as provided in subparagraph (B), in the case of any periodic payment or nonperiodic distributions which is to be delivered outside of the United States and any possession of the United States, no election may be made under subsection (a)(2) or (b)(2) with respect to such payment.

(B) Exception.—Subparagraph (A) shall not apply if the recipient certifies to the payor, in such manner as the Secretary may prescribe, that such person is not—

(i) a United States citizen or a resident alien of the United States, or

(ii) an individual to whom section 877 applies.

(f) Withholding to Be Treated as Wage Withholding Under section 3402 for Other Purposes.—For purposes of this chapter (and so much of subtitle F as relates to this chapter)—

(1) any designated distribution (whether or not an election under this section applies to such distribution) shall be treated as if it were wages paid by an employer to an employee with respect to which there has been withholding under section 3402, and

(2) in the case of any designated distribution not subject to withholding under this section by reason of an election under this section, the amount withheld shall be treated as zero.

Recent Amendments to IRC §3405

Pension Protection Act (Pub. L. No. 109-280), as follows:

● **Sunset Provision.** Act §811, provides:

SEC. 811. PENSIONS AND INDIVIDUAL RETIREMENT ARRANGEMENT PROVISIONS OF ECONOMIC GROWTH AND TAX RELIEF RECONCILIATION ACT OF 2001 MADE PERMANENT.

Title IX of the Economic Growth and Tax Relief Reconciliation Act of 2001 [Pub. L. No. 107-16] shall not apply to the provisions of, and amendments made by, subtitles A through F [§§601–666] of title VI of such Act (relating to pension and individual retirement arrangement provisions).

Economic Growth and Tax Relief Reconciliation Act of 2001 (Pub. L. No. 107-16), as follows:

● IRC §3405(c)(3) was amended by Act §641(a)(1)(D)(ii). Eff. for distributions after Dec. 31, 2001. See Act §641(f)(3) for a special rule. IRC §3405(c)(3) prior to amendment:

(3) Eligible rollover distributions.—For purposes of this subsection, the term "eligible rollover distribution" has the meaning given such term by §402(f)(2)(A) (or in the case of an annuity contract under §403(b), a distribution from such contract described in §402(f)(2)(A)).

● IRC §3405(d)(2)(B) was amended by Act §641(a)(1)(D)(iii) by striking "or" at the end of cl. (ii), by replacing the period at the end of cl. (iii) with ", or", and by adding new cl. (iv). Eff. generally for distributions after Dec. 31, 2001. [*Ed. Note:* see Act §641(f)(3) for a special rule.]

● **Sunset Provision.** Act §901, as amended by Pub. L. No. 111-312, §101(a)(1), provides the sunset rule below. But see Pub. L. No. 109-280, §811, and Pub. L. No. 111-148, §10909(c), as amended by Pub. L. No. 111-312, §101(b)(1).

SEC. 901. SUNSET OF PROVISIONS OF ACT.

(a) In general. All provisions of, and amendments made by, this Act shall not apply—

(1) to taxable, plan, or limitation years beginning after December 31, 2012, or

(2) in the case of title V, to estates of decedents dying, gifts made, or generation skipping transfers, after December 31, 2012.

(b) Application of certain laws.—The Internal Revenue Code of 1986 and the Employee Retirement Income Security Act of 1974 shall be applied and administered to years, estates, gifts, and transfers described in subsection (a) as if the provisions and amendments described in subsection (a) had never been enacted.

---

* * *

Subtitle D—Miscellaneous Excise Taxes
* * *

Chapter 34—Taxes on Certain Insurance Policies
* * *

Subchapter B—Insured and Self-Insured Health Plans

Editor's Note

Caution: IRC §4375, below, added by Pub. L. No. 111-148, §6301, applies to each policy year ending after September 30, 2012, but does not apply to policy years ending after September 30, 2019.

SEC. 4375. HEALTH INSURANCE.

(a) Imposition of Fee.—There is hereby imposed on each specified health insurance policy for each policy year ending after September 30, 2012, a fee equal to the product of $2 ($1 in the case of policy years ending during fiscal year 2013) multiplied by the average number of lives covered under the policy.

(b) Liability for Fee.—The fee imposed by subsection (a) shall be paid by the issuer of the policy.

(c) Specified Health Insurance Policy.—For purposes of this section:

(1) **In general.**—Except as otherwise provided in this section, the term "specified health insurance policy" means any accident or health insurance policy (including a policy under a group health plan) issued with respect to individuals residing in the United States.

(2) **Exemption for certain policies.**—The term "specified health insurance policy" does not include any insurance if substantially all of its coverage is of excepted benefits described in section 9832(c).

(3) **Treatment of prepaid health coverage arrangements.**—

(A) In general.—In the case of any arrangement described in subparagraph (B), such arrangement shall be treated as a specified health insurance policy, and the person referred to in such subparagraph shall be treated as the issuer.

(B) Description of arrangements.—An arrangement is described in this subparagraph if under such arrangement fixed payments or premiums are received as consideration for any person's agreement to provide or arrange for the provision of accident or health coverage to residents of the United States, regardless of how such coverage is provided or arranged to be provided.

(d) Adjustments for Increases in Health Care Spending.—In the case of any policy year ending in any fiscal year beginning after September 30, 2014, the dollar amount in effect under subsection (a) for such policy year shall be equal to the sum of such dollar amount for policy years ending in the previous fiscal year (determined after the application of this subsection), plus an amount equal to the product of—

(1) such dollar amount for policy years ending in the previous fiscal year, multiplied by

(2) the percentage increase in the projected per capita amount of National Health Expenditures, as most recently published by the Secretary before the beginning of the fiscal year.

(e) Termination.—This section shall not apply to policy years ending after September 30, 2019.

Amendments to IRC §4375

Patient Protection and Affordable Care Act, 2010 (Pub. L. No. 111-148), as follows:

● IRC §4375 was added by Act §6301(e)(2)(A). Eff. on date of enactment of this Act [enacted: Mar. 23, 2010]. *Note*: IRC §4375 applies to policy years ending after Sept. 30, 2012, but does not apply to policy years ending after Sept. 30, 2019.

Editor's Note

Caution: IRC §4376, below, added by Pub. L. No. 111-148, §6301, applies to each plan year ending after September 30, 2012, but does not apply to plan years ending after September 30, 2019.

SEC. 4376. SELF-INSURED HEALTH PLANS.

(a) Imposition of Fee.—In the case of any applicable self-insured health plan for each plan year ending after September 30, 2012, there is hereby imposed a fee equal to $2 ($1 in the case of plan years ending during fiscal year 2013) multiplied by the average number of lives covered under the plan.

(b) Liability for Fee.—

(1) **In general.**—The fee imposed by subsection (a) shall be paid by the plan sponsor.

(2) **Plan sponsor.**—For purposes of paragraph (1) the term "plan sponsor" means—

(A) the employer in the case of a plan established or maintained by a single employer,

(B) the employee organization in the case of a plan established or maintained by an employee organization,

(C) in the case of—

(i) a plan established or maintained by 2 or more employers or jointly by 1 or more employers and 1 or more employee organizations,

(ii) a multiple employer welfare arrangement, or

(iii) a voluntary employees' beneficiary association described in section 501(c)(9), the association, committee, joint board of trustees, or other similar group of representatives of the parties who establish or maintain the plan, or

(D) the cooperative or association described in subsection (c)(2)(F) in the case of a plan established or maintained by such a cooperative or association.

(c) Applicable Self-insured Health Plan.—For purposes of this section, the term "applicable self-insured health plan" means any plan for providing accident or health coverage if—

(1) any portion of such coverage is provided other than through an insurance policy, and

(2) such plan is established or maintained—

(A) by 1 or more employers for the benefit of their employees or former employees,

(B) by 1 or more employee organizations for the benefit of their members or former members,

(C) jointly by 1 or more employers and 1 or more employee organizations for the benefit of employees or former employees,

(D) by a voluntary employees' beneficiary association described in section 501(c)(9),

(E) by any organization described in section 501(c)(6), or

(F) in the case of a plan not described in the preceding subparagraphs, by a multiple employer welfare arrangement (as defined in section 3(40) of Employee Retirement Income Security Act of 1974), a rural electric cooperative (as defined in section 3(40)(B)(iv) of such Act), or a rural telephone cooperative association (as defined in section 3(40)(B)(v) of such Act).

(d) Adjustments for Increases in Health Care Spending.—In the case of any plan year ending in any fiscal year beginning after September 30, 2014, the dollar amount in effect under subsection (a) for such plan year shall be equal to the sum of such dollar amount for plan years ending in the previous fiscal year (determined after the application of this subsection), plus an amount equal to the product of—

(1) such dollar amount for plan years ending in the previous fiscal year, multiplied by

(2) the percentage increase in the projected per capita amount of National Health Expenditures, as most recently published by the Secretary before the beginning of the fiscal year.

(e) Termination.—This section shall not apply to plan years ending after September 30, 2019.

Amendments to IRC §4376

Patient Protection and Affordable Care Act, 2010 (Pub. L. No. 111-148), as follows:

• IRC §4376 was added by Act §6301(e)(2)(A). Eff. on date of enactment of this Act [enacted: Mar. 23, 2010]. *Note:* IRC §4376 applies to plan years ending after Sept. 30, 2012, and does not apply to plan years ending after Sept. 30, 2019.

> **Editor's Note**
>
> **Caution**: IRC §4377, below, added by Pub. L. No. 111-148, §6301, applies to each policy year ending after September 30, 2012, but does not apply to policy years ending after September 30, 2019.

SEC. 4377. DEFINITIONS AND SPECIAL RULES.

(a) Definitions.—For purposes of this subchapter—

(1) Accident and health coverage.—The term "accident and health coverage" means any coverage which, if provided by an insurance policy, would cause such policy to be a specified health insurance policy (as defined in section 4375(c)).

(2) Insurance policy.—The term "insurance policy" means any policy or other instrument whereby a contract of insurance is issued, renewed, or extended.

(3) United States.—The term "United States" includes any possession of the United States.

(b) Treatment of Governmental Entities.—

(1) In general.—For purposes of this subchapter—

(A) the term "person" includes any governmental entity, and

(B) notwithstanding any other law or rule of law, governmental entities shall not be exempt from the fees imposed by this subchapter except as provided in paragraph (2).

(2) Treatment of exempt governmental programs.—In the case of an exempt governmental program, no fee shall be imposed under section 4375 or section 4376 on any covered life under such program.

(3) Exempt governmental program defined.—For purposes of this subchapter, the term "exempt governmental program" means—

(A) any insurance program established under title XVIII of the Social Security Act,

(B) the medical assistance program established by title XIX or XXI of the Social Security Act,

(C) any program established by Federal law for providing medical care (other than through insurance policies) to individuals (or the spouses and dependents thereof) by reason of such individuals being members of the Armed Forces of the United States or veterans, and

(D) any program established by Federal law for providing medical care (other than through insurance policies) to members of Indian tribes (as defined in section 4(d) of the Indian Health Care Improvement Act).

(c) Treatment as Tax.—For purposes of subtitle F, the fees imposed by this subchapter shall be treated as if they were taxes.

(d) No Cover Over to Possessions.—Notwithstanding any other provision of law, no amount collected under this subchapter shall be covered over to any possession of the United States.

Amendments to IRC §4377

Patient Protection and Affordable Care Act, 2010 (Pub. L. No. 111-148), as follows:
● IRC §4377 was added by Act §6301(e)(2)(A). Eff. on date of enactment of this Act [enacted: Mar. 23, 2010]. *Note:* IRC §4377 applies to policy years ending after Sept. 30, 2012, and does not apply to policy years ending after Sept. 30, 2019.

---

* * *

Chapter 42—Private Foundations and Certain Other Tax-Exempt Organizations
* * *

Subchapter D—Failure by Certain Charitable Organizations to Meet Certain Qualification Requirements

SEC. 4958. TAXES ON EXCESS BENEFIT TRANSACTIONS.

(a) Initial Taxes.—

(1) On the disqualified person.—There is hereby imposed on each excess benefit transaction a tax equal to 25 percent of the excess benefit. The tax imposed by this paragraph shall be paid by any disqualified person referred to in subsection (f)(1) with respect to such transaction.

(2) On the management.—In any case in which a tax is imposed by paragraph (1), there is hereby imposed on the participation of any organization manager in the excess benefit transaction, knowing that it is such a transaction, a tax equal to 10 percent of the excess benefit, unless such participation is not willful and is due to reasonable cause. The tax imposed by this paragraph shall be paid by any organization manager who participated in the excess benefit transaction.

(b) Additional Tax on the Disqualified Person.— In any case in which an initial tax is imposed by subsection (a)(1) on an excess benefit transaction and the excess benefit involved in such transaction is not corrected within the taxable period, there is hereby imposed a tax equal to 200 percent of the excess benefit involved. The tax imposed by this subsection

shall be paid by any disqualified person referred to in subsection (f)(1) with respect to such transaction.

(c) Excess Benefit Transaction; Excess Benefit.— For purposes of this section—

(1) Excess benefit transaction.—

(A) In general.—The term "excess benefit transaction" means any transaction in which an economic benefit is provided by an applicable tax-exempt organization directly or indirectly to or for the use of any disqualified person if the value of the economic benefit provided exceeds the value of the consideration (including the performance of services) received for providing such benefit. For purposes of the preceding sentence, an economic benefit shall not be treated as consideration for the performance of services unless such organization clearly indicated its intent to so treat such benefit.

(B) Excess benefit.—The term "excess benefit" means the excess referred to in subparagraph (A).

(2) Special rules for donor advised funds.—In the case of any donor advised fund (as defined in section 4966(d)(2))—

(A) the term "excess benefit transaction" includes any grant, loan, compensation, or other similar payment from such fund to a person described in subsection (f)(7) with respect to such fund, and

(B) the term "excess benefit" includes, with respect to any transaction described in subparagraph (A), the amount of any such grant, loan, compensation, or other similar payment.

(3) Special rules for supporting organizations.—

(A) In general.—In the case of any organization described in section 509(a)(3)—

(i) the term "excess benefit transaction" includes—

(I) any grant, loan, compensation, or other similar payment provided by such organization to a person described in subparagraph (B), and

(II) any loan provided by such organization to a disqualified person (other than an organization described in subparagraph (C)(ii)), and

(ii) the term "excess benefit" includes, with respect to any transaction described in clause (i), the amount of any such grant, loan, compensation, or other similar payment.

(B) Person described.—A person is described in this subparagraph if such person is—

(i) a substantial contributor to such organization,

(ii) a member of the family (determined under section 4958(f)(4)) of an individual described in clause (i), or

(iii) a 35-percent controlled entity (as defined in section 4958(f)(3) by substituting "persons described in clause (i) or (ii) of section 4958(c)(3)(B)" for "personsdescribed in subparagraph (A) or (B) ofparagraph (1)" in subparagraph (A)(i) thereof).

(C) Substantial contributor.—For purposes of this paragraph—

(i) In general.—The term "substantial contributor" means any person who contributed or bequeathed an aggregate amount of more than $5,000 to the organization, if such amount is more than 2 percent of the total contributions and bequests received by the organization before the close of the taxable year of the organization in which the contribution or bequest is received by the organization from such person. In the case of a trust, such term also means the creator of the trust. Rules similar to the rules of subparagraphs (B) and (C) of section 507(d)(2) shall apply for purposes of this subparagraph.

(ii) Exception.—Such term shall not include—

(I) any organization described in paragraph (1), (2), or (4) of section 509(a), and

(II) any organization which is treated as described in such paragraph (2) by reason of the last sentence of section 509(a) and which is a supported organization (as defined in section 509(f)(3)) of the organization to which subparagraph (A) applies.

(4) Authority to include certain other private inurement.—To the extent provided in regulations prescribed by the Secretary, the term "excess benefit transaction" includes any transaction in which the amount of any economic benefit provided to or for the use of a disqualified person is determined in whole or in part by the revenues of 1 or more activities of the organization but only if such transaction results in inurement not permitted under paragraph (3) or (4) of section 501(c), as the case may be. In the case of any such transaction, the excess benefit shall be the amount of the inurement not so permitted.

(d) Special Rules.—For purposes of thissection—

(1) Joint and several liability.—If more than 1 person is liable for any tax imposed by subsection (a) or subsection (b), all such persons shall be jointly and severally liable for such tax.

(2) Limit for management.—With respect to any 1 excess benefit transaction, the maximum amount of the tax imposed by subsection (a)(2) shall not exceed $20,000.

(e) Applicable Tax-Exempt Organization.—For purposes of this subchapter, the term "applicable tax-exempt organization" means—

> **Editor's Note**
>
> IRC §4958(e)(1), below, as amended by Pub. L. No. 111-148, §1322, is effective on the date of enactment (enacted: March 23, 2010).

(1) any organization which (without regard to any excess benefit) would be described in paragraph (3), (4), or (29) of section 501(c) and exempt from tax under section 501(a), and

(2) any organization which was described in paragraph (1) at any time during the 5-year period ending on the date of the transaction. Such term shall not include a private foundation (as defined in section 509(a)).

(f) Other Definitions.—For purposes of this section—

(1) Disqualified person.—The term "disqualified person" means, with respect to any transaction—

(A) any person who was, at any time during the 5-year period ending on the date of such transaction, in a position to exercise substantial influence over the affairs of the organization,

(B) a member of the family of an individual described in subparagraph (A),

(C) a 35-percent controlled entity,

(D) any person who is described in subparagraph (A), (B), or (C) with respect to an organization described in section 509(a)(3) and organized and operated exclusively for the benefit of, to perform the functions of, or to carry out the purposes of the applicable tax-exempt organization,

(E) which involves a donor advised fund (as defined in section 4966(d)(2)), any person who is described in paragraph (7) with respect to such donor advised fund (as so defined), and

(F) which involves a sponsoring organization (as defined in section 4966(d)(1)), any person who is described in paragraph (8) with respect to such sponsoring organization (as so defined).

(2) Organization manager.—The term "organization manager" means, with respect to any applicable tax-exempt organization, any officer, director, or trustee of such organization (or any individual having powers or responsibilities similar to those of officers, directors, or trustees of the organization).

(3) 35-percent controlled entity.—

(A) In general.—The term "35-percent controlled entity" means—

(i) a corporation in which persons described in subparagraph (A) or (B) of paragraph (1) own more than 35 percent of the total combined voting power,

(ii) a partnership in which such persons own more than 35 percent of the profits interest, and

IRC Sec. 4958(f)(3)(A)(ii)

(iii) a trust or estate in which such persons own more than 35 percent of the beneficial interest.

(B) Constructive ownership rules.—Rules similar to the rules of paragraphs (3) and (4) of section 4946(a) shall apply for purposes of this paragraph.

(4) Family members.—The members of an individual's family shall be determined under section 4946(d); except that such members also shall include the brothers and sisters (whether by the whole or half blood) of the individual and their spouses.

(5) Taxable period.—The term "taxable period" means, with respect to any excess benefit transaction, the period beginning with the date on which the transaction occurs and ending on the earliest of—

(A) the date of mailing a notice of deficiency under section 6212 with respect to the tax imposed by subsection (a)(1), or

(B) the date on which the tax imposed by subsection (a)(1) is assessed.

(6) Correction.—The terms "correction" and "correct" mean, with respect to any excess benefit transaction, undoing the excess benefit to the extent possible, and taking any additional measures necessary to place the organization in a financial position not worse than that in which it would be if the disqualified person were dealing under the highest fiduciary standards, except that in the case of any correction of an excess benefit transaction described in subsection (c)(2), no amount repaid in a manner prescribed by the Secretary may be held in any donor advised fund.

(7) Donors and donor advisors.—For purposes of paragraph (1)(E), a person is described in this paragraph if such person—

(A) is described in section 4966(d)(2)(A)(iii),

(B) is a member of the family of an individual described in subparagraph (A), or

(C) is a 35-percent controlled entity (as defined in paragraph (3) by substituting "persons described in subparagraph (A) or (B) of paragraph (7)" for "persons described in subparagraph (A) or (B) of paragraph (1)" in subparagraph (A)(i) thereof).

(8) Investment advisors.—For purposes of paragraph (1)(F)—

(A) In general.—A person is described in this paragraph if such person—

(i) is an investment advisor,

(ii) is a member of the family of an individual described in clause (i), or

(iii) is a 35-percent controlled entity (as defined in paragraph (3) by substituting "persons described in clause (i) or (ii) of paragraph (8)(A)" for "persons described in subparagraph (A) or (B) of paragraph (1)" in subparagraph (A)(i) thereof).

(B) Investment advisor defined.—For purposes of subparagraph (A), the term "investment advisor" means, with respect to any sponsoring organization (as defined in section 4966(d)(1)), any person (other than an employee of such organization) compensated by such organization for managing the investment of, or providing investment advice with respect to, assets maintained in donor advised funds (as defined in section 4966(d)(2)) owned by such organization.

Recent Amendments to IRC §4958

Patient Protection and Affordable Care Act, 2010 (Pub. L. No. 111-148), as follows:

• IRC §4958(e)(1) was amended by Act §1322(h)(3) by substituting "(3), (4), or (29)" for "(3) or (4)". Eff. on date of enactment of this Act [enacted: Mar. 23, 2010].

Tax Technical Corrections Act of 2007 (Pub. L. No. 110-172), as follows:

• IRC §4958(c)(3)(A)(i)(II) was amended by Act §3(i)(1) by substituting "subparagraph (C)(ii)" for "paragraph (1), (2), or (4) of section 509(a)". Eff. as if included in Pub. L. No. 109-280, §1242 [eff. for transactions occurring after July. 25, 2006].

• IRC §4958(c)(3)(C)(ii) was amended by Act §3(i)(2). Eff. as if included in Pub. L. No. 109-280, §1242 [eff. for transactions occurring after July. 25, 2006]. IRC §4958(c)(3)(C)(ii) prior to amendment:

(ii) Exception—Such term shall not include any organization described in paragraph (1), (2), or (4) of section 509(a).

Pension Protection Act of 2006 (Pub. L. No. 109-280), as follows:

• IRC §4958(c) was amended by Act §1232(b)(1) by redesignating para. (2) as para. (3), and by adding new para. (2). Eff. for transactions occurring after Aug. 17, 2006.

• IRC §4958(c), as amended by Act §1232(b)(1), was amended by Act §1242(b) by redesignating para. (3) as para. (4), and by adding new para. (3). Eff. for transactions occurring after Jul. 25, 2006.

• IRC §4958(d)(2) was amended by Act §1212(a)(3) by replacing "$10,000" with "$20,000." Eff. tax years beginning after Aug. 17, 2006.

• IRC §4958(f)(1) was amended by Act §1232(a)(1) by striking "and" at the end of subpara. (B), by replacing the period at the end of subpara. (C) with a comma, and by adding new subparas. (D) and (E). Eff. for transactions occurring after Aug. 17, 2006.

• IRC §4958(f)(1), as amended by Act §1232(a)(1), was amended by Act §1242(a) by redesignating subparas. (D) and (E) as subparas. (E) and (F), respectively, and by adding new subpara. (D). Eff. for transaction occurring after Aug. 17, 2006.

• IRC §4958(f) was amended by Act §1232(a)(2) by adding new paras. (7) and (8). Eff. for transactions occurring after Aug. 17, 2006.

• IRC §4958(f)(6) was amended by Act §1232(b)(2) by inserting ", except that in the case of any correction of an excess benefit transaction described in subsection (c)(2), no amount repaid in a manner prescribed by the Secretary may be held in any donor advised fund" after "standards". Eff. for transactions occurring after Aug. 17, 2006.

---

* * *

Subchapter F—Tax Shelter Transactions

SEC. 4965. EXCISE TAX ON CERTAIN TAX-EXEMPT ENTITIES ENTERING INTO PROHIBITED TAX SHELTER TRANSACTIONS.

(a) Being a Party to and Approval of Prohibited Transactions.—

(1) Tax-exempt entity.—

(A) In general.—If a transaction is a prohibited tax shelter transaction at the time any tax-exempt entity described in paragraph (1), (2), or (3) of subsection (c) becomes a party to the transaction, such entity shall pay a tax for the taxable year in which the entity becomes such a party and any subsequent taxable year in the amount determined under subsection (b)(1).

(B) Post-transaction determination.—If any tax-exempt entity described in paragraph (1), (2), or (3) of subsection (c) is a party to a subsequently listed transaction at any time during a taxable year, such entity shall pay a tax for such taxable year in the amount determined under subsection (b)(1).

(2) Entity manager.—If any entity manager of a tax-exempt entity approves such entity as (or otherwise causes such entity to be) a party to a prohibited tax shelter transaction at any time during the taxable year and knows or has reason to know that the transaction is a prohibited tax shelter transaction, such manager shall pay a tax for such taxable year in the amount determined under subsection (b)(2).

(b) Amount of Tax.—

(1) Entity.—In the case of a tax-exempt entity—

(A) In general.—Except as provided in subparagraph (B), the amount of the tax imposed under subsection (a)(1) with respect to any transaction for a taxable year shall be an amount equal to the product of the highest rate of tax under section 11, and the greater of—

(i) the entity's net income (after taking into account any tax imposed by this subtitle (other than by this section) with respect to such transaction) for such taxable year which—

(I) in the case of a prohibited tax shelter transaction (other than a subsequently listed transaction), is attributable to such transaction, or

(II) in the case of a subsequently listed transaction, is attributable to such transaction and which is properly allocable to the period beginning on the later of the date such transaction is identified by guidance as a listed transaction by the Secretary or the first day of the taxable year, or

(ii) 75 percent of the proceeds received by the entity for the taxable year which—

(I) in the case of a prohibited tax shelter transaction (other than a subsequently listed transaction), are attributable to such transaction, or

(II) in the case of a subsequently listed transaction, are attributable to such transaction and which are properly allocable to the period beginning on the later of the date such transaction is identified by guidance as a listed transaction by the Secretary or the first day of the taxable year.

(B) Increase in tax for certain knowing transactions.—In the case of a tax-exempt entity which knew, or had reason to know, a transaction was a prohibited tax shelter transaction at the time the entity became a party to the transaction, the amount of the tax imposed under subsection (a)(1)(A) with respect to any transaction for a taxable year shall be the greater of—

(i) 100 percent of the entity's net income (after taking into account any tax imposed by this subtitle (other than by this section) with respect to the prohibited tax shelter transaction) for such taxable year which is attributable to the prohibited tax shelter transaction, or

(ii) 75 percent of the proceeds received by the entity for the taxable year which are attributable to the prohibited tax shelter transaction.

This subparagraph shall not apply to any prohibited tax shelter transaction to which a tax-exempt entity became a party on or before the date of the enactment of this section.

(2) Entity manager.—In the case of each entity manager, the amount of the tax imposed under subsection (a)(2) shall be $20,000 for each approval (or other act causing participation) described in subsection (a)(2).

(c) Tax-Exempt Entity.—For purposes of this section, the term "tax-exempt entity" means an entity which is—

(1) described in section 501(c) or 501(d),

(2) described in section 170(c) (other than the United States),

(3) an Indian tribal government (within the meaning of section 7701(a)(40)),

(4) described in paragraph (1), (2), or (3) of section 4979(e),

(5) a program described in section 529,

(6) an eligible deferred compensation plan described in section 457(b) which is maintained by an employer described in section 457(e)(1)(A), or

(7) an arrangement described in section 4973(a).

(d) Entity Manager.—For purposes of this section, the term "entity manager" means—

(1) in the case of an entity described in paragraph (1), (2), or (3) of subsection (c)—

(A) the person with authority or responsibility similar to that exercised by an officer, director, or trustee of an organization, and

(B) with respect to any act, the person having authority or responsibility with respect to such act, and

(2) in the case of an entity described in paragraph (4), (5), (6), or (7) of subsection (c), the person who

IRC Sec. 4965(d)(2)

approves or otherwise causes the entity to be a party to the prohibited tax shelter transaction.

(e) Prohibited Tax Shelter Transaction; Subsequently Listed Transaction.—For purposes of this section—

  (1) Prohibited tax shelter transaction.—

  (A) In general.—The term "prohibited tax shelter transaction" means—

   (i) any listed transaction, and

   (ii) any prohibited reportable transaction.

  (B) Listed transaction.—The term "listed transaction" has the meaning given such term by section 6707A(c)(2).

  (C) Prohibited reportable transaction.—The term "prohibited reportable transaction" means any confidential transaction or any transaction with contractual protection (as defined under regulationsprescribed by the Secretary) which is a reportable transaction (as defined in section 6707A(c)(1)).

  (2) Subsequently listed transaction.—The term "subsequently listed transaction" means any transaction to which a tax-exempt entity is a party and which is determined by the Secretary to be a listed transaction at any time after the entity has become a party to the transaction. Such term shall not include a transaction which is a prohibited reportable transaction at the time the entity became a party to the transaction.

(f) Regulatory Authority.—The Secretary is authorized to promulgate regulations which provide guidance regarding the determination of the allocation of net income or proceeds of a tax-exempt entity attributable to a transaction to various periods, including before and after the listing of the transaction or the date which is 90 days after the date of the enactment of this section.

(g) Coordination With Other Taxes and Penalties.—The tax imposed by this section is in addition to any other tax, addition to tax, or penalty imposed under this title.

Amendments to IRC §4965

Tax Technical Corrections Act of 2007 (Pub. L. No. 110-172), as follows:
• IRC §4965(c)(6) was amended by Act §11(a)(30) by substituting "section 457(e)(1)(A)" for "section 4457(e)(1)(A)". Eff. on date of enactment [enacted: Dec. 29, 2007].

Tax Increase Prevention and Reconciliation Act of 2005 (Pub. L. No. 109-222), as follows:
• IRC §4965 was added by Act §516(a). Eff. tax years ending after May 17, 2006, for transactions before, on, or after such date, except that no tax under IRC §4965(a) shall apply with respect to income or proceeds properly allocable to any period ending on or before the date that is 90 days after May 17, 2006.

---

* * *

Chapter 43—Qualified Pension, etc., Plans

SEC. 4971. TAXES ON FAILURE TO MEET MINIMUM FUNDING STANDARDS.

(a) Initial Tax.—If at any time during any taxable year an employer maintains a plan to which section 412 applies, there is hereby imposed for the taxable year a tax equal to—

  (1) in the case of a single-employer plan, 10 percent of the aggregate unpaid minimum required contributions for all plan years remaining unpaid as of the end of any plan year ending with or within the taxable year, and

  (2) in the case of a multiemployer plan, 5 percent of the accumulated funding deficiency determined under section 431 as of the end of any plan year ending with or within the taxable year.

(b) Additional Tax.—If—

  (1) a tax is imposed under subsection (a)(1) on any unpaid minimum required contribution and such amount remains unpaid as of the close of the taxable period, or

  (2) a tax is imposed under subsection (a)(2) on any accumulated funding deficiency and the accumulated funding deficiency is not corrected within the taxable period, there is hereby imposed a tax equal to 100 percent of the unpaid minimum required contribution or accumulated funding deficiency, whichever is applicable, to the extent not so paid or corrected.

(c) Definitions.—For purposes of this section—

  (1) Accumulated funding deficiency.—The term "accumulated funding deficiency" has the meaning given to such term by section 431.

  (2) Correct.—The term "correct" means, with respect to an accumulated funding deficiency, the contribution, to or under the plan, of the amount necessary to reduce such accumulated funding deficiency as of the end of a plan year in which such deficiency arose to zero.

  (3) Taxable period.—The term "taxable period" means, with respect to an accumulated funding deficiency or unpaid minimum required contribution, whichever is applicable, the period beginning with the end of a plan year in which there is an accumulated funding deficiency or unpaid minimum required contribution, whichever is applicable and ending on the earlier of—

  (A) the date of mailing of a notice of deficiency with respect to the tax imposed by subsection (a), or

  (B) the date on which the tax imposed by subsection (a) is assessed.

  (4) Unpaid minimum required contribution.—

  (A) In general.—The term "unpaid minimum required contribution" means, with respect to any plan year, any minimum required contribution under section 430 for the plan year which is not paid on or before the due date (as determined under section 430(j)(1)) for the plan year.

(B) Ordering rule.—Any payment to or under a plan for any plan year shall be allocated first to unpaid minimum required contributions for all preceding plan years on a first-in, first-out basis and then to the minimum required contribution under section 430 for the plan year.

(d) Notification of the Secretary of Labor.—Before issuing a notice of deficiency with respect to the tax imposed by subsection (a) or (b), the Secretary shall notify the Secretary of Labor and provide him a reasonable opportunity (but not more than 60 days)—

(1) to require the employer responsible for contributing to or under the plan to eliminate the accumulated funding deficiency or unpaid minimum required contribution, whichever is applicable, or

(2) to comment on the imposition of such tax.

In the case of a multiemployer plan which is in reorganization under section 418, the same notice and opportunity shall be provided to the Pension Benefit Guaranty Corporation.

(e) Liability for Tax.—

(1) In general.—Except as provided in paragraph (2), the tax imposed by subsection (a), (b), or (f) shall be paid by the employer responsible for contributing to or under the plan the amount described in section 412(a)(2).

Editor's Note

Caution: IRC §4971(e)(2), as follows, was amended by Pub. L. No. 109-280, §212(b)(2)(A)–(B) (as corrected by Pub. L. No. 110-458, §102(b)(3)(A)), generally applicable to plan years beginning after 2007. For sunset provision of Pub. L. No. 109-280, §221(c), see the amendment notes to this section for Pub. L. No. 109-280.

---

(2) Joint and several liability where employer member of controlled group.—

(A) In general.—If an employer referred to in paragraph (1) is a member of a controlled group, each member of such group shall be jointly and severally liable for the tax imposed by subsection (a), (b), (f), or (g).

(B) Controlled group.—For purposes of subparagraph (A), the term "controlled group" means any group treated as a single employer under subsection (b), (c), (m), or (o) of section 414.

(f) Failure to Pay Liquidity Shortfall.—

(1) In general.—In the case of a plan to which section 430(j)(4) applies, there is hereby imposed a tax of 10 percent of the excess (if any) of—

(A) the amount of the liquidity shortfall for any quarter, over

(B) the amount of such shortfall which is paid by the required installment under section 430(j) for such quarter (but only if such installment is paid on or before the due date for such installment).

(2) Additional tax.—If the plan has a liquidity shortfall as of the close of any quarter and as of the close of each of the following 4 quarters, there is hereby imposed a tax equal to 100 percent of the amount on which tax was imposed by paragraph (1) for such first quarter.

(3) Definitions and special rule.—

(A) Liquidity shortfall; quarter.—For purposes of this subsection, the terms "liquidity shortfall" and "quarter" have the respective meanings given such terms by section 412(m)(5).

(B) Special rule.—If the tax imposed by paragraph (2) is paid with respect to any liquidity shortfall for any quarter, no further tax shall be imposed by this subsection on such shortfall for such quarter.

(4) Waiver by Secretary.—If the taxpayer establishes to the satisfaction of the Secretary that—

(A) the liquidity shortfall described in paragraph (1) was due to reasonable cause and not willful neglect, and

(B) reasonable steps have been taken to remedy such liquidity shortfall,

the Secretary may waive all or part of the tax imposed by this subsection.

Editor's Note

Caution: IRC §4971(g) was redesignated as (h), and new (g) was added, as follows, by Pub. L. No. 109-280, §212(b)(1), generally effective for plan years beginning after 2007. For sunset provision of Pub. L. No. 109-280, §221(c), see the amendment notes to this section for Pub. L. No. 109-280.

(g) Multiemployer Plans in Endangered or Critical Status.—

(1) In general.—Except as provided in this subsection—

(A) no tax shall be imposed under this section for a taxable year with respect to a multiemployer plan if, for the plan years ending with or within the taxable year, the plan is in critical status pursuant to section 432, and

IRC Sec. 4971(g)(1)(A)

(B) any tax imposed under this subsection for a taxable year with respect to a multiemployer plan if, for the plan years ending with or within the taxable year, the plan is in endangered status pursuant to section 432 shall be in addition to any other tax imposed by this section.

(2) Failure to comply with funding improvement or rehabilitation plan.—

(A) In general.—If any funding improvement plan or rehabilitation plan in effect under section 432 with respect to a multiemployer plan requires an employer to make a contribution to the plan, there is hereby imposed a tax on each failure of the employer to make the required contribution within the time required under such plan.

(B) Amount of tax.—The amount of the tax imposed by subparagraph (A) shall be equal to the amount of the required contribution the employer failed to make in a timely manner.

(C) Liability for tax.—The tax imposed by subparagraph (A) shall be paid by the employer responsible for contributing to or under the rehabilitation plan which fails to make the contribution.

(3) Failure to meet requirements for plans in endangered or critical status.—If—

(A) a plan which is in seriously endangered status fails to meet the applicable benchmarks by the end of the funding improvement period, or

(B) a plan which is in critical status either—

(i) fails to meet the requirements of section 432(e) by the end of the rehabilitation period, or

(ii) has received a certification under section 432(b)(3)(A)(ii) for 3 consecutive plan years that the plan is not making the scheduled progress in meeting its requirements under the rehabilitation plan,

the plan shall be treated as having an accumulated funding deficiency for purposes of this section for the last plan year in such funding improvement, rehabilitation, or 3-consecutive year period (and each succeeding plan year until such benchmarks or requirements are met) in an amount equal to the greater of the amount of the contributions necessary to meet such benchmarks or requirements or the amount of such accumulated funding deficiency without regard to this paragraph.

(4) Failure to adopt rehabilitation plan.—

(A) In general.—In the case of a multiemployer plan which is in critical status, there is hereby imposed a tax on the failure of such plan to adopt a rehabilitation plan within the time prescribed under section 432.

(B) Amount of tax.—The amount of the tax imposed under subparagraph (A) with respect to any

plan sponsor for any taxable year shall be the greater of—

(i) the amount of tax imposed under subsection (a) for the taxable year (determined without regard to this subsection), or

(ii) the amount equal to $1,100 multiplied by the number of days during the taxable year which are included in the period beginning on the day following the close of the 240-day period described in section 432(e)(1)(A) and ending on the day on which the rehabilitation plan is adopted.

(C) Liability for tax.—

(i) In general.—The tax imposed by subparagraph (A) shall be paid by each plan sponsor.

(ii) Plan sponsor.—For purposes of clause (i), the term "plan sponsor" has the meaning given such term by section 432(i)(9).

(5) Waiver.—In the case of a failure described in paragraph (2) or (3) which is due to reasonable cause and not to willful neglect, the Secretary may waive part or all of the tax imposed by this subsection. For purposes of this paragraph, reasonable cause includes unanticipated and material market fluctuations, the loss of a significant contributing employer, or other factors to the extent that the payment of tax under this subsection with respect to the failure would be excessive or otherwise inequitable relative to the failure involved.

(6) Terms used in section 432.—For purposes of this subsection, any term used in this subsection which is also used in section 432 shall have the meaning given such term by section 432.

Editor's Note

Caution: Former IRC §4971(g) was redesignated as IRC §4971(h), as follows, by Pub. L. No. 109-280, §212(b)(1), applicable in general to plan years beginning after 2007. For sunset provision, see the amendment notes to this section for Pub. L. No. 109-280.

(h) Cross References.—For disallowance of deductions for taxes paid under this section, see section 275.

For liability for tax in case of an employer party to collective bargaining agreement, see section 413(b)(6).

For provisions concerning notification of Secretary of Labor of imposition of tax under this section, waiver of the tax imposed by subsection (b), and other coordination between Secretary of the Treasury and Secretary of Labor with respect to compliance with this section, see section 3002(b) of title III of the Employee Retirement Income Security Act of 1974.

Recent Amendments to IRC §4971

Worker, Retiree, and Employer Recovery Act of 2008 (Pub. L. No. 110-458), as follows:

- IRC §4971(b)(1) was amended by Act §101(d)(2)(F)(i) by substituting "minimum required" for "required minimum". Eff. as if included in Pub. L. No. 109-280, §114, as amended by Act §101(d)(3) [eff. for plan years beginning after 2007].
- IRC §4971(c)(3) was amended by Act §101(d)(2)(F)(ii) by inserting "or unpaid minimum required contribution, whichever is applicable" after "accumulated funding deficiency" each place it appeared. Eff. as if included in Pub. L. No. 109-280, §114, as amended by Act §101(d)(3) [eff. for plan years beginning after 2007].
- IRC §4971(d)(1) was amended by Act §101(d)(2)(F)(ii) by inserting "or unpaid minimum required contribution, whichever is applicable" after "accumulated funding deficiency". Eff. as if included in Pub. L. No. 109-280, §114, as amended by Act §101(d)(3) [eff. for plan years beginning after 2007].
- IRC §4971(e)(1) was amended by Act §101(d)(2)(F)(iii) by substituting "section 412(a)(2)" for "section 412(a)(1)(A)". Eff. as if included in Pub. L. No. 109-280, §114, as amended by Act §101(d)(3) [eff. for plan years beginning after 2007].
- IRC §4971(g)(4)(B)(ii) was amended by Act §102(b)(2)(I)(i) by substituting "day following the close of" for "first day of". Eff. as if included in Pub. L. 109-280, §212 [eff. generally with respect to plan years beginning after 2007].
- IRC §4971(g)(4)(C)(ii) was amended by Act §102(b)(2)(I)(ii). Eff. as if included in Pub. L. 109-280, §212 [eff. generally with respect to plan years beginning after 2007]. IRC §4971(g)(4)(C)(ii) prior to amendment:

    (ii) Plan sponsor.—For purposes of clause (i), the term "plan sponsor" in the case of a multiemployer plan means the association, committee, joint board of trustees, or other similar group of representatives of the parties who establish or maintain the plan.

Pension Protection Act of 2006 (Pub. L. No. 109-280), as follows:

- IRC §4971(a)–(b) were amended by Act §114(e)(1). Eff. generally Aug. 17, 2006, with transition relief for certain multiemployer plans [for plan years after 2007, eff. date as amended by Pub. L. No. 110-458, §101(d)(3)]. See Act §214 for exemption for certain multiemployer plans. For special rules for certain plans, see Act §§104 through 106, below. IRC §4971(a)–(b) prior to amendment:

    (a) Initial tax.—For each taxable year of an employer who maintains a plan to which section 412 applies, there is hereby imposed a tax of 10 percent (5 percent in the case of multiemployer plan) on the amount of the accumulated funding deficiency under the plan, determined as of the end of the plan year ending with or within such taxable year.

    (b) Additional tax.—In any case in which an initial tax is imposed by subsection (a) on an accumulated funding deficiency and such accumulated funding deficiency is not corrected within the taxable period, there is hereby imposed a tax equal to 100 percent of such accumulated funding deficiency to the extent not corrected.

- IRC §4971(c) was amended by Act §114(e)(A)–(B) by replacing in para. (1) "the last two sentences of §412(a)" with "§431", and by adding a new para. (4). Eff. Aug. 17, 2006 [for plan years after 2007, eff. date as amended by Pub. L. No. 110-458, §101(d)(3)].
- IRC §4971(e)(1) was amended by Act §114(e)(3) by replacing "§412(b)(3)(A)" with "§412(a)(1)(A)." Eff. Aug. 17, 2006 [for plan years after 2007, eff. date as amended by Pub. L. No. 110-458, §101(d)(3)].
- IRC §4971(c)(2)[(e)(2)] was amended by Act §212(b)(2)(A)–(B) (as corrected by Pub. L. No. 110-458, §102(b)(3)(A)) by replacing "In the case of a plan other than a multiemployer plan, if the" with "If an", and by replacing "or (f)" with "(f), or (g)". Eff. generally for plan years beginning after 2007. [*Ed. Note*: for special rules, see Act §212(e)(2)–(3). For transition relief for amendments for certain benefits funded under an agreement approved by the PBGC, see Act §206.]

- IRC §4971(f)(1) was amended by Act §114(e)(4)(A)–(B) by replacing "§412(m)(5)" with "§430(j)(4)", and by replacing "§412(m)" with "§430(j)." Eff. Aug. 17, 2006.
- IRC §4971 was amended by Act §212(b)(1) by redesignating former subsec. (g) as subsec. (h), and by adding new subsec. (g). Eff. generally for plan years beginning after 2007. [*Ed. Note*: for special rules, see Act §212(e)(2) and (3). For transition relief for certain benefits funded under an agreement approved by the PBGC, see Act §206.]
- **Other Provision.** Act §104 provides:

    Sec. 104. Special Rule for Multiple Employer Plans of Certain Cooperatives.

    (a) General rule.—Except as provided in this section, if a plan in existence on July 26, 2005, was an eligible cooperative plan for its plan year which includes July 26, 2005, amendments made by Act sections 101 through 107 and sections 111 through 116 will not apply to plan years beginning before the earlier of—

    (1) the first plan year for which the plan ceases to be an eligible cooperative plan, or (2) January 1, 2017.

    (b) Interest rate.—In applying ERISA section 302(b)(5)(B) and IRC section 412(b)(5)(B) (as in effect before amendments made by Pub. L. No. 109-280) to an eligible cooperative plan for plan years beginning after December 31, 2007, and before the first plan year to which such amendments apply, the third segment rate determined under ERISA section 303(h)(2)(C)(iii) and IRC section 430(h)(2)(C)(iii) (as added by Pub. L. No. 109-280) will be used in lieu of the interest rate otherwise used.

    (c) Eligible cooperative plan defined.—For purposes of Act section 104, a plan shall be treated as an eligible cooperative plan for a plan year if the plan is maintained by more than 1 employer and at least 85 percent of the employers are—

    (1) rural cooperatives (as defined in IRC section 401(k)(7)(B) without regard to clause (iv) thereof), or (2) organizations which are—

    (A) cooperative organizations described in IRC section 1381(a) which are more than 50-percent owned by agricultural producers or by cooperatives owned by agricultural producers, or

    (B) more than 50-percent owned, or controlled by, one or more cooperative organizations described in subparagraph (A).

    A plan shall also be treated as an eligible cooperative plan for any plan year for which it is described in ERISA section 210(a) and is maintained by a rural telephone cooperative association described in ERISA section 3(40)(B)(v).

- **Other Provision.** Act section 105 provides:

    Sec. 105. Temporary Relief for Certain PBGC Settlement Plans.

    (a) General rule.—Except as provided in Act section 105, if a plan in existence on July 26, 2005, was a PBGC settlement plan as such date, the amendments made by sections 101 through 107 and sections 111 through 116 will not apply to plan years beginning before January 1, 2014.

    (b) Interest rate.—In applying ERISA section 302(b)(5)(B) and IRC section 412(b)(5)(B) (as in effect before the amendments made by Pub. L. No. 109-280), to a PBGC settlement plan for plan years beginning after December 31, 2007, and before January 1, 2014, the third segment rate determined under ERISA section 303(h)(2)(C)(iii) and IRC section 430(h)(2)(C)(iii) (as added by Pub. L. No. 109-280) shall be used in lieu of the interest rate otherwise used.

    (c) PBGC settlement plan.—For purposes of this section, the term "PBGC settlement plan" means a defined benefit plan (other than a multiemployer plan) to which ERISA section 302 and IRC section 412 apply and—

    (1) which was sponsored by an employer which was in bankruptcy, giving rise to a claim by the PBGC of not greater than $150,000,000, and the sponsorship of which was assumed by another employer that was not a member of the same controlled group as the bankrupt sponsor and the claim of the PBGC was settled or withdrawn in connection with the assumption of the sponsorship, or (2) which, by agreement with the PBGC, was spun off from a plan subsequently terminated by the PBGC under ERISA section 4042.

IRC Sec. 4971(h)

● **Other Provision.** Act section 106 provides:

Sec. 106. Special Rules for Plans of Certain Government Contractors.

(a) General rule.—Except as provided in Act section 106, if a plan is an eligible government contractor plan, Act sections 101 through 107 and sections 111 through 116 will not apply to plan years beginning before the earliest of—

(1) the first plan year for which the plan ceases to be an eligible government contractor plan, (2) the effective date of the Cost Accounting Standards Pension Harmonization Rule, or (3) January 1, 2011.

(b) Interest rate.—In applying ERISA section 302(b)(5)(B) and IRC section 412(b)(5)(B) (as in effect before the amendments made by Pub. L. No. 109-280), to a PBGC settlement plan for plan years beginning after December 31, 2007, and before January 1, 2014, the third segment rate determined under ERISA section 303(h)(2)(C)(iii) and IRC section 430(h)(2)(C)(iii) (as added by Pub. L. No. 109-280) shall be used in lieu of the interest rate otherwise used.

(c) Eligible government contractor plan defined.—For purposes of Act section 106, a plan shall be treated as an eligible government contractor plan if it is maintained by a corporation or a member of the same affiliated group (as defined by IRC section 1504(a)), whose primary source of revenue is derived from business performed under contracts with the United States that are subject to the Federal Acquisition Regulations (Chapter 1 of Title 48, C.F.R.) and that are also subject to the Defense Federal Acquisition Regulation Supplement (Chapter 2 of Title 48, C.F.R.), and whose revenue derived from such business in the previous fiscal year exceeded $5,000,000,000, and whose pension plan costs that are assignable under those contracts are subject to sections 412 and 413 of the Cost Accounting Standards (48 C.F.R. 9904.412 and 9904.413).

(d) Cost accounting standards pension harmonization rule.—The Cost Accounting Standards Board shall review and revise sections 412 and 413 of the Cost Accounting Standards (48 C.F.R. 9904.412 and 9904.413) to harmonize the minimum required contribution under ERISA of eligible government contractor plans and government reimbursable pension plan costs not later than January 1, 2010. Any final rule adopted by the Cost Accounting Standards Board shall be deemed the Cost Accounting Standards Pension Harmonization Rule.

● **Other Provision.** Act §114(g)(2), added by Pub. L. No. 110-458, §101(d)(3), provides:

(2) Excise Tax.—The amendments made by subsection (e) shall apply to taxable years beginning after 2007, but only with respect to plan years described in paragraph (1) which end with or within any such taxable year.

● **Other Provision—Effective Date.** Act §212(e)(1), as amended by Pub. L. No. 110-458, §102(b)(3)(B), provides:

(1) The amendments made by this section shall apply with respect to plan years beginning after 2007, except that the amendments made by subsection (b) shall apply to taxable years beginning after 2007, but only with respect to plan years beginning after 2007 which end with or within any such taxable year.

● **Sunset Rule.** Act §221(c) provides:

(c) Sunset

(1) In general.—Except as provided in this subsection, notwithstanding any other provision of this Act, the provisions of, and the amendments made by, sections 201(b), 202, and 212 shall not apply to plan years beginning after December 31, 2014.

(2) Funding improvement and rehabilitation plans.—If a plan is operating under a funding improvement or rehabilitation plan under section 305 of such Act or 432 of such Code for its last year beginning before January 1, 2015, such plan shall continue to operate under such funding improvement or rehabilitation plan during any period after December 31, 2014, such funding improvement or rehabilitation plan is in effect and all provisions of such Act or Code relating to the opera-

tion of such funding improvement or rehabilitation plan shall continue in effect during such period.

SEC. 4972. TAX ON NONDEDUCTIBLE CONTRIBUTIONS TO QUALIFIED EMPLOYER PLANS.

(a) Tax Imposed.—In the case of any qualified employer plan, there is hereby imposed a tax equal to 10 percent of the nondeductible contributions under the plan (determined as of the close of the taxable year of the employer).

(b) Employer Liable for Tax.—The tax imposed by this section shall be paid by the employer making the contributions.

(c) Nondeductible Contributions.—For purposes of this section—

(1) In general.—The term "nondeductible contributions" means, with respect to any qualified employer plan, the sum of—

(A) the excess (if any) of—

(i) the amount contributed for the taxable year by the employer to or under such plan, over

(ii) the amount allowable as a deduction under section 404 for such contributions, (determined without regard to subsection (e) thereof), and

(B) the amount determined under this subsection for the preceding taxable year reduced by the sum of—

(i) the portion of the amount so determined returned to the employer during the taxable year, and

(ii) the portion of the amount so determined deductible under section 404 for the taxable year (determined without regard to subsection (e) thereof).

(2) Ordering rule for section 404.—For purposes of paragraph (1), the amount allowable as a deduction under section 404 for any taxable year shall be treated as—

(A) first from carryforwards to such taxable year from preceding taxable years (in order of time), and

(B) then from contributions made during such taxable year.

(3) Contributions which may be returned to employer.—In determining the amount of nondeductible contributions for any taxable year, there shall not be taken into account any contribution for such taxable year which is distributed to the employer in a distribution described in section 4980(c)(2)(B)(ii) if such distribution is made on or before the last day on which a contribution may be made for such taxable year under section 404(a)(6).

(4) Special rule for self-employed individuals.—For purposes of paragraph (1), if—

(A) the amount which is required to be contributed to a plan under section 412 on behalf of an individual who is an employee (within the meaning of section 401(c)(1)), exceeds

(B) the earned income (within the meaning of section 404(a)(8)) of such individual derived from the trade or business with respect to which such plan is established,

such excess shall be treated as an amount allowable as a deduction under section 404.

(5) Pre-1987 contributions.—The term "nondeductible contribution" shall not include any contribution made for a taxable year beginning before January 1, 1987.

(6) Exceptions.—In determining the amount of nondeductible contributions for any taxable year, there shall not be taken into account—

(A) so much of the contributions to 1 or more defined contribution plans which are not deductible when contributed solely because of section 404(a)(7) as does not exceed the amount of contributions described in section 401(m)(4)(A), or

(B) so much of the contributions to a simple retirement account (within the meaning of section 408(p)) of a simple plan (within the meaning of section 401(k)(11)) which are not deductible when contributed solely because such contributions are not made in connection with a trade or business of the employer.

For purposes of subparagraph (A), the deductible limits under section 404(a)(7) shall first be applied to amounts contributed to a defined benefit plan and then to amounts described in subparagraph (A). Subparagraph (B) shall not apply to contributions made on behalf of the employer or a member of the employer's family (as defined in section 447(e)(1)).

(7) Defined benefit plan exception.—In determining the amount of nondeductible contributions for any taxable year, an employer may elect for such year not to take into account any contributions to a defined benefit plan except, in the case of a multiemployer plan, to the extent that such contributions exceed the full-funding limitation (as defined in section 431(c)(6)). For purposes of this paragraph, the deductible limits under section 404(a)(7) shall first be applied to amounts contributed to defined contribution plans and then to amounts described in this paragraph. If an employer makes an election under this paragraph for a taxable year, paragraph (6) shall not apply to such employer for such taxable year.

(d) Definitions.—For purposes of this section—

(1) Qualified employer plan.—

(A) In general.—The term "qualified employer plan" means—

(i) any plan meeting the requirements of section 401(a) which includes a trust exempt from tax under section 501(a),

(ii) an annuity plan described in section 403(a),

(iii) any simplified employee pension (within the meaning of section 408(k)),

(iv) any simple retirement account (within the meaning of section 408(p)).

(B) Exemption for governmental and tax exempt plans.—The term "qualified employer plan" does not include a plan described in subparagraph (A) or (B) of section 4980(c)(1).

(2) Employer.—In the case of a plan which provides contributions or benefits for employees some or all of whom are self-employed individuals within the meaning of section 401(c)(1), the term "employer" means the person treated as the employer under section 401(c)(4).

Recent Amendments to IRC §4972

Pension Protection Act of 2006 (Pub. L. No. 109-280), as follows:

● IRC §4972(c)(6)(A) was amended by Act §803(c). Eff. for contributions for tax years beginning after Dec. 31, 2005. IRC §4972(c)(6)(A) prior to amendment:

(A) so much of the contributions to 1 or more defined contribution plans which are not deductible when contributed solely because of section 404(a)(7) as does not exceed the greater of—

(i) the amount of contributions not in excess of 6 percent of compensation (within the meaning of section 404(a) and as adjusted under section 404(a)(12)) paid or accrued (during the taxable year for which the contributions were made) to beneficiaries under the plans, or

(ii) the amount of contributions described in section 401(m)(4)(A), or.

● IRC §4972(c)(7) was amended by Act §114(e)(5) by replacing "except to the extent that such contributions exceed the full-funding limitation (as defined in §412(c)(7), determined without regard to subparagraph (A)(i)(I) thereof)" with "except, in the case of a multiemployer plan, to the extent that such contributions exceed the full-funding limitation (as defined in §431(c)(6))." Eff. Aug. 17, 2006 [eff. for plan years after 2007, eff. date as amended by Pub. L. No. 110-458, §101(d)(3)].

● **Sunset Provision.** Act §811, provides:

SEC. 811. PENSIONS AND INDIVIDUAL RETIREMENT ARRANGEMENT PROVISIONS OF ECONOMIC GROWTH AND TAX RELIEF RECONCILIATION ACT OF 2001 MADE PERMANENT.

Title IX of the Economic Growth and Tax Relief Reconciliation Act of 2001 [Pub. L. No. 107-16] shall not apply to the provisions of, and amendments made by, subtitles A through F [§§601–666] of title VI of such Act (relating to pension and individual retirement arrangement provisions).

Working Families Tax Relief Act of 2004 (Pub. L. No. 108-311), as follows:

● §4972(c)(6)(A)(ii) was amended by Act §404(c). Eff. years beginning after Dec. 31, 2001, as if included in the provision of Pub. L. No. 107-16 to which it relates. §4972(c)(6)(A)(ii) prior to amendment:

(ii) the sum of—

(I) the amount of contributions described in section 401(m)(4)(A), plus

(II) the amount of contributions described in section 402(g)(3)(A), or.

IRC Sec. 4972(d)(2)

Economic Growth and Tax Relief Reconciliation Act of 2001 (Pub. L. No. 107-16), as follows:

- IRC §4972(c)(6)(B)(i) was amended by Act §616(b)(2)(B) by replacing "(within the meaning of §404(a))" with "(within the meaning of §404(a) and as adjusted under §404(a)(12))." Eff. years beginning after Dec. 31, 2001.
- IRC §4972(c)(6), as amended by Act §616, was amended by Act §637(a) by striking "and" at the end of subpara. (A), by replacing the period at the end of subpara. (B) with ", or", and adding new subpara. (C). Eff. tax years beginning after Dec. 31, 2001. [*Ed. Note*: see Act §637(c) for a special rule.]
- IRC §4972(c)(6), as amended by Act §637(a), was amended by Act §637(b) by adding a new sentence at the end. Eff. tax years beginning after Dec. 31, 2001.
- IRC §4972(c)(6), as amended by Act §§616 and 637, was amended by Act §652(b)(1)–(4) (as amended by Pub. L. No. 108-311, §408(b)(9)) by striking subpara. (A) and redesignating subparas. (B) and (C) as (A) and (B), respectively; by striking the first sentence following subpara. (B) (as redesignated); by replacing "subparagraph (B)" each place it appears in the next to last sentence with "subparagraph (A)"; and by replacing "Subparagraph (C)" in the last sentence with "Subparagraph (B)". Eff. plan years beginning after Dec. 31, 2001. IRC §4972(c)(6) prior to amendment:

(6) Exceptions.—In determining the amount of nondeductible contributions for any taxable year, there shall not be taken into account—
(A) contributions that would be deductible under section 404(a)(1)(D) if the plan had more than 100 participants if—
(i) the plan is covered under section 4021 of the Employee Retirement Income Security Act of 1974,
(ii) the plan is terminated under section 4041(b) of such Act on or before the last day of the taxable year,
(B) so much of he contributions to 1 or more defined contribution plans which are not deductible when contributed solely because of section 404(a)(7) as does not exceed the greater of—
(i) the amount of contributions not in excess of 6 percent of compensation (within the meaning of section 404(a) and as adjusted under section 404(a)(12)) paid or accrued (during the taxable year for which the contributions were made) to the beneficiaries under the plans, or
(ii) the sum of—
(I) the amount or contributions described in section 401(m)(4), plus
(II) the amount of contributions described in section 402(g)(3)(A), or
(C) so much of the contributions to a simple retirement account (within the meaning of section 408(p)) or a simple plan (within the meaning of section 401(k)(11)) which are not deductible when contributed solely because such contributions are not made in connection with a trade or business of the employer.
If 1 or more defined benefit plans were taken into account in determining the amount allowable as a deduction under section 404 for contributions to any defined contribution plan, subparagraph (B) shall apply only if such defined benefit plans are described in section 404(a)(1)(D). For purposes of subparagraph (B), the deductible limits under section 404(a)(7) shall first be applied to amounts contributed to a defined benefit plan and then to amounts described in subparagraph (B). Subparagraph (C) shall not apply to contributions made on behalf of the employer or a member of the employer's family (as defined in section 447(e)(1)).

- IRC §4972(c) was amended by Act §653(a) by adding new para. (7). Eff. years beginning after Dec. 31, 2001.
- **Sunset Provision.** Act §901, as amended by Pub. L. No. 111-312, §101(a)(1), provides the sunset rule below. But see Pub. L. No. 109-280, §811, and Pub. L. No. 111-148, §10909(c), as amended by Pub. L. No. 111-312, §101(b)(1).
  SEC. 901. SUNSET OF PROVISIONS OF ACT.
  (a) In general. All provisions of, and amendments made by, this Act shall not apply—
  (1) to taxable, plan, or limitation years beginning after December 31, 2012, or
  (2) in the case of title V, to estates of decedents dying, gifts made, or generation skipping transfers, after December 31, 2012.

(b) Application of certain laws.—The Internal Revenue Code of 1986 and the Employee Retirement Income Security Act of 1974 shall be applied and administered to years, estates, gifts, and transfers described in subsection (a) as if the provisions and amendments described in subsection (a) had never been enacted.

SEC. 4973. TAX ON EXCESS CONTRIBUTIONS TO CERTAIN TAX-FAVORED ACCOUNTS AND ANNUITIES.

(a) Tax Imposed.—In the case of—

(1) an individual retirement account (within the meaning of section 408(a)),

(2) an Archer MSA (within the meaning of section 220(d)),

(3) an individual retirement annuity (within the meaning of section 408(b)), a custodial account treated as an annuity contract under section 403(b)(7)(A) (relating to custodial accounts for regulated investment company stock),

(4) a Coverdell education savings account (as defined in section 530), or

(5) a health savings account (within the meaning of section 223(d)),

there is imposed for each taxable year a tax in an amount equal to 6 percent of the amount of the excess contributions to such individual's accounts or annuities (determined as of the close of the taxable year). The amount of such tax for any taxable year shall not exceed 6 percent of the value of the account or annuity (determined as of the close of the taxable year). In the case of an endowment contract described in section 408(b), the tax imposed by this section does not apply to any amount allocable to life, health, accident, or other insurance under such contract. The tax imposed by this subsection shall be paid by such individual.

(b) Excess Contributions.—For purposes of this section, in the case of individual retirement accounts or individual retirement annuities, the term "excess contributions" means the sum of—

(1) the excess (if any) of—

(A) the amount contributed for the taxable year to the accounts or for the annuities (other than a contribution to a Roth IRA or a rollover contribution described in section 402(c), 403(a)(4), 403(b)(8), or 408(d)(3), or 457(e)(16)), over

(B) the amount allowable as a deduction under section 219 for such contributions, and

(2) the amount determined under this subsection for the preceding taxable year, reduced by the sum of—

(A) the distributions out of the account for the taxable year which were included in the gross income of the payee under section 408(d)(1),

(B) the distributions out of the account for the taxable year to which section 408(d)(5) applies, and

(C) the excess (if any) of the maximum amount allowable as a deduction under section 219 for the taxable year over the amount contributed (determined without regard to section 219(f)(6)) to the accounts or for the annuities (including the amount contributed to a Roth IRA) for the taxable year.

For purposes of this subsection, any contribution which is distributed from the individual retirement account or the individual retirement annuity in a distribution to which section 408(d)(4) applies shall be treated as an amount not contributed. For purposes of paragraphs (1)(B) and (2)(C), the amount allowable as a deduction under section 219 shall be computed without regard to section 219(g).

(c) Section 403(b) Contracts.—For purposes of this section, in the case of a custodial account referred to in subsection (a)(3), the term "excess contributions" means the sum of—

(1) the excess (if any) of the amount contributed for the taxable year to such account (other than a rollover contribution described in section 403(b)(8) or 408(d)(3)(A)(iii)), over the lesser of the amount excludable from gross income under section 403(b) or the amount permitted to be contributed under the limitations contained in section 415 (or under whichever such section is applicable, if only one is applicable), and

(2) the amount determined under this subsection for the preceding taxable year, reduced by—

(A) the excess (if any) of the lesser of (i) the amount excludable from gross income under section 403(b) or (ii) the amount permitted to be contributed under the limitations contained in section 415 over the amount contributed to the account for the taxable year (or under whichever such section is applicable, if only one is applicable), and

(B) the sum of the distributions out of the account (for all prior taxable years) which are included in gross income under section 72(e).

(d) Excess Contributions to Archer MSAs.—For purposes of this section, in the case of Archer MSAs (within the meaning of section 220(d)), the term "excess contributions" means the sum of—

(1) the aggregate amount contributed for the taxable year to the accounts (other than rollover contributions described in section 220(f)(5)) which is neither excludable from gross income under section 106(b) nor allowable as a deduction under section 220 for such year, and

(2) the amount determined under this subsection for the preceding taxable year, reduced by the sum of—

(A) the distributions out of the accounts which were included in gross income under section 220(f)(2), and

(B) the excess (if any) of—

(i) the maximum amount allowable as a deduction under section 220(b)(1) (determined without regard to section 106(b)) for the taxable year, over

(ii) the amount contributed to the accounts for the taxable year.

For purposes of this subsection, any contribution which is distributed out of the Archer MSA in a distribution to which section 220(f)(3) or section 138(c)(3) applies shall be treated as an amount not contributed.

(e) Excess Contributions to Coverdell Education Savings Accounts.—For purposes of this section—

Editor's Note

Caution: IRC §4973(e)(1), as follows, was amended by Pub. L. No. 107-16. For sunset provision, see the amendment notes to this section for Pub. L. No. 107-16.

---

(1) In general.—In the case of Coverdell education savings accounts maintained for the benefit of any one beneficiary, the term "excess contributions" means the sum of—

(A) the amount by which the amount contributed for the taxable year to such accounts exceeds $2,000 (or, if less, the sum of the maximum amounts permitted to be contributed under section 530(c) by the contributors to such accounts for such year); and

(B) the amount determined under this subsection for the preceding taxable year, reduced by the sum of—

(i) the distributions out of the accounts for the taxable year (other than rollover distributions); and

(ii) the excess (if any) of the maximum amount which may be contributed to the accounts for the taxable year over the amount contributed to the accounts for the taxable year.

(2) Special rules.—For purposes of paragraph (1), the following contributions shall not be taken into account:

(A) Any contribution which is distributed out of the Coverdell education savings account in a distribution to which section 530(d)(4)(C) applies.

(B) Any rollover contribution.

(f) Excess Contributions to Roth IRAs.—For purposes of this section, in the case of contributions to a Roth IRA (within the meaning of section 408A(b)), the term "excess contributions" means the sum of—

(1) the excess (if any) of—

(A) the amount contributed for the taxable year to Roth IRAs (other than a qualified rollover contribution described in section 408A(e)), over

(B) the amount allowable as a contribution under sections 408A(c)(2) and (c)(3), and

(2) the amount determined under this subsection for the preceding taxable year, reduced by the sum of—

(A) the distributions out of the accounts for the taxable year, and

(B) the excess (if any) of the maximum amount allowable as a contribution under sections 408A(c)(2) and (c)(3) for the taxable year over the amount contributed by the individual to all individual retirement plans for the taxable year.

For purposes of this subsection, any contribution which is distributed from a Roth IRA in a distribution described in section 408(d)(4) shall be treated as an amount not contributed.

(g) Excess Contributions to Health Savings Accounts.—For purposes of this section, in the case of health savings accounts (within the meaning of section 223(d)), the term "excess contributions" means the sums of—

(1) the aggregate amount contributed for the taxable year to the accounts (other than a rollover contribution described in section 220(f)(5) or section 223(f)(5)) which is neither excludable from gross income under section 106(d) nor allowable as a deduction under section 223 for such year, and

(2) the amount determined under this subsection for the preceding taxable year, reduced by the sum of—

(A) the distributions out of the accounts which were included in gross income under section 223(f)(2), and

(B) the excess (if any) of—

(i) the maximum amount allowable as a deduction under section 223(b) (determined without regard to section 106(d)) for the taxable year, over

(ii) the amount contributed to the accounts for the taxable year.

For purposes of this subsection, any contribution which is distributed out of the health savings account in a distribution to which section 223(f)(3) applies shall be treated as an amount not contributed.

Recent Amendments to IRC §4973

Pension Protection Act of 2006 (Pub. L. No. 109-280), as follows:
● Sunset Provision. Act §811, provides:

SEC. 811. PENSIONS AND INDIVIDUAL RETIREMENT ARRANGEMENT PROVISIONS OF ECONOMIC GROWTH AND TAX RELIEF RECONCILIATION ACT OF 2001 MADE PERMANENT.
Title IX of the Economic Growth and Tax Relief Reconciliation Act of 2001 [Pub. L. No. 107-16] shall not apply to the provisions of, and amendments made by, subtitles A through F [§§601–666] of title VI of such Act (relating to pension and individual retirement arrangement provisions).
● **Other Provision.** Act §1304(a) provides:
  (a) Permanent Extension of Modifications.—Section 901 of the Economic Growth and Tax Relief Reconciliation Act of 2001 [Pub. L. No. 107-16] (relating to sunset provisions) shall not apply to section 402 of such Act (relating to modifications to qualified tuition programs).
Working Families Tax Relief Act of 2004 (Pub. L. No. 108-311), as follows:
● IRC §4973(c) was amended by Act §408(a)(22) by replacing "subsection (a)(2)" with "subsection (a)(3)." Eff. Oct. 4, 2004.
Medicare Prescription Drug, Improvement, and Modernization Act of 2003 (Pub. L. No. 108-173), as follows:
● IRC §4973(a) was amended by Act §1201(e)(1) by striking "or" at the end of subsec. (a)(3), by inserting "or" at the end of subsec. (a)(4), and by inserting new para. (5). Eff. tax years beginning after Dec. 31, 2003.
● IRC §4973(g) was amended by Act §1201(e)(2) by adding new subsec. (g). Eff. tax years beginning after Dec. 31, 2003.
Pub. L. No. 107-22, as follows:
● IRC §4973(a) was amended by Act §1(b)(1)(C) by replacing "an education individual retirement" with "a Coverdell education savings." Eff. Jul. 26, 2001.
● IRC §4973(e) was amended by Act §1(b)(2)(B) by replacing "education individual retirement" each place it appears with "Coverdell education savings." Eff. Jul. 26, 2001.
● IRC §4973(e) was amended by Act §1(b)(4) by replacing in the heading "Education individual retirement" with "Coverdell education savings." Eff. Jul. 26, 2001.
Economic Growth and Tax Relief Reconciliation Act of 2001 (Pub. L. No. 107-16), as follows:
● IRC §4973(b)(1)(A) was amended by Act §641(e)(11) by replacing "or 408(d)(3)" with "408(d)(3), or 457(e)(16)." Eff. for distributions after Dec. 31, 2001. [*Ed. Note:* see Act §641(f)(3) for a special rule.]
● IRC §4973(e)(1)(A) was amended by Act §401(a)(2) by replacing "$500" with "$2,000." Eff. tax years beginning after Dec. 31, 2001.
● IRC §4973(e)(1) was amended by Act §401(g)(2)(D) by adding "and" at the end of subpara. (A), by striking subpara. (B), and by redesignating subpara. (C) as subpara. (B). Eff. tax years beginning after Dec. 31, 2001. IRC §4973(e)(1)(B) prior to being stricken:
  (B) if any amount is contributed (other than a contributions described in section 530(b)(2)(B)) during such year to a qualified State tuition program for the benefit of such beneficiary, any amount contributed to such accounts for such taxable year; and
● IRC §4973(e) was amended by Act §402(a)(4)(A) by replacing "qualified State tuition" each place it appeared with "qualified tuition." Eff. tax years beginning after Dec. 31, 2001.
● **Sunset Provision.** Act §901, as amended by Pub. L. No. 111-312, §101(a)(1), provides the sunset rule below. But see Pub. L. No. 109-280, §811, and Pub. L. No. 111-148, §10909(c), as amended by Pub. L. No. 111-312, §101(b)(1).
  SEC. 901. SUNSET OF PROVISIONS OF ACT.
  (a) In general. All provisions of, and amendments made by, this Act shall not apply—
  (1) to taxable, plan, or limitation years beginning after December 31, 2012, or
  (2) in the case of title V, to estates of decedents dying, gifts made, or generation skipping transfers, after December 31, 2012.
  (b) Application of certain laws.—The Internal Revenue Code of 1986 and the Employee Retirement Income Security Act of 1974 shall be applied and administered to years, estates, gifts, and transfers described in subsection (a) as if the

provisions and amendments described in subsection (a) had never been enacted.

SEC. 4974. EXCISE TAX ON CERTAIN ACCUMULATIONS IN QUALIFIED RETIREMENT PLANS.

(a) General Rule.—If the amount distributed during the taxable year of the payee under any qualified retirement plan or any eligible deferred compensation plan (as defined in section 457(b)) is less than the minimum required distribution for such taxable year, there is hereby imposed a tax equal to 50 percent of the amount by which such minimum required distribution exceeds the actual amount distributed during the taxable year. The tax imposed by this section shall be paid by the payee.

(b) Minimum Required Distribution.—For purposes of this section, the term "minimum required distribution" means the minimum amount required to be distributed during a taxable year under section 401(a)(9), 403(b)(10), 408(a)(6), 408(b)(3), or 457(d)(2), as the case may be, as determined under regulations prescribed by the Secretary.

(c) Qualified Retirement Plan.—For purposes of this section, the term "qualified retirement plan" means—

(1) a plan described in section 401(a) which includes a trust exempt from tax under section 501(a),

(2) an annuity plan described in section 403(a),

(3) an annuity contract described in section 403(b),

(4) an individual retirement account described in section 408(a), or

(5) an individual retirement annuity described in section 408(b).

Such term includes any plan, contract, account, or annuity which, at any time, has been determined by the Secretary to be such a plan, contract, account, or annuity.

(d) Waiver of Tax in Certain Cases.—If the taxpayer establishes to the satisfaction of the Secretary that—

(1) the shortfall described in subsection (a) in the amount distributed during any taxable year was due to reasonable error, and

(2) reasonable steps are being taken to remedy the shortfall, the Secretary may waive the tax imposed by subsection (a) for the taxable year.

SEC. 4975. TAX ON PROHIBITED TRANSACTIONS.

(a) Initial Taxes on Disqualified Person.—There is hereby imposed a tax on each prohibited transaction. The rate of tax shall be equal to 15 percent of the amount involved with respect to the prohibited transaction for each year (or part thereof) in the taxable period. The tax imposed by this subsection shall be paid by any disqualified person who participates in the prohibited transaction (other than a fiduciary acting only as such).

(b) Additional Taxes on Disqualified Person.—In any case in which an initial tax is imposed by subsection (a) on a prohibited transaction and the transaction is not corrected within the taxable period, there is hereby imposed a tax equal to 100 percent of the amount involved. The tax imposed by this subsection shall be paid by any disqualified person who participated in the prohibited transaction (other than a fiduciary acting only as such).

(c) Prohibited Transaction.—

(1) General rule.—For purposes of this section, the term "prohibited transaction" means any direct or indirect—

(A) sale or exchange, or leasing, of any property between a plan and a disqualified person;

(B) lending of money or other extension of credit between a plan and a disqualified person;

(C) furnishing of goods, services, or facilities between a plan and a disqualified person;

(D) transfer to, or use by or for the benefit of, a disqualified person of the income or assets of a plan;

(E) act by a disqualified person who is a fiduciary whereby he deals with the income or assets of a plan in his own interest or for his own account; or

(F) receipt of any consideration for his own personal account by any disqualified person who is a fiduciary from any party dealing with the plan in connection with a transaction involving the income or assets of the plan.

(2) Special exemption.—The Secretary shall establish an exemption procedure for purposes of this subsection. Pursuant to such procedure, he may grant a conditional or unconditional exemption of any disqualified person or transaction or class of disqualified persons or transactions, from all or part of the restrictions imposed by paragraph (1) of this subsection. Action under this subparagraph may be taken only after consultation and coordination with the Secretary of Labor. The Secretary may not grant an exemption under this paragraph unless he finds that such exemption is—

(A) administratively feasible,

(B) in the interests of the plan and of its participants and beneficiaries, and

(C) protective of the rights of participants and beneficiaries of the plan.

Before granting an exemption under this paragraph, the Secretary shall require adequate notice to be given

IRC Sec. 4975(c)(2)(C)

to interested persons and shall publish notice in the Federal Register of the pendency of such exemption and shall afford interested persons an opportunity to present views. No exemption may be granted under this paragraph with respect to a transaction described in subparagraph (E) or (F) of paragraph (1) unless the Secretary affords an opportunity for hearing and makes a determination on the record with respect to the findings required under subparagraphs (A), (B), and (C) of this paragraph, except that in lieu of such hearing the Secretary may accept any record made by the Secretary of Labor with respect to an application for exemption under section 408(a) of title I of the Employee Retirement Income Security Act of 1974.

(3) Special rule for individual retirement accounts.—An individual for whose benefit an individual retirement account is established and his beneficiaries shall be exempt from the tax imposed by this section with respect to any transaction concerning such account (which would otherwise be taxable under this section) if, with respect to such transaction, the account ceases to be an individual retirement account by reason of the application of section 408(e)(2)(A) or if section 408(e)(4) applies to such account.

(4) Special rule for Archer MSAs.—An individual for whose benefit an Archer MSA (within the meaning of section 220(d)) is established shall be exempt from the tax imposed by this section with respect to any transaction concerning such account (which would otherwise be taxable under this section) if section 220(e)(2) applies to such transaction.

(5) Special rule for Coverdell education savings accounts.—An individual for whose benefit a Coverdell education savings account is established and any contributor to such account shall be exempt from the tax imposed by this section with respect to any transaction concerning such account (which would otherwise be taxable under this section) if section 530(d) applies with respect to such transaction.

(6) Special Rule for Health Savings Accounts.—An individual for whose benefit a health savings account (within the meaning of section 223(d)) is established shall be exempt from the tax imposed by this section with respect to any transaction concerning such account (which would otherwise be taxable under this section) if, with respect to such transaction, the account ceases to be a health savings account by reason of the application of section 223(e)(2) to such account.

(d) Exemptions.—Except as provided in subsection (f)(6), the prohibitions provided in subsection (c) shall not apply to—

(1) any loan made by the plan to a disqualified person who is a participant or beneficiary of the plan if such loan—

(A) is available to all such participants or beneficiaries on a reasonably equivalent basis,

(B) is not made available to highly compensated employees (within the meaning of section 414(q) of the Internal Revenue Code of 1986) in an amount greater than the amount made available to other employees,

(C) is made in accordance with specific provisions regarding such loans set forth in the plan,

(D) bears a reasonable rate of interest, and

(E) is adequately secured;

(2) any contract, or reasonable arrangement, made with a disqualified person for office space, or legal, accounting, or other services necessary for the establishment or operation of the plan, if no more than reasonable compensation is paid therefor;

(3) any loan to a leveraged employee stock ownership plan (as defined in subsection (e)(7)), if—

(A) such loan is primarily for the benefit of participants and beneficiaries of the plan, and

(B) such loan is at a reasonable rate of interest, and any collateral which is given to a disqualified person by the plan consists only of qualifying employer securities (as defined in subsection (e)(8));

(4) the investment of all or part of a plan's assets in deposits which bear a reasonable interest rate in a bank or similar financial institution supervised by the United States or a State, if such bank or other institution is a fiduciary of such plan and if—

(A) the plan covers only employees of such bank or other institution and employees of affiliates of such bank or other institution, or

(B) such investment is expressly authorized by a provision of the plan or by a fiduciary (other than such bank or institution or affiliates thereof) who is expressly empowered by the plan to so instruct the trustee with respect to such investment;

(5) any contract for life insurance, health insurance, or annuities with one or more insurers which are qualified to do business in a State if the plan pays no more than adequate consideration, and if each such insurer or insurers is—

(A) the employer maintaining the plan, or

(B) a disqualified person which is wholly owned (directly or indirectly) by the employer establishing the plan, or by any person which is a disqualified person with respect to the plan, but only if the total premiums and annuity considerations written by such insurers for life insurance, health insurance, or annuities for all plans (and their employers) with respect to which such insurers are disqualified persons (not including premiums or annuity considerations written by the employer maintaining the plan) do not exceed 5 percent of the total premiums and annuity considerations written for all lines of insurance in that year by such insurers (not including premiums or annuity considerations written by the employer maintaining the plan);

(6) the provision of any ancillary service by a bank or similar financial institution supervised by the United States or a State, if such service is provided at not more than reasonable compensation, if such bank or other institution is a fiduciary of such plan, and if—

(A) such bank or similar financial institution has adopted adequate internal safeguards which assure that the provision of such ancillary service is consistent with sound banking and financial practice, as determined by Federal or State supervisory authority, and

(B) the extent to which such ancillary service is provided is subject to specific guidelines issued by such bank or similar financial institution (as determined by the Secretary after consultation with Federal and State supervisory authority), and under such guidelines the bank or similar financial institution does not provide such ancillary service—

(i) in an excessive or unreasonable manner, and

(ii) in a manner that would be inconsistent with the best interests of participants and beneficiaries of employee benefit plans;

(7) the exercise of a privilege to convert securities, to the extent provided in regulations of the Secretary, but only if the plan receives no less than adequate consideration pursuant to such conversion;

(8) any transaction between a plan and a common or collective trust fund or pooled investment fund maintained by a disqualified person which is a bank or trust company supervised by a State or Federal agency or between a plan and a pooled investment fund of an insurance company qualified to do business in a State if—

(A) the transaction is a sale or purchase of an interest in the fund,

(B) the bank, trust company, or insurance company receives not more than reasonable compensation, and

(C) such transaction is expressly permitted by the instrument under which the plan is maintained, or by a fiduciary (other than the bank, trust company, or insurance company, or an affiliate thereof) who has authority to manage and control the assets of the plan;

(9) receipt by a disqualified person of any benefit to which he may be entitled as a participant or beneficiary in the plan, so long as the benefit is computed and paid on a basis which is consistent with the terms of the plan as applied to all other participants and beneficiaries;

(10) receipt by a disqualified person of any reasonable compensation for services rendered, or for the reimbursement of expenses properly and actually incurred, in the performance of his duties with the plan, but no person so serving who already receives full-time pay from an employer or an association of employers, whose employees are participants in the plan, or from an employee organization whose members are participants in such plan shall receive compensation from such fund, except for reimbursement of expenses properly and actually incurred;

(11) service by a disqualified person as a fiduciary in addition to being an officer, employee, agent, or other representative of a disqualified person;

(12) the making by a fiduciary of a distribution of the assets of the trust in accordance with the terms of the plan if such assets are distributed in the same manner as provided under section 4044 of title IV of the Employee Retirement Income Security Act of 1974 (relating to allocation of assets);

(13) any transaction which is exempt from section 406 of such Act by reason of section 408(e) of such Act (or which would be so exempt if such section 406 applied to such transaction) or which is exempt from section 406 of such Act by reason of section 408(b)(12) of such Act;

(14) any transaction required or permitted under part 1 of subtitle E of title IV or section 4223 of the Employee Retirement Income Security Act of 1974, but this paragraph shall not apply with respect to the application of subsection (c)(1)(E) or (F);

(15) a merger of multiemployer plans, or the transfer of assets or liabilities between multiemployer plans, determined by the Pension Benefit Guaranty Corporation to meet the requirements of section 4231 of such Act, but this paragraph shall not apply with respect to the application of subsection (c)(1)(E) or (F);

(16) a sale of stock held by a trust which constitutes an individual retirement account under section 408(a) to the individual for whose benefit such account is established if—

(A) such stock is in a bank (as defined in section 581) or a depository institution holding company (as defined in section 3(w)(1) of the Federal Deposit Insurance Act (12 U.S.C. 1813(w)(1)),

(B) such stock is held by such trust as of the date of the enactment of this paragraph,

(C) such sale is pursuant to an election under section 1362(a) by such bank or company,

(D) such sale is for fair market value at the time of sale (as established by an independent appraiser) and the terms of the sale are otherwise at least as favorable to such trust as the terms that would apply on a sale to an unrelated party,

(E) such trust does not pay any commissions, costs, or other expenses in connection with the sale, and

IRC Sec. 4975(d)(16)(E)

(F) the stock is sold in a single transaction for cash not later than 120 days after the S corporation election is made;

(17) Any transaction in connection with the provision of investment advice described in subsection (e)(3)(B) to a participant or beneficiary in a plan that permits such participant or beneficiary to direct the investment of plan assets in an individual account, if—

(A) the transaction is—

(i) the provision of the investment advice to the participant or beneficiary of the plan with respect to a security or other property available as an investment under the plan,

(ii) the acquisition, holding, or sale of a security or other property available as an investment under the plan pursuant to the investment advice, or

(iii) the direct or indirect receipt of fees or other compensation by the fiduciary adviser or an affiliate thereof (or any employee, agent, or registered representative of the fiduciary adviser or affiliate) in connection with the provision of the advice or in connection with an acquisition, holding, or sale of a security or other property available as an investment under the plan pursuant to the investment advice; and

(B) the requirements of subsection (f)(8) are met;

(18) any transaction involving the purchase or sale of securities, or other property (as determined by the Secretary of Labor), between a plan and a disqualified person (other than a fiduciary described in subsection (e)(3)) with respect to a plan if—

(A) the transaction involves a block trade,

(B) at the time of the transaction, the interest of the plan (together with the interests of any other plans maintained by the same plan sponsor), does not exceed 10 percent of the aggregate size of the block trade,

(C) the terms of the transaction, including the price, are at least as favorable to the plan as an arm's length transaction, and

(D) the compensation associated with the purchase and sale is not greater than the compensation associated with an arm's length transaction with an unrelated party;

(19) any transaction involving the purchase or sale of securities, or other property (as determined by the Secretary of Labor), between a plan and a disqualified person if—

(A) the transaction is executed through an electronic communication network, alternative trading system, or similar execution system or trading venue subject to regulation and oversight by—

(i) the applicable Federal regulating entity, or

(ii) such foreign regulatory entity as the Secretary of Labor may determine by regulation,

(B) either—

(i) the transaction is effected pursuant to rules designed to match purchases and sales at the best price available through the execution system in accordance with applicable rules of the Securities and Exchange Commission or other relevant governmental authority, or

(ii) neither the execution system nor the parties to the transaction take into account the identity of the parties in the execution of trades,

(C) the price and compensation associated with the purchase and sale are not greater than the price and compensation associated with an arm's length transaction with an unrelated party,

(D) if the disqualified person has an ownership interest in the system or venue described in subparagraph (A), the system or venue has been authorized by the plan sponsor or other independent fiduciary for transactions described in this paragraph, and

(E) not less than 30 days prior to the initial transaction described in this paragraph executed through any system or venue described in subparagraph (A), a plan fiduciary is provided written or electronic notice of the execution of such transaction through such system or venue;

(20) transactions described in subparagraphs (A), (B), and (D) of subsection (c)(1) between a plan and a person that is a disqualified person other than a fiduciary (or an affiliate) who has or exercises any discretionary authority or control with respect to the investment of the plan assets involved in the transaction or renders investment advice (within the meaning of subsection (e)(3)(B)) with respect to those assets, solely by reason of providing services to the plan or solely by reason of a relationship to such a service provider described in subparagraph (F), (G), (H), or (I) of subsection (e)(2), or both, but only if in connection with such transaction the plan receives no less, nor pays no more, than adequate consideration;

(21) any foreign exchange transactions, between a bank or broker-dealer (or any affiliate of either) and a plan (as defined in this section) with respect to which such bank or broker-dealer (or affiliate) is a trustee, custodian, fiduciary, or other disqualified person person [sic], if—

(A) the transaction is in connection with the purchase, holding, or sale of securities or other investment assets (other than a foreign exchange transaction unrelated to any other investment in securities or other investment assets),

(B) at the time the foreign exchange transaction is entered into, the terms of the transaction are not

IRC Sec. 4975(d)(16)(F)

less favorable to the plan than the terms generally available in comparable arm's length foreign exchange transactions between unrelated parties, or the terms afforded by the bank or broker-dealer (or any affiliate of either) in comparable arm's-length foreign exchange transactions involving unrelated parties,

(C) the exchange rate used by such bank or broker-dealer (or affiliate) for a particular foreign exchange transaction does not deviate by more than 3 percent from the interbank bid and asked rates for transactions of comparable size and maturity at the time of the transaction as displayed on an independent service that reports rates of exchange in the foreign currency market for such currency, and

(D) the bank or broker-dealer (or any affiliate of either) does not have investment discretion, or provide investment advice, with respect to the transaction;

(22) any transaction described in subsection (c)(1)(A) involving the purchase and sale of a security between a plan and any other account managed by the same investment manager, if—

(A) the transaction is a purchase or sale, for no consideration other than cash payment against prompt delivery of a security for which market quotations are readily available,

(B) the transaction is effected at the independent current market price of the security (within the meaning of section 270.17a-7(b) of title 17, Code of Federal Regulations),

(C) no brokerage commission, fee (except for customary transfer fees, the fact of which is disclosed pursuant to subparagraph (D)), or other remuneration is paid in connection with the transaction,

(D) a fiduciary (other than the investment manager engaging in the cross-trades or any affiliate) for each plan participating in the transaction authorizes in advance of any cross-trades (in a document that is separate from any other written agreement of the parties) the investment manager to engage in cross trades at the investment manager's discretion, after such fiduciary has received disclosure regarding the conditions under which cross trades may take place (but only if such disclosure is separate from any other agreement or disclosure involving the asset management relationship), including the written policies and procedures of the investment manager described in subparagraph (H),

(E) each plan participating in the transaction has assets of at least $100,000,000, except that if the assets of a plan are invested in a master trust containing the assets of plans maintained by employers in the same controlled group (as defined in section 407(d)(7) of the Employee Retirement Income Security Act of 1974), the master trust has assets of at least $100,000,000,

(F) the investment manager provides to the plan fiduciary who authorized cross trading under subparagraph (D) a quarterly report detailing all cross trades executed by the investment manager in which the plan participated during such quarter, including the following information, as applicable: (i) the identity of each security bought or sold; (ii) the number of shares or units traded; (iii) the parties involved in the cross-trade; and (iv) trade price and the method used to establish the trade price,

(G) the investment manager does not base its fee schedule on the plan's consent to cross trading, and no other service (other than the investment opportunities and cost savings available through a cross trade) is conditioned on the plan's consent to cross trading,

(H) the investment manager has adopted, and cross-trades are effected in accordance with, written cross-trading policies and procedures that are fair and equitable to all accounts participating in the cross-trading program, and that include a description of the manager's pricing policies and procedures, and the manager's policies and procedures for allocating cross trades in an objective manner among accounts participating in the cross-trading program, and

(I) the investment manager has designated an individual responsible for periodically reviewing such purchases and sales to ensure compliance with the written policies and procedures described in subparagraph (H), and following such review, the individual shall issue an annual written report no later than 90 days following the period to which it relates signed under penalty of perjury to the plan fiduciary who authorized cross trading under subparagraph (D) describing the steps performed during the course of the review, the level of compliance, and any specific instances of non-compliance.

The written report shall also notify the plan fiduciary of the plan's right to terminate participation in the investment manager's cross-trading program at any time; or

(23) except as provided in subsection (f)(11), a transaction described in subparagraph (A), (B), (C), or (D) of subsection (c)(1) in connection with the acquisition, holding, or disposition of any security or commodity, if the transaction is corrected before the end of the correction period.

(e) Definitions.—

(1) Plan.—For purposes of this section, the term "plan" means—

(A) a trust described in section 401(a) which forms a part of a plan, or a plan described in section 403(a), which trust or plan is exempt from tax under section 501(a),

(B) an individual retirement account described in section 408(a),

IRC Sec. 4975(e)(1)(B)

(C) an individual retirement annuity described in section 408(b),

(D) an Archer MSA described in section 220(d),

(E) a health savings account described in section 223(d),

(F) a Coverdell education savings account described in section 530, or

(G) a trust, plan, account, or annuity which, at any time, has been determined by the Secretary to be described in any preceding subparagraph of this paragraph.

(2) Disqualified person.—For purposes of this section, the term "disqualified person" means a person who is—

(A) a fiduciary;

(B) a person providing services to the plan;

(C) an employer any of whose employees are covered by the plan;

(D) an employee organization any of whose members are covered by the plan;

(E) an owner, direct or indirect, of 50 percent or more of—

   (i) the combined voting power of all classes of stock entitled to vote or the total value of shares of all classes of stock of a corporation,

   (ii) the capital interest or the profits interest of a partnership, or

   (iii) the beneficial interest of a trust or unincorporated enterprise,

which is an employer or an employee organization described in subparagraph (C) or (D);

(F) a member of the family (as defined in paragraph (6)) of any individual described in subparagraph (A), (B), (C), or (E);

(G) a corporation, partnership, or trust or estate of which (or in which) 50 percent or more of—

   (i) the combined voting power of all classes of stock entitled to vote or the total value of shares of all classes of stock of such corporation,

   (ii) the capital interest or profits interest of such partnership, or

   (iii) the beneficial interest of such trust or estate, is owned directly or indirectly, or held by persons described in subparagraph (A), (B), (C), (D), or (E);

(H) an officer, director (or an individual having powers or responsibilities similar to those of officers or directors), a 10 percent or more shareholder, or a highly compensated employee (earning 10 percent or more of the yearly wages of an employer) of a person described in subparagraph (C), (D), (E), or (G); or

(I) a 10 percent or more (in capital or profits) partner or joint venturer of a person described in subparagraph (C), (D), (E), or (G).

The Secretary, after consultation and coordination with the Secretary of Labor or his delegate, may by regulation prescribe a percentage lower than 50 percent for subparagraphs (E) and (G) and lower than 10 percent for subparagraphs (H) and (I).

(3) Fiduciary.—For purposes of this section, the term "fiduciary" means any person who—

(A) exercises any discretionary authority or discretionary control respecting management of such plan or exercises any authority or control respecting management or disposition of its assets,

(B) renders investment advice for a fee or other compensation, direct or indirect, with respect to any moneys or other property of such plan, or has any authority or responsibility to do so, or

(C) has any discretionary authority or discretionary responsibility in the administration of such plan.

Such term includes any person designated under section 405(c)(1)(B) of the Employee Retirement Income Security Act of 1974.

(4) Stockholdings.—For purposes of paragraphs (2)(E)(i), and (G)(i) there shall be taken into account indirect stockholdings which would be taken into account under section 267(c), except that, for purposes of this paragraph, section 267(c)(4) shall be treated as providing that the members of the family of an individual are the members within the meaning of paragraph (6).

(5) Partnerships; trusts.—For purposes of paragraphs (2)(E)(ii) and (iii), (G)(ii) and (iii), and (I) the ownership of profits or beneficial interests shall be determined in accordance with the rules for constructive ownership of stock provided in section 267(c) (other than paragraph (3) thereof), except that section 267(c)(4) shall be treated as providing that the members of the family of an individual are the members within the meaning of paragraph (6).

(6) Members of family.—For purposes of paragraph (2)(F), the family of any individual shall include his spouse, ancestor, lineal descendant, and any spouse of a lineal descendant.

(7) Employee stock ownership plan.—The term "employee stock ownership plan" means a defined contribution plan—

(A) which is a stock bonus plan which is qualified, or a stock bonus and a money purchase plan both of which are qualified under section 401(a) and which are designed to invest primarily in qualifying employer securities; and

(B) which is otherwise defined in regulations prescribed by the Secretary.

IRC Sec. 4975(e)(1)(C)

A plan shall not be treated as an employee stock ownership plan unless it meets the requirements of section 409(h), section 409(o), and, if applicable, section 409(n), 409(p), and section 664(g) and, if the employer has a registration-type class of securities (as defined in section409(e)(4)), it meets the requirements of section 409(e).

(8) Qualifying employer security.—The term "qualifying employer security" means an employer security within the meaning of section 409(*l*).

If any moneys or other property of a plan are invested in shares of an investment company registered under the Investment Company Act of 1940, the investment shall not cause that investment company or that investment company's investment adviser or principal underwriter to be treated as a fiduciary or a disqualified person for purposes of this section, except when an investment company or its investment adviser or principal underwriter acts in connection with a plan covering employees of the investment company, its investment adviser, or its principal underwriter.

(9) Section made applicable to withdrawal liability payment funds.—For purposes of this section—

   (A) In general.—The term "plan" includes a trust described in section 501(c)(22).

   (B) Disqualified person.—In the case of any trust to which this section applies by reason of subparagraph (A), the term "disqualified person" includes any person who is a disqualified person with respect to any plan to which such trust is permitted to make payments under section 4223 of the Employee Retirement Income Security Act of 1974.

(f) Other Definitions and Special Rules.—For purposes of this section—

(1) Joint and several liability.—If more than one person is liable under subsection (a) or (b) with respect to any one prohibited transaction, all such persons shall be jointly and severally liable under such subsection with respect to such transaction.

(2) Taxable period.—The term "taxable period" means, with respect to any prohibited transaction, the period beginning with the date on which the prohibited transaction occurs and ending on the earliest of—

   (A) the date of mailing of a notice of deficiency with respect to the tax imposed by subsection (a) under section 6212,

   (B) the date on which the tax imposed by subsection (a) is assessed, or

   (C) the date on which correction of the prohibited transaction is completed.

(3) Sale or exchange; encumbered property.—A transfer of real or personal property by a disqualified person to a plan shall be treated as a sale or exchange if the property is subject to a mortgage or similar lien which the plan assumes or if it is subject to a mortgage or similar lien which a disqualified person placed on the property within the 10-year period ending on the date of the transfer.

(4) Amount involved.—The term "amount involved" means, with respect to a prohibited transaction, the greater of the amount of money and the fair market value of the other property given or the amount of money and the fair market value of the other property received; except that, in the case of services described in paragraphs (2) and (10) of subsection (d) the amount involved shall be only the excess compensation. For purposes of the preceding sentence, the fair market value—

   (A) in the case of the tax imposed by subsection (a), shall be determined as of the date on which the prohibited transaction occurs; and

   (B) in the case of the tax imposed by subsection (b), shall be the highest fair market value during the taxable period.

(5) Correction.—The terms "correction" and "correct" mean, with respect to a prohibited transaction, undoing the transaction to the extent possible, but in any case placing the plan in a financial position not worse than that in which it would be if the disqualified person were acting under the highest fiduciary standards.

(6) Exemptions not to apply to certain transactions.—

   (A) In general.—In the case of a trust described in section 401(a) which is part of a plan providing contributions or benefits for employees some or all of whom are owner-employees (as defined in section 401(c)(3)), the exemptions provided by subsection (d) (other than paragraphs (9) and (12)) shall not apply to a transaction in which the plan directly or indirectly—

      (i) lends any part of the corpus or income of the plan to,

      (ii) pays any compensation for personal services rendered to the plan to, or

      (iii) acquires for the plan any property from, or sells any property to, any such owner-employee, a member of the family (as defined in section 267(c)(4)) of any such owner-employee, or any corporation in which any such owner-employee owns, directly or indirectly, 50 percent or more of the total combined voting power of all classes of stock entitled to vote or 50 percent or more of the total value of shares of all classes of stock of the corporation.

   (B) Special rules for shareholder-employees, etc.—

      (i) In general.—For purposes of subparagraph (A), the following shall be treated as owner-employees:

IRC Sec. 4975(f)(6)(B)(i)

(I) A shareholder-employee.

(II) A participant or beneficiary of an individual retirement plan (as defined in section 7701(a)(37)).

(III) An employer or association of employees which establishes such an individual retirement plan under section 408(c).

(ii) Exception for certain transactions involving shareholder-employees.—Subparagraph (A)(iii) shall not apply to a transaction which consists of a sale of employer securities to an employee stock ownership plan (as defined in subsection (e)(7)) by a shareholder-employee, a member of the family (as defined in section 267(c)(4)) of such shareholder-employee, or a corporation in which such a shareholder-employee owns stock representing a 50 percent or greater interest described in subparagraph (A).

(iii) Loan exception.—For purposes of subparagraph (A)(i), the term "owner-employee" shall only include a person described in subclause (II) or (III) of clause (i).

(C) Shareholder-employee.—For purposes of subparagraph (B), the term "shareholder-employee" means an employee or officer of an S corporation who owns (or is considered as owning within the meaning of section 318(a)(1)) more than 5 percent of the outstanding stock of the corporation on any day during the taxable year of such corporation.

(7) S corporation repayment of loans for qualifying employer securities.—A plan shall not be treated as violating the requirements of section 401 or 409 or subsection (e)(7), or as engaging in a prohibited transaction for purposes of subsection (d)(3), merely by reason of any distribution (as described in section 1368(a)) with respect to S corporation stock that constitutes qualifying employer securities, which in accordance with the plan provisions is used to make payments on a loan described in subsection (d)(3) the proceeds of which were used to acquire such qualifying employer securities (whether or not allocated to participants). The preceding sentence shall not apply in the case of a distribution which is paid with respect to any employer security which is allocated to a participant unless the plan provides that employer securities with a fair market value of not less than the amount of such distribution are allocated to such participant for the year which (but for the preceding sentence) such distribution would have been allocated to such participant.

(8) Provision of investment advice to participant and beneficiaries.—

(A) In general.—The prohibitions provided in subsection (c) shall not apply to transactions described in subsection (d)(17) if the investment advice provided by a fiduciary adviser is provided under an eligible investment advice arrangement.

(B) Eligible investment advice arrangement.—For purposes of this paragraph, the term "eligible investment advice arrangement" means an arrangement—

(i) which either—

(I) provides that any fees (including any commission or other compensation) received by the fiduciary adviser for investment advice or with respect to the sale, holding, or acquisition of any security or other property for purposes of investment of plan assets do not vary depending on the basis of any investment option selected, or

(II) uses a computer model under an investment advice program meeting the requirements of subparagraph (C) in connection with the provision of investment advice by a fiduciary adviser to a participant or beneficiary, and

(ii) with respect to which the requirements of subparagraphs (D), (E), (F), (G), (H), and (I) are met.

(C) Investment advice program using computer model.—

(i) In general.—An investment advice program meets the requirements of this subparagraph if the requirements of clauses (ii), (iii), and (iv) are met.

(ii) Computer model.—The requirements of this clause are met if the investment advice provided under the investment advice program is provided pursuant to a computer model that—

(I) applies generally accepted investment theories that take into account the historic returns of different asset classes over defined periods of time,

(II) utilizes relevant information about the participant, which may include age, life expectancy, retirement age, risk tolerance, other assets or sources of income, and preferences as to certain types of investments,

(III) utilizes prescribed objective criteria to provide asset allocation portfolios comprised of investment options available under the plan,

(IV) operates in a manner that is not biased in favor of investments offered by the fiduciary adviser or a person with a material affiliation or contractual relationship with the fiduciary adviser, and

(V) takes into account all investment options under the plan in specifying how a participant's account balance should be invested and is not inappropriately weighted with respect to any investment option.

(iii) Certification.—

(I) In general.—The requirements of this clause are met with respect to any investment advice program if an eligible investment expert certifies, prior to the utilization of the computer model and in accordance with rules prescribed by the Secretary of Labor, that the computer model meets the requirements of clause (ii).

(II) Renewal of certifications.—If, as determined under regulations prescribed by the Secretary of Labor, there are material modifications to a computer model, the requirements of this clause are met only if a certification described in subclause (I) is obtained with respect to the computer model as so modified.

(III) Eligible investment expert.—The term "eligible investment expert" means any person which meets such requirements as the Secretary of Labor may provide and which does not bear any material affiliation or contractual relationship with any investment adviser or a related person thereof (or any employee, agent, or registered representative of the investment adviser or related person).

(iv) Exclusivity of recommendation.—The requirements of this clause are met with respect to any investment advice program if—

(I) the only investment advice provided under the program is the advice generated by the computer model described in clause (ii), and

(II) any transaction described in [subsection] (d)(17)(A)(ii) occurs solely at the direction of the participant or beneficiary.

Nothing in the preceding sentence shall preclude the participant or beneficiary from requesting investment advice other than that described in clause (i), but only if such request has not been solicited by any person connected with carrying out the arrangement.

(D) Express authorization by separate fiduciary.— The requirements of this subparagraph are met with respect to an arrangement if the arrangement is expressly authorized by a plan fiduciary other than the person offering the investment advice program, any person providing investment options under the plan, or any affiliate of either.

(E) Audits.—

(i) In general.—The requirements of this subparagraph are met if an independent auditor, who has appropriate technical training or experience and proficiency and so represents in writing—

(I) conducts an annual audit of the arrangement for compliance with the requirements of this paragraph, and

(II) following completion of the annual audit, issues a written report to the fiduciary who authorized use of the arrangement which presents its specific findings regarding compliance of the arrangement with the requirements of this paragraph.

(ii) Special rule for individual retirement and similar plans.—In the case of a plan described in

subparagraphs (B) through (F) (and so much of subparagraph (G) as relates to such subparagraphs) of subsection (e)(1), in lieu of the requirements of clause (i), audits of the arrangement shall be conducted at such times and in such manner as the Secretary of Labor may prescribe.

(iii) Independent auditor.—For purposes of this subparagraph, an auditor is considered independent if it is not related to the person offering the arrangement to the plan and is not related to any person providing investment options under the plan.

(F) Disclosure.—The requirements of this subparagraph are met if—

(i) the fiduciary adviser provides to a participant or a beneficiary before the initial provision of the investment advice with regard to any security or other property offered as an investment option, a written notification (which may consist of notification by means of electronic communication)—

(I) of the role of any party that has a material affiliation or contractual relationship with the fiduciary adviser in the development of the investment advice program and in the selection of investment options available under the plan,

(II) of the past performance and historical rates of return of the investment options available under the plan,

(III) of all fees or other compensation relating to the advice that the fiduciary adviser or any affiliate thereof is to receive (including compensation provided by any third party) in connection with the provision of the advice or in connection with the sale, acquisition, or holding of the security or other property,

(IV) of any material affiliation or contractual relationship of the fiduciary adviser or affiliates thereof in the security or other property,

(V) the manner, and under what circumstances, any participant or beneficiary information provided under the arrangement will be used or disclosed,

(VI) of the types of services provided by the fiduciary adviser in connection with the provision of investment advice by the fiduciary adviser,

(VII) that the adviser is acting as a fiduciary of the plan in connection with the provision of the advice, and

(VIII) that a recipient of the advice may separately arrange for the provision of advice by another adviser, that could have no material affiliation with and receive no fees or other compensation in connection with the security or other property, and

(ii) at all times during the provision of advisory services to the participant or beneficiary, the fiduciary adviser—

IRC Sec. 4975(f)(8)(F)(ii)

(I) maintains the information described in clause (i) in accurate form and in the manner described in subparagraph (H),

(II) provides, without charge, accurate information to the recipient of the advice no less frequently than annually,

(III) provides, without charge, accurate information to the recipient of the advice upon request of the recipient, and

(IV) provides, without charge, accurate information to the recipient of the advice concerning any material change to the information required to be provided to the recipient of the advice at a time reasonably contemporaneous to the change in information.

(G) Other conditions.—The requirements of this subparagraph are met if—

(i) the fiduciary adviser provides appropriate disclosure, in connection with the sale, acquisition, or holding of the security or other property, in accordance with all applicable securities laws,

(ii) the sale, acquisition, or holding occurs solely at the direction of the recipient of the advice,

(iii) the compensation received by the fiduciary adviser and affiliates thereof in connection with the sale, acquisition, or holding of the security or other property is reasonable, and

(iv) the terms of the sale, acquisition, or holding of the security or other property are at least as favorable to the plan as an arm's length transaction would be.

(H) Standards for presentation of information.—

(i) In general.—The requirements of this subparagraph are met if the notification required to be provided to participants and beneficiaries under subparagraph (F)(i) is written in a clear and conspicuous manner and in a manner calculated to be understood by the average plan participant and is sufficiently accurate and comprehensive to reasonably apprise such participants and beneficiaries of the information required to be provided in the notification.

(ii) Model form for disclosure of fees and other compensation.—The Secretary of Labor shall issue a model form for the disclosure of fees and other compensation required in subparagraph (F)(i)(III) which meets the requirements of clause (i).

(I) Maintenance for 6 years of evidence of compliance.—The requirements of this subparagraph are met if a fiduciary adviser who has provided advice referred to in subparagraph (A) maintains, for a period of not less than 6 years after the provision of the advice, any records necessary for determining whether the requirements of the pre-

ceding provisions of this paragraph and of subsection (d)(17) have been met. A transaction prohibited under subsection (c) shall not be considered to have occurred solely because the records are lost or destroyed prior to the end of the 6-year period due to circumstances beyond the control of the fiduciary adviser.

(J) Definitions.—For purposes of this paragraph and subsection (d)(17)—

(i) Fiduciary adviser.—The term "fiduciary adviser" means, with respect to a plan, a person who is a fiduciary of the plan by reason of the provision of investment advice referred to in subsection (e)(3)(B) by the person to a participant or beneficiary of the plan and who is—

(I) registered as an investment adviser under the Investment Advisers Act of 1940 (15 U.S.C. 80b-1 et seq.) or under the laws of the State in which the fiduciary maintains its principal office and place of business,

(II) a bank or similar financial institution referred to in subsection (d)(4) or a savings association (as defined in section 3(b)(1) of the Federal Deposit Insurance Act (12 U.S.C. 1813(b)(1)), but only if the advice is provided through a trust department of the bank or similar financial institution or savings association which is subject to periodic examination and review by Federal or State banking authorities,

(III) an insurance company qualified to do business under the laws of a State,

(IV) a person registered as a broker or dealer under the Securities Exchange Act of 1934 (15 U.S.C. 78a et seq.),

(V) an affiliate of a person described in any of subclauses (I) through (IV), or

(VI) an employee, agent, or registered representative of a person described in subclauses (I) through (V) who satisfies the requirements of applicable insurance, banking, and securities laws relating to the provision of the advice.

For purposes of this title, a person who develops the computer model described in subparagraph (C)(ii) or markets the investment advice program or computer model shall be treated as a person who is a fiduciary of the plan by reason of the provision of investment advice referred to in subsection (e)(3)(B) to a participant or beneficiary and shall be treated as a fiduciary adviser for purposes of this paragraph and subsection (d)(17), except that the Secretary of Labor may prescribe rules under which only 1 fiduciary adviser may elect to be treated as a fiduciary with respect to the plan.

(ii) Affiliate.—The term "affiliate" of another entity means an affiliated person of the entity (as defined in section 2(a)(3) of the Investment Company Act of 1940 (15 U.S.C. 80a-2(a)(3))).

IRC Sec. 4975(f)(8)(F)(ii)(I)

(iii) Registered representative.—The term "registered representative" of another entity means a person described in section 3(a)(18) of the Securities Exchange Act of 1934 (15 U.S.C. 78c(a)(18)) (substituting the entity for the broker or dealer referred to in such section) or a person described in section 202(a)(17) of the Investment Advisers Act of 1940 (15 U.S.C. 80b-2(a)(17)) (substituting the entity for the investment adviser referred to in such section).

(9) Block trade.—The term "block trade" means any trade of at least 10,000 shares or with a market value of at least $200,000 which will be allocated across two or more unrelated client accounts of a fiduciary.

(10) Adequate consideration.—The term "adequate consideration" means—

(A) in the case of a security for which there is a generally recognized market—

(i) the price of the security prevailing on a national securities exchange which is registered under section 6 of the Securities Exchange Act of 1934, taking into account factors such as the size of the transaction and marketability of the security, or

(ii) if the security is not traded on such a national securities exchange, a price not less favorable to the plan than the offering price for the security as established by the current bid and asked prices quoted by persons independent of the issuer and of the party in interest, taking into account factors such as the size of the transaction and marketability of the security, and

(B) in the case of an asset other than a security for which there is a generally recognized market, the fair market value of the asset as determined in good faith by a fiduciary or fiduciaries in accordance with regulations prescribed by the Secretary of Labor.

(11) Correction period.—

(A) In general.—For purposes of subsection (d)(23), the term "correction period" means the 14-day period beginning on the date on which the disqualified person discovers, or reasonably should have discovered, that the transaction would (without regard to this paragraph and subsection (d)(23)) constitute a prohibited transaction.

(B) Exceptions.—

(i) Employer securities.—Subsection (d)(23) does not apply to any transaction between a plan and a plan sponsor or its affiliates that involves the acquisition or sale of an employer security (as defined in section 407(d)(1) of the Employee Retirement Income Security Act of 1974) or the acquisition, sale, or lease of employer real property (as defined in section 407(d)(2) of such Act).

(ii) Knowing prohibited transaction.—In the case of any disqualified person, subsection (d)(23) does not apply to a transaction if, at the time the transaction is entered into, the disqualified person knew (or reasonably should have known) that the transaction would (without regard to this paragraph) constitute a prohibited transaction.

(C) Abatement of tax where there is a correction.—If a transaction is not treated as a prohibited transaction by reason of subsection (d)(23), then no tax under subsections (a) and (b) shall be assessed with respect to such transaction, and if assessed the assessment shall be abated, and if collected shall be credited or refunded as an overpayment.

(D) Definitions.—For purposes of this paragraph and subsection (d)(23)—

(i) Security.—The term "security" has the meaning given such term by section 475(c)(2) (without regard to subparagraph (F)(iii) and the last sentence thereof).

(ii) Commodity.—The term "commodity" has the meaning given such term by section 475(e)(2) (without regard to subparagraph (D)(iii) thereof).

(iii) Correct.—The term "correct" means, with respect to a transaction—

(I) to undo the transaction to the extent possible and in any case to make good to the plan or affected account any losses resulting from the transaction, and

(II) to restore to the plan or affected account any profits made through the use of assets of the plan.

(g) Application of Section.—This section shall not apply—

(1) in the case of a plan to which a guaranteed benefit policy (as defined in section 401(b)(2)(B) of the Employee Retirement Income Security Act of 1974) is issued, to any assets of the insurance company, insurance service, or insurance organization merely because of its issuance of such policy;

(2) to a governmental plan (within the meaning of section 414(d)); or

(3) to a church plan (within the meaning of section 414(e)) with respect to which the election provided by section 410(d) has not been made.

In the case of a plan which invests in any security issued by an investment company registered under the Investment Company Act of 1940, the assets of such plan shall be deemed to include such security but shall not, by reason of such investment, be deemed to include any assets of such company.

(h) Notification of Secretary of Labor.—Before sending a notice of deficiency with respect to the tax

IRC Sec. 4975(h)

imposed by subsection (a) or (b), the Secretary shall notify the Secretary of Labor and provide him a reasonable opportunity to obtain a correction of the prohibited transaction or to comment on the imposition of such tax.

(i) Cross Reference.—For provisions concerning coordination procedures between Secretary of Labor and Secretary of Treasury with respect to application of tax imposed by this section and for authority to waive imposition of the tax imposed by subsection (b), see section 3003 of the Employee Retirement Income Security Act of 1974.

Recent Amendments to IRC §4975

Worker, Retiree, and Employer Recovery Act of 2008 (Pub. L. No. 110-458), as follows:

- IRC §4975(d)(17) was amended by Act §106(a)(2)(A) by substituting "that permits" for "and that permits". Eff. with respect to advice referred to in IRC §4975(e)(3)(B) provided after Dec. 31, 2006.
- IRC §4975(d)(18) was amended by Act §106(b)(2)(A) by substituting "disqualified person" for "party in interest" and by substituting "subsection (e)(3)" for "subsection (e)(3)(B)" in the matter preceding subpara. (A). Eff. for transactions occurring after Aug. 17, 2006.
- IRC §4975(d) was amended by Act §106(b)(2)(B)–(C) by substituting "disqualified person" for "party in interest" each place it appeared in paras. (19), (20), and (21); and by striking "or less" in para. (21)(C). Eff. for transactions occurring after Aug. 17, 2006.
- IRC §4975(f)(8) was amended by Act §106(a)(2)(B)(i)–(v) by substituting "subsection (d)(17)" for "subsection (b)(14)" in subpara. (A); by substituting "(d)(17)(A)(ii)" for "subsection (b)(14)(B)(ii)" in subpara. (C)(iv)(II); by substituting "fiduciary adviser," for "financial adviser" in subpara. (F)(i)(I); by substituting "subsection (c)" for "section 406" in subpara. (I); by substituting "a participant" for "the participant" each place it appeared and by inserting "referred to in subsection (e)(3)(B)" after "investment advice" in subpara. (J)(i) in the matter preceding subcl. (I); and by substituting "subsection (d)(4)" for "section 408(b)(4)" in subpara. (J)(II). Eff. with respect to advice referred to in IRC §4975(e)(3)(B) provided after Dec. 31, 2006.
- IRC §4975(f)(11)(B)(i) was amended by Act §106(c)(1)–(2) by inserting "of the Employee Retirement Income Security Act of 1974" after "section 407(d)(1)", and by inserting "of such Act" after "section 407(d)(2)" in subpara. (B)(i). Eff. with respect to advice referred to in IRC §4975(e)(3)(B) provided after Dec. 31, 2006.

Pension Protection Act of 2006 (Pub. L. No. 109-280), as follows:

- IRC §4975(d) was amended by Act §601(b)(1)(A)–(C) by striking "or" at the end of para. (15); by replacing the period at the end of para. (16) with ";or" [sic] and by adding new para. (17). Eff. with respect to advice referred to in IRC §4975(c)(3)(B)[(e)(3)(B)] provided after Dec. 31, 2006.
- IRC §4975(d), as amended, was amended by Act §611(a)(2)(A) by striking "or" at the end of para. (16) and the period at the end of para. (17), and adding new para. (18). Eff. for transactions occurring after Aug. 17, 2006.
- IRC §4975(d), as amended, was amended by Act §611(c)(2) by striking "or" at the end of para. (17); by striking the period at the end of para. (18) and adding ", or"; and by adding new para. (19). Eff. for transactions occurring after Aug. 17, 2006.
- IRC §4975(d), as amended, was amended by Act §611(d)(2)(A) by striking "or" at the end of para. (18); by striking the period at the end of para. (19) and adding ", or"; and by adding new para. (20). Eff. for transactions occurring after Aug. 17, 2006.
- IRC §4975(d), as amended, was amended by Act §611(e)(2) by striking "or" at the end of para. (19); by striking the period at the

end of para. (20) and adding ", or"; and by adding new para. (21). Eff. for transactions occurring after Aug. 17, 2006.
- IRC §4975(d), as amended, was amended by Act §611(g)(2) by striking "or" at the end of para. (20); by striking the period at the end of para. (21) and adding ", or"; and by adding new para. (22). Eff. for transactions occurring after Aug. 17, 2006.
- IRC §4975(d), as amended, was amended by Act §612(b)(1) by striking "or" at the end of para. (21); by striking the period at the end of para. (22) and adding ", or"; and by adding new para. (23). Eff. for any transaction which the fiduciary or disqualified person discovers, or reasonably should have discovered, after Aug. 17, 2006, constitutes a prohibited transaction.
- IRC §4975(f) was amended by Act §601(b)(2) by adding new para. (8). Eff. with respect to advice referred to in IRC §4975(c)(3)(B)[(e)(3)(B)] provided after Dec. 31, 2006.
- IRC §4975(f) was amended by Act §611(a)(2)(B) by adding new para. (9). Eff. for transactions occurring after Aug. 17, 2006.
- IRC §4975(f) was amended by Act §611(d)(2)(B) by adding new para. (10). Eff. for transactions occurring after Aug. 17, 2006.
- IRC §4975(f) was amended by Act §612(b)(2) by adding new para. (11). Eff. for any transaction which the fiduciary or disqualified person discovers, or reasonably should have discovered, after Aug. 17, 2006, constitutes a prohibited transaction.
- **Sunset Provision.** Act §811, provides:

> **SEC. 811. PENSIONS AND INDIVIDUAL RETIREMENT ARRANGEMENT PROVISIONS OF ECONOMIC GROWTH AND TAX RELIEF RECONCILIATION ACT OF 2001 MADE PERMANENT.**
>
> Title IX of the Economic Growth and Tax Relief Reconciliation Act of 2001 [Pub. L. No. 107-16] shall not apply to the provisions of, and amendments made by, subtitles A through F [§§601–666] of title VI of such Act (relating to pension and individual retirement arrangement provisions).

Gulf Opportunity Zone Act of 2005 (Pub. L. No. 109-135), as follows:

- IRC §4975(d)(16) was amended by Act §413(a)(2)(A)–(B) by inserting "or a depository institution holding company (as defined in section 3(w)(1) of the Federal Deposit Insurance Act (12 U.S.C. 1813(w)(1))" after "a bank (as defined in §581)" in subpara. (A), and by inserting "or company" after "such bank" in subpara. (C). Eff. Oct. 22, 2004, as if included in the provision of Pub. L. No. 108-357 to which it relates.

American Jobs Creation Act of 2004 (Pub. L. No. 108-357), as follows:

- IRC §4975(d) was amended by Act §233(c) by striking "or" at the end of para. (14); by striking the period at the end of para. (15) and adding "; or"; and by adding new para. (16). Eff. Oct. 22, 2004.
- IRC §4975(f) was amended by Act §240(a) by adding new para. (7). Eff. for distributions with respect to S corporation stock made after Dec. 31, 1997.

Medicare Prescription Drug, Improvement, and Modernization Act of 2003 (Pub. L. No. 108-173), as follows:

- IRC §4975(c) was amended by Act §1201(f)(1) by adding new para. (6). Eff. tax years beginning after Dec. 31, 2003.
- IRC §4975(e)(1) were amended by Act §1201(f)(2) by redesignating subparas. (E) and (F) as (F) and (G), respectively, and adding new subpara. (E). Eff. tax years beginning after Dec. 31, 2003.

Pub. L. No. 107-22, as follows:

- IRC §4975(c) was amended by Act §1(b)(1)(D) by replacing "an education individual retirement" with "a Coverdell education savings." Eff. Jul. 26, 2001.
- IRC §4975(c)(5) was amended by Act §1(b)(3)(D) by replacing "Education individual retirement" with "Coverdell education savings." Eff. Jul. 26, 2001.
- IRC §4975(e) was amended by Act §1(b)(1)(D) by replacing "an education individual retirement" with "a Coverdell education savings." Eff. Jul. 26, 2001.

Economic Growth and Tax Relief Reconciliation Act of 2001 (Pub. L. No. 107-16), as follows:

- IRC §4975(e)(7) was amended by Act §656(b) by adding ", §409(p)," after "409(n)" in last sentence. Eff. plan years beginning after Dec. 31, 2004. [*Ed. Note*: for an exception for certain ESOPs, see Act §656(d)(2).]

• IRC §4975(f)(6)(B) was amended by Act §612(a) by adding new cl. (iii). Eff. years beginning after Dec. 31, 2001.
• **Sunset Provision.** Act §901, as amended by Pub. L. No. 111-312, §101(a)(1), provides the sunset rule below. But see Pub. L. No. 109-280, §811, and Pub. L. No. 111-148, §10909(c), as amended by Pub. L. No. 111-312, §101(b)(1).

SEC. 901. SUNSET OF PROVISIONS OF ACT.

(a) **In general.** All provisions of, and amendments made by, this Act shall not apply—

(1) to taxable, plan, or limitation years beginning after December 31, 2012, or

(2) in the case of title V, to estates of decedents dying, gifts made, or generation skipping transfers, after December 31, 2012.

(b) **Application of certain laws.**—The Internal Revenue Code of 1986 and the Employee Retirement Income Security Act of 1974 shall be applied and administered to years, estates, gifts, and transfers described in subsection (a) as if the provisions and amendments described in subsection (a) had never been enacted.

SEC. 4976. TAXES WITH RESPECT TO FUNDED WELFARE BENEFIT PLANS.

(a) **General Rule.**—If—

(1) an employer maintains a welfare benefit fund, and

(2) there is a disqualified benefit provided during any taxable year,

there is hereby imposed on such employer a tax equal to 100 percent of such disqualified benefit.

(b) **Disqualified Benefit.**—For purposes of subsection (a)—

(1) **In general.**—The term "disqualified benefit" means—

(A) any post-retirement medical benefit or life insurance benefit provided with respect to a key employee if a separate account is required to be established for such employee under section 419A(d) and such payment is not from such account,

(B) any post-retirement medical benefit or life insurance benefit provided with respect to an individual in whose favor discrimination is prohibited unless the plan meets the requirements of section 505(b) with respect to such benefit (whether or not such requirements apply to such plan), and

(C) any portion of a welfare benefit fund reverting to the benefit of the employer.

(2) **Exception for collective bargaining plans.**—Paragraph (1)(B) shall not apply to any plan maintained pursuant to an agreement between employee representatives and 1 or more employers if the Secretary finds that such agreement is a collective bargaining agreement and that the benefits referred to in paragraph (1)(B) were the subject of good faith bargaining between such employee representatives and such employer or employers.

(3) **Exception for nondeductible contributions.**—Paragraph (1)(C) shall not apply to any

amount attributable to a contribution to the fund which is not allowable as a deduction under section 419 for the taxable year or any prior taxable year (and such contribution shall not be included in any carryover under section 419(d)).

(4) **Exception for certain amounts charged against existing reserve.**—Subparagraphs (A) and (B) of paragraph (1) shall not apply to post-retirement benefits charged against an existing reserve for post-retirement medical or life insurance benefits (as defined in section 512(a)(3)(E)) or charged against the income on such reserve.

(c) **Definitions.**—For purposes of this section, the terms used in this section shall have the same respective meanings as when used in subpart D of part I of subchapter D of chapter 1.

SEC. 4977. TAX ON CERTAIN FRINGE BENEFITS PROVIDED BY AN EMPLOYER.

(a) **Imposition of Tax.**—In the case of an employer to whom an election under this section applies for any calendar year, there is hereby imposed a tax for such calendar year equal to 30 percent of the excess fringe benefits.

(b) **Excess Fringe Benefits.**—For purposes of subsection (a), the term "excess fringe benefits" means, with respect to any calendar year—

(1) the aggregate value of the fringe benefits provided by the employer during the calendar year which were not includible in gross income under paragraphs (1) and (2) of section 132(a), over

(2) 1 percent of the aggregate amount of compensation—

(A) which was paid by the employer during such calendar year to employees, and

(B) was includible in gross income for purposes of chapter 1.

(c) **Effect of Election on Section 132(a).**—If—

(1) an election under this section is in effect with respect to an employer for any calendar year, and

(2) at all times on or after January 1, 1984, and before the close of the calendar year involved, substantially all of the employees of the employer were entitled to employee discounts on goods or services provided by the employer in 1 line of business,

for purposes of paragraphs (1) and (2) of section 132(a) (but not for purposes of section 132(h)) all employees of any line of business of the employer which was in existence on January 1, 1984, shall be treated as employees of the line of business referred to in paragraph (2).

(d) **Period of Election.**—An election under this section shall apply to the calendar year for which made and all subsequent calendar years unless revoked by the employer.

(e) **Treatment of Controlled Groups.**—All employees treated as employed by a single employer under subsection (b), (c), or (m) of section 414 shall be treated as employed by a single employer for purposes of this section.

(f) **Section to Apply Only to Employment Within the United States.**—Except as otherwise provided in regulations, this section shall apply only with respect to employment within the United States.

SEC. 4978. TAX ON CERTAIN DISPOSITIONS BY EMPLOYEE STOCK OWNERSHIP PLANS AND CERTAIN COOPERATIVES.

(a) **Tax on Dispositions of Securities to Which Section 1042 Applies Before Close of Minimum Holding Period.**—If, during the 3-year period after the date on which the employee stock ownership plan or eligible worker-owned cooperative acquired any qualified securities in a sale to which section 1042 applied or acquired any qualified employer securities in a qualified gratuitous transfer to which section 664(g) applied, such plan or cooperative disposes of any qualified securities and—

(1) the total number of shares held by such plan or cooperative after such disposition is less than the total number of employer securities held immediately after such sale, or

(2) except to the extent provided in regulations, the value of qualified securities held by such plan or cooperative after such disposition is less than 30 percent of the total value of all employer securities as of such disposition (60 percent of the total value of all employer securities as of such disposition in the case of any qualified employer securities acquired in a qualified gratuitous transfer to which section 664(g) applied),

there is hereby imposed a tax on the disposition equal to the amount determined under subsection(b).

(b) **Amount of Tax.**—

(1) **In general.**—The amount of tax imposed by subsection (a) shall be equal to 10 percent of the amount realized on the disposition.

(2) **Limitation.**—The amount realized taken into account under paragraph (1) shall not exceed that portion allocable to qualified securities acquired in the sale to which section 1042 applied or acquired in a qualified gratuitous transfer to which section 664(g) applied determined as if such securities were disposed of—

(A) first from qualified securities to which section 1042 applied or to which section 664(g) applied acquired during the 3-year period ending on the date of the disposition, beginning with the securities first so acquired, and

(B) then from any other employer securities.

If subsection (d) applies to a disposition, the disposition shall be treated as made from employer securities in the opposite order of the preceding sentence.

(3) **Distributions to employees.**—The amount realized on any distribution to an employee for less than fair market value shall be determined as if the qualified security had been sold to the employee at fair market value.

(c) **Liability for Payment of Taxes.**—The tax imposed by this subsection shall be paid by—

(1) the employer, or

(2) the eligible worker-owned cooperative,

that made the written statement described in section 664(g)(1)(E) or in section 1042(b)(3) (as the case may be).

(d) **Section Not to Apply to Certain Dispositions.**—

(1) **Certain distributions to employees.**—This section shall not apply with respect to any distribution of qualified securities (or sale of such securities) which is made by reason of—

(A) the death of the employee,

(B) the retirement of the employee after the employee has attained 59½ years of age,

(C) the disability of the employee (within the meaning of section 72(m)(7)), or

(D) the separation of the employee from service for any period which results in a 1-year break in service (within the meaning of section 411(a)(6)(A)).

(2) **Certain reorganizations.**—In the case of any exchange of qualified securities in any reorganization described in section 368(a)(1) for stock of another corporation, such exchange shall not be treated as a disposition for purposes of this section.

(3) **Liquidation of corporation into cooperative.**—In the case of any exchange of qualified securities pursuant to the liquidation of the corporation issuing qualified securities into the eligible worker-owned cooperative in a transaction which meets the requirements of section 332 (determined by substituting "100 percent" for "80 percent" each place it appears in section 332(b)(1)), such exchange shall not be treated as a disposition for purposes of this section.

(4) **Dispositions to meet diversification requirements.**—This section shall not apply to any disposition of qualified securities which is required under section 401(a)(28).

(e) **Definitions and Special Rules.**—For purposes of this section—

(1) **Employee stock ownership plan.**—The term "employee stock ownership plan" has the meaning given such term by section 4975(e)(7).

IRC Sec. 4977(e)

(2) Qualified securities.—The term "qualified securities" has the meaning given such term by section 1042(c)(1); except that such section shall be applied without regard to subparagraph (B) thereof for purposes of applying this section and section 4979A with respect to securities acquired in a qualified gratuitous transfer (as defined in section 664(g)(1)).

(3) Eligible worker-owned cooperative.—The term "eligible worker-owned cooperative" has the meaning given such term by section 1042(c)(2).

(4) Disposition.—The term "disposition" includes any distribution.

(5) Employer securities.—The term "employer securities" has the meaning given to such term by section 409(*l*).

Recent Amendments to IRC §4978

Working Families Tax Relief Act of 2004 (Pub. L. No. 108-311), as follows:
• IRC §4978(a)(2) was amended by Act §408(a)(23) by replacing "60 percent" with "(60 percent)". Eff. Oct. 4, 2004.

SEC. 4979. TAX ON CERTAIN EXCESS CONTRIBUTIONS.

(a) General Rule.—In the case of any plan, there is hereby imposed a tax for the taxable year equal to 10 percent of the sum of—

(1) any excess contributions under such plan for the plan year ending in such taxable year, and

(2) any excess aggregate contributions under the plan for the plan year ending in such taxable year.

(b) Liability for Tax.—The tax imposed by subsection (a) shall be paid by the employer.

(c) Excess Contributions.—For purposes of this section, the term "excess contributions" has the meaning given such term by sections 401(k)(8)(B), 408(k)(6)(C), and 501(c)(18).

(d) Excess Aggregate Contribution.—For purposes of this section, the term "excess aggregate contribution" has the meaning given to such term by section 401(m)(6)(B). For purposes of determining excess aggregate contributions under an annuity contract described in section 403(b), such contract shall be treated as a plan described in subsection (e)(1).

(e) Plan.—For purposes of this section, the term "plan" means—

(1) a plan described in section 401(a) which includes a trust exempt from tax under section 501(a),

(2) any annuity plan described in section 403(a),

(3) any annuity contract described in section 403(b),

(4) a simplified employee pension of an employer which satisfies the requirements of section 408(k), and

(5) a plan described in section 501(c)(18).

Such term includes any plan which, at any time, has been determined by the Secretary to be such a plan.

(f) No Tax Where Excess Distributed Within Specified Period After Close of Year.—

(1) In general.—No tax shall be imposed under this section on any excess contribution or excess aggregate contribution, as the case may be, to the extent such contribution (together with any income allocable thereto through the end of the plan year for which the contribution was made) is distributed (or, if forfeitable, is forfeited) before the close of the first 2½ months (6 months in the case of an excess contribution or excess aggregate contribution to an eligible automatic contribution arrangement (as defined in section 414(w)(3))) of the following plan year.

(2) Year of inclusion.—Any amount distributed as provided in paragraph (1) shall be treated as earned and received by the recipient in the recipient's taxable year in which such distributions were made.

Recent Amendments to IRC §4979

Pension Protection Act of 2006 (Pub. L. No. 109-280), as follows:
• IRC §4979(f) was amended by Act §902(e)(1)(A)–(B) by adding "(6 months in the case of an excess contribution or excess aggregate contribution to an eligible automatic contribution arrangement (as defined in §414(w)(3)))" after "2 months" in para. (1); and by replacing "2 months of" in the heading with "specified period after". Eff. plan years beginning after Dec. 31, 2007.
• IRC §4979(f)(1) was amended by Act §902(e)(3)(A) by adding "through the end of the plan year for which the contribution was made" after "thereto." Eff. plan years beginning after Dec. 31, 2007.
• IRC §4979(f)(2) was amended by Act §902(e)(2). Eff. plan years beginning after Dec. 31, 2007. IRC §4979(f)(2) prior to amendment:
   (2) Year of inclusion.—
   (A) In general.—Except as provided in subparagraph (B), any amount distributed as provided in paragraph (1) shall be treated as received and earned by the recipient in his taxable year for which such contribution was made.
   (B) De minimis distributions.—If the total excess contributions and excess aggregate contributions distributed to a recipient under a plan for any plan year are less than $100, such distributions (and any income allocable thereto) shall be treated as earned and received by the recipient in his taxable year in which such distributions were made.

SEC. 4979A. TAX ON CERTAIN PROHIBITED ALLOCATIONS OF QUALIFIED SECURITIES.

(a) Imposition of Tax.—If—

(1) there is a prohibited allocation of qualified securities by any employee stock ownership plan or eligible worker-owned cooperative, or

(2) there is an allocation described in section 664(g)(5)(A), there is hereby imposed a tax on such allocation equal to 50 percent of the amount involved,

(3) there is any allocation of employer securities which violates the provisions of section 409(p), or a nonallocation year described in subsection (e)(2)(C) with respect to an employee stock ownership plan, or

(4) any synthetic equity is owned by a disqualified person in any nonallocation year,

there is hereby imposed a tax on such allocation or ownership equal to 50 percent of the amount involved.

(b) Prohibited Allocation.—For purposes of this section, the term "prohibited allocation" means—

(1) any allocation of qualified securities acquired in a sale to which section 1042 applies which violates the provisions of section 409(n), and

(2) any benefit which accrues to any person in violation of the provisions of section 409(n).

(c) Liability for Tax.—The tax imposed by this section shall be paid by—

(1) in the case of an allocation referred to in paragraph (1) or (2) of subsection (a), by—

(A) the employer sponsoring such plan, or

(B) the eligible worker-owed cooperative,

which made the written statement described in section 664(g)(1)(E) or in section 1042(b)(3)(B) (as the case may be), and

(2) in the case of an allocation of ownership referred to in paragraph (3) or (4) of subsection (a), by the S corporation the stock in which was so allocated or owned.

(d) Special Statute of Limitations for Tax Attributable to Certain Allocations.—The statutory period for the assessment of any tax imposed by this section on an allocation described in subsection (a)(2) of qualified employer securities shall not expire before the date which is 3 years from the later of—

(1) the 1st allocation of such securities in connection with a qualified gratuitous transfer (as defined in section 664(g)(1)), or

(2) the date on which the Secretary is notified of the allocation described in subsection (a)(2).

(e) Definitions and Special Rules.—For purposes of this section.—

(1) Definitions.—Except as provided in paragraph (2), terms used in this section have the same respective meanings as when used in sections 409 and 4978.

(2) Special rules relating to tax imposed by reason of paragraph (3) or (4) of subsection (a).—

(A) Prohibited allocations.—The amount involved with respect to any tax imposed by reason

of subsection (a)(3) is the amount allocated to the account of any person in violation of section 409(p)(1).

(B) Synthetic equity.—The amount involved with respect to any tax imposed by reason of subsection (a)(4) is the value of the shares on which the synthetic equity is based.

(C) Special rule during first non-allocation year.— For purposes of subparagraph (A), the amount involved for the first nonallocation year of any employee stock ownership plan shall be determined by taking into account the total value of all the deemed-owned shares of all disqualified persons with respect to such plan.

(D) Statute of limitations.—The statutory period for the assessment of any tax imposed by this section by reason of paragraphs (3) or (4) of subsection (a) shall not expire before the date which is 3 years from the later of—

(i) the allocation or ownership referred to in such paragraph giving rise to such tax, or

(ii) the date on which the Secretary is notified of such allocation or ownership.

Recent Amendments to IRC §4979A

Pension Protection Act of 2006 (Pub. L. No. 109-280), as follows:

● **Sunset Provision.** Act §811, provides:
  SEC. 811. PENSIONS AND INDIVIDUAL RETIRE-MENT ARRANGEMENT PROVISIONS OF ECONOMIC GROWTH AND TAX RELIEF RECONCILIATION ACT OF 2001 MADE PERMANENT.
  Title IX of the Economic Growth and Tax Relief Reconciliation Act of 2001 [Pub. L. No. 107-16] shall not apply to the provisions of, and amendments made by, subtitles A through F [§§601–666] of title VI of such Act (relating to pension and individual retirement arrangement provisions).

Economic Growth and Tax Relief Reconciliation Act of 2001 (Pub. L. No. 107-16), as follows:
● IRC §4979A(a) was amended by Act §656(c)(1)(A)–(B) by striking "or" at the end of para. (1); striking all that follows para. (2); and adding new paras. (2)–(4). Eff. plan years beginning after Dec. 31, 2004. For an exception for certain ESOPs, see Act §656(d)(2). IRC §4979A(a)(2) prior to amendment:
  (2) there is hereby imposed a tax on such allocation equal to 50 percent of the amount involved.
● IRC §4979A(c) was amended by Act §656(c)(2). Eff. plan years beginning after Dec. 31, 2004. For an exception for certain ESOPs, see Act §656(d)(2). IRC §4979A(c) prior to amendment:
  (c) Liability for tax.— The tax imposed by this section shall be paid by—
  (1) the employer sponsoring such plan, or
  (2) the eligible worker-owned cooperative, which made the written statement described in section 664(g)(1)(E) or in section 1042(b)(3)(B) (as the case may be).
● IRC §4979A(e) was amended by Act §656(c)(3). Eff. plan years beginning after Dec. 31, 2004. [*Ed. Note*: for an exception for certain ESOPs, see Act §656(d)(2).] IRC §4979A(e) prior to amendment:
  (e) Definitions.— Terms used in this section have the same respective meaning as when used in section 4978.
● **Sunset Provision.** Act §901, as amended by Pub. L. No. 111-312, §101(a)(1), provides the sunset rule below. But see Pub. L. No. 109-280, §811, and Pub. L. No. 111-148, §10909(c), as amended by Pub. L. No. 111-312, §101(b)(1).

SEC. 901. SUNSET OF PROVISIONS OF ACT.

(a) In general. All provisions of, and amendments made by, this Act shall not apply—

(1) to taxable, plan, or limitation years beginning after December 31, 2012, or

(2) in the case of title V, to estates of decedents dying, gifts made, or generation skipping transfers, after December 31, 2012.

(b) Application of certain laws.—The Internal Revenue Code of 1986 and the Employee Retirement Income Security Act of 1974 shall be applied and administered to years, estates, gifts, and transfers described in subsection (a) as if the provisions and amendments described in subsection (a) had never been enacted.

SEC. 4980. TAX ON REVERSION OF QUALIFIED PLAN ASSETS TO EMPLOYER.

(a) Imposition of Tax.—There is hereby imposed a tax of 20 percent of the amount of any employer reversion from a qualified plan.

(b) Liability for Tax.—The tax imposed by subsection (a) shall be paid by the employer maintaining the plan.

(c) Definitions and Special Rules.—For purposes of this section—

(1) Qualified plan.—The term "qualified plan" means any plan meeting the requirements of section 401(a) or 403(a), other than—

(A) a plan maintained by an employer if such employer has, at all times, been exempt from tax under subtitle A, or

(B) a governmental plan (within the meaning of section 414(d)).

Such term shall include any plan which, at any time, has been determined by the Secretary to be a qualified plan.

(2) Employer reversion.—

(A) In general.—The term "employer reversion" means the amount of cash and the fair market value of other property received (directly or indirectly) by an employer from the qualified plan.

(B) Exceptions.—The term "employer reversion" shall not include—

(i) except as provided in regulations, any amount distributed to or on behalf of any employee (or his beneficiaries) if such amount could have been so distributed before termination of such plan without violating any provision of section 401,

(ii) any distribution to the employer which is allowable under section 401(a)(2)—

(I) in the case of a multiemployer plan, by reason of mistakes of law or fact or the return of any withdrawal liability payment,

(II) in the case of a plan other than a multiemployer plan, by reason of mistake of fact, or

(III) in the case of any plan, by reason of the failure of the plan to initially qualify or the failure of contributions to be deductible, or

(iii) any transfer described in section 420(f)(2)(B)(ii)(II).

(3) Exception for employee stock ownership plans.—

(A) In general.—If, upon an employer reversion from a qualified plan, any applicable amount is transferred from such plan to an employee stock ownership plan described in section 4975(e)(7) or a tax credit employee stock ownership plan (as described in section 409), such amount shall not be treated as an employer reversion for purposes of this section (or includible in the gross income of the employer) if the requirements of subparagraphs (B), (C), and (D) are met.

(B) Investment in employer securities.—The requirements of this subparagraph are met if, within 90 days after the transfer (or such longer period as the Secretary may prescribe), the amount transferred is invested in employer securities (as defined in section 409(*l*)) or used to repay loans used to purchase such securities.

(C) Allocation requirements.—The requirements of this subparagraph are met if the portion of the amount transferred which is not allocated under the plan to accounts of participants in the plan year in which the transfer occurs—

(i) is credited to a suspense account and allocated from such account to accounts of participants no less rapidly than ratably over a period not to exceed 7 years, and

(ii) when allocated to accounts of participants under the plan, is treated as an employer contribution for purposes of section 415(c), except that—

(I) the annual addition (as determined under section 415(c)) attributable to each such allocation shall not exceed the value of such securities as of the time such securities were credited to such suspense account, and

(II) no additional employer contributions shall be permitted to an employee stock ownership plan described in subparagraph (A) of the employer before the allocation of such amount.

The amount allocated in the year of transfer shall not be less than the lesser of the maximum amount allowable under section 415 or 1/8 of the amount attributable to the securities acquired. In the case of dividends on securities held in the suspense account, the requirements of this subparagraph are met only if the dividends are allocated to accounts of participants or paid to participants in proportion to their accounts, or used to repay loans used to purchase employer securities.

(D) Participants.—The requirements of this subparagraph are met if at least half of the participants

IRC Sec. 4980(c)(3)(D)

in the qualified plan are participants in the employee stock ownership plan (as of the close of the 1st plan year for which an allocation of the securities is required).

(E) Applicable amount.—For purposes of this paragraph, the term "applicable amount" means any amount which—

(i) is transferred after March 31, 1985, and before January 1, 1989, or

(ii) is transferred after December 31, 1988, pursuant to a termination which occurs after March 31, 1985, and before January 1, 1989.

(F) No credit or deduction allowed.—No credit or deduction shall be allowed under chapter 1 for any amount transferred to an employee stock ownership plan in a transfer to which this paragraph applies.

(G) Amount transferred to include income thereon, etc.—The amount transferred shall not be treated as meeting the requirements of subparagraphs (B) and (C) unless amounts attributable to such amount also meet such requirements.

(4) Time for payment of tax.—For purposes of subtitle F, the time for payment of the tax imposed by subsection (a) shall be the last day of the month following the month in which the employer reversion occurs.

(d) Increase in Tax for Failure to Establish Replacement Plan or Increase Benefits.—

(1) In general.—Subsection (a) shall be applied by substituting "50 percent" for "20 percent" with respect to any employer reversion from a qualified plan unless—

(A) the employer establishes or maintains a qualified replacement plan, or

(B) the plan provides benefit increases meeting the requirements of paragraph (3).

(2) Qualified replacement plan.—For purposes of this subsection, the term "qualified replacement plan" means a qualified plan established or maintained by the employer in connection with a qualified plan termination (hereinafter referred to as the "replacement plan") with respect to which the following requirements are met:

(A) Participation requirement.—At least 95 percent of the active participants in the terminated plan who remain as employees of the employer after the termination are active participants in the replacement plan.

(B) Asset transfer requirement.—

(i) 25 percent cushion.—A direct transfer from the terminated plan to the replacement plan is made before any employer reversion, and the transfer is in an amount equal to the excess (if any) of—

(I) 25 percent of the maximum amount which the employer could receive as an employer reversion without regard to this subsection, over

(II) the amount determined under clause (ii).

(ii) Reduction for increase in benefits.—The amount determined under this clause is an amount equal to the present value of the aggregate increases in the accrued benefits under the terminated plan of any participants or beneficiaries pursuant to a plan amendment which—

(I) is adopted during the 60-day period ending on the date of termination of the qualified plan, and

(II) takes effect immediately on the termination date.

(iii) Treatment of amount transferred.—In the case of the transfer of any amount under clause (i)—

(I) such amount shall not be includible in the gross income of the employer,

(II) no deduction shall be allowable with respect to such transfer, and

(III) such transfer shall not be treated as an employer reversion for purposes of this section.

(C) Allocation requirements.—

(i) In general.—In the case of any defined contribution plan, the portion of the amount transferred to the replacement plan under subparagraph (B)(i) is—

(I) allocated under the plan to the accounts of participants in the plan year in which the transfer occurs, or

(II) credited to a suspense account and allocated from such account to accounts of participants no less rapidly than ratably over the 7-plan-year period beginning with the year of the transfer.

(ii) Coordination with section 415 limitation.—If, by reason of any limitation under section 415, any amount credited to a suspense account under clause (i)(II) may not be allocated to a participant before the close of the 7-year period under such clause—

(I) such amount shall be allocated to the accounts of other participants, and

(II) if any portion of such amount may not be allocated to other participants by reason of any such limitation, shall be allocated to the participant as provided in section 415.

(iii) Treatment of income.—Any income on any amount credited to a suspense account under clause (i)(II) shall be allocated to accounts of participants no less rapidly than ratably over the remainder of the period determined under such clause (after application of clause (ii)).

(iv) Unallocated amounts at termination.—If any amount credited to a suspense account under clause (i)(II) is not allocated as of the termination date of the replacement plan—

(I) such amount shall be allocated to the accounts of participants as of such date, except that any amount which may not be allocated by reason of any limitation under section 415 shall be allocated to the accounts of other participants, and

(II) if any portion of such amount may not be allocated to other participants under subclause (I) by reason of such limitation, such portion shall be treated as an employer reversion to which this section applies.

(3) Pro rata benefit increases.—

(A) In general.—The requirements of this paragraph are met if a plan amendment to the terminated plan is adopted in connection with the termination of the plan which provides pro rata increases in the accrued benefits of all qualified participants which—

(i) have an aggregate present value not less than 20 percent of the maximum amount which the employer could receive as an employer reversion without regard to this subsection, and

(II) take effect immediately on the termination date.

(B) Pro rata increase.—For purposes of subparagraph (A), a pro rata increase is an increase in the present value of the accrued benefit of each qualified participant in an amount which bears the same ratio to the aggregate amount determined under subparagraph (A)(i) as—

(i) the present value of such participant's accrued benefit (determined without regard to this subsection), bears to

(ii) the aggregate present value of accrued benefits of the terminated plan (as so determined).

Notwithstanding the preceding sentence, the aggregate increases in the present value of the accrued benefits of qualified participants who are not active participants shall not exceed 40 percent of the aggregate amount determined under subparagraph (A)(i) by substituting "equal to" for "not less than".

(4) Coordination with other provisions.—

(A) Limitations.—A benefit may not be increased under paragraph (2)(B)(ii) or (3)(A), and an amount may not be allocated to a participant under paragraph (2)(C), if such increase or allocation would result in a failure to meet any requirement under section 401(a)(4) or 415.

(B) Treatment as employer contributions.—Any increase in benefits under paragraph (2)(B)(ii) or (3)(A), or any allocation of any amount (or income

allocable thereto) to any account under paragraph (2)(C), shall be treated as an annual benefit or annual addition for purposes of section 415.

(C) 10-year participation requirement.—Except as provided by the Secretary, section 415(b)(5)(D) shall not apply to any increase in benefits by reason of this subsection to the extent that the application of this subparagraph does not discriminate in favor of highly compensated employees (as defined in section 414(q)).

(5) Definitions and special rules.—For purposes of this subsection—

(A) Qualified participant.—The term "qualified participant" means an individual who—

(i) is an active participant,

(ii) is a participant or beneficiary in pay status as of the termination date,

(iii) is a participant not described in clause (i) or (ii)—

(I) who has a nonforfeitable right to an accrued benefit under the terminated plan as of the termination date, and

(II) whose service, which was creditable under the terminated plan, terminated during the period beginning 3 years before the termination date and ending with the date on which the final distribution of assets occurs, or

(iv) is a beneficiary of a participant described in clause (iii)(II) and has a nonforfeitable right to an accrued benefit under the terminated plan as of the termination date.

(B) Present value.—Present value shall be determined as of the termination date and on the same basis as liabilities of the plan are determined on termination.

(C) Reallocation of increase.—Except as provided in paragraph (2)(C), if any benefit increase is reduced by reason of the last sentence of paragraph (3)(A)(ii) or paragraph (4), the amount of such reduction shall be allocated to the remaining participants on the same basis as other increases (and shall be treated as meeting any allocation requirements of this subsection).

(D) Plans taken into account.—For purposes of determining whether there is a qualified replacement plan under paragraph (2), the Secretary may provide that—

(i) 2 or more plans may be treated as 1 plan, or

(ii) a plan of a successor employer may be taken into account.

(E) Special rule for participation requirement.— For purposes of paragraph (2)(A), all employers treated as 1 employer under section 414(b), (c), (m), or (o) shall be treated as 1 employer.

IRC Sec. 4980(d)(5)(E)

(6) Subsection not to apply to employer in bankruptcy.—This subsection shall not apply to an employer who, as of the termination date of the qualified plan, is in bankruptcy liquidation under chapter 7 of title 11 of the United States Code or in similar proceedings under State law.

Recent Amendments to IRC §4980

Worker, Retiree, and Employer Recovery Act of 2008 (Pub. L. No. 110-458), as follows:
- IRC §4980(c)(2)(B)(i)–(iii) was amended by Act §108(i)(3) by striking "or" at the end of clause (i), by substituting ", or" for the period at the end of clause (ii), and by adding clause (iii). Eff. as if included in Pub. L. No. 109-280, §841 [eff. for transfers after Aug. 17, 2008].

Pension Protection Act of 2006 (Pub. L. No. 109-280), as follows:
- IRC §4980(c)(3)(A) was amended by Act §901(a)(2)(C) by replacing "if—" and all the follows with "if the requirements of subparagraphs (B), (C), and (D) are met.". Eff. generally for plan years beginning after Dec. 31, 2006, with a special rule for collectively bargained plans. [*Ed. Note*: see Act §901(c).] IRC §4980(c)(3)(A) prior to amendment:
  (i) the requirements of subparagraphs (B), (C), and (D) are met, and
  (ii) under the plan, employer securities to which subparagraph (B) applies must, except to the extent necessary to meet the requirements of section 401(a)(28), remain in the plan until distribution to participants in accordance with the provisions of such plan.

SEC. 4980A. TAX ON EXCESS DISTRIBUTIONS FROM QUALIFIED RETIREMENT PLANS. [Repealed.]

SEC. 4980B. FAILURE TO SATISFY CONTINUATION COVERAGE REQUIREMENTS OF GROUP HEALTH PLANS.

(a) General Rule.—There is hereby imposed a tax on the failure of a group health plan to meet the requirements of subsection (f) with respect to any qualified beneficiary.

(b) Amount of Tax.—

(1) **In general.**—The amount of the tax imposed by subsection (a) on any failure with respect to a qualified beneficiary shall be $100 for each day in the noncompliance period with respect to such failure.

(2) **Noncompliance period.**—For purposes of this section, the term "noncompliance period" means, with respect to any failure, the period—

(A) beginning on the date such failure first occurs, and

(B) ending on the earlier of—

(i) the date such failure is corrected, or

(ii) the date which is 6 months after the last day in the period applicable to the qualified beneficiary under subsection (f)(2)(B) (determined without regard to clause (iii) thereof).

If a person is liable for tax under subsection (e)(1)(B) by reason of subsection (e)(2)(B) with respect to any failure, the noncompliance period for such person with respect to such failure shall not begin before the 45th day after the written request described in subsection (e)(2)(B) is provided to such person.

(3) **Minimum tax for noncompliance period where failure discovered after notice of examination.**—Notwithstanding paragraphs (1) and (2) of subsection (c)—

(A) In general.—In the case of 1 or more failures with respect to a qualified beneficiary—

(i) which are not corrected before the date a notice of examination of income tax liability is sent to the employer, and

(ii) which occurred or continued during the period under examination,

the amount of tax imposed by subsection (a) by reason of such failures with respect to such beneficiary shall not be less than the lesser of $2,500 or the amount of tax which would be imposed by subsection (a) without regard to such paragraphs.

(B) Higher minimum tax where violations are more than de minimis.—To the extent violations by the employer (or the plan in the case of a multiemployer plan) for any year are more than de minimis, subparagraph (A) shall be applied by substituting "$15,000" for "$2,500" with respect to the employer (or such plan).

(c) **Limitations on Amount of Tax.**—

(1) **Tax not to apply where failure not discovered exercising reasonable diligence.**—No tax shall be imposed by subsection (a) on any failure during any period for which it is established to the satisfaction of the Secretary that none of the persons referred to in subsection (e) knew, or exercising reasonable diligence would have known, that such failure existed.

(2) **Tax not to apply to failures corrected within 30 days.**—No tax shall be imposed by subsection (a) on any failure if—

(A) such failure was due to reasonable cause and not to willful neglect, and

(B) such failure is corrected during the 30-day period beginning on the 1st date any of the persons referred to in subsection (e) knew, or exercising reasonable diligence would have known, that such failure existed.

(3) **$100 limit on amount of tax for failures on any day with respect to a qualified beneficiary.**—

(A) In general.—Except as provided in subparagraph (B), the maximum amount of tax imposed by subsection (a) on failures on any day during the noncompliance period with respect to a qualified beneficiary shall be $100.

(B) Special rule where more than 1 qualified beneficiary.—If there is more than 1 qualified beneficiary with respect to the same qualifying event, the maximum amount of tax imposed by subsection (a) on all failures on any day during the noncompliance period with respect to such qualified beneficiaries shall be $200.

(4) Overall limitation for unintentional failures.—In the case of failures which are due to reasonable cause and not to willful neglect—

(A) Single employer plans.—

(i) In general.—In the case of failures with respect to plans other than multiemployer plans, the tax imposed by subsection (a) for failures during the taxable year of the employer shall not exceed the amount equal to the lesser of—

(I) 10 percent of the aggregate amount paid or incurred by the employer (or predecessor employer) during the preceding taxable year for group health plans, or

(II) $500,000.

(ii) Taxable years in the case of certain controlled groups.—For purposes of this subparagraph, if not all persons who are treated as a single employer for purposes of this section have the same taxable year, the taxable years taken into account shall be determined under principles similar to the principles of section 1561.

(B) Multiemployer plans.—

(i) In general.—In the case of failures with respect to a multiemployer plan, the tax imposed by subsection (a) for failures during the taxable year of the trust forming part of such plan shall not exceed the amount equal to the lesser of—

(I) 10 percent of the amount paid or incurred by such trust during such taxable year to provide medical care (as defined in section 213(d)) directly or through insurance, reimbursement, or otherwise, or

(II) $500,000.

For purposes of the preceding sentence, all plans of which the same trust forms a part shall be treated as 1 plan.

(ii) Special rule for employers required to pay tax.—If an employer is assessed a tax imposed by subsection (a) by reason of a failure with respect to a multiemployer plan, the limit shall be determined under subparagraph (A) (and not under this subparagraph) and as if such plan were not a multiemployer plan.

(C) Special rule for persons providing benefits.—In the case of a person described in subsection (e)(1)(B) (and not subsection (e)(1)(A)), the aggregate amount of tax imposed by subsection (a) for failures during a taxable year with respect to all plans shall not exceed $2,000,000.

(5) Waiver by Secretary.—In the case of a failure which is due to reasonable cause and not to willful neglect, the Secretary may waive part or all of the tax imposed by subsection (a) to the extent that the payment of such tax would be excessive relative to the failure involved.

(d) Tax Not to Apply to Certain Plans.—This section shall not apply to—

(1) any failure of a group health plan to meet the requirements of subsection (f) with respect to any qualified beneficiary if the qualifying event with respect to such beneficiary occurred during the calendar year immediately following a calendar year during which all employers maintaining such plan normally employed fewer than 20 employees on a typical business day.

(2) any governmental plan (within the meaning of section 414(d)), or

(3) any church plan (within the meaning of section 414(e)).

(e) Liability for Tax.—

(1) In general.—Except as otherwise provided in this subsection, the following shall be liable for the tax imposed by subsection (a) on a failure:

(A) (i) In the case of a plan other than a multiemployer plan, the employer.

(ii) In the case of a multiemployer plan, the plan.

(B) Each person who is responsible (other than in a capacity as an employee) for administering or providing benefits under the plan and whose act or failure to act caused (in whole or in part) the failure.

(2) Special rules for persons described in paragraph (1)(b).—

(A) No liability unless written agreement.—Except in the case of liability resulting from the application of subparagraph (B) of this paragraph, a person described in subparagraph (B) (and not in subparagraph (A)) of paragraph (1) shall be liable for the tax imposed by subsection (a) on any failure only if such person assumed (under a legally enforceable written agreement) responsibility for the performance of the act to which the failure relates.

(B) Failure to cover qualified beneficiaries where current employees are covered.—A person shall be treated as described in paragraph (1)(B) with respect to a qualified beneficiary if—

(i) such person provides coverage under a group health plan for any similarly situated beneficiary under the plan with respect to whom a qualifying event has not occurred, and

IRC Sec. 4980B(e)(2)(B)(i)

(ii) the—

(I) employer or plan administrator, or

(II) in the case of a qualifying event described in subparagraph (C) or (E) of subsection (f)(3) where the person described in clause (i) is the plan administrator, the qualified beneficiary,

submits to such person a written request that such person make available to such qualified beneficiary the same coverage which such person provides to the beneficiary referred to in clause (i).

(f) Continuation Coverage Requirements of Group Health Plans.—

(1) In general.—A group health plan meets the requirements of this subsection only if the coverage of the costs of pediatric vaccines (as defined under section 2162 of the Public Health Service Act) is not reduced below the coverage provided by the plan as of May 1, 1993, and only if each qualified beneficiary who would lose coverage under the plan as a result of a qualifying event is entitled to elect, within the election period, continuation coverage under the plan.

(2) Continuation coverage.—For purposes of paragraph (1), the term "continuation coverage" means coverage under the plan which meets the following requirements:

(A) Type of benefit coverage.—The coverage must consist of coverage which, as of the time the coverage is being provided, is identical to the coverage provided under the plan to similarly situated beneficiaries under the plan with respect to whom a qualifying event has not occurred. If coverage under the plan is modified for any group of similarly situated beneficiaries, the coverage shall also be modified in the same manner for all individuals who are qualified beneficiaries under the plan pursuant to this subsection in connection with such group.

(B) Period of coverage.—The coverage must extend for at least the period beginning on the date of the qualifying event and ending not earlier than the earliest of the following:

(i) Maximum required period.—

(I) General rule for terminations and reduced hours.—In the case of a qualifying event described in paragraph (3)(B), except as provided in subclause (II), the date which is 18 months after the date of the qualifying event.

(II) Special rule for multiple qualifying events.—If a qualifying event (other than a qualifying event described in paragraph (3)(F)) occurs during the 18 months after the date of a qualifying event described in paragraph (3)(B), the date which is 36 months after the date of the qualifying event described in paragraph (3)(B).

(III) Special rule for certain bankruptcy proceedings.—In the case of a qualifying event de-

scribed in paragraph (3)(F) (relating to bankruptcy proceedings), the date of the death of the covered employee or qualified beneficiary (described in subsection (g)(1)(D)(iii)), or in the case of the surviving spouse or dependent children of the covered employee, 36 months after the date of the death of the covered employee.

(IV) General rule for other qualifying events.—In the case of a qualifying event not described in paragraph (3)(B) or (3)(F), the date which is 36 months after the date of the qualifying event.

Editor's Note

IRC §4980B(f)(2)(B)(i)(V)–(VI), as follows, were amended by Pub. L. No. 111-344, applicable to periods of coverage that would (without regard to the amendments made by this section) end on or after December 31, 2010.

(V) Special rule for PBGC recipients.—In the case of a qualifying event described in paragraph (3)(B) with respect to a covered employee who (as of such qualifying event) has a nonforfeitable right to a benefit any portion of which is to be paid by the Pension Benefit Guaranty Corporation under title IV of the Employee Retirement Income Security Act of 1974, notwithstanding subclause (I) or (II), the date of the death of the covered employee, or in the case of the surviving spouse or dependent children of the covered employee, 24 months after the date of the death of the covered employee. The preceding sentence shall not require any period of coverage to extend beyond ~~December 31, 2010~~ *February 12, 2011*.

(VI) Special rule for TAA-eligible individuals.—In the case of a qualifying event described in paragraph (3)(B) with respect to a covered employee who is (as of the date that the period of coverage would, but for this subclause or subclause (VII), otherwise terminate under subclause (I) or (II)) a TAA-eligible individual (as defined in paragraph (5)(C)(iv)(II)), the period of coverage shall not terminate by reason of subclause (I) or (II), as the case may be, before the later of the date specified in such subclause or the date on which such individual ceases to be such a TAA-eligible individual. The preceding sentence shall not require any period of coverage to extend beyond ~~December 31, 2010~~ *February 12, 2011*.

(VII) Medicare entitlement followed by qualifying event.—In the case of a qualifying event described in paragraph (3)(B) that occurs less than 18 months after the date the covered employee became entitled to benefits under title XVIII of the Social Security Act, the period of coverage for qualified beneficiaries other than the covered employee shall not terminate under this clause before the close of the 36-month period beginning on the date the covered employee became so entitled.

(VIII) Special rule for disability.—In the case of a qualified beneficiary who is determined, under title II or XVI of the Social Security Act, to have been disabled at any time during the first 60 days of continuation coverage under this section, any reference in subclause (I) or (II) to 18 months with respect to such event is deemed a reference to 29 months, (with respect to all qualified beneficiaries), but only if the qualified beneficiary has provided notice of such determination under paragraph (6)(C) before the end of such 18 months.

(ii) End of plan.—The date on which the employer ceases to provide any group health plan to any employee.

(iii) Failure to pay premium.—The date on which coverage ceases under the plan by reason of a failure to make timely payment of any premium required under the plan with respect to the qualified beneficiary. The payment of any premium (other than any payment referred to in the last sentence of subparagraph (C)) shall be considered to be timely if made within 30 days after the date due or within such longer period as applies to or under the plan.

(iv) Group health plan coverage or Medicare entitlement.—The date on which the qualified beneficiary first becomes, after the date of the election—

(I) covered under any other group health plan (as an employee or otherwise) which does not contain any exclusion or limitation with respect to any preexisting condition of such beneficiary (other than such an exclusion or limitation which does not apply to (or is satisfied by) such beneficiary by reason of Chapter 100 of this title, part 7 of subtitle B of title I of the Employee Retirement Income Security Act of 1974, or title XXVII of the Public Health Services Act), or

(II) in the case of a qualified beneficiary other than a qualified beneficiary described in subsection (g)(1)(D) entitled to benefits under title XVIII of the Social Security Act.

(v) Termination of extended coverage for disability.—In the case of a qualified beneficiary who is disabled at any time during the first 60 days of continuation coverage under this section, the month that begins more than 30 days after the date of the final determination under title II or XVI of the Social Security Act that the qualified beneficiary is no longer disabled.

(C) Premium requirements.—The plan may require payment of a premium for any period of continuation coverage, except that such premium—

(i) shall not exceed 102 percent of the applicable premium for such period, and

(ii) may, at the election of the payor, be made in monthly installments.

In no event may the plan require the payment of any premium before the day which is 45 days after the day on which the qualified beneficiary made the initial election for continuation coverage. In the case of an individual described in the last sentence of subparagraph (B)(i), any reference in clause (i) of this subparagraph to "102 percent" is deemed a reference to "150 percent" for any month after the 18th month of continuation coverage described in subclause (I) or (II) of subparagraph (B)(i).

(D) No requirement of insurability.—The coverage may not be conditioned upon, or discriminate on the basis of lack of, evidence of insurability.

(E) Conversion option.—In the case of a qualified beneficiary whose period of continuation coverage expires under subparagraph (B)(i), the plan must, during the 180-day period ending on such expiration date, provide to the qualified beneficiary the option of enrollment under a conversion health plan otherwise generally available under the plan.

(3) Qualifying event.—For purposes of this subsection, the term "qualifying event means, with respect to any covered employee, any of the following events which, but for the continuation coverage required under this subsection, would result in the loss of coverage of a qualified beneficiary—

(A) The death of the covered employee.

(B) The termination (other than by reason of such employee's gross misconduct), or reduction of hours, of the covered employee's employment.

(C) The divorce or legal separation of the covered employee from the employee's spouse.

(D) The covered employee becoming entitled to benefits under title XVIII of the Social Security Act.

(E) A dependent child ceasing to be a dependent child under the generally applicable requirements of the plan.

(F) A proceeding in a case under title 11, United States Code, commencing on or after July 1, 1986, with respect to the employer from whose employment the covered employee retired at any time.

In the case of an event described in subparagraph (F), a loss of coverage includes a substantial elimination of coverage with respect to a qualified beneficiary described in subsection (g)(1)(D) within one year before or after the date of commencement of the proceeding.

(4) Applicable premium.—For purposes of this subsection—

(A) In general.—The term "applicable premium" means, with respect to any period of continuation coverage of qualified beneficiaries, the cost to the plan for such period of the coverage for similarly situated beneficiaries with respect to whom a qualifying event has not occurred (without regard to whether such cost is paid by the employer or employee).

(B) Special rule for self-insured plans.—To the extent that a plan is a self-insured plan—

(i) In general.—Except as provided in clause (ii), the applicable premium for any period of continuation coverage of qualified beneficiaries shall be equal to a reasonable estimate of the cost of providing coverage for such period for similarly situated beneficiaries which—

(I) is determined on an actuarial basis, and

(II) takes into account such factors as the Secretary may prescribe in regulations.

(ii) Determination on basis of past cost.—If a plan administrator elects to have this clause apply, the applicable premium for any period of continuation coverage of qualified beneficiaries shall be equal to—

(I) the cost to the plan for similarly situated beneficiaries for the same period occurring during the preceding determination period under subparagraph (C), adjusted by

(II) the percentage increase or decrease in the implicit price deflator of the gross national product (calculated by the Department of Commerce and published in the Survey of Current Business) for the 12-month period ending on the last day of the sixth month of such preceding determination period.

(iii) Clause (ii) not to apply where significant change.—A plan administrator may not elect to have clause (ii) apply in any case in which there is any significant difference between the determination period and the preceding determination period, in coverage under, or in employees covered by, the plan. The determination under the preceding sentence for any determination period shall be made at the same time as the determination under subparagraph (C).

(C) Determination period.—The determination of any applicable premium shall be made for a period of 12 months and shall be made before the beginning of such period.

(5) Election.—For purposes of this subsection—

(A) Election period.—The term "election period" means the period which—

(i) begins not later than the date on which coverage terminates under the plan by reason of a qualifying event,

(ii) is of at least 60 days' duration, and

(iii) ends not earlier than 60 days after the later of—

(I) the date described in clause (i), or

(II) in the case of any qualified beneficiary who receives notice under paragraph (6)(D), the date of such notice.

(B) Effect of election on other beneficiaries.—Except as otherwise specified in an election, any election of continuation coverage by a qualified beneficiary described in subparagraph (A)(i) or (B) of subsection (g)(1) shall be deemed to include an election of continuation coverage on behalf of any other qualified beneficiary who would lose coverage under the plan by reason of the qualifying event. If there is a choice among types of coverage under the plan, each qualified beneficiary is entitled to make a separate selection among such types of coverage.

(C) Temporary extension of COBRA election period for certain individuals.—

(i) In general.—In the case of a nonelecting TAA-eligible individual and notwithstanding subparagraph (A), such individual may elect continuation coverage under this subsection during the 60-day period that begins on the first day of the month in which the individual becomes a TAA-eligible individual, but only if such election is made not later than 6 months after the date of the TAA-related loss of coverage.

(ii) Commencement of coverage; no reachback.—Any continuation coverage elected by a TAA-eligible individual under clause (i) shall commence at the beginning of the 60-day election period described in such paragraph and shall not include any period prior to such 60-day election period.

(iii) Preexisting conditions.—With respect to an individual who elects continuation coverage pursuant to clause (i), the period—

(I) beginning on the date of the TAA-related loss of coverage, and

(II) ending on the first day of the 60-day election period described in clause (i),

shall be disregarded for purposes of determining the 63-day periods referred to in section 9801(c)(2), section 701(c)(2) of the Employee Retirement Income Security Act of 1974, and section 2701(c)(2) of the Public Health Service Act.

(iv) Definitions.—For purposes of this subsection:

(I) Nonelecting TAA-eligible individual.—The term "nonelecting TAA-eligible individual" means a TAA-eligible individual who has a TAA-related loss of coverage and did not elect continuation coverage under this subsection during the TAA-related election period.

(II) TAA-eligible individual.—The term "TAA-eligible individual" means an eligible TAA recipient (as defined in paragraph (2) of section 35(c)) and an eligible alternative TAA recipient (as defined in paragraph (3) of such section).

(III) TAA-related election period.—The term "TAA-related election period" means, with respect to a TAA-related loss of coverage, the 60-day election period under this subsection which is a direct consequence of such loss.

(IV) TAA-related loss of coverage.—The term "TAA-related loss of coverage" means, with respect to an individual whose separation from employment gives rise to being an TAA-eligible individual, the loss of health benefits coverage associated with such separation.

(6) **Notice requirement**.—In accordance with regulations prescribed by the Secretary—

(A) The group health plan shall provide, at the time of commencement of coverage under the plan, written notice to each covered employee and spouse of the employee (if any) of the rights provided under this subsection.

(B) The employer of an employee under a plan must notify the plan administrator of a qualifying event described in subparagraph (A), (B), (D), or (F) of paragraph (3) with respect to such employee within 30 days (or, in the case of a group health plan which is a multiemployer plan, such longer period of time as may be provided in the terms of the plan) of the date of the qualifying event.

(C) Each covered employee or qualified beneficiary is responsible for notifying the plan administrator of the occurrence of any qualifying event described in subparagraph (C) or (E) of paragraph (3) within 60 days after the date of the qualifying event and each qualified beneficiary who is determined, under title II or XVI of the Social Security Act, to have been disabled at any time during the first 60 days of continuation coverage under this section is responsible for notifying the plan administrator of such determination within 60 days after the date of the determination and for notifying the plan administrator within 30 days of the date of any final determination under such title or titles that the qualified beneficiary is no longer disabled.

(D) The plan administrator shall notify—

(i) in the case of a qualifying event described in subparagraph (A), (B), (D), or (F) of paragraph (3), any qualified beneficiary with respect to such event, and

(ii) in the case of a qualifying event described in subparagraph (C) or (E) of paragraph (3) where the covered employee notifies the plan administrator under subparagraph (C), any qualified beneficiary with respect to such event, of such beneficiary's rights under this subsection.

The requirements of subparagraph (B) shall be considered satisfied in the case of a multiemployer plan in connection with a qualifying event described in paragraph (3)(B) if the plan provides that the determination of the occurrence of such qualifying event will be made by the plan administrator. For purposes of subparagraph (D), any notification shall be made within 14 days (or, in the case of a group health plan which is a multiemployer plan, such longer period of time as may be provided in the terms of the plan) of the date on which the plan administrator is notified under subparagraph (B) or (C), whichever is applicable, and any such notification to an individual who is a qualified beneficiary as the spouse of the covered employee shall be treated as notification to all other qualified beneficiaries residing with such spouse at the time such notification is made.

(7) **Covered employee**.—For purposes of this subsection, the term "covered employee" means an individual who is (or was) provided coverage under a group health plan by virtue of the performance of services by the individual for 1 or more persons maintaining the plan (including as an employee defined in section 401(c)(1)).

(8) **Optional extension of required periods**.—A group health plan shall not be treated as failing to meet the requirements of this subsection solely because the plan provides both—

(A) that the period of extended coverage referred to in paragraph (2)(B) commences with the date of the loss of coverage, and

(B) that the applicable notice period provided under paragraph (6)(B) commences with the date of the loss of coverage.

(g) **Definitions**.—For purposes of this section—

(1) **Qualified beneficiary**.—

(A) **In general**.—The term "qualified beneficiary" means, with respect to a covered employee under a group health plan, any other individual who, on the day before the qualifying event for that employee, is a beneficiary under the plan—

(i) as the spouse of the covered employee, or

(ii) as the dependent child of the employee.

Such term shall also include a child who is born to or placed for adoption with the covered employee during the period of continuation coverage under this section.

(B) Special rule for terminations and reduced employment.—In the case of a qualifying event described in subsection (f)(3)(B), the term "qualified beneficiary" includes the covered employee.

IRC Sec. 4980B(g)(1)(B)

(C) Exception for nonresident aliens.—Notwithstanding subparagraphs (A) and (B), the term "qualified beneficiary" does not include an individual whose status as a covered employee is attributable to a period in which such individual was a nonresident alien who received no earned income (within the meaning of section 911(d)(2)) from the employer which constituted income from sources within the United States (within the meaning of section 861(a)(3)). If an individual is not a qualified beneficiary pursuant to the previous sentence, a spouse or dependent child of such individual shall not be considered a qualified beneficiary by virtue of the relationship of the individual.

(D) Special rule for retirees and widows.—In the case of a qualifying event described in subsection (f)(3)(F), the term "qualified beneficiary" includes a covered employee who had retired on or before the date of substantial elimination of coverage and any other individual who, on the day before such qualifying event, is a beneficiary under the plan—

(i) as the spouse of the covered employee,

(ii) as the dependent child of the covered employee, or

(iii) as the surviving spouse of the covered employee.

(2) Group health plan.—The term "group health plan" has the meaning given such term by section 5000(b)(1). Such term shall not include any plan substantially all of the coverage under which is for qualified long-term care services (as defined in section 7702B(c)).

(3) Plan administrator.—The term "plan administrator" has the meaning given the term "administrator" by section 3(16)(A) of the Employee Retirement Income Security Act of 1974.

(4) Correction.—A failure of a group health plan to meet the requirements of subsection (f) with respect to any qualified beneficiary shall be treated as corrected if—

(A) such failure is retroactively undone to the extent possible, and

(B) the qualified beneficiary is placed in a financial position which is as good as such beneficiary would have been in had such failure not occurred.

For purposes of applying subparagraph (B), the qualified beneficiary shall be treated as if he had elected the most favorable coverage in light of the expenses he incurred since the failure first occurred.

Recent Amendments to IRC §4980B

Omnibus Trade Act of 2010 (Pub. L. No. 111-344), as follows:
• IRC §4980B(f)(2)(B)(i)(V)–(VI) were amended by Act §116(b)(1)–(2) by striking "December 31, 2010" and inserting "February 12, 2011". Eff. for periods of coverage which would

(without regard to the amendments made by this section) end on or after Dec. 31, 2010.

TAA Health Coverage Improvement Act of 2009 (Pub. L. No. 111-5), as follows:
• IRC §4980B(f)(2)(B)(i) was amended by Act, Div. B, §1899F(b)(1)–(2) by substituting "(VI) Special Rule For Disability.—In the case of a qualified beneficiary" for "In the case of a qualified beneficiary"; redesignating subcls. (V) and (VI) as subcls. (VII) and (VIII), respectively; and adding new subcls. (V) and (VI). Eff. for periods of coverage which would (without regard to the amendments made by this section) end on or after date of enactment [enacted: Feb. 17, 2009].

Trade Act of 2002 (Pub. L. No. 107-210), as follows:
• IRC §4980B(f)(5) was amended by Act §203(e)(3) by adding new subpara. (C). Eff. Aug. 6, 2002.

SEC. 4980C. REQUIREMENTS FOR ISSUERS OF QUALIFIED LONG-TERM CARE INSURANCE CONTRACTS.

(a) **General Rule.**—There is hereby imposed on any person failing to meet the requirements of subsection (c) or (d) a tax in the amount determined under subsection (b).

(b) **Amount.**—

(1) **In general.**—The amount of the tax imposed by subsection (a) shall be $100 per insured for each day any requirement of subsection (c) or (d) is not met with respect to each qualified long-term care insurance contract.

(2) **Waiver.**—In the case of a failure which is due to reasonable cause and not to willful neglect, the Secretary may waive part or all of the tax imposed by subsection (a) to the extent that payment of the tax would be excessive relative to the failure involved.

(c) **Responsibilities.**—The requirements of this subsection are as follows:

(1) **Requirements of model provisions.**—

(A) Model regulation.—The following requirements of the model regulation must be met:

(i) Section 13 (relating to application forms and replacement coverage).

(ii) Section 14 (relating to reporting requirements), except that the issuer shall also report at least annually the number of claims denied during the reporting period for each class of business (expressed as a percentage of claims denied), other than claims denied for failure to meet the waiting period or because of any applicable preexisting condition.

(iii) Section 20 (relating to filing requirements for marketing).

(iv) Section 21 (relating to standards for marketing), including inaccurate completion of medical histories, other than sections 21C(1) and 21C(6) thereof, except that—

(I) in addition to such requirements, no person shall, in selling or offering to sell a qualified long-term care insurance contract, misrepresent a material fact; and

(II) no such requirements shall include a requirement to inquire or identify whether a prospective applicant or enrollee for long-term care insurance has accident and sickness insurance.

(v) Section 22 (relating to appropriateness of recommended purchase).

(vi) Section 24 (relating to standard line of coverage).

(vii) Section 25 (relating to requirement to deliver shopper's guide).

(B) Model Act.—The following requirements of the model Act must be met:

(i) Section 6F (relating to right to return), except that such section shall also apply to denials of applications and any refund shall be made within 30 days of the return or denial.

(ii) Section 6G (relating to outline of coverage).

(iii) Section 6H (relating to requirements for certificates under group plans).

(iv) Section 6I (relating to policy summary).

(v) Section 6J (relating to monthly reports on accelerated death benefits).

(vi) Section 7 (relating to incontestability period).

(C) Definitions.—For purposes of this paragraph, the terms "model regulation" and "model Act" have the meanings given such terms by section 7702B(g)(2)(B).

(2) Delivery of policy.—If an application for a qualified long-term care insurance contract (or for a certificate under such a contract for a group) is approved, the issuer shall deliver to the applicant (or policyholder or certificate holder) the contract (or certificate) of insurance not later than 30 days after the date of the approval.

(3) Information on denials of claims.—If a claim under a qualified long-term care insurance contract is denied, the issuer shall, within 60 days of the date of a written request by the policyholder or certificate holder (or representative)—

(A) provide a written explanation of the reasons for the denial, and

(B) make available all information directly relating to such denial.

(d) Disclosure.—The requirements of this subsection are met if the issuer of a long-term care insurance policy discloses in such policy and in the outline of coverage required under subsection (c)(1)(B)(ii) that the policy is intended to be a qualified long-term care insurance contract under section 7702B(b).

(e) Qualified Long-Term Care Insurance Contract Defined.—For purposes of this section, the term "qualified long-term care insurance contract" has the meaning given such term by section 7702B.

(f) Coordination With State Requirements.—If a State imposes any requirement which is more stringent than the analogous requirement imposed by this section or section 7702B(g), the requirement imposed by this section or section 7702B(g) shall be treated as met if the more stringent State requirement is met.

SEC. 4980D. FAILURE TO MEET CERTAIN GROUP HEALTH PLAN REQUIREMENTS.

(a) General Rule.—There is hereby imposed a tax on any failure of a group health plan to meet the requirements of chapter 100 (relating to group health plan requirements).

(b) Amount of Tax.—

(1) In general.—The amount of the tax imposed by subsection (a) on any failure shall be $100 for each day in the noncompliance period with respect to each individual to whom such failure relates.

(2) Noncompliance period.—For purposes of this section, the term "noncompliance period" means, with respect to any failure, the period—

(A) beginning on the date such failure first occurs, and

(B) ending on the date such failure is corrected.

(3) Minimum tax for noncompliance period where failure discovered after notice of examination.—Notwithstanding paragraphs (1) and (2) of subsection (c)—

(A) In general.—In the case of 1 or more failures with respect to an individual—

(i) which are not corrected before the date a notice of examination of income tax liability is sent to the employer, and

(ii) which occurred or continued during the period under examination, the amount of tax imposed by subsection (a) by reason of such failures with respect to such individual shall not be less than the lesser of $2,500 or the amount of tax which would be imposed by subsection (a) without regard to such paragraphs.

(B) Higher minimum tax where violations are more than de minimis.—To the extent violations for which any person is liable under subsection (e) for any year are more than de minimis, subparagraph (A) shall be applied by substituting "$15,000" for "$2,500" with respect to such person.

(C) Exception for church plans.—This paragraph shall not apply to any failure under a church plan (as defined in section 414(e)).

(c) Limitations on Amount of Tax.—

(1) Tax not to apply where failure not discovered exercising reasonable diligence.—No tax shall be imposed by subsection (a) on any failure during any period for which it is established to the satisfaction of the Secretary that the person otherwise liable for such tax did not know, and exercising reasonable diligence would not have known, that such failure existed.

(2) Tax not to apply to failures corrected within certain periods.—No tax shall be imposed by subsection (a) on any failure if—

(A) such failure was due to reasonable cause and not to willful neglect, and

(B) (i) in the case of a plan other than a church plan (as defined in section 414(e)), such failure is corrected during the 30-day period beginning on the 1st date the person otherwise liable for such tax knew, or exercising reasonable diligence would have known, that such failure existed, and

(ii) in the case of a church plan (as so defined), such failure is corrected before the close of the correction period (determined under the rules of section 414(e)(4)(C)).

(3) Overall limitation for unintentional failures.—In the case of failures which are due to reasonable cause and not to willful neglect—

(A) Single employer plans.—

(i) In general.—In the case of failures with respect to plans other than specified multiple employer health plans, the tax imposed by subsection (a) for failures during the taxable year of the employer shall not exceed the amount equal to the lesser of—

(I) 10 percent of the aggregate amount paid or incurred by the employer (or predecessor employer) during the preceding taxable year for group health plans, or

(II) $500,000.

(ii) Taxable years in the case of certain controlled groups.—For purposes of this subparagraph, if not all persons who are treated as a single employer for purposes of this section have the same taxable year, the taxable years taken into account shall be determined under principles similar to the principles of section 1561.

(B) Specified multiple employer health plans.—

(i) In general.—In the case of failures with respect to a specified multiple employer health plan, the tax imposed by subsection (a) for failures during the taxable year of the trust forming part of such plan shall not exceed the amount equal to the lesser of—

(I) 10 percent of the amount paid or incurred by such trust during such taxable year to provide medical care (as defined in section 9832(d)(3)) directly or through insurance, reimbursement, or otherwise, or

(II) $500,000.

For purposes of the preceding sentence, all plans of which the same trust forms a part shall be treated as 1 plan.

(ii) Special rule for employers required to pay tax.—If an employer is assessed a tax imposed by subsection (a) by reason of a failure with respect to a specified multiple employer health plan, the limit shall be determined under subparagraph (A) (and not under this subparagraph) and as if such plan were not a specified multiple employer health plan.

(4) Waiver by Secretary.—In the case of a failure which is due to reasonable cause and not to willful neglect, the Secretary may waive part or all of the tax imposed by subsection (a) to the extent that the payment of such tax would be excessive relative to the failure involved.

(d) Tax Not to Apply to Certain Insured Small Employer Plans.—

(1) In general.—In the case of a group health plan of a small employer which provides health insurance coverage solely through a contract with a health insurance issuer, no tax shall be imposed by this section on the employer on any failure (other than a failure attributable to section 9811) which is solely because of the health insurance coverage offered by such issuer.

(2) Small employer.—

(A) In general.—For purposes of paragraph (1), the term "small employer" means, with respect to a calendar year and a plan year, an employer who employed an average of at least 2 but not more than 50 employees on business days during the preceding calendar year and who employs at least 2 employees on the first day of the plan year. For purposes of the preceding sentence, all persons treated as a single employer under subsection (b), (c), (m), or (o) of section 414 shall be treated as 1 employer.

(B) Employers not in existence in preceding year.—In the case of an employer which was not in existence throughout the preceding calendar year, the determination of whether such employer is a small employer shall be based on the average number of employees that it is reasonably expected such employer will employ on business days in the current calendar year.

(C) Predecessors.—Any reference in this paragraph to an employer shall include a reference to any predecessor of such employer.

(3) Health insurance coverage; health insurance issuer.—For purposes of paragraph (1), the terms "health insurance coverage" and "health insurance issuer" have the respective meanings given such terms by section 9832.

(e) Liability for Tax.—The following shall be liable for the tax imposed by subsection (a) on a failure:

(1) Except as otherwise provided in this subsection, the employer.

(2) In the case of a multiemployer plan, the plan.

(3) In the case of a failure under section 9803 (relating to guaranteed renewability) with respect to a plan described in subsection (f)(2)(B), the plan.

(f) Definitions.—For purposes of this section—

(1) Group health plan.—The term "group health plan" has the meaning given such term by section 9832(a).

(2) Specified multiple employer health plan.—The term "specified multiple employer health plan" means a group health plan which is—

(A) any multiemployer plan, or

(B) any multiple employer welfare arrangement (as defined in section 3(40) of the Employee Retirement Income Security Act of 1974, as in effect on the date of the enactment of this section).

(3) Correction.—A failure of a group health plan shall be treated as corrected if—

(A) such failure is retroactively undone to the extent possible, and

(B) the person to whom the failure relates is placed in a financial position which is as good as such person would have been in had such failure not occurred.

Recent Amendments to IRC §4980D

Gulf Opportunity Zone Act of 2005 (Pub. L. No. 109-135), as follows:
• IRC §4980D(a) was amended by Act §412(w)(w) by replacing "plans" with "plan." Eff. Dec. 21, 2005.

SEC. 4980E. FAILURE OF EMPLOYER TO MAKE COMPARABLE ARCHER MSA CONTRIBUTIONS.

(a) General Rule.—In the case of an employer who makes a contribution to the Archer MSA of any employee with respect to coverage under a high deductible health plan of the employer during a calendar year, there is hereby imposed a tax on the failure of such employer to meet the requirements of subsection (d) for such calendar year.

(b) Amount of Tax.—The amount of the tax imposed by subsection (a) on any failure for any calendar year is the amount equal to 35 percent of the aggregate amount contributed by the employer to

Archer MSAs of employees for taxable years of such employees ending with or within such calendar year.

(c) Waiver by Secretary.—In the case of a failure which is due to reasonable cause and not to willful neglect, the Secretary may waive part or all of the tax imposed by subsection (a) to the extent that the payment of such tax would be excessive relative to the failure involved.

(d) Employer Required to Make Comparable MSA Contributions for All Participating Employees.—

(1) In general.—An employer meets the requirements of this subsection for any calendar year if the employer makes available comparable contributions to the Archer MSAs of all comparable participating employees for each coverage period during such calendar year.

(2) Comparable contributions.—

(A) In general.—For purposes of paragraph (1), the term "comparable contributions" means contributions—

(i) which are the same amount, or

(ii) which are the same percentage of the annual deductible limit under the high deductible health plan covering the employees.

(B) Part-year employees.—In the case of an employee who is employed by the employer for only a portion of the calendar year, a contribution to the Archer MSA of such employee shall be treated as comparable if it is an amount which bears the same ratio to the comparable amount (determined without regard to this subparagraph) as such portion bears to the entire calendar year.

(3) Comparable participating employees.—For purposes of paragraph (1), the term "comparable participating employees" means all employees—

(A) who are eligible individuals covered under any high deductible health plan of the employer, and

(B) who have the same category of coverage. For purposes of subparagraph (B), the categories of coverage are self-only and family coverage.

(4) Part-time employees.—

(A) In general.—Paragraph (3) shall be applied separately with respect to part-time employees and other employees.

(B) Part-time employee.—For purposes of subparagraph (A), the term "part-time employee" means any employee who is customarily employed for fewer than 30 hours per week.

(e) Controlled Groups.—For purposes of this section, all persons treated as a single employer under subsection (b), (c), (m), or (o) of section 414 shall be treated as 1 employer.

IRC Sec. 4980E(e)

(f) Definitions.—Terms used in this section which are also used in section 220 have the respective meanings given such terms in section 220.

Recent Amendments to IRC §4980E

Job Creation and Worker Assistance Act of 2002 (Pub. L. No. 107-147), as follows:

• IRC §4980E heading was amended by Act §417(17)(A). Eff. Mar. 9, 2002. IRC §4980E, heading, prior to amendment:
   SEC. 4980E. FAILURE OF EMPLOYER TO MAKE COMPARABLE MEDICAL SAVINGS ACCOUNT CONTRIBUTIONS.

SEC. 4980F. FAILURE OF APPLICABLE PLANS REDUCING BENEFIT ACCRUALS TO SATISFY NOTICE REQUIREMENTS.

(a) Imposition of Tax.—There is hereby imposed a tax on the failure of any applicable pension plan to meet the requirements of subsection (e) with respect to any applicable individual.

(b) Amount of Tax.—

   (1) In general.—The amount of the tax imposed by subsection (a) on any failure with respect to any applicable individual shall be $100 for each day in the noncompliance period with respect to such failure.

   (2) Noncompliance period.—For purposes of this section, the term "noncompliance period" means, with respect to any failure, the period beginning on the date the failure first occurs and ending on the date the notice to which the failure relates is provided or the failure is otherwise corrected.

(c) Limitations on Amount of Tax.—

   (1) Tax not to apply where failure not discovered and reasonable diligence exercised.—No tax shall be imposed by subsection (a) on any failure during any period for which it is established to the satisfaction of the Secretary that any person subject to liability for the tax under subsection (d) did not know that the failure existed and exercised reasonable diligence to meet the requirements of subsection (e).

   (2) Tax not to apply to failures corrected within 30 days.—No tax shall be imposed by subsection (a) on any failure if—

      (A) any person subject to liability for the tax under subsection (d) exercised reasonable diligence to meet the requirements of subsection (e), and

      (B) such person provides the notice described in subsection (e) during the 30-day period beginning on the first date such person knew, or exercising reasonable diligence would have known, that such failure existed.

   (3) Overall limitation for unintentional failures.—

      (A) In general.—If the person subject to liability for tax under subsection (d) exercised reasonable

diligence to meet the requirements of subsection (e), the tax imposed by subsection (a) for failures during the taxable year of the employer (or, in the case of a multiemployer plan, the taxable year of the trust forming part of the Plan) shall not exceed $500,000. For purposes of the preceding sentence, all multiemployer plans of which the same trust forms a part shall be treated as 1 plan.

      (B) Taxable years in the case of certain controlled groups.—For purposes of this paragraph, if all persons who are treated as a single employer for purposes of this section do not have the same taxable year, the taxable years taken into account shall be determined under principles similar to the principles of §1561.

   (4) Waiver by secretary.—In the case of a failure which is due to reasonable cause and not to willful neglect, the Secretary may waive part or all of the tax imposed by subsection (a) to the extent that the payment of such tax would be excessive or otherwise inequitable relative to the failure involved.

(d) Liability for Tax.—The following shall be liable for the tax imposed by subsection (a):

   (1) In the case of a plan other than a multiemployer plan, the employer.

   (2) In the case of a multiemployer plan, the plan.

(e) Notice Requirements for Plans Significantly Reducing Benefit Accruals.—

   (1) In general.—If an applicable pension plan is amended to provide for a significant reduction in the rate of future benefit accrual, the plan administrator shall provide the notice described in paragraph (2) to each applicable individual (and to each employee organization representing applicable individuals) and to each employer who has an obligation to contribute to the plan.

   (2) Notice.—The notice required by paragraph (1) shall be written in a manner calculated to be understood by the average plan participant and shall provide sufficient information (as determined in accordance with regulations prescribed by the Secretary) to allow applicable individuals to understand the effect of the plan amendment. The Secretary may provide a simplified form of notice for or exempt from any notice requirement, a plan—

      (A) which has fewer than 100 participants who have accrued a benefit under the plan, or

      (B) which offers participants the option to choose between the new benefit formula and the old benefit formula.

   (3) Timing of notice.—Except as provided in regulations, the notice required by paragraph (1) shall be provided within a reasonable time before the effective date of the plan amendment.

   (4) Designees.—Any notice under paragraph (1) may be provided to a person designated, in writing, by the person to which it would otherwise be provided.

(5) Notice before adoption of amendment.—A plan shall not be treated as filing to meet the requirements of paragraph (1) merely because notice is provided before the adoption of the plan amendment if no material modification of the amendment occurs before the amendment is adopted.

(f) Definitions and Special Rules.—For purposes of this section—

(1) Applicable individual.—The term "applicable individual" means, with respect to any plan amendment —

(A) each participant in the plan, and

(B) any beneficiary who is an alternate payee (within the meaning of section 414(p)(8)) under an applicable qualified domestic relations order (within the meaning of section 414(p)(1)(A)),

whose rate of future benefit accrual under the plan may reasonably be expected to be significantly reduced by such plan amendment.

(2) Applicable pension plan.—The term "applicable pension plan" means—

(A) any defined benefit plan described in section 401(a) which includes a trust exempt from tax under section 501(a), or

(B) an individual account plan which is subject to the funding standards of section 412.

Such term shall not include a governmental plan (within the meaning of section 414(d)) or a church plan (within the meaning of section 414(e)) with respect to which the election provided by section 410(d) has not been made.

(3) Early retirement.—A plan amendment which eliminates or reduces any early retirement benefit or retirement-type subsidy (within the earning of section 411(d)(6)(B)(i)) shall be treated as having the effect of reducing the rate of future benefit accrual.

(g) New Technologies.—The Secretary may by regulations allow any notice under subsection (e) to be provided by using new technologies.

Recent Amendments to IRC §4980F

Pension Protection Act of 2006 (Pub. L. No. 109-280), as follows:
- IRC §4980F(e)(1) was amended by Act §502(c)(2) by adding before the period at the end "and to each employer who has an obligation to contribute to the plan". Eff. plan years beginning after Dec. 31, 2007.

Job Creation and Worker Assistance Act of 2002 (Pub. L. No. 107-247), as follows:
- IRC §4980F(e)(1) was amended by Act §411(u)(1)(A) by replacing "written notice" with "the notice described in paragraph (2)". Eff. for plan amendments taking effect on or after June 7, 2001, as if included in the provision of Pub. L. No. 107-16 to which it relates.

- IRC §4980F(f)(2)(A) was amended by Act §411(u)(1)(B). Eff. for plan amendments taking effect on or after June 7, 2001, as if included in the provision of Pub. L. No. 107-16 to which it relates. IRC §4980F(f)(2)(A) prior to amendment:

(A) any defined benefit plan, or

- IRC §4980F(f)(3) was amended by Act §411(u)(1)(C) by striking "significantly" before "reduces" and "reducing", respectively, each place it appeared. Eff. for plan amendments taking effect on or after June 7, 2001, as if included in the provision of Pub. L. No. 107-16 to which it relates.

Economic Growth and Tax Relief Reconciliation Act of 2001 (Pub. L. No. 107-16), as follows:

- IRC §4980F was added by Act §659(a)(1). Eff. generally for plan amendments taking effect on or after June 7, 2001. [*Ed. Note:* see Act §659(c)(2)–(3), as amended by Pub. L. No. 107-147, §411(u)(3), for transition rules.]

- **Sunset Rule.** To comply with the Congressional Budget Act of 1974, §901 of Pub. L. No. 107-16 provides that all provisions of, and amendments made by, the Act will not apply to taxable, plan, or limitation years beginning after December 31, 2010. *But see* Pension Protection Act of 2006 (Pub. L. No. 109-280), §811 (sunset rule does not apply to Pub. L. No. 107-16, §§601–666 (relating to pensions and individual retirement arrangement provisions)).

SEC. 4980G. FAILURE OF EMPLOYER TO MAKE COMPARABLE HEALTH SAVINGS ACCOUNT CONTRIBUTIONS.

(a) General Rule.—In the case of an employer who makes a contribution to the health savings account of any employee during a calendar year, there is hereby imposed a tax on the failure of such employer to meet the requirements of subsection (b) for such calendar year.

(b) Rules and Requirements.—Rules and requirements similar to the rules and requirements of section 4980E shall apply for purposes of this section.

(c) Regulations.—The Secretary shall issue regulations to carry out the purposes of this section, including regulations providing special rules for employers who make contributions to Archer MSAs and health savings accounts during the calendar year.

(d) Exception.—For purposes of applying section 4980E to a contribution to a health savings account of an employee who is not a highly compensated employee (as defined in section 414(q)), highly compensated employees shall not be treated as comparable participating employees.

Recent Amendments to IRC §4980G

Tax Relief and Health Care Act of 2006 (Pub. L. No. 109-432), as follows:

- IRC §4980G was amended by Act §306(a) by adding new subsec. (d). Eff. tax years beginning after Dec. 31, 2006.

Medicare Prescription Drug, Improvement, and Modernization Act of 2003 (Pub. L. No. 108-173), as follows:

IRC Sec. 4980G(d)

• IRC §4980G was added by Act §1201(d)(4)(A). Eff. tax years beginning after Dec. 31, 2003.

SEC. 4980H. SHARED RESPONSIBILITY FOR EMPLOYERS REGARDING HEALTH COVERAGE.

(a) Large Employers Not Offering Health Coverage.—If—

(1) any applicable large employer fails to offer to its full-time employees (and their dependents) the opportunity to enroll in minimum essential coverage under an eligible employer-sponsored plan (as defined in section 5000A(f)(2)) for any month, and

(2) at least one full-time employee of the applicable large employer has been certified to the employer under section 1411 of the Patient Protection and Affordable Care Act as having enrolled for such month in a qualified health plan with respect to which an applicable premium tax credit or cost-sharing reduction is allowed or paid with respect to the employee,

then there is hereby imposed on the employer an assessable payment equal to the product of the applicable payment amount and the number of individuals employed by the employer as full-time employees during such month.

(b) Large Employers Offering Coverage With Employees Who Qualify for Premium Tax Credits or Cost-sharing Reductions.—

(1) In general.—If—

(A) an applicable large employer offers to its full-time employees (and their dependents) the opportunity to enroll in minimum essential coverage under an eligible employer-sponsored plan (as defined in section 5000A(f)(2)) for any month, and

(B) 1 or more full-time employees of the applicable large employer has been certified to the employer under section 1411 of the Patient Protection and Affordable Care Act as having enrolled for such month in a qualified health plan with respect to which an applicable premium tax credit or cost-sharing reduction is allowed or paid with respect to the employee,

then there is hereby imposed on the employer an assessable payment equal to the product of the num-

ber of full-time employees of the applicable large employer described in subparagraph (B) for such month and an amount equal to 1/12 of $3,000.

(2) Overall limitation.—The aggregate amount of tax determined under paragraph (1) with respect to all employees of an applicable large employer for any month shall not exceed the product of the applicable payment amount and the number of individuals employed by the employer as full-time employees during such month.

~~(3) Special rules for employers providing free choice vouchers.—No assessable payment shall be imposed under paragraph (1) for any month with respect to any employee to whom the employer provides a free choice voucher under section 10108 of the Patient Protection and Affordable Care Act for such month.~~

(c) Definitions and Special Rules.—For purposes of this section—

(1) Applicable payment amount.—The term "applicable payment amount" means, with respect to any month, 1/12 of $2,000.

(2) Applicable larger employer.—

(A) In general.—The term "applicable large employer" means, with respect to a calendar year, an employer who employed an average of at least 50 full-time employees on business days during the preceding calendar year.

(B) Exemption for certain employers.—

(i) In general.—An employer shall not be considered to employ more than 50 full-time employees if—

(I) the employer's workforce exceeds 50 full-time employees for 120 days or fewer during the calendar year, and

(II) the employees in excess of 50 employed during such 120-day period were seasonal workers.

(ii) Definition of seasonal workers.—The term "seasonal worker" means a worker who performs labor or services on a seasonal basis as defined by the Secretary of Labor, including workers covered by section 500.20(s)(1) of title 29, Code of Federal Regulations and retail workers employed exclusively during holiday seasons.

(C) Rules for determining employer size.—For purposes of this paragraph—

(i) Application of Aggregation Rule for Employers.—All persons treated as a single employer under subsection (b), (c), (m), or (o) of section 414 of the Internal Revenue Code of 1986 shall be treated as 1 employer.

(ii) Employers not in existence in preceding year.—In the case of an employer which was not in existence throughout the preceding calendar year, the determination of whether such employer is an applicable large employer shall be based on the average number of employees that it is reasonably expected such employer will employ on business days in the current calendar year.

(iii) Predecessors.—Any reference in this subsection to an employer shall include a reference to any predecessor of such employer.

(D) Application of employer size to assessable penalties.—

(i) In general.—The number of individuals employed by an applicable large employer as full-time employees during any month shall be reduced by 30 solely for purposes of calculating—

(I) the assessable payment under subsection (a), or

(II) the overall limitation under subsection (b)(2).

(ii) Aggregation.—In the case of persons treated as 1 employer under subparagraph (C)(i), only 1 reduction under subclause (I) or (II) shall be allowed with respect to such persons and such reduction shall be allocated among such persons ratably on the basis of the number of full-time employees employed by each such person.

(E) Full-time equivalents treated as full-time employees.—Solely for purposes of determining whether an employer is an applicable large employer under this paragraph, an employer shall, in addition to the number of full-time employees for any month otherwise determined, include for such month a number of full-time employees determined by dividing the aggregate number of hours of service of employees who are not full-time employees for the month by 120.

(3) Applicable premium tax credit and cost-sharing reduction.—The term "applicable premium tax credit and cost-sharing reduction" means—

(A) any premium tax credit allowed under section 36B,

(B) any cost-sharing reduction under section 1402 of the Patient Protection and Affordable Care Act, and

(C) any advance payment of such credit or reduction under section 1412 of such Act.

(4) Full-time employee.—

(A) In general.—The term "full-time employee" means, with respect to any month, an employee who is employed on average at least 30 hours of service per week.

(B) Hours of service.—The Secretary, in consultation with the Secretary of Labor, shall prescribe such regulations, rules, and guidance as may be necessary to determine the hours of service of an employee, including rules for the application of this paragraph to employees who are not compensated on an hourly basis.

(5) Inflation adjustment.—

(A) In general.—In the case of any calendar year after 2014, each of the dollar amounts in subsection (b) and paragraph (1) shall be increased by an amount equal to the product of—

(i) such dollar amount, and

(ii) the premium adjustment percentage (as defined in section 1302(c)(4) of the Patient Protection and Affordable Care Act) for the calendar year.

(B) Rounding.—If the amount of any increase under subparagraph (A) is not a multiple of $10, such increase shall be rounded to the next lowest multiple of $10.

(6) Other definitions.—Any term used in this section which is also used in the Patient Protection and Affordable Care Act shall have the same meaning as when used in such Act.

(7) Tax nondeductible.—For denial of deduction for the tax imposed by this section, see section 275(a)(6).

(d) Administration and Procedure.—

(1) In general.—Any assessable payment provided by this section shall be paid upon notice and demand by the Secretary, and shall be assessed and collected in the same manner as an assessable penalty under subchapter B of chapter 68.

(2) Time payment.—The Secretary may provide for the payment of any assessable payment provided by this section on an annual, monthly, or other periodic basis as the Secretary may prescribe.

(3) Coordination with credits, etc.—The Secretary shall prescribe rules, regulations, or guidance for the repayment of any assessable payment (including interest) if such payment is based on the allowance or payment of an applicable premium tax credit or cost-sharing reduction with respect to an employee, such allowance or payment is subsequently disallowed, and the assessable payment would not have been required to be made but for such allowance or payment.

Amendments to §4980H

Department of Defense and Full-Year Continuing Appropriations Act, 2011 (Pub. L. No. 112-10), as follows:

IRC Sec. 4980H(d)(3)

• IRC §4980H(b)(3) was stricken by Act §1858(b)(4). Eff. as if included in the provisions of, and the amendments made by, the Patient Protection and Affordable Care Act to which they relate [Ed. Note: for months beginning after Dec. 31, 2013].

Health Care and Education Reconciliation Act of 2010 (Pub. L. No. 111-152), as follows:

• IRC §4980H(b) was struck by Act §1003(d). Eff. on date of enactment [enacted: Mar. 30, 2010]. *Note:* IRC §4980H is applicable to months beginning after Dec. 31, 2013. IRC §4980H(b) before being struck:

  (b) Large Employers With Waiting Periods Exceeding 60 Days.—

  (1) In general.—In the case of any applicable large employer which requires an extended waiting period to enroll in any minimum essential coverage under an employer-sponsored plan (as defined in section 5000A(f)(2)), there is hereby imposed on the employer an assessable payment of $600 for each full-time employee of the employer to whom the extended waiting period applies.

  (2) Extended waiting period.—The term "extended waiting period" means any waiting period (as defined in section 2701(b)(4) of the Public Health Service Act) which exceeds 60 days.

• IRC §4980H(c)–(e) were redesignated by Act §1003(d) as subsecs. (b)–(d), respectively. Eff. on date of enactment [enacted: Mar. 30, 2010]. *Note:* IRC §4980H is applicable to months beginning after Dec. 31, 2013.

• IRC §4980H(c)(1) (before redesignation) was amended by Act §1003(b)(1) by substituting "an amount equal to 1/12 of $3,000" for "400 percent of the applicable payment amount" in the flush text following subsec. (c)(1)(B). Eff. on date of enactment [enacted: Mar. 30, 2010]. *Note:* IRC §4980H is applicable to months beginning after Dec. 31, 2013.

• IRC §4980H(d)(1) (before redesignation) was amended by Act §1003(b)(2) by substituting "$2,000" for "$750". Eff. on date of enactment [enacted: Mar. 30, 2010]. *Note:* IRC §4980H is applicable to months beginning after Dec. 31, 2013.

• IRC §4908H(d)(2)(D) (before redesignation) was amended by Act §1003(a). Eff. on date of enactment [enacted: Mar. 30, 2010]. *Note:* IRC §4980H is applicable to months beginning after Dec. 31, 2013. IRC §4908H(d)(2)(D) prior to amendment:

  (D) Application to construction industry employers.—In the case of any employer the substantial annual gross receipts of which are attributable to the construction industry—

  (i) subparagraph (A) shall be applied by substituting "who employed an average of at least 5 full-time employees on business days during the preceding calendar year and whose annual payroll expenses exceed $250,000 for such preceding calendar year" for "who employed an average of at least 50 full-time employees on business days during the preceding calendar year", and

  (ii) subparagraph (B) shall be applied by substituting "5" for "50"."

• IRC §4980H(d)(2)(E) (before redesignation) was amended by Act §1003(c) by adding subpara. (E). Eff. on date of enactment [enacted: Mar. 30, 2010]. *Note:* IRC §4980H is applicable to months beginning after Dec. 31, 2013.

• IRC §4980H(d)(5)(A) (before redesignation) was amended by Act §1003(b)(3) by substituting "subsection (b) and paragraph (1)" for "subsection (b)(2) and (d)(1)". Eff. on date of enactment [enacted: Mar. 30, 2010]. *Note:* IRC §4980H is applicable to months beginning after Dec. 31, 2013.

Patient Protection and Affordable Care Act, 2010 (Pub. L. No. 111-148), as follows:

• IRC §4980H was added by Act §1513(a). Eff. for months beginning after Dec. 31, 2013.

• IRC §4980H(b) was amended by Act §10106(e). Eff. for months beginning after Dec. 31, 2013. IRC §4980H(b) prior to amendment:

  (b) Large Employers with Waiting Periods Exceeding 30 Days.—

  (1) In general.—In the case of any applicable large employer which requires an extended waiting period to enroll in any minimum essential coverage under an employer-sponsored plan (as defined in section 5000A(f)(2)), there is hereby im-

posed on the employer an assessable payment, in the amount specified in paragraph (2), for each full-time employee of the employer to whom the extended waiting period applies.

  (2) Amount.—For purposes of paragraph (1), the amount specified in this paragraph for a full-time employee is—

  (A) in the case of an extended waiting period which exceeds 30 days but does not exceed 60 days, $400, and

  (B) in the case of an extended waiting period which exceeds 60 days, $600.

  (3) Extended waiting period.—The term "extended waiting period" means any waiting period (as defined in section 2701(b)(4) of the Public Health Service Act) which exceeds 30 days.

• IRC §4980H(c)(3) was added by Act §10108(i)(1)(A). Eff. for months beginning after Dec. 31, 2013.

• IRC §4980H(d)(2)(D) was added by Act §10106(f)(2). Eff. for months beginning after Dec. 31, 2013.

• IRC §4980H(d)(4)(A) was amended by Act §10106(f)(1) by inserting ", with respect to any month," after "means". Eff. on date of enactment of this Act [Mar. 23, 2010]. *Note:* IRC §4980H is applicable to months beginning after Dec. 31, 2013.

> ### Editor's Note
>
> **Caution**: IRC §4980I, below, added by Pub. L. No. 111-148, §9001, and amended by Pub. L. No. 111-148, §10901, and Pub. L. No. 111-152, §1401, is effective for taxable years beginning after December 31, 2017.

SEC. 4980I. EXCISE TAX ON HIGH COST EMPLOYER-SPONSORED HEALTH COVERAGE.

(a) Imposition of Tax.—If—

(1) an employee is covered under any applicable employer-sponsored coverage of an employer at any time during a taxable period, and

(2) there is any excess benefit with respect to the coverage,

there is hereby imposed a tax equal to 40 percent of the excess benefit.

(b) Excess Benefit.—For purposes of this section—

(1) In general.—The term "excess benefit" means, with respect to any applicable employer-sponsored coverage made available by an employer to an employee during any taxable period, the sum of the excess amounts determined under paragraph (2) for months during the taxable period.

(2) Monthly excess amount.—The excess amount determined under this paragraph for any month is the excess (if any) of—

(A) the aggregate cost of the applicable employer-sponsored coverage of the employee for the month, over

(B) an amount equal to 1/12 of the annual limitation under paragraph (3) for the calendar year in which the month occurs.

(3) Annual limitation.—For purposes of this subsection—

(A) In general.—The annual limitation under this paragraph for any calendar year is the dollar limit determined under subparagraph (C) for the calendar year.

(B) Applicable annual limitation.—

(i) In general.—Except as provided in clause (ii), the annual limitation which applies for any month shall be determined on the basis of the type of coverage (as determined under subsection (f)(1)) provided to the employee by the employer as of the beginning of the month.

(ii) Multiemployer plan coverage.—Any coverage provided under a multiemployer plan (as defined in section 414(f)) shall be treated as coverage other than self-only coverage.

(C) Applicable dollar limit.—

(i) 2018—In the case of 2018, the dollar limit under this subparagraph is—

(I) in the case of an employee with self-only coverage, $10,200 multiplied by the health cost adjustment percentage (determined by only taking into account self-only coverage), and

(II) in the case of an employee with coverage other than self-only coverage, $27,500 multiplied by the health cost adjustment percentage (determined by only taking into account coverage other than self-only coverage).

(ii) Health cost adjustment percentage.—For purposes of clause (i), the health cost adjustment percentage is equal to 100 percent plus the excess (if any) of—

(I) the percentage by which the per employee cost for providing coverage under the Blue Cross/Blue Shield standard benefit option under the Federal Employees Health Benefits Plan for plan year 2018 (determined by using the benefit package for such coverage in 2010) exceeds such cost for plan year 2010, over

(II) 55 percent.

(iii) Age and gender adjustment.—

(I) In general.—The amount determined under subclause (I) or (II) of clause (i), whichever is applicable, for any taxable period shall be increased by the amount determined under subclause (II).

(II) Amount determined.—The amount determined under this subclause is an amount equal to the excess (if any) of—

(aa) the premium cost of the Blue Cross/Blue Shield standard benefit option under the Federal Employees Health Benefits Plan for the type of coverage provided such individual in such taxable period if priced for the age and gender characteristics of all employees of the individual's employer, over

(bb) that premium cost for the provision of such coverage under such option in such taxable period if priced for the age and gender characteristics of the national workforce.

(iv) Exception for certain individuals.—In the case of an individual who is a qualified retiree or who participates in a plan sponsored by an employer the majority of whose employees covered by the plan are engaged in a high-risk profession or employed to repair or install electrical or telecommunications lines—

(I) the dollar amount in clause (i)(I) shall be increased by $1,650, and

(II) the dollar amount in clause (i)(II) shall be increased by $3,450.

(v) Subsequent years.—In the case of any calendar year after 2018, each of the dollar amounts under clauses (i) (after the application of clause (ii)) and (iv) shall be increased to the amount equal to such amount as in effect for the calendar year preceding such year, increased by an amount equal to the product of—

(I) such amount as so in effect, multiplied by

(II) the cost-of-living adjustment determined under section 1(f)(3) for such year (determined by substituting the calendar year that is 2 years before such year for "1992" in subparagraph (B) thereof), increased by 1 percentage point in the case of determinations for calendar years beginning before 2020.

If any amount determined under this clause is not a multiple of $50, such amount shall be rounded to the nearest multiple of $50.

(c) Liability To Pay Tax.—

(1) In general.—Each coverage provider shall pay the tax imposed by subsection (a) on its applicable share of the excess benefit with respect to an employee for any taxable period.

(2) Coverage provider.—For purposes of this subsection, the term "coverage provider" means each of the following:

(A) Health insurance coverage.—If the applicable employer-sponsored coverage consists of coverage under a group health plan which provides health insurance coverage, the health insurance issuer.

(B) HSA and MSA contributions.—If the applicable employer-sponsored coverage consists of coverage under an arrangement under which the employer makes contributions described in subsection (b) or (d) of section 106, the employer.

(C) Other coverage.—In the case of any other applicable employer-sponsored coverage, the person that administers the plan benefits.

(3) Applicable share.—For purposes of this subsection, a coverage provider's applicable share of an

IRC Sec. 4980I(c)(3)

excess benefit for any taxable period is the amount which bears the same ratio to the amount of such excess benefit as—

(A) the cost of the applicable employer-sponsored coverage provided by the provider to the employee during such period, bears to

(B) the aggregate cost of all applicable employer-sponsored coverage provided to the employee by all coverage providers during such period.

(4) Responsibility to calculate tax and applicable shares.—

(A) In general.—Each employer shall—

(i) calculate for each taxable period the amount of the excess benefit subject to the tax imposed by subsection (a) and the applicable share of such excess benefit for each coverage provider, and

(ii) notify, at such time and in such manner as the Secretary may prescribe, the Secretary and each coverage provider of the amount so determined for the provider.

(B) Special rule for multiemployer plans.—In the case of applicable employer-sponsored coverage made available to employees through a multiemployer plan (as defined in section 414(f)), the plan sponsor shall make the calculations, and provide the notice, required under subparagraph (A).

(d) Applicable Employer-Sponsored Coverage; Cost.—For purposes of this section—

(1) Applicable employer-sponsored coverage.—

(A) In general.—The term "applicable employer-sponsored coverage" means, with respect to any employee, coverage under any group health plan made available to the employee by an employer which is excludable from the employee's gross income under section 106, or would be so excludable if it were employer-provided coverage (within the meaning of such section 106).

(B) Exceptions.—The term "applicable employer-sponsored coverage" shall not include—

(i) any coverage (whether through insurance or otherwise) described in section 9832(c)(1) (other than subparagraph (G) thereof) or for long-term care, or

(ii) any coverage under a separate policy, certificate, or contract of insurance which provides benefits substantially all of which are for treatment of the mouth (including any organ or structure within the mouth) or for treatment of the eye, or

(iii) *any coverage described in section 9832(c)(3) the payment for which is not excludable from gross income and for which a deduction under section 162(l) is not allowable.*

(C) overage includes employee paid portion.— Coverage shall be treated as applicable employer-

sponsored coverage without regard to whether the employer or employee pays for the coverage.

(D) Self-employed individual.—In the case of an individual who is an employee within the meaning of section 401(c)(1), coverage under any group health plan providing health insurance coverage shall be treated as applicable employer-sponsored coverage if a deduction is allowable under section 162(l) with respect to all or any portion of the cost of the coverage.

(E) Governmental plans included.—Applicable employer-sponsored coverage shall include coverage under any group health plan established and maintained primarily for its civilian employees by the Government of the United States, by the government of any State or political subdivision thereof, or by any agency or instrumentality of any such government.

(2) Determination of cost.—

(A) In general.—The cost of applicable employer-sponsored coverage shall be determined under rules similar to the rules of section 4980B(f)(4), except that in determining such cost, any portion of the cost of such coverage which is attributable to the tax imposed under this section shall not be taken into account and the amount of such cost shall be calculated separately for self-only coverage and other coverage. In the case of applicable employer-sponsored coverage which provides coverage to retired employees, the plan may elect to treat a retired employee who has not attained the age of 65 and a retired employee who has attained the age of 65 as similarly situated beneficiaries.

(B) Health FSAs.—In the case of applicable employer-sponsored coverage consisting of coverage under a flexible spending arrangement (as defined in section 106(c)(2)), the cost of the coverage shall be equal to the sum of—

(i) the amount of employer contributions under any salary reduction election under the arrangement, plus

(ii) the amount determined under subparagraph (A) with respect to any reimbursement under the arrangement in excess of the contributions described in clause (i).

(C) Archer MSAs and HSAs.—In the case of applicable employer-sponsored coverage consisting of coverage under an arrangement under which the employer makes contributions described in subsection (b) or (d) of section 106, the cost of the coverage shall be equal to the amount of employer contributions under the arrangement.

(D) Allocation on a monthly basis.—If cost is determined on other than a monthly basis, the cost shall be allocated to months in a taxable period on such basis as the Secretary may prescribe.

IRC Sec. 4980I(c)(3)

(3) Employee.—The term "employee" includes any former employee, surviving spouse, or other primary insured individual.

(e) Penalty for Failure To Properly Calculate Excess Benefit.—

(1) In general.—If, for any taxable period, the tax imposed by subsection (a) exceeds the tax determined under such subsection with respect to the total excess benefit calculated by the employer or plan sponsor under subsection (c)(4)—

(A) each coverage provider shall pay the tax on its applicable share (determined in the same manner as under subsection (c)(4)) of the excess, but no penalty shall be imposed on the provider with respect to such amount, and

(B) the employer or plan sponsor shall, in addition to any tax imposed by subsection (a), pay a penalty in an amount equal to such excess, plus interest at the underpayment rate determined under section 6621 for the period beginning on the due date for the payment of tax imposed by subsection (a) to which the excess relates and ending on the date of payment of the penalty.

(2) Limitations on penalty.—

(A) Penalty not to apply where failure not discovered exercising reasonable diligence.—No penalty shall be imposed by paragraph (1)(B) on any failure to properly calculate the excess benefit during any period for which it is established to the satisfaction of the Secretary that the employer or plan sponsor neither knew, nor exercising reasonable diligence would have known, that such failure existed.

(B) Penalty not to apply to failures corrected within 30 days.—No penalty shall be imposed by paragraph (1)(B) on any such failure if—

(i) such failure was due to reasonable cause and not to willful neglect, and

(ii) such failure is corrected during the 30-day period beginning on the 1st date that the employer knew, or exercising reasonable diligence would have known, that such failure existed

(C) Waiver by Secretary.—In the case of any such failure which is due to reasonable cause and not to willful neglect, the Secretary may waive part or all of the penalty imposed by paragraph (1), to the extent that the payment of such penalty would be excessive or otherwise inequitable relative to the failure involved.

(f) Other definitions and special rules.—For purposes of this section—

(1) Coverage determinations.—

(A) In general.—Except as provided in subparagraph (B), an employee shall be treated as having self-only coverage with respect to any applicable employer-sponsored coverage of an employer.

(B) Minimum essential coverage.—An employee shall be treated as having coverage other than self-only coverage only if the employee is enrolled in coverage other than self-only coverage in a group health plan which provides minimum essential coverage (as defined in section 5000A(f)) to the employee and at least one other beneficiary, and the benefits provided under such minimum essential coverage do not vary based on whether any individual covered under such coverage is the employee or another beneficiary.

(2) Qualified retiree.—The term "qualified retiree" means any individual who—

(A) is receiving coverage by reason of being a retiree,

(B) has attained age 55, and

(C) is not entitled to benefits or eligible for enrollment under the Medicare program under title XVIII of the Social Security Act.

(3) Employees engaged in high-risk profession.—The term "employees engaged in a high-risk profession" means law enforcement officers (as such term is defined in section 1204 of the Omnibus Crime Control and Safe Streets Act of 1968), employees in fire protection activities (as such term is defined in section 3(y) of the Fair Labor Standards Act of 1938), individuals who provide out-of-hospital emergency medical care (including emergency medical technicians, paramedics, and first-responders), individuals whose primary work is longshore work (as defined in section 258(b) of the Immigration and Nationality Act (8 U.S.C. 1288(b)), determined without regard to paragraph (2) thereof), and individuals engaged in the construction, mining, agriculture (not including food processing), forestry, and fishing industries. Such term includes an employee who is retired from a high-risk profession described in the preceding sentence, if such employee satisfied the requirements of such sentence for a period of not less than 20 years during the employee's employment.

(4) Group health plan.—The term "group health plan" has the meaning given such term by section 5000(b)(1).

(5) Health insurance coverage; health insurance issuer.—

(A) Health insurance coverage.—The term "health insurance coverage" has the meaning given such term by section 9832(b)(1) (applied without regard to subparagraph (B) thereof, except as provided by the Secretary in regulations).

(B) Health insurance issuer.—The term "health insurance issuer" has the meaning given such term by section 9832(b)(2).

(6) Person that administers the plan benefits.— The term "person that administers the plan benefits" shall include the plan sponsor if the plan sponsor administers benefits under the plan.

(7) Plan sponsor.—The term "plan sponsor" has the meaning given such term in section 3(16)(B) of the Employee Retirement Income Security Act of 1974.

(8) Taxable period.—The term "taxable period" means the calendar year or such shorter period as the Secretary may prescribe. The Secretary may have different taxable periods for employers of varying sizes.

(9) Aggregation rules.—All employers treated as a single employer under subsection (b), (c), (m), or (o) of section 414 shall be treated as a single employer.

(10) Denial of deduction.—For denial of a deduction for the tax imposed by this section, see section 275(a)(6).

(g) Regulations.—The Secretary shall prescribe such regulations as may be necessary to carry out this section.

Amendments to IRC §4980I

Health Care and Education Reconciliation Act of 2010 (Pub. L. No. 111-152), as follows:

• IRC §4980I(b)(3)(B) was amended by Act §1401(a)(1) by substituting "(i) In General.—Except as provided in clause (ii), the annual" for "The annual" and by adding clause (ii). Eff. on date of enactment of this Act [Mar. 30, 2010]. *Note:* IRC §4980I is applicable for tax years beginning after Dec. 31, 2017.

• IRC §4980I(b)(3)(C) was amended by Act §1401(a)(2)(A) by striking "Except as provided in subparagraph (D)—" in the matter preceding cl. (i). Eff. on date of enactment of this Act [Mar. 30, 2010]. *Note:* IRC §4980I is applicable for tax years beginning after Dec. 31, 2017.

• IRC §4980I(b)(3)(C)(i) was amended by Act §1401(a)(2)(B)(i) by substituting "2018" for "2013" in heading and text. Eff. on date of enactment of this Act [Mar. 30, 2010]. *Note:* IRC §4980I is applicable for tax years beginning after Dec. 31, 2017.

• IRC §4980I(b)(3)(C)(i)(I) was amended by Act §1401(a)(2)(B)(ii) by substituting "$10,200 multiplied by the health cost adjustment percentage (determined by only taking into account self-only coverage)" for "$8,500". Eff. on date of enactment of this Act [Mar. 30, 2010]. *Note:* IRC §4980I is applicable for tax years beginning after Dec. 31, 2017.

• IRC §4980I(b)(3)(C)(i)(II) was amended by Act §1401(a)(2)(B)(iii) by substituting "$27,500 multiplied by the health cost adjustment percentage (determined by only taking into account coverage other than self-only coverage)" for "$23,000". Eff. on date of enactment of this Act [Mar. 30, 2010]. *Note:* IRC §4980I is applicable for tax years beginning after Dec. 31, 2017.

• IRC §4980I(b)(3)(C)(ii)–(iii) were amended by Act §1401(a)(2)(C) by redesignating clauses (ii)–(iii) as clauses (iv)–(v), respectively, and by adding new clauses (ii) and (iii). Eff. on date of enactment of this Act [Mar. 30, 2010]. *Note:* IRC §4980I is applicable for tax years beginning after Dec. 31, 2017.

• IRC §4980I(b)(3)(C)(iv) (as redesignated) was amended by Act §1401(a)(2)(D)(i) by inserting "covered by the plan" after "whose employees"; striking subclauses (I) and (II); and adding new subclauses (I) and (II). Eff. on date of enactment of this Act [Mar. 30, 2010]. *Note:* IRC §4980I is applicable for tax years beginning after Dec. 31, 2017. IRC §4980I(b)(3)(C)(iv) prior to being struck:

    (I) the dollar amount in clause (i)(I) (determined after the application of subparagraph (D)) shall be increased by $1,350, and

    (II) the dollar amount in clause (i)(II) (determined after the application of subparagraph (D)) shall be increased by $3,000.

• IRC §4980I(b)(3)(v) (as redesignated) was amended by Act §1401(a)(2)(E) by substituting "2018" for "2013"; substituting "clauses (i) (after the application of clause (ii)) and (iv)" for "clauses (i) and (ii)"; and inserting "in the case of determinations for calendar years beginning before 2010" after "1 percentage point". Eff. on date of enactment of this Act [Mar. 30, 2010]. *Note:* IRC §4980I is applicable for tax years beginning after Dec. 31, 2017.

• IRC §4980I(b)(3)(D) was stricken by Act §1401(a)(3). Eff. on date of enactment of this Act [Mar. 30, 2010]. *Note:* IRC §4980I is applicable for tax years beginning after Dec. 31, 2017. IRC §4980I(b)(3)(D) prior to being struck:

    (D) Transition rule for states with highest coverage costs.—
    (i) In general.—If an employee is a resident of a high cost State on the first day of any month beginning in 2013, 2014, or 2015, the annual limitation under this paragraph for such month with respect to such employee shall be an amount equal to the applicable percentage of the annual limitation (determined without regard to this subparagraph or subparagraph (C)(ii)).
    (ii) Applicable percentage.—The applicable percentage is 120 percent for 2013, 110 percent for 2014, and 105 percent for 2015.
    (iii) High cost state.—The term "high cost State" means each of the 17 States which the Secretary of Health and Human Services, in consultation with the Secretary, estimates had the highest average cost during 2012 for employer-sponsored coverage under health plans. The Secretary's estimate shall be made on the basis of aggregate premiums paid in the State for such health plans, determined using the most recent data available as of August 31, 2012.

• IRC §4980I(d)(1)(B) was amended by Act §1401(a)(4) by redesignating cl. (ii) as cl. (iii) and adding new cl. (ii). Eff. on date of enactment of this Act [Mar. 30, 2010]. *Note:* IRC §4980I is applicable for tax years beginning after Dec. 31, 2017.

• IRC §4980I(d)(3) was added by Act §1401(a)(5). Eff. on date of enactment of this Act [Mar. 30, 2010]. *Note:* IRC §4980I is applicable for tax years beginning after Dec. 31, 2017.

Patient Protection and Affordable Care Act, 2010 (Pub. L. No. 111-148), as follows:

• IRC §4980I was added by Act §9001(a). Eff. for taxable years beginning after Dec. 31, 2012. *Note:* Act §9001(c) was amended by Pub. L. No. 111-152, §1401(b) by striking "2012" and inserting "2017"; thus, extending the effective date of IRC §4980I to Dec. 31, 2017.

• IRC §4980I(f)(3) was amended by Act §10901(a) and (b) by inserting "individuals whose primary work is longshore work (as defined in section 258(b) of the Immigration and Nationality Act (8 U.S.C. 1288(b)), determined without regard to paragraph (2) thereof)," before "and individuals engaged in the construction, mining"; and by striking "section 9832(c)(1)(A)" and inserting "section 9832(c)(1) (other than subparagraph (G) thereof)". Eff. for taxable years beginning after Dec. 31, 2012. *Note:* Act §9001(c) was amended by Pub. L. No. 111-152, §1401(b) by striking "2012" and inserting "2017"; thus, extending the effective date of IRC §4980I to Dec. 31, 2017.

---

* * *

Chapter 45—Provisions Relating to Expatriated Entities

SEC. 4985. STOCK COMPENSATION OF INSIDERS IN EXPATRIATED CORPORATIONS.

(a) Imposition of Tax.—In the case of an individual who is a disqualified individual with respect to any expatriated corporation, there is hereby imposed on such person a tax equal to—

(1) the rate of tax specified in section (h)(1)(C), multiplied by

(2) the value (determined under subsection (b)) of the specified stock compensation held (directly or indirectly) by or for the benefit of such individual or a member of such individual's family (as defined in section 267) at any time during the 12-month period beginning on the date which is 6 months before the expatriation date.

(b) Value.—For purposes of subsection (a)—

(1) In general.—The value of specified stock compensation shall be—

(A) in the case of a stock option (or other similar right) or a stock appreciation right, the fair value of such option or right, and

(B) in any other case, the fair market value of such compensation.

(2) Date for determining value.—The determination of value shall be made—

(A) in the case of specified stock compensation held on the expatriation date, on such date,

(B) in the case of such compensation which is canceled during the 6 months before the expatriation date, on the day before such cancellation, and

(C) in the case of such compensation which is granted after the expatriation date, on the date such compensation is granted.

(c) Tax to Apply Only If Shareholder Gain Recognized.—Subsection (a) shall apply to any disqualified individual with respect to an expatriated corporation only if gain (if any) on any stock in such corporation is recognized in whole or part by any shareholder by reason of the acquisition referred to in section 7874(a)(2)(B)(i) with respect to such corporation.

(d) Exception Where Gain Recognized on Compensation.—Subsection (a) shall not apply to—

(1) any stock option which is exercised on the expatriation date or during the 6-month period before such date and to the stock acquired in such exercise, if income is recognized under section 83 on or before the expatriation date with respect to the stock acquired pursuant to such exercise, and

(2) any other specified stock compensation which is exercised, sold, exchanged, distributed, cashed-out, or otherwise paid during such period in a transaction in which income, gain, or loss is recognized in full.

(e) Definitions.—For purposes of this section—

(1) Disqualified individual.—The term "disqualified individual" means, with respect to a corporation, any individual who, at any time during the 12-month period beginning on the date which is 6 months before the expatriation date—

(A) is subject to the requirements of section 16(a) of the Securities Exchange Act of 1934 with respect to such corporation or any member of the expanded affiliated group which includes such corporation, or

(B) would be subject to such requirements if such corporation or member were an issuer of equity securities referred to in such section.

(2) Expatriated corporation; expatriation date.—

(A) Expatriated corporation.—The term "expatriated corporation" means any corporation which is an expatriated entity (as defined in section 7874(a)(2)). Such term includes any predecessor or successor of such a corporation.

(B) Expatriation date.—The term "expatriation date" means, with respect to a corporation, the date on which the corporation first becomes an expatriated corporation.

(3) Specified stock compensation.—

(A) In general.—The term "specified stock compensation" means payment (or right to payment) granted by the expatriated corporation (or by any member of the expanded affiliated group which includes such corporation) to any person in connection with the performance of services by a disqualified individual for such corporation or member if the value of such payment or right is based on (or determined by reference to) the value (or change in value) of stock in such corporation (or any such member).

(B) Exceptions.—Such term shall not include—

(i) any option to which part II of subchapter D of chapter 1 applies, or

(ii) any payment or right to payment from a plan referred to in section 280G(b)(6).

(4) Expanded affiliated group.—The term "expanded affiliated group" means an affiliated group (as defined in section 1504(a) without regard to section 1504(b)(3)); except that section 1504(a) shall be applied by substituting "more than 50 percent" for "at least 80 percent" each place it appears.

(f) Special Rules.—For purposes of this section—

(1) Cancellation of restriction.—The cancellation of a restriction which by its terms will never lapse shall be treated as a grant.

(2) Payment or reimbursement of tax by corporation treated as specified stock compensation.—Any payment of the tax imposed by this section directly or indirectly by the expatriated corporation or by any member of the expanded affiliated group which includes such corporation—

(A) shall be treated as specified stock compensation, and

(B) shall not be allowed as a deduction under any provision of chapter 1.

IRC Sec. 4985(f)(2)(B)

(3) Certain restrictions ignored.—Whether there is specified stock compensation, and the value thereof, shall be determined without regard to any restriction other than a restriction which by its terms will never lapse.

(4) Property transfers.—Any transfer of property shall be treated as a payment and any right to a transfer of property shall be treated as a right to a payment.

(5) Other administrative provisions.—For purposes of subtitle F, any tax imposed by this section shall be treated as a tax imposed by subtitle A.

(g) Regulations.—The Secretary shall prescribe such regulations as may be necessary or appropriate to carry out the purposes of this section.

Amendments to IRC §4985

American Jobs Creation Act of 2004 (Pub. L. No. 108-357), as follows:
- IRC §4985 was added by Act §802(a). Eff. Mar. 3, 2003, except that periods before such date shall not be taken into account in applying the periods in IRC §4985(a) and (e)(1).

---

* * *

Chapter 46—Golden Parachute Payments

SEC. 4999. GOLDEN PARACHUTE PAYMENTS.

(a) Imposition of Tax. There is hereby imposed on any person who receives an excess parachute payment a tax equal to 20 percent of the amount of such payment.

(b) Excess Parachute Payment Defined. For purposes of this section, the term "excess parachute payment" has the meaning given to such term by section 280G(b).

(c) Administrative Provisions.

(1) Withholding. In the case of any excess parachute payment which is wages (within the meaning of section 3401) the amount deducted and withheld under section 3402 shall be increased by the amount of the tax imposed by this section on such payment.

(2) Other administrative provisions. For purposes of subtitle F, any tax imposed by this section shall be treated as a tax imposed by subtitle A.

Chapter 47—Certain Group Health Plans

SEC. 5000. CERTAIN GROUP HEALTH PLANS.

(a) Imposition of Tax.—There is hereby imposed on any employer (including a self-employed person) or employee organization that contributes to a nonconforming group health plan a tax equal to 25 percent of the employer's or employee organization's expenses incurred during the calendar year for each group health plan to which the employer (including a self-employed person) or employee organization contributes.

(b) Group Health Plan and Large Group Health Plan.—For purposes of this section—

(1) Group health plan.—The term "group health plan" means a plan (including a self-insured plan) of, or contributed to by, an employer (including a self-employed person) or employee organization to provide health care (directly or otherwise) to the employees, former employees, the employer, others associated with the employer in a business relationship, or their families.

(2) Large group health plan.—The term "large group health plan" means a plan of, or contributed to by, an employer or employee organization (including a self-insured plan) to provide health care (directly or otherwise) to the employees, former employees, the employer, others associated or formerly associated with the employer in a business relationship, or their families, that covers employees of at least one employer that normally employed at least 100 employees on a typical business day during the previous calendar year. For purposes of the preceding sentence—

(A) all employers treated as a single employer under subsection (a) or (b) of section 52 shall be treated as a single employer.

(B) all employees of the members of an affiliated service group (as defined in section 414(m)) shall be treated as employed by a single employer, and

(C) leased employees (as defined in section 414(n)(2)) shall be treated as employees of the person for whom they perform services to the extent they are so treated under section 414(n).

(c) Nonconforming Group Health Plan.—For purposes of this section, the term "nonconforming group health plan" means a group health plan or large group health plan that at any time during a calendar year does not comply with the requirements of subparagraphs (A) and (C) or subparagraph (B), respectively, of paragraph (1), or with the requirements of paragraph (2), of section 1862(b) of the Social Security Act.

(d) Government Entities.—For purposes of this section, the term "employer" does not include a Federal or other governmental entity.

Chapter 48—Maintenance of Minimum Essential Coverage

Editor's Note

Caution: IRC §5000A, below, added by Pub. L. No. 111-148, §1501, and amended by Pub. L. No. 111-148, §10106(b), Pub. L. No. 111-152, §§1002 and 1004, and Pub. L. No. 111-159, §2, is effective for taxable years ending after December 31, 2013.

SEC. 5000A. REQUIREMENT TO MAINTAIN MINIMUM ESSENTIAL COVERAGE.

(a) Requirement To Maintain Minimum Essential Coverage.—An applicable individual shall for each month beginning after 2013 ensure that the individual, and any dependent of the individual who is an applicable individual, is covered under minimum essential coverage for such month.

(b) Shared Responsibility Payment.—

(1) In general.—If a taxpayer who is an applicable individual, or an applicable individual for whom the taxpayer is liable under paragraph (3), fails to meet the requirement of subsection (a) for 1 or more months, then, except as provided in subsection (e), there is hereby imposed on the taxpayer a penalty with respect to such failures in the amount determined under subsection (c).

(2) Inclusion with return.—Any penalty imposed by this section with respect to any month shall be included with a taxpayer's return under chapter 1 for the taxable year which includes such month.

(3) Payment of penalty.—If an individual with respect to whom a penalty is imposed by this section for any month—

(A) is a dependent (as defined in section 152) of another taxpayer for the other taxpayer's taxable year including such month, such other taxpayer shall be liable for such penalty, or

(B) files a joint return for the taxable year including such month, such individual and the spouse of such individual shall be jointly liable for such penalty.

(c) Amount of Penalty.—

(1) In general.—The amount of the penalty imposed by this section on any taxpayer for any taxable year with respect to failures described in subsection (b)(1) shall be equal to the lesser of—

(A) the sum of the monthly penalty amounts determined under paragraph (2) for months in the taxable year during which 1 or more such failures occurred, or

(B) an amount equal to the national average premium for qualified health plans which have a bronze level of coverage, provide coverage for the applicable family size involved, and are offered through Exchanges for plan years beginning in the calendar year with or within which the taxable year ends.

(2) Monthly penalty amounts.—For purposes of paragraph (1)(A), the monthly penalty amount with respect to any taxpayer for any month during which any failure described in subsection (b)(1) occurred is an amount equal to of the greater of the following amounts:

(A) Flat dollar amounts.—An amount equal to the lesser of—

(i) the sum of the applicable dollar amounts for all individuals with respect to whom such failure occurred during such month, or

(ii) 300 percent of the applicable dollar amount (determined without regard to paragraph (3)(C)) for the calendar year with or within which the taxable year ends.

(B) Percentage of income.—An amount equal to the following percentage of the excess of the taxpayer's household income for the taxable year over the amount of gross income specified in section 6012(a)(1) with respect to the taxpayer for the taxable year:

(i) 1.0 percent for taxable years beginning in 2014.

(ii) 2.0 percent for taxable years beginning in 2015.

(iii) 2.5 percent for taxable years beginning after 2015.

(3) Applicable dollar amount.—For purposes of paragraph (1)—

(A) In general.—Except as provided in subparagraphs (B) and (C), the applicable dollar amount is $695.

(B) Phase in.—The applicable dollar amount is $95 for 2014 and $325 for 2015.

(C) Special rule for individuals under age 18.—If an applicable individual has not attained the age of 18 as of the beginning of a month, the applicable dollar amount with respect to such individual for the month shall be equal to one-half of the applicable dollar amount for the calendar year in which the month occurs.

(D) Indexing of amount.—In the case of any calendar year beginning after 2016, the applicable dollar amount shall be equal to $695, increased by an amount equal to—

(i) $695, multiplied by

(ii) the cost-of-living adjustment determined under section 1(f)(3) for the calendar year, determined by substituting "calendar year 2015" for "calendar year 1992" in subparagraph (B) thereof.

If the amount of any increase under clause (i) is not a multiple of $50, such increase shall be rounded to the next lowest multiple of $50.

(4) Terms Relating To Income and Families.— For purposes of this section—

(A) Family size.—The family size involved with respect to any taxpayer shall be equal to the number of individuals for whom the taxpayer is allowed a deduction under section 151 (relating to allowance of deduction for personal exemptions) for the taxable year.

(B) Household income.—The term "household income" means, with respect to any taxpayer for any taxable year, an amount equal to the sum of—

(i) the modified adjusted gross income of the taxpayer, plus

(ii) the aggregate modified adjusted gross incomes of all other individuals who—

(I) were taken into account in determining the taxpayer's family size under paragraph (1), and

(II) were required to file a return.

(C) Modified adjusted gross income.—The term "modified adjusted gross income" means adjusted gross income increased by—

(i) any amount excluded from gross income under section 911, and

(ii) any amount of interest received or accrued by the taxpayer during the taxable year which is exempt from tax.

(d) Applicable Individual.—For purposes of this section—

(1) In general.—The term "applicable individual" means, with respect to any month, an individual other than an individual described in paragraph (2), (3), or (4).

(2) Religious exemptions.—

(A) Religious conscience exemption.—Such term shall not include any individual for any month if such individual has in effect an exemption under section 1311(d)(4)(H) of the Patient Protection and Affordable Care Act which certifies that such individual is—

(i) a member of a recognized religious sect or division thereof which is described in section 1402(g)(1), and

(ii) an adherent of established tenets or teachings of such sect or division as described in such section.

(B) Health care sharing ministry.—

(i) In general.—Such term shall not include any individual for any month if such individual is a member of a health care sharing ministry for the month.

(ii) Health care sharing ministry.—The term "health care sharing ministry" means an organization—

(I) which is described in section 501(c)(3) and is exempt from taxation under section 501(a),

(II) members of which share a common set of ethical or religious beliefs and share medical expenses among members in accordance with those beliefs and without regard to the State in which a member resides or is employed,

(III) members of which retain membership even after they develop a medical condition,

(IV) which (or a predecessor of which) has been in existence at all times since December 31, 1999, and medical expenses of its members have been shared continuously and without interruption since at least December 31, 1999, and

(V) which conducts an annual audit which is performed by an independent certified public accounting firm in accordance with generally accepted accounting principles and which is made available to the public upon request.

(3) Individuals not lawfully present.—Such term shall not include an individual for any month if for the month the individual is not a citizen or national of the United States or an alien lawfully present in the United States.

(4) Incarcerated individuals.—Such term shall not include an individual for any month if for the month the individual is incarcerated, other than incarceration pending the disposition of charges.

(e) Exemptions.—No penalty shall be imposed under subsection (a) with respect to—

(1) Individuals who cannot afford coverage.—

(A) In general.—Any applicable individual for any month if the applicable individual's required contribution (determined on an annual basis) for coverage for the month exceeds 8 percent of such individual's household income for the taxable year described in section 1412(b)(1)(B) of the Patient Protection and Affordable Care Act. For purposes of applying this subparagraph, the taxpayer's household income shall be increased by any exclusion from gross income for any portion of the required contribution made through a salary reduction arrangement.

(B) Required contribution.—For purposes of this paragraph, the term "required contribution" means—

(i) in the case of an individual eligible to purchase minimum essential coverage consisting of coverage through an eligible-employer-sponsored plan, the portion of the annual premium which would be paid by the individual (without regard to whether paid through salary reduction or otherwise) for self-only coverage, or

(ii) in the case of an individual eligible only to purchase minimum essential coverage described in subsection (f)(1)(C), the annual premium for the lowest cost bronze plan available in the individual market through the Exchange in the State in the rating area in which the individual resides (without regard to whether the individual purchased a qualified health plan through the Exchange), reduced by the amount of the credit allowable under section 36B for the taxable year (determined as if the individual was covered by a qualified health plan offered through the Exchange for the entire taxable year).

(C) Special rules for individuals related to employees.—For purposes of subparagraph (B)(i), if an applicable individual is eligible for minimum essential coverage through an employer by reason of a relationship to an employee, the determination under subparagraph (A) shall be made by reference to required contribution of the employee.

(D) Indexing.—In the case of plan years beginning in any calendar year after 2014, subparagraph (A) shall be applied by substituting for "8 percent" the percentage the Secretary of Health and Human Services determines reflects the excess of the rate of premium growth between the preceding calendar year and 2013 over the rate of income growth for such period.

(2) **Taxpayers with income below filing threshold.**—Any applicable individual for any month during a calendar year if the individual's household income for the taxable year described in section 1412(b)(1)(B) of the Patient Protection and Affordable Care Act is the amount of gross income specified in section 6012(a)(1) with respect to the taxpayer.

(3) **Members of Indian tribes.**—Any applicable individual for any month during which the individual is a member of an Indian tribe (as defined in section 45A(c)(6)).

(4) **Months during short coverage gaps.**—

(A) In general.—Any month the last day of which occurred during a period in which the applicable individual was not covered by minimum essential coverage for a continuous period of less than 3 months.

(B) Special rules.—For purposes of applying this paragraph—

(i) the length of a continuous period shall be determined without regard to the calendar years in which months in such period occur,

(ii) if a continuous period is greater than the period allowed under subparagraph (A), no exception shall be provided under this paragraph for any month in the period, and

(iii) if there is more than 1 continuous period described in subparagraph (A) covering months in a calendar year, the exception provided by this paragraph shall only apply to months in the first of such periods.

The Secretary shall prescribe rules for the collection of the penalty imposed by this section in cases where continuous periods include months in more than 1 taxable year.

(5) **Hardships.**—Any applicable individual who for any month is determined by the Secretary of Health and Human Services under section 1311(d)(4)(H) to have suffered a hardship with respect to the capability to obtain coverage under a qualified health plan.

(f) **Minimum Essential Coverage.**—For purposes of this section—

(1) **In general.**—The term "minimum essential coverage" means any of the following:

(A) Government sponsored programs.—Coverage under—

(i) the Medicare program under part A of title XVIII of the Social Security Act,

(ii) the Medicaid program under title XIX of the Social Security Act,

(iii) the CHIP program under title XXI of the Social Security Act,

(iv) medical coverage under chapter 55 of title 10, United States Code, including coverage under the TRICARE program;

(v) a health care program under chapter 17 or 18 of title 38, United States Code, as determined by the Secretary of Veterans Affairs, in coordination with the Secretary of Health and Human Services and the Secretary,

(vi) a health plan under section 2504(e) of title 22, United States Code (relating to Peace Corps volunteers); or

(vii) the Nonappropriated Fund Health Benefits Program of the Department of Defense, established under section 349 of the National Defense Authorization Act for Fiscal Year 1995 (Public Law 103-337; 10 U.S.C. 1587 note).

(B) Employer-sponsored plan.—Coverage under an eligible employer-sponsored plan.

(C) Plans in the individual market.—Coverage under a health plan offered in the individual market within a State.

(D) Grandfathered health plan.—Coverage under a grandfathered health plan.

(E) Other coverage.—Such other health benefits coverage, such as a State health benefits risk pool,

IRC Sec. 5000A(f)(1)(E)

as the Secretary of Health and Human Services, in coordination with the Secretary, recognizes for purposes of this subsection.

(2) Eligible employer-sponsored plan.—The term "eligible employer-sponsored plan" means, with respect to any employee, a group health plan or group health insurance coverage offered by an employer to the employee which is—

(A) a governmental plan (within the meaning of section 2791(d)(8) of the Public Health Service Act), or

(B) any other plan or coverage offered in the small or large group market within a State.

Such term shall include a grandfathered health plan described in paragraph (1)(D) offered in a group market.

(3) Excepted benefits not treated as minimum essential coverage.—The term "minimum essential coverage" shall not include health insurance coverage which consists of coverage of excepted benefits—

(A) described in paragraph (1) of subsection (c) of section 2791 of the Public Health Service Act; or

(B) described in paragraph (2), (3), or (4) of such subsection if the benefits are provided under a separate policy, certificate, or contract of insurance.

(4) Individuals residing outside United States or residents of territories.—Any applicable individual shall be treated as having minimum essential coverage for any month—

(A) if such month occurs during any period described in subparagraph (A) or (B) of section 911(d)(1) which is applicable to the individual, or

(B) if such individual is a bona fide resident of any possession of the United States (as determined under section 937(a)) for such month.

(5) Insurance-related terms.—Any term used in this section which is also used in title I of the Patient Protection and Affordable Care Act shall have the same meaning as when used in such title.

(g) Administration and Procedure.—

(1) In general.—The penalty provided by this section shall be paid upon notice and demand by the Secretary, and except as provided in paragraph (2), shall be assessed and collected in the same manner as an assessable penalty under subchapter B of chapter 68.

(2) Special rules.—Notwithstanding any other provision of law—

(A) Waiver of criminal penalties.—In the case of any failure by a taxpayer to timely pay any penalty imposed by this section, such taxpayer shall not be subject to any criminal prosecution or penalty with respect to such failure.

(B) Limitations on liens and levies.—The Secretary shall not—

(i) file notice of lien with respect to any property of a taxpayer by reason of any failure to pay the penalty imposed by this section, or

(ii) levy on any such property with respect to such failure.

Amendments to §5000A

Pub. L. No. 111-173, 2010, as follows:

● IRC §5000A(f)(1)(A)(v) was amended by Act §1(a). Eff. as if included in §1501(b) of Pub. L. No. 111-148. IRC §5000A(f)(1)(A)(v) prior to amendment:

(v) the veteran's health care program under chapter 17 of title 38, United States Code;

TRICARE Affirmation Act, 2010 (Pub. L. No. 111-159), as follows:

● IRC §5000A(f)(1)(A) was amended by Act §2(a) by striking cl. (iv) and inserting new cl. (iv); striking "or" at the end of clause (v); substituting "; or" for the period at the end of cl. (vi); and adding cl. (vii). Eff. as if included in Pub. L. No. 111-148, §1501(b), and shall be executed immediately after the amendments made by such section. IRC §5000A(f)(1)(A)(iv) prior to being struck:

(iv) the TRICARE for Life program,.

Health Care and Education Reconciliation Act of 2010 (Pub. L. No. 111-152), as follows:

● IRC §5000A(c)(2)(B) was amended by Act §1002(a)(1)(A) by inserting "the excess of" before "the taxpayer's household income"; and inserting "for the taxable year over the amount of gross income specified in section 6012(a)(1) with respect to the taxpayer" before "for the taxable year" in the matter preceding clause (i). Eff. on date of enactment of this Act [enacted: Mar. 30, 2010].

● IRC §5000A(c)(2)(B)(i) was amended by Act §1002(a)(1)(B) by substituting "1.0" for "0.5". Eff. on date of enactment of this Act [enacted: Mar. 30, 2010].

● IRC §5000A(c)(2)(B)(ii) was amended by Act §1002(a)(1)(C) by substituting "2.0" for "1.0". Eff. on date of enactment of this Act [enacted: Mar. 30, 2010].

● IRC §5000A(c)(2)(B)(iii) was amended by Act §1002(a)(1)(D) by substituting "2.5" for "2.0". Eff. on date of enactment of this Act [enacted: Mar. 30, 2010].

● IRC §5000A(c)(3)(A) was amended by Act §1002(a)(2)(A) by substituting "$695" for "$750". Eff. on date of enactment of this Act [enacted: Mar. 30, 2010].

● IRC §5000A(c)(3)(B) was amended by Act §1002(a)(2)(B) by substituting "$325" for "$495". Eff. on date of enactment of this Act [enacted: Mar. 30, 2010].

● IRC §5000A(c)(3)(D) was amended by Act §1002(a)(2)(C) by substituting "$695" for "$750" in the matter preceding cl. (i) and in cl. (i). Eff. on date of enactment of this Act [enacted: Mar. 30, 2010].

● IRC §5000A(c)(4)[B](i) was amended by Act §1004(a)(1)(C) by substituting "modified adjusted gross" for "modified gross". Eff. on date of enactment of this Act [enacted: Mar. 30, 2010].

● IRC §5000A(c)(4)[B](ii) was amended by Act §1004(a)(1)(C) by substituting "modified adjusted gross" for "modified gross". Eff. on date of enactment of this Act [enacted: Mar. 30, 2010].

● IRC §5000A(c)(4)(C) was amended by Act §1004(a)(2)(B). Eff. on date of enactment of this Act [enacted: Mar. 30, 2010]. IRC §5000A(c)(4)(C) prior to amendment:

(C) Modified Gross Income.—The term "modified gross income" means gross income—

(i) decreased by the amount of any deduction allowable under paragraph (1), (3), (4), or (10) of section 62(a),

(ii) increased by the amount of interest received or accrued during the taxable year which is exempt from tax imposed by this chapter, and

(iii) determined without regard to sections 911, 931, and 933.

- IRC §5000A(c)(4)(D) was amended by Act §1002(b)(1). Eff. on date of enactment of this Act [enacted: Mar. 30, 2010]. IRC §5000A(c)(4)(D) prior to being struck:

  (D) Poverty Line.—

  (i) In General.—The term "poverty line" has the meaning given that term in section 2110(c)(5) of the Social Security Act (42 U.S.C. 1397jj(c)(5)).

  (ii) Poverty Line Use.—In the case of any taxable year ending with or within a calendar year, the poverty line used shall be the most recently published poverty line as of the 1st day of such calendar year.

- IRC §5000A(e)(2) was amended by Act §1002(b)(2) by substituting "Below Filing Threshold" for "Under 100 Percent Of Poverty Line"; and substituting "the amount of gross income specified in section 6012(a)(1) with respect to the taxpayer." for "less than 100 percent of the poverty line for the size of the family involved (determined in the same manner as under subsection (b)(4)).". Eff. on date of enactment of this Act [enacted: Mar. 30, 2010].

Patient Protection and Affordable Care Act, 2010 (Pub. L. No. 111-148), as follows:

- IRC §5000A was added by Act §1501(b). Eff. for taxable years ending after Dec. 31, 2013.

- IRC §5000A(b)(1) was amended by Act §10106(b)(1). Eff. for taxable years ending after Dec. 31, 2013. IRC §5000A(b)(1) prior to amendment:

  (1) In general.—If an applicable individual fails to meet the requirement of subsection (a) for 1 or more months during any calendar year beginning after 2013, then, except as provided in subsection (d), there is hereby imposed a penalty with respect to the individual in the amount determined under subsection (c).

- IRC §5000A(c)(1)–(2) were amended by Act §10106(b)(2). Eff. for taxable years ending after Dec. 31, 2013. IRC §5000A(c)(1)–(2) prior to amendment:

  (c) **Amount of Penalty**—

  (1) In general.—The penalty determined under this subsection for any month with respect to any individual is an amount equal to 1/12 of the applicable dollar amount for the calendar year.

  (2) Dollar limitation.—The amount of the penalty imposed by this section on any taxpayer for any taxable year with respect to all individuals for whom the taxpayer is liable under subsection (b)(3) shall not exceed an amount equal to 300 percent the applicable dollar amount (determined without regard to paragraph (3)(C)) for the calendar year with or within which the taxable year ends.

- IRC §5000A(e)(1)(C) was amended by Act §10106(d). Eff. for taxable years ending after Dec. 31, 2013. IRC §5000A(e)(1)(C) prior to amendment:

  (C) Special rules for individuals related to employees.—For purposes of subparagraph (B)(i), if an applicable individual is eligible for minimum essential coverage through an employer by reason of a relationship to an employee, the determination shall be made by reference to the affordability of the coverage to the employee.

---

* * *

Subtitle F—Procedure and Administration

Chapter 61—Information and Returns

Subchapter A—Returns and Records
* * *

Part III—Information Returns

Subpart A—Information Concerning Persons Subject to Special Provisions
* * *

SEC. 6039. RETURNS REQUIRED IN CONNECTION WITH CERTAIN OPTIONS.

(a) **Requirement of reporting.** Every corporation—

(1) which in any calendar year transfers to any person a share of stock pursuant to such person's exercise of an incentive stock option, or

(2) which in any calendar year records (or has by its agent recorded) a transfer of the legal title of a share of stock acquired by the transferor pursuant to his exercise of an option described in section 423(c) (relating to special rule where option price is between 85 percent and 100 percent of value of stock),

shall, for such calendar year, make a return at such time and in such manner, and setting forth such information, as the Secretary may be regulations prescribe.

(b) **Statements to be furnished to persons with respect to whom information is reported.**—Every corporation making a return under subsection (a) shall furnish to each person whose name is set forth in such return a written statement setting forth such information as the Secretary may by regulations prescribe. The written statement required under the preceding sentence shall be furnished to such person on or before January 31 of the year following the calendar year for which the return under subsection (a) was made.

(c) **Special Rules.**—For purposes of this section—

(1) **Treatment by employer to be determinative.**—Any option which the corporation treats as an incentive stock option, or an option granted under an employee stock purchase plan shall be deemed to be such an option.

(2) **Subsection (a)(2) applies only to first transfer described therein.**—A statement is required by reason of a transfer described in subsection (a)(2) of a share only with respect to the first transfer of such share by the person who exercised the option.

(3) **Identification of stock.**—Any corporation which transfers any share of stock pursuant to the exercise of any option described in subsection (a)(2) shall identify such stock in a manner adequate to carry out the purposes of this section.

(d) **Cross references.** For definition of—

(1) the term "incentive stock option", see section 422(b).

(2) the term "employee stock purchase plan", see section 423(b).

IRC Sec. 6039(d)(2)

Recent Amendments to §6039

Tax Relief and Health Care Act of 2006 (Pub. L. No. 109-432), as follows:
- IRC §6039, heading, was amended by Act §403(c)(3) by substituting "Returns" for "Information". Eff. for calendar years beginning after the date of the enactment [Enacted: Dec. 20, 2006].
- IRC §6039(a), heading, was amended by Act §403(c)(4) by substituting "Requirement of Reporting" for "Furnishing of Information". Eff. for calendar years beginning after the date of the enactment [Enacted: Dec. 20, 2006].
- IRC §6039(a) was amended by Act §403(a) by amending the material following para. (2), which read as follows prior to amendment: "shall (on or before January 31 of the following calendar year) furnish to such person a written statement in such manner and setting forth such information as the Secretary may by regulations prescribe." Eff. for calendar years beginning after the date of the enactment [Enacted: Dec. 20, 2006].
- IRC §6039(b)–(d) were amended by Act §403(b) by redesignating subsecs. (b)–(c) as subsecs. (c)–(d), respectively, and adding new subsec. (b). Eff. for calendar years beginning after the date of the enactment [Enacted: Dec. 20, 2006].

* * *

SEC. 6039D. RETURNS AND RECORDS WITH RESPECT TO CERTAIN FRINGE BENEFIT PLANS.

(a) In General.—Every employer maintaining a specified fringe benefit plan during any year beginning after December 31, 1984, for any portion of which the applicable exclusion applies, shall file a return (at such time and in such manner as the Secretary shall by regulations prescribe) with respect to such plan showing for such year—

(1) the number of employees of the employer,

(2) the number of employees of the employer eligible to participate under the plan,

(3) the number of employees participating under the plan,

(4) the total cost of the plan during the year,

(5) the name, address, and taxpayer identification number of the employer and the type of business in which the employer is engaged, and

(6) the number of highly compensated employees among the employees described in paragraphs (1), (2), and (3).

(b) Recordkeeping Requirement.—Each employer maintaining a specified fringe benefit plan during any year shall keep such records as may be necessary for purposes of determining whether the requirements of the applicable exclusion are met.

(c) Additional Information When Required by the Secretary.—Any employer—

(1) who maintains a specified fringe benefit plan during any year for which a return is required under subsection (a), and

(2) who is required by the Secretary to file an additional return for such year,

shall file such additional return. Such additional return shall be filed at such time and in such manner as the Secretary shall prescribe and shall contain such information as the Secretary shall prescribe. The Secretary may require returns under this subsection only from a representative group of employers.

(d) Definitions and Special Rules.—For purposes of this section.—

(1) Specified fringe benefit plan.—The term "specified fringe benefit plan" means any plan under section 79, 105, 106, 120, 125, 127, 129, or 137.

(2) Applicable exclusion.—The term "applicable exclusion" means, with respect to any specified fringe benefit plan, the section specified under paragraph (1) under which benefits under such plan are excludable from gross income.

(3) Special rule for multiemployer plans.—In the case of a multiemployer plan, the plan shall be required to provide any information required by this section which the Secretary determines, on the basis of the agreement between the plan and employer, is held by the plan (and not the employer).

* * *

SEC. 6039I. RETURNS AND RECORDS WITH RESPECT TO EMPLOYER-OWNED LIFE INSURANCE CONTRACTS.

(a) In General.—Every applicable policyholder owning 1 or more employer-owned life insurance contracts issued after the date of the enactment of this section shall file a return (at such time and in such manner as the Secretary shall by regulations prescribe) showing for each year such contracts are owned—

(1) the number of employees of the applicable policyholder at the end of the year,

(2) the number of such employees insured under such contracts at the end of the year,

(3) the total amount of insurance in force at the end of the year under such contracts,

(4) the name, address, and taxpayer identification number of the applicable policyholder and the type of business in which the policyholder is engaged, and

(5) that the applicable policyholder has a valid consent for each insured employee (or, if all such consents are not obtained, the number of insured employees for whom such consent was not obtained).

(b) Recordkeeping Requirement.—Each applicable policyholder owning 1 or more employer-owned life insurance contracts during any year shall keep such records as may be necessary for purposes of determining whether the requirements of this section and section 101(j) are met.

(c) Definitions.—Any term used in this section which is used in section 101(j) shall have the same meaning given such term by section 101(j).

Amendments to IRC §6039I

Pension Protection Act of 2006 (Pub. L. No. 109-280), as follows:

• IRC §6039I was added by Act §863(b). Eff. for life insurance contracts issued after Aug. 17, 2006, except for a contract issued after such date pursuant to an IRC §1035 exchange for a contract issued on or prior to that date. Any material increase in the death benefit or other material change shall cause the contract to be treated as a new contract except that, in the case of a master contract (within the meaning of IRC §264(f)(4)(E)), the addition of covered lives shall be treated as a new contract only with respect to such additional covered lives.

* * *

Subpart B—Information Concerning Transactions With Other Persons

SEC. 6041. INFORMATION AT SOURCE.

> ### Editor's Note
> IRC §6041(a), as follows, was amended by Pub. L. No. 112-9, effective for payments made after December 31, 2011.

(a) Payments of $600 or More.—All persons engaged in a trade or business and making payment in the course of such trade or business to another person, of rent, salaries, wages, ~~amounts in consideration for property~~, premiums, annuities, compensations, remunerations, emoluments, or other ~~gross proceeds,~~ fixed or determinable gains, profits, and income (other than payments to which section 6042(a)(1), 6044(a)(1), 6047(e)[d], 6049(a), or 6050N(a) applies, and other than payments with respect to which a statement is required under the authority of section 6042(a)(2), 6044(a)(2), or 6045), or $600 or more in any taxable year, or, in the case of such payments made by the United States, the officers or employees of the United States having information as to such payments and required to make returns in regard thereto by the regulations hereinafter provided for, shall render a true and accurate return to the Secretary, under such regulations and in such form and manner and to such extent as may be prescribed by the Secretary, setting forth the amount of such ~~gross proceeds,~~ gains, profits, and income, and the name and address of the recipient of such payment.

(b) Collection of Foreign Items.—In the case of collections of items (not payable in the United States) of interest upon the bonds of foreign countries and interest upon the bonds of and dividends from foreign corporations by any person undertaking as a matter of business or for profit the collection of foreign payments of such interest or dividends by means of coupons, checks, or bills of exchange, such person shall make a return according to the forms or regulations prescribed by the Secretary, setting forth the amount paid and the name and address of the recipient of each such payment.

(c) Recipient to Furnish Name and Address.—When necessary to make effective the provisions of this section, the name and address of the recipient of income shall be furnished upon demand of the person paying the income.

(d) Statements to Be Furnished to Persons With Respect to Whom Information Is Required.—Every person required to make a return under subsection (a) shall furnish to each person with respect to whom such a return is required a written statement showing—

(1) the name, address, and phone number of the information contact of the person required to make such return, and

(2) the aggregate amount of payments to the person required to be shown on the return.

The written statement required under the preceding sentence shall be furnished to the person on or before January 31 of the year following the calendar year for which the return under subsection (a) was required to be made. To the extent provided in regulations prescribed by the Secretary, this subsection shall also apply to persons required to make returns under subsection (b).

(e) Section Does Not Apply to Certain Tips.—This section shall not apply to tips with respect to which section 6053(a) (relating to reporting of tips) applies.

(f) Section Does Not Apply to Certain Health Arrangements.—This section shall not apply to any payment for medical care (as defined in section 213(d)) made under—

(1) a flexible spending arrangement (as defined in section 106(c)(2)), or

(2) a health reimbursement arrangement which is treated as employer-provided coverage under an accident or health plan for purposes of section 106.

(g) Nonqualified Deferred Compensation.—Subsection (a) shall apply to—

(1) any deferrals for the year under a nonqualified deferred compensation plan (within the meaning of section 409A(d)), whether or not paid, except that this paragraph shall not apply to deferrals which are required to be reported under section 6051(a)(13) (without regard to any de minimis exception), and

(2) any amount includible under section 409A and which is not treated as wages under §3401(a).

IRC Sec. 6041(g)(2)

Editor's Note

Caution: Former IRC §6041(h), below, was added by Pub. L. No. 111-240 to be applicable to payments made after December 31, 2010, and stricken by Pub. L. No. 112-9, applicable to payments made after December 31, 2010.

(h) Treatment of Rental Property Expense Payments [Stricken].—

　　(1) In general.—Solely for purposes of subsection (a) and except as provided in paragraph (2), a person receiving rental income from real estate shall be considered to be engaged in a trade or business of renting property.

　　(2) Exceptions.—Paragraph (1) shall not apply to—

　　(A) any individual, including any individual who is an active member of the uniformed services or an employee of the intelligence community (as defined in section 121(d)(9)(C)(iv)), if substantially all rental income is derived from renting the principal residence (within the meaning of section 121) of such individual on a temporary basis,

　　(B) any individual who receives rental income of not more than the minimal amount, as determined under regulations prescribed by the Secretary, and

　　(C) any other individual for whom the requirements of this section would cause hardship, as determined under regulations prescribed by the Secretary.

Editor's Note

Caution: Former IRC §6041(h) was added by Pub. L. No. 111-148 to be applicable to payments made after December 31, 2011, and redesignated by Pub. L. No. 111-240 as IRC §6041(i), below, to be applicable to payments made after December 31, 2010. IRC §6041(i) was stricken by Pub. L. No. 112-9, applicable to payments made after December 31, 2011.

(i) Application to Corporations [Stricken].—Notwithstanding any regulation prescribed by the Secretary before the date of the enactment of this subsection, for purposes of this section the term "person" includes any corporation that is not an organization exempt from tax under section 501(a).

Editor's Note

Caution: Former IRC §6041(i) was added by Pub. L. No. 111-148 to be applicable to payments made after December 31, 2011, and redesignated by Pub. L. No. 111-240 as IRC §6041(j), below, to be applicable to payments made after December 31, 2010. IRC §6041(j) was stricken by Pub. L. No. 112-9, applicable to payments made after December 31, 2011.

(j) Regulations.—The Secretary may prescribe such regulations and other guidance as may be appropriate or necessary to carry out the purposes of this section, including the rules to prevent duplicative reporting of transactions.

Recent Amendments to IRC §6041

Comprehensive 1099 Taxpayer Protection and Repayment of Exchange Subsidy Overpayments Act of 2011 (Pub. L. No. 112-9), as follows:
- IRC §6041(a) was amended by Act §2(b) by striking "amounts in consideration for property," and by striking "gross proceeds," both places it appears. Eff. for payments made after Dec. 31, 2011.
- IRC §6041(h)–(i) were stricken by Act §9006(a). Eff. for payments made after Dec. 31, 2011.

Patient Protection and Affordable Care Act, 2010 (Pub. L. No. 111-148), as follows:
- IRC §6041(a) was amended by Act §9006(b) by inserting "amounts in consideration for property," after "wages,", by inserting "gross proceeds," after "emoluments, or other", and by inserting "gross proceeds," after "setting forth the amount of such". Eff. for payments made after Dec. 31, 2011.
- IRC §6041(h)–(i) were added by Act §9006(a). Eff. for payments made after Dec. 31, 2011.

American Jobs Creation Act of 2004 (Pub. L. No. 108-357), as follows:
- IRC §6041 was amended by Act §885(b)(3) by adding new subsec. (g). Eff. generally for amounts deferred after Dec. 31, 2004. [*Ed. Note:* see Act §885(d)(2) and (3), (e), and (f) for special rules.]

Medicare Prescription Drug, Improvement, and Modernization Act of 2003 (Pub. L. No. 108-173), as follows:
- IRC §6041 was amended by Act §1203(a) by adding new subsec. (f). Eff. for payments made after Dec. 31, 2002.

---

* * *

SEC. 6047. INFORMATION RELATING TO CERTAIN TRUSTS AND ANNUITY PLANS.

(a) Trustees and Insurance Companies.—The trustee of a trust described in section 401(a) which is exempt from tax under section 501(a) to which contributions have been paid under a plan on behalf of any owner-employee (as defined in section 401(c)(3)), and each insurance company or other person which is the issuer of a contract purchased by such a trust, or purchased under a plan described in section 403(a), contributions for which have been paid on behalf of any owner-employee, shall file such returns (in such form and at such times), keep such records, make such identification of contracts and funds (and accounts within such funds), and supply such information, as the Secretary shall by forms or regulations prescribe.

(b) Owner-Employees.—Every individual on whose behalf contributions have been paid as an owner-employee (as defined in section 401(c)(3))—

(1) to a trust described in section 401(a) which is exempt from tax under section 501(a), or

(2) to an insurance company or other person under a plan described in section 403(a),

shall furnish the trustee, insurance company, or other person, as the case may be, such information at such times and in such form and manner as the Secretary shall prescribe by forms or regulations.

(c) Other Programs.—To the extent provided by regulations prescribed by the Secretary, the provisions of this section apply with respect to any payment described in section 219 and to transaction of any trust described in section 408(a) or under an individual retirement annuity described in section 408(b).

(d) Reports by Employers, Plan Administrators, etc.—

(1) **In general.**—The Secretary shall by forms or regulations require that—

(A) the employer maintaining, or the plan administrator (within the meaning of section 414(g)) of, a plan from which designated distributions (as defined in section 3405(e)(1)) may be made, and

(B) any person issuing any contract under which designated distributions (as so defined) may be made,

make returns and reports regarding such plan (or contract) to the Secretary, to the participants and beneficiaries of such plan (or contract), and to such other persons as the Secretary may by regulations prescribe. No return or report may be required under the preceding sentence with respect to distributions to any person during any year unless such distributions aggregate $10 or more.

(2) **Form, etc., of reports.**—Such reports shall be in such form, made at such time, and contain such information as the Secretary may prescribe by forms or regulations.

(e) Employee Stock Ownership Plans.—The Secretary shall require—

(1) any employer maintaining, or the plan administrator (within the meaning of section 414(g)) of, an employee stock ownership plan which holds stock with respect to which section 404(k) applies to dividends paid on such stock, or

(2) both such employer or plan administrator,

to make returns and reports regarding such plan, transaction, or loan to the Secretary and to such other persons as the Secretary may prescribe. Such returns and reports shall be made in such form, shall be made at such time, and shall contain such information as the Secretary may prescribe.

(f) Designated Roth Contributions.—The Secretary shall require the plan administrator of each applicable retirement plan (as defined in section 402A) to make such returns and reports regarding designated Roth contributions (as defined in section 402A) to the Secretary, participants and beneficiaries of the plan, and such other persons as the Secretary may prescribe.

(g) Cross References.—

(1) For provisions relating to penalties for failure to file a return required by this section, see sections 6652(e), 6721, and 6722.

(2) For criminal penalty for furnishing fraudulent information, see section 7207.

(3) For provisions relating to penalty for failure to comply with the provisions of subsection (d), see section 6704.

Recent Amendments to IRC §6047

Pension Protection Act of 2006 (Pub. L. No. 109-280), as follows:

● **Sunset Provision.** Act §811, provides:
  SEC. 811. PENSIONS AND INDIVIDUAL RETIRE-MENT ARRANGEMENT PROVISIONS OF ECONOMIC GROWTH AND TAX RELIEF RECONCILIATION ACT OF 2001 MADE PERMANENT.
  Title IX of the Economic Growth and Tax Relief Reconciliation Act of 2001 [Pub. L. No. 107-16] shall not apply to the provisions of, and amendments made by, subtitles A through F [§§601–666] of title VI of such Act (relating to pension and individual retirement arrangement provisions).

Economic Growth and Tax Relief Reconciliation Act of 2001 (Pub. L. No. 107-16), as follows:
● IRC §6047 was amended by Act §617(d)(2) by redesignating subsec. (f) as subsec. (g) and adding new subsec.(f). Eff. tax years beginning after Dec. 31, 2005.
● **Sunset Provision.** Act §901, as amended by Pub. L. No. 111-312, §101(a)(1), provides the sunset rule below. But see Pub. L. No. 109-280, §811, and Pub. L. No. 111-148, §10909(c), as amended by Pub. L. No. 111-312, §101(b)(1).
  SEC. 901. SUNSET OF PROVISIONS OF ACT.
  (a) In general. All provisions of, and amendments made by, this Act shall not apply—
  (1) to taxable, plan, or limitation years beginning after December 31, 2012, or
  (2) in the case of title V, to estates of decedents dying, gifts made, or generation skipping transfers, after December 31, 2012.
  (b) Application of certain laws.—The Internal Revenue Code of 1986 and the Employee Retirement Income Security Act of 1974 shall be applied and administered to years, estates, gifts, and transfers described in subsection (a) as if the provisions and amendments described in subsection (a) had never been enacted.

---

* * *

SEC. 6050Q. CERTAIN LONG-TERM CARE BENEFITS.

(a) Requirement of Reporting.—Any person who pays long-term care benefits shall make a return, according to the forms or regulations prescribed by the Secretary, setting forth—

(1) the aggregate amount of such benefits paid by such person to any individual during any calendar year,

(2) whether or not such benefits are paid in whole or in part on a per diem or other periodic basis without regard to the expenses incurred during the period to which the payments relate,

(3) the name, address, and TIN of such individual, and

(4) the name, address, and TIN of the chronically ill or terminally ill individual on account of whose condition such benefits are paid.

(b) Statements to Be Furnished to Persons With Respect to Whom Information Is Required.—Every person required to make a return under subsection (a) shall furnish to each individual whose name, address, and phone number of the information contact is required to be set forth in such return a written statement showing—

(1) the name, address, and phone number of the information contact of the person making the payments, and

(2) the aggregate amount of long-term care benefits paid to the individual which are required to be shown on such return.

The written statement required under the preceding sentence shall be furnished to the individual on or before January 31 of the year following the calendar year for which the return under subsection (a) was required to be made.

(c) Long-Term Care Benefits.—For purposes of this section, the term "long-term care benefit" means—

(1) any payment under a product which is advertised, marketed, or offered as long-term care insurance, and

(2) any payment which is excludable from gross income by reason of section 101(g).

* * *

SEC. 6050T. RETURNS RELATING TO CREDIT FOR HEALTH INSURANCE COSTS OF ELIGIBLE INDIVIDUALS.

(a) Requirement of Reporting.—Every person who is entitled to receive payments for any month of any calendar year under section 7527 (relating to advance payment of credit for health insurance costs of eligible individuals) with respect to any certified individual (as defined in section 7527(c)) shall, at such time as the Secretary may prescribe, make the return described in subsection (b) with respect to each such individual.

(b) Form and Manner of Returns.—A return is described in this subsection if such return—

(1) is in such form as the Secretary may prescribe, and

(2) contains—

(A) the name, address, and TIN of each individual referred to in subsection (a),

(B) the number of months for which amounts were entitled to be received with respect to such individual under section 7527 (relating to advance payment of credit for health insurance costs of eligible individuals),

(C) the amount entitled to be received for each such month, and

(D) such other information as the Secretary may prescribe.

(c) Statements to Be Furnished to Individuals With Respect to Whom Information Is Required.—Every person required to make a return under subsection (a) shall furnish to each individual whose name is required to be set forth in such return a written statement showing—

(1) the name and address of the person required to make such return and the phone number of the information contact for such person, and

(2) the information required to be shown on the return with respect to such individual.

The written statement required under the preceding sentence shall be furnished on or before January 31 of the year following the calendar year for which the return under subsection (a) is required to be made.

Recent Amendments to IRC §6050T

Trade Act of 2002 (Pub. L. No. 107-210), as follows:
● IRC §6050T was added by Act §202(c)(1). Eff. Aug. 6, 2002.

SEC. 6050U. CHARGES OR PAYMENTS FOR QUALIFIED LONG-TERM CARE INSURANCE CONTRACTS UNDER COMBINED ARRANGEMENTS.

(a) Requirement of Reporting.—Any person who makes a charge against the cash value of an annuity contract, or the cash surrender value of a life insurance contract, which is excludible from gross income under section 72(e)(11) shall make a return, according to the forms or regulations prescribed by the Secretary, setting forth—

(1) the amount of the aggregate of such charges against each such contract for the calendar year,

(2) the amount of the reduction in the investment in each such contract by reason of such charges, and

(3) the name, address, and TIN of the individual who is the holder of each such contract.

(b) Statements to be Furnished to Persons With Respect to Whom Information Is Required.—Every person required to make a return under subsection (a) shall furnish to each individual whose name is required to be set forth in such return a written statement showing—

(1) the name, address, and phone number of the information contact of the person making the payments, and

(2) the information required to be shown on the return with respect to such individual.

The written statement required under the preceding sentence shall be furnished to the individual on or before January 31 of the year following the calendar year for which the return under subsection (a) was required to be made.

Amendments to IRC §6050U

Pension Protection Act of 2006 (Pub. L. No. 109-280), as follows:

● IRC §6050U was added by Act §844(d)(1). Eff. for charges made after Dec. 31, 2009.

---

* * *

Subpart C—Information Regarding Wages Paid Employees

SEC. 6051. RECEIPTS FOR EMPLOYEES.

(a) Requirement.—Every person required to deduct and withhold from an employee a tax under section 3101 or 3402, or who would have been required to deduct and withhold a tax under section 3402 (determined without regard to subsection (n)) if the employee had claimed no more than one withholding exemption, or every employer engaged in a trade or business who pays remuneration for services performed by an employee, including the cash value of such remuneration paid in any medium other than cash, shall furnish to each such employee in respect of the remuneration paid by such person to such employee during the calendar year, on or before January 31 of the succeeding year, or, if his employment is terminated before the close of such calendar year, within 30 days after the date of receipt of a written request from the employee if each 30-day period ends before January 31, a written statement showing the following:

(1) the name of such person,

(2) the name of the employee (and his social security account number if wages as defined in section 3121(a) have been paid),

(3) the total amount of wages as defined in section 3401(a),

(4) the total amount deducted and withheld as tax under section 3402,

(5) the total amount of wages as defined in section 3121(a),

(6) the total amount deducted and withheld as tax under section 3101,

---

> #### Editor's Note
>
> IRC §6051(a)(7) was repealed by Pub. L. No. 111-226, effective for tax years beginning after December 31, 2010.

~~**(7)** the total amount paid to the employee under section 3507 (relating to advance payment of earned income credit),~~ [Repealed]

(8) the total amount of elective deferrals (within the meaning of section 402(g)(3)) and compensation deferred under section 457, including the amount of designated Roth contributions (as defined in section 402A),

(9) the total amount incurred for dependent care assistance with respect to such employee under a dependent care assistance program described in section 129(d),

(10) in the case of an employee who is a member of the Armed Forces of the United States, such employee's earned income as determined for purposes of section 32 (relating to earned income credit),

(11) the amount contributed to any Archer MSA (as defined in section 220(d)) of such employee or such employer's spouse,

(12) the amount contributed to any health savings account (as defined in section 223(d)) of such employee or such employee's spouse,

(13) the total amount of deferrals for the year under a nonqualified deferred compensation plan (within the meaning of section 409A(d)), and

---

> #### Editor's Note
>
> IRC §6051(a)(14), below, added by Pub. L. No. 111-148, §9002, is effective for taxable years beginning after December 31, 2010.

---

(14) the aggregate cost (determined under rules similar to the rules of section 4980B(f)(4)) of applicable employer-sponsored coverage (as defined in section 4980I(d)(1)), except that this paragraph shall not apply to—

(A) coverage to which paragraphs (11) and (12) apply, or

(B) the amount of any salary reduction contributions to a flexible spending arrangement (within the meaning of section 125).

In the case of compensation paid for service as a member of a uniformed service, the statement shall show, in lieu of the amount required to be shown by paragraph (5), the total amount of wages as defined in section 3121(a), computed in accordance with such section and section 3121(i)(2). In the case of compensation paid for service as a volunteer or volunteer leader within the meaning of the Peace Corps Act, the statement shall show, in lieu of the amount required to be shown by paragraph (5), the total amount of wages as defined in section 3121(a), computed in accordance with such section and section 3121(i)(3). In the case of tips received by an employee in the course of his employment, the amounts required to be shown by paragraphs (3) and (5) shall include only such tips as are included in statements furnished to the employer pursuant to section 6053(a). The amounts required to be shown by paragraph (5) shall not include wages which are exempted pursuant to sections 3101(c) and 3111(c) from the taxes imposed by sections 3101 and 3111. In the case of the amounts required to be shown by paragraph (13), the Secretary may (by regulation) establish a minimum amount of deferrals below which paragraph (13) does not apply.

(b) Special Rule as to Compensation of Members of Armed Forces.—In the case of compensation paid for service as a member of the Armed Forces, the statement required by subsection (a) shall be furnished if any tax was withheld during the calendar year under section 3402, or if any of the compensation paid during such year is includible in gross income under chapter 1, or if during the calendar year any amount was required to be withheld as tax under section 3101. In lieu of the amount required to be shown by paragraph (3) of subsection (a), such statement shall show as wages paid during the calendar year the amount of such compensation paid during the calendar year which is not excluded from gross income under chapter 1 (whether or not such compensation constituted wages as defined in section 3401(a)).

(c) Additional Requirements.—The statements required to be furnished pursuant to this section in respect of any remuneration shall be furnished at such other times, shall contain such other information, and shall be in such form as the Secretary may by regulations prescribe. The statements required under this section shall also show the proportion of the total amount withheld as tax under section 3101 which is for financing the cost of hospital insurance benefits under part A of title XVIII of the Social Security Act.

(d) Statements to Constitute Information Returns.—A duplicate of any statement made pursuant to this section and in accordance with regulations prescribed by the Secretary shall, when required by such regulations, be filed with the Secretary.

(e) Railroad Employees.—

(1) Additional requirement.—Every person required to deduct and withhold tax under section 3201 from an employee shall include on or with the statement required to be furnished such employee under subsection (a) a notice concerning the provisions of this title with respect to the allowance of a credit or refund of the tax on wages imposed by section 3101(b) and the tax on compensation imposed by section 3201 or 3211 which is treated as a tax on wages imposed by section 3101(b).

(2) Information to be supplied to employees.—Each person required to deduct and withhold tax under section 3201 during any year from an employee who has also received wages during such year subject to the tax imposed by section 3101(b) shall, upon request of such employee, furnish to him a written statement showing—

(A) the total amount of compensation with respect to which the tax imposed by section 3201 was deducted,

(B) the total amount deducted as tax under section 3201, and

(C) the portion of the total amount deducted as tax under section 3201 which is for financing the cost of hospital insurance under part A of title XVIII of the Social Security Act.

(f) Statements Required in Case of Sick Pay Paid by Third Parties.—

(1) Statements required from payor.—

(A) In general.—If, during any calendar year, any person makes a payment of third-party sick pay to an employee, such person shall, on or before January 15 of the succeeding year, furnish a written statement to the employer in respect of whom such payment was made showing—

(i) the name and, if there is withholding under section 3402(o), the social security number of such employee,

(ii) the total amount of the third-party sick pay paid to such employee during the calendar year, and

(iii) the total amount (if any) deducted and withheld from such sick pay under section 3402.

For purposes of the preceding sentence, the term "third-party sick pay" means any sick pay (as defined in section 3402(o)(2)(C)) which does not constitute wages for purposes of chapter 24 (determined without regard to section 3402(o)(1)).

(B) Special rules.—

(i) Statements are in lieu of other reporting requirements.—The reporting requirements of subparagraph (A) with respect to any payments shall, with respect to such payments, be in lieu of the requirements of subsection (a) and of section 6041.

(ii) Penalties made applicable.—For purposes of sections 6674 and 7204, the statements required

IRC Sec. 6051(a)(14)(B)

to be furnished by subparagraph (A) shall be treated as statements required under this section to be furnished to employees.

(2) Information required to be furnished by employer.—Every employer who receives a statement under paragraph (1)(A) with respect to sick pay paid to any employee during any calendar year shall, on or before January 31 of the succeeding year, furnish a written statement to such employee showing—

(A) the information shown on the statement furnished under paragraph (1)(A), and

(B) if any portion of the sick pay is excludable from gross income under section 104(a)(3), the portion which is not so excludable and the portion which is so excludable.

To the extent practicable, the information required under the preceding sentence shall be furnished on or with the statement (if any) required under subsection (a).

Recent Amendments to IRC §6051

Pub. L. No. 111-226, as follows:
- IRC §6051(a)(7) was repealed by Act §219(a)(3). Eff. for taxable years beginning after Dec. 31, 2010. IRC §6051(a)(7) prior to repeal:
  (7) the total amount paid to the employee under section 3507 (relating to advance payment of earned income credit),

Patient Protection and Affordable Care Act, 2010 (Pub. L. No. 111-148), as follows:
- IRC §6051(a)(14) was added by Act §9002(a). Eff. for taxable years beginning after Dec. 31, 2010.

Pension Protection Act of 2006 (Pub. L. No. 109-280), as follows:
- Sunset Provision. Act §811, provides:
  SEC. 811. PENSIONS AND INDIVIDUAL RETIREMENT ARRANGEMENT PROVISIONS OF ECONOMIC GROWTH AND TAX RELIEF RECONCILIATION ACT OF 2001 MADE PERMANENT.
  Title IX of the Economic Growth and Tax Relief Reconciliation Act of 2001 [Pub. L. No. 107-16] shall not apply to the provisions of, and amendments made by, subtitles A through F [§§601–666] of title VI of such Act (relating to pension and individual retirement arrangement provisions).

American Jobs Creation Act of 2004 (Pub. L. No. 108-357), as follows:
- IRC §6051(a) was amended by Act §885(b)(1)(A) by striking "and" at the end of para. (11); by replacing the period at the end of para. (12) with ", and"; and adding new para. (13). Eff. for amounts deferred after Dec. 31, 2004. See Act §885(d)(2)–(3), (e)–(f) for special rules.
- IRC §6051(a) was amended by Act §885(b)(1)(B) by adding at the end new sentence. Eff. for amounts deferred after Dec. 31, 2004. [*Ed. Note*: see Act §885(d)(2)–(3), (e)–(f) for special rules.]

Medicare Prescription Drug, Improvement, and Modernization Act of 2003 (Pub. L. No. 108-173), as follows:
- IRC §6051(a) was amended by Act §1201(d)(3) by striking "and" at the end of para. (10); by replacing the period at the end of para. (11) with ", and"; and adding new para. (12). Eff. tax years beginning after Dec. 31, 2003.

Economic Growth and Tax Relief Reconciliation Act of 2001 (Pub. L. No. 107-16), as follows:
- IRC §6051(a)(8) was amended by Act §617(d)(1) by inserting ", including the amount of designated Roth contributions (as defined in §402A)" before the comma at the end. Eff. tax years beginning after Dec. 31, 2005.

- **Sunset Provision.** Act §901, as amended by Pub. L. No. 111-312, §101(a)(1), provides the sunset rule below. But see Pub. L. No. 109-280, §811, and Pub. L. No. 111-148, §10909(c), as amended by Pub. L. No. 111-312, §101(b)(1).

SEC. 901. SUNSET OF PROVISIONS OF ACT.

(a) In general. All provisions of, and amendments made by, this Act shall not apply—

(1) to taxable, plan, or limitation years beginning after December 31, 2012, or

(2) in the case of title V, to estates of decedents dying, gifts made, or generation skipping transfers, after December 31, 2012.

(b) Application of certain laws.—The Internal Revenue Code of 1986 and the Employee Retirement Income Security Act of 1974 shall be applied and administered to years, estates, gifts, and transfers described in subsection (a) as if the provisions and amendments described in subsection (a) had never been enacted.

SEC. 6052. RETURNS REGARDING PAYMENT OF WAGES IN THE FORM OF GROUP-TERM LIFE INSURANCE.

(a) Requirement of Reporting.—Every employer who during any calendar year provides group-term life insurance on the life of an employee during part or all of such calendar year under a policy (or policies) carried directly or indirectly by such employer shall make a return according to the forms or regulations prescribed by the Secretary, setting forth the cost of such insurance and the name and address of the employee on whose life such insurance is provided, but only to the extent that the cost of such insurance is includible in the employee's gross income under section 79(a). For purposes of this section, the extent to which the cost of group-term life insurance is includible in the employee's gross income under section 79(a) shall be determined as if the employer were the only employer paying such employee remuneration in the form of such insurance.

(b) Statements to Be Furnished to Employees With Respect to Whom Information Is Required.—Every employer required to make a return under subsection (a) shall furnish to each employee whose name is required to be set forth in such return a written statement showing the cost of the group-term life insurance shown on such return. The written statement required under the preceding sentence shall be furnished to the employee on or before January 31 of the year following the calendar year for which the return under subsection (a) was required to be made.

* * *

Subpart D—Information Regarding Health Insurance Coverage

Editor's Note

Caution: IRC §6055, below, added by Pub. L. No. 111-148, §1502(a), is effective for calendar years beginning after 2013.

SEC. 6055. REPORTING OF HEALTH INSURANCE COVERAGE.

(a) In General.—Every person who provides minimum essential coverage to an individual during a calendar year shall, at such time as the Secretary may prescribe, make a return described in subsection (b).

(b) Form and Manner of Return.—

(1) In general.—A return is described in this subsection if such return—

(A) is in such form as the Secretary may prescribe, and

(B) contains—

(i) the name, address and TIN of the primary insured and the name and TIN of each other individual obtaining coverage under the policy,

(ii) the dates during which such individual was covered under minimum essential coverage during the calendar year,

(iii) in the case of minimum essential coverage which consists of health insurance coverage, information concerning—

(I) whether or not the coverage is a qualified health plan offered through an Exchange established under section 1311 of the Patient Protection and Affordable Care Act, and

(II) in the case of a qualified health plan, the amount (if any) of any advance payment under section 1412 of the Patient Protection and Affordable Care Act of any cost-sharing reduction under section 1402 of such Act or of any premium tax credit under section 36B with respect to such coverage, and

(iv) such other information as the Secretary may require.

(2) Information relating to employer-provided coverage.—If minimum essential coverage provided to an individual under subsection (a) consists of health insurance coverage of a health insurance issuer provided through a group health plan of an employer, a return described in this subsection shall include—

(A) the name, address, and employer identification number of the employer maintaining the plan,

(B) the portion of the premium (if any) required to be paid by the employer, and

(C) if the health insurance coverage is a qualified health plan in the small group market offered through an Exchange, such other information as the Secretary may require for administration of the credit under section 45R (relating to credit for employee health insurance expenses of small employers).

(c) Statements to be Furnished to Individuals With Respect to Whom Information Is Reported.—

(1) In general.—Every person required to make a return under subsection (a) shall furnish to each individual whose name is required to be set forth in such return a written statement showing—

(A) the name and address of the person required to make such return and the phone number of the information contact for such person, and

(B) the information required to be shown on the return with respect to such individual.

(2) Time for furnishing statements.—The written statement required under paragraph (1) shall be furnished on or before January 31 of the year following the calendar year for which the return under subsection (a) was required to be made.

(d) Coverage Provided by Governmental Units.—In the case of coverage provided by any governmental unit or any agency or instrumentality thereof, the officer or employee who enters into the agreement to provide such coverage (or the person appropriately designated for purposes of this section) shall make the returns and statements required by this section.

(e) Minimum Essential Coverage.—For purposes of this section, the term "minimum essential coverage" has the meaning given such term by section 5000A(f).

Amendments to IRC §6055

Patient Protection and Affordable Care Act, 2010 (Pub. L. No. 111-148), as follows:
• IRC §6055 was added by Act §1502(a). Eff. for calendar years beginning after 2013.

Editor's Note

Caution: IRC §6056, below, added by Pub. L. No. 111-148, §1514, and amended by Pub. L. No. 111-148, §§10106 and 10108, and Pub. L. No. 112-10, is effective for periods beginning after December 31, 2013. For details, see amendment notes in this section.

SEC. 6056. CERTAIN EMPLOYERS REQUIRED TO REPORT ON HEALTH INSURANCE COVERAGE.

(a) In General.—Every applicable large employer required to meet the requirements of section 4980H with respect to its full-time employees during a calendar year shall, at such time as the Secretary may prescribe, make a return described in subsection (b).

(b) Form and Manner of Return.—A return is described in this subsection if such return—

(1) is in such form as the Secretary may prescribe, and

(2) contains—

(A) the name, date, and employer identification number of the employer,

(B) a certification as to whether the employer offers to its full-time employees (and their dependents) the opportunity to enroll in minimum essential coverage under an eligible employer-sponsored plan (as defined in section 5000A(f)(2)),

(C) if the employer certifies that the employer did offer to its full-time employees (and their dependents) the opportunity to so enroll—

(i) the length of any waiting period (as defined in section 2701(b)(4) of the Public Health Service Act) with respect to such coverage,

(ii) the months during the calendar year for which coverage under the plan was available,

(iii) the monthly premium for the lowest cost option in each of the enrollment categories under the plan, and

(iv) the employer's share of the total allowed costs of benefits provided under the plan.

(D) the number of full-time employees for each month during the calendar year,

(E) the name, address, and TIN of each full-time employee during the calendar year and the months (if any) during which such employee (and any dependents) were covered under any such health benefits plans, and

(F) such other information as the Secretary may require.

The Secretary shall have the authority to review the accuracy of the information provided under this subsection, including the applicable large employer's share under paragraph (2)(C)(iv).

(c) Statements to be Furnished to Individuals With Respect to Whom Information Is Reported.—

(1) In general.—Every person required to make a return under subsection (a) shall furnish to each full-time employee whose name is required to be set forth in such return under subsection (b)(2)(E) a written statement showing—

(A) the name and address of the person required to make such return and the phone number of the information contact for such person, and

(B) the information required to be shown on the return with respect to such individual.

(2) Time for furnishing statements.—The written statement required under paragraph (1) shall be furnished on or before January 31 of the year following the calendar year for which the return under subsection (a) was required to be made.

(d) Coordination With Other Requirements.—To the maximum extent feasible, the Secretary may provide that—

(1) any return or statement required to be provided under this section may be provided as part of any return or statement required under section 6051 or 6055, and

(2) in the case of an applicable large employer offering health insurance coverage of a health insurance issuer, the employer may enter into an agreement with the issuer to include information required under this section with the return and statement required to be provided by the issuer under section 6055.

(e) Coverage Provided by Governmental Units.—In the case of any applicable large employer which is a governmental unit or any agency or instrumentality thereof, the person appropriately designated for purposes of this section shall make the returns and statements required by this section.

(f) Definitions.—For purposes of this section, any term used in this section which is also used in section 4980H shall have the meaning given such term by section 4980H.

Amendments to IRC §6056

Department of Defense and Full-Year Continuing Appropriations Act, 2011 (Pub. L. No. 112-10), as follows:

- IRC §6056(a) was amended by Act §1858(b)(5)(A) by striking "and every offering employer". Eff. as if included in the provision of, and the amendments made by, the provision of Pub. L. No. 111-148 to which it relates [eff. for periods beginning after Dec. 31, 2013].
- IRC §6056(b)(2)(C) was amended by Act §1858(b)(5)(B)(i)–(iv) by striking "in the case of an applicable large employer," in cl. (i), by inserting "and" at the end of cl. (iii), by striking "and" at the end of cl. (iv) and by striking cl. (v). ". Eff. as if included in the provision of, and the amendments made by, the provision of Pub. L. No. 111-148 to which it relates [eff. for periods beginning after Dec. 31, 2013]. IRC §6056(b)(2)(C)(v) before being struck:

  (v) in the case of an offering employer, the option for which the employer pays the largest portion of the cost of the plan and the portion of the cost paid by the employer in each of the enrollment categories under such option,

- IRC §6056(d)(2) was amended by Act §1858(b)(5)(C) by striking "or offering employer". Eff. as if included in the provision of, and the amendments made by, the provision of Pub. L. No. 111-148 to which it relates [eff. for periods beginning after Dec. 31, 2013].
- IRC §6056(e) was amended by Act §1858(b)(5)(C) by striking "or offering employer". Eff. as if included in the provision of, and the amendments made by, the provision of Pub. L. No. 111-148 to which it relates [eff. for periods beginning after Dec. 31, 2013].

• IRC §6056(f) was amended by Act §1858(b)(5)(D). Eff. as if included in the provision of, and the amendments made by, the provision of Pub. L. No. 111-148 to which it relates [eff. for periods beginning after Dec. 31, 2013]. IRC §6056(f) prior to amendment:

  (f) Definitions.—For purposes of this section—

  (1) Offering employer.—

  (A) In general.—The term "offering employer" means any offering employer (as defined in section 10108(b) of the Patient Protection and Affordable Care Act) if the required contribution (within the meaning of section 5000A(e)(1)(B)(i)) of any employee exceeds 8 percent of the wages (as defined in section 3121(a)) paid to such employee by such employer.

  (B) Indexing.— In the case of any calendar year beginning after 2014, the 8 percent under subparagraph (A) shall be adjusted for the calendar year to reflect the rate of premium growth between the preceding calendar year and 2013 over the rate of income growth for such period.

  (2) Other definitions.—Any term used in this section which is also used in section 4980H shall have the meaning given such term by section 4980H.

Patient Protection and Affordable Care Act, 2010 (Pub. L. No. 111-148), as follows:

• IRC §6056 was added by Act §1514(a). Eff. for periods beginning after Dec. 31, 2013.

• IRC §6056, heading, was amended by Act §10108(j)(3)(A) by substituting "Certain" for "Large". Eff. for periods beginning after Dec. 31, 2013.

• IRC §6056(a) was amended by Act §10108(j)(1) by inserting "and every offering employer" before "shall". Eff. for periods beginning after Dec. 31, 2013.

• IRC §6056(b) was amended by Act §10106(g) by adding a flush sentence at the end. Eff. date of the enactment of this Act [Mar. 23, 2010].

• IRC §6056(b)(2)(C) was amended by Act §10108(j)(3)(B) by inserting "in the case of an applicable large employer," before "the length" in cl. (i); striking " 'and" at the end of cl. (iii); subsituting "employer" for "applicable large employer" in cl. (iv); inserting " 'and" at the end of cl. (iv); and adding cl. (v). Eff. for periods beginning after Dec. 31, 2013.

• IRC §6056(d)(2) was amended by Act §10108(j)(3)(C) by inserting "or offering employer" after "applicable large employer". Eff. for periods beginning after Dec. 31, 2013.

• IRC §6056(e) was amended by Act §10108(j)(3)(D) by inserting "or offering employer" after "applicable large employer". Eff. for periods beginning after Dec. 31, 2013.

• IRC §6056(f) was amended by Act §10108(j)(2). Eff. for periods beginning after Dec. 31, 2013. IRC §6056(f) prior to amendment:

  (f) Definitions.—For purposes of this section, any term used in this section which is also used in section 4980H shall have the meaning given such term by section 4980H.

Subpart E—Registration of and Information Concerning Pension, etc., Plans

SEC. 6057. ANNUAL REGISTRATION, ETC.

(a) Annual Registration.—

(1) **General rule.**—Within such period after the end of a plan year as the Secretary may by regulations prescribe, the plan administrator (within the meaning of section 414(g)) of each plan to which the vesting standards of section 203 of part 2 of subtitle B of title I of the Employee Retirement Income Security Act of 1974 applies for such plan year shall file a registration statement with the Secretary.

(2) **Contents.**—The registration statement required by paragraph (1) shall set forth—

(A) the name of the plan,

(B) the name and address of the plan administrator,

(C) the name and taxpayer identifying number of each participant in the plan—

  (i) who, during such plan year, separated from the service covered by the plan,

  (ii) who is entitled to a deferred vested benefit under the plan as of the end of such plan year, and

  (iii) with respect to whom retirement benefits were not paid under the plan during such plan year,

(D) the nature, amount and form of the deferred vested benefit to which such participant is entitled, and

(E) such other information as the Secretary may require.

At the time he files the registration statement under this subsection, the plan administrator shall furnish evidence satisfactory to the Secretary that he has complied with the requirement contained in subsection (e).

(b) Notification of Change in Status.—Any plan administrator required to register under subsection (a) shall also notify the Secretary, at such times as may be prescribed by regulations, of—

(1) any change in the name of the plan,

(2) any change in the name or address of the plan administrator,

(3) the termination of the plan, or

(4) the merger or consolidation of the plan with any other plan or its division into two or more plans.

(c) Voluntary Reports.—To the extent provided in regulations prescribed by the Secretary, the Secretary may receive from—

(1) any plan to which subsection (a) applies, and

(2) any other plan (including any governmental plan or church plan (within the meaning of section 414)), such information (including information relating to plan years beginning before January 1, 1974) as the plan administrator may wish to file with respect to the deferred vested benefit rights of any participant separated from the service covered by the plan during any plan year.

(d) Transmission of Information to Commissioner of Social Security.—The Secretary shall transmit copies of any statements, notifications, reports, or other information obtained by him under this section to the Commissioner of Social Security.

(e) Individual Statement to Participant.—Each plan administrator required to file a registration statement under subsection (a) shall, before the expiration of the time prescribed for the filing of such registration statement, also furnish to each participant described in subsection (a)(2)(C) an individual statement setting forth the information with respect to such participant required to be contained in such registration statement. Such statement shall also include a notice to the participant of any benefits which are forfeitable if the participant dies before a certain date.

(f) Regulations.—

(1) In general.—The Secretary, after consultation with the Commissioner of Social Security, may prescribe such regulations as may be necessary to carry out the provisions of this section.

(2) Plans to which more than one employer contributes.—This section shall apply to any plan to which more than one employer is required to contribute only to the extent provided in regulations prescribed under this subsection.

(g) Cross References.—For provisions relating to penalties for failure to register or furnish statements required by this section, see section 6652(d) and section 6690.

For coordination between Department of the Treasury and the Department of Labor with regard to administration of this section see section 3004 of the Employee Retirement Income Security Act of 1974.

SEC. 6058. INFORMATION REQUIRED IN CONNECTION WITH CERTAIN PLANS OF DEFERRED COMPENSATION.

(a) In General.—Every employer who maintains a pension, annuity, stock bonus, profit-sharing or other funded plan of deferred compensation described in part I of subchapter D of chapter 1, or the plan administrator (within the meaning of section 414(g)) of the plan, shall file an annual return stating such information as the Secretary may by regulations prescribe with respect to the qualification, financial condition, and operations of the plan; except that, in the discretion of the Secretary, the employer may be relieved from stating in its return any information which is reported in other returns.

(b) Actuarial Statement in Case of Mergers, etc.—Not less than 30 days before a merger, consolidation, or transfer of assets or liabilities of a plan described in subsection (a) to another plan, the plan administrator (within the meaning of section 414(g)) shall file an actuarial statement of valuation evidencing compliance with the requirements of section 401(a)(12).

(c) Employer.—For purposes of this section, the term "employer" includes a person described in section 401(c)(4) and an individual who establishes an individual retirement plan.

(d) Coordination With Income Tax Returns, etc.—An individual who establishes an individual retirement plan shall not be required to file a return under this section with respect to such plan for any taxable year for which there is—

(1) no special IRP tax, and

(2) no plan activity other than—

(A) the making of contributions (other than rollover contributions), and

(B) the making of distributions.

(e) Special IRP Tax Defined.—For purposes of this section, the term "special IRP tax" means a tax imposed by—

(1) section 408(f),

(2) section 4973, or

(3) section 4974.

(f) Cross References.—For provisions relating to penalties for failure to file a return required by this section, see section 6652(e).

For coordination between the Department of the Treasury and the Department of Labor with respect to the information required under this section, see section 3004 of title III of the Employee Retirement Income Security Act of 1974.

SEC. 6059. PERIODIC REPORT OF ACTUARY.

(a) General Rule.—The actuarial report described in subsection (b) shall be filed by the plan administrator (as defined in section 414(g)) of each defined benefit plan to which section 412 applies, for the first plan year for which section 412 applies to the plan and for each third plan year thereafter (or more frequently if the Secretary determines that more frequent reports are necessary).

(b) Actuarial Report.—The actuarial report of a plan required by subsection (a) shall be prepared and signed by an enrolled actuary (within the meaning of section 7701(a)(35)) and shall contain—

(1) a description of the funding method and actuarial assumptions used to determine costs under the plan,

(2) a certification of the contribution necessary to reduce the minimum required contribution determined under section 430, or the accumulated funding deficiency determined under section 431, to zero,

(3) a statement—

(A) that to the best of his knowledge the report is complete and accurate, and

(B) the requirements for reasonable actuarial assumptions under section 430(h)(1) or 431(c)(3), whichever are applicable, have been complied with.

(4) such other information as may be necessary to fully and fairly disclose the actuarial position of the plan, and

(5) such other information regarding the plan as the Secretary may by regulations require.

(c) Time and Manner of Filing.—The actuarial report and statement required by this section shall be filed at the time and in the manner provided by regulations prescribed by the Secretary.

(d) Cross Reference.—For coordination between the Department of the Treasury and the Department of Labor with respect to the report required to be filed under this section, see section 3004 of title III of the Employee Retirement Income Security Act of 1974.

Recent Amendments to IRC §6059

Pension Protection Act of 2006 (Pub. L. No. 109-280), as follows:
• IRC section 6059(b) was amended by Act section 114(f)(1)–(2) by replacing "the accumulated funding deficiency (as defined in section 412(a))" in paragraph (2) with "the minimum required contribution determined under section 430, or the accumulated funding deficiency determined under section 431,"; and by striking para. (3)(B) and adding a new para. (3)(B). Eff. Aug. 17, 2006 [for plan years after 2007, eff. date as amended by Pub. L. No. 110-458, section 101(d)(3)]. [*Ed. Note*: for special rules for certain plans, see Act §§104–106.] IRC §6059(b)(3)(B) prior to amendment:

> (B) the requirements of section 412(c) (relating to reasonable actuarial assumptions) have been complied with.

---

* * *

Subchapter B—Miscellaneous Provisions
* * *

SEC. 6103. CONFIDENTIALITY AND DISCLOSURE OF RETURNS AND RETURN INFORMATION.

* * *

(*l*) Disclosure of Return and Return Information for Purposes Other than Tax Administration.—

* * *

(2) Disclosure of returns and return information to the Department of Labor and Pension Benefit Guaranty Corporation.—The Secretary may, upon written request, furnish returns and return information to the proper officers and employees of the Department of Labor and Pension Benefit Guaranty Corporation for purposes of, but only to the extent necessary in, the administration of titles I and IV of the Employee Retirement Income Security Act of 1974.

* * *

(18) Disclosure of return information for purposes of carrying out a program for advance payment of credit for health insurance costs of eligible individuals.—The Secretary may disclose to providers of health insurance for any certified individual (as defined in section 7527(c)) return information with

respect to such certified individual only to the extent necessary to carry out the program established by section 7527 (relating to advance payment of credit for health insurance costs of eligible individuals).

* * *

> ### Editor's Note
>
> IRC §6103(*l*)(21), below, added by Pub. L. No. 111-148, §1414, and amended by Pub. L. No. 111-152, §1004, is effective on the date of the enactment of Pub. L. No. 111-148 (enacted: March 23, 2010).

---

(21) Disclosure of return information to carry out eligibility requirements for certain programs.—

(A) In general.—The Secretary, upon written request from the Secretary of Health and Human Services, shall disclose to officers, employees, and contractors of the Department of Health and Human Services return information of any taxpayer whose income is relevant in determining any premium tax credit under section 36B or any cost-sharing reduction under section 1402 of the Patient Protection and Affordable Care Act or eligibility for participation in a State Medicaid program under title XIX of the Social Security Act, a State's children's health insurance program under title XXI of the Social Security Act, or a basic health program under section 1331 of Patient Protection and Affordable Care Act. Such return information shall be limited to—

(i) taxpayer identity information with respect to such taxpayer,

(ii) the filing status of such taxpayer,

(iii) the number of individuals for whom a deduction is allowed under section 151 with respect to the taxpayer (including the taxpayer and the taxpayer's spouse),

(iv) the modified adjusted gross income (as defined in section 36B) of such taxpayer and each of the other individuals included under clause (iii) who are required to file a return of tax imposed by chapter 1 for the taxable year,

(v) such other information as is prescribed by the Secretary by regulation as might indicate whether the taxpayer is eligible for such credit or reduction (and the amount thereof), and

(vi) the taxable year with respect to which the preceding information relates or, if applicable, the fact that such information is not available.

(B) Information to exchange and state agencies.— The Secretary of Health and Human Services may disclose to an Exchange established under the Patient Protection and Affordable Care Act or its contractors, or to a State agency administering a State program described in subparagraph (A) or its contractors, any inconsistency between the information provided by the Exchange or State agency to the Secretary and the information provided to the Secretary under subparagraph (A).

(C) Restriction of use of disclosed information.— Return information disclosed under subparagraph (A) or (B) may be used by officers, employees, and contractors of the Department of Health and Human Services, an Exchange, or a State agency only for the purposes of, and to the extent necessary in—

(i) establishing eligibility for participation in the Exchange, and verifying the appropriate amount of, any credit or reduction described in subparagraph (A),

(ii) determining eligibility for participation in the State programs described in subparagraph (A).

* * *

Recent Amendments to IRC §6103 (as Excerpted)

Health Care and Education Reconciliation Act of 2010 (Pub. L. No. 111-152), as follows:
- IRC §6103(*l*)(21)(A)(iv) was amended by Act §1004(a)(1)(B) by substituting "modified adjusted gross" for "modified gross". Eff. on date of enactment of this Act [date of enactment: Mar. 30, 2010].

Patient Protection and Affordable Care Act, 2010 (Pub. L. No. 111-148), as follows:
- IRC §6103(*l*)(21) was added by Act §1414(a)(1). Eff. on date of enactment of this Act [date of enactment: Mar. 23, 2010].

Trade Act of 2002 (Pub. L. No. 107-210), as follows:
- IRC §6103(l)(18) was added by Act §202(b)(1). Eff. Aug. 6, 2002.

SEC. 6104. PUBLICITY OF INFORMATION REQUIRED FROM CERTAIN EXEMPT ORGANIZATIONS AND CERTAIN TRUSTS.

(a) Inspection of Applications for Tax Exemption or Notice of Status.

(1) Public inspection.

(A) Organizations described in section 501 or 527. An organization described in section 501(c) or (d) is exempt from taxation under section 501(a) for any taxable year or a political organization is exempt from taxation under section 527 for any taxable year, the application filed by the organization with respect to which the Secretary made his determination that such organization was entitled to exemption under section 501(a) or notice of status filed by the organization under section 527(i), together with any papers submitted in support of such application or notice, and any letter or other document issued by the Internal Revenue Service with respect to such application or notice

shall be open to public inspection at the national office of the Internal Revenue Service. In the case of any application or notice filed after the date of the enactment of this subparagraph, a copy of such application or notice and such letter or document shall be open to public inspection at the appropriate field office of the Internal Revenue Service (determined under regulations prescribed by the Secretary). Any inspection under this subparagraph may be made at such times, and in such manner, as the Secretary shall by regulations prescribe. After the application of any organization for exemption from taxation under section 501(a) has been opened to public inspection under this subparagraph, the Secretary shall, on the request of any person with respect to such organization, furnish a statement indicating the subsection and paragraph of section 501 which it has been determined describes such organization.

(B) Pension, etc., plans. The following shall be open to public inspection at such times and in such places as the Secretary may prescribe:

(i) any application filed with respect to the qualification of a pension, profit-sharing, or stock bonus plan under section 401(a) or 403(a) or, an individual retirement account described in section 408(a), or an individual retirement annuity described in section 408(b),

(ii) any application filed with respect to the exemption from tax under section 501(a) of an organization forming part of a plan or account referred to in clause (i),

(iii) any papers submitted in support of an application referred to in clause (i) or (ii), and

(iv) any letter or other document issued by the Internal Revenue Service and dealing with the qualification referred to in clause (i) or the exemption from tax referred to in clause (ii).

Except in the case of a plan participant, this subparagraph shall not apply to any plan referred to in clause (i) having not more than 25 participants.

(C) Certain names and compensation not to be opened to public inspection. In the case of any application, document, or other papers, referred to in subparagraph (B), information from which the compensation (including deferred compensation) of any individual may be ascertained shall not be open to public inspection under subparagraph (B).

(D) Withholding of certain other information. Upon request of the organization submitting any supporting papers described in subparagraph (A) or (B), the Secretary shall withhold from public inspection any information contained therein which he determines relates to any trade secret, patent, process, style of work, or apparatus, of the organization, if he determines that public disclosure of such information would adversely affect

IRC Sec. 6104(a)(1)(D)

the organization. The Secretary shall withhold from public inspection any information contained in supporting papers described in subparagraph (A) or (B) the public disclosure of which he determines would adversely affect the national defense.

(2) Inspection by committees of Congress. Section 6103(f) shall apply with respect to—

(A) the application for exemption of any organization described in section 501(c) or (d) which is exempt from taxation under section 501(a) for any taxable year or notice of status of any political organization which is exempt from taxation under section 527 for any taxable year, and any application referred to in subparagraph (B) of subsection (a)(1) of this section, and

(B) any other papers which are in the possession of the Secretary and which relate to such application,

as if such papers constituted returns.

(3) Information available on Internet and in person.

(A) In general. The Secretary shall make publicly available, on the Internet and at the offices of the Internal Revenue Service—

(i) a list of all political organizations which file a notice with the Secretary under section 527(i), and

(ii) the name, address, electronic mailing address, custodian of records, and contact person for such organization.

(B) Time to make information available. The Secretary shall make available the information required under subparagraph (A) not later than 5 business days after the Secretary receives a notice from a political organization under section 527(i).

(b) Inspection of Annual Returns. The information required to be furnished by sections 6033, 6034, and 6058, together with the names and addresses of such organizations and trusts, shall be made available to the public at such times and in such places as the Secretary may prescribe. Nothing in this subsection shall authorize the Secretary to disclose the name or address of any contributor to any organization or trust (other than a private foundation, as defined in section 509(a) or a political organization exempt from taxation under section 527) which is required to furnish such information. In the case of an organization described in section 501(d), this subsection shall not apply to copies referred to in section 6031(b) with respect to such organization. In the case of a trust which is required to file a return under section 6034(a), this subsection shall not apply to information regarding beneficiaries which are not organizations described in section 170(c). Any annual return which is filed under section 6011 by an organization described in section 501(c)(3) and which relates to any

tax imposed by section 511 (relating to imposition of tax on unrelated business income of charitable, etc., organizations) shall be treated for purposes of this subsection in the same manner as if furnished under section 6033.

(c) Publication to State Officials.

(1) General rule for charitable organizations. In the case of any organization which is described in section 501(c)(3) and exempt from taxation under section 501(a), or has applied under section 508(a) for recognition as an organization described in section 501(c)(3), the Secretary at such times and in such manner as he may by regulations prescribe shall—

(A) notify the appropriate State officer of a refusal to recognize such organization as an organization described in section 501(c)(3), or of the operation of such organization in a manner which does not meet, or no longer meets, the requirements of its exemption,

(B) notify the appropriate State officer of the mailing of a notice of deficiency of tax imposed under section 507 or chapter 41 or 42, and

(C) at the request of such appropriate State officer, make available for inspection and copying such returns, filed statements, records, reports, and other information, relating to a determination under subparagraph (A) or (B) as are relevant to any determination under State law.

(2) Disclosure of proposed actions related to charitable organizations.

(A) Specific notifications. In the case of an organization to which paragraph (1) applies, the Secretary may disclose to the appropriate State officer—

(i) a notice of proposed refusal to recognize such organization as an organization described in section 501(c)(3) or a notice of proposed revocation of such organization's recognition as an organization exempt from taxation,

(ii) the issuance of a letter of proposed deficiency of tax imposed under section 507 or chapter 41 or 42, and

(iii) the names, addresses, and taxpayer identification numbers of organizations which have applied for recognition as organizations described in section 501(c)(3).

(B) Additional disclosures. Returns and return information of organizations with respect to which information is disclosed under subparagraph (A) may be made available for inspection by or disclosed to an appropriate State officer.

(C) Procedures for disclosure. Information may be inspected or disclosed under subparagraph (A) or (B) only—

(i) upon written request by an appropriate State officer, and

(ii) for the purpose of, and only to the extent necessary in, the administration of State laws regulating such organizations.

Such information may only be inspected by or disclosed to a person other than the appropriate State officer if such person is an officer or employee of the State and is designated by the appropriate State officer to receive the returns or return information under this paragraph on behalf of the appropriate State officer.

(D) Disclosures other than by request. The Secretary may make available for inspection or disclose returns and return information of an organization to which paragraph (1) applies to an appropriate State officer of any State if the Secretary determines that such returns or return information may constitute evidence of noncompliance under the laws within the jurisdiction of the appropriate State officer.

(3) Disclosure with respect to certain other exempt organizations. Upon written request by an appropriate State officer, the Secretary may make available for inspection or disclosure returns and return information of any organization described in section 501(c) (other than organizations described in paragraph (1) or (3) thereof) for the purpose of, and only to the extent necessary in, the administration of State laws regulating the solicitation or administration of the charitable funds or charitable assets of such organizations. Such information may only be inspected by or disclosed to a person other than the appropriate State officer if such person is an officer or employee of the State and is designated by the appropriate State officer to receive the returns or return information under this paragraph on behalf of the appropriate State officer.

(4) Use in civil judicial and administrative proceedings. Returns and return information disclosed pursuant to this subsection may be disclosed in civil administrative and civil judicial proceedings pertaining to the enforcement of State laws regulating such organizations in a manner prescribed by the Secretary similar to that for tax administration proceedings under section 6103(h)(4).

(5) No disclosure if impairment. Returns and return information shall not be disclosed under this subsection, or in any proceeding described in paragraph (4), to the extent that the Secretary determines that such disclosure would seriously impair Federal tax administration.

(6) Definitions. For purposes of this subsection—

(A) Return and return information. The terms "return" and "return information" have the respective meanings given to such terms by section 6103(b).

(B) Appropriate State officer. The term "appropriate State officer" means—

(i) the State attorney general,

(ii) the State tax officer,

(iii) in the case of an organization to which paragraph (1) applies, any other State official charged with overseeing organizations of the type described in section 501(c)(3), and

(iv) in the case of an organization to which paragraph (3) applies, the head of an agency designated by the State attorney general as having primary responsibility for overseeing the solicitation of funds for charitable purposes.

(d) Public Inspection of Certain Annual Returns, Reports, Applications for Exemption, and Notices of Status.

(1) In general. In the case of an organization described in subsection (c) or (d) of section 501 and exempt from taxation under section 501(a) or an organization exempt from taxation under section 527(a)—

(A) a copy of—

(i) the annual return filed under section 6033 (relating to returns by exempt organizations) by such organization,

(ii) any annual return which is filed under section 6011 by an organization described in section 501(c)(3) and which relates to any tax imposed by section 511 (relating to imposition of tax on unrelated business income of charitable, etc., organizations),

(iii) if the organization filed an application for recognition of exemption under section 501 or notice of status under section 527(i), the exempt status application materials or any notice materials of such organization, and

(iv) the reports filed under section 527(j) (relating to required disclosure of expenditures and contributions) by such organization,

shall be made available by such organization for inspection during regular business hours by any individual at the principal office of such organization and, if such organization regularly maintains 1 or more regional or district offices having 3 or more employees, at each such regional or district office, and

(B) upon request of an individual made at such principal office or such a regional or district office, a copy of such annual return, reports, and exempt status application materials or such notice materials shall be provided to such individual without charge other than a reasonable fee for any reproduction and mailing costs.

The request described in subparagraph (B) must be made in person or in writing. If such request is made in person, such copy shall be provided immediately and, if made in writing, shall be provided within 30 days.

(2) 3-year limitation on inspection of returns. Paragraph (1) shall apply to an annual return filed under section 6011 or 6033 only during the 3-year period beginning on the last day prescribed for filing such return (determined with regard to any extension of time for filing).

(3) Exceptions from disclosure requirement.

(A) Nondisclosure of contributors, etc. In the case of an organization which is not a private foundation (within the meaning of section 509(a)) or a political organization exempt from taxation under section 527, paragraph (1) shall not require the disclosure of the name or address of any contributor to the organization. In the case of an organization described in section 501(d), paragraph (1) shall not require the disclosure of the copies referred to in section 6031(b) with respect to such organization.

(B) Nondisclosure of certain other information. Paragraph (1) shall not require the disclosure of any information if the Secretary withheld such information from public inspection under subsection (a)(1)(D).

(4) Limitation on providing copies. Paragraph (1)(B) shall not apply to any request if, in accordance with regulations promulgated by the Secretary, the organization has made the requested documents widely available, or the Secretary determines, upon application by an organization, that such request is part of a harassment campaign and that compliance with such request is not in the public interest.

(5) Exempt status application materials. For purposes of paragraph (1), the term "exempt status application materials" means the application for recognition of exemption under section 501 and any papers submitted in support of such application and any letter or other document issued by the Internal Revenue Service with respect to such application.

(6) Notice materials. For purposes of paragraph (1), the term "notice materials" means the notice of status filed under section 527(i) and any papers submitted in support of such notice and any letter or other document issued by the Internal Revenue Service with respect to such notice.

[(7)](6) Disclosure of reports by Internal Revenue Service. Any report filed by an organization under section 527(j) (relating to required disclosure of expenditures and contributions) shall be made available to the public at such times and in such places as the Secretary may prescribe.

[(8)](6) Application to nonexempt charitable trusts and nonexempt private foundations. The organizations referred to in paragraphs (1) and (2) of section 6033(d) shall comply with the requirements of this subsection relating to annual returns filed under section 6033 in the same manner as the organizations referred to in paragraph (1).

(e) [Stricken.]

Recent Amendments to IRC §6104

Tax Technical Corrections Act of 2007 (Pub. L. No. 110-172), as follows:

- IRC §6104(b) was amended by Act §3(g)(1) by striking "Information" after "Annual" in the heading and by adding the sentence at the end. Eff. as if included in Pub. L. No. 109-280, §1225 [eff. for returns filed after Aug. 17, 2006].
- IRC §6104(d)(1)(A)(ii) was amended by Act §3(g)(2). Eff. as if included in Pub. L. No. 109-280, §1225 [eff. for returns filed after Aug. 17, 2006]. IRC §6104(d)(1)(A)(ii) prior to amendment:

  (ii) any annual return filed under section 6011 which relates to any tax imposed by section 511 (relating to imposition of tax on unrelated business income of charitable, etc., organizations) by such organization, but only if such organization is described in section 501(c)(3),

- IRC §6104(d)(2) was amended by Act §3(g)(3) by substituting "section 6011 or 6033" for "section 6033". Eff. as if included in Pub. L. No. 109-280, §1225 [eff. for returns filed after Aug. 17, 2006].

Pension Protection Act of 2006 (Pub. L. No. 109-280), as follows:

- IRC §6104(b) was amended by Act §1201(b)(3) by adding a new sentence at the end. Eff. for returns for tax years beginning after Dec. 31, 2006.
- IRC §6104(c) was amended by Act §1224(a) by striking para. (2) and adding new paras. (2) through (6). Eff. Aug. 17, 2006, but does not apply to requests made before that date. IRC §6014(c)(2) prior to amendment:

  (2) Appropriate state officer.—For purposes of this subsection, the term "appropriate State officer" means the State attorney general, State tax officer, or any State official charged with overseeing organizations of the type described in section 501(c)(3).

- IRC §6041(c)(1) was amended by Act §1224(b)(4) by inserting in the heading "for charitable organizations" after "rule". Eff. Aug. 17, 2006, but does not apply to requests made before such date.
- IRC §6041(d)(1)(A) was amended by Act §1225(a) by redesignating cls. (ii) and (iii) as cls. (iii) and (iv), respectively, and by adding a new cl. (ii). Eff. for returns filed after Aug. 17, 2006.

Pub. L. No. 107-276, as follows:

- IRC §6104(b) was amended by Act §3(b)(1) by striking "6012(a)(6)," after "to be furnished by sections". Eff. for returns for tax years beginning after June 30, 2000, as if included in the amendments made by Pub. L. No. 106-230.
- IRC §6041(d)(1)(A)(i) was amended by Act §3(b)(2)(A) by striking "or §6012(a)(6) (relating to returns by political organizations)" after "by exempt organizations)". Eff. for returns for tax years beginning after June 30, 2000, as if included in the amendments made by Pub. L. No. 106-230.
- IRC §6041(d)(2) was amended by Act §3(b)(2)(B) by striking "or §6012(a)(6)" after "§6033." Eff. for returns for tax years beginning after June 30, 2000, as if included in the amendments made by Pub. L. No. 106-230.

---

* * *

Chapter 65—Abatements, Credits, and Refunds

Subchapter B—Rules of Special Application

* * *

SEC. 6432. COBRA PREMIMUM ASSISTANCE.

(a) In General.—The person to whom premiums are payable under COBRA continuation coverage shall be reimbursed as provided in subsection (c) for the amount of premiums not paid by assistance eligible individuals by reason of section 3001(a) of title III of division B of the American Recovery and Reinvestment Act of 2009.

(b) Person Entitled to Reimbursement.—For purposes of subsection (a), except as otherwise provided by the Secretary, the person to whom premiums are payable under COBRA continuation coverage shall be treated as being—

(1) in the case of any group health plan which is a multiemployer plan (as defined in section 3(37) of the Employee Retirement Income Security Act of 1974), the plan,

(2) in the case of any group health plan not described in paragraph (1)—

(A) which is subject to the COBRA continuation provisions contained in—

(i) the Internal Revenue Code of 1986,

(ii) the Employee Retirement Income Security Act of 1974,

(iii) the Public Health Service Act, or

(iv) title 5, United States Code, or

(B) under which some or all of the coverage is not provided by insurance, the employer maintaining the plan, and

(3) in the case of any group health plan not described in paragraph (1) or (2), the insurer providing the coverage under the group health plan.

(c) Method of Reimbursement.—Except as otherwise provided by the Secretary—

(1) Treatment as payment of payroll taxes.— Each person entitled to reimbursement under subsection (a) (and filing a claim for such reimbursement at such time and in such manner as the Secretary may require) shall be treated for purposes of this title and section 1324(b)(2) of title 31, United States Code, as having paid to the Secretary, on the date that the assistance eligible individual's premium payment is received, payroll taxes in an amount equal to the portion of such reimbursement which relates to such premium. To the extent that the amount treated as paid under the preceding sentence exceeds the amount of such person's liability for such taxes, the Secretary shall credit or refund such excess in the same manner as if it were an overpayment of such taxes.

(2) Overstatements.—Any overstatement of the reimbursement to which a person is entitled under this section (and any amount paid by the Secretary as a result of such overstatement) shall be treated as an underpayment of payroll taxes by such person and may be assessed and collected by the Secretary in the same manner as payroll taxes.

(3) Reimbursement contingent on payment of remaining premium.—No reimbursement may be made under this section to a person with respect to any assistance eligible individual until after the reduced premium required under section 3001(a)(1)(A) of title III of division B of the American Recovery and Reinvestment Act of 2009 with respect to such individual has been received.

(d) Definitions.—For purpose of this section—

(1) Payroll taxes.—The term "payroll taxes" means—

(A) amounts required to be deducted and withheld for the payroll period under section 3402 (relating to wage withholding),

(B) amounts required to be deducted for the payroll period under section 3102 (relating to FICA employee taxes), and

(C) amounts of the taxes imposed for the payroll period under section 3111 (relating to FICA employer taxes).

(2) Person.—The term "person" includes any governmental entity.

(e) Employer Determination of Qualifying Event as Involuntary Termination.—For purposes of this section, in any case in which—

(1) based on a reasonable interpretation of section 3001(a)(3)(C) of division B of the American Recovery and Reinvestment Act of 2009 and administrative guidance thereunder, an employer determines that the qualifying event with respect to COBRA continuation coverage for an individual was involuntary termination of a covered employee's employment, and

(2) the employer maintains supporting documentation of the determination, including an attestation by the employer of involuntary termination with respect to the covered employee,

the qualifying event for the individual shall be deemed to be involuntary termination of the covered employee's employment.

(f) Reporting.—Each person entitled to reimbursement under subsection (a) for any period shall submit such reports (at such time and in such manner) as the Secretary may require, including—

(1) an attestation of involuntary termination of employment for each covered employee on the basis of whose termination entitlement to reimbursement is claimed under subsection (a),

(2) a report of the amount of payroll taxes offset under subsection (a) for the reporting period and the estimated offsets of such taxes for the subsequent reporting period in connection with reimbursements under subsection (a), and

(3) a report containing the TINs of all covered employees, the amount of subsidy reimbursed with

IRC Sec. 6432(f)(3)

respect to each covered employee and qualified beneficiaries, and a designation with respect to each covered employee as to whether the subsidy reimbursement is for coverage of 1 individual or 2 or more individuals.

(g) Regulations.—The Secretary shall issue such regulations or other guidance as may be necessary or appropriate to carry out this section, including—

(1) the requirement to report information or the establishment of other methods for verifying the correct amounts of reimbursements under this section, and

(2) the application of this section to group health plans that are multiemployer plans (as defined in section 3(37) of the Employee Retirement Income Security Act of 1974).

Amendments to IRC §6432

Continuing Extension Act of 2010 (Pub. L. No. 111-157), as follows:
- **Rules Related to COBRA Premium Extension.** Act §3(b) added para. (18) to Pub. L. No. 111-5, Div. B, §3001(a) (see below for Pub. L. No. 111-5, Div. B, §3001(a)(1)–(10), as amended) provided:
    (18) Rules Related to April and May 2010 Extension.—In the case of an individual who, with regard to coverage described in paragraph (10)(B), experiences a qualifying event related to a termination of employment on or after April 1, 2010 and prior to the date of the enactment of this paragraph, rules similar to those in paragraphs (4)(A) and (7)(C) shall apply with respect to all continuation coverage, including State continuation coverage programs.

Temporary Extension Act of 2010 (Pub. L. No. 111-144), as follows:
- IRC §6432(a) was amended by Act §3(b)(5)(C)(i) by substituting "section 3001(a) of title III of division B of the American Recovery and Reinvestment Act of 2009" for "section 3002(a) of the Health Insurance Assistance for the Unemployed Act of 2009". Eff. as if included in Pub. L. No. 111-5, Div. B, §3001 [generally effective for premiums for periods of coverage beginning on or after Feb. 17, 2009].
- IRC §6432(c)(3) was amended by Act §3(b)(5)(C)(ii) by substituting "section 3001(a)(1)(A) of title III of division B of the American Recovery and Reinvestment Act of 2009" for "section 3002(a)(1)(A) of such Act". Eff. as if included in Pub. L. No. 111-5, Div. B, §3001 [generally effective for premiums for periods of coverage beginning on or after Feb. 17, 2009].
- IRC §6432(e)–(f) were amended by Act §3(b)(5)(C)(iii) by redesignating subsecs. (e) and (f) as subsecs. (f) and (g), respectively, and adding new subsec. (e). Eff. as if included in Pub. L. No. 111-5, Div. B, §3001 [generally effective for premiums for periods of coverage beginning on or after Feb. 17, 2009].
- **Other Provision.** Act §3(b)(1)(B), which added para. (17) to Pub. L. No. 111-5, Div. B, §3001(a) (see below for Pub. L. No. 111-5, Div. B, §3001(a)(1)–(10), as amended) provided:
    (17) Special Rules in case of individuals losing coverage because of a reduction of hours.—
    (A) New election period.—
    (i) In general.—For the purposes of the COBRA continuation provisions, in the case of an individual described in subparagraph (C) who did not make (or who made and discontinued) an election of COBRA continuation coverage on the basis of the reduction of hours of employment, the involuntary termination of employment of such individual on or after the date of the enactment of this paragraph shall be treated as a qualifying event.
    (ii) Counting COBRA duration period from previous qualifying event.—In any case of an individual referred to in clause

(i), the period of such individual's continuation coverage shall be determined as though the qualifying event were the reduction of hours of employment.
(iii) Construction.—Nothing in this paragraph shall be construed as requiring an individual referred to in clause (i) to make a payment for COBRA continuation coverage between the reduction of hours and the involuntary termination of employment.
(iv) Preexisting conditions.—With respect to an individual referred to in clause (i) who elects COBRA continuation coverage pursuant to such clause, rules similar to the rules in paragraph (4)(C) shall apply.
(B) Notices.—In the case of an individual described in subparagraph (C), the administrator of the group health plan (or other entity) involved shall provide, during the 60-day period beginning on the date of such individual's involuntary termination of employment, an additional notification described in paragraph (7)(A), including information on the provisions of this paragraph. Rules similar to the rules of paragraph (7) shall apply with respect to such notification.
(C) Individuals described.—Individuals described in this subparagraph are individuals who are assistance eligible individuals on the basis of a qualifying event consisting of a reduction of hours occurring during the period described in paragraph (3)(A) followed by an involuntary termination of employment insofar as such involuntary termination of employment occurred on or after the date of the enactment of this paragraph.

Department of Defense Appropriations Act, 2010 (Pub. L. No. 111-118), as follows:
- **Rules Related to COBRA Premium Extension.** Act Div. B, §1010, as amended by Pub. L. No. 111-144, §3(b)(2), which added para. (16) to Pub. L. No. 111-5, Div. B, §3001(a) (see below for Pub. L. No. 111-5, Div. B, §3001(a)(1)–(10), as amended) provided:
    (16) Rules related to 2009 extension.—
    (A) Election to pay premiums retroactively and maintain COBRA coverage.—In the case of any premium for a period of coverage during an assistance eligible individual's transition period, such individual shall be treated for purposes of any COBRA continuation provision as having timely paid the amount of such premium if—
    (i) such individual was covered under the COBRA continuation coverage to which such premium relates for the period of coverage immediately preceding such transition period, and
    (ii) such individual pays, the amount of such premium, after the application of paragraph (1)(A), by the latest of—
    (I) 60 days after the date of the enactment of this paragraph,
    (II) 30 days after the date of provision of the notification required under subparagraph (D)(ii), or
    (III) the end of the period described in section 4980B(f)(2)(B)(iii) of the Internal Revenue Code of 1986.
    (B) Refunds and credits for retroactive premium assistance eligibility.—In the case of an assistance eligible individual who pays, with respect to any period of COBRA continuation coverage during such individual's transition period, the premium amount for such coverage without regard to paragraph (1)(A), rules similar to the rules of paragraph (12)(E) shall apply.
    (C) Transition period.—
    (i) In general.—For purposes of this paragraph, the term "transition period" means, with respect to any assistance eligible individual, any period of coverage if—
    (I) such assistance eligible individual experienced an involuntary termination that was a qualifying event prior to the date of the enactment of the Department of Defense Appropriations Act, 2010; and
    (II) paragraph (1)(A) applies to such period by reason of the amendment made by section 1010(b) of the Department of Defense Appropriations Act, 2010.
    (ii) Construction.—Any period during the period described in subclauses (I) and (II) of clause (i) for which the applicable premium has been paid pursuant to subparagraph (A) shall be treated as a period of coverage referred to in such paragraph, irrespective of any failure to timely pay the applicable premium (other than pursuant to subparagraph (A)) for such period.

(D) Notification.—

(i) In general.—In the case of an individual who was an assistance eligible individual at any time on or after October 31, 2009, or experiences a qualifying event (consisting of termination of employment) relating to COBRA continuation coverage on or after such date, the administrator of the group health plan (or other entity) involved shall provide an additional notification with information regarding the amendments made by section 1010 of the Department of Defense Appropriations Act, 2010, within 60 days after the date of the enactment of such Act or, in the case of a qualifying event occurring after such date of enactment, consistent with the timing of notifications under paragraph (7)(A).

(ii) To individuals who lost assistance.—In the case of an assistance eligible individual described in subparagraph (A)(i) who did not timely pay the premium for any period of coverage during such individual's transition period or paid the premium for such period without regard to paragraph (1)(A), the administrator of the group health plan (or other entity) involved shall provide to such individual, within the first 60 days of such individual's transition period, an additional notification with information regarding the amendments made by section 1010 of the Department of Defense Appropriations Act, 2010, including information on the ability under subparagraph (A) to make retroactive premium payments with respect to the transition period of the individual in order to maintain COBRA continuation coverage.

(iii) Application of rules.—Rules similar to the rules of paragraph (7) shall apply with respect to notifications under this subparagraph.

American Recovery and Reinvestment Tax Act of 2009 (Pub. L. No. 111-5), as follows:

- IRC §6432 was added by Act, Div. B, §3001(a)(12)(A). Eff. generally for premiums for periods of coverage beginning on or after Feb. 17, 2009.

- **Other Provision.** Act Div. B, §3001(a)(1)–(11), *as amended by* Pub. L. No. 111-118, Div. B, §1010, Pub. L. No, 111-144, §3(a) and (b)(1)–(4), *and* Pub. L. No. 111-157, §3(a), provided:

SEC. 3001. PREMIUM ASSISTANCE FOR COBRA BENEFITS.

(a) Premium Assistance for COBRA Continuation Coverage for Individuals and Their Families.

(1)

(A) Reduction of Premiums Payable.—In the case of any premium for a period of coverage beginning on or after the date of the enactment of this Act for COBRA continuation coverage with respect to any assistance eligible individual, such individual shall be treated for purposes of any COBRA continuation provision as having paid the amount of such premium if such individual pays (or a person other than such individual's employer pays on behalf of such individual) 35 percent of the amount of such premium (as determined without regard to this subsection).

(B) Plan Enrollment Option.—

(i) In General.—Notwithstanding the COBRA continuation provisions, an assistance eligible individual may, not later than 90 days after the date of notice of the plan enrollment option described in this subparagraph, elect to enroll in coverage under a plan offered by the employer involved, or the employee organization involved (including, for this purpose, a joint board of trustees of a multiemployer trust affiliated with one or more multiemployer plans), that is different than coverage under the plan in which such individual was enrolled at the time the qualifying event occurred, and such coverage shall be treated as COBRA continuation coverage for purposes of the applicable COBRA continuation coverage provision.

(ii) Requirements.—An assistance eligible individual may elect to enroll in different coverage as described in clause (i) only if—

(I) the employer involved has made a determination that such employer will permit assistance eligible individuals to enroll in different coverage as provided for this subparagraph;

(II) the premium for such different coverage does not exceed the premium for coverage in which the individual was enrolled at the time the qualifying event occurred;

(III) the different coverage in which the individual elects to enroll is coverage that is also offered to the active employees of the employer at the time at which such election is made; and

(IV) the different coverage is not—

(aa) coverage that provides only dental, vision, counseling, or referral services (or a combination of such services);

(bb) a flexible spending arrangement (as defined in section 106(c)(2) of the Internal Revenue Code of 1986); or

(cc) coverage that provides coverage for services or treatments furnished in an on-site medical facility maintained by the employer and that consists primarily of first-aid services, prevention and wellness care, or similar care (or a combination of such care).

(C) Premium Reimbursement.—For provisions providing the balance of such premium, see section 6432 of the Internal Revenue Code of 1986, as added by paragraph (12).

(2) Limitation of period of premium assistance.—

(A) In general.—Paragraph (1)(A) shall not apply with respect to any assistance eligible individual for months of coverage beginning on or after the earlier of—

(i) the first date that such individual is eligible for coverage under any other group health plan (other than coverage consisting of only dental, vision, counseling, or referral services (or a combination thereof), coverage under a flexible spending arrangement (as defined in section 106(c)(2) of the Internal Revenue Code of 1986), or coverage of treatment that is furnished in an on-site medical facility maintained by the employer and that consists primarily of first-aid services, prevention and wellness care, or similar care (or a combination thereof)) or is eligible for benefits under title XVIII of the Social Security Act, or

(ii) the earliest of—

(I) the date which is 15 months after the first day that paragraph (1)(A) applies with respect to such individual,

(II) the date following the expiration of the maximum period of continuation coverage required under the applicable CO-BRA continuation coverage provision, or

(III) the date following the expiration of the period of continuation coverage allowed under paragraph (4)(B)(ii).

(B) Timing of eligibility for additional coverage.—For purposes of subparagraph (A)(i), an individual shall not be treated as eligible for coverage under a group health plan before the first date on which such individual could be covered under such plan.

(C) Notification requirement.—An assistance eligible individual shall notify in writing the group health plan with respect to which paragraph (1)(A) applies if such paragraph ceases to apply by reason of subparagraph (A)(i). Such notice shall be provided to the group health plan in such time and manner as may be specified by the Secretary of Labor.

(3) Assistance eligible individual.—For purposes of this section, the term "assistance eligible individual" means any qualified beneficiary if—

(A) such qualified beneficiary is eligible for COBRA continuation coverage related to a qualifying event occurring during the period that begins with September 1, 2008, and ends with May 31, 2010,

(B) such qualified beneficiary elects such coverage, and

(C) the qualifying event with respect to the COBRA continuation coverage consists of the involuntary termination of the covered employee's employment and occurred during such period or consists of a reduction of hours followed by such an involuntary termination of employment during such period (as described in paragraph (17)(C)).

(4) Extension of election period and effect on coverage.—

(A) In general.—For purposes of applying section 605(a) of the Employee Retirement Income Security Act of 1974, section 4980B(f)(5)(A) of the Internal Revenue Code of 1986, section 2205(a) of the Public Health Service Act, and section 8905a(c)(2) of title 5, United States Code, in the case of an individual who does not have an election of COBRA continuation coverage in effect on the date of the enactment of this Act but who would be an assistance eligible individual if such election were so in effect, such individual may elect the COBRA continuation coverage under the COBRA continua-

IRC Sec. 6432(g)(2)

tion coverage provisions containing such sections during the period beginning on the date of the enactment of this Act and ending 60 days after the date on which the notification required under paragraph (7)(C) is provided to such individual.

(B) Commencement of coverage; no reach-back.—Any COBRA continuation coverage elected by a qualified beneficiary during an extended election period under subparagraph (A)—

(i) shall commence with the first period of coverage beginning on or after the date of the enactment of this Act, and

(ii) shall not extend beyond the period of COBRA continuation coverage that would have been required under the applicable COBRA continuation coverage provision if the coverage had been elected as required under such provision.

(C) Preexisting conditions.—With respect to a qualified beneficiary who elects COBRA continuation coverage pursuant to subparagraph (A), the period—

(i) beginning on the date of the qualifying event, and

(ii) ending with the beginning of the period described in subparagraph (B)(i),

shall be disregarded for purposes of determining the 63-day periods referred to in section 701(c)(2) of the Employee Retirement Income Security Act of 1974, section 9801(c)(2) of the Internal Revenue Code of 1986, and section 2701(c)(2) of the Public Health Service Act.

(5) Expedited review of denials of premium assistance.—In any case in which an individual requests treatment as an assistance eligible individual and is denied such treatment by the group health plan, the Secretary of Labor (or the Secretary of Health and Human Services in connection with COBRA continuation coverage which is provided other than pursuant to part 6 of subtitle B of title I of the Employee Retirement Income Security Act of 1974), in consultation with the Secretary of the Treasury, shall provide for expedited review of such denial. An individual shall be entitled to such review upon application to such Secretary in such form and manner as shall be provided by such Secretary. Such Secretary shall make a determination regarding such individual's eligibility within 15 business days after receipt of such individual's application for review under this paragraph. Either Secretary's determination upon review of the denial shall be de novo and shall be the final determination of such Secretary. A reviewing court shall grant deference to such Secretary's determination. The provisions of this paragraph, paragraphs (1) through (4), and paragraph (7) shall be treated as provisions of title I of the Employee Retirement Income Security Act of 1974 for purposes of part 5 of subtitle B of such title. In addition to civil actions that may be brought to enforce applicable provisions of such Act or other laws, the appropriate Secretary or an affected individual may bring a civil action to enforce such determinations and for appropriate relief. In addition, such Secretary may assess a penalty against a plan sponsor or health insurance issuer of not more than $110 per day for each failure to comply with such determination of such Secretary after 10 days after the date of the plan sponsor's or issuer's receipt of the determination.

(6) Disregard of subsidies for purposes of federal and state programs.—Notwithstanding any other provision of law, any premium reduction with respect to an assistance eligible individual under this subsection shall not be considered income or resources in determining eligibility for, or the amount of assistance or benefits provided under, any other public benefit provided under Federal law or the law of any State or political subdivision thereof.

(7) Notices to individuals.—

(A) General notice.—

(i) In general.—In the case of notices provided under section 606(a)(4) of the Employee Retirement Income Security Act of 1974 (29 U.S.C. 1166(4)), section 4980B(f)(6)(D) of the Internal Revenue Code of 1986, section 2206(4) of the Public Health Service Act (42 U.S.C. 300bb-6(4)), or section 8905a(f)(2)(A) of title 5, United States Code, with respect to individuals who, during the period described in paragraph (3)(A), have a qualifying event relating to COBRA continuation coverage, the requirements of such sections shall not be treated as met unless such notices include an additional notification to the recipient of—

(I) the availability of premium reduction with respect to such coverage under this subsection, and

(II) the option to enroll in different coverage if the employer permits assistance eligible individuals to elect enrollment in different coverage (as described in paragraph (1)(B)).

(ii) Alternative notice.—In the case of COBRA continuation coverage to which the notice provision under such sections does not apply, the Secretary of Labor, in consultation with the Secretary of the Treasury and the Secretary of Health and Human Services, shall, in consultation with administrators of the group health plans (or other entities) that provide or administer the COBRA continuation coverage involved, provide rules requiring the provision of such notice.

(iii) Form.—The requirement of the additional notification under this subparagraph may be met by amendment of existing notice forms or by inclusion of a separate document with the notice otherwise required.

(B) Specific requirements.—Each additional notification under subparagraph (A) shall include—

(i) the forms necessary for establishing eligibility for premium reduction under this subsection,

(ii) the name, address, and telephone number necessary to contact the plan administrator and any other person maintaining relevant information in connection with such premium reduction,

(iii) a description of the extended election period provided for in paragraph (4)(A),

(iv) a description of the obligation of the qualified beneficiary under paragraph (2)(C) to notify the plan providing continuation coverage of eligibility for subsequent coverage under another group health plan or eligibility for benefits under title XVIII of the Social Security Act and the penalty provided under section 6720C of the Internal Revenue Code of 1986 for failure to so notify the plan,

(v) a description, displayed in a prominent manner, of the qualified beneficiary's right to a reduced premium and any conditions on entitlement to the reduced premium, and

(vi) a description of the option of the qualified beneficiary to enroll in different coverage if the employer permits such beneficiary to elect to enroll in such different coverage under paragraph (1)(B).

(C) Notice in connection with extended election periods.—In the case of any assistance eligible individual (or any individual described in paragraph (4)(A)) who became entitled to elect COBRA continuation coverage before the date of the enactment of this Act, the administrator of the group health plan (or other entity) involved shall provide (within 60 days after the date of enactment of this Act) for the additional notification required to be provided under subparagraph (A) and failure to provide such notice shall be treated as a failure to meet the notice requirements under the applicable COBRA continuation provision.

(D) Model notices.—Not later than 30 days after the date of enactment of this Act—

(i) the Secretary of the Labor, in consultation with the Secretary of the Treasury and the Secretary of Health and Human Services, shall prescribe models for the additional notification required under this paragraph (other than the additional notification described in clause (ii)), and

(ii) in the case of any additional notification provided pursuant to subparagraph (A) under section 8905a(f)(2)(A) of title 5, United States Code, the Office of Personnel Management shall prescribe a model for such additional notification.

(8) Regulations.—The Secretary of the Treasury may prescribe such regulations or other guidance as may be necessary or appropriate to carry out the provisions of this subsection, including the prevention of fraud and abuse under this subsection, except that the Secretary of Labor and the Secretary of Health and Human Services may prescribe such regulations (including interim final regulations) or other guidance as may be necessary or appropriate to carry out the provisions of paragraphs (5), (7), and (9).

(9) Outreach.—The Secretary of Labor, in consultation with the Secretary of the Treasury and the Secretary of Health and Human Services, shall provide outreach consisting of public education and enrollment assistance relating to premium re-

IRC Sec. 6432(g)(2)

duction provided under this subsection. Such outreach shall target employers, group health plan administrators, public assistance programs, States, insurers, and other entities as determined appropriate by such Secretaries. Such outreach shall include an initial focus on those individuals electing continuation coverage who are referred to in paragraph (7)(C). Information on such premium reduction, including enrollment, shall also be made available on websites of the Departments of Labor, Treasury, and Health and Human Services.

(10) Definitions.—For purposes of this section—

(A) Administrators.—The term "administrator" has the meaning given such term in section 3(16)(A) of the Employee Retirement Income Security Act of 1974.

(B) COBRA continuation coverage.—The term "COBRA continuation coverage" means continuation coverage provided pursuant to part 6 of subtitle B of title I of the Employee Retirement Income Security Act of 1974 (other than under section 609), title XXII of the Public Health Service Act, section 4980B of the Internal Revenue Code of 1986 (other than subsection (f)(1) of such section insofar as it relates to pediatric vaccines), or section 8905a of title 5, United States Code, or under a State program that provides comparable continuation coverage. Such term does not include coverage under a health flexible spending arrangement under a cafeteria plan within the meaning of section 125 of the Internal Revenue Code of 1986.

(C) COBRA continuation provision.—The term "COBRA continuation provision" means the provisions of law described in subparagraph (B).

(D) Covered employee.—The term "covered employee" has the meaning given such term in section 607(2) of the Employee Retirement Income Security Act of 1974.

(E) Qualified beneficiary.—The term "qualified beneficiary" has the meaning given such term in section 607(3) of the Employee Retirement Income Security Act of 1974.

(F) Group health plan.—The term "group health plan" has the meaning given such term in section 607(1) of the Employee Retirement Income Security Act of 1974.

(G) State.—The term "State" includes the District of Columbia, the Commonwealth of Puerto Rico, the Virgin Islands, Guam, American Samoa, and the Commonwealth of the Northern Mariana Islands.

(H) Period of coverage.—Any reference in this subsection to a period of coverage shall be treated as a reference to a monthly or shorter period of coverage with respect to which premiums are charged with respect to such coverage.

(11) Reports.—

(A) Interim reports.—The Secretary of the Treasury shall submit an interim report to the Committee on Education and Labor, the Committee on Ways and Means, and the Committee on Energy and Commerce of the House of Representatives and the Committee on Health, Education, Labor, and Pensions and the Committee on Finance of the Senate regarding the premium reduction provided under this subsection that includes—

(i) the number of individuals provided such assistance as of the date of the report; and

(ii) the total amount of expenditures incurred (with administrative expenditures noted separately) in connection with such assistance as of the date of the report.

(B) Final reports.—As soon as practicable after the last period of COBRA continuation coverage for which premium reduction is provided under this section, the Secretary of the Treasury shall submit a final report to each Committee referred to in subparagraph (A) that includes—

(i) the number of individuals provided premium reduction under this section;

(ii) the average dollar amount (monthly and annually) of premium reductions provided to such individuals; and

(iii) the total amount of expenditures incurred (with administrative expenditures noted separately) in connection with premium reduction under this section.

• **Other Provision.** Act Div. B, §3001(a)(12)(E), provided:

(E) Special rule.—

(i) In general.—In the case of an assistance eligible individual who pays, with respect to the first period of COBRA continu-

ation coverage to which subsection (a)(1)(A) applies or the immediately subsequent period, the full premium amount for such coverage, the person to whom such payment is payable shall—

(I) make a reimbursement payment to such individual for the amount of such premium paid in excess of the amount required to be paid under subsection (a)(1)(A); or

(II) provide credit to the individual for such amount in a manner that reduces one or more subsequent premium payments that the individual is required to pay under such subsection for the coverage involved.

(ii) Reimbursing employer.—A person to which clause (i) applies shall be reimbursed as provided for in section 6432 of the Internal Revenue Code of 1986 for any payment made, or credit provided, to the employee under such clause.

(iii) Payment or credits.—Unless it is reasonable to believe that the credit for the excess payment in clause (i)(II) will be used by the assistance eligible individual within 180 days of the date on which the person receives from the individual the payment of the full premium amount, a person to which clause (i) applies shall make the payment required under such clause to the individual within 60 days of such payment of the full premium amount. If, as of any day within the 180-day period, it is no longer reasonable to believe that the credit will be used during that period, payment equal to the remainder of the credit outstanding shall be made to the individual within 60 days of such day.

• **Other Provision.** Pub. L. No. 111-118, Div. B, §1010(c), as amended by Pub. L. No. 111-144, §3(b)(2), which added para. (16) to §3001(a) of Pub. L. No. 111-5, Div. B, provided:

(16) Rules related to 2009 extension.—

(A) Election to Pay Premiums Retroactively and Maintain COBRA Coverage.—In the case of any premium for a period of coverage during an assistance eligible individual's transition period, such individual shall be treated for purposes of any COBRA continuation provision as having timely paid the amount of such premium if—

(i) such individual was covered under the COBRA continuation coverage to which such premium relates for the period of coverage immediately preceding such transition period, and

(ii) such individual pays, the amount of such premium, after the application of paragraph (1)(A), by the latest of—

(I) 60 days after the date of the enactment of this paragraph,

(II) 30 days after the date of provision of the notification required under subparagraph (D)(ii), or

(III) the end of the period described in section 4980B(f)(2)(B)(iii) of the Internal Revenue Code of 1986.

(B) Refunds and credits for retroactive premium assistance eligibility.—In the case of an assistance eligible individual who pays, with respect to any period of COBRA continuation coverage during such individual's transition period, the premium amount for such coverage without regard to paragraph (1)(A), rules similar to the rules of paragraph (12)(E) shall apply.

(C) Transition period.—

(i) In general.—For purposes of this paragraph, the term "transition period" means, with respect to any assistance eligible individual, any period of coverage if—

(I) such assistance eligible individual experienced an involuntary termination that was a qualifying event prior to the date of the enactment of the Department of Defense Appropriations Act, 2010; and

(II) paragraph (1)(A) applies to such period by reason of the amendment made by section 1010(b) of the Department of Defense Appropriations Act, 2010.

(ii) Construction.—Any period during the period described in subclauses (I) and (II) of clause (i) for which the applicable premium has been paid pursuant to subparagraph (A) shall be treated as a period of coverage referred to in such paragraph, irrespective of any failure to timely pay the applicable premium (other than pursuant to subparagraph (A)) for such period.

(D) Notification.—

(i) In general.—In the case of an individual who was an assistance eligible individual at any time on or after October 31, 2009, or experiences a qualifying event (consisting of termination of employment) relating to COBRA continuation coverage on or after such date, the administrator of the group health plan (or other entity) involved shall provide an additional notification with information regarding the amendments made by section 1010 of the Department of Defense Appropriations Act, 2010, within 60 days after the date of the enactment of such Act or, in the case of a qualifying event occurring after such date of enactment, consistent with the timing of notifications under paragraph (7)(A).

(ii) To individuals who lost assistance.—In the case of an assistance eligible individual described in subparagraph (A)(i) who did not timely pay the premium for any period of coverage during such individual's transition period or paid the premium for such period without regard to paragraph (1)(A), the administrator of the group health plan (or other entity) involved shall provide to such individual, within the first 60 days of such individual's transition period, an additional notification with information regarding the amendments made by section 1010 of the Department of Defense Appropriations Act, 2010, including information on the ability under subparagraph (A) to make retroactive premium payments with respect to the transition period of the individual in order to maintain COBRA continuation coverage.

(iii) Application of rules.—Rules similar to the rules of paragraph (7) shall apply with respect to notifications under this subparagraph.

- **Other Provision.** Act Div. B, §3001(b), provided:

  (b) Elimination of Premium Subsidy for High-Income Individuals.—

  (1) Recapture of subsidy for high-income individuals.—If—

  (A) premium assistance is provided under this section with respect to any COBRA continuation coverage which covers the taxpayer, the taxpayer's spouse, or any dependent (within the meaning of section 152 of the Internal Revenue Code of 1986, determined without regard to subsections (b)(1), (b)(2), and (d)(1)(B) thereof) of the taxpayer during any portion of the taxable year, and

  (B) the taxpayer's modified adjusted gross income for such taxable year exceeds $125,000 ($250,000 in the case of a joint return),

  then the tax imposed by chapter 1 of such Code with respect to the taxpayer for such taxable year shall be increased by the amount of such assistance.

  (2) Phase-in of recapture.—

  (A) In General.—In the case of a taxpayer whose modified adjusted gross income for the taxable year does not exceed $145,000 ($290,000 in the case of a joint return), the increase in the tax imposed under paragraph (1) shall not exceed the phase-in percentage of such increase (determined without regard to this paragraph).

  (B) Phase-In Percentage.—For purposes of this subsection, the term "phase-in percentage" means the ratio (expressed as a percentage) obtained by dividing—

  (i) the excess of described in subparagraph (B) of paragraph (1), by

  (ii) $20,000 ($40,000 in the case of a joint return).

  (3) Option for high-income individuals to wave assistance and avoid recapture.—Notwithstanding subsection (a)(3), an individual shall not be treated as an assistance eligible individual for purposes of this section and section 6432 of the Internal Revenue Code of 1986 if such individual—

  (A) makes a permanent election (at such time and in such form and manner as the Secretary of the Treasury may prescribe) to waive the right to the premium assistance provided under this section, and

  (B) notifies the entity to whom premiums are reimbursed under section 6432(a) of such Code of such election.

  (4) Modified adjusted gross income.—For purposes of this subsection, the term "modified adjusted gross income" means the adjusted gross income (as defined in section 62 of the Internal Revenue Code of 1986) of the taxpayer for the taxable year increased by any amount excluded from gross income under section 911, 931, or 933 of such Code.

  (5) Credits not allowed against tax, etc.—For purposes determining regular tax liability under section 26(b) of such Code, the increase in tax under this subsection shall not be treated as a tax imposed under chapter 1 of such Code.

(6) Regulations.—The Secretary of the Treasury shall issue such regulations or other guidance as are necessary or appropriate to carry out this subsection, including requirements that the entity to whom premiums are reimbursed under section 6432(a) of the Internal Revenue Code of 1986 report to the Secretary, and to each assistance eligible individual, the amount of premium assistance provided under subsection (a) with respect to each such individual.

(7) Effective date.—The provisions of this subsection shall apply to taxable years ending after the date of the enactment of this Act [Enacted: Feb. 17, 2009].

---

* * *

Chapter 68—Additions to the Tax, Additional Amounts, and Assessable Penalties

Subchapter A—Additions to the Tax and Additional Amounts

Part I—General Provisions

* * *

SEC. 6652. FAILURE TO FILE CERTAIN INFORMATION RETURNS, REGISTRATION STATEMENTS, ETC.

* * *

(d) Annual Registration and Other Notification by Pension Plan.—

(1) Registration.—In the case of any failure to file a registration statement required under section 6057(a) (relating to annual registration of certain plans) which includes all participants required to be included in suchstatement, on the date prescribed therefor(determined without regard to any extension of time for filing), unless it is shown that such failure is due to reasonable cause, there shall be paid (on notice and demand by the Secretary and in the same manner as tax) by the person failing so to file, an amount equal to $1 for each participant with respect to whom there is a failure to file, multiplied by the number of days during which such failure continues, but the total amount imposed under this paragraph on any person for any failure to file with respect to any plan year shall not exceed $5,000.

(2) Notification of change of status.—In the case of failure to file a notification required under section 6057(b) (relating to notification of change of status) on the date prescribed therefor (determined without regard to any extension of time for filing), unless it is shown that such failure is due to reasonable cause, there shall be paid (on notice and demand by the Secretary in the same manner as tax) by the person failing so to file, $1 for each day during which such failure continues, but the total amounts imposed under this paragraph on any person for failure to file any notification shall not exceed $1,000.

(e) Information Required in Connection With Certain Plans of Deferred Compensation, etc.—In the case of failure to file a return or statement required under section 6058 (relating to information required in connection with certain plans of deferred compensation), 6047 (relating to information relating to certain trusts and annuity and bond purchase plans), or 6039D (relating to returns and records with respect to certain fringe benefit plans) on the date and in the manner prescribed therefor (determined with regard to any extension of time for filing), unless it is shown that such failure is due to reasonable cause, there shall be paid (on notice and demand by the Secretary and in the same manner as tax) by the person failing so to file, $25 for each day during which such failure continues, but the total amount imposed under this subsection on any person for failure to file any return shall not exceed $15,000. This subsection shall not apply to any return or statement which is an information return described in section 6724(d)(1)(C)(ii) or a payee statement described in section 6724(d)(2)(Y).

* * *

(g) Information Required in Connection With Deductible Employee Contributions.—In the case of failure to make a report required by section 219(f)(4) which contains the information required by such section on the date prescribed therefor (determined with regard to any extension of time for filing), there shall be paid (on notice and demand by the Secretary and in the same manner as tax) by the person failing so to file, an amount equal to $25 for each participant with respect to whom there was a failure to file such information, multiplied by the number of years during which such failure continues, but the total amount imposed under this subsection on any person for failure to file shall not exceed $10,000. No penalty shall be imposed under this subsection for any failure which is shown to be due to reasonable cause and not willful neglect.

(h) Failure to Give Notice to Recipients of Certain Pension, etc., Distributions.—In the case of each failure to provide a notice as required by section 3405(e)(10)(B), at the time prescribed therefor, unless it is shown that such failure is due to reasonable cause and not to willful neglect, there shall be paid, on notice and demand of the Secretary and in the same manner as tax, by the person failing to provide such notice, an amount equal to $10 for each such failure, but the total amount imposed on such person for all such failures during any calendar year shall not exceed $5,000.

(i) Failure to Give Written Explanation to Recipients of Certain Qualifying Rollover Distributions.—In the case of each failure to provide a written explanation as required by section 401(f), at the time prescribed therefor, unless it is shown that such failure is due to reasonable cause and not to willful neglect, there shall be paid, on notice and demand of the Secretary and in the same manner as tax, by the person failing to provide such written explanation, an amount equal to $100 for each such failure, but the

total amount imposed on such person for all such failures during any calendar year shall not exceed $50,000.

* * *

Part II—Accuracy-Related and Fraud Penalties

SEC. 6662. IMPOSITION OF ACCURACY-RELATED PENALTY ON UNDERPAYMENTS.

(a) Imposition of Penalty.—If this section applies to any portion of an underpayment of tax required to be shown on a return, there shall be added to the tax an amount equal to 20 percent of the portion of the underpayment to which this section applies.

(b) Portion of Underpayment to Which Section Applies.—This section shall apply to the portion of any underpayment which is attributable to 1 or more of the following:

* * *

(4) Any substantial overstatement of pension liabilities.

* * *

This section shall not apply to any portion of an underpayment on which a penalty is imposed under section 6663. Except as provided in paragraph (1) or (2)(B) of section 6662A(e), this section shall not apply to the portion of any underpayment which is attributable to a reportable transaction understatement on which a penalty is imposed under section 6662A.

(c) Negligence.—For purposes of this section, the term "negligence" includes any failure to make a reasonable attempt to comply with the provisions of this title, and the term "disregard" includes any careless, reckless, or intentional disregard.

* * *

(f) Substantial Overstatement of Pension Liabilities.—

(1) In general.—For purposes of this section, there is a substantial overstatement of pension liabilities if the actuarial determination of the liabilities taken into account for purposes of computing the deduction under paragraph (1) or (2) of section 404(a) is 200 percent or more of the amount determined to be the correct amount of such liabilities.

(2) Limitation.—No penalty shall be imposed by reason of subsection (b)(4) unless the portion of the underpayment for the taxable year attributable to substantial overstatements of pension liabilities exceeds $1,000.

* * *

Recent Amendments to IRC §6662 (as Excerpted)

American Jobs Creation Act of 2004 (Pub. L. No. 108-357), as follows:

IRC Sec. 6662(f)(2)

● IRC §6662 was amended by Act §812(e)(1) in the heading. Eff. tax years ending after Oct. 22, 2004. IRC §6662 heading prior to amendment:

SEC. 6662. IMPOSITION OF ACCURACY-RELATED PENALTY.

Gulf Opportunity Zone Act of 2005 (Pub. L. No. 109-135), as follows:

● IRC §6662(b) was amended by Act §403(x)(1) by adding new sentence at the end. Eff. tax years ending after Oct. 22, 2004, as if included in the provision in Pub. L. No. 108-357 to which it relates.

* * *

Subchapter B—Assessable Penalties

Part I—General Provisions
* * *

SEC. 6690. FRAUDULENT STATEMENT OR FAILURE TO FURNISH STATEMENT TO PLAN PARTICIPANT.

Any person required under section 6057(e) to furnish a statement to a participant who willfully furnishes a false or fraudulent statement, or who willfully fails to furnish a statement in the manner, at the time, and showing the information required under section 6057(e), or regulations prescribed thereunder, shall for each such act, or for each such failure, be subject to a penalty under this subchapter of $50, which shall be assessed and collected in the same manner as the tax on employers imposed by section 3111.

SEC. 6692. FAILURE TO FILE ACTUARIAL REPORT.

The plan administrator (as defined in section 414(g)) of each defined benefit plan to which section 412 applies who fails to file the report required by section 6059 at the time and in the manner required by section 6059, shall pay a penalty of $1,000 for each such failure unless it is shown that such failure is due to reasonable cause.

SEC. 6693. FAILURE TO PROVIDE REPORTS ON CERTAIN TAX-FAVORED ACCOUNTS OR ANNUITIES; PENALTIES RELATING TO DESIGNATED NONDEDUCTIBLE CONTRIBUTIONS.

(a) Reports.—

(1) In general.—If a person required to file a report under a provision referred to in paragraph (2) fails to file such report at the time and in the manner required by such provision, such person shall pay a penalty of $50 for each failure unless it is shown that such failure is due to reasonable cause.

(2) Provisions.—The provisions referred to in this paragraph are—

(A) subsections (i) and (*l*) of section 408 (relating to individual retirement plans),

(B) section 220(h) (relating to Archer MSAs),

(C) Section 223(h) (relating to health savings accounts),

(D) section 529(d) (relating to qualified tuition programs), and

(E) section 530(h) (relating to Coverdell education savings accounts).

This subsection shall not apply to any report which is an information return described in section 6724(d)(1)(C)(i) or a payee statement described in section 6724(d)(2)(W). This subsection shall not apply to any report which is an information return described in section 6724(d)(1)(C)(i) or a payee statement described in section 6724(d)(2)(X).

(b) Penalties Relating to Nondeductible Contributions.—

(1) Overstatement of designated nondeductible contributions.—Any individual who—

(A) is required to furnish information under section 408(o)(4) as to the amount of designated nondeductible contributions made for any taxable year, and

(B) overstates the amount of such contributions made for such taxable year, shall pay a penalty of $100 for each such overstatement unless it is shown that such overstatement is due to reasonable cause.

(2) Failure to file form.—Any individual who fails to file a form required to be filed by the Secretary under section 408(o)(4) shall pay a penalty of $50 for each such failure unless it is shown that such failure is due to reasonable cause.

(c) Penalties Relating to Simple Retirement Accounts.—

(1) Employer penalties.—An employer who fails to provide 1 or more notices required by section 408(*l*)(2)(C) shall pay a penalty of $50 for each day on which such failures continue.

(2) Trustee and issuer penalties.—A trustee or issuer who fails—

(A) to provide 1 or more statements required by the last sentence of section 408(i) shall pay a penalty of $50 for each day on which such failures continue, or

(B) to provide 1 or more summary descriptions required by section 408(*l*)(2)(B) shall pay a penalty of $50 for each day on which such failures continue.

(3) Reasonable cause exception.—No penalty shall be imposed under this subsection with respect to any failure which the taxpayer shows was due to reasonable cause.

(d) Deficiency Procedures Not to Apply.—Subchapter B of chapter 63 (relating to deficiency procedures for income, estate, gift, and certain excise tax) does not apply to the assessment or collection of any penalty imposed by this section.

Recent Amendments to IRC §6693

Pension Protection Act of 2006 (Pub. L. No. 109-280), as follows:

- **Other Provision.** Act §1304(a) provides:

  (a) Permanent Extension of Modifications.—Section 901 of the Economic Growth and Tax Relief Reconciliation Act of 2001 [Pub. L. No. 107-16] (relating to sunset provisions) shall not apply to section 402 of such Act (relating to modifications to qualified tuition programs).

Medicare Prescription Drug, Improvement, and Modernization Act of 2003 (Pub. L. No. 108-173), as follows:

- IRC §6693(a)(2) was amended by Act §1201(g) by redesignating subparas. (C) and (D) as subparas. (D) and (E), respectively, and by adding a new subpara. (C). Eff. tax years beginning after Dec. 31, 2003.

Pub. L. No. 107-22, as follows:

- IRC §6693(a)(2)(D) was amended by Act §1(b)(2)(C) by replacing "education individual retirement" with "Coverdell education savings." Eff. Jul. 26, 2001.

Economic Growth and Tax Relief Reconciliation Act of 2001 (Pub. L. No. 107-16), as follows:

- IRC §6693(a)(2)(C) was amended by Act §402(a)(4)(A) by replacing "qualified State tuition" with "qualified tuition." Eff. for tax years beginning after Dec. 31, 2001.

- **Sunset Provision.** Act §901, as amended by Pub. L. No. 111-312, §101(a)(1), provides the sunset rule below. But see Pub. L. No. 109-280, §811, and Pub. L. No. 111-148, §10909(c), as amended by Pub. L. No. 111-312, §101(b)(1).

  SEC. 901. SUNSET OF PROVISIONS OF ACT.

  (a) In general. All provisions of, and amendments made by, this Act shall not apply—

  (1) to taxable, plan, or limitation years beginning after December 31, 2012, or

  (2) in the case of title V, to estates of decedents dying, gifts made, or generation skipping transfers, after December 31, 2012.

  (b) Application of certain laws.—The Internal Revenue Code of 1986 and the Employee Retirement Income Security Act of 1974 shall be applied and administered to years, estates, gifts, and transfers described in subsection (a) as if the provisions and amendments described in subsection (a) had never been enacted.

---

* * *

SEC. 6704. FAILURE TO KEEP RECORDS NECESSARY TO MEET REPORTING REQUIREMENTS UNDER SECTION 6047(d).

(a) Liability for Penalty. Any person who—

(1) has a duty to report or may have a duty to report any information under section 6047(d), and

(2) fails to keep such records as may be required by regulations prescribed under section 6047(d) for the purpose of providing the necessary data base for either current reporting or future reporting, shall pay a penalty for each calendar year for which there is any failure to keep such records.

(b) Amount of Penalty.

(1) In general. The penalty of any person for any calendar year shall be $50, multiplied by the number of individuals with respect to whom such failure occurs in such year.

(2) Maximum amount. The penalty under this section of any person for any calendar year shall not exceed $50,000.

(c) Exceptions.

(1) Reasonable cause. No penalty shall be imposed by this section on any person for any failure which is shown to be due to reasonable cause and not to willful neglect.

(2) Inability to correct previous failure. No penalty shall be imposed by this section on any failure by a person if such failure is attributable to a prior failure which has been penalized under this section and with respect to which the person has made all reasonable efforts to correct the failure.

(3) Pre-1983 failures. No penalty shall be imposed by this section on any person for any failure which is attributable to a failure occurring before January 1, 1983, if the person has made all reasonable efforts to correct such pre-1983 failure.

* * *

Editor's Note

IRC §6720C, below, as amended by Pub. L. No. 111-144, §3(b)(5)(D), is effective as if included in Pub. L. No. 111-5, Div. B, §3001 [effective for failures occurring after the date of enactment (enacted Feb. 17, 2009)].

SEC. 6720C. PENALTY FOR FAILURE TO NOTIFY HEALTH PLAN OF CESSATION OF ELIGIBLITY FOR COBRA PREMIUM ASSISTANCE.

(a) In General.—Any person required to notify a group health plan under section 3001(a)(2)(C) of title III of division B of the American Recovery and Reinvestment Act of 2009 who fails to make such a notification at such time and in such manner as the Secretary of Labor may require shall pay a penalty of 110 percent of the premium reduction provided under such section after termination of eligibility under such subsection.

(b) Reasonable Cause Exception.—No penalty shall be imposed under subsection (a) with respect to any failure if it is shown that such failure is due to reasonable cause and not to willful neglect.

Amendments to IRC §6720C

Temporary Extension Act of 2010 (Pub. L. No. 111-144), as follows:

- IRC §6720C(a) was amended by Act §3(b)(5)(D) by substituting "section 3001(a)(2)(C) of title III of division B of the American

Recovery and Reinvestment Act of 2009" for "section 3002(a)(2)(C)" of the Health Insurance Assistance for the Unemployed Act of 2009". Eff. as if included in Pub. L. No. 111-5, Div. B, §3001 [effective for failures occurring after date of enactment (enacted: Feb. 17, 2009)]. See amendment notes for IRC §6432 for text of Pub. L. No. 111-5, Div. B, §3001, as amended.

American Recovery and Reinvestment Tax Act of 2009 (Pub. L. No. 111-5), as follows:

• IRC §6720C was added by Act Div. B, §3001(a)(13)(A). Eff. for failures occurring after enactment of this Act [enacted: Feb. 17, 2009]. See amendment notes for IRC §6432 for text of Pub. L. No. 111-5, Div. B, §3001, as amended.

* * *

Chapter 76—Judicial Proceedings
* * *

Subchapter C—The Tax Court
* * *

Part IV—Declaratory Judgments

SEC. 7476. DECLARATORY JUDGMENTS RELATING TO QUALIFICATION OF CERTAIN RETIREMENT PLANS.

(a) Creation of Remedy.—In the case of actual controversy involving—

(1) a determination by the Secretary with respect to the initial qualification or continuing qualification of a retirement plan under subchapter D of chapter 1, or

(2) a failure by the Secretary to make a determination with respect to—

(A) such initial qualification, or

(B) such continuing qualification if the controversy arises from a plan amendment or plan termination,

upon the filing of an appropriate pleading, the Tax Court may make a declaration with respect to such initial qualification or continuing qualification. Any such declaration shall have the force and effect of a decision of the Tax Court and shall be reviewable as such. For purposes of this section, a determination with respect to a continuing qualification includes any revocation of or other change in a qualification.

(b) Limitations.—

(1) Petitioner.—A pleading may be filed under this section only by a petitioner who is the employer, the plan administrator, an employee who has qualified under regulations prescribed by the Secretary as an interested party for purposes of pursuing administrative remedies within the Internal Revenue Service, or the Pension Benefit Guaranty Corporation.

(2) Notice.—For purposes of this section, the filing of a pleading by any petitioner may be held by the Tax Court to be premature, unless the petitioner establishes to the satisfaction of the court that he has complied with the requirements prescribed by regulations of the Secretary with respect to notice to other interested parties of the filing of the request for a determination referred to in subsection (a).

(3) Exhaustion of administrative remedies.— The Tax Court shall not issue a declaratory judgment or decree under this section in any proceeding unless it determines that the petitioner has exhausted administrative remedies available to him within the Internal Revenue Service. A petitioner shall not be deemed to have exhausted his administrative remedies with respect to failure by the Secretary to make a determination with respect to initial qualification or continuing qualification of a retirement plan before the expiration of 270 days after the request for such determination was made.

(4) Plan put into effect.—No proceeding may be maintained under this section unless the plan (and, in the case of a controversy involving the continuing qualification of the plan because of an amendment to the plan, the amendment) with respect to which a decision of the Tax Court is sought has been put into effect before the filing of the pleading. A plan or amendment shall not be treated as not being in effect merely because under the plan the funds contributed to the plan may be refunded if the plan (or the plan as so amended) is found to be not qualified.

(5) Time for bringing action.—If the Secretary sends by certified or registered mail notice of his determination with respect to the qualification of the plan to the persons referred to in paragraph (1) (or, in the case of employees referred to in paragraph (1), to any individual designated under regulations prescribed by the Secretary as a representative of such employee), no proceeding may be initiated under this section by any person unless the pleading is filed before the ninety-first day after the day after such notice is mailed to such person (or to his designated representative, in the case of an employee).

(c) Retirement Plan.—For purposes of this section, the term "retirement plan" means—

(1) a pension, profit-sharing, or stock bonus plan described in section 401(a) or a trust which is part of such a plan, or

(2) an annuity plan described in section 403(a).

(d) Cross Reference.—For provisions concerning intervention by Pension Benefit Guaranty Corporation and Secretary of Labor in actions brought under this section and right of Pension Benefit Guaranty Corporation to bring action, see section 3001(c) of subtitle A of title III of the Employee Retirement Income Security Act of 1974.

* * *

Chapter 77—Miscellaneous Provisions

SEC. 7508. TIME FOR PERFORMING CERTAIN ACTS POSTPONED BY REASON OF SERVICE IN COMBAT ZONE OR CONTINGENCY OPERATION.

(a) Time to Be Disregarded.—In the case of an individual serving in the Armed Forces of the United States, or serving in support of such Armed Forces, in an area designated by the President of the United States by Executive order as a "combat zone" for purposes of section 112, or when deployed outside the United States away from the individual's permanent duty station while participating in an operation designated by the Secretary of Defense as a contingency operation (as defined in section 101(a)(13) of Title 10, United States Code) or which became such a contingency operation by operation of law at any time during the period designated by the President by Executive order as the period of combatant activities in such zone for purposes of such section or at any time during the period of such contingency operation, or hospitalized as a result of injury received while serving in such an area or operation during such time, the period of service in such area or operation, plus the period of continuous qualified hospitalization attributable to such injury, and the next 180 days thereafter, shall be disregarded in determining, under the internal revenue laws, in respect of any tax liability (including any interest, penalty, additional amount, or addition to the tax) of such individual—

(1) Whether any of the following acts was performed within the time prescribed therefor:

(A) Filing any return of income, estate, gift, employment, or excise tax;

(B) Payment of any income, estate, gift, employment, or excise tax or any installment thereof or of any other liability to the United States in respect thereof;

(C) Filing a petition with the Tax Court for redetermination of a deficiency, or for review of a decision rendered by the Tax Court;

(D) Allowance of a credit or refund of any tax;

(E) Filing a claim for credit or refund of any tax;

(F) Bringing suit upon any such claim for credit or refund;

(G) Assessment of any tax;

(H) Giving or making any notice or demand for the payment of any tax, or with respect to any liability to the United States in respect of any tax;

(I) Collection, by the Secretary, by levy or otherwise, of the amount of any liability in respect of any tax;

(J) Bringing suit by the United States, or any officer on its behalf, in respect of any liability in respect of any tax; and

(K) Any other act required or permitted under the internal revenue laws specified by the Secretary;

(2) The amount of any credit or refund.

* * *

Recent Amendments to IRC §7508 (as Excerpted)

Katrina Emergency Tax Relief Act of 2005 (Pub. L. No. 109-73), as follows:
● IRC §7508(a)(1)(A)–(B) were amended by Act §403(a). Eff. for any period for performing an act which has not expired before Aug. 25, 2005. IRC §7508(a)(1)(A)–(B) prior to amendment:
   (A) Filing any return of income, estate, or gift tax (except income tax withheld at source and income tax imposed by subtitle C or any other law superseded thereby);
   (B) Payment of any income, estate, or gift tax (except income tax withheld at source and income tax imposed by subtitle C or any law superseded thereby) or any installment thereof or of any other liability to the United States in respect thereof;

Military Family Tax Relief Act of 2003 (Pub. L. No. 108-121), as follows:
● IRC §7508(a) was amended by Act §104(a)(1) by inserting ", or when deployed outside the United States away from the individual's permanent duty station while participating in an operation designated by the Secretary of Defense as a contingency operation (as defined in section 101(a)(13) of title 10, United States Code) or which became such a contingency operation by operation of law" after "§112". Eff. for any period for performing an act which has not expired before Nov. 11, 2003.
● IRC §7508(a) was amended by Act §104(a)(2) by inserting in the first sentence "or at any time during the period of such contingency operation" after "for purposes of such section". Eff. for any period for performing an act which has not expired before Nov. 11, 2003.
● IRC §7508(a) was amended by Act §104(a)(3) by inserting "or operation" after "such an area". Eff. for any period for performing an act which has not expired before Nov. 11, 2003.
● IRC §7508(a) was amended by Act §104(a)(4) and by inserting "or operation" after "such area". Eff. for any period for performing an act which has not expired before Nov. 11, 2003.
● IRC §7508 was amended by Act §104(b)(2) by inserting in the heading "OR CONTINGENCY OPERATION" after "COMBAT ZONE." Eff. for any period for performing an act which has not expired before Nov. 11, 2003.

Victims of Terrorism Tax Relief Act of 2001 (Pub. L. No. 107-134), as follows:
● IRC §7508(a)(1)(K) was amended by Act §112(b) by striking "in regulations prescribed under this section" after "specified." Eff. for disasters and terroristic or military actions occurring on or after Sept. 11, 2001, with respect to any action of the Secretary of the Treasury, Secretary of Labor, or PBGC occurring on or after Oct. 23, 2002.

SEC. 7508A. AUTHORITY TO POSTPONE CERTAIN DEADLINES BY REASON OF PRESIDENTIALLY DECLARED DISASTER OR TERRORISTIC OR MILITARY ACTIONS.

(a) In General.—In the case of a taxpayer determined by the Secretary to be affected by a federally declared disaster (as defined by section 165(h)(3)(C)(i)) or a terroristic or military action (as defined in section 692(c)(2)), the Secretary may specify a period of up to one year that may be disregarded in determining, under the internal revenue laws, in respect of any tax liability of such taxpayer—

(1) whether any of the acts described in paragraph (1) of section 7508(a) were performed within the time prescribed therefore determined without regard to extension under any other provision of this subtitle for periods after the date (determined by the Secretary) of such disaster or action),

(2) the amount of any interest, penalty, additional amount, or addition to the tax for periods after such date, and

(3) the amount of any credit or refund.

(b) Special Rules Regarding Pensions, etc.—In the case of a pension or other employee benefit plan, or any sponsor, administrator, participant, beneficiary, or other person with respect to such plan, affected by a disaster or action described in subsection (a), the Secretary may specify a period of up to 1 year which may be disregarded in determining the date by which any action is required or permitted to be completed under this title. No plan shall be treated as failing to be operated in accordance with the terms of the plan solely as the result of disregarding any period by reason of the preceding sentence.

(c) Special Rules for Overpayments.—The rules of section 7508(b) shall apply for purposes of this section.

Recent Amendments to IRC §7508A

Tax Extenders and Alternative Minimum Tax Relief Act of 2008 (Pub. L. No. 110-343), as follows:
● IRC §7508A(a) was amended by Act, Div. C, §706(a)(2)(D)(vii) by striking "Presidentially declared disaster (as defined in section 1033(h)(3))" and inserting "federally declared disaster (as defined by section 165(h)(3)(C)(i))". Eff. for disasters declared in tax years beginning after Dec. 31, 2007.

Victims of Terrorism Tax Relief Act of 2001 (Pub. L. No. 107-134), as follows:
● IRC §7508A was amended by Act §112(a). Eff. for disasters and terroristic or military actions occurring on or after Sept. 11, 2001, with respect to any action of the Secretary of the Treasury, Secretary of Labor, or PBGC occurring on or after Oct. 23, 2002. IRC §7508A prior to amendment:

> **SEC. 7508A. AUTHORITY TO POSTPONE CERTAIN TAX-RELATED DEADLINES BY REASON OF PRESIDENTIALLY DECLARED DISASTER.**
> **(a) In general.**—In the case of a taxpayer determined by the Secretary to be affected by a Presidentially declared disaster (as defined by section 1033(h)(3)), the Secretary may prescribe regulations under which a period of up to 120 days may be disregarded in determining, under the internal revenue laws, in respect of any tax liability (including any penalty, additional amount, or addition to the tax) of such taxpayer—
> (1) whether any of the acts described in paragraph (1) of section 7508(a) were performed within the time prescribed therefore, and
> (2) the amount of any credit or refund.
> **(b) Interest on overpayments and underpayments.**—Subsection (a) shall not apply for the purpose of determining interest on any overpayment or underpayment.

Economic Growth and Tax Relief Reconciliation Act of 2001 (Pub. L. No. 107-16), as follows:
● IRC §7508A was amended by Act §802(a) by replacing "90 days" with "120 days." Eff. June 7, 2001.
● **Sunset Provision.** Act §901, as amended by Pub. L. No. 111-312, §101(a)(1), provides the sunset rule below. But see Pub. L.

No. 109-280, §811, and Pub. L. No. 111-148, §10909(c), as amended by Pub. L. No. 111-312, §101(b)(1).

> **SEC. 901. SUNSET OF PROVISIONS OF ACT.**
> **(a) In general.** All provisions of, and amendments made by, this Act shall not apply—
> (1) to taxable, plan, or limitation years beginning after December 31, 2012, or
> (2) in the case of title V, to estates of decedents dying, gifts made, or generation skipping transfers, after December 31, 2012.
> **(b) Application of certain laws.**—The Internal Revenue Code of 1986 and the Employee Retirement Income Security Act of 1974 shall be applied and administered to years, estates, gifts, and transfers described in subsection (a) as if the provisions and amendments described in subsection (a) had never been enacted.

---

* * *

SEC. 7527. ADVANCE PAYMENT OF CREDIT FOR HEALTH INSURANCE COSTS OF ELIGIBLE INDIVIDUALS.

(a) General Rule.—Not later than August 1, 2003, the Secretary shall establish a program for making payments on behalf of certified individuals to providers of qualified health insurance (as defined in section 35(e)) for such individuals.

> ### *Editor's Note*
> IRC §7527(b), as follows, was amended by Pub. L. No. 111-344, applicable to coverage months beginning after December 31, 2010.

(b) Limitation on Advance Payments During Any Taxable Year.—The Secretary may make payments under subsection (a) only to the extent that the total amount of such payments made on behalf of any individual during the taxable year does not exceed 65 percent (80 percent in the case of eligible coverage months beginning before ~~January 1, 2011~~ *February 13, 2011*) of the amount paid by the taxpayer for coverage of the taxpayer and qualifying family members under qualified health insurance for eligible coverage months beginning in the taxable year.

(c) Certified Individual.—For purposes of this section, the term "certified individual" means any individual for whom a qualified health insurance costs credit eligibility certificate is in effect.

(d) Qualified Health Insurance Costs Eligibility Certificate.—

(1) In general.—For purposes of this section, the term "qualified health insurance costs eligibility certificate" means any written statement that an individual is an eligible individual (as defined in section 35(c)) if such statement provides such information as the Secretary may require for purposes of this section and—

(A) in the case of an eligible TAA recipient (as defined in section 35(c)(2)) or an eligible alternative TAA recipient (as defined in section 35(c)(3)), is certified by the Secretary of Labor (or by any other person or entity designated by the Secretary), or

(B) in the case of an eligible PBGC pension recipient (as defined in section 35(c)(4)), is certified by the Pension Benefit Guaranty Corporation (or by any other person or entity designated by the Secretary).

Editor's Note

IRC §7527(d)(2), as follows, was amended by Pub. L. No. 111-344, effective for certificates issued after December 31, 2010.

---

(2) Inclusion of certain information. —In the case of any statement described in paragraph (1) which is issued before ~~January 1, 2011~~ *February 13, 2011,* such statement shall not be treated as a qualified health insurance costs credit eligibility certificate unless such statement includes—

(A) the name, address, and telephone number of the State office or offices responsible for providing the individual with assistance with enrollment in qualified health insurance (as defined in section 35(e)),

(B) a list of the coverage options that are treated as qualified health insurance (as so defined) by the State in which the individual resides, and

(C) in the case of a TAA-eligible individual (as defined in section 4980B(f)(5)(C)(iv)(II)), a statement informing the individual that the individual has 63 days from the date that is 7 days after the date of the issuance of such certificate to enroll in such insurance without a lapse in creditable coverage (as defined in section 9801(c)).

Editor's Note

IRC §7527(e), as follows, was amended by Pub. L. No. 111-344, applicable to coverage months beginning after December 31, 2010.

(e) Payment for Premiums Due Prior to Commencement of Advance Payments.—In the case of eligible coverage months beginning before ~~January 1, 2011~~ *February 13, 2011*—

(1) In general.—The program established under subsection (a) shall provide that the Secretary shall make 1 or more retroactive payments on behalf of a certified individual in an aggregate amount equal to 80 percent of the premiums for coverage of the taxpayer and qualifying family members under qualified health insurance for eligible coverage months (as de-

fined in section 35(b)) occurring prior to the first month for which an advance payment is made on behalf of such individual under subsection (a).

(2) Reduction of payment for amounts received under national emergency grants.—The amount of any payment determined under paragraph (1) shall be reduced by the amount of any payment made to the taxpayer for the purchase of qualified health insurance under a national emergency grant pursuant to section 173(f) of the Workforce Investment Act of 1998 for a taxable year including the eligible coverage months described in paragraph (1).

Amendments to IRC §7527

Omnibus Trade Act of 2010 (Pub. L. No. 111-344), as follows:
- IRC §7527(b) was amended by Act §111(b) by striking "January 1, 2011" and inserting "February 13, 2011". Eff. for coverage months beginning after Dec. 31, 2010.
- IRC §7527(d)(2) was amended by Act §118(a) by striking "January 1, 2011" and inserting "February 13, 2011". Eff. for certificates issued after Dec. 31, 2010.
- IRC §7527(e) was amended by Act §112(a) by striking "January 1, 2011" and inserting "February 13, 2011". Eff. for coverage months beginning after Dec. 31, 2010.

TAA Health Coverage Improvement Act of 2009 (Pub. L. No. 111-5), as follows:
- IRC §7527(b) was amended by Act, Div. B, §1899A(a)(2) by inserting "(80 percent in the case of eligible coverage months beginning before January 1, 2011)" after "65 percent". Eff. for coverage months beginning on or after the first day of the first month beginning 60 days after date of enactment [enacted: Feb. 17, 2009].
- IRC §7527(d) was amended by Act, Div. B, §1899H(a). Eff. for certificates issued after the date that is 6 months after date of enactment [enacted: Feb. 17, 2009]. IRC §7527(d) prior to amendment:

  (d) Qualified Health Insurance Costs Credit Eligibility Certificate.—For purposes of this section, the term "qualified health insurance costs credit eligibility certificate" means any written statement that an individual is an eligible individual (as defined in section 35(c)) if such statement provides such information as the Secretary may require for purposes of this section and—

  (1) in the case of an eligible TAA recipient (as defined in section 35(c)(2)) or an eligible alternative TAA recipient (as defined in section 35(c)(3)), is certified by the Secretary of Labor (or by any other person or entity designated by the Secretary), or

  (2) in the case of an eligible PBGC pension recipient (as defined in section 35(c)(4)), is certified by the Pension Benefit Guaranty Corporation (or by any other person or entity designated by the Secretary).

- IRC §7527(e) was added by Act, Div. B, §1899B(a). Eff. for coverage months beginning after Dec. 31, 2008.

Trade Act of 2002 (Pub. L. No. 107-210), as follows:
- IRC §7527 was added by Act §202(a). Eff. Aug. 6, 2002.

---

* * *

Chapter 79—Definitions

SEC. 7701. DEFINITIONS.

(a) When Used in This Title, Where Not Otherwise Distinctly Expressed or Manifestly Incompatible With the Intent Thereof—

(1) Person. The term "person" shall be construed to mean and include an individual, a trust, estate, partnership, association, company or corporation.

(2) Partnership and partner. The term "partnership" includes a syndicate, group, pool, joint venture, or other unincorporated organization, through or by means of which any business, financial operation, or venture is carried on, and which is not, within the meaning of this title, a trust or estate or a corporation; and the term "partner" includes a member in such a syndicate, group, pool, joint venture, or organization.

(3) Corporation. The term "corporation" includes associations, joint-stock companies, and insurance companies.

(4) Domestic. The term "domestic" when applied to a corporation or partnership means created or organized in the United States or under the law of the United States or of any State unless, in the case of a partnership, the Secretary provides otherwise by regulations.

(5) Foreign. The term "foreign" when applied to a corporation or partnership means a corporation or partnership which is not domestic.

(6) Fiduciary. The term "fiduciary" means a guardian, trustee, executor, administrator, receiver, conservator, or any person acting in any fiduciary capacity for any person.

(7) Stock. The term "stock" includes shares in an association, joint-stock company, or insurance company.

(8) Shareholder. The term "shareholder" includes a member in an association, joint-stock company, or insurance company.

(9) United States. The term "United States" when used in a geographical sense includes only the States and the District of Columbia.

(10) State. The term "State" shall be construed to include the District of Columbia, where such construction is necessary to carry out provisions of this title.

(11) Secretary of the Treasury and Secretary.

(A) Secretary of the Treasury. The term "Secretary of the Treasury" means the Secretary of the Treasury, personally, and shall not include any delegate of his.

(B) Secretary. The term "Secretary" means the Secretary of the Treasury or his delegate.

(12) Delegate.

(A) In general. The term "or his delegate"—

(i) when used with reference to the Secretary of the Treasury, means any officer, employee, or agency of the Treasury Department duly authorized by the Secretary of the Treasury directly, or indirectly by one or more redelegations of authority, to perform the function mentioned or described in the context; and

(ii) when used with reference to any other official of the United States, shall be similarly construed.

(B) Performance of certain functions in Guam or American Samoa. The term "delegate," in relation to the performance of functions in Guam or American Samoa with respect to the taxes imposed by chapters 1, 2, and 21, also includes any officer or employee of any other department or agency of the United States, or of any possession thereof, duly authorized by the Secretary (directly, or indirectly by one or more redelegations of authority) to perform such functions.

(13) Commissioner. The term "Commissioner" means the Commissioner of Internal Revenue.

(14) Taxpayer. The term "taxpayer" means any person subject to any internal revenue tax.

(15) Military or naval forces and armed forces of the United States. The term "military or naval forces of the United States" and the term "Armed Forces of the United States" each includes all regular and reserve components of the uniformed services which are subject to the jurisdiction of the Secretary of Defense, the Secretary of the Army, the Secretary of the Navy, or the Secretary of the Air Force, and each term also includes the Coast Guard. The members of such forces include commissioned officers and personnel below the grade of commissioned officers in such forces.

(16) Withholding agent. The term "withholding agent" means any person required to deduct and withhold any tax under the provisions of sections 1441, 1442, 1443, or 1461.

(17) Husband and wife. As used in sections 682 and 2516, if the husband and wife therein referred to are divorced, wherever appropriate to the meaning of such sections, the term "wife" shall be read "former wife" and the term "husband" shall be read "former husband"; and, if the payments described in such sections are made by or on behalf of the wife or former wife to the husband or former husband instead of vice versa, wherever appropriate to the meaning of such sections, the term "husband" shall be read "wife" and the term "wife" shall be read "husband."

(18) International organization. The term "international organization" means a public international organization entitled to enjoy privileges, exemptions, and immunities as an international organization under the International Organizations Immunities Act (22 U.S.C. 288–288f).

(19) Domestic building and loan association. The term "domestic building and loan association" means a domestic building and loan association, a domestic savings and loan association, and a Federal savings and loan association—

(A) which either (i) is an insured institution within the meaning of section 401(a) of the National Housing Act (12 U.S.C., sec. 1724(a)), or (ii) is subject by law to supervision and examination by State or Federal authority having supervision over such associations;

(B) the business of which consists principally of acquiring the savings of the public and investing in loans; and

(C) at least 60 percent of the amount of the total assets of which (at the close of the taxable year) consists of—

(i) cash,

(ii) obligations of the United States or of a State or political subdivision thereof, and stock or obligations of a corporation which is an instrumentality of the United States or of a State or political subdivision thereof, but not including obligations the interest on which is excludable from gross income under section 103,

(iii) certificates of deposit in, or obligations of, a corporation organized under a State law which specifically authorizes such corporation to insure the deposits or share accounts of member associations,

(iv) loans secured by a deposit or share of a member,

(v) loans (including redeemable ground rents, as defined in section 1055) secured by an interest in real property which is (or, from the proceeds of the loan, will become) residential real property or real property used primarily for church purposes, loans made for the improvement of residential real property or real property used primarily for church purposes, provided that for purposes of this clause, residential real property shall include single or multifamily dwellings, facilities in residential developments dedicated to public use or property used on a nonprofit basis for residents, and mobile homes not used on a transient basis,

(vi) loans secured by an interest in real property located within an urban renewal area to be developed for predominantly residential use under an urban renewal plan approved by the Secretary of Housing and Urban Development under part A or part B of title I of the Housing Act of 1949, as amended, or located within any area covered by a program eligible for assistance under section 103 of the Demonstration Cities and Metropolitan Development Act of 1966, as amended, and loans made for the improvement of any such real property,

(vii) loans secured by an interest in educational, health, or welfare institutions or facilities, including structures designed or used primarily for residential purposes for students, residents, and persons under care, employees, or members of the staff of such institutions or facilities,

(viii) property acquired through the liquidation of defaulted loans described in clause (v), (vi), or (vii),

(ix) loans made for the payment of expenses of college or university education or vocational training, in accordance with such regulations as may be prescribed by the Secretary,

(x) property used by the association in the conduct of the business described in subparagraph (B), and

(xi) any regular or residual interest in a REMIC, but only in the proportion which the assets of such REMIC consist of property described in any of the preceding clauses of this subparagraph; except that if 95 percent or more of the assets of such REMIC are assets described in clauses (i) through (x), the entire interest in the REMIC shall qualify.

At the election of the taxpayer, the percentage specified in this subparagraph shall be applied on the basis of the average assets outstanding during the taxable year, in lieu of the close of the taxable year, computed under regulations prescribed by the Secretary. For purposes of clause (v), if a multifamily structure securing a loan is used in part for nonresidential purposes, the entire loan is deemed a residential real property loan if the planned residential use exceeds 80 percent of the property's planned use (determined as of the time the loan is made). For purposes of clause (v), loans made to finance the acquisition or development of land shall be deemed to be loans secured by an interest in residential real property if, under regulations prescribed by the Secretary, there is reasonable assurance that the property will become residential real property within a period of 3 years from the date of acquisition of such land; but this sentence shall not apply for any taxable year unless, within such 3-year period, such land becomes residential real property. For purposes of determining whether any interest in a REMIC qualifies under clause (xi), any regular interest in another REMIC held by such REMIC shall be treated as a loan described in a preceding clause under principles similar to the principles of clause (xi); except that, if such REMIC's are part of a tiered structure, they shall be treated as 1 REMIC for purposes of clause (xi).

(20) Employee. For the purpose of applying the provisions of section 79 with respect to group-term life insurance purchased for employees, for the purpose of applying the provisions of sections 104, 105, and 106 with respect to accident and health insurance or accident and health plans, and for the purpose of applying the provisions of subtitle A with respect to contributions to or under a stock bonus, pension, profit-sharing, or annuity plan, and with respect to distributions under such a plan, or by a trust forming part of such a plan, and for purposes of applying section 125 with respect to cafeteria plans, the term "employee" shall include a full-time life insurance salesman who is considered an employee for the purpose of chapter 21, or in the case of services performed before January 1, 1951, who would be considered an employee if his services were performed during 1951.

(21) Levy. The term "levy" includes the power of distraint and seizure by any means.

(22) Attorney General. The term "Attorney General" means the Attorney General of the United States.

(23) Taxable year. The term "taxable year" means the calendar year, or the fiscal year ending during such calendar year, upon the basis of which the taxable income is computed under subtitle A. "Taxable year" means, in the case of a return made for a fractional part of a year under the provisions of subtitle A or under regulations prescribed by the Secretary, the period for which such return is made.

(24) Fiscal year. The term "fiscal year" means an accounting period of 12 months ending on the last day of any month other than December.

(25) Paid or incurred, paid or accrued. The terms "paid or incurred" and "paid or accrued" shall be construed according to the method of accounting upon the basis of which the taxable income is computed under subtitle A.

(26) Trade or business. The term "trade or business" includes the performance of the functions of a public office.

(27) Tax Court. The term "Tax Court" means the United States Tax Court.

(28) Other terms. Any term used in this subtitle with respect to the application of, or in connection with, the provisions of any other subtitle of this title shall have the same meaning as in such provisions.

(29) Internal Revenue Code. The term "Internal Revenue Code of 1986" means this title, and the term "Internal Revenue Code of 1939" means the Internal Revenue Code enacted February 10, 1939, as amended.

(30) United States person. The term "United States person" means—

(A) a citizen or resident of the United States,

(B) a domestic partnership,

(C) a domestic corporation,

(D) any estate (other than a foreign estate, within the meaning of paragraph (31)), and

(E) any trust if—

(i) a court within the United States is able to exercise primary supervision over the administration of the trust, and

(ii) one or more United States persons have the authority to control all substantial decisions of the trust.

(31) Foreign estate or trust.

(A) Foreign estate. The term "foreign estate" means an estate the income of which, from sources without the United States which is not effectively connected with the conduct of a trade or business

within the United States, is not includible in gross income under subtitle A.

(B) Foreign trust. The term "foreign trust" means any trust other than a trust described in subparagraph (E) of paragraph (30).

(32) Cooperative bank. The term "cooperative bank" means an institution without capital stock organized and operated for mutual purposes and without profit, which—

(A) either—

(i) is an insured institution within the meaning of section 401(a) of the National Housing Act (12 U.S.C., sec. 1724(a)), or

(ii) is subject by law to supervision and examination by State or Federal authority having supervision over such institutions, and

(B) meets the requirements of subparagraphs (B) and (C) of paragraph (19) of this subsection (relating to definition of domestic building and loan association).

In determining whether an institution meets the requirements referred to in subparagraph (B) of this paragraph, any reference to an association or to a domestic building and loan association contained in paragraph (19) shall be deemed to be a reference to such institution.

(33) Regulated public utility. The term "regulated public utility" means—

(A) A corporation engaged in the furnishing or sale of—

(i) electric energy, gas, water, or sewerage disposal services, or

(ii) transportation (not included in subparagraph (C)) on an intrastate, suburban, municipal, or interurban electric railroad, on an intrastate, municipal, or suburban trackless trolley system, or on a municipal or suburban bus system, or

(iii) transportation (not included in clause (ii)) by motor vehicle—if the rates for such furnishing or sale, as the case may be, have been established or approved by a State or political subdivision thereof, by an agency or instrumentality of the United States, by a public service or public utility commission or other similar body of the District of Columbia or of any State or political subdivision thereof, or by a foreign country or an agency or instrumentality or political subdivision thereof.

(B) A corporation engaged as a common carrier in the furnishing or sale of transportation of gas by pipe line, if subject to the jurisdiction of the Federal Energy Regulatory Commission.

(C) A corporation engaged as a common carrier (i) in the furnishing or sale of transportation by railroad, if subject to the jurisdiction of the Surface

Transportation Board, or (ii) in the furnishing or sale of transportation of oil or other petroleum products (including shale oil) by pipe line, if subject to the jurisdiction of the Federal Energy Regulatory Commission or if the rates for such furnishing or sale are subject to the jurisdiction of a public service or public utility commission or other similar body of the District of Columbia or of any State.

(D) A corporation engaged in the furnishing or sale of telephone or telegraph service, if the rates for such furnishing or sale meet the requirements of subparagraph (A).

(E) A corporation engaged in the furnishing or sale of transportation as a common carrier by air, subject to the jurisdiction of the Secretary of Transportation.

(F) A corporation engaged in the furnishing or sale of transportation by a water carrier subject to jurisdiction under subchapter II of chapter 135 of title 49.

(G) A rail carrier subject to part A of subtitle IV of title 49, if (i) substantially all of its railroad properties have been leased to another such railroad corporation or corporations by an agreement or agreements entered into before January 1, 1954, (ii) each lease is for a term of more than 20 years, and (iii) at least 80 percent or more of its gross income (computed without regard to dividends and capital gains and losses) for the taxable year is derived from such leases and from sources described in subparagraphs (A) through (F), inclusive. For purposes of the preceding sentence, an agreement for lease of railroad properties entered into before January 1, 1954, shall be considered to be a lease including such term as the total number of years of such agreement may, unless sooner terminated, be renewed or continued under the terms of the agreement, and any such renewal or continuance under such agreement shall be considered part of the lease entered into before January 1, 1954.

(H) A common parent corporation which is a common carrier by railroad subject to part A of subtitle IV of title 49 if at least 80 percent of its gross income (computed without regard to capital gains or losses) is derived directly or indirectly from sources described in subparagraphs (A) through (F), inclusive. For purposes of the preceding sentence, dividends and interest, and income from leases described in subparagraph (G), received from a regulated public utility shall be considered as derived from sources described in subparagraphs (A) through (F), inclusive, if the regulated public utility is a member of an affiliated group (as defined in section 1504) which includes the common parent corporation.

The term "regulated public utility" does not (except as provided in subparagraphs (G) and (H)) include a corporation described in subparagraphs (A) through (F), inclusive, unless 80 percent or more of its gross income (computed without regard to dividends and capital gains and losses) for the taxable year is derived from sources described in subparagraphs (A) through (F), inclusive. If the taxpayer establishes to the satisfaction of the Secretary that (i) its revenue from regulated rates described in subparagraph (A) or (D) and its revenue derived from unregulated rates are derived from the operation of a single interconnected and coordinated system or from the operation of more than one such system, and (ii) the unregulated rates have been and are substantially as favorable to users and consumers as are the regulated rates, then such revenue from such unregulated rates shall be considered, for purposes of the preceding sentence, as income derived from sources described in subparagraph (A) or (D).

(34) **[Repealed.]**

(35) Enrolled actuary. The term "enrolled actuary" means a person who is enrolled by the Joint Board for the Enrollment of Actuaries established under subtitle C of the title III of the Employee Retirement Income Security Act of 1974.

(36) Tax return preparer.

(A) In general. The term "tax return preparer" means any person who prepares for compensation, or who employs one or more persons to prepare for compensation, any return of tax imposed by this title or any claim for refund of tax imposed by this title. For purposes of the preceding sentence, the preparation of a substantial portion of a return or claim for refund shall be treated as if it were the preparation of such return or claim for refund.

(B) Exceptions. A person shall not be an "tax return preparer" merely because such person—

(i) furnishes typing, reproducing, or other mechanical assistance,

(ii) prepares a return or claim for refund of the employer (or of an officer or employee of the employer) by whom he is regularly and continuously employed,

(iii) prepares as a fiduciary a return or claim for refund for any person, or

(iv) prepares a claim for refund for a taxpayer in response to any notice of deficiency issued to such taxpayer or in response to any waiver of restriction after the commencement of an audit of such taxpayer or another taxpayer if a determination in such audit of such other taxpayer directly or indirectly affects the tax liability of such taxpayer.

(37) Individual retirement plan. The term "individual retirement plan" means—

(A) an individual retirement account described in section 408(a), and

IRC Sec. 7701(a)(37)(A)

(B) an individual retirement annuity described in section 408(b).

(38) Joint return. The term "joint return" means a single return made jointly under section 6013 by a husband and wife.

(39) Persons residing outside United States. If any citizen or resident of the United States does not reside in (and is not found in) any United States judicial district, such citizen or resident shall be treated as residing in the District of Columbia for purposes of any provision of this title relating to—

(A) jurisdiction of courts, or

(B) enforcement of summons.

(40) Indian tribal government.

(A) In general. The term "Indian tribal government" means the governing body of any tribe, band, community, village, or group of Indians, or (if applicable) Alaska Natives, which is determined by the Secretary, after consultation with the Secretary of the Interior, to exercise governmental functions.

(B) Special rule for Alaska natives. No determination under subparagraph (A) with respect to Alaska Natives shall grant or defer any status or powers other than those enumerated in section 7871. Nothing in the Indian Tribal Governmental Tax Status Act of 1982, or in the amendments made thereby, shall validate or invalidate any claim by Alaska Natives of sovereign authority over lands or people.

(41) TIN. The term "TIN" means the identifying number assigned to a person under section 6109.

(42) Substituted basis property. The term "substituted basis property" means property which is—

(A) transferred basis property, or

(B) exchanged basis property.

(43) Transferred basis property. The term "transferred basis property" means property having a basis determined under any provision of subtitle A (or under any corresponding provision of prior income tax law) providing that the basis shall be determined in whole or in part by reference to the basis in the hands of the donor, grantor, or other transferor.

(44) Exchanged basis property. The term "exchanged basis property" means property having a basis determined under any provision of subtitle A (or under any corresponding provision of prior income tax law) providing that the basis shall be determined in whole or in part by reference to other property held at any time by the person for whom the basis is to be determined.

(45) Nonrecognition transaction. The term "nonrecognition transaction" means any disposition of property in a transaction in which gain or loss is not recognized in whole or in part for purposes of subtitle A.

(46) Determination of whether there is a collective bargaining agreement. In determining whether there is a collective bargaining agreement between employee representatives and 1 or more employers, the term "employee representatives" shall not include any organization more than one-half of the members of which are employees who are owners, officers, or executives of the employer. An agreement shall not be treated as a collective bargaining agreement unless it is a bona fide agreement between bona fide employee representatives and 1 or more employers.

Editor's Note

Caution: IRC §7701(a)(47), as follows, was added by Pub. L. No. 107-16, §542(e)(3), applicable to estates of decedents dying after December 31, 2009. Pub. L. No. 111-312, §301(a), removed IRC §7701(a)(47), effective for decedents dying, and transfers made, after December 31, 2009. See the amendment notes to this section for Pub. L. No. 111-312 for a special election for estates of decedents dying in 2010. For the amended sunset rule of Pub. L. No. 107-16, see the amendment notes to this section for Pub. L. No. 107-16.

---

(47) Executor. The term "executor" means the executor or administrator of the decedent, or, if there is no executor or administrator appointed, qualified, and acting within the United States, then any person in actual or constructive possession of any property of the decedent.

(48) Off-highway vehicles.

(A) Off-highway transportation vehicles.

(i) In general. A vehicle shall not be treated as a highway vehicle if such vehicle is specially designed for the primary function of transporting a particular type of load other than over the public highway and because of this special design such vehicle's capability to transport a load over the public highway is substantially limited or impaired.

(ii) Determination of vehicle's design. For purposes of clause (i), a vehicle's design is determined solely on the basis of its physical characteristics.

(iii) Determination of substantial limitation or impairment. For purposes of clause (i), in determining whether substantial limitation or impairment exists, account may be taken of factors such as the size of the vehicle, whether such vehicle is subject to the licensing, safety, and other requirements applicable to highway vehicles, and whether such vehicle can transport a load at a sustained speed of at least 25 miles per hour. It is immaterial that a vehicle can transport a greater load off the public highway than such vehicle is permitted to transport over the public highway.

(B) Nontransportation trailers and semitrailers. A trailer or semitrailer shall not be treated as a highway vehicle if it is specially designed to function only as an enclosed stationary shelter for the carrying on of an off-highway function at an off-highway site.

(49) Qualified blood collector organization. The term "qualified blood collector organization" means an organization which is—

(A) described in section 501(c)(3) and exempt from tax under section 501(a),

(B) primarily engaged in the activity of the collection of human blood,

(C) registered with the Secretary for purposes of excise tax exemptions, and

(D) registered by the Food and Drug Administration to collect blood.

(50) Termination of United States citizenship.

(A) In general. An individual shall not cease to be treated as a United States citizen before the date on which the individual's citizenship is treated as relinquished under section 877A(g)(4).

(B) Dual citizens. Under regulations prescribed by the Secretary, subparagraph (A) shall not apply to an individual who became at birth a citizen of the United States and a citizen of another country.

(b) Definition of Resident Alien and Nonresident Alien.

(1) In general. For purposes of this title (other than subtitle B)—

(A) Resident alien. An alien individual shall be treated as a resident of the United States with respect to any calendar year if (and only if) such individual meets the requirements of clause (i), (ii), or (iii):

(i) Lawfully admitted for permanent residence. Such individual is a lawful permanent resident of the United States at any time during such calendar year.

(ii) Substantial presence test. Such individual meets the substantial presence test of paragraph (3).

(iii) First year election. Such individual makes the election provided in paragraph (4).

(B) Nonresident alien. An individual is a nonresident alien if such individual is neither a citizen of the United States nor a resident of the United States (within the meaning of subparagraph (A)).

(2) Special rules for first and last year of residency.

(A) First year of residency.

(i) In general. If an alien individual is a resident of the United States under paragraph (1)(A) with respect to any calendar year, but was not a resident of the United States at any time during the preceding calendar year, such alien individual shall be treated as a resident of the United States only for the portion of such calendar year which begins on the residency starting date.

(ii) Residency starting date for individuals lawfully admitted for permanent residence. In the case of an individual who is a lawfully permanent resident of the United States at any time during the calendar year, but does not meet the substantial presence test of paragraph (3), the residency starting date shall be the first day in such calendar year on which he was present in the United States while a lawful permanent resident of the United States.

(iii) Residency starting date for individuals meeting substantial presence test. In the case of an individual who meets the substantial presence test of paragraph (3) with respect to any calendar year, the residency starting date shall be the first day during such calendar year on which the individual is present in the United States.

(iv) Residency starting date for individuals making first year election. In the case of an individual who makes the election provided by paragraph (4) with respect to any calendar year, the residency starting date shall be the 1st day during such calendar year on which the individual is treated as a resident of the United States under that paragraph.

(B) Last year of residency. An alien individual shall not be treated as a resident of the United States during a portion of any calendar year if—

(i) such portion is after the last day in such calendar year on which the individual was present in the United States (or, in the case of an individual described in paragraph (1)(A)(i), the last day on which he was so described),

(ii) during such portion the individual has a closer connection to a foreign country than to the United States, and

(iii) the individual is not a resident of the United States at any time during the next calendar year.

(C) Certain nominal presence disregarded.

(i) In general. For purposes of subparagraphs (A)(iii) and (B), an individual shall not be treated as present in the United States during any period for which the individual establishes that he has a closer connection to a foreign country than to the United States.

IRC Sec. 7701(b)(2)(C)(i)

(ii) Not more than 10 days disregarded. Clause (i) shall not apply to more than 10 days on which the individual is present in the United States.

(3) Substantial presence test.

(A) In general. Except as otherwise provided in this paragraph, an individual meets the substantial presence test of this paragraph with respect to any calendar year (hereinafter in this subsection referred to as the "current year") if—

(i) such individual was present in the United States on at least 31 days during the calendar year, and

(ii) the sum of the number of days on which such individual was present in the United States during the current year and the 2 preceding calendar years (when multiplied by the applicable multiplier determined under the following table) equals or exceeds 183 days:

In the case of days in:	The applicable multiplier is:
Current year	1
1st preceding year	⅓
2nd preceding year	⅙

(B) Exception where individual is present in the United States during less than one-half of current year and closer connection to foreign country is established. An individual shall not be treated as meeting the substantial presence test of this paragraph with respect to any current year if—

(i) such individual is present in the United States on fewer than 183 days during the current year, and

(ii) it is established that for the current year such individual has a tax home (as defined in section 911(d)(3) without regard to the second sentence thereof) in a foreign country and has a closer connection to such foreign country than to the United States.

(C) Subparagraph (B) not to apply in certain cases. Subparagraph (B) shall not apply to any individual with respect to any current year if at any time during such year—

(i) such individual had an application for adjustment of status pending, or

(ii) such individual took other steps to apply for status as a lawful permanent resident of the United States.

(D) Exception for exempt individuals or for certain medical conditions. An individual shall not be treated as being present in the United States on any day if—

(i) such individual is an exempt individual for such day, or

(ii) such individual was unable to leave the United States on such day because of a medical condition which arose while such individual was present in the United States.

(4) First-year election.

(A) An alien individual shall be deemed to meet the requirements of this subparagraph if such individual—

(i) is not a resident of the United States under clause (i) or (ii) of paragraph (1)(A) with respect to a calendar year (hereinafter referred to as the "election year"),

(ii) was not a resident of the United States under paragraph (1)(A) with respect to the calendar year immediately preceding the election year,

(iii) is a resident of the United States under clause (ii) of paragraph (1)(A) with respect to the calendar year immediately following the election year, and

(iv) is both—

(I) present in the United States for a period of at least 31 consecutive days in the election year, and

(II) present in the United States during the period beginning with the first day of such 31-day period and ending with the last day of the election year (hereinafter referred to as the "testing period") for a number of days equal to or exceeding 75 percent of the number of days in the testing period (provided that an individual shall be treated for purposes of this subclause as present in the United States for a number of days during the testing period not exceeding 5 days in the aggregate, notwithstanding his absence from the United States on such days).

(B) An alien individual who meets the requirements of subparagraph (A) shall, if he so elects, be treated as a resident of the United States with respect to the election year.

(C) An alien individual who makes the election provided by subparagraph (B) shall be treated as a resident of the United States for the portion of the election year which begins on the 1st day of the earliest testing period during such year with respect to which the individual meets the requirements of clause (iv) of subparagraph (A).

(D) The rules of subparagraph (D)(i) of paragraph (3) shall apply for purposes of determining an individual's presence in the United States under this paragraph.

(E) An election under subparagraph (B) shall be made on the individual's tax return for the election year, provided that such election may not be made before the individual has met the substantial presence test of paragraph (3) with respect to the calendar year immediately following the election year.

(F) An election once made under subparagraph (B) remains in effect for the election year, unless revoked with the consent of the Secretary.

(5) Exempt individual defined. For purposes of this subsection—

(A) In general. An individual is an exempt individual for any day if, for such day, such individual is—

(i) a foreign government-related individual,

(ii) a teacher or trainee,

(iii) a student, or

(iv) a professional athlete who is temporarily in the United States to compete in a charitable sports event described in section 274(l)(1)(B).

(B) Foreign government-related individual. The term "foreign government-related individual" means any individual temporarily present in the United States by reason of—

(i) diplomatic status, or a visa which the Secretary (after consultation with the Secretary of State) determines represents full-time diplomatic or consular status for purposes of this subsection,

(ii) being a full-time employee of an international organization, or

(iii) being a member of the immediate family of an individual described in clause (i) or (ii).

(C) Teacher or trainee. The term "teacher or trainee" means any individual—

(i) who is temporarily present in the United States under subparagraph (J), (M), or (Q) of section 101(15) of the Immigration and Nationality Act (other than as a student), and

(ii) who substantially complies with the requirements for being so present.

(D) Student. The term "student" means any individual—

(i) who is temporarily present in the United States—

(I) under subparagraph (F) or (M) of section 101(15) of the Immigration and Nationality Act, or

(II) as a student under subparagraph (J), (M), or (Q) of such section 101(15), and

(ii) who substantially complies with the requirements for being so present.

(E) Special rules for teachers, trainees, and students.

(i) Limitation on teachers and trainees. An individual shall not be treated as an exempt individual by reason of clause (ii) of subparagraph (A) for the current year if, for any 2 calendar years during the preceding 6 calendar years, such person

was an exempt person under clause (ii) or (iii) of subparagraph (A). In the case of an individual all of whose compensation is described in section 872(b)(3), the preceding sentence shall be applied by substituting "4 calendar years" for "2 calendar years".

(ii) Limitation on students. For any calendar year after the 5th calendar year for which an individual was an exempt individual under clause (ii) or (iii) of subparagraph (A), such individual shall not be treated as an exempt individual by reason of clause (iii) of subparagraph (A), unless such individual establishes to the satisfaction of the Secretary that such individual does not intend to permanently reside in the United States and that such individual meets the requirements of subparagraph (D)(ii).

(6) Lawful permanent resident. For purposes of this subsection, an individual is a lawful permanent resident of the United States at any time if—

(A) such individual has the status of having been lawfully accorded the privilege of residing permanently in the United States as an immigrant in accordance with the immigration laws, and

(B) such status has not been revoked (and has not been administratively or judicially determined to have been abandoned).

An individual shall cease to be treated as a lawful permanent resident of the United States if such individual commences to be treated as a resident of a foreign country under the provisions of a tax treaty between the United States and the foreign country, does not waive the benefits of such treaty applicable to residents of the foreign country, and notifies the Secretary of the commencement of such treatment.

(7) Presence in the United States. For purposes of this subsection—

(A) In general. Except as provided in subparagraph (B), (C), or (D) an individual shall be treated as present in the United States on any day if such individual is physically present in the United States at any time during such day.

(B) Commuters from Canada or Mexico. If an individual regularly commutes to employment (or self-employment) in the United States from a place of residence in Canada or Mexico, such individual shall not be treated as present in the United States on any day during which he so commutes.

(C) Transit between 2 foreign points. If an individual, who is in transit between 2 points outside the United States, is physically present in the United States for less than 24 hours, such individual shall not be treated as present in the United States on any day during such transit.

(D) Crew members temporarily present. An individual who is temporarily present in the United

IRC Sec. 7701(b)(7)(D)

States on any day as a regular member of the crew of a foreign vessel engaged in transportation between the United States and a foreign country or a possession of the United States shall not be treated as present in the United States on such day unless such individual otherwise engages in any trade or business in the United States on such day.

(8) Annual statements. The Secretary may prescribe regulations under which an individual who (but for subparagraph (B) or (D) of paragraph (3)) would meet the substantial presence test of paragraph (3) is required to submit an annual statement setting forth the basis on which such individual claims the benefits of subparagraph (B) or (D) of paragraph (3), as the case may be.

(9) Taxable year.

(A) In general. For purposes of this title, an alien individual who has not established a taxable year for any prior period shall be treated as having a taxable year which is the calendar year.

(B) Fiscal year taxpayer. If—

(i) an individual is treated under paragraph (1) as a resident of the United States for any calendar year, and

(ii) after the application of subparagraph (A), such individual has a taxable year other than a calendar year, he shall be treated as a resident of the United States with respect to any portion of a taxable year which is within such calendar year.

(10) Coordination with section 877. If—

(A) an alien individual was treated as a resident of the United States during any period which includes at least 3 consecutive calendar years (hereinafter referred to as the "initial residency period"), and

(B) such individual ceases to be treated as a resident of the United States but subsequently becomes a resident of the United States before the close of the 3rd calendar year beginning after the close of the initial residency period,

such individual shall be taxable for the period after the close of the initial residency period and before the day on which he subsequently became a resident of the United States in the manner provided in section 877(b). The preceding sentence shall apply only if the tax imposed pursuant to section 877(b) exceeds the tax which, without regard to this paragraph, is imposed pursuant to section 871.

(11) Regulations. The Secretary shall prescribe such regulations as may be necessary or appropriate to carry out the purposes of this subsection.

(c) Includes and Including. The terms "includes" and "including" when used in a definition contained in this title shall not be deemed to exclude other things otherwise within the meaning of the term defined.

(d) Commonwealth of Puerto Rico. Where not otherwise distinctly expressed or manifestly incompatible with the intent thereof, references in this title to possessions of the United States shall be treated as also referring to the Commonwealth of Puerto Rico.

(e) Treatment of Certain Contracts for Providing Services, Etc. For purposes of chapter 1—

(1) In general. A contract which purports to be a service contract shall be treated as a lease of property if such contract is properly treated as a lease of property, taking into account all relevant factors including whether or not—

(A) the service recipient is in physical possession of the property,

(B) the service recipient controls the property,

(C) the service recipient has a significant economic or possessory interest in the property,

(D) the service provider does not bear any risk of substantially diminished receipts or substantially increased expenditures if there is nonperformance under the contract,

(E) the service provider does not use the property concurrently to provide significant services to entities unrelated to the service recipient, and

(F) the total contract price does not substantially exceed the rental value of the property for the contract period.

(2) Other arrangements. An arrangement (including a partnership or other pass-thru entity) which is not described in paragraph (1) shall be treated as a lease if such arrangement is properly treated as a lease, taking into account all relevant factors including factors similar to those set forth in paragraph (1).

(3) Special rules for contracts or arrangements involving solid waste disposal, energy, and clean water facilities.

(A) In general. Notwithstanding paragraphs (1) and (2), and except as provided in paragraph (4), any contract or arrangement between a service provider and a service recipient—

(i) with respect to—

(I) the operation of a qualified solid waste disposal facility,

(II) the sale to the service recipient of electrical or thermal energy produced at a cogeneration or alternative energy facility, or

(III) the operation of a water treatment works facility, and

(ii) which purports to be a service contract, shall be treated as a service contract.

(B) Qualified solid waste disposal facility. For purposes of subparagraph (A), the term "qualified solid waste disposal facility" means any facility if such facility provides solid waste disposal services for residents of part or all of 1 or more governmental units and substantially all of the solid waste processed at such facility is collected from the general public.

(C) Cogeneration facility. For purposes of subparagraph (A), the term "cogeneration facility" means a facility which uses the same energy source for the sequential generation of electrical or mechanical power in combination with steam, heat, or other forms of useful energy.

(D) Alternative energy facility. For purposes of subparagraph (A), the term "alternative energy facility" means a facility for producing electrical or thermal energy if the primary energy source for the facility is not oil, natural gas, coal, or nuclear power.

(E) Water treatment works facility. For purposes of subparagraph (A), the term "water treatment works facility" means any treatment works within the meaning of section 212(2) of the Federal Water Pollution Control Act.

(4) Paragraph (3) not to apply in certain cases.

(A) In general. Paragraph (3) shall not apply to any qualified solid waste disposal facility, cogeneration facility, alternative energy facility, or water treatment works facility used under a contract or arrangement if—

(i) the service recipient (or a related entity) operates such facility,

(ii) the service recipient (or a related entity) bears any significant financial burden if there is nonperformance under the contract or arrangement (other than for reasons beyond the control of the service provider),

(iii) the service recipient (or a related entity) receives any significant financial benefit if the operating costs of such facility are less than the standards of performance or operation under the contract or arrangement, or

(iv) the service recipient (or a related entity) has an option to purchase, or may be required to purchase, all or a part of such facility at a fixed and determinable price (other than for fair market value).

For purposes of this paragraph, the term "related entity" has the same meaning as when used in section 168(h).

(B) Special rules for application of subparagraph (A) with respect to certain rights and allocations under the contract. For purposes of subparagraph (A), there shall not be taken into account—

(i) any right of a service recipient to inspect any facility, to exercise any sovereign power the service recipient may possess, or to act in the event of a breach of contract by the service provider, or

(ii) any allocation of any financial burden or benefits in the event of any change in any law.

(C) Special rules for application of subparagraph (A) in the case of certain events.

(i) Temporary shut-downs, etc. For purposes of clause (ii) of subparagraph (A), there shall not be taken into account any temporary shut-down of the facility for repairs, maintenance, or capital improvements, or any financial burden caused by the bankruptcy or similar financial difficulty of the service provider.

(ii) Reduced costs. For purposes of clause (iii) of subparagraph (A), there shall not be taken into account any significant financial benefit merely because payments by the service recipient under the contract or arrangement are decreased by reason of increased production or efficiency or the recovery of energy or other products.

(5) Exception for certain low-income housing. This subsection shall not apply to any property described in clause (i), (ii), (iii), or (iv) of section 1250(a)(1)(B) (relating to low-income housing) if—

(A) such property is operated by or for an organization described in paragraph (3) or (4) of section 501(c), and

(B) at least 80 percent of the units in such property are leased to low-income tenants (within the meaning of section 167(k)(3)(B)) (as in effect on the day before the date of the enactment of the Revenue Reconciliation Act of 1990).

(6) Regulations. The Secretary may prescribe such regulations as may be necessary or appropriate to carry out the provisions of this subsection.

(f) Use of Related Persons or Pass-Thru Entities. The Secretary shall prescribe such regulations as may be necessary or appropriate to prevent the avoidance of those provisions of this title which deal with—

(1) the linking of borrowing to investment, or

(2) diminishing risks,

through the use of related persons, pass-thru entities, or other intermediaries.

(g) Clarification of Fair Market Value in the Case of Nonrecourse Indebtedness. For purposes of subtitle A, in determining the amount of gain or loss (or deemed gain or loss) with respect to any property, the fair market value of such property shall be treated as being not less than the amount of any nonrecourse indebtedness to which such property is subject.

(h) Motor Vehicle Operating Leases.

(1) In general. For purposes of this title, in the case of a qualified motor vehicle operating agreement which contains a terminal rental adjustment clause—

IRC Sec. 7701(h)(1)

(A) such agreement shall be treated as a lease if (but for such terminal rental adjustment clause) such agreement would be treated as a lease under this title, and

(B) the lessee shall not be treated as the owner of the property subject to an agreement during any period such agreement is in effect.

(2) Qualified motor vehicle operating agreement defined. For purposes of this subsection—

(A) In general. The term "qualified motor vehicle operating agreement" means any agreement with respect to a motor vehicle (including a trailer) which meets the requirements of subparagraphs (B), (C), and (D) of this paragraph.

(B) Minimum liability of lessor. An agreement meets the requirements of this subparagraph if under such agreement the sum of—

(i) the amount the lessor is personally liable to repay, and

(ii) the net fair market value of the lessor's interest in any property pledged as security for property subject to the agreement,

equals or exceeds all amounts borrowed to finance the acquisition of property subject to the agreement. There shall not be taken into account under clause (ii) any property pledged which is property subject to the agreement or property directly or indirectly financed by indebtedness secured by property subject to the agreement.

(C) Certification by lessee; notice of tax ownership. An agreement meets the requirements of this subparagraph if such agreement contains a separate written statement separately signed by the lessee—

(i) under which the lessee certifies, under penalty of perjury, that it intends that more than 50 percent of the use of the property subject to such agreement is to be in a trade or business of the lessee, and

(ii) which clearly and legibly states that the lessee has been advised that it will not be treated as the owner of the property subject to the agreement for Federal income tax purposes.

(D) Lessor must have no knowledge that certification is false. An agreement meets the requirements of this subparagraph if the lessor does not know that the certification described in subparagraph (C)(i) is false.

(3) Terminal rental adjustment clause defined.

(A) In general. For purposes of this subsection, the term "terminal rental adjustment clause" means a provision of an agreement which permits or requires the rental price to be adjusted upward or downward by reference to the amount realized

by the lessor under the agreement upon sale or other disposition of such property.

(B) Special rule for lessee dealers. The term "terminal rental adjustment clause" also includes a provision of an agreement which requires a lessee who is a dealer in motor vehicles to purchase the motor vehicle for a predetermined price and then resell such vehicle where such provision achieves substantially the same results as a provision described in subparagraph (A).

(i) Taxable Mortgage Pools.

(1) Treated as separate corporations. A taxable mortgage pool shall be treated as a separate corporation which may not be treated as an includible corporation with any other corporation for purposes of section 1501.

(2) Taxable mortgage pool defined. For purposes of this title—

(A) In general. Except as otherwise provided in this paragraph, a taxable mortgage pool is any entity (other than a REMIC) if—

(i) substantially all of the assets of such entity consists of debt obligations (or interests therein) and more than 50 percent of such debt obligations (or interests) consists of real estate mortgages (or interests therein),

(ii) such entity is the obligor under debt obligations with 2 or more maturities, and

(iii) under the terms of the debt obligations referred to in clause (ii) (or underlying arrangement), payments on such debt obligations bear a relationship to payments on the debt obligations (or interests) referred to in clause (i).

(B) Portion of entities treated as pools. Any portion of an entity which meets the definition of subparagraph (A) shall be treated as a taxable mortgage pool.

(C) Exception for domestic building and loan. Nothing in this subsection shall be construed to treat any domestic building and loan association (or portion thereof) as a taxable mortgage pool.

(D) Treatment of certain equity interests. To the extent provided in regulations, equity interest of varying classes which correspond to maturity classes of debt shall be treated as debt for purposes of this subsection.

(3) Treatment of certain REIT's. If—

(A) a real estate investment trust is a taxable mortgage pool, or

(B) a qualified REIT subsidiary (as defined in section 856(i)(2)) of a real estate investment trust is a taxable mortgage pool,

under regulations prescribed by the Secretary, adjustments similar to the adjustments provided in section

IRC Sec. 7701(h)(1)(A)

860E(d) shall apply to the shareholders of such real estate investment trust.

(j) Tax Treatment of Federal Thrift Savings Fund

(1) **In general.** For purposes of this title—

(A) the Thrift Savings Fund shall be treated as a trust described in section 401(a) which is exempt from taxation under section 501(a);

(B) any contribution to, or distribution from, the Thrift Savings Fund shall be treated in the same manner as contributions to or distributions from such a trust; and

(C) subject to section 401(k)(4)(B) and any dollar limitation on the application of section 402(e)(3), contributions to the Thrift Savings Fund shall not be treated as distributed or made available to an employee or Member nor as a contribution made to the Fund by an employee or Member merely because the employee or Member has, under the provisions of subchapter III of chapter 84 of title 5, United States Code, and section 8351 of such title 5, an election whether the contribution will be made to the Thrift Savings Fund or received by the employee or Member in cash.

(2) **Nondiscrimination requirements.** Notwithstanding any other provision of law, the Thrift Savings Fund is not subject to the nondiscrimination requirements applicable to arrangements described in section 401(k) or to matching contributions (as described in section 401(m)), so long as it meets the requirements of this section.

(3) **Coordination with Social Security Act.** Paragraph (1) shall not be construed to provide that any amount of the employee's or Member's basic pay which is contributed to the Thrift Savings Fund shall not be included in the term "wages" for the purposes of section 209 of the Social Security Act or section 3121(a) of this title.

(4) **Definitions.** For purposes of this subsection, the terms "Member", "employee", and "Thrift Savings Fund" shall have the same respective meanings as when used in subchapter III of chapter 84 of title 5, United States Code.

(5) **Coordination with other provisions of law.** No provision of law not contained in this title shall apply for purposes of determining the treatment under this title of the Thrift Savings Fund or any contribution to, or distribution from, such Fund.

(k) Treatment of Certain Amounts Paid to Charity. In the case of any payment which, except for section 501(b) of the Ethics in Government Act of 1978, might be made to any officer or employee of the Federal Government but which is made instead on behalf of such officer or employee to an organization described in section 170(c)—

(1) such payment shall not be treated as received by such officer or employee for all purposes of this title and for all purposes of any tax law of a State or political subdivision thereof, and

(2) no deduction shall be allowed under any provision of this title (or of any tax law of a State or political subdivision thereof) to such officer or employee by reason of having such payment made to such organization.

For purposes of this subsection, a Senator, a Representative in, or a Delegate or Resident Commissioner to, the Congress shall be treated as an officer or employee of the Federal Government.

(*l*) Regulations Relating to Conduit Arrangements. The Secretary may prescribe regulations recharacterizing any multiple-party financing transaction as a transaction directly among any 2 or more of such parties where the Secretary determines that such recharacterization is appropriate to prevent avoidance of any tax imposed by this title.

(m) Designation of Contract Markets. Any designation by the Commodity Futures Trading Commission of a contract market which could not have been made under the law in effect on the day before the date of the enactment of the Commodity Futures Modernization Act of 2000 shall apply for purposes of this title except to the extent provided in regulations prescribed by the Secretary.

(n) Convention or Association of Churches. For purposes of this title, any organization which is otherwise a convention or association of churches shall not fail to so qualify merely because the membership of such organization includes individuals as well as churches or because individuals have voting rights in such organization.

Editor's Note

IRC §7701(o), below, added by Pub. L. No. 111-152, §1409, is effective for transactions entered into after the date of enactment of the Act (enacted: March 30, 2010).

(o) Clarification of Economic Substance Doctrine.—

(1) **Application of doctrine.—**In the case of any transaction to which the economic substance doctrine is relevant, such transaction shall be treated as having economic substance only if—

(A) the transaction changes in a meaningful way (apart from Federal income tax effects) the taxpayer's economic position, and

(B) the taxpayer has a substantial purpose (apart from Federal income tax effects) for entering into such transaction.

(2) **Special rule where taxpayer relies on profit potential.—**

(A) In general.—The potential for profit of a transaction shall be taken into account in determining whether the requirements of subparagraphs (A) and (B) of paragraph (1) are met with respect to the transaction only if the present value of the reasonably expected pre-tax profit from the transaction is substantial in relation to the present value of the expected net tax benefits that would be allowed if the transaction were respected.

(B) Treatment of fees and foreign taxes.—Fees and other transaction expenses shall be taken into account as expenses in determining pre-tax profit under subparagraph (A). The Secretary shall issue regulations requiring foreign taxes to be treated as expenses in determining pre-tax profit in appropriate cases.

(3) State and local tax benefits.—For purposes of paragraph (1), any State or local income tax effect which is related to a Federal income tax effect shall be treated in the same manner as a Federal income tax effect.

(4) Financial accounting benefits.—For purposes of paragraph (1)(B), achieving a financial accounting benefit shall not be taken into account as a purpose for entering into a transaction if the origin of such financial accounting benefit is a reduction of Federal income tax.

(5) Definitions and special rules.—For purposes of this subsection—

(A) Economic substance doctrine.—The term "economic substance doctrine" means the common law doctrine under which tax benefits under subtitle A with respect to a transaction are not allowable if the transaction does not have economic substance or lacks a business purpose.

(B) Exception for personal transactions of individuals.—In the case of an individual, paragraph (1) shall apply only to transactions entered into in connection with a trade or business or an activity engaged in for the production of income.

(C) Determination of application of doctrine not affected.—The determination of whether the economic substance doctrine is relevant to a transaction shall be made in the same manner as if this subsection had never been enacted.

(D) Transaction.—The term "transaction" includes a series of transactions.

(p) Cross References.

(1) Other definitions. For other definitions, see the following sections of Title 1 of the United States Code:

(1) Singular as including plural, section 1.

(2) Plural as including singular, section 1.

(3) Masculine as including feminine, section 1.

(4) Officer, section 1.

(5) Oath as including affirmation, section 1.

(6) County as including parish, section 2.

(7) Vessel as including all means of water transportation, section 3.

(8) Vehicle as including all means of land transportation, section 4.

(9) Company or association as including successors and assigns, section 5.

(2) Effect of cross references. For effect of cross references in this title, see section 7806(a).

Recent Amendments to IRC §7701

Tax Relief, Unemployment Insurance Reauthorization, and Job Creation Act of 2010 (Pub. L. No. 111-312), as follows:

• IRC §7701(a)(47) was removed by Act §301(a). Eff. for estates of decedents dying, and transfers made, after Dec. 31, 2009. See Act §301(c), below, for a special election for decedents dying in 2010. IRC §7701(a)(47) prior to removal:

(47) Executor.—The term "executor" means the executor or administrator of the decedent, or, if there is no executor or administrator appointed, qualified, and acting within the United States, then any person in actual or constructive possession of any property of the decedent.

• Other Provision. Act §301 provides:

SEC. 301. REINSTATEMENT OF ESTATE TAX; REPEAL OF CARRYOVER BASIS.

(a) In General.—Each provision of law amended by subtitle A or E of title V of the Economic Growth and Tax Relief Reconciliation Act of 2001 [Ed. Note: IRC §§121, 684, 1014, 1022, 1040, 1221, 1246, 1291, 1296, 2210, 2664, 6018, 6019, 6075, 6716, 7701.] is amended to read as such provision would read if such subtitle had never been enacted.

(b) Conforming Amendment.—On and after January 1, 2011, paragraph (1) of section 2505(a) of the Internal Revenue Code of 1986 <<NOTE: 26 USC 2505.>> is amended to read as such paragraph would read if section 521(b)(2) of the Economic Growth and Tax Relief Reconciliation Act of 2001 had never been enacted.

(c) Special Election With Respect to Estates of Decedents Dying in 2010.—Notwithstanding subsection (a), in the case of an estate of a decedent dying after December 31, 2009, and before January 1, 2011, the executor (within the meaning of section 2203 of the Internal Revenue Code of 1986) may elect to apply such Code as though the amendments made by subsection (a) do not apply with respect to chapter 11 of such Code and with respect to property acquired or passing from such decedent (within the meaning of section 1014(b) of such Code). Such election shall be made at such time and in such manner as the Secretary of the Treasury or the Secretary's delegate shall provide. Such an election once made shall be revocable only with the consent of the Secretary of the Treasury or the Secretary's delegate. For purposes of section 2652(a)(1) of such Code, the determination of whether any property is subject to the tax imposed by such chapter 11 shall be made without regard to any election made under this subsection.

(d) Extension of Time for Performing Certain Acts.—

(1) Estate tax.—In the case of the estate of a decedent dying after December 31, 2009, and before the date of the enactment of this Act, the due date for—

(A) filing any return under section 6018 of the Internal Revenue Code of 1986 (including any election required to be made on such a return) as such section is in effect after the date of the enactment of this Act without regard to any election under subsection (c),

(B) making any payment of tax under chapter 11 of such Code, and

(C) making any disclaimer described in section 2518(b) of such Code of an interest in property passing by reason of the death of such decedent,

shall not be earlier than the date which is 9 months after the date of the enactment of this Act.

(2) Generation-skipping tax.—In the case of any generation-skipping transfer made after December 31, 2009, and before the date of the enactment of this Act, the due date for filing any return under section 2662 of the Internal Revenue Code of 1986 (including any election required to be made on such a return) shall not be earlier than the date which is 9 months after the date of the enactment of this Act.

(e) Effective Date.—Except as otherwise provided in this section, the amendments made by this section shall apply to estates of decedents dying, and transfers made, after December 31, 2009.

- **Other Provision.** Act §304 provides:

    SEC. 304. APPLICATION OF EGTRRA SUNSET TO THIS TITLE.

    Section 901 of the Economic Growth and Tax Relief Reconciliation Act of 2001 shall apply to the amendments made by this title.

Health Care and Education Reconciliation Act of 2010 (Pub. L. No. 111-152), as follows:

- IRC §7701(o) (former) was redesignated as (p) and new subsec. (o) was added by Act §1409(a). Eff. for transactions entered into after the date of the enactment of the Act [enacted: Mar. 30, 2010].

Heroes Earnings Assistance and Relief Tax Act of 2008 (Pub. L. No. 110-245), as follows:

- IRC §7701(a)(50) was added by Act §301(c)(1). Eff. for any individual whose expatriation date is on or after the date of enactment [enacted: June 17, 2008], see Act §301(g)(1).
- IRC §7701(b)(6) was amended by Act §301(c)(2)(B) by adding the sentence at the end. Eff. for any individual whose expatriation date is on or after the date of enactment [enacted: June 17, 2008], see Act §301(g)(1).
- IRC §7701(n)–(p) were amended by Act §301(c)(2)(C) by striking subsec. (n) and redesignating subsecs. (o) and (p) as subsecs. (n) and (o), respectively. Eff. for any individual whose expatriation date is on or after the date of enactment [enacted: June 17, 2008], see Act §301(g)(1). IRC §7701(n) prior to amendment:

    (n) Special Rules for Determining When an Individual Is No Longer a United States Citizen or Long-Term Resident—For purposes of this chapter—

    (1) United States Citizens—An individual who would (but for this paragraph) cease to be treated as a citizen of the United States shall continue to be treated as a citizen of the United States until such individual—

    (A) gives notice of an expatriating act (with the requisite intent to relinquish citizenship) to the Secretary of State, and

    (B) provides a statement in accordance with section 6039G (if such a statement is otherwise required).

    (2) Long-Term Residents—A long-term resident (as defined in section 877(e)(2)) who would (but for this paragraph) be described in section 877(e)(1) shall be treated as a lawful permanent resident of the United States and as not described in section 877(e)(1) until such individual—

    (A) gives notice of termination of residency (with the requisite intent to terminate residency) to the Secretary of Homeland Security, and

    (B) provides a statement in accordance with section 6039G (if such a statement is otherwise required).

Small Business Tax Relief Act of 2007 (Pub. L. No. 110-28), as follows:

- IRC §7701(a)(36) was amended by Act §8246(a)(1)(A) by striking "income" each place it appeared in the heading and text. Eff. for returns prepared after May 25, 2007.
- IRC §7701(a)(36)(A) was amended by Act §8246(a)(1)(B) by substituting "this title" for "subtitle A" each place it appeared. Eff. for returns prepared after May 25, 2007.

Pension Protection Act of 2006 (Pub. L. No. 109-280), as follows:

- IRC §7701(a)(49) was added by Act §1207(f). Eff. Jan. 1, 2007.
- IRC §7701(o)–(p) was amended by Act §1222 by redesignating subsec. (o) as subsec. (p) and adding new subsec. (o). Eff. Aug. 17, 2006.

Gulf Opportunity Zone Act of 2005 (Pub. L. No. 109-135), as follows:

- IRC §7701(n) was amended by Act §403(v)(2). Eff. as if included in the provision of Pub. L. No. 108-357 to which it relates (§804). IRC §7701(n) prior to amendment:

    (n) Special Rules for Determining When an Individual Is No Longer a United States Citizen or Long-Term Resident—

    An individual who would (but for this subsection) cease to be treated as a citizen or resident of the United States shall continue to be treated as a citizen or resident of the United States, as the case may be, until such individual—

    (1) gives notice of an expatriating act or termination of residency (with the requisite intent to relinquish citizenship or terminate residency) to the Secretary of State or the Secretary of Homeland Security, and

    (2) provides a statement in accordance with section 6039G.

American Jobs Creation Act of 2004 (Pub. L. No. 108-357), as follows:

- IRC §7701(a)(19)(C)(xi) was amended by Act §835(b)(10) by striking "and any regular interest in a FASIT," and by striking "or FASIT" each place it appeared. Eff. Jan. 1, 2005, except for any FASIT in existence on Oct. 22, 2004, to the extent that regular interests issued by the FASIT before such date continue to remain outstanding in accordance with the original terms of issuance.
- IRC §7701(a)(48) was added by Act §852(a). Eff. Oct. 22, 2004, except for taxes imposed under subchapter B of chapter 31 and part III of subchapter A of chapter 32, the amendment applies to taxable periods beginning after Oct. 22, 2004, see Act §852(c).
- IRC §7701(i)(2)(A) was amended by Act §835(b)(11) by striking "or a FASIT". Eff. Jan. 1, 2005, except for any FASIT in existence on Oct. 22, 2004, to the extent that regular interests issued by the FASIT before such date continue to remain outstanding in accordance with the original terms of issuance.
- IRC §7701(n)–(o) were amended by Act §804(b) by redesignating subsec. (n) as subsec. (o) and adding subsec. (n). Eff. for individuals who expatriate after June 3, 2004.

Working Families Tax Relief Act of 2004 (Pub. L. No. 108-311), as follows:

- IRC §7701(a)(17) was amended by Act §207(24) by substituting "682" for "152(b)(4), 682," . Eff. for taxable years beginning after Dec. 31, 2004.

Economic Growth and Tax Relief Reconciliation Act of 2001 (Pub. L. No. 107-16), as follows:

- IRC §7701(a)(47) was added by Act §542(e)(3). Eff. for estates of decedents dying after Dec. 31, 2009.
- **Sunset Provision.** Act §901, as amended by Pub. L. No. 111-312, §101(a)(1), provides the sunset rule below. But see Pub. L. No. 109-280, §811, and Pub. L. No. 111-148, §10909(c), as amended by Pub. L. No. 111-312, §101(b)(1).

    SEC. 901. SUNSET OF PROVISIONS OF ACT.

    (a) In general. All provisions of, and amendments made by, this Act shall not apply—

    (1) to taxable, plan, or limitation years beginning after December 31, 2012, or

    (2) in the case of title V, to estates of decedents dying, gifts made, or generation skipping transfers, after December 31, 2012.

    (b) Application of certain laws.—The Internal Revenue Code of 1986 and the Employee Retirement Income Security Act of 1974 shall be applied and administered to years, estates, gifts, and transfers described in subsection (a) as if the provisions and amendments described in subsection (a) had never been enacted.

SEC. 7702. LIFE INSURANCE CONTRACT DEFINED.

(a) General Rule. For purposes of this title, the term "life insurance contract" means any contract which is a life insurance contract under the applicable law, but only if such contract—

(1) meets the cash value accumulation test of subsection (b), or

(2) (A) meets the guideline premium requirements of subsection (c), and

(B) falls within the cash value corridor of subsection (d).

(b) Cash Value Accumulation Test for Subsection (a)(1).

(1) In general. A contract meets the cash value accumulation test of this subsection if, by the terms of the contract, the cash surrender value of such contract may not at any time exceed the net single premium which would have to be paid at such time to fund future benefits under the contract.

(2) Rules for applying paragraph (1). Determinations under paragraph (1) shall be made—

(A) on the basis of interest at the greater of an annual effective rate of 4 percent or the rate or rates guaranteed on issuance of the contract,

(B) on the basis of the rules of subparagraph (B)(i) (and, in the case of qualified additional benefits, subparagraph (B)(ii)) of subsection (c)(3), and

(C) by taking into account under subparagraphs (A) and (D) of subsection (e)(1) only current and future death benefits and qualified additional benefits.

(c) Guideline Premium Requirements. For purposes of this section—

(1) In general. A contract meets the guideline premium requirements of this subsection if the sum of the premiums paid under such contract does not at any time exceed the guideline premium limitation as of such time.

(2) Guideline premium limitation. The term "guideline premium limitation" means, as of any date, the greater of—

(A) the guideline single premium, or

(B) the sum of the guideline level premiums to such date.

(3) Guideline single premium.

(A) In general. The term "guideline single premium" means the premium at issue with respect to future benefits under the contract.

(B) Basis on which determination is made. The determination under subparagraph (A) shall be based on

(i) reasonable mortality charges which meet the requirements (if any) prescribed in regulations and which (except as provided in regulations) do not exceed the mortality charges specified in the prevailing commissioners standard tables (as defined in section 807(d)(5)) as of the time the contract is issued,

(ii) any reasonable charges (other than mortality charges) which (on the basis of the company's experience, if any, with respect to similar contracts) are reasonably expected to be actually paid, and

(iii) interest at the greater of an annual effective rate of 6 percent or the rate or rates guaranteed on issuance of the contract.

(C) When determination made. Except as provided in subsection (f)(7), the determination under subparagraph (A) shall be made as of the time the contract is issued.

(D) Special rules for subparagraph (B)(ii).—

(i) Charges not specified in the contract. If any charge is not specified in the contract, the amount taken into account under subparagraph (B)(ii) for such charge shall be zero.

(ii) New companies, etc. If any company does not have adequate experience for purposes of the determination under subparagraph (B)(ii), to the extent provided in regulations, such determination shall be made on the basis of the industry-wide experience.

(4) Guideline level premium. The term "guideline level premium" means the level annual amount, payable over a period not ending before the insured attains age 95, computed on the same basis as the guideline single premium, except that paragraph (3)(B)(iii) shall be applied by substituting "4 percent" for "6 percent".

(d) Cash Value Corridor for Purposes of Subsection (a)(2)(B). For purposes of this section—

(1) In general. A contract falls within the cash value corridor of this subsection if the death benefit under the contract at any time is not less than the applicable percentage of the cash surrender value.

(2) Applicable percentage.

In the case of an insured with an attained age as of the beginning of the contract year of:		The applicable percentage shall decrease by a ratable portion for each full year:	
More than:	But not more than:	From:	To:
0	40	250	250

IRC Sec. 7702(a)(1)

40	45	250	215
45	50	215	185
50	55	185	150
55	60	150	130
60	65	130	120
65	70	120	115
70	75	115	105
75	90	105	105
90	95	105	100

(e) Computational Rules.

(1) In general. For purposes of this section (other than subsection (d))—

(A) the death benefit (and any qualified additional benefit) shall be deemed not to increase,

(B) the maturity date, including the date on which any benefit described in subparagraph (C) is payable, shall be deemed to be no earlier than the day on which the insured attains age 95, and no later than the day on which the insured attains age 100,

(C) the death benefits shall be deemed to be provided until the maturity date determined by taking into account subparagraph (B), and

(D) the amount of any endowment benefit (or sum of endowment benefits, including any cash surrender value on the maturity date determined by taking into account subparagraph (B)) shall be deemed not to exceed the least amount payable as a death benefit at any time under the contract.

(2) Limited increases in death benefit permitted. Notwithstanding paragraph (1)(A)

(A) for purposes of computing the guideline level premium, an increase in the death benefit which is provided in the contract may be taken into account but only to the extent necessary to prevent a decrease in the excess of the death benefit over the cash surrender value of the contract,

(B) for purposes of the cash value accumulation test, the increase described in subparagraph (A) may be taken into account if the contract will meet such test at all times assuming that the net level reserve (determined as if level annual premiums were paid for the contract over a period not ending before the insured attains age 95) is substituted for the net single premium

(C) for purposes of the cash value accumulation test, the death benefit increases may be taken into account if the contract—

(i) has an initial death benefit of $5,000 or less and a maximum death benefit of $25,000 or less,

(ii) provides for a fixed predetermined annual increase not to exceed 10 percent of the initial death benefit or 8 percent of the death benefit at the end of the preceding year, and

(iii) was purchased to cover payment of burial expenses or in connection with prearranged funeral expenses.

For purposes of subparagraph (C), the initial death benefit of a contract shall be determined by treating all contracts issued to the same contract owner as 1 contract.

(f) Other Definitions and Special Rules. For purposes of this section—

(1) Premiums paid.

(A) In general. The term "premiums paid" means the premiums paid under the contract less amounts (other than amounts includible in gross income) to which section 72(e) applies and less any excess premiums with respect to which there is a distribution described in subparagraph (B) or (E) of paragraph (7) and any other amounts received with respect to the contract which are specified in regulations.

(B) Treatment of certain premiums returned to policyholder. If, in order to comply with the requirements of subsection (a)(2)(A), any portion of any premium paid during any contract year is returned by the insurance company (with interest) within 60 days after the end of a contract year, the amount so returned (excluding interest) shall be deemed to reduce the sum of the premiums paid under the contract during such year.

(C) Interest returned includible in gross income. Notwithstanding the provisions of section 72(e), the amount of any interest returned as provided in subparagraph (B) shall be includible in the gross income of the recipient.

(2) Cash values.

(A) Cash surrender value. The cash surrender value of any contract shall be its cash value determined without regard to any surrender charge, policy loan, or reasonable termination dividends.

(B) Net surrender value. The net surrender value of any contract shall be determined with regard to surrender charges but without regard to any policy loan.

(3) **Death benefit.** The term "death benefit" means the amount payable by reason of the death of the insured (determined without regard to any qualified additional benefits).

(4) **Future benefits.** The term "future benefits" means death benefits and endowment benefits.

(5) **Qualified additional benefits.**

(A) In general. The term "qualified additional benefits" means any—

(i) guaranteed insurability,

(ii) accidental death or disability benefit,

(iii) family term coverage,

(iv) disability waiver benefit, or

(v) other benefit prescribed under regulations.

(B) Treatment of qualified additional benefits. For purposes of this section, qualified additional benefits shall not be treated as future benefits under the contract, but the charges for such benefits shall be treated as future benefits.

(C) Treatment of other additional benefits. In the case of any additional benefit which is not a qualified additional benefit—

(i) such benefit shall not be treated as a future benefit, and

(ii) any charge for such benefit which is not prefunded shall not be treated as a premium.

(6) **Premium payments not disqualifying contract.** The payment of a premium which would result in the sum of the premiums paid exceeding the guideline premium limitation shall be disregarded for purposes of subsection (a)(2) if the amount of such premium does not exceed the amount necessary to prevent the termination of the contract on or before the end of the contract year (but only if the contract will have no cash surrender value at the end of such extension period).

(7) **Adjustments.**

(A) In general. If there is a change in the benefits under (or in other terms of) the contract which was not reflected in any previous determination or adjustment made under this section, there shall be proper adjustments in future determinations made under this section.

(B) Rule for certain changes during first 15 years. If—

(i) a change described in subparagraph (A) reduces benefits under the contract,

(ii) the change occurs during the 15-year period beginning on the issue date of the contract, and

(iii) a cash distribution is made to the policyholder as a result of such change,

section 72 (other than subsection (e)(5) thereof) shall apply to such cash distribution to the extent it does not exceed the recapture ceiling determined under subparagraph (C) or (D) (whichever applies).

(C) Recapture ceiling where change occurs during first 5 years. If the change referred to in subparagraph (B)(ii) occurs during the 5-year period beginning on the issue date of the contract, the recapture ceiling is—

(i) in the case of a contract to which subsection (a)(1) applies, the excess of—

(I) the cash surrender value of the contract, immediately before the reduction, over

(II) the net single premium (determined under subsection (b)), immediately after the reduction, or

(ii) in the case of a contract to which subsection (a)(2) applies, the greater of—

(I) the excess of the aggregate premiums paid under the contract, immediately before the reduction, over the guideline premium limitation for the contract (determined under subsection (c)(2), taking into account the adjustment described in subparagraph (A)), or

(II) the excess of the cash surrender value of the contract, immediately before the reduction, over the cash value corridor of subsection (d) (determined immediately after the reduction).

(D) Recapture ceiling where change occurs after 5th year and before 16th year. If the change referred to in subparagraph (B) occurs after the 5-year period referred to under subparagraph (C), the recapture ceiling is the excess of the cash surrender value of the contract, immediately before the reduction, over the cash value corridor of subsection (d) (determined immediately after the reduction and whether or not subsection (d) applies to the contract).

(E) Treatment of certain distributions made in anticipation of benefit reductions. Under regulations prescribed by the Secretary, subparagraph (B) shall apply also to any distribution made in anticipation of a reduction in benefits under the contract. For purposes of the preceding sentence, appropriate adjustments shall be made in the provisions of subparagraphs (C) and (D); and any distribution which reduces the cash surrender value of a contract and which is made within 2 years before a reduction in benefits under the contract shall be treated as made in anticipation of such reduction.

(8) **Correction of errors.** If the taxpayer establishes to the satisfaction of the Secretary that—

(A) the requirements described in subsection (a) for any contract year were not satisfied due to reasonable error, and

(B) reasonable steps are being taken to remedy the error,

the Secretary may waive the failure to satisfy such requirements.

(9) Special rule for variable life insurance contracts. In the case of any contract which is a variable contract (as defined in section 817), the determination of whether such contract meets the requirements of subsection (a) shall be made whenever the death benefits under such contract change but not less frequently than once during each 12-month period.

(g) Treatment of Contracts Which Do Not Meet Subsection (a) Test.

(1) Income inclusion.

(A) In general. If at any time any contract which is a life insurance contract under the applicable law does not meet the definition of life insurance contract under subsection (a), the income on the contract for any taxable year of the policyholder shall be treated as ordinary income received or accrued by the policyholder during such year.

(B) Income on the contract. For purposes of this paragraph, the term "income on the contract" means, with respect to any taxable year of the policyholder, the excess of—

(i) the sum of

(I) the increase in the net surrender value of the contract during the taxable year, and

(II) the cost of life insurance protection provided under the contract during the taxable year, over

(ii) the premiums paid (as defined in subsection (f)(1)) under the contract during the taxable year.

(C) Contracts which cease to meet definition. If, during any taxable year of the policyholder, a contract which is a life insurance contract under the applicable law ceases to meet the definition of life insurance contract under subsection (a), the income on the contract for all prior taxable years shall be treated as received or accrued during the taxable year in which such cessation occurs.

(D) Cost of life insurance protection. For purposes of this paragraph, the cost of life insurance protection provided under the contract shall be the lesser of—

(i) the cost of individual insurance on the life of the insured as determined on the basis of uniform premiums (computed on the basis of 5-year age brackets) prescribed by the Secretary by regulations, or

(ii) the mortality charge (if any) stated in the contract.

(2) Treatment of amount paid on death of insured. If any contract which is a life insurance contract under the applicable law does not meet the definition of life insurance contract under subsection (a), the excess of the amount paid by the reason of the death of the insured over the net surrender value of the contract shall be deemed to be paid under a life insurance contract for purposes of section 101 and subtitle B.

(3) Contract continues to be treated as insurance contract. If any contract which is a life insurance contract under the applicable law does not meet the definition of life insurance contract under subsection (a), such contract shall, notwithstanding such failure, be treated as an insurance contract for purposes of this title.

(h) Endowment Contracts Receive Same Treatment.

(1) In general. References in subsections (a) and (g) to a life insurance contract shall be treated as including references to a contract which is an endowment contract under the applicable law.

(2) Definition of endowment contract. For purposes of this title (other than paragraph (1)), the term "endowment contract" means a contract which is an endowment contract under the applicable law and which meets the requirements of subsection (a).

(i) Transitional Rule for Certain 20-Pay Contracts.

(1) In general. In the case of a qualified 20-pay contract, this section shall be applied by substituting "3 percent" for "4 percent" in subsection (b)(2).

(2) Qualified 20-pay contract. For purposes of paragraph (1), the term "qualified 20-pay contract" means any contract which—

(A) requires at least 20 nondecreasing annual premium payments, and

(B) is issued pursuant to an existing plan of insurance.

(3) Existing plan of insurance. For purposes of this subsection, the term "existing plan of insurance" means, with respect to any contract, any plan of insurance which was filed by the company issuing such contract in 1 or more States before September 28, 1983, and is on file in the appropriate State for such contract.

(j) Certain Church Self-Funded Death Benefit Plans Treated as Life Insurance.

(1) In general. In determining whether any plan or arrangement described in paragraph (2) is a life insurance contract, the requirement of subsection (a) that the contract be a life insurance contract under applicable law shall not apply.

(2) Description. For purposes of this subsection, a plan or arrangement is described in this paragraph if—

IRC Sec. 7702(j)(2)

(A) such plan or arrangement provides for the payment of benefits by reason of the death of the individuals covered under such plan or arrangement, and

(B) such plan or arrangement is provided by a church for the benefit of its employees and their beneficiaries, directly or through an organization described in section 414(e)(3)(A) or an organization described in section 414(e)(3)(B)(ii).

(3) Definitions. For purposes of this subsection—

(A) Church. The term "church" means a church or a convention or association of churches.

(B) Employee. The term "employee" includes an employee described in section 414(e)(3)(B).

(k) Regulations. The Secretary shall prescribe such regulations as may be necessary or appropriate to carry out the purposes of this section.

SEC. 7702A. MODIFIED ENDOWMENT CONTRACT DEFINED.

(a) General Rule. For purposes of section 72, the term "modified endowment contract" means any contract meeting the requirements of section 7702—

(1) which—

(A) is entered into on or after June 21, 1988, and

(B) fails to meet the 7-pay test of subsection (b), or

(2) which is received in exchange for a contract described in paragraph (1) or this paragraph.

(b) 7-Pay Test. For purposes of subsection (a), a contract fails to meet the 7-pay test of this subsection if the accumulated amount paid under the contract at any time during the 1st 7 contract years exceeds the sum of the net level premiums which would have been paid on or before such time if the contract provided for paid-up future benefits after the payment of 7 level annual premiums.

(c) Computational Rules.

(1) In general. Except as provided in this subsection, the determination under subsection (b) of the 7 level annual premiums shall be made—

(A) as of the time the contract is issued, and

(B) by applying the rules of section 7702(b)(2) and of section 7702(e) (other than paragraph (2)(C) thereof), except that the death benefit provided for the 1st contract year shall be deemed to be provided until the maturity date without regard to any scheduled reduction after the 1st 7 contract years.

(2) Reduction in benefits during 1st 7 years.

(A) In general. If there is a reduction in benefits under the contract within the 1st 7 contract years,

this section shall be applied as if the contract had originally been issued at the reduced benefit level.

(B) Reductions attributable to nonpayment of premiums. Any reduction in benefits attributable to the nonpayment of premiums due under the contract shall not be taken into account under subparagraph (A) if the benefits are reinstated within 90 days after the reduction in such benefits.

(3) Treatment of material changes.

(A) In general. If there is a material change in the benefits under (or in other terms of) the contract which was not reflected in any previous determination under this section, for purposes of this section—

(i) such contract shall be treated as a new contract entered into on the day on which such material change takes effect, and

(ii) appropriate adjustments shall be made in determining whether such contract meets the 7-pay test of subsection (b) to take into account the cash surrender value under the contract.

(B) Treatment of certain benefit increases. For purposes of subparagraph (A), the term "material change" includes any increase in the death benefit under the contract or any increase in, or addition of, a qualified additional benefit under the contract. Such term shall not include—

(i) any increase which is attributable to the payment of premiums necessary to fund the lowest level of the death benefit and qualified additional benefits payable in the 1st 7 contract years (determined after taking into account death benefit increases described in subparagraph (A) or (B) of section 7702(e)(2)) or to crediting of interest or other earnings (including policyholder dividends) in respect of such premiums, and

(ii) to the extent provided in regulations, any cost-of-living increase based on an established broad-based index if such increase is funded ratably over the remaining period during which premiums are required to be paid under the contract.

(4) Special rule for contracts with death benefits of $10,000 or less. In the case of a contract—

(A) which provides an initial death benefit of $10,000 or less, and

(B) which requires at least 7 nondecreasing annual premium payments, each of the 7 level annual premiums determined under subsection (b) (without regard to this paragraph) shall be increased by $75. For purposes of this paragraph, the contract involved and all contracts previously issued to the same policyholder by the same company shall be treated as one contract.

(5) Regulatory authority for certain collection expenses. The Secretary may by regulations prescribe rules for taking into account expenses solely attributable to the collection of premiums paid more frequently than annually.

(6) Treatment of certain contracts with more than one insured. If—

(A) a contract provides a death benefit which is payable only upon the death of 1 insured following (or occurring simultaneously with) the death of another insured, and

(B) there is a reduction in such death benefit below the lowest level of such death benefit provided under the contract during the 1st 7 contract years, this section shall be applied as if the contract had originally been issued at the reduced benefit level.

(d) Distributions Affected. If a contract fails to meet the 7-pay test of subsection (b), such contract shall be treated as failing to meet such requirements only in the case of—

(1) distributions during the contract year in which the failure takes effect and during any subsequent contract year, and

(2) under regulations prescribed by the Secretary, distributions (not described in paragraph (1)) in anticipation of such failure.

For purposes of the preceding sentence, any distribution which is made within 2 years before the failure to meet the 7-pay test shall be treated as made in anticipation of such failure.

(e) Definitions. For purposes of this section—

(1) Amount paid.

(A) In general. The term "amount paid" means—

(i) the premiums paid under the contract, reduced by

(ii) amounts to which section 72(e) applies (determined without regard to paragraph (4)(A) thereof) but not including amounts includible in gross income.

(B) Treatment of certain premiums returned. If, in order to comply with the requirements of subsection (b), any portion of any premium paid during any contract year is returned by the insurance company (with interest) within 60 days after the end of such contract year, the amount so returned (excluding interest) shall be deemed to reduce the sum of the premiums paid under the contract during such contract year.

(C) Interest returned includible in gross income. Notwithstanding the provisions of section 72(e), the amount of any interest returned as provided in subparagraph (B) shall be includible in the gross income of the recipient.

(2) Contract year. The term "contract year" means the 12-month period beginning with the 1st

month for which the contract is in effect, and each 12-month period beginning with the corresponding month in subsequent calendar years.

(3) Other terms. Except as otherwise provided in this section, terms used in this section shall have the same meaning as when used in section 7702.

Recent Amendments to §7702A

Job Creation and Worker Assistance Act of 2002 (Pub. L. No. 107-147), as follows:

● IRC §7702A(c)(3)(A)(ii): Act §416(f) provides that amendments made by Pub. L. No. 106-554, §318(a)(2), are repealed and IRC §7702A(c)(3)(A)(ii) shall read and be applied as if the amendment had not been enacted. Eff. Mar. 9, 2002. [*Ed. Note*: in IRC §7702A(c)(3)(A)(ii), Pub. L. No. 106-544, §318(a)(2), struck "under the contract" and inserted "under the old contract". Eff. as if included in the amendments made by Pub. L. No. 100-647, §5012.]

SEC. 7702B. TREATMENT OF QUALIFIED LONG-TERM CARE INSURANCE.

(a) In General.—For purposes of this title—

(1) a qualified long-term care insurance contract shall be treated as an accident and health insurance contract,

(2) amounts (other than policyholder dividends, as defined in section 808, or premium refunds) received under a qualified long-term care insurance contract shall be treated as amounts received for personal injuries and sickness and shall be treated as reimbursement for expenses actually incurred for medical care (as defined in section 213(d)),

(3) any plan of an employer providing coverage under a qualified long-term care insurance contract shall be treated as an accident and health plan with respect to such coverage,

(4) except as provided in subsection (e)(3), amounts paid for a qualified long-term care insurance contract providing the benefits described in subsection (b)(2)(A) shall be treated as payments made for insurance for purposes of section 213(d)(1)(D), and

(5) a qualified long-term care insurance contract shall be treated as a guaranteed renewable contract subject to the rules of section 816(e).

(b) Qualified Long-Term Care Insurance Contract.—For purposes of this title—

(1) In general.—The term "qualified long-term care insurance contract" means any insurance contract if—

(A) the only insurance protection provided under such contract is coverage of qualified long-term care services,

(B) such contract does not pay or reimburse expenses incurred for services or items to the extent that such expenses are reimbursable under title

XVIII of the Social Security Act or would be so reimbursable but for the application of a deductible or coinsurance amount,

(C) such contract is guaranteed renewable,

(D) such contract does not provide for a cash surrender value or other money that can be—

(i) paid, assigned, or pledged as collateral for a loan, or

(ii) borrowed, other than as provided in subparagraph (E) or paragraph (2)(C),

(E) all refunds of premiums, and all policyholder dividends or similar amounts, under such contract are to be applied as a reduction in future premiums or to increase future benefits, and

(F) such contract meets the requirements of subsection (g).

(2) Special rules.—

(A) Per diem, etc. payments permitted.—A contract shall not fail to be described in subparagraph (A) or (B) of paragraph (1) by reason of payments being made on a per diem or other periodic basis without regard to the expenses incurred during the period to which the payments relate.

(B) Special rules relating to Medicare.—

(i) Paragraph (1)(B) shall not apply to expenses which are reimbursable under title XVIII of the Social Security Act only as a secondary payor.

(ii) No provision of law shall be construed or applied so as to prohibit the offering of a qualified long-term care insurance contract on the basis that the contract coordinates its benefits with those provided under such title.

(C) Refunds of premiums.—Paragraph (1)(E) shall not apply to any refund on the death of the insured, or on a complete surrender or cancellation of the contract, which cannot exceed the aggregate premiums paid under the contract. Any refund on a complete surrender or cancellation of the contract shall be includible in gross income to the extent that any deduction or exclusion was allowable with respect to the premiums.

(c) Qualified Long-Term Care Services.—For purposes of this section—

(1) In general.—The term "qualified long-term care services" means necessary diagnostic, preventive, therapeutic, curing, treating, mitigating, and rehabilitative services, and maintenance or personal care services, which—

(A) are required by a chronically ill individual, and

(B) are provided pursuant to a plan of care prescribed by a licensed health care practitioner.

(2) Chronically ill individual.—

(A) In general.—The term "chronically ill individual" means any individual who has been certified by a licensed health care practitioner as—

(i) being unable to perform (without substantial assistance from another individual) at least 2 activities of daily living for a period of at least 90 days due to a loss of functional capacity,

(ii) having a level of disability similar (as determined under regulations prescribed by the Secretary in consultation with the Secretary of Health and Human Services) to the level of disability described in clause (i), or

(iii) requiring substantial supervision to protect such individual from threats to health and safety due to severe cognitive impairment.

Such term shall not include any individual otherwise meeting the requirements of the preceding sentence unless within the preceding 12-month period a licensed health care practitioner has certified that such individual meets such requirements.

(B) Activities of daily living.—For purposes of subparagraph (A), each of the following is an activity of daily living:

(i) Eating.

(ii) Toileting.

(iii) Transferring.

(iv) Bathing.

(v) Dressing.

(vi) Continence.

A contract shall not be treated as a qualified long-term care insurance contract unless the determination of whether an individual is a chronically ill individual described in subparagraph (A)(i) takes into account at least 5 of such activities.

(3) Maintenance or personal care services.—The term "maintenance or personal care services" means any care the primary purpose of which is the provision of needed assistance with any of the disabilities as a result of which the individual is a chronically ill individual (including the protection from threats to health and safety due to severe cognitive impairment).

(4) Licensed health care practitioner.—The term "licensed health care practitioner" means any physician (as defined in section 1861(r)(1) of the Social Security Act) and any registered professional nurse, licensed social worker, or other individual who meets such requirements as may be prescribed by the Secretary.

(d) Aggregate Payments in Excess of Limits.—

(1) In general.—If the aggregate of—

(A) the periodic payments received for any period under all qualified long-term care insurance contracts which are treated as made for qualified long-term care services for an insured, and

(B) the periodic payments received for such period which are treated under section 101(g) as paid by reason of the death of such insured,

exceeds the per diem limitation for such period, such excess shall be includible in gross income without regard to section 72. A payment shall not be taken into account under subparagraph (B) if the insured is a terminally ill individual (as defined in section 101(g)) at the time the payment is received.

(2) Per diem limitation.—For purposes of paragraph (1), the per diem limitation for any period is an amount equal to the excess (if any) of—

(A) the greater of—

(i) the dollar amount in effect for such period under paragraph (4), or

(ii) the costs incurred for qualified long-term care services provided for the insured for such period, over

(B) the aggregate payments received as reimbursements (through insurance or otherwise) for qualified long-term care services provided for the insured during such period.

(3) Aggregation rules.—For purposes of this subsection—

(A) all persons receiving periodic payments described in paragraph (1) with respect to the same insured shall be treated as 1 person, and

(B) the per diem limitation determined under paragraph (2) shall be allocated first to the insured and any remaining limitation shall be allocated among the other such persons in such manner as the Secretary shall prescribe.

(4) Dollar amount.—The dollar amount in effect under this subsection shall be $175 per day (or the equivalent amount in the case of payments on another periodic basis).

(5) Inflation adjustment.—In the case of a calendar year after 1997, the dollar amount contained in paragraph (4) shall be increased at the same time and in the same manner as amounts are increased pursuant to section 213(d)(10).

(6) Periodic payments.—For purposes of this subsection, the term "periodic payment" means any payment (whether on a periodic basis or otherwise) made without regard to the extent of the costs incurred by the payee for qualified long-term care services.

(e) Treatment of Coverage Provided as Part of a Life Insurance or Annuity Contract.—Except as otherwise provided in regulations prescribed by the Secretary, in the case of any long-term care insurance coverage (whether or not qualified) provided by a rider on or as part of a life insurance contract or an annuity contract—

(1) In general.—This title shall apply as if the portion of the contract providing such coverage is a separate contract.

(2) Denial of deduction under section 213.—No deduction shall be allowed under section 213(a) for any payment made for coverage under a qualified long-term care insurance contract if such payment is made as a charge against the cash surrender value of a life insurance contract or the cash value of an annuity contract.

(3) Portion defined.—For purposes of this subsection, the term "portion" means only the terms and benefits under a life insurance contract or annuity contract that are in addition to the terms and benefits under the contract without regard to long-term care insurance coverage.

(4) Annuity contracts to which paragraph (1) does not apply.—For purposes of this subsection, none of the following shall be treated as an annuity contract:

(A) A trust described in section 401(a) which is exempt from tax under section 501(a).

(B) A contract—

(i) purchased by a trust described in subparagraph (A),

(ii) purchased as part of a plan described in section 403(a),

(iii) described in section 403(b),

(iv) provided for employees of a life insurance company under a plan described in section 818(a)(3), or

(v) from an individual retirement account or an individual retirement annuity.

(C) A contract purchased by an employer for the benefit of the employee (or the employee's spouse).

Any dividend described in section 404(k) which is received by a participant or beneficiary shall, for purposes of this paragraph, be treated as paid under a separate contract to which subparagraph (B)(i) applies.

(f) Treatment of Certain State-Maintained Plans.—

(1) In general.—If—

(A) an individual receives coverage for qualified long-term care services under a State long-term care plan, and

(B) the terms of such plan would satisfy the requirements of subsection (b) were such plan an insurance contract, such plan shall be treated as a qualified long-term care insurance contract for purposes of this title.

(2) State long-term care plan.—For purposes of paragraph (1), the term "State long-term care plan" means any plan—

(A) which is established and maintained by a State or an instrumentality of a State,

(B) which provides coverage only for qualified long-term care services, and

(C) under which such coverage is provided only to—

(i) employees and former employees of a State (or any political subdivision or instrumentality of a State),

(ii) the spouses of such employees, and

(iii) individuals bearing a relationship to such employees or spouses which is described in any of subparagraphs (A) through (G) of section 152(d)(2).

(g) Consumer Protections Provisions.—

(1) In general.—The requirements of this subsection are met with respect to any contract if the contract meets—

(A) the requirements of the model regulation and model Act described in paragraph (2),

(B) the disclosure requirement of paragraph (3), and

(C) the requirements relating to nonforfeitability under paragraph (4).

(2) Requirements of model regulation and Act.—

(A) In general.—The requirements of this paragraph are met with respect to any contract if such contract meets—

(i) Model regulation.—The following requirements of the model regulation:

(I) Section 7A (relating to guaranteed renewal or noncancellability), and the requirements of section 6B of the model Act relating to such section 7A.

(II) Section 7B (relating to prohibitions on limitations and exclusions).

(III) Section 7C (relating to extension of benefits).

(IV) Section 7D (relating to continuation or conversion of coverage).

(V) Section 7E (relating to discontinuance and replacement of policies).

(VI) Section 8 (relating to unintentional lapse).

(VII) Section 9 (relating to disclosure), other than section 9F thereof.

(VIII) Section 10 (relating to prohibitions against post-claims underwriting).

(IX) Section 11 (relating to minimum standards).

(X) Section 12 (relating to requirement to offer inflation protection), except that any requirement for a signature on a rejection of inflation protection shall permit the signature to be on an application or on a separate form.

(XI) Section 23 (relating to prohibition against preexisting conditions and probationary periods in replacement policies or certificates).

(ii) Model Act.—The following requirements of the model Act:

(I) Section 6C (relating to preexisting conditions).

(II) Section 6D (relating to prior hospitalization).

(B) Definitions.—For purposes of this paragraph—

(i) Model provisions.—The terms "model regulation" and "model Act" mean the long-term care insurance model regulation, and the long-term care insurance model Act, respectively, promulgated by the National Association of Insurance Commissioners (as adopted as of January 1993).

(ii) Coordination.—Any provision of the model regulation or model Act listed under clause (i) or (ii) of subparagraph (A) shall be treated as including any other provision of such regulation or Act necessary to implement the provision.

(iii) Determination.—For purposes of this section and section 4980C, the determination of whether any requirement of a model regulation or the model Act has been met shall be made by the Secretary.

(3) Disclosure requirement.—The requirement of this paragraph is met with respect to any contract if such contract meets the requirements of section 4980C(d).

(4) Nonforfeiture requirements.—

(A) In general.—The requirements of this paragraph are met with respect to any level premium contract, if the issuer of such contract offers to the policyholder, including any group policyholder, a nonforfeiture provision meeting the requirements of subparagraph (B).

(B) Requirements of provision.—The nonforfeiture provision required under subparagraph (A) shall meet the following requirements:

(i) The nonforfeiture provision shall be appropriately captioned.

(ii) The nonforfeiture provision shall provide for a benefit available in the event of a default in the payment of any premiums and the amount of the benefit may be adjusted subsequent to being initially granted only as necessary to reflect changes in claims, persistency, and interest as reflected in changes in rates for premium paying contracts approved by the appropriate State regulatory agency for the same contract form.

(iii) The nonforfeiture provision shall provide at least one of the following:

(I) Reduced paid-up insurance.

(II) Extended term insurance.

(III) Shortened benefit period.

(IV) Other similar offerings approved by the appropriate State regulatory agency.

(5) Cross reference.—For coordination of the requirements of this subsection with State requirements, see section 4980C(f).

Recent Amendments to IRC §7702B

Pension Protection Act of 2006 (Pub. L. No. 109-280), as follows:
- IRC §7702B(e) was amended by Act §844(c). Eff. for contracts issued after Dec. 31, 1996, but only with respect to tax years beginning after Dec. 31, 2009. IRC §7702B(e) prior to amendment:
  (e) Treatment of coverage provided as part of a life insurance contract.—Except as otherwise provided in regulations prescribed by the Secretary, in the case of any long-term care insurance coverage (whether or not qualified) provided by a rider on or as part of a life insurance contract—
  (1) In general.—This title shall apply as if the portion of the contract providing such coverage is a separate contract.
  (2) Application of section 7702.—Section 7702(c)(2) (relating to the guideline premium limitation) shall be applied by increasing the guideline premium limitation with respect to a life insurance contract, as of any date—
  (A) by the sum of any charges (but not premium payments) against the life insurance contract's cash surrender value (within the meaning of section 7702(f)(2)(A)) for such coverage made to that date under the contract, less
  (B) any such charges the imposition of which reduces the premiums paid for the contract (within the meaning of section 7702(f)(1)).
  (3) Application of section 213.—No deduction shall be allowed under section 213(a) for charges against the life insurance contract's cash surrender value described in paragraph (2), unless such charges are includible in income as a result of the application of section 72(e)(10) and the rider is a qualified long-term care insurance contract under subsection (b).
  (4) Portion defined.—For purposes of this subsection, the term "portion" means only the terms and benefits under a life insurance contract that are in addition to the terms under the contract without regard to long-term care insurance coverage.
- IRC §7702B(e)(1), prior to amendment by Act §844(c), was amended by Act §844(f) by replacing "section" with "title." Eff. for contracts issued after Dec. 31, 1996, as if included in Pub. L. No. 104-191, §321(a).

Working Families Tax Relief Act of 2004 (Pub. L. No. 108-311), as follows:
- IRC §7702B(f)(2)(C)(iii) was amended by Act §207(25) by replacing "paragraphs (1) through (8) of §152(a)" with "subparagraphs (A) through (G) of §152(d)(2)." Eff. tax years beginning after Dec. 31, 2004.

---

* * *

Subtitle I—Trust Fund Code

Chapter 98—Trust Fund Code

Subchapter A—Establishment of Trust Funds

SEC. 9511. PATIENT-CENTERED OUTCOMES RESEARCH TRUST FUND.

(a) Creation of Trust Fund.—There is established in the Treasury of the United States a trust fund to be known as the "Patient-Centered Outcomes Research Trust Fund" (hereafter in this section referred to as the "PCORTF"), consisting of such amounts as may be appropriated or credited to such Trust Fund as provided in this section and section 9602(b).

(b) Transfers to Fund.—

(1) Appropriation.—There are hereby appropriated to the Trust Fund the following:

(A) For fiscal year 2010, $10,000,000.

(B) For fiscal year 2011, $50,000,000.

(C) For fiscal year 2012, $150,000,000.

(D) For fiscal year 2013—

(i) an amount equivalent to the net revenues received in the Treasury from the fees imposed under subchapter B of chapter 34 (relating to fees on health insurance and self-insured plans) for such fiscal year; and

(ii) $150,000,000.

(E) For each of fiscal years 2014, 2015, 2016, 2017, 2018, and 2019—

(i) an amount equivalent to the net revenues received in the Treasury from the fees imposed under subchapter B of chapter 34 (relating to fees on health insurance and self-insured plans) for such fiscal year; and

(ii) $150,000,000.

The amounts appropriated under subparagraphs (A), (B), (C), (D)(ii), and (E)(ii) shall be transferred from the general fund of the Treasury, from funds not otherwise appropriated.

(2) Trust fund transfers.—In addition to the amounts appropriated under paragraph (1), there shall be credited to the PCORTF the amounts transferred under section 1183 of the Social Security Act.

(3) Limitation on transfers to PCORTF.—No amount may be appropriated or transferred to the PCORTF on and after the date of any expenditure from the PCORTF which is not an expenditure permitted under this section. The determination of whether an expenditure is so permitted shall be made without regard to—

(A) any provision of law which is not contained or referenced in this chapter or in a revenue Act, and

(B) whether such provision of law is a subsequently enacted provision or directly or indirectly seeks to waive the application of this paragraph.

(c) Trustee.—The Secretary of the Treasury shall be a trustee of the PCORTF.

(d) Expenditures From Fund.—

(1) Amounts available to the patient-centered outcomes research institute.—Subject to paragraph (2), amounts in the PCORTF are available, without further appropriation, to the Patient-Centered Outcomes Research Institute established under section 1181(b) of the Social Security Act for carrying out part D of title XI of the Social Security Act (as in effect on the date of enactment of such Act).

(2) Transfer of funds.—

(A) In general.—The trustee of the PCORTF shall provide for the transfer from the PCORTF of 20 percent of the amounts appropriated or credited to the PCORTF for each of fiscal years 2011 through 2019 to the Secretary of Health and Human Services to carry out section 937 of the Public Health Service Act.

(B) Availability.—Amounts transferred under subparagraph (A) shall remain available until expended.

(C) Requirements.—Of the amounts transferred under subparagraph (A) with respect to a fiscal year, the Secretary of Health and Human Services shall distribute—

(i) 80 percent to the Office of Communication and Knowledge Transfer of the Agency for Healthcare Research and Quality (or any other relevant office designated by Agency for Healthcare Research and Quality) to carry out the activities described in section 937 of the Public Health Service Act; and

(ii) 20 percent to the Secretary to carry out the activities described in such section 937.

(e) Net Revenues.—For purposes of this section, the term "net revenues" means the amount estimated by the Secretary of the Treasury based on the excess of—

(1) the fees received in the Treasury under subchapter B of chapter 34, over

(2) the decrease in the tax imposed by chapter 1 resulting from the fees imposed by such subchapter.

(f) Termination.—No amounts shall be available for expenditure from the PCORTF after September 30, 2019, and any amounts in such Trust Fund after such date shall be transferred to the general fund of the Treasury.

Recent Amendments to IRC §9511

Patient Protection and Affordable Care Act (Pub. L. No. 111-148), as follows:

● IRC §9511 was added by Act §6301(e)(1)(A). Eff. date of enactment [enacted: Mar. 23, 2010].

Subtitle J—Coal Industry Health Benefits

Chapter 99—Coal Industry Health Benefits

Subchapter A—Definitions of General Applicability

SEC. 9701. DEFINITIONS OF GENERAL APPLICABILITY.

(a) Plans and Funds.—For purposes of this chapter—

(1) UMWA benefit plan.—

(A) In general.—The term "UMWA Benefit Plan" means a plan—

(i) which is described in section 404(c), or a continuation thereof; and

(ii) which provides health benefits to retirees and beneficiaries of the industry which maintained the 1950 UMWA Pension Plan.

(B) 1950 UMWA benefit plan.—The term "1950 UMWA Benefit Plan" means a UMWA Benefit Plan, participation in which is substantially limited to individuals who retired before 1976.

(C) 1974 UMWA benefit plan.—The term "1974 UMWA Benefit Plan" means a UMWA Benefit Plan, participation in which is substantially limited to individuals who retired on or after January 1, 1976.

(2) 1950 UMWA pension plan.—The term "1950 UMWA Pension Plan" means a pension plan described in section 404(c) (or a continuation thereof), participation in which is substantially limited to individuals who retired before 1976.

(3) 1974 UMWA pension plan.—The term "1974 UMWA Pension Plan" means a pension plan described in section 404(c) (or a continuation thereof), participation in which is substantially limited to individuals who retired in 1976 and thereafter.

(4) 1992 UMWA benefit plan.—The term "1992 UMWA Benefit Plan" means the plan referred to in section 9713A.

(5) Combined fund.—The term "Combined Fund" means the United Mine Workers of America Combined Benefit Fund established under section 9702.

(b) Agreements.—For purposes of this section—

(1) Coal wage agreement.—The term "coal wage agreement" means—

(A) the National Bituminous Coal Wage Agreement, or

(B) any other agreement entered into between an employer in the coal industry and the United Mine Workers of America that required or requires one or both of the following:

(i) the provision of health benefits to retirees of such employer, eligibility for which is based on years of service credited under a plan established by the settlors and described in section 404(c) or a continuation of such plan; or

(ii) contributions to the 1950 UMWA Benefit Plan or the 1974 UMWA Benefit Plan, or any predecessor thereof.

(2) Settlors.—The term "settlors" means the United Mine Workers of America and the Bituminous Coal Operators' Association, Inc. (referred to in this chapter as the "BCOA").

(3) National Bituminous Coal Wage Agreement.—The term "National Bituminous Coal Wage Agreement" means a collective bargaining agreement negotiated by the BCOA and the United Mine Workers of America.

(c) Terms Relating to Operators.—For purposes of this section—

(1) Signatory operator.—The term "signatory operator" means a person which is or was a signatory to a coal wage agreement.

(2) Related persons.—

(A) In general.—A person shall be considered to be a related person to a signatory operator if that person is—

(i) a member of the controlled group of corporations (within the meaning of section 52(a)) which includes such signatory operator;

(ii) a trade or business which is under common control (as determined under section 52(b)) with such signatory operator; or

(iii) any other person who is identified as having a partnership interest or joint venture with a signatory operator in a business within the coal industry, but only if such business employed eligible beneficiaries, except that this clause shall not apply to a person whose only interest is as a limited partner.

A related person shall also include a successor in interest of any person described in clause (i), (ii), or (iii).

(B) Time for determination.—The relationships described in clauses (i), (ii), and (iii) of subparagraph (A) shall be determined as of July 20, 1992, except that if, on July 20, 1992, a signatory operator is no longer in business, the relationships shall be determined as of the time immediately before such operator ceased to be in business.

(3) 1988 agreement operator.—The term "1988 agreement operator" means—

(A) a signatory operator which was a signatory to the 1988 National Bituminous Coal Wage Agreement,

(B) an employer in the coal industry which was a signatory to an agreement containing pension and health care contribution and benefit provisions which are the same as those contained in the 1988 National Bituminous Coal Wage Agreement, or

(C) an employer from which contributions were actually received after 1987 and before July 20, 1992, by the 1950 UMWA Benefit Plan or the 1974 UMWA Benefit Plan in connection with employment in the coal industry during the period covered by the 1988 National Bituminous Coal Wage Agreement.

(4) Last signatory operator.—The term "last signatory operator" means, with respect to a coal industry retiree, a signatory operator which was the most recent coal industry employer of such retiree.

(5) Assigned operator.—The term "assigned operator" means, with respect to an eligible beneficiary defined in section 9703(f), the signatory operator to which liability under subchapter B with respect to the beneficiary is assigned under section 9706.

(6) Operators of dependent beneficiaries.—For purposes of this chapter, the signatory operator, last signatory operator, or assigned operator of any eligible beneficiary under this chapter who is a coal industry retiree shall be considered to be the signatory operator, last signatory operator, or assigned operator with respect to any other individual who is an eligible beneficiary under this chapter by reason of a relationship to the retiree.

(7) Business.—For purposes of this chapter, a person shall be considered to be in business if such person conducts or derives revenue from any business activity, whether or not in the coal industry.

(8) Successor in interest.—

(A) Safe harbor.—The term "successor in interest" shall not include any person who—

(i) is an unrelated person to an eligible seller described in subparagraph (C); and

(ii) purchases for fair market value assets, or all of the stock, of a related person to such seller, in a bona fide, arm's-length sale.

(B) Unrelated person.—The term "unrelated person" means a purchaser who does not bear a relationship to the eligible seller described in section 267(b).

(C) Eligible seller.—For purposes of this paragraph, the term "eligible seller" means an assigned operator described in section 9704(j)(2) or a related person to such assigned operator.

(d) Enactment Date.—For purposes of this chapter, the term "enactment date" means the date of the enactment of this chapter.

IRC Sec. 9701(d)

Subchapter B—Combined Benefit Fund

Part I—Establishment and Benefits

SEC. 9702. ESTABLISHMENT OF THE UNITED MINE WORKERS OF AMERICA COMBINED BENEFIT FUND.

(a) Establishment.—

(1) In general.—As soon as practicable (but not later than 60 days) after the enactment date, the persons described in subsection (b) shall designate the individuals to serve as trustees. Such trustees shall create a new private plan to be known as the United Mine Workers of America Combined Benefit Fund.

(2) Merger of retiree benefit plans.—As of February 1, 1993, the settlors of the 1950 UMWA Benefit Plan and the 1974 UMWA Benefit Plan shall cause such plans to be merged into the Combined Fund, and such merger shall not be treated as an employer withdrawal for purposes of any 1988 coal wage agreement.

(3) Treatment of plan.—The Combined Fund shall be—

(A) a plan described in section 302(c)(5) of the Labor Management Relations Act, 1947 (29 U.S.C. 186(c)(5)),

(B) an employee welfare benefit plan within the meaning of section 3(1) of the Employee Retirement Income Security Act of 1974 (29 U.S.C. 1002(1)), and

(C) a multiemployer plan within the meaning of section 3(37) of such Act (29 U.S.C. 1002(37)).

(4) Tax treatment.—For purposes of this title, the Combined Fund and any related trust shall be treated as an organization exempt from tax under section 501(a).

(b) Board of Trustees.—

(1) In general.—For purposes of subsection (a), the board of trustees for the Combined Fund shall be appointed as follows:

(A) 2 individuals who represent employers in the coal mining industry shall be designated by the BCOA;

(B) 2 individuals designated by the United Mine Workers of America; and

(C) 3 individuals selected by the individuals appointed under subparagraphs (A) and (B).

(2) Successor trustees.—Any successor trustee shall be appointed in the same manner as the trustee being succeeded. The plan establishing the Combined Fund shall provide for the removal of trustees.

(3) Special rule.—If the BCOA ceases to exist, any trustee or successor under paragraph (1)(A) shall be designated by the 3 employers who were members of the BCOA on the enactment date and who have been assigned the greatest number of eligible beneficiaries under section 9706.

(c) Plan Year.—The first plan year of the Combined Fund shall begin February 1, 1993, and end September 30, 1993. Each succeeding plan year shall begin on October 1 of each calendar year.

SEC. 9703. PLAN BENEFITS.

(a) In General.—Each eligible beneficiary of the Combined Fund shall receive—

(1) health benefits described in subsection (b), and

(2) in the case of an eligible beneficiary described in subsection (f)(1), death benefits coverage described in subsection (c).

(b) Health Benefits.—

(1) In general.—The trustees of the Combined Fund shall provide health care benefits to each eligible beneficiary by enrolling the beneficiary in a health care services plan which undertakes to provide such benefits on a prepaid risk basis. The trustees shall utilize all available plan resources to ensure that, consistent with paragraph (2), coverage under the managed care system shall to the maximum extent feasible be substantially the same as (and subject to the same limitations of) coverage provided under the 1950 UMWA Benefit Plan and the 1974 UMWA Benefit Plan as of January 1, 1992.

(2) Plan payment rates.—

(A) In general.—The trustees of the Combined Fund shall negotiate payment rates with the health care services plans described in paragraph (1) for each plan year which are in amounts which—

(i) vary as necessary to ensure that beneficiaries in different geographic areas have access to a uniform level of health benefits; and

(ii) result in aggregate payments for such plan year from the Combined Fund which do not exceed the total premium payments required to be paid to the Combined Fund under section 9704(a) for the plan year, adjusted as provided in subparagraphs (B) and (C).

(B) Reductions.—The amount determined under subparagraph (A)(ii) for any plan year shall be reduced—

(i) by the aggregate death benefit premiums determined under section 9704(c) for the plan year, and

(ii) by the amount reserved for plan administration under subsection (d).

(C) Increases.—The amount determined under subparagraph (A)(ii) shall be increased—

(i) by any reduction in the total premium payments required to be paid under section 9704(a) by reason of transfers described in section 9705,

(ii) by any carryover to the plan year from any preceding plan year which—

(I) is derived from amounts described in section 9704(e)(3)(B)(i), and

(II) the trustees elect to use to pay benefits for the current plan year, and

(iii) any interest earned by the Combined Fund which the trustees elect to use to pay benefits for the current plan year.

(3) Qualified providers.—The trustees of the Combined Fund shall not enter into an agreement under paragraph (1) with any provider of services which is of a type which is required to be certified by the Secretary of Health and Human Services when providing services under title XVIII of the Social Security Act unless the provider is so certified.

(4) Effective date.—Benefits shall be provided under paragraph (1) on and after February 1, 1993.

(c) Death Benefits Coverage.—

(1) In general.—The trustees of the Combined Fund shall provide death benefits coverage to each eligible beneficiary described in subsection (f)(1) which is identical to the benefits provided under the 1950 UMWA Pension Plan or 1974 UMWA Pension Plan, whichever is applicable, on July 20, 1992. Such coverage shall be provided on and after February 1, 1993.

(2) Termination of coverage.—The 1950 UMWA Pension Plan and the 1974 UMWA Pension Plan shall each be amended to provide that death benefits coverage shall not be provided to eligible beneficiaries on and after February 1, 1993. This paragraph shall not prohibit such plans from subsequently providing death benefits not described in paragraph (1).

(d) Reserves for Administration.—The trustees of the Combined Fund may reserve for each plan year, for use in payment of the administrative costs of the Combined Fund, an amount not to exceed 5 percent of the premiums to be paid to the Combined Fund under section 9704(a) during the plan year.

(e) Limitation on Enrollment.—The Combined Fund shall not enroll any individual who is not receiving benefits under the 1950 UMWA Benefit Plan or the 1974 UMWA Benefit Plan as of July 20, 1992.

(f) Eligible Beneficiary.—For purposes of this subchapter, the term "eligible beneficiary" means an individual who—

(1) is a coal industry retiree who, on July 20, 1992, was eligible to receive, and receiving, benefits from the 1950 UMWA Benefit Plan or the 1974 UMWA Benefit Plan, or

(2) on such date was eligible to receive, and receiving, benefits in either such plan by reason of a relationship to such retiree.

Part II—Financing

SEC. 9704. LIABILITY OF ASSIGNED OPERATORS.

(a) Annual Premiums.—Each assigned operator shall pay to the Combined Fund for each plan year beginning on or after February 1, 1993, an annual premium equal to the sum of the following three premiums—

(1) the health benefit premium determined under subsection (b) for such plan year, plus

(2) the death benefit premium determined under subsection (c) for such plan year, plus

(3) the unassigned beneficiaries premium determined under subsection (d) for such plan year.

Any related person with respect to an assigned operator shall be jointly and severally liable for any premium required to be paid by such operator.

IRC Sec. 9704(a)(3)

(b) Health Benefit Premium.—For purposes of this chapter—

(1) In general.—The health benefit premium for any plan year for any assigned operator shall be an amount equal to the product of the per beneficiary premium for the plan year multiplied by the number of eligible beneficiaries assigned to such operator under section 9706.

(2) Per beneficiary premium.—The Commissioner of Social Security shall calculate a per beneficiary premium for each plan year beginning on or after February 1, 1993, which is equal to the sum of—

(A) the amount determined by dividing—

(i) the aggregate amount of payments from the 1950 UMWA Benefit Plan and the 1974 UMWA Benefit Plan for health benefits (less reimbursements but including administrative costs) for the plan year beginning July 1, 1991, for all individuals covered under such plans for such plan year, by

(ii) the number of such individuals, plus

(B) the amount determined under subparagraph (A) multiplied by the percentage (if any) by which the medical component of the Consumer Price Index for the calendar year in which the plan year begins exceeds such component for 1992.

(3) Adjustments for Medicare reductions.—If, by reason of a reduction in benefits under title XVIII of the Social Security Act, the level of health benefits under the Combined Fund would be reduced, the trustees of the Combined Fund shall increase the per beneficiary premium for the plan year in which the reduction occurs and each subsequent plan year by the amount necessary to maintain the level of health benefits which would have been provided without such reduction.

(c) Death Benefit Premium.—The death benefit premium for any plan year for any assigned operator shall be equal to the applicable percentage of the amount, actuarially determined, which the Combined Fund will be required to pay during the plan year for death benefits coverage described in section 9703(c).

(d) Unassigned Beneficiaries Premium.

(1) Plan years ending on or before September 30, 2006.—For plan years ending on or before September 30, 2006, the unassigned beneficiaries premium for any assigned operator shall be equal to the applicable percentage of the product of the per beneficiary premium for the plan year multiplied by the number of eligible beneficiaries who are not assigned under section 9706 to any person for such plan year.

(2) Plan years beginning on or after October 1, 2006.—

(A) In general.—For plan years beginning on or after October 1, 2006, subject to subparagraph (B), there shall be no unassigned beneficiaries pre-

mium, and benefit costs with respect to eligible beneficiaries who are not assigned under section 9706 to any person for any such plan year shall be paid from amounts transferred under section 9705(b).

(B) Inadequate transfers.—If, for any plan year beginning on or after October 1, 2006, the amounts transferred under section 9705(b) are less than the amounts required to be transferred to the Combined Fund under subsection (h)(2)(A) or (i) of section 402 of the Surface Mining Control and Reclamation Act of 1977 (30 U.S.C. 1232)), then the unassigned beneficiaries premium for any assigned operator shall be equal to the operator's applicable percentage of the amount required to be so transferred which was not so transferred.

(e) Premium Accounts; Adjustments.—

(1) Accounts.—The trustees of the Combined Fund shall establish and maintain 3 separate accounts for each of the premiums described in subsections (b), (c), and (d). Such accounts shall be credited with the premiums received and debited with expenditures allocable to such premiums.

(2) Allocations.—

(A) Administrative expenses.—Administrative costs for any plan year shall be allocated to premium accounts under paragraph (1) on the basis of expenditures (other than administrative costs) from such accounts during the preceding plan year.

(B) Interest.—Interest shall be allocated to the account established for health benefit premiums.

(3) Shortfalls and surpluses.—

(A) In general.—Except as provided in subparagraph (B), if, for any plan year, there is a shortfall or surplus in any premium account, the premium for the following plan year for each assigned operator shall be proportionately reduced or increased, whichever is applicable, by the amount of such shortfall or surplus.

(B) Exception.—Subparagraph (A) shall not apply to any surplus in the health benefit premium account or the unassigned beneficiaries premium account which is attributable to—

(i) the excess of the premiums credited to such account for a plan year over the benefits (and administrative costs) debited to such account for the plan year, but such excess shall only be available for purposes of the carryover described in section 9703(b)(2)(C)(ii) (relating to carryovers of premiums not used to provide benefits), or

(ii) interest credited under paragraph (2)(B) for the plan year or any preceding plan year.

(C) No authority for increased payments. Nothing in this paragraph shall be construed to allow expenditures for health care benefits for any plan year in excess of the limit under section 9703(b)(2).

(f) Applicable Percentage.—For purposes of this section—

(1) In general.—The term "applicable percentage" means, with respect to any assigned operator, the percentage determined by dividing the number of eligible beneficiaries assigned under section 9706 to such operator by the total number of eligible beneficiaries assigned under section 9706 to all such operators (determined on the basis of assignments as of October 1, 1993).

(2) Annual adjustments.—In the case of any plan year beginning on or after October 1, 1994, the applicable percentage for any assigned operator shall be redetermined under paragraph (1) by making the following changes to the assignments as of October 1, 1993:

(A) Such assignments shall be modified to reflect any changes during the period beginning October 1, 1993, and ending on the last day of the preceding plan year pursuant to the appeals process under section 9706(f).

(B) The total number of assigned eligible beneficiaries shall be reduced by the eligible beneficiaries of assigned operators which (and all related persons with respect to which) had ceased business (within the meaning of section 9701(c)(6)) during the period described in subparagraph (A).

(g) Payment of Premiums.—

(1) In general.—The annual premium under subsection (a) for any plan year shall be payable in 12 equal monthly installments, due on the twenty-fifth day of each calendar month in the plan year. In the case of the plan year beginning February 1, 1993, the annual premium under subsection (a) shall be added to such premium for the plan year beginning October 1, 1993.

(2) Deductibility.—Any premium required by this section shall be deductible without regard to any limitation on deductibility based on the prefunding of health benefits.

(h) Information.—The trustees of the Combined Fund shall, not later than 60 days after the enactment date, furnish to the Commissioner of Social Security information as to the benefits and covered beneficiaries under the fund, and such other information as the Secretary may require to compute any premium under this section.

(i) Transition Rules.—

(1) 1988 agreement operators.—

(A) 1st year costs.—During the plan year of the Combined Fund beginning February 1, 1993, the 1988 agreement operators shall make contributions to the Combined Fund in amounts necessary to pay benefits and administrative costs of the Combined Fund incurred during such year, reduced by the amount transferred to the Combined Fund under section 9705(a) on February 1, 1993.

(B) Deficits from merged plans.—During the period beginning February 1, 1993, and ending September 30, 1994, the 1988 agreement operators shall make contributions to the Combined Fund as are necessary to pay off the expenses accrued (and remaining unpaid) by the 1950 UMWA Benefit Plan and the 1974 UMWA Benefit Plan as of February 1, 1993, reduced by the assets of such plans as of such date.

(C) Failure.—If any 1988 agreement operator fails to meet any obligation under this paragraph, any contributions of such operator to the Combined Fund or any other plan described in section 404(c) shall not be deductible under this title until such time as the failure is corrected.

(D) Premium reductions.—

(i) 1st year payments.—In the case of a 1988 agreement operator making contributions under subparagraph (A), the premium of such operator under subsection (a) shall be reduced by the amount paid under subparagraph (A) by such operator for the plan year beginning February 1, 1993.

(ii) Deficit payments.—In the case a 1988 agreement operator making contributions under subparagraph (B), the premium of such operator under subsection (a) shall be reduced by the amounts which are paid to the Combined Fund by reason of claims arising in connection with the 1950 UMWA Benefit Plan and the 1974 UMWA Benefit Plan as of February 1, 1993, including claims based on the "evergreen clause" found in the language of the 1950 UMWA Benefit Plan and the 1974 UMWA Benefit Plan, and which are allocated to such operator under subparagraph (E).

(iii) Limitation.—Clause (ii) shall not apply to the extent the amounts paid exceed the contributions.

(iv) Plan years.—Premiums under subsection (a) shall be reduced for the first plan year for which amounts described in clause (i) or (ii) are available and for any succeeding plan year until such amounts are exhausted.

(E) Allocations of contributions and refunds.—Contributions under subparagraphs (A) and (B), and premium reductions under subparagraph (D)(ii), shall be made ratably on the basis of aggregate contributions made by such operators under the applicable 1988 coal wage agreements as of January 31, 1993.

(2) 1st plan year.—In the case of the plan year of the Combined Fund beginning February 1, 1993—

(A) the premiums under subsections (a)(1) and (a)(3) shall be 67 percent of such premiums without regard to this paragraph, and

(B) the premiums under subsection (a) shall be paid as provided in subsection (g).

(3) Startup costs.—The 1950 UMWA Benefit Plan and the 1974 UMWA Benefit Plan shall pay the costs of the Combined Fund incurred before February 1, 1993. For purposes of this section, such costs shall be treated as administrative expenses incurred for the plan year beginning February 1, 1993.

(j) Prepayment of Premium Liability.—

(1) In general.—If—

(A) a payment meeting the requirements of paragraph (3) is made to the Combined Fund by or on behalf of—

(i) any assigned operator to which this subsection applies, or

(ii) any related person to any assigned operator described in clause (i), and

(B) the common parent of the controlled group of corporations described in paragraph (2)(B) is jointly and severally liable for any premium under this section which (but for this subsection) would be required to be paid by the assigned operator or related person,

then such common parent (and no other person) shall be liable for such premium.

(2) Assigned operators to which subsection applies.—

(A) In general.—This subsection shall apply to any assigned operator if—

(i) the assigned operator (or a related person to the assigned operator)—

(I) made contributions to the 1950 UMWA Benefit Plan and the 1974 UMWA Benefit Plan for employment during the period covered by the 1988 agreement; and

(II) is not a 1988 agreement operator,

(ii) the assigned operator (and all related persons to the assigned operator) are not actively engaged in the production of coal as of July 1, 2005, and

(iii) the assigned operator was, as of July 20, 1992, a member of a controlled group of corporations described in subparagraph (B).

(B) Controlled group of corporations.—A controlled group of corporations is described in this subparagraph if the common parent of such group is a corporation the shares of which are publicly traded on a United States exchange.

(C) Coordination with repeal of assignments.—A person shall not fail to be treated as an assigned

operator to which this subsection applies solely because the person ceases to be an assigned operator by reason of section 9706(h)(1) if the person otherwise meets the requirements of this subsection and is liable for the payment of premiums under section 9706(h)(3).

(D) Controlled group.—For purposes of this subsection, the term "controlled group of corporations" has the meaning given such term by section 52(a).

(3) Requirements.—A payment meets the requirements of this paragraph if—

(A) the amount of the payment is not less than the present value of the total premium liability under this chapter with respect to the Combined Fund of the assigned operators or related persons described in paragraph (1) or their assignees, as determined by the operator's or related person's enrolled actuary (as defined in section 7701(a)(35)) using actuarial methods and assumptions each of which is reasonable and which are reasonable in the aggregate, as determined by such enrolled actuary;

(B) such enrolled actuary files with the Secretary of Labor a signed actuarial report containing—

(i) the date of the actuarial valuation applicable to the report; and

(ii) a statement by the enrolled actuary signing the report that, to the best of the actuary's knowledge, the report is complete and accurate and that in the actuary's opinion the actuarial assumptions used are in the aggregate reasonably related to the experience of the operator and to reasonable expectations; and

(C) 90 calendar days have elapsed after the report required by subparagraph (B) is filed with the Secretary of Labor, and the Secretary of Labor has not notified the assigned operator in writing that the requirements of this paragraph have not been satisfied.

(4) Use of prepayment.—The Combined Fund shall—

(A) establish and maintain an account for each assigned operator or related person by, or on whose behalf, a payment described in paragraph (3) was made,

(B) credit such account with such payment (and any earnings thereon), and

(C) use all amounts in such account exclusively to pay premiums that would (but for this subsection) be required to be paid by the assigned operator.

Upon termination of the obligations for the premium liability of any assigned operator or related person for which such account is maintained, all funds remaining in such account (and earnings thereon) shall be refunded to such person as may be designated by the common parent described in paragraph (1)(B).

IRC Sec. 9704(i)(2)(A)

Tax Relief and Health Care Act of 2006 (Pub. L. No. 109-432), as follows:

- IRC §9704(d) was amended by Act, Div. C, §212(a)(2)(A). Eff. plan years of the Combined Fund beginning after Sept. 30, 2006. IRC §9704(d) prior to amendment:

    (d) Unassigned beneficiaries premium.—The unassigned beneficiaries premium for any plan year for any assigned operator shall be equal to the applicable percentage of the product of the per beneficiary premium for the plan year multiplied by the number of eligible beneficiaries who are not assigned under section 9706 to any person for such plan year.

- IRC §9704(e)(1) was amended by Act, Div. C, §212(a)(2)(B)(i) by inserting "and amounts transferred under §9705(b)" after "premiums received". Eff. plan years of the Combined Fund beginning after Sept. 30, 2006.

- IRC §9704(e)(3)(A) was amended by Act, Div. C, §212(a)(2)(B)(ii) by adding the sentence at the end. Eff. plan years of the Combined Fund beginning after Sept. 30, 2006.

- IRC §9704(f)(2)(C) was amended by Act, Div. C, §212(a)(2)(C) by adding subpara. (C). Eff. plan years of the Combined Fund beginning after Sept. 30, 2006.

- IRC §9704(j) was added by Act, Div. C, §211(a). Eff. plan years of the Combined Fund beginning after Sept. 30, 2006.

SEC. 9705. TRANSFERS.

(a) Transfer of Assets From 1950 UMWA Pension Plan.—

(1) In general.—From the funds reserved under paragraph (2), the board of trustees of the 1950 UMWA Pension Plan shall transfer to the Combined Fund—

(A) $70,000,000 on February 1, 1993,

(B) $70,000,000 on October 1, 1993, and

(C) $70,000,000 on October 1, 1994.

(2) Reservation.—Immediately upon the enactment date, the board of trustees of the 1950 UMWA Pension Plan shall segregate $210,000,000 from the general assets of the plan. Such funds shall be held in the plan until disbursed pursuant to paragraph (1). Any interest on such funds shall be deposited into the general assets of the 1950 UMWA Pension Plan.

(3) Use of funds.—Amounts transferred to the Combined Fund under paragraph (1) shall—

(A) in the case of the transfer on February 1, 1993, be used to proportionately reduce the premium of each assigned operator under section 9704(a) for the plan year of the Fund beginning February 1, 1993, and

(B) in the case of any other such transfer, be used to proportionately reduce the unassigned beneficiary premium under section 9704(a)(3) and the death benefit premium under section 9704(a)(2) of each assigned operator for the plan year in which transferred and for any subsequent plan year in which such funds remain available.

Such funds may not be used to pay any amounts required to be paid by the 1988 agreement operators under section 9704(i)(1)(B).

(4) Tax treatment; validity of transfer.—

(A) No deduction.—No deduction shall be allowed under this title with respect to any transfer pursuant to paragraph (1), but such transfer shall not adversely affect the deductibility (under applicable provisions of this title) of contributions previously made by employers, or amounts hereafter contributed by employers, to the 1950 UMWA Pension Plan, the 1950 UMWA Benefit Plan, the 1974 UMWA Pension Plan, the 1974 UMWA Benefit Plan, the 1992 UMWA Benefit Plan, or the Combined Fund.

(B) Other tax provisions.—Any transfer pursuant to paragraph (1)—

(i) shall not be treated as an employer reversion from a qualified plan for purposes of section 4980, and

(ii) shall not be includible in the gross income of any employer maintaining the 1950 UMWA Pension Plan.

(5) Treatment of transfer.—Any transfer pursuant to paragraph (1) shall not be deemed to violate, or to be prohibited by, any provision of law, or to cause the settlors, joint board of trustees, employers or any related person to incur or be subject to liability, taxes, fines, or penalties of any kind whatsoever.

(b) Transfers.—

(1) In general.—The Combined Fund shall include any amount transferred to the Fund under subsections (h) and (i) of section 402 of the Surface Mining Control and Reclamation Act of 1977 (30 U.S.C. 1232(h)).

(2) Use of funds.—Any amount transferred under paragraph (1) for any fiscal year shall be used to pay benefits and administrative costs of beneficiaries of the Combined Fund or for such other purposes as are specifically provided in the Acts described in paragraph (1).

Tax Relief and Health Care Act of 2006 (Pub. L. No. 109-432), as follows:

- IRC §9705(b) was amended by Act, Div. C, §212(a)(1)(C) by striking "From Abandoned Mine Reclamation Fund" in the heading. Eff. plan years of the Combined Fund beginning after Sept. 30, 2006.

- IRC §9705(b)(1) was amended by Act, Div. C, §212(a)(1)(A) by substituting "subsections (h) and (i) of §402" for "§402(h)". Eff. plan years of the Combined Fund beginning after Sept. 30, 2006.

- IRC §9705(b)(2) was amended by Act, Div. C, §212(a)(1)(B). Eff. plan years of the Combined Fund beginning after Sept. 30, 2006. IRC §9705(b)(2) prior to being stricken:

    (2) Use of funds.—Any amount transferred under paragraph (1) for any fiscal year shall be used to proportionately reduce the unassigned beneficiary premium under §9704(a)(3) of each assigned operator for the plan year in which transferred.

SEC. 9706. ASSIGNMENT OF ELIGIBLE BENEFICIARIES.

(a) **In General.**—For purposes of this chapter, the Commissioner of Social Security shall, before October 1, 1993, assign each coal industry retiree who is an eligible beneficiary to a signatory operator which (or any related person with respect to which) remains in business in the following order:

(1) First, to the signatory operator which—

(A) was a signatory to the 1978 coal wage agreement or any subsequent coal wage agreement, and

(B) was the most recent signatory operator to employ the coal industry retiree in the coal industry for at least 2 years.

(2) Second, if the retiree is not assigned under paragraph (1), to the signatory operator which—

(A) was a signatory to the 1978 coal wage agreement or any subsequent coal wage agreement, and

(B) was the most recent signatory operator to employ the coal industry retiree in the coal industry.

(3) Third, if the retiree is not assigned under paragraph (1) or (2), to the signatory operator which employed the coal industry retiree in the coal industry for a longer period of time than any other signatory operator prior to the effective date of the 1978 coal wage agreement.

(b) **Rules Relating to Employment and Reassignment Upon Purchase.**—For purposes of subsection (a)—

(1) **Aggregation rules.**—

(A) Related person.—Any employment of a coal industry retiree in the coal industry by a signatory operator shall be treated as employment by any related persons to such operator.

(B) Certain employment disregarded.—Employment with—

(i) a person which is (and all related persons with respect to which are) no longer in business, or

(ii) a person during a period during which such person was not a signatory to a coal wage agreement, shall not be taken into account.

(2) **Reassignment upon purchase.**—If a person becomes a successor of an assigned operator after the enactment date, the assigned operator may transfer the assignment of an eligible beneficiary under subsection (a) to such successor, and such successor shall be treated as the assigned operator with respect to such eligible beneficiary for purposes of this chapter. Notwithstanding the preceding sentence, the assigned operator transferring such assignment (and any re-

lated person) shall remain the guarantor of the benefits provided to the eligible beneficiary under this chapter. An assigned operator shall notify the trustees of the Combined Fund of any transfer described in this paragraph.

(c) **Identification of Eligible Beneficiaries.**—The 1950 UMWA Benefit Plan and the 1974 UMWA Benefit Plan shall, by the later of October 1, 1992, or the twentieth day after the enactment date, provide to the Commissioner of Social Security a list of the names and social security account numbers of each eligible beneficiary, including each deceased eligible beneficiary if any other individual is an eligible beneficiary by reason of a relationship to such deceased eligible beneficiary. In addition, the plans shall provide, where ascertainable from plan records, the names of all persons described in subsection (a) with respect to any eligible beneficiary or deceased eligible beneficiary.

(d) **Cooperation by Other Agencies and Persons.**—

(1) **Cooperation.**—The head of any department, agency, or instrumentality of the United States shall cooperate fully and promptly with the Commissioner of Social Security in providing information which will enable the Commissioner to carry out his responsibilities under this section.

(2) **Providing of information.**—

(A) In general.—Notwithstanding any other provision of law, including section 6103, the head of any other agency, department, or instrumentality shall, upon receiving a written request from the Commissioner of Social Security in connection with this section, cause a search to be made of the files and records maintained by such agency, department, or instrumentality with a view to determining whether the information requested is contained in such files or records. The Commissioner shall be advised whether the search disclosed the information requested, and, if so, such information shall be promptly transmitted to the Commissioner, except that if the disclosure of any requested information would contravene national policy or security interests of the United States, or the confidentiality of census data, the information shall not be transmitted and the Commissioner shall be so advised.

(B) Limitation.—Any information provided under subparagraph (A) shall be limited to information necessary for the Commissioner to carry out his duties under this section.

(3) **Trustees.**—The trustees of the Combined Fund, the 1950 UMWA Benefit Plan, the 1974 UMWA Benefit Plan, the 1950 UMWA Pension Plan, and the 1974 UMWA Pension Plan shall fully and promptly cooperate with the Commissioner in furnishing, or assisting the Commissioner to obtain, any

information the Commissioner needs to carry out the Commissioner's responsibilities under this section.

(e) Notice by Secretary.—

(1) Notice to fund.—The Commissioner of Social Security shall advise the trustees of the Combined Fund of the name of each person identified under this section as an assigned operator, and the names and social security account numbers of eligible beneficiaries with respect to whom he is identified.

(2) Other notice.—The Commissioner of Social Security shall notify each assigned operator of the names and social security account numbers of eligible beneficiaries who have been assigned to such person under this section and a brief summary of the facts related to the basis for such assignments.

(f) Reconsideration by Commissioner.—

(1) In general.—Any assigned operator receiving a notice under subsection (e)(2) with respect to an eligible beneficiary may, within 30 days of receipt of such notice, request from the Commissioner of Social Security detailed information as to the work history of the beneficiary and the basis of the assignment.

(2) Review.—An assigned operator may, within 30 days of receipt of the information under paragraph (1), request review of the assignment. The Commissioner of Social Security shall conduct such review if the Commissioner finds the operator provided evidence with the request constituting a prima facie case of error.

(3) Results of review.—

(A) Error.—If the Commissioner of Social Security determines under a review under paragraph (2) that an assignment was in error—

(i) the Commissioner shall notify the assigned operator and the trustees of the Combined Fund and the trustees shall reduce the premiums of the operator under section 9704 by (or if there are no such premiums, repay) all premiums paid under section 9704 with respect to the eligible beneficiary, and

(ii) the Commissioner shall review the beneficiary's record for reassignment under subsection (a).

(B) No error.—If the Commissioner of Social Security determines under a review conducted under paragraph (2) that no error occurred, the Commissioner shall notify the assigned operator.

(4) Determinations.—Any determination by the Commissioner of Social Security under paragraph (2) or (3) shall be final.

(5) Payment pending review.—An assigned operator shall pay the premiums under section 9704 pending review by the Commissioner of Social Security or by a court under this subsection.

(6) Private actions.—Nothing in this section shall preclude the right of any person to bring a separate civil action against another person for responsibility for assigned premiums, notwithstanding any prior decision by the Commissioner.

(g) Confidentiality of Information.—Any person to which information is provided by the Commissioner of Social Security under this section shall not disclose such information except in any proceedings related to this section. Any civil or criminal penalty which is applicable to an unauthorized disclosure under section 6103 shall apply to any unauthorized disclosure under this section.

(h) Assignments as of October 1, 2007.—

(1) In general.—Subject to the premium obligation set forth in paragraph (3), the Commissioner of Social Security shall—

(A) revoke all assignments to persons other than 1988 agreement operators for purposes of assessing premiums for plan years beginning on and after October 1, 2007; and

(B) make no further assignments to persons other than 1988 agreement operators, except that no individual who becomes an unassigned beneficiary by reason of subparagraph (A) may be assigned to a 1988 agreement operator.

(2) Reassignment upon purchase.—This subsection shall not be construed to prohibit the reassignment under subsection (b)(2) of an eligible beneficiary.

(3) Liability of persons during three fiscal years beginning on and after October 1, 2007.—In the case of each of the fiscal years beginning on October 1, 2007, 2008, and 2009, each person other than a 1988 agreement operator shall pay to the Combined Fund the following percentage of the amount of annual premiums that such person would otherwise be required to pay under section 9704(a), determined on the basis of assignments in effect without regard to the revocation of assignments under paragraph (1)(A):

(A) For the fiscal year beginning on October 1, 2007, 55 percent.

(B) For the fiscal year beginning on October 1, 2008, 40 percent.

(C) For the fiscal year beginning on October 1, 2009, 15 percent.

Recent Amendments to IRC §9706

Tax Relief and Health Care Act of 2006 (Pub. L. No. 109-432), as follows:

● IRC §9706 was amended by Act, Division C, §212(a)(3) by adding new subsec. (h). Eff. plan years of the Combined Fund beginning after Sept. 30, 2006.

Part III—Enforcement

SEC. 9707. FAILURE TO PAY PREMIUM.

(a) Failures to Pay.—

(1) Premiums for eligible beneficiaries.—There is hereby imposed a penalty on the failure of any assigned operator to pay any premium required to be paid under section 9704 with respect to any eligible beneficiary.

(2) Contributions required under the mining laws.—There is hereby imposed a penalty on the failure of any person to make a contribution required under section 402(h)(5)(B)(ii) of the Surface Mining Control and Reclamation Act of 1977 to a plan referred to in section 402(h)(2)(C) of such Act. For purposes of applying this section, each such required monthly contribution for the hours worked of any individual shall be treated as if it were a premium required to be paid under section 9704 with respect to an eligible beneficiary.

(b) Amount of Penalty.—The amount of the penalty imposed by subsection (a) on any failure with respect to any eligible beneficiary shall be $100 per day in the noncompliance period with respect to any such failure.

(c) Noncompliance Period.—For purposes of this section, the term "noncompliance period" means, with respect to any failure to pay any premium or installment thereof, the period—

(1) beginning on the due date for such premium or installment, and

(2) ending on the date of payment of such premium or installment.

(d) Limitations on Amount of Penalty.—

(1) In general.—No penalty shall be imposed by subsection (a) on any failure during any period for which it is established to the satisfaction of the Secretary of the Treasury that none of the persons responsible for such failure knew, or exercising reasonable diligence, would have known, that such failure existed.

(2) Corrections.—No penalty shall be imposed by subsection (a) on any failure if—

(A) such failure was due to reasonable cause and not to willful neglect, and

(B) such failure is corrected during the 30-day period beginning on the 1st date that any of the persons responsible for such failure knew, or exercising reasonable diligence would have known, that such failure existed.

(3) Waiver.—In the case of a failure that is due to reasonable cause and not to willful neglect, the Sec-

retary of the Treasury may waive all or part of the penalty imposed by subsection (a) for failures to the extent that the Secretary determines, in his sole discretion, that the payment of such penalty would be excessive relative to the failure involved.

(e) Liability for Penalty.—The person failing to meet the requirements of section 9704 shall be liable for the penalty imposed by subsection (a).

(f) Treatment.—For purposes of this title, the penalty imposed by this section shall be treated in the same manner as the tax imposed by section 4980B.

Recent Amendments to IRC §9707

Tax Relief and Health Care Act of 2006 (Pub. L. No. 109-432), as follows:

● IRC §9707(a) was amended by Act, Div. C, §213(b)(1). Eff. Dec. 20, 2006. IRC §9707(a) prior to amendment:

   (a) General rule.— There is hereby imposed a penalty on the failure of any assigned operator to pay any premium required to be paid under section 9704 with respect to any eligible beneficiary.

Part IV—Other Provisions

SEC. 9708. EFFECT ON PENDING CLAIMS OR OBLIGATIONS.

All liability for contributions to the Combined Fund that arises on and after February 1, 1993, shall be determined exclusively under this chapter, including all liability for contributions to the 1950 UMWA Benefit Plan and the 1974 UMWA Benefit Plan for coal production on and after February 1, 1993. However, nothing in this chapter is intended to have any effect on any claims or obligations arising in connection with the 1950 UMWA Benefit Plan and the 1974 UMWA Benefit Plan as of February 1, 1993, including claims or obligations based on the "evergreen" clause found in the language of the 1950 UMWA Benefit Plan and the 1974 UMWA Benefit Plan. This chapter shall not be construed to affect any rights of subrogation of any 1988 agreement operator with respect to contributions due to the 1950 UMWA Benefit Plan or the 1974 UMWA Benefit Plan as of February 1, 1993.

Subchapter C—Health Benefits of Certain Miners

Part I—Individual Employer Plans

SEC. 9711. CONTINUED OBLIGATIONS OF INDIVIDUAL EMPLOYER PLANS.

(a) Coverage of Current Recipients.—The last signatory operator of any individual who, as of February 1, 1993, is receiving retiree health benefits from an individual employer plan maintained pursuant to a 1978 or subsequent coal wage agreement shall con-

IRC Sec. 9707

tinue to provide health benefits coverage to such individual and the individual's eligible beneficiaries which is substantially the same as (and subject to all the limitations of) the coverage provided by such plan as of January 1, 1992. Such coverage shall continue to be provided for as long as the last signatory operator (and any related person) remains in business.

(b) Coverage of Eligible Recipients.—

(1) In general.—The last signatory operator of any individual who, as of February 1, 1993, is not receiving retiree health benefits under the individual employer plan maintained by the last signatory operator pursuant to a 1978 or subsequent coal wage agreement, but has met the age and service requirements for eligibility to receive benefits under such plan as of such date, shall, at such time as such individual becomes eligible to receive benefits under such plan, provide health benefits coverage to such individual and the individual's eligible beneficiaries which is described in paragraph (2). This paragraph shall not apply to any individual who retired from the coal industry after September 30, 1994, or any eligible beneficiary of such individual.

(2) Coverage.—Subject to the provisions of subsection (d), health benefits coverage is described in this paragraph if it is substantially the same as (and subject to all the limitations of) the coverage provided by the individual employer plan as of January 1, 1992. Such coverage shall continue for as long as the last signatory operator (and any related person) remains in business.

(c) Joint and Several Liability of Related Persons.—

(1) In general.—Except as provided in paragraph (2), each related person of a last signatory operator to which subsection (a) or (b) applies shall be jointly and severally liable with the last signatory operator for the provision of health care coverage described in subsection (a) or (b).

(2) Liability limited if security provided.—If—

(A) security meeting the requirements of paragraph (3) is provided by or on behalf of—

(i) any last signatory operator which is an assigned operator described in section 9704(j)(2), or

(ii) any related person to any last signatory operator described in clause (i), and

(B) the common parent of the controlled group of corporations described in section 9704(j)(2)(B) is jointly and severally liable for the provision of health care under this section which, but for this paragraph, would be required to be provided by the last signatory operator or related person,

then, as of the date the security is provided, such common parent (and no other person) shall be liable for the provision of health care under this section

which the last signatory operator or related person would otherwise be required to provide. Security may be provided under this paragraph without regard to whether a payment was made under section 9704(j).

(3) Security.—Security meets the requirements of this paragraph if—

(A) the security—

(i) is in the form of a bond, letter of credit, or cash escrow,

(ii) is provided to the trustees of the 1992 UMWA Benefit Plan solely for the purpose of paying premiums for beneficiaries who would be described in section 9712(b)(2)(B) if the requirements of this section were not met by the last signatory operator, and

(iii) is in an amount equal to 1 year of liability of the last signatory operator under this section, determined by using the average cost of such operator's liability during the prior 3 calendar years;

(B) the security is in addition to any other security required under any other provision of this title; and

(C) the security remains in place for 5 years.

(4) Refunds of security.—The remaining amount of any security provided under this subsection (and earnings thereon) shall be refunded to the last signatory operator as of the earlier of—

(A) the termination of the obligations of the last signatory operator under this section, or

(B) the end of the 5-year period described in paragraph (4)(C).

(d) Managed Care and Cost Containment.—The last signatory operator shall not be treated as failing to meet the requirements of subsection (a) or (b) if benefits are provided to eligible beneficiaries under managed care and cost containment rules and procedures described in section 9712(c) or agreed to by the last signatory operator and the United Mine Workers of America.

(e) Treatment of Noncovered Employees.—The existence, level, and duration of benefits provided to former employees of a last signatory operator (and their eligible beneficiaries) who are not otherwise covered by this chapter and who are (or were) covered by a coal wage agreement shall only be determined by, and shall be subject to, collective bargaining, lawful unilateral action, or other applicable law.

(f) Eligible Beneficiary.—For purposes of this section, the term "eligible beneficiary" means any individual who is eligible for health benefits under a plan described in subsection (a) or (b) by reason of the individual's relationship with the retiree described in such subsection (or to an individual who, based on service and employment history at the time of death, would have been so described but for such death).

IRC Sec. 9711(f)

(g) Rules Applicable to This Part and Part II.— For purposes of this part and part II—

(1) Successor.—The term "last signatory operator" shall include a successor in interest of such operator.

(2) Reassignment upon purchase.—If a person becomes a successor of a last signatory operator after the enactment date, the last signatory operator may transfer any liability of such operator under this chapter with respect to an eligible beneficiary to such successor, and such successor shall be treated as the last signatory operator with respect to such eligible beneficiary for purposes of this chapter. Notwithstanding the preceding sentence, the last signatory operator transferring such assignment (and any related person) shall remain the guarantor of the benefits provided to the eligible beneficiary under this chapter. A last signatory operator shall notify the trustees of the 1992 UMWA Benefit Plan of any transfer described in this paragraph.

Recent Amendments to IRC §9711

Tax Relief and Health Care Act of 2006 (Pub. L. No. 109-432), as follows:
- IRC §9711(c) was amended by Act, Div. C, §211(b). Eff. Dec. 20, 2006. IRC §9711(c) prior to amendment:

    (c) Joint and several liability of related persons.—Each related person of a last signatory operator to which subsection (a) or (b) applies shall be jointly and severally liable with the last signatory operator for the provision of health care coverage described in subsection (a) or (b).

Part II—1992 UMWA Benefit Plan

SEC. 9712. ESTABLISHMENT AND COVERAGE OF 1992 UMWA BENEFIT PLAN.

(a) Creation of Plan.—

(1) In general.—As soon as practicable after the enactment date, the settlors shall create a separate private plan which shall be known as the United Mine Workers of America 1992 Benefit Plan. For purposes of this title, the 1992 UMWA Benefit Plan shall be treated as an organization exempt from taxation under section 501(a). The settlors shall be responsible for designing the structure, administration and terms of the 1992 UMWA Benefit Plan, and for appointment and removal of the members of the board of trustees. The board of trustees shall initially consist of five members and shall thereafter be the number set by the settlors.

(2) Treatment of plan.—The 1992 UMWA Benefit Plan shall be—

(A) a plan described in section 302(c)(5) of the Labor Management Relations Act, 1947 (29 U.S.C. 186(c)(5)),

(B) an employee welfare benefit plan within the meaning of section 3(1) of the Employee Retirement Income Security Act of 1974 (29 U.S.C. 1002(1)), and

(C) a multiemployer plan within the meaning of section 3(37) of such Act (29 U.S.C. 1002(37)).

(3) Transfers under other federal statutes.—

(A) In general.—The 1992 UMWA Benefit Plan shall include any amount transferred to the plan under subsections (h) and (i) of section 402 of the Surface Mining Control and Reclamation Act of 1977 (30 U.S.C. 1232).

(B) Use of funds.—Any amount transferred under subparagraph (A) for any fiscal year shall be used to provide the health benefits described in subsection (c) with respect to any beneficiary for whom no monthly per beneficiary premium is paid pursuant to paragraph (1)(A) or (3) of subsection (d).

(4) Special rule for 1993 plan.—

(A) In general.—The plan described in section 402(h)(2)(C) of the Surface Mining Control and Reclamation Act of 1977 (30 U.S.C. 1232(h)(2)(C)) shall include any amount transferred to the plan under subsections (h) and (i) of the Surface Mining Control and Reclamation Act of 1977 (30 U.S.C. 1232).

(B) Use of funds.—Any amount transferred under subparagraph (A) for any fiscal year shall be used to provide the health benefits described in section 402(h)(2)(C)(i) of the Surface Mining Control and Reclamation Act of 1977 (30 U.S.C. 1232(h)(2)(C)(i)) to individuals described in section 402(h)(2)(C) of such Act (30 U.S.C. 1232(h)(2)(C)).

(b) Coverage Requirement.—

(1) In general.—The 1992 UMWA Benefit Plan shall only provide health benefits coverage to any eligible beneficiary who is not eligible for benefits under the Combined Fund and shall not provide such coverage to any other individual.

(2) Eligible beneficiary.—For purposes of this section, the term "eligible beneficiary" means an individual who—

(A) but for the enactment of this chapter, would be eligible to receive benefits from the 1950 UMWA Benefit Plan or the 1974 UMWA Benefit Plan, based upon age and service earned as of February 1, 1993; or

(B) with respect to whom coverage is required to be provided under section 9711, but who does not receive such coverage from the applicable last signatory operator or any related person,

and any individual who is eligible for benefits by reason of a relationship to an individual described in subparagraph (A) or (B). In no event shall the 1992 UMWA Benefit Plan provide health benefits coverage to any eligible beneficiary who is a coal industry retiree who retired from the coal industry after September 30, 1994, or any beneficiary of such individual.

(c) Health Benefits.—

(1) In general.—The 1992 UMWA Benefit Plan shall provide health care benefits coverage to each eligible beneficiary which is substantially the same as (and subject to all the limitations of) coverage provided under the 1950 UMWA Benefit Plan and the 1974 UMWA Benefit Plan as of January 1, 1992.

(2) Managed care.—The 1992 UMWA Benefit Plan shall develop managed care and cost containment rules which shall be applicable to the payment of benefits under this subsection. Application of such rules shall not cause the plan to be treated as failing to meet the requirements of this subsection. Such rules shall preserve freedom of choice while reinforcing managed care network use by allowing a point of service decision as to whether a network medical provider will be used. Major elements of such rules may include, but are not limited to, elements described in paragraph (3).

(3) Major elements of rules.—Elements described in this paragraph are—

(A) implementing formulary for drugs and subjecting the prescription program to a rigorous review of appropriate use,

(B) obtaining a unit price discount in exchange for patient volume and preferred provider status with the amount of the potential discount varying by geographic region,

(C) limiting benefit payments to physicians to the allowable charge under title XVIII of the Social Security Act, while protecting beneficiaries from balance billing by providers,

(D) utilizing, in the claims payment function "appropriateness of service" protocols under title XVIII of the Social Security Act if more stringent,

(E) creating mandatory utilization review (UR) procedures, but placing the responsibility to follow such procedures on the physician or hospital, not the beneficiaries,

(F) selecting the most efficient physicians and state-of-the-art utilization management techniques, including ambulatory care techniques, for medical services delivered by the managed care network, and

(G) utilizing a managed care network provider system, as practiced in the health care industry, at the time medical services are needed (point-of-service) in order to receive maximum benefits available under this subsection.

(4) Last signatory operators.—The board of trustees of the 1992 UMWA Benefit Plan shall permit any last signatory operator required to maintain an individual employer plan under section 9711 to utilize the managed care and cost containment rules and programs developed under this subsection if the operator elects to do so.

(5) Standards of quality.—Any managed care system or cost containment adopted by the board of trustees of the 1992 UMWA Benefit Plan or by a last signatory operator may not be implemented unless it is approved by, and meets the standards of quality adopted by, a medical peer review panel, which has been established—

(A) by the settlors, or

(B) by the United Mine Workers of America and a last signatory operator or group of operators.

Standards of quality shall include accessibility to medical care, taking into account that accessibility requirements may differ depending on the nature of the medical need.

(d) Guarantee of Benefits.—

(1) In general.—All 1988 last signatory operators shall be responsible for financing the benefits described in subsection (c) by meeting the following requirements in accordance with the contribution requirements established in the 1992 UMWA Benefit Plan:

(A) The payment of a monthly per beneficiary premium by each 1988 last signatory operator for each eligible beneficiary of such operator who is described in subsection (b)(2) and who is receiving benefits under the 1992 UMWA Benefit Plan.

(B) The provision of a security (in the form of a bond, letter of credit, or cash escrow) in an amount equal to a portion of the projected future cost to the 1992 UMWA Benefit Plan of providing health benefits for eligible and potentially eligible beneficiaries attributable to the 1988 last signatory operator.

(C) If the amounts transferred under subsection (a)(3) are less than the amounts required to be transferred to the 1992 UMWA Benefit Plan under subsections (h) and (i) of section 402 of the Surface Mining Control and Reclamation Act of 1977 (30 U.S.C. 1232), the payment of an additional backstop premium by each 1988 last signatory operator which is equal to such operator's share of the amounts required to be so transferred but which were not so transferred, determined on the basis of the number of eligible and potentially eligible beneficiaries attributable to the operator.

(2) Adjustments.—The 1992 UMWA Benefit Plan shall provide for—

(A) annual adjustments of the per beneficiary premium to cover changes in the cost of providing benefits to eligible beneficiaries, and

(B) adjustments as necessary to the annual backstop premium to reflect changes in the cost of

IRC Sec. 9712(d)(2)(B)

providing benefits to eligible beneficiaries for whom per beneficiary premiums are not paid.

(3) Additional liability.—Any last signatory operator who is not a 1988 last signatory operator shall pay the monthly per beneficiary premium under paragraph(1)(A) for each eligible beneficiary described in such paragraph attributable to that operator.

(4) Joint and several liability.—A 1988 last signatory operator or last signatory operator described in paragraph (3), and any related person to any such operator, shall be jointly and severally liable with such operator for any amount required to be paid by such operator under this section. The provisions of section 9711(c)(2) shall apply to any last signatory operator described in such section (without regard to whether security is provided under such section, a payment is made under section 9704(j), or both) and if security meeting the requirements of section 9711(c)(3) is provided, the common parent described in section 9711(c)(2)(B) shall be exclusively responsible for any liability for premiums under this section which, but for this sentence, would be required to be paid by the last signatory operator or any related person.

(5) Deductibility.—Any premium required by this section shall be deductible without regard to any limitation on deductibility based on the prefunding of health benefits.

(6) 1988 last signatory operator.—For purposes of this section, the term "1988 last signatory operator" means a last signatory operator which is a 1988 agreement operator.

Recent Amendments to IRC §9712

Tax Relief and Health Care Act of 2006 (Pub. L. No. 109-432), as follows:

- IRC §9712(a) was amended by Act, Div. C, §212(b)(1) by adding new paras. (3) and (4). Eff. Dec. 20, 2006.
- IRC §9712(d)(1) was amended by Act, Div. C, §212(b)(2)(A). Eff. fiscal years beginning on or after Oct. 1, 2010. IRC §9712(d)(1) prior to amendment:

  (1) In general.—All 1988 last signatory operators shall be responsible for financing the benefits described in subsection (c), in accordance with contribution requirements established in the 1992 UMWA Benefit Plan. Such contribution requirements, which shall be applied uniformly to each 1988 last signatory operator, on the basis of the number of eligible and potentially eligible beneficiaries attributable to each operator, shall include:

  (A) the payment of an annual prefunding premium for all eligible and potentially eligible beneficiaries attributable to a 1988 last signatory operator,

  (B) the payment of a monthly per beneficiary premium by each 1988 last signatory operator for each eligible beneficiary of such operator who is described in subsection (b)(2) and who is receiving benefits under the 1992 UMWA Benefit Plan, and

  (C) the provision of security (in the form of a bond, letter of credit or cash escrow) in an amount equal to a portion of the projected future cost to the 1992 UMWA Benefit Plan of providing health benefits for eligible and potentially eligible beneficiaries attributable to the 1988 last signatory operator. If a 1988 last signatory operator is unable to provide the security

required the 1992 UMWA Benefit Plan shall require the operator to pay an annual prefunding premium that is greater than the premium otherwise applicable.

- IRC §9712(d)(2)(B) was amended by Act, Div. C, §212(b)(2)(B)(i) by substituting "backstop" for "prefunding". Eff. fiscal years beginning on or after Oct. 1, 2010.
- IRC §9712(d)(3) was amended by Act, Div. C, §212(b)(2)(B)(ii) by substituting "paragraph (1)(A)" for "paragraph (1)(B)". Eff. fiscal years beginning on or after Oct. 1, 2010.
- IRC §9712(d)(4) was amended by Act, Div. C, §211(c) by adding the sentence at the end. Eff. Dec. 20, 2006.

Subchapter D—Other Provisions

SEC. 9721. CIVIL ENFORCEMENT.

The provisions of section 4301 of the Employee Retirement Income Security Act of 1974 shall apply, in the same manner as any claim arising out of an obligation to pay withdrawal liability under subtitle E of title IV of such Act, to any claim—

(1) arising out of an obligation to pay any amount required to be paid by this chapter; or

(2) arising out of an obligation to pay any amount required by section 402(h)(5)(B)(ii) of the Surface Mining Control and Reclamation Act of 1977 (30 U.S.C. 1232(h)(5)(B)(ii)).

Recent Amendments to IRC §9721

Tax Relief and Health Care Act of 2006 (Pub. L. No. 109-432), as follows:

- IRC §9721 was amended by Act, Div. C, §213(b)(2). Eff. Dec. 20, 2006. IRC §9721 prior to amendment:

  SEC. 9721. CIVIL ENFORCEMENT.
  The provisions of section 4301 of the Employee Retirement Income Security Act of 1974 shall apply to any claim arising out of an obligation to pay any amount required to be paid by this chapter in the same manner as any claim arising out of an obligation to pay withdrawal liability under subtitle E of title IV of such Act. For purposes of the preceding sentence, a signatory operator and related persons shall be treated in the same manner as employers.

---

* * *

Subtitle K—Group Health Plan Requirements

Chapter 100—Group Health Plan Requirements

Subchapter A—Requirements Relating to Portability, Access, and Renewability

SEC. 9801. INCREASED PORTABILITY THROUGH LIMITATION ON PREEXISTING CONDITION EXCLUSIONS.

(a) Limitation on Preexisting Condition Exclusion Period; Crediting for Periods of Previous Coverage.—Subject to subsection (d), a group health plan may, with respect to a participant or beneficiary, impose a preexisting condition exclusion only if—

(1) such exclusion relates to a condition (whether physical or mental), regardless of the cause of the condition, for which medical advice, diagnosis, care, or treatment was recommended or received within the 6-month period ending on the enrollment date;

(2) such exclusion extends for a period of not more than 12 months (or 18 months in the case of a late enrollee) after the enrollment date; and

(3) the period of any such preexisting condition exclusion is reduced by the length of the aggregate of the periods of creditable coverage (if any) applicable to the participant or beneficiary as of the enrollment date.

(b) Definitions.—For purposes of this section—

(1) Preexisting condition exclusion.—

(A) In general.—The term "preexisting condition exclusion" means, with respect to coverage, a limitation or exclusion of benefits relating to a condition based on the fact that the condition was present before the date of enrollment for such coverage, whether or not any medical advice, diagnosis, care, or treatment was recommended or received before such date.

(B) Treatment of genetic information.—For purposes of this section, genetic information shall not be treated as a condition described in subsection (a)(1) in the absence of a diagnosis of the condition related to such information.

(2) Enrollment date.—The term "enrollment date" means, with respect to an individual covered under a group health plan, the date of enrollment of the individual in the plan or, if earlier, the first day of the waiting period for such enrollment.

(3) Late enrollee.—The term "late enrollee" means, with respect to coverage under a group health plan, a participant or beneficiary who enrolls under the plan other than during—

(A) the first period in which the individual is eligible to enroll under the plan, or

(B) a special enrollment period under subsection (f).

(4) Waiting period.—The term "waiting period" means, with respect to a group health plan and an individual who is a potential participant or beneficiary in the plan, the period that must pass with respect to the individual before the individual is eligible to be covered for benefits under the terms of the plan.

(c) Rules Relating to Crediting Previous Coverage.—

(1) Creditable coverage defined.—For purposes of this part, the term "creditable coverage" means, with respect to an individual, coverage of the individual under any of the following:

(A) A group health plan.

(B) Health insurance coverage.

(C) Part A or part B of title XVIII of the Social Security Act.

(D) Title XIX of the Social Security Act, other than coverage consisting solely of benefits under section 1928.

(E) Chapter 55 of title 10, United States Code.

(F) A medical care program of the Indian Health Service or of a tribal organization.

(G) A State health benefits risk pool.

(H) A health plan offered under chapter 89 of title 5, United States Code.

(I) A public health plan (as defined in regulations).

(J) A health benefit plan under section 5(e) of the Peace Corps Act (22 U.S.C. 2504(e)).

Such term does not include coverage consisting solely of coverage of excepted benefits (as defined in section 9832(c)).

(2) Not counting periods before significant breaks in coverage.—

(A) In general.—A period of creditable coverage shall not be counted, with respect to enrollment of an individual under a group health plan, if, after such period and before the enrollment date, there was a 63-day period during all of which the individual was not covered under any creditable coverage.

(B) Waiting period not treated as a break in coverage.—For purposes of subparagraph (A) and subsection (d)(4), any period that an individual is in a waiting period for any coverage under a group health plan or is in an affiliation period shall not be taken into account in determining the continuous period under subparagraph (A).

(C) Affiliation period.—

(i) **In general.**—For purposes of this section, the term "affiliation period" means a period which, under the terms of the health insurance coverage offered by the health maintenance organization, must expire before the health insurance coverage becomes effective. During such an affiliation period, the organization is not required to provide health care services or benefits and no premium shall be charged to the participant or beneficiary.

(ii) **Beginning.**—Such period shall begin on the enrollment date.

(iii) **Runs concurrently with waiting periods.**—Any such affiliation period shall run concurrently with any waiting period under the plan.

IRC Sec. 9801(c)(2)(C)(iii)

(D) TAA-eligible individuals.—In the case of plan years beginning before ~~January 1, 2011~~ *February 13, 2011*—

(i) TAA pre-certification period rule.—In the case of a TAA-eligible individual, the period beginning on the date the individual has a TAA-related loss of coverage and ending on the date which is 7 days after the date of the issuance by the Secretary (or by any person or entity designated by the Secretary) of a qualified health insurance costs credit eligibility certificate for such individual for purposes of section 7527 shall not be taken into account in determining the continuous period under subparagraph (A).

(ii) Definitions.—The terms "TAA-eligible individual" and "TAA-related loss of coverage" have the meanings given such terms in section 4980B(f)(5)(C)(iv).

(3) Method of crediting coverage.—

(A) Standard method.—Except as otherwise provided under subparagraph (B), for purposes of applying subsection (a)(3), a group health plan shall count a period of creditable coverage without regard to the specific benefits for which coverage is offered during the period.

(B) Election of alternative method.—A group health plan may elect to apply subsection (a)(3) based on coverage of any benefits within each of several classes or categories of benefits specified in regulations rather than as provided under subparagraph (A). Such election shall be made on a uniform basis for all participants and beneficiaries. Under such election a group health plan shall count a period of creditable coverage with respect to any class or category of benefits if any level of benefits is covered within such class or category.

(C) Plan notice.—In the case of an election with respect to a group health plan under subparagraph (B), the plan shall—

(i) prominently state in any disclosure statements concerning the plan, and state to each enrollee at the time of enrollment under the plan, that the plan has made such election, and

(ii) include in such statements a description of the effect of this election.

(4) Establishment of period.—Periods of creditable coverage with respect to an individual shall be established through presentation of certifications described in subsection (e) or in such other manner as may be specified in regulations.

(d) Exceptions.—

(1) Exclusion not applicable to certain newborns.—Subject to paragraph (4), a group health plan may not impose any preexisting condition exclusion in the case of an individual who, as of the last day of the 30-day period beginning with the date of birth, is covered under creditable coverage.

(2) Exclusion not applicable to certain adopted children.—Subject to paragraph (4), a group health plan may not impose any preexisting condition exclusion in the case of a child who is adopted or placed for adoption before attaining 18 years of age and who, as of the last day of the 30-day period beginning on the date of the adoption or placement for adoption, is covered under creditable coverage. The previous sentence shall not apply to coverage before the date of such adoption or placement for adoption.

(3) Exclusion not applicable to pregnancy.—For purposes of this section, a group health plan may not impose any preexisting condition exclusion relating to pregnancy as a preexisting condition.

(4) Loss if break in coverage.—Paragraphs (1) and (2) shall no longer apply to an individual after the end of the first 63-day period during all of which the individual was not covered under any creditable coverage.

(e) Certifications and Disclosure of Coverage.—

(1) Requirement for certification of period of creditable coverage.—

(A) In general.—A group health plan shall provide the certification described in subparagraph (B)—

(i) at the time an individual ceases to be covered under the plan or otherwise becomes covered under a COBRA continuation provision,

(ii) in the case of an individual becoming covered under such a provision, at the time the individual ceases to be covered under such provision, and

(iii) on the request on behalf of an individual made not later than 24 months after the date of cessation of the coverage described in clause (i) or (ii), whichever is later.

The certification under clause (i) may be provided, to the extent practicable, at a time consistent with notices required under any applicable COBRA continuation provision.

(B) Certification.—The certification described in this subparagraph is a written certification of—

(i) the period of creditable coverage of the individual under such plan and the coverage under such COBRA continuation provision, and

(ii) the waiting period (if any) (and affiliation period, if applicable) imposed with respect to the individual for any coverage under such plan.

(C) Issuer compliance.—To the extent that medical care under a group health plan consists of health insurance coverage offered in connection with the plan, the plan is deemed to have satisfied the certification requirement under this paragraph if the issuer provides for such certification in accordance with this paragraph.

(2) Disclosure of information on previous benefits.—

(A) In general.—In the case of an election described in subsection (c)(3)(B) by a group health plan, if the plan enrolls an individual for coverage under the plan and the individual provides a certification of coverage of the individual under paragraph (1)—

(i) upon request of such plan, the entity which issued the certification provided by the individual shall promptly disclose to such requesting plan information on coverage of classes and categories of health benefits available under such entity's plan, and

(ii) such entity may charge the requesting plan or issuer for the reasonable cost of disclosing such information.

(3) Regulations.—The Secretary shall establish rules to prevent an entity's failure to provide information under paragraph (1) or (2) with respect to previous coverage of an individual from adversely affecting any subsequent coverage of the individual under another group health plan or health insurance coverage.

(f) Special Enrollment Periods.—

(1) Individuals losing other coverage.—A group health plan shall permit an employee who is eligible, but not enrolled, for coverage under the terms of the plan (or a dependent of such an employee if the dependent is eligible, but not enrolled, for coverage under such terms) to enroll for coverage under the terms of the plan if each of the following conditions is met:

(A) The employee or dependent was covered under a group health plan or had health insurance coverage at the time coverage was previously offered to the employee or individual.

(B) The employee stated in writing at such time that coverage under a group health plan or health insurance coverage was the reason for declining enrollment, but only if the plan sponsor (or the health insurance issuer offering health insurance coverage in connection with the plan) required such a statement at such time and provided the employee with notice of such requirement (and the consequences of such requirement) at such time.

(C) The employee's or dependent's coverage described in subparagraph (A)—

(i) was under a COBRA continuation provision and the coverage under such provision was exhausted; or

(ii) was not under such a provision and either the coverage was terminated as a result of loss of eligibility for the coverage (including as a result of legal separation, divorce, death, termination of employment, or reduction in the number of hours of employment) or employer contributions towards such coverage were terminated.

(D) Under the terms of the plan, the employee requests such enrollment not later than 30 days after the date of exhaustion of coverage described in subparagraph (C)(i) or termination of coverage or employer contribution described in subparagraph (C)(ii).

(2) For dependent beneficiaries.—

(A) In general.—If—

(i) a group health plan makes coverage available with respect to a dependent of an individual,

(ii) the individual is a participant under the plan (or has met any waiting period applicable to becoming a participant under the plan and is eligible to be enrolled under the plan but for a failure to enroll during a previous enrollment period), and

(iii) a person becomes such a dependent of the individual through marriage, birth, or adoption or placement for adoption,

the group health plan shall provide for a dependent special enrollment period described in subparagraph (B) during which the person (or, if not otherwise enrolled, the individual) may be enrolled under the plan as a dependent of the individual, and in the case of the birth or adoption of a child, the spouse of the individual may be enrolled as a dependent of the individual if such spouse is otherwise eligible for coverage.

(B) Dependent special enrollment period.—The dependent special enrollment period under this subparagraph shall be a period of not less than 30 days and shall begin on the later of—

(i) the date dependent coverage is made available, or

(ii) the date of the marriage, birth, or adoption or placement for adoption (as the case may be) described in subparagraph (A)(iii).

(C) No waiting period.—If an individual seeks coverage of a dependent during the first 30 days of such a dependent special enrollment period, the coverage of the dependent shall become effective—

(i) in the case of marriage, not later than the first day of the first month beginning after the date the completed request for enrollment is received;

(ii) in the case of a dependent's birth, as of the date of such birth; or

(iii) in the case of a dependent's adoption or placement for adoption, the date of such adoption or placement for adoption.

IRC Sec. 9801(f)(2)(C)(iii)

(3) Special rules relating to Medicaid and CHIP.—

(A) In general.—A group health plan shall permit an employee who is eligible, but not enrolled, for coverage under the terms of the plan (or a dependent of such an employee if the dependent is eligible, but not enrolled, for coverage under such terms) to enroll for coverage under the terms of the plan if either of the following conditions is met:

(i) Termination of Medicaid or CHIP coverage.—The employee or dependent is covered under a Medicaid plan under title XIX of the Social Security Act or under a State child health plan under title XXI of such Act and coverage of the employee or dependent under such a plan is terminated as a result of loss of eligibility for such coverage and the employee requests coverage under the group health plan not later than 60 days after the date of termination of such coverage.

(ii) Eligibility for employment assistance under Medicaid or CHIP.—The employee or dependent becomes eligible for assistance, with respect to coverage under the group health plan under such Medicaid plan or State child health plan (including under any waiver or demonstration project conducted under or in relation to such a plan), if the employee requests coverage under the group health plan not later than 60 days after the date the employee or dependent is determined to be eligible for such assistance.

(B) Employee outreach and disclosure.—

(i) Outreach to employees regarding availability of Medicaid and CHIP coverage.—

(I) In general.—Each employer that maintains a group health plan in a State that provides medical assistance under a State Medicaid plan under title XIX of the Social Security Act, or child health assistance under a State child health plan under title XXI of such Act, in the form of premium assistance for the purchase of coverage under a group health plan, shall provide to each employee a written notice informing the employee of potential opportunities then currently available in the State in which the employee resides for premium assistance under such plans for health coverage of the employee or the employee's dependents. For purposes of compliance with this clause, the employer may use any State- specific model notice developed in accordance with section 701(f)(3)(B)(i)(II) of the Employee Retirement Income Security Act of 1974 (29 U.S.C. 1181(f)(3)(B)(i)(II)).

(II) Option to provide concurrent with provision of plan materials to employee.—An employer may provide the model notice applicable to the State in which an employee resides concurrent with the furnishing of materials notifying the employee of health plan eligibility, concurrent with materials provided to the employee in connection with an open season or election process conducted under the plan, or concurrent with the furnishing of the summary plan description as provided in section 104(b) of the Employee Retirement Income Security Act of 1974 (29 U.S.C. 1024).

(ii) Disclosure about group health plan benefits to states for Medicaid and CHIP eligible individuals.—In the case of a participant or beneficiary of a group health plan who is covered under a Medicaid plan of a State under title XIX of the Social Security Act or under a State child health plan under title XXI of such Act, the plan administrator of the group health plan shall disclose to the State, upon request, information about the benefits available under the group health plan in sufficient specificity, as determined under regulations of the Secretary of Health and Human Services in consultation with the Secretary that require use of the model coverage coordination disclosure form developed under section 311(b)(1)(C) of the Children's Health Insurance Program Reauthorization Act of 2009, so as to permit the State to make a determination (under paragraph (2)(B), (3), or (10) of section 2105(c) of the Social Security Act or otherwise) concerning the cost-effectiveness of the State providing medical or child health assistance through premium assistance for the purchase of coverage under such group health plan and in order for the State to provide supplemental benefits required under paragraph (10)(E) of such section or other authority.

Recent Amendments to IRC §9801

Omnibus Trade Act of 2010 (Pub. L. No. 111-344), as follows:
- IRC §9801(c)(2)(D) was amended by Act §114(a) by striking "January 1, 2011" and inserting "February 13, 2011". Eff. for plan years beginning after Dec. 31, 2010.

TAA Health Coverage Improvement Act of 2009 (Pub. L. No. 111-5), as follows:
- IRC §9801(c)(2)(D) was added by Act, Div. B, §1899D(a). Eff. for plan years beginning after date of enactment [enacted: Feb. 17, 2009].

Children's Health Insurance Program Reauthoriza-tion Act of 2009 (Pub. L. No. 111-3), as follows:
- IRC §9801(f)(3) was added by Act §311(a). See Act §3, below, for effective date.
- **Other Provision—Effective Date.** Act §3 provides:

> SEC. 3. GENERAL EFFECTIVE DATE; EXCEPTION FOR STATE LEGISLATION; CONTINGENT EFFECTIVE DATE; RELIANCE ON LAW.
> (a) **General Effective Date.**—Unless otherwise provided in this Act, subject to subsections (b) through (d), this Act (and the amendments made by this Act) shall take effect on April 1, 2009, and shall apply to child health assistance and medical assistance provided on or after that date.
> (b) **Exception for State Legislation.**—In the case of a State plan under title XIX or State child health plan under XXI of the Social Security Act, which the Secretary of Health and Human Services determines requires State legislation in order for the respective plan to meet one or more additional requirements imposed by amendments made by this Act, the respective plan shall not be regarded as failing to comply with the

requirements of such title solely on the basis of its failure to meet such an additional requirement before the first day of the first calendar quarter beginning after the close of the first regular session of the State legislature that begins after the date of enactment of this Act. For purposes of the previous sentence, in the case of a State that has a 2-year legislative session, each year of the session shall be considered to be a separate regular session of the State legislature.

(c) Coordination of CHIP Funding for Fiscal Year 2009.—Notwithstanding any other provision of law, insofar as funds have been appropriated under section 2104(a)(11), 2104(k), or 2104(*l*) of the Social Security Act, as amended by section 201 of Public Law 110-173, to provide allotments to States under CHIP for fiscal year 2009—

(1) any amounts that are so appropriated that are not so allotted and obligated before April 1, 2009 are rescinded; and

(2) any amount provided for CHIP allotments to a State under this Act (and the amendments made by this Act) for such fiscal year shall be reduced by the amount of such appropriations so allotted and obligated before such date.

(d) Reliance on Law.—With respect to amendments made by this Act (other than title VII) that become effective as of a date—

(1) such amendments are effective as of such date whether or not regulations implementing such amendments have been issued; and

(2) Federal financial participation for medical assistance or child health assistance furnished under title XIX or XXI, respectively, of the Social Security Act on or after such date by a State in good faith reliance on such amendments before the date of promulgation of final regulations, if any, to carry out such amendments (or before the date of guidance, if any, regarding the implementation of such amendments) shall not be denied on the basis of the State>s failure to comply with such regulations or guidance.

SEC. 9802. PROHIBITING DISCRIMINATION AGAINST INDIVIDUAL PARTICIPANTS AND BENEFICIARIES BASED ON HEALTH STATUS.

(a) In Eligibility to Enroll.—

(1) In general.—Subject to paragraph (2), a group health plan may not establish rules for eligibility (including continued eligibility) of any individual to enroll under the terms of the plan based on any of the following factors in relation to the individual or a dependent of the individual:

(A) Health status.

(B) Medical condition (including both physical and mental illnesses).

(C) Claims experience.

(D) Receipt of health care.

(E) Medical history.

(F) Genetic information.

(G) Evidence of insurability (including conditions arising out of acts of domestic violence).

(H) Disability.

(2) No application to benefits or exclusions.—To the extent consistent with section 9801, paragraph (1) shall not be construed—

(A) to require a group health plan to provide particular benefits (or benefits with respect to a specific procedure, treatment, or service) other than those provided under the terms of such plan; or

(B) to prevent such a plan from establishing limitations or restrictions on the amount, level, extent, or nature of the benefits or coverage for similarly situated individuals enrolled in the plan or coverage.

(3) Construction.—For purposes of paragraph (1), rules for eligibility to enroll under a plan include rules defining any applicable waiting periods for such enrollment.

(b) In Premium Contributions.—

(1) In general.—A group health plan may not require any individual (as a condition of enrollment or continued enrollment under the plan) to pay a premium or contribution which is greater than such premium or contribution for a similarly situated individual enrolled in the plan on the basis of any factor described in subsection (a)(1) in relation to the individual or to an individual enrolled under the plan as a dependent of the individual.

(2) Construction.—Nothing in paragraph (1) shall be construed—

(A) to restrict the amount that an employer may be charged for coverage under a group health plan except as provided in paragraph (3); or

(B) to prevent a group health plan from establishing premium discounts or rebates or modifying otherwise applicable copayments or deductibles in return for adherence to programs of health promotion and disease prevention.

(3) No group-based discrimination on basis of genetic information.—

(A) In general.—For purposes of this section, a group health plan may not adjust premium or contribution amounts for the group covered under such plan on the basis of genetic information.

(B) Rule of construction.—Nothing in subparagraph (A) or in paragraphs (1) and (2) of subsection (d) shall be construed to limit the ability of a group health plan to increase the premium for an employer based on the manifestation of a disease or disorder of an individual who is enrolled in the plan. In such case, the manifestation of a disease or disorder in one individual cannot also be used as genetic information about other group members and to further increase the premium for the employer.

(c) Genetic Testing.—

(1) Limitation on requesting or requiring genetic testing.—A group health plan may not request or require an individual or a family member of such individual to undergo a genetic test.

(2) Rule of construction.—Paragraph (1) shall not be construed to limit the authority of a health care professional who is providing health care services to an individual to request that such individual undergo a genetic test.

(3) Rule of construction regarding payment.—

(A) In general.—Nothing in paragraph (1) shall be construed to preclude a group health plan from obtaining and using the results of a genetic test in making a determination regarding payment (as such term is defined for the purposes of applying the regulations promulgated by the Secretary of Health and Human Services under part C of title XI of the Social Security Act and section 264 of the Health Insurance Portability and Accountability Act of 1996, as may be revised from time to time) consistent with subsection (a).

(B) Limitation.—For purposes of subparagraph (A), a group health plan may request only the minimum amount of information necessary to accomplish the intended purpose.

(4) Research exception.—Notwithstanding paragraph (1), a group health plan may request, but not require, that a participant or beneficiary undergo a genetic test if each of the following conditions is met:

(A) The request is made pursuant to research that complies with part 46 of title 45, Code of Federal Regulations, or equivalent Federal regulations, and any applicable State or local law or regulations for the protection of human subjects in research.

(B) The plan clearly indicates to each participant or beneficiary, or in the case of a minor child, to the legal guardian of such beneficiary, to whom the request is made that—

(i) compliance with the request is voluntary; and

(ii) non-compliance will have no effect on enrollment status or premium or contribution amounts.

(C) No genetic information collected or acquired under this paragraph shall be used for underwriting purposes.

(D) The plan notifies the Secretary in writing that the plan is conducting activities pursuant to the exception provided for under this paragraph, including a description of the activities conducted.

(E) The plan complies with such other conditions as the Secretary may by regulation require for activities conducted under this paragraph.

(d) Prohibition on Collection of Genetic Information.—

(1) In general.—A group health plan shall not request, require, or purchase genetic information for underwriting purposes (as defined in section 9832).

(2) Prohibition on collection of genetic information prior to enrollment.—A group health plan

shall not request, require, or purchase genetic information with respect to any individual prior to such individual's enrollment under the plan or in connection with such enrollment.

(3) Incidental collection.—If a group health plan obtains genetic information incidental to the requesting, requiring, or purchasing of other information concerning any individual, such request, requirement, or purchase shall not be considered a violation of paragraph (2) if such request, requirement, or purchase is not in violation of paragraph (1).

(e) Application to All Plans.—The provisions of subsections (a)(1)(F), (b)(3), (c), and (d) and subsection (b)(1) and section 9801 with respect to genetic information, shall apply to group health plans without regard to section 9831(a)(2).

(f) Special Rules for Church Plans.—A church plan (as defined in section 414(e)) shall not be treated as failing to meet the requirements of this section solely because such plan requires evidence of good health for coverage of—

(1) both any employee of an employer with 10 or less employees (determined without regard to section 414(e)(3)(C)) and any self-employed individual, or

(2) any individual who enrolls after the first 90 days of initial eligibility under the plan.

This subsection shall apply to a plan for any year only if the plan included the provisions described in the preceding sentence on July 15, 1997, and at all times thereafter before the beginning of such year.

(f)[g] Genetic Information of a Fetus or Embryo.—Any reference in this chapter to genetic information concerning an individual or family member of an individual shall—

(1) with respect to such an individual or family member of an individual who is a pregnant woman, include genetic information of any fetus carried by such pregnant woman; and

(2) with respect to an individual or family member utilizing an assisted reproductive technology, include genetic information of any embryo legally held by the individual or family member.

Recent Amendments to IRC §9802

Genetic Information Nondiscrimination Act of 2008 (Pub. L. No. 110-233), as follows:

• IRC §9802(b)(2)(A) was amended by Act §103(a)(1) by inserting before the semicolon "except as provided in paragraph (3)". Eff. for group health plans for plan years beginning after the date that is one year after the date of enactment [enacted: May 21, 2008].

• IRC §9802(b)(3) was added by Act §103(a)(2). Eff. for group health plans for plan years beginning after the date that is one year after the date of enactment [enacted: May 21, 2008].

• IRC §9802(c) was redesignated as subsec. (f) by Act §103(b). Eff. for group health plans for plan years beginning after the date that is one year after the date of enactment [enacted: May 21, 2008].

- IRC §9802(c)–(e) were added by Act §103(b). Eff. for group health plans for plan years beginning after the date that is one year after the date of enactment [enacted: May 21, 2008].
- IRC §9802(f)[g] was added by Act §103(c). Eff. for group health plans for plan years beginning after the date that is one year after the date of enactment [enacted: May 21, 2008].
- **Other Provision.** Act §103(f)(1) provides:
    (1) Regulations. The Secretary of the Treasury shall issue final regulations or other guidance not later than 12 months after the date of the enactment of this Act to carry out the amendments made by this section.

SEC. 9803. GUARANTEED RENEWABILITY IN MULTIEMPLOYER PLANS AND CERTAIN MULTIPLE EMPLOYER WELFARE ARRANGEMENTS.

(a) In General.—A group health plan which is a multiemployer plan (as defined in section 414(f)) or which is a multiple employer welfare arrangement may not deny an employer continued access to the same or different coverage under such plan, other than—

(1) for nonpayment of contributions;

(2) for fraud or other intentional misrepresentation of material fact by the employer;

(3) for noncompliance with material plan provisions;

(4) because the plan is ceasing to offer any coverage in a geographic area;

(5) in the case of a plan that offers benefits through a network plan, because there is no longer any individual enrolled through the employer who lives, resides, or works in the service area of the network plan and the plan applies this paragraph uniformly without regard to the claims experience of employers or a factor described in section 9802(a)(1) in relation to such individuals or their dependents; or

(6) for failure to meet the terms of an applicable collective bargaining agreement, to renew a collective bargaining or other agreement requiring or authorizing contributions to the plan, or to employ employees covered by such an agreement.

(b) Multiple Employer Welfare Arrangement.— For purposes of subsection (a), the term "multiple employer welfare arrangement" has the meaning given such term by section 3(40) of the Employee Retirement Income Security Act of 1974, as in effect on the date of the enactment of this section.

Subchapter B—Other Requirements

SEC. 9811. STANDARDS RELATING TO BENEFITS FOR MOTHERS AND NEWBORNS.

(a) Requirements for Minimum Hospital Stay Following Birth.—

(1) **In general.**—A group health plan may not—

(A) except as provided in paragraph (2)—

(i) restrict benefits for any hospital length of stay in connection with childbirth for the mother or newborn child, following a normal vaginal delivery, to less than 48 hours, or

(ii) restrict benefits for any hospital length of stay in connection with childbirth for the mother or newborn child, following a caesarean section, to less than 96 hours; or

(B) require that a provider obtain authorization from the plan or the issuer for prescribing any length of stay required under subparagraph (A) (without regard to paragraph (2)).

(2) **Exception.**—Paragraph (1)(A) shall not apply in connection with any group health plan in any case in which the decision to discharge the mother or her newborn child prior to the expiration of the minimum length of stay otherwise required under paragraph (1)(A) is made by an attending provider in consultation with the mother.

(b) Prohibitions.—A group health plan may not—

(1) deny to the mother or her newborn child eligibility, or continued eligibility, to enroll or to renew coverage under the terms of the plan, solely for the purpose of avoiding the requirements of this section;

(2) provide monetary payments or rebates to mothers to encourage such mothers to accept less than the minimum protections available under this section;

(3) penalize or otherwise reduce or limit the reimbursement of an attending provider because such provider provided care to an individual participant or beneficiary in accordance with this section;

(4) provide incentives (monetary or otherwise) to an attending provider to induce such provider to provide care to an individual participant or beneficiary in a manner inconsistent with this section; or

(5) subject to subsection (c)(3), restrict benefits for any portion of a period within a hospital length of stay required under subsection (a) in a manner which is less favorable than the benefits provided for any preceding portion of such stay.

(c) Rules of Construction.—

(1) Nothing in this section shall be construed to require a mother who is a participant or beneficiary—

(A) to give birth in a hospital; or

(B) to stay in the hospital for a fixed period of time following the birth of her child.

(2) This section shall not apply with respect to any group health plan which does not provide benefits for hospital lengths of stay in connection with childbirth for a mother or her newborn child.

(3) Nothing in this section shall be construed as preventing a group health plan from imposing deduct-

IRC Sec. 9811(c)(3)

ibles, coinsurance, or other cost-sharing in relation to benefits for hospital lengths of stay in connection with childbirth for a mother or newborn child under the plan, except that such coinsurance or other cost-sharing for any portion of a period within a hospital length of stay required under subsection (a) may not be greater than such coinsurance or cost-sharing for any preceding portion of such stay.

(d) Level and Type of Reimbursements.—Nothing in this section shall be construed to prevent a group health plan from negotiating the level and type of reimbursement with a provider for care provided in accordance with this section.

(e) Preemption; Exception for Health Insurance Coverage in Certain States.—The requirements of this section shall not apply with respect to health insurance coverage if there is a State law (including a decision, rule, regulation, or other State action having the effect of law) for a State that regulates such coverage that is described in any of the following paragraphs:

(1) Such State law requires such coverage to provide for at least a 48-hour hospital length of stay following a normal vaginal delivery and at least a 96-hour hospital length of stay following a caesarean section.

(2) Such State law requires such coverage to provide for maternity and pediatric care in accordance with guidelines established by the American College of Obstetricians and Gynecologists, the American Academy of Pediatrics, or other established professional medical associations.

(3) Such State law requires, in connection with such coverage for maternity care, that the hospital length of stay for such care is left to the decision of (or required to be made by) the attending provider in consultation with the mother.

SEC. 9812. PARITY IN MENTAL HEALTH AND SUBSTANCE USE DISORDER BENEFITS

(a) In General.—

(1) Aggregate lifetime limits.—In the case of a group health plan that provides both medical and surgical benefits and mental health or substance use disorder benefits—

(A) No lifetime limit.—If the plan does not include an aggregate lifetime limit on substantially all medical and surgical benefits, the plan may not impose any aggregate lifetime limit on mental health or substance use disorder benefits.

(B) Lifetime Limit.—If the plan includes an aggregate lifetime limit on substantially all medical and surgical benefits (in this paragraph referred to as the "applicable lifetime limit"), the plan shall either—

(i) apply the applicable lifetime limit both to the medical and surgical benefits to which it otherwise would apply and to mental health and substance use disorder benefits and not distinguish in the application of such limit between such medical and surgical benefits and mental health and substance use disorder benefits; or

(ii) not include any aggregate lifetime limit on mental health or substance use disorder benefits that is less than the applicable lifetime limit.

(C) Rule in case of different limits.—In the case of a plan that is not described in subparagraph (A) or (B) and that includes no or different aggregate lifetime limits on different categories of medical and surgical benefits, the Secretary shall establish rules under which subparagraph (B) is applied to such plan with respect to mental health and substance use disorder benefits by substituting for the applicable lifetime limit an average aggregate lifetime limit that is computed taking into account the weighted average of the aggregate lifetime limits applicable to such categories.

(2) Annual limits.—In the case of a group health plan that provides both medical and surgical benefits and mental health or substance use disorder benefits—

(A) No annual limit.—If the plan does not include an annual limit on substantially all medical and surgical benefits, the plan may not impose any annual limit on mental health or substance use disorder benefits.

(B) Annual limit.—If the plan includes an annual limit on substantially all medical and surgical benefits (in this paragraph referred to as the "applicable annual limit"), the plan shall either—

(i) apply the applicable annual limit both to medical and surgical benefits to which it otherwise would apply and to mental health and substance use disorder benefits and not distinguish in the application of such limit between such medical and surgical benefits and mental health and substance use disorder benefits; or

(ii) not include any annual limit on mental health or substance use disorder benefits that is less than the applicable annual limit.

(C) Rule in case of different limits.—In the case of a plan that is not described in subparagraph (A) or (B) and that includes no or different annual limits on different categories of medical and surgical benefits, the Secretary shall establish rules under which subparagraph (B) is applied to such plan with respect to mental health and substance use disorder benefits by substituting for the applicable annual limit an average annual limit that is computed taking into account the weighted average of the annual limits applicable to such categories.

(3) Financial requirements and treatment limitations.—

(A) In General.—In the case of a group health plan that provides both medical and surgical benefits and mental health or substance use disorder benefits, such plan shall ensure that—

(i) the financial requirements applicable to such mental health or substance use disorder benefits are no more restrictive than the predominant financial requirements applied to substantially all medical and surgical benefits covered by the plan, and there are no separate cost sharing requirements that are applicable only with respect to mental health or substance use disorder benefits; and

(ii) the treatment limitations applicable to such mental health or substance use disorder benefits are no more restrictive than the predominant treatment limitations applied to substantially all medical and surgical benefits covered by the plan and there are no separate treatment limitations that are applicable only with respect to mental health or substance use disorder benefits.

(B) Definitions.—In this paragraph:

(i) Financial requirement.—The term "financial requirement" includes deductibles, copayments, coinsurance, and out-of-pocket expenses, but excludes an aggregate lifetime limit and an annual limit subject to paragraphs (1) and (2),

(ii) Predominant.—A financial requirement or treatment limit is considered to be predominant if it is the most common or frequent of such type of limit or requirement.

(iii) Treatment limitation.—The term "treatment limitation" includes limits on the frequency of treatment, number of visits, days of coverage, or other similar limits on the scope or duration of treatment.

(4) **Availability of plan information.**—The criteria for medical necessity determinations made under the plan with respect to mental health or substance use disorder benefits shall be made available by the plan administrator in accordance with regulations to any current or potential participant, beneficiary, or contracting provider upon request. The reason for any denial under the plan of reimbursement or payment for services with respect to mental health or substance use disorder benefits in the case of any participant or beneficiary shall, on request or as otherwise required, be made available by the plan administrator to the participant or beneficiary in accordance with regulations.

(5) **Out-of-network providers.**—In the case of a plan that provides both medical and surgical benefits and mental health or substance use disorder benefits, if the plan provides coverage for medical or surgical benefits provided by out-of-network providers, the plan shall provide coverage for mental health or substance use disorder benefits provided by out-of-network providers in a manner that is consistent with the requirements of this section.

(b) **Construction.**—Nothing in this section shall be construed—

(1) as requiring a group health plan to provide any mental health or substance use disorder benefits; or

(2) in the case of a group health plan that provides mental health or substance use disorder benefits, as affecting the terms and conditions of the plan relating to such benefits under the plan, except as provided in subsection (a).

(c) **Exemptions.**—

(1) Small employer exemption.—

(A) In general.—This section shall not apply to any group health plan for any plan year of a small employer.

(B) Small employer.—For purposes of subparagraph (A), the term "small employer" means, with respect to a calendar year and a plan year, an employer who employed an average of at least 2 (or 1 in the case of an employer residing in a State that permits small groups to include a single individual) but not more than 50 employees on business days during the preceding calendar year. For purposes of the preceding sentence, all persons treated as a single employer under subsection (b), (c), (m), or (o) of section 414 shall be treated as 1 employer and rules similar to rules of subparagraphs (B) and (C) of section 4980D(d)(2) shall apply.

(2) **Cost exemption.**—

(A) In General.—With respect to a group health plan, if the application of this section to such plan results in an increase for the plan year involved of the actual total costs of coverage with respect to medical and surgical benefits and mental health and substance use disorder benefits under the plan (as determined and certified under subparagraph (C)) by an amount that exceeds the applicable percentage described in subparagraph (B) of the actual total plan costs, the provisions of this section shall not apply to such plan during the following plan year, and such exemption shall apply to the plan for 1 plan year. An employer may elect to continue to apply mental health and substance use disorder parity pursuant to this section with respect to the group health plan involved regardless of any increase in total costs.

(B) Applicable Percentage.—With respect to a plan, the applicable percentage described in this subparagraph shall be—

(i) 2 percent in the case of the first plan year in which this section is applied; and

(ii) 1 percent in the case of each subsequent plan year.

(C) Determinations by actuaries.—Determinations as to increases in actual costs under a plan for

IRC Sec. 9812(c)(2)(C)

purposes of this section shall be made and certified by a qualified and licensed actuary who is a member in good standing of the American Academy of Actuaries. All such determinations shall be in a written report prepared by the actuary. The report, and all underlying documentation relied upon by the actuary, shall be maintained by the group health plan for a period of 6 years following the notification made under subparagraph (E).

(D) 6-Month determinations.—If a group health plan seeks an exemption under this paragraph, determinations under subparagraph (A) shall be made after such plan has complied with this section for the first 6 months of the plan year involved.

(E) Notification.—

(i) In General.—A group health plan that, based upon a certification described under subparagraph (C), qualifies for an exemption under this paragraph, and elects to implement the exemption, shall promptly notify the Secretary, the appropriate State agencies, and participants and beneficiaries in the plan of such election.

(ii) Requirement.—A notification to the Secretary under clause (i) shall include—

(I) a description of the number of covered lives under the plan involved at the time of the notification, and as applicable, at the time of any prior election of the cost-exemption under this paragraph by such plan;

(II) for both the plan year upon which a cost exemption is sought and the year prior, a description of the actual total costs of coverage with respect to medical and surgical benefits and mental health and substance use disorder benefits under the plan; and

(III) for both the plan year upon which a cost exemption is sought and the year prior, the actual total costs of coverage with respect to mental health and substance use disorder benefits under the plan.

(iii) Confidentiality.—A notification to the Secretary under clause (i) shall be confidential. The Secretary shall make available, upon request and on not more than an annual basis, an anonymous itemization of such notifications, that includes—

(I) a breakdown of States by the size and type of employers submitting such notification; and

(II) a summary of the data received under clause (ii).

(F) Audits by appropriate agencies.—To determine compliance with this paragraph, the Secretary may audit the books and records of a group health plan relating to an exemption, including any actuarial reports prepared pursuant to subpara-

graph (C), during the 6 year period following the notification of such exemption under subparagraph (E). A State agency receiving a notification under subparagraph (E) may also conduct such an audit with respect to an exemption covered by such notification.

(d) **Separate Application to Each Option Offered.**—In the case of a group health plan that offers a participant or beneficiary two or more benefit package options under the plan, the requirements of this section shall be applied separately with respect to each such option.

(e) **Definitions.**—For purposes of this section:

(1) **Aggregate lifetime limit.**—The term "aggregate lifetime limit" means, with respect to benefits under a group health plan, a dollar limitation on the total amount that may be paid with respect to such benefits under the plan with respect to an individual or other coverage unit.

(2) **Annual limit.**—The term "annual limit" means, with respect to benefits under a group health plan, a dollar limitation on the total amount of benefits that may be paid with respect to such benefits in a 12-month period under the plan with respect to an individual or other coverage unit.

(3) **Medical or surgical benefits.**—The term "medical or surgical benefits" means benefits with respect to medical or surgical services, as defined under the terms of the plan, but does not include mental health or substance use disorder benefits.

(4) **Mental health benefits.**—The term "mental health benefits" means benefits with respect to services for mental health conditions, as defined under the terms of the plan and in accordance with applicable Federal and State law.

(5) **Substance use disorder benefits.**—The term "substance use disorder benefits" means benefits with respect to services for substance use disorders, as defined under the terms of the plan and in accordance with applicable Federal and State law.

(f) **[Stricken.]**

Recent Amendments to IRC §9812

Paul Wellstone and Pete Domenici Mental Health Parity and Addiction Equity Act of 2008 (Pub. L. No. 110-343), as follows:

● IRC §9812 was amended by Act, Div. C, §512(g) in the heading by substituting "Parity In Mental Health and Substance Use Disorder Benefits" for "Parity in the Application of Certain Limits to Mental Health Benefits". Eff. on date of enactment [enacted: Oct. 3, 2008].

● IRC §9812 was amended by Act, Div. C, §512(c)(6), (7), by substituting "mental health and substance use disorder benefits" for "mental health benefits" each place it appeared in subsec. (a)(1)(B)(i), (a)(1)(C), (a)(2)(B)(i), and (a)(2)(C), and by substituting "mental health or substance use disorder benefits" for "mental health benefits" in any other provision. Eff. for group health plans for plan years beginning after date that is 1 year after date of enactment [enacted: Oct. 3, 2008], regardless of whether regulations have been issued to carry out such amendments by such effective date.

- IRC §9812(a)(3)–(5) were added by Act, Div. C, §512(c)(1). Eff. for group health plans for plan years beginning after date that is 1 year after date of enactment [enacted: Oct. 3, 2008], regardless of whether regulations have been issued to carry out such amendments by such effective date.
- IRC §9812(b)(2) was amended by Act, Div. C, §512(c)(2). Eff. for group health plans for plan years beginning after date that is 1 year after date of enactment [enacted: Oct. 3, 2008], regardless of whether regulations have been issued to carry out such amendments by such effective date. IRC §9812(b)(2) prior to amendment:

  (b) Construction Nothing in this section shall be construed—
  (1) as requiring a group health plan to provide any mental health benefits; or
  (2) in the case of a group health plan that provides mental health benefits, as affecting the terms and conditions (including cost sharing, limits on numbers of visits or days of coverage, and requirements relating to medical necessity) relating to the amount, duration, or scope of mental health benefits under the plan, except as specifically provided in subsection (a) (in regard to parity in the imposition of aggregate lifetime limits and annual limits for mental health benefits).
- IRC §9812(c)(1) was amended by Act, Div. C, §512(c)(3)(A). Eff. for group health plans for plan years beginning after date that is 1 year after date of enactment [enacted: Oct. 3, 2008], regardless of whether regulations have been issued to carry out such amendments by such effective date. IRC §9812(c)(1) prior to amendment:

  (1) Small employer exemption.—This section shall not apply to any group health plan for any plan year of a small employer (as defined in section 4980D(d)(2)).
- IRC §9812(c)(2) was amended by Act, Div. C, §512(c)(3)(B). Eff. for group health plans for plan years beginning after date that is 1 year after date of enactment [enacted: Oct. 3, 2008], regardless of whether regulations have been issued to carry out such amendments by such effective date. IRC §9812(c)(2) prior to amendment:

  (2) Increased cost exemption.—This section shall not apply with respect to a group health plan if the application of this section to such plan results in an increase in the cost under the plan of at least 1 percent.
- IRC §9812(e)(4) was repealed and new paras. (4) and (5) were added by Act, Div. C, §512(c)(4). Eff. for group health plans for plan years beginning after date that is 1 year after date of enactment [enacted: Oct. 3, 2008], regardless of whether regulations have been issued to carry out such amendments by such effective date. IRC §9812(e)(4) prior to repeal:

  (4) Mental health benefits.—The term "mental health benefits" means benefits with respect to mental health services, as defined under the terms of the plan, but does not include benefits with respect to treatment of substance abuse or chemical dependency.
- IRC §9812(f) was repealed by Act, Div. C, §512(c)(5). Eff. Jan. 1, 2009. IRC §9812(f) prior to repeal:

  (f) Application of section.—This section shall not apply to benefits for services furnished—
  (1) on or after September 30, 2001, and before January 10, 2002,
  (2) on or after January 1, 2004, and before the date of the enactment of the Working Families Tax Relief Act of 2004,
  (3) on or after January 1, 2008, and before the date of the enactment of the Heroes Earnings Assistance and Relief Tax Act of 2008, and
  (4) after December 31, 2008.
- Other Provision. Act, Div. C, §512(e)(2), as amended by Pub. L. No. 110-460, §1, provides:

  (2) SPECIAL RULE FOR COLLECTIVE BARGAINING AGREEMENTS.—In the case of a group health plan maintained pursuant to one or more collective bargaining agreements between employee representatives and one or more employers ratified before the date of the enactment of this Act, the amendments made by this section shall not apply to plan years beginning before the later of—
  (A) the date on which the last of the collective bargaining agreements relating to the plan terminates (determined without regard to any extension thereof agreed to after the date of the enactment of this Act), or
  (B) January 1, 2010.
  For purposes of subparagraph (A), any plan amendment made pursuant to a collective bargaining agreement relating to the plan which amends the plan solely to conform to any requirement added by this section shall not be treated as a termination of such collective bargaining agreement.

Heroes Earnings Assistance and Relief Tax Act of 2008 (Pub. L. No. 110-245), as follows:
- IRC §9812(f)(3) was deleted and new paras. (3) and (4) were added by Act §401(a). Eff. on the date of enactment [enacted: June 17, 2008].

Tax Relief and Health Care Act of 2006 (Pub. L. No. 109-432), as follows:
- IRC §9812(f)(3) was amended by Act, Division A, §115(a) by replacing "2006" with "2007". Eff. Dec. 20, 2006.

Pub. L. No. 109-151, as follows:
- IRC §9812(f)(3) was amended by Act §1(c) by replacing "December 31, 2005" with "December 31, 2006." Eff. Dec. 30, 2005.

Working Families Tax Relief Act of 2004 (Pub. L. No. 108-311), as follows:
- IRC §9812(f) was amended by Act §302(a)(1)–(2) by striking "and" at the end of para. (1) and para. (2), and adding new paras. (2) and (3). Eff. Oct. 4, 2004. IRC §9812(f)(2) prior being stricken:

  (2) after December 31, 2003.

Job Creation and Worker Assistance Act of 2002 (Pub. L. No. 107-147), as follows:
- IRC §9812(f) was amended by Act §610(a). Eff. plan years beginning after Dec. 31, 2000. IRC §9812(f) prior to amendment:

  (f) Sunset.—This section shall not apply to benefits for services furnished on or after December 31, 2002.

Pub. L. No. 107-116, as follows:
- IRC §9812(f) was amended by Act §701(c) by replacing "September 30, 2001" with "December 31, 2002." Eff. Jan. 10, 2002.

SEC. 9813. COVERAGE OF DEPENDENT STUDENTS ON MEDICALLY NECESSARY LEAVE OF ABSENCE.

(a) Medically Necessary Leave of Absence.—In this section, the term "medically necessary leave of absence" means, with respect to a dependent child described in subsection (b)(2) in connection with a group health plan, a leave of absence of such child from a postsecondary educational institution (including an institution of higher education as defined in section 102 of the Higher Education Act of 1965), or any other change in enrollment of such child at such an institution, that—

(1) commences while such child is suffering from a serious illness or injury;

(2) is medically necessary; and

(3) causes such child to lose student status for purposes of coverage under the terms of the plan or coverage.

(b) Requirement to Continue Coverage.—

(1) In general.—In the case of a dependent child described in paragraph (2), a group health plan shall not terminate coverage of such child under such plan due to a medically necessary leave of absence before the date that is the earlier of—

(A) the date that is 1 year after the first day of the medically necessary leave of absence; or

(B) the date on which such coverage would otherwise terminate under the terms of the plan.

(2) Dependent child described.—A dependent child described in this paragraph is, with respect to a group health plan, a beneficiary under the plan who—

(A) is a dependent child, under the terms of the plan, of a participant or beneficiary under the plan; and

(B) was enrolled in the plan, on the basis of being a student at a postsecondary educational institution (as described in subsection (a)), immediately before the first day of the medically necessary leave of absence involved.

(3) Certification by physician.—Paragraph (1) shall apply to a group health plan only if the plan, or the issuer of health insurance coverage offered in connection with the plan, has received written certification by a treating physician of the dependent child which states that the child is suffering from a serious illness or injury and that the leave of absence (or other change of enrollment) described in subsection (a) is medically necessary.

(c) Notice.—A group health plan shall include, with any notice regarding a requirement for certification of student status for coverage under the plan, a description of the terms of this section for continued coverage during medically necessary leaves of absence. Such description shall be in language which is understandable to the typical plan participant.

(d) No Change in Benefits.—A dependent child whose benefits are continued under this section shall be entitled to the same benefits as if (during the medically necessary leave of absence) the child continued to be a covered student at the institution of higher education and was not on a medically necessary leave of absence.

(e) Continued Application in Case of Changed Coverage.—If—

(1) a dependent child of a participant or beneficiary is in a period of coverage under a group health plan, pursuant to a medically necessary leave of absence of the child described in subsection (b);

(2) the manner in which the participant or beneficiary is covered under the plan changes, whether through a change in health insurance coverage or health insurance issuer, a change between health insurance coverage and self-insured coverage, or otherwise; and

(3) the coverage as so changed continues to provide coverage of beneficiaries as dependent children,

this section shall apply to coverage of the child under the changed coverage for the remainder of the period of the medically necessary leave of absence of the

dependent child under the plan in the same manner as it would have applied if the changed coverage had been the previous coverage.

Amendments to IRC §9813

Michelle's Law (Pub. L. No. 110-381), as follows:
- IRC §9813 was added by Act §2(c). Eff. for plan years beginning on or after the date that is 1 year after the date of enactment [enacted: Oct. 9, 2008] and to medically necessary leaves of absence beginning during such plan years.

> **Editor's Note**
> IRC §9815, below, added by Pub. L. No. 111-148, §1563(f) (as redesignated by Pub. L. No. 111-148, §10107(b)(1)), is effective March 23, 2010.

SEC. 9815. ADDITIONAL MARKET REFORMS.

(a) General Rule.—Except as provided in subsection (b)—

(1) the provisions of part A of title XXVII of the Public Health Service Act (as amended by the Patient Protection and Affordable Care Act) shall apply to group health plans, and health insurance issuers providing health insurance coverage in connection with group health plans, as if included in this subchapter; and

(2) to the extent that any provision of this subchapter conflicts with a provision of such part A with respect to group health plans, or health insurance issuers providing health insurance coverage in connection with group health plans, the provisions of such part A shall apply.

(b) Exception.—Notwithstanding subsection (a), the provisions of sections 2716 and 2718 of title XXVII of the Public Health Service Act (as amended by the Patient Protection and Affordable Care Act) shall not apply with respect to self-insured group health plans, and the provisions of this subchapter shall continue to apply to such plans as if such sections of the Public Health Service Act (as so amended) had not been enacted.

Recent Amendments to §9815

Patient Protection and Affordable Care Act (Pub. L. No. 111-148), as follows:
- IRC §9815 was added by Act §1563(f) (as redesignated by Act §10107(b)(1)). Eff. Mar. 23, 2010.

Subchapter C—General Provisions

SEC. 9831. GENERAL EXCEPTIONS.

(a) Exception for Certain Plans.—The requirements of this chapter shall not apply to—

(1) any governmental plan, and

(2) any group health plan for any plan year if, on the first day of such plan year, such plan has less than 2 participants who are current employees.

(b) Exception for Certain Benefits.—The requirements of this chapter shall not apply to any group health plan in relation to its provision of excepted benefits described in section 9832(c)(1).

(c) Exception for Certain Benefits if Certain Conditions Met.—

(1) Limited, excepted benefits.—The requirements of this chapter shall not apply to any group health plan in relation to its provision of excepted benefits described in section 9832(c)(2) if the benefits—

(A) are provided under a separate policy, certificate, or contract of insurance; or

(B) are otherwise not an integral part of the plan.

(2) Noncoordinated, excepted benefits.—The requirements of this chapter shall not apply to any group health plan in relation to its provision of excepted benefits described in section 9832(c)(3) if all of the following conditions are met:

(A) The benefits are provided under a separate policy, certificate, or contract of insurance.

(B) There is no coordination between the provision of such benefits and any exclusion of benefits under any group health plan maintained by the same plan sponsor.

(C) Such benefits are paid with respect to an event without regard to whether benefits are provided with respect to such an event under any group health plan maintained by the same plan sponsor.

(3) Supplemental excepted benefits.—The requirements of this chapter shall not apply to any group health plan in relation to its provision of excepted benefits described in section 9832(c)(4) if the benefits are provided under a separate policy, certificate, or contract of insurance.

SEC. 9832. DEFINITIONS.

(a) Group Health Plan.—For purposes of this chapter, the term "group health plan" has the meaning given to such term by section 5000(b)(1).

(b) Definitions Relating to Health Insurance.—For purposes of this chapter—

(1) Health insurance coverage.—

(A) In general.—Except as provided in subparagraph (B), the term "health insurance coverage" means benefits consisting of medical care (provided directly, through insurance or reimbursement, or otherwise) under any hospital or medical service policy or certificate, hospital or medical service plan contract, or health maintenance organization contract offered by a health insurance issuer.

(B) No application to certain excepted benefits.—In applying subparagraph (A), excepted benefits described in subsection (c)(1) shall not be treated as benefits consisting of medical care.

(2) Health insurance issuer.—The term "health insurance issuer" means an insurance company, insurance service, or insurance organization (including a health maintenance organization, as defined in paragraph (3)) which is licensed to engage in the business of insurance in a State and which is subject to State law which regulates insurance (within the meaning of section 514(b)(2) of the Employee Retirement Income Security Act of 1974, as in effect on the date of the enactment of this section). Such term does not include a group health plan.

(3) Health maintenance organization.—The term "health maintenance organization" means—

(A) a Federally qualified health maintenance organization (as defined in section 1301(a) of the Public Health Service Act (42 U.S.C. 300e(a)),

(B) an organization recognized under State law as a health maintenance organization, or

(C) a similar organization regulated under State law for solvency in the same manner and to the same extent as such a health maintenance organization.

(c) Excepted Benefits.—For purposes of this chapter, the term "excepted benefits" means benefits under one or more (or any combination thereof) of the following:

(1) Benefits not subject to requirements.—

(A) Coverage only for accident, or disability income insurance, or any combination thereof.

(B) Coverage issued as a supplement to liability insurance.

(C) Liability insurance, including general liability insurance and automobile liability insurance.

(D) Workers' compensation or similar insurance.

(E) Automobile medical payment insurance.

(F) Credit-only insurance.

(G) Coverage for on-site medical clinics.

(H) Other similar insurance coverage, specified in regulations, under which benefits for medical care are secondary or incidental to other insurance benefits.

(2) Benefits not subject to requirements if offered separately.—

(A) Limited scope dental or vision benefits.

(B) Benefits for long-term care, nursing home care, home health care, community-based care, or any combination thereof.

IRC Sec. 9832(c)(2)(B)

(C) Such other similar, limited benefits as are specified in regulations.

(3) Benefits not subject to requirements if offered as independent, noncoordinated benefits.—

(A) Coverage only for a specified disease or illness.

(B) Hospital indemnity or other fixed indemnity insurance.

(4) Benefits not subject to requirements if offered as separate insurance policy.—Medicare supplemental health insurance (as defined under section 1882(g)(1) of the Social Security Act), coverage supplemental to the coverage provided under chapter 55 of title 10, United States Code, and similar supplemental coverage provided to coverage under a group health plan.

(d) Other Definitions.—For purposes of this chapter—

(1) COBRA continuation provision.—The term "COBRA continuation provision" means any of the following:

(A) Section 4980B, other than subsection (f)(1) thereof insofar as it relates to pediatric vaccines.

(B) Part 6 of subtitle B of title I of the Employee Retirement Income Security Act of 1974 (29 U.S.C. 1161 et seq.), other than section 609 of such Act.

(C) Title XXII of the Public Health Service Act. *

(2) Governmental plan.—The term "governmental plan" has the meaning given such term by section 414(d).

(3) Medical care.—The term "medical care" has the meaning given such term by section 213(d) determined without regard to—

(A) paragraph (1)(C) thereof, and

(B) so much of paragraph (1)(D) thereof as relates to qualified long-term care insurance.

(4) Network plan.—The term "network plan" means health insurance coverage of a health insurance issuer under which the financing and delivery of medical care are provided, in whole or in part, through a defined set of providers under contract with the issuer.

(5) Placed for adoption defined.—The term "placement", or being "placed", for adoption, in connection with any placement for adoption of a child with any person, means the assumption and retention by such person of a legal obligation for total or partial support of such child in anticipation of adoption of such child. The child's placement with such person terminates upon the termination of such legal obligation.

(6) Family member.—The term "family member" means, with respect to any individual—

(A) a dependent (as such term is used for purposes of section 9801(f)(2)) of such individual, and

(B) any other individual who is a first-degree, second-degree, third-degree, or fourth-degree relative of such individual or of an individual described in subparagraph (A).

(7) Genetic information.—

(A) In general.—The term "genetic information" means, with respect to any individual, information about—

(i) such individual's genetic tests,

(ii) the genetic tests of family members of such individual, and

(iii) the manifestation of a disease or disorder in family members of such individual.

(B) Inclusion of genetic services and participation in genetic research.—Such term includes, with respect to any individual, any request for, or receipt of, genetic services, or participation in clinical research which includes genetic services, by such individual or any family member of such individual.

(C) Exclusions.—The term "genetic information" shall not include information about the sex or age of any individual.

(8) Genetic test.—

(A) In general.—The term "genetic test" means an analysis of human DNA, RNA, chromosomes, proteins, or metabolites, that detects genotypes, mutations, or chromosomal changes.

(B) Exceptions.—The term "genetic test" does not mean—

(i) an analysis of proteins or metabolites that does not detect genotypes, mutations, or chromosomal changes, or

(ii) an analysis of proteins or metabolites that is directly related to a manifested disease, disorder, or pathological condition that could reasonably be detected by a health care professional with appropriate training and expertise in the field of medicine involved.

(9) Genetic services.—The term "genetic services" means—

(A) a genetic test;

(B) genetic counseling (including obtaining, interpreting, or assessing genetic information); or

(C) genetic education.

(10) Underwriting purposes.—The term "underwriting purposes" means, with respect to any group health plan, or health insurance coverage offered in connection with a group health plan—

(A) rules for, or determination of, eligibility (including enrollment and continued eligibility) for benefits under the plan or coverage;

(B) the computation of premium or contribution amounts under the plan or coverage;

(C) the application of any pre-existing condition exclusion under the plan or coverage; and

(D) other activities related to the creation, renewal, or replacement of a contract of health insurance or health benefits.

Recent Amendments to IRC §9832

Genetic Information Nondiscrimination Act of 2008 (Pub. L. No. 110-233), as follows:

● IRC §9832(d)(6)–(10) were added by Act §103(d). Eff. for group health plans for plan years beginning after the date that is one year after the date of enactment [enacted: May 21, 2008], see Act §103(f)(2).

● **Other Provision.** Act §103(f)(1) provides:

(1) Regulations. The Secretary of the Treasury shall issue final regulations or other guidance not later than 12 months after the date of enactment of this Act to carry out the amendments made by this section.

SEC. 9833. REGULATIONS.

The Secretary, consistent with section 104 of the Health Care Portability and Accountability Act of 1996, may promulgate such regulations as may be necessary or appropriate to carry out the provisions of this chapter. The Secretary may promulgate any interim final rules as the Secretary determines are appropriate to carry out this chapter.

SEC. 9834. ENFORCEMENT.

For the imposition of tax on any failure of a group health plan to meet the requirements of this chapter, see section 4980D.

Amendments to §9834

Genetic Information Nondiscrimination Act of 2008 (Pub. L. No. 110-233), as follows:

● IRC §9834 was added by Act §103(e)(1). Eff. for group health plans for plan years beginning after the date that is one year after the date of enactment [enacted: May 21, 2008], see Act §103(f)(2).

Part 3

Public Health Service Act Excerpts as Amended by the Patient Protection and Affordable Care Act (Enacted March 23, 2010) and Other Legislation

Public Health Service Act After PPACA
Finding List

Editor's Note: The following are selected provisions of the Public Health Service Act as amended by the Patient Protection and Affordable Care Act and other legislation.

Section

42 U.S.C.   PHSA

Title 42—Public Health and Welfare

Editor's Note

Part 3 contains excerpts from the Public Health Service Act (PHSA), title XXVII (42 USC §§300gg et seq.), as amended by the Patient Protection and Affordable Care Act (PPACA) (Pub. L. No. 111-148; enacted March 23, 2010) and other legislation. The individual and group market changes made to PHSA by PPACA apply to group health plans and health insurance issuers providing health insurance coverage in connection with such plans as if the provisions were included in ERISA and the tax Code.[1] The PHSA sections incorporated by reference are §§2701 through 2728. PHSA §§2701 through 2719A are substantially new, although those sections include some provisions of prior law. PHSA §§2722 through 2728 are renumbered sections of prior law with some changes.

For a list of the PHSA sections reproduced here and a list of the PHSA sections as they are codified in Title 42 of the U.S. Code, see the PHSA Finding List above.

For the corresponding PHSA sections prior to the enactment of PPACA, see Part 4.

PART A—INDIVIDUAL AND GROUP MARKET REFORMS

Editor's Note

Caution: PHSA §2701, as follows, is effective for plan years beginning on or after January 1, 2014.

SEC. 2701. FAIR HEALTH INSURANCE PREMIUMS.

(a) **Prohibiting Discriminatory Premium Rates.—**

(1) **In general.—**With respect to the premium rate charged by a health insurance issuer for health insurance coverage offered in the individual or small group market—

(A) such rate shall vary with respect to the particular plan or coverage involved only by—

(i) whether such plan or coverage covers an individual or family;

(ii) rating area, as established in accordance with paragraph (2);

(iii) age, except that such rate shall not vary by more than 3 to 1 for adults (consistent with section 2707(c)); and

(iv) tobacco use, except that such rate shall not vary by more than 1.5 to 1; and

(B) such rate shall not vary with respect to the particular plan or coverage involved by any other factor not described in subparagraph (A).

(2) **Rating area.—**

(A) In general.—Each State shall establish 1 or more rating areas within that State for purposes of applying the requirements of this title.

(B) Secretarial review.—The Secretary shall review the rating areas established by each State under subparagraph (A) to ensure the adequacy of such areas for purposes of carrying out the requirements of this title. If the Secretary determines a State's rating areas are not adequate, or that a State does not establish such areas, the Secretary may establish rating areas for that State.

(3) **Permissible age bands.—**The Secretary, in consultation with the National Association of Insurance Commissioners, shall define the permissible age bands for rating purposes under paragraph (1)(A)(iii).

(4) **Application of variations based on age or tobacco use.—**With respect to family coverage under a group health plan or health insurance coverage, the rating variations permitted under clauses (iii) and (iv) of paragraph (1)(A) shall be applied based on the portion of the premium that is attributable to each family member covered under the plan or coverage.

(5) **Special rule for large group market.—**If a State permits health insurance issuers that offer coverage in the large group market in the State to offer such coverage through the State Exchange (as provided for under section 1312(f)(2)(B) of the Patient Protection and Affordable Care Act), the provisions of this subsection shall apply to all coverage offered in such market (other than self-insured group health plans offered in such market) in the State.

[(b) Not enacted.]

---

[1] ERISA §715; IRC §9815.

Selected Provisions of PHSA After Amendment by PPACA. For sections prior to PPACA, see Part 4.

Amendments to PHSA §2701

Patient Protection and Affordable Care Act, 2010 (Pub. L. No. 111-148), as follows:

- **Note on Redesignation:** PHSA §2701 (former) was redesignated as PHSA §2704 by Act §1201(2). Eff. for plan years beg. on or after Jan. 1, 2014, see Act §1255, as redesignated by Act §10103(f)(1).
- PHSA §2701 was added by Act §1201(4). Eff. for plan years beg. on or after Jan. 1, 2014, Act §1255, as redesignated by Act §10103(f)(1).
- PHSA §2701(a)(5) was amended by Act §10103(a) by adding "(other than self-insured group health plans offered in such market)" after "such market". Eff. for plan years beg. on or after Jan. 1, 2014, Act §1255, as amended by Act §10103(e) and redesignated by Act §10103(f)(1).

Other Provision. Act §1251, as amended by Act §10103(d) and by Pub. L. No. 111-152, §2301(a), eff. on date of enactment, see Act §10103(e), provides:

SEC. 1251. PRESERVATION OF RIGHT TO MAINTAIN EXISTING COVERAGE

(a) No Changes to Existing Coverage.—

(1) In general.—Nothing in this Act (or an amendment made by this Act) shall be construed to require that an individual terminate coverage under a group health plan or health insurance coverage in which such individual was enrolled on the date of enactment of this Act.

(2) Continuation of coverage.—Except as provided in paragraph (3), with respect to a group health plan or health insurance coverage in which an individual was enrolled on the date of enactment of this Act, this subtitle and subtitle A (and the amendments made by such subtitles) shall not apply to such plan or coverage, regardless of whether the individual renews such coverage after such date of enactment.

(3) Application of certain provisions.—The provisions of sections 2715 and 2718 of the Public Health Service Act (as added by subtitle A) shall apply to grandfathered health plans for plan years beginning on or after the date of enactment of this Act.

(4) Application of certain provisions.—

(A) In general.—The following provisions of the Public Health Service Act (as added by this title) shall apply to grandfathered health plans for plan years beginning with the first plan year to which such provisions would otherwise apply:

(i) Section 2708 (relating to excessive waiting periods).

(ii) Those provisions of section 2711 relating to lifetime limits.

(iii) Section 2712 (relating to rescissions).

(iv) Section 2714 (relating to extension of dependent coverage).

(B) Provisions applicable only to group health plans.—

(i) Provisions described.—Those provisions of section 2711 relating to annual limits and the provisions of section 2704 (relating to pre-existing condition exclusions) of the Public Health Service Act (as added by this subtitle [Pub. L. No. 111-148, Title I, Subtitle C—Quality Health Insurance Coverage for All Americans]) shall apply to grandfathered health plans that are group health plans for plan years beginning with the first plan year to which such provisions otherwise apply.

(ii) Adult child coverage.—For plan years beginning before January 1, 2014, the provisions of section 2714 of the Public Health Service Act (as added by this subtitle [Pub. L. No. 111-148, Title I, Subtitle C—Quality Health Insurance Coverage for All Americans]) shall apply in the case of an adult child with respect to a grandfathered health plan that is a group health plan only if such adult child is not eligible to enroll in an eligible employer-sponsored health plan (as defined in section 5000A(f)(2) of the Internal Revenue Code of 1986) other than such grandfathered health plan.

(b) Allowance for Family Members to Joint Current Coverage.—With respect to a group health plan or health insurance

coverage in which an individual was enrolled on the date of enactment of this Act and which is renewed after such date, family members of such individual shall be permitted to enroll in such plan or coverage if such enrollment is permitted under the terms of the plan in effect as of such date of enactment.

(c) Allowance for New Employees to Join Current Plan.—A group health plan that provides coverage on the date of enactment of this Act may provide for the enrolling of new employees (and their families) in such plan, and this subtitle and subtitle A (and the amendments made by such subtitles) shall not apply with respect to such plan and such new employees (and their families).

(d) Effect on Collective Bargaining Agreements.—In the case of health insurance coverage maintained pursuant to one or more collective bargaining agreements between employee representatives and one or more employers that was ratified before the date of enactment of this Act, the provisions of this subtitle and subtitle A (and the amendments made by such subtitles) shall not apply until the date on which the last of the collective bargaining agreements relating to the coverage terminates. Any coverage amendment made pursuant to a collective bargaining agreement relating to the coverage which amends the coverage solely to conform to any requirement added by this subtitle or subtitle A (or amendments) shall not be treated as a termination of such collective bargaining agreement.

(e) Definition.—In this title, the term "grandfathered health plan" means any group health plan or health insurance coverage to which this section applies.

Other Provision. Act §1252 provides:

SEC. 1252—RATING REFORMS MUST APPLY UNIFORMLY TO ALL HEALTH INSURANCE ISSUERS AND GROUP HEALTH PLANS.

Any standard or requirement adopted by a State pursuant to this title [Title I—Quality, Affordable Health Care for All Americans], or any amendment made by this title, shall be applied uniformly to all health plans in each insurance market to which the standard and requirements apply. The preceding sentence shall also apply to a State standard or requirement relating to the standard or requirement required by this title (or any such amendment) that is not the same as the standard or requirement but that is not preempted under section 1321(d).

Department of Veterans Affairs and Housing and Urban Development, and Independent Agencies Appropriations Act, 1997 (Pub. L. No. 104-204), as follows:

- PHSA §2701 (former) was amended by Act §604(a)(2), (b)(2). Eff. for group health plans for plan years beg. on or after Jan. 1, 1998.

Health Insurance Portability and Accountability Act of 1996 (Pub. L. No. 104-191), as follows:

- PHSA §2701 (former) was added by Act §102(a). Eff. generally for group health plans, and health insurance coverage offered in connection with group health plans, for plan years beg. after June 30, 1997, see Act §102(c).

> ### *Editor's Note*
>
> **Caution:** PHSA §2702, as follows, is effective for plan years beginning on or after January 1, 2014.

SEC. 2702. GUARANTEED AVAILABILITY OF COVERAGE.

(a) Guaranteed Issuance of Coverage in the Individual and Group Market.—Subject to subsections (b) through (e), each health insurance issuer that offers health insurance coverage in the individual or group market in a State must accept every employer and individual in the State that applies for such coverage.

Selected Provisions of PHSA After Amendment by PPACA. For sections prior to PPACA, see Part 4.

(b) Enrollment.—

(1) Restriction.—A health insurance issuer described in subsection (a) may restrict enrollment in coverage described in such subsection to open or special enrollment periods.

(2) Establishment.—A health insurance issuer described in subsection (a) shall, in accordance with the regulations promulgated under paragraph (3), establish special enrollment periods for qualifying events (under section 603 of the Employee Retirement Income Security Act of 1974).

(3) Regulations.—The Secretary shall promulgate regulations with respect to enrollment periods under paragraphs (1) and (2).

(c) Special Rules for Network Plans.—

(1) In general.—In the case of a health insurance issuer that offers health insurance coverage in the group and individual market through a network plan, the issuer may—

(A) limit the employers that may apply for such coverage to those with eligible individuals who live, work, or reside in the service area for such network plan; and

(B) within the service area of such plan, deny such coverage to such employers and individuals if the issuer has demonstrated, if required, to the applicable State authority that—

(i) it will not have the capacity to deliver services adequately to enrollees of any additional groups or any additional individuals because of its obligations to existing group contract holders and enrollees, and

(ii) it is applying this paragraph uniformly to all employers and individuals without regard to the claims experience of those individuals, employers and their employees (and their dependents) or any health status-related factor relating to such individuals[,] employees and dependents.

(2) 180-day suspension upon denial of coverage.—An issuer, upon denying health insurance coverage in any service area in accordance with paragraph (1)(B), may not offer coverage in the group or individual market within such service area for a period of 180 days after the date such coverage is denied.

(d) Application of Financial Capacity Limits.—

(1) In general.—A health insurance issuer may deny health insurance coverage in the group or individual market if the issuer has demonstrated, if required, to the applicable State authority that—

(A) it does not have the financial reserves necessary to underwrite additional coverage; and

(B) it is applying this paragraph uniformly to all employers and individuals in the group or individual market in the State consistent with applicable State law and without regard to the claims experience of those individuals, employers and their employees (and their dependents) or any health status-related factor relating to such individuals, employees and dependents.

(2) 180-day suspension upon denial of coverage.—A health insurance issuer upon denying health insurance coverage in connection with group health plans in accordance with paragraph (1) in a State may not offer coverage in connection with group health plans in the group or individual market in the State for a period of 180 days after the date such coverage is denied or until the issuer has demonstrated to the applicable State authority, if required under applicable State law, that the issuer has sufficient financial reserves to underwrite additional coverage, whichever is later. An applicable State authority may provide for the application of this subsection on a service-area-specific basis.

Amendments to PHSA §2702

Patient Protection and Affordable Care Act, 2010 (Pub. L. No. 111-148), as follows:

● **Note on Redesignation:** PHSA §2702 (former) was redesignated as PHSA §2705 by Act §1201(3)(B). Eff. for plan years beg. on or after Jan. 1, 2014, see Act §1255, as redesignated by Act §10103(f)(1).

● PHSA §2702 heading and subsecs. (a) and (b) were added by Act §1201(4). Eff. for plan years beg. on or after Jan. 1, 2014, Act §1255, as redesignated by Act §10103(f)(1).

● PHSA §2711 (former) was redesignated by Act §1001(3) as PHSA §2731 (former), amended by Act §1563(c)(8)(A)–(E), as redesignated by Act §10107(b)(1), and transferred to PHSA §2702 by Act §1563(c)(8)(F), as redesignated by Act §10107(b)(1).

● PHSA §2702 was amended by Act §1563(c)(8)(F), as redesignated by Act §10107(b)(1), by amending PHSA §2731 (former) as follows: striking the heading and all that followed through subsec. (b); in subsec. (c)(1), in the matter preceding subpara. (A) striking "small group" and inserting "group and individual", and in subpara. (B), in the matter preceding cl. (i), by inserting "and individuals" after "employers", in cl. (i), inserting "or any additional individuals" after "additional groups", in cl. (ii), by striking "without regard to the claims experience of those employers and their employees (and their dependents) or any health status-related factor relating to such" and inserting "and individuals without regard to the claims experience of those individuals, employers and their employees (and their dependents) or any health status-related factor relating to such individuals"; in subsec. (c), para. (2), striking "small group" and inserting "group or individual"; in subsec. (d), by striking "small group" each place it appeared and inserting "group or individual", in para. (1)(B), striking "all employers" and inserting "all employers and individuals", striking "those employers" and inserting "those individuals, employers", and striking "such employees" and inserting "such individuals, employees"; striking subsecs. (e) and (f); and transferring such section (as amended) (i.e., subsecs. (b)–(f)) to the end of PHSA §2702 (as added by Act §1201(4). Eff. for plan years beg. on or after Jan. 1, 2014, see Act §1255, as redesignated by Act §10103(f)(1).

Health Insurance Portability and Accountability Act of 1996 (Pub. L. No. 104-191), as follows:

● PHSA §2702 (former) was added by Act §102(a). Eff. generally for group health plans, and health insurance coverage offered in connection with group health plans, for plan years beg. after June 30, 1997.

> ### Editor's Note
>
> **Caution:** PHSA §2703, as follows, is effective for plan years beginning on or after January 1, 2014.

SEC. 2703. GUARANTEED RENEWABILITY OF COVERAGE.

(a) In General.—Except as provided in this section, if a health insurance issuer offers health insurance coverage in the individual or group market, the issuer must renew or continue in force such coverage at the option of the plan sponsor or the individual, as applicable.

(b) General Exceptions.—A health insurance issuer may nonrenew or discontinue health insurance coverage offered in connection with a health insurance coverage offered in the group or individual market based only on one or more of the following:

(1) Nonpayment of premiums.—The plan sponsor, or individual, as applicable, has failed to pay premiums or contributions in accordance with the terms of the health insurance coverage or the issuer has not received timely premium payments.

(2) Fraud.—The plan sponsor, or individual, as applicable, has performed an act or practice that constitutes fraud or made an intentional misrepresentation of material fact under the terms of the coverage.

(3) Violation of participation or contribution rates.—In the case of a group health plan, the plan sponsor has failed to comply with a material plan provision relating to employer contribution or group participation rules, pursuant to applicable State law.

(4) Termination of coverage.—The issuer is ceasing to offer coverage in such market in accordance with subsection (c) and applicable State law.

(5) Movement outside service area.—In the case of a health insurance issuer that offers health insurance coverage in the market through a network plan, there is no longer any enrollee in connection with such plan who lives, resides, or works in the service area of the issuer (or in the area for which the issuer is authorized to do business) and, in the case of the small group market, the issuer would deny enrollment with respect to such plan under section 2711(c)(1)(A).

(6) Association membership ceases.—In the case of health insurance coverage that is made available in the small or large group market (as the case may be) only through one or more bona fide associations, the membership of an employer in the association (on the basis of which the coverage is provided) ceases but only if such coverage is terminated under this paragraph uniformly without regard to any health status-related factor relating to any covered individual.

(c) Requirements for Uniform Termination of Coverage.—

(1) Particular type of coverage not offered.—In any case in which an issuer decides to discontinue offering a particular type of group or individual health insurance coverage, coverage of such type may be discontinued by the issuer in accordance with applicable State law in such market only if—

(A) the issuer provides notice to each plan sponsor, or individual, as applicable, provided coverage of this type in such market (and participants and beneficiaries covered under such coverage) of such discontinuation at least 90 days prior to the date of the discontinuation of such coverage;

(B) the issuer offers to each plan sponsor, or individual, as applicable, provided coverage of this type in such market, the option to purchase all (or, in the case of the large group market, any) other health insurance coverage currently being offered by the issuer to a group health plan or individual health insurance coverage in such market; and

(C) in exercising the option to discontinue coverage of this type and in offering the option of coverage under subparagraph (B), the issuer acts uniformly without regard to the claims experience of those sponsors or individuals, as applicable, or any health status-related factor relating to any participants or beneficiaries covered or new participants or beneficiaries who may become eligible for such coverage.

(2) Discontinuance of all coverage.—

(A) In general.—In any case in which a health insurance issuer elects to discontinue offering all health insurance coverage in the individual or group market, or all markets, in a State, health insurance coverage may be discontinued by the issuer only in accordance with applicable State law and if—

(i) the issuer provides notice to the applicable State authority and to each plan sponsor, or individual, as applicable[,] (and participants and beneficiaries covered under such coverage) of such discontinuation at least 180 days prior to the date of the discontinuation of such coverage; and

(ii) all health insurance issued or delivered for issuance in the State in such market (or markets)

Selected Provisions of PHSA After Amendment by PPACA. For sections prior to PPACA, see Part 4.

are discontinued and coverage under such health insurance coverage in such market (or markets) is not renewed.

(B) Prohibition on market reentry.—In the case of a discontinuation under subparagraph (A) in a market, the issuer may not provide for the issuance of any health insurance coverage in the market and State involved during the 5-year period beginning on the date of the discontinuation of the last health insurance coverage not so renewed.

(d) Exception for Uniform Modification of Coverage.—At the time of coverage renewal, a health insurance issuer may modify the health insurance coverage for a product offered to a group health plan—

(1) in the large group market; or

(2) in the small group market if, for coverage that is available in such market other than only through one or more bona fide associations, such modification is consistent with State law and effective on a uniform basis among group health plans with that product.

(e) Application to Coverage Offered Only Through Associations.—In applying this section in the case of health insurance coverage that is made available by a health insurance issuer in the small or large group market to employers only through one or more associations, a reference to "plan sponsor" is deemed, with respect to coverage provided to an employer member of the association, to include a reference to such employer.

Amendments to PHSA §2703

Patient Protection and Affordable Care Act, 2010 (Pub. L. No. 111-148), as follows:

- **Note on redesignation:** PHSA §2712 (former) was redesignated by Act §1001(3) as PHSA §2732 (former), amended by Act §1563(c)(9)(A)–(C) (as redesignated by Act §10107(b)(1)), and transferred to PHSA §2703 by Act §1563(c)(9)(D) (as redesignated by Act §10107(b)(1)).

- PHSA §2703 heading and subsec. (a) were added by Act §1201(4). Eff. for plan years beg. on or after Jan. 1, 2014, Act §1255, as redesignated by Act §10103(f)(1).

- PHSA §2703 was amended by Act §1563(c)(9) (as redesignated by Act §10107(b)(1)) by amending PHSA §2732 as follows: by striking the heading and all the followed through subsec. (a); in subsec. (b), in the matter preceding paras. (1) and (2), by striking "group health plan in the small or large group market" and inserting "health insurance coverage offered in the group or individual market", in para. (1), by inserting ", or individual, as applicable," after "plan sponsor", and striking para. (3) and inserting new para. (3); and transferring such section, as amended, to the end of PHSA §2703, as added by Act §1201(4). Eff. for plan years beg. on or after Jan. 1, 2014, Act §1255, as redesignated by Act §10103(f)(1).

SEC. 2704. PROHIBITION OF PREEXISTING CONDITION EXCLUSIONS OR OTHER DISCRIMINATION BASED ON HEALTH STATUS.

(a) In General.—A group health plan and a health insurance issuer offering group or individual health insurance coverage may not impose any preexisting condition exclusion with respect to such plan or coverage.

(b) Definitions.—For purposes of this part—

(1) Preexisting condition exclusion.—

(A) In general.—The term "preexisting condition exclusion" means, with respect to coverage, a limitation or exclusion of benefits relating to a condition based on the fact that the condition was present before the date of enrollment for such coverage, whether or not any medical advice, diagnosis, care, or treatment was recommended or received before such date.

(B) Treatment of genetic information.—Genetic information shall not be treated as a condition described in subsection (a)(1) in the absence of a diagnosis of the condition related to such information.

(2) Enrollment date.—The term "enrollment date" means, with respect to an individual covered under a group health plan or health insurance coverage, the date of enrollment of the individual in the plan or coverage or, if earlier, the first day of the waiting period for such enrollment.

(3) Late enrollee.—The term "late enrollee" means, with respect to coverage under a group health plan, a participant or beneficiary who enrolls under the plan other than during—

(A) the first period in which the individual is eligible to enroll under the plan, or

(B) a special enrollment period under subsection (f).

(4) Waiting period.—The term "waiting period" means, with respect to a group health plan and an individual who is a potential participant or beneficiary in the plan, the period that must pass with respect to the individual before the individual is eligible to be covered for benefits under the terms of the plan.

(c) Rules Relating to Crediting Previous Coverage.—

(1) Creditable coverage defined.—For purposes of this title, the term "creditable coverage" means, with respect to an individual, coverage of the individual under any of the following:

(A) A group health plan.

(B) Health insurance coverage.

(C) Part A or part B of title XVIII of the Social Security Act.

(D) Title XIX of the Social Security Act, other than coverage consisting solely of benefits under section 1928.

(E) Chapter 55 of title 10, United States Code.

(F) A medical care program of the Indian Health Service or of a tribal organization.

(G) A State health benefits risk pool.

(H) A health plan offered under chapter 89 of title 5, United States Code.

(I) A public health plan (as defined in regulations).

(J) A health benefit plan under section 5(e) of the Peace Corps Act (22 U.S.C. 2504(e)).

Such term does not include coverage consisting solely of coverage of excepted benefits (as defined in section 2791(c)).

(2) Not counting periods before significant breaks in coverage.—

(A) In general.—A period of creditable coverage shall not be counted, with respect to enrollment of an individual under a group or individual health plan, if, after such period and before the enrollment date, there was a 63-day period during all of which the individual was not covered under any creditable coverage.

(B) Waiting period not treated as a break in coverage.—For purposes of subparagraph (A) and subsection (d)(4), any period that an individual is in a waiting period for any coverage under a group or individual health plan (or for group health insurance coverage) or is in an affiliation period (as defined in subsection (g)(2)) shall not be taken into account in determining the continuous period under subparagraph (A).

(C) TAA-eligible individuals.—In the case of plan years beginning before January 1, 2011—

(i) TAA pre-certification period rule. In the case of a TAA-eligible individual, the period beginning on the date the individual has a TAA-related loss of coverage and ending on the date that is 7 days after the date of the issuance by the Secretary (or by any person or entity designated by the Secretary) of a qualified health insurance costs credit eligibility certificate for such individual for purposes of section 7527 of the Internal Revenue Code of 1986 shall not be taken into account in determining the continuous period under subparagraph (A).

(ii) Definitions. The terms "TAA-eligible individual" and "TAA-related loss of coverage" have the meanings given such terms in section 2205(b)(4).

(3) Method of crediting coverage.—

(A) Standard method.—Except as otherwise provided under subparagraph (B), for purposes of applying subsection (a)(3), a group health plan, and a health insurance issuer offering group or individual health insurance coverage, shall count a period of creditable coverage without regard to the specific benefits covered during the period.

(B) Election of alternative method.—A group health plan, or a health insurance issuer offering group or individual health insurance, may elect to apply subsection (a)(3) based on coverage of benefits within each of several classes or categories of benefits specified in regulations rather than as provided under subparagraph (A). Such election shall be made on a uniform basis for all participants and beneficiaries. Under such election a group health plan or issuer shall count a period of creditable coverage with respect to any class or category of benefits if any level of benefits is covered within such class or category.

(C) Plan notice.—In the case of an election with respect to a group health plan under subparagraph (B) (whether or not health insurance coverage is provided in connection with such plan), the plan shall—

(i) prominently state in any disclosure statements concerning the plan, and state to each enrollee at the time of enrollment under the plan, that the plan has made such election, and

(ii) include in such statements a description of the effect of this election.

(D) Issuer notice.—In the case of an election under subparagraph (B) with respect to health insurance coverage offered by an issuer in the individual or group [group] market, the issuer—

(i) shall prominently state in any disclosure statements concerning the coverage, and to each employer at the time of the offer or sale of the coverage, that the issuer has made such election, and

(ii) shall include in such statements a description of the effect of such election.

(4) Establishment of period.—Periods of creditable coverage with respect to an individual shall be established through presentation of certifications described in subsection (e) or in such other manner as may be specified in regulations.

Selected Provisions of PHSA After Amendment by PPACA. For sections prior to PPACA, see Part 4.

(d) Exceptions.—

(1) Exclusion not applicable to certain newborns.—Subject to paragraph (4), a group health plan, and a health insurance issuer offering group or individual health insurance coverage, may not impose any preexisting condition exclusion in the case of an individual who, as of the last day of the 30-day period beginning with the date of birth, is covered under creditable coverage.

(2) Exclusion not applicable to certain adopted children.—Subject to paragraph (4), a group health plan, and a health insurance issuer offering group or individual health insurance coverage, may not impose any preexisting condition exclusion in the case of a child who is adopted or placed for adoption before attaining 18 years of age and who, as of the last day of the 30-day period beginning on the date of the adoption or placement for adoption, is covered under creditable coverage. The previous sentence shall not apply to coverage before the date of such adoption or placement for adoption.

(3) Exclusion not applicable to pregnancy.—A group health plan, and health insurance issuer offering group or individual health insurance coverage, may not impose any preexisting condition exclusion relating to pregnancy as a preexisting condition.

(4) Loss if break in coverage.—Paragraphs (1) and (2) shall no longer apply to an individual after the end of the first 63-day period during all of which the individual was not covered under any creditable coverage.

(e) Certifications and Disclosure of Coverage.—

(1) Requirement for certification of period of creditable coverage.—

(A) In general.—A group health plan, and a health insurance issuer offering group or individual health insurance coverage, shall provide the certification described in subparagraph (B)—

(i) at the time an individual ceases to be covered under the plan or otherwise becomes covered under a COBRA continuation provision,

(ii) in the case of an individual becoming covered under such a provision, at the time the individual ceases to be covered under such provision, and

(iii) on the request on behalf of an individual made not later than 24 months after the date of cessation of the coverage described in clause (i) or (ii), whichever is later. The certification under clause (i) may be provided, to the extent practicable, at a time consistent with notices required under any applicable COBRA continuation provision.

(B) Certification.—The certification described in this subparagraph is a written certification of—

(i) the period of creditable coverage of the individual under such plan and the coverage (if any) under such COBRA continuation provision, and

(ii) the waiting period (if any) (and affiliation period, if applicable) imposed with respect to the individual for any coverage under such plan.

(C) Issuer compliance.—To the extent that medical care under a group health plan consists of group health insurance coverage, the plan is deemed to have satisfied the certification requirement under this paragraph if the health insurance issuer offering the coverage provides for such certification in accordance with this paragraph.

(2) Disclosure of information on previous benefits.—In the case of an election described in subsection (c)(3)(B) by a group health plan or health insurance issuer, if the plan or issuer enrolls an individual for coverage under the plan and the individual provides a certification of coverage of the individual under paragraph (1)—

(A) upon request of such plan or issuer, the entity which issued the certification provided by the individual shall promptly disclose to such requesting plan or issuer information on coverage of classes and categories of health benefits available under such entity's plan or coverage, and

(B) such entity may charge the requesting plan or issuer for the reasonable cost of disclosing such information.

(3) Regulations.—The Secretary shall establish rules to prevent an entity's failure to provide information under paragraph (1) or (2) with respect to previous coverage of an individual from adversely affecting any subsequent coverage of the individual under another group health plan or health insurance coverage.

(f) Special Enrollment Periods.—

(1) Individuals losing other coverage.—A group health plan, and a health insurance issuer offering group health insurance coverage in connection with a group health plan, shall permit an employee who is eligible, but not enrolled, for coverage under the terms of the plan (or a dependent of such an employee if the dependent is eligible, but not enrolled, for coverage under such terms) to enroll for coverage under the terms of the plan if each of the following conditions is met:

(A) The employee or dependent was covered under a group health plan or had health insurance coverage at the time coverage was previously offered to the employee or dependent.

(B) The employee stated in writing at such time that coverage under a group health plan or health insurance coverage was the reason for declining enrollment, but only if the plan sponsor or issuer (if applicable) required such a statement at such time and provided the employee with notice of such requirement (and the consequences of such requirement) at such time.

(C) The employee's or dependent's coverage described in subparagraph (A)—

(i) was under a COBRA continuation provision and the coverage under such provision was exhausted; or

(ii) was not under such a provision and either the coverage was terminated as a result of loss of eligibility for the coverage (including as a result of legal separation, divorce, death, termination of employment, or reduction in the number of hours of employment) or employer contributions toward such coverage were terminated.

(D) Under the terms of the plan, the employee requests such enrollment not later than 30 days after the date of exhaustion of coverage described in subparagraph (C)(i) or termination of coverage or employer contribution described in subparagraph (C)(ii).

(2) For dependent beneficiaries.—

(A) In general.—If—

(i) a group health plan makes coverage available with respect to a dependent of an individual,

(ii) the individual is a participant under the plan (or has met any waiting period applicable to becoming a participant under the plan and is eligible to be enrolled under the plan but for a failure to enroll during a previous enrollment period), and

(iii) a person becomes such a dependent of the individual through marriage, birth, or adoption or placement for adoption,
the group health plan shall provide for a dependent special enrollment period described in subparagraph (B) during which the person (or, if not otherwise enrolled, the individual) may be enrolled under the plan as a dependent of the individual, and in the case of the birth or adoption of a child, the spouse of the individual may be enrolled as a dependent of the individual if such spouse is otherwise eligible for coverage.

(B) Dependent special enrollment period.—A dependent special enrollment period under this subparagraph shall be a period of not less than 30 days and shall begin on the later of—

(i) the date dependent coverage is made available, or

(ii) the date of the marriage, birth, or adoption or placement for adoption (as the case may be) described in subparagraph (A)(iii).

(C) No waiting period.—If an individual seeks to enroll a dependent during the first 30 days of such a dependent special enrollment period, the coverage of the dependent shall become effective—

(i) in the case of marriage, not later than the first day of the first month beginning after the date the completed request for enrollment is received;

(ii) in the case of a dependent's birth, as of the date of such birth; or

(iii) in the case of a dependent's adoption or placement for adoption, the date of such adoption or placement for adoption.

(3) Special rules for application in case of Medicaid and CHIP.—

(A) In general.—A group health plan, and a health insurance issuer offering group health insurance coverage in connection with a group health plan, shall permit an employee who is eligible, but not enrolled, for coverage under the terms of the plan (or a dependent of such an employee if the dependent is eligible, but not enrolled, for coverage under such terms) to enroll for coverage under the terms of the plan if either of the following conditions is met:

(i) Termination of Medicaid or CHIP coverage.—The employee or dependent is covered under a Medicaid plan under title XIX of the Social Security Act or under a State child health plan under title XXI of such Act and coverage of the employee or dependent under such a plan is terminated as a result of loss of eligibility for such coverage and the employee requests coverage under the group health plan (or health insurance coverage) not later than 60 days after the date of termination of such coverage.

(ii) Eligibility for employment assistance under Medicaid or CHIP.—The employee or dependent becomes eligible for assistance, with respect to coverage under the group health plan or health insurance coverage, under such Medicaid plan or State child health plan (including under any waiver or demonstration project conducted under or in relation to such a plan), if the employee requests coverage under the group health plan or health insurance coverage not later than 60 days after the date the employee or dependent is determined to be eligible for such assistance.

(B) Coordination with Medicaid and CHIP.—

(i) Outreach to employees regarding availability of Medicaid and CHIP coverage.—

(I) In general.—Each employer that maintains a group health plan in a State that provides medical assistance under a State Medicaid plan under title XIX of the Social Security Act, or child health assistance under a State child health plan under title XXI of such Act, in the form of premium assistance for the purchase of coverage under a group health plan, shall provide to each employee a written notice informing the employee of potential opportunities then currently available in the

Selected Provisions of PHSA After Amendment by PPACA. For sections prior to PPACA, see Part 4.

PHSA Sec. 2704(f)(1)(B)

State in which the employee resides for premium assistance under such plans for health coverage of the employee or the employee's dependents. For purposes of compliance with this subclause, the employer may use any State-specific model notice developed in accordance with section 701(f)(3)(B)(i)(II) of the Employee Retirement Income Security Act of 1974 (29 U.S.C. 1181(f)(3)(B)(i)(II)).

(II) Option to provide concurrent with provision of plan materials to employee.—An employer may provide the model notice applicable to the State in which an employee resides concurrent with the furnishing of materials notifying the employee of health plan eligibility, concurrent with materials provided to the employee in connection with an open season or election process conducted under the plan, or concurrent with the furnishing of the summary plan description as provided in section 104(b) of the Employee Retirement Income Security Act of 1974.

(ii) Disclosure about group health plan benefits to States for Medicaid and CHIP eligible individuals.—In the case of an enrollee in a group health plan who is covered under a Medicaid plan of a State under title XIX of the Social Security Act or under a State child health plan under title XXI of such Act, the plan administrator of the group health plan shall disclose to the State, upon request, information about the benefits available under the group health plan in sufficient specificity, as determined under regulations of the Secretary of Health and Human Services in consultation with the Secretary that require use of the model coverage coordination disclosure form developed under section 311(b)(1)(C) of the Children's Health Insurance Reauthorization Act of 2009, so as to permit the State to make a determination (under paragraph (2)(B), (3), or (10) of section 2105(c) of the Social Security Act or otherwise) concerning the cost-effectiveness of the State providing medical or child health assistance through premium assistance for the purchase of coverage under such group health plan and in order for the State to provide supplemental benefits required under paragraph (10)(E) of such section or other authority.

(g) Use of Affiliation Period by HMOs as Alternative to Preexisting Condition Exclusion.—

(1) In general.—A health maintenance organization which offers health insurance coverage in connection with a group health plan and which does not impose any preexisting condition exclusion allowed under subsection (a) with respect to any particular coverage option may impose an affiliation period for such coverage option, but only if—

(A) such period is applied uniformly without regard to any health status-related factors; and

(B) such period does not exceed 2 months (or 3 months in the case of a late enrollee).

(2) Affiliation period.—

(A) Defined.—For purposes of this title, the term "affiliation period" means a period which, under the terms of the health insurance coverage offered by the health maintenance organization, must expire before the health insurance coverage becomes effective. The organization is not required to provide health care services or benefits during such period and no premium shall be charged to the participant or beneficiary for any coverage during the period.

(B) Beginning.—Such period shall begin on the enrollment date.

(C) Runs concurrently with waiting periods.—An affiliation period under a plan shall run concurrently with any waiting period under the plan.

(3) Alternative methods.—A health maintenance organization described in paragraph (1) may use alternative methods, from those described in such paragraph, to address adverse selection as approved by the State insurance commissioner or official or officials designated by the State to enforce the requirements of this part for the State involved with respect to such issuer.

Amendments to PHSA §2704

Patient Protection and Affordable Care Act, 2010 (Pub. L. No. 111-148), as follows:

- **Note on redesignation:** PHSA §2704 was redesignated by Act §1201(2) from PHSA §2701 (former) and renamed.

- PHSA §2704, as redesignated, was amended by Act §1563(c)(1) (as redesignated by Act §10107(b)(1)) in subsec. (c), para. (2) by striking "group health plan" each place it appeared and inserting "group or individual health plan", in para. (3) by striking "group health insurance" each place it appeared and inserting "group or individual health insurance", and in subpara (D), by striking "small or large" and inserting "individual or group"; in subsec. (d) by striking "group health insurance" each place it appeared and inserting "group or individual health insurance". Eff. for plan years beg. on or after Jan. 1, 2014; except, as applicable to enrollees under age 19, eff. for plan years beg. on or after 6 months after date of enactment [date of enactment: Mar. 23, 2010]. Act §1255, as amended by Act §10103(e) and redesignated by Act §10103(f)(1).

TAA Health Coverage Improvement Act of 2009 (Pub. L. No. 111-5), as follows:

- PHSA §2701(c)(2)(C) (former) was added by Act Div. B, §1899D(c). Eff. for plan years beg. after date of enactment [enacted: Feb. 17, 2009].

Children's Health Insurance Program Reauthorization Act of 2009 (Pub. L. No. 111-3), as follows:

- PHSA §2701(f)(3) (former) was added by Act §311(b)(2). See effective date note to ERISA §701.

Health Insurance Portability and Accountability Act of 1996 (Pub. L. No. 104-191), as follows:

- PHSA §2701 (former) was added by Act §102(a). Eff. with respect to group health plans, and health insurance coverage offered in connection with group health plans, for plan years beginning after June 30, 1997.

Selected Provisions of PHSA After Amendment by PPACA. For sections prior to PPACA, see Part 4.

SEC. 2705. PROHIBITING DISCRIMINATION AGAINST INDIVIDUAL PARTICIPANTS AND BENEFICIARIES BASED ON HEALTH STATUS.

(a) In General.—A group health plan and a health insurance issuer offering group or individual health insurance coverage may not establish rules for eligibility (including continued eligibility) of any individual to enroll under the terms of the plan or coverage based on any of the following health status-related factors in relation to the individual or a dependent of the individual:

(1) Health status.

(2) Medical condition (including both physical and mental illnesses).

(3) Claims experience.

(4) Receipt of health care.

(5) Medical history.

(6) Genetic information.

(7) Evidence of insurability (including conditions arising out of acts of domestic violence).

(8) Disability.

(9) Any other health status-related factor determined appropriate by the Secretary.

(b) In Premium Contributions.—

(1) In general.—A group health plan, and a health insurance issuer offering group or individual health insurance coverage, may not require any individual (as a condition of enrollment or continued enrollment under the plan) to pay a premium or contribution which is greater than such premium or contribution for a similarly situated individual enrolled in the plan on the basis of any health status-related factor in relation to the individual or to an individual enrolled under the plan as a dependent of the individual.

(2) Construction.—Nothing in paragraph (1) shall be construed—

(A) to restrict the amount that an employer or individual may be charged for coverage under a group health plan except as provided in paragraph (3) or individual health coverage, as the case may be; or

(B) to prevent a group health plan, and a health insurance issuer offering group health insurance coverage, from establishing premium discounts or rebates or modifying otherwise applicable copayments or deductibles in return for adherence to programs of health promotion and disease prevention.

(3) No group-based discrimination on basis of genetic information.—

(A) In general.—For purposes of this section, a group health plan, and health insurance issuer offering group or individual health insurance coverage, may not adjust premium or contribution amounts for the group covered under such plan on the basis of genetic information.

(B) Rule of construction.—Nothing in subparagraph (A) or in paragraphs (1) and (2) of subsection (d) shall be construed to limit the ability of a health insurance issuer offering group or individual health insurance coverage to increase the premium for an employer based on the manifestation of a disease or disorder of an individual who is enrolled in the plan. In such case, the manifestation of a disease or disorder in one individual cannot also be used as genetic information about other group members and to further increase the premium for the employer.

(c) Genetic Testing.—

(1) Limitation on requesting or requiring genetic testing.—A group health plan, and a health insurance issuer offering health insurance coverage in connection with a group health plan, shall not request or require an individual or a family member of such individual to undergo a genetic test.

(2) Rule of construction.—Paragraph (1) shall not be construed to limit the authority of a health care professional who is providing health care services to an individual to request that such individual undergo a genetic test.

(3) Rule of construction regarding payment.—

(A) In general.—Nothing in paragraph (1) shall be construed to preclude a group health plan, or a health insurance issuer offering health insurance coverage in connection with a group health plan, from obtaining and using the results of a genetic test in making a determination regarding payment (as such term is defined for the purposes of applying the regulations promulgated by the Secretary under part C of title XI of the Social Security Act and section 264 of the Health Insurance Portability and Accountability Act of 1996, as may be revised from time to time) consistent with subsection (a).

(B) Limitation.—For purposes of subparagraph (A), a group health plan, or a health insurance issuer offering health insurance coverage in connection with a group health plan, may request only the minimum amount of information necessary to accomplish the intended purpose.

(4) Research exception.—Notwithstanding paragraph (1), a group health plan, or a health insurance

Selected Provisions of PHSA After Amendment by PPACA. For sections prior to PPACA, see Part 4.

issuer offering health insurance coverage in connection with a group health plan, may request, but not require, that a participant or beneficiary undergo a genetic test if each of the following conditions is met:

(A) The request is made pursuant to research that complies with part 46 of title 45, Code of Federal Regulations, or equivalent Federal regulations, and any applicable State or local law or regulations for the protection of human subjects in research.

(B) The plan or issuer clearly indicates to each participant or beneficiary, or in the case of a minor child, to the legal guardian of such beneficiary, to whom the request is made that—

(i) compliance with the request is voluntary; and

(ii) non-compliance will have no effect on enrollment status or premium or contribution amounts.

(C) No genetic information collected or acquired under this paragraph shall be used for underwriting purposes.

(D) The plan or issuer notifies the Secretary in writing that the plan or issuer is conducting activities pursuant to the exception provided for under this paragraph, including a description of the activities conducted.

(E) The plan or issuer complies with such other conditions as the Secretary may by regulation require for activities conducted under this paragraph.

(d) Prohibition on Collection of Genetic Information.—

(1) In general.—A group health plan, and a health insurance issuer offering health insurance coverage in connection with a group health plan, shall not request, require, or purchase genetic information for underwriting purposes (as defined in section 2791).

(2) Prohibition on collection of genetic information prior to enrollment.—A group health plan, and a health insurance issuer offering health insurance coverage in connection with a group health plan, shall not request, require, or purchase genetic information with respect to any individual prior to such individual's enrollment under the plan or coverage in connection with such enrollment.

(3) Incidental collection.—If a group health plan, or a health insurance issuer offering health insurance coverage in connection with a group health plan, obtains genetic information incidental to the requesting, requiring, or purchasing of other information concerning any individual, such request, requirement, or purchase shall not be considered a violation of paragraph (2) if such request, requirement, or purchase is not in violation of paragraph (1).

(e) Application to All Plans.—The provisions of subsections (a)(6), (b)(3), (c) , and (d) and subsection

(b)(1) and section 2704 with respect to genetic information, shall apply to group health plans and health insurance issuers without regard to section 2735(a).

(f) Genetic Information of a Fetus or Embryo.— Any reference in this part to genetic information concerning an individual or family member of an individual shall—

(1) with respect to such an individual or family member of an individual who is a pregnant woman, include genetic information of any fetus carried by such pregnant woman; and

(2) with respect to an individual or family member utilizing an assisted reproductive technology, include genetic information of any embryo legally held by the individual or family member.

[(g)—(i)]

(j) Programs of Health Promotion or Disease Prevention.—

(1) General provisions.—

(A) General rule.—For purposes of subsection (b)(2)(B), a program of health promotion or disease prevention (referred to in this subsection as a "wellness program") shall be a program offered by an employer that is designed to promote health or prevent disease that meets the applicable requirements of this subsection.

(B) No conditions based on health status factor.— If none of the conditions for obtaining a premium discount or rebate or other reward for participation in a wellness program is based on an individual satisfying a standard that is related to a health status factor, such wellness program shall not violate this section if participation in the program is made available to all similarly situated individuals and the requirements of paragraph (2) are complied with.

(C) Conditions based on health status factor.—If any of the conditions for obtaining a premium discount or rebate or other reward for participation in a wellness program is based on an individual satisfying a standard that is related to a health status factor, such wellness program shall not violate this section if the requirements of paragraph (3) are complied with.

(2) Wellness programs not subject to requirements.—If none of the conditions for obtaining a premium discount or rebate or other reward under a wellness program as described in paragraph (1)(B) are based on an individual satisfying a standard that is related to a health status factor (or if such a wellness program does not provide such a reward), the wellness program shall not violate this section if participation in the program is made available to all similarly situated individuals. The following programs shall not have to comply with the requirements of paragraph (3) if participation in the program is made available to all similarly situated individuals:

(A) A program that reimburses all or part of the cost for memberships in a fitness center.

(B) A diagnostic testing program that provides a reward for participation and does not base any part of the reward on outcomes.

(C) A program that encourages preventive care related to a health condition through the waiver of the copayment or deductible requirement under group health plan for the costs of certain items or services related to a health condition (such as pre-natal care or well-baby visits).

(D) A program that reimburses individuals for the costs of smoking cessation programs without re-gard to whether the individual quits smoking.

(E) A program that provides a reward to individu-als for attending a periodic health education semi-nar.

(3) Wellness programs subject to require-ments.—If any of the conditions for obtaining a pre-mium discount, rebate, or reward under a wellness program as described in paragraph (1)(C) is based on an individual satisfying a standard that is related to a health status factor, the wellness program shall not violate this section if the following requirements are complied with:

(A) The reward for the wellness program, together with the reward for other wellness programs with respect to the plan that requires satisfaction of a standard related to a health status factor, shall not exceed 30 percent of the cost of employee-only coverage under the plan. If, in addition to employ-ees or individuals, any class of dependents (such as spouses or spouses and dependent children) may participate fully in the wellness program, such re-ward shall not exceed 30 percent of the cost of the coverage in which an employee or individual and any dependents are enrolled. For purposes of this paragraph, the cost of coverage shall be deter-mined based on the total amount of employer and employee contributions for the benefit package un-der which the employee is (or the employee and any dependents are) receiving coverage. A reward may be in the form of a discount or rebate of a premium or contribution, a waiver of all or part of a cost-sharing mechanism (such as deductibles, copayments, or coinsurance), the absence of a sur-charge, or the value of a benefit that would other-wise not be provided under the plan. The Secretar-ies of Labor, Health and Human Services, and the Treasury may increase the reward available under this subparagraph to up to 50 percent of the cost of coverage if the Secretaries determine that such an increase is appropriate.

(B) The wellness program shall be reasonably de-signed to promote health or prevent disease. A program complies with the preceding sentence if the program has a reasonable chance of improving the health of, or preventing disease in, participat-ing individuals and it is not overly burdensome, is not a subterfuge for discriminating based on a health status factor, and is not highly suspect in the method chosen to promote health or prevent dis-ease.

(C) The plan shall give individuals eligible for the program the opportunity to qualify for the reward under the program at least once each year.

(D) The full reward under the wellness program shall be made available to all similarly situated individuals. For such purpose, among other things:

(i) The reward is not available to all similarly situated individuals for a period unless the well-ness program allows—

(I) for a reasonable alternative standard (or waiver of the otherwise applicable standard) for obtaining the reward for any individual for whom, for that period, it is unreasonably difficult due to a medical condition to satisfy the otherwise appli-cable standard; and

(II) for a reasonable alternative standard (or waiver of the otherwise applicable standard) for obtaining the reward for any individual for whom, for that period, it is medically inadvisable to at-tempt to satisfy the otherwise applicable standard.

(ii) If reasonable under the circumstances, the plan or issuer may seek verification, such as a statement from an individual's physician, that a health status factor makes it unreasonably difficult or medically inadvisable for the individual to sat-isfy or attempt to satisfy the otherwise applicable standard.

(E) The plan or issuer involved shall disclose in all plan materials describing the terms of the well-ness program the availability of a reasonable alter-native standard (or the possibility of waiver of the otherwise applicable standard) required under sub-paragraph (D). If plan materials disclose that such a program is available, without describing its terms, the disclosure under this subparagraph shall not be required.

(k) Existing Programs.—Nothing in this section shall prohibit a program of health promotion or dis-ease prevention that was established prior to the date of enactment of this section and applied with all applicable regulations, and that is operating on such date, from continuing to be carried out for as long as such regulations remain in effect.

(l) Wellness Program Demonstration Project.—

(1) In general.—Not later than July 1, 2014, the Secretary, in consultation with the Secretary of the Treasury and the Secretary of Labor, shall establish a 10-State demonstration project under which partici-pating States shall apply the provisions of subsection (j) to programs of health promotion offered by a

Selected Provisions of PHSA After Amendment by PPACA. For sections prior to PPACA, see Part 4.

health insurance issuer that offers health insurance coverage in the individual market in such State.

(2) Expansion of demonstration project.—If the Secretary, in consultation with the Secretary of the Treasury and the Secretary of Labor, determines that the demonstration project described in paragraph (1) is effective, such Secretaries may, beginning on July 1, 2017 expand such demonstration project to include additional participating States.

(3) Requirements.—

(A) Maintenance of coverage.—The Secretary, in consultation with the Secretary of the Treasury and the Secretary of Labor, shall not approve the participation of a State in the demonstration project under this section unless the Secretaries determine that the State's project is designed in a manner that—

(i) will not result in any decrease in coverage; and

(ii) will not increase the cost to the Federal Government in providing credits under section 36B of the Internal Revenue Code of 1986 or cost-sharing assistance under section 1402 of the Patient Protection and Affordable Care Act.

(B) Other requirements.—States that participate in the demonstration project under this subsection—

(i) may permit premium discounts or rebates or the modification of otherwise applicable copayments or deductibles for adherence to, or participation in, a reasonably designed program of health promotion and disease prevention;

(ii) shall ensure that requirements of consumer protection are met in programs of health promotion in the individual market;

(iii) shall require verification from health insurance issuers that offer health insurance coverage in the individual market of such State that premium discounts—

(I) do not create undue burdens for individuals insured in the individual market;

(II) do not lead to cost shifting; and

(III) are not a subterfuge for discrimination;

(iv) shall ensure that consumer data is protected in accordance with the requirements of section 264(c) of the Health Insurance Portability and Accountability Act of 1996 (42 U.S.C. 1320d-2 note); and

(v) shall ensure and demonstrate to the satisfaction of the Secretary that the discounts or other rewards provided under the project reflect the expected level of participation in the wellness program involved and the anticipated effect the program will have on utilization or medical claim costs.

(m) Report.—

(1) In general.—Not later than 3 years after the date of enactment of the Patient Protection and Affordable Care Act, the Secretary, in consultation with the Secretary of the Treasury and the Secretary of Labor, shall submit a report to the appropriate committees of Congress concerning—

(A) the effectiveness of wellness programs (as defined in subsection (j)) in promoting health and preventing disease;

(B) the impact of such wellness programs on the access to care and affordability of coverage for participants and non-participants of such programs;

(C) the impact of premium-based and cost-sharing incentives on participant behavior and the role of such programs in changing behavior; and

(D) the effectiveness of different types of rewards.

(2) Data collection.—In preparing the report described in paragraph (1), the Secretaries shall gather relevant information from employers who provide employees with access to wellness programs, including State and Federal agencies.

(n) Regulations.—Nothing in this section shall be construed as prohibiting the Secretaries of Labor, Health and Human Services, or the Treasury from promulgating regulations in connection with this section.

Amendments to PHSA §2705

Patient Protection and Affordable Care Act, 2010 (Pub. L. No. 111-148), as follows:

• **Note on Redesignation:** PHSA §2705 (former) was redesignated as PHSA §2526 by Act §1001(2). Eff. for plan years beg. on or after the date that is 6 months after date of enactment [date of enactment: Mar. 23, 2010], see Act §1004(a).

• PHSA §2705 was added by Act §1201(4). Eff. for plan years beg. on or after Jan. 1, 2014, see Act §1255, as redesignated by Act §10103(f)(1).

• PHSA §2702 (former) was amended by Act §1201(3)(A). Eff. for plan years beg. on or after Jan. 1, 2014, see Act §1255, as redesignated by Act §10103(f)(1).

• PHSA §2705 was amended by Act §1201(3)(B) by transferring the amended portion of PHSA §2702 (former) to subsec. (a). Eff. for plan years beg. on or after Jan. 1, 2014, see Act §1255, as redesignated by Act §10103(f)(1).

> ### *Editor's Note*
>
> **Caution:** PHSA §2706, as follows, is effective for plan years beginning on or after January 1, 2014.

SEC. 2706. NONDISCRIMINATION IN HEALTH CARE.

(a) Providers.—A group health plan and a health insurance issuer offering group or individual health insurance coverage shall not discriminate with respect to participation under the plan or coverage against any health care provider who is acting within the scope of that provider's license or certification under applicable State law. This section shall not require that a group health plan or health insurance issuer contract with any health care provider willing to abide by the terms and conditions for participation established by the plan or issuer. Nothing in this section shall be construed as preventing a group health plan, a health insurance issuer, or the Secretary from establishing varying reimbursement rates based on quality or performance measures.

(b) Individuals.—The provisions of section 1558 of the Patient Protection and Affordable Care Act (relating to non-discrimination) shall apply with respect to a group health plan or health insurance issuer offering group or individual health insurance coverage.

Amendments to PHSA §2706

Patient Protection and Affordable Care Act, 2010 (Pub. L. No. 111-148), as follows:

• **Note on Redesignation:** PHSA §2706 (former) was redesignated as PHSA §2727 by Act §1001(2). Eff. for plan years beg. on or after the date that is 6 months after date of enactment [date of enactment: Mar. 23, 2010], see Act §1004(a).

• PHSA §2706 was amended by Act §1201(4). Eff. for plan years beg. on or after Jan. 1, 2014, Act §1255, as redesignated by Act §10103(f)(1).

SEC. 2707. COMPREHENSIVE HEALTH INSURANCE COVERAGE.

(a) Coverage for Essential Health Benefits Package.—A health insurance issuer that offers health insurance coverage in the individual or small group market shall ensure that such coverage includes the essential health benefits package required under section 1302(a) of the Patient Protection and Affordable Care Act.

(b) Cost-Sharing Under Group Health Plans.—A group health plan shall ensure that any annual cost-sharing imposed under the plan does not exceed the limitations provided for under paragraphs (1) and (2) of section 1302(c).

(c) Child-Only Plans.—If a health insurance issuer offers health insurance coverage in any level of coverage specified under section 1302(d) of the Patient Protection and Affordable Care Act, the issuer shall also offer such coverage in that level as a plan in which the only enrollees are individuals who, as of

the beginning of a plan year, have not attained the age of 21.

(d) Dental Only.—This section shall not apply to a plan described in section 1302(d)(2)(B)(ii)(I).

Amendments to PHSA §2707

Patient Protection and Affordable Care Act, 2010 (Pub. L. No. 111-148), as follows:

• **Note on Redesignation:** PHSA §2707 (former) was redesignated by Act §1001(2) as PHSA §2728. Eff. for plan years beg. on or after the date that is 6 months after date of enactment [date of enactment: Mar. 23, 2010], see Act §1004(a).

• PHSA §2707 was added by Act §1201(4). Eff. for plan years beg. on or after Jan. 1, 2014, Act §1255, as redesignated by Act §10103(f)(1).

SEC. 2708. PROHIBITION ON EXCESSIVE WAITING PERIODS.

A group health plan and a health insurance issuer offering group health insurance coverage shall not apply any waiting period (as defined in section 2704(b)(4)) that exceeds 90 days.

Amendments to PHSA §2708

Patient Protection and Affordable Care Act, 2010 (Pub. L. No. 111-148), as follows:

• PHSA §2708 was added by Act §1201(4). Eff. for plan years beg. on or after Jan. 1, 2014, see Act §1255, as redesignated by Act §10103(f)(1).

• PHSA §2708 was amended by Act §10103(b) by striking "or individual". Eff. for plan years beg. on or after Jan. 1, 2014, see Act §1255, as redesignated by Act §10103(f)(1).

SEC. 2709. COVERAGE FOR INDIVIDUALS PARTICIPATING IN APPROVED CLINICAL TRIALS.

(a) Coverage.—

(1) In general.—If a group health plan or a health insurance issuer offering group or individual health insurance coverage provides coverage to a qualified individual, then such plan or issuer—

Selected Provisions of PHSA After Amendment by PPACA. For sections prior to PPACA, see Part 4.

(A) may not deny the individual participation in the clinical trial referred to in subsection (b)(2);

(B) subject to subsection (c), may not deny (or limit or impose additional conditions on) the coverage of routine patient costs for items and services furnished in connection with participation in the trial; and

(C) may not discriminate against the individual on the basis of the individual's participation in such trial.

(2) Routine patient costs.—

(A) Inclusion.—For purposes of paragraph (1)(B), subject to subparagraph (B), routine patient costs include all items and services consistent with the coverage provided in the plan (or coverage) that is typically covered for a qualified individual who is not enrolled in a clinical trial.

(B) Exclusion.—For purposes of paragraph (1)(B), routine patient costs does not include—

(i) the investigational item, device, or service, itself;

(ii) items and services that are provided solely to satisfy data collection and analysis needs and that are not used in the direct clinical management of the patient; or

(iii) a service that is clearly inconsistent with widely accepted and established standards of care for a particular diagnosis.

(3) Use of in-network providers.—If one or more participating providers is participating in a clinical trial, nothing in paragraph (1) shall be construed as preventing a plan or issuer from requiring that a qualified individual participate in the trial through such a participating provider if the provider will accept the individual as a participant in the trial.

(4) Use of out-of-network.—Notwithstanding paragraph (3), paragraph (1) shall apply to a qualified individual participating in an approved clinical trial that is conducted outside the State in which the qualified individual resides.

(b) Qualified Individual Defined.—For purposes of subsection (a), the term "qualified individual" means an individual who is a participant or beneficiary in a health plan or with coverage described in subsection (a)(1) and who meets the following conditions:

(1) The individual is eligible to participate in an approved clinical trial according to the trial protocol with respect to treatment of cancer or other life-threatening disease or condition.

(2) Either—

(A) the referring health care professional is a participating health care provider and has concluded that the individual's participation in such trial would be appropriate based upon the individual

meeting the conditions described in paragraph (1); or

(B) the participant or beneficiary provides medical and scientific information establishing that the individual's participation in such trial would be appropriate based upon the individual meeting the conditions described in paragraph (1).

(c) Limitations on Coverage.—This section shall not be construed to require a group health plan, or a health insurance issuer offering group or individual health insurance coverage, to provide benefits for routine patient care services provided outside of the plan's (or coverage's) health care provider network unless out-of-network benefits are otherwise provided under the plan (or coverage).

(d) Approved Clinical Trial Defined.—

(1) In general.—In this section, the term "approved clinical trial" means a phase I, phase II, phase III, or phase IV clinical trial that is conducted in relation to the prevention, detection, or treatment of cancer or other life-threatening disease or condition and is described in any of the following subparagraphs:

(A) Federally funded trials.—The study or investigation is approved or funded (which may include funding through in-kind contributions) by one or more of the following:

(i) The National Institutes of Health.

(ii) The Centers for Disease Control and Prevention.

(iii) The Agency for Health Care Research and Quality.

(iv) The Centers for Medicare & Medicaid Services.

(v) cooperative group or center of any of the entities described in clauses (i) through (iv) or the Department of Defense or the Department of Veterans Affairs.

(vi) A qualified non-governmental research entity identified in the guidelines issued by the National Institutes of Health for center support grants.

(vii) Any of the following if the conditions described in paragraph (2) are met:

(I) The Department of Veterans Affairs.

(II) The Department of Defense.

(III) The Department of Energy.

(B) The study or investigation is conducted under an investigational new drug application reviewed by the Food and Drug Administration.

(C) The study or investigation is a drug trial that is exempt from having such an investigational new drug application.

(2) Conditions for Departments.—The conditions described in this paragraph, for a study or investigation conducted by a Department, are that the study or investigation has been reviewed and approved through a system of peer review that the Secretary determines—

(A) to be comparable to the system of peer review of studies and investigations used by the National Institutes of Health, and

(B) assures unbiased review of the highest scientific standards by qualified individuals who have no interest in the outcome of the review.

(e) Life-Threatening Condition Defined.—In this section, the term "life-threatening condition" means any disease or condition from which the likelihood of death is probable unless the course of the disease or condition is interrupted.

(f) Construction.—Nothing in this section shall be construed to limit a plan's or issuer's coverage with respect to clinical trials.

(g) Application to FEHBP.—Notwithstanding any provision of chapter 89 of title 5, United States Code, this section shall apply to health plans offered under the program under such chapter.

(h) Preemption.—Notwithstanding any other provision of this Act, nothing in this section shall preempt State laws that require a clinical trials policy for State regulated health insurance plans that is in addition to the policy required under this section.

Amendments to PHSA §2709

Patient Protection and Affordable Care Act, 2010 (Pub. L. No. 111-148), as follows:
• PHSA §2709 was added by Act §10103(c). Eff. for plan years beg. on or after Jan. 1, 2014, see Act §1255 (as redesignated by Act §10103(f)(1).

Editor's Note

PHSA §2709 [2710], as follows, is effective for plan years beginning on or after September 23, 2010.

SEC. 2709 [2710]. DISCLOSURE OF INFORMATION.

(a) Disclosure of Information by Health Plan Issuers.—In connection with the offering of any health insurance coverage to a small employer or an individual, a health insurance issuer—

(1) shall make a reasonable disclosure to such employer, or individual, as applicable, as part of its solicitation and sales materials, of the availability of information described in subsection (b), and

(2) upon request of such a employer, or individual, as applicable, provide such information.

(b) Information Described.—

(1) In general.—Subject to paragraph (3), with respect to a health insurance issuer offering health insurance coverage to a employer, or individual, as applicable, information described in this subsection is information concerning—

(A) the provisions of such coverage concerning issuer's right to change premium rates and the factors that may affect changes in premium rates; and

(B) the benefits and premiums available under all health insurance coverage for which the employer, or individual, as applicable, is qualified.

(2) Form of information.—Information under this subsection shall be provided to employers, or individuals, as applicable, in a manner determined to be understandable by the average employer, or individual, as applicable, and shall be sufficient to reasonably inform employers, or individuals, as applicable, of their rights and obligations under the health insurance coverage.

(3) Exception.—An issuer is not required under this section to disclose any information that is proprietary and trade secret information under applicable law.

Amendments to PHSA §2709 [2710]

Patient Protection and Affordable Care Act, 2010 (Pub. L. No. 111-148), as follows:
• **Note on Redesignation:** PHSA §2713 (former) was redesignated by Act §1001(3) as PHSA §2733, and amended, redesignated (as PHSA §2709) and transferred by Act §1563(c)(10) (as redesignated by Act §10107(b)(1)). Eff. for plan years beg. on or after date that is 6 months after date of enactment [date of enactment: Mar. 23, 2010].

Editor's Note

PHSA §2711, as follows, is effective for plan years beginning on or after September 23, 2010.

SEC. 2711. NO LIFETIME OR ANNUAL LIMITS.

(a) Prohibition.—

(1) In General.—A group health plan and a health insurance issuer offering group or individual health insurance coverage may not establish—

(A) lifetime limits on the dollar value of benefits for any participant or beneficiary; or

(B) except as provided in paragraph (2), annual limits on the dollar value of benefits for any participant or beneficiary.

Selected Provisions of PHSA After Amendment by PPACA. For sections prior to PPACA, see Part 4.

(2) Annual Limits Prior to 2014.—With respect to plan years beginning prior to January 1, 2014, a group health plan and a health insurance issuer offering group or individual health insurance coverage may only establish a restricted annual limit on the dollar value of benefits for any participant or beneficiary with respect to the scope of benefits that are essential health benefits under section 1302(b) of the Patient Protection and Affordable Care Act, as determined by the Secretary. In defining the term "restricted annual limit" for purposes of the preceding sentence, the Secretary shall ensure that access to needed services is made available with a minimal impact on premiums.

(b) Per Beneficiary Limits.—Subsection (a) shall not be construed to prevent a group health plan or health insurance coverage from placing annual or lifetime per beneficiary limits on specific covered benefits that are not essential health benefits under section 1302(b) of the Patient Protection and Affordable Care Act, to the extent that such limits are otherwise permitted under Federal or State law.

Amendments to PHSA §2711

Patient Protection and Affordable Care Act, 2010 (Pub. L. No. 111-148), as follows:
- **Note on Redesignation:** PHSA §2711 (former) was redesignated by Act §1001(3) as PHSA §2731 and amended, redesignated, and transferred to PHSA §2702 by Act §1563(c)(8) (as redesignated by Act §10107(b)(1)).
- PHSA §2711 was added by Act §1001(5) and amended by Act §10101(a) by replacing the entire text. Eff. for plan years beginning 6 months after date of enactment [date of enactment: Mar. 23, 2010], see Act §1004(a).

> #### *Editor's Note*
> PHSA §2712, as follows, is effective for plan years beginning on or after September 23, 2010.

SEC. 2712. PROHIBITION ON RESCISSIONS.

A group health plan and a health insurance issuer offering group or individual health insurance coverage shall not rescind such plan or coverage with respect to an enrollee once the enrollee is covered under such plan or coverage involved, except that this section shall not apply to a covered individual who has performed an act or practice that constitutes fraud or makes an intentional misrepresentation of material fact as prohibited by the terms of the plan or coverage. Such plan or coverage may not be cancelled except with prior notice to the enrollee, and only as permitted under section 2702(c) or 2742(b).

Amendments to PHSA §2712

Patient Protection and Affordable Care Act, 2010 (Pub. L. No. 111-148), as follows:

- **Note on Redesignation:** PHSA §2712 (former) was redesignated as PHSA §2732 by Act §1001(3), and amended, redesignated, and transferred to PHSA §2703 by Act §1563(c)(9) (as redesignated by Act §10107(b)(1)).
- PHSA §2712 was added by Act §1001(5). Eff. for plan years beginning on or after date that is 6 months after date of enactment [date of enactment: Mar. 23, 2010], see Act §1004(a).

> #### *Editor's Note*
> PHSA §2713, as follows, is effective for plan years beginning on or after September 23, 2010.

SEC. 2713. COVERAGE OF PREVENTIVE HEALTH SERVICES.

(a) In General.—A group health plan and a health insurance issuer offering group or individual health insurance coverage shall, at a minimum provide coverage for and shall not impose any cost sharing requirements for—

(1) evidence-based items or services that have in effect a rating of "A" or "B" in the current recommendations of the United States Preventive Services Task Force;

(2) immunizations that have in effect a recommendation from the Advisory Committee on Immunization Practices of the Centers for Disease Control and Prevention with respect to the individual involved; and

(3) with respect to infants, children, and adolescents, evidence-informed preventive care and screenings provided for in the comprehensive guidelines supported by the Health Resources and Services Administration.

(4) with respect to women, such additional preventive care and screenings not described in paragraph (1) as provided for in comprehensive guidelines supported by the Health Resources and Services Administration for purposes of this paragraph.

(5) for the purposes of this Act, and for the purposes of any other provision of law, the current recommendations of the United States Preventive Service Task Force regarding breast cancer screening, mammography, and prevention shall be considered the most current other than those issued in or around November 2009.

Nothing in this subsection shall be construed to prohibit a plan or issuer from providing coverage for services in addition to those recommended by United States Preventive Services Task Force or to deny coverage for services that are not recommended by such Task Force.

(b) Interval.—

(1) In general.—The Secretary shall establish a minimum interval between the date on which a recommendation described in subsection (a)(1) or (a)(2) or a guideline under subsection (a)(3) is issued and the plan year with respect to which the requirement described in subsection (a) is effective with respect to the service described in such recommendation or guideline.

(2) Minimum.—The interval described in paragraph (1) shall not be less than 1 year.

(c) Value-Based Insurance Design.—The Secretary may develop guidelines to permit a group health plan and a health insurance issuer offering group or individual health insurance coverage to utilize value-based insurance designs.

Amendments to PHSA §2713

Patient Protection and Affordable Care Act, 2010 (Pub. L. No. 111-148), as follows:
- **Note on Redesignation:** PHSA §2713 (former) was redesignated by Act §1001(3) as PHSA §2733, and amended, redesignated, and transferred to PHSA §2709 by Act §1563(c)(10) (as redesignated by Act §10107(b)(1)).
- PHSA §2713 was added by Act §1001(5). Eff. for plan years beginning on or after date that is 6 months after date of enactment [date of enactment: Mar. 23, 2010], see Act §1004(a).

> ### *Editor's Note*
>
> PHSA §2714, as follows, is effective for plan years beginning on or after September 23, 2010.

SEC. 2714. EXTENSION OF DEPENDENT COVERAGE.

(a) In General.—A group health plan and a health insurance issuer offering group or individual health insurance coverage that provides dependent coverage of children shall continue to make such coverage available for an adult child until the child turns 26 years of age. Nothing in this section shall require a health plan or a health insurance issuer described in the preceding sentence to make coverage available for a child of a child receiving dependent coverage.

(b) Regulations.—The Secretary shall promulgate regulations to define the dependents to which coverage shall be made available under subsection (a).

(c) Rule of Construction.—Nothing in this section shall be construed to modify the definition of "dependent" as used in the Internal Revenue Code of 1986 with respect to the tax treatment of the cost of coverage.

Amendments to PHSA §2714

Health Care and Education Reconciliation Act of 2010 (Pub. L. No. 111-152), as follows:

- PHSA §2714(a) was amended by Act §2301(b) by striking "(who is not married)". Eff. Mar. 30, 2010.

Patient Protection and Affordable Care Act, 2010 (Pub. L. No. 111-148), as follows:
- PHSA §2714 was added by Act §1001(5). Eff. for plan years beginning on or after date that is 6 months after date of enactment [date of enactment: Mar. 23, 2010], see Act §1004(a).

> ### *Editor's Note*
>
> PHSA §2715, as follows, is effective for plan years beginning on or after September 23, 2010.

SEC. 2715. DEVELOPMENT AND UTILIZATION OF UNIFORM EXPLANATION OF COVERAGE DOCUMENTS AND STANDARDIZED DEFINITIONS.

(a) In General.—Not later than 12 months after the date of enactment of the Patient Protection and Affordable Care Act, the Secretary shall develop standards for use by a group health plan and a health insurance issuer offering group or individual health insurance coverage, in compiling and providing to applicants, enrollees, and policyholders or certificate holders a summary of benefits and coverage explanation that accurately describes the benefits and coverage under the applicable plan or coverage. In developing such standards, the Secretary shall consult with the National Association of Insurance Commissioners (referred to in this section as the "NAIC"), a working group composed of representatives of health insurance-related consumer advocacy organizations, health insurance issuers, health care professionals, patient advocates including those representing individuals with limited English proficiency, and other qualified individuals.

(b) Requirements.—The standards for the summary of benefits and coverage developed under subsection (a) shall provide for the following:

(1) Appearance.—The standards shall ensure that the summary of benefits and coverage is presented in a uniform format that does not exceed 4 pages in length and does not include print smaller than 12-point font.

(2) Language.—The standards shall ensure that the summary is presented in a culturally and linguistically appropriate manner and utilizes terminology understandable by the average plan enrollee.

(3) Contents.—The standards shall ensure that the summary of benefits and coverage includes—

(A) uniform definitions of standard insurance terms and medical terms (consistent with subsection (g)) so that consumers may compare health insurance coverage and understand the terms of coverage (or exception to such coverage);

Selected Provisions of PHSA After Amendment by PPACA. For sections prior to PPACA, see Part 4.

(B) a description of the coverage, including cost sharing for—

(i) each of the categories of the essential health benefits described in subparagraphs (A) through (J) of section 1302(b)(1) of the Patient Protection and Affordable Care Act; and

(ii) other benefits, as identified by the Secretary;

(C) the exceptions, reductions, and limitations on coverage;

(D) the cost-sharing provisions, including deductible, coinsurance, and co-payment obligations;

(E) the renewability and continuation of coverage provisions;

(F) a coverage facts label that includes examples to illustrate common benefits scenarios, including pregnancy and serious or chronic medical conditions and related cost sharing, such scenarios to be based on recognized clinical practice guidelines;

(G) a statement of whether the plan or coverage—

(i) provides minimum essential coverage (as defined under section 5000A(f) of the Internal Revenue Code 1986); and

(ii) ensures that the plan or coverage share of the total allowed costs of benefits provided under the plan or coverage is not less than 60 percent of such costs;

(H) a statement that the outline is a summary of the policy or certificate and that the coverage document itself should be consulted to determine the governing contractual provisions; and

(I) a contact number for the consumer to call with additional questions and an Internet web address where a copy of the actual individual coverage policy or group certificate of coverage can be reviewed and obtained.

(c) Periodic Review and Updating.—The Secretary shall periodically review and update, as appropriate, the standards developed under this section.

(d) Requirement To Provide.—

(1) In general.—Not later than 24 months after the date of enactment of the Patient Protection and Affordable Care Act, each entity described in paragraph (3) shall provide, prior to any enrollment restriction, a summary of benefits and coverage explanation pursuant to the standards developed by the Secretary under subsection (a) to—

(A) an applicant at the time of application;

(B) an enrollee prior to the time of enrollment or reenrollment, as applicable; and

(C) a policyholder or certificate holder at the time of issuance of the policy or delivery of the certificate.

(2) Compliance.—An entity described in paragraph (3) is deemed to be in compliance with this section if the summary of benefits and coverage described in subsection (a) is provided in paper or electronic form.

(3) Entities in general.—An entity described in this paragraph is—

(A) a health insurance issuer (including a group health plan that is not a self-insured plan) offering health insurance coverage within the United States; or

(B) in the case of a self-insured group health plan, the plan sponsor or designated administrator of the plan (as such terms are defined in section 3(16) of the Employee Retirement Income Security Act of 1974).

(4) Notice of modifications.—If a group health plan or health insurance issuer makes any material modification in any of the terms of the plan or coverage involved (as defined for purposes of section 102 of the Employee Retirement Income Security Act of 1974) that is not reflected in the most recently provided summary of benefits and coverage, the plan or issuer shall provide notice of such modification to enrollees not later than 60 days prior to the date on which such modification will become effective.(e) Preemption.—The standards developed under subsection (a) shall preempt any related State standards that require a summary of benefits and coverage that provides less information to consumers than that required to be provided under this section, as determined by the Secretary.

(f) Failure To Provide.—An entity described in subsection (d)(3) that willfully fails to provide the information required under this section shall be subject to a fine of not more than $1,000 for each such failure. Such failure with respect to each enrollee shall constitute a separate offense for purposes of this subsection.

(g) Development of Standard Definitions.—

(1) In general.—The Secretary shall, by regulation, provide for the development of standards for the definitions of terms used in health insurance coverage, including the insurance-related terms described in paragraph (2) and the medical terms described in paragraph (3).

(2) Insurance-related terms.—The insurance-related terms described in this paragraph are premium, deductible, co-insurance, co-payment, out-of-pocket limit, preferred provider, non-preferred provider, out-of-network co-payments, UCR (usual, customary and reasonable) fees, excluded services, grievance and appeals, and such other terms as the Secretary determines are important to define so that consumers may compare health insurance coverage and understand the terms of their coverage.

(3) Medical terms.—The medical terms described in this paragraph are hospitalization, hospital outpatient care, emergency room care, physician services, prescription drug coverage, durable medical equipment, home health care, skilled nursing care, rehabilitation services, hospice services, emergency medical transportation, and such other terms as the Secretary determines are important to define so that consumers may compare the medical benefits offered by health insurance and understand the extent of those medical benefits (or exceptions to those benefits).

Amendments to PHSA §2715

Patient Protection and Affordable Care Act, 2010 (Pub. L. No. 111-148), as follows:

- PHSA §2715(a) was amended by Act §10101(b) by striking "and providing to enrollees" and inserting "and providing to applicants, enrollees, and policyholders or certificate holders". Eff. for plan years beg. on or after the date that is 6 months after date of enactment [date of enactment: Mar. 23, 2010], see Act §1004(a). PHSA §2715 was added by Act §1001(5). Eff. for plan years beg. on or after the date that is 6 months after date of enactment [date of enactment: Mar. 23, 2010], see Act §1004(a).

> ***Editor's Note***
>
> PHSA §2715A, as follows, is effective for plan years beginning on or after September 23, 2010.

SEC. 2715A. PROVISION OF ADDITIONAL INFORMATION.

A group health plan and a health insurance issuer offering group or individual health insurance coverage shall comply with the provisions of section 1311(e)(3) of the Patient Protection and Affordable Care Act, except that a plan or coverage that is not offered through an Exchange shall only be required to submit the information required to the Secretary and the State insurance commissioner, and make such information available to the public.

Amendments to PHSA §2715A

Patient Protection and Affordable Care Act, 2010 (Pub. L. No. 111-148), as follows:

- PHSA §2715A was added by Act §10101(c). Eff. for plan years beg. on or after the date that is 6 months after date of enactment [date of enactment: Mar. 23, 2010], see Act §1004(a).

> ***Editor's Note***
>
> PHSA §2716, as follows, is effective for plan years beginning on or after September 23, 2010.

SEC. 2716. PROHIBITION ON DISCRIMINATION IN FAVOR OF HIGHLY COMPENSATED INDIVIDUALS.

(a) In General.—A group health plan (other than a self-insured plan) shall satisfy the requirements of section 105(h)(2) of the Internal Revenue Code of 1986 (relating to prohibition on discrimination in favor of highly compensated individuals).

(b) Rules and Definitions.—For purposes of this section—

(1) Certain rules to apply.—Rules similar to the rules contained in paragraphs (3), (4), and (8) of section 105(h) of such Code shall apply.

(2) Highly compensated individual.—The term "highly compensated individual" has the meaning given such term by section 105(h)(5) of such Code.

Amendments to PHSA §2716

Patient Protection and Affordable Care Act, 2010 (Pub. L. No. 111-148), as follows:
- PHSA §2716 was added by Act §1001(5). Eff. for plan years beg. on or after date that is 6 months after date of enactment [date of enactment: Mar. 23, 2010], see Act §1004(a).
- PHSA §2716 was amended by Act §10101(d) by replacing the entire text. Eff. for plan years beg. on or after date that is 6 months after date of enactment [date of enactment: Mar. 23, 2010], see Act §1004(a).

> ***Editor's Note***
>
> PHSA §2717, as follows, is effective for plan years beginning on or after September 23, 2010.

SEC. 2717. ENSURING THE QUALITY OF CARE.

(a) Quality Reporting.—

(1) In general.—Not later than 2 years after the date of enactment of the Patient Protection and Affordable Care Act, the Secretary, in consultation with experts in health care quality and stakeholders, shall develop reporting requirements for use by a group health plan, and a health insurance issuer offering group or individual health insurance coverage, with respect to plan or coverage benefits and health care provider reimbursement structures that—

(A) improve health outcomes through the implementation of activities such as quality reporting,

Selected Provisions of PHSA After Amendment by PPACA. For sections prior to PPACA, see Part 4.

effective case management, care coordination, chronic disease management, and medication and care compliance initiatives, including through the use of the medical homes model as defined for purposes of section 3602 of the Patient Protection and Affordable Care Act, for treatment or services under the plan or coverage;

(B) implement activities to prevent hospital readmissions through a comprehensive program for hospital discharge that includes patient-centered education and counseling, comprehensive discharge planning, and post discharge reinforcement by an appropriate health care professional;

(C) implement activities to improve patient safety and reduce medical errors through the appropriate use of best clinical practices, evidence based medicine, and health information technology under the plan or coverage; and

(D) implement wellness and health promotion activities.

(2) Reporting requirements.—

(A) In general.—A group health plan and a health insurance issuer offering group or individual health insurance coverage shall annually submit to the Secretary, and to enrollees under the plan or coverage, a report on whether the benefits under the plan or coverage satisfy the elements described in subparagraphs (A) through (D) of paragraph (1).

(B) Timing of reports.—A report under subparagraph (A) shall be made available to an enrollee under the plan or coverage during each open enrollment period.

(C) Availability of reports.—The Secretary shall make reports submitted under subparagraph (A) available to the public through an Internet website.

(D) Penalties.—In developing the reporting requirements under paragraph (1), the Secretary may develop and impose appropriate penalties for noncompliance with such requirements.

(E) Exceptions.—In developing the reporting requirements under paragraph (1), the Secretary may provide for exceptions to such requirements for group health plans and health insurance issuers that substantially meet the goals of this section.

(b) Wellness and Prevention Programs.—For purposes of subsection (a)(1)(D), wellness and health promotion activities may include personalized wellness and prevention services, which are coordinated, maintained or delivered by a health care provider, a wellness and prevention plan manager, or a health, wellness or prevention services organization that conducts health risk assessments or offers ongoing face-to-face, telephonic or web-based intervention efforts for each of the program's participants, and which may include the following wellness and prevention efforts:

(1) Smoking cessation.

(2) Weight management.

(3) Stress management.

(4) Physical fitness.

(5) Nutrition.

(6) Heart disease prevention.

(7) Healthy lifestyle support.

(8) Diabetes prevention.

(c) Protection of Second Amendment Gun Rights.—

(1) Wellness and prevention programs.—A wellness and health promotion activity implemented under subsection (a)(1)(D) may not require the disclosure or collection of any information relating to—

(A) the presence or storage of a lawfully-possessed firearm or ammunition in the residence or on the property of an individual; or

(B) the lawful use, possession, or storage of a firearm or ammunition by an individual.

(2) Limitation on data collections.—None of the authorities provided to the Secretary under the Patient Protection and Affordable Care Act or an amendment made by that Act shall be construed to authorize or may be used for the collection of any information relating to—

(A) the lawful ownership or possession of a firearm or ammunition;

(B) the lawful use of a firearm or ammunition; or

(C) the lawful storage of a firearm or ammunition.

(3) Limitation on databases or data banks.—None of the authorities provided to the Secretary under the Patient Protection and Affordable Care Act or an amendment made by that Act shall be construed to authorize or may be used to maintain records of individual ownership or possession of a firearm or ammunition.

(4) Limitation on determination of premium rates or eligibility for health insurance.—A premium rate may not be increased, health insurance coverage may not be denied, and a discount, rebate, or reward offered for participation in a wellness program may not be reduced or withheld under any health benefit plan issued pursuant to or in accordance with the Patient Protection and Affordable Care Act or an amendment made by that Act on the basis of, or on reliance upon—

(A) the lawful ownership or possession of a firearm or ammunition; or

(B) the lawful use or storage of a firearm or ammunition.

(5) Limitation on data collection requirements for individuals.—No individual shall be required to disclose any information under any data collection activity authorized under the Patient Protection and Affordable Care Act or an amendment made by that Act relating to—

(A) the lawful ownership or possession of a firearm or ammunition; or

(B) the lawful use, possession, or storage of a firearm or ammunition.

(d) **Regulations.**—Not later than 2 years after the date of enactment of the Patient Protection and Affordable Care Act, the Secretary shall promulgate regulations that provide criteria for determining whether a reimbursement structure is described in subsection (a).

(e) **Study and Report.**—Not later than 180 days after the date on which regulations are promulgated under subsection (c), the Government Accountability Office shall review such regulations and conduct a study and submit to the Committee on Health, Education, Labor, and Pensions of the Senate and the Committee on Energy and Commerce of the House of Representatives a report regarding the impact the activities under this section have had on the quality and cost of health care.

Amendments to PHSA §2717

Patient Protection and Affordable Care Act, 2010 (Pub. L. No. 111-148), as follows:

- PHSA §2717 was added by Act §1001(5). Eff. for plan years beg. on or after date that is 6 months after date of enactment [date of enactment: Mar. 23, 2010], see Act §1004(a).
- PHSA §2717 was amended by Act §10101(e) by redesignating subsecs. (c) and (d) as subsecs. (d) and (e) and adding new subsec. (c). Eff. for plan years beg. on or after date that is 6 months after date of enactment [date of enactment: Mar. 23, 2010], see Act §1004(a).

> ### Editor's Note
>
> PHSA §2718, as follows, is effective for plan years beginning on or after September 23, 2010.

SEC. 2718. BRINGING DOWN THE COST OF HEALTH CARE COVERAGE.

(a) **Clear Accounting for Costs.**—A health insurance issuer offering group or individual health insurance coverage (including a grandfathered health plan) shall, with respect to each plan year, submit to the Secretary a report concerning the ratio of the incurred loss (or incurred claims) plus the loss adjustment expense (or change in contract reserves) to earned premiums. Such report shall include the percentage of total premium revenue, after accounting for collections or receipts for risk adjustment and risk corridors and payments of reinsurance, that such coverage expends—

(1) on reimbursement for clinical services provided to enrollees under such coverage;

(2) for activities that improve health care quality; and

(3) on all other non-claims costs, including an explanation of the nature of such costs, and excluding Federal and State taxes and licensing or regulatory fees.

The Secretary shall make reports received under this section available to the public on the Internet website of the Department of Health and Human Services.

(b) **Ensuring That Consumers Receive Value for Their Premium Payments.**—

(1) **Requirement to provide value for premium payments.**—

(A) Requirement.—Beginning not later than January 1, 2011, a health insurance issuer offering group or individual health insurance coverage (including a grandfathered health plan) shall, with respect to each plan year, provide an annual rebate to each enrollee under such coverage, on a pro rata basis, if the ratio of the amount of premium revenue expended by the issuer on costs described in paragraphs (1) and (2) of subsection (a) to the total amount of premium revenue (excluding Federal and State taxes and licensing or regulatory fees and after accounting for payments or receipts for risk adjustment, risk corridors, and reinsurance under sections 1341, 1342, and 1343 of the Patient Protection and Affordable Care Act) for the plan year (except as provided in subparagraph (B)(ii)), is less than—

(i) with respect to a health insurance issuer offering coverage in the large group market, 85 percent, or such higher percentage as a State may by regulation determine; or

(ii) with respect to a health insurance issuer offering coverage in the small group market or in the individual market, 80 percent, or such higher percentage as a State may by regulation determine, except that the Secretary may adjust such percentage with respect to a State if the Secretary determines that the application of such 80 percent may destabilize the individual market in such State.

(B) Rebate amount.—

(i) Calculation of amount.—The total amount of an annual rebate required under this paragraph shall be in an amount equal to the product of—

(I) the amount by which the percentage described in clause (i) or (ii) of subparagraph (A) exceeds the ratio described in such subparagraph; and

(II) the total amount of premium revenue (excluding Federal and State taxes and licensing or regulatory fees and after accounting for payments

Selected Provisions of PHSA After Amendment by PPACA. For sections prior to PPACA, see Part 4.

or receipts for risk adjustment, risk corridors, and reinsurance under sections 1341, 1342, and 1343 of the Patient Protection and Affordable Care Act) for such plan year.

(ii) Calculation based on average ratio.—Beginning on January 1, 2014, the determination made under subparagraph (A) for the year involved shall be based on the averages of the premiums expended on the costs described in such subparagraph and total premium revenue for each of the previous 3 years for the plan.

(2) Consideration in setting percentages.—In determining the percentages under paragraph (1), a State shall seek to ensure adequate participation by health insurance issuers, competition in the health insurance market in the State, and value for consumers so that premiums are used for clinical services and quality improvements.

(3) Enforcement.—The Secretary shall promulgate regulations for enforcing the provisions of this section and may provide for appropriate penalties.

(c) Definitions.—Not later than December 31, 2010, and subject to the certification of the Secretary, the National Association of Insurance Commissioners shall establish uniform definitions of the activities reported under subsection (a) and standardized methodologies for calculating measures of such activities, including definitions of which activities, and in what regard such activities, constitute activities described in subsection (a)(2). Such methodologies shall be designed to take into account the special circumstances of smaller plans, different types of plans, and newer plans.

(d) Adjustments.—The Secretary may adjust the rates described in subsection (b) if the Secretary determines appropriate on account of the volatility of the individual market due to the establishment of State Exchanges.

(e) Standard Hospital Charges.—Each hospital operating within the United States shall for each year establish (and update) and make public (in accordance with guidelines developed by the Secretary) a list of the hospital's standard charges for items and services provided by the hospital, including for diagnosis-related groups established under section 1886(d)(4) of the Social Security Act.

Amendments to PHSA §2718

Patient Protection and Affordable Care Act, 2010 (Pub. L. No. 111-148), as follows:

• PHSA §2718 was added by Act §1001(5). Eff. for plan years beg. on or after date that is 6 months after date of enactment [date of enactment: Mar. 23, 2010], see Act §1004(a).

• PHSA §2718 was amended by Act §10101(f) by replacing the entire text. Eff. for plan years beg. on or after date that is 6 months after date of enactment [date of enactment: Mar. 23, 2010], see Act §1004(a).

> **Editor's Note**
>
> PHSA §2719, as follows, is effective for plan years beginning on or after September 23, 2010.

SEC. 2719. APPEALS PROCESS.

(a) Internal Claims Appeals.—

(1) In general.—A group health plan and a health insurance issuer offering group or individual health insurance coverage shall implement an effective appeals process for appeals of coverage determinations and claims, under which the plan or issuer shall, at a minimum—

(A) have in effect an internal claims appeal process;

(B) provide notice to enrollees, in a culturally and linguistically appropriate manner, of available internal and external appeals processes, and the availability of any applicable office of health insurance consumer assistance or ombudsman established under section 2793 to assist such enrollees with the appeals processes; and

(C) allow an enrollee to review their file, to present evidence and testimony as part of the appeals process, and to receive continued coverage pending the outcome of the appeals process.

(2) Established processes.—To comply with paragraph (1)—

(A) a group health plan and a health insurance issuer offering group health coverage shall provide an internal claims and appeals process that initially incorporates the claims and appeals procedures (including urgent claims) set forth at section 2560.503-1 of title 29, Code of Federal Regulations, as published on November 21, 2000 (65 Fed. Reg. 70256), and shall update such process in accordance with any standards established by the Secretary of Labor for such plans and issuers; and

(B) a health insurance issuer offering individual health coverage, and any other issuer not subject to subparagraph (A), shall provide an internal claims and appeals process that initially incorporates the claims and appeals procedures set forth under applicable law (as in existence on the date of enactment of this section), and shall update such process in accordance with any standards established by the Secretary of Health and Human Services for such issuers.

(b) External Review.—A group health plan and a health insurance issuer offering group or individual health insurance coverage—

(1) shall comply with the applicable State external review process for such plans and issuers that, at a minimum, includes the consumer protections set forth in the Uniform External Review Model Act promulgated by the National Association of Insurance Commissioners and is binding on such plans; or

(2) shall implement an effective external review process that meets minimum standards established by the Secretary through guidance and that is similar to the process described under paragraph (1)—

(A) if the applicable State has not established an external review process that meets the requirements of paragraph (1); or

(B) if the plan is a self-insured plan that is not subject to State insurance regulation (including a State law that establishes an external review process described in paragraph (1)).

(c) Secretary Authority.—The Secretary may deem the external review process of a group health plan or health insurance issuer, in operation as of the date of enactment of this section, to be in compliance with the applicable process established under subsection (b), as determined appropriate by the Secretary.

Amendments to PHSA §2719

Patient Protection and Affordable Care Act, 2010 (Pub. L. No. 111-148), as follows:

- PHSA §2719 was added by Act §1001(5). Eff. for plan years beg. on or after date that is 6 months after date of enactment [date of enactment: Mar. 23, 2010], see Act §1004(a).
- PHSA §2719 was amended by Act §10101(g) by replacing the entire text. Eff. for plan years beg. on or after date that is 6 months after date of enactment [date of enactment: Mar. 23, 2010], see Act §1004(a).

> ### Editor's Note
> PHSA §2719A, as follows, is effective for plan years beginning on or after September 23, 2010.

SEC. 2719A. PATIENT PROTECTIONS.

(a) Choice of Health Care Professional.—If a group health plan, or a health insurance issuer offering group or individual health insurance coverage, requires or provides for designation by a participant, beneficiary, or enrollee of a participating primary care provider, then the plan or issuer shall permit each participant, beneficiary, and enrollee to designate any participating primary care provider who is available to accept such individual.

(b) Coverage of Emergency Services.—

(1) In general.—If a group health plan, or a health insurance issuer offering group or individual health insurance issuer, provides or covers any benefits with respect to services in an emergency department of a hospital, the plan or issuer shall cover

emergency services (as defined in paragraph (2)(B))—

(A) without the need for any prior authorization determination;

(B) whether the health care provider furnishing such services is a participating provider with respect to such services;

(C) in a manner so that, if such services are provided to a participant, beneficiary, or enrollee—

(i) by a nonparticipating health care provider with or without prior authorization; or

(ii)(I) such services will be provided without imposing any requirement under the plan for prior authorization of services or any limitation on coverage where the provider of services does not have a contractual relationship with the plan for the providing of services that is more restrictive than the requirements or limitations that apply to emergency department services received from providers who do have such a contractual relationship with the plan; and

(II) if such services are provided out-of-network, the cost-sharing requirement (expressed as a copayment amount or coinsurance rate) is the same requirement that would apply if such services were provided in-network;

(D) without regard to any other term or condition of such coverage (other than exclusion or coordination of benefits, or an affiliation or waiting period, permitted under section 2701 of this Act, section 701 of the Employee Retirement Income Security Act of 1974, or section 9801 of the Internal Revenue Code of 1986, and other than applicable cost-sharing).

(2) Definitions.—In this subsection:

(A) Emergency medical condition.—The term "emergency medical condition" means a medical condition manifesting itself by acute symptoms of sufficient severity (including severe pain) such that a prudent layperson, who possesses an average knowledge of health and medicine, could reasonably expect the absence of immediate medical attention to result in a condition described in clause (i), (ii), or (iii) of section 1867(e)(1)(A) of the Social Security Act.

(B) Emergency services.—The term "emergency services" means, with respect to an emergency medical condition—

(i) a medical screening examination (as required under section 1867 of the Social Security Act) that is within the capability of the emergency department of a hospital, including ancillary services routinely available to the emergency department to evaluate such emergency medical condition, and

(ii) within the capabilities of the staff and facilities available at the hospital, such further medical examination and treatment as are required under section 1867 of such Act to stabilize the patient.

(C) Stabilize.—The term "to stabilize", with respect to an emergency medical condition (as defined in subparagraph (A)), has the meaning give in section 1867(e)(3) of the Social Security Act (42 U.S.C. 1395dd(e)(3)).

(c) Access to Pediatric Care.—

(1) Pediatric care.—In the case of a person who has a child who is a participant, beneficiary, or enrollee under a group health plan, or health insurance coverage offered by a health insurance issuer in the group or individual market, if the plan or issuer requires or provides for the designation of a participating primary care provider for the child, the plan or issuer shall permit such person to designate a physician (allopathic or osteopathic) who specializes in pediatrics as the child's primary care provider if such provider participates in the network of the plan or issuer.

(2) Construction.—Nothing in paragraph (1) shall be construed to waive any exclusions of coverage under the terms and conditions of the plan or health insurance coverage with respect to coverage of pediatric care.

(d) Patient Access to Obstetrical and Gynecological Care.—

(1) General rights.—

(A) Direct access.—A group health plan, or health insurance issuer offering group or individual health insurance coverage, described in paragraph (2) may not require authorization or referral by the plan, issuer, or any person (including a primary care provider described in paragraph (2)(B)) in the case of a female participant, beneficiary, or enrollee who seeks coverage for obstetrical or gynecological care provided by a participating health care professional who specializes in obstetrics or gynecology. Such professional shall agree to otherwise adhere to such plan's or issuer's policies and procedures, including procedures regarding referrals and obtaining prior authorization and providing services pursuant to a treatment plan (if any) approved by the plan or issuer.

(B) Obstetrical and gynecological care.—A group health plan or health insurance issuer described in paragraph (2) shall treat the provision of obstetrical and gynecological care, and the ordering of related obstetrical and gynecological items and services, pursuant to the direct access described under subparagraph (A), by a participating health care professional who specializes in obstetrics or gynecology as the authorization of the primary care provider.

(2) Application of paragraph.—A group health plan, or health insurance issuer offering group or individual health insurance coverage, described in this paragraph is a group health plan or coverage that—

(A) provides coverage for obstetric or gynecologic care; and

(B) requires the designation by a participant, beneficiary, or enrollee of a participating primary care provider.

(3) Construction.—Nothing in paragraph (1) shall be construed to—

(A) waive any exclusions of coverage under the terms and conditions of the plan or health insurance coverage with respect to coverage of obstetrical or gynecological care; or

(B) preclude the group health plan or health insurance issuer involved from requiring that the obstetrical or gynecological provider notify the primary care health care professional or the plan or issuer of treatment decisions.

Amendments to PHSA §2719A

Patient Protection and Affordable Care Act, 2010 (Pub. L. No. 111-148), as follows:
- PHSA §2719A was added by Act §10101(h). Eff. for plan years beg. on or after date that is 6 months after date of enactment [date of enactment: Mar. 23, 2010], see Act §1004(a).

> *Editor's Note*
>
> PHSA §2722, as follows, is effective for plan years beginning on or after September 23, 2010.

SEC. 2722. EXCLUSION OF CERTAIN PLANS.

(a) Limitation on Application of Provisions Relating to Group Health Plans.—

(1) In general.—The requirements of subparts 1 and 2 shall apply with respect to group health plans only—

(A) subject to paragraph (2), in the case of a plan that is a nonfederal governmental plan, and

(B) with respect to health insurance coverage offered in connection with a group health plan (including such a plan that is a church plan or a governmental plan).

(2) Treatment of nonfederal governmental plans.—

(A) Election to be excluded.—Except as provided in subparagraph (D) or (E), if the plan sponsor of a nonfederal governmental plan which is a group health plan to which the provisions of subparts 1 and 2 otherwise apply makes an election under this subparagraph (in such form and manner as the Secretary may by regulations prescribe), then the requirements of such subparts insofar as they apply directly to group health plans (and not merely to group health insurance coverage) shall not apply to such governmental plans for such period except as provided in this paragraph.

(B) Period of election.—An election under subparagraph (A) shall apply—

(i) for a single specified plan year, or

(ii) in the case of a plan provided pursuant to a collective bargaining agreement, for the term of such agreement.

An election under clause (i) may be extended through subsequent elections under this paragraph.

(C) Notice to enrollees.—Under such an election, the plan shall provide for—

(i) notice to enrollees (on an annual basis and at the time of enrollment under the plan) of the fact and consequences of such election, and

(ii) certification and disclosure of creditable coverage under the plan with respect to enrollees in accordance with section 2701(e) [42 USCS §300gg(e)].

(D) Election not applicable to requirements concerning genetic information.—The election described in subparagraph (A) shall not be available with respect to the provisions of subsections (a)(1)(F), (b)(3), (c), and (d) of section 2702 and the provisions of sections 2701 and 2702(b) to the extent that such provisions apply to genetic information.

(E) Election not applicable.—The election described in subparagraph (A) shall not be available with respect to the provisions of subparts I and II [1 and 2].

(b) **Exception for Certain Benefits.**—The requirements of subparts 1 and 2 shall not apply to any individual coverage or any group health plan (or group health insurance coverage) in relation to its provision of excepted benefits described in section 2791(c)(1).

(c) **Exception for Certain Benefits if Certain Conditions Met.—**

(1) **Limited, excepted benefits.**—The requirements of subparts 1 and 2 shall not apply to any individual coverage or any group health plan (and group health insurance coverage offered in connection with a group health plan) in relation to its provision of excepted benefits described in section 2791(c)(2) if the benefits—

(A) are provided under a separate policy, certificate, or contract of insurance; or

(B) are otherwise not an integral part of the plan.

(2) **Noncoordinated, excepted benefits.**—The requirements of subparts 1 and 2 shall not apply to any individual coverage or any group health plan (and group health insurance coverage offered in connection with a group health plan) in relation to its provision of excepted benefits described in section 2791(c)(3) if all of the following conditions are met:

(A) The benefits are provided under a separate policy, certificate, or contract of insurance.

(B) There is no coordination between the provision of such benefits and any exclusion of benefits under any group health plan maintained by the same plan sponsor.

(C) Such benefits are paid with respect to an event without regard to whether benefits are provided with respect to such an event under any group health plan maintained by the same plan sponsor or, with respect to individual coverage, under any health insurance coverage maintained by the same health insurance issuer.

(3) **Supplemental excepted benefits.**—The requirements of this part shall not apply to any individual coverage or any group health plan (and group health insurance coverage) in relation to its provision of excepted benefits described in section 2791(c)(4) if the benefits are provided under a separate policy, certificate, or contract of insurance.

(d) **Treatment of Partnerships. For purposes of this part—**

(1) **Treatment as a group health plan.**—Any plan, fund, or program which would not be (but for this subsection) an employee welfare benefit plan and which is established or maintained by a partnership, to the extent that such plan, fund, or program provides medical care (including items and services paid for as medical care) to present or former partners in the partnership or to their dependents (as defined under the terms of the plan, fund, or program), directly or through insurance, reimbursement, or otherwise, shall be treated (subject to paragraph (2)) as an employee welfare benefit plan which is a group health plan.

(2) **Employer.**—In the case of a group health plan, the term "employer" also includes the partnership in relation to any partner.

(3) **Participants of group health plans.**—In the case of a group health plan, the term "participant" also includes—

(A) in connection with a group health plan maintained by a partnership, an individual who is a partner in relation to the partnership, or

(B) in connection with a group health plan maintained by a self-employed individual (under which one or more employees are participants), the self-employed individual,

Selected Provisions of PHSA After Amendment by PPACA. For sections prior to PPACA, see Part 4.

PHSA Sec. 2722(a)(2)(A)

if such individual is, or may become, eligible to receive a benefit under the plan or such individual's beneficiaries may be eligible to receive any such benefit.

Amendments to PHSA §2722

Patient Protection and Affordable Care Act, 2010 (Pub. L. No. 111-148), as follows:

- **Note on Redesignation:** PHSA §2721 (former) was redesignated as PHSA §2735 by Act §1001(4), and further redesignated as PHSA §2722 by Act §1563(c)(12)(D) (as redesignated by Act §10107(b)(1)).

- PHSA §2735 (former) was amended by Act §1563(a)(1) and (c)(12)(A) by striking subsec. (a). Eff. for plan years beg. on or after date that is 6 months after enactment [date of enactment: Mar. 23, 2010], see Act §1004(a). PHSA §2735(a) prior to deletion:

    (a) **Exception for certain small group health plans.** The requirements of subparts 1 and 3 shall not apply to any group health plan (and health insurance coverage offered in connection with a group health plan) for any plan year if, on the first day of such plan year, such plan has less than 2 participants who are current employees.

- PHSA §2735 (former) was amended further by Act §1563(a)(2) (as redesignated) in subsec. (b), para. (1), striking "1 through 3" and inserting "1 and 2", in para. (2), subpara. (A), striking "subparagraph (D)" and inserting "subparagraph (D) or (E)", striking "1 through 3" and inserting "1 and 2"; adding new subpara. (E); by Act §1563(a)(3) in subsec. (c), striking "1 through 3 shall not apply to any group" and inserting "1 and 2 shall not apply to any individual coverage or any group"; and by Act §1563(a)(4) in subsec. (d), para. (1), striking "1 through 3 shall not apply to any group" and inserting "1 and 2 shall not apply to any individual coverage or any group", in para. (2), striking "1 through 3 shall not apply to any group" and inserting "1 and 2 shall not apply to any individual coverage or any group", in subpara (C), by inserting "or, with respect to individual coverage, under any health insurance coverage maintained by the same health insurance issuer", and para. (3), striking "any group" and inserting "any individual coverage or any group". Eff. for plan years beg. on or after date that is 6 months after enactment [date of enactment: Mar. 23, 2010], see Act §1004(a). *Note:* Act §1563(a)(2)(B)(iii) (as redesignated) was amended by Act §10107(a) by striking "subpart 1" and inserting "subparts I and II" in new subpara. (E).

- PHSA §2735 (former) was amended by Act §1563(c)(12) by striking subsec. (a); striking "subparts 1 through 3" each place that such appears and inserting "subpart 1"; redesignating subsecs. (b)–(e) as (a)–(d); and redesignating PHSA §2735 (as redesignated) as PHSA §2722. Eff. for plan years beg. on or after date that is 6 months after enactment [date of enactment: Mar. 23, 2010], Act §1004(a).

Departments of Veterans Affairs and Housing and Urban Development, and Independent Agencies Appropriations Act, 1997 (Pub. L. No. 104-204), as follows:

- PHSA §2721(a) (former) was amended by Act §604(b)(1)(A) by substituting "subparts 1 and 3" for "subparts 1 and 2". Eff. for group health plans for plan years beg. on or after Jan. 1, 1998, see Act §604(c).

- PHSA §2721(b)–(d) (former) were amended by Act §604(b)(1)(B) by substituting "subparts 1 through 3" for "subparts 1 and 2" wherever appearing. Eff. for group health plans for plan years beg. on or after Jan. 1, 1998, see Act §604(c).

Health Insurance Portability and Accountability Act of 1996 (Pub. L. No. 104-191), as follows:

- PHSA §2721 (former) was added by Act §102(a). Eff. for group health plans, and health insurance coverage offered in connection with group health plans, for plan years beg. after June 30, 1997, except as otherwise provided, see Act §102(c).

> ### *Editor's Note*
>
> PHSA §2723, as follows, is effective for plan years beginning on or after September 23, 2010.

SEC. 2723. ENFORCEMENT.

(a) State Enforcement.—

(1) State authority.—Subject to section 2723 [2724], each State may require that health insurance issuers that issue, sell, renew, or offer health insurance coverage in the State in the individual or group market meet the requirements of this part with respect to such issuers.

(2) Failure to implement provisions.—In the case of a determination by the Secretary that a State has failed to substantially enforce a provision (or provisions) in this part with respect to health insurance issuers in the State, the Secretary shall enforce such provision (or provisions) under subsection (b) insofar as they relate to the issuance, sale, renewal, and offering of health insurance coverage in connection with group health plans or individual health insurance coverage in such State.

(b) Secretarial Enforcement Authority.—

(1) Limitation.—The provisions of this subsection shall apply to enforcement of a provision (or provisions) of this part only—

(A) as provided under subsection (a)(2); and

(B) with respect to individual health insurance coverage or group health plans that are non-Federal governmental plans.

(2) Imposition of penalties.—In the cases described in paragraph (1)—

(A) In general.—Subject to the succeeding provisions of this subsection, any non-Federal governmental plan that is a group health plan and any health insurance issuer that fails to meet a provision of this part applicable to such plan or issuer is subject to a civil money penalty under this subsection.

(B) Liability for penalty. In the case of a failure by—

(i) a health insurance issuer, the issuer is liable for such penalty, or

(ii) a group health plan that is a non-Federal governmental plan which is—

(I) sponsored by 2 or more employers, the plan is liable for such penalty, or

(II) not so sponsored, the employer is liable for such penalty.

(C) Amount of penalty.—

Selected Provisions of PHSA After Amendment by PPACA. For sections prior to PPACA, see Part 4.

(i) In general.—The maximum amount of penalty imposed under this paragraph is $ 100 for each day for each individual with respect to which such a failure occurs.

(ii) Considerations in imposition.—In determining the amount of any penalty to be assessed under this paragraph, the Secretary shall take into account the previous record of compliance of the entity being assessed with the applicable provisions of this part and the gravity of the violation.

(iii) Limitations.—

(I) Penalty not to apply where failure not discovered exercising reasonable diligence. No civil money penalty shall be imposed under this paragraph on any failure during any period for which it is established to the satisfaction of the Secretary that none of the entities against whom the penalty would be imposed knew, or exercising reasonable diligence would have known, that such failure existed.

(II) Penalty not to apply to failures corrected within 30 days. No civil money penalty shall be imposed under this paragraph on any failure if such failure was due to reasonable cause and not to willful neglect, and such failure is corrected during the 30-day period beginning on the first day any of the entities against whom the penalty would be imposed knew, or exercising reasonable diligence would have known, that such failure existed.

(D) Administrative review.—

(i) Opportunity for hearing.—The entity assessed shall be afforded an opportunity for hearing by the Secretary upon request made within 30 days after the date of the issuance of a notice of assessment. In such hearing the decision shall be made on the record pursuant to section 554 of title 5, United States Code. If no hearing is requested, the assessment shall constitute a final and unappealable order.

(ii) Hearing procedure.—If a hearing is requested, the initial agency decision shall be made by an administrative law judge, and such decision shall become the final order unless the Secretary modifies or vacates the decision. Notice of intent to modify or vacate the decision of the administrative law judge shall be issued to the parties within 30 days after the date of the decision of the judge. A final order which takes effect under this paragraph shall be subject to review only as provided under subparagraph (E).

(E) Judicial review.—

(i) Filing of action for review.—Any entity against whom an order imposing a civil money penalty has been entered after an agency hearing under this paragraph may obtain review by the United States district court for any district in which such entity is located or the United States District Court for the District of Columbia by filing a notice of appeal in such court within 30 days from the date of such order, and simultaneously sending a copy of such notice by registered mail to the Secretary.

(ii) Certification of administrative record.—The Secretary shall promptly certify and file in such court the record upon which the penalty was imposed.

(iii) Standard for review.—The findings of the Secretary shall be set aside only if found to be unsupported by substantial evidence as provided by section 706(2)(E) of title 5, United States Code.

(iv) Appeal.—Any final decision, order, or judgment of the district court concerning such review shall be subject to appeal as provided in chapter 83 of title 28 of such Code.

(F) Failure to pay assessment; maintenance of action.—

(i) Failure to pay assessment.—If any entity fails to pay an assessment after it has become a final and unappealable order, or after the court has entered final judgment in favor of the Secretary, the Secretary shall refer the matter to the Attorney General who shall recover the amount assessed by action in the appropriate United States district court.

(ii) Nonreviewability.—In such action the validity and appropriateness of the final order imposing the penalty shall not be subject to review.

(G) Payment of penalties.—Except as otherwise provided, penalties collected under this paragraph shall be paid to the Secretary (or other officer) imposing the penalty and shall be available without appropriation and until expended for the purpose of enforcing the provisions with respect to which the penalty was imposed.

(3) Enforcement authority relating to genetic discrimination.—

(A) General rule.—In the cases described in paragraph (1), notwithstanding the provisions of paragraph (2)(C), the succeeding subparagraphs of this paragraph shall apply with respect to an action under this subsection by the Secretary with respect to any failure of a health insurance issuer in connection with a group health plan, to meet the requirements of subsection (a)(1)(F), (b)(3), (c), or (d) of section 2702 or section 2701 or 2702(b)(1) with respect to genetic information in connection with the plan.

(B) Amount.—

(i) In general.—The amount of the penalty imposed under this paragraph shall be $ 100 for each day in the noncompliance period with respect to each participant or beneficiary to whom such failure relates.

(ii) Noncompliance period.—For purposes of this paragraph, the term "noncompliance period" means, with respect to any failure, the period—

(I) beginning on the date such failure first occurs; and

(II) ending on the date the failure is corrected.

(C) Minimum penalties where failure discovered.—Notwithstanding clauses (i) and (ii) of subparagraph (D):

(i) In general.—In the case of 1 or more failures with respect to an individual—

(I) which are not corrected before the date on which the plan receives a notice from the Secretary of such violation; and

(II) which occurred or continued during the period involved;

the amount of penalty imposed by subparagraph (A) by reason of such failures with respect to such individual shall not be less than $ 2,500.

(ii) Higher minimum penalty where violations are more than de minimis.—To the extent violations for which any person is liable under this paragraph for any year are more than de minimis, clause (i) shall be applied by substituting "$ 15,000" for "$ 2,500" with respect to such person.

(D) Limitations.—

(i) Penalty not to apply where failure not discovered exercising reasonable diligence.—No penalty shall be imposed by subparagraph (A) on any failure during any period for which it is established to the satisfaction of the Secretary that the person otherwise liable for such penalty did not know, and exercising reasonable diligence would not have known, that such failure existed.

(ii) Penalty not to apply to failures corrected within certain periods.—No penalty shall be imposed by subparagraph (A) on any failure if—

(I) such failure was due to reasonable cause and not to willful neglect; and

(II) such failure is corrected during the 30-day period beginning on the first date the person otherwise liable for such penalty knew, or exercising reasonable diligence would have known, that such failure existed.

(iii) Overall limitation for unintentional failures.—In the case of failures which are due to reasonable cause and not to willful neglect, the penalty imposed by subparagraph (A) for failures shall not exceed the amount equal to the lesser of—

(I) 10 percent of the aggregate amount paid or incurred by the employer (or predecessor em-

ployer) during the preceding taxable year for group health plans; or

(II) $ 500,000.

(E) Waiver by Secretary.—In the case of a failure which is due to reasonable cause and not to willful neglect, the Secretary may waive part or all of the penalty imposed by subparagraph (A) to the extent that the payment of such penalty would be excessive relative to the failure involved.

Amendments to PHSA §2723

Patient Protection and Affordable Care Act, 2010 (Pub. L. No. 111-148), as follows:
- **Note on Redesignation.** PHSA §2722 (former) was redesignated as PHSA §2736 by Act §1001 (4) and further redesignated as PHSA §2723 by Act §1563(c)(13)(C) (as redesignated by Act §10107(b)(1)).
- PHSA §2736 (former) was amended by Act §1563(c)(13) in subsec. (a), para. (1) by striking "small or large group markets" and inserting "individual or group market"; and in para. (2) by inserting "or individual health insurance coverage" after "group health plans"; and in subsec. (b)(1)(B) by inserting "individual health insurance coverage or" after "respect to". Eff. for plan years beg. on or after date that is 6 months from date of enactment [date of enactment: Mar. 23, 2010], see Act §1004(a).

Genetic Information Nondiscrimination Act of 2008 (Pub. L. No. 110-233), as follows:
- PHSA §2722(b)(3) (former) was added by Act §102(a)(5). Eff. generally for plan years beg. 1 year after date of enactment [date of enactment: May 21, 2008].

Departments of Veterans Affairs and Housing and Urban Development, and Independent Agencies Appropriations Act, 1997 (Pub. L. No. 104-204), as follows:
- PHSA §2722 (former) was amended by Act §604(a)(2). Eff. for group health plans for plan years beg. on or after Jan. 1, 1998, see Act §604(c).

Health Insurance Portability and Accountability Act of 1996 (Pub. L. No. 104-191), as follows:
- PHSA §2722 (former) was added by Act §102(a). Eff. for group health plans, and health insurance coverage offered in connection with group health plans, for plan years beg. after June 30, 1997, except as otherwise provided, see Act §102(c).

> ### *Editor's Note*
> PHSA §2724, as follows, is effective for plan years beginning on or after September 23, 2010.

SEC. 2724. PREEMPTION; STATE FLEXIBILITY; CONSTRUCTION.

(a) Continued Applicability of State Law With Respect to Health Insurance Issuers.—

(1) In general.—Subject to paragraph (2) and except as provided in subsection (b), this part and part C insofar as it relates to this part shall not be construed to supersede any provision of State law which establishes, implements, or continues in effect any standard or requirement solely relating to health insurance issuers in connection with individual or group health insurance coverage except to the extent that such standard or requirement prevents the application of a requirement of this part.

(2) Continued preemption with respect to group health plans.—Nothing in this part shall be construed to affect or modify the provisions of section 514 of the Employee Retirement Income Security Act of 1974 with respect to group health plans.

(b) Special Rules in Case of Portability Requirements.—

(1) In general.—Subject to paragraph (2), the provisions of this part relating to health insurance coverage offered by a health insurance issuer supersede any provision of State law which establishes, implements, or continues in effect a standard or requirement applicable to imposition of a preexisting condition exclusion specifically governed by section 701 which differs from the standards or requirements specified in such section.

(2) Exceptions.—Only in relation to health insurance coverage offered by a health insurance issuer, the provisions of this part do not supersede any provision of State law to the extent that such provision—

(i) substitutes for the reference to "6-month period" in section 2701(a)(1) a reference to any shorter period of time;

(ii) substitutes for the reference to "12 months" and "18 months" in section 2701(a)(2) a reference to any shorter period of time;

(iii) substitutes for the references to "63" days in sections 2701(c)(2)(A) and 2701(d)(4)(A) a reference to any greater number of days;

(iv) substitutes for the reference to "30-day period" in sections 2701(b)(2) and 2701(d)(1) a reference to any greater period;

(v) prohibits the imposition of any preexisting condition exclusion in cases not described in section 2701(d) or expands the exceptions described in such section;

(vi) requires special enrollment periods in addition to those required under section 2701(f); or

(vii) reduces the maximum period permitted in an affiliation period under section 2701(g)(1)(B).

(c) Rules of Construction.—Nothing in this part (other than section 2704) shall be construed as requiring a group health plan or health insurance coverage to provide specific benefits under the terms of such plan or coverage.

(d) Definitions.—For purposes of this section—

(1) State law.—The term "State law" includes all laws, decisions, rules, regulations, or other State action having the effect of law, of any State. A law of the United States applicable only to the District of Columbia shall be treated as a State law rather than a law of the United States.

(2) State.—The term "State" includes a State (including the Northern Mariana Islands), any political subdivisions of a State or such Islands, or any agency or instrumentality of either.

Amendments to PHSA §2724

Patient Protection and Affordable Care Act, 2010 (Pub. L. No. 111-148), as follows:

● **Note on Redesignation:** PHSA §2723 (former) was redesignated as PHSA §2737 by Act §1001(4) and further redesignated as PHSA §2724 by Act §1563(c)(14)(B) (as redesignated by Act §10107(b)(1)).

● PHSA §2737 (former) was amended by Act §1563(c)(14)(A) (as redesignated) by inserting "individual or" before "group health insurance". Eff. for plan years beg. on or after date that is 6 months after date of enactment [date of enactment: Mar. 23, 2010], see Act §1004(a).

Department of Veterans Affairs and Housing and Urban Development, and Independent Agencies Appropriations Act, 1997 (Pub. L. No. 104-204), as follows:

● PHSA §2723 (former) was amended by Act §604(b)(2) in subsec. (c) by inserting "(other than section 300gg-4 of this title)" after "part". Eff. in general for group health plans for plan years beg. on or after Jan. 1, 1998, Act §604(c).

Health Insurance Portability and Accountability Act of 1996 (Pub. L. No. 104-191), as follows:

● PHSA §2723 (former) was added by Act §102(a). Eff. generally for group health plans, and health insurance coverage offered in connection with group health plans, for plan years beg. after June 30, 1997, except as otherwise provided, Act §102(c).

> **Editor's Note**
>
> PHSA §2725, as follows, is effective for plan years beginning on or after September 23, 2010.

SEC. 2725. STANDARDS RELATING TO BENEFITS FOR MOTHERS AND NEWBORNS.

(a) Requirements for Minimum Hospital Stay Following Birth.—

(1) In general.—A group health plan, and a health insurance issuer offering group or individual health insurance coverage, may not—

(A) except as provided in paragraph (2)—

(i) restrict benefits for any hospital length of stay in connection with childbirth for the mother or newborn child, following a normal vaginal delivery, to less than 48 hours, or

(ii) restrict benefits for any hospital length of stay in connection with childbirth for the mother or newborn child, following a cesarean section, to less than 96 hours, or

(B) require that a provider obtain authorization from the plan or the issuer for prescribing any length of stay required under subparagraph (A) (without regard to paragraph (2)).

Selected Provisions of PHSA After Amendment by PPACA. For sections prior to PPACA, see Part 4.

(2) Exception.—Paragraph (1)(A) shall not apply in connection with any group health plan or health insurance issuer in any case in which the decision to discharge the mother or her newborn child prior to the expiration of the minimum length of stay otherwise required under paragraph (1)(A) is made by an attending provider in consultation with the mother.

(b) Prohibitions.—A group health plan, and a health insurance issuer offering group or individual health insurance coverage, may not—

(1) deny to the mother or her newborn child eligibility, or continued eligibility, to enroll or to renew coverage under the terms of the plan or coverage, solely for the purpose of avoiding the requirements of this section;

(2) provide monetary payments or rebates to mothers to encourage such mothers to accept less than the minimum protections available under this section;

(3) penalize or otherwise reduce or limit the reimbursement of an attending provider because such provider provided care to an individual participant or beneficiary in accordance with this section;

(4) provide incentives (monetary or otherwise) to an attending provider to induce such provider to provide care to an individual participant or beneficiary in a manner inconsistent with this section; or

(5) subject to subsection (c)(3), restrict benefits for any portion of a period within a hospital length of stay required under subsection (a) in a manner which is less favorable than the benefits provided for any preceding portion of such stay.

(c) Rules of Construction.—

(1) Nothing in this section shall be construed to require a mother who is a participant or beneficiary—

(A) to give birth in a hospital; or

(B) to stay in the hospital for a fixed period of time following the birth of her child.

(2) This section shall not apply with respect to any group health plan, or any health insurance issuer offering group or individual health insurance coverage, which does not provide benefits for hospital lengths of stay in connection with childbirth for a mother or her newborn child.

(3) Nothing in this section shall be construed as preventing a group health plan or health insurance issuer from imposing deductibles, coinsurance, or other cost-sharing in relation to benefits for hospital lengths of stay in connection with childbirth for a mother or newborn child under the plan (or under health insurance coverage offered in connection with a group health plan), except that such coinsurance or other cost-sharing for any portion of a period within a hospital length of stay required under subsection (a) may not be greater than such coinsurance or cost-sharing for any preceding portion of such stay.

(d) Notice.—A group health plan under this part shall comply with the notice requirement under section 711(d) of the Employee Retirement Income Security Act of 1974 with respect to the requirements of this section as if such section applied to such plan.

(e) Level and Type of Reimbursements.—Nothing in this section shall be construed to prevent a group health plan or a health insurance issuer offering group or individual health insurance coverage from negotiating the level and type of reimbursement with a provider for care provided in accordance with this section.

(f) Preemption; Exception for Health Insurance Coverage in Certain States.—

(1) In general.—The requirements of this section shall not apply with respect to health insurance coverage if there is a State law (as defined in section 2723(d)(1)) for a State that regulates such coverage that is described in any of the following subparagraphs:

(A) Such State law requires such coverage to provide for at least a 48-hour hospital length of stay following a normal vaginal delivery and at least a 96- hour hospital length of stay following a cesarean section.

(B) Such State law requires such coverage to provide for maternity and pediatric care in accordance with guidelines established by the American College of Obstetricians and Gynecologists, the American Academy of Pediatrics, or other established professional medical associations.

(C) Such State law requires, in connection with such coverage for maternity care, that the hospital length of stay for such care is left to the decision of (or required to be made by) the attending provider in consultation with the mother.

(2) Construction.—Section 2723(a)(1) shall not be construed as superseding a State law described in paragraph (1).

Amendments to PHSA §2725

Patient Protection and Affordable Care Act, 2010 (Pub. L. No. 111-148), as follows:

- Note on Redesignation: PHSA §2704 (former) was redesignated as PHSA §2725 by Act §1001(2). Act §1562, which amended this section, was redesignated as Act §1563 by Act §10107(b)(1).

- PHSA §2725 was amended by Act §1563(c)(3) (as redesignated) in subsec. (a) by striking "health insurance issuer offering group health insurance coverage" and inserting "health insurance issuer offering group or individual health insurance coverage"; in subsec. (b), by striking "health insurance issuer offering group health insurance coverage in connection with a group health plan" and inserting "health insurance issuer offering group or individual health insurance coverage", in para. (1), by striking "plan" and inserting "plan or coverage"; in subsec. (c), in para. (2), by striking "group health insurance coverage offered by a health insurance issuer" and inserting "health insurance issuer offering group or individual health insurance coverage" and, in para. (3), by striking "issuer" and inserting "health insurance issuer"; in subsec. (e), by striking "health insurance issuer offering group health insurance coverage" and inserting "health insurance issuer offering group or individual health insurance coverage. Eff. for plan years beg. on or after date that is 6 months after date of enactment [date of enactment: Mar. 23, 2010], see Act §1004(a).

Department of Veterans Affairs and Housing and Urban Development, and Independent Agencies Appropriations Act, 1997 (Pub. L. No. 104-204), as follows:

● PHSA §2704 (former) was added by Act §604(a)(3). Eff. generally for group health plans for plan years beg. on or after Jan. 1, 1998, see Act §604(c).

> ### Editor's Note
>
> PHSA §2726, as follows, is effective for plan years beginning on or after September 23, 2010.

SEC. 2726. PARITY IN MENTAL HEALTH AND SUBSTANCE USE DISORDER BENEFITS.

(a) In General.—

(1) Aggregate lifetime limits.—In the case of a group health plan or a health insurance issuer offering group or individual health insurance coverage that provides both medical and surgical benefits and mental health or substance use disorder benefits—

(A) Noo lifetime limit.—If the plan or coverage does not include an aggregate lifetime limit on substantially all medical and surgical benefits, the plan or coverage may not impose any aggregate lifetime limit on mental health or substance use disorder benefits.

(B) Lifetime limit.—If the plan or coverage includes an aggregate lifetime limit on substantially all medical and surgical benefits (in this paragraph referred to as the "applicable lifetime limit"), the plan or coverage shall either—

(i) apply the applicable lifetime limit both to the medical and surgical benefits to which it otherwise would apply and to mental health and substance use disorder benefits and not distinguish in the application of such limit between such medical and surgical benefits and mental health and substance use disorder benefits; or

(ii) not include any aggregate lifetime limit on mental health or substance use disorder benefits that is less than the applicable lifetime limit.

(C) Rule in case of different limits.—In the case of a plan or coverage that is not described in subparagraph (A) or (B) and that includes no or different aggregate lifetime limits on different categories of medical and surgical benefits, the Secretary shall establish rules under which subparagraph (B) is applied to such plan or coverage with respect to

mental health and substance use disorder benefits by substituting for the applicable lifetime limit an average aggregate lifetime limit that is computed taking into account the weighted average of the aggregate lifetime limits applicable to such categories.

(2) Annual limits.—In the case of a group health plan or a health insurance issuer offering group or individual health insurance coverage that provides both medical and surgical benefits and mental health or substance use disorder benefits—

(A) No annual limit.—If the plan or coverage does not include an annual limit on substantially all medical and surgical benefits, the plan or coverage may not impose any annual limit on mental health or substance use disorder benefits.

(B) Annual limit.—If the plan or coverage includes an annual limit on substantially all medical and surgical benefits (in this paragraph referred to as the "applicable annual limit"), the plan or coverage shall either—

(i) apply the applicable annual limit both to medical and surgical benefits to which it otherwise would apply and to mental health and substance use disorder benefits and not distinguish in the application of such limit between such medical and surgical benefits and mental health and substance use disorder benefits; or

(ii) not include any annual limit on mental health or substance use disorder benefits that is less than the applicable annual limit.

(C) Rule in case of different limits.—In the case of a plan or coverage that is not described in subparagraph (A) or (B) and that includes no or different annual limits on different categories of medical and surgical benefits, the Secretary shall establish rules under which subparagraph (B) is applied to such plan or coverage with respect to mental health and substance use disorder benefits by substituting for the applicable annual limit an average annual limit that is computed taking into account the weighted average of the annual limits applicable to such categories.

(3) Financial requirements and treatment limitations.—

(A) In general.—In the case of a group health plan or a health insurance issuer offering group or individual health insurance coverage that provides both medical and surgical benefits and mental health or substance use disorder benefits, such plan or coverage shall ensure that—

(i) the financial requirements applicable to such mental health or substance use disorder benefits are no more restrictive than the predominant financial requirements applied to substantially all medical and surgical benefits covered by the plan (or coverage), and there are no separate cost sharing requirements that are applicable only with respect to mental health or substance use disorder benefits; and

(ii) the treatment limitations applicable to such mental health or substance use disorder benefits are no more restrictive than the predominant treatment limitations applied to substantially all medical and surgical benefits covered by the plan (or coverage) and there are no separate treatment limitations that are applicable only with respect to mental health or substance use disorder benefits.

(B) Definitions.—In this paragraph:

(i) Financial requirement.—The term "financial requirement" includes deductibles, copayments, coinsurance, and out-of-pocket expenses, but excludes an aggregate lifetime limit and an annual limit subject to paragraphs (1) and (2).

(ii) Predominant.—A financial requirement or treatment limit is considered to be predominant if it is the most common or frequent of such type of limit or requirement.

(iii) Treatment limitation.—The term "treatment limitation" includes limits on the frequency of treatment, number of visits, days of coverage, or other similar limits on the scope or duration of treatment.

(4) **Availability of plan information.**—The criteria for medical necessity determinations made under the plan with respect to mental health or substance use disorder benefits (or the health insurance coverage offered in connection with the plan with respect to such benefits) shall be made available by the plan administrator (or the health insurance issuer offering such coverage) in accordance with regulations to any current or potential participant, beneficiary, or contracting provider upon request. The reason for any denial under the plan (or coverage) of reimbursement or payment for services with respect to mental health or substance use disorder benefits in the case of any participant or beneficiary shall, on request or as otherwise required, be made available by the plan administrator (or the health insurance issuer offering such coverage) to the participant or beneficiary in accordance with regulations.

(5) **Out-of-network providers.**—In the case of a plan or coverage that provides both medical and surgical benefits and mental health or substance use disorder benefits, if the plan or coverage provides coverage for medical or surgical benefits provided by out-of-network providers, the plan or coverage shall provide coverage for mental health or substance use disorder benefits provided by out-of-network providers in a manner that is consistent with the requirements of this section.

(b) **Construction.**—Nothing in this section shall be construed—

(1) as requiring a group health plan or a health insurance issuer offering group or individual health insurance coverage to provide any mental health or substance use disorder benefits; or

(2) in the case of a group health plan or a health insurance issuer offering group or individual health insurance coverage that provides mental health or substance use disorder benefits, as affecting the terms and conditions of the plan or coverage relating to such benefits under the plan or coverage, except as provided in subsection (a).

(c) **Exemptions.**—

(1) **Small employer exemption.**—This section shall not apply to any group health plan and a health insurance issuer offering group or individual health insurance coverage for any plan year of a small employer (as defined in section 2791(e)(4), except that for purposes of this paragraph such term shall include employers with 1 employee in the case of an employer residing in a State that permits small groups to include a single individual).

(2) **Cost exemption.**—

(A) In general.—With respect to a group health plan or a health insurance issuer offering group or individual health insurance coverage, if the application of this section to such plan (or coverage) results in an increase for the plan year involved of the actual total costs of coverage with respect to medical and surgical benefits and mental health and substance use disorder benefits under the plan (as determined and certified under subparagraph (C)) by an amount that exceeds the applicable percentage described in subparagraph (B) of the actual total plan costs, the provisions of this section shall not apply to such plan (or coverage) during the following plan year, and such exemption shall apply to the plan (or coverage) for 1 plan year. An employer may elect to continue to apply mental health and substance use disorder parity pursuant to this section with respect to the group health plan (or coverage) involved regardless of any increase in total costs.

(B) Applicable percentage.—With respect to a plan (or coverage), the applicable percentage described in this subparagraph shall be—

(i) 2 percent in the case of the first plan year in which this section is applied; and

(ii) 1 percent in the case of each subsequent plan year.

(C) Determinations by actuaries.—Determinations as to increases in actual costs under a plan (or coverage) for purposes of this section shall be made and certified by a qualified and licensed actuary who is a member in good standing of the American Academy of Actuaries. All such determinations shall be in a written report prepared by the actuary. The report, and all underlying documentation relied upon by the actuary, shall be maintained by the group health plan or health insurance issuer for a period of 6 years following the notification made under subparagraph (E).

(D) 6-month determinations.—If a group health plan (or a health insurance issuer offering coverage in connection with a group health plan) seeks an exemption under this paragraph, determinations under subparagraph (A) shall be made after such plan (or coverage) has complied with this section for the first 6 months of the plan year involved.

(E) Notification.—

(i) In general.—A group health plan (or a health insurance issuer offering coverage in connection with a group health plan) that, based upon a certification described under subparagraph (C), qualifies for an exemption under this paragraph, and elects to implement the exemption, shall promptly notify the Secretary, the appropriate State agencies, and participants and beneficiaries in the plan of such election.

(ii) Requirement.—A notification to the Secretary under clause (i) shall include—

(I) a description of the number of covered lives under the plan (or coverage) involved at the time of the notification, and as applicable, at the time of any prior election of the cost-exemption under this paragraph by such plan (or coverage);(II) for both the plan year upon which a cost exemption is sought and the year prior, a description of the actual total costs of coverage with respect to medical and surgical benefits and mental health and substance use disorder benefits under the plan; and

(III) for both the plan year upon which a cost exemption is sought and the year prior, the actual total costs of coverage with respect to mental health and substance use disorder benefits under the plan.

(iii) Confidentiality.—A notification to the Secretary under clause (i) shall be confidential. The Secretary shall make available, upon request and on not more than an annual basis, an anonymous itemization of such notifications, that includes—

(I) a breakdown of States by the size and type of employers submitting such notification; and

(II) a summary of the data received under clause (ii).

(F) Audits by appropriate agencies.—To determine compliance with this paragraph, the Secretary may audit the books and records of a group health plan or health insurance issuer relating to an exemption, including any actuarial reports prepared pursuant to subparagraph (C), during the 6 year period following the notification of such exemption under subparagraph (E). A State agency

receiving a notification under subparagraph (E) may also conduct such an audit with respect to an exemption covered by such notification.

(d) Separate Application to Each Option Offered.—In the case of a group health plan that offers a participant or beneficiary two or more benefit package options under the plan, the requirements of this section shall be applied separately with respect to each such option.

(e) Definitions.—For purposes of this section—

(1) Aggregate lifetime limit.—The term "aggregate lifetime limit" means, with respect to benefits under a group health plan or health insurance coverage, a dollar limitation on the total amount that may be paid with respect to such benefits under the plan or health insurance coverage with respect to an individual or other coverage unit.

(2) Annual limit.—The term "annual limit" means, with respect to benefits under a group health plan or health insurance coverage, a dollar limitation on the total amount of benefits that may be paid with respect to such benefits in a 12-month period under the plan or health insurance coverage with respect to an individual or other coverage unit.

(3) Medical or surgical benefits.—The term "medical or surgical benefits" means benefits with respect to medical or surgical services, as defined under the terms of the plan or coverage (as the case may be), but does not include mental health benefits.

(4) Mental health benefits.—The term "mental health benefits" means benefits with respect to services for mental health conditions, as defined under the terms of the plan and in accordance with applicable Federal and State law.

(5) Substance use disorder benefits.—The term "substance use disorder benefits" means benefits with respect to services for substance use disorders, as defined under the terms of the plan and in accordance with applicable Federal and State law.

Amendments to PHSA §2726

Patient Protection and Affordable Care Act, 2010 (Pub. L. No. 111-148), as follows:

• Note on Redesignation: This section originally was enacted as PHSA §2705. It was redesignated as PHSA §2726 by Act §1001(2). Act §1562, which amends this section, was redesignated as Act §1563 by Act §10107(b)(1).

• PHSA §2726 was amended by Act §1563(c)(4) (as redesignated) in subsec. (a), by striking "(or health insurance coverage offered in connection with such a plan)" each place it appears and inserting "or a health insurance issuer offering group or individual health insurance coverage"; in subsec. (b), by striking "(or health insurance coverage offered in connection with such a plan)" each place it appears and inserting "or a health insurance issuer offering group or individual health insurance coverage"; in subsec. (c), para. (1), by striking "(and group health insurance coverage offered in connection with a group health plan)" and inserting "and a health insurance issuer offering group or individual health insurance coverage"; in para. (2), by striking "(or health insurance coverage offered in connection with such a plan)" each place it appeared and inserting "or a health insurance issuer offering group or individual health insurance coverage". Eff. for plan years beg. on or after date that is 6 months after date of enactment [date of enactment: Mar. 23, 2010].

Emergency Economic Stabilization Act of 2008 (Pub. L. No. 110-343), as follows:

- PHSA §2705(a)(3)–(5) (former) were added by Act Div. C, §512(b)(1).*

- PHSA §2705(b)(2) (former) was amended by Act §512(b)(2).*

- PHSA §2705(c) (former) was amended by Act §512(b)(3) in para. (1) by inserting before the period: "(as defined in section 2791(e)(4), except that for purposes of this paragraph such term shall include employers with 1 employee in the case of an employer residing in a State that permits small groups to include a single individual)"; and by striking para. (2) and inserting new para. (2).*

- PHSA §2705(e) (former) was amended by Act §512(b)(4) by striking para. (4) and inserting new paras. (4)–(7).*

*See Effective Date Note in amendment notes to ERISA §712 for this Act.

Heroes Earnings Assistance and Relief Tax Act of 2008 (Pub. L. No. 110-245), as follows:

- PHSA §2726(f) (former) was amended by Act 401(c) by striking "services furnished after December 31, 2007" and inserting "services furnished—(1) on or after January 1, 2008, and before the date of the enactment of the Heroes Earnings Assistance and Relief Tax Act of 2008, and (2) after December 31, 2008.". See note on sunset provision in amendment notes to ERISA §712 for this Act.

Tax Relief and Health Care Act of 2006 (Pub. L. No. 109-432), as follows:

- PHSA §2705(f)(former) was amended by Act, Div. A, §115(c) by striking "2006" and inserting "2007". Eff. Dec. 20, 2006.

Retirement Preservation Act of 2006 (Pub. L. No. 109-151), as follows:

- PHSA §2705(f)(former) was amended by Act §1(b) by striking "December 31, 2005" and inserting "December 31, 2006". Eff. Dec. 30, 2005.

Working Families Tax Relief Act of 2004 (Pub. L. No. 108-311), as follows:

- PHSA §2705(f) (former) was amended by Act §302(c) by striking "on or after December 31, 2004" and inserting "after December 31, 2005". Eff. Oct. 4, 2004.

Mental Health Parity Reauthorization Act of 2003 (Pub. L. No. 108-197), as follows:

- PHSA §2705(f) (former) was amended by Act §2(b) by striking "December 31, 2003" and inserting "December 31, 2004". Eff. Dec. 19, 2003.

Mental Health Parity Reauthorization Act of 2002 (Pub. L. No. 107-313), as follows:

- PHSA §2705(f) (former) was amended by Act §2(b) by striking "December 31, 2002" and inserting "December 31, 2003". Eff. Dec. 2, 2002.

Department of Labor, Health and Human Services, and Education, and Related Agencies Appropriations Act of 2002 (Pub. L. No. 107-116), as follows:

- PHSA §2705(f) (former) was amended by Act §701(b) by substituting "December 31, 2002" for "September 30, 2001". Eff. Jan. 10, 2002.

Department of Veterans Affairs and HUD, and Independent Agencies Appropriations Act, 1997 (Pub. L. No. 104-204), as follows:

- PHSA §2705(f) (former) was added by Act §703(a). Eff. with respect to group health plans for plan years beg. on or after Jan. 1, 1998.

> ### *Editor's Note*
>
> PHSA §2727, as follows, is effective for plan years beginning on or after September 23, 2010.

SEC. 2727. REQUIRED COVERAGE FOR RECONSTRUCTIVE SURGERY FOLLOWING MASTECTOMIES.

The provisions of section 713 of the Employee Retirement Income Security Act of 1974 shall apply to group health plans, and [] health insurance issuers offering group or individual health insurance coverage, as if included in this subpart.

Amendments to PHSA §2727

Patient Protection and Affordable Care Act, 2010 (Pub. L. No. 111-148), as follows:

- **Note on Redesignation:** PHSA §2706 (former) was redesignated as PHSA §2727 by Act §1001(2). Act §1562, which amends this section, was redesignated as Act §1563 by Act §10107(b)(1).

- PHSA §2727 was amended by Act §1563(c)(5) (as redesignated) by striking "health insurance issuers providing health insurance coverage in connection with group health plans" and inserting "and health insurance issuers offering group or individual health insurance coverage". Eff. for plan years beg. on or after date that is 6 months after date of enactment [date of enactment: Mar. 23, 2010], see Act §1004(a).

Women's Health and Cancer Rights Act of 1998 (Pub. L. No. 105-277), as follows:

- PHSA §2706 (former) was added by Act, Title IX, §903(a). Eff. in general for group health plans for plan years beg. on or after date of enactment [date of enactment: Oct. 21, 1998].

- **Other Provision. Effective Date for Collective Bargaining Agreements.** Act, Title IX, §903(c) provides:

  * * *

  (B) Special rule for collective bargaining agreements.—In the case of a group health plan maintained pursuant to 1 or more collective bargaining agreements between employee representatives and 1 or more employers, any plan amendment made pursuant to a collective bargaining agreement relating to the plan which amends the plan solely to conform to any requirement added by the amendment made by subsection (a) shall not be treated as a termination of such collective bargaining agreement.

> ### *Editor's Note*
>
> PHSA §2728, as follows, is effective for plan years beginning on or after September 23, 2010.

SEC. 2728. COVERAGE OF DEPENDENT STUDENTS ON MEDICALLY NECESSARY LEAVE OF ABSENCE.

(a) Medically Necessary Leave of Absence.—In this section, the term "medically necessary leave of absence" means, with respect to a dependent child

---

described in subsection (b)(2) in connection with a group health plan or individual health insurance coverage, a leave of absence of such child from a post-secondary educational institution (including an institution of higher education as defined in section 102 of the Higher Education Act of 1965), or any other change in enrollment of such child at such an institution, that—

(1) commences while such child is suffering from a serious illness or injury;

(2) is medically necessary; and

(3) causes such child to lose student status for purposes of coverage under the terms of the plan or coverage.

(b) Requirement To Continue Coverage.—

(1) In general.—In the case of a dependent child described in paragraph (2), a group health plan, or a health insurance issuer that offers group or individual health insurance coverage, shall not terminate coverage of such child under such plan or health insurance coverage due to a medically necessary leave of absence before the date that is the earlier of—

(A) the date that is 1 year after the first day of the medically necessary leave of absence; or

(B) the date on which such coverage would otherwise terminate under the terms of the plan or health insurance coverage.

(2) Dependent child described.—A dependent child described in this paragraph is, with respect to a group health plan or individual health insurance coverage, a beneficiary under the plan who—

(A) is a dependent child, under the terms of the plan or coverage, of a participant or beneficiary under the plan or coverage; and

(B) was enrolled in the plan or coverage, on the basis of being a student at a postsecondary educational institution (as described in subsection (a)), immediately before the first day of the medically necessary leave of absence involved.

(3) Certification by physician.—Paragraph (1) shall apply to a group health plan or individual health insurance coverage only if the plan or issuer of the coverage has received written certification by a treating physician of the dependent child which states that the child is suffering from a serious illness or injury and that the leave of absence (or other change of enrollment) described in subsection (a) is medically necessary.

(c) Notice.—A group health plan, and a health insurance issuer that offers group or individual health insurance coverage, shall include, with any notice regarding a requirement for certification of student status for coverage under the plan or coverage, a description of the terms of this section for continued coverage during medically necessary leaves of ab-

sence. Such description shall be in language which is understandable to the typical plan participant.

(d) No Change in Benefits.—A dependent child whose benefits are continued under this section shall be entitled to the same benefits as if (during the medically necessary leave of absence) the child continued to be a covered student at the institution of higher education and was not on a medically necessary leave of absence.

(e) Continued Application in Case of Changed Coverage.—If—

(1) a dependent child of a participant or beneficiary is in a period of coverage under a group health plan or individual health insurance coverage, pursuant to a medically necessary leave of absence of the child described in subsection (b);

(2) the manner in which the participant or beneficiary is covered under the plan changes, whether through a change in health insurance coverage or health insurance issuer, a change between health insurance coverage and self-insured coverage, or otherwise; and

(3) the coverage as so changed continues to provide coverage of beneficiaries as dependent children, this section shall apply to coverage of the child under the changed coverage for the remainder of the period of the medically necessary leave of absence of the dependent child under the plan in the same manner as it would have applied if the changed coverage had been the previous coverage.

Amendments to PHSA §2728

Patient Protection and Affordable Care Act, 2010 (Pub. L. No. 111-148), as follows:

• **Note on Redesignation:** PHSA §2707 (former) was redesignated as PHSA §2728 by Act §1001(2). Act §1562, which amends this section, was redesignated as Act §1563 by Act §10107(b)(1).

• PHSA §2728(a) was amended by Act §1563(c)(6)(A) by striking "health insurance coverage offered in connection with such plan" and inserting "individual health insurance coverage". Eff. for plan years beg. on or after date that is 6 months after date of enactment [date of enactment: Mar. 23, 2010], Act §1004(a).

• PHSA §2728(b) was amended by Act §1563(c)(6)(B) in para. (1) by striking "or a health insurance issuer that provides health insurance coverage in connection with a group health plan" and inserting "or a health insurance issuer that offers group or individual health insurance coverage"; in para. (2) by striking "health insurance coverage offered in connection with the plan" and inserting "individual health insurance coverage"; and in para. (3) by striking "health insurance coverage offered by an issuer in connection with such plan" and inserting "individual health insurance coverage". Eff. for plan years beg. on or after date that is 6 months after date of enactment [date of enactment: Mar. 23, 2010], Act §1004(a).

• PHSA §2728(c) was amended by Act §1563(c)(6)(C) by striking "health insurance issuer providing health insurance coverage in connection with a group health plan" and inserting "health insurance issuer that offers group or individual health insurance coverage". Eff. for plan years beg. on or after date that is 6 months after date of enactment [date of enactment: Mar. 23, 2010], Act §1004(a).

• PHSA §2728(e)(1) was amended by Act §1563(c)(6)(D) by striking "health insurance coverage offered in connection with such

Selected Provisions of PHSA After Amendment by PPACA. For sections prior to PPACA, see Part 4.

a plan" and inserting "individual health insurance coverage". Eff. for plan years beg. on or after date that is 6 months after date of enactment [date of enactment: Mar. 23, 2010], Act §1004(a).

Michelle's Law (Pub. L. No. 110-381), as follows:
• PHSA §2707 (former) was added by Act §2(b)(1). Eff. for plan years beg. on or after date that is one year after date of the enactment [date of enactment: Oct. 9, 2008] and to medically necessary leaves of absence beg. during such plan years.

PART B—INDIVIDUAL MARKET RULES

SEC. 2741. GUARANTEED AVAILABILITY OF INDIVIDUAL HEALTH INSURANCE COVERAGE TO CERTAIN INDIVIDUALS WITH PRIOR GROUP COVERAGE.

(a) Guaranteed Availability.—

(1) In general.—Subject to the succeeding subsections of this section and section 2744, each health insurance issuer that offers health insurance coverage (as defined in section 2791(b)(1) in the individual market in a State may not, with respect to an eligible individual (as defined in subsection (b)) desiring to enroll in individual health insurance coverage—

(A) decline to offer such coverage to, or deny enrollment of, such individual; or

(B) impose any preexisting condition exclusion (as defined in section 2701(b)(1)(A)) with respect to such coverage.

(2) Substitution by State of acceptable alternative mechanism.—The requirement of paragraph (1) shall not apply to health insurance coverage offered in the individual market in a State in which the State is implementing an acceptable alternative mechanism under section 2744.

(b) Eligible Individual Defined.—In this part, the term "eligible individual" means an individual—

(1)(A) for whom, as of the date on which the individual seeks coverage under this section, the aggregate of the periods of creditable coverage (as defined in section 2701(c)) is 18 or more months and (B) whose most recent prior creditable coverage was under a group health plan, governmental plan, or church plan (or health insurance coverage offered in connection with any such plan);

(2) who is not eligible for coverage under (A) a group health plan, (B) part A or part B of title XVIII of the Social Security Act, or (C) a State plan under title XIX of such Act (or any successor program), and does not have other health insurance coverage;

(3) with respect to whom the most recent coverage within the coverage period described in paragraph (1)(A) was not terminated based on a factor described in paragraph (1) or (2) of section 2712(b) (relating to nonpayment of premiums or fraud);

(4) if the individual had been offered the option of continuation coverage under a COBRA continuation

provision or under a similar State program, who elected such coverage; and

(5) who, if the individual elected such continuation coverage, has exhausted such continuation coverage under such provision or program.

(c) Alternative Coverage Permitted Where No State Mechanism.—

(1) In general.—In the case of health insurance coverage offered in the individual market in a State in which the State is not implementing an acceptable alternative mechanism under section 2744, the health insurance issuer may elect to limit the coverage offered under subsection (a) so long as it offers at least two different policy forms of health insurance coverage both of which—

(A) are designed for, made generally available to, and actively marketed to, and enroll both eligible and other individuals by the issuer; and

(B) meet the requirement of paragraph (2) or (3), as elected by the issuer.

For purposes of this subsection, policy forms which have different cost-sharing arrangements or different riders shall be considered to be different policy forms.

(2) Choice of most popular policy forms.—The requirement of this paragraph is met, for health insurance coverage policy forms offered by an issuer in the individual market, if the issuer offers the policy forms for individual health insurance coverage with the largest, and next to largest, premium volume of all such policy forms offered by the issuer in the State or applicable marketing or service area (as may be prescribed in regulation) by the issuer in the individual market in the period involved.

(3) Choice of 2 policy forms with representative coverage.—

(A) In general.—The requirement of this paragraph is met, for health insurance coverage policy forms offered by an issuer in the individual market, if the issuer offers a lower-level coverage policy form (as defined in subparagraph (B)) and a higher-level coverage policy form (as defined in subparagraph (C)) each of which includes benefits substantially similar to other individual health insurance coverage offered by the issuer in that State and each of which is covered under a method described in section 2744(c)(3)(A) (relating to risk adjustment, risk spreading, or financial subsidization).

(B) Lower-level of coverage described.—A policy form is described in this subparagraph if the actuarial value of the benefits under the coverage is at least 85 percent but not greater than 100 percent of a weighted average (described in subparagraph (D)).

(C) Higher-level of coverage described.—A policy form is described in this subparagraph if—

(i) the actuarial value of the benefits under the coverage is at least 15 percent greater than the actuarial value of the coverage described in subparagraph (B) offered by the issuer in the area involved; and

(ii) the actuarial value of the benefits under the coverage is at least 100 percent but not greater than 120 percent of a weighted average (described in subparagraph (D)).

(D) Weighted average.—For purposes of this paragraph, the weighted average described in this subparagraph is the average actuarial value of the benefits provided by all the health insurance coverage issued (as elected by the issuer) either by that issuer or by all issuers in the State in the individual market during the previous year (not including coverage issued under this section), weighted by enrollment for the different coverage.

(4) Election.—The issuer elections under this subsection shall apply uniformly to all eligible individuals in the State for that issuer. Such an election shall be effective for policies offered during a period of not shorter than 2 years.

(5) Assumptions.—For purposes of paragraph (3), the actuarial value of benefits provided under individual health insurance coverage shall be calculated based on a standardized population and a set of standardized utilization and cost factors.

(d) Special Rules for Network Plans.—

(1) In general.—In the case of a health insurance issuer that offers health insurance coverage in the individual market through a network plan, the issuer may—

(A) limit the individuals who may be enrolled under such coverage to those who live, reside, or work within the service area for such network plan; and

(B) within the service area of such plan, deny such coverage to such individuals if the issuer has demonstrated, if required, to the applicable State authority that—

(i) it will not have the capacity to deliver services adequately to additional individual enrollees because of its obligations to existing group contract holders and enrollees and individual enrollees, and

(ii) it is applying this paragraph uniformly to individuals without regard to any health status-related factor of such individuals and without regard to whether the individuals are eligible individuals.

(2) 180-day suspension upon denial of coverage.—An issuer, upon denying health insurance coverage in any service area in accordance with paragraph (1)(B), may not offer coverage in the individual

market within such service area for a period of 180 days after such coverage is denied.

(e) Application of Financial Capacity Limits.—

(1) In general.—A health insurance issuer may deny health insurance coverage in the individual market to an eligible individual if the issuer has demonstrated, if required, to the applicable State authority that—

(A) it does not have the financial reserves necessary to underwrite additional coverage; and

(B) it is applying this paragraph uniformly to all individuals in the individual market in the State consistent with applicable State law and without regard to any health status-related factor of such individuals and without regard to whether the individuals are eligible individuals.

(2) 180-day suspension upon denial of coverage.—An issuer upon denying individual health insurance coverage in any service area in accordance with paragraph (1) may not offer such coverage in the individual market within such service area for a period of 180 days after the date such coverage is denied or until the issuer has demonstrated, if required under applicable State law, to the applicable State authority that the issuer has sufficient financial reserves to underwrite additional coverage, whichever is later. A State may provide for the application of this paragraph on a service-area-specific basis.

(e)[(f)] Market requirements.—

(1) In general.—The provisions of subsection (a) shall not be construed to require that a health insurance issuer offering health insurance coverage only in connection with group health plans or through one or more bona fide associations, or both, offer such health insurance coverage in the individual market.

(2) Conversion policies.—A health insurance issuer offering health insurance coverage in connection with group health plans under this title shall not be deemed to be a health insurance issuer offering individual health insurance coverage solely because such issuer offers a conversion policy.

(f)[(g)] Construction.—Nothing in this section shall be construed—

(1) to restrict the amount of the premium rates that an issuer may charge an individual for health insurance coverage provided in the individual market under applicable State law; or

(2) to prevent a health insurance issuer offering health insurance coverage in the individual market from establishing premium discounts or rebates or modifying otherwise applicable copayments or deductibles in return for adherence to programs of health promotion and disease prevention.

Amendments to PHSA §2741

Health Insurance Portability and Accountability Act of 1996 (Pub. L. No. 104-191), as follows:

Selected Provisions of PHSA After Amendment by PPACA. For sections prior to PPACA, see Part 4.

- PHSA §2741 was added by Act §111(a). See effective date note below.
- **Other Provision. Effective Date.** Act §111(b) provided:
  (b) Effective Date.—
  (1) In general.—Except as provided in this subsection, part B of title XXVII of the Public Health Service Act (as inserted by subsection (a)) shall apply with respect to health insurance coverage offered, sold, issued, renewed, in effect, or operated in the individual market after June 30, 1997, regardless of when a period of creditable coverage occurs.
  (2) Application of certification rules.—The provisions of section 102(d)(2) of this Act shall apply to section 2743 of the Public Health Service Act in the same manner as it applies to section 2701(e) of such Act.

SEC. 2742. GUARANTEED RENEWABILITY OF INDIVIDUAL HEALTH INSURANCE COVERAGE.

(a) In General.—Except as provided in this section, a health insurance issuer that provides individual health insurance coverage to an individual shall renew or continue in force such coverage at the option of the individual.

(b) General Exceptions.—A health insurance issuer may nonrenew or discontinue health insurance coverage of an individual in the individual market based only on one or more of the following:

(1) Nonpayment of premiums.—The individual has failed to pay premiums or contributions in accordance with the terms of the health insurance coverage or the issuer has not received timely premium payments.

(2) Fraud.—The individual has performed an act or practice that constitutes fraud or made an intentional misrepresentation of material fact under the terms of the coverage.

(3) Termination of plan.—The issuer is ceasing to offer coverage in the individual market in accordance with subsection (c) and applicable State law.

(4) Movement outside service area.—In the case of a health insurance issuer that offers health insurance coverage in the market through a network plan, the individual no longer resides, lives, or works in the service area (or in an area for which the issuer is authorized to do business) but only if such coverage is terminated under this paragraph uniformly without regard to any health status-related factor of covered individuals.

(5) Association membership ceases.—In the case of health insurance coverage that is made available in the individual market only through one or more bona fide associations, the membership of the individual in the association (on the basis of which the coverage is provided) ceases but only if such coverage is terminated under this paragraph uniformly without regard to any health status-related factor of covered individuals.

(c) Requirements for Uniform Termination of Coverage.—

(1) Particular type of coverage not offered.—In any case in which an issuer decides to discontinue offering a particular type of health insurance coverage offered in the individual market, coverage of such type may be discontinued by the issuer only if—

(A) the issuer provides notice to each covered individual provided coverage of this type in such market of such discontinuation at least 90 days prior to the date of the discontinuation of such coverage;

(B) the issuer offers to each individual in the individual market provided coverage of this type, the option to purchase any other individual health insurance coverage currently being offered by the issuer for individuals in such market; and

(C) in exercising the option to discontinue coverage of this type and in offering the option of coverage under subparagraph (B), the issuer acts uniformly without regard to any health status-related factor of enrolled individuals or individuals who may become eligible for such coverage.

(2) Discontinuance of all coverage.—

(A) In general.—Subject to subparagraph (C), in any case in which a health insurance issuer elects to discontinue offering all health insurance coverage in the individual market in a State, health insurance coverage may be discontinued by the issuer only if—

(i) the issuer provides notice to the applicable State authority and to each individual of such discontinuation at least 180 days prior to the date of the expiration of such coverage, and

(ii) all health insurance issued or delivered for issuance in the State in such market are discontinued and coverage under such health insurance coverage in such market is not renewed.

(B) Prohibition on market reentry.—In the case of a discontinuation under subparagraph (A) in the individual market, the issuer may not provide for the issuance of any health insurance coverage in the market and State involved during the 5-year period beginning on the date of the discontinuation of the last health insurance coverage not so renewed.

(d) Exception for Uniform Modification of Coverage.—At the time of coverage renewal, a health insurance issuer may modify the health insurance coverage for a policy form offered to individuals in the individual market so long as such modification is consistent with State law and effective on a uniform basis among all individuals with that policy form.

(e) Application to Coverage Offered Only Through Associations.—In applying this section in the case of health insurance coverage that is made available by a health insurance issuer in the individual market to individuals only through one or more associations, a reference to an "individual" is deemed to include a reference to such an association (of which the individual is a member).

Amendments to PHSA §2742

Health Insurance Portability and Accountability Act of 1996 (Pub. L. No. 104-191), as follows:

• PHSA §2742 was added by Act §111(a). See effective date note below.

• **Other Provision. Effective Date.** Act §111(b) provided:

    (b) Effective Date.—

    (1) In general.—Except as provided in this subsection, part B of title XXVII of the Public Health Service Act (as inserted by subsection (a)) shall apply with respect to health insurance coverage offered, sold, issued, renewed, in effect, or operated in the individual market after June 30, 1997, regardless of when a period of creditable coverage occurs.

    (2) Application of certification rules.—The provisions of section 102(d)(2) of this Act shall apply to section 2743 of the Public Health Service Act in the same manner as it applies to section 2701(e) of such Act.

SEC. 2743. CERTIFICATION OF COVERAGE.

The provisions of section 2701(e) shall apply to health insurance coverage offered by a health insurance issuer in the individual market in the same manner as it applies to health insurance coverage offered by a health insurance issuer in connection with a group health plan in the small or large group market.

Amendments to PHSA §2743

Health Insurance Portability and Accountability Act of 1996 (Pub. L. No. 104-191), as follows:

• PHSA §2743 was added by Act §111(a). See effective date note below.

• **Other Provision. Effective Date.** Act §111(b) provided:

    (b) Effective Date.—

    (1) In general.—Except as provided in this subsection, part B of title XXVII of the Public Health Service Act (as inserted by subsection (a)) shall apply with respect to health insurance coverage offered, sold, issued, renewed, in effect, or operated in the individual market after June 30, 1997, regardless of when a period of creditable coverage occurs.

    (2) Application of certification rules.—The provisions of section 102(d)(2) of this Act shall apply to section 2743 of the Public Health Service Act in the same manner as it applies to section 2701(e) of such Act.

SEC. 2744. STATE FLEXIBILITY IN INDIVIDUAL MARKET REFORMS.

(a) Waiver of Requirements Where Implementation of Acceptable Alternative Mechanism.—

(1) In general.—The requirements of section 2741 shall not apply with respect to health insurance coverage offered in the individual market in the State so long as a State is found to be implementing, in accordance with this section and consistent with section 2762(b), an alternative mechanism (in this section referred to as an "acceptable alternative mechanism")—

(A) under which all eligible individuals are provided a choice of health insurance coverage;

(B) under which such coverage does not impose any preexisting condition exclusion with respect to such coverage;

(C) under which such choice of coverage includes at least one policy form of coverage that is comparable to comprehensive health insurance coverage offered in the individual market in such State or that is comparable to a standard option of coverage available under the group or individual health insurance laws of such State; and

(D) in a State which is implementing—

    (i) a model act described in subsection (c)(1),

    (ii) a qualified high risk pool described in subsection (c)(2), or

    (iii) a mechanism described in subsection (c)(3).

(2) Permissible Forms of mechanisms.—A private or public individual health insurance mechanism (such as a health insurance coverage pool or programs, mandatory group conversion policies, guaranteed issue of one or more plans of individual health insurance coverage, or open enrollment by one or more health insurance issuers), or combination of such mechanisms, that is designed to provide access to health benefits for individuals in the individual market in the State in accordance with this section may constitute an acceptable alternative mechanism.

(b) Application of Acceptable Alternative Mechanisms.—

(1) Presumption.—

(A) In general.—Subject to the succeeding provisions of this subsection, a State is presumed to be implementing an acceptable alternative mechanism in accordance with this section as of July 1, 1997, if, by not later than April 1, 1997, the chief executive officer of a State—

    (i) notifies the Secretary that the State has enacted or intends to enact (by not later than January 1, 1998, or July 1, 1998, in the case of a State described in subparagraph (B)(ii)) any necessary legislation to provide for the implementation of a mechanism reasonably designed to be an acceptable alternative mechanism as of January 1, 1998, (or, in the case of a State described in subparagraph (B)(ii), July 1, 1998); and

    (ii) provides the Secretary with such information as the Secretary may require to review the mechanism and its implementation (or proposed implementation) under this subsection.

(B) Delay permitted for certain states.—

    (i) Effect of delay.—In the case of a State described in clause (ii) that provides notice under

---

Selected Provisions of PHSA After Amendment by PPACA. For sections prior to PPACA, see Part 4.

subparagraph (A)(i), for the presumption to continue on and after July 1, 1998, the chief executive officer of the State by April 1, 1998—

(I) must notify the Secretary that the State has enacted any necessary legislation to provide for the implementation of a mechanism reasonably designed to be an acceptable alternative mechanism as of July 1, 1998; and

(II) must provide the Secretary with such information as the Secretary may require to review the mechanism and its implementation (or proposed implementation) under this subsection.

(ii) States described.—A State described in this clause is a State that has a legislature that does not meet within the 12-month period beginning on the date of enactment of this Act.

(C) Continued application.—In order for a mechanism to continue to be presumed to be an acceptable alternative mechanism, the State shall provide the Secretary every 3 years with information described in subparagraph (A)(ii) or (B)(i)(II) (as the case may be).

(2) Notice.—If the Secretary finds, after review of information provided under paragraph (1) and in consultation with the chief executive officer of the State and the insurance commissioner or chief insurance regulatory official of the State, that such a mechanism is not an acceptable alternative mechanism or is not (or no longer) being implemented, the Secretary—

(A) shall notify the State of—

(i) such preliminary determination, and "(ii) the consequences under paragraph (3) of a failure to implement such a mechanism; and

(B) shall permit the State a reasonable opportunity in which to modify the mechanism (or to adopt another mechanism) in a manner so that may be an acceptable alternative mechanism or to provide for implementation of such a mechanism.

(3) Final determination.—If, after providing notice and opportunity under paragraph (2), the Secretary finds that the mechanism is not an acceptable alternative mechanism or the State is not implementing such a mechanism, the Secretary shall notify the State that the State is no longer considered to be implementing an acceptable alternative mechanism and that the requirements of section 2741 shall apply to health insurance coverage offered in the individual market in the State, effective as of a date specified in the notice.

(4) Limitation on secretarial authority.—The Secretary shall not make a determination under paragraph (2) or (3) on any basis other than the basis that a mechanism is not an acceptable alternative mechanism or is not being implemented.

(5) Future adoption of mechanisms.—If a State, after January 1, 1997, submits the notice and information described in paragraph (1), unless the Secretary makes a finding described in paragraph (3) within the 90-day period beginning on the date of submission of the notice and information, the mechanism shall be considered to be an acceptable alternative mechanism for purposes of this section, effective 90 days after the end of such period, subject to the second sentence of paragraph (1).

(c) Provision Related to Risk.—

(1) Adoption of NAIC models.—The model act referred to in subsection (a)(1)(D)(i) is the Small Employer and Individual Health Insurance Availability Model Act (adopted by the National Association of Insurance Commissioners on June 3, 1996) insofar as it applies to individual health insurance coverage or the Individual Health Insurance Portability Model Act (also adopted by such Association on such date).

(2) Qualified high risk pool.—For purposes of subsection(a)(1)(D)(ii), a "qualified high risk pool" described in this paragraph is a high risk pool that—

(A) provides to all eligible individuals health insurance coverage (or comparable coverage) that does not impose any preexisting condition exclusion with respect to such coverage for all eligible individuals, and

(B) provides for premium rates and covered benefits for such coverage consistent with standards included in the NAIC Model Health Plan for Uninsurable Individuals Act (as in effect as of the date of the enactment of this title).

(3) Other mechanisms.—For purposes of subsection (a)(1)(D)(iii), a mechanism described in this paragraph—

(A) provides for risk adjustment, risk spreading, or a risk spreading mechanism (among issuers or policies of an issuer) or otherwise provides for some financial subsidization for eligible individuals, including through assistance to participating issuers; or

(B) is a mechanism under which each eligible individual is provided a choice of all individual health insurance coverage otherwise available.

Amendments to PHSA §2744

Departments of Veterans Affairs and HUD, and Independent Agencies Appropriations Act, 1997 (Pub. L. No. 104-204), as follows:
● PHSA §2744(a)(1) was amended by Act §605(b)(1) by striking "2746(b)" and inserting "2762(b)". Eff. for health insurance coverage in the individual market on or after Jan. 1, 1998.
Health Insurance Portability and Accountability Act of 1996 (Pub. L. No. 104-191), as follows:
● PHSA §2744 was added by Act §111(a). See effective date note below.
● **Other Provision—Effective Date.** Act §111(b) provided:
   (b) Effective Date.—
   (1) In general.—Except as provided in this subsection, part B of title XXVII of the Public Health Service Act (as inserted by

subsection (a)) shall apply with respect to health insurance coverage offered, sold, issued, renewed, in effect, or operated in the individual market after June 30, 1997, regardless of when a period of creditable coverage occurs.

(2) Application of certification rules.—The provisions of section 102(d)(2) of this Act shall apply to section 2743 of the Public Health Service Act in the same manner as it applies to section 2701(e) of such Act.

SEC. 2745. RELIEF FOR HIGH RISK POOLS.

(a) Seed Grants to States.—The Secretary shall provide from the funds appropriated under subsection (d)(1)(A) a grant of up to $1,000,000 to each State that has not created a qualified high risk pool as of the date of enactment of the State High Risk Pool Funding Extension Act of 2006 for the State's costs of creation and initial operation of such a pool.

(b) Grants for Operational Losses.—

(1) **In general.**—In the case of a State that has established a qualified high risk pool that—

(A) restricts premiums charged under the pool to no more than 200 percent of the premium for applicable standard risk rates;

(B) offers a choice of two or more coverage options through the pool; and

(C) has in effect a mechanism reasonably designed to ensure continued funding of losses incurred by the State in connection with operation of the pool after the end of the last fiscal year for which a grant is provided under this paragraph; the Secretary shall provide, from the funds appropriated under paragraphs (1)(B)(i) and (2)(A) of subsection (d) and allotted to the State under paragraph (2), a grant for the losses incurred by the State in connection with the operation of the pool.

(2) **Allotment.**—Subject to paragraph (4), the amounts appropriated under paragraphs (1)(B)(i) and (2)(A) of subsection (d) for a fiscal year shall be allotted and made available to the States (or the entities that operate the high risk pool under applicable State law) that qualify for a grant under paragraph (1) as follows:

(A) An amount equal to 40 percent of such appropriated amount for the fiscal year shall be allotted in equal amounts to each qualifying State that is one of the 50 States or the District of Columbia and that applies for a grant under this subsection.

(B) An amount equal to 30 percent of such appropriated amount for the fiscal year shall be allotted among qualifying States that apply for such a grant so that the amount allotted to such a State bears the same ratio to such appropriated amount as the number of uninsured individuals in the State bears to the total number of uninsured individuals (as determined by the Secretary) in all qualifying States that so apply.

(C) An amount equal to 30 percent of such appropriated amount for the fiscal year shall be allotted among qualifying States that apply for such a grant so that the amount allotted to a State bears the same ratio to such appropriated amount as the number of individuals enrolled in health care coverage through the qualified high risk pool of the State bears to the total number of individuals so enrolled through qualified high risk pools (as determined by the Secretary) in all qualifying States that so apply.

(3) **Special rule for pools charging higher premiums.**—In the case of a qualified high risk pool of a State which charges premiums that exceed 150 percent of the premium for applicable standard risks, the State shall use at least 50 percent of the amount of the grant provided to the State to carry out this subsection to reduce premiums for enrollees.

(4) **Limitation for territories.**—In no case shall the aggregate amount allotted and made available under paragraph (2) for a fiscal year to States that are not the 50 States or the District of Columbia exceed $1,000,000.

(c) Bonus Grants for Supplemental Consumer Benefits.—

(1) **In general.**—In the case of a State that is one of the 50 States or the District of Columbia, that has established a qualified high risk pool, and that is receiving a grant under subsection (b)(1), the Secretary shall provide, from the funds appropriated under paragraphs (1)(B)(ii) and (2)(B) of subsection (d) and allotted to the State under paragraph (3), a grant to be used to provide supplemental consumer benefits to enrollees or potential enrollees (or defined subsets of such enrollees or potential enrollees) in qualified high risk pools.

(2) **Benefits.**—A State shall use amounts received under a grant under this subsection to provide one or more of the following benefits:

(A) Low-income premium subsidies.

(B) A reduction in premium trends, actual premiums, or other cost-sharing requirements.

(C) An expansion or broadening of the pool of individuals eligible for coverage, such as through eliminating waiting lists, increasing enrollment caps, or providing flexibility in enrollment rules.

(D) Less stringent rules, or additional waiver authority, with respect to coverage of pre-existing conditions.

(E) Increased benefits.

(F) The establishment of disease management programs.

(3) **Allotment; limitation.**—The Secretary shall allot funds appropriated under paragraphs (1)(B)(ii) and (2)(B) of subsection (d) among States qualifying

for a grant under paragraph (1) in a manner specified by the Secretary, but in no case shall the amount so allotted to a State for a fiscal year exceed 10 percent of the funds so appropriated for the fiscal year.

(4) Rule of construction.—Nothing in this subsection shall be construed to prohibit a State that, on the date of the enactment of the State High Risk Pool Funding Extension Act of 2006, is in the process of implementing a program to provide benefits of the type described in paragraph (2), from being eligible for a grant under this subsection.

(d) Funding.—

(1) Appropriation for fiscal year 2006.—There are authorized to be appropriated for fiscal year 2006—

(A) $15,000,000 to carry out subsection (a); and

(B) $75,000,000, of which, subject to paragraph (4)—

(i) two-thirds of the amount appropriated shall be made available for allotments under subsection (b)(2); and

(ii) one-third of the amount appropriated shall be made available for allotments under subsection (c)(3).

(2) Authorization of appropriations for fiscal years 2007 through 2010.—There are authorized to be appropriated $75,000,000 for each of fiscal years 2007 through 2010, of which, subject to paragraph (4)—

(A) two-thirds of the amount appropriated for a fiscal year shall be made available for allotments under subsection (b)(2); and

(B) one-third of the amount appropriated for a fiscal year shall be made available for allotments under subsection (c)(3).

(3) Availability.—Funds appropriated for purposes of carrying out this section for a fiscal year shall remain available for obligation through the end of the following fiscal year.

(4) Reallotment.—If, on June 30 of each fiscal year for which funds are appropriated under paragraph (1)(B) or (2), the Secretary determines that all the amounts so appropriated are not allotted or otherwise made available to States, such remaining amounts shall be allotted and made available under subsection (b) among States receiving grants under subsection (b) for the fiscal year based upon the allotment formula specified in such subsection.

(5) No entitlement.—Nothing in this section shall be construed as providing a State with an entitlement to a grant under this section.

(e) Applications.—To be eligible for a grant under this section, a State shall submit to the Secretary an application at such time, in such manner, and containing such information as the Secretary may require.

(f) Annual Report.—The Secretary shall submit to Congress an annual report on grants provided under this section. Each such report shall include information on the distribution of such grants among States and the use of grant funds by States.

(g) Definitions.—In this section:

(1) Qualified high risk pool.—

(A) In general.—The term "qualified high risk pool" has the meaning given such term in section 2744(c)(2), except that a State may elect to meet the requirement of subparagraph (A) of such section (insofar as it requires the provision of coverage to all eligible individuals) through providing for the enrollment of eligible individuals through an acceptable alternative mechanism (as defined for purposes of section 2744) that includes a high risk pool as a component.

[(B) Not enacted.]

(2) Standard risk rate.—The term "standard risk rate" means a rate—

(A) determined under the State high risk pool by considering the premium rates charged by other health insurers offering health insurance coverage to individuals in the insurance market served;

(B) that is established using reasonable actuarial techniques; and

(C) that reflects anticipated claims experience and expenses for the coverage involved.

(3) State.—The term "State" means any of the 50 States and the District of Columbia and includes Puerto Rico, the Virgin Islands, Guam, American Samoa, and the Northern Mariana Islands.

Amendments to PHSA §2745

State High Risk Pool Funding Extension Act of 2006 (Pub. L. No. 109-172), as follows:
● PHSA §2745 was amended by Act §2. Eff. on enactment [date of enactment: Feb. 10, 2006].

Trade Act of 2002 (Pub. L. No. 107-210), as follows:
● PHSA §2745 was added by Act Div. A, §201(b). Eff. on enactment [date of enactment: Aug. 6, 2002].

SEC. 2751. STANDARDS RELATING TO BENEFITS FOR MOTHERS AND NEWBORNS.

(a) In General.—The provisions of 2704 of this title (other than subsections (d) and (f)) shall apply to health insurance coverage offered by a health insurance issuer in the individual market in the same manner as it applies to health insurance coverage offered by a health insurance issuer in connection with a group health plan in the small or large group market.

(b) Notice Requirement.—A health insurance issuer under this part shall comply with the notice requirement under 711(d) of the Employee Retirement Income Security Act with respect to the requirements referred to in subsection (a) of this section as if such section applied to such issuer and such issuer were a group health plan.

(c) Preemption; Exception for Health Insurance Coverage in Certain States.—

(1) In general.—The requirements of this section shall not apply with respect to health insurance coverage if there is a State law (as defined in 2723(d)(1)) for a State that regulates such coverage that is described in any of the following subparagraphs:

(A) Such State law requires such coverage to provide for at least a 48-hour hospital length of stay following a normal vaginal delivery and at least a 96-hour hospital length of stay following a cesarean section.

(B) Such State law requires such coverage to provide for maternity and pediatric care in accordance with guidelines established by the American College of Obstetricians and Gynecologists, the American Academy of Pediatrics, or other established professional medical associations.

(C) Such State law requires, in connection with such coverage for maternity care, that the hospital length of stay for such care is left to the decision of (or required to be made by) the attending provider in consultation with the mother.

(2) Construction.—Section 2762(a) of this title shall not be construed as superseding a State law described in paragraph (1).

Amendments to PHSA §2751

Departments of Veterans Affairs and HUD, and Independent Agencies Appropriations Act, 1997 (Pub. L. No. 104-204), as follows:
• PHSA §2751 was added by Act §605(a)(4). Eff. for health insurance coverage offered, sold, issued, renewed, in effect, or operated in the individual market on or after Jan. 1, 1998, Act §605(c).

SEC. 2752. REQUIRED COVERAGE FOR RECONSTRUCTIVE SURGERY FOLLOWING MASTECTOMIES.

The provisions of section 2706 shall apply to health insurance coverage offered by a health insurance issuer in the individual market in the same manner as they apply to health insurance coverage offered by a health insurance issuer in connection with a group health plan in the small or large group market.

Amendments to PHSA §2752

Tax and Trade Relief Extension Act of 1998 (Pub. L. No. 105-277), as follows:
• PHSA §2752 was added by Act, Title IX, §903(b). Eff. for plan years beg. on or after date enacted [date of enactment: Oct. 21,

1998], with a special rule for collective bargaining agreements, see Act §903(c).

SEC. 2753. PROHIBITION OF HEALTH DISCRIMINATION ON THE BASIS OF GENETIC INFORMATION.

(a) Prohibition on Genetic Information as a Condition of Eligibility.—

(1) In general.—A health insurance issuer offering health insurance coverage in the individual market may not establish rules for the eligibility (including continued eligibility) of any individual to enroll in individual health insurance coverage based on genetic information.

(2) Rule of construction.—Nothing in paragraph (1) or in paragraphs (1) and (2) of subsection (e) shall be construed to preclude a health insurance issuer from establishing rules for eligibility for an individual to enroll in individual health insurance coverage based on the manifestation of a disease or disorder in that individual, or in a family member of such individual where such family member is covered under the policy that covers such individual.

(b) Prohibition on Genetic Information in Setting Premium Rates.—

(1) In general.—A health insurance issuer offering health insurance coverage in the individual market shall not adjust premium or contribution amounts for an individual on the basis of genetic information concerning the individual or a family member of the individual.

(2) Rule of construction.—Nothing in paragraph (1) or in paragraphs (1) and (2) of subsection (e) shall be construed to preclude a health insurance issuer from adjusting premium or contribution amounts for an individual on the basis of a manifestation of a disease or disorder in that individual, or in a family member of such individual where such family member is covered under the policy that covers such individual. In such case, the manifestation of a disease or disorder in one individual cannot also be used as genetic information about other individuals covered under the policy issued to such individual and to further increase premiums or contribution amounts.

(c) Prohibition on Genetic Information as Preexisting Condition.—

(1) In general.—A health insurance issuer offering health insurance coverage in the individual market may not, on the basis of genetic information, impose any preexisting condition exclusion (as defined in section 2701(b)(1)(A)) with respect to such coverage.

(2) Rule of construction.—Nothing in paragraph (1) or in paragraphs (1) and (2) of subsection (e) shall be construed to preclude a health insurance issuer from imposing any preexisting condition exclusion

---

Selected Provisions of PHSA After Amendment by PPACA. For sections prior to PPACA, see Part 4.

for an individual with respect to health insurance coverage on the basis of a manifestation of a disease or disorder in that individual.

(d) Genetic Testing.—

(1) Limitation on requesting or requiring genetic testing.—A health insurance issuer offering health insurance coverage in the individual market shall not request or require an individual or a family member of such individual to undergo a genetic test.

(2) Rule of construction.—Paragraph (1) shall not be construed to limit the authority of a health care professional who is providing health care services to an individual to request that such individual undergo a genetic test.

(3) Rule of construction regarding payment.—

(A) In general.—Nothing in paragraph (1) shall be construed to preclude a health insurance issuer offering health insurance coverage in the individual market from obtaining and using the results of a genetic test in making a determination regarding payment (as such term is defined for the purposes of applying the regulations promulgated by the Secretary under part C of title XI of the Social Security Act and section 264 of the Health Insurance Portability and Accountability Act of 1996, as may be revised from time to time) consistent with subsection (a) and (c).

(B) Limitation.—For purposes of subparagraph (A), a health insurance issuer offering health insurance coverage in the individual market may request only the minimum amount of information necessary to accomplish the intended purpose.

(4) Research exception.—Notwithstanding paragraph (1), a health insurance issuer offering health insurance coverage in the individual market may request, but not require, that an individual or a family member of such individual undergo a genetic test if each of the following conditions is met:

(A) The request is made pursuant to research that complies with part 46 of title 45, Code of Federal Regulations, or equivalent Federal regulations, and any applicable State or local law or regulations for the protection of human subjects in research.

(B) The issuer clearly indicates to each individual, or in the case of a minor child, to the legal guardian of such child, to whom the request is made that—

(i) compliance with the request is voluntary; and

(ii) non-compliance will have no effect on enrollment status or premium or contribution amounts.

(C) No genetic information collected or acquired under this paragraph shall be used for underwriting purposes.

(D) The issuer notifies the Secretary in writing that the issuer is conducting activities pursuant to

the exception provided for under this paragraph, including a description of the activities conducted.

(E) The issuer complies with such other conditions as the Secretary may by regulation require for activities conducted under this paragraph.

(e) Prohibition on Collection of Genetic Information.—

(1) In general.—A health insurance issuer offering health insurance coverage in the individual market shall not request, require, or purchase genetic information for underwriting purposes (as defined in section 2791).

(2) Prohibition on collection of genetic information prior to enrollment.—A health insurance issuer offering health insurance coverage in the individual market shall not request, require, or purchase genetic information with respect to any individual prior to such individual's enrollment under the plan in connection with such enrollment.

(3) Incidental collection.—If a health insurance issuer offering health insurance coverage in the individual market obtains genetic information incidental to the requesting, requiring, or purchasing of other information concerning any individual, such request, requirement, or purchase shall not be considered a violation of paragraph (2) if such request, requirement, or purchase is not in violation of paragraph (1).

(f) Genetic Information of a Fetus or Embryo.— Any reference in this part to genetic information concerning an individual or family member of an individual shall—

(1) with respect to such an individual or family member of an individual who is a pregnant woman, include genetic information of any fetus carried by such pregnant woman; and

(2) with respect to an individual or family member utilizing an assisted reproductive technology, include genetic information of any embryo legally held by the individual or family member.

Amendments to PHSA §2753

Genetic Information Nondiscrimination Act of 2008 (Pub. L. No. 110-233), as follows:

● PHSA §2753 was added by Act Title 1, §102(b)(1)(B). See effective date below.

● **Other Provision—Effective Date.** Act Title 1, §102(d)(2) provided:

(2) Effective date.—The amendments made by this section shall apply—

(A) with respect to group health plans, and health insurance coverage offered in connection with group health plans, for plan years beginning after the date that is 1 year after the date of enactment of this Act; and

(B) with respect to health insurance coverage offered, sold, issued, renewed, in effect, or operated in the individual market after the date that is 1 year after the date of enactment of this Act.

SEC. 2753[2754]. COVERAGE OF DEPENDENT STUDENTS ON MEDICALLY NECESSARY LEAVE OF ABSENCE.

The provisions of section 2707 shall apply to health insurance coverage offered by a health insurance issuer in the individual market in the same manner as they apply to health insurance coverage offered by a health insurance issuer in connection with a group health plan in the small or large group market.

Amendments to PHSA §2753[2754]

Michelle's Law (Pub. L. No. 110-381), as follows:
• PHSA §2753[2754] was added by Act §2(b)(2). Eff. for plan years beg. on or after date that is one year after date of the enactment [date of enactment: Oct. 9, 2008] and to medically necessary leaves of absence beginning during such plan years.

SEC. 2761. ENFORCEMENT.

(a) State Enforcement.—

(1) State authority.—Subject to section 2762, each State may require that health insurance issuers that issue, sell, renew, or offer health insurance coverage in the State in the individual market meet the requirements established under this part with respect to such issuers.

(2) Failure to implement requirements.—In the case of a State that fails to substantially enforce the requirements set forth in this part with respect to health insurance issuers in the State, the Secretary shall enforce the requirements of this part under subsection (b) insofar as they relate to the issuance, sale, renewal, and offering of health insurance coverage in the individual market in such State.

(b) Secretarial Enforcement Authority.—The Secretary shall have the same authority in relation to enforcement of the provisions of this part with respect to issuers of health insurance coverage in the individual market in a State as the Secretary has under section 2722(b)(2), and section 2722(b)(3) with respect to violations of genetic nondiscrimination provisions, in relation to the enforcement of the provisions of part A with respect to issuers of health insurance coverage in the small group market in the State.

Amendments to PHSA §2761

Genetic Information Nondiscrimination Act of 2008 (Pub. L. No. 110-233), as follows:
• PHSA §2761(b) was amended by Act §102(b)(2). See effective date below. PHSA §2761(b) prior to amendment:
  (b) Secretarial Enforcement Authority.—The Secretary shall have the same authority in relation to enforcement of the provisions of this part with respect to issuers of health insurance

coverage in the individual market in a State as the Secretary has under section 2722(b)(2) in relation to the enforcement of the provisions of part A with respect to issuers of health insurance coverage in the small group market in the State.
• **Other Provision—Effective Date.** Act §102(d)(2) provided:
  (2) Effective date.—The amendments made by this section shall apply—
  (A) with respect to group health plans, and health insurance coverage offered in connection with group health plans, for plan years beginning after the date that is 1 year after the date of enactment of this Act [date of enactment: May 21, 2008]; and
  (B) with respect to health insurance coverage offered, sold, issued, renewed, in effect, or operated in the individual market after the date that is 1 year after the date of enactment of this Act [date of enactment: May 21, 2008].

Departments of Veterans Affairs and HUD, and Independent Agencies Appropriations Act, 1997 (Pub. L. No. 104-204), as follows:
• **Note on Redesignation:** This section originally was enacted as PHSA §2745. It was redesignated by Act, Title 6, §605(a)(2) as PHSA §2761.
• PHSA §2745 (former) was amended by Act Title 6, §605(b)(2) by striking "2746" and inserting "2762". Eff. for health insurance coverage offered, sold, issued, renewed, in effect, or operated in the individual market on or after Jan. 1, 1998.

Health Insurance Portability and Accountability Act of 1996 (Pub. L. No. 104-191), as follows:
• PHSA §2745 (former) was added by Act Title I, §111(a). Eff. in general for health insurance coverage offered, sold, issued, renewed, in effect, or operated in the individual market after June 30, 1997, regardless of when a period of creditable coverage occurs.

> **Editor's Note**
>
> PHSA §2762, as follows, is effective March 23, 2010.

SEC. 2762. PREEMPTION AND APPLICATION.

(a) In General.—Subject to subsection (b), nothing in this part (or part C insofar as it applies to this part) shall be construed to prevent a State from establishing, implementing, or continuing in effect standards and requirements unless such standards and requirements prevent the application of a requirement of this part.

(b) Rules of Construction.—

(1) Nothing in this part (or part C insofar as it applies to this part shall be construed to affect or modify the provisions of section 514 of the Employee Retirement Income Security Act of 1974 (29 U.S.C. 1144).

(2) Nothing in this part (other than section 2751 shall be construed as requiring health insurance coverage offered in the individual market to provide specific benefits under the terms of such coverage.

(c) Application of part A Provisions.—

(1) In general.—The provisions of part A shall apply to health insurance issuers providing health

Selected Provisions of PHSA After Amendment by PPACA. For sections prior to PPACA, see Part 4.

insurance coverage in the individual market in a State as provided for in such part.

(2) Clarification.—To the extent that any provision of this part conflicts with a provision of part A with respect to health insurance issuers providing health insurance coverage in the individual market in a State, the provisions of such part A shall apply.

Amendments to PHSA §2762

Patient Protection and Affordable Care Act, 2010 (Pub. L. No. 111-148), as follows:

● PHSA §2762 was amended by Act §1563(c)(15) (as redesignated by Act §10107(b)(1)) by inserting "AND APPLICATION" in the heading, and by adding subsec. (c). Eff. on enactment [date of enactment: Mar. 23, 2010].

Departments of Veterans Affairs and HUD, and Independent Agencies Appropriations Act, 1997 (Pub. L. No. 104-204), as follows:

● **Note on Redesignation:** This section originally was enacted as PHSA §2746. It was redesignated by Act Title 6, §605(a)(2) as PHSA §2762.

● PHSA §2746 (former) was amended by Act Title 6, §605(b)(3) by inserting "(1)" after the dash, and by adding PHSA 2746(b)(2). Eff. for health insurance coverage offered, sold, issued, renewed, in effect, or operated in the individual market on or after Jan. 1, 1998.

Health Insurance Portability and Accountability Act of 1996 (Pub. L. No. 104-191), as follows:

● PHSA §2746 (former) was added by Act, Title I, §111(a). Eff. in general for health insurance coverage offered, sold, issued, renewed, in effect, or operated in the individual market after June 30, 1997, regardless of when a period of creditable coverage occurs.

SEC. 2763. GENERAL EXCEPTIONS.

(a) Exception for Certain Benefits.—The requirements of this part shall not apply to any health insurance coverage in relation to its provision of excepted benefits described in section 2791(c)(1).

(b) Exception for Certain Benefits if Certain Conditions Met.—The requirements of this part shall not apply to any health insurance coverage in relation to its provision of excepted benefits described in paragraph (2), (3), or (4) of section 2791(c) if the benefits are provided under a separate policy, certificate, or contract of insurance.

Amendments to PHSA §2763

Departments of Veterans Affairs and HUD, and Independent Agencies Appropriations Act, 1997 (Pub. L. No. 104-204), as follows:

● **Note on Redesignation:** This section originally was enacted as PHSA §2747. It was redesignated by Act Title 6, §605(a)(2) as PHSA §2763. Eff. for health insurance coverage offered, sold, issued, renewed, in effect, or operated in the individual market on or after Jan. 1, 1998.

Health Insurance Portability and Accountability Act of 1996 (Pub. L. No. 104-191), as follows:

● PHSA §2747 (former) was added by Act Title I, §111(a). Eff. in general for health insurance coverage offered, sold, issued, renewed, in effect, or operated in the individual market after June 30, 1997, regardless of when a period of creditable coverage occurs.

PART C—DEFINITIONS; MISCELLANEOUS PROVISIONS

> ### *Editor's Note*
> PHSA §2791, as follows, is effective March 23, 2010.

SEC. 2791. DEFINITIONS.

(a) Group Health Plan.—

(1) Definition.—The term "group health plan" means an employee welfare benefit plan (as defined in section 3(1) of the Employee Retirement Income Security Act of 1974) to the extent that the plan provides medical care (as defined in paragraph (2)) and including items and services paid for as medical care) to employees or their dependents (as defined under the terms of the plan) directly or through insurance, reimbursement, or otherwise.

(2) Medical care.—The term "medical care" means amounts paid for—

(A) the diagnosis, cure, mitigation, treatment, or prevention of disease, or amounts paid for the purpose of affecting any structure or function of the body,

(B) amounts paid for transportation primarily for and essential to medical care referred to in subparagraph (A), and

(C) amounts paid for insurance covering medical care referred to in subparagraphs (A) and (B).

(3) Treatment of certain plans as group health plan for notice provision.—A program under which creditable coverage described in subparagraph (C), (D), (E), or (F) of section 2701(c)(1) is provided shall be treated as a group health plan for purposes of applying section 2701(e).

(b) Definitions Relating to Health Insurance.—

(1) Health insurance coverage.—The term "health insurance coverage" means benefits consisting of medical care (provided directly, through insurance or reimbursement, or otherwise and including items and services paid for as medical care) under any hospital or medical service policy or certificate, hospital or medical service plan contract, or health maintenance organization contract offered by a health insurance issuer.

(2) Health insurance issuer.—The term "health insurance issuer" means an insurance company, insurance service, or insurance organization (including a health maintenance organization, as defined in paragraph (3)) which is licensed to engage in the business of insurance in a State and which is subject to State law which regulates insurance (within the meaning of section 514(b)(2) of the Employee Retirement Income Security Act of 1974). Such term does not include a group health plan.

(3) Health maintenance organization.—The term "health maintenance organization" means—

(A) a Federally qualified health maintenance organization (as defined in section 1301(a)),

(B) an organization recognized under State law as a health maintenance organization, or

(C) a similar organization regulated under State law for solvency in the same manner and to the same extent as such a health maintenance organization.

(4) Group health insurance coverage.—The term "group health insurance coverage" means, in connection with a group health plan, health insurance coverage offered in connection with such plan.

(5) Individual health insurance coverage.—The term "individual health insurance coverage" means health insurance coverage offered to individuals in the individual market, but does not include short-term limited duration insurance.

(c) Excepted Benefits.—For purposes of this title, the term "excepted benefits" means benefits under one or more (or any combination thereof) of the following:

(1) Benefits not subject to requirements.—

(A) Coverage only for accident, or disability income insurance, or any combination thereof.

(B) Coverage issued as a supplement to liability insurance.

(C) Liability insurance, including general liability insurance and automobile liability insurance.

(D) Workers' compensation or similar insurance.

(E) Automobile medical payment insurance.

(F) Credit-only insurance.

(G) Coverage for on-site medical clinics.

(H) Other similar insurance coverage, specified in regulations, under which benefits for medical care are secondary or incidental to other insurance benefits.

(2) Benefits not subject to requirements if offered separately.—

(A) Limited scope dental or vision benefits.

(B) Benefits for long-term care, nursing home care, home health care, community-based care, or any combination thereof.

(C) Such other similar, limited benefits as are specified in regulations.

(3) Benefits not subject to requirements if offered as independent, noncoordinated benefits.—

Selected Provisions of PHSA After Amendment by PPACA. For sections prior to PPACA, see Part 4.

(A) Coverage only for a specified disease or illness.

(B) Hospital indemnity or other fixed indemnity insurance.

(4) Benefits not subject to requirements if offered as separate insurance policy.—Medicare supplemental health insurance (as defined under section 1882(g)(1) of the Social Security Act), coverage supplemental to the coverage provided under chapter 55 of title 10, United States Code, and similar supplemental coverage provided to coverage under a group health plan.

(d) Other Definitions.—

(1) Applicable State authority.—The term "applicable State authority" means, with respect to a health insurance issuer in a State, the State insurance commissioner or official or officials designated by the State to enforce the requirements of this title for the State involved with respect to such issuer.

(2) Beneficiary.—The term "beneficiary" has the meaning given such term under section 3(8) of the Employee Retirement Income Security Act of 1974.

(3) Bona fide association.—The term "bona fide association" means, with respect to health insurance coverage offered in a State, an association which—

(A) has been actively in existence for at least 5 years;

(B) has been formed and maintained in good faith for purposes other than obtaining insurance;

(C) does not condition membership in the association on any health status-related factor relating to an individual (including an employee of an employer or a dependent of an employee);

(D) makes health insurance coverage offered through the association available to all members regardless of any health status-related factor relating to such members (or individuals eligible for coverage through a member);

(E) does not make health insurance coverage offered through the association available other than in connection with a member of the association; and

(F) meets such additional requirements as may be imposed under State law.

(4) COBRA continuation provision.—The term "COBRA continuation provision" means any of the following:

(A) Section 4980B of the Internal Revenue Code of 1986, other than subsection (f)(1) of such section insofar as it relates to pediatric vaccines.

(B) Part 6 of subtitle B of title I of the Employee Retirement Income Security Act of 1974, other than section 609 of such Act.

(C) Title XXII of this Act.

(5) Employee.—The term "employee" has the meaning given such term under section 3(6) of the Employee Retirement Income Security Act of 1974.

(6) Employer.—The term "employer" has the meaning given such term under section 3(5) of the Employee Retirement Income Security Act of 1974, except that such term shall include only employers of two or more employees.

(7) Church plan.—The term "church plan" has the meaning given such term under section 3(33) of the Employee Retirement Income Security Act of 1974.

(8) Governmental plan.—

(A) The term "governmental plan" has the meaning given such term under section 3(32) of the Employee Retirement Income Security Act of 1974 and any Federal governmental plan.

(B) Federal governmental plan.—The term "Federal governmental plan" means a governmental plan established or maintained for its employees by the Government of the United States or by any agency or instrumentality of such Government.

(C) Non-Federal governmental plan.—The term "non-Federal governmental plan" means a governmental plan that is not a Federal governmental plan.

(9) Health status-related factor.—The term "health status-related factor" means any of the factors described in section 2702(a)(1).

(10) Network plan.—The term "network plan" means health insurance coverage of a health insurance issuer under which the financing and delivery of medical care (including items and services paid for as medical care) are provided, in whole or in part, through a defined set of providers under contract with the issuer.

(11) Participant.—The term "participant" has the meaning given such term under section 3(7) of the Employee Retirement Income Security Act of 1974.

(12) Placed for adoption defined.—The term "placement", or being "placed", for adoption, in connection with any placement for adoption of a child with any person, means the assumption and retention by such person of a legal obligation for total or partial support of such child in anticipation of adoption of such child. The child's placement with such person terminates upon the termination of such legal obligation.

(13) Plan sponsor.—The term "plan sponsor" has the meaning given such term under section 3(16)(B) of the Employee Retirement Income Security Act of 1974.

(14) State.—The term "State" means each of the several States, the District of Columbia, Puerto Rico, the Virgin Islands, Guam, American Samoa, and the Northern Mariana Islands.

(15) Family member.—The term "family member" means, with respect to any individual—

(A) a dependent (as such term is used for purposes of section 2701(f)(2)) of such individual; and

(B) any other individual who is a first-degree, second-degree, third-degree, or fourth-degree relative of such individual or of an individual described in subparagraph (A).

(16) Genetic information.—

(A) In general.—The term "genetic information" means, with respect to any individual, information about—

(i) such individual's genetic tests,

(ii) the genetic tests of family members of such individual, and

(iii) the manifestation of a disease or disorder in family members of such individual.

(B) Inclusion of genetic services and participation in genetic research.—Such term includes, with respect to any individual, any request for, or receipt of, genetic services, or participation in clinical research which includes genetic services, by such individual or any family member of such individual.

(C) Exclusions.—The term "genetic information" shall not include information about the sex or age of any individual.

(17) Genetic test.—

(A) In general.—The term "genetic test" means an analysis of human DNA, RNA, chromosomes, proteins, or metabolites, that detects genotypes, mutations, or chromosomal changes.

(B) Exceptions.—The term "genetic test" does not mean—

(i) an analysis of proteins or metabolites that does not detect genotypes, mutations, or chromosomal changes; or

(ii) an analysis of proteins or metabolites that is directly related to a manifested disease, disorder, or pathological condition that could reasonably be detected by a health care professional with appropriate training and expertise in the field of medicine involved.

(18) Genetic services.—The term "genetic services" means—

(A) a genetic test;

(B) genetic counseling (including obtaining, interpreting, or assessing genetic information); or

(C) genetic education.

(19) Underwriting purposes.—The term "underwriting purposes" means, with respect to any group health plan, or health insurance coverage offered in connection with a group health plan—

(A) rules for, or determination of, eligibility (including enrollment and continued eligibility) for benefits under the plan or coverage;

(B) the computation of premium or contribution amounts under the plan or coverage;

(C) the application of any pre-existing condition exclusion under the plan or coverage; and

(D) other activities related to the creation, renewal, or replacement of a contract of health insurance or health benefits.

(20) Qualified health plan.—The term "qualified health plan" has the meaning given such term in section 1301(a) of the Patient Protection and Affordable Care Act.

(21) Exchange.—The term "Exchange" means an American Health Benefit Exchange established under section 1311 of the Patient Protection and Affordable Care Act.

(e) Definitions Relating to Markets and Small Employers.—For purposes of this title:

(1) Individual market.—

(A) In general.—The term "individual market" means the market for health insurance coverage offered to individuals other than in connection with a group health plan.

(B) Treatment of very small groups.—

(i) In general.—Subject to clause (ii), such terms [term] includes coverage offered in connection with a group health plan that has fewer than two participants as current employees on the first day of the plan year.

(ii) State exception.—Clause (i) shall not apply in the case of a State that elects to regulate the coverage described in such clause as coverage in the small group market.

(2) Large employer.—The term "large employer" means, in connection with a group health plan with respect to a calendar year and a plan year, an employer who employed an average of at least 101 employees on business days during the preceding calendar year and who employs at least 2 employees on the first day of the plan year.

(3) Large group market.—The term "large group market" means the health insurance market under which individuals obtain health insurance coverage (directly or through any arrangement) on behalf of themselves (and their dependents) through a group health plan maintained by a large employer.

(4) Small employer.—The term "small employer" means, in connection with a group health

Selected Provisions of PHSA After Amendment by PPACA. For sections prior to PPACA, see Part 4.

PHSA Sec. 2791(d)(14)

plan with respect to a calendar year and a plan year, an employer who employed an average of at least 1 but not more than 50 employees on business days during the preceding calendar year and who employs at least 1 employees on the first day of the plan year.

(5) Small group market.—The term "small group market" means the health insurance market under which individuals obtain health insurance coverage (directly or through any arrangement) on behalf of themselves (and their dependents) through a group health plan maintained by a small employer.

(6) Application of certain rules in determination of employer size.—For purposes of this subsection—

(A) Application of aggregation rule for employers.—all [All] persons treated as a single employer under subsection (b), (c), (m), or (o) of section 414 of the Internal Revenue Code of 1986 shall be treated as 1 employer.

(B) Employers not in existence in preceding year.—In the case of an employer which was not in existence throughout the preceding calendar year, the determination of whether such employer is a small or large employer shall be based on the average number of employees that it is reasonably expected such employer will employ on business days in the current calendar year.

(C) Predecessors.—Any reference in this subsection to an employer shall include a reference to any predecessor of such employer.

Amendments to PHSA §2791

Patient Protection and Affordable Care Act, 2010 (Pub. L. No. 111-148), as follows:
- PHSA §2791(d)(20)–(21) were added by Act §1563(b) (as redesignated by Act §10107(b)(1)). Eff. on enactment [date of enactment: Mar. 23, 2010].
- PHSA §2791(e) was amended by Act §1563(c)(16) (as redesignated by Act §10107(b)(1)) in para. (2) by striking "51" and inserting "101"; and in para. (4) by striking "at least 2" each place it appeared and inserting "at least 1", and striking "50" and inserting "100". Eff. on enactment [date of enactment: Mar. 23, 2010].

Genetic Information Nondiscrimination Act of 2008 (Pub. L. No. 110-233), as follows:
- PHSA §2791(d)(15)–(19) were added by Act §102(a)(4). Eff. for group health plans, and health insurance coverage offered in connection with group health plans, for plan years beg. after June 21, 2009, and for health insurance coverage offered, sold, issued, renewed, in effect, or operated in the individual market after June 21, 2009.

Health Insurance Portability and Accountability Act of 1996 (Pub. L. No. 104-191), as follows:
- PHSA §2791 was added by Act, Title I, §102(a). Eff. in general for group health plans, and health insurance coverage offered in connection with group health plans, for plan years beg. after June 30, 1997.

SEC. 2792. REGULATIONS.

The Secretary, consistent with section 104 of the Health Care Portability and Accountability Act of 1996, may promulgate such regulations as may be necessary or appropriate to carry out the provisions of this title. The Secretary may promulgate any interim final rules as the Secretary determines are appropriate to carry out this title.

Amendments to PHSA §2792

Health Insurance Portability and Accountability Act of 1996 (Pub. L. No. 104-191), as follows:
- PHSA §2792 was added by Act, Title I, §102(a). Eff. in general for group health plans, and health insurance coverage offered in connection with group health plans, for plan years beg. after June 30, 1997.

> ### Editor's Note
> PHSA §2793, as follows, is effective March 23, 2010.

SEC. 2793. HEALTH INSURANCE CONSUMER INFORMATION.

(a) In General.—The Secretary shall award grants to States to enable such States (or the Exchanges operating in such States) to establish, expand, or provide support for—

(1) offices of health insurance consumer assistance; or

(2) health insurance ombudsman programs.

(b) Eligibility.—

(1) In general.—To be eligible to receive a grant, a State shall designate an independent office of health insurance consumer assistance, or an ombudsman, that, directly or in coordination with State health insurance regulators and consumer assistance organizations, receives and responds to inquiries and complaints concerning health insurance coverage with respect to Federal health insurance requirements and under State law.

(2) Criteria.—A State that receives a grant under this section shall comply with criteria established by the Secretary for carrying out activities under such grant.

(c) Duties.—The office of health insurance consumer assistance or health insurance ombudsman shall—

(1) assist with the filing of complaints and appeals, including filing appeals with the internal appeal or grievance process of the group health plan or health insurance issuer involved and providing information about the external appeal process;

(2) collect, track, and quantify problems and inquiries encountered by consumers;

(3) educate consumers on their rights and responsibilities with respect to group health plans and health insurance coverage;

(4) assist consumers with enrollment in a group health plan or health insurance coverage by providing information, referral, and assistance; and

(5) resolve problems with obtaining premium tax credits under section 36B of the Internal Revenue Code of 1986.

(d) Data Collection.—As a condition of receiving a grant under subsection (a), an office of health insurance consumer assistance or ombudsman program shall be required to collect and report data to the Secretary on the types of problems and inquiries encountered by consumers. The Secretary shall utilize such data to identify areas where more enforcement action is necessary and shall share such information with State insurance regulators, the Secretary of Labor, and the Secretary of the Treasury for use in the enforcement activities of such agencies.

(e) Funding.—

(1) Initial funding.—There is hereby appropriated to the Secretary, out of any funds in the Treasury not otherwise appropriated, $ 30,000,000 for the first fiscal year for which this section applies to carry out this section. Such amount shall remain available without fiscal year limitation.

(2) Authorization for subsequent years.—There is authorized to be appropriated to the Secretary for each fiscal year following the fiscal year described in paragraph (1), such sums as may be necessary to carry out this section.

Amendments to PHSA §2793

Patient Protection and Affordable Care Act, 2010 (Pub. L. No. 111-148), as follows:
- PHSA §2793 was added by Act §1002. Eff. on enactment [date of enactment: Mar. 23, 2010], see Act §1004(b).

> *Editor's Note*
>
> PHSA §2794, as follows, is effective March 23, 2010.

SEC. 2794. ENSURING THAT CONSUMERS GET VALUE FOR THEIR DOLLARS.

(a) Initial Premium Review Process.—

(1) In general.—The Secretary, in conjunction with States, shall establish a process for the annual review, beginning with the 2010 plan year and subject to subsection (b)(2)(A), of unreasonable increases in premiums for health insurance coverage.

(2) Justification and disclosure.—The process established under paragraph (1) shall require health insurance issuers to submit to the Secretary and the relevant State a justification for an unreasonable premium increase prior to the implementation of the increase. Such issuers shall prominently post such information on their Internet websites. The Secretary shall ensure the public disclosure of information on such increases and justifications for all health insurance issuers.

(b) Continuing Premium Review Process.—

(1) Informing Secretary of premium increase patterns.—As a condition of receiving a grant under subsection (c)(1), a State, through its Commissioner of Insurance, shall—

(A) provide the Secretary with information about trends in premium increases in health insurance coverage in premium rating areas in the State; and

(B) make recommendations, as appropriate, to the State Exchange about whether particular health insurance issuers should be excluded from participation in the Exchange based on a pattern or practice of excessive or unjustified premium increases.

(2) Monitoring by Secretary of premium increases.—

(A) In general.—Beginning with plan years beginning in 2014, the Secretary, in conjunction with the States and consistent with the provisions of subsection (a)(2), shall monitor premium increases of health insurance coverage offered through an Exchange and outside of an Exchange.

(B) Consideration in opening exchange.—In determining under section 1312(f)(2)(B) of the Patient Protection and Affordable Care Act whether to offer qualified health plans in the large group market through an Exchange, the State shall take into account any excess of premium growth outside of the Exchange as compared to the rate of such growth inside the Exchange.

(c) Grants in Support of Process.—

(1) Premium review grants during 2010 through 2014.—The Secretary shall carry out a program to award grants to States during the 5-year period beginning with fiscal year 2010 to assist such States in carrying out subsection (a), including—

(A) in reviewing and, if appropriate under State law, approving premium increases for health insurance coverage;

(B) in providing information and recommendations to the Secretary under subsection (b)(1); and

(C) in establishing centers (consistent with subsection (d)) at academic or other nonprofit institutions to collect medical reimbursement information from health insurance issuers, to analyze and organize such information, and to make such information available to such issuers, health care providers, health researchers, health care policy makers, and the general public.

Selected Provisions of PHSA After Amendment by PPACA. For sections prior to PPACA, see Part 4.

(2) Funding.—

(A) In general.—Out of all funds in the Treasury not otherwise appropriated, there are appropriated to the Secretary $250,000,000, to be available for expenditure for grants under paragraph (1) and subparagraph (B).

(B) Further availability for insurance reform and consumer protection.—If the amounts appropriated under subparagraph (A) are not fully obligated under grants under paragraph (1) by the end of fiscal year 2014, any remaining funds shall remain available to the Secretary for grants to States for planning and implementing the insurance reforms and consumer protections under part A.

(C) Allocation.—The Secretary shall establish a formula for determining the amount of any grant to a State under this subsection. Under such formula—

(i) the Secretary shall consider the number of plans of health insurance coverage offered in each State and the population of the State; and

(ii) no State qualifying for a grant under paragraph (1) shall receive less than $1,000,000, or more than $5,000,000 for a grant year.

(d) Medical Reimbursement Data Centers.—

(1) Functions.—A center established under subsection (c)(1)(C) shall—

(A) develop fee schedules and other database tools that fairly and accurately reflect market rates for medical services and the geographic differences in those rates;

(B) use the best available statistical methods and data processing technology to develop such fee schedules and other database tools;

(C) regularly update such fee schedules and other database tools to reflect changes in charges for medical services;

(D) make health care cost information readily available to the public through an Internet website that allows consumers to understand the amounts that health care providers in their area charge for particular medical services; and

(E) regularly publish information concerning the statistical methodologies used by the center to analyze health charge data and make such data available to researchers and policy makers.

(2) Conflicts of interest.—A center established under subsection (c)(1)(C) shall adopt by-laws that ensures that the center (and all members of the governing board of the center) is independent and free from all conflicts of interest. Such by-laws shall ensure that the center is not controlled or influenced by, and does not have any corporate relation to, any individual or entity that may make or receive payments for health care services based on the center's analysis of health care costs.

(3) **Rule of construction.**—Nothing in this subsection shall be construed to permit a center established under subsection (c)(1)(C) to compel health insurance issuers to provide data to the center.

Amendments to PHSA §2794

Patient Protection and Affordable Care Act, 2010 (Pub. L. No. 111-148), as follows:

● PHSA §2794 was added by Act §1003. Eff. on enactment [date of enactment: Mar. 23, 2010], see Act §1004(b).

● PHSA §2794(c)(1) was amended by Act §10101(i)(1) in subpara. (A) by striking "and" at the end; in subpara. (B), by striking the period and inserting "; and"; and adding subpara. (C). Eff. on enactment [date of enactment: Mar. 23, 2010], see Act §1004(b).

● PHSA §2794(d) was added by Act §10101(i)(2). Eff. on enactment [date of enactment: Mar. 23, 2010], see Act §1004(b).

Editor's Note
PHSA §2794[2795], as follows, is effective March 23, 2010.

SEC. 2794 [2795]. UNIFORM FRAUD AND ABUSE REFERRAL FORMAT.

The Secretary shall request the National Association of Insurance Commissioners to develop a model uniform report form for private health insurance issuer seeking to refer suspected fraud and abuse to State insurance departments or other responsible State agencies for investigation. The Secretary shall request that the National Association of Insurance Commissioners develop recommendations for uniform reporting standards for such referrals.

Amendments to PHSA §2794[2795]

Patient Protection and Affordable Care Act, 2010 (Pub. L. No. 111-148), as follows:

● PHSA §2794[2795] was added by Act §6603. Eff. on enactment [date of enactment: Mar. 23, 2010].

Part 4

Public Health Service Act Excerpts
Prior to Enactment of the Patient Protection
and Affordable Care Act

Public Health Service Act, Selected Provisions Prior to PPACA
Finding List

Editor's Note: The following are selected provisions of the Public Health Service Act as they appeared prior to enactment of the Patient Protection and Affordable Care Act.

Section

42 U.S.C.   PHSA

Title 42—Public Health and Welfare

Editor's Note

Part 4 contains excerpts from the Public Health Service Act (PHSA) (42 USC §§300gg et seq.), *prior to* amendment by the Patient Protection and Affordable Care Act (PPACA) (Pub. L. No. 111-148; enacted March 23, 2010) and other legislation.

For a list of the PHSA sections reproduced here, see the PHSA Prior to PPACA Finding List above.

For PHSA sections as amended by PPACA, see Part 3.

PART A—GROUP MARKET REFORMS

SEC. 2701. INCREASED PORTABILITY THROUGH LIMITATION ON PREEXISTING CONDITION EXCLUSIONS.

(a) **Limitation on preexisting condition exclusion period; crediting for periods of previous coverage.**—Subject to subsection (d), a group health plan, and a health insurance issuer offering group health insurance coverage, may, with respect to a participant or beneficiary, impose a preexisting condition exclusion only if—

(1) such exclusion relates to a condition (whether physical or mental), regardless of the cause of the condition, for which medical advice, diagnosis, care, or treatment was recommended or received within the 6-month period ending on the enrollment date;

(2) such exclusion extends for a period of not more than 12 months (or 18 months in the case of a late enrollee) after the enrollment date; and

(3) the period of any such preexisting condition exclusion is reduced by the aggregate of the periods of creditable coverage (if any, as defined in subsection (c)(1)) applicable to the participant or beneficiary as of the enrollment date.

(b) **Definitions.**—For purposes of this part—

(1) **Preexisting condition exclusion.—**

(A) In general.—The term "preexisting condition exclusion" means, with respect to coverage, a limitation or exclusion of benefits relating to a condition based on the fact that the condition was present before the date of enrollment for such coverage, whether or not any medical advice, diagnosis, care, or treatment was recommended or received before such date.

(B) Treatment of genetic information.—Genetic information shall not be treated as a condition described in subsection (a)(1) in the absence of a diagnosis of the condition related to such information.

(2) **Enrollment date.**—The term "enrollment date" means, with respect to an individual covered under a group health plan or health insurance coverage, the date of enrollment of the individual in the plan or coverage or, if earlier, the first day of the waiting period for such enrollment.

(3) **Late enrollee.**—The term "late enrollee" means, with respect to coverage under a group health plan, a participant or beneficiary who enrolls under the plan other than during—

(A) the first period in which the individual is eligible to enroll under the plan, or

(B) a special enrollment period under subsection (f).

(4) **Waiting period.**—The term "waiting period" means, with respect to a group health plan and an individual who is a potential participant or beneficiary in the plan, the period that must pass with respect to the individual before the individual is eligible to be covered for benefits under the terms of the plan.

(c) **Rules Relating to Crediting Previous Coverage.—**

(1) **Creditable coverage defined.**—For purposes of this title, the term "creditable coverage" means, with respect to an individual, coverage of the individual under any of the following:

(A) A group health plan.

(B) Health insurance coverage.

(C) Part A or part B of title XVIII of the Social Security Act.

(D) Title XIX of the Social Security Act, other than coverage consisting solely of benefits under section 1928.

(E) Chapter 55 of title 10, United States Code.

(F) A medical care program of the Indian Health Service or of a tribal organization.

(G) A State health benefits risk pool.

(H) A health plan offered under chapter 89 of title 5, United States Code.

(I) A public health plan (as defined in regulations).

(J) A health benefit plan under section 5(e) of the Peace Corps Act (22 U.S.C. 2504(e)).

Such term does not include coverage consisting solely of coverage of excepted benefits (as defined in section 2791(c)).

(2) Not counting periods before significant breaks in coverage.—

(A) In general.—A period of creditable coverage shall not be counted, with respect to enrollment of an individual under a group health plan, if, after such period and before the enrollment date, there was a 63-day period during all of which the individual was not covered under any creditable coverage.

(B) Waiting period not treated as a break in coverage.—For purposes of subparagraph (A) and subsection (d)(4), any period that an individual is in a waiting period for any coverage under a group health plan (or for group health insurance coverage) or is in an affiliation period (as defined in subsection (g)(2)) shall not be taken into account in determining the continuous period under subparagraph (A).

Editor's Note

PHSA §2701(c)(2)(C), below, as amended by Pub. L. No. 111-344, §114(c), is effective for plan years beginning after December 31, 2010.

(C) TAA-eligible individuals.—In the case of plan years beginning before February 13, 2011—

(i) TAA pre-certification period rule.—In the case of a TAA-eligible individual, the period beginning on the date the individual has a TAA-related loss of coverage and ending on the date that is 7 days after the date of the issuance by the Secretary (or by any person or entity designated by the Secretary) of a qualified health insurance costs credit eligibility certificate for such individual for purposes of section 7527 of the Internal Revenue Code of 1986 shall not be taken into account in determining the continuous period under subparagraph (A).

(ii) Definitions.—The terms "TAA-eligible individual" and "TAA-related loss of coverage" have the meanings given such terms in section 2205(b)(4).

(3) Method of crediting coverage.—

(A) Standard method.—Except as otherwise provided under subparagraph (B), for purposes of applying subsection (a)(3), a group health plan, and a health insurance issuer offering group health insurance coverage, shall count a period of creditable coverage without regard to the specific benefits covered during the period.

(B) Election of alternative method.—A group health plan, or a health insurance issuer offering group health insurance, may elect to apply subsection (a)(3) based on coverage of benefits within each of several classes or categories of benefits specified in regulations rather than as provided under subparagraph (A). Such election shall be made on a uniform basis for all participants and beneficiaries. Under such election a group health plan or issuer shall count a period of creditable coverage with respect to any class or category of benefits if any level of benefits is covered within such class or category.

(C) Plan notice.—In the case of an election with respect to a group health plan under subparagraph (B) (whether or not health insurance coverage is provided in connection with such plan), the plan shall—

(i) prominently state in any disclosure statements concerning the plan, and state to each enrollee at the time of enrollment under the plan, that the plan has made such election, and

(ii) include in such statements a description of the effect of this election.

(D) Issuer notice.—In the case of an election under subparagraph (B) with respect to health insurance coverage offered by an issuer in the small or large group market, the issuer—

(i) shall prominently state in any disclosure statements concerning the coverage, and to each employer at the time of the offer or sale of the coverage, that the issuer has made such election, and

(ii) shall include in such statements a description of the effect of such election.

(4) Establishment of period.—Periods of creditable coverage with respect to an individual shall be established through presentation of certifications described in subsection (e) or in such other manner as may be specified in regulations.

(d) Exceptions.—

(1) Exclusion not applicable to certain newborns.—Subject to paragraph (4), a group health plan, and a health insurance issuer offering group health insurance coverage, may not impose any pre-existing condition exclusion in the case of an individual who, as of the last day of the 30-day period beginning with the date of birth, is covered under creditable coverage.

(2) Exclusion not applicable to certain adopted children.—Subject to paragraph (4), a group health plan, and a health insurance issuer offering group health insurance coverage, may not impose any pre-existing condition exclusion in the case of a child who is adopted or placed for adoption before attaining 18 years of age and who, as of the last day of the 30-day

Selected Provisions of PHSA Prior to Amendment by PPACA. For sections after PPACA and other legislation, see Part 3.

period beginning on the date of the adoption or placement for adoption, is covered under creditable coverage. The previous sentence shall not apply to coverage before the date of such adoption or placement for adoption.

(3) Exclusion not applicable to pregnancy.—A group health plan, and health insurance issuer offering group health insurance coverage, may not impose any preexisting condition exclusion relating to pregnancy as a preexisting condition.

(4) Loss if break in coverage.—Paragraphs (1) and (2) shall no longer apply to an individual after the end of the first 63-day period during all of which the individual was not covered under any creditable coverage.

(e) Certifications and Disclosure of Coverage.—

(1) Requirement for certification of period of creditable coverage.—

(A) In general.—A group health plan, and a health insurance issuer offering group health insurance coverage, shall provide the certification described in subparagraph (B)—

(i) at the time an individual ceases to be covered under the plan or otherwise becomes covered under a COBRA continuation provision,

(ii) in the case of an individual becoming covered under such a provision, at the time the individual ceases to be covered under such provision, and

(iii) on the request on behalf of an individual made not later than 24 months after the date of cessation of the coverage described in clause (i) or (ii), whichever is later.

The certification under clause (i) may be provided, to the extent practicable, at a time consistent with notices required under any applicable COBRA continuation provision.

(B) Certification.—The certification described in this subparagraph is a written certification of—

(i) the period of creditable coverage of the individual under such plan and the coverage (if any) under such COBRA continuation provision, and

(ii) the waiting period (if any) (and affiliation period, if applicable) imposed with respect to the individual for any coverage under such plan.

(C) Issuer compliance.—To the extent that medical care under a group health plan consists of group health insurance coverage, the plan is deemed to have satisfied the certification requirement under this paragraph if the health insurance issuer offering the coverage provides for such certification in accordance with this paragraph.

(2) Disclosure of information on previous benefits.—In the case of an election described in subsection (c)(3)(B) by a group health plan or health insurance issuer, if the plan or issuer enrolls an individual for coverage under the plan and the individual provides a certification of coverage of the individual under paragraph (1)—

(A) upon request of such plan or issuer, the entity which issued the certification provided by the individual shall promptly disclose to such requesting plan or issuer information on coverage of classes and categories of health benefits available under such entity's plan or coverage, and

(B) such entity may charge the requesting plan or issuer for the reasonable cost of disclosing such information.

(3) Regulations.—The Secretary shall establish rules to prevent an entity's failure to provide information under paragraph (1) or (2) with respect to previous coverage of an individual from adversely affecting any subsequent coverage of the individual under another group health plan or health insurance coverage.

(f) Special Enrollment Periods.—

(1) Individuals losing other coverage.—A group health plan, and a health insurance issuer offering group health insurance coverage in connection with a group health plan, shall permit an employee who is eligible, but not enrolled, for coverage under the terms of the plan (or a dependent of such an employee if the dependent is eligible, but not enrolled, for coverage under such terms) to enroll for coverage under the terms of the plan if each of the following conditions is met:

(A) The employee or dependent was covered under a group health plan or had health insurance coverage at the time coverage was previously offered to the employee or dependent.

(B) The employee stated in writing at such time that coverage under a group health plan or health insurance coverage was the reason for declining enrollment, but only if the plan sponsor or issuer (if applicable) required such a statement at such time and provided the employee with notice of such requirement (and the consequences of such requirement) at such time.

(C) The employee's or dependent's coverage described in subparagraph (A)—

(i) was under a COBRA continuation provision and the coverage under such provision was exhausted; or

(ii) was not under such a provision and either the coverage was terminated as a result of loss of eligibility for the coverage (including as a result of legal separation, divorce, death, termination of employment, or reduction in the number of hours of employment) or employer contributions toward such coverage were terminated.

Selected Provisions of PHSA Prior to Amendment by PPACA. For sections after PPACA and other legislation, see Part 3.

(D) Under the terms of the plan, the employee requests such enrollment not later than 30 days after the date of exhaustion of coverage described in subparagraph (C)(i) or termination of coverage or employer contribution described in subparagraph (C)(ii).

(2) For dependent beneficiaries.—

(A) In general.—If—

(i) a group health plan makes coverage available with respect to a dependent of an individual,

(ii) the individual is a participant under the plan (or has met any waiting period applicable to becoming a participant under the plan and is eligible to be enrolled under the plan but for a failure to enroll during a previous enrollment period), and

(iii) a person becomes such a dependent of the individual through marriage, birth, or adoption or placement for adoption, the group health plan shall provide for a dependent special enrollment period described in subparagraph (B) during which the person (or, if not otherwise enrolled, the individual) may be enrolled under the plan as a dependent of the individual, and in the case of the birth or adoption of a child, the spouse of the individual may be enrolled as a dependent of the individual if such spouse is otherwise eligible for coverage.

(B) Dependent special enrollment period.—A dependent special enrollment period under this subparagraph shall be a period of not less than 30 days and shall begin on the later of—

(i) the date dependent coverage is made available, or

(ii) the date of the marriage, birth, or adoption or placement for adoption (as the case may be) described in subparagraph (A)(iii).

(C) No waiting period.—If an individual seeks to enroll a dependent during the first 30 days of such a dependent special enrollment period, the coverage of the dependent shall become effective—

(i) in the case of marriage, not later than the first day of the first month beginning after the date the completed request for enrollment is received;

(ii) in the case of a dependent's birth, as of the date of such birth; or

(iii) in the case of a dependent's adoption or placement for adoption, the date of such adoption or placement for adoption.

(3) Special rules for application in case of Medicaid and CHIP.—

(A) In general.—A group health plan, and a health insurance issuer offering group health insurance coverage in connection with a group health plan, shall permit an employee who is eligible, but not enrolled, for coverage under the terms of the plan (or a dependent of such an employee if the dependent is eligible, but not enrolled, for coverage under such terms) to enroll for coverage under the terms of the plan if either of the following conditions is met:

(i) Termination of Medicaid or CHIP coverage.—The employee or dependent is covered under a Medicaid plan under title XIX of the Social Security Act or under a State child health plan under title XXI of such Act and coverage of the employee or dependent under such a plan is terminated as a result of loss of eligibility for such coverage and the employee requests coverage under the group health plan (or health insurance coverage) not later than 60 days after the date of termination of such coverage.

(ii) Eligibility for employment assistance under Medicaid or CHIP.—The employee or dependent becomes eligible for assistance, with respect to coverage under the group health plan or health insurance coverage, under such Medicaid plan or State child health plan (including under any waiver or demonstration project conducted under or in relation to such a plan), if the employee requests coverage under the group health plan or health insurance coverage not later than 60 days after the date the employee or dependent is determined to be eligible for such assistance.

(B) Coordination with Medicaid and CHIP.—

(i) Outreach to employees regarding availability of Medicaid and CHIP coverage.—

(I) In general.—Each employer that maintains a group health plan in a State that provides medical assistance under a State Medicaid plan under title XIX of the Social Security Act, or child health assistance under a State child health plan under title XXI of such Act, in the form of premium assistance for the purchase of coverage under a group health plan, shall provide to each employee a written notice informing the employee of potential opportunities then currently available in the State in which the employee resides for premium assistance under such plans for health coverage of the employee or the employee's dependents. For purposes of compliance with this subclause, the employer may use any State-specific model notice developed in accordance with section 701(f)(3)(B)(i)(II) of the Employee Retirement Income Security Act of 1974 (29 U.S.C. 1181(f)(3)(B)(i)(II)).

(II) Option to provide concurrent with provision of plan materials to employee.—An employer may provide the model notice applicable to the State in which an employee resides concurrent with the furnishing of materials notifying the employee of health plan eligibility, concurrent with materials provided to the employee in connection with an open season or election process conducted under the plan, or concurrent with the furnishing of the summary plan description as provided in section 104(b) of the Employee Retirement Income Security Act of 1974.

(ii) Disclosure about group health plan benefits to States for Medicaid and CHIP eligible individuals.—In the case of an enrollee in a group health plan who is covered under a Medicaid plan of a State under title XIX of the Social Security Act or under a State child health plan under title XXI of such Act, the plan administrator of the group health plan shall disclose to the State, upon request, information about the benefits available under the group health plan in sufficient specificity, as determined under regulations of the Secretary of Health and Human Services in consultation with the Secretary that require use of the model coverage coordination disclosure form developed under section 311(b)(1)(C) of the Children's Health Insurance Reauthorization Act of 2009, so as to permit the State to make a determination (under paragraph (2)(B), (3), or (10) of section 2105(c) of the Social Security Act or otherwise) concerning the cost-effectiveness of the State providing medical or child health assistance through premium assistance for the purchase of coverage under such group health plan and in order for the State to provide supplemental benefits required under paragraph (10)(E) of such section or other authority.

(g) Use of Affiliation Period by HMOs as Alternative to Preexisting Condition Exclusion.—

(1) In general.—A health maintenance organization which offers health insurance coverage in connection with a group health plan and which does not impose any preexisting condition exclusion allowed under subsection (a) with respect to any particular coverage option may impose an affiliation period for such coverage option, but only if—

(A) such period is applied uniformly without regard to any health status-related factors; and

(B) such period does not exceed 2 months (or 3 months in the case of a late enrollee).

(2) Affiliation period.—

(A) Defined.—For purposes of this title, the term "affiliation period" means a period which, under the terms of the health insurance coverage offered by the health maintenance organization, must expire before the health insurance coverage becomes effective. The organization is not required to provide health care services or benefits during such period and no premium shall be charged to the participant or beneficiary for any coverage during the period.

(B) Beginning.—Such period shall begin on the enrollment date.

(C) Runs concurrently with waiting periods.—An affiliation period under a plan shall run concurrently with any waiting period under the plan.

(3) Alternative methods.—A health maintenance organization described in paragraph (1) may use alternative methods, from those described in such paragraph, to address adverse selection as approved by the State insurance commissioner or official or officials designated by the State to enforce the requirements of this part for the State involved with respect to such issuer.

SEC. 2702. PROHIBITING DISCRIMINATION AGAINST INDIVIDUAL PARTICIPANTS AND BENEFICIARIES BASED ON HEALTH STATUS.

(a) Ineligibility to Enroll.—

(1) In general.—Subject to paragraph (2), a group health plan, and a health insurance issuer offering group health insurance coverage in connection with a group health plan, may not establish rules for eligibility (including continued eligibility) of any individual to enroll under the terms of the plan based on any of the following health status-related factors in relation to the individual or a dependent of the individual:

(A) Health status.

(B) Medical condition (including both physical and mental illnesses).

(C) Claims experience.

(D) Receipt of health care.

(E) Medical history.

(F) Genetic information.

(G) Evidence of insurability (including conditions arising out of acts of domestic violence).

(H) Disability.

(2) No application to benefits or exclusions.— To the extent consistent with section 701, paragraph (1) shall not be construed—

(A) to require a group health plan, or group health insurance coverage, to provide particular benefits other than those provided under the terms of such plan or coverage, or

(B) to prevent such a plan or coverage from establishing limitations or restrictions on the amount, level, extent, or nature of the benefits or coverage for similarly situated individuals enrolled in the plan or coverage.

(3) Construction.—For purposes of paragraph (1), rules for eligibility to enroll under a plan include rules defining any applicable waiting periods for such enrollment.

(b) In Premium Contributions.—

(1) In general.—A group health plan, and a health insurance issuer offering health insurance coverage in connection with a group health plan, may not require any individual (as a condition of enrollment or continued enrollment under the plan) to pay a premium or contribution which is greater than such premium or contribution for a similarly situated individual enrolled in the plan on the basis of any health status-related factor in relation to the individual or to an individual enrolled under the plan as a dependent of the individual.

(2) Construction.—Nothing in paragraph (1) shall be construed—

(A) to restrict the amount that an employer may be charged for coverage under a group health plan except as provided in paragraph (3); or

(B) to prevent a group health plan, and a health insurance issuer offering group health insurance coverage, from establishing premium discounts or rebates or modifying otherwise applicable copayments or deductibles in return for adherence to programs of health promotion and disease prevention.

(3) No group-based discrimination on basis of genetic information.—

(A) In general.—For purposes of this section, a group health plan, and health insurance issuer offering group health insurance coverage in connection with a group health plan, may not adjust premium or contribution amounts for the group covered under such plan on the basis of genetic information.

(B) Rule of construction.—Nothing in subparagraph (A) or in paragraphs (1) and (2) of subsection (d) shall be construed to limit the ability of a health insurance issuer offering health insurance coverage in connection with a group health plan to increase the premium for an employer based on the manifestation of a disease or disorder of an individual who is enrolled in the plan. In such case, the manifestation of a disease or disorder in one individual cannot also be used as genetic information about other group members and to further increase the premium for the employer.

(c) Genetic Testing.—

(1) Limitation on requesting or requiring genetic testing.—A group health plan, and a health insurance issuer offering health insurance coverage in connection with a group health plan, shall not request or require an individual or a family member of such individual to undergo a genetic test.

(2) Rule of construction.—Paragraph (1) shall not be construed to limit the authority of a health care professional who is providing health care services to an individual to request that such individual undergo a genetic test.

(3) Rule of construction regarding payment.—

(A) In general.—Nothing in paragraph (1) shall be construed to preclude a group health plan, or a

health insurance issuer offering health insurance coverage in connection with a group health plan, from obtaining and using the results of a genetic test in making a determination regarding payment (as such term is defined for the purposes of applying the regulations promulgated by the Secretary under part C of title XI of the Social Security Act and section 264 of the Health Insurance Portability and Accountability Act of 1996, as may be revised from time to time) consistent with subsection (a).

(B) Limitation.—For purposes of subparagraph (A), a group health plan, or a health insurance issuer offering health insurance coverage in connection with a group health plan, may request only the minimum amount of information necessary to accomplish the intended purpose.

(4) Research exception.—Notwithstanding paragraph (1), a group health plan, or a health insurance issuer offering health insurance coverage in connection with a group health plan, may request, but not require, that a participant or beneficiary undergo a genetic test if each of the following conditions is met:

(A) The request is made pursuant to research that complies with part 46 of title 45, Code of Federal Regulations, or equivalent Federal regulations, and any applicable State or local law or regulations for the protection of human subjects in research.

(B) The plan or issuer clearly indicates to each participant or beneficiary, or in the case of a minor child, to the legal guardian of such beneficiary, to whom the request is made that—

(i) compliance with the request is voluntary; and

(ii) non-compliance will have no effect on enrollment status or premium or contribution amounts.

(C) No genetic information collected or acquired under this paragraph shall be used for underwriting purposes.

(D) The plan or issuer notifies the Secretary in writing that the plan or issuer is conducting activities pursuant to the exception provided for under this paragraph, including a description of the activities conducted.

(E) The plan or issuer complies with such other conditions as the Secretary may by regulation require for activities conducted under this paragraph.

(d) Prohibition on Collection of Genetic Information.—

(1) In general.—A group health plan, and a health insurance issuer offering health insurance coverage in connection with a group health plan, shall not request, require, or purchase genetic information for underwriting purposes (as defined in section 2791).

(2) Prohibition on collection of genetic information prior to enrollment.—A group health plan,

Selected Provisions of PHSA Prior to Amendment by PPACA. For sections after PPACA and other legislation, see Part 3.

PHSA Sec. 2702(b)(1)

and a health insurance issuer offering health insurance coverage in connection with a group health plan, shall not request, require, or purchase genetic information with respect to any individual prior to such individual's enrollment under the plan or coverage in connection with such enrollment.

(3) Incidental collection.—If a group health plan, or a health insurance issuer offering health insurance coverage in connection with a group health plan, obtains genetic information incidental to the requesting, requiring, or purchasing of other information concerning any individual, such request, requirement, or purchase shall not be considered a violation of paragraph (2) if such request, requirement, or purchase is not in violation of paragraph (1).

(e) Application to All Plans.—The provisions of subsections (a)(1)(F), (b)(3), (c) , and (d) and subsection (b)(1) and section 2701 with respect to genetic information, shall apply to group health plans and health insurance issuers without regard to section 2721(a).

(f) Genetic Information of a Fetus or Embryo.— Any reference in this part to genetic information concerning an individual or family member of an individual shall—

(1) with respect to such an individual or family member of an individual who is a pregnant woman, include genetic information of any fetus carried by such pregnant woman; and

(2) with respect to an individual or family member utilizing an assisted reproductive technology, include genetic information of any embryo legally held by the individual or family member.

SEC. 2704. STANDARDS RELATING TO BENEFITS FOR MOTHERS AND NEWBORNS.

(a) Requirements for Minimum Hospital Stay Following Birth.—

(1) In general.—A group health plan, and a health insurance issuer offering group health insurance coverage, may not—

(A) except as provided in paragraph (2)—

(i) restrict benefits for any hospital length of stay in connection with childbirth for the mother or newborn child, following a normal vaginal delivery, to less than 48 hours, or

(ii) restrict benefits for any hospital length of stay in connection with childbirth for the mother or newborn child, following a cesarean section, to less than 96 hours, or

(B) require that a provider obtain authorization from the plan or the issuer for prescribing any length of stay required under subparagraph (A) (without regard to paragraph (2)).

(2) Exception.—Paragraph (1)(A) shall not apply in connection with any group health plan or health insurance issuer in any case in which the decision to discharge the mother or her newborn child prior to the expiration of the minimum length of stay otherwise required under paragraph (1)(A) is made by an attending provider in consultation with the mother.

(b) Prohibitions.—A group health plan, and a health insurance issuer offering group health insurance coverage in connection with a group health plan, may not—

(1) deny to the mother or her newborn child eligibility, or continued eligibility, to enroll or to renew coverage under the terms of the plan, solely for the purpose of avoiding the requirements of this section;

(2) provide monetary payments or rebates to mothers to encourage such mothers to accept less than the minimum protections available under this section;

(3) penalize or otherwise reduce or limit the reimbursement of an attending provider because such provider provided care to an individual participant or beneficiary in accordance with this section;

(4) provide incentives (monetary or otherwise) to an attending provider to induce such provider to provide care to an individual participant or beneficiary in a manner inconsistent with this section; or

(5) subject to subsection (c)(3), restrict benefits for any portion of a period within a hospital length of stay required under subsection (a) in a manner which is less favorable than the benefits provided for any preceding portion of such stay.

(c) Rules of Construction.—

(1) Nothing in this section shall be construed to require a mother who is a participant or beneficiary—

(A) to give birth in a hospital; or

(B) to stay in the hospital for a fixed period of time following the birth of her child.

(2) This section shall not apply with respect to any group health plan, or any group health insurance coverage offered by a health insurance issuer, which does not provide benefits for hospital lengths of stay in connection with childbirth for a mother or her newborn child.

(3) Nothing in this section shall be construed as preventing a group health plan or issuer from imposing deductibles, coinsurance, or other cost-sharing in relation to benefits for hospital lengths of stay in connection with childbirth for a mother or newborn child under the plan (or under health insurance coverage offered in connection with a group health plan), except that such coinsurance or other cost-sharing for any portion of a period within a hospital length of stay required under subsection (a) may not be greater than such coinsurance or cost-sharing for any preceding portion of such stay.

(d) Notice.—A group health plan under this part shall comply with the notice requirement under section 711(d) of the Employee Retirement Income Security Act of 1974 with respect to the requirements of this section as if such section applied to such plan.

(e) Level and type of reimbursements.—Nothing in this section shall be construed to prevent a group health plan or a health insurance issuer offering group health insurance coverage from negotiating the level and type of reimbursement with a provider for care provided in accordance with this section.

(f) Preemption; Exception for Health Insurance Coverage in Certain States.—

(1) In general.—The requirements of this section shall not apply with respect to health insurance coverage if there is a State law (as defined in section 2723(d)(1)) for a State that regulates such coverage that is described in any of the following subparagraphs:

(A) Such State law requires such coverage to provide for at least a 48-hour hospital length of stay following a normal vaginal delivery and at least a 96-hour hospital length of stay following a cesarean section.

(B) Such State law requires such coverage to provide for maternity and pediatric care in accordance with guidelines established by the American College of Obstetricians and Gynecologists, the American Academy of Pediatrics, or other established professional medical associations.

(C) Such State law requires, in connection with such coverage for maternity care, that the hospital length of stay for such care is left to the decision of (or required to be made by) the attending provider in consultation with the mother.

(2) Construction.—Section 2723(a)(1) shall not be construed as superseding a State law described in paragraph (1).

SEC. 2705. PARITY IN MENTAL HEALTH AND SUBSTANCE USE DISORDER BENEFITS.

(a) In general.—

(1) Aggregate lifetime limits.—In the case of a group health plan (or health insurance coverage offered in connection with such a plan) that provides both medical and surgical benefits and mental health or substance use disorder benefits—

(A) No lifetime limit.—If the plan or coverage does not include an aggregate lifetime limit on substantially all medical and surgical benefits, the plan or coverage may not impose any aggregate lifetime limit on mental health or substance use disorder benefits.

(B) Lifetime limit.—If the plan or coverage includes an aggregate lifetime limit on substantially all medical and surgical benefits (in this paragraph referred to as the "applicable lifetime limit"), the plan or coverage shall either—

(i) apply the applicable lifetime limit both to the medical and surgical benefits to which it otherwise would apply and to mental health and substance use disorder benefits and not distinguish in the application of such limit between such medical and surgical benefits and mental health and substance use disorder benefits; or

(ii) not include any aggregate lifetime limit on mental health or substance use disorder benefits that is less than the applicable lifetime limit.

(C) Rule in case of different limits.—In the case of a plan or coverage that is not described in subparagraph (A) or (B) and that includes no or different aggregate lifetime limits on different categories of medical and surgical benefits, the Secretary shall establish rules under which subparagraph (B) is applied to such plan or coverage with respect to mental health and substance use disorder benefits by substituting for the applicable lifetime limit an average aggregate lifetime limit that is computed taking into account the weighted average of the aggregate lifetime limits applicable to such categories.

(2) Annual limits.—In the case of a group health plan (or health insurance coverage offered in connection with such a plan) that provides both medical and surgical benefits and mental health or substance use disorder benefits—

(A) No annual limit.—If the plan or coverage does not include an annual limit on substantially all medical and surgical benefits, the plan or coverage may not impose any annual limit on mental health or substance use disorder benefits.

(B) Annual limit.—If the plan or coverage includes an annual limit on substantially all medical and surgical benefits (in this paragraph referred to as the "applicable annual limit"), the plan or coverage shall either—

(i) apply the applicable annual limit both to medical and surgical benefits to which it otherwise would apply and to mental health and substance use disorder benefits and not distinguish in the application of such limit between such medical and surgical benefits and mental health and substance use disorder benefits; or

(ii) not include any annual limit on mental health or substance use disorder benefits that is less than the applicable annual limit.

(C) Rule in case of different limits.—In the case of a plan or coverage that is not described in subparagraph (A) or (B) and that includes no or different annual limits on different categories of medical and surgical benefits, the Secretary shall establish

Selected Provisions of PHSA Prior to Amendment by PPACA. For sections after PPACA and other legislation, see Part 3.

rules under which subparagraph (B) is applied to such plan or coverage with respect to mental health and substance use disorder benefits by substituting for the applicable annual limit an average annual limit that is computed taking into account the weighted average of the annual limits applicable to such categories.

(3) Financial requirements and treatment limitations.—

(A) In general.—In the case of a group health plan (or health insurance coverage offered in connection with such a plan) that provides both medical and surgical benefits and mental health or substance use disorder benefits, such plan or coverage shall ensure that—

(i) the financial requirements applicable to such mental health or substance use disorder benefits are no more restrictive than the predominant financial requirements applied to substantially all medical and surgical benefits covered by the plan (or coverage), and there are no separate cost sharing requirements that are applicable only with respect to mental health or substance use disorder benefits; and

(ii) the treatment limitations applicable to such mental health or substance use disorder benefits are no more restrictive than the predominant treatment limitations applied to substantially all medical and surgical benefits covered by the plan (or coverage) and there are no separate treatment limitations that are applicable only with respect to mental health or substance use disorder benefits.

(B) Definitions.—In this paragraph:

(i) Financial requirement.—The term "financial requirement" includes deductibles, copayments, coinsurance, and out-of-pocket expenses, but excludes an aggregate lifetime limit and an annual limit subject to paragraphs (1) and (2).

(ii) Predominant.—A financial requirement or treatment limit is considered to be predominant if it is the most common or frequent of such type of limit or requirement.

(iii) Treatment limitation.—The term "treatment limitation" includes limits on the frequency of treatment, number of visits, days of coverage, or other similar limits on the scope or duration of treatment.

(4) Availability of plan information.—The criteria for medical necessity determinations made under the plan with respect to mental health or substance use disorder benefits (or the health insurance coverage offered in connection with the plan with respect to such benefits) shall be made available by the plan administrator (or the health insurance issuer offering such coverage) in accordance with regulations to any current or potential participant, beneficiary, or con-

tracting provider upon request. The reason for any denial under the plan (or coverage) of reimbursement or payment for services with respect to mental health or substance use disorder benefits in the case of any participant or beneficiary shall, on request or as otherwise required, be made available by the plan administrator (or the health insurance issuer offering such coverage) to the participant or beneficiary in accordance with regulations.

(5) Out-of-network providers.—In the case of a plan or coverage that provides both medical and surgical benefits and mental health or substance use disorder benefits, if the plan or coverage provides coverage for medical or surgical benefits provided by out-of-network providers, the plan or coverage shall provide coverage for mental health or substance use disorder benefits provided by out-of-network providers in a manner that is consistent with the requirements of this section.

(b) Construction.—Nothing in this section shall be construed—

(1) as requiring a group health plan (or health insurance coverage offered in connection with such a plan) to provide any mental health or substance use disorder benefits; or

(2) in the case of a group health plan (or health insurance coverage offered in connection with such a plan) that provides mental health or substance use disorder benefits, as affecting the terms and conditions of the plan or coverage relating to such benefits under the plan or coverage, except as provided in subsection (a).

(c) Exemptions.—

(1) Small employer exemption.—This section shall not apply to any group health plan (and group health insurance coverage offered in connection with a group health plan) for any plan year of a small employer (as defined in section 2791(e)(4), except that for purposes of this paragraph such term shall include employers with 1 employee in the case of an employer residing in a State that permits small groups to include a single individual).

(2) Cost exemption.—

(A) In general.—With respect to a group health plan (or health insurance coverage offered in connection with such a plan), if the application of this section to such plan (or coverage) results in an increase for the plan year involved of the actual total costs of coverage with respect to medical and surgical benefits and mental health and substance use disorder benefits under the plan (as determined and certified under subparagraph (C)) by an amount that exceeds the applicable percentage described in subparagraph (B) of the actual total plan costs, the provisions of this section shall not apply to such plan (or coverage) during the following plan year, and such exemption shall apply to the plan (or coverage) for 1 plan year. An employer may elect to continue to apply mental health and substance use disorder parity pursuant to this section with respect to the group health plan (or coverage) involved regardless of any increase in total costs.

(B) Applicable percentage.—With respect to a plan (or coverage), the applicable percentage described in this subparagraph shall be—

(i) 2 percent in the case of the first plan year in which this section is applied; and

(ii) 1 percent in the case of each subsequent plan year.

(C) Determinations by actuaries.—Determinations as to increases in actual costs under a plan (or coverage) for purposes of this section shall be made and certified by a qualified and licensed actuary who is a member in good standing of the American Academy of Actuaries. All such determinations shall be in a written report prepared by the actuary. The report, and all underlying documentation relied upon by the actuary, shall be maintained by the group health plan or health insurance issuer for a period of 6 years following the notification made under subparagraph (E).

(D) 6-month determinations.—If a group health plan (or a health insurance issuer offering coverage in connection with a group health plan) seeks an exemption under this paragraph, determinations under subparagraph (A) shall be made after such plan (or coverage) has complied with this section for the first 6 months of the plan year involved.

(E) Notification.—

(i) In general.—A group health plan (or a health insurance issuer offering coverage in connection with a group health plan) that, based upon a certification described under subparagraph (C), qualifies for an exemption under this paragraph, and elects to implement the exemption, shall promptly notify the Secretary, the appropriate State agencies, and participants and beneficiaries in the plan of such election.

(ii) Requirement.—A notification to the Secretary under clause (i) shall include—

(I) a description of the number of covered lives under the plan (or coverage) involved at the time of the notification, and as applicable, at the time of any prior election of the cost-exemption under this paragraph by such plan (or coverage);

(II) for both the plan year upon which a cost exemption is sought and the year prior, a description of the actual total costs of coverage with respect to medical and surgical benefits and mental health and substance use disorder benefits under the plan; and

(III) for both the plan year upon which a cost exemption is sought and the year prior, the actual total costs of coverage with respect to mental health and substance use disorder benefits under the plan.

(iii) Confidentiality.—A notification to the Secretary under clause (i) shall be confidential. The Secretary shall make available, upon request and on not more than an annual basis, an anonymous itemization of such notifications, that includes—

(I) a breakdown of States by the size and type of employers submitting such notification; and

(II) a summary of the data received under clause (ii).

(F) Audits by appropriate agencies.—To determine compliance with this paragraph, the Secretary may audit the books and records of a group health plan or health insurance issuer relating to an exemption, including any actuarial reports prepared pursuant to subparagraph (C), during the 6 year period following the notification of such exemption under subparagraph (E). A State agency receiving a notification under subparagraph (E) may also conduct such an audit with respect to an exemption covered by such notification.

(d) Separate Application to Each Option Offered.—In the case of a group health plan that offers a participant or beneficiary two or more benefit package options under the plan, the requirements of this section shall be applied separately with respect to each such option.

(e) Definitions.—For purposes of this section—

(1) Aggregate lifetime limit.—The term "aggregate lifetime limit" means, with respect to benefits under a group health plan or health insurance coverage, a dollar limitation on the total amount that may be paid with respect to such benefits under the plan or health insurance coverage with respect to an individual or other coverage unit.

(2) Annual limit.—The term "annual limit" means, with respect to benefits under a group health plan or health insurance coverage, a dollar limitation on the total amount of benefits that may be paid with respect to such benefits in a 12-month period under the plan or health insurance coverage with respect to an individual or other coverage unit.

(3) Medical or surgical benefits.—The term "medical or surgical benefits" means benefits with respect to medical or surgical services, as defined under the terms of the plan or coverage (as the case may be), but does not include mental health benefits.

(4) Mental health benefits.—The term "mental health benefits" means benefits with respect to services for mental health conditions, as defined under the terms of the plan and in accordance with applicable Federal and State law.

(5) Substance use disorder benefits.—The term "substance use disorder benefits" means benefits with respect to services for substance use disorders, as defined under the terms of the plan and in accordance with applicable Federal and State law.

SEC. 2706. REQUIRED COVERAGE FOR RECONSTRUCTIVE SURGERY FOLLOWING MASTECTOMIES.

The provisions of section 713 of the Employee Retirement Income Security Act of 1974 shall apply to group health plans, and health insurance issuers providing health insurance coverage in connection with group health plans, as if included in this subpart.

SEC. 2707. COVERAGE OF DEPENDENT STUDENTS ON MEDICALLY NECESSARY LEAVE OF ABSENCE.

(a) **Medically Necessary Leave of Absence.**—In this section, the term "medically necessary leave of absence" means, with respect to a dependent child described in subsection (b)(2) in connection with a group health plan or health insurance coverage offered in connection with such plan, a leave of absence of such child from a postsecondary educational institution (including an institution of higher education as defined in section 102 of the Higher Education Act of 1965, or any other change in enrollment of such child at such an institution, that—

(1) **commences while such child is suffering from a serious illness or injury;**

(2) is medically necessary; and

(3) causes such child to lose student status for purposes of coverage under the terms of the plan or coverage.

(b) **Requirement to Continue Coverage.**—

(1) **In general.**—In the case of a dependent child described in paragraph (2), a group health plan, or a health insurance issuer that provides health insurance coverage in connection with a group health plan, shall not terminate coverage of such child under such plan or health insurance coverage due to a medically necessary leave of absence before the date that is the earlier of—

(A) the date that is 1 year after the first day of the medically necessary leave of absence; or

(B) the date on which such coverage would otherwise terminate under the terms of the plan or health insurance coverage.

(2) **Dependent child described.**—A dependent child described in this paragraph is, with respect to a group health plan or health insurance coverage offered in connection with the plan, a beneficiary under the plan who—

(A) is a dependent child, under the terms of the plan or coverage, of a participant or beneficiary under the plan or coverage; and

(B) was enrolled in the plan or coverage, on the basis of being a student at a postsecondary educational institution (as described in subsection (a)), immediately before the first day of the medically necessary leave of absence involved.

(3) **Certification by physician.**—Paragraph (1) shall apply to a group health plan or health insurance coverage offered by an issuer in connection with such plan only if the plan or issuer of the coverage has received written certification by a treating physician of the dependent child which states that the child is suffering from a serious illness or injury and that the leave of absence (or other change of enrollment) described in subsection (a) is medically necessary.

(c) **Notice.**—A group health plan, and a health insurance issuer providing health insurance coverage in connection with a group health plan, shall include, with any notice regarding a requirement for certification of student status for coverage under the plan or coverage, a description of the terms of this section for continued coverage during medically necessary leaves of absence. Such description shall be in language which is understandable to the typical plan participant.

(d) **No Change in Benefits.**—A dependent child whose benefits are continued under this section shall be entitled to the same benefits as if (during the medically necessary leave of absence) the child continued to be a covered student at the institution of higher education and was not on a medically necessary leave of absence.

(e) **Continued Application in Case of Changed Coverage.**—If—

(1) a dependent child of a participant or beneficiary is in a period of coverage under a group health plan or health insurance coverage offered in connection with such a plan, pursuant to a medically necessary leave of absence of the child described in subsection (b);

(2) the manner in which the participant or beneficiary is covered under the plan changes, whether through a change in health insurance coverage or health insurance issuer, a change between health insurance coverage and self-insured coverage, or otherwise; and

(3) the coverage as so changed continues to provide coverage of beneficiaries as dependent children,

this section shall apply to coverage of the child under the changed coverage for the remainder of the period of the medically necessary leave of absence of the dependent child under the plan in the same manner as it would have applied if the changed coverage had been the previous coverage.

SEC. 2711. GUARANTEED AVAILABLITY OF COVERAGE FOR EMPLOYERS IN THE GROUP MARKET.

(a) Issuance of Coverage in the Small Group Market.—

(1) In general.—Subject to subsections (c) through (f), each health insurance issuer that offers health insurance coverage in the small group market in a State—

(A) must accept every small employer (as defined in section 2791(e)(4)) in the State that applies for such coverage; and

(B) must accept for enrollment under such coverage every eligible individual (as defined in paragraph (2)) who applies for enrollment during the period in which the individual first becomes eligible to enroll under the terms of the group health plan and may not place any restriction which is inconsistent with section 2702 on an eligible individual being a participant or beneficiary.

(2) Eligible individual defined.—For purposes of this section, the term "eligible individual" means, with respect to a health insurance issuer that offers health insurance coverage to a small employer in connection with a group health plan in the small group market, such an individual in relation to the employer as shall be determined—

(A) in accordance with the terms of such plan,

(B) as provided by the issuer under rules of the issuer which are uniformly applicable in a State to small employers in the small group market, and

(C) in accordance with all applicable State laws governing such issuer and such market.

(b) Assuring Access in the Large Group Market.—

(1) Reports to HHS.—The Secretary shall request that the chief executive officer of each State submit to the Secretary, by not later December 31, 2000, and every 3 years thereafter a report on—

(A) the access of large employers to health insurance coverage in the State, and

(B) the circumstances for lack of access (if any) of large employers (or one or more classes of such employers) in the State to such coverage.

(2) Triennial reports to Congress.—The Secretary, based on the reports submitted under paragraph (1) and such other information as the Secretary may use, shall prepare and submit to Congress, every 3 years, a report describing the extent to which large employers (and classes of such employers) that seek health insurance coverage in the different States are able to obtain access to such coverage. Such report shall include such recommendations as the Secretary determines to be appropriate.

(3) GAO report on large employer access to health insurance coverage.—The Comptroller General shall provide for a study of the extent to which classes of large employers in the different States are able to obtain access to health insurance coverage and the circumstances for lack of access (if any) to such coverage. The Comptroller General shall submit to Congress a report on such study not later than 18 months after the date of the enactment of this title.

(c) Special Rules for Network Plans.—

(1) In general.—In the case of a health insurance issuer that offers health insurance coverage in the small group market through a network plan, the issuer may—

(A) limit the employers that may apply for such coverage to those with eligible individuals who live, work, or reside in the service area for such network plan; and

(B) within the service area of such plan, deny such coverage to such employers if the issuer has demonstrated, if required, to the applicable State authority that—

(i) it will not have the capacity to deliver services adequately to enrollees of any additional groups because of its obligations to existing group contract holders and enrollees, and

(ii) it is applying this paragraph uniformly to all employers without regard to the claims experience of those employers and their employees (and their dependents) or any health status-related factor relating to such employees and dependents.

(2) 180-day suspension upon denial of coverage.—An issuer, upon denying health insurance coverage in any service area in accordance with paragraph (1)(B), may not offer coverage in the small group market within such service area for a period of 180 days after the date such coverage is denied.

(d) Application of Financial Capacity Limits.—

(1) In general.—A health insurance issuer may deny health insurance coverage in the small group market if the issuer has demonstrated, if required, to the applicable State authority that—

(A) it does not have the financial reserves necessary to underwrite additional coverage; and

(B) it is applying this paragraph uniformly to all employers in the small group market in the State consistent with applicable State law and without regard to the claims experience of those employers and their employees (and their dependents) or any health status-related factor relating to such employees and dependents.

(2) 180-day suspension upon denial of coverage.—A health insurance issuer upon denying health insurance coverage in connection with group health plans in accordance with paragraph (1) in a State may

Selected Provisions of PHSA Prior to Amendment by PPACA. For sections after PPACA and other legislation, see Part 3.

not offer coverage in connection with group health plans in the small group market in the State for a period of 180 days after the date such coverage is denied or until the issuer has demonstrated to the applicable State authority, if required under applicable State law, that the issuer has sufficient financial reserves to underwrite additional coverage, whichever is later. An applicable State authority may provide for the application of this subsection on a service-area-specific basis.

(e) Exception to Requirement for Failure to Meet Certain Minimum Participation or Contribution Rules.—

(1) In general.—Subsection (a) shall not be construed to preclude a health insurance issuer from establishing employer contribution rules or group participation rules for the offering of health insurance coverage in connection with a group health plan in the small group market, as allowed under applicable State law.

(2) Rules defined.—For purposes of paragraph (1)—

(A) the term "employer contribution rule" means a requirement relating to the minimum level or amount of employer contribution toward the premium for enrollment of participants and beneficiaries; and

(B) the term "group participation rule" means a requirement relating to the minimum number of participants or beneficiaries that must be enrolled in relation to a specified percentage or number of eligible individuals or employees of an employer.

(f) Exception for Coverage Offered Only to Bona Fide Association Members.—Subsection (a) shall not apply to health insurance coverage offered by a health insurance issuer if such coverage is made available in the small group market only through one or more bona fide associations (as defined in section 2791(d)(3)).

SEC. 2712. GUARANTEED RENEWABILITY OF COVERAGE FOR EMPLOYERS IN THE GROUP MARKET.

(a) In general.—Except as provided in this section, if a health insurance issuer offers health insurance coverage in the small or large group market in connection with a group health plan, the issuer must renew or continue in force such coverage at the option of the plan sponsor of the plan.

(b) General Exceptions.—A health insurance issuer may nonrenew or discontinue health insurance coverage offered in connection with a group health plan in the small or large group market based only on one or more of the following:

(1) Nonpayment of premiums.—The plan sponsor has failed to pay premiums or contributions in accordance with the terms of the health insurance coverage or the issuer has not received timely premium payments.

(2) Fraud.—The plan sponsor has performed an act or practice that constitutes fraud or made an intentional misrepresentation of material fact under the terms of the coverage.

(3) Violation of participation or contribution rules.—The plan sponsor has failed to comply with a material plan provision relating to employer contribution or group participation rules, as permitted under section 2711(e) in the case of the small group market or pursuant to applicable State law in the case of the large group market.

(4) Termination of coverage.—The issuer is ceasing to offer coverage in such market in accordance with subsection (c) and applicable State law.

(5) Movement outside service area.—In the case of a health insurance issuer that offers health insurance coverage in the market through a network plan, there is no longer any enrollee in connection with such plan who lives, resides, or works in the service area of the issuer (or in the area for which the issuer is authorized to do business) and, in the case of the small group market, the issuer would deny enrollment with respect to such plan under section 2711(c)(1)(A).

(6) Association membership ceases.—In the case of health insurance coverage that is made available in the small or large group market (as the case may be) only through one or more bona fide associations, the membership of an employer in the association (on the basis of which the coverage is provided) ceases but only if such coverage is terminated under this paragraph uniformly without regard to any health status-related factor relating to any covered individual.

(c) Requirements for Uniform Termination of Coverage.—

(1) Particular type of coverage not offered.—In any case in which an issuer decides to discontinue offering a particular type of group health insurance coverage offered in the small or large group market, coverage of such type may be discontinued by the issuer in accordance with applicable State law in such market only if—

(A) the issuer provides notice to each plan sponsor provided coverage of this type in such market (and participants and beneficiaries covered under such coverage) of such discontinuation at least 90 days prior to the date of the discontinuation of such coverage;

(B) the issuer offers to each plan sponsor provided coverage of this type in such market, the option to purchase all (or, in the case of the large group market, any) other health insurance coverage currently being offered by the issuer to a group health plan in such market; and

(C) in exercising the option to discontinue coverage of this type and in offering the option of coverage under subparagraph (B), the issuer acts uniformly without regard to the claims experience of those sponsors or any health status-related factor relating to any participants or beneficiaries covered or new participants or beneficiaries who may become eligible for such coverage.

(2) Discontinuance of all coverage.—

(A) In general.—In any case in which a health insurance issuer elects to discontinue offering all health insurance coverage in the small group market or the large group market, or both markets, in a State, health insurance coverage may be discontinued by the issuer only in accordance with applicable State law and if—

(i) the issuer provides notice to the applicable State authority and to each plan sponsor (and participants and beneficiaries covered under such coverage) of such discontinuation at least 180 days prior to the date of the discontinuation of such coverage; and

(ii) all health insurance issued or delivered for issuance in the State in such market (or markets) are discontinued and coverage under such health insurance coverage in such market (or markets) is not renewed.

(B) Prohibition on market reentry.—In the case of a discontinuation under subparagraph (A) in a market, the issuer may not provide for the issuance of any health insurance coverage in the market and State involved during the 5-year period beginning on the date of the discontinuation of the last health insurance coverage not so renewed.

(d) Exception for uniform modification of coverage.—At the time of coverage renewal, a health insurance issuer may modify the health insurance coverage for a product offered to a group health plan—

(1) in the large group market; or

(2) in the small group market if, for coverage that is available in such market other than only through one or more bona fide associations, such modification is consistent with State law and effective on a uniform basis among group health plans with that product.

(e) Application to Coverage Offered Only Through Associations.—In applying this section in the case of health insurance coverage that is made available by a health insurance issuer in the small or large group market to employers only through one or more associations, a reference to "plan sponsor" is deemed, with respect to coverage provided to an employer member of the association, to include a reference to such employer.

SEC. 2713. DISCLOSURE OF INFORMATION.

(a) Disclosure of Information by Health Plan Issuers.—In connection with the offering of any health insurance coverage to a small employer, a health insurance issuer—

(1) shall make a reasonable disclosure to such employer, as part of its solicitation and sales materials, of the availability of information described in subsection (b), and

(2) upon request of such a small employer, provide such information.

(b) Information Described.—

(1) In general.—Subject to paragraph (3), with respect to a health insurance issuer offering health insurance coverage to a small employer, information described in this subsection is information concerning—

(A) the provisions of such coverage concerning issuer's right to change premium rates and the factors that may affect changes in premium rates;

(B) the provisions of such coverage relating to renewability of coverage;

(C) the provisions of such coverage relating to any preexisting condition exclusion; and

(D) the benefits and premiums available under all health insurance coverage for which the employer is qualified.

(2) Form of information.—Information under this subsection shall be provided to small employers in a manner determined to be understandable by the average small employer, and shall be sufficient to reasonably inform small employers of their rights and obligations under the health insurance coverage.

(3) Exception.—An issuer is not required under this section to disclose any information that is proprietary and trade secret information under applicable law.

SEC. 2721. EXCLUSION OF CERTAIN PLANS.

(a) Exception for Certain Small Group Health Plans.—The requirements of subparts 1 and 3 shall not apply to any group health plan (and health insurance coverage offered in connection with a group health plan) for any plan year if, on the first day of such plan year, such plan has less than 2 participants who are current employees.

(b) Limitation on Application of Provisions Relating to Group Health Plans.—

(1) In general.—The requirements of subparts 1 through 3 shall apply with respect to group health plans only—

(A) subject to paragraph (2), in the case of a plan that is a nonfederal governmental plan, and

(B) with respect to health insurance coverage offered in connection with a group health plan (including such a plan that is a church plan or a governmental plan).

(2) Treatment of nonfederal governmental plans.—

(A) Election to be excluded.—Except as provided in subparagraph (D), if the plan sponsor of a nonfederal governmental plan which is a group health plan to which the provisions of subparts 1 through 3 otherwise apply makes an election under this subparagraph (in such form and manner as the Secretary may by regulations prescribe), then the requirements of such subparts insofar as they apply directly to group health plans (and not merely to group health insurance coverage) shall not apply to such governmental plans for such period except as provided in this paragraph.

(B) Period of election.—An election under subparagraph (A) shall apply—

(i) for a single specified plan year, or

(ii) in the case of a plan provided pursuant to a collective bargaining agreement, for the term of such agreement.

An election under clause (i) may be extended through subsequent elections under this paragraph.

(C) Notice to enrollees.—Under such an election, the plan shall provide for—

(i) notice to enrollees (on an annual basis and at the time of enrollment under the plan) of the fact and consequences of such election, and

(ii) certification and disclosure of creditable coverage under the plan with respect to enrollees in accordance with section 2701(e).

(D) Election not applicable to requirements concerning genetic information.—The election described in subparagraph (A) shall not be available with respect to the provisions of subsections (a)(1)(F), (b)(3), (c), and (d) of section 2702 and the provisions of sections 2701 and 2702(b) to the extent that such provisions apply to genetic information.

(c) Exception for Certain Benefits.—The requirements of subparts 1 through 3 shall not apply to any group health plan (or group health insurance coverage) in relation to its provision of excepted benefits described in section 2791(c)(1).

(d) Exception for Certain Benefits if Certain Conditions Met.—

(1) Limited, excepted benefits.—The requirements of subparts 1 through 3 shall not apply to any group health plan (and group health insurance coverage offered in connection with a group health plan) in relation to its provision of excepted benefits described in section 2791(c)(2) if the benefits—

(A) are provided under a separate policy, certificate, or contract of insurance; or

(B) are otherwise not an integral part of the plan.

(2) Noncoordinated, excepted benefits.—The requirements of subparts 1 through 3 shall not apply to any group health plan (and group health insurance coverage offered in connection with a group health plan) in relation to its provision of excepted benefits described in section 2791(c)(3) if all of the following conditions are met:

(A) The benefits are provided under a separate policy, certificate, or contract of insurance.

(B) There is no coordination between the provision of such benefits and any exclusion of benefits under any group health plan maintained by the same plan sponsor.

(C) Such benefits are paid with respect to an event without regard to whether benefits are provided with respect to such an event under any group health plan maintained by the same plan sponsor.

(3) Supplemental excepted benefits.—The requirements of this part shall not apply to any group health plan (and group health insurance coverage) in relation to its provision of excepted benefits described in section 2791(c)(4) if the benefits are provided under a separate policy, certificate, or contract of insurance.

(e) Treatment of Partnerships.—For purposes of this part—

(1) Treatment as a group health plan.—Any plan, fund, or program which would not be (but for this subsection) an employee welfare benefit plan and which is established or maintained by a partnership, to the extent that such plan, fund, or program provides medical care (including items and services paid for as medical care) to present or former partners in the partnership or to their dependents (as defined under the terms of the plan, fund, or program), directly or through insurance, reimbursement, or otherwise, shall be treated (subject to paragraph (2)) as an employee welfare benefit plan which is a group health plan.

(2) Employer.—In the case of a group health plan, the term 'employer' also includes the partnership in relation to any partner.

(3) Participants of group health plans.—In the case of a group health plan, the term "participant" also includes—

(A) in connection with a group health plan maintained by a partnership, an individual who is a partner in relation to the partnership, or

(B) in connection with a group health plan maintained by a self-employed individual (under which one or more employees are participants), the self-employed individual, if such individual is, or may become, eligible to receive a benefit under the plan or such individual's beneficiaries may be eligible to receive any such benefit.

SEC. 2722. ENFORCEMENT.

(a) State Enforcement.—

(1) State authority.—Subject to section 2723, each State may require that health insurance issuers that issue, sell, renew, or offer health insurance coverage in the State in the small or large group markets meet the requirements of this part with respect to such issuers.

(2) Failure to implement provisions.—In the case of a determination by the Secretary that a State has failed to substantially enforce a provision (or provisions) in this part with respect to health insurance issuers in the State, the Secretary shall enforce such provision (or provisions) under subsection (b) insofar as they relate to the issuance, sale, renewal, and offering of health insurance coverage in connection with group health plans in such State.

(b) Secretarial Enforcement Authority.—

(1) Limitation.—The provisions of this subsection shall apply to enforcement of a provision (or provisions) of this part only—

(A) as provided under subsection (a)(2); and

(B) with respect to group health plans that are non-Federal governmental plans.

(2) Imposition of penalties.—In the cases described in paragraph (1)—

(A) In general.—Subject to the succeeding provisions of this subsection, any non-Federal governmental plan that is a group health plan and any health insurance issuer that fails to meet a provision of this part applicable to such plan or issuer is subject to a civil money penalty under this subsection.

(B) Liability for penalty.—In the case of a failure by—

(i) a health insurance issuer, the issuer is liable for such penalty, or

(ii) a group health plan that is a non-Federal governmental plan which is—

(I) sponsored by 2 or more employers, the plan is liable for such penalty, or

(II) not so sponsored, the employer is liable for such penalty.

(C) Amount of penalty.—

(i) In general.—The maximum amount of penalty imposed under this paragraph is $100 for each day for each individual with respect to which such a failure occurs.

(ii) Considerations in imposition.—In determining the amount of any penalty to be assessed under this paragraph, the Secretary shall take into account the previous record of compliance of the entity being assessed with the applicable provisions of this part and the gravity of the violation.

(iii) Limitations.—

(I) Penalty not to apply where failure not discovered exercising reasonable diligence. No civil money penalty shall be imposed under this paragraph on any failure during any period for which it is established to the satisfaction of the Secretary that none of the entities against whom the penalty would be imposed knew, or exercising reasonable diligence would have known, that such failure existed.

(II) Penalty not to apply to failures corrected within 30 days. No civil money penalty shall be imposed under this paragraph on any failure if such failure was due to reasonable cause and not to willful neglect, and such failure is corrected during the 30-day period beginning on the first day any of the entities against whom the penalty would be imposed knew, or exercising reasonable diligence would have known, that such failure existed.

(D) Administrative review.—

(i) Opportunity for hearing.—The entity assessed shall be afforded an opportunity for hearing by the Secretary upon request made within 30 days after the date of the issuance of a notice of assessment. In such hearing the decision shall be made on the record pursuant to section 554 of title 5, United States Code. If no hearing is requested, the assessment shall constitute a final and unappealable order.

(ii) Hearing procedure.—If a hearing is requested, the initial agency decision shall be made by an administrative law judge, and such decision shall become the final order unless the Secretary modifies or vacates the decision. Notice of intent to modify or vacate the decision of the administrative law judge shall be issued to the parties within 30 days after the date of the decision of the judge. A final order which takes effect under this paragraph shall be subject to review only as provided under subparagraph (E).

(E) Judicial review.—

(i) Filing of action for review.—Any entity against whom an order imposing a civil money penalty has been entered after an agency hearing under this paragraph may obtain review by the United States district court for any district in which such entity is located or the United States District Court for the District of Columbia by filing a notice of appeal in such court within 30 days from the date of such order, and simultaneously sending a copy of such notice by registered mail to the Secretary.

Selected Provisions of PHSA Prior to Amendment by PPACA. For sections after PPACA and other legislation, see Part 3.

(ii) Certification of administrative record.—The Secretary shall promptly certify and file in such court the record upon which the penalty was imposed.

(iii) Standard for review.—The findings of the Secretary shall be set aside only if found to be unsupported by substantial evidence as provided by section 706(2)(E) of title 5, United States Code.

(iv) Appeal.—Any final decision, order, or judgment of the district court concerning such review shall be subject to appeal as provided in chapter 83 of title 28 of such Code.

(F) Failure to pay assessment; maintenance of action.—

(i) Failure to pay assessment.—If any entity fails to pay an assessment after it has become a final and unappealable order, or after the court has entered final judgment in favor of the Secretary, the Secretary shall refer the matter to the Attorney General who shall recover the amount assessed by action in the appropriate United States district court.

(ii) Nonreviewability.—In such action the validity and appropriateness of the final order imposing the penalty shall not be subject to review.

(G) Payment of penalties.—Except as otherwise provided, penalties collected under this paragraph shall be paid to the Secretary (or other officer) imposing the penalty and shall be available without appropriation and until expended for the purpose of enforcing the provisions with respect to which the penalty was imposed.

(3) Enforcement authority relating to genetic discrimination.—

(A) General rule.—In the cases described in paragraph (1), notwithstanding the provisions of paragraph (2)(C), the succeeding subparagraphs of this paragraph shall apply with respect to an action under this subsection by the Secretary with respect to any failure of a health insurance issuer in connection with a group health plan, to meet the requirements of subsection (a)(1)(F), (b)(3), (c), or (d) of section 2702 or section 2701 or 2702(b)(1) with respect to genetic information in connection with the plan.

(B) Amount.—

(i) In general.—The amount of the penalty imposed under this paragraph shall be $100 for each day in the noncompliance period with respect to each participant or beneficiary to whom such failure relates.

(ii) Noncompliance period.—For purposes of this paragraph, the term "noncompliance period" means, with respect to any failure, the period—

(I) beginning on the date such failure first occurs; and

(II) ending on the date the failure is corrected.

(C) Minimum penalties where failure discovered.—Notwithstanding clauses (i) and (ii) of subparagraph (D):

(i) In general.—In the case of 1 or more failures with respect to an individual—

(I) which are not corrected before the date on which the plan receives a notice from the Secretary of such violation; and

(II) which occurred or continued during the period involved;

the amount of penalty imposed by subparagraph (A) by reason of such failures with respect to such individual shall be not less than $2,500.

(ii) Higher minimum penalty where violations are more than de minimis.—To the extent violations for which any person is liable under this paragraph for any year are more than de minimis, clause (i) shall be applied by substituting "$15,000" for "$2,500" with respect to such person.

(D) Limitations.—

(i) Penalty not to apply where failure not discovered exercising reasonable diligence. No penalty shall be imposed by subparagraph (A) on any failure during any period for which it is established to the satisfaction of the Secretary that the person otherwise liable for such penalty did not know, and exercising reasonable diligence would not have known, that such failure existed.

(ii) Penalty not to apply to failures corrected within certain periods. No penalty shall be imposed by subparagraph (A) on any failure if—

(I) such failure was due to reasonable cause and not to willful neglect; and

(II) such failure is corrected during the 30-day period beginning on the first date the person otherwise liable for such penalty knew, or exercising reasonable diligence would have known, that such failure existed.

(iii) Overall limitation for unintentional failures. In the case of failures which are due to reasonable cause and not to willful neglect, the penalty imposed by subparagraph (A) for failures shall not exceed the amount equal to the lesser of—

(I) 10 percent of the aggregate amount paid or incurred by the employer (or predecessor employer) during the preceding taxable year for group health plans; or

(II) $500,000.

(E) Waiver by Secretary.—In the case of a failure which is due to reasonable cause and not to willful neglect, the Secretary may waive part or all of the penalty imposed by subparagraph (A) to the extent that the payment of such penalty would be excessive relative to the failure involved.

SEC. 2723. PREEMPTION; STATE FLEXIBILITY; CONSTRUCTION.

(a) Continued Applicability of State Law With Respect to Health Insurance Issuers.—

(1) In general.—Subject to paragraph (2) and except as provided in subsection (b), this part and part C insofar as it relates to this part shall not be construed to supersede any provision of State law which establishes, implements, or continues in effect any standard or requirement solely relating to health insurance issuers in connection with group health insurance coverage except to the extent that such standard or requirement prevents the application of a requirement of this part.

(2) Continued preemption with respect to group health plans.—Nothing in this part shall be construed to affect or modify the provisions of section 514 of the Employee Retirement Income Security Act of 1974 with respect to group health plans.

(b) Special Rules in Case of Portability Requirements.—

(1) In general.—Subject to paragraph (2), the provisions of this part relating to health insurance coverage offered by a health insurance issuer supersede any provision of State law which establishes, implements, or continues in effect a standard or requirement applicable to imposition of a preexisting condition exclusion specifically governed by section 701 which differs from the standards or requirements specified in such section.

(2) Exceptions.—Only in relation to health insurance coverage offered by a health insurance issuer, the provisions of this part do not supersede any provision of State law to the extent that such provision—

(i) substitutes for the reference to "6-month period" in section 2701(a)(1) a reference to any shorter period of time;

(ii) substitutes for the reference to "12 months" and "18 months" in section 2701(a)(2) a reference to any shorter period of time;

(iii) substitutes for the references to "63" days in sections 2701(c)(2)(A) and 2701(d)(4)(A) a reference to any greater number of days;

(iv) substitutes for the reference to "30-day period" in sections 2701(b)(2) and 2701(d)(1) a reference to any greater period;

(v) prohibits the imposition of any preexisting condition exclusion in cases not described in section 2701(d) or expands the exceptions described in such section;

(vi) requires special enrollment periods in addition to those required under section 2701(f); or

(vii) reduces the maximum period permitted in an affiliation period under section 2701(g)(1)(B).

(c) Rules of Construction.—Nothing in this part (other than section 2704) shall be construed as requiring a group health plan or health insurance coverage to provide specific benefits under the terms of such plan or coverage.

(d) Definitions.—For purposes of this section—

(1) State law.—The term "State law" includes all laws, decisions, rules, regulations, or other State action having the effect of law, of any State. A law of the United States applicable only to the District of Columbia shall be treated as a State law rather than a law of the United States.

(2) State.—The term "State" includes a State (including the Northern Mariana Islands), any political subdivisions of a State or such Islands, or any agency or instrumentality of either.

PART B—INDIVIDUAL MARKET REFORMS

* * *

SEC. 2762. PREEMPTION.

(a) In General.—Subject to subsection (b), nothing in this part (or part C insofar as it applies to this part) shall be construed to prevent a State from establishing, implementing, or continuing in effect standards and requirements unless such standards and requirements prevent the application of a requirement of this part.

(b) Rules of Construction.—

(1) Nothing in this part (or part C insofar as it applies to this part shall be construed to affect or modify the provisions of section 514 of the Employee Retirement Income Security Act of 1974 (29 U.S.C. 1144).

(2) Nothing in this part (other than section 2751) shall be construed as requiring health insurance coverage offered in the individual market to provide specific benefits under the terms of such coverage.

* * *

PART C—DEFINITIONS; MISCELLANEOUS PROVISIONS

SEC. 2791. DEFINITIONS.

(a) Group Health Plan.—

(1) Definition.—The term "group health plan" means an employee welfare benefit plan (as defined in section 3(1) of the Employee Retirement Income Security Act of 1974 to the extent that the plan provides medical care (as defined in paragraph (2)) and including items and services paid for as medical care) to employees or their dependents (as defined under the

Selected Provisions of PHSA Prior to Amendment by PPACA. For sections after PPACA and other legislation, see Part 3.

terms of the plan) directly or through insurance, reimbursement, or otherwise.

(2) Medical care.—The term "medical care" means amounts paid for—

(A) the diagnosis, cure, mitigation, treatment, or prevention of disease, or amounts paid for the purpose of affecting any structure or function of the body,

(B) amounts paid for transportation primarily for and essential to medical care referred to in subparagraph (A), and

(C) amounts paid for insurance covering medical care referred to in subparagraphs (A) and (B).

(3) Treatment of certain plans as group health plan for notice provision.—A program under which creditable coverage described in subparagraph (C), (D), (E), or (F) of section 2701(c)(1) is provided shall be treated as a group health plan for purposes of applying section 2701(e).

(b) Definitions Relating to Health Insurance.—

(1) Health insurance coverage.—The term "health insurance coverage" means benefits consisting of medical care (provided directly, through insurance or reimbursement, or otherwise and including items and services paid for as medical care) under any hospital or medical service policy or certificate, hospital or medical service plan contract, or health maintenance organization contract offered by a health insurance issuer.

(2) Health insurance issuer.—The term "health insurance issuer" means an insurance company, insurance service, or insurance organization (including a health maintenance organization, as defined in paragraph (3)) which is licensed to engage in the business of insurance in a State and which is subject to State law which regulates insurance (within the meaning of section 514(b)(2) of the Employee Retirement Income Security Act of 1974). Such term does not include a group health plan.

(3) Health maintenance organization.—The term "health maintenance organization" means—

(A) a Federally qualified health maintenance organization (as defined in section 1301(a)),

(B) an organization recognized under State law as a health maintenance organization, or

(C) a similar organization regulated under State law for solvency in the same manner and to the same extent as such a health maintenance organization.

(4) Group health insurance coverage.—The term "group health insurance coverage" means, in connection with a group health plan, health insurance coverage offered in connection with such plan.

(5) Individual health insurance coverage.—The term "individual health insurance coverage" means

health insurance coverage offered to individuals in the individual market, but does not include short-term limited duration insurance.

(c) Excepted Benefits.—For purposes of this title, the term "excepted benefits" means benefits under one or more (or any combination thereof) of the following:

(1) Benefits not subject to requirements.

(A) Coverage only for accident, or disability income insurance, or any combination thereof.

(B) Coverage issued as a supplement to liability insurance.

(C) Liability insurance, including general liability insurance and automobile liability insurance.

(D) Workers' compensation or similar insurance.

(E) Automobile medical payment insurance.

(F) Credit-only insurance.

(G) Coverage for on-site medical clinics.

(H) Other similar insurance coverage, specified in regulations, under which benefits for medical care are secondary or incidental to other insurance benefits.

(2) Benefits not subject to requirements if offered separately.

(A) Limited scope dental or vision benefits.

(B) Benefits for long-term care, nursing home care, home health care, community-based care, or any combination thereof.

(C) Such other similar, limited benefits as are specified in regulations.

(3) Benefits not subject to requirements if offered as independent, noncoordinated benefits.

(A) Coverage only for a specified disease or illness.

(B) Hospital indemnity or other fixed indemnity insurance.

(4) Benefits not subject to requirements if offered as separate insurance policy.—Medicare supplemental health insurance (as defined under section 1882(g)(1) of the Social Security Act), coverage supplemental to the coverage provided under chapter 55 of title 10, United States Code, and similar supplemental coverage provided to coverage under a group health plan.

(d) Other Definitions.—

(1) Applicable State authority.—The term "applicable State authority" means, with respect to a health insurance issuer in a State, the State insurance commissioner or official or officials designated by the State to enforce the requirements of this title for the State involved with respect to such issuer.

Selected Provisions of PHSA Prior to Amendment by PPACA. For sections after PPACA and other legislation, see Part 3.

(2) Beneficiary.—The term "beneficiary" has the meaning given such term under section 3(8) of the Employee Retirement Income Security Act of 1974.

(3) Bona fide association.—The term "bona fide association" means, with respect to health insurance coverage offered in a State, an association which—

(A) has been actively in existence for at least 5 years;

(B) has been formed and maintained in good faith for purposes other than obtaining insurance;

(C) does not condition membership in the association on any health status-related factor relating to an individual (including an employee of an employer or a dependent of an employee);

(D) makes health insurance coverage offered through the association available to all members regardless of any health status-related factor relating to such members (or individuals eligible for coverage through a member);

(E) does not make health insurance coverage offered through the association available other than in connection with a member of the association; and

(F) meets such additional requirements as may be imposed under State law.

(4) COBRA continuation provision.—The term "COBRA continuation provision" means any of the following:

(A) Section 4980B of the Internal Revenue Code of 1986, other than subsection (f)(1) of such section insofar as it relates to pediatric vaccines.

(B) Part 6 of subtitle B of title I of the Employee Retirement Income Security Act of 1974, other than section 609 of such Act.

(C) Title XXII of this Act.

(5) Employee.—The term "employee" has the meaning given such term under section 3(6) of the Employee Retirement Income Security Act of 1974.

(6) Employer.—The term "employer" has the meaning given such term under section 3(5) of the Employee Retirement Income Security Act of 1974, except that such term shall include only employers of two or more employees.

(7) Church plan.—The term "church plan" has the meaning given such term under section 3(33) of the Employee Retirement Income Security Act of 1974.

(8) Governmental plan.

(A) The term "governmental plan" has the meaning given such term under section 3(32) of the Employee Retirement Income Security Act of 1974 and any Federal governmental plan.

(B) Federal governmental plan. The term "Federal governmental plan" means a governmental plan established or maintained for its employees by the Government of the United States or by any agency or instrumentality of such Government.

(C) Non-Federal governmental plan. The term "non-Federal governmental plan" means a governmental plan that is not a Federal governmental plan.

(9) Health status-related factor.—The term "health status-related factor" means any of the factors described in section 2702(a)(1).

(10) Network plan.—The term "network plan" means health insurance coverage of a health insurance issuer under which the financing and delivery of medical care (including items and services paid for as medical care) are provided, in whole or in part, through a defined set of providers under contract with the issuer.

(11) Participant.—The term "participant" has the meaning given such term under section 3(7) of the Employee Retirement Income Security Act of 1974.

(12) Placed for adoption defined.—The term "placement", or being "placed", for adoption, in connection with any placement for adoption of a child with any person, means the assumption and retention by such person of a legal obligation for total or partial support of such child in anticipation of adoption of such child. The child's placement with such person terminates upon the termination of such legal obligation.

(13) Plan sponsor.—The term "plan sponsor" has the meaning given such term under section 3(16)(B) of the Employee Retirement Income Security Act of 1974.

(14) State.—The term "State" means each of the several States, the District of Columbia, Puerto Rico, the Virgin Islands, Guam, American Samoa, and the Northern Mariana Islands.

(15) Family member.—The term "family member" means, with respect to any individual—

(A) a dependent (as such term is used for purposes of section 2701(f)(2)) of such individual; and

(B) any other individual who is a first-degree, second-degree, third-degree, or fourth-degree relative of such individual or of an individual described in subparagraph (A).

(16) Genetic information.

(A) In general. The term "genetic information" means, with respect to any individual, information about—

(i) such individual's genetic tests,

(ii) the genetic tests of family members of such individual, and

(iii) the manifestation of a disease or disorder in family members of such individual.

Selected Provisions of PHSA Prior to Amendment by PPACA. For sections after PPACA and other legislation, see Part 3.

PHSA Sec. 2791(d)(2)

(B) Inclusion of genetic services and participation in genetic research. Such term includes, with respect to any individual, any request for, or receipt of, genetic services, or participation in clinical research which includes genetic services, by such individual or any family member of such individual.

(C) Exclusions. The term "genetic information" shall not include information about the sex or age of any individual.

(17) Genetic test.

(A) In general. The term "genetic test" means an analysis of human DNA, RNA, chromosomes, proteins, or metabolites, that detects genotypes, mutations, or chromosomal changes.

(B) Exceptions. The term "genetic test" does not mean—

(i) an analysis of proteins or metabolites that does not detect genotypes, mutations, or chromosomal changes; or

(ii) an analysis of proteins or metabolites that is directly related to a manifested disease, disorder, or pathological condition that could reasonably be detected by a health care professional with appropriate training and expertise in the field of medicine involved.

(18) Genetic services.—The term "genetic services" means—

(A) a genetic test;

(B) genetic counseling (including obtaining, interpreting, or assessing genetic information); or

(C) genetic education.

(19) Underwriting purposes.—The term "underwriting purposes" means, with respect to any group health plan, or health insurance coverage offered in connection with a group health plan—

(A) rules for, or determination of, eligibility (including enrollment and continued eligibility) for benefits under the plan or coverage;

(B) the computation of premium or contribution amounts under the plan or coverage;

(C) the application of any pre-existing condition exclusion under the plan or coverage; and

(D) other activities related to the creation, renewal, or replacement of a contract of health insurance or health benefits.

(e) Definitions Relating to Markets and Small Employers.—For purposes of this title:

(1) Individual market.

(A) In general. The term "individual market" means the market for health insurance coverage offered to individuals other than in connection with a group health plan.

(B) Treatment of very small groups.

(i) In general. Subject to clause (ii), such terms includes coverage offered in connection with a group health plan that has fewer than two participants as current employees on the first day of the plan year.

(ii) State exception. Clause (i) shall not apply in the case of a State that elects to regulate the coverage described in such clause as coverage in the small group market.

(2) Large employer.—The term "large employer" means, in connection with a group health plan with respect to a calendar year and a plan year, an employer who employed an average of at least 51 employees on business days during the preceding calendar year and who employs at least 2 employees on the first day of the plan year.

(3) Large group market.—The term "large group market" means the health insurance market under which individuals obtain health insurance coverage (directly or through any arrangement) on behalf of themselves (and their dependents) through a group health plan maintained by a large employer.

(4) Small employer.—The term "small employer" means, in connection with a group health plan with respect to a calendar year and a plan year, an employer who employed an average of at least 2 but not more than 50 employees on business days during the preceding calendar year and who employs at least 2 employees on the first day of the plan year.

(5) Small group market.—The term "small group market" means the health insurance market under which individuals obtain health insurance coverage (directly or through any arrangement) on behalf of themselves (and their dependents) through a group health plan maintained by a small employer.

(6) Application of certain rules in determination of employer size.—For purposes of this subsection—

(A) Application of aggregation rule for employers. all [All] persons treated as a single employer under subsection (b), (c), (m), or (o) of section 414 of the Internal Revenue Code of 1986 shall be treated as 1 employer.

(B) Employers not in existence in preceding year. In the case of an employer which was not in existence throughout the preceding calendar year, the determination of whether such employer is a small or large employer shall be based on the average number of employees that it is reasonably expected such employer will employ on business days in the current calendar year.

(C) Predecessors. Any reference in this subsection to an employer shall include a reference to any predecessor of such employer.

* * *

Selected Provisions of PHSA Prior to Amendment by PPACA. For sections after PPACA and other legislation, see Part 3.

PHSA Sec. 2791(e)(6)(C)

Part 5

Joint Committee on Taxation,

General Explanation of Tax

Legislation Enacted in the

111th Congress: Health Care Provisions

GENERAL EXPLANATION OF TAX LEGISLATION ENACTED IN THE 111TH CONGRESS

Prepared by the Staff

of the

JOINT COMMITTEE ON TAXATION

MARCH 2011

JCS–2–11

* * *

XII

XIII

XIV

XV

XVI

* * *

PART EIGHT: HEALTH CARE PROVISIONS

PATIENT PROTECTION AND AFFORDABLE CARE ACT (PUBLIC LAW 111–148),[685] HEALTH CARE AND EDUCATION RECONCILIATION ACT OF 2010 (PUBLIC LAW 111–152),[686] AN ACT TO CLARIFY THE HEALTH CARE PROVIDED BY THE SECRETARY OF VETERANS AFFAIRS THAT CONSTITUTES MINIMUM ESSENTIAL COVERAGE (PUBLIC LAW 111–173),[687] AND MEDICARE AND MEDICAID EXTENDERS ACT OF 2010 (PUBLIC LAW 111–309)[688]

PATIENT PROTECTION AND AFFORDABLE CARE ACT

TITLE I—QUALITY, AFFORDABLE HEALTH CARE FOR ALL AMERICANS

A. Tax Exemption for Certain Member-Run Health Insurance Issuers (sec. 1322[689] of the Act and new sec. 501(c)(29) and sec. 6033 of the Code)

---

[685] H.R. 3590. The bill originated as the Service Members Home Ownership Tax Act of 2009 and passed the House on the suspension calendar on October 8, 2009. The House Ways and Means Committee reported H.R. 3200 on October 14, 2009 (H.R. Rep. No. 111–299 (part II)). The Senate Finance Committee reported S. 1796 on October 19, 2009 (S. Rep. No. 111–89). The House passed H.R. 3962 on November 7, 2009. The Senate passed H.R. 3590 with an amendment substituting the text of the Patient Protection and Affordable Care Act on December 24, 2009. The House agreed to the Senate amendment on March 21, 2010. The President signed the bill on March 23, 2010.

[686] H.R. 4872. The bill passed the House on March 21, 2010. The Senate passed the bill with amendments on March 25, 2010. The House agreed to the Senate amendments on March 25, 2010. The President signed the bill on March 30, 2010.

For a technical explanation of the bills prepared by the staff of the Joint Committee on Taxation, see *Technical Explanation of the Revenue Provisions of the "Reconciliation Act of 2010," as Amended, in Combination with the "Patient Protection and Affordable Care Act"* (JCX–18–10), March 21, 2010.

[687] H.R. 5014. The bill passed the House on the suspension calendar on May 12, 2010. The Senate passed the bill by unanimous consent on May 18, 2010. The President signed the bill on May 27, 2010.

Pub. L. No. 111–173, which amends section 5000A(f)(1)(A) of the Code, as added by section 1501(b) of the Patient Protection and Affordable Care Act, is described *infra* in a footnote in section H of title I of the Patient Protection and Affordable Care Act of Part Eight.

[688] H.R. 4994. The bill passed the House on the suspension calendar on April 14, 2010. The Senate passed the bill with amendments by unanimous consent on December 8, 2010. The House agreed to the Senate amendments on the suspension calendar on December 9, 2010. The President signed the bill on December 15, 2010.

Pub. L. No. 111–309, which amends section 36B(f)(2)(B) of the Code, is described *infra* in section C of title I of the Patient Protection and Affordable Care Act of Part Eight.

[689] Section 1322 of the Patient Protection and Affordable Care Act, Pub. L. No. 111–148, as amended by section 10104.

253

Present Law

In general

Although present law provides that certain limited categories of organizations that offer insurance may qualify for exemption from Federal income tax, present law generally does not provide tax-exempt status for newly established, member-run nonprofit health insurers that are established and funded pursuant to the Consumer Oriented, Not-for-Profit Health Plan program created under the Act and described below.

Taxation of insurance companies

Taxation of stock and mutual companies providing health insurance

Present law provides special rules for determining the taxable income of insurance companies (subchapter L of the Code). Both mutual insurance companies and stock insurance companies are subject to Federal income tax under these rules. Separate sets of rules apply to life insurance companies and to property and casualty insurance companies. Insurance companies are subject to Federal income tax at regular corporate income tax rates.

An insurance company that provides health insurance is subject to Federal income tax as either a life insurance company or as a property and casualty insurance company, depending on its mix of lines of business and on the resulting portion of its reserves that are treated as life insurance reserves. For Federal income tax purposes, an insurance company is treated as a life insurance company if the sum of its (1) life insurance reserves and (2) unearned premiums and unpaid losses on noncancellable life, accident or health contracts not included in life insurance reserves, comprise more than 50 percent of its total reserves.[690]

Life insurance companies

A life insurance company, whether stock or mutual, is taxed at regular corporate rates on its life insurance company taxable income (LICTI). LICTI is life insurance gross income reduced by life insurance deductions.[691] An alternative tax applies if a company has a net capital gain for the taxable year, if such tax is less than the tax that would otherwise apply. Life insurance gross income is the sum of (1) premiums, (2) decreases in reserves, and (3) other amounts generally includible by a taxpayer in gross income. Methods for determining reserves for Federal income tax purposes generally are based on reserves prescribed by the National Association of Insurance Commissioners for purposes of financial reporting under State regulatory rules.

Because deductible reserves might be viewed as being funded proportionately out of taxable and tax-exempt income, the net increase and net decrease in reserves are computed by reducing the ending balance of the reserve items by a portion of tax-exempt in-

---

[690] Sec. 816(a).
[691] Sec. 801.

254

terest (known as a proration rule).[692] Similarly, a life insurance company is allowed a dividends-received deduction for intercorporate dividends from nonaffiliates only in proportion to the company's share of such dividends.[693]

Property and casualty insurance companies

The taxable income of a property and casualty insurance company is determined as the sum of the amount earned from underwriting income and from investment income (as well as gains and other income items), reduced by allowable deductions.[694] For this purpose, underwriting income and investment income are computed on the basis of the underwriting and investment exhibit of the annual statement approved by the National Association of Insurance Commissioners.[695]

Underwriting income means premiums earned during the taxable year less losses incurred and expenses incurred.[696] Losses incurred include certain unpaid losses (reported losses that have not been paid, estimates of losses incurred but not reported, resisted claims, and unpaid loss adjustment expenses). Present law limits the deduction for unpaid losses to the amount of discounted unpaid losses, which are discounted using prescribed discount periods and a prescribed interest rate, to take account partially of the time value of money.[697] Any net decrease in the amount of unpaid losses results in income inclusion, and the amount included is computed on a discounted basis.

In calculating its reserve for losses incurred, a proration rule requires that a property and casualty insurance company must reduce the amount of losses incurred by 15 percent of (1) the insurer's tax-exempt interest, (2) the deductible portion of dividends received (with special rules for dividends from affiliates), and (3) the increase for the taxable year in the cash value of life insurance, endowment, or annuity contracts the company owns (sec. 832(b)(5)). This rule reflects the fact that reserves are generally funded in part from tax-exempt interest, from wholly or partially deductible dividends, or from other untaxed amounts.

Tax exemption for certain organizations

In general

Section 501(a) generally provides for exemption from Federal income tax for certain organizations. These organizations include: (1) qualified pension, profit sharing, and stock bonus plans described in section 401(a); (2) religious and apostolic organizations described

---

[692] Secs. 807(b)(2)(B) and (b)(1)(B).

[693] Secs. 805(a)(4), 812. Fully deductible dividends from affiliates are excluded from the application of this proration formula (so long as such dividends are not themselves distributions from tax-exempt interest or from dividend income that would not be fully deductible if received directly by the taxpayer). In addition, the proration rule includes in prorated amounts the increase for the taxable year in policy cash values of life insurance policies and annuity and endowment contracts owned by the company (the inside buildup on which is not taxed).

[694] Sec. 832.

[695] Sec. 832(b)(1)(A).

[696] Sec. 832(b)(3). In determining premiums earned, the company deducts from gross premiums the increase in unearned premiums for the year (sec. 832(b)(4)(B)). The company is required to reduce the deduction for increases in unearned premiums by 20 percent, reflecting the matching of deferred expenses to deferred income.

[697] Sec. 846.

255

in section 501(d); and (3) organizations described in section 501(c). Sections 501(c) describes 28 different categories of exempt organizations, including: charitable organizations (section 501(c)(3)); social welfare organizations (section 501(c)(4)); labor, agricultural, and horticultural organizations (section 501(c)(5)); professional associations (section 501(c)(6)); and social clubs (section 501(c)(7)).[698]

Insurance organizations described in section 501(c)

Although most organizations that engage principally in insurance activities are not exempt from Federal income tax, certain organizations that engage in insurance activities are described in section 501(c) and exempt from tax under section 501(a). Section 501(c)(8), for example, describes certain fraternal beneficiary societies, orders, or associations operating under the lodge system or for the exclusive benefit of their members that provide for the payment of life, sick, accident, or other benefits to the members or their dependents. Section 501(c)(9) describes certain voluntary employees' beneficiary associations that provide for the payment of life, sick, accident, or other benefits to the members of the association or their dependents or designated beneficiaries. Section 501(c)(12)(A) describes certain benevolent life insurance associations of a purely local character. Section 501(c)(15) describes certain small non-life insurance companies with annual gross receipts of no more than $600,000 ($150,000 in the case of a mutual insurance company). Section 501(c)(26) describes certain membership organizations established to provide health insurance to certain high-risk individuals.[699] Section 501(c)(27) describes certain organizations established to provide workmen's compensation insurance.

Certain section 501(c)(3) organizations

Certain health maintenance organizations (HMOs) have been held to qualify for tax exemption as charitable organizations described in section 501(c)(3). In *Sound Health Association v. Com-*

---

[698] Certain organizations that operate on a cooperative basis are taxed under special rules set forth in Subchapter T of the Code. The two principal criteria for determining whether an entity is operating on a cooperative basis are: (1) ownership of the cooperative by persons who patronize the cooperative (e.g., the farmer members of a cooperative formed to market the farmers' produce); and (2) return of earnings to patrons in proportion to their patronage. In general, cooperative members are those who participate in the management of the cooperative and who share in patronage capital. For Federal income tax purposes, a cooperative that is taxed under the Subchapter T rules generally computes its income as if it were a taxable corporation, with one exception—the cooperative may deduct from its taxable income distributions of patronage dividends. In general, patronage dividends are the profits of the cooperative that are rebated to its patrons pursuant to a preexisting obligation of the cooperative to do so. Certain farmers' cooperatives described in section 521 are authorized to deduct not only patronage dividends from patronage sources, but also dividends on capital stock and certain distributions to patrons from nonpatronage sources.

Separate from the Subchapter T rules, the Code provides tax exemption for certain cooperatives. Section 501(c)(12), for example, provides that certain rural electric and telephone cooperative are exempt from tax under section 501(a), provided that 85 percent or more of the cooperative's income consists of amounts collected from members for the sole purpose of meeting losses or expenses, and certain other requirements are met.

[699] When section 501(c)(26) was enacted in 1996, the House Ways and Means Committee, in reporting out the bill, stated as its reasons for change: "The Committee believes that eliminating the uncertainty concerning the eligibility of certain State health insurance risk pools for tax-exempt status will assist States in providing medical care coverage for their uninsured high-risk residents." H.R. Rep. No. 104–496, Part I, "Health Coverage Availability and Affordability Act of 1996," 104th Cong., 2d Sess., March 25, 1996, 124. See also Joint Committee on Taxation, *General Explanation of Tax Legislation Enacted in the 104th Congress* (JCS–12–96), December 18, 1996, p. 351.

256

missioner,[700] the Tax Court held that a staff model HMO qualified as a charitable organization. A staff model HMO generally employs its own physicians and staff and serves its subscribers at its own facilities. The court concluded that the HMO satisfied the section 501(c)(3) community benefit standard, as its membership was open to almost all members of the community. Although membership was limited to persons who had the money to pay the fixed premiums, the court held that this was not disqualifying, because the HMO had a subsidized premium program for persons of lesser means to be funded through donations and Medicare and Medicaid payments. The HMO also operated an emergency room open to all persons regardless of income. The court rejected the government's contention that the HMO conferred primarily a private benefit to its subscribers, stating that when the potential membership is such a broad segment of the community, benefit to the membership is benefit to the community.

In *Geisinger Health Plan v. Commissioner,*[701] the court applied the section 501(c)(3) community benefit standard to an individual practice association (IPA) model HMO. In the IPA model, health care generally is provided by physicians practicing independently in their own offices, with the IPA usually contracting on behalf of the physicians with the HMO. Reversing a Tax Court decision, the court held that the HMO did not qualify as charitable, because the community benefit standard requires that an HMO be an actual provider of health care rather than merely an arranger or deliverer of health care, which is how the court viewed the IPA model in that case.

More recently, in *IHC Health Plans, Inc. v. Commissioner,*[702] the court ruled that three affiliated HMOs did not operate primarily for the benefit of the community they served. The organizations in the case did not provide health care directly, but provided group insurance that could be used at both affiliated and non-affiliated providers. The court found that the organizations primarily performed a risk-bearing function and provided virtually no free or below-cost health care services. In denying charitable status, the court held that a health-care provider must make its services available to all in the community plus provide additional community or public benefits.[703] The benefit must either further the function of government-funded institutions or provide a service that would not likely be provided within the community but for the subsidy. Further, the additional public benefit conferred must be sufficient to give rise to a strong inference that the public benefit is the primary purpose for which the organization operates.[704]

Certain organizations providing commercial-type insurance

Section 501(m) provides that an organization may not be exempt from tax under section 501(c)(3) (generally, charitable organizations) or section 501(c)(4) (social welfare organizations) unless no substantial part of its activities consists of providing commercial-

---

[700] 71 T.C. 158 (1978), *acq.* 1981–2 C.B. 2.
[701] 985 F.2d 1210 (3rd Cir. 1993), *rev'g* T.C. Memo. 1991–649.
[702] 325 F.3d 1188 (10th Cir. 2003).
[703] *Ibid.* at 1198.
[704] *Ibid.*

257

type insurance. For this purpose, commercial-type insurance excludes, among other things: (1) insurance provided at substantially below cost to a class of charitable recipients; and (2) incidental health insurance provided by an HMO of a kind customarily provided by such organizations.

When section 501(m) was enacted in 1986, the following reasons for the provision were stated: "The committee is concerned that exempt charitable and social welfare organizations that engaged in insurance activities are engaged in an activity whose nature and scope is so inherently commercial that tax exempt status is inappropriate. The committee believes that the tax-exempt status of organizations engaged in insurance activities provides an unfair competitive advantage to these organizations. The committee further believes that the provision of insurance to the general public at a price sufficient to cover the costs of insurance generally constitutes an activity that is commercial. In addition, the availability of tax-exempt status . . . has allowed some large insurance entities to compete directly with commercial insurance companies. For example, the Blue Cross/Blue Shield organizations historically have been treated as tax-exempt organizations described in sections 501(c)(3) or (4). This group of organizations is now among the largest health care insurers in the United States. Other tax-exempt charitable and social welfare organizations engaged in insurance activities also have a competitive advantage over commercial insurers who do not have tax-exempt status. . . ."[705]

Unrelated business income tax

Most organizations that are exempt from tax under section 501(a) are subject to the unrelated business income tax rules of sections 511 through 515. The unrelated business income tax generally applies to income derived from a trade or business regularly carried on by the organization that is not substantially related to the performance of the organization's tax-exempt functions. Certain types of income are specifically exempt from the unrelated business income tax, such as dividends, interest, royalties, and certain rents, unless derived from debt-financed property or from certain 50-percent controlled subsidiaries.

Explanation of Provision

In general

The provision authorizes $6 billion in funding for, and instructs the Secretary of Health and Human Services ("HHS") to establish, the Consumer Operated and Oriented Plan (the "program") to foster the creation of qualified nonprofit health insurance issuers to offer qualified health plans in the individual and small group markets in the States in which the issuers are licensed to offer such plans. Federal funds are to be distributed as loans to assist with start-up costs and grants to assist in meeting State solvency requirements.

---

[705] H.R. Rep. No. 99–426, "Tax Reform Act of 1985," Report of the Committee on Ways and Means, 99th Cong., 1st Sess., December 7, 1985, 664. See also Joint Committee on Taxation, *General Explanation of the Tax Reform Act of 1986* (JCS–10–87), May 4, 1987, p. 584.

Under the provision, the Secretary of HHS must require any person receiving a loan or grant under the program to enter into an agreement with the Secretary of HHS requiring the recipient of funds to meet and continue to meet any requirement under the provision for being treated as a qualified nonprofit health insurance issuer, and any requirements to receive the loan or grant. The provision also requires that the agreement prohibit the use of loan or grant funds for carrying on propaganda or otherwise attempting to influence legislation or for marketing.

If the Secretary of HHS determines that a grant or loan recipient failed to meet the requirements described in the preceding paragraph, and failed to correct such failure within a reasonable period from when the person first knew (or reasonably should have known) of such failure, then such person must repay the Secretary of HHS an amount equal to 110 percent of the aggregate amount of the loans and grants received under the program, plus interest on such amount for the period during which the loans or grants were outstanding. The Secretary of HHS must notify the Secretary of the Treasury of any determination of a failure that results in the termination of the grantee's Federal tax-exempt status.

Qualified nonprofit health insurance issuers

The provision defines a qualified nonprofit health insurance issuer as an organization that meets the following requirements:

1. The organization is organized as a nonprofit, member corporation under State law;

2. Substantially all of its activities consist of the issuance of qualified health plans in the individual and small group markets in each State in which it is licensed to issue such plans;

3. None of the organization, a related entity, or a predecessor of either was a health insurance issuer as of July 16, 2009;

4. The organization is not sponsored by a State or local government, any political subdivision thereof, or any instrumentality of such government or political subdivision;

5. Governance of the organization is subject to a majority vote of its members;

6. The organization's governing documents incorporate ethics and conflict of interest standards protecting against insurance industry involvement and interference;

7. The organization must operate with a strong consumer focus, including timeliness, responsiveness, and accountability to its members, in accordance with regulations to be promulgated by the Secretary of HHS;

8. Any profits made must be used to lower premiums, improve benefits, or for other programs intended to improve the quality of health care delivered to its members;

9. The organization meets all other requirements that other issuers of qualified health plans are required to meet in any State in which it offers a qualified health plan, including solvency and licensure requirements, rules on payments to providers, rules on network adequacy, rate and form filing rules, and any applicable State premium assessments. Additionally, the organization must coordinate with certain other State insurance reforms under the Act; and

259

10. The organization does not offer a health plan in a State until that State has in effect (or the Secretary of HHS has implemented for the State), the market reforms required by part A of title XXVII of the Public Health Service Act ("PHSA"), as amended by the Act.

Tax exemption for qualified nonprofit health insurance issuers

An organization receiving a grant or loan under the program qualifies for exemption from Federal income tax under section 501(a) of the Code with respect to periods during which the organization is in compliance with the above-described requirements of the program and with the terms of any program grant or loan agreement to which such organization is a party. Such organizations also are subject to organizational and operational requirements applicable to certain section 501(c) organizations, including the prohibitions on private inurement and political activities, the limitation on lobbying activities, taxation of excess benefit transactions (section 4958), and taxation of unrelated business taxable income under section 511.

Program participants are required to file an application for exempt status with the IRS in such manner as the Secretary of the Treasury may require, and are subject to annual information reporting requirements. In addition, such an organization is required to disclose on its annual information return the amount of reserves required by each State in which it operates and the amount of reserves on hand.

Effective Date

The provision is effective on the date of enactment (March 23, 2010).

B. Tax Exemption for Entities Established Pursuant to Transitional Reinsurance Program for Individual Market in Each State (sec. 1341 [706] of the Act)

Present Law

Although present law provides that certain limited categories of organizations that offer insurance may qualify for exemption from Federal income tax, present law does not provide tax-exempt status for transitional nonprofit reinsurance entities created under the Senate bill and described below.

Explanation of Provision

In general, issuers of health benefit plans that are offered in the individual market would be required to contribute to a temporary reinsurance program for individual policies that is administered by a nonprofit reinsurance entity. Such contributions would begin January 1, 2014, and continue for a 36-month period. The provision requires each State, no later than January 1, 2014, to adopt a rein-

---

[706] Section 1341 of the Patient Protection and Affordable Care Act, Pub. L. No. 111–148, as amended by section 10104.

260

surance program based on a model regulation and to establish (or enter into a contract with) one or more applicable reinsurance entities to carry out the reinsurance program under the provision. For purposes of the provision, an applicable reinsurance entity is a not-for-profit organization (1) the purpose of which is to help stabilize premiums for coverage in the individual market in a State during the first three years of operation of an exchange for such markets within the State, and (2) the duties of which are to carry out the reinsurance program under the provision by coordinating the funding and operation of the risk-spreading mechanisms designed to implement the reinsurance program. A State may have more than one applicable reinsurance entity to carry out the reinsurance program in the State, and two or more States may enter into agreements to allow a reinsurer to operate the reinsurance program in those States.

An applicable reinsurance entity established under the provision is exempt from Federal income tax. Notwithstanding an applicable reinsurance entity's tax-exempt status, it is subject to tax on unrelated business taxable income under section 511 as if such entity were described in section 511(a)(2).

Effective Date

The provision is effective on the date of enactment (March 23, 2010).

C. Refundable Tax Credit Providing Premium Assistance for Coverage Under a Qualified Health Plan (secs. 1401, 1411, and 1412 [707] of the Act and sec. 208 of Pub. L. No. 111–309 and new sec. 36B of the Code)

Present Law

Currently there is no tax credit that is generally available to low or middle income individuals or families for the purchase of health insurance. Some individuals may be eligible for health coverage through State Medicaid programs which consider income, assets, and family circumstances. However, these Medicaid programs are not in the Code.

Health coverage tax credit

Certain individuals are eligible for the health coverage tax credit ("HCTC"). The HCTC is a refundable tax credit equal to 80 percent of the cost of qualified health coverage paid by an eligible individual. In general, eligible individuals are individuals who receive a trade adjustment allowance (and individuals who would be eligible to receive such an allowance but for the fact that they have not exhausted their regular unemployment benefits), individuals eligible for the alternative trade adjustment assistance program, and individuals over age 55 who receive pension benefits from the Pension Benefit Guaranty Corporation. The HCTC is available for "qualified health insurance," which includes certain employer-based

---

[707] Sections 1401, 1411, and 1412 of the Patient Protection and Affordable Care Act, Pub. L. No. 111–148, as amended by sections 10104, 10105, and 10107, are further amended by section 1001 of the Health Care and Education Reconciliation Act of 2010, Pub. L. No. 111–152.

261

insurance, certain State-based insurance, and in some cases, insurance purchased in the individual market.

The credit is available on an advance basis through a program established and administered by the Treasury Department. The credit generally is delivered as follows: the eligible individual sends his or her portion of the premium to the Treasury, and the Treasury then pays the full premium (the individual's portion and the amount of the refundable tax credit) to the insurer. Alternatively, an eligible individual is also permitted to pay the entire premium during the year and claim the credit on his or her income tax return.

Individuals entitled to Medicare and certain other governmental health programs, covered under certain employer-subsidized health plans, or with certain other specified health coverage are not eligible for the credit.

COBRA continuation coverage premium reduction

The Consolidated Omnibus Reconciliation Act of 1985 ("COBRA")[708] requires that a group health plan must offer continuation coverage to qualified beneficiaries in the case of a qualifying event (such as a loss of employment). A plan may require payment of a premium for any period of continuation coverage. The amount of such premium generally may not exceed 102 percent of the "applicable premium" for such period and the premium must be payable, at the election of the payor, in monthly installments.

Section 3001 of the American Recovery and Reinvestment Act of 2009,[709] as amended by the Department of Defense Appropriations Act, 2010,[710] and the Temporary Extension Act of 2010[711] provides that, for a period not exceeding 15 months, an assistance eligible individual is treated as having paid any premium required for COBRA continuation coverage under a group health plan if the individual pays 35 percent of the premium. Thus, if the assistance eligible individual pays 35 percent of the premium, the group health plan must treat the individual as having paid the full premium required for COBRA continuation coverage, and the individual is entitled to a subsidy for 65 percent of the premium. An assistance eligible individual generally is any qualified beneficiary who elects COBRA continuation coverage and the qualifying event with respect to the covered employee for that qualified beneficiary is a loss of group health plan coverage on account of an involuntary termination of the covered employee's employment (for other than gross misconduct).[712] In addition, the qualifying event must occur during the period beginning September 1, 2008, and ending March 31, 2010.

---

[708] Pub. L. No. 99–272.

[709] Pub. L. No. 111–5.

[710] Pub. L. No. 111–118.

[711] Pub. L. No. 111–144.

[712] TEA expanded eligibility for the COBRA subsidy to include individuals who experience a loss of coverage on account of a reduction in hours of employment followed by the involuntary termination of employment of the covered employee. For an individual entitled to COBRA because of a reduction in hours and who is then subsequently involuntarily terminated from employment, the termination is considered a qualifying event for purposes of the COBRA subsidy, as long as the termination occurs during the period beginning on the date following TEA's date of enactment and ending on date of enactment (March 31, 2010).

262

The COBRA continuation coverage subsidy also applies to temporary continuation coverage elected under the Federal Employees Health Benefits Program and to continuation health coverage under State programs that provide coverage comparable to continuation coverage. The subsidy is generally delivered by requiring employers to pay the subsidized portion of the premium for assistance eligible individuals. The employer then treats the payment of the subsidized portion as a payment of employment taxes and offsets its employment tax liability by the amount of the subsidy. To the extent that the aggregate amount of the subsidy for all assistance eligible individuals for which the employer is entitled to a credit for a quarter exceeds the employer's employment tax liability for the quarter, the employer can request a tax refund or can claim the credit against future employment tax liability.

There is an income limit on the entitlement to the COBRA continuation coverage subsidy. Taxpayers with modified adjusted gross income exceeding $145,000 (or $290,000 for joint filers), must repay any subsidy received by them, their spouse, or their dependant, during the taxable year. For taxpayers with modified adjusted gross incomes between $125,000 and $145,000 (or $250,000 and $290,000 for joint filers), the amount of the subsidy that must be repaid is reduced proportionately. The subsidy is also conditioned on the individual not being eligible for certain other health coverage. To the extent that an eligible individual receives a subsidy during a taxable year to which the individual was not entitled due to income or being eligible for other health coverage, the subsidy overpayment is repaid on the individual's income tax return as additional tax. However, in contrast to the HCTC, the subsidy for COBRA continuation coverage may only be claimed through the employer and cannot be claimed at the end of the year on an individual tax return.

Explanation of Provision

Premium assistance credit

The provision creates a refundable tax credit (the "premium assistance credit") for eligible individuals and families who purchase health insurance through an exchange.[713] The premium assistance credit, which is refundable and payable in advance directly to the insurer, subsidizes the purchase of certain health insurance plans through an exchange.

Under the provision, to receive advance payment of the premium assistance credit, an eligible individual enrolls in a plan offered through an exchange and reports his or her income to the exchange. Based on the information provided to the exchange, the individual receives a premium assistance credit based on income and the Treasury pays the premium assistance credit amount directly to the insurance plan in which the individual is enrolled. The individual then pays to the plan in which he or she is enrolled the dollar difference between the premium tax credit amount and the

---

[713] Individuals enrolled in multi-state plans, pursuant to section 1334 of the Patient Protection and Affordable Care Act, Pub. L. No. 111–148, are also eligible for the credit.

263

total premium charged for the plan.[714] Individuals who fail to pay
all or part of the remaining premium amount are given a mandatory three-month grace period prior to an involuntary termination
of their participation in the plan. Initial eligibility for the premium
assistance credit is based on the individual's income for the tax
year ending two years prior to the enrollment period. Individuals
(or couples) who experience a change in marital status or other
household circumstance, experience a decrease in income of more
than 20 percent, or receive unemployment insurance, may update
eligibility information or request a redetermination of their tax
credit eligibility.

The premium assistance credit is generally available for individuals (single or joint filers) with household incomes between 100
and 400 percent of the Federal poverty level ("FPL") for the family
size involved.[715] Individuals who are not eligible for certain other
health insurance, including certain health insurance through an
employer or a spouse's employer, may not be eligible for the credit.
Household income is defined as the sum of: (1) the taxpayer's modified adjusted gross income, plus (2) the aggregate modified adjusted
gross incomes of all other individuals taken into account in determining that taxpayer's family size (but only if such individuals are
required to file a tax return for the taxable year). Modified adjusted gross income is defined as adjusted gross income increased
by: (1) the amount (if any) normally excluded by section 911 (the
exclusion from gross income for citizens or residents living abroad),
plus (2) any tax-exempt interest received or accrued during the tax
year. To be eligible for the premium assistance credit, taxpayers
who are married (within the meaning of section 7703) must file a
joint return. Individuals who are listed as dependents on a return
are ineligible for the premium assistance credit.

As described in Table 1 below, premium assistance credits are
available on a sliding scale basis for individuals and families with
household incomes between 100 and 400 percent of FPL to help offset the cost of private health insurance premiums. The premium
assistance credit amount is determined based on the percentage of
income the cost of premiums represents, rising from two percent of
income for those at 100 percent of FPL for the family size involved
to 9.5 percent of income for those at 400 percent of FPL for the
family size involved. Beginning in 2014, the percentages of income
are indexed to the excess of premium growth over income growth
for the preceding calendar year. Beginning in 2018, if the aggregate
amount of premium assistance credits and cost-sharing reductions[716] exceeds 0.504 percent of the gross domestic product for
that year, the percentage of income is also adjusted to reflect the
excess (if any) of premium growth over the rate of growth in the
consumer price index for the preceding calendar year. For purposes

---

[714] Although the credit is generally payable in advance directly to the insurer, individuals may
choose to purchase health insurance out-of-pocket and claim the credit at the end of the taxable
year. The amount of the reduction in premium is required to be included with each bill sent
to the individual.

[715] Individuals who are lawfully present in the United States but are not eligible for Medicaid
because of their immigration status are treated as having a household income equal to 100 percent of FPL (and thus eligible for the premium assistance credit) as long as their household income does not actually exceed 100 percent of FPL.

[716] As described in section 1402 of the Patient Protection and Affordable Care Act, Pub. L.
No. 111–148.

of calculating family size, individuals who are in the country illegally are not included.

Premium assistance credits, or any amounts that are attributable to them, cannot be used to pay for abortions for which federal funding is prohibited. Premium assistance credits are not available for months in which an individual has a free choice voucher (as defined in section 10108 of the Act).

The low income premium credit phase-out

The premium assistance credit increases, on a sliding scale in a linear manner, as shown in the table below.

Household Income (expressed as a percent of poverty line)	Initial Premium (percentage)	Final Premium (percentage)
100% through 133%	2.0	2.0
133% through 150%	3.0	4.0
150% through 200%	4.0	6.3
200% through 250%	6.3	8.05
250% through 300%	8.05	9.5
300% through 400%	9.5	9.5

The premium assistance credit amount is tied to the cost of the second lowest-cost silver plan (adjusted for age) which: (1) is in the rating area where the individual resides, (2) is offered through an exchange in the area in which the individual resides, and (3) provides self-only coverage in the case of an individual who purchases self-only coverage, or family coverage in the case of any other individual. If the plan in which the individual enrolls offers benefits in addition to essential health benefits,[717] even if the State in which the individual resides requires such additional benefits, the portion of the premium that is allocable to those additional benefits is disregarded in determining the premium assistance credit amount.[718] Premium assistance credits may be used for any plan purchased through an exchange, including bronze, silver, gold and platinum level plans and, for those eligible,[719] catastrophic plans.

Minimum essential coverage and employer offer of health insurance coverage

Generally, if an employee is offered minimum essential coverage[720] in the group market, including employer-provided health insurance coverage, the individual is ineligible for the premium tax credit for health insurance purchased through a State exchange.

If an employee is offered unaffordable coverage by his or her employer or the plan's share of the total allowed cost of benefits is less than 60 percent of such costs, the employee can be eligible for the premium tax credit, but only if the employee declines to enroll in the coverage and satisfies the conditions for receiving a tax credit

---

[717] As defined in section 1302(b) of the Patient Protection and Affordable Care Act, Pub. L. No. 111–148.

[718] A similar rule applies to additional benefits that are offered in multi-State plans, under section 1334 of the Patient Protection and Affordable Care Act, Pub. L. No. 111–148.

[719] Those eligible to purchase catastrophic plans either must have not reached the age of 30 before the beginning of the plan year, or have certification of an affordability or hardship exemption from the individual responsibility payment, as described in new sections 5000A(e)(1) and 5000A(e)(5), respectively.

[720] As defined in section 5000A(f) of the Patient Protection and Affordable Care Act, Pub. L. No. 111–148.

through an exchange. Unaffordable is defined as coverage with a premium required to be paid by the employee that is more than 9.5 percent of the employee's household income, based on the self-only coverage.[721] The percentage of income that is considered unaffordable is indexed in the same manner as the percentage of income is indexed for purposes of determining eligibility for the credit (as discussed above). The Secretary of the Treasury is informed of the name and employer identification number of every employer that has one or more employees receiving a premium tax credit.

No later than five years after the date of the enactment of the provision the Comptroller General must conduct a study of whether the percentage of household income used for purposes of determining whether coverage is affordable is the appropriate level, and whether such level can be lowered without significantly increasing the costs to the Federal Government and reducing employer-provided health coverage. The Secretary reports the results of such study to the appropriate committees of Congress, including any recommendations for legislative changes.

Procedures for determining eligibility

In order to receive an advance payment of the premium assistance credit, exchange participants must provide to the exchange certain information from their tax return from two years prior during the open enrollment period for coverage during the next calendar year. For example, if an individual applies for a premium assistance credit for 2014, the individual must provide a tax return from 2012 during the 2103 open enrollment period. The Internal Revenue Service ("IRS") is authorized to disclose to HHS limited tax return information to verify a taxpayer's income based on the most recent return information available to establish eligibility for advance payment of the premium tax credit. Existing privacy and safeguard requirements apply. Individuals who do not qualify for advance payment of the premium tax credit on the basis of their prior year income may apply for the premium tax credit based on specified changes in circumstances. For individuals and families who did not file a tax return in the prior tax year, the Secretary of HHS will establish alternative income documentation that may be provided to determine income eligibility for advance payment of the premium tax credit.

The Secretary of HHS must establish a program for determining whether or not individuals are eligible to: (1) enroll in an exchange-offered health plan; (2) receive advance payment of a premium assistance credit; and (3) establish that their coverage under an employer-sponsored plan is unaffordable. The program must provide for the following: (1) the details of an individual's application process; (2) the details of how public entities are to make determinations of individuals' eligibility; (3) procedures for deeming individuals to be eligible; and, (4) procedures for allowing individuals with limited English proficiency to have proper access to exchanges.

In applying for enrollment in an exchange-offered health plan, an individual applicant is required to provide individually identifiable

---

[721] The 9.5 percent amount is indexed for calendar years beginning after 2014.

information, including name, address, date of birth, and citizenship or immigration status. In the case of an individual applying to receive advance payment of a premium assistance credit, the individual is required to submit to the exchange income and family size information and information regarding changes in marital or family status or income. Personal information provided to the exchange is submitted to the Secretary of HHS. In turn, the Secretary of HHS submits the applicable information to the Social Security Commissioner, Homeland Security Secretary, and Treasury Secretary for verification purposes. The Secretary of HHS is notified of the results following verification, and notifies the exchange of such results. The provision specifies actions to be undertaken if inconsistencies are found. The Secretary of HHS, in consultation with the Social Security Commissioner, the Secretary of Homeland Security, and the Treasury Secretary must establish procedures for appealing determinations resulting from the verification process, and redetermining eligibility on a periodic basis.

An employer must be notified if one of its employees is determined to be eligible for a premium assistance credit because the employer does not provide minimal essential coverage through an employer-sponsored plan, or the employer does offer such coverage but it is not affordable or does not provide minimum value. The notice must include information about the employer's potential liability for payments under section 4980H and that terminating or discriminating against an employee because he or she received a credit or subsidy is in violation of the Fair Labor Standards Act.[722] An employer is generally not entitled to information about its employees who qualify for the premium assistance credit. Employers may, however, be notified of the name of the employee and whether his or her income is above or below the threshold used to measure the affordability of the employer's health insurance coverage.

Personal information submitted for verification may be used only to the extent necessary for verification purposes and may not be disclosed to anyone not identified in this provision. Any person, who submits false information due to negligence or disregard of any rule, and without reasonable cause, is subject to a civil penalty of not more than $25,000. Any person who intentionally provides false information will be fined not more than $250,000. Any person who knowingly and willfully uses or discloses confidential applicant information will be fined not more than $25,000. Any fines imposed by this provision may not be collected through a lien or levy against property, and the section does not impose any criminal liability.

The provision requires the Secretary of HHS, in consultation with the Secretaries of the Treasury and Labor, to conduct a study to ensure that the procedures necessary to administer the determination of individuals' eligibility to participate in an exchange, to receive advance payment of premium assistance credits, and to obtain an individual responsibility exemption, adequately protect employees' rights of privacy and employers' rights to due process. The results of the study must be reported by January 1, 2013, to the appropriate committees of Congress.

---

[722] Pub. L. No. 75–718.

Reconciliation

If the premium assistance received through an advance payment exceeds the amount of credit to which the taxpayer is entitled, the excess advance payment is treated as an increase in tax. For persons with household income below 500% of the FPL, the amount of the increase in tax is limited as shown in the table below (one half of the applicable dollar amount shown below for unmarried individuals who are not surviving spouses or filing as heads of households).[723]

Household income (expressed as a percent of poverty line)	Applicable dollar amount
Less than 200%	$600
At least 200% but less than 250%	1,000
At least 250% but less than 300%	1,500
At least 300% but less than 350%	2,000
At least 350% but less than 400%	2,500
At least 400% but less than 450%	3,000
At least 450% but less than 500%	3,500

If the premium assistance received through an advance payment is less than the amount of the credit to which the taxpayer is entitled, the shortfall is treated as a reduction in tax.

The eligibility for and amount of advance payment of premium assistance is determined in advance of the coverage year, on the basis of household income and family size from two years prior, and the monthly premiums for qualified health plans in the individual market in which the taxpayer, spouse and any dependent enroll in an exchange. Any advance premium assistance is paid during the year for which coverage is provided by the exchange. In the subsequent year, the amount of advance premium assistance is required to be reconciled with the allowable refundable credit for the year of coverage. Generally, this would be accomplished on the tax return filed for the year of coverage, based on that year's actual household income, family size, and premiums. Any adjustment to tax resulting from the difference between the advance premium assistance and the allowable refundable tax credit would be assessed as additional tax or a reduction in tax on the tax return.

Separately, the provision requires that the exchange, or any person with whom it contracts to administer the insurance program, must report to the Secretary with respect to any taxpayer's participation in the health plan offered by the Exchange. The information to be reported is information necessary to determine whether a person has received excess advance payments, identifying information about the taxpayer (such as name, taxpayer identification number, months of coverage) and any other person covered by that policy; the level of coverage purchased by the taxpayer; the total premium charged for the coverage, as well as the aggregate advance payments credited to that taxpayer; and information provided to the Exchange for the purpose of establishing eligibility for the program, including changes of circumstances of the taxpayer since first pur-

---

[723] Medicare and Medicaid Extenders Act of 2010, Pub. L. No. 111–309, sec. 208. Prior to the Medicare and Medicaid Extenders Act of 2010, for persons whose household income was below 400% of the FPL, the amount of the increase in tax was limited to $400 ($250 for unmarried individuals who are not surviving spouses or filing as heads of households).

268

chasing the coverage. Finally, the party submitting the report must provide a copy to the taxpayer whose information is the subject of the report.

Effective Date

The provision is effective for taxable years ending after December 31, 2013.

D. Reduced Cost-Sharing for Individuals Enrolling in Qualified Health Plans (secs. 1402, 1411, and 1412 of the Act [724])

Present Law

Currently there is no tax credit that is generally available to low or middle income individuals or families for the purchase of health insurance. Some individuals may be eligible for health coverage through State Medicaid programs which consider income, assets, and family circumstances. However, these Medicaid programs are not in the Code.

Health coverage tax credit

Certain individuals are eligible for the HCTC. The HCTC is a refundable tax credit equal to 80 percent of the cost of qualified health coverage paid by an eligible individual. In general, eligible individuals are individuals who receive a trade adjustment allowance (and individuals who would be eligible to receive such an allowance but for the fact that they have not exhausted their regular unemployment benefits), individuals eligible for the alternative trade adjustment assistance program, and individuals over age 55 who receive pension benefits from the Pension Benefit Guaranty Corporation. The HCTC is available for "qualified health insurance," which includes certain employer-based insurance, certain State-based insurance, and in some cases, insurance purchased in the individual market.

The credit is available on an advance basis through a program established and administered by the Treasury Department. The credit generally is delivered as follows: the eligible individual sends his or her portion of the premium to the Treasury, and the Treasury then pays the full premium (the individual's portion and the amount of the refundable tax credit) to the insurer. Alternatively, an eligible individual is also permitted to pay the entire premium during the year and claim the credit on his or her income tax return.

Individuals entitled to Medicare and certain other governmental health programs, covered under certain employer-subsidized health plans, or with certain other specified health coverage are not eligible for the credit.

---

[724] Sections 1401, 1411 and 1412 of the Patient Protection and Affordable Care Act, Pub. L. No. 111–148, as amended by section 10104, is further amended by section 1001 of the Health Care and Education Reconciliation Act of 2010, Pub. L. No. 111–152.

269

COBRA continuation coverage premium reduction

COBRA[725] requires that a group health plan must offer continuation coverage to qualified beneficiaries in the case of a qualifying event (such as a loss of employment). A plan may require payment of a premium for any period of continuation coverage. The amount of such premium generally may not exceed 102 percent of the "applicable premium" for such period and the premium must be payable, at the election of the payor, in monthly installments.

Section 3001 of the American Recovery and Reinvestment Act of 2009,[726] as amended by the Department of Defense Appropriations Act, 2010,[727] and the Temporary Extension Act of 2010[728] provides that, for a period not exceeding 15 months, an assistance eligible individual is treated as having paid any premium required for COBRA continuation coverage under a group health plan if the individual pays 35 percent of the premium. Thus, if the assistance eligible individual pays 35 percent of the premium, the group health plan must treat the individual as having paid the full premium required for COBRA continuation coverage, and the individual is entitled to a subsidy for 65 percent of the premium. An assistance eligible individual generally is any qualified beneficiary who elects COBRA continuation coverage and the qualifying event with respect to the covered employee for that qualified beneficiary is a loss of group health plan coverage on account of an involuntary termination of the covered employee's employment (for other than gross misconduct).[729] In addition, the qualifying event must occur during the period beginning September 1, 2008, and ending March 31, 2010.

The COBRA continuation coverage subsidy also applies to temporary continuation coverage elected under the Federal Employees Health Benefits Program and to continuation health coverage under State programs that provide coverage comparable to continuation coverage. The subsidy is generally delivered by requiring employers to pay the subsidized portion of the premium for assistance eligible individuals. The employer then treats the payment of the subsidized portion as a payment of employment taxes and offsets its employment tax liability by the amount of the subsidy. To the extent that the aggregate amount of the subsidy for all assistance eligible individuals for which the employer is entitled to a credit for a quarter exceeds the employer's employment tax liability for the quarter, the employer can request a tax refund or can claim the credit against future employment tax liability.

There is an income limit on the entitlement to the COBRA continuation coverage subsidy. Taxpayers with modified adjusted gross income exceeding $145,000 (or $290,000 for joint filers), must repay any subsidy received by them, their spouse, or their dependant,

---

[725] Pub. L. No. 99–272.
[726] Pub. L. No. 111–5.
[727] Pub. L. No. 111–118.
[728] Pub. L. No. 111–144.
[729] TEA expanded eligibility for the COBRA subsidy to include individuals who experience a loss of coverage on account of a reduction in hours of employment followed by the involuntary termination of employment of the covered employee. For an individual entitled to COBRA because of a reduction in hours and who is then subsequently involuntarily terminated from employment, the termination is considered a qualifying event for purposes of the COBRA subsidy, as long as the termination occurs during the period beginning on the date following TEA's date of enactment and ending on March 31, 2010.

270

during the taxable year. For taxpayers with modified adjusted gross incomes between $125,000 and $145,000 (or $250,000 and $290,000 for joint filers), the amount of the subsidy that must be repaid is reduced proportionately. The subsidy is also conditioned on the individual not being eligible for certain other health coverage. To the extent that an eligible individual receives a subsidy during a taxable year to which the individual was not entitled due to income or being eligible for other health coverage, the subsidy overpayment is repaid on the individual's income tax return as additional tax. However, in contrast to the HCTC, the subsidy for COBRA continuation coverage may only be claimed through the employer and cannot be claimed at the end of the year on an individual tax return.

Explanation of Provision

Cost-sharing subsidy

A cost-sharing subsidy is provided to reduce annual out-of-pocket cost-sharing for individuals and households between 100 and 400 of percent FPL (for the family size involved). The reductions are made in reference to the dollar cap on annual deductibles for high deductable health plans in section 223(c)(2)(A)(ii) (currently $5,000 for self-only coverage and $10,000 for family coverage). For individuals with household income of more than 100 but not more than 200 percent of FPL, the out-of-pocket limit is reduced by two-thirds. For those between 201 and 300 percent of FPL by one-half, and for those between 301 and 400 percent of FPL by one-third.

The cost-sharing subsidy that is provided must buy out any difference in cost-sharing between the qualified health insurance purchased and the actuarial values specified below. For individuals between 100 and 150 percent of FPL (for the family size involved), the subsidy must bring the value of the plan to not more than 94 percent actuarial value. For those between 150 and 200 percent of FPL, the subsidy must bring the value of the plan to not more than 87 percent actuarial value. For those between 201 and 250 percent of FPL, the subsidy must bring the value of the plan to not more than 73 percent actuarial value. For those between 251 and 400 percent of FPL, the subsidy must bring the value of the plan to not more than 70 percent actuarial value. The determination of cost-sharing subsidies will be made based on data from the same taxable year as is used for determining advance credits under section 1412 of the Act (and not the taxable year used for determining premium assistance credits under section 36B). The amount received by an insurer as a cost-sharing subsidy on behalf of an individual, as well as any out-of-pocket spending by the individual, counts towards the out-of-pocket limit. Individuals enrolled in multi-state plans, pursuant to section 1334 of the Act, are eligible for the subsidy.

In addition to adjusting actuarial values, plans must further reduce cost-sharing for low-income individuals as specified below. For individuals between 100 and 150 percent of FPL (for the family size involved) the plan's share of the total allowed cost of benefits provided under the plan must be 94 percent. For those between 151 and 200 percent of FPL, the plan's share must be 87 percent, and

271

for those between 201 and 250 percent of FPL the plan's share must be 73 percent.

The cost-sharing subsidy is available only for those months in which an individual receives an affordability credit under new section 36B.[730]

As with the premium assistance credit, if the plan in which the individual enrolls offers benefits in addition to essential health benefits,[731] even if the State in which the individual resides requires such additional benefits, the reduction in cost-sharing does not apply to the additional benefits. In addition, individuals enrolled in both a qualified health plan and a pediatric dental plan may not receive a cost-sharing subsidy for the pediatric dental benefits that are included in the essential health benefits required to be provided by the qualified health plan. Cost-sharing subsidies, and any amounts that are attributable to them, cannot be used to pay for abortions for which federal funding is prohibited.

The Secretary of HHS must establish a program for determining whether individuals are eligible to claim a cost-sharing credit. The program must provide for the following: (1) the details of an individual's application process; (2) the details of how public entities are to make determinations of individuals' eligibility; (3) procedures for deeming individuals to be eligible; and, (4) procedures for allowing individuals with limited English proficiency proper access to exchanges.

In applying for enrollment, an individual claiming a cost-sharing subsidy is required to submit to the exchange income and family size information and information regarding changes in marital or family status or income. Personal information provided to the exchange is submitted to the Secretary of HHS. In turn, the Secretary of HHS submits the applicable information to the Social Security Commissioner, Homeland Security Secretary, and Treasury Secretary for verification purposes. The Secretary of HHS is notified of the results following verification, and notifies the exchange of such results. The provision specifies actions to be undertaken if inconsistencies are found. The Secretary of HHS, in consultation with the Treasury Secretary, Homeland Security Secretary, and Social Security Commissioner, must establish procedures for appealing determinations resulting from the verification process, and redetermining eligibility on a periodic basis.

The Secretary of HHS notifies the plan that the individual is eligible and the plan reduces the cost-sharing by reducing the out-of-pocket limit under the provision. The plan notifies the Secretary of HHS of cost-sharing reductions and the Secretary of HHS makes periodic and timely payments to the plan equal to the value of the reductions in cost-sharing. The provision authorizes the Secretary of HHS to establish a capitated payment system with appropriate risk adjustments.

An employer must be notified if one of its employees is determined to be eligible for a cost-sharing subsidy. The notice must include information about the employer's potential liability for payments under section 4980H and explicit notice that hiring, termi-

---

[730] Section 1401 of the Patient Protection and Affordable Care Act, Pub. L. No. 111–148.

[731] As defined in section 1302(b) of the Patient Protection and Affordable Care Act, Pub. L. No. 111–148.

272

nating, or otherwise discriminating against an employee because he or she received a credit or subsidy is in violation of the Fair Labor Standards Act.[732] An employer is generally not entitled to information about its employees who qualify for the premium assistance credit or the cost-sharing subsidy. Employers may, however, be notified of the name of an employee and whether his or her income is above or below the threshold used to measure the affordability of the employer's health insurance coverage.

The Secretary of the Treasury is informed of the name and employer identification number of every employer that has one or more employees receiving a cost-sharing subsidy.

The provision implements special rules for Indians (as defined by the Indian Health Care Improvement Act) and undocumented aliens. The provision prohibits cost-sharing reductions for individuals who are not lawfully present in the United States, and such individuals are not taken into account in determining the family size involved.

The provision defines any term used in this section that is also used by section 36B as having the same meaning as defined by the latter. The provision also denies subsidies to dependents, with respect to whom a deduction under section 151 is allowable to another taxpayer for a taxable year beginning in the calendar year in which the individual's taxable year begins. Further, the provision does not permit a subsidy for any month that is not treated as a coverage month.

Effective Date

The provision is effective on the date of enactment (March 23, 2010).

E. Disclosures to Carry Out Eligibility Requirements for Certain Programs (Sec. 1414[733] of the Act and sec. 6103 of the Code)

Present Law

Section 6103 provides that returns and return information are confidential and may not be disclosed by the IRS, other Federal employees, State employees, and certain others having access to such information except as provided in the Internal Revenue Code. Section 6103 contains a number of exceptions to the general rule of nondisclosure that authorize disclosure in specifically identified circumstances. For example, section 6103 provides for the disclosure of certain return information for purposes of establishing the appropriate amount of any Medicare Part B premium subsidy adjustment.

Section 6103(p)(4) requires, as a condition of receiving returns and return information, that Federal and State agencies (and certain other recipients) provide safeguards as prescribed by the Sec-

---

[732] Pub. L. No. 75–718.

[733] Section 1414 of the Patient Protection and Affordable Care Act, Pub. L. No. 111–148, is amended by section 1004 of the Health Care and Education Reconciliation Act of 2010, Pub. L. No. 111–152.

273

retary of the Treasury by regulation to be necessary or appropriate to protect the confidentiality of returns or return information. Unauthorized disclosure of a return or return information is a felony punishable by a fine not exceeding $5,000 or imprisonment of not more than five years, or both, together with the costs of prosecution.[734] The unauthorized inspection of a return or return information is punishable by a fine not exceeding $1,000 or imprisonment of not more than one year, or both, together with the costs of prosecution.[735] An action for civil damages also may be brought for unauthorized disclosure or inspection.[736]

Explanation of Provision

Individuals will submit income information to an exchange as part of an application process in order to claim the cost-sharing reduction and the tax credit on an advance basis. The Department of HHS serves as the centralized verification agency for information submitted by individuals to the exchanges with respect to the reduction and the tax credit to the extent provided on an advance basis. The IRS is permitted to substantiate the accuracy of income information that has been provided to HHS for eligibility determination.

Specifically, upon written request of the Secretary of HHS, the IRS is permitted to disclose the following return information of any taxpayer whose income is relevant in determining the amount of the tax credit or cost-sharing reduction, or eligibility for participation in the specified State health subsidy programs (i.e., a State Medicaid program under title XIX of the Social Security Act, a State's children's health insurance program under title XXI of such Act, or a basic health program under section 2228 of such Act): (1) taxpayer identity; (2) the filing status of such taxpayer; (3) the modified adjusted gross income (as defined in new sec. 36B of the Code) of such taxpayer, the taxpayer's spouse and of any dependants who are required to file a tax return; (4) such other information as is prescribed by Treasury regulation as might indicate whether such taxpayer is eligible for the credit or subsidy (and the amount thereof); and (5) the taxable year with respect to which the preceding information relates, or if applicable, the fact that such information is not available. HHS is permitted to disclose to an exchange or its contractors, or to the State agency administering the health subsidy programs referenced above (and their contractors) any inconsistency between the information submitted and IRS records.

The disclosed return information may be used only for the purposes of, and only to the extent necessary in, establishing eligibility for participation in the exchange, verifying the appropriate amount of the tax credit, and cost-sharing subsidy, or eligibility for the specified State health subsidy programs.

Recipients of the confidential return information are subject to the safeguard protections and civil and criminal penalties for unau-

---

[734] Sec. 7213.
[735] Sec. 7213A.
[736] Sec. 7431.

274

thorized disclosure and inspection. The IRS is required to make an accounting for all disclosures.

Effective Date

The provision is effective on the date of enactment (March 23, 2010).

F. Premium Tax Credit and Cost-Sharing Reduction Payments Disregarded for Federal and Federally Assisted Programs (sec. 1415 of the Act)

Present Law

There is no tax credit that is generally available to low or middle income individuals or families for the purchase of health insurance.

Explanation of Provision

Any premium assistance tax credits and cost-sharing subsidies provided to an individual under the Act are disregarded for purposes of determining that individual's eligibility for benefits or assistance, or the amount or extent of benefits and assistance, under any Federal program or under any State or local program financed in whole or in part with Federal funds. Specifically, any amount of premium tax credit provided to an individual is not counted as income, and cannot be taken into account as resources for the month of receipt and the following two months. Any cost sharing subsidy provided on the individual's behalf is treated as made to the health plan in which the individual is enrolled and not to the individual.

Effective Date

The provision is effective on the date of enactment (March 23, 2010).

G. Small Business Tax Credit (sec. 1421 [737] of the Act and new sec. 45R of the Code)

Present Law

The Code does not provide a tax credit for employers that provide health coverage for their employees. The cost to an employer of providing health coverage for its employees is generally deductible as an ordinary and necessary business expense for employee compensation.[738] In addition, the value of employer-provided health insurance is not subject to employer-paid Federal Insurance Contributions Act ("FICA") tax.

The Code generally provides that employees are not taxed on the value of employer-provided health coverage under an accident or

---

[737] Section 1421 of the Patient Protection and Affordable Care Act, Pub. L. No. 111–148, is amended by section 10105 of the Patient Protection and Affordable Care Act, Pub. L. No. 111–152.

[738] Sec. 162. However, see special rules in sections 419 and 419A for the deductibility of contributions to welfare benefit plans with respect to medical benefits for employees and their dependents.

275

health plan.[739] That is, these benefits are excluded from gross income. In addition, medical care provided under an accident or health plan for employees, their spouses, and their dependents generally is excluded from gross income.[740] Active employees participating in a cafeteria plan may be able to pay their share of premiums on a pre-tax basis through salary reduction.[741] Such salary reduction contributions are treated as employer contributions and thus also are excluded from gross income.

Reasons for Change

The Congress supports additional incentives and assistance to encourage small business employers with low-wage employees to provide health insurance coverage to their employees. Providing health insurance coverage is particularly challenging for these small business employers. In particular, the cost of health insurance may be disproportionately large as a portion of payroll expenses. The tax credit for qualified employee health coverage expenses is designed to make the provision of health insurance coverage by small business employers of low-wage employees more affordable.

Explanation of Provisions

Small business employers eligible for the credit

Under the provision, a tax credit is provided for a qualified small employer for nonelective contributions to purchase health insurance for its employees. A qualified small employer for this purpose generally is an employer with no more than 25 full-time equivalent employees ("FTEs") employed during the employer's taxable year, and whose employees have annual full-time equivalent wages that average no more than $50,000. However, the full amount of the credit is available only to an employer with 10 or fewer FTEs and whose employees have average annual full-time equivalent wages from the employer of not more than $25,000. These wage limits are indexed to the Consumer Price Index for Urban Consumers ("CPI–U") for years beginning in 2014.

Under the provision, an employer's FTEs are calculated by dividing the total hours worked by all employees during the employer's tax year by 2080. For this purpose, the maximum number of hours that are counted for any single employee is 2080 (rounded down to the nearest whole number). Wages are defined in the same manner as under section 3121(a) (as determined for purposes of FICA taxes but without regard to the dollar limit for covered wages) and the average wage is determined by dividing the total wages paid by the small employer by the number of FTEs (rounded down to the nearest $1,000).

The number of hours of service worked by, and wages paid to, a seasonal worker of an employer is not taken into account in determining the full-time equivalent employees and average annual wages of the employer unless the worker works for the employer on more than 120 days during the taxable year. For purposes of the

---

[739] Sec 106.
[740] Sec. 105(b).
[741] Sec. 125.

276

credit the term 'seasonal worker' means a worker who performs labor or services on a seasonal basis as defined by the Secretary of Labor, including workers covered by 29 CFR sec. 500.20(s)(1) and retail workers employed exclusively during holiday seasons.

The contributions must be provided under an arrangement that requires the eligible small employer to make a nonelective contribution on behalf of each employee who enrolls in certain defined qualifying health insurance offered to employees by the employer equal to a uniform percentage (not less than 50 percent) of the premium cost of the qualifying health plan.

The credit is only available to offset actual tax liability and is claimed on the employer's tax return. The credit is not payable in advance to the taxpayer or refundable. Thus, the employer must pay the employees' premiums during the year and claim the credit at the end of the year on its income tax return. The credit is a general business credit, and can be carried back for one year and carried forward for 20 years. The credit is available for tax liability under the alternative minimum tax.

Years the credit is available

Under the provision, the credit is initially available for any taxable year beginning in 2010, 2011, 2012, or 2013. Qualifying health insurance for claiming the credit for this first phase of the credit is health insurance coverage within the meaning of section 9832, which is generally health insurance coverage purchased from an insurance company licensed under State law.

For taxable years beginning in years after 2013, the credit is only available to a qualified small employer that purchases health insurance coverage for its employees through a State exchange and is only available for a maximum coverage period of two consecutive taxable years beginning with the first year in which the employer or any predecessor first offers one or more qualified plans to its employees through an exchange.[742]

The maximum two-year coverage period does not take into account any taxable years beginning in years before 2014. Thus a qualified small employer could potentially qualify for this credit for six taxable years, four years under the first phase and two years under the second phase.

Calculation of credit amount

Only nonelective contributions by the employer are taken into account in calculating the credit. Therefore, any amount contributed pursuant to a salary reduction arrangement under a cafeteria plan within the meaning of section 125 is not treated as an employer contribution for purposes of this credit. The credit is equal to the lesser of the following two amounts multiplied by an applicable tax credit percentage: (1) the amount of contributions the employer made on behalf of the employees during the taxable year for the qualifying health coverage and (2) the amount of contributions that the employer would have made during the taxable year if each employee had enrolled in coverage with a small business benchmark

---

[742] Sec. 1301 of the Patient Protection and Affordable Care Act, Pub. L. No. 111–148, provides the requirements for a qualified health plan purchased through the exchange.

277

premium. As discussed above, this tax credit is only available if this uniform percentage is at least 50 percent.

For the first phase of the credit (any taxable years beginning in 2010, 2011, 2012, or 2013), the applicable tax credit percentage is 35 percent. The benchmark premium is the average total premium cost in the small group market for employer-sponsored coverage in the employer's State. The premium and the benchmark premium vary based on the type of coverage provided to the employee (e.g., single or family).

For taxable years beginning in years after 2013, the applicable tax credit percentage is 50 percent. The benchmark premium is the average premium cost in the small group market in the rating area in which the employee enrolls in coverage. The premium and the benchmark premium vary based on the type of coverage being provided to the employee (e.g., single or family).

The credit is reduced for an employer with between 10 and 25 FTEs. The amount of this reduction is equal to the amount of the credit (determined before any reduction) multiplied by a fraction, the numerator is the number of FTEs of the employer in excess of 10 and the denominator of which is 15. The credit is also reduced for an employer for whom the average wages per employee is between $25,000 and $50,000. The amount of this reduction is equal to the amount of the credit (determined before any reduction) multiplied by a fraction, the numerator of which is the average annual wages of the employer in excess of $25,000 and the denominator is $25,000. For an employer with both more than 10 FTEs and average annual wages in excess of $25,000, the reduction is the sum of the amount of the two reductions.

Tax exempt organizations as qualified small employers

Any organization described in section 501(c) which is exempt under section 501(a) that otherwise qualifies for the small business tax credit is eligible to receive the credit. However, for tax-exempt organizations, the applicable percentage for the credit during the first phase of the credit (any taxable year beginning in 2010, 2011, 2012, or 2013) is limited to 25 percent and the applicable percentage for the credit during the second phase (taxable years beginning in years after 2013) is limited to 35 percent. The small business tax credit is otherwise calculated in the same manner for tax-exempt organizations that are qualified small employers as the tax credit is calculated for all other qualified small employers. However, for tax-exempt organizations, instead of being a general business credit, the small business tax credit is a refundable tax credit limited to the amount of the payroll taxes of the employer during the calendar year in which the taxable year begins. For this purpose, payroll taxes of an employer means: (1) the amount of income tax required to be withheld from its employees' wages; (2) the amount of hospital insurance tax under section 3101(b) required to be withheld from its employees' wages; and (3) the amount of the hospital insurance tax under section 3111(b) imposed on the employer.

Special rules

The employer is entitled to a deduction under section 162 equal to the amount of the employer contribution minus the dollar

278

amount of the credit. For example, if a qualified small employer pays 100 percent of the cost of its employees' health insurance coverage and the tax credit under this provision is 50 percent of that cost, the employer is able to claim a section 162 deduction for the other 50 percent of the premium cost.

The employer is determined by applying the employer aggregations rules in section 414(b), (c), and (m). In addition, the definition of employee includes a leased employee within the meaning of section 414(n).[743]

Self-employed individuals, including partners and sole proprietors, two percent share-holders of an S Corporation, and five percent owners of the employer (within the meaning of section 416(i)(1)(B)(i)) are not treated as employees for purposes of this credit. There is also a special rule to prevent sole proprietorships from receiving the credit for the owner and their family members. Thus, no credit is available for any contribution to the purchase of health insurance for these individuals and these individuals are not taken into account in determining the number of FTEs or average full-time equivalent wages.

The Secretary of is directed to prescribe such regulations as may be necessary to carry out the provisions of new section 45R, including regulations to prevent the avoidance of the two-year limit on the credit period for the second phase of the credit through the use of successor entities and the use of the limit on the number of employees and the amount of average wages through the use of multiple entities. The Secretary of the Treasury, in consultation with the Secretary of Labor, is directed to prescribe such regulations, rules, and guidance as may be necessary to determine the hours of service of an employee for purposes of determining FTEs, including rules for the employees who are not compensated on an hourly basis.

Effective Date

The provision is effective for taxable years beginning after December 31, 2009.

H. Excise Tax on Individuals Without Essential Health Benefits Coverage (sec. 1501[744] of the Act and sec. 1 of Pub. L. No. 111–173 and new sec. 5000A of the Code)

---

[743] Section 414(b) provides that, for specified employee benefit purposes, all employees of all corporations which are members of a controlled group of corporations are treated as employed by a single employer. There is a similar rule in section 414(c) under which all employees of trades or businesses (whether or not incorporated) which are under common are treated under regulations as employed by a single employer, and, in section 414(m), under which employees of an affiliated service group (as defined in that section) are treated as employed by a single employer. Section 414(n) provides that leased employees, as defined in that section, are treated as employees of the service recipient for specified purposes. Section 414(o) authorizes the Treasury to issue regulations to prevent avoidance of the certain requirement under sections 414(m) and (n).

[744] Section 1501 of the Patient Protection and Affordable Care Act, Pub. L. No. 111–148, as amended by section 10106, is further amended by section 1002 of the Health Care and Education Reconciliation Act of 2010, Pub. L. No. 111–152.

279

Present Law

Federal law does not require individuals to have health insurance. Only the Commonwealth of Massachusetts, through its statewide program, requires that individuals have health insurance (although this policy has been considered in other states, such as California, Maryland, Maine, and Washington). All adult residents of Massachusetts are required to have health insurance that meets "minimum creditable coverage" standards if it is deemed "affordable" at their income level under a schedule set by the board of the Commonwealth Health Insurance Connector Authority ("Connector"). Individuals report their insurance status on State income tax forms. Individuals can file hardship exemptions from the mandate; persons for whom there are no affordable insurance options available are not subject to the requirement for insurance coverage.

For taxable year 2007, an individual without insurance and who was not exempt from the requirement did not qualify under Massachusetts law for a State income tax personal exemption. For taxable years beginning on or after January 1, 2008, a penalty is levied for each month an individual is without insurance. The penalty consists of an amount up to 50 percent of the lowest premium available to the individual through the Connector. The penalty is reported and paid by the individual with the individual's Massachusetts State income tax return at the same time and in the same manner as State income taxes. Failure to pay the penalty results in the same interest and penalties as apply to unpaid income tax.

Explanation of Provision

Personal responsibility requirement

Beginning January, 2014, non-exempt U.S. citizens and legal residents are required to maintain minimum essential coverage. Minimum essential coverage includes government sponsored programs, eligible employer-sponsored plans, plans in the individual market, grandfathered group health plans and grandfathered health insurance coverage, and other coverage as recognized by the Secretary of HHS in coordination with the Secretary of the Treasury. Government sponsored programs include Medicare, Medicaid, Children's Health Insurance Program, coverage for members of the U.S. military,[745] veterans health care,[746] and health care for Peace Corps volunteers.[747] Eligible employer-sponsored plans include: governmental plans,[748] church plans,[749] grandfathered plans and other group health plans offered in the small or large group market within a State. Minimum essential coverage does not include coverage that consists of certain HIPAA excepted benefits.[750] Other

---

[745] 10 U.S.C. sec. 55 and 38 U.S.C. sec. 1781.

[746] Section 5000A is amended by Pub. L. No. 111–173 to clarify that minimum essential coverage includes any health care program under section 17 or 18 of Title 38 of the United States Code, as determined by the Secretary of Veterans Affairs, in coordination with the Secretary of HHS and the Secretary of Treasury.

[747] 22 U.S.C. sec. 2504(e).

[748] ERISA sec. 3(32).

[749] ERISA sec. 3(33).

[750] 42 U.S.C. sec. 300gg–91(c)(1). HIPAA excepted benefits include: (1) coverage only for accident, or disability income insurance; (2) coverage issued as a supplement to liability insurance; (3) liability insurance, including general liability insurance and automobile liability insurance;

Continued

280

HIPAA excepted benefits that do not constitute minimum essential coverage if offered under a separate policy, certificate or contract of insurance include long term care, limited scope dental and vision benefits, coverage for a disease or specified illness, hospital indemnity or other fixed indemnity insurance or Medicare supplemental health insurance.[751]

Individuals are exempt from the requirement for months they are incarcerated, not legally present in the United States or maintain religious exemptions. Those who are exempt from the requirement due to religious reasons must be members of a recognized religious sect exempting them from self-employment taxes[752] and adhere to tenets of the sect. Individuals residing[753] outside of the United States are deemed to maintain minimum essential coverage. If an individual is a dependent[754] of another taxpayer, the other taxpayer is liable for any penalty payment with respect to the individual.

Penalty

Individuals who fail to maintain minimum essential coverage in 2016 are subject to a penalty equal to the greater of: (1) 2.5 percent of the excess of the taxpayer's household income for the taxable year over the threshold amount of income required for income tax return filing for that taxpayer under section 6012(a)(1);[755] or (2) $695 per uninsured adult in the household. The fee for an uninsured individual under age 18 is one-half of the adult fee for an adult. The total household penalty may not exceed 300 percent of the per adult penalty ($2,085). The total annual household payment may not exceed the national average annual premium for bronze level health plan offered through the Exchange that year for the household size.

This per adult annual penalty is phased in as follows: $95 for 2014; $325 for 2015; and $695 in 2016. For years after 2016, the $695 amount is indexed to CPI–U, rounded to the next lowest $50. The percentage of income is phased in as follows: one percent for 2014; two percent in 2015; and 2.5 percent beginning after 2015. If a taxpayer files a joint return, the individual and spouse are jointly liable for any penalty payment.

The penalty applies to any period the individual does not maintain minimum essential coverage and is determined monthly. The penalty is an excise tax that is assessed in the same manner as an assessable penalty under the enforcement provisions of subtitle F of the Code.[756] As a result, it is assessable without regard to the

---

(4) workers' compensation or similar insurance; (5) automobile medical payment insurance; (6) credit-only insurance; (7) coverage for on-site medical clinics; and (8) other similar insurance coverage, specified in regulations, under which benefits for medical care are secondary or incidental to other insurance benefits.

[751] 42 U.S.C. sec. 300gg–91(c)(2–4).

[752] Sec. 1402(g)(1).

[753] Sec. 911(d)(1).

[754] Sec. 152.

[755] Generally, in 2010, the filing threshold is $9,350 for a single person or a married person filing separately and is $18,700 for married filing jointly. IR–2009–93, Oct. 15, 2009.

[756] IRS authority to assess and collect taxes is generally provided in subtitle F, "Procedure and Administration" in the Code. That subtitle establishes the rules governing both how taxpayers are required to report information to the IRS and pay their taxes as well as their rights. It also establishes the duties and authority of the IRS to enforce the Code, including civil and criminal penalties.

281

restrictions of section 6213(b). Although assessable and collectible under the Code, the IRS authority to use certain collection methods is limited. Specifically, the filing of notices of liens and levies otherwise authorized for collection of taxes does not apply to the collection of this penalty. In addition, the statute waives criminal penalties for non-compliance with the requirement to maintain minimum essential coverage. However, the authority to offset refunds or credits is not limited by the provision.

Individuals who cannot afford coverage because their required contribution for employer-sponsored coverage or, with respect to whom, the lowest cost bronze plan in the local Exchange exceeds eight percent of household income for the year are exempt from the penalty.[757] In years after 2014, the eight percent exemption is increased by the amount by which premium growth exceeds income growth. For employees, and individuals who are eligible for minimum essential coverage through an employer by reason of a relationship to an employee, the determination of whether coverage is affordable to the employee and any such individual is made by reference to the required contribution of the employees for self-only coverage. Individuals are liable for penalties imposed with respect to their dependents (as defined in section 152). An individual filing a joint return with a spouse is jointly liable for any penalty imposed with respect to the spouse. Taxpayers with income below the income tax filing threshold[758] are also exempt from the penalty for failure to maintain minimum essential coverage. All members of Indian tribes[759] are exempt from the penalty.

No penalty is assessed for individuals who do not maintain health insurance for a period of three months or less during the taxable year. If an individual exceeds the three month maximum during the taxable year, the penalty for the full duration of the gap during the year is applied. If there are multiple gaps in coverage during a calendar year, the exemption from penalty applies only to the first such gap in coverage. The Secretary of the Treasury shall provide rules when a coverage gap includes months in multiple calendar years. Individuals may also apply to the Secretary of HHS for a hardship exemption due to hardship in obtaining coverage.[760] Residents of the possessions[761] of the United States are treated as being covered by acceptable coverage.

Family size is the number of individuals for whom the taxpayer is allowed a personal exemption. Household income is the sum of the modified adjusted gross incomes of the taxpayer and all individuals accounted for in the family size required to file a tax return for that year. Modified adjusted gross income means adjusted gross

---

[757] In the case of an individual participating in a salary reduction arrangement, the taxpayer's household income is increased by any exclusion from gross income for any portion of the required contribution to the premium. The required contribution to the premium is the individual contribution to coverage through an employer or in the purchase of a bronze plan through the Exchange.

[758] Generally, in 2010, the filing threshold is $9,350 for a single person or a married person filing separately and is $18,700 for married filing jointly. IR–2009–93, Oct. 15, 2009.

[759] Tribal membership is defined in section 45A(c)(6).

[760] Sec. 1311(d)(4)(H).

[761] Sec. 937(a).

282

income increased by all tax-exempt interest and foreign earned income.[762]

Effective Date

The provision is effective for taxable years beginning after December 31, 2013.

I. Reporting of Health Insurance Coverage (sec. 1502 of the Act and new sec. 6055 and sec. 6724(d) of the Code)

Present Law

Insurer reporting of health insurance coverage

No provision.

Penalties for failure to comply with information reporting requirements

Present law imposes a variety of information reporting requirements on participants in certain transactions.[763] These requirements are intended to assist taxpayers in preparing their income tax returns and help the IRS determine whether such returns are correct and complete. Failure to comply with the information reporting requirements may result in penalties, including: a penalty for failure to file the information return,[764] a penalty for failure to furnish payee statements,[765] and a penalty for failure to comply with various other reporting requirements.[766]

The penalty for failure to file an information return generally is $50 for each return for which such failure occurs. The total penalty imposed on a person for all failures during a calendar year cannot exceed $250,000. Additionally, special rules apply to reduce the per-failure and maximum penalty where the failure is corrected within a specified period.

The penalty for failure to provide a correct payee statement is $50 for each statement with respect to which such failure occurs, with the total penalty for a calendar year not to exceed $100,000. Special rules apply that increase the per-statement and total penalties where there is intentional disregard of the requirement to furnish a payee statement.

Explanation of Provision

Under the provision, insurers (including employers who self-insure) that provide minimum essential coverage[767] to any individual during a calendar year must report certain health insurance coverage information to both the covered individual and to the IRS. In the case of coverage provided by a governmental unit, or any agency or instrumentality thereof, the reporting requirement ap-

---

[762] Sec. 911.
[763] Secs. 6031 through 6060.
[764] Sec. 6721.
[765] Sec. 6722.
[766] Sec. 6723. The penalty for failure to comply timely with a specified information reporting requirement is $50 per failure, not to exceed $100,000 for a calendar year.
[767] As defined in section 5000A of the Patient Protection and Affordable Care Act, Pub. L. No. 111–148, as amended by section 10106, as further amended by section 1002 of the Health Care and Education Reconciliation Act of 2010, Pub. L. No. 111–152.

283

plies to the person or employee who enters into the agreement to provide the health insurance coverage (or their designee).

The information required to be reported includes: (1) the name, address, and taxpayer identification number of the primary insured, and the name and taxpayer identification number of each other individual obtaining coverage under the policy; (2) the dates during which the individual was covered under the policy during the calendar year; (3) whether the coverage is a qualified health plan offered through an exchange; (4) the amount of any premium tax credit or cost-sharing reduction received by the individual with respect to such coverage; and (5) such other information as the Secretary may require.

To the extent health insurance coverage is provided through an employer-sponsored group health plan, the insurer is also required to report the name, address and employer identification number of the employer, the portion of the premium, if any, required to be paid by the employer, and any other information the Secretary may require to administer the new tax credit for eligible small employers.

The insurer is required to report the above information, along with the name, address and contact information of the reporting insurer, to the covered individual on or before January 31 of the year following the calendar year for which the information is required to be reported to the IRS.

The provision amends the information reporting provisions of the Code to provide that an insurer who fails to comply with these new reporting requirements is subject to the penalties for failure to file an information return and failure to furnish payee statements, respectively.

The IRS is required, not later than June 30 of each year, in consultation with the Secretary of HHS, to provide annual notice to each individual who files an income tax return and who fails to enroll in minimum essential coverage. The notice is required to include information on the services available through the exchange operating in the individual's State of residence.

Effective Date

The provision is effective for calendar years beginning after 2013.

J. Shared Responsibility for Employers (sec. 1513 [768] of the Act and new sec. 4980H of the Code)

Present Law

Currently, there is no Federal requirement that employers offer health insurance coverage to employees or their families. However, as with other compensation, the cost of employer-provided health coverage is a deductible business expense under section 162 of the

---

[768] Section 1513 of the Patient Protection and Affordable Care Act, Pub. L. No. 111–148, as amended by section 10106, is further amended by section 1003 of the Health Care and Education Reconciliation Act of 2010, Pub. L. No. 111–152.

284

Code.[769] In addition, employer-provided health insurance coverage is generally not included in an employee's gross income.[770]

Employees participating in a cafeteria plan may be able to pay the portion of premiums for health insurance coverage not otherwise paid for by their employers on a pre-tax basis through salary reduction.[771] Such salary reduction contributions are treated as employer contributions for purposes of the Code, and are thus excluded from gross income.

One way that employers can offer employer-provided health insurance coverage for purposes of the tax exclusion is to offer to reimburse employees for the premiums for health insurance purchased by employees in the individual health insurance market. The payment or reimbursement of employees' substantiated individual health insurance premiums is excludible from employees' gross income.[772] This reimbursement for individual health insurance premiums can also be paid through salary reduction under a cafeteria plan.[773] However, this offer to reimburse individual health insurance premiums constitutes a group health plan.

The Employee Retirement Income Security Act of 1974 ("ERISA")[774] preempts State law relating to certain employee benefit plans, including employer-sponsored health plans. While ERISA specifically provides that its preemption rule does not exempt or relieve any person from any State law which regulates insurance, ERISA also provides that an employee benefit plan is not deemed to be engaged in the business of insurance for purposes of any State law regulating insurance companies or insurance contracts. As a result of this ERISA preemption, self-insured employer-sponsored health plans need not provide benefits that are mandated under State insurance law.

While ERISA does not require an employer to offer health benefits, it does require compliance if an employer chooses to offer health benefits, such as compliance with plan fiduciary standards, reporting and disclosure requirements, and procedures for appealing denied benefit claims. There are other Federal requirements for health plans which include, for example, rules for health care continuation coverage.[775] The Code imposes an excise tax on group health plans that fail to meet these other requirements.[776] The excise tax generally is equal to $100 per day per failure during the period of noncompliance and is imposed on the employer sponsoring the plan.

Under Medicaid, States may establish "premium assistance" programs, which pay a Medicaid beneficiary's share of premiums for employer-sponsored health coverage. Besides being available to the beneficiary through his or her employer, the coverage must be comprehensive and cost-effective for the State. An individual's enroll-

---

[769] Sec. 162. However see special rules in sections 419 and 419A for the deductibility of contributions to welfare benefit plans with respect to medical benefits for employees and their dependents.

[770] Sec. 106.

[771] Sec. 125.

[772] Rev. Rul. 61–146 (1961–2 CB 25).

[773] Prop. Treas. Reg. sec. 1.125–1(m).

[774] Pub. L. No. 93–406.

[775] These rules were added to ERISA and the Code by the Consolidated Omnibus Budget Reconciliation Act of 1985, Pub. L. No. 99–272.

[776] Sec. 4980B.

285

ment in an employer plan is considered cost-effective if paying the premiums, deductibles, coinsurance and other cost-sharing obligations of the employer plan is less expensive than the State's expected cost of directly providing Medicaid-covered services. States are also required to provide coverage for those Medicaid-covered services that are not included in the private plans. A 2007 analysis showed that 12 States had Medicaid premium assistance programs as authorized under current law.

Explanation of Provision

An applicable large employer that does not offer coverage for all its full-time employees, offers minimum essential coverage that is unaffordable, or offers minimum essential coverage that consists of a plan under which the plan's share of the total allowed cost of benefits is less than 60 percent, is required to pay a penalty if any full-time employee is certified to the employer as having purchased health insurance through a state exchange with respect to which a tax credit or cost-sharing reduction is allowed or paid to the employee.

Applicable large employer

An employer is an applicable large employer with respect to any calendar year if it employed an average of at least 50 full-time employees during the preceding calendar year. For purposes of the provision, "employer" includes any predecessor employer. An employer is not treated as employing more than 50 full-time employees if the employer's workforce exceeds 50 full-time employees for 120 days or fewer during the calendar year and the employees that cause the employer's workforce to exceed 50 full-time employees are seasonal workers. A seasonal worker is a worker who performs labor or services on a seasonal basis (as defined by the Secretary of Labor), including retail workers employed exclusively during the holiday season and workers whose employment is, ordinarily, the kind exclusively performed at certain seasons or periods of the year and which, from its nature, may not be continuous or carried on throughout the year.[777]

In counting the number of employees for purposes of determining whether an employer is an applicable large employer, a full-time employee (meaning, for any month, an employee working an average of at least 30 hours or more each week) is counted as one employee and all other employees are counted on a pro-rated basis in accordance with regulations prescribed by the Secretary. The number of full-time equivalent employees that must be taken into account for purposes of determining whether the employer exceeds the threshold is equal to the aggregate number of hours worked by non-full-time employees for the month, divided by 120 (or such other number based on an average of 30 hours of service each week as the Secretary may prescribe in regulations).

The Secretary, in consultation with the Secretary of Labor, is directed to issue, as necessary, rules, regulations and guidance to de-

---

[777] 29 C.F.R. section 500.20(s)(1). Under section 5000.20(s)(1), a worker who moves from one seasonal activity to another, while employed in agriculture or performing agricultural labor, is employed on a seasonal basis even though he may continue to be employed during a major portion of the year.

termine an employee's hours of service, including rules that apply to employees who are not compensated on an hourly basis.

The aggregation rules of section 414(b), (c), (m), and (o) apply in determining whether an employer is an applicable large employer. The determination of whether an employer that was not in existence during the preceding calendar year is an applicable large employer is made based on the average number of employees that it is reasonably expected to employ on business days in the current calendar year.

Penalty for employers not offering coverage

An applicable large employer who fails to offer its full-time employees and their dependents the opportunity to enroll in minimum essential coverage under an employer-sponsored plan for any month is subject to a penalty if at least one of its full-time employees is certified to the employer as having enrolled in health insurance coverage purchased through a State exchange with respect to which a premium tax credit or cost-sharing reduction is allowed or paid to such employee or employees. The penalty for any month is an excise tax equal to the number of full-time employees over a 30-employee threshold during the applicable month (regardless of how many employees are receiving a premium tax credit or cost-sharing reduction) multiplied by one-twelfth of $2,000. In the case of persons treated as a single employer under the provision, the 30-employee reduction in full-time employees is made from the total number of full-time employees employed by such persons (i.e., only one 30-person reduction is permitted per controlled group of employers) and is allocated among such persons in relation to the number of full-time employees employed by each such person.

For example, in 2014, Employer A fails to offer minimum essential coverage and has 100 full-time employees, ten of whom receive a tax credit for the year for enrolling in a State exchange-offered plan. For each employee over the 30-employee threshold, the employer owes $2,000, for a total penalty of $140,000 ($2,000 multiplied by 70 ((100–30)). This penalty is assessed on an annual, monthly, or periodic basis as the Secretary may prescribe.

For calendar years after 2014, the $2,000 amount is increased by the percentage (if any) by which the average per capita premium for health insurance coverage in the United States for the preceding calendar year (as estimated by the Secretary of HHS no later than October 1 of the preceding calendar year) exceeds the average per capita premium for 2013 (as determined by the Secretary of HHS), rounded down to the nearest $10.

Penalty for employees receiving premium credits

An applicable large employer who offers, for any month, its full-time employees and their dependents the opportunity to enroll in minimum essential coverage under an employer-sponsored plan is subject to a penalty if any full-time employee is certified to the employer as having enrolled in health insurance coverage purchased through a State exchange with respect to which a premium tax credit or cost-sharing reduction is allowed or paid to such employee or employees.

287

The penalty is an excise tax that is imposed for each employee who receives a premium tax credit or cost-sharing reduction for health insurance purchased through a State exchange. For each full-time employee receiving a premium tax credit or cost-sharing subsidy through a State exchange for any month, the employer is required to pay an amount equal to one-twelfth of $3,000. The penalty for each employer for any month is capped at an amount equal to the number of full-time employees during the month (regardless of how many employees are receiving a premium tax credit or cost-sharing reduction) in excess of 30, multiplied by one-twelfth of $2,000. In the case of persons treated as a single employer under the provision, the 30-employee reduction in full-time employees for purposes of calculating the maximum penalty is made from the total number of full-time employees employed by such persons (i.e., only one 30-person reduction is permitted per controlled group of employers) and is allocated among such persons in relation to the number of full-time employees employed by each such person.

For example, in 2014, Employer A offers health coverage and has 100 full-time employees, 20 of whom receive a tax credit for the year for enrolling in a State exchange offered plan. For each employee receiving a tax credit, the employer owes $3,000, for a total penalty of $60,000. The maximum penalty for this employer is capped at the amount of the penalty that it would have been assessed for a failure to provide coverage, or $140,000 ($2,000 multiplied by 70 ((100–30)). Since the calculated penalty of $60,000 is less than the maximum amount, Employer A pays the $60,000 calculated penalty. This penalty is assessed on an annual, monthly, or periodic basis as the Secretary may prescribe.

For calendar years after 2014, the $3,000 and $2,000 amounts are increased by the percentage (if any) by which the average per capita premium for health insurance coverage in the United States for the preceding calendar year (as estimated by the Secretary of HHS no later than October 1 of the preceding calendar year) exceeds the average per capita premium for 2013 (as determined by the Secretary of HHS), rounded down to the nearest $10.

Time for payment, deductibility of excise taxes, restrictions on assessment

The excise taxes imposed under this provision are payable on an annual, monthly or other periodic basis as the Secretary of the Treasury may prescribe. The excise taxes imposed under this provision for employees receiving premium tax credits are not deductible under section 162 as a business expense. The restrictions on assessment under section 6213 are not applicable to the excise taxes imposed under the provision.

Employer offer of health insurance coverage

Under the provision, as under current law, an employer is not required to offer health insurance coverage. If an employee is offered health insurance coverage by his or her employer and chooses to enroll in the coverage, the employer-provided portion of the coverage is excluded from gross income. The tax treatment is the same whether the employer offers coverage outside of a State exchange or the employer offers a coverage option through a State exchange.

288

Definition of coverage

As a general matter, if an employee is offered affordable minimum essential coverage under an employer-sponsored plan, the individual is ineligible for a premium tax credit and cost sharing reductions for health insurance purchased through a State exchange.

Unaffordable coverage

If an employee is offered minimum essential coverage by their employer that is either unaffordable or that consists of a plan under which the plan's share of the total allowed cost of benefits is less than 60 percent, however, the employee is eligible for a premium tax credit and cost sharing reductions, but only if the employee declines to enroll in the coverage and purchases coverage through the exchange instead. Unaffordable is defined as coverage with a premium required to be paid by the employee that is more than 9.5 percent of the employee's household income (as defined for purposes of the premium tax credits), based on the self-only coverage. This percentage of the employee's income is indexed to the per capita growth in premiums for the insured market as determined by the Secretary of HHS. The employee must seek an affordability waiver from the State exchange and provide information as to family income and the lowest cost employer option offered to them. The State exchange then provides the waiver to the employee. The employer penalty applies for any employee(s) receiving an affordability waiver.

For purposes of determining if coverage is unaffordable, required salary reduction contributions are treated as payments required to be made by the employee. However, if an employee is reimbursed by the employer for any portion of the premium for health insurance coverage purchased through the exchange, including any reimbursement through salary reduction contributions under a cafeteria plan, the coverage is employer-provided and the employee is not eligible for premium tax credits or cost-sharing reductions. Thus, an individual is not permitted to purchase coverage through the exchange, apply for the premium tax credit, and pay for the individual's portion of the premium using salary reduction contributions under the cafeteria plan of the individual's employer.

An employer must be notified if one of its employees is determined to be eligible for a premium assistance credit or a cost-sharing reduction because the employer does not provide minimal essential coverage through an employer-sponsored plan, or the employer does offer such coverage but it is not affordable or the plan's share of the total allowed cost of benefits is less than 60 percent. The notice must include information about the employer's potential liability for payments under section 4980H. The employer must also receive notification of the appeals process established for employers notified of potential liability for payments under section 4980H. An employer is generally not entitled to information about its employees who qualify for the premium assistance credit or cost-sharing reductions; however, the appeals process must provide an employer the opportunity to access the data used to make the determination of an employee's eligibility for a premium assistance credit or cost-sharing reduction, to the extent allowable by law.

289

The Secretary is required to prescribe rules, regulations or guidance for the repayment of any assessable payment (including interest) if the payment is based on the allowance or payment of a premium tax credit or cost-sharing reduction with respect to an employee that is subsequently disallowed and with respect to which the assessable payment would not have been required to have been made in the absence of the allowance or payment.

Effect of medicaid enrollment

A Medicaid-eligible individual can always choose to leave the employer's coverage and enroll in Medicaid, and an employer is not required to pay a penalty for any employees enrolled in Medicaid.

Study and reporting on employer responsibility requirements

The Secretary of Labor is required to study whether employee wages are reduced by reason of the application of the employer responsibility requirements, using the National Compensation Survey published by the Bureau of Labor Statistics. The Secretary of Labor is to report the results of this study to the Committee on Ways and Means of the House of Representatives and the Committee on Finance of the Senate.

Effective Date

The provision is effective for months beginning after December 31, 2013.

K. Reporting of Employer Health Insurance Coverage (sec. 1514 of the Act and new sec. 6056 and sec. 6724(d) of the Code)

Present Law

Employer reporting of health insurance coverage

No provision.

Penalties for failure to comply with information reporting requirements

Present law imposes a variety of information reporting requirements on participants in certain transactions.[778] These requirements are intended to assist taxpayers in preparing their income tax returns and help the IRS determine whether such returns are correct and complete. Failure to comply with the information reporting requirements may result in penalties, including: a penalty for failure to file the information return,[779] a penalty for failure to furnish payee statements,[780] and a penalty for failure to comply with various other reporting requirements.[781]

The penalty for failure to file an information return generally is $50 for each return for which such failure occurs. The total penalty imposed on a person for all failures during a calendar year cannot

---

[778] Secs. 6031 through 6060.
[779] Sec. 6721.
[780] Sec. 6722.
[781] Sec. 6723. The penalty for failure to comply timely with a specified information reporting requirement is $50 per failure, not to exceed $100,000 for a calendar year.

290

exceed $250,000. Additionally, special rules apply to reduce the per-failure and maximum penalty where the failure is corrected within a specified period.

The penalty for failure to provide a correct payee statement is $50 for each statement with respect to which such failure occurs, with the total penalty for a calendar year not to exceed $100,000. Special rules apply that increase the per-statement and total penalties where there is intentional disregard of the requirement to furnish a payee statement.

Explanation of Provision

Under the provision, each applicable large employer subject to the employer responsibility provisions of new section 4980H and each "offering employer" must report certain health insurance coverage information to both its full-time employees and to the IRS. An offering employer is any employer who offers minimum essential coverage [782] to its employees under an eligible employer-sponsored plan and who pays any portion of the costs of such plan, but only if the required employer contribution of any employee exceeds eight percent of the wages paid by the employer to the employee. In the case of years after 2014, the eight percent is indexed to reflect the rate of premium growth over income growth between 2013 and the preceding calendar year. In the case of coverage provided by a governmental unit, or any agency or instrumentality thereof, the reporting requirement applies to the person or employee appropriately designated for purposes of making the returns and statements required by the provision.

The information required to be reported includes: (1) the name, address and employer identification number of the employer; (2) a certification as to whether the employer offers its full-time employees and their dependents the opportunity to enroll in minimum essential coverage under an eligible employer-sponsored plan; (3) the number of full-time employees of the employer for each month during the calendar year; (4) the name, address and taxpayer identification number of each full-time employee employed by the employer during the calendar year and the number of months, if any, during which the employee (and any dependents) was covered under a plan sponsored by the employer during the calendar year; and (5) such other information as the Secretary may require.

Employers who offer the opportunity to enroll in minimum essential coverage must also report: (1) in the case of an applicable large employer, the length of any waiting period with respect to such coverage; (2) the months during the calendar year during which the coverage was available; (3) the monthly premium for the lowest cost option in each of the enrollment categories under the plan; (4) the employer's share of the total allowed costs of benefits under the plan; and (5), in the case of an offering employer, the option for which the employer pays the largest position of the cost of the plan and the portion of the cost paid by the employer in each of the enrollment categories under each option.

---

[782] As defined in section 5000A of the Patient Protection and Affordable Care Act, Pub. L. No. 111–148, as amended by section 10106, as further amended by section 1002 of the Health Care and Education Reconciliation Act of 2010, Pub. L. No. 111–152.

291

The employer is required to report to each full-time employee the above information required to be reported with respect to that employee, along with the name, address and contact information of the reporting employer, on or before January 31 of the year following the calendar year for which the information is required to be reported to the IRS.

The provision amends the information reporting provisions of the Code to provide that an employer who fails to comply with these new reporting requirements is subject to the penalties for failure to file an information return and failure to furnish payee statements, respectively.

To the maximum extent feasible, the Secretary may provide that any information return or payee statement required to be provided under the provision may be provided as part of any return or statement required under new sections 6051[783] or 6055[784] and, in the case of an applicable large employer or offering employer offering health insurance coverage of a health insurance issuer, the employer may enter into an agreement with the issuer to include the information required by the provision with the information return and payee statement required under new section 6055.

The Secretary has the authority, in coordination with the Secretary of Labor, to review the accuracy of the information reported by the employer, including the employer's share of the total allowed costs of benefits under the plan.

Effective Date

The provision is effective for periods beginning after December 31, 2013.

L. Offering of Qualified Health Plans Through Cafeteria Plans (sec. 1515 of the Act and sec. 125 of the Code)

Present Law

Currently, there is no Federal requirement that employers offer health insurance coverage to employees or their families. However, as with other compensation, the cost of employer-provided health coverage is a deductible business expense under section 162 of the Code.[785] In addition, employer-provided health insurance coverage is generally not included in an employee's gross income.[786]

Definition of a cafeteria plan

If an employee receives a qualified benefit (as defined below) based on the employee's election between the qualified benefit and a taxable benefit under a cafeteria plan, the qualified benefit gen-

---

[783] For additional information on new section 6051, see the explanation of section 9002 of the Patient Protection and Affordable Care Act, Pub. L. No. 111–148, "Inclusion of Employer-Sponsored Health Coverage on W–2."

[784] For additional information on new section 6055, see the explanation of section 1502 of the Patient Protection and Affordable Care Act, Pub. L. No. 111–148, "Reporting of Health Insurance Coverage."

[785] Sec. 162. However see special rules in sections 419 and 419A for the deductibility of contributions to welfare benefit plans with respect to medical benefits for employees and their dependents.

[786] Sec. 106.

292

erally is not includable in gross income.[787] However, if a plan offering an employee an election between taxable benefits (including cash) and nontaxable qualified benefits does not meet the requirements for being a cafeteria plan, the election between taxable and nontaxable benefits results in gross income to the employee, regardless of what benefit is elected and when the election is made.[788] A cafeteria plan is a separate written plan under which all participants are employees, and participants are permitted to choose among at least one permitted taxable benefit (for example, current cash compensation) and at least one qualified benefit. Finally, a cafeteria plan must not provide for deferral of compensation, except as specifically permitted in sections 125(d)(2)(B), (C), or (D).

Qualified benefits

Qualified benefits under a cafeteria plan are generally employer-provided benefits that are not includable in gross income under an express provision of the Code. Examples of qualified benefits include employer-provided health insurance coverage, group term life insurance coverage not in excess of $50,000, and benefits under a dependent care assistance program. In order to be excludable, any qualified benefit elected under a cafeteria plan must independently satisfy any requirements under the Code section that provides the exclusion. However, some employer-provided benefits that are not includable in gross income under an express provision of the Code are explicitly not allowed in a cafeteria plan. These benefits are generally referred to as nonqualified benefits. Examples of nonqualified benefits include scholarships;[789] employer-provided meals and lodging;[790] educational assistance;[791] and fringe benefits.[792] A plan offering any nonqualified benefit is not a cafeteria plan.[793]

Payment of health insurance premiums through a cafeteria plan

Employees participating in a cafeteria plan may be able to pay the portion of premiums for health insurance coverage not otherwise paid for by their employers on a pre-tax basis through salary reduction.[794] Such salary reduction contributions are treated as employer contributions for purposes of the Code, and are thus excluded from gross income.

One way that employers can offer employer-provided health insurance coverage for purposes of the tax exclusion is to offer to reimburse employees for the premiums for health insurance purchased by employees in the individual health insurance market. The payment or reimbursement of employees' substantiated individual health insurance premiums is excludible from employees'

---

[787] Sec. 125(a).
[788] Prop. Treas. Reg. sec. 1.125–1(b).
[789] Sec. 117.
[790] Sec. 119.
[791] Sec. 127.
[792] Sec. 132.
[793] Prop. Treas. Reg. sec. 1.125–1(q). Long-term care services, contributions to Archer Medical Savings Accounts, group term life insurance for an employee's spouse, child or dependent, and elective deferrals to section 403(b) plans are also nonqualified benefits.
[794] Sec. 125.

293

gross income.[795] This reimbursement for individual health insurance premiums can also be paid for through salary reduction under a cafeteria plan.[796] This offer to reimburse individual health insurance premiums constitutes a group health plan.

Explanation of Provision

Under the provision, reimbursement (or direct payment) for the premiums for coverage under any qualified health plan (as defined in section 1301(a) of the Act) offered through an Exchange established under section 1311 of the Act is a qualified benefit under a cafeteria plan if the employer is a qualified employer. Under section 1312(f)(2) of the Act, a qualified employer is generally a small employer that elects to make all its full-time employees eligible for one or more qualified plans offered in the small group market through an Exchange.[797] Otherwise, reimbursement (or direct payment) for the premiums for coverage under any qualified health plan offered through an Exchange is not a qualified benefit under a cafeteria plan. Thus, an employer that is not a qualified employer cannot offer to reimburse an employee for the premium for a qualified plan that the employee purchases through the individual market in an Exchange as a health insurance coverage option under its cafeteria plan.

Effective Date

This provision applies to taxable years beginning after December 31, 2013.

M. Conforming Amendments (sec. 1563 of the Act and new sec. 9815 of the Code)

Present Law

The Health Insurance Portability and Accountability Act of 1996 ("HIPAA")[798] imposes a number of requirements with respect to group health coverage that are designed to provide protections to health plan participants. These protections include limitations on exclusions from coverage based on pre-existing conditions; the prohibition of discrimination on the basis of health status; guaranteed renewability in multiemployer plans and certain employer welfare arrangements; standards relating to benefits for mother and newborns; parity in the application of certain limits to mental health benefits; and coverage of dependent students on medically necessary leave of absence. The requirements are enforced through the Code, ERISA,[799] and the PHSA.[800] The HIPAA requirements in the Code are in chapter 100 of Subtitle K, Group Health Plan Requirements.

---

[795] Rev. Rul. 61–146, 1961–2 CB 25.

[796] Prop. Treas. Reg. sec. 1.125–1(m).

[797] Beginning in 2017, each State may allow issuers of health insurance coverage in the large group market in a state to offer qualified plans in the large group market. In that event, a qualified employer includes a small employer that elects to make all its full-time employees eligible for one or more qualified plans offered in the large group market through an Exchange.

[798] Pub. L. No. 104–191.

[799] Pub. L. No. 93–406.

[800] 42 U.S.C. 6A.

294

A group health plan is defined as a plan (including a self-insured plan) of, or contributed to by, an employer (including a self-employed person) or employee organization to provide health care (directly or otherwise) to the employees, former employees, the employer, others associated or formerly associated with the employer in a business relationship, or their families.[801]

The Code imposes an excise tax on group health plans which fail to meet the HIPAA requirements.[802] The excise tax is equal to $100 per day during the period of noncompliance and is generally imposed on the employer sponsoring the plan if the plan fails to meet the requirements. The maximum tax that can be imposed during a taxable year cannot exceed the lesser of: (1) 10 percent of the employer's group health plan expenses for the prior year; or (2) $500,000. No tax is imposed if the Secretary determines that the employer did not know, and in exercising reasonable diligence would not have known, that the failure existed.

Explanation of Provision

The provision adds new Code section 9815 which provides that the provisions of part A of title XXVII of the PHSA (as amended by the Act) apply to group health plans, and health insurance issuers providing health insurance coverage in connection with group health plans, as if included in Subchapter B of Chapter 100 of the Code. To the extent that any HIPAA provision of the Code conflicts with a provision of part A of title XXVII of the PHSA with respect to group health plans, or health insurance issuers providing health insurance coverage in connection with group health plans, the provisions of such part A generally apply.

The provisions of part A of title XXVII of the PHSA added by section 1001 of the Act that are incorporated by reference in new section 9815 include the following: section 2711 (No lifetime or annual limits); section 2712 (Prohibition on rescissions); section 2713 (Coverage of preventive health services); section 2714 (Extension of dependent coverage); section 2715 (Development and utilization of uniform explanation of coverage documents and standardized definitions); section 2716 (Prohibition of discrimination in favor of highly compensated individuals); section 2717 (Ensuring the quality of care); section 2718 (Bringing down the cost of health care coverage); and section 2719 (Appeals process). These new sections of the PHSA, which relate to individual and group market reforms, are effective six months after the date of enactment (March 23, 2010).

The provisions of part A of title XXVII of the PHSA added by section 1201 of the Act that are incorporated by reference in new section 9815 include the following: section 2704 (Prohibition of pre-existing condition exclusions or other discrimination based on health status); section 2701 (Fair health insurance premiums); section 2702 (Guaranteed availability of coverage) section 2703 (Guaranteed renewability of coverage); section 2705 (Prohibiting discrimination against individual participants and beneficiaries based

---

[801] The requirements do not apply to any governmental plan or any group health plan that has fewer than two participants who are current employees.

[802] Sec. 4980D.

295

on health status); section 2706 (Non-discrimination in health care); section 2707 (Comprehensive health insurance coverage); and section 2708 (Prohibition on excessive waiting periods). These new sections of the PHSA, which relate to general health insurance reforms, are effective for plan years beginning on or after January 1, 2014.

New section 9815 specifies that section 2716 (Prohibition of discrimination based on salary) and 2718 (Bringing down the cost of health coverage) of title XXVII of the PHSA (as amended by the Act) do not apply under the Code provisions of HIPAA with respect to self-insured group health plans.

As a result of incorporating these PHSA provisions by reference, the excise tax that applies in the event of a violation of present law HIPAA requirements also applies in the event of a violation of these new requirements.

Effective Date

This provision is effective on the date of enactment (March 23, 2010).

TITLE III—IMPROVING THE QUALITY AND EFFICIENCY OF HEALTHCARE

A. Disclosures to Carry Out the Reduction of Medicare Part D Subsidies for High Income Beneficiaries (sec. 3308(b)(2) of the Act and sec. 6103 of the Code)

Present Law

Section 6103 provides that returns and return information are confidential and may not be disclosed by the IRS, other Federal employees, State employees, and certain others having access to such information except as provided in the Code. Section 6103 contains a number of exceptions to the general rule of nondisclosure that authorize disclosure in specifically identified circumstances. For example, section 6103 provides for the disclosure of certain return information for purposes of establishing the appropriate amount of any Medicare Part B premium subsidy adjustment.

Specifically, upon written request from the Commissioner of Social Security, the IRS may disclose the following limited return information of a taxpayer whose premium, according to the records of the Secretary, may be subject to adjustment under section 1839(i) of the Social Security Act (relating to Medicare Part B):

   • Taxpayer identity information with respect to such taxpayer;
   • The filing status of the taxpayer;
   • The adjusted gross income of such taxpayer;
   • The amounts excluded from such taxpayer's gross income under sections 135 and 911 to the extent such information is available;
   • The interest received or accrued during the taxable year which is exempt from the tax imposed by chapter 1 to the extent such information is available;

296

- The amounts excluded from such taxpayer's gross income by sections 931 and 933 to the extent such information is available;
- Such other information relating to the liability of the taxpayer as is prescribed by the Secretary by regulation as might indicate that the amount of the premium of the taxpayer may be subject to an adjustment and the amount of such adjustment; and
- The taxable year with respect to which the preceding information relates.

This return information may be used by officers, employees, and contractors of the Social Security Administration only for the purposes of, and to the extent necessary in, establishing the appropriate amount of any Medicare Part B premium subsidy adjustment.

Section 6103(p)(4) requires, as a condition of receiving returns and return information, that Federal and State agencies (and certain other recipients) provide safeguards as prescribed by the Secretary by regulation to be necessary or appropriate to protect the confidentiality of returns or return information. Unauthorized disclosure of a return or return information is a felony punishable by a fine not exceeding $5,000 or imprisonment of not more than five years, or both, together with the costs of prosecution.[803] The unauthorized inspection of a return or return information is punishable by a fine not exceeding $1,000 or imprisonment of not more than one year, or both, together with the costs of prosecution.[804] An action for civil damages also may be brought for unauthorized disclosure or inspection.[805]

Explanation of Provision

Upon written request from the Commissioner of Social Security, the IRS may disclose the following limited return information of a taxpayer whose Medicare Part D premium subsidy, according to the records of the Secretary, may be subject to adjustment:

- Taxpayer identity information with respect to such taxpayer;
- The filing status of the taxpayer;
- The adjusted gross income of such taxpayer;
- The amounts excluded from such taxpayer's gross income under sections 135 and 911 to the extent such information is available;
- The interest received or accrued during the taxable year which is exempt from the tax imposed by chapter 1 to the extent such information is available;
- The amounts excluded from such taxpayer's gross income by sections 931 and 933 to the extent such information is available;
- Such other information relating to the liability of the taxpayer as is prescribed by the Secretary by regulation as might indicate that the amount of the Part D premium of the tax-

---

[803] Sec. 7213.
[804] Sec. 7213A.
[805] Sec. 7431.

297

payer may be subject to an adjustment and the amount of such adjustment; and
  • The taxable year with respect to which the preceding information relates.

This return information may be used by officers, employees, and contractors of the Social Security Administration only for the purposes of, and to the extent necessary in, establishing the appropriate amount of any Medicare Part D premium subsidy adjustment.

For purposes of both the Medicare Part B premium subsidy adjustment and the Medicare Part D premium subsidy adjustment, the provision provides that the Social Security Administration may redisclose only taxpayer identity and the amount of premium subsidy adjustment to officers and employees and contractors of the Centers for Medicare and Medicaid Services, and officers and employees of the Office of Personnel Management and the Railroad Retirement Board. This redisclosure is permitted only to the extent necessary for the collection of the premium subsidy amount from the taxpayers under the jurisdiction of the respective agencies.

Further, the Social Security Administration may redisclose the return information received under this provision to officers and employees of the Department of HHS to the extent necessary to resolve administrative appeals of the Part B and Part D subsidy adjustments and to officers and employees of the Department of Justice to the extent necessary for use in judicial proceedings related to establishing and collecting the appropriate amount of any Medicare Part B or Medicare Part D premium subsidy adjustments.

Effective Date

The provision is effective on the date of enactment (March 23, 2010).

TITLE VI—TRANSPARENCY AND PROGRAM INTEGRITY

A. Patient-Centered Outcomes Research Trust Fund; Financing for Trust Fund (sec. 6301 of the Act and new secs. 4375, 4376, 4377, and 9511 of the Code)

Present Law

No provision.

Reasons for Change

The Congress believes that comparative effectiveness research is a public good and that a sustained investment in such research is needed to improve the quality of information about the relative strengths and weaknesses of various health care items, services and systems to allow physicians and patients to make more informed health care decisions. To insure that there are sufficient amounts of public and private funds dedicated to this purpose, and to insulate such funding from inappropriate outside influence, the Congress believes that it is appropriate to establish a trust fund, impose fees on health insurance plans and receive transfer payments from Medicare, and have such amounts in the fund dedicated to finance comparative effectiveness research.

Explanation of Provision

Patient-Centered Outcomes Research Trust Fund

Under new section 9511, there is established in the Treasury of the United States a trust fund, the Patient Centered Outcomes Research Trust Fund ("PCORTF"), to carry out the provisions in the Act relating to comparative effectiveness research. The PCORTF is funded in part from fees imposed on health plans under new sections 4375 through 4377.

Fee on insured and self-insured health plans

Insured plans

Under new section 4375, a fee is imposed on each specified health insurance policy. The fee is equal to two dollars (one dollar in the case of policy years ending during fiscal year 2013) multiplied by the average number of lives covered under the policy. For any policy year beginning after September 30, 2014, the dollar amount is equal to the sum of: (1) the dollar amount for policy years ending in the preceding fiscal year, plus (2) an amount equal to the product of (A) the dollar amount for policy years ending in the preceding fiscal year, multiplied by (B) the percentage increase in the projected per capita amount of National Health Expenditures, as most recently published by the Secretary before the beginning of the fiscal year. The issuer of the policy is liable for payment of the fee. A specified health insurance policy includes any accident or health insurance policy [806] issued with respect to individuals residing in the United States. [807] An arrangement under which fixed payments of premiums are received as consideration for a person's agreement to provide, or arrange for the provision of, accident or health coverage to residents of the United States, regardless of how such coverage is provided or arranged to be provided, is treated as a specified health insurance policy. The person agreeing to provide or arrange for the provision of coverage is treated as the issuer.

Self-insured plans

In the case of an applicable self-insured health plan, new Code section 4376 imposes a fee equal to two dollars (one dollar in the case of policy years ending during fiscal year 2013) multiplied by the average number of lives covered under the plan. For any policy year beginning after September 30, 2014, the dollar amount is equal to the sum of: (1) the dollar amount for policy years ending in the preceding fiscal year, plus (2) an amount equal to the prod-

---

[806] A specified health insurance policy does not include insurance if substantially all of the coverage provided under such policy consists of excepted benefits described in section 9832(c). Examples of excepted benefits described in section 9832(c) are coverage for only accident, or disability insurance, or any combination thereof; liability insurance, including general liability insurance and automobile liability insurance; workers' compensation or similar insurance; automobile medical payment insurance; coverage for on-site medical clinics; limited scope dental or vision benefits; benefits for long term care, nursing home care, community based care, or any combination thereof; coverage only for a specified disease or illness; hospital indemnity or other fixed indemnity insurance; and Medicare supplemental coverage.

[807] Under the provision, the United States includes any possession of the United States.

uct of (A) the dollar amount for policy years ending in the preceding fiscal year, multiplied by (B) the percentage increase in the projected per capita amount of National Health Expenditures, as most recently published by the Secretary before the beginning of the fiscal year. The plan sponsor is liable for payment of the fee. For purposes of the provision, the plan sponsor is: the employer in the case of a plan established or maintained by a single employer or the employee organization in the case of a plan established or maintained by an employee organization. In the case of: (1) a plan established or maintained by two or more employers or jointly by one of more employers and one or more employee organizations, (2) a multiple employer welfare arrangement, or (3) a voluntary employees' beneficiary association described in Code section 501(c)(9) ("VEBA"), the plan sponsor is the association, committee, joint board of trustees, or other similar group of representatives of the parties who establish or maintain the plan. In the case of a rural electric cooperative or a rural telephone cooperative, the plan sponsor is the cooperative or association.

Under the provision, an applicable self-insured health plan is any plan providing accident or health coverage if any portion of such coverage is provided other than through an insurance policy and such plan is established or maintained: (1) by one or more employers for the benefit of their employees or former employees, (2) by one or more employee organizations for the benefit of their members or former members, (3) jointly by one or more employers and one or more employee organizations for the benefit of employees or former employees, (4) by a VEBA, (5) by any organization described in section 501(c)(6) of the Code, or (6) in the case of a plan not previously described, by a multiple employer welfare arrangement (as defined in section 3(40) of ERISA, a rural electric cooperative (as defined in section 3(40)(B)(iv) of ERISA), or a rural telephone cooperative association (as defined in section 3(40)(B)(v) of ERISA).

Other special rules

Governmental entities are generally not exempt from the fees imposed under the provision. There is an exception for exempt governmental programs including, Medicare, Medicaid, SCHIP, and any program established by Federal law for proving medical care (other than through insurance policies) to members of the Armed Forces, veterans, or members of Indian tribes.

No amount collected from the fee on health insurance and self-insured plans is covered over to any possession of the United States. For purposes of the Code's procedure and administration rules, the fee imposed under the provision is treated as a tax. The fees imposed under new sections 4375 and 4376 do not apply to plan years ending after September 31, 2019.

Effective Date

The fee on health insurance and self-insured plans is effective with respect to policies and plans for portions of policy or plan years ending after September 30, 2012.

300

TITLE IX—REVENUE PROVISIONS

A. Excise Tax on High Cost Employer-Sponsored Health Coverage (sec. 9001 [808] of the Act and new sec. 4980I of the Code)

Present Law

Taxation of insurance companies

Current law provides special rules for determining the taxable income of insurance companies (subchapter L of the Code). Separate sets of rules apply to life insurance companies and to property and casualty insurance companies. Insurance companies generally are subject to Federal income tax at regular corporate income tax rates.

An insurance company that provides health insurance is subject to Federal income tax as either a life insurance company or as a property insurance company, depending on its mix of lines of business and on the resulting portion of its reserves that are treated as life insurance reserves. For Federal income tax purposes, an insurance company is treated as a life insurance company if the sum of its (1) life insurance reserves and (2) unearned premiums and unpaid losses on noncancellable life, accident or health contracts not included in life insurance reserves, comprise more than 50 percent of its total reserves.[809]

Some insurance providers may be exempt from Federal income tax under section 501(a) if specific requirements are satisfied. Section 501(c)(8), for example, describes certain fraternal beneficiary societies, orders, or associations operating under the lodge system or for the exclusive benefit of their members that provide for the payment of life, sick, accident, or other benefits to the members or their dependents. Section 501(c)(9) describes certain voluntary employees' beneficiary associations that provide for the payment of life, sick, accident, or other benefits to the members of the association or their dependents or designated beneficiaries. Section 501(c)(12)(A) describes certain benevolent life insurance associations of a purely local character. Section 501(c)(15) describes certain small non-life insurance companies with annual gross receipts of no more than $600,000 ($150,000 in the case of a mutual insurance company). Section 501(c)(26) describes certain membership organizations established to provide health insurance to certain high-risk individuals. Section 501(c)(27) describes certain organizations established to provide workmen's compensation insurance. A health maintenance organization that is tax-exempt under section 501(c)(3) or (4) is not treated as providing prohibited [810] commercial-type insurance, in the case of incidental health insurance provided by the health maintenance organization that is of a kind customarily provided by such organizations.

---

[808] Section 9001 of the Patient Protection and Affordable Care Act, Pub. L. No. 111–148, as amended by section 10901, is further amended by section 1401 of the Health Care and Education Reconciliation Act of 2010, Pub. L. No. 111–152.

[809] Sec. 816(a).

[810] Sec. 501(m).

301

Treatment of employer-sponsored health coverage

As with other compensation, the cost of employer-provided health coverage is a deductible business expense under section 162.[811] Employer-provided health insurance coverage is generally not included in an employee's gross income.

In addition, employees participating in a cafeteria plan may be able to pay the portion of premiums for health insurance coverage not otherwise paid for by their employers on a pre-tax basis through salary reduction.[812] Such salary reduction contributions are treated as employer contributions for Federal income purposes, and are thus excluded from gross income.

Employers may agree to reimburse medical expenses of their employees (and their spouses and dependents), not covered by a health insurance plan, through flexible spending arrangements which allow reimbursement not in excess of a specified dollar amount (either elected by an employee under a cafeteria plan or otherwise specified by the employer). Reimbursements under these arrangements are also excludible from gross income as employer-provided health coverage.

A flexible spending arrangement for medical expenses under a cafeteria plan ("Health FSA") is an unfunded arrangement under which employees are given the option to reduce their current cash compensation and instead have the amount made available for use in reimbursing the employee for his or her medical expenses.[813] Health FSAs that are funded on a salary reduction basis are subject to the requirements for cafeteria plans, including a requirement that amounts remaining under a Health FSA at the end of a plan year must be forfeited by the employee (referred to as the "use-it-or-lose-it rule").[814]

Alternatively, the employer may specify a dollar amount that is available for medical expense reimbursement. These arrangements are commonly called Health Reimbursement Arrangements ("HRAs"). Some of the rules applicable to HRAs and Health FSAs are similar (e.g., the amounts in the arrangements can only be used to reimburse medical expenses and not for other purposes), but the rules are not identical. In particular, HRAs cannot be funded on a salary reduction basis and the use-it-or-lose-it rule does not apply. Thus, amounts remaining at the end of the year may be carried forward to be used to reimburse medical expenses in following years.[815]

Current law provides that individuals with a high deductible health plan (and generally no other health plan) may establish and make tax-deductible contributions to a health savings account ("HSA"). An HSA is subject to a condition that the individual is covered under a high deductible health plan (purchased either

---

[811] Sec. 162. However see special rules in section 419 and 419A for the deductibility of contributions to welfare benefit plans with respect to medical benefits for employees and their dependents.

[812] Sec. 125.

[813] Sec. 125. Prop. Treas. Reg. sec. 1.125–5 provides rules for Health FSAs. There is a similar type of flexible spending arrangement for dependent care expenses.

[814] Sec. 125(d)(2). A cafeteria plan is permitted to allow a grace period not to exceed two and one-half months immediately following the end of the plan year during which unused amounts may be used. Notice 2005–42, 2005–1 C.B. 1204.

[815] Guidance with respect to HRAs, including the interaction of FSAs and HRAs in the case of an individual covered under both, is provided in Notice 2002–45, 2002–2 C.B. 93.

302

through the individual market or through an employer). Subject to certain limitations,[816] contributions made to an HSA by an employer, including contributions made through a cafeteria plan through salary reduction, are excluded from income (and from wages for payroll tax purposes). Contributions made by individuals are deductible for income tax purposes, regardless of whether the individuals itemize. Like an HSA, an Archer MSA is a tax-exempt trust or custodial account to which tax-deductible contributions may be made by individuals with a high deductible health plan; however, only self-employed individuals and employees of small employers are eligible to have an Archer MSA. Archer MSAs provide tax benefits similar to, but generally not as favorable as, those provided by HSAs for individuals covered by high deductible health plans.[817]

ERISA[818] preempts State law relating to certain employee benefit plans, including employer-sponsored health plans. While ERISA specifically provides that its preemption rule does not exempt or relieve any person from any State law which regulates insurance, ERISA also provides that an employee benefit plan is not deemed to be engaged in the business of insurance for purposes of any State law regulating insurance companies or insurance contracts. As a result of this ERISA preemption, self-insured employer-sponsored health plans need not provide benefits that are mandated under State insurance law.

While ERISA does not require an employer to offer health benefits, it does require compliance if an employer chooses to offer health benefits, such as compliance with plan fiduciary standards, reporting and disclosure requirements, and procedures for appealing denied benefit claims. ERISA was amended (as well as the PHSA and the Code) by COBRA[819] and HIPAA,[820] which added other Federal requirements for health plans, including rules for health care continuation coverage, limitations on exclusions from coverage based on preexisting conditions, and a few benefit requirements such as minimum hospital stay requirements for mothers following the birth of a child.

COBRA requires that a group health plan offer continuation coverage to qualified beneficiaries in the case of a qualifying event (such as a loss of employment).[821] A plan may require payment of a premium for any period of continuation coverage. The amount of

---

[816] For 2010, the maximum aggregate annual contribution that can be made to an HSA is $3,050 in the case of self-only coverage and $6,150 in the case of family coverage. The annual contribution limits are increased for individuals who have attained age 55 by the end of the taxable year (referred to as "catch-up contributions"). In the case of policyholders and covered spouses who are age 55 or older, the HSA annual contribution limit is greater than the otherwise applicable limit by $1,000 in 2009 and thereafter. Contributions, including catch-up contributions, cannot be made once an individual is enrolled in Medicare.

[817] In addition to being limited to self-employed individuals and employees of small employers, the definition of a high deductible health plan for an Archer MSA differs from that for an HSA. After 2007, no new contributions can be made to Archer MSAs except by or on behalf of individuals who previously had made Archer MSA contributions and employees who are employed by a participating employer.

[818] Pub. L. No. 93–406.

[819] Pub. L. No. 99–272.

[820] Pub. L. No. 104–191.

[821] A group health plan is defined as a plan (including a self-insured plan) of, or contributed to by, an employer (including a self-employed person) or employee organization to provide health care (directly or otherwise) to the employees, former employees, the employer, others associated or formerly associated with the employer in a business relationship, or their families. The COBRA requirements are enforced through the Code, ERISA, and the PHSA.

303

such premium generally may not exceed 102 percent of the "applicable premium" for such period and the premium must be payable, at the election of the payor, in monthly installments. The applicable premium for any period of continuation coverage means the cost to the plan for such period of coverage for similarly situated non-COBRA beneficiaries with respect to whom a qualifying event has not occurred, and is determined without regard to whether the cost is paid by the employer or employee. There are special rules for determining the applicable premium in the case of self-insured plans. Under the special rules for self-insured plans, the applicable premium generally is equal to a reasonable estimate of the cost of providing coverage for similarly situated beneficiaries which is determined on an actuarial basis and takes into account such other factors as the Secretary of the Treasury may prescribe in regulations.

Current law imposes an excise tax on group health plans that fail to meet HIPAA and COBRA requirements.[822] The excise tax generally is equal to $100 per day per failure during the period of noncompliance and is imposed on the employer sponsoring the plan.

Deduction for health insurance costs of self-employed individuals

Under current law, self-employed individuals may deduct the cost of health insurance for themselves and their spouses and dependents.[823] The deduction is not available for any month in which the self-employed individual is eligible to participate in an employer-subsidized health plan. Moreover, the deduction may not exceed the individual's earned income from self-employment. The deduction applies only to the cost of insurance (i.e., it does not apply to out-of-pocket expenses that are not reimbursed by insurance). The deduction does not apply for self-employment tax purposes. For purposes of the deduction, a more-than-two-percent-shareholder-employee of an S corporation is treated the same as a self-employed individual. Thus, the exclusion for employer provided health care coverage does not apply to such individuals, but they are entitled to the deduction for health insurance costs as if they were self-employed.

Deductibility of excise taxes

In general, excise taxes may be deductible under section 162 of the Code if such taxes are paid or incurred in carrying on a trade or business, and are not within the scope of the disallowance of deductions for certain taxes enumerated in section 275 of the Code.

Explanation of Provision

The provision imposes an excise tax on insurers if the aggregate value of employer-sponsored health insurance coverage for an employee (including, for purposes of the provision, any former employee, surviving spouse and any other primary insured individual) exceeds a threshold amount. The tax is equal to 40 percent of the aggregate value that exceeds the threshold amount. For 2018, the

---

[822] Secs. 4980B and 4980D.
[823] Sec. 162(l).

304

threshold amount is $10,200 for individual coverage and $27,500 for family coverage, multiplied by the health cost adjustment percentage (as defined below) and increased by the age and gender adjusted excess premium amount (as defined below).

The health cost adjustment percentage is designed to increase the thresholds in the event that the actual growth in the cost of U.S. health care between 2010 and 2018 exceeds the projected growth for that period. The health cost adjustment percentage is equal to 100 percent plus the excess, if any, of (1) the percentage by which the per employee cost of coverage under the Blue Cross/Blue Shield standard benefit option under the Federal Employees Health Benefits Plan ("standard FEHBP coverage")[824] for plan year 2018 (as determined using the benefit package for standard FEHBP coverage for plan year 2010) exceeds the per employee cost of standard FEHBP coverage for plan year 2010; over (2) 55 percent. In 2019, the threshold amounts, after application of the health cost adjustment percentage in 2018, if any, are indexed to the CPI-U, as determined by the Department of Labor, plus one percentage point, rounded to the nearest $50. In 2020 and thereafter, the threshold amounts are indexed to the CPI-U as determined by the Department of Labor, rounded to the nearest $50.

For each employee (other than for certain retirees and employees in high risk professions, whose thresholds are adjusted under rules described below), the age and gender adjusted excess premium amount is equal to the excess, if any, of (1) the premium cost of standard FEHBP coverage for the type of coverage provided to the individual if priced for the age and gender characteristics of all employees of the individual's employer over (2) the premium cost, determined under procedures proscribed by the Secretary, for that coverage if priced for the age and gender characteristics of the national workforce.

For example, if the growth in the cost of health care during the period between 2010 and 2018, calculated by reference to the growth in the per employee cost of standard FEHBP coverage during that period (holding benefits under the standard FEBHP plan constant during the period) is 57 percent, the threshold amounts for 2018 will be $10,200 for individual coverage and $27,500 for family coverage, multiplied by 102 percent (100 percent plus the excess of 57 percent over 55 percent), or $10,404 for individual coverage and $28,050 for family coverage. In 2019, the new threshold amounts of $10,404 for individual coverage and $28,050 for family coverage are indexed for CPI–U, plus one percentage point, rounded to the nearest $50. Beginning in 2020, the threshold amounts are indexed to the CPI–U, rounded to the nearest $50.

The new threshold amounts (as indexed) are then increased for any employee by the age and gender adjusted excess premium amount, if any. For an employee with individual coverage in 2019, if standard FEHBP coverage priced for the age and gender characteristics of the workforce of the employee's employer is $11,400 and

---

[824] For purposes of determining the health cost adjustment percentage in 2018 and the age and gender adjusted excess premium amount in any year, in the event the standard Blue Cross/Blue Shield option is not available under the Federal Employees Health Benefit Plan for such year, the Secretary will determine the health cost adjustment percentage by reference to a substantially similar option available under the Federal Employees Health Benefit Plan for that year.

305

the Secretary estimates that the premium cost for individual standard FEHBP coverage priced for the age and gender characteristics
of the national workforce is $10,500, the threshold for that em-
ployee is increased by $900 ($11,400 less $10,500) to $11,304
($10,404 plus $900).

The excise tax is imposed pro rata on the issuers of the insurance. In the case of a self-insured group health plan, a Health FSA
or an HRA, the excise tax is paid by the entity that administers
benefits under the plan or arrangement ("plan administrator").
Where the employer acts as plan administrator to a self-insured
group health plan, a Health FSA or an HRA, the excise tax is paid
by the employer. Where an employer contributes to an HSA or an
Archer MSA, the employer is responsible for payment of the excise
tax, as the insurer.

Employer-sponsored health insurance coverage is health coverage
under any group health plan offered by an employer to an employee without regard to whether the employer provides the coverage (and thus the coverage is excludable from the employee's
gross income) or the employee pays for the coverage with after-tax
dollars. Employer-sponsored health insurance coverage includes
coverage under any group health plan established and maintained
primarily for the civilian employees of the Federal government or
any of its agencies or instrumentalities and, except as provided
below, of any State government or political subdivision thereof or
by any of agencies or instrumentalities of such government or subdivision.

Employer-sponsored health insurance coverage includes both
fully-insured and self-insured health coverage excludable from the
employee's gross income, including, in the self-insured context, on-
site medical clinics that offer more than a de minimis amount of
medical care to employees and executive physical programs. In the
case of a self-employed individual, employer-sponsored health insurance coverage is coverage for any portion of which a deduction
is allowable to the self-employed individual under section 162(l).

In determining the amount by which the value of employer-sponsored health insurance coverage exceeds the threshold amount, the
aggregate value of all employer-sponsored health insurance coverage is taken into account, including coverage in the form of reimbursements under a Health FSA or an HRA, contributions to an
HSA or Archer MSA, and, except as provided below, other supplementary health insurance coverage. The value of employer-sponsored coverage for long term care and the following benefits described in section 9832(c)(1) that are excepted from the portability,
access and renewability requirements of HIPAA are not taken into
account in the determination of whether the value of health coverage exceeds the threshold amount: (1) coverage only for accident
or disability income insurance, or any combination of these cov-
erages; (2) coverage issued as a supplement to liability insurance;
(3) liability insurance, including general liability insurance and
automobile liability insurance; (4) workers' compensation or similar
insurance; (5) automobile medical payment insurance; (5) credit-
only insurance; and (6) other similar insurance coverage, specified
in regulations, under which benefits for medical care are secondary
or incidental to other insurance benefits.

306

The value of employer-sponsored health insurance coverage does not include the value of independent, noncoordinated coverage described in section 9832(c)(3) as excepted from the portability, access and renewability requirements of HIPAA if that coverage is purchased exclusively by the employee with after-tax dollars (or, in the case of a self-employed individual, for which a deduction under section 162(l) is not allowable). The value of employer-sponsored health insurance coverage does include the value of such coverage if any portion of the coverage is employer-provided (or, in the case of a self-employed individual, if a deduction is allowable for any portion of the payment for the coverage). Coverage described in section 9832(c)(3) is coverage only for a specified disease or illness or for hospital or other fixed indemnity health coverage. Fixed indemnity health coverage pays fixed dollar amounts based on the occurrence of qualifying events, including but not limited to the diagnosis of a specific disease, an accidental injury or a hospitalization, provided that the coverage is not coordinated with other health coverage.

Finally, the value of employer-sponsored health insurance coverage does not include any coverage under a separate policy, certificate, or contract of insurance which provides benefits substantially all of which are for treatment of the mouth (including any organ or structure within the mouth) or for treatment of the eye.

Calculation and proration of excise tax and reporting requirements

Applicable threshold

In general, the individual threshold applies to any employee covered by employer-sponsored health insurance coverage. The family threshold applies to an employee only if such individual and at least one other beneficiary are enrolled in coverage other than self-only coverage under an employer-sponsored health insurance plan that provides minimum essential coverage (as determined for purposes of the individual responsibility requirements) and under which the benefits provided do not vary based on whether the covered individual is the employee or other beneficiary.

For all employees covered by a multiemployer plan, the family threshold applies regardless of whether the individual maintains individual or family coverage under the plan. For purposes of the provision, a multiemployer plan is an employee health benefit plan to which more than one employer is required to contribute, which is maintained pursuant to one or more collective bargaining agreements between one or more employee organizations and more than one employer.

Amount of applicable premium

Under the provision, the aggregate value of all employer-sponsored health insurance coverage, including any supplementary health insurance coverage not excluded from the value of employer-sponsored health insurance, is generally calculated in the same manner as the applicable premiums for the taxable year for the employee determined under the rules for COBRA continuation coverage, but without regard to the excise tax. If the plan provides for

307

the same COBRA continuation coverage premium for both individual coverage and family coverage, the plan is required to calculate separate individual and family premiums for this purpose. In determining the coverage value for retirees, employers may elect to treat pre-65 retirees together with post-65 retirees.

Value of coverage in the form of Health FSA reimbursements

In the case of a Health FSA from which reimbursements are limited to the amount of the salary reduction, the value of employer-sponsored health insurance coverage is equal to the dollar amount of the aggregate salary reduction contributions for the year. To the extent that the Health FSA provides for employer contributions in excess of the amount of the employee's salary reduction, the value of the coverage generally is determined in the same manner as the applicable premium for COBRA continuation coverage. If the plan provides for the same COBRA continuation coverage premium for both individual coverage and family coverage, the plan is required to calculate separate individual and family premiums for this purpose.

Amount subject to the excise tax and reporting requirement

The amount subject to the excise tax on high cost employer-sponsored health insurance coverage for each employee is the sum of the aggregate premiums for health insurance coverage, the amount of any salary reduction contributions to a Health FSA for the taxable year, and the dollar amount of employer contributions to an HSA or an Archer MSA, minus the dollar amount of the threshold. The aggregate premiums for health insurance coverage include all employer-sponsored health insurance coverage including coverage for any supplementary health insurance coverage. The applicable premium for health coverage provided through an HRA is also included in this aggregate amount.

Under a separate rule,[825] an employer is required to disclose the aggregate premiums for health insurance coverage for each employee on his or her annual Form W-2.

Under the provision, the excise tax is allocated pro rata among the insurers, with each insurer responsible for payment of the excise tax on an amount equal to the amount subject to the total excise tax multiplied by a fraction, the numerator of which is the amount of employer-sponsored health insurance coverage provided by that insurer to the employee and the denominator of which is the aggregate value of all employer-sponsored health insurance coverage provided to the employee. In the case of a self-insured group health plan, a Health FSA or an HRA, the excise tax is allocated to the plan administrator. If an employer contributes to an HSA or an Archer MSA, the employer is responsible for payment of the excise tax, as the insurer. The employer is responsible for calculating the amount subject to the excise tax allocable to each insurer and plan administrator and for reporting these amounts to each insurer, plan administrator and the Secretary, in such form and at such time as the Secretary may prescribe. Each insurer and

---

[825] See the explanation of section 9002 of the Patient Protection and Affordable Care Act, Pub. L. No. 111-148, "Inclusion of Cost of Employer Sponsored Health Coverage on W-2."

308

plan administrator is then responsible for calculating, reporting and paying the excise tax to the IRS on such forms and at such time as the Secretary may prescribe.

For example, if in 2018 an employee elects family coverage under a fully-insured health care policy covering major medical and dental with a value of $31,000, the health cost adjustment percentage for that year is 100 percent, and the age and gender adjusted excess premium amount for the employee is $600, the amount subject to the excise tax is $2,900 ($31,000 less the threshold of $28,100 ($27,500 multiplied by 100 percent and increased by $600)). The employer reports $2,900 as taxable to the insurer, which calculates and remits the excise tax to the IRS.

Alternatively, if in 2018 an employee elects family coverage under a fully-insured major medical policy with a value of $28,500 and contributes $2,500 to a Health FSA, the employee has an aggregate health insurance coverage value of $31,000. If the health cost adjustment percentage for that year is 100 percent and the age and gender adjusted excess premium amount for the employee is $600, the amount subject to the excise tax is $2,900 ($31,000 less the threshold of $28,100 ($27,500 multiplied by 100 percent and increased by $600)). The employer reports $2,666 ($2,900 × $28,500/$31,000) as taxable to the major medical insurer which then calculates and remits the excise tax to the IRS. If the employer uses a third-party administrator for the Health FSA, the employer reports $234 ($2,900 × $2,500/$31,000) to the administrator and the administrator calculates and remits the excise tax to the IRS. If the employer is acting as the plan administrator of the Health FSA, the employer is responsible for calculating and remitting the excise tax on the $234 to the IRS.

Penalty for underreporting liability for tax to insurers

If the employer reports to insurers, plan administrators and the IRS a lower amount of insurance cost subject to the excise tax than required, the employer is subject to a penalty equal to the sum of any additional excise tax that each such insurer and administrator would have owed if the employer had reported correctly and interest attributable to that additional excise tax as determined under Code section 6621 from the date that the tax was otherwise due to the date paid by the employer. This may occur, for example, if the employer undervalues the aggregate premium and thereby lowers the amount subject to the excise tax for all insurers and plan administrators (including the employer, when acting as plan administrator of a self-insured plan).

The penalty will not apply if it is established to the satisfaction of the Secretary that the employer neither knew, nor exercising reasonable diligence would have known, that the failure existed. In addition, no penalty will be imposed on any failure corrected within the 30–day period beginning on the first date that the employer knew, or exercising reasonable diligence, would have known, that the failure existed, so long as the failure is due to reasonable cause and not to willful neglect. All or part of the penalty may be waived by the Secretary in the case of any failure due to reasonable cause and not to willful neglect, to the extent that the payment of the

309

penalty would be excessive or otherwise inequitable relative to the failure involved.

The penalty is in addition to the amount of excise tax owed, which may not be waived.

Increased thresholds for certain retirees and individuals in high-risk professions

The threshold amounts are increased for an individual who has attained age of 55 who is non-Medicare eligible and receiving employer-sponsored retiree health coverage or who is covered by a plan sponsored by an employer the majority of whose employees covered by the plan are engaged in a high risk profession or employed to repair or install electrical and telecommunications lines. For these individuals, the threshold amount in 2018 is increased by (1) $1,650 for individual coverage or $3,450 for family coverage and (2) the age and gender adjusted excess premium amount (as defined above). In 2019, the additional $1,650 and $3,450 amounts are indexed to the CPI–U, plus one percentage point, rounded to the nearest $50. In 2020 and thereafter, the additional threshold amounts are indexed to the CPI–U, rounded to the nearest $50.

For purposes of this rule, employees considered to be engaged in a high risk profession are law enforcement officers, employees who engage in fire protection activities, individuals who provide out-of-hospital emergency medical care (including emergency medical technicians, paramedics, and first-responders), individuals whose primary work is longshore work, and individuals engaged in the construction, mining, agriculture (not including food processing), forestry, and fishing industries. A retiree with at least 20 years of employment in a high risk profession is also eligible for the increased threshold.

Under this provision, an individual's threshold cannot be increased by more than $1,650 for individual coverage or $3,450 for family coverage (indexed as described above) and the age and gender adjusted excess premium amount, even if the individual would qualify for an increased threshold both on account of his or her status as a retiree over age 55 and as a participant in a plan that covers employees in a high risk profession.

Deductibility of excise tax

Under the provision, the amount of the excise tax imposed is not deductible for Federal income tax purposes.

Regulatory authority

The Secretary is directed to prescribe such regulations as may be necessary to carry out the provision.

Effective Date

The provision is effective for taxable years beginning after December 31, 2017.

310

B. Inclusion of Cost of Employer-Sponsored Health Coverage on W-2 (sec. 9002 of the Act and sec. 6051 of the Code)

Present Law

In many cases, an employer pays for all or a portion of its employees' health insurance coverage as an employee benefit. This benefit often includes premiums for major medical, dental, and other supplementary health insurance coverage. Under present law, the value of employer-provided health coverage is not required to be reported to the IRS or any other Federal agency. The value of the employer contribution to health coverage is excludible from an employee's income.[826]

Under current law, every employer is required to furnish each employee and the Federal government with a statement of compensation information, including wages, paid by the employer to the employee, and the taxes withheld from such wages during the calendar year. The statement, made on the Form W-2, must be provided to each employee by January 31 of the succeeding year. There is no requirement that the employer report the total value of employer-sponsored health insurance coverage on the Form W-2,[827] although some employers voluntarily report the amount of salary reduction under a cafeteria plan resulting in tax-free employee benefits in box 14.

Explanation of Provision

Under the provision, an employer is required to disclose on each employee's annual Form W-2 the value of the employee's health insurance coverage sponsored by the employer. If an employee enrolls in employer-sponsored health insurance coverage under multiple plans, the employer must disclose the aggregate value of all such health coverage (excluding the value of any salary reduction contribution to a health flexible spending arrangement). For example, if an employee enrolls in employer-sponsored health insurance coverage under a major medical plan and a health reimbursement arrangement, the employer is required to report the total value of the combination of both of these health plans. For this purpose, employers generally use the same value for all similarly situated employees receiving the same category of coverage (such as single or family health insurance coverage).

To determine the value of employer-sponsored health insurance coverage, the employer calculates the applicable premiums for the taxable year for the employee under the rules for COBRA continuation coverage under section 4980B(f)(4) (and accompanying Treasury regulations), including the special rule for self-insured plans. The value that the employer is required to report is the portion of the aggregate premium. If the plan provides for the same COBRA continuation coverage premium for both individual coverage and family coverage, the plan would be required to calculate separate individual and family premiums for this purpose.

---

[826] Sec. 106.

[827] Any portion of employer sponsored coverage that is paid for by the employee with after-tax contributions is included as wages on the W-2 Form.

311

Effective Date

The provision is effective for taxable years beginning after December 31, 2010.

C. Distributions for Medicine Qualified Only if for Prescribed Drug or Insulin (sec. 9003 of the Act and secs. 105, 106, 220, and 223 of the Code)

Present Law

Individual deduction for medical expenses

Expenses for medical care, not compensated for by insurance or otherwise, are deductible by an individual under the rules relating to itemized deductions to the extent the expenses exceed 7.5 percent of adjusted gross income ("AGI").[828] Medical care generally is defined broadly as amounts paid for diagnoses, cure, mitigation, treatment or prevention of disease, or for the purpose of affecting any structure of the body.[829] However, any amount paid during a taxable year for medicine or drugs is explicitly deductible as a medical expense only if the medicine or drug is a prescribed drug or is insulin.[830] Thus, any amount paid for medicine available without a prescription ("over-the-counter medicine") is not deductible as a medical expense, including any medicine recommended by a physician.[831]

Exclusion for employer-provided health care

The Code generally provides that employees are not taxed on (that is, may exclude from gross income) the value of employer-provided health coverage under an accident or health plan.[832] In addition, any reimbursements under an accident or health plan for medical care expenses for employees, their spouses, and their dependents generally are excluded from gross income.[833] An employer may agree to reimburse expenses for medical care of its employees (and their spouses and dependents), not covered by a health insurance plan, through a flexible spending arrangement ("FSA") which allows reimbursement not in excess of a specified dollar amount. Such dollar amount is either elected by an employee under a cafeteria plan ("Health FSA") or otherwise specified by the employer under an HRA. Reimbursements under these arrangements are also excludible from gross income as employer-provided health coverage. The general definition of medical care without the explicit limitation on medicine applies for purposes of the exclusion for employer-provided health coverage and medical care.[834] Thus, under an HRA or under a Health FSA, amounts paid for prescription and

---

[828] Sec. 213(a).
[829] Sec. 213(d). There are certain limitations on the general definition including a rule that cosmetic surgery or similar procedures are generally not medical care.
[830] Sec. 213(b).
[831] Rev. Rul. 2003–58, 2003–1 CB 959.
[832] Sec 106.
[833] Sec. 105(b).
[834] Sec. 105(b) provides that reimbursements for medical care within the meaning of section 213(d) pursuant to employer-provided health coverage are excludible from gross income. The definition of medical care in section 213(d) does not include the prescription drug limitation in section 213(b).

312

over-the-counter medicine are treated as medical expenses, and re-imbursements for such amounts are excludible from gross income.

Medical savings arrangements

Present law provides that individuals with a high deductible health plan (and generally no other health plan) purchased either through the individual market or through an employer may estab-lish and make tax-deductible contributions to a health savings ac-count ("HSA").[835] Subject to certain limitations,[836] contributions made to an HSA by an employer, including contributions made through a cafeteria plan through salary reduction, are excluded from income (and from wages for payroll tax purposes). Contribu-tions made by individuals are deductible for income tax purposes, regardless of whether the individuals itemize. Distributions from an HSA that are used for qualified medical expenses are excludible from gross income.[837] The general definition of medical care with-out the explicit limitation on medicine also applies for purposes of this exclusion.[838] Similar rules apply for another type of medical savings arrangement called an Archer MSA.[839] Thus, a distribution from a HSA or an Archer MSA used to purchase over-the-counter medicine also is excludible as an amount used for qualified medical expenses.

Explanation of Provision

Under the provision, with respect to medicines, the definition of medical expense for purposes of employer-provided health coverage (including HRAs and Health FSAs), HSAs, and Archer MSAs, is conformed to the definition for purposes of the itemized deduction for medical expenses, except that prescribed drug is determined without regard to whether the drug is available without a prescrip-tion. Thus, under the provision, the cost of over-the-counter medi-cines may not be reimbursed with excludible income through a Health FSA, HRA, HSA, or Archer MSA, unless the medicine is prescribed by a physician.

Effective Date

The provision is effective for expenses incurred after December 31, 2010.

---

[835] Sec. 223.

[836] For 2009, the maximum aggregate annual contribution that can be made to an HSA is $3,000 in the case of self-only coverage and $5,950 in the case of family coverage ($3,050 and $6,150 for 2010). The annual contribution limits are increased for individuals who have attained age 55 by the end of the taxable year (referred to as "catch-up contributions"). In the case of policyholders and covered spouses who are age 55 or older, the HSA annual contribution limit is greater than the otherwise applicable limit by $1,000 in 2009 and thereafter. Contributions, including catch-up contributions, cannot be made once an individual is enrolled in Medicare.

[837] Sec. 223(f).

[838] Sec. 223(d)(2).

[839] Sec. 220.

313

D. Increase in Additional Tax on Distributions from HSAs Not Used for Medical Expenses (sec. 9004 of the Act and secs. 220 and 223 of the Code)

Present Law

Health savings account

Present law provides that individuals with a high deductible health plan (and generally no other health plan) may establish and make tax-deductible contributions to a health savings account ("HSA").[840] An HSA is a tax-exempt account held by a trustee or custodian for the benefit of the individual. An HSA is subject to a condition that the individual is covered under a high deductible health plan (purchased either through the individual market or through an employer). The decision to create and fund an HSA is made on an individual-by-individual basis and does not require any action on the part of the employer.

Subject to certain limitations, contributions made to an HSA by an employer, including contributions made through a cafeteria plan through salary reduction, are excluded from income (and from wages for payroll tax purposes). Contributions made by individuals are deductible for income tax purposes, regardless of whether the individuals itemize their deductions on their tax return (rather than claiming the standard deduction). Income from investments made in HSAs is not taxable and the overall income is not taxable upon disbursement for medical expenses.

For 2010, the maximum aggregate annual contribution that can be made to an HSA is $3,050 in the case of self-only coverage and $6,150 in the case of family coverage. The annual contribution limits are increased for individuals who have attained age 55 by the end of the taxable year (referred to as "catch-up contributions"). In the case of policyholders and covered spouses who are age 55 or older, the HSA annual contribution limit is greater than the otherwise applicable limit by $1,000 in 2010 and thereafter. Contributions, including catch-up contributions, cannot be made once an individual is enrolled in Medicare.

A high deductible health plan is a health plan that has an annual deductible that is at least $1,200 for self-only coverage or $2,400 for family coverage for 2010 and that limits the sum of the annual deductible and other payments that the individual must make with respect to covered benefits to no more than $5,950 in the case of self-only coverage and $11,900 in the case of family coverage for 2010.

Distributions from an HSA that are used for qualified medical expenses are excludible from gross income. Distributions from an

---

[840] An individual with other coverage in addition to a high deductible health plan is still eligible for an HSA if such other coverage is "permitted insurance" or "permitted coverage." Permitted insurance is: (1) insurance if substantially all of the coverage provided under such insurance relates to (a) liabilities incurred under worker's compensation law, (b) tort liabilities, (c) liabilities relating to ownership or use of property (e.g., auto insurance), or (d) such other similar liabilities as the Secretary may prescribe by regulations; (2) insurance for a specified disease or illness; and (3) insurance that provides a fixed payment for hospitalization. Permitted coverage is coverage (whether provided through insurance or otherwise) for accidents, disability, dental care, vision care, or long-term care. With respect to coverage for years beginning after December 31, 2006, certain coverage under a Health FSA is disregarded in determining eligibility for an HSA.

314

HSA that are not used for qualified medical expenses are includible in gross income. An additional 10 percent tax is added for all HSA disbursements not made for qualified medical expenses. The additional 10-percent tax does not apply, however, if the distribution is made after death, disability, or attainment of age of Medicare eligibility (currently, age 65). Unlike reimbursements from a flexible spending arrangement or health reimbursement arrangement, distributions from an HSA are not required to be substantiated by the employer or a third party for the distributions to be excludible from income.

As in the case of individual retirement arrangements,[841] the individual is the beneficial owner of his or her HSA, and thus the individual is required to maintain books and records with respect to the expense and claim the exclusion for a distribution from the HSA on their tax return. The determination of whether the distribution is for a qualified medical expense is subject to individual self-reporting and IRS enforcement.

Archer medical savings account

An Archer MSA is also a tax-exempt trust or custodial account to which tax-deductible contributions may be made by individuals with a high deductible health plan.[842] Archer MSAs provide tax benefits similar to, but generally not as favorable as, those provided by HSAs for individuals covered by high deductible health plans. The main differences include: (1) only self-employed individuals and employees of small employers are eligible to have an Archer MSA; (2) for Archer MSA purposes, a high deductible health plan is a health plan with (a) an annual deductible for 2010 of at least $2,000 and no more than $3,000 in the case of self-only coverage and at least $4,050 and no more than $6,050 in the case of family coverage and (b) maximum out-of pocket expenses for 2010 of no more than $4,050 in the case of self-only coverage and no more than $7,400 in the case of family coverage; and (3) the additional tax on distributions not used for medical expenses is 15 percent rather than 10 percent. After 2007, no new contributions can be made to Archer MSAs except by or on behalf of individuals who previously had made Archer MSA contributions and employees who are employed by a participating employer.

Explanation of Provision

The additional tax on distributions from an HSA or an Archer MSA that are not used for qualified medical expenses is increased to 20 percent of the disbursed amount.

Effective Date

The change is effective for disbursements made during tax years starting after December 31, 2010.

---

[841] Sec. 408.
[842] Sec. 220.

315

E. Limitation on Health Flexible Spending Arrangements under Cafeteria Plans (sec. 9005 [843] of the Act and sec. 125 of the Code)

Present law

Exclusion from income for employer-provided health coverage

The Code generally provides that the value of employer-provided health coverage under an accident or health plan is excludible from gross income.[844] In addition, any reimbursements under an accident or health plan for medical care expenses for employees, their spouses, and their dependents generally are excluded from gross income.[845] The exclusion applies both to health coverage in the case in which an employer absorbs the cost of employees' medical expenses not covered by insurance (i.e., a self-insured plan) as well as in the case in which the employer purchases health insurance coverage for its employees. There is no limit on the amount of employer-provided health coverage that is excludible. A similar rule excludes employer-provided health insurance coverage from the employees' wages for payroll tax purposes.[846]

Employers may also provide health coverage in the form of an agreement to reimburse medical expenses of their employees (and their spouses and dependents), not reimbursed by a health insurance plan, through flexible spending arrangements which allow reimbursement for medical care not in excess of a specified dollar amount (either elected by an employee under a cafeteria plan or otherwise specified by the employer). Health coverage provided in the form of one of these arrangements is also excludible from gross income as employer-provided health coverage under an accident or health plan.[847]

Qualified benefits

Qualified benefits under a cafeteria plan are generally employer-provided benefits that are not includable in gross income under an express provision of the Code. Examples of qualified benefits include employer-provided health coverage, group term life insurance coverage not in excess of $50,000, and benefits under a dependent care assistance program. In order to be excludable, any qualified benefit elected under a cafeteria plan must independently satisfy any requirements under the Code section that provides the exclusion. However, some employer-provided benefits that are not includable in gross income under an express provision of the Code are explicitly not allowed in a cafeteria plan. These benefits are generally referred to as nonqualified benefits. Examples of non-

---

[843] Section 9005 of the Patient Protection and Affordable Care Act, Pub. L. No. 111–148, as amended by section 10902, is further amended by section 1403 of the Health Care and Education Reconciliation Act of 2010, Pub. L. No. 111–152.

[844] Sec. 106. Health coverage provided to active members of the uniformed services, military retirees, and their dependents are excludable under section 134. That section provides an exclusion for "qualified military benefits," defined as benefits received by reason of status or service as a member of the uniformed services and which were excludable from gross income on September 9, 1986, under any provision of law, regulation, or administrative practice then in effect.

[845] Sec. 105(b).

[846] Secs. 3121(a)(2), and 3306(a)(2). See also section 3231(e)(1) for a similar rule with respect to compensation for purposes of Railroad Retirement Tax.

[847] Sec. 106.

qualified benefits include scholarships;[848] employer-provided meals and lodging;[849] educational assistance;[850] and fringe benefits.[851] A plan offering any nonqualified benefit is not a cafeteria plan.[852]

Flexible spending arrangement under a cafeteria plan

A flexible spending arrangement for medical expenses under a cafeteria plan ("Health FSA") is health coverage in the form of an unfunded arrangement under which employees are given the option to reduce their current cash compensation and instead have the amount of the salary reduction contributions made available for use in reimbursing the employee for his or her medical expenses.[853] Health FSAs are subject to the general requirements for cafeteria plans, including a requirement that amounts remaining under a Health FSA at the end of a plan year must be forfeited by the employee (referred to as the "use-it-or-lose-it rule").[854] A Health FSA is permitted to allow a grace period not to exceed two and one-half months immediately following the end of the plan year during which unused amounts may be used.[855] A Health FSA can also include employer flex-credits which are non-elective employer contributions that the employer makes for every employee eligible to participate in the employer's cafeteria plan, to be used only for one or more tax excludible qualified benefits (but not as cash or a taxable benefit).[856]

A flexible spending arrangement including a Health FSA (under a cafeteria plan) is generally distinguishable from other employer-provided health coverage by the relationship between the value of the coverage for a year and the maximum amount of reimbursement reasonably available during the same period. A flexible spending arrangement for health coverage generally is defined as a benefit program which provides employees with coverage under which specific incurred medical care expenses may be reimbursed (subject to reimbursement maximums and other conditions) and the maximum amount of reimbursement reasonably available is less than 500 percent of the value of such coverage.[857]

Health reimbursement arrangement

Rather than offering a Health FSA through a cafeteria plan, an employer may specify a dollar amount that is available for medical expense reimbursement. These arrangements are commonly called HRAs. Some of the rules applicable to HRAs and Health FSAs are similar (e.g., the amounts in the arrangements can only be used to reimburse medical expenses and not for other purposes), but the rules are not identical. In particular, HRAs cannot be funded on a salary reduction basis and the use-it-or-lose-it rule does not apply.

---

[848] Sec. 117.

[849] Sec. 119.

[850] Sec. 127.

[851] Sec. 132.

[852] Prop. Treas. Reg. sec. 1.125–1(q). Long-term care services, contributions to Archer Medical Savings Accounts, group term life insurance for an employee's spouse, child or dependent, and elective deferrals to section 403(b) plans are also nonqualified benefits.

[853] Sec. 125 and Prop. Treas. Reg. sec. 1.125–5.

[854] Sec. 125(d)(2) and Prop. Treas. Reg. sec. 1.125–5(c).

[855] Notice 2005–42, 2005–1 C.B. 1204 and Prop. Treas. Reg. sec. 1.125–1(e).

[856] Prop. Treas. Reg. sec. 1–125–5(b).

[857] Sec. 106(c)(2) and Prop. Treas. Reg. sec. 1.125–5(a).

317

Thus, amounts remaining at the end of the year may be carried forward to be used to reimburse medical expenses in following years.[858]

Explanation of Provision

Under the provision, in order for a Health FSA to be a qualified benefit under a cafeteria plan, the maximum amount available for reimbursement of incurred medical expenses of an employee, the employee's dependents, and any other eligible beneficiaries with respect to the employee, under the Health FSA for a plan year (or other 12-month coverage period) must not exceed $2,500.[859] The $2,500 limitation is indexed to CPI–U, with any increase that is not a multiple of $50 rounded to the next lowest multiple of $50 for years beginning after December 31, 2013.

A cafeteria plan that does not include this limitation on the maximum amount available for reimbursement under any FSA is not a cafeteria plan within the meaning of section 125. Thus, when an employee is given the option under a cafeteria plan maintained by an employer to reduce his or her current cash compensation and instead have the amount of the salary reduction be made available for use in reimbursing the employee for his or her medical expenses under a Health FSA, the amount of the reduction in cash compensation pursuant to a salary reduction election must be limited to $2,500 for a plan year.

It is intended that regulations would require all cafeteria plans of an employer to be aggregated for purposes of applying this limit. The employer for this purpose is determined after applying the employer aggregation rules in section 414(b), (c), (m), and (o).[860] In the event of a plan year or coverage period that is less than 12 months, it is intended that the limit be required to be prorated.

The provision does not limit the amount permitted to be available for reimbursement under employer-provided health coverage offered through an HRA, including a flexible spending arrangement within the meaning of section 106(c)(2), that is not part of a cafeteria plan.

Effective Date

The provision is effective for taxable year beginning after December 31, 2012.

---

[858] Guidance with respect to HRAs, including the interaction of FSAs and HRAs in the case of an individual covered under both, is provided in Notice 2002–45, 2002–2 C.B. 93.

[859] The provision does not change the present law treatment as described in Prop. Treas. Reg. section 1.125–5 for dependent care flexible spending arrangements or adoption assistance flexible spending arrangements.

[860] Section 414(b) provides that, for specified employee benefit purposes, all employees of all corporations which are members of a controlled group of corporations are treated as employed by a single employer. There is a similar rule in section 414(c) under which all employees of trades or businesses (whether or not incorporated) which are under common control are treated under regulations as employed by a single employer, and, in section 414(m), under which employees of an affiliated service group (as defined in that section) are treated as employed by a single employer. Section 414(o) authorizes the Treasury to issue regulations to prevent avoidance of the requirements under section 414(m). Section 125(g)(4) applies this rule to cafeteria plans.

318

F. Expansion of Information Reporting Requirements (sec. 9006 of the Act and sec. 6041 of the Code) [861]

Present Law

Present law imposes a variety of information reporting requirements on participants in certain transactions.[862] These requirements are intended to assist taxpayers in preparing their income tax returns and to help the IRS determine whether such returns are correct and complete.

The primary provision governing information reporting by payors requires an information return by every person engaged in a trade or business who makes payments aggregating $600 or more in any taxable year to a single payee in the course of that payor's trade or business.[863] Payments subject to reporting include fixed or determinable income or compensation, but do not include payments for goods or certain enumerated types of payments that are subject to other specific reporting requirements.[864] The payor is required to provide the recipient of the payment with an annual statement showing the aggregate payments made and contact information for the payor.[865] The regulations generally except from reporting, payments to corporations, exempt organizations, governmental entities, international organizations, or retirement plans.[866] However, the following types of payments to corporations must be reported: Medical and healthcare payments;[867] fish purchases for cash;[868] attorney's fees;[869] gross proceeds paid to an attorney;[870] substitute payments in lieu of dividends or tax-exempt interest;[871] and payments by a Federal executive agency for services.[872]

Failure to comply with the information reporting requirements results in penalties, which may include a penalty for failure to file the information return,[873] and a penalty for failure to furnish

---

[861] This description is based upon the discussion at page 334 in S. Rep. No. 111–89, *Final Committee Report of the Senate Finance Committee on "America's Healthy Future Act of 2009,"* published October 21, 2009.

[862] Secs. 6031 through 6060.

[863] Sec. 6041(a). The information return is generally submitted electronically as a Form–1099 or Form–1096, although certain payments to beneficiaries or employees may require use of Forms W–3 or W–2, respectively. Treas. Reg. sec. 1.6041–1(a)(2).

[864] Sec. 6041(a) requires reporting as to "other fixed or determinable gains, profits, and income (other than payments to which section 6042(a)(1), 6044(a)(1), 6047(c), 6049(a) or 6050N(a) applies and other than payments with respect to which a statement is required under authority of section 6042(a), 6044(a)(2) or 6045)[.]" These excepted payments include most interest, royalties, and dividends.

[865] Sec. 6041(d).

[866] Treas. Reg. sec. 1.6041–3(p). Certain for-profit health provider corporations are not covered by this general exception, including those organizations providing billing services for such companies.

[867] Sec. 6050T.

[868] Sec. 6050R.

[869] Sec. 6045(f)(1) and (2); Treas. Reg. secs. 1.6041–1(d)(2) and 1.6045–5(d)(5).

[870] *Ibid.*

[871] Sec. 6045(d).

[872] Sec. 6041(d)(3).

[873] Sec. 6721. The penalty for the failure to file an information return generally is $50 for each return for which such failure occurs. The total penalty imposed on a person for all failures during a calendar year cannot exceed $250,000. Additionally, special rules apply to reduce the per-failure and maximum penalty where the failure is corrected within a specified period.

319

payee statements [874] or failure to comply with other various reporting requirements.[875]

Detailed rules are provided for the reporting of various types of investment income, including interest, dividends, and gross proceeds from brokered transactions (such as a sale of stock).[876] In general, the requirement to file Form 1099 applies with respect to amounts paid to U.S. persons and is linked to the backup withholding rules of section 3406. Thus, a payor of interest, dividends or gross proceeds generally must request that a U.S. payee (other than certain exempt recipients) furnish a Form W–9 providing that person's name and taxpayer identification number.[877] That information is then used to complete the Form 1099.

Explanation of Provision

Under the provision, a business is required to file an information return for all payments aggregating $600 or more in a calendar year to a single payee (other than a payee that is a tax-exempt corporation), notwithstanding any regulation promulgated under section 6041 prior to the date of enactment (March 23, 2010). The payments to be reported include gross proceeds paid in consideration for property or services. However, the provision does not override specific provisions elsewhere in the Code that except certain payments from reporting, such as securities or broker transactions as defined under section 6045(a) and the regulations thereunder.

Effective Date

The provision is effective for payments made after December 31, 2011.

G. Additional Requirements for Charitable Hospitals (sec. 9007 [878] of the Act and sec. 501(c), new sec. 4959, and sec. 6033 of the Code)

Present Law

Tax exemption

Charitable organizations, i.e., organizations described in section 501(c)(3), generally are exempt from Federal income tax, are eligible to receive tax deductible contributions,[879] have access to tax-exempt financing through State and local governments (described in

---

[874] Sec. 6722. The penalty for failure to provide a correct payee statement is $50 for each statement with respect to which such failure occurs, with the total penalty for a calendar year not to exceed $100,000. Special rules apply that increase the per-statement and total penalties where there is intentional disregard of the requirement to furnish a payee statement.

[875] Sec. 6723. The penalty for failure to timely comply with a specified information reporting requirement is $50 per failure, not to exceed $100,000 for a calendar year.

[876] Secs. 6042 (dividends), 6045 (broker reporting) and 6049 (interest) and the Treasury regulations thereunder.

[877] See Treas. Reg. sec. 31.3406(h)–3.

[878] Section 9007 of the Patient Protection and Affordable Care Act, Pub. L. No. 111–148, is amended by section 10903 of the Patient Protection and Affordable Care Act, Pub. L. No. 111–152.

[879] Sec. 170.

320

more detail below),[880] and generally are exempt from State and local taxes. A charitable organization must operate primarily in pursuit of one or more tax-exempt purposes constituting the basis of its tax exemption.[881] The Code specifies such purposes as religious, charitable, scientific, educational, literary, testing for public safety, to foster international amateur sports competition, or for the prevention of cruelty to children or animals. In general, an organization is organized and operated for charitable purposes if it provides relief for the poor and distressed or the underprivileged.[882]

The Code does not provide a per se exemption for hospitals. Rather, a hospital qualifies for exemption if it is organized and operated for a charitable purpose and otherwise meets the requirements of section 501(c)(3).[883] The promotion of health has been recognized by the IRS as a charitable purpose that is beneficial to the community as a whole.[884] It includes not only the establishment or maintenance of charitable hospitals, but clinics, homes for the aged, and other providers of health care.

Since 1969, the IRS has applied a "community benefit" standard for determining whether a hospital is charitable.[885] According to Revenue Ruling 69–545, community benefit can include, for example: maintaining an emergency room open to all persons regardless of ability to pay; having an independent board of trustees composed of representatives of the community; operating with an open medical staff policy, with privileges available to all qualifying physicians; providing charity care; and utilizing surplus funds to improve the quality of patient care, expand facilities, and advance medical training, education and research. Beginning in 2009, hospitals generally are required to submit information on community benefit on their annual information returns filed with the IRS.[886] Present law does not include sanctions short of revocation of tax-exempt status for hospitals that fail to satisfy the community benefit standard.

Although section 501(c)(3) hospitals generally are exempt from Federal tax on their net income, such organizations are subject to the unrelated business income tax on income derived from a trade or business regularly carried on by the organization that is not substantially related to the performance of the organization's tax-exempt functions.[887] In general, interest, rents, royalties, and annu-

---

[880] Sec. 145.

[881] Treas. Reg. sec. 1.501(c)(3)–1(c)(1).

[882] Treas. Reg. sec. 1.501(c)(3)–1(d)(2).

[883] Although nonprofit hospitals generally are recognized as tax-exempt by virtue of being "charitable" organizations, some might qualify for exemption as educational or scientific organizations because they are organized and operated primarily for medical education and research purposes.

[884] Rev. Rul. 69–545, 1969–2 C.B. 117; see also Restatement (Second) of Trusts secs. 368, 372 (1959); see Bruce R. Hopkins, *The Law of Tax-Exempt Organizations*, sec. 6.3 (8th ed. 2003) (discussing various forms of health-care providers that may qualify for exemption under section 501(c)(3)).

[885] Rev. Rul. 69–545, 1969–2 C.B. 117. From 1956 until 1969, the IRS applied a "financial ability" standard, requiring that a charitable hospital be "operated to the extent of its financial ability for those not able to pay for the services rendered and not exclusively for those who are able and expected to pay." Rev. Rul. 56–185, 1956–1 C.B. 202.

[886] IRS Form 990, Schedule H.

[887] Secs. 511–514.

321

ities are excluded from the unrelated business income of tax-exempt organizations.[888]

Charitable contributions

In general, a deduction is permitted for charitable contributions, including charitable contributions to tax-exempt hospitals, subject to certain limitations that depend on the type of taxpayer, the property contributed, and the donee organization. The amount of deduction generally equals the fair market value of the contributed property on the date of the contribution. Charitable deductions are provided for income, estate, and gift tax purposes.[889]

Tax-exempt financing

In addition to issuing tax-exempt bonds for government operations and services, State and local governments may issue tax-exempt bonds to finance the activities of charitable organizations described in section 501(c)(3). Because interest income on tax-exempt bonds is excluded from gross income, investors generally are willing to accept a lower pre-tax rate of return on such bonds than they might otherwise accept on a taxable investment. This, in turn, lowers the cost of capital for the users of such financing. Both capital expenditures and limited working capital expenditures of charitable organizations described in section 501(c)(3) generally may be financed with tax-exempt bonds. Private, nonprofit hospitals frequently are the beneficiaries of this type of financing.

Bonds issued by State and local governments may be classified as either governmental bonds or private activity bonds. Governmental bonds are bonds the proceeds of which are primarily used to finance governmental functions or which are repaid with governmental funds. Private activity bonds are bonds in which the State or local government serves as a conduit providing financing to nongovernmental persons (e.g., private businesses or individuals). For these purposes, the term "nongovernmental person" generally includes the Federal government and all other individuals and entities other than States or local governments, including section 501(c)(3) organizations. The exclusion from income for interest on State and local bonds does not apply to private activity bonds, unless the bonds are issued for certain permitted purposes ("qualified private activity bonds") and other Code requirements are met.

Reporting and disclosure requirements

Exempt organizations are required to file an annual information return, stating specifically the items of gross income, receipts, disbursements, and such other information as the Secretary may prescribe.[890] Section 501(c)(3) organizations that are classified as public charities must file Form 990 (Return of Organization Exempt

---

[888] Sec. 512(b).

[889] Secs. 170, 2055, and 2522, respectively.

[890] Sec. 6033(a). An organization that has not received a determination of its tax-exempt status, but that claims tax-exempt status under section 501(a), is subject to the same annual reporting requirements and exceptions as organizations that have received a tax-exemption determination.

322

From Income Tax),[891] including Schedule A, which requests information specific to section 501(c)(3) organizations. Additionally, an organization that operates at least one facility that is, or is required to be, licensed, registered, or similarly recognized by a state as a hospital must complete Schedule H (Form 990), which requests information regarding charity care, community benefits, bad debt expense, and certain management company and joint venture arrangements of a hospital.

An organization described in section 501(c) or (d) generally is also required to make available for public inspection for a period of three years a copy of its annual information return (Form 990) and exemption application materials.[892] This requirement is satisfied if the organization has made the annual return and exemption application widely available (e.g., by posting such information on its website).[893]

Explanation of Provision

Additional requirements for section 501(c)(3) hospitals [894]

In general

The provision establishes new requirements applicable to section 501(c)(3) hospitals. The new requirements are in addition to, and not in lieu of, the requirements otherwise applicable to an organization described in section 501(c)(3). The requirements generally apply to any section 501(c)(3) organization that operates at least one hospital facility. For purposes of the provision, a hospital facility generally includes: (1) any facility that is, or is required to be, licensed, registered, or similarly recognized by a State as a hospital; and (2) any other facility or organization the Secretary of the Treasury (the "Secretary"), in consultation with the Secretary of HHS and after public comment, determines has the provision of hospital care as its principal purpose. To qualify for tax exemption under section 501(c)(3), an organization subject to the provision is required to comply with the following requirements with respect to each hospital facility operated by such organization.

Community health needs assessment

Each hospital facility is required to conduct a community health needs assessment at least once every three taxable years and adopt an implementation strategy to meet the community needs identified through such assessment. The assessment may be based on current information collected by a public health agency or non-profit organizations and may be conducted together with one or more other organizations, including related organizations. The assessment process must take into account input from persons who represent the broad interests of the community served by the hospital facility, including those with special knowledge or expertise of public health issues. The hospital must disclose in its annual informa-

---

[891] Social welfare organizations, labor organizations, agricultural organizations, horticultural organizations, and business leagues are subject to the generally applicable Form 990, Form 990–EZ, and Form 990–T annual filing requirements.

[892] Sec. 6104(d).

[893] Sec. 6104(d)(4); Treas. Reg. sec. 301.6104(d)-2(b).

[894] No inference is intended regarding whether an organization satisfies the present law community benefit standard.

323

tion report to the IRS (i.e., Form 990 and related schedules) how it is addressing the needs identified in the assessment and, if all identified needs are not addressed, the reasons why (e.g., lack of financial or human resources). Each hospital facility is required to make the assessment widely available. Failure to complete a community health needs assessment in any applicable three-year period results in a penalty on the organization equal to $50,000. For example, if a facility does not complete a community health needs assessment in taxable years one, two or three, it is subject to the penalty in year three. If it then fails to complete a community health needs assessment in year four, it is subject to another penalty in year four (for failing to satisfy the requirement during the three-year period beginning with taxable year two and ending with taxable year four). An organization that fails to disclose how it is meeting needs identified in the assessment is subject to existing incomplete return penalties.[895]

Financial assistance policy

Each hospital facility is required to adopt, implement, and widely publicize a written financial assistance policy. The financial assistance policy must indicate the eligibility criteria for financial assistance and whether such assistance includes free or discounted care. For those eligible for discounted care, the policy must indicate the basis for calculating the amounts that will be billed to such patients. The policy must also indicate how to apply for such assistance. If a hospital does not have a separate billing and collections policy, the financial assistance policy must also indicate what actions the hospital may take in the event of non-response or non-payment, including collections action and reporting to credit rating agencies. Each hospital facility also is required to adopt and implement a policy to provide emergency medical treatment to individuals. The policy must prevent discrimination in the provision of emergency medical treatment, including denial of service, against those eligible for financial assistance under the facility's financial assistance policy or those eligible for government assistance.

Limitation on charges

Each hospital facility is permitted to bill for emergency or other medically necessary care provided to individuals who qualify for financial assistance under the facility's financial assistance policy no more than the amounts generally billed to individuals who have insurance covering such care. A hospital facility may not use gross charges (i.e., "chargemaster" rates) when billing individuals who qualify for financial assistance. It is intended that amounts billed to those who qualify for financial assistance may be based on either the best, or an average of the three best, negotiated commercial rates, or Medicare rates.

Collection processes

Under the provision, a hospital facility (or its affiliates) may not undertake extraordinary collection actions (even if otherwise permitted by law) against an individual without first making reason-

---

[895] Sec. 6652.

324

able efforts to determine whether the individual is eligible for assistance under the hospital's financial assistance policy. Such extraordinary collection actions include lawsuits, liens on residences, arrests, body attachments, or other similar collection processes. The Secretary is directed to issue guidance concerning what constitutes reasonable efforts to determine eligibility. It is intended that for this purpose, "reasonable efforts" includes notification by the hospital of its financial assistance policy upon admission and in written and oral communications with the patient regarding the patient's bill, including invoices and telephone calls, before collection action or reporting to credit rating agencies is initiated.

Reporting and disclosure requirements

The provision includes new reporting and disclosure requirements. Under the provision, the Secretary or the Secretary's delegate is required to review information about a hospital's community benefit activities (currently reported on Form 990, Schedule H) at least once every three years. The provision also requires each organization to which the provision applies to file with its annual information return (i.e., Form 990) a copy of its audited financial statements (or, in the case of an organization the financial statements of which are included in a consolidated financial statement with other organizations, such consolidated financial statements).

The provision requires the Secretary, in consultation with the Secretary of HHS, to submit annually a report to Congress with information regarding the levels of charity care, bad debt expenses, unreimbursed costs of means-tested government programs, and unreimbursed costs of non-means tested government programs incurred by private tax-exempt, taxable, and governmental hospitals, as well as the costs incurred by private tax-exempt hospitals for community benefit activities. In addition, the Secretary, in consultation with the Secretary of HHS, must conduct a study of the trends in these amounts, and submit a report on such study to Congress not later than five years from date of enactment (March 23, 2010).

Effective Date

Except as provided below, the provision is effective for taxable years beginning after the date of enactment (March 23, 2010). The community health needs assessment requirement is effective for taxable years beginning after the date which is two years after the date of enactment (March 23, 2010).[896] The excise tax on failures to satisfy the community health needs assessment requirement is effective for failures occurring after the date of enactment (March 23, 2010).

---

[896] For example, assume the date of enactment is April 1, 2010. A calendar year taxpayer would test whether it meets the community health needs assessment requirement in the taxable year ending December 31, 2013. To avoid the penalty, the taxpayer must have satisfied the community health needs assessment requirements in 2011, 2012, or 2013.

325

H. Imposition of Annual Fee on Branded Prescription Pharmaceutical Manufacturers and Importers (sec. 9008 [897] of the Act)

Present Law

There are two Medicare trust funds under present law, the Hospital Insurance ("HI") fund and the Supplementary Medical Insurance ("SMI") fund.[898] The HI trust fund is primarily funded through payroll tax on covered earnings. Employers and employees each pay 1.45 percent of wages, while self-employed workers pay 2.9 percent of a portion of their net earnings from self-employment. Other HI trust fund revenue sources include a portion of the Federal income taxes paid on Social Security benefits, and interest paid on the U.S. Treasury securities held in the HI trust fund. For the SMI trust fund, transfers from the general fund of the Treasury represent the largest source of revenue, but additional revenues include monthly premiums paid by beneficiaries, and interest paid on the U.S. Treasury securities held in the SMI trust fund.

Present law does not impose a fee creditable to the Medicare trust funds on companies that manufacture or import prescription drugs for sale in the United States.

Explanation of Provision

The provision imposes a fee on each covered entity engaged in the business of manufacturing or importing branded prescription drugs for sale to any specified government program or pursuant to coverage under any such program for each calendar year beginning after 2010. Fees collected under the provision are credited to the Medicare Part B trust fund.

The aggregate annual fee for all covered entities is the applicable amount. The applicable amount is $2.5 billion for calendar year 2011, $2.8 billion for calendar years 2012 and 2013, $3 billion for calendar years 2014 through 2016, $4 billion for calendar year 2017, $4.1 billion for calendar year 2018, and $2.8 billion for calendar year 2019 and thereafter. The aggregate fee is apportioned among the covered entities each year based on such entity's relative share of branded prescription drug sales taken into account during the previous calendar year. The Secretary of the Treasury will establish an annual payment date that will be no later than September 30 of each calendar year.

The Secretary of the Treasury will calculate the amount of each covered entity's fee for each calendar year by determining the relative market share for each covered entity. A covered entity's relative market share for a calendar year is the covered entity's branded prescription drug sales taken into account during the preceding calendar year as a percentage of the aggregate branded prescription drug sales of all covered entities taken into account during the preceding calendar year. The percentage of branded pre-

---

[897] Section 9008 of the Patient Protection and Affordable Care Act, Pub. L. No. 111–148, is amended by section 1404 of the Health Care and Education Reconciliation Act of 2010, Pub. L. No. 111–152.

[898] See 2009 Annual Report of the Boards of Trustees of the Federal Hospital Insurance and Federal Supplementary Medical Insurance Trust Funds, available at *http://www.cms.hhs.gov/ReportsTrustFunds/downloads/tr2009.pdf.*

326

scription drug sales that are taken into account during any calendar year with respect to any covered entity is: (1) zero percent of sales not more than $5 million, (2) 10 percent of sales over $5 million but not more than $125 million, (3) 40 percent of sales over $125 million but not more than $225 million, (4) 75 percent of sales over $225 million but not more than $400 million, and (5) 100 percent of sales over $400 million.

For purposes of the provision, a covered entity is any manufacturer or importer with gross receipts from branded prescription drug sales. All persons treated as a single employer under section 52(a) or (b) or under section 414(m) or 414(o) will be treated as a single covered entity for purposes of the provision. In applying the single employer rules under 52(a) and (b), foreign corporations will not be excluded. If more than one person is liable for payment of the fee imposed by this provision, all such persons are jointly and severally liable for payment of such fee. It is anticipated that the Secretary may require each covered entity to identify each member of the group that is treated as a single covered entity under the provision.

Under the provision, branded prescription drug sales are sales of branded prescription drugs made to any specified government program or pursuant to coverage under any such program. The term branded prescription drugs includes any drug which is subject to section 503(b) of the Federal Food, Drug, and Cosmetic Act and for which an application was submitted under section 505(b) of such Act, and any biological product the license for which was submitted under section 351(a) of the Public Health Service Act. Branded prescription drug sales, as defined under the provision, does not include sales of any drug or biological product with respect to which an orphan drug tax credit was allowed for any taxable year under section 45C. The exception for orphan drug sales does not apply to any drug or biological product after such drug or biological product is approved by the Food and Drug Administration for marketing for any indication other than the rare disease or condition with respect to which the section 45C credit was allowed.

Specified government programs under the provision are: (1) the Medicare Part D program under part D of title XVIII of the Social Security Act; (2) the Medicare Part B program under part B of title XVIII of the Social Security Act; (3) the Medicaid program under title XIX of the Social Security Act; (4) any program under which branded prescription drugs are procured by the Department of Veterans Affairs; (5) any program under which branded prescription drugs are procured by the Department of Defense; and (6) the TRICARE retail pharmacy program under section 1074g of title 10, United States Code.

The Secretary of HHS, the Secretary of Veterans Affairs, and the Secretary of Defense will report to the Secretary of the Treasury, at a time and in such a manner as the Secretary of the Treasury prescribes, the total branded prescription drug sales for each covered entity with respect to each specified government program under such Secretary's jurisdiction. The provision includes specific information to be included in the reports by the respective Secretaries for each specified government program.

327

The fees imposed under the provision are treated as excise taxes with respect to which only civil actions for refunds under the provisions of subtitle F will apply. Thus, the fees may be assessed and collected using the procedures in subtitle F without regard to the restrictions on assessment in section 6213.

The Secretary of the Treasury has authority to publish guidance as necessary to carry out the purposes of this provision.[899] It is anticipated that the Secretary of the Treasury will publish guidance related to the determination of the fee under this section. For example, the Secretary may publish initial determinations, allow a notice and comment period, and then provide notice and demand for payment of the fee. It is also anticipated that the Secretary of the Treasury will provide guidance as to the determination of the fee in situations involving mergers, acquisitions, business divisions, bankruptcy, or any other situations where guidance is necessary to account for sales taken into account for determining the fee for any calendar year.

The fees imposed under the provision are not deductible for U.S. income tax purposes.

Effective Date

The provision is effective for calendar years beginning after December 31, 2010.

I. Imposition of Annual Fee on Medical Device Manufacturers and Importers (sec. 9009 [900] of the Act)

Repeal

The provision of the Patient Protection and Affordable Care Act imposing an annual fee on manufacturers and importers of medical devices is repealed by the Health Care and Education Reconciliation Act of 2010.

Effective Date

The repeal is effective as of the date of enactment (March 23, 2010) of the Patient Protection and Affordable Care Act.

J. Imposition of Annual Fee on Health Insurance Providers (sec. 9010 [901] of the Act)

Present Law

Present law provides special rules for determining the taxable income of insurance companies (subchapter L of the Code). Separate sets of rules apply to life insurance companies and to property and

---

[899] Notice 2010–71 provided initial guidance on the annual fee imposed under this provision, including procedures for filing Form 8947, Report of Branded Prescription Drug Information. Notice 2011–9 supersedes Notice 2010–71 and provides guidance on the methodology that will be used for calculating the allocation of the branded prescription drug fee and requests public comments.

[900] Section 9009 of the Patient Protection and Affordable Care Act, Pub. L. No. 111–148, is repealed by section 1405(d) of the Health Care and Education Reconciliation Act of 2010, Pub. L. No. 111–152.

[901] Section 9010 of the Patient Protection and Affordable Care Act, Pub. L. No. 111–148, as amended by section 10905, is further amended by section 1406 of the Health Care and Education Reconciliation Act of 2010, Pub. L. No. 111–152.

328

casualty insurance companies. Insurance companies are subject to Federal income tax at regular corporate income tax rates.

An insurance company that provides health insurance is subject to Federal income tax as either a life insurance company or as a property insurance company, depending on its mix of lines of business and on the resulting portion of its reserves that are treated as life insurance reserves. For Federal income tax purposes, an insurance company is treated as a life insurance company if the sum of its (1) life insurance reserves and (2) unearned premiums and unpaid losses on noncancellable life, accident or health contracts not included in life insurance reserves, comprise more than 50 percent of its total reserves.[902]

Some insurance providers may be exempt from Federal income tax under section 501(a) if specific requirements are satisfied. Section 501(c)(8), for example, describes certain fraternal beneficiary societies, orders, or associations operating under the lodge system or for the exclusive benefit of their members that provide for the payment of life, sick, accident, or other benefits to the members or their dependents. Section 501(c)(9) describes certain voluntary employees' beneficiary associations that provide for the payment of life, sick, accident, or other benefits to the members of the association or their dependents or designated beneficiaries. Section 501(c)(12)(A) describes certain benevolent life insurance associations of a purely local character. Section 501(c)(15) describes certain small non-life insurance companies with annual gross receipts of no more than $600,000 ($150,000 in the case of a mutual insurance company). Section 501(c)(26) describes certain membership organizations established to provide health insurance to certain high-risk individuals. Section 501(c)(27) describes certain organizations established to provide workmen's compensation insurance.

An excise tax applies to premiums paid to foreign insurers and reinsurers covering U.S. risks.[903] The excise tax is imposed on a gross basis at the rate of one percent on reinsurance and life insurance premiums, and at the rate of four percent on property and casualty insurance premiums. The excise tax does not apply to premiums that are effectively connected with the conduct of a U.S. trade or business or that are exempted from the excise tax under an applicable income tax treaty. The excise tax paid by one party cannot be credited if, for example, the risk is reinsured with a second party in a transaction that is also subject to the excise tax.

IRS authority to assess and collect taxes is generally provided in subtitle F of the Code (secs. 6001–7874), relating to procedure and administration. That subtitle establishes the rules governing both how taxpayers are required to report information to the IRS and to pay their taxes, as well as their rights. It also establishes the duties and authority of the IRS to enforce the Federal tax law, and sets forth rules relating to judicial proceedings involving Federal tax.

---

[902] Sec. 816(a).
[903] Secs. 4371–4374.

329

Explanation of Provision

Under the provision, an annual fee applies to any covered entity engaged in the business of providing health insurance with respect to United States health risks. The fee applies for calendar years beginning after 2013. The aggregate annual fee for all covered entities is the applicable amount. The applicable amount is $8 billion for calendar year 2014, $11.3 billion for calendar years 2015 and 2016, $13.9 billion for calendar year 2017, and $14.3 billion for calendar year 2018. For calendar years after 2018, the applicable amount is indexed to the rate of premium growth.

The annual payment date for a calendar year is determined by the Secretary of the Treasury, but in no event may be later than September 30 of that year.

Under the provision, the aggregate annual fee is apportioned among the providers based on a ratio designed to reflect relative market share of U.S. health insurance business. For each covered entity, the fee for a calendar year is an amount that bears the same ratio to the applicable amount as (1) the covered entity's net premiums written during the preceding calendar year with respect to health insurance for any United States health risk, bears to (2) the aggregate net written premiums of all covered entities during such preceding calendar year with respect to such health insurance.

The provision requires the Secretary of the Treasury to calculate the amount of each covered entity's fee for the calendar year, determining the covered entity's net written premiums for the preceding calendar year with respect to health insurance for any United States health risk on the basis of reports submitted by the covered entity and through the use of any other source of information available to the Treasury Department. It is intended that the Treasury Department be able to rely on published aggregate annual statement data to the extent necessary, and may use annual statement data and filed annual statements that are publicly available to verify or supplement the reports submitted by covered entities.

Net written premiums is intended to mean premiums written, including reinsurance premiums written, reduced by reinsurance ceded, and reduced by ceding commissions. Net written premiums do not include amounts arising under arrangements that are not treated as insurance (i.e., in the absence of sufficient risk shifting and risk distribution for the arrangement to constitute insurance).[904]

The amount of net premiums written that are taken into account for purposes of determining a covered entity's market share is subject to dollar thresholds. A covered entity's net premiums written during the calendar year that are not more than $25 million are not taken into account for this purpose. With respect to a covered entity's net premiums written during the calendar year that are more than $25 million but not more than $50 million, 50 percent are taken into account, and 100 percent of net premiums written in excess of $50 million are taken into account.

After application of the above dollar thresholds, a special rule provides an exclusion, for purposes of determining an otherwise

---

[904] See *Helvering v. Le Gierse*, 312 U.S. 531 (1941).

330

covered entity's market share, of 50 percent of net premiums written that are attributable to the exempt activities[905] of a health insurance organization that is exempt from Federal income tax[906] by reason of being described in section 501(c)(3) (generally, a public charity), section 501(c)(4) (generally, a social welfare organization), section 501(c)(26) (generally, a high-risk health insurance pool), or section 501(c)(29) (a consumer operated and oriented plan ("CO-OP") health insurance issuer).

A covered entity generally is an entity that provides health insurance with respect to United States health risks during the calendar year in which the fee under this section is due. Thus for example, an insurance company subject to tax under part I or II of subchapter L, an organization exempt from tax under section 501(a), a foreign insurer that provides health insurance with respect to United States health risks, or an insurer that provides health insurance with respect to United States health risks under Medicare Advantage, Medicare Part D, or Medicaid, is a covered entity under the provision except as provided in specific exceptions.

Specific exceptions are provided to the definition of a covered entity. A covered entity does not include an employer to the extent that the employer self-insures the health risks of its employees. For example, a manufacturer that enters into a self-insurance arrangement with respect to the health risks of its employees is not treated as a covered entity. As a further example, an insurer that sells health insurance and that also enters into a self-insurance arrangement with respect to the health risks of its own employees is treated as a covered entity with respect to its health insurance business, but is not treated as a covered entity to the extent of the self-insurance of its own employees' health risks.

A covered entity does not include any governmental entity. For this purpose, it is intended that a governmental entity includes a county organized health system entity that is an independent public agency organized as a nonprofit under State law and that contracts with a State to administer State Medicaid benefits through local care providers or HMOs.

A covered entity does not include an entity that (1) qualifies as nonprofit under applicable State law, (2) meets the private inurement and limitation on lobbying provisions described in section 501(c)(3), and (3) receives more than 80 percent of its gross revenue from government programs that target low-income, elderly, or disabled populations (including Medicare, Medicaid, the State Children's Health Insurance Plan ("SCHIP"), and dual-eligible plans).

A covered entity does not include an organization that qualifies as a VEBA under section 501(c)(9) that is established by an entity other than the employer (i.e., a union) for the purpose of providing health care benefits. This exclusion does not apply to multi-employer welfare arrangements ("MEWAs").

---

[905] The exempt activities for this purpose are activities other than activities of an unrelated trade or business defined in section 513.

[906] Section 501(m) of the Code provides that an organization described in section 501(c)(3) or (4) is exempt from Federal income tax only if no substantial part of its activities consists of providing commercial-type insurance. Thus, an organization otherwise described in section 501(c)(3) or (4) that is taxable (under the Federal income tax rules) by reason of section 501(m) is not eligible for the 50-percent exclusion under the insurance fee.

331

For purposes of the provision, all persons treated as a single employer under section 52(a) or (b) or section 414(m) or (o) are treated as a single covered entity (or as a single employer, for purposes of the rule relating to employers that self-insure the health risks of employees), and otherwise applicable exclusion of foreign corporations under those rules is disregarded. However, the exceptions to the definition of a covered entity are applied on a separate entity basis, not taking into account this rule. If more than one person is liable for payment of the fee by reason of being treated as a single covered entity, all such persons are jointly and severally liable for payment of the fee.

A United States heath risk means the health risk of an individual who is a U.S. citizen, is a U.S. resident within the meaning of section 7701(b)(1)(A) (whether or not located in the United States), or is located in the United States, with respect to the period that the individual is located there. In general, it is intended that risks in the following lines of business reported on the annual statement as prescribed by the National Association of Insurance Commissioners and as filed with the insurance commissioners of the States in which insurers are licensed to do business constitute health risks for this purpose: comprehensive (hospital and medical), vision, dental, Federal Employees Health Benefit plan, title XVIII Medicare, title XIX Medicaid, and other health.

For purposes of the provision, health insurance does not include coverage only for accident, or disability income insurance, or a combination thereof. Health insurance does not include coverage only for a specified disease or illness, nor does health insurance include hospital indemnity or other fixed indemnity insurance. Health insurance does not include any insurance for long-term care or any Medicare supplemental health insurance (as defined in section 1882(g)(1) of the Social Security Act).

For purposes of procedure and administration under the rules of Subtitle F of the Code, the fee under this provision is treated as an excise tax with respect to which only civil actions for refund under Subtitle F apply. The Secretary of the Treasury may redetermine the amount of a covered entity's fee under the provision for any calendar year for which the statute of limitations remains open.

For purposes of section 275, relating to the nondeductibility of specified taxes, the fee is considered to be a nondeductible tax described in section 275(a)(6).

A reporting rule applies under the provision. A covered entity is required to report to the Secretary of the Treasury the amount of its net premiums written during any calendar year with respect to health insurance for any United States health risk.

A penalty applies for failure to report, unless it is shown that the failure is due to reasonable cause. The amount of the penalty is $10,000 plus the lesser of (1) $1,000 per day while the failure continues, or (2) the amount of the fee imposed for which the report was required. The penalty is treated as a penalty for purposes of subtitle F of the Code, must be paid on notice and demand by the Treasury Department and in the same manner as tax, and with respect to which only civil actions for refund under procedures of subtitle F apply. The reported information is not treated as taxpayer information under section 6103.

An accuracy-related penalty applies in the case of any understatement of a covered entity's net premiums written. For this purpose, an understatement is the difference between the amount of net premiums written as reported on the return filed by the covered entity and the amount of net premiums written that should have been reported on the return. The penalty is equal to the amount of the fee that should have been paid in the absence of an understatement over the amount of the fee determined based on the understatement. The accuracy-related penalty is subject to the provisions of subtitle F of the Code that apply to assessable penalties imposed under Chapter 68.

The provision provides authority for the Secretary of the Treasury to publish guidance necessary to carry out the purposes of the provision and to prescribe regulations necessary or appropriate to prevent avoidance of the purposes of the provision, including inappropriate actions taken to qualify as an exempt entity under the provision.

Effective Date

The annual fee is required to be paid in each calendar year beginning after December 31, 2013. The fee under the provision is determined with respect to net premiums written after December 31, 2012, with respect to health insurance for any United States health risk.

K. Study and Report of Effect on Veterans Health Care (sec. 9011 of the Act)

Present Law

No provision.

Explanation of Provision

The provision requires the Secretary of Veterans Affairs to conduct a study on the effect (if any) of the fees assessed on manufacturers and importers of branded prescription drugs, manufacturers and importers of medical devices, and health insurance providers on (1) the cost of medical care provided to veterans and (2) veterans' access to branded prescription drugs and medical devices.

The Secretary of Veterans Affairs will report the results of the study to the Committee on Ways and Means of the House of Representatives and to the Committee on Finance of the Senate no later than December 31, 2012.

Effective Date

The provision is effective on the date of enactment (March 23, 2010).

333

L. Repeal Business Deduction for Federal Subsidies for Certain Retiree Prescription Drug Plans (sec. 9012[907] of the Act and sec. 139A of the Code)

Present Law

In general

Sponsors[908] of qualified retiree prescription drug plans are eligible for subsidy payments from the Secretary of HHS with respect to a portion of each qualified covered retiree's gross covered prescription drug costs ("qualified retiree prescription drug plan subsidy").[909] A qualified retiree prescription drug plan is employment-based retiree health coverage[910] that has an actuarial value at least as great as the Medicare Part D standard plan for the risk pool and that meets certain other disclosure and recordkeeping requirements.[911] These qualified retiree prescription drug plan subsidies are excludable from the plan sponsor's gross income for the purposes of regular income tax and alternative minimum tax (including the adjustment for adjusted current earnings).[912]

Subsidy amounts

For each qualifying covered retiree enrolled for a coverage year in a qualified retiree prescription drug plan, the qualified retiree prescription drug plan subsidy is equal to 28 percent of the portion of the allowable retiree costs paid by the plan sponsor on behalf of the retiree that exceed the cost threshold but do not exceed the cost limit. A "qualifying covered retiree" is an individual who is eligible for Medicare but not enrolled in either a Medicare Part D prescription drug plan or a Medicare Advantage-Prescription Drug plan, but who is covered under a qualified retiree prescription drug plan. In general, allowable retiree costs are, with respect to prescription drug costs under a qualified retiree prescription drug plan, the part of the actual costs paid by the plan sponsor on behalf of a qualifying covered retiree under the plan.[913] Both the threshold and limit are indexed to the percentage increase in Medicare per capita

---

[907] Section 9012 of the Patient Protection and Affordable Care Act, Pub. L. No. 111–148, is amended by section 1407 of the Health Care and Education Reconciliation Act of 2010, Pub. L. No. 111–152.

[908] The identity of the plan sponsor is determined in accordance with section 16(B) of ERISA, except that for cases where a plan is maintained jointly by one employer and an employee organization, and the employer is the primary source of financing, the employer is the plan sponsor.

[909] Sec. 1860D–22 of the Social Security Act (SSA), 42 U.S.C. sec. 1395w–132.

[910] Employment-based retiree health coverage is health insurance coverage or other coverage of health care costs (whether provided by voluntary insurance coverage or pursuant to statutory or contractual obligation) for Medicare Part D eligible individuals (their spouses and dependents) under group health plans based on their status as retired participants in such plans. For purposes of the subsidy, group health plans generally include employee welfare benefit plans (as defined in section 607(1) of ERISA) that provide medical care (as defined in section 213(d)), Federal and State governmental plans, collectively bargained plans, and church plans.

[911] In addition to meeting the actuarial value standard, the plan sponsor must also maintain and provide the Secretary of HHS access to records that meet the Secretary of HHS's requirements for purposes of audits and other oversight activities necessary to ensure the adequacy of prescription drug coverage and the accuracy of payments made to eligible individuals under the plan. In addition, the plan sponsor must disclose to the Secretary of HHS whether the plan meets the actuarial equivalence requirement and if it does not, must disclose to retirees the limitations of their ability to enroll in Medicare Part D and that non-creditable coverage enrollment is subject to penalties such as fees for late enrollment. 42 U.S.C. sec. 1395w–132(a)(2).

[912] Sec. 139A.

[913] For purposes of calculating allowable retiree costs, actual costs paid are net of discounts, chargebacks, and average percentage rebates, and exclude administrative costs.

334

prescription drug costs; the cost threshold was $250 in 2006 ($310 in 2010) and the cost limit was $5,000 in 2006 ($6,300 in 2010).[914]

Expenses relating to tax-exempt income

In general, no deduction is allowed under any provision of the Code for any expense or amount which would otherwise be allowable as a deduction if such expense or amount is allocable to a class or classes of exempt income.[915] Thus, expenses or amount paid or incurred with respect to the subsidies excluded from income under section 139A would generally not be deductible. However, a provision under section 139A specifies that the exclusion of the qualified retiree prescription drug plan subsidy from income is not taken into account in determining whether any deduction is allowable with respect to covered retiree prescription drug expenses that are taken into account in determining the subsidy payment. Therefore, under present law, a taxpayer may claim a business deduction for covered retiree prescription drug expenses incurred notwithstanding that the taxpayer excludes from income qualified retiree prescription drug plan subsidies allocable to such expenses.

Explanation of Provision

The provision eliminates the rule that the exclusion for subsidy payments is not taken into account for purposes of determining whether a deduction is allowable with respect to retiree prescription drug expenses. Thus, under the provision, the amount otherwise allowable as a deduction for retiree prescription drug expenses is reduced by the amount of the excludable subsidy payments received.

For example, assume a company receives a subsidy of $28 with respect to eligible drug expenses of $100. The $28 is excludable from income under section 139A, and the amount otherwise allowable as a deduction is reduced by the $28. Thus, if the company otherwise meets the requirements of section 162 with respect to its eligible drug expenses, it would be entitled to an ordinary business expense deduction of $72.

Effective Date

The provision is effective for taxable years beginning after December 31, 2012.

M. Modify the Itemized Deduction for Medical Expenses (sec. 9013 of the Act and sec. 213 of the Code)

Present Law

Regular income tax

For regular income tax purposes, individuals are allowed an itemized deduction for unreimbursed medical expenses, but only to the extent that such expenses exceed 7.5 percent of AGI.[916]

---

[914] *http://www.cms.hhs.gov/MedicareAdvtgSpecRateStats/Downloads/Announcement2010.pdf.* Retrieved on March 19, 2010.
[915] Sec. 265(a) and Treas. Reg. sec. 1.265–1(a).
[916] Sec. 213.

335

This deduction is available both to insured and uninsured individuals; thus, for example, an individual with employer-provided health insurance (or certain other forms of tax-subsidized health benefits) may also claim the itemized deduction for the individual's medical expenses not covered by that insurance if the 7.5 percent AGI threshold is met. The medical deduction encompasses health insurance premiums to the extent they have not been excluded from taxable income through the employer exclusion or self-insured deduction.

Alternative minimum tax

For purposes of the alternative minimum tax ("AMT"), medical expenses are deductible only to the extent that they exceed 10 percent of AGI.

Explanation of Provision

This provision increases the threshold for the itemized deduction for unreimbursed medical expenses from 7.5 percent of AGI to 10 percent of AGI for regular income tax purposes. However, for the years 2013, 2014, 2015 and 2016, if either the taxpayer or the taxpayer's spouse turns 65 before the end of the taxable year, the increased threshold does not apply and the threshold remains at 7.5 percent of AGI. The provision does not change the AMT treatment of the itemized deduction for medical expenses.

Effective Date

The provision is effective for taxable years beginning after December 31, 2012.

N. Limitation on Deduction for Remuneration Paid by Health Insurance Providers (sec. 9014 of the Act and sec. 162 of the Code)

Present Law

An employer generally may deduct reasonable compensation for personal services as an ordinary and necessary business expense. Section 162(m) provides explicit limitations on the deductibility of compensation expenses in the case of corporate employers.

Section 162(m)

In general

The otherwise allowable deduction for compensation paid or accrued with respect to a covered employee of a publicly held corporation[917] is limited to no more than $1 million per year.[918] The deduction limitation applies when the deduction would otherwise be taken. Thus, for example, in the case of compensation resulting from a transfer of property in connection with the performance of services, such compensation is taken into account in applying the

---

[917] A corporation is treated as publicly held if it has a class of common equity securities that is required to be registered under section 12 of the Securities Exchange Act of 1934.

[918] Sec. 162(m). This deduction limitation applies for purposes of the regular income tax and the alternative minimum tax.

deduction limitation for the year for which the compensation is deductible under section 83 (i.e., generally the year in which the employee's right to the property is no longer subject to a substantial risk of forfeiture).

Covered employees

Section 162(m) defines a covered employee as (1) the chief executive officer of the corporation (or an individual acting in such capacity) as of the close of the taxable year and (2) the four most highly compensated officers for the taxable year (other than the chief executive officer). Treasury regulations under section 162(m) provide that whether an employee is the chief executive officer or among the four most highly compensated officers should be determined pursuant to the executive compensation disclosure rules promulgated under the Securities Exchange Act of 1934 ("Exchange Act").

In 2006, the Securities and Exchange Commission amended certain rules relating to executive compensation, including which executive officers' compensation must be disclosed under the Exchange Act. Under the new rules, such officers consist of (1) the principal executive officer (or an individual acting in such capacity), (2) the principal financial officer (or an individual acting in such capacity), and (3) the three most highly compensated executive officers, other than the principal executive officer or financial officer. In response to the Securities and Exchange Commission's new disclosure rules, the IRS issued updated guidance on identifying which employees are covered by section 162(m).[919]

Remuneration subject to the limit

Unless specifically excluded, the deduction limitation applies to all remuneration for services, including cash and the cash value of all remuneration (including benefits) paid in a medium other than cash. If an individual is a covered employee for a taxable year, the deduction limitation applies to all compensation not explicitly excluded from the deduction limitation, regardless of whether the compensation is for services as a covered employee and regardless of when the compensation was earned. The $1 million cap is reduced by excess parachute payments (as defined in sec. 280G, discussed below) that are not deductible by the corporation.

Certain types of compensation are not subject to the deduction limit and are not taken into account in determining whether other compensation exceeds $1 million. The following types of compensation are not taken into account: (1) remuneration payable on a commission basis; (2) remuneration payable solely on account of the attainment of one or more performance goals if certain outside director and shareholder approval requirements are met ("performance-based compensation"); (3) payments to a tax-qualified retirement plan (including salary reduction contributions); (4) amounts that are excludable from the executive's gross income (such as employer-provided health benefits and miscellaneous fringe benefits[920]); and

---

[919] Notice 2007–49, 2007–25 I.R.B. 1429.
[920] Sec. 132.

337

(5) any remuneration payable under a written binding contract which was in effect on February 17, 1993.

Remuneration does not include compensation for which a deduction is allowable after a covered employee ceases to be a covered employee. Thus, the deduction limitation often does not apply to deferred compensation that is otherwise subject to the deduction limitation (e.g., is not performance-based compensation) because the payment of compensation is deferred until after termination of employment.

Executive compensation of employers participating in the Troubled Assets Relief Program

In general

Under section 162(m)(5), the deduction limit is reduced to $500,000 in the case of otherwise deductible compensation of a covered executive for any applicable taxable year of an applicable employer.

An applicable employer means any employer from which one or more troubled assets are acquired under the "troubled assets relief program" ("TARP") established by the Emergency Stabilization Act of 2008[921] ("EESA") if the aggregate amount of the assets so acquired for all taxable years (including assets acquired through a direct purchase by the Treasury Department, within the meaning of section 113(c) of Title I of EESA) exceeds $300,000,000. However, such term does not include any employer from which troubled assets are acquired by the Treasury Department solely through direct purchases (within the meaning of section 113(c) of Title I of EESA). For example, if a firm sells $250,000,000 in assets through an auction system managed by the Treasury Department, and $100,000,000 to the Treasury Department in direct purchases, then the firm is an applicable employer. Conversely, if all $350,000,000 in sales take the form of direct purchases, then the firm would not be an applicable employer.

Unlike section 162(m), an applicable employer under this provision is not limited to publicly held corporations (or even limited to corporations). For example, an applicable employer could be a partnership if the partnership is an employer from which a troubled asset is acquired. The aggregation rules of section 414(b) and (c) apply in determining whether an employer is an applicable employer. However, these rules are applied disregarding the rules for brother-sister controlled groups and combined groups in sections 1563(a)(2) and (3). Thus, this aggregation rule only applies to parent-subsidiary controlled groups. A similar controlled group rule applies for trades and businesses under common control.

The result of this aggregation rule is that all corporations in the same controlled group are treated as a single employer for purposes of identifying the covered executives of that employer and all compensation from all members of the controlled group are taken into account for purposes of applying the $500,000 deduction limit. Further, all sales of assets under the TARP from all members of the controlled group are considered in determining whether such sales exceed $300,000,000.

---

[921] Pub. L. No. 110–343.

An applicable taxable year with respect to an applicable employer means the first taxable year which includes any portion of the period during which the authorities for the TARP established under EESA are in effect (the "authorities period") if the aggregate amount of troubled assets acquired from the employer under that authority during the taxable year (when added to the aggregate amount so acquired for all preceding taxable years) exceeds $300,000,000, and includes any subsequent taxable year which includes any portion of the authorities period.

A special rule applies in the case of compensation that relates to services that a covered executive performs during an applicable taxable year but that is not deductible until a later year ("deferred deduction executive remuneration"), such as nonqualified deferred compensation. Under the special rule, the unused portion (if any) of the $500,000 limit for the applicable tax year is carried forward until the year in which the compensation is otherwise deductible, and the remaining unused limit is then applied to the compensation.

For example, assume a covered executive is paid $400,000 in cash salary by an applicable employer in 2008 (assuming 2008 is an applicable taxable year) and the covered executive earns $100,000 in nonqualified deferred compensation (along with the right to future earnings credits) payable in 2020. Assume further that the $100,000 has grown to $300,000 in 2020. The full $400,000 in cash salary is deductible under the $500,000 limit in 2008. In 2020, the applicable employer's deduction with respect to the $300,000 will be limited to $100,000 (the lesser of the $300,000 in deductible compensation before considering the special limitation, and $500,000 less $400,000, which represents the unused portion of the $500,000 limit from 2008).

Deferred deduction executive remuneration that is properly deductible in an applicable taxable year (before application of the limitation under the provision) but is attributable to services performed in a prior applicable taxable year is subject to the special rule described above and is not double-counted. For example, assume the same facts as above, except that the nonqualified deferred compensation is deferred until 2009 and that 2009 is an applicable taxable year. The employer's deduction for the nonqualified deferred compensation for 2009 would be limited to $100,000 (as in the example above). The limit that would apply under the provision for executive remuneration that is in a form other than deferred deduction executive remuneration and that is otherwise deductible for 2009 is $500,000. For example, if the covered executive is paid $500,000 in cash compensation for 2009, all $500,000 of that cash compensation would be deductible in 2009 under the provision.

Covered executive

The term covered executive means any individual who is the chief executive officer or the chief financial officer of an applicable employer, or an individual acting in that capacity, at any time during a portion of the taxable year that includes the authorities period. It also includes any employee who is one of the three highest compensated officers of the applicable employer for the applicable taxable year (other than the chief executive officer or the chief fi-

339

nancial officer and only taking into account employees employed during any portion of the taxable year that includes the authorities period).[922]

Executive remuneration

The provision generally incorporates the present law definition of applicable employee remuneration. However, the present law exceptions for remuneration payable on commission and performance-based compensation do not apply for purposes of the $500,000 limit. In addition, the $500,000 limit only applies to executive remuneration which is attributable to services performed by a covered executive during an applicable taxable year. For example, assume the same facts as in the example above, except that the covered executive also receives in 2008 a payment of $300,000 in nonqualified deferred compensation that was attributable to services performed in 2006. Such payment is not treated as executive remuneration for purposes of the $500,000 limit.

Taxation of insurance companies

Present law provides special rules for determining the taxable income of insurance companies (subchapter L of the Code). Separate sets of rules apply to life insurance companies and to property and casualty insurance companies. Insurance companies are subject to Federal income tax at regular corporate income tax rates. An insurance company generally may deduct compensation paid in the course of its trade or business.

Explanation of Provision

Under the provision, no deduction is allowed for remuneration which is attributable to services performed by an applicable individual for a covered health insurance provider during an applicable taxable year to the extent that such remuneration exceeds $500,000. As under section 162(m)(5) for remuneration from TARP participants, the exceptions for performance based remuneration, commissions, or remuneration under existing binding contracts do not apply. This $500,000 deduction limitation applies without regard to whether such remuneration is paid during the taxable year or a subsequent taxable year. In applying this rule, rules similar to those in section 162(m)(5)(A)(ii) apply. Thus in the case of remuneration that relates to services that an applicable individual performs during a taxable year but that is not deductible until a later year, such as nonqualified deferred compensation, the unused portion (if any) of the $500,000 limit for the year is carried forward until the year in which the compensation is otherwise deductible, and the remaining unused limit is then applied to the compensation.

---

[922] The determination of the three highest compensated officers is made on the basis of the shareholder disclosure rules for compensation under the Exchange Act, except to the extent that the shareholder disclosure rules are inconsistent with the provision. Such shareholder disclosure rules are applied without regard to whether those rules actually apply to the employer under the Exchange Act. If an employee is a covered executive with respect to an applicable employer for any applicable taxable year, the employee will be treated as a covered executive for all subsequent applicable taxable years (and will be treated as a covered executive for purposes of any subsequent taxable year for purposes of the special rule for deferred deduction executive remuneration).

340

In determining whether the remuneration of an applicable individual for a year exceeds $500,000, all remuneration from all members of any controlled group of corporations (within the meaning of section 414(b)), other businesses under common control (within the meaning of section 414(c)), or affiliated service group (within the meaning of sections 414(m) and (o)) are aggregated.

Covered health insurance provider and applicable taxable year

An insurance provider is a covered health insurance provider if at least 25 percent of the insurance provider's gross premium income from health business is derived from health insurance plans that meet the minimum creditable coverage requirements in the bill ("covered health insurance provider"). A taxable year is an applicable taxable year for an insurance provider if an insurance provider is a covered insurance provider for any portion of the taxable year. Employers with self-insured plans are excluded from the definition of covered health insurance provider.

Applicable individual

Applicable individuals include all officers, employees, directors, and other workers or service providers (such as consultants) performing services for or on behalf of a covered health insurance provider. Thus, in contrast to the general rules under section 162(m) and the special rules executive compensation of employers participating in the TARP program, the limitation on the deductibility of remuneration from a covered health insurance provided is not limited to a small group of officers and covered executives but generally applies to remuneration of all employees and service providers. If an individual is an applicable individual with respect to a covered health insurance provider for any taxable year, the individual is treated as an applicable individual for all subsequent taxable years (and is treated as an applicable individual for purposes of any subsequent taxable year for purposes of the special rule for deferred remuneration).

Effective Date

The provision is effective for remuneration paid in taxable years beginning after 2012 with respect to services performed after 2009.

O. Additional Hospital Insurance Tax on High Income Taxpayers (sec. 9015 [923] of the Act and new secs. 1401 and 3101 of the Code)

Present Law

Federal Insurance Contributions Act tax

The Federal Insurance Contributions Act imposes tax on employers based on the amount of wages paid to an employee during the year. The tax imposed is composed of two parts: (1) the old age, survivors, and disability insurance ("OASDI") tax equal to 6.2 per-

---

[923] Section 9015 of the Patient Protection and Affordable Care Act, Pub. L. No. 111–148, is amended by section 10906.

341

cent of covered wages up to the taxable wage base ($106,800 in 2010); and (2) the HI tax amount equal to 1.45 percent of covered wages. Generally, covered wages means all remuneration for employment, including the cash value of all remuneration (including benefits) paid in any medium other than cash. Certain exceptions from covered wages are also provided. In addition to the tax on employers, each employee is subject to FICA taxes equal to the amount of tax imposed on the employer.

The employee portion of the FICA tax generally must be withheld and remitted to the Federal government by the employer.[924] The employer generally is liable for the amount of this tax whether or not the employer withholds the amount from the employee's wages.[925] In the event that the employer fails to withhold from an employee, the employee generally is not liable to the IRS for the amount of the tax. However, if the employer pays its liability for the amount of the tax not withheld, the employer generally has a right to collect that amount from the employee. Further, if the employer deducts and pays the tax the employer is indemnified against the claims and demands of any person for the amount of any payment of the tax made by the employer.[926]

Self-Employment Contributions Act tax

As a parallel to FICA taxes, the Self-Employment Contributions Act ("SECA") imposes taxes on the net income from self employment of self employed individuals. The rate of the OASDI portion of SECA taxes is equal to the combined employee and employer OASDI FICA tax rates and applies to self employment income up to the FICA taxable wage base. Similarly, the rate of the HI portion is the same as the combined employer and employee HI rates and there is no cap on the amount of self employment income to which the rate applies.[927]

For purposes of computing net earnings from self employment, taxpayers are permitted a deduction equal to the product of the taxpayer's earnings (determined without regard to this deduction) and one-half of the sum of the rates for OASDI (12.4 percent) and HI (2.9 percent), i.e., 7.65 percent of net earnings. This deduction reflects the fact that the FICA rates apply to an employee's wages, which do not include FICA taxes paid by the employer, whereas the self-employed individual's net earnings are economically equivalent to an employee's wages plus the employer share of FICA taxes.

---

[924] Sec. 3102(a).

[925] Sec. 3102(b).

[926] *Ibid.*

[927] For purposes of computing net earnings from self employment, taxpayers are permitted a deduction equal to the product of the taxpayer's earnings (determined without regard to this deduction) and one-half of the sum of the rates for OASDI (12.4 percent) and HI (2.9 percent), i.e., 7.65 percent of net earnings. This deduction reflects the fact that the FICA rates apply to an employee's wages, which do not include FICA taxes paid by the employer, whereas the self-employed individual's net earnings are economically equivalent to an employee's wages plus the employer share of FICA taxes.

342

Explanation of Provision

Additional HI tax on employee portion of HI tax

Calculation of additional tax

The employee portion of the HI tax is increased by an additional tax of 0.9 percent on wages [928] received in excess of the threshold amount. However, unlike the general 1.45 percent HI tax on wages, this additional tax is on the combined wages of the employee and the employee's spouse, in the case of a joint return. The threshold amount is $250,000 in the case of a joint return or surviving spouse, $125,000 in the case of a married individual filing a separate return, and $200,000 in any other case.

Liability for the additional HI tax on wages

As under present law, the employer is required to withhold the additional HI tax on wages but is liable for the tax if the employer fails to withhold the amount of the tax from wages, or collect the tax from the employee if the employer fails to withhold. However, in determining the employer's requirement to withhold and liability for the tax, only wages that the employee receives from the employer in excess of $200,000 for a year are taken into account and the employer must disregard the amount of wages received by the employee's spouse. Thus, the employer is only required to withhold on wages in excess of $200,000 for the year, even though the tax may apply to a portion of the employee's wages at or below $200,000, if the employee's spouse also has wages for the year, they are filing a joint return, and their total combined wages for the year exceed $250,000.

For example, if a taxpayer's spouse has wages in excess of $250,000 and the taxpayer has wages of $100,000, the employer of the taxpayer is not required to withhold any portion of the additional tax, even though the combined wages of the taxpayer and the taxpayer's spouse are over the $250,000 threshold. In this instance, the employer of the taxpayer's spouse is obligated to withhold the additional 0.9-percent HI tax with respect to the $50,000 above the threshold with respect to the wages of $250,000 for the taxpayer's spouse.

In contrast to the employee portion of the general HI tax of 1.45 percent of wages for which the employee generally has no direct liability to the IRS to pay the tax, the employee is also liable for this additional 0.9-percent HI tax to the extent the tax is not withheld by the employer. The amount of this tax not withheld by an employer must also be taken into account in determining a taxpayer's liability for estimated tax.

Additional HI for self-employed individuals

This same additional HI tax applies to the HI portion of SECA tax on self-employment income in excess of the threshold amount. Thus, an additional tax of 0.9 percent is imposed on every self-employed individual on self-employment income [929] in excess of the threshold amount.

---

[928] Sec. 3121(a).
[929] Sec. 1402(b).

343

As in the case of the additional HI tax on wages, the threshold amount for the additional SECA HI tax is $250,000 in the case of a joint return or surviving spouse, $125,000 in the case of a married individual filing a separate return, and $200,000 in any other case. The threshold amount is reduced (but not below zero) by the amount of wages taken into account in determining the FICA tax with respect to the taxpayer. No deduction is allowed under section 164(f) for the additional SECA tax, and the deduction under 1402(a)(12) is determined without regard to the additional SECA tax rate.

Effective Date

The provision applies to remuneration received and taxable years beginning after December 31, 2012.

P. Modification of Section 833 Treatment of Certain Health Organizations (sec. 9016 of the Act and sec. 833 of the Code)

Present Law

A property and casualty insurance company is subject to tax on its taxable income, generally defined as its gross income less allowable deductions (sec. 832). For this purpose, gross income includes underwriting income and investment income, as well as other items. Underwriting income is the premiums earned on insurance contracts during the year, less losses incurred and expenses incurred. The amount of losses incurred is determined by taking into account the discounted unpaid losses. Premiums earned during the year is determined taking into account a 20-percent reduction in the otherwise allowable deduction, intended to represent the allocable portion of expenses incurred in generating the unearned premiums (sec. 832(b)(4)(B)).

Present law provides that an organization described in sections 501(c)(3) or (4) of the Code is exempt from tax only if no substantial part of its activities consists of providing commercial-type insurance (sec. 501(m)). When this rule was enacted in 1986,[930] special rules were provided under section 833 for Blue Cross and Blue Shield organizations providing health insurance that (1) were in existence on August 16, 1986; (2) were determined at any time to be tax-exempt under a determination that had not been revoked; and (3) were tax-exempt for the last taxable year beginning before January 1, 1987 (when the present-law rule became effective), provided that no material change occurred in the structure or operations of the organizations after August 16, 1986, and before the close of 1986 or any subsequent taxable year. Any other organization is eligible for section 833 treatment if it meets six requirements set forth in section 833(c): (1) substantially all of its activities involve providing health insurance; (2) at least 10 percent of

---

[930] See H. Rep. 99–426, Tax Reform Act of 1985, (December 7, 1985), p. 664. The Committee stated, "[T]he availability of tax-exempt status under [then-]present law has allowed some large insurance entities to compete directly with commercial insurance companies. For example, the Blue Cross/Blue Shield organizations historically have been treated as tax-exempt organizations described in sections 501(c)(3) or (4). This group of organizations is now among the largest health care insurers in the United States." See also Joint Committee on Taxation, *General Explanation of the Tax Reform Act of 1986*, JCS–10–87 (May 4, 1987), pp. 583–592.

344

its health insurance is provided to individuals and small groups (not taking into account Medicare supplemental coverage); (3) it provides continuous full-year open enrollment for individuals and small groups; (4) for individuals, it provides full coverage of pre-existing conditions of high-risk individuals and coverage without regard to age, income, or employment of individuals under age 65; (5) at least 35 percent of its premiums are community rated; and (6) no part of its net earnings inures to the benefit of any private shareholder or individual.

Section 833 provides a deduction with respect to health business of such organizations. The deduction is equal to 25 percent of the sum of (1) claims incurred, and liabilities incurred under cost-plus contracts, for the taxable year, and (2) expenses incurred in connection with administration, adjustment, or settlement of claims or in connection with administration of cost-plus contracts during the taxable year, to the extent this sum exceeds the adjusted surplus at the beginning of the taxable year. Only health-related items are taken into account.

Section 833 provides an exception for such an organization from the application of the 20-percent reduction in the deduction for increases in unearned premiums that applies generally to property and casualty companies.

Section 833 provides that such an organization is taxable as a stock property and casualty insurer under the Federal income tax rules applicable to property and casualty insurers.

Explanation of Provision

The provision limits eligibility for the rules of section 833 to those organizations meeting a medical loss ratio standard of 85 percent for the taxable year. Thus, under the provision, an organization that does not meet the 85-percent standard is not allowed the 25-percent deduction and the exception from the 20-percent reduction in the unearned premium reserve deduction under section 833.

For this purpose, an organization's medical loss ratio is determined as the percentage of total premium revenue expended on reimbursement for clinical services that are provided to enrollees under the organization's policies during the taxable year, as reported under section 2718 of the PHSA.[931]

It is intended that the medical loss ratio under this provision be determined on an organization-by-organization basis, not on an affiliated or other group basis, and that Treasury Department guid-

---

[931] See Wednesday, March 24, 2010, Senate Floor statement of Senator Baucus relating to this provision, 156 Cong. Rec. S1989, stating in part, "First, it was our intention that, in calculating the medical loss ratios, these entities could include both the cost of reimbursement for clinical services provided to the individuals they insure and the cost of activities that improve health care quality. Determining the medical loss ratio under this provision using those two types of costs is consistent with the calculation of medical loss ratios elsewhere in the legislation. This determination would be made on an annual basis and would only affect the application of the special deductions for that year. Second, it was our intention that the only consequence for not meeting the medical loss ratio threshold would be that the 25 percent deduction for claims and expenses and the exception from the 20 percent reduction in the deduction for unearned premium reserves would not be allowed. The entity would still be treated as a stock property and casualty insurance company." A technical correction may be necessary so that the statute reflects this intent.

345

ance be promulgated promptly to carry out the purposes of the provision.

Effective Date

The provision is effective for taxable years beginning after December 31, 2009.

Q. Excise Tax on Indoor Tanning Services (sec. 9017 [932] of the Act and new sec. 5000B of the Code)

Present Law

There is no tax on indoor tanning services under present law.

Explanation of Provision

In general

The provision imposes a tax on each individual on whom indoor tanning services are performed. The tax is equal to 10 percent of the amount paid for indoor tanning services.

For purposes of the provision, indoor tanning services are services employing any electronic product designed to induce skin tanning and which incorporate one or more ultraviolet lamps and intended for the irradiation of an individual by ultraviolet radiation, with wavelengths in air between 200 and 400 nanometers. Indoor tanning services do not include any phototherapy service performed by a licensed medical professional.

Payment of tax

The tax is paid by the individual on whom the indoor tanning services are performed. The tax is collected by each person receiving a payment for tanning services on which a tax is imposed. If the tax is not paid by the person receiving the indoor tanning services at the time the payment for the service is received, the person performing the procedure pays the tax.

Payment of the tax is remitted quarterly to the Secretary by the person collecting the tax. The Secretary is given discretion over the manner of the payment.

Effective Date

The provision applies to tanning services performed on or after July 1, 2010.

---

[932] Section 9017 of the Patient Protection and Affordable Care Act, Pub. L. No. 111–148, as amended by section 10907.

346

R. Exclusion of Health Benefits Provided by Indian Tribal Governments (sec. 9021 of the Act and new sec. 139D of the Code)

Present Law

Present law generally provides that gross income includes all income from whatever source derived.[933] Exclusions from income are provided, however, for certain health care benefits.

Exclusion from income for employer-provided health coverage

Employees generally are not taxed on (that is, may "exclude" from gross income) the value of employer-provided health coverage under an accident or health plan.[934] In addition, any reimbursements under an accident or health plan for medical care expenses for employees, their spouses, and their dependents generally are excluded from gross income.[935] As with cash or other compensation, the amount paid by employers for employer-provided health coverage is a deductible business expense. Unlike other forms of compensation, however, if an employer contributes to a plan providing health coverage for employees (and the employees' spouses and dependents), the value of the coverage and all benefits (including reimbursements) in the form of medical care under the plan are excludable from the employees' income for income tax purposes.[936] The exclusion applies both to health coverage in the case in which an employer absorbs the cost of employees' medical expenses not covered by insurance (i.e., a self-insured plan) as well as in the case in which the employer purchases health insurance coverage for its employees. There is no limit on the amount of employer-provided health coverage that is excludable.

In addition, employees participating in a cafeteria plan may be able to pay the portion of premiums for health insurance coverage not otherwise paid for by their employers on a pre-tax basis through salary reduction.[937] Such salary reduction contributions are treated as employer contributions and thus also are excluded from gross income.

Employers may agree to reimburse medical expenses of their employees (and their spouses and dependents), not covered by a health insurance plan, through flexible spending arrangements which allow reimbursement not in excess of a specified dollar amount (either elected by an employee under a cafeteria plan or otherwise specified by the employer). Reimbursements under these arrangements are also excludible from gross income as employer-provided health coverage.

---

[933] Sec. 61.
[934] Sec 106.
[935] Sec. 105(b).
[936] Secs. 104, 105, 106, 125. A similar rule excludes employer provided health insurance coverage and reimbursements for medical expenses from the employees' wages for payroll tax purposes under sections 3121(a)(2), and 3306(a)(2). Health coverage provided to active members of the uniformed services, military retirees, and their dependents are excludable under section 134. That section provides an exclusion for "qualified military benefits," defined as benefits received by reason of status or service as a member of the uniformed services and which were excludable from gross income on September 9, 1986, under any provision of law, regulation, or administrative practice then in effect.
[937] Sec. 125.

347

The general welfare exclusion

Under the general welfare exclusion doctrine, certain payments made to individuals are excluded from gross income. The exclusion has been interpreted to cover payments by governmental units under legislatively provided social benefit programs for the promotion of the general welfare.[938]

The general welfare exclusion generally applies if the payments: (1) are made from a governmental fund, (2) are for the promotion of general welfare (on the basis of the need of the recipient), and (3) do not represent compensation for services.[939] A representative of the IRS recently expressed the view that the general welfare exclusion does not apply to persons with significant income or assets, and that any such extension would represent a departure from well-established administrative practice.[940] The representative further expressed the view that application of the general welfare exclusion to an Indian tribal government providing coverage or benefits to tribal members is dependent upon the structure and administration of the particular program.[941]

Explanation of Provision

The provision allows an exclusion from gross income for the value of specified Indian tribe health care benefits. The exclusion applies to the value of: (1) health services or benefits provided or purchased by the Indian Health Service ("IHS"), either directly or indirectly, through a grant to or a contract or compact with an Indian tribe or tribal organization or through programs of third par-

---

[938] See, e.g., Rev. Rul. 78–170, 1978–1 C.B. 24 (government payments to assist low-income persons with utility costs are not income); Rev. Rul. 76–395, 1976–2 C.B. 16, 17 (government grants to assist low-income city inhabitants to refurbish homes are not income); Rev. Rul. 76–144, 1976–1 C.B. 17 (government grants to persons eligible for relief under the Disaster Relief Act of 1974 are not income); Rev. Rul. 74–153, 1974–1 C.B. 20 (government payments to assist adoptive parents with support and maintenance of adoptive children are not income); Rev. Rul. 74–205, 1974–1 C.B. 20 (replacement housing payments received by individuals under the Housing and Urban Development Act of 1968 are not includible in gross income); Gen. Couns. Mem. 34506 (May 26, 1971) (federal mortgage assistance payments excluded from income under general welfare exception); Rev. Rul. 57–102, 1957–1 C.B. 26 (government benefits paid to blind persons are not income). The courts have also acknowledged the existence of this doctrine. See, e.g., *Bailey v. Commissioner*, 88 T.C. 1293, 1299–1301 (1987) (new building façade paid for by urban renewal agency on taxpayer's property under façade grant program not considered payments under general welfare doctrine because awarded without regard to any need of the recipients); *Graff v. Commissioner*, 74 TC 743, 753–754 (1980) (court acknowledged that rental subsidies under Housing Act were excludable under general welfare doctrine but found that payments at issue made by HUD on taxpayer landlord's behalf were taxable income to him), *affd. per curiam* 673 F.2d 784 (5th Cir. 1982).

[939] See Rev. Rul. 98–19, 1998–1 C.B. 840 (excluding relocation payments made by local governments to those whose homes were damaged by floods). Recent guidance as to whether the need of the recipient (taken into account under the second requirement of the general welfare exclusion) must be based solely on financial means or whether the need can be based on a variety of other considerations including health, educational background, or employment status, has been mixed. Chief Couns. Adv. 200021036 (May 25, 2000) (excluding state adoption assistant payments made to individuals adopting special needs children without regard to financial means of parents; the children were considered to be the recipients); Priv. Ltr. Rul. 200632005 (April 13, 2006) (excluding payments made by Tribe to members based on multiple factors of need pursuant to housing assistance program); Chief Couns. Adv. 200648027 (Jul 25, 2006) (excluding subsidy payments based on financial need of recipient made by state to certain participants in state health insurance program to reduce cost of health insurance premiums).

[940] Testimony of Sarah H. Ingram, Commissioner, Tax Exempt and Government Entities, Internal Revenue Service, before the Senate Committee on Indian Affairs, *Oversight Hearing to Examine the Federal Tax Treatment of Health Care Benefits Provided by Tribal Governments to Their Citizens*, September 17, 2009.

[941] *Ibid.*

348

ties funded by the IHS; [942] (2) medical care (in the form of provided or purchased medical care services, accident or health insurance or an arrangement having the same effect, or amounts paid directly or indirectly, to reimburse the member for expenses incurred for medical care) provided by an Indian tribe or tribal organization to a member of an Indian tribe, including the member's spouse or dependents; [943] (3) accident or health plan coverage (or an arrangement having the same effect) provided by an Indian tribe or tribal organization for medical care to a member of an Indian tribe, including the member's spouse or dependents; and (4) any other medical care provided by an Indian tribe or tribal organization that supplements, replaces, or substitutes for the programs and services provided by the Federal government to Indian tribes or Indians.

This provision does not apply to any amount which is deducted or excluded from gross income under another provision of the Code.

No change made by the provision is intended to create an inference with respect to the exclusion from gross income of benefits provided prior to the date of enactment (March 23, 2010). Additionally, no inference is intended with respect to the tax treatment of other benefits provided by an Indian tribe or tribal organization not covered by this provision.

Effective Date

The provision applies to benefits and coverage provided after the date of enactment (March 23, 2010).

S. Establishment of SIMPLE Cafeteria Plans for Small Businesses (sec. 9022 of the Act and sec. 125 of the Code)

Present Law

Definition of a cafeteria plan

If an employee receives a qualified benefit (as defined below) based on the employee's election between the qualified benefit and a taxable benefit under a cafeteria plan, the qualified benefit generally is not includable in gross income. [944] However, if a plan offering an employee an election between taxable benefits (including cash) and nontaxable qualified benefits does not meet the requirements for being a cafeteria plan, the election between taxable and nontaxable benefits results in gross income to the employee, re-

---

[942] The term "Indian tribe" means any Indian tribe, band, nation, pueblo, or other organized group or community, including any Alaska Native village, or regional or village corporation, as defined by, or established pursuant to, the Alaska Native Claims Settlement Act (43 U.S.C. 1601 et seq.), which is recognized as eligible for the special programs and services provided by the United States to Indians because of their status as Indians. The term "tribal organization" has the same meaning as such term in section 4(l) of the Indian Self-Determination and Education Assistance Act (25 U.S.C. 450b(1)).

[943] The terms "accident or health insurance" and "accident or health plan" have the same meaning as when used in section 105. The term "medical care" is the same as the definition under section 213. For purposes of the provision, dependents are determined under section 152, but without regard to subsections (b)(1), (b)(2), and (d)(1)(B). Section 152(b)(1) generally provides that if an individual is a dependent of another taxpayer during a taxable year such individual is treated as having no dependents for such taxable year. Section 152(b)(2) provides that a married individual filing a joint return with his or her spouse is not treated as a dependent of a taxpayer. Section 152(d)(1)(B) provides that a "qualifying relative" (i.e., a relative that qualifies as a dependent) does not include a person whose gross income for the calendar year in which the taxable year begins equals or exceeds the exempt amount (as defined under section 151).

[944] Sec. 125(a).

349

gardless of what benefit is elected and when the election is made.[945] A cafeteria plan is a separate written plan under which all participants are employees, and participants are permitted to choose among at least one permitted taxable benefit (for example, current cash compensation) and at least one qualified benefit. Finally, a cafeteria plan must not provide for deferral of compensation, except as specifically permitted in sections 125(d)(2)(B), (C), or (D).

Qualified benefits

Qualified benefits under a cafeteria plan are generally employer-provided benefits that are not includable in gross income under an express provision of the Code. Examples of qualified benefits include employer-provided health insurance coverage, group term life insurance coverage not in excess of $50,000, and benefits under a dependent care assistance program. In order to be excludable, any qualified benefit elected under a cafeteria plan must independently satisfy any requirements under the Code section that provides the exclusion. However, some employer-provided benefits that are not includable in gross income under an express provision of the Code are explicitly not allowed in a cafeteria plan. These benefits are generally referred to as nonqualified benefits. Examples of nonqualified benefits include scholarships;[946] employer-provided meals and lodging;[947] educational assistance;[948] and fringe benefits.[949] A plan offering any nonqualified benefit is not a cafeteria plan.[950]

Employer contributions through salary reduction

Employees electing a qualified benefit through salary reduction are electing to forego salary and instead to receive a benefit that is excludible from gross income because it is provided by employer contributions. Section 125 provides that the employee is treated as receiving the qualified benefit from the employer in lieu of the taxable benefit. For example, active employees participating in a cafeteria plan may be able to pay their share of premiums for employer-provided health insurance on a pre-tax basis through salary reduction.[951]

Nondiscrimination requirements

Cafeteria plans and certain qualified benefits (including group term life insurance, self-insured medical reimbursement plans, and dependent care assistance programs) are subject to nondiscrimination requirements to prevent discrimination in favor of highly compensated individuals generally as to eligibility for benefits and as to actual contributions and benefits provided. There are also rules to prevent the provision of disproportionate benefits to key employees (within the meaning of section 416(i)) through a cafeteria

---

[945] Prop. Treas. Reg. sec. 1.125–1(b).
[946] Sec. 117.
[947] Sec. 119.
[948] Sec. 127.
[949] Sec. 132.
[950] Prop. Treas. Reg. sec. 1.125–1(q). Long-term care services, contributions to Archer Medical Savings Accounts, group term life insurance for an employee's spouse, child or dependent, and elective deferrals to section 403(b) plans are also nonqualified benefits.
[951] Sec. 125.

350

plan.[952] Although the basic purpose of each of the nondiscrimination rules is the same, the specific rules for satisfying the relevant nondiscrimination requirements, including the definition of highly compensated individual,[953] vary for cafeteria plans generally and for each qualified benefit. An employer maintaining a cafeteria plan in which any highly compensated individual participates must make sure that both the cafeteria plan and each qualified benefit satisfies the relevant nondiscrimination requirements, as a failure to satisfy the nondiscrimination rules generally results in a loss of the tax exclusion by the highly compensated individuals.

Explanation of Provision

Under the provision, an eligible small employer is provided with a safe harbor from the nondiscrimination requirements for cafeteria plans as well as from the nondiscrimination requirements for specified qualified benefits offered under a cafeteria plan, including group term life insurance, benefits under a self insured medical expense reimbursement plan, and benefits under a dependent care assistance program. Under the safe harbor, a cafeteria plan and the specified qualified benefits are treated as meeting the specified nondiscrimination rules if the cafeteria plan satisfies minimum eligibility and participation requirements and minimum contribution requirements.

Eligibility requirement

The eligibility requirement is met only if all employees (other than excludable employees) are eligible to participate, and each employee eligible to participate is able to elect any benefit available under the plan (subject to the terms and conditions applicable to all participants). However, a cafeteria plan will not fail to satisfy this eligibility requirement merely because the plan excludes employees who (1) have not attained the age of 21 (or a younger age provided in the plan) before the close of a plan year, (2) have fewer than 1,000 hours of service for the preceding plan year, (3) have not completed one year of service with the employer as of any day during the plan year, (4) are covered under an agreement that the Secretary of Labor finds to be a collective bargaining agreement if there is evidence that the benefits covered under the cafeteria plan were the subject of good faith bargaining between employee rep-

---

[952] A key employee generally is an employee who, at any time during the year is (1) a five-percent owner of the employer, or (2) a one-percent owner with compensation of more than $150,000 (not indexed for inflation), or (3) an officer with compensation more than $160,000 (for 2010). A special rule limits the number of officers treated as key employees. If the employer is a corporation, a five-percent owner is a person who owns more than five percent of the outstanding stock or stock possessing more than five percent of the total combined voting power of all stock. If the employer is not a corporation, a five-percent owner is a person who owns more than five percent of the capital or profits interest. A one-percent owner is determined by substituting one percent for five percent in the preceding definitions. For purposes of determining employee ownership in the employer, certain attribution rules apply.

[953] For cafeteria plan purposes, a "highly compensated individual" is (1) an officer, (2) a five-percent shareholder, (3) an individual who is highly compensated, or (4) the spouse or dependent of any of the preceding categories. A "highly compensated participant" is a participant who falls in any of those categories. "Highly compensated" is not defined for this purpose. Under section 105(h), a self-insured medical expense reimbursement plan must not discriminate in favor of a "highly compensated individual," defined as (1) one of the five highest paid officers, (2) a 10–percent shareholder, or (3) an individual among the highest paid 25 percent of all employees. Under section 129 for a dependent care assistance program, eligibility for benefits, and the benefits and contributions provided, generally must not discriminate in favor of highly compensated employees within the meaning of section 414(q).

351

resentatives and the employer, or (5) are described in section 410(b)(3)(C) (relating to nonresident aliens working outside the United States). An employer may have a shorter age and service requirement but only if such shorter service or younger age applies to all employees.

Minimum contribution requirement

The minimum contribution requirement is met if the employer provides a minimum contribution for each nonhighly compensated employee (employee who is not a highly compensated employee [954] or a key employee (within the meaning of section 416(i))) in addition to any salary reduction contributions made by the employee. The minimum must be available for application toward the cost of any qualified benefit (other than a taxable benefit) offered under the plan. The minimum contribution is permitted to be calculated under either the nonelective contribution method or the matching contribution method, but the same method must be used for calculating the minimum contribution for all nonhighly compensated employees. The minimum contribution under the nonelective contribution method is an amount equal to a uniform percentage (not less than two percent) of each eligible employee's compensation for the plan year, determined without regard to whether the employees makes any salary reduction contribution under the cafeteria plan. The minimum matching contribution is the lesser of 100 percent of the amount of the salary reduction contribution elected to be made by the employee for the plan year or six percent of the employee's compensation for the plan year. Compensation for purposes of this minimum contribution requirement is compensation with the meaning of section 414(s).

A simple cafeteria plan is permitted to provide for the matching contributions in addition to the minimum required but only if matching contributions with respect to salary reduction contributions for any highly compensated employee or key employee are not made at a greater rate than the matching contributions for any nonhighly compensated employee. Nothing in this provision prohibits an employer from making contributions to provide qualified benefits under the plan in addition to the required contributions.

Eligible employer

An eligible small employer under the provision is, with respect to any year, an employer who employed an average of 100 or fewer employees on business days during either of the two preceding years. For purposes of the provision, a year may only be taken into account if the employer was in existence throughout the year. If an employer was not in existence throughout the preceding year, the determination is based on the average number of employees that it is reasonably expected such employer will employ on business days in the current year. If an employer was an eligible employer for any year and maintained a simple cafeteria plan for its employ-

---

[954] Section 414(q) generally defines a highly compensated employee as an employee (1) who was a five-percent owner during the year or the preceding year, or (2) who had compensation of $110,000 (for 2010) or more for the preceding year. An employer may elect to limit the employees treated as highly compensated employees based upon their compensation in the preceding year to the highest paid 20 percent of employees in the preceding year. Five-percent owner is defined by cross-reference to the definition of key employee in section 416(i).

352

ees for such year, then, for each subsequent year during which the employer continues, without interruption, to maintain the cafeteria plan, the employer is deemed to be an eligible small employer until the employer employs an average of 200 or more employees on business days during any year preceding any such subsequent year.

The determination of whether an employer is an eligible small employer is determined by applying the controlled group rules of sections 52(a) and (b) under which all members of the controlled group are treated as a single employer. In addition, the definition of employee includes leased employees within the meaning of sections 414(n) and (o).[955]

Effective Date

The provision is effective for taxable years beginning after December 31, 2010.

T. Investment Credit for Qualifying Therapeutic Discovery Projects (sec. 9023 of the Act and new sec. 48D of the Code)

Present Law

Present law provides for a research credit equal to 20 percent (14 percent in the case of the alternative simplified credit) of the amount by which the taxpayer's qualified research expenses for a taxable year exceed its base amount for that year.[956] Thus, the research credit is generally available with respect to incremental increases in qualified research.

A 20-percent research tax credit is also available with respect to the excess of (1) 100 percent of corporate cash expenses (including grants or contributions) paid for basic research conducted by universities (and certain nonprofit scientific research organizations) over (2) the sum of (a) the greater of two minimum basic research floors plus (b) an amount reflecting any decrease in nonresearch giving to universities by the corporation as compared to such giving during a fixed-base period, as adjusted for inflation. This separate credit computation is commonly referred to as the "university basic research credit."[957]

Finally, a research credit is available for a taxpayer's expenditures on research undertaken by an energy research consortium. This separate credit computation is commonly referred to as the "energy research credit." Unlike the other research credits, the energy research credit applies to all qualified expenditures, not just those in excess of a base amount.

---

[955] Section 52(b) provides that, for specified purposes, all employees of all corporations which are members of a controlled group of corporations are treated as employed by a single employer. However, section 52(b) provides certain modifications to the control group rules including substituting 50 percent ownership for 80 percent ownership as the measure of control. There is a similar rule in section 52(c) under which all employees of trades or businesses (whether or not incorporated) which are under common control are treated under regulations as employed by a single employer. Section 414(n) provides rules for specified purposes when leased employees are treated as employed by the service recipient and section 414(o) authorizes the Treasury to issue regulations to prevent avoidance of the requirements of section 414(n).

[956] Sec. 41.

[957] Sec. 41(e).

353

The research credit, including the university basic research credit and the energy research credit, expired for amounts paid or incurred after December 31, 2009.[958]

Qualified research expenses eligible for the research tax credit
consist of: (1) in-house expenses of the taxpayer for wages and supplies attributable to qualified research; (2) certain time-sharing
costs for computer use in qualified research; and (3) 65 percent of
amounts paid or incurred by the taxpayer to certain other persons
for qualified research conducted on the taxpayer's behalf (so-called
contract research expenses).[959] Notwithstanding the limitation for
contract research expenses, qualified research expenses include 100
percent of amounts paid or incurred by the taxpayer to an eligible
small business, university, or Federal laboratory for qualified energy research.

Present law also provides a 50-percent credit[960] for expenses related to human clinical testing of drugs for the treatment of certain
rare diseases and conditions, generally those that afflict less than
200,000 persons in the United States. Qualifying expenses are
those paid or incurred by the taxpayer after the date on which the
drug is designated as a potential treatment for a rare disease or
disorder by the Food and Drug Administration ("FDA") in accordance with section 526 of the Federal Food, Drug, and Cosmetic Act.

Present law does not provide a credit specifically designed to encourage investment in new therapies relating to diseases.

Explanation of Provision

In general

The provision establishes a 50-percent nonrefundable investment
tax credit for qualified investments in qualifying therapeutic discovery projects. The provision allocates $1 billion during the two-
year period 2009 through 2010 for the program. The Secretary, in
consultation with the Secretary of HHS, will award certifications
for qualified investments. The credit is available only to companies
having 250 or fewer employees.[961]

A "qualifying therapeutic discovery project" is a project which is
designed to develop a product, process, or therapy to diagnose,
treat, or prevent diseases and afflictions by: (1) conducting pre-clin-
ical activities, clinical trials, clinical studies, and research protocols, or (2) by developing technology or products designed to diagnose diseases and conditions, including molecular and companion
drugs and diagnostics, or to further the delivery or administration
of therapeutics.

---

[958] Sec. 41(h). The research credit, including the university basic research credit and the energy research credit, was extended for two years through 2011, in section 731 of the Tax Relief,
Unemployment Insurance Reauthorization, and Job Creation Act of 2010, Pub. L. No. 111–312,
described in Part Sixteen of this document.

[959] Under a special rule, 75 percent of amounts paid to a research consortium for qualified
research are treated as qualified research expenses eligible for the research credit (rather than
65 percent under the general rule of section 41(b)(3) governing contract research expenses) if
(1) such research consortium is a tax-exempt organization that is described in section 501(c)(3)
(other than a private foundation) or section 501(c)(6) and is organized and operated primarily
to conduct scientific research, and (2) such qualified research is conducted by the consortium
on behalf of the taxpayer and one or more persons not related to the taxpayer. Sec. 41(b)(3)(C).

[960] Sec. 45C.

[961] The number of employees is determined taking into account all businesses of the taxpayer
at the time it submits an application, and is determined taking into account the rules for determining a single employer under section 52(a) or (b) or section 414(m) or (o).

354

The qualified investment for any taxable year is the aggregate amount of the costs paid or incurred in such year for expenses necessary for and directly related to the conduct of a qualifying therapeutic discovery project. The qualified investment for any taxable year with respect to any qualifying therapeutic discovery project does not include any cost for: (1) remuneration for an employee described in section 162(m)(3), (2) interest expense, (3) facility maintenance expenses, (4) a service cost identified under Treas. Reg. Sec. 1.263A–1(e)(4), or (5) any other expenditure as determined by the Secretary as appropriate to carry out the purposes of the provision.

Companies must apply to the Secretary to obtain certification for qualifying investments.[962] The Secretary, in determining qualifying projects, will consider only those projects that show reasonable potential to: (1) result in new therapies to treat areas of unmet medical need or to prevent, detect, or treat chronic or acute disease and conditions, (2) reduce long-term health care costs in the United States, or (3) significantly advance the goal of curing cancer within a 30-year period. Additionally, the Secretary will take into consideration which projects have the greatest potential to: (1) create and sustain (directly or indirectly) high quality, high paying jobs in the United States, and (2) advance the United States' competitiveness in the fields of life, biological, and medical sciences.

Qualified therapeutic discovery project expenditures do not qualify for the research credit, orphan drug credit, or bonus depreciation.[963] If a credit is allowed for an expenditure related to property subject to depreciation, the basis of the property is reduced by the amount of the credit. Additionally, expenditures taken into account in determining the credit are nondeductible to the extent of the credit claimed that is attributable to such expenditures.

Election to receive grant in lieu of tax credit

Taxpayers may elect to receive credits that have been allocated to them in the form of Treasury grants equal to 50 percent of the qualifying investment. Any such grant is not includible in the taxpayer's gross income.

In making grants under this section, the Secretary of the Treasury is to apply rules similar to the rules of section 50. In applying such rules, if an investment ceases to be a qualified investment, the Secretary of the Treasury shall provide for the recapture of the appropriate percentage of the grant amount in such manner as the Secretary of the Treasury determines appropriate. The Secretary of the Treasury shall not make any grant under this section to: (1) any Federal, State, or local government (or any political subdivision, agency, or instrumentality thereof), (2) any organization described in section 501(c) and exempt from tax under section 501(a), (3) any entity referred to in paragraph (4) of section 54(j), or (4) any partnership or other pass-thru entity any partner (or other

---

[962] The Secretary must take action to approve or deny an application within 30 days of the submission of such application.

[963] Any expenses for the taxable year that are qualified research expenses under section 41(b) are taken into account in determining base period research expenses for purposes of computing the research credit under section 41 for subsequent taxable years.

355

holder of an equity or profits interest) of which is described in paragraph (1), (2), or (3).

Effective Date

The provision applies to expenditures paid or incurred after December 31, 2008, in taxable years beginning after December 31, 2008.

TITLE X—STRENGTHENING QUALITY, AFFORDABLE HEALTH CARE FOR ALL AMERICANS

A. Study of Geographic Variation in Application of FPL (sec. 10105 of the Act)

Present Law

No provision.

Explanation of Provision

The Secretary of HHS is instructed to conduct a study on the feasibility and implication of adjusting the application of the FPL under the provisions enacted in the Act for different geographical areas so as to reflect disparities in the cost of living among different areas in the United States, including the territories. If the Secretary deems such an adjustment feasible, then the study should include a methodology for implementing the adjustment. The Secretary is required to report the results of the study to Congress no later than January 1, 2013. The provision requires that special attention be paid to the impact of disparities between the poverty levels and the cost of living in the territories and the impact of this disparity on the expansion of health coverage in the territories. The territories are the Commonwealth of Puerto Rico, the U.S. Virgin Islands, Guam, the Commonwealth of the Northern Mariana Islands, American Samoa, and any other territory or possession of the United States.

Effective Date

The provision is effective on the date of enactment (March 23, 2010).

B. Free Choice Vouchers (sec. 10108 of the Act and sec. 139D of the Code)

Present Law

No provision.

Explanation of Provision

Provision of vouchers

Employers offering minimum essential coverage through an eligible employer-sponsored plan and paying a portion of that coverage must provide qualified employees with a voucher whose value can be applied to purchase of a health plan through the Exchange. Qualified employees are employees whose required contribution for employer sponsored minimum essential coverage exceeds eight percent, but does not exceed 9.8 percent of the employee's household income for the taxable year and the employee's total household income does not exceed 400 percent of the poverty line for the family. In addition, the employee must not participate in the employer's health plan.

The value of the voucher is equal to the dollar value of the employer contribution to the employer offered health plan. If multiple plans are offered by the employer, the value of the voucher is the dollar amount that would be paid if the employee chose the plan for which the employer would pay the largest percentage of the premium cost.[964] The value of the voucher is for self-only coverage unless the individual purchases family coverage in the Exchange. Under the provision, for purposes of calculating the dollar value of the employer contribution, the premium for any health plan is determined under rules similar to the rules of section 2204 of PHSA, except that the amount is adjusted for age and category of enrollment in accordance with regulations established by the Secretary.

In the case of years after 2014, the eight percent and the 9.8 percent are indexed to the excess of premium growth over income growth for the preceding calendar year.

Use of vouchers

Vouchers can be used in the Exchange towards the monthly premium of any qualified health plan in the Exchange. The value of the voucher to the extent it is used for the purchase of a health plan is not includable in gross income. If the value of the voucher exceeds the premium of the health plan chosen by the employee, the employee is paid the excess value of the voucher. The excess amount received by the employee is includible in the employee's gross income.

If an individual receives a voucher, the individual is disqualified from receiving any tax credit or cost sharing credit for the purchase of a plan in the Exchange. Similarly, if any employee receives a free choice voucher, the employer is not be assessed a shared responsibility payment on behalf of that employee.[965]

Definition of terms

The terms used for this provision have the same meaning as any term used in the provision for the requirement to maintain minimum essential coverage (section 1501 of the Act and new section 5000A). Thus for example, the terms "household income," "poverty line," "required contribution," and "eligible employer-sponsored plan" have the same meaning for both provisions. Thus, the re-

---

[964] For example, if an employer offering the same plans for $200 and $300 offers a flat $180 contribution for all plans, a contribution of 90 percent for the $200 plan and a contribution of 60 percent for the $300 plan, and the value of the voucher would equal the value of the contribution to the $200 since it received a 90 percent contribution, a value of $180. However, if the firm offers a $150 contribution to the $200 plan (75 percent) and a $200 contribution to the $300 plan (67 percent), the value of the voucher is based on the plan receiving the greater percentage paid by the employer and would be $150. If a firm offers health plans with monthly premiums of $200 and $300 and provides a payment of 60 percent of any plan purchased, the value of the voucher will be 60 percent the higher premium plan, in this case, 60 percent of $300 or $180.

[965] Section 1513 of the Patient Protection and Affordable Care Act, Pub. L. No. 111–148, and new Code section 4980H.

357

quired contribution includes the amount of any salary reduction contribution.

Effective Date

The provision is effective after December 31, 2013.

C. Exclusion for Assistance Provided to Participants in State Student Loan Repayment Programs for Certain Health Professionals (sec. 10908 of the Act and sec. 108(f)(4) of the Code)

Present Law

Gross income generally includes the discharge of indebtedness of the taxpayer. Under an exception to this general rule, gross income does not include any amount from the forgiveness (in whole or in part) of certain student loans, provided that the forgiveness is contingent on the student's working for a certain period of time in certain professions for any of a broad class of employers.

Student loans eligible for this special rule must be made to an individual to assist the individual in attending an educational institution that normally maintains a regular faculty and curriculum and normally has a regularly enrolled body of students in attendance at the place where its education activities are regularly carried on. Loan proceeds may be used not only for tuition and required fees, but also to cover room and board expenses. The loan must be made by (1) the United States (or an instrumentality or agency thereof), (2) a State (or any political subdivision thereof), (3) certain tax-exempt public benefit corporations that control a State, county, or municipal hospital and whose employees have been deemed to be public employees under State law, or (4) an educational organization that originally received the funds from which the loan was made from the United States, a State, or a tax-exempt public benefit corporation.

In addition, an individual's gross income does not include amounts from the forgiveness of loans made by educational organizations (and certain tax-exempt organizations in the case of refinancing loans) out of private, nongovernmental funds if the proceeds of such loans are used to pay costs of attendance at an educational institution or to refinance any outstanding student loans (not just loans made by educational organizations) and the student is not employed by the lender organization. In the case of such loans made or refinanced by educational organizations (or refinancing loans made by certain tax-exempt organizations), cancellation of the student loan must be contingent upon the student working in an occupation or area with unmet needs, and such work must be performed for, or under the direction of, a tax-exempt charitable organization or a governmental entity.

Finally, an individual's gross income does not include any loan repayment amount received under the National Health Service Corps loan repayment program or certain State loan repayment programs.

358

Explanation of Provision

The provision modifies the gross income exclusion for amounts received under the National Health Service Corps loan repayment program or certain State loan repayment programs to include any amount received by an individual under any State loan repayment or loan forgiveness program that is intended to provide for the increased availability of health care services in underserved or health professional shortage areas (as determined by the State).

Effective Date

The provision is effective for amounts received by an individual in taxable years beginning after December 31, 2008.

D. Expansion of Adoption Credit and the Exclusion from Gross Income for Employer-Provided Adoption Assistance (sec. 10909 of the Act and secs. 23 and 137 of the Code)

Present Law

Tax credit

Non-special needs adoptions

Generally a nonrefundable tax credit is allowed for qualified adoption expenses paid or incurred by a taxpayer subject to the maximum credit. The maximum credit is $12,170 per eligible child for taxable years beginning in 2010. An eligible child is an individual who: (1) has not attained age 18; or (2) is physically or mentally incapable of caring for himself or herself. The maximum credit is applied per child rather than per year. Therefore, while qualified adoption expenses may be incurred in one or more taxable years, the tax credit per adoption of an eligible child may not exceed the maximum credit.

Special needs adoptions

In the case of a special needs adoption finalized during a taxable year, the taxpayer may claim as an adoption credit the amount of the maximum credit minus the aggregate qualified adoption expenses with respect to that adoption for all prior taxable years. A special needs child is an eligible child who is a citizen or resident of the United States whom a State has determined: (1) cannot or should not be returned to the home of the birth parents; and (2) has a specific factor or condition (such as the child's ethnic background, age, or membership in a minority or sibling group, or the presence of factors such as medical conditions, or physical, mental, or emotional handicaps) because of which the child cannot be placed with adoptive parents without adoption assistance.

Qualified adoption expenses

Qualified adoption expenses are reasonable and necessary adoption fees, court costs, attorneys fees, and other expenses that are: (1) directly related to, and the principal purpose of which is for, the legal adoption of an eligible child by the taxpayer; (2) not incurred in violation of State or Federal law, or in carrying out any surrogate parenting arrangement; (3) not for the adoption of the child

359

of the taxpayer's spouse; and (4) not reimbursed (e.g., by an employer).

Phase-out for higher-income individuals

The adoption credit is phased out ratably for taxpayers with modified adjusted gross income between $182,520 and $222,520 for taxable years beginning in 2010. Under present law, modified adjusted gross income is the sum of the taxpayer's adjusted gross income plus amounts excluded from income under sections 911, 931, and 933 (relating to the exclusion of income of U.S. citizens or residents living abroad; residents of Guam, American Samoa, and the Northern Mariana Islands; and residents of Puerto Rico, respectively).

EGTRRA sunset [966]

For taxable years after 2010, the adoption credit will be reduced to a maximum credit of $6,000 for special needs adoptions and no tax credit for non-special needs adoptions. Also, the credit phase-out range will revert to the pre-EGTRRA levels (i.e., a ratable phase-out between modified adjusted gross income between $75,000 and $115,000). Finally, the adoption credit will be allowed only to the extent the individual's regular income tax liability exceeds the individual's tentative minimum tax, determined without regard to the minimum foreign tax credit.

Exclusion for employer-provided adoption assistance

An exclusion from the gross income of an employee is allowed for qualified adoption expenses paid or reimbursed by an employer under an adoption assistance program. For 2010, the maximum exclusion is $12,170. Also for 2010, the exclusion is phased out ratably for taxpayers with modified adjusted gross income between $182,520 and $222,520. Modified adjusted gross income is the sum of the taxpayer's adjusted gross income plus amounts excluded from income under Code sections 911, 931, and 933 (relating to the exclusion of income of U.S. citizens or residents living abroad; residents of Guam, American Samoa, and the Northern Mariana Islands; and residents of Puerto Rico, respectively). For purposes of this exclusion, modified adjusted gross income also includes all employer payments and reimbursements for adoption expenses whether or not they are taxable to the employee.

Adoption expenses paid or reimbursed by the employer under an adoption assistance program are not eligible for the adoption credit. A taxpayer may be eligible for the adoption credit (with respect to qualified adoption expenses he or she incurs) and also for the exclusion (with respect to different qualified adoption expenses paid or reimbursed by his or her employer).

Because of the EGTRRA sunset, the exclusion for employer-provided adoption assistance does not apply to amounts paid or incurred after December 31, 2010.

---

[966] "EGTRRA" refers to the Economic Growth and Tax Relief Reconciliation Act of 2001, Pub. L. No. 107–16.

360

Explanation of Provision

Tax credit

For 2010, the maximum credit is increased to $13,170 per eligible child (a $1,000 increase). This increase applies to both non-special needs adoptions and special needs adoptions. Also, the adoption credit is made refundable.

The new dollar limit and phase-out of the adoption credit are adjusted for inflation in taxable years beginning after December 31, 2010.

The EGTRRA sunset is delayed for one year (i.e., the sunset becomes effective for taxable years beginning after December 31, 2011).

Adoption assistance program

The maximum exclusion is increased to $13,170 per eligible child (a $1,000 increase).

The new dollar limit and income limitations of the employer-provided adoption assistance exclusion are adjusted for inflation in taxable years beginning after December 31, 2010.

The EGTRRA sunset is delayed for one year (i.e., the sunset becomes effective for taxable years beginning after December 31, 2011).[967]

Effective Date

The provisions generally are effective for taxable years beginning after December 31, 2009.

HEALTH CARE AND EDUCATION RECONCILIATION ACT OF 2010

A. Adult Dependents (sec. 1004 of the Act and secs. 105, 162, 401, and 501 of the Code)

Present Law

Definition of dependent for exclusion for employer-provided health coverage

The Code generally provides that employees are not taxed on (that is, may "exclude" from gross income) the value of employer-provided health coverage under an accident or health plan.[968] This exclusion applies to coverage for personal injuries or sickness for employees (including retirees), their spouses and their dependents.[969] In addition, any reimbursements under an accident or health plan for medical care expenses for employees (including retirees), their spouses, and their dependents (as defined in section 152) generally are excluded from gross income.[970] Section 152 defines a dependent as a qualifying child or qualifying relative.

---

[967] Section 101(b) of the Tax Relief, Unemployment Insurance Reauthorization, and Job Creation Act of 2010 terminated the amendments made by this provision for taxable years beginning after December 31, 2011, without regard to the EGTRRA sunset.

[968] Sec 106.

[969] Treas. Reg. sec. 1.106–1.

[970] Sec. 105(b).

361

Under section 152(c), a child generally is a qualifying child of a taxpayer if the child satisfies each of five tests for the taxable year: (1) the child has the same principal place of abode as the taxpayer for more than one-half of the taxable year; (2) the child has a specified relationship to the taxpayer; (3) the child has not yet attained a specified age; (4) the child has not provided over one-half of their own support for the calendar year in which the taxable year of the taxpayer begins; and (5) the qualifying child has not filed a joint return (other than for a claim of refund) with their spouse for the taxable year beginning in the calendar year in which the taxable year of the taxpayer begins. A tie-breaking rule applies if more than one taxpayer claims a child as a qualifying child. The specified relationship is that the child is the taxpayer's son, daughter, stepson, stepdaughter, brother, sister, stepbrother, stepsister, or a descendant of any such individual. With respect to the specified age, a child must be under age 19 (or under age 24 in the case of a full-time student). However, no age limit applies with respect to individuals who are totally and permanently disabled within the meaning of section 22(e)(3) at any time during the calendar year. Other rules may apply.

Under section 152(d), a qualifying relative means an individual that satisfies four tests for the taxable year: (1) the individual bears a specified relationship to the taxpayer; (2) the individual's gross income for the calendar year in which such taxable year begins is less than the exemption amount under section 151(d); (3) the taxpayer provides more than one-half the individual's support for the calendar year in which the taxable year begins; and (4) the individual is not a qualifying child of the taxpayer or any other taxpayer for any taxable year beginning in the calendar year in which such taxable year begins. The specified relationship test for qualifying relative is satisfied if that individual is the taxpayer's: (1) child or descendant of a child; (2) brother, sister, stepbrother or stepsister; (3) father, mother or ancestor of either; (4) stepfather or stepmother; (5) niece or nephew; (6) aunt or uncle; (7) in-law; or (8) certain other individuals, who for the taxable year of the taxpayer, have the same principal place of abode as the taxpayer and are members of the taxpayer's household.[971]

Employers may agree to reimburse medical expenses of their employees (and their spouses and dependents), not covered by a health insurance plan, through flexible spending arrangements which allow reimbursement not in excess of a specified dollar amount (either elected by an employee under a cafeteria plan or otherwise specified by the employer). Reimbursements under these arrangements are also excludible from gross income as employer-provided health coverage. The same definition of dependents applies for purposes of flexible spending arrangements.

Deduction for health insurance premiums of self-employed individuals

Under present law, self-employed individuals may deduct the cost of health insurance for themselves and their spouses and de-

---

[971] Generally, same-sex partners do not qualify as dependents under section 152. In addition, same-sex partners are not recognized as spouses for purposes of the Code. The Defense of Marriage Act, Pub. L. No. 104–199.

362

pendents. The deduction is not available for any month in which the self-employed individual is eligible to participate in an employer-subsidized health plan. Moreover, the deduction may not exceed the individual's self-employment income. The deduction applies only to the cost of insurance (i.e., it does not apply to out-of-pocket expenses that are not reimbursed by insurance). The deduction does not apply for self-employment tax purposes. For purposes of the deduction, a more than two percent shareholder-employee of an S corporation is treated the same as a self-employed individual. Thus, the exclusion for employer-provided health care coverage does not apply to such individuals, but they are entitled to the deduction for health insurance costs as if they were self-employed.

Voluntary Employees' Beneficiary Associations

A VEBA is a tax-exempt entity that is a part of a plan for providing life, sick or accident benefits to its members or their dependents or designated beneficiaries.[972] No part of the net earnings of the association inures (other than through the payment of life, sick, accident or other benefits) to the benefit of any private shareholder or individual. A VEBA may be funded with employer contributions or employee contributions or a combination of employer contributions and employee contributions. The same definition of dependent applies for purposes of receipt of medical benefits through a VEBA.

Qualified plans providing retiree health benefits

A qualified pension or annuity plan can establish and maintain a separate account to provide for the payment of sickness, accident, hospitalization, and medical expenses for retired employees, their spouses and their dependents ("401(h) account"). An employer's contributions to a 401(h) account must be reasonable and ascertainable, and retiree health benefits must be subordinate to the retirement benefits provided by the plan. In addition, it must be impossible, at any time prior to the satisfaction of all retiree health liabilities under the plan, for any part of the corpus or income of the 401(h) account to be (within the taxable year or thereafter) used for, or diverted to, any purpose other than providing retiree health benefits and, upon satisfaction of all retiree health liabilities, the plan must provide that any amount remaining in the 401(h) account be returned to the employer.

Explanation of Provision

The provision amends section 105(b) to extend the general exclusion for reimbursements for medical care expenses under an employer-provided accident or health plan to any child of an employee who has not attained age 27 as of the end of the taxable year. This change is also intended to apply to the exclusion for employer-proved coverage under an accident or health plan for injuries or sickness for such a child. A parallel change is made for VEBAs and 401(h) accounts.

The provision similarly amends section 162(l) to permit self-employed individuals to take a deduction for the cost of health insur-

---

[972] Secs. 419(e) and 501(c)(9).

363

ance for any child of the taxpayer who has not attained age 27 as of the end of the taxable year.

For purposes of the provision, "child" means an individual who is a son, daughter, stepson, stepdaughter or eligible foster child of the taxpayer.[973] An eligible foster child means an individual who is placed with the taxpayer by an authorized placement agency or by judgment, decree, or other order of any court of competent jurisdiction.

Effective Date

The provision is effective as of the date of enactment (March 30, 2010).

B. Unearned Income Medicare Contribution (sec. 1402 of the Act and new sec. 1411 of the Code)

Present Law

Social Security benefits and certain Medicare benefits are financed primarily by payroll taxes on covered wages. FICA imposes tax on employers based on the amount of wages paid to an employee during the year. The tax imposed is composed of two parts: (1) the OASDI tax equal to 6.2 percent of covered wages up to the taxable wage base ($106,800 in 2010); and (2) the Medicare hospital insurance ("HI") tax amount equal to 1.45 percent of covered wages. In addition to the tax on employers, each employee is subject to FICA taxes equal to the amount of tax imposed on the employer. The employee level tax generally must be withheld and remitted to the Federal government by the employer.

As a parallel to FICA taxes, SECA imposes taxes on the net income from self-employment of self-employed individuals. The rate of the OASDI portion of SECA taxes is equal to the combined employee and employer OASDI FICA tax rates and applies to self-employment income up to the FICA taxable wage base. Similarly, the rate of the HI portion is the same as the combined employer and employee HI rates and there is no cap on the amount of self-employment income to which the rate applies.[974]

Explanation of Provision

In general

In the case of an individual, estate, or trust an unearned income Medicare contribution tax is imposed. No provision is made for the transfer of the tax imposed by this provision from the General Fund of the United States Treasury to any Trust Fund.

---

[973] Sec. 152(f)(1). Under section 152(f)(1), a legally adopted child of the taxpayer or an individual who is lawfully placed with the taxpayer for legal adoption by the taxpayer is treated as a child of the taxpayer by blood.

[974] For purposes of computing net earnings from self employment, taxpayers are permitted a deduction equal to the product of the taxpayer's earnings (determined without regard to this deduction) and one-half of the sum of the rates for OASDI tax (12.4 percent) and HI tax (2.9 percent), i.e., 7.65 percent of net earnings. This deduction reflects the fact that the FICA rates apply to an employee's wages, which do not include FICA taxes paid by the employer, whereas the self-employed individual's net earnings are economically equivalent to an employee's wages plus the employer share of FICA taxes.

364

In the case of an individual, the tax is 3.8 percent of the lesser of net investment income or the excess of modified adjusted gross income over the threshold amount.

The threshold amount is $250,000 in the case of a joint return or surviving spouse, $125,000 in the case of a married individual filing a separate return, and $200,000 in any other case.

Modified adjusted gross income is adjusted gross income increased by the amount excluded from income as foreign earned income under section 911(a)(1) (net of the deductions and exclusions disallowed with respect to the foreign earned income).

In the case of an estate or trust, the tax is 3.8 percent of the lesser of undistributed net investment income or the excess of adjusted gross income (as defined in section 67(e)) over the dollar amount at which the highest income tax bracket applicable to an estate or trust begins.

The tax does not apply to a non-resident alien or to a trust all the unexpired interests in which are devoted to charitable purposes. The tax also does not apply to a trust that is exempt from tax under section 501 or a charitable remainder trust exempt from tax under section 664.

The tax is subject to the individual estimated tax provisions. The tax is not deductible in computing any tax imposed by subtitle A of the Internal Revenue Code (relating to income taxes).

Net investment income

Net investment income is investment income reduced by the deductions properly allocable to such income.

Investment income is the sum of (i) gross income from interest, dividends, annuities, royalties, and rents (other than income derived in the ordinary course of any trade or business to which the tax does not apply), (ii) other gross income derived from any trade or business to which the tax applies, and (iii) net gain (to the extent taken into account in computing taxable income) attributable to the disposition of property other than property held in a trade or business to which the tax does not apply.[975]

In the case of a trade or business, the tax applies if the trade or business is a passive activity with respect to the taxpayer or the trade or business consists of trading financial instruments or commodities (as defined in section 475(e)(2)). The tax does not apply to other trades or businesses.

In the case of the disposition of a partnership interest or stock in an S corporation, gain or loss is taken into account only to the extent gain or loss would be taken into account by the partner or shareholder if the entity had sold all its properties for fair market value immediately before the disposition. Thus, only net gain or loss attributable to property held by the entity which is not property attributable to an active trade or business is taken into account.[976]

---

[975] Gross income does not include items, such as interest on tax-exempt bonds, veterans' benefits, and excluded gain from the sale of a principal residence, which are excluded from gross income under the income tax.

[976] For this purpose, a business of trading financial instruments or commodities is not treated as an active trade or business.

365

Income, gain, or loss on working capital is not treated as derived from a trade or business. Investment income does not include distributions from a qualified retirement plan or amounts subject to SECA tax.

Effective Date

The provision applies to taxable years beginning after December 31, 2012.

C. Excise Tax on Medical Device Manufacturers[977] (sec. 1405 of the Act and new sec. 4191 of the Code)

Present Law

Chapter 32 imposes excise taxes on sales by manufacturers of certain products. Terms and procedures related to the imposition, payment, and reporting of these excise taxes are included in various provisions within the Code.

Certain sales are exempt from the excise tax imposed on manufacturers. Exempt sales include sales (1) for use by the purchaser for further manufacture, or for resale to a second purchaser in further manufacture, (2) for export or for resale to a second purchaser for export, (3) for use by the purchaser as supplies for vessels or aircraft, (4) to a State or local government for the exclusive use of a State or local government, (5) to a nonprofit educational organization for its exclusive use, or (6) to a qualified blood collector organization for such organization's exclusive use in the collection, storage, or transportation of blood.[978] If an article is sold free of tax for resale to a second purchaser for further manufacture or for export, the exemption will not apply unless, within the six-month period beginning on the date of sale by the manufacturer, the manufacturer receives proof that the article has been exported or resold for the use in further manufacturing.[979] In general, the exemptions will not apply unless the manufacturer, the first purchaser, and the second purchaser are registered with the Secretary of the Treasury.

The lease of an article is generally considered to be a sale of such article.[980] Special rules apply for the imposition of tax to each lease payment. Rules are also imposed that treat the use of articles subject to tax by manufacturers, producers, or importers of such articles, as sales for the purpose of imposition of certain excise taxes.[981]

There are also rules for determining the price of an article on which excise tax is imposed.[982] These rules provide for: (1) the inclusion of containers, packaging, and certain transportation charges in the price, (2) determining a constructive sales price if an article is sold for less than the fair market price, and (3) deter-

---

[977] The excise tax on medical devices as imposed by this provision replaces the annual fee on medical device manufacturers and importers under section 9009 of the Patient Protection and Affordable Care Act.
[978] Sec. 4221(a).
[979] Sec. 4221(b).
[980] Sec. 4217(a).
[981] Sec. 4218.
[982] Sec. 4216.

366

mining the tax due in the case of partial payments or installment sales.

A credit or refund is generally allowed for overpayments of manufacturers excise taxes.[983] Overpayments may occur when tax-paid articles are sold for export and for certain specified uses and resales, when there are price adjustments, and where tax paid articles are subject to further manufacture. Generally, no credit or refund of any overpayment of tax is allowed or made unless the person who paid the tax establishes one of four prerequisites: (1) the tax was not included in the price of the article or otherwise collected from the person who purchased the article; (2) the tax was repaid to the ultimate purchaser of the article; (3) for overpayments due to specified uses and resales, the tax has been repaid to the ultimate vendor or the person has obtained the written consent of such ultimate vendor; or (4) the person has filed with the Secretary of the Treasury the written consent of the ultimate purchaser of the article to the allowance of the credit or making of the refund.[984]

Explanation of Provision

Under the provision, a tax equal to 2.3 percent of the sale price is imposed on the sale of any taxable medical device by the manufacturer, producer, or importer of such device. A taxable medical device is any device, defined in section 201(h) of the Federal Food, Drug, and Cosmetic Act,[985] intended for humans. The excise tax does not apply to eyeglasses, contact lenses, hearing aids, and any other medical device determined by the Secretary to be of a type that is generally purchased by the general public at retail for individual use. The Secretary may determine that a specific medical device is exempt under the provision if the device is generally sold at retail establishments (including over the internet) to individuals for their personal use. The exemption for such items is not limited by device class as defined in section 513 of the Federal Food, Drug, and Cosmetic Act. For example, items purchased by the general public at retail for individual use could include Class I items such as certain bandages and tipped applicators, Class II items such as certain pregnancy test kits and diabetes testing supplies, and Class III items such as certain denture adhesives and snake bite kits. Such items would only be exempt if they are generally designed and sold for individual use. It is anticipated that the Secretary will publish a list of medical device classifications[986] that are of a type generally purchased by the general public at retail for individual use.

---

[983] Sec. 6416.

[984] Sec. 6416(a).

[985] 21 U.S.C. 321. Section 201(h) defines device as an instrument, apparatus, implement, machine, contrivance, implant, in vitro reagent, or other similar or related article, including any component, part, or accessory, which is (1) recognized in the official National Formulary, or the United States Pharmacopeia, or any supplement to them, (2) intended for use in the diagnosis of disease or other conditions, or in the cure, mitigation, treatment, or prevention of disease, in man or other animals, or (3) intended to affect the structure or any function of the body of man or other animals, and which does not achieve its primary intended purposes through chemical action within or on the body of man or other animals and which is not dependent upon being metabolized for the achievement of its primary intended purposes.

[986] Medical device classifications are found in Title 21 of the Code of Federal Regulations, Parts 862–892.

367

The present law manufacturers excise tax exemptions for further manufacture and for export apply to tax imposed under this provision; however exemptions for use as supplies for vessels or aircraft, and for sales to State or local governments, nonprofit educational organizations, and qualified blood collector organizations are not applicable.

The provision repeals section 9009 of the Patient Protection and Affordable Care Act (relating to an annual fee on medical device manufacturers and importers).

Effective Date

The provision applies to sales after December 31, 2012.

The repeal of section 9009 of Patient Protection and Affordable Care Act is effective on the date of enactment of the Patient Protection and Affordable Care Act (March 30, 2010).

D. Elimination of Unintended Application of Cellulosic Biofuel Producer Credit (sec. 1408 of the Act and sec. 40 of the Code)

Present Law

The "cellulosic biofuel producer credit" is a nonrefundable income tax credit for each gallon of qualified cellulosic fuel production of the producer for the taxable year. The amount of the credit is generally $1.01 per gallon.[987]

"Qualified cellulosic biofuel production" is any cellulosic biofuel which is produced by the taxpayer and which is: (1) sold by the taxpayer to another person (a) for use by such other person in the production of a qualified cellulosic biofuel mixture in such person's trade or business (other than casual off-farm production), (b) for use by such other person as a fuel in a trade or business, or (c) who sells such cellulosic biofuel at retail to another person and places such cellulosic biofuel in the fuel tank of such other person; or (2) used by the producer for any purpose described in (1)(a), (b), or (c).

"Cellulosic biofuel" means any liquid fuel that (1) is produced in the United States and used as fuel in the United States, (2) is derived from any lignocellulosic or hemicellulosic matter that is available on a renewable or recurring basis, and (3) meets the registration requirements for fuels and fuel additives established by the Environmental Protection Agency ("EPA") under section 211 of the Clean Air Act. The cellulosic biofuel producer credit cannot be claimed unless the taxpayer is registered by the IRS as a producer of cellulosic biofuel.

Cellulosic biofuel eligible for the section 40 credit is precluded from qualifying as biodiesel, renewable diesel, or alternative fuel for purposes of the applicable income tax credit, excise tax credit, or payment provisions relating to those fuels.[988]

Because it is a credit under section 40(a), the cellulosic biofuel producer credit is part of the general business credits in section 38.

---

[987] In the case of cellulosic biofuel that is alcohol, the $1.01 credit amount is reduced by the credit amount of the alcohol mixture credit, and for ethanol, the credit amount for small ethanol producers, as in effect at the time the cellulosic biofuel fuel is produced.

[988] See secs. 40A(d)(1), 40A(f)(3), and 6426(h).

368

However, the credit can only be carried forward three taxable years after the termination of the credit. The credit is also allowable against the alternative minimum tax. Under section 87, the credit is included in gross income. The cellulosic biofuel producer credit terminates on December 31, 2012.

The kraft process for making paper produces a byproduct called black liquor, which has been used for decades by paper manufacturers as a fuel in the papermaking process. Black liquor is composed of water, lignin and the spent chemicals used to break down the wood. The amount of the biomass in black liquor varies. The portion of the black liquor that is not consumed as a fuel source for the paper mills is recycled back into the papermaking process. Black liquor has ash content (mineral and other inorganic matter) significantly above that of other fuels.

In an informal Chief Counsel Advice ("CCA"), the IRS has concluded that black liquor is a liquid fuel from biomass and may qualify for the cellulosic biofuel producer credit, as well as the refundable alternative fuel mixture credit.[989] A taxpayer cannot claim both the alternative fuel mixture credit and the cellulosic biofuel producer credit. The alternative fuel credits and payment provisions expired December 31, 2009.

Explanation of Provision

The provision modifies the cellulosic biofuel producer credit to exclude fuels with significant water, sediment, or ash content, such as black liquor. Consequently, credits will cease to be available for these fuels. Specifically, the provision excludes from the definition of cellulosic biofuel any fuels that (1) are more than four percent (determined by weight) water and sediment in any combination, or (2) have an ash content of more than one percent (determined by weight). Water content (including both free water and water in solution with dissolved solids) is determined by distillation, using for example ASTM method D95 or a similar method suitable to the specific fuel being tested. Sediment consists of solid particles that are dispersed in the liquid fuel and is determined by centrifuge or extraction using, for example, ASTM method D1796 or D473 or similar method that reports sediment content in weight percent. Ash is the residue remaining after combustion of the sample using a specified method, such as ASTM D3174 or a similar method suitable for the fuel being tested.

Effective Date

The provision is effective for fuels sold or used on or after January 1, 2010.

---

[989] Chief Couns. Adv. 200941011 (June 30, 2009). The Code provides for a tax credit of 50 cents for each gallon of alternative fuel used to produce an alternative fuel mixture that is used or sold for use as a fuel. (sec. 6426(e)). Under Notice 2006–92, an alternative fuel mixture is a mixture of alternative fuel and a taxable fuel (such as diesel) that contains at least 0.1 percent taxable fuel. Liquid fuel derived from biomass is an alternative fuel (sec. 6426(d)(2)(G)). Diesel fuel has been added to black liquor to qualify for the alternative mixture credit and the mixture is burned in a recovery boiler as fuel. Persons that have an alternative fuel mixture credit amount in excess of their taxable fuel excise tax liability may make a claim for payment from the Treasury in the amount of the excess.

369

E. Codification of Economic Substance Doctrine and Imposition of Penalties (sec. 1409 of the Act and secs. 6662, 6662A, 6664, 6676, and 7701 of the Code)

Present Law

In general

The Code provides detailed rules specifying the computation of taxable income, including the amount, timing, source, and character of items of income, gain, loss, and deduction. These rules permit both taxpayers and the government to compute taxable income with reasonable accuracy and predictability. Taxpayers generally may plan their transactions in reliance on these rules to determine the Federal income tax consequences arising from the transactions.

In addition to the statutory provisions, courts have developed several doctrines that can be applied to deny the tax benefits of a tax-motivated transaction, notwithstanding that the transaction may satisfy the literal requirements of a specific tax provision. These common-law doctrines are not entirely distinguishable, and their application to a given set of facts is often blurred by the courts, the IRS, and litigants. Although these doctrines serve an important role in the administration of the tax system, they can be seen as at odds with an objective, "rule-based" system of taxation.

One common-law doctrine applied over the years is the "economic substance" doctrine. In general, this doctrine denies tax benefits arising from transactions that do not result in a meaningful change to the taxpayer's economic position other than a purported reduction in Federal income tax.[990]

Economic substance doctrine

Courts generally deny claimed tax benefits if the transaction that gives rise to those benefits lacks economic substance independent of U.S. Federal income tax considerations—notwithstanding that the purported activity actually occurred. The Tax Court has described the doctrine as follows:

> The tax law . . . requires that the intended transactions have economic substance separate and distinct from economic benefit achieved solely by tax reduction. The doctrine of economic substance becomes applicable, and a judicial remedy is warranted, where a taxpayer seeks to claim tax benefits, unin-

---

[990] See, e.g., *ACM Partnership v.* Commissioner, 157 F.3d 231 (3d Cir. 1998), *aff'g* 73 T.C.M. (CCH) 2189 (1997), *cert.* denied 526 U.S. 1017 (1999); *Klamath Strategic Investment Fund, LLC v. United States,* 472 F. Supp. 2d 885 (E.D. Texas 2007), *aff'd* 568 F.3d 537 (5th Cir. 2009); *Coltec Industries, Inc. v. United States,* 454 F.3d 1340 (Fed. Cir. 2006), *vacating and remanding* 62 Fed. Cl. 716 (2004) (slip opinion pp. 123–124, 128); *cert. denied,* 127 S. Ct. 1261 (Mem.) (2007).

Closely related doctrines also applied by the courts (sometimes interchangeable with the economic substance doctrine) include the "sham transaction doctrine" and the "business purpose doctrine." *See, e.g., Knetsch v. United States,* 364 U.S. 361 (1960) (denying interest deductions on a "sham transaction" that lacked "commercial economic substance"). Certain "substance over form" cases involving tax-indifferent parties, in which courts have found that the substance of the transaction did not comport with the form asserted by the taxpayer, have also involved examination of whether the change in economic position that occurred, if any, was consistent with the form asserted, and whether the claimed business purpose supported the particular tax benefits that were claimed. *See, e.g., TIFD III–E, Inc. v. United States,* 459 F.3d 220 (2d Cir. 2006); *BB&T Corporation v. United States,* 2007–1 USTC P 50,130 (M.D.N.C. 2007), aff'd 523 F.3d 461 (4th Cir. 2008). Although the Second Circuit found for the government in *TIFD III–E, Inc.,* on remand to consider issues under section 704(e), the District Court found for the taxpayer. See, *TIFD III–E Inc. v. United States,* No. 3:01–cv–01839, 2009 WL 3208650 (D. Conn. Oct. 23, 2009).

370

tended by Congress, by means of transactions that serve no economic purpose other than tax savings.[991]

Business purpose doctrine

A common law doctrine that often is considered together with the economic substance doctrine is the business purpose doctrine. The business purpose doctrine involves an inquiry into the subjective motives of the taxpayer—that is, whether the taxpayer intended the transaction to serve some useful non-tax purpose. In making this determination, some courts have bifurcated a transaction in which activities with non-tax objectives have been combined with unrelated activities having only tax-avoidance objectives, in order to disallow the tax benefits of the overall transaction.[992]

Application by the courts

Elements of the doctrine

There is a lack of uniformity regarding the proper application of the economic substance doctrine.[993] Some courts apply a conjunctive test that requires a taxpayer to establish the presence of both economic substance (i.e., the objective component) and business purpose (i.e., the subjective component) in order for the transaction to survive judicial scrutiny.[994] A narrower approach used by some courts is to conclude that either a business purpose or economic substance is sufficient to respect the transaction.[995] A third approach regards economic substance and business purpose as "simply more precise factors to consider" in determining whether a transaction has any practical economic effects other than the creation of tax benefits.[996]

One decision by the Court of Federal Claims questioned the continuing viability of the doctrine. That court also stated that "the use of the 'economic substance' doctrine to trump 'mere compliance

---

[991] *ACM Partnership v.* Commissioner, 73 T.C.M. at 2215.

[992] See, *ACM Partnership v.* Commissioner, 157 F.3d at 256 n.48.

[993] "The casebooks are glutted with [economic substance] tests. Many such tests proliferate because they give the comforting illusion of consistency and precision. They often obscure rather than clarify." *Collins v.* Commissioner, 857 F.2d 1383, 1386 (9th Cir. 1988).

[994] See, e.g., *Pasternak v.* Commissioner, 990 F.2d 893, 898 (6th Cir. 1993) ("The threshold question is whether the transaction has economic substance. If the answer is yes, the question becomes whether the taxpayer was motivated by profit to participate in the transaction."). See also, *Klamath Strategic Investment Fund v.* United States, 568 F. 3d 537, (5th Cir. 2009) (even if taxpayers may have had a profit motive, a transaction was disregarded where it did not in fact have any realistic possibility of profit and funding was never at risk).

[995] See, e.g., *Rice's Toyota World v.* Commissioner, 752 F.2d 89, 91–92 (4th Cir. 1985) ("To treat a transaction as a sham, the court must find that the taxpayer was motivated by no business purposes other than obtaining tax benefits in entering the transaction, and, second, that the transaction has no economic substance because no reasonable possibility of a profit exists."); *IES Industries v.* United States, 253 F.3d 350, 358 (8th Cir. 2001) ("In determining whether a transaction is a sham for tax purposes [under the Eighth Circuit test], a transaction will be characterized as a sham if it is not motivated by any economic purpose outside of tax considerations (the business purpose test), and if it is without economic substance because no real potential for profit exists (the economic substance test)."). As noted earlier, the economic substance doctrine and the sham transaction doctrine are similar and sometimes are applied interchangeably. For a more detailed discussion of the sham transaction doctrine, see, e.g., Joint Committee on Taxation, *Study of Present-Law Penalty and Interest Provisions as Required by Section 3801 of the Internal Revenue Service Restructuring and Reform Act of 1998 (including Provisions Relating to Corporate Tax Shelters)* (JCS–3–99), p. 182.

[996] See, e.g., *ACM Partnership v. Commissioner*, 157 F.3d at 247; *James v. Commissioner*, 899 F.2d 905, 908 (10th Cir. 1995); *Sacks v. Commissioner*, 69 F.3d 982, 985 (9th Cir. 1995) ("Instead, the consideration of business purpose and economic substance are simply more precise factors to consider . . . We have repeatedly and carefully noted that this formulation cannot be used as a 'rigid two-step analysis'.")

371

with the Code' would violate the separation of powers" though that court also found that the particular transaction at issue in the case did not lack economic substance. The Court of Appeals for the Federal Circuit ("Federal Circuit Court") overruled the Court of Federal Claims decision, reiterating the viability of the economic substance doctrine and concluding that the transaction in question violated that doctrine.[997] The Federal Circuit Court stated that "[w]hile the doctrine may well also apply if the taxpayer's sole subjective motivation is tax avoidance even if the transaction has economic substance, [footnote omitted], a lack of economic substance is sufficient to disqualify the transaction without proof that the taxpayer's sole motive is tax avoidance."[998]

Nontax economic benefits

There also is a lack of uniformity regarding the type of non-tax economic benefit a taxpayer must establish in order to demonstrate that a transaction has economic substance. Some courts have denied tax benefits on the grounds that a stated business benefit of a particular structure was not in fact obtained by that structure.[999] Several courts have denied tax benefits on the grounds that the subject transactions lacked profit potential.[1000] In addition, some courts have applied the economic substance doctrine to disallow tax benefits in transactions in which a taxpayer was exposed to risk and the transaction had a profit potential, but the court concluded that the economic risks and profit potential were insignificant when compared to the tax benefits.[1001] Under this analysis, the taxpayer's profit potential must be more than nominal. Conversely, other courts view the application of the economic substance doctrine as requiring an objective determination of whether a "reasonable possibility of profit" from the transaction existed apart from the tax benefits.[1002] In these cases, in assessing whether a reason-

---

[997] Coltec Industries, Inc. v. United States, 62 Fed. Cl. 716 (2004) (slip opinion at 123–124, 128); vacated and remanded, 454 F.3d 1340 (Fed. Cir. 2006), cert. denied, 127 S. Ct. 1261 (Mem.) (2007).

[998] The Federal Circuit Court stated that "when the taxpayer claims a deduction, it is the taxpayer who bears the burden of proving that the transaction has economic substance." The Federal Circuit Court quoted a decision of its predecessor court, stating that "Gregory v. Helvering requires that a taxpayer carry an unusually heavy burden when he attempts to demonstrate that Congress intended to give favorable tax treatment to the kind of transaction that would never occur absent the motive of tax avoidance." The Court also stated that "while the taxpayer's subjective motivation may be pertinent to the existence of a tax avoidance purpose, all courts have looked to the objective reality of a transaction in assessing its economic substance." Coltec Industries, Inc. v. United States, 454 F.3d at 1355, 1356.

[999] See, e.g., Coltec Industries v. United States, 454 F.3d 1340 (Fed. Cir. 2006). The court analyzed the transfer to a subsidiary of a note purporting to provide high stock basis in exchange for a purported assumption of liabilities, and held these transactions unnecessary to accomplish any business purpose of using a subsidiary to manage asbestos liabilities. The court also held that the purported business purpose of adding a barrier to veil-piercing claims by third parties was not accomplished by the transaction. 454 F.3d at 1358–1360 (Fed. Cir. 2006).

[1000] See, e.g., Knetsch, 364 U.S. at 361; Goldstein v. Commissioner, 364 F.2d 734 (2d Cir. 1966) (holding that an unprofitable, leveraged acquisition of Treasury bills, and accompanying prepaid interest deduction, lacked economic substance).

[1001] See, e.g., Goldstein v. Commissioner, 364 F.2d at 739–40 (disallowing deduction even though taxpayer had a possibility of small gain or loss by owning Treasury bills); Sheldon v. Commissioner, 94 T.C. 738, 768 (1990) (stating that "potential for gain . . . is infinitesimally nominal and vastly insignificant when considered in comparison with the claimed deductions").

[1002] See, e.g., Rice's Toyota World v. Commissioner, 752 F.2d 89, 94 (4th Cir. 1985) (the economic substance inquiry requires an objective determination of whether a reasonable possibility of profit from the transaction existed apart from tax benefits); Compaq Computer Corp. v. Commissioner, 277 F.3d 778, 781 (5th Cir. 2001) (applied the same test, citing Rice's Toyota World);

Continued

372

able possibility of profit exists, it may be sufficient if there is a nominal amount of pre-tax profit as measured against expected tax benefits.

Financial accounting benefits

In determining whether a taxpayer had a valid business purpose for entering into a transaction, at least two courts have concluded that financial accounting benefits arising from tax savings do not qualify as a non-tax business purpose.[1003] However, based on court decisions that recognize the importance of financial accounting treatment, taxpayers have asserted that financial accounting benefits arising from tax savings can satisfy the business purpose test.[1004]

Tax-indifferent parties

A number of cases have involved transactions structured to allocate income for Federal tax purposes to a tax-indifferent party, with a corresponding deduction, or favorable basis result, to a taxable person. The income allocated to the tax-indifferent party for tax purposes was structured to exceed any actual economic income to be received by the tax indifferent party from the transaction. Courts have sometimes concluded that this particular type of transaction did not satisfy the economic substance doctrine.[1005] In other cases, courts have indicated that the substance of a transaction did not support the form of income allocations asserted by the taxpayer and have questioned whether asserted business purpose or other standards were met.[1006]

Penalty regime

General accuracy-related penalty

An accuracy-related penalty under section 6662 applies to the portion of any underpayment that is attributable to (1) negligence, (2) any substantial understatement of income tax, (3) any substantial valuation misstatement, (4) any substantial overstatement of pension liabilities, or (5) any substantial estate or gift tax valuation understatement. If the correct income tax liability exceeds that reported by the taxpayer by the greater of 10 percent of the correct tax or $5,000 (or, in the case of corporations, by the lesser of (a) 10 percent of the correct tax (or $10,000 if greater) or (b) $10 million), then a substantial understatement exists and a penalty may

---

IES Industries v. United States, 253 F.3d 350, 354 (8th Cir. 2001); *Wells Fargo & Company v. United States*, No. 06–628T, 2010 WL 94544, at *57–58 (Fed. Cl. Jan. 8, 2010).

[1003] See *American Electric Power, Inc. v. United States*, 136 F. Supp. 2d 762, 791–92 (S.D. Ohio 2001), *aff'd*, 326 F.3d.737 (6th Cir. 2003) and *Wells Fargo & Company v. United States*, No. 06–628T, 2010 WL 94544, at *59 (Fed. Cl. Jan. 8, 2010).

[1004] See, e.g., Joint Committee on Taxation, *Report of Investigation of Enron Corporation and Related Entities Regarding Federal Tax and Compensation Issues, and Policy Recommendations* (JSC–3–03), February, 2003 ("Enron Report"), Volume III at C–93, 289. Enron Corporation relied on *Frank Lyon Co. v. United States*, 435 U.S. 561, 577–78 (1978), and *Newman v. Commissioner*, 902 F.2d 159, 163 (2d Cir. 1990), to argue that financial accounting benefits arising from tax savings constitute a good business purpose.

[1005] See, e.g., *ACM Partnership v. Commissioner*, 157 F.3d 231 (3d Cir. 1998), *aff'g* 73 T.C.M. (CCH) 2189 (1997), *cert. denied* 526 U.S. 1017 (1999).

[1006] See, e.g., *TIFD III–E, Inc. v. United States*, 459 F.3d 220 (2d Cir. 2006). Although the Second Circuit found for the government in *TIFD III–E, Inc.*, on remand to consider issues under section 704(e), the District Court found for the taxpayer. See, *TIFD III–E Inc. v. United States*, No. 3:01–cv–01839, 2009 WL 3208650 (Oct. 23, 2009).

373

be imposed equal to 20 percent of the underpayment of tax attributable to the understatement.[1007] The section 6662 penalty is increased to 40 percent in the case of gross valuation misstatements as defined in section 6662(h). Except in the case of tax shelters,[1008] the amount of any understatement is reduced by any portion attributable to an item if (1) the treatment of the item is supported by substantial authority, or (2) facts relevant to the tax treatment of the item were adequately disclosed and there was a reasonable basis for its tax treatment. The Treasury Secretary may prescribe a list of positions which the Secretary believes do not meet the requirements for substantial authority under this provision.

The section 6662 penalty generally is abated (even with respect to tax shelters) in cases in which the taxpayer can demonstrate that there was "reasonable cause" for the underpayment and that the taxpayer acted in good faith.[1009] The relevant regulations for a tax shelter provide that reasonable cause exists where the taxpayer "reasonably relies in good faith on an opinion based on a professional tax advisor's analysis of the pertinent facts and authorities [that] . . . unambiguously concludes that there is a greater than 50-percent likelihood that the tax treatment of the item will be upheld if challenged" by the IRS.[1010] For transactions other than tax shelters, the relevant regulations provide a facts and circumstances test, the most important factor generally being the extent of the taxpayer's effort to assess the proper tax liability. If a taxpayer relies on an opinion, reliance is not reasonable if the taxpayer knows or should have known that the advisor lacked knowledge in the relevant aspects of Federal tax law, or if the taxpayer fails to disclose a fact that it knows or should have known is relevant. Certain additional requirements apply with respect to the advice.[1011]

Listed transactions and reportable avoidance transactions

In general

A separate accuracy-related penalty under section 6662A applies to any "listed transaction" and to any other "reportable transaction" that is not a listed transaction, if a significant purpose of such transaction is the avoidance or evasion of Federal income

---

[1007] Sec. 6662.

[1008] A tax shelter is defined for this purpose as a partnership or other entity, an investment plan or arrangement, or any other plan or arrangement if a significant purpose of such partnership, other entity, plan, or arrangement is the avoidance or evasion of Federal income tax. Sec. 6662(d)(2)(C).

[1009] Sec. 6664(c).

[1010] Treas. Reg. sec. 1.6662–4(g)(4)(i)(B); Treas. Reg. sec. 1.6664–4(c).

[1011] See Treas. Reg. Sec. 1.6664–4(c). In addition to the requirements applicable to taxpayers under the regulations, advisors may be subject to potential penalties under section 6694 (applicable to return preparers), and to monetary penalties and other sanctions under Circular 230 (which provides rules governing persons practicing before the IRS). Under Circular 230, if a transaction is a "covered transaction" (a term that includes listed transactions and certain non-listed reportable transactions) a "more likely than not" confidence level is required for written tax advice that may be relied upon by a taxpayer for the purpose of avoiding penalties, and certain other standards must also be met. Treasury Dept. Circular 230 (Rev. 4–2008) Sec. 10.35. For other tax advice, Circular 230 generally requires a lower "realistic possibility" confidence level or a "non-frivolous" confidence level coupled with advising the client of any opportunity to avoid the accuracy related penalty under section 6662 by adequate disclosure. Treasury Dept. Circular 230 (Rev. 4–2008) Sec. 10.34.

374

tax [1012] (hereinafter referred to as a "reportable avoidance transaction"). The penalty rate and defenses available to avoid the penalty vary depending on whether the transaction was adequately disclosed.

Both listed transactions and other reportable transactions are allowed to be described by the Treasury Department under section 6011 as transactions that must be reported, and section 6707A(c) imposes a penalty for failure to adequately report such transactions under section 6011. A reportable transaction is defined as one that the Treasury Secretary determines is required to be disclosed because it is determined to have a potential for tax avoidance or evasion. [1013] A listed transaction is defined as a reportable transaction which is the same as, or substantially similar to, a transaction specifically identified by the Secretary as a tax avoidance transaction for purposes of the reporting disclosure requirements. [1014]

Disclosed transactions

In general, a 20-percent accuracy-related penalty is imposed on any understatement attributable to an adequately disclosed listed transaction or reportable avoidance transaction. [1015] The only exception to the penalty is if the taxpayer satisfies a more stringent reasonable cause and good faith exception (hereinafter referred to as the "strengthened reasonable cause exception"), which is described below. The strengthened reasonable cause exception is available only if the relevant facts affecting the tax treatment were adequately disclosed, there is or was substantial authority for the claimed tax treatment, and the taxpayer reasonably believed that the claimed tax treatment was more likely than not the proper treatment. A "reasonable belief" must be based on the facts and law as they exist at the time that the return in question is filed, and not take into account the possibility that a return would not be audited. Moreover, reliance on professional advice may support a "reasonable belief" only in certain circumstances. [1016]

Undisclosed transactions

If the taxpayer does not adequately disclose the transaction, the strengthened reasonable cause exception is not available (i.e., a strict liability penalty generally applies), and the taxpayer is subject to an increased penalty equal to 30 percent of the understatement. [1017] However, a taxpayer will be treated as having adequately disclosed a transaction for this purpose if the IRS Commissioner has separately rescinded the separate penalty under section 6707A for failure to disclose a reportable transaction. [1018] The IRS Commissioner is authorized to do this only if the failure does not relate to a listed transaction and only if rescinding the penalty would promote compliance and effective tax administration. [1019]

[1012] Sec. 6662A(b)(2).
[1013] Sec. 6707A(c)(1).
[1014] Sec. 6707A(c)(2).
[1015] Sec. 6662A(a).
[1016] Section 6664(d)(3)(B) does not allow a reasonable belief to be based on a "disqualified opinion" or on an opinion from a "disqualified tax advisor."
[1017] Sec. 6662A(c).
[1018] Sec. 6664(d).
[1019] Sec. 6707A(d).

375

A public entity that is required to pay a penalty for an undisclosed listed or reportable transaction must disclose the imposition of the penalty in reports to the SEC for such periods as the Secretary specifies. The disclosure to the SEC applies without regard to whether the taxpayer determines the amount of the penalty to be material to the reports in which the penalty must appear, and any failure to disclose such penalty in the reports is treated as a failure to disclose a listed transaction. A taxpayer must disclose a penalty in reports to the SEC once the taxpayer has exhausted its administrative and judicial remedies with respect to the penalty (or if earlier, when paid).[1020]

Determination of the understatement amount

The penalty is applied to the amount of any understatement attributable to the listed or reportable avoidance transaction without regard to other items on the tax return. For purposes of this provision, the amount of the understatement is determined as the sum of: (1) the product of the highest corporate or individual tax rate (as appropriate) and the increase in taxable income resulting from the difference between the taxpayer's treatment of the item and the proper treatment of the item (without regard to other items on the tax return);[1021] and (2) the amount of any decrease in the aggregate amount of credits which results from a difference between the taxpayer's treatment of an item and the proper tax treatment of such item.

Except as provided in regulations, a taxpayer's treatment of an item will not take into account any amendment or supplement to a return if the amendment or supplement is filed after the earlier of when the taxpayer is first contacted regarding an examination of the return or such other date as specified by the Secretary.[1022]

Strengthened reasonable cause exception

A penalty is not imposed under section 6662A with respect to any portion of an understatement if it is shown that there was reasonable cause for such portion and the taxpayer acted in good faith. Such a showing requires: (1) adequate disclosure of the facts affecting the transaction in accordance with the regulations under section 6011;[1023] (2) that there is or was substantial authority for such treatment; and (3) that the taxpayer reasonably believed that such treatment was more likely than not the proper treatment. For this purpose, a taxpayer will be treated as having a reasonable belief with respect to the tax treatment of an item only if such belief: (1) is based on the facts and law that exist at the time the tax return (that includes the item) is filed; and (2) relates solely to the taxpayer's chances of success on the merits and does not take into account the possibility that (a) a return will not be audited, (b) the

---

[1020] Sec. 6707A(e).

[1021] For this purpose, any reduction in the excess of deductions allowed for the taxable year over gross income for such year, and any reduction in the amount of capital losses which would (without regard to section 1211) be allowed for such year, will be treated as an increase in taxable income. Sec. 6662A(b).

[1022] Sec. 6662A(e)(3).

[1023] See the previous discussion regarding the penalty for failing to disclose a reportable transaction.

376

treatment will not be raised on audit, or (c) the treatment will be resolved through settlement if raised.[1024]

A taxpayer may (but is not required to) rely on an opinion of a tax advisor in establishing its reasonable belief with respect to the tax treatment of the item. However, a taxpayer may not rely on an opinion of a tax advisor for this purpose if the opinion (1) is provided by a "disqualified tax advisor" or (2) is a "disqualified opinion."

Disqualified tax advisor

A disqualified tax advisor is any advisor who: (1) is a material advisor [1025] and who participates in the organization, management, promotion, or sale of the transaction or is related (within the meaning of section 267(b) or 707(b)(1)) to any person who so participates; (2) is compensated directly or indirectly [1026] by a material advisor with respect to the transaction; (3) has a fee arrangement with respect to the transaction that is contingent on all or part of the intended tax benefits from the transaction being sustained; or (4) as determined under regulations prescribed by the Secretary, has a disqualifying financial interest with respect to the transaction.

A material advisor is considered as participating in the "organization" of a transaction if the advisor performs acts relating to the development of the transaction. This may include, for example, preparing documents: (1) establishing a structure used in connection with the transaction (such as a partnership agreement); (2) describing the transaction (such as an offering memorandum or other statement describing the transaction); or (3) relating to the registration of the transaction with any Federal, state, or local government body.[1027] Participation in the "management" of a transaction means involvement in the decision-making process regarding any business activity with respect to the transaction. Participation in the "promotion or sale" of a transaction means involvement in the marketing or solicitation of the transaction to others. Thus, an advisor who provides information about the transaction to a potential participant is involved in the promotion or sale of a transaction, as is any advisor who recommends the transaction to a potential participant.

[1024] Sec. 6664(d).

[1025] The term "material advisor" means any person who provides any material aid, assistance, or advice with respect to organizing, managing, promoting, selling, implementing, or carrying out any reportable transaction, and who derives gross income in excess of $50,000 in the case of a reportable transaction substantially all of the tax benefits from which are provided to natural persons ($250,000 in any other case). Sec. 6111(b)(1).

[1026] This situation could arise, for example, when an advisor has an arrangement or understanding (oral or written) with an organizer, manager, or promoter of a reportable transaction that such party will recommend or refer potential participants to the advisor for an opinion regarding the tax treatment of the transaction.

[1027] An advisor should not be treated as participating in the organization of a transaction if the advisor's only involvement with respect to the organization of the transaction is the rendering of an opinion regarding the tax consequences of such transaction. However, such an advisor may be a "disqualified tax advisor" with respect to the transaction if the advisor participates in the management, promotion, or sale of the transaction (or if the advisor is compensated by a material advisor, has a fee arrangement that is contingent on the tax benefits of the transaction, or as determined by the Secretary, has a continuing financial interest with respect to the transaction). See Notice 2005–12, 2005–1 C.B. 494, regarding disqualified compensation arrangements.

377

Disqualified opinion

An opinion may not be relied upon if the opinion: (1) is based on unreasonable factual or legal assumptions (including assumptions as to future events); (2) unreasonably relies upon representations, statements, findings or agreements of the taxpayer or any other person; (3) does not identify and consider all relevant facts; or (4) fails to meet any other requirement prescribed by the Secretary.

Coordination with other penalties

Any understatement upon which a penalty is imposed under section 6662A is not subject to the accuracy related penalty for underpayments under section 6662.[1028] However, that understatement is included for purposes of determining whether any understatement (as defined in sec. 6662(d)(2)) is a substantial understatement under section 6662(d)(1).[1029] Thus, in the case of an understatement (as defined in sec. 6662(d)(2)), the amount of the understatement (determined without regard to section 6662A(e)(1)(A)) is increased by the aggregate amount of reportable transaction understatements for purposes of determining whether the understatement is a substantial understatement. The section 6662(a) penalty applies only to the excess of the amount of the substantial understatement (if any) after section 6662A(e)(1)(A) is applied over the aggregate amount of reportable transaction understatements.[1030] Accordingly, every understatement is penalized, but only under one penalty provision.

The penalty imposed under section 6662A does not apply to any portion of an understatement to which a fraud penalty applies under section 6663 or to which the 40-percent penalty for gross valuation misstatements under section 6662(h) applies.[1031]

Erroneous claim for refund or credit

If a claim for refund or credit with respect to income tax (other than a claim relating to the earned income tax credit) is made for an excessive amount, unless it is shown that the claim for such excessive amount has a reasonable basis, the person making such claim is subject to a penalty in an amount equal to 20 percent of the excessive amount.[1032]

The term "excessive amount" means the amount by which the amount of the claim for refund for any taxable year exceeds the amount of such claim allowable for the taxable year.

This penalty does not apply to any portion of the excessive amount of a claim for refund or credit which is subject to a penalty imposed under the accuracy related or fraud penalty provisions (including the general accuracy related penalty, or the penalty with respect to listed and reportable transactions, described above).

[1028] Sec. 6662(b) (flush language). In addition, section 6662(b) provides that section 6662 does not apply to any portion of an underpayment on which a fraud penalty is imposed under section 6663.

[1029] Sec. 6662A(e)(1).

[1030] Sec. 6662(d)(2)(A) (flush language).

[1031] Sec. 6662A(e)(2).

[1032] Sec. 6676.

378

Reasons for Change

Tax avoidance transactions have relied upon the interaction of highly technical tax law provisions to produce tax consequences not contemplated by Congress. When successful, taxpayers who engage in these transactions enlarge the tax gap by gaining unintended tax relief and by undermining the overall integrity of the tax system.

A strictly rule-based tax system cannot efficiently prescribe the appropriate outcome of every conceivable transaction that might be devised and is, as a result, incapable of preventing all unintended consequences. Thus, many courts have long recognized the need to supplement tax rules with anti-tax-avoidance standards, such as the economic substance doctrine, in order to assure the Congressional purpose is achieved. The Congress recognizes that the IRS has achieved a number of recent successes in litigation. The Congress believes it is still desirable to provide greater clarity and uniformity in the application of the economic substance doctrine in order to improve its effectiveness at deterring unintended consequences.

The Congress believes that a stronger penalty under section 6662 should be imposed on understatements attributable to non-economic substance and similar transactions, to improve compliance by deterring taxpayers from entering such transactions. The Congress is concerned that under present law there is a potential to avoid penalties in such cases (based for example on certain levels of tax advice), and that the potential that a taxpayer in such cases may pay only the tax due plus interest is not a sufficient deterrent. The Congress therefore believes it is appropriate to impose a new strict liability penalty in such cases.

Explanation of Provision

The provision clarifies and enhances the application of the economic substance doctrine. Under the provision, new section 7701(o) provides that in the case of any transaction [1033] to which the economic substance doctrine is relevant, such transaction is treated as having economic substance only if (1) the transaction changes in a meaningful way (apart from Federal income tax effects) the taxpayer's economic position, and (2) the taxpayer has a substantial purpose (apart from Federal income tax effects) for entering into such transaction. The provision provides a uniform definition of economic substance, but does not alter the flexibility of the courts in other respects.

The determination of whether the economic substance doctrine is relevant to a transaction is made in the same manner as if the provision had never been enacted. Thus, the provision does not change present law standards in determining when to utilize an economic substance analysis. [1034]

[1033] The term "transaction" includes a series of transactions.

[1034] If the realization of the tax benefits of a transaction is consistent with the Congressional purpose or plan that the tax benefits were designed by Congress to effectuate, it is not intended that such tax benefits be disallowed. See, e.g., Treas. Reg. sec. 1.269–2, stating that characteristic of circumstances in which an amount otherwise constituting a deduction, credit, or other allowance is not available are those in which the effect of the deduction, credit, or other allowance would be to distort the liability of the particular taxpayer when the essential nature

379

The provision is not intended to alter the tax treatment of certain basic business transactions that, under longstanding judicial and administrative practice are respected, merely because the choice between meaningful economic alternatives is largely or entirely based on comparative tax advantages. Among [1035] these basic transactions are (1) the choice between capitalizing a business enterprise with debt or equity; [1036] (2) a U.S. person's choice between utilizing a foreign corporation or a domestic corporation to make a foreign investment; [1037] (3) the choice to enter a transaction or series of transactions that constitute a corporate organization or reorganization under subchapter C; [1038] and (4) the choice to utilize a related-party entity in a transaction, provided that the arm's length standard of section 482 and other applicable concepts are satisfied.[1039] Leasing transactions, like all other types of transactions, will continue to be analyzed in light of all the facts and circumstances.[1040] As under present law, whether a particular transaction meets the requirements for specific treatment under any of these provisions is a question of facts and circumstances. Also, the fact that a transaction meets the requirements for specific treatment under any provision of the Code is not determinative of whether a transaction or series of transactions of which it is a part has economic substance.[1041]

The provision does not alter the court's ability to aggregate, disaggregate, or otherwise recharacterize a transaction when applying the doctrine. For example, the provision reiterates the present-law ability of the courts to bifurcate a transaction in which inde-

---

of the transaction or situation is examined in the light of the basic purpose or plan which the deduction, credit, or other allowance was designed by the Congress to effectuate. Thus, for example, it is not intended that a tax credit (e.g., section 42 (low-income housing credit), section 45 (production tax credit), section 45D (new markets tax credit), section 47 (rehabilitation credit), section 48 (energy credit), etc.) be disallowed in a transaction pursuant to which, in form and substance, a taxpayer makes the type of investment or undertakes the type of activity that the credit was intended to encourage.

[1035] The examples are illustrative and not exclusive.

[1036] See, e.g., *John Kelley Co. v. Commissioner,* 326 U.S. 521 (1946) (respecting debt characterization in one case and not in the other, based on all the facts and circumstances).

[1037] See, e.g., *Sam Siegel v. Commissioner,* 45. T.C. 566 (1966), acq. 1966–2 C.B. 3. But see *Commissioner v. Bollinger,* 485 U.S. 340 (1988) (agency principles applied to title-holding corporation under the facts and circumstances).

[1038] See, e.g., *Rev. Proc. 2010–3 2010–1 I.R.B. 110, Secs. 3.01(38), (39), (40), and (42)* (IRS will not rule on certain matters relating to incorporations or reorganizations unless there is a "significant issue"); *compare Gregory v. Helvering.* 293 U.S. 465 (1935).

[1039] See, e.g., *National Carbide v. Commissioner,* 336 U.S. 422 (1949), *Moline Properties v. Commissioner,* 319 U.S. 435 (1943); *compare, e.g. Aiken Industries, Inc. v. Commissioner,* 56 T.C. 925 (1971), acq., 1972–2 C.B. 1; *Commissioner v. Bollinger,* 485 U.S. 340 (1988); see also sec. 7701(l).

[1040] See, e.g., *Frank Lyon Co. v. Commissioner,* 435 U.S. 561 (1978); *Hilton v. Commissioner,* 74 T.C. 305, aff'd, 671 F. 2d 316 (9th Cir. 1982), *cert. denied,* 459 U.S. 907 (1982); *Coltec Industries v. United States,* 454 F.3d 1340 (Fed. Cir. 2006), *cert. denied,* 127 S. Ct. 1261 (Mem) (2007); *BB&T Corporation v. United States,* 2007–1 USTC P 50,130 (M.D.N.C. 2007), aff'd, 523 F.3d 461 (4th Cir. 2008); *Wells Fargo & Company v. United States,* No. 06–628T, 2010 WL 94544, at *60 (Fed. Cl. Jan. 8, 2010) (distinguishing leasing case *Consolidated Edison Company of New York,* No. 06–305T, 2009 WL 3418533 (Fed. Cl. Oct. 21, 2009) by observing that "considerations of economic substance are factually specific to the transaction involved").

[1041] As examples of cases in which courts have found that a transaction does not meet the requirements for the treatment claimed by the taxpayer under the Code, or does not have economic substance, See, e.g., *BB&T Corporation v. United States,* 2007–1 USTC P 50,130 (M.D.N.C. 2007) aff'd, 523 F.3d 461 (4th Cir. 2008); *Tribune Company and Subsidiaries v. Commissioner,* 125 T.C. 110 (2005); *H.J. Heinz Company and Subsidiaries v. United States,* 76 Fed. Cl. 570 (2007); *Coltec Industries, Inc. v. United States,* 454 F.3d 1340 (Fed. Cir. 2006), *cert. denied* 127 S. Ct. 1261 (Mem.) (2007); *Long Term Capital Holdings LP v. United States,* 330 F. Supp. 2d 122 (D. Conn. 2004), aff'd, 150 Fed. Appx. 40 (2d Cir. 2005); *Klamath Strategic Investment Fund, LLC v. United States,* 472 F. Supp. 2d 885 (E.D. Texas 2007); aff'd, 568 F. 3d 537 (5th Cir. 2009); *Santa Monica Pictures LLC v. Commissioner,* 89 T.C.M. 1157 (2005).

380

pendent activities with non-tax objectives are combined with an unrelated item having only tax-avoidance objectives in order to disallow those tax-motivated benefits.[1042]

Conjunctive analysis

The provision clarifies that the economic substance doctrine involves a conjunctive analysis—there must be an inquiry regarding
the objective effects of the transaction on the taxpayer's economic
position as well as an inquiry regarding the taxpayer's subjective
motives for engaging in the transaction. Under the provision, a
transaction must satisfy both tests, i.e., the transaction must
change in a meaningful way (apart from Federal income tax effects)
the taxpayer's economic position and the taxpayer must have a
substantial non-Federal-income-tax purpose for entering into such
transaction, in order for a transaction to be treated as having economic substance. This clarification eliminates the disparity that exists among the Federal circuit courts regarding the application of
the doctrine, and modifies its application in those circuits in which
either a change in economic position or a non-tax business purpose
(without having both) is sufficient to satisfy the economic substance
doctrine.[1043]

Non-Federal-income-tax business purpose

Under the provision, a taxpayer's non-Federal-income-tax purpose [1044] for entering into a transaction (the second prong in the
analysis) must be "substantial." For purposes of this analysis, any
State or local income tax effect which is related to a Federal income tax effect is treated in the same manner as a Federal income
tax effect. Also, a purpose of achieving a favorable accounting treatment for financial reporting purposes is not taken into account as
a non-Federal-income-tax purpose if the origin of the financial accounting benefit is a reduction of Federal income tax.[1045]

[1042] See, e.g., *Coltec Industries, Inc. v. United States,* 454 F.3d 1340 (Fed. Cir. 2006), *cert. denied* 127 S. Ct. 1261 (Mem.) (2007) ("the first asserted business purpose focuses on the wrong
transaction—the creation of Garrison as a separate subsidiary to manage asbestos liabilities. .
. . [W]e must focus on the transaction that gave the taxpayer a high basis in the stock and thus
gave rise to the alleged benefit upon sale") 454 F.3d 1340, 1358 (Fed. Cir. 2006). See also *ACM
Partnership v. Commissioner,* 157 F.3d at 256 n.48; *Minnesota Tea Co. v. Helvering,* 302 U.S.
609, 613 (1938) ("A given result at the end of a straight path is not made a different result
because reached by following a devious path.").

[1043] The provision defines "economic substance doctrine" as the common law doctrine under
which tax benefits under subtitle A with respect to a transaction are not allowable if the transaction does not have economic substance or lacks a business purpose. Thus, the definition includes any doctrine that denies tax benefits for lack of economic substance, for lack of business
purpose, or for lack of both.

[1044] See, e.g., Treas. Reg. sec. 1.269–2(b) (stating that a distortion of tax liability indicating
the principal purpose of tax evasion or avoidance might be evidenced by the fact that "the transaction was not undertaken for reasons germane to the conduct of the business of the taxpayer").
Similarly, in *ACM Partnership v. Commissioner,* 73 T.C.M. (CCH) 2189 (1997), the court stated:
  Key to [the determination of whether a transaction has economic substance] is that the transaction must be rationally related to a useful nontax purpose that is plausible in light of the
taxpayer's conduct and useful in light of the taxpayer's economic situation and intentions. Both
the utility of the stated purpose and the rationality of the means chosen to effectuate it must
be evaluated in accordance with commercial practices in the relevant industry. A rational relationship between purpose and means ordinarily will not be found unless there was a reasonable
expectation that the nontax benefits would be at least commensurate with the transaction costs.
[citations omitted]

[1045] Claiming that a financial accounting benefit constitutes a substantial non-tax purpose
fails to consider the origin of the accounting benefit (i.e., reduction of taxes) and significantly
diminishes the purpose for having a substantial non-tax purpose requirement. *See, e.g., American Electric Power, Inc. v. United States,* 136 F. Supp. 2d 762, 791–92 (S.D. Ohio 2001) ("AEP's
intended use of the cash flows generated by the [corporate-owned life insurance] plan is irrele-

381

Profit potential

Under the provision, a taxpayer may rely on factors other than profit potential to demonstrate that a transaction results in a meaningful change in the taxpayer's economic position or that the taxpayer has a substantial non-Federal-income-tax purpose for entering into such transaction. The provision does not require or establish a minimum return that will satisfy the profit potential test. However, if a taxpayer relies on a profit potential, the present value of the reasonably expected pre-tax profit must be substantial in relation to the present value of the expected net tax benefits that would be allowed if the transaction were respected.[1046] Fees and other transaction expenses are taken into account as expenses in determining pre-tax profit. In addition, the Secretary is to issue regulations requiring foreign taxes to be treated as expenses in determining pre-tax profit in appropriate cases.[1047]

Personal transactions of individuals

In the case of an individual, the provision applies only to transactions entered into in connection with a trade or business or an activity engaged in for the production of income.

Other rules

No inference is intended as to the proper application of the economic substance doctrine under present law. The provision is not intended to alter or supplant any other rule of law, including any common-law doctrine or provision of the Code or regulations or other guidance thereunder; and it is intended the provision be construed as being additive to any such other rule of law.

As with other provisions in the Code, the Secretary has general authority to prescribe rules and regulations necessary for the enforcement of the provision.[1048]

Penalty for underpayments and understatements attributable to transactions lacking economic substance

The provision imposes a new strict liability penalty under section 6662 for an underpayment attributable to any disallowance of claimed tax benefits by reason of a transaction lacking economic substance, as defined in new section 7701(o), or failing to meet the requirements of any similar rule of law.[1049] The penalty rate is 20 percent (increased to 40 percent if the taxpayer does not adequately disclose the relevant facts affecting the tax treatment in

---

vant to the subjective prong of the economic substance analysis. If a legitimate business purpose for the use of the tax savings 'were sufficient to breathe substance into a transaction whose only purpose was to reduce taxes, [then] every sham tax-shelter device might succeed,'") (citing Winn-Dixie v. Commissioner, 113 T.C. 254, 287 (1999)); aff'd, 326 F3d 737 (6th Cir. 2003).

[1046] See, e.g., *Rice's Toyota World v. Commissioner,* 752 F.2d at 94 (the economic substance inquiry requires an objective determination of whether a reasonable possibility of profit from the transaction existed apart from tax benefits); *Compaq Computer Corp. v. Commissioner,* 277 F.3d at 781 (applied the same test, *citing Rice's Toyota World);* IES Industries v. United States, 253 F.3d at 354 (the application of the objective economic substance test involves determining whether there was a "reasonable possibility of profit . . . apart from tax benefits.").

[1047] There is no intention to restrict the ability of the courts to consider the appropriate treatment of foreign taxes in particular cases, as under present law.

[1048] Sec. 7805(a).

[1049] It is intended that the penalty would apply to a transaction the tax benefits of which are disallowed as a result of the application of the similar factors and analysis that is required under the provision for an economic substance analysis, even if a different term is used to describe the doctrine.

382

the return or a statement attached to the return). An amended return or supplement to a return is not taken into account if filed after the taxpayer has been contacted for audit or such other date as is specified by the Secretary. No exceptions (including the reasonable cause rules) to the penalty are available. Thus, under the provision, outside opinions or in-house analysis would not protect a taxpayer from imposition of a penalty if it is determined that the transaction lacks economic substance or fails to meet the requirements of any similar rule of law. Similarly, a claim for refund or credit that is excessive under section 6676 due to a claim that is lacking in economic substance or failing to meet the requirements of any similar rule of law is subject to the 20 percent penalty under that section, and the reasonable basis exception is not available.

The penalty does not apply to any portion of an underpayment on which a fraud penalty is imposed.[1050] The new 40-percent penalty for nondisclosed transactions is added to the penalties to which section 6662A will not also apply.[1051]

As described above, under the provision, the reasonable cause and good faith exception of present law section 6664(c)(1) does not apply to any portion of an underpayment which is attributable to a transaction lacking economic substance, as defined in section 7701(o), or failing to meet the requirements of any similar rule of law. Likewise, the reasonable cause and good faith exception of present law section 6664(d)(1) does not apply to any portion of a reportable transaction understatement which is attributable to a transaction lacking economic substance, as defined in section 7701(o), or failing to meet the requirements of any similar rule of law.

Effective Date

The provision applies to transactions entered into after the date of enactment and to underpayments, understatements, and refunds and credits attributable to transactions entered into after the date of enactment of the Act (March 30, 2010).

F. Time for Payment of Corporate Estimated Taxes (sec. 1410 of the Act and sec. 6655 of the Code)

Present Law

In general, corporations are required to make quarterly estimated tax payments of their income tax liability.[1052] For a corporation whose taxable year is a calendar year, these estimated tax payments must be made by April 15, June 15, September 15, and December 15. In the case of a corporation with assets of at least $1 billion (determined as of the end of the preceding taxable year), payments due in July, August, or September, 2014, are increased

---

[1050] As under present law, the penalties under section 6662 (including the new penalty) do not apply to any portion of an underpayment on which a fraud penalty is imposed.

[1051] As revised by the provision, new section 6662A(e)(2)(b) provides that section 6662A will not apply to any portion of an understatement due to gross valuation misstatement under section 6662(h) or nondisclosed noneconomic substance transactions under new section 6662(i).

[1052] Sec. 6655.

383

to 157.75 percent of the payment otherwise due and the next required payment is reduced accordingly.[1053]

Explanation of Provision [1054]

The provision increases the required payment of estimated tax otherwise due in July, August, or September, 2014, by 15.75 percentage points.

Effective Date

The provision is effective on the date of enactment (March 30, 2010).

[1053] Hiring Incentives to Restore Employment Act, Pub. L. No. 111–147, sec. 561, par. (1); Act to extend the Generalized System of Preferences and the Andean Trade Preference Act, and for other purposes, Pub. L. No. 111–124, sec. 4; Worker, Homeownership, and Business Assistance Act of 2009, Pub. L. No. 111–92, sec. 18; Joint resolution approving the renewal of import restrictions contained in the Burmese Freedom and Democracy Act of 2003, and for other purposes, Pub. L. No. 111–42, sec. 202(b)(1).

[1054] All of the public laws enacted in the 111th Congress affecting this provision are described in Part Twenty-One of this document.

Part 6

Indexes

Index to ERISA, IRC, and Related Regulations

	ERISA[1]	IRC[1]	Treas. Regs.[2] (26 CFR)	DOL & PBGC Regs.[2,3] (29 CFR)	HHS Regs. (45 CFR)
-A-					
Abandoned plans, termination of				2578.1	
Individual account plans				2578.1	
Rollovers				2550.404a-3	
Terminal report				2520.103-13	
Accident and health plans (*see* **Health benefits**)					
Accrued benefit					
Accrual requirements	204	411(b)	1.411(b)-1	2530.204-1	
Accrual computation period				2530.204-2	
Alternative methods				2530.204-3	
Period of service			1.410(a)-7(e)		
Definition	3(23)	411(a)(7)	1.411(a)-7		
Reduction in future accruals, notice of	204(h)	4980F	54.4980F-1		
Accrued liability	3(29)		p1.412(c)(4)-1		
Accumulated funding deficiency (*see also* Funding standard)	302(a)	412(a)			
Excise tax		4971(c)(1)	54.4971-1		
Correction			54.4971-2		
Multiple employers			p54.4971-3(b)		
Active participant		219(g)(5)–(7)	p1.219-2		
Actuarial assumptions					
Funding	302(c)(3)	412(c)(3)	p1.412(b)-1(h)		
Interest	302(b)(5)	412(b)(5)	p1.412(b)-1(e)		
Lump sum					
Participant's benefit	203(e)(2)	411(a)(11)(A)–(B)	1.417(e)-1(d)		
Spouse's benefit	205(g)(3)	417(e)(3)	1.417(e)-1(d)		
Multiemployer mass withdrawal	4281				
Single-employer plan	4044				
Specified in plan		401(a)(25)			
Withdrawal liability	4213				
Actuarial cost method					
Definition	3(31)		1.412(c)(1)-1		

[1]Regulatory references in this index are included for researching convenience. Text of the regulations can be found in *ERISA Regulations, 2012 Edition* (BNA).
[2]The prefix **p** indicates a proposed regulation.
[3]Regulations marked with an asterisks (*) indicate a PBGC regulation.

	ERISA[1]	IRC[1]	Treas. Regs.[2] (26 CFR)	DOL & PBGC Regs.[2,3] (29 CFR)	HHS Regs. (45 CFR)
Funding, use of	302(c)(1)	412(c)(1)	1.412(c)(1)-1		
Shortfall method			1.412(c)(1)-2		
Actuarial report/ information					
Contents	103(a), (d)	6059	301.6059-1(c)		
Failure to file		6692	301.6692-1		
Filed with Secretary of Labor in electronic format	104(b)(5)				
Form not required	109(b)			2520.104-42	
Actuarial valuation					
Pension plan					
Funding	302(c)(2), (9)	412(c)(2), (9)	1.412(c)(2)-1 p1.412(c)(9)-1		
Welfare plan, funded		419A(c)			
Actuary					
Definition	103(a)(4)(C) 3043	7701(a)(35)			
Enrollment of	3041–42			20 CFR pt. 901	
Adequate consideration	3(18)				
Administration of ERISA					
Agency coordination					
Department of Labor	506, 3004			2530.200a-1–3	
Department of Treasury	3004				
Funding requirement	3002				
IRS determination letters	3001				
Participation requirements	3002				
Prohibited transactions	3003				
QDROs	206(d)(3)(N)	401(n) 414(p)(13)	1.401(a)-13(g)		
Vesting requirements	3002				
Department of Labor	507				
IRS		7476	601.201(n)(9)		
Affiliate of employer	407(d)(7)				
Affiliated service group		414(m)	p1.414(m)-1–4 p1.414(o)-1		
Age discrimination				29 CFR pt. 1625	
Pension plans					
Accruals and allocations		411(b)	p1.411(b)-2		
Maximum	202(a)(2)	410(a)(2)	1.410(a)-4 p1.410(a)-4A	29 CFR pt. 1625	

For an Index to PHSA sections after amendment by PPACA and other legislation (Part 3), see separate PHSA Index following this Index.

	ERISA[1]	**IRC**[1]	**Treas. Regs.**[2] **(26 CFR)**	**DOL & PBGC Regs.**[2,3] **(29 CFR)**	**HHS Regs. (45 CFR)**
Minimum	202(a)(1)	410(a)(1)	1.410(a)-3 1.411(a)-5(b)	2530.202-2	
Airlines					
Defined benefit plan funding	4022(h)				
Air pilots' plan		410(b)(3)(B)	1.410(b)-1(c)(2)		
Aliens, nonresident					
Deductions for foreign plans		404A	p1.404A-1-7		
Exclusion from					
ERISA	4(b)(4)				
Health care continuation		4980B(g)(1)			
Qualified plans		410(b)(3)(C)	1.410(b)-1(c)(3) 1.410(b)-6(c)		
Simplified employee pensions		408(k)(2)	p1.408-7(d)(4)		
Tax-deferred annuities		403(b)(12)			
Allocation and delegation of fiduciary responsibilities	402(b)–(c)				
Allocation of assets	4044			pt. 4044*	
Valuation of benefits	4044				
Multiemployer plans (mass withdrawal)				4281.12–.18*	
Single-employer plans				4044.41–.75*	
Amendments					
Pre-ERISA plans			1.401-5		
Procedure for	402(b)(3)				
Reducing benefits	204(g)	411(d)(6)	1.411(d)-3		
Retroactive		401(b)	1.401(b)-1		
Approval of	203(a)(3)(C) 302(c)(8)	411(a)(3)(C) 412(c)(8)			
Reversion of surplus assets	4044(d)(2)			4044.3*	
Security for	307	401(a)(29) 436(f)(1)			
Annual addition		415(c)(2)	1.415(c)-1(b)		
Annual report					
Contents				2520.103-1	
Bank or insurance carrier				2520.103-9	
Group insurance arrangement				2520.103-2	
Electronic filing				2520.104a-2	

[1]Regulatory references in this index are included for researching convenience. Text of the regulations can be found in *ERISA Regulations, 2012 Edition* (BNA).
[2]The prefix **p** indicates a proposed regulation.
[3]Regulations marked with an asterisks (*) indicate a PBGC regulation.

	ERISA[1]	IRC[1]	Treas. Regs.[2] (26 CFR)	DOL & PBGC Regs.[2,3] (29 CFR)	HHS Regs. (45 CFR)
Exemption for certain investments				2520.103-12	
PBGC	4008				
Plan administrator to					
Department of Labor	101(b)(1) 103, 104 502(c)(2)			2520.103 2520.104 2520.104a-5–6 2560.502c-2 2570.60–.88	
IRS (*see* Annual return)					
PBGC	4065			pt. 4065*	
Secretary of Labor	513(b)				
Annual return (IRS)					
Cafeteria plan		6039D			
Disclosure of					
Pension plan return		6104(b)			
Private foundation		6104(d)			
Educational assistance		6039D			
Group legal services plan		6039D			
Disclosure of return		6104(b)			
ERISA registration		6057(a)			
Qualified plan		6058(a)			
Tax on failure to file		6652(d)–(e)			
Annuity					
Annuity starting date		72(c)(4)			
Spouse's survivor benefit	205(h)(2)	417(f)(2)			
Corporate-owned		72(s)(6)–(7)			
Definition		401(g)			
Distribution of		402			
Distributions from					
Penalty for premature		72(q)			
Required		72(s)			
Estate tax on		2039			
Exclusion ratio		72(b), (d)(1)	1.72-4		
Immediate annuity		72(u)(4)			
Investment in contract		72(c)(1)	1.72-6, -7 p1.72-6		
Before 1987		72(e)(8)(D)			
Lump sum, in lieu of		72(h)			
Modified endowment contract		72(v)			

For an Index to PHSA sections after amendment by PPACA and other legislation (Part 3), see separate PHSA Index following this Index.

	ERISA[1]	IRC[1]	Treas. Regs.[2] (26 CFR)	DOL & PBGC Regs.[2,3] (29 CFR)	HHS Regs. (45 CFR)
Defined		7702A			
Taxation of		72(v)	1.403(a)-1		
Treatment of qualified annuity plan		72(e)(10)–(12)			
Taxation of recipient		61(a)(9), 72(d)	1.61-11 1.72-1–18		
Employee contributions		72(b), (f) 72(m)(2), (10)	1.72-13 1.72(e)-1T		
Qualified annuity plan		403(a)			
Tax-deferred (403(b)) annuity	403(b)				
Transfer of		72(e)(4)(C) 72(g)	1.72-10		
Treated as plan		401(f)			
Withholding from		3405			
Anti-cutback rules		411(d)(6)	1.411(d)(6)-3, -4		
Assignment or alienation					
Health plan, to Medicaid	609(b)				
Pension plan (*see also* Qualified domestic relations order)	206(d)	401(a)(13)	p1.401(a)-13		
Vacation plan				2509.78-1	
Association health plans, reserve		419A(c)(6)			
Attorney's fees					
Multiemployer plans	502(g), 4301(e)				
Single-employer plans	4070(e)				
Title I	502(g)				
Audit requirement	103(a)(3)			2520.103-1	
Exceptions	103(a)(3)(A)			2520.103-3, 4	
Independent accountant	103(a)(3)(D)			2509.75-9	
Limitations on scope	103(a)(3)(C)			2520.103-8	
Waiver, small plans				2520.104-46	
Automatic enrollment (or automatic contribution arrangement)					
Eligible combined plans	210(e)(3)				
Excess contributions		4979(f)(1) 401(m)(13)			
Nondiscrimination testing		401(m)(12)			
Preemption of state law	514(e)				
Requirements		401(k)(13)			
Top-heavy exception		416(g)(4)(H)			

[1]Regulatory references in this index are included for researching convenience. Text of the regulations can be found in *ERISA Regulations, 2012 Edition* (BNA).
[2]The prefix **p** indicates a proposed regulation.
[3]Regulations marked with an asterisks (*) indicate a PBGC regulation.

	ERISA[1]	IRC[1]	Treas. Regs.[2] (26 CFR)	DOL & PBGC Regs.[2,3] (29 CFR)	HHS Regs. (45 CFR)
Withdrawal of contributions		414(w)			

-B-

	ERISA[1]	IRC[1]	Treas. Regs.[2] (26 CFR)	DOL & PBGC Regs.[2,3] (29 CFR)	HHS Regs. (45 CFR)
Bank					
Definition		408(n)	54.4975-6(b)(4)		
ESOP distribution		409(h)(3)			
Investment manager	3(38)(B)				
Prohibited transaction exemptions					
Ancillary services	408(b)(6)	4975(d)(6)		2550.408b-6	
Common or collective trust	408(b)(8)	4975(d)(8)			
Deposits	408(b)(4)	4975(d)(4)		2550.408b-4	
Reports by	103(a)(2) 103(b)(3)(G)			2520.103-9	
Bankruptcy					
Funding lien	302(f)	412(n)			
IRA contributions by employees		219(b)(5)(C)			
PBGC benefit guarantee	4022(g)				
PBGC lien priority	4068(c)(2)–(4)				
Retiree health continuation	602(2)(A) 603(6) 607(3)(C)	4980B(f)(2) 4980B(f)(3) 4980B(g)(1)			
Beneficiary	3(8)				
Benefit liabilities					
Amount of unfunded	4001(a)(18)				
Definition	4001(a)(16)				
Outstanding amount of	4001(a)(19)				
Benefit plan investor	3(42)				
Benefit statement	105				
Black lung benefit trusts		501(c)(2)(D)			
Black-out periods	502			2560.502c-2, -5 to -8 2570.61, .64, .94; 2570.130– .141	
Fiduciary liability (*see also* Fiduciary)	404(c)(1)				
Notice					
Exception for one-participant plans	101(i)(8)(B)				

For an Index to PHSA sections after amendment by PPACA and other legislation (Part 3), see separate PHSA Index following this Index.

	ERISA[1]	IRC[1]	Treas. Regs.[2] (26 CFR)	DOL & PBGC Regs.[2,3] (29 CFR)	HHS Regs. (45 CFR)
Notice				2520.101-3	
Bonding of plan officials	412			2580.412	
Maximum amount	412(a)				
Bonding of brokers and dealers	412(a)(2)				
Break in service				2530.200b-4	
Amendment of rules					
Eligibility			1.410(a)-7		
Vesting			1.411(a)-7(d)		
Eligibility to participate	202(b)	410(a)(5)	1.410(a)-5(c), -8 1.410(a)-8T(c)(2)	2530.202-2(c)	
Maternity/paternity absence					
Eligibility	203(b)(3)	411(a)(6)			
Vesting	203(a)(3)	411(a)(6)	1.411(a)-6(c)	2530.203-2(d)	
Bus companies					
Funding defined benefit plans	302(d)(9)A)	412(I)(9)(A)			

-C-

	ERISA[1]	IRC[1]	Treas. Regs.[2] (26 CFR)	DOL & PBGC Regs.[2,3] (29 CFR)	HHS Regs. (45 CFR)
Cafeteria plans		125	1.125-2T p1.125-1–2		
Annual return		6039D			
Discrimination		125(b), (c)	p1.125-1, Q-19		
Effect of FMLA			1.125-3		
Health flexible spending arrangements		125(i)			
Permitted change			1.125-4		
Qualified benefits, defined		125(f)			
Simple cafeteria plans for small business		125(j)			
Written plan required		125(d)(1)	p1.125-1, Q-3		
Cash balance plans					
Age discrimination protection	204(b)(5) (A)(i)	411(b)(5)(A)(i)			
Conversions	204(b)(5)(B)(v)(I)	411(b)(5)(B)(v)(I)			
Interest credits	204(b)(5)(B)(i)(I)	411(b)(5)(B)(i)(I)			
Nondiscrimination cross testing			1.401(a)(4)-3 1.401(a)(4)-9 p1.411(b)-2		
Cash or deferred arrangements					
Actual deferral percentage		401(k)(3)	1.401(k)-2		

[1]Regulatory references in this index are included for researching convenience. Text of the regulations can be found in *ERISA Regulations, 2012 Edition* (BNA).
[2]The prefix **p** indicates a proposed regulation.
[3]Regulations marked with an asterisks (*) indicate a PBGC regulation.

	ERISA[1]	IRC[1]	Treas. Regs.[2] (26 CFR)	DOL & PBGC Regs.[2,3] (29 CFR)	HHS Regs. (45 CFR)
Safe harbor		401(k)(12)	1.401(k)-3		
Contribution limit		401(k)(3)			
Coverage and participation requirements		401(a)(26) 401(k)(2)(D) 401(k)(3)(A)(i) 410(b)	1.401(k)-1(b)		
Definition			1.401(k)-1(a)(2)(i) 1.401(k)-1(a)(4)		
Definitions of certain terms			1.401(k)-6		
Distributions					
Hardship		401(k)(2)(B)(i)(IV)	1.401(k)-1(d)(3)		
Limitation		401(k)(2)(B)	1.401(k)-1(d)		
Plan Termination			1.401(k)-1(d)(4)		
Qualified plan requirement			1.401(k)-1(e)		
Severance from employment			1.401(k)-1(d)(2)		
Elections			1.401(k)-1(a)(3)		
Elective deferral limit		402(g)	1.402(g)-1		
Qualification requirement		401(a)(30)	1.401(a)-30		
Equivalencies				2530.200b-3	
Excess contributions, excise tax on		4979	54.4979-1		
Matching contributions (*see* Matching contributions)					
Nondiscrimination requirements			1.401(k)-1(b)		
Nonforfeitability			1.401(k)-1(c)		
Plans permitted to include			1.401(k)-1(a)(1)		
Pre-ERISA plans	2006(b)	401(k)(6)	1.401(k)-6		
Roth contributions to		402A	1.401(k)-2(b)(2)(vi)(C)		
Actual contribution percentage			1.401(m)-2(b)		
Actual deferral percentage			1.401(k)-2(b)		
Definitions			1.401(k)-6 1.401(m)-5		
Rules			1.401(k)-1(f)		
Safe harbor plans		401(k)(12)			
SIMPLE 401(k)		401(k)(11)	1.401(k)-4		

For an Index to PHSA sections after amendment by PPACA and other legislation (Part 3), see separate PHSA Index following this Index.

	ERISA[1]	IRC[1]	Treas. Regs.[2] (26 CFR)	DOL & PBGC Regs.[2,3] (29 CFR)	HHS Regs. (45 CFR)
Simplified employee pension		408(k)(6)	1.408-7 p1.408-7		
Top-heavy plans		416	1.416-1		
Catch-up contributions		414(v) 457(e)(18)	1.402(g)-2 1.414(v)-1		
Church					
Convention or association of churches		7701(o)			
Church plan					
Compensation benefit limit waiver		415(b)(11)			
Definition	3(33)	414(e)	1.414(e)-1		
Elective deferral limit		402(g)(2)			
Exclusion from ERISA	4(b)(2)				
Election to be ERISA plan		410(d)	1.410(d)-1		
Health plan continuation, exclusion	601(b)	4980B(d)(3)			
Life insurance, group-term		79(d)(7)			
Qualified plans					
Contribution limit		415(c)(7)			
Correction period for		414(e)(4)			
Domestic relations orders		414(p)(9), (11)			
Funding		412(h)(4)			
Participation		410(c)(1)(B)	1.410(d)-1		
Required beginning date		401(a)(9)(C)			
Retirement income accounts		403(b)(9)			
Contributions		404(a)(10)			
Vesting		411(e)			
Real property held by		514(c)(9)(C)(iv)			
Section 457 exclusion		457(e)(13)			
UBIT exemption, debt-financed income		514(c)(9)(C)			
Civil enforcement					
Title I	502				
Annual report, failure to file	502(c)(2)			2560.502c-2 2570.60-.88	
DOL enforcement request	502(b)(1)			2560.502-1	
Hearings	502(c)(5)			2570.90-.101	

[1]Regulatory references in this index are included for researching convenience. Text of the regulations can be found in *ERISA Regulations, 2012 Edition* (BNA).
[2]The prefix **p** indicates a proposed regulation.
[3]Regulations marked with an asterisks (*) indicate a PBGC regulation.

	ERISA[1]	IRC[1]	Treas. Regs.[2] (26 CFR)	DOL & PBGC Regs.[2,3] (29 CFR)	HHS Regs. (45 CFR)
Medicare/Medicaid Coverage Data Bank	502(a)(7)				
Penalties	502(c)(8)			2560.502c-4 2560.502c-8 2570.130–.141 2570.160–.171 2575.502c-5, -6	
Prohibited transaction penalty (welfare plans)	502(i)			2560.502i-1 2570.1–.12	
Title IV					
Multiemployer plans	4301				
Single-employer plans	4070				
Civil procedure—findings	3(40)			2570.150–.159	
Claims procedure	503			2560.503-1	
Class-year plan vesting	203(a)(3)(D)	411(a)(3)(D)			
COBRA continuation (*see* Health benefits, Continuation of)					
Co-fiduciary liability	405			2509.75-5	
Collective bargaining agreement		7701(a)(46)	301.7701-17T	2510.3-40	
Collectively bargained plans					
Accident or health plan (self-insured)		105(h)(3)(B)	1.105-1(c)(2)		
Defined—plans established and maintained under	3(40)(A)			2510.3-40	
Dependent care assistance		129(d)(3)			
Educational assistance program		127(b)(2)			
Group legal services		120(c)(2)	1.120-3(b)(3) p1.120-2(h)(3)		
Group-term life insurance plan		79(d)(3)(B)			
Pension plans					
Participation		401(a)(26)(D) 410(b)(3)	1.401(a)(26)-6(b) 1.410(b)-1(c)(1) 1.410(b)-6(d)(2)		
Qualification of		401(a)			
Requirements for		413(a)			
Termination of	4041(a)(3)				
Top-heavy plan exception		416(i)(4)			
Vesting		413(c)(3)	1.413-2(d)		
TRA '84 effect on		7701(a)(46)	301.7701-17T		

For an Index to PHSA sections after amendment by PPACA and other legislation (Part 3), see separate PHSA Index following this Index.

	ERISA[1]	IRC[1]	Treas. Regs.[2] (26 CFR)	DOL & PBGC Regs.[2,3] (29 CFR)	HHS Regs. (45 CFR)
Welfare benefits, funded		419A(f)(5) 505(a)(2)			
Collective net worth					
Payment of single-employer plan liability	4062(d)				
PBGC lien	4068(f)(1)				
Commerce					
Definition	3(11)				
Employer/employee organization engaged in	4(a), 4021(a)(1)				
Common or collective trust					
IRAs		408(e)(6)	1.408-2(b)(5)		
Prohibited transaction exemption	408(b)(8)	4975(d)(8)			
Reporting	103(a), (b)			2520.103-3 2520.103-5 2520.103-9	
Company-owned life insurance		101(j)			
Comparability of plans		401(a)(5)	1.401(a)(4)-8–9		
Compensation					
Definition		414(s) 415(c)(3)	1.414(s)-1 1.415(c)-2		
Gross income, inclusion in		61(a)(1)	1.61-2		
Highly compensated		414(q)	1.414(q)-1T		
IRA		219(f)(1)			
Key employee		416(i)(1)(D)			
Limit on deductible remuneration		162(m)	1.162-27		
Deductions		404(l)			
Property transferred in respect of services		83	1.83-1–8		
Self-employed individuals		414(s)(2)	1.414(s)-1(g)		
VEBAs		505(b)(7)			
Consolidated returns		1563			
Constructive ownership of stock		318			
Contributions (*see also* Employee contributions; Funding standard)					
Aggregating plans			1.415(f)-1		
Compensation, definition			1.415(c)-2		
Cost-of-living adjustments			1.415(d)-1		
Discontinuance of		411(d)(3)	1.411(d)-2		

[1]Regulatory references in this index are included for researching convenience. Text of the regulations can be found in *ERISA Regulations, 2012 Edition* (BNA).
[2]The prefix **p** indicates a proposed regulation.
[3]Regulations marked with an asterisks (*) indicate a PBGC regulation.

	ERISA[1]	IRC[1]	Treas. Regs.[2] (26 CFR)	DOL & PBGC Regs.[2,3] (29 CFR)	HHS Regs. (45 CFR)
Limitations					
Defined benefit		415(b)(1)	1.415(b)-1		
Defined contribution		415(c)(1)	1.415(c)-1		
Annual additions		415(c)	1.415(c)-1(b)		
Multiemployer plan (*see also* Multiemployer plan, Funding)					
Collection actions	502(g)(2)				
Obligation to pay	515				
Single-employer plans					
Annual payment	302(c)(10) 303(j)	412(c)(10) 430(j)(11)			
Lien for failure to make	302(f), 303(k)	412(n), 430(k)			
Quarterly payments	302(e) 303(j)(3)	412(m) 430(j)(3)			
Timing of	302(c)(10) 303(j)(1) 4001(b)(2)(A)	412(c)(10) 430(j)(1)			
Controlled group					
Change in					
Qualified plans		401(a)(26)(E) 410(b)(6)(C)	1.410(b)-2(f)		
Single-employer plan	4069(b)				
Withdrawal liability	4218(1)				
Collective net worth	4062(d)(1)			4062.4–.6*	
Compensation			1.415-2(g)(2)		
Consolidated returns		1563			
Contributions					
Liability for	302(c)(11) 303(b)(2)	412(c)(11) 412(b)(2)			
Lien for failure to pay	302(f) 303(k)(1)	412(n)(1) 430(k)(1)			
Tax for funding deficiency		4971(e)(2)	54.4971-1		
Definition					
Funding	302(f)(6)(B) 303(k)(6)(C)	412(n)(6)(B) 430(k)(6)(C)			
General rule		1563			
Multiemployer plan liability	4001(b)(1)				
Qualified plan requirements	3(40)(b)	414(b)–(c)	1.414(c)-1		
Single-employer plan liability	4001(a)(14) 4062				

For an Index to PHSA sections after amendment by PPACA and other legislation (Part 3), see separate PHSA Index following this Index.

	ERISA[1]	IRC[1]	Treas. Regs.[2] (26 CFR)	DOL & PBGC Regs.[2,3] (29 CFR)	HHS Regs. (45 CFR)
Employer securities	407(d)(1)	409(*l*)			
Fringe benefits		414(t)			
Funding waiver	303(d)(2) 302(c)(5)(B)	412(d)(5) 412(c)(15)			
Health benefits (self-insured)		105(h)(8)	1.105-11(f)		
Leased employees		414(n)			
Maximum benefits/ contributions		415(h)	1.415(c)-2(g)(2)		
Participation and vesting	210(c)–(d)	414(b)–(c)	1.414(c)-1	2530.210	
PBGC liability					
Lien for	4068			4068.1–.4*	
Multiple employer plans	4063(b), 4064(a)				
Premiums	4007(e)(2)				
Single-employer plans	4062(a)			pt. 4062*	
Welfare plans		414(t)			
Corporate governance				2509.94-2	
Corporate-owned life insurance		101(j)			
Cost of living arrangement		415(k)(2)			
Coverage (*see* Participation, Minimum requirements)					
Coverage, exclusion of plans from					
Accrual requirements		411(e)			
Fiduciary requirements	401				
Funding requirements	301	412(h)			
Joint and survivor requirements	201	401(a)(11)		2530.201-1–2	
Participation	201	410(c)		2530.201-1–2	
Prohibited transactions	401	4975(g)			
Title I	4(b)				
Title IV	4021				
Vesting requirements	201	411(e)		2530.201-1–2	
Coverdell Education Savings Accounts		530			
Criminal offenses					
Coercive interference	511				
Defenses	108				
Felon prohibited as service provider	411				
Reporting, disclosure violations	501				

[1]Regulatory references in this index are included for researching convenience. Text of the regulations can be found in *ERISA Regulations, 2012 Edition* (BNA).
[2]The prefix **p** indicates a proposed regulation.
[3]Regulations marked with an asterisks (*) indicate a PBGC regulation.

	ERISA[1]	IRC[1]	Treas. Regs.[2] (26 CFR)	DOL & PBGC Regs.[2,3] (29 CFR)	HHS Regs. (45 CFR)
State criminal statutes not preempted	514(b)(4)				
Current liability	302(d)(7)	412(l)(7)			
Current value	3(26)				
Custodial accounts					
IRA	403(b)(3)(B)	408(h)	1.408-2(d)	2550.403b-1	
Self-employed individual	403(b)(3)(A)	401(f)		2550.403b-1	
Tax-deferred annuities		403(b)(7)			

-D-

	ERISA[1]	IRC[1]	Treas. Regs.[2] (26 CFR)	DOL & PBGC Regs.[2,3] (29 CFR)	HHS Regs. (45 CFR)
Death benefits					
Incidental					
IRA		408(a)(6) 408(b)(3)	1.408-2(b)(7)		
Qualified plan		401(a)(9)(G)	1.401(a)(9)-2		
Tax-deferred annuities		403(b)(10)	1.403(b)-1(c)		
Declaratory judgments					
Qualification of plan	3001	7476			
Deductible employee contributions		72(o)			
Deductions					
Combination of defined benefit and defined contribution plans		404(a)(7)			
Compensation for services		162(a)(1)			
Compensation, annual		404(l)			
Contributions to plans					
Annuities		404(a)(2)	1.404(a)-8		
Compensation limit		404(l)			
ESOPs		404(a)(9) 404(k)	1.404(k)-1T		
Independent contractors		404(d)	1.404(d)-1T		
Multiple plans		404(a)(7)	1.404(a)-13		
Nonqualified plan		404(a)(5)	1.404(a)-12		
Pension plan		404(a)(1) 404(o)	1.404(a)-1–10		
Profit-sharing plan		404(a)(3)	1.404(a)-9		
SEPs		404(h)	p1.404(h)-1		
SIMPLE plans		404(m)			
Stock bonus plan		404(a)(3)	1.404(a)-9		
Timing of deduction		404(a)(6)	1.404(a)(6)-1		

For an Index to PHSA sections after amendment by PPACA and other legislation (Part 3), see separate PHSA Index following this Index.

	ERISA[1]	IRC[1]	Treas. Regs.[2] (26 CFR)	DOL & PBGC Regs.[2,3] (29 CFR)	HHS Regs. (45 CFR)
Dividends paid, ESOP securities		404(k)	1.404(k)-1T		
Foreign plan		404(a)(4) 404A	1.404(a)-11 p1.404A-1–7		
Multiemployer plan, maximum		404(a)(1)(D)			
PBGC liability		404(g)	1.404(g)-1		
Self-employed individuals					
Group health plan		162(l)			
Qualified plans		404(a)(8) 404(e)	1.404(a)(8)-1T 1.404(e)-1, -1A		
SIMPLE plans		404(m)			
Single-employer plans		404(o)			
Trade or business expenses		162(a)			
Travel expenses		162(a)(2)			
Welfare benefit plan, funded		419			
Withdrawal liability		404(g)	1.404(g)-1		
Deferred compensation plan					
Nonqualified (*see also* Nonqualified deferred compensation)					
Deductions		404(a)(5)	1.404(a)-12		
Substantial risk of forfeiture		83(c)			
Taxation of employees		402(b)	1.402(b)-1		
State and local government (*see also* Governmental plans)		457	1.457-1–12		
Tax-exempt organizations		457	1.457-1–12		
Deficit reduction contribution	302(d)(2)	412(*l*)(2)			
Defined benefit plans	3(35)	414(j)			
Adjusted funding target attainment percentage	206(g)(9)(B)	436(j)(2)		4043.36* 4043.69*	
After-tax employee contributions		402(c)(2)(A)			
Annual report	103(a)(1)(B)				
At-risk plans		430(i)	1.430(i)-1		
Benefit limits					
Average compensation		415(b)(3)	1.415(b)-1(a)(5)		
Contingent event benefits	206(g)(1)	436(b)(1)	1.436-1(b)		
Lump-sum calculation		415(b)(2)(E)(ii)			

[1]Regulatory references in this index are included for researching convenience. Text of the regulations can be found in *ERISA Regulations, 2012 Edition* (BNA).
[2]The prefix **p** indicates a proposed regulation.
[3]Regulations marked with an asterisks (*) indicate a PBGC regulation.

	ERISA[1]	IRC[1]	Treas. Regs.[2] (26 CFR)	DOL & PBGC Regs.[2,3] (29 CFR)	HHS Regs. (45 CFR)
Benefits limit		415(b)	1.415(b)-1		
Disqualification			1.415(g)-1		
Combined plans	210(e)	414(x)			
Conversion to hybrid plans	203(f), 204(b)(5)	411(a)(13), (b)(5)			
Distributions					
Lump sum	206(g)(3)	436(d)			
Working retirement	3(2)(A)	401(a)(36)	1.401(a)-1(b)		
Distributions, forms of			1.411(d)-4		
Excess pension assets					
Defined		420(e)(2)			
Transfer to multiem-ployer health		420(e)(5)			
Transfer to retiree health		420(f)		4043.37* 4043.70*	
Funding					
Annual funding notice	101(f)			p2520.101-5	
Minimum required contribution	302(a)(2)	412(a)(2)			
Underfunded plans	206(g)	436			
Waiver of minimum funding standards	302(c)(1)	412(c)(1)			
Medical benefits account		401(h), 420			
Separate account within		414(k)			
Defined contribution plan	3(34)	401(k), 414(i), 415(k)			
Annual additions		415(c)(2)	1.415(c)-1		
Disqualification of plan or trust			1.415(g)-1		
Combined plans	210(e)	414(x)			
Diversification	204(j)	401(a)(35)	1.401(a)(35)-1		
Safe harbor requirement			1.401(k)-3, p1.401(k)-3, 1.401(m)-3, p1.401(m)-3		
Department store		132(j)(2)			
Dependent care					
Credit		21			
Dependent care assistance programs		129			
Discrimination		129(d)(2), (8)			
Exclusion from income		129(a), (b)			
Dependent defined		152	54.9815-2714T		
Designated Roth accounts		402(A)	1.402A-1		

For an Index to PHSA sections after amendment by PPACA and other legislation (Part 3), see separate PHSA Index following this Index.

	ERISA[1]	IRC[1]	Treas. Regs.[2] (26 CFR)	DOL & PBGC Regs.[2,3] (29 CFR)	HHS Regs. (45 CFR)
Reporting and recordkeeping			1.402A-2		
Roth IRAs, coordination with			1.408A-10		
Taxable rollovers to		402A(d)(5)			
Determination letters (IRS)					
Declaratory judgment		7476			
Defined			601.201		
Disqualifications	3002				
Notice of determination			601.201 1.7476-3		
Notice to employees	3001(a)				
Notice to interested parties			1.7476-2		
Procedure	3001				
Disability insurance					
ERISA exclusion	4(b)(3)				
Disabled		72(m)(7)			
Disclosure (*see also* Reports and returns to)					
Alternative compliance	110				
Participants and beneficiaries	101(a)			2520.101-1	
Benefit statement	105, 209				
Failure to furnish	502(c)(1)(B)	6690			
Summary annual report	104(b)(3)			2520.104b-10	
Summary plan description	102			2520.102-1–5	
Written request from	104(b)(4)			2520.104b-1, -30	
Public					
By DOL	106				
By IRS		6103, 6104			
Qualification application					
To law enforcement officials		6103(i)(3), (7)			
To PBGC		6103(*l*)(2)			
To public		6104(a)(1)(B)			
Discrimination					
Cafeteria plan		125(b), (c), (g)	p1.125-1		
Dependent care assistance		129(d)			
Educational assistance program		127(b)(2)	1.127-2(e)		
Fringe benefits		132(j)(1)			
Group legal services		505(b)			

[1]Regulatory references in this index are included for researching convenience. Text of the regulations can be found in *ERISA Regulations, 2012 Edition* (BNA).
[2]The prefix **p** indicates a proposed regulation.
[3]Regulations marked with an asterisk (*) indicate a PBGC regulation.

	ERISA[1]	IRC[1]	Treas. Regs.[2] (26 CFR)	DOL & PBGC Regs.[2,3] (29 CFR)	HHS Regs. (45 CFR)
Health benefits (self-insured)		105(h)	1.105-11(c)		
Life insurance, group-term		79(d)	1.79-4T		
Qualified plans		401(a)(4)–(5)	1.401(a)(4)-1–13		
Amendments			1.401(a)(4)-5		
Benefits, rights, features			1.401(a)(4)-4		
Cash balance plans			1.401(a)(4)-8(c)(3)		
Coverage, minimum		410(b)	1.410(b)-1–10		
Cross-testing			1.401(a)(4)-8		
Defined benefit plan			1.401(a)(4)-3		
Contributory			1.401(a)(4)-6		
Defined contribution plan			1.401(a)(4)-2		
Early retirement window benefits			1.401(a)(4)-3(f) 1.401(a)(4)-4(d)		
Employee contributions		401(m)	1.401(m)-1(a), (b)		
Floor-offset arrangements			1.401(a)(4)-8(d)		
Former employees			1.401(a)(4)-10		
Governmental plans			1.401(a)(4)-13(b)		
Matching contributions		401(m)	1.401(m)-1(a), (b)		
Optional forms			1.401(a)-4		
Plan aggregation			1.401(a)(4)-9		
Restructuring			1.401(a)(4)-9		
Service-crediting rules			1.401(a)(4)-11(d)		
Target benefit plans			1.401(a)(4)-8(b) 1.401(a)(4)-13		
Uniform points formula			1.401(a)(4)-2(b)(3)		
Vesting		411(d)(1)	1.401(a)(4)-11(c)		
SEPs		408(k)(3)	p1.408-7		
Tax-deferred annuities		403(b)(12)			
Termination	4044(b)(4)			4044.17(d)*	
VEBA		505(b)			
Welfare plan, funded		505(b)			
Distribution of benefits					
Cash or deferred arrangements		401(k)(2)	1.401(k)-1(d)		
Charitable IRAs		408(d)(8)			
Early distribution, tax on					
Annuity		72(q)			

	ERISA[1]	IRC[1]	Treas. Regs.[2] (26 CFR)	DOL & PBGC Regs.[2,3] (29 CFR)	HHS Regs. (45 CFR)
Excess deferrals		402(g)(2)(C)	1.402(g)-1(e)(8)		
IRA		72(t)			
Qualified plan		72(t)			
Form of benefit, protection of			1.411(d)-4		
Relative values of optional form			1.401(a)-20, Q&A16 1.417(a)(3)-1(d)(2)(ii)		
Life insurance, value of			1.402(a)-1		
Lump sums, mandatory	203(e) 204(d), (e)	411(a)(11) 411(a)(7)(B)			
Military, active duty		72(t)(2)(G)			
Notice and consent period	205(c)(7)(A)	417(a)(6)(A)			
Phased retirement			p1.401(a)-3		
Required distributions					
Annuities		72(s)			
Failure to make		4974	54.4974-1–2		
IRA		408(a)(6) 408(b)(3)	1.408-8		
Qualified plan		401(a)(9), 401(a)(14)	1.401(a)(9)-0–9		
Section 457 plan	206	457(d)	1.457-6		
Tax-deferred annuities		403(b)(10)–(11)	1.403(b)-3		
Waiver, temporary		401(a)(9)(H)			
Restrictions and valuations			1.411(a)-11 p1.411(a)-11(f), 1.417(e)-1, p1.417(e)-1		
Spouse's benefits	205(g)				
Working retirement	3(2)	401(a)(36)			
Diversification	404(a)(1)(C)			2550.404a-1	

-E-

	ERISA[1]	IRC[1]	Treas. Regs.[2] (26 CFR)	DOL & PBGC Regs.[2,3] (29 CFR)	HHS Regs. (45 CFR)
Earliest retirement age		417(f)(3)			
Early retiree reinsurance program					pt. 149
Early retirement subsidies					
Accrual	204(b)(1)(H)	411(b)(1)(H)			
Reduction of	204(h)(2)	411(d)(6)(B)			
Earned income (self-employed)		401(c)(2)			

[1]Regulatory references in this index are included for researching convenience. Text of the regulations can be found in *ERISA Regulations, 2012 Edition* (BNA).
[2]The prefix **p** indicates a proposed regulation.
[3]Regulations marked with an asterisks (*) indicate a PBGC regulation.

	ERISA[1]	IRC[1]	Treas. Regs.[2] (26 CFR)	DOL & PBGC Regs.[2,3] (29 CFR)	HHS Regs. (45 CFR)
Economically targeted investments				2509.94-1	
Economic substance doctrine		7701(o)		2509.94-1	
Educational IRA (*see* Coverdell Education Savings Accounts)					
Education loans, interest on		221			
Education or training					
Educational assistance		127(c)(1)			
Annual return (IRS)		6039D			
Definition		127(b)			
Exclusion from income		127(a), (d)			
Scholarships		117	1.117-1–5		
Working condition fringe		132(j)(8)			
Effective dates					
ERISA					
Collectively bargained plans	1017(c), (h)				
Fiduciary requirements	414				
Funding requirements	308, 1013				
Participation requirements	211, 1017				
Regulations, authority to promulgate	111(c)				
Spouse's benefits	211, 1017				
Title IV	4402				
Vesting	211				
Multiemployer Pension Plan Amendments Act	1017, 4402(e)–(g)				
Elective deferrals (*see also* Cash or deferred arrangements)					
Definition		401(m)(4)(B) 402(g)(3)	1.402(g)-1(b)		
Limitation on		402(g)	1.402(g)-1		
Qualification requirement		401(a)(30)	1.401(a)-30		
Top-heavy plans			1.416-1 M-20		
Eligibility to participate		401(a)(3)			
Minimum age and service		410(a)	1.410(a)-1–9 1.410(b)-6(b)		
Quarterly testing		401(a)(6)			
Employee (*see also* Self-employed individuals)					

For an Index to PHSA sections after amendment by PPACA and other legislation (Part 3), see separate PHSA Index following this Index.

	ERISA[1]	IRC[1]	Treas. Regs.[2] (26 CFR)	DOL & PBGC Regs.[2,3] (29 CFR)	HHS Regs. (45 CFR)
Affiliated service group		414(m)	p1.414(m)-1–4		
Definition					
ERISA	3(6)				
Fringe benefits		132(f)(5), (h)			
Leased employees		414(n)			
Life insurance salesman		7701(a)(20)			
Regulations concerning		414(o)			
Employee benefit plan	3(3)			2510.3-3	
Employee contributions					
Benefit derived from	204(c)(2)	411(c)(2)			
Computing (annuities)		72(f)			
Deductible		72(o)			
Designation as		414(h)(1)			
Discrimination		401(m)	1.401(m)-1(a), (b)		
Governmental plan, pick-up		414(h)(2)			
Mandatory					
Allocation of assets to	4044(a)(2)				
Definition	204(c)(2)	411(c)(2)(C)			
Withdrawal of	203(a)(3)	411(a)(3)(D)			
Plan asset treatment				2510.3-102	
Exemption		501(c)(18)	1.501(c)(18)-1		
Recovery of		72(e)(8)			
Separate contract for		72(d)(2)			
Surplus assets attributable to	4044(d)(3)				
Vesting	203(a)(1)	411(a)(1)			
Voluntary					
Allocation of assets to	4044(a)(1)			4044.11*	
Defined benefit plan	204(c)(4)	411(d)(5)			
Employee discount (*see also* Fringe benefits)		132(a)(2)			
Employee organization	3(4)				
Employee pension benefit plan	3(2)			2510.3-2	
Employee representative		7701(a)(46)			
Employee stock purchase plan, defined		423(b)	1.423-2		
Employee welfare benefit plan	3(1)			2510.3-1	
Employer					
Definition	3(5)				

[1]Regulatory references in this index are included for researching convenience. Text of the regulations can be found in *ERISA Regulations, 2012 Edition* (BNA).
[2]The prefix **p** indicates a proposed regulation.
[3]Regulations marked with an asterisks (*) indicate a PBGC regulation.

	ERISA[1]	IRC[1]	Treas. Regs.[2] (26 CFR)	DOL & PBGC Regs.[2,3] (29 CFR)	HHS Regs. (45 CFR)
Partnership	4001(b)(1)				
Sole proprietor	4001(b)(1)				
Employer real property					
Acquisition of	407			2550.407a-1, -2	
Definition	407(d)(2)				
Prohibited transaction	406(a)(2)				
Diversification	404(a)(2)			2550.404a-1(b)(2)(i)	
Exemption	408(e)	4975(d)(13)		2550.408e	
Qualifying	407(d)(4)				
Transition rule	414(c)				
Employer securities					
Acquisition of	407			2550.407a-1, -2	
Diversification	404(a)(2)				
Definition	407(d)(1)	409(*l*)		2550.407d-5	
Marketable obligation	407(e)			2550.407d-5(b)	
Net unrealized appreciation		402(e)(4), 402(j)	1.402(a)-1(b) p1.402(a)-1(b)		
Prohibited transaction	406(a)(2)				
Exemptions	408(b)(12), (e)	4975(d)(13)		2550.408e	
Publicly traded partnership	407(d)(5)				
Qualifying	407(d)(5), (f)	4975(e)(8)		2550.407d-5	
Registration-type class of		409(e)(4)			
Stock	407(d)(5), (f)(1)				
Voting rights		401(a)(22) 409(e) 4975(e)(7)			
Entry date	202(a)(4)	410(a)(4)			
ESOP					
Appraisal		401(a)(28)			
Bank, maintained by		409(h)(3)			
Coverage, minimum			1.410(b)-7(c)(2)		
Deduction limits		404(a)(9), (k)	1.404(k)-1T		
Reacquisition of stock		162(k)	1.162(k)-1 1.404(k)-3		
Definition	407(c)(6)	4975(e)(7)		2550.407d-6	
Distributions					
Change in options		411(d)(6)(C)	1.411(d)-4, Q-2		
Early		72(t)(2)			
Required		409(h), (o)			
Diversification		401(a)(28)			

For an Index to PHSA sections after amendment by PPACA and other legislation (Part 3), see separate PHSA Index following this Index.

	ERISA[1]	IRC[1]	Treas. Regs.[2] (26 CFR)	DOL & PBGC Regs.[2,3] (29 CFR)	HHS Regs. (45 CFR)
Dividends paid					
Deduction		404(k)	1.404(k)-1T, p1.404(k)-2		
Mandatory distribution		411(a)(11)			
Reports		6047(e)			
Taxation of		72(e)(5)(D)			
Leveraged ESOP	408(b)(3)	4975(d)(3)		2550.408b-3	
Maximum allocations		415(c)(6)	1.415(c)-2(f)		
Prohibited transaction exemptions	408(b)(3) 408(e)	4975(d)(3) 4975(d)(13)		2550.408b-3 2550.408c-2	
Put option		409(h) 4975(e)(7)			
Reports		6047(e)			
Reversion transferred to		4980(c)(3)			
Sale of stock to					
Nonrecognition of gain		1042			
S Corporation securities		4975(f)(7)	1.409(p)-1		
Spouse's survivor benefits	205(b)(2)	401(a)(11)			
Tax credit ESOP					
Cash distribution option		401(a)(23) 409(h)(2)			
Contribution allocation		409(b)			
Definition		409(a)	1.423-2		
Eligibility/coverage		410(b)(2)	1.410(b)-7		
Gain or loss on contributed securities		409(m)			
Holding period		409(d)			
Vesting		409(c)			
Voting rights		401(a)(22) 409(e) 4975(e)(7)			
Evasion of liability					
Multiemployer plan	4212(c)				
Single-employer plan	4069				
Excess benefit plan					
Definition	3(36)				
Unfunded excluded from ERISA	4(b)(5) 4021(b)(8)				
Excess benefit transactions		4958			
Excess contributions, tax on		4979	54.4979-1		

[1]Regulatory references in this index are included for researching convenience. Text of the regulations can be found in *ERISA Regulations, 2012 Edition* (BNA).
[2]The prefix **p** indicates a proposed regulation.
[3]Regulations marked with an asterisks (*) indicate a PBGC regulation.

	ERISA[1]	IRC[1]	Treas. Regs.[2] (26 CFR)	DOL & PBGC Regs.[2,3] (29 CFR)	HHS Regs. (45 CFR)
Excess deferrals, refund of (*see also* Elective deferrals)		401(k)(8) 402(g)(2)	1.401(k)-2(b)(2)(v) 1.402(g)-1(e) 1.415(c)-1(b)		
Exclusive purpose/benefit	404(a)(1)	401(a)(2)			
Exculpatory provisions	410(a)				
Exempt organizations		501(c)			
Black Lung trust		501(c)(21)			
Group legal services (*see also* Group legal services plan)		501(c)(20)			
Pension plan, employee contributions only		501(c)(18)	1.501(c)(18)-1		
Plans of					
Cash or deferred arrangement		401(k)(4)(B)	1.401(k)-1(e)(4)		
Deferred compensation plan		457	1.457-1–4		
Profit-sharing plan		401(a)(27)			
Qualified plans		501(a)			
Retired miners' accident or health benefits trust		501(c)(21)			
Supplemental unemployment benefits (SUB) trust		501(c)(17)			
Expatriated corporations, insider stock compensation		4985			
Expatriation, election to defer tax		877A			

-F-

	ERISA[1]	IRC[1]	Treas. Regs.[2] (26 CFR)	DOL & PBGC Regs.[2,3] (29 CFR)	HHS Regs. (45 CFR)
Family and Medical Leave Act (FMLA)					
Cafeteria plan, effect on			1.125-3		
Felony conviction	411				
Fiduciary responsibility					
Actions under Title IV	4023				
Anuity provider, selection of	404(a)(1)(B)			2550.404a-4	
Bonding	412(a)				
Breach					
Co-fiduciary liability	405			2509.75-5, -8	
Knowing participation in	502(i)			**p**2560.502i-1	
Liability for	409				

For an Index to PHSA sections after amendment by PPACA and other legislation (Part 3), see separate PHSA Index following this Index.

	ERISA[1]	IRC[1]	Treas. Regs.[2] (26 CFR)	DOL & PBGC Regs.[2,3] (29 CFR)	HHS Regs. (45 CFR)
Penalty for	502(i)			p2560.502i-1	
Statute of limitations	413				
Definition	3(21)	4975(e)(3)		2509.75-4, -8 2510.3-21	
Duties of (*see also* Prudence)	404			2550.404a-1	
Exculpatory provisions	410				
Felon prohibited as	411				
Insurance or indemnification	410(b)			2509.75-4	
Investments, economically targeted	403, 404			2509.08-1	
Participant-directed accounts (*see* Participant-directed accounts)					
Prohibited transactions (*see* Prohibited transactions)					
Financial statement					
Form not required	109(b)				
Requirement for	103(a)–(b)			2520.103-1	
Firefighters plans (*see* Police and firefighters plans)					
Five-percent owner					
Definition		416(i)(1)(B)(i)			
Distributions, required		401(a)(9)			
Payments before age 59½		72(m)(5)			
Flexible spending arrangements (FSAs)—military		125(h)			
Foreign affiliate, American employees of		406	1.406-1		
Foreign deferred compensation plan, deduction for		404A	p1.404A-1–7		
Foreign employment of U.S. citizens					
Domestic subsidiary		407	1.407-1		
Foreign affiliate		406	1.406-1		
Foreign investments	404(b)			2550.404b-1	
Forfeitable benefits, statement of (*see also* Vesting)	105(c)				
Forfeitures (*see also* Vesting)		401(a)(8) 401(a)(19)			
Forms	109				

[1]Regulatory references in this index are included for researching convenience. Text of the regulations can be found in *ERISA Regulations, 2012 Edition* (BNA).
[2]The prefix **p** indicates a proposed regulation.
[3]Regulations marked with an asterisks (*) indicate a PBGC regulation.

	ERISA[1]	IRC[1]	Treas. Regs.[2] (26 CFR)	DOL & PBGC Regs.[2,3] (29 CFR)	HHS Regs. (45 CFR)
Fringe benefits					
Athletic facility		132(j)(4)			
Automobile, personal use			1.61-21		
Auto salesmen		132(j)(3)	1.132-5(o)		
Bicycle commuting		132(f)(1)(D) (5)(F)			
Commuter highway vehicle		132(f)(1)(A) 132(f)(5)(B)			
Controlled group		414(t)			
De minimis fringe		132(e)	1.132-6		
Discrimination		132(j)(1)	1.132-8		
Eating facility		132(e)(2)	1.132-7		
Educational or training benefits (*see* Education or training)					
Employee		132(f)(5)(E), (h)	1.132-1(b)		
Gross income, inclusion in		61(a)(1)	1.61-21		
Gym		132(j)(4)			
Highly compensated employee		132(j)(6)	1.132-8(f)		
Meals and lodging, employer convenience		119	1.119-1		
No-additional-cost service		132(b)	1.132-2		
Parking, qualified		132(f)(1)(C) 132(f)(5)(C)			
Qualified employee discount		132(c)	1.132-3		
Qualified moving expense reimbursement		132(g)			
Qualified transportation fringe		132(f)			
Qualified tuition program		529			
Subchapter S corporation		1372			
Tax on excess		4977			
Transit pass		132(f)(1)(B) 132(f)(5)(A)			
Working condition fringe		132(d)	1.132-5		
Frozen deposits (*see also* Rollovers)		402(c)(7)			
Fund					
PBGC	4001(a)(5)				
Welfare benefit fund		419(e)			
Funded current liability percentage	302(d)(8)	412(*l*)(8)			

For an Index to PHSA sections after amendment by PPACA and other legislation (Part 3), see separate PHSA Index following this Index.

	ERISA[1]	IRC[1]	Treas. Regs.[2] (26 CFR)	DOL & PBGC Regs.[2,3] (29 CFR)	HHS Regs. (45 CFR)
Funding policy	402(b)(1)				
Financial statement, inclusion in	103(b)(2)			2520.103-1	
Funding standard prior to Pension Protection Act of 2006 (*see also* Funding under Pension Protection Act of 2006)					
Agency coordination	3002				
Alternative deficit reduc-tion contribution	302(d)(12)(A)	412(*l*)(12)(A)			
Alternative minimum funding standard	305	412(g)	**p**1.412(g)-1		
Anticipation of benefit increases payable in the future	302(c)(12)	412(c)(12)			
Current liability, mortality tables	302(d)(7)	412(*l*)(7)	1.412(*l*)(7)-1		
Due date for contributions					
Annual	302(c)(10)	412(c)(10)			
Quarterly	302(e)(3)	412(m)(3)			
Failure to meet					
Excise tax		4971	54.4971-1		
Lien	302(f)	412(n)			
Notice to participants	101(d)				
Notice to PBGC	302(f)(4)	412(n)(4)		4043.31*	
Full funding limit					
Deduction limit	302(a)(1)				
Definition	302(c)(7)	412(c)(7)			
Effect on funding	302(c)(6)	412(c)(6)			
Multiemployer plan	302(b)(7)	412(b)(7)			
Funding standard account	302(b)	412(b)			
Interest rates	302(b)(5)	412(b)(5)			
Special rule through 2007	302(b)(5)(B) (ii)(II)	412(b)(5)(B) (ii)(II)			
Liquidity requirement	302(e)(5)	412(m)(5)			
Required installments (quarterly)	302(e)	412(m)			
Unfunded current liability	302(d)(8)	412(*l*)(8)			
Multiemployer plan, notice of	101(f)				
Unfunded mortality increase amount	302(d)(10)	412(*l*)(10)			

[1]Regulatory references in this index are included for researching convenience. Text of the regulations can be found in *ERISA Regulations, 2012 Edition* (BNA).
[2]The prefix **p** indicates a proposed regulation.
[3]Regulations marked with an asterisks (*) indicate a PBGC regulation.

	ERISA[1]	IRC[1]	Treas. Regs.[2] (26 CFR)	DOL & PBGC Regs.[2,3] (29 CFR)	HHS Regs. (45 CFR)
Waivers and variances (*see also* Waived funding deficiency)					
Application for, due date of	303(d)(1)	412(d)(4)			
Benefit increases	304(b)	412(f)			
Extension of amortization periods	304	412(e)			
Grant of waiver	303	412(d)			
Interest on	303(a)(1)	412(d)(1)			
Notice of	303(e) 304(c)	412(f)(4)			
Security for	306	412(f)(3)			
Funding under Pension Protection Act of 2006					
Multiemployer plans					
Actuary	305(b)(3)	432(b)(3)			
Critical status	305(b)(2)	432(b)(2)			
Endangered status	305(b)(1), (c)	432(b)(1)			
Excise tax on endangered plans		4971(g)(2)			
Insolvent plans	4245	418E			
Minimum funding standards	304	431			
Notice requirements	101(k)				
Rehabilitation plans	305(e)	432(e)			
Special rules	304(b)(8)	431(b)(8)			
Single-employer plans	303	430			
Alternate required installments	303(c)(7)				
Minimum required contribution					
Credit balances	303(f)	430(f)	1.430(f)-1		
Funding target percentage	303(d)	430(d)	1.430(d)-1		
Plan assets, valuation	303(g)	430(g)	1.430(g)-1		
Shortfall amortization installments	303(c)(2)	430(c)(2)			
Special rules for 2008, 2009, and 2010		436(j)(3)[4]			
Target normal cost	303(b)	430(b)	1.430(d)-1		
Waiver for business hardship	302(c)(1)	412(c)(1)			
Mortality table					
Current liability			1.431(c)(6)-1		

For an Index to PHSA sections after amendment by PPACA and other legislation (Part 3), see separate PHSA Index following this Index.

	ERISA[1]	IRC[1]	Treas. Regs.[2] (26 CFR)	DOL & PBGC Regs.[2,3] (29 CFR)	HHS Regs. (45 CFR)
Present value			1.430(h)(3)-1		
Plan specific substitute, present value			1.430(h)(3)-2		
Underfunded plans					
Amendment limits	305(d)(1)(B)	432(d)(1)(B)			
Contingent events benefits	206(g)(1)	436(b)	1.436-1(b)		
Exception, new plans	206(g)(6)	436(g)			
Lump sum distributions	206(d)(3)	436(d)	1.436-1(d)		
Nonqualified deferred compensation		409A(b)(3)			
Notice requirements	101(j)				
PBGC, financial report to	4010(b)(1), (d)				
PBGC, variable rate premium	4006(a)(3)(E)(iii)				
Shutdown benefits	206(g)(1)	436(b)	1.436-1(b)		

-G-

	ERISA[1]	IRC[1]	Treas. Regs.[2] (26 CFR)	DOL & PBGC Regs.[2,3] (29 CFR)	HHS Regs. (45 CFR)
Garnishment					
Qualified domestic relations order not	206(d)(3)(M)				
Genetic information— nondiscrimination	502(c)(9) 702(b)(2)(A), (b)(3), (c)–(e) 733(d)(5)–(9)	9802(b)(3)(c)– (f)[g]	54.9802-3T	2590.702-1	
Golden parachute payments		280G	1.280G-1		
Coordination with remuneration limit		162(m)(4)			
Government contracts, study on	3032				
Governmental plans					
Congressional study of	3031				
Definition	3(32)	414(d)			
Early retirement incentive, voluntary		457(e)(11)(D)			
Defined		457(e)(11)(D)(ii)			
Payments from		457(e)(11)(D)(i)			
Severance pay plan, treated as		457(e)(11)(D)(i)			
Welfare plan, treated as	3(2)(B)				

[1]Regulatory references in this index are included for researching convenience. Text of the regulations can be found in *ERISA Regulations, 2012 Edition* (BNA).
[2]The prefix **p** indicates a proposed regulation.
[3]Regulations marked with an asterisks (*) indicate a PBGC regulation.

	ERISA[1]	IRC[1]	Treas. Regs.[2] (26 CFR)	DOL & PBGC Regs.[2,3] (29 CFR)	HHS Regs. (45 CFR)
Employment retention plans					
Defined		457(f)(4)(C), (D)			
Welfare plan, treated as	3(2)(B)				
Exclusion of					
Title I	4(b)(1)				
Title IV	4021(b)(2)				
Group trust, participation in		401(a)(24)			
Health and long-term care insurance, distributions for		402(l)			
Health plan continuation, tax exclusion		4980B(d)(2)			
Indian tribes	3(32)	414(d)			
Coverage, exception	4021(b)(14)				
Qualified plans					
Domestic relations order		414(p)(9), (11)			
Participant's deceased beneficiary, expenses of		105(j)			
Participation		410(c)(1)(A)			
Permissive service credit		403(b)(13) 415(n) 457(e)(17)			
Pick-up of employee contributions		414(h)(2)			
Police and firefighter plans (see Police and firefighters plans)					
Required beginning date		401(a)(9)(C)			
Survivor annuity		401(a)(11), 417			
Top-heavy exception		401(a)(10)(B)			
Vesting		411(e)			
Gross income		61	1.61-2–21		
Group health plan (*see also* Health benefits)	607(1)	5000(b)(1)			
Definitions	733				
Enrollment periods				2590.701-6 p2590.701-6	
Family and Medical Leave Act				p2590.701-8	
Grandfathered health plans			54.9815-1251T	2590.715-1251	147.140
Guaranteed renewability in multiemployer plans	703	9803			

For an Index to PHSA sections after amendment by PPACA and other legislation (Part 3), see separate PHSA Index following this Index.

	ERISA[1]	IRC[1]	Treas. Regs.[2] (26 CFR)	DOL & PBGC Regs.[2,3] (29 CFR)	HHS Regs. (45 CFR)
Health factor, discrimination based on	702			2590.702	
Internal claims and appeals				2590.715-2719	
Large group health plan		5000(b)(2)			
Limits			54.9815-2711T		147.126
Mental health parity	712	9812	54.9812-1T	2590.712	
Mothers and newborns	711	9811		2590.711	
Nonconforming group health plan		5000(c)			
Penalty for failure to meet portability and other requirements		4980D			
Portability (limitation on preexisting condition exclusion)	701, 2701	9801	54.9815-2704T	2590.701-3	147.108
Creditable coverage			54.9801-4, p54.9801-4	2590.701-4, p2590.701-4	
Evidence of			54.9801-5, p54.9801-5	2590.701-5, p2590.701-5	
Definitions			54.9801-2	2590.701-2	
Enrollment periods, special			54.9801-6, p54.9801-6	2590.701-6, p2590.701-6	
Family and Medical Leave Act, interaction with			p54.9801-7	p2590.701-8	
Group health plans, special rules			54.9831-1, p54.9831-1	2590.732, p2590.732	
Preemption			54.9815-1251T	2590.731	
Preexisting condition exclusion, limit on period of			54.9801-3 54.9815-2704T	2590.701-3	
HMO affiliation period				2590.701-7	
Preemption	731(a)			2590.731	
Preventative services			54.9815-2713T(b)(1)	2590.715-2713(b)(1)	
Prohibition of discrimination based on health status	702	9802	54.9802-1		
Church plans			54.9802-2		
Regulations	734	9806			
Rescissions, prohibition on			54.9815-2712T		147.128
Small group health plan	732			2590.732 p2590.732	
Special rules	732				
Students	714				
Group legal services plan					

[1]Regulatory references in this index are included for researching convenience. Text of the regulations can be found in *ERISA Regulations, 2012 Edition* (BNA).

[2]The prefix **p** indicates a proposed regulation.

[3]Regulations marked with an asterisks (*) indicate a PBGC regulation.

	ERISA[1]	IRC[1]	Treas. Regs.[2] (26 CFR)	DOL & PBGC Regs.[2,3] (29 CFR)	HHS Regs. (45 CFR)
Annual report (IRS)		6039D			
Discrimination		120(c)(1), 505	**p**1.120-2(e)		
Exclusion from income		120			
Exemption for trust		501(c)(20)			
Application required		505(c)			
Highly compensated employee		505(b)(5)			
Notice to IRS		505(c)	1.120-3		
Written plan requirement		120(b)	**p**1.120-2(b)		
Group life insurance (*see* Life insurance, Group)					
Group trust		401(a)(24)			
Guaranteed benefit policy	401(b)(2)				
Guaranteed benefits (PBGC)					
Aggregate limit	4022B				
Multiemployer plans					
Benefit amendments	4022A(b)				
Insolvent plans	4022A(a)				
Monthly limit	4022A(c)				
Nonbasic benefits	4022A(d)				
Supplemental guarantee	4022A(g)(2)				
Single-employer plans	4022				
Bankruptcy	4022(g), 4044(e)				
Benefit amendments	4022(b)(1) 4022(b)(7)			4022.24–.26*	
Disqualified plan	4022(b)(6)			4022.27*	
Majority owner	4022(b)(5)				
Monthly limit	4022(b)(3)			4022.22–.23*	
Nonbasic benefits	4022(c)				
Qualified preretirement survivor annuity	4022(e)				
Substantial owner	4022(b)(5) 4021(b)(9), (d)			Part 4022*	
Uniformed service				4022.11*	
Gym or athletic facility		132(j)(4)			

-H-

	ERISA[1]	IRC[1]	Treas. Regs.[2] (26 CFR)	DOL & PBGC Regs.[2,3] (29 CFR)	HHS Regs. (45 CFR)
Hawaii Prepaid Health Care Act	514(b)(5)				
Health benefits (*see also* Welfare benefit plan)					

For an Index to PHSA sections after amendment by PPACA and other legislation (Part 3), see separate PHSA Index following this Index.

	ERISA[1]	IRC[1]	Treas. Regs.[2] (26 CFR)	DOL & PBGC Regs.[2,3] (29 CFR)	HHS Regs. (45 CFR)
Account in pension plan (*see also* Retiree health account)		401(h)	1.401(a)(4)-1(c)(14) 1.401-14(b)		
Adopted children, coverage required	609(c)				
Cafeteria plan		125(g)(2)	1.125-2T p1.125-1, Q-17		
Continuation of (COBRA)					
Benefit, type of	602(1)	4980B(f)(2)(A)	54.4980B-1		
Church plan, exclusion		4980B(d)(3)	54.4980B-2, Q-4(b)		
Conversion	602(5)	4980B(f)(2)(E)	54.4980B-7, Q-8		
Correction		4980B(g)(4)			
Coverage	601	4980B(d)	54.4980B-2		
Covered employee	607(2)	4980B(f)(7)	54.4980B-3, Q-2		
Death of employee	603(1)	4980B(f)(3)	54.4980B-4, Q-1		
Definitions				2590.701-2	
Dependent child	603(5)	4980B(g)(1)(A)	54.4980B-3		147.120
Disabled individual	602(2)(A), (3) 606(a)(3)	4980B(f)(2)(B) 4980B(f)(6)(C)	54.4980B-7, Q-5		
Divorce	603(3)	4980B(f)(3)(C)	54.4980B-4, Q-1		
Election of	605	4980B(f)(5)	54.4980B-6		
Temporary extension for TAA-eligible individuals	605, 701(c)(2)(C)	4980B(f)(5)(C)			
Enrollment, special periods	701(f)				
Failure to notify health plan of cessation of eligibility		6720C			
Indian		139D			
Insurability	602(4)	4980B(f)(2)(D)			
Medicare (*see* Medicare)					
Multiemployer plan	606(a)(2) 606(a)(3) 606(b)–(c) 607(5)	4980B(f)(6)(B) 4980B(f)(6)(C) 4980B(f)(6)(D) 4980B(f)(8)	54.4980B-2, Q-3 54.4980B-9, Q-9–10		
Notice of	606	4980B(f)(6)	54.4980B-6	2590.606-1–4	
Pediatric vaccine	609(d)	4980B(f)(1)			
Penalty, failure to notify	502(c)(1)		54.4980B-1, Q-9		
Period of	602(2)	4980B(f)(2)(B)	54.4980B-7		
Pre-existing condition	701	9801, 9815	54.9815-2704T	2590.701-1–7	147.108
Premium	602(3) 604	4980B(f)(2)(C) 4980B(f)(4)	54.4980B-8		

[1]Regulatory references in this index are included for researching convenience. Text of the regulations can be found in *ERISA Regulations, 2012 Edition* (BNA).
[2]The prefix **p** indicates a proposed regulation.
[3]Regulations marked with an asterisks (*) indicate a PBGC regulation.

	ERISA[1]	IRC[1]	Treas. Regs.[2] (26 CFR)	DOL & PBGC Regs.[2,3] (29 CFR)	HHS Regs. (45 CFR)
Premium assistance		139C	6432		
Qualified beneficiary	607(3)	4980B(g)(1)	54.4980B-3		147.120
Qualifying event	603	4980B(f)(3)	54.4980B-4		
Retirees, bankruptcy	602(2)(A)(iii) 603(6) 607(3)(C)	4980B(f)(2)(B) 4980B(f)(3)(F) 4980B(g)(1)	54.4980B-4, Q-1 54.4980B-7, Q-4		
Tax		4980B(a)–(e)	54.4980B-2, Q-10		
Termination of employment	603(2)	4980B(f)(3)(B)	54.4980B-4, Q-1 54.4980B-7, Q-4		
Credits for health insurance costs		35, 36B, 6050T 7527			
Discrimination		105(h)	1.105-11(c)		
Exclusion from income					
Employer contributions to		106	p1.106-1		
Payments from		104(a)(3), 105(b)	1.105-1(a)		
Inclusion in income		105(a)	1.105-1(a)		
Medicaid (*see* Medicaid)					
Medicare (*see* Medicare)					
Public safety officers, retired		402(*l*)			
Reimbursements for medicine		106(f)			
S corporation shareholder		162(*l*)(5)			
Self-employed individual		162(*l*)			
Health care reform					
Credits					
Refundable credit for premium assistance		36B			
Small employers		45R			
Definitions		4377			
Employers and group health plans					
Excise tax on high-cost coverage		4980I			
Failure to provide employee coverage		4980H			
Reporting individual coverage		6055, 6056			
Self-insured plan, fee based on average number of lives covered		4376			
Treatment as tax		4377(c)			
ERISA, relation to PHSA	715				

For an Index to PHSA sections after amendment by PPACA and other legislation (Part 3), see separate PHSA Index following this Index.

	ERISA[1]	IRC[1]	Treas. Regs.[2] (26 CFR)	DOL & PBGC Regs.[2,3] (29 CFR)	HHS Regs. (45 CFR)
Health insurance issuers					
Deduction for compensation		162(m)(6)			
Fee per policy		4375			
Treatment as tax		4377(c)			
Reporting individual coverage		6055			
Individuals					
Minimum essential coverage		5000A(f)			147.140
Requirement of coverage		5000A			149.35
Patient-Centered Outcomes Research Trust Fund		9511			
Tax code, relation to PHSA		9815			54.9815-2714T 54.9815-2251T 54.9815-2704T 54.9815-2711T 54.9815-2712T 54.9815-2719AT
Web portal					pt. 159
Health savings accounts					
Comparable contributions		4980G	54.4980G-4		
Failure to make			54.4980G-1		
Contributions for 55 and over		223(b)(3)			
Coordination with other contributions		223(b)(4)			
Deductions—limitations		223(a), (b)			
Definitions		223(c), (d)			
Distributions—tax treatment		223(f)			
Highly compensated employee					
Definition					
Cafeteria plan		125(d)			
Cash or deferred arrangement		401(k)(5)			
Fringe benefits		132(j)(6)			
Group legal services		505(b)(5)			
Qualified plans		414(q)	1.414(q)-1T		
VEBA		505(b)(5)			
Discrimination in favor of (*see* Discrimination)					
Loans to	408(b)(1)	4975(d)(1)		2550.408b-1	

[1]Regulatory references in this index are included for researching convenience. Text of the regulations can be found in *ERISA Regulations, 2012 Edition* (BNA).
[2]The prefix **p** indicates a proposed regulation.
[3]Regulations marked with an asterisks (*) indicate a PBGC regulation.

	ERISA[1]	IRC[1]	Treas. Regs.[2] (26 CFR)	DOL & PBGC Regs.[2,3] (29 CFR)	HHS Regs. (45 CFR)
Highly compensated individual					
Cafeteria plan		125(e)(2)			
Health benefits (self-insured)		105(h)(5)	1.105-11(d)		
Highly compensated participants		125(e)(1)	p1.125-1, Q-13		
Hours of service	202(a)(3)	410(a)(3)(C)		2530.200b-2–3	
Hybrid retirement plans		411	1.411(a)(13)-1 1.411(b)(5)-1		

-I-

	ERISA[1]	IRC[1]	Treas. Regs.[2] (26 CFR)	DOL & PBGC Regs.[2,3] (29 CFR)	HHS Regs. (45 CFR)
Incentive stock option (*see* **Stock options, Incentive**)					
Income on the contract		72(u)(2)(A)			
Independent contractors					
Deferred compensation, deduction		404(d)	1.404(d)-1T		
Nonprofit organizations		457(e)(12)			
Indian tribal plans (*see* **Governmental plans**)					
Indicia of ownership outside U.S.	404(b)			2550.404b-1	
Individual account plan					
Contribution limits		415(c)			
Definition	3(34), 4021(c)(1)	414(i)			
Eligible individual account plan					
Definition	407(d)(3)				
Diversification	404(a)(2) 407(a)(2)			2550.404a-1(b)(2)(i)	
Employer securities	408(e)			2550.408e	
Exclusion from					
Funding requirements	301(a)(8)	412(h)(1)			
Title IV	4021(b)(1)				
Safe harbor for distributions from terminated				2550.404a-3	
Termination				2578.1	
Individual retirement account/annuity (IRA)					
Active duty reservists/ national guardsmen		72(t)(2)(G)			

For an Index to PHSA sections after amendment by PPACA and other legislation (Part 3), see separate PHSA Index following this Index.

	ERISA[1]	IRC[1]	Treas. Regs.[2] (26 CFR)	DOL & PBGC Regs.[2,3] (29 CFR)	HHS Regs. (45 CFR)
Automatic rollover safe harbor				2550.404a-2	
Charitable distributions		408(d)(8)			
Collectibles, investment in		408(m)	p1.408-10		
Contributions					
Employees of bankrupt employer		219(b)(5)(C)			
Contribution to					
Deductible		219			
Nondeductible		408(o)	p1.219-1		
Recharacterized			1.408A-5		
Reporting nondeductible contributions		6693(b)	301.6693-1		
Coverdell Education Savings Accounts		530			
Custodial accounts	403(b)(3)	408(h)	1.408-2(d)	2550.403b-1(a)(3)(ii)	
Death benefits		408(a)(6) 408(b)(3)	1.408-8		
Deductible amount, limitation		219(b), (g)			
Deemed IRAs under qualified employer plans		408(q)	1.408(q)-1		
Definition		408(a)–(b)	1.408-2		
Distribution from					
Early		72(t)			
Minimum		408(a)(6) 408(b)(3)	1.408-8		
Tax for failure to distribute		4974	54.4974-1		
Endowment contract		408(e)(5)	1.408-3(e)		
Excess contributions, tax on		4973	p54.4973-1		
Exemption from tax		408(e)(1)	1.408-1(b)		
Income limit, indexed for inflation (Roth IRA)		219(g)(8) 408A(c)(3)[D]			
Investments			1.408-2		
Nonbank trustees			1.408-2(e), 1.408-2T(e)(8)		
PBGC assistance	4009				
Income limit, indexed for inflation (Roth IRA)		219(g)(8) 408A(c)(3)[D]			
Investments			1.408-2		

[1]Regulatory references in this index are included for researching convenience. Text of the regulations can be found in *ERISA Regulations, 2012 Edition* (BNA).
[2]The prefix **p** indicates a proposed regulation.
[3]Regulations marked with an asterisks (*) indicate a PBGC regulation.

	ERISA[1]	IRC[1]	Treas. Regs.[2] (26 CFR)	DOL & PBGC Regs.[2,3] (29 CFR)	HHS Regs. (45 CFR)
Nonbank trustees			1.408-2(e), 1.408-2T(e)(8)		
PBGC assistance	4009				
Pledging		408(e)(4)	1.408-1(c)(4)		
Prohibited transaction	408(e)(2)	408, 4975(c)(3), (d)	1.408-1(c)(3)		
Report to IRS					
Annual		408(i)	1.408-5(c)(2)		
Nondeductible contributions		408(o)(4)			
Penalty for failure to file		6693	301.6693-1		
Rollovers (*see* Rollovers)					
Roth IRA		408A	1.408A-4T		
Income limit, indexed for inflation		408A(c)(3)(D)			
Rollover from qualified plans		408A(c)(3)(B)			
Simplified employee pension (*see also* Simplified employee pension (SEP))		219(b)(2)			
Taxation of					
Borrowing on annuity contract		408(e)(3)			
Distributions before age 59½		72(t)			
Excess contributions		4973			
Failure to distribute		4974			
Individual retirement plan		7701(a)(37)			
Industry or activity affecting commerce	3(12)				
Insurance company					
General accounts	401				
Guaranteed benefit policy	401(b)(2)				
Investment manager	3(38)				
Plan assets	401(b)(2)				
Prohibited transaction exemptions					
Insurance company plan	408(b)(5)	4975(d)(5)			
Pooled investment fund	408(b)(8)	4975(d)(8)			
Report	103(a)(2) 103(b)(3) 103(e)			2520.103-2, -5 2520.103-4, -9	
Separate account					
Definition	3(17)				

For an Index to PHSA sections after amendment by PPACA and other legislation (Part 3), see separate PHSA Index following this Index.

	ERISA[1]	IRC[1]	Treas. Regs.[2] (26 CFR)	DOL & PBGC Regs.[2,3] (29 CFR)	HHS Regs. (45 CFR)
Plan assets	401(b)(2)				
Report	103(a)(2), (b)(3)			2520.103-4	
Insurance contract plan	301(b)				
Insurer	401(b)(2)(A)				
Integration (*see* Social Security integration)					
Interference					
Coercive interference	511				
Rights protected by ERISA	510				
Inurement of plan assets	403(c)	401(a)(2)			
Investigative authority, DOL and other agencies	504				
Investment company, registered					
Definition	3(38)(B)(i)				
Fiduciary status	3(21)(B)				
Plan assets	401(b)(1)				
Investment manager					
Appointment	402(c)(3) 403(a)(2) 405(d)(1)			2509.75-5 2550.403a-1(c)(2)	
Definition	3(38)			2509.75-5	
Investment policy				2509.94-2	
Liability of other fiduciary	405(d)			2509.75-8	
Proxy voting guidelines				2509.94-2	
State registered investment advisors, filing requirements				2510.3-38	

-J-

	ERISA[1]	IRC[1]	Treas. Regs.[2] (26 CFR)	DOL & PBGC Regs.[2,3] (29 CFR)	HHS Regs. (45 CFR)
Joint and survivor annuity (*see* Spouse's benefits)					
Jurisdiction					
PBGC					
Suits against	4003(f)				
Suits by	4003(e)(3)				
Single-employer plan terminations	4070(c)				
Termination actions	4042(f)				
Title I	502(e)–(f)				

[1]Regulatory references in this index are included for researching convenience. Text of the regulations can be found in *ERISA Regulations, 2012 Edition* (BNA).
[2]The prefix **p** indicates a proposed regulation.
[3]Regulations marked with an asterisks (*) indicate a PBGC regulation.

	ERISA[1]	IRC[1]	Treas. Regs.[2] (26 CFR)	DOL & PBGC Regs.[2,3] (29 CFR)	HHS Regs. (45 CFR)

-K-

	ERISA[1]	IRC[1]	Treas. Regs.[2] (26 CFR)	DOL & PBGC Regs.[2,3] (29 CFR)	HHS Regs. (45 CFR)
Keogh plan (*see* Self-employed individuals)					
Key employee		416(i)(1)			
Cafeteria plan		125(b)(2)			
Life insurance		79(d)(6)			
Loans to		72(p)(3)			
Medical account, qualified plan		401(h)			
Postretirement medical or life insurance		419A(d)			
Top-heavy plans		416(i)(1)	1.416-1		

-L-

	ERISA[1]	IRC[1]	Treas. Regs.[2] (26 CFR)	DOL & PBGC Regs.[2,3] (29 CFR)	HHS Regs. (45 CFR)
Labor union (*see* Employee organization)					
Large group health plan		5000(b)(2)			
Leased employees		414(n)	p1.414(o)-1		
Liens					
Contribution payments, unpaid	303(k)	412(n), 430(k)			
PBGC liability	4068				
Life insurance (*see also* Welfare benefit plan, Funded)					
Cost of		79(d)	1.79-1(d)		
Definition			1.79-1(a)		
Discrimination		79(d)	1.79-4T		
Exclusion of proceeds		101	1.101-1–7		
FICA tax treatment		3121(a)(2)(C)			
Group		79, 6052			
Post-retirement		79(d)(6)	1.79-2(b)		
Funding limit		419A(d)			
Premiums, taxation of		79(a)			
Valuation of, when distributed from qualified plan			1.402(a)-1		
Life insurance benefit		419A(f)(3)			
Line of business (*see* Separate line of business)					
Loans to participants					

For an Index to PHSA sections after amendment by PPACA and other legislation (Part 3), see separate PHSA Index following this Index.

	ERISA[1]	IRC[1]	Treas. Regs.[2] (26 CFR)	DOL & PBGC Regs.[2,3] (29 CFR)	HHS Regs. (45 CFR)
Prohibited transaction exemption	408(b)(1)	4975(d)(1)		2550.408b-1	
Spousal consent to	205(c)(4)	417(a)(4)			
Surviving spouse's rights	205(e)(3) 205(k)	417(c)(3) 417(f)(5)			
Treated as distributions		72(p)	1.72(p)-1		
Long-term care insurance		6050U			
Lump sum distributions					
Involuntary, limit on	203(e) 205(g)	411(a)(11), 417(e)	1.417(e)-1		
Taxation of (*see* Taxation of distributions)					
Terminated multiemployer plan	4041A(f)				

-M-

	ERISA[1]	IRC[1]	Treas. Regs.[2] (26 CFR)	DOL & PBGC Regs.[2,3] (29 CFR)	HHS Regs. (45 CFR)
Mandatory contributions, employee (*see* Employee contributions)					
Maritime industry					
Day of service				2530.200b-7–8	
Participation requirement	202(a)(3)(D)	410(a)(3)(D)		2530.200b-6	
Suspension of benefits				2530.203-3	
Year of participation	204(b)(3)	411(b)(4)		2530.200b-6(e)	
Matching contributions					
Actual contribution percentage		401(m)	1.401(m)-2		
Definitions		401(m)(4)	1.401(m)-5		
Employee contributions			1.401(m)-1		
Forfeiture of	203(a)(3)(F)	411(a)(3)(G)			
Safe harbor			1.401(m)-3		
Maternity/paternity absence					
Participation	202(b)(5)	410(a)(5)	1.410(a)-9		
Vesting	203(b)(3)(E)	411(a)(6)	1.410(a)-9		
Maximum benefits, contributions					
Church plan		415(c)(7)	1.415(c)-1(d)		
Combined plans		415(f)	1.415(f)-1		
Deduction limit		404(j)			
Defined benefit plan		415(b)	1.415(b)-1		
Defined contribution plan		415(c)	1.415(c)-1		

---

[1]Regulatory references in this index are included for researching convenience. Text of the regulations can be found in *ERISA Regulations, 2012 Edition* (BNA).

[2]The prefix **p** indicates a proposed regulation.

[3]Regulations marked with an asterisks (*) indicate a PBGC regulation.

	ERISA[1]	IRC[1]	Treas. Regs.[2] (26 CFR)	DOL & PBGC Regs.[2,3] (29 CFR)	HHS Regs. (45 CFR)
Employee stock ownership plan		415(c)(6)	1.415(c)-1(f)		
Medical benefits		415(*l*)	1.415(c)-1(e)		
Qualification requirement		401(a)(16)	1.401(a)-16		
Top-heavy plan		416(h)	1.416-1, M		
Welfare benefit plan, funded		419A	1.415(c)-1(e)		
Meals and lodging (*see* Fringe Benefits, Meals and lodging)					
Medicaid					
Assignment of participant's rights to					
Preemption exception	514(b)(8)				
State Medicaid program	609(b)				
Medical benefits		419A(f)(2)			
Medical benefits for retirees					
Limits on		415(*l*), 419A(d)			
Pension plan account		401(h)	1.401-14(c)(2)		
Medical expense (deductibility)		213	1.213-1 et seq.		
Medical reimbursement plan (self-insured)		105(h)	1.105-11		
Medical Savings Accounts (Archer MSAs)					
Cafeteria plan		125			
Deduction		62(a)(16) 220(a), (c)			
Earnings (exemption)		220(e)			
Excess contributions		4973			
Exclusion from income		106(b)			
Failure to match contributions (penalty)		4980E(d)			
Prohibited transactions		4975			
Medicare					
Continuation coverage	601	4980B(f)			
End of coverage	602(2)(A) 602(2)(D)	4980B(f)(2)(B)			
Qualifying event	603(4)	4980B(f)(3)(D)			
Coordination with health plans		5000			
Civil enforcement	502(a)(7)				
Civil penalty	502(c)(4)				

For an Index to PHSA sections after amendment by PPACA and other legislation (Part 3), see separate PHSA Index following this Index.

	ERISA[1]	IRC[1]	Treas. Regs.[2] (26 CFR)	DOL & PBGC Regs.[2,3] (29 CFR)	HHS Regs. (45 CFR)
Medicare Advantage MSA		138			
Medicare+Choice MSA (*see* Medicare Advantage MSA)					
Mental health parity and substance use disorder benefits, group health plans	712	9812	54.9812-1T	2590.712	
Mergers and transfers					
Multiemployer plans					
Asset transfers	4234				
Between multiemployer plans	4231	414(*l*)		4231.2–.3*	
Change in bargaining representative	4235				
Overburden credit	4244(g)	418C(g)			
With single-employer plan	4232	414(*l*)			
Single-employer plans	208	401(a)(12), 414(*l*)	1.401(a)-12 1.414(*l*)-1		
Military, benefits for		134 401(a)(37) 403(b)(14) 414(u)(9) 457(g)(4) 530(d)(9)			
Minimum benefits, top-heavy plan		416(c)	1.416-1		
Minimum funding standard (*see* Funding standard)					
Missing participants (*see* Termination—pension plan)					
Money purchase plan					
Designation of		401(a)(27)			
Employer securities, put option		401(a)(22)			
Mothers and newborns	711			2590.711	
Multiemployer plan					
Civil penalties	502(c)(8), 4302			2560.502c-8	
Civil suits	4301				
Contributions					
Deduction limit		404(a)(1)			
Contributions to					
Delinquent, collection of	502(g)(2)				
Mistaken contributions and withdrawal liability payments			1.401(a)(2)-1		

[1]Regulatory references in this index are included for researching convenience. Text of the regulations can be found in *ERISA Regulations, 2012 Edition* (BNA).
[2]The prefix **p** indicates a proposed regulation.
[3]Regulations marked with an asterisks (*) indicate a PBGC regulation.

	ERISA[1]	IRC[1]	Treas. Regs.[2] (26 CFR)	DOL & PBGC Regs.[2,3] (29 CFR)	HHS Regs. (45 CFR)
Obligation to pay	515				
Definition	3(37), 4001(a)(3)	414(f)	1.414(f)-1	2510.3-37	
Delinquent contributions, action for	502(g)(2)				
Election of plan status	4303	414(f)(5), (6)			
Revocation of	3(37)(G)	414(f)(6)			
Excess pension assets, transferred to retiree health plan		420(e)(5)			
Financial assistance (PBGC)					
Amount payable	4061				
Application for	4245(f)	418E(f)			
Funding, effect on	301(d) 304(b)	412(k) 431(b)(7)(F)			
Payment by PBGC	4261				
Funding (*see* Funding under Pension Protection Act of 2006)					
Funding (*see also* Funding standard)					
Amortization periods, pre-1980	302(b)(6)	412(b)(6)			
Expanded smoothing period and solvency test	304(b)(8)(B)–(C)				
Financial assistance, effect on	301(d) 304(b)(7)(F)	412(k) 431(b)(7)(F)			
Full funding limit	302(b)(7) 304(b)(7)	412(b)(7) 431(b)(7)			
Minimum funding	210(a)(3)	413(b)(5)–(6)			
Net investment losses, amortization of	304(b)(8)(A)				
Reorganization	302(a)(3) 302(b)(7) 304(a)(2) 304(b)(7)(B)	412(a) 412(b)(7) 431(a)(2) 431(b)(7)(B)			
Terminated plan	301(c)	412(j)			
Withdrawal liability	302(b)(7) 304(b)(7)	412(b)(7) 431(b)(7)			
Health benefits (*see also* Health benefits)					
Continuation, tax		4980B(c)(4)			
Mandatory disaggregation			1.401(a)(26)-2(d)(ii)(B)		

For an Index to PHSA sections after amendment by PPACA and other legislation (Part 3), see separate PHSA Index following this Index.

	ERISA[1]	IRC[1]	Treas. Regs.[2] (26 CFR)	DOL & PBGC Regs.[2,3] (29 CFR)	HHS Regs. (45 CFR)
Medicare/Medicaid coordination (*see* Medicare)					
Mergers and transfers (*see* Mergers and transfers)					
Minimum contribution requirement	4243	418B			
Minimum participation, exception		401(a)(26)	1.401(a)(26)-1(b)(2)		
Net experience loss, deferral of	302(b)(7)(F) 304(b)(7)(E)	412(b)(7)(F) 431(b)(7)(E)			
Notice, annual funding	101(f)(2)(B)(ii)(II)			2520.101-4	
Notice, reduction in accruals	204(h)	4980F(e)			
Overburden credit	4244	418C			
Participation, minimum	210(a)(1)	413(b)(1)		2530.210	
Partition	4233				
Plan information on request	101(k) 502(c)			2520.101-6	
Plan sponsor	4001(a)(10)				
Reducing future accruals	204(h)(1)	4980F(e)(1)			
Reorganization	4241–4244A	418–418D			
Reduction in benefits	203(a)(3)(E)	411(a)(3)			
Service forfeitable	203(a)(3)	411(a)(3)			
Single-employer election, revocation	3(37)(G)	414(f)(6)			
Successor plan	4231				
Summary report to employers, employee organizations	104(d)				
Suspension of benefits	203(a)(3)(B)	411(a)(3)(B)		2530.203-3	
Termination of					
Benefit reductions	4281				
Definition of	4041A				
Vesting, minimum	210(a)(2)	413(b)(4)		2530.203-1	
Vesting service	203(b)(1)	411(a)(4)(G)		2530.203-2	
Welfare plans, IRS returns		6039D(d)(3)			
Whistleblower protection for employer	510				
Multiple annuity starting dates			1.415(b)-1(b)(1) 1.415(b)-2		
Multiple employer plan					
Eligible combined plans				210(e)	

[1]Regulatory references in this index are included for researching convenience. Text of the regulations can be found in *ERISA Regulations, 2012 Edition* (BNA).
[2]The prefix **p** indicates a proposed regulation.
[3]Regulations marked with an asterisks (*) indicate a PBGC regulation.

	ERISA[1]	IRC[1]	Treas. Regs.[2] (26 CFR)	DOL & PBGC Regs.[2,3] (29 CFR)	HHS Regs. (45 CFR)
Participation, vesting, funding	210(b)	413(c)		2530.210	
Maintained by controlled group	210(c)				
Substantial employer					
Liability of	4063			4063.1*	
Notice of	4066				
Withdrawal of	4063				
Termination of	4064				
Multiple employer welfare arrangement					
Cease and desist orders and seizure orders	521				
Definition	3(40)				
False statements	519				
Preemption, exception from	514(b)(6), 520				

-N-

	ERISA[1]	IRC[1]	Treas. Regs.[2] (26 CFR)	DOL & PBGC Regs.[2,3] (29 CFR)	HHS Regs. (45 CFR)
Named fiduciary	402(a)(2)			2509.75-5	
Net premiums		72(u)(2)(B)			
No-additional-cost service		132(b)			
Non-basic benefits (*see also* Guaranteed benefits (PBGC))	4001(a)(7)				
Nondeductible contributions		408(o), 4972 6693(b)(1)			
Nondiscrimination testing		401(a)(4), (5)			
Nonforfeitable (*see also* **Vesting**)	3(19)				
Nonforfeitable benefit	4001(a)(8)				
Non-key employee		416(i)(2)			
Nonqualified deferred compensation		409A	1.409A-1 to -6 p1.409A-4		
Foreign corporations, partnerships		457A			
Reporting		6041(g)			
Non-resident aliens		871			
Application of basis rules		72(w), 83(c)(4)			
Nonvested participant					
Participation break in service	202(b)(4)	410(a)(5)(D)	1.410(a)-5(c)(4)		
Vesting break in service	203(b)(3)	411(a)(6)		2530.203-2(d)	
Normal cost					

For an Index to PHSA sections after amendment by PPACA and other legislation (Part 3), see separate PHSA Index following this Index.

	ERISA[1]	IRC[1]	Treas. Regs.[2] (26 CFR)	DOL & PBGC Regs.[2,3] (29 CFR)	HHS Regs. (45 CFR)
Definition	3(28)				
Funding	302(b)(2)(A)	412(b)(2)(A)			
Normal retirement age	3(24)	411(a)(8)			
Accrual after					
Defined benefit plan		411(b)(1)(H)			
Defined contribution plan		411(b)(2)			
Defined		411(a)(8)	1.411(a)-7(b)		
Normal retirement benefit	3(22)	411(a)(9)			
Notices					
Additional premium, plans subject to	4011				
Blackout periods	101(i)				
Distress termination					
Benefit distribution	4041(c)(3)(B)			4041.46*	
Distress termination notice	4041(c)(2)(A)			4041.43*	
Intent to terminate	4041(a)(2) 4041(c)(1)(A)			4041.41*	
PBGC determination of distress	4041(b)(2)(C)			4041.44*	
PBGC determination of sufficiency/ insufficiency	4041(c)(2)(C)			4041.47*	
Plan benefits	4041(b)(2)(B)			4041.44*	
Post-distribution certification	4041(b)(3)(B)			4041.48(b)*	
Distribution from terminated plan		401(a)(20)			
Electronic media			1.401(a)-21 1.401(a)-20, Q-16, 36		
Eligible rollover distributions		402(f)	1.402(f)-1		
Failure to meet minimum funding standard					
Participants and beneficiaries	101(d)				
PBGC	302(f)(4)(A) 303(k)(4)(A) 4071	412(n)(4)(A) 430(k)(4)(A)		4043.31*	
Reportable events (PBGC)	4043			pt. 4043*	
Significant reduction in rate of future benefit accrual		4980F			
Standard termination					

[1]Regulatory references in this index are included for researching convenience. Text of the regulations can be found in *ERISA Regulations, 2012 Edition* (BNA).
[2]The prefix **p** indicates a proposed regulation.
[3]Regulations marked with an asterisks (*) indicate a PBGC regulation.

	ERISA[1]	IRC[1]	Treas. Regs.[2] (26 CFR)	DOL & PBGC Regs.[2,3] (29 CFR)	HHS Regs. (45 CFR)
Information on request	4041(c)(2)(D)				
Intent to terminate	4041(a)(2) 4041(b)(1)(A)			4041.21*	
Noncompliance	4041(b)(2)(C)			4041.26*	
Plan benefits	4041(b)(2)(B)			4041.22–.23*	
Post-distribution certification	4041(b)(3)(B)			4041.29*	
Standard termination notice	4041(b)(2)(A)			4041.24*	
Transfer of excess pension assets to health benefits account	101(e)				

-O-

	ERISA[1]	IRC[1]	Treas. Regs.[2] (26 CFR)	DOL & PBGC Regs.[2,3] (29 CFR)	HHS Regs. (45 CFR)
One-participant plan, defined	101(i)(8)(B)	401(a)(35)(E)(iv)			
Optional forms of benefits, relative values			1.417(a)(3)-1		
Outstanding claim for withdrawal liability	4001(a)(12)				
Owner-employees (*see also* Self-employed individuals)					
Contributions on behalf of		401(c)(5)			
Definition		72(m)(6) 401(c)(3)			
Plan for		401(a)(10) 401(d)			
Prohibited transactions	408(d)	4975(d)			
Return for plan covering		6047			
Failure to file penalty		6704			
Taxation of distributions			1.72-17, 17A		

-P-

	ERISA[1]	IRC[1]	Treas. Regs.[2] (26 CFR)	DOL & PBGC Regs.[2,3] (29 CFR)	HHS Regs. (45 CFR)
Parachute payments		280G	1.280G-1		
Parking (*see* Fringe benefits)					
Partial termination, vesting on		411(d)(3)			
Participant	3(7)				
Participant-directed accounts					2550.404c-1 p2550.404c-1
Blackout period exception	404(c)			2550.404c-1	
Default investments	404(c)(5)			2550.404c-5	

For an Index to PHSA sections after amendment by PPACA and other legislation (Part 3), see separate PHSA Index following this Index.

	ERISA[1]	IRC[1]	Treas. Regs.[2] (26 CFR)	DOL & PBGC Regs.[2,3] (29 CFR)	HHS Regs. (45 CFR)
Fiduciary requirements for disclosure				2550.404a-5	
Participant or beneficiary directed investments, suspension of	404(c)(4)				
Participation (pension plans)					
Less than 10 years		415(b)(5)	1.415(b)-1(g)		
Minimum requirements		401(a)(26)–410			
Cash or deferred arrangement		401(k)(2)(D) 401(k)(3)(A)(i)	1.401(k)-1(e)(5) 1.401(k)-1(b)(1)		
Defined benefit plan		401(a)(26)	1.401(a)(26)-1		
Excludable employees			1.410(b)-6		
Qualified plans	202	401(a)(3) 401(a)(6), 410(a)	1.410(a)-3, 3T	2530.202-1–2	
SIMPLE plan		408(p)(4)			
Simplified employee pension		408(k)(2)	**p**1.408-7		
Tax-deferred annuities		403(b)(12)			
Taxation of highly compensated		402(b)(4)			
Party in interest (*see also* Prohibited transactions)					
Definition	3(14)	4975(e)(2)			
Report of transactions with	103(b)			2520.103-6(b)(3)	
PBGC					
Advisory committee	4002(h)				
Annual report	4008				
Appeals procedure				pt. 4003*	
Audits by	4003(a)				
Authority to require certain information	4010				
Benefit valuation				4044.52*	
Board of directors	4002(d)				
Borrowing authority	4003(c)				
Bylaws	4002(f)			pt. 4002*	
Civil actions against	4003(f)				
Civil actions by	4003(e)				
Corporate powers	4002(b)				
Debt collection				pt. 4903*	
Deduction for payments to		404(g)	1.404(g)-1		
Director	4002(a)				

[1]Regulatory references in this index are included for researching convenience. Text of the regulations can be found in *ERISA Regulations, 2012 Edition* (BNA).
[2]The prefix **p** indicates a proposed regulation.
[3]Regulations marked with an asterisks (*) indicate a PBGC regulation.

	ERISA[1]	IRC[1]	Treas. Regs.[2] (26 CFR)	DOL & PBGC Regs.[2,3] (29 CFR)	HHS Regs. (45 CFR)
Disasters, special rules	4002(i)				
Establishment	4002(a)				
Failure to notify	4071				
Filing, electronic				4000.3–.4, .23, .29*	
Requirement				4010.3–.9*	
Freedom of Information Act (FOIA) rules				4901*	
Confidential information				pt. 4901*	
Funds of	4005(a)				
Loans from	4005(g)				
Voting stock	4005(h)				
Guaranteed benefits (*see* Guaranteed benefits (PBGC))					
Investigatory authority	4003(a)				
IRS disclosure to		6103(*l*)(2)			
Liens					
Funding	302(f)(5) 303(k)(5)	412(n)(5) 430(k)(15)			
Termination	4068				
Missing participants	4050			4050.2*	
Mortality assumptions				4044.53* 4281.14*	
Mortality rate table				pt. 4044, Appendix A*	
Multiemployer plan (*see* Multiemployer plan)					
Operation	4003				
Recover ratio	4044(c)(3)(A)				
Retirement rate category				pt. 4044, Table 1-10*	
Submissions to				4000.1–.3*	
Subpoena authority	4003(b)–(c)				
Tax exemption	4002(g)(1)				
Termination of plans (*see* Termination—pension plan)					
Pension plans (*see also* Defined benefit plans or Annuity)					
Actuarial report (*see* Actuarial report)					
Definition	3(2)			2510.3-2	
Financial statement	103(b)(2)–(3)			2520.103-1(b)	

For an Index to PHSA sections after amendment by PPACA and other legislation (Part 3), see separate PHSA Index following this Index.

	ERISA[1]	IRC[1]	Treas. Regs.[2] (26 CFR)	DOL & PBGC Regs.[2,3] (29 CFR)	HHS Regs. (45 CFR)
Forfeitures under		401(a)(8)			
Funding (*see* Funding standard)					
Qualifying rollover distributions from		401(a)(31)			
Spouse's survivor benefits (*see* Spouse's benefits)					
Withholding by		3405			
Working retirement	3(2)	401(a)(36)			
Person	3(9) 4001(a)(20)				
Plan	3(3)	4975(e)(1)		2510.3-3	
Plan administrator					
Annual report (*see* Annual report by)					
Definition	3(16)(A) 4001(a)(1)	414(g) 4980B(g)(3)	1.414(g)-1		
Felon prohibited as	411				
Plan assets				2509.75-2	
Definition	3(42)			2510.3-101	
Employee contributions				2510.3-102	
Government mortgage pools				2510.3-101(i)	
Group trust				2510.3-101(h)(1)(i)	
Insurance	401(b)(2)			2510.3-101(h)(1)(iii)	
Investment company	401(b)(1)			2510.3-101(a)(2)	
Operating company				2510.3-101(c)	
Real estate operating company				2510.3-101(e)	
Trust requirement				2550.403a-1(b)(3)	
Venture capital operating company				2510.3-101(d)	
Plan sponsor					
Definition	3(16)(B)				
Multiemployer plan	4001(a)(10)				
Plan year	3(39)				
Plant shutdown, unpredictable event benefits (*see* Single-employer plan)					
Police and firefighters plans					
Coverage		401(a)(26)(H)	1.401(a)(26)-6(d)		
Maximum benefits		415(b)(2)(G)–(H)	1.415(b)-1(d)(3)		
Postponement of deadlines		7508(a), 7508A			

[1]Regulatory references in this index are included for researching convenience. Text of the regulations can be found in *ERISA Regulations, 2012 Edition* (BNA).
[2]The prefix **p** indicates a proposed regulation.
[3]Regulations marked with an asterisks (*) indicate a PBGC regulation.

	ERISA[1]	IRC[1]	Treas. Regs.[2] (26 CFR)	DOL & PBGC Regs.[2,3] (29 CFR)	HHS Regs. (45 CFR)
Predecessor employer, plan of	210(b)	414(a)			
Preemption of state laws	514				
Premiums—PBGC					
Alternative schedules	4006(b)				
Approved by Congress	4006(a)(3)(C)–(D)				
Multiemployer plans	4022A(f)				
Designated payor	4007(e)			4007.12*	
Due dates				4007.11*	
Electronic filing				4000.3, .4, .23, .29*, 4007.3*	
Exemptions	4006			4006.5*	
Late filing penalty				4007.8*	
Late payment, interest				4007.7*	
Multiemployer plans	4006				
Study of	4022A(f)				
Nonbasic benefits	4006(a)(5)				
Participant, defined				4006.6*	
Participant in multiple plans	4006(a)(3)(B)				
Payment of	4007			4007*	
Date of filing				4007.5*	
Overpayment refunds, interest on	4007(b)(2)				
Recordkeeping				4007.10*	
Short plan year				4006.5(f)*, 4006.2*	
Single-employer plans	4006			4006.1*, .3–.5* 4007*	
Small plans	4006(a)(3)(H)				
Preretirement survivor annuity (see Spouse's benefits)					
Present value					
Definition	3(27)				
Lump sum	203(e)(2)	411(a)(11)			
Pre-tax profits	4068(f)(2)				
Profit-sharing plan					
Profits requirement eliminated		401(a)(27)			
Prohibited transactions					
Agency coordination	3003				
Civil penalty	502(i)			2560.502i-1	

For an Index to PHSA sections after amendment by PPACA and other legislation (Part 3), see separate PHSA Index following this Index.

	ERISA[1]	IRC[1]	Treas. Regs.[2] (26 CFR)	DOL & PBGC Regs.[2,3] (29 CFR)	HHS Regs. (45 CFR)
Procedures for assessment				2570.1–.12	
Contributed property	406(c)	4975(f)(3)			
Criminal offenses (*see* Criminal offenses)					
Definition of	406(a)(1)	4975(c)(1)			
Employer real property	406(a)(2), 407			2550.407a-1, 2	
Employer securities	406(a)(2), 407			2550.407a-1, 2	
Excise tax		4975(a)–(b)			
Exemptions	408	4975(d)			
Application for				2570.30–.52	
Bank ancillary services	408(b)(6)	4975(d)(6)		2550.408b-6	
Bank common or collective trust	408(b)(8)	4975(d)(8)			
Bank deposits	408(b)(4)	4975(d)(4)		2550.408b-4	
Block trading	408(b)(15)	4975(d)(18), (f)(9)			
Class exemptions	408(a)	4975(c)(2)		2570.30–.52	
Conversion of securities	408(b)(7)	4975(d)(7)			
Correction period for securities and commodities transactions	408(b)(20)	4975(f)(11)			
Cross trading	408(b)(19)	4975(d)(22)		2550.408b-19	
Electronic communication network, transactions with parties in interest	408(b)(16)	4975(d)(19)			
Employee or officer of party in interest	408(c)(3)	4975(d)(11)			
Employer securities	408(e)			2550.408e	
ESOPs	408(b)(3)	4975(d)(3)		2550.408b-3	
Fiduciary as participant	408(c)(1)	4975(d)(9)			
Fiduciary compensation	408(c)(2)	4975(d)(10)		2550.408c-2	
Foreign exchange transactions	408(b)(18)	4975(d)(21)			
Individual exemptions	408(a)	4975(c)(2)		2570.30–.52	
Individual retirement accounts		4975(d)(16)	1.408-1(c)(3)		
Insurance company plan	408(b)(5)	4975(d)(5)			
Insurance company pooled investment fund	408(b)(8)	4975(d)(8)			
Investment advice	408(b)(14), (g)	4975(d)(17), (f)(8)			

[1]Regulatory references in this index are included for researching convenience. Text of the regulations can be found in *ERISA Regulations, 2012 Edition* (BNA).
[2]The prefix **p** indicates a proposed regulation.
[3]Regulations marked with an asterisks (*) indicate a PBGC regulation.

	ERISA[1]	IRC[1]	Treas. Regs.[2] (26 CFR)	DOL & PBGC Regs.[2,3] (29 CFR)	HHS Regs. (45 CFR)
Loans to participants	408(b)(1)	4975(d)(1)		2550.408b-1	
Merger, multiemployer plans	408(b)(11)	4975(d)(15)			
Multiemployer withdrawal liability	408(b)(10) 4219(d)	4975(d)(14)			
Owner-employee	408(d)	4975(f)(16)(A)			
Service providers	408(b)(17)	4975(d)(20)			
Services	408(b)(2)	4975(d)(2)		2550.408b-2	
Shareholder-employee	408(d)	4975(f)(6)			
Termination, pension plan	408(b)(9)	4975(d)(12)			
Fiduciary, transaction involving	406(b)	4975(c)(1), (e)(2)(A), (e)(3)		2550.408b-2(e)	
Party in interest transaction	406(a)(1)				
Civil penalty	502(i)			2560.502i-1	
Correction period	408(b)(20)	4975(d)(23), (f)(11)			
Excise tax		4975(a)–(b)			
Procedure for assessment of civil penalty				2570.1–.12	
Transactions with plan (*see* Prohibited transactions, Exemptions)					
Proxy voting				2509.08-2, 2509.94-2	
Prudence	404(a)(1)				
Economically targeted investments				2509.94-1	
Investment policy				2509.94-2	
Public Health Service Act (*see* PHSA Index)					
Public safety employees		72(t)(10), 402(*l*)			

-Q-

	ERISA[1]	IRC[1]	Treas. Regs.[2] (26 CFR)	DOL & PBGC Regs.[2,3] (29 CFR)	HHS Regs. (45 CFR)
Qualified beneficiary	607(3)	4980B(g)(1)	54.4980B-3		
Qualified benefit		125(f)	p1.125-2, Q-4		
Qualified domestic relations order		414(p)	1.401(a)-13(g)		
Subsequent orders				2520.206	
Qualified employee discount		132(c)	1.132-3		

For an Index to PHSA sections after amendment by PPACA and other legislation (Part 3), see separate PHSA Index following this Index.

	ERISA[1]	IRC[1]	Treas. Regs.[2] (26 CFR)	DOL & PBGC Regs.[2,3] (29 CFR)	HHS Regs. (45 CFR)
Qualified joint and survivor annuity (*see also* Spouse's benefits)		401(a)(11) 417	1.401(a)-11 1.417(e)-1 1.401(a)-11 1.417(a)(3)-1 1.401(a)-20, p1.401(a)-20		
Qualified medical child support order					
Civil actions to enforce	502(a)(7)				
Compliance with required	609				
Definition	609(a)(2)				
National medical support notice				2590.609-2	
Preemption exception	514(b)(7)				
Qualified moving expense reimbursement		132(g)			
Qualified preretirement survivor annuity (*see also* Spouse's benefits)		401(a)(11) 417	1.401(a)-11 1.417(e)-1		
Qualified public accountant (*see also* Audit requirement)	103(a)(3)			2509.75-9	
Qualified replacement plan	404(d)(1)	4980(d)			
Qualified transportation fringe		132(f)	1.132-9		

-R-

	ERISA[1]	IRC[1]	Treas. Regs.[2] (26 CFR)	DOL & PBGC Regs.[2,3] (29 CFR)	HHS Regs. (45 CFR)
Railroad retirement plans					
Social Security integration		401(*l*)(6)	1.401(*l*)-4		
Taxation of benefits		72(r)			
Real estate operating company				2510.3-101(e)	
Records, retention of	107, 209				
Use of electronic media				2520.107-1	
Refunds (*see also* Reversion of surplus assets)					
Employer contributions	403(c)(2)	401(a)(2)			
Excess deferral (*see* Excess deferrals, refund of)					
Withdrawal liability	403(c)(2), (3) 4221(d)	401(a)(2)		4219.31–.32*	
Regulations (DOL)	505				
Relative	3(15)				
Remedial amendment period		401(b)			

[1]Regulatory references in this index are included for researching convenience. Text of the regulations can be found in *ERISA Regulations, 2012 Edition* (BNA).
[2]The prefix **p** indicates a proposed regulation.
[3]Regulations marked with an asterisks (*) indicate a PBGC regulation.

	ERISA[1]	IRC[1]	Treas. Regs.[2] (26 CFR)	DOL & PBGC Regs.[2,3] (29 CFR)	HHS Regs. (45 CFR)
Reorganization index	4001(a)(9)	418(b)			
Reorganization— multiemployer plan	4241–4244A	418–418D			
Repayment of benefits	204(e)				
Reportable events (PBGC)	4043			pt. 4043*	
Reportable transaction (DOL)	103(b)(3)			2520.103-10	
Reports and returns to (*see also* Disclosure; Notices)					
Department of Labor					
Alternative compliance	110				
Annual report	103			2520.103-1–12	
Disclosure of	106				
Forms	109				
Requirement for	101(b)–(c)			2520.101-1	
Summary plan description	102(a)–(b)			2520.104a-1	
IRS					
Actuarial report		6059, 6692			
Annual return		6057(a), 6058(a) 6652(e)			
Cafeteria plan		6039D			
Change of status		6057(b) 6652(d)(2)			
Credit for health insurance costs		6050T			
Educational assistance program		6039D			
Failure to file, penalty		6652			
Group legal services plan		6039D			
Individual retirement accounts		6047 6652(e), (g) 6704 6724(d)			
Merger		6057(b) 6058(b) 6652(d)(2)			
Multiemployer welfare plan		6039D(d)(3)			
Nondeductible IRA contribution		408(o)(4) 6923(b)			
Owner-employee, plan covering		6047, 6704			
Participant					

For an Index to PHSA sections after amendment by PPACA and other legislation (Part 3), see separate PHSA Index following this Index.

[1]Regulatory references in this index are included for researching convenience. Text of the regulations can be found in *ERISA Regulations, 2012 Edition* (BNA).

[2]The prefix **p** indicates a proposed regulation.

[3]Regulations marked with an asterisks (*) indicate a PBGC regulation.

	ERISA[1]	IRC[1]	Treas. Regs.[2] (26 CFR)	DOL & PBGC Regs.[2,3] (29 CFR)	HHS Regs. (45 CFR)
Required		401(a)(31)	1.401(a)(31)-1		
Written explanation		401(a)(31)	1.402(f)-1		
Eligible retirement plan		402(c)(8)			
Eligible rollover distribution		402(f)(2)(A)			
Explanation of			**p**1.402(f)-1		
Frozen deposits		402(c)(7) 408(d)(3)(F)			
Individual retirement account		408(d)(3)	1.408-4(b)		
Nonspouse beneficiary, distribution to IRA of		402(c)(11)			
Notice to PBGC of distribution from terminated plan		401(a)(20)			
Reports to participants		402(f), 6652(i)	1.402(f)-1		
Requirements for		402(c)	1.402(a)(5)-1T		
Spouse, distribution to		402(c)(9)	**p**1.402(e)-2(e)(2)		
Tax deferred (403(b)) annuity		403(b)(8)			
Withholding		3405	31.3405(c)-1		
Written explanation		402(f)	1.402(f)-1		
Roth IRA (*see also* Cash or deferred arrangements or individual retirement accounts)		408A	1.408A-4T		
Rollover from retirement plan to		408A(e)			

-S-

	ERISA[1]	IRC[1]	Treas. Regs.[2] (26 CFR)	DOL & PBGC Regs.[2,3] (29 CFR)	HHS Regs. (45 CFR)
S corporation		1372			
Contributions to ESOPs		404(a)(9)(C)			
Health benefits for shareholder-employees		162(*l*)(5)			
Loans to shareholder-employees	408(d)	4975(f)(6)			
Salary reduction					
Dependent care		129(d)(8)(B)			
Qualified plans (*see* Cash or deferred arrangements)					
Regulations	2006				
Sale of assets (*see also* Controlled group, Change in)					

For an Index to PHSA sections after amendment by PPACA and other legislation (Part 3), see separate PHSA Index following this Index.

	ERISA[1]	IRC[1]	Treas. Regs.[2] (26 CFR)	DOL & PBGC Regs.[2,3] (29 CFR)	HHS Regs. (45 CFR)
Cash or deferred arrangement		401(k)(10)			
Withdrawal liability	4204, 4225(a)			pt. 4204*	
Saver's credit		25B			
Scholarships (*see also* Education or training)					
Taxation		117	1.117-1–5		
Seasonal industry					
Service for participation	202(a)(3)(B)	410(a)(3)(B)			
Service for vesting	203(b)(2)	411(a)(5)	1.410(a)-5(b)		
Year of participation	204(b)(3)	411(b)(4)			
Secretary (Title I)	3(13)				
Secretary of Treasury	4001(b)(2)(B)				
Security (*see also* Employer securities)	3(20)				
Self-employed individuals (*see also* Owner-employees)					
Cash or deferred arrangements, partnership			1.401(k)-1(a)(6)		
Compensation		414(s)(2)			
Custodial accounts	403(b)(3)	401(f)		2550.403b-1(a)(3)	
Deduction limits					
Health insurance		162(*l*)			
Qualified plan		404(a)(8) 404(e)	1.404(a)(8)-1T 1.404(e)-1, -1A		
Definition		401(c)(1)(B)			
Dependent care assistance		129(e)(3)			
Earned income of		401(c)(2) 404(a)(8)(B) 416(i)(3)(B)	1.404(e)-1(h)(3) 1.404(e)- 1A(i)(3)		
Educational assistance program		127(c)(2)			
Fishermen		401(c)(6)			
Group legal services plan		120(d)(1)	p1.120-2		
Health benefits					
Deduction		162(*l*)			
Nonemployee status		105(g)			
Qualified plan (Keogh plan)		401(c)(1)(A) 402(i) 416(i)(3)(A)			
Taxation of lump sum distributions to			1.72-18		
Separability	509				

---

[1]Regulatory references in this index are included for researching convenience. Text of the regulations can be found in *ERISA Regulations, 2012 Edition* (BNA).
[2]The prefix **p** indicates a proposed regulation.
[3]Regulations marked with an asterisks (*) indicate a PBGC regulation.

	ERISA[1]	IRC[1]	Treas. Regs.[2] (26 CFR)	DOL & PBGC Regs.[2,3] (29 CFR)	HHS Regs. (45 CFR)
Separate line of business					
Coverage, qualified plan		410(b)(5)	1.410(b)-6(e)		
Aggregation, permissive			1.410(b)-7(d)(4)		
Definition		414(r)	1.414(r)-1–11		
Title I	502(e)(2)				
Title IV					
Contempt (PBGC)	4003(c)				
Multiemployer plan	4301(d)				
Single-employer plan	4070(b)–(c)				
Service requirements					
Computation periods				2530.200b-1	
Equivalencies				2530.200b-3	
Hour of service				2530.200b-2	
Participation	202	410(a)	1.410(a)-1–9 1.410(a)-3T **p**1.410(a)-4A 1.410(a)-8T, -9T	2530.202-1–2	
Vesting	203(a)(2)	411(a)(2)		2530.203-1, -2	
Severance pay arrangements					
Nonprofit organization		457(e)(11)			
Pension plan	3(2)(B)			2510.3-2(b)	
Welfare plan	3(1)			2510.3-1(a)(3)	
SIMPLE plans					
Cash or deferred arrangements		401(k)(11)			
Contributions and distributions		402(b)			
Deductibility of contributions		219(b)(4)			
Definition		408(p)			
Early distributions		72(t)(6)			
Employer contributions		404(m)			
Employment taxes		3121(a)(5)(H)			
Reports		408(*l*)(2)			
Rollovers		408(d)(3)(G)			
Simplified employee pension (SEP)					
Contribution limit		219(b)(2), 402(h)			
Deduction		404(h)	**p**1.404(h)-1		
Definition		408(k)	**p**1.408-7		
Maximum contribution		408(j)			

For an Index to PHSA sections after amendment by PPACA and other legislation (Part 3), see separate PHSA Index following this Index.

	ERISA[1]	IRC[1]	Treas. Regs.[2] (26 CFR)	DOL & PBGC Regs.[2,3] (29 CFR)	HHS Regs. (45 CFR)
Reports		408(*l*), 6693(a)	p1.408-9		
Top-heavy plan		416(i)(6)			
Single-employer plan					
Definition	3(41), 4001(a)(15)				
Funding of (*see* Funding under Pension Protection Act of 2006)					
Plant shutdown, unpredictable contingent event benefits	101(j) 206(g), (h) 4022(b)(8)	436(b)	1.436-1(b)		
PBGC Premiums	4006(a)(3)(A)(i)			pt. 4006*	
Termination of (*see* Termination—pension plan)					
Valuation				4044.41–.75*	
Social Security integration					
Benefit decrease prohibited	206(b)	401(a)(15)			
Defined benefit plan		401(a)(5)(D) 401(*l*)(3)	1.401(*l*)-3		
Defined contribution plan		401(*l*)(2)	1.401(*l*)-2		
Funding impact	302(c)(4) 304(c)(4)	412(c)(4) 431(c)(4)			
Permitted disparity (integration)		401(a)(5) 401(*l*)	1.401(a)(4)-7 1.401(a)(5)-1 1.401(*l*)-1–6		
Railroad plans		401(*l*)(6)	1.401(*l*)-4		
Social Security increase	206(b)	401(a)(15)			
Top-heavy plan		401(*l*)(5)(E) 416(e)			
Split-dollar life insurance		61	1.61-22 1.83-3 1.83-6 1.301-1		
Split-dollar loans			1.7872-15		
Spouse's benefits					
Cash out of	205(g)	417(e)			
Divorced spouse (*see also* Qualified domestic relations order)		414(p)(5)			
Qualified joint and survivor annuity	205	401(a)(11)	1.401(a)-11 1.401(a)-20		
Definition	205(d)	417(b)			
Required explanation of			1.417(a)(3)-1		
Waiver of	205(c)	417(a)			
Qualified optional survivor annuity	205(d)(2)	417(g)			

[1]Regulatory references in this index are included for researching convenience. Text of the regulations can be found in *ERISA Regulations, 2012 Edition* (BNA).
[2]The prefix **p** indicates a proposed regulation.
[3]Regulations marked with an asterisks (*) indicate a PBGC regulation.

	ERISA[1]	IRC[1]	Treas. Regs.[2] (26 CFR)	DOL & PBGC Regs.[2,3] (29 CFR)	HHS Regs. (45 CFR)
Qualified preretirement survivor annuity	205	401(a)(11), 417(c)	1.401(a)-20		
Definition	205(e)	417(c)			
Required explanation of			1.417(a)(3)-1		
Requirement	205	401(a)(11)			
Transfer of options to		424(c)(4)			
Waiver of	205(c)	417(a)			
Start-up costs		45E			
State, defined	3(10)				
State law, preemption	514				
Statute of limitations					
ESOP, sale of stock to		1042(f)			
Multiemployer plan—Title IV	4301(f)				
PBGC					
Suits against	4003(f)(5)				
Suits by	4003(e)(6)				
Single-employer plan—Title IV	4070(f)				
Title I	413				
Stock bonus plan					
Distribution requirements		401(a)(23) 409(o)			
Put option		401(a)(23) 409(h)			
Voting pass-through		401(a)(22) 409(e)			
Stock options					
Corporate reorganizations		424	1.424-1		
Deductions for		421(a)(2)			
Disqualifying disposition		421(b)	1.424-1		
Employee stock purchase plans		423			
Estate, exercise by		421(c)			
Incentive (or statutory)		421, 422			
Defined			1.421-1(b), 1.422-2		
Definitions of terms			1.424-1		
Disqualifying transfer			1.421-2(b)		
Employment requirement, failure to satisfy			1.422-1(c)		
Exercise			1.421-1(f)		
Exercise by estate			1.421-2(c)		

For an Index to PHSA sections after amendment by PPACA and other legislation (Part 3), see separate PHSA Index following this Index.

	ERISA[1]	IRC[1]	Treas. Regs.[2] (26 CFR)	DOL & PBGC Regs.[2,3] (29 CFR)	HHS Regs. (45 CFR)
General rules			1.421-2, 1.4221		
Holding period, failure to satisfy			1.422-1(b)		
Limit, $100,000			1.422-4		
Option, defined			1.421-1(a)		
Option price			1.421-1(e)		
Permissible provisions			1.422-5		
Qualifying transfer			1.421-2(a)		
Return requirement		6039	1.6039-1–2		
Stock and voting stock			1.421-1(d)		
Stockholder approval			1.422-3		
Time and date of granting			1.421-1(c)		
Nonstatutory, taxation of		83	1.83-7		
Subpoena					
PBGC	4003(b)–(c)				
Secretary of Labor	504				
Substance use disorder benefits (*see* Mental health policy)					
Successor plan (*see also* Predecessor employer, plan of)					
Definition	4021(a)				
Multiemployer plan	4231(d)				
Summary annual report	104(b)(3) 109(c)			2520.104b-10	
Electronic filing				2520.104a-2	
Summary of material modifications	102(a)(2) 104(a)–(b)			2520.104a-8	
Summary plan description					
Contents of	102(b)			2520.102-3	
Department of Labor, filing	101(b)(1)			2520.101-1 2520.104b-1–3	
Disclosure of	106				
Form of	109(b)–(c)				
Participant, furnishing to	101(a)(1) 102(a)(1) 104(b)			2520.101-1 2520.104b-2, -4	
Failure to provide	502(c)(1)				
Supplemental unemploy-ment benefits (SUB) trust					
Deductions for		419			

[1]Regulatory references in this index are included for researching convenience. Text of the regulations can be found in *ERISA Regulations, 2012 Edition* (BNA).
[2]The prefix **p** indicates a proposed regulation.
[3]Regulations marked with an asterisks (*) indicate a PBGC regulation.

	ERISA[1]	IRC[1]	Treas. Regs.[2] (26 CFR)	DOL & PBGC Regs.[2,3] (29 CFR)	HHS Regs. (45 CFR)
Exemption of		501(c)(17)			
Application for		505(c)			
Limits on contributions to		419A			
Notice to IRS		505(c)			
Suspension of benefits	203(a)(3)	411(a)(3)(B)	1.411(c)-1(f) p1.411(c)-1(f)	2530.203-3	

<h1 style="text-align:center">-T-</h1>

	ERISA[1]	IRC[1]	Treas. Regs.[2] (26 CFR)	DOL & PBGC Regs.[2,3] (29 CFR)	HHS Regs. (45 CFR)
Target benefit plan, accrual		411(b)(2)(B)			
Taxation of distributions					
Annuities		72	1.72-1–18		
Distribution from		403(a)	1.403(a)-1, -2 p1.403(a)-1, -2		
Distribution of		402(e)	1.402(a)-1(a)		
Employer securities		402(e)(4), 402(j)	1.402(a)-1(b)		
Foreign trust		402(d)	1.402(c)-1		
Lump sum distributions		402(e)(4)(D)			
Definition		402(e)	p1.402(e)-2		
Nonexempt plan		402(b), 403(c)	1.402(b)-1 1.403(c)-1		
Nonresident aliens		402(e)(2)			
Qualified domestic relations order		402(e)(1)			
Tax-exempt organizations			1.457-1–12		
Early retirement incentive					
Defined		457(e)(11)(D)(ii)			
Payments from		457(e)(11)(D)(i)			
Severance pay plan, treated as		457(e)(11)(D)(i)			
Welfare plan, treated as	3(2)(B)				
Eligible employer		457(e)(1)(B)			
Employment retention plan					
Defined		457(f)(4)(C)			
Welfare plan, treated as	3(2)(B)				
Tax-sheltered annuities					
Custodial accounts		403(b)(5), (7)			
Definitions			1.403(b)-2		
Discrimination		403(b)(12)			
Distributions					
Early, before age 59$\frac{1}{2}$		72(t)			
Required		403(b)(10)–(11)			

For an Index to PHSA sections after amendment by PPACA and other legislation (Part 3), see separate PHSA Index following this Index.

	ERISA[1]	IRC[1]	Treas. Regs.[2] (26 CFR)	DOL & PBGC Regs.[2,3] (29 CFR)	HHS Regs. (45 CFR)
Taxation of		72, 402(b) 403(b), (c)	1.403(b)-1–11		
Tax on failure to distribute		4974			
Elective deferrals, limit on		402(g) 403(b)(1)(E)	1.402(g)-1(d) 1.403(b)-1(b)(3)		
Excess contributions, tax on		4973, 4979	54.4979-1		
Exclusion for contributions to purchase			1.403(b)-3		
Maximum contributions		403(b)(2) 415(c)(4)	1.403(b)-1(d)–(g)		
Nondiscrimination testing			1.403(b)-5		
Termination—pension plan (*see also* PBGC)					
Allocation of assets	403(d), 4044(a)			pt. 4044*	
Annuity contracts, purchase	502(a)(9)				
Cessation of operations	4062(e)			4062.8*	
Civil actions					
Multiemployer plan	4301				
Single-employer plan	4070				
Controlled group, cessation or change in membership of	4041(b)(5)				
Discrimination	4044(b)(5)			4044.17(d)*	
Multiemployer plan					
Amendment ceasing accruals	4041A(a)(1)				
Benefit reductions	4281				
Conversion to defined contribution plan	4041A(a)(3)				
Date of	4041A(b) 4048(b)				
Definition of termination	4041A				
Funding	301(c), 4041A(e)	412(e)(4)			
Lump sum distributions from	4041A(f)(1)				
Mass withdrawal	4041A(a)				
Missing participants	4050(c)				
Payment of benefits after	4041A(c), (f)				
Multiple employer plan	4064				
Partial termination	4062(e)	411(d)(3)		4062.8*	

[1]Regulatory references in this index are included for researching convenience. Text of the regulations can be found in *ERISA Regulations, 2012 Edition* (BNA).
[2]The prefix **p** indicates a proposed regulation.
[3]Regulations marked with an asterisks (*) indicate a PBGC regulation.

	ERISA[1]	IRC[1]	Treas. Regs.[2] (26 CFR)	DOL & PBGC Regs.[2,3] (29 CFR)	HHS Regs. (45 CFR)
Exceptions	403(b)			2550.403b-1(a)	
Insurance contract		401(f)		2550.403b-1(a)(2)	
Plan asset entity				2550.403a-1(b)(3)	
Required	403(a)	401(a)		2550.403a-1	
Street name or nominee				2550.403a-1(b)(1)	
Trustee					
Allocation of responsibilities	405(b)				
Co-trustee liability	405(b)			2509.75-5	
Designation of	403(a)			2550.403a-1(c)	
Felon prohibited as	411				
Liability	405(d)(2)				
Trustee responsibility	405(c)(3)				

-U-

	ERISA[1]	IRC[1]	Treas. Regs.[2] (26 CFR)	DOL & PBGC Regs.[2,3] (29 CFR)	HHS Regs. (45 CFR)
Uncollectible withdrawal liability fund	4005(d)				
Unfunded accrued liability	3(30)				
Unfunded current liability	302(d)(8)(A)	412(*l*)(8)(A)			
Unfunded guaranteed benefits	4001(a)(17)				
Unfunded new liability amount	302(d)(4)	412(*l*)(4)			
Unfunded old liability amount	302(d)(3)	412(*l*)(3)			
Unfunded vested benefits					
Determination of				4006.4*	
PBGC variable rate premium				4006.4*	
Withdrawal liability	4213(c)			4211.2*	
Mass withdrawal				4219.2*	
Uniformed Services Retirement Pay, Reduced		122			
United Mine Workers Fund					
Deduction for contribution to		404(c)	1.404(c)-1		
Health benefits		9701–9722			
Unpredictable contingent event amount	302(d)(5)	412(*l*)(5)			

[1]Regulatory references in this index are included for researching convenience. Text of the regulations can be found in *ERISA Regulations, 2012 Edition* (BNA).
[2]The prefix **p** indicates a proposed regulation.
[3]Regulations marked with an asterisks (*) indicate a PBGC regulation.

	ERISA[1]	IRC[1]	Treas. Regs.[2] (26 CFR)	DOL & PBGC Regs.[2,3] (29 CFR)	HHS Regs. (45 CFR)
Unpredictable contingent event benefit	206(g)(1) 302(d)(7)(B)	412(*l*)(7)(B) 436(b)			
Unrelated party					
Definition	4204(d)				
Sale of assets to	4204, 4225(a)				

-V-

	ERISA[1]	IRC[1]	Treas. Regs.[2] (26 CFR)	DOL & PBGC Regs.[2,3] (29 CFR)	HHS Regs. (45 CFR)
Vacation pay					
Deduction		404(a)(5)	1.404(b)-1T		
Nonprofit organizations		457(e)(11)			
Welfare plan status	3(1)			2510.3-1(a)(2)	
Payroll practice exception				2510.3-1(b)(3)	
VEBA (voluntary employees beneficiary association)					
Discrimination		505(b)			
Employee-pay-all plan		419A(f)(5)			
Exemption from tax		501(c)(9)	1.501(c)(9)-1–8		
Application required		505(c)			
Geographic locale restriction			p1.501(c)(9)-2(d)		
Requirements for		505			
Notice to IRS		505(c)			
Venue					
Multiemployer plans—Title IV	4301(d)				
PBGC					
Single-employer plan termination	4070(c)				
Suits against	4003(f)(2)				
Suits by	4003(e)(2)				
Title I suits	502(e)(2), 502(k)				
Vesting					
Agency coordination of rules	3002				
Benefit accrual, age discrimination	204(b)(5)	411(b)(5)			
Break in service	203(b)(3)	411(a)(6)		2530.203-2(d)	
Changes in	203(c)	411(a)(10)		2530.203-2(c)	
Church plan		410(d), 411(e)	1.410(d)-1		
Class year plan	203(a)(3)(D)(iv)	411(a)(3)(D)			

For an Index to PHSA sections after amendment by PPACA and other legislation (Part 3), see separate PHSA Index following this Index.

	ERISA[1]	IRC[1]	Treas. Regs.[2] (26 CFR)	DOL & PBGC Regs.[2,3] (29 CFR)	HHS Regs. (45 CFR)
Controlled group	210(c)–(d)	414(b)–(c)	1.414(b)-1 1.414(c)-1–5	2530.210(d)	
Effective date	211				
Employee contributions	203(a)(1)	411(a)(1)			
Employer nonelective contributions					
Defined benefit	203(a)(2)(A)	411(a)(2)(A)			
Defined contribution	203(a)(2)(B)	411(a)(2)(B)			
Government plan		411(e)			
Maternity/paternity absence	203(b)(3)(E)	411(a)(6)(E)	1.410(a)-9		
Minimum vesting schedules	203(a)(2)	411(a)(2)			
Multiemployer plan	210(a)(2)	413(b)(4)		2530.210(d)–(e)	
Vesting service	203(b)(1)	411(a)(4)			
Multiple employer plan	210(a)(2)	413(c)(3)		2530.210(c)	
Partial termination of plan		411(d)(3)			
Requirement for	203	401(a)(7)		2530.203-1, -2	
Seasonal industry	203(b)(2)(C)	411(a)(5)(C)			
Statement of forfeitable benefits	105(c)				
Tax-credit ESOP		409(c)			
Termination of plan		411(d)(3)			
Top-heavy		416(b)			
Variance from, temporary	207, 1012				
Year of service	203(b)(2)	411(a)(5)			

-W-

	ERISA[1]	IRC[1]	Treas. Regs.[2] (26 CFR)	DOL & PBGC Regs.[2,3] (29 CFR)	HHS Regs. (45 CFR)
Wages		3121(a), 3401(a)			
Waived funding deficiency (*see also* Funding standard)					
Amortization	302(b)(2)	412(b)(2)(C)			
Credit for	302(b)(3)	412(b)(3)(C)			
Definition	302(c)(3), 303(c)	412(c)(3)			
Security for	302(c)(4) 306	412(c)(4)			
Welfare benefit		419(e)(2)			
Welfare benefit fund		419(e)(1)			
Fund		419(e)(3)			
Welfare benefit plan					

[1]Regulatory references in this index are included for researching convenience. Text of the regulations can be found in *ERISA Regulations, 2012 Edition* (BNA).
[2]The prefix **p** indicates a proposed regulation.
[3]Regulations marked with an asterisks (*) indicate a PBGC regulation.

	ERISA[1]	IRC[1]	Treas. Regs.[2] (26 CFR)	DOL & PBGC Regs.[2,3] (29 CFR)	HHS Regs. (45 CFR)
Controlled group		414(t)			
Definition	3(1)			2510.3-1	
Exceptions			1.419A(f)(6)-1	2510.3-1(b)–(k)	
Financial statement	103(b)			2520.103-1, -2	
Funded (*see also* VEBA)					
Actuarial certification		419A(c)(5)			
Collectively bargained		419A(f)(5)			
Deduction limit		419(b)			
Discrimination		505(b)			
Limitation on additions to		419A			
Method having effect of plan		419(f)			
Qualified asset account		419A			
Tax on disqualified benefits		4976			
Payroll practices exception				2510.3-1(b)	
Termination of	403(d)(2)				
Withdrawal—multiemployer plan					
Amendments relating to					
Notice to employers	4214(b)				
PBGC approval of	4220			pt. 4220*	
Retroactive effect	4214(a)				
Arbitration of disputes	4221			pt. 4221*	
Building, construction industry					
Complete withdrawal	4203(b)				
Partial withdrawal	4208(d)(1)				
Cessation before effective date	4217				
Complete withdrawal	4203				
Abatement	4207			4207.3*	
Building and construction	4203(b)				
Date of	4203(e)				
Entertainment industry	4203(c)				
Resumption of operations	4207			pt. 4207*	
Sale of assets	4204			pt. 4204*	
Trucking industry	4203(d)				
Corporate reorganization	4218(1)				

For an Index to PHSA sections after amendment by PPACA and other legislation (Part 3), see separate PHSA Index following this Index.

[1]Regulatory references in this index are included for researching convenience. Text of the regulations can be found in *ERISA Regulations, 2012 Edition* (BNA).

[2]The prefix **p** indicates a proposed regulation.

[3]Regulations marked with an asterisks (*) indicate a PBGC regulation.

	ERISA[1]	IRC[1]	Treas. Regs.[2] (26 CFR)	DOL & PBGC Regs.[2,3] (29 CFR)	HHS Regs. (45 CFR)
Definition of	4205				
Liability, adjustment for	4206				
Reduction of	4208			pt. 4208*	
Retail food industry	4205(c)				
Subsequent withdrawal	4206			pt. 4206*	
Prohibited transaction exemption	408(b)(10) 4219(d)	4975(d)(14)			
Sale of assets					
Limitation on liability	4225(a), (e)				
Purchaser's liability	4204(b)(1)				
Unrelated party	4204(d)				
Variances, PBGC	4204(c)			pt. 4204*	
Withdrawal as result of	4204(a)				
Service of process	4301(d)				
Statute of limitations	4301(f)				
Successor employer	4218				
Withdrawal from multiple employer plan	4063			4062.1*, 4063.1*	
Withdrawal of employee contributions	206(c) 203(a)(3)	401(a)(19) 411(a)(3)			
Withholding					
Eligible rollover distributions		3405(c)	35.3405(c)-1		
Pension payments		3405(a), (b)	35.3405-1T		
Working condition fringe (*see* Fringe benefits)					
Written plan					
Compliance with	404(a)(1)				
Required					
Cafeteria plans		125(d)(1)	**p**1.125-1, Q-3		
Dependent care assistance plan		129(d)(1)			
Educational assistance program		127(b)(1)			
Employee benefit plans	402(a)(1)				

-Y-

	ERISA[1]	IRC[1]	Treas. Regs.[2] (26 CFR)	DOL & PBGC Regs.[2,3] (29 CFR)	HHS Regs. (45 CFR)
Year of credited service	4022A(c)(3)				
Year of participation	204(b)(4)	411(b)(4)		2530.204-1, -4	
Year of service				2530.200b-1	
Eligibility to participate	202(a)(3)	410(a)(3)	1.410(a)-5(a)	2530.202-2	

For an Index to PHSA sections after amendment by PPACA and other legislation (Part 3), see separate PHSA Index following this Index.

	ERISA[1]	IRC[1]	Treas. Regs.[2] (26 CFR)	DOL & PBGC Regs.[2,3] (29 CFR)	HHS Regs. (45 CFR)
Equivalencies				2530.200b-3	
Tax-deferred annuity		403(b)(4)	1.403(b)-1(f)		
Vesting	203(b)(2)	411(a)(5)	1.411(a)-6(a)	2530.203-2	

[1]Regulatory references in this index are included for researching convenience. Text of the regulations can be found in *ERISA Regulations, 2012 Edition* (BNA).
[2]The prefix **p** indicates a proposed regulation.
[3]Regulations marked with an asterisks (*) indicate a PBGC regulation.

Index to Public Health Service Act (PHSA), as Amended by the Patient Protection and Affordable Care Act (Enacted March 23, 2010) and Other Legislation

	PHSA[1]
-A-	
Annual limits	2711
Appeals process	2719
Availability of coverage, guaranteed	2702
Availability to individuals with prior group coverage, guaranteed —Network plans	2741(d)
Availability to individuals with prior group coverage, guaranteed —Waiver for states with alternative mechanism	2744
-C-	
Certification of coverage	2743
Clinical trials	2709
-D-	
Definitions	2791
Dependent coverage	2714
Dependent students, coverage of	2728, 2753[2754]
Disclosure requirements —Additional information from plan or coverage not offered through exchange	2715A
Disclosure requirements —Health plan issuers	2709[2710]
—Standardized definitions	2715
—Uniform explanation of coverage	2715
Discrimination based on health status	2704
-E-	
Emergency services, coverage of	2719A(b)
Enforcement	2723
Essential health benefits package	2707(a)
Excepted benefits	2763, 2791(c)

[1] For a list of the PHSA sections (amended by PPACA and other legislation) as codified in Title 42 of the U.S. Code, see the PHSA Finding List on page xlvii.

This Index covers Part 3, Public Health Service Act, Selected Provisions as Amended by the Patient Protection and Affordable Care Act (Enacted Mar. 23, 2010) and Other Legislation

	PHSA[1]
-R-	
Rebate to enrollees	2718(b), (d)
Renewability of coverage, guaranteed	2742
Reporting requirements, standards	2717(a)
Rescission of coverage	2712
-U-	
Uniform fraud and abuse referral format	2794[2795]
-W-	
Waiting periods	2708
Wellness and prevention programs	2717(b)